YOUR CLEAR PATH TO SUCCESS IN THE PSYCHO...

P9-DGF-832

Unifying themes help you make sense of it all. In Chapter 1, the authors introduce seven themes that reappear as you move from chapter to chapter. Use these themes as a framework for organizing information as you learn.

Putting It in Perspective sections at the end of each chapter put the chapters' contents into perspective by recalling the book's seven overarching themes—helping you think about important topics in new ways.

Featured Studies found in every chapter give you an over-the-shoulder look at interesting, real-life research—showing you how psychologists conduct and report their research.

Personal Applications in every chapter give you practical advice that will be helpful in improving your academic performance and your daily life.

Critical Thinking Applications in every chapter offer specific, concrete ways to improve your thinking skills. You'll have opportunities to practice your newly learned skills on chapter material.

Web Links appear throughout every chapter. This book is a rich resource for expanding your knowledge of psychology topics online. Carefully selected by Web expert Vincent Hevern (the Internet editor for the *Society for the Teaching of Psychology*) and author Doug McCann, the book's Web links help you clarify your understanding of psychology and learn about current research. Because Web addresses change frequently, we recommend that you access these links through the book Web site (accessible at http://www.themesandvariations.nelson.com) where the URLs are periodically updated.

FIRST CANADIAN EDITION

Psychology

themes & variations

FIRST CANADIAN EDITION

Psychology

themes & variations

WAYNE WEITEN

University of Nevada, Las Vegas

DOUG McCANN

York University

With Critical Thinking Applications by **DIANE F. HALPERN**

Claremont McKenna College

THOMSON

NELSON

Australia   Canada   Mexico   Singapore   Spain   United Kingdom   United States

THOMSON

NELSON

Psychology: Themes and Variations

First Canadian Edition
by Wayne Weiten and Doug McCann

Associate Vice-President, Editorial Director:
Evelyn Veitch

Publisher:
Joanna Cotton

Senior Marketing Manager:
Wayne Morden

Senior Developmental Editor:
Lesley Mann

Photo Researcher:
Indu Ghuman

Permissions Cooordinator:
Indu Ghuman

Production Editor:
Anne Macdonald

Copy Editor:
Valerie Adams

Proofreader:
Kelli Howey

Indexer:
Belle Wong

Senior Production Coordinator:
Hedy Sellers

Design Director:
Ken Phipps

Interior Design:
Tammy Gay

Cover Design:
Johanna Liburd

Cover Image:
Latchezar Boyadjiev/
L.B. Glass Studios

Compositor:
Brenda Prangley

Printer:
Quebecor World

Library and Archives Canada Cataloguing in Publication

Weiten, Wayne, 1950–
        Psychology: themes and variations / Wayne Weiten, Douglas McCann.—1st Canadian ed.

Includes bibliographical references and index.
ISBN 0-17-625142-1

1. Psychology—Textbooks.
I. McCann, Douglas, 1951–
II. Title.

BF121.W38 2006   150
C2005-907442-6

About the Cover The work of Bulgarian-born Latchezar Boyadjiev has been exhibited at the Sandra Ainsley Gallery in Toronto and other galleries in North America. He writes, "The main focus of my work is to create dynamic shapes supported by sensual lines that will gradually evolve from an idea on paper to a sculpture in glass—and combined with light it will have a powerful impact on the viewer. I want my work to become a part of modern architecture and a contemporary environment, to reflect the era in which we live" (from http://www.latchezarboyadjiev.com). Boyadjiev's work was selected for the cover of this book to suggest the mind-body relationship studied in psychology: the play of light through the solid glass symbolizes the interaction of the mind with the physical properties of the brain. This concept is continued through the chapter-opening photos used in the text. They feature other works by Boyadjiev and have been especially selected to reflect the themes of the chapters. For example, the sculpture used for Chapter 8, Language and Thought, is entitled "Conversation." "Transition" appears with Chapter 11, Human Development Across the Life Span. "Joy" accompanies Chapter 10, Motivation and Emotion. This beautiful array of images helps convey the book's subtitle—*Themes and Variations*.

For Nancy
D.M.

Beth,
This one is for you
W.W.

Brief Contents

To the Instructor — xvii

Acknowledgments — xxxi

To the Student — xxxiii

What Should Introductory Psychology

Students Know About the Internet? — xxxvii

Chapter 1 The Evolution of Psychology — 1

PERSONAL APPLICATION • Improving Academic Performance — 31
CRITICAL THINKING APPLICATION • Developing Critical Thinking Skills: An Introduction — 36

Chapter 2 The Research Enterprise in Psychology — 40

PERSONAL APPLICATION • Finding and Reading Journal Articles — 69
CRITICAL THINKING APPLICATION • The Perils of Anecdotal Evidence: "I Have a Friend Who ..." — 72

Chapter 3 The Biological Bases of Behaviour — 76

PERSONAL APPLICATION • Evaluating the Concept of "Two Minds in One" — 117
CRITICAL THINKING APPLICATION • Building Better Brains: The Perils of Extrapolation — 120

Chapter 4 Sensation and Perception — 124

PERSONAL APPLICATION • Appreciating Art and Illusion — 169
CRITICAL THINKING APPLICATION • Recognizing Contrast Effects: It's All Relative — 175

Chapter 5 Variations in Consciousness — 180

PERSONAL APPLICATION • Addressing Practical Questions about Sleep and Dreams — 216
CRITICAL THINKING APPLICATION • Is Alcoholism a Disease? The Power of Definitions — 220

Chapter 6 Learning — 224

PERSONAL APPLICATION • Achieving Self-Control Through Behaviour Modification — 258
CRITICAL THINKING APPLICATION • Manipulating Emotions: Pavlov and Persuasion — 262

Chapter 7 Human Memory — 266

PERSONAL APPLICATION • Improving Everyday Memory — 301
CRITICAL THINKING APPLICATION • Understanding the Fallibility of Eyewitness Accounts — 305

Chapter 8 Language and Thought — 310

PERSONAL APPLICATION • Understanding Pitfalls in Reasoning about Decisions — 340
CRITICAL THINKING APPLICATION • Shaping Thought with Language: "Only a Naïve Moron Would Believe That" — 344

Chapter 9 Intelligence and Psychological Testing — 348

PERSONAL APPLICATION • Understanding Creativity — 383
CRITICAL THINKING APPLICATION • The Intelligence Debate, Appeals to Ignorance, and Reification — 386

Chapter 10 Motivation and Emotion — 390

PERSONAL APPLICATION • Exploring the Ingredients of Happiness — 428
CRITICAL THINKING APPLICATION • Analyzing Arguments: Making Sense out of Controversy — 432

Chapter 11 Human Development across the Life Span — 436

PERSONAL APPLICATION • Understanding Gender Differences — 481
CRITICAL THINKING APPLICATION • Are Fathers Essential to Children's Well-Being? — 486

Chapter 12 Personality: Theory, Research, and Assessment — 490

PERSONAL APPLICATION • Understanding Personality Assessment — 525
CRITICAL THINKING APPLICATION • Hindsight in Everyday Analyses of Personality — 530

Chapter 13 Stress, Coping, and Health — 534

PERSONAL APPLICATION • Improving Coping and Stress Management — 566
CRITICAL THINKING APPLICATION • Thinking Rationally About Health Statistics and Decisions — 570

Chapter 14 Psychological Disorders — 574

PERSONAL APPLICATION • Understanding Eating Disorders — 614
CRITICAL THINKING APPLICATION • Working with Probabilities in Thinking about Mental Illness — 617

Chapter 15 Treatment of Psychological Disorders — 622

PERSONAL APPLICATION • Looking for a Therapist — 654
CRITICAL THINKING APPLICATION • From Crisis to Wellness—But Was It the Therapy? — 658

Chapter 16 Social Behaviour — 662

PERSONAL APPLICATION • Understanding Prejudice — 698
CRITICAL THINKING APPLICATION • Whom Can You Trust? Analyzing Credibility and Social Influence Tactics — 702

Appendix A: Answers to Concept Checks and Practice Tests — A-1

Appendix B: Statistical Methods — A-9

Appendix C: Industrial/Organizational Psychology — A-17

Appendix D: Evaluating the Quality of Web-Based Resources — A-29

Glossary — G-1

References — R-1

Name Index — I-1

Subject Index — I-14

Contents

To the Instructor   xvii

Acknowledgments   xxxi

To the Student   xxxiii

What Should Introductory Psychology
Students Know About the Internet?   xxxvii

Chapter 1
The Evolution of Psychology   1

**From Speculation to Science: How
Psychology Developed**   3
  A New Science Is Born: The Contributions of Wundt and Hall 3
  The Battle of the "Schools" Begins: Structuralism versus
    Functionalism   4
  Watson Alters Psychology's Course as Behaviourism
    Makes Its Debut   6
  Freud Brings the Unconscious into the Picture   8
  Skinner Questions Free Will as Behaviourism Flourishes   9
  The Humanists Revolt   11
  Psychology in Canada   12
  Psychology Comes of Age as a Profession   14
  Featured Study • Bullying in Canadian Schoolyards   15
  Psychology Returns to Its Roots: Renewed Interest in
    Cognition and Physiology   16
  Psychology Broadens Its Horizons: Increased Interest
    in Cultural Diversity   18
  Psychology Adapts: The Emergence of Evolutionary
    Psychology   19

Psychology Today: Vigorous and Diversified   21
  Research Areas in Psychology   24
  Professional Specialties in Psychology   24

Putting It in Perspective: Seven Key Themes   26
  Themes Related to Psychology as a Field of Study   26
  Themes Related to Psychology's Subject Matter   28

***Personal Application •* Improving Academic
Performance**   31
  Developing Sound Study Habits   31
  Improving Your Reading   33
  Getting More out of Lectures   33
  Improving Test-Taking Strategies   34

***Critical Thinking Application •* Developing Critical
Thinking Skills: An Introduction**   36
  The Skills of Critical Thinking   36
  The Attitude of a Critical Thinker   36
  The Need to Teach Critical Thinking   36
  An Example   36

Recap   38

Practice Test   39

Chapter 2
The Research Enterprise in Psychology   40

The Scientific Approach to Behaviour   42
  Goals of the Scientific Enterprise   42
  Steps in a Scientific Investigation   44
  Featured Study • Can Fear Increase Sexual Attraction?   46
  Advantages of the Scientific Approach   47

Looking for Causes: Experimental Research   48
  Independent and Dependent Variables   48
  Experimental and Control Groups   48
  Extraneous Variables   49
  Variations in Designing Experiments   50
  Advantages and Disadvantages of Experimental Research   51

Looking for Links: Descriptive/Correlational Research   52
  Naturalistic Observation   52
  Case Studies   52
  Surveys   54
  Advantages and Disadvantages of Descriptive/
    Correlational Research   55

Looking for Conclusions: Statistics and Research   57
  Descriptive Statistics   57
  Inferential Statistics   60

Looking for Flaws: Evaluating Research   62
  Sampling Bias   62
  Placebo Effects   63
  Distortions in Self-Report Data   64
  Experimenter Bias   64

Looking at Ethics: Do the Ends Justify the Means?   65
  Ethical Guidelines for Research in Psychology in Canada   66

Putting It in Perspective   67

***Personal Application •* Finding and Reading
Journal Articles**   69
  The Nature of Technical Journals   69
  Finding Journal Articles   69
  Reading Journal Articles   70

***Critical Thinking Application •* The Perils of
Anecdotal Evidence: "I Have a Friend Who ..."**   72

Recap   74

Practice Test   75

Chapter 3
The Biological Bases of Behaviour   76

Communication in the Nervous System   78
  Nervous Tissue: The Basic Hardware   78
  The Neural Impulse: Using Energy to Send Information   79
  The Synapse: Where Neurons Meet   80
  Neurotransmitters and Behaviour   84

Organization of the Nervous System   **87**
   The Peripheral Nervous System   87
   The Central Nervous System   88

Looking Inside the Brain: Research Methods   **90**
   Electrical Recordings   90
   Lesioning   91
   Electrical Stimulation of the Brain   91
   Brain-Imaging Procedures   92
   Featured Study • Searching for the Self in the Brain   94

The Brain and Behaviour   **95**
   The Hindbrain   95
   The Midbrain   95
   The Forebrain   97
   The Plasticity of the Brain   101

Right Brain/Left Brain: Cerebral Laterality   **102**
   Bisecting the Brain: Split-Brain Research   102
   Hemispheric Specialization in the Intact Brain   104

The Endocrine System: Another Way to Communicate   **105**

Heredity and Behaviour: Is It All in the Genes?   **107**
   Basic Principles of Genetics   107
   Investigating Hereditary Influence: Research Methods   109
   The Interplay of Heredity and Environment   112

The Evolutionary Bases of Behaviour   **113**
   Darwin's Insights   113
   Subsequent Refinements to Evolutionary Theory   114
   Behaviours as Adaptive Traits   115

Putting It in Perspective   **116**

***Personal Application* • Evaluating the
Concept of "Two Minds in One"**   **117**
   Cerebral Specialization and Cognitive Processes   117
   Complexities and Qualifications   118

***Critical Thinking Application* • Building Better
Brains: The Perils of Extrapolation**   **120**
   The Key Findings on Neural Development   120
   The Risks of Overextrapolation   120

Recap   **122**

Practice Test   **123**

Chapter 4
Sensation and Perception   **124**

Psychophysics: Basic Concepts and Issues   **127**
   Thresholds: Looking for Limits   127
   Weighing the Differences: The JND   128
   Psychophysical Scaling   128
   Signal-Detection Theory   128
   Perception without Awareness   129
   Sensory Adaptation   130

Our Sense of Sight: The Visual System   **131**
   The Stimulus: Light   131
   The Eye: A Living Optical Instrument   132
   The Retina: The Brain's Envoy in the Eye   133
   Vision and the Brain   136
   Viewing the World in Colour   140
   Perceiving Forms, Patterns, and Objects   142
   Perceiving Depth or Distance   148
   Perceptual Constancies in Vision   149
   The Power of Misleading Cues: Optical Illusions   150
   Vision for Perception and Vision for Action   153

Our Sense of Hearing: The Auditory System   **155**
   The Stimulus: Sound   155
   Human Hearing Capacities   156
   Sensory Processing in the Ear   156
   Auditory Perception: Theories of Hearing   157
   Auditory Localization: Perceiving Sources of Sound   159
   Music and Its Effects   159
   Featured Study • Decoding Speech Prosody:
     Do Music Lessons Help?   161

Our Chemical Senses: Taste and Smell   **162**
   Taste: The Gustatory System   162
   Smell: The Olfactory System   164

Our Sense of Touch: Sensory Systems in the Skin   **165**
   Feeling Pressure   165
   Feeling Pain   165

Our Other Senses   **167**
   The Kinesthetic System   167
   The Vestibular System   167

Putting It in Perspective   **168**

***Personal Application* • Appreciating Art and Illusion** **169**

***Critical Thinking Application* • Recognizing
Contrast Effects: It's All Relative**   **175**

Recap   **177**

Practice Test   **179**

Chapter 5
Variations in Consciousness   **180**

The Nature of Consciousness   **182**
   Variations in Levels of Awareness   182
   Consciousness and Brain Activity   182

Biological Rhythms and Sleep   **183**
   The Role of Circadian Rhythms   183
   Ignoring Circadian Rhythms   184
   Melatonin and Circadian Rhythms   185

The Sleep and Waking Cycle   **186**
   Cycling through the Stages of Sleep   186
   Age Trends in Sleep   188
   Culture and Sleep   189
   The Neural Bases of Sleep   190
   Doing without: Sleep Deprivation   191
   Featured Study • Gauging the Impact of Sleep
     Deprivation in College Students   192
   Problems in the Night: Sleep Disorders   193

The World of Dreams   **197**
   The Contents of Dreams   197
   Links between Dreams and Waking Life   198
   Culture and Dreams   199
   Theories of Dreaming   199

Hypnosis: Altered Consciousness or Role Playing?   **201**
   Hypnotic Induction and Susceptibility   201
   Hypnotic Phenomena   202
   Theories of Hypnosis   203

Meditation: Pure Consciousness or Relaxation?   **204**
   Physiological Correlates   205
   Long-Term Benefits   205

Altering Consciousness with Drugs   **206**
   Principal Abused Drugs and Their Effects   206

Factors Influencing Drug Effects   209
Mechanisms of Drug Action   210
Drug Dependence   212
Drugs and Health   212

Putting It in Perspective   **214**

Personal Application • **Addressing Practical Questions about Sleep and Dreams**   **216**
Common Questions about Sleep   216
Common Questions about Dreams   218

Critical Thinking Application • **Is Alcoholism a Disease? The Power of Definitions**   **220**
The Power to Make Definitions   220
Definitions, Labels, and Circular Reasoning   221

Recap   **222**

Practice Test   **223**

Chapter 6
Learning   224

Classical Conditioning   **227**
Pavlov's Demonstration: "Psychic Reflexes"   227
Terminology and Procedures   228
Classical Conditioning in Everyday Life   229
Featured Study • Sex and the Single Quail   232
Basic Processes in Classical Conditioning   233

Operant Conditioning   **236**
Thorndike's Law of Effect   237
Skinner's Demonstration: It's All a Matter of Consequences   237
Terminology and Procedures   237
Basic Processes in Operant Conditioning   238
Reinforcement: Consequences That Strengthen Responses   242
Intermittent Reinforcement: Effects of Basic Schedules   242
Positive Reinforcement versus Negative Reinforcement   244
Negative Reinforcement and Avoidance Behaviour   245
Punishment: Consequences That Weaken Responses   246

Changing Directions in the Study of Conditioning   **249**
Recognizing Biological Constraints on Conditioning   249
Recognizing Cognitive Processes in Conditioning   251

Observational Learning   **253**
Basic Processes   253
Acquisition versus Performance   254
Applications   254

Putting It in Perspective   **255**

Personal Application • **Achieving Self-Control Through Behaviour Modification**   **258**
Specifying Your Target Behaviour   258
Gathering Baseline Data   258
Designing Your Program   259
Executing and Evaluating Your Program   261
Ending Your Program   261

Critical Thinking Application • **Manipulating Emotions: Pavlov and Persuasion**   **262**
Classical Conditioning in Advertising   262
Classical Conditioning in Business Negotiations   262
Classical Conditioning in the World of Politics   263
Becoming More Aware of Classical Conditioning Processes   263

Recap   **264**

Practice Test   **265**

Chapter 7
Human Memory   266

Encoding: Getting Information into Memory   **269**
The Role of Attention   269
Levels of Processing   270
Enriching Encoding   271

Storage: Maintaining Information in Memory   **273**
Sensory Memory   273
Short-Term Memory   275
Long-Term Memory   276
Featured Study • How Accurate Are Flashbulb Memories?   277
Are Short-Term Memory and Long-Term Memory Really Separate?   278
How Is Knowledge Represented and Organized in Memory?   279

Retrieval: Getting Information Out of Memory   **282**
Using Cues to Aid Retrieval   282
Reinstating the Context of an Event   283
Reconstructing Memories and the Misinformation Effect   284
Source Monitoring and Reality Monitoring   285

Forgetting: When Memory Lapses   **286**
How Quickly We Forget: Ebbinghaus's Forgetting Curve   286
Measures of Forgetting   286
Why We Forget   287
The Repressed Memories Controversy   290

In Search of the Memory Trace: The Physiology of Memory   **294**
The Biochemistry of Memory   294
The Neural Circuitry of Memory   294
The Anatomy of Memory   295

Are There Multiple Memory Systems?   **296**
Implicit versus Explicit Memory   296
Declarative versus Procedural Memory   297
Semantic versus Episodic Memory   298
Prospective versus Retrospective Memory   298

Putting It in Perspective   **300**

Personal Application • **Improving Everyday Memory**   **301**
Engage in Adequate Rehearsal   301
Schedule Distributed Practice and Minimize Interference   301
Emphasize Deep Processing and Organize Information   302
Enrich Encoding with Verbal Mnemonics   302
Enrich Encoding with Visual Mnemonics   303

Critical Thinking Application • **Understanding the Fallibility of Eyewitness Accounts**   **305**
The Contribution of Hindsight Bias   306
The Contribution of Overconfidence   306
Strategies to Reduce Overconfidence   306

Recap   **307**

Practice Test   **309**

Chapter 8
Language and Thought   310

Language: Turning Thoughts into Words   **312**
What Is Language?   312
The Structure of Language   313
Milestones in Language Development   314
Featured Study • Babbling in the Manual Mode   315
Learning More than One Language: Bilingualism   318

Can Animals Develop Language? 321
Language in Evolutionary Context 322
Theories of Language Acquisition 323
Culture, Language, and Thought 325

Problem Solving: In Search of Solutions 326
Types of Problems 326
Barriers to Effective Problem Solving 326
Approaches to Problem Solving 329
Culture, Cognitive Style, and Problem Solving 332

Decision Making: Choices and Chances 335
Making Choices: Selecting an Alternative 335
Taking Chances: Factors Weighed in Risky Decisions 336
Heuristics in Judging Probabilities 337
The Tendency to Ignore Base Rates 337
The Conjunction Fallacy 338
Evolutionary Analyses of Flaws in Human Decision Making 338

Putting It in Perspective 339

Personal Application • **Understanding Pitfalls in Reasoning about Decisions** 340
The Gambler's Fallacy 340
The Law of Small Numbers 340
Overestimating the Improbable 341
Confirmation Bias and Belief Perseverance 341
The Overconfidence Effect 342
The Effects of Framing 342

Critical Thinking Application • **Shaping Thought with Language: "Only a Naïve Moron Would Believe That"** 344
Semantic Slanting 344
Name-Calling 345

Recap 346

Practice Test 347

Chapter 9
Intelligence and Psychological Testing 348

Key Concepts in Psychological Testing 351
Principal Types of Tests 351
Standardization and Norms 351
Reliability 353
Validity 353

The Evolution of Intelligence Testing 356
Galton's Studies of Hereditary Genius 356
Binet's Breakthrough 356
Terman and the Stanford-Binet 356
Wechsler's Innovations 357
Intelligence Testing Today 357

Basic Questions about Intelligence Testing 358
What Kinds of Questions Are on Intelligence Tests? 358
What Do Modern IQ Scores Mean? 358
Do Intelligence Tests Measure Potential or Knowledge? 360
Do Intelligence Tests Have Adequate Reliability? 360
Do Intelligence Tests Have Adequate Validity? 361
Do Intelligence Tests Predict Vocational Success? 362
Are IQ Tests Widely Used in Other Cultures? 362

Extremes of Intelligence 363
Mental Retardation 363
Giftedness 364

Heredity and Environment as Determinants of Intelligence 367
Evidence for Hereditary Influence 367
Evidence for Environmental Influence 369
The Interaction of Heredity and Environment 370
Cultural Differences in IQ Scores 371
Featured Study • Racial Stereotypes and Test Performance 374

New Directions in the Assessment and Study of Intelligence 376
Increasing Emphasis on Specific Abilities 376
Exploring Biological Indexes of Intelligence 377
Investigating Cognitive Processes in Intelligent Behaviour 379
Expanding the Concept of Intelligence 380
Measuring Emotional Intelligence 381

Putting It in Perspective 382

Personal Application • **Understanding Creativity** 383
The Nature of Creativity 383
Measuring Creativity 383
Correlates of Creativity 384

Critical Thinking Application • **The Intelligence Debate, Appeals to Ignorance, and Reification** 386
Appeal to Ignorance 386
Reification 387

Recap 388

Practice Test 389

Chapter 10
Motivation and Emotion 390

Motivational Theories and Concepts 392
Drive Theories 392
Incentive Theories 393
Evolutionary Theories 394
The Range and Diversity of Human Motives 394

The Motivation of Hunger and Eating 395
Biological Factors in the Regulation of Hunger 395
Environmental Factors in the Regulation of Hunger 397
Eating and Weight: The Roots of Obesity 399

Sexual Motivation and Behaviour 403
Determinants of Sexual Desire 403
Evolutionary Analyses of Human Sexual Behaviour 405
Featured Study • Evolution, Culture, and Mating Priorities 407
The Mystery of Sexual Orientation 409
The Human Sexual Response 413

Affiliation: In Search of Belongingness 414

Achievement: In Search of Excellence 415
Individual Differences in the Need for Achievement 416
Situational Determinants of Achievement Behaviour 416

The Elements of Emotional Experience 418
The Cognitive Component: Subjective Feelings 418
The Physiological Component: Diffuse and Multifaceted 419
The Behavioural Component: Nonverbal Expressiveness 422
Culture and the Elements of Emotion 422

Theories of Emotion 424
James–Lange Theory 424
Cannon–Bard Theory 425
Schachter's Two-Factor Theory 425
Evolutionary Theories of Emotion 426

Putting It in Perspective | 427

Personal Application • Exploring the
Ingredients of Happiness | 428
   How Happy Are People? 428
   Factors That Do Not Predict Happiness 428
   Moderately Good Predictors of Happiness 429
   Strong Predictors of Happiness 430
   Conclusions about Subjective Well-Being 431

Critical Thinking Application • Analyzing
Arguments: Making Sense out of Controversy | 432
   The Anatomy of an Argument 432
   Common Fallacies 433
   Evaluating the Strength of Arguments 433

Recap | 434

Practice Test | 435

Chapter 11
Human Development across the Life Span | 436

Progress before Birth: Prenatal Development | 439
   The Course of Prenatal Development 439
   Environmental Factors and Prenatal Development 440

The Wondrous Years of Childhood | 444
   Exploring the World: Motor Development 444
   Easy and Difficult Babies: Differences in Temperament 446
   Early Emotional Development: Attachment 448
   Becoming Unique: Personality Development 451
   The Growth of Thought: Cognitive Development 453
   The Development of Moral Reasoning 460

The Transition of Adolescence | 462
   Puberty and the Growth Spurt 463
   Time of Turmoil? 464
   Featured Study • Youth Suicide in Canada's First Nations 465
   The Search for Identity 467

The Expanse of Adulthood | 469
   Personality Development 469
   Transitions in Family Life 470
   Aging and Physical Changes 473
   Aging and Cognitive Changes 474

Putting It in Perspective | 480

Personal Application • Understanding
Gender Differences | 481
   How Do the Sexes Differ in Behaviour? 481
   Biological Origins of Gender Differences 482
   Environmental Origins of Gender Differences 484
   Conclusion 485

Critical Thinking Application • Are Fathers
Essential to Children's Well-Being? | 486
   The Basic Argument 486
   Evaluating the Argument 486

Recap | 488

Practice Test | 489

Chapter 12
Personality: Theory, Research, and Assessment | 490

The Nature of Personality | 492
   Defining Personality: Consistency and Distinctiveness 492

Personality Traits: Dispositions and Dimensions 492
The Five-Factor Model of Personality Traits 493

Psychodynamic Perspectives | 494
   Freud's Psychoanalytic Theory 494
   Jung's Analytical Psychology 500
   Adler's Individual Psychology 501
   Evaluating Psychodynamic Perspectives 503

Behavioural Perspectives | 504
   Skinner's Ideas Applied to Personality 504
   Bandura's Social Cognitive Theory 505
   Mischel and the Person–Situation Controversy 507
   Evaluating Behavioural Perspectives 507

Humanistic Perspectives | 508
   Rogers's Person-Centred Theory 508
   Featured Study • The Pope Is Watching You:
     Effects on Self-Concept 510
   Maslow's Theory of Self-Actualization 511
   Evaluating Humanistic Perspectives 512

Biological Perspectives | 514
   Eysenck's Theory 514
   Behavioural Genetics and Personality 515
   The Evolutionary Approach to Personality 516
   Evaluating Biological Perspectives 517

Contemporary Empirical Approaches to Personality | 520
   Sensation Seeking: Life in the Fast Lane 520
   Self-Monitoring: Life as Theatre 520

Culture and Personality | 521

Putting It in Perspective | 523

Personal Application • Understanding
Personality Assessment | 525
   The Uses of Personality Scales 525
   Self-Report Inventories 525
   Projective Tests 528

Critical Thinking Application • Hindsight in
Everyday Analyses of Personality | 530
   The Prevalence of Hindsight Bias 530
   Hindsight and Personality 530
   Other Implications of "20/20 Hindsight" 531

Recap | 532

Practice Test | 533

Chapter 13
Stress, Coping, and Health | 534

The Nature of Stress | 536
   Stress as an Everyday Event 537
   Appraisal: Stress Lies in the Eye of the Beholder 537

Major Types of Stress | 537
   Frustration 537
   Conflict 538
   Change 539
   Pressure 540

Responding to Stress | 541
   Emotional Responses 541
   Physiological Responses 543
   Behavioural Responses 544

The Effects of Stress on Psychological Functioning | 549
   Impaired Task Performance 549

Burnout 549
Post-Traumatic Stress Disorders 550
Psychological Problems and Disorders 550
Positive Effects 551

The Effects of Stress on Physical Health **552**
Type A Personality, Hostility, and Heart Disease 552
Emotional Reactions, Depression, and Heart Disease 553
Stress, Other Diseases, and Immune Functioning 554
Featured Study • Connecting Stress to the Common Cold 555
Sizing Up the Link between Stress and Illness 556

Factors Moderating the Impact of Stress **557**
Social Support 557
Optimism and Conscientiousness 558

Health-Impairing Behaviour **558**
Smoking 558
Poor Nutritional Habits 559
Lack of Exercise 560
Alcohol and Drug Use 560
Behaviour and AIDS 560
How Does Health-Impairing Behaviour Develop? 562

Reactions to Illness **563**
Deciding to Seek Treatment 563
Communicating with Health Providers 563
Adhering to Medical Advice 564

Putting It in Perspective **565**

Personal Application • Improving Coping
and Stress Management **566**
Reappraisal: Ellis's Rational Thinking 566
Using Humour as a Stress Reducer 567
Releasing Pent-Up Emotions 567
Managing Hostility and Forgiving Others 567
Learning to Relax 568
Minimizing Physiological Vulnerability 568

Critical Thinking Application • Thinking
Rationally about Health Statistics and Decisions **570**
Evaluating Statistics on Health Risks 570
Thinking Systematically about Health Decisions 570

Recap **572**

Practice Test **573**

Chapter 14
Psychological Disorders **574**

**Abnormal Behaviour: Myths, Realities,
and Controversies** **576**
The Medical Model Applied to Abnormal Behaviour 576
Criteria of Abnormal Behaviour 577
Stereotypes of Psychological Disorders 578
Psychodiagnosis: The Classification of Disorders 579
The Prevalence of Psychological Disorders 579

Anxiety Disorders **582**
Generalized Anxiety Disorder 582
Phobic Disorder 582
Panic Disorder and Agoraphobia 582
Obsessive-Compulsive Disorder 583
Post-Traumatic Stress Disorder (PTSD) 584
Etiology of Anxiety Disorders 584

Somatoform Disorders **586**
Somatization Disorder 587

Conversion Disorder 587
Hypochondriasis 587
Etiology of Somatoform Disorders 588

Dissociative Disorders **589**
Dissociative Amnesia and Fugue 589
Dissociative Identity Disorder 589
Etiology of Dissociative Disorders 589

Mood Disorders **590**
Major Depressive Disorder 591
Bipolar Disorder 592
Etiology of Mood Disorders 593
Featured Study • Does Negative Thinking
Cause Depression? 595

Schizophrenic Disorders **598**
General Symptoms 598
Subtypes, Course, and Outcome 599
Etiology of Schizophrenia 601

Personality Disorders **605**
Diagnostic Problems 606
Antisocial Personality Disorder 606

Psychological Disorders and the Law **610**
Insanity 610

Culture and Pathology **611**
Are Equivalent Disorders Found around the World? 611
Are Symptom Patterns Culturally Invariant? 612

Putting It in Perspective **612**
Personal Application • Understanding
Eating Disorders **614**
Anorexia Nervosa 614
Bulimia Nervosa 614
History, Prevalence, and Course 615
Etiology of Eating Disorders 616

Critical Thinking Application • Working with
Probabilities in Thinking about Mental Illness **617**

Recap **620**

Practice Test **621**

Chapter 15
Treatment of Psychological Disorders **622**

The Elements of the Treatment Process **624**
Treatments: How Many Types Are There? 624
Clients: Who Seeks Therapy? 625
Therapists: Who Provides Professional Treatment? 625

Insight Therapies **627**
Psychoanalysis 627
Client-Centred Therapy 629
Cognitive Therapy 631
Group Therapy 632
Evaluating Insight Therapies 633

Behaviour Therapies **635**
Systematic Desensitization 636
Aversion Therapy 636
Social Skills Training 637
Evaluating Behaviour Therapies 638

Biomedical Therapies **638**
Treatment with Drugs 639
Electroconvulsive Therapy (ECT) 642

Current Trends and Issues in Treatment   **646**
Blending Approaches to Treatment   646
Featured Study • Combining Insight Therapy
and Medication   647
Increasing Multicultural Sensitivity in Treatment   648

Institutional Treatment in Transition   **649**
Disenchantment with Mental Hospitals   650
Deinstitutionalization   650
Mental Illness, the Revolving Door, and Homelessness   651

Putting It in Perspective   **652**

Personal Application • **Looking for a Therapist**   **654**
Where Do You Find Therapeutic Services?   654
Is the Therapist's Profession or Sex Important?   654
Is Treatment Always Expensive?   655
Is the Therapist's Theoretical Approach Important?   656
What Should You Look for in a Prospective Therapist?   656
What If There Isn't Any Progress?   657
What Is Therapy Like?   657

Critical Thinking Application • **From Crisis
to Wellness—But Was It the Therapy?**   **658**

Recap   **660**

Practice Test   **661**

Chapter 16
Social Behaviour   **662**

Person Perception: Forming Impressions of Others   **664**
Effects of Physical Appearance   665
Cognitive Schemas   666
Stereotypes   666
Subjectivity in Person Perception   667
An Evolutionary Perspective on Bias in Person
Perception   668

Attribution Processes: Explaining Behaviour   **669**
Internal versus External Attributions   669
Attributions for Success and Failure   670
Bias in Attribution   670
Culture and Attributional Tendencies   672

Close Relationships: Liking and Loving   **674**
Key Factors in Attraction   674
Perspectives on the Mystery of Love   676
Culture and Close Relationships   678
An Evolutionary Perspective on Attraction   679

Attitudes: Making Social Judgments   **679**
Components and Dimensions of Attitudes   679
Attitudes and Behaviour   680
Trying to Change Attitudes: Factors in Persuasion   681
Theories of Attitude Formation and Change   684

Conformity and Obedience: Yielding to Others   **687**
Conformity   688
Obedience   689
Featured Study • "I Was Just Following Orders"   689
Cultural Variations in Conformity and Obedience   691

Behaviour in Groups: Joining with Others   **692**
Behaviour Alone and in Groups: The Case of the
Bystander Effect   693
Group Productivity and Social Loafing   693
Decision Making in Groups   694

Putting It in Perspective   **697**

Personal Application • **Understanding Prejudice**   **698**
Stereotyping and Subjectivity in Person Perception   698
Biases in Attribution   699
Forming and Preserving Prejudicial Attitudes   700
Dividing the World into Ingroups and Outgroups   700

Critical Thinking Application • **Whom Can You Trust?**
Analyzing Credibility and Social Influence Tactics   **702**
Evaluating Credibility   702
Recognizing Social Influence Strategies   703

Recap   **704**

Practice Test   **705**

**Appendix A: Answers to Concept
Checks and Practice Tests**   **A-1**

Appendix B: Statistical Methods   **A-9**

**Appendix C: Industrial/
Organizational Psychology**   **A-17**

**Appendix D: Evaluating the
Quality of Web-Based Resources**   **A-29**

Glossary   **G-1**

References   **R-1**

Name Index   **I-1**

Subject Index   **I-14**

To the Instructor

Welcome to the first Canadian edition of *Psychology: Themes and Variations*. In this edition we decided to build upon the considerable strengths of the U.S. text by increasing its relevance to a Canadian university audience. We have added over 300 new references to Canadian research and the Canadian context, supplied relevant Canadian statistics, and highlighted issues of particular concern to Canadians, such as bilingualism, cultural diversity, First Nations peoples' issues, and the contribution of women to Canadian psychology and Canadian life.

We have also added new Featured Studies executed by prominent Canadian researchers, and have supplied introductory vignettes for each chapter to provide an immediate and compelling Canadian context for the chapter's material. Topics of these vignettes include the group of women who succeeded in having women in Canada officially declared persons, eccentric Canadian geniuses who display various types of high intelligence, high-profile cases of bullying and spousal abuse, and the use of CIA-funded brainwashing techniques in Canadian psychiatric institutions.

If we had to sum up in a single sentence what we hope will distinguish this text, that sentence would be this: We set out to create a *paradox* instead of a *compromise*. Let's elaborate. An introductory psychology text must satisfy two disparate audiences: professors and students. Because of the tension between the divergent needs and preferences of these audiences, textbook authors usually indicate that they have attempted to strike a compromise between being theoretical versus practical, comprehensive versus comprehensible, research oriented versus applied, rigorous versus accessible, and so forth. However, we believe that many of these dichotomies are false. As Kurt Lewin once remarked, "What could be more practical than a good theory?" Similarly, is rigorous really the opposite of accessible? Not in our dictionary. We think that many of the antagonistic goals that we strive for in our textbooks only *seem* incompatible and that we may not need to make compromises as often as we assume.

In our estimation, a good introductory textbook is a paradox in that it integrates characteristics and goals that appear contradictory. With this in mind, we have endeavoured to write a text that is paradoxical in three ways. First, in surveying psychology's broad range of content, we have tried to show that its interests are characterized by both diversity *and* unity. Second, we have emphasized both research

and application and how they work in harmony. Finally, we have aspired to write a compelling book that is challenging to think about *and* easy to learn from. Let's take a closer look at these goals.

Goals

1. *To show both the unity and the diversity of psychology's subject matter.* Students entering an introductory psychology course are often unaware of the immense diversity of subjects studied by psychologists. We find this diversity to be part of psychology's charm, and throughout the book we highlight the enormous range of questions and issues addressed by psychology. Of course, psychology's diversity proves disconcerting for some students who see little continuity between such disparate areas of research as physiology, motivation, cognition, and abnormal behaviour. Indeed, in this era of specialization, even some psychologists express concern about the fragmentation of the field. Since we believe that the subfields of psychology overlap considerably, we emphasize their common core, portraying psychology as an integrated whole.

2. *To illuminate the process of research and its intimate link to application.* For us, a research-oriented book is not one that bulges with summaries of many studies but one that enhances students' appreciation of the logic and excitement of empirical inquiry. We want students to appreciate the strengths of the empirical approach and to see scientific psychology as a creative effort to solve intriguing behavioural puzzles. For this reason, the text emphasizes not only *what* psychologists know (and don't know) but *how* they attempt to find out. The book examines in some detail and encourages students to adopt the skeptical attitude of a scientist and to think critically about claims regarding behaviour. Throughout the book, we also share the practical implications of the work of psychologists, satisfying students' desire for concrete, personally useful information.

3. *To make the text challenging to think about and easy to learn from.* Perhaps most of all, we have sought to create a *book of ideas* rather than a compendium of studies. We consistently emphasize concepts and theories over facts, and focus on major issues and tough questions that cut across the subfields of psychology (e.g., the extent to which behaviour is governed by nature, nurture, and their interaction), as opposed to parochial debates (such as the merits of averaging versus adding in impression formation).

Challenging students to think also means urging them to confront the complexity and ambiguity of psychological knowledge. Hence, the text doesn't skirt around grey areas, unresolved questions, and theoretical controversies. Instead, it encourages readers to contemplate open-ended questions, to examine their assumptions about behaviour, and to apply psychological concepts to their own lives. Our goal is not simply to describe psychology but to stimulate students' intellectual growth.

Admittedly, these goals are ambitious. If you're skeptical, you have every right to be. Let us explain how we have tried to realize these objectives.

Special Features

A variety of unusual features each contributes in its own way to the book's paradoxical nature. These special elements include unifying themes, Featured Studies, Personal Application sections, Critical Thinking Application sections, a didactic illustration program, Web Links and other Internet-related features, an integrated running glossary, Concept Checks, Preview Questions, interim Reviews of Key Points, and Practice Tests.

Unifying Themes

Chapter 1 introduces seven key ideas that serve as unifying themes throughout the text. The themes serve several purposes. First, they provide threads of continuity across chapters that help students see the connections among various areas of research in psychology. Second, as the themes evolve over the course of the book, they provide a forum for a relatively sophisticated discussion of enduring issues in psychology, thus helping to make this a "book of ideas." Third, the themes focus a spotlight on a number of basic insights about psychology and its subject matter that should leave lasting impressions on your students.

In selecting the themes, the question we asked ourselves (and other professors) was "What do we really want students to remember five years from now?" The resulting themes are grouped into two sets.

THEMES RELATED TO PSYCHOLOGY AS A FIELD OF STUDY

Theme 1: Psychology is empirical. This theme is used to enhance the student's appreciation of psychology's scientific nature and to demonstrate the advantages of empiricism over uncritical common sense and speculation. We also use this theme to encourage the reader to adopt a scientist's skeptical attitude and to engage in more critical thinking about information of all kinds.

Theme 2: Psychology is theoretically diverse. Students are often confused by psychology's theoretical pluralism and view it as a weakness. We don't downplay or apologize for the field's theoretical diversity, because we honestly believe that it is one of psychology's greatest strengths. Throughout the book, we provide concrete examples of how clashing theories have stimulated productive research, how converging on a question from several perspectives can yield increased understanding, and how competing theories are sometimes reconciled in the end.

Theme 3: Psychology evolves in a sociohistorical context. This theme emphasizes that psychology is embedded in the ebb and flow of everyday life. The text shows how the spirit of the times has often shaped psychology's evolution and how progress in psychology leaves its mark on our society.

THEMES RELATED TO PSYCHOLOGY'S SUBJECT MATTER

Theme 4: Behaviour is determined by multiple causes. Throughout the book, we emphasize, and repeatedly illustrate, that behavioural processes are complex and that multifactorial causation is the rule. This theme is used to discourage simplistic, single-cause thinking and to encourage more critical reasoning.

Theme 5: Behaviour is shaped by cultural heritage. This theme is intended to enhance students' appreciation of how cultural factors moderate psychological processes and how the viewpoint of one's own culture can distort one's interpretation of the behaviour of people from other cultures. The discussions that elaborate on this theme do not simply celebrate diversity. They strike a careful balance—that accurately reflects the research in this area—highlighting both cultural variations *and* similarities in behaviour.

Theme 6: Heredity and environment jointly influence behaviour. Repeatedly discussing this theme permits us to air out the nature versus nurture issue in all its complexity. Over a series of chapters, students gradually learn how biology shapes behaviour, how experience shapes behaviour, and how scientists estimate the relative importance of each. Along the way, students will gain an in-depth appreciation of what it means when we say that heredity and environment interact.

Theme 7: People's experience of the world is highly subjective. All of us tend to forget the extent to which people view the world through their own personal lenses. This theme is used to explain the principles that underlie the subjectivity of human experience, to clarify its implications, and to repeatedly remind the readers that their view of the world is not the only legitimate view.

After introducing all seven themes in Chapter 1, we discuss different sets of themes in each chapter, as they are relevant to the subject matter. The connections between a chapter's content and the unifying themes are highlighted in a standard section near the end of the chapter, in which we reflect on the "lessons to be learned" from the chapter. The discussions of the unifying themes are largely confined to these sections, titled "Putting It in Perspective." We have not tried to make every chapter illustrate a certain number of themes. Rather, the themes were allowed to emerge naturally, and we found that two to five surfaced in any given chapter. The chart below shows which themes are highlighted in each chapter. Numbered, colour-coded icons at the beginning of each "Putting It in Perspective" section indicate the specific themes featured in each chapter.

Unifying Themes Highlighted in Each Chapter

Chapter	Theme						
	1 Empiricism	2 Theoretical Diversity	3 Sociohistorical Context	4 Multifactorial Causation	5 Cultural Heritage	6 Heredity and Environment	7 Subjectivity of Experience
1. The Evolution of Psychology	1	2	3	4	5	6	7
2. The Research Enterprise in Psychology	1						7
3. The Biological Bases of Behaviour	1			4		6	
4. Sensation and Perception		2			5		7
5. Variations in Consciousness		2	3		5		7
6. Learning			3			6	
7. Human Memory		2		4			7
8. Language and Thought	1				5	6	7
9. Intelligence and Psychological Testing			3		5	6	
10. Motivation and Emotion		2	3	4	5	6	
11. Human Development across the Life Span		2	3	4	5	6	
12. Personality: Theory, Research, and Assessment		2	3				
13. Stress, Coping, and Health				4			7
14. Psychological Disorders			3	4	5	6	
15. Treatment of Psychological Disorders		2			5		
16. Social Behaviour	1				5		7

Featured Studies

Each chapter includes a Featured Study that provides a relatively detailed but clear summary of a particular piece of research. Each Featured Study is presented in the conventional purpose-method-results-discussion format seen in journal articles, followed by a comment in which we discuss why the study is featured (to illustrate a specific method, raise ethical issues, and so forth). By showing research methods in action, we hope to improve students' understanding of how research is done while also giving them a painless introduction to the basic format of journal articles. Additionally, the Featured Studies show how complicated research can be, so students can better appreciate why scientists may disagree about the meaning of a study. The Featured Studies are fully incorporated into the flow of discourse in the text and are *not* presented as optional boxes.

In selecting the Featured Studies, we assembled a mixture of classic and recent studies that illustrate a wide variety of methods. To make them enticing, we tilted our selections in favour of those that students find interesting. Thus, readers will encounter explorations of sleep deprivation among college students, the effects of fear on sexual attraction, gender differences in mating priorities, and the effects of stress on susceptibility to the common cold. This edition includes several new Featured Studies selected to reflect some of the groundbreaking work being conducted by Canadian psychologists, including studies of infant babbling and studies of suicide rates among First Nations youth.

Personal Applications

To reinforce the pragmatic implications of theory and research stressed throughout the text, each chapter closes with a Personal Application section that highlights the practical side of psychology. Each Personal Application devotes three to six *pages* of text (rather than the usual box) to a single issue that should be of special interest to many of your students. Although most of the Personal Application sections have a "how to" character, they continue to review studies and summarize data in much the same way as the main body of each chapter. Thus, they portray research and application not as incompatible polarities but as two sides of the same coin. Many of the Personal Applications—such as those on finding and reading journal articles, understanding art and illusion, and improving stress management—provide topical coverage unusual for an introductory text.

Critical Thinking Applications

A great deal of unusual coverage can also be found in the Critical Thinking Applications that follow the Personal Applications. Conceived by Diane Halpern (Claremont McKenna College), a leading authority on critical thinking, these applications are based on the assumption that critical thinking skills can be taught. They do not simply review research critically, as is typically the case in other introductory texts. Instead, they introduce and model a host of critical thinking *skills*, such as looking for contradictory evidence or alternative explanations; recognizing anecdotal evidence, circular reasoning, hindsight bias, reification, weak analogies, and false dichotomies; evaluating arguments systematically; and working with cumulative and conjunctive probabilities.

The specific skills discussed in the Critical Thinking Applications are listed in the accompanying table on page xxi, where they are organized into five categories using a taxonomy developed by Halpern (1994). In each chapter, some of these skills are applied to topics and issues related to the chapter's content. For instance, in the chapter that covers drug abuse (Chapter 5), the concept of alcoholism is used to highlight the immense power of definitions and to illustrate how circular reasoning can seem so seductive. Skills that are particularly important may surface in more than one chapter, so students see them applied in a variety of contexts. For example, in Chapter 7 students learn how hindsight bias can contaminate memory, and in Chapter 12 they see how hindsight can distort analyses of personality. Repeated practice across chapters should help students to spontaneously recognize the relevance of specific critical thinking skills when they encounter certain types of information. The skills approach taken to critical thinking and the content it has spawned are unprecedented for an introductory psychology text.

A Didactic Illustration Program

When Wayne Weiten first outlined his plans for the U.S. edition of the text, he wanted every aspect of the illustration program to have a genuine didactic purpose. He was intimately involved in planning every detail of the illustration program. We kept this approach in developing this Canadian edition. We have endeavoured to create a program of figures, diagrams, photos, and tables that work hand-in-hand with the prose to strengthen and clarify the main points in the text.

The most obvious results of this didactic approach to illustration are the six summary spreads that combine tabular information, photos, diagrams, and sketches to provide well-organized overviews of key ideas in the areas of history, learning, development, personality theory, psychopathology, and psychotherapy. But we hope you will also notice the

Taxonomy of Skills Covered in the Critical Thinking Applications

Verbal Reasoning Skills	
Understanding the way definitions shape how people think about issues	Chapter 5
Identifying the source of definitions	Chapter 5
Avoiding the nominal fallacy in working with definitions and labels	Chapter 5
Understanding the way language can influence thought	Chapter 8
Recognizing semantic slanting	Chapter 8
Recognizing name-calling and anticipatory name-calling	Chapter 8
Recognizing and avoiding reification	Chapter 9
Argument/Persuasion Analysis Skills	
Understanding the elements of an argument	Chapter 10
Recognizing and avoiding common fallacies, such as irrelevant reasons, circular reasoning, slippery slope reasoning, weak analogies, and false dichotomies	Chapters 10 and 11
Evaluating arguments systematically	Chapter 10
Recognizing and avoiding appeals to ignorance	Chapter 9
Understanding how Pavlovian conditioning can be used to manipulate emotions	Chapter 6
Developing the ability to detect conditioning procedures used in the media	Chapter 6
Recognizing social influence strategies	Chapter 16
Judging the credibility of an information source	Chapter 16
Skills in Thinking as Hypothesis Testing	
Looking for alternative explanations for findings and events	Chapters 1, 9, and 11
Looking for contradictory evidence	Chapters 1, 3, and 9
Recognizing the limitations of anecdotal evidence	Chapters 2 and 15
Understanding the need to seek disconfirming evidence	Chapter 7
Understanding the limitations of correlational evidence	Chapters 11 and 13
Understanding the limitations of statistical significance	Chapter 13
Recognizing situations in which placebo effects might occur	Chapter 15
Skills in Working with Likelihood and Uncertainty	
Utilizing base rates in making predictions and evaluating probabilities	Chapter 13
Understanding cumulative probabilities	Chapter 14
Understanding conjunctive probabilities	Chapter 14
Understanding the limitations of the representativeness heuristic	Chapter 14
Understanding the limitations of the availability heuristic	Chapter 14
Recognizing situations in which regression toward the mean may occur	Chapter 15
Understanding the limits of extrapolation	Chapter 3
Decision-Making and Problem-Solving Skills	
Using evidence-based decision making	Chapter 2
Recognizing the bias in hindsight analysis	Chapters 7 and 12
Seeking information to reduce uncertainty	Chapter 13
Making risk–benefit assessments	Chapter 13
Generating and evaluating alternative courses of action	Chapter 13
Recognizing overconfidence in human cognition	Chapter 7
Understanding the limitations and fallibility of human memory	Chapter 7
Understanding how contrast effects can influence judgments and decisions	Chapter 4
Recognizing when extreme comparitors are being used	Chapter 4

subtleties of the illustration program. For instance, diagrams of important concepts (conditioning, synaptic transmission, experimental design, and so forth) are often repeated in several chapters (with variations) to highlight connections among research areas and to enhance students' mastery of key ideas. Numerous easy-to-understand graphs of research results underscore psychology's foundation in research, and photos and diagrams often bolster each other (e.g., see the treatment of classical conditioning in Chapter 6). Colour is used carefully as an organizational device, and visual schematics are used to simplify hard-to-visualize concepts (e.g., see Figure 9.15, which explains reaction range for intelligence, on page 371). All of these efforts were made in the service of one master: the desire to make this an inviting book that is easy to learn from.

Internet-Related Features

The Internet is rapidly altering the landscape of modern life, and students clearly need help dealing with the information explosion in cyberspace. To assist them, this text has three features. First, Web expert Vincent Hevern (Le Moyne College), the Internet editor for the Society for the Teaching of Psychology, has written a concise preface that explains the essentials of the Internet to the uninitiated. This preface, which follows the student preface, briefly explains URLs, domain names, hyperlinks, search engines, and so forth. Second, cognizant of the highly variable quality and frequently questionable validity of much of the information available on the Web, Dr. Hevern was asked to write an essay on how to critically evaluate Web sites and online resource materials. His highly informative essay is found in the back of the book in Appendix D. Third, Professor Hevern was asked to evaluate hundreds of psychology-related sites on the Web and come up with some recommended sites that appear to provide reasonably accurate, balanced, and empirically sound information. Short descriptions of these recommended Web sites (called Web Links) are dispersed throughout the chapters, adjacent to related topical coverage. In the Canadian edition, we supplemented and sometimes changed other recommended Web sites to reflect the Canadian context and research. Through the Web Links provided in this text, students will have access to fundamental and applied research and research groups in Canada and around the world. Insofar as students are interested in visiting these sites, we recommend that they do so through the *Psychology: Themes & Variations* home page at the Thomson Nelson Web site **http://www.themesand variations.nelson.com**. Links to all the recommended

Web sites are maintained there, and the Nelson Webmaster periodically updates the URLs.

Integrated Running Glossary

An introductory text should place great emphasis on acquainting students with psychology's technical language—not for the sake of jargon, but because a great many of the key terms are also cornerstone concepts (e.g., *independent variable*, *reliability*, and *cognitive dissonance*). This text handles terminology with a running glossary embedded in the prose itself. The terms are set off in ***boldface italics***, and the definitions follow in **boldface roman type**. This approach retains the two advantages of a conventional running glossary: vocabulary items are made salient, and their definitions are readily accessible. However, the approach does so without interrupting the flow of discourse, while eliminating redundancy between text matter and marginal entries.

Concept Checks

To help students assess their mastery of important ideas, Concept Checks are sprinkled throughout the book (two to four per chapter). In keeping with the goal of making this a book of ideas, the Concept Checks challenge students to apply ideas instead of testing rote memory. For example, in Chapter 6 the reader is asked to analyze realistic examples of conditioning and identify conditioned stimuli and responses, reinforcers, and schedules of reinforcement. Many of the Concept Checks require the reader to put together ideas introduced in different sections of the chapter. For instance, in Chapter 2 students are asked to look for various types of deficiencies in hypothetical studies, and in Chapter 4 students are asked to identify parallels between vision and hearing. Some of the Concept Checks are quite challenging, but students find them engaging, and they report that the answers (available in Appendix A) are often illuminating.

Preview Questions and Reviews of Key Points

To help students organize and remember important ideas, each chapter includes five to eight sets of Preview Questions and companion Reviews of Key Points. Generally speaking, the Preview Questions are found at the beginning of each major section in a chapter, in the margin, adjacent to a level-one heading; the Reviews of Key Points are found at the end of each major section, just before the next level-one heading. Of course, some exceptions to this rule-of-thumb had to be made to accommodate very long or very brief sections under level-one headings. The Preview Questions are short, thought-provoking learning objectives that should help students focus on the key issues in each section. Each Review of Key Points is an interim summary that addresses the issues posed in the preceding Preview Questions. Interspersing these reviews throughout the chapters permits students to check their understanding of each section's main ideas immediately after finishing the section instead of waiting until the end of the chapter. This approach also allows students to work with more modest-sized chunks of information.

Practice Tests

Each chapter ends with a 15-item multiple-choice Practice Test that should give students a realistic assessment of their mastery of that chapter and valuable practice taking the type of test that many of them will face in the classroom (if the instructor uses the Test Bank). This feature grew out of some research that Weiten conducted on students' use of textbook pedagogical devices (see Weiten, Guadagno, & Beck, 1996). This research indicated that students pay scant attention to some standard pedagogical devices. When Weiten grilled his students to gain a better understanding of this finding, it quickly became apparent that students are very pragmatic about pedagogy. Essentially, their refrain was "We want study aids that will help us pass the next test." They should be very realistic, as most of the items were taken from previous editions of the Test Bank (these items do not appear in the Test Bank for this edition).

In addition to the special features just described, the text includes a variety of more conventional, "tried and true" features. The back of the book contains a standard *alphabetical glossary*. Opening *outlines* preview each chapter, and a thorough *Recap of Key Ideas* appears at the end of each chapter, along with lists of *Key Terms* and *Key People* (important theorists and researchers). We make frequent use of *italics for emphasis,* and we depend on *frequent headings* to maximize organizational clarity. The preface for students describes these pedagogical devices in more detail.

Content

The text is divided into 16 chapters, which follow a traditional ordering. The chapters are not grouped into sections or parts, primarily because such groupings can limit your options if you want to reorganize the order of topics. The chapters are written in a way that facilitates organizational flexibility, as we assume that some chapters might be omitted or presented in a different order.

The topical coverage in the text is relatively conventional, but there are some subtle departures from the norm. For instance, Chapter 1 presents a relatively "meaty" discussion of the evolution of ideas in psychology. This coverage of history lays the foundation for many of the crucial ideas emphasized in subsequent chapters. The historical perspective is also our way of reaching out to the students who find that psychology just isn't what they expected it to be. If we want students to contemplate the mysteries of behaviour, we must begin by clearing up the biggest mysteries of them all: "Where did these rats, statistics, synapses, and JNDs come from, what could they possibly have in common, and why doesn't this course bear any resemblance to what I anticipated?" We use history as a vehicle to explain how psychology evolved into its modern form and why misconceptions about its nature are so common.

We also devote an entire chapter (Chapter 2) to the scientific enterprise—not just the mechanics of research methods but the logic behind them. We believe that an appreciation of the nature of empirical evidence can contribute greatly to improving students' critical thinking skills. Ten years from now, many of the "facts" reported in this book will have changed, but an understanding of the methods of science will remain invaluable. An introductory psychology course, by itself, isn't going to make a student think like a scientist, but we can't think of a better place to start the process. Essential statistical concepts are introduced in Chapter 2, but no effort is made to teach actual calculations. For those who emphasize statistics, Appendix B expands on statistical concepts.

New to the Canadian Edition

The following list of specific chapter changes highlights some of the key new topics and examples that have been included in the Canadian edition.

Chapter 1: The Evolution of Psychology

- The new opening vignette describes the Reena Virk case and links it to leading Canadian research on bullying.
- The new Featured Study, "Bullying in Canadian Schoolyards," links to the opening vignette, showing how psychology relates to peoples' everyday lives and introducing students to the use of a particular research methodology (naturalistic observation).
- A new section, "Psychology in Canada," looks at the history of the discipline here, from the first departments to the establishment of the Canadian Psychological Association. Brenda Milner is profiled

as a leading Canadian researcher, while Figure 1.2 looks at three other women pioneers in Canadian psychology.

- The continuing relevance of Donald Hebb's pioneering work in cognition, with its focus on physiological and neuropsychological perspectives, is discussed in the section entitled "Psychology Returns to Its Roots."
- Table 1.3 sets out recipients of the CPA Donald O. Hebb Award for Distinguished Contributions to Psychology as a Science and provides page references in the text where some of the recipients' work is discussed.

Chapter 2: The Research Enterprise in Psychology

- The opening vignette explores reactions to the 2004 tsunami and a troubling domestic violence incident to discuss how different kinds of research are used to answer questions about human behaviour.
- A new Featured Study, "Can Fear Increase Sexual Attraction?" examines the classic experiment by Dutton and Aron set on bridges over the Capilano River; the study is referenced throughout the chapter and in other chapters as new concepts can be applied to it (for example, Schachter's two-factor theory of emotion in Chapter 11).
- New examples are included in the section entitled "Looking at Ethics"—such as the author's own undergraduate experience in a conformity study, the Tuskegee syphilis study in the United States, and the CIA-funded experiments at the Allen Memorial Institute in Montreal.
- A new section details "Ethical Guidelines for Research in Psychology in Canada"; Table 2.5 lists the key principles set out by the CPA.

Chapter 3: The Biological Bases of Behaviour

- The new opening vignette previews the pioneering work of Canadian psychologists, with a close look at Sandra Witelson's work on Einstein's brain and John Connolly's use of EEG responses to prove rehabilitation was possible for a brain-injured man in an apparent vegetative state.
- Donald Hebb's analysis of the neural basis of behaviour, and its continuing importance today, is detailed in the section "Integrating Signals: Neural Networks."
- Wilder Penfield's pioneering work mapping functions of the brain is discussed in the section "Electrical Stimulation of the Brain."
- A new Featured Study, "Searching for the Self in the Brain," looks at how a team of Canadian researchers used PET scans to determine what areas of the brain were activated when partici-

pants were asked to encode information with reference to their "self."

- Recent Canadian research includes Doug Crawford's studies of the role of the parietal cortex, Bryan Kolb's work on the brain's ability to change structure and function, Maryse Lassonde's studies of the corpus callosum's role in integrating communication between the two brain hemispheres, and Doreen Kimura's conclusions about gender and cognitive differences.

Chapter 4: Sensation and Perception

- The new opening vignette looks at experiments by scientists associated with the Canadian Space Agency on the vestibular system and the role interpreting visual cues has on spatial orientation, determining body position, and sensory adaptation to microgravity.
- Darwin Muir's work on the impact of the deprivation of early visual stimulation on mature development is discussed in the section "Information Processing in the Visual Cortex."
- A new section, "Multiple Methods in Vision Research," looks at the different research methods and technologies available for research.
- A new section on "Music and Its Effects" has been added.
- A new Featured Study, "Decoding Speech Prosody: Do Music Lessons Help?" looks at whether musical training can help individuals interpret emotions conveyed in the speech of others.
- Robert Melzak's research on pain, including the development of the McGill Pain Questionnaire, is discussed in the section "Puzzles in Pain Perception."

Chapter 5: Variations in Consciousness

- The new opening vignette looks at proposed Canadian legislation decriminalizing marijuana and Statistics Canada data on the hours of sleep Canadians are getting—two examples of topics related to consciousness that are covered in the chapter.
- Canadian data on shift work and its impact on health are included in the section "Ignoring Circadian Rhythms."
- The discussion of insomnia treatment considers studies on the efficacy of cognitive behavioural therapy done by Charles Morin and his colleagues.
- Canadian research on the relationship between stress and dreams and on lucid dreaming is highlighted in the section entitled "Links between Dreams and Waking Life."
- A section dealing with the indirect effects of drug abuse discusses Canadian research on the effects of alcohol—from intentions toward engaging

in unsafe sex to playing a causal role in relationship conflict.

Chapter 6: Learning
- The opening vignette discusses Wayne Gretzky's well-known superstitions and phobias as examples of operant conditioning and classical conditioning.
- The section "Conditioning and Physiological Responses" discusses Shepard Siegel's work on how classical conditioning contributes to increasing drug tolerance.
- A discussion of positive and negative punishment has been added.
- The section "Observational Learning" includes an expanded discussion of Albert Bandura's background and achievements, including a detailed look at how his Bobo doll experiments explored aggression in children and led to later studies on the links between television viewing and violence.

Chapter 7: Human Memory
- The opening vignette looks at time travel and memory, Endel Tulving's distinction between semantic and episodic memory, and Canadian data on memory impairment.
- The section entitled "The Role of Attention" discusses Lynn Hasher's work on automatic and effortful memory processing.
- Canadian research examined in this chapter includes Alan Paivio's dual-coding theory, Nick Kuiper's work on self-referent encoding, and Mark Baldwin's exploration of how relational schemas affect our processing of information about ourselves and others.
- A discussion on reinstating the context of an event outlines how state and mood affect recall of events, summarizing work by Fergus Craik, Eric Eich, Stephen Porter, and others.
- Canadian scholarship on eyewitness testimony is detailed in the Critical Thinking Application.

Chapter 8: Language and Thought
- The new opening vignette looks at language issues in Canada, from the Official Languages Bill of the Trudeau era and the growth of language immersion programs in schools to Ellen Bialystok's studies of the cognitive benefits of bilingual education.
- The importance of the cognitive revolution is discussed, with explicit references to its overlapping treatment in Chapters 7, 11, 14, and 16.
- Janet Werker's pioneering studies in the development of language in infants are explored in the section "Milestones in Language Development."
- The new Featured Study, "Babbling in the Manual Mode," looks at Petitto and Marentette's research that suggests babbling reflects not the developing motor portions of the infant's brain, but rather the maturation of the infant's developing language capacity.
- Substantial material on bilingualism has been added.

Chapter 9: Intelligence and Psychological Testing
- The new opening vignette puts forward questions about the nature of intelligence, looking at careers as diverse as those of Nobel Prize–winner Gerhard Herzberg and eccentric golfer Moe Norman. Implications of when differences in intelligence are perceived are also considered, with a look at two child prodigies and the case of a 14-year-old girl sterilized in 1959.
- The development of Canadian norms for intelligence testing (WAIS-III in Canada) is detailed in the section entitled "Standardization and Norms."
- Judy Lupart and Michael Pyryt's work on the "hidden gifted" is introduced in the section "Giftedness and Achievement in Life."
- The section entitled "Cultural Differences in IQ Scores" takes a critical look at the controversial theories of J. Phillipe Rushton and some of the reactions of Canadians to his theories.
- A measure for emotional intelligence in children and adolescents, developed by James Parker and colleagues, is described in the section "Measuring Emotional Intelligence."

Chapter 10: Motivation and Emotion
- The new opening vignette looks at Canadian athletes Chantal Petitclerc and Perdita Felicien, exploring the motivations underlying their achievements and the emotions arising from success or failure in their goals.
- Recent Canadian research discussed in this chapter includes Donald Taylor's study of street kids and their difficulties establishing definable goals; dieting rates among Canadian children; work on dietary restraint by Urbszat, Herman, and Polivy and by Jennifer Mills; sexual assault rates in Canada; McCann and Sato's study of the link between depression and overinvestment in dependent relations; and Richard Sorrentino's theory of uncertainty orientation as an aspect of motivation.
- Herman and Polivy's inhibitory norm model of social influence on eating is detailed in the section "Environmental Factors in the Regulation of Hunger."
- Obesity rates are discussed, based on results from the Canadian Community Health Survey.
- New research and examples are included in the "Eating Disorders" section, including David Pierce and Frank Epling's work on activity anorexia.

- Recent data on the sexual behaviour of Canadian teenagers is introduced in the section "Determinants of Sexual Desire," and changes in Canadian attitudes toward homosexuality are outlined in the section entitled "The Mystery of Sexual Orientation."

Chapter 11: Human Development across the Life Span

- The new opening vignette addresses students directly with an invitation to think about lifespan development, and looks at issues ranging from the achievements of Craig Kielburger, a young activist for children's rights, to the abolition of mandatory retirement in many Canadian provinces.
- The goals of McCain and Mustard's *Early Years Report*, reviewing current knowledge about neuroscience and early childhood development, are discussed in the section "The Wondrous Years of Childhood."
- A new subsection on neo-Piagetian theories has been added, examining Juan Pascual-Leone's theory of M-capacity and his reinterpretation of Piaget's developmental stages, and explaining Robbie Case's view of cognitive development, including his *Staircase* model.
- The section "What Do Children Understand about the Mind?" explores Lalonde and Chandler's work proposing an interpretive theory of mind that signals a child's progression to a mature understanding of how the mind works.
- Data on youth suicide and attempted suicide rates in Canada are critically analyzed, accompanied by new Figure 11.16 on adolescent suicide; additional studies of First Nations' suicide rates introduce the new Featured Study "Youth Suicide in Canada's First Nations."
- The section "Aging and Physical Changes" looks at studies on Alzheimer's disease by Murtha and colleagues (selective attention deficits relating to inhibition) and Rich and colleagues (language-based semantic impairments affecting the retrieval stage).
- Troyer and Rich's development of the Multifactorial Memory Questionnaire (MMQ) to assess metamemory (awareness of the functioning of one's own memory) is detailed in the section "Aging and Cognitive Changes."
- Canadian statistics provided throughout the chapter include rates of happiness and dysfunctional behaviours in the lives of young Canadians; rates for marriage, common-law relationships, and divorce; and the number of single-parent families in Canada.

Chapter 12: Personality: Theory, Research, and Assessment

- The new opening vignette considers the mystery of personality through examples of individuals whose personalities led them to unique accomplishments: Dan Matthews and Jason Hamilton, Canadian soldiers awarded for courage in Afghanistan, and pioneering feminist Nellie McClung, who fought for the right of Canadian women to be considered "persons" under the law.
- Sampo Paunonen's exploration of the nature and implications of the "Big Five" is discussed in the section "The Five-Factor Model of Personality Traits."
- The omission of a concept students may know through popular culture is addressed with a brief mention of the Electra complex (and the fact that it was not endorsed by Freud).
- Norman Endler's interactional approach to personality is discussed in the section "Mischel and the Person–Situation Controversy."
- The importance of Rogers's person-centred theory of personality is articulated in the section "Humanistic Perspectives," leading to an introduction to the new Featured Study by McGill's Mark Baldwin and his colleagues, "The Pope Is Watching You: Effects on Self-Concept."

Chapter 13: Stress, Coping, and Health

- The opening vignette examines stress experienced by Canadian university students, including statistics and coping strategies for exam-time stress; the work of stress pioneers at Canadian universities, including Hans Selye and Hymie Anisman, is previewed.
- Canadian scholarship introduced in the chapter includes Anisman and Merali's analysis of the different factors underlying an individual's response to a stressor; the development of Peacock and Wong' s Stress Appraisal Measure; DeLongis's consideration of whether positive spousal support can offset negative relationship strain during illness; and research of various scholars on the tendency to engage in risky sexual behaviours.
- Background on Hans Selye's accomplishments and eminence has been added to the section "Responding to Stress."
- Endler and Parker's development of the Coping Inventory for Stressful Situations (CISS) is outlined in the section on behavioural responses to stress.
- Canadian statistics are provided throughout the chapter, including work–life stress reports, data on job-related stress, the link between stress and health outcomes, mortality rates from heart disease, smoking rates, and exercise rates.

Chapter 14: Psychological Disorders

- The new opening vignette examines General Roméo Dallaire's experience with post-traumatic stress disorder, and presents data on PTSD in the military.
- An overview of rates and costs of psychological disorders in Canada is included.
- Findings by Moretti and by Kirsch and Kuiper on gender differences in depression disorders are discussed.
- Robert Hare's work on psychopathy is examined in the section "Antisocial Personality Disorder."
- A detailed look at how psychological defences have been used in the Canadian legal system is included in the section entitled "Psychological Disorders and the Law."

Chapter 15: Treatment of Psychological Disorders

- The new opening vignette looks at abuses of psychotherapeutic treatment in Canada, from Dr. Ewen Cameron's unethical thought-control experiments to the use of LSD on maximum-security psychiatric patients in Ontario.
- Canadian statistics introduced to the chapter include a 2005 poll on attitudes toward caring for mental as well as physical health, findings on which medical professionals are consulted by patients seeking medical help for psychological problems, the percentage of Canadians reporting use of tranquillizers and antidepressants, and rates of deinstitutionalization of patients in mental hospitals.
- Sources for practical advice on mental health issues have been added, including issues to consider when seeking therapy, clinical and counselling psychology programs accredited by the CPA, and pharmacological treatments for anxiety disorders and their side effects.
- Donald Meichenbaum's innovative contributions to cognitive-behavioural therapies are discussed in detail, including his development of self-instructional training and risk assessment guidelines for evaluating suicidal patients.
- Background on Canada's diverse population, with a close look at psychological disorders experienced by First Nations people, is included in the section "Increasing Multicultural Sensitivity in Treatment"; Hertzsprung and Dobson's arguments for increased diversity training are described.

Chapter 16: Social Behaviour

- The new opening vignette looks at stereotyping and discrimination in Canada, beginning with a recent example of segregation in Quebec.

- Karen Dion's findings on the positive attributes of attractiveness are outlined.
- Mark Zanna's work on self-fulfilling prophecy as an aspect of our perception of others is described in the discussion on stereotypes.
- The discussion of conformity and obedience describes Zimbardo's Stanford prison experiment and relates it to American mistreatment of Iraqi prisoners and an atrocity committed by Canadian peacekeepers in Somalia.
- A discussion of implicit (underground) prejudice has been added to the Personal Application, "Understanding Prejudice."

Writing Style

In writing this text, we attempted a down-to-earth, conversational writing style; effective communication is always the paramount goal. Our intent is to talk *with* the reader rather than throw information *at* the reader. To clarify concepts and maintain students' interest, we frequently provide concrete examples that students can relate to. As much as possible, we avoid using technical jargon when ordinary language serves just as well.

Making learning easier depends, above all else, on clear, well-organized writing. For this reason, we've worked hard to ensure that chapters, sections, and paragraphs are organized in a logical manner, so that key ideas stand out in sharp relief against supportive information.

Student Supplements

Concept Charts for Study and Review

To help your students organize and assimilate the main ideas contained in the text, we have created a booklet of Concept Charts that is included with each new copy of the text. This booklet contains a two-page Concept Chart for each chapter. Each Concept Chart provides a detailed visual map of the key ideas found in the main body of that chapter. These colour-coded, hierarchically organized charts create snapshots of the chapters that should allow your students to quickly see the relationships among ideas and sections.

ThomsonNOW™

This online diagnostic tool identifies each student's unique needs with a Pretest that generates a personalized Study Plan for each chapter, helping students focus on concepts they're having the most difficulty mastering. Students then take a Posttest to measure their understanding of the material. An instructor

Gradebook is available to track and monitor student progress. A key component of the Study Plan is the inclusion of visually and pedagogically rich modules that begin with clearly stated learning objectives, followed by knowledge-building animations with audio to present key concepts. Modules also include discovery activities and self-check quizzes that confirm students' understanding of the module material.

Study Guide (by Richard Stalling and Ronald Wasden, and adapted by Andrew Howell)

An exceptionally thorough *Study Guide* is available to help your students master the information in the text.

The review of key ideas for each chapter is made up of an engaging mixture of matching exercises, fill-in-the-blank items, free-response questions, and programmed learning. Each review is organized around learning objectives. The *Study Guide* is closely coordinated with the *Test Bank,* as the same learning objectives guided the construction of the questions in the *Test Bank.* The *Study Guide* also includes a review of key terms, a review of key people, and a self-test for each chapter in the text.

Psyk.Trek™ 3.0: A Multimedia Introduction to Psychology

Psyk.Trek 3.0 is a multimedia supplement that will provide students with new opportunities for active learning and reach out to "visual learners" with greatly increased efficacy. *Psyk.Trek* is intended to give students a second pathway to learning much of the content of introductory psychology. Although it does not cover all of the content of the introductory course, we think you will see that a great many key concepts and principles can be explicated *more effectively* in an interactive audio-visual medium than in a textbook.

The revised *Psyk.Trek 3.0* includes three new interactive Learning Modules: 6d, "Forgetting"; 9e, "Attachment"; and 12e, "Conformity and Obedience," bringing the total to 65 modules. Based on user feedback, we have included new pedagogy, such as bulleted learning objectives at the beginning of each module, multiple-choice tests at the end of each module, unit-level exams, and one critical thinking exercise per unit. For the first time, *Psyk.Trek* is available either on CD-ROM or online, with a new, easier-to-use interface. Students using the CD-ROM are able to e-mail and print results from quizzes and simulations. These results can flow into an instructor gradebook for those using the web-based version of *Psyk.Trek.*

Psyk.Trek 3.0 consists of four components. The main component is a set of 65 *Interactive Learning Modules* that present the core content of psychology in a whole new way. These tutorials include thousands of graphics, hundreds of photos, hundreds of animations, approximately four hours of narration, 35 carefully selected videos, and about 160 uniquely visual concept checks and quizzes. The *Simulations* allow students to explore complex psychological phenomena in depth. They are highly interactive, experiential demonstrations that will enhance students' appreciation of research methods. Three new modules can be found on *Psyk.Trek 3.0.* A *Multimedia Glossary* allows students to look up over 800 psychological terms, access hundreds of pronunciations of obscure words, and pull up hundreds of related diagrams, photos, and videos. The *Video Selector* allows students to directly access the 35 video segments that are otherwise embedded in the Interactive Learning Modules.

The key strength of *Psyk.Trek* is its ability to give students new opportunities for active learning outside of the classroom. For example, students can run themselves through re-creations of classic experiments to see the complexities of data collection in action. Or they can play with visual illusions on screen in ways that will make them doubt their own eyes. Or they can stack colour filters on screen to demonstrate the nature of subtractive colour mixing. *Psyk.Trek* is intended to supplement and complement *Psychology: Themes and Variations.* For instance, after reading about operant conditioning in the text, a student could work through three interactive tutorials on operant principles, watch three videos, (including historic footage of B. F. Skinner shaping a rat), and then try to shape Morphy, the virtual rat, in one of the simulations.

Instructor Supplements

The teaching/learning package that has been developed to supplement *Psychology: Themes and Variations* also includes many other useful tools. The development of all its parts was carefully coordinated so that they are mutually supported. Moreover, the materials have been created and written by highly experienced, top-flight professors we have worked hard to recruit.

Instructor's Resource Manual (coordinated by Randolph Smith)

A talented roster of professors has contributed to the *Instructor's Resource Manual (IRM)* in their respective areas of expertise. The *IRM* was developed under the guidance of Randolph Smith, the editor of the journal *Teaching of Psychology.* It contains a diverse array of materials designed to facilitate efforts to teach the introductory course and includes the following sections:

- The *Instructor's Manual* contains a wealth of detailed suggestions for lecture topics, class demonstrations, exercises, discussion questions, and suggested readings, organized around the content of each chapter in the text. It also highlights the connections between the text coverage and *Psyk.Trek* content and features an expanded collection of masters for class handouts.
- *Strategies for Effective Teaching,* by Joseph Lowman (University of North Carolina), discusses practical issues such as what to put in a course syllabus, how to handle the first class meeting, how to cope with large classes, and how to train and organize teaching assistants.
- *AV Media for Introductory Psychology,* by Russ Watson (College of DuPage), provides a comprehensive, up-to-date critical overview of educational films relevant to the introductory course.
- *The Use of Computers in Teaching Introductory Psychology,* by Susan J. Shapiro and Michael Shapiro (Indiana University–East), offers a thorough listing of computer materials germane to the introductory course and analyzes their strengths and weaknesses.
- *Integrating Writing into Introductory Psychology,* by Jane Jegerski (Elmhurst College), examines the writing-across-the-curriculum movement and provides suggestions and materials for specific writing assignments chapter by chapter.
- *Crossing Borders/Contrasting Behaviours: Using Cross-Cultural Comparisons to Enrich the Introductory Psychology Course,* by Bill Hill and Michael Reiner (Kennesaw State University), discusses the movement toward "internationalizing" the curriculum and provides suggestions for lectures, exercises, and assignments that can add a cross-cultural flavour to the introductory course.
- *Teaching Introductory Psychology with the World Wide Web,* by Michael R. Snyder (University of Alberta), discusses how to work Internet assignments into the introductory course and provides a guide to many psychology-related sites on the World Wide Web.
- *Using InfoTrac® in Introductory Psychology* by Randolph Smith discusses how to make effective use of the *InfoTrac* subscription that is made available to students with this text. *InfoTrac College Edition* is an online database of recent full-text articles from hundreds of scholarly and popular periodicals.

Test Bank (by S. A. Hensch, and adapted by Lynne Honey)

The test bank that accompanies the text was adapted for Canadian readers by Lynne Honey of Grant MacEwan College. She has paid particular attention to ensuring the questions reflect the material in the Canadian edition while matching the outstanding U.S. original in the scope, effectiveness, and accuracy of test items. A careful effort has been made to ensure personal names used in the questions reflect Canada's ethnic diversity, underscoring the fact that psychology is for everyone. The questions are closely tied to chapter learning objectives and to the lists of key terms and key people found in both the text and the *Study Guide.* The items are categorized as (a) factual, (b) conceptual/applied, (c) integrative, or (d) critical thinking questions. All essay-type questions are accompanied by suggested answers.

Computerized Test Items

Electronic versions of the *Test Bank* are available for a variety of computer configurations. The *ExamView* software is user-friendly and allows teachers to insert their own questions and to customize those provided.

Test Bank, Volume II

This alternative test bank allows professors to draw from an entirely new set of questions, offering more varied test materials and ensuring students are challenged by fresh items. Each chapter has 100 to 125 multiple-choice questions.

Multimedia Manager PowerPoint Presentation (adapted by Dax Urbszat)

Adapted for the Canadian edition by Dax Urbszat, of the University of Toronto, this CD-ROM includes text-specific lecture outlines, a high resolution digital version of each figure and illustration from the text, videos, and animations. These graphics can be combined with your own material to create powerful, personal media-enhanced presentations.

Transparencies (by Susan Shapiro)

A collection of *text-specific transparencies* has been created to enhance visual presentations in the classroom. The development of the transparencies was supervised by Susan Shapiro (Indiana University–East), who has great expertise in the use of visual media in the classroom. She has done a terrific job making the transparencies clear, readable, pedagogically sound, and technically accurate. A second set of transparencies from other Thomson psychology texts is also available.

Challenging Your Preconceptions: Thinking Critically About Psychology (by Randolph Smith)

This brief paperback book is a wonderful introduction to critical thinking as it applies to psychological issues. Written by Randolph Smith (Ouachita Baptist University), this book helps students apply their critical thinking skills to a variety of topics, including hypnosis, advertising, misleading statistics, IQ testing, gender differences, and memory bias. Each chapter ends with critical thinking challenges that give students opportunities to practise their critical thinking skills.

Culture and Modern Life (by David Matsumoto)

If you emphasize cultural diversity in your course, this is an ideal supplementary book. Written by David Matsumoto (San Francisco State University), a leading authority on cross-cultural psychology, this brief paperback will help students appreciate how cultural factors affect psychological processes. It includes chapters on self, social behaviour, gender, work, and abnormal psychology.

Psychology: Themes & Variations Web site http://www.themesandvariations.nelson.com

Both students and faculty will find a wealth of useful materials at the *Psychology: Themes & Variations* Web site. If you haven't done so already, we encourage you to visit the site and experience the rich diversity of resources that are available there, including practice quizzes, tutorials, Web links, simulations, critical thinking activities, flash cards, interactive exercises, and suggested readings available through InfoTrac.

Wayne Weiten
Doug McCann

Acknowledgments for the Canadian Edition

Working on this first Canadian edition of *Psychology: Themes and Variations* has proven to be a pleasure. Wayne Weiten's text was a joy to work with, and his support and advice for the Canadian edition were invaluable. There was much to learn but Thomson Nelson facilitated the learning from beginning to end. Creating a text such as this is a complicated challenge, and I am indebted to a group of dedicated professionals at Thomson Nelson for all the assistance they provided. Joanna Cotton, publisher, provided the spark and enthusiasm for the project and continued her support throughout. Lesley Mann, senior developmental editor, was a constant guide through the intricacies of producing and publishing a text. Valerie Adams was a superb copyeditor whose expertise was much appreciated. Production editor Anne Macdonald worked with tireless good humour to ensure all the deadlines were met. Photo and permissions researcher Indu Ghuman rose to every challenge, finding marvellous illustrations for the new content in the text. The proofreading skills of Kelli Howey, the support of Wayne Morden, marketing manager, and the work of other Thomson Nelson staff (including Lenore Spence, Katherine Goodes, and Susan Calvert) have contributed to the text. I am also indebted to Paul Saundercook. He was the book representative who first introduced me to the Weiten text and who assured me that if I read that book it would be the last time I would have to choose a text to use. He was right, and I always enjoy talking hockey with him.

A host of psychologists deserve thanks for the contributions they made to this adaptation. I am grateful to Vic Catano of Saint Mary's University for revision of the appendix on I/O psychology; Andrew Howell for his work on the Study Guide; Lynne Honey for adapting the Test Bank; Dax Urbszat for taking on the PowerPoint Slides and accompanying Lecture Outlines; and Lisa Best for her work on the Self-Study Assessment Questions found in ThomsonNOW™.

I would also like to thank the many reviewers and chapter consultants who provided insightful and constructive critiques of various portions of the manuscript:

Noushine Afshar, Langara College
George Alder, Simon Fraser University
Lisa Best, University of New Brunswick–Saint John
Wendy Bourque, University of New Brunswick–Fredericton
Dianne Crisp, Kwantlen University College
Hank Davis, University of Guelph
Shannon Gadbois, Brandon University
Lyle Grant, Athabasca University
Carla Gunn, University of New Brunswick–Fredericton
Mark Holder, University of British Columbia, Okanagan
Lynne Honey, Grant MacEwan College
Melike Schalomon, Grant MacEwan College
Heather Schellinck, Dalhousie University
Dax Urbszat, University of Toronto

In working on the first Canadian edition, I was fortunate to be surrounded by a world-class group of colleagues who were more than willing to talk to me about issues in psychology and to give generously of their time and expertise. They include Gordon Flett, Chris Green, Alex Rutherford, Hiroshi Ono, Thomas Teo, Maxine Wintre, Ann-Marie Wall, Henny Westra, Frances Wilkinson, Janice Johnson, Laurence Harris, Doug Crawford, Regina Schuller, and Richard Lalonde. Lalonde in particular was helpful as always in contributing ideas and enthusiasm for the teaching of introductory psychology. Two research assistants, Stephanie Mears and Cynthia Wong, along with my secretary Eda Muia, were extremely helpful in producing tables and figures and running down facts and references. Thanks to Aubrey for the advice on music and Pamela for the Web site help. I would also like to thank all the Canadian researchers I contacted who made their ideas readily available to me. Thanks also to Norm Endler; his legendary aoristic red pen still affects my work.

During the time the book was in preparation, I was fortunate to have the support and enthusiasm of a small group who made the task easy and enjoyable. Thanks to Tuck and Check for allowing me to try out language and ideas at our daily 5 a.m. get-togethers. Thanks to David for pulling out all the stops in helping us all out; I hope the picture is enough. Thanks to Harry for his ideas and feedback. It was always a pleasure to answer his questions about "The Book." I trust he will forgive me for all the missed karate and snowboarding; these are important together times for me. In the end, as always, it comes down to the ineffable Nancy. Thanks for getting it started, for sharing, and for keeping the motivation for research and writing going when it seemed to stop. Her enthusiasm for and knowledge of pedagogy never fails to inspire.

Doug McCann

To the Student

Welcome to your introductory psychology textbook. In most university and college courses, students spend more time with their textbooks than with their professors, so it helps if students *like* their textbooks. Making textbooks likable, however, is a tricky proposition. By its very nature, a textbook must introduce students to many complicated concepts, ideas, and theories. If it doesn't, it isn't much of a textbook, and instructors won't choose to use it. Nevertheless, in writing this book we've tried to make it as likable as possible without compromising the academic content that your instructor demands. We've especially tried to keep in mind your need for a clear, well-organized presentation that makes the important material stand out and yet is interesting to read. Above all else, we hope you find this book challenging to think about and easy to learn from.

Before you plunge into your first chapter, let's look at the book's key features. Becoming familiar with how the book works will help you to get more out of it.

Key Features

You're about to embark on a journey into a new domain of ideas. Your text includes some important features that are intended to highlight certain aspects of psychology's landscape.

Unifying Themes

To help you make sense of a complex and diverse field of study, seven themes are introduced in Chapter 1 and reappear in a number of variations as we move from chapter to chapter. These unifying themes are meant to provoke thought about important issues and to highlight the connections between chapters. They are discussed at the end of each chapter in a section called "Putting It in Perspective."

Featured Studies

Every chapter includes a Featured Study, which is an in-depth look at an interesting piece of research. The Featured Studies are presented much as if they were journal articles. We hope they will enhance your understanding of how psychologists conduct and report their research.

Personal Applications

Toward the end of each chapter you'll find a Personal Application section that shows how psychology is relevant to everyday life. Some of these sections provide concrete, practical advice that could be helpful to you in your educational endeavours, such as those on improving academic performance, improving everyday memory, and achieving self-control. So, you may want to jump ahead and read some of these Personal Applications early.

Critical Thinking Applications

Each Personal Application is followed by a two-page Critical Thinking Application that teaches and models basic critical thinking skills. We think you will find these sections refreshing and interesting. Like the Personal Applications, they are part of the text's basic content and should be read (unless you are told otherwise by your instructor). Although the "facts" of psychology will gradually change after you take this course (thanks to scientific progress), the critical thinking skills modelled in these sections should prove valuable for many years to come.

Web Links and Internet Essays

To help make this book a rich resource guide, we have included dozens of Web Links, which are recommended Web sites that can provide you with additional information on many topics. Many of the recommended sites were selected by Professor Vincent Hevern, who sought out resources that are interesting and that provide accurate, empirically sound information. Others were researched specifically for their relevance to Canadian students. The Web Links are dispersed throughout the chapters, adjacent to related topical coverage. While Web Links include the site URLs, we recommend that if you are interested in visiting these sites, you do so through the *Psychology: Themes & Variations* home page at **http://www.themesandvariations.nelson.com.** Links to all the recommended Web sites are maintained there and the Nelson Webmaster periodically updates the URLs. By the way, if you are not particularly sophisticated about the Internet, it is strongly suggested that you read Professor Hevern's essay on Internet basics, which follows this preface. And even if you *are* sophisticated about the Internet, you can probably benefit from reading Appendix D, which discusses how to evaluate the quality and credibility of Web-based resources.

Learning Aids

This text contains a great deal of information. A number of learning aids have been incorporated into the book to help you digest it all.

An *outline* at the beginning of each chapter provides you with an overview of the topics covered in that chapter. Think of the outlines as road maps, and bear in mind that it's easier to reach a destination if you know where you're going.

Headings serve as road signs in your journey through each chapter. Four levels of headings are used to make it easy to see the organization of each chapter.

Preview Questions, found at the beginning of major sections, can help you focus on the key issues in the material you are about to read.

Reviews of Key Points, found at the end of major sections, are interim summaries that permit you to check your understanding of a section's main ideas immediately after finishing the section.

Italics (without boldface) are used liberally throughout the text to emphasize crucial points.

Key terms are identified with ***italicized boldface*** type to alert you that these are important vocabulary items that are part of psychology's technical language. The key terms, with page references, are also listed at the end of the chapter.

An *integrated running glossary* provides an on-the-spot definition of each key term as it's introduced in the text. These formal definitions are printed in **boldface** type. Becoming familiar with psychology's terminology is an essential part of learning about the field. The integrated running glossary should make this learning process easier.

Concept Checks are sprinkled throughout the chapters to let you test your mastery of important ideas. Generally, they ask you to integrate or organize a number of key ideas, or to apply ideas to real-world situations. Although they're meant to be engaging and fun, they do check conceptual *understanding,* and some are challenging. But if you get stuck, don't worry; the answers (and explanations, where they're needed) are in the back of the book in Appendix A.

Illustrations in the text are important elements in your complete learning package. Some illustrations provide enlightening diagrams of complicated concepts; others furnish examples that help flesh out ideas or provide concise overviews of research results. Careful attention to the tables and figures in the book will help you understand the material discussed in the text.

A *Chapter Recap* at the end of each chapter provides a summary of the chapter's *Key Ideas,* a list of *Key Terms,* and a list of *Key People* (important theorists and researchers). It's wise to read over these review materials to make sure you've digested the information in the chapter.

Each chapter ends with a 15-item *Practice Test* that should give you a realistic assessment of your mastery of that chapter and valuable practice in taking multiple-choice tests. Answers to these Practice Tests are included at the back of the book in Appendix A.

An *alphabetical glossary* is provided in the back of the book. Most key terms are formally defined in the integrated running glossary only when they are first introduced. So if you run into a technical term a second time and can't remember its meaning, it may be easier to look it up in the alphabetical glossary than to try to find the definition where the term was originally introduced.

A Few Footnotes

Psychology textbooks customarily identify the studies, theoretical treatises, books, and articles that information comes from. These *citations* occur (1) when names are followed by a date in parentheses, as in "Smith (1993) found that ..." or (2) when names and dates are provided together within parentheses, as in "In one study (Smith, Miller, & Jones, 2001), the researchers attempted to ..." All of the cited publications are listed by author in the alphabetized *References* section in the back of the book. The citations and references are a necessary part of a book's scholarly and scientific foundation. Practically speaking, however, you'll probably want to glide right over them as you read. You definitely don't need to memorize the names and dates. The only names you may need to know are the handful listed under Key People in each Chapter Recap (unless your instructor mentions a personal favourite that you should know).

Concept Charts for Study and Review

Your text should be accompanied by a booklet of Concept Charts that are designed to help you organize and master the main ideas contained in each chapter. Each Concept Chart provides a detailed visual map of the key ideas found in the main body of that chapter. Seeing how it all fits together should help you to better understand each chapter. You can use these charts to preview chapters, to get a handle on how key ideas fit together, to double-check your mastery of the chapters, and to memorize the crucial principles in chapters.

Psyk.Trek™ 3.0: A Multimedia Introduction to Psychology

Psyk.Trek 3.0, available in both CD-ROM and online format, is an enormously powerful learning tool that can enhance your understanding of many complex processes and theories, provide you with an alternative way to assimilate many crucial concepts, and add a little more fun to your journey through introductory psychology. *Psyk.Trek* has been designed to supplement and complement your textbook. We strongly encourage you to use it. The CD icons that you will see in many of the headings in the upcoming chapters refer to the content of *Psyk.Trek*. An icon indicates that the textbook topic referred to in the heading is covered in the Interactive Learning Modules or Simulations found on *Psyk.Trek*. The relevant simulations (Sim1, Sim2, and so forth) and the relevant Interactive Learning Modules (1a, 1b, 1c, and so forth) are listed to the right of the icons.

A Word About the Study Guide

A *Study Guide* is available to accompany this text. It was written by two of Wayne Weiten's former professors, who introduced him to psychology years ago, and adapted for the Canadian edition by Andrew

Howell of Grant MacEwan College. They have done a great job of organizing review materials to help you master the information in the book. You should seriously consider using it to help you study.

A Final Word

We are pleased to be a part of your first journey into the world of psychology, and sincerely hope that you'll find the book as thought provoking and as easy to learn from as we've tried to make it. If you have any comments or advice on the book, please write in care of the publisher (Thomson Nelson, 1120 Birchmount Road, Toronto, Ontario, M1K 5G4). You can be sure we'll pay careful attention to your feedback. Finally, we wish you good luck. We hope you enjoy your course and learn a great deal.

Wayne Weiten
Doug McCann

 W W W   **O N   T H E   W E B**

For additional resources on the topics covered in this text, visit the *Psychology: Themes and Variations* Web site, where you will find practice quizzes, tutorials, Web links, simulations, critical thinking activities, flash cards, interactive exercises, and suggested readings available through INFOTRAC.

http://www.themesandvariations.nelson.com

 http://hed.nelson.com

Go to this site for the link to ThomsonNOW™, your one-stop study shop. Take a Pretest for this chapter and ThomsonNOW™ will generate a personalized Study Plan based on your test results! The Study Plan will identify the topics you need to review and direct you to online resources to help you master those topics. You can then take a Posttest to help you determine the concepts you have mastered and what you still need work on.

What Should Introductory Psychology Students Know About the Internet?

by Vincent W. Hevern, Le Moyne College

After dinner one night, Wayne Weiten, an author of this textbook, challenged me: Using no more than three pages, could I tell introductory psychology students the most important things they need to know about the Internet? Wait a minute, I thought, that's tough! I've been using the Net intensively for more than seven years in teaching and research with undergraduates, so I know there's an awful lot to talk about. But, after a couple of days I decided to accept his challenge. So, I'm going to share with you here what I believe to be the really important stuff about the Internet ("the Net")—information that should make your life as a student easier and, in the end, help you to learn even more about the fascinating world of psychology.

General Comments About the Internet

We now know that something of a fundamental change in the way people exchange ideas and information took place during the 1990s. For over 20 years, the Internet had been the tool of a relatively small group of lab scientists communicating mostly with each other. Suddenly, in the mid-1990s, the Net began to expand rapidly beyond the research laboratory. It first reached tens and then hundreds of millions of people as vast numbers of computers, large and small, were interconnected to form what is often called *cyberspace*. In the 21st century, learning to navigate the Internet will become as crucial as learning to read or to write—most of us will probably use the Net in some form at work or at home for the rest of our lives.

So, what are some basic notions necessary to understanding the Internet and how it works? Let me propose briefly eight crucial ideas.

1. *The goal of the Internet is communication—the rapid exchange of information—between people separated from each other.* Electronic mail (e-mail) and the World Wide Web (WWW, or just "the Web") are currently the two most important ways of communicating in cyberspace, even though the Net also uses other formats to do so.

2. *Every piece of information on the Net—every Web page, every graphic, every movie or sound, every e-mail box—has a unique, short, and structured address called a URL (or uniform resource locator).* The URL for this text's Student Resources is:
http://www.themesandvariations.nelson.com /student

This example shows the three elements of a URL: (a) to the left of the double forward slashes (//) is the protocol that tells the Net how to transfer the information. Here it is *http:* which means "use hypertext transfer protocol"—the most frequent protocol on the Net; (b) to the right of the double slashes up to the first forward slash (/) is the *domain name* that indicates which computer on the Net from which to get the information. Here the name of the computer is "www.themesandvariations.nelson.com"; (c) finally, everything after the first forward slash is called the *pathway* which indicates where the information is located within that particular computer. Here the pathway comprises the location "student."

3. *The foundation of the Web rests on hypertext links ("hyperlinks"), which are contained within documents (or "Web pages") displayed online.* A hyperlink is a highlighted word, phrase, or graphic image within an onscreen document that refers to some other document or Web page elsewhere. Part of every hyperlink on a computer screen includes the URL for the document that is hidden from view but stored within the computer displaying the document. Users can easily move from one document to another on screen because of hypertext links and their URLs.

4. *Pay attention to the last element of the domain name (the "domain" itself), which indicates what type of organization sponsors the link.* Important domains are *.ca* (Canadian Web sites), *.com* (commercial businesses), *.edu* (U.S. colleges and universities), *.gc* and *.gov* (Canadian and U.S. federal governmental agencies), and *.org* (non-profit organizations).

5. *The Internet is too large for any one individual to know all the important resources that can be found there.* Users, even experienced ones, often need help to find what they're looking for. In the chapters ahead, you will find many recommended Web sites that we have carefully selected based on their quality and their suitability for undergraduates. In making these selections, we emphasize quality over quantity and strive to send you to excellent gateway sites that are rich in links to related sites. We hope these suggested Web links help you begin to explore the field of psychology on the Internet.

6. *URLs are relatively unstable.* Many Web sites are moved or changed each year, as new computer systems are installed to replace older ones. Thus, links or URLs that are good one day may be useless the next. If you want to check out a recommended Web site, we suggest that you do so through the *Psychology: Themes and Variations*, First Canadian Edition home

page at the Thomson Nelson Web site (**http://www. themesandvariations.nelson.com**). Links to all of the recommended Web sites will be maintained there, and the Nelson Webmaster will periodically update the URLs.

7. *The Web is a worldwide democracy on which anyone can post materials.* Hence, the quality of information found online varies tremendously. Some material is first-rate, up-to-date, and backed up by good research and professional judgment. But a great deal of information online is junk—based on poor or invalid research and filled with many errors. Frankly, some sites are downright wacky, and others are run by hucksters and hatemongers. Thus, users need to learn to tell the difference between reputable and disreputable Web resources (see Appendix D in the back of the book).

8. *Knowledge has a monetary value.* Although the Internet started out as a non-commercial enterprise where almost everything was free, things have changed swiftly. Owners of knowledge (the holders of commercial "copyrights") usually expect to be paid for sharing what they own over the Net. Thus, many commercial businesses, such as the publishers of academic journals or books, either do not make journal articles available online or expect users to pay some type of fee for accessing their materials. Cognizant of this problem, the publisher of this text has entered into an agreement with a major online resource for magazine and journal articles and other types of information called *InfoTrac.* Your text may have come bundled with a subscription to *InfoTrac,* which provides easy access to full-text versions of thousands of periodicals. If you received an *InfoTrac* subscription with this book, it would be wise to take advantage of this valuable resource.

Some Suggestions for Action

In light of these ideas, how might you approach the Internet? What should you do to make the most of your time online? Let's review some general suggestions for exploring the Internet.

1. *Learn to navigate the Net before you get an assignment requiring you to do so.* If you've never used the Net before, start now to get a feel for it. Consider doing what lots of students do: Ask a friend who knows the Net to work with you directly so you can quickly get personal experience in cyberspace. What if you "hate" computers or they make you uncomfortable? Recent research has shown that students' fears of using computers tend to diminish once they get some practical experience in the course of a single semester.

2. *Learn how the software browser on your computer works.* The two most popular Web browser programs, Netscape Navigator and Microsoft Internet Explorer, are filled with many simple tricks and helpful short-cuts. Ask your friends or the computer consultants at school. Learning the tricks makes Net-based research much easier. (Hint: Find out what happens when you hold down the right-hand mouse button on a PC or the whole button on a Mac once you have the cursor on top of a hyperlink.)

3. *Get to know the different types of online help to find resources on the Web.* These resources currently fall into three general categories: (a) *General guides or directories* like Yahoo! (http://www.yahoo.ca) are similar to the Yellow Pages for telephones. You ask the online guide to show you what's listed in its directory under a category heading you supply. (b) *Search engines* such as Google (http://www.google.com) or AllTheWeb (http://www.alltheweb.com/), and *meta-search engines* such as ProFusion (http://www. profusion.com/) are huge databases that generally collect the names and URLs of millions of pages on the Net, along with many lines of text from these pages. They can be searched by either keywords or phrases and provide ranked listings of Web pages that contain the search target words or phrases. (c) *Expert subject guides* such as Russ Dewey's *PsychWeb* (http://www.psychwww.com/) or Jeffrey Browndyke's *Neuropsychology Central* (http://www.neuropsychology central.com/) provide links to online resources in more narrow or specific fields. Volunteer specialists who claim to be experts on the topic select the links.

4. *Check very carefully everything you type online because even the slightest error in spelling a URL or an e-mail address will cause a failure to retrieve the Web page or to deliver the e-mail message.* Remember that computers are stupid and will do exactly and only what you tell them to do. They don't read minds.

Using the Internet in Psychology

Here are five specific suggestions to help students of psychology when using the Net.

1. *Plan what to look for before going online.* Too many psychology students jump right to the Web when they're given a research task, before giving careful thought to what they're looking for. They easily get frustrated because the Web doesn't seem to have anything about the topic. It would be better (a) to think about the subject you are researching and what specifically you want to learn about that topic, (b) to recall what you already know that relates to the topic, especially psychological concepts and vocabulary words associated with the topic, and

(c) to devise a strategy for getting the information you desire. Consult your school's reference library staff or your teachers for suggestions.

2. *Do not rely on the Internet as your principal or only source of data or references in a research project* (especially if you want a good grade). The Net may be easy to use, but your teachers will expect you to cite journal articles, books, and other printed sources more than you cite Internet materials in research. Developing your library skills is essential.

3. *As noted before, don't expect to find many full-text journal articles or other copyrighted commercial materials online for free.* Consult your school's reference librarians about online access to such materials. You are more likely to uncover government reports, specialized technical materials from non-profit organizations, current news and opinion, and general sorts of information rather than findings of specific research studies (although, if the findings were recently in the news, you may find some news reports describing the research).

4. *Learn to recognize the characteristics of a good online resource site.* Good sites have Webmasters or editors personally identified by name and affiliation. Such persons may be professionals or staff members at a reputable institution such as a hospital or university. These sites tend to provide a broad set of resources, are balanced and reasonably objective in their content, and avoid sensational or one-sided viewpoints. Reputable sites tend not to promote specific products or services for money—or, if they do, they acknowledge that there are other resources that people may want to consider. The challenge of evaluating the quality of online resources is such an important skill for students to master so we have included a much more detailed discussion of this matter in Appendix D.

5. *If you contact anyone online for help, be courteous.* Introduce yourself as you would if you were standing in a faculty member's office. Give your name, your school, and a full statement of what help you are asking for and what you've tried to do that hasn't worked. Don't demand that someone help you. Be sure you've done adequate research on your own before contacting an expert on the Web. And don't be surprised if your request for help is turned down by a Webmaster or editor. Frankly, he or she has already done a lot of volunteer work by editing the site online.

I hope some of these ideas and suggestions help. The Internet offers an awesome array of learning resources related to psychology. Welcome to an exciting new world of discovery.

FIRST CANADIAN EDITION

Psychology

themes & variations

CHAPTER 1

Latchezar Boyadjiev, *Source,* L.B. Glass Studios

From Speculation to Science: How Psychology Developed
A New Science Is Born: The Contributions of Wundt and Hall
The Battle of the "Schools" Begins: Structuralism versus
 Functionalism
Watson Alters Psychology's Course as Behaviourism Makes Its
 Debut
Freud Brings the Unconscious into the Picture
Skinner Questions Free Will as Behaviourism Flourishes
The Humanists Revolt
Psychology in Canada
Psychology Comes of Age as a Profession
Featured Study • Bullying in Canadian Schoolyards
Psychology Returns to Its Roots: Renewed Interest in Cognition and
 Physiology
Psychology Broadens Its Horizons: Increased Interest in Cultural
 Diversity
Psychology Adapts: The Emergence of Evolutionary Psychology

Psychology Today: Vigorous and Diversified
Research Areas in Psychology
Professional Specialties in Psychology

Putting It in Perspective: Seven Key Themes
Themes Related to Psychology as a Field of Study
Themes Related to Psychology's Subject Matter

Personal Application • **Improving Academic Performance**
Developing Sound Study Habits
Improving Your Reading
Getting More Out of Lectures
Improving Test-Taking Strategies

Critical Thinking Application • **Developing Critical
Thinking Skills: An Introduction**
The Skills of Critical Thinking
The Attitude of a Critical Thinker
The Need to Teach Critical Thinking
An Example

Recap

Practice Test

The Evolution of Psychology

According to her mother, Suman, Reena Virk was a troubled 14-year-old girl who desperately wanted to fit in. Reena had a difficult time living in Victoria, British Columbia. She rebelled against parental authority and had been bullied frequently. Things were difficult but somehow she managed. On the night of November 14, 1997, things took a more serious turn. According to testimony at the original trial, Reena had wanted to be part of Kelly Ellard's group—Reena and Kelly were acquainted but were not friends. Reena was invited out the night of November 14 to be with members of the group. That night she was swarmed and beaten by the group, consisting of eight youths, including Kelly Ellard. The group consisted of seven girls aged 14–16 and one male aged 16. She managed to escape from them but was dragged by two of the group members to a nearby waterway. Her body was found one week later by police divers a kilometre or so away from where she was beaten. After a series of trials, Ellard was sentenced on July 7, 2005, to life in prison with no chance for parole for seven years (Carmichael, 2005).

The circumstances surrounding Reena's death received national attention in Canada. Canadians were outraged by the events. Reena's life and death along with those of other high-profile bullying casualties, like Dawn-Marie Wesley of Mission, British Columbia, have focused society's attention on bullying and related violent acts. The circumstances surrounding Dawn's suicide were the subject of Lynn Glazier's recent documentary *It's a Girl's World*. The film was broadcast nationally in Canada and provoked considerable debate and reflection. What was particularly noteworthy to many Canadians was that in both of these cases most of the perpetrators were young girls. Bullying by means of physical aggression had been thought to be the province of young males. These and other events made it clear that bullying could quickly escalate to physical harm and that while boys might be the more frequent physical aggressors, girls were not averse to employing physical violence in their attempts to intimidate others. While the group members in these cases were brought to justice, there are countless bullying episodes that go unreported, cases in which the victims, often very young children, suffer alone.

These and similar high-profile events served to motivate and energize researchers in psychology to attempt to document and understand such acts in the hope of attenuating their occurrence. Canadian psychologists are at the forefront of this research effort. Some, such as Marlene Moretti of Simon Fraser University, Tracy Vaillancourt of McMaster University, Debra Pepler of York University, and Wendy Craig of Queen's University, have made important contributions to the growing scientific literature on bullying. We will read more about their research and advice for children and parents regarding bullying in Chapters 11 and 16. We will summarize their findings and their suggestions regarding what to do about such episodes. In this chapter, as in all chapters, we include a Featured Study. Featured Studies give you a look at interesting and relevant real-life research. They show you how psychologists conduct and report their research. The Featured Study in this chapter, on page 15, is by Craig and Pepler (1997) on bullying.

One of the reasons that students and researchers are drawn to psychology is in terms of what it can offer in such circumstances. Psychologists seek to describe, explain, and predict the occurrence of such behaviour. By the rigorous application of scientific methods, psychologists can often offer possible explanations for such behaviour as well as suggestions about what to do about it immediately in order to cope with it and prevent its occurrence in the future.

As you begin your course in Introductory Psychology and start reading this text, you may be wondering, "What is psychology?" Your initial answer to this question is likely to bear little resemblance to the picture of psychology that will emerge as you work your way through this book. Many students at the beginning associate psychology with the study of abnormal psychology. While abnormal psychology is an important component, psychology is about much more than that.

Modern psychology ranges widely in its investigations, looking at divergent topics such as work, sleep, stress, trauma, and brain function. It covers situations in which you work as a member of a group, such as an Olympic gold medal–winning hockey team, and situations in which individual motivation is key. As you progress through this book, you will see that the range and diversity of psychology's subject matter are enormous.

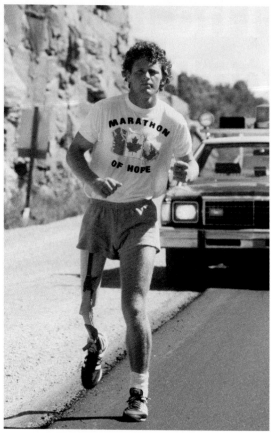

When we took our first courses in psychology, we were surprised to learn that psychology is about a great many things other than abnormal psychology. It's also about how people are able to perceive colour, how hunger is regulated by the brain, whether chimpanzees can use language to communicate, what causes bullying and aggression and how you can protect yourself, and a multitude of other topics. We are confident that you will come away from this text with a new appreciation for the subject matter of psychology and what it can do for you. Psychology is practical, but it is more than that—it is a way of thinking.

We are all exposed to claims about psychological issues. You see reports in the newspapers and on television programs. In some cases the sources are quite authoritative, such as CBC's *The Nature of Things* with David Suzuki. Sometimes the validity of the material is less clear. We hope that as a result of reading this text you will be in a position to think critically about such matters and to be motivated to approach psychological issues in the same way that a psychologist would. As a science, psychology demands that researchers ask precise questions about such issues and that they test their ideas through systematic observation. Psychology provides a way of building knowledge that is relatively accurate and

dependable. As you will see in the text, psychologists study an amazing variety of topics.

Mental illness, rats running in mazes, the physiology of hunger, the mysteries of love, creativity, and prejudice—what ties all these subjects together in a single discipline? How did psychology come to be so diverse? Why is it so different from what most people expect? If psychology is a social science, why do psychologists study subjects such as brain chemistry and the physiological basis of vision? To answer these questions, we begin our introduction to psychology by retracing its development. By seeing how psychology grew and changed, you will discover why it has the shape it does today.

After our journey into psychology's past, we will examine a formal definition of psychology. We'll also look at psychology as it is today—a sprawling, multifaceted science and profession. To help keep psychology's diversity in perspective, the chapter concludes with a discussion of seven unifying themes that will serve as connecting threads in the chapters to come. Finally, in the chapter's Personal Application we'll review research that gives insights on how to be an effective student, and in the Critical Thinking Application we'll discuss how critical thinking skills can be enhanced.

From Speculation to Science: How Psychology Developed

Psychology's story is one of people groping toward a better understanding of themselves. As psychology has evolved, its focus, methods, and explanatory models have changed. In this section we'll look at how psychology has developed from philosophical speculations about the mind into a modern science. A pictorial overview of the highlights of psychology's history can be found on pages 22–23.

The term *psychology* comes from two Greek words, *psyche*, meaning the soul, and *logos*, referring to the study of a subject. These two Greek roots were first put together to define a topic of study in the 16th century, when *psyche* was used to refer to the soul, spirit, or mind, as distinguished from the body (Boring, 1966). Not until the early 18th century did the term *psychology* gain more than rare usage among scholars. By that time it had acquired its literal meaning, "the study of the mind."

Of course, people have always wondered about the mysteries of the mind. In that sense, psychology is as old as the human race. But it was only a little over a hundred years ago that psychology emerged as a scientific discipline.

A New Science Is Born: The Contributions of Wundt and Hall 1A

Psychology's intellectual parents were the disciplines of philosophy and physiology. By the 1870s a small number of scholars in both fields were actively exploring questions about the mind. How are bodily sensations turned into a mental awareness of the outside world? Are people's perceptions of the world accurate reflections of reality? How do mind and body interact? The philosophers and physiologists who were interested in the mind viewed such questions as fascinating issues within their respective fields. It was a German professor, Wilhelm Wundt (1832–1920), who eventually changed this view. Wundt mounted a campaign to make psychology an independent discipline rather than a stepchild of philosophy or physiology.

The time and place were right for Wundt's appeal. German universities were in a healthy period of expansion, so resources were available for new disciplines. Furthermore, the intellectual climate favoured the scientific approach that Wundt advocated. Hence, his proposals were well received by the academic community. In 1879 Wundt succeeded in establishing the first formal laboratory for research in psychology at the University of Leipzig. In deference to this landmark event, historians have christened 1879 as psychology's "date of birth." Soon afterward, in 1881, Wundt established the first journal devoted to publishing research on psychology. All in all, Wundt's campaign was so successful that today he is widely characterized as the founder of psychology.

Wundt's conception of psychology was influential for decades. Borrowing from his training in physiology, Wundt (1874) declared that the new psychology should be a science modelled after fields such as physics and chemistry. What was the subject matter of the new science? According to Wundt, psychology's primary focus was consciousness—the awareness of immediate experience. Thus, psychology became the scientific study of conscious experience. This orientation kept psychology focused on the mind and mental processes. But it demanded that the methods psychologists used to investigate the mind be as scientific as those of chemists or physicists.

Wundt was a tireless, dedicated scholar who generated an estimated 54 000 pages of books and articles in his career (Bringmann & Balk, 1992).

PREVIEW QUESTIONS
- What were Wundt's and Hall's key ideas and accomplishments?
- What were the chief tenets of structuralism and functionalism?
- What was the main idea underlying behaviourism?

The establishment of the first research laboratory in psychology by Wilhelm Wundt (far right) marked the birth of psychology as a modern science.

Archives of the History of American Psychology, University of Akron, Akron, Ohio.

Figure 1.1

Early research laboratories in North America. This map highlights the location and year of founding for the first 24 psychological research labs established in North American colleges and universities. As the colour coding shows, a great many of these labs were founded by the students of Wilhelm Wundt, G. Stanley Hall, and William James. (Based on Garvey, 1929; Hilgard, 1987)

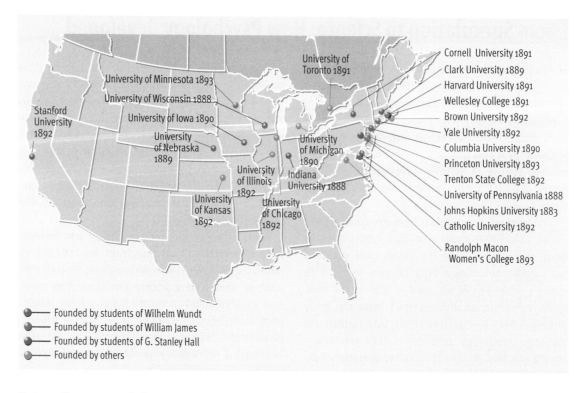

University of Minnesota 1893
University of Wisconsin 1888
University of Iowa 1890
University of Nebraska 1889
Stanford University 1892
University of Illinois 1892
University of Kansas 1892
University of Chicago 1892
University of Michigan 1890
Indiana University 1888
University of Toronto 1891

Cornell University 1891
Clark University 1889
Harvard University 1891
Wellesley College 1891
Brown University 1892
Yale University 1892
Columbia University 1890
Princeton University 1893
Trenton State College 1892
University of Pennsylvania 1888
Johns Hopkins University 1883
Catholic University 1892
Randolph Macon Women's College 1893

— Founded by students of Wilhelm Wundt
— Founded by students of William James
— Founded by students of G. Stanley Hall
— Founded by others

> *Physiology informs us about those life phenomena that we perceive by our external senses. In psychology, the person looks upon himself as from within and tries to explain the interrelations of those processes that this internal observation discloses.*
> WILHELM WUNDT
> *1832–1920*

Web Link 1.1

History of Psychology
http://psych.athabascau.ca/html/aupr/history.shtml

This site maintained by the Department of Psychology at Athabasca University contains links to many articles and sites focusing on the history of psychology.

Note: You can access all Web Links from the Web site for this text (http://www.themesandvariations.nelson.com).

Outstanding young scholars came to Leipzig to study under Wundt. Many of Wundt's students then fanned out across Germany and North America, establishing the research laboratories that formed the basis for the new, independent science of psychology. Indeed, it was in North America that Wundt's new science grew by leaps and bounds.

Between 1883 and 1893, some 24 new psychological research laboratories sprang up in the United States and Canada, at the schools shown in Figure 1.1 (Benjamin, 2000). Many of the laboratories were started by Wundt's students, or by his students' students.

G. Stanley Hall (1846–1924), who studied briefly with Wundt, was a particularly important contributor to the rapid growth of psychology in America. Toward the end of the 19th century, Hall reeled off a series of "firsts" for American psychology. To begin with, he established America's first research laboratory in psychology at Johns Hopkins University in 1883. Four years later he launched America's first psychology journal. Furthermore, in 1892 he was the driving force behind the establishment of the American Psychological Association (APA) and was elected its first president. Today the APA is the world's largest organization devoted to the advancement of psychology, with over 155 000 members and affiliates. Hall never envisioned such a vast membership when he and 26 others set up their new organization. Two early psychologists from the University of Toronto, James Mark Baldwin and James Gibson Hume, were among those who attended meetings designed to establish the American Psychological Association (Greene, 2004; Hoff, 1992). Psychology in Canada and some of the figures who were important in the establishment of it will be discussed later in this chapter.

Exactly why Americans took to psychology so quickly is hard to say. Perhaps it was because America's relatively young universities were more open to new disciplines than were the older, more tradition-bound universities in Europe. In any case, although psychology was born in Germany, it blossomed into adolescence in America. Like many adolescents, however, the young science was about to enter a period of turbulence and turmoil.

The Battle of the "Schools" Begins: Structuralism versus Functionalism

While reading about how psychology became a science, you might have imagined that psychologists became a unified group of scholars who busily added new discoveries to an uncontested store of "facts." In reality, no science works that way. Competing schools of thought exist in most scientific disciplines. Sometimes the disagreements among these schools are sharp. Such diversity in thought is natural and often stimulates enlightening debate. In psychology, the first two major schools of thought, structuralism and functionalism, were entangled in the field's first great intellectual battle.

Structuralism emerged through the leadership of Edward Titchener, an Englishman who emigrated to the United States in 1892 and taught for decades at Cornell University. Although Titchener earned his degree in Wundt's Leipzig laboratory and expressed great admiration for Wundt's work, he brought his own version of Wundt's psychology to America (Hilgard, 1987; Thorne & Henley, 1997). **Structuralism was based on the notion that the task of psychology is to analyze consciousness into its basic elements and investigate how these elements are related.** Just as physicists were studying how matter is made up of basic particles, the structuralists wanted to identify and examine the fundamental components of conscious experience, such as sensations, feelings, and images.

Although the structuralists explored many questions, most of their work concerned sensation and perception in vision, hearing, and touch. To examine the contents of consciousness, the structuralists depended on the method of **introspection, or the careful, systematic self-observation of one's own conscious experience.** As practised by the structuralists, introspection required training to make the subject—the person being studied—more objective and more aware. Once trained, subjects were typically exposed to auditory tones, optical illusions, and visual stimuli under carefully controlled and systematically varied conditions and were asked to analyze what they experienced. Limitations associated with the use of introspection were a factor that contributed to the demise of structuralism. If you depend solely on an individual's reflection to document a phenomenon, there is no independent objective evaluation of that claim.

The functionalists took a different view of psychology's task. **Functionalism was based on the belief that psychology should investigate the function or purpose of consciousness, rather than its structure.** The chief impetus for the emergence of functionalism was the work of William James (1842–1910), a brilliant American scholar (and brother of novelist Henry James). James's formal training was in medicine. However, he did not find medicine to be intellectually challenging, and he felt he was too sickly to pursue a medical practice (Ross, 1991). Hence, when an opportunity arose in 1872, he joined the faculty of Harvard University to pursue a less arduous career in academia. Medicine's loss proved to be psychology's gain, as James quickly became an intellectual giant in the field. James's landmark book, *Principles of Psychology* (1890), became standard reading for generations of psychol-ogists and is perhaps the most influential text in the history of psychology (Weiten & Wight, 1992).

James's thinking illustrates how psychology, like any field, is deeply embedded in a network of cultural and intellectual influences. James had been impressed with Charles Darwin's (1859, 1871) concept of *natural selection*. According to the principle of **natural selection, heritable characteristics that provide a survival or reproductive advantage are more likely than alternative characteristics to be passed on to subsequent generations and thus come to be "selected" over time.** This cornerstone notion of Darwin's evolutionary theory suggested that the typical characteristics of a species must serve some purpose. Applying this idea to humans, James (1890) noted that consciousness obviously is an important characteristic of our species. Hence, he contended that psychology should investigate the functions rather than the *structure* of consciousness.

James also argued that the structuralists' approach missed the real nature of conscious experience. Consciousness, he argued, consists of a continuous *flow* of thoughts. In analyzing consciousness into its "elements," the structuralists were looking at static points in that flow. James wanted to understand the flow itself, which he called the "stream of consciousness."

Whereas structuralists naturally gravitated to the laboratory, functionalists were more interested in how people adapt their behaviour to the demands of the real world around them. This practical slant led them to introduce new subjects into psychology. Instead of focusing on sensation and perception, functionalists such as James McKeen Cattell and John Dewey began to investigate mental testing, patterns of development in children, the effectiveness of educational practices, and behavioural differences between the sexes. These new topics may have played a role in attracting the first women into the field of psychology. Some of these women played critical roles in the developing science of psychology. Mary Washburn was the first woman in the United States to receive a Ph.D. in psychology. She was the author of the book *The Animal Mind* (1908), which served as a precursor to behaviourism, a theoretical approach discussed on page 6. Another pioneering female psychologist, Leta Hollingworth, did important work on children's intelligence and was influential in debunking some of the theories current at the time that were proposed to explain why women were "inferior" to men. Mary Whiton Calkins, who studied with William James, went on to become the first woman to serve as president of the

❝*It is just free water of consciousness that psychologists resolutely overlook.*❞
WILLIAM JAMES
1842–1910

W W W

Web Link 1.2

Mind and Body: René Descartes to William James
http://serendip.brynmawr.edu/ Mind/Table.html

Designed originally to celebrate psychology's first century as an independent discipline, this online exhibition traces three historical themes: the mind–body problem posed in the 17th century by philosopher René Descartes, the rise of experimental psychology, and the beginnings of psychology in America.

The Evolution of Psychology

"The time seems to have come when psychology must discard all references to consciousness."

JOHN B. WATSON
1878–1958

Web Link 1.3

History and Philosophy of Psychology Web Resources
http://www.psych.yorku.ca/orgs/resource.htm

Professor Christopher Green of York University has assembled a wide range of Web-based materials relating to psychology's theoretical and historical past, including a collection of sites focused on specific individuals. Web pages devoted to key figures mentioned in this chapter (such as Mary Whiton Calkins, William James, B. F. Skinner, and Margaret Floy Washburn) can be accessed here. It contains lists of and links to hundreds of classic papers in psychology. It has been in operation since the late 1990s and to date has received over 10 million hits. If you need a classic important paper, you will likely find it here. It even includes a link to the floor plans and a description of the first experimental psychology laboratory established in Canada (1891 at the University of Toronto).

American Psychological Association. You can learn more about women in psychology by visiting the American Psychological Society's Web page for the Society for the Psychology of Women Heritage Site (http://www.psych.yorku.ca/femhop/). The site is maintained by York University psychologist Alexandra Rutherford.

The impassioned advocates of structuralism and functionalism saw themselves as fighting for high stakes: the definition and future direction of the new science of psychology. Their war of ideas continued energetically for many years. Who won? Most historians give the edge to functionalism. Although both schools of thought gradually faded away, functionalism fostered the development of two descendants that have dominated modern psychology: behaviourism and applied psychology.

Watson Alters Psychology's Course as Behaviourism Makes Its Debut

 1A 5B

The debate between structuralism and functionalism was only the prelude to other fundamental controversies in psychology. In the early 1900s, another major school of thought appeared that dramatically altered the course of psychology. Founded by John B. Watson (1878–1958), *behaviourism* **is a theoretical orientation based on the premise that scientific psychology should study only observable behaviour.** It is important to understand what a radical change this definition represents. Watson (1913, 1919) was proposing that psychologists abandon the study of consciousness altogether and focus exclusively on behaviours that they could observe directly. In essence, he was redefining what scientific psychology should be about.

Why did Watson argue for such a fundamental shift in direction? Because to him, the power of the scientific method rested on the idea of verifiability. In principle, scientific claims can always be verified (or disproved) by anyone who is able and willing to make the required observations. However, this power depends on studying things that can be observed objectively. Otherwise, the advantage of using the scientific approach—replacing vague speculation and personal opinion with reliable, exact knowledge—is lost. For Watson, mental processes were not a proper subject for scientific study because they are ultimately private events. After all, no one can see or touch another's thoughts. Consequently, if psychology were to be a science, it would have to give

up consciousness as its subject matter and become instead the *science of behaviour*.

Behaviour **refers to any overt (observable) response or activity by an organism.** Watson asserted that psychologists could study anything that people do or say—shopping, playing chess, eating, complimenting a friend—but they could not study scientifically the thoughts, wishes, and feelings that might accompany these observable behaviours.

Watson's radical reorientation of psychology did not end with his redefinition of its subject matter. He also staked out a rather extreme position on one of psychology's oldest and most fundamental questions: the issue of nature versus nurture. This age-old debate is concerned with whether behaviour is determined mainly by genetic inheritance ("nature") or by environment and experience ("nurture"). To oversimplify, the question is this: Is a great concert pianist or a master criminal born, or made? Watson argued that each is made, not born. In other words, he downplayed the importance of heredity, maintaining that behaviour is governed primarily by the environment. Indeed, he boldly claimed:

Give me a dozen healthy infants, well-formed, and my own special world to bring them up in and I'll guarantee to take any one at random and train him to become any type of specialist I might select—doctor, lawyer, artist, merchant-chief, and yes, even beggar-man and thief, regardless of his talents, penchants, tendencies, abilities, vocations and race of his ancestors. I am going beyond my facts and I admit it, but so have the advocates of the contrary and they have been doing it for many thousands of years. (Watson, 1924, p. 82)

For obvious reasons, Watson's tongue-in-cheek challenge was never put to a test. Although this widely cited quotation overstated and oversimplified Watson's views on the nature–nurture issue (Todd & Morris, 1992), his writings contributed to the strong environmental slant that became associated with behaviourism (Horowitz, 1992).

The behaviourists eventually came to view psychology's mission as an attempt to relate overt behaviours ("responses") to observable events in the environment ("stimuli"). **A *stimulus* is any detectable input from the environment.** Stimuli can range from light and sound waves to such complex inputs as the words on this page, advertisements on TV, or sarcastic remarks from a friend. Because the behaviourists investigated stimulus–response relationships, the behavioural approach is often referred to as *stimulus–response (S–R) psychology*.

Although it met resistance and skepticism in some quarters, Watson's behavioural point of view gradually took hold (Samelson, 1981, 1994). Actually, psychology had already been edging away imperceptibly from the study of consciousness toward the study of behaviour for two decades before Watson made his case for behaviourism (Leahey, 1992). The gradual emergence of behaviourism was partly attributable to an important discovery made around the turn of the last century by Ivan Pavlov, a Russian physiologist. As you'll learn in Chapter 6, Pavlov (1906) showed that dogs could be trained to salivate in response to an auditory stimulus such as a tone. This deceptively simple demonstration provided insight into how stimulus–response bonds are formed. Such bonds were exactly what behaviourists wanted to investigate, so Pavlov's discovery paved the way for their work.

Behaviourism's stimulus–response approach contributed to the rise of animal research in psychology. Having deleted consciousness from their scope of concern, behaviourists no longer needed to study human subjects who could report on their mental processes. Many psychologists thought that animals would make better research subjects anyway. One key reason was that experimental research is often more productive if experimenters can exert considerable *control* over their subjects. Otherwise, too many complicating factors enter into the picture and contaminate the experiment. Obviously, a researcher can exert much more control over a laboratory rat or pigeon than over a human subject, who arrives at a lab with years of uncontrolled experience and who will probably insist on going home at night. Thus, the discipline that had begun its life a few decades earlier as the study of the mind now found itself heavily involved in the study of simple responses made by laboratory animals.

Although Watson's views shaped the evolution of psychology for many decades, his ideas did not go unchallenged. In Germany opposition came from an emerging school of thought called *Gestalt* psychology. The Gestalt theorists, who were primarily concerned with perception (we'll discuss their ideas in Chapter 4), argued that psychology should continue to study conscious experience rather than overt behaviour. Another alternative conception of psychology emerged from Austria, where an obscure physician named Sigmund Freud had been contemplating the mysteries of unconscious mental processes. We'll look at Freud's ideas next.

REVIEW OF KEY POINTS

- Psychology's intellectual parents were 19th-century philosophy and physiology, disciplines that shared an interest in the mysteries of the mind.
- Psychology became an independent discipline when Wilhelm Wundt established the first psychological research laboratory in 1879 at Leipzig, Germany. He defined psychology as the scientific study of consciousness.
- The new discipline grew rapidly in North America in the late 19th century, as illustrated by G. Stanley Hall's career.
- Hall established America's first research lab in psychology and founded the American Psychological Association.
- The structuralists, led by Edward Titchener, believed that psychology should use introspection to analyze consciousness into its basic elements.
- The functionalists, inspired by the ideas of William James, believed that psychology should focus on the purpose and adaptive functions of consciousness. Functionalism paved the way for behaviourism and applied psychology.
- Behaviourists, led by John B. Watson, argued that psychology should study only observable behaviour. Thus, they campaigned to redefine psychology as the science of behaviour.
- Emphasizing the importance of the environment over heredity, the behaviourists began to explore stimulus–response relationships, often using laboratory animals as subjects.

CONCEPT CHECK 1.1

Understanding the Implications of Major Theories: Wundt, James, and Watson

Check your understanding of the implications of some of the major theories reviewed in this chapter by indicating who is likely to have made each of the statements quoted below. Choose from the following theorists: (a) Wilhelm Wundt, (b) William James, and (c) John B. Watson. You'll find the answers in Appendix A in the back of the book.

_____ 1. "Our conclusion is that we have no real evidence of the inheritance of traits. I would feel perfectly confident in the ultimately favourable outcome of careful upbringing of a healthy, well-formed baby born of a long line of crooks, murderers and thieves, and prostitutes."

_____ 2. "The book which I present to the public is an attempt to mark out a new domain of science.... The new discipline rests upon anatomical and physiological foundations.... The experimental treatment of psychological problems must be pronounced from every point of view to be in its first beginnings."

_____ 3. "Consciousness, then, does not appear to itself chopped up in bits. Such words as 'chain' or 'train' do not describe it fitly.... It is nothing jointed; it flows. A 'river' or 'stream' are the metaphors by which it is most naturally described."

Freud Brings the Unconscious into the Picture

 1A, 10A

- What did Freud have to say about the unconscious and sexuality, and why were his ideas so controversial?
- How did Freudian theory affect the mainstream of psychology?
- What basic principle of behaviour did Skinner emphasize?
- What did Skinner do to stir up controversy?
- What was the impetus for the emergence of humanism?
- Where and when did academic psychology emerge in Canada?

"*The unconscious is the true psychical reality; in its innermost nature it is as much unknown to us as the reality of the external world.*"
SIGMUND FREUD
1856–1939

Sigmund Freud (1856–1939) was an Austrian physician who early in his career dreamed of achieving fame by making an important discovery. His determination was such that in medical school he dissected 400 male eels to prove for the first time that they had testes. His work with eels did not make him famous, but his subsequent work with people did. Indeed, his theories made him one of the most controversial intellectual figures of modern times.

Freud's (1900, 1933) approach to psychology grew out of his efforts to treat mental disorders. In his medical practice, Freud treated people troubled by psychological problems such as irrational fears, obsessions, and anxieties with an innovative procedure he called *psychoanalysis* (described in detail in Chapter 15). Decades of experience probing into his patients' lives provided much of the inspiration for Freud's theory. He also gathered material by looking inward and examining his own anxieties, conflicts, and desires.

His work with patients and his own self-exploration persuaded Freud of the existence of what he called the unconscious. According to Freud, **the *unconscious* contains thoughts, memories, and desires that are well below the surface of conscious aware-**ness but that nonetheless exert great influence on behaviour. Freud based his concept of the unconscious on a variety of observations. For instance, he noticed that seemingly meaningless slips of the tongue (such as "I decided to take a summer school curse") often appeared to reveal a person's true feelings. He also noted that his patients' dreams often seemed to express important feelings they were unaware of. Knitting these and other observations together, Freud eventually concluded that psychological disturbances are largely caused by personal conflicts existing at an unconscious level. More generally, his ***psychoanalytic theory* attempts to explain personality, motivation, and mental disorders by focusing on unconscious determinants of behaviour.**

Freud's concept of the unconscious was not entirely new (Rieber, 1998). However, it was a major departure from the prevailing belief that people are fully aware of the forces affecting their behaviour. In arguing that behaviour is governed by unconscious forces, Freud made the disconcerting suggestion that people are not masters of their own minds. Other aspects of Freud's theory also stirred up debate. For instance, he proposed that behaviour is greatly influenced by how people cope with their sexual urges. At a time when people were far less comfortable discussing sexual issues than they are today, even scien-

A portrait taken at the famous Clark University psychology conference, September 1909. Pictured are Freud, G. Stanley Hall, and four of Freud's students and associates. Seated, left to right: Freud, Hall, and Carl Jung; standing: Abraham Brill, Ernest Jones, and Sandor Ferenczi.

Courtesy of the Clark University Archives.

tists were offended and scandalized by Freud's emphasis on sex. Small wonder, then, that Freud was soon engulfed in controversy.

In part because of its controversial nature, Freud's theory gained influence only very slowly. However, he gradually won acceptance within medicine, attracting prominent followers such as Carl Jung and Alfred Adler. Important public recognition from psychology came in 1909, when G. Stanley Hall invited Freud to give a series of lectures at Clark University in Massachusetts (see the photo on page 8).

By 1920 psychoanalytic theory was widely known around the world, but it continued to meet with considerable resistance in psychology (Fancher, 2000). Why? The main reason was that it conflicted with the spirit of the times in psychology. Many psychologists were becoming uncomfortable with their earlier focus on conscious experience and were turning to the less murky subject of observable behaviour. If they felt that conscious experience was inaccessible to scientific observation, you can imagine how they felt about trying to study unconscious experience. Most psychologists contemptuously viewed psychoanalytic theory as unscientific speculation that would eventually fade away (Hornstein, 1992).

They turned out to be wrong. Psychoanalytic ideas steadily gained credence in the culture at large, influencing thought in medicine, the arts, and literature (Rieber, 1998). According to Hornstein (1992), by the 1940s, "Psychoanalysis was becoming so popular that it threatened to eclipse psychology entirely" (p. 258). Thus, the widespread popular acceptance of psychoanalytic theory essentially forced psychologists to apply their scientific methods to the topics Freud had studied: personality, motivation, and abnormal behaviour. As they turned to these topics, many of them saw merit in some of Freud's notions (Rosenzweig, 1985). Although psychoanalytic theory continued to generate heated debate, it survived to become an influential theoretical perspective. Today, many psychoanalytic concepts have filtered into the mainstream of psychology (Westen, 1998).

Skinner Questions Free Will as Behaviourism Flourishes 1A, 10B

While psychoanalytic thought was slowly gaining a foothold within psychology, a young psychologist from Harvard, B.F. Skinner (1904–1990), was emerging as a central figure in behaviourism and the history of psychology. Skinner had set out to be a writer but concluded that he had "nothing important to say"

B.F. Skinner created considerable controversy when he asserted that free will is an illusion.

(1967, p. 395). However, he had many important things to say within psychology about behaviour.

Although Skinner was influenced by Watson's methodological behaviourism and by Pavlov's work on conditioned reflexes, he eventually developed a system based on his own philosophy of *radical behaviourism* that represented a departure from earlier forms of behaviourism and neo-behaviourism (Rutherford, in press).

Skinner did not deny the existence of internal, mental events but he redefined them as private events and did not think that they should be given special status when explaining behaviour. Skinner noted that these private events are much more difficult to study and much of his own science of behaviour is based on public observable events. Although they could be studied scientifically, he believed that there was little need to do so.

According to Skinner, if the stimulus of food is followed by the response of eating, we can fully describe what is happening without making any guesses about whether the animal is experiencing hunger. Like Watson, Skinner also emphasized how environmental factors mould behaviour. Although he repeatedly acknowledged that an organism's behaviour is influenced by its biological endowment, he argued that psychology could understand and predict behaviour adequately without resorting to physiological explanations (Delprato & Midgley, 1992).

Web Link 1.4

Museum of the History of Psychological Instrumentation
http://www.chss.montclair.edu/psychology/museum/

You can examine instruments and complex apparatus used by psychological researchers in the discipline's early decades in this "cybermuseum" maintained by Edward J. Haupt and Thomas Perera of Montclair State University.

"I submit that what we call the behaviour of the human organism is no more free than its digestion."
B.F. SKINNER
1904–1990

The Evolution of Psychology

The fundamental principle of behaviour documented by Skinner is deceptively simple: Organisms tend to repeat responses that lead to positive outcomes, and they tend not to repeat responses that lead to neutral or negative outcomes. Despite its simplicity, this principle turns out to be quite powerful. Working primarily with laboratory rats and pigeons, Skinner showed that he could exert remarkable control over the behaviour of animals by manipulating the outcomes of their responses. He was even able to train animals to perform unnatural behaviours. For example, he once trained some pigeons to play ping-pong! Skinner's followers eventually showed that the principles uncovered in their animal research could be applied to complex human behaviours as well. Behavioural principles are now widely used in factories, schools, prisons, mental hospitals, and a variety of other settings (see Chapter 6).

Skinner's ideas had repercussions that went far beyond the debate among psychologists about what they should study. Skinner spelled out the full implications of his findings in his book *Beyond Freedom and Dignity* (1971). There he asserted that all behaviour is fully governed by external stimuli. In other words, your behaviour is determined in predictable ways by lawful principles, just as the flight of an arrow is governed by the laws of physics. Thus, if you believe that your actions are the result of conscious decisions, you're wrong. According to Skinner, people are controlled by their environment, not by themselves. In short, Skinner arrived at the conclusion that *free will is an illusion*.

As you can readily imagine, such a disconcerting view of human nature was not universally acclaimed. Like Freud, Skinner was the target of harsh criticism. Much of this criticism stemmed from misinterpretations of his ideas that were disseminated in the popular press (Rutherford, 2000). For example, his analysis of free will was often misconstrued as an attack on the concept of a free society—which it was not—and he was often mistakenly condemned for advocating an undemocratic "scientific police state" (Dinsmoor, 1992).

There is no doubt that Skinner significantly impacted the developing field of psychology. But his influence went beyond academia. Some of his books topped the popular bestsellers' lists. According to Alexandra Rutherford, a Canadian psychologist specializing in the history of psychology, at the height of his influence his was a household name. Coverage of Skinner appeared in magazines and newspapers, and on radio and television. He himself popularized some of his ideas by writing for mass consumer magazines. For example, he wrote an article on the topic of the "Baby in a Box" for the *Ladies' Home Journal* in

1947. His development of mechanical teaching machines was widely covered by the popular press. He also published a fictional account of the application of his principles of operant conditioning to produce a utopian society in his book *Walden Two* in 1948. Not everyone was pleased by his message. According to Rutherford, the public furor over his messages reached its greatest heights upon publication of his book *Beyond Freedom and Dignity* in 1971.

It seems clear that Skinner and his ideas influenced both academia and the general population to a degree matched by few psychologists. For many laypersons, for a time at least, Skinner was the face of psychology. Whatever the exact nature of the relationship between Skinner and the general public, it seems quite clear that it was not a simple one. As Rutherford (2003) points out, the influence was most likely a bi-directional one. As she notes, "Skinner was both a product of the American context and a challenger of some of its most prized ideals" (p. 20). This interrelationship and Skinner's impact will become clearer in Chapter 6.

Despite all the controversy, however, behaviourism flourished as the dominant school of thought in psychology during the 1950s and 1960s (Gilgen, 1982). And when 93 psychology department chairpersons were surveyed in 1990 about the field's most important contributors (Estes, Coston, & Fournet, 1990), Skinner was ranked at the top of the list (see Table 1.1).

Table (1.1) Important Figures in the History of Psychology

In a 1990 survey, 93 chairpersons of psychology departments ranked psychology's most important contributors (Estes, Coston, & Fournet, 1990, as cited in Korn et al., 1991). As you can see, B. F. Skinner edged out Sigmund Freud for the top ranking. Although these ratings of scholarly eminence are open to considerable debate, the data should give you some idea of the relative impact of various figures in the history of psychology.

Rank	Individual	Rank Points
1	B. F. Skinner	508
2	Sigmund Freud	459
3	William James	372
4	Jean Piaget	237
5	G. Stanley Hall	216
6	Wilhelm Wundt	203
7	Carl Rogers	192
8	John B. Watson	188
9	Ivan Pavlov	152
10	E. L. Thorndike	124

SOURCE: Adapted from Korn, J. H., Davis, R., & Davis, S. F. (1991). Historians' and chairpersons' judgments of eminence among psychologists. *American Psychologist, 46,* 789–792. Copyright © 1991 by the American Psychological Association. Adapted with permission.

Table 1.2 Overview of Six Contemporary Theoretical Perspectives in Psychology

Perspective and Its Influential Period	Principal Contributors	Subject Matter	Basic Premise
Behavioural (1913–present)	John B. Watson Ivan Pavlov B. F. Skinner	Effects of environment on the overt behaviour of humans and animals	Only observable events (stimulus–response relations) can be studied scientifically.
Psychoanalytic (1900–present)	Sigmund Freud Carl Jung Alfred Adler	Unconscious determinants of behaviour	Unconscious motives and experiences in early childhood govern personality and mental disorders.
Humanistic (1950s–present)	Carl Rogers Abraham Maslow	Unique aspects of human experience	Humans are free, rational beings with the potential for personal growth, and they are fundamentally different from animals.
Cognitive (1950s–present)	Jean Piaget Noam Chomsky Herbert Simon	Thoughts; mental processes	Human behaviour cannot be fully understood without examining how people acquire, store, and process information.
Biological (1950s–present)	James Olds Roger Sperry David Hubel Torsten Wiesel	Physiological basis of behaviour in humans and animals	An organism's functioning can be explained in terms of the bodily structures and biochemical processes that underlie behaviour.
Evolutionary (1980s–present)	David Buss Martin Daly Margo Wilson Leda Cosmides John Tooby	Evolutionary basis of behaviour in humans and animals	Behaviour patterns have evolved to solve adaptive problems; natural selection favours behaviours that enhance reproductive success.

The Humanists Revolt

 1A, 10C

By the 1950s, behaviourism and psychoanalytic theory had become the most influential schools of thought in psychology. However, many psychologists found these theoretical orientations unappealing. The principal charge hurled at both schools was that they were "dehumanizing." Psychoanalytic theory was attacked for its belief that behaviour is dominated by primitive, sexual urges. Behaviourism was criticized for its preoccupation with the study of simple animal behaviour. Both theories were criticized because they suggested that people are not masters of their own destinies. Above all, many people argued, both schools of thought failed to recognize the unique qualities of *human* behaviour.

Beginning in the 1950s, the diverse opposition to behaviourism and psychoanalytic theory blended into a loose alliance that eventually became a new school of thought called "humanism" (Bühler & Allen, 1972). In psychology, **humanism is a theoretical orientation that emphasizes the unique qualities of humans, especially their freedom and their potential for personal growth**. Some of the key differences between the humanistic, psychoanalytic, and behavioural viewpoints are summarized in Table 1.2, which compares six influential contemporary theoretical perspectives in psychology.

Humanists take an *optimistic* view of human nature. They maintain that people are not pawns of either their animal heritage or environmental circumstances. Furthermore, they say, because humans are fundamentally different from other animals, research on animals has little relevance to the understanding of human behaviour. The most prominent architects of the humanistic movement have been Carl Rogers (1902–1987) and Abraham Maslow (1908–1970). Rogers (1951) argued that human behaviour is governed primarily by each individual's sense of self, or "self-concept"—which animals presumably lack. Both he and Maslow (1954) maintained that to fully understand people's behaviour, psychologists must take into account the fundamental human drive toward personal growth. They asserted that people have a basic need to continue to evolve as human beings and to fulfill their potentials. In fact, the humanists argued that many psychological disturbances are the result of thwarting these uniquely human needs.

It seems to me that at bottom each person is asking, 'Who am I, really?' How can I get in touch with this real self, underlying all my surface behaviour? How can I become myself?
CARL ROGERS
1902–1987

The Evolution of Psychology **11**

Understanding the Implications of Major Theories: Freud, Skinner, and Rogers

Check your understanding of the implications of some of the major theories reviewed in this chapter by indicating who is likely to have made each of the statements quoted below. Choose from the following: (a) Sigmund Freud, (b) B. F. Skinner, and (c) Carl Rogers. You'll find the answers in Appendix A at the back of the book.

_____ **1.** "In the traditional view, a person is free.... He can therefore be held responsible for what he does and justly punished if he offends. That view, together with its associated practices, must be re-examined when a scientific analysis reveals unsuspected controlling relations between behaviour and environment."

_____ **2.** "He that has eyes to see and ears to hear may convince himself that no mortal can keep a secret. If the lips are silent, he chatters with his fingertips; betrayal oozes out of him at every pore. And thus the task of making conscious the most hidden recesses of the mind is one which it is quite possible to accomplish."

_____ **3.** "I do not have a Pollyanna view of human nature.... Yet one of the most refreshing and invigorating parts of my experience is to work with [my clients] and to discover the strongly positive directional tendencies which exist in them, as in all of us, at the deepest levels."

Fragmentation and dissent have reduced the influence of humanism in recent decades, although some advocates are predicting a renaissance for the humanistic movement (Taylor, 1999). To date, the humanists' greatest contribution to psychology has probably been their innovative treatments for psychological problems and disorders. More generally, the humanists have argued eloquently for a different picture of human nature than those implied by psychoanalysis and behaviourism (Wertz, 1998).

Psychology in Canada

While Wundt is credited with establishing the first experimental laboratory in psychology in Leipzig, Germany, in 1879, North American psychology was not far behind. G. Stanley Hall established the first experimental laboratory in psychology in 1883 at Johns Hopkins University in Baltimore, Maryland. The first experimental laboratory in the British Empire was established by James Mark Baldwin at the University of Toronto in 1891. While this date marks the birth of experimental psychology in Canada, psychology began as an academic topic in Canadian universities before then. The first psychology course offered at a Canadian university was likely at Dalhousie in 1838 (Wright & Myers, 1982). According to Wright and Myers (1982), the teaching of psychology at universities in Canada became more common in the 1850s, beginning then at McGill University in Montreal and the University of Toronto. In many cases, however, these first courses in psychology were taught through philosophy departments (Greene, 2004; Hoff, 1992; Kenwood, 1999; Pols, 2002). As elsewhere, psychology in Canada had its beginnings in philosophy (Hagman, 1999; Kenwood, 1999; Jung, 1999; Tolman, 1999). The first distinct academic department of psychology was established at McGill University in 1924, with the University of Toronto (in 1926), the University of Western Ontario (in 1931), and University of Manitoba (in 1936) not far behind (Wright & Myers, 1982). Growth in work conducted and in the number of psychology departments continued over the decades (e.g., Dalhousie in 1948 and University of British Columbia in 1958), especially the period of growth paralleling the increase in the number of new universities established in the 1960s and 1970s (e.g., separate psychology departments at York University in 1962 and at Trent University in 1964). During these years, growth in graduate training (i.e., master's and Ph.D. degrees) in psychology also flourished.

The beginnings of experimental psychology in Canada were far from quiescent. James Mark Baldwin accepted a position at the University of Toronto in 1889. Baldwin was born in South Carolina and before completing his Ph.D. at Princeton University had spent some time working in Wundt's lab in Leipzig (Greene, 2004). He applied to fill an opening in the University of Toronto's philosophy department, and his main competition at the time was James Gibson Hume, who had received his undergraduate training at the University of Toronto. Baldwin was clearly the better candidate but was opposed by many both at the university and in the community because of his citizenship and the opposition of the "nativist" group (Greene, 2002, 2004; Hoff, 1992; Myers, 1982). In fact, even the provincial government and the premier of Ontario, Oliver Mowat, became involved. In the end, Baldwin was offered the job and another position was given to Hume (Greene, 2002). Baldwin did establish the first experimental laboratory but left the University of Toronto, his departure due at least in part to the difficulties he had in getting support for the laboratory. Baldwin became a major contributor to the literature in psychology and was involved in the founding of the American Psychological Association in 1892 and several prestigious psychological journals (Johnson, 2000). Hume remained at the University of Toronto, although his career was less stellar and was rife with controversy (Greene, 2002).

The years have given evidence of many significant trends in Canadian psychology in terms of research (e.g., Pols, 2002), its administration (e.g., Wright, 1992a), and the role of women (see Storm & Gurevich, 2001). The Canadian Psychological Association was formed in 1939 (see the Special Issue of *Canadian Psychology* published in 1992 on the 50th anniversary of CPA's formation; Wright, 1992a, 1992b, 1992c). It was established to advance psychology as a science (Ferguson, 1993) and continues to play a vital role in psychology in Canada. It has a current membership of 5357 (CPA, 2004: for more information on the CPA, visit its Web site at http://www.cpa.ca/).

While there were few female students or professors in Canadian psychology in the beginning, things have changed dramatically over the years (Wright, 1992c). In fact, recent data suggest that women are now in the majority in graduate programs in psychology (Boatswain, Brown, Fiksenbaum, Goldstein, Greenglass, Nadler, & Pyke, 2001). In the last decade or so, across disciplines, the number of female university teachers has increased by over 50%. According to a recent survey by Statistics Canada, in the 2002–03 academic year women made up about 30% of full–time professors (Statistics Canada, 2005d).

Few psychologists have made any more important contribution to psychology in Canada than Brenda Milner of McGill University. She obtained her Ph.D. in psychology from McGill and has taught at the University of Montreal and at McGill. She has made crucial contributions to our understanding of memory and was one of the founders of neuropsychology in Canada. We discuss some of her contributions in Chapters 3 and 7. Three other women who have made significant contributions to psychology in Canada are profiled in Figure 1.2.

Mary Salter Ainsworth	Mary Wright	Doreen Kimura

Mary Salter Ainsworth (1913–1999) was one of the most important figures in developmental psychology in the last century. Although born in Ohio, she moved to Toronto at the age of four and earned her Ph.D. from the University of Toronto. She lectured at the University of Toronto and then joined the Canadian Women's Army Corps where she attained the rank of major. After the war, she returned to teaching at the University of Toronto. She married another student of that university and went with him to London, England, while he completed his studies. There she worked with John Bowlby, who was interested in attachment. She later went on to a position at Johns Hopkins University and made important contributions to attachment theory and the study of developmental psychology. She retired in 1984 from the University of Virginia.

Mary Wright was a professor of psychology at the University of Western Ontario, retiring in 1980. She was a developmental psychologist who made important contributions to educational psychology and developmental training at the University of Western Ontario, establishing a laboratory preschool there that now bears her name. She served during World War II in the Canadian Children's Service in charge of training child-care workers. She is a historian of academic psychology in Canada (Wright & Myers, 1982), she served as president of the Ontario Psychological Association (OPA; 1951–1952), and she was the first female president of the Canadian Psychological Association (1968–1969). She has received numerous honourary degrees and awards, including two Distinguished Contribution Awards from the OPA and the CPA Gold Medal Award for Distinguished Lifetime Contribution to Canadian Psychology.

Doreen Kimura is currently a visiting professor at Simon Fraser University. Before that, she was a professor of psychology at the University of Western Ontario for 30 years. She received her undergraduate and graduate training at McGill University. She has made significant and sustained contributions to the study of the brain including neuromotor mechanisms in human communication and sex differences in cognition. She is also active in the area of promoting academic freedom; she was the founding president (1992–1993) of the Society for Academic Freedom and Scholarship and remains active in that organization. She is a fellow of the Royal Society of Canada and was honoured in 1985 by the CPA with its Donald O. Hebb Award for Distinguished Contributions to Psychology as a Science.

Dan Grogan Photography

Image courtesy of Huron University College

Image courtesy of Dr. Doreen Kimura

Figure 1.2

Women pioneers in Canadian psychology.
These three female psychologists represent just some of the different forms of significant contributions women have made to psychology in Canada.

Sources: Bretherton, I., & Main, M. (2000). Mary Dinsmore Salter Ainsworth (1913–1999). *American Psychologist, 55,* 1148–1149 [Ainsworth]; Wright, M. J. (1993). Women Groundbreakers in Canadian Psychology: World War II and its aftermath. *Canadian Psychology, 33,* 14–26 [Wright]; SFU home page document retrieved March 15, 2005, from http://www.sfu.ca/~dkimura/dkhome.htm, profile by Science.ca, retrieved March 15, 2005 from http://www.science.ca/scientists/scientistprofile.php?pID=10, and Society for Academic Freedom and Scholarship, http://www.safs.ca/academic.html [Kimura].

Psychology Comes of Age as a Profession

 1A

The 1950s also saw psychology come of age as a profession. As you know, psychology is not all pure science. It has a highly practical side. Many psychologists provide a variety of professional services to the public. Their work falls within the domain of ***applied psychology,*** **the branch of psychology concerned with everyday, practical problems**.

This branch of psychology, so prominent today, was actually slow to develop (Benjamin et al., 2003). The first applied arm of psychology to emerge was *clinical psychology*. As practised today, ***clinical psychology*** **is the branch of psychology concerned with the diagnosis and treatment of psychological problems and disorders**. In the early days, however, the emphasis was almost exclusively on psychological testing, and few psychologists were involved in clinical work. Although the first psychological clinic was established as early as 1896, by 1937 only about one in five members of the American Psychological Association reported an interest in clinical psychology (Goldenberg, 1983).

Clinicians were a small minority in a field devoted primarily to research.

That picture was about to change with dramatic swiftness. The impetus was a world war. During World War II (1939–1945), many academic psychologists were pressed into service as clinicians. They were needed to screen military recruits and to treat soldiers suffering from trauma. Many of these psychologists (often to their surprise) found the clinical work to be challenging and rewarding, and a substantial portion continued to do clinical work after the war. More significant, some 40 000 American veterans returned to seek postwar treatment in Veterans Administration (VA) hospitals for their psychological scars. With the demand for clinicians far greater than the supply, the VA stepped in to finance many new training programs in clinical psychology. These programs, emphasizing training in the treatment of psychological disorders as well as psychological testing, proved attractive. Within a few years, about half the new Ph.D.s in psychology were specializing in clinical psychology and most went on to offer professional services to the public (Goldenberg, 1983). Thus, during the 1950s the prewar orphan of applied/professional psychology rapidly matured into a robust, powerful adult.

In the halls of academia, many traditional research psychologists were alarmed by the professionalization of the field. They argued that the energy and resources previously devoted to research would be diluted. Because of conflicting priorities, tensions between the research and professional arms of psychology have continued to grow. Although the American Psychological Association continues to work diligently to represent both the scientific and professional branches of psychology, recent decades have brought complaints from many researchers that the APA has come to be dominated by clinicians. In 1988 this rift stimulated some research psychologists to form a new organization, the American Psychological Society (APS), to serve exclusively as an advocate for the science of psychology. In Canada, similar concerns regarding the direction of the Canadian Psychological Association led to the formation of the Canadian Society for Brain, Behaviour and Cognitive Science (CSBBCS; see http://www.csbbcs.org/) in the early 1990s.

Despite these conflicts, the professionalization of psychology has continued at a steady pace. In fact, the trend has spread into additional areas of psychology. Today the broad umbrella of applied psychology covers a variety of professional specialties, including school psychology, industrial and organizational psychology, and counselling psychology. Whereas psychologists

Bullying in Canadian Schoolyards

Prior to the research program initiated by Pepler and Craig, much of the research on bullying utilized questionnaire methodologies in which students would be asked questions about their experiences with bullying as victims or bullies in such events. In their research program, Pepler and Craig employed a naturalistic method in which they videotaped elementary school children during the schoolday on the school playground. In this study, the authors look at the behaviour observed in bullying episodes.

Method

Participants. The participants in this study were 34 teacher-nominated aggressive and 31 teacher-nominated socially competent children who had been videotaped on the school playground during unstructured lunch and recess activities. These children (average age 9.9 years) were a subset of the entire original sample of videotaped children who had all participated in bullying episodes either as a victim or bully. In the study, target children wore microphones that could pick up their conversations.

Measures. Children were categorized as socially competent or aggressive as a result of ratings made by their teachers, which were then verified by ratings made by their classmates.

Procedure. The videotapes were viewed and content coded by two trained experimenters. The similarity of the raters' judgments was assessed and found to be satisfactory. The raters made many types of judgments that were divided into four broad categories: nature of the bullying, individual characteristics of bullies and victims, social interactional factors, and social ecology (e.g., location and covertness of the episode).

Results

This is a very large study with many significant and interesting results, only a few of which can be mentioned here. There were over 300 bullying episodes identified in the 48 hours of taping. Half of the episodes involved verbal aggression (50%); physical aggression (29%) and a combination of physical and verbal aggression (21%) accounted for the rest of the episodes. Boys were involved in bullying at a rate about double that of girls. Interestingly, those with aggressive reputations (being identified as an aggressive child) did not seem to be engaged in more bullying than those who were seen as socially competent. Bullying does not seem to take place in an isolated social setting: peers were involved to some extent (as aggressors, witnesses, etc.) 85% of the time.

Discussion

The study was designed in part to demonstrate the viability of naturalistic observation in research on bullying. The results of the study suggest this is an effective tool for use in bullying research. The results also indicated the degree to which bullying is a social phenomenon, with most episodes involving peers. According to the authors, this is critical information in attempts to develop anti-bullying programs in schools.

Comment

This study was selected not only because it is an excellent example of the use of a particular methodology—naturalistic observation—in psychological research but also because it illustrates the fact that psychologists often do research on topics that affect people's everyday lives. While you will see many examples of basic theory testing research throughout the text, psychologists also do research on issues that have direct application to our lives. Some research, of course, does both simultaneously.

While naturalistic observation as a research technique has many advantages, including allowing the researchers to document an important phenomenon outside of the constraints of the laboratory, it does not allow for clear causal statement regarding the phenomenon under investigation. In many cases, the use of naturalistic observation allows the researchers to observe behaviour that is uncontaminated by the intervention of the scientists. One question you might have about this study by Craig and Pepler is the effect that wearing a microphone might have had on the behaviour of the children. Craig and Pepler maintain that the children habituated readily to the microphones and that they did not affect their behaviour. You might want to think about whether or not it would affect your own behaviour under similar circumstances.

At the very beginning of the chapter we indicated that recent research in bullying has highlighted bullying by girls. This recent focus on girls and bullying is likely the result of several factors. While males overall have been found to be more involved in serious violence than females, the rate of violence involving females seems to be increasing at a faster rate than that for males (Moretti & Odgers, 2002). In addition, the term *bullying* in the past has been used primarily to refer to physical aggression. More recently, its meaning has been expanded to include relational and control-oriented bullying often associated with the interpersonal relations of girls. Finally, recent high-profile cases of bullying involving girls have alerted researchers and the Canadian public to its dangers. ■

Investigators: Wendy M. Craig (Queen's University) and Debra J. Pepler (York University)

Source: Observations of Bullying and Victimization in the School Yard. *Canadian Journal of School Psychology*, 1997, *13*, 41–60.

were once almost exclusively academics, the vast majority of today's psychologists devote some of their time to providing professional services.

In Canada clinical psychologists are licensed and governed by the various provincial and territorial colleges of and boards of examiners in psychology. The Web sites of these organizations contain information about practice, standards, and relevant legislation. In some circumstances, these organizations may be responsible for disciplinary action toward a psychologist. For an example, visit the College of Psychologists of British Columbia Web page at http://www.collegeofpsychologists.bc.ca for some of these details regarding practice in British Columbia.

Psychology Returns to Its Roots: Renewed Interest in Cognition and Physiology

While applied psychology has blossomed in recent decades, research has continued to evolve. Ironically, two of the relatively recent trends in research hark back a century to psychology's beginning, when psychologists were principally interested in consciousness and physiology. Today psychologists are showing renewed interest in consciousness (now called "cognition") and the physiological bases of behaviour.

Cognition **refers to the mental processes involved in acquiring knowledge**. In other words, cognition involves thinking or conscious experience. For many decades, the dominance of behaviourism discouraged investigation of "unobservable" mental processes, and most psychologists showed little interest in cognition (Maudler, 2002). During the 1950s and 1960s, however, research on cognition slowly began to change (Miller, 2003). The research of Swiss psychologist Jean Piaget (1954) focused increased attention on the study of children's cognitive development, while the work of Noam Chomsky (1957) elicited new interest in the psychological underpinnings of language. Around the same time, Herbert Simon and his colleagues (Newell, Shaw, & Simon, 1958) began influential, groundbreaking research on problem solving that eventually led to a Nobel Prize for Simon (in 1978). These advances sparked a surge of interest in cognitive processes.

Since then, cognitive theorists have argued that psychology must study internal mental events to fully understand behaviour (Gardner, 1985; Neisser, 1967). Advocates of the *cognitive perspective* point out that people's manipulations of mental images surely influence how they behave. Consequently, focusing exclusively on overt behaviour yields an incomplete picture of why individuals behave as they do. Equally important, psychologists investigating decision making, reasoning, and problem solving have shown that methods can be devised to study cognitive processes scientifically. Although the methods are different from those used in psychology's early days, modern research on the inner workings of the mind has put the psyche back in psychology. In fact, many observers maintain that the cognitive perspective has become the dominant perspective in contemporary psychology—and some interesting data support this assertion, as can be seen in Figure 1.3 (Robins, Gosling, & Craik, 1999).

The 1950s and 1960s also saw many discoveries that highlighted the interrelations among mind, body, and behaviour (Thompson & Zola, 2003). For example, Canadian psychologist James Olds (1956) demonstrated that electrical stimulation of the brain could evoke emotional responses such as pleasure and rage in animals. Other work, which eventually earned a Nobel Prize for Roger Sperry (in 1981), showed that the right and left halves of the brain are specialized to handle different types of mental tasks (Gazzaniga, Bogen, & Sperry, 1965). The 1960s also brought the publication of David Hubel and Torsten Wiesel's (1962, 1963) Nobel Prize–winning work on how visual signals are processed in the brain.

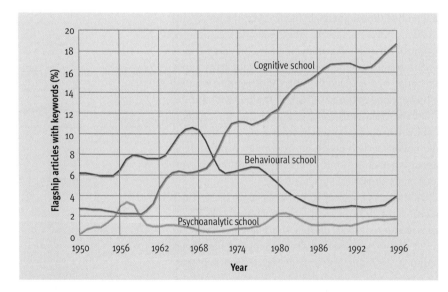

Figure 1.3

The relative prominence of three major schools of thought in psychology. To estimate the relative influence of various theoretical orientations in recent decades, Robins, Gosling, and Craik (1999) analyzed the subject matter of four prestigious general publications in psychology, measuring the percentage of articles relevant to each school of thought. Obviously, their approach is just one of many ways one might gauge the prominence of various theoretical orientations in psychology. Nonetheless, the data are thought provoking. Their findings suggest that the cognitive perspective surpassed the behavioural perspective in influence sometime around 1970. As you can see, the psychoanalytic perspective has always had a modest impact on the mainstream of psychology.

Source: Adapted from Robins, R. W., Gosling, S. D., & Craik, K. H. (1999). An empirical analysis of trends in psychology. *American Psychologist, 54,* 117–128. Copyright © 1999 by the American Psychological Association. Reprinted by permission of the author.

One important figure in this area was Donald Hebb. He was a professor of psychology at McGill University in Montreal whose pioneering ideas are credited with highlighting the importance of physiological and neuropsychological perspectives and as having paved the way for the recent cognitive revolution in psychology (Klein, 1999). In fact, some have claimed recently that Hebb's early work provides the long-sought-after integrative approach for psychology (Posner & Rothbart, 2004).

Born in Nova Scotia, Hebb began his academic career as a school principal and part-time student in psychology at McGill University. He later went to work on his Ph.D. with Lashley, a pioneer in physiological psychology at Harvard. After obtaining his Ph.D. and pursuing some important other educational experiences, he returned to Montreal and joined the faculty of the psychology department at McGill, where he became chair of the department in 1948 (Klein, 1999). His seminal book, *The Organization of Behavior: A Neuropsychological Theory*, appeared in 1949 and immediately attracted the interest of international scholars. According to Klein (1999), Hebb's book "made McGill University a North American mecca for scientists interested in brain mechanisms of behaviour ... and steered contemporary psychology onto a more fruitful path" (p. 1).

Hebb's emphasis on the importance of the brain in behaviour provided an important counterweight to that time's dominance of the behaviourist models. He argued that the locus of behaviour should be sought in the brain. One of the pivotal concepts he introduced was the cell assembly. Hebb suggested that repeated stimulation leads to the development of cell assemblies. These cell assemblies resemble cognitive units that together or in concert with other cell assemblies facilitate behaviour. His ideas suggested how neural networks might work and be organized. He proposed that the key to understanding this was activity at the neuronal level. According to many, his innovative ideas set the stage for contemporary developments in cognition and neuroscience and underscored the importance of the neuropsychological approach to understanding behaviour (Posner & Rothbart, 2004; Wikelgren, 1999).

We will return to Hebb's ideas in later chapters and we will see his influence in various areas of psychology. His conception of the link between brain and behaviour, although over 50 years old, continues to influence contemporary thinking. His significance to the shape of contemporary psychology has been acknowledged internationally. His stature in Canadian psychology has been acknowledged by the Canadian Psychological Association, which

Donald Hebb's pioneering ideas highlighted the importance of physiological and neuropsychological perspectives.

Courtesy of the McGill University Archives

named one of its most prestigious awards the "Donald O. Hebb Award for Distinguished Contributions to Psychology as a Science." The award is given annually to a Canadian psychologist who has made significant and sustained contributions to the science of psychology. A list of recipients of the award and their institutional affiliations is given in Table 1.3. We will consider the impact of their work throughout the text.

Discoveries in the 1950s and 1960s stimulated an increase in research on the biological bases of behaviour. Advocates of the biological perspective maintain that much of human and animal behaviour can be explained in terms of the bodily structures and biochemical processes that allow organisms to behave. In the 19th century the young science of psychology had a heavy physiological emphasis. Thus, the recent interest in the biological bases of behaviour represents another return to psychology's heritage.

Although adherents of the cognitive and biological perspectives haven't done as much organized campaigning for their viewpoints as the proponents of the older, traditional schools of thought have, these newer perspectives have become important theoretical orientations in modern psychology. They are increasingly influential regarding what psychology should study and how. The cognitive and biological perspectives are compared to other contemporary theoretical perspectives in Table 1.2 (p. 11).

Table 1.3 Recipients of the CPA Donald O. Hebb Award for Distinguished Contributions to Psychology as a Science

Year of Award	Name of Recipient	Institutional Affiliation	Further Discussion in Text
2005	David Wolfe	University of Western Ontario	p. 48
2004	Albert S. Bregman	McGill University	
2003	David Regan	York University	
2002	Kenneth D. Craig	University of Toronto	
2001	Kenneth Dion	University of Toronto	p. 678
2000	Bryan Kolb	University of Lethbridge	p. 101
1999	Byron P. Rourke	University of Windsor	
1998	John W. Berry	Queen's University	p. 362
1997	Norman S. Endler	York University	pp. 507, 545, 576, 592, 625, 643
1996	Peter Suedfeld	University of British Columbia	
1995	Anthony Phillips	University of British Columbia	
1994	Franco Lepore	University of Montreal	
1993	Mark Zanna	University of Waterloo	pp. 667, 680, 686
1992	Peter Dodwell	Queen's University	p. 141
1991	Adrien Pinard	University of Montreal	
1990	Zenon Pylyshyn	University of Western Ontario	
1989	Not awarded		
1988	Philip Bryden	University of Waterloo	
1987	Fergus I. M. Craik	University of Toronto	pp. 94, 268, 270, 271, 283
1986	Ronald Melzack	McGill University	p. 166
1985	Doreen Kimura	University of Western Ontario	pp. 13, 106
1984	Wallace Lambert	McGill University	pp. 319, 320
1983	Endel Tulving	University of Toronto	pp. 94, 267, 268, 282, 283, 297
1982	Allan U. Paivio	University of Western Ontario	p. 272
1981	Brenda Milner	McGill University	pp. 13, 53, 77, 90, 91, 154, 267, 295, 296, 438, 491
1980	Donald O. Hebb	McGill University	pp. 13, 77, 83, 84, 91, 96, 320, 545, 623, 667

Source: Adapted from the Canadian Psychological Association (n.d.). *CPA Awards*. Retrieved February 21, 2005, from http://www.cpa.ca/recip.html. Reprinted by permission of the Canadian Psychological Association.

Psychology Broadens Its Horizons: Increased Interest in Cultural Diversity

Throughout psychology's history, most researchers have worked under the assumption that they were seeking to identify general principles of behaviour that would be applicable to all of humanity. In reality, however, psychology has largely been a Western (North American and European) enterprise (Gergen et al., 1996). The vast preponderance of psychology's research has been conducted in the United States by middle- and upper-class white psychologists who have used mostly middle- and upper-class white males as subjects (Hall, 1997; Segall et al., 1990). Traditionally, Western psychologists have paid scant attention to how well their theories and research might apply to non-Western cultures, to ethnic minorities in Western societies, or even to women as opposed to men.

Why has the focus of Western psychology been so narrow? A host of factors have probably contributed (Albert, 1988; Segall, Lonner, & Berry, 1998). First, cross-cultural research is costly, difficult, and time-consuming. It has always been cheaper, easier, and more convenient for academic psychologists to study the middle-class white students enrolled in their schools. Second, some psychologists worry that cultural comparisons may inadvertently foster stereotypes of various cultural groups, many of which already have a long history of being victimized by prejudice. Third, *ethnocentrism*—**the tendency to view one's own group as superior to others and as the standard for judging the worth of foreign ways**—may have contributed to Western psychologists' lack of interest in other cultures.

Despite these considerations, in recent years Western psychologists have begun to recognize that their neglect of cultural variables has diminished the value of their work, and they are devoting increased attention to culture as a determinant of behaviour. What brought about this shift? Some of the impetus probably came from the sociopolitical upheavals of the 1960s and 1970s (Bronstein & Quina, 1988). The civil rights movement, the women's movement, and the gay rights movement all raised doubts about whether psychology had dealt adequately with human diversity. Above all else, however, the new interest in culture appears attributable to two recent trends: (1) advances in communication, travel, and international trade have "shrunk" the world and increased global interdependence, bringing more and more North Americans and Europeans into contact with people from non-Western cultures, and (2) the ethnic makeup of the Western world has become an increasingly diverse multicultural mosaic. A recent survey by Statistics Canada gives a snapshot of Canada's increasing diversity (Chard & Badets, 2004), and some of the results are shown in Figure 1.4. These data report on respondents' ethnic ancestry by generational status. (First generational status refers to respondents born outside Canada; second generational status includes respondents born in Canada with at least one parent born outside Canada; and third generational status includes respondents born in Canada, both of whose parents were also born in Canada). The survey shows, among other things, increasing ethnic diversity in those with first generational status.

These realities have prompted more and more Western psychologists to broaden their horizons and incorporate cultural factors into their theories and research (Adamopoulos & Lonner, 2001; Miller, 1999). These psychologists are striving to study previously underrepresented groups of subjects to test the generality of earlier findings and to catalogue both the differences and similarities among cultural groups. They are working to increase knowledge of

SOURCE: Adapted from Statistics Canada. Chard, J., & Badets, J. (2004). Ethnic Identification in Canada: Data from the Ethnic Diversity Survey. Paper presented at the Canadian Population Survey Annual Meetings, June 4, 2004. Retrieved March 15, 2005, from http://www.canpopsoc.org/2004/secure/chardCPS.ppt.

Figure 1.4

Ethnic ancestry by generational status.

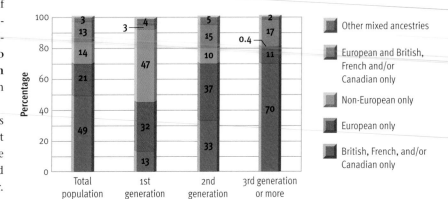

how culture is transmitted through socialization practices and how culture colours one's view of the world. They are seeking to learn how people cope with cultural change and to find ways to reduce misunderstandings and conflicts in intercultural interactions. In addition, they are trying to enhance understanding of how cultural groups are affected by prejudice, discrimination, and racism. In all these efforts, they are striving to understand the unique experiences of culturally diverse people *from the point of view of those people.* These efforts to ask new questions, study new groups, and apply new perspectives promise to enrich the discipline of psychology in the 21st century (Lehman, Chiu, & Schaller, 2004; Matsumoto, 2003; Sue, 2003).

Psychology Adapts: The Emergence of Evolutionary Psychology

Another development in psychology has been the emergence of evolutionary psychology, a theoretical perspective that is likely to be influential in the years to come. This renewed focus on evolutionary principles in psychology has its roots in earlier human and comparative research. We previously mentioned the impact that Darwin's ideas had on William James and early functionalism. Evolutionary psychologists assert that the patterns of behaviour seen in a species are products of evolution in the same way that anatomical characteristics are. *Evolutionary psychology* **examines behavioural processes in terms of their adaptive value for members of a species over the course of many generations.** The basic premise of evolutionary psychology is that natural selection favours behaviours that enhance organisms' reproductive success—that is, passing on genes to the next generation. Thus, if a species is highly aggressive, evolutionary psychologists argue that it's because aggressiveness conveys a survival or reproductive advantage for members of that species, so genes that promote aggressiveness are more likely to be passed on to the next generation. Although evolutionary psychologists have a natural interest in animal behaviour, they have not been bashful about analyzing the evolutionary bases of human behaviour. As La Cerra and Kurzban (1995) put it, "The human mind was sculpted by natural selection, and it is this evolved organ that constitutes the subject matter of psychology" (p. 63).

Consider, for instance, evolutionary psychologists' analysis of differences between males and females in visual-spatial ability. On the average, males tend to perform slightly better than females on most visual-spatial tasks, including tasks involving mental rotation of images and navigation in space (Halpern, 2000; see Chapter 11). Canadian psychologist Irwin Silverman and his colleagues at York University maintain that these gender differences originated in human evolution as a result of the sex-based division of labour in ancient hunting and gathering societies (Silverman & Phillips, 1998; Silverman et al., 2000). According to this analysis, males' superiority in mental rotation and navigation developed because the chore of hunting was largely assigned to men over the course of human history, and these skills would have facilitated success on hunting trips and thus been favoured by natural selection. In contrast, women in ancient societies generally had responsibility for *gathering* food rather than hunting it. Hence, Silverman and Eals (1992) hypothesized that females ought to be superior to males on spatial skills that would have facilitated gathering, such as memory for locations, which is exactly what they found in a series of four studies. Thus, evolutionary psychologists explain gender differences in spatial ability—and many other aspects of human behaviour—in terms of how such abilities evolved to meet the adaptive pressures faced by our ancestors.

Looking at behavioural patterns in terms of their evolutionary significance is not an entirely new idea (Graziano, 1995). As noted earlier, William James and other functionalists were influenced by Darwin's concept of natural selection over a century ago. Until recently, however, applications of evolutionary concepts to *psychological* processes were piecemeal, half-hearted, and not particularly well received. The 1960s and 1970s brought major breakthroughs in the field of evolutionary biology (Hamilton, 1964; Trivers, 1971, 1972; Williams, 1966), but these advances had little immediate impact in psychology. The situation began to change in the 1980s. A growing cadre of evolutionary psychologists, led by David Buss (1985, 1988, 1989), Martin Daly and Margo Wilson (1985, 1988), and Leda Cosmides and John Tooby (Cosmides & Tooby, 1989; Tooby & Cosmides, 1989), published widely cited studies on a broad range of topics, including mating preferences, jealousy, aggression, sexual behaviour, language, decision making, personality, and development. In 1989–1990, Buss, Daly, Wilson, Cosmides, and Tooby gathered at the Center for Advanced Study in the Behavioral Sciences in Palo Alto, California, to sketch out an ambitious research agenda for evolutionary psychology (Buss, 1999). By the mid-1990s, it became clear that psychology was witnessing the birth of its first major, new theoretical perspective since the cognitive revolution in the 1950s and 1960s.

As with all prominent theoretical perspectives in psychology, evolutionary theory has its critics (Caporael & Brewer, 1995; Gould, 1993; Lickliter & Honeycutt, 2003; Plotkin, 2004; Rose & Rose, 2000). Among other things, they argue that many evolutionary hypotheses are untestable and that evolutionary explanations are post hoc, speculative accounts for obvious behavioural phenomena. However, evolutionary psychologists have articulated persuasive rebuttals to these and other criticisms (Bereczkei, 2000; Buss & Reeves, 2003; Conway & Schaller, 2002), and the evolutionary perspective is rapidly gaining acceptance. Advocates of the evolutionary approach have heralded it as an "immense advance over traditional perspectives" (Masters, 1995, p. 65), a "revolutionary scientific paradigm" (Buss, 1995, p. 85), and a "renaissance in the sciences of mind" (La Cerra & Kurzban, 1995, p. 62). These proclamations will probably prove to be overly enthusiastic, as is often the case when a new school of thought strives to establish its identity. Nonetheless, evolutionary psychology undeniably provides a thought-provoking, innovative perspective that is rapidly gaining influence and promises to shake things up.

Our review of psychology's past has shown the field's evolution. We have seen psychology develop from philosophical speculation into a rigorous science committed to research. We have seen how a highly visible professional arm involved in mental health services emerged from this science. We have seen how psychology's focus on physiology is rooted in its 19th-century origins. We have seen how and why psychologists began conducting research on lower animals. We have seen how psychology has evolved from the study of mind and body to the study of behaviour. And we have seen how the investigation of mind and body has been welcomed back into the mainstream of modern psychology. We have seen how various theoretical schools have defined the scope and mission of psychology in different ways. We have seen how psychology's interests have expanded and become increasingly diverse. Above all else, we have seen that psychology is a growing, evolving intellectual enterprise.

Psychology's history is already rich, but its story has barely begun. The century or so that has elapsed since Wilhelm Wundt put psychology on a scientific footing is only an eyeblink of time in human history. What has been discovered during those years, and what remains unknown, is the subject of the rest of this book.

REVIEW OF KEY POINTS

- Stimulated by the demands of World War II, clinical psychology grew rapidly in the 1950s. Thus, psychology became a profession as well as a science. This movement toward professionalization eventually spread to other areas in psychology.

- During the 1950s and 1960s, advances in the study of cognition led to renewed interest in mental processes, as psychology returned to its roots. Advocates of the cognitive perspective argue that human behaviour cannot be fully understood without considering how people think.

- The 1950s and 1960s also saw advances in research on the physiological bases of behaviour. Advocates of the biological perspective assert that human and animal behaviour can be explained in terms of the bodily structures and biochemical processes that allow organisms to behave.

- In the 1980s, Western psychologists, who had previously been rather provincial, developed a greater interest in how cultural factors influence behaviour. This trend was sparked in large part by growing global interdependence and by increased cultural diversity in Western societies.

- The 1990s witnessed the emergence of a new theoretical perspective called evolutionary psychology. The central premises of this new school of thought are that patterns of behaviour are the product of evolutionary forces and that natural selection favours behaviours that enhance reproductive success.

Psychology Today: Vigorous and Diversified

We began this chapter with an informal description of what psychology is about. Now that you have a feel for how psychology has developed, you can better appreciate a definition that does justice to the field's modern diversity: *Psychology* **is the science that studies behaviour and the physiological and cognitive processes that underlie it, and it is the profession that applies the accumulated knowledge of this science to practical problems**.

Psychology's vigorous presence in modern society is also demonstrated by the great variety of settings in which psychologists work. Psychologists were once found almost exclusively in the halls of academia. Today, however, colleges and universities are the primary work setting for fewer than one-third of North American psychologists. The remaining two-thirds work in hospitals, clinics, police departments, research institutes, government agencies, business and industry, schools, nursing homes, counselling centres, and private practice. Figure 1.5 shows the distribution of psychologists employed in various categories of settings.

Clearly, contemporary psychology is a multifaceted field, a fact that is especially apparent when we consider the many areas of specialization within psychology today. Let's look at the current areas of specialization in both the science and the profession of psychology.

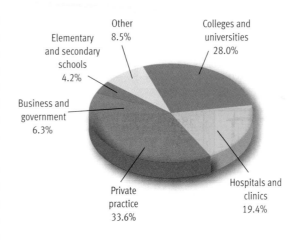

Elementary and secondary schools 4.2%

Other 8.5%

Colleges and universities 28.0%

Business and government 6.3%

Private practice 33.6%

Hospitals and clinics 19.4%

Figure 1.5

Employment of psychologists by setting. The work settings in which psychologists are employed have become very diverse. Survey data on the primary employment setting of APA members indicates that one-third are in private practice (compared to 12% in 1976) and only 28% work in colleges and universities (compared to 47% in 1976). These data may slightly underestimate the percentage of psychologists in academia, given the competition between APA and APS to represent research psychologists.

Based on *2000 APA Directory Survey*.

PREVIEW QUESTIONS

- What evidence suggests that psychology is a vigorous, growing discipline?
- What are the main areas of research in psychology?
- What are the four professional specialties in psychology?
- How do clinical psychology and psychiatry differ?

Web Link 1.5

American Psychological Association (APA)
http://www.apa.org/

The APA Web site is a treasure trove of resources on psychology in all its rich diversity. The section for the public includes electronic pamphlets on practical topics such as depression, aging, and anger. A wealth of information on career possibilities in the field is also available here.

Figure 1.6

Major research areas in contemporary psychology.
Most research psychologists specialize in one of the seven broad areas described here. The figures in the pie chart reflect the percentage of academic and research psychologists belonging to APA who identify each area as their primary interest.

Based on 2000 APA Directory Survey.

Psychometrics 4.8%
Personality 4.2%
Cognitive 7.7%
Developmental 23.4%
Physiological 9.7%
Social 21.1%
Experimental 12.6%
Other 16.5%

Area	Focus of research
Developmental psychology	Looks at human development across the life span. Developmental psychology once focused primarily on child development but today devotes a great deal of research to adolescence, adulthood, and old age.
Social psychology	Focuses on interpersonal behaviour and the role of social forces in governing behaviour. Typical topics include attitude formation, attitude change, prejudice, conformity, attraction, aggression, intimate relationships, and behaviour in groups.
Experimental psychology	Encompasses the traditional core of topics that psychology focused on heavily in its first half-century as a science: sensation, perception, learning, conditioning, motivation, and emotion. The name experimental psychology is somewhat misleading, as this is not the only area in which experiments are done. Psychologists working in all the areas listed here conduct experiments.
Physiological psychology	Examines the influence of genetic factors on behaviour and the role of the brain, nervous system, endocrine system, and bodily chemicals in the regulation of behaviour.
Cognitive psychology	Focuses on "higher" mental processes, such as memory, reasoning, information processing, language, problem solving, decision making, and creativity.
Personality	Is interested in describing and understanding individuals' consistency in behaviour, which represents their personality. This area of interest is also concerned with the factors that shape personality and with personality assessment.
Psychometrics	Is concerned with the measurement of behaviour and capacities, usually through the development of psychological tests. Psychometrics is involved with the design of tests to assess personality, intelligence, and a wide range of abilities. It is also concerned with the development of new techniques for statistical analysis.

Web Link 1.6

Canadian Psychological Association (CPA)
http://www.cpa.ca/

This Web site contains information about the CPA and what it does. In addition, it provides information about upcoming events and conferences, psychology Web links, links to the provincial and territorial psychological associations, careers in psychology, how to obtain the services of a psychologist, and much more.

Research Areas in Psychology

Although most psychologists receive broad training that provides them with knowledge about many areas of psychology, they usually specialize when it comes to doing research. Such specialization is necessary because the subject matter of psychology has become so vast over the years. Today it is virtually impossible for anyone to stay abreast of the new research in all specialties. Specialization is also necessary because specific skills and training are required to do research in some areas.

The seven major research areas in modern psychology are (1) developmental psychology, (2) social psychology, (3) experimental psychology, (4) physiological psychology, (5) cognitive psychology, (6) personality, and (7) psychometrics. Figure 1.6 describes these areas briefly and shows the percentage of research psychologists in the APA who identify each area as their primary interest. As you can see, social psychology and developmental psychology have become especially active areas of research.

Professional Specialties in Psychology

Applied psychology consists of four clearly identified areas of specialization: (1) clinical psychology, (2) counselling psychology, (3) educational and school psychology, and (4) industrial and organizational psychology. Descriptions of these specialties can be found in Figure 1.7, along with the percentage of professional psychologists in the APA who are working in each area. As the graphic indicates, clinical psychology is the most prominent and widely practised professional specialty in the field.

The data in Figures 1.6 and 1.7 are based on APA members' reports of their single, principal area of specialization. However, many psychologists work on both research and application. Some academic psychologists work as consultants, therapists, and counsellors on a part-time basis. Similarly, some applied psychologists conduct basic research on issues related to their specialty. For example, many clinical psychologists are involved in research on the nature and causes of abnormal behaviour.

1933 Sigmund Freud's influence continues to build as he publishes *New Introductory Lectures on Psychoanalysis.*

1936 Hans Selye introduces concept of stress into the language of science.

1941–1945 Rapid growth in clinical psychology begins in response to huge demand for clinical services created by World War II and its aftermath.

1943 Clark Hull advocates modified behaviourism, which permits careful inferences about unobservable internal states.

1947 Kenneth and Mamie Clark publish work on prejudice that is cited in landmark 1954 U.S. Supreme Court decision outlawing segregation.

1949 Donald O. Hebb publishes *The Organization of Behavior.*

1950 Erik Erikson writes *Childhood and Society,* in which he extends Freud's theory of development across the life span.

1951 Carl Rogers helps launch humanistic movement with publication of *Client-Centered Therapy.*

1953 B. F. Skinner publishes his influential *Science and Human Behavior,* advocating radical behaviourism similar to Watson's.

1954 Abraham Maslow's *Motivation and Personality* helps fuel humanistic movement.

1956 The cognitive revolution is launched at watershed conference where Herbert Simon, George Miller, and Noam Chomsky report three major advances in just one day.

1961–1964 Roger Sperry's split-brain research and work by David Hubel and Torsten Wiesel on how cortical cells respond to light help rejuvenate the biological perspective in psychology.

1963 Stanley Milgram conducts controversial study of obedience to authority, which may be the most famous single study in psychology's history.

1971 B. F. Skinner creates furor over radical behaviourism with his controversial book *Beyond Freedom and Dignity.*

1974 Eleanor Maccoby and Carol Jacklin publish their landmark review of research on gender differences, which galvanizes research in this area.

1978 Herbert Simon wins Nobel Prize (in economics) for research on cognition.

1980s Increased global interdependence and cultural diversity in Western societies spark surge of interest in how cultural factors mould behaviour.

1981 Roger Sperry wins Nobel Prize (in physiology and medicine) for split-brain studies.

1988 Research psychologists form the American Psychological Society (APS) to serve as an advocate for the science of psychology.

1930 **1940** **1950** **1960** **1970** **1980** **1990**

The Evolution of Psychology

Figure 1.6

Major research areas in contemporary psychology.
Most research psychologists specialize in one of the seven broad areas described here. The figures in the pie chart reflect the percentage of academic and research psychologists belonging to APA who identify each area as their primary interest.

Based on *2000 APA Directory Survey.*

Area	Focus of research
Developmental psychology	Looks at human development across the life span. Developmental psychology once focused primarily on child development but today devotes a great deal of research to adolescence, adulthood, and old age.
Social psychology	Focuses on interpersonal behaviour and the role of social forces in governing behaviour. Typical topics include attitude formation, attitude change, prejudice, conformity, attraction, aggression, intimate relationships, and behaviour in groups.
Experimental psychology	Encompasses the traditional core of topics that psychology focused on heavily in its first half-century as a science: sensation, perception, learning, conditioning, motivation, and emotion. The name experimental psychology is somewhat misleading, as this is not the only area in which experiments are done. Psychologists working in all the areas listed here conduct experiments.
Physiological psychology	Examines the influence of genetic factors on behaviour and the role of the brain, nervous system, endocrine system, and bodily chemicals in the regulation of behaviour.
Cognitive psychology	Focuses on "higher" mental processes, such as memory, reasoning, information processing, language, problem solving, decision making, and creativity.
Personality	Is interested in describing and understanding individuals' consistency in behaviour, which represents their personality. This area of interest is also concerned with the factors that shape personality and with personality assessment.
Psychometrics	Is concerned with the measurement of behaviour and capacities, usually through the development of psychological tests. Psychometrics is involved with the design of tests to assess personality, intelligence, and a wide range of abilities. It is also concerned with the development of new techniques for statistical analysis.

Web Link 1.6

Canadian Psychological Association (CPA)
http://www.cpa.ca/

This Web site contains information about the CPA and what it does. In addition, it provides information about upcoming events and conferences, psychology Web links, links to the provincial and territorial psychological associations, careers in psychology, how to obtain the services of a psychologist, and much more.

Research Areas in Psychology

Although most psychologists receive broad training that provides them with knowledge about many areas of psychology, they usually specialize when it comes to doing research. Such specialization is necessary because the subject matter of psychology has become so vast over the years. Today it is virtually impossible for anyone to stay abreast of the new research in all specialties. Specialization is also necessary because specific skills and training are required to do research in some areas.

The seven major research areas in modern psychology are (1) developmental psychology, (2) social psychology, (3) experimental psychology, (4) physiological psychology, (5) cognitive psychology, (6) personality, and (7) psychometrics. Figure 1.6 describes these areas briefly and shows the percentage of research psychologists in the APA who identify each area as their primary interest. As you can see, social psychology and developmental psychology have become especially active areas of research.

Professional Specialties in Psychology

Applied psychology consists of four clearly identified areas of specialization: (1) clinical psychology, (2) counselling psychology, (3) educational and school psychology, and (4) industrial and organizational psychology. Descriptions of these specialties can be found in Figure 1.7, along with the percentage of professional psychologists in the APA who are working in each area. As the graphic indicates, clinical psychology is the most prominent and widely practised professional specialty in the field.

The data in Figures 1.6 and 1.7 are based on APA members' reports of their single, principal area of specialization. However, many psychologists work on both research and application. Some academic psychologists work as consultants, therapists, and counsellors on a part-time basis. Similarly, some applied psychologists conduct basic research on issues related to their specialty. For example, many clinical psychologists are involved in research on the nature and causes of abnormal behaviour.

why psychologists began conducting research on lower animals. We have seen how psychology has evolved from the study of mind and body to the study of behaviour. And we have seen how the investigation of mind and body has been welcomed back into the mainstream of modern psychology. We have seen how various theoretical schools have defined the scope and mission of psychology in different ways. We have seen how psychology's interests have expanded and become increasingly diverse. Above all else, we have seen that psychology is a growing, evolving intellectual enterprise.

Psychology's history is already rich, but its story has barely begun. The century or so that has elapsed since Wilhelm Wundt put psychology on a scientific footing is only an eyeblink of time in human history. What has been discovered during those years, and what remains unknown, is the subject of the rest of this book.

REVIEW OF KEY POINTS

● Stimulated by the demands of World War II, clinical psychology grew rapidly in the 1950s. Thus, psychology became a profession as well as a science. This movement toward professionalization eventually spread to other areas in psychology.

● During the 1950s and 1960s, advances in the study of cognition led to renewed interest in mental processes, as psychology returned to its roots. Advocates of the cognitive perspective argue that human behaviour cannot be fully understood without considering how people think.

● The 1950s and 1960s also saw advances in research on the physiological bases of behaviour. Advocates of the biological perspective assert that human and animal behaviour can be explained in terms of the bodily structures and biochemical processes that allow organisms to behave.

● In the 1980s, Western psychologists, who had previously been rather provincial, developed a greater interest in how cultural factors influence behaviour. This trend was sparked in large part by growing global interdependence and by increased cultural diversity in Western societies.

● The 1990s witnessed the emergence of a new theoretical perspective called evolutionary psychology. The central premises of this new school of thought are that patterns of behaviour are the product of evolutionary forces and that natural selection favours behaviours that enhance reproductive success.

Psychology Today: Vigorous and Diversified

We began this chapter with an informal description of what psychology is about. Now that you have a feel for how psychology has developed, you can better appreciate a definition that does justice to the field's modern diversity: **Psychology is the science that studies behaviour and the physiological and cognitive processes that underlie it, and it is the profession that applies the accumulated knowledge of this science to practical problems.**

Psychology's vigorous presence in modern society is also demonstrated by the great variety of settings in which psychologists work. Psychologists were once found almost exclusively in the halls of academia. Today, however, colleges and universities are the primary work setting for fewer than one-third of North American psychologists. The remaining two-thirds work in hospitals, clinics, police departments, research institutes, government agencies, business and industry, schools, nursing homes, counselling centres, and private practice. Figure 1.5 shows the distribution of psychologists employed in various categories of settings.

Clearly, contemporary psychology is a multifaceted field, a fact that is especially apparent when we consider the many areas of specialization within psychology today. Let's look at the current areas of specialization in both the science and the profession of psychology.

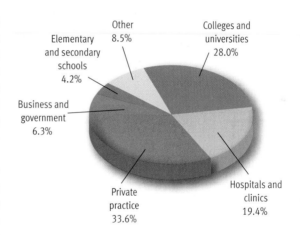

Figure 1.5

Employment of psychologists by setting. The work settings in which psychologists are employed have become very diverse. Survey data on the primary employment setting of APA members indicates that one-third are in private practice (compared to 12% in 1976) and only 28% work in colleges and universities (compared to 47% in 1976). These data may slightly underestimate the percentage of psychologists in academia, given the competition between APA and APS to represent research psychologists.

Based on 2000 APA Directory Survey.

PREVIEW QUESTIONS

● What evidence suggests that psychology is a vigorous, growing discipline?

● What are the main areas of research in psychology?

● What are the four professional specialties in psychology?

● How do clinical psychology and psychiatry differ?

Web Link 1.5

American Psychological Association (APA)
http://www.apa.org/

The APA Web site is a treasure trove of resources on psychology in all its rich diversity. The section for the public includes electronic pamphlets on practical topics such as depression, aging, and anger. A wealth of information on career possibilities in the field is also available here.

1875 First demonstration laboratories are set up independently by William James (at Harvard) and Wilhelm Wundt (at the University of Leipzig).

1879 Wilhelm Wundt establishes first research laboratory in psychology at Leipzig, Germany.

1881 Wilhelm Wundt establishes first journal devoted to research in psychology.

1883 G. Stanley Hall establishes America's first research laboratory in psychology at Johns Hopkins University.

1890 William James publishes his seminal work, *The Principles of Psychology*.

1891 James Mark Baldwin establishes the first experimental laboratory in psychology in Canada at the University of Toronto.

1892 G. Stanley Hall founds American Psychological Association.

1904 Ivan Pavlov shows how conditioned responses are created, paving the way for stimulus–response psychology.

1905 Alfred Binet develops first successful intelligence test in France.

1908 Margaret Washburn publishes *The Animal Mind*, which serves as an impetus for behaviourism.

1909 Sigmund Freud's increasing influence receives formal recognition as G. S. Hall invites Freud to give lectures at Clark University.

1913 John B. Watson writes classic behaviourism manifesto, arguing that psychology should study only observable behaviour.

1914 Leta Hollingworth publishes pioneering work on the psychology of women.

1914–1918 Widespread intelligence testing is begun by military during World War I.

1916 Lewis Terman publishes Stanford-Binet Intelligence Scale, which becomes the world's foremost intelligence test.

1920s Gestalt psychology nears its peak influence.

THE PRINCIPLES OF PSYCHOLOGY

William James

1880   1890   1900   1910   1920

Putting It in Perspective: Seven Key Themes

PREVIEW QUESTIONS

- What is the purpose of the text's unifying themes?
- What are the first three themes that elucidate the nature of psychology?
- What are the remaining four themes that emphasize crucial insights about behaviour?

Web Link 1.9

Approaches to Psychology
http://www.ryerson.ca/~glassman/approach.html

Maintained at Ryerson Polytechnic University in Toronto, this site provides access to an electronic version of the book *Approaches to Psychology* by William E. Glassman. This e-book is organized around the various theoretical orientations that guide thinking in contemporary psychology. Visitors will find concise overviews of the biological, behavioural, cognitive, psychoanalytic, and humanistic perspectives in psychology.

The enormous breadth and diversity of psychology make it a challenging subject for the beginning student. In the pages ahead you will be introduced to many areas of research and a multitude of ideas, concepts, and principles. Fortunately, ideas are not all created equal. Some are far more important than others. In this section, we will highlight seven fundamental themes that will reappear in a number of variations as we move from one area of psychology to another in this text. You have already met some of these key ideas in our review of psychology's past and present. Now we will isolate them and highlight their significance. In the remainder of the book these ideas serve as organizing themes to provide threads of continuity across chapters and to help you see the connections among the various areas of research in psychology.

In studying psychology, you are learning about both behaviour and the scientific discipline that investigates it. Accordingly, our seven themes come in two sets. The first set consists of statements highlighting crucial aspects of psychology as a way of thinking and as a field of study. The second set consists of broad generalizations about psychology's subject matter: behaviour and the cognitive and physiological processes that underlie it.

Themes Related to Psychology as a Field of Study

Looking at psychology as a field of study, we see three crucial ideas: (1) psychology is empirical, (2) psychology is theoretically diverse, and (3) psychology evolves in a sociohistorical context. Let's look at each of these ideas in more detail.

Theme 1: Psychology Is Empirical

Everyone tries to understand behaviour. Most of us have our own personal answers to questions such as why some people are hard workers, why some are overweight, and why others stay in demeaning relationships. If all of us are amateur psychologists, what makes scientific psychology different? The critical difference is that psychology is empirical. This aspect of psychology is fundamental, and virtually every page of this book reflects it.

What do we mean by empirical? ***Empiricism is the premise that knowledge should be acquired through observation.*** This premise is crucial to the scientific method that psychology embraced in the late 19th century. To say that psychology is empirical means that its conclusions are based on direct observation rather than on reasoning, speculation, traditional beliefs, or common sense. Psychologists are not content with having ideas that sound plausible. They conduct research to test their ideas. Is intelligence higher, on average, in some social classes than in others? Are men more aggressive than women? Psychologists find a way to make direct, objective, and precise observations to answer such questions.

The empirical approach requires a certain attitude—a healthy brand of skepticism. Empiricism is a tough taskmaster. It demands data and documentation. Psychologists' commitment to empiricism means that they must learn to think critically about generalizations concerning behaviour. If someone asserts that people tend to get depressed around Christmas, a psychologist is likely to ask, "How many people get depressed? In what population? In comparison to what baseline rate of depression? How is depression defined?" Their skeptical attitude means that psychologists are trained to ask, "Where's the evidence? How do you know?" If psychology's empirical orientation rubs off on you (and we hope it does), you will be asking similar questions by the time you finish this book.

Theme 2: Psychology Is Theoretically Diverse

Although psychology is based on observation, a string of unrelated observations would not be terribly enlightening. Psychologists do not set out to just collect isolated facts; they seek to explain and understand what they observe. To achieve these goals they must construct theories. **A *theory* is a system of interrelated ideas used to explain a set of observations.** In other words, a theory links apparently unrelated observations and tries to explain them. As an example, consider Sigmund Freud's observations about slips of the tongue, dreams, and psychological disturbances. On the surface, these observations appear unrelated. By devising the concept of the unconscious, Freud created a theory that links and explains these seemingly unrelated aspects of behaviour.

Our review of psychology's past should have made one thing abundantly clear: Psychology is marked by theoretical diversity. Why do we have so many competing points of view? One reason is that no single theory can adequately explain everything

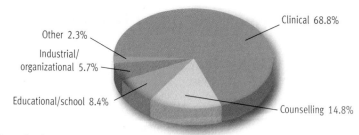

Figure 1.7

Principal professional specialties in contemporary psychology. Most psychologists who deliver professional services to the public specialize in one of the four areas described here. The figures in the pie chart reflect the percentage of APA members delivering professional services who identify each area as their chief specialty.

Based on 2000 APA Directory Survey.

Pie chart labels: Clinical 68.8%, Counselling 14.8%, Educational/school 8.4%, Industrial/organizational 5.7%, Other 2.3%

Specialty	Focus of professional practice
Clinical psychology	Clinical psychologists are concerned with the evaluation, diagnosis, and treatment of individuals with psychological disorders, as well as treatment of less severe behavioural and emotional problems. Principal activities include interviewing clients, psychological testing, and providing group or individual psychotherapy.
Counselling psychology	Counselling psychology overlaps with clinical psychology in that specialists in both areas engage in similar activities—interviewing, testing, and providing therapy. However, counselling psychologists usually work with a somewhat different clientele, providing assistance to people struggling with everyday problems of moderate severity. Thus, they often specialize in family, marital, or career counselling.
Educational and school psychology	Educational psychologists work to improve curriculum design, achievement testing, teacher training, and other aspects of the educational process. School psychologists usually work in elementary or secondary schools, where they test and counsel children having difficulties in school and aid parents and teachers in solving school-related problems.
Industrial and organizational psychology	Psychologists in this area perform a wide variety of tasks in the world of business and industry. These tasks include running human resources departments, working to improve staff morale and attitudes, striving to increase job satisfaction and productivity, examining organizational structures and procedures, and making recommendations for improvements.

Some people are confused about the difference between clinical psychology and psychiatry. The confusion is understandable, as both clinical psychologists and psychiatrists are involved in analyzing and treating psychological disorders. Although some overlap exists between the two professions, the training and educational requirements for the two are quite different. Clinical psychologists go to graduate school to earn one of several doctoral degrees (Ph.D., Ed.D., or Psy.D.) in order to enjoy full status in their profession. Psychiatrists go to medical school for their postgraduate education, where they receive general training in medicine and earn an M.D. degree. They then specialize by completing residency training in psychiatry at a hospital. Clinical psychologists and psychiatrists also differ in the way they tend to approach the treatment of mental disorders, as we will see in Chapter 15. To summarize, *psychiatry* **is a branch of medicine concerned with the diagnosis and treatment of psychological problems and disorders**. In contrast, clinical psychology takes a nonmedical approach to such problems.

REVIEW OF KEY POINTS

● Contemporary psychology is a diversified science and profession that has grown rapidly in recent decades. The main work settings for contemporary psychologists are (1) private practice, (2) colleges and universities, and (3) hospitals and clinics.

● Major areas of research in modern psychology include developmental psychology, social psychology, experimental psychology, physiological psychology, cognitive psychology, personality, and psychometrics.

● Applied psychology encompasses four professional specialties: clinical psychology, counselling psychology, educational and school psychology, and industrial and organizational psychology.

● Although clinical psychology and psychiatry share some of the same interests, they are different professions with different types of training. Psychiatrists are physicians who specialize in the diagnosis and treatment of mental disorders, whereas clinical psychologists take a nonmedical approach to psychological problems.

Web Link 1.7

Marky Lloyd's Career Page
http://www.psywww.com/careers/index.htm

For those who think they might want to find a job or career in psychology or a related field, Marky Lloyd of Georgia Southern University has put together a fine set of resources to help in both planning and making choices.

Web Link 1.8

A Student's Guide to Careers in the Helping Professions
http://www.lemoyne.edu/OTRP/otrpresources/helping-online.html

Written by Melissa J. Himeline of the University of North Carolina at Asheville, this online guide provides detailed career information for 15 of the most important helping professions that psychology majors often consider entering.

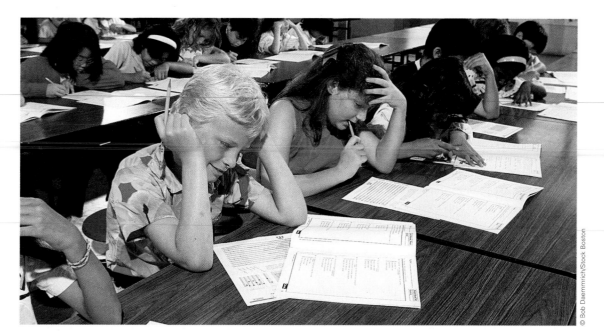

Social trends and values have shaped the evolution of psychology and progress in psychology has left its mark on everyday life in our society. For example, standardized psychological tests are pervasive in our educational system, where they exert great influence over students' lives.

© Bob Daemmrich/Stock Boston

that is known about behaviour. Sometimes different theories focus on different aspects of behaviour—that is, different collections of observations. Sometimes there is simply more than one way to look at something. Is the glass half empty or half full? Obviously, it is both. To take an example from another science, physicists wrestled for years with the nature of light. Is it a wave, or is it a particle? In the end, it proved useful to think of light sometimes as a wave and sometimes as a particle. Similarly, if a business executive lashes out at her employees with stinging criticism, is she releasing pent-up aggressive urges (a psychoanalytic view)? Is she making a habitual response to the stimulus of incompetent work (a behavioural view)? Or is she scheming to motivate her employees by using "mind games" (a cognitive view)? In some cases, all three of these explanations might have some validity. In short, it is an oversimplification to expect that one view has to be right while all others are wrong. Life is rarely that simple.

Students are often troubled by psychology's many conflicting theories, which they view as a weakness. However, contemporary psychologists increasingly recognize that theoretical diversity is a strength rather than a weakness (Hilgard, 1987). As we proceed through this text, you will see how differing theoretical perspectives often provide a more complete understanding of behaviour than could be achieved by any one perspective alone.

Theme 3: Psychology Evolves in a Sociohistorical Context

Science is often seen as an "ivory tower" undertaking, isolated from the ebb and flow of everyday life. In reality, however, psychology and other sciences do not exist in a cultural vacuum. Dense interconnections exist between what happens in psychology and what happens in society at large (Altman, 1990; Braginsky, 1985; Danziger, 1990). Trends, issues, and values in society influence psychology's evolution. Similarly, progress in psychology affects trends, issues, and values in society. To put it briefly, psychology develops in a *sociohistorical* (social and historical) context.

Our review of psychology's past is filled with examples of how social trends have left their imprint on psychology. In the late 19th century, psychology's rapid growth as a laboratory science was due, in part, to its fascination with physics as the model discipline. Thus, the spirit of the times fostered a scientific approach rather than a philosophical approach to the investigation of the mind. Similarly, Freud's groundbreaking ideas emerged out of a specific sociohistorical context. Cultural values in Freud's era encouraged the suppression of sexuality. Hence, people tended to feel guilty about their sexual urges to a much greater extent than is common today. This situation clearly contributed to Freud's emphasis on unconscious sexual conflicts. As another example, consider the impact of World War II on the development of psychology as a profession. The rapid growth of professional psychology was largely due to the war-related surge in the demand for clinical services. Hence, World War II reshaped the landscape of psychology in a remarkably short time. Finally, in recent years we have seen how growing global interdependence and increased cultural diversity have prompted psychologists to focus

The Evolution of Psychology

new attention on cultural factors as determinants of behaviour.

If we reverse our viewpoint, we can see that psychology has in turn left its mark on society. Consider, for instance, the pervasive role of mental testing in modern society. Your own career success may depend in part on how well you weave your way through a complex maze of intelligence and achievement tests made possible (to the regret of some) by research in psychology. As another example of psychology's impact on society, consider the influence that various theorists have had on parenting styles. Trends in childrearing practices have been shaped by the ideas of John B. Watson, Sigmund Freud, B. F. Skinner, and Carl Rogers—not to mention a host of additional psychologists yet to be discussed. In short, society and psychology influence each other in complex ways. In the chapters to come, we will frequently have occasion to notice this dynamic relationship.

Themes Related to Psychology's Subject Matter

Looking at psychology's subject matter, we see four additional crucial ideas: (4) behaviour is determined by multiple causes, (5) behaviour is shaped by cultural heritage, (6) heredity and environment jointly influence behaviour, and (7) people's experience of the world is highly subjective.

Theme 4: Behaviour Is Determined by Multiple Causes

As psychology has matured, it has provided more and more information about the forces that govern behaviour. This growing knowledge has led to a deeper appreciation of a simple but important fact: Behaviour is exceedingly complex, and most aspects of behaviour are determined by multiple causes.

Although the complexity of behaviour may seem self-evident, people usually think in terms of single causes. Thus, they offer explanations such as "Andrea flunked out of school because she is lazy." Or they assert that "teenage pregnancies are increasing because of all the sex in the media." Single-cause explanations are sometimes accurate as far as they go, but they usually are incomplete. In general, psychologists find that behaviour is governed by a complex network of interacting factors, an idea referred to as the *multifactorial causation of behaviour*.

As a simple illustration, consider the multiple factors that might influence your performance in your introductory psychology course. Relevant personal factors might include your overall intelligence, your

reading ability, your memory skills, your motivation, and your study skills. In addition, your grade could be affected by numerous situational factors, including whether you like your psychology professor, whether you like your assigned text, whether the class meets at a good time for you, whether your work schedule is light or heavy, and whether you're having any personal problems.

As you proceed through this book, you will learn that complexity of causation is the rule rather than the exception. If we expect to understand behaviour, we usually have to take into account multiple determinants.

Theme 5: Behaviour Is Shaped by Cultural Heritage

Among the multiple determinants of human behaviour, cultural factors are particularly prominent. Just as psychology evolves in a sociohistorical context, so, too, do individuals. People's cultural backgrounds exert considerable influence over their behaviour. What is culture? It's the human-made part of the environment. More specifically, *culture* **refers to the widely shared customs, beliefs, values, norms, institutions, and other products of a community that are transmitted socially across generations.** Culture is a broad construct, encompassing everything from a society's legal system to its assumptions about family roles, from its dietary habits to its political ideals, from its technology to its attitudes about time, from its modes of dress to its spiritual beliefs, and from its art and music to its unspoken rules about sexual liaisons. We tend to think of culture as belonging to entire societies or broad ethnic groups within societies—which it does—but the concept can also be applied to small groups (a tiny Aboriginal tribe in Australia, for example) and to nonethnic groups (gay/homosexual culture, for instance).

Much of a person's cultural heritage is invisible (Brislin, 1993, 2000). Assumptions, ideals, attitudes, beliefs, and unspoken rules exist in people's minds and may not be readily apparent to outsiders. Moreover, because a cultural background is widely shared, members feel little need to discuss it with others and often take it for granted. For example, you probably don't spend much time thinking about the importance of living in rectangular rooms, trying to minimize body odour, limiting yourself to one spouse at a time, or using credit cards to obtain material goods and services. Although we generally fail to appreciate its influence, our cultural heritage has a pervasive impact on our thoughts, feelings, and behaviour.

Let's look at a couple of examples of this influence. In North America, when people are invited to dinner in someone's home, they generally show

Web Link 1.10

Encyclopedia of Psychology
http://www.psychology.org/

This "encyclopedia," developed by psychology faculty at Jacksonville State University, is actually a collection of over 2000 links to Web pages around the world on psychological matters. The links related to the history of the field and careers in psychology are extensive, as are the links relating to theories and publications in psychology.

their appreciation of their host's cooking efforts by eating all of the food they are served. In India, this behaviour would be insulting to the host, as guests are expected to leave some food on their plates. The leftover food acknowledges the generosity of the host, implying that he or she provided so much food the guest could not eat it all (Moghaddam, Taylor, & Wright, 1993). Cultures also vary in their emphasis on punctuality. In North America, we expect people to show up for meetings on time; if someone is more than 10 to 15 minutes late we begin to get upset. We generally strive to be on time, and many of us are quite proud of our precise and dependable punctuality. However, in many Asian and Latin American countries, social obligations that arise at the last minute are given just as much priority as scheduled commitments. Hence, people often show up for important meetings an hour or two late with little remorse, and they may be quite puzzled by the consternation of their Western visitors (Brislin, 2000).

These examples may seem trivial, but as you will see in upcoming chapters, culture can also influence crucial matters, such as educational success, mental health, and vulnerability to physical illnesses.

Although the influence of culture is everywhere, generalizations about cultural groups must always be tempered by the realization that great diversity also exists within any society or ethnic group. Researchers may be able to pinpoint genuinely useful insights about Ethiopian, Korean, or Ukrainian culture, for example, but it would be foolish to assume that all Ethiopians, Koreans, or Ukrainians exhibit identical behaviour. It is also important to realize that both differences and similarities in behaviour occur across cultures. As we will see repeatedly, psychological processes are characterized by both cultural variance and invariance. Caveats aside, if we hope to achieve a sound understanding of human behaviour, we need to consider cultural determinants.

Theme 6: Heredity and Environment Jointly Influence Behaviour

Are individuals who they are—athletic or artistic, quick-tempered or calm, shy or outgoing, energetic or laid back—because of their genetic inheritance or because of their upbringing? This question about the importance of nature versus nurture, or heredity versus environment, has been asked in one form or another since ancient times. Historically, the nature-versus-nurture question was framed as an all-or-none proposition. In other words, theorists argued that personal traits and abilities are governed either entirely by heredity or entirely by environment. John B. Watson, for instance, asserted that person-

ality and ability depend almost exclusively on an individual's environment. In contrast, Sir Francis Galton, a pioneer in mental testing, maintained that personality and ability depend almost entirely on genetic inheritance.

Today, most psychologists agree that heredity and environment are both important. A century of research has shown that genetics and experience jointly influence an individual's intelligence, temperament, personality, and susceptibility to many psychological disorders (Grigorenko & Sternberg, 2003; Plomin, 2004). If we ask whether individuals are born or made, psychology's answer is "Both." This does not mean that nature versus nurture is a dead issue. Lively debate about the relative influence of genetics and experience continues unabated. Furthermore, psychologists are actively seeking to understand the complex ways in which genetic inheritance and experience interact to mould behaviour.

Theme 7: People's Experience of the World Is Highly Subjective

Even elementary perception—for example, of sights and sounds—is not a passive process. People actively process incoming stimulation, selectively focusing on some aspects of that stimulation while ignoring others. Moreover, they impose organization on the stimuli that they pay attention to. These tendencies combine to make perception personalized and subjective.

The subjectivity of perception was demonstrated nicely in a classic study by Hastorf and Cantril (1954). They showed students at Princeton and Dartmouth universities a film of a recent football game between the two schools. The students were told to watch for rules infractions. Both groups saw the same film, but the Princeton students "saw" the Dartmouth players engage in twice as many infractions as the Dartmouth students "saw." The investigators concluded that the game "actually was many different games and that each version of the events that transpired was just as 'real' to a particular person as other versions were to other people" (Hastorf & Cantril, 1954). In this study, the subjects' perceptions were swayed by their motives. It shows how people sometimes see what they *want* to see.

Other studies reveal that people also tend to see what they expect to see. For example, Harold Kelley (1950) showed how perceptions of people are influenced by their reputation. Kelley told students that their class would be taken over by a new lecturer, whom they would be asked to evaluate later. Before the class, the students were given a short description of the incoming instructor, with one important variation. Half the students were led to expect a "warm"

Understanding the Seven Key Themes

Check your understanding of the seven key themes introduced in the chapter by matching the vignettes with the themes they exemplify. You'll find the answers in Appendix A.

Themes

1. Psychology is empirical.

2. Psychology is theoretically diverse.

3. Psychology evolves in a sociohistorical context.

4. Behaviour is determined by multiple causes.

5. Behaviour is shaped by cultural heritage.

6. Heredity and environment jointly influence behaviour.

7. People's experience of the world is highly subjective.

Vignettes

_____ **a.** Several or more theoretical models of emotion have contributed to our overall understanding of the dynamics of emotion.

_____ **b.** According to the stress-vulnerability model, some people are at greater risk for developing certain psychological disorders for genetic reasons. Whether these people actually develop the disorders depends on how much stress they experience in their work, families, or other areas of their lives.

_____ **c.** Physical health and illness seem to be influenced by a complex constellation of psychological, biological, and social system variables.

_____ **d.** One of the difficulties in investigating the effects of drugs on consciousness is that individuals tend to have different experiences with a given drug because of their different expectations.

Figure 1.8

Manipulating person perception. Read the accompanying description of Mr. Blank carefully. If you were about to hear him give a lecture, would this description bias your perceptions of him? You probably think not, but when Kelley (1950) altered one adjective in this description (replacing the word *warm* with *cold*), the change had a dramatic impact on subjects' ratings of the guest lecturer.

SOURCE: Description from Kelley, H. H. (1950). The warm-cold variable in first impressions of persons. *Journal of Personality, 8*, 431–439. Copyright © 1950 by the Ecological Society of America. Reprinted by permission.

Mr. Blank is a graduate student in the Department of Economics and Social Science here at M.I.T. He has had three semesters of teaching experience in psychology at another college. This is his first semester teaching Ec. 70. He is 26 years old, a veteran, and married. People who know him consider him to be a very warm person, industrious, critical, practical, and determined.

Elisa Cicinelli/Index Stock Imagery

person, while the other half were led to expect a "cold" one (see Figure 1.8). All the subjects were exposed to the same 20 minutes of lecture and interaction with the new instructor. However, the group of subjects who expected a warm person rated the instructor as more considerate, sociable, humorous, good natured, informal, and humane than the subjects in the group who had expected a cold person.

Thus, it is clear that motives and expectations colour people's experiences. To some extent, individuals see what they want to see or what they expect to see. This subjectivity in perception turns out to explain a variety of behavioural tendencies that would otherwise be perplexing (Pronin, Lin, & Ross, 2002; Pronin, Gilovich, & Ross, 2004).

Human subjectivity is precisely what the scientific method is designed to counteract. In using the scientific approach, psychologists strive to make their observations as objective as possible. In some respects, overcoming subjectivity is what science is all about. Left to their own subjective experience, people might still believe that the earth is flat and that the sun revolves around it. Thus, psychologists are committed to the scientific approach because they believe it is the most reliable route to accurate knowledge.

Now that you have been introduced to the text's organizing themes, let's turn to an example of how psychological research can be applied to the challenges of everyday life. In our first Personal Application, we'll focus on a subject that should be highly relevant to you: how to be a successful student. In the Critical Thinking Application that follows it, we discuss the nature and importance of critical thinking skills.

REVIEW OF KEY POINTS

- As we examine psychology in all its many variations, we will emphasize seven key ideas as unifying themes. First, psychology is empirical because psychologists base their conclusions on observation through research rather than reasoning or common sense.

- Psychology is theoretically diverse, as there are many competing schools of thought in the field. This diversity has fuelled progress and is a strength rather than a weakness. Psychology also evolves in a sociohistorical context, as trends, issues, and values in society influence what goes on in psychology, and vice versa.

- Behaviour is determined by multiple causes, as most aspects of behaviour are influenced by complex networks of interacting factors. Although cultural heritage is often taken for granted, it has a pervasive impact on people's thoughts, feelings, and behaviour.

- Lively debate about the relative importance of nature versus nurture continues, but it is clear that heredity and environment jointly influence behaviour. People's experience of the world is highly subjective, as they sometimes see what they want to see or what they expect to see.

Improving Academic Performance

Answer the following "true" or "false."

____ **1** It's a good idea to study in as many different locations (your bedroom or kitchen, the library, lounges around school, and so forth) as possible.

____ **2** If you have a professor who delivers chaotic, hard-to-follow lectures, there is little point in attending class.

____ **3** Cramming the night before an exam is an effective method of study.

____ **4** In taking lecture notes, you should try to be a "human tape recorder" (that is, write down everything your professor says).

____ **5** You should never change your answers to multiple-choice questions, because your first hunch is your best hunch.

All of the above statements are false. If you answered them all correctly, you may have already acquired the kinds of skills and habits that facilitate academic success. If so, however, you are not typical. Today, many students enter university with poor study skills and habits—and it's not entirely their fault. The educational system generally provides minimal instruction on good study techniques. In this first Application, we will try to remedy this situation to some extent by reviewing some insights that psychology offers on how to improve academic performance. We will discuss how to promote better study habits, how to enhance reading efforts, how to get more out of lectures, and how to improve test-taking strategies. You may also want to jump ahead and read the Personal Application for Chapter 7, which focuses on how to improve everyday memory.

Developing Sound Study Habits

Effective study is crucial to success in university. Although you may run into a few classmates who boast about getting good grades without studying, you can be sure that if they perform well on exams, they do study. Students who claim otherwise simply want to be viewed as extremely bright rather than as studious.

Learning can be immensely gratifying, but studying usually involves hard work. The first step toward effective study habits is to face up to this reality. You don't have to feel guilty if you don't look forward to studying. Most students don't. Once you accept the premise that studying doesn't come naturally, it should be apparent that you need to set up an organized program to promote adequate study. According to Siebert (1995), such a program should include the following considerations:

1. *Set up a schedule for studying.* If you wait until the urge to study strikes you, you may still be waiting when the exam rolls around. Thus, it is important to allocate definite times to studying. Review your various time obligations (work, chores, and so on) and figure out in advance when you can study. When allotting certain times to studying, keep in mind that you need to be wide awake and alert. Be realistic about how long you can study at one time before you wear down from fatigue. Allow time for study breaks—they can revive sagging concentration.

It's important to write down your study schedule. A written schedule serves as a reminder and increases your commitment to following it. You should begin by setting up a general schedule for the quarter or semester, like the one in Figure 1.9. Then, at the beginning of each week, plan the specific assignments that you intend to

Figure 1.9

One student's general activity schedule for a semester. Each week the student fills in the specific assignments to work on during each study period.

Weekly Activity Schedule

	Monday	Tuesday	Wednesday	Thursday	Friday	Saturday	Sunday
8 A.M.						Work	
9 A.M.	History	Study	History	Study	History	Work	
10 A.M.	Psychology	French	Psychology	French	Psychology	Work	
11 A.M.	Study	French	Study	French	Study	Work	
NOON	Math	Study	Math	Study	Math	Work	Study
1 P.M.							Study
2 P.M.	Study	English	Study	English	Study		Study
3 P.M.	Study	English	Study	English	Study		Study
4 P.M.							
5 P.M.							
6 P.M.	Work	Study	Study	Work			Study
7 P.M.	Work	Study	Study	Work			Study
8 P.M.	Work	Study	Study	Work			Study
9 P.M.	Work	Study	Study	Work			Study
10 P.M.	Work			Work			

work on during each study session. This approach to scheduling should help you avoid cramming for exams at the last minute. Cramming is an ineffective study strategy for most students (Underwood, 1961; Zechmeister & Nyberg, 1982). It will strain your memorization capabilities, can tax your energy level, and may stoke the fires of test anxiety.

In planning your weekly schedule, try to avoid the tendency to put off working on major tasks such as term papers and reports. Time-management experts such as Alan Lakein (1996) point out that many people tend to tackle simple, routine tasks first, saving larger tasks for later when they supposedly will have more time. This common tendency leads many individuals to repeatedly delay working on major assignments until it's too late to do a good job. A good way to avoid this trap is to break major assignments down into smaller component tasks that can be scheduled individually.

Research on the differences between successful and unsuccessful students suggests that successful students monitor and regulate their use of time more effectively (Allgood et al., 2000). You can assess other aspects of your time-management practices by responding to the questionnaire in Figure 1.10.

2. *Find a place to study where you can concentrate.* Where you study is also important. The key is to find a place where distractions are likely to be minimal. Most people cannot study effectively while the TV or stereo is on or while other people are talking. Don't depend on willpower to carry you through such distractions. It's much easier to plan ahead and avoid the distractions altogether. In fact, you would be wise to set up one or two specific places used solely for study (Hettich, 1998).

3. *Reward your studying.* One reason that it is so difficult to be motivated to study regularly is that the payoffs often lie in the distant future. The ultimate reward, a degree, may be years away. Even short-term rewards, such as an A in the course, may be weeks or months away. To combat this problem, it helps to give yourself immediate, tangible rewards for studying, such as

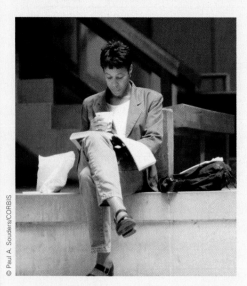

Some locations are far more conducive to successful studying than others.

Figure 1.10

Assessing your time management. This brief questionnaire (from LeBoeuf, 1980) is designed to evaluate the quality of one's time management. It should allow you to get a rough handle on how well you manage your time.

How Well Do You Manage Your Time?

Listed below are ten statements that reflect generally accepted principles of good time management. Answer these items by circling the response most characteristic of how you perform. Please be honest. No one will know your answers except you.

1 Each day I set aside a small amount of time for planning and thinking about my responsibilities.
0. Almost never 1. Sometimes 2. Often 3. Almost always

2 I set specific, written goals and put deadlines on them.
0. Almost never 1. Sometimes 2. Often 3. Almost always

3 I make a daily "to do" list, arrange items in order of importance, and try to get the important items done as soon as possible.
0. Almost never 1. Sometimes 2. Often 3. Almost always

4 I am aware of the 80/20 rule and use it. (The 80/20 rule states that 80% of your effectiveness will generally come from achieving only 20% of your goals.)
0. Almost never 1. Sometimes 2. Often 3. Almost always

5 I keep a loose schedule to allow for crises and the unexpected.
0. Almost never 1. Sometimes 2. Often 3. Almost always

6 I delegate everything I can to others.
0. Almost never 1. Sometimes 2. Often 3. Almost always

7 I try to handle each piece of paper only once.
0. Almost never 1. Sometimes 2. Often 3. Almost always

8 I eat a light lunch so I don't get sleepy in the afternoon.
0. Almost never 1. Sometimes 2. Often 3. Almost always

9 I make an active effort to keep common interruptions (visitors, meetings, telephone calls) from continually disrupting my work day.
0. Almost never 1. Sometimes 2. Often 3. Almost always

10 I am able to say no to others' requests for my time that would prevent my completing important tasks.
0. Almost never 1. Sometimes 2. Often 3. Almost always

To get your score, give yourself	If you scored	
3 points for each "almost always"	0–15	Better give some thought to managing your time.
2 points for each "often"		
1 point for each "sometimes"	16–20	You're doing OK, but there's room for improvement.
0 points for each "almost never"	21–25	Very good.
Add up your points to get your total score.	26–30	You cheated!

SOURCE: From the questionnaire "Managing Time Means Managing Yourself," by LeBoeuf, 1980, p. 45. *Business Horizons Magazine*, 1980, 23 (1) February, Table 3. Reprinted with permission from Business Horizons. Copyright © 1980 by the Board of Trustees of Indiana University, Kelley School of Business.

a snack, TV show, or phone call to a friend. Thus, you should set realistic study goals for yourself and then reward yourself when you meet them. The systematic manipulation of rewards involves harnessing the principles of *behaviour modification* described by B. F. Skinner and other behavioural psychologists. These principles are covered in the Chapter 6 Personal Application.

Improving Your Reading

Much of your study time is spent reading and absorbing information. These efforts must be active. Many students deceive themselves into thinking that they are studying by running a marker through a few sentences here and there in their text. If they do so without thoughtful selectivity, they are simply turning a textbook into a colouring book. Research suggests that highlighting selected textbook material is a useful strategy—if students are reasonably effective in identifying the main ideas in the material and if they subsequently review the main ideas they have highlighted (Caverly, Orlando, & Mullen, 2000).

You can use a number of methods to actively attack your reading assignments. One of the more widely taught strategies is Robinson's (1970) SQ3R method. *SQ3R is a study system designed to promote effective reading, which includes five steps: survey, question, read, recite, and review*. SQ3R stands for the five steps in the procedure: survey, question, read, recite, and review.

Step 1: Survey. Before you plunge into the reading itself, glance over the topic headings in the chapter. If you know where the chapter is going, you can better appreciate and organize the information you are about to read.

Step 2: Question. Once you have an overview of your reading assignment, you should proceed through it one section at a time. Take a look at the heading of the first section and convert it into a question. Doing so is usually quite simple. If the heading is "Prenatal Risk Factors," your question should be "What are sources of risk during prenatal development?" If the

heading is "Stereotyping," your question should be "What is stereotyping?" Asking these questions gets you actively involved in your reading and helps you identify the main ideas.

Step 3: Read. Only now, in the third step, are you ready to sink your teeth into the reading. Read only the specific section that you have decided to tackle. Read it with an eye toward answering the question you have just formulated. If necessary, reread the section until you can answer that question. Decide whether the segment addresses any other important questions and answer them as well.

Step 4: Recite. Now that you can answer the key question for the section, recite the answer out loud to yourself in your own words. Don't move on to the next section until you understand the main ideas of the current section. You may want to write down these ideas for review later. When you have fully digested the first section, you may go on to the next. Repeat steps 2 through 4 with the next section. Once you have mastered the crucial points there, you can go on again.

Step 5: Review. When you have read the entire chapter, refresh your memory by going back over the key points. Repeat your questions and try to answer them without consulting your book or notes. This review should fortify your retention of the main ideas. It should also help you see how the main ideas are related.

The SQ3R method should probably be applied to many texts on a paragraph-by-paragraph basis. Obviously, doing so will require you to formulate some questions without the benefit of topic headings. If you don't have enough headings, you can simply reverse the order of steps 2 and 3. Read the paragraph first and then formulate a question that addresses the basic idea of the paragraph. Then work at answering the question in your own words. The point is that you can be flexible in your use of the SQ3R technique.

Using the SQ3R method does not automatically lead to improved mastery of text-

book reading assignments. It won't be effective unless it is applied diligently and skillfully, and it tends to be more helpful to students with low to medium reading ability (Caverly, Orlando, & Mullen, 2000). Any strategy that facilitates active processing of text material, the identification of key ideas, and effective review of these ideas should enhance your reading.

Besides topic headings, your textbooks may contain various other learning aids you can use to improve your reading. If a book provides a chapter outline, chapter summary, learning objectives, or preview questions, don't ignore them. They can help you recognize the important points in the chapter. Graphic organizers (such as the Concept Checks available for this text) can enhance understanding of text material (Nist & Holschuh, 2000). A lot of effort and thought goes into formulating these and other textbook learning aids. It is wise to take advantage of them.

Getting More Out of Lectures

Although lectures are sometimes boring and tedious, it is a simple fact that poor class attendance is associated with poor grades. For example, in one study, Lindgren (1969) found that absences from class were much more common among "unsuccessful" students (grade average C– or below) than among "successful" students (grade average B or above), as shown in Figure 1.11. Even when you have an instructor who delivers hard-to-follow lectures, it is still important to go to class. If nothing else, you can get a feel for how the instructor thinks, which can help you anticipate the content of exams and respond in the manner expected by your professor.

Fortunately, most lectures are reasonably coherent. Studies indicate that attentive note taking is associated with enhanced learning and performance in university classes (Titsworth & Kiewra, 2004; Williams & Eggert, 2002). However, research also shows that many students' lecture notes are surprisingly incomplete, with the average student often recording less than 40% of the crucial ideas in a lecture (Armbruster, 2000). Thus,

Figure 1.11

Attendance and grades. When Lindgren (1969) compared the class attendance of successful students (B average or above) and unsuccessful students (C– average or below), he found a clear association between poor attendance and poor grades.

SOURCE: Adapted from Lindgren, H. C. (1969). *The psychology of college success: A dynamic approach.* New York: John Wiley & Sons, Inc. Copyright © 1969 by Henry Clay Lindgren. Adapted by permission of H. C. Lindgren.

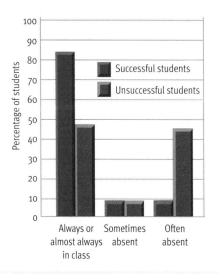

the key to getting more out of lectures is to stay motivated, stay attentive, and expend the effort to make your notes as complete as possible. Books on study skills (Longman & Atkinson, 2002; Sotiriou, 2002) offer a number of suggestions on how to take good-quality lecture notes, some of which are summarized here:

- Extracting information from lectures requires *active listening*. Focus full attention on the speaker. Try to anticipate what's coming and search for deeper meanings.

- When course material is especially complex, it is a good idea to prepare for the lecture by *reading ahead* on the scheduled subject in your text. Then you have less brand-new information to digest.

- You are not supposed to be a human tape recorder. Insofar as possible, try to write down the lecturer's thoughts *in your own words*. Doing so forces you to organize the ideas in a way that makes sense to you. In taking notes, pay attention to clues about what is most important. These clues may range from subtle hints, such as an instructor repeating a point, to not-so-subtle hints, such as an instructor saying, "You'll run into this again."

- *Asking questions* during lectures can be helpful. Doing so keeps you actively involved in the lecture and allows you to clarify points that you may have misun-

derstood. Many students are more bashful about asking questions than they should be. They don't realize that most professors welcome questions.

Improving Test-Taking Strategies

Let's face it—some students are better than others at taking tests. **Testwiseness is the ability to use the characteristics and format of a cognitive test to maximize one's score.** Students clearly vary in test-

wiseness, and such variations are reflected in performance on exams (Geiger, 1997; Rogers & Yang, 1996). Testwiseness is not a substitute for knowledge of the subject matter. However, skill in taking tests can help you show what you know when it is critical to do so (Flippo, Becker, & Wark, 2000).

A number of myths exist about the best way to take tests. For instance, it is widely believed that students shouldn't go back and change their answers to multiple-choice questions. Benjamin, Cavell, and Shallenberger (1984) found this to be the dominant belief among university *faculty* as well as students (see Figure 1.12). However, the old adage that "your first hunch is your best hunch on tests" has been shown to be wrong. Empirical studies clearly and consistently indicate that, over the long run, changing answers pays off. Benjamin and his colleagues reviewed 20 studies on this issue; their findings are presented in Figure 1.13. As you can see, answer changes that go from a wrong answer to a right answer outnumber changes that go from a right answer to a wrong one by a sizable margin. The popular belief that answer changing is harmful is probably attributable to painful memories of right-to-wrong changes. In any case, you can see how it pays to be familiar with sound test-taking strategies.

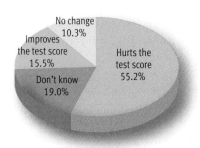

Figure 1.12

Beliefs about the effects of answer changing on tests. Ludy Benjamin and his colleagues (1984) asked 58 college faculty whether changing answers on tests is a good idea. Like most students, the majority of the faculty felt that answer changing usually hurts a student's test score, even though the research evidence contradicts this belief (see Figure 1.13).

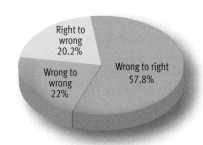

Figure 1.13

Actual effects of changing answers on multiple-choice tests. When the data from all the relevant studies were combined by Benjamin et al. (1984), they indicated that answer changing on tests generally increased rather than reduced students' test scores. It is interesting to note the contrast between beliefs about answer changing (see Figure 1.12) and the actual results of this practice.

General Tips

The principles of testwiseness were first described by Millman, Bishop, and Ebel (1965). Let's look at some of their general ideas:

- If efficient time use appears crucial, set up a mental schedule for progressing through the test. Make a mental note to check whether you're one-third finished when a third of your time is gone.
- Don't waste time pondering difficult-to-answer questions excessively. If you have no idea at all, just guess and go on. If you need to devote a good deal of time to the question, skip it and mark it so you can return to it later if time permits.
- Adopt the appropriate level of sophistication for the test. Don't read things into questions. Sometimes students make things more complex than they were intended to be. Often, simple-looking questions are just what they appear to be.
- If you complete all of the questions and still have some time remaining, review the test. Make sure that you have recorded your answers correctly. If you were unsure of some answers, go back and reconsider them.

Tips for Multiple-Choice Exams

Sound test-taking strategies are especially important with multiple-choice (and true-false) questions. These types of questions often include clues that may help you converge on the correct answer (Mentzer, 1982; Weiten, 1984). You may be able to improve your performance on such tests by considering the following points (Flippo, 2000):

- As you read the stem of each multiple choice question, anticipate the answer if you can, before looking at the options. If the answer you anticipated is among the options, it is likely to be the correct one.
- Always read each question completely. Continue reading even if you find your anticipated answer among the options. A more complete option may be farther down the list.
- Learn how to quickly eliminate options that are highly implausible. Many questions have only two plausible options, accompanied by "throwaway" options for filler. You should work at spotting these implausible options so that you can quickly discard them and narrow your task.
- Be alert to the fact that information relevant to one question is sometimes given away in another test item.
- On items that have "all of the above" as an option, if you know that just two of the options are correct, you should choose "all of the above." If you are confident that one of the options is incorrect, you should eliminate this option and "all of the above" and choose from the remaining options.
- Options that represent broad, sweeping generalizations tend to be incorrect. You should be vigilant for words such as always, never, necessarily, only, must, completely, totally, and so forth that create these improbable assertions.
- In contrast, options that represent carefully qualified statements tend to be correct. Words such as often, sometimes, perhaps, may, and generally tend to show up in these well-qualified statements.

Tips for Essay Exams

Little research has been done on testwiseness as it applies to essay exams. That's because there are relatively few clues to take advantage of in the essay format. Nonetheless, various books (Flippo, 2000; Pauk, 1990; Walter & Siebert, 1990) offer tips based on expert advice, including the following:

- Time is usually a crucial factor on essay tests. Therefore, you should begin by looking over the questions and making time allocations on the basis of (1) your knowledge, (2) the time required to answer each question, and (3) the points awarded for answering each question. It's usually a good idea to answer the questions that you know best first.
- Many students fail to appreciate the importance of good organization in their essay responses. If your instructor can't follow where you are going with your answers, you won't get many points. Test essays are often poorly organized because students feel pressured for time and plunge into answering questions without any planning. It will pay off in the long run if you spend a minute getting organ-ized first. Also, many examiners appreciate it if you make your organization quite explicit by using headings or by numbering the points you're making.
- In many courses you'll learn a great deal of jargon or technical terminology. Demonstrate your learning by using this technical vocabulary in your essay answers.

In summary, sound study skills and habits are crucial to academic success. Intelligence alone won't do the job (although it certainly helps). Good academic skills do not develop overnight. They are acquired gradually, so be patient with yourself. Fortunately, tasks such as reading textbooks, writing papers, and taking tests get easier with practice. Ultimately, we think you'll find that the rewards—knowledge, a sense of accomplishment, and progress toward a degree—are worth the effort.

REVIEW OF KEY POINTS

- To foster sound study habits, you should devise a written study schedule and reward yourself for following it. You should also try to find one or two specific places for studying that are relatively free of distractions.
- You should use active reading techniques to select the most important ideas from the material you read. SQ3R is one approach to active reading that can be helpful if it is used diligently.
- The key to good note taking is to strive to make lecture notes as complete as possible. It's important to use active listening techniques and to record lecturers' ideas in your own words. It also helps if you read ahead to prepare for lectures and ask questions as needed.
- Being an effective student requires sound test-taking skills. In general, it's a good idea to devise a schedule for progressing through an exam, to adopt the appropriate level of sophistication, to avoid wasting time on troublesome questions, and to review your answers whenever time permits.
- On multiple-choice tests it is wise to anticipate answers, to read questions completely, and to quickly eliminate implausible options. Options that represent carefully qualified assertions are more likely to be correct than options that create sweeping generalizations.
- On essay tests, it is wise to start with questions you know, to emphasize good organization, and to use technical vocabulary when it is appropriate.

Developing Critical Thinking Skills: An Introduction

If you ask any group of professors, parents, employers, or politicians, "What is the most important outcome of an education?", the most popular answer is likely to be "the development of the ability to think critically." **Critical thinking is the use of cognitive skills and strategies that increase the probability of a desirable outcome**. Such outcomes would include good career choices, effective decisions in the workplace, wise investments, and so forth. In the long run, critical thinkers should have more desirable outcomes than people who are not skilled in critical thinking (Halpern, 1998, 2003). Critical thinking is purposeful, reasoned, goal-directed thinking that involves solving problems, formulating inferences, working with probabilities, and making carefully thought-out decisions. Here are some of the skills exhibited by critical thinkers:

- They understand and use the principles of scientific investigation. (How can the effectiveness of punishment as a disciplinary procedure be determined?)
- They apply the rules of formal and informal logic. (If most people disapprove of sex sites on the World Wide Web, then why are these sites so popular?)
- They think effectively in terms of probabilities. (What is the likelihood of being able to predict who will commit a violent crime?)
- They carefully evaluate the quality of information. (Can I trust the claims made by this politician?)
- They analyze arguments for the soundness of the conclusions. (Does the rise in drug use mean that a stricter drug policy is needed?)

The topic of thinking has a long history in psychology, dating back to Wilhelm Wundt in the 19th century. Modern cognitive psychologists have found that a useful model of critical thinking has at least two components: (1) knowledge of the skills of critical thinking—the *cognitive component*, and (2) the attitude or disposition of a critical thinker—the *emotional or affective* component. Both are needed for effective critical thinking.

The Skills of Critical Thinking

Instruction in critical thinking is based on two assumptions: (1) a set of skills or strategies exists that students can learn to recognize and apply in appropriate contexts; (2) if the skills are applied appropriately, students will become more effective thinkers. Critical thinking skills that would be useful in any context might include understanding how reasons and evidence support or refute conclusions; distinguishing among facts, opinions, and reasoned judgments; using principles of likelihood and uncertainty when thinking about probabilistic events; generating multiple solutions to problems and working systematically toward a desired goal; and understanding how causation is determined. This list provides some typical examples of what is meant by the term *critical thinking skills*. Because these skills are useful in a wide variety of contexts, they are sometimes called *transcontextual skills*.

The Attitude of a Critical Thinker

It is of little use to know the skills of critical thinking if you are unwilling to exert the hard mental work to use them or if you have a sloppy or careless attitude toward thinking. A critical thinker is willing to plan, flexible in thinking, persistent, able to admit mistakes and make corrections, and mindful of the thinking process. The use of the word *critical* represents the notion of a critique or evaluation of thinking processes and outcomes. It is not meant to be negative (as in a "critical person") but rather to convey that critical thinkers are vigilant about their thinking.

The Need to Teach Critical Thinking

Decades of research on instruction in critical thinking have shown that the skills and attitudes of critical thinking need to be deliberately and consciously taught, because they often do not develop by themselves with standard instruction in a content area (Nisbett, 1993). For this reason, each chapter in this text ends with a "Critical Thinking Application." The material presented in each of these Critical Thinking Applications relates to the chapter topics, but the focus is on how to think about a particular issue, line of research, or controversy. Because the emphasis is on the thinking process, you may be asked to consider conflicting interpretations of data, judge the credibility of information sources, or generate your own testable hypotheses. The specific critical thinking skills highlighted in each Application are summarized in a table so that they are easily identified. Some of the skills will show up in multiple chapters because the goal is to help you spontaneously select the appropriate critical thinking skills when you encounter new information. Repeated practice with selected skills across chapters should help you develop this ability.

An Example

As explained in the main body of the chapter, *evolutionary psychology* is emerging as an influential school of thought. As one example of evolutionary theorizing in psychology, we looked at evolutionary analyses of gender differences in spatial abilities. To show you how critical thinking skills can be applied to psychological issues, let's re-examine the evolutionary explanation of gender differences in spatial talents, expand on it slightly, and then use some critical thinking strategies to evaluate this explanation.

Evolutionary psychologists explain gender differences in spatial abilities in terms of how they presumably evolved to meet the adaptive pressures faced by our ancient ancestors (Silverman & Eals, 1992; Silverman & Phillips, 1998). These Canadian psychologists focus on how natural selection would have favoured certain skills that would have been adaptive in hunting and gathering societies, as most of the human race's time on earth has been spent in such societal arrangements. Specifically, they assert that the typical division of labour between the sexes in hunting and gathering societies created different adaptive pressures for males and females. For example, it is believed that in such societies adult males often travelled long distances to hunt, while the women and children stayed closer to home to gather food. This was an efficient division of labour because women spent much of their adult lives pregnant, nursing, or caring for the young and, therefore, could not travel long distances. Building on these assumptions, evolutionary theorists assert that males tend to perform somewhat better than females on visual-spatial tasks involving mental rotation of images (see Figure 1.14), mental reconstruction of figures, map reading, and maze learning because these skills would have fostered success in the hunting tasks traditionally handled by males (by helping them to traverse long distances, aim projectiles at prey, and so forth). In contrast, the theorists argue that females exhibit a slight superiority on tasks measuring memory for locations because this talent would have fostered success in the foraging and gathering tasks traditionally handled by females.

How can you critically evaluate these claims? If your first thought was that you need more information, good for you, because you are already showing an aptitude for critical thinking. Some additional information about gender differences in

Figure 1.14

An example of a spatial task involving mental rotation. Spatial reasoning tasks can be divided into a variety of subtypes. Studies indicate that males perform slightly better than females on most, but not all, spatial tasks. The tasks on which males are superior often involve mentally rotating objects, such as in the problem shown here. In this problem, the person has to figure out which object on the right (A through E) could be a rotation of the object at the left.

Source: Stafford, R. E., & Gullikson, H. (1962). *Identical Blocks*, Form AA.

A   Ⓑ   C   D   E

"B" is the correct answer.

cognitive abilities is presented in Chapter 11 of this text. You also need to develop the habit of asking good questions, such as, "Are there alternative explanations for these results? Are there contradictory data?" Let's briefly consider each of these questions.

Are there alternative explanations for gender differences in spatial skills? Well, there certainly are other explanations for males' superiority on most spatial tasks. For example, one could attribute this finding to the gender-typed activities that males are encouraged to engage in more than females, such as playing with building blocks, Lego sets, Lincoln Logs, and various types of construction sets, as well as a host of spatially oriented video games. These gender-typed activities appear to provide boys with more practice than girls on most types of spatial tasks (Voyer, Nolan, & Voyer, 2000), and experience with spatial activities appears to enhance spatial skills (Lizarraga & Ganuza, 2003). If we can explain gender differences in spatial abilities in terms of disparities in

the everyday activities of males and females, we may have no need to appeal to natural selection.

Are there data that run counter to the evolutionary explanation for modern gender differences in spatial skills? Again, the answer is yes. Some scholars who have studied hunting and gathering societies suggest that women often travelled long distances to gather food and that women were often involved in hunting (Adler, 1993). In addition, women wove baskets and clothing and worked on other tasks that required spatial thinking (Halpern, 1997). Moreover—think about it—men on long hunting trips obviously needed to develop a good memory for locations or they might never have returned home. So, there is room for some argument about exactly what kinds of adaptive pressures males and females faced in ancient hunting and gathering societies.

Thus, you can see how considering alternative explanations and contradictory evidence weakens the evolutionary explanation of gender differences in spatial abilities. The questions we raised about alternative explanations and contradictory data are two generic critical thinking questions that can be asked in a wide variety of contexts. The answers to these questions do *not* prove that evolutionary psychologists are wrong in their explanation of gender differences in visual-spatial skills, but they do weaken the evolutionary explanation. In thinking critically about psychological issues, you will see that it makes more sense to talk about the *relative strength of an argument,* as opposed to whether an argument is right or wrong, because we will be dealing with complex issues that rarely lend themselves to being correct or incorrect.

Table 1.4 Critical Thinking Skills Discussed in This Application

Skill	Description
Looking for alternative explanations for findings and events	In evaluating explanations, the critical thinker explores whether there are other explanations that could also account for the findings or events under scrutiny.
Looking for contradictory evidence	In evaluating the evidence presented on an issue, the critical thinker attempts to look for contradictory evidence that may have been left out of the debate.

RECAP

Key Ideas

From Speculation to Science: How Psychology Developed

● Psychology's intellectual parents were 19th-century philosophy and physiology, which shared an interest in the mysteries of the mind. Psychology was born as an independent discipline when Wilhelm Wundt established the first psychological research laboratory in 1879 at Leipzig, Germany. He argued that psychology should be the scientific study of consciousness.

● The structuralists believed that psychology should use introspection to analyze consciousness into its basic elements. Functionalists, such as William James, believed that psychology should focus on the purpose and adaptive functions of consciousness.

● Behaviourists, led by John B. Watson, argued that psychology should study only observable behaviour. Thus, they campaigned to redefine psychology as the science of behaviour. Emphasizing the importance of the environment over heredity, they began to explore stimulus–response relationships, often using laboratory animals as subjects.

● Sigmund Freud's psychoanalytic theory emphasized the unconscious determinants of behaviour and the importance of sexuality. Freud's ideas were controversial, and they met with resistance in academic psychology.

● Behaviourism continued as a powerful force in psychology, boosted greatly by B. F. Skinner's research. Skinner in his research emphasized observable behaviour, and he generated controversy by arguing that free will is an illusion.

● Finding both behaviourism and psychoanalysis unsatisfactory, advocates of a new theoretical orientation called humanism became influential in the 1950s. Humanism, led by Abraham Maslow and Carl Rogers, emphasized humans' freedom and potential for personal growth.

● The first experimental laboratory in Canada was established in 1891 at the University of Toronto in 1891 by James Mark Baldwin. Rapid growth in Canadian psychology has been evident over the last century.

● Stimulated by the demands of World War II, clinical psychology grew rapidly in the 1950s. Thus, psychology became a profession as well as a science. This movement toward professionalization eventually spread to other areas in psychology.

● During the 1950s and 1960s, advances in the study of cognitive processes and the physiological bases of behaviour led to renewed interest in cognition and physiology, as psychology returned to its original roots.

● In the 1980s, Western psychologists, who had previously been rather provincial, developed a greater interest in how cultural factors influence thoughts, feelings, and behaviour. This trend was sparked in large part by growing global interdependence and by increased cultural diversity in Western societies.

● The 1990s witnessed the emergence of a new theoretical perspective called evolutionary psychology. The central premise of this new school of thought is that patterns of behaviour are the product of evolutionary forces, just as anatomical characteristics are shaped by natural selection.

Psychology Today: Vigorous and Diversified

● Contemporary psychology is a diversified science and profession that has grown rapidly in recent decades. Major areas of research in modern psychology include developmental psychology, social psychology, experimental psychology, physiological psychology, cognitive psychology, personality, and psychometrics.

● Applied psychology encompasses four professional specialties: clinical psychology, counselling psychology, educational and school psychology, and industrial and organizational psychology.

Putting It in Perspective: Seven Key Themes

● As we examine psychology in all its many variations, we will emphasize seven key ideas as unifying themes. Looking at psychology as a field of study, our three key themes are (1) psychology is empirical, (2) psychology is theoretically diverse, and (3) psychology evolves in a sociohistorical context.

● Looking at psychology's subject matter, the remaining four themes are (4) behaviour is determined by multiple causes, (5) behaviour is shaped by cultural heritage, (6) heredity and environment jointly influence behaviour, and (7) people's experience of the world is highly subjective.

Personal Application • Improving Academic Performance

● To foster sound study habits, you should devise a written study schedule and reward yourself for following it. You should also try to find one or two specific places for studying that are relatively free of distractions.

● You should use active reading techniques to select the most important ideas from the material you read. SQ3R, one approach to active reading, breaks a reading assignment into manageable segments and requires that you understand each segment before you move on.

● Good note taking can help you get more out of lectures. It's important to use active listening techniques and to record lecturers' ideas in your own words.

● Being an effective student also requires sound test-taking skills. In general, it's a good idea to devise a schedule for progressing through an exam, to adopt the appropriate level of sophistication, to avoid wasting time on troublesome questions, and to review your answers whenever time permits.

Critical Thinking Application • Developing Critical Thinking Skills: An Introduction

● Critical thinking is the use of cognitive skills and strategies that increase the probability of a desirable outcome. Critical thinking is purposeful, reasoned thinking. A critical thinker is flexible, persistent, able to admit mistakes, and mindful of the thinking process.

● Evolutionary psychologists have attributed contemporary gender differences in spatial abilities to the sex-based division of labour in hunting and gathering societies. However, alternative explanations have been offered for these differences, focusing on the gender-typed activities that modern males and females engage in. There also are contradictory data regarding the adaptive pressures faced by females and males in hunting and gathering societies.

Key Terms

Applied psychology, 14
Behaviour, 6
Behaviourism, 6
Clinical psychology, 14
Cognition, 16
Critical thinking, 36
Culture, 28
Empiricism, 26
Ethnocentrism, 19
Evolutionary psychology, 19
Functionalism, 5
Humanism, 11
Introspection, 5
Natural selection, 5
Psychiatry, 25
Psychoanalytic theory, 8
Psychology, 21
SQ3R, 33
Stimulus, 6
Structuralism, 5
Testwiseness, 34
Theory, 26
Unconscious, 8

Key People

Sigmund Freud, 8
G. Stanley Hall, 4
Donald Hebb, 17
William James, 5
Brenda Milner, 13
Carl Rogers, 11
B. F. Skinner, 9
John B. Watson, 6
Wilhelm Wundt, 3

PRACTICE TEST

1. For which of the following is Wilhelm Wundt primarily known?
   A. the establishment of the first formal laboratory for research in psychology
   B. the distinction between mind and body as two separate entities
   C. the discovery of how signals are conducted along nerves in the body
   D. the development of the first formal program for training in psychotherapy

2. G. Stanley Hall is noteworthy in the history of psychology because he:
   A. established the first American research laboratory in psychology.
   B. launched America's first psychological journal.
   C. was the driving force behind the establishment of the American Psychological Association.
   D. did all of the above.

3. Which of the following approaches might William James criticize for examining a movie frame by frame instead of seeing the motion in the motion picture?
   A. structuralism
   B. functionalism
   C. dualism
   D. humanism

4. Fred, a tennis coach, insists that he can make any reasonably healthy individual into an internationally competitive tennis player. Fred is echoing the thoughts of:
   A. Sigmund Freud.
   B. John B. Watson.
   C. Abraham Maslow.
   D. William James.

5. Which of the following approaches might suggest that forgetting to pick his mother up at the airport was Henry's unconscious way of saying that he did not welcome her visit?
   A. psychoanalytic
   B. behavioural
   C. humanistic
   D. cognitive

6. Which of the following is a statement with which Skinner's followers would agree?
   A. Most behaviour is controlled by unconscious forces.
   B. The goal of behaviour is self-actualization.
   C. Nature is more influential than nurture.
   D. Free will is an illusion.

7. Which of the following approaches has the most optimistic view of human nature?
   A. humanism
   B. behaviourism
   C. psychoanalysis
   D. structuralism

8. Which of the following historical events created a demand for clinicians that was far greater than the supply?
   A. World War I
   B. the Depression
   C. World War II
   D. the Korean War

9. The tendency to view one's own group as superior to others and as the standard for judging the worth of foreign ways is known as:
   A. behaviourism.
   B. ethnocentrism.
   C. humanism.
   D. functionalism.

10. The study of the endocrine system and genetic mechanisms would most likely be undertaken by a(n):
    A. clinical psychologist.
    B. physiological psychologist.
    C. social psychologist.
    D. educational psychologist.

11. The fact that psychologists do not all agree about the nature and development of personality demonstrates:
    A. that there are many ways of looking at the same phenomenon.
    B. the fundamental inability of psychologists to work together in developing a single theory.
    C. the failure of psychologists to communicate with one another.
    D. the possibility that personality may simply be incomprehensible.

12. A multifactorial causation approach to behaviour suggests that:
    A. most behaviours can be explained best by single-cause explanations.
    B. most behaviour is governed by a complex network of interrelated factors.
    C. data must be subjected to rigorous statistical analysis in order to make sense.
    D. explanations of behaviour tend to build up from the simple to the complex in a hierarchical manner.

13. Psychology's answer to the question of whether we are born or made tends to be:
    A. we are born.
    B. we are made.
    C. we are both born and made.
    D. neither.

14. In regard to changing answers on multiple-choice tests, research indicates that _____ changes tend to be more common than other types of changes.
    A. wrong to right
    B. right to wrong
    C. wrong to wrong

15. Critical thinking skills:
    A. are abstract abilities that cannot be identified.
    B. usually develop spontaneously through normal content instruction.
    C. usually develop spontaneously without any instruction.
    D. need to be deliberately taught, because they often do not develop by themselves with standard content instruction.

16. Donald Hebb is a well-known Canadian psychologist who did research in which of the following areas of psychology?
    A. developmental psychology
    B. social psychology
    C. neuropsychology
    D. clinical psychology

   See Appendix A for answers to this Practice Test.

WWW ON THE WEB

For additional resources on the topics covered in this chapter, visit the *Psychology: Themes and Variations* Web site, where you will find practice quizzes, tutorials, Web links, simulations, critical thinking activities, flash cards, interactive exercises, and suggested readings available through INFOTRAC.

   http://www.themesandvariations.nelson.com

 Thomson NOW! http://hed.nelson.com

Go to this site for the link to ThomsonNOW™, your one-stop study shop. Take a Pretest for this chapter and ThomsonNOW™ will generate a personalized Study Plan based on your test results! The Study Plan will identify the topics you need to review and direct you to online resources to help you master those topics. You can then take a Posttest to help you determine the concepts you have mastered and what you still need work on.

CHAPTER 2

Latchezar Boyadjiev, *The Witness*, L.B. Glass Studios

The Scientific Approach to Behaviour
Goals of the Scientific Enterprise
Steps in a Scientific Investigation
Featured Study • Can Fear Increase Sexual Attraction?
Advantages of the Scientific Approach

Looking for Causes: Experimental Research
Independent and Dependent Variables
Experimental and Control Groups
Extraneous Variables
Variations in Designing Experiments
Advantages and Disadvantages of Experimental Research

Looking for Links: Descriptive/Correlational Research
Naturalistic Observation
Case Studies
Surveys
Advantages and Disadvantages of Descriptive/Correlational
    Research

Looking for Conclusions: Statistics and Research
Descriptive Statistics
Inferential Statistics

Looking for Flaws: Evaluating Research
Sampling Bias
Placebo Effects
Distortions in Self-Report Data
Experimenter Bias

Looking at Ethics: Do the Ends Justify the Means?
Ethical Guidelines for Research in Psychology in Canada

Putting It in Perspective

Personal Application • **Finding and Reading Journal
Articles**
The Nature of Technical Journals
Finding Journal Articles
Reading Journal Articles

Critical Thinking Application • **The Perils of Anecdotal
Evidence: "I Have a Friend Who ..."**

Recap

Practice Test

The Research Enterprise in Psychology

We both remember well our first course in psychology. If you are now like we were then, one of the reasons you are taking this course is because you want to understand better why people behave in the ways that they do. You likely have many questions about human behaviour, yours and that of others, that you hope you can answer after you read this book. Where do these answers come from? In Chapter 1 you learned that psychology is a scientific enterprise in which formal research methods are employed in an attempt to answer such questions. Is it possible to provide answers to all these questions? Some of the questions you have may concern intimate and personal emotions and feelings you have about yourself. Are psychologists able to scientifically examine emotions or to evaluate explanations of how and why they occur? You may be concerned about things happening around you such as the level of violence in society and you may be wondering if psychology has discovered anything about these issues that can be used to lessen their frequency. If so, how do psychologists evaluate the effectiveness of any interventions designed to help?

For example, consider your reactions and emotions when you first heard about the tsunami devastation in countries such as Indonesia, India, and Sri Lanka that occurred just after Christmas Day in 2004. Your emotional reactions may have ranged from shock, to horror, to sadness. Think also about the more positive reactions such as relief and pride you may have had when it became clear that Canadians were more than willing to give money and other resources to aid relief in the area either as a result of their own personal initiative or in response to benefits such as CBC's *Canada for Asia* concert held on January 13, 2005. Canadian musician Tom Cochrane is credited with initiating the benefit concert and with securing the involvement of musicians such as Barenaked Ladies, actors such as Mike Myers, and personalities such as Don Cherry (Rayner, 2005). You may be curious about how psychologists do research into such personal emotions and whether they have been able to offer any answers concerning where they come from.

Most of us are very concerned about the level of aggression in society, especially in the context of personal relationships. The media are frequently filled with reports of relationship abuse (Brown, 2005). For example, according to all reports, Tony Brookes had a long history of spousal abuse before he beat and tried to shoot his wife in the food court of a busy building in downtown Toronto on August 26, 2004. Fortunately, his gun jammed. After fleeing the scene, Brookes took a female McMaster University student hostage at gunpoint outside Union Station. At this point no one knew whether his gun was operational or not. He was later shot and killed by Emergency

Reuters/Mike Cassese/Landov

Canadians donated millions for tsunami victims as a result of the Concert for Asia and other benefits.

Task Force sniper Gord Lusby (Diebel & Roy, 2005). What do we know about the nature of domestic and relationship violence and is there anything we can do about it? What do we know about the types of emotions that Officer Lusby and the many onlookers were feeling as the events took place?

Questions, questions, questions—we all have questions about behaviour. Perhaps the most basic question is how can we investigate these and other questions. Although we will touch briefly on some of the research on emotions and relationship violence, this chapter is about the more basic question of how research in psychology is conducted. As you learned in Chapter 1, psychology is empirical. Psychologists use a variety of research methods in answering questions about human behaviour. Different types of questions may call for different types of research strategies. Part of the creativity involved in psychology is figuring out

how to make systematic observations that will shed light on the puzzles and questions that concern them.

In this chapter, we will examine the scientific approach to the study of behaviour and then look at the specific research methods that psychologists use most frequently. We'll also see why psychologists use statistics in their research. After you learn how research is done, you'll also learn how *not* to do it. That is, we'll review some common flaws in doing research.

Finally, we will take a look at ethical issues in behavioural research. In the Personal Application, you'll learn how to find and read journal articles that report on research. In the chapter's Critical Thinking Application, we'll examine the nature and validity of anecdotal evidence. As we consider and learn about the research enterprise in psychology, we will highlight some attempts to answer some of our questions about research on emotions and relationship violence.

The Scientific Approach to Behaviour

PREVIEW QUESTIONS
- What are the goals of the scientific enterprise?
- What are the key steps required by a scientific investigation?
- What are the principal advantages of the scientific approach?

Goals of the Scientific Enterprise

Psychologists and other scientists share three sets of interrelated goals: measurement and description, understanding and prediction, and application and control.

1. *Measurement and description.* Science's commitment to observation requires that an investigator figure out a way to measure the phenomenon under study. For example, if you were interested in the effects of different situations on emotion, you would have to first develop some means of measuring emotions. Thus, the first goal of psychology is to develop measurement techniques that make it possible to describe behaviour clearly and precisely.

2. *Understanding and prediction.* A higher-level goal of science is understanding. Scientists believe that they understand events when they can explain the reasons for the occurrence of the events. To evaluate their understanding, scientists make and test predictions called hypotheses. **A *hypothesis* is a tentative statement about the relationship between two or more variables. *Variables* are any measurable conditions, events, characteristics, or behaviours that are controlled or observed in a study.** If we hypothesized that physiological arousal would affect emotions as did the authors of our Featured Study, Dutton and Aron (see page 46), the variables in our study would be physiological arousal and emotional state.

3. *Application and control.* Ultimately, many scientists hope that the information they gather will be of some practical value in helping to solve everyday problems. Once people understand a phenomenon, they often can exert more control over it. Today, the profession of psychology attempts to apply research findings to practical problems in schools, businesses, factories, and mental hospitals. For example, a clinical psychologist might use what we know about typical, everyday emotions to assist individuals suffering from emotional disorders. In the Featured Study, you will see how one group of researchers employed these concepts in their examination of emotions. A psychologist might use what he or she knows about the roots and nature of violence in relationships to design a treatment program with the objective of lowering the probability of such violence in the future. Of course, to be sure such an intervention program works, the psychologist might design a scientific examination of the intervention's effectiveness.

How do theories help scientists to achieve their goals? As noted in Chapter 1, psychologists do not set out just to collect isolated facts about relationships between variables. To build toward a better understanding of behaviour, they construct theories. **A *theory* is a system of interrelated ideas used to explain a set of observations.** For example, using a handful of concepts, such as children's cognitive development, semantics, and parental interaction, Canada Research Chair Susan Graham at the University of Calgary attempted to explain some important characteristics of language development. (e.g., Graham, Kilbreath, & Welder, 2004). We will discuss language development in Chapter 11. For your interest, the Canada Research Chair program was developed by the government of Canada to highlight and support the research efforts of excellent researchers across Canada—we will describe the research of several of these prestigious award-winners throughout the text. For a list of some of the current Canada Research Chairs and their areas of study, see Table 2.1 (for a complete list of Canada Research Chairs go to www.chairs.gc.ca).

Thus, by integrating apparently unrelated facts and principles into a coherent whole, theories permit psychologists to make the leap from the *description* of behaviour to the *understanding* of behaviour. Moreover, the enhanced understanding afforded by theories guides future research by generating new predictions and suggesting new lines of inquiry (Higgins, 2004).

A scientific theory must be testable, as the cornerstone of science is its commitment to putting ideas to an empirical test. Most theories are too complex to be tested all at once. For example, it would be impossible to devise a single study that could test all the many facets of evolutionary theory. Rather, in a typical study, investigators test one or two specific

Table 2.1 Selected List of Recent Canada Research Chairs in Psychology

Name	Institution	Research Area	Further Discussion in Text
Hymie Anisman	Carleton University	Behavioural Neurosciences	p. 536
Michel Bédard	Lakehead University	Aging and Health	
Michel Boivin	Université Laval	Children's Social Development	
Lori Buchanan	University of Windsor	Psycholinguistics	
Kim Cornish	McGill University	Neuropsychology and Education	
Brian Cox	University of Manitoba	Mood and Anxiety Disorders	pp. 582, 585
Amedeo D'Angiulli	University College of the Cariboo	Early Intervention and Child Development	
Serge Desmarais	University of Guelph	Applied Social Psychology	
Roger Dixon	University of Alberta	Cognition and Aging	
James Donckert	University of Waterloo	Cognitive Neurosciences	
Mark Ellenbogen	Concordia University	Development Psychopathology	
Gordon Flett	York University	Personality and Health	p. 594
Mel Goodale	University of Western Ontario	Visual Neuroscience	pp. 153, 154, 155
Susan Graham	University of Calgary	Language and Cognitive Development	p. 43
Stevan Harnad	Université du Québec à Montréal	Cognitive Science	
Lisa Kalynchuk	University of Saskatchewan	Behavioural Neurosciences	
Valerie Kuhlmeier	Queen's University	Cognitive Development	
Michael Leiter	Acadia University	Occupational Health and Well-Being	p. 550
Cheryl McCormick	Brock University	Behavioural Neuroscience	
Robert McDonald	University of Lethbridge	Behavioural Neuroscience	
Patrick McGrath	Dalhousie University	Pediatric Pain	
James Parker	Trent University	Emotion and Health	pp. 381, 382, 545
Linda Parker	Wilfrid Laurier University	Behavioural Neurosciences	
Keith Stanovich	University of Toronto	Applied Cognitive Science	
Janet Werker	University of British Columbia	Language Acquisition	pp. 314, 315
Stephen Wright	Simon Fraser University	Social Psychology	p. 320

SOURCE: From Canada Research Chairs, retrieved April 7, 2005, from http://www.chairs.gc.ca.

hypotheses derived from a theory. If their findings support the hypotheses, confidence in the theory that the hypotheses were derived from grows. If their findings fail to support the hypotheses, confidence in the theory diminishes, and the theory may be revised or discarded (see Figure 2.1). Thus, theory construction is a gradual, iterative process that is always subject to revision.

Steps in a Scientific Investigation

Curiosity about a question provides the point of departure for any kind of investigation, scientific or otherwise. Scientific investigations, however, are *systematic*. They follow an orderly pattern described below in steps 1 through 5. They are reflected in the Featured Study by University of British Columbia researchers Donald Dutton and Arthur Aron on the effects of fear arousal on sexual attraction (Dutton & Aron, 1974). You should read the Featured Study on page 46 before continuing with this section.

Step 1: Formulate a Testable Hypothesis

The first step in a scientific investigation is to translate a theory or an intuitive idea into a testable hypothesis. Normally, hypotheses are expressed as predictions. In their research, Dutton and Aron predict that increased arousal would heighten the sexual attraction of their research participants to members of the opposite sex to whom they were just introduced. This hypothesis was based on previous work on emotions, such as that by Schachter (1964).

To be testable, scientific hypotheses must be formulated precisely, and the variables under study must be clearly defined. Researchers achieve these clear formulations by providing operational definitions of the relevant variables. An *operational definition* **describes the actions or operations that will be used to measure or control a variable.** Operational definitions—which may be quite different from concepts' dictionary definitions—establish precisely what is meant by each variable in the context of a study.

To illustrate, let's examine some of the operational definitions used by Dutton and Aron. They measured sexual attraction in Study 1 in two ways: first, by evaluating the amount of sexual imagery in participants' responses to a projective measure, the Thematic Apperception Test (you will learn more about the nature of projective tests in Chapter 12); and second, by assessing the number of participants in various conditions who called the experimental confederate (i.e., the male or female they had just met after crossing the bridge) after the experiment had ended.

Step 2: Select the Research Method and Design the Study

The second step in a scientific investigation is to figure out how to put the hypothesis to an empirical

Figure **2.1**

Theory construction. A good theory will generate a host of testable hypotheses. In a typical study, only one or a few of these hypotheses can be evaluated. If the evidence supports the hypotheses, our confidence in the theory they were derived from generally grows. If the hypotheses are not supported, confidence in the theory decreases and revisions to the theory may be made to accommodate the new findings. If the hypotheses generated by a theory consistently fail to garner empirical support, the theory may be discarded altogether. Thus, theory construction and testing is a gradual process.

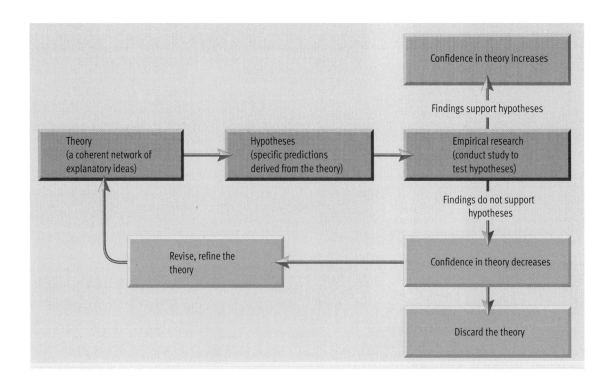

test. The research method chosen depends to a large degree on the nature of the question under study. The various methods—experiments, case studies, surveys, naturalistic observation, and so forth—each have advantages and disadvantages. The researcher has to ponder the pros and cons and then select the strategy that appears to be the most appropriate and practical. In this case, Dutton and Aron decided that they would use an experiment. Once researchers have chosen a general method, they must make detailed plans for executing their study. Thus, Dutton and Aron had to decide what kind of experiment they would conduct, who their participants would be, how many participants they needed, and where they would get their participants. ***Participants,* or *subjects,* are the persons or animals whose behaviour is systematically observed in a study.** For their study, Dutton and Aron decided to use males crossing either a high (high-anxiety or -arousal) or low (low-anxiety or -arousal) bridge across the Capilano River in North Vancouver, British Columbia.

Step 3: Collect the Data

The third step in the research enterprise is to collect the data. Thus, Dutton and Aron collected sexual imagery and recorded the number of calls to the confederate after participants crossed one of the bridges. Researchers use a variety of ***data collection techniques,* which are procedures for making empirical observations and measurements** (see Table 2.2).

Step 4: Analyze the Data and Draw Conclusions

The observations made in a study are usually converted into numbers, which constitute the raw data of the study. Researchers use *statistics* to analyze their data and to decide whether their hypotheses have been supported. Thus, statistics play an essential role in the scientific enterprise.

Step 5: Report the Findings

Scientific progress can be achieved only if researchers share their findings with one another and with the general public. Therefore, the final step in a scientific investigation is to write up a concise summary of the study and its findings. Typically, researchers prepare a report that is delivered at a scientific meeting and submitted to a journal for publication. **A *journal* is a periodical that publishes technical and scholarly material, usually in a narrowly defined area of inquiry.** The study by Dutton and Aron was published in the *Journal of Personality and Social Psychology* in 1974. This journal is one of the most prestigious journals in that area of research.

The process of publishing scientific studies allows other experts to evaluate and critique new research findings. Sometimes this process of critical evaluation discloses flaws in a study. If the flaws are serious enough, the results may be discounted or discarded.

This evaluation process is a major strength of the scientific approach because it gradually weeds out erroneous findings.

www

Web Link 2.1

PubMed
http://www.ncbi.nlm.nih.gov/PubMed/

Few commercial databases of journal articles or abstracts in the health sciences are available online for no charge. However, the National Library of Medicine has opened the 9 million items of MEDLINE's abstracts and references to anyone wanting to research within the scientific literature of medical journals, including some important psychology publications.

Table 2.2 Key Data Collection Techniques in Psychology

Technique	Description
Direct observation	Observers are trained to watch and record behaviour as objectively and precisely as possible. They may use some instrumentation, such as a stopwatch or video recorder.
Questionnaire	Subjects are administered a series of written questions designed to obtain information about attitudes, opinions, and specific aspects of their behaviour.
Interview	A face-to-face dialogue is conducted to obtain information about specific aspects of a subject's behaviour.
Psychological test	Subjects are administered a standardized measure to obtain a sample of their behaviour. Tests are usually used to assess mental abilities or personality traits.
Physiological recording	An instrument is used to monitor and record a specific physiological process in a subject. Examples include measures of blood pressure, heart rate, muscle tension, and brain activity.
Examination of archival records	The researcher analyzes existing institutional records (the archives), such as census, economic, medical, legal, educational, and business records.

Can Fear Increase Sexual Attraction?

Investigators: Donald G. Dutton
and Arthur P. Aron
(University of British
Columbia)

Source: Some evidence for
heightened sexual attraction
under conditions of high
anxiety, *Journal of
Personality and Social
Psychology*, 1974, *30*,
510–517.

In Chapter 10 you will learn more about various theories of emotion. One theory proposed by Schachter (1964) suggests that salient environmental cues can be used to provide emotional labels for physiological arousal. This suggests that you might relabel a naturally occurring emotion such as fear or anxiety as another emotion if cues relevant to that other emotion were highly salient. In previous work, Aron (1970) had proposed that even unambiguous emotions such as fear or anxiety can, under specific conditions, be relabelled as sexual attraction. The specific hypothesis being tested was that an attractive female would be seen as more attractive "by males who encounter her while they experience a strong emotion (fear) than by males not experiencing a strong emotion" (Dutton & Aron, 1974, p. 511).

Method

Participants. The participants were males between the ages of 18 and 35 who chose to cross alone either of two bridges spanning the Capilano River in North Vancouver. The "control" bridge was low, solid, and unlikely to arouse much fear or anxiety in the participants. The "experimental," high–fear-arousing bridge was a high suspension bridge with a "tendency to tilt, sway, and wobble, creating the impression that one is about to fall over the side" (p. 511).

Materials. Participants were asked to complete portions of the Thematic Apperception Test (TAT). The TAT is a projective test. We will discuss the nature of projective tests more fully in Chapter 12. Briefly, projective tests ask participants to respond to vague, ambiguous stimuli in ways that may reveal the participants' needs, feelings, and personality traits. In this case, the participants' responses to the TAT were scored to reveal the degree of sexual imagery in their responses. See Figure 12.19 (page 529) for an example of stimuli used in the TAT.

Design. There were two *independent* variables in the experiment. Participants were approached after they crossed either the high, fear-arousing bridge or the low, nonarousing bridge (first independent variable). The participants were approached by either a male or female confederate (second independent variable). Whether they were approached by the male or female was randomly determined.

Procedure. After crossing the bridge, the males were met by a male or female confederate (someone working for the researchers engaging in predetermined behaviours). The confederates individually approached a participant and asked him to fill out a short questionnaire. Included was a measure of sexual imagery taken from the Thematic Apperception Test (TAT). Participants were then offered the confederate's phone number to call later in the day if they wanted more explanation about the study. It was assumed that if participants called more after crossing the high than the low bridge, then they had been more attracted to the female confederate, mislabelling their fear as sexual attraction. The *dependent* variables in the study were the degree of sexual imagery in participants' responses to the TAT and the proportion of participants who crossed each bridge who called the confederate later.

Results

The results were just as the researchers had predicted. Participants who crossed the high bridge and who were met by the female confederate evidenced more sexual arousal in their TAT stories than did those who crossed the low bridge (average scores of 2.47 versus 1.41). In addition, a higher proportion of males who took the confederate's phone number called the female confederate back if they had crossed the high as compared to the low bridge. If the participants were met by a male confederate, not only were they less likely to call him later on, but whether they crossed the high or low bridge did not seem to affect call-back rates.

Discussion

The results of the study suggest that naturally occurring emotions can be relabelled as other emotions if salient and relevant environmental cues are present. Results such as these provide support for theories such as Schachter's (1964), suggesting that arousal combines with cognitive labelling to produce distinct emotions. You will learn more about this and other perspectives on emotion in later chapters.

Comment

This study was featured because it addresses an interesting question using a reasonably straightforward experimental design. It was selected in particular because it employed a very naturalistic experimental procedure using participants who were not recruited from undergraduate courses in psychology. The fact that some research is conducted in relatively artificial settings and employs only first-year psychology students are two criticisms sometimes made of research in psychology. A recent review by York University psychologist Maxine Wintre and her colleagues (Wintre, North, & Sugar, 2001) revealed that there has been no decrease in the use of undergraduate research participants despite the latter criticism. Wintre's paper also includes a review of the types of criticisms given toward this practice. In the case of the research conducted by Dutton and Aron, the researchers conducted three studies, only one of which was a traditional laboratory-based experiment (Study 3, which was not discussed here). The best research strategy might be to use a variety of research methods and settings so that you can take advantage of the strengths of each methodology. The study also illustrates the importance of collecting empirical data to answer psychological questions. We wonder how many of you would have predicted the findings before you read about the study? A well-conducted set of experiments can serve to increase our confidence in the validity and reliability of the findings. ■

Advantages of the Scientific Approach

Science is certainly not the only method that can be used to draw conclusions about behaviour. Everyone uses logic, casual observation, and good old-fashioned common sense. Because the scientific method often requires painstaking effort, it seems reasonable to ask what advantages make it worth the trouble.

Basically, the scientific approach offers two major advantages. The first is its clarity and precision. Commonsense notions about behaviour tend to be vague and ambiguous. Consider the old adage "Spare the rod and spoil the child." What exactly does this generalization about childrearing amount to? How severely should children be punished if parents are not to "spare the rod"? How do we assess whether a child qualifies as "spoiled"? The scientific approach requires that people specify *exactly* what they are talking about when they formulate hypotheses. This clarity and precision enhances communication about important ideas.

The second and perhaps greatest advantage offered by the scientific approach is its relative intolerance of error. Scientists are trained to be skeptical. They subject their ideas to empirical tests. They also scrutinize one another's findings with a critical eye. They demand objective data and thorough documentation before they accept ideas. When the findings of two studies conflict, the scientist tries to figure out why, usually by conducting additional research.

All this is not to say that science has an exclusive copyright on truth. However, the scientific approach does tend to yield more accurate and dependable information than casual analyses and armchair speculation do. Knowledge of scientific data can thus provide a useful benchmark against which to judge claims and information from other kinds of sources.

Now that we have had an overview of how the scientific enterprise works, we can focus on how specific research methods are used. ***Research methods consist of various approaches to the observation, measurement, manipulation, and control of variables in empirical studies.*** In other words, they are general strategies for conducting studies. No single research method is ideal for all purposes and situations. Much of the ingenuity in research involves selecting and tailoring the method to the question at hand. The next two sections of this chapter discuss the two basic types of methods used in psychology: *experimental research methods* and *descriptive/correlational research methods.*

REVIEW OF KEY POINTS

- The scientific approach assumes that there are laws of behaviour that can be discovered through empirical research. The goals of the science of psychology include (1) the measurement and description of behaviour, (2) the understanding and prediction of behaviour, and (3) the application of this knowledge to the task of controlling behaviour.
- By integrating apparently unrelated facts into a coherent whole, theories permit psychologists to make the leap from the description of behaviour to the understanding of behaviour. Confidence in a theory increases when hypotheses derived from it are supported by research.
- A scientific investigation follows a systematic pattern that includes five steps: (1) formulate a testable hypothesis, (2) select the research method and design the study, (3) collect the data, (4) analyze the data and draw conclusions, and (5) report the findings.
- Scientists use operational definitions to clarify what their variables mean. They depend on statistics to analyze their data. The two major advantages of the scientific approach are its clarity in communication and its relative intolerance of error.

Looking for Causes: Experimental Research

PREVIEW QUESTIONS

● What is the difference between an independent variable and a dependent variable?

● What is the purpose of experimental and control groups?

● What are extraneous variables and confounded variables?

● How can experiments vary in format?

● How did Dutton and Aron use the experimental method to evaluate the role of arousal in emotional experience?

● What are the strengths and weaknesses of experimental research?

The *experiment* **is a research method in which the investigator manipulates a variable under carefully controlled conditions and observes whether any changes occur in a second variable as a result.** The experiment is a relatively powerful procedure that allows researchers to detect cause-and-effect relationships. Psychologists depend on this method more than any other.

Although its basic strategy is straightforward, in practice the experiment is a fairly complicated technique. A well-designed experiment must take into account a number of factors that could affect the clarity of the results. To see how an experiment is designed, let's use Dutton and Aron's study as an example.

Independent and Dependent Variables

The purpose of an experiment is to find out whether changes in one variable (let's call it *X*) cause changes in another variable (let's call it *Y*). To put it more concisely, we want to find out *how X affects Y*. In this formulation, we refer to *X* as the *independent variable* and to *Y* as the *dependent variable*.

An *independent variable* **is a condition or event that an experimenter varies in order to see its impact on another variable.** The independent variable is the variable that the experimenter controls or manipulates. It is hypothesized to have some effect on the dependent variable, and the experiment is conducted to verify this effect. **The** *dependent variable* **is the variable that is thought to be affected by manipulation of the independent variable.** In psychology studies, the dependent variable is usually a measurement of some aspect of the participants' behaviour. The independent variable is called *independent* because it is *free* to be varied by the experimenter. The dependent variable is called *dependent* because it is thought to *depend* (at least in part) on manipulations of the independent variable.

In Dutton and Aron's experiment in the Featured Study (p. 46), one independent variable was the anxiety or arousal level of the participants. Participants crossing the high bridge were assumed and found to have higher levels of arousal than did those crossing the low bridge. After crossing the bridge, participants were asked to complete the TAT and were given the means to call the experimental confederate later as measures of sexual attraction. Participants' sexual imagery scores on the TAT and whether or not they called the confederate later were the dependent measures.

Experimental and Control Groups

In an experiment the investigator typically assembles two groups of subjects who are treated differently with regard to the independent variable. These two groups are referred to as the experimental group and the control group. **The** *experimental group* **consists of the subjects who receive some special treatment in regard to the independent variable. The** *control group* **consists of similar subjects who do** *not* **receive the special treatment given to the experimental group.**

Consider, for example, a study conducted by David Wolfe and his colleagues (Wolfe, Wekerle, Scott, Straatman, Grasely, and Reitzel-Jaffe, 2003) from the University of Western Ontario. Wolfe was interested in the effects of treatment on dating abuse on the part of male and female teens who were at risk of abusive relationships based on their own history of maltreatment. All the participants were teens who had suffered maltreatment and who were under a protection, supervision, or wardship order. Recent theories had linked previous maltreatment with aggression in one's own current relationships. Half of the participants were assigned to a psychoeducational treatment program (an 18-session intervention including skill- and learning-based approaches), while the other half of the participants were those who received the existing standard Child Protection Services program consisting of social worker visits and basic shelter and care. In this case, those teens receiving the standard program, who did not receive the special intervention program, comprised the control group. The researchers found that the intervention was effective in reducing the frequency and severity of the teens' experience of abuse in relationships with others. (For more information on relationship violence and its prevention, see the Web site developed by David Wolfe and his colleagues at http://www.thefourthr.ca/.)

It is crucial that the experimental and control groups in a study be alike, except for the different treatment that they receive in regard to the independent variable. This stipulation brings us to the logic that underlies the experimental method. If the two groups are alike in all respects *except for the variation created by the manipulation of the independent variable,* any differences between the two groups on the dependent variable *must be due to the manipulation of the independent variable.* In this way researchers isolate the effect of the independent variable on the dependent variable.

Extraneous Variables

 SIM1, 1B

As we have seen, the logic of the experimental method rests on the assumption that the experimental and control groups are alike except for their treatment in regard to the independent variable. Any other differences between the two groups can cloud the situation and make it impossible to draw conclusions about how the independent variable affects the dependent variable.

In practical terms, of course, it is impossible to ensure that two groups of participants are exactly alike in *every* respect. The experimental and control groups have to be alike only on dimensions relevant to the dependent variable. Thus, Dutton and Aron did not need to worry about whether their two groups were similar in hair colour, height, or interest in music, as these variables were unlikely to influence the dependent variable of emotion.

Instead, experimenters concentrate on ensuring that the experimental and control groups are alike on a limited number of variables that could have a bearing on the results of the study. These variables are called extraneous, secondary, or nuisance variables. *Extraneous variables* **are any variables other than the independent variable that seem likely to influence the dependent variable in a specific study.**

In the Dutton and Aron study, one extraneous variable would have been the participants' personality or risk-taking propensity. Why? Because the males could choose to cross the high or low bridge themselves, different types of people may have decided to cross the high (perhaps sports enthusiasts or risk takers) and the low (more cautious) bridge and participant personality might by itself affect the sexual attraction measures. For example, high risk takers might have been more likely to call the female confederate than more cautious persons regardless of which bridge they crossed. Here, personality and arousal would have been confounded. You might wish to take a moment to think about how you might redo the experiment in a way that would make this problem less of an issue in this case (you will see below how the experimenters decided to rid themselves of this potential confound). **A** *confounding of variables* **occurs when two variables are linked together in a way that makes it difficult**

CONCEPT **CHECK 2.1**

Recognizing Independent and Dependent Variables

Check your understanding of the experimental method by identifying the independent variable (IV) and dependent variable (DV) in the following investigations. Note that one study has two IVs and another has two DVs. You'll find the answers in Appendix A in the back of the book.

1. A researcher is interested in how heart rate and blood pressure are affected by viewing a violent film sequence as opposed to a nonviolent film sequence.

IV _____

DV _____

2. An organizational psychologist develops a new training program to improve clerks' courtesy to customers in a large chain of retail stores. She conducts an experiment to see whether the training program leads to a reduction in the number of customer complaints.

IV _____

DV _____

3. A researcher wants to find out how stimulus complexity and stimulus contrast (light/dark variation) affect infants' attention to stimuli. He manipulates stimulus complexity and stimulus contrast and measures how long infants stare at various stimuli.

IV _____

DV _____

4. A social psychologist investigates the impact of group size on subjects' conformity in response to group pressure.

IV _____

DV _____

to sort out their specific effects. When an extraneous variable is confounded with an independent variable, a researcher cannot tell which is having what effect on the dependent variable.

Unanticipated confoundings of variables have wrecked innumerable experiments. That is why so much care, planning, and forethought must go into designing an experiment. One of the key qualities that separates a talented experimenter from a mediocre one is the ability to foresee troublesome extraneous variables and control them to avoid confoundings.

Experimenters use a variety of safeguards to control for extraneous variables. For instance, subjects are usually assigned to the experimental and control groups randomly. *Random assignment* **of subjects occurs when all subjects have an equal chance of being assigned to any group or condition in the study.** When experimenters distribute subjects into groups through some random procedure, they can be reasonably confident that the groups will be similar in most ways.

How did Dutton and Aron deal with the potential confounding of personality differences between those who crossed the high and low bridges and the intended variable of differences in arousal or anxiety? They conducted a second study employing a procedure very much like that used in Study 1 except that all the participants were males who crossed only the high bridge. To look at the effect of arousal on sexual attraction, the confederates approached one-half of the participants immediately after they crossed the high bridge, and were then given the dependent measures with the other half of the participants contacted about ten minutes after they had crossed the bridge. The authors reasoned that the latter group would be less aroused than those who had just crossed the bridge—after all, they had ten minutes to rest and calm down—so that any observed differences in sexual arousal and/or proportion of participants calling the confederate later on the phone would not likely be due to personality differences (because all had chosen to cross the same bridge) but to differences in arousal. In this follow-up study, only a female confederate was used. As illustrated in Table 2.3, those participants contacted immediately after crossing the bridge showed evidence of greater sexual attraction than did those contacted ten minutes later. As you can see, there is a great deal of creativity and art to conducting an experiment well. You will encounter many other examples of this type of creativity as you read through the text.

Variations in Designing Experiments

 Sim1, 1b

Some experiments are conducted with a simple design, with just one independent variable and one dependent variable. For example, the study conducted by Wolfe and his colleagues included just one independent variable: whether the teens were or were not receiving the specially designed intervention program. Actually, many variations are possible in conducting experiments. These variations warrant a brief mention.

First, it is sometimes advantageous to use only one group of subjects who serve as their own control group. The effects of the independent variable are evaluated by exposing this single group to two different conditions—an experimental condition and a control condition. For example, imagine that you wanted to study the effects of loud music on typing performance (see Figure 2.2). You could have a group of participants work on a typing task while loud music was played (experimental condition) and in the absence of music (control condition). This approach would ensure that the participants in the experimental and control conditions would be alike on any extraneous variables involving their personal characteristics, such as motivation or typing skill. After all, the same people would be studied in both conditions.

Second, it is possible to manipulate more than one independent variable in a single experiment. Researchers often manipulate two or three independent variables to examine their joint effects on the dependent variable. Of course, after reading the Featured Study you know that arousal wasn't the only independent variable manipulated by Dutton and Aron. Dutton and Aron included two independent variables in their study. Participants were chosen after crossing the high or low bridge (first independent variable) and were met on the other side by a male or female confederate (second independent variable). Their hypothesis was that arousal will heighten sexual attraction only if there are situation cues relevant to sexual attraction. In this case, assuming mostly heterosexual participants, arousal should increase sexual attraction primarily in the context of the female confederate. The main advantage of this approach is that it permits the experimenter to see whether two variables interact. An *interaction* means that the effect of one variable depends on the effect of another. In the case of Dutton and Aron's experiment, arousal affected sexual attraction only when the males were met on the other side of the bridge by the female confederate, just as their hypothesis predicted.

Third, it is also possible to use more than one dependent variable in a single study. Researchers frequently use a number of dependent variables to get a more complete picture of how experimental manipulations affect subjects' behaviour. This is precisely what Dutton and Aron did. They used both a questionnaire (i.e., the TAT) and a behavioural measure (i.e., calling the confederate) of sexual attraction.

Table 2.3 Results from Study Two of Dutton and Aron's (1974) Research on Fear and Emotion

	Participants Approached Immediately	Participants Approached after 10 Minutes
Sexual imagery	2.99	1.92
Proportion calling female confederate	65%	30%

Source: Dutton, D.G. & Aron, A.P. (1974). Some evidence for heightened sexual attraction under conditions of high anxiety, *Journal of Personality and Social Psychology, 30*, pp. 510–517. Published by the American Psychological Association. Reprinted with permission.

Present   Absent

Room temperature

Normal

High

Figure 2.2

Manipulation of two independent variables in an experiment. As this example shows, when two independent variables are manipulated in a single experiment, the researcher has to compare four groups of subjects (or conditions) instead of the usual two. The main advantage of this procedure is that it allows an experimenter to see whether two variables interact.

Advantages and Disadvantages of Experimental Research

The experiment is a powerful research method. Its principal advantage is that it permits conclusions about cause-and-effect relationships between variables. Researchers are able to draw these conclusions about causation because the precise control available in the experiment allows them to isolate the relationship between the independent variable and the dependent variable, while neutralizing the effects of extraneous variables. No other research method can duplicate this strength of the experiment. This advantage is why psychologists usually prefer to use the experimental method whenever possible.

For all its power, however, the experiment has limitations. One problem is that experiments are often artificial. Because experiments require great control over proceedings, researchers must often construct simple, contrived situations to test their hypotheses experimentally. For example, to investigate decision making in juries, psychologists have conducted many experiments in which subjects read a brief summary of a trial and then record their individual "verdicts"

of innocence or guilt. This approach allows the experimenter to manipulate a variable, such as the race of the defendant, to see whether it affects the participants' verdicts. However, critics have pointed out that having a participant read a short case summary and make an individual decision cannot really compare to the complexities of real trials (Weiten & Diamond, 1979). In actual court cases, jurors may spend weeks listening to confusing testimony while making subtle judgments about the credibility of witnesses. They then retire for hours of debate to arrive at a group verdict, which is quite different from rendering an individual decision. Many researchers have failed to do justice to this complex process in their laboratory experiments. When experiments are highly artificial, doubts arise about the applicability of findings to everyday behaviour outside the experimental laboratory.

Another disadvantage is that the experimental method can't be used to explore some research questions. Psychologists are frequently interested in the effects of factors that cannot be manipulated as independent variables because of ethical concerns or practical realities. In some cases manipulations of variables are difficult or impossible. For example, you might want to know whether being brought up in an urban as opposed to a rural area affects people's values. An experiment would require you to randomly assign similar families to live in urban and rural areas, which obviously is impossible to do. To explore this question, you would have to use descriptive/correlational research methods, which we turn to next.

REVIEW OF KEY POINTS

● Experimental research involves the manipulation of an independent variable to determine its effect on a dependent variable. This research is usually done by comparing experimental and control groups, which must be alike in regard to important extraneous variables.

● Any differences between the groups in the dependent variable ought to be due to manipulation of the independent variable, as long as there are no confounds. Variables are said to be confounded when they vary together so that researchers cannot isolate the effect of the independent variable on the dependent variable.

● Experimental designs may vary. For example, sometimes an experimental group serves as its own control group. And many experiments have more than one independent variable or more than one dependent variable.

● Some of these variations were seen in the Featured Study, which examined the effects of level of fear or anxiety on sexual attraction.

● An experiment is a powerful research method that permits conclusions about cause-and-effect relationships between variables. However, the experimental method is often not usable for a specific problem, and many experiments tend to be artificial.

Web Link 2.3

Psychological Research on the Net
http://psych.hanover.edu/research/exponnet.html

This site, sponsored by the American Psychological Society, is a jumping off point for people interested in participating in ongoing research projects that are collecting data over the Internet. Visitors will find a host of opportunities for taking part in genuine research.

Looking for Links: Descriptive/Correlational Research

PREVIEW QUESTIONS

- How did Levine and Norenzayan (1999) use naturalistic observation to estimate the pace of life in different cultures?
- How can case studies be used to look for general principles of behaviour?
- Why do researchers use surveys?
- What are the strengths and weaknesses of descriptive/correlational research?

In some situations psychologists cannot exert experimental control over the variables they want to study for either ethical or practical reasons. For example, if you were interested in the effects of nutritious and non-nutritious maternal diets on the health of babies, you would never try to get some expectant mothers to follow poor nutritional habits. In such situations, investigators must rely on *descriptive/correlational research methods*. These methods include naturalistic observation, case studies, and surveys. What distinguishes these methods is that the researcher cannot manipulate the variables under study. This lack of control means that these methods cannot be used to demonstrate cause-and-effect relationships between variables. *Descriptive/correlational methods permit investigators to only describe patterns of behaviour and discover links or associations between variables.* That is not to suggest that associations are unimportant. You'll see in this section that information on associations between variables can be extremely valuable in our efforts to understand behaviour.

Naturalistic Observation

Does the pace of everyday life vary substantially from one culture to the next? Do people operate at a different speed in, say, Germany as opposed to Canada or Brazil? Are factors such as economic vitality and climate related to differences in the pace of life? These are the kinds of questions that intrigued Robert V. Levine and Ara Norenzayan (1999), who compared the pace of life in 31 countries around the world. Perhaps they could have devised an experiment to examine this question, but they wanted to focus on the pace of life in the real world rather than in the laboratory.

To study the pace of life, Levine and Norenzayan (1999) had to come up with concrete ways to measure it—their operational definition of the concept. The measure they chose depended on *naturalistic observation*. **In naturalistic observation a researcher engages in careful observation of behaviour without intervening directly with the subjects.** In this instance, the researchers observed (1) the average walking speed in downtown locations, (2) the accuracy of public clocks, and (3) the speed with which postal clerks completed a simple request. Their collection of data on walking speed illustrates the careful planning required to execute naturalistic observation effectively. In the main downtown area of each city, they had to find two

flat, unobstructed, uncrowded 60-foot (18-metre) walkways where they could unobtrusively time pedestrians during normal business hours. Only adult pedestrians walking alone and not window shopping were timed. In most cities, the observations continued until 35 men and 35 women had been timed.

Levine and Norenzayan conducted their naturalistic observations in 31 countries, typically using the largest city in each country as the locale for their research. Their data suggest that the pace of life is fastest in the countries of Western Europe (e.g., Switzerland, Ireland, Germany) and in Japan. Using archival data, they also conducted correlational analyses to see whether variations in the pace of life were associated with factors such as climate, economic vitality, or population size. Among other things, they found that the pace of life was faster in colder climates and in countries that were more economically productive. It is interesting to note that Canada ranked 17th in pace of life based on this measure in their rankings of 31 countries. The slowest pace was observed in Mexico and Indonesia.

This type of research is called *naturalistic* because behaviour is allowed to unfold naturally (without interference) in its natural environment—that is, the setting in which it would normally occur. The major strength of naturalistic observation is that it allows researchers to study behaviour under conditions that are less artificial than in experiments. A major problem with this method is that researchers often have trouble making their observations unobtrusively so they don't affect their participants' behaviour.

Case Studies

What portion of people who commit suicide suffer from psychological disorders? Which disorders are most common among victims of suicide? In health-care visits during the final month of their lives, do people who commit suicide communicate their intent to do so? A research team in Finland wanted to investigate the psychological characteristics of people who take their own lives (Henriksson et al., 1993; Isometsa et al., 1995). Other researchers had explored these questions, but the Finnish team planned a comprehensive, national study of unprecedented scope. Their initial sample consisted of all the known suicides in Finland for an entire year.

The research team decided that their question called for a case study approach. **A *case study* is an**

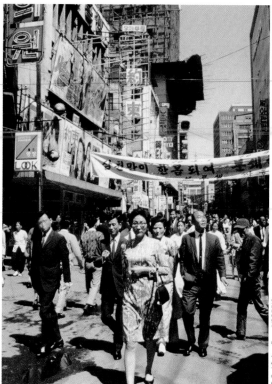

Naturalistic observation can be complex and challenging, as the study by Levine and Norenzayan (1999) illustrates. One of their measures of the pace of life in 31 cultures involved estimating people's walking speed in downtown locations. To reduce the influence of confounding factors, they had to find sidewalks that were unobstructed, uncrowded, not dominated by window shoppers, and so forth. Moreover, they had to find reasonably comparable locations in 31 very different types of cities.

in-depth investigation of an individual subject. When this method is applied to victims of suicide, the case studies are called *psychological autopsies*. A variety of data collection techniques can be used in case studies. In normal circumstances, when the participants are not deceased, typical techniques include interviewing the subjects, interviewing people who are very close to the subjects, direct observation of the subjects, examination of records, and psychological testing. In this study, the investigators conducted thorough interviews with the families of the suicide victims and with the health-care professionals who had treated them. The researchers also examined the suicide victims' medical, psychiatric, and social agency records, as well as relevant police investigations and forensic reports. Comprehensive case reports were then assembled for each person who committed suicide.

These case studies revealed that in 93% of the suicides the victim suffered from a significant psychological disorder (Henriksson et al., 1993). The most common diagnoses, by a large margin, were depression and alcohol dependence. In 571 cases, victims had a health-care appointment during the last four weeks of their lives, but only 22% of these people discussed the possibility of suicide during their final visit (Isometsa et al., 1995). Even more surprising, the sample included 100 people who saw a health professional on the same day they killed themselves,

yet only 21% of these individuals raised the issue of suicide. The investigators concluded that mental illness is a contributing factor in virtually all completed suicides and that the vast majority of suicidal people do not spontaneously reveal their intentions to health-care professionals.

Clinical psychologists, who diagnose and treat psychological problems, routinely do case studies of their clients (see Figure 2.3). When clinicians assemble a case study for diagnostic purposes, they generally are *not* conducting empirical research. Case study *research* typically involves investigators analyzing a collection of case studies to look for patterns that permit general conclusions.

Case studies are particularly well suited for investigating certain phenomena, such as psychological disorders and neuropsychological issues. For example, Brenda Milner of McGill University made important contributions to our knowledge about the importance of the temporal lobes of the brain in memory and the existence of multiple memory systems in the brain by using this method. She made extensive use of her case study of a patient known as H.M. in her early work (Milner, Corking, & Teuber, 1968). (We will discuss this and other work in neuropsychology and memory in Chapters 3 and 7.)

Case studies can also provide compelling, real-life illustrations that bolster a hypothesis or theory. However, the main problem with case studies is that

Web Link 2.4

PSYCLine: Your Guide to Psychology and Social Science Journals on the Web
http://www.psycline.org/ journals/psycline.html

Relatively few journals actually post their articles online for free. But this searchable index to the online sites of more than 1900 psychology journals may lead you to recent tables of contents or abstracts or help you identify research resources on more unusual topics in psychology.

```
Case Study                    Page 2
     Jennie is a 21-year-old single college
student with no prior psychiatric history.
She was admitted to a short-term psychi-
atric ward from a hospital emergency room
with a chief complaint of "I think I was
psychotic." For several months prior to
her admission she reported a series of
"strange experiences." These included
religious experiences, increased anxiety,
a conviction that other students were
conspiring against her, visual distor-
tions, auditory hallucinations, and grand-
iose delusions. During the week prior to
admission, the symptoms gradually worsened,
and eventually she became agitated and
disorganized.
     A number of stressful events preceded
this decompensation. A maternal aunt, a
strong and central figure in her family,
had died four months previously. As a
college senior, she was struggling with
decisions about her career choices fol-
lowing graduation. She was considering
applying to graduate programs but was
unable to decide which course of study
she preferred. She was very much involved
with her boyfriend, also a college senior.
He, too, was struggling with anxiety
about graduation, and it was not clear
that their relationship would continue.
The patient also reported feeling pres-
sured and overextended.
     The patient's older sister had suffered
two psychotic episodes. This sister had
slowly deteriorated, particularly after
```

Figure 2.3

An example of a case study report. As this example illustrates, case studies are particularly appropriate for clinical situations in which efforts are made to diagnose and treat psychological problems. Usually, one case study does not provide much basis for deriving general laws of behaviour. However, if you examine a series of case studies involving similar problems, you can look for threads of consistency that may yield general conclusions.

Source: Greenfield, D. (1985). *The psychotic patient: Medication and psychotherapy.* New York: The Free Press. Copyright © 1985 by David Greenfield. Reprinted by permission of the author.

they can be highly subjective. Information from several sources must be knit together in an impressionistic way. In this process, clinicians and researchers may focus selectively on information that fits with their expectations, which usually reflect their theoretical slant. Thus, it is relatively easy for investigators to see what they expect to see in case study research.

Surveys

One research method that many of us are frequently exposed to is the survey. **In a *survey*, researchers use questionnaires or interviews to gather information** about specific aspects of participants' behaviour. Large companies may survey the buying habits of specific segments of the buying public. Political parties often do extensive polling before they call an election or propose specific legislation. As such, surveys are often used to obtain information on aspects of behaviour that are difficult to observe directly. Surveys also make it relatively easy to collect data on attitudes and opinions from large samples of participants.

Many of you may have taken a course in psychology because you are interested in clinical psychology, helping others through the assessment and treatment of mental disorders. You may have wondered how prevalent such disorders are. A recent Statistics Canada (2003c) survey may help to answer some of these questions. The rates of the specific disorders illustrated in Table 2.4 were based on data collected by Statistics Canada between May and December 2002. The survey respondents consisted of about 37 000 Canadians, ages 15 and up, living in all provinces. The prevalence rates in the sample were then applied to the population of Canada to get estimates of countrywide numbers.

The survey revealed many interesting and important findings relating to gender and age differences in rates of specific disorders. Such surveys yield important information concerning mental health status and may assist in treatment planning and allocation of resources. A survey well done can be an important research tool.

The major problem with surveys is that they depend on self-report data. As we'll discuss later, intentional deception, wishful thinking, memory lapses, and poorly worded questions can distort participants' verbal reports about their behaviour (Krosnick, 1999). In addition, not all surveys are conducted with care. One problem discussed in more detail later in the chapter is that of sampling bias. A survey is characterized by sampling bias if the sample on which it is based is not representative of the population that it is intended to describe. Statistics Canada goes to great lengths to conduct its surveys properly. You should critically evaluate surveys you are exposed to. For example, some popular Web sites invite students to rate the teaching ability of their professors. But what do we know about the sample upon which the results are based? One of this book's authors, looking at his own ratings, was struck by the fact that less than 100 students rated him on the site. He often teaches up to 1000 students a year and the site gives ratings for the past few years. Exactly who is doing the rating? Do only specific types of students do these ratings (e.g., males, A students, C students)? Are these students represen-

Table 2.4 Mental Disorder Prevalence Rates Based on the Canadian Community Health Survey, 2002

	Total		Males		Females	
	Number	%	Number	%	Number	%
Major depression	1 120 000	4.5	420 000	3.4	700 000	5.5
Mania disorder	190 000	0.8	90 000	0.7	100 000	0.8
Any mood	**1 210 000**	**4.9**	**460 000**	**3.8**	**750 000**	**5.9**
Panic disorder	400 000	1.6	130 000	1.1	270 000	2.1
Agoraphobia	180 000	0.7	40 000	0.4	140 000	1.1
Social anxiety disorder (social phobia)	750 000	3.0	310 000	2.6	430 000	3.4
Any anxiety	**1 180 000**	**4.7**	**440 000**	**3.6**	**740 000**	**5.8**
Alcohol dependence	640 000	2.6	470 000	3.8	170 000	1.3
Illicit drugs dependence	170 000	0.7	120 000	1.0	50 000	0.4
Substance dependence	**740 000**	**3.0**	**540 000**	**4.4**	**200 000**	**1.6**
Total—Any measured disorder or substance dependence	**2 600 000**	**10.4**	**1 190 000**	**9.7**	**1 410 000**	**11.1**

SOURCE: Adapted from the Statistics Canada publication, *The Daily*, Catalogue 11–001, Statistics Canada (2003, September 3), "Canadian Community Health Survey: Mental health and well-being," *The Daily*, retrieved April 7, 2005 from http://www.statcan.ca/Daily/English/030903/d030903a.htm.

tative of the students in his classes? He'd like to think so—the ratings are very high! But before he made any important career decisions based on this data he would need to know a great deal more about the sample characteristics.

Advantages and Disadvantages of Descriptive/Correlational Research

Descriptive/correlational research methods have advantages and disadvantages, which are compared to the strengths and weaknesses of experimental research in Figure 2.4. As a whole, the foremost advantage of these methods is that they give researchers a way to explore questions that could not be examined with experimental procedures. For example, after-the-fact analyses would be the only ethical way to investigate the possible link between poor maternal nutrition and birth defects in humans. In a similar vein, if researchers hope to learn how urban and rural upbringing relate to people's values, they have to depend on descriptive methods,

CONCEPT **CHECK 2.2**

Matching Research Methods to Questions

Check your understanding of the uses and strengths of various research methods by figuring out which method would be optimal for investigating the following questions about behavioural processes. Choose from the following methods: (a) experiment, (b) naturalistic observation, (c) case study, and (d) survey. Indicate your choice (by letter) next to each question. You'll find the answers in Appendix A in the back of the book.

_____ **1.** Are people's attitudes about nuclear disarmament related to their social class or education?

_____ **2.** Do people who suffer from anxiety disorders share similar early childhood experiences?

_____ **3.** Do troops of baboons display territoriality—that is, do they mark off an area as their own and defend it from intrusion by other baboons?

_____ **4.** Can the presence of food-related cues (delicious-looking desserts in advertisements, for example) cause an increase in the amount of food that people eat?

Figure 2.4

Comparison of major research methods. This chart pulls together a great deal of information on key research methods in psychology and gives a simple example of how each method might be applied in research on aggression. As you can see, the various research methods each have their strengths and weaknesses.

since they can't control where subjects grow up. Thus, *descriptive/correlational research broadens the scope of phenomena that psychologists are able to study.*

Unfortunately, descriptive methods have one significant disadvantage: Investigators cannot control events to isolate cause and effect. *Consequently, correlational research cannot demonstrate conclusively that two variables are causally related.* As an example, consider the cross-cultural investigation of the pace of life that we discussed earlier. Although Levine and Norenzayan (1999) found an association between

colder climates and a faster pace of life, their data do not permit us to conclude that a cold climate *causes* a culture to move at a faster pace. Too many factors were left uncontrolled in the study. For example, we do not know how similar the cold and warm cities were. Climate could co-vary with some other factors, such as modernization or economic vitality, that might have led to the observed differences in the pace of life. In correlational studies assessing the relationship between two variables, you never know if the correlation between them is actually

Overview of key research methods in psychology

Research method		Description	Example	Advantages	Disadvantages
Experiment		Manipulation of an independent variable under carefully controlled conditions to see whether any changes occur in a dependent variable	Youngsters are randomly assigned to watch a violent or nonviolent film, and their aggression is measured in a laboratory situation	Precise control over variables; ability to draw conclusions about cause-and-effect relationships	Contrived situations often artificial; ethical concerns and practical realities preclude experiments on many important questions
Naturalistic observation		Careful, usually prolonged observation of behaviour without direct intervention	Youngsters' spontaneous acts of aggression during recreational activities are observed unobtrusively and recorded	Minimizes artificiality; can be good place to start when little is known about phenomena under study	Often difficult to remain unobtrusive; can't explain why certain patterns of behaviour were observed
Case studies		In-depth investigation of a single participant using direct interview, direct observation, and other data collection techniques	Detailed case histories are worked up for youngsters referred to counselling because of excessive aggressive behaviour	Well-suited for study of certain phenomena; can provide compelling illustrations to support a theory	Subjectivity makes it easy to see what one expects to see based on one's theoretical slant; clinical samples often unrepresentative
Surveys		Use of questionnaires or interviews to gather information about specific aspects of participants' behaviour	Youngsters are given questionnaire that describes hypothetical scenarios and are asked about the likelihood of aggressive behaviour	Can gather data on difficult-to-observe aspects of behaviour; relatively easy to collect data from large samples	Self-report data often unreliable, due to intentional deception, social desirability bias, response sets, memory lapses, and wishful thinking

due to the relationship between each of them and some third variable you did not even measure. For example, if you took all the students in your school and correlated their heights and weights, you would likely find a strong association. All you can conclude is that they are related to each other; you cannot draw any conclusions about which factor causes the other. In fact, they are both likely due to some other factor you did not consider, such as age or nutrition. These and related issues are discussed in the next section.

Looking for Conclusions: Statistics and Research

Whether researchers use experimental or correlational methods, they need some way to make sense of their data. **Statistics is the use of mathematics to organize, summarize, and interpret numerical data.** Statistical analyses permit researchers to draw conclusions based on their observations. Many students find statistics intimidating, but statistics are an integral part of modern life. Although you may not realize it, you are bombarded with statistics nearly every day. When you read about economists' projections for inflation, when you check a baseball player's batting average, when you see the popularity ratings of television shows, you are dealing with statistics. In this section, we will examine a few basic statistical concepts that will help you understand the research discussed throughout this book. For the most part, we won't concern ourselves with the details of statistical *computations*. These details and some additional statistical concepts are discussed in Appendix B at the back of the book. At this juncture, we will discuss only the purpose, logic, and value of the two basic types of statistics: descriptive statistics and inferential statistics.

Descriptive Statistics

Descriptive statistics are used to organize and summarize data. They provide an overview of numerical data. Key descriptive statistics include measures of central tendency, measures of variability, and the coefficient of correlation. Let's take a brief look at each of these.

Central Tendency

In summarizing numerical data, researchers often want to know what constitutes a typical or average score. To answer this question, they use three meas-

ures of central tendency: the median, the mean, and the mode. **The *median* is the score that falls exactly in the centre of a distribution of scores.** Half of the scores fall above the median and half fall below it. **The *mean* is the arithmetic average of the scores in a distribution.** It is obtained by adding up all the scores and dividing by the total number of scores. Finally, **the *mode* is the most frequent score in a distribution.**

In general, the mean is the most useful measure of central tendency because additional statistical manipulations can be performed on it that are not possible with the median or mode. However, the mean is sensitive to extreme scores in a distribution, which can sometimes make the mean misleading. To illustrate, imagine that you're interviewing for a sales position at a company. Unbeknownst to you, the company's five salespeople earned the following incomes in the previous year: $20 000, $20 000, $25 000, $35 000, and $200 000. You ask how much the typical salesperson earns in a year. The sales director proudly announces that her five salespeople earned a *mean* income of $60 000 last year (the calculations are shown in Figure 2.5). However, before you order that expensive new sports car, you had better inquire about the *median* and *modal* income for the sales staff. In this case, one extreme score ($200 000) has inflated the mean, making it unrepresentative of the sales staff's earnings. In this instance, the median ($25 000) and the mode ($20 000) both provide better estimates of what you are likely to earn.

Variability

In describing a set of data, it is often useful to have some estimate of the variability among the scores.

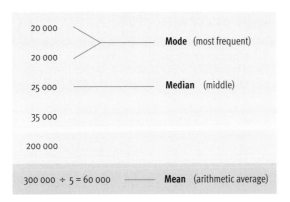

20 000	
20 000	**Mode** (most frequent)
25 000	**Median** (middle)
35 000	
200 000	
300 000 ÷ 5 = 60 000	**Mean** (arithmetic average)

Figure 2.5

Measures of central tendency. The three measures of central tendency usually converge, but that is not always the case, as these data illustrate. Which measure is most useful depends on the nature of the data. Generally, the mean is the best index of central tendency, but in this instance the median is more informative.

Speed (kilometres per hour)

Set A Perfection Boulevard	Set B Wild Street
70	42
68	74
66	100
74	56
76	84
80	74
72	78
66	50
68	46
60	96
70 — **Mean** — 70	
5.74 — **Standard deviation** — 20.78	

Figure 2.6

Variability and the standard deviation. Although these two sets of data produce the same mean, or average, an observer on Wild Street would see much more variability in the speeds of individual cars than an observer on Perfection Boulevard would. As you can see, the standard deviation for set B is higher than that for set A because of the greater variability in set B.

Variability refers to how much the scores in a data set vary from each other and from the mean. The *standard deviation* is an index of the amount of variability in a set of data. When variability is great, the standard deviation will be relatively large. When variability is low, the standard deviation will be smaller. This relationship is apparent if you examine the two sets of data in Figure 2.6. The mean is the same for both sets of scores, but variability clearly is greater in set B than in set A. This greater variability yields a higher standard deviation for set B than for set A. Estimates of variability play a crucial role when researchers use statistics to decide whether the results of their studies support their hypotheses.

Correlation

A *correlation* exists when two variables are related to each other. Investigators often want to quantify the strength of an association between two variables, such as between class attendance and course grade, or between cigarette smoking and physical disease. In this effort, they depend extensively on a useful descriptive statistic: the correlation coefficient. **The correlation coefficient is a numerical index of the degree of relationship between two variables.** A correlation coefficient indicates (1) the direction (positive or negative) of the relationship and (2) how strongly the two variables are related.

Positive versus Negative Correlation A *positive correlation* indicates that two variables co-vary in the *same* direction. This means that high scores on variable X are associated with high scores on variable Y and that low scores on variable X are associated with low scores on variable Y. For example, there is a positive correlation between high school grade point average (GPA) and subsequent university GPA. That is, people who do well in high school tend to do well in university, and those who perform poorly in high school tend to perform poorly in university (see Figure 2.7).

In contrast, a *negative* correlation indicates that two variables co-vary in the *opposite* direction. This means that people who score high on variable X tend to score low on variable Y, whereas those who score low on X tend to score high on Y. For example, in most university courses there is a negative correlation between how frequently students are absent and how well they perform on exams. Students who have a high number of absences tend to get low exam scores, while students who have a low number of absences tend to earn higher exam scores (see Figure 2.7). The nature of positive and negative correlations is also discussed and illustrated through the use of scatterplots in Appendix B (see page A–13).

If a correlation is negative, a minus sign (–) is always placed in front of the coefficient. If a correlation is positive, a plus sign (+) may be placed in front of the coefficient, or the coefficient may be shown with no sign. Thus, if there's no sign, the correlation is positive.

Strength of the Correlation Whereas the positive or negative sign indicates the direction of an association, the *size of the coefficient* indicates the *strength* of an association between two variables. The coefficient can vary between 0 and +1.00 (if positive) or between

Positive correlation

High scores on *X* are associated with high scores on *Y*, and low scores on *X* are associated with low scores on *Y*.

High school GPA — University GPA

High school GPA — University GPA

Negative correlation

High scores on *X* are associated with low scores on *Y*, and low scores on *X* are associated with high scores on *Y*.

Absences — Exam scores

Absences — Exam scores

Figure 2.7

Positive and negative correlation. Notice that the terms *positive* and *negative* refer to the direction of the relationship between two variables, not to its strength. Variables are positively correlated if they tend to increase and decrease together and are negatively correlated if one tends to increase when the other decreases.

0 and –1.00 (if negative). A coefficient near zero indicates no relationship between the variables; that is, high or low scores on variable *X* show no consistent relationship to high or low scores on variable *Y*. A coefficient of +1.00 or –1.00 indicates a perfect, one-to-one correspondence between the two variables. Most correlations fall between these extremes.

The closer the correlation to either –1.00 or +1.00, the stronger the relationship (see Figure 2.8). Thus, a correlation of 0.90 represents a stronger tendency for variables to be associated than a correlation of 0.40 does. Likewise, a correlation of –0.75 represents a stronger relationship than a correlation of –0.45. Keep in mind that the *strength* of a correlation depends only on the size of the coefficient. The positive or negative sign simply indicates the direction of the relationship. Therefore, a correlation of –0.60 reflects a stronger relationship than a correlation of +0.30.

Computation of correlation coefficients allowed Levine and Norenzayan (1999) to determine whether associations existed between various predictor variables and the pace of life in their cross-cultural study. For example, they found a robust correlation of +0.74 between a measure of economic vitality (gross domestic product per capita) and overall pace, but they found a negligible correlation (–0.07) between population size and the pace of life. Thus, statistical analyses permitted them to precisely quantify the associations between important cultural factors and the pace of life.

Correlation and Prediction You may recall that one of the key goals of scientific research is accurate *prediction*. A close link exists between the magnitude of a correlation and the power it gives scientists to make predictions. *As a correlation increases in strength (gets closer to either –1.00 or +1.00), the ability to predict one variable based on knowledge of the other variable increases.*

To illustrate, consider how university or college admissions tests (such as the SAT or ACT) are used to predict performance. When students' admissions test scores and first-year university GPA are correlated, researchers generally find moderate positive correlations in the 0.40s and 0.50s (Gregory, 1996). Because of this relationship, university admissions committees can predict with modest accuracy how well prospective students will do at university. Admittedly,

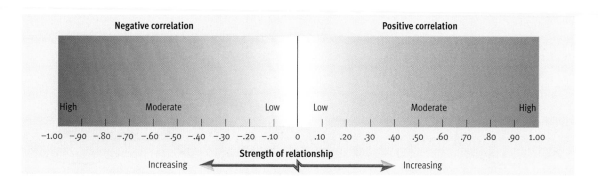

Negative correlation

High — Moderate — Low

Positive correlation

Low — Moderate — High

–1.00 –.90 –.80 –.70 –.60 –.50 –.40 –.30 –.20 –.10   0   .10 .20 .30 .40 .50 .60 .70 .80 .90 1.00

Strength of relationship

Increasing ← → Increasing

Figure 2.8

Interpreting correlation coefficients. The magnitude of a correlation coefficient indicates the strength of the relationship between two variables. The sign (plus or minus) indicates whether the correlation is positive or negative. The closer the coefficient comes to +1.00 or –1.00, the stronger the relationship between the variables.

Understanding Correlation

Check your understanding of correlation by interpreting the meaning of the correlation in item 1 and by guessing the direction (positive or negative) of the correlations in item 2. You'll find the answers in Appendix A.

1. Researchers have found a substantial positive correlation between youngsters' self-esteem and their academic achievement (measured by grades in school). Check any acceptable conclusions based on this correlation.

    _____ **a.** Low grades cause low self-esteem.

    _____ **b.** There is an association between self-esteem and academic achievement.

    _____ **c.** High self-esteem causes high academic achievement.

    _____ **d.** High ability causes both high self-esteem and high academic achievement.

    _____ **e.** Youngsters who score low in self-esteem tend to get low grades, and those who score high in self-esteem tend to get high grades.

2. Indicate whether you would expect the following correlations to be positive or negative.

    _____ **a.** The correlation between age and visual acuity (among adults).

    _____ **b.** The correlation between years of education and income.

    _____ **c.** The correlation between shyness and the number of friends one has.

the predictive power of these admissions tests is *far* from perfect. But it's substantial enough to justify the use of the tests as one factor in making admissions decisions. However, if this correlation were much higher, say 0.90, admissions tests could predict with superb accuracy how students would perform. In contrast, if this correlation were much lower, say 0.20, the tests' prediction of performance at university would be so poor that it would be unreasonable to consider the test scores in admissions decisions.

Correlation and Causation Although a high correlation allows us to predict one variable from another, it does not tell us whether a cause-and-effect relationship exists between the two variables. The problem is that variables can be highly correlated even though they are not causally related. For example, there is a substantial positive correlation between the size of young children's feet and the size of their vocabulary. That is, larger feet are associated with a larger vocabulary. Obviously, increases in foot size do not *cause* increases in vocabulary size. Nor do increases in vocabulary size cause increases in foot size. Instead, both are caused by a third variable: an increase in the children's age.

When we find that variables X and Y are correlated, we can safely conclude only that X and Y are related. We do not know *how* X and Y are related. We do not know whether X causes Y or Y causes X or whether both are caused by a third variable. For example, survey studies have found a positive correlation between smoking and the risk of experiencing a major depressive disorder (Breslau, Kilbey, & Andreski, 1991, 1993). Although it's clear that there is an association between smoking and depression, it's hard to tell what's causing what. The investigators acknowledge that they don't know whether smoking makes people more vulnerable to depression or whether depression increases the tendency to smoke. Moreover, they note that they can't rule out the possibility that both are caused by a third variable (Z). Perhaps anxiety and neuroticism increase the likelihood of both taking up smoking and becoming depressed. The plausible causal relationships in this case are diagrammed in Figure 2.9, which illustrates the "third variable problem" in interpreting correlations. This is a common problem in research, and you'll see this type of diagram again when we discuss other correlations. Thus, it is important to remember that *correlation is not equivalent to causation*.

Inferential Statistics

After researchers have summarized their data with descriptive statistics, they still need to decide whether their data support their hypotheses. ***Inferential statistics*** are used to interpret data and

Figure 2.9

Three possible causal relations between correlated variables. If variables X and Y are correlated, does X cause Y, does Y cause X, or does some hidden third variable, Z, account for the changes in both X and Y? As the relationship between smoking and depression illustrates, a correlation alone does not provide the answer. We will encounter this problem of interpreting the meaning of correlations frequently in this text.

draw conclusions. Working with the laws of probability, researchers use inferential statistics to evaluate the possibility that their results might be due to the fluctuations of chance.

To illustrate this process, envision a hypothetical experiment. A computerized tutoring program (the independent variable) is designed to increase sixth graders' reading achievement (the dependent variable). Our hypothesis is that program participants (the experimental group) will score higher than non-participants (the control group) on a standardized reading test given near the end of the school year. Let's assume that we compare 60 subjects in each group. We obtain the following results, reported in terms of participants' grade-level scores for reading:

Control group		Experimental group
6.3	Mean	6.8
1.4	Standard deviation	2.4

We hypothesized that the training program would produce higher reading scores in the experimental group than in the control group. Sure enough, that is indeed the case. However, we have to ask ourselves a critical question: Is this observed difference between the two groups large enough to support our hypothesis? That is, do the higher scores in the experimental group reflect the effect of the training program? Or could a difference of this size have occurred by chance? If our results could easily have occurred by chance, they don't provide meaningful support for our hypothesis.

When statistical calculations indicate that research results are not likely to be due to chance, the results are said to be *statistically significant.* You will probably hear your psychology professor use this phrase quite frequently. In discussing research, it is routine to note that "statistically significant differences were found." In statistics, the word *significant* has a precise and special meaning. **Statistical significance is said to exist when the probability that the observed findings are due to chance is very low.** "Very low" is usually defined as fewer than 5 chances in 100, which is referred to as the 0.05 level of significance.

Notice that in this special usage, *significant* does not mean "important," or even "interesting." Statistically significant findings may or may not be theoretically significant or practically significant. They simply are research results that are unlikely to be due to chance.

You don't need to be concerned here with the details of how statistical significance is calculated.

However, it is worth noting that a key consideration is the amount of variability in the data. That is why the standard deviation, which measures variability, is such an important statistic. When the necessary computations are made for our hypothetical experiment, the difference between the two groups does *not* turn out to be statistically significant. Thus, our results would not be adequate to demonstrate that our tutoring program leads to improved reading achievement. Psychologists have to do this kind of statistical analysis as part of virtually every study. Thus, inferential statistics are an integral element in the research enterprise.

Statistics even provide you with a way of combining the results of several experiments that have examined the same issues. In *meta-analysis* the results of findings obtained in several studies are integrated to allow for conclusions regarding the set of observed results. For example, you may be aware of several studies that have examined the effects of insight therapy for the treatment of depression. Through the use of meta-analysis you can generate conclusions regarding the size of the therapeutic effects.

REVIEW OF KEY POINTS

- Psychologists use descriptive statistics to organize and summarize their numerical data. The mean, median, and mode are widely used measures of central tendency. The mean tends to be the most useful of these indexes, but it can be distorted by extreme scores. Variability is usually measured with the standard deviation, which increases as the variability in a data set grows.

- Correlations may be either positive (when two variables co-vary in the same direction) or negative (when two variables co-vary in the opposite direction). The closer a correlation is to either +1.00 or −1.00, the stronger the association is.

- As a correlation increases in strength, the ability to predict one variable based on knowledge of the other variable increases. However, a correlation is no assurance of causation. When variables are correlated, we do not know whether *X* causes *Y*, or *Y* causes *X*, or a third variable causes both.

- Hypothesis testing involves deciding whether observed findings support the researcher's hypothesis. Findings are statistically significant only when they are unlikely to be due to chance.

Looking for Flaws: Evaluating Research

PREVIEW QUESTIONS
- What is sampling bias?
- What are placebo effects and how can you guard against them?
- What is the social desirability bias?
- What are response sets?
- What is experimenter bias, and how can you guard against it?

Scientific research is a more reliable source of information than casual observation or popular belief. However, it would be wrong to conclude that all published research is free of errors. As we just saw, when researchers report statistically significant differences at the 0.05 level, there are 5 chances in 100 that the results really are a misleading byproduct of chance fluctuation. This probability is pretty low, but it's not zero. Moreover, scientists' effort to minimize the probability of obtaining significant differences when none really exist increases the likelihood of the opposite mistake—failing to find significant differences when the groups really are different. Thus, even when research is conducted in a sound fashion, there's still a small chance of erroneous conclusions. Above and beyond this problem, we need to recognize that scientists are fallible human beings who do not conduct flawless research. Their personal biases in designing and interpreting studies can also distort research results (MacCoun, 1998).

For these reasons, researchers are reluctant to settle scientific questions on the basis of just one empirical study. Instead, important questions usually generate a flurry of studies to see whether key findings will stand the test of replication. *Replication* **is the repetition of a study to see whether the earlier results are duplicated.** The replication process helps science identify and purge erroneous findings. While the contradictory findings that sometimes emerge from replications can be confusing to those reading the research, replication is an essential check on the accuracy of scientific findings. It sometimes can lead to new theories and advances.

Sampling Bias

A *sample* **is the collection of subjects selected for observation in an empirical study.** In contrast, **the** *population* **is the much larger collection of animals or people** (from which the sample is drawn) that researchers want to generalize about (see Figure 2.10). For example, when political pollsters attempt to predict elections, all the voters in a jurisdiction represent the population, and the voters who are actually surveyed constitute the sample. If a researcher was interested in the ability of six-year-old children to form concepts, those six-year-olds actually studied would be the sample, and all similar six-year-old children (perhaps those in modern, Western cultures) would be the population.

The strategy of observing a limited sample in order to generalize about a much larger population rests on the assumption that the sample is reasonably *representative* of the population. A sample is representative if its composition is similar to the composition of the population. *Sampling bias* **exists when a sample is not representative of the population from which it was drawn.** When a sample is not representative, generalizations about the population may be inaccurate. For instance, if a political pollster were to survey only people in posh shopping areas frequented by the wealthy, the pollster's generalizations about the voting public as a whole would be off the mark.

Figure 2.10

The relationship between the population and the sample. The process of drawing inferences about a population based on a sample only works if the sample is reasonably representative of the population. A sample is representative if its demographic makeup is similar to that of the population, as shown on the left. If some groups in the population are overrepresented or underrepresented in the sample, as shown on the right, inferences about the population may be skewed or inaccurate.

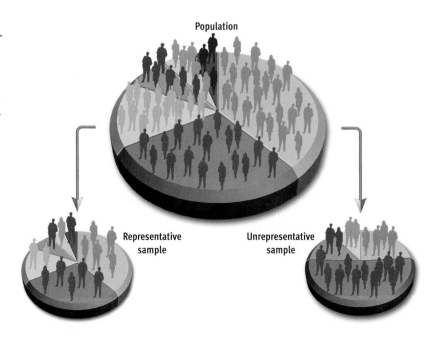

Population

Representative sample

Unrepresentative sample

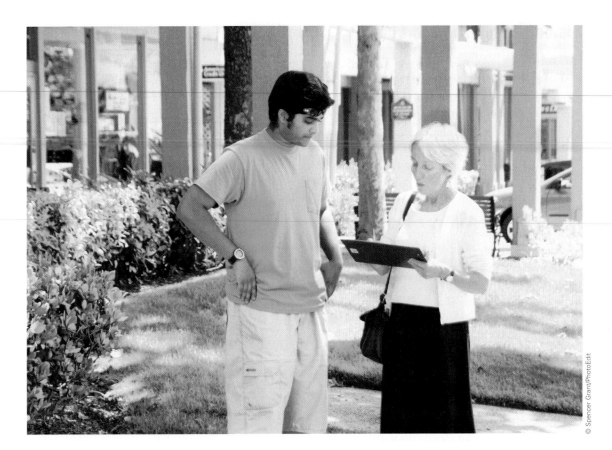

Before accepting the results of a survey poll, one should know something about how the poll was conducted. A polling could, for instance, contain sampling bias. Opinions collected solely from middle-class people but generalized to the voting public as a whole would be an example of such bias.

As we discussed in Chapter 1, historically, psychologists have tended to undersample women, ethnic minorities, and people from non-Western cultures. They have also tended to neglect older adults, while depending much too heavily on white, middle- and upper-class university and college students. This excessive reliance on students may not be all that problematic for some research questions, but it certainly seems likely to distort results in many research areas (Sears, 1986). In general, then, when you have doubts about the results of a study, the first thing to examine is the composition of the sample.

Placebo Effects

In pharmacology, a *placebo* is a substance that resembles a drug but has no actual pharmacological effect. In studies that assess the effectiveness of medications, placebos are given to some subjects to control for the effects of a treacherous extraneous variable: participants' expectations. Placebos are used because researchers know that participants' expectations can influence their feelings, reactions, and behaviour (Stewart-Williams, 2004). **Thus, *placebo effects* occur when participants' expectations lead them to experience some change even though they receive empty, fake, or ineffectual treatment.** In medicine, placebo effects are well documented (Quitkin, 1999). Many physicians tell of patients being "cured" by prescriptions of sugar pills. Similarly, psychologists have found that participants' expectations can be powerful determinants of their perceptions and behaviour when they are under the microscope in an empirical study.

For example, placebo effects have been seen in research on meditation. A number of studies have found that meditation can improve people's energy level, mental and physical health, and happiness (Alexander et al., 1990; Carrington, 1987; Reibel et al., 2001). However, in many of the early studies of meditation, researchers assembled their experimental groups with volunteer subjects eager to learn meditation. Most of these subjects *wanted* and *expected* meditation to have beneficial effects. Their positive expectations may have coloured their subsequent ratings of their energy level, happiness, and so on. Better-designed studies have shown that meditation can be beneficial (see Chapter 5). However, placebo effects have probably exaggerated these benefits in some studies (Shapiro, 1987).

Researchers should guard against placebo effects whenever subjects are likely to have expectations that a treatment will affect them in a certain way.

Distortions in Self-Report Data

Research psychologists often work with *self-report data,* consisting of subjects' verbal accounts of their behaviour. This is the case whenever questionnaires, interviews, or personality inventories are used to measure variables. Self-report methods can be quite useful, taking advantage of the fact that people have a unique opportunity to observe themselves full-time (Baldwin, 2000). However, self-reports can be plagued by several kinds of distortion.

One of the most problematic of these distortions is **the *social desirability bias,* which is a tendency to give socially approved answers to questions about oneself.** Subjects who are influenced by this bias work overtime trying to create a favourable impression (Holtgraves, 2004). For example, many survey respondents will report that they voted in an election or gave to a charity when in fact it is possible to determine that they did not (Granberg & Holmberg, 1991). Respondents influenced by social desirability bias also tend to report that they are healthier, happier, and less prejudiced than other types of evidence would suggest.

Other problems can also produce distortions in self-report data (Krosnick, 1999; Schuman & Kalton, 1985). Respondents misunderstand questionnaire items surprisingly often, and the way questions are worded can shape subjects' responses (Schwarz, 1999). Memory errors can undermine the accuracy of verbal reports. Response sets are yet another problem. **A *response set* is a tendency to respond to questions in a particular way that is unrelated to the content of the questions.** For example, some people tend to agree with nearly everything on a questionnaire (Krosnick & Fabrigar, 1998). Obviously, distortions like these can produce inaccurate results. Although researchers have devised ways to neutralize these problems—such as carefully pretesting survey instruments—we should be cautious in drawing conclusions from self-report data (Schaeffer, 2000).

Experimenter Bias

As scientists, psychologists try to conduct their studies in an objective, unbiased way so that their own views will not influence the results. However, objectivity is a *goal* that scientists strive for, not an accomplished fact that can be taken for granted (MacCoun, 1998). In reality, most researchers have an emotional investment in the outcome of their research. Often they are testing hypotheses that they have developed themselves and that they would like to see supported by the data. It is understandable, then, that *experimenter bias* is a possible source of error in research.

***Experimenter bias* occurs when a researcher's expectations or preferences about the outcome of a study influence the results obtained.** Experimenter bias can slip through to influence studies in many subtle ways. One problem is that researchers, like others, sometimes *see what they want to see.* For instance, when experimenters make apparently honest mistakes in recording subjects' responses, the mistakes tend to be heavily slanted in favour of supporting the hypothesis (O'Leary, Kent, & Kanowitz, 1975).

Research by Robert Rosenthal (1976) suggests that experimenter bias may lead researchers to unintentionally influence the behaviour of their subjects. In one study, Rosenthal and Fode (1963) recruited undergraduate psychology students to serve as the "experimenters." The students were told that they would be collecting data for a study of how participants rated the success of people portrayed in photographs. In a pilot study, photos were selected that generated (on the average) neutral ratings on a scale extending from –10 (extreme failure) to +10 (extreme success). Rosenthal and Fode then manipulated the expectancies of their experimenters. Half of them were told that, based on pilot data, they would probably obtain average ratings of –5. The other half were led to expect average ratings of +5. The experimenters were forbidden from conversing with their subjects except for reading some standardized instructions. Even though the photographs were exactly the same for both groups, the experimenters who *expected* positive ratings *obtained* significantly higher ratings than those who expected negative ratings.

How could the experimenters have swayed the participants' ratings? According to Rosenthal, the experimenters may have unintentionally influenced their subjects by sending subtle nonverbal signals as the experiment progressed. Without realizing it, they may have smiled, nodded, or sent other positive cues when participants made ratings that were in line with the experimenters' expectations. Thus, experimenter bias may influence both researchers' observations and their subjects' behaviour (Rosenthal, 1994, 2002).

The problems associated with experimenter bias can be neutralized by using a double-blind procedure. **The *double-blind procedure* is a research**

Courtesy of Robert Rosenthal

"*Quite unconsciously, a psychologist interacts in subtle ways with the people he is studying so that he may get the response he expects to get.*"
ROBERT ROSENTHAL

strategy in which neither subjects nor experimenters know which subjects are in the experimental or control groups. It's not particularly unusual for participants to be "blind" about their treatment condition. However, the double-blind procedure keeps the experimenter in the dark as well. Of course, a member of the research team who isn't directly involved with subjects keeps track of who is in which group.

Looking at Ethics: Do the Ends Justify the Means?

When we took our first course in psychology, as is often the case now, as students we were required to participate in research studies as part of that course. One of us chose and showed up at the appointed time for a study on ESP. When he arrived, he was shown a black curtain and was told that behind the curtain a famous psychic was sitting who would telepathically transmit a set of numbers between 1 and 10 and it was the research participant's job to identify the numbers on a series of trials. He was told that others would be taking part simultaneously and, to ensure privacy, everyone would be taken to different cubicles and would communicate via an intercom. Each time a trial began, he heard the others give their guesses first, with his guess coming last. He gave the study his all because he was very interested in psychology.

Once the experiment was over, he was told that, surprise, the experiment was not about ESP but was an experiment in conformity. There were no other participants. What he heard were tape-recorded voices and the purpose was to see if the numbers guessed by the other "participants" would influence his own judgments. At that point he felt a number of emotions, ranging from relief to embarrassment.

Should researchers be allowed to play with your feelings in this way? Should they be permitted to deceive subjects in such a manner? Is this the cost that must be paid to advance scientific knowledge? As these questions indicate, the research enterprise sometimes presents scientists with difficult ethical dilemmas. *These dilemmas reflect concern about the possibility for inflicting harm on participants.* In psychological research, the major ethical concerns

centre on the use of deception and guidelines for the participation of humans and animals in psychological research.

While ethical abuses are the exceptions, they can often be very serious. In the Tuskegee Syphilis Study carried out in the United States from 1932 to 1972, a group of black men who had contracted syphilis were enrolled in the study but were never told they had the disease and the doctors conducting the study never treated them for it. Or consider the secret CIA-funded experiments carried out at the Allan Memorial Institute in Montreal in the 1950s and '60s. The abuses inflicted on the unsuspecting patients are horrifying, such as being left in drug-induced comas for days at a time. Patients were not informed about the nature of the research and it was typically carried out without their consent. This set of experiments was thankfully exposed in the 1970s. This research is discussed more fully in Chapter 15.

Elaborate deception, such as that experienced by one of the authors in his first research in psychology, has been fairly common in psychological research since the 1960s, especially in the area of social psychology (Epley & Huff, 1998; Korn, 1997). Critics argue against the use of deception on several grounds (Baumrind, 1985; Kelman, 1982; Ortmann & Hertwig, 1997). First, they assert that deception is only a nice word for lying, which they see as inherently immoral. Second, they argue that by deceiving unsuspecting participants, psychologists may undermine many individuals' trust in others. Third, they point out that many deceptive studies produce distress for participants who were not forewarned about

Web Link 2.7

The Troubling Legacy of the Tuskegee Syphilis Study
http://www.med.virginia.edu/
hs-library/historical/apology/
index.html

The enduring damage of unethical scientific and medical research—here seen in the infamous 1932–1972 Tuskegee Syphilis Study among 399 poor black men in Alabama—is detailed in several government reports and a rare presidential apology to the victims.

Yale University

"Who are the cruel and inhumane ones, the behavioural scientists whose research on animals led to the cures of the anorexic girl and the vomiting child, or those leaders of the radical animal activists who are making an exciting career of trying to stop all such research and are misinforming people by repeatedly asserting that it is without any value?"
NEAL MILLER

that possibility. Specifically, subjects may experience great stress during a study or be made to feel foolish when the true nature of a study is explained. Those who defend the use of deception in research maintain that many important issues could not be investigated if experimenters were not permitted to sometimes mislead participants (Broder, 1998). While there may be no easy answers to questions concerning such matters as deception and the use of animals in psychological research, it is clear that psychologists and their professional associations are very serious about protecting the rights of clients and research participants. In this section we will review some of the ethical guidelines that oversee research in psychology in Canada.

Ethical Guidelines for Research in Psychology in Canada

In Chapter 1 we introduced you to the major organization for psychology in Canada, the Canadian Psychological Association (CPA). Like its more senior counterpart in the United States, the American Psychological Association, the CPA has spent a great deal of effort developing ethical guidelines to inform psychological research. While the CPA's statements on this issue are quite detailed (the interested reader is referred to the Canadian Code of Ethics for Psychologists, http://www.cpa.ca/ethics.html), we will refer to the four principles underlying the CPA's ethical guidelines. The general principles and their relative ranking of importance are illustrated in Table 2.5.

Some of the background of the development of the Canadian Psychological Association's ethical guidelines are discussed in a paper by University of Manitoba psychologist John Adair (2001). Some of the similarities and differences between the CPA's and APA's codes of ethics have been considered

Table 2.5 Ethics in Research

Key Principles in Psychological Research, as set forth by the Canadian Psychological Association (2000), are illustrated here. These principles are designed to ensure the welfare both of human and animal participants:

- Principle I: Respect for the Dignity of Persons.
- Principle II: Responsible Caring.
- Principle III: Integrity in Relationships.
- Principle IV: Responsibility to Society.

SOURCE: Canadian Psychological Association (2000), *Canadian Code of Ethics for Psychologists*, 3rd ed., retrieved April 8, 2005, from http://www.cpa.ca/ethics2000.html.

by the University of Regina's Thomas Hadjistavropoulos and his colleagues (Hadjistavropoulos, Mally, Sharpe, Green, & Fuchs-Lacelle, 2002). A special issue of the journal *Canadian Psychology* (Volume 39, Issue 3) published in 1998 was devoted to the topic of the code of ethics.

The CPA ethical principles deal with how people with whom the psychologist comes into contact should be treated. All such persons should be treated with dignity and the psychologist should ensure that their value is not dependent upon culture, race, nationality, or other such factors. Psychologists have a responsibility to protect the rights, privacy, personal liberty, and self-determination of others. Psychologists are also expected to be especially vigilant to safeguards to protect the vulnerable (e.g., children) and to ensure in all cases that freedom of consent is assured. Psychologists should take all available measures to ensure that their activities will benefit (or at least, do no harm to) those with whom they interact in a professional capacity. Psychologists should emphasize integrity in their relationships with their clients, students, and research participants. Finally, psychologists must recognize that psychology has a responsibility to society to increase knowledge and promote the welfare of all human beings.

The principles also have implications for psychologists who employ animals in their research. For example, every effort must be made to minimize the discomfort felt by such participants and to ensure that animals will not be used unless there is a strong expectation that the results will benefit both humans and animals. Additional guidelines regarding the treatment of animals have been developed by the Canadian Council on the Care of Animals (see http://www.ccac.ca). This national organization is responsible for setting guidelines for the care and use of animals in research.

In Canadian universities great care is taken in the application of high ethical standards to research conducted by their members. Before students participate in university-sponsored research, that research must be approved at a variety of levels. Most psychology departments have their own research ethics boards or committees to approve research. It is also typical that the research has to be approved by a committee at the university level consisting of members from various academic departments and groups. Finally, most university research conducted in Canada is funded by the federal government by the Social Sciences and Humanities Research Council, the National Sciences and Engineering Research Council, and/or the Canadian Institutes of Health

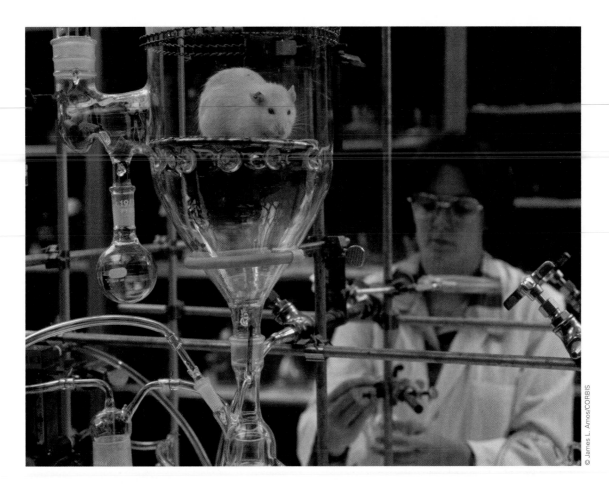

The use of rats and other animals in scientific research is now a major ethical issue. Researchers claim that experiments on animals often yield results and knowledge beneficial to humankind. Opponents maintain that humans have no right to subject animals to harm for research purposes. What is your view?

© James L. Amos/CORBIS

Research. These three federal funding agencies, known collectively as the Tri-Council, have formulated their own set of ethical standards that must be reflected for any research to be eligible for funding (see http://www.pre.ethics.gc.ca).

While many of these decisions are not easy, such as the use of animals in research, psychologists hope that ethical guidelines such as those described here will promote responsible and ethical treatment of all clients and research participants.

Putting It in Perspective

Two of our seven unifying themes have emerged strongly in this chapter. First, the entire chapter is a testimonial to the idea that psychology is empirical. Second, the discussion of methodological flaws in research provides numerous examples of how people's experience of the world can be highly subjective. Let's examine each of these points in more detail.

As explained in Chapter 1, the empirical approach entails testing ideas, basing conclusions on systematic observation, and relying on a healthy brand of skepticism. All those features of the empirical approach have been apparent in our review of the research enterprise in psychology.

As you have seen, psychologists test their ideas by formulating clear hypotheses that involve predictions about relations between variables. They then use a variety of research methods to collect data so they can see whether their predictions are supported. The data collection methods are designed to make researchers' observations systematic and precise. The entire venture is saturated with skepticism. Psychologists are impressed only by research results that are highly unlikely to have occurred by chance. In planning and executing their research, they are constantly on the lookout for methodological flaws. They publish their findings so that other experts can subject their methods and conclusions to critical scrutiny.

PREVIEW QUESTIONS
- How has this chapter demonstrated that psychology is empirical?
- How has this chapter illustrated the subjectivity of human experience?

Collectively, these procedures represent the essence of the empirical approach.

The subjectivity of personal experience became apparent in the discussion of methodological problems, especially placebo effects and experimenter bias. When subjects report beneficial effects from a fake treatment (the placebo), it's because they expected to see these effects. As pointed out in Chapter 1, psychologists and other scientists are not immune to the effects of subjective experience. Although they are trained to be objective, even scientists may see what they expect to see or what they want to see. This is one reason that the empirical approach emphasizes precise measurement and a skeptical attitude. The highly subjective nature of experience is exactly what the empirical approach attempts to neutralize.

The publication of empirical studies allows us to apply a critical eye to the research enterprise. However, you cannot critically analyze studies unless you know where and how to find them. In the upcoming Personal Application, we will discuss where studies are published, how to find studies on specific topics, and how to read research reports. In the subsequent Critical Thinking Application, we'll analyze the shortcomings of anecdotal evidence, which should help you to appreciate the value of empirical evidence.

REVIEW OF KEY POINTS

- Research sometimes raises complex ethical issues. Critics argue that it is unethical to deceive subjects and to expose animals to harmful treatments. Those who defend deception in research argue that many important issues could not be investigated without misleading subjects.

- Psychologists who defend animal research argue that it has brought major advances that are worth the costs. The CPA has formulated ethical principles to serve as guidelines for researchers who employ humans and animals in their research.

- Two of the book's unifying themes are apparent in this chapter's discussion of the research enterprise in psychology: psychology is empirical, and people's experience of the world is highly subjective.

PERSONAL APPLICATION

Finding and Reading Journal Articles

Answer the following "yes" or "no."

___ **1** I have read about scientific studies in newspapers and magazines and sometimes wondered, "How did they come to those conclusions?"

___ **2** When I go to the library, I often have difficulty figuring out how to find information based on research.

___ **3** I have tried to read scientific reports and found them to be too technical and difficult to understand.

If you responded "yes" to any of the above statements, you have struggled with the information explosion in the sciences. We live in a research-oriented society. The number of studies conducted in most sciences is growing at a dizzying pace. This expansion has been particularly spectacular in psychology. Moreover, psychological research increasingly commands attention from the popular press because it is often relevant to people's personal concerns.

This Personal Application is intended to help you cope with the information explosion in psychology. It assumes that there may come a time when you need to examine original psychological research. Perhaps it will be in your role as a student (working on a term paper, for instance), in another role (parent, teacher, nurse, administrator), or merely out of curiosity. In any case, this Personal Application explains the nature of technical journals and discusses how to find and read articles in them. You can learn more about how to use library resources in psychology from an excellent little book titled *Library Use: A Handbook for Psychology* (Reed & Baxter, 1992, 2003).

The Nature of Technical Journals

As you will recall from earlier in the chapter, a *journal* is a periodical that publishes tech-

nical and scholarly material, usually in a narrowly defined area of inquiry. Scholars in most fields—whether economics, chemistry, education, or psychology—publish the bulk of their work in these journals. Journal articles represent the core of intellectual activity in any academic discipline.

In general, journal articles are written for other professionals in the field. Hence, authors assume that their readers are other interested economists or chemists or psychologists. Because journal articles are written in the special language unique to a particular discipline, they are often difficult for nonprofessionals to understand. You will be learning a great deal of psychology's special language in this course, which will improve your ability to understand articles in psychology journals.

In psychology, most journal articles are reports that describe original empirical studies. These reports permit researchers to disseminate their findings to the scientific community. Another common type of article is the review article. *Review articles* summarize and reconcile the findings of a large number of studies on a specific issue. Some psychology journals also publish comments or critiques of previously published research, book reviews, theoretical treatises, and descriptions of methodological innovations.

Finding Journal Articles **1e**

Reports of psychological research are commonly mentioned in newspapers and popular magazines. These summaries can be helpful to readers, but they often embrace the most sensational conclusions that might be drawn from the research. They also tend to include many oversimplifications and factual errors. Hence, if a study mentioned in the press is of interest to you, you may want to track down the orig-

inal article to ensure that you get accurate information.

Most discussions of research in the popular press do not mention where you can find the original technical article. However, there is a way to find out. A computerized database called PsycINFO makes it possible to locate journal articles by specific researchers or scholarly work on specific topics. This huge, online database, which is updated constantly, contains brief summaries, or *abstracts*, of journal articles, books, and chapters in edited books, reporting, reviewing, or theorizing about psychological research. Over 1800 journals are checked regularly to select items for inclusion. The abstracts are concise—about 75 to 175 words. They briefly describe the hypotheses, methods, results, and conclusions of the studies. Each abstract should allow you to determine whether an article is relevant to your interests. If it is, you should be able to find the article in your library (or to order it) because a complete bibliographic reference is provided.

Although news accounts of research rarely mention where a study was published, they often mention the name of the researcher. If you have this information, the easiest way to find a specific article is to search PsycINFO for materials published by that researcher. For example, let's say you read a news report that summarizes an interesting study on whether alcohol hangovers affect managerial effectiveness in the business world that was published by Siegfried Streufert in the mid-1990s. To track down the original article, you would search for journal articles authored by Streufert. Given that you know the approximate year of publication, you could select the PsycINFO option to narrow your search to materials published between 1990 and 1996. If you conducted this search, you would turn up the list of eight articles shown in Figure 2.11. The sixth item in the list appears to be the article you are interested in. Figure 2.12 shows what you would see if you clicked to obtain the Abstract and Citation for this article. As you can see, the abstract shows that the original report was published in the October 1995 issue of *Alcoholism: Clinical and Experimental Research.* Armed with this information, you could obtain the article easily.

You can also search PsycINFO for research literature on particular topics, such as achievement motivation, aggressive behaviour, alcoholism, appetite disorders, or artistic ability. These computerized literature searches can be much more powerful, precise, and thorough than traditional, manual searches in a library. PsycINFO can sift through a couple million articles in a matter of seconds to identify *all* the articles on a subject, such as alcoholism. Obviously, there is no way you can match this efficiency stumbling around in the stacks at your library. Moreover, the computer allows you to pair up topics to swiftly narrow your search to exactly those issues that interest you.

The PsycINFO database can be accessed online at many libraries or via the Internet (see Web Link 2.2 on p. 47 for a description of PsycINFO Direct). The database is also available at some libraries that have the information stored on CD-ROM discs. This version of the database is updated monthly. The summaries contained in PsycINFO can also be found in a monthly print journal called *Psychological Abstracts,* but fewer and fewer libraries are subscribing to this traditional publication because it cannot match the swift and efficient search capabilities of PsycINFO.

Reading Journal Articles

Once you find the journal articles you want to examine, you need to know how to decipher them. You can process the information in such articles more efficiently if you understand how they are organized. Depending on your needs and purpose, you may want to simply skim through some of the sections. Journal articles follow a fairly standard organization, which includes the following sections and features.

Abstract

Most journals print a concise summary at the beginning of each article. This abstract allows readers scanning the journal to quickly decide whether articles are relevant to their interests.

Introduction

The introduction presents an overview of the problem studied in the research. It mentions relevant theories and quickly reviews previous research that bears on the problem, usually citing shortcomings in previous research that necessitate the present study. This review of the current state of knowledge on the topic usually progresses to a specific and precise statement regarding the hypotheses under investigation.

Method

The method section provides a thorough description of the research methods used in

Figure 2.11

Searching PsycINFO. If you searched PsycINFO for journal articles authored by Siegfried Streufert during the period of 1990–1996, the database would return the eight titles shown here. For each article, you can click to see its abstract or its full PsycINFO record (the abstract plus subject descriptors and other details). In some cases (depending on the version of PsycINFO that your library has ordered) you can even click to see the *full text* of some articles (those articles that appeared in journals published by APA in recent years).

SOURCE: Sample search reprinted with permission of the American Psychological Association, publisher of the PsycINFO® database. Copyright © 1887–present, American Psychological Association. All rights reserved. For more information contact psycinfo.apa.org.

found 8 documents, (8 returned).
for Your Query : *(streufert, siegfried):Author*

1. **Effects of alcohol intoxication on risk taking, strategy, and error rate in visuomotor performance.**
   By Streufert, Siegfried; Pogash, Rosanne M.; Roache, John D.; Gingrich, Dennis; et al
   Journal of Applied Psychology. 1992 Aug Vol 77(4) 515-524
   Abstract and Citation | Full PsycINFO Record | Full Text of Article

2. **Age and management team performance.**
   By Streufert, Siegfried; Pogash, Rosanne; Piasecki, Mary; Post, Gerald M.
   Psychology & Aging. 1990 Dec Vol 5(4) 551-559
   Abstract and Citation | Full PsycINFO Record | Full Text of Article

3. **Authoring of complex learning environments: Design considerations for dynamic simulations.**
   By Breuer, Klaus; Streufert, Siegfried
   Journal of Structural Learning. 1996 Nov Vol 12(4) 315-321
   Abstract and Citation | Full PsycINFO Record

4. **Effects of alprazolam on complex human functioning.**
   By Streufert, Siegfried; Satish, Usha; Pogash, Rosanne; Gingrich, Dennis; et al
   Journal of Applied Social Psychology. 1996 Nov Vol 26(21) 1912-1930
   Abstract and Citation | Full PsycINFO Record

5. **Effects of caffeine deprivation on complex human functioning.**
   By Streufert, Siegfried; Pogash, Rosanne; Miller, Jill; Gingrich, Dennis; et al
   Psychopharmacology. 1995 Apr Vol 118(4) 377-384
   Abstract and Citation | Full PsycINFO Record

6. **Alcohol hangover and managerial effectiveness.**
   By Streufert, Siegfried; Pogash, Rosanne; Braig, Daniela; Gingrich, Dennis; et al
   Alcoholism: Clinical & Experimental Research. 1995 Oct Vol 19(5) 1141-1146
   Abstract and Citation | Full PsycINFO Record

7. **Alcohol and management performance.**
   By Streufert, Siegfried; Pogash, Rosanne; Roache, John; Severs, Walter; et al
   Journal of Studies on Alcohol. 1994 Mar Vol 55(2) 230-238
   Abstract and Citation | Full PsycINFO Record

8. **Alcohol and complex functioning.**
   By Streufert, Siegfried; Pogash, Rosanne M.; Gingrich, Dennis; Kantner, Anne; et al
   Journal of Applied Social Psychology. 1993 Jun Vol 23(11) 847-866
   Abstract and Citation | Full PsycINFO Record

Figure 2.12

Example of a PsycINFO abstract. This information is what you would see if you clicked to see the abstract of item 6 in the list shown in Figure 2.11. It is a typical abstract from the online PsycINFO database. Each abstract in PsycINFO provides a summary of a specific journal article, book, or chapter in an edited book, and complete bibliographical information. (It is also possible to combine topics in a PsycINFO search to pinpoint articles dealing with specific topics. For example, combining a search for articles on marijuana and articles on memory to yield a smaller subset of articles on marijuana and memory.)

TITLE	Alcohol hangover and managerial effectiveness.
ABSTRACT	21 male managers who normally drank moderate amounts of alcohol participated in a placebo-controlled, double-blind, crossover experiment to determine whether alcohol-induced hangovers would influence managerial/professional task performance characteristics. Ss consumed either placebo or alcoholic drinks to attain a breath alcohol level of 0.10 during the evening before participation in Strategic Management Simulations. By the following morning, breath alcohol levels were measured at 0.00. Questionnaire responses indicated considerable hangover discomfort. Responses to semantic differential evaluative scales suggested that Ss evaluated their own managerial performance in the simulation setting as impaired. However, multiple measures of decision-making performance obtained in the simulation task did not show any deterioration of functioning. (PsycINFO Database Record © 2000 APA, all rights reserved)
AUTHOR	*Streufert, Siegfried;* Pogash, Rosanne; Braig, Daniela; Gingrich, Dennis; et al
AFFILIATION	Pennsylvania State U, Coll of Medicine, Dept of Behavioral Science, Hershey, USA
SOURCE	Alcoholism: Clinical & Experimental Research. 1995 Oct Vol 19(5) 1141-1146

the study. Information is provided on the subjects used, the procedures followed, and the data collection techniques employed. This description is made detailed enough to permit another researcher to attempt to replicate the study.

Results

The data obtained in the study are reported in the results section. This section often creates problems for novice readers because it includes complex statistical analyses, figures, tables, and graphs. This section does *not* include any inferences based on the data, as such conclusions are supposed to follow in the next section. Instead, it simply contains a concise summary of the raw data and the statistical analyses.

Discussion

In the discussion section you will find the conclusions drawn by the author(s). In contrast to the results section, which is a straightforward summary of empirical observations, the discussion section allows for interpretation and evaluation of the data. Implications for theory and factual knowledge in the discipline are discussed. Conclusions are usually qualified carefully, and any limitations in the study may be acknowledged. This section may also include suggestions for future research on the issue.

References

At the end of each article you will find a list of bibliographic references for any studies cited. This list permits you to examine firsthand other relevant studies mentioned in the article. The references list is often a rich source of leads about other articles that are germane to the topic that you are looking into.

For additional hints on reading journal articles, see the paper published by two psychologists writing at the University of Waterloo, Christian Jordan and Mark Zanna (1999).

REVIEW OF KEY POINTS

- Journals publish technical and scholarly material. Usually they are written for other professionals in a narrow area of inquiry. In psychology, most journal articles are reports of original research.
- PsycINFO is a computerized database that contains brief summaries of newly published journal articles, books, and chapters in edited books. Works on specific topics and publications by specific authors can be found by using the search mechanisms built into the database.
- Computerized literature searches can be much more powerful and precise than manual searches. The information contained in PsycINFO is also available in a monthly print journal called *Psychological Abstracts*.
- Journal articles are easier to understand if one is familiar with the standard format. Most articles include six elements: abstract, introduction, method, results, discussion, and references.

CHAPTER ③

Latchezar Boyadjiev, *Transformation,* L.B. Glass Studios

Communication in the Nervous System
Nervous Tissue: The Basic Hardware
The Neural Impulse: Using Energy to Send Information
The Synapse: Where Neurons Meet
Neurotransmitters and Behaviour

Organization of the Nervous System
The Peripheral Nervous System
The Central Nervous System

Looking Inside the Brain: Research Methods
Electrical Recordings
Lesioning
Electrical Stimulation of the Brain
Brain-Imaging Procedures
Featured Study • Searching for the Self in the Brain

The Brain and Behaviour
The Hindbrain
The Midbrain
The Forebrain
The Plasticity of the Brain

Right Brain/Left Brain: Cerebral Laterality
Bisecting the Brain: Split-Brain Research
Hemispheric Specialization in the Intact Brain

The Endocrine System: Another Way to Communicate

Heredity and Behaviour: Is It All in the Genes?
Basic Principles of Genetics
Investigating Hereditary Influence: Research Methods
The Interplay of Heredity and Environment

The Evolutionary Bases of Behaviour
Darwin's Insights
Subsequent Refinements to Evolutionary Theory
Behaviours as Adaptive Traits

Putting It in Perspective

Personal Application • **Evaluating the Concept of "Two Minds in One"**
Cerebral Specialization and Cognitive Processes
Complexities and Qualifications

Critical Thinking Application • **Building Better Brains: The Perils of Extrapolation**
The Key Findings on Neural Development
The Risks of Overextrapolation

Recap

Practice Test

PRACTICE TEST

1. A tentative prediction about the relationship between two variables is:
   A. a confounding of variables.
   B. an operational definition.
   C. a theory.
   D. a hypothesis.

2. Researchers must describe the actions that will be taken to measure or control each variable in their studies. In other words, they must:
   A. provide operational definitions of their variables.
   B. decide if their studies will be experimental or correlational.
   C. use statistics to summarize their findings.
   D. decide how many subjects should participate in their studies.

3. A researcher found that clients who were randomly assigned to same-sex groups participated more in group therapy sessions than clients who were randomly assigned to co-ed groups. In this experiment, the independent variable was:
   A. the amount of participation in the group therapy sessions.
   B. whether or not the group was co-ed.
   C. the clients' attitudes toward group therapy.
   D. how much the clients' mental health improved.

4. A researcher wants to see whether a protein-enriched diet will enhance the maze-running performance of rats. One group of rats are fed the high-protein diet for the duration of the study; the other group continues to receive ordinary rat chow. In this experiment, the diet fed to the two groups of rats is the _____ variable.
   A. correlated
   B. control
   C. dependent
   D. independent

5. In a study of the effect of a new teaching technique on students' achievement test scores, an important extraneous variable would be the students':
   A. hair colour.
   B. athletic skills.
   C. IQ scores.
   D. sociability.

6. Whenever you have a cold, you rest in bed, take Aspirin, and drink plenty of fluids. You can't determine which remedy is most effective because of which of the following problems?
   A. sampling bias
   B. distorted self-report data
   C. confounding of variables
   D. experimenter bias

7. A psychologist monitors a group of nursery-school children, recording each instance of altruistic behaviour as it occurs. The psychologist is using:
   A. the experimental method.
   B. naturalistic observation.
   C. case studies.
   D. the survey method.

8. Among the advantages of descriptive/correlational research is (are):
   A. it allows investigators to isolate cause and effect.
   B. it permits researchers to study variables that would be impossible to manipulate.
   C. it can demonstrate conclusively that two variables are causally related.
   D. a and b.

9. Which of the following correlation coefficients would indicate the strongest relationship between two variables?
   A. 0.58
   B. 0.19
   C. –0.97
   D. –0.05

10. When psychologists say that their results are statistically significant, they mean that the results:
    A. have important practical applications.
    B. have important implications for scientific theory.
    C. are unlikely to be due to the fluctuations of chance.
    D. all of the above.

11. Sampling bias exists when:
    A. the sample is representative of the population.
    B. the sample is not representative of the population.
    C. two variables are confounded.
    D. the effect of the independent variable can't be isolated.

12. The problem of experimenter bias can be avoided by:
    A. not informing subjects of the hypothesis of the experiment.
    B. telling the subjects that there are no "right" or "wrong" answers.
    C. using a research strategy in which neither subjects nor experimenter know which subjects are in the experimental and control groups.
    D. having the experimenter use only nonverbal signals when communicating with the subjects.

13. Critics of deception in research have assumed that deceptive studies are harmful to subjects. The empirical data on this issue suggest that:
    A. many deceptive studies do produce significant distress for subjects who were not forewarned about the possibility of deception.
    B. most participants in deceptive studies report that they enjoyed the experience and didn't mind being misled.
    C. deceptive research seriously undermines subjects' trust in others.
    D. a and c.

14. PsycINFO is:
    A. a new journal that recently replaced *Psychological Abstracts*.
    B. a computerized database containing abstracts of articles, chapters, and books reporting psychological research.
    C. a reference book that explains the format and techniques for writing journal articles.
    D. a computerized database containing information about studies that have not yet been published.

15. Anecdotal evidence:
    A. is often concrete, vivid, and memorable.
    B. tends to influence people.
    C. is fundamentally flawed and unreliable.
    D. is all of the above.

    See Appendix A for answers to this Practice Test.

 ON THE WEB

For additional resources on the topics covered in this chapter, visit the *Psychology: Themes and Variations* Web site, where you will find practice quizzes, tutorials, Web links, simulations, critical thinking activities, flash cards, interactive exercises, and suggested readings available through INFOTRAC.

http://www.themesandvariations.nelson.com

 http://hed.nelson.com

Go to this site for the link to ThomsonNOW™, your one-stop study shop. Take a Pretest for this chapter and ThomsonNOW™ will generate a personalized Study Plan based on your test results! The Study Plan will identify the topics you need to review and direct you to online resources to help you master those topics. You can then take a Posttest to help you determine the concepts you have mastered and what you still need work on.

CHAPTER 3

Latchezar Boyadjiev, *Transformation*, L.B. Glass Studios

Communication in the Nervous System
Nervous Tissue: The Basic Hardware
The Neural Impulse: Using Energy to Send Information
The Synapse: Where Neurons Meet
Neurotransmitters and Behaviour

Organization of the Nervous System
The Peripheral Nervous System
The Central Nervous System

Looking Inside the Brain: Research Methods
Electrical Recordings
Lesioning
Electrical Stimulation of the Brain
Brain-Imaging Procedures
Featured Study • Searching for the Self in the Brain

The Brain and Behaviour
The Hindbrain
The Midbrain
The Forebrain
The Plasticity of the Brain

Right Brain/Left Brain: Cerebral Laterality
Bisecting the Brain: Split-Brain Research
Hemispheric Specialization in the Intact Brain

The Endocrine System: Another Way to Communicate

Heredity and Behaviour: Is It All in the Genes?
Basic Principles of Genetics
Investigating Hereditary Influence: Research Methods
The Interplay of Heredity and Environment

The Evolutionary Bases of Behaviour
Darwin's Insights
Subsequent Refinements to Evolutionary Theory
Behaviours as Adaptive Traits

Putting It in Perspective

***Personal Application* • Evaluating the Concept of "Two Minds in One"**
Cerebral Specialization and Cognitive Processes
Complexities and Qualifications

***Critical Thinking Application* • Building Better Brains: The Perils of Extrapolation**
The Key Findings on Neural Development
The Risks of Overextrapolation

Recap

Practice Test

RECAP

Key Ideas

The Scientific Approach to Behaviour

● The scientific approach assumes that there are laws of behaviour that can be discovered through empirical research. The goals of the science of psychology include (1) the measurement and description of behaviour, (2) the understanding and prediction of behaviour, and (3) the application of this knowledge to the task of controlling behaviour.

● A scientific investigation follows a systematic pattern that includes five steps: (1) formulate a testable hypothesis, (2) select the research method and design the study, (3) collect the data, (4) analyze the data and draw conclusions, and (5) report the findings. The two major advantages of the scientific approach are its clarity in communication and its relative intolerance of error.

● By integrating apparently unrelated facts into a coherent whole, theories permit psychologists to make the leap from the description of behaviour to understanding behaviour.

Looking for Causes: Experimental Research

● Experimental research involves the manipulation of an independent variable to ascertain its effect on a dependent variable. This research is usually done by comparing experimental and control groups, which must be alike in regard to important extraneous variables.

● Experimental designs may vary. For example, sometimes an experimental group serves as its own control group. And many experiments have more than one independent variable or more than one dependent variable. Some of these variations were seen in the Featured Study, in which more than one independent variable was used.

● An experiment is a powerful research method that permits conclusions about cause-and-effect relationships between variables. However, the experimental method is often not usable for a specific problem, and many experiments tend to be artificial.

Looking for Links: Descriptive/Correlational Research

● Psychologists rely on descriptive/correlational research when they are unable to manipulate the variables they want to study. Key descriptive methods include naturalistic observation, case studies, and surveys.

● Descriptive/correlational research methods allow psychologists to explore issues that might not be open to experimental investigation. However, these research methods cannot demonstrate cause-and-effect relationships.

Looking for Conclusions: Statistics and Research

● Psychologists use descriptive statistics, such as measures of central tendency and variability, to organize and summarize their numerical data. The mean, median, and mode are widely used measures of central tendency. Variability is usually measured with the standard deviation.

● Correlations may be either positive (when two variables co-vary in the same direction) or negative (when two variables co-vary in opposite directions). The closer a correlation is to either +1.00 or –1.00, the stronger the association. Higher correlations yield greater predictability. However, a correlation is no assurance of causation.

● Hypothesis testing involves deciding whether observed findings support the researcher's hypothesis. Findings are statistically significant only when they are unlikely to be due to chance.

Looking for Flaws: Evaluating Research

● Scientists often try to replicate research findings to double-check their validity. Sampling bias occurs when a sample is not representative of the population of interest. Placebo effects occur when subjects' expectations cause them to change their behaviour in response to a fake treatment.

● Distortions in self-reports are a source of concern whenever questionnaires and personality inventories are used to collect data. Experimenter bias occurs when researchers' expectations and desires distort their observations or unintentionally influence their subjects' behaviour.

Looking at Ethics: Do the Ends Justify the Means?

● Research sometimes raises complex ethical issues. In psychology, the key questions concern the use of deception with human subjects and the use of harmful or painful manipulations with animal subjects. The CPA has formulated ethical principles to serve as guidelines for researchers.

Putting It in Perspective

● Two of the book's unifying themes are apparent in this chapter's discussion of the research enterprise in psychology: psychology is empirical, and people's experience of the world can be highly subjective.

Personal Application • Finding and Reading Journal Articles

● Journals publish technical and scholarly material. Usually they are written for other professionals in a narrow area of inquiry.

● PsycINFO is a computerized database that contains brief summaries of published journal articles, books, and chapters in edited books. Works on specific topics and publications by specific authors can be found by using the search mechanisms built into the database.

● Journal articles are easier to understand if one is familiar with the standard format. Most articles include six elements: abstract, introduction, method, results, discussion, and references.

Critical Thinking Application • The Perils of Anecdotal Evidence: "I Have a Friend Who ..."

● Anecdotal evidence consists of personal stories about specific incidents and experiences. Anecdotes often influence people because they tend to be concrete, vivid, and memorable.

● However, anecdotal evidence is usually based on the equivalent of a single case study, which is not an adequate sample, and there are no safeguards to reduce the distortion often found in self-report data. Many anecdotes are inaccurate, second-hand reports of others' experiences. Effective critical thinking depends on evidence-based decision making.

Key Terms

Anecdotal evidence, 72
Case study, 52
Confounding of variables, 49
Control group, 48
Correlation, 58
Correlation coefficient, 58
Data collection techniques, 45
Dependent variable, 48
Descriptive statistics, 57
Double-blind procedure, 64
Experiment, 48
Experimental group, 48
Experimenter bias, 64
Extraneous variables, 49
Hypothesis, 42
Independent variable, 48
Inferential statistics, 60
Journal, 45
Mean, 57
Median, 57
Mode, 57
Naturalistic observation, 52

Operational definition, 44
Participants, 45
Placebo effects, 63
Population, 62
Random assignment, 49
Replication, 62
Research methods, 47
Response set, 64
Sample, 62
Sampling bias, 62
Social desirability bias, 64
Standard deviation, 58
Statistical significance, 61
Statistics, 57
Subjects, 45
Survey, 54
Theory, 42
Variability, 58
Variables, 42

Key People

Arthur Aron, 46
Donald Dutton, 46
Neal Miller, 66
Robert Rosenthal, 64
David Wolfe, 48

rable. Indeed, people tend to be influenced by anecdotal information even when they are explicitly forewarned that the information is *not* representative (Hammill, Wilson, & Nisbett, 1980). Many politicians are keenly aware of the power of anecdotes and they frequently rely on a single vivid story rather than solid data to sway voters' views. However, anecdotal evidence is fundamentally flawed (Ruscio, 2002; Stanovich, 2004).

What, exactly, is wrong with anecdotal evidence? Let's use some of the concepts introduced in the main body of the chapter to analyze the shortcomings of anecdotal evidence. First, in the language of research designs, the anecdotal experiences of one family resemble a single *case study*. The story they tell about their experiences with joint custody may be quite interesting, but their experiences—good or bad—cannot be used to generalize to other couples. Why not? Because they are only one family, and they may be unusual in some way that affects how well they manage joint custody. To draw general conclusions based on the case study approach, you need a systematic series of case studies, so you can look for threads of consistency. A single family is a sample size of one, which surely is not large enough to derive broad principles that would apply to other families.

Second, anecdotal evidence is similar to *self-report data,* which can be distorted for a variety of reasons, such as people's tendency to give socially approved information about themselves (the *social desirability bias*). When researchers use tests and surveys to gather self-report data, they can take steps to reduce or assess the impact of distortions in their data, but there are no comparable safeguards with anecdotal evidence. Thus, the family that appears in your courtroom may be eager to make a good impression and unknowingly slant their story accordingly.

Anecdotes are often inaccurate and riddled with embellishments. We will see in Chapter 7 that memories of personal experiences are far more malleable and far less reliable than widely assumed (Roediger, Wheeler, & Rajaram, 1993). And, although it would not be an issue in this case, in other situations *anecdotal evidence often consists of stories that people have heard about others' experiences*. Hearsay evidence is not accepted in courtrooms for good reason. As stories are passed on from one person to another, they often become increasingly distorted and inaccurate.

Can you think of any other reasons for being wary of anecdotal evidence? After reading the chapter, perhaps you thought about the possibility of *sampling bias*. Do you think that the lawyer will pick a couple at random from all those who have been awarded joint custody? It seems highly unlikely. If she wants you to award joint custody, she will find a couple for whom this arrangement worked very well; and if she wants you to award sole custody to her client, she will find a couple whose inability to make joint custody work had dire consequences for their children. One reason people love to work with anecdotal evidence is that it is so readily manipulated; they can usually find an anecdote or two to support their position, whether or not these anecdotes are representative of most people's experiences.

If the testimony of one family cannot be used in making this critical custody decision, what sort of evidence should you be looking for? One goal of effective critical thinking is to make decisions based on solid evidence. This process is called *evidence-based decision making*. In this case, you would need to consider the overall experiences of a large sample of families who have tried joint custody arrangements. In general, across many different families, did the children in joint custody develop well? Was there a disproportionately high rate of emotional problems or other signs of stress for the children or the parents? Was the percentage of families who returned to court at a later date to change their joint custody arrangements higher than for other types of custody arrangements? You can probably think of additional information that you would want to collect regarding the outcomes of various custody arrangements.

In examining research reports, many people recognize the need to evaluate the evidence by looking for the types of flaws described in the main body of the chapter (sampling bias, experimenter bias, and so forth). Curiously, though, many of the same people then fail to apply the same principles of good evidence to their personal decisions in everyday life. The tendency to rely on the anecdotal experiences of a small number of people is sometimes called the *"I have a friend who" syndrome,* because no matter what the topic is, it seems that someone will provide a personal story about a friend as evidence for his or her particular point of view. In short, when you hear people support their assertions with personal stories, a little skepticism is in order.

Table **2.6** Critical Thinking Skills Discussed in This Application	
Skill	**Description**
Recognizing the limitations of anecdotal evidence	The critical thinker is wary of anecdotal evidence, which consists of personal stories used to support one's assertions. Anecdotal evidence tends to be unrepresentative, inaccurate, and unreliable.
Using evidence-based decision making	The critical thinker understands the need to seek sound evidence to guide decisions in everyday life.

Figure 2.12

Example of a PsycINFO abstract. This information is what you would see if you clicked to see the abstract of item 6 in the list shown in Figure 2.11. It is a typical abstract from the online PsycINFO database. Each abstract in PsycINFO provides a summary of a specific journal article, book, or chapter in an edited book, and complete bibliographical information. (It is also possible to combine topics in a PsycINFO search to pinpoint articles dealing with specific topics. For example, combining a search for articles on marijuana and articles on memory to yield a smaller subset of articles on marijuana and memory.)

TITLE	Alcohol hangover and managerial effectiveness.
ABSTRACT	21 male managers who normally drank moderate amounts of alcohol participated in a placebo-controlled, double-blind, crossover experiment to determine whether alcohol-induced hangovers would influence managerial/professional task performance characteristics. Ss consumed either placebo or alcoholic drinks to attain a breath alcohol level of 0.10 during the evening before participation in Strategic Management Simulations. By the following morning, breath alcohol levels were measured at 0.00. Questionnaire responses indicated considerable hangover discomfort. Responses to semantic differential evaluative scales suggested that Ss evaluated their own managerial performance in the simulation setting as impaired. However, multiple measures of decision-making performance obtained in the simulation task did not show any deterioration of functioning. (PsycINFO Database Record © 2000 APA, all rights reserved)
AUTHOR	*Streufert, Siegfried;* Pogash, Rosanne; Braig, Daniela; Gingrich, Dennis; et al
AFFILIATION	Pennsylvania State U, Coll of Medicine, Dept of Behavioral Science, Hershey, USA
SOURCE	Alcoholism: Clinical & Experimental Research. 1995 Oct Vol 19(5) 1141-1146

the study. Information is provided on the subjects used, the procedures followed, and the data collection techniques employed. This description is made detailed enough to permit another researcher to attempt to replicate the study.

Results

The data obtained in the study are reported in the results section. This section often creates problems for novice readers because it includes complex statistical analyses, figures, tables, and graphs. This section does *not* include any inferences based on the data, as such conclusions are supposed to follow in the next section. Instead, it simply contains a concise summary of the raw data and the statistical analyses.

Discussion

In the discussion section you will find the conclusions drawn by the author(s). In contrast to the results section, which is a straightforward summary of empirical observations, the discussion section allows for interpretation and evaluation of the data. Implications for theory and factual knowledge in the discipline are discussed. Conclusions are usually qualified carefully, and any limitations in the study may be acknowledged. This section may also include suggestions for future research on the issue.

References

At the end of each article you will find a list of bibliographic references for any studies cited. This list permits you to examine firsthand other relevant studies mentioned in the article. The references list is often a rich source of leads about other articles that are germane to the topic that you are looking into.

For additional hints on reading journal articles, see the paper published by two psychologists writing at the University of Waterloo, Christian Jordan and Mark Zanna (1999).

REVIEW OF KEY POINTS

- Journals publish technical and scholarly material. Usually they are written for other professionals in a narrow area of inquiry. In psychology, most journal articles are reports of original research.

- PsycINFO is a computerized database that contains brief summaries of newly published journal articles, books, and chapters in edited books. Works on specific topics and publications by specific authors can be found by using the search mechanisms built into the database.

- Computerized literature searches can be much more powerful and precise than manual searches. The information contained in PsycINFO is also available in a monthly print journal called *Psychological Abstracts.*

- Journal articles are easier to understand if one is familiar with the standard format. Most articles include six elements: abstract, introduction, method, results, discussion, and references.

The Perils of Anecdotal Evidence: "I Have a Friend Who ..."

Here's a tough problem. Suppose you are the judge in a family law court. As you look over the cases that will come before you today, you see that one divorcing couple has managed to settle almost all of the important decisions with minimal conflict—such as who gets the house, who gets the car and the dog, and who pays which bills. However, there is one crucial issue left: Each parent wants custody of the children, and because they could not reach an agreement on their own, the case is now in your court. You will need the wisdom of the legendary King Solomon for this decision. How can you determine what is in the best interests of the children?

Child custody decisions have major consequences for all of the parties involved. As you review the case records, you see that both parents are loving and competent, so there are no obvious reasons for selecting one parent over the other as the primary caretaker. In considering various alternatives, you mull over the possibility of awarding *joint custody,* an arrangement in which the children spend half their time with each parent, instead of the more usual arrangement where one parent has primary custody and the other has visitation rights. Joint custody seems to have some obvious benefits, but you are not sure how well these arrangements actually work. Will the children feel more attached to both parents if the parents share custody equally? Or will the children feel hassled by always moving around, perhaps spending half the week at one parent's home and half at the other parent's home? Can parents who are already feuding over child custody issues make these complicated arrangements work? Or is joint custody just too disruptive to everyone's life? You really don't know the answer to any of these vexing questions.

Anecdotes readily sway people because they often are concrete, vivid, and memorable.

One of the lawyers involved in the case knows that you are thinking about the possibility of joint custody. She also understands that you want more information about how well joint custody tends to work before you render a decision. To help you make up your mind, she tells you about a divorced couple that has had a joint custody arrangement for many years and offers to have them appear in court to describe their experiences "firsthand." They and their children can answer any questions you might have about the pros and cons of joint custody. They should be in the best position to know how well joint custody works because they are living it. Sounds like a reasonable plan. What do you think?

Hopefully, you said, "No, No, No!" What's wrong with asking someone who's been there how well joint custody works? The crux of the problem is that the evidence a single family brings to the question of joint custody is **anecdotal evidence, which consists of personal stories about specific incidents and experiences.** Anecdotal evidence can be very seductive. For example, one study found that psychology majors' choices of future courses to enroll in were influenced more by a couple of students' brief anecdotes than by extensive statistics on many other students' ratings of the courses from the previous term (Borgida & Nisbett, 1977). Anecdotes readily sway people because they often are concrete, vivid, and memo-

The Biological Bases of Behaviour

Most people seem to have an almost endless fascination with the human brain. And why not? It is assumed to be the basis of most of what differentiates us from other mammals—language, reasoning, consciousness, the self, and many other human qualities and characteristics. When it is working well, so are we. When it encounters difficulties, the problems can be both overwhelming and intriguing, and these problems generate many questions about the brain. Why do people with Alzheimer's forget central things about themselves and those they love, perhaps even being unable to recognize their own spouse or children? If someone suffers a stroke, why does language sometimes disappear, but not always? Why does the accompanying paralysis show up on the opposite side of the body relative to the side of the brain in which the stroke occurred? Why are athletes such as Toronto Maple Leaf Eric Lindros so disoriented after suffering a concussion? The study of the brain and its connections to behaviour is one of the focal topics in this chapter.

There are few more rapidly developing areas of research than biological approaches to psychology, especially neuropsychology, the study of the brain. The study of the brain is one of those areas of psychology where Canadian researchers have made pivotal discoveries (Hayman-Abello, Hayman-Abello, & Rourke, 2003). After reading this chapter, you will be familiar with the pioneering contributions of senior Canadian scholars such as Wilder Penfield, Donald Hebb, and Brenda Milner. Even before you read this chapter, however, you may have heard about the work of neuroscientists such as McMaster University's Sandra Witelson or Dalhousie University's John Connolly.

Sandra Witelson, who is well known for her research and for having one of the most extensive collections of preserved human brains, was given the opportunity to study one of the world's most famous brains—that of Albert Einstein. The tale of how Einstein's brain got to Witelson is fascinating in itself and has been the subject of numerous articles and Carolyn Abraham's (2002) recent book *Possessing Genius*. Einstein died in April 1955 from a ruptured

aneurysm for which he had previously refused surgery. His brain was removed by Tom Harvey, a hospital pathologist. It was injected with formalin to preserve it at that time. Einstein's eyes were taken by his friend Henry Abrams, an ophthalmologist, who kept them in a safety deposit box. Einstein was eventually cremated, and Harvey took the brain with him. Over the years, he had donated some small pieces of the brain for analysis but was waiting for the right person who could conduct a scientific examination of the brain. Eventually, Harvey read about the scientific work of Sandra Witelson and offered her the brain. He drove across the border in 1996 with Einstein's brain in the trunk of his car and delivered it to her.

Witelson examined and measured the pieces of the brain and examined photos originally taken of the brain. She compared the results of her examination of Einstein's brain with other "control" brains she had in her laboratory. Witelson found that Einstein's brain seemed highly similar overall to most other brains; it was about the same size and weight (Witelson, Kigar, & Harvey, 1999). But there were a couple of important exceptions, including a wider parietal region and distinct sylvian fissure. Witelson speculated that these differences made sense in light of Einstein's intellect and approach to science: "Visuospatial cognition, mathematical thought, and imagery of movement are strongly dependent on this region. Einstein's exceptional intellect in these cognitive domains and his self-described mode of scientific thinking may be related to the atypical anatomy in his inferior parietal lobules" (Witelson et al., 1999, p. 2152).

One of the enduring mysteries in the study of the brain is in terms of localization of function—discovering which parts of the brain are associated with specific behaviours and functions. In this chapter you will learn about the parts of the brain and their functions. We will also describe the wide range of techniques that neuroscientists have to assist them in their research. One traditional method was to examine the electrical activity of the brain through EEG recordings.

Dalhousie's John Connolly used EEG to unravel the mystery surrounding one of the brains he became involved with. This brain was also remarkable, but it was remarkable in quite a different way. It belonged to a young man who had general aphasia and whose cognitive status could not be ascertained in traditional ways. While working at a bar, the 21-year-old man was stabbed in the head, more specifically in the left temporal region, with a 30-cm knife. At the hospital, the staff needed to determine whether he would benefit from rehabilitation; it seemed that he was in a vegetative state and that recovery was unlikely. Rehabilitation seemed not to be warranted. But no one really knew his cognitive status, because he could not communicate in any way with others. The possibility existed that he was alert but trapped in an unresponsive body, a victim of locked-in syndrome. Connolly devised an inno-vative method (Connolly & D'Arcy, 2000) of assessing the patient's status by recording EEG responses to carefully selected stimuli that were presented to the patient (Connolly, Mate-Kole, & Joyce, 1999). As we will describe later in this chapter, the brain responds with measurable electrical activity when stimulated. On the basis of this assessment, Connolly and his colleagues were optimistic about the patient's chances for recovery. Rehabilitation was successfully reinstated and the patient experienced substantial recovery.

While much of the research you will read about in this chapter is not as dramatic as these two examples, it has the potential for unlocking some of the mysteries of the brain and improving the lives of individuals suffering from various types of disorders. The research discussed in this chapter will consider the countless ways that biology is fundamental to the study of behaviour.

Communication in the Nervous System

PREVIEW QUESTIONS
- What are the key parts of the neuron, and what are their functions?
- What is an action potential?
- How does synaptic transmission take place?
- Which neurotransmitters regulate which aspects of behaviour?

Imagine that you are watching a scary movie. As the tension mounts, your palms sweat and your heart beats faster. You begin shovelling popcorn into your mouth, carelessly spilling some in your lap. If someone were to ask you what you are doing at this moment, you would probably say, "Nothing—just watching the movie." Yet some highly complex processes are occurring without your thinking about them. A stimulus (the light from the screen) is striking your eye. Almost instantaneously, your brain is interpreting the light stimulus, and signals are flashing to other parts of your body, leading to a flurry of activity. Your sweat glands are releasing perspiration, your heartbeat is quickening, and muscular movements are enabling your hand to find the popcorn and, more or less successfully, lift it to your mouth.

Even in this simple example, you can see that behaviour depends on rapid information processing. Information travels almost instantaneously from your eye to your brain, from your brain to the muscles of your arm and hand, and from your palms back to your brain. In essence, your nervous system is a complex communication network in which signals are constantly being transmitted, received, and integrated. The nervous system handles information, just as the circulatory system handles blood. In this section, we take a close look at communication in the nervous system.

Nervous Tissue: The Basic Hardware

Your nervous system is living tissue composed of cells. The cells in the nervous system fall into two major categories: *glia* and *neurons*. Glia are cells found throughout the nervous system that provide structural support, nourishment, and insulation for neurons. Glia cells are also involved in the removal of waste. Glia (literally "glue") help maintain the chemical environment of the neurons, which promotes more efficient signalling in the nervous system (Kandel, 2000). **Neurons are individual cells in the nervous system that receive, integrate, and transmit information.** They are the basic links that permit communication within the nervous system. The vast majority of them communicate only with other neurons. However, a small minority receive signals from outside the nervous system (from sensory organs) or carry messages from the nervous system to the muscles that move the body.

A highly simplified drawing of two "typical" neurons is shown in Figure 3.1. Actually, neurons come in such a tremendous variety of types and shapes that no single drawing can adequately represent them. Trying to draw the "typical" neuron is like trying to draw the "typical" tree. In spite of this diversity, the drawing in Figure 3.1 highlights some common features of neurons.

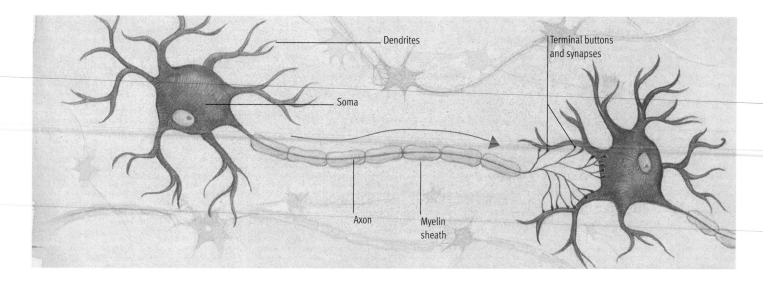

The *soma,* or cell body, contains the cell nucleus and much of the chemical machinery common to most cells (*soma* is Greek for "body"). The rest of the neuron is devoted exclusively to handling information. The neurons in Figure 3.1 have a number of branched, feeler-like structures called *dendritic trees* (*dendrite* is a Greek word for "tree"). Each individual branch is a *dendrite.* **Dendrites are the parts of a neuron that are specialized to receive information.** Most neurons receive information from many other cells—sometimes thousands of others—and so have extensive dendritic trees.

From the many dendrites, information flows into the cell body and then travels away from the soma along the *axon* (from the Greek for "axle"). **The *axon* is a long, thin fibre that transmits signals away from the soma to other neurons or to muscles or glands.** Axons may be quite long (sometimes over a metre), and they may branch off to communicate with a number of other cells.

In humans, many axons are wrapped in cells with a high concentration of a white, fatty substance called *myelin.* **The *myelin sheath* is insulating material, derived from glial cells, that encases some axons.** The myelin sheath speeds up the transmission of signals that move along axons. If an axon's myelin sheath deteriorates, its signals may not be transmitted effectively. The loss of muscle control seen with the disease *multiple sclerosis* is due to a degeneration of myelin sheaths (Schwartz & Westbrook, 2000).

The axon ends in a cluster of **terminal buttons, which are small knobs that secrete chemicals called neurotransmitters.** These chemicals serve as messengers that may activate neighbouring neurons. The points at which neurons interconnect are called *synapses.* **A *synapse* is a junction where informa-tion is transmitted from one neuron to another** (*synapse* is from the Greek for "junction").

To summarize, information is received at the dendrites, is passed through the soma and along the axon, and is transmitted to the dendrites of other cells at meeting points called synapses. Unfortunately, this nice, simple picture has more exceptions than the Income Tax Act. For example, some neurons do not have an axon, while others have multiple axons. Also, although neurons typically synapse on the dendrites of other cells, they may also synapse on a soma or an axon. Despite these and other complexities, however, the fundamental function of neurons is clear: they are the nervous system's input–output devices that transmit, receive, and integrate informational signals.

The Neural Impulse: Using Energy to Send Information

What happens when a neuron is stimulated? What is the nature of the signal—the *neural impulse*—that moves through the neuron? These were the questions that Alan Hodgkin and Andrew Huxley set out to answer in their groundbreaking experiments with axons removed from squid. Why did they choose to work with squid axons? Because the squid has a pair of "giant" axons that are about a hundred times larger than those in humans (which still makes them only about as thick as a human hair). Their large size permitted Hodgkin and Huxley to insert fine wires called *microelectrodes* into them. By using the microelectrodes to record the electrical activity in individual neurons, Hodgkin and Huxley unravelled the mystery of the neural impulse.

Figure 3.1

Structure of the neuron.
Neurons are the communication links of the nervous system. This diagram highlights the key parts of a neuron, including specialized receptor areas (dendrites), the cell body (soma), the axon fibre along which impulses are transmitted, and the terminal buttons, which release chemical messengers that carry signals to other neurons. Neurons vary considerably in size and shape and are usually densely interconnected.

The Neuron at Rest: A Tiny Battery

Hodgkin and Huxley (1952) learned that the neural impulse is a complex electrochemical reaction. Both inside and outside the neuron are fluids containing electrically charged atoms and molecules called *ions*. The cell membrane is semi-permeable, permitting movement of some ions. Positively charged sodium and potassium ions and negatively charged chloride ions flow back and forth across the cell membrane, but they do not cross at the same rate. The difference in flow rates leads to a slightly higher concentration of negatively charged ions inside the cell. The resulting voltage means that the neuron at rest is a tiny battery, a store of potential energy. **The *resting potential* of a neuron is its stable, negative charge when the cell is inactive.** As shown in Figure 3.2(a), this charge is about –70 millivolts, roughly one-twentieth of the voltage of a flashlight battery.

The Action Potential

As long as the voltage of a neuron remains constant, the cell is quiet, and no messages are being sent. When the neuron is stimulated, channels in its cell membrane open, briefly allowing positively charged sodium ions to rush in, as shown in Figure 3.2(c). For an instant, the neuron's charge is less negative, or even positive, creating an action potential (Koester & Siegelbaum, 2000). **An *action potential* is a very brief shift in a neuron's electrical charge that travels along an axon.** The firing of an action potential is reflected in the voltage spike shown in Figure 3.2(b). Like a spark travelling along a trail of gunpowder, the voltage change races down the axon.

After the firing of an action potential, the channels in the cell membrane that opened to let in sodium close up, as shown in Figure 3.2(d) and (e). Some time is needed before they are ready to open again, and until that time the neuron cannot fire. **The *absolute refractory period* is the minimum length of time after an action potential during which another action potential cannot begin.** This "down time" isn't very long, only 1 or 2 milliseconds. It is followed by a brief *relative refractory period*. During the relative refractory period, the neuron can fire, but its threshold for firing is elevated, so more intense stimulation is required to initiate an action potential.

The All-or-None Law

The neural impulse is an all-or-none proposition, like firing a gun. You can't half-fire a gun. The same is true of the neuron's firing of action potentials. Either the neuron fires or it doesn't, and its action potentials are

all the same size (Kandel, 2000). That is, weaker stimuli do not produce smaller action potentials.

Even though the action potential is an all-or-nothing event, neurons *can* convey information about the strength of a stimulus. They do so by varying the *rate* at which they fire action potentials. In general, a stronger stimulus will cause a cell to fire a more rapid volley of neural impulses than a weaker stimulus will.

Various neurons transmit neural impulses at different speeds. For example, thicker axons transmit neural impulses more rapidly than thinner ones do. Although neural impulses do not travel as fast as electricity along a wire, they *are* very fast, moving at up to 100 metres per second, which is equivalent to more than 300 kilometres per hour. The entire, complicated process of neural transmission takes only a few thousandths of a second. In the time it has taken you to read this description of the neural impulse, billions of such impulses have been transmitted in your nervous system!

The Synapse: Where Neurons Meet

In the nervous system, the neural impulse functions as a signal. For that signal to have any meaning for the system as a whole, it must be transmitted from the neuron to other cells. As noted earlier, this transmission takes place at special junctions called *synapses*, which depend on *chemical* messengers.

Sending Signals: Chemicals as Couriers

A "typical" synapse is shown in Figure 3.3. The first thing that you should notice is that the two neurons don't actually touch. They are separated by the **synaptic cleft, a microscopic gap between the terminal button of one neuron and the cell membrane of another neuron.** Signals have to cross this gap to permit neurons to communicate. In this situation, the neuron that sends a signal across the gap is called the *presynaptic neuron*, and the neuron that receives the signal is called the *postsynaptic neuron*.

How do messages travel across the gaps between neurons? The arrival of an action potential at an axon's terminal buttons triggers the release of **neurotransmitters—chemicals that transmit information from one neuron to another.** Within the buttons, most of these chemicals are stored in small sacs, called *synaptic vesicles*. The neurotransmitters are released when a vesicle fuses with the membrane of the presynaptic cell and its contents spill into the synaptic cleft. After their release, neurotransmitters

Figure 3.2

The neural impulse. The electric charge of a neuron can be measured with a pair of electrodes connected to an oscilloscope. **(a)** At rest, the neuron is like a tiny wet battery with a resting potential of about −70 millivolts. **(b)** When a neuron is stimulated, a sharp jump in its electric potential occurs, resulting in a spike on the oscilloscope recording of the neuron's electrical activity. This change in voltage, called an action potential, travels along the axon.
(c) Biochemical changes propel the action potential along the axon. An action potential begins when sodium gates in the membrane of an axon open, permitting positively charged sodium ions to flow into the axon. **(d)** The potassium gates have opened to let potassium ions flow outward. At the next point along the axon membrane, sodium gates open and the process is repeated, thus allowing the action potential to move along the axon.
(e) This blowup of the voltage spike associated with an action potential depicts how these biochemical changes relate to the electrical activity of the cell.

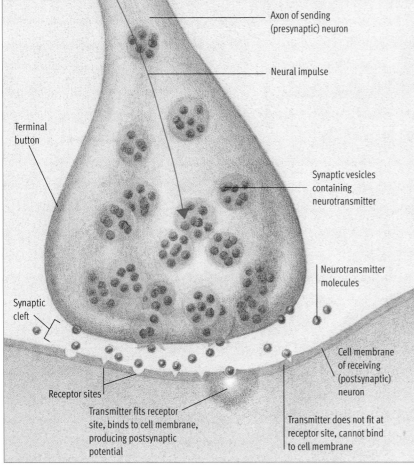

Axon of sending
(presynaptic) neuron

Neural impulse

Terminal
button

Synaptic vesicles
containing
neurotransmitter

Neurotransmitter
molecules

Synaptic
cleft

Cell membrane
of receiving
(postsynaptic)
neuron

Receptor sites

Transmitter fits receptor
site, binds to cell membrane,
producing postsynaptic
potential

Transmitter does not fit at
receptor site, cannot bind
to cell membrane

Figure 3.3

The synapse. When a neural impulse reaches an axon's terminal buttons, it triggers the release of chemical messengers called neurotransmitters. The neurotransmitter molecules diffuse across the synaptic cleft and bind to receptor sites on the postsynaptic neuron. A specific neurotransmitter can bind only to receptor sites that its molecular structure will fit into, much like a key must fit a lock.

diffuse across the synaptic cleft to the membrane of the receiving cell. There they may bind with special molecules in the postsynaptic cell membrane at various *receptor sites*. These sites are specifically "tuned" to recognize and respond to some neurotransmitters but not to others.

Receiving Signals: Postsynaptic Potentials

When a neurotransmitter and a receptor molecule combine, reactions in the cell membrane cause a *postsynaptic potential (PSP),* **a voltage change at a receptor site on a postsynaptic cell membrane.** Postsynaptic potentials do *not* follow the all-or-none

law as action potentials do. Instead, postsynaptic potentials are *graded.* That is, they vary in size and they increase or decrease the *probability* of a neural impulse in the receiving cell in proportion to the amount of voltage change.

Two types of messages can be sent from cell to cell: excitatory and inhibitory. **An *excitatory PSP* is a positive voltage shift that increases the likelihood that the postsynaptic neuron will fire action potentials. An *inhibitory PSP* is a negative voltage shift that decreases the likelihood that the postsynaptic neuron will fire action potentials.** The direction of the voltage shift, and thus the nature of the PSP (excitatory or inhibitory), depends on which receptor sites are activated in the postsynaptic neuron (Kandel, 2000).

The excitatory or inhibitory effects produced at a synapse last only a fraction of a second. Then neurotransmitters drift away from receptor sites or are inactivated by enzymes that metabolize (convert) them into inactive forms. Most are reabsorbed into the presynaptic neuron through *reuptake,* **a process in which neurotransmitters are sponged up from the synaptic cleft by the presynaptic membrane.** Reuptake allows synapses to recycle their materials. Reuptake and the other key processes in synaptic transmission are summarized in Figure 3.4.

Integrating Signals: Neural Networks

A neuron may receive a symphony of signals from *thousands* of other neurons. The same neuron may pass its messages along to thousands of neurons as well. Thus, a neuron must do a great deal more than simply relay messages it receives. It must *integrate* signals arriving at many synapses before it "decides" whether to fire a neural impulse. If enough excitatory PSPs occur in a neuron, the electrical currents can add up, causing the cell's voltage to reach the threshold at which an action potential will be fired. However, if many inhibitory PSPs also occur, they will tend to cancel the effects of excitatory PSPs. Thus, the state of the neuron is a weighted balance between excitatory and inhibitory influences (Kandel & Siegelbaum, 2000).

As Rita Carter (1998, p. 19) has pointed out in *Mapping the Mind,* "The firing of a single neuron is not enough to create the twitch of an eyelid in sleep, let alone a conscious impression.... Millions of neurons must fire in unison to produce the most trifling thought." Most neurons are interlinked in complex chains, pathways, circuits, and networks. Our perceptions, thoughts, and actions depend on *patterns* of neural activity in elaborate neural networks. These

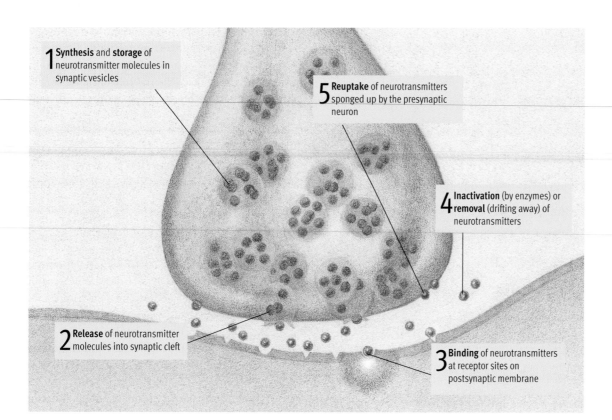

1 **Synthesis** and **storage** of neurotransmitter molecules in synaptic vesicles

5 **Reuptake** of neurotransmitters sponged up by the presynaptic neuron

4 **Inactivation** (by enzymes) or **removal** (drifting away) of neurotransmitters

2 **Release** of neurotransmitter molecules into synaptic cleft

3 **Binding** of neurotransmitters at receptor sites on postsynaptic membrane

Figure 3.4

Overview of synaptic transmission. The main elements in synaptic transmission are summarized here, superimposed on a blowup of the synapse seen in Figure 3.3. The five key processes involved in communication at synapses are (1) synthesis and storage, (2) release, (3) binding, (4) inactivation or removal, and (5) reuptake of neurotransmitters. As you'll see in this chapter and the remainder of the book, the effects of many phenomena—such as pain, drug use, and some diseases—can be explained in terms of how they alter one or more of these processes (usually at synapses releasing a specific neurotransmitter).

networks consist of interconnected neurons that frequently fire together or sequentially to perform certain functions (Song et al., 2005). The links in these networks are fluid, as new synaptic connections may be made while some old connections wither away (Hua & Smith, 2004). Ironically, the *elimination of old synapses* appears to play a larger role in the sculpting of neural networks than the *creation of new synapses*. The nervous system normally forms more synapses than needed and then gradually eliminates the less active synapses. For example, the number of synapses in the human visual cortex peaks at around age one and then declines, as diagrammed in Figure 3.5 (Huttenlocher, 1994). Thus, *synaptic pruning* is a key process in the formation of the neural networks that are crucial to communication in the nervous system.

The linkage of neurons to form networks was the focus of the work of McGill University's Donald Hebb (to whom you were introduced in Chapter 1). Hebb's influential text *The Organization of Behavior* (Hebb, 1949) contained his analysis of the neural basis of behaviour and served to highlight his view that understanding the brain and its processes was fundamental to understanding behaviour. He realized that neurons do not act alone in influencing behaviour but that they are linked in complex networks or *cell assemblies*. One of his important contributions was the *Hebbian Learning Rule* specifying how these linkages might operate and come about.

In his well-known neurophysiological postulate he said, "When an axon of cell A is near enough to excite a cell B and repeatedly or persistently takes part in firing it, some growth process or metabolic change takes place in one or both cells such that A's efficiency, as one of the cells firing B, is increased" (Hebb, 1949, p. 62). Thus, one neuron stimulating

CONCEPT **CHECK 3.1**

Understanding Nervous System Hardware Using Metaphors

A useful way to learn about the structures and functions of parts of the nervous system is through metaphors. Check your understanding of the basic components of the nervous system by matching the metaphorical descriptions below with the correct terms in the following list: (a) glia, (b) neuron, (c) soma, (d) dendrite, (e) axon, (f) myelin, (g) terminal button, (h) synapse. You'll find the answers in Appendix A.

_____ **1.** Like a tree. Also, each branch is a telephone wire that carries incoming messages to you.

_____ **2.** Like the insulation that covers electrical wires.

_____ **3.** Like a silicon chip in a computer that receives and transmits information between input and output devices as well as between other chips.

_____ **4.** Like an electrical cable that carries information.

_____ **5.** Like the maintenance personnel who keep things clean and in working order so the operations of the enterprise can proceed.

_____ **6.** Like the nozzle at the end of a hose, from which water is squirted.

_____ **7.** Like a railroad junction, where two trains may meet.

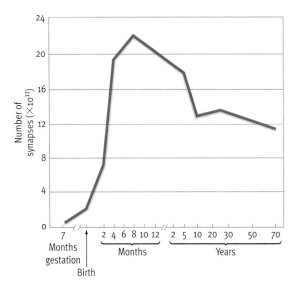

24

20

16

Number of
synapses (×10¹¹)

12

8

4

0

7
Months
gestation

Birth

2 4 6 8 10 12

Months

2 5 10 20 30   50 70

Years

Figure 3.5

Synaptic pruning. This graph summarizes data on the estimated number of synapses in the human visual cortex as a function of age (Huttenlocher, 1994). As you can see, the number of synapses in this area of the brain peaks around age one and then mostly declines over the course of the life span. This decline reflects the process of *synaptic pruning*, which involves the gradual elimination of less active synapses.

Source: Data based on Huttenlocher, P.R. (1994). Synaptogenesis in human cerebral cortex. In G. Dawson & K.W. Fischer (Eds.), *Human behavior and the developing brain*. New York: Guilford Press. Graphic adapted from Kolb, B. & Whishaw, I. Q. (2001). *An introduction to brain and behavior*. New York: Worth Publishers.

Web Link 3.2

Molecular Neurobiology: A Gallery of Animations
http://www.neuroguide.com/cajal _gallery.html

Site editor and physician Neil Busis brings together a set of QuickTime animations demonstrating activities at the molecular level of the synapse, such as the fusion of synaptic vesicles with the presynaptic membrane.

another neuron repeatedly produces changes in the synapse; learning has taken place. These ideas were foreshadowed by Hebb's earlier work on his master's thesis conducted in 1932 (Milner, 2003).

Although Hebb could not specify the exact character of the changes (Posner & Rothbart, 2004), he did speculate about their metabolic nature. His ideas are often referred to as the Hebb Synapse and continue to influence work today (Hinton, 2003; Milner, 2003; Sejnowski, 2003). Hebb's 1949 text set the stage for a focus on neurophysiology and has been listed as number four of the 100 most influential publications in cognitive science (Tees, 2003). Remarkably, over 50 years after its publication, it has been recently reissued (Hebb, 2002) and continues to serve as an important resource in neuroscience.

Neurotransmitters and Behaviour

2B, 4D

As we have seen, the nervous system relies on chemical couriers to communicate information between neurons. These *neurotransmitters* are fundamental to behaviour, playing a key role in everything from muscle movements to moods and mental health.

You might guess that the nervous system would require only two neurotransmitters—one for excitatory potentials and one for inhibitory potentials. In reality, there are nine well-established, classic (small-molecule) transmitters, about 40 additional neuropeptide chemicals that function, at least part-time, as neurotransmitters, and a handful of recently recognized "novel" neurotransmitters (Snyder, 2002). As scientists continue to discover new and increasingly diverse transmitter substances, they are being forced to re-evaluate their criteria regarding what qualifies as a neurotransmitter (Snyder & Ferris, 2000).

Specific neurotransmitters work at specific kinds of synapses. You may recall that transmitters deliver their messages by binding to receptor sites on the postsynaptic membrane. However, a transmitter cannot bind to just any site. The binding process operates much like a lock and key, as was shown in Figure 3.3 (page 82). Just as a key has to fit a lock to work, a transmitter has to fit into a receptor site for binding to occur. Hence, specific transmitters can deliver signals only at certain locations on cell membranes.

Why are there many neurotransmitters, each of which works only at certain synapses? This variety and specificity reduces cross-talk between densely packed neurons, making the nervous system's communication more precise. Let's briefly review some of the most interesting findings about how neurotransmitters regulate behaviour, which are summarized in Table 3.1.

Acetylcholine

The discovery that cells communicate by releasing chemicals was first made in connection with the transmitter *acetylcholine* (ACh). ACh has been found throughout the nervous system. It is the only transmitter between motor neurons and voluntary muscles. Every move you make—typing, walking, talking, breathing—depends on ACh released to your muscles by motor neurons (Kandel & Siegelbaum, 2000). ACh appears to contribute to attention, arousal, and perhaps memory.

The activity of ACh (and other neurotransmitters) may be influenced by other chemicals in the brain. Although synaptic receptor sites are sensitive to specific neurotransmitters, sometimes they can be "fooled" by other chemical substances. For example, if you smoke tobacco, some of your ACh synapses will be stimulated by the nicotine that arrives in your brain. At these synapses, the nicotine acts like ACh itself. It binds to receptor sites for ACh, causing postsynaptic potentials (PSPs). In technical language, nicotine is an ACh agonist. **An *agonist* is a chemical that mimics the action of a neurotransmitter.**

Table 3.1 Common Neurotransmitters and Some of Their Functions

Neurotransmitter	Functions and Characteristics
Acetylcholine (ACh)	Activates motor neurons controlling skeletal muscles Contributes to the regulation of attention, arousal, and memory Some ACh receptors stimulated by nicotine
Dopamine (DA)	Contributes to control of voluntary movement, pleasurable emotions Decreased levels associated with Parkinson's disease Overactivity at DA synapses associated with schizophrenia Cocaine and amphetamines elevate activity at DA synapses
Norepinephrine (NE)	Contributes to modulation of mood and arousal Cocaine and amphetamines elevate activity at NE synapses
Serotonin	Involved in regulation of sleep and wakefulness, eating, aggression Abnormal levels may contribute to depression and obsessive-compulsive disorder Prozac and similar antidepressant drugs affect serotonin circuits
GABA	Serves as widely distributed inhibitory transmitter Valium and similar antianxiety drugs work at GABA synapses
Endorphins	Resemble opiate drugs in structure and effects Contribute to pain relief and perhaps to some pleasurable emotions

Not all chemicals that fool synaptic receptors are agonists. Some chemicals bind to receptors but fail to produce a PSP (the key slides into the lock, but it doesn't work). In effect, they temporarily *block* the action of the natural transmitter by occupying its receptor sites, rendering them unusable. Thus, they act as antagonists. **An *antagonist* is a chemical that opposes the action of a neurotransmitter.** For example, the drug *curare* is an ACh antagonist. It blocks action at the same ACh synapses that are fooled by nicotine. As a result, muscles are unable to move. Some South American natives use a form of curare on arrows. If they wound an animal, the curare blocks the synapses from nerve to muscle, paralyzing the animal.

Monoamines

 2B, 4D

The *monoamines* include three neurotransmitters: dopamine, norepinephrine, and serotonin. Neurons using these transmitters regulate many aspects of everyday behaviour. Dopamine (DA), for example, is used by neurons that control voluntary movements. The degeneration of such neurons apparently causes *Parkinsonism,* a disease marked by tremors, muscular rigidity, and reduced control over voluntary movements (DeLong, 2000).

Although other neurotransmitters are also involved, serotonin-releasing neurons appear to play a prominent role in the regulation of sleep and wakefulness (Vodelholzer et al., 1998) and eating behaviour (Blundell & Halford, 1998). There also is considerable

evidence that neural circuits using serotonin modulate aggressive behaviour in animals (Bernhardt, 1997), and some preliminary evidence relating serotonin activity to aggression and impulsive behaviour in humans (Dolan, Anderson, & Deakin, 2001; Nelson & Chiavegatto, 2001; Douzenis et al., 2004).

Abnormal levels of monoamines in the brain have been related to the development of certain psychological disorders. For example, people who suffer from depression appear to have lowered levels of activation at norepinephrine (NE) and serotonin synapses. Although a host of other biochemical changes may also contribute to depression, abnormalities at NE and serotonin synapses appear to play a central role, as most antidepressant drugs exert their main effects at these synapses (Sher & Mann, 2003; Thase, Jindel, & Howland, 2002).

In a similar fashion, abnormalities in activity at dopamine synapses have been implicated in the development of *schizophrenia*. This severe mental illness is marked by irrational thought, hallucinations, poor contact with reality, and deterioration of routine adaptive behaviour. Afflicting roughly 1% of the population, schizophrenia requires hospitalization more often than any other psychological disorder (see Chapter 14). Studies suggest, albeit with many complications, that overactivity at DA synapses is the neurochemical basis for schizophrenia. Why? Primarily because the therapeutic drugs that tame schizophrenic symptoms are known to be DA antagonists that reduce the neurotransmitter's activity (Tamminga & Carlsson, 2003).

Web Link 3.3

Neurosciences on the Internet
http://www.neuroguide.com/
Dr. Neil Busis has gathered what appears to be the largest collection of neuroscience links currently on the Web and provides a search engine to help visitors.

Temporary alterations at monoamine synapses also appear to account for the powerful effects of some widely abused drugs, including amphetamines and cocaine. Amphetamines and cocaine seem to exert most of their effects by creating a storm of increased activity at dopamine and norepinephrine synapses (Gold & Miller, 1997; Repetto & Gold, 2005; King & Ellinwood, 2005).

GABA

Another group of transmitters consists of *amino acids*. Two of these, *gamma-aminobutyric acid* (GABA) and *glycine*, are notable in that they seem to produce only *inhibitory* postsynaptic potentials. Some transmitters, such as ACh and NE, are versatile. They can produce either excitatory or inhibitory PSPs, depending on the synaptic receptors they bind to. However, GABA and glycine appear to have inhibitory effects at virtually all synapses where either is present. GABA receptors are widely distributed in the brain and may be present at 40% of all synapses. GABA appears to be responsible for much of the inhibition in the central nervous system. Studies also suggest that GABA contributes to the regulation of anxiety in humans and that it plays a central role in the expression of seizures (Charney et al., 1996; Shank, Smith-Swintosky, & Twyman, 2000; Skolnick, 2003).

Endorphins

In 1970, after a horseback-riding accident, Candace Pert, a graduate student in neuroscience, lay in a hospital bed receiving frequent shots of *morphine*, a painkilling drug derived from the opium plant. This experience left her with a driving curiosity about how morphine works. A few years later, she and Solomon Snyder rocked the scientific world by showing that *morphine exerts its effects by binding to specialized receptors in the brain* (Pert & Snyder, 1973).

This discovery raised a perplexing question: Why would the brain be equipped with receptors for morphine, a powerful, addictive opiate drug not normally found in the body? It occurred to Pert and others that the nervous system must have its own, endogenous (internally produced) morphine-like substances. Investigators dubbed these as-yet undiscovered substances *endorphins*—**internally produced chemicals that resemble opiates in structure and effects.** A search for the body's natural opiate ensued. In short order, a number of endogenous, opiate-like substances were identified (Hughes et al., 1975). Subsequent studies revealed that endorphins and their receptors are widely distributed in the human body and that they clearly contribute to the modula-

tion of pain, as well as a variety of other phenomena (Basbaum & Jessell, 2000).

In this section we have highlighted just a few of the more interesting connections between neurotransmitters and behaviour. These highlights barely begin to convey the rich complexity of biochemical processes in the nervous system. Most aspects of behaviour are probably regulated by several types of transmitters. To further complicate matters, researchers are finding fascinating *interactions* between various neurotransmitter systems such as serotonin and dopamine circuits (Smith et al., 1997; Fraser et al., 2003). Although scientists have learned a great deal about neurotransmitters and behaviour, much still remains to be discovered.

REVIEW OF KEY POINTS

● Behaviour depends on complex information processing in the nervous system. Cells in the nervous system receive, integrate, and transmit information.

● Neurons are the basic communication links. They normally transmit a neural impulse along an axon to a synapse with another neuron. The neural impulse is a brief change in a neuron's electrical charge that moves along an axon. An action potential is an all-or-none event. Neurons convey information about the strength of a stimulus by variations in their rate of firing.

● Action potentials trigger the release of chemicals called neurotransmitters that diffuse across a synapse to communicate with other neurons. Transmitters bind with receptors in the postsynaptic cell membrane, causing excitatory or inhibitory PSPs.

● Whether the postsynaptic neuron fires a neural impulse depends on the balance of excitatory and inhibitory PSPs. Our thoughts and actions depend on patterns of activity in neural circuits and networks.

● The transmitter ACh plays a key role in muscular movement. Serotonin circuits may contribute to the regulation of sleep, eating, and aggression. Depression is associated with reduced activation at norepinephrine and serotonin synapses.

● Schizophrenia has been linked to overactivity at dopamine synapses. Cocaine and amphetamines appear to exert their main effects by altering activity at DA and NE synapses. GABA is an important inhibitory transmitter. Endorphins, which resemble opiates, contribute to pain relief.

"When human beings engage in various activities, it seems that neuro-juices are released that are associated with either pain or pleasure."
CANDACE PERT

"Brain research of the past decade, especially the study of neurotransmitters, has proceeded at a furious pace, achieving progress equal in scope to all the accomplishments of the preceding 50 years—and the pace of discovery continues to accelerate."
SOLOMON SNYDER

Linking Brain Chemistry to Behaviour

Check your understanding of relations between brain chemistry and behaviour by indicating which neurotransmitters have been linked to the phenomena listed below. Choose your answers from the following list: (a) acetylcholine, (b) norepinephrine, (c) dopamine, (d) serotonin, (e) endorphins. Indicate your choice (by letter) in the spaces on the left. You'll find the answers in Appendix A.

_____ **1.** A transmitter involved in the regulation of sleep, eating, and aggression.

_____ **2.** The two monoamines that have been linked to depression.

_____ **3.** Chemicals that resemble opiate drugs in structure and that are involved in pain relief.

_____ **4.** A neurotransmitter for which abnormal levels have been implicated in schizophrenia.

_____ **5.** The only neurotransmitter between motor neurons and voluntary muscles

Organization of the Nervous System

Clearly, communication in the nervous system is fundamental to behaviour. So far we have looked at how individual cells communicate with one another. In this section, we examine the organization of the nervous system as a whole.

Experts estimate that there are roughly *100 billion* neurons in the human brain (Kandel, 2000). The multitudes of neurons in your nervous system have to work together to keep information flowing effectively. To see how the nervous system is organized to accomplish this end, we will divide it into parts. In many instances, the parts will be divided once again. Figure 3.6 presents an organizational chart that shows the relationships of all the parts of the nervous system.

The Peripheral Nervous System

 2B, 8C

The first and most important division separates the *central nervous system* (the brain and spinal cord) from the *peripheral nervous system* (see Figure 3.7). **The *peripheral nervous system* is made up of all those nerves that lie outside the brain and spinal cord. *Nerves* are bundles of neuron fibres (axons) that are routed together in the peripheral nervous system.** This portion of the nervous system is just what it sounds like: the part that extends outside the central nervous system. The peripheral nervous system can be subdivided into the *somatic nervous system* and the *autonomic nervous system*.

PREVIEW QUESTIONS
- What are the subdivisions of the peripheral nervous system?
- What is the difference between afferent and efferent nerves?
- What does the autonomic nervous system regulate, and what are its subdivisions?
- What is the central nervous system made up of?

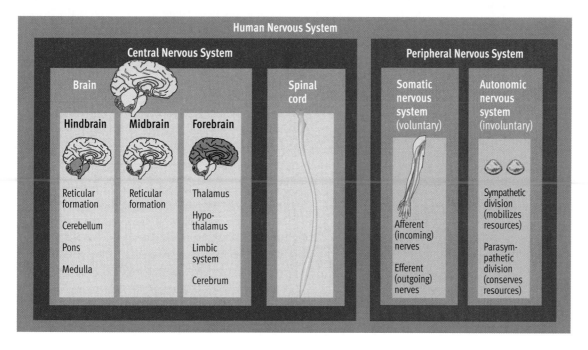

Figure 3.6

Organization of the human nervous system. This overview of the human nervous system shows the relationships of its various parts and systems. The brain is traditionally divided into three regions: the hindbrain, the midbrain, and the forebrain. The reticular formation runs through both the midbrain and the hindbrain on its way up and down the brainstem. These and other parts of the brain are discussed in detail later in the chapter. The peripheral nervous system is made up of the somatic nervous system, which controls voluntary muscles and sensory receptors, and the autonomic nervous system, which controls the involuntary activities of smooth muscles, blood vessels, and glands.

The Somatic Nervous System

The *somatic nervous system* is made up of nerves that connect to voluntary skeletal muscles and to sensory receptors. These nerves are the cables that carry information from receptors in the skin, muscles, and joints to the central nervous system and that carry commands from the CNS to the muscles. These functions require two kinds of nerve fibres. *Afferent nerve fibres* are axons that carry information inward to the central nervous system from the periphery of the body. *Efferent nerve fibres* are axons that carry information outward from the central nervous system to the periphery of the body. Each body nerve contains many axons of each type. Thus, somatic nerves are "two-way streets" with incoming (afferent) and outgoing (efferent) lanes. The somatic nervous system lets you feel the world and move around in it.

The Autonomic Nervous System

The *autonomic nervous system (ANS)* is made up of nerves that connect to the heart, blood vessels, smooth muscles, and glands. As its name hints, the autonomic system is a separate (autonomous) system, although it is ultimately governed by the central nervous system. The autonomic nervous system controls automatic, involuntary, visceral functions that people don't normally think about, such as heart rate, digestion, and perspiration (see Figure 3.8).

Figure 3.7

The central and peripheral nervous systems.
The central nervous system consists of the brain and the spinal cord. The peripheral nervous system consists of the remaining nerves that fan out throughout the body. The peripheral nervous system is divided into the somatic nervous system, which is shown in red, and the autonomic nervous system, which is shown in blue.

Source: Graphic from Nairne, J. (2000). *Psychology: The adaptive mind.* Belmont, CA: Wadsworth. © 2000 Wadsworth Publishing. Reprinted by permission.

The autonomic nervous system mediates much of the physiological arousal that occurs when people experience emotions. For example, imagine that you are walking home alone one night when a seedy-looking character falls in behind you and begins to follow you. If you feel threatened, your heart rate and breathing will speed up. Your blood pressure may surge, you may get goosebumps, and your palms may begin to sweat. These difficult-to-control reactions are aspects of autonomic arousal.

Walter Cannon (1932), one of the first psychologists to study this reaction, called it the *fight-or-flight response.* Cannon carefully monitored this response in cats—after confronting them with dogs. He concluded that organisms generally respond to threat by preparing physiologically for attacking (fight) or fleeing (flight) from the enemy. Unfortunately, as you will see in Chapter 13, this fight-or-flight response can backfire if stress leaves a person in a chronic state of autonomic arousal. According to McGill's Hans Selye (1974), prolonged autonomic arousal can eventually contribute to the development of physical diseases.

The autonomic nervous system can be subdivided into two branches: the sympathetic division and the parasympathetic division (see Figure 3.8). **The *sympathetic division* is the branch of the autonomic nervous system that mobilizes the body's resources for emergencies.** It creates the fight-or-flight response. Activation of the sympathetic division slows digestive processes and drains blood from the periphery, lessening bleeding in the case of an injury. Key sympathetic nerves send signals to the adrenal glands, triggering the release of hormones that ready the body for exertion. In contrast, **the *parasympathetic division* is the branch of the autonomic nervous system that generally conserves bodily resources.** It activates processes that allow the body to save and store energy. For example, actions by parasympathetic nerves slow heart rate, reduce blood pressure, and promote digestion.

The Central Nervous System

The central nervous system is the portion of the nervous system that lies within the skull and spinal column (see Figure 3.7). Thus, **the *central nervous system (CNS)* consists of the brain and the spinal cord.** It is protected by enclosing sheaths called the *meninges* (hence *meningitis,* the name for the disease in which the meninges become inflamed). In addition, the central nervous system is bathed in its own special nutritive "soup," the cerebrospinal fluid. **The *cerebrospinal fluid (CSF)* nourishes the brain and**

provides a protective cushion for it. The hollow cavities in the brain that are filled with CSF are called *ventricles* (see Figure 3.9).

The Spinal Cord

The *spinal cord* connects the brain to the rest of the body through the peripheral nervous system. Although the spinal cord looks like a cable from which the somatic nerves branch, it is part of the central nervous system. Like the brain, it is enclosed by the meninges and bathed in CSF. In short, the spinal cord is an extension of the brain.

The spinal cord runs from the base of the brain to just below the level of the waist. It houses bundles of axons that carry the brain's commands to peripheral nerves and that relay sensations from the periphery of the body to the brain. Many forms of paralysis result from spinal cord damage, a fact that underscores the critical role the spinal cord plays in transmitting signals from the brain to the motor neurons that move the body's muscles.

The Brain

The crowning glory of the central nervous system is, of course, the *brain*. Anatomically, the brain is the part of the central nervous system that fills the upper portion of the skull. Although it weighs only about 1.5 kilograms and could be held in one hand, the brain contains billions of interacting cells that integrate information from inside and outside the body, coordinate the body's actions, and enable human beings to talk, think, remember, plan, create, and dream.

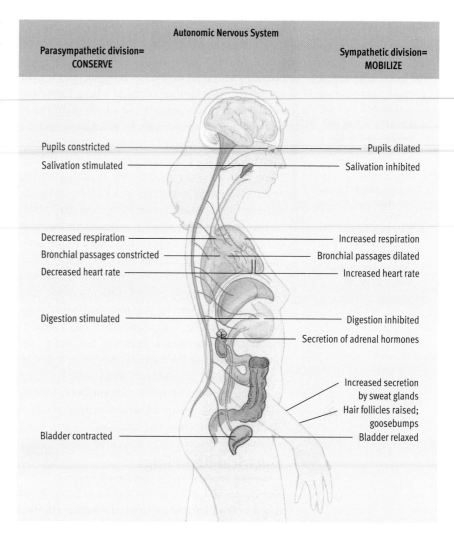

Autonomic Nervous System

Parasympathetic division= **CONSERVE**

Sympathetic division= **MOBILIZE**

Pupils constricted — Pupils dilated
Salivation stimulated — Salivation inhibited

Decreased respiration — Increased respiration
Bronchial passages constricted — Bronchial passages dilated
Decreased heart rate — Increased heart rate

Digestion stimulated — Digestion inhibited
— Secretion of adrenal hormones

Increased secretion by sweat glands
Hair follicles raised; goosebumps
Bladder contracted — Bladder relaxed

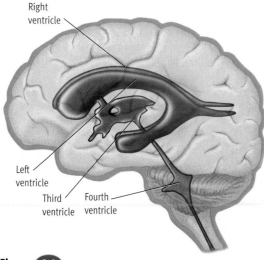

Right ventricle

Left ventricle

Third ventricle   Fourth ventricle

Figure 3.9

The ventricles of the brain. Cerebrospinal fluid (CSF) circulates around the brain and the spinal cord. The hollow cavities in the brain filled with CSF are called ventricles. The four ventricles in the human brain are depicted here.

SOURCE: Graphic adapted from Starr, C. & Taggart, R. (1998). *Biology: The unity and diversity of life.* Belmont, CA: Wadsworth. © 1998 Wadsworth Publishing. Reprinted by permission.

Because of its central importance for behaviour, the brain is the subject of the next three sections of the chapter. We begin by looking at the remarkable methods that have enabled researchers to unlock some of the brain's secrets.

REVIEW OF KEY POINTS

● The nervous system can be divided into two main subdivisions, the central nervous system and the peripheral nervous system. The central nervous system consists of the brain and spinal cord.

● The peripheral nervous system consists of the nerves that lie outside the brain and spinal cord. It can be subdivided into the somatic nervous system, which connects to muscles and sensory receptors, and the autonomic nervous system, which connects to blood vessels, smooth muscles, and glands.

● The autonomic nervous system mediates the largely automatic arousal that accompanies emotion and the fight-or-flight response to stress. The ANS is divided into the sympathetic division, which mobilizes bodily resources, and the parasympathetic division, which conserves bodily resources.

Figure 3.8

The autonomic nervous system (ANS). The ANS is composed of the nerves that connect to the heart, blood vessels, smooth muscles, and glands. The ANS is divided into the sympathetic division, which mobilizes bodily resources in times of need, and the parasympathetic division, which conserves bodily resources. Some of the key functions controlled by each division of the ANS are summarized in the diagram.

Looking Inside the Brain: Research Methods

PREVIEW QUESTIONS

- What is an EEG and what is its output?
- How are lesioning and electrical stimulation used to study brain function?
- Which brain-imaging procedures provide information about brain structure or brain function?
- What have brain-imaging studies told us about how the brain processes information related to the self?

Scientists who want to find out how parts of the brain are related to behaviour are faced with a formidable task. The geography, or *structure*, of the brain can be mapped out relatively easily by examining and dissecting brains removed from animals or from deceased humans who have donated their bodies to science. Mapping of brain *function*, however, requires a working brain. Thus, special research methods are needed to discover relations between brain activity and behaviour.

Investigators who conduct research on the brain or other parts of the nervous system are called *neuroscientists*. Often, brain research involves collaboration by neuroscientists from several disciplines, including anatomy, physiology, biology, pharmacology, neurology, neurosurgery, psychiatry, and psychology. Neuroscientists use many specialized techniques to investigate connections between the brain and behaviour. Among the methods they have depended on most heavily are electrical recordings, lesioning, and electrical stimulation. In addition, brain-imaging techniques have enhanced neuroscientists' ability to observe brain structure and function.

Electrical Recordings 2c

The electrical activity of the brain can be recorded, much as Hodgkin and Huxley recorded the electrical activity of individual neurons. Recordings of single cells in the brain have proven valuable, but scientists also need ways to record the simultaneous activity of many of the billions of neurons in the brain.

Fortunately, in 1929 a German psychiatrist named Hans Berger invented a machine that could record broad patterns of brain electrical activity. **The *electroencephalograph (EEG)* is a device that monitors the electrical activity of the brain over time by means of recording electrodes attached to the surface of the scalp** (see Figure 3.10). An EEG electrode sums and amplifies electric potentials occurring in many thousands of brain cells.

Usually, many recording electrodes are attached (with paste) at various places on the skull. The resulting EEG recordings are translated into line tracings, commonly called *brain waves*. These brain-wave recordings provide a useful overview of the electrical activity in the brain. Different brain-wave patterns are associated with different states of mental activity (Martin, 1991; Westbrook, 2000), as shown in Figure 3.10. The EEG is often used in the clinical diagnosis of brain damage and neurological disorders. In research applications, the EEG can be used to identify patterns of brain activity that occur when participants engage in specific behaviours or experience specific emotions. For example, in one study, researchers using EEG recordings found interesting correlations between specific types of anxiety and distinct patterns of regional brain activity (Heller et al., 1997). Overall, EEG technology has contributed greatly to our understanding of brain–behaviour relations (Eastman, 2004; Rosler, 2005), and as you'll see in Chapter 5, the EEG has been invaluable to researchers exploring the physiology of sleep.

Wilder Penfield and Brenda Milner, pioneers in neuroscience in Canada.

McGill University Archives, Photographic Collection PR000632. Portrait: Wilder Penfield, Director of the Montreal Neurological Institute, 1938–1960.

John Kenney/*The Gazette* (Montreal)

Awake
Low-voltage,
high-frequency
brain waves

50 mv

1 second

Drowsy
Higher-voltage,
slower-frequency
brain waves

**Deep,
dreamless sleep**
High-voltage,
low-frequency
brain waves

© Richard T. Nowitz/Phototake

Lesioning

Brain tumours, strokes, head injuries, and other misfortunes often produce brain damage in people. Many major insights about brain–behaviour relations have resulted from observations of behavioural changes in people who have suffered damage in specific brain areas. This type of research approach, as we discussed in Chapter 2, is referred to as the case study method. One of the most famous case studies of an individual suffering from specific brain damage was conducted by Brenda Milner. Milner was a Ph.D. student of Donald Hebb at McGill University and studied some of Wilder Penfield's patients. The patient she studied is referred to as H.M.

H.M. suffered from epilepsy as a child, a condition that was attributed by some to a childhood biking accident. As part of his treatment, H.M. had portions of his brain removed, including his medial temporal lobe, involving substantial portions of his hippocampus and amygdala. Although the surgery did help reduce his convulsions, it had some negative effects. After his surgery he suffered from a particular form of amnesia (Scolville & Milner, 1957) referred to as anterograde amnesia. He had good memory for events that occurred in the years before the surgery but he could not form new long-term memories: "He did not know where objects in constant use were kept, and his mother stated that he would read the same magazines over and over again without finding their contents familiar" (Milner, 1965, p. 104). He did, however, have a normal short-term memory. We will discuss the distinctions between short- and long-term memory more fully in Chapter 7, but short-term memory is a limited-capacity memory store that can maintain unrehearsed information for about 20 seconds.

Milner's work with patients such as H.M. and her other research was pivotal in establishing the role of the medial structures of the temporal lobes in memory and the existence of multiple memory systems. We will consider the idea of multiple memory systems in Chapter 7.

Doing research with patients who have suffered brain damage has its limitations. Subjects are not plentiful, and neuroscientists can't control the location or severity of their subjects' brain damage. Furthermore, variations in the participants' histories create a host of extraneous variables that make it difficult to isolate cause-and-effect relationships between brain damage and behaviour.

To study the relations between brain and behaviour more precisely, scientists sometimes observe what happens when specific brain structures in animals are purposely disabled. *Lesioning* **involves destroying a piece of the brain**. It is typically done by inserting an electrode into a brain structure and passing a high-frequency electric current through it to burn the tissue and disable the structure.

Lesioning requires researchers to get an electrode to a particular place buried deep inside the brain. They do so with a stereotaxic instrument, a device used to implant electrodes at precise locations in the brain. The use of this surgical device is described in Figure 3.11. Of course, appropriate anesthetics are used to minimize pain and discomfort for the animals. The lesioning of brain structures in animals has proven invaluable in neuroscientists' research on brain functioning.

Electrical Stimulation of the Brain

Electrical stimulation of the brain (ESB) involves **sending a weak electric current into a brain structure**

y axis calibrating knob

x axis calibrating knob

Calibration scale

Electrode carrier

z axis calibrating knob

Nose bar

Figure 3.11

An anesthetized rat in a stereotaxic instrument. This rat is undergoing brain surgery. After consulting a detailed map of the rat brain, researchers use the control knobs on the apparatus to position an electrode along the three axes (x, y, and z) shown in the upper-left corner. This precise positioning allows researchers to implant the electrode in an exact location in the rat's brain.

Figure 3.12

CT technology. CT scans can be used in research to examine aspects of brain structure. They provide computer-enhanced X-rays of horizontal slices of the brain.

to stimulate (activate) it. The current is delivered through an electrode, but the current is different from that used in lesioning. This sort of electrical stimulation does not exactly duplicate normal signals in the brain. However, it is usually a close enough approximation to activate the brain structures in which the electrodes are lodged. If areas deep within the brain are to be stimu-

lated, the electrodes are implanted with the same stereotaxic techniques used in lesioning procedures.

Most ESB research is conducted with animals. However, ESB is occasionally used on humans in the context of brain surgery required for medical purposes (see Moriarty et al., 2001 for an example). After a patient's skull is opened, the surgeons may stimulate areas to map the individual patient's brain (to some extent, each of us is unique), so that they don't slice through critical areas. ESB research has led to advances in the understanding of many aspects of brain–behaviour relations (Berman, 1991; Yudofsky, 1999).

Wilder Penfield was a gifted neurosurgeon and pioneer in neuroscience and the mapping of the functions of the brain (Penfield, 1977). One of his many accomplishments was the founding of the world-famous Montreal Neurological Institute (http://www.mni.mcgill.ca/). One of Penfield's specialties was the surgical treatment of epilepsy (Penfield & Jasper, 1964). During neurosurgery, the patient would remain conscious and alert. Working with more than 1000 such patients, Penfield was able to stimulate portions of the brain with a mild electrical probe. By carefully recording and categorizing his patients' responses, and making reports of memories, sounds, and so on as a result of the stimulation, he was able to systematically map out many of the functions of the brain.

Brain-Imaging Procedures 2c

In recent decades, the invention of new brain-imaging devices has led to spectacular advances in science's ability to look into the brain (Dougherty &

(a) The patient's head is positioned in a large cylinder, as shown here.

(b) An X-ray beam and X-ray detector rotate around the patient's head, taking multiple X-rays of a horizontal slice of the patient's brain.

(c) A computer combines X-rays to create an image of a horizontal slice of the brain. This scan shows a tumour (in red) on the right.

X-ray source

X-ray detector

Rauch, 2003). The *CT (computerized tomography) scan* is a computer-enhanced X-ray of brain structure. Multiple X-rays are shot from many angles, and the computer combines the readings to create a vivid image of a horizontal slice of the brain (see Figure 3.12). The entire brain can be visualized by assembling a series of images representing successive slices of the brain. Of the new brain-imaging techniques, the CT scan is the least expensive, and it has been widely used in research. For example, many researchers have used CT scans to look for abnormalities in brain structure among people suffering from specific types of mental illness (Andreasen, 2001; G. N. Smith et al., 1997).

In research on how brain and behaviour are related, *PET (positron emission tomography) scanning* is proving especially valuable (Nahas et al., 1998). Whereas CT scans can portray only brain *structure,* PET scans can examine brain *function,* mapping actual *activity* in the brain over time. In PET scans, radioactively tagged chemicals are introduced into the brain. They serve as markers of blood flow or metabolic activity in the brain, which can be monitored with X-rays. Thus, a PET scan can provide a colour-coded map indicating which areas of the brain become active when subjects clench their fist, sing, or contemplate the mysteries of the universe (see Figure 3.13). In this way, neuroscientists are using PET scans to better pinpoint the brain areas that handle various types of mental activities (Craik et al., 1999; Raichle, 1994). Because PET scans monitor chemical processes, they can also be used to study the activity of specific neurotransmitters. For example, PET scans have helped researchers determine how cocaine affects activity in dopamine circuits in the human brain (Oswald et al., 2005). This chapter's Featured Study (see page 94) involves the

Figure 3.13

PET scans. PET scans are used to map brain activity rather than brain structure. They provide colour-coded maps that show areas of high activity in the brain over time. The PET scan shown here pinpointed two areas of high activity (indicated by the red and green colours) when a research participant worked on a verbal short-term memory task.

use of PET scans to determine the location of self-referent encoding in the brain.

The *MRI (magnetic resonance imaging) scan* uses magnetic fields, radio waves, and computerized enhancement to map out brain structure. MRI scans provide much better images of brain structure than CT scans (Bohning et al., 1998), producing three-dimensional pictures of the brain that have remarkably high resolution (see Figure 3.14a). *Functional magnetic resonance imaging (fMRI)* consists of several new variations on MRI technology that monitor blood and oxygen flow in the brain to identify areas of high activity (Dougherty & Rauch, 2003). This technology is exciting because it can provide both *functional and structural* information in the same image and monitor changes in brain activity in real time (see Figure 3.14b). For example, using fMRI scans researchers have identified patterns of brain activity associated with cocaine craving in cocaine addicts (Wexler et al., 2001). MRI technology has proven extremely valuable in behavioural research in the last decade.

Figure 3.14

MRI scans. (a) MRI scans can be used to produce remarkably high-resolution pictures of brain structure. A vertical view of a brain from the left side is shown here. **(b)** Like PET scans, functional MRIs can monitor chemical activity in the brain. This image shows regions of the brain that were activated by the visual stimulus of a flashing light.

The Biological Bases of Behaviour

Searching for the Self in the Brain

Investigators: Fergus I.M. Craik (University of Toronto, Rotman Research Institute), Tara M. Moroz (University of Toronto), Morris Moscovitch (University of Toronto, Rotman Research Institute), Donald Struss (University of Toronto, Rotman Research Institute), Gordon Winocur (University of Toronto, Rotman Research Institute), Endel Tulving (Rotman Research Institute), and Shitij Kapur (Rotman Research Institute, Clarke Institute of Psychiatry)

Source: In search of the self: A positron emission tomography study, *Psychological Science*, 1999, *10*, 26–34.

When facing an upcoming examination, students tend to look for specific study habits and test-taking strategies that might help them perform better on the exam. When we discuss memory in Chapter 7, we will look at many factors that have been found to enhance memory, including what has been referred to as *depth of processing.* According to a theory developed by University of Toronto researchers (Craik & Lockhart, 1972; Craik & Tulving, 1975), deeper and more elaborative encoding leads to better memory. Encoding refers to the process of forming a memory code, putting information into memory. The theory suggests that the more elaborate or rich the encoding, the better the memory is. For example, imagine you were given the following list of words to remember: *moderate, aoristic, perfectionist, moody.* One way to try to encode the information would be to focus on *structural* characteristics of the words, such as what font they are printed in, or on their *phonemic* characteristics, how they sound. Both of these are relatively shallow encoding strategies. As you might expect, a deeper encoding strategy in which you focus on the meaning of the words (*semantic encoding*) leads to enhanced memory. Research has found that an even better, deeper encoding strategy is *self-referent* encoding, in which you relate the to-be-remembered material to yourself (e.g., does the word "perfectionist" describe you?).

Previous PET scan research had shown that deep, semantic-type encoding is associated with the activation of the left prefrontal cortex and that this area is associated with the processing of meaning. While the self-task is an example of deeper, more elaborative semantic encoding, it differs from the other two semantic encoding tasks because it involves the self. One of the authors' objectives in this research was to determine what areas of the brain were activated when the processing task involved the self, when participants were encoding words with the task of determining if the trait words described them. They speculated that this latter task might involve activation of the right prefrontal cortex, which might be the area in the brain where the self is represented.

Method

Participants. Eight right-handed participants (four males and four females) were recruited for the study.

Procedure. Research participants were presented with eight lists of personality traits that they were asked to encode using four encoding tasks (two lists for each task): self-task—participants judged how well the word described them; other task—how well the word described a famous Canadian (Brian Mulroney, Prime Minister at the time); general task—how socially desirable the trait was; and a syllable task—how many syllables were in each word. While the first three tasks all involve some type of more elaborative encoding, the last clearly does not. However, only one task explicitly involves the self. Participants were also given a later test to examine their memory for the words. While participants were performing the encoding tasks, relative regional cerebral blood flow was measured (PET scan).

Results. The results indicated that the three semantic encoding tasks (i.e., self, general, and social desirability) were associated with better recognition memory for the trait words than was the less elaborate syllable task. The self-task words were associated with somewhat better memory than the other two semantic tasks. These results confirm what researchers in the area had found before: that deeper encoding leads to better memory. The self-related condition was also associated with the fastest recognition reaction time. The blood flow data were analyzed in two ways. The first analysis showed that all three semantic tasks were associated with increased left prefrontal activity as compared to the syllable task. All three tasks, then, involve some form of deeper, semantic-type encoding. The second, alternative PET scan analysis showed that the self-condition only was associated with increased right prefrontal activity.

Discussion

This study suggested some fascinating conclusions to the authors regarding the self and its representation in the brain. The self may in fact be represented in two ways. The first is a generalized *conceptual self* that is similar to the other context-free schemas that constitute our cognitive system. This is consistent with the similarity in left prefrontal activation produced by the three semantic tasks. The self also may be represented in a more specialized way, related to episodic memory retrieval. In Chapter 7 we discuss the distinctions between episodic and semantic memory in more detail.

Comment

This study was featured because it provides a relatively simple example of how brain-imaging technologies have yielded new insights about brain–behaviour relations. Science depends on observation. Improvements in our ability to observe the brain have resulted in increased knowledge of how brain structure and function are related to psychological phenomena. This study by itself will not allow us to identify the location of the self in the brain, but it does give us some insight into how the brain functions in specific ways when the self is implicated. This is an issue of continuing interest. More recent fMRI research by Kelley, Macrae, Wyland, Caglar, Inati, and Heatherton (2002) has supported and extended this research by showing that processing related to the self is clearly dissociable from other types of semantic encoding such as that used in the current study. These types of questions can be answered only through more research. Thus, scientific inquiry is an endless process in which new knowledge stimulates new questions. ■

The Brain and Behaviour

Now that we have examined selected techniques of brain research, let's look at what researchers have discovered about the functions of various parts of the brain.

The brain can be divided into three major regions: the hindbrain, the midbrain, and the forebrain. The principal structures found in each of these regions are listed in the organizational chart of the nervous system in Figure 3.6 (page 87). You can see where these regions are located in the brain by looking at Figure 3.15. They can be found easily in relation to the *brainstem*. The brainstem looks like its name—it appears to be a stem from which the rest of the brain "flowers," like a head of cauliflower. At its lower end it is contiguous with the spinal cord. At its higher end it lies deep within the brain.

We'll begin at the brain's lower end, where the spinal cord joins the brainstem. As we proceed upward, notice how the functions of brain structures go from the regulation of basic bodily processes to the control of "higher" mental processes.

coughing, and salivating. The *pons* (literally "bridge") includes a bridge of fibres that connects the brainstem with the cerebellum. The pons also contains several clusters of cell bodies involved with sleep and arousal.

The *cerebellum* (literally "little brain") is a relatively large and deeply folded structure located adjacent to the back surface of the brainstem. The cerebellum is critical to the coordination of movement and to the sense of equilibrium, or physical balance (Ghez & Thach, 2000). Although the actual commands for muscular movements come from higher brain centres, the cerebellum plays a key role in organizing the sensory information that guides these movements. It is your cerebellum that allows you to hold your hand out to the side and then smoothly bring your finger to a stop on your nose. This is a useful roadside test for drunken driving because the cerebellum is one of the structures first depressed by alcohol. Damage to the cerebellum disrupts fine motor skills, such as those involved in writing, typing, or playing a musical instrument.

PREVIEW QUESTIONS

- What are some functions of the medulla, pons, and cerebellum?
- What are some functions of the midbrain and which structure is the brain's relay centre?
- What does the hypothalamus regulate?
- What are some functions of the limbic system?
- What is each lobe in the brain known for?
- What does it mean to say that the brain is characterized by "plasticity"?

The Hindbrain

The *hindbrain* includes the cerebellum and two structures found in the lower part of the brainstem: the medulla and the pons. The *medulla*, which attaches to the spinal cord, has charge of largely unconscious but vital functions, including circulating blood, breathing, maintaining muscle tone, and regulating reflexes such as sneezing,

The Midbrain

The *midbrain* is the segment of the brainstem that lies between the hindbrain and the forebrain. The midbrain contains an area that is concerned with integrating sensory processes, such as vision and hearing (Stein, Wallace, & Stanford, 2000). An important system of dopamine-releasing neurons that projects into various higher brain centres origi-

Figure 3.15

Structures and areas in the human brain. (Top left) This photo of a human brain shows many of the structures discussed in this chapter. (Top right) The brain is divided into three major areas: the hindbrain, midbrain, and forebrain. These subdivisions actually make more sense for the brains of other animals than of humans. In humans, the forebrain has become so large it makes the other two divisions look trivial. However, the hindbrain and midbrain aren't trivial; they control such vital functions as breathing, waking, and maintaining balance. (Bottom) This cross-section of the brain highlights key structures and some of their principal functions. As you read about the functions of a brain structure, such as the corpus callosum, you may find it helpful to visualize it.

Wadsworth Collection

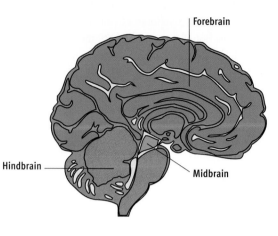

Forebrain

Hindbrain

Midbrain

Cerebrum
Responsible for sensing, thinking, learning, emotion, consciousness, and voluntary movement

Corpus callosum
Bridge of fibres passing information between the two cerebral hemispheres

Amygdala
Part of limbic system involved in emotion and aggression

Thalamus
Relay centre for cortex; handles incoming and outgoing signals

Hypothalamus
Responsible for regulating basic biological needs: hunger, thirst, temperature control

Cerebellum
Structure that coordinates fine muscle movement, balance

Pituitary gland
"Master" gland that regulates other endocrine glands

Brainstem

Hippocampus
Part of limbic system involved in learning and memory

Spinal cord
Responsible for transmitting information between brain and rest of body; handles simple reflexes

Reticular formation
Group of fibres that carry stimulation related to sleep and arousal through brainstem

Medulla
Responsible for regulating largely unconscious functions such as breathing and circulation

Pons
Involved in sleep and arousal

nates in the midbrain. Among other things, this dopamine system is involved in the performance of voluntary movements. The decline in dopamine synthesis that causes Parkinsonism is due to degeneration of a structure located in the midbrain (DeLong, 2000).

Running through both the hindbrain and the midbrain is the *reticular formation* (see Figure 3.15). Lying at the central core of the brainstem, the reticular formation contributes to the modulation of muscle reflexes, breathing, and pain perception (Saper, 2000). It is best known, however, for its role in the regulation of sleep and arousal. Activity in the ascending fibres of the reticular formation contributes to arousal (Coenen, 1998).

The Forebrain 2E, 2F

The *forebrain* is the largest and most complex region of the brain, encompassing a variety of structures, including the thalamus, hypothalamus, limbic system, and cerebrum (consult Figure 3.15 once again). The thalamus, hypothalamus, and limbic system form the core of the forebrain. All three structures are located near the top of the brainstem. Above them is the *cerebrum*—the seat of complex thought. The wrinkled surface of the cerebrum is the *cerebral cortex*—the outer layer of the brain, which looks like a cauliflower.

The Thalamus: A Way Station 2E

The *thalamus* is a structure in the forebrain through which all sensory information (except smell) must pass to get to the cerebral cortex. This way station is made up of clusters of cell bodies, or somas. Each cluster is concerned with relaying sensory information to a particular part of the cortex. However, it would be a mistake to characterize the thalamus as nothing more than a passive relay station. The thalamus also appears to play an active role in integrating information from various senses.

The Hypothalamus: A Regulator of Biological Needs 2E

The *hypothalamus* is a structure found near the base of the forebrain that is involved in the regulation of basic biological needs. The hypothalamus lies beneath the thalamus (*hypo* means "under," making the hypothalamus the area under the thalamus). Although no larger than a kidney bean, the hypothalamus contains various clusters of cells that have many key functions. One such function is to control the autonomic nervous system (Iversen, Iversen, & Saper, 2000). In addition, the hypothalamus serves as a vital link between the brain and the endocrine system (a network of hormone-producing glands, discussed later in this chapter).

The hypothalamus plays a major role in the regulation of basic biological drives related to survival, including the so-called "four F's": fighting, fleeing, feeding, and mating. For example, when researchers lesion the lateral areas (the sides) of the hypothalamus, animals lose interest in eating. The animals must be fed intravenously or they starve, even in the presence of abundant food. In contrast, when electrical stimulation (ESB) is used to *activate* the lateral hypothalamus, animals eat constantly and gain weight rapidly (Grossman et al., 1978; Keesey & Powley, 1975). Does this mean that the lateral hypothalamus is the "hunger centre" in the brain? Not necessarily. The regulation of hunger turns out to be complex and multifaceted, as you'll see in Chapter 10. Nonetheless, the hypothalamus clearly contributes to the control of hunger and other basic biological processes, including thirst and temperature regulation (Kupfermann, Kandel, & Iversen, 2000).

The Limbic System: The Seat of Emotion 2E

The *limbic system* is a loosely connected network of structures located roughly along the border between the cerebral cortex and deeper subcortical areas (hence the term *limbic*, which means "edge"). First described by Paul MacLean (1954), the limbic system is *not* a well-defined anatomical system with clear boundaries. Indeed, scientists disagree about which structures should be included in the limbic system (Van Hoesen, Morecraft, & Semendeferi, 1996). Broadly defined, the limbic system includes parts of the thalamus and hypothalamus, the hippocampus, the amygdala, and other structures. The limbic system is involved in the regulation of emotion, memory, and motivation.

The hippocampus and adjacent structures clearly play a role in memory processes, although the exact nature of that role is the subject of debate (Squire & Knowlton, 2000). Some theorists believe that the hippocampal region is responsible for the consolidation of memories for factual information (Gluck & Myers, 1997). In any event, many other brain structures contribute to memory processes, so the hippocampus is only one element in a complex system (see Chapter 7).

Similarly, there is ample evidence linking the limbic system to the experience of emotion, but the exact mechanisms of control are not yet well understood (Mega et al., 1997; Paradiso et al., 1997). Recent evidence suggests that the *amygdala* may play a central role in the learning of fear responses (Mori et al., 1999; Armony & LeDoux, 2000). The limbic system is also one of the areas in the brain that appears to be rich in emotion-tinged "pleasure centres." This intriguing possibility first surfaced, quite by chance, in brain stimulation research with rats conducted by James Olds and Peter Milner (1954).

James Olds had come to McGill University to work with Donald Hebb as a post-doctoral fellow. He had earlier read Hebb's 1949 text and was influenced by Hebb's ideas. James Olds and Peter Milner (1954) accidentally discovered that a rat would press a lever repeatedly to send brief bursts of electrical stimulation to a specific spot in its brain where an electrode was implanted (see Figure 3.16). They thought that they had inserted the electrode in the rat's reticular formation. However, they learned later that the electrode had been bent during implantation and ended up elsewhere (probably in the hypothalamus). Much to their surprise, the rat kept coming back for more self-stimulation in this area. Subsequent studies showed that rats and monkeys would press a lever *thousands of times per hour,* until they sometimes collapsed from exhaustion, to stimulate certain brain sites. Although the experimenters obviously couldn't ask the animals about it, they *inferred* that the animals were experiencing some sort of pleasure.

Where are the self-stimulation centres located in the brain? Many self-stimulation sites have been found in the limbic system (Olds & Fobes, 1981). The heaviest concentration appears to be where the *medial forebrain bundle* (a bundle of axons) passes through the hypothalamus. The medial forebrain bundle is rich in dopamine-releasing neurons. The rewarding effects of ESB at self-stimulation sites may be largely mediated by the activation of these dopamine circuits (Nakajima & Patterson, 1997). The rewarding, pleasurable effects of opiate and stimulant drugs (cocaine and amphetamines) may also depend on excitation of this dopamine system, although this conclusion is the subject of some debate (Gratton, 1996; Wise, 1999). In any event, it is clear that this dopamine system is *not* the ultimate biological basis for *all* reward (Berridge & Robinson, 1998). That is not surprising, as the brain is never that simple. Nonetheless, recent evidence suggests that the so-called "pleasure centres" in the brain may not be anatomical centres so much as neural circuits releasing dopamine.

The Cerebrum: The Seat of Complex Thought

The *cerebrum* is the largest and most complex part of the human brain. It includes the brain areas that are responsible for the most complex mental activities, including learning, remembering, thinking, and consciousness itself. **The *cerebral cortex* is the convoluted outer layer of the cerebrum.** The cortex is folded and bent, so that its large surface area—about 1400 cm^2—can be packed into the limited volume of the skull (Hubel & Wiesel, 1979).

Figure 3.16

Electrical stimulation of the brain (ESB) in the rat. Olds and Milner (1954) were using an apparatus like that depicted here when they discovered self-stimulation centres, or "pleasure centres," in the brain of a rat. In this set-up, the rat's lever pressing earns brief electrical stimulation that is sent to a specific spot in the rat's brain where an electrode has been implanted.

Suspending elastic band

Stimulation to animal

Lever pressing activates stimulator

Lever

Stimulator

The cerebral hemispheres and the corpus callosum. (Left) As this photo shows, the longitudinal fissure running down the middle of the brain (viewed from above) separates the left and right halves of the cerebral cortex. (Right) In this drawing the cerebral hemispheres have been "pulled apart" to reveal the corpus callosum. This band of fibres is the communication bridge between the right and left halves of the human brain.

Corpus callosum

The cerebrum is divided into two halves called hemispheres. Hence, **the *cerebral hemispheres* are the right and left halves of the cerebrum** (see Figure 3.17). The hemispheres are separated in the centre of the brain by a longitudinal fissure that runs from the front to the back of the brain. This fissure descends to a thick band of fibres called the *corpus callosum* (also shown in Figure 3.17). **The *corpus callosum* is the structure that connects the two cerebral hemispheres.** We'll discuss the functional specialization of the cerebral hemispheres in the next section of this chapter. Each cerebral hemisphere is divided into four parts called *lobes*. To some extent, each of these lobes is dedicated to specific purposes. The location of these lobes can be seen in Figure 3.18.

The *occipital lobe,* at the back of the head, includes the cortical area, where most visual signals are sent and visual processing is begun. This area is called the *primary visual cortex.* We will discuss how it is organized in Chapter 4.

The *parietal lobe* is forward of the occipital lobe. It includes the area that registers the sense of touch, called the *primary somatosensory cortex.* Various sections of this area receive signals from different regions of the body. When ESB is delivered in these parietal lobe areas, people report physical sensations—as if someone actually touched them on the arm or cheek, for example. The parietal lobe is also involved in integrating visual input and in monitoring the body's position in space. York University neuroscientist Doug Crawford has examined the role of the parietal cortex in enabling us to reach for and

grasp objects with so much proficiency. He suggests that the parietal cortex mediates the visual control of reaching (Crawford, Medendorp, & Marotta, 2004).

The *temporal lobe* (meaning "near the temples") lies below the parietal lobe. Near its top, the temporal lobe contains an area devoted to auditory processing, called the *primary auditory cortex.* As we will see momentarily, damage to an area in the temporal lobe on the left side of the brain can impair the comprehension of speech and language.

Continuing forward, we find the *frontal lobe,* the largest lobe in the human brain. It contains the principal areas that control the movement of muscles, called the *primary motor cortex.* ESB applied in these areas can cause actual muscle contractions. The amount of motor cortex allocated to the control of a body part depends not on the part's size but on the diversity and precision of its movements. Thus, more of the cortex is given to parts we have fine control over, such as fingers, lips, and the tongue. Less of the cortex is devoted to larger parts that make crude movements, such as the thighs and shoulders (see Figure 3.19).

The portion of the frontal lobe to the front of the motor cortex, which is called the *prefrontal cortex* (see the inset in Figure 3.19), is something of a mystery. This area is disproportionately large in humans, accounting for about 28% of the human cerebral cortex (Shimamura, 1996). In light of this fact, it was once assumed to house the highest, most abstract intellectual functions, but this view was eventually dismissed as an oversimplification. Still, recent studies suggest that the prefrontal cortex *does* contribute to

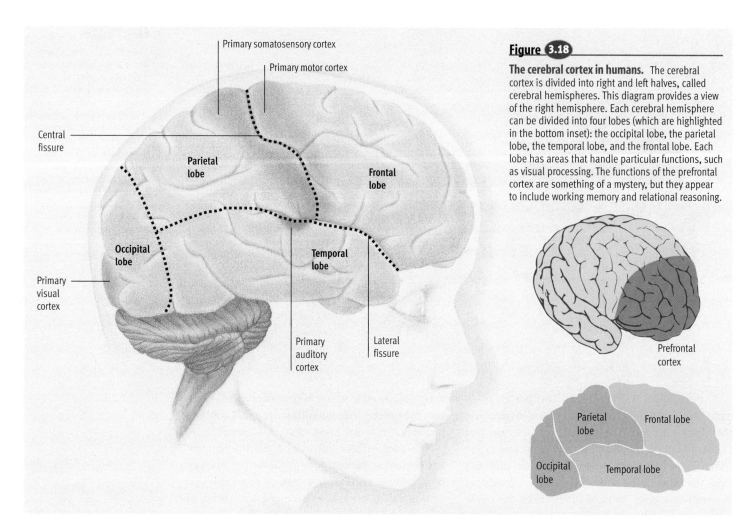

Primary somatosensory cortex

Primary motor cortex

Central fissure

Parietal lobe

Frontal lobe

Occipital lobe

Temporal lobe

Primary visual cortex

Primary auditory cortex

Lateral fissure

Figure 3.18

The cerebral cortex in humans. The cerebral cortex is divided into right and left halves, called cerebral hemispheres. This diagram provides a view of the right hemisphere. Each cerebral hemisphere can be divided into four lobes (which are highlighted in the bottom inset): the occipital lobe, the parietal lobe, the temporal lobe, and the frontal lobe. Each lobe has areas that handle particular functions, such as visual processing. The functions of the prefrontal cortex are something of a mystery, but they appear to include working memory and relational reasoning.

Prefrontal cortex

Parietal lobe

Frontal lobe

Occipital lobe

Temporal lobe

Figure 3.19

The primary motor cortex. This diagram shows the amount of motor cortex devoted to the control of various muscles and limbs. The anatomical features in the drawing are distorted because their size is proportional to the amount of cortex devoted to their control. As you can see, more of the cortex is allocated to muscle groups that must make relatively precise movements.

SOURCE: Graphic from Sternberg, R. J. (2001). *Psychology: In search of the human mind.* Fort Worth: Harcourt. Reprinted by permission of Wadsworth Publishing.

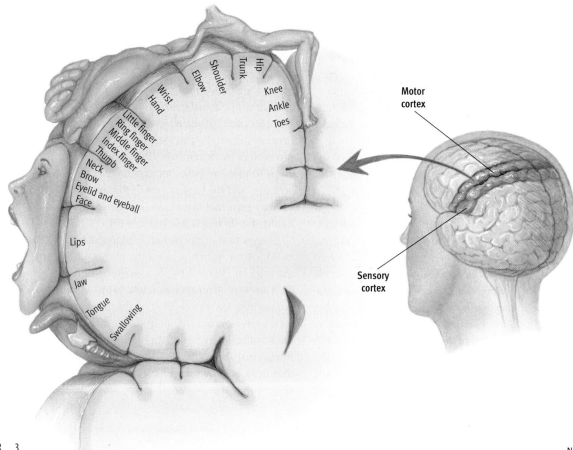

Hip
Trunk
Shoulder
Elbow
Wrist
Hand
Little finger
Ring finger
Middle finger
Index finger
Thumb
Neck
Brow
Eyelid and eyeball
Face
Lips
Jaw
Tongue
Swallowing

Knee
Ankle
Toes

Motor cortex

Sensory cortex

an impressive variety of higher-order functions, such as memory for temporal sequences (Kresner, 1998); working memory, which is a temporary buffer that processes current information (Goldman-Rakic, 1993, 1998); and reasoning about relations between objects and events (Huettel, Mack, & McCarthy, 2002; Waltz et al., 1999). Its contribution to working memory and relational reasoning have led some theorists to suggest that the prefrontal cortex houses some sort of "executive control system," which is thought to monitor, organize, and direct thought processes (Kimberg, D'Esposito, & Farah, 1997; Shimamura, 1995). Consistent with this hypothesis, people who suffer damage in the prefrontal cortex often show deficits in planning, paying attention, and getting organized (Fuster, 1996).

The Plasticity of the Brain

It was once believed that significant changes in the anatomy and organization of the brain were limited to early periods of development in both humans and animals. However, according to University of Lethbridge behavioural neuroscientist Bryan Kolb, research has gradually demonstrated that the anatomical structure and functional organization of the brain are more "plastic" or malleable than widely assumed (Kolb, Gibb, & Robinson, 2003; Kolb & Whishaw, 1998; Recanzone, 2000). According to Kolb, *brain plasticity* refers to "the brain's ability to change structure and function" (Kolb & Whishaw, 1998, p. 44). He suggests that experience is an important stimulant of brain plasticity and that experience affects dendritic length, synapse formation, and altered metabolic activity.

Conclusions about brain plasticity in general are based on several lines of research. First, studies have shown that aspects of experience can sculpt features of brain structure. For example, neuroimaging studies have shown that an area in the somatosensory cortex that receives input from the fingers of the left hand is enlarged in string musicians who constantly use the left hand to finger the strings of their instruments (Elbert et al., 1995). In a similar vein, researchers find greater dendritic branching and synaptic density in rats raised in a stimulating, enriched environment, as opposed to a dull, barren environment (Rosenzweig & Bennet, 1996; see the Critical Thinking Application at the end of the chapter).

Second, research has shown that damage to incoming sensory pathways or the destruction of brain tissue can lead to neural reorganization. For example, when scientists amputated the third finger in an owl monkey, the part of its cortex that formerly responded to the third finger gradually became responsive to the second and fourth fingers (Kaas, 2000). Neural reorganization has also been seen in response to brain damage as healthy neurons attempt to compensate for the loss of nearby neurons (Cao et al., 1994; Gilbert, 1993).

Third, recent studies indicate that the adult brain can generate new neurons (Gage, 2002). Until recently it was believed that the brain formed all its neurons by infancy at the latest. However, new evidence suggests that adult humans can form new neurons in the hippocampus (Eriksson et al., 1998). Furthermore, Elizabeth Gould and her colleagues (1999, 2002) have found that adult monkeys form *thousands* of new brain cells each day in deep subcortical areas. These new neurons then migrate to areas in the cortex where they sprout axons and form new synapses with existing neurons.

In sum, research suggests that the brain is not "hard wired" the way a computer is. It appears that the neural wiring of the brain is flexible and constantly evolving. That said, this plasticity is not unlimited. Rehabilitation efforts with people who have suffered severe brain damage clearly demonstrate that there are limits on the extent to which the brain can rewire itself (Zillmer & Spiers, 2001). And the evidence suggests that the brain's plasticity declines with age (Rains, 2002). Younger brains are more malleable than older brains. Still, the neural circuits of the brain show substantial plasticity, which certainly helps organisms adapt to their environments.

REVIEW OF KEY POINTS

- The brain has three major regions: the hindbrain, midbrain, and forebrain. Structures in the hindbrain include the medulla, pons, and cerebellum. These structures handle essential functions such as breathing, circulation, coordination of movement, and the rhythm of sleep and arousal.

- The midbrain contributes to the coordination of sensory processes. Deterioration of an area in the midbrain has been implicated as a factor in Parkinson's disease.

- The forebrain includes many structures that handle higher functions. The thalamus is primarily a relay station. The hypothalamus is involved in the regulation of basic biological drives such as hunger and sex.

- The limbic system is a network of loosely connected structures located along the border between the cortex and deeper subcortical areas. It includes the hippocampus, which appears to play a role in memory, the amygdala, which is involved in the regulation of emotion, and areas rich in self-stimulation sites.

- The cerebrum is the brain area implicated in most complex mental activities. The cortex is the cerebrum's convoluted outer layer, which is subdivided into four lobes.

- These lobes and their primary known functions are the occipital lobe (vision), the parietal lobe (touch), the temporal lobe (hearing), and the frontal lobe (movement of the body). The prefrontal cortex may contribute to working memory and relational reasoning. The structure and function of the brain appears to be more plastic than widely appreciated.

Right Brain/Left Brain: Cerebral Laterality

PREVIEW QUESTIONS

● How was the left hemisphere originally implicated in the control of language?

● How are sensory and motor information routed to the two hemispheres?

● What did split-brain research reveal about the right and left hemispheres of the brain?

● How do scientists study hemispheric specialization in normal subjects, and what have they learned?

As we noted a moment ago, the cerebrum—the seat of complex thought—is divided into two separate hemispheres (see Figure 3.17 on page 99). Recent decades have seen an exciting flurry of research on the specialized abilities of the right and left cerebral hemispheres. Some theorists have gone so far as to suggest that we really have two brains in one!

Hints of this hemispheric specialization have been available for many years, from cases in which one side of a person's brain has been damaged. The left hemisphere was implicated in the control of language as early as 1861, by Paul Broca, a French surgeon. Broca was treating a patient who had been unable to speak for 30 years. After the patient died, Broca showed that the probable cause of his speech deficit was a localized lesion on the left side of the frontal lobe. Since then, many similar cases have shown that this area of the brain—known as *Broca's area*—plays an important role in the *production* of speech (see Figure 3.20). Another major language centre—*Wernicke's area*—was identified in the temporal lobe of the left hemisphere in 1874. Damage in Wernicke's area (see Figure 3.20) usually leads to problems with the *comprehension* of language.

Evidence that the left hemisphere usually processes language led scientists to characterize it as the "dominant" hemisphere. Because thoughts are usually coded in terms of language, the left hemisphere was given the lion's share of credit for handling the "higher" mental processes, such as reasoning, remembering, planning, and problem solving. Meanwhile, the right hemisphere came to be viewed as the "nondominant," or "dumb," hemisphere, lacking any special functions or abilities.

This characterization of the left and right hemispheres as major and minor partners in the brain's work began to change in the 1960s. It all started with landmark research by Roger Sperry, Michael Gazzaniga, and their colleagues who studied "split-brain" patients: individuals whose cerebral hemispheres had been surgically disconnected (Gazzaniga, 1970; Gazzaniga, Bogen, & Sperry, 1965; Levy, Trevarthen, & Sperry, 1972; Sperry, 1982). In 1981 Sperry received a Nobel Prize in physiology/medicine for this work.

Bisecting the Brain: Split-Brain Research

 SIM2, 2F

In *split-brain surgery* the bundle of fibres that connects the cerebral hemispheres (the corpus callosum) is cut to reduce the severity of epileptic seizures. It is a radical procedure that is chosen only in exceptional cases that have not responded to other forms of treatment. But the surgery provides scientists with an unusual opportunity to study people who have had their brain literally split in two.

To appreciate the logic of split-brain research, you need to understand how sensory and motor information is routed to and from the two hemispheres. *Each hemisphere's primary connections are to the opposite side of the body.* Thus, the left hemisphere controls, and communicates with, the right hand, right arm, right leg, right eyebrow, and so on. In contrast, the right hemisphere controls, and communicates with, the left side of the body.

Vision and hearing are more complex. Both eyes deliver information to both hemispheres, but there still is a separation of input. Stimuli in the right half of the *visual field* are registered by receptors on the left side of each eye, which send signals to the left hemisphere. Stimuli in the left half of the visual field are transmitted by both eyes to the right hemisphere (see Figure 3.21). Auditory inputs to each ear also go to both hemispheres. However, connections to the opposite hemisphere are stronger or more immediate. That is, sounds presented exclusively to the right ear (through headphones) are registered in the left hemisphere first, while sounds presented to the left ear are registered more quickly in the right hemisphere.

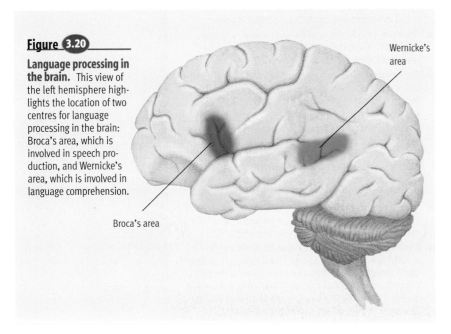

Figure 3.20

Language processing in the brain. This view of the left hemisphere highlights the location of two centres for language processing in the brain: Broca's area, which is involved in speech production, and Wernicke's area, which is involved in language comprehension.

Wernicke's area

Broca's area

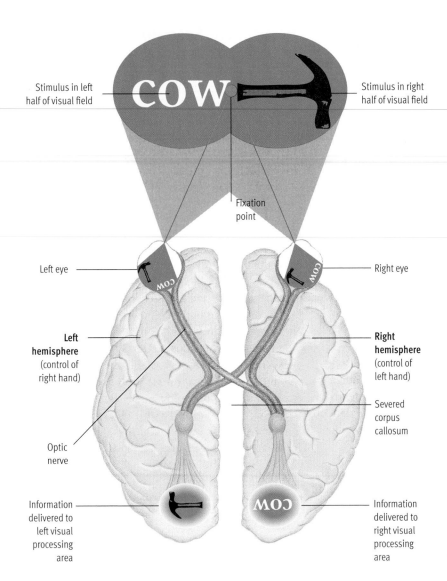

Stimulus in left half of visual field

COW

Stimulus in right half of visual field

Fixation point

Left eye

Right eye

Left hemisphere (control of right hand)

Right hemisphere (control of left hand)

Optic nerve

Severed corpus callosum

Information delivered to left visual processing area

Information delivered to right visual processing area

Figure 3.21

Visual input in the split brain.
If a participant stares at a fixation point, the point divides the subject's visual field into right and left halves. Input from the right visual field (a picture of a hammer in this example) strikes the left side of each eye and is transmitted to the left hemisphere. Input from the left visual field strikes the right side of each eye and is transmitted to the right hemisphere. Normally, the hemispheres share the information from the two halves of the visual field, but in split-brain patients, the corpus callosum is severed, and the two hemispheres cannot communicate. Hence, the experimenter can present a visual stimulus to just one hemisphere at a time.

Both the left and right hemispheres of the brain have been found to have their own specialized forms of intellect.
ROGER SPERRY

For the most part, people don't notice this asymmetric, "crisscrossed" organization because the two hemispheres are in close communication with each other. Information received by one hemisphere is readily shared with the other via the corpus callosum. However, when the two hemispheres are surgically disconnected, the functional specialization of the brain becomes apparent.

In their classic study of split-brain patients, Gazzaniga, Bogen, and Sperry (1965) presented visual stimuli such as pictures, symbols, and words in a single visual field (the left or the right), so that the stimuli would be sent to only one hemisphere. The stimuli were projected onto a screen in front of the participants, who stared at a fixation point (a spot) in the centre of the screen (see Figure 3.22). The images were flashed to the right or the left of the fixation point for only a split second. Thus, the subjects did not have a chance to move their eyes, and the stimuli were glimpsed in only one visual field.

When pictures were flashed in the right visual field and thus sent to the left hemisphere, the split-brain subjects were able to name and describe the objects depicted (such as a cup or spoon). However, the subjects were *not* able to name and describe the

Figure 3.22

Experimental apparatus in split-brain research.
On the left is a special slide projector that can present images very briefly, before the subject's eyes can move and thus change the visual field. Images are projected on one side of the screen to present stimuli to just one hemisphere. The portion of the apparatus beneath the screen is constructed to prevent participants from seeing objects that they may be asked to handle with their right or left hand, another procedure that can be used to send information to just one hemisphere.

The Biological Bases of Behaviour

Web Link 3.6

The Society for Neuroscience

http://web.sfn.org/Template.cfm?
Section=PublicResources

The largest scientific association devoted solely to the study of the nervous system and its functioning has gathered a host of materials that will introduce visitors to the latest research on a full spectrum of brain-related topics.

same objects when they were flashed in the left visual field and sent to the right hemisphere. In a similar fashion, an object placed out of view in the right hand (communicating with the left hemisphere) could be named. However, the same object placed in the left hand (right hemisphere) could not be. These findings supported the notion that language is housed in the left hemisphere.

Although the split-brain subjects' right hemisphere was not able to speak up for itself, further tests revealed that it *was* processing the information presented. If subjects were given an opportunity to *point out a picture* of an object they had held in their left hand, they were able to do so. They were also able to point out pictures that had been flashed to the left visual field. Furthermore, the right hemisphere (left hand) turned out to be *superior* to the left hemisphere (right hand) in assembling little puzzles and copying drawings, even though the subjects were right-handed. These findings provided the first compelling demonstration that the right hemisphere has its own special talents. Subsequent studies of additional split-brain patients showed the right hemisphere to be better than the left on a variety of visual–spatial tasks, including discriminating colours, arranging blocks, and recognizing faces.

Hemispheric Specialization in the Intact Brain

SIM2, 2F

The problem with the split-brain operation, of course, is that it creates an abnormal situation. The vast majority of us remain "neurologically intact." Moreover, the surgery is done only with people who suffer from prolonged, severe cases of epilepsy. These people may have had somewhat atypical brain organization even before the operation. Thus, theorists couldn't help wondering whether it was safe to generalize broadly from the split-brain studies. For this reason, researchers developed methods that allowed them to study cerebral specialization in the intact brain.

Maryse Lassonde of the University of Montreal has been an active researcher in examining the effects of agenesis of the corpus callosum. In some of her research, much like Sperry and his colleagues, she has recruited callosotomized (corpus callosum severed surgically) as well as acallosal (born without an intact corpus callosum) participants in order to examine the operation of the two hemispheres (De Guise, Del Pesce, Foschi, Quattrini, Papo, & Lassonde, 1999). More recently, along with her colleague Elaine De Guise, Lassonde has conducted

CONCEPT **CHECK 3.3**

Relating Disorders to the Nervous System

Imagine that you are working as a neuropsychologist at a clinic. You are involved in the diagnosis of the cases described below. You are asked to identify the probable cause(s) of the disorders in terms of nervous system malfunctions. Based on the information in this chapter, indicate the probable location of any brain damage or the probable disturbance of neurotransmitter activity. The answers can be found in the back of the book in Appendix A.

Case 1. Miriam is exhibiting language deficits. In particular, she does not seem to comprehend the meaning of words.

_____

_____

Case 2. Camille displays tremors and muscular rigidity and is diagnosed as having Parkinsonism.

_____

_____

Case 3. Ricardo, a 28-year-old computer executive, has gradually seen his strength and motor coordination deteriorate badly. He is diagnosed as having multiple sclerosis.

_____

_____

Case 4. Wendy is highly irrational, has poor contact with reality, and reports hallucinations. She is given a diagnosis of schizophrenic disorder.

_____

_____

similar research with children of different ages (6 to 16 years of age), all of whom have intact corpus callosums (De Guise & Lassonde, 2001). Younger children often show limitations in hemispheric communication because their callosum has not yet reached functional maturity.

In one study, De Guise and Lassonde (2001) presented four age groups of children (6–8, 9–11, 12–14, and 15–16) with a visuomotor task to learn on a computer. In a condition where the skills to be learned to successfully perform the task involved bihemispheric integration, only the older children (12 and above) tended to perform well. Only a mature corpus callosum allowed for sufficient integration of information between hemispheres. The authors suggest that findings such as these emphasize the "crucial role of the [corpus callosum] in transfer and integration of a procedural visuomotor skill" (p. 254). This doesn't mean that the younger children are not able to transfer information between hemispheres but that they showed deficits in learning a task that involved integration of information from both hemispheres.

Another method involves looking at *perceptual asymmetries*—**left–right imbalances between the cerebral hemispheres in the speed of visual or auditory processing**. As we just discussed, it is possible to present visual stimuli to just one visual field at a time. In normal individuals, the input sent to one hemisphere is quickly shared with the other. However, subtle differences in the "abilities" of the two hemispheres can be detected by precisely measuring how long it takes subjects to recognize different types of stimuli.

For instance, when *verbal* stimuli are presented to the right visual field (and thus sent to the *left hemisphere* first), they are identified more quickly and more accurately than when they are presented to the left visual field (and sent to the right hemisphere

first). The faster reactions in the left hemisphere presumably occur because it can recognize verbal stimuli on its own, while the right hemisphere has to take extra time to "consult" the left hemisphere. In contrast, the *right hemisphere* is faster than the left on *visual–spatial* tasks, such as locating a dot or recognizing a face (Bradshaw, 1989; Bryden, 1982).

Researchers have also used a variety of other approaches to explore hemispheric specialization in normal people. For the most part, their findings have converged nicely with the results of the split-brain studies (Reuter-Lorenz & Miller, 1998). Overall, the findings suggest that the two hemispheres are specialized, with each handling certain types of cognitive tasks better than the other (Carballis, 2003; Gazzaniga, 2000; Springer & Deutsch, 1998). *The left hemisphere usually is better on tasks involving verbal processing, such as language, speech, reading, and writing. The right hemisphere exhibits superiority on many tasks involving nonverbal processing, such as most spatial, musical, and visual recognition tasks.*

Cerebral lateralization is a burgeoning area of research that has broad implications, which we will discuss further in the Personal Application at the end of the chapter. For now, however, let's leave the brain and turn our attention to the endocrine system.

REVIEW OF KEY POINTS

- The cerebrum is divided into right and left hemispheres connected by the corpus callosum. Evidence that the left cerebral hemisphere usually processes language led scientists to view it as the dominant hemisphere.
- However, studies of split-brain patients revealed that the right and left halves of the brain each have unique talents, with the right hemisphere being specialized to handle visual–spatial functions.
- Studies of perceptual asymmetries in normal subjects also showed that the left hemisphere is better equipped to handle verbal processing, whereas the right hemisphere is more adept at nonverbal processing.

The Endocrine System: Another Way to Communicate

The major way the brain communicates with the rest of the body is through the nervous system. However, the body has a second communication system that is also important to behaviour. **The *endocrine system* consists of glands that secrete chemicals into the bloodstream that help control bodily functioning.** The messengers in this communication network are called hormones. ***Hormones* are the chemical substances released by the endocrine glands.** In a way, hormones are like neurotransmitters in the nervous system. They are stored for subse-

quent release as chemical messengers, and once released, they diffuse through the bloodstream and bind to special receptors on target cells. In fact, some chemical substances do double duty, functioning as hormones when they're released in the endocrine system and as neurotransmitters in the nervous system (norepinephrine, for example). However, there are some important differences between hormones and neurotransmitters. Neural messages generally are transmitted short distances with lightning speed (measured in milliseconds) along very specific

PREVIEW QUESTIONS

- What does the endocrine system consist of?
- What are hormones, and how do they resemble and differ from neurotransmitters?
- What is the master gland of the endocrine system?
- What are some aspects of behaviour regulated by hormones?

Figure 3.23

The endocrine system.
This graphic depicts most of the major endocrine glands. The endocrine glands secrete hormones into the bloodstream. These chemicals regulate a variety of physical functions and affect many aspects of behaviour.

SOURCE: Graphic from Starr, C. & Taggart, R. (1998). *Biology: The unity and diversity of life.* Belmont, CA: Wadsworth. © 1998 Wadsworth Publishing. Reprinted by permission.

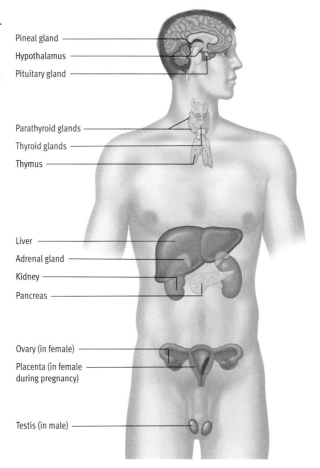

Pineal gland
Hypothalamus
Pituitary gland

Parathyroid glands
Thyroid glands
Thymus

Liver
Adrenal gland
Kidney
Pancreas

Ovary (in female)
Placenta (in female during pregnancy)

Testis (in male)

pressure. And pancreatic hormone (insulin) is essential for cells to use sugar from the blood. Hormone release tends to be *pulsatile.* That is, hormones tend to be released several times per day in brief bursts or pulses that last only a few minutes. The levels of many hormones increase and decrease in a rhythmic pattern throughout the day.

Much of the endocrine system is controlled by the nervous system through the *hypothalamus.* This structure at the base of the forebrain has intimate connections with the pea-sized *pituitary gland.* **The pituitary gland releases a great variety of hormones that fan out around the body, stimulating actions in the other endocrine glands.** In this sense, the pituitary is the "master gland" of the endocrine system, although the hypothalamus is the real power behind the throne.

The intermeshing of the nervous system and the endocrine system can be seen in the fight-or-flight response described earlier. In times of stress, the hypothalamus sends signals along two pathways—through the autonomic nervous system and through the pituitary gland—to the adrenal glands (Clow, 2001). In response, the adrenal glands secrete hormones that radiate throughout the body, preparing it to cope with an emergency (see Chapter 13). The communication between the brain and the endocrine system is not a one-way street, as hormonal fluctuations can trigger responses in the brain. For example, hormones secreted by the adrenal medulla in response to stress can signal the hypothalamus to inhibit further hormone output. The levels of many hormones are regulated through *negative feedback systems.* When a hormone increases to a certain level, signals are sent to the hypothalamus or the relevant endocrine gland to reduce or stop further secretion of that hormone.

Hormones play important roles in modulating human physiological development. For example, among the more interesting hormones released by the pituitary are the *gonadotropins,* which affect the *gonads,* or sexual glands. Prior to birth, these hormones direct the formation of the external sexual organs in the developing fetus (Breedlove, 1992). Thus, your sexual identity as a male or female was shaped during prenatal development by the actions of hormones. At puberty, increased levels of sexual hormones are responsible for the emergence of secondary sexual characteristics, such as male facial hair and female breasts (Susman, Dorn, & Schiefelbein, 2003). The actions of other hormones are responsible for the spurt in physical growth that occurs around puberty (see Chapter 11).

These developmental effects of hormones illustrate how genetic programming has a hand in behaviour. Obviously, the hormonal actions that shaped your sex

pathways, whereas hormonal messages often travel to distant cells at a much slower speed (measured in seconds and minutes) and tend to be less specific, as they can act on many target cells throughout the body.

As we will see, hormones have important effects on our body. They may even be the basis of some of the cognitive differences observed between males and females. According to Simon Fraser University neuroscientist Doreen Kimura, cognitive gender differences such as males' greater spatial ability and females' greater verbal fluency may be caused, in part, by the early effects of sex hormones on brain organization (Kimura, 1992, 2004). Hormonal differences may result in the fact that the "environment is acting on differently wired brains in boys and girls" (Kimura, 1992, p. 119). We will discuss some of the evidence for gender differences in cognitive abilities more fully in later chapters.

The major endocrine glands are shown in Figure 3.23. Some hormones are released in response to changing conditions in the body and act to regulate those conditions. For example, hormones released by the stomach and intestines help control digestion. Kidney hormones play a part in regulating blood were determined by your genetic makeup. Similarly, the hormonal changes in early adolescence that launched your growth spurt and aroused your interest in sexuality were preprogrammed over a decade earlier by your genetic inheritance. Which brings us to the role of heredity in shaping behaviour.

Heredity and Behaviour: Is It All in the Genes?

As you have learned throughout this chapter, your biological makeup is intimately related to your behaviour. That is why your genetic inheritance, which shapes your biological makeup, may have much to do with your behaviour. Most people realize that physical characteristics such as height, hair colour, blood type, and eye colour are largely shaped by heredity. But what about psychological characteristics, such as intelligence, moodiness, impulsiveness, and shyness? To what extent are people's behavioural qualities moulded by their genes? These questions are the central focus of *behavioural genetics*—an interdisciplinary field that studies the influence of genetic factors on behavioural traits.

As we saw in Chapter 1, questions about the relative importance of heredity versus environment are very old ones in psychology. However, research in behavioural genetics has grown by leaps and bounds since the 1970s, and this research has shed new light on the age-old nature-versus-nurture debate. Ironically, although behavioural geneticists have mainly sought to demonstrate the influence of heredity on behaviour, their recent work has also highlighted the importance of the environment, as we shall see in this section.

Basic Principles of Genetics

Every cell in your body contains enduring messages from your mother and father. These messages are found on the *chromosomes* that lie within the nucleus of each cell.

Chromosomes and Genes

Chromosomes are strands of DNA (deoxyribonucleic acid) molecules that carry genetic information (see Figure 3.24). Every cell in humans, except the sex cells (sperm and eggs), contains 46 chromosomes. These chromosomes operate in 23 pairs, with one chromosome of each pair being contributed by each parent. Parents make this contribution when fertilization creates a *zygote,* a single cell formed by the union of a sperm and an egg. The sex cells that form a zygote each have 23 chromosomes; together they contribute the 46 chromosomes that appear in the zygote and in all the body cells that develop

from it. Each chromosome in turn contains thousands of biochemical messengers called genes. *Genes are DNA segments that serve as the key functional units in hereditary transmission.*

If all offspring are formed by a union of the parents' sex cells, why aren't family members identical clones? The reason is that a single pair of parents can produce an extraordinary variety of combinations of chromosomes. When sex cells form in each parent, it is a matter of chance as to which member of each chromosome pair ends up in the sperm or egg. Each parent's 23 chromosome pairs can be scrambled in over 8 million (2^{23}) different ways, yielding roughly 70 trillion (2^{46}) possible configurations when sperm and egg unite. Actually, this is a conservative estimate. It doesn't take into account complexities such as *mutations* (changes in the genetic code) or *crossing over* during sex-cell formation (an interchange of material between chromosomes). Thus, genetic transmission is a complicated process, and everything is a matter of probability. Except for identical twins, each person ends up with a unique genetic blueprint.

Like chromosomes, genes operate in pairs, with one gene of each pair coming from each parent. **In the *homozygous condition*, the two genes in a specific pair are the same. In the *heterozygous condition*, the two genes in a specific pair are different** (see Figure 3.25). In the simplest scenario, a single pair of genes determines a trait. Attached versus detached earlobes provide a nice example. When both parents contribute a gene for the same type of earlobe (the *homozygous* condition), the child will have an earlobe of that type. When the parents contribute genes for different types of earlobes (the *heterozygous* condition), one gene in the pair—called the *dominant gene*—overrides or masks the other, called the *recessive gene*. Thus, **a *dominant gene* is one that is expressed when paired genes are different. A**

Figure 3.24

Genetic material. This series of enlargements shows the main components of genetic material. (Top) In the nucleus of every cell are chromosomes, which carry the information needed to construct new human beings. (Centre) Chromosomes are threadlike strands of DNA that carry thousands of genes, the functional units of hereditary transmission. (Bottom) DNA is a spiralled double chain of molecules that can copy itself to reproduce.

PREVIEW QUESTIONS

- What are the basic mechanisms of hereditary transmission?
- What is the difference between one's genotype and phenotype?
- How are family studies conducted, and what can they reveal?
- How are twin studies conducted, and what have they revealed about intelligence and personality?
- How do adoption studies assess the role of genetics and environment?
- What is genetic mapping, and how will it facilitate behavioural genetics research?

Cell

Nucleus

Chromosomes

DNA

Figure 3.25

Homozygous and heterozygous genotypes. Like chromosomes, genes operate in pairs, with one gene in each pair coming from each parent. When paired genes are the same, they are said to be homozygous. When paired genes are different, they are said to be heterozygous. Whether people have attached or detached earlobes is determined by a single pair of genes. In the heterozygous condition, genes for detached earlobes are dominant over genes for attached earlobes.

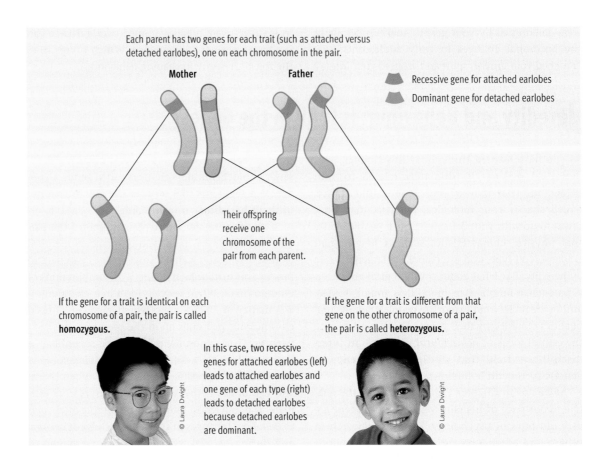

Each parent has two genes for each trait (such as attached versus detached earlobes), one on each chromosome in the pair.

Mother   Father

Recessive gene for attached earlobes
Dominant gene for detached earlobes

Their offspring receive one chromosome of the pair from each parent.

If the gene for a trait is identical on each chromosome of a pair, the pair is called **homozygous.**

If the gene for a trait is different from that gene on the other chromosome of a pair, the pair is called **heterozygous.**

In this case, two recessive genes for attached earlobes (left) leads to attached earlobes and one gene of each type (right) leads to detached earlobes because detached earlobes are dominant.

© Laura Dwight

recessive gene **is one that is masked when paired genes are different**. In the case of earlobes, genes for detached earlobes are dominant over genes for attached earlobes.

Because genes operate in pairs, a child has a 50% probability of inheriting a specific gene in a particular gene pair from each parent. Hence, the *genetic relatedness* of parents and children is said to be 50%. The genetic relatedness of other types of relatives can be calculated in the same way; the results are shown in Figure 3.26. As you can see, genetic relatedness ranges from 100% for identical twins down to 6.25% for second cousins. The numbers in Figure 3.26 are purely theoretical, and for a variety of complicated reasons they underestimate the actual genetic overlap among people. But the key to the concept of genetic relatedness is that members of a family share more of the same genes than nonmembers, and closer relatives share a larger proportion of genes than more distant relatives. These realities explain why family members tend to resemble one another and why this resemblance tends to be greater among closer relatives.

Genotype versus Phenotype

It might seem that two parents with the same manifest trait, such as detached earlobes, should always produce offspring with that trait. However, that isn't always the case. For instance, two parents with detached earlobes can produce a child with attached earlobes. This happens because there are unexpressed recessive genes in the family's gene pool—in this case, genes for attached earlobes.

This point brings us to the distinction between genotype and phenotype. *Genotype* **refers to a person's genetic makeup.** *Phenotype* **refers to the ways in which a person's genotype is manifested in observable characteristics.** Different genotypes (such as two genes for detached earlobes as opposed to one gene for detached and one for attached) can yield the same phenotype (detached earlobes). Genotype is determined at conception and is fixed forever. In contrast, phenotypic characteristics (hair colour, for instance) may change over time. They may also be modified by environmental factors.

Genotypes translate into phenotypic characteristics in a variety of ways. Not all gene pairs operate according to the principles of dominance. In some instances, when paired genes are different, they produce a blend, an "averaged out" phenotype. In other cases, paired genes that are different strike another type of compromise, and both characteristics show up phenotypically. In the case of type AB blood, for example, one gene is for type A and the other is for type B.

Polygenic Inheritance

Most human characteristics appear to be *polygenic traits,* **or characteristics that are influenced by more than one pair of genes.** For example, three to five gene pairs are thought to interactively determine skin colour. Complex physical abilities, such as motor coordination, may be influenced by tangled interactions among a great many pairs of genes. Most psychological characteristics that appear to be affected by heredity seem to involve complex polygenic inheritance (Plomin et al., 2001).

Investigating Hereditary Influence: Research Methods

How do behavioural geneticists and other scientists disentangle the effects of genetics and experience to determine whether heredity affects behavioural traits? Researchers have designed special types of studies to assess the impact of heredity. Of course, with humans they are limited to correlational rather than experimental methods, as they cannot manipulate genetic variables by assigning subjects to mate with each other (this approach, called *selective breeding,* is used in animal studies). The three most important methods in human research are family studies, twin studies, and adoption studies. After examining these classic methods of research, we'll discuss the impact of new developments in genetic mapping.

Family Studies

In *family studies* researchers assess hereditary influence by examining blood relatives to see how much they resemble one another on a specific trait. If heredity affects the trait under scrutiny, researchers should find phenotypic similarity among relatives. Furthermore, they should find more similarity among relatives who share more genes. For instance, siblings should exhibit more similarity than cousins.

Illustrative of this method are the numerous family studies conducted to assess the contribution of heredity to the development of schizophrenic disorders. These disorders strike approximately 1% of the population, yet as Figure 3.27 reveals, 9% of the siblings of schizophrenic patients exhibit schizophrenia themselves (Gottesman, 1991). Thus, these first-degree relatives of schizophrenic patients show a risk for the disorder that is nine times higher than normal. This risk is greater than that observed for more distantly related, second-degree relatives, such as nieces and nephews (4%), who, in turn, are at greater risk than third-degree relatives, such as second cousins (2%). This pattern of results is consistent with the hypothesis that genetic

inheritance influences the development of schizophrenic disorders (Gottesman & Moldin, 1998; Ho, Black, & Andreasen, 2003).

Family studies can indicate whether a trait runs in families. However, this correlation does not provide conclusive evidence that the trait is influenced by heredity. Why not? Because family members generally share not only genes but also similar environments. Furthermore, closer relatives are more likely to live together than more distant relatives. Thus, genetic similarity and environmental similarity *both* tend to be greater for closer relatives. Either of these confounded variables could be responsible when greater phenotypic similarity is found in closer relatives. Family studies can offer useful insights about the possible impact of heredity, but they cannot provide definitive evidence.

Twin Studies

Twin studies can yield better evidence about the possible role of genetic factors. In *twin studies* researchers assess hereditary influence by comparing the resemblance of identical twins and fraternal twins with respect to a trait. The logic of twin studies hinges on the genetic relatedness of identical and fraternal twins (see Figure 3.28). *Identical (monozygotic) twins emerge from one zygote that splits for unknown reasons.* Thus, they have exactly the same genotype; their genetic relatedness is 100%. *Fraternal (dizygotic)*

Relationship		Degree of relatedness
Identical twins		100%
Fraternal twins Brother or sister Parent or child	First-degree relatives	50%
Grandparent or grandchild Uncle, aunt, nephew, or niece Half-brother or half-sister	Second-degree relatives	25%
First cousin	Third-degree relatives	12.5%
Second cousin	Fourth-degree relatives	6.25%
Unrelated		0%

Figure 3.26

Genetic relatedness.
Research on the genetic bases of behaviour takes advantage of the different degrees of genetic relatedness between various types of relatives. If heredity influences a trait, relatives who share more genes should be more similar with regard to that trait than are more distant relatives, who share fewer genes. Comparisons involving various degrees of biological relationships will come up frequently in later chapters.

Figure 3.27

Family studies of risk for schizophrenic disorders.
First-degree relatives of schizophrenic patients have an elevated risk of developing a schizophrenic disorder (Gottesman, 1991). For instance, the risk for siblings of schizophrenic patients is about 9% instead of the baseline 1% for unrelated people. Second- and third-degree relatives have progressively smaller elevations in risk for this disorder. Although these patterns of risk do not prove that schizophrenia is partly inherited, they are consistent with this hypothesis.

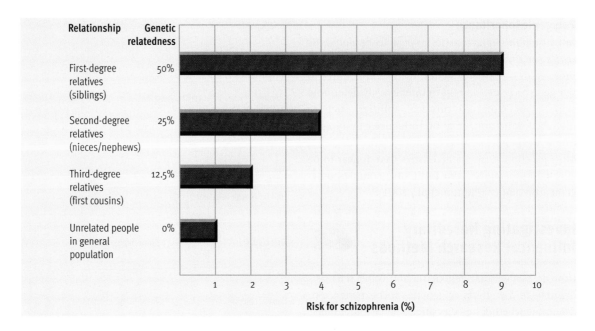

twins **result when two eggs are fertilized simultaneously by different sperm cells, forming two separate zygotes.** Fraternal twins are no more alike in genetic makeup than any two siblings born to a pair of parents at different times. Their genetic relatedness is only 50%.

Fraternal twins provide a useful comparison to identical twins because in both cases the twins usually grow up in the same home, at the same time, exposed to the same configuration of relatives, neighbours, peers, teachers, events, and so forth. Thus, both kinds of twins normally develop under equally similar environmental conditions. However, identical twins share more genetic kinship than fraternal twins. Consequently, if sets of identical twins tend to exhibit more similarity on a trait than sets of fraternal twins do, it is reasonable to infer that this greater similarity is *probably* due to heredity rather than environment.

Twin studies have been conducted to assess the impact of heredity on a variety of traits. Some representative results are summarized in Figure 3.29. The higher correlations found for identical twins indicate that they tend to be more similar to each other than fraternal twins on measures of general intelligence (McGue et al., 1993) and measures of specific personality traits, such as extraversion (Loehlin, 1992). These results support the notion that intelligence and personality are influenced to some degree by genetic makeup. However, the fact that identical twins are far from identical in intelligence and personality also shows that environment influences these characteristics.

Adoption Studies

Adoption studies **assess hereditary influence by examining the resemblance between adopted children and both their biological and their adoptive parents.** Generally, adoptees are used as subjects in this type of study only if they were given up for adoption in early infancy and were raised without having contact with their biological parents. The logic underlying the adoption study approach is quite simple. If adopted children resemble their biological parents on a trait, even though they were not raised by them, genetic factors probably influence that trait. In contrast, if adopted children resemble their adoptive parents, even though they inherited no genes from them, environmental factors probably influence the trait.

In recent years, adoption studies have contributed to science's understanding of how genetics and the environment influence intelligence. The research shows modest similarity between adopted children and their biological parents, as indicated by an average correlation of 0.22 (Grigorenko, 2000). Interestingly, adopted children resemble their adoptive parents just as much (also an average correlation of about 0.20). These findings suggest that both heredity and environment have an influence on intelligence.

The Cutting Edge: Genetic Mapping

While behavioural geneticists have recently made great progress in documenting the influence of heredity on behaviour, *molecular geneticists,* who study the biochemical bases of genetic inheritance, have made even more spectacular advances in their

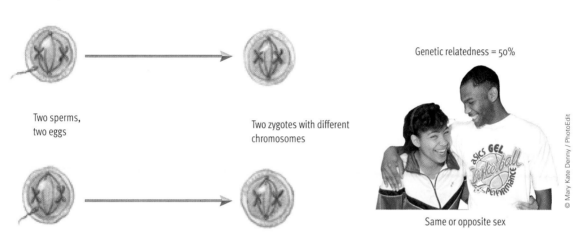

Identical (monozygotic) twins

One sperm, one egg → Zygote divides → Two zygotes with identical chromosomes

Genetic relatedness = 100%

Same sex only

© Marina Jefferson/Taxi/Getty Images

Figure 3.28

Identical versus fraternal twins. Identical (monozygotic) twins emerge from one zygote that splits, so their genetic relatedness is 100%. Fraternal (dizygotic) twins emerge from two separate zygotes, so their genetic relatedness is only 50%.

Source: Adapted from Kalat, J. (1996). *Introduction to psychology*, 4th edition, © 1996 Belmont, CA: Wadsworth. Reprinted by permission.

Fraternal (dizygotic) twins

Two sperms, two eggs → Two zygotes with different chromosomes

Genetic relatedness = 50%

Same or opposite sex

© Mary Kate Denny / PhotoEdit

efforts to unravel the genetic code. ***Genetic mapping is the process of determining the location and chemical sequence of specific genes on specific chromosomes.*** New methods of manipulating DNA are now allowing scientists to create detailed physical maps of the genetic material on chromosomes in plants, animals, and humans. The Human Genome Project, a huge international enterprise, has produced a working draft of the sequence of all 3 billion letters of DNA in the human genome, and the chromosomal location of almost all human genes has been identified (Kelsoe, 2004). Gene maps, by themselves, do not reveal which genes govern which traits. However, the compilation of a precise genetic atlas will fuel a quantum leap in the ability of scientists to pinpoint links between specific genes and specific traits and disorders. For example, medical researchers have already identified the genes responsible for cystic fibrosis, Huntington's chorea, and muscular dystrophy. Many medical researchers predict that genetic mapping will ultimately lead to revolutionary

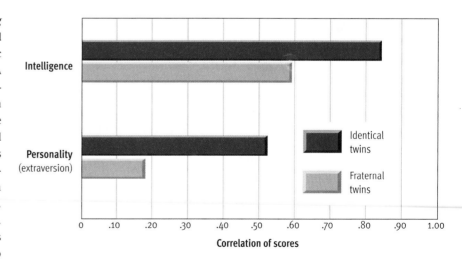

Figure 3.29

Twin studies of intelligence and personality. Identical twins tend to be more similar than fraternal twins (as reflected in higher correlations) with regard to intelligence and specific personality traits, such as extraversion. These findings suggest that intelligence and personality are influenced by heredity. (Intelligence data from McGue et al., 1993; extraversion data based on Loehlin, 1992)

The Pennsylvania State University Center for Development and Health Genetics

❝*The transformation of the social and behavioural sciences from environmentalism to biological determinism is happening so fast that I find I more often have to say, 'Yes, genetic influences are substantial, but environmental influences are important, too.'*❞

ROBERT PLOMIN

advances in the diagnosis and treatment of physical diseases (Collins & McKusick, 2001).

Will genetic mapping permit researchers to discover the genetic basis for intelligence, extraversion, musical ability, and other *behavioural* traits? Perhaps someday, but progress is likely to be painstakingly slow (Cowan, Kopinski, & Hyman, 2002; Plomin & McGuffin, 2003). Virtually all behavioural traits appear to be *polygenic* and are shaped by many genes rather than a single gene. Because of these and a host of other complexities, scientists are not likely to find a single gene that controls intelligence, extraversion, or musical talent (Plomin & Crabbe, 2000). The challenge will be to identify specific constellations of genes that each exert modest influence over particular aspects of behaviour.

The Interplay of Heredity and Environment

We began this section by asking, is it all in the genes? When it comes to behavioural traits, the answer clearly is no. According to Robert Plomin (1993, 2004), perhaps the leading behavioural genetics researcher in the last decade, what scientists find again and again is that heredity and experience jointly influence most aspects of behaviour. Moreover, their effects are interactive—genetics and experience play off each other (Gottesman & Hanson, 2005; Rutter & Silberg, 2002; Rutter, 1997).

For example, consider what researchers have learned about the development of schizophrenic disorders. Although the evidence indicates that genetic factors influence the development of schizophrenia, it does *not* appear that anyone directly inherits the disorder itself. Rather, what people appear to inherit is a certain degree of *vulnerability* to the disorder (McDonald & Murphy, 2003; Paris, 1999). Whether this vulnerability is ever converted into an actual disorder depends on each person's experiences in life. As we will discuss in Chapter 14, certain types of stressful experience seem to evoke the disorder in people who are more vulnerable to it. Thus, as Danielle Dick and Richard Rose (2002) put it in a major review of behavioural genetics research, "We inherit dispositions, not destinies."

REVIEW OF KEY POINTS

● The endocrine system consists of the glands that secrete hormones, which are chemicals involved in the regulation of basic bodily processes. The control centres for the endocrine system are the hypothalamus and the pituitary gland.

● Hormones regulate many aspects of behaviour, such as the fight-or-flight response, and many aspects of physiological development, such as sexual differentiation.

● The basic units of genetic transmission are genes housed on chromosomes. Genes operate in pairs, and, when heterozygous, one may be dominant and one recessive. Genotypes are translated into phenotypes in many ways. Most behavioural qualities appear to involve polygenic inheritance.

● Researchers assess hereditary influence through a variety of methods, including family studies, twin studies, adoption studies, and genetic mapping. Family studies cannot provide conclusive evidence that a trait is influenced by heredity. Twin studies can provide much better evidence.

● Research indicates that most behavioural qualities are influenced jointly by heredity and environment, which play off of each other in complex interactions.

CONCEPT **CHECK 3.4**

Recognizing Hereditary Influence

Check your understanding of the methods scientists use to explore hereditary influences on specific behavioural traits by filling in the blanks in the descriptive statements below. The answers can be found in the back of the book in Appendix A.

1. The findings from family studies indicate that heredity may influence a trait if _____ show more trait similarity than _____.

2. The findings from twin studies suggest that heredity influences a trait if _____ show more trait similarity than _____.

3. The findings from adoption studies suggest that heredity influences a trait if children adopted at a young age share more trait similarity with their _____ than their _____.

4. The findings from family studies, twin studies, or adoption studies suggest that heredity does not influence a trait when _____ is not related to _____.

The Evolutionary Bases of Behaviour

To round out our look at the biological bases of behaviour, we need to discuss how evolutionary forces have shaped many aspects of human and animal behaviour. As you may recall from Chapter 1, *evolutionary psychology* is a major new theoretical perspective in the field that analyzes behavioural processes in terms of their adaptive significance. In this section, we will outline some basic principles of evolutionary theory and relate them to animal behaviour. These ideas will create a foundation for forthcoming chapters, where we'll see how these principles can enhance our understanding of many aspects of human behaviour.

Darwin's Insights

Charles Darwin, the legendary British naturalist, was *not* the first person to describe the process of evolution. Well before Darwin's time, other biologists who had studied the earth's fossil record noted that various species appeared to have undergone gradual changes over the course of a great many generations. What Darwin (1859) contributed in his landmark book, *The Origin of Species,* was a creative, new explanation for *how and why* evolutionary changes unfold over time. He identified *natural selection* as the mechanism that orchestrates the process of evolution.

The mystery that Darwin set out to solve was complicated. He wanted to explain how the characteristics of a species might change over generations and why these changes tended to be surprisingly adaptive. In other words, he wanted to shed light on why organisms tend to have characteristics that serve them well in the context of their environments. For example, how did giraffes acquire their long necks that allow them to reach high into acacia trees to secure their main source of food? Darwin's explanation for the seemingly purposive nature of evolution centred on four crucial insights.

First, he noted that organisms vary in endless ways, such as size, speed, strength, aspects of appearance, visual abilities, hearing capacities, digestive processes, cell structure, and so forth. Second, he noted that some of these characteristics are heritable—that is, they are passed down from one generation to the next. Although genes and chromosomes had not yet been discovered, the concept of heredity was well established. In Darwin's theory, variations in hereditary traits provide the crude materials for evolution. Third, borrowing from the work of Thomas Malthus, he noted that organisms tend to

produce offspring at a pace that outstrips the local availability of food supplies, living space, and other crucial resources. As a population increases and resources dwindle, the competition for precious resources intensifies. Thus, it occurred to Darwin—and this was his grand insight—that variations in hereditary traits might affect organisms' ability to obtain the resources necessary for survival and reproduction. Fourth, building on this insight, Darwin argued that if a specific heritable trait contributes to an organism's survival or reproductive success, organisms with that trait should produce more offspring than those without the trait (or those with less of the trait), and the prevalence of that trait should gradually increase over generations—resulting in evolutionary change.

Although evolution is widely characterized as a matter of "survival of the fittest," Darwin recognized from the beginning that survival is only important insofar as it relates to reproductive success. Indeed, in evolutionary theory, **fitness refers to the reproductive success (number of descendants) of an individual organism relative to the average reproductive success in the population.** *Variations in reproductive success are what really fuels evolutionary change.* But survival is crucial because organisms typically need to mature and thrive before they can reproduce. So, Darwin theorized that there ought to be two ways in which traits might contribute to evolution: by providing either a survival advantage or a reproductive advantage. For example, a turtle's shell has great protective value that provides a survival advantage. In contrast, a firefly's emission of light is a courtship overture that provides a reproductive advantage.

To summarize, the principle of **natural selection posits that heritable characteristics that provide a survival or reproductive advantage are more likely than alternative characteristics to be passed on to subsequent generations and thus come to be "selected" over time.** Please note that the process of natural selection works on *populations* rather than *organisms*. Evolution occurs when the gene pool in a population changes gradually as a result of selection pressures.

Darwin's theory was highly controversial for at least two reasons: (a) it suggested that the awe-inspiring diversity of life is the result of an unplanned, natural process rather than divine creation, and (b) it implied that humans are not unique and that they share a common ancestry with other

PREVIEW QUESTIONS
- What were Darwin's four key insights?
- Can adaptations linger in a population even if they are no longer adaptive?
- How do evolutionary theorists explain self-sacrifice?
- How can behaviours be adaptive?

© Bettmann/CORBIS

"*Can we doubt (remembering that many more individuals are born than can possibly survive) that individuals having any advantage, however slight, over others, would have the best chance of surviving and procreating their kind? . . . This preservation of favourable variations and the rejection of injurious variations, I call Natural Selection.*"
CHARLES DARWIN

Photo by John Dominis/Time Life Pictures/Getty Images

The fight-or-flight response discussed earlier in the chapter (see page 88) is an example of a behaviour that provides a survival advantage. Although traits that convey a survival advantage can contribute to evolution, it is variations in reproductive fitness that ultimately fuel evolutionary change.

species. Nonetheless, Darwin's theory eventually gained considerable acceptance because it provided a compelling explanation for how the characteristics of various species gradually changed over many generations and for the functional, adaptive direction of these changes.

Subsequent Refinements to Evolutionary Theory

Although Darwin's evolutionary theory quickly acquired many articulate advocates, it also remained controversial for decades. One legitimate objection was that the theory did not provide an adequate explanation for the details of the inheritance process. This shortcoming was gradually rectified. Gregor Mendel's previously ignored work on patterns of inheritance started attracting attention around 1900. Research building on his insights led to major advances in the understanding of heredity over the next several decades. By 1937, these advances were sufficient to permit Theodore Dobzhansky to write a fairly comprehensive and convincing account of the evolutionary process in genetic terms. Dobzhansky's synthesis of Darwinian natural selection and Mendelian genetics was enormously influential, and by the 1950s the core tenets of evolutionary theory enjoyed widespread acceptance among scientists.

Contemporary models of evolution recognize that natural selection operates on the gene pool of a population. The makeup of a gene pool is also shaped by genetic drift, mutations, and gene flow. *Genetic drift* consists of random fluctuation in gene frequencies over generations, as a result of chance alone. **A *mutation* is a spontaneous, heritable change in a piece of DNA that occurs in an indi-**vidual organism.** Mutations are unpredictable errors in DNA replication. Although infrequent, mutations increase the variability in a gene pool and give natural selection new genetic material to work with. Most mutations are not beneficial, but the minority that prove adaptive are increasingly passed on to subsequent generations. *Gene flow* occurs when gene frequencies in a population shift because some individuals leave the population (emigration) and others enter it (immigration). Gene flow operates to keep neighbouring populations genetically similar. It can counterbalance gene pool differences between populations that have developed as a result of genetic drift, mutation, and natural selection. Conversely, when the gene flow between populations is minimal, the populations may evolve in divergent directions. This divergence can eventually contribute to the emergence of new species.

Adaptations are the key product of the process of evolution. **An *adaptation* is an inherited characteristic that increased in a population (through natural selection) because it helped solve a problem of survival or reproduction during the time it emerged.** Because of the gradual, incremental nature of evolution, adaptations sometimes linger in a population even though they no longer provide a survival or reproductive advantage. For example, as noted earlier, the physiological arousal associated with the "fight or flight response" that aided humans' survival in more primitive times appears to be more detrimental than adaptive today, as it leads to a variety of stress-related diseases (see Chapter 13). Similarly, humans show a taste preference for fatty substances that was adaptive in an era of hunting and gathering, when dietary fat was a scarce source of important calories. However, in our modern world, where dietary fat is typically available in abundance, this taste preference leads many people to consume too much fat, resulting in obesity, heart disease, and other health problems. Thus, the preference for fatty foods has become a liability for human survival (although its impact on reproductive success is more difficult to gauge). Organisms' environments often undergo changes so that adaptations that were once beneficial become obsolete. As you will see, evolutionary psychologists have found that many aspects of human nature reflect the adaptive demands faced by our ancient ancestors rather than contemporary demands. Of course, as natural selection continues to work, these formerly adaptive traits should gradually be eliminated, but the process is extremely slow.

In recent decades, theorists have broadened Darwin's original concept of reproductive fitness to better explain a variety of phenomena. For example, traditional evolutionary theory had difficulty explaining self-sacrifice. If organisms try to maximize their reproductive success, why does a blackbird risk death to signal the approach of a hawk to others in the flock? And why would a tribesman risk life and limb to race into a burning hut to save young children? In 1964, W. D. Hamilton proposed the theory of *inclusive fitness* to explain the paradox of self-sacrifice. According to Hamilton, an organism may contribute to passing on its genes by sacrificing itself to save others that share the same genes. Helping behaviour that evolves as members of a species protect their own offspring, for example, can be extended to other, more distantly related members of the species. Thus, **inclusive fitness is the sum of an individual's own reproductive success plus the effects the organism has on the reproductive success of related others.** The concept of inclusive fitness suggests that the probability of self-sacrifice decreases as the degree of relatedness between a helper and potential recipients declines, a prediction that has been supported in studies of organisms as diverse as ground squirrels (Sherman, 1981) and humans (Burnstein, Crandall, & Kitayama, 1994).

Behaviours as Adaptive Traits

Scholarly analyses of evolution have focused primarily on the evolution of *physical characteristics* in the animal kingdom, but from the very beginning, Darwin recognized that natural selection was applicable to *behavioural traits* as well. Studying the evolution of behaviour is more difficult than studying the evolution of physical traits because behaviour is more transient—crucial behaviours by an organism may occur infrequently and may not last long. For example, female wood frogs are sexually receptive just one night per year. Additionally, although the fossil record *can* leave clues about past organisms' behaviour (such as its prey or nesting habits), it leaves much more detailed information about organisms' physical characteristics. Nonetheless, it is clear that a species' typical patterns of behaviour often reflect evolutionary solutions to adaptive problems.

Let's look at some additional examples of how evolution has shaped organisms' behaviour. Avoiding predators is a nearly universal problem for organisms. Because of natural selection, many species, such as the grasshopper, have developed physical characteristics that allow them to blend in with their environments, making detection by predators more difficult. Many organisms also engage in elaborate *behavioural manoeuvres* to hide themselves. For example, the grasshopper pictured below has dug itself a small trench in which to hide and has used its midlegs to pull pebbles over its back (Alcock, 1998). This clever hiding behaviour is just as much a product of evolution as the grasshopper's remarkable camouflage.

The "stotting" behaviour exhibited by Thomson's gazelles when they spot a cheetah is another example of a behavioural adaptation. The cheetah is a feared predator that elicits evasive actions in Thomson's gazelles. But as the gazelles start to flee, they often

Web Link 3.7

Human Behavior and Evolution Society
http://www.hbes.com/

The HBES is an interdisciplinary organization devoted to the exploration of human behaviour from the perspective of evolutionary theory. This site provides a particularly rich set of links to published and online materials and organizations dealing with the evolutionary perspective on behaviour.

The behaviour that helps the grasshopper on the left hide from predators is a product of evolution, just like the physical characteristics that help it blend in with its surroundings. As explained in the text, the stotting behaviour exhibited by Thomson's gazelles is adaptive in that it is intended to deter the pursuit of predators.

slow up briefly to *stot*—that is, they jump high into the air with all four legs held straight and their white rump fully displayed. Slowing up when fleeing may not sound adaptive, but research has revealed that gazelles stot to signal to the cheetah that they have spotted the predator, they are off and running, and they will be difficult to catch. Consistent with this interpretation, stotting increases the likelihood that a cheetah will abandon its pursuit of a gazelle (Caro, 1986). Thus, stotting is a behavioural adaptation, in that it enhances the probability of survival by deterring pursuit and saves precious energy that may be needed to evade another predator.

Many behavioural adaptations are designed to improve organisms' chances of reproductive success.

Consider, for instance, the wide variety of species in which females actively choose which male to mate with. In many such species, females demand material goods and services from males in return for copulation opportunities. For example, in one type of moth, males have to spend hours extracting sodium from mud puddles, which they then transfer to prospective mates, who use it to supply their larvae with an important nutritional element (Smedley & Eisner, 1996). In the black-tipped hangingfly, females insist on a nuptial gift of food before they mate. They reject suitors bringing unpalatable food, and they tie the length of subsequent copulation to the size of the nuptial gift (Thornhill, 1976).

Putting It in Perspective

PREVIEW QUESTIONS
- How did this chapter demonstrate that heredity and environment shape behaviour interactively?
- How did this chapter illustrate multifactorial causation?
- How did this chapter clarify the empirical nature of psychology?

Three of our seven themes stood out in this chapter: (1) heredity and environment jointly influence behaviour, (2) behaviour is determined by multiple causes, and (3) psychology is empirical. Let's look at each of these points.

In Chapter 1, when it was first emphasized that heredity and environment jointly shape behaviour, you may have been a little perplexed about how your genes could be responsible for your sarcastic wit or your interest in art. In fact, there are no genes for behaviour per se. Experts do not expect to find genes for sarcasm or artistic interest, for example. Insofar as your hereditary endowment plays a role in your behaviour, it does so *indirectly,* by moulding the physiological machine that you work with. Thus, your genes influence your physiological makeup, which in turn influences your personality, temperament, intelligence, interests, and other traits. Bear in mind, however, that genetic factors do not operate in a vacuum. Genes exert their effects in an environmental context. The impact of genetic makeup depends on environment, and the impact of environment depends on genetic makeup.

The empirical nature of psychology was apparent in the numerous discussions of the specialized research methods used to study the physiological bases of behaviour. As you know, the empirical approach depends on precise observation. Throughout this chapter, you've seen how investigators have come up with innovative methods to observe and measure elusive phenomena such as electrical activity in the brain, neural impulses, brain function, cerebral specialization, and the impact of heredity on behaviour. The point is that empirical methods are the lifeblood of the scientific enterprise. When researchers figure out how to better observe something, their new methods usually facilitate major advances in our scientific knowledge. That is why brain-imaging techniques and genetic mapping hold such exciting promise.

The importance of empiricism will also be apparent in the upcoming Personal Application and Critical Thinking Application that follow. In both you'll see that it is important to learn to distinguish between scientific findings and conjecture based on those findings.

REVIEW OF KEY POINTS
- Darwin argued that if a heritable trait contributes to an organism's survival or reproductive success, organisms with that trait should produce more offspring than those without the trait and that the prevalence of that trait should gradually increase over generations—thanks to natural selection.
- Because of the gradual, incremental nature of evolution, adaptations sometimes linger in a population even though they no longer provide a survival or reproductive advantage. Hamilton proposed the theory of inclusive fitness to explain the paradox of self-sacrifice.
- Theorists have focused primarily on the evolution of *physical characteristics* in the animal kingdom, but from the very beginning Darwin recognized that natural selection was applicable to *behavioural traits* as well.
- Three of the book's unifying themes stand out in this chapter. First, we saw how heredity interacts with experience to govern behaviour. Second, the discussions of biological factors underlying schizophrenia highlighted the multifactorial causation of behaviour. Third, we saw how innovations in research methods often lead to advances in knowledge, underscoring the empirical nature of psychology.

Evaluating the Concept of "Two Minds in One"

Answer the following "true" or "false."

____ **1** The right and left brains give people two minds in one.

____ **2** Each half of the brain has its own special mode of thinking.

____ **3** Some people are left-brained while others are right-brained.

____ **4** Schools should devote more effort to teaching the overlooked right side of the brain.

Do people have two minds in one that think differently? Do some people depend on one side of the brain more than the other? Is the right side of the brain neglected? These questions are too complex to resolve with a simple true or false, but in this Application we'll take a closer look at the issues involved in these proposed applications of the findings on cerebral specialization. You'll learn that some of these ideas are plausible, but in many cases the hype has outstripped the evidence.

Earlier, we described Roger Sperry's Nobel Prize–winning research with split-brain patients, whose right and left hemispheres were disconnected (to reduce epileptic seizures). The split-brain studies showed that the previously underrated right hemisphere has some special talents of its own. This discovery detonated an explosion of research on cerebral laterality.

Cerebral Specialization and Cognitive Processes

 SIM2, 2F

Using a variety of methods, scientists have compiled mountains of data on the specialized abilities of the right and left hemispheres. These findings have led to extensive theorizing about how the right and left brains might be related to cognitive processes. Some of the more intriguing ideas include the following:

1. *The two hemispheres are specialized to process different types of cognitive tasks* (Corballis, 1991; Ornstein, 1977). The findings of many researchers have been widely interpreted as showing that the left hemisphere handles verbal tasks, including language, speech, writing, math, and logic, while the right hemisphere handles nonverbal tasks, including spatial problems, music, art, fantasy, and creativity. These conclusions have attracted a great deal of public interest and media attention. For example, Figure 3.30 shows a *Newsweek* artist's depiction of how the brain divides its work.

2. *Each hemisphere has its own independent stream of consciousness* (Bogen, 1985, 2000; Pucetti, 1981). For instance, Joseph Bogen has asserted, "Pending further evidence, I believe that each of us has two minds in one

person" (Hooper & Teresi, 1986, p. 221). Supposedly, this duality of consciousness goes largely unnoticed because of the considerable overlap between the experiences of each independent mind. Ultimately, though, the apparent unity of consciousness is but an illusion.

3. *The two hemispheres have different modes of thinking* (Banich & Heller, 1998; Joseph, 1992). According to this notion, the documented differences between the hemispheres in dealing with verbal and nonverbal materials are due to more basic differences in *how* the hemispheres process information. The standard version of this theory holds that the reason the left hemisphere handles verbal material well is that it is analytic, abstract, rational, logical, and linear. In contrast, the right hemisphere is thought to be better equipped

Figure 3.30

Popular conceptions of hemispheric specialization. As this *Newsweek* diagram illustrates, depictions of hemispheric specialization in the popular press have often been oversimplified.

Source: Cartoon courtesy of Roy Doty.

HOW THE BRAIN DIVIDES ITS WORK

to handle spatial and musical material because it is synthetic, concrete, nonrational, intuitive, and holistic. Robert Ornstein (1997) characterizes hemispheric differences in cognitive processing somewhat differently, asserting that the left hemisphere focuses on details while the right hemisphere responds to global patterns and the big picture.

4. *People vary in their reliance on one hemisphere as opposed to the other* (Bakan, 1971; Zenhausen, 1978). Allegedly, some people are "left-brained." Their greater dependence on their left hemisphere supposedly makes them analytic, rational, and logical. Other people are "right-brained." Their greater use of their right hemisphere supposedly makes them intuitive, holistic, and irrational. Being right-brained or left-brained is thought to explain many personal characteristics, such as whether an individual likes to read, is good with maps, or enjoys music. This notion of "brainedness" has even been used to explain occupational choice. Supposedly, right-brained people are more likely to become artists or musicians, while left-brained people are more likely to become writers or scientists.

5. *Schools should place more emphasis on teaching the right side of the brain* (Kitchens, 1991; Prince, 1978). "A real reform of the educational system will not occur until individual teachers learn to understand the true duality of their students' minds," says Thomas Blakeslee (1980, p. 59). Those sympathetic to his view assert that schools overemphasize logical, analytical left-hemisphere thinking (required by English, math, and science) while short-changing intuitive, holistic right-hemisphere thinking (required by art and music). These educators have concluded that modern schools turn out an excess of left-brained graduates. They advocate curriculum reform to strengthen the right side of the brain in their students. This line of thinking has also spawned quite a collection of popular self-help books, such as *Whole-Brain Thinking* (Wonder, 1992), *Unleashing the Right Side of the Brain* (Williams & Stockmyer, 1987), and *Workout for the Balanced Brain* (Carter & Russell, 2001).

Complexities and Qualifications SIM2, 2F

The ideas just outlined are the source of considerable debate among psychologists and neuroscientists. These ideas are intriguing and have clearly captured the imagination of the general public. However, the research on cerebral specialization is complex, and doubts have been raised about many of these ideas (Efron, 1990; Springer & Deutsch, 1998). Let's examine each point.

1. There *is* ample evidence that the right and left hemispheres are specialized to handle different types of cognitive tasks, *but only to a degree* (Brown & Kosslyn, 1993; Corballis, 2003). While at the University of Western Ontario, Doreen Kimura (1973) compared the abilities of the right and left hemispheres to quickly recognize letters, words, faces, and melodies in a series of perceptual asymmetry studies, like those described earlier in the chapter. She found that the superiority of one hemisphere over the other was usually quite modest, as you can see in Figure 3.31, which shows superiority ratios for four cognitive tasks.

Furthermore, in normal individuals, the hemispheres don't work alone. As Hellige (1993) notes, "In the intact brain, it is unlikely that either hemisphere is ever completely uninvolved in ongoing processing" (p. 23). Most tasks probably engage *both* hemispheres, albeit to different degrees (Beeman & Chiarello, 1998; Ornstein, 1997). For instance, imagine that you are asked the following question: "In what direction are you headed if you start north and make two right turns and a left turn?" In answering this question, you're confronted with a *spatial* task that should engage the right hemisphere. However, first you have to process the wording of the question, a *language* task that should engage the left hemisphere.

Furthermore, people differ in their patterns of cerebral specialization (Springer & Deutsch, 1998). Some people display little specialization—that is, their hemispheres seem to have equal abilities on various types of tasks. Others even reverse the usual specialization, so that verbal processing might be housed in the right hemisphere. These unusual patterns are especially common among left-handed people (Josse & Tzourio-Mazoyer, 2004). For example, when Rasmussen and Milner (1977) tested subjects for the localization of speech, they found bilateral representation in 15% of the left-handers. They found a reversal of the usual specialization (speech handled by the right hemisphere) in another 15% of

Figure 3.31

Relative superiority of one brain hemisphere over the other in studies of perceptual asymmetry.
These performance ratios from a study by Doreen Kimura (1973) show the degree to which one hemisphere was "superior" to the other on each type of task in one study of normal participants. For example, the right hemisphere was 20% better than the left hemisphere in quickly recognizing melodic patterns (ratio 1.2 to 1). Most differences in the performance of the two hemispheres are quite small. (Data from Kimura, 1973)

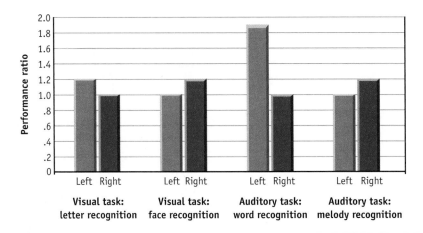

Figure 3.32

Handedness and patterns of speech localization. Left-handed people tend to show more variety in cerebral specialization and more bilateral representation than right-handers. For example, speech processing is almost always localized in the left hemisphere of right-handed subjects. However, Rasmussen and Milner (1977) found the usual pattern of speech localization in only 70% of their left-handed subjects. (Data from Rasmussen & Milner, 1977)

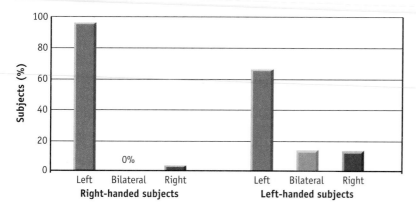

the left-handed subjects (see Figure 3.32). These variations in cerebral specialization are not well understood. However, they clearly indicate that the functional specialization of the cerebral hemispheres is not set in concrete.

2. The evidence for the idea that people have a separate stream of consciousness in each hemisphere is weak. There *are* clear signs of such duality among *split-brain patients* (Bogen, 1990; Mark, 1996). But this duality is probably a unique byproduct of the radical procedure that they have undergone—the surgical disconnection of their hemispheres (Bradshaw, 1981). In fact, many theorists have been impressed by the degree to which even split-brain patients mostly experience *unity* of consciousness. There is little empirical basis for the idea that people have two independent streams of awareness neatly housed in the right and left halves of the brain.

3. Similarly, there is little direct evidence to support the notion that each hemisphere has its own mode of thinking, or *cognitive style* (Bradshaw, 1989). This notion is plausible and there *is* some supportive evidence, but the evidence is inconsistent and more research is needed (Gordon, 1990; Reuter-Lorenz & Miller, 1998). One key problem with this idea is that aspects of cognitive

style have proven difficult to define and measure (Brownell & Gardner, 1981). For instance, there is debate about the meaning of analytic versus synthetic thinking, or linear versus holistic thinking.

4. The evidence on the assertion that some people are left-brained while others are right-brained is inconclusive at best (Hellige, 1990). This notion has some plausibility—*if* it means only that some people consistently display more activation of one hemisphere than the other. However, researchers have yet to develop reliable measures of these possible "preferences" in cerebral activation. Hence, there are no convincing data linking braineduess to musical ability, occupational choice, or the like (Springer & Deutsch, 1998).

5. The idea that schools should be reformed to better exercise the right side of the brain represents intriguing but wild speculation. In neurologically intact people it is impossible to teach just one hemisphere at a time (J. Levy, 1985). Many sound arguments exist for reforming schools to encourage more holistic, intuitive thinking, but these arguments have nothing to do with cerebral specialization.

In summary, the theories linking cerebral specialization to cognitive processes are highly speculative. There's nothing wrong

with theoretical speculation. Unfortunately, the tentative, conjectural nature of these ideas about cerebral specialization has gotten lost in the popular book descriptions of research on the right and left hemispheres (Coren, 1992). Popular writers continue to churn out allegedly scientific books, applying brain lateralization concepts to a host of new topics on which there often is little or no real evidence. Thus, one can find books on how to have right-brain sex (Wells, 1991), develop right-brain social skills (Snyder, 1989), and lose weight with a right-brain diet (Sommer, 1987). Commenting on this popularization, Hooper and Teresi (1986) note, "A widespread cult of the right brain ensued, and the duplex house that Sperry built grew into the K mart of brain science. Today our hairdresser lectures us about the 'Two Hemispheres of the Brain,'" (p. 223). Cerebral specialization is an important and intriguing area of research. However, it is unrealistic to expect that the hemispheric divisions in the brain will provide a biological explanation for every dichotomy or polarity in modes of thinking.

REVIEW OF KEY POINTS

- Split-brain research stimulated speculation about relations between cerebral specialization and cognitive processes. Some theorists believe that each hemisphere has its own stream of consciousness and mode of thinking, which are applied to specific types of cognitive tasks.

- Some theorists also believe that people vary in their reliance on the right and left halves of the brain and that schools should work more to exercise the right half of the brain.

- The cerebral hemispheres *are* specialized for handling different cognitive tasks, but only to a degree, as most tasks engage both hemispheres. Moreover, people vary in their patterns of hemispheric specialization.

- Evidence for duality in consciousness divided along hemispheric lines is weak. Evidence on whether people vary in braineduess and whether the two hemispheres vary in cognitive style is inconclusive.

- There is no way to teach only one hemisphere of the brain, so a "right-brain curriculum" is pointless. Popular ideas about the right and left brain have gone far beyond the actual research findings.

The Biological Bases of Behaviour

Building Better Brains:
The Perils of Extrapolation

Summarizing the implications of recent research in neuroscience, science writer Ronald Kotulak (1996) concluded, "The first three years of a child's life are critically important to brain development" (pp. ix–x). In some countries, well-intended educational groups and elected officials have argued for the creation of schools for infants on the grounds that enriched educational experiences during infancy will lead to enhanced neural development.

What are these practical, new discoveries about the brain that will permit parents and educators to optimize infants' brain development? Well, we will discuss the pertinent research momentarily, but it is not as new or as practical as suggested in many quarters. Unfortunately, as we saw in our discussion of research on hemispheric specialization, the hype in the media has greatly outstripped the realities of what scientists have learned in the laboratory (Chance, 2001).

This focus on the brain led many child-care advocates and educational reformers to use research in neuroscience as the rationale for the policies they sought to promote, as a host of books on "brain-based learning" were published (see Jensen, 2000; Sousa, 2000; Sprenger, 2001). The people advocating these ideas have good intentions, but the neuroscience rationale has been stretched to the breaking point. The result? An enlightening case study in the perils of overextrapolation.

The Key Findings on Neural Development

The education and child-care reformers who have used brain science as the basis for their campaigns have primarily cited two key findings: the discovery of critical periods in neural development and the demonstration that rats raised in "enriched environments" have more synapses than rats raised in "impoverished environments." Let's look at each of these findings.

A *critical period* **is a limited time span in the development of an organism when it is optimal for certain capacities to emerge because the organism is especially responsive to certain experiences.** The seminal research on critical periods in neural development was conducted by Torsten Wiesel and David Hubel (1963, 1965) in the 1960s. They showed that if an eye of a newborn kitten is sutured shut early in its development (typically the first four to six weeks), the kitten will become permanently blind in that eye, but if the eye is covered for the same amount of time at later ages (after four months) blindness does not result. Such studies show that certain types of visual input are necessary during a critical period of development, or neural pathways between the eye and brain will not form properly. Basically, what happens is that the inactive synapses from the closed eye are displaced by the active synapses from the open eye. Critical periods have been found for other aspects of neural development and in other species, but a great deal remains to be learned. Based on this type of research, some educational and child-care reformers have argued that the first three years of life are a critical period for human neural development.

The pioneering work on environment and brain development was begun in the 1960s by Mark Rosenzweig and his colleagues (1961, 1962). They raised some rats in an impoverished environment (housed individually in small, barren cages) and other rats in an enriched environment (housed in groups of 10 to 12 in larger cages, with a variety of objects available for exploration), as shown in Figure 3.33. They found that the rats raised in the enriched environment performed better on problem-

solving tasks than the impoverished rats and had slightly heavier brains and a thicker cerebral cortex in some areas of the brain. Subsequent research by William Greenough demonstrated that enriched environments resulted in heavier and thicker cortical areas by virtue of producing denser dendritic branching, more synaptic contacts, and richer neural networks (Greenough, 1975; Greenough & Volkmar, 1973). Based on this type of research, some child-care reformers have argued that human infants need to be brought up in enriched environments during the critical period before age three, to promote synapse formation and to optimize the development of their emerging neural circuits.

The findings on critical periods and the effects of enriched environments were genuine breakthroughs in neuroscience, but they certainly aren't *new* findings, as suggested by various political action groups. Moreover, one can raise many doubts about whether this research can serve as a meaningful guide for decisions about parenting practices, daycare programs, educational policies, and welfare reform (Thompson & Nelson, 2001).

The Risks of Overextrapolation

Extrapolation occurs when an effect is estimated by extending beyond some known values or conditions. Extrapolation is a normal process, but some extrapolations are conservative, plausible projections drawn from directly relevant data, whereas others are wild leaps of speculation based on loosely related data. The extrapolations made regarding the educational implications of critical periods and environmental effects on synapse formation are highly conjectural *overextrapolations*. The studies that highlighted the possible importance

Figure 3.33

Enriched environments in the study of rats' neural development. In the studies by Rosenzweig and colleagues (1961, 1962), rats raised in an impoverished environment were housed alone in small cages, whereas rats raised in enriched environments were housed in groups and were given playthings that were changed daily. Although the enriched conditions provided more stimulating environments than what laboratory rats normally experience, they may not be any more stimulating than rats' natural habitats. Thus, the "enriched" condition may reveal more about the importance of normal stimulation than about the benefits of extra stimulation (Gopnik, Meltzoff, & Kuhl, 1999).

of early experience in animals have all used extreme conditions to make their comparisons, such as depriving an animal of all visual input or raising it in stark isolation. In light of the findings, it seems plausible to speculate that children probably need normal stimulation to experience normal brain development. However, great difficulty arises when these findings are extended to conclude that adding *more* stimulation to a normal environment will be beneficial to brain development (Shatz, 1992).

The ease with which people fall into the trap of overextrapolating has been particularly apparent in recent recommendations that infants listen to classical music to enhance their brain development. These recommendations have been derived from two studies that showed that university students' performance on spatial reasoning tasks was enhanced slightly for about 10–15 minutes after listening to a brief Mozart recording (Rauscher, Shaw, & Ky, 1993, 1995). This peculiar finding, dubbed the "Mozart effect," has proven difficult to replicate, as shown in studies by researchers from the University of Toronto (Thompson, Schellenberg, & Husain, 2001) and others (McKelvie & Low, 2002; Steele, 2003). The pertinent point here is that there was no research on how classical music affects *infants,* no research relating classical music to *brain development,* and no research on anyone showing *lasting effects.* Nonetheless, many people were quick to extrapolate the shaky findings on the Mozart effect to infants' brain development.

As discussed in Chapter 1, thinking critically about issues often involves asking questions such as: What is missing from this debate? Is there any contradictory evidence? In this case, there is some contradictory evidence that is worthy of consideration. The basis for advocating infant educational programs is the belief that the brain is malleable during the hypothesized critical period of birth to age three but not at later ages. However, Greenough's work on synaptic formation and other lines of research suggest that the brain remains somewhat malleable throughout life, responding to stimulation into old age (Thompson & Nelson, 2001). Thus, advocates for the aged could just as readily argue for new educational initiatives for the elderly to help them maximize their intellectual potential. Another problem is the implicit assumption that greater synaptic density is associated with greater intelligence. As noted earlier in the chapter, there is evidence that infant animals and humans begin life with an overabundance of synaptic connections and that learning involves selective *pruning* of inactive synapses (Huttenlocher, 2004; Rakic, Bourgeois, & Goldman-Rakic, 1994). Thus, in the realm of synapses, more may *not* be better.

In conclusion, there may be many valid reasons for increasing educational programs for infants, but research in neuroscience does not appear to provide a clear rationale for much in the way of specific infant care policies (Bruer, 2002). One problem in evaluating these proposals is that few people want to argue against high-quality child-care or education. But modern societies need to allocate their limited resources to the programs that appear most likely to have beneficial effects, so even intuitively appealing ideas need to be subjected to critical scrutiny.

Table 3.2 Critical Thinking Skills Discussed in This Application

Skill	Description
Understanding the limits of extrapolation	The critical thinker appreciates that extrapolations are based on certain assumptions, vary in plausibility, and ultimately involve speculation.
Looking for contradictory evidence	In evaluating the evidence presented on an issue, the critical thinker attempts to look for contradictory evidence that may have been left out of the debate.

RECAP

Key Ideas

Communication in the Nervous System

● Neurons are the basic communication links in the nervous system. They normally transmit a neural impulse (an electric current) along an axon to a synapse with another neuron. The neural impulse is a brief change in a neuron's electrical charge that moves along an axon. It is an all-or-none event.

● Action potentials trigger the release of chemicals called neurotransmitters that diffuse across a synapse to communicate with other neurons. Transmitters bind with receptors in the postsynaptic cell membrane, causing excitatory or inhibitory PSPs. Most neurons are linked in neural pathways, circuits, and networks.

● ACh plays a key role in muscular movement. Disturbances in the activity of the monoamine transmitters have been related to the development of depression and schizophrenia. GABA is a widely distributed inhibitory transmitter. Endorphins contribute to the relief of pain.

Organization of the Nervous System

● The nervous system can be divided into the central nervous system and the peripheral nervous system. The central nervous system consists of the brain and spinal cord.

● The peripheral nervous system can be subdivided into the somatic nervous system, which connects to muscles and sensory receptors, and the autonomic nervous system, which connects to blood vessels, smooth muscles, and glands.

Looking Inside the Brain: Research Methods

● The EEG can record broad patterns of electrical activity in the brain. Lesioning involves destroying a piece of the brain. Another technique is electrical stimulation of areas in the brain in order to activate them. In recent years, new brain-imaging procedures have been developed, including CT scans, PET scans, MRI scans, and fMRI scans.

The Brain and Behaviour

● The brain has three major regions: the hindbrain, midbrain, and forebrain. Structures in the hindbrain and midbrain handle essential functions. The thalamus is primarily a relay station. The hypothalamus is involved in the regulation of basic biological drives such as hunger and sex.

● The limbic system is involved in emotion, motivation, and memory. The cortex is the cerebrum's convoluted outer layer, which is subdivided into occipital, parietal, temporal, and frontal lobes. The brain's organization is somewhat malleable.

Right Brain/Left Brain: Cerebral Laterality

● The cerebrum is divided into right and left hemispheres connected by the corpus callosum.

Studies of split-brain patients and perceptual asymmetries have revealed that the right and left halves of the brain each have unique talents.

The Endocrine System: Another Way to Communicate

● The endocrine system consists of the glands that secrete hormones, which are chemicals involved in the regulation of basic bodily processes. The control centres for the endocrine system are the hypothalamus and the pituitary gland.

Heredity and Behaviour: Is It All in the Genes?

● The basic units of genetic transmission are genes housed on chromosomes. Most behavioural qualities appear to involve polygenic inheritance. Researchers assess hereditary influence through a variety of methods, including family studies, twin studies, adoption studies, and genetic mapping.

The Evolutionary Bases of Behaviour

● Darwin argued that if a heritable trait contributes to an organism's survival or reproductive success, organisms with that trait should produce more offspring than those without the trait and the prevalence of that trait should gradually increase over generations—thanks to natural selection.

● Darwin recognized from the beginning that natural selection was applicable to behavioural traits as well as physical traits.

Putting It in Perspective

● Three of the book's unifying themes stand out in this chapter. First, we saw how heredity interacts with experience to govern behaviour. Second, the discussions of biological factors underlying schizophrenia highlighted the multifactorial causation of behaviour. Third, we saw how innovations in research methods often lead to advances in knowledge, underscoring the empirical nature of psychology.

Personal Application • Evaluating the Concept of "Two Minds in One"

● The cerebral hemispheres are specialized for handling different cognitive tasks, but only to a degree, and people vary in their patterns of hemispheric specialization. Evidence on whether people vary in brainedness and whether the two hemispheres vary in cognitive style is inconclusive.

Critical Thinking Application • Building Better Brains: The Perils of Extrapolation

● Although some education and child-care reformers have used research in neuroscience as the basis for their campaigns, research has not demonstrated that birth to age three is a critical period for human neural development or that

specific enrichment programs can enhance brain development. These assertions are highly conjectural overextrapolations from existing data.

Key Terms

Absolute refractory period, 80
Action potential, 80
Adaptation, 114
Adoption studies, 110
Afferent nerve fibres, 88
Agonist, 84
Antagonist, 85
Autonomic nervous system (ANS), 88
Axon, 79
Behavioural genetics, 107
Central nervous system (CNS), 88
Cerebral cortex, 98
Cerebral hemispheres, 99
Cerebrospinal fluid (CSF), 88
Chromosomes, 107
Corpus callosum, 99
Critical period, 120
Dendrites, 79
Dominant gene, 107
Efferent nerve fibres, 88
Electrical stimulation of the brain (ESB), 91
Electroencephalograph (EEG), 90
Endocrine system, 105
Endorphins, 86
Excitatory PSP, 82
Family studies, 109
Fitness, 113
Forebrain, 97
Fraternal (dizygotic) twins, 109
Genes, 107
Genetic mapping, 111
Genotype, 108
Heterozygous condition, 107
Hindbrain, 95
Homozygous condition, 107
Hormones, 105
Hypothalamus, 97
Identical (monozygotic) twins, 109
Inclusive fitness, 115
Inhibitory PSP, 82
Lesioning, 91
Limbic system, 97
Midbrain, 95
Mutation, 114
Myelin sheath, 79
Natural selection, 113
Nerves, 87
Neurons, 78
Neurotransmitters, 80
Parasympathetic division, 88
Perceptual asymmetries, 105
Peripheral nervous system, 87
Phenotype, 108
Pituitary gland, 106
Polygenic traits, 109
Postsynaptic potential (PSP), 82
Recessive gene, 108
Resting potential, 80
Reuptake, 82
Soma, 79
Somatic nervous system, 88
Split-brain surgery, 102
Sympathetic division, 88
Synapse, 79
Synaptic cleft, 80
Terminal buttons, 79
Thalamus, 97
Twin studies, 109
Zygote, 107

Key People

Doug Crawford, 99
Charles Darwin, 113
Michael Gazzaniga, 102
Donald Hebb, 83
Alan Hodgkin, 79
Andrew Huxley, 79
Doreen Kimura, 106
Bryan Kolb, 101
Maryse Lassonde, 104
Brenda Milner, 90
James Olds, 98
Wilder Penfield, 90
Candace Pert, 86
Robert Plomin, 112
Solomon Snyder, 86
Roger Sperry, 102

PRACTICE TEST

1. A neural impulse is initiated when a neuron's charge momentarily becomes less negative, or even positive. This event is called:
   A. an action potential.
   B. a resting potential.
   C. impulse facilitation.
   D. inhibitory.

2. Neurons convey information about the strength of stimuli by varying:
   A. the size of their action potentials.
   B. the velocity of their action potentials.
   C. the rate at which they fire action potentials.
   D. all of the above.

3. Alterations in activity at dopamine synapses have been implicated in the development of:
   A. anxiety.
   B. schizophrenia.
   C. Alzheimer's disease.
   D. nicotine addiction.

4. Jim just barely avoided a head-on collision on a narrow road. With heart pounding, hands shaking, and body perspiring, Jim recognizes that these are signs of the body's fight-or-flight response, which is controlled by the:
   A. empathetic division of the peripheral nervous system.
   B. parasympathetic division of the autonomic nervous system.
   C. somatic division of the peripheral nervous system.
   D. sympathetic division of the autonomic nervous system.

5. The hindbrain consists of the:
   A. endocrine system and the limbic system.
   B. reticular formation.
   C. thalamus, hypothalamus, and cerebrum.
   D. cerebellum, medulla, and pons.

6. Juan is watching a basketball game. The neural impulses from his eyes will ultimately travel to his primary visual cortex, but first they must pass through the:
   A. amygdala.
   B. hypothalamus.
   C. thalamus.
   D. pons.

7. The _____ lobe is to hearing as the occipital lobe is to vision.
   A. frontal
   B. temporal
   C. parietal
   D. cerebellar

8. Paul has profound difficulty producing spoken language. If his problem is attributable to brain damage, the damage would probably be found in:
   A. the cerebellum.
   B. Sperry's area.
   C. Broca's area.
   D. Wernicke's area.

9. Sounds presented to the right ear are registered:
   A. only in the right hemisphere.
   B. only in the left hemisphere.
   C. more quickly in the right hemisphere.
   D. more quickly in the left hemisphere.

10. In people whose corpus callosums have not been severed, verbal stimuli are identified more quickly and more accurately:
    A. when sent to the right hemisphere first.
    B. when sent to the left hemisphere first.

    C. when presented to the left visual field.
    D. when presented auditorally rather than visually.

11. Hormones are to the endocrine system as _____ are to the nervous system.
    A. nerves
    B. synapses
    C. neurotransmitters
    D. action potentials

12. Jenny has brown hair and blue eyes and is 175 cm tall. What is being described is Jenny's:
    A. genotype.
    B. phenotype.
    C. somatotype.
    D. physiognomy.

13. Adopted children's similarity to their biological parents is generally attributed to _____; adopted children's similarity to their adoptive parents is generally attributed to _____.
    A. heredity; the environment
    B. the environment; heredity
    C. the environment; the environment
    D. heredity; heredity

14. A spontaneous, heritable change or error in DNA replication is called:
    A. genetic drift.
    B. gene flow.
    C. an adaptation.
    D. a mutation.

15. For which of the following assertions is the empirical evidence strongest?
    A. The two cerebral hemispheres are specialized to handle different types of cognitive tasks.
    B. People have a separate stream of consciousness in each hemisphere.
    C. Each hemisphere has its own cognitive style.
    D. Some people are right-brained, while others are left-brained.

    See Appendix A for answers to this Practice Test.

---

www **ON THE WEB**

For additional resources on the topics covered in this chapter, visit the *Psychology: Themes and Variations* Web site, where you will find practice quizzes, tutorials, Web links, simulations, critical thinking activities, flash cards, interactive exercises, and suggested readings available through INFOTRAC.

http://www.themesandvariations.nelson.com

 http://hed.nelson.com

Go to this site for the link to ThomsonNOW™, your one-stop study shop. Take a Pretest for this chapter and ThomsonNOW™ will generate a personalized Study Plan based on your test results! The Study Plan will identify the topics you need to review and direct you to online resources to help you master those topics. You can then take a Posttest to help you determine the concepts you have mastered and what you still need work on.

The Canadian Space Agency and NASA collaborated on an investigation of the role of visual cues in spatial orientation using the VEG (Virtual Environment Generator) headgear.

in *sensation/perception* research, particularly in the area of binocular vision and human spatial orientation (Howard & Templeton, 1966; Howard & Rogers, 1995). Along with other colleagues such as Laurence Harris, Howard has used tilting/sideways rooms and airplane flights that involve parabolic flight paths in order to experience normal, hyper-, and micro-gravity environments (Jenkin, Dyde, Jenkin, Howard, & Harris, 2003; Jenkin, Dyde, Zacher, Zikovitz, Jenkin, Allison, Howard, & Harris, in press). Ordinarily people can rely on three types of cues to determine which way is up: visual, gravity, and body direction. In space, astronauts are primarily dependent upon visual cues and body orientation. Using the tilting/sideways room they are able to isolate the three types of cues and have found that body orientation cannot help establish the direction of up (Jenkin et al., 2003). This suggests that the astronaut is dependent upon visual cues. Their future research will examine the nature of visual features that might maximize the astronaut's ability to determine accurately and efficiently the direction of up. The success of this research will depend on basic findings in the areas of sensation and perception.

performance, and motion sickness. There may be discontinuity between sensory information derived from the vestibular system (organs in the inner ear) and visual cues. The research was designed, in part, to examine the role of vision in determining body position and sensory adaptation to micro-gravity. Some phases of the research were carried out using NASA's Virtual Environment Generator, which was worn by the astronauts and which created a virtual visual environment (Canadian Space Agency, n.d., c).

Long before he was involved in space research, Ian Howard was known internationally as a pioneer

Sensation and perception are the topics of this chapter. Many people tend to use the terms *sensation* and *perception* as being interchangeable terms. For psychologists, however, they refer to related but distinct aspects of our contact with our environment. **Sensation is the stimulation of sense organs. Perception is the selection, organization, and inter-**

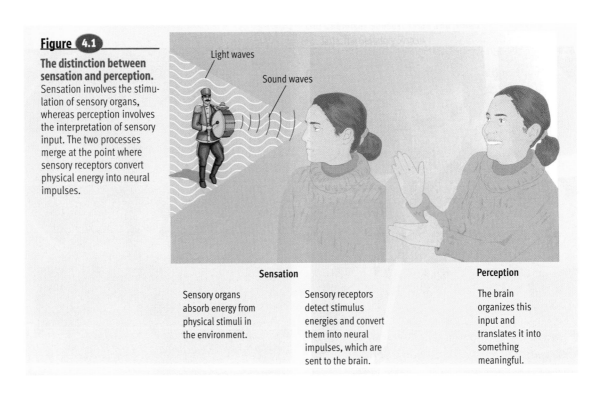

Figure 4.1

The distinction between sensation and perception. Sensation involves the stimulation of sensory organs, whereas perception involves the interpretation of sensory input. The two processes merge at the point where sensory receptors convert physical energy into neural impulses.

Light waves

Sound waves

Sensation

Sensory organs absorb energy from physical stimuli in the environment.

Sensory receptors detect stimulus energies and convert them into neural impulses, which are sent to the brain.

Perception

The brain organizes this input and translates it into something meaningful.

Sensation and Perception

While most students are probably aware of the fact that there is a Canadian astronaut program and that some have flown aboard the space shuttles into space, perhaps fewer know about the existence of the Canadian Space Agency and its role in coordinating Canadian involvement in space exploration and space-related research.

The Canadian Space Agency's mandate includes, among other things, the objective of promoting and facilitating space-related research. One of the first Canadian experiments carried out was an experiment on the manufacture of mirrors. If you can believe it, the experiment was designed by two Ottawa high-school students. It was carried out in 1985 on the first flight of Shuttle *Atlantis*. In 1993 experiments on the vestibular system designed by McGill's Dr. Douglas Watt were conducted (Canadian Space Agency, n.d., b). In 1997 sleep experiments developed by Toronto sleep researcher Dr. Harvey Moldofsky were carried out aboard Shuttle *Atlantis* (Canadian Space Agency, n.d., a). You will learn more about the scientific investigation of sleep in Chapter 5.

Canadian space psychology is a rapidly developing area of research and, according to the University of British Columbia's Peter Seudfeld (2003), includes examination of such matters as the effects of isolated and extreme environments and the nature and effects of multicultural interactions. Also important in understanding how astronauts will function in space is recent sensation/perception research. The space shuttle flights themselves have been the scene of some of these experiments. For example, in 1998 experiments designed by Canadian psychologist Ian Howard in collaboration with Massachusetts Institute of Technology's Charles Oman (Canadian Space Agency, n.d., c) examined the role of visual cues in spatial orientation. The research was directed at an important problem facing astronauts in space: While on earth gravity provides important cues for people's judgments concerning the spatial orientation of their bodies (which way is up?), in space astronauts can't depend on gravity as a cue—they lose sense of what is up and what is down. Among other problems, this can lead to disorientation, difficulty in task

Marc Garneau and Roberta Bondar were among the first Canadian astronauts to have joined one of NASA's space missions.

Reprinted by permission of The Canadian Space Agency, http://www.space.gc.ca

The Canadian Space Agency and NASA collaborated on an investigation of the role of visual cues in spatial orientation using the VEG (Virtual Environment Generator) headgear.

performance, and motion sickness. There may be discontinuity between sensory information derived from the vestibular system (organs in the inner ear) and visual cues. The research was designed, in part, to examine the role of vision in determining body position and sensory adaptation to micro-gravity. Some phases of the research were carried out using NASA's Virtual Environment Generator, which was worn by the astronauts and which created a virtual visual environment (Canadian Space Agency, n.d., c).

Long before he was involved in space research, Ian Howard was known internationally as a pioneer

in *sensation/perception* research, particularly in the area of binocular vision and human spatial orientation (Howard & Templeton, 1966; Howard & Rogers, 1995). Along with other colleagues such as Laurence Harris, Howard has used tilting/sideways rooms and airplane flights that involve parabolic flight paths in order to experience normal, hyper-, and micro-gravity environments (Jenkin, Dyde, Jenkin, Howard, & Harris, 2003; Jenkin, Dyde, Zacher, Zikovitz, Jenkin, Allison, Howard, & Harris, in press). Ordinarily people can rely on three types of cues to determine which way is up: visual, gravity, and body direction. In space, astronauts are primarily dependent upon visual cues and body orientation. Using the tilting/sideways room they are able to isolate the three types of cues and have found that body orientation cannot help establish the direction of up (Jenkin et al., 2003). This suggests that the astronaut is dependent upon visual cues. Their future research will examine the nature of visual features that might maximize the astronaut's ability to determine accurately and efficiently the direction of up. The success of this research will depend on basic findings in the areas of sensation and perception.

Sensation and perception are the topics of this chapter. Many people tend to use the terms *sensation* and *perception* as being interchangeable terms. For psychologists, however, they refer to related but distinct aspects of our contact with our environment. **Sensation is the stimulation of sense organs. Perception is the selection, organization, and inter-**

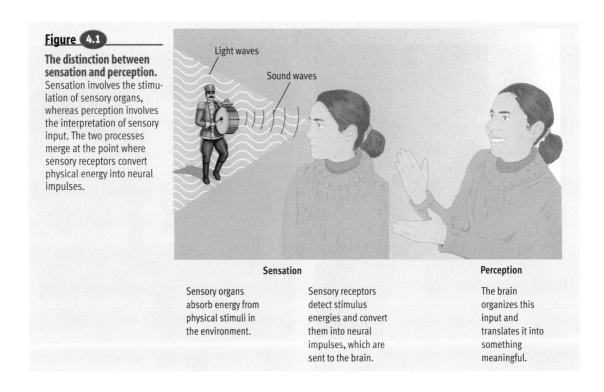

Figure 4.1

The distinction between sensation and perception. Sensation involves the stimulation of sensory organs, whereas perception involves the interpretation of sensory input. The two processes merge at the point where sensory receptors convert physical energy into neural impulses.

Light waves

Sound waves

Sensation

Sensory organs absorb energy from physical stimuli in the environment.

Sensory receptors detect stimulus energies and convert them into neural impulses, which are sent to the brain.

Perception

The brain organizes this input and translates it into something meaningful.

PRACTICE TEST

1. A neural impulse is initiated when a neuron's charge momentarily becomes less negative, or even positive. This event is called:
   A. an action potential.
   B. a resting potential.
   C. impulse facilitation.
   D. inhibitory.

2. Neurons convey information about the strength of stimuli by varying:
   A. the size of their action potentials.
   B. the velocity of their action potentials.
   C. the rate at which they fire action potentials.
   D. all of the above.

3. Alterations in activity at dopamine synapses have been implicated in the development of:
   A. anxiety.
   B. schizophrenia.
   C. Alzheimer's disease.
   D. nicotine addiction.

4. Jim just barely avoided a head-on collision on a narrow road. With heart pounding, hands shaking, and body perspiring, Jim recognizes that these are signs of the body's fight-or-flight response, which is controlled by the:
   A. empathetic division of the peripheral nervous system.
   B. parasympathetic division of the autonomic nervous system.
   C. somatic division of the peripheral nervous system.
   D. sympathetic division of the autonomic nervous system.

5. The hindbrain consists of the:
   A. endocrine system and the limbic system.
   B. reticular formation.
   C. thalamus, hypothalamus, and cerebrum.
   D. cerebellum, medulla, and pons.

6. Juan is watching a basketball game. The neural impulses from his eyes will ultimately travel to his primary visual cortex, but first they must pass through the:
   A. amygdala.
   B. hypothalamus.
   C. thalamus.
   D. pons.

7. The _____ lobe is to hearing as the occipital lobe is to vision.
   A. frontal
   B. temporal
   C. parietal
   D. cerebellar

8. Paul has profound difficulty producing spoken language. If his problem is attributable to brain damage, the damage would probably be found in:
   A. the cerebellum.
   B. Sperry's area.
   C. Broca's area.
   D. Wernicke's area.

9. Sounds presented to the right ear are registered:
   A. only in the right hemisphere.
   B. only in the left hemisphere.
   C. more quickly in the right hemisphere.
   D. more quickly in the left hemisphere.

10. In people whose corpus callosums have not been severed, verbal stimuli are identified more quickly and more accurately:
    A. when sent to the right hemisphere first.
    B. when sent to the left hemisphere first.
    C. when presented to the left visual field.
    D. when presented auditorally rather than visually.

11. Hormones are to the endocrine system as _____ are to the nervous system.
    A. nerves
    B. synapses
    C. neurotransmitters
    D. action potentials

12. Jenny has brown hair and blue eyes and is 175 cm tall. What is being described is Jenny's:
    A. genotype.
    B. phenotype.
    C. somatotype.
    D. physiognomy.

13. Adopted children's similarity to their biological parents is generally attributed to _____; adopted children's similarity to their adoptive parents is generally attributed to _____.
    A. heredity; the environment
    B. the environment; heredity
    C. the environment; the environment
    D. heredity; heredity

14. A spontaneous, heritable change or error in DNA replication is called:
    A. genetic drift.
    B. gene flow.
    C. an adaptation.
    D. a mutation.

15. For which of the following assertions is the empirical evidence strongest?
    A. The two cerebral hemispheres are specialized to handle different types of cognitive tasks.
    B. People have a separate stream of consciousness in each hemisphere.
    C. Each hemisphere has its own cognitive style.
    D. Some people are right-brained, while others are left-brained.

See Appendix A for answers to this Practice Test.

 ON THE WEB

For additional resources on the topics covered in this chapter, visit the *Psychology: Themes and Variations* Web site, where you will find practice quizzes, tutorials, Web links, simulations, critical thinking activities, flash cards, interactive exercises, and suggested readings available through INFOTRAC.

http://www.themesandvariations.nelson.com

 http://hed.nelson.com

Go to this site for the link to ThomsonNOW™, your one-stop study shop. Take a Pretest for this chapter and ThomsonNOW™ will generate a personalized Study Plan based on your test results! The Study Plan will identify the topics you need to review and direct you to online resources to help you master those topics. You can then take a Posttest to help you determine the concepts you have mastered and what you still need work on.

CHAPTER 4

Latchezar Boyadjiev, *Vision,* L.B. Glass Studios

Psychophysics: Basic Concepts and Issues
Thresholds: Looking for Limits
Weighing the Differences: The JND
Psychophysical Scaling
Signal-Detection Theory
Perception without Awareness
Sensory Adaptation

Our Sense of Sight: The Visual System
The Stimulus: Light
The Eye: A Living Optical Instrument
The Retina: The Brain's Envoy in the Eye
Vision and the Brain
Viewing the World in Colour
Perceiving Forms, Patterns, and Objects
Perceiving Depth or Distance
Perceptual Constancies in Vision
The Power of Misleading Cues: Optical Illusions
Vision for Perception and Vision for Action

Our Sense of Hearing: The Auditory System
The Stimulus: Sound
Human Hearing Capacities
Sensory Processing in the Ear
Auditory Perception: Theories of Hearing
Auditory Localization: Perceiving Sources of Sound
Music and Its Effects
Featured Study • Decoding Speech Prosody: Do Music Lessons Help?

Our Chemical Senses: Taste and Smell
Taste: The Gustatory System
Smell: The Olfactory System

Our Sense of Touch: Sensory Systems in the Skin
Feeling Pressure
Feeling Pain

Our Other Senses
The Kinesthetic System
The Vestibular System

Putting It in Perspective

Personal Application • **Appreciating Art and Illusion**

Critical Thinking Application • **Recognizing Contrast Effects: It's All Relative**

Recap

Practice Test

pretation of sensory input. Sensation involves the absorption of energy, such as light or sound waves, by sensory organs, such as the ears and eyes. Perception involves organizing and translating sensory input into something meaningful, such as your best friend's face or other environmental stimuli (see Figure 4.1).

We'll begin our discussion of sensation and perception by examining some general concepts that are rel-

evant to all the senses. Next, we'll examine individual senses, in each case beginning with the sensory aspects and working our way through to the perceptual aspects. The chapter's Personal Application explores how principles of visual perception come into play in art and illusion. The Critical Thinking Application discusses how perceptual contrasts can be manipulated in persuasive efforts.

Psychophysics: Basic Concepts and Issues

As you may recall from Chapter 1, the first experimental psychologists were interested mainly in sensation and perception. They called their area of interest *psychophysics—***the study of how physical stimuli are translated into psychological experience.** A particularly important contributor to psychophysics was Gustav Fechner, who published a seminal work on the subject in 1860. Fechner was a German scientist working at the University of Leipzig, where Wilhelm Wundt later founded the first formal laboratory and journal devoted to psychological research.

Thresholds: Looking for Limits

Sensation begins with a *stimulus,* any detectable input from the environment. What counts as detectable, though, depends on who or what is doing the detecting. For instance, you might not be able to detect a weak odour that is readily apparent to your dog. Thus, Fechner wanted to know: For any given sense, what is the weakest detectable stimulus? For example, what is the minimum amount of light needed for a person to see that there is light?

Implicit in Fechner's question is a concept central to psychophysics: the threshold. **A *threshold* is a dividing point between energy levels that do and do not have a detectable effect.** For example, hardware stores sell a gadget with a photocell that automatically turns a lamp on when a room gets dark. The level of light intensity at which the gadget clicks on is its threshold.

An *absolute threshold* **for a specific type of sensory input is the minimum amount of stimulation that an organism can detect.** Absolute thresholds define the boundaries of an organism's sensory capabilities. Fechner and his contemporaries used a variety of methods to determine humans' absolute threshold for detecting light. They discovered that absolute thresholds are anything but absolute. When lights of varying intensity are flashed at a subject, there

is no single stimulus intensity at which the subject jumps from no detection to completely accurate detection. Instead, as stimulus intensity increases, subjects' probability of responding to stimuli *gradually* increases, as shown in red in Figure 4.2. Thus, researchers had to arbitrarily define the absolute threshold as the stimulus intensity *detected 50% of the time.*

Using this definition, investigators found that under ideal conditions, human abilities to detect weak stimuli are greater than appreciated. Some concrete examples of the absolute thresholds for various senses can be seen in Table 4.1. For example, on a clear, dark night, in the absence of other distracting lights, you could see the light of a candle burning 50 kilometres in the distance! Of course, we're talking about ideal conditions—you would have to go out to the middle of nowhere to find the darkness required to put this assertion to a suitable test.

PREVIEW QUESTIONS
- How is stimulus intensity related to absolute thresholds?
- What is a JND, and where does it fit in with Weber's and Fechner's laws?
- What is the central idea of signal-detection theory?
- What is the practical significance of subliminal perception?
- What is sensory adaptation?

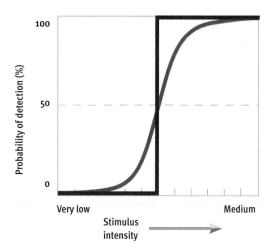

Figure 4.2

The absolute threshold. If absolute thresholds were truly absolute, then at threshold intensity the probability of detecting a stimulus would jump from 0 to 100%, as graphed here in blue. In reality, the chances of detecting a stimulus increase gradually with stimulus intensity, as shown in red. Accordingly, an "absolute" threshold is defined as the intensity level at which the probability of detection is 50%.

Table 4.1 Examples of Absolute Thresholds

Sense	Absolute Threshold
Vision	A candle flame seen at 50 kilometres on a dark clear night
Hearing	The tick of a watch under quiet conditions at 6 metres
Taste	One teaspoon (5 mL) of sugar in 7.5 litres of water
Smell	One drop of perfume diffused into entire volume of a six-room apartment
Touch	The wing of a fly falling on your cheek from a distance of 1 centimetre

Source: Galanter, E. (1962). Contemporary psychophysics. In R. Brown (Ed.), *New directions in psychology*. New York: Holt, Rinehart & Winston. © 1962 Eugene Galanter. Reprinted by permission.

Weighing the Differences: The JND

Fechner was also interested in people's sensitivity to differences between stimuli. A *just noticeable difference (JND)* **is the smallest difference in the amount of stimulation that a specific sense can detect.** JNDs are close cousins of absolute thresholds. In fact, an absolute threshold is simply the just noticeable difference from nothing (no stimulus input). JNDs vary by sense and the smallest detectable difference is a fairly stable proportion of the size of the original stimulus.

This principle was first demonstrated by Fechner's brother-in-law, Ernst Weber, and came to be known as Weber's law. **Weber's law states that the size of a just noticeable difference is a constant proportion of the size of the initial stimulus.** This constant proportion is called the *Weber fraction*. Weber's law applies not only to weight perception but to all the senses. However, different fractions apply to different types of sensory input. For example, the Weber fraction for lifting weights is approximately 1/30. That means that you should be just able to detect the difference between a 300-gram weight and a 310-gram weight (the JND for 300 grams is 10 grams). If you started with a 900-gram weight, however, you would not be able to tell the difference between it and a 910-gram weight. Why? Because the JND for 900 grams is 30 grams (1/30 of 90). In general, then, as stimuli increase in magnitude, the JND becomes larger.

Psychophysical Scaling

If one light has twice the energy of another, do you necessarily perceive it as twice as bright? When asked to make this kind of judgment, you are being asked

The method of just noticeable differences consists in determining how much the weights have to differ so that they can just be discriminated.
GUSTAV FECHNER

Archives of the History of American Psychology, University of Akron, Akron, Ohio

to *scale* the magnitude of sensory experiences. In his work on the scaling of sensory experiences, Fechner used the JND as his unit of measurement. His work yielded a principle that came to be known as *Fechner's law,* **which states that the magnitude of a sensory experience is proportional to the number of JNDs that the stimulus causing the experience is above absolute threshold.**

An important ramification of Fechner's law is that constant increments in stimulus intensity produce smaller and smaller increases in the *perceived* magnitude of sensation. This principle is easy to illustrate. Imagine that you're in a dark room with a single lamp that has three bulbs of the same wattage. You turn a switch, and one bulb lights. After a dark room, the difference is striking. Turn again, and a second bulb comes on. The amount of light is doubled, but the room does not seem twice as bright. When you turn the third bulb on, it adds just as much light as the first or second, but you barely notice the difference. Thus, three equal increases in stimulus intensity (the amount of light) produce progressively smaller differences in the magnitude of sensation (perceived brightness).

What all this means is that perceptions can't be measured on absolute scales. In the domain of sensory experience, virtually everything is relative.

Signal-Detection Theory

This insight applies not only to sensory scaling but to sensory thresholds as well. *Signal-detection theory* **proposes that the detection of stimuli involves decision processes as well as sensory processes, which are both influenced by a variety of factors besides stimulus intensity** (Egan, 1975; Swets, Tanner, & Birdsall, 1961).

Imagine that you are monitoring a radar screen, looking for signs of possible enemy aircraft. Your mission is to detect signals that represent approaching airplanes as quickly and as accurately as possible. In this situation, there are four possible outcomes, which are outlined in Figure 4.3: *hits* (detecting signals when they are present), *misses* (failing to detect signals when they are present), *false alarms* (detecting signals when they are not present), and *correct rejections* (not detecting signals when they are absent). Given these possibilities, signal-detection theory attempts to account for the influence of decision-making processes on stimulus detection. In detecting weak signals on the radar screen, you will often have to decide whether a faint signal represents an airplane or whether you're just imagining that it does. Your responses will depend in part on the *criterion* you set for how sure you must feel before you react.

Setting this criterion involves higher mental processes rather than raw sensation and depends on your expectations and on the consequences of missing a signal or of reporting a false alarm.

According to signal-detection theory, your performance will also depend on the level of "noise" in the system (Kubovy, Epstein, & Gepshtein, 2003). Noise comes from all the irrelevant stimuli in the environment and the neural activity they elicit. Noise is analogous to the background static on a radio station. The more noise in the system, the harder it will be for you to pick up a weak signal. Variations in noise provide another reason why sensory thresholds depend on more than just the intensity of stimuli. In comparison to classical models of psychophysics, signal-detection theory is better equipped to explain some of the complexities of perceived experience in the real world.

Perception without Awareness

The concepts of thresholds and detectability lie at the core of an interesting debate: Can sensory stimuli that fall beneath the threshold of awareness still influence behaviour? This issue centres on the concept of *subliminal perception*—**the registration of sensory input without conscious awareness** (*limen* is another term for threshold, so *subliminal* means below threshold). This question might be just another technical issue in the normally staid world of psychophysics, except that subliminal perception has become tied up in highly charged controversies relating to money, sex, religion, and rock music.

The controversy began in 1957 when an executive named James Vicary placed hidden messages such as "Eat popcorn" in a film showing at a theatre in New Jersey. The messages were superimposed on only a few frames of the film, so that they flashed by quickly and imperceptibly. Nonetheless, Vicary claimed in the press that popcorn sales increased by 58%, and a public outcry ensued (McConnell, Cutler, & McNeil, 1958). Since then, Wilson Bryan Key, a former advertising executive and faculty member, has written several books claiming that sexual words and drawings are embedded subliminally in magazine advertisements to elicit favourable unconscious reactions from consumers (Key, 1973, 1976, 1980). One such advertisement discussed by Key is shown in Figure 4.4. If you look closely, you'll find the word SEX embedded in the ice cubes. Taking the sexual manipulation theme a step further, entrepreneurs are now marketing music audiotapes containing subliminal messages that are supposed to help people seduce unsuspecting listeners. Subliminal self-help

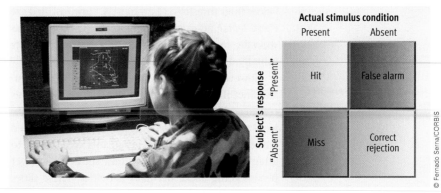

Figure 4.3

Possible outcomes in signal-detection theory. This diagram shows the four outcomes that are possible in attempting to detect the presence of weak signals. The criterion you set for how confident you want to feel before reporting a signal will affect your responding. For example, if you require high confidence before reporting a signal, you will minimize false alarms, but you'll be more likely to miss some signals.

tapes intended to facilitate weight loss, sleep, memory, self-esteem, and the like have become a multi-million-dollar industry. Religious overtones were added to this controversy in the 1980s when subliminal messages encouraging devil worship were allegedly found in rock music played *backward* (Vokey & Read, 1985).

Can listening to Led Zeppelin's "Stairway to Heaven" promote Satanic rituals? Can your sexual urges be manipulated by messages hidden under music? Can advertisers influence your product preferences with subliminal stimuli? Those who are concerned about subliminal messages assert that such messages are likely to be persuasive because people supposedly are defenceless against appeals operating

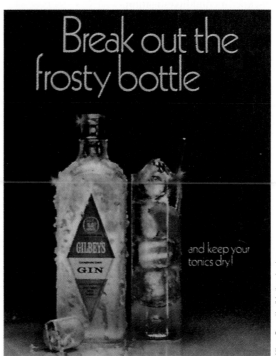

Figure 4.4

Subliminal advertising: Is it all in the eye of the beholder? If you look closely at the ice cubes in this ad, you will see the word SEX spelled out. Former advertising executive Wilson Bryan Key (1973) claims advertisers routinely place subliminal stimuli in their ads. Marketing companies maintain that people are merely reading things into their ads, much like you might see familiar forms in clouds. Although subliminal perception appears to be a genuine phenomenon, Thomas Creed (1987) has pinpointed a host of fallacies in Key's analysis, which he characterizes as pseudoscience.

below their threshold of awareness. How justified are these fears? Research on subliminal perception was sporadic in the 1960s and 1970s because scientists initially dismissed the entire idea as preposterous.

However, empirical studies have begun to accumulate since the 1980s. For example, Jon Krosnick and his colleagues (1992) set out to determine whether subjects' attitudes toward a target person could be shaped without their awareness. Participants were asked to attentively view a series of slides showing a target person going about her daily activities. These slides were preceded by very brief (13/1000 of a second) subliminal presentations of photos expected to arouse positive emotions (a bridal couple, a pair of kittens, and so on) or negative emotions (a skull, a werewolf, and so on). After the slide presentations, subjects rated the target person on various dimensions. The researchers found statistically significant differences in participants' attitudes toward the target person that reflected the type of subliminal photos they had seen. Thus, subliminal inputs produced measurable, although small, effects in subjects who subsequently reported that they did not consciously register the stimuli.

Since the 1980s, a host of other studies have also found support for the existence of subliminal perception (Abrams, Klinger, & Greenwald, 2002; De Houwer, 2001; Dijksterhuis, 2004; Monahan, Murphy, & Zajonc, 2000). Hence, according to researchers such as Philip Merikle at the University of Waterloo and others (Loftus & Klinger, 1992; Merikle & Daneman, 1998), the dominant view today is that subliminal perception is a genuine phenomenon that is worthy of experimental investigation.

So, should we be worried about the threat of subliminal persuasion? The research to date suggests that there is little reason for concern. The effects of subliminal stimuli turn out to be nearly as subliminal as the stimuli themselves. Subliminal stimulation generally produces weak effects (De Houwer, Hendrickx, & Baeyens, 1997; Kihlstrom, Barnhardt, & Tataryn, 1992). These effects can be detected only by very precise measurement, under carefully controlled laboratory conditions, in which subjects are asked to focus their undivided attention on visual or auditory materials that contain the subliminal stimuli. Although these effects are theoretically interesting, they appear unlikely to have much practical importance.

Sensory Adaptation

The process of sensory adaptation is yet another factor that influences registration of sensory input. **Sensory adaptation is a gradual decline in sensitivity to prolonged stimulation.** For example, let's say you find that the garbage in your kitchen has started to smell. If you stay in the kitchen without removing the garbage, the stench will soon start to fade. In reality, the stimulus intensity of the odour is stable, but with continued exposure, your *sensitivity* to it decreases. Sensory adaptation is a pervasive aspect of everyday life. When you put on your clothes in the morning, you feel them initially, but the sensation quickly fades. Similarly, if you jump reluctantly into a pool of cold water, you'll probably find that the water temperature feels fine in a few moments after you *adapt* to it.

Sensory adaptation is an automatic, built-in process that keeps people tuned in to the *changes* rather than the *constants* in their sensory input. It allows people to ignore the obvious and focus on changes in their environment that may signal threats to safety. Thus, as its name suggests, sensory adaptation probably is a behavioural adaptation that has been sculpted by natural selection. Sensory adaptation also shows once again that there is no one-to-one correspondence between sensory input and sensory experience.

The general points we've reviewed so far begin to suggest the complexity of the relationships between the world outside and people's perceived experience of it. As we review each of the principal sensory systems in detail, we'll see repeatedly that people's experience of the world depends on both the physical stimuli they encounter and their active processing of stimulus inputs. We begin our exploration of the senses with vision—the sense that most people think of as nearly synonymous with a direct perception of reality. The case is actually quite different, as you'll see.

REVIEW OF KEY POINTS

- Psychophysicists use a variety of methods to relate sensory inputs to subjective perception. They have found that absolute thresholds are not really absolute.

- Weber's law states that the size of a just noticeable difference is a constant proportion of the size of the initial stimulus. Fechner's law asserts that larger and larger increases in stimulus intensity are required to produce just noticeable differences in the magnitude of sensation.

- According to signal-detection theory, the detection of sensory inputs is influenced by noise in the system and by decision-making strategies. Signal-detection theory replaces Fechner's sharp threshold with the concept of detectability and emphasizes that factors besides stimulus intensity influence detectability.

- In recent years, a host of researchers, using very different conceptual approaches, have demonstrated that perception can occur without awareness. However, research indicates that the effects of subliminal perception are relatively weak and of little or no practical concern.

- Prolonged stimulation may lead to sensory adaptation, which involves a reduction in sensitivity to constant stimulation.

Our Sense of Sight: The Visual System

"Seeing is believing." Good ideas are "bright," and a good explanation is "illuminating." This section is an "overview." Do you see the point? As these common expressions show, humans are visual animals. People rely heavily on their sense of sight, and they virtually equate it with what is trustworthy (seeing is believing). Although it is taken for granted, you'll see (there it is again) that the human visual system is amazingly complex. Furthermore, as in all sensory domains, what people "sense" and what they "perceive" may be quite different.

The Stimulus: Light

For people to see, there must be light. *Light* is a form of electromagnetic radiation that travels as a wave, moving, naturally enough, at the speed of light. As Figure 4.5(a) shows, light waves vary in *amplitude* (height) and in *wavelength* (the distance between peaks). Amplitude affects mainly the perception of brightness, while wavelength affects mainly the perception of colour. The lights humans normally see are mixtures of several wavelengths. Hence, light can also vary in its *purity* (how varied the mix is). Purity influences perception of the saturation, or richness, of colours. Saturation is difficult to describe, but if you glance at Figure 4.6, you'll find it clearly illustrated. Of course, most objects do not emit light, they reflect it (the sun, lamps, and fireflies being some exceptions).

PREVIEW QUESTIONS
- What are the three properties of light?
- What do the lens and pupil contribute to visual functioning?
- What are the functions of rods and cones?
- How do visual receptive fields typically function?
- How are visual signals routed from the eye to the primary visual cortex?
- What are feature detectors?

Figure 4.5

Light, the physical stimulus for vision. **(a)** Light waves vary in amplitude and wavelength. **(b)** Within the spectrum of visible light, amplitude (corresponding to physical intensity) affects mainly the experience of brightness. Wavelength affects mainly the experience of colour, and purity is the key determinant of saturation. **(c)** If white light (such as sunlight) passes through a prism, the prism separates the light into its component wavelengths, creating a rainbow of colours. However, visible light is only the narrow band of wavelengths to which human eyes happen to be sensitive.

Saturation

Figure 4.6

Saturation. Variations in saturation are difficult to describe, but you can see examples for two colours here.

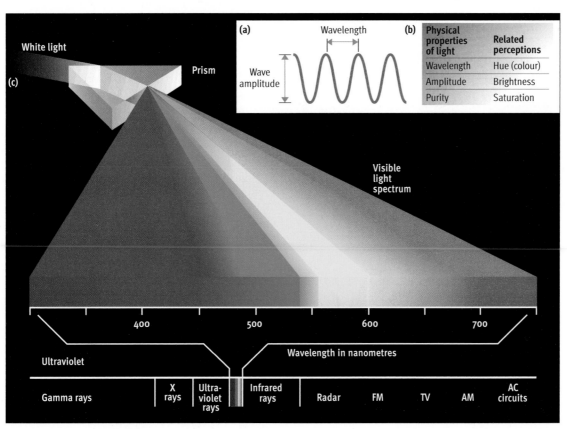

Physical properties of light	Related perceptions
Wavelength	Hue (colour)
Amplitude	Brightness
Purity	Saturation

What most people call light includes only the wavelengths that humans can see. But as Figure 4.5(c) shows, the visible spectrum is only a slim portion of the total range of wavelengths. Vision is a filter that permits people to sense but a fraction of the real world. Other animals have different capabilities and so live in a quite different visual world. For example, many insects can see shorter wavelengths than humans can see, in the *ultraviolet* spectrum, whereas many fish and reptiles can see longer wavelengths, in the *infrared* spectrum. Although the sense of sight depends on light waves, for people to *see*, incoming visual input must be converted into neural impulses that are sent to the brain. Let's investigate how this transformation is accomplished.

The Eye: A Living Optical Instrument

The eyes serve two main purposes: They channel light to the neural tissue that receives it, called the *retina,* and they house that tissue. The structure of the eye is shown in Figure 4.7. Each eye is a living optical instru-

ment that creates an image of the visual world on the light-sensitive retina lining its inside back surface.

Light enters the eye through a transparent "window" at the front, the *cornea.* The cornea and the crystalline *lens,* located behind it, form an upside-down image of objects on the retina. It might seem disturbing that the image is upside down, but the brain knows the rule for relating positions on the retina to the corresponding positions in the world.

The *lens* is the transparent eye structure that focuses the light rays falling on the retina. The lens is made up of relatively soft tissue, capable of adjustments that facilitate a process called accommodation. *Accommodation* occurs when the curvature of the lens adjusts to alter visual focus. When you focus on a close object, the lens of your eye gets fatter (rounder) to give you a clear image. When you focus on distant objects, the lens flattens out to give you a better image of them.

A number of common visual deficiencies are caused by focusing problems or by defects in the lens (Guyton, 1991). For example, **in *nearsightedness,* close objects are seen clearly but distant objects appear blurry** because the focus of light from distant

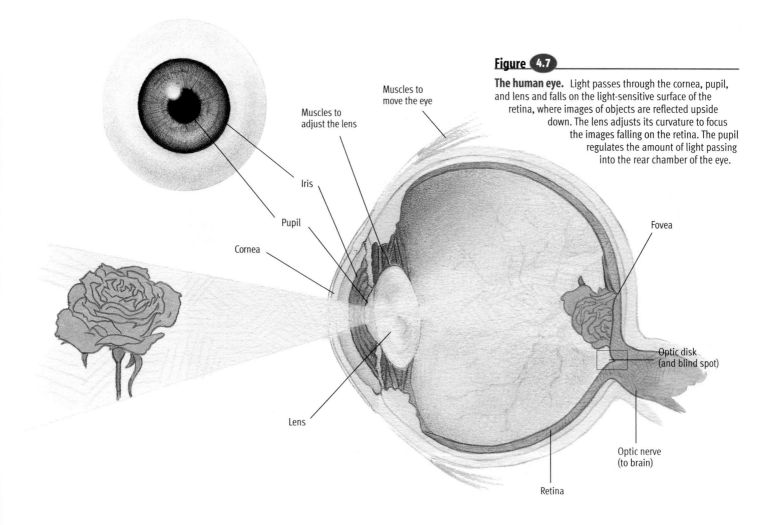

Figure 4.7

The human eye. Light passes through the cornea, pupil, and lens and falls on the light-sensitive surface of the retina, where images of objects are reflected upside down. The lens adjusts its curvature to focus the images falling on the retina. The pupil regulates the amount of light passing into the rear chamber of the eye.

Muscles to move the eye

Muscles to adjust the lens

Iris

Pupil

Cornea

Lens

Fovea

Optic disk (and blind spot)

Optic nerve (to brain)

Retina

objects falls a little short of the retina (see Figure 4.8). This focusing problem occurs when the cornea or lens bends light too much, or when the eyeball is too long. **In *farsightedness*, distant objects are seen clearly but close objects appear blurry** because the focus of light from close objects falls behind the retina. This focusing problem typically occurs when the eyeball is too short.

The eye can make adjustments to alter the amount of light reaching the retina. The *iris* is the coloured ring of muscle surrounding the *pupil,* or black centre of the eye. **The *pupil* is the opening in the centre of the iris that helps regulate the amount of light passing into the rear chamber of the eye.** When the pupil constricts, it lets less light into the eye, but it sharpens the image falling on the retina. When the pupil dilates (opens), it lets more light in, but the image is less sharp. In bright light, the pupils constrict to take advantage of the sharpened image. But in dim light, the pupils dilate; image sharpness is sacrificed to allow more light to fall on the retina so that more remains visible.

The Retina: The Brain's Envoy in the Eye

Nearsightedness

Farsightedness

Craig McClain

The *retina* **is the neural tissue lining the inside back surface of the eye; it absorbs light, processes images, and sends visual information to the brain.** You may be surprised to learn that the retina *processes* images. But it's a piece of the central nervous system that happens to be located in the eyeball. Much as

the spinal cord is a complicated extension of the brain, the retina is the brain's envoy in the eye. Although the retina is only a paper-thin sheet of neural tissue, it contains a complex network of specialized cells arranged in layers, as shown in Figure 4.9.

Figure 4.8

Nearsightedness and farsightedness. These pictures simulate how a scene might look to nearsighted and farsighted people. Nearsightedness occurs because light from distant objects focuses in front of the retina. Farsightedness is due to the opposite situation—light from close objects focuses behind the retina.

Figure 4.9

The retina. The close-up shows the several layers of cells in the retina. The cells closest to the back of the eye (the rods and cones) are the receptor cells that actually detect light. The intervening layers of cells receive signals from the rods and cones and form circuits that begin the process of analyzing incoming information before it is sent to the brain. These cells feed into many optic fibres, all of which head toward the "hole" in the retina where the optic nerve leaves the eye—the point known as the optic disk (which corresponds to the blind spot).

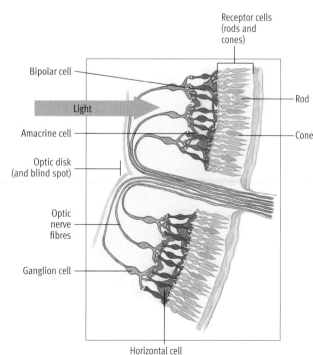

Receptor cells (rods and cones)

Bipolar cell

Light

Amacrine cell

Optic disk (and blind spot)

Optic nerve fibres

Ganglion cell

Rod

Cone

Horizontal cell

The axons that run from the retina to the brain converge at the **optic disk, a hole in the retina where the optic nerve fibres exit the eye.** Because the optic disk is a *hole* in the retina, you cannot see the part of an image that falls on it. It is therefore known as the *blind spot.* You may not be aware that you have a blind spot in each eye, as each normally compensates for the blind spot of the other.

Visual Receptors: Rods and Cones

The retina contains millions of receptor cells that are sensitive to light. Surprisingly, these receptors are located in the innermost layer of the retina. Hence, light must pass through several layers of cells before it gets to the receptors that actually detect it. Interestingly, only about 10% of the light arriving at the cornea reaches these receptors (Leibovic, 1990). The retina contains two types of receptors, *rods* and *cones.* Their names are based on their shapes, as rods are elongated and cones are stubbier. Rods outnumber cones by a huge margin, as humans have 100–125 million rods, but only 5–6.4 million cones (Frishman, 2001).

Cones are specialized visual receptors that play a key role in daylight vision and colour vision. The cones handle most of our daytime vision, because bright lights dazzle the rods. The special sensitivities of cones also allow them to play a major role in the perception of colour. However, cones do not respond well to dim light, which is why you don't see colour very well in low illumination. Nonetheless, cones provide better *visual acuity*—that is, sharpness and precise detail—than rods. Cones are concentrated most heavily in the centre of the retina and quickly fall off in density toward its periphery. **The *fovea* is a tiny spot in the centre of the retina that contains** only cones; visual acuity is greatest at this spot. When you want to see something sharply, you usually move your eyes to centre the object in the fovea.

Rods are specialized visual receptors that play a key role in night vision and peripheral vision. Rods handle night vision because they are more sensitive than cones to dim light. They handle the lion's share of peripheral vision because they greatly outnumber cones in the periphery of the retina. The density of the rods is greatest just outside the fovea and gradually decreases toward the periphery of the retina. Because of the distribution of rods, when you want to see a faintly illuminated object in the dark, it's best to look slightly above or below the place it should be. Averting your gaze this way moves the image from the cone-filled fovea, which requires more light, to the rod-dominated area just outside the fovea, which requires less light. This trick of averted vision is well known to astronomers, who use it to study dim objects viewed through the eyepiece of a telescope.

Dark and Light Adaptation

You've probably noticed that when you enter a dark theatre on a bright day, you stumble around almost blindly. But within minutes you can make your way about quite well in the dim light. This adjustment is called *dark adaptation*—**the process in which the eyes become more sensitive to light in low illumination.** Figure 4.10 maps out the course of this process. The declining absolute thresholds over time indicate that you require less and less light to see. Dark adaptation is virtually complete in about 30 minutes, with considerable progress occurring in the first 10 minutes. The curve (in Figure 4.10) that charts this progress consists of two segments because cones adapt more rapidly than rods (Walraven et al., 1990).

When you emerge from a dark theatre on a sunny day, you need to squint to ward off the overwhelming brightness, and the reverse of dark adaptation occurs. *Light adaptation* **is the process whereby the eyes become less sensitive to light in high illumination.** As with dark adaptation, light adaptation improves your visual acuity under the prevailing circumstances. Both types of adaptation are due in large part to chemical changes in the rods and cones, but neural changes in the receptors and elsewhere in the retina also contribute (Frumkes, 1990).

Information Processing in the Retina

In processing visual input, the retina transforms a pattern of light falling onto it into a very different representation of the visual scene. Light striking the

Figure 4.10

The process of dark adaptation.
The declining thresholds over time indicate that your visual sensitivity is improving, as less and less light is required to see. Visual sensitivity improves markedly during the first 5 to 10 minutes after entering a dark room, as the eye's bright-light receptors (the cones) rapidly adapt to low light levels. However, the cones' adaptation, which is plotted in purple, soon reaches its limit, and further improvement comes from the rods' adaptation, which is plotted in red. The rods adapt more slowly than the cones, but they are capable of far greater visual sensitivity in low levels of light.

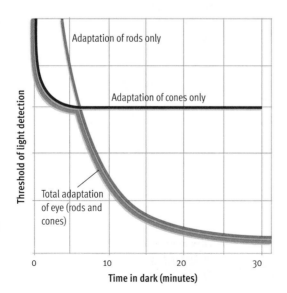

retina's receptors (rods and cones) triggers neural signals that pass into the intricate network of cells in the retina, which in turn send impulses along the *optic nerve*—a collection of axons that connect the eye with the brain (see Figure 4.9). These axons, which depart from the eye through the optic disk, carry visual information, encoded as a stream of neural impulses, to the brain.

A great deal of complex information processing goes on in the retina itself before visual signals are sent to the brain. Ultimately, the information from over 100 million rods and cones converges to travel along "only" 1 million axons in the optic nerve (Slaughter, 1990). The collection of rod and cone receptors that funnel signals to a particular visual cell in the retina (or ultimately in the brain) make up that cell's *receptive field*. Thus, **the *receptive field of a visual cell* is the retinal area that, when stimulated, affects the firing of that cell.**

Receptive fields in the retina come in a variety of shapes and sizes. Particularly common are circular fields with a centre-surround arrangement (Tessier-Lavigne, 2000). In these receptive fields, light falling in the centre has the opposite effect of light falling in the surrounding area (see Figure 4.11). For example, the rate of firing of a visual cell might be *increased* by light in the *centre* of its receptive field and *decreased* by light in the *surrounding area,* as Figure 4.11 shows. Other visual cells may work in just the opposite way. Either way, when receptive fields are stimulated, retinal cells send signals both toward the brain and *laterally* (sideways) toward nearby visual cells. These lateral signals allow visual cells in the retina to have interactive effects on each other.

Lateral antagonism (also known as lateral inhibition) is the most basic of these interactive effects. ***Lateral antagonism* occurs when neural activity in a cell opposes activity in surrounding cells.** Lateral antagonism is responsible for the opposite effects that occur when light falls on the inner versus outer portions of centre-surround receptive fields. Lateral antagonism allows the retina to compare the light falling in a specific area against general lighting. This means that the visual system can compute the *relative* amount of light at a point instead of reacting to *absolute* levels of light. This attention to *contrast* is

Figure 4.11

Receptive fields in the retina. Visual cells' receptive fields—made up of rods and cones in the retina—are often circular with a centre-surround arrangement, so that light striking the centre of the field produces the opposite result of light striking the surround. In the receptive field depicted here, light in the centre produces excitatory effects (symbolized by green at the synapse) and increased firing in the visual cell, whereas light in the surround produces inhibitory effects (symbolized by red at the synapse) and decreased firing. However, the arrangement in other receptive fields may be just the opposite. Note that no light **(a)** and light in both centre and surround **(d)** produce similar baseline rates of firing. This visual cell is more sensitive to *contrast* than to absolute levels of light. In **(b)** and **(c)** there is a contrast between the light falling on the centre versus the surround, producing increased or decreased activity in the visual cell.

NEL

Sensation and Perception **135**

Understanding Sensory Processes in the Retina

Check your understanding of sensory receptors in the retina by completing the following exercises. Consult Appendix A for the answers.

1. The receptors for vision are rods and cones in the retina. These two types of receptors have many important differences, which are compared systematically in the chart below. Fill in the missing information to finish the chart.

Dimension	Rods	Cones
Physical shape	Elongated	
Number in the retina		5–6.4 million
Area of the retina in which they are dominant receptor	Periphery	
Critical to colour vision		
Critical to peripheral vision		No
Sensitivity to dim light	Strong	
Speed of dark adaptation		Rapid

2. The text notes that lateral antagonism in the retina is the probable cause of the illusory dark spots seen in the intersections of the Hermann grid (consult Figure 4.12). Try to construct an explanation of how lateral antagonism might account for this phenomenon. This is no small challenge, so don't feel bad if you have to consult Appendix A for the answer. Hint: The centre-surround receptive fields shown in Figure 4.11 are crucial to the explanation. It will help if you draw a centre-surround receptive field at one of the intersections in the grid and another adjacent to it.

exactly what is needed because most of the crucial information needed to recognize objects in a visual scene is contained in the pattern of contrasts (Tessier-Lavigne, 2000). If you look at Figure 4.12, you will

Figure 4.12

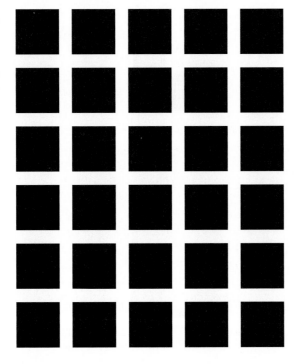

The Hermann grid. If you look at this grid, you will see dark spots at the intersections of the white bars, except in the intersection you're staring at directly. This illusion is due to lateral antagonism (see Concept Check 4.1).

experience a perplexing illusion attributable to lateral antagonism in the ganglion cells of the retina.

Vision and the Brain

Light falls on the eye, but you see with your brain. Although the retina does an unusual amount of information processing for a sensory organ, visual input is meaningless until it is processed in the brain.

Visual Pathways to the Brain

How does visual information get to the brain? Axons leaving the back of each eye form the optic nerves, which travel to the **optic chiasm—the point at which the optic nerves from the inside half of each eye cross over and then project to the opposite half of the brain.** This arrangement ensures that signals from both eyes go to both hemispheres of the brain. Thus, as Figure 4.13 shows, axons from the left half of each retina carry signals to the left side of the brain, and axons from the right half of each retina carry information to the right side of the brain.

After reaching the optic chiasm, the optic nerve fibres diverge along two pathways. The main pathway projects into the thalamus, the brain's major relay station. Here, about 90% of the axons from the retinas synapse in the *lateral geniculate nucleus* (LGN). Visual signals are processed in the LGN and then distributed to areas in the occipital lobe that make up the *primary visual cortex* (see Figure 4.13). The second visual pathway leaving the optic chiasm branches off to an area in the midbrain called the *superior colliculus* before travelling through the thalamus and on to the occipital lobe. The principal function of the second pathway appears to be the coordination of visual input with other sensory input (Casanova et al., 2001; Stein & Meredith, 1993).

The main visual pathway is subdivided into two more specialized pathways called the *magnocellular* and *parvocellular* channels (based on the layers of the LGN they synapse in). These channels engage in **parallel processing, which involves simultaneously extracting different kinds of information from the same input.** For example, the parvocellular channel handles the perception of colour, while the magnocellular channel processes information regarding brightness (Wurtz & Kandel, 2000). Of course, this brief description hardly does justice to the immense complexity of visual processing in the brain.

Information Processing in the Visual Cortex

Most visual input eventually arrives in the primary visual cortex, located in the occipital lobe. Explaining

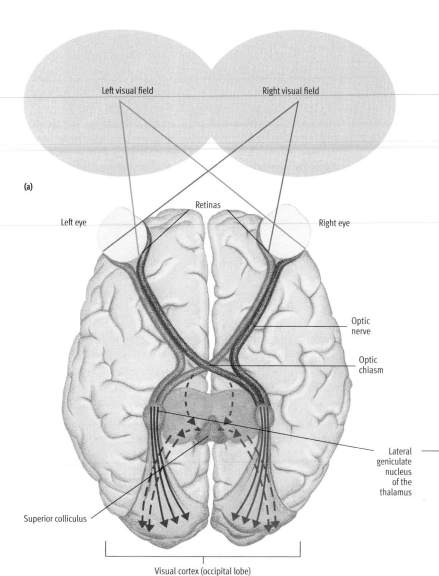

(a)

Left visual field   Right visual field

Retinas

Left eye   Right eye

Optic nerve

Optic chiasm

Lateral geniculate nucleus of the thalamus

Superior colliculus

Visual cortex (occipital lobe)

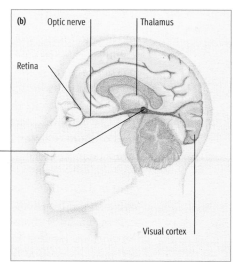

(b)   Optic nerve   Thalamus

Retina

Visual cortex

© Ira Wyman/CORBIS Sygma

Figure 4.13

Visual pathways through the brain. **(a)** Input from the right half of the visual field strikes the left side of each retina and is transmitted to the left hemisphere (shown in red). Input from the left half of the visual field strikes the right side of each retina and is transmitted to the right hemisphere (shown in green). The nerve fibres from each eye meet at the optic chiasm, where fibres from the inside half of each retina cross over to the opposite side of the brain. After reaching the optic chiasm, the major visual pathway projects through the lateral geniculate nucleus in the thalamus and onto the primary visual cortex (shown with solid lines). A second pathway detours through the superior colliculus and then projects through the thalamus and onto the primary visual cortex (shown with dotted lines). **(b)** This inset shows a vertical view of how the optic pathways project through the thalamus and onto the visual cortex in the back of the brain (the two pathways mapped out in diagram **(a)** are virtually indistinguishable from this angle).

how the cortical cells in this area respond to light once posed a perplexing problem. Researchers investigating the question placed microelectrodes in the primary visual cortex of animals to record action potentials from individual cells. They would flash spots of light in the retinal receptive fields that the cells were thought to monitor, but there was rarely any response.

According to David Hubel and Torsten Wiesel (1962, 1963), they discovered the solution to this mystery quite by accident. One of the projector slides they used to present a spot to a cat had a crack in it. The spot elicited no response, but when they removed the slide, the crack moved through the cell's receptive field, and the cell fired like crazy in response to the moving dark line. It turns out that individual cells in the primary visual cortex don't really respond much to little spots—they are much more sensitive to lines, edges, and other more complicated stimuli. Armed with new slides, Hubel and Wiesel embarked on years of painstaking study of

the visual cortex (see Figure 4.14). Their work eventually earned them a Nobel Prize in 1981. Hubel, who was born in Windsor, Ontario, moved to Montreal with his family while he was a child. He went to university and medical school at McGill University. As we stated in Chapter 3, important work was being carried out in the 1940s and 1950s at the Montreal Neurological Institute by Wilder Penfield, Herbert Jasper, and others. Hubel's continued interest in the workings of the nervous system and the brain was influenced by the pioneering work of Penfield and his co-workers (Nobel Prize, n.d.).

Hubel and Wiesel (1962, 1979) identified various types of specialized cells in the primary visual cortex that respond to different stimuli. For example, *simple cells* respond best to a line of the correct width, oriented at the correct angle, and located in the correct position in its receptive field. *Complex cells* also care about width and orientation, but they respond to any position in their receptive fields. Some complex

❝One can now begin to grasp the significance of the great number of cells in the visual cortex. Each cell seems to have its own specific duties.❞
DAVID HUBEL

Figure 4.14

Hubel and Wiesel's procedure for studying the activity of neurons in the visual cortex. As the cat is shown various stimuli, a microelectrode records the firing of a neuron in the cat's visual cortex. The figure shows the electrical responses of a visual cell apparently "programmed" to respond to lines oriented vertically.

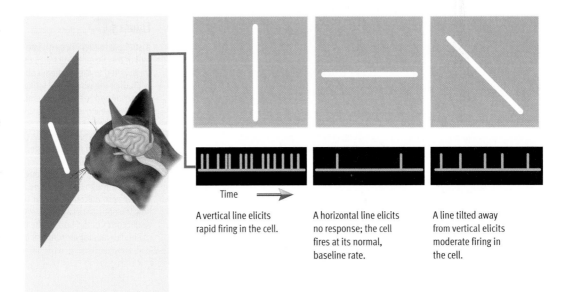

Time →

A vertical line elicits rapid firing in the cell.

A horizontal line elicits no response; the cell fires at its normal, baseline rate.

A line tilted away from vertical elicits moderate firing in the cell.

cells are most responsive if a line sweeps across their receptive field—but only if it's moving in the "right" direction. The key point of all this is that the cells in the visual cortex seem to be highly specialized. They have been characterized as *feature detectors,* **neurons that respond selectively to very specific features of more complex stimuli.** According to some theorists, most visual stimuli could ultimately be represented by combinations of lines such as those registered by these feature detectors (Maguire, Weisstein, & Klymenko, 1990).

Research by Dalhousie University psychologist Darwin Muir (Muir & Mitchell, 1975) suggests that organisms deprived of specific types of stimulation early in the development of their cortex may show selective visual deficits in the future. In this research, when he confined the early visual stimulation (up to four months) of cats to either vertical or horizontal lines only, he found that their ability to discriminate lines orthogonal to those with which they were raised was relatively poor. Thus, if cats were raised in an environment in which they were exposed only to vertical lines, then they performed more poorly on discrimination tasks involving horizontal lines than those involving vertical lines. This is in contrast to cats who had been raised normally, cats raised alternately with horizontal and vertical lines, or cats raised in environments with no bias toward type of line, all of which performed equally well with both types of lines. These and other findings suggest that significant disruptions in visual input for humans early in their lives, due, for example, to certain eye diseases, might lead to permanent perceptual deficits.

As signals move further along in the visual processing system, neurons become even more specialized or fussy about what turns them on, and the stimuli that activate them become more and more complex. For example, researchers have identified cells in the temporal lobe (along the *what* pathway) of monkeys and humans that respond best to pictures of faces (Levine, 2001; Rolls & Tovee, 1995). This incredible specificity has led researchers to joke that they may eventually find a cell that only recognizes one's grandmother (Cowey, 1994). The discovery of neurons that respond to facial stimuli raises an obvious question: Why does the cortex have face detectors? Theorists are far from sure, but one line of thinking is that the ability to quickly recognize faces—such as those of friends or foes—probably has had adaptive significance over the course of evolution (Desimone, 1991). Thus, natural selection may have wired the brains of some species to quickly respond to faces.

In any event, the discovery of the *what pathway* and the neurons inside it that respond specifically to faces has shed new light on visual disorders that have perplexed scientists for decades. For example, some people exhibit *visual agnosia*—**an inability to recognize objects**—even though their eyes function just fine. This previously baffling condition now has a plausible explanation—it is probably the result of damage somewhere along the visual pathway that handles object recognition (Zeki, 1993).

Multiple Methods in Vision Research

As we discussed in Chapter 3, researchers interested in examining neurological functioning use a wide array of methods in their attempts to understand the operation of the brain. These include contemporary technologies such as functional magnetic resonance imaging (fMRI) as well as classic techniques such as observing the performance of individuals who have suffered specific types of brain damage. This is equally true of neuroscientists interested in vision. Throughout Chapter 4 you will read about research employing technologies such as fMRI or the use of microelectrodes, as in the research of Hubel and Wiesel. Vision researchers often complement this type of research by observations of the performance of individuals suffering from brain damage. For example, consider research on the *McCollough effect*.

The McCollough effect is a well-known afterimage phenomenon that differs from other colour afterimage effects because it is contingent upon both colour and pattern/form (i.e., line orientation). After alternating between the two circles on the top of Figure 4.15, if you were then asked to look at a circle like that at the bottom left of Figure 4.15, but one composed only of black and white lines, you would see an afterimage resembling the one illustrated in the bottom left of the figure. The colours you would see are complements of the colours in which the line pattern (vertical or horizontal) was presented in the top.

Several groups of Canadian researchers, including Peter Dodwell from Queen's University (Dodwell & Humphrey, 1990) and Keith Humphrey and his colleagues from the University of Western Ontario (Humphrey, James, Gati, Menon, & Goodale, 1999), have conducted research on the McCollough effect using a variety of contemporary and classic methods. For example, in addition to fMRI results, Humphrey and Goodale (1998) reviewed the results of experiments using individuals who suffered from visual agnosia. These patients had brain damage such that while they could perceive colour, they could not consciously perceive contour (line) orientation. Despite this deficit, they experienced the McCollough effect. This result, along with other available findings, suggests that the effect is mediated by the area of the brain known as *V1*, or the primary visual cortex, and that it does not depend upon conscious form perception. The authors used these results to speculate on the nature of conscious visual experience.

REVIEW OF KEY POINTS

- Light varies in terms of wavelength, amplitude, and purity. Light enters the eye through the cornea and pupil and is focused upside down on the retina by the lens. Distant objects appear blurry to nearsighted people and close objects appear blurry to farsighted people.
- The retina is the neural tissue in the eye that absorbs light, processes images, and sends visual signals to the brain. Cones, which are concentrated in the fovea, play a key role in daylight vision and colour perception. Rods, which have their greatest density just outside the fovea, are critical to night vision and peripheral vision. Dark adaptation and light adaptation both involve changes in the retina's sensitivity to light, allowing the eye to adapt to changes in illumination.

- The retina transforms light into neural impulses that are sent to the brain via the optic nerve. Receptive fields are areas in the retina that affect the firing of visual cells. They vary in shape and size, but centre-surround arrangements are common. The optic nerves from the inside half of each eye cross at the optic chiasm and then project to the opposite half of the brain.

- Two visual pathways engage in parallel processing and send signals to different areas of the primary visual cortex. The main pathway is routed through the LGN in the thalamus. After processing in the primary visual cortex, visual information is shuttled along the *what* and *where* pathways to other cortical areas.

- Nobel Prize–winning research by Hubel and Wiesel suggests that the visual cortex contains cells that function as feature detectors. The discovery of the *what pathway* and the neurons inside it that respond specifically to faces have shed new light on visual disorders that have perplexed scientists for decades.

- Vision researchers employ multiple, converging methods when trying to explain the role of the brain in visual experience. This was illustrated with recent research on the McCollough effect.

Figure 4.15

The McCollough effect.
An illustration of typical induction and testing conditions for the McCollough effect. Subjects would view the vertical red-and-black grating alternating with the horizontal green-and-black grating for a few minutes. After such induction, black-and-white vertical gratings would appear green and horizontal gratings would appear pink (as in the simulated aftereffect shown in the lower left of the figure). Black-and-white oblique test gratings, as in the lower right of the figure, would not appear coloured.

SOURCE: Humphrey, G. K., and Goodale, M.A. (1998). Probing unconscious visual processing with the McCollough Effect. *Consciousness and Cognition, 7*, 494–519. Reprinted by permission of Elsevier.

PREVIEW QUESTIONS

- How are additive and subtractive colour mixing different?
- How have the trichromatic and opponent process theories been reconciled to explain colour vision?
- What is feature analysis, and what is the difference between top-down and bottom-up processing?
- What was the basic premise of Gestalt psychology?
- What are the Gestalt principles of form perception?
- How do perceptual hypotheses contribute to form perception?

Viewing the World in Colour

So far, we've considered only how the visual system deals with light and dark. Let's journey now into the world of colour. On the one hand, you can see perfectly well without seeing in colour. Many animals get by with little or no colour vision, and no one seemed to suffer back when all photographs, movies, or TV shows were in black and white. On the other hand, colour clearly adds rich information to our perception of the world. Colour vision may have evolved because it facilitates identification of objects, perhaps improving our ability to find fruit in the forest (Mollon, 1989). Although the purpose of colour vision remains elusive, scientists have learned a great deal about the mechanisms underlying the perception of colour.

The Stimulus for Colour

As noted earlier, the lights people see are mixtures of various wavelengths. Perceived colour is primarily a function of the dominant wavelength in these mixtures. In the visible spectrum, lights with the longest wavelengths appear red, whereas those with the shortest appear violet. Notice the word *appear*. Colour is a psychological interpretation. It's not a physical property of light itself.

Although wavelength wields the greatest influence, perception of colour depends on complex blends of all three properties of light. Wavelength is most closely related to hue, amplitude to brightness, and purity to saturation. These three dimensions of colour are illustrated in the *colour solid* shown in Figure 4.16.

As a colour solid demonstrates systematically, people can perceive many different colours. Indeed, experts estimate that humans can discriminate

among roughly a million colours (Boynton, 1990). Most of these diverse variations are the result of mixing a few basic colours. There are two kinds of colour mixture: subtractive and additive. **Subtractive colour mixing works by removing some wavelengths of light, leaving less light than was originally there.** You probably became familiar with subtractive mixing as a child when you mixed yellow and blue paints to make green. Paints yield subtractive mixing because pigments *absorb* most wavelengths, selectively reflecting specific wavelengths that give rise to particular colours. Subtractive colour mixing can also be demonstrated by stacking colour filters. If you look through a sandwich of yellow and blue cellophane filters, they will block out certain wavelengths. The middle wavelengths that are left will look green.

Additive colour mixing works by superimposing lights, putting more light in the mixture than exists in any one light by itself. If you shine red, green, and blue spotlights on a white surface, you'll have an additive mixture. As Figure 4.17 shows, additive and subtractive mixtures of the same colours produce different results. Human processes of colour perception parallel additive colour mixing much more closely than subtractive mixing, as you'll see in the following discussion of theories of colour vision.

Trichromatic Theory of Colour Vision

The *trichromatic theory* of colour vision (*tri* for "three," *chroma* for "colour") was first stated by Thomas Young and modified later by Hermann von Helmholtz (1852). The **trichromatic theory of colour vision holds that the human eye has three types of receptors with differing sensitivities to different light wavelengths.** Helmholtz theorized

Figure 4.16

The colour solid. The colour solid shows how colour varies along three perceptual dimensions: brightness (increasing from the bottom to the top of the solid), hue (changing around the solid's perimeter), and saturation (increasing toward the periphery of the solid).

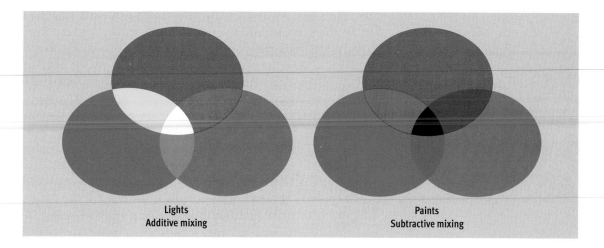

Figure 4.17

Lights
Additive mixing

Paints
Subtractive mixing

Additive versus subtractive colour mixing. Lights mix additively because all the wavelengths contained in each light reach the eye. If red, blue, and green lights are projected onto a white screen, they produce the colours shown on the left, with white at the intersection of all three lights. If paints of the same three colours were combined in the same way, the subtractive mixture would produce the colours shown on the right, with black at the intersection of all three colours.

that the eye contains specialized receptors sensitive to the specific wavelengths associated with red, green, and blue. According to this model, people can see all the colours of the rainbow because the eye does its own "colour mixing" by varying the ratio of neural activity among these three types of receptors.

Most of the known facts about colour blindness also meshed well with trichromatic theory. *Colour blindness* encompasses a variety of deficiencies in the ability to distinguish among colours. Colour blindness occurs much more frequently in males than in females. Actually, the term colour *blindness* is somewhat misleading, since complete blindness to differences in colours is quite rare. Most people who are colour blind are *dichromats;* that is, they make do with only two colour channels. There are three types of dichromats, and each type is insensitive to a different colour (red, green, or blue, although the latter is rare) (Gouras, 1991). The three deficiencies seen among dichromats support the notion that there are three channels for colour vision, as proposed by trichromatic theory.

Opponent Process Theory of Colour Vision

Although trichromatic theory explained some facets of colour vision well, it ran aground in other areas. Consider complementary afterimages, for instance. *Complementary colours* are pairs of colours that produce grey tones when mixed together. The various pairs of complementary colours can be arranged in a *colour circle,* such as the one in Figure 4.18. If you stare at a strong colour and then look at a white background, you'll see an *afterimage*—a visual image that persists after a stimulus is removed. The colour of the afterimage will be the *complement* of the colour you originally stared at. Trichromatic theory cannot account for the appearance of complementary afterimages.

Here's another peculiarity to consider. If you ask people to describe colours but restrict them to using three names, they run into difficulty. For example, using only red, green, and blue, they simply don't feel comfortable describing yellow as "reddish green." However, if you let them have just one more name, they usually choose yellow; they can then describe any colour quite well (Gordon & Abramov, 2001). If colours are reduced to three channels, why are four colour names required to describe the full range of possible colours?

In an effort to answer questions such as these, Ewald Hering proposed the *opponent process theory* in 1878. The *opponent process theory* of colour vision holds that colour perception depends on receptors that make antagonistic responses to three pairs of colours. The three pairs of opponent colours posited by Hering were red versus green, yellow versus blue, and black versus white. The antagonistic processes in this theory provide plausible explanations for complementary afterimages and the need for four names (red, green, blue, and yellow) to describe colours. Opponent process theory also explains some aspects of colour blindness. For instance, it can

Web Link 4.2

The Joy of Visual Perception: A Web Book
http://www.yorku.ca/eye/
thejoy.htm

This site shows the Internet at its best. Peter Kaiser of York University has crafted a comprehensive guide to human colour vision, supplying plenty of graphics and demonstrations to help visitors understand what laboratory research in psychology has learned about visual perception.

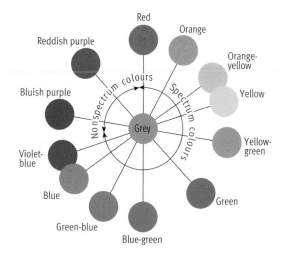

Figure 4.18

The colour circle and complementary colours. Colours opposite each other on this colour circle are complements, or "opposites." Additively, mixing complementary colours produces grey. Opponent process principles help explain this effect as well as the other peculiarities of complementary colours noted in the text.

Short-wavelength "blue" cones

Medium-wavelength "green" cones

Long-wavelength "red" cones

Receptor sensitivity (percentage of maximum response)

Wavelength (nanometres)

Source: Wald, G., & Brown, P.K. (1965). Human color vision and color blindness. *Symposium Cold Spring Harbor Laboratory of Quantitative Biology, 30,* 345–359 (p. 351). Copyright © 1965. Reprinted by permission of the author.

Figure 4.19

Three types of cones.
Research has identified three types of cones that show varied sensitivity to different wavelengths of light. As the graph shows, these three types of cones correspond only roughly to the red, green, and blue receptors predicted by trichromatic theory, so it is more accurate to refer to them as cones sensitive to short, medium, and long wavelengths.

Figure 4.20

Reconciling theories of colour vision. Contemporary explanations of colour vision include aspects of both the trichromatic and opponent process theories. As predicted by trichromatic theory, there are three types of receptors for colour—cones sensitive to short, medium, and long wavelengths. However, these cones are organized into receptive fields that excite or inhibit the firing of higher-level visual cells in the retina, thalamus, and cortex. As predicted by opponent process theory, some of these cells respond in antagonistic ways to blue versus yellow, red versus green, and black versus white.

explain why dichromats typically find it hard to distinguish either green from red or yellow from blue.

Reconciling Theories of Colour Vision 3D

Advocates of trichromatic theory and opponent process theory argued about the relative merits of their models for almost a century. Most researchers assumed that one theory must be wrong and the other must be right. In recent decades, however, it has become clear that *it takes both theories to explain colour vision.* Eventually a physiological basis for both theories was found. Research that earned George Wald a Nobel Prize demonstrated that *the eye has three types of cones,* with each type being most sensitive to a different band of wavelengths, as shown

in Figure 4.19 (Lennie, 2000; Wald, 1964). The three types of cones represent the three different colour receptors predicted by trichromatic theory.

Researchers also discovered a biological basis for opponent processes. They found cells in the retina, the LGN, and the visual cortex *that respond in opposite ways to red versus green and blue versus yellow* (DeValois & Jacobs, 1984; Zrenner et al., 1990). For example, there are ganglion cells in the retina that are excited by green and inhibited by red. Other ganglion cells in the retina work in just the opposite way, as predicted in opponent process theory.

In summary, the perception of colour appears to involve sequential stages of information processing (Hurvich, 1981). The receptors that do the first stage of processing (the cones) seem to follow the principles outlined in trichromatic theory. In later stages of processing, at least some cells in the retina, the LGN, and the visual cortex seem to follow the principles outlined in opponent process theory (see Figure 4.20). As you can see, vigorous theoretical debate about colour vision produced a solution that went beyond the contributions of either theory alone.

Perceiving Forms, Patterns, and Objects   3C, 3E

The drawing in Figure 4.21 is a poster for a circus act involving a trained seal. Take a good look at it. What do you see?

No doubt you see a seal balancing a ball on its nose and a trainer holding a fish and a whip. But

Figure 4.21

A poster for a trained seal act. Or is it? The picture is an ambiguous figure, which can be interpreted as either of two scenes, as explained in the text.

suppose you had been told that the drawing is actually a poster for a costume ball. Would you have perceived it differently?

If you focus on the idea of a costume ball (stay with it a minute if you still see the seal and trainer), you will probably see a costumed man and woman in Figure 4.21. She's handing him a hat, and he has a sword in his right hand. This tricky little sketch was made ambiguous quite intentionally. It's a *reversible figure,* **a drawing that is compatible with two interpretations that can shift back and forth.** Another classic reversible figure is shown in Figure 4.22. What do you see? A rabbit or a duck? It all depends on how you look at the drawing.

The key point is simply this: The same visual input can result in radically different perceptions. No one-to-one correspondence exists between sensory input and what you perceive. This is a principal reason that people's experience of the world is subjective. Perception involves much more than passively receiving signals from the outside world. It involves the interpretation of sensory input. To some extent, this interpretive process can be influenced by manipulating people's expectations. For example, information given to you about the drawing of the "circus act involving a trained seal" created a *perceptual set*—a readiness to perceive a stimulus in a

particular way. A perceptual set creates a certain slant in how someone interprets sensory input.

Form perception also depends on the *selection* of sensory input—that is, what people focus their attention on (Chun & Wolfe, 2001). A visual scene may include many objects and forms. Some of them may capture viewers' attention while others may not. This fact has been demonstrated in dramatic fashion in studies of *inattentional blindness,* which involves the failure to see fully visible objects or events in a visual display. In one such study (Simons & Chabris, 1999), participants watched a video of a group of people in white shirts passing a basketball that was laid over another video of people in black shirts passing a basketball (the two videos were partially transparent). The observers were instructed to focus on one of the two teams and press a key whenever that team passed the ball. Thirty seconds into the task, a woman carrying an umbrella clearly walked through the scene for four seconds. You might guess that this bizarre development would be noticed by virtually all the observers, but 44% of the participants failed to see the woman. Moreover, when someone in a gorilla suit strolled through the same scene, even more subjects (73%) missed the unexpected event! Inattentional blindness has been attributed to subjects having a perceptual set that leads them to focus most of their attention on a specific feature in a scene (such as the basketball passes) while neglecting other facets of the scene (Most et al., 2001). Inattentional blindness may account for many automobile accidents; people often say "I looked right there, but never saw them" (Shermer, 2004).

An understanding of how people perceive forms and objects also requires knowledge of how people *organize* their visual inputs. Several influential approaches to this issue emphasize *feature analysis.*

Feature Analysis: Assembling Forms 3c

The information received by your eyes would do you little good if you couldn't recognize objects and forms—ranging from words on a page to mice in your cellar and friends in the distance. According to some theories, perceptions of form and pattern entail *feature analysis* (Lindsay & Norman, 1977; Maguire et al., 1990). *Feature analysis* **is the process of detecting specific elements in visual input and assembling them into a more complex form.** In other words, you start with the components of a form, such as lines, edges, and corners, and build them into perceptions of squares, triangles, stop signs, bicycles, ice cream cones, and telephones. An application of this model of form perception is diagrammed in Figure 4.23.

Figure 4.22

Another ambiguous figure. What animal do you see here? As the text explains, two very different perceptions are possible. This ambiguous figure was devised around 1900 by Joseph Jastrow, a prominent psychologist at the turn of the 20th century (Block & Yuker, 1992).

Web Link 4.3

Sensation and Perception Tutorials
http://psych.hanover.edu/Krantz/sen_tut.html

John Krantz of Hanover College has assembled a collection of quality tutorials on sensation and perception. Topics covered include receptive fields, depth perception, Gestalt laws, and the use of perceptual principles in art.

Figure **4.23**

Feature analysis in form perception. One vigorously debated theory of form perception is that the brain has cells that respond to specific aspects or features of stimuli, such as lines and angles. Neurons functioning as higher-level analyzers then respond to input from these "feature detectors." The more input each analyzer receives, the more active it becomes. Finally, other neurons weigh signals from these analyzers and make a "decision" about the stimulus. In this way perception of a form is arrived at by assembling elements from the bottom up.

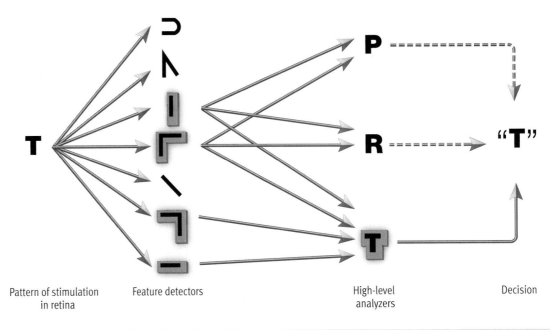

| Pattern of stimulation in retina | Feature detectors | High-level analyzers | Decision |

Top-down processing

Formulate perceptual hypothesis about the nature of the stimulus as a whole

Select and examine features to check hypothesis

Recognize stimulus

Recognize stimulus

Combine specific features into more complex forms

Detect specific features of stimulus

Bottom-up processing

Figure 4.24

Bottom-up versus top-down processing. As explained in these diagrams, bottom-up processing progresses from individual elements to whole elements, whereas top-down processing progresses from the whole to the individual elements.

Figure 4.25

Subjective contours. Our perception of the triangle on the right and the circle on the left results from subjective contours that are not really there. The effect is so powerful, the triangle and circle appear lighter than the background, which they are not. To demonstrate the illusory nature of these contours for yourself, cover the red circles that mark off the triangle. You'll see that the triangle disappears.

Feature analysis assumes that form perception involves *bottom-up processing,* **a progression from individual elements to the whole** (see Figure 4.24). The plausibility of this model was bolstered greatly when Hubel and Wiesel showed that cells in the visual cortex operate as highly specialized feature detectors. Indeed, their findings strongly suggested that at least some aspects of form perception involve feature analysis.

Can feature analysis provide a complete account of how people perceive forms? Clearly not. A crucial problem for the theory is that form perception often does not involve bottom-up processing. In fact, there is ample evidence that perceptions of form frequently involve *top-down processing,* **a progression from the whole to the elements** (see Figure 4.24).

For example, there is evidence that people can perceive a word before its individual letters, a phenomenon that has to reflect top-down processing (Johnston & McClelland, 1974). If readers depended exclusively on bottom-up processing, they would have to analyze the features of letters in words to recognize them and then assemble the letters into words. This would be a terribly time-consuming task and would slow down reading speed to a snail's pace.

Subjective contours are another phenomenon traditionally attributed to top-down processing, although that view is changing. The phenomenon of *subjective contours* **is the perception of contours where none actually exist.** Consider, for instance, the triangle shown in Figure 4.25. We see the contours of the triangle easily, even though no physical edges or lines are present. It is hard to envision how feature detectors could detect edges that are not really there, so most theorists have argued that bottom-up models of form perception are unlikely to account for subjective contours. Until recently, the prevailing view was that subjective contours depend on viewing stimulus configurations as wholes and then filling in the blanks (Rock, 1986). However, researchers have demonstrated that feature detectors *do* respond to the edges in subjective contours (Peterhans & von der Heydt, 1991). At present, neural theories of subjective contours that emphasize bottom-up processing or both types of processing are under investigation, with promising results (Gunn et al., 2000; Lesher, 1995). In sum, it appears that both top-down and bottom-up processing have their niches in form perception.

Looking at the Whole Picture: Gestalt Principles

Top-down processing is clearly at work in the principles of form perception described by the Gestalt psychologists. As mentioned in Chapter 1, *Gestalt psychology* was an influential school of thought that emerged out of Germany during the first half of the 20th century. (*Gestalt* is a German word for "form" or "shape.") Gestalt psychologists repeatedly demonstrated that the whole can be greater than the sum of its parts.

A simple example of this principle is the *phi phenomenon,* first described by Max Wertheimer in 1912. **The *phi phenomenon* is the illusion of movement created by presenting visual stimuli in rapid succession.** You encounter examples of the phi phenomenon nearly every day. For example, movies and TV consist of separate still pictures projected rapidly one after the other. You see smooth motion, but in reality the "moving" objects merely take slightly different positions in successive frames. Viewed as a whole, a movie has a property (motion) that isn't evident in any of its parts (the individual frames). The Gestalt psychologists formulated a series of principles that describe how the visual system organizes a scene into discrete forms. Let's examine some of these principles.

Figure and Ground Take a look at Figure 4.26. Do you see the figure as two silhouetted faces against a white background, or as a white vase against a black background? This reversible figure illustrates the Gestalt principle of *figure and ground.* Dividing visual displays into figure and ground is a fundamental way in which people organize visual perceptions (Baylis & Driver, 1995). The *figure* is the thing being looked at, and the *ground* is the background against which it stands. Figures seem to have more substance and shape, appear closer to the viewer, and

Figure 4.26

The principle of figure and ground. Whether you see two faces or a vase depends on which part of this drawing you see as figure and which as background. Although this reversible drawing allows you to switch back and forth between two ways of organizing your perception, you can't perceive the drawing both ways at once.

seem to stand out in front of the ground. More often than not, your visual field may contain many figures sharing a background. The following Gestalt principles relate to how these elements are grouped into higher-order figures (Palmer, 2003).

Proximity Things that are near one another seem to belong together. The black dots in the upper left panel of Figure 4.27(a) could be grouped into vertical columns or horizontal rows. However, people tend to perceive rows because of the effect of proximity (the dots are closer together horizontally).

Closure People often group elements to create a sense of *closure,* or completeness. Thus, you may "complete" figures that actually have gaps in them. This principle is demonstrated in the upper right panel of Figure 4.27(b).

Similarity People also tend to group stimuli that are similar. This principle is apparent in Figure 4.27(c), where viewers group elements of similar lightness into the number 2.

Simplicity The Gestaltists' most general principle was the law of *Pragnanz,* which translates from German as "good form." The idea is that people tend to group elements that combine to form a good figure. This

"The fundamental 'formula' of Gestalt theory might be expressed in this way: There are wholes, the behaviour of which is not determined by that of their individual elements."
MAX WERTHEIMER

Figure 4.27

Gestalt principles of perceptual organization. Gestalt principles help explain some of the factors that influence form perception. **(a) Proximity:** These dots might well be organized in vertical columns rather than horizontal rows, but because of proximity (the dots are closer together horizontally), they tend to be perceived in rows. **(b) Closure:** Even though the figures are incomplete, you fill in the blanks and see a circle and a dog. **(c) Similarity:** Because of similarity of colour, you see dots organized into the number 2 instead of a random array. If you did not group similar elements, you wouldn't see the number 2 here. **(d) Simplicity:** You could view this as a complicated 11-sided figure, but given the preference for simplicity, you are more likely to see it as an overlapping rectangle and triangle. **(e) Continuity:** You tend to group these dots in a way that produces a smooth path rather than an abrupt shift in direction.

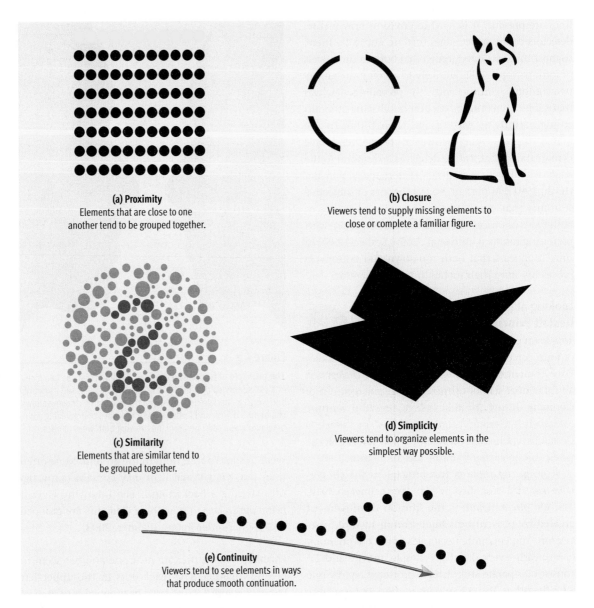

(a) Proximity
Elements that are close to one another tend to be grouped together.

(b) Closure
Viewers tend to supply missing elements to close or complete a familiar figure.

(c) Similarity
Elements that are similar tend to be grouped together.

(d) Simplicity
Viewers tend to organize elements in the simplest way possible.

(e) Continuity
Viewers tend to see elements in ways that produce smooth continuation.

principle is somewhat vague in that it's often difficult to spell out what makes a figure "good" (Biederman, Hilton, & Hummel, 1991). Some theorists maintain that goodness is largely a matter of simplicity, asserting that people tend to organize forms in the simplest way possible (see Figure 4.27d).

Continuity The principle of continuity reflects people's tendency to follow in whatever direction they've been led. Thus, people tend to connect points that result in straight or gently curved lines that create "smooth" paths, as shown in the bottom panel of Figure 4.27(e). Although Gestalt psychology is no longer an active theoretical orientation in modern psychology, its influence is still felt in the study of perception (Banks & Krajicek, 1991). The Gestalt psychologists raised many important questions that still occupy researchers, and they left a legacy of many

useful insights about form perception that have stood the test of time (Sharps & Wertheimer, 2000).

Formulating Perceptual Hypotheses

The Gestalt principles provide some indications of how people organize visual input. However, scientists are still one step away from understanding how these organized perceptions result in a representation of the real world. Understanding the problem requires distinguishing between two kinds of stimuli: distal and proximal (Hochberg, 1988). **Distal stimuli are stimuli that lie in the distance (that is, in the world outside the body).** In vision, these are the objects that you're looking at. They are "distant" in that your eyes don't touch them. What your eyes do "touch" are the images formed by patterns of light falling on your retinas. These images are the **proximal stimuli, the stimulus energies that impinge directly**

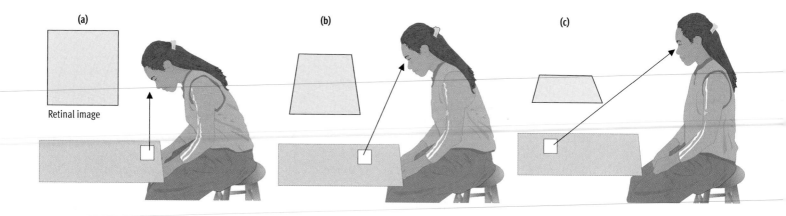

(a)   (b)   (c)

Retinal image

on sensory receptors. The distinction is important, because there are great differences between the objects you perceive and the stimulus energies that represent them.

In visual perception, the proximal stimuli are distorted, two-dimensional versions of their actual, three-dimensional counterparts. For example, consider the distal stimulus of a square such as the one in Figure 4.28. If the square is lying on a desk in front of you, it is actually projecting a trapezoid (the proximal stimulus) onto your retinas, because the top of the square is farther from your eyes than the bottom. Obviously, the trapezoid is a distorted representation of the square. If what people have to work with is so distorted a picture, how do they get an accurate view of the world out there?

One explanation is that people bridge the gap between distal and proximal stimuli by constantly making and testing *hypotheses* about what's out there in the real world (Gregory, 1973). Thus, **a *perceptual hypothesis* is an inference about which distal stimuli could be responsible for the proximal stimuli sensed.** In effect, people make educated guesses about what form could be responsible for a pattern of sensory stimulation. The square in Figure 4.28 may project a trapezoidal image on your retinas, but your perceptual system "guesses" correctly that it's a square—and that's what you see.

Let's look at another ambiguous drawing to further demonstrate the process of making a perceptual hypothesis. Figure 4.29 is a famous reversible figure, first published as a cartoon in a humour magazine. Perhaps you see a drawing of a young woman looking back over her right shoulder. Alternatively, you might see an old woman with her chin down on her chest. The ambiguity exists because there isn't enough information to force your perceptual system to accept only one of these hypotheses. Incidentally, studies show that people who are led to *expect* the young woman or the old woman generally see the one they

expect (Leeper, 1935). This is another example of how perceptual sets influence what people see.

Psychologists have used a variety of reversible figures to study how people formulate perceptual hypotheses. Another example can be seen in Figure 4.30, which shows the *Necker cube.* The shaded surface can appear as either the front or the rear of the transparent cube. If you look at the cube for a while, your

Figure 4.29

A famous reversible figure. What do you see? Consult the text to learn what the two possible interpretations of this figure are.

Figure 4.30

The Necker cube. The tinted surface of this reversible figure can become either the front or the back of the cube.

Figure 4.28

Distal and proximal stimuli. Proximal stimuli are often distorted, shifting representations of distal stimuli in the real world. If you look directly down at a small, square piece of paper on a desk **(a)**, the distal stimulus (the paper) and the proximal stimulus (the image projected on your retina) will both be square. But as you move the paper away on the desktop, as shown in **(b)** and **(c),** the square distal stimulus projects an increasingly trapezoidal image on your retina, making the proximal stimulus more and more distorted. Nevertheless, you continue to perceive a square.

perception will alternate between these possibilities. People tend to experience a similar shift back and forth between two perceptions when they view the image in Figure 4.31.

The *context* in which something appears often guides people's perceptual hypotheses. To illustrate, take a look at Figure 4.32. What do you see? You probably saw the words "THE CAT." But look again; the middle characters in both words are identical. You identified an "H" in the first word and an "A" in the second because of the surrounding letters, which created an expectation—another example of top-down processing in visual perception. The power of expectations explains why typographocal errors like those in this sentence often pass unoberved (Lachman, 1996).

Perceiving Depth or Distance

More often than not, forms and figures are objects in space. Spatial considerations add a third dimension to visual perception. **Depth perception involves interpretation of visual cues that indicate how near or far away objects are.** To make judgments of distance, people rely on quite a variety of clues, which can be classified into two types: binocular and monocular (Hochberg, 1988; Proffit & Caudek, 2003).

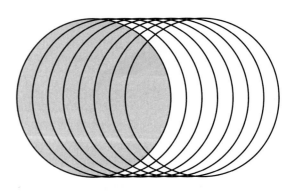

Figure 4.31

Another reversible figure. The tinted surface of this reversible figure can become either the closer or farther end of the "tube." People's perceptions of this stimulus tend to dynamically go back and forth between these interpretations.

THE CAT

Figure 4.32

Context effects. The context in which a stimulus is seen can affect your perceptual hypotheses

Binocular Cues

Because the eyes are set apart, each eye has a slightly different view of the world. **Binocular depth cues are clues about distance based on the differing views of the two eyes.** "Stereo" viewers like the Viewmaster toy you may have had as a child make use of this principle by presenting slightly different flat images of the same scene to each eye. The brain then supplies the "depth," and you perceive a three-dimensional scene.

The principal binocular depth cue is *retinal disparity*, which refers to the fact that objects project images to slightly different locations on the right and left retinas, so the right and left eyes see slightly different views of the object. The closer an object gets, the greater the disparity between the images seen by each eye. Thus, retinal disparity increases as objects come closer, providing information about distance. Another binocular cue is *convergence*, **which involves sensing the eyes converging toward each other as they focus on closer objects.**

Monocular Cues

Monocular depth cues **are clues about distance based on the image in either eye alone.** There are two kinds of monocular cues to depth. One kind is the result of active use of the eye in viewing the world. For example, as an object comes closer, you may sense the accommodation (the change in the curvature of the lens) that must occur for the eye to adjust its focus. Furthermore, if you cover one eye and move your head from side to side, closer objects appear to move more than distant objects. In a similar vein, you may notice when driving along a highway that nearby objects (such as fenceposts along the road) appear to move by more rapidly than objects that are farther away (such as trees in the distance). Thus, you get cues about depth from **motion parallax, which involves images of objects at different distances moving across the retina at different rates.**

The other kind of monocular cues are *pictorial depth cues—clues about distance that can be given in a flat picture.* There are many pictorial cues to depth, which is why some paintings and photographs seem so realistic that you feel you can climb right into them. Six prominent pictorial depth cues are described and illustrated in Figure 4.33. *Linear*

perspective is a depth cue reflecting the fact that lines converge in the distance. Because details are too small to see when they are far away, *texture gradients* can provide information about depth. If an object comes between you and another object, it must be closer to you, a cue called *interposition. Relative size* is a cue because closer objects appear larger. *Height in plane* reflects the fact that distant objects appear higher in a picture. Finally, the familiar effects of shadowing make *light and shadow* useful in judging distance. Research also suggests that application of pictorial depth cues to pictures varies to some degree across cultures (Berry et al., 1992; Hudson, 1960).

Perceptual Constancies in Vision

When a person approaches you from a distance, his or her image on your retinas gradually changes in size. Do you perceive that the person is growing right before your eyes? Of course not. Your perceptual

Figure 4.33

Pictorial cues to depth.
Six pictorial depth cues are explained and illustrated here. Although one cue stands out in each photo, in most visual scenes several pictorial cues are present. Try looking at the light-and-shadow picture upside down. The change in shadowing reverses what you see.

Linear perspective Parallel lines that run away from the viewer seem to get closer together.

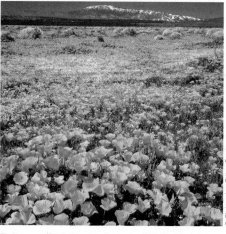

Texture gradient A texture is coarser for near areas and finer for more distant ones.

Interposition The shapes of near objects overlap or mask those of more distant ones.

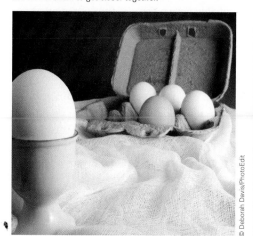

Relative size If separate objects are expected to be of the same size, the larger ones are seen as closer.

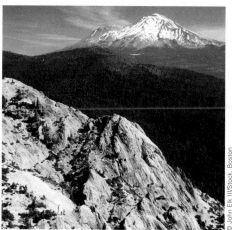

Height in plane Near objects are low in the visual field; more distant ones are higher up.

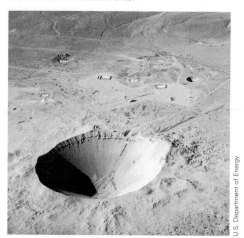

Light and shadow Patterns of light and dark suggest shadows that can create an impression of three-dimensional forms.

Recognizing Pictorial Depth Cues

Painters routinely attempt to create the perception of depth on a flat canvas by using pictorial depth cues. Figure 4.33 describes and illustrates six pictorial depth cues, most of which are apparent in Vincent van Gogh's colourful piece *Corridor in the Asylum* (1889). Check your understanding of depth perception by trying to spot the depth cues in the painting.

In the list below, check off the depth cues used by van Gogh. The answers can be found in the back of the book in Appendix A. You can learn more about how artists use the principles of visual perception in the Personal Application at the end of this chapter.

van Gogh, Vincent, *Corridor in the Asylum* (1889), gouache and watercolour, 24 3/8 × 18 1/2 inches (61.5 × 47 cm). Metropolitan Museum of Art. Bequest of Abby Aldrich Rockefeller, 1948. (48.190.2) Photograph © 1998 The Metropolitan Museum of Art.

_____ **1.** Interposition   _____ **4.** Relative size

_____ **2.** Height in plane   _____ **5.** Light and shadow

_____ **3.** Texture gradient   _____ **6.** Linear perspective

system constantly makes allowances for this variation in visual input. The task of the perceptual system is to provide an accurate rendition of distal stimuli based on distorted, ever-changing proximal stimuli. In doing so, it relies in part on perceptual constancies. A *perceptual constancy* **is a tendency to experience a stable perception in the face of continually changing sensory input.** Among other things, people tend to view objects as having a stable size, shape, brightness, hue, and location in space.

The Power of Misleading Cues: Optical Illusions

 SIM 3, 3G

In general, perceptual constancies, depth cues, and principles of visual organization (such as the Gestalt laws) help people perceive the world accurately. Sometimes, however, perceptions are based on inappropriate assumptions, and *optical illusions* can result. **An *optical illusion* involves an apparently inexplicable discrepancy between the appearance of a visual stimulus and its physical reality.**

One famous optical illusion is the *Müller-Lyer* illusion, shown in Figure 4.34. The two vertical lines in this figure are equally long, but they certainly don't look that way. Why not? Several mechanisms probably play a role (Day, 1965; Gregory, 1978). The figure on the left looks like the outside of a building, thrust toward the viewer, while the one on the right looks like an inside corner, thrust away (see Figure 4.35). The vertical line in the left figure therefore seems closer. If two lines cast equally long retinal images but one seems closer, the closer one is assumed to be shorter. Thus, the Müller-Lyer illusion may result from

a combination of size constancy processes and misperception of depth. As we saw earlier with regard to the McCollough effect, visual illusions can be useful to probe the nature of visual systems and visual processing. Daniel Meegan of the University of Guelph and his colleagues (Meegan, Glazebrook, Dhillon, Trembly, Welsh, & Elliott, 2004) have used the Müller-Lyer illusion to derive conclusions regarding the nature of visual representations underlying perception, motor control, and planning.

The geometric illusions shown in Figure 4.36 also demonstrate that visual stimuli can be highly deceptive. The *Ponzo illusion*, which is shown at the top of Figure 4.36, appears to result from the same factors at work in the Müller-Lyer illusion (Coren & Girgus, 1978). The upper and lower horizontal lines are the same length, but the upper one appears longer. This illusion probably occurs because the converging lines

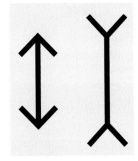

Figure 4.34

The Müller-Lyer illusion.
Go ahead, measure them: the two vertical lines are of equal length.

Figure 4.35

Explaining the Müller-Lyer illusion. The figure on the left seems to be closer, since it looks like an outside corner, thrust toward you, whereas the figure on the right looks like an inside corner thrust away from you. Given retinal images of the same length, you assume that the "closer" line is shorter.

convey linear perspective, a key depth cue suggesting that the upper line lies farther away. Figure 4.37 shows a drawing by Stanford University psychologist Roger Shepard (1990) that creates a similar illusion. The second monster appears much larger than the first, even though they are really identical in size.

Adelbert Ames designed a striking illusion that makes use of misperception of distance. It's called, appropriately enough, the *Ames room.* It's a specially contrived room built with a trapezoidal rear wall and a sloping floor and ceiling. When viewed from the correct point, as in the picture, it looks like an ordinary rectangular room (see Figure 4.38). But in reality, the left corner is much taller and much farther from the viewer than the right corner. Hence, bizarre illusions unfold in the Ames room. People standing in the right corner appear to be giants, while those standing in the left corner appear to be midgets. Even more disconcerting, a person who walks across the room from right to left appears to

shrink before your eyes! The Ames room creates these misperceptions by toying with the perfectly reasonable assumption that the room is vertically and horizontally rectangular.

Impossible figures create another form of illusion. **Impossible figures are objects that can be represented in two-dimensional pictures but cannot exist in three-dimensional space.** These figures may look fine at first glance, but a closer look reveals that they are geometrically inconsistent or impossible. Three widely studied impossible figures are shown in Figure 4.39, and a more recent impossible figure created by Roger Shepard (1990) can be seen in Figure 4.40. Notice that specific portions of these figures are reasonable, but they don't add up to a sensible whole. The parts don't interface properly. The initial illusion that the figures make sense is probably a result of bottom-up processing. You perceive specific features of the figure as acceptable but are baffled as they are built into a whole.

Figure 4.36

Four geometric illusions. **Ponzo:** The horizontal lines are the same length. **Poggendorff:** The two diagonal segments lie on the same straight line. **Upside-down T:** The vertical and horizontal lines are the same length. **Zollner:** The long diagonals are all parallel (try covering up some of the short diagonal lines if you don't believe it).

Figure 4.37

A monster of an illusion. The principles underlying the Ponzo illusion also explain the striking illusion seen here, in which two identical monsters appear to be quite different in size.

Source: Shepard, R. N. (1990). *Mind sights.* New York: W. H. Freeman. Copyright © 1990 by Roger N. Shepard. Used by permission of Henry Holt & Co., LLC.

Wayne Weiten

Figure **4.38**

The Ames room. The diagram below shows the room as it is actually constructed. However, the viewer assumes that the room is rectangular, and the image cast on the retina is consistent with this hypothesis. Because of this reasonable perceptual hypothesis, the normal perceptual adjustments made to preserve size constancy lead to the illusions described in the text. For example, naïve viewers "conclude" that one boy is much larger than the other, when in fact he is merely closer.

Figure 4.39

Three classic impossible figures. The figures are impossible, yet they clearly exist—on the page. What makes them impossible is that they appear to be three-dimensional representations yet are drawn in a way that frustrates mental attempts to "assemble" their features into possible objects. It's difficult to see the drawings simply as lines lying in a plane—even though this perceptual hypothesis is the only one that resolves the contradiction.

Obviously, illusions such as impossible figures and their real-life relative, the Ames room, involve a conspiracy of cues intended to deceive the viewer. Many visual illusions, however, occur quite naturally. A well-known example is the *moon illusion.* The full moon appears to be much smaller when overhead than when looming on the horizon (see the photo on page 153). As with many of the other illusions we have discussed, the moon illusion appears to be due mainly to size constancy effects coupled with the misperception of distance (Coren & Aks, 1990; Kaufman & Rock, 1962). The moon illusion shows that optical illusions are part of everyday life. Indeed, many people are virtually addicted to an optical illusion called television (an illusion of movement created by a series of still images presented in quick succession).

Cross-cultural studies have uncovered some interesting differences among cultural groups in their propensity to see certain illusions. For example, Segall, Campbell, and Herskovits (1966) found that people from a variety of non-Western cultures are less susceptible to the Müller-Lyer illusion than Western samples. What could account for this difference? The most plausible explanation is that in the West, we live in a "carpentered world" dominated by straight lines, right angles, and rectangular rooms, buildings, and furniture. Thus, our experience prepares us to readily view the Müller-Lyer figures as inside and outside corners of buildings—inferences that help foster the illusion (Segall et al., 1990). In contrast, people in many non-Western cultures, such as the Zulu (see the photo on page 153) who were tested by Segall and associates (1966), live in a less carpentered world, making them less prone to see the Müller-Lyer figures as building corners. Although there is some debate about the matter, cultural differences in illusion susceptibility suggest that people's

Figure 4.40

Another impossible figure. This impossible figure, drawn by Stanford University psychologist Roger Shepard (1990), seems even more perplexing than the classic impossible figure that it is based on (the one seen in the middle of Figure 4.39).

Source: Shepard, R. N. (1990). *Mind sights.* New York: W. H. Freeman. Copyright © 1990 by Roger N. Shepard. Used by permission of Henry Holt & Co., LLC.

perceptual inferences can be shaped by experience (Segall et al., 1990).

What do optical illusions reveal about visual perception? They drive home the point that people go through life formulating perceptual hypotheses about what lies out there in the real world. The fact that these are only hypotheses becomes especially striking when the hypotheses are wrong, as they are with illusions. Optical illusions also show how contextual factors such as depth cues shape perceptual hypotheses. Finally, like ambiguous figures, illusions clearly demonstrate that human perceptions are not simple reflections of objective reality. Once again, we see that perception of the world is subjective. These insights do not apply to visual perception only. We will encounter these lessons again as we examine other sensory systems, such as hearing.

Vision for Perception and Vision for Action

If you think about some of the theories and research discussed in this chapter and in Chapter 3 in the section on the brain, it should be apparent that there is a great deal of cross-fertilization between the two areas. Recent work by Mel Goodale and his colleagues at the University of Western Ontario (Goodale & Humphrey, 2001; Goodale & Milner, 1992, 2004) is a good illustration of this point.

Web Link 4.5

The Moon Illusion Explained
http://facstaff.uww.edu/mccreadd/index.html

Don McCready, professor emeritus at the University of Wisconsin (Whitewater), addresses the age-old puzzle of why the moon appears much larger at the horizon than overhead. He uses a helpful collection of illustrations in a comprehensive review of alternative theories.

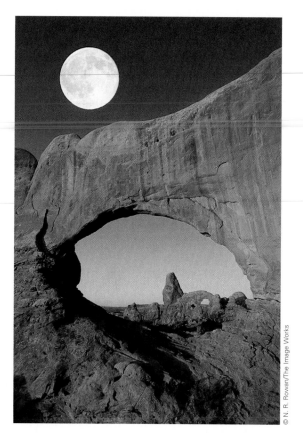

A puzzling perceptual illusion common in everyday life is the moon illusion: The moon looks larger when at the horizon than when overhead.

Unlike people in Western nations, the Zulus live in a culture where straight lines and right angles are scarce, if not entirely absent. Thus, they are not affected by such phenomena as the Müller-Lyer illusion nearly as much as people raised in environments that abound with rectangular structures.

Goodale (Goodale & Humphrey, 2001) distinguishes between two functions that vision serves. The first is to create an internal representation or model of the external world. This function is the subject of most of the research that we have discussed so far in this chapter. If you think about some of the things you might do as a result of being able to see the external world, it might give you a hint as to the nature of the second function that Goodale emphasized. The second function is not concerned with perceiving objects per se but with the related process of controlling your actions that are directed at those objects. Thus, if you are standing next to your best friend, one function of vision relates to creating an internal representation of that person and the second relates to guiding your actions in your attempt, for example, to pat him or her on the back as a means of congratulating. The first visual process is referred to as *vision for perception* and the second as *vision for action*. Goodale and his colleagues were led to this formulation by the work of previous researchers and through observation of the deficits shown by individuals who suffered specific types of brain damage, such as that experienced by an individual referred to as DF (Goodale & Milner, 1992, 2004).

DF had suffered a tragic accident. She was young, well educated, and fluent in several languages. She was living at the time in Milan with her partner, Carlo. One day while taking a shower, she was overcome by carbon monoxide fumes—the water was heated by a propane heater. As a result of the carbon monoxide poisoning, she suffered brain damage. DF had difficulty with her vision, seeing things and

Mel Goodale is internationally known for his work in the area of vision and neuroscience. He holds the Canada Research Chair in Visual Neuroscience in the Departments of Psychology and Physiology at the University of Western Ontario. In 1999 he was awarded the D. O. Hebb Award by the Canadian Society for Brain, Behaviour, and Cognitive Science and was made a Fellow of the Royal Society of Canada in 2001.

making sense out of them. Her visual problems were quite remarkable. She could see the surface detail of objects and their colour but she could not use their form or contours to identify them. For example, although she could see grids of lines projected onto a screen, she could not tell whether they were vertical or horizontal: "[DF] has never regained a full and integrated experience of the visual world. The world she sees still lacks shape and form. [DF] is unable to identify objects on the basis of their form alone" (Goodale & Milner, 2004, p. 9). DF was unable to copy simple drawings but could draw them from memory (see Figure 4.41). The drawings in Figure 4.41 show that her problems resulted from difficulties in perceptual organization, not in a "failure of the visual input to invoke the stored representation of the objects" (Goodale & Humphrey, 2001, p. 319). Her inability to recognize common objects is known as *agnosia*.

DF's neurological deficits were highly selective. For example, her motor abilities were intact. While testing DF one day, Goodale and Milner were struck by her ability to grasp a pencil they had placed in front of her while not being able to identify it. They wondered how she could perform all the motor acts dependent on vision that enabled her to grasp the

Figure 4.41

Samples of drawings made by DF. The left column shows examples of line drawings that were shown to DF, the right column shows some of DF's drawings of the objects from memory, and the middle column shows examples of DF's copies of the line drawings shown in the left column.

Source: Goodale, M.A, & Humphrey, G.K. (2001). Separate visual systems for action and perception. In E. Bruce Goldstein (Ed.), *Blackwell handbook of perception* (pp. 311–343). Oxford, UK: Blackwell Publishers Inc. (page 320).

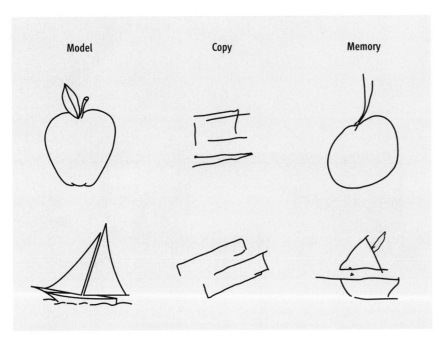

Model   Copy   Memory

object, while still being unable to identify it. She had to be using some kind of vision. They went on to test DF's abilities systematically in the laboratory. Drawing upon earlier work by Ungerleider and Mishkin (1982) and his own (Goodale & Westwood, 2004) current work and that of others, Goodale suggested that these two types of vision follow different pathways in the brain. The two pathways (see Figure 4.42) are a *dorsal stream* for the visual control of action and a *ventral stream* for perception of the external world.

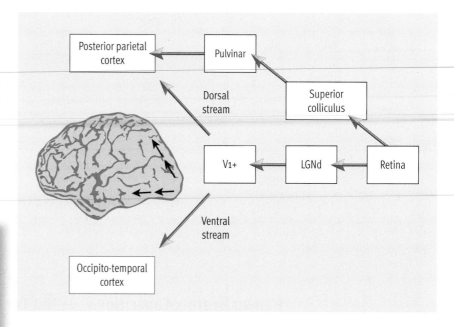

Figure 4.42

Schematic representation of the two streams of visual processing in the human cerebral cortex. The retina sends projections to the dorsal part of the lateral geniculate nucleus in the thalamus, which projects in turn to the primary visual cortex (V1). Within the cerebral cortex, the ventral stream (red) arises from early visual areas (V1+) and projects to regions in the occipito-temporal cortex. The dorsal stream (blue) also arises from early visual areas but projects instead to the posterior parietal cortex. The posterior parietal cortex also receives visual input from the superior colliculus through the pulvinar.

SOURCE: Adapted from Goodale, M. A. & Westwood, D. A. (2004). An evolving view of duplex vision: Separate but interacting cortical pathways for perception and action. *Current Opinion in Neurobiology, 14*, 203–211.

Our Sense of Hearing: The Auditory System

Stop reading for a moment, close your eyes, and listen carefully. What do you hear?

Chances are, you'll discover that you're immersed in sounds: street noises, a high-pitched laugh from the next room, the hum of a fluorescent lamp, perhaps some background music you put on a while ago but forgot about. As this little demonstration shows, physical stimuli producing sound are present almost constantly, but you're not necessarily aware of these sounds.

Like vision, the auditory (hearing) system provides input about the world "out there," but not until incoming information is processed by the brain. A distal stimulus—a screech of tires, someone laughing, the hum of the refrigerator—produces a proximal stimulus in the form of sound waves reaching the ears. The perceptual system must somehow transform this stimulation into the psychological experience of hearing. We'll begin our discussion of hearing by looking at the stimulus for auditory experience: sound.

The Stimulus: Sound

Sound waves are vibrations of molecules, which means that they must travel through some physical medium, such as air. They move at a fraction of the speed of light. Sound waves are usually generated by vibrating objects, such as a guitar string, a loudspeaker cone, or your vocal cords. However, sound waves can also be generated by forcing air past a chamber (as in a pipe organ), or by suddenly releasing a burst of air (as when you clap).

Like light waves, sound waves are characterized by their *amplitude*, their *wavelength*, and their *purity* (see Figure 4.43). The physical properties of amplitude, wavelength, and purity affect mainly the perceived (psychological) qualities of loudness, pitch, and timbre, respectively. However, the physical properties of sound interact in complex ways to produce perceptions of these sound qualities (Hirsh & Watson, 1996).

(a) Wavelength

Amplitude

Air pressure

(b)

Physical properties of sound	Related perceptions
Amplitude	Loudness
Frequency	Pitch
Purity	Timbre

Figure 4.43

Sound, the physical stimulus for hearing. **(a)** Like light, sound travels in waves—in this case, waves of air pressure. A smooth curve would represent a pure tone, such as that produced by a tuning fork. Most sounds, however, are complex. For example, the wave shown here is for middle C played on a piano. The sound wave for the same note played on a violin would have the same wavelength (or frequency) as this one, but the "wrinkles" in the wave would be different, corresponding to the differences in timbre between the two sounds. **(b)** The table shows the main relations between objective aspects of sound and subjective perceptions.

Human Hearing Capacities

Wavelengths of sound are described in terms of their *frequency,* which is measured in cycles per second, or *hertz (Hz).* For the most part, higher frequencies are perceived as having higher pitch. That is, if you strike the key for high C on a piano, it will produce higher-frequency sound waves than the key for low C. Although the perception of pitch depends mainly on frequency, the amplitude of the sound waves also influences it.

Just as the visible spectrum is only a portion of the total spectrum of light, so, too, what people can hear is only a portion of the available range of sounds. Humans can hear sounds ranging from a low of 20 Hz up to a high of about 20 000 Hz. Sounds at either end of this range are harder to hear, and sensitivity to high-frequency tones declines as adults grow older. Other organisms have different capabilities. Low-frequency sounds under 10 Hz are audible to homing pigeons, for example. At the other extreme, bats and porpoises can hear frequencies well above 20 000 Hz.

In general, the greater the amplitude of sound waves, the louder the sound perceived. Whereas frequency is measured in hertz, amplitude is measured in *decibels (dB).* The relationship between decibels (which measure a physical property of sound) and loudness (a psychological quality) is complex. A rough rule of thumb is that perceived loudness doubles about every 10 decibels (Stevens, 1955). To make this idea less abstract, Figure 4.44 shows approximate decibel levels for a wide range of common sounds. Very loud sounds can jeopardize the quality of your hearing. Even brief exposure to sounds over 120 decibels can be painful and may cause damage to your auditory system (Henry, 1984).

As shown in Figure 4.44, the absolute thresholds for the weakest sounds people can hear differ for sounds of various frequencies. The human ear is most sensitive to sounds at frequencies near 2000 Hz. That is, these frequencies yield the lowest absolute thresholds. To summarize, amplitude is the principal determinant of loudness, but loudness ultimately depends on an interaction between amplitude and frequency.

People are also sensitive to variations in the purity of sounds. The purest sound is one that has only a single frequency of vibration, such as that produced by a tuning fork. Most everyday sounds are complex mixtures of many frequencies. The purity or complexity of a sound influences how *timbre* is perceived. To understand timbre, think of a note with precisely the same loudness and pitch played on a French horn and then on a violin. The difference you perceive in the sounds is a difference in timbre.

Sensory Processing in the Ear

Like your eyes, your ears channel energy to the neural tissue that receives it. Figure 4.45 shows that the human ear can be divided into three sections: the external ear, the middle ear, and the inner ear. Sound is conducted differently in each section. The external ear depends on the *vibration of air molecules.* The middle ear depends on the *vibration of movable bones.* And the inner ear depends on *waves in a fluid,* which are finally converted into a stream of neural signals sent to the brain (Moore, 2001).

The *external ear* consists mainly of the *pinna,* a sound-collecting cone. When you cup your hand behind your ear to try to hear better, you are augmenting that cone. Many animals have large external ears that they can aim directly toward a sound source. However, humans can adjust their aim only crudely, by turning their heads. Sound waves collected by the pinna are funnelled along the auditory canal toward the *eardrum,* a taut membrane that vibrates in response.

In the *middle ear,* the vibrations of the eardrum are transmitted inward by a mechanical chain made up of the three tiniest bones in your body (the hammer, anvil, and stirrup), known collectively as the *ossicles.* The ossicles form a three-stage lever system that converts relatively large movements with little force into smaller motions with greater force. The ossicles serve to amplify tiny changes in air pressure.

The *inner ear* consists largely of the **cochlea, a fluid-filled, coiled tunnel that contains the receptors for hearing.** The term *cochlea* comes from the

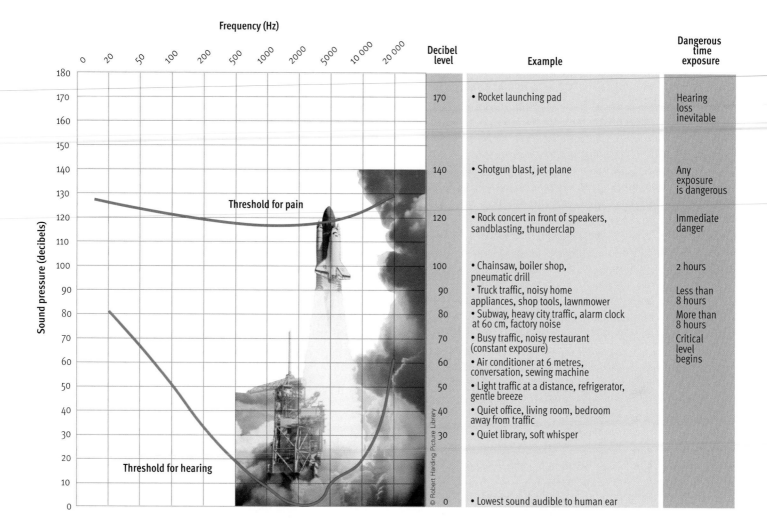

Frequency (Hz)

| | 0 | 20 | 50 | 100 | 200 | 500 | 1000 | 2000 | 5000 | 10 000 | 20 000 |

Sound pressure (decibels)

Threshold for pain

Threshold for hearing

© Robert Harding Picture Library

Decibel level	Example	Dangerous time exposure
170	• Rocket launching pad	Hearing loss inevitable
140	• Shotgun blast, jet plane	Any exposure is dangerous
120	• Rock concert in front of speakers, sandblasting, thunderclap	Immediate danger
100	• Chainsaw, boiler shop, pneumatic drill	2 hours
90	• Truck traffic, noisy home appliances, shop tools, lawnmower	Less than 8 hours
80	• Subway, heavy city traffic, alarm clock at 60 cm, factory noise	More than 8 hours
70	• Busy traffic, noisy restaurant (constant exposure)	Critical level begins
60	• Air conditioner at 6 metres, conversation, sewing machine	
50	• Light traffic at a distance, refrigerator, gentle breeze	
40	• Quiet office, living room, bedroom away from traffic	
30	• Quiet library, soft whisper	
0	• Lowest sound audible to human ear	

Figure 4.44

Sound pressure and auditory experience. The threshold for human hearing (graphed in green) is a function of both sound pressure (decibel level) and frequency. Human hearing is keenest for sounds at a frequency of about 2000 Hz; at other frequencies, higher decibel levels are needed to produce sounds people can detect. On the other hand, the human threshold for pain (graphed in red) is almost purely a function of decibel level. Some common sounds corresponding to various decibel levels are listed to the right of the graph, together with the amount of time at which exposure to higher levels becomes dangerous.

SOURCE: Decibel level examples from Atkinson, R. L., Atkinson, R. C., Smith, E. F., & Hilgard, E. R. (1987). *Introduction to Psychology*. San Diego: Harcourt. Reprinted by permission of Wadsworth Publishing.

Greek word for a spiral-shelled snail, which this chamber resembles (see Figure 4.45). Sound enters the cochlea through the *oval window*, which is vibrated by the ossicles. The ear's neural tissue, analogous to the retina in the eye, lies within the cochlea. This tissue sits on the basilar membrane that divides the cochlea into upper and lower chambers. **The *basilar membrane*, which runs the length of the spiralled cochlea, holds the auditory receptors.** The auditory receptors are called *hair cells* because of the tiny bundles of hairs that protrude from them. Waves in the fluid of the inner ear stimulate the hair cells. Like the rods and cones in the eye, the hair cells convert this physical stimulation into neural impulses that are sent to the brain (Hudspeth, 2000).

These signals are routed through the thalamus to the auditory cortex, which is located mostly in the temporal lobes of the brain. Studies demonstrate that the auditory cortex has specialized cells—similar to the feature detectors found in the visual cortex— that have special sensitivity to certain features of

sound (Pickles, 1988). Evidence also suggests that the parallel processing of input seen in the visual system also occurs in the auditory pathways (Rouiller, 1997).

Auditory Perception: Theories of Hearing

Theories of hearing need to account for how sound waves are physiologically translated into the perceptions of pitch, loudness, and timbre. To date, most of the theorizing about hearing has focused on the perception of pitch, which is reasonably well understood. Researchers' understanding of loudness and timbre perception is primitive by comparison. Hence, we'll limit our coverage to theories of pitch perception.

Two theories have dominated the debate on pitch perception: *place theory* and *frequency theory*. You'll be able to follow the development of these theories more easily if you can imagine the spiralled cochlea unravelled, so that the basilar membrane becomes a long, thin sheet, lined with about 25 000 individual hair cells (see Figure 4.46).

Figure 4.45

The human ear. Converting sound pressure to information processed by the nervous system involves a complex relay of stimuli. Waves of air pressure create vibrations in the eardrum, which in turn cause oscillations in the tiny bones in the inner ear (the hammer, anvil, and stirrup). As they are relayed from one bone to the next, the oscillations are magnified and then transformed into pressure waves moving through a liquid medium in the cochlea. These waves cause the basilar membrane to oscillate, stimulating the hair cells that are the actual auditory receptors (see Figure 4.46).

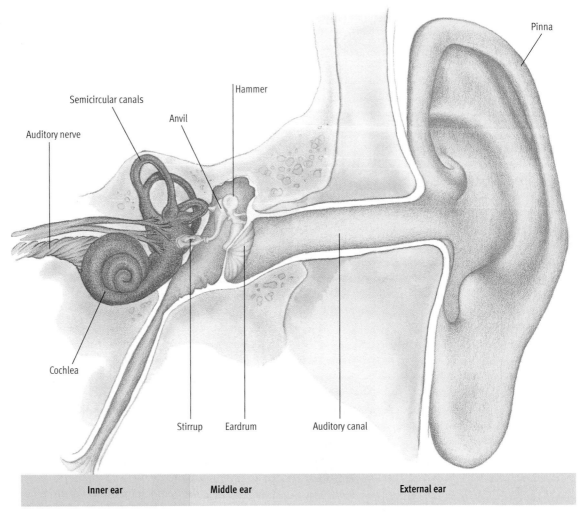

Semicircular canals

Auditory nerve

Hammer

Anvil

Pinna

Cochlea

Stirrup

Eardrum

Auditory canal

Inner ear

Middle ear

External ear

Place Theory

Long ago, Hermann von Helmholtz (1863) proposed that specific sound frequencies vibrate specific portions of the basilar membrane, producing distinct pitches, just as plucking specific strings on a harp produces sounds of varied pitch. This model, called *place theory,* **holds that perception of pitch corresponds to the vibration of different portions, or places, along the basilar membrane.** Place theory assumes that hair cells at various locations respond independently and that different sets of hair cells are vibrated by different sound frequencies. The brain then detects the frequency of a tone according to which area along the basilar membrane is most active.

Frequency Theory

Other theorists in the 19th century proposed an alternative theory of pitch perception, called frequency theory (Rutherford, 1886). *Frequency theory* **holds that perception of pitch corresponds to the rate, or frequency, at which the entire basilar membrane vibrates.** This theory views the basilar membrane as more like a drumhead than a harp. According to frequency theory, the whole membrane vibrates in unison in response to sounds. However, a particular sound frequency, say 3000 Hz, causes the basilar membrane to vibrate at a corresponding rate of 3000 times per second. The brain detects the frequency of a tone by the rate at which the auditory nerve fibres fire.

Reconciling Place and Frequency Theories

The competition between these two theories is reminiscent of the dispute between the trichromatic and opponent process theories of colour vision. As with that argument, the debate between place and frequency theories generated roughly a century of research. Although both theories proved to have some flaws, *both turned out to be valid in part.*

Helmholtz's place theory was basically on the mark except for one detail. The hair cells along the basilar membrane are not independent. They vibrate together, as suggested by frequency theory. The actual pattern of vibration, described in Nobel Prize–winning research by Georg von Békésy (1947), is a travelling wave that moves along the basilar membrane. Place theory is correct, however, in that the wave peaks at a particular place, depending on the frequency of the sound wave.

Frequency theory was also found to be flawed when investigators learned that neurons are hard pressed to fire at a maximum rate of about 1000 impulses per second. How, then, can frequency theory account for the translation of 4000 Hz sound waves, which would require 4000 impulses per second? The answer, suggested by Wever and Bray (1937), is that groups of hair cells operate according to the volley principle. The **volley principle holds that groups of auditory nerve fibres fire neural impulses in rapid succession, creating volleys of impulses.** These volleys exceed the 1000-per-second limit. Studies suggest that auditory nerves can team up like this to generate volleys of up to 5000 impulses per second (Zwislocki, 1981).

Although the original theories had to be revised, the current thinking is that pitch perception depends on both place and frequency coding of vibrations along the basilar membrane (Goldstein, 1996). Sounds under 1000 Hz appear to be translated into pitch through frequency coding. For sounds between 1000 and 5000 Hz, pitch perception seems to depend on a combination of frequency and place coding. Sounds over 5000 Hz seem to be handled through place coding only. Again we find that theories that were pitted against each other for decades are complementary rather than contradictory.

Auditory Localization: Perceiving Sources of Sound

You're driving down a street when suddenly you hear a siren wailing in the distance. As the wail grows louder, you glance around, cocking your ear to the sound. Where is it coming from? Behind you? In front of you? From one side? This example illustrates a common perceptual task called **auditory localization—locating the source of a sound in space.** The process of recognizing where a sound is coming from is analogous to recognizing depth or distance in vision. Both processes involve spatial aspects of sensory input. The fact that human ears are set *apart* contributes to auditory localization, just as the separation of the eyes contributes to depth perception.

Many features of sounds can contribute to auditory localization, but two cues are particularly important: the intensity (loudness) and the timing of sounds arriving at each ear (Yost, 2001). For example, a sound source to one side of the head produces a

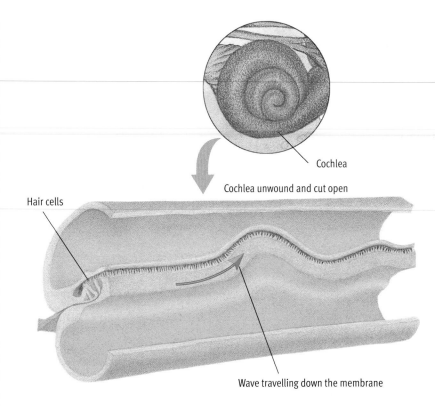

Figure 4.46

The basilar membrane. This graphic shows how the cochlea might look if it were unwound and cut open to reveal the basilar membrane, which is covered with thousands of hair cells (the auditory receptors). Pressure waves in the fluid filling the cochlea cause oscillations to travel in waves down the basilar membrane, stimulating the hair cells to fire. Although the entire membrane vibrates, as predicted by frequency theory, the point along the membrane where the wave peaks depends on the frequency of the sound stimulus, as suggested by place theory.

greater intensity at the ear nearer to the sound. This difference is due partly to the loss of sound intensity with distance. Another factor at work is the "shadow," or partial sound barrier, cast by the head itself (see Figure 4.47). The intensity difference between the two ears is greatest when the sound source is well to one side. The human perceptual system uses this difference as a clue in localizing sounds. Because the path to the farther ear is longer, a sound takes longer to reach that ear. This fact means that sounds can be localized by comparing the timing of their arrival at each ear. Such comparison of the timing of sounds is remarkably sensitive. People can detect timing differences as small as 1/100 000 of a second (Durlach & Colburn, 1978).

Music and Its Effects

Our auditory system provides us with one way to experience and relate to the world. In terms of our auditory experiences, music is something that most of us enjoy. Although we may disagree somewhat in

The psychic activities, by which we arrive at the judgment that a certain object of a certain character exists before us at a certain place, are generally not conscious activities but unconscious ones. . . . It may be permissible to designate the psychic acts of ordinary perception as unconscious inferences.
HERMANN VON HELMHOLTZ

Sensation and Perception

Comparing Vision and Hearing

Check your understanding of both vision and audition by comparing key aspects of sensation and perception in these senses. The dimensions of comparison are listed in the first column below. The second column lists the answers for the sense of vision. Fill in the answers for the sense of hearing in the third column. The answers can be found in Appendix A in the back of the book.

Dimension	Vision	Hearing
1. Stimulus	*Light waves*	
2. Elements of stimulus and related perceptions	*Wavelength, hue* *Amplitude/brightness* *Purity/saturation*	
3. Receptors	*Rods and cones*	
4. Location of receptors	*Retina*	
5. Main location of processing in brain	*Occipital lobe , visual cortex*	
6. Spatial aspect of perception	*Depth perception*	

terms of our musical preferences, music is important to most of us. Canadian researchers in the psychology of music have been active in examining several features of this experience, such as processes of perceptual organization in the perception of tonality (Smith & Shmuckler, 2004) and the effects that music has on us. We often seek out musical experiences because they affect our mood, make us feel happier, or calm us down. It has even been suggested that music can enhance our spatial abilities—the so-called Mozart effect (Rauscher, Shaw, & Ky, 1993). While there is some disagreement on what produces this effect (Thompson, Schellenberg, & Husain, 2001), the fact that music influences us in many ways should not be a surprise. But, what about all those years of practising the piano that you endured? Did they have any effect beyond improving your piano playing or causing conflict with your parents? A recent review of work in the area of brain plasticity by the University of Montreal's Isabelle Peretz and McGill's Robert Zatorre (Peretz & Zatorre, 2005) suggests that music training can induce functional and morphological changes in the brain. In addition, recent research by University of Toronto psychologist William Thompson suggests that music training and lessons may facilitate your sensitivity to human emotions reflected in speech prosody. Speech prosody refers to the musical aspects of speech, such as intonation (melody) and stress and timing (rhythm). This research is our Featured Study for Chapter 4.

Figure 4.47

Cues in auditory localization. A sound coming from the left reaches the left ear sooner than the right. When the sound reaches the right ear, it is also less intense because it has travelled a greater distance and because it is in the sound shadow produced by the listener's head. These cues are used to localize the sources of sound in space.

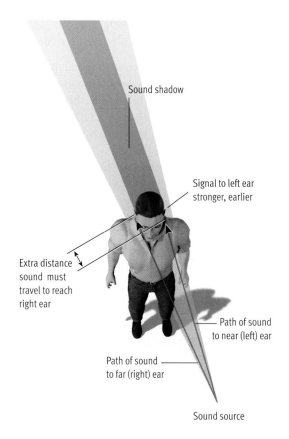

Sound shadow

Signal to left ear stronger, earlier

Extra distance sound must travel to reach right ear

Path of sound to near (left) ear

Path of sound to far (right) ear

Sound source

REVIEW OF KEY POINTS

- Sound varies in terms of wavelength (frequency), amplitude, and purity. These properties affect mainly perceptions of pitch, loudness, and timbre, respectively. The human ear is most sensitive to sounds around 2000 Hz. Even brief exposure to sounds over 120 decibels can be painful and damaging.

- Sound is transmitted through the external ear via air conduction to the middle ear, where sound waves are translated into the vibration of tiny bones called ossicles. In the inner ear, fluid conduction vibrates hair cells along the basilar membrane in the cochlea. These hair cells are the receptors for hearing.

- Place theory proposed that pitch perception depends on where vibrations occur along the basilar membrane. Frequency theory countered with the idea that pitch perception depends on the rate at which the basilar membrane vibrates. Modern evidence suggests that these theories are complementary rather than incompatible.

- Auditory localization involves locating the source of a sound in space. People pinpoint where sounds have come from by comparing inter-ear differences in the intensity and timing of sounds.

- There is evidence to suggest that exposure to music does more than temporarily affect our moods. It may increase our ability to perform certain tasks and to correctly identify emotions in the speech of others.

Decoding Speech Prosody: Do Music Lessons Help?

Thompson and his colleagues expected to find positive transfer from past music training to an individual's ability to decode or correctly identify emotions conveyed by prosody in speech. A connection between music and emotional experience has been documented in the past, as has a connection between emotion and speech prosody. Speech prosody refers "to the musical aspects of speech, including its *melody* (intonation) and its *rhythm* (stress and timing) (p. 48)." The researchers suggested that there are parallels between music and speech in terms of how emotions are expressed. Accordingly, they reasoned the musical training would enhance a person's ability to decode emotions from speech.

Method

Participants. Three studies were conducted. We will present the third study for illustrative purposes. In the study, 43 seven-year-old children, none of whom had any formal musical/arts training, were recruited. The experimenters arranged that 30 of the children were given one year of formal training in keyboard, drama, or singing at the Royal Conservatory of Music in Toronto. The remaining 13 children did not take part in this arts training.

Stimuli. The stimuli consisted of four neutral sentences (e.g., "The chairs are made of wood"), each spoken in four different ways to convey the emotions of happiness, fear, sadness, or anger. The sentences were presented to the children in English or an unfamiliar language, Tagalog, resulting in 16 sentences (four sentences times four emotions) for each language, for a total of 32 spoken sentences. Tagalog is a language spoken in the Philippines by about 25% of the population. In addition, musical analogues using musical tone sequences were prepared for each of the 32 spoken sentences. The construction of the musical analogues is quite fascinating, and interested students should read the journal article by Thompson and his colleagues to learn more about how this is accomplished.

Measures and Apparatus. The sentences and tone sequences were presented by a computer while the children listened through earphones. The children were asked to choose which of a pair of descriptions (e.g., happy or sad) applied to what they heard. For the tone sequences, the children were given an imagination task. They were asked to imagine the tonal sequence was a sentence spoken by the computer and that they should decide if the computer sounded, for example, sad or happy.

Results

As you might expect, children's identification of emotions was better for spoken sentences than for tonal analogues, and better for English than for Tagalog sentences. What about the effects of training? First, for happy/sad sentences everyone did extremely well and so there were no differences in identification accuracy between participant groups. For the fearful/angry sentences, the music-training (particularly the keyboard group) and drama-training groups were better able to identify the correct emotion than was the no-training group.

Discussion

It is instructive to put the results of the third study together with the results of the other two studies Thompson and his colleagues conducted. The participants in the first two studies were university students who had no musical training or at least eight years of musical training. Once again, the results suggested that musical training enhanced participants' ability to decode emotions conveyed by speech prosody. In terms of the specific results of the third study, you might wonder why drama lessons facilitated this ability and singing lessons did not. The authors report that the drama lessons taken by the children "focused specifically on training the speaking voice and the use of prosody" while the "singing lessons emphasize non-prosodic uses of the voice" (p. 58). Why were there no training effects for happy/sad sentences? These distinctions were so easy that most of the children got most of them correct. This is referred to as a ceiling effect. Here, the identifications were so easy that the training had no additional room to positively affect performance.

Comment

The study of sensation and perception is one of the oldest areas of scientific research in psychology. Yet this study shows that there are still fascinating areas of inquiry that remain unexplored. It just takes some creativity and insight to recognize them. This research also illustrates the importance of using more than one way to examine an issue. The fact that very similar results were obtained with children and adult samples with varying lengths of training increases the authors' confidence in the results. ■

Investigators: William Forde Thompson, E. Glenn Schellenberg, & Gabriela Husain (University of Toronto at Mississauga).

Source: Decoding speech prosody: Do music lessons help? *Emotion,* 2004, 4, 46–64.

Our Chemical Senses: Taste and Smell

PREVIEW QUESTIONS
- Where are the receptors for taste?
- How many basic tastes are there?
- How do people vary in taste sensitivity?
- Where are the receptors for smell?
- Are there primary odours?
- How well do people perform when asked to name odours?

Psychologists have devoted most of their attention to the visual and auditory systems. Although less is known about the chemical senses, taste and smell also play a critical role in people's experience of the world. Let's take a brief look at what psychologists have learned about **the *gustatory system*—the sensory system for taste**—and its close cousin, **the *olfactory system*—the sensory system for smell.**

Taste: The Gustatory System

True wine lovers go through an elaborate series of steps when they are served a good bottle of wine. Typically, they begin by drinking a little water to cleanse their palate. Then they sniff the cork from the wine bottle, swirl a small amount of the wine around in a glass, and sniff the odour emerging from the glass. Finally, they take a sip of the wine, rolling it around in their mouth for a short time before swallowing it. At last they are ready to confer their approval or disapproval. Is all this activity really a meaningful way to put the wine to a sensitive test? Or is it just a harmless ritual passed on through tradition? You'll find out in this section.

The physical stimuli for the sense of taste are chemical substances that are soluble (dissolvable in water). The gustatory receptors are clusters of taste cells found in the *taste buds* that line the trenches around tiny bumps on the tongue (see Figure 4.48). When these cells absorb chemicals dissolved in saliva, they trigger neural impulses that are routed through the thalamus to the cortex. Interestingly, taste cells have a short life, spanning only about ten days, and they are constantly being replaced. New cells are born at the edge of the taste bud and migrate inward to die at the centre.

It's generally (but not universally) agreed that there are four *primary tastes:* sweet, sour, bitter, and salty (Buck, 2000). Sensitivity to these tastes is distributed somewhat unevenly across the tongue, but the variations in sensitivity are quite small and highly complicated (Bartoshuk, 1993b; see Figure 4.48). Although taste cells respond to more than one of the primary tastes, they typically respond best to a specific taste (DiLorenzo & Youngentob, 2003). Perceptions of taste quality appear to depend on complex *patterns* of neural activity initiated by taste receptors (Erickson, DiLorenzo, & Woodbury, 1994).

Some basic taste preferences appear to be innate and to be automatically regulated by physiological mechanisms. In humans, for instance, newborn infants react positively to sweet tastes and negatively to strong concentrations of bitter, salty, or sour tastes (Lipsitt & Behl, 1990). To some extent, these innate

Figure 4.48

The tongue and taste. **(a)** Taste buds line the trenches around tiny bumps on the tongue called papillae (see the inset). **(b)** There are three types of papillae, which are distributed on the tongue as shown here. The taste buds found in each type of papillae show slightly different sensitivities to the four basic tastes, as mapped out in the graph at the top. Thus, sensitivity to the primary tastes varies across the tongue, but these variations are small, and all four primary tastes can be detected wherever there are taste receptors.

SOURCE: Adapted from Bartoshuk, L. M. (1993). Genetic and pathological taste variation: What can we learn from animal models and human disease? In D. Chadwick, J. Marsh, & J. Goode (Eds.), *The molecular basis of smell and taste transduction* (pp. 251–267). New York: John Wiley & Sons, Inc.

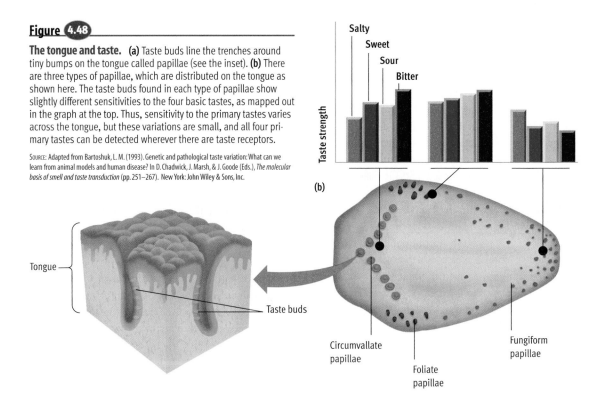

Figure **4.49**

Culture and taste preferences. Taste preferences are largely learned, and they vary dramatically from one society to the next, as these examples demonstrate.

Grubs. For most North Americans, the thought of eating a worm would be totally unthinkable. For the Asmat of New Guinea, however, a favourite delicacy is the plump, white, 5-cm larva or beetle grub.

Fish eyes. For some Inuit children, raw fish eyes are like candy. Here you see a young girl using the Inuit's all-purpose knife to gouge out the eye of an already-filleted Arctic fish.

Blood. Several tribes in East Africa supplement their diet with fresh blood that is sometimes mixed with milk. They obtain the blood by puncturing a cow's jugular vein with a sharp arrow. The blood–milk drink provides a rich source of protein and iron.

taste preferences are flexible, changing to accommodate the body's nutritional needs (Scott, 1990).

Although some basic aspects of taste perception may be innate, taste preferences are largely learned and heavily influenced by social processes (Rozin, 1990). Most parents are aware of this fact and intentionally try—with varied success—to mould their children's taste preferences early in life (Patrick et al., 2005). This extensive social influence contributes greatly to the striking ethnic and cultural disparities found in taste preferences (Kittler & Sucher, 1998). Foods that are a source of disgust in Western cultures—such as worms, fish eyes, and blood—may be delicacies in other cultures (see Figure 4.49). Indeed, Rozin (1990) asserts that feces may be the only universal source of taste-related disgust in humans. To a large degree, variations in taste preferences depend on what one has been exposed to (Capaldi & VandenBos, 1991; Zellner, 1991). Exposure to various foods varies along ethnic lines because different cultures have different traditions in food preparation, different agricultural resources, different climates to work with, and so forth.

Research by Linda Bartoshuk and others reveals that people vary considerably in their sensitivity to certain tastes. These differences depend in part on the density of taste buds on the tongue, which appears to be a matter of genetic inheritance (Bartoshuk, 1993a). People characterized as *supertasters* tend to have about four times as many taste buds per square centimetre as people at the other end of the spectrum, who are called *nontasters* (Miller

& Reedy, 1990). Women are more likely to be supertasters than men are (Bartoshuk, Duffy, & Miller, 1994). Supertasters and nontasters respond similarly to many foods, but supertasters are much more sensitive to certain sweet and bitter substances. For example, supertasters react far more strongly to the chemical (capsaicin) in hot peppers (Tepper & Nurse, 1997). Some psychologists speculate that the gender gap in this trait may have evolutionary significance. Over the course of evolution, women have generally been more involved than men in feeding children. Increased reactivity to sweet and bitter tastes would have been adaptive in that it would have made women more sensitive to the relatively scarce high-caloric foods (which often taste sweet) needed for survival and to the toxic substances (which often taste bitter) that hunters and gatherers needed to avoid.

So far, we've been discussing taste, but what we are really interested in is the *perception of flavour.* Odour contributes greatly to flavour (Lawless, 2001). Although taste and smell are distinct sensory systems, they interact extensively. The ability to identify flavours declines noticeably when odour cues are absent. You might have noticed this interaction when you ate a favourite meal while enduring a severe head cold. The food probably tasted bland, because your stuffy nose impaired your sense of smell.

Now that we've explored the dynamics of taste, we can return to our question about the value of the wine-tasting ritual. This elaborate ritual is indeed an authentic way to put wine to a sensitive test. The

❝*Good and bad are so intimately associated with taste and smell that we have special words for the experiences (e.g., repugnant, foul). The immediacy of the pleasure makes it seem absolute and thus inborn. This turns out to be true for taste but not for smell.*❞
LINDA BARTOSHUK

aftereffects associated with sensory adaptation make it wise to cleanse one's palate before tasting the wine. Sniffing the cork, and the wine in the glass, is important because odour is a major determinant of flavour. Swirling the wine in the glass helps release the wine's odour. And rolling the wine around in your mouth is especially critical, because it distributes the wine over the full diversity of taste cells. It also forces the wine's odour up into the nasal passages. Thus, each action in this age-old ritual makes a meaningful contribution to the tasting.

Smell: The Olfactory System

In many ways, the sense of smell is much like the sense of taste. The physical stimuli are chemical substances—volatile ones that can evaporate and be carried in the air. These chemical stimuli are dissolved in fluid—specifically, the mucus in the nose. The receptors for smell are *olfactory cilia,* hairlike structures located in the upper portion of the nasal passages (see Figure 4.50). They resemble taste cells in that they have a short life (30–60 days) and are constantly being replaced (Buck, 2000). Olfactory receptors have axons that synapse with cells in the olfactory bulb and then are routed directly to various areas in the cortex. This arrangement is unique. Smell is the only sensory system in which incoming information is not routed through the thalamus before it projects to the cortex. Research by Linda Buck and Richard Axel (1991) has served to clarify some of the mechanisms involved in odour recognition. They have discovered a gene set consisting of 1000 different genes that affect the operation of our olfactory receptor cells. These olfactory receptor cells are highly specialized in that each has the ability to detect only a very limited number of odours. Axel and Buck were awarded the 2004 Nobel Prize in Physiology or Medicine for their work (Nobel Prize, n.d.).

Odours cannot be classified as neatly as tastes, since efforts to identify primary odours have proven unsatisfactory (Doty, 1991). If primary odours exist, there must be a fairly large number of them. Most olfactory receptors respond to a wide range of odours (Doty, 2001). Hence, the perception of various odours probably depends on a great many types of receptors that are uniquely responsive to specific chemical structures (Bartoshuk & Beauchamp, 1994). Like the other senses, the sense of smell shows sensory adaptation. The perceived strength of an odour usually fades to less than half its original strength within about four minutes (Cain, 1988).

Humans can distinguish among about 10 000 different odours (Axel, 1995). However, when people

Figure 4.50

The olfactory system. Odour molecules travel through the nasal passages and stimulate olfactory cilia. An enlargement of these hairlike olfactory receptors is shown in the inset. The olfactory nerves transmit neural impulses through the olfactory bulb to the brain.

are asked to identify the sources of specific odours (such as smoke or soap), their performance is rather mediocre. For some unknown reason, people have a hard time attaching names to odours (Cowart & Rawson, 2001). Gender differences have been found in the ability to identify odours, as females tend to be somewhat more accurate than males on odour recognition tasks (de Wijk, Schab, & Cain, 1995).

REVIEW OF KEY POINTS

- The taste buds are sensitive to four basic tastes: sweet, sour, bitter, and salty. Sensitivity to these tastes is distributed unevenly across the tongue, but the variations are small.

- Taste preferences are largely learned and are heavily influenced by one's cultural background. The perception of flavour is influenced greatly by the odour of food.

- Like taste, smell is a chemical sense. Chemical stimuli activate receptors, called olfactory cilia, which line the nasal passages. Most of these receptors respond to more than one odour.

- Recent research has discovered a family of genes that seem to be responsible for olfaction.

Web Link 4.7

Seeing, Hearing, and Smelling the World
http://www.hhmi.org/senses/

Hosted by the Howard Hughes Medical Institute, this site provides a graphically attractive review of what scientific research has discovered about human sensory systems, with suggestions about where research will be moving in the future.

Our Sense of Touch: Sensory Systems in the Skin

If there is any sense that people trust almost as much as sight, it is the sense of touch. Yet, like all the senses, touch involves converting the sensation of physical stimuli into a psychological experience—and it can be fooled.

The physical stimuli for touch are mechanical, thermal, and chemical energy that impinge on the skin. These stimuli can produce perceptions of tactile stimulation (the pressure of touch against the skin), warmth, cold, and pain. The human skin is saturated with at least six types of sensory receptors. To some degree, these different types of receptors are specialized for different functions, such as the registration of pressure, heat, cold, and so forth. However, these distinctions are not as clear as researchers had originally expected (Sinclair, 1981).

Feeling Pressure

If you've been to a mosquito-infested picnic lately, you'll appreciate the need to quickly know where tactile stimulation is coming from. The sense of touch is set up to meet this need for tactile localization with admirable precision and efficiency. Cells in the nervous system that respond to touch are sensitive to specific patches of skin. These skin patches, which vary considerably in size, are the functional equivalents of *receptive fields* in vision. Like visual receptive fields, they often involve a centre-surround arrangement (see Figure 4.51). Thus, stimuli falling in the centre produce the opposite effect of stimuli falling in the surrounding area (Kandel & Jessell, 1991). If a stimulus is applied continuously to a specific spot on the skin, the perception of pressure gradually fades. Hence, sensory adaptation occurs in the perception of touch, as it does in other sensory systems.

The nerve fibres that carry incoming information about tactile stimulation are routed through the spinal cord to the brainstem. There, the fibres from each side of the body cross over mostly to the opposite side of the brain. The tactile pathway then projects through the thalamus and onto the *somatosensory cortex* in the brain's parietal lobe. Some cells in the somatosensory cortex function like the *feature detectors* discovered in vision (Gardner & Kandel, 2000). They respond to specific features of touch, such as a movement across the skin in a particular direction.

Feeling Pain

As unpleasant as pain is, the sensation of pain is crucial to survival. Pain is a marvellous warning system. It tells people when they should stop shovelling snow, or it lets them know that they have a pinched nerve that requires treatment. However, chronic pain is a frustrating, demoralizing affliction that affects millions of people and is a major factor in lost productivity (Gatchel & Maddrey, 2004; Turk, 1994). Thus, there are pressing practical reasons for psychologists' keen interest in the perception of pain.

Pathways to the Brain

The receptors for pain are mostly free nerve endings in the skin. Pain messages are transmitted to the brain via two types of pathways that pass through different areas in the thalamus (Willis, 1985). One is a *fast pathway* that registers localized pain and relays it to the cortex in a fraction of a second. This is the system that hits you with sharp pain when you first cut your finger. The second system uses a *slow pathway* that lags a second or two behind the fast system. This pathway (which also carries information about temperature) conveys the less localized, longer-lasting, aching or burning pain that comes after the initial injury. The slow pathway depends on thin, unmyelinated neurons called *C fibres,* whereas the fast pathway is mediated by thicker, myelinated neurons called *A-delta fibres* (see Figure 4.52).

Puzzles in Pain Perception

As with other perceptions, pain is not an automatic result of certain types of stimulation. The perception of pain can be influenced greatly by expectations, personality, mood, and other factors involving higher mental processes (Turk & Okifuji, 2003; Rollman, 1992; Stalling, 1992). The subjective nature of pain is illustrated by placebo effects. As we saw in Chapter 2, many people suffering from pain report relief when given a placebo—an inert "sugar pill" that is presented to them as if it were a painkilling drug (Stewart-Williams, 2004; Vase, Riley, & Price, 2002).

Further evidence regarding the subjective quality of pain has come from studies that have found ethnic and cultural differences in the pain associated with childbirth (Jordan, 1983) and the experience of chronic pain (Bates, Edwards, & Anderson, 1993). According to Melzack and Wall (1982), culture does not affect the process of pain perception so much as

PREVIEW QUESTIONS

- How are tactile data routed to the brain?
- How are the two pathways for pain different?
- What does a useful theory of pain perception need to explain?
- How does the physiological evidence relate to gate-control theory?

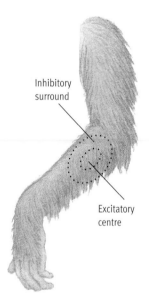

Inhibitory surround

Excitatory centre

Figure 4.51

Receptive field for touch. A receptive field for touch is an area on the skin surface that, when stimulated, affects the firing of a cell that responds to pressure on the skin. Shown here is a centre-surround receptive field for a cell in the thalamus of a monkey.

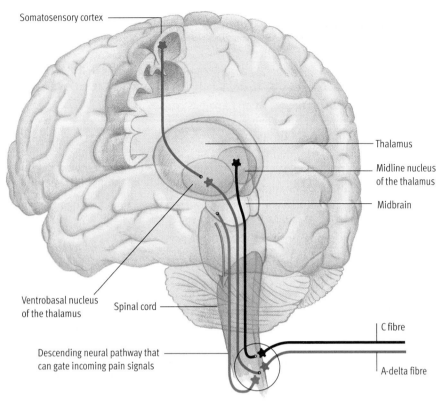

Somatosensory cortex

Thalamus

Midline nucleus of the thalamus

Midbrain

Ventrobasal nucleus of the thalamus

Spinal cord

C fibre

Descending neural pathway that can gate incoming pain signals

A-delta fibre

Figure 4.52

The two pathways for pain signals. Pain signals are sent from receptors to the brain along the two pathways depicted here. The fast pathway, shown in red, and the slow pathway, shown in black, depend on different types of nerve fibres and are routed through different parts of the thalamus. The gate-control mechanism posited by Melzack and Wall (1965) apparently depends on descending signals originating in an area of the midbrain (the pathway shown in green).

the willingness to tolerate certain types of pain, a conclusion echoed by Zatzick and Dimsdale (1990).

The psychological element in pain perception becomes clear when something distracts your attention from pain and the hurting temporarily disappears. For example, imagine that you've just hit your thumb with a hammer and it's throbbing with pain. Suddenly, your child cries out that there's a fire in the laundry room. As you race to deal with this emergency, you forget all about the pain in your thumb.

As you can see, then, tissue damage that sends pain impulses on their way to the brain doesn't necessarily result in the experience of pain. Cognitive and emotional processes that unfold in higher brain centres can somehow block pain signals coming from peripheral receptors. Thus, any useful explanation of pain perception must be able to answer a critical question: How does the central nervous system block incoming pain signals?

In an influential effort to answer this question, McGill University psychologists Ronald Melzack and Patrick Wall (1965) devised the gate-control theory of pain. *Gate-control theory* **holds that incoming pain sensations must pass through a "gate" in the spinal cord that can be closed, thus blocking ascending pain signals.** The gate in this model is not an anatomical structure but a pattern of neural activity that inhibits incoming pain signals. Melzack and Wall suggested that this imaginary gate can be closed by

signals from peripheral receptors or by signals from the brain. They theorized that the latter mechanism can help explain how factors such as attention and expectations can shut off pain signals. Melzack has continued his research on pain and is well known for his development of the McGill Pain Questionnaire, which is one of the most important tools for research on pain (Melzack, 1975). Most recently, along with York University pain researcher Joel Katz, Melzack has examined the puzzle of phantom-limb pain, in which patients continue to "feel" the missing limb, including pain in the nonexistent limb (Melzack & Katz, 2004). Melzack's (2001) recent neuromatrix theory of pain suggests that pain is a multidimensional phenomenon, produced by many influences.

As a whole, research suggests that the concept of a gating mechanism for pain has merit (Craig & Rollman, 1999). However, relatively little support has been found for the neural circuitry originally hypothesized by Melzack and Wall in the 1960s. Other neural mechanisms, discovered after gate-control theory was proposed, appear to be responsible for blocking the perception of pain.

One of these discoveries was the identification of endorphins. As discussed in Chapter 3, *endorphins* are the body's own natural morphine-like painkillers. Studies suggest that the release of endorphins underlies the pain-relieving effects of placebo drugs (Fields & Levine, 1984). The analgesic effects that can be achieved through the ancient Chinese art of acupuncture may likewise involve endorphins (Murray, 1995). Endorphins are widely distributed in the central nervous system. Scientists are still working out the details of how they suppress pain (Zubieta et al., 2001).

The other discovery involved the identification of a descending neural pathway that mediates the suppression of pain (Basbaum & Jessell, 2000). This pathway appears to originate in an area of the midbrain called the *periaqueductal gray (PAG)*. Neural activity in this pathway is probably initiated by endorphins acting on PAG neurons, which eventually trigger impulses sent down neural circuits that mostly release serotonin. These circuits synapse in the spinal cord, where they appear to release more endorphins, thus inhibiting the activity of neurons that would normally transmit incoming pain impulses to the brain (see Figure 4.52). The painkilling effects of morphine appear to be at least partly attributable to activity in this descending pathway, as cutting the fibres in this pathway reduces the analgesic effects of morphine (Jessell & Kelly, 1991). In contrast, activation of this pathway by electrical stimulation of the brain can produce an analgesic effect. Clearly, this pathway plays a central role in gating incoming pain signals.

Comparing Taste, Smell, and Touch

Check your understanding of taste, smell, and touch by comparing these sensory systems on the dimensions listed in the first column below. A few answers are supplied; see whether you can fill in the rest. The answers can be found in Appendix A.

Dimension	Taste	Smell	Touch
1. Stimulus		*Volatile chemicals in the air*	
2. Receptors			*Many (at least 6) types*
3. Location of receptors		*Upper areas of nasal passages*	
4. Basic elements of perception	*Sweet, sour, salty, bitter*		

Our Other Senses

We have discussed the dynamics of sensation and perception in five sensory domains—vision, hearing, taste, smell, and touch. Since it is widely known that humans have five senses, that should wrap up our coverage, right? Wrong! People have still other sensory systems: the kinesthetic system (which monitors positions of the body) and the vestibular system (sense of balance).

The Kinesthetic System

The *kinesthetic system* monitors the positions of the various parts of the body. To some extent, you know where your limbs are because you commanded the muscles that put them there. Nonetheless, the kinesthetic system allows you to double-check these locations. Where are the receptors for your kinesthetic sense? Some reside in the joints, indicating how much they are bending. Others reside within the muscles, registering their tautness, or extension. Most kinesthetic stimulation is transmitted to the brain along the same pathway as tactile stimulation. However, the two types of information are kept separate (Vierck, 1978).

The Vestibular System

When you're jolting along in a bus, the world outside the bus window doesn't seem to jump about as your head bounces up and down. Yet a movie taken with a camera fastened to the bus would show a bouncing world. How are you and the camera different? Unlike the camera, you are equipped with a *vestibular system,* **which responds to gravity and keeps you informed of your body's location in space.** The vestibular system provides the sense of balance, or equilibrium, compensating for changes in the body's position.

The vestibular system shares space in the inner ear with the auditory system. The *semicircular canals* (consult Figure 4.45 on page 158 once again) make up the largest part of the vestibular system. They look like three inner tubes joined at the base. Any rotational motion of the head is uniquely represented by a combination of fluid flows in the semicircular canals (Kelly, 1991). These shifts in fluid are detected by hair cells similar to those found along the basilar membrane in the cochlea (Goldberg & Hudspeth, 2000). Your perceptual system integrates the vestibular input about your body's position with information from other senses. After all, you can see where you are and you know where you've instructed your muscles to take you.

This integration of sensory input raises a point that merits emphasis as we close our tour of the human sensory systems. Although we have discussed the various sensory domains separately, it's important to remember that all the senses send signals to the same brain, where the information is pooled. We have already encountered examples of sensory integration. For example, it's at work when the sight and smell of food influence taste. *Sensory integration is the norm in perceptual experience.* For instance, when you sit around a campfire, you *see* it blazing, you *hear* it crackling, you *smell* it burning, and you feel the *touch* of its warmth. If you cook something over it, you may even *taste* it. Thus, perception involves building a unified model of the world out of integrated input from all the senses (Stein, Wallace, & Stanford, 2001).

PREVIEW QUESTIONS
- What does the kinesthetic system monitor?
- What does the vestibular system do?
- Where is the vestibular system located?

Putting It in Perspective

PREVIEW QUESTIONS

● How did this chapter demonstrate the value of theoretical diversity?

● How did this chapter clarify the subjective nature of human experience?

● How did this chapter illustrate the importance of cultural influences?

In this chapter, three of our unifying themes stand out in sharp relief. Let's discuss the value of theoretical diversity first. Contradictory theories about behaviour can be disconcerting and frustrating for theorists, researchers, teachers, and students alike. Yet this chapter provides two dramatic demonstrations of how theoretical diversity can lead to progress in the long run. For decades, the trichromatic and opponent process theories of colour vision and the place and frequency theories of pitch perception were viewed as fundamentally incompatible. As you know, in each case the evidence eventually revealed that both theories were needed to fully explain the sensory processes that each sought to explain individually. If it hadn't been for these theoretical debates, current understanding of colour vision and pitch perception might be far more primitive, as the understanding of timbre still is.

Our coverage of sensation and perception should also have enhanced your appreciation of why human experience of the world is highly subjective. As ambiguous figures and optical illusions clearly show, there is no one-to-one correspondence between sensory input and perceived experience of the world. Perception is an active process in which people organize and interpret the information received by the senses. These interpretations are shaped by a host of factors, including the environmental context and perceptual sets. Small wonder, then, that people often perceive the same event in very different ways.

Finally, this chapter provided numerous examples of how cultural factors can shape behaviour—in an area of research where one might expect to find little cultural influence. Most people are not surprised to learn that there are cultural differences in attitudes, values, social behaviour, and development. But perception is widely viewed as a basic, universal process that should be invariant across cultures. In most respects it is, as the similarities among cultural groups in perception far outweigh the differences. Nonetheless, we saw cultural variations in depth perception, susceptibility to illusions, taste preferences, and pain tolerance. Thus, even a fundamental, heavily physiological process such as perception can be modified to some degree by one's cultural background.

The following Personal Application demonstrates the subjectivity of perception once again. It focuses on how painters have learned to use the principles of visual perception to achieve a variety of artistic goals.

REVIEW OF KEY POINTS

● Sensory receptors in the skin respond to pressure, temperature, and pain. Tactile localization depends on receptive fields similar to those seen for vision. Some cells in the somatosensory cortex appear to function like feature detectors.

● Pain signals are sent to the brain along two pathways that are characterized as fast and slow. The perception of pain is highly subjective and may be influenced by mood, attention, and culture. Gate-control theory holds that incoming pain signals can be blocked in the spinal cord. Endorphins and a descending neural pathway appear responsible for the suppression of pain by the central nervous system.

● The kinesthetic system monitors the position of various body parts. Kinesthetic receptors, located in the joints and muscles, send signals to the brain along the same pathway as tactile stimulation. The sense of balance depends primarily on activity in the semicircular canals in the vestibular system.

● This chapter underscored three of our unifying themes: the value of theoretical diversity, the subjective nature of human experience, and the influence of culture on behaviour.

PERSONAL APPLICATION

Appreciating Art and Illusion

Answer the following multiple-choice question: Artistic works such as paintings:

____ **a** render an accurate picture of reality.

____ **b** create an illusion of reality.

____ **c** provide an interpretation of reality.

____ **d** make us think about the nature of reality.

____ **e** all of the above.

The answer to this question is (e), "all of the above." Historically, artists have pursued many and varied purposes, including each of those listed in the question (Goldstein, 2001). To realize their goals, they have had to use a number of principles of perception—sometimes quite deliberately, and sometimes not. Let's use the example of painting to explore the role of perceptual principles in art and illusion.

The goal of most early painters was to produce a believable picture of reality. This goal immediately created a problem familiar to most of us who have attempted to draw realistic pictures: The real world is three-dimensional, but a canvas or a sheet of paper is flat. Paradoxically, then, painters who set out to re-create reality have to do so by creating an *illusion* of three-dimensional reality.

Prior to the Renaissance, efforts to create a convincing illusion of reality were relatively awkward by modern standards. Why? Because artists did not understand how to use the full range of depth cues. This is apparent in Figure 4.53, a religious scene painted around 1300. The painting clearly lacks a sense of depth. The people seem paper-thin. They have no real position in space.

Although earlier artists made some use of depth cues, Renaissance artists manipulated the full range of pictorial depth cues and really harnessed the crucial cue of linear perspective (Solso, 1994). Figure 4.54 dramatizes the resulting transition in art.

Figure 4.53

Master of the Arrest of Christ (detail, central part) by S. Francesco, Assisi, Italy (circa 1300). Notice how the paucity of depth cues makes the painting seem flat and unrealistic.

It shows a scene depicted by Gentile and Giovanni Bellini, Italian Renaissance painters. It seems much more realistic and lifelike than the painting in Figure 4.53. Notice how the buildings on the sides converge to make use of linear perspective. Additionally, distant objects are smaller than nearby ones, an application of relative size. This painting also uses height in plane, light and shadow, and interposition. By taking fuller advantage of pictorial depth cues, Renaissance artists enhanced the illusion of reality in paintings.

In the centuries since the Renaissance, painters have adopted a number of viewpoints about the portrayal of reality. For instance, the Impressionists of the 19th century did not want to re-create the photographic "reality" of a scene. They set out to interpret a viewer's fleeting perception or *impression* of reality. To accomplish this end, they worked with colour in unprecedented ways.

Consider, for instance, Claude Monet, a French Impressionist who began to work with separate daubs of pure, bright colours that blurred together to create an alternating perceptual experience. If you view his paintings up close, you see only a shimmering mass of colour. When you step back, however, the adjacent colours begin to blend, and forms begin to take shape, as you can see in Figure 4.55. Monet achieved this duality through careful use of colour mixing and by working systematically with complementary colours.

CHAPTER 5

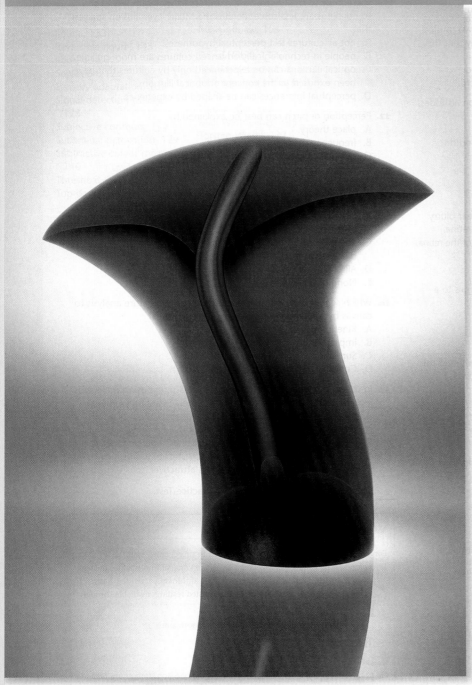

Latchezar Boyadjiev, *Wave*, L.B. Glass Studios

The Nature of Consciousness
    Variations in Levels of Awareness
    Consciousness and Brain Activity

Biological Rhythms and Sleep
    The Role of Circadian Rhythms
    Ignoring Circadian Rhythms
    Melatonin and Circadian Rhythms

The Sleep and Waking Cycle
    Cycling through the Stages of Sleep
    Age Trends in Sleep
    Culture and Sleep
    The Neural Bases of Sleep
    Doing without: Sleep Deprivation
    Featured Study • Gauging the Impact of Sleep Deprivation in
      College Students
    Problems in the Night: Sleep Disorders

The World of Dreams
    The Contents of Dreams
    Links between Dreams and Waking Life
    Culture and Dreams
    Theories of Dreaming

Hypnosis: Altered Consciousness or Role Playing?
    Hypnotic Induction and Susceptibility
    Hypnotic Phenomena
    Theories of Hypnosis

Meditation: Pure Consciousness or Relaxation?
    Physiological Correlates
    Long-Term Benefits

Altering Consciousness with Drugs
    Principal Abused Drugs and Their Effects
    Factors Influencing Drug Effects
    Mechanisms of Drug Action
    Drug Dependence
    Drugs and Health

Putting It in Perspective

***Personal Application* • Addressing Practical Questions
about Sleep and Dreams**
    Common Questions about Sleep
    Common Questions about Dreams

***Critical Thinking Application* • Is Alcoholism a Disease?**
The Power of Definitions
    The Power to Make Definitions
    Definitions, Labels, and Circular Reasoning

Recap

Practice Test

PRACTICE TEST

1. In psychophysical research, the absolute threshold has been arbitrarily defined as:
   A. the stimulus intensity that can be detected 100% of the time.
   B. the stimulus intensity that can be detected 50% of the time.
   C. the minimum amount of difference in intensity needed to tell two stimuli apart.
   D. a constant proportion of the size of the initial stimulus.

2. A tone-deaf person would probably not be able to tell two musical notes apart unless they were very different. We could say that this person has a relatively large:
   A. just noticeable difference.   C. absolute threshold.
   B. relative threshold.   D. detection threshold.

3. In their study of the influence of subliminal perception on attitudes, Krosnick and his colleagues (1992) found:
   A. absolutely no evidence of such influence.
   B. overwhelming evidence that subliminal stimuli can and do influence subjects' attitudes.
   C. that subliminal stimuli do not really exist.
   D. small but measurable effects.

4. In farsightedness:
   A. close objects are seen clearly but distant objects appear blurry.
   B. the focus of light from close objects falls behind the retina.
   C. the focus of light from distant objects falls a little short of the retina.
   D. a and b.
   E. a and c.

5. The collection of rod and cone receptors that funnel signals to a particular visual cell in the retina make up that cell's:
   A. blind spot.   C. opponent process field.
   B. optic disk.   D. receptive field.

6. The visual pathway that has been characterized as _____ travels through the dorsal stream to the parietal lobes, whereas the pathway that has been labelled the _____ travels through the ventral stream to the temporal lobes.
   A. the *what* pathway; the *where* pathway
   B. the *where* pathway; the *what* pathway
   C. the *opponent process* pathway; the *trichromatic* pathway
   D. the *trichromatic* pathway; the *opponent process* pathway

7. Which theory would predict that the Canadian flag would have a green and black afterimage?
   A. subtractive colour mixing
   B. opponent process theory
   C. additive colour mixing
   D. trichromatic theory

8. The illusion of movement created by presenting visual stimuli in rapid succession is called:
   A. convergence.
   B. retinal disparity.
   C. motion parallax.
   D. the phi phenomenon.

9. In a painting, train tracks may look as if they go off into the distance because the artist draws the tracks as converging lines, a monocular cue to depth known as:
   A. interposition.   C. convergence.
   B. texture gradient.   D. linear perspective.

10. Which of the following would be expected to produce the phi phenomenon?
    A. music training
    B. staring at a bright red colour and then closing your eyes

C. scanning rapidly in sequence through a series of pictures you took of your best friend water skiing
D. listening to several rapidly played musical notes each separated by a semitone

11. The facts that cultural groups with little exposure to roads are less susceptible to the Ponzo illusion and that those with less exposure to buildings are less susceptible to the Müller-Lyer illusion suggest that:
    A. not all cultures test perceptual hypotheses.
    B. people in technologically advanced cultures are more gullible.
    C. optical illusions can be experienced only by cultures that have been exposed to the concept of optical illusions.
    D. perceptual inferences can be shaped by experience.

12. Perception of pitch can best be explained by:
    A. place theory.
    B. frequency theory.
    C. both place theory and frequency theory.
    D. neither theory.

13. In what way(s) is the sense of taste like the sense of smell?
    A. There are four primary stimulus groups for both senses.
    B. Both systems are routed through the thalamus on the way to the cortex.
    C. The physical stimuli for both senses are chemical substances dissolved in fluid.
    D. All of the above.
    E. None of the above.

14. Which school of painting applied the theory of feature analysis to canvas by building figures out of simple features?
    A. Kineticism
    B. Impressionism
    C. Surrealism
    D. Cubism

15. In the study by Kenrick and Gutierres (1980), exposing male subjects to a TV show dominated by extremely beautiful women:
    A. had no effect on their ratings of the attractiveness of a prospective date.
    B. increased their ratings of the attractiveness of a prospective date.
    C. decreased their ratings of the attractiveness of a prospective date.
    D. increased their ratings of their own attractiveness.

See Appendix A for answers to this Practice Test.

 ON THE WEB

For additional resources on the topics covered in this chapter, visit the *Psychology: Themes and Variations* Web site, where you will find practice quizzes, tutorials, Web links, simulations, critical thinking activities, flash cards, interactive exercises, and suggested readings available through INFOTRAC.

http://www.themesandvariations.nelson.com

 http://hed.nelson.com

Go to this site for the link to ThomsonNOW™, your one-stop study shop. Take a Pretest for this chapter and ThomsonNOW™ will generate a personalized Study Plan based on your test results! The Study Plan will identify the topics you need to review and direct you to online resources to help you master those topics. You can then take a Posttest to help you determine the concepts you have mastered and what you still need work on.

CHAPTER 5

Latchezar Boyadjiev, *Wave,* L.B. Glass Studios

The Nature of Consciousness
Variations in Levels of Awareness
Consciousness and Brain Activity

Biological Rhythms and Sleep
The Role of Circadian Rhythms
Ignoring Circadian Rhythms
Melatonin and Circadian Rhythms

The Sleep and Waking Cycle
Cycling through the Stages of Sleep
Age Trends in Sleep
Culture and Sleep
The Neural Bases of Sleep
Doing without: Sleep Deprivation
Featured Study • Gauging the Impact of Sleep Deprivation in
    College Students
Problems in the Night: Sleep Disorders

The World of Dreams
The Contents of Dreams
Links between Dreams and Waking Life
Culture and Dreams
Theories of Dreaming

Hypnosis: Altered Consciousness or Role Playing?
Hypnotic Induction and Susceptibility
Hypnotic Phenomena
Theories of Hypnosis

Meditation: Pure Consciousness or Relaxation?
Physiological Correlates
Long-Term Benefits

Altering Consciousness with Drugs
Principal Abused Drugs and Their Effects
Factors Influencing Drug Effects
Mechanisms of Drug Action
Drug Dependence
Drugs and Health

Putting It in Perspective

Personal Application • **Addressing Practical Questions
about Sleep and Dreams**
Common Questions about Sleep
Common Questions about Dreams

Critical Thinking Application • **Is Alcoholism a Disease?
The Power of Definitions**
The Power to Make Definitions
Definitions, Labels, and Circular Reasoning

Recap

Practice Test

Perceptual hypothesis, 147
Perceptual set, 143
Phi phenomenon, 145
Pictorial depth cues, 149
Place theory, 158
Proximal stimuli, 146
Psychophysics, 127
Pupil, 133
Receptive field of a visual
  cell, 135
Retina, 133
Reversible figure, 143
Rods, 134
Sensation, 126
Sensory adaptation, 130
Signal-detection theory,
  128
Subjective contours, 144
Subliminal perception, 129
Subtractive colour mixing,
  140
Threshold, 127
Top-down processing, 144

Trichromatic theory, 140
Vestibular system, 167
Visual agnosia, 138
Volley principle, 159
Weber's law, 128

Key People

Linda Bartoshuk, 163
Mel Goodale, 154
Gustav Fechner, 127
David Hubel, 137
Ronald Melzack, 166
Hermann von Helmholtz,
  158
Patrick Wall, 166
Max Wertheimer, 145
Torsten Wiesel, 137

RECAP

Key Ideas

Psychophysics: Basic Concepts and Issues

● Absolute thresholds are not really absolute. Fechner's law asserts that larger and larger increases in stimulus intensity are required to produce just noticeable differences in the magnitude of sensation.

● According to signal-detection theory, the detection of sensory inputs is influenced by noise in the system and by decision-making strategies. In recent years, it has become apparent that perception can occur without awareness. Prolonged stimulation may lead to sensory adaptation.

Our Sense of Sight: The Visual System

● Light varies in terms of wavelength, amplitude, and purity. Light enters the eye through the cornea and pupil and is focused on the retina by the lens. Rods and cones are the visual receptors found in the retina. Cones play a key role in daylight vision and colour perception, and rods are critical to night vision and peripheral vision. Dark and light adaptation both involve changes in the retina's sensitivity to light.

● The retina transforms light into neural impulses that are sent to the brain via the optic nerve. Receptive fields are areas in the retina that affect the firing of visual cells. Two visual pathways, which engage in parallel processing, send signals through the thalamus to the primary visual cortex. From there, visual signals are shuttled along pathways that have been characterized as the *what* and *where* pathways.

● Perceptions of colour (hue) are primarily a function of light wavelength, while amplitude affects brightness and purity affects saturation. Perceptions of many varied colours depend on processes that resemble additive colour mixing. The evidence now suggests that both the trichromatic and opponent process theories are necessary to account for colour vision.

● Form perception depends on the selection and interpretation of visual inputs. According to feature analysis theories, people detect specific elements in stimuli and build them into forms through bottom-up processing. However, evidence suggests that form perception also involves top-down processing.

● Gestalt psychology emphasized that the whole may be greater than the sum of its parts (features), as illustrated by Gestalt principles of form perception. Other approaches to form perception emphasize that people develop perceptual hypotheses about the distal stimuli that could be responsible for the proximal stimuli that are sensed.

● Depth perception depends primarily on monocular cues. Binocular cues such as retinal disparity and convergence can also contribute to depth perception.

● Perceptual constancies help viewers deal with the ever-shifting nature of proximal stimuli. Optical illusions demonstrate that perceptual hypotheses can be inaccurate and that perceptions are not simple reflections of objective reality.

Our Sense of Hearing: The Auditory System

● Sound varies in terms of wavelength (frequency), amplitude, and purity. These properties affect mainly perceptions of pitch, loudness, and timbre, respectively. Auditory signals are transmitted through the thalamus to the auditory cortex in the temporal lobe.

● Modern evidence suggests that place theory and frequency theory are complementary rather than incompatible explanations of pitch perception. People pinpoint the source of sounds by comparing inter-ear differences in the intensity and timing of sounds.

● Exposure to music has been found to affect our emotions. In addition, as revealed in the Featured Study, music training affects our ability to decode emotions in the speech of others.

Our Chemical Senses: Taste and Smell

● The taste buds are sensitive to four basic tastes: sweet, sour, bitter, and salty. Taste preferences are largely learned and are heavily influenced by one's cultural background. Supertasters are more sensitive to bitter and sweet tastes than others are.

● Like taste, smell is a chemical sense. Chemical stimuli activate olfactory receptors lining the nasal passages. Most of these receptors respond to more than one odour. Humans exhibit surprising difficulty attaching names to odours.

Our Sense of Touch: Sensory Systems in the Skin

● Sensory receptors in the skin respond to pressure, temperature, and pain. Pain signals are sent to the brain along two pathways characterized as fast and slow. The perception of pain is highly subjective and may be influenced by mood, attention, personality, and culture. Gate-control theory holds that incoming pain signals can be blocked in the spinal cord. Endorphins and a descending neural pathway appear responsible for the suppression of pain by the central nervous system.

Our Other Senses

● The kinesthetic system monitors the position of various body parts. The sense of balance depends on activity in the vestibular system.

Putting It in Perspective

● This chapter underscored three of our unifying themes: the value of theoretical diversity, the subjective nature of human experience, and the influence of culture on behaviour.

Personal Application • Appreciating Art and Illusion

● The principles of visual perception are often applied to artistic endeavours. Painters routinely use pictorial depth cues to make their scenes more lifelike. Colour mixing, feature analysis, Gestalt principles, reversible figures, and impossible figures have also been used in influential paintings.

Critical Thinking Application • Recognizing Contrast Effects: It's All Relative

● The study of perception often highlights the relativity of experience. This relativity can be manipulated by arranging for contrast effects. Critical thinking is enhanced by an awareness of how comparitors can distort many judgments.

Key Terms

Absolute threshold, 127
Additive colour mixing, 140
Afterimage, 141
Auditory localization, 159
Basilar membrane, 157
Binocular depth cues, 148
Bottom-up processing, 144
Cochlea, 156
Colour blindness, 141
Comparitors, 176
Complementary colours, 141
Cones, 134
Convergence, 148
Dark adaptation, 134
Depth perception, 148
Distal stimuli, 146
Door-in-the-face technique, 175
Farsightedness, 133
Feature analysis, 143
Feature detectors, 138
Fechner's law, 128

Fovea, 134
Frequency theory, 158
Gate-control theory, 166
Gustatory system, 162
Impossible figures, 151
Just noticeable difference (JND), 128
Kinesthetic system, 167
Lateral antagonism, 135
Lens, 132
Light adaptation, 134
Monocular depth cues, 148
Motion parallax, 149
Nearsightedness, 132
Olfactory system, 162
Opponent process theory, 141
Optic chiasm, 136
Optic disk, 134
Optical illusion, 150
Parallel processing, 136
Perception, 126
Perceptual constancy, 150

Figure 4.65

Contrast effects in visual perception.
This composition by Joseph Albers shows how one colour can be perceived differently when contrasted against different backgrounds. The top X looks yellow and the bottom X looks brown, but they're really the same colour.

SOURCE: Albers, Joseph. *Interaction of Color.* Copyright © 1963 and reprinted by permission of the publisher, Yale University Press.

Figure 4.66

Contrast effects in judgments of physical attractiveness. Participants rated their own physical attractiveness under two conditions. In the experimental condition, the ratings occurred after subjects were exposed to a series of photos depicting very attractive models. The resulting contrast effects led to lower self-ratings in this condition. (Data based on Thornton & Moore, 1993)

assertion that everything is relative raises the issue of *relative to what?* **Comparitors are people, objects, events, and other standards used as a baseline for comparison in making judgments.** It is fairly easy to manipulate many types of judgments by selecting *extreme* comparitors that may be unrepresentative.

The influence of extreme comparitors was demonstrated in a couple of interesting studies of judgments of physical attractiveness. In one study, undergraduate males were asked to rate the attractiveness of an average-looking female (who was described as a potential date for another male in the dorm) presented in a photo either just before or just after the participants watched a TV show dominated by strikingly beautiful women (Kenrick & Gutierres, 1980). The female was viewed as less attractive when the ratings were obtained just after the men had seen gorgeous women cavorting on TV as opposed to when they hadn't. In another investigation (Thornton and Moore, 1993), both male and female participants rated *themselves* as less attractive after being exposed to many pictures of extremely attractive models (see Figure 4.66). Thus, contrast effects can influence important social judgments that are likely to affect how people feel about themselves and others.

Anyone who understands how easily judgments can be manipulated by a careful choice of comparitors could influence your thinking. For example, a politician who is caught in some illegal or immoral act could sway public opinion by bringing to mind (perhaps subtly) the fact that many other politicians have committed acts that were much worse. When considered against a backdrop of more extreme comparitors, the politician's transgression will probably seem less offensive. A defence lawyer could use a similar strategy in an attempt to obtain a lighter sentence for a client by comparing the client's offence to much more serious crimes. And a realtor who wants to sell you an expensive house that will require huge mortgage payments will be quick to mention other homeowners who have taken on even larger mortgages.

In summary, critical thinking is facilitated by conscious awareness of the way comparitors can influence and perhaps distort a wide range of judgments. In particular, it pays to be vigilant about the possibility that others may manipulate contrast effects in their persuasive efforts. One way to reduce the influence of contrast effects is to consciously consider comparitors that are both worse and better than the event you are judging, as a way of balancing the effects of the two extremes.

Table 4.2 Critical Thinking Skills Discussed in This Application

Skill	Description
Understanding how contrast effects can influence judgments and decisions	The critical thinker appreciates how striking contrasts can be manipulated to influence many types of judgments.
Recognizing when extreme comparitors are being used	The critical thinker is on the lookout for extreme comparitors that distort judgments.

Recognizing Contrast Effects: It's All Relative

You're sitting at home one night, when the phone rings. It's Simone, an acquaintance from school who needs help with a recreational program for youngsters that she runs for the local park district. She tries to persuade you to volunteer four hours of your time every Friday night throughout the school year to supervise the volleyball program. The thought of giving up your Friday nights and adding this sizable obligation to your already busy schedule makes you cringe with horror. You politely explain to Simone that you can't possibly afford to give up that much time and you won't be able to help her. She accepts your rebuff graciously, but the next night she calls again. This time she wants to know whether you would be willing to supervise volleyball every third Friday. You still feel like it's a big obligation that you really don't want to take on, but the new request seems much more reasonable than the original one. So, with a sigh of resignation, you agree to Simone's request.

What's wrong with this picture? Well, there's nothing wrong with volunteering your time for a good cause, but you just succumbed to a social influence strategy called the *door-in-the face technique*. The **door-in-the-face technique involves making a large request that is likely to be turned down as a way to increase the chances that people will agree to a smaller request later** (see Figure 4.64). The name for this strategy is derived from the expectation that the initial request will be quickly rejected (hence, the door is slammed in the salesperson's face). Although they may not be familiar with the strategy's name, many people use this manipulative tactic. For example, a husband who wants to coax his frugal wife into agreeing to buy a $25 000 sports car might begin by proposing that they purchase a $44 000 sports car. By the time the wife talks her husband out of the $44 000 car, the $25 000 price tag may look quite reasonable to her—which is what the husband wanted all along.

Research has demonstrated that the door-in-the-face technique is a highly effective persuasive strategy (Cialdini, 2001). One of the reasons it works so well is that it depends on a simple and pervasive perceptual principle. As noted in our discussion of psychophysical scaling (see p. 128), in the domain of perceptual experience, *everything is relative*. This relativity means that people are easily swayed by *contrast effects*. For example, lighting a match or a small candle in a dark room will produce a burst of light that seems quite bright, but if you light the same match or candle in a well-lit room, you may not even detect the additional illumination. The relativity of perception is apparent in the painting by Josef Albers shown in Figure 4.65. The two X's are exactly the same colour, but the X in the top half looks yellow, whereas the X in the bottom half looks brown. These varied perceptions occur because of contrast effects—the two X's are contrasted against different background colours.

The same principles of relativity and contrast that operate when we are making judgments about the intensity or colour of visual stimuli also affect the way we make judgments in a wide variety of domains. For example, a 185-cm basketball player, who is really quite tall, can look downright small when surrounded by teammates who are all over 200 cm. And a salary of $30 000 per year for your first full-time job may seem like a princely sum, until a close friend gets an offer of $55 000 a year. The

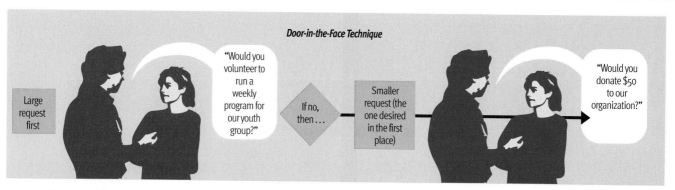

Figure 4.64

The door-in-the-face technique. The door-in-the-face technique is a frequently used compliance strategy in which you begin with a large request and work down to the smaller request you are really after. It depends in part on contrast effects.

Figure 4.62

Victor Vasarely's *Vega-Tek* (1969). In this painting, Vasarely manipulates a host of depth cues to create the image of a sphere inflating.

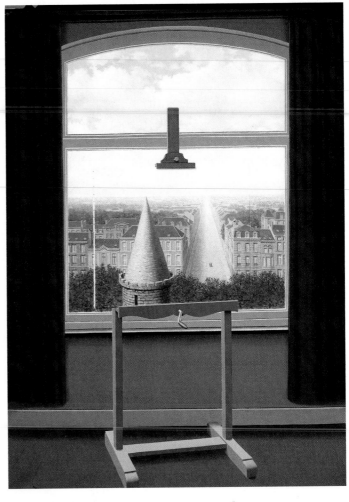

Figure 4.63

René Magritte's *Les Promenades d'Euclide* (1955). Notice how the pair of nearly identical triangles look quite different in different contexts.

While Escher and Vasarely challenged viewers to think about perception, Belgian artist René Magritte challenged people to think about the conventions of painting. Many of his works depict paintings on an easel, with the "real" scene continuing unbroken at the edges. The painting in Figure 4.63 is such a picture within a picture. In addition, there are two identical triangles in the painting. One represents a road and the other a nearby tower. Notice how the identical triangles are perceived differently because of the variations in *context*.

Ultimately, Magritte's painting blurs the line between the real world and the illusory world created by the artist, suggesting that there is no line—that everything is an illusion. In this way, Magritte "framed" the ageless, unanswerable question: What is reality?

REVIEW OF KEY POINTS

- The principles of visual perception are often applied to artistic endeavours. Prior to the Renaissance, efforts to create a convincing illusion of three-dimensional reality were awkward because artists did not understand how to use depth cues. After the Renaissance, painters began to routinely use pictorial depth cues to make their scenes more lifelike.

- Nineteenth-century painters, such as the Impressionists, manipulated colour in creative, new ways. The Cubists were innovative in manipulating form, as they applied the theory of feature analysis to canvas. The Surrealists toyed with reality, exploring the world of fantasy and dreams.

- Modern artists such as Escher and Vasarely have tried to stimulate viewers to think about the process of perception. Among other things, Escher worked with the Necker cube and the impossible triangle.

Figure 4.60

Escher's lithograph *Waterfall* (1961). Escher's use of depth cues and impossible triangles deceives the brain into seeing water flow uphill.

Figure 4.61

Escher's *Belvedere* (1958).

This lithograph depicts an impossible figure inspired by the Necker cube. The cube appears in the architecture of the building, in the model held by the boy on the bench, and in the drawing lying at his feet.

Escher's 1958 lithograph *Belvedere,* shown in Figure 4.61. You have to look carefully to realize that this is another impossible figure. Note that the top storey runs at a right angle from the first storey. Note also how the pillars are twisted around. The pillars that start on one side of the building end up supporting the second storey on the other side! Escher's debt to the Necker cube is manifested in several places. Notice, for instance, the drawing of a Necker cube on the floor next to the seated boy (on the lower left).

Like Escher, Victor Vasarely challenged viewers to think about the process of perception. A Hungarian artist, Vasarely pioneered an approach called Kinetic Art because of his interest in creating illusions of motion. Like Georges Seurat, he went about his work with scientific precision. His paintings are based on optical illusions, as squares seem to advance and recede, or spheres seem to inflate and deflate. For example, note how Vasarely used a variety of depth cues to convey the look of a sphere inflating in his painting *Vega-Tek,* shown in Figure 4.62.

Figure **4.58**

Marcel Duchamp's *Nude Descending a Staircase, No 2* (1912). This painting uses the Gestalt principles of continuity and common fate.

Figure 4.59

Salvador Dali's *The Hallucinogenic Toreador* (1969–1970).
This surrealistic painting includes a reversible figure (the bullfighter is made up of Venus de Milo statues). Gestalt principles are crucial to the perception of the bull and the dalmatian near the bottom of the painting.

The Surrealists toyed with reality in a different way. Influenced by Sigmund Freud's writings on the unconscious, the Surrealists explored the world of dreams and fantasy. Specific elements in their paintings are often depicted realistically, but the strange juxtaposition of elements yields a disconcerting irrationality reminiscent of dreams. A prominent example of this style is Salvador Dali's *The Hallucinogenic Toreador*, shown in Figure 4.59. Notice the reversible figure near the centre of the painting. The bullfighter is made up of Venus de Milo sculptures. Dali often used reversible figures to enhance the ambiguity of his bizarre visions.

Perhaps no one has been more creative in manipulating perceptual ambiguity than M. C. Escher, a modern Dutch artist. Escher's chief goal was to stimulate viewers to think about the nature of reality and the process of visual perception itself. Interestingly, Escher readily acknowledged his debt to psychology as a source of inspiration (Teuber, 1974). He followed the work of the Gestalt psychologists carefully and would even cite specific journal articles that served as the point of departure for his works. For example, *Waterfall*, a 1961 lithograph by Escher, is an impossible figure that appears to defy the law of gravity (see Figure 4.60). The puzzling problem here is that a level channel of water terminates in a waterfall that "falls" into the *same* channel two levels "below." This drawing is made up of two impossible triangles. In case you need help seeing them, the waterfall itself forms one side of each triangle.

The Necker cube, a reversible figure mentioned earlier, was the inspiration for career. The Cubists didn't try to *portray* reality so much as to *reassemble* it. They attempted to reduce everything to combinations of geometric forms (lines, circles, triangles, rectangles, and such) laid out in a flat space, lacking depth. In a sense, *they applied the theory of feature analysis to canvas,* as they built their figures out of simple features.

The resulting paintings were decidedly unrealistic, but the painters would leave realistic fragments that provided clues about the subject. Picasso liked to challenge his viewers to decipher the subject of his paintings. Take a look at the painting in Figure 4.57 and see whether you can figure out what Picasso was portraying.

The work in Figure 4.57 is titled *Violin and Grapes*. Note how Gestalt principles of perceptual organization are at work to create these forms. Proximity and similarity serve to bring the grapes together in the bottom right corner. Closure accounts for your being able to see the essence of the violin.

Other Gestalt principles are the key to the effect achieved in the painting in Figure 4.58. This painting, by Marcel Duchamp, a French artist who blended Cubism and a style called Futurism, is titled *Nude Descending a Staircase*. The effect clearly depends on the Gestalt principle of continuity.

Figure 4.57

***Violin and Grapes* by Pablo Picasso (1912).** This painting makes use of the Gestalt principles of proximity, similarity, and closure.

PERSONAL APPLICATION

Appreciating Art and Illusion

Answer the following multiple-choice question: Artistic works such as paintings:

____ **a** render an accurate picture of reality.

____ **b** create an illusion of reality.

____ **c** provide an interpretation of reality.

____ **d** make us think about the nature of reality.

____ **e** all of the above.

The answer to this question is (e), "all of the above." Historically, artists have pursued many and varied purposes, including each of those listed in the question (Goldstein, 2001). To realize their goals, they have had to use a number of principles of perception—sometimes quite deliberately, and sometimes not. Let's use the example of painting to explore the role of perceptual principles in art and illusion.

The goal of most early painters was to produce a believable picture of reality. This goal immediately created a problem familiar to most of us who have attempted to draw realistic pictures: The real world is three-dimensional, but a canvas or a sheet of paper is flat. Paradoxically, then, painters who set out to re-create reality have to do so by creating an *illusion* of three-dimensional reality.

Prior to the Renaissance, efforts to create a convincing illusion of reality were relatively awkward by modern standards. Why? Because artists did not understand how to use the full range of depth cues. This is apparent in Figure 4.53, a religious scene painted around 1300. The painting clearly lacks a sense of depth. The people seem paper-thin. They have no real position in space.

Although earlier artists made some use of depth cues, Renaissance artists manipulated the full range of pictorial depth cues and really harnessed the crucial cue of linear perspective (Solso, 1994). Figure 4.54 dramatizes the resulting transition in art.

Figure 4.53

Master of the Arrest of Christi **(detail, central part) by S. Francesco, Assisi, Italy (circa 1300).** Notice how the paucity of depth cues makes the painting seem flat and unrealistic.

Scala/Art Resource, New York

It shows a scene depicted by Gentile and Giovanni Bellini, Italian Renaissance painters. It seems much more realistic and lifelike than the painting in Figure 4.53. Notice how the buildings on the sides converge to make use of linear perspective. Additionally, distant objects are smaller than nearby ones, an application of relative size. This painting also uses height in plane, light and shadow, and interposition. By taking fuller advantage of pictorial depth cues, Renaissance artists enhanced the illusion of reality in paintings.

In the centuries since the Renaissance, painters have adopted a number of viewpoints about the portrayal of reality. For instance, the Impressionists of the 19th century did not want to re-create the photographic "reality" of a scene. They set out to interpret a viewer's fleeting perception or *impression* of reality. To accomplish this end, they worked with colour in unprecedented ways.

Consider, for instance, Claude Monet, a French Impressionist who began to work with separate daubs of pure, bright colours that blurred together to create an alternating perceptual experience. If you view his paintings up close, you see only a shimmering mass of colour. When you step back, however, the adjacent colours begin to blend, and forms begin to take shape, as you can see in Figure 4.55. Monet achieved this duality through careful use of colour mixing and by working systematically with complementary colours.

Figure 4.54

Brera Predica di S. Marco Pinacoteca **by Gentile and Giovanni Bellini (circa 1480).** In this painting, the Italian Renaissance artists use a number of depth cues—including linear perspective, relative size, height in plane, light and shadow, and interposition—to enhance the illusion of three-dimensional reality.

Figure 4.55

Claude Monet's *Palazzo da Mula, Venice* **(1908).** The French Impressionist Monet often used complementary colours to achieve his visual effects.

Similar methods were used even more precisely and systematically by Georges Seurat, a French artist who used a technique called *pointillism*. Seurat carefully studied what scientists knew about the composition of colour in the 1880s, and then applied this knowledge in a calculated, laboratory-like manner. Indeed, critics in his era dubbed him the "little chemist." Seurat constructed his paintings out of tiny dots of pure, intense colours. He used additive colour mixing, a departure from the norm in painting, which usually depends on subtractive mixing of pigments. A famous result of Seurat's "scientific" approach to painting was his renowned *Sunday Afternoon on the Island of La Grande Jatte* (see Figure 4.56). As the work of Seurat illustrates, modernist painters were moving away from attempts to re-create the world as it is literally seen.

If 19th-century painters liberated colour, their successors at the turn of the 20th century liberated form. This was particularly true of the Cubists. Cubism was begun in 1909 by Pablo Picasso, a Spanish artist who went on to experiment with other styles in his prolific

Variations in Consciousness

Although Canadians and Americans are often lumped together as representing highly similar cultures and societies, it wouldn't likely take you long to think of some important ways in which we differ. We have universal health care; they do not. This is a key issue when Canadians think of what symbolizes us as a nation. Remember the results of the recent 2004 search for the Greatest Canadian produced by the CBC? The number-one Greatest Canadian was Tommy Douglas, the originator of universal health care in Canada. If the recent past is any indicator, we also play hockey better than the Americans do. Witness the success of our men's and women's Olympic hockey teams in the 2002 Olympic Games in Salt Lake City, and the success of the Canadian Junior Hockey team in winning gold at the World Championships in 2005.

Another area of social policy on which we differ relates to the recent proposal to decriminalize marijuana possession. In November 2004 the federal government proposed legislation to decriminalize the possession of small amounts of marijuana. In part, the legislation suggests replacing existing criminal sanctions with fines for possession of small amounts of the drug. This is not a proposal viewed favourably by the U.S. government (Canadian Government, 2005). The legislation is controversial in Canada, too, a controversy that will likely be fuelled by the killing of four RCMP officers raiding a marijuana-growing operation on March 3, 2005, near Mayerthorpe, Alberta (Harding & Walton, 2005). In light of this tragedy, the federal government promised to crack down on marijuana grow-ops (Clark & Freeze, 2005).

While there are differences between Canadians and Americans, one thing that we likely share is the pace of modern life and complaints about a lack of sleep. Recent surveys by Statistics Canada (Williams, 2001) reveal that many Canadians (47%) report that they have cut down on the number of hours they sleep each night in the hope of squeezing more into their busy days. But what does it matter? What's a little irritability? For some, the consequences of sleep disturbance can be significant indeed. William Dement (1999), a pioneer in sleep research, states that many of the major industrial accidents that we hear about occur after midnight, implicating the effects of shift work and sleep deprivation. Sometimes even when we do have the opportunity to sleep, the quality of the sleep may suffer. Twenty-five percent of Canadians report that they have trouble falling or staying asleep (Williams, 2001), but it seems that certain groups are getting their eight hours of sleep. The survey also shows that there are age trends in terms of number of hours of sleep. Canadians between 15 and 24 years of age and those over 65 seem to get the most sleep, an average of 8.5 hours per night.

What do these two topics—illegal drugs and sleep—have in common? Both of these general topics, along with many more important topics, are covered in this chapter on consciousness. At this point, you may be wondering what is meant by *consciousness*, a term that has to be broad enough to include these and other topics. Consciousness is also quite dynamic, as we tend to drift into and out of different states over the course of a day. We begin by considering the nature of consciousness in general. Then we will discuss specific states of consciousness that have intrigued psychologists for decades.

The Nature of Consciousness

PREVIEW QUESTIONS

- What is consciousness?
- What did Freud have to say about levels of awareness?
- Is there any awareness during sleep?
- How might consciousness be adaptive?
- How are variations in consciousness associated with EEG activity?

Consciousness is the awareness of internal and external stimuli. Your consciousness includes (1) your awareness of external events ("The professor just asked me a difficult question about medieval history"), (2) your awareness of your internal sensations ("My heart is racing and I'm beginning to sweat"), (3) your awareness of your self as the unique being having these experiences ("Why me?"), and (4) your awareness of your thoughts about these experiences ("I'm going to make a fool of myself!"). To put it more concisely, consciousness is personal awareness.

The contents of your consciousness are continually changing. Recognizing this fact, William James (1902) christened this continuous flow the *stream of consciousness*. Constant shifting and changing seem to be part of the essential nature of consciousness.

Variations in Levels of Awareness

Whereas William James emphasized the stream of consciousness, Sigmund Freud (1900) wanted to examine what went on beneath the surface of this stream. As explained in Chapter 1, Freud argued that people's feelings and behaviour are influenced by *unconscious* needs, wishes, and conflicts that lie below the surface of conscious awareness. According to Freud, the stream of consciousness has depth. Conscious and unconscious processes are different *levels of awareness*. Thus, Freud was one of the first theorists to recognize that consciousness is not an all-or-none phenomenon.

Since Freud's time, research has shown that people continue to maintain some awareness during sleep and even when they are put under anesthesia for surgery. How do we know? Because some stimuli can still penetrate awareness. For example, people under surgical anesthesia occasionally hear comments made during their surgery, which they later repeat to their surprised surgeons (Bennett, 1993; Merikle & Daneman, 1996). Other research indicates that while people are asleep they remain aware of external events to some degree (Campbell, 2000; Evans, 1990). A good example is the new parent who can sleep through a loud thunderstorm or a buzzing alarm clock but who immediately hears the muffled sound of the baby crying down the hall. The parent's selective sensitivity to sounds means that some mental processing must be going on even during sleep.

Why do humans experience consciousness? Like other aspects of human nature, consciousness must have evolved because it helped our ancient ancestors survive and reproduce (Ornstein & Dewan, 1991).

That said, there is plenty of debate about exactly how consciousness proved adaptive (Guzeldere, Flanagan, & Hardcastle, 2000).

Consciousness and Brain Activity

Consciousness does not arise from any distinct structure in the brain but rather from activity in distributed networks of neural pathways (Kinsbourne, 1997). Thus, one of the best physiological indicators of variations in consciousness is the EEG, which records activity from broad swaths of the cortex. **The *electroencephalograph* (EEG) is a device that monitors the electrical activity of the brain over time by means of recording electrodes attached to the surface of the scalp.** Ultimately, the EEG summarizes the rhythm of cortical activity in the brain in terms of line tracings called *brain waves*. These brain-wave tracings vary in *amplitude* (height) and *frequency* (cycles per second, abbreviated *cps*). You can see what brain waves look like if you glance ahead to Figure 5.4 on page 187. Human brain-wave activity is usually divided into four principal bands based on the frequency of the brain waves. These bands, named after letters in the Greek alphabet, are *beta* (13–24 cps), *alpha* (8–12 cps), *theta* (4–7 cps), and *delta* (under 4 cps).

Different patterns of EEG activity are associated with different states of consciousness, as is summarized in Table 5.1. For instance, when you are alertly engaged in problem solving, beta waves tend to dominate. When you are relaxed and resting, alpha waves increase. When you slip into deep, dreamless sleep, delta waves become more prevalent. Although these correlations are far from perfect, changes in EEG activity are closely related to variations in consciousness (Wallace & Fisher, 1999).

As we discussed in Chapter 2, measures of association such as correlations between mental states and

Table 5.1
EEG Patterns Associated with States of Consciousness

EEG pattern	Frequency (cps)	Typical States of Consciousness
Beta (β)	13–24	Normal waking thought, alert problem solving
Alpha (α)	8–12	Deep relaxation, blank mind, meditation
Theta (θ)	4–7	Light sleep
Delta (Δ)	less than 4	Deep

brain waves don't allow you to make firm statements regarding causation. We do not know based on such measures whether changes in mental states cause brain wave changes or vice versa. Also, it could be that some third factor such as signals coming from a subcortical structure of the brain is causing both (see Figure 5.1).

Measures of brain-wave activity have provided investigators with a method for mapping out the mysterious state of consciousness called sleep. As we will see in the next two sections of the chapter, this state turns out to be far more complex and varied than you might expect.

Figure 5.1

The correlation between mental states and electrical activity in the brain. As discussed in Chapter 2, correlations alone do not establish causation. For example, there are strong correlations between drowsiness and a particular pattern of cortical activity, as reflected by EEG brain waves. But does drowsiness cause a change in cortical activity, or do changes in cortical activity cause drowsiness? Or does some third variable account for the changes in both?

REVIEW OF KEY POINTS

● William James emphasized that consciousness is a continually changing stream of mental activity. Consciousness varies along a continuum of levels of awareness.

● Consciousness may have evolved because it allowed humans to think through the possible consequences of their actions and avoid some negative consequences. People maintain some degree of awareness during sleep and sometimes while under anesthesia.

● Brain waves vary in amplitude and frequency (cps) and are divided into four bands: beta, alpha, theta, and delta. Variations in consciousness are related to variations in brain activity, as measured by the EEG.

Biological Rhythms and Sleep

According to University of Ottawa psychologist Joseph De Koninck, the past three decades have increasingly demonstrated the critical impact that sleep has on many of the important processes and tasks that we engage in every day (De Koninck, 1997). This work has also indicated the important links between sleep quality and the body's natural rhythm. Canadian sleep research labs have played an important role in much of this research. For a list of some of the sleep centres across Canada, visit the Web site for the Canadian Sleep Society (http://www.css.to/).

Variations in consciousness are shaped in part by biological rhythms. Rhythms pervade the world around us. The daily alternation of light and darkness, the annual pattern of the seasons, and the phases of the moon all reflect this rhythmic quality of repeating cycles. Humans, many other animals, and even plants display biological rhythms that are tied to these planetary rhythms (Foster, 2004). **Biological rhythms are periodic fluctuations in physiological functioning.** The existence of these rhythms means that organisms have internal "biological clocks" that somehow monitor the passage of time.

The Role of Circadian Rhythms

Circadian rhythms **are the 24-hour biological cycles found in humans and many other species.** In humans, circadian rhythms are particularly influential in the regulation of sleep (Lavie, 2001). However, daily cycles also produce rhythmic variations in blood pressure, urine production, hormonal secretions, and other physical functions (see Figure 5.2), as well as alertness, short-term memory, and other aspects of cognitive performance (Czeisler & Khalsa, 2005; Van Dongen & Dinges, 2005). For instance, body temperature varies rhythmically in a daily cycle, usually peaking in the afternoon and reaching its low point in the depths of the night.

Research indicates that people generally fall asleep as their body temperature begins to drop and awaken as it begins to ascend once again (Kumar, 2004). Investigators have concluded that circadian rhythms can leave individuals physiologically primed to fall asleep most easily at a particular time of day (Richardson, 1993). This optimal time varies from person to person,

PREVIEW QUESTIONS

● What are biological rhythms?

● How are circadian rhythms related to falling asleep?

● Which physiological structures control our biological clocks?

● How are circadian rhythms related to jet lag?

● How do rotating work shifts tend to affect sleep?

● What are the pros and cons of using melatonin as a sleep aid?

Figure **5.2**

Examples of circadian rhythms. These graphs show how alertness, core body temperature, and the secretion of growth hormone typically fluctuate in a 24-hour rhythm. Note how alertness tends to diminish with declining body temperature.

SOURCE: Adapted from Coleman, R. (1986). *Wide awake at 3:00 A.M.* New York: W. H. Freeman. Copyright © 1986 by Richard M. Coleman. Used with the permission of Henry Holt & Co., LLC.

depending on their schedules, but it's interesting to learn that each individual may have an "ideal" time for going to bed. This ideal bedtime may also promote better quality sleep during the night (Akerstedt et al., 1997), which is interesting in light of evidence that sleep *quality* may be more strongly correlated with health and well-being than the sheer quantity of sleep (Pilcher, Ginter, & Sadowsky, 1997).

To study biological clocks, researchers have monitored physiological processes while subjects are cut off from exposure to the cycle of day and night and all other external time cues. These studies have demonstrated that circadian rhythms generally persist even when external time cues are eliminated. However, when people are isolated in this way, their cycles run a little longer than normal, about 24.2 hours on the average (Czeisler et al., 2005). Investigators aren't sure why this drift toward a longer cycle occurs, but it is not apparent under normal circumstances because daily exposure to light *readjusts* people's biological clocks.

In fact, researchers have worked out many of the details regarding how the day–night cycle resets biological clocks. When exposed to light, some receptors in the retina send direct inputs to a small structure in the hypothalamus called the *suprachiasmatic nucleus (SCN)* (Gooley & Saper, 2005). According to Simon Fraser University sleep researcher Ralph Mistlberger and his colleague Mary Harrington, the SCN sends signals to the nearby *pineal gland,* whose secretion of the hormone *melatonin* plays a key role in adjusting biological clocks (Harrington & Mistlberger, 2000).

Much of the research in this area has been focused on exploring the neural mechanisms linked with circadian rhythms (Rusak & Zucker, 1979). While research has implicated the role of this central circadian pacemaker, Dalhousie psychologist Benjamin Rusak suggests that mammalian circadian systems are more complex and that a more multifaceted structure might be a more appropriate model (Rusak, 1990). Circadian rhythms in humans actually appear to be regulated by *multiple* internal clocks, with a central pacemaker located in the SCN (Foster, 2004).

Ignoring Circadian Rhythms

What happens when you ignore your biological clock and go to sleep at an unusual time? Typically, the quality of your sleep suffers. Getting out of sync with your circadian rhythms also causes *jet lag*. When you fly across several time zones, your biological clock keeps time as usual, even though official clock time changes. You then go to sleep at the "wrong" time and are likely to experience difficulty falling asleep and poor-quality sleep. This inferior sleep, which can continue to occur for several days, can make you feel fatigued, sluggish, and irritable during the daytime (Arendt, Stone, & Skene, 2005). Moreover, chronic jet lag appears to be associated with measurable deficits in cognitive performance (Cho et al., 2000).

People differ in how quickly they can reset their biological clocks to compensate for jet lag, but a rough rule of thumb is that the readjustment process takes about a day for each time zone crossed (Moline, 1993). In addition, the speed of readjustment depends on the direction travelled. Generally, it's easier to fly westward and lengthen your day than it is to fly eastward and shorten it (Arendt et al., 2005). This east–west disparity in jet lag is sizable enough to have an impact on the performance of sports teams. Studies have found that teams flying westward perform significantly better than teams flying eastward in professional baseball (Recht, Lew, & Schwartz, 1995; see Figure 5.3) and college football (Worthen & Wade, 1999).

Of course, you don't have to hop on a jet to get out of sync with your biological clock. For many of us, going to work means something other than the standard workday. Nearly one-third of Canadian workers (30% of males and 26% of females) surveyed in 2001 reported that they worked on some type of shift-work schedule (Statistics Canada, 2002c). For most, shift work does not represent a choice but rather a job requirement. Some of you as students may be working part-time as shift workers to support your studies. If you are a shift worker, then you know it can have important effects on you. Studies show that workers get less total sleep and poorer-quality sleep when they go on rotating shifts. It can also increase their accident proneness and their mental and physical health (Cruz, dell Rocco, & Hackworth, 2000; Hossain & Shapiro, 1999). Canadian shift workers report more stress and a lower sense of mastery or control (Statistics Canada, 2002c), as well as lower-quality sleep (Williams, 2001). University of British Columbia psychologist Stanley Coren (1996) suggests that the sleep lost when the clock is set ahead in the spring shift to

Daylight Savings Time is associated with an increase in traffic accidents for the week after the switch.

Melatonin and Circadian Rhythms

As scientists have come to appreciate the importance of circadian rhythms, they have begun to look for new ways to help people harness their daily rhythms. A promising line of research has focused on giving people small doses of the hormone melatonin, which appears to regulate the human biological clock. The evidence from a number of studies suggests that melatonin *can* reduce the effects of jet lag by helping travellers resynchronize their biological clocks, but the research results are inconsistent (Arendt & Skene, 2005; Takahashi et al., 2002). Research also suggests that melatonin may have some utility as a mild sedative (Hughes & Badia, 1997; Lavie, 1997). The pattern of responsiveness to melatonin suggests that melatonin can facilitate daytime naps but may have limited value in the treatment of nighttime insomnia (Czeisler et al., 2000).

Web Link 5.1

NSF Center for Biological Timing
http://www.cbt.virginia.edu/

The role of biological rhythms in the functioning of living organisms has become an important focus of both medical and psychological research. This centre's online tutorial about biological timing, or "chronobiology," is a broad and well-illustrated introduction to this field.

REVIEW OF KEY POINTS

- The cycle of sleep and wakefulness is influenced considerably by circadian rhythms. Exposure to light resets biological clocks by affecting the activity of the suprachiasmatic nucleus and the pineal gland, which secretes the hormone melatonin.

- Ignoring your biological clock by going to sleep at an unusual time may have a negative effect on your sleep. Being out of sync with circadian rhythms is one reason for jet lag and for the unpleasant nature of rotating shift work.

- Melatonin may have value in efforts to alleviate the effects of jet lag and it may be an effective sedative in some situations.

Figure 5.3

Effects of direction travelled on the performance of professional baseball teams. To gain some insight into the determinants of jet lag, Recht, Lew, and Schwartz (1995) analyzed the performance of visiting teams in major league baseball over a three-year period. In baseball, visiting teams usually play 3–4 games in each destination city, so there are plenty of games in which the visiting team has not travelled the day before. These games, which served as a baseline for comparison, were won by the visiting team 46% of the time. Consistent with the observation that flying west creates less jet lag than flying east, visiting teams that flew westward the day (or night) before performed only slightly worse, winning 44% of the time. In contrast, visiting teams that flew eastward the day before won only 37% of their games, presumably because flying east and shortening one's day creates greater jet lag.

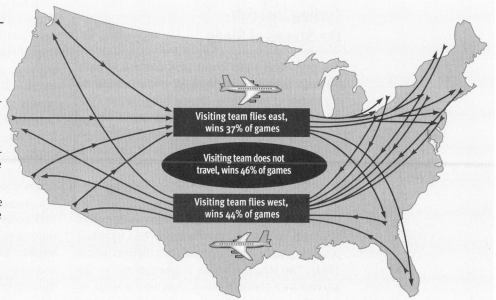

SOURCE: Adapted from Kalat, J.W. (2001). *Biological psychology.* Belmont, CA: Wadsworth. Reprinted by permission.

The Sleep and Waking Cycle

PREVIEW QUESTIONS

- What happens when people fall asleep?
- How is REM sleep different from non-REM sleep?
- How do sleep stages evolve over the course of a night's sleep?
- How does age affect patterns of sleeping?
- Which aspects of sleep are influenced by culture?
- Which brain centres and neurotransmitters are involved in the modulation of sleep?

Although it is a familiar state of consciousness, sleep is widely misunderstood. Generally, people consider sleep to be a single, uniform state of physical and mental inactivity, during which the brain is "shut down" (Dement, 2003). In reality, sleepers experience quite a bit of physical and mental activity throughout the night. Scientists have learned a great deal about sleep since the landmark discovery of REM sleep in the 1950s.

The advances in psychology's understanding of sleep are the result of hard work by researchers who have spent countless nighttime hours watching other people sleep. This work is done in sleep laboratories, where volunteer subjects come to spend the night. Sleep labs have one or more "bedrooms" in which the subjects retire, usually after being hooked up to a variety of physiological recording devices. In addition to an EEG, the other two crucial devices are an *electromyograph (EMG),* **which records muscular activity and tension, and an** *electrooculograph (EOG),* **which records eye movements** (Carskadon & Rechtschaffen, 2005). Typically, other instruments are also used to monitor heart rate, breathing, pulse rate, and body temperature. The researchers observe the sleeping subject through a window (or with a video camera) from an adjacent room, where they also monitor their elaborate physiological recording equipment (see the photo above). For most people, it takes just one night to adapt to the strange bedroom and the recording devices and return to their normal mode of sleeping (Carskadon & Dement, 1994).

Researchers in a sleep laboratory can observe subjects while using elaborate equipment to record physiological changes during sleep. This kind of research has disclosed that sleep is a complex series of physical and mental states.

the person has slept, where the person is in his or her circadian cycle, the amount of noise or light in the sleep environment, and the person's age, desire to fall asleep, boredom level, recent caffeine or drug intake, and stress level, among other things (Broughton, 1994). In any event, stage 1 is a brief transitional stage of light sleep that usually lasts only a few (1–7) minutes. Breathing and heart rate slow as muscle tension and body temperature decline. The alpha waves that probably dominated EEG activity just before falling asleep give way to lower-frequency EEG activity in which theta waves are prominent (see Figure 5.4). *Hypnic jerks,* those brief muscular contractions that occur as people fall asleep, generally occur during stage 1 drowsiness (Broughton, 1994).

As the sleeper descends through stages 2, 3, and 4 of the cycle, respiration rate, heart rate, muscle tension, and body temperature continue to decline. During stage 2, which typically lasts about 10–25 minutes, brief bursts of higher-frequency brain waves, called *sleep spindles,* appear against a background of mixed EEG activity (refer to Figure 5.4 once again). Gradually, brain waves become higher in amplitude and slower in frequency, as the body moves into a deeper form of sleep, called slow-wave sleep. **Slow-wave sleep (SWS) consists of sleep stages 3 and 4, during which high-amplitude, low-frequency delta waves become prominent in EEG recordings.** Typically, individuals reach slow-wave sleep in about a half-hour and stay there for roughly 30 minutes. Then the cycle reverses itself and the sleeper gradually moves back upward through the lighter stages. That's when things start to get especially interesting.

Cycling through the Stages of Sleep

Not only does sleep occur in a context of daily rhythms, but subtler rhythms are evident within the experience of sleep itself. During sleep, people cycle through a series of five stages. Let's take a look at what researchers have learned about the changes that occur during each of these stages (Carskadon & Dement, 2005).

Stages 1–4

Although it may only take a few minutes, the onset of sleep is gradual and there is no obvious transition point between wakefulness and sleep (Rechtschaffen, 1994). The length of time it takes people to fall asleep varies considerably. It depends on quite an array of factors, including how long it has been since

REM Sleep

When sleepers reach what should be stage 1 once again, they usually go into the *fifth* stage of sleep, which is most widely known as *REM sleep*. As we have seen, REM is an abbreviation for the *rapid eye movements* prominent during this stage of sleep. In a sleep lab, researchers use an electrooculograph to monitor these lateral (side-to-side) movements that occur beneath the sleeping person's closed eyelids. However, they can be seen with the naked eye if you closely watch someone in the REM stage of sleep (little ripples move back and forth across his or her closed eyelids).

REM sleep was discovered accidentally in the 1950s in Nathaniel Kleitman's lab at the University of Chicago (Aserinsky & Kleitman, 1953; Dement, 2005). After hooking sleep study participants to an apparatus designed to measure eye movements for the first time, the researchers noticed very rapid eye movements at some points during sleep. At first, they thought the rapid movements recorded by the machine were errors—due to using an old and possibly defective machine. Only when they decided to walk in and personally observe sleeping participants were they convinced the rapid eye movements were real. In retrospect, it is amazing that no one had discovered the rapid eye movements before. The term *REM sleep* was coined by grad student William Dement, who went on to become one of the world's foremost sleep researchers. The REM stage tends to be a "deep" stage of sleep in the conventional sense that people are relatively hard to awaken from it (although arousal thresholds vary during REM). The REM stage is also marked by irregular breathing and pulse rate. Muscle tone is extremely relaxed—so much so that bodily movements are minimal and the sleeper is virtually paralyzed. *Although REM is a relatively deep stage of sleep, EEG activity is dominated by high-frequency beta waves that resemble those observed when people are alert and awake* (see Figure 5.4 again).

This paradox is probably related to the association between REM sleep and dreaming. As noted earlier, when subjects are awakened during various stages of sleep and asked whether they are dreaming, most dream reports come from the REM stage (Dement, 1978; McCarley, 1994). Although REM dreams may be more frequent, vivid, and memorable (Pace-Schott, 2005), there is evidence to suggest that mentation or dreaming does occur in non-REM sleep periods too. Recent research by Tore Nielsen of l'Université de Montréal and his colleagues (Esposito, Nielsen, & Paquette, 2004; Nielsen, 2000) has begun to explore the similarities and differences between REM and non-REM dreaming. They have been interested in examining whether recall of dreams from both REM and non-REM sleep is explained better by assuming the existence of a single dream generator or two different dream generators.

Based on earlier research on waking states supporting a connection between lowered alpha wave rates and cognitive activity, Esposito and colleagues (2004) reasoned that a decrease in alpha power during sleep might be a "marker" of dreaming activity that is remembered upon being awakened from that particular sleep stage. If similar relationships were found between alpha power and mentation in both REM and non-REM sleep (in this case, stage 2 sleep), the researchers suggest that this would indicate support for a one-generator model. The authors conclude that their results provide some support for the one-generator model. This research is still in its early stages and the authors note existence of one potential confound in their research—the REM and stage 2 results came from different groups of participants, and the interpretation of the findings is complicated by potential inter-subject differences. An additional direction of this research would be to determine the nature of the mechanism that is responsible for the dream recall and brain wave effects (Esposito et al., 2004).

Carlyle Smith, a psychology professor at Trent University, is a prominent sleep researcher who has been active in examining the relations between brain

Figure 5.4

EEG patterns in sleep and wakefulness. Characteristic brain waves vary depending on one's state of consciousness. Generally, as people move from an awake state through deeper stages of sleep, their brain waves decrease in frequency (cycles per second) and increase in amplitude (height). However, brain waves during REM sleep resemble "wide-awake" brain waves.

SOURCE: Adapted from Hauri, P. (1982). *Current concepts: The sleep disorders.* Kalamazoo, MI: The Upjohn Company. Reprinted by permission.

**Figure labels (right side):**

Awake — Low-voltage, high-frequency beta waves

Drowsy — Alpha waves prominent

Theta waves

Stage 1 sleep — Theta waves prominent

Sleep spindle

Stage 2 sleep — Sleep spindles and mixed EEG activity

Slow-wave sleep (stage 3 and stage 4 sleep) — Progressively more delta waves (stage 4 shown)

REM sleep — Low-voltage, high-frequency waves

50 μV · 1 second

"Sleep deprivation is a major epidemic in our society. . . . Americans spend so much time and energy chasing the American dream, that they don't have much time left for actual dreaming."
WILLIAM DEMENT

functioning in sleep and memory (Smith, 1996, 2003). His research suggests that brain activity during sleep is central to consolidation of information acquired during the day. He also suggests that different stages of sleep may be implicated in memory for different types of tasks or information. For example, stage 2 sleep may be important for consolidation of procedural motor-type tasks, while REM sleep may be important for complex logic-type tasks (Nader & Smith, 2003; Smith & Fazekas, 1997).

While sleep is important for learning, it may be that different types of sleep are important for different types of learning. This is an important consideration given that there are changes in sleep as we age. Smith's current research is examining the links between age, sleep, and memory (Trent University, 2005).

To summarize, ***REM sleep* is a relatively deep stage of sleep marked by rapid eye movements, high-frequency, low-amplitude brain waves, and vivid dreaming.** It is such a special stage of sleep that the other four stages are often characterized simply as "non-REM sleep." ***Non-REM (NREM) sleep* consists of sleep stages 1 through 4, which are marked by an absence of rapid eye movements, relatively little dreaming, and varied EEG activity.**

Repeating the Cycle

During the course of a night, people usually repeat the sleep cycle about four times. As the night wears on, the cycle changes gradually. The first REM period is relatively short, lasting only a few minutes. Subsequent REM periods get progressively longer, peaking at around 40–60 minutes in length. Additionally, NREM intervals tend to get shorter, and descents into NREM stages usually become more shallow. These trends can be seen in Figure 5.5, which provides an overview of a typical night's sleep cycle. These trends mean that most slow-wave sleep occurs early in the sleep cycle and that REM sleep tends to pile up in the second half of the sleep cycle. Summing across the entire cycle, young adults typically spend about 20% of their sleep time in slow-wave sleep and another 20% in REM sleep.

Age Trends in Sleep

Age alters the sleep cycle. What we have described so far is the typical pattern for young adults. Children, however, display different patterns (Bootzin et al., 2001; Roffwarg, Muzio, & Dement, 1966). Newborns will sleep six to eight times in a 24-hour period, often

Figure 5.5

An overview of the cycle of sleep. The white line charts how a typical, healthy, young adult moves through the various stages of sleep during the course of a night. This diagram also shows how dreams and rapid eye movements tend to coincide with REM sleep, whereas posture changes occur between REM periods (because the body is nearly paralyzed during REM sleep). Notice how the person cycles into REM four times, as descents into NREM sleep get shallower and REM periods get longer. Thus, slow-wave sleep is prominent early in the night, while REM sleep dominates the second half of a night's sleep. Although these patterns are typical, keep in mind that sleep patterns vary from one person to another and that they change with age.

exceeding a total of 16 hours of sleep. Fortunately for parents, during the first several months much of this sleep begins to get consolidated into one particularly long nighttime sleep period (Webb, 1992a). Interestingly, infants spend much more of their sleep time in the REM stage than adults do. In the first few months, REM accounts for about 50% of babies' sleep, as compared to 20% of adults' sleep.

During the remainder of the first year, the REM portion of infants' sleep declines to roughly 30% (Ohayon et al., 2004). The REM portion of sleep continues to decrease gradually until it levels off at about 20% (see Figure 5.6). During adulthood, gradual, age-related changes in sleep continue. Although the proportion of REM sleep remains fairly stable (Bliwise, 2005), the percentage of slow-wave sleep declines dramatically and the percentage of time spent in stage 1 increases slightly, with these trends stronger in men than in women (Bliwise, 2005). These shifts toward lighter sleep *may* contribute to the increased frequency of nighttime awakenings seen among the elderly. As Figure 5.6 shows, the average amount of total sleep time also declines with advancing age. However, these averages mask important variability, as total sleep *increases* with age in a substantial minority of older people (Webb, 1992a).

Culture and Sleep

Although age clearly affects the nature and structure of sleep itself, the psychological and physiological experience of sleep does not appear to vary systematically across cultures. Cultural disparities in sleep are limited to more peripheral matters, such as sleeping arrangements and napping customs. For example, there are cultural differences in *co-sleeping,* the practice of children and parents sleeping together (McKenna, 1993). In modern Western societies, co-sleeping is actively discouraged. In contrast, co-sleeping is more widely accepted in Japanese culture, which emphasizes interdependence and group harmony (Latz et al., 1999). Around the world as a whole, co-sleeping is normative (Ball, Hooker, & Kelly, 2000). Strong pressure against co-sleeping appears to be largely an urban, Western phenomenon.

Napping practices also vary along cultural lines. In many societies, shops close and activities are curtailed in the afternoon to permit people to enjoy a one- to two-hour midday nap. These "siesta cultures" are found mostly in tropical regions of the world (Webb & Dinges, 1989). There, this practice is adaptive in that it allows people to avoid working during the hottest part of the day.

Web Link 5.2

The Sleep Well
http://www.stanford.edu/~dement/

Leading sleep researcher William Dement of Stanford University offers a major Internet resource centre on sleep and sleeping disorders.

The last REM period of the night has the fastest eye movements and may be the period from which dreams are best remembered.

Figure 5.6

Changes in sleep patterns over the life span. Both the total amount of sleep per night and the portion of sleep that is REM sleep change with age. Sleep patterns change most dramatically during infancy, with total sleep time and amount of REM sleep declining sharply in the first two years of life. After a noticeable drop in the average amount of sleep in adolescence, sleep patterns remain relatively stable, although total sleep and slow-wave sleep continue to decline gradually with age.

SOURCE: Adapted from an updated revision of a figure in Roffwarg, H. P., Muzio, J. N., & Dement, W. C. (1966). Ontogenetic development of human sleep-dream cycle. *Science, 152*, 604–609. Copyright © 1966 by the American Association for the Advancement of Science. Adapted and revised by permission of the authors.

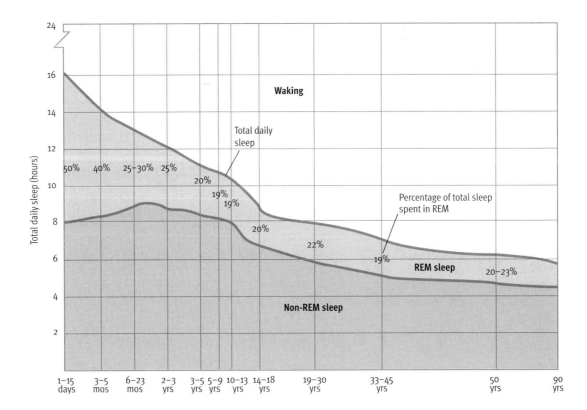

The Neural Bases of Sleep

The rhythm of sleep and waking appears to be regulated by subcortical structures that lie deep within the brain. One brain structure that is important to sleep and wakefulness is the *reticular formation* in the core of the brainstem (Steriade, 2005). **The *ascending reticular activating system (ARAS)* consists of the afferent fibres running through the reticular formation that influence physiological arousal.** As you can see in Figure 5.7, the ARAS projects diffusely into many areas of the cortex. When these ascending fibres are cut in the brainstem of a cat, the result is continuous sleep (Moruzzi, 1964). Electrical stimulation along the same pathways produces arousal and alertness.

Although the ARAS contributes to the neural regulation of sleep and waking, many other brain structures are also involved (Hobson, 1995). For example, activity in the pons and adjacent areas in the midbrain seems to be critical to the generation of REM sleep (Siegel, 2005). Specific areas in the medulla, thalamus, hypothalamus, and limbic system have also been implicated in the control of sleep and waking (see Figure 5.7). Thus, the ebb and flow of sleep and waking is regulated through activity in a *constellation* of interacting brain centres.

Efforts to identify the neurotransmitters involved in the regulation of sleep and waking have uncovered similar diffusion of responsibility. Serotonin and GABA appear to play especially important roles in the regulation of sleep. However, a variety of other neurotransmitters—norepinephrine, dopamine, and acetylcholine—clearly influence the course of sleep and arousal, and several other chemicals play contributing roles (Jones, 2005; Mendelson, 2001). In summary, no single structure in the brain serves as a "sleep centre," nor does any one neurotransmitter serve as a "sleep chemical." Instead, sleep depends on the interplay of many neural centres and neurotransmitters.

REVIEW OF KEY POINTS

- Research on sleep is typically done in laboratories where volunteers come to spend the night. Participants are hooked up to an EEG, EOG, EMG, and instruments that monitor heart rate, respiration, pulse rate, and body temperature.

- When people fall asleep, they evolve through a series of stages in cycles of approximately 90 minutes. Slow-wave sleep consists of stages 3 and 4, during which delta waves are prominent. During the REM stage, sleepers experience rapid eye movements, brain waves that are characteristic of waking thought, and vivid dreaming. The sleep cycle tends to be repeated about four times a night, as REM sleep gradually becomes more predominant and NREM sleep dwindles.

- The REM portion of sleep declines during childhood, levelling off at around 20%. During adulthood, slow-wave sleep declines. Total sleep time decreases for most elderly people, although it increases for some. Culture appears to have little impact on the physiological experience of sleep, but it does influence napping patterns and sleeping arrangements, such as co-sleeping.

- The neural bases of sleep are complex. Arousal depends on activity in the ascending reticular activating system, but a constellation of brain structures and neurotransmitters contribute to regulation of the sleep and waking cycle.

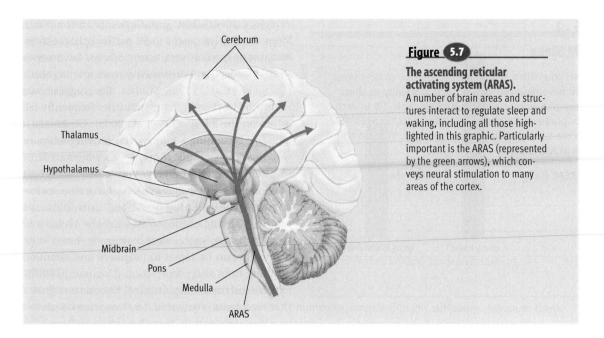

Figure **5.7**

The ascending reticular activating system (ARAS).
A number of brain areas and structures interact to regulate sleep and waking, including all those highlighted in this graphic. Particularly important is the ARAS (represented by the green arrows), which conveys neural stimulation to many areas of the cortex.

Cerebrum

Thalamus

Hypothalamus

Midbrain

Pons

Medulla

ARAS

Doing without: Sleep Deprivation

Scientific research on sleep deprivation presents something of a paradox. On the one hand, research suggests that sleep deprivation is not as detrimental as one might expect. On the other hand, evidence suggests that sleep deprivation may be a major social problem, undermining efficiency at work and contributing to countless accidents.

Complete Deprivation

What happens when people go completely without sleep for a period of days? As you might expect, complete deprivation of sleep has negative effects on participants' mood and on their performance on both cognitive and perceptual-motor tasks (Pilcher & Huffcutt, 1996). However, these negative effects tend to be modest, and many researchers have been impressed by how *well* sleep-deprived subjects can perform if they are motivated to do so (Anch et al., 1988). The effects of complete sleep deprivation would probably be more severe except that most people have a hard time going very long without sleep. Most experience great difficulty getting beyond a third or fourth sleepless day.

Partial Deprivation

Partial sleep deprivation, or *sleep restriction,* occurs when people make do with substantially less sleep than normal over a period of time. Partial deprivation occurs far more often in everyday life than complete sleep deprivation. Indeed, many sleep experts believe that much of North American society chronically suffers from partial sleep deprivation (Walsh,

Dement, & Dinges, 2005). It appears that more and more people are trying to squeeze additional waking hours out of their days as they attempt to juggle work, family, household, and school responsibilities, leading William Dement to comment that most of us "no longer know what it feels like to be fully alert" (Toufexis, 1990, p. 79).

How serious are the effects of partial sleep deprivation? Studies suggest that the effects depend on the amount of sleep lost and on the nature of the task at hand (Bonnet, 2000). Negative effects are most likely when subjects are asked to work on long-lasting, difficult, or monotonous tasks, or when subjects are asked to restrict their sleep to under five hours for many nights (Gillberg & Akerstedt, 1998). Interestingly, people often do not appreciate the degree to which sleep deprivation has a negative impact on their functioning, a finding that is apparent in our Featured Study for this chapter.

Our Featured Study is representative of a great deal of recent research suggesting that the effects of sleep deprivation are not as benign as widely believed. Studies indicate that partial sleep deprivation can impair individuals' attention, reaction time, motor coordination, and decision making (Dinges, Rogers, & Baynard, 2005). Evidence suggests that sleep deprivation contributes to errors in medical treatment by physicians in training (medical residents), who often work 80–100 hours a week without adequate rest (Weinger & Ancoli-Israel, 2002). Sleep deprivation has also been blamed for a large proportion of transportation accidents and mishaps in the workplace (Walsh et al., 2005). For example, sleepiness appears to be a contributing factor in roughly 20% of motor

PREVIEW QUESTIONS
- What are the effects of sleep deprivation?
- What is known about the causes and prevalence of insomnia?
- What is the role of sedative drugs in the treatment of insomnia?
- What are the symptoms of narcolepsy? Sleep apnea? Nightmares? Night terrors? Somnambulism?

A large number of traffic accidents occur because drivers get drowsy or fall asleep at the wheel. Although the effects of sleep deprivation seem innocuous, sleep loss can be deadly.

W W W

Web Link 5.3

National Sleep Foundation
http://www.sleepfoundation.org/

This attractive, well-organized site houses a great deal of information on sleep. Highlights include an interactive test to assess your sleep habits; electronic pamphlets on practical sleep topics, such as strategies for shift workers, the dangers of drowsy driving, and reducing jet lag; and extensive coverage of the full range of sleep disorders.

Figure 5.9

The effects of REM deprivation on sleep. This graph plots how often researchers had to awaken a subject over the course of three nights of REM deprivation. Notice how the awakenings rapidly became more frequent during the course of each night and from night to night. This pattern of awakenings illustrates how a REM-deprived subject tends to compensate by repeatedly slipping back into REM sleep.

SOURCE: Adapted from Borbely, A. (1986). *Secrets of sleep* (English translation). New York: Basic Books. Copyright © 1986 by Basic Books. Reprinted by permission of Basic Books, Inc.

problem to those who haven't struggled with it, but it can be a very unpleasant malady. Insomniacs have to endure the agony of watching their precious sleep time tick away as they toss and turn in restless frustration. Moreover, insomnia is associated with daytime fatigue, impaired functioning, an elevated risk for accidents, reduced productivity, absenteeism at work, depression, and increased health problems (Benca, 2001; Edinger & Means, 2005).

Prevalence Estimates of the prevalence of insomnia vary considerably because surveys have to depend on respondents' highly subjective judgments of whether their sleep is adequate. Another complicating consideration is that nearly everyone suffers *occasional* sleep difficulties because of stress, disruptions of biological rhythms, or other temporary circumstances. Fortunately, these problems clear up spontaneously for most people. Caveats aside, the best estimates suggest that about 34%–35% of adults report problems with insomnia and about half of these people (15%–17%) suffer from severe or fre-

quent insomnia (Zorick & Walsh, 2000). The prevalence of insomnia increases with age and is about 50% more common in women than in men (Partinen & Hublin, 2005).

Some people may suffer from "pseudo-insomnia," or *sleep state misperception,* which means that they just *think* they are getting an inadequate amount of sleep (Edinger & Krystal, 2003). When actually monitored in a sleep clinic, about 5% of insomniac patients show sound patterns of sleep (Hauri, 2000). In one well-known case of exaggerated complaining, a British insomniac claimed that he hadn't slept in 10 years! When invited to stay at a sleep clinic for observation, he seemed determined to prove his chronic sleeplessness. However, on the second night he nodded out for 20 minutes. By the fourth night, he could barely keep his eyes open, and soon he was snoring blissfully for hours (Oswald & Adam, 1980). Misperceptions of sleep efficiency are not unique to pseudo-insomniacs. Many people underestimate how much sleep they get (Reynolds et al., 1991). The discrepancy between individuals' feelings about how much they sleep and objective reality shows once again that states of consciousness are highly subjective.

Causes Insomnia has many causes (Hauri, 2002; Roehrs, Zorick, & Roth, 2000; Roth & Drake, 2004). In some cases, excessive anxiety and tension prevent relaxation and keep people awake. Insomnia is frequently a side effect of emotional problems, such as depression, or of significant stress, such as pressures at work. Understandably, health problems such as back pain, ulcers, and asthma can lead to insomnia. The use of certain drugs, especially such stimulants as cocaine and amphetamines, may also lead to problems in sleeping.

Treatment The most common approach to the treatment of insomnia is prescription of sedative drugs

were minimal and unenlightening. However, the participants' self-ratings yielded more interesting data, as the
sleep-deprived subjects rated their effort, concentration, and performance significantly *higher* than the nondeprived subjects did.

Discussion

Although the sleep-deprived group performed substantially worse on the cognitive test, their subjective estimates of their effort, concentration, and performance
were inconsistent with this reality. Thus, the investigators conclude that "college students are not aware of
the extent to which sleep deprivation impairs their
ability to complete cognitive tasks successfully" (p. 125).

Comment

This study was selected for its straightforward examination of a practical issue that is obviously relevant to students' lives. The negative impact of sleep deprivation
on the participants' cognitive functioning was striking.
The study also provides yet another demonstration that

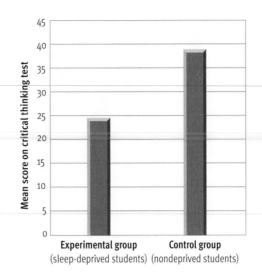

Figure 5.8

**Effect of sleep deprivation
on cognitive performance.**
Experimental subjects in the
Pilcher and Walters (1997)
study underwent 24 hours of
sleep deprivation prior to
taking the Watson-Glaser
Critical Thinking Appraisal.
As you can see, their performance on this cognitive test was
clearly inferior to that of the
control subjects, who had not
experienced sleep deprivation.

human experience is highly subjective. Although sleep-
deprived subjects showed clear impairment on an
objective measure of their cognitive performance, they
felt that their performance was fine. ■

laboratory studies, subjects were awakened over a
period of nights whenever they began to go into the
REM stage. These subjects usually got a decent
amount of sleep in NREM stages, but they were selectively deprived of REM sleep.

What are the effects of REM deprivation? The evidence indicates that it has little impact on daytime
functioning and task performance, but it *does* have
some interesting effects on subjects' patterns of
sleeping (Bonnet, 2005). As the nights go by in REM-
deprivation studies, it becomes necessary to awaken
the subjects more and more often to deprive them of
their REM sleep, because they spontaneously shift
into REM more and more frequently. In one study,
researchers had to awaken a subject 64 times by the
third night of REM deprivation, as shown in Figure 5.9
(Borbely, 1986). Furthermore, when a REM-deprivation
experiment comes to an end and subjects are allowed
to sleep without interruption, they experience a
"rebound effect." That is, they spend extra time in
REM periods for one to three nights to make up for
their REM deprivation (Bonnet, 2005).

Similar results have been observed when subjects
have been selectively deprived of slow-wave sleep
(Klerman, 1993). As the nights go by, more awakenings are required to prevent SWS, and after deprivation of SWS people experience a rebound effect
(Borbely & Achermann, 2005). In fact, by some standards, the need for slow-wave sleep appears to be even
more pressing than the need for REM sleep, which
may explain why, in a typical night's sleep, people get

lots of SWS first, and then load up on REM sleep
(Borbely, 1994). What do theorists make of these spontaneous pursuits of REM and slow-wave sleep? They
conclude that people must have specific *needs* for REM
and slow-wave sleep—and rather strong needs, at that
(Borbely & Achermann, 2000). As we discussed earlier,
some recent studies suggest that REM and perhaps
slow-wave sleep contribute to firming up learning that
takes place during the day—a process called *memory
consolidation* (Smith, 2003; Stickgold, 2005; Stickgold,
James, & Hobson, 2000; Stickgold et al., 2000).

Problems in the Night:
Sleep Disorders

Not everyone is able to consistently enjoy the luxury
of a good night's sleep. In this section we will briefly
discuss what is currently known about a variety of
sleep disorders.

Insomnia

Insomnia is the most common sleep disorder. ***Insomnia
refers to chronic problems in getting adequate sleep.***
It occurs in three basic patterns: (1) difficulty in falling
asleep initially, (2) difficulty in remaining asleep, and
(3) persistent early-morning awakening. Difficulty
falling asleep is the most common problem among
young people, whereas trouble staying asleep and early-
morning awakenings are the most common syndromes
among middle-aged and elderly people (Hublin &
Partinen, 2002). Insomnia may sound like a minor

A large number of traffic accidents occur because drivers get drowsy or fall asleep at the wheel. Although the effects of sleep deprivation seem innocuous, sleep loss can be deadly.

w (W) W

Web Link 5.3

National Sleep Foundation
http://www.sleepfoundation.org/
This attractive, well-organized site houses a great deal of information on sleep. Highlights include an interactive test to assess your sleep habits; electronic pamphlets on practical sleep topics, such as strategies for shift workers, the dangers of drowsy driving, and reducing jet lag; and extensive coverage of the full range of sleep disorders.

Figure 5.9

The effects of REM deprivation on sleep. This graph plots how often researchers had to awaken a subject over the course of three nights of REM deprivation. Notice how the awakenings rapidly became more frequent during the course of each night and from night to night. This pattern of awakenings illustrates how a REM-deprived subject tends to compensate by repeatedly slipping back into REM sleep.

SOURCE: Adapted from Borbely, A. (1986). *Secrets of sleep* (English translation). New York: Basic Books. Copyright © 1986 by Basic Books. Reprinted by permission of Basic Books, Inc.

problem to those who haven't struggled with it, but it can be a very unpleasant malady. Insomniacs have to endure the agony of watching their precious sleep time tick away as they toss and turn in restless frustration. Moreover, insomnia is associated with daytime fatigue, impaired functioning, an elevated risk for accidents, reduced productivity, absenteeism at work, depression, and increased health problems (Benca, 2001; Edinger & Means, 2005).

Prevalence Estimates of the prevalence of insomnia vary considerably because surveys have to depend on respondents' highly subjective judgments of whether their sleep is adequate. Another complicating consideration is that nearly everyone suffers *occasional* sleep difficulties because of stress, disruptions of biological rhythms, or other temporary circumstances. Fortunately, these problems clear up spontaneously for most people. Caveats aside, the best estimates suggest that about 34%–35% of adults report problems with insomnia and about half of these people (15%–17%) suffer from severe or fre-

quent insomnia (Zorick & Walsh, 2000). The prevalence of insomnia increases with age and is about 50% more common in women than in men (Partinen & Hublin, 2005).

Some people may suffer from "pseudo-insomnia," or *sleep state misperception,* which means that they just *think* they are getting an inadequate amount of sleep (Edinger & Krystal, 2003). When actually monitored in a sleep clinic, about 5% of insomniac patients show sound patterns of sleep (Hauri, 2000). In one well-known case of exaggerated complaining, a British insomniac claimed that he hadn't slept in 10 years! When invited to stay at a sleep clinic for observation, he seemed determined to prove his chronic sleeplessness. However, on the second night he nodded out for 20 minutes. By the fourth night, he could barely keep his eyes open, and soon he was snoring blissfully for hours (Oswald & Adam, 1980). Misperceptions of sleep efficiency are not unique to pseudo-insomniacs. Many people underestimate how much sleep they get (Reynolds et al., 1991). The discrepancy between individuals' feelings about how much they sleep and objective reality shows once again that states of consciousness are highly subjective.

Causes Insomnia has many causes (Hauri, 2002; Roehrs, Zorick, & Roth, 2000; Roth & Drake, 2004). In some cases, excessive anxiety and tension prevent relaxation and keep people awake. Insomnia is frequently a side effect of emotional problems, such as depression, or of significant stress, such as pressures at work. Understandably, health problems such as back pain, ulcers, and asthma can lead to insomnia. The use of certain drugs, especially such stimulants as cocaine and amphetamines, may also lead to problems in sleeping.

Treatment The most common approach to the treatment of insomnia is prescription of sedative drugs

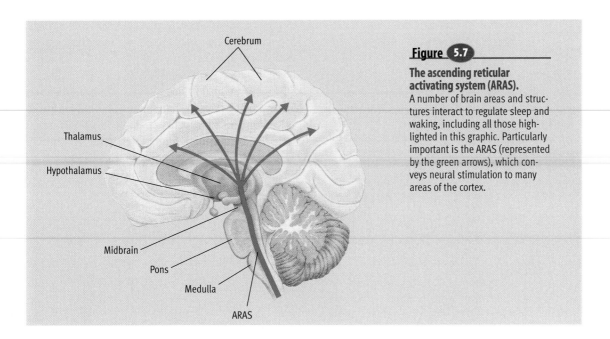

Figure 5.7

The ascending reticular activating system (ARAS).
A number of brain areas and structures interact to regulate sleep and waking, including all those highlighted in this graphic. Particularly important is the ARAS (represented by the green arrows), which conveys neural stimulation to many areas of the cortex.

Labels: Cerebrum, Thalamus, Hypothalamus, Midbrain, Pons, Medulla, ARAS

Doing without: Sleep Deprivation

Scientific research on sleep deprivation presents something of a paradox. On the one hand, research suggests that sleep deprivation is not as detrimental as one might expect. On the other hand, evidence suggests that sleep deprivation may be a major social problem, undermining efficiency at work and contributing to countless accidents.

Complete Deprivation

What happens when people go completely without sleep for a period of days? As you might expect, complete deprivation of sleep has negative effects on participants' mood and on their performance on both cognitive and perceptual-motor tasks (Pilcher & Huffcutt, 1996). However, these negative effects tend to be modest, and many researchers have been impressed by how *well* sleep-deprived subjects can perform if they are motivated to do so (Anch et al., 1988). The effects of complete sleep deprivation would probably be more severe except that most people have a hard time going very long without sleep. Most experience great difficulty getting beyond a third or fourth sleepless day.

Partial Deprivation

Partial sleep deprivation, or *sleep restriction,* occurs when people make do with substantially less sleep than normal over a period of time. Partial deprivation occurs far more often in everyday life than complete sleep deprivation. Indeed, many sleep experts believe that much of North American society chronically suffers from partial sleep deprivation (Walsh,

Dement, & Dinges, 2005). It appears that more and more people are trying to squeeze additional waking hours out of their days as they attempt to juggle work, family, household, and school responsibilities, leading William Dement to comment that most of us "no longer know what it feels like to be fully alert" (Toufexis, 1990, p. 79).

How serious are the effects of partial sleep deprivation? Studies suggest that the effects depend on the amount of sleep lost and on the nature of the task at hand (Bonnet, 2000). Negative effects are most likely when subjects are asked to work on long-lasting, difficult, or monotonous tasks, or when subjects are asked to restrict their sleep to under five hours for many nights (Gillberg & Akerstedt, 1998). Interestingly, people often do not appreciate the degree to which sleep deprivation has a negative impact on their functioning, a finding that is apparent in our Featured Study for this chapter.

Our Featured Study is representative of a great deal of recent research suggesting that the effects of sleep deprivation are not as benign as widely believed. Studies indicate that partial sleep deprivation can impair individuals' attention, reaction time, motor coordination, and decision making (Dinges, Rogers, & Baynard, 2005). Evidence suggests that sleep deprivation contributes to errors in medical treatment by physicians in training (medical residents), who often work 80–100 hours a week without adequate rest (Weinger & Ancoli-Israel, 2002). Sleep deprivation has also been blamed for a large proportion of transportation accidents and mishaps in the workplace (Walsh et al., 2005). For example, sleepiness appears to be a contributing factor in roughly 20% of motor

PREVIEW QUESTIONS

● What are the effects of sleep deprivation?

● What is known about the causes and prevalence of insomnia?

● What is the role of sedative drugs in the treatment of insomnia?

● What are the symptoms of narcolepsy? Sleep apnea? Nightmares? Night terrors? Somnambulism?

Comparing REM and NREM Sleep

A table here could have provided you with a systematic comparison of REM sleep and NREM sleep, but that would have deprived you of the opportunity to check your understanding of these sleep phases by creating your own table. Fill in each of the blanks below with a word or phrase highlighting the differences between REM and NREM sleep with regard to the various characteristics specified. You can find the answers in the back of the book in Appendix A.

Characteristic	REM sleep	NREM sleep
1. Type of EEG activity		
2. Eye movements		
3. Dreaming		
4. Depth (difficulty in awakening)		
5. Percentage of total sleep (in adults)		
6. Increases or decreases (as percentage of sleep) during childhood		
7. Timing in sleep cycle (dominates early or late)		

vehicle accidents (MacLean, Davies, & Thiele, 2003). Sleep deprivation seems to be particularly problematic among truck drivers, young drivers, drivers with sleep disorders, and drivers who work rotating shifts (Lyznicki et al., 1998). Studies also suggest that nighttime workers in many industries frequently fall asleep on the job (Roehrs et al., 2005). Obviously, if a person is running a punch press, driving a bus, or working as an air traffic controller, a momentary lapse in attention could be very, very costly. In recent years, a number of major disasters, such as the nuclear accidents at Three Mile Island and Chernobyl, the running aground of the Exxon *Valdez* in Alaska, and the *Challenger* space shuttle tragedy have been blamed in part on lapses in judgment and attention resulting from sleep deprivation (Doghramji, 2001). Experts such as Stanley Coren (1996) have *estimated* that accidents attributed to drowsiness induced by sleep deprivation cost the U.S. economy over US$56 billion annually, lead to the loss of over 52 million work days each year, and result in over 24 000 deaths per year.

Selective Deprivation

The unique quality of REM sleep led researchers to look into the effects of a special type of partial sleep deprivation—*selective deprivation*. In a number of

FEATURED STUDY

Gauging the Impact of Sleep Deprivation in College Students

Investigators: June J. Pilcher and Amy S. Walters (Bradley University)

Source: How sleep deprivation affects psychological variables related to college students' cognitive performance. *Journal of American College Health*, 1997, *46*, 121–126.

Whether it's because they want to fit in more time for partying or for studying, university and college students routinely deprive themselves of sleep. This study assessed the effects of 24 hours of sleep deprivation on students' cognitive performance and attempted to identify some factors, such as negative mood or poor attention, that might contribute to any decrements in cognitive functioning. The investigators also wanted to see whether sleep deprivation altered participants' ability to make accurate assessments of their concentration, effort, and performance.

Method

Participants. Volunteers were solicited from five psychology classes. Of the original 65 volunteers, 44 (26 women and 18 men) completed the study. Their mean age was 20.5 years.

Measures. Cognitive performance was evaluated with the Watson-Glaser Critical Thinking Appraisal, a challenging standardized test that resembles the normal tests college students encounter. Mood was assessed with the Profile of Mood States, and attention was meas-

ured with the Cognitive Interference Questionnaire. The participants also rated their effort, concentration, and performance on seven-point scales.

Procedure. After a normal day with no napping, participants reported to a sleep lab at 10 P.M. on a Friday night. At that time, the students were randomly assigned to the experimental (sleep-deprived) and control (nondeprived) groups. Members of the control group were sent home and instructed to get about eight hours of sleep. The sleep-deprived subjects remained at the lab, where they watched movies, played video and board games, and worked on personal projects, under the supervision of research assistants. The participants in both groups completed the various tests and other measures on Saturday at 10 A.M.

Results

As anticipated, the sleep-deprived group scored significantly lower on the measure of cognitive performance (see Figure 5.8). Contrary to expectation, the differences between the two groups on the Profile of Mood States and the Cognitive Interference Questionnaire (sleeping pills). *Benzodiazepine medications,* which exert their effects at GABA synapses, are the most widely prescribed sedatives. These drugs are fairly effective in helping people fall asleep more quickly, and they reduce nighttime awakenings and increase total sleep (Mendelson, 2005). Nonetheless, sedative drugs may be used to combat insomnia *too* frequently. Many sleep experts argue that in the past physicians prescribed sleeping pills far too readily. As a result of this criticism, prescriptions for sleeping pills have declined significantly in recent decades (Walsh & Scweitzer, 1999). Nonetheless, about 5%–15% of adults still use sleep medication with some regularity (Hublin & Partinen, 2002).

Sedatives can be a poor long-term solution for insomnia for a number of reasons (Roehrs & Roth, 2000; Wesson et al., 2005). One problem is that sedatives have carryover effects that can make people drowsy and sluggish the next day and can lead to memory decrements. They can also cause an overdose in combination with alcohol or opiate drugs. Although the abuse of sleeping medications appears to be less common than widely assumed, there are legitimate concerns about people becoming physically dependent on sedatives (Ballenger, 2000). Moreover, with continued use sedatives gradually become less effective, so some people increase their dose to higher levels, creating a vicious circle of escalating dependency and daytime sluggishness (Lader, 2002; see Figure 5.10). Ironically, most sedatives also interfere with the normal cycle of sleep. Although they promote sleep, most sedatives decrease the proportion of time spent in slow-wave sleep, and some of the older drugs also reduce REM sleep (Nishino, Mignot, & Dement, 1995). Fortunately, the newer generation of sedatives such as zolpidem (trade name: Ambien) reduce some of the problems associated with traditional sleeping pills (Sanger, 2004). People suffering from insomnia can also turn to melatonin, the hormone that has been used to treat jet lag, which is available over the counter in the United States. Research indicates that melatonin can function as a mild sedative and that it has some value in the treatment of insomnia (Turck & Gillete, 2004).

In conclusion, sedatives *do* have an important place in the treatment of insomnia, but they need to be used cautiously and conservatively. They should be used primarily for short-term treatment (two to four weeks) of sleep problems. Beyond discouraging overreliance on drugs, it is difficult to generalize about how insomnia should be treated, because its many causes call for different solutions.

Treatment programs based in psychology have also been shown to be useful. Relaxation procedures and behavioural interventions can be helpful for many individuals (Morin, 2002, 2005; Stepanski, 2000). Recent studies suggest that behavioural treatments are just as effective as medication in the short term and that behavioural interventions produce more long-lasting benefits than drug therapies (Morin et al., 1999; Smith et al., 2002). Charles Morin and his colleagues at Laval University in Montreal have been actively involved in exploring the effects of psychological treatments such as cognitive behavioural therapy (CBT) for insomnia (Morin, Bastien, & Savard, 2003). In a meta-analysis of recent clinical trials, they concluded that CBT can have real benefits for many individuals suffering from insomnia. They suggest that as many as 70–80% of individuals suffering from primary insomnia may benefit in some way from CBT-based treatment. They caution, however, that not all become good sleepers. Cognitive therapies generally emphasize recognizing and changing negative thoughts and maladaptive beliefs. Some additional insights about how to combat insomnia are presented in the Personal Application at the end of this chapter. Cognitive behavioural therapy is discussed in greater detail in Chapter 15.

Other Sleep Problems

Although insomnia is the most common difficulty associated with sleep, people are plagued by many other types of sleep problems as well. Let's briefly look at the symptoms, causes, and prevalence of five additional sleep problems, as described by Kryger, Roth, and Dement (2005) and Bootzin et al. (2001).

Narcolepsy **is a disease marked by sudden and irresistible onsets of sleep during normal waking periods.** A person suffering from narcolepsy goes directly from wakefulness into REM sleep, usually for a

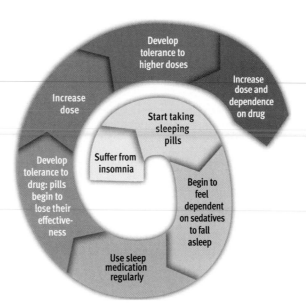

Figure 5.10

The vicious circle of dependence on sleeping pills.
Because of the body's ability to develop tolerance to drugs, using sedatives routinely to "cure" insomnia can lead to a vicious circle of escalating dependency as larger and larger doses of the sedative are needed to produce the same effect.

Web Link 5.4

Sleep Medicine Homepage
http://www.users.cloud9.net/~thorpy/

This site, assembled by sleep–wake specialist Michael J. Thorpy (Montefiore Medical Center), brings together a broad range of Internet links regarding sleep in all its aspects, as well as clinical problems associated with disruptions in normal sleep and waking patterns.

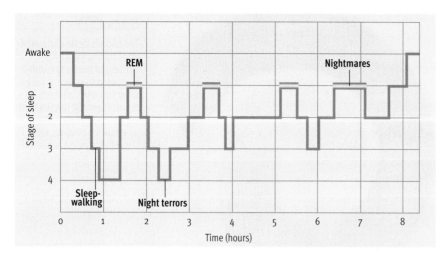

Figure 5.11

Sleep problems and the cycle of sleep. Different sleep problems tend to occur at different points in the sleep cycle. Whereas sleepwalking and night terrors are associated with slow-wave sleep, nightmares are associated with the heightened dream activity of REM sleep.

short period of time (10–20 minutes). This is a potentially dangerous condition, since some victims fall asleep instantly, even while driving a car or operating machinery. Narcolepsy is relatively infrequent, as it is seen in only about 0.05% of the population (Partinen & Hublin, 2005). Its causes are not well understood, but some people appear to be genetically predisposed to the disease (Mignot, 2000). Stimulant drugs have been used to treat this condition with modest success (Guilleminault & Fromherz, 2005). But as you will see in our upcoming discussion of drugs, stimulants carry many problems of their own.

Sleep apnea **involves frequent, reflexive gasping for air that awakens a person and disrupts sleep.** Some victims are awakened from their sleep hundreds of times a night. Apnea occurs when a person literally stops breathing for a minimum of 10 seconds. This disorder, which is usually accompanied by loud snoring, is seen in about 2% of women and about 4% of men between the ages of 30 and 60 (Bassiri & Guilleminault, 2000). As you might expect, sleep apnea often leads to insomnia as a side effect. Apnea may be treated with surgery or drug therapy.

Nightmares **are anxiety-arousing dreams that lead to awakening, usually from REM sleep** (see Figure 5.11). Typically, a person who awakens from a nightmare recalls a vivid dream and may have difficulty getting back to sleep. There is evidence that nightmares are associated with measures of an individual's well-being. Montreal psychologists and sleep researchers A. L. Zadra and D. C. Donderi (2000) found significant correlations between number of nightmares and measures of well-being, including neuroticism, trait anxiety, state anxiety, and depression. Although about 10% of adults have occasional nightmares, these frightening episodes are mainly a problem among children. Most youngsters have occasional nightmares, but *persistent* nightmares may reflect an emotional disturbance. If a child's nightmares are frequent and unpleasant, counselling may

prove helpful. Otherwise, treatment is unnecessary, as most children outgrow the problem.

Night terrors **(also called sleep terrors) are abrupt awakenings from NREM sleep accompanied by intense autonomic arousal and feelings of panic.** Night terrors, which can produce remarkable accelerations of heart rate, usually occur during stage 4 sleep early in the night, as shown in Figure 5.11 (Nielsen & Zadra, 2000). Victims typically let out a piercing cry, bolt upright, and then stare into space. They do not usually recall a coherent dream, although they may remember a simple, frightening image. The panic normally fades quickly, and a return to sleep is fairly easy. Night terrors occur in adults, but they are especially common in children ages three to eight. Night terrors are *not* indicative of an emotional disturbance. Treatment may not be necessary, as night terrors are often a temporary problem.

Somnambulism, **or sleepwalking, occurs when a person arises and wanders about while remaining asleep.** Sleepwalking tends to occur during the first two hours of sleep, when individuals are in slow-wave sleep (see Figure 5.11). Episodes may last from 15 seconds to 30 minutes (Aldrich, 2000). Sleepwalkers may awaken during their journey, or they may return to bed without any recollection of their excursion. The causes of this unusual disorder are unknown, although it appears to have a genetic predisposition (Keefauver & Guilleminault, 1994). Sleepwalking does not appear to be a manifestation of underlying emotional or psychological problems (Mahowald, 1993). However, sleepwalkers *are* prone to accidents. In light of this reality, it is important to note that, contrary to popular myth, it is safe to awaken people (gently) from a sleepwalking episode—much safer than letting them wander about.

REVIEW OF KEY POINTS

- The effects of sleep deprivation depend on a variety of factors. Our Featured Study showed that college students underestimate the impact of sleep deprivation. Increased sleepiness can be a significant problem that appears to contribute to many transportation accidents and mishaps at work. Research on selective sleep deprivation suggests that people need REM sleep and slow-wave sleep.

- Many people are troubled by sleep disorders. Insomnia has a variety of causes. Sleeping pills generally are a poor solution. The optimal treatment for insomnia depends on its apparent cause.

- Narcolepsy is a disease marked by sudden, irresistible onsets of sleep during normal waking periods. Sleep apnea involves frequent gasping for air, which occurs when people stop breathing. Night terrors are abrupt awakenings from NREM sleep accompanied by panic, whereas nightmares are anxiety-arousing dreams that typically awaken one from REM sleep. Somnambulism typically occurs during slow-wave sleep.

The World of Dreams

For the most part, dreams are not taken very seriously in Western societies. Paradoxically, though, Robert Van de Castle (1994) points out that dreams have sometimes changed the world. For example, Van de Castle describes how René Descartes's philosophy of dualism, Frederick Banting's discovery of insulin, Elias Howe's refinement of the sewing machine, Mohandas Gandhi's strategy of nonviolent protest, and Lyndon Johnson's withdrawal from the 1968 U.S. presidential race were all inspired by dreams. He also explains how Mary Shelley's *Frankenstein* and Robert Louis Stevenson's *The Strange Case of Dr. Jekyll and Mr. Hyde* emerged out of their dream experiences. In his wide-ranging discussion, Van de Castle also relates how the Surrealist painter Salvador Dali characterized his works as "dream photographs," and how legendary filmmakers Ingmar Bergman, Orson Welles, and Federico Fellini all drew on their dreams in making their films. Thus, Van de Castle concludes that "dreams have had a dramatic influence on almost every important aspect of our culture and history" (p. 10).

What exactly is a dream? This question is more complex and controversial than you might guess (Pagel et al., 2001). The conventional view is that dreams are mental experiences during REM sleep that have a storylike quality, include vivid visual imagery, are often bizarre, and are regarded as perceptually real by the dreamer (Antrobus, 1993). However, theorists have begun to question virtually every aspect of this characterization. Decades of research on the contents of dreams, which we will discuss momentarily, has shown that dreams are not as bizarre as widely assumed (Cartwright, 1994). Recent years have seen renewed interest in the fact that dreams are not the exclusive property of REM sleep (Antrobus, 2000). Moreover, studies that have focused on dream reports from non-REM stages of sleep have found that these dreams appear to be less vivid, visual, and storylike than REM dreams (Verdone, 1993). And research suggests that dreamers realize they are dreaming more often than previously thought and that mental processes during sleep are more similar to waking thought processes than is widely assumed (Kahan & LaBerge, 1994, 1996). Thus, the concept of dreaming is undergoing some revision in scientific circles.

The Contents of Dreams

What do people dream about? Overall, dreams are not as exciting as advertised. Perhaps dreams are seen as exotic because people are more likely to remember their more bizarre nighttime dramas (De Koninck, 2000). After analyzing the contents of more than 10 000 dreams, Calvin Hall (1966) concluded that most dreams are relatively mundane. They tend to unfold in familiar settings with a cast of characters dominated by family, friends, and colleagues.

Certain themes tend to be more common than others in dreams. In a large recent study, sleep researchers from the University of Montreal, Trent University, and the University of Alberta administered the Typical Dreams Questionnaire to over 1000 first-year Canadian university students. The dream themes and their frequency reported by those students are shown in Figure 5.12.

Take a look at the results in Figure 5.12. Do the dreams of these students seem similar to yours? The most frequent types of dreams related to "being chased or pursued, but not physically injured" and "sexual experiences." In addition to the general frequency of different types of dreams, the researchers obtained several other interesting results. There were significant differences between males and females. Several dream types demonstrated gender differences with the affective tone of the dreams differentiating males and females. The dreams distinctly associated with males tended to be positive in nature, while those associated with females tended to be more negative, including dreams with themes related to phobias (snakes, spiders), performance anxiety (failure), and control (loss of control). There were also some differences in dream prevalence across student samples. For example, the theme of "being half awake and paralyzed" distinguished McGill students from the other samples, and the theme of "finding money" differentiated students from Alberta. Participants were also asked how many nightmares they recalled and, on average, they recalled almost one every two weeks! Overall, however, the study revealed substantial consistency of dream content over age, region, and gender.

Relatively little research has been done on developmental trends in dream reports, but the available data suggest that children's dreams are different from adults' dreams (Foulkes, 1982, 1999). For one thing, the rate of dream recall after REM awakenings is only 20%–30% until ages 9–11, when the recall rate begins to approach adult levels (typically around 80%). Dream reports from children under age five mostly consist of static, bland images with no storyline.

PREVIEW QUESTIONS

● What is a dream, and how are views on this question changing?
● What is known about the contents of people's dreams?
● Can external events affect the content of dreams?
● How does culture affect dream recall and dream content?
● How do the Freudian, cognitive, and activation-synthesis models view dreams?

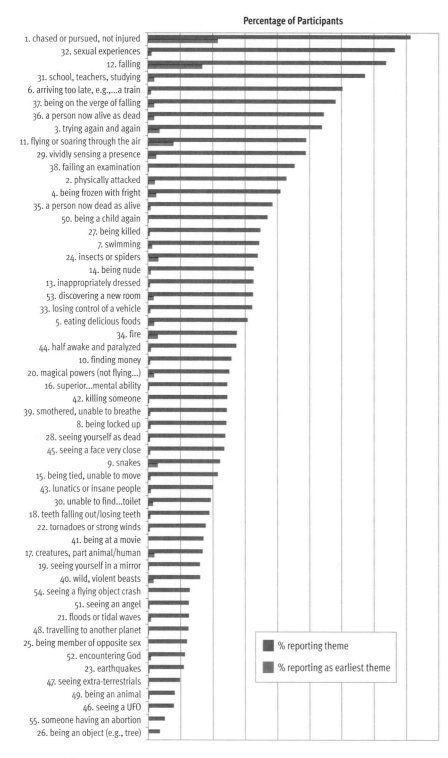

Percentage of Participants

1. chased or pursued, not injured
32. sexual experiences
12. falling
31. school, teachers, studying
6. arriving too late, e.g.,...a train
37. being on the verge of falling
36. a person now alive as dead
3. trying again and again
11. flying or soaring through the air
29. vividly sensing a presence
38. failing an examination
2. physically attacked
4. being frozen with fright
35. a person now dead as alive
50. being a child again
27. being killed
7. swimming
24. insects or spiders
14. being nude
13. inappropriately dressed
53. discovering a new room
33. losing control of a vehicle
5. eating delicious foods
34. fire
44. half awake and paralyzed
10. finding money
20. magical powers (not flying...)
16. superior...mental ability
42. killing someone
39. smothered, unable to breathe
8. being locked up
28. seeing yourself as dead
45. seeing a face very close
9. snakes
15. being tied, unable to move
43. lunatics or insane people
30. unable to find...toilet
18. teeth falling out/losing teeth
22. tornadoes or strong winds
41. being at a movie
17. creatures, part animal/human
19. seeing yourself in a mirror
40. wild, violent beasts
54. seeing a flying object crash
51. seeing an angel
21. floods or tidal waves
48. travelling to another planet
25. being member of opposite sex
52. encountering God
23. earthquakes
47. seeing extra-terrestrials
49. being an animal
46. seeing a UFO
55. someone having an abortion
26. being an object (e.g., tree)

■ % reporting theme
■ % reporting as earliest theme

Figure 5.12

The typical dreams of Canadian university students. This figure shows the percentage of participants reporting each of the 55 dream themes.

Source: Nielsen, T.A., Zadra, A., Simard, V., Saucier, S., Stenstrom, P., Smith, C., & Kuiken, D. (2003). The Typical Dreams of Canadian University Students. *Dreaming, Vol. 13*, Issue 4, p. 216. Copyright © 2003 by the American Psychological Association. Reprinted with permission.

Children ages five to eight report dream narratives, but they are not well developed, and common adult themes of aggression and misfortune are notably infrequent. The contents of children's dreams don't become adultlike until around ages 11–13. These findings suggest that dreaming is a cognitive ability that develops gradually, like other cognitive abilities.

Links between Dreams and Waking Life

Though dreams seem to belong in a world of their own, what people dream about is affected by what is going on in their lives (Kramer, 1994). If you're struggling with financial problems, worried about an upcoming exam, or sexually attracted to a classmate, these themes may very well show up in your dreams. As Domhoff (2001) puts it, "dream content in general is continuous with waking conceptions and emotional preoccupations" (p. 13). Does stress show up in dreams? Does the stress of exams show up in the dreams of students? Answers to the effect of stress on stress-themed content seem to be mixed. In one recent study, University of Ottawa researchers found that students who were experiencing stress concerning upcoming exams (Delorme, Lortie-Lussier, & De Koninck, 2002) did not necessarily have more exam-themed dreams. The relation of daily stress to dreams may depend on a variety of factors, including the nature of the stressor. The authors note that not all stressors are the same, and that particular types of stressors such as imminent surgery might be more likely to affect dream content than impending exams. It seems that not all daytime events are equally likely to affect dream content. Freud noticed long ago that the contents of waking life often tended to spill into dreams; he labelled this spillover the *day residue*.

On occasion, the content of dreams can also be affected by stimuli experienced while one is dreaming (De Koninck, 2000). For example, William Dement sprayed water on one hand of sleeping subjects while they were in the REM stage (Dement & Wolpert, 1958). Subjects who weren't awakened by the water were awakened by the experimenter a short time later and asked what they had been dreaming about. Dement found that 42% of the subjects had incorporated the water into their dreams. They said that they had dreamt that they were in rainfalls, floods, baths, swimming pools, and the like. Some people report that they occasionally experience the same sort of phenomenon at home when the sound of their alarm clock fails to awaken them. The alarm is incorporated into their dream as a loud engine or a siren, for instance. As with day residue, the incorporation of external stimuli into dreams shows that people's dream world is not entirely separate from their real world.

Sometimes people may realize they are dreaming while still in the dream state. These are often referred to as "lucid dreams." In some of these dreams, the dreamer may be able to exert some control over the dream. According to members of the Dream and Nightmare Laboratory established in Montreal's Sacré-Coeur Hospital in 1991 (Lucid Dreaming, 2005), it has been suggested that lucid dreaming might be useful in the treatment of nightmares. To be useful, however, the therapist must be able to somehow control or influence the onset of the lucid dreams. Thus, one of the issues here is the induction of lucid dreaming for therapeutic use. Antonio Zadra, a University of Montreal psychologist and member of the Dream and Nightmare Laboratory, has done research on lucid dreaming induction (Zadra, Donderi, & Pihl, 1992). It may be easier to induce lucid dreaming in some individuals than in others.

Culture and Dreams

Striking cross-cultural variations occur in beliefs about the nature of dreams and the importance attributed to them. In modern Western society, people typically make a distinction between the "real" world they experience while awake and the "imaginary" world they experience while dreaming. Some people realize that events in the real world can affect their dreams, but few believe that events in their dreams hold any significance for their waking life. Although a small minority of individuals take their dreams seriously, in Western cultures dreams are largely written off as insignificant, meaningless meanderings of the unconscious (Tart, 1988).

In many non-Western cultures, however, dreams are viewed as important sources of information about oneself, about the future, or about the spiritual world (Kracke, 1991). Although no culture confuses dreams with waking reality, many view events in dreams as another type of reality that may be just as important as, or perhaps even more important than,

events experienced while awake. Among Australian aborigines, for example, "Dreaming is the focal point of traditional aboriginal existence and simultaneously determines their way of life, their culture, and their relationship to the physical and spiritual environment" (Dawson, 1993, p. 1).

In regard to dream content, both similarities and differences occur across cultures in the types of dreams that people report (Domhoff, 2005b; Hunt, 1989). Some basic dream themes appear to be nearly universal (falling, being pursued, having sex). However, the contents of dreams vary some from one culture to another because people in different societies deal with different worlds while awake. For example, in a 1950 study of the Siriono, a hunting-and-gathering people of the Amazon who were almost always hungry and spent most of their time in a grim search for food, *half* of the reported dreams focused on hunting, gathering, and eating food (D'Andrade, 1961). Shared systems for interpreting the contents of dreams also vary from one society to another. Table 5.2 lists a number of common dream interpretations among the Toraja of Indonesia (Hollan, 1989). Although some of these interpretations (example: standing on mountaintop = becoming a leader) might be common in other societies, some clearly are peculiar to Toraja society (example: buffalo in the rice fields = rats will eat the rice harvest).

Theories of Dreaming

Many theories have been proposed to explain why people dream. Sigmund Freud (1900), who analyzed clients' dreams in therapy, believed that the principal purpose of dreams is *wish fulfillment*. He thought that people fulfill ungratified needs from waking hours through wishful thinking in dreams. For

❝*[Dreams are] the royal road to the unconscious.*❞
SIGMUND FREUD

Table 5.2 Examples of Common Dream Interpretations among the Toraja of Indonesia

"Good" Dreams	Interpretation	"Bad" Dreams	Interpretation
Receive gold	Good rice harvest	Buffalo in the rice fields	Rats will eat rice harvest
Carry pig or buffalo meat	Good rice harvest	Naked	Get sick
Act "crazy"	Receive wealth	Enter burial cave	Die
Objects are thrown at dreamer	Rain will fall	Carried off by an ancestor	Die
Stand on mountaintop	Become a leader	Objects are stolen/lost/carried away	Lose those objects
Steal objects	Receive those objects/become wealthy		
Swim in ocean or river	Receive wealth	House burns or is destroyed	Lose wealth/become poor
Jump over or cross water	Become wise/clever		
Gored by a buffalo	Buy a buffalo		

SOURCE: Adapted from Hollan, D. (1989). The personal use of dream beliefs in the Toraja Highlands. *Ethos, 17*, 166–186. Copyright © 1989 by the American Anthropological Association. Reproduced by permission. Not for further reproduction.

"One function of dreams may be to restore our sense of competence. . . . It is also probable that in times of stress, dreams have more work to do in resolving our problems and are thus more salient and memorable."
ROSALIND CARTWRIGHT

Dr. Cartwright obtained her undergraduate and master's training at the University of Toronto. She is currently Chair of Psychology at Rush-Presbyterian-St. Luke's Medical Centre in Chicago and serves on the Scientific and Professional Advisory Board of the False Memory Syndrome Foundation (http://www.fmsfonline.org).

example, someone who is sexually frustrated might have highly erotic dreams, while an unsuccessful person might dream about great accomplishments. Although these examples involve blatant wishful thinking, Freud asserted that the wish-fulfilling quality of many dreams may not be readily apparent because the true meaning of dreams may be disguised. Freud's influential theory sounded plausible when it was proposed over 100 years ago, but research has not provided much support for Freud's conception of dreaming (Fisher & Greenberg, 1996).

Other theorists, such as Rosalind Cartwright (1977; Cartwright & Lamberg, 1992), have proposed that dreams provide an opportunity to work through everyday problems. According to her *cognitive, problem-solving view,* there is considerable continuity between waking and sleeping thought. Proponents of this view believe that dreams allow people to engage in creative thinking about problems because dreams are not restrained by logic or realism. Consistent with this view, Cartwright (1991) has found that women going through divorce frequently dream about divorce-related problems. Cartwright's analysis is thought provoking, but critics point out that just because people dream about problems from their waking life doesn't mean they are dreaming up solutions (Blagrove, 1992, 1996). Nonetheless, recent research showing that sleep can enhance learning (Walker & Stickgold, 2004) adds new credibility to the problem-solving view of dreams (Cartwright, 2004).

J. Allan Hobson and Robert McCarley argue that dreams are simply the byproduct of bursts of activity emanating from subcortical areas in the brain (Hobson & McCarley, 1977; Hobson, Pace-Schott, & Stickgold, 2000; Hobson, 2002). Their *activation-synthesis model* proposes that dreams are side effects of the neural activation that produces "wide awake" brain waves during REM sleep. According to this model, neurons firing periodically in lower brain centres send random signals to the cortex (the seat of complex thought). The cortex supposedly synthesizes (constructs) a dream to make sense out of these signals. The activation-synthesis model does *not* assume that dreams are meaningless. As Hobson (1988) puts it, "Dreams are as meaningful as they can be under the adverse working conditions of the brain in REM sleep" (p. 214). In contrast to the theories of Freud and Cartwright, this theory obviously downplays the role of emotional factors as determinants of dreams. Like other theories of dreams, the activation-synthesis model has its share of critics. They point out that the model cannot accommodate the fact that dreaming occurs outside of REM sleep and that the contents of dreams are considerably more meaningful than the model would predict (Domhoff, 2005a; Foulkes, 1996).

These approaches, summarized in Figure 5.13, are only three out of a host of theories about the functions of dreams. All these theories are based more on conjecture than solid evidence, and none of them has been tested adequately. In part, this is because the private, subjective nature of dreams makes it difficult to put the theories to an empirical test. Thus, the purpose of dreaming remains a mystery.

Figure 5.13

Three theories of dreaming. Dreams can be explained in a variety of ways. Freud stressed the wish-fulfilling function of dreams. Cartwright emphasizes the problem-solving function of dreams. Hobson and McCarley assert that dreams are merely a byproduct of periodic neural activation. All three theories are speculative and have their critics.

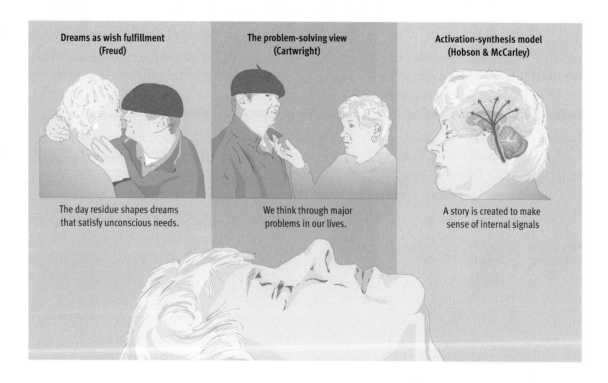

Dreams as wish fulfillment (Freud)
The day residue shapes dreams that satisfy unconscious needs.

The problem-solving view (Cartwright)
We think through major problems in our lives.

Activation-synthesis model (Hobson & McCarley)
A story is created to make sense of internal signals

- The conventional view is that dreams are mental experiences during REM sleep that have a storylike quality, include vivid imagery, are often bizarre, and are regarded as real by the dreamer, but theorists have begun to question many aspects of this view.

- Researchers have found modest differences between men and women in dream content that seem to reflect conventional gender roles. The content of one's dreams may be affected by what is going on in one's life and by external stimuli that are experienced during the dream.

- In many non-Western cultures, dreams are viewed as important sources of information. Cultures vary in beliefs about the nature of dreams, dream recall, dream content, and dream interpretation.

- Freud argued that the principal purpose of dreams is wish fulfillment. Cartwright has articulated a problem-solving view, whereas Hobson and McCarley assert that dreams are side effects of the neural activation seen during REM sleep. Ultimately, theories of dreaming remain largely untested.

Hypnosis: Altered Consciousness or Role Playing?

Hypnosis has a long and chequered history. According to hypnosis researcher Nicholas Spanos of Carleton University, some believe that there are even events described in the Old and New Testaments that refer to hypnosis-like phenomena (Spanos & Chaves, 1991). In terms of more contemporary events, however, the recent history of hypnosis begins with a flamboyant 18th-century Austrian physician by the name of Franz Anton Mesmer. Working in Paris, Mesmer claimed to cure people of illnesses through an elaborate routine involving a "laying on of hands." Mesmer had some complicated theories about how he had harnessed "animal magnetism." However, we know today that he had simply stumbled onto the power of suggestion. It was rumoured that the French government offered him a princely amount of money to disclose how he effected his cures. He refused, probably because he didn't really know. Eventually he was dismissed as a charlatan and run out of town by the local authorities. Although officially discredited, Mesmer inspired followers—practitioners of "mesmerism"—who continued to ply their trade. To this day, our language preserves the memory of Franz Mesmer: When we are under the spell of an event or a story, we are "mesmerized."

Eventually, a Scottish physician, James Braid, became interested in the trancelike state that could be induced by the mesmerists. It was Braid who popularized the term *hypnotism* in 1843, borrowing it from the Greek word for sleep. Braid thought that hypnotism could be used to produce anesthesia for surgeries. However, just as hypnosis was catching on as a general anesthetic, more powerful and reliable chemical anesthetics were discovered, and interest in hypnotism dwindled.

Since then, hypnotism has led a curious dual existence. On the one hand, it has been the subject of numerous scientific studies. Furthermore, it has enjoyed considerable use as a clinical tool by physicians, dentists, and psychologists for over a century and has empirically supported value in the treatment of a variety of psychological and physical maladies (Lynn et al., 2000; Spiegel, Greenleaf, & Spiegel, 2000). On the other hand, however, an assortment of entertainers and quacks have continued in the less respectable tradition of mesmerism, using hypnotism for parlour tricks and chicanery. It is little wonder, then, that many myths about hypnosis have come to be widely accepted (see Figure 5.14). In this section, we'll work on clearing up some of the confusion surrounding hypnosis.

Hypnotic Induction and Susceptibility

Hypnosis **is a systematic procedure that typically produces a heightened state of suggestibility.** It may also lead to passive relaxation, narrowed attention, and enhanced fantasy. If only in popular films, virtually everyone has seen a *hypnotic induction* enacted with a swinging pendulum. Actually many techniques can be used for inducing hypnosis (Meyer, 1992). Usually, the hypnotist will suggest to the subject that he or she is relaxing. Repetitively, softly, subjects are told that they are getting tired, drowsy, or sleepy. Often, the hypnotist vividly describes bodily sensations that should be occurring. Subjects are told that their arms are going limp, their feet are getting warm, their eyelids are getting heavy. Gradually, most subjects succumb and become hypnotized.

People differ in how well they respond to hypnotic induction. Ernest and Josephine Hilgard have done extensive research on this variability in *hypnotic susceptibility.* Not everyone can be hypnotized.

PREVIEW QUESTIONS
- What is the history of hypnosis?
- What are some correlates of hypnotic susceptibility?
- What are some prominent hypnotic phenomena?
- What lines of evidence support the role-playing theory of hypnosis?
- What is Hilgard's explanation for how hypnosis works?

Hypnosis: Myth and Reality

If you think . . .	The reality is . . .
Relaxation is an important feature of hypnosis.	It's not. Hypnosis has been induced during vigorous exercise.
It's mostly just compliance.	Many highly motivated subjects fail to experience hypnosis.
It's a matter of willful faking.	Physiological responses indicate that hypnotized subjects generally are not lying.
It has something to do with a sleeplike state.	It does not. Hypnotized subjects are fully awake.
Responding to hypnosis is like responding to a placebo.	Placebo responsiveness and hypnotizability are not correlated.
People who are hypnotized lose control of themselves.	Subjects are perfectly capable of saying no or terminating hypnosis.
Hypnosis can enable people to "relive" the past.	Age-regressed adults behave like adults play-acting as children.
When hypnotized, people can remember more accurately.	Hypnosis may actually muddle the distinction between memory and fantasy and may artificially inflate confidence.
Hypnotized people do not remember what happened during the session.	Posthypnotic amnesia does not occur spontaneously.
Hypnosis can enable people to perform otherwise impossible feats of strength, endurance, learning, and sensory acuity.	Performance following hypnotic suggestions for increased muscle strength, learning, and sensory acuity does not exceed what can be accomplished by motivated subjects outside hypnosis.

Figure 5.14

Misconceptions regarding hypnosis. Mistaken ideas about the nature of hypnosis are common. Some widely believed myths about hypnosis are summarized here along with more accurate information on each point, based on an article by Michael Nash (2001), a prominent hypnosis researcher. Many of these myths and realities are discussed in more detail in the text.

Source: Adapted from Nash, M. R. (2001, July). The truth and the hype of hypnosis. *Scientific American, 285,* 36–43. Copyright © 2001 by Scientific American, Inc.

About 10% of the population doesn't respond well at all. At the other end of the continuum, about 10% of people are exceptionally good hypnotic subjects (Hilgard, 1965). Responsiveness to hypnosis is a stable, measurable trait. It can be estimated pretty effectively with the Stanford Hypnotic Susceptibility Scale (SHSS) or its derivative, the Harvard Group Scale of Hypnotic Susceptibility (Perry, Nadon, & Button, 1992). The distribution of scores on the SHSS is graphed in Figure 5.15.

Research has recently demonstrated that people who are responsive to suggestion under hypnosis are just as responsive to suggestion without being hypnotized (Braffman & Kirsch, 1999). In other words, their "hypnotic susceptibility" is not unique to hypnosis and is part of a broader trait that Kirsch and Braffman (2001) characterize as *imaginative suggestibility*. Kirsch and Braffman argue that future research should focus on measuring the determinants and repercussions of this broader trait. It remains to be seen whether this proposal will enhance our understanding of why some people are more responsive to hypnosis than others.

Hypnotic Phenomena

Many interesting effects can be produced through hypnosis. Some of the more prominent include:

1. *Anesthesia.* Under the influence of hypnosis, some participants can withstand treatments that would normally cause considerable pain (Patterson, 2004). As a result, some physicians and dentists have used hypnosis as a substitute for anesthetic drugs. Admittedly, drugs are far more reliable pain relievers,

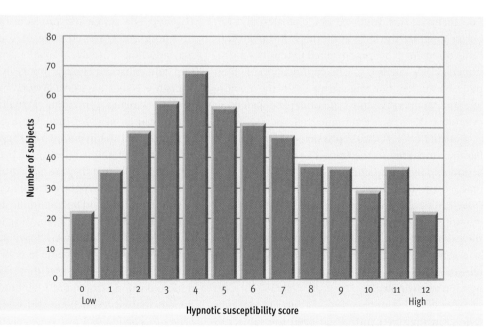

Figure 5.15

Variation in hypnotic susceptibility. This graph shows the distribution of scores of more than 500 subjects on the Stanford Hypnotic Susceptibility Scale. As you can see, responsiveness to hypnotism varies widely, and many people are not very susceptible to hypnotic induction.

Source: Adapted from Hilgard, E. (1965). *Hypnotic susceptibility.* San Diego: Harcourt Brace Jovanovich. Copyright © 1965 by Ernest R. Hilgard. Reprinted by permission of Ernest R. Hilgard.

making hypnosis something of a scientific curiosity as a solo treatment for acute pain (Gibson & Heap, 1991). Nonetheless, hypnosis can be a surprisingly effective anesthetic in the treatment of both acute and chronic pain (Patterson & Jensen, 2003).

2. *Sensory distortions and hallucinations.* Hypnotized participants may be led to experience auditory or visual hallucinations (Spiegel, 2003). They may hear sounds or see things that are not there, or fail to hear or see stimuli that are present. In one study, for instance, hypnotized participants were induced to "see" a cardboard box that blocked their view of a television (Spiegel et al., 1985). Subjects may also have their sensations distorted so that something sweet tastes sour or an unpleasant odour smells fragrant.

3. *Disinhibition.* Generally, it is difficult to get hypnotized participants to do things that they would normally consider unacceptable. Nonetheless, hypnosis *can* sometimes reduce inhibitions that would normally prevent subjects from acting in ways that they would see as socially undesirable. In experiments, hypnotized participants have been induced to throw what they believed to be nitric acid into the face of a research assistant. Similarly, stage hypnotists are sometimes successful in getting people to disrobe in public. One lay hypnotist even coaxed a man into robbing a bank (Deyoub, 1984). This disinhibition effect may occur simply because hypnotized people feel that they cannot be held responsible for their actions while they are hypnotized.

4. *Posthypnotic suggestions and amnesia.* Suggestions made during hypnosis may influence a subject's later behaviour (Barnier, 2002). The most common posthypnotic suggestion is the creation of posthypnotic amnesia. That is, participants are told that they will remember nothing that happened while they were hypnotized. Such subjects usually claim to remember nothing, as ordered. However, when pressed, many of these subjects acknowledge that they have not really forgotten the information (Kirsch & Lynn, 1998).

Theories of Hypnosis

Although a number of theories have been developed to explain hypnosis, it is still not well understood. One popular view is that hypnotic effects occur because participants are put into a special, altered state of consciousness, called a *hypnotic trance*. Although hypnotized subjects may feel as though they are in an altered state, their patterns of EEG activity cannot be distinguished from their EEG patterns in normal waking states (Dixon & Laurence, 1992; Orne & Dinges, 1989). The failure to find any special physiological changes associated with hypnosis has led some theorists to conclude that hypnosis is a normal state of consciousness that is simply characterized by dramatic role playing.

Hypnosis as Role Playing

Theodore Barber (1979) and Carleton University's Nicholas Spanos (1986; Spanos & Coe, 1992) have been the leading advocates of the view that hypnosis produces a normal mental state in which suggestible people act out the role of a hypnotic subject and behave as they think hypnotized people are supposed to. According to this notion, it is subjects' role expectations that produce hypnotic effects, rather than a special trancelike state of consciousness.

Two lines of evidence support the role-playing view. First, many of the seemingly amazing effects of hypnosis have been duplicated by nonhypnotized participants or have been shown to be exaggerated (Kirsch, 1997). For example, much has been made of the fact that hypnotized subjects can be used as "human planks," but it turns out that nonhypnotized subjects can easily match this feat (Barber, 1986). In a similar vein, anecdotal reports that hypnosis can enhance memory have not stood up well to empirical testing. Although hypnosis may occasionally facilitate recall in some people, experimental studies have tended to find that hypnotized participants make more memory errors than nonhypnotized participants, even though they often feel more confident about their recollections (McConkey, 1992; Scoboria et al., 2002). These findings suggest that no special state of consciousness is required to explain hypnotic feats.

The second line of evidence involves demonstrations that hypnotized participants are often acting out a role. For example, Martin Orne (1951) regressed

Web Link 5.5

States of Consciousness
http://www.psywww.com/asc/asc.html

PsychWeb, Russ Dewey's (Georgia Southern University) superb resource page, hosts this fine collection of scientifically grounded guides to three topics that too often provoke nonsensical claims: hypnosis, out-of-body experiences, and dreaming.

"Thousands of books, movies, and professional articles have woven the concept of 'hypnotic trance' into the common knowledge. And yet there is almost no scientific support for it."
THEODORE BARBER

Some feats performed under hypnosis can be performed equally well by nonhypnotized subjects. Here "the Amazing Kreskin" demonstrates that proper positioning is the only requirement for the famous human plank feat.

Courtesy of Ernest R. Hilgard

"Many psychologists argue that the hypnotic trance is a mirage. It would be unfortunate if this skeptical view were to gain such popularity that the benefits of hypnosis are denied to the numbers of those who could be helped.**"**
ERNEST HILGARD

hypnotized subjects back to their sixth birthday and asked them to describe it. They responded with detailed descriptions that appeared to represent great feats of hypnosis-enhanced memory. However, instead of accepting this information at face value, Orne compared it with information that he had obtained from the subjects' parents. It turned out that many of the participants' memories were inaccurate and invented! Many other studies have also found that age-regressed subjects' recall of the distant past tends to be more fanciful than factual (Green, 1999; Perry, Kusel, & Perry, 1988). Thus, the role-playing explanation of hypnosis suggests that situational factors lead some subjects to act out a certain role in a highly cooperative manner.

Hypnosis as an Altered State of Consciousness

Despite the doubts raised by role-playing explanations, many prominent theorists still maintain that hypnotic effects are attributable to a special, altered state of consciousness (Beahrs, 1983; Fromm, 1979, 1992; Hilgard, 1986; Spiegel, 1995, 2003). These theorists argue that it is doubtful that role playing can explain all hypnotic phenomena. For instance, they assert that even the most cooperative subjects are unlikely to endure surgery without a drug anesthetic just to please their physician and live up to their expected role. They also cite studies in which hypnotized participants have continued to display hypnotic responses when they thought they were alone and not being observed (Perugini et al., 1998). If hypnotized participants were merely acting, they would drop the act when alone.

The most impressive research undermining the role-playing view has come from recent brain-imaging studies, which suggest that hypnotized participants experience changes in brain activity that appear consistent with their reports of hypnosis-induced

hallucinations (Spiegel, 2003) or pain suppression (Hofbauer et al., 2001).

The most influential explanation of hypnosis as an altered state of awareness has been offered by Ernest Hilgard (1986, 1992). According to Hilgard, hypnosis creates a *dissociation* in consciousness. **Dissociation is a splitting off of mental processes into two separate, simultaneous streams of awareness.** In other words, Hilgard theorizes that hypnosis splits consciousness into two streams. One stream is in communication with the hypnotist and the external world, while the other is a difficult-to-detect "hidden observer." Hilgard believes that many hypnotic effects are a product of this divided consciousness. For instance, he suggests that a hypnotized subject might appear unresponsive to pain because the pain isn't registered in the portion of consciousness that communicates with other people.

One appealing aspect of Hilgard's theory is that *divided consciousness* is a common, normal experience. For example, people will often drive a car a great distance, responding to traffic signals and other cars, with no recollection of having consciously done so. In such cases, consciousness is clearly divided between driving and the person's thoughts about other matters. Interestingly, this common experience has long been known as *highway hypnosis*. In this condition, there is even an "amnesia" for the component of consciousness that drove the car, similar to posthypnotic amnesia. In summary, Hilgard presents hypnosis as a plausible variation in consciousness that has continuity with everyday experience.

The debate about whether hypnosis involves an altered or normal state of consciousness appears likely to continue for the foreseeable future (Kihlstrom, 1998a; Kirsch & Lynn, 1998). As you will see momentarily, a similar debate has dominated the scientific discussion of meditation.

Meditation: Pure Consciousness or Relaxation?

PREVIEW QUESTIONS
- What is meditation and how is it practised?
- How does meditation affect physiological responding?
- What's the evidence on the long-term benefits of meditation?

Recent years have seen growing interest in the ancient discipline of meditation. *Meditation* refers to a family of practices that train attention to heighten awareness and bring mental processes under greater voluntary control. There are many approaches to meditation. In North America, the most widely practised approaches are those associated with yoga, Zen, and transcendental meditation (TM). All three of these approaches are rooted in Eastern religions (Hinduism,

Buddhism, and Taoism). However, meditation has been practised throughout history as an element of all religious and spiritual traditions, including Judaism and Christianity. Moreover, the practice of meditation can be largely divorced from religious beliefs. In fact, most North Americans who meditate have only vague ideas regarding its religious significance. Of interest to psychology is the fact that meditation involves a deliberate effort to alter consciousness.

Most meditative techniques are deceptively simple. For example, in TM a person is supposed to sit in a comfortable position with eyes closed and silently focus attention on a *mantra*. A mantra is a specially assigned Sanskrit word that is personalized to each meditator. This exercise in mental self-discipline is to be practised twice daily for about 20 minutes. The technique has been described as "diving from the active surface of the mind to its quiet depths" (Bloomfield & Kory, 1976, p. 49). Most proponents of TM believe it involves an altered state of "pure consciousness" that has many unique benefits. Many skeptics counter that meditation is only an effective relaxation technique. Let's look at the evidence.

Physiological Correlates

What happens when an experienced meditator goes into the meditative state? One intriguing finding is that alpha waves and theta waves become more prominent in EEG recordings. Many studies also find that subjects' heart rate, skin conductance, respiration rate, oxygen consumption, and carbon dioxide elimination decline (see Figure 5.16; Dillbeck & Orme-Johnson, 1987; Fenwick, 1987; Travis, 2001). Taken together, these changes suggest that meditation leads to a potentially beneficial physiological state characterized by suppression of bodily arousal. However, debate continues about whether there are physiological changes associated with meditation that are unique to a special state of consciousness (Shear & Jevning, 1999; Travis & Pearson, 2000).

To shed new light on this lingering question, some researchers have begun to use new brain-imaging technologies in an effort to identify the neural circuits that are affected by meditation (Newberg, Alavi, Baime, Pourdehnad, Santanna, & D'Aquili, 2001).

Long-Term Benefits

What about the long-term benefits that have been claimed for meditation? Research suggests that meditation may have some value in reducing the effects of stress (Anderson et al., 1999; Winzelberg & Luskin, 1999). In particular, regular meditation is associated with lower levels of some "stress hormones" (Infante et al., 2001) and enhanced immune response (Davidson et al., 2003). Research also suggests that meditation can improve mental health while reducing anxiety and drug abuse (Alexander et al., 1994). Other studies report that meditation may have beneficial effects on blood pressure (Barnes,

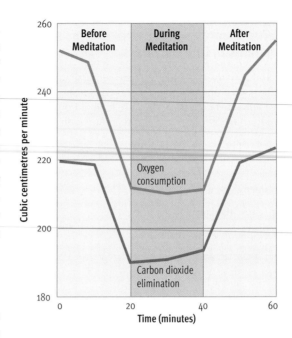

Figure 5.16

The suppression of physiological arousal during transcendental meditation. The physiological changes shown in the graph are evidence of physical relaxation during the meditative state. However, critics argue that similar changes may also be produced by systematic relaxation procedures.

SOURCE: Adapted from Wallace, R. K., & Benson, H. (1972, February). The physiology of meditation. *Scientific American, 226*, 85–90. Graphic redrawn from illustration on p. 86 by Lorelle A. Raboni. Copyright © 1972 by Scientific American, Inc.

Treiber, & Davis, 2001), self-esteem (Emavardhana & Tori, 1997), mood and one's sense of control (Easterlin & Cardena, 1999), happiness (Smith, Compton, & West, 1995), and overall physical health and well-being (Reibel et al., 2001). One recent study even reported that regular meditation led to increased creativity and intelligence in a sample of high school students (So & Orme-Johnson, 2001). At first glance these results are profoundly impressive, but they need to be viewed with some caution. At least some of these effects may be just as attainable through systematic relaxation or other mental focusing procedures (Shapiro, 1984; Smith, 1975). Critics also wonder whether placebo effects, sampling bias, and other methodological problems may contribute to some of the reported benefits of meditation (Bishop, 2002; Canter, 2003; Caspi & Burleson, 2005). In a recent and relatively enthusiastic review of meditation research, the authors acknowledge that many meditation studies "do not use rigorous research design (including lack of randomization, lack of followup, and imprecise measurement of constructs) and sometimes are based on small samples" (Shapiro, Schwartz, & Santerre, 2002).

In summary, it seems safe to conclude that meditation is a potentially worthwhile relaxation strategy. And it's entirely possible that meditation involves much more than mere relaxation, as meditation advocates insist. Certainly, it is hard to envision mere relaxation providing such a diverse constellation of benefits. At present, however, there is great debate about the notion that meditation produces a unique state of "pure consciousness" and healthy skepticism about some of its alleged long-term benefits.

Relating EEG Activity to Variations in Consciousness

Early in the chapter we emphasized the intimate relationship between brain activity and variations in consciousness. Check your understanding of this relationship by indicating the kind of EEG activity (alpha, beta, theta, or delta) that would probably be dominant in each of the following situations. The answers are in Appendix A.

_____ **1.** You are playing a video game.

_____ **2.** You are deep in meditation.

_____ **3.** You have just fallen asleep.

_____ **4.** You are sleepwalking across the lawn.

_____ **5.** You are in the midst of a terrible nightmare.

REVIEW OF KEY POINTS

● Hypnosis has had a long and curious history since the era of mesmerism in the 18th century. Hypnotic susceptibility is a stable trait. It is only weakly correlated with personality, but highly hypnotizable people tend to score somewhat higher than others in absorption and imaginativeness. Hypnosis can produce anesthesia, sensory distortions, disinhibition, and posthypnotic amnesia.

● One approach to hypnosis is to view it as a normal state of consciousness in which subjects assume a hypnotic role. Another approach asserts that hypnosis leads to an altered state in which consciousness is split into two streams of awareness.

● Meditation refers to a family of practices that train attention to heighten awareness and bring mental processes under greater voluntary control. Evidence suggests that meditation leads to a potentially beneficial physiological state characterized by suppression of bodily arousal. However, some experts suggest that the benefits of meditation are not unique to meditation and are a product of any effective relaxation procedure.

Altering Consciousness with Drugs

PREVIEW QUESTIONS

● What are the principal categories of abused drugs, and what are their main effects?

● What kinds of factors influence drug experiences?

● Where do drugs exert their effects in the brain?

● What is the difference between physical and psychological dependence?

● What are the three ways in which abused drugs can harm health?

● What are the health risks associated with the use of marijuana and MDMA?

Like hypnosis and meditation, drugs are commonly used in deliberate efforts to alter consciousness. In this section, we focus on the use of drugs for nonmedical purposes, commonly referred to as "drug abuse" or "recreational drug use." Drug abuse reaches into every corner of modern society. Although some modest declines occurred in the overall abuse of drugs during the 1980s and early 1990s, survey data indicate that illicit drug use has mostly been increasing since the 1960s (Winick & Norman, 2005). In spite of extraordinary efforts to reduce drug abuse, it seems reasonable to conclude that widespread recreational drug use is here to stay for the foreseeable future.

As with other controversial social problems, recreational drug use often inspires more rhetoric than reason. For instance, a former president of the American Medical Association made headlines when he declared that marijuana "makes a man of 35 sexually like a man of 70." In reality, the research findings do not support this assertion. This influential physician later retracted his statement, admitting that he had made it simply to campaign against marijuana use (Leavitt, 1995). Unfortunately, such scare tactics can backfire by undermining the credibility of drug education efforts.

Recreational drug use involves personal, moral, political, and legal issues that are not matters for science to resolve. However, the more knowledgeable you are about drugs, the more informed your decisions and opinions about them will be. Accordingly, this section describes the types of drugs that are most commonly used for recreational purposes and summarizes their effects on consciousness, behaviour, and health.

Principal Abused Drugs and Their Effects 4c

The drugs that people use recreationally are *psychoactive*. **Psychoactive drugs are chemical substances that modify mental, emotional, or behavioural functioning.** Not all psychoactive drugs produce effects that lead to recreational use. Generally, people prefer drugs that elevate their mood or produce other pleasurable alterations in consciousness.

A recent survey on addictions, the 2004 Canadian Addiction Survey (CAS), was released by Health Canada and the Canadian Centre of Substance Abuse (CCSA). It shows the prevalence and use of various drugs (see Table 5.3). In addition to telling us about the general usage of various drug across Canada, the survey also revealed several other important findings. In general, drug use has increased over the past decade. For example, the rate of cannabis use has doubled since 1994. The current rate of cannabis use by those aged 15–17 is 30%, and for those aged 18–19 the rate is 47%. While most Canadians over 15 drink, most are not problem drinkers and do so in moderation. Many of those surveyed, over 30%, however, did report that their own drinking or that

Table **5.3** Overview of Major CAS Indicators

	CAN	NL	PE	NS	NB	QC	ON	NB	SK	AB	BC	***
N =	**13 909**	1001	1000	1002	1000	1003	1000	1502	1000	2401	3000	
Alcohol												
Current drinkers–past year	**79.3**	73.9	70.2	76.0	73.8	82.3	78.7	76.5	78.2	79.5	79.3	**
Drinking Type												
Abstainer–never in life	**7.3**	9.5	8.6	7.1	10.1	6.2	8.3	7.1	4.7	6.5	6.9	**
Former drinker–not in past year	**13.7**	17.1	21.5	17.2	16.5	11.7	13.3	17.0	17.5	14.3	14.1	**
Light infrequent–past year	**38.7**	34.4	36.9	40.1	39.8	39.0	37.8	40.0	43.6	40.5	37.9	**
Light frequent–past year	**27.7**	16.5	15.2	18.3	16.0	33.8	28.3	21.1	19.5	23.4	27.8	**
Heavy infrequent–past year	**5.6**	11.5	9.6	9.2	9.1	3.7	5.0	7.2	7.8	7.5	6.0	**
Heavy frequent–past year	**7.1**	11.1	8.2	8.1	8.5	5.7	5.7	7.3	7.7	6.9	7.3	**
Monthly heavy drinking	**20.2**	26.1	18.3	20.8	20.6	20.7	19.6	20.9	18.9	21.0	19.3	**
Exceeded drinking guidelines	**17.8**	20.1	15.2	17.6	17.5	18.6	17.6	16.2	16.7	17.8	17.6	NS
Exceeded drinking guidelines[1]	**22.6**	27.3	21.7	23.3	23.7	22.7	22.6	21.4	21.5	22.5	22.4	NS
AUDIT hazardous drinking	**13.6**	16.9	14.8	15.8	14.1	11.9	13.7	15.1	13.8	15.3	13.4	NS
Other drug use												
Cannabis–lifetime	**44.5**	38.5	36.5	43.4	42.1	46.4	40.4	44.6	41.0	48.7	52.1	**
Cannabis–past year	**14.1**	11.6	10.7	14.4	11.1	15.8	12.4	13.4	11.4	15.4	16.8	**
Any drug (incl. cannabis)–life	**45.1**	38.5	36.9	43.7	42.5	47.3	40.9	44.8	41.3	49.3	52.7	**
Any drug (incl. cannabis)–past year	**14.5**	11.7	10.7	14.5	11.1	16.4	12.6	13.7	11.8	15.9	17.5	**
Any drug (excl. cannabis)–life	**16.5**	8.3	11.9	13.4	10.8	18.1	14.0	14.8	14.2	18.7	23.0	**
Any drug (excl. cannabis)–past year	**3.0**	1.4^Q	2.2^Q	2.3^Q	1.5^Q	4.0	2.3^Q	2.6	2.8^Q	3.3	4.0	**
Cocaine/crack–life	**10.6**	3.7	5.5	7.1	4.2	12.2	8.7	8.9	8.0	12.3	16.3	**
Cocaine/crack–past year	**1.9**	0.9	1.1^Q	1.1^Q	S	2.5^Q	1.3^Q	2.0^Q	1.7^Q	2.4^Q	2.6^Q	**
Speed–life	**6.4**	1.2^Q	3.3^Q	3.2^Q	4.5	8.9	5.5	4.5	4.0	6.1	7.3	**
Ecstasy–life	**4.1**	1.5^Q	2.6^Q	3.4^Q	1.9^Q	3.7	3.7	2.6^Q	3.1^Q	5.1	6.5	**
Hallucinogens–life	**11.4**	6.2	9.1	10.6	7.3	11.0	10.5	10.6	9.3	12.3	16.5	**
Inhalants–life	**1.3**	0.7^Q	1.4^Q	1.1^Q	1.0^Q	2.1^Q	S	1.6^Q	1.6^Q	1.6^Q	1.7^Q	NS
Alcohol and drug-related harms												
Any alcohol harm (to self)[2] — past year	**8.8**	7.2	9.3	8.7	7.3	8.4	9.1	7.6	8.9	9.5	9.1	NS
Any alcohol harm (from others)[3] — past year	**32.7**	29.7	33.6	32.1	31.4	30.2	31.8	36.2	35.7	38.0	35.4	**
Any drug harm (to self)[4] — past year	**17.5**	20.3	15.9	19.9	14.7	21.6	12.9	19.2	24.4	18.4	17.6	NS

[1] Among past-year drinkers (N = 10696); [2] among past-year drinkers (N = 10696); [3] among respondents 18 years and older (N = 13328); [4] among past-year illicit drug users (cannabis included; N = 1909)

NS not significant; * p<.05; ** p<.01; ^{Q} Qualified release due to high sampling variability; S estimate surpressed

Source: Adapted from the Statistics Canada, Health Canada, and Canadian Executive Council on Addictions publication (2004, November), *A national survey of Canadians' use of alcohol and other drugs: Prevalence of Use and Related Harms.* Ottawa: Canadian Centre on Substance Abuse (CCSA). Retrieved March 11, 2005 from http://www.ccsa.ca/pdf/ccsa-004804-2004.pdf.

of others created personal harm ranging from verbal abuse, to family problems, to physical assault.

The principal types of recreational drugs are described in Table 5.4. The table lists representative drugs in each of six categories. It also summarizes how the drugs are taken, their medical uses, their effects on consciousness, and their common side effects (based on Julien, 2001; Levinthal, 2002; Lowinson et al., 2005). The six categories of psychoactive drugs that we will focus on are narcotics, sedatives, stimulants, hallucinogens, cannabis, and alcohol. We will also discuss one specific drug that is not listed in the table (because it does not fit into traditional drug categories) but that cannot be ignored in light of its escalating popularity: MDMA, better known as "ecstasy."

***Narcotics,* or *opiates,* are drugs derived from opium that are capable of relieving pain.** The main drugs in this category are heroin and morphine, although less potent opiates such as codeine, Demerol, and methadone are also abused. In sufficient dosages these drugs can produce an overwhelming

Drugs	Methods of Ingestion	Principal Medical Uses	Desired Effects	Potential Short-Term Side Effects
Narcotics (opiates) Morphine Heroin	Injected, smoked, oral	Pain relief	Euphoria, relaxation, anxiety reduction, pain relief	Lethargy, drowsiness, nausea, impaired coordination, impaired mental functioning, constipation
Sedatives Barbiturates (e.g., Seconal) Nonbarbiturates (e.g., Quaalude)	Oral, injected	Sleeping pill, anticonvulsant	Euphoria, relaxation, anxiety reduction, reduced inhibitions	Lethargy, drowsiness, severely impaired coordination, impaired mental functioning, emotional swings, dejection
Stimulants Amphetamines Cocaine	Oral, sniffed, injected, freebased, smoked	Treatment of hyperactivity and narcolepsy, local anesthetic (cocaine only)	Elation, excitement, increased alertness, increased energy, reduced fatigue	Increased blood pressure and heart rate, increased talkativeness, restlessness, irritability, insomnia, reduced appetite, increased sweating and urination, anxiety, paranoia, increased aggressiveness, panic
Hallucinogens LSD Mescaline Psilocybin	Oral	None	Increased sensory awareness, euphoria, altered perceptions, hallucinations, insightful experiences	Dilated pupils, nausea, emotional swings, paranoia, jumbled thought processes, impaired judgment, anxiety, panic reaction
Cannabis Marijuana Hashish THC	Smoked, oral	Treatment of glaucoma and chemotherapy-induced nausea and vomiting; other uses under study	Mild euphoria, relaxation, altered perceptions, enhanced awareness	Bloodshot eyes, elevated heart rate, dry mouth, reduced short-term memory, sluggish motor coordination, sluggish mental functioning, anxiety
Alcohol	Drinking	None	Mild euphoria, relaxation, anxiety reduction, reduced inhibitions	Severely impaired coordination, impaired mental functioning, increased urination, emotional swings, depression, quarrelsomeness, hangover

sense of euphoria or well-being. This euphoric effect has a relaxing, "Who cares?" quality that makes the high an attractive escape from reality. Frequent side effects include lethargy, nausea, and impaired mental and motor functioning.

Sedatives are sleep-inducing drugs that tend to decrease central nervous system (CNS) activation and behavioural activity. People abusing sedatives, or "downers," generally consume larger doses than are prescribed for medical purposes. The desired effect is a euphoria similar to that produced by drinking large amounts of alcohol. Feelings of tension or dejection are replaced by a relaxed, pleasant state of intoxication, accompanied by loosened inhibitions. Prominent side effects include drowsiness, unpredictable emotional swings, and severe impairments in motor coordination and mental functioning.

Stimulants are drugs that tend to increase central nervous system activation and behavioural activity. Stimulants range from mild, widely available drugs such as caffeine and nicotine, to stronger, carefully regulated ones such as cocaine. We will focus on cocaine and amphetamines. Cocaine is a natural substance that comes from the coca shrub. In contrast, amphetamines are synthesized in a pharmaceutical laboratory. Cocaine and amphetamines have fairly similar effects, except that cocaine produces a briefer high. Stimulants produce a euphoria very different from that created by narcotics or sedatives. They produce a buoyant, elated, energetic "I can conquer the world!" feeling accompanied by increased alertness. In recent years, cocaine and amphetamines have become available in much more potent (and dangerous) forms than before. "Freebasing" is a chemical treatment used to extract nearly pure cocaine from ordinary street cocaine. "Crack" is the most widely distributed byproduct of this process, consisting of chips of pure cocaine that are usually smoked. Amphetamines are increasingly sold as a crystalline powder, called "crank," that may be snorted or injected intravenously. Drug dealers are also beginning to market a smokable form of methamphetamine called "ice." Side effects of stimulants vary with dosage and potency but may include restlessness, anxiety, paranoia, and insomnia.

Hallucinogens are a diverse group of drugs that have powerful effects on mental and emotional functioning, marked most prominently by distor-

Web Link 5.6

Web of Addictions

http://www.well.com/user/woa/

From the earliest days of the World Wide Web, this page at *The Well* has been regularly recognized as a primary source for accurate and responsible information about alcohol and other drugs.

tions in sensory and perceptual experience. The principal hallucinogens are LSD, mescaline, and psilocybin. These drugs have similar effects, although they vary in potency. Hallucinogens produce euphoria, increased sensory awareness, and a distorted sense of time. In some users, they lead to profound, dream-like, "mystical" feelings that are difficult to describe. The latter effect is why they have been used in religious ceremonies for centuries in some cultures. Unfortunately, at the other end of the emotional spectrum hallucinogens can also produce night-marish feelings of anxiety and paranoia, commonly called a "bad trip." Other side effects include impaired judgment and jumbled thought processes.

Cannabis **is the hemp plant from which mari-juana, hashish, and THC are derived.** Marijuana is a mixture of dried leaves, flowers, stems, and seeds taken from the plant. Hashish comes from the plant's resin. Smoking is the usual route of ingestion for both marijuana and hashish. THC, the active chemical ingredient in cannabis, can be synthesized for research purposes (for example, to give to ani-mals, who can't very well smoke marijuana). When smoked, cannabis has an immediate impact that may last several hours. The desired effects of the drug are a mild, relaxed euphoria and enhanced sensory awareness. Unintended effects may include anxiety, sluggish mental functioning, and impaired memory.

Alcohol **encompasses a variety of beverages containing ethyl alcohol,** such as beers, wines, and distilled spirits. The concentration of ethyl alcohol varies from about 4% in most beers to 40% in 80-proof liquor—and occasionally more in higher-proof liquors. When people drink heavily, the central effect is a relaxed euphoria that temporarily boosts self-esteem, as problems seem to melt away and inhi-bitions diminish. Common side effects include severe impairments in mental and motor functioning, mood swings, and quarrelsomeness. Alcohol is the most widely used recreational drug in our society. Because alcohol is legal, many people use it casually without even thinking of it as a drug.

MDMA **is a compound drug related to both amphetamines and hallucinogens, especially mescaline.** MDMA was originally formulated in 1912 but was not widely used in North America until the 1990s, when as *ecstasy* it became popular in the context of raves and dance clubs. MDMA produces a short-lived high that typically lasts a few hours or more. Users report that they feel warm, friendly, euphoric, sensual, insightful, and empathetic, but alert and energetic. Problematic side effects include increased blood pressure, muscle tension, sweating, blurred vision, insomnia, and transient anxiety.

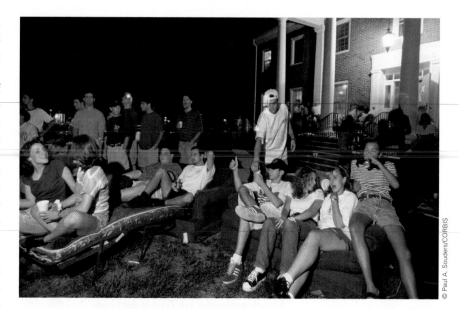

© Paul A. Souders/CORBIS

Overindulging in alcohol is particularly widespread among university students.

Factors Influencing Drug Effects

The drug effects summarized in Table 5.4 (see page 208) are the *typical* ones. Drug effects can vary from person to person and even for the same person in different situations. The impact of any drug depends in part on the user's age, mood, motivation, person-ality, previous experience with the drug, body weight, and physiology. The dose and potency of a drug, the method of administration, and the setting in which a drug is taken also influence its effects (Leavitt, 1995). Our theme of *multifactorial causation* clearly applies to the effects of drugs.

So, too, does our theme emphasizing the *subjec-tivity of experience*. Expectations are potentially pow-erful factors that can influence the user's perceptions of a drug's effects. You may recall from our discus-sion of placebo effects in Chapter 2 that some people who are misled to *think* that they are drinking alcohol show signs of intoxication (Wilson, 1982). If people *expect* a drug to make them feel giddy, serene, or profound, their expectation may contribute to the feelings they experience.

A drug's effects can also change as the person's body develops a tolerance for the chemical as a result of continued use. *Tolerance* **refers to a progressive decrease in a person's responsiveness to a drug.** Tolerance usually leads people to consume larger and larger doses of a drug to attain the effects they desire. Most drugs produce tolerance effects, but some do so more rapidly than others. For example, tolerance to alcohol usually builds slowly, while tolerance to heroin increases much more quickly. Table 5.5 indicates whether various categories of drugs tend to produce tolerance rapidly or gradually.

Drugs	Tolerance	Risk of Physical Dependence	Risk of Psychological Dependence	Fatal Overdose Potential	Health Risks
Narcotics (opiates)	Rapid	High	High	High	Infectious diseases, accidents, immune suppression
Sedatives	Rapid	High	High	High	Accidents
Stimulants	Rapid	Moderate	High	Moderate to high	Sleep problems, malnutrition, nasal damage, hypertension, respiratory disease, stroke, liver disease, heart attack
Hallucinogens	Gradual	None	Very low	Very low	Accidents
Cannabis	Gradual	None	Low to moderate	Very low	Accidents, lung cancer, respiratory disease, pulmonary disease
Alcohol	Gradual	Moderate	Moderate	Low to high	Accidents, liver disease, malnutrition, brain damage, neurological disorders, heart disease, stroke, hypertension, ulcers, cancer, birth defects

Figure 5.17

Stimulant drugs and neurotransmitter activity.
Like other psychoactive drugs, amphetamines and cocaine alter neurotransmitter activity at specific synapses. Amphetamines primarily increase the release of dopamine (DA) and norepinephrine (NE) and secondarily inhibit the reuptake of these neurotransmitters. Cocaine slows the reuptake process at DA, NE, and serotonin synapses. The psychological and behavioural effects of the drugs have largely been attributed to their impact on dopamine circuits, but recent evidence suggests that altered activity in serotonin circuits may play a larger role in the cocaine high than previously suspected (Julien, 2001).

Mechanisms of Drug Action 4D

Most drugs have effects that reverberate throughout the body. However, psychoactive drugs work primarily by altering neurotransmitter activity in the brain. As we discussed in Chapter 3, neurotransmitters are chemicals that transmit information between neurons at junctions called *synapses*.

The actions of amphetamines and cocaine illustrate how drugs have selective, multiple effects on neurotransmitter activity (see Figure 5.17). Amphetamines exert their main effects on two of the monoamine neurotransmitters: norepinephrine (NE) and dopamine (DA). Indeed, the name *amphetamines* reflects the kinship between these drugs and the *monoamines*. Amphetamines mainly increase the release of DA and NE by presynaptic neurons. They also interfere with the reuptake of DA and NE from synaptic clefts (Cami & Farre, 2003). These actions serve to increase the levels of dopamine and norepinephrine at the affected synapses. Cocaine shares some of these actions, which is why cocaine and amphetamines produce similar stimulant effects. Cocaine mainly blocks reuptake at DA, NE, and serotonin synapses. For both amphetamines and cocaine, elevated activity in certain *dopamine circuits* is believed to be crucial to the drug's pleasurable, rewarding effects (Volkow et al., 2004).

The cellular mechanisms underlying stimulant drugs' effects also explain why cocaine and amphetamine highs are often followed by an emotional crash, marked by depression and exhaustion (see Figure 5.18). The slowing of reuptake leaves more neurotransmitter in the affected synapses to stimulate increased activity, but it also gives enzymes that metabolize the neurotransmitter more opportunity to swoop in and inactivate more of the neurotransmitter, and there is more opportunity for the neurotransmitter to drift away from affected synapses. Hence, the use of cocaine or amphetamines can eventually lead to a depletion of dopamine and norepinephrine. This depletion appears to be the cause of the emotional crash experienced by many users.

The effects of other drugs can also be explained in terms of their impact on specific types of neurotransmitter activity. Sedatives are thought to exert their key effects by increasing activity at GABA synapses (Brady, Myrick, & Malcolm, 1999). Changes in GABA activity are also thought to be the main culprit underlying alcohol intoxication, although alcohol has additional effects on dopamine, serotonin, and other neurotransmitter systems (Moak & Anton, 1999). The finding that alcohol and sedatives converge on many of the same (GABA) synapses probably explains why these drugs are *synergistic*. Drugs are said to be synergistic when their combined effect is greater than the sum of their individual effects. Synergistic effects explain why the combination of

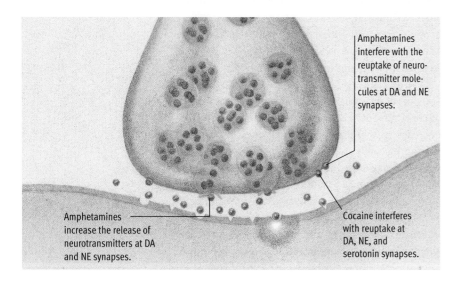

Amphetamines interfere with the reuptake of neurotransmitter molecules at DA and NE synapses.

Amphetamines increase the release of neurotransmitters at DA and NE synapses.

Cocaine interferes with reuptake at DA, NE, and serotonin synapses.

alcohol and sedatives has caused many fatal overdoses by depressing CNS activity excessively.

The discovery of endorphins (the body's internally produced opiate-like chemicals) has led to new insights about the actions of narcotic drugs (see Chapter 3). These drugs apparently bind to specific subtypes of endorphin receptors, and their actions at these receptor sites indirectly elevate dopamine activity (Cami & Farre, 2003). Scientists have recently found receptors in the brain for THC, the active chemical ingredient in marijuana (Stephens, 1999), which are called cannabinoid receptors. They have also found an internally produced chemical, christened *anandamide* (from a Sanskrit word for internal bliss), that activates these receptors (Wiley, 1999). Researchers are still working out the details, but it appears that the THC from marijuana "hijacks" the brain's cannabinoid receptors (Piomelli, 2004).

Although specific drugs exert their initial effects in the brain on a wide variety of neurotransmitter systems, many theorists believe that virtually all abused drugs eventually increase activity in a particular neural pathway, called the *mesolimbic dopamine pathway* (Nestler & Malenka, 2004). This neural circuit,

which runs from the midbrain, through the *nucleus accumbens,* and on to the prefrontal cortex (see Figure 5.19), has been characterized as a "reward pathway." Increased dopamine release along this pathway is thought to be the principal source of the reinforcing effects of most abused drugs (Volkow, Fowler, & Wang, 2004).

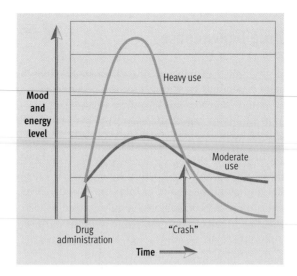

Figure 5.18

The "crash" after use of cocaine or amphetamines. Stimulant drugs induce an emotional high that is often followed by an emotional letdown called a "crash." Larger doses of the drugs tend to precipitate bigger crashes. As the text explains, the crash is attributable to the depletion of certain neurotransmitters.

Figure 5.19

The "reward pathway" in the brain. The neural circuits shown here in purple make up the *mesolimbic dopamine pathway.* Axons in this pathway run from an area in the midbrain through the medial forebrain bundle to the *nucleus accumbens* and on to the prefrontal cortex. Recreational drugs affect a variety of neurotransmitter systems, but theorists believe that heightened dopamine activity in this pathway—especially the portion running from the midbrain to the nucleus accumbens—is responsible for the reinforcing effects of most abused drugs.

SOURCE: Adapted from Kalat, J. W. (2001). *Biological psychology.* Belmont, CA: Wadsworth. Reprinted by permission.

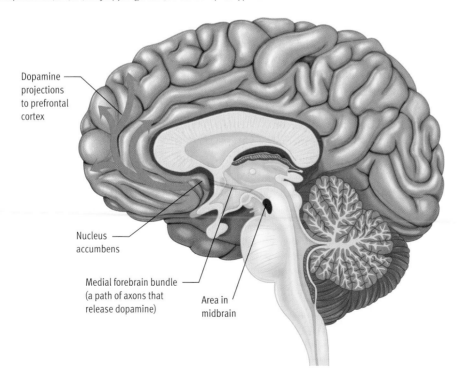

Variations in Consciousness

Drug Dependence

People can become either physically or psychologically dependent on a drug. Physical dependence is a common problem with narcotics, sedatives, alcohol, and stimulants. *Physical dependence* **exists when a person must continue to take a drug to avoid withdrawal illness.** The symptoms of withdrawal illness depend on the specific drug. Withdrawal from heroin, barbiturates, and alcohol can produce fever, chills, tremors, convulsions, vomiting, cramps, diarrhea, and severe aches and pains. Withdrawal from stimulants can lead to a more subtle syndrome, marked by fatigue, apathy, irritability, depression, and feelings of disorientation.

McMaster University psychologist Shepard Siegel has found that some of the withdrawal symptoms experienced by addicts are conditioned responses that are elicited by stimuli that have been paired with the drug in the past (McDonald & Siegel, 2004; Siegel, 2002). This means when addicts are presented with cues typically associated with drug injections in the past they may experience withdrawal symptoms. Thus, if an addict always injects in a particular room, entering the room itself may produce withdrawal symptoms. You will learn more about the process of classical conditioning and about conditioned responses in Chapter 6. In general, classical conditioning is a type of learning in which a stimulus has acquired the capacity to evoke a response that was originally evoked by another stimulus. According to Siegel (2002), conditioning is implicated in dependency in many ways. For example, the situational cues present in the situation in which a drug is typically injected may contribute to the individual's increased tolerance of the drug. This has been termed the "situational specificity of tolerance" (Siegel, 1976).

Psychological dependence **exists when a person must continue to take a drug to satisfy intense mental and emotional craving for the drug.** Psychological dependence is more subtle than physical dependence, but the need it creates can be powerful. Cocaine, for instance, can produce an overwhelming psychological need for continued use. Psychological dependence is possible with all recreational drugs, although it seems rare for hallucinogens.

Both types of dependence are established gradually with repeated use of a drug. It was originally assumed that only physical dependence has a physiological basis, but theorists now believe that both types of dependence reflect alterations in synaptic transmission (Di Chara, 1999; Self, 1997). Dysregulation in the mesolimbic dopamine pathway appears to be the chief factor underlying drug craving and addiction (Nestler & Malenka, 2004). Drugs vary in their potential for creating either physical or psychological dependence. Table 5.5 (see page 210) provides estimates of the risk of each kind of dependence for the six categories of recreational drugs covered in our discussion.

Drugs and Health

The use of recreational drugs can be damaging to health. The harmful effects of drugs were illustrated dramatically in a widely cited study of rats that were given unlimited access to heroin or cocaine (Bozarth & Wise, 1985). In this study, the rats "earned" drug injections delivered through tubes implanted in their bodies by pressing a lever in an experimental chamber. Even though unlimited food and water were available, rats on cocaine lost an average of 29% of their body weight. Their health deteriorated rapidly, and by the end of the 30-day study 90% of them had died. The health of the rats on heroin deteriorated less rapidly, but 36% of them also died during the course of the study. As is true for many human drug users, serious aversive effects did not deter the rats from continuing their "drug abuse." Many of the rats on cocaine experienced severe and highly unpleasant seizures. However, they would resume their lever pressing as soon as they stopped writhing from convulsions!

In humans, recreational drug use can affect health in a variety of ways. The three principal ways are by triggering an overdose, by producing various types of physiological damage (direct effects), and by causing health-impairing behaviour (indirect effects).

Overdose

Any drug can be fatal if a person takes enough of it, but some drugs are much more dangerous than others. Table 5.5 shows estimates of the risk of accidentally consuming a lethal overdose of each listed drug. Drugs that are CNS depressants—sedatives, narcotics, and alcohol—carry the greatest risk of overdose. It's important to remember that these drugs are synergistic with each other, so many overdoses involve lethal *combinations* of CNS depressants. What happens when a person overdoses on these drugs? The respiratory system usually grinds to a halt, producing coma, brain damage, and death within a brief period.

Fatal overdoses with CNS stimulants usually involve a heart attack, stroke, or cortical seizure. Deaths due to overdoses of stimulant drugs used to be relatively infrequent, but cocaine overdoses have increased sharply as more people have experimented with freebasing, smoking crack, and other more dangerous modes of ingestion (Repetto & Gold, 2005).

Direct Effects

In some cases, drugs cause tissue damage directly. For example, snorting cocaine can damage nasal membranes. Cocaine can also alter cardiovascular functioning in ways that increase the risk of heart attack and stroke, and crack smoking is associated with a host of respiratory problems (Gourevitch & Arnsten, 2005; Weaver & Schnoll, 1999). Long-term, excessive alcohol consumption is associated with an elevated risk for a wide range of serious health problems, including liver damage, ulcers, hypertension, stroke, heart disease, neurological disorders, and some types of cancer (Mack, Franklin, & Frances, 2003; Moak & Anton, 1999).

Indirect Effects

The negative effects of drugs on physical health are often indirect results of the drugs' impact on attitudes, intentions, and behaviour. For instance, people using stimulants tend not to eat or sleep properly. Sedatives increase the risk of accidental injuries because they severely impair motor coordination. People who abuse downers often trip down stairs, fall off stools, and suffer other mishaps. Tara MacDonald of Queen's University, in a series of studies, has found that alcohol can affect students' intentions to engage in risky sexual behaviour, including unprotected sex (MacDonald, Fong, Zanna, & Martineau, 2000; MacDonald, MacDonald, Zanna, & Fong, 2000). For example, intoxicated students who were sexually aroused reported more favourable intentions toward having unprotected sex. According to University of Waterloo researchers (MacDonald, Zanna, & Holmes, 2000), alcohol can also play a causal role in relationship conflict, a result which mirrors some of the harm results reported in the Canadian Abuse Survey. That survey also suggested that physical abuse was frequently associated with alcohol intoxication. Of course, not everyone who becomes intoxicated becomes violent. According to McGill psychologist Robert Pihl and his colleagues (Pihl, Assaad, & Hoaken, 2003), there are certain types of people who are more at risk for intoxicated aggression than are other types of people.

Many drugs impair driving ability, increasing the risk of automobile accidents. Alcohol, for instance, may contribute to roughly 40% of all automobile fatalities (Liu et al., 1997). In 2004, the Ontario Provincial Police reported an increase over 2003 in alcohol-related collisions and deaths. It is unclear whether this increase represents a trend because,

overall, the alcohol-related incidents have decreased since 1997 (Mitchell, 2005). Intravenous drug users risk contracting infectious diseases that can be spread by unsterilized needles. In recent years, acquired immune deficiency syndrome (AIDS) has been transmitted at an alarming rate through the population of intravenous drug users (Des Jarlais, Hagan, & Friedman, 2005).

The major health risks (other than overdose) of various recreational drugs are listed in the sixth column of Table 5.5. As you can see, alcohol appears to have the most diverse negative effects on physical health. The irony, of course, is that alcohol is the only recreational drug listed that is legal.

Controversies Concerning Marijuana

The possible health risks associated with marijuana use have generated considerable debate in recent years. The preponderance of evidence suggests that heavy use of marijuana *probably* increases the risk for respiratory and pulmonary disease, including lung cancer (Tashkin, 2002). Reasonably convincing evidence also indicates that marijuana increases the risk of automobile accidents (Ramaekers, Robbe, & O'Hanlon, 2000). These dangers are listed in Table 5.5, but many other widely publicized dangers are omitted because the findings on these other risks have been exaggerated or remain debatable. Here is a brief overview of the evidence on some of these controversies.

- *Does marijuana reduce one's immune response?* Research with animals clearly demonstrates that cannabis can suppress various aspects of immune system response (Cabral & Petitt, 1998. However, infectious diseases do *not* appear to be more common among marijuana smokers than among nonsmokers. Hence, marijuana's effect on immune functioning apparently is too small to have any practical importance (Hall, Solowij, & Lemon, 1994; Hollister, 1988).

- *Does marijuana lead to impotence and sterility in men?* Cannabis appears to produce a small, reversible decline in sperm count among male smokers and may have temporary effects on hormone levels (Bloodworth, 1987). Citing these findings, the popular media have frequently implied that marijuana therefore makes men sterile and impotent. However, the evidence suggests that marijuana has little lasting impact on male smokers' fertility or sexual functioning (Grinspoon & Bakalar, 1997).

- *Does marijuana have long-term negative effects on cognitive functioning?* It has long been known that marijuana has a negative impact on attention and memory while users are high, but until recently studies had failed to find any permanent cognitive deficits attributable to cannabis use. However, a spate of recent studies using more elaborate and precise assessments of cognitive functioning *have* found an association between chronic, heavy marijuana use and measurable impairments in attention and memory that show up when users are not high (Ehrenreich et al., 1999; Solowij et al., 2002). That said, the cognitive deficits that have been observed are very modest and certainly not disabling, and one study found that the deficits vanished after a month of marijuana abstinence (Pope, Gruber, & Yurgelun-Todd, 2001; Pope et al., 2001). More research is needed, but the recent studies in this area provide some cause for concern.

New Findings Regarding Ecstasy

Like marijuana, ecstasy is viewed as a harmless drug in some quarters, but accumulating empirical evidence is beginning to alter that perception. Research on MDMA is in its infancy, so conclusions about its risks must be tentative. MDMA does not appear to be especially addictive, but psychological dependence clearly can become a problem for some people.

MDMA has been implicated in cases of stroke and heart attack, seizures, heat stroke, and liver damage, but its exact contribution is hard to gauge, given all the other drugs that MDMA users typically consume and the fact that ecstasy often contains contaminants (Grob & Poland, 2005; Scholey et al., 2004). Chronic, heavy use of ecstasy appears to be associated with sleep disorders, depression, and elevated anxiety and hostility (Morgan, 2000). Moreover, studies of former MDMA users suggest that ecstasy may have subtle, long-term effects on cognitive functioning (Parrott, 2000). Quite a few studies have found memory deficits in former users (Bhattachary & Powell, 2001; Rogers et al., 2003). Other studies have found decreased performance on laboratory tasks requiring attention and learning (Gouzoulis-Mayfrank et al., 2000). Thus, although a great deal of additional research is needed, the preliminary evidence suggests that MDMA may be more harmful than widely assumed. According to recent media reports (Sallot, 2005), Canada appears to be playing a major role in ecstasy production. While Canada used to be employed as a transit point for some of the ingredients, currently it appears that more labs are being set up to produce it. In fact, the increased production in Canada has become a problem for the U.S. government, which has targeted this issue as an emerging threat (Sallot, 2005).

Putting It in Perspective

PREVIEW QUESTIONS
- How did this chapter show that psychology evolves in a sociohistorical context?
- How did this chapter illustrate the subjective nature of human experience?
- How did this chapter illustrate the importance of cultural influences?
- How did this chapter highlight psychology's theoretical diversity?

This chapter highlights four of our unifying themes. First, we can see how psychology evolves in a sociohistorical context. Psychology began as the science of consciousness in the 19th century, but consciousness proved difficult to study empirically. Research on consciousness dwindled after John B. Watson and others redefined psychology as the science of behaviour. However, in the 1960s people began to turn inward, showing a new interest in altering consciousness through drug use, meditation, hypnosis, and biofeedback. Psychologists responded to these social trends by beginning to study variations in consciousness in earnest. This renewed interest in consciousness shows how social forces can have an impact on psychology's evolution.

A second theme that predominates in this chapter is the idea that people's experience of the world is highly subjective. We encountered this theme at the start of the chapter when we mentioned the difficulty that people have describing their states of consciousness. The subjective nature of consciousness was apparent elsewhere in the chapter, as well. For instance, we found that the alterations of consciousness produced by drugs depend significantly on personal expectations.

Third, we saw once again how culture moulds some aspects of behaviour. Although the basic physiological process of sleep appears largely invariant from one society to another, culture influences certain aspects of sleep habits and has a dramatic impact on whether people remember their dreams and how they interpret and feel about their dreams. If not for space constraints, we might also have discussed cross-cultural differences in patterns of recreational drug use, which vary considerably from one society to the next.

Finally, the chapter illustrates psychology's theoretical diversity. We discussed conflicting theories about dreams, hypnosis, and meditation. For the most part, we did not see these opposing theories converging toward reconciliation, as we did in the areas of sensation and perception. However, it's important to emphasize that rival theories do not always merge neatly into tidy models of behaviour. Many theoretical controversies go on indefinitely. This fact does not negate the value of theoretical diversity. While it's always nice to resolve a theoretical debate, the debate itself can advance knowledge by stimulating and guiding empirical research.

Indeed, our upcoming Personal Application demonstrates that theoretical debates need not be resolved in order to advance knowledge. Many theoretical controversies and enduring mysteries remain in the study of sleep and dreams. Nonetheless, researchers have accumulated a great deal of practical information on these topics, which we'll discuss in the next few pages.

REVIEW OF KEY POINTS

- The principal categories of abused drugs are narcotics, sedatives, stimulants, hallucinogens, cannabis, and alcohol. Although it's possible to describe the typical effects of various drugs, the actual effect on any individual depends on a host of factors, including subjective expectations and tolerance to the drug.

- Psychoactive drugs exert their main effects in the brain, where they alter neurotransmitter activity at synaptic sites in a variety of ways. For example, amphetamines increase the release of DA and NE, and like cocaine, they slow reuptake at DA and NE synapses. The mesolimbic dopamine pathway may mediate the reinforcing effects of most abused drugs.

- Recreational drug use can prove harmful to health by producing an overdose, by causing tissue damage, or by increasing health-impairing behaviour. The chances of accidentally consuming a lethal overdose are greatest for the CNS depressants and cocaine. Direct tissue damage occurs most frequently with alcohol and cocaine. The health risks of marijuana have generated debate. Preliminary evidence suggests that MDMA may be more dangerous than widely assumed.

- Four of our unifying themes were highlighted in this chapter. We saw that psychology evolves in a sociohistorical context, that experience is highly subjective, that culture influences many aspects of behaviour, and that psychology is characterized by extensive theoretical diversity.

Addressing Practical Questions about Sleep and Dreams

Indicate whether the following statements are "true" or "false."

____ **1** Naps rarely have a refreshing effect.

____ **2** Some people never dream.

____ **3** When people cannot recall their dreams, it's because they are trying to repress them.

____ **4** Only an expert in symbolism, such as a psychoanalytic therapist, can interpret the real meaning of dreams.

These assertions were all drawn from the Sleep and Dreams Information Questionnaire (Palladino & Carducci, 1984), which measures practical knowledge about sleep and dreams. Are they true or false? You'll see in this Application.

Common Questions about Sleep

How much sleep do people need? The average amount of daily sleep for young adults is 7.5 hours. However, there is considerable variability in how long people sleep. Based on a synthesis of data from many studies, Webb (1992b) estimates that sleep time is normally distributed as shown in Figure 5.20. Thus, sleep needs vary from person to person. That said, many sleep experts believe that most people would function more effectively if they increased their amount of sleep (Maas, 1998).

Can short naps be refreshing? Some naps are beneficial and some are not. The effectiveness of napping varies from person to person. Also, the benefits of any specific nap depend on the time of day and the amount of sleep one has had recently (Dinges, 1993). On the negative side, naps are not very *efficient* ways to sleep because you're often just getting into the deeper stages of sleep when your naptime is up. Another potential problem is that overly long naps or naps that occur too close to bedtime can disrupt nighttime sleep (Thorpy & Yager, 2001).

Nonetheless, many highly productive people (including Thomas Edison, Winston Churchill, and John F. Kennedy) have made effective use of naps. On the positive side, most naps enhance subsequent alertness and task performance and reduce sleepiness (Takahashi et al., 2004). In conclusion, naps can be refreshing for most people (so the first statement opening this Application is false), and they can pay off in the long run if they don't interfere with nighttime sleep.

How do alcohol and drugs affect sleep? Obviously, stimulants such as cocaine and amphetamines make it difficult to sleep. More surprising is the finding that most of the CNS depressants that facilitate sleep (such as alcohol, analgesics, sedatives, and tranquillizers) actually disrupt the normal sleep cycle. The principal problem is that they reduce the time spent in REM sleep and slow-wave sleep (Carskadon & Dement,

2005). Unfortunately, these are the sleep stages that appear to be most important to a refreshing night's sleep.

Is there such a thing as sleep learning? Yes, but it won't get you through university. Studies show that cognitive responding to external stimuli can occur during the lighter stages (1 and 2) of sleep (Ogilvie, Wilkinson, & Allison, 1989). This and other lines of evidence suggest that sleep learning is a legitimate possibility (Eich, 1990). However, studies indicate that people have minimal ability to assimilate information of any complexity into memory while asleep (Badia, 1990). It would be nice if people could learn Spanish by listening to an audiotape while they slept, but the evidence indicates that trying to do so is pointless.

Can people learn to awaken without an alarm clock? Some people who have consistent sleep habits find themselves awak-

Figure 5.20

Variation in sleep needs. Based on data from a variety of sources, Webb (1992b) estimates that average sleep length among young adults is distributed normally, as shown here. Although most young adults sleep an average of 6.5 to 8.5 hours per night, some people need less and some people need more sleep.

SOURCE: Adapted from Webb, W. B. (1992). *Sleep, the gentle tyrant* (2nd Ed.). Bolton, MA: Anker Publishing Co. Copyright © 1992 by Anker Publishing Co. Adapted by permission.

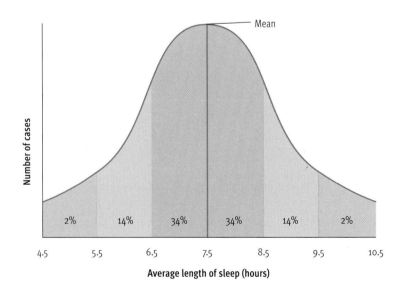

ening on their own just before their alarm clock goes off. This phenomenon is fairly common and presumably reflects the influence of circadian rhythms. A smaller number of people claim that they can reliably awaken themselves at predetermined, nonhabitual times. However, when some of these people have been tested carefully in sleep laboratories, their performance has been inconsistent (Zepelin, 1993). Thus, people who claim that they have an adjustable internal alarm clock are probably exaggerating its reliability.

What do yawning and snoring have to do with sleep? Yawning is a universal phenomenon seen in all cultural groups—not to mention other mammals, birds, fish, and reptiles (Baenninger, 1997). Contrary to popular belief, yawning is not a response to a build-up of carbon dioxide or a shortage of oxygen. However, as reputed, yawning *is* correlated with sleepiness and boredom, although the association with sleepiness may not be as strong as widely assumed. Whether yawning facilitates or impedes sleep, or has no effect, is not yet known (Provine, 1993). According to one theory, the principal function of yawning is to modify cortical arousal in situations where there is little external stimulation (Baenninger, 1997). The most fascinating and perplexing facet of yawning is that it is contagious—seeing others yawn creates a powerful urge to follow suit. Contagious yawning is not well understood, although Provine (1989) argues that it is a neurologically programmed, reflexive response.

Snoring is a common phenomenon seen in roughly 30%–40% of adults (Hoffstein, 2005). Snoring increases after age 35, occurs in men more than women, and is more frequent among people who are overweight (Kryger, 1993; Stoohs et al., 1998). Many factors, including colds, allergies, smoking, and some drugs, can contribute to snoring, mainly by forcing people to breathe through their mouths while sleeping. Some people who snore loudly disrupt their own sleep as well as that of their bed partners. It can be difficult to prevent snoring in some people, whereas others are able to reduce their snoring by simply losing weight or by

People typically get very upset when they have difficulty falling asleep. Unfortunately, the emotional distress tends to make it even harder for people to get to sleep.

sleeping on their side instead of their back (Lugaresi et al., 1994). Snoring may seem like a trivial problem, but it is associated with sleep apnea and cardiovascular disease, and it may have considerably more medical significance than most people realize (Dement & Vaughn, 1999).

What can be done to avoid sleep problems? There are many ways to improve your chances of getting satisfactory sleep (see Figure 5.21). Most of them involve developing sensible daytime habits that won't interfere with sleep (see Maas, 1998; Stepanski & Wyatt, 2003; Thorpy & Yager, 2001; Zarcone, 2000). For example, if you've been having trouble sleeping at night, it's wise to avoid daytime naps, so you will be tired when bedtime arrives. Some people find that daytime exercise helps them fall asleep more readily at bedtime (King et al., 1997). Of course, the exercise should be part of a regular regimen that doesn't leave one sore or aching.

It's also a good idea to minimize consumption of stimulants such as caffeine or nicotine. Because coffee and cigarettes aren't prescription drugs, people don't appreciate how much the stimulants they contain can heighten physical arousal. Many foods (such as chocolate) and beverages (such as cola

Figure 5.21

Suggestions for better sleep. In his book *Power Sleep*, James Maas (1998) offers the following advice for people concerned about enhancing their sleep. Maas argues convincingly that good daytime habits can make all the difference in the world to the quality of one's sleep.

SOURCE: Adapted from Maas, J. B. (1998). *Power sleep*. New York: Random House. Copyright © 1998 by James B. Mass, Ph. D. Reprinted by permission of Villard Books, a division of Random House, Inc.

1. Reduce stress as much as possible.
2. Exercise to stay fit.
3. Keep mentally stimulated during the day.
4. Eat a proper diet.
5. Stop smoking.
6. Reduce caffeine intake.
7. Avoid alcohol near bedtime.
8. Take a warm bath before bed.
9. Maintain a relaxing atmosphere in the bedroom.
10. Establish a bedtime ritual.
11. Have pleasurable sexual activity.
12. Clear your mind at bedtime.
13. Try some bedtime relaxation techniques.
14. Avoid trying too hard to get to sleep.
15. Learn to value sleep.

drinks) contain more caffeine than people realize. Also, bear in mind that ill-advised eating habits can interfere with sleep. Try to avoid going to bed hungry, uncomfortably stuffed, or soon after eating foods that disagree with you.

In addition to these prudent habits, two other preventive measures are worth mentioning. First, try to establish a reasonably regular bedtime. This habit will allow you to take advantage of your circadian rhythm, so you'll be trying to fall asleep when your body is primed to cooperate. Second, create a favourable environment for sleep. This advice belabours what should be obvious, but many people fail to heed it. Make sure you have a good bed that is comfortable for you. Take steps to ensure that your bedroom is quiet enough and that the humidity and temperature are to your liking.

What can be done about insomnia? First, don't panic if you run into a little trouble sleeping. An overreaction to sleep problems can begin a vicious circle of escalating problems, like that depicted in Figure 5.22. If you jump to the conclusion that you are becoming an insomniac, you may approach sleep with anxiety that will aggravate the problem. The harder you work at falling asleep, the less success you're likely to have. As noted earlier, temporary sleep problems are common and generally clear up on their own.

One sleep expert, Dianne Hales (1987), lists 101 suggestions for combating insomnia in her book *How to Sleep Like a Baby*. Many involve "boring yourself to sleep" by playing alphabet games, reciting poems, or listening to your clock. Another recommended strategy is to engage in some not-so-engaging activity. For instance, you might try reading your dullest textbook. It could turn out to be a superb sedative. Whatever you think about, try to avoid ruminating about the current stresses and problems in your life. Research has shown that the tendency to ruminate is one of the key factors contributing to insomnia (Kales et al., 1984), as the data in Figure 5.23 show.

Anything that relaxes you—whether it's music, meditation, prayer, or a warm bath—can aid you in falling asleep. Experts have also devised systematic relaxation procedures that can make relaxation efforts more effective. You may want to learn about techniques such as *progressive relaxation* (Jacobson, 1938), *autogenic training* (Schultz & Luthe, 1959), or the *relaxation response* (Benson & Klipper, 1988).

Common Questions about Dreams

Does everyone dream? Yes. Some people just don't *remember* their dreams. However, when these people are brought into a sleep lab and awakened from REM sleep, they report having been dreaming—much to their surprise. Thus, statement 2 at the start of this Application is false. Scientists have studied a small number of people who have sustained brain damage in the area of the pons that has wiped out their REM sleep, but even these people report dreams (Klosch & Kraft, 2005).

Why don't some people remember their dreams? The evaporation of dreams appears to be quite normal. Given the lowered level of awareness during sleep, it's understandable that memory of dreams is mediocre. Dream recall is best when people are awakened during or very soon after a dream (Goodenough, 1991). Most of the time, people who *do* recall dreams upon waking are remembering either their *last* dream from their final REM period or a dream that awakened them earlier in the night. Hobson's (1989) educated guess is that people probably forget 95%–99% of their dreams. This forgetting is natural and is not due to repression, so statement 3 is also false. People who never remember their dreams probably have a sleep pattern that puts too much time between their last REM/dream period and awakening, so even their last dream is forgotten.

Can people improve their recall of dreams? Yes. Most people don't have any significant reason to work at recalling their dreams, so

Figure 5.22

The vicious circle of anxiety and sleep difficulty. Anxiety about sleep difficulties leads to poorer sleep, which increases anxiety further, which in turn leads to even greater difficulties in sleeping.

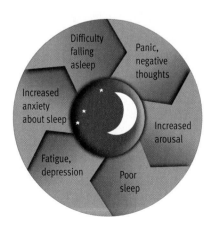

Figure 5.23

Thoughts and emotions associated with insomnia. This graph depicts the percentage of insomniacs and control subjects reporting various presleep feelings and thoughts. Insomniacs' tendency to ruminate about their problems contributes to their sleep difficulties.

Source: Data from Kales, A., & Kales, J. D. (1984). *Evaluation and treatment of insomnia.* New York: Oxford University Press. Copyright © 1984 by Oxford University Press. Reprinted by permission.

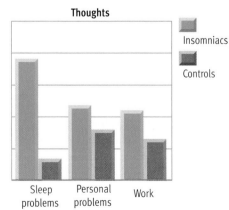

they just let them float away. However, many people have found that they can remember more dreams if they merely place that goal uppermost in their minds as they go to sleep (Goodenough, 1991). Dream recall is also aided by making a point of trying to remember dreams upon first awakening, before opening one's eyes or getting out of bed.

Are dreams instantaneous? No. It has long been speculated that dreams flash through consciousness almost instantaneously. According to this notion, complicated plots that would require 20 minutes to think through in waking life could bolt through the dreaming mind in a second or two. However, modern research shows that this isn't the case (Weinstein, Schwartz, & Arkin, 1991).

Do dreams require interpretation? Most theorists would say yes, but interpretation may not be as difficult as generally assumed. People have long believed that dreams are symbolic and that it is necessary to interpret the symbols to understand the meaning of dreams. Freud, for instance, made a distinction between the *manifest content* and the *latent content* of a dream. The **manifest content consists of the plot of a dream at a surface level. The *latent content* refers to the hidden or disguised meaning of the events in the plot.** Thus, a Freudian therapist might equate such dream events as walking into a tunnel or riding a horse with sexual intercourse.

Freudian theorists assert that dream interpretation is a complicated task requiring considerable knowledge of symbolism. However, many dream theorists argue that symbolism in dreams is less deceptive and mysterious than Freud thought (Faraday, 1974; Foulkes, 1985; Hall, 1979). Calvin Hall makes the point that dreams require some interpretation simply because they are more visual than verbal. That is, pictures need to be translated into ideas. According to Hall, dream symbolism is highly personal and the dreamer may be the person best equipped to decipher a dream (statement 4 is also false). Thus, it is not unreasonable for you to try to interpret your own dreams. Unfortunately, you'll never know whether you're "correct," because there is no definitive way to judge the validity of different dream interpretations.

Can people learn to influence their dreams? Quite possibly, but it is not easy. Researchers in a number of studies have instructed subjects to try to dream about a particular topic. Subjects have been successful often enough to suggest that some dream control is possible (Nikles et al., 1998). However, there have been many failures as well, suggesting that dream control may be fairly difficult (Tart, 1990).

What is lucid dreaming? Generally, when people dream, they are not aware that they are dreaming. Occasionally, however, some people experience "lucid" dreams in which they recognize that they are dreaming. Typically, normal dreams become lucid when people puzzle over something bizarre in a dream and recognize that they must be dreaming. **In *lucid dreams* people can think clearly about the circumstances of waking life and the fact that they are dreaming, yet they remain asleep in the midst of a vivid dream.** Perhaps the most intriguing aspect of this dual consciousness is that people can often exert some control over the events unfolding in their lucid dreams (LaBerge, 1990; Tart, 1988).

Reports of lucid dreams have a long history, but the inability of one person to experience another person's dream has always made it difficult to verify the existence of these exotic, paradoxical dreams (LaBerge, 1988). However, Stephen LaBerge reasoned that if lucid dreamers can act deliberately in their dreams, they should be able to make prearranged special eye movements to signal the occurrence of lucid dreams while being carefully monitored with physiological recording devices in a sleep lab. The ability to send such signals while dreaming would provide evidence of some degree of lucidity. This clever utilization of modern sleep monitoring techniques has allowed LaBerge and his colleagues to gather objective evidence that lucid dreaming is a genuine phenomenon that usually occurs during the REM stage (LaBerge et al., 1981). The ability of lucid dreamers to communicate with sleep researchers while dreaming may provide new opportunities for investigators to explore the world of dreams (Kahan & LaBerge, 1994).

Could a shocking dream be fatal? According to folklore, if you fall from a height in a dream you'd better wake up on the plunge downward, for if you hit the bottom the shock to your system will be so great that you will actually die in your sleep. Think about this one for a moment. *If* it were a genuine problem, who would have reported it? You can be sure that no one has ever testified to experiencing a fatal dream. This myth presumably exists because many people do awaken during the downward plunge, thinking that they've averted a close call. A study by Barrett (1988–1989) suggests that dreams of one's own death are relatively infrequent. However, people do have such dreams—and live to tell about them.

REVIEW OF KEY POINTS

- People's sleep needs vary in a normal distribution. The value of short naps depends on many factors, including one's biological rhythm. Alcohol and many other widely used drugs have a negative effect on sleep.

- Sleep learning is possible, but only in primitive ways. People's internal alarm clocks are not as reliable as often claimed. Yawning appears to be associated with boredom and sleepiness but is not well understood. Snoring occurs exclusively during sleep, increases after age 35, and may have more medical significance than most people realize.

- People can do many things to avoid or reduce sleep problems. Mostly, it's a matter of developing good daytime habits that do not interfere with sleep. Individuals troubled by transient insomnia should avoid panic, pursue effective relaxation, and try distracting themselves so they don't work too hard at falling asleep.

- Everyone dreams, but some people don't remember their dreams, probably because of the nature of their sleep cycle. Dream recall can be improved, and some people have even been taught to influence the course of their dreams.

- Freud distinguished between the manifest and latent content of dreams and asserted that dreams require interpretation. Most theorists agree that dreams require some interpretation, but doing so may not be as complicated as Freud assumed.

- In lucid dreams, people consciously recognize that they are dreaming and exert some control over the events in their dreams. Dreams are not instantaneous, and there's no evidence that they can be fatal.

CRITICAL THINKING APPLICATION

Is Alcoholism a Disease?
The Power of Definitions

Alcoholism is a major problem in most, perhaps all, societies. As we saw in the main body of the chapter, alcohol is a dangerous drug. Alcoholism destroys countless lives, tears families apart, and is associated with an elevated risk for a host of physical maladies (Johnson & Ait–Daoud, 2005). With the huge numbers of problem drinkers in our society, it seems likely that alcoholism has touched the lives of most of us.

In almost every discussion about alcoholism someone will ask, "Is alcoholism a disease?" If alcoholism is a disease, it is a strange one, because the alcoholic is the most direct cause of his or her own sickness. If alcoholism is *not* a disease, then what else might it be? Over the course of history, alcoholism has been categorized under many labels, from a personal weakness to a crime, a sin, a mental disorder, and a physical illness (Meyer, 1996). Each of these definitions carries important personal, social, political, and economic implications.

Consider, for instance, the consequences of characterizing alcoholism as a disease. If that is the case, then alcoholics should be treated like diabetics, heart patients, or victims of other physical illnesses. That is, they should be viewed with sympathy and should be given appropriate medical and therapeutic interventions to foster recovery from their illness. These treatments should be covered by medical insurance and delivered by health care professionals. Just as important, if alcoholism is defined as a disease, it should lose much of its stigma. After all, we don't blame people with diabetes or heart disease for their illnesses. Yes, alcoholics admittedly contribute to their own disease (by drinking too much), but so do many victims of diabetes and heart disease, who eat the wrong foods, fail to control their weight, and so forth (McLellan et al., 2000). And, as is the case with many physical illnesses, one can inherit a genetic vulnerability to alcoholism (Lin & Anthenelli, 2005), so it is difficult to argue that alcoholism is caused solely by one's behaviour.

However, if alcoholism is defined as a personal failure or a moral weakness, alcoholics are less likely to be viewed with sympathy and compassion. They might be admonished to quit drinking, be put in prison, or be punished in some other way. These responses to their alcoholism would be administered primarily by the legal system rather than the health care system, as medical interventions are not designed to remedy moral failings.

The key point here is that definitions lie at the centre of many complex debates, and they can have profound and far-reaching implications. People tend to think of definitions as insignificant, arbitrary, abstruse sets of words found buried in the obscurity of thick dictionaries compiled by ivory tower intellectuals. Well, much of this characterization may be accurate, but definitions are *not* insignificant. They are vested with enormous power to shape how people think about important issues. And an endless array of issues boil down to matters of definition. For example, the next time you hear people arguing over whether a particular movie is pornographic or whether spanking is child abuse, you'll find it helps to focus the debate on clarifying the definitions of the crucial concepts.

The Power to Make Definitions

So, how can we resolve the debate about whether alcoholism is a disease? Scientists generally try to resolve their debates by conducting research to achieve a better understanding of the phenomena under scrutiny. You may have noticed already that the assertion "We need more research on this issue …" is a frequent refrain in this text. Is more research the answer in this case? For once, the answer is "no." There is no conclusive way to determine whether alcoholism is a disease. It is not as though there is a "right" answer to this question that we can discover through more and better research.

The question of whether alcoholism is a disease is a *matter of definition:* Does alcoholism fit the currently accepted definition of what constitutes a disease? If you consult medical texts or dictionaries, you will find that *disease is typically defined as an impairment in the normal functioning of an organism that alters its vital functions.* Given that alcoholism clearly impairs people's normal functioning and disrupts a variety of vital functions (see Figure 5.24), it seems reasonable to characterize it as a disease, and this has been the dominant view since the middle of the 20th century (Maltzman, 1994; Meyer, 1996). Still, many critics express vigorous doubts about the wisdom of defining alcoholism as a disease (Peele, 2000). They often raise a question that comes up frequently in arguments about definitions: Who should have the power to make the definition? In this case, the power lies in the hands of the medical community, which seems sensible, given that disease is a medical concept. But some critics argue that the medical community has a strong bias in favour of defining conditions as diseases because this creates new markets and fuels economic growth for the health industry (Nikelly, 1994). Thus, debate about whether alcoholism is a disease seems likely to continue for the indefinite future.

To summarize, definitions generally do not emerge out of research. They are typically crafted by experts or authorities in a specific field who try to reach a consensus about how to best define a particular concept. Thus, in analyzing the validity of a definition, you need to look not only at the definition itself but at where it came from. Who decided what the definition should be? Does the source of the definition seem legitimate and appropriate? Did the authorities who formulated the definition have any biases that should be considered?

Definitions, Labels, and Circular Reasoning

There is one additional point about definitions that is worth discussing. Perhaps because definitions are imbued with so much power, people have an interesting tendency to incorrectly use them as *explanations* for the phenomena they describe. This logical error, which equates *naming* something with *explaining* it, is sometime called the *nominal fallacy*. Names and labels that are used as explanations may sound reasonable at first glance, but definitions do not really have any explanatory value; they simply specify what certain terms mean. Consider an example. Let's say your friend, Frank, has a severe drinking problem. You are sitting around with some other friends discussing why Frank drinks so much. Rest assured, at least one of these friends will assert that "Frank drinks too much because he is an alcoholic." This is circular reasoning, which is just as useless as explaining that Frank is an alcoholic because he drinks too much. It tells us nothing about *why* Frank has a drinking problem. The diagnostic labels that are used in the classification of mental disorders—labels such as schizophrenia, depression, autism, and obsessive-compulsive disorder—seem to invite this type of circular reasoning. For example, people often say things like "That person is delusional because she is schizophrenic," or "He is afraid of small, enclosed places because he is claustrophobic." These statements are just as logical as saying "She is a redhead because she has red hair." The logical fallacy of mistaking a label for an explanation will get us as far in our understanding as a dog gets in chasing its own tail.

Figure 5.24

Physiological malfunctions associated with alcoholism. This chart amply demonstrates that alcoholism is associated with a diverse array of physiological maladies. In and of itself, however, this information does not settle the argument about whether alcoholism should be regarded as a disease. It all depends on one's definition of what constitutes a disease.

Source: Edlin, G., & Golanty, E. (1992). *Health and wellness: A holistic approach.* Boston: Jones & Bartlett. Copyright © 1992 by Jones & Bartlett Publishers, Inc. www.jbpub.com. Reprinted by permission.

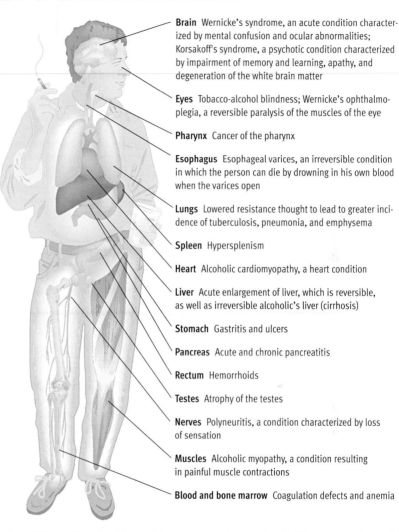

Brain Wernicke's syndrome, an acute condition characterized by mental confusion and ocular abnormalities; Korsakoff's syndrome, a psychotic condition characterized by impairment of memory and learning, apathy, and degeneration of the white brain matter

Eyes Tobacco-alcohol blindness; Wernicke's ophthalmoplegia, a reversible paralysis of the muscles of the eye

Pharynx Cancer of the pharynx

Esophagus Esophageal varices, an irreversible condition in which the person can die by drowning in his own blood when the varices open

Lungs Lowered resistance thought to lead to greater incidence of tuberculosis, pneumonia, and emphysema

Spleen Hypersplenism

Heart Alcoholic cardiomyopathy, a heart condition

Liver Acute enlargement of liver, which is reversible, as well as irreversible alcoholic's liver (cirrhosis)

Stomach Gastritis and ulcers

Pancreas Acute and chronic pancreatitis

Rectum Hemorrhoids

Testes Atrophy of the testes

Nerves Polyneuritis, a condition characterized by loss of sensation

Muscles Alcoholic myopathy, a condition resulting in painful muscle contractions

Blood and bone marrow Coagulation defects and anemia

Table 5.6 Critical Thinking Skills Discussed in This Application

Skill	Description
Understanding the way definitions shape how people think about issues	The critical thinker appreciates the enormous power of definitions and the need to clarify definitions in efforts to resolve disagreements.
Identifying the source of definitions	The critical thinker recognizes the need to determine who has the power to make specific definitions and to evaluate their credibility.
Avoiding the nominal fallacy in working with definitions and labels	The critical thinker understands that labels do not have explanatory value.

RECAP

Key Ideas

The Nature of Consciousness
● Consciousness is the continually changing stream of mental activity. There is some degree of awareness during sleep and sometimes even when patients are under anesthesia.

● Consciousness clearly is adaptive, but the question of exactly why it evolved is open to debate. Variations in consciousness are related to brain activity, as measured by the EEG.

Biological Rhythms and Sleep
● The cycle of sleep and wakefulness is influenced by circadian rhythms. Exposure to light resets biological clocks by affecting the activity of the suprachiasmatic nucleus and the pineal gland, which secretes melatonin.

● Being out of sync with circadian rhythms is one reason for jet lag and for the unpleasant nature of rotating shift work. Melatonin may have some value in treating jet lag and other sleep problems, but more research is needed.

The Sleep and Waking Cycle
● During a night's sleep, you evolve through a series of stages in cycles of approximately 90 minutes. During the REM stage you experience rapid eye movements, brain waves characteristic of waking thought, and vivid dreaming. The sleep cycle tends to be repeated four times in a night, as REM sleep gradually becomes more predominant and NREM sleep dwindles.

● The REM portion of sleep declines during childhood, levelling off at around 20%. During adulthood, slow-wave sleep declines. Culture appears to have little impact on the physiological experience of sleep, but it does influence sleeping arrangements and napping patterns.

● People often underestimate the impact of sleep deprivation. Going without sleep appears to contribute to many transportation accidents and mishaps at work. Research on selective sleep deprivation suggests that people need REM sleep and slow-wave sleep.

● Many people are troubled by sleep disorders. Foremost among these disorders is insomnia, which has a variety of causes. Other common sleep problems include narcolepsy, sleep apnea, night terrors, nightmares, and somnambulism.

The World of Dreams
● The conventional view is that dreams are mental experiences during REM sleep that have a storylike quality, include vivid imagery, are often bizarre, and are regarded as real by the dreamer, but theorists have begun to question many aspects of this view.

● The content of one's dreams may be affected by one's age and gender, events in one's life, and external stimuli experienced during the dream. There are variations across cultures in dream recall, content, and interpretation.

● Freud argued that the purpose of dreams is wish fulfillment. Cartwright has articulated a problem-solving view, whereas Hobson and McCarley assert that dreams are side effects of the neural activation seen during REM sleep.

Hypnosis: Altered Consciousness or Role Playing?
● Hypnosis has a long and curious history. People vary greatly in their susceptibility to hypnosis. Among other things, hypnosis can produce anesthesia, sensory distortions, disinhibition, and posthypnotic amnesia.

● There are two major theoretical approaches to hypnosis that view it either as an altered state of consciousness or as a normal state of consciousness in which subjects assume a hypnotic role.

Meditation: Pure Consciousness or Relaxation?
● Evidence suggests that meditation leads to a potentially beneficial physiological state characterized by suppression of bodily arousal. However, the long-term benefits of meditation may not be unique to meditation and critics are worried about methodological flaws in meditation research.

Altering Consciousness with Drugs
● Recreational drug use involves an effort to alter consciousness with psychoactive drugs. Psychoactive drugs exert their main effects in the brain, where they alter neurotransmitter activity in a variety of ways. The mesolimbic dopamine pathway may mediate the reinforcing effects of most abused drugs.

● Drugs vary in their potential for psychological and physical dependence. Likewise, the dangers to health vary depending on the drug. Recreational drug use can prove harmful to health by producing an overdose, by causing tissue damage, or by increasing health-impairing behaviour.

Putting It in Perspective
● Four of our unifying themes were highlighted in this chapter. We saw that psychology evolves in a sociohistorical context, that experience is highly subjective, that culture influences many aspects of behaviour, and that psychology is characterized by theoretical diversity.

Personal Application • Addressing Practical Questions about Sleep and Dreams
● People's sleep needs vary, and the value of short naps depends on many factors. Sleep learning is possible, but only in primitive ways. People's internal alarm clocks are not as reliable as often claimed.

● People can do many things to avoid or reduce sleep problems. Mostly, it's a matter of developing good daytime habits that do not interfere with sleep. Individuals troubled by transient insomnia should avoid panic, pursue relaxation, and try distracting themselves.

● Everyone dreams, but some people cannot remember their dreams, probably because of the nature of their sleep cycle. In lucid dreams, people consciously recognize that they are dreaming and exert some control over the events in their dreams. Most theorists believe that dreams require some interpretation, but this may not be as complicated as once assumed.

Critical Thinking Application • Is Alcoholism a Disease? The Power of Definitions
● Like many questions, the issue of whether alcoholism should be regarded as a disease is a matter of definition. In evaluating the validity of a definition, one should look not only at the definition but also at where it came from. People have a tendency to use definitions as explanations for the phenomena they describe, but doing so involves circular reasoning.

Key Terms

Alcohol, 209
Ascending reticular activating system (ARAS), 190
Biological rhythms, 183
Cannabis, 209
Circadian rhythms, 183
Dissociation, 204
Electroencephalograph (EEG), 182
Electromyograph (EMG), 186
Electrooculograph (EOG), 186
Hallucinogens, 208
Hypnosis, 201
Insomnia, 193
Latent content, 219
Lucid dreams, 219
Manifest content, 219
MDMA, 209
Meditation, 204
Narcolepsy, 195
Narcotics, 207
Night terrors, 196
Nightmares, 196
Non-REM (NREM) sleep, 188
Opiates, 207
Physical dependence, 212
Psychoactive drugs, 206
Psychological dependence, 212
REM sleep, 188
Sedatives, 208
Sleep apnea, 196
Slow-wave sleep (SWS), 186
Somnambulism, 196
Stimulants, 208
Tolerance, 209

Key People

Theodore Barber, 203
Rosalind Cartwright, 200
William Dement, 188
Sigmund Freud, 199
Calvin Hall, 197
Ernest Hilgard, 204
J. Allan Hobson, 200
William James, 182
Shepard Siegel, 212
Nicholas Spanos, 201

PRACTICE TEST

1. An EEG would indicate primarily _____ activity while you take this test.
   A. alpha
   B. beta
   C. delta
   D. theta

2. Other things being equal, which of the following flights would lead to the greatest difficulty with jet lag?
   A. northward
   B. southward
   C. eastward
   D. westward

3. Slow-wave sleep consists of stages _____ of sleep and is dominated by _____ waves.
   A. 1 and 2; beta
   B. 2 and 3; alpha
   C. 3 and 4; delta
   D. 1 and 2; delta

4. As the sleep cycle evolves through the night, people tend to:
   A. spend more time in REM sleep and less time in NREM sleep.
   B. spend more time in NREM sleep and less time in REM sleep.
   C. spend a more or less equal amount of time in REM sleep and NREM sleep.
   D. spend more time in stage 4 sleep and less time in REM sleep.

5. Newborn infants spend about _____% of their sleep time in REM, while adults spend about _____% of their sleep time in REM.
   A. 20; 50
   B. 50; 20
   C. 20; 20
   D. 50; 50

6. Tamara has taken part in a three-day study in which she was awakened every time she went into REM sleep. Now that she is home sleeping without interference, it is likely that she will:
   A. exhibit psychotic symptoms for a few nights.
   B. experience severe insomnia for about a week.
   C. spend extra time in REM sleep for a few nights.
   D. spend less time in REM sleep for a few nights.

7. Which of the following generally occurs during REM sleep?
   A. sleep apnea
   B. somnambulism
   C. night terrors
   D. nightmares

8. Which of the following is *not* true of cultural influences on dream experiences?
   A. The ability to recall dreams is fairly consistent across cultures.
   B. In some cultures, people are held responsible for their dream actions.
   C. In many cultures, dreams are seen as a window into the spiritual world.
   D. People in some cultures believe that dreams provide information about the future.

9. The activation-synthesis theory of dreaming contends that:
   A. dreams are simply the byproduct of bursts of activity in the brain.
   B. dreams provide an outlet for energy invested in socially undesirable impulses.
   C. dreams represent the brain's attempt to process information taken in during waking hours.
   D. dreams are an attempt to restore a neurotransmitter balance within the brain.

10. A common driving experience is "highway hypnosis," in which one's consciousness seems to be divided between the driving itself and one's conscious train of thought. This phenomenon is consistent with the idea that hypnosis is:
    A. an exercise in role playing.
    B. a dissociated state of consciousness.
    C. a goal-directed fantasy.
    D. not an altered state of consciousness.

11. Stimulant is to depressant as:
    A. cocaine is to alcohol.
    B. mescaline is to barbiturates.
    C. caffeine is to amphetamines.
    D. alcohol is to barbiturates.

12. Amphetamines work by increasing the levels of _____ in a variety of ways.
    A. GABA and glycine
    B. melatonin
    C. acetylcholine
    D. norepinephrine and dopamine

13. Which of the following drugs would be most likely to result in a fatal overdose?
    A. LSD
    B. mescaline
    C. marijuana
    D. sedatives

14. Which of the following is a true statement about naps?
    A. Daytime naps invariably lead to insomnia.
    B. Daytime naps are invariably refreshing and an efficient way to rest.
    C. Daytime naps are not very efficient ways to sleep, but their effects are sometimes beneficial.
    D. Taking many naps during the day can substitute for a full night's sleep.

15. Definitions:
    A. generally emerge out of research.
    B. often have great explanatory value.
    C. generally exert little influence over how people think.
    D. are usually constructed by experts or authorities in a specific field.

    See Appendix A for answers to this Practice Test.

 ON THE WEB

For additional resources on the topics covered in this chapter, visit the *Psychology: Themes and Variations* Web site, where you will find practice quizzes, tutorials, Web links, simulations, critical thinking activities, flash cards, interactive exercises, and suggested readings available through INFOTRAC.

http://www.themesandvariations.nelson.com

 http://hed.nelson.com

Go to this site for the link to ThomsonNOW™, your one-stop study shop. Take a Pretest for this chapter and ThomsonNOW™ will generate a personalized Study Plan based on your test results! The Study Plan will identify the topics you need to review and direct you to online resources to help you master those topics. You can then take a Posttest to help you determine the concepts you have mastered and what you still need work on.

CHAPTER 6

Classical Conditioning
Pavlov's Demonstration: "Psychic Reflexes"
Terminology and Procedures
Classical Conditioning in Everyday Life
Featured Study • Sex and the Single Quail
Basic Processes in Classical Conditioning

Operant Conditioning
Thorndike's Law of Effect
Skinner's Demonstration: It's All a Matter of Consequences
Terminology and Procedures
Basic Processes in Operant Conditioning
Reinforcement: Consequences That Strengthen Responses
Intermittent Reinforcement: Effects of Basic Schedules
Positive Reinforcement versus Negative Reinforcement
Negative Reinforcement and Avoidance Behaviour
Punishment: Consequences That Weaken Responses

Changing Directions in the Study of Conditioning
Recognizing Biological Constraints on Conditioning
Recognizing Cognitive Processes in Conditioning

Observational Learning
Basic Processes
Acquisition versus Performance
Applications

Putting It in Perspective

Personal Application • **Achieving Self-Control Through Behaviour Modification**
Specifying Your Target Behaviour
Gathering Baseline Data
Designing Your Program
Executing and Evaluating Your Program
Ending Your Program

Critical Thinking Application • **Manipulating Emotions: Pavlov and Persuasion**
Classical Conditioning in Advertising
Classical Conditioning in Business Negotiations
Classical Conditioning in the World of Politics
Becoming More Aware of Classical Conditioning Processes

Recap

Practice Test

Latchezar Boyadjiev, *Independence,* L.B. Glass Studios

Learning

- You're sitting in the waiting room of your dentist's office. You cringe when you hear the whirring of a dental drill coming from the next room.
- A four-year-old boy pinches his hand in one of his toys and curses loudly. His mother looks up in dismay and says to his father, "Where did he pick up that kind of language?"
- A young girl goes to the front closet, takes out a chain leash for her dog, and jingles the chain loudly. The dog leaps off the couch and comes running, wagging its tail with excitement.
- A seal waddles across the stage, bows ceremoniously, and "doffs his cap" by flipping it into the air and catching it in his mouth. The spectators at the aquatic show clap appreciatively as the trainer tosses the seal a fish as a reward.
- The crowd hushes as an Olympic diver prepares to execute her dive. In a burst of motion she propels herself into the air and glides smoothly through a dazzling corkscrew somersault.

What do all of these scenarios have in common? At first glance, very little. They are a diverse collection of events, some trivial, some impressive. However, they do share one common thread: *They all involve learning.* This may surprise you. When most people think of learning, they envision students reading textbooks or novices working to acquire a specific skill, such as riding a bicycle or skiing. Although such activities do involve learning, they represent only the tip of the iceberg in psychologists' eyes.

Perhaps we can illustrate some of the range of phenomena covered by what psychologists refer to by the term *learning* by telling you some things you may not know about hockey icon Wayne Gretzky. As a player, his talents were legendary. For example, on December 30, 1981, he put the puck into an empty net in a game against the Philadelphia Flyers, giving the Edmonton Oilers the victory. The goal he scored not only won the game for his team but also secured his place in hockey history because it was his 50th goal, a goal scored in his 39th game ("50 Goals," n.d.). It broke the record of Montreal's Rocket Richard who had first scored 50 goals in 50 games— a record no one expected to be broken. Breaking this record was unexpected by most, but not by Wayne's father, Walter, his greatest supporter. When Wayne phoned his father after the game, Walter gave his congratulations and remarked, "What took you so long?" (Gretzky & Reilly, 1990, p. 61).

Gretzky went on to win four Stanley Cups with Edmonton and then to revitalize hockey in Los Angeles as a member of the L.A. Kings. After his playing career was over, he became a part owner of an NHL team, and as general manager guided Canada's men's hockey team to an Olympic gold

Wayne Gretzky had many superstitions while playing hockey. He is well known for tucking in his jersey before each game. His superstitions also affected the way he put on his equipment for the game and what he ate just before the game.

medal in 2002, Canada's first in 50 years. But, you may be wondering, what does Gretzky have to do with learning? The most obvious answer is to point to his skill as a player. While there is no doubt that he has great natural ability, he goes to great lengths to point out the importance of the practice and skill acquisition training sessions conducted when he was young by his father. In addition, as a player, Gretzky was extremely superstitious: He ate the same food each day before a game; when on a scoring streak, he often would not cut his hair; he always tucked in only the right side of his hockey jersey; he would not let his stick touch other players' sticks or cross each other; and he put on his equipment exactly the same way each time he dressed for a game. You may even have superstitions of your own—perhaps a favourite pen to use when writing an exam or a lucky shirt to wear when flying in an airplane.

Superstitions like these are often the result of obtaining a reward after engaging in some behaviour. Boston Bruins hockey legend Phil Esposito was known for always wearing a black turtleneck under his hockey jersey. It all began before one game when he put on a turtleneck because he was suffering from a cold. That night he scored a hat trick, and so wore a turtleneck under his uniform every game until he retired ("Esposito's Turtleneck," n.d.) Athletes frequently believe that if they repeat the behaviour, such as wearing the black turtleneck, the good luck will continue, thus giving them an edge over the competition (Todd, 2003). As we will discuss later in the chapter, this is a prototypic example of what psychologists are referring to when they use the term *learning*—in this case, a type of learning known as *operant conditioning*.

One more characteristic about Gretzky is noteworthy in connection with a chapter on learning. Gretzky was afraid to fly (Gretzky & Reilly, 1990). He frequently rented limousines to take him to hockey games in other cities if it was possible to get there by car in time. When he had to fly, his team-mates sometimes had to sit on him in his seat to keep him there. He later found sitting in the cockpit more comfortable—it seemed to ease his fear of flying. Such fears are termed *phobias*. Phobias are irrational fears of specific objects or situations and are often the result of another learning process termed *classical conditioning*. Phobias are relatively common. A study for the Public Health Agency of Canada (Antony & Swinson, 1996) gave lifetime prevalence rates for simple phobias at about 11%. You will also learn more about phobias in Chapter 14.

The study of learning is about more than phobias and superstitions and has had a long and important history in psychology. ***Learning* refers to a relatively durable change in behaviour or knowledge that is due to experience.** This broad definition means that learning is one of the most fundamental concepts in all of psychology. Learning includes the acquisition of knowledge and skills, but it also shapes personal habits, such as nail biting; personality traits, such as shyness; emotional responses, such as a fear of storms; and personal preferences, such as a taste for tacos or a distaste for formal clothes. Much of your behaviour is the result of learning. If it were possible to strip away your learned responses, little behaviour would be left. You would not be able to read this book, find your way home, or cook yourself a hamburger. You would be about as complex and exciting as a turnip.

Although we depend on learning, it is *not* an exclusively human process. Most organisms are capable of learning. Even the lowly flatworm can acquire a learned response. As this chapter unfolds, you may be surprised to see that much of the research on learning has been conducted using animals as subjects. Why? Mainly because researchers can exert much better experimental control over animal subjects than human subjects. As we saw in Chapter 1, that was one of the reasons why the noted behaviourist John B. Watson advocated the study of animal behaviour. For the most part, Watson's plan has worked out well. Decades of research have shown that many principles of learning discovered in animal research apply quite well to humans.

In this chapter, we will focus most of our attention on a specific kind of learning: conditioning. *Conditioning* involves learning associations between events that occur in an organism's environment. In investigating conditioning, psychologists study learning at a very fundamental level. This strategy has paid off with fruitful insights that have laid the foundation for the study of more complex forms of learning, including learning by means of observation. In the Personal Application, you'll see how you can harness the principles of conditioning to improve your self-control. The Critical Thinking Application shows how conditioning procedures can be used to manipulate emotions.

Classical Conditioning

Do you go weak in the knees at the thought of standing on the roof of a tall building? Does your heart race when you imagine encountering a harmless garter snake? If so, you can understand, at least to some degree, what it's like to have a phobia. **Phobias are irrational fears of specific objects or situations.** Mild phobias are commonplace (Eaton, Dryman, & Weissman, 1991). Over the years, students in our classes have described their phobic responses to a diverse array of stimuli, including bridges, elevators, tunnels, heights, dogs, cats, bugs, snakes, professors, doctors, strangers, thunderstorms, and germs. If you have a phobia, you may have wondered how you managed to acquire such a perplexing fear. Chances are, it was through classical conditioning (Antony & McCabe, 2003).

Classical conditioning is a type of learning in which a stimulus acquires the capacity to evoke a response that was originally evoked by another stimulus. The process was first described around 1900 by Ivan Pavlov, and it is sometimes called **Pavlovian conditioning** in tribute to him. The term *conditioning* comes from Pavlov's determination to discover the "conditions" that produce this kind of learning.

Pavlov's Demonstration: "Psychic Reflexes"

Ivan Pavlov was a prominent Russian physiologist who did Nobel Prize–winning research on digestion. According to York University psychologist and historian Ray Fancher (1979), Pavlov was something of a "classic" himself—he was an absent-minded but brilliant professor obsessed with his research. He was absent-minded about many things including money, sometimes forgetting to pick up his pay for months. He rarely carried money with him. One exception

Surrounded by his research staff, the great Russian physiologist Ivan Pavlov (centre, white beard) demonstrates his famous classical conditioning experiment with dogs.

was on his first trip to New York where he was mugged of $800—a great deal of money in those days. If he was absent-minded about money, he was very serious about his work. Legend has it that Pavlov once reprimanded an assistant who arrived late for an experiment because of trying to avoid street fighting in the midst of the Russian Revolution. The assistant defended his tardiness, saying, "But Professor, there's a revolution going on with shooting in the streets!" Pavlov supposedly replied, "What the hell difference does a revolution make when you've work to do in the laboratory? Next time there's a revolution, get up earlier!" Apparently, dodging bullets wasn't an adequate excuse for delaying the march of scientific progress (Fancher, 1979; Gantt, 1975).

Pavlov was studying the role of saliva in the digestive processes of dogs when he stumbled onto what he called "psychic reflexes" (Pavlov, 1906). Like many great discoveries, Pavlov's was partly accidental, although he had the insight to recognize its significance. His subjects were dogs restrained in harnesses in an experimental chamber (see Figure 6.1). Their saliva was collected by means of a surgically implanted tube in the salivary gland. Pavlov would present meat powder to a dog and then collect the resulting saliva. As his research progressed, he noticed that dogs accustomed to the procedure would start salivating *before* the meat powder was presented. For instance, they would salivate in response to a clicking sound made by the device that was used to present the meat powder.

Intrigued by this unexpected finding, Pavlov decided to investigate further. To clarify what was happening, he paired the presentation of the meat powder with various stimuli that would stand out in the laboratory situation. For instance, in some experiments he used a simple auditory stimulus—the presentation of a tone. After the tone and the meat powder had been presented together a number of times, the tone was presented alone. What happened? The dogs responded by salivating to the sound of the tone alone.

What was so significant about a dog salivating when a tone was presented? The key is that the tone started out as a *neutral* stimulus. That is, it did not originally produce the response of salivation. However, Pavlov managed to change that by pairing the tone with a stimulus (meat powder) that did produce the salivation response. Through this process, the tone acquired the capacity to trigger the response of salivation. What Pavlov had demonstrated was how

PREVIEW QUESTIONS
- What happens in classical conditioning?
- What are the key elements in this type of learning?
- What types of emotional responses are modulated by classical conditioning?
- What are some physiological processes governed by classical conditioning?
- How are conditioned responses acquired and weakened?
- What is higher-order conditioning?

Web Link 6.1

Phobias
http://www.cpa.ca/factsheets/phobias.htm

For more information on phobias and how to deal with them, head to this page of the Canadian Psychological Association's Web site.

Next time there's a revolution, get up earlier!
IVAN PAVLOV

Figure 6.1

Classical conditioning apparatus. An experimental arrangement similar to the one depicted here (taken from Yerkes & Morgulis, 1909) has typically been used in demonstrations of classical conditioning, although Pavlov's original set-up (see inset) was quite a bit simpler. The dog is restrained in a harness. A tone is used as the conditioned stimulus (CS), and the presentation of meat powder is used as the unconditioned stimulus (UCS). The tube inserted into the dog's salivary gland allows precise measurement of its salivation response. The pen and rotating drum of paper on the left are used to maintain a continuous record of salivary flow. (Inset) The less elaborate set-up that Pavlov originally used to collect saliva on each trial is shown here (Goodwin, 1991).

Sources: Figure 6.1: Adapted from Yerkes, R. M., & Morgulis, S. (1909), "The Method of Pavlov in Animal Psychology," *Psychological Bulletin, 6,* 257–273. American Psychological Association. Inset: From Goodwin, C. J., "Misportraying Pavlov's Apparatus," 1991. *American Journal of Psychology 104* (1), 135–141. © 1991 by the Board of Trustees of the University of Illinois.

learned associations—which were viewed as the basic building blocks of the entire learning process—were formed by events in an organism's environment. Based on this insight, he built a broad theory of learning that attempted to explain aspects of emotion, temperament, neuroses, and language (Windholz, 1997).

Terminology and Procedures 5A

There is a special vocabulary associated with classical conditioning. It often looks intimidating to the uninitiated, but it's really not all that mysterious. The bond Pavlov noted between the meat powder and salivation was a natural, unlearned association. It did not have to be created through conditioning. It is therefore called an *unconditioned* association. Thus, **the *unconditioned stimulus (UCS)* is a stimulus that evokes an unconditioned response without previous conditioning. The *unconditioned response (UCR)* is an unlearned reaction to an unconditioned stimulus that occurs without previous conditioning.**

In contrast, the link between the tone and salivation was established through conditioning. It is there-

fore called a *conditioned* association. Thus, **the *conditioned stimulus (CS)* is a previously neutral stimulus that has, through conditioning, acquired the capacity to evoke a conditioned response. The *conditioned response (CR)* is a learned reaction to a conditioned stimulus that occurs because of previous conditioning.** Ironically, the names for the four key elements in classical conditioning (the UCS, UCR, CS, and CR) are the byproduct of a poor translation of Pavlov's writing into English. Pavlov actually used the words condition*al* and uncondition*al* to refer to these concepts (Todes, 1997).

To avoid possible confusion, it is worth noting that the unconditioned response and conditioned response often consist of the same behaviour, although there may be subtle differences between them. In Pavlov's initial demonstration, the UCR and CR were both salivation. When evoked by the UCS (meat powder), salivation was an unconditioned response. When evoked by the CS (the tone), salivation was a conditioned response. The procedures involved in classical conditioning are outlined in Figure 6.2.

Pavlov's "psychic reflex" came to be called the *conditioned reflex*. Classically conditioned responses have traditionally been characterized as reflexes and are said to be *elicited* (**drawn forth**) because most of them are relatively automatic or involuntary. However, research in recent decades has demonstrated that classical conditioning is involved in a wider range of human and animal behaviour than previously appreciated, including some types of nonreflexive responding (Allan, 1998). Finally, **a *trial* in classical conditioning consists of any presentation of a stimulus or pair of stimuli.** Psychologists are interested in how many trials are required to establish a particular conditioned bond. The number needed to form an association varies considerably. Although classical conditioning generally proceeds gradually, it *can* occur quite rapidly, sometimes in just one pairing of the CS and UCS.

Classical Conditioning in Everyday Life

In laboratory experiments on classical conditioning, researchers have generally worked with extremely simple responses. Besides salivation, frequently studied favourites include eyelid closure, knee jerks, the flexing of various limbs, and fear responses. The study of such simple responses has proven both practical and productive. However, these responses do not even begin to convey the rich diversity of everyday behaviours regulated by classical conditioning. Let's look at some examples of classical conditioning taken from everyday life.

Conditioned Fears

Classical conditioning often plays a key role in shaping emotional responses such as fears. Phobias are a good example of such responses. Case studies of patients suffering from phobias suggest that many irrational fears can be traced back to experiences that involve classical conditioning (Ayres, 1998; McAllister & McAllister, 1995). Wayne Gretzky's fear of flying is a good example. While not giving any evidence of being aware of the formal principles of Pavlov's classical conditioning, Gretzky in his autobiography (Gretzky & Reilly, 1990) refers to a couple of early experiences that fit with conditioning theory. It is easy to imagine how such conditioning can occur outside of the laboratory. For example, one of our students was troubled by a bridge phobia so severe that she couldn't drive on highways because of all the viaducts that had to be crossed. She was able to pinpoint as the source of her phobia something that had happened during her childhood (see Figure 6.3). Whenever her family drove to visit her grandmother,

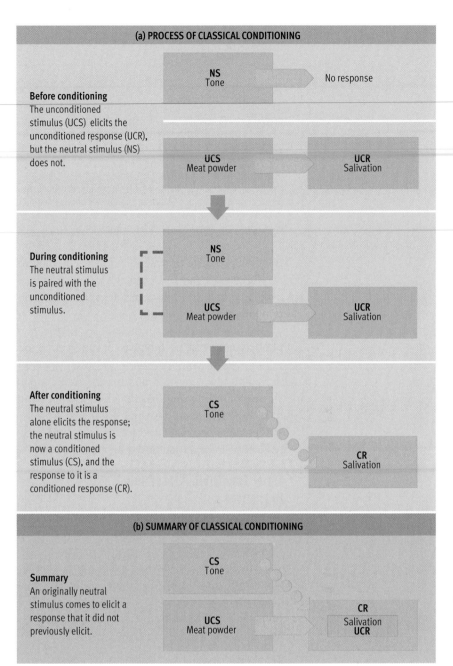

Figure 6.2

The sequence of events in classical conditioning. **(a)** Moving downward, this series of three panels outlines the sequence of events in classical conditioning, using Pavlov's original demonstration as an example. **(b)** As we encounter other examples of classical conditioning throughout the book, we will see many diagrams like the one in this panel, which will provide snapshots of specific instances of classical conditioning.

they had to cross a little-used, rickety, dilapidated bridge out in the countryside. Her father, in a misguided attempt at humour, made a major production out of these crossings. He would stop short of the bridge and carry on about the enormous danger. Obviously, he thought the bridge was safe or he wouldn't have driven across it. However, the naïve young girl was terrified by her father's scare tactics.

Figure 6.3

Classical conditioning of a fear response. Many emotional responses that would otherwise be puzzling can be explained by classical conditioning. In the case of one woman's bridge phobia, the fear originally elicited by her father's scare tactics became a conditioned response to the stimulus of bridges.

Hence, the bridge became a conditioned stimulus eliciting great fear. Unfortunately, the fear spilled over to *all* bridges. Forty years later she was still carrying the burden of this phobia.

Everyday fear responses that are less severe than phobias may also be products of classical conditioning. For instance, if you cringe when you hear the sound of a dentist's drill, this response is due to classical conditioning. In this case, the pain you have experienced from dental drilling is the UCS. This pain has been paired with the sound of the drill, which became a CS eliciting your cringe.

Other Conditioned Emotional Responses

Classical conditioning is not limited to producing unpleasant emotions such as fear. Many pleasant emotional responses are also acquired through classical conditioning. Consider the following example, described by a woman who wrote a letter to newspaper columnist Bob Greene about the news that a company was bringing back a discontinued product—Beemans gum. She wrote:

That was the year I met Charlie. I guess first love is always the same.... Charlie and I went out a lot. He chewed Beemans gum and he smoked.... We would go to all the passion pits—the drive-in movies and the places to park. We did a lot of necking, but we always stopped at a certain point. Charlie wanted to get married when we got out of high school ... [but] Charlie and I drifted apart. We both ended up getting married to different people.

And the funny thing is ... for years the combined smell of cigarette smoke and Beemans gum made my knees weak. Those two smells were Charlie to me. When I would smell the Beemans and the cigarette smoke, I could feel the butterflies dancing all over my stomach.

The writer clearly had a unique and long-lasting emotional response to the smell of Beemans gum

and cigarettes. Her experiences led to a connection between these stimuli and her emotional reaction. Her reactions that were originally derived from her assignations with Charlie were later elicited by stimuli associated with Charlie at the time. The credit for this *pleasant* response goes to classical conditioning (see Figure 6.4).

Advertising campaigns often try to take advantage of classical conditioning. Advertisers frequently pair their products with UCSs that elicit pleasant emotions (Till & Priluck, 2000). The most common strategy is to present a product in association with an attractive person or enjoyable surroundings (see Figure 6.5). Advertisers hope that these pairings will make their products conditioned stimuli that evoke good feelings. For example, Kodak used a child playing with puppies in one of its TV commercials to help associate warm feelings with its film products. Advertisers also may pair their products with well-known, popular celebrities.

Conditioning and Physiological Responses

Classical conditioning affects not only overt behaviours but physiological processes as well. Consider, for example, your body's immune functioning. When an infectious agent invades your body, your immune system attempts to repel the invasion by producing specialized proteins called *antibodies*. The critical importance of the immune response becomes evident when the immune system is disabled, as occurs with the disease AIDS (acquired immune deficiency syndrome).

Figure 6.4

Classical conditioning and romance. Pleasant emotional responses can be acquired through classical conditioning, as illustrated by one woman's unusual conditioned response to the aroma of Beemans gum and cigarette smoke.

Recent advances have revealed that the functioning of the immune system can be influenced by psychological factors, including conditioning (Ader, 2001). Robert Ader and Nicholas Cohen (1984, 1993) have shown that classical conditioning procedures can lead to *immunosuppression*—a decrease in the production of antibodies. In a typical study, animals are injected with a drug (the UCS) that *chemically* causes immunosuppression while they are simultaneously given an unusual-tasting liquid to drink (the CS). Days later, after the chemical immunosuppression has ended, some of the animals are re-exposed to the CS by giving them the unusual-tasting solution. Measurements of antibody production indicate that animals exposed to the CS show a reduced immune response (see Figure 6.6).

Immune resistance is only one example of the subtle physiological processes that can be influenced by classical conditioning. Studies suggest that classical conditioning can also elicit *allergic reactions* (MacQueen et al., 1989) and that classical conditioning contributes to the growth of *drug tolerance* and the experience of withdrawal symptoms when drug use is halted (McDonald & Seigel, 2004; Siegel, 2001). You may recall that we introduced you to the work of McMaster University's Shepard Siegel in Chapter 5. Siegel suggests that the events that occur during administration of a drug and the context of the drug use may come to serve as CSs for drug-related effects. In Chapter 5 we also discussed the concept of drug tolerance. Continued use of drugs may lead to increased drug tolerance in which increasing amounts of the drug are needed to produce the same effect. Drug use leads the body to produce compensatory responses in an attempt to counteract or compensate for the effects of the drug on the body. The greater the compensatory response, the more of the drug that is needed to produce the same effect.

One factor that may contribute to increased tolerance results from classical conditioning, associating predrug contextual cues with the effects of the drug. Imagine, for example, a particular drug user who always takes the drug in a specific setting: alone, in a park, at night, by the swings. That setting (a predrug CS), for example, may become associated with the drug's effects (UCS) and the body's compensatory responses (UCRs).

The contextual cues (in the park, by the swings) may themselves come to elicit (conditioned) compensatory responses that contribute to the development of tolerance for the drug. "When the drug is administered repeatedly in the context of the usual

Figure 6.5

Classical conditioning in advertising. Many advertisers attempt to make their products conditioned stimuli that elicit pleasant emotional responses by pairing their products with attractive or popular people or sexual imagery.

predrug cues, these cues elicit a CCR that attenuates the drug effect. As the drug is administered more and more often, and the CCR grows in strength, the attenuation of the drug effect becomes more pronounced" (Seigel, 2002, p. 4). In addition, when the drug user is in the company of the cues associated with drug use but not administering the drug itself, withdrawal symptoms may be produced (McDonald & Siegel, 2004).

Recently, researchers have shown an interest in how classical conditioning modulates sexual responding (Pfaus, Kippin, & Centeno, 2001), which brings us to our Featured Study.

Figure 6.6

Classical conditioning of immunosuppression. When a neutral stimulus is paired with a drug that chemically causes immunosuppression, it can become a CS that elicits immunosuppression on its own. Thus, even the immune response can be influenced by classical conditioning.

Figure 6.9

Acquisition, extinction, and spontaneous recovery. During acquisition, the strength of the dog's conditioned response (measured by the amount of salivation) increases rapidly and then levels off near its maximum. During extinction, the CR declines erratically until it's extinguished. After a "rest" period in which the dog is not exposed to the CS, a spontaneous recovery occurs, and the CS once again elicits a (weakened) CR. Repeated presentations of the CS alone re-extinguish the CR, but after another "rest" interval, a weaker spontaneous recovery occurs.

Extinction: Weakening Conditioned Responses

Fortunately, a newly formed stimulus–response bond does not necessarily last indefinitely. If it did, learning would be inflexible, and organisms would have difficulty adapting to new situations. Instead, the right circumstances produce *extinction*, **the gradual weakening and disappearance of a conditioned response tendency.**

What leads to extinction in classical conditioning? The consistent presentation of the conditioned stimulus *alone*, without the unconditioned stimulus. For example, when Pavlov consistently presented *only* the tone to a previously conditioned dog, the tone gradually lost its capacity to elicit the response of salivation. Such a sequence of events is depicted in the yellow portion of Figure 6.9, which graphs the amount of salivation by a dog over a series of conditioning trials. Note how the salivation response declines during extinction.

How long does it take to extinguish a conditioned response? That depends on many factors, but particularly the strength of the conditioned bond when extinction begins. Some conditioned responses extinguish quickly, while others are difficult to weaken.

Spontaneous Recovery: Resurrecting Responses

Some conditioned responses display the ultimate in tenacity by "reappearing from the dead" after having been extinguished. Learning theorists use the term *spontaneous recovery* to describe such a resurrection from the graveyard of conditioned associations. *Spontaneous recovery* **is the reappearance of an extinguished response after a period of nonexposure to the conditioned stimulus.**

Pavlov (1927) observed this phenomenon in some of his pioneering studies. He fully extinguished a dog's CR of salivation to a tone and then returned the dog to its home cage for a "rest interval" (a period of nonexposure to the CS). On a subsequent day, when the dog was brought back to the experimental chamber for retesting, the tone was sounded and the salivation response reappeared. Although it had returned, the rejuvenated response was weak. The salivation was less than when the response was at its peak strength. If Pavlov consistently presented the CS by itself again, the response re-extinguished quickly. However, in some of the dogs the response made still another spontaneous recovery (typically even weaker than the first) after they had spent another period in their cages (consult Figure 6.9 once again).

Recent studies have also demonstrated that if a response is extinguished in a different environment than it was acquired, the extinguished response will reappear if the animal is returned to the original environment where acquisition took place (Bouton, 1994). This phenomenon, called the *renewal effect,* along with the evidence on spontaneous recovery, suggests that extinction somehow suppresses a conditioned response rather than erasing a learned association. In other words, *extinction does not appear to lead to unlearning* (Bouton & Nelson, 1998). The theoretical meaning of spontaneous recovery and the renewal effect is complex and the subject of some debate. However, their practical meaning is quite simple: Even if you manage to rid yourself of an unwanted conditioned response (such as cringing when you hear a dental drill), there is an excellent chance that it may make a surprise reappearance later.

Stimulus Generalization

After conditioning has occurred, organisms often show a tendency to respond not only to the exact CS used but also to other, similar stimuli. For example, Pavlov's dogs might have salivated in response to a different-sounding tone, or you might cringe at the sound of a jeweller's as well as a dentist's drill. These are examples of stimulus generalization. *Stimulus generalization* **occurs when an organism that has learned a response to a specific stimulus responds in the same way to new stimuli that are similar to the original stimulus.** Generalization is adaptive given that organisms rarely encounter the exact same stimulus more than once (Thomas, 1992). Stimulus generalization is also commonplace. We have already discussed a real-life example: the woman who acquired a bridge phobia during her childhood because her father scared her

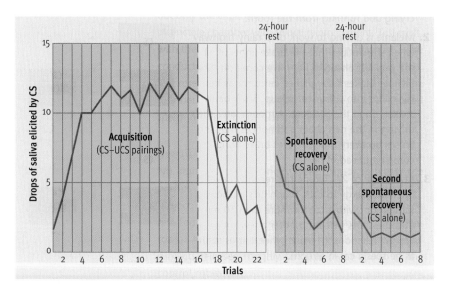

Comment

This study was featured because it highlights the growing influence of the evolutionary perspective in psychology. Researchers are increasingly investigating Pavlovian conditioning by trying to discern its adaptive significance (Hollis, 1997). This research is also extremely interesting for what it implies about human sexual functioning. Psychologists have long suspected that stimuli routinely paired with sex, such as seductive nightgowns, mood music, lit candles, and the like, probably become conditioned stimuli that elicit arousal, but this hypothesis is not readily investigated in the laboratory with human subjects. Elucidating the role of classical conditioning in sexual functioning may also shed new light on how humans' sexual tastes can go awry in the form of *fetishes* for inanimate objects. If quail can be conditioned to find a red light or a distinctive chamber arousing, it seems likely that humans may be conditioned to be aroused by objects such as shoes, boots, leather, and undergarments. ■

Basic Processes in Classical Conditioning

Classical conditioning is often portrayed as a mechanical process that inevitably leads to a certain result. This view reflects the fact that most conditioned responses are reflexive and difficult to control—Pavlov's dogs would have been hard pressed to withhold their salivation. Similarly, most people with phobias have great difficulty suppressing their fear. However, this vision of classical conditioning as an "irresistible force" is misleading because it fails to consider the many factors involved in classical conditioning (Kehoe & Macrae, 1998). In this section, we'll look at basic processes in classical conditioning to expand on the rich complexity of this form of learning.

Acquisition: Forming New Responses

We have already discussed *acquisition* without attaching a formal name to the process. **Acquisition refers to the initial stage of learning something.** Pavlov theorized that the acquisition of a conditioned response depends on *stimulus contiguity*. Stimuli are contiguous if they occur together in time and space.

Stimulus contiguity is important, but learning theorists now realize that contiguity alone doesn't automatically produce conditioning (Miller & Grace, 2003). People are bombarded daily by countless stimuli that could be perceived as being paired, yet only some of these pairings produce classical conditioning. Consider the woman who developed a conditioned emotional reaction to the smell of Beemans gum and cigarettes. There were no doubt other stimuli that shared contiguity with her boyfriend, Charlie. He smoked, so ashtrays were probably present, but she doesn't get weak in the knees at the sight of an ashtray.

If conditioning does not occur to all the stimuli present in a situation, what determines its occurrence? Evidence suggests that stimuli that are novel, unusual, or especially intense have more potential to become CSs than routine stimuli, probably because they are more likely to stand out among other stimuli (Hearst, 1988).

CONCEPT CHECK 6.1

Identifying Elements in Classical Conditioning

Check your understanding of classical conditioning by trying to identify the unconditioned stimulus (UCS), unconditioned response (UCR), conditioned stimulus (CS), and conditioned response (CR) in each of the examples below. Fill in the diagram next to each example. You'll find the answers in Appendix A in the back of the book.

1. Sam is three years old. One night his parents build a roaring fire in the family room fireplace. The fire spits out a large ember that hits Sam in the arm, giving him a nasty burn that hurts a great deal for several hours. A week later, when Sam's parents light another fire in the fireplace, Sam becomes upset and fearful, crying and running from the room.

2. Melanie is driving to work on a rainy highway when she notices that the brake lights of all the cars just ahead of her have come on. She hits her brakes but watches in horror as her car glides into a four-car pileup. She's badly shaken up in the accident. A month later she's driving in the rain again and notices that she tenses up every time she sees brake lights come on ahead of her.

3. At the age of 24, Tyrone has recently developed an allergy to cats. When he's in the same room with a cat for more than 30 minutes, he starts wheezing. After a few such allergic reactions, he starts wheezing as soon as he sees a cat in a room.

Figure 6.9

Acquisition, extinction, and spontaneous recovery. During acquisition, the strength of the dog's conditioned response (measured by the amount of salivation) increases rapidly and then levels off near its maximum. During extinction, the CR declines erratically until it's extinguished. After a "rest" period in which the dog is not exposed to the CS, a spontaneous recovery occurs, and the CS once again elicits a (weakened) CR. Repeated presentations of the CS alone re-extinguish the CR, but after another "rest" interval, a weaker spontaneous recovery occurs.

Extinction: Weakening Conditioned Responses

Fortunately, a newly formed stimulus–response bond does not necessarily last indefinitely. If it did, learning would be inflexible, and organisms would have difficulty adapting to new situations. Instead, the right circumstances produce *extinction*, **the gradual weakening and disappearance of a conditioned response tendency.**

What leads to extinction in classical conditioning? The consistent presentation of the conditioned stimulus *alone,* without the unconditioned stimulus. For example, when Pavlov consistently presented *only* the tone to a previously conditioned dog, the tone gradually lost its capacity to elicit the response of salivation. Such a sequence of events is depicted in the yellow portion of Figure 6.9, which graphs the amount of salivation by a dog over a series of conditioning trials. Note how the salivation response declines during extinction.

How long does it take to extinguish a conditioned response? That depends on many factors, but particularly the strength of the conditioned bond when extinction begins. Some conditioned responses extinguish quickly, while others are difficult to weaken.

Spontaneous Recovery: Resurrecting Responses

Some conditioned responses display the ultimate in tenacity by "reappearing from the dead" after having been extinguished. Learning theorists use the term *spontaneous recovery* to describe such a resurrection from the graveyard of conditioned associations. **Spontaneous recovery is the reappearance of an extinguished response after a period of nonexposure to the conditioned stimulus.**

Pavlov (1927) observed this phenomenon in some of his pioneering studies. He fully extinguished a dog's CR of salivation to a tone and then returned the dog to its home cage for a "rest interval" (a period of nonexposure to the CS). On a subsequent day, when the dog was brought back to the experimental chamber for retesting, the tone was sounded and the salivation response reappeared. Although it had returned, the rejuvenated response was weak. The salivation was less than when the response was at its peak strength. If Pavlov consistently presented the CS by itself again, the response re-extinguished quickly. However, in some of the dogs the response made still another spontaneous recovery (typically even weaker than the first) after they had spent another period in their cages (consult Figure 6.9 once again).

Recent studies have also demonstrated that if a response is extinguished in a different environment than it was acquired, the extinguished response will reappear if the animal is returned to the original environment where acquisition took place (Bouton, 1994). This phenomenon, called the *renewal effect,* along with the evidence on spontaneous recovery, suggests that extinction somehow suppresses a conditioned response rather than erasing a learned association. In other words, *extinction does not appear to lead to unlearning* (Bouton & Nelson, 1998). The theoretical meaning of spontaneous recovery and the renewal effect is complex and the subject of some debate. However, their practical meaning is quite simple: Even if you manage to rid yourself of an unwanted conditioned response (such as cringing when you hear a dental drill), there is an excellent chance that it may make a surprise reappearance later.

Stimulus Generalization

After conditioning has occurred, organisms often show a tendency to respond not only to the exact CS used but also to other, similar stimuli. For example, Pavlov's dogs might have salivated in response to a different-sounding tone, or you might cringe at the sound of a jeweller's as well as a dentist's drill. These are examples of stimulus generalization. **Stimulus generalization occurs when an organism that has learned a response to a specific stimulus responds in the same way to new stimuli that are similar to the original stimulus.** Generalization is adaptive given that organisms rarely encounter the exact same stimulus more than once (Thomas, 1992). Stimulus generalization is also commonplace. We have already discussed a real-life example: the woman who acquired a bridge phobia during her childhood because her father scared her

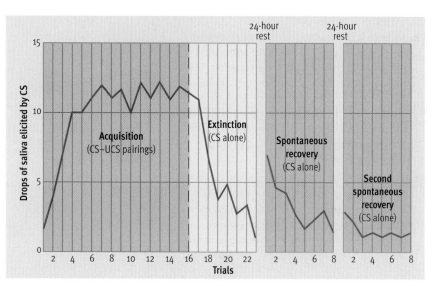

Recent advances have revealed that the functioning of the immune system can be influenced by psychological factors, including conditioning (Ader, 2001). Robert Ader and Nicholas Cohen (1984, 1993) have shown that classical conditioning procedures can lead to *immunosuppression*—a decrease in the production of antibodies. In a typical study, animals are injected with a drug (the UCS) that *chemically* causes immunosuppression while they are simultaneously given an unusual-tasting liquid to drink (the CS). Days later, after the chemical immunosuppression has ended, some of the animals are re-exposed to the CS by giving them the unusual-tasting solution. Measurements of antibody production indicate that animals exposed to the CS show a reduced immune response (see Figure 6.6).

Immune resistance is only one example of the subtle physiological processes that can be influenced by classical conditioning. Studies suggest that classical conditioning can also elicit *allergic reactions* (MacQueen et al., 1989) and that classical conditioning contributes to the growth of *drug tolerance* and the experience of withdrawal symptoms when drug use is halted (McDonald & Seigel, 2004; Siegel, 2001). You may recall that we introduced you to the work of McMaster University's Shepard Siegel in Chapter 5. Siegel suggests that the events that occur during administration of a drug and the context of the drug use may come to serve as CSs for drug-related effects. In Chapter 5 we also discussed the concept of drug tolerance. Continued use of drugs may lead to increased drug tolerance in which increasing amounts of the drug are needed to produce the same effect. Drug use leads the body to produce compensatory responses in an attempt to counteract or compensate for the effects of the drug on the body. The greater the compensatory response, the more of the drug that is needed to produce the same effect.

One factor that may contribute to increased tolerance results from classical conditioning, associating predrug contextual cues with the effects of the drug. Imagine, for example, a particular drug user who always takes the drug in a specific setting: alone, in a park, at night, by the swings. That setting (a predrug CS), for example, may become associated with the drug's effects (UCS) and the body's compensatory responses (UCRs).

The contextual cues (in the park, by the swings) may themselves come to elicit (conditioned) compensatory responses that contribute to the development of tolerance for the drug. "When the drug is administered repeatedly in the context of the usual predrug cues, these cues elicit a CCR that attenuates the drug effect. As the drug is administered more and more often, and the CCR grows in strength, the attenuation of the drug effect becomes more pronounced" (Seigel, 2002, p. 4). In addition, when the drug user is in the company of the cues associated with drug use but not administering the drug itself, withdrawal symptoms may be produced (McDonald & Siegel, 2004).

Recently, researchers have shown an interest in how classical conditioning modulates sexual responding (Pfaus, Kippin, & Centeno, 2001), which brings us to our Featured Study.

Figure **6.5**

Classical conditioning in advertising. Many advertisers attempt to make their products conditioned stimuli that elicit pleasant emotional responses by pairing their products with attractive or popular people or sexual imagery.

CS Products (e.g., beer)		
UCS Attractive person		CR Pleasant emotional response UCR

© Bill Aron/PhotoEdit

CS Unusual-tasting liquid		
UCS Injection of immuno-suppressive drug		CR Immuno-suppression UCR

Figure **6.6**

Classical conditioning of immunosuppression. When a neutral stimulus is paired with a drug that chemically causes immunosuppression, it can become a CS that elicits immunosuppression on its own. Thus, even the immune response can be influenced by classical conditioning.

Sex and the Single Quail

Investigators: Michael Domjan (University of Texas, Austin), Elisabeth Blesbois, and John Williams (Institut National de Recherche Agronomique, Centre de Tours, France)

Source: The adaptive significance of sexual conditioning: Pavlovian control of sperm release. *Psychological Science*, 1998, *9*, 411–415.

Previous research had shown that male Japanese quail could be conditioned to become sexually aroused by an originally neutral stimulus. The neutral stimulus—a red light—was paired with opportunities to copulate with a female. These pairings eventually made the red light a CS that elicited excitement in the male subjects—and led them to copulate more quickly if females were made available in the presence of the red light (Domjan, 1992, 1994). The present study examined the evolutionary significance of this type of sexual conditioning. The investigators hypothesized that this type of conditioning might have a favourable impact on organisms' reproductive fitness by increasing the quantity or quality of sperm released.

Method

Subjects. Twenty-nine adult male Japanese quail were used in the experiment. Fifteen came from a line of experimental animals previously bred for high sociality and 14 from a line bred for low emotionality.

Apparatus. The conditioned stimulus was a distinctive chamber (painted white with a wire mesh floor) in which the males were given copulation opportunities. On test trials, the subjects' semen was collected by allowing them to mount a taxidermically prepared artificial female made of terrycloth and polyester fibre.

Procedure. The subjects in the experimental group went through six conditioning trials, each of which involved giving them access to a receptive female in the distinctive chamber (see Figure 6.7). The subjects in the control group were given similar opportunities for copulation, but in their home cages. Thus, both groups received equivalent handling and sexual opportunities, but only the experimental group learned to associate the distinctive chamber with sexual reinforcement. Test trials, with the artificial female in the distinctive chamber, were conducted after the fourth and sixth conditioning trials. The researchers measured semen volume, estimated the number of spermatozoa per ejaculate, and evaluated sperm quality (the percentage of viable sperm).

Results

No significant differences were found between the groups in sperm quality. However, the experimental subjects ejaculated a greater volume of semen, which resulted in the release of a greater number of spermatozoa. As you can see in Figure 6.8, the experimental subjects released roughly twice as many sperm as the control subjects.

Figure 6.7

Classical conditioning of sexual arousal. Working with quail, Domjan and his colleagues (1998) paired the neutral stimulus of a distinctive chamber with a receptive female and the opportunity to copulate. Hence, the chamber became a conditioned stimulus that elicited a conditioned response of sexual arousal.

Discussion

The physiological mechanisms underlying the enhanced sperm release will require further investigation. Domjan and his colleagues speculate that the conditioned stimulus *may* have elicited greater muscular contractions during ejaculation. Obviously, a conditioned response that results in the ejaculation of a greater number of spermatozoa should facilitate the fertilization of eggs and result in increased offspring. Thus, the investigators conclude that their study "demonstrates an important way in which Pavlovian conditioning can alter reproductive fitness" (pp. 412–413).

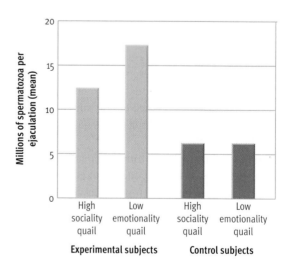

Figure 6.8

Effect of classical conditioning on sperm release. The conditioning of sexual arousal in the two experimental groups clearly enhanced sperm release in these groups, as compared to the two control groups.

Source: Adapted from Domjan, M., Blesbois, E., & Williams, J. (1998). The adaptive significance of sexual conditioning: Pavlovian control of sperm release. *Psychological Science, 9*, 411–415. Blackwell Publishers. Adapted by permission.

whenever they went over a particular old bridge. The original CS for her fear was that specific bridge, but her fear was ultimately *generalized* to all bridges.

The likelihood and amount of generalization to a new stimulus depend on the similarity between the new stimulus and the original CS (Balsam, 1988). The basic law governing generalization is this: *The more similar new stimuli are to the original CS, the greater the generalization.* This principle can be quantified in graphs called *generalization gradients,* such as those shown in Figure 6.10. These generalization gradients map out how a dog conditioned to salivate to a tone of 1200 hertz might respond to other tones. As you can see, the strength of the generalization response declines as the similarity between the new stimuli and the original CS decreases.

Stimulus Discrimination 5B

Stimulus discrimination is just the opposite of stimulus generalization. **Stimulus discrimination occurs when an organism that has learned a response to a specific stimulus does *not* respond in the same way to new stimuli that are similar to the original stimulus.** Like generalization, discrimination is adaptive in that an animal's survival may hinge on its being able to distinguish friend from foe, or edible from poisonous food (Thomas, 1992). Organisms can gradually learn to discriminate between an original CS and similar stimuli if they have adequate experience with both. For instance, let's say your pet dog runs around, excitedly wagging its tail, whenever it hears your car pull up in the driveway. Initially it will probably respond to *all* cars that pull into the driveway (stimulus generalization). However, if there is anything distinctive about the sound of your car, your dog may gradually respond with excitement to only your car and not to other cars (stimulus discrimination).

The development of stimulus discrimination usually requires that the original CS (your car) continue to be paired with the UCS (your arrival) while similar stimuli (the other cars) not be paired with the UCS. As with generalization, a basic law governs discrimination: *The less similar new stimuli are to the original CS, the greater the likelihood (and ease) of discrimination.* Conversely, if a new stimulus is quite similar to the original CS, discrimination will be relatively difficult to learn. What happens to a generalization gradient when an organism learns a discrimination? The generalization gradient gradually narrows around the original CS, which means that the organism is generalizing to a smaller and smaller range of similar stimuli (consult Figure 6.10 again).

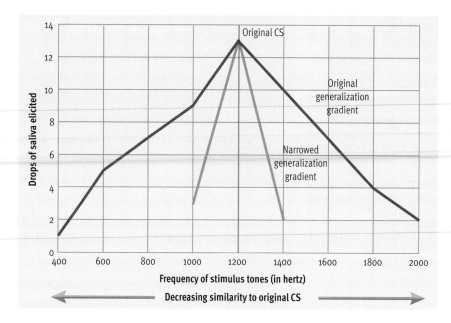

Figure 6.10

Generalization gradients. In a study of stimulus generalization, an organism is typically conditioned to respond to a specific CS, such as a 1200-hertz tone, and then is tested with similar stimuli, such as other tones between 400 and 2000 hertz. Graphs of the organism's responding are called *generalization gradients.* The graphs normally show, as depicted here, that generalization declines as the similarity between the original CS and the new stimuli decreases. When an organism gradually learns to *discriminate* between a CS and similar stimuli, the generalization gradient tends to narrow around the original CS.

Higher-Order Conditioning 5B

Imagine that you were to conduct the following experiment. First, you condition a dog to salivate in response to the sound of a tone by pairing the tone with meat powder. Once the tone is firmly established as a CS, you pair the tone with a new stimulus, let's say a red light, for 15 trials. You then present the red light alone, without the tone. Will the dog salivate in response to the red light?

The answer is "yes." Even though the red light has never been paired with the meat powder, it will acquire the capacity to elicit salivation by virtue of being paired with the tone (see Figure 6.11). This is a demonstration of **higher-order conditioning, in which a conditioned stimulus functions as if it were an unconditioned stimulus.** Higher-order conditioning shows that classical conditioning does not depend on the presence of a genuine, natural UCS. An already established CS will do just fine. In higher-order conditioning, new conditioned responses are built on the foundation of already established conditioned responses. Many human conditioned responses are the product of higher-order conditioning (Rescorla, 1980). The phenomenon of higher-order conditioning greatly extends the reach of classical conditioning.

Figure 6.11

Higher-order conditioning.
Higher-order conditioning involves a two-phase process. In the first phase, a neutral stimulus (such as a tone) is paired with an unconditioned stimulus (such as meat powder) until it becomes a conditioned stimulus that elicits the response originally evoked by the UCS (such as salivation). In the second phase, another neutral stimulus (such as a red light) is paired with the previously established CS, so that it also acquires the capacity to elicit the response originally evoked by the UCS.

REVIEW OF KEY POINTS

- Learning is defined as a relatively durable change in behaviour or knowledge due to experience. Classical conditioning explains how a neutral stimulus can acquire the capacity to elicit a response originally elicited by another stimulus. This kind of conditioning was originally described by Ivan Pavlov, who conditioned dogs to salivate in response to the sound of a tone.

- In classical conditioning, the unconditioned stimulus (UCS) is a stimulus that elicits an unconditioned response without previous conditioning. The unconditioned response (UCR) is an unlearned reaction to an unconditioned stimulus that occurs without previous conditioning. The conditioned stimulus (CS) is a previously neutral stimulus that has acquired the capacity to elicit a conditioned response. The conditioned response (CR) is a learned reaction to a conditioned stimulus.

- Classically conditioned responses are said to be elicited. Many kinds of everyday responses are regulated through classical conditioning, including phobias, mild fears, and pleasant emotional responses. Even subtle physiological responses such as immune system functioning respond to classical conditioning. Our Featured Study showed that sexual arousal can be influenced by Pavlovian conditioning and that this process may have adaptive significance.

- Stimulus contiguity plays a key role in the acquisition of new conditioned responses. A conditioned response may be weakened and extinguished entirely when the CS is no longer paired with the UCS. In some cases, spontaneous recovery occurs, and an extinguished response reappears after a period of nonexposure to the CS.

- Conditioning may generalize to additional stimuli that are similar to the original CS.

- The opposite of generalization is discrimination, which involves not responding to stimuli that resemble the original CS. When an organism learns a discrimination, the generalization gradient narrows around the original CS. Higher-order conditioning occurs when a CS functions as if it were a UCS.

Operant Conditioning

PREVIEW QUESTIONS

- How did Thorndike's law of effect anticipate Skinner's findings?
- What are the key elements in operant conditioning?
- How do organisms acquire new responses through operant conditioning?
- What is resistance to extinction, and why does it matter?
- How does stimulus control fit into operant responding?
- How do primary and secondary reinforcers differ?

Even Pavlov recognized that classical conditioning is not the only form of conditioning. Classical conditioning best explains reflexive responding that is largely controlled by stimuli that *precede* the response. However, humans and other animals make a great many responses that don't fit this description. Consider the response that you are engaging in right now: studying. It is definitely not a reflex (life might be easier if it were). The stimuli that govern it (exams and grades) do not precede it. Instead, your studying is mainly influenced by stimulus events that *follow* the response—specifically, its *consequences*.

In the 1930s, this kind of learning was christened *operant conditioning* by B. F. Skinner. The term was derived from his belief that in this type of responding, an organism "operates" on the environment instead of simply reacting to stimuli. Learning occurs because responses come to be influenced by the outcomes that follow them. Thus, **operant conditioning is a form of learning in which responses come to be controlled by their consequences.** Learning theorists originally distinguished between classical and operant conditioning on the grounds that the former regulated reflexive, involuntary responses, whereas the latter governed voluntary responses. This distinction holds up much of the time, but it is not absolute. Research in recent decades has shown that classical conditioning sometimes contributes to the regulation of voluntary behaviour, that operant conditioning can influence involuntary, visceral responses, and that the two types of conditioning jointly and interactively govern some aspects of behaviour (Allan, 1998; Turkkan, 1989). Indeed, some theorists have argued that classical and operant conditioning should just be viewed as two different aspects of a single learning process (Donahoe & Vegas, 2004).

Thorndike's Law of Effect

Another name for operant conditioning is *instrumental learning*, a term introduced earlier by Edward L. Thorndike (1913). Thorndike wanted to emphasize that this kind of responding is often *instrumental* in obtaining some desired outcome. His pioneering work provided the foundation for many of the ideas proposed later by Skinner (Chance, 1999). Thorndike began studying animal learning around the turn of the last century. Setting out to determine whether animals could think, he conducted some classic studies of problem solving in cats. In these studies, a hungry cat was placed in a small cage or "puzzle box" with food available just outside. The cat could escape to obtain the food by performing a specific response, such as pulling a wire or depressing a lever (see Figure 6.12). After each escape, the cat was rewarded with a small amount of food and then returned to the cage for another trial. Thorndike monitored how long it took the cat to get out of the box over a series of trials. If the cat could think, Thorndike reasoned, there would be a sudden drop in the time required to escape when the cat recognized the solution to the problem.

Instead of a sudden drop, Thorndike observed a gradual, uneven decline in the time it took cats to escape from his puzzle boxes (see the graph in Figure 6.12). The decline in solution time showed that the cats *were learning*. But the gradual nature of this decline suggested that this learning did *not* depend on thinking and understanding. Instead, Thorndike attributed this learning to a principle he called the *law of effect*. According to the ***law of effect, if a response in the presence of a stimulus leads to satisfying effects, the association between the stimulus and the response is strengthened.*** Thorndike viewed instrumental learning as a mechanical process in which successful responses are gradually "stamped in" by their favourable effects. His law of effect became the cornerstone of Skinner's theory of operant conditioning, although Skinner used different terminology.

Skinner's Demonstration: It's All a Matter of Consequences

Like Pavlov, Skinner (1953, 1969, 1984) conducted some deceptively simple research that became enormously influential (Lattal, 1992). Ironically, he got off to an inauspicious start. His first book, *The Behavior of Organisms* (1938), sold only 80 copies in its first four years in print. Nonetheless, he went on to become,

in the words of historian Albert Gilgen (1982), "without question the most famous American psychologist in the world" (p. 97). You may recall that we discussed Alexandra Rutherford's analysis of the popularization of some of Skinner's work in Chapter 1. He was a very recognizable face to North Americans and wrote popular as well as scientific articles.

The fundamental principle of operant conditioning is uncommonly simple and was anticipated by Thorndike's law of effect. *Skinner demonstrated that organisms tend to repeat those responses that are followed by favourable consequences.* This fundamental principle is embodied in Skinner's concept of reinforcement. ***Reinforcement occurs when an event following a response increases an organism's tendency to make that response.*** In other words, a response is strengthened because it leads to rewarding consequences (see Figure 6.13).

The principle of reinforcement may be simple, but it is immensely powerful. Skinner and his followers have shown that much of everyday behaviour is regulated by reinforcement. For example, you put money in a pop vending machine and you get a soft drink back as a result. Paradoxically, though, this principle emerged out of Skinner's research on the behaviour of rats and pigeons in exceptionally simple situations. Let's look at that research.

Terminology and Procedures

Like Pavlov, Skinner created a prototype experimental procedure that has been repeated (with variations) thousands of times. In his research Skinner typically used pigeons or rats. They made ideal participants for his research where the focus was on observable behaviour, although Hank Davis from the

Figure 6.12

The learning curve of one of Thorndike's cats. The inset shows one of Thorndike's puzzle boxes. The cat had to perform three separate acts to escape the box, including depressing the pedal on the right. The learning curve shows how the cat's escape time declined gradually over a number of trials.

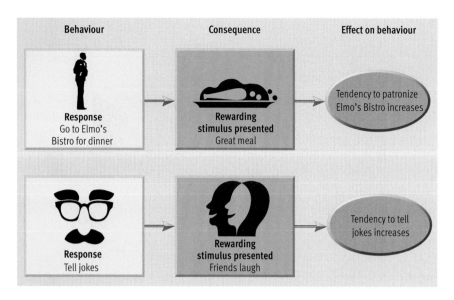

Behaviour	Consequence	Effect on behaviour

Response
Go to Elmo's
Bistro for dinner

**Rewarding
stimulus presented**
Great meal

Tendency to patronize
Elmo's Bistro increases

Response
Tell jokes

**Rewarding
stimulus presented**
Friends laugh

Tendency to tell
jokes increases

Figure 6.13

Reinforcement in operant conditioning. According to Skinner, reinforcement occurs when a response is followed by rewarding consequences and the organism's tendency to make the response increases. The two examples diagrammed here illustrate the basic premise of operant conditioning—that voluntary behaviour is controlled by its consequences. These examples involve positive reinforcement (for a comparison of positive and negative reinforcement, see Figure 6.18 on page 245).

Courtesy of B. F. Skinner

"*Operant conditioning shapes behavior as a sculptor shapes a lump of clay.*"
B.F. SKINNER

University of Guelph suggests that psychologists may have underestimated the rat's intelligence (Davis, 1996). In the typical procedure, a rat or a pigeon is placed in an *operant chamber* that has come to be better known as a "Skinner box." **An *operant chamber,* or *Skinner box,* is a small enclosure in which an animal can make a specific response that is recorded while the consequences of the response are systematically controlled.** In the boxes designed for rats, the main response made available is pressing a small lever mounted on one side wall (see Figure 6.14). In the boxes made for pigeons, the designated response is pecking a small disk mounted on a side wall. Because operant responses *tend* to be voluntary, they are said to be *emitted* rather than *elicited*. **To *emit* means to send forth.**

The Skinner box permits the experimenter to control the reinforcement contingencies that are in effect for the animal. ***Reinforcement contingencies are the circumstances or rules that determine whether responses lead to the presentation of reinforcers.*** Typically, the experimenter manipulates whether positive consequences occur when the animal makes the designated response. The main positive consequence is usually delivery of a small bit of food into a food cup mounted in the chamber. Because the animals are deprived of food for a while prior to the experimental session, their hunger virtually ensures that the food serves as a reinforcer.

The key dependent variable in most research on operant conditioning is the subjects' *response rate* over time. An animal's rate of lever pressing or disk pecking in the Skinner box is monitored continuously by a device known as a cumulative recorder (see Figure 6.14). **The *cumulative recorder* creates a graphic record of responding and reinforcement in a Skinner box**

as a function of time. The recorder works by means of a roll of paper that moves at a steady rate underneath a movable pen. When there is no responding, the pen stays still and draws a straight horizontal line, reflecting the passage of time. Whenever the designated response occurs, however, the pen moves upward a notch. The pen's movements produce a graphic summary of the animal's responding over time. The pen also makes slash marks to record the delivery of each reinforcer.

The results of operant-conditioning studies are usually portrayed in graphs. In these graphs, the horizontal axis is used to mark the passage of time, while the vertical axis is used to plot the accumulation of responses, as shown in Figure 6.15. In interpreting these graphs, the key consideration is the *slope* of the line that represents the record of responding. *A rapid response rate produces a steep slope, whereas a slow response rate produces a shallow slope.* Because the response record is cumulative, the line never goes down. It can only go up as more responses are made or flatten out if the response rate slows to zero. The magnifications shown in Figure 6.15 show how slope and response rate are related.

Basic Processes in Operant Conditioning SIM4, 5c

Although the principle of reinforcement is strikingly simple, many other processes involved in operant conditioning make this form of learning just as complex as classical conditioning. In fact, some of the *same* processes are involved in both types of conditioning. In this section, we'll discuss how the processes of acquisition, extinction, generalization, and discrimination occur in operant conditioning.

Acquisition and Shaping SIM4, 5c

As in classical conditioning, *acquisition* in operant conditioning refers to the initial stage of learning some new pattern of responding. However, the procedures used to establish a tendency to emit an operant response are different from those used to create the typical conditioned response. Operant responses are usually established through a gradual process called ***shaping,* which consists of the reinforcement of closer and closer approximations of a desired response.**

Shaping is necessary when an organism does not, on its own, emit the desired response. One of our colleagues used shaping to help her housetrain her new puppy. Because the dog, named Meisje, was small and quiet, she had difficulty in determining when the puppy needed to go outside. She thought that she would train the puppy to ring a bell, but of course puppies do not naturally ring bells. So she began to shape the puppy by rewarding him as he came progressively closer to the bell, finally reinforcing Meisje's behaviour only when he rang the bell with his nose. He now can communicate his needs to her easily. She reports a couple of other interesting effects. When she leaves town, she can readily find someone to dog-sit her puppy because no matter where he stays, she brings along the bell and he can let the caretaker know when he needs to go outside. Curiously, however, at home, she finds herself frequently getting up and running to the back door whenever she hears any bell—she suspects the puppy may be ringing the bell just to see her run to the back door.

Shaping was an important component of Skinner's research. For example, when a rat is first placed in a Skinner box, it may not press the lever at all. In this case an experimenter begins shaping by releasing food pellets whenever the rat moves toward the lever. As this response becomes more frequent, the experimenter starts requiring a closer approximation of the desired response, possibly releasing food only when the rat actually touches the lever. As reinforcement increases the rat's tendency to touch the lever, the rat will spontaneously press the lever on occasion, finally providing the experimenter with an opportunity to reinforce the designated response. These reinforcements will gradually increase the rate of lever pressing.

The mechanism of shaping is the key to training animals to perform impressive tricks. When you go to a zoo, circus, or marine park and see bears riding bicycles, monkeys playing the piano, and whales leaping through hoops, you are witnessing the results

Figure 6.14

Skinner box and cumulative recorder. **(a)** This diagram highlights some of the key features of an operant chamber, or Skinner box. In this apparatus designed for rats, the response under study is lever pressing. Food pellets, which may serve as reinforcers, are delivered into the food cup on the right. The speaker and light permit manipulations of visual and auditory stimuli, and the electric grid gives the experimenter control over aversive consequences (shock) in the box. **(b)** A cumulative recorder connected to the box keeps a continuous record of responses and reinforcements. A small segment of a cumulative record is shown here. The entire process is automatic as the paper moves with the passage of time; each lever press moves the pen up a step, and each reinforcement is marked with a slash. **(c)** This photo shows the real thing—a rat being conditioned in a Skinner box. Note the food dispenser on the left, which was omitted from the diagram.

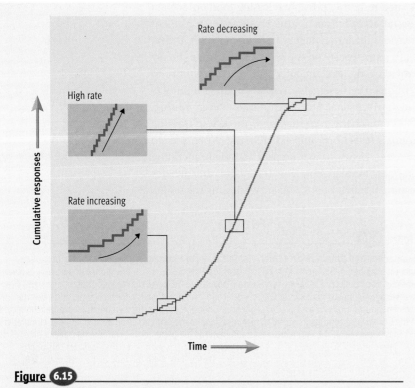

Figure 6.15

A graphic portrayal of operant responding. The results of operant conditioning are often summarized in a graph of cumulative responses over time. The insets magnify small segments of the curve to show how an increasing response rate yields a progressively steeper slope (bottom); a high, steady response rate yields a steep, stable slope (middle); and a decreasing response rate yields a progressively flatter slope (top).

food when the rat presses the lever. When the extinction process is begun, a brief surge often occurs in the rat's responding, followed by a gradual decline in response rate until it approaches zero.

A key issue in operant conditioning is how much *resistance to extinction* an organism will display when reinforcement is halted. **Resistance to extinction occurs when an organism continues to make a response after delivery of the reinforcer has been terminated.** The greater the resistance to extinction, the longer the responding will continue. Thus, if a researcher stops giving reinforcement for lever pressing and the response tapers off slowly, the response shows high resistance to extinction. However, if the response tapers off quickly, it shows relatively little resistance to extinction.

Resistance to extinction may sound like a matter of purely theoretical interest, but it's actually quite practical. People often want to strengthen a response in such a way that it will be relatively resistant to extinction. For instance, most parents want to see their child's studying response survive even if the child hits a rocky stretch when studying doesn't lead to reinforcement (good grades). In a similar fashion, a casino wants to see patrons continue to gamble, even if they encounter a lengthy losing streak. Thus, a high degree of resistance to extinction can be desirable in many situations. Resistance to extinction depends on a variety of factors. Chief among them is the *schedule of reinforcement* used during acquisition, a matter that we will discuss a little later in this chapter.

Stimulus Control: Generalization and Discrimination

Operant responding is ultimately controlled by its consequences, as organisms learn response–outcome (R–O) associations (Colwill, 1993). However, stimuli that *precede* a response can also exert considerable influence over operant behaviour. When a response is consistently followed by a reinforcer in the presence of a particular stimulus, that stimulus comes to serve as a "signal" indicating that the response is likely to lead to a reinforcer. Once an organism learns the signal, it tends to respond accordingly (Honig & Alsop, 1992). For example, a pigeon's disk pecking may be reinforced only when a small light behind the disk is lit. When the light is out, pecking does not lead to the reward. Pigeons quickly learn to peck the disk only when it is lit. The light that signals the availability of reinforcement is called a discriminative stimulus. **Discriminative stimuli are cues that influence operant behaviour by indicating the probable consequences (reinforcement or nonreinforcement) of a response.**

of shaping. To demonstrate the power of shaping techniques, Skinner once trained some pigeons so that they appeared to play Ping-Pong. They would run about on opposite ends of a Ping-Pong table and peck the ball back and forth. Keller and Marian Breland, a couple of psychologists influenced by Skinner, went into the business of training animals for advertising and entertainment purposes. One of their better known feats was shaping "Priscilla, the Fastidious Pig" to turn on a radio, eat at a kitchen table, put dirty clothes in a hamper, run a vacuum, and then "go shopping" with a shopping cart. Of course, Priscilla picked the sponsor's product off the shelf in her shopping expedition (Breland & Breland, 1961).

Extinction

 SIM4, 5c

In operant conditioning, *extinction* refers to the gradual weakening and disappearance of a response tendency because the response is no longer followed by a reinforcer. Extinction begins in operant conditioning whenever previously available reinforcement is stopped. In laboratory studies with rats, this usually means that the experimenter stops delivering

Courtesy of Animal Behavior Enterprises, Inc.

© Gerald Davis by permission of Karen Davis

Shaping—an operant technique in which an organism is rewarded for closer and closer approximations of the desired response—is used in teaching both animals and humans. It is the main means of training animals to perform unnatural tricks. Breland and Breland's (1961) famous subject, "Priscilla, the Fastidious Pig," is shown on the left.

Discriminative stimuli play a key role in the regulation of operant behaviour. For example, birds learn that hunting for worms is likely to be reinforced after a rain. Human social behaviour is also regulated extensively by discriminative stimuli. Consider the behaviour of asking someone out for a date. Many people emit this response only cautiously, after receiving many signals (such as eye contact, smiles, encouraging conversational exchanges) that reinforcement (a favourable answer) is fairly likely.

Reactions to a discriminative stimulus are governed by the processes of *stimulus generalization* and *stimulus discrimination,* just like reactions to a CS in classical conditioning. For instance, envision a cat that comes running into the kitchen whenever it hears the sound of a can opener because that sound has become a discriminative stimulus signalling a good chance of its getting fed. If the cat also responded to the sound of a new kitchen appliance (say, a blender), this response would represent *generalization*—responding to a new stimulus as if it were the original. *Discrimination* would occur if the cat learned to respond only to the can opener and not to the blender.

As you have learned in this section, the processes of acquisition, extinction, generalization, and discrimination in operant conditioning parallel these same processes in classical conditioning. Table 6.1 compares these processes in the two kinds of conditioning.

Table **6.1** Comparison of Basic Processes in Classical and Operant Conditioning

Process and Definition	Description in Classical Conditioning	Description in Operant Conditioning
Acquisition: The initial stage of learning	CS and UCS are paired, gradually resulting in CR.	Responding gradually increases because of reinforcement, possibly through shaping.
Extinction: The gradual weakening and disappearance of a conditioned response tendency	CS is presented alone until it no longer elicits CR.	Responding gradually slows and stops after reinforcement is terminated.
Stimulus generalization: An organism's responding to stimuli other than the original stimulus used in conditioning	CR is elicited by new stimulus that resembles original CS.	Responding increases in the presence of new stimulus that resembles discriminative stimulus.
Stimulus discrimination: An organism's response to stimuli that are similar to the original stimulus used in conditioning	CR is not elicited by new stimulus that resembles original CS.	Responding does not increase in the lack of presence of new stimulus that resembles the original discriminative stimulus.

Web Link 6.4

http://www.behavior.org/

Cambridge Center for Behavioral Studies
A team of behavioural analysts and researchers affiliated with this nonprofit organization have crafted a rich site devoted to scientific applications of the behavioural approach. Some of the practical topics covered here include behavioural approaches to parenting, education, organizational management, and pet training.

PREVIEW QUESTIONS

- What are the typical effects of various schedules of reinforcement?

- How do researchers study choice in operant behaviour, and what have they discovered?

- How do positive and negative reinforcement differ?

- How does two-process theory explain the persistence of avoidance behaviour?

- What is the difference between negative reinforcement and punishment?

- What are some side effects of punishment and some factors that influence its efficacy?

Reinforcement: Consequences That Strengthen Responses

Although it is convenient to equate reinforcement with reward and the experience of pleasure, strict behaviourists object to this practice. Why? Because the experience of pleasure is an unobservable event that takes place within an organism. As explained in Chapter 1, most behaviourists believe that scientific assertions must be limited to what can be observed.

In keeping with this orientation, Skinner said that reinforcement occurs whenever an outcome strengthens a response, as measured by an increase in the rate of responding. This definition avoids the issue of what the organism is feeling and focuses on observable events. Thus, the central process in reinforcement is the *strengthening of a response tendency*. To know whether an event is reinforcing, researchers must make it contingent on a response and observe whether the rate of this response increases after the supposed reinforcer has been presented.

Thus, reinforcement is defined *after the fact*, in terms of its *effect* on behaviour. Something that is clearly reinforcing for an organism at one time may not function as a reinforcer later (Catania, 1992). Food will reinforce lever pressing by a rat only if the rat is hungry. Similarly, something that serves as a reinforcer for one person may not function as a reinforcer for another person. For example, parental approval is a potent reinforcer for most children, but not all.

Delayed Reinforcement

In operant conditioning, a favourable outcome is much more likely to strengthen a response if the outcome follows *immediately*. If a delay occurs between a response and the positive outcome, the response may not be strengthened. Furthermore, studies show that the longer the delay between the designated response and the delivery of the reinforcer, the more slowly conditioning proceeds (Church, 1989; Mazur, 1993).

Conditioned Reinforcement

Operant theorists make a distinction between unlearned, or primary, reinforcers as opposed to conditioned, or secondary, reinforcers. **Primary reinforcers are events that are inherently reinforcing because they satisfy biological needs.** A given species has a limited number of primary reinforcers because they are closely tied to physiological needs. In humans, primary reinforcers include food, water, warmth, sex, and perhaps affection expressed through hugging and close bodily contact.

***Secondary, or conditioned, reinforcers* are events that acquire reinforcing qualities by being associated** with primary reinforcers. The events that function as secondary reinforcers vary among members of a species because they depend on learning. Examples of common secondary reinforcers in humans include money, good grades, attention, flattery, praise, and applause.

REVIEW OF KEY POINTS

- Operant conditioning involves largely voluntary responses that are governed by their consequences. Thorndike paved the way for Skinner's work by investigating instrumental conditioning and describing the law of effect.

- Skinner pioneered the study of operant conditioning, working mainly with rats and pigeons in Skinner boxes. He demonstrated that organisms tend to repeat those responses that are followed by reinforcers. Operant responses are said to be emitted.

- The key dependent variable in operant conditioning is the rate of response over time, which is tracked by a device called a cumulative recorder. When responding over time is shown graphically, steep slopes indicate rapid responding.

- New operant responses can be shaped by gradually reinforcing closer and closer approximations of the desired response. Shaping is the key to training animals to perform impressive tricks. In operant conditioning, extinction occurs when reinforcement for a response is terminated and the rate of that response declines. There are variations in resistance to extinction.

- Operant responses are regulated by discriminative stimuli that are cues for the likelihood of obtaining reinforcers. These stimuli are subject to the same processes of generalization and discrimination that occur in classical conditioning.

- The central process in reinforcement is the strengthening of a response. Delayed reinforcement slows the process of conditioning. Primary reinforcers are unlearned; they are closely tied to the satisfaction of physiological needs. In contrast, secondary reinforcers acquire their reinforcing quality through conditioning.

Intermittent Reinforcement: Effects of Basic Schedules

Organisms make innumerable responses that do not lead to favourable consequences. It would be nice if people were reinforced every time they took an exam, watched a movie, hit a golf shot, asked for a date, or made a sales call. However, in the real world most responses are reinforced only some of the time. How does this fact affect the potency of reinforcers? To find out, operant psychologists have devoted an enormous amount of attention to how *intermittent schedules of reinforcement* influence operant behaviour (Ferster & Skinner, 1957; Skinner, 1938, 1953).

A *schedule of reinforcement* **determines which occurrences of a specific response result in the presentation of a reinforcer.** The simplest pattern is continuous reinforcement. *Continuous reinforcement* **occurs when every instance of a designated response is reinforced**. In the laboratory, experimenters often use continuous reinforcement to shape and establish a new response before moving on to more realistic schedules involving intermittent reinforcement. *Intermittent, or partial, reinforcement* **occurs when a designated response is reinforced only some of the time**.

Which do you suppose leads to longer-lasting effects—being reinforced every time you emit a response, or being reinforced only some of the time? Studies show that, given an equal number of reinforcements, *intermittent* reinforcement makes a response more resistant to extinction than continuous reinforcement does (Falls, 1998; Schwartz & Robbins, 1995). In other words, organisms continue responding longer after removal of reinforcers when a response has been reinforced only *some* of the time. In fact, schedules of reinforcement that provide only sporadic delivery of reinforcers can yield great resistance to extinction. This finding explains why behaviours that are reinforced only occasionally—such as youngsters' temper tantrums—can be very durable and difficult to eliminate.

Reinforcement schedules come in many varieties, but four particular types of intermittent schedules have attracted the most interest. These schedules are described here along with examples drawn from the laboratory and everyday life (see Figure 6.16 for additional examples).

Ratio schedules require the organism to make the designated response a certain number of times to gain each reinforcer. **With a *fixed-ratio (FR) schedule*, the reinforcer is given after a fixed number of nonreinforced responses.** *Examples:* (1) A rat is reinforced for every tenth lever press. (2) A salesperson receives a bonus for every fourth set of encyclopedias sold. **With a *variable-ratio (VR) schedule*, the reinforcer is given after a variable number of nonreinforced responses.** The number of nonreinforced responses varies around a predetermined average. *Examples:* (1) A rat is reinforced for every tenth lever press on the average. The exact number of responses required for reinforcement varies from one time to the next. (2) A slot machine in a casino pays off once every six tries on the average. The number of nonwinning responses between payoffs varies greatly from one time to the next.

Interval schedules require a time period to pass between the presentation of reinforcers. **With a *fixed-interval (FI) schedule*, the reinforcer is given for the first response that occurs after a fixed time interval has elapsed.** *Examples:* (1) A rat is reinforced for the first lever press after a two-minute interval

Fixed

Variable

Ratio

Interval

has elapsed and then must wait two minutes before being able to earn the next reinforcement. (2) A man washing his clothes periodically checks to see whether each load is finished. The reward (clean clothes) is available only after a fixed time interval (corresponding to how long the washer takes to complete a cycle) has elapsed, and checking responses during the interval are not reinforced. **With a *variable-interval (VI) schedule*, the reinforcer is given for the first response after a variable time interval has elapsed.** The interval length varies around a predetermined average. *Examples:* (1) A rat is reinforced for the first lever press after a one-minute interval has elapsed, but the following intervals are three minutes, two minutes, four minutes, and so on—with an average length of two minutes. (2) A person repeatedly dials a busy phone number (getting through is the reinforcer).

More than 50 years of research has yielded an enormous volume of data on how these schedules of reinforcement are related to patterns of responding (Williams, 1988; Zeiler, 1977). Some of the more prominent findings are summarized in Figure 6.17, which depicts typical response patterns generated by each schedule. For example, with fixed-interval schedules, a pause in responding usually occurs after each reinforcer is delivered, and then responding gradually increases to a rapid rate at the end of the interval. This pattern of behaviour yields a "scalloped" response curve. In general, ratio schedules tend to produce more rapid responding than interval

Figure 6.16

Reinforcement schedules in everyday life. Complex human behaviours are regulated by schedules of reinforcement. Piecework in factories is reinforced on a fixed-ratio schedule. Playing slot machines is based on variable-ratio reinforcement. Watching the clock at work is rewarded on a fixed-interval basis (the arrival of quitting time is the reinforcer). Surfers waiting for a big wave are rewarded on a variable-interval basis.

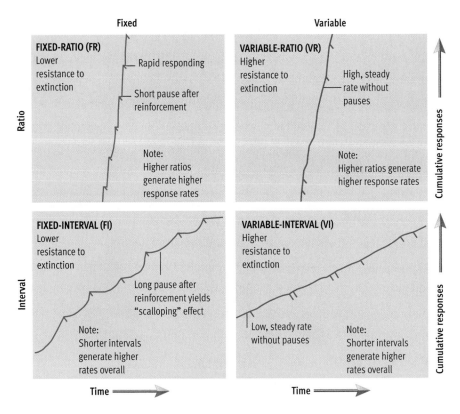

	Fixed	Variable

Ratio

FIXED-RATIO (FR)
Lower resistance to extinction

— Rapid responding

— Short pause after reinforcement

Note:
Higher ratios generate higher response rates

VARIABLE-RATIO (VR)
Higher resistance to extinction

High, steady rate without pauses

Note:
Higher ratios generate higher response rates

Interval

FIXED-INTERVAL (FI)
Lower resistance to extinction

Long pause after reinforcement yields "scalloping" effect

Note:
Shorter intervals generate higher rates overall

VARIABLE-INTERVAL (VI)
Higher resistance to extinction

Low, steady rate without pauses

Note:
Shorter intervals generate higher rates overall

Cumulative responses

Time →

Figure 6.17

Schedules of reinforcement and patterns of response.
Each type of reinforcement schedule tends to generate a characteristic pattern of responding. In general, ratio schedules tend to produce more rapid responding than interval schedules (note the steep slopes of the FR and VR curves). In comparison to fixed schedules, variable schedules tend to yield steadier responding (note the smoother lines for the VR and VI schedules on the right) and greater resistance to extinction.

schedules. Why? Because faster responding leads to reinforcement sooner when a ratio schedule is in effect. Variable schedules tend to generate steadier response rates and greater resistance to extinction than their fixed counterparts.

Most of the research on reinforcement schedules was conducted on rats and pigeons in Skinner boxes. However, the available evidence suggests that humans react to schedules of reinforcement in much the same way as animals (De Villiers, 1977; Perone, Galizio, & Baron, 1988). For example, when animals are placed on ratio schedules, shifting to a higher ratio (that is,

requiring more responses per reinforcement) tends to generate faster responding. Managers of factories that pay on a piecework basis (a fixed-ratio schedule) have seen the same reaction in humans. Shifting to a higher ratio (more pieces for the same pay) usually stimulates harder work and greater productivity (although workers often complain).

There are many other parallels between animals' and humans' reactions to different schedules of reinforcement. For instance, with rats and pigeons, variable-ratio schedules yield steady responding and great resistance to extinction. Similar effects are routinely observed among people who gamble. Most gambling is reinforced according to variable-ratio schedules, which tend to produce rapid, steady responding and great resistance to extinction—exactly what casino operators want. The scalloped response curve seen when animals are placed on a fixed-interval schedule is also seen when humans work under this schedule. For example, consider what happens when the exams in a course occur every three weeks (a fixed-interval schedule). There's usually a pause in responding (studying) after each reinforcer (exam), and responding becomes very rapid (cramming) as each interval comes to an end.

Of course, animals don't match their responding to the realities of reinforcement perfectly, but they come surprisingly close (B. A. Williams, 1994).

Positive Reinforcement versus Negative Reinforcement 5E, 5F

According to Skinner, reinforcement can take two forms, which he called *positive reinforcement* and *negative reinforcement*. **Positive reinforcement occurs when a response is strengthened because it is followed by**

CONCEPT **CHECK 6.2**

Recognizing Schedules of Reinforcement

Check your understanding of schedules of reinforcement in operant conditioning by indicating the type of schedule that would be in effect in each of the examples below. In the spaces on the left, fill in CR for continuous reinforcement, FR for fixed-ratio, VR for variable-ratio, FI for fixed-interval, and VI for variable-interval. The answers can be found in Appendix A in the back of the book.

_____ **1.** Sarah is paid on a commission basis for selling computer systems. She gets a bonus for every third sale.

_____ **2.** Juan's parents let him earn some pocket money by doing yard work approximately once a week.

_____ **3.** Martha is fly-fishing. Think of each time that she casts her line as the response that may be rewarded.

_____ **4.** Jamal, who is in the fourth grade, gets a gold star from his teacher for every book he reads.

_____ **5.** Skip, a professional baseball player, signs an agreement that his salary increases will be renegotiated every third year.

the presentation of a rewarding stimulus. Thus far, for purposes of simplicity, our examples of reinforcement have involved positive reinforcement. Good grades, tasty meals, paycheques, scholarships, promotions, nice clothes, nifty cars, attention, and flattery are all positive reinforcers.

In contrast, **negative reinforcement occurs when a response is strengthened because it is followed by the removal of an aversive (unpleasant) stimulus**. Don't let the word *negative* confuse you. Negative reinforcement *is* reinforcement. As with all reinforcement, it involves a favourable outcome that *strengthens* a response tendency. However, this strengthening takes place because a response leads to the *removal of an aversive stimulus* rather than the arrival of a pleasant stimulus (see Figure 6.18).

In laboratory studies, negative reinforcement is usually accomplished as follows. While a rat is in a Skinner box, a moderate electric shock is delivered to the animal through the floor of the box. When the rat presses the lever, the shock is turned off for a period of time. Thus, lever pressing leads to removal of an aversive stimulus (shock). Although this sequence of events is different from those for positive reinforcement, it reliably strengthens the rat's lever-pressing response.

Everyday human behaviour is regulated extensively by negative reinforcement. Consider a handful of examples. You rush home in the winter to get out of the cold. You clean house to get rid of a disgusting mess. You give in to your child's begging to halt the whining. You take medication to get rid of pain or discomfort. You give in to a roommate or spouse to bring an unpleasant argument to an end.

Negative Reinforcement and Avoidance Behaviour

You have probably noticed that many people tend to avoid facing awkward situations, difficult challenges, and sticky personal problems. Consistent reliance on avoidance is not a very effective coping strategy. How do people learn to rely on such a strategy? In large part, it may be through negative reinforcement.

Escape Learning

The roots of avoidance lie in escape learning. **In *escape learning* an organism acquires a response that decreases or ends some aversive stimulation.** Psychologists often study escape learning in the laboratory with rats that are conditioned in a *shuttle box*. The shuttle box has two compartments connected by a doorway, which can be opened and closed by the experimenter, as depicted in Figure 6.19(a). In a typical study, an animal is placed in one compartment and an electric current in the floor of that chamber is turned on, with the doorway open. The animal learns to escape the shock by running to the other compartment. This escape response leads to the removal of an aversive stimulus (shock), so it is strengthened through negative reinforcement. If you were to leave a party where you were getting picked on by peers, you would be engaging in an escape response. Escape learning doesn't necessarily entail leaving the scene of the aversive stimulation. Any behaviour that decreases or ends aversive stimulation (e.g., turning on the air conditioner to get rid of stifling heat) represents escape learning.

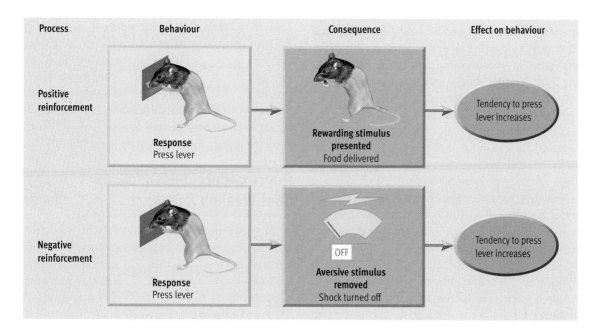

Figure 6.18

Positive reinforcement versus negative reinforcement. In positive reinforcement, a response leads to the presentation of a rewarding stimulus. In negative reinforcement, a response leads to the removal of an aversive stimulus. Both types of reinforcement involve favourable consequences and both have the same effect on behaviour: The organism's tendency to emit the reinforced response is strengthened.

Figure **6.19**

Escape and avoidance learning. **(a)** Escape and avoidance learning are often studied with a shuttle box like that shown here. Warning signals, shock, and the animal's ability to flee from one compartment to another can be controlled by the experimenter. **(b)** According to Mowrer's two-process theory, avoidance begins because classical conditioning creates a conditioned fear that is elicited by the warning signal (panel 1). Avoidance continues because it is maintained by operant conditioning (panel 2). Specifically, the avoidance response is strengthened through negative reinforcement, since it leads to removal of the conditioned fear.

(a)

Light

(b) **1. Classical conditioning**

CS Light		
UCS Shock		**CR** Fear **UCR**

2. Operant conditioning (negative reinforcement)

Response Run away	→	**Aversive stimulus removed** Conditioned fear reduced

Avoidance Learning 5F

Escape learning often leads to avoidance learning. **In** ***avoidance learning*** **an organism acquires a response that prevents some aversive stimulation from occurring.** In laboratory studies of avoidance learning, the experimenter simply gives the animal a signal that shock is forthcoming. The typical signal is a light that goes on a few seconds prior to the shock. At first the rat runs only when shocked (escape learning). Gradually, however, the animal learns to run to the safe compartment as soon as the light comes on, demonstrating avoidance learning. Similarly, if you were to quit going to parties because of your concern about being picked on, this would represent avoidance learning. Turning on air conditioning *before* a room gets hot would also represent avoidance learning.

Avoidance learning presents an interesting puzzle for learning theorists. Avoidance responses tend to be long-lasting even though the mechanism of continuing reinforcement is obscure. For example, when

an animal in a shuttle box learns to avoid shock entirely, it seems to have no opportunity for continued negative reinforcement. After all, the animal can't remove shock that never occurs. In theory, the avoidance response should gradually extinguish, because it is no longer followed by the removal of an aversive stimulus. However, avoidance responses usually remain strong. The best explanation of this paradox appears to be the two-process theory of avoidance, which integrates the processes of classical and operant conditioning (Miller, 1951; Mowrer, 1947; Rescorla & Solomon, 1967).

Two-Process Theory of Avoidance 5F

According to the two-process theory, the warning light that goes on in the shuttle box becomes a CS (through classical conditioning) eliciting conditioned fear in the animal. The behaviour of fleeing to the other side of the box is an operant response that produces negative reinforcement, even after shock is no longer experienced, *because it reduces conditioned fear.* In short, two-process theory appears to solve our riddle by asserting that the avoidance response removes an *internal* aversive stimulus—conditioned fear—rather than an external aversive stimulus, such as shock. This idea is diagrammed in Figure 6.19(b).

There are some "holes" in the two-process theory and some alternative theories that provide better explanations for certain aspects of avoidance behaviour (Bolles & Fanselow, 1980; Hineline, 1981). Nonetheless, the two-process theory remains "the standard against which all other explanations of avoidance behavior are always measured" (Domjan, 1998, p. 255). One of its strengths is that it provides a simple, compelling account for why avoidance behaviours—such as phobias—are so resistant to extinction (Levis, 1989). According to two-process theory, phobias are highly resistant to extinction for two reasons. First, a phobia usually leads to an avoidance response that earns negative reinforcement each time it is made. Second, avoidance behaviour prevents opportunities to extinguish the phobic conditioned response because the person doesn't get much exposure to the conditioned (phobic) stimulus.

Punishment: Consequences That Weaken Responses 5E

Reinforcement is defined in terms of its consequences. It *increases* an organism's tendency to make a certain response. Are there also consequences that *decrease* an organism's tendency to make a particular response? Yes. In Skinner's model of operant behaviour, such consequences are called *punishment.*

In our discussion of reinforcement we saw that there were two types of reinforcement: positive reinforcement and negative reinforcement. As with reinforcement, a distinction is made in punishment between positive and negative punishment. They have in common the essential feature of punishment: *punishment occurs when an event following a response weakens the tendency to make that response.*

Positive punishment **involves the presentation of an aversive stimulus** (e.g., spanking a child for misbehaving). In a Skinner box, the administration of punishment is very simple. When a rat presses the lever or a pigeon pecks the disk, it receives a brief shock. This procedure usually leads to a rapid decline in the animal's response rate (Dinsmoor, 1998). In most examples punishment typically involves presentation of an aversive stimulus. However, *negative punishment* **involves the removal of a rewarding stimulus.** For example, when a child misbehaves the parent may take away the child's opportunity to watch a favourite television program. Here the misbehaviour weakens because something rewarding is taken away from the child. In this example, although the television program did not lead to the behaviour, its removal should serve to lessen the misbehaviour because the child finds the program rewarding.

The concept of punishment in operant conditioning is confusing to many students on two counts. First, they often confuse it with negative reinforcement, which is entirely different. Negative reinforcement involves the *removal* of an aversive stimulus, thereby *strengthening* a response. Punishment, on the other hand, involves the *presentation* of an aversive stimulus, thereby *weakening* a response. Thus, punishment and

negative reinforcement are opposite procedures that yield opposite effects on behaviour (see Figure 6.20).

The second source of confusion involves the tendency to equate punishment with *disciplinary procedures* used by parents, teachers, and other authority figures. In the operant model, punishment occurs any time undesirable consequences weaken a response tendency. Defined in this way, the concept of punishment goes far beyond things like parents spanking children and teachers handing out detentions. Although punishment in operant conditioning encompasses far more than disciplinary acts, it *is* used frequently for disciplinary purposes. In light of this reality, it is worth looking at the research on punishment as a disciplinary measure.

Side Effects of Physical Punishment

About three-quarters of parents report that they sometimes spank their children (Straus & Stewart, 1999), but quite a bit of controversy exists about the wisdom of using physical punishment. Opponents of corporal punishment argue that it produces many unintended and undesirable side effects (Hyman, 1996; Lytton, 1997; Straus, 2000). These views were bolstered by a recent, comprehensive review of the empirical research on physical punishment with children. Summarizing the results of 88 studies, Elizabeth Thompson Gershoff (2002) concluded that physical punishment is associated with poor-quality parent–child relations, elevated aggression, delinquency, and behavioural problems in youngsters, and is associated with an increased likelihood of children being abused. Moreover, she concluded that these effects can carry over into adulthood, as studies find

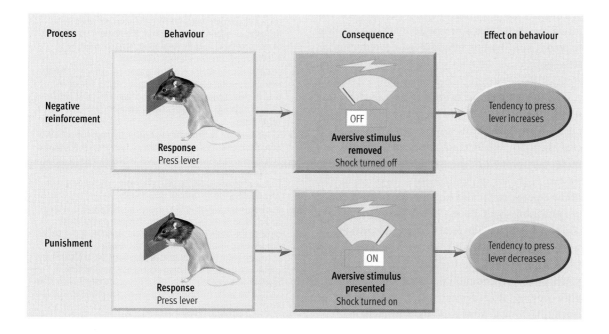

Figure 6.20

Comparison of negative reinforcement and punishment. Although punishment can occur when a response leads to the removal of a rewarding stimulus (negative punishment), it more typically involves the presentation of an aversive stimulus (positive punishment). Students often confuse positive punishment with negative reinforcement because they associate both with aversive stimuli. However, as this diagram shows, punishment and negative reinforcement represent opposite procedures that have opposite effects on behaviour.

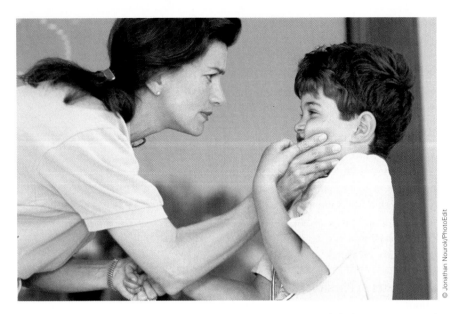

Although physical punishment is frequently administered to suppress aggressive behaviour, in the long run it actually is associated with an increase in aggressive behaviour.

increased aggression, criminal behaviour, mental health problems, and child abuse among adults who were physically punished as children.

In the wake of Gershoff's (2002) stinging indictment of physical punishment, critics have raised some doubts about her conclusions, arguing for example that her review failed to distinguish between the effects of frequent, harsh, heavy-handed physical punishment and the effects of occasional, mild spankings, used as a backup when other disciplinary strategies fail (Baumrind, Larzelere, & Cowan, 2002). Critics also point out that the evidence linking spanking to negative effects is correlational, and correlation is no assurance of causation (Kazdin & Benjet, 2003). This is clearly an issue in need of further theoretical and empirical work.

Although punishment is probably overused in disciplinary efforts, it does have a role to play. The following guidelines summarize evidence on how to make punishment effective while reducing its side effects:

1. *Apply punishment swiftly.* A delay in delivering punishment—like a delay in delivering reinforcement—tends to undermine its impact (Abramowitz & O'Leary, 1990). When a mother says, "Wait until your father gets home …" she is making a fundamental mistake in the use of punishment. This problem with delayed punishment also explains the ineffectiveness of punishing a pet hours after it has misbehaved, when the owner finally returns home. For instance, it won't do any good to hit your dog with a newspaper while shoving its face in the feces it previously left on your carpet. This common punishment doesn't teach your dog to stop defecating on your carpet—it teaches the dog to keep its face out of its feces.

2. *Use punishment just severe enough to be effective.* The intensity of punishment is a two-edged sword. Severe punishments usually are more effective in weakening unwanted responses. However, they also increase the likelihood of undesirable side effects. Thus, it's best to use the least severe punishment that seems likely to have the necessary impact (Powell, Symbaluk, & MacDonald, 2002).

3. *Make punishment consistent.* If you want to eliminate a response, you should punish the response every time it occurs. When parents are inconsistent about punishing a particular behaviour, they create more confusion than learning (Acker & O'Leary, 1996).

4. *Explain the punishment.* When children are punished, the reason for their punishment should be explained as fully as possible, given the constraints of their age. Punishment combined with reasoning is more effective than either alone (Larzelere et al., 1996; Parke, 2002). The more that children understand why they were punished, the more effective the punishment tends to be.

5. *Use noncorporal punishments, such as withdrawal of privileges.* Given the concerns about physical punishment, many experts argue that noncorporal punishments are a more prudent means to achieve disciplinary goals. For example, Kazdin and Benjet (2003, p. 103) assert that "mild noncorporal punishments such as a brief time out from reinforcement or short-term loss of privileges in the context of praise and rewards can accomplish the goals for which spanking is usually employed." In contrast, withdrawing valued privileges can give children hours to contemplate the wisdom of changing their ways.

REVIEW OF KEY POINTS

- Schedules of reinforcement influence patterns of operant responding. Continuous reinforcement occurs when every designated response is reinforced. Intermittent schedules of reinforcement include fixed-ratio, variable-ratio, fixed-interval, and variable-interval schedules.

- Intermittent schedules produce greater resistance to extinction than similar continuous schedules. Ratio schedules tend to yield higher rates of response than interval schedules. Shorter intervals and higher ratios are associated with faster responding.

- Responses can be strengthened either through the presentation of positive reinforcers or through the removal of negative reinforcers. Negative reinforcement regulates escape and avoidance learning. The two-process theory provides the best explanation of avoidance behaviour and may shed light on why phobias are so difficult to eliminate.

- Punishment involves unfavourable consequences that lead to a decline in response strength. Positive punishment involves the application of aversive consequences and negative punishment involves the removal of a reward. Problems associated with the application of punishment as a disciplinary procedure include emotional side effects and increased aggressive behaviour. To be effective, punishment of children should be swift, consistent, explained, nonphysical, and just severe enough to have an impact.

Recognizing Outcomes in Operant Conditioning

Check your understanding of the various types of consequences that can occur in operant conditioning by indicating whether the examples below involve positive reinforcement (PR), negative reinforcement (NR), positive punishment (PP), negative punishment (NP), or extinction (E). The answers can be found in Appendix A.

_____ **1.** Antonio gets a speeding ticket and is fined.

_____ **2.** Diane's supervisor compliments her on her hard work.

_____ **3.** Harry shows up to work late for the fifth day in a row and his boss takes away his health club privileges, which Harry used each noon hour.

_____ **4.** Audrey lets her dog out so she won't have to listen to its whimpering.

_____ **5.** Richard shoots up heroin to ward off tremors and chills associated with heroin withdrawal.

_____ **6.** Sharma constantly complains about minor aches and pains to obtain sympathy from colleagues at work. Three co-workers who share an office with her decide to ignore her complaints instead of responding with sympathy.

Changing Directions in the Study of Conditioning

As you learned in Chapter 1, science is constantly evolving and changing in response to new research and new thinking. Such change has certainly occurred in the study of conditioning. In this section, we will examine two major changes in thinking about conditioning. First, we'll consider the recent recognition that an organism's biological heritage can limit or channel conditioning. Second, we'll discuss the increased appreciation of the role of cognitive processes in conditioning.

Recognizing Biological Constraints on Conditioning

Learning theorists have traditionally assumed that the fundamental laws of conditioning have great generality—that they apply to a wide range of species. Although no one ever suggested that hamsters could learn physics, until the 1960s most psychologists assumed that associations could be conditioned between any stimulus an organism could register and any response it could make. However, findings in recent decades have demonstrated that there are limits to the generality of conditioning principles—limits imposed by an organism's biological heritage.

Instinctive Drift: The Case of the Miserly Raccoons

One biological constraint on learning is instinctive drift. *Instinctive drift* **occurs when an animal's innate response tendencies interfere with conditioning processes.** Instinctive drift was first described by the Brelands, the operant psychologists who went into the business of training animals for commercial purposes (Breland & Breland, 1966). They have

described many amusing examples of their "failures" to control behaviour through conditioning. For instance, they once were training some raccoons to deposit coins in a piggy bank. They were successful in shaping the raccoons to pick up a coin and put it into a small box, using food as the reinforcer. However, when they gave the raccoons a couple of coins, an unexpected problem arose: The raccoons wouldn't give the coins up! In spite of the reinforcers available for depositing the coins, they would sit and rub the coins together like so many little misers.

What had happened to disrupt the conditioning program? Apparently, associating the coins with food had brought out the raccoons' innate food-washing behaviour. Raccoons often rub things together to clean them. The Brelands report that they have run into this sort of instinct-related interference on many occasions with a wide variety of species.

Conditioned Taste Aversion: The "Sauce Béarnaise Syndrome"

A number of years ago, a prominent psychologist, Martin Seligman, dined out with his wife and enjoyed a steak with sauce béarnaise. About six hours afterward, he developed a wicked case of stomach flu and endured severe nausea. Subsequently, when he ordered sauce béarnaise, he was chagrined to discover that its aroma alone nearly made him throw up.

Seligman's experience was not unique. Many people develop aversions to food that has been followed by nausea from illness, alcohol intoxication, or food poisoning. However, Seligman was puzzled by what he called his "sauce béarnaise syndrome" (Seligman & Hager, 1972). On the one hand, it appeared to be the straightforward result of classical

PREVIEW QUESTIONS
- What is instinctive drift?
- Why are conditioned taste aversions so easy to acquire?
- Why are some phobias much more common than others?
- To what degree are the laws of learning universal across species?
- How does the predictive value of a CS affect conditioning?
- Are responses that are followed by favourable consequences always strengthened?

"*Taste aversions do not fit comfortably within the present framework of classical or instrumental conditioning: These aversions selectively seek flavors to the exclusion of other stimuli. Interstimulus intervals are a thousandfold too long.*"

JOHN GARCIA

conditioning. A neutral stimulus (the sauce) had been paired with an unconditioned stimulus (the flu), which caused an unconditioned response (the nausea). Hence, the sauce béarnaise became a conditioned stimulus eliciting nausea (see Figure 6.21).

On the other hand, Seligman recognized that his aversion to béarnaise sauce seemed to violate certain basic principles of conditioning. First, the lengthy delay of 6 hours between the CS (the sauce) and the UCS (the flu) should have prevented conditioning from occurring. In laboratory studies, a delay of more than *30 seconds* between the CS and UCS makes it difficult to establish a conditioned response, yet this conditioning occurred in just one pairing. Second, why was it that *only* the béarnaise sauce became a CS eliciting nausea? Why not other stimuli that were present in the restaurant? Shouldn't plates, knives, tablecloths, or his wife, for example, also trigger Seligman's nausea?

The riddle of Seligman's sauce béarnaise syndrome was solved by John Garcia (1989) and his colleagues. They conducted a series of studies on *conditioned taste aversion* (Garcia, Clarke, & Hankins, 1973; Garcia & Koelling, 1966; Garcia & Rusiniak, 1980). In these studies, they manipulated the kinds of stimuli preceding the onset of nausea and other noxious experiences in rats, using radiation to artificially induce the nausea (see Figure 6.22). They found that when taste cues were followed by nausea, rats quickly acquired conditioned taste aversions. However, when taste cues were followed by other types of noxious stimuli (such as shock), rats did *not* develop conditioned taste aversions. Furthermore, visual and auditory stimuli followed by nausea also failed to produce conditioned aversions. In short, Garcia and his co-workers found that it was almost impossible to create certain associations, whereas taste–nausea associations (and odour–nausea associations) were almost impossible to prevent.

What is the theoretical significance of this unique readiness to make connections between taste and nausea? Garcia argues that it is a byproduct of the evolutionary history of mammals. Animals that consume poisonous foods and survive must learn not to repeat their mistakes. Natural selection will favour organisms that quickly learn what *not* to eat. Thus,

evolution may have biologically programmed some organisms to learn certain types of associations more easily than others.

Preparedness and Phobias

According to Martin Seligman, evolution has also programmed organisms to acquire certain fears more readily than others, because of a phenomenon he calls *preparedness*. **Preparedness involves a species-specific predisposition to be conditioned in certain ways and not others.** Seligman (1971) believes that preparedness can explain why certain phobias are vastly more common than others. People tend to develop phobias to snakes, spiders, heights, and darkness relatively easily. However, even after painful experiences with hammers, knives, hot stoves, and electrical outlets, phobic fears of these objects are infrequent. What characteristics do common phobic objects share? Most were once genuine threats to our ancestors. Consequently, a fear response to such objects has survival value for our species. According to Seligman, evolutionary forces gradually programmed humans to acquire conditioned fears of these objects easily and rapidly. Laboratory simulations of phobic conditioning, like those of Dalhousie's Vincent LoLordo, have provided some support for the concept of preparedness (LoLordo & Droungas, 1989; Mineka & Hamida, 1998). We will return to a discussion of some of Seligman's other work in Chapter 14. Based on some of his other conditioning research, Seligman has developed the theory of learned helplessness and depression (Seligman, 1974). As LoLordo (2001) suggests, Seligman's learned helplessness theory of

Figure 6.22

Garcia and Koelling's research on conditioned taste aversion. In a landmark series of studies, Garcia and Koelling (1966) demonstrated that some stimulus–response associations are much easier to condition than others. Their apparatus is depicted here. Rats drink saccharin-flavoured water out of the tube on the right. When they make contact with the tube, they may trigger a bright light and buzzer, or a brief electric shock, or radiation exposure that will make them nauseated. This set-up allowed Garcia and Koelling to pair various types of stimuli, as discussed in your text.

Figure 6.21

Conditioned taste aversion. Taste aversions can be established through classical conditioning, as in the "sauce béarnaise syndrome." However, as the text explains, taste aversions can be acquired in ways that seem to violate basic principles of classical conditioning.

Tom McCarthy/SKA

People tend to develop phobias to snakes very easily but to electrical outlets rarely, even though the latter are just as dangerous. Preparedness theory can explain this paradox.

depression came as a result of research on "fundamental learning mechanisms" in animals.

Evolutionary Perspectives on Learning

Clearly, several lines of research suggest that there are species-specific biological constraints on conditioning. So, what is the current thinking on the idea that the laws of learning are *universal* across various species? The predominant view among learning theorists seems to be that the basic mechanisms of learning are *similar* across species but that these mechanisms have sometimes been modified in the course of evolution as species have adapted to the specialized demands of their environments (Shettleworth, 1998). According to this view, learning is a very general process because the neural substrates of learning and the basic problems confronted by various organisms are much the same across species. For example, developing the ability to recognize stimuli that signal important events is probably adaptive for virtually any organism. However, given that different organisms confront different adaptive problems to survive and reproduce, it makes sense that learning has evolved along somewhat different paths in different species (Hollis, 1997; Sherry, 1992).

Some evolutionary psychologists take this line of reasoning one step further. The consensus view just described assumes that an organism's biological heritage—which has been shaped by natural selection— places certain constraints on the learning process. The more radical view espoused by some theorists is that there is no such thing as *the* learning process. Rather, there are many learning processes, sculpted by evolution, as specialized mechanisms designed to solve particular types of adaptive problems for particular species. For example, C. R. Gallistel (2000) asserts, "Most theorizing assumes that there is a general-purpose learning process in the brain.... this assumption is equivalent to assuming that there is a general-purpose sensory organ" (p. 1179). According to this more radical view, the adaptive problems faced by different types of organisms are extraordinarily diverse and often have little in common. For example, the problems faced by a migratory bird that needs to navigate its way over thousands of kilometres, a star-nosed mole that needs to detect worms underground, and a male squirrel monkey that needs to remember the locations of females about to enter into estrus are entirely different. Hence, the solutions to these problems depend on highly specialized learning mechanisms that were crafted by evolution to meet the unique needs of various species. Thus, some evolutionary psychologists completely reject the idea that there are universal laws of learning.

Recognizing Cognitive Processes in Conditioning

Pavlov, Skinner, and their followers traditionally viewed conditioning as a mechanical process in which stimulus–response associations are stamped in by experience. Learning theorists asserted that if creatures such as flatworms can be conditioned, conditioning can't depend on higher mental processes. Although this viewpoint did not go entirely unchallenged (e.g., Tolman, 1922, 1932, 1938), mainstream theories of conditioning did not allocate a major role to cognitive processes. In recent decades, however, research findings have led theorists to shift toward more cognitive explanations of conditioning. Let's review some of these findings and the theories that have resulted.

Signal Relations

The cognitive element in conditioning is especially prominent in research conducted by Robert Rescorla

Distinguishing between Classical Conditioning and Operant Conditioning

Check your understanding of the usual differences between classical conditioning and operant conditioning by indicating the type of conditioning process involved in each of the following examples. In the space on the left, place a C if the example involves classical conditioning, an O if it involves operant conditioning, or a B if it involves both. The answers can be found in Appendix A.

_____ **1.** Whenever Midori takes her dog out for a walk, she wears the same old blue windbreaker. Eventually, she notices that her dog becomes excited whenever she puts on this windbreaker.

_____ **2.** The Creatures are a successful rock band with three hit albums to their credit. They begin their world tour featuring many new, unreleased songs, all of which draw silence from their concert fans. The same fans cheer wildly when the Creatures play any of their old hits. Gradually, the band reduces the number of new songs it plays and starts playing more of the old standbys.

_____ **3.** When Cindy and Mel first fell in love, they listened constantly to the Creatures' hit song "Transatlantic Obsession." Although several years have passed, whenever they hear this song they experience a warm, romantic feeling.

_____ **4.** For nearly 20 years Ralph has worked as a machinist in the same factory. His new supervisor is never satisfied with his work and criticizes him constantly. After a few weeks of heavy criticism, he experiences anxiety whenever he arrives at work. He starts calling in sick more and more frequently to evade this anxiety.

University of Pennsylvania

"Pavlovian conditioning is a sophisticated and sensible mechanism by which organisms represent the world.... I encourage students to think of animals as behaving like little statisticians.... They really are very finely attuned to small changes in the likelihood of events."
ROBERT RESCORLA

(1978, 1980; Rescorla & Wagner, 1972). Rescorla asserts that environmental stimuli serve as signals and that some stimuli are better, or more dependable, signals than others. Hence, he has manipulated *signal relations* in classical conditioning—that is, CS–UCS relations that influence whether a CS is a good signal. A "good" signal is one that allows accurate prediction of the UCS.

In essence, Rescorla manipulates the *predictive value* of a conditioned stimulus. How does he do so? He varies the proportion of trials in which the CS and UCS are paired. Consider the following example. A tone and shock are paired 20 times for one group of rats. Otherwise, these rats are never shocked. For these rats the CS (tone) and UCS (shock) are paired in 100% of the experimental trials. Another group of rats also receive 20 pairings of the tone and shock. However, the rats in this group are also exposed to the shock on 20 other trials when the tone does *not* precede it. For this group, the CS and UCS are paired in only 50% of the trials. Thus, the two groups of rats have had an equal number of CS–UCS pairings, but the CS is a better signal or predictor of shock for the 100% CS–UCS group than for the 50% CS–UCS group.

What did Rescorla find when he tested the two groups of rats for conditioned fear? He found that the CS elicits a much stronger response in the 100% CS–UCS group than in the 50% CS–UCS group. Given that the two groups have received an equal number of CS–UCS pairings, this difference must be due to the greater predictive power of the CS for the 100% group. Numerous studies of signal relations have shown that the predictive value of a CS is an influential factor governing classical conditioning (Rescorla, 1978).

Response–Outcome Relations and Reinforcement

Studies of response–outcome relations and reinforcement also highlight the role of cognitive processes in conditioning. Imagine that on the night before an important exam you study hard while repeatedly playing a Sum 41 song. The next morning you earn an A on your exam. Does this result strengthen your tendency to play Sum 41's music before exams? Probably not. Chances are, you will recognize the logical relation between the response of studying hard and the reinforcement of a good grade, and only the response of studying will be strengthened (Killeen, 1981).

Thus, reinforcement is *not* automatic when favourable consequences follow a response. People actively reason out the relations between responses and the outcomes that follow. When a response is followed by a desirable outcome, the response is more likely to be strengthened if the person thinks that the response *caused* the outcome. You might guess that only humans would engage in this causal reasoning. However, evidence suggests that under the right circumstances even pigeons can learn to recognize causal relations between responses and outcomes (Killeen, 1981).

In sum, modern, reformulated models of conditioning view it as a matter of detecting the *contingencies* among environmental events (Matute & Miller, 1998). According to these theories, organisms actively try to figure out what leads to what (the contingencies) in the world around them. Stimuli are viewed as signals that help organisms minimize their aversive experiences and maximize their pleasant experiences. The new, cognitively oriented theories of conditioning are quite a departure from older theories that depicted conditioning as a mindless, mechanical process. We can also see this new emphasis on cognitive processes in our next subject, observational learning.

Observational Learning

Can classical and operant conditioning account for all learning? Absolutely not. Consider how people learn a fairly basic skill such as driving a car. They do not hop naïvely into an automobile and start emitting random responses until one leads to favourable consequences. On the contrary, most people learning to drive know exactly where to place the key and how to get started. How are these responses acquired? Through *observation*. Most new drivers have years of experience observing others drive, and they put those observations to work. Learning through observation accounts for a great deal of learning in both animals and humans.

Observational learning occurs when an organism's responding is influenced by the observation of others, who are called models. This process has been investigated extensively by Albert Bandura (1977, 1986). Bandura's theory and research on observational learning is one of the pivotal contributions to the psychology of learning in the past few decades. Interestingly, Bandura, who was born in Alberta and did his undergraduate studies at the University of British Columbia, began his career in psychology almost by chance (Evans, 1989). He commuted to classes with friends who were early risers so he found himself with morning class periods to fill. One of the courses available was in psychology and the rest, as they say, is history. Bandura's insights on the mediating role of modelling or observational learning came from his analysis of the differences between animal and human learning. The literature on human conditioning suggested to him at the time that for humans "representation of the connection between action and consequence is an important determinant of whether or not a change will occur" (Evans, 1980, p. 161). While this might seem obvious to us now, it was not an insight that was compatible with the prevailing orientation of learning theory at the time.

Bandura does not see observational learning as entirely separate from classical and operant conditioning. Instead, he asserts that it greatly extends the reach of these conditioning processes. Whereas previous conditioning theorists emphasized the organism's direct experience, Bandura has demonstrated that both classical and operant conditioning can take place vicariously through observational learning.

Essentially, observational learning involves being conditioned indirectly by virtue of observing another's conditioning (see Figure 6.23). To illustrate, suppose you observe a friend behaving assertively with a car salesperson. You see your friend's assertive behaviour reinforced by the exceptionally good buy she gets on the car. Your own tendency to behave assertively with salespeople might well be strengthened as a result. Notice that the reinforcement is experienced by your friend, not you. The good buy should strengthen your friend's tendency to bargain assertively, but your tendency to do so may also be strengthened indirectly.

Basic Processes

Bandura has identified four key processes that are crucial in observational learning. The first two—attention and retention—highlight the importance of the type of cognition he was referring to in the quote above in this type of learning.

● *Attention.* To learn through observation, you must pay attention to another person's behaviour and its consequences.

● *Retention.* You may not have occasion to use an observed response for weeks, months, or even years. Hence, you must store a mental representation of what you have witnessed in your memory.

● *Reproduction.* Enacting a modelled response depends on your ability to reproduce the response by converting your stored mental images into overt behaviour. This may not be easy for some responses. For example, most people cannot execute a breath-

Photo courtesy of Albert Bandura

Most human behavior is learned by observation through modeling.
ALBERT BANDURA

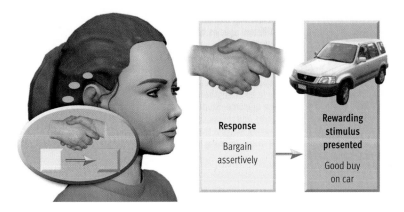

Figure 6.23

Observational learning.

In observational learning, an observer attends to and stores a mental representation of a model's behaviour (e.g., assertive bargaining) and its consequences (e.g., a good buy on a car). If the observer sees the modelled response lead to a favourable outcome, the observer's tendency to emit the modelled response will be strengthened.

Web Link 6.5

Studies on Aggression

http://psychclassics.yorku.ca/ Bandura/bobo.htm

At York University professor Chris Green's Web site you can access a copy of one of Albert Bandura's classic studies on aggression (Bandura et al., 1961).

Web Link 6.6

Albert Bandura

http://www.emory.edu/ EDUCATION/mfp/bandurabio.html

This site offers an excellent biography of Albert Bandura.

The Bobo doll was employed in Bandura's well-known research on observational learning and aggression.

taking windmill dunk after watching Steve Nash do it in a basketball game.

• *Motivation.* Finally, you are unlikely to reproduce an observed response unless you are motivated to do so. Your motivation depends on whether you encounter a situation in which you believe that the response is likely to pay off for you.

Observational learning has proven especially valuable in explaining complex human behaviours, but animals can also learn through observation. A simple example is the thieving behaviour of the English titmouse, a small bird renowned for its early-morning raids on its human neighbours. The titmouse has learned how to open cardboard caps on bottles of milk delivered to the porches of many homes in England. Having opened the bottle, the titmouse skims the cream from the top of the milk. This clever learned behaviour has been passed down from one generation of titmouse to the next through observational learning.

Acquisition versus Performance

Bandura points out that people have many learned responses that they may or may not perform, depending on the situation. Thus, he distinguishes between the *acquisition* of a learned response and the *performance* of that response. He maintains that reinforcement affects which responses are actually

Photos courtesy of Albert Bandura

performed more than which responses are acquired. People emit those responses that they think are likely to be reinforced. For instance, you may study hard for a course in which the professor gives fair exams, because you expect studying to lead to reinforcement in the form of a good grade. In contrast, you may hardly open the text for a course in which the professor gives arbitrary, unpredictable exams, because you do not expect studying to be reinforced. Your performance is different in the two situations because you think the reinforcement contingencies are different. Thus, like Skinner, Bandura asserts that reinforcement is a critical determinant of behaviour. However, Bandura maintains that reinforcement influences performance rather than learning per se.

Applications

It is the power of observational learning that makes television such an influential determinant of behaviour. Along with his colleague and first graduate student Richard Walters (later a professor at the University of Waterloo), Bandura was an early advocate of the application of learning principles to explain aggression in children (Bandura & Walters, 1959, 1963). Young children are especially impressionable, and extensive evidence indicates that they pick up many responses—including aggressive behaviours—from viewing models on TV (Huston & Wright, 1982; Liebert & Sprafkin, 1988). Bandura conducted a series of classic experiments on aggression often referred to as the "Bobo doll" experiments (Bandura, 1965; Bandura, Ross, & Ross, 1961, 1963). In these and other studies, Bandura showed that children would imitate aggressive behaviour directed toward a Bobo doll (a large, inflatable toy clown) by an adult model. Children who saw the model rewarded were more likely than children who saw the model punished for the aggression to aggress (i.e., performance) themselves toward the Bobo doll when left alone with it. However, all the children behaved aggressively (i.e., acquisition) if they were offered a reward for imitating the model's behaviour. This early research by Bandura suggested a connection between children watching violence on television and their own aggressiveness. A recent review of the literature by University of Toronto psychologist Jonathan Freedman has confirmed the link between viewing media violence and aggressiveness (Freedman, 2002). The causal connection between media violence and aggression is still being debated.

Bandura's theory of observational learning also explains why physical punishment tends to increase aggressive behaviour in children, even when it is intended to do just the opposite. Parents who depend on physical punishment often punish a child for hitting other children—by hitting the child. The parents may sincerely intend to reduce the child's aggressive behaviour, but they are unwittingly serving as models of such behaviour. Although they may tell the child that "hitting people won't accomplish anything," they are in the midst of hitting the child in order to accomplish something. Because parents usually accomplish their immediate goal of stopping the child's hitting, the child witnesses the reinforcement of aggressive behaviour. In this situation, actions speak louder than words—because of observational learning. Because of the significance of Bandura's modelling research, the Bobo doll has achieved a type of stardom on its own. Bandura states that when he visits and lectures at other universities, the hosts often place Bobo dolls close to the stage and that people frequently bring him Bobo dolls to autograph (Evans, 1989). More recently, Bandura has examined the concepts of self-efficacy and human agency and their implications for society

(Bandura, 2001). We will consider some of his work on self-efficacy and agency in Chapter 12.

Clearly, observational learning plays an important role in regulating behaviour. It represents a third major type of learning that builds on the first two types—classical conditioning and operant conditioning. These three basic types of learning are summarized and compared in a pictorial table on pages 256–257.

Observational learning occurs in both humans and animals. For example, the English titmouse has learned how to break into containers to swipe cream from its human neighbours and this behaviour has been passed across generations through observational learning. In a similar vein, children acquire a diverse array of responses from role models.

Putting It in Perspective

Two of our seven unifying themes stand out in this chapter. First, you can see how nature and nurture interactively govern behaviour. Second, looking at psychology in its sociohistorical context, you can see how progress in psychology spills over to affect trends and values in society at large. Let's examine each of these points in more detail.

In regard to nature versus nurture, research on learning clearly demonstrates the enormous power of the environment in shaping behaviour. Pavlov's model of classical conditioning shows how experiences can account for everyday fears and other emotional responses. Skinner's model of operant conditioning shows how reinforcement and punishment can mould everything from a child's bed-time whimpering to an adult's restaurant preferences. Indeed, many learning theorists once believed that *all* aspects of behaviour could be explained in terms of environmental determinants. In recent decades, however, evidence on instinctive drift, conditioned taste aversion, and preparedness has shown that there are biological constraints on conditioning. Thus, even in explanations of learning—an area once dominated by nurture theories—we see once again that heredity and environment jointly influence behaviour.

The history of research on conditioning also shows how progress in psychology can seep into every corner of society. For example, the behaviourists' ideas about reinforcement and punishment have influenced patterns of discipline in our society. Research on operant conditioning has also affected management styles in the business world, leading to an increased emphasis on positive reinforcement. In the educational arena, the concept of individualized, programmed learning is a spin-off from behavioural research. The fact that the principles of conditioning are routinely applied in homes, businesses, schools, and factories clearly shows that psychology is not an ivory tower endeavour.

In the upcoming Personal Application, you will see how you can apply the principles of conditioning to improve your self-control, as we discuss the techniques of behaviour modification.

PREVIEW QUESTIONS
- How did this chapter demonstrate that nature and nurture jointly influence behaviour?
- How did this chapter show that psychology evolves in a sociohistorical context?

REVIEW OF KEY POINTS
- In observational learning, an organism is conditioned vicariously by watching a model's conditioning. Both classical and operant conditioning can occur through observational learning, which depends on the processes of attention, retention, reproduction, and motivation.
- According to Bandura, reinforcement influences which of several already acquired responses one will perform more than it influences the acquisition of new responses.
- Observational learning can account for the influence of mass media (such as television) on behaviour. The principles of observational learning have also been used to explain why physical punishment increases aggressive behaviour.
- Two of our key themes were especially apparent in our coverage of learning and conditioning. One theme involves the interaction of heredity and environment in learning. The other involves the way progress in psychology affects society at large.

Three Types of Learning

Type of learning	Procedure	Diagram	Result

Classical conditioning

Ivan Pavlov

A neutral stimulus (for example, a tone) is paired with an unconditioned stimulus (such as food) that elicits an unconditioned response (salivation).

CS
Tone

UCS
Meat powder

CR
Salivation
UCR

The neutral stimulus becomes a conditioned stimulus that elicits the conditioned response (for example, a tone triggers salivation).

Operant conditioning

B. F. Skinner

In a stimulus situation, a response is followed by favourable consequences (reinforcement) or unfavourable consequences (punishment).

Response
Press lever

Rewarding or aversive stimulus presented or removed
Food delivery or shock

If reinforced, the response is strengthened (emitted more frequently); if punished, the response is weakened (emitted less frequently).

Observational learning

Albert Bandura

An observer attends to a model's behaviour (for example, aggressive bargaining) and its consequences (for example, a good buy on a car).

Response
Bargain assertively

Rewarding stimulus presented
Good buy on car

The observer stores a mental representation of the modelled response; the observer's tendency to emit the response may be strengthened or weakened, depending on the consequences observed.

Typical kinds of responses	Examples in animals	Examples in humans

Mostly (but not always) involuntary reflexes and visceral responses

Dogs learn to salivate to the sound of a tone that has been paired with meat powder.

© Bettmann/CORBIS

Political candidates draw on the power of classical conditioning when they associate with popular celebrities who elicit positive feelings among many voters.

© Jim Young/Reuters/CORBIS

Mostly (but not always) voluntary, spontaneous responses

Trained animals perform remarkable feats because they have been reinforced for gradually learning closer and closer approximations of responses they do not normally emit.

© Gerald Davis by permission of Karen Davis

Casino patrons tend to exhibit high, steady rates of gambling, as most games of chance involve complex variable-ratio schedules of reinforcement.

© Bob Krist/CORBIS

A young boy performs a response that he has acquired through observational learning.

© Laura Dwight/CORBIS

Mostly voluntary responses, often consisting of novel and complex sequences

An English titmouse learns to break into milk bottles by observing the thievery of other titmice.

© J. Markham/Bruce Coleman, Inc.

RECAP

Key Ideas

Classical Conditioning

● Classical conditioning explains how a neutral stimulus can acquire the capacity to elicit a response originally evoked by another stimulus. This kind of conditioning was originally described by Ivan Pavlov.

● Many kinds of everyday responses are regulated through classical conditioning, including phobias, fears, and pleasant emotional responses. Even physiological responses such as immune and sexual functioning respond to classical conditioning.

● A conditioned response may be weakened and extinguished entirely when the CS is no longer paired with the UCS. In some cases, spontaneous recovery occurs, and an extinguished response reappears after a period of nonexposure to the CS.

● Conditioning may generalize to additional stimuli that are similar to the original CS. The opposite of generalization is discrimination, which involves not responding to stimuli that resemble the original CS. Higher-order conditioning occurs when a CS functions as if it were a UCS, to establish new conditioning.

Operant Conditioning

● Operant conditioning involves largely voluntary responses that are governed by their consequences. Following the lead of E. L. Thorndike, B. F. Skinner investigated this form of conditioning, working mainly with rats and pigeons in Skinner boxes.

● The key dependent variable in operant conditioning is the rate of response over time. When this responding is shown graphically, steep slopes indicate rapid responding. New operant responses can be shaped by gradually reinforcing closer and closer approximations of the desired response. In operant conditioning, extinction occurs when reinforcement for a response is terminated and the rate of that response declines.

● Operant responses are regulated by discriminative stimuli that are cues for the likelihood of obtaining reinforcers. These stimuli are subject to the same processes of generalization and discrimination that occur in classical conditioning.

● Delayed reinforcement slows the process of conditioning. Primary reinforcers are unlearned; secondary reinforcers acquire their reinforcing quality through conditioning.

● Intermittent schedules of reinforcement produce greater resistance to extinction than similar continuous schedules. Ratio schedules tend to yield higher rates of response than interval schedules. Shorter intervals and higher ratios are associated with faster responding.

● Responses can be strengthened through either the presentation of positive reinforcers or the removal of negative reinforcers. Negative reinforcement regulates escape and avoidance learning. The two-process theory provides the best explanation of avoidance behaviour and may shed light on why phobias are so difficult to eliminate.

● Positive and negative punishment involve consequences that lead to a decline in response strength. Some of the problems associated with punishment as a disciplinary procedure are emotional side effects and increased aggressive behaviour.

Changing Directions in the Study of Conditioning

● The findings on instinctive drift, conditioned taste aversion, and preparedness have led to the recognition that there are species-specific biological constraints on conditioning. Some evolutionary psychologists argue that learning processes vary considerably across species.

● Studies of signal relations in classical conditioning and response–outcome relations in operant conditioning suggest that cognitive processes play a larger role in conditioning than originally believed.

Observational Learning

● In observational learning, an organism is conditioned by watching a model's conditioning. Both classical and operant conditioning can occur through observational learning, which depends on the processes of attention, retention, reproduction, and motivation.

● Observational learning can account for the influence of mass media (such as television) on behaviour. The principles of observational learning have also been used to explain why physical punishment increases aggressive behaviour.

Putting It in Perspective

● Two of our key themes were especially apparent in our coverage of learning and conditioning. One theme involves the interaction of heredity and environment in learning. The other involves the way progress in psychology affects society at large.

Personal Application • Achieving Self-Control Through Behaviour Modification

● The first step in self-modification is specifying the target behaviour to be increased or decreased. The second step is gathering baseline data.

● The third step is to design a program, using procedures such as reinforcement, control of antecedents, and punishment. The fourth step involves executing and evaluating your program. The final step is to determine how and when you will phase out your program.

Critical Thinking Application • Manipulating Emotions: Pavlov and Persuasion

● Advertisers routinely pair their products with stimuli that seem likely to elicit positive emotions or other specific feelings. The practice of taking customers out to dinner or to major events also takes advantage of Pavlovian conditioning. Politicians also work to pair themselves with positive events. The best defence against these tactics is to become more aware of efforts to manipulate your emotions.

Key Terms

Acquisition, 233
Antecedents, 259
Avoidance learning, 246
Behaviour modification, 258
Behavioural contract, 261
Classical conditioning, 227
Conditioned reinforcers, 242
Conditioned response (CR), 228
Conditioned stimulus (CS), 228
Continuous reinforcement, 243
Cumulative recorder, 238
Discriminative stimuli, 240
Elicit, 229
Emit, 238
Escape learning, 245
Extinction, 234
Fixed-interval (FI) schedule, 243
Fixed-ratio (FR) schedule, 243
Higher-order conditioning, 235
Instinctive drift, 249
Instrumental learning, 237
Intermittent reinforcement, 243
Law of effect, 237
Learning, 226
Negative punishment, 247
Negative reinforcement, 245
Observational learning, 253
Operant chamber, 238
Operant conditioning, 236

Partial reinforcement, 243
Pavlovian conditioning, 227
Phobias, 227
Positive punishment, 247
Positive reinforcement, 244
Preparedness, 250
Primary reinforcers, 242
Punishment, 247
Reinforcement, 237
Reinforcement contingencies, 238
Resistance to extinction, 240
Schedule of reinforcement, 242
Secondary reinforcers, 242
Shaping, 238
Skinner box, 238
Spontaneous recovery, 234
Stimulus discrimination, 235
Stimulus generalization, 234
Token economy, 260
Trial, 229
Unconditioned response (UCR), 228
Unconditioned stimulus (UCS), 228
Variable-interval (VI) schedule, 243
Variable-ratio (VR) schedule, 243

Key People

Albert Bandura, 253
John Garcia, 250
Ivan Pavlov, 227
Robert Rescorla, 252
Martin Seligman, 249
B. F. Skinner, 238
E. L. Thorndike, 237

business tactic. One of us has a friend who uses his Toronto Blue Jays season tickets solely for entertaining business clients. He maintains that the cost of the tickets is more than offset by the increased business this practice brings him. This practice pairs the host with both pleasant feelings and the excitement of a big event.

It is worth noting that these strategies take advantage of other processes besides classical conditioning. They also make use of the *reciprocity norm*—the social rule that one should pay back in kind what one receives from others (Cialdini, 2001). Thus, wining and dining clients creates a sense of obligation that they should reciprocate their hosts' generosity—presumably in their business dealings.

Classical Conditioning in the World of Politics

Like advertisers, candidates running for election need to influence the attitudes of many people quickly, subtly, and effectively—and they depend on classical conditioning to help them do so. For example, have you noticed how politicians show up at an endless variety of pleasant public events (such as the opening of a new mall) that often have nothing to do with their public service? When a sports team wins some sort of championship, local politicians are drawn like flies to the subsequent celebrations. Past prime ministers have made a practice of calling the Grey Cup winners. It is noteworthy that they do this during the post-game celebrations when many Canadians are watching the festivities on TV, ensuring the prime minister maximum coverage. They want to pair themselves with these positive events, so that they are associated with pleasant emotions.

Election campaign ads use the same techniques as commercial ads. Candidates are paired with popular celebrities, wholesome families, pleasant music, and symbols of patriotism. Cognizant of the power of classical conditioning, politicians also exercise great care to ensure that they are not paired with people or events that might trigger negative feelings.

The ultimate political perversion of the principles of classical conditioning probably occurred in Nazi Germany. The Nazis used many propaganda techniques to create prejudice toward Jews and members of other targeted groups (such as Gypsies). One such strategy was the repeated pairing of disgusting, repulsive images with stereotypical pictures of Jews. For example, the Nazis would show alternating pictures of rats or roaches crawling over filthy garbage and stereotypical Jewish faces, so that the two images would become associated in the minds of the viewers. Thus, the German population was conditioned to have negative emotional reactions to Jews and to associate them with vermin subject to extermination. The Nazis reasoned that if people would not hesitate to exterminate rats and roaches, then why not human beings associated with these vermin?

Becoming More Aware of Classical Conditioning Processes

How effective are the efforts to manipulate people's emotions through Pavlovian conditioning? It's hard to say. In the real world, these strategies are always used in combination with other persuasive tactics, which creates multiple confounds that make it difficult to assess the impact of the Pavlovian techniques (Walther et al., 2005). Laboratory research can eliminate these confounds, but surprisingly little research on these strategies has been published, and virtually all of it has dealt with advertising. The advertising studies suggest that classical conditioning can be effective and leave enduring imprints on consumers' attitudes (Grossman & Till, 1998; Shimp, Stuart, & Engle, 1991; Walther & Grigoriadis, 2003), but a great deal

Political candidates are very savvy about the potential power of classical conditioning. For example, they like to be seen in public with popular celebrities who elicit positive feelings among many voters.

of additional research is needed. Given the monumental sums that advertisers spend using these techniques, it seems reasonable to speculate that individual companies have data on their specific practices to demonstrate their efficacy, but these data are not made available to the public.

What can you do to reduce the extent to which your emotions are manipulated through Pavlovian procedures? Well, you could turn off your radio and TV, close up your magazines, stop your newspaper, disconnect your modem, and withdraw into a media-shielded shell, but that hardly seems realistic for most people. Realistically, the best defence is to make a conscious effort to become more aware of the pervasive attempts to condition your emotions and attitudes. Some research on persuasion suggests that *to be forewarned is to be forearmed* (Pfau et al., 1990). In other words, if you know how media sources try to manipulate you, you should be more resistant to their strategies.

Table 6.2 Critical Thinking Skills Discussed in This Application

Skill	Description
Understanding how Pavlovian conditioning can be used to manipulate emotions	The critical thinker understands how stimuli can be paired together to create automatic associations that people may not be aware of.
Developing the ability to detect conditioning procedures used in the media	The critical thinker can recognize Pavlovian conditioning tactics in commercial and political advertisements.

RECAP

Key Ideas

Classical Conditioning

● Classical conditioning explains how a neutral stimulus can acquire the capacity to elicit a response originally evoked by another stimulus. This kind of conditioning was originally described by Ivan Pavlov.

● Many kinds of everyday responses are regulated through classical conditioning, including phobias, fears, and pleasant emotional responses. Even physiological responses such as immune and sexual functioning respond to classical conditioning.

● A conditioned response may be weakened and extinguished entirely when the CS is no longer paired with the UCS. In some cases, spontaneous recovery occurs, and an extinguished response reappears after a period of nonexposure to the CS.

● Conditioning may generalize to additional stimuli that are similar to the original CS. The opposite of generalization is discrimination, which involves not responding to stimuli that resemble the original CS. Higher-order conditioning occurs when a CS functions as if it were a UCS, to establish new conditioning.

Operant Conditioning

● Operant conditioning involves largely voluntary responses that are governed by their consequences. Following the lead of E. L. Thorndike, B. F. Skinner investigated this form of conditioning, working mainly with rats and pigeons in Skinner boxes.

● The key dependent variable in operant conditioning is the rate of response over time. When this responding is shown graphically, steep slopes indicate rapid responding. New operant responses can be shaped by gradually reinforcing closer and closer approximations of the desired response. In operant conditioning, extinction occurs when reinforcement for a response is terminated and the rate of that response declines.

● Operant responses are regulated by discriminative stimuli that are cues for the likelihood of obtaining reinforcers. These stimuli are subject to the same processes of generalization and discrimination that occur in classical conditioning.

● Delayed reinforcement slows the process of conditioning. Primary reinforcers are unlearned; secondary reinforcers acquire their reinforcing quality through conditioning.

● Intermittent schedules of reinforcement produce greater resistance to extinction than similar continuous schedules. Ratio schedules tend to yield higher rates of response than interval schedules. Shorter intervals and higher ratios are associated with faster responding.

● Responses can be strengthened through either the presentation of positive reinforcers or the removal of negative reinforcers. Negative reinforcement regulates escape and avoidance learning. The two-process theory provides the best explanation of avoidance behaviour and may shed light on why phobias are so difficult to eliminate.

● Positive and negative punishment involve consequences that lead to a decline in response strength. Some of the problems associated with punishment as a disciplinary procedure are emotional side effects and increased aggressive behaviour.

Changing Directions in the Study of Conditioning

● The findings on instinctive drift, conditioned taste aversion, and preparedness have led to the recognition that there are species-specific biological constraints on conditioning. Some evolutionary psychologists argue that learning processes vary considerably across species.

● Studies of signal relations in classical conditioning and response–outcome relations in operant conditioning suggest that cognitive processes play a larger role in conditioning than originally believed.

Observational Learning

● In observational learning, an organism is conditioned by watching a model's conditioning. Both classical and operant conditioning can occur through observational learning, which depends on the processes of attention, retention, reproduction, and motivation.

● Observational learning can account for the influence of mass media (such as television) on behaviour. The principles of observational learning have also been used to explain why physical punishment increases aggressive behaviour.

Putting It in Perspective

● Two of our key themes were especially apparent in our coverage of learning and conditioning. One theme involves the interaction of heredity and environment in learning. The other involves the way progress in psychology affects society at large.

Personal Application • Achieving Self-Control Through Behaviour Modification

● The first step in self-modification is specifying the target behaviour to be increased or decreased. The second step is gathering baseline data.

● The third step is to design a program, using procedures such as reinforcement, control of antecedents, and punishment. The fourth step involves executing and evaluating your program. The final step is to determine how and when you will phase out your program.

Critical Thinking Application • Manipulating Emotions: Pavlov and Persuasion

● Advertisers routinely pair their products with stimuli that seem likely to elicit positive emotions or other specific feelings. The practice of taking customers out to dinner or to major events also takes advantage of Pavlovian conditioning. Politicians also work to pair themselves with positive events. The best defence against these tactics is to become more aware of efforts to manipulate your emotions.

Key Terms

Acquisition, 233
Antecedents, 259
Avoidance learning, 246
Behaviour modification, 258
Behavioural contract, 261
Classical conditioning, 227
Conditioned reinforcers, 242
Conditioned response (CR), 228
Conditioned stimulus (CS), 228
Continuous reinforcement, 243
Cumulative recorder, 238
Discriminative stimuli, 240
Elicit, 229
Emit, 238
Escape learning, 245
Extinction, 234
Fixed-interval (FI) schedule, 243
Fixed-ratio (FR) schedule, 243
Higher-order conditioning, 235
Instinctive drift, 249
Instrumental learning, 237
Intermittent reinforcement, 243
Law of effect, 237
Learning, 226
Negative punishment, 247
Negative reinforcement, 245
Observational learning, 253
Operant chamber, 238
Operant conditioning, 236
Partial reinforcement, 243
Pavlovian conditioning, 227
Phobias, 227
Positive punishment, 247
Positive reinforcement, 244
Preparedness, 250
Primary reinforcers, 242
Punishment, 247
Reinforcement, 237
Reinforcement contingencies, 238
Resistance to extinction, 240
Schedule of reinforcement, 242
Secondary reinforcers, 242
Shaping, 238
Skinner box, 238
Spontaneous recovery, 234
Stimulus discrimination, 235
Stimulus generalization, 234
Token economy, 260
Trial, 229
Unconditioned response (UCR), 228
Unconditioned stimulus (UCS), 228
Variable-interval (VI) schedule, 243
Variable-ratio (VR) schedule, 243

Key People

Albert Bandura, 253
John Garcia, 250
Ivan Pavlov, 227
Robert Rescorla, 252
Martin Seligman, 249
B. F. Skinner, 238
E. L. Thorndike, 237

Manipulating Emotions: Pavlov and Persuasion

With all due respect to the great Ivan Pavlov, when we focus on his demonstration that dogs can be trained to slobber in response to a tone, it is easy to lose sight of the importance of classical conditioning. At first glance, most people do not see a relationship between Pavlov's slobbering dogs and anything that they are even remotely interested in. However, in the main body of the chapter, we saw that classical conditioning actually contributes to the regulation of many important aspects of behaviour, including fears, phobias, and other emotional reactions; immune function and other physiological processes; food preferences; and even sexual arousal. In this Application you will learn that classical conditioning is routinely used to manipulate emotions in persuasive efforts. If you watch TV, you have been subjected to Pavlovian techniques. An understanding of these techniques can help you recognize when your emotions are being manipulated by advertisers, politicians, and the media.

Perhaps the most interesting aspect of classically conditioned emotional responses is that people often are unaware of the origin of these responses, or even that they feel the way they do. Consistent with this observation, research by Jim Olson of the University of Western Ontario has shown that attitudes can be shaped through classical conditioning without participants' conscious awareness (Olson & Fazio, 2001; Walther, Nagengast, & Trasselli, 2005). The key to the process is simply to manipulate the automatic, subconscious associations that people make in response to various stimuli. Let's look at how this manipulation is done in advertising, business negotiations, and the world of politics.

Classical Conditioning in Advertising

The art of manipulating people's associations has been perfected by the advertising industry (Till & Priluck, 2000). Advertisers consistently endeavour to pair the products they are peddling with stimuli that seem likely to elicit positive emotional responses. An extensive variety of stimuli are used for this purpose. Products are paired with well-liked celebrity spokespersons (Wayne Gretzky is a popular choice, promoting a car company and a fast food company); depictions of warm, loving families; beautiful pastoral scenery; cute, cuddly pets; enchanting, rosy-cheeked children; upbeat, pleasant music; opulent surroundings that reek of wealth; and, above all else, extremely attractive models—especially, glamorous, alluring women (Reichert, 2003; Reichert & Lambiase, 2003). Advertisers also like to pair their products with exciting events, such as the Stanley Cup or Grey Cup, and cherished symbols, such as flags and the Olympic rings insignia.

Advertisers mostly seek to associate their products with stimuli that evoke pleasurable feelings of a general sort, but in some cases they try to create more specific associations. For example, cigarette brands sold mainly to men are frequently paired with tough-looking men in rugged settings to create an association between the cigarettes and masculinity. In contrast, cigarette brands that are mainly marketed to women are paired with images that evoke feelings of femininity. In a similar vein, manufacturers of designer jeans typically seek to forge associations between their products and things that are young, urban, and hip. Advertisers marketing expensive automobiles or platinum credit cards pair their products with symbols of affluence, luxury, and privilege, such as mansions, butlers, and dazzling jewellery.

Classical Conditioning in Business Negotiations

In the world of business interactions, two standard practices are designed to get customers to make an association between one's business and pleasurable feelings. The first is to take customers out to dinner at fine restaurants. The provision of delicious food and fine wine in a luxurious environment is a powerful unconditioned stimulus that reliably elicits pleasant feelings that are likely to be associated with one's host. The second practice is the strategy of entertaining customers at major events, such as concerts and hockey games. Over the last decade, many sports arenas have largely been rebuilt with vastly more "luxury skyboxes" to accommodate this

The practice of taking customers out to dinner at expensive, luxurious restaurants takes advantage of the process of classical conditioning.

Control of Antecedents. A worthwhile strategy for decreasing the occurrence of an undesirable response may be to identify its antecedents and avoid exposure to them. This strategy is especially useful when you are trying to decrease the frequency of a consummatory response, such as smoking or eating. In the case of overeating, for instance, the easiest way to resist temptation is to avoid having to face it. Thus, you might stay away from enticing restaurants, minimize time spent in your kitchen, shop for groceries just after eating (when willpower is higher), and avoid purchasing favourite foods. Control of antecedents can also be helpful in a program to increase studying. The key often lies in *where* you study. You can reduce excessive socializing by studying somewhere devoid of people. Similarly, you can reduce loafing by studying someplace where there is no TV, stereo, or phone to distract you.

Punishment. The strategy of decreasing unwanted behaviour by punishing yourself for that behaviour is an obvious option that people tend to overuse. The biggest problem with punishment in a self-modification effort is that it is difficult to follow through and punish yourself. Nonetheless, there may be situations in which your manipulations of reinforcers need to be bolstered by the threat of punishment.

If you're going to use punishment, keep two guidelines in mind. First, do not use punishment alone. Use it in conjunction with positive reinforcement. If you set up a program in which you can earn only negative consequences, you probably won't stick to it. Second, use a relatively mild punishment so that you will actually be able to administer it to yourself. Nurnberger and Zimmerman (1970) developed a creative method of self-punishment. They had subjects write out a cheque to an organization they hated (e.g., the campaign of a political candidate whom they despised). The cheque was held by a third party who mailed it if subjects failed to meet their behavioural goals. Such a punishment is relatively harmless, but it can serve as a strong source of motivation.

Executing and Evaluating Your Program

Once you have designed your program, the next step is to put it to work by enforcing the contingencies that you have carefully planned. During this period, you need to continue to accurately record the frequency of your target behaviour so you can evaluate your progress. The success of your program depends on your not "cheating." The most common form of cheating is to reward yourself when you have not actually earned it.

You can do two things to increase the likelihood that you will comply with your program. One is to make up a *behavioural contract*—**a written agreement outlining a promise to adhere to the contingencies of a behaviour modification program**. The formality of signing such a contract in front of friends or family seems to make many people take their program more seriously. You can further reduce the likelihood of cheating by having someone other than you dole out the reinforcers and punishments.

Behaviour modification programs often require some fine-tuning, so don't be surprised if you need to make a few adjustments. Several flaws are especially common in designing self-modification programs. Among those that you should look out for are (1) depending on a weak reinforcer, (2) permitting lengthy delays between appropriate behaviour and delivery of reinforcers, and (3) trying to do too much too quickly by setting unrealistic goals. Often, a small revision or two can turn a failing program around and make it a success.

Ending Your Program

Generally, when you design your program you should spell out the conditions under which you will bring it to an end. Doing so involves setting terminal goals such as reaching a certain weight, studying with a certain regularity, or going without cigarettes for a certain length of time. Often, it is a good idea to phase out your program by planning a gradual reduction in the frequency or potency of your reinforcement for appropriate behaviour.

If your program is successful, it may fade away without a conscious decision on your part. Often, new, improved patterns of behaviour become self-maintaining. Responses such as eating right, exercising regularly, and studying diligently may become habitual. Whether or not you end your program intentionally, you should always be prepared to reinstitute the program if you find yourself slipping back to your old patterns of behaviour.

REVIEW OF KEY POINTS

- In behaviour modification, the principles of learning are used to change behaviour directly. Behaviour modification techniques can be used to increase one's self-control. The first step in self-modification involves specifying the overt target behaviour to be increased or decreased.

- The second step involves gathering baseline data about the initial rate of the target response and identifying any typical antecedents and consequences associated with the behaviour.

- The third step is to design a program. If you are trying to increase the strength of a response, you'll depend on positive reinforcement. The reinforcement contingencies should spell out exactly what you have to do to earn your reinforcer. A number of strategies can be used to decrease the strength of a response, including reinforcement, control of antecedents, and punishment.

- The fourth step involves executing and evaluating your program. Self-modification programs often require some fine-tuning. The final step is to determine how and when you will phase out your program.

reward yourself for behaving properly. Although the basic strategy is quite simple, doing it skillfully involves a number of considerations.

Selecting a Reinforcer. To use positive reinforcement, you need to find a reward that will be effective for you. Reinforcement is subjective—what is reinforcing for one person may not be reinforcing for another. Figure 6.26 lists questions you can ask yourself to help you determine your personal reinforcers. Be sure to be realistic and choose a reinforcer that is really available to you.

Figure 6.26

Selecting a reinforcer. Finding a good reinforcer to use in a behaviour modification program can require a lot of thought. The questions listed here can help people identify their personal reinforcers.

SOURCE: Adapted from Watson, D. L., & Tharp, R. G. (1997). *Self-directed behavior: Self-modification for personal adjustment.* Belmont, CA: Wadsworth. Reprinted by permission.

1. What will be the rewards of achieving your goal?
2. What kind of praise do you like to receive, from yourself and others?
3. What kinds of things do you like to have?
4. What are your major interests?
5. What are your hobbies?
6. What people do you like to be with?
7. What do you like to do with those people?
8. What do you do for fun?
9. What do you do to relax?
10. What do you do to get away from it all?
11. What makes you feel good?
12. What would be a nice present to receive?
13. What kinds of things are important to you?
14. What would you buy if you had an extra $20? $50? $100?
15. On what do you spend your money each week?
16. What behaviours do you perform every day? (Don't overlook the obvious or commonplace.)
17. Are there any behaviours you usually perform instead of the target behaviour?
18. What would you hate to lose?
19. Of the things you do every day, which would you hate to give up?
20. What are your favourite daydreams and fantasies?
21. What are the most relaxing scenes you can imagine?

You don't have to come up with spectacular new reinforcers that you've never experienced before. *You can use reinforcers that you are already getting.* However, you have to restructure the contingencies so that you get them only if you behave appropriately. For example, if you normally buy two compact discs per week, you might make these purchases contingent on studying a certain number of hours during the week. Making yourself earn rewards that you used to take for granted is often a useful strategy in a self-modification program.

Arranging the Contingencies. Once you have chosen your reinforcer, you have to set up reinforcement contingencies. These contingencies will describe the exact behavioural goals that must be met and the reinforcement that may then be awarded. For example, in a program to increase exercise, you might make spending $50 on clothes (the reinforcer) contingent on having jogged 25 kilometres during the week (the target behaviour).

Try to set behavioural goals that are both challenging and realistic. You want your goals to be challenging so that they lead to improvement in your behaviour. However, setting unrealistically high goals—a common mistake in self-modification—often leads to unnecessary discouragement.

You also need to be concerned about doling out too much reinforcement. If reinforcement is too easy to get, you may become *satiated,* and the reinforcer may lose its motivational power. For example, if you were to reward yourself with virtually all the compact discs you wanted, this reinforcer would lose its incentive value.

One way to avoid the satiation problem is to put yourself on a token economy. A *token economy* is a system for doling out symbolic reinforcers that are exchanged later for a variety of genuine reinforcers. Thus, you might develop a point system for exercise behaviour, accumulating points that can be spent on compact discs, movies, restaurant meals, and so forth (see Figure 6.27).

Decreasing Response Strength

Let's turn now to the challenge of reducing the frequency of an undesirable response. You can go about this task in a number of

Figure 6.27

Example of a token economy. This token economy was set up to strengthen three types of exercise behaviour (jogging, tennis, and sit-ups). The person can exchange the tokens earned for four types of reinforcers that require different numbers of tokens. A token economy allows for immediate reinforcement (you can award yourself tokens each time you exercise) and it can allow you to employ a variety of reinforcers.

Response earning tokens

Response	Amount	Number of tokens
Jogging	1 km	4
Jogging	2 km	8
Jogging	4 km	16
Tennis	1 hour	4
Tennis	2 hours	8
Sit-ups	25	1
Sit-ups	50	2

Redemption value of tokens

Reinforcer	Tokens required
Purchase one compact disc of your choice	30
Go to movie	50
Go to nice restaurant	100
Take special weekend trip	500

ways. Your principal options include reinforcement, control of antecedents, and punishment.

Reinforcement. Reinforcers can be used in an indirect way to decrease the frequency of a response. This may sound paradoxical, since you have learned that reinforcement strengthens a response. The trick lies in how you define the target behaviour. For example, in the case of overeating you might define your target behaviour as eating more than 1600 calories a day (an excess response that you want to decrease) or eating fewer than 1600 calories a day (a deficit response that you want to increase). You can choose the latter definition and reinforce yourself whenever you eat fewer than 1600 calories in a day. Thus, you can reinforce yourself for not emitting a response, or for emitting it less, and thereby decrease a response through reinforcement.

tain time interval. Thus, you might count the daily frequency of snapping at your children, smoking cigarettes, or biting your fingernails. If studying is your target behaviour, you will probably monitor hours of study. If you want to modify your eating, you will probably keep track of how many calories you consume. Whatever the unit of measurement, *it is crucial to gather accurate data.* You should keep permanent written records, and it is usually best to portray these records graphically (see Figure 6.25).

Second, you need to monitor the antecedents of your target behaviour. **Antecedents are events that typically precede the target response.** Often these events play a major role in evoking your target behaviour. For example, if your target is overeating, you might discover that the bulk of your overeating occurs late in the evening while you watch TV. If you can pinpoint this kind of antecedent–response connection, you may be able to design your program to circumvent or break the link.

Third, you need to monitor the typical consequences of your target behaviour. Try to identify the reinforcers that are maintaining an undesirable target behaviour or the unfavourable outcomes that are suppressing a desirable target behaviour. In trying to identify reinforcers, remember that avoidance behaviour is usually maintained by negative reinforcement. That is, the payoff for avoidance is usually the removal of something aversive, such as anxiety or a threat to self-esteem. You should also take into account the fact that a response may not be reinforced every time, as most behaviour is maintained by intermittent reinforcement.

Designing Your Program

Once you have selected a target behaviour and gathered adequate baseline data, it is time to plan your intervention program. Generally speaking, your program will be designed either to increase or to decrease the frequency of a target response.

Increasing Response Strength

Efforts to increase the frequency of a target response depend largely on the use of positive reinforcement. In other words, you

Figure 6.25

Example of record keeping in a self-modification program. Graphic records are ideal for tracking progress in behaviour modification efforts. The records shown here illustrate what people would be likely to track in a behaviour modification program for weight loss.

Overeating is just one of the many types of maladaptive behaviour that can be changed with a self-modification program.

Typical kinds of responses	Examples in animals	Examples in humans

Mostly (but not always) involuntary reflexes and visceral responses

Dogs learn to salivate to the sound of a tone that has been paired with meat powder.

© Bettmann/CORBIS

Political candidates draw on the power of classical conditioning when they associate with popular celebrities who elicit positive feelings among many voters.

© Jim Young/Reuters/CORBIS

Mostly (but not always) voluntary, spontaneous responses

Trained animals perform remarkable feats because they have been reinforced for gradually learning closer and closer approximations of responses they do not normally emit.

© Gerald Davis by permission of Karen Davis

Casino patrons tend to exhibit high, steady rates of gambling, as most games of chance involve complex variable-ratio schedules of reinforcement.

© Bob Krist/CORBIS

A young boy performs a response that he has acquired through observational learning.

© Laura Dwight/CORBIS

Mostly voluntary responses, often consisting of novel and complex sequences

An English titmouse learns to break into milk bottles by observing the thievery of other titmice.

© J. Markham/Bruce Coleman, Inc.

Achieving Self-Control Through Behaviour Modification

Answer the following "yes" or "no."

____ 1 Do you have a hard time passing up food, even when you're not hungry?

____ 2 Do you wish you studied more often?

____ 3 Would you like to cut down on your smoking or drinking?

____ 4 Do you experience difficulty in getting yourself to exercise regularly?

____ 5 Do you wish you had more willpower?

If you answered "yes" to any of these questions, you have struggled with the challenge of self-control. This Personal Application discusses how you can use the techniques of behaviour modification to improve your self-control. If you stop to think about it, self-control—or rather a lack of it—underlies many of the personal problems that people struggle with in everyday life.

Behaviour modification is a systematic approach to changing behaviour through the application of the principles of conditioning. Advocates of behaviour modification assume that behaviour is a product of learning, conditioning, and environmental control. They further assume that *what is learned can be unlearned.* Thus, they set out to "recondition" people to produce more desirable patterns of behaviour.

The technology of behaviour modification has been applied with great success in schools, businesses, hospitals, factories, child-care facilities, prisons, and mental health centres (Kazdin, 1982, 2001; O'Donohue, 1998; Rachman, 1992). Moreover, behaviour modification techniques have proven particularly valuable in efforts to improve self-control. Our discussion will borrow liberally from an excellent book on self-modification by David Watson and Roland Tharp (2002). We will discuss five steps in the process of self-modification, which are outlined in Figure 6.24.

Specifying Your Target Behaviour

The first step in a self-modification program is to specify the target behaviour(s) that you want to change. Behaviour modification can be applied only to a clearly defined, overt response, yet many people have difficulty pinpointing the behaviour they hope to alter. They tend to describe their problems in terms of unobservable personality *traits* rather than overt *behaviours.* For example, asked what behaviour he would like to change, a man might say, "I'm too irritable." That may be true, but it is of little help in designing a self-modification program. To use a behavioural approach, vague statements about traits need to be translated into precise descriptions of specific target behaviours.

To identify target responses, you need to ponder past behaviour or closely observe future behaviour and list specific *examples* of responses that lead to the trait description. For instance, the man who regards himself as "too irritable" might identify two overly frequent responses, such as arguing with his wife and snapping at his children. These are specific behaviours for which he could design a self-modification program.

Gathering Baseline Data

The second step in behaviour modification is to gather baseline data. You need to systematically observe your target behaviour for a period of time (usually a week or two) before you work out the details of your program. In gathering your baseline data, you need to monitor three things.

First, you need to determine the initial response level of your target behaviour. After all, you can't tell whether your program is working effectively unless you have a baseline for comparison. In most cases, you would simply keep track of how often the target response occurs in a cer-

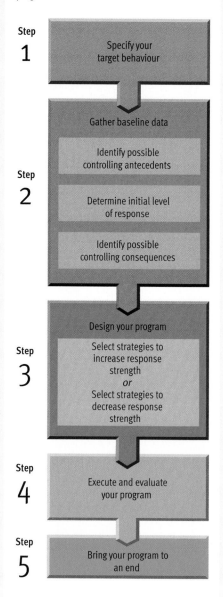

Figure 6.24

Steps in a self-modification program.
This flowchart provides an overview of the five steps necessary to execute a self-modification program.

Step 1 — Specify your target behaviour

Step 2
- Gather baseline data
- Identify possible controlling antecedents
- Determine initial level of response
- Identify possible controlling consequences

Step 3
- Design your program
- Select strategies to increase response strength
  or
- Select strategies to decrease response strength

Step 4 — Execute and evaluate your program

Step 5 — Bring your program to an end

PRACTICE TEST

1. After repeated pairings of a tone with meat powder, Pavlov found that a dog will salivate when the tone is presented. Salivation to the tone is a(n):
   A. unconditioned stimulus.
   B. unconditioned response.
   C. conditioned stimulus.
   D. conditioned response.

2. Sam's wife always wears the same black nightgown whenever she is "in the mood" for sexual relations. Sam becomes sexually aroused as soon as he sees his wife in the nightgown. For Sam, the night-gown is a(n):
   A. unconditioned stimulus.
   B. unconditioned response.
   C. conditioned stimulus.
   D. conditioned response.

3. When ten-year-old Amir broke his brother's favourite toy, his parents decided to take away his favourite toy for one week. This conse-quence is best described as a
   A. positive punishment
   B. negative punishment
   C. positive reinforcement.
   D. negative reinforcement

4. The phenomenon of higher-order conditioning shows that:
   A. only a genuine, natural UCS can be used to establish a CR.
   B. auditory stimuli are easier to condition than visual stimuli.
   C. visual stimuli are easier to condition than auditory stimuli.
   D. an already established CS can be used in the place of a natural UCS.

5. Which of the following statements is (are) true?
   A. Classical conditioning regulates reflexive, involuntary responses exclusively.
   B. Operant conditioning regulates voluntary responses exclusively.
   C. The distinction between the two types of conditioning is not absolute, with both types jointly and interactively governing some aspects of behaviour.
   D. a and b.

6. A pigeon in a Skinner box is pecking the disk at a high, steady rate. The graph portraying this pigeon's responding will have:
   A. a steep, unchanging slope.
   B. a shallow, unchanging slope.
   C. a progressively steeper slope.
   D. a progressively shallower slope.

7. A primary reinforcer has _____ reinforcing properties; a sec-ondary reinforcer has _____ reinforcing properties.
   A. biological; acquired
   B. conditioned; unconditioned
   C. potent; weak
   D. immediate; delayed

8. The steady, rapid responding of a person playing a slot machine is an example of the pattern of responding typically generated on a _____ schedule.
   A. fixed-ratio   C. fixed-interval
   B. variable-ratio   D. variable-interval

9. Positive reinforcement _____ the rate of responding; negative reinforcement _____ the rate of responding.
   A. increases; decreases
   B. decreases; increases
   C. increases; increases
   D. decreases; decreases

10. According to the two-process theory, a fear response is acquired due to _____ conditioning; it is maintained due to _____ conditioning.
    A. classical; operant
    B. operant; classical
    C. classical; classical
    D. operant; operant

11. Nolan used to love tequila. However, a few weeks ago he drank way too much tequila and became very, very sick. His tendency to drink tequila has since declined dramatically. In operant terms, this sequence of events represents:
    A. avoidance learning.
    B. negative reinforcement.
    C. escape learning.
    D. punishment.

12. According to Rescorla, the strength of a conditioned response depends on:
    A. the number of trials in which the CS and UCS are paired.
    B. the number of trials in which the CS is presented alone.
    C. the percentage of trials in which the CS and UCS are paired.
    D. resistance to extinction.

13. Skinner maintained that reinforcement determines the acquisition of a response; Bandura maintains that reinforcement determines the _____ of a response.
    A. acquisition
    B. development
    C. performance
    D. generalization

14. The link between physical punishment and subsequent aggressive behaviour is probably best explained by:
    A. observational learning.
    B. noncontingent reinforcement.
    C. resistance to extinction.
    D. positive punishment.

15. The *second* step in a self-modification program is to:
    A. specify the target behaviour.
    B. design your program.
    C. gather baseline data.
    D. set up a behavioural contract.

    See Appendix A for answers to this Practice Test.

 ON THE WEB

For additional resources on the topics covered in this chapter, visit the *Psychology: Themes and Variations* Web site, where you will find practice quizzes, tutorials, Web links, simulations, critical thinking activities, flash cards, interactive exercises, and suggested readings available through INFOTRAC.

http://www.themesandvariations.nelson.com

 http://hed.nelson.com

Go to this site for the link to ThomsonNOW™, your one-stop study shop. Take a Pretest for this chapter and ThomsonNOW™ will generate a personalized Study Plan based on your test results! The Study Plan will identify the topics you need to review and direct you to online resources to help you master those topics. You can then take a Posttest to help you determine the concepts you have mastered and what you still need work on.

CHAPTER 7

Latchezar Boyadjiev, *Diversion*, L.B. Glass Studios

Encoding: Getting Information into Memory
The Role of Attention
Levels of Processing
Enriching Encoding

Storage: Maintaining Information in Memory
Sensory Memory
Short-Term Memory
Long-Term Memory
Featured Study • How Accurate Are Flashbulb Memories?
Are Short-Term Memory and Long-Term Memory Really Separate?
How Is Knowledge Represented and Organized in Memory?

Retrieval: Getting Information Out of Memory
Using Cues to Aid Retrieval
Reinstating the Context of an Event
Reconstructing Memories and the Misinformation Effect
Source Monitoring and Reality Monitoring

Forgetting: When Memory Lapses
How Quickly We Forget: Ebbinghaus's Forgetting Curve
Measures of Forgetting
Why We Forget
The Repressed Memories Controversy

In Search of the Memory Trace: The Physiology of Memory
The Biochemistry of Memory
The Neural Circuitry of Memory
The Anatomy of Memory

Are There Multiple Memory Systems?
Implicit versus Explicit Memory
Declarative versus Procedural Memory
Semantic versus Episodic Memory
Prospective versus Retrospective Memory

Putting It in Perspective

Personal Application • **Improving Everyday Memory**
Engage in Adequate Rehearsal
Schedule Distributed Practice and Minimize Interference
Emphasize Deep Processing and Organize Information
Enrich Encoding with Verbal Mnemonics
Enrich Encoding with Visual Mnemonics

Critical Thinking Application • **Understanding the Fallibility of Eyewitness Accounts**
The Contribution of Hindsight Bias
The Contribution of Overconfidence
Strategies to Reduce Overconfidence

Recap

Practice Test

Human Memory

Have you ever thought about the possibility of travelling through time? The concept is fascinating and has been the subject of several books and movies. Do you happen to remember the name of the British author who wrote *The Time Machine*? You might have seen the movie adaptation that came out in 2002—if you saw the movie, do you remember whom you saw it with? The 2002 film was a remake of an earlier version released in 1960. When casting the 2002 movie, the producers decided to cast a bit part for one of the leading actors who starred in the 1960 film—he was cast as a salesperson in a flower shop in the 2002 release. Those familiar with the actor may have reacted upon seeing him in the 2002 film, recognizing the face but not able to place him or remember his name. In fact, when this occurs we often respond by suggesting that the name is on the tip of our tongue. In this case, if they tried hard enough, they might remember that his name was Alan Young. This casting was clearly intentional on the part of the producers and they were hoping to make contact with the memory of some of the older members of the audience. These types of events have likely happened to most of you and reveal how intimately our memory is tied up with our everyday experiences. Time travel is related to memory in at least one other way. In fact, time travel itself, while clearly fascinating, isn't as rare as you might think; in fact, most of us can do it and if you think carefully about it, it shouldn't surprise you to know that such time travel is intimately linked with the nature of our cognition and memory systems.

It is the nature of our cognitive and memory processes that allow us all to travel through time (Roberts, 2002; Tulving, 1983, 1993). We can go backwards to remember specific events that happened to us, such as attending a screening of *The Time Machine* and the people with whom we attended the movie. Other memories are not tied to us personally, but may relate more to general knowledge such as what the word "machine" means or who wrote the original novel—it was H. G. Wells in 1895. These two kinds of memory—memory for general information and memory for personal events—were labelled *semantic* and *episodic* memory, respectively, by University of Toronto psychologist Endel Tulving (1972). Tulving's well-known patient referred to as K. C. gives a dramatic example of the distinction between these types of memories. Unfortunately, K. C. suffered serious brain damage in 1981 after a motorcycle accident. But you might never realize it if you restricted yourself to asking him questions such as "Who wrote *The Time Machine*?" After the accident, K. C.'s semantic memory for facts was unimpaired. He was not distinguishable from anyone else and frequently outperformed normal undergraduates at the University of Toronto on various cognitive/perceptual tasks. What was impaired, however, was his episodic memory: No matter how hard he tries he cannot remember anything that has ever happened *to him* (Tulving, 2001). We will discuss in much more detail the notion of types of memory and the theories and work of Endel Tulving in this chapter. Tulving is an internationally recognized expert in the nature of memory. He was awarded the Donald O. Hebb award by the Canadian Psychological Association in 1983 and was just awarded, along with neuroscientist Brenda Milner of McGill University, the 2005 Gairdner Award. Interestingly, while not a criterion for the award, both researchers study memory.

Of course, we are not constrained to the past in our time travelling. Our cognitive systems also allow us to experience the present and to travel forward in time to plan and anticipate things in the future. Some of these characteristics are unique to humans. William Roberts (2002) of the University of Western Ontario argues that animals are "stuck in time," as they have no episodic memory or ability to anticipate events far in the future. It is episodic memory, of course, that affords humans the ability to "time travel" (Tulving, 1993). Memory is a fascinating topic relevant to our everyday lives. For most of us, memory is not a concern. For some, however, memory—or rather lack of it—is a priority issue.

Process	Encoding	Storage	Retrieval
Definition	Involves forming a memory code	Involves maintaining encoded information in memory over time	Involves recovering information from memory stores
Analogy to information processing by a computer	Entering data through keyboard	Saving data in file on hard disk	Calling up file and displaying data on monitor

Figure 7.1

Three key processes in memory. Memory depends on three sequential processes: encoding, storage, and retrieval. Some theorists have drawn an analogy between these processes and elements of information processing by computers, as depicted here. The analogies for encoding and retrieval work pretty well, but the storage analogy is somewhat misleading. When information is stored on a hard drive, it remains unchanged indefinitely and you can retrieve an exact copy. As you will learn in this chapter, memory storage is a much more dynamic process. Our memories change over time and are rough reconstructions rather than exact copies of past events.

In a recent Statistics Canada (2002b) survey focusing on Canadians with some type of disability, one out of seven reported a significant disability, and of those 15 and older, 12.3% reported significant memory impairment and confusion. While this problem increased with age, it was not entirely restricted to the elderly. There are, however, specific memory deficits associated with aging. While we will deal more specifically with aging and issues such as Alzheimer's disease in Chapter 11, it is noteworthy that Endel Tulving joins other Canadian memory researchers, such as Fergus Craik, Lynn Hasher, Gordon Winocur, and Morris Moscovitch, at the Rotman Research Institute at the Baycrest Centre for Geriatric Care in Toronto. This is one of the leading centres for memory and aging research in the world. One of its programs, known as the Memory-Link program, is headed by psychologist Brian Richards. This program aims to teach amnesiacs skills that enable them to employ external devices such as Palm Pilots in order to compensate for their memory disabilities (Baycrest Centre, 2004).

In this chapter we focus on the nature of our memory systems. As the preceding discussion suggests, memory involves more than taking information in and storing it in some mental compartment. In fact, psychologists probing the workings of memory have had to grapple with three enduring questions: (1) How does information get *into* memory? (2) How is information *maintained* in memory? and (3) How is information pulled *back out* of memory? These three questions correspond to the three key processes involved in memory (see Figure 7.1): *encoding* (getting information in), *storage* (maintaining it), and *retrieval* (getting it out).

Encoding **involves forming a memory code.** For example, when you form a memory code for a word, you might emphasize how it looks, how it sounds, or what it means. Encoding usually requires attention. *Storage* **involves maintaining encoded information in memory over time.** Psychologists have focused much of their memory research on trying to identify just what factors help or hinder memory storage. Information storage isn't enough to guarantee that you'll remember something. You need to be able to get information out of storage. *Retrieval* **involves recovering information from memory stores.** Research issues concerned with retrieval include the study of how people search memory and why some retrieval strategies are more effective than others.

Most of this chapter is devoted to an examination of memory encoding, storage, and retrieval. As you'll see, these basic processes help explain the ultimate puzzle in the study of memory: why people forget. Just as memory involves more than storage, forgetting involves more than "losing" something from the memory store. Forgetting may be due to deficiencies in any of the three key processes in memory—encoding, storage, or retrieval. After our discussion of forgetting, we will take a brief look at the physiological bases of memory. Finally, we will discuss the theoretical controversy about whether there are separate memory systems for different types of information. The chapter's Personal Application provides some practical advice on how to improve your memory. The Critical Thinking Application discusses some reasons why memory is less reliable than people assume it to be.

Encoding: Getting Information into Memory

Have you ever been introduced to someone and then realized only 30 seconds into your interaction that you had already "forgotten" his or her name? More often than not, this familiar kind of forgetting results from a failure to form a memory code for the name. When you're introduced to people, you're often busy sizing them up and thinking about what you're going to say. With your attention diverted in this way, names go in one ear and out the other. You don't remember them because they aren't encoded for storage into memory. Psychologists have observed a similar phenomenon in the laboratory, which they have dubbed the *next-in-line effect*. If participants in a small group take turns speaking to the group, subsequent memory tests reveal that the subjects tend to not recall much of what was said just before they took their turn (Bond, Pitre, & Van Leeuwen, 1991). Why? Because when participants are next in line to speak, they are too preoccupied rehearsing to pay attention to what is being said.

Like the problem of forgetting people's names just after you've met them, the next-in-line effect illustrates that active encoding is a crucial process in memory. In this section, we discuss the role of attention in encoding, various types of encoding, and ways to enrich the encoding process.

The Role of Attention

Although there are some fascinating exceptions, you generally need to pay attention to information if you intend to remember it (Lachter, Forster, & Ruthruff, 2004; Craik et al., 1996; Mulligan, 1998). For example, if you sit through a class lecture but pay little attention to it, you're unlikely to remember much of what the professor had to say.

Attention **involves focusing awareness on a narrowed range of stimuli or events.** If you pause to devote a little attention to the matter, you'll realize that selective attention is critical to everyday functioning. If your attention were distributed equally among all stimulus inputs, life would be utter chaos. If you weren't able to filter out most of the potential stimulation around you, you wouldn't be able to read a book, converse with a friend, or even carry on a coherent train of thought.

Attention is often likened to a *filter* that screens out most potential stimuli while allowing a select few to pass through into conscious awareness. However, a great deal of debate has been devoted to *where* the filter is located in the information-processing system. The key issue in this debate is whether stimuli are screened out *early*, during sensory input, or *late*, after the brain has processed the meaning or significance of the input (see Figure 7.2).

Evidence on the "cocktail party phenomenon" suggests the latter. For example, imagine a young woman named Claudia at a crowded party where many conversations are taking place. Claudia is paying attention to her conversation with a friend and filtering out the other conversations. However, if someone in another conversation mentions her name, Claudia may notice it, even though she has been ignoring that conversation. In experimental simulations of this situation about 35% of participants report hearing their own name (Wood & Cowan, 1995). If selection is early, how can these people register input they've been blocking out? This cocktail party phenomenon suggests that attention involves *late* selection, based on the *meaning* of input.

PREVIEW QUESTIONS
- What does attention have to do with memory?
- What types of encoding produce deeper processing?
- How do levels of processing relate to retention?
- How does elaboration enhance encoding?
- How does the use of visual imagery improve memory?
- What is self-referent encoding?

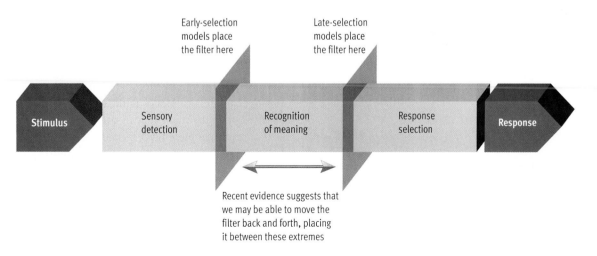

Early-selection models place the filter here

Late-selection models place the filter here

| Stimulus | Sensory detection | Recognition of meaning | Response selection | Response |

Recent evidence suggests that we may be able to move the filter back and forth, placing it between these extremes

Figure 7.2

Models of selective attention. Early-selection models propose that input is filtered before meaning is processed. Late-selection models hold that filtering occurs after the processing of meaning. There is evidence to support early, late, and intermediate selection, suggesting that the location of the attentional filter may not be fixed.

Which view is supported by the weight of scientific evidence—early selection or late selection? Studies have found ample evidence for *both* as well as for intermediate selection (Cowan, 1988; Posner & DiGirolamo, 2000). These findings have led some theorists to conclude that the location of the attention filter may be flexible rather than fixed (Shiffrin, 1988).

Wherever filtering occurs, it is clear that people have difficulty if they attempt to focus their attention on two or more inputs simultaneously. For example, if Claudia tried to continue her original conversation while also monitoring the other conversation in which she was mentioned, she would struggle in her efforts to attend to both conversations and would remember less of her original conversation. Studies by University of Toronto professor and Rotman Research Institute member Fergus Craik indicate that when participants are forced to divide their attention between memory encoding and some other task, large reductions in memory performance are seen (Craik, 2001; Craik & Kester, 2000). He has also conducted important work with Ellen Bialystok on bilingualism (Craik & Bialystok, 2005) and has made important contributions to the literature on cognition and aging. We will consider work on bilingualism in Chapter 10 and Craik's contributions to aging in Chapter 11.

Other work has demonstrated that the negative effects of divided attention are not limited to memory. Divided attention can have a negative impact on the performance of quite a variety of tasks, especially when the tasks are complex or unfamiliar (Pashler, Johnston, & Ruthruff, 2001). This principle appears to apply to the controversy about the advisability of driving while conversing on a cellular telephone. One recent study of a simulated driving task suggests that cellular conversations double the chances of missing traffic signals and slow reactions to signals that are detected (Strayer & Johnston, 2001).

Attention and deficits related to it may help us understand some of the cognitive difficulties faced by some of the elderly. University of Toronto psychologist Lynn Hasher and her colleagues (Hasher & Zacks, 1974) suggest that while much of the information we want to remember is encoded as a result of *effortful processing*, some types of information may be acquired more *automatically*. In the first type of processing, you are picking up information because you are intentionally attempting to do so, such as when you are listening to your psychology professor's inspiring lectures. Other information, such as the frequency of word use (e.g., whether the word *bacon* or *pastrami* occurs more frequently in English), is picked up without your intending to do so (Hasher & Zacks, 1974). People are surprisingly accurate at answering questions about matters like word frequency without remembering how they acquired the knowledge. Under some circumstances, that type of information may be very important. The ability to answer questions based on each type of processing has been found to be a function of several factors, including circadian patterns and age (May, Hasher, & Foong, 2005).

Levels of Processing

Attention is critical to the encoding of memories, but not all attention is created equal. You can attend to things in different ways, focusing on different aspects of the stimulus input. According to some theorists, these qualitative differences in *how* people attend to information are the main factors influencing how much they remember. Fergus Craik and Robert Lockhart (1972), both from the University of Toronto, proposed an important model in this area. In their formulation, they argue that different rates of forgetting occur because some methods of encoding create more durable memory codes than others.

Craik and Lockhart propose that incoming information can be processed at different levels. For instance, they maintain that in dealing with verbal information, people engage in three progressively deeper levels of processing: structural, phonemic, and semantic encoding (see Figure 7.3). *Structural encoding* is relatively shallow processing that emphasizes the physical structure of the stimulus. For example, if words are flashed on a screen, structural encoding registers such things as how they were

Figure 7.3

Levels-of-processing theory. According to Craik (2002) and Lockhart and Craik (1972, 1990), structural, phonemic, and semantic encoding— which can be elicited by questions such as those shown on the right—involve progressively deeper levels of processing, which should result in more durable memories.

Level of processing	Type of encoding	Example of questions used to elicit appropriate encoding
Shallow processing	*Structural encoding:* emphasizes the physical structure of the stimulus	Is the word written in capital letters?
Intermediate processing	*Phonemic encoding:* emphasizes what a word sounds like	Does the word rhyme with weight?
Deep processing	*Semantic encoding:* emphasizes the meaning of verbal input	Would the word fit in the sentence: "He met a _____ on the street"?

Depth of processing

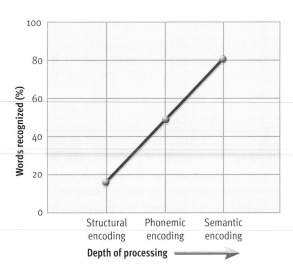

Figure 7.4

Retention at three levels of processing. In accordance with levels-of-processing theory, Craik and Tulving (1975) found that structural, phonemic, and semantic encoding, which involve progressively deeper levels of processing, led to progressively better retention. (Data from Craik & Tulving, 1975)

printed (capital, lowercase, and so on) or the length of the words (how many letters). Further analysis may result in *phonemic encoding,* which emphasizes what a word sounds like. Phonemic encoding involves naming or saying (perhaps silently) the words. Finally, *semantic encoding* emphasizes the meaning of verbal input; it involves thinking about the objects and actions the words represent. **Levels-of-processing theory proposes that deeper levels of processing result in longer-lasting memory codes.**

In one experimental test of levels-of-processing theory, Craik and Tulving (1975) compared the durability of structural, phonemic, and semantic encoding. They directed subjects' attention to particular aspects of briefly presented stimulus words by asking them questions about various characteristics of the words (see Figure 7.3). The questions were designed to engage the subjects in different levels of processing. The key hypothesis was that retention of the stimulus words would increase as subjects moved from structural to phonemic to semantic encoding. After responding to 60 words, the subjects received an unexpected test of their memory for the words. As predicted, the subjects' recall was low after structural encoding, notably better after phonemic encoding, and highest after semantic encoding (see Figure 7.4).

The hypothesis that deeper processing leads to enhanced memory has been replicated in many studies (Koriat & Melkman, 1987; Lockhart & Craik, 1990). Nonetheless, the levels-of-processing model is not without its weaknesses. Critics ask, what exactly

is a "level" of processing? And how do we determine whether one level is deeper than another? Craik and Lockhart had hoped that the *time required for processing* would prove to be a good indicator of depth. However, Craik and Tulving (1975) found that it's possible to design a task in which structural encoding takes longer than semantic encoding. This finding indicates that processing time is not a reliable index of depth of processing. Thus, the levels in levels-of-processing theory remain vaguely defined.

Enriching Encoding

Structural, phonemic, and semantic encoding do not exhaust the options when it comes to forming memory codes. There are other dimensions to encoding, dimensions that can enrich the encoding process and thereby improve memory.

Elaboration

Semantic encoding can often be enhanced through a process called elaboration. **Elaboration is linking a stimulus to other information at the time of encoding.** For example, let's say you read that phobias are often caused by classical conditioning, and you apply this idea to your own fear of spiders. In doing so, you are engaging in elaboration. The additional associations created by elaboration usually help people remember information. Differences in elaboration can help explain why different approaches to semantic processing result in varied amounts of retention (Craik & Tulving, 1975; Willoughby, Motz, & Wood, 1997).

Elaboration often consists of thinking of examples that illustrate an idea. The value of examples was demonstrated in a study in which subjects read 32 paragraphs of information about a fictitious African country (Palmere et al., 1983). Each paragraph communicated one main idea, which was followed by no example, one example, two examples, or three examples. The effect of examples on memory was dramatic. As you can see in Figure 7.5, additional examples led to better memory. In this study, the examples were provided to the students, but self-generated examples created through elaboration would probably be even more valuable in enhancing memory.

Visual Imagery

Imagery—the creation of visual images to represent the words to be remembered—can also be used to enrich encoding. Of course, some words are easier to create images for than others. If you were asked to remember the word *juggler,* you could readily form an

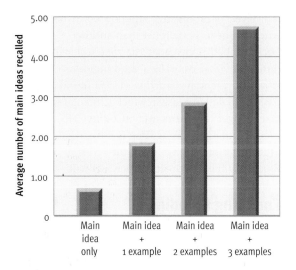

Figure 7.5

Effects of examples on retention of ideas. Palmere et al. (1983) manipulated the number of examples provided to illustrate the main idea of various paragraphs. As the number of examples increased from none to three, so did participants' retention of the main ideas. These results are consistent with the notion that elaboration enhances retention. (Data from Palmere et al., 1983)

image of someone juggling balls. However, if you were asked to remember the word *truth,* you would probably have more difficulty forming a suitable image. The difference is that *juggler* refers to a concrete object, whereas *truth* refers to an abstract concept. The University of Western Ontario's Allan Paivio (1969) points out that it is easier to form images of concrete objects than of abstract concepts. He believes that this ease of image formation affects memory.

The beneficial effect of imagery on memory was demonstrated in a study by Paivio, Smythe, and Yuille (1968). They asked subjects to learn a list of 16 pairs of words. They manipulated whether the words were concrete, high-imagery words or abstract, low-imagery words. In terms of imagery potential, the list contained four types of pairings: high–high (*juggler–dress*), high–low (*letter–effort*), low–high (*duty–hotel*), and low–low (*quality–necessity*). Figure 7.6 shows the recall for each type of pairing. The impact of imagery is quite evident. The best recall was of high–high pairings, and the worst recall was of low–low pairings, showing that high-imagery words are easier to remember than low-imagery words. Similar results were observed in a more recent study that controlled for additional confounding factors (Paivio, Khan, & Begg, 2000).

According to Paivio (1986), imagery facilitates memory because it provides a second kind of memory code, and two codes are better than one. His **dual-coding theory** holds that memory is enhanced by forming **semantic and visual codes, since either can lead**

to recall. Although some aspects of dual-coding theory have been questioned, it's clear that the use of mental imagery can enhance memory in many situations (Marschark, 1992; McCauley, Eskes, & Moscovitch, 1996).

Self-Referent Encoding

Making material *personally* meaningful can also enrich encoding. For example, if you ride a bus regularly, you've probably heard the driver call out the names of the stops day in and day out for months. Do you remember all of the stops? If you haven't made an effort to memorize them, probably not. But you could probably list those that you've used, or even the ones where your friends get on or off. People's recall of information tends to be slanted in favour of material that is personally relevant (Kahan & Johnson, 1992).

Self-referent encoding involves deciding how or whether information is personally relevant. This approach to encoding was compared to structural, phonemic, and semantic encoding in a study by University of Calgary psychologists Rogers, Kuiper, and Kirker (1977). Like Craik and Tulving (1975), these researchers manipulated encoding by asking their subjects certain kinds of questions. To induce self-referent encoding, subjects were asked to decide

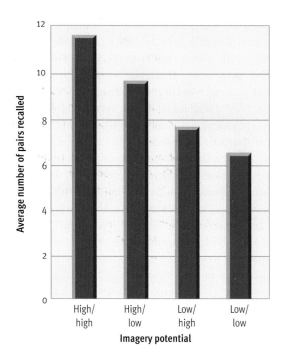

Figure 7.6

The effect of visual imagery on retention. Participants given pairs of words to remember showed better recall for high-imagery pairings than for low-imagery pairings, demonstrating that visual imagery can enrich encoding. (Data from Paivio, Smythe, & Yuille, 1968)

whether adjectives flashed on a screen applied to them personally. The results showed that self-referent encoding led to improved recall of the adjectives. Self-referent encoding appears to enhance recall by promoting additional elaboration and better organization of information (Symons & Johnson, 1997). Nick Kuiper (Kuiper & Rogers, 1979), now at the University of Western Ontario, has gone on to use the self-referent encoding to show that people who are depressed differ from nondepressed people in the content of their self-concept or self-prototype. Depressed people have more negative content as part of their self-prototype (Kuiper & Derry, 1981). We will review some of the research findings with regard to self-concept and depression in Chapter 14.

The value of self-referent encoding demonstrates once again that encoding plays a critical role in memory. But encoding is only one of the three key processes in memory. We turn next to the process of storage, which for many people is virtually synonymous with memory.

REVIEW OF KEY POINTS

● Three key processes contribute to memory: encoding, storage, and retrieval. The next-in-line effect illustrates that active encoding is crucial to memory.

● Attention, which facilitates encoding, is inherently selective and has been compared to a filter. The cocktail party phenomenon suggests that input is screened late in mental processing. The empirical evidence indicates that people may have some flexibility in where they place their attention filter.

● According to levels-of-processing theory, the kinds of memory codes people create depend on which aspects of a stimulus are emphasized. Structural, phonemic, and semantic encoding emphasize the structure, sound, and meaning of words, respectively.

● Deeper processing results in better recall of information. Structural, phonemic, and semantic encoding represent progressively deeper levels of processing.

● Elaboration enriches encoding by linking a stimulus to other information, such as examples of an idea. The creation of visual images to represent words can enrich encoding. Visual imagery may help by creating two memory codes rather than just one. Encoding that emphasizes personal self-reference may be especially useful in facilitating retention.

Storage: Maintaining Information in Memory

In their efforts to understand memory storage, theorists have historically related it to the technologies of their age (Roediger, 1980). One of the earliest models used to explain memory storage was the wax tablet. Both Aristotle and Plato compared memory to a block of wax that differed in size and hardness for various individuals. Remembering, according to this analogy, was like stamping an impression into the wax. As long as the image remained in the wax, the memory would remain intact.

Modern theories of memory reflect the technological advances of the 20th century. For example, many theories formulated at the dawn of the computer age drew an analogy between information storage by computers and information storage in human memory (Atkinson & Shiffrin, 1968, 1971; Broadbent, 1958; Waugh & Norman, 1965). The main contribution of these *information-processing theories* was to subdivide memory into three separate memory stores (Estes, 1999; Pashler & Carrier, 1996). The names for these stores and their exact characteristics varied some from one theory to the next. For purposes of simplicity, we'll organize our discussion around the model devised by Atkinson and Shiffrin, which proved to be the most influential of the information-processing theories. According to their model, incoming information passes through two temporary storage buffers—the sensory store and short-term store—before it is trans-

ferred into a long-term store (see Figure 7.7). Like the wax tablet before it, the information-processing model of memory is a metaphor; the three memory stores are not viewed as anatomical structures in the brain, but rather as functionally distinct types of memory.

Sensory Memory

The *sensory memory* preserves information in its original sensory form for a brief time, usually only a fraction of a second. Sensory memory allows the

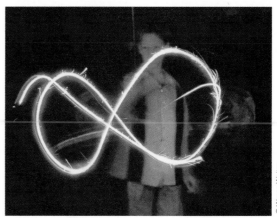

Because the image of the sparkler persists briefly in sensory memory, when the sparkler is moved fast enough, the blending of afterimages causes people to see a continuous stream of light instead of a succession of individual points.

PREVIEW QUESTIONS

● What is sensory memory?

● What is the duration and capacity of the short-term store?

● What are the components of working memory?

● Is long-term storage permanent?

● Why have some theorists questioned the distinction between short-term and long-term memory?

● How is information organized and represented in memory?

Figure 7.7

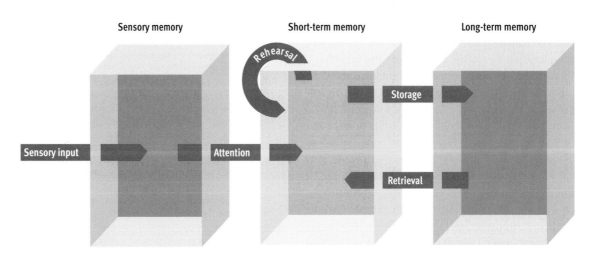

The Atkinson and Shiffrin model of memory storage. Atkinson and Shiffrin (1971) proposed that memory is made up of three information stores. *Sensory memory* can hold a large amount of information just long enough (a fraction of a second) for a small portion of it to be selected for longer storage. *Short-term memory* has a limited capacity, and unless aided by rehearsal, its storage duration is brief. *Long-term memory* can store an apparently unlimited amount of information for indeterminate periods.

sensation of a visual pattern, sound, or touch to linger for a brief moment after the sensory stimulation is over. In the case of vision, people really perceive an *afterimage* rather than the actual stimulus. You can demonstrate the existence of afterimages for yourself by rapidly moving a lighted sparkler or flashlight in circles in the dark. If you move a sparkler fast enough, you should see a complete circle even though the light source is only a single point (see the photo on page 273). The sensory memory preserves the sensory image long enough for you to perceive a continuous circle rather than separate points of light.

The brief preservation of sensations in sensory memory gives you additional time to try to recognize stimuli. However, you'd better take advantage of sensory storage immediately, because it doesn't last long. This fact was demonstrated in a classic experiment by George Sperling (1960). His subjects saw three rows of letters flashed on a screen for just $1/20$ of a second. A tone following the exposure signalled which row of letters the subject should report to the experimenter (see Figure 7.8). Subjects were fairly accurate when the signal occurred immediately. However, their accuracy steadily declined as the delay of the tone increased to 1 second. Why? Because the memory trace in the visual sensory store decays in about $1/4$ of a second. Memory traces in the auditory sensory store also appear to last less than a second (Massaro & Loftus, 1996).

Figure 7.8

Sperling's (1960) study of sensory memory. After the participants had fixated on the cross, the letters were flashed on the screen just long enough to create a visual afterimage. High, medium, and low tones signalled which row of letters to report. Because subjects had to rely on the afterimage to report the letters, Sperling (1960) was able to measure how rapidly the afterimage disappeared by varying the delay between the display and the signal to report.

Short-Term Memory 6B

Short-term memory (STM) is a limited-capacity store that can maintain unrehearsed information for up to about 20 seconds. In contrast, information stored in long-term memory may last weeks, months, or years. However, there is a way that you can maintain information in your short-term store indefinitely. How? Primarily, by engaging in **rehearsal**—the **process of repetitively verbalizing or thinking about the information.** You surely have used the rehearsal process on many occasions. For instance, when you look up a phone number, you probably recite it over and over until you can dial it. Rehearsal keeps recycling the information through your short-term memory. In theory, this recycling could go on forever, but in reality something eventually distracts you and breaks the rehearsal loop.

Durability of Storage 6B

Without rehearsal, information in short-term memory is lost in less than 20 seconds (Wickens, 1999; Nairne, 2003). This rapid loss was demonstrated in a study by Peterson and Peterson (1959). They measured how long undergraduates could remember three consonants if they couldn't rehearse them. To prevent rehearsal, the Petersons required the students to count backward by threes from the time the consonants were presented until they saw a light that signalled the

recall test (see Figure 7.9). Their results showed that subjects' recall accuracy was pretty dismal after only 15 seconds. Other approaches to the issue have suggested that the typical duration of STM storage may even be shorter (Baddely, 1986). Theorists originally believed that the loss of information from short-term memory was due purely to time-related *decay* of memory traces, but follow-up research showed that *interference* from competing material also contributes (Lewandowsky, Duncan, & Brown, 2004; Nairne, 2002).

Capacity of Storage 6B

Short-term memory is also limited in the number of items it can hold. The small capacity of STM was pointed out by George Miller (1956) in a famous paper called "The Magical Number Seven, Plus or Minus Two: Some Limits on Our Capacity for Processing Information." Miller noticed that people could recall only about seven items in tasks that required them to remember unfamiliar material. The common thread in these tasks, Miller argued, was that they required the use of STM. The limited capacity of STM constrains people's ability to perform tasks in which they need to mentally juggle various pieces of information (Baddeley & Hitch, 1974).

You can increase the capacity of your short-term memory by combining stimuli into larger, possibly higher-order units, called *chunks* (Simon, 1974). **A *chunk* is a group of familiar stimuli stored as a single unit.** You can demonstrate the effect of

Web Link 7.1

The Magical Number Seven, Plus or Minus Two
http://www.well.com/user/smalin/miller.html

In 1956, Princeton psychology professor George A. Miller published one of the most famous papers in the history of psychology: "The Magical Number Seven, Plus or Minus Two: Some Limits on Our Capacity for Processing Information." At this site, you'll find a copy of the original text with tables so you can see why this is such an important research milestone in psychology.

Warning
Green signal light: trial about to begin

Stimulus presentation
3 letters and a 3-digit number

"CJL 547"

Retention interval
Subject counts backward by threes for intervals of 3 to 18 seconds

547...
544...
541...
538...
535...

Recall signal and report
Red signal light: recall letters

"CJL ?"

Time (seconds)

Figure 7.9

Peterson and Peterson's (1959) study of short-term memory. After a warning light was flashed, the participants were given three consonants to remember. The researchers prevented rehearsal by giving the subjects a three-digit number at the same time and telling them to count backward by three from that number until given the signal to recall the letters. By varying the amount of time between stimulus presentation and recall, Peterson and Peterson (1959) were able to measure how quickly information is lost from short-term memory.

The Magical Number Seven, Plus or Minus Two.
GEORGE MILLER

chunking by asking someone to recall a sequence of 12 letters grouped in the following way:

NF - BCT - VC - BCIB - M

As you read the letters aloud, pause at the hyphens. Your subject will probably attempt to remember each letter separately because there are no obvious groups or chunks. But a string of 12 letters is too long for STM, so errors are likely. Now present the same string of letters to another person, but place the pauses in the following locations:

NFB - CTV - CBC - IBM

The letters now form four familiar chunks that should occupy only four slots in STM, resulting in successful recall (Bower & Springston, 1970).

To successfully chunk the letters I B M, a subject must first recognize these letters as a familiar unit. This familiarity has to be stored somewhere in long-term memory. Hence, in this case information was transferred from long-term into short-term memory. This is not unusual. People routinely draw information out of their long-term memory banks to evaluate and understand information that they are working with in short-term memory.

Short-Term Memory as "Working Memory"

Research eventually uncovered a number of problems with the original model of short-term memory (Bower, 2000). Among other things, studies showed that short-term memory is *not* limited to phonemic encoding as originally thought and that decay is *not* the only process responsible for the loss of information from STM. These and other findings suggested that short-term memory involves more than a simple rehearsal buffer, as originally envisioned. To make sense of such findings, Alan Baddeley (1986, 1989, 1992) proposed a more complex, modularized model of short-term memory that characterizes it as "working memory."

The original conception of working memory consisted of three components, but Baddeley (2001) has recently added a fourth element (see Figure 7.10). The first is the *phonological rehearsal loop* that represented all of STM in earlier models. This component is at work when you use recitation to temporarily hold on to a phone number. The second component in working memory is a *visuospatial sketchpad* that permits people to temporarily hold and manipulate visual images. This component is at work when you try to mentally rearrange the furniture in your bedroom. The third component is an *executive control system*. It controls the deployment of attention, switching the focus of attention and dividing attention as needed. The fourth component is the *episodic buffer,* a temporary, limited–capacity store that allows the various components of working memory to integrate information and that serves as an interface between working memory and long-term memory.

The two key characteristics that originally defined short-term memory—small capacity and short storage duration—are still present in the concept of working memory. However, Baddeley's model accounts for evidence that STM handles a greater variety of functions and depends on more complicated processes than previously thought.

Long-Term Memory

Long-term memory (LTM) **is an unlimited capacity store that can hold information over lengthy periods of time.** Unlike sensory and short-term memory, which have very brief storage durations, LTM can store information indefinitely. In fact, one point of view is that all information stored in long-term memory is stored there *permanently.* According to this view, forgetting occurs only because people sometimes cannot *retrieve* needed information from LTM.

The notion that LTM storage may be permanent is certainly intriguing. A couple of interesting lines of research have seemed to provide compelling evidence of permanent storage. However, each line of research turns out to be less compelling than it appears at first glance. The first line of research consisted of some landmark studies conducted by Canadian neuroscientist

Figure 7.10
_____

Short-term memory as working memory. This diagram depicts the revised model of the short-term store proposed by Alan Baddeley. According to Baddeley (2001), working memory includes four components: a phonological rehearsal loop, a visuospatial sketchpad, an executive control system, and an episodic buffer.

Wilder Penfield in the 1960s (we referred to some of Penfield's work at the Montreal Neurological Institute in Chapter 3). He reported triggering long-lost memories through electrical stimulation of the brain (ESB) during brain surgeries (Penfield & Perot, 1963). When Penfield used ESB (see Chapter 3) to map brain function in patients undergoing surgery for epilepsy, he found that stimulation of the temporal lobe sometimes elicited vivid descriptions of events long past. Patients would describe events that apparently came from their childhood—such as "being in a lumberyard" or "watching Mom make a phone call"—as if they were there once again. Penfield and others inferred that these descriptions were exact playbacks of long-lost memories unearthed by electrical stimulation of the brain.

The second line of research centres on the phenomenon of *flashbulb memories,* **which are unusually vivid and detailed recollections of momentous events.** For instance, many people remember exactly where they were, what they were doing, and how they felt when they learned of the death of John F. Kennedy or Princess Diana. A more recent example concerns the events surrounding the terrorist attacks that took place in the United States on September 11, 2001; the events were traumatic for people all over the world. The vivid detail of people's memories of such events—especially those from decades ago—would seem to provide a striking example of permanent storage.

So, why don't these lines of evidence demonstrate that LTM storage is permanent? Let's look at each. Closer scrutiny eventually showed that the remarkable "memories" activated by ESB in Penfield's studies often included major distortions or factual impossibilities. For instance, the person who recalled being in a lumberyard had never actually been to one. The ESB-induced recollections of Penfield's subjects apparently were hallucinations, dreams, or loose reconstructions of events rather than exact replays of the past (Squire, 1987). In a similar vein,

© AP/Wide World Photos

subsequent research has undermined the notion that flashbulb memories represent an instance of permanent storage. A study conducted by Peter Lee and Norman Brown (2003) with University of Alberta students shortly after the terrorist attacks in September 2001 also argued against the existence of any type of "special encoding" mechanism or process for these types of memories. Although flashbulb memories tend to be strong, vivid, and detailed, studies suggest that they are neither as accurate nor as special as once believed (Neisser & Harsch, 1992; Schmolck, Buffalo, & Squire, 2000; Talarico & Rubin, 2003). Like other memories, they become less detailed and complete with time and are often inaccurate (McCloskey, 1992; Weaver, 1993). This observation brings us to our Featured Study for this chapter, which examines the accuracy of students' flashbulb memories of the announcement of the verdict in the 1995 O. J. Simpson murder trial.

Flashbulb memories are vivid and detailed recollections of momentous events. For example, many people will long remember exactly where they were and how they felt when they learned about the terrorist attacks on the World Trade Center.

How Accurate Are Flashbulb Memories?

FEATURED STUDY

Studies have yielded somewhat inconsistent findings regarding the accuracy of flashbulb memories. When researchers have chosen to evaluate participants' memories 7 to 12 months after a momentous event, distortions invariably are found in some subjects, but one could characterize subjects' overall memory performance as reasonably accurate. However, when researchers have chosen to assess flashbulb memories after a time span of about three years, participants' accuracy has been mediocre. This discrepancy could simply mean that

flashbulb memories fade with time—like other memories—but other explanations for the discrepant findings could not be ruled out because the relevant studies focused on different notable events, used different types of samples, and varied methods of measuring memory accuracy. Hence, the present research was designed to examine both time intervals in a single study that focused on the same event. The event was the announcement of the verdict in the O. J. Simpson murder trial, which had held the world spellbound for months in 1995.

Investigators: H. Schmolck, E. A. Buffalo, and L. R. Squire (University of California, San Diego)

Source: Memory distortions develop over time: Recollections of the O. J. Simpson trial verdict after 15 and 32 months. *Psychological Science,* 2000, *11,* 39–45.

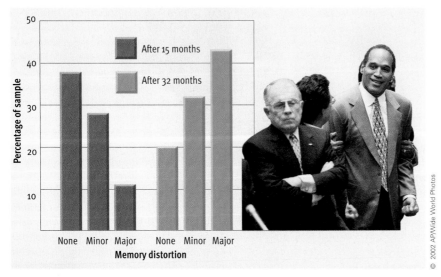

Figure 7.11

Accuracy of flashbulb memories. Schmolck, Buffalo, and Squire (2000) assessed the accuracy of participants' flashbulb memories of the announcement of the O. J. Simpson murder trial verdict after 15 and 32 months. As you can see, there was a substantial deterioration in subjects' recollections between 15 and 32 months, and distorted memories were quite common after 32 months. (Note: The two sets of numbers do not add up to 100% because the graph does not include subjects who were scored as "don't remember.")

Source: Schmolck, H., Buffalo, E. A., & Squire, L. R. (2000). Memory distortions develop over time: Recollections of the O. J. Simpson trial verdict after 15 and 32 months. *Psychological Science, 11,* 39–45. Blackwell Publishers. Reprinted by permission.

Method

Participants. Students in an undergraduate psychology class completed a questionnaire three days after the announcement of the Simpson verdict. The subjects were then divided into two groups that were matched for the intensity of their reported emotional reactions and for whether they agreed with the verdict. One group was contacted 15 months after the verdict and the other group was contacted 32 months after the verdict. The follow-up questionnaires were completed by 28 members of the first group (evaluated at 15 months) and 35 members of the second group (evaluated at 32 months). At follow-up, roughly 80% of the subjects in both groups met the usual criteria (based on Brown & Kulik, 1977) for having a flashbulb memory of the Simpson verdict announcement.

Materials. The questionnaire administered three days after the verdict and many months later asked sub-jects nine specific questions about their experiences, such as: What time was it when you first heard the news of the verdict? Where were you? What were you doing? Who told you? Participants were also asked to write a paragraph describing how they heard about the verdict and to rate their emotional reaction to it and their agreement with it. The follow-up questionnaire also asked participants to rate how confident they were about the accuracy of their recollections.

Results

The principal finding was that recollections containing no distortions predominated at 15 months, whereas recollections containing major distortions predominated at 32 months. After a 32-month time interval, over 40% of subjects' recollections contained major distortions and more than 30% contained minor distortions (see Figure 7.11). Interestingly, 61% of the subjects who exhibited major memory distortions indicated that they had high confidence in their recollections.

Discussion

The authors conclude that flashbulb memories fade gradually over time, just like other memories, and that flashbulb memories are not all that accurate just three years after a momentous event. They also interpret their findings as undermining the notion that flashbulb memories have special characteristics that make them less vulnerable to forgetting than ordinary memories.

Comment

This research was featured because it examined a very timely question in light of the September 2001 terrorist attacks in the United States. If ever there was a momentous event that ought to create indelible memories, it ought to be the 9/11 attacks. Many flashbulb memory investigations were launched in the aftermath of the traumatic assaults on the World Trade Center. They also suggest that flashbulb memories fade over time (Talarico & Rubin, 2003). This study was also featured because it demonstrates that human memory is not as reliable as we assume it to be, a conclusion that will be echoed throughout this chapter. ■

Returning to the question at hand, the results of our Featured Study clearly conflict with the hypothesis that memory storage is permanent. Although the possibility cannot be ruled out completely, there is no convincing evidence that memories are stored away permanently and that forgetting is all a matter of retrieval failure (Payne & Blackwell, 1998; Schacter, 1996).

Are Short-Term Memory and Long-Term Memory Really Separate?

The partitioning of memory into the sensory, short-term, and long-term stores has dominated thinking about memory for many decades, but over the years

Comparing the Memory Stores

Check your understanding of the three memory stores by filling in the blanks in the table below. The answers can be found in the back of the book in Appendix A.

Feature	Sensory memory	Short-term memory	Long-term memory
Main encoding format	*copy of input*		*largely semantic*
Storage capacity	*limited*	*up to 20 seconds*	
Storage duration			

some theorists have expressed doubts about whether there really are separate memory stores. A handful of theorists have questioned the concept of sensory memory on the grounds that it may be nothing more than perceptual processes at work, rather than memory. A larger number of theorists have questioned the concept of short-term memory on the grounds that it really isn't all that different from long-term memory (Crowder, 1993; Healy & McNamara, 1996; Nairne, 1996). The view of short-term memory and long-term memory as independent systems was originally based, in part, on the belief that they depended on different types of encoding and were subject to different mechanisms of forgetting. STM was thought to depend on *phonemic* encoding (based on sound), whereas LTM encoding was thought to be largely *semantic* (based on meaning). Information loss from STM was believed to be mostly due to time-related *decay*, whereas *interference* was viewed as the principal mechanism of LTM forgetting. However, decades of research have undermined both of these distinctions, as both semantic encoding and interference effects have been found in research on short-term memory (Meiser & Klauer, 1999; Walker & Hulme, 1999).

How do theorists who doubt the existence of separate memory stores view the structure of memory? Their views vary considerably (Nairne, 2002). One perspective is to view short-term memory as a tiny and constantly changing portion of long-term memory that happens to be in a heightened state of activation (Cowan, 1995, 1999). Other, more radical views assert that there is a single, unitary, "generic" memory store that is governed by one set of rules and processes (Nairne, 2001). The outcome of the debate about whether there are separate memory stores is difficult to predict. At present, the multiple stores viewpoint remains dominant, but alternative approaches are becoming increasingly influential.

How Is Knowledge Represented and Organized in Memory? 6B

Over the years memory researchers have wrestled endlessly with another major question relating to memory storage: How is knowledge represented and organized in memory? In other words, what forms do our mental representations of information take? Most theorists seem to agree that our mental representations probably take a variety of forms, depending on the nature of the material that needs to be tucked away in memory.

Clustering and Conceptual Hierarchies 6B

If you were to memorize the list of 60 words in Figure 7.12, your recall of the list at a later time would demonstrate how the mind spontaneously organizes information stored in memory. Each of the words in this list fits into one of four categories: animals, men's names, vegetables, or professions. Bousfield (1953) showed that subjects recalling this list engage in clustering. *Clustering* **is the tendency to remember similar or related items in groups.** Even though the words are not presented in organized groups, you would tend to remember them in bunches that belong in the same category.

Figure 7.12

Clustering. The words in this list fall into four categories: animals, men's names, vegetables, and professions. Even when the words are presented in mixed order, people tend to recall them in these groupings. This phenomenon is called clustering.

SOURCE: Adapted from Bousfield, W. A. (1953). The occurrence of clustering in the recall of randomly arranged associates. *Journal of General Psychology, 49*, 229–240. Published by Heldref Publications. Reprinted with permission of the Helen Dwight Reid Education Foundation.

Giraffe	Plumber	Owen	Lettuce
Parsnip	Otto	Parsley	Donkey
Zebra	Noah	Otter	Blacksmith
Radish	Chipmunk	Grocer	Eggplant
Diver	Adam	Badger	Garlic
Broker	Chemist	Camel	Wildcat
Spinach	Turnip	Baboon	Jason
Baker	Simon	Florist	Leopard
Woodchuck	Howard	Rhubarb	Printer
Dancer	Milkman	Melon	Bernard
Weasel	Gerard	Mustard	Carrot
Pumpkin	Panther	Wallace	Sherman
Amos	Oswald	Dentist	Waiter
Typist	Druggist	Muskrat	Moses
Byron	Reindeer	Mushroom	Cabbage

Web Link 7.2

Memory Principles
http://www.mtsu.edu/~studskl/
mem.html

This brief overview of practical guidelines for improving recall of academic material is maintained by Carolyn Hopper at Middle Tennessee State University. Ten basic principles are outlined succinctly. Elsewhere at this site you will find other worthwhile materials intended to help students improve their study techniques.

Web Link 7.3

Mind Tools—Tools for Improving Your Memory
http://www.mindtools.com/
memory.html

The Mind Tools site details practical techniques to help people improve their cognitive efficiency in many areas. The subpage dedicated to memory functioning offers an excellent collection of suggestions for ways to enhance memory.

as they radiate outward from a rock tossed into a pond. Consider again the semantic network shown in Figure 7.14. If subjects see the word *red*, words that are closely linked to it (such as *orange*) should be easier to recall than words that have longer links (such as *sunrises*).

Connectionist Networks and Parallel Distributed Processing (PDP) Models

Instead of taking their cue from how computers process information, *connectionist models* of memory take their inspiration from how neural networks appear to handle information. As we noted in our discussion of visual perception in Chapter 4, the human brain appears to depend extensively on *parallel distributed processing*—that is, simultaneous processing of the same information that is spread across networks of neurons. Based on this insight and basic findings about how neurons operate, **connectionist, or parallel distributed processing (PDP), models assume that cognitive processes depend on patterns of activation in highly interconnected computational networks that resemble neural networks** (McClelland, 2000; McClelland & Rumelhart, 1985; McClelland & Rogers, 2003; Smolensky, 1995). A PDP system consists of a large network of interconnected computing units, or *nodes*, that operate much like neurons. These nodes may be inactive or they may send either excitatory or inhibitory signals to other units. Like an individual neuron, a specific node's level of activation reflects the weighted balance of excitatory and inhibitory inputs from many other units. Given this framework, *PDP models assert that specific memories correspond to particular patterns of activation in these networks* (McClelland, 1992). Connectionist networks bear some superficial resemblance

to semantic networks, but there is a crucial difference. In semantic networks, specific nodes represent specific concepts or pieces of knowledge. In connectionist networks, a piece of knowledge is represented by a particular *pattern* of activation across an entire network. Thus, the information lies in the strengths of the *connections*, which is why the PDP approach is called "connectionism."

REVIEW OF KEY POINTS

- Information-processing theories of memory assert that people have three kinds of memory stores: a sensory memory, a short-term memory, and a long-term memory. The sensory store preserves information in its original form, probably for only a fraction of a second.

- Short-term memory has a limited capacity of about seven chunks of information. STM can maintain unrehearsed information for up to about 20 seconds. Short-term memory is working memory, and it appears to involve more than a simple rehearsal loop. According to Baddeley, working memory also includes a visuospatial sketchpad, an executive control system, and an episodic buffer.

- Long-term memory is an unlimited capacity store that may hold information indefinitely. Penfield's ESB research and the existence of flashbulb memories suggest that LTM storage may be permanent, but the evidence is not convincing. Our Featured Study showed that flashbulb memories are not as accurate as claimed. Some theorists have questioned the distinction between short-term and long-term memory.

- Information in long-term memory can be organized in simple clusters or multilevel classification systems called conceptual hierarchies. A schema is an organized cluster of knowledge about a particular object or sequence of events.

- Semantic networks consist of concepts joined by pathways. Research suggests that activation spreads along the paths of semantic networks to activate closely associated words. Parallel distributed processing models of memory assert that specific memories correspond to particular patterns of activation in connectionist networks.

Retrieval: Getting Information Out of Memory

PREVIEW QUESTIONS

- What does the tip-of-the-tongue phenomenon reveal about memory?
- Why does reinstating the context of an event aid in its recall?
- What is the misinformation effect?
- How can source-monitoring errors shed light on eyewitness suggestibility and inadvertent plagiarism?
- What is reality monitoring?

Entering information into long-term memory is a worthy goal, but an insufficient one if you can't get the information back out again when you need it. Some theorists maintain that understanding retrieval is the key to understanding human memory (Roediger, 2000). Understanding retrieval may also be important to success in your studies. When you study for your exams you are attempting to encode the information in such a way that it is stored in your long-term memory so that it will be there when you need it. As most of us know, however, we don't get all the questions correct. What does this indicate? Tulving distinguished between the *availability* and *accessibility* of information in memory (Tulving & Pearlstone, 1966).

You might not be able to answer a particular question because the information is unavailable (no longer present in the memory system) or because it is not accessible (present in the system but not accessible to you at the moment). The information may not be accessible because the cues you are using in your attempt to answer the question are not effective.

Using Cues to Aid Retrieval

The *tip-of-the-tongue phenomenon*—the temporary inability to remember something you know, accompanied by a feeling that it's just out of reach—is a common experience that is typically triggered by predict, but either way it is apparent that information stored in memory is often organized around schemas.

It is important to note that not only do we have schemas about physical settings like professors' offices, but we also have schemas about specific people, types of people, and social events. We will consider representations of specific others and types of persons in Chapter 16 when we discuss social psychology. Relational schemas are particularly important because, according to some, they may be related to a variety of disorders. Mark Baldwin of McGill University terms these representations of typical events surrounding interpersonal interactions *relational schemas* (Baldwin, 1992). He suggests that these relational schemas represent *regularities* in your interpersonal experience much in the same way that your office schema represents regularities in your exposure to offices. These relational schemas affect the way you process information about others and yourself and influence your expectations and beliefs about yourself. They may partially underlie low self-esteem and social anxiety (Baldwin, Baccus, & Fitzsimons, 2004; Baldwin & Main, 2001). For example, if you enter a situation expecting that the others in that context will dislike and reject you, you may interpret ambiguous cues in a way that reflects badly on you and then act in a way that serves to elicit negative reactions from others. Research by York University psychologist Doug McCann suggests that this very cycle emerges for people with depression (McCann, 1990).

Semantic Networks

Of course, not all information fits neatly into conceptual hierarchies or schemas. Much knowledge seems to be organized into less systematic frameworks, called semantic networks (Collins & Loftus, 1975). A *semantic network* consists of nodes representing concepts, joined together by pathways that link related concepts. A small semantic network is shown in Figure 7.14. The ovals are the nodes, and the words inside the ovals are the interlinked concepts. The lines connecting the nodes are the pathways. A more detailed figure would label the pathways to show how the concepts are related to one another. However, in this instance, the relations should be fairly clear. The length of each pathway represents the degree of association between two concepts. Shorter pathways imply stronger associations.

Semantic networks have proven useful in explaining why thinking about one word (such as *butter*) can make a closely related word (such as *bread*) easier to remember (Meyer & Schvaneveldt, 1976). According to Collins and Loftus (1975), when people think about a word, their thoughts naturally go to related words. These theorists call this process *spreading activation* within a semantic network. They assume that activation spreads out along the pathways of the semantic network surrounding the word. They also theorize that the strength of this activation decreases as it travels outward, much as ripples decrease in size

Figure 7.14

A semantic network. Much of the organization of long-term memory depends on networks of associations among concepts. In this highly simplified depiction of a fragment of a semantic network, the shorter the line linking any two concepts, the stronger the association between them. The colouration of the concept boxes represents activation of the concepts. This is how the network might look just after a person hears the words *fire engine*.

SOURCE: Adapted from Collins, A. M., & Loftus, E. F. (1975). A spreading activation theory of semantic processing. *Psychological Review, 82,* 407–428. Copyright © 1975 by the American Psychological Association. Adapted by permission of the authors.

as they radiate outward from a rock tossed into a pond. Consider again the semantic network shown in Figure 7.14. If subjects see the word *red,* words that are closely linked to it (such as *orange*) should be easier to recall than words that have longer links (such as *sunrises*).

Connectionist Networks and Parallel Distributed Processing (PDP) Models

Instead of taking their cue from how computers process information, *connectionist models* of memory take their inspiration from how neural networks appear to handle information. As we noted in our discussion of visual perception in Chapter 4, the human brain appears to depend extensively on *parallel distributed processing*—that is, simultaneous processing of the same information that is spread across networks of neurons. Based on this insight and basic findings about how neurons operate, **connectionist, or *parallel distributed processing (PDP)*, models assume that cognitive processes depend on patterns of activation in highly interconnected computational networks that resemble neural networks** (McClelland, 2000; McClelland & Rumelhart, 1985; McClelland & Rogers, 2003; Smolensky, 1995). A PDP system consists of a large network of interconnected computing units, or *nodes,* that operate much like neurons. These nodes may be inactive or they may send either excitatory or inhibitory signals to other units. Like an individual neuron, a specific node's level of activation reflects the weighted balance of excitatory and inhibitory inputs from many other units. Given this framework, *PDP models assert that specific memories correspond to particular patterns of activation in these networks* (McClelland, 1992). Connectionist networks bear some superficial resemblance

to semantic networks, but there is a crucial difference. In semantic networks, specific nodes represent specific concepts or pieces of knowledge. In connectionist networks, a piece of knowledge is represented by a particular *pattern* of activation across an entire network. Thus, the information lies in the strengths of the *connections,* which is why the PDP approach is called "connectionism."

REVIEW OF KEY POINTS

- Information-processing theories of memory assert that people have three kinds of memory stores: a sensory memory, a short-term memory, and a long-term memory. The sensory store preserves information in its original form, probably for only a fraction of a second.

- Short-term memory has a limited capacity of about seven chunks of information. STM can maintain unrehearsed information for up to about 20 seconds. Short-term memory is working memory, and it appears to involve more than a simple rehearsal loop. According to Baddeley, working memory also includes a visuospatial sketchpad, an executive control system, and an episodic buffer.

- Long-term memory is an unlimited capacity store that may hold information indefinitely. Penfield's ESB research and the existence of flashbulb memories suggest that LTM storage may be permanent, but the evidence is not convincing. Our Featured Study showed that flashbulb memories are not as accurate as claimed. Some theorists have questioned the distinction between short-term and long-term memory.

- Information in long-term memory can be organized in simple clusters or multilevel classification systems called conceptual hierarchies. A schema is an organized cluster of knowledge about a particular object or sequence of events.

- Semantic networks consist of concepts joined by pathways. Research suggests that activation spreads along the paths of semantic networks to activate closely associated words. Parallel distributed processing models of memory assert that specific memories correspond to particular patterns of activation in connectionist networks.

Retrieval: Getting Information Out of Memory

Entering information into long-term memory is a worthy goal, but an insufficient one if you can't get the information back out again when you need it. Some theorists maintain that understanding retrieval is the key to understanding human memory (Roediger, 2000). Understanding retrieval may also be important to success in your studies. When you study for your exams you are attempting to encode the information in such a way that it is stored in your long-term memory so that it will be there when you need it. As most of us know, however, we don't get all the questions correct. What does this indicate? Tulving distinguished between the *availability* and *accessibility* of information in memory (Tulving & Pearlstone, 1966).

You might not be able to answer a particular question because the information is unavailable (no longer present in the memory system) or because it is not accessible (present in the system but not accessible to you at the moment). The information may not be accessible because the cues you are using in your attempt to answer the question are not effective.

Using Cues to Aid Retrieval

The *tip-of-the-tongue phenomenon*—**the temporary inability to remember something you know, accompanied by a feeling that it's just out of reach**—is a common experience that is typically triggered by

Comparing the Memory Stores

Check your understanding of the three memory stores by filling in the blanks in the table below. The answers can be found in the back of the book in Appendix A.

Feature	Sensory memory	Short-term memory	Long-term memory
Main encoding format	*copy of input*		*largely semantic*
Storage capacity	*limited*	*up to 20 seconds*	
Storage duration			

some theorists have expressed doubts about whether there really are separate memory stores. A handful of theorists have questioned the concept of sensory memory on the grounds that it may be nothing more than perceptual processes at work, rather than memory. A larger number of theorists have questioned the concept of short-term memory on the grounds that it really isn't all that different from long-term memory (Crowder, 1993; Healy & McNamara, 1996; Nairne, 1996). The view of short-term memory and long-term memory as independent systems was originally based, in part, on the belief that they depended on different types of encoding and were subject to different mechanisms of forgetting. STM was thought to depend on *phonemic* encoding (based on sound), whereas LTM encoding was thought to be largely *semantic* (based on meaning). Information loss from STM was believed to be mostly due to time-related *decay,* whereas *interference* was viewed as the principal mechanism of LTM forgetting. However, decades of research have undermined both of these distinctions, as both semantic encoding and interference effects have been found in research on short-term memory (Meiser & Klauer, 1999; Walker & Hulme, 1999).

How do theorists who doubt the existence of separate memory stores view the structure of memory? Their views vary considerably (Nairne, 2002). One perspective is to view short-term memory as a tiny and constantly changing portion of long-term memory that happens to be in a heightened state of activation (Cowan, 1995, 1999). Other, more radical views assert that there is a single, unitary, "generic" memory store that is governed by one set of rules and processes (Nairne, 2001). The outcome of the debate about whether there are separate memory stores is difficult to predict. At present, the multiple stores viewpoint remains dominant, but alternative approaches are becoming increasingly influential.

How Is Knowledge Represented and Organized in Memory? 6B

Over the years memory researchers have wrestled endlessly with another major question relating to memory storage: How is knowledge represented and organized in memory? In other words, what forms do our mental representations of information take? Most theorists seem to agree that our mental representations probably take a variety of forms, depending on the nature of the material that needs to be tucked away in memory.

Clustering and Conceptual Hierarchies 6B

If you were to memorize the list of 60 words in Figure 7.12, your recall of the list at a later time would demonstrate how the mind spontaneously organizes information stored in memory. Each of the words in this list fits into one of four categories: animals, men's names, vegetables, or professions. Bousfield (1953) showed that subjects recalling this list engage in clustering. *Clustering* **is the tendency to remember similar or related items in groups.** Even though the words are not presented in organized groups, you would tend to remember them in bunches that belong in the same category.

Figure 7.12

Clustering. The words in this list fall into four categories: animals, men's names, vegetables, and professions. Even when the words are presented in mixed order, people tend to recall them in these groupings. This phenomenon is called clustering.

SOURCE: Adapted from Bousfield, W. A. (1953). The occurrence of clustering in the recall of randomly arranged associates. *Journal of General Psychology, 49,* 229–240. Published by Heldref Publications. Reprinted with permission of the Helen Dwight Reid Education Foundation.

Giraffe	Plumber	Owen	Lettuce
Parsnip	Otto	Parsley	Donkey
Zebra	Noah	Otter	Blacksmith
Radish	Chipmunk	Grocer	Eggplant
Diver	Adam	Badger	Garlic
Broker	Chemist	Camel	Wildcat
Spinach	Turnip	Baboon	Jason
Baker	Simon	Florist	Leopard
Woodchuck	Howard	Rhubarb	Printer
Dancer	Milkman	Melon	Bernard
Weasel	Gerard	Mustard	Carrot
Pumpkin	Panther	Wallace	Sherman
Amos	Oswald	Dentist	Waiter
Typist	Druggist	Muskrat	Moses
Byron	Reindeer	Mushroom	Cabbage

Professor Smith's office is shown in this photo. Follow the instructions in the text to learn how Brewer and Treyens (1981) used it in a study of memory.

Schemas 6B

Imagine that you've just visited Professor Smith's office, which is shown in the adjacent photo. Take a brief look at the photo and then cover it up. Now pretend that you want to describe Professor Smith's office to a friend. Write down what you saw in the office (the picture).

After you finish, compare your description with the picture. Chances are, your description will include elements—books or filing cabinets, for instance—that were *not* in the office. This common phenomenon demonstrates how *schemas* can influence memory.

A *schema* **is an organized cluster of knowledge about a particular object or event abstracted from previous experience with the object or event.** For example, university students have schemas for what professors' offices are like. When Brewer and Treyens (1981) tested the recall of 30 subjects who had briefly visited the office shown in the photo, most subjects recalled the desks and chairs, but few recalled the wine bottle or the picnic basket, which aren't part of a typical office schema. Moreover, nine subjects in the Brewer and Treyens study falsely recalled that the office contained books. Perhaps you made the same mistake.

These results suggest that *people are more likely to remember things that are consistent with their schemas than things that are not.* Although this principle seems applicable much of the time, the inverse is also true: *people sometimes exhibit better recall of things that violate their schema-based expectations* (Rojahn & Pettigrew, 1992; Koriat, Goldsmith, & Pansky, 2000). If information really clashes with a schema, it may attract extra attention and deeper processing and become very memorable. Thus, the impact of schemas on memory can be difficult to

Factual information is routinely represented in categories, and when possible, this information is organized into conceptual hierarchies. A *conceptual hierarchy* **is a multilevel classification system based on common properties among items.** A conceptual hierarchy that a person might construct for minerals can be found in Figure 7.13. According to Gordon Bower (1970), organizing information into a conceptual hierarchy can improve recall dramatically.

SOURCE: Adapted from Bower, G. (1970). Organizational factors in memory. *Cognitive Psychology, 1* (1), 18–46. Copyright © 1970 Elsevier Science (USA), reproduced with permission from the publisher.

Figure 7.13

Conceptual hierarchies and long-term memory. Some types of information can be organized into a multilevel hierarchy of concepts, like the one shown here, which was studied by Bower and others (1969). They found that subjects remember more information when they organize it into a conceptual hierarchy.

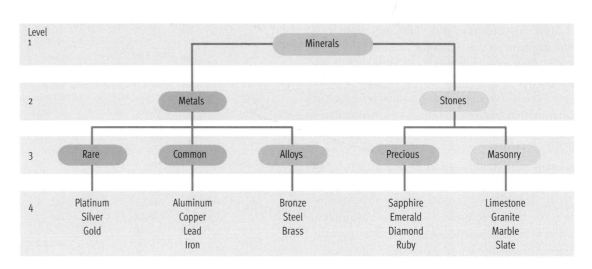

a name that one can't quite recall. Most people experience this temporary frustration about once a week, although its occurrence increases with age (A. Brown, 1991; Burke & Shafto, 2004). The tip-of-the-tongue phenomenon clearly constitutes a failure in retrieval. However, the exact mechanisms underlying this failure are the subject of debate, as a host of explanations have been proposed for the tip-of-the-tongue phenomenon (Schwartz, 1999).

Fortunately, memories can often be jogged with *retrieval cues*—stimuli that help gain access to memories. This was apparent when Roger Brown and David McNeill (1966) studied the tip-of-the-tongue phenomenon. They gave subjects definitions of obscure words and asked them to come up with the words. Brown and McNeill found that subjects groping for obscure words were correct in guessing the first letter of the missing word 57% of the time. This figure far exceeds chance and shows that partial recollections are often headed in the right direction.

Reinstating the Context of an Event

Another principle of memory articulated by Tulving was the *encoding specificity principle*. He suggested that your memory for information would be better when the conditions during encoding and retrieval were similar (Tulving & Thompson, 1973). According to Tulving (1983, p. 223), cues used at retrieval will facilitate recall "if and only if the information about them and about their relation to the to-be-remembered words is stored at the same time" as the to-be-remembered information. Of course, this is more likely the more similar the encoding and retrieval conditions.

Let's test your memory: What did you have for breakfast two days ago? If you can't immediately answer, you might begin by imagining yourself sitting at the breakfast table. Trying to recall an event by putting yourself back in the context in which it occurred involves working with *context cues* to aid retrieval.

Context cues often facilitate the retrieval of information (Smith, 1988). Most people have experienced the effects of context cues on many occasions. For instance, when people return after a number of years to a place where they used to live, they typically are flooded with long-forgotten memories. Or consider how often you have gone from one room to another to get something (scissors, perhaps), only to discover that you can't remember what you were after. However, when you return to the first room (the original context), you suddenly recall what it was ("Of course, the scissors!"). These examples illustrate the potentially powerful effects of context cues on memory. This even seems to hold true with

regard to encoding information while scuba-diving! The information is better remembered underwater rather than on dry land if that matches the context in which it was encoded (Godden & Baddeley, 1975).

The technique of reinstating the context of an event has been used effectively in legal investigations to enhance eyewitness recall (Chandler & Fisher, 1996). The eyewitness may be encouraged to retrieve information about a crime by replaying the sequence of events. The value of reinstating the context of an event may account for how hypnosis occasionally stimulates eyewitness recall (Meyer, 1992). The hypnotist usually attempts to reinstate the context of the event by telling the witness to imagine being at the scene of the crime once again. Unfortunately, research suggests that hypnosis often increases subjects' tendencies to report *incorrect* information (Lynn, Neuschatz, & Fite, 2002; McConkey, Barnier, & Sheehan, 1998). Concerns about the accuracy of hypnosis-aided recall have led courts to be cautious about allowing hypnosis-aided recollections as admissible testimony.

This principle extends beyond the effects of reinstating the context; it also seems to be true for *state-* and *mood*-dependent effects too. According to Fergus Craik (Brown & Craik, 2000) and others, the effects of matching the person's *internal* state of encoding at the retrieval phase is just a special case of the encoding specificity principle. For example, if you encoded information while intoxicated, your recall should be facilitated by attempting to retrieve the information while in a similar state (Brown & Craik, 2000). According to University of British Columbia psychologist Eric Eich (Schooler & Eich, 2000), similar effects are observed when considering the match or mismatch between the emotional state at encoding and retrieval of the individual attempting to retrieve the information (Eich & Metcalfe, 1989). Eich maintains that state-dependent memory effects are more readily observed for free-recall conditions than for recognition or cued-recall tests where retrieval cues are more abundant (Eich, 1980). According to University of British Columbia psychologists Gayla Swihart and John Yuille and Dalhousie's Stephen Porter (Swihart, Yuille, and Porter, 1999), some of these effects may account for *red-outs*, or amnesia by the perpetrators of violent crime for the crime itself. For example, if the abuse or crime was carried out in a state of rage, retrieval when in a condition of normal arousal may be attenuated. Stephen Porter (Porter, Spencer, & Birt, 2003) has also shown that negative emotions may increase one's susceptibility to false memories in the context of the misinformation effect, which we discuss next.

"One reason most of us, as jurors, place so much faith in eyewitness testimony is that we are unaware of how many factors influence its accuracy."

ELIZABETH LOFTUS

Figure 7.15

A story used in a study of reconstructive memory by Bartlett (1932). Subjects recalling the story tended to change details and to "remember" elements not in the original at all.

SOURCE: Excerpt from Bartlett, F. C. (1932). *Remembering: A study in experimental and social psychology.* New York: Cambridge University Press, p. 65. Copyright © 1932. Reprinted with the permission of Cambridge University Press.

Reconstructing Memories and the Misinformation Effect

When you retrieve information from long-term memory, you're not able to pull up a "mental videotape" that provides an exact replay of the past. To some extent, your memories are sketchy *reconstructions* of the past that may be distorted and may include details that did not actually occur (Roediger, Wheeler, & Rajaram, 1993). The reconstructive nature of memory was first highlighted many years ago by Sir Frederic Bartlett, a prominent English psychologist. Bartlett (1932) had his subjects read the tale "War of the Ghosts," which is reproduced in Figure 7.15. Subjects read the story twice and waited 15 minutes. Then they were asked to write down the tale as best they could recall it.

What did Bartlett find? As you might expect, subjects condensed the story, leaving out boring details. Of greater interest was Bartlett's discovery that subjects frequently *changed* the tale to some extent. The canoe became a boat or the two young men were hunting beavers instead of seals. Subjects often introduced entirely *new elements* and twists. For instance, in one case, the death at the end was attributed to fever and the character was described as "foaming at the mouth" (instead of "something black came out of his mouth"). Bartlett concluded that the distortions in recall occurred because subjects recon-

structed the tale to fit with their established schemas. Modern schema theories also emphasize the reconstructive nature of memory (Hirt, McDonald, & Markman, 1998). These theories propose that part of what people recall about an event is the details of that particular event and part is a reconstruction of the event based on their schemas.

Research by Elizabeth Loftus (1979, 1992) and others on the *misinformation effect* has shown that reconstructive distortions show up frequently in eyewitness testimony. Studies of the misinformation effect include three stages. In the first stage, subjects view an event. In the second stage, they are exposed to information about this event, some of which is misleading. In the third stage, their recall of the original event is tested to see if the post-event misinformation altered their memory of the original event. For example, in one study Loftus and Palmer (1974) showed subjects a videotape of an automobile accident. Subjects were then "grilled" as if they were providing eyewitness testimony, and biasing information was introduced. Some subjects were asked, "How fast were the cars going when they *hit* each other?" Other subjects were asked, "How fast were the cars going when they *smashed into* each other?" A week later, subjects' recall of the accident was tested and they were asked whether they remembered seeing any broken glass in the accident (there was none). Subjects who had earlier been asked about the cars *smashing into* each other were more likely to "recall" broken glass. Why would they add this detail to their reconstructions of the accident? Probably because broken glass is consistent with their schema for cars *smashing* together (see Figure 7.16).

The misinformation effect has been replicated in numerous studies by Loftus and other researchers (Ayers & Reder, 1998; Lindsay, 1993; Loftus, 2003). Indeed, the effect is difficult to escape, as even subjects who have been forewarned can be swayed by post-event misinformation (Koriat, Goldsmith, & Pansky, 2000). However, there is considerable debate about the mechanisms underlying the effect (Ceci & Bruck, 1993). Loftus (1979) has argued for an "overwriting" explanation in which the new misinformation destroys and replaces the original memory of the event (much like saving a new version of a file on a computer). An alternative explanation is that the new misinformation interferes with the retrieval of the original memory (Chandler, 1991). Other theorists argue that subjects can access both the original memory and the altered memory but have difficulty distinguishing which one was the original (Lindsay & Johnson, 1989). This explanation attributes the misinformation effect to difficulties in *source moni-*

WAR OF THE GHOSTS

One night two young men from Egulac went down to the river to hunt seals, and while they were there it became foggy and calm. Then they heard war cries, and they thought: "Maybe this is a war party." They escaped to the shore, and hid behind a log. Now canoes came up, and they heard the noise of paddles, and saw one canoe coming up to them. There were five men in the canoe, and they said:

"What do you think? We wish to take you along. We are going up the river to make war on the people."

One of the young men said: "I have no arrows."

"Arrows are in the canoe," they said.

"I will not go along. I might be killed. My relatives do not know where I have gone. But you," he said, turning to the other, "may go with them."

So one of the young men went, but the other returned home.

And the warriors went up to the river to a town on the other side of Kalama. The people came down to the water, and they began to fight, and many were killed. But presently the young man heard one of the warriors say: "Quick, let us go home: that Indian has been hit." Now he thought: "Oh, they are ghosts." He did not feel sick, but they said he had been shot.

So the canoes went back to Egulac and the young man went ashore to his house, and made a fire. And he told everybody and said: "Behold I accompanied the ghosts, and we went to fight. Many of our fellows were killed, and many of those who attacked us were killed. They said I was hit, and I did not feel sick."

He told it all, and then he became quiet. When the sun rose he fell down. Something black came out of his mouth. His face became contorted. The people jumped up and cried.

He was dead.

toring, an interesting memory process that we'll discuss next. A review of the extensive evidence on the misinformation effect concluded that all three proposed mechanisms probably contribute to this phenomenon (Ayers & Reder, 1998).

Source Monitoring and Reality Monitoring

The misinformation effect appears to be due, in part, to the unreliability of source monitoring (Mitchell & Johnson, 2000). *Source monitoring* **is the process of making attributions about the origins of memories.** Marcia Johnson and her colleagues maintain that source monitoring is a crucial facet of memory retrieval that contributes to many of the mistakes that people make in reconstructing their experiences (Johnson, 1996; Johnson, Hashtroudi, & Lindsay, 1993). According to Johnson, memories are not tagged with labels that specify their sources. Hence, when people pull up specific memory records, they have to make decisions *at the time of retrieval* about where the memories came from (e.g., "Did I read that in *The Globe and Mail* or *The Peterborough Examiner?*"). Much of the time, these decisions are so easy and automatic, people make them without being consciously aware of the source-monitoring process. In other instances, however, they may consciously struggle to pinpoint the source of a memory. A *source-monitoring error* **occurs when a memory derived from one source is misattributed to another source.** For example, you might attribute something that your roommate said to your psychology professor, or something you heard on David Suzuki's *The Nature of Things* to your psychology textbook. Inaccurate memories that reflect source-monitoring errors may seem quite compelling, and people often feel quite confident about their authenticity even though the recollections really are inaccurate (Lampinen, Neuschatz, & Payne, 1999).

Source-monitoring errors appear to be commonplace and may shed light on many interesting memory phenomena. For instance, in studies of eyewitness suggestibility, some subjects have gone so far as to insist that they "remember" seeing something that was only verbally suggested to them. Most theories have a hard time explaining how people can have memories of events that they never actually saw or experienced, but this paradox doesn't seem all that perplexing when it is explained as a source-monitoring error (Lindsay et al., 2004). The source-monitoring approach can also make sense of *cryptomnesia*—inadvertent plagiarism that occurs when people come up with an idea that they think is original, when they

were actually exposed to it earlier (Bredart, Lampinen, & Defeldre, 2003). Source-monitoring errors also appear to underlie the common tendency for people to mix up fictional information from novels and movies with factual information from news reports and personal experiences (Marsh, Meade, & Roediger, 2003).

Marcia Johnson's source-monitoring theory has built and expanded on an earlier concept that she called *reality monitoring*, which she now views as a subtype of source monitoring. *Reality monitoring* **refers to the process of deciding whether memories are based on external sources (one's perceptions of actual events) or internal sources (one's thoughts and imaginations).** People engage in reality monitoring when they reflect on whether something actually happened or they only thought about it happening.

REVIEW OF KEY POINTS

● The tip-of-the-tongue phenomenon shows that recall is often guided by partial information about a word. Reinstating the context of an event can facilitate recall. This factor may account for cases in which hypnosis appears to aid recall of previously forgotten information. However, hypnosis seems to increase people's tendency to report incorrect information.

● Memories are not exact replicas of past experiences. As Bartlett showed many years ago, memory is partially reconstructive. Research on the misinformation effect shows that information learned after an event can alter one's memory of it.

● Source monitoring is the process of making attributions about the origins of memories. Source-monitoring errors appear to be common and may explain why people sometimes "recall" something that was only suggested to them or something they only imagined. Reality monitoring involves deciding whether memories are based on perceptions of actual events or on just thinking about the events.

Leading question asked during witness testimony	Possible schemas activated	Response of subjects asked one week later, "Did you see any broken glass?" (There was none.)
"About how fast were the cars going when they hit each other?"		"Yes"—14%
"About how fast were the cars going when they smashed into each other?"		"Yes"—32%

Figure 7.16

The misinformation effect. In an experiment by Loftus and Palmer (1974), participants who were asked leading questions in which cars were described as *hitting* or *smashing* each other were prone to recall the same accident differently one week later, demonstrating the reconstructive nature of memory.

Denise Applewhite/Communications Department, Princeton University

"Our long-term goal is to develop ways of determining which aspects of mental experience create one's sense of a personal past and one's conviction (accurate or not) that memories, knowledge, beliefs, attitudes, and feelings are tied to reality in a veridical fashion."
MARCIA K. JOHNSON

Forgetting: When Memory Lapses

PREVIEW QUESTIONS

- What did Ebbinghaus discover about how quickly people forget?
- What are the three methods for measuring retention?
- What is the difference between the decay and interference explanations of forgetting?
- When are retrieval failures likely to occur?
- Why do some experts believe that recovered memories of childhood sexual abuse are mostly genuine, while other experts are skeptical?

Why do people forget information—even information they would like to remember? Many theorists believe that there isn't one simple answer to this question. They point to the complex, multifaceted nature of memory and assert that forgetting can be caused by deficiencies in encoding, storage, retrieval, or some combination of these processes.

How Quickly We Forget: Ebbinghaus's Forgetting Curve 6D

The first person to conduct scientific studies of forgetting was Hermann Ebbinghaus. He published a series of insightful memory studies way back in 1885. Ebbinghaus studied only one subject—himself. To give himself lots of new material to memorize, he invented *nonsense syllables*—consonant-vowel-consonant arrangements that do not correspond to words (such as BAF, XOF, VIR, and MEQ). He wanted to work with meaningless materials that would be uncontaminated by his previous learning.

Ebbinghaus was a remarkably dedicated researcher. For instance, in one study he went through over 14 000 practice repetitions, as he tirelessly memorized 420 lists of nonsense syllables (Slamecka, 1985). He tested his memory of these lists after various time intervals. Figure 7.17 shows what he found. This diagram, called a *forgetting curve,* **graphs retention and forgetting over time.** Ebbinghaus's forgetting curve shows a precipitous drop in retention during the first few hours after the nonsense syllables were memorized. Thus, he concluded that most forgetting occurs very rapidly after learning something.

That's a depressing conclusion. What is the point of memorizing information if you're going to forget it all right away? Fortunately, subsequent research showed that Ebbinghaus's forgetting curve was unusually steep (Postman, 1985). Forgetting isn't usually quite as swift or as extensive as Ebbinghaus thought. One problem was that he was working with such meaningless material. When subjects memorize more meaningful material, such as prose or poetry, forgetting curves aren't nearly as steep. Studies of how well people recall their high school classmates suggest that forgetting curves for autobiographical information are much shallower (Bahrick, 2000). Also, different methods of measuring forgetting yield varied estimates of how quickly people forget. This variation underscores the importance of the methods used to measure forgetting, the matter we turn to next.

Measures of Forgetting SIM5, SIM6

To study forgetting empirically, psychologists need to be able to measure it precisely. Measures of forgetting inevitably measure retention as well. *Retention* **refers to the proportion of material retained (remembered).** In studies of forgetting, the results may be reported in terms of the amount forgotten or the amount retained. In these studies, the *retention interval* is the length of time between the presentation of materials to be remembered and the measurement of forgetting. The three principal methods used to measure forgetting are recall, recognition, and relearning (Lockhart, 1992).

Who is the current premier of Manitoba? What movie won the Academy Award for best picture last year? These questions involve recall measures of retention. **A *recall* measure of retention requires subjects to reproduce information on their own without any cues.** If you were to take a recall test on a list of 25 words you had memorized, you would simply be told to write down on a blank sheet of paper as many of the words as you could remember.

In contrast, in a recognition test you might be shown a list of 100 words and asked to choose the 25 words that you had memorized. **A *recognition* measure of retention requires subjects to select previously learned information from an array of options.** Subjects not only have cues to work with, they have the answers right in front of them. In educational testing, essay questions and fill-in-the-blanks questions are recall measures of retention.

Figure 7.17

Ebbinghaus's forgetting curve for nonsense syllables. From his experiments on himself, Ebbinghaus concluded that forgetting is extremely rapid immediately after the original learning and then levels off. Although this generalization remains true, subsequent research has shown that forgetting curves for nonsense syllables are unusually steep. (Data from Ebbinghaus, 1885)

Multiple-choice, true-false, and matching questions are recognition measures.

If you're like most students, you probably prefer multiple-choice tests over essay tests. This preference is understandable, because evidence shows that recognition measures tend to yield higher scores than recall measures of memory for the same information (Lockhart, 2000). This reality was demonstrated many decades ago by Luh (1922), who measured subjects' retention of nonsense syllables with both a recognition test and a recall test. As Figure 7.18 shows, subjects' performance on the recognition measure was far superior to their performance on the recall measure. There are two ways of looking at this disparity between recall and recognition tests. One view is that recognition tests are especially *sensitive* measures of retention. The other view is that recognition tests are excessively *easy* measures of retention.

Actually, there is no guarantee that a recognition test will be easier than a recall test. This tends to be the case, but the difficulty of a recognition test can vary greatly, depending on the number, similarity, and plausibility of the options provided as possible answers. To illustrate, see whether you know the answer to the following multiple-choice question:

The capital of Nunavut is:
a. Umingmaktok
b. Rankin Inlet
c. Igloolik
d. Iqaluit

Retention (%) — Retention interval (20 min., 1 hour, 4 hours, 1 day, 2 days)

Recognition

Recall

Figure 7.18

Recognition versus recall in the measurement of retention.
Luh (1922) had participants memorize lists of nonsense syllables and then measured their retention with either a recognition test or a recall test at various intervals up to two days. As you can see, the forgetting curve for the recall test was quite steep, whereas the recognition test yielded much higher estimates of subjects' retention. (Data from Luh, 1922)

Many students who aren't from Nunavut find this a fairly difficult question. The answer is Iqaluit. Now take a look at the next question:

The capital of Nunavut is:
a. London
b. New York
c. Tokyo
d. Iqaluit

Virtually anyone can answer this question because the incorrect options are readily dismissed. Although this illustration is a bit extreme, it shows that two recognition measures of the same information can be dramatically different in difficulty.

The third method of measuring forgetting is relearning. **A *relearning* measure of retention requires a subject to memorize information a second time to determine how much time or how many practice trials are saved by having learned it before.** Subjects' *savings scores* provide an estimate of their retention. Relearning measures can detect retention that is overlooked by recognition tests (Crowder & Greene, 2000).

Why We Forget 6D

Measuring forgetting is only the first step in the long journey toward explaining why forgetting occurs. In this section, we explore the possible causes of forgetting, looking at factors that may affect encoding, storage, and retrieval processes.

Ineffective Encoding

A great deal of forgetting may only *appear* to be forgetting. The information in question may never have been inserted into memory in the first place. Since you can't really forget something you never learned, this phenomenon is sometimes called *pseudoforgetting*. People usually assume that they know what a penny looks like, but most have actually failed to encode this information. When presented with a picture of a real penny and some realistic fakes, however, most people have difficulty picking out the real penny. This is a good example of pseudoforgetting: pseudoforgetting is usually due to *lack of attention*. Although we handle them every day, most of us do not really look at pennies closely.

Even when memory codes *are* formed for new information, subsequent forgetting may be the result of ineffective or inappropriate encoding (Brown & Craik, 2000). The research on levels of processing shows that some approaches to encoding lead to more forgetting than others (Craik & Tulving, 1975). For example, if you're distracted while you read your

"*Left to itself every mental content gradually loses its capacity for being revived.... Facts crammed at examination time soon vanish.*"
HERMANN EBBINGHAUS

textbooks, you may be doing little more than saying the words to yourself. This is *phonemic encoding,* which is inferior to *semantic encoding* for retention of verbal material. When you can't remember the information that you've read, your forgetting may be due to ineffective encoding.

Decay

Instead of focusing on encoding, decay theory attributes forgetting to the impermanence of memory *storage.* **Decay theory proposes that forgetting occurs because memory traces fade with time.** The implicit assumption is that decay occurs in the physiological mechanisms responsible for memories. According to decay theory, the mere passage of time produces forgetting. This notion meshes nicely with commonsense views of forgetting.

As we noted earlier, evidence suggests that decay does contribute to the loss of information from the sensory and short-term memory stores. However, the critical task for theories of forgetting is to explain the loss of information from long-term memory. Researchers have *not* been able to demonstrate that decay causes LTM forgetting (Slamecka, 1992).

If decay theory is correct, the principal cause of forgetting should be the passage of time. In studies of long-term memory, however, researchers have repeatedly found that time passage is not as influential as what happens during the time interval. Research has shown that forgetting depends not on the amount of time that has passed since learning but on the amount, complexity, and type of information that subjects have had to assimilate *during* the retention interval. The negative impact of competing information on retention is called *interference.*

Interference

Interference theory **proposes that people forget information because of competition from other material.** Although demonstrations of decay in long-term memory have remained elusive, hundreds of studies have shown that interference influences forgetting (Anderson & Neely, 1996; Bjork, 1992; Bower, 2000). In many of these studies, researchers have controlled interference by varying the *similarity* between the original material given to subjects (the test material) and the material studied in the intervening period. Interference is assumed to be greatest when intervening material is most similar to the test material. Decreasing the similarity should reduce interference and cause less forgetting. This is exactly what McGeoch and McDonald (1931) found in an influential study. They had subjects memorize test material that consisted of a list of two-syllable adjectives. They varied the similarity of intervening learning by having subjects then memorize one of five lists. In order of decreasing similarity to the test material, they were synonyms of the test words, antonyms of the test words, unrelated adjectives, nonsense syllables, and numbers. Later, subjects' recall of the test material was measured. Figure 7.19 shows that as the similarity of the intervening material decreased, the amount of forgetting also decreased—because of reduced interference.

McMaster University psychologist Larry Jacoby states that there are two kinds of interference: *retroactive* interference and *proactive* interference (Jacoby, Hessels, & Bopp, 2001). **Retroactive interference occurs when new information impairs the retention of previously learned information.** Retroactive interference occurs between the original learning and the retest on that learning, during the retention interval (see Figure 7.20). For example, the interference manipulated by McGeoch and McDonald (1931) was retroactive interference. In contrast, **proactive interference occurs when previously learned information interferes with the retention of new information.** Proactive interference is rooted in learning that comes *before* exposure to the test material.

Figure 7.19

Effects of interference. According to interference theory, more interference from competing information should produce more forgetting. McGeoch and McDonald (1931) controlled the amount of interference with a learning task by varying the similarity of an intervening task. The results were consistent with interference theory. The amount of interference is greatest at the left of the graph, as is the amount of forgetting. As interference decreases (moving to the right on the graph), retention improves. (Data from McGeoch & McDonald, 1931)

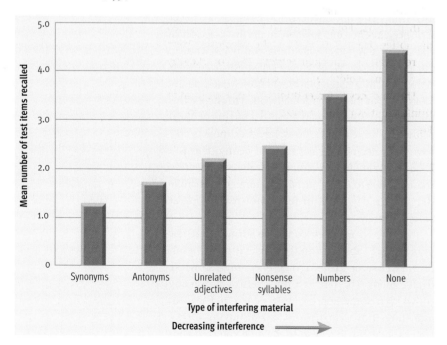

Bar graph. Y-axis: Mean number of test items recalled (0 to 5.0). X-axis: Type of interfering material — Synonyms, Antonyms, Unrelated adjectives, Nonsense syllables, Numbers, None. Decreasing interference →

Retrieval Failure

People often remember things that they were unable to recall at an earlier time. This phenomenon may be obvious only during struggles with the tip-of-the-tongue phenomenon, but it happens frequently. In fact, a great deal of forgetting may be due to breakdowns in the process of retrieval.

Why does an effort to retrieve something fail on one occasion and succeed on another? That's a tough question. As we suggested earlier in our discussion of context- and state-dependent encoding, one theory is that retrieval failures may be more likely when a mismatch occurs between retrieval cues and the encoding of the information you're searching for. According to Tulving and Thomson (1973), a good retrieval cue is consistent with the original encoding of the information to be recalled. For example, if the sound of a word—its phonemic quality—was emphasized during encoding, an effective retrieval cue should emphasize the sound of the word. If the meaning of the word was emphasized during encoding, semantic cues should be best.

A general statement of the principle at work here was formulated by Tulving and Thomson (1973). **The *encoding specificity principle* states that the value of a retrieval cue depends on how well it corresponds to the memory code** (Tulving & Thompson, 1973). This principle provides one explanation for the inconsistent success of retrieval efforts.

Another line of research also indicates that memory is influenced by the "fit" between the processing during encoding and retrieval. ***Transfer-appropriate processing* occurs when the initial processing of information is similar to the type of processing required by the subsequent measure of retention.** For example, Morris, Bransford, and Franks (1977) gave subjects a list of words and a task that required either semantic or phonemic processing. Retention was measured with recognition tests that emphasized either the meaning or the sound of the words. Semantic processing yielded higher retention when the testing emphasized semantic factors, while phonemic processing yielded higher retention when the testing emphasized phonemic factors. Thus, retrieval failures are more likely when there is a poor fit between the processing done during encoding and the processing invoked by the measure of retention (Roediger & Guynn, 1996).

Motivated Forgetting

Many years ago, Sigmund Freud (1901) came up with an entirely different explanation for retrieval failures.

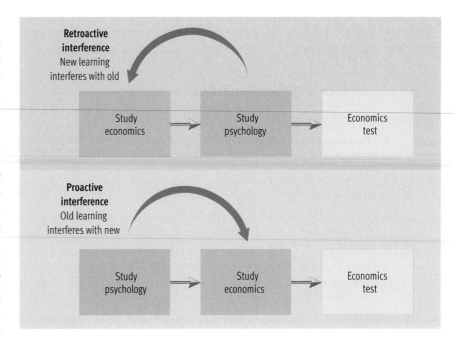

Figure 7.20

Retroactive and proactive interference. Retroactive interference occurs when learning produces a "backward" effect, reducing recall of previously learned material. Proactive interference occurs when learning produces a "forward" effect, reducing recall of subsequently learned material. For example, if you were to prepare for an economics test and then study psychology, the interference from the psychology study would be retroactive interference. However, if you studied psychology first and then economics, the interference from the psychology study would be proactive interference.

As we noted in Chapter 1, Freud asserted that people often keep embarrassing, unpleasant, or painful memories buried in their unconscious. For example, a person who was deeply wounded by perceived slights at a childhood birthday party might suppress all recollection of that party. In his therapeutic work with patients, Freud recovered many such buried memories. He theorized that the memories were there all along, but their retrieval was blocked by unconscious avoidance tendencies.

The tendency to forget things one doesn't want to think about is called *motivated forgetting*, or to use Freud's terminology, *repression*. In Freudian theory, **repression refers to keeping distressing thoughts and feelings buried in the unconscious** (see Chapter 12). Although it is difficult to demonstrate the operation of repression in laboratory studies (Holmes, 1990), a number of experiments suggest that people don't remember anxiety-laden material as readily as emotionally neutral material, just as Freud proposed (Guenther, 1988; Reisner, 1998). Thus, when you forget unpleasant things such as a dental appointment, a promise to help a friend move, or a term paper deadline, motivated forgetting *may* be at work.

Figuring Out Forgetting

Check your understanding of why people forget by identifying the probable causes of forgetting in each of the following scenarios. Choose from (a) motivated forgetting (repression), (b) decay, (c) ineffective encoding, (d) proactive interference, (e) retroactive interference, or (f) retrieval failure. You will find the answers in Appendix A.

_____ **1.** Ellen can't recall the reasons for the Charlottetown Accord because she was daydreaming when it was discussed in her political science class.

_____ **2.** Rufus hates his job at Taco Heaven and is always forgetting when he is scheduled to work.

_____ **3.** Ray's new assistant in the shipping department is named John Cocker. Ray keeps calling him Joe, mixing him up with the rock singer Joe Cocker.

_____ **4.** Tania studied history on Sunday morning and sociology on Sunday evening. It's Monday, and she's struggling with her history test because she keeps mixing up prominent historians with influential sociologists.

The Repressed Memories Controversy

Although the concept of repression has been around for a century, interest in this phenomenon has surged in recent years, thanks to a spate of prominent reports involving the return of individuals' long-lost memories of sexual abuse and other traumas during childhood. The media have been flooded with reports of adults accusing their parents, teachers, and neighbours of horrific child abuse decades earlier, based on previously repressed memories of these travesties. For the most part, these parents, teachers, and neighbours have denied the allegations. Many of them have seemed genuinely baffled by the accusations, which have torn some previously happy families apart (Gudjonsson, 2001; Wylie, 1998). In an effort to make sense of the charges, some accused parents have argued that their children's recollections are false memories created inadvertently by well-intentioned therapists through the power of suggestion.

The controversy surrounding repressed memories is complex and difficult to sort out. The crux of the problem is that child abuse usually takes place behind closed doors. In the absence of corroborative evidence, there is no way to reliably distinguish genuine recovered memories from false ones. A handful of recovered memory incidents have been substantiated by independent witnesses or belated admissions of guilt from the accused (Brewin, 2003; Bull, 1999; Duggal & Sroufe, 1998; Reisner, 1998; Schooler, 1999). But in the vast majority of cases, the allegations of abuse have been vehemently denied,

and independent corroboration has not been available. What do psychologists and psychiatrists have to say about the authenticity of repressed memories? They are sharply divided on the issue.

Many psychologists and psychiatrists, especially clinicians involved in the treatment of psychological disorders, largely accept recovered memories of abuse at face value (Banyard & Williams, 1999; Briere & Conte, 1993; Herman, 1992, 1994; Terr, 1994; Skinner, 2001; Whitfield, 1995). They assert that sexual abuse in childhood is far more widespread than most people realize. For example, a recent, large-scale survey (MacMillan et al., 1997), using a random sample of 9953 residents of Ontario, found that 12.8% of the females and 4.3% of the males reported that they had been victims of sexual abuse during childhood (see Figure 7.21). They further assert that there is ample evidence that it is common for people to bury traumatic incidents in their unconscious (Del Monte, 2000; Karon & Widener, 1997; Wilshack et al., 2002). For instance, in one widely cited study, L. M. Williams (1994) followed up on 129 female children who had been brought to a hospital emergency room for treatment of sexual abuse. When interviewed approximately 17 years later about a variety of things, including their history of sexual abuse, 38% of the women failed to report the original incident, which Williams largely attributed to amnesia for the incident. In a recent

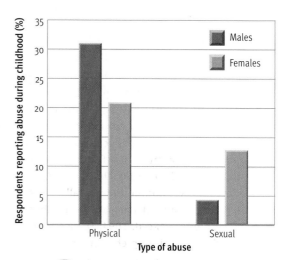

Figure 7.21

Estimates of the prevalence of childhood physical and sexual abuse. In one of the better efforts to estimate the prevalence of child abuse, MacMillan and her colleagues (1997) questioned a random sample of almost 10 000 adults living in Ontario about whether they were abused during childhood. As you can see, males were more likely to have experienced physical abuse and females were more likely to have suffered from sexual abuse. The data support the assertion that millions of people have been victimized by childhood sexual abuse, which is far from rare. (Based on data from MacMillan et al., 1997) study of psychiatric patients hospitalized for post-traumatic or dissociative disorders (see Chapter 14), one-third of those who reported childhood sexual abuse said that they experienced complete amnesia for the abuse at some point in their lives (Chu et al., 1999). According to Freyd (1996), sexual abuse by a parent evokes coping efforts that attempt to block awareness of the abuse because that awareness would interfere with normal attachment processes. The clinicians who accept the authenticity of recovered memories of abuse attribute the recent upsurge in recovered memories to therapists' and clients' increased sensitivity to an issue that people used to be reluctant to discuss.

In contrast, many other psychologists, especially memory researchers, have expressed skepticism about the recent upsurge of recovered memories of abuse (Kihlstrom, 2004; Loftus, 1998, 2003; Lynn & Nash, 1994; McNally, 2003). They point out that the women in the Williams (1994) study may have failed to report their earlier sexual abuse for a variety of reasons besides amnesia, including embarrassment, poor rapport with the interviewer, normal forgetfulness, or a conscious preference not to revisit painful experiences from the past (Loftus, Garry, & Feldman, 1998; Pope & Hudson, 1998). Many memory researchers are also skeptical about retrospective self-reports of amnesia—such as those seen in the Chu et al. (1999) study—because self-assessments of personal memory are often distorted and because it is difficult to distinguish between a period when a memory was not *accessed* versus a period when a memory was not *available* due to repression (Belli et al., 1998; Schooler, 1999).

The skeptics do *not* say that people are lying about their previously repressed memories. Rather, they maintain that some suggestible people wrestling with emotional problems have been convinced by persuasive therapists that their emotional problems must be the result of abuse that occurred years before. Critics blame a minority of therapists who presumably have good intentions but who operate under the dubious assumption that virtually all psychological problems are attributable to childhood sexual abuse (Lindsay & Read, 1994; Spanos, 1994). Using hypnosis, dream interpretation, and leading questions, they supposedly prod and probe patients until they inadvertently create the memories of abuse that they are searching for (Lynn et al., 2003). Consistent with this view, Yapko (1994) reviews evidence that some therapists are (1) overly prone to see signs of abuse where none has occurred, (2) unsophisticated about the extent to which memories can be distorted, and (3) naïve about how much their expectations and beliefs can influence their patients' efforts to achieve self-understanding.

Tom Rutherford (shown here with his wife, Joyce) received a US$1 million settlement in a suit against a church therapist and a Springfield, Missouri, church in a false memory case. Under the church counsellor's guidance, the Rutherfords' daughter, Beth, had "recalled" childhood memories of having been raped repeatedly by her minister father, gotten pregnant, and undergone a painful coat-hanger abortion. Her father lost his job and was ostracized. After he later revealed he'd had a vasectomy when Beth was age four, and a physical exam revealed that at age 23 she was still a virgin, the memories were shown to be false.

Psychologists who doubt the authenticity of repressed memories support their analysis by pointing to discredited cases of recovered memories (Brown, Goldstein, & Bjorklund, 2000). For example, with the help of a church counsellor, one woman recovered memories of how her minister father had repeatedly raped her, gotten her pregnant, and then aborted the pregnancy with a coat-hanger; however, subsequent evidence revealed that the woman was still a virgin and that her father had had a vasectomy years before (Loftus, 1997; Testa, 1996). The skeptics also point to published case histories that clearly involved suggestive questioning and to cases in which patients have recanted recovered memories of sexual abuse (see Figure 7.22) after realizing that these memories were implanted by their therapists (Goldstein & Farmer, 1993; Loftus, 1994; Shobe & Schooler, 2001).

Those who question the accuracy of repressed memories also point to findings on the misinformation effect, research on source-monitoring errors, and other studies that demonstrate the relative ease of creating "memories" of events that never happened (Lindsay et al., 2004; Loftus, 2003). For example, working with college students, Ira Hyman and his colleagues have managed to implant recollections of fairly substantial events (such as spilling a punch bowl at a wedding, being in a grocery store when the fire sprinkler system went off, being hospitalized for an earache) in about 25% of their subjects, just by asking them to elaborate on events supposedly reported by their parents (Hyman, Husband, & Billings, 1995; Hyman & Kleinknecht, 1999).

A Case History of Recovered Memories Recanted

Suffering from a prolonged bout of depression and desperate for help, Melody Gavigan, 39, a computer specialist from Long Beach, California, checked herself into a local psychiatric hospital. As Gavigan recalls the experience, her problems were just beginning. During five weeks of treatment there, a family and marriage counsellor repeatedly suggested that her depression stemmed from incest during her childhood. While at first Gavigan had no recollection of any abuse, the therapist kept prodding. "I was so distressed and needed help so desperately, I latched on to what he was offering me," she says. "I accepted his answers."

When asked for details, she wrote page after page of what she believed were emerging repressed memories. She told about running into the yard after being raped in the bathroom. She incorporated into another lurid rape scene an actual girlhood incident, in which she had dislocated a shoulder. She went on to recall being molested by her father when she was only a year old—as her diapers were being changed—and sodomized by him at five. Following what she says was the therapist's advice, Gavigan confronted her father with her accusations, severed her relationship with him, moved away, and formed an incest survivors' group.

But she remained uneasy. Signing up for a college psychology course, she examined her newfound memories more carefully and concluded that they were false. Now Gavigan has begged her father's forgiveness and filed a lawsuit against the psychiatric hospital for the pain that she and her family suffered.

Figure **7.22**

A case of recovered memories recanted. Revelations of repressed memories of sexual abuse are viewed with skepticism in some quarters. One reason is that some people who have recovered previously repressed recollections of child abuse have subsequently realized that their "memories" were the product of suggestion. A number of case histories, such as the one summarized here (from Jaroff, 1993), have demonstrated that therapists who relentlessly search for memories of child abuse in their patients sometimes instill the memories they are seeking.

SOURCE: Jaroff, L. (1993, November 29). Lies of the mind. *Time*, pp. 52–59. Copyright © 1993 Time Inc. Reprinted by permission.

In a similar vein, Roediger and McDermott (1995, 2000) have devised a simple laboratory paradigm involving the learning of word lists that is remarkably reliable in producing memory illusions. In this paradigm, a series of lists of 15 words are presented to participants, who are asked to recall the words immediately after each list is presented and are given a recognition measure of their retention at the end of the session. The trick is that each list consists of a set of words (such as *bed, rest, awake, tired*) that are strongly associated with another target word that is not on the list (in this case, *sleep*). When subjects *recall* the words on each list, they remember the nonpresented target word over 50% of the time, and when they are given the final *recognition* test, they typically indicate that about 80% of the nonstudied target words were presented in the lists (see Figure 7.23).

The trivial memory illusions created in this experiment may seem a far cry from the vivid, detailed recollections of previously forgotten sexual abuse that have generated the repressed memories controversy. But these false memories can be reliably created in normal, healthy participants in a matter of minutes, with little effort and no pressure or misleading information. Thus, the Roediger and McDermott paradigm provides a dramatic demonstration of how easy it is to get people to remember that they saw something they really didn't see. The simplicity and reliability of the paradigm are also permitting investigators to explore personal correlates of the tendency to falsely remember target words. For example, researchers who have used this paradigm have found an elevated rate of false recollections among women who have reported recovering memories of abuse (Clancy et al., 2000) and among victims of emotional trauma (Zoellner et al., 2000).

Skepticism about the validity of recovered memories of abuse has also been fuelled by the following observations and research findings:

- Many repressed memories of abuse have been recovered under the influence of hypnosis. However, an extensive body of research indicates that hypnosis tends to increase memory distortions while paradoxically making people feel more confident about their recollections (Lynn et al., 1997, 2002; Whitehouse et al., 1988).

- Many repressed memories of abuse have been recovered through therapists' dream interpretations. But as you learned in Chapter 5, dream interpretation depends on highly subjective guesswork that cannot be verified. Moreover, research shows that bogus dream interpretations can lead normal subjects to believe that they actually experienced the events suggested in the dream analyses (Loftus, 2000; Loftus & Mazzoni, 1998).

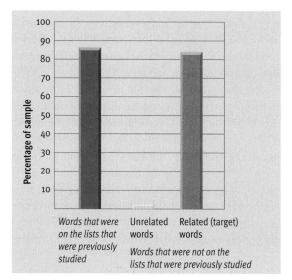

Figure **7.23**

The prevalence of false memories observed by Roediger and McDermott (1995). The graph shown here summarizes the recognition test results in Study 1 conducted by Roediger and McDermott (1995). Participants correctly identified words that had been on the lists that they had studied 86% of the time and misidentified unrelated words that had not been on the lists only 2% of the time, indicating that they were paying careful attention to the task. Nonetheless, they mistakenly reported that they "remembered" related target words that were *not* on the lists 84% of the time—a remarkably high prevalence of false memories. (Data from Roediger & McDermott, 1995)

- Some recovered memories have described incidents of abuse that occurred before the victim reached the age of three. However, when adults are asked to recall their earliest memories, their oldest recollections typically don't go back that far (Bruce, Dolan, & Phillips-Grant, 2000; Eacott & Crawley, 1998).

Of course, psychologists who believe in recovered memories have mounted rebuttals to the numerous arguments raised by the skeptics. For example, Kluft (1999) argues that a recantation of a recovered memory of abuse does not prove that the memory was false. Gleaves (1994) points out that individuals with a history of sexual abuse often vacillate between denying and accepting that the abuse occurred. Harvey (1999) argues that laboratory demonstrations that it is easy to create false memories have involved insignificant memory distortions that do not resemble the emotionally wrenching recollections of sexual abuse that have been recovered in therapy (Gleaves et al., 2004). Olio (1994) concludes that "The possibility of implanting entire multiple scenarios of horror that differ markedly from the individual's experience, such as memories of childhood abuse in an individual who does not have a trauma history, remains an unsubstantiated hypothesis" (p. 442). Moreover, even if one accepts the assertion that therapists *can* create false memories of abuse in their patients, some critics have noted that there is virtually no direct evidence on how often this occurs and no empirical basis for the claim that there has been an *epidemic* of such cases (Berliner & Briere, 1999; Calof, 1998; Leavitt, 2001; Wilsnack et al., 2002; Pope & Brown, 1996).

Although both sides seem genuinely concerned about the welfare of the people involved, the debate about recovered memories of sexual abuse has grown increasingly bitter and emotionally charged (Lindsay, 1998; Pope, 1996). So, what can we conclude about the recovered memories controversy? It seems pretty clear that therapists can unknowingly create false memories in their patients and that a significant portion of recovered memories of abuse are the product of suggestion. But it also seems likely that some cases of recovered memories are authentic (Brown, Scheflin, & Whitfield, 1999; Lindsay & Read, 2001). At this point, we don't have adequate data to estimate what proportion of recovered memories of abuse fall in each category (Brown, Scheflin, & Hammond, 1998; Gow, 1999). Thus, the matter needs to be addressed with great caution. On the one hand, people should be extremely careful about accepting recovered memories of abuse in the absence of convincing corroboration. On the other hand, recovered memories of abuse cannot be summarily

dismissed, and it would be tragic if the repressed memories controversy made people overly skeptical about the all-too-real problem of childhood sexual abuse.

The repressed memories controversy deserves one last comment regarding its impact on memory research and scientific conceptions of memory. The controversy has helped inspire a great deal of research that has increased our understanding of just how fragile, fallible, malleable, and subjective human memory is. It is presumptuous to trust memory—whether recovered or not—to provide accurate recollections of the past. Moreover, the implicit dichotomy underlying the repressed memories debate—that some memories are true, whereas others are false—is misleading and oversimplified. Research demonstrates that all our memories are imperfect reconstructions of the past that are subject to many types of distortion. Although Schacter (1999) has argued convincingly that the imperfections of memory may be adaptive in the long run, the fact remains that memory is surprisingly unreliable.

Web Link 7.4

False Memory Syndrome Foundation (FMSF) Online
http://www.fmsfonline.org/

This site marshals evidence that recovered memories of childhood abuse are often false, therapist induced, and grounded in shoddy and nonobjective scientific claims. Dealing with perhaps the most bitterly contested topic in current psychology, the FMSF has elicited fierce opposition, as the material presented at the site described in Web Link 7.5 demonstrates.

Web Link 7.5

"False Memory Syndrome" Facts
http://fmsf.com

Social worker and psychotherapist Linda Chapman, editor of the online *Wounded Healer Journal*, has brought together scientific and clinical evidence that "false memory syndrome" is a misleading label and that adults may indeed recover repressed memories of childhood abuse.

REVIEW OF KEY POINTS

- Ebbinghaus's early studies of nonsense syllables suggested that people forget very rapidly. Subsequent research showed that Ebbinghaus's forgetting curve was exceptionally steep.

- Forgetting can be measured by asking people to recall, recognize, or relearn information. Different methods of measuring retention often produce different estimates of forgetting. Recognition measures tend to yield higher estimates of retention than recall measures.

- Some forgetting, including pseudoforgetting, is due to ineffective encoding of information. Decay theory proposes that forgetting occurs spontaneously with the passage of time. It has proven difficult to show that decay occurs in long-term memory.

- Interference theory proposes that people forget information because of competition from other material. Proactive interference occurs when old learning interferes with new information. Retroactive interference occurs when new learning interferes with old information.

- Forgetting may also be a matter of retrieval failure. According to the encoding specificity principle, the effectiveness of a retrieval cue depends on how well it corresponds to the memory code that represents the stored item.

- Repression involves the motivated forgetting of painful or unpleasant memories. Recent years have seen a surge of reports of recovered memories of sexual abuse in childhood. The authenticity of these repressed memories is the subject of controversy because empirical studies have demonstrated that it is not all that difficult to create false memories.

- The evidence suggests that therapists can unknowingly create false memories in their patients and that a significant portion of recovered memories of abuse are the product of suggestion. But it also seems likely that some cases of recovered memories are authentic.

In Search of the Memory Trace: The Physiology of Memory

PREVIEW QUESTIONS
- What do synaptic transmission and hormonal fluctuations have to do with memory?
- What type of memory has been explained in terms of a localized neural circuit?
- Which brain structures appear to be involved in memory?

For decades, neuroscientists have ventured forth in search of the physiological basis for memory, often referred to as the "memory trace." On several occasions scientists have been excited by new leads, only to be led down blind alleys. For example, as we noted earlier, Montreal neurosurgeon Wilder Penfield's work with electrical stimulation of the brain during surgery suggested that the cortex houses exact tape recordings of past experiences (Penfield & Perot, 1963). At the time, scientists believed that this was a major advance. Ultimately, it was not.

Similarly, James McConnell rocked the world of science when he reported that he had chemically transferred a specific memory from one flatworm to another. McConnell (1962) created a conditioned reflex (contraction in response to light) in flatworms and then transferred RNA (a basic molecular constituent of all living cells) from trained worms to untrained worms. The untrained worms showed evidence of "remembering" the conditioned reflex. McConnell boldly speculated that in the future, chemists might be able to formulate pills containing the information for Physics 201 or History 101! Unfortunately, the RNA transfer studies proved difficult to replicate (Rilling, 1996). Today, more than 30 years after McConnell's "breakthrough," we are still a long way from breaking the chemical code for memory.

Investigators continue to explore a variety of leads about the physiological bases for memory. In light of past failures, these lines of research should probably be viewed with guarded optimism, but we'll look at some of the more promising approaches. You may want to consult Chapter 3 if you need to refresh your memory about the physiological processes and structures discussed in this section.

The Biochemistry of Memory

One line of research suggests that memory formation results in *alterations in synaptic transmission* at specific sites. According to this view, specific memories depend on biochemical changes that occur at specific synapses. Like McConnell, Eric Kandel (2001) and his colleagues have studied conditioned reflexes in a simple organism—a sea slug. In research that earned a Nobel Prize for Kandel, they showed that specific forms of learning in the sea slug result in an increase or decrease in the release of neurotransmitters by presynaptic neurons (Kandel & Schwartz, 1982; Kennedy, Hawkins, & Kandel, 1992). Kandel believes that durable changes in synaptic transmis-

sion may be the neural building blocks of more complex memories as well. Of course, critics point out that it's risky to generalize from marine mollusks to humans.

Manipulations that alter hormone levels shortly after an organism has learned a new response can affect memory storage in a variety of animals. These hormonal changes can either facilitate or impair memory, depending on the specific hormone and the amount of change (McGaugh & Roozendaal, 2002; McGaugh, Roozendaal, & Cahill, 2000). James McGaugh (2002, 2004) theorizes that hormones influence memory storage by modulating activity in the amygdala and a variety of neurotransmitter systems in the brain. Other animal studies suggest that adequate protein synthesis is necessary for the formation of memories (Rose, 1992; Rosenzweig, 1996; Dudai, 2004; Luft et al., 2004). For example, the administration of drugs that interfere with protein synthesis impairs long-term memory storage in chicks and rats.

The Neural Circuitry of Memory

Richard F. Thompson (1989, 1992, 2005) and his colleagues have shown that specific memories may depend on *localized neural circuits* in the brain. In other words, memories may create unique, reusable pathways in the brain along which signals flow. Thompson has traced the pathway that accounts for a rabbit's memory of a conditioned eyeblink response. The key link in this circuit is a microscopic spot in the *cerebellum*, a structure in the hindbrain (see Figure 7.24). When this spot is destroyed, the conditioned stimulus no longer elicits the eyeblink response, even though the unconditioned stimulus still does (Steinmetz, 1998). This finding does *not* mean that the cerebellum is the key to all memory. Other memories presumably create entirely different pathways in other areas of the brain. The key implication of this work is that it may be possible to map out specific neural circuits that correspond to at least some types of specific memories.

Evidence on *long-term potentiation* also supports the idea that memory traces consist of specific neural circuits. **Long-term potentiation (LTP) is a long-lasting increase in neural excitability at synapses along a specific neural pathway.** Thus far, researchers have produced LTP artificially by sending a burst of high-frequency electrical stimulation along a neural pathway (Racine & deJonge, 1988). Many theorists suspect that natural events produce the same sort of potentiated neural circuit when a memory is formed (Martinez, Barea-Rodriguez, & Derrick, 1998).

In some cases, memory formation may stimulate neural growth and the emergence of new neural circuits (Rosenzweig, 1996). For instance, new branches in the dendritic trees of certain neurons are found in rats that learn to run a series of mazes (Greenough, 1985). As you may recall from Chapter 3, dendritic trees are specialized to receive signals from other neurons. Hence, increased dendritic branching probably leads to the formation of additional synapses and the creation of new neural pathways. These new neural circuits may reflect the storage of learned information.

The Anatomy of Memory 6c

Cases of *organic amnesia*—extensive memory loss due to head injury—are another source of clues about the physiological bases of memory (Mayes, 1992). There are two basic types of amnesia: retrograde and anterograde (see Figure 7.25). *Retrograde amnesia* **involves the loss of memories for events that occurred prior to the onset of amnesia.** For example, a 25-year-old gymnast who sustains a head trauma might find the prior three years, or seven years, or her entire lifetime erased. *Anterograde amnesia* **involves the loss of memories for events that occur after the onset of amnesia.** For instance, after her accident, the injured gymnast might suffer impaired ability to remember people she meets, where she has parked her car, and so on.

The study of anterograde amnesia has proven to be an especially rich source of information about the brain and memory. One well-known case that we referred to in Chapters 1 and 3, that of a man referred to as H. M., has been followed by McGill's Brenda Milner and her colleagues since 1953 (Corkin, 1984; Milner, Corkin, & Teuber, 1968; Scoville & Milner, 1957). H. M. had surgery to relieve debilitating epileptic seizures. Unfortunately, the surgery inadvertently wiped out most of his ability to form long-term memories. H. M.'s short-term memory is fine, but he has no recollection of anything that has happened since 1953 (other than about the most recent 20–30 seconds of his life). He doesn't recognize the doctors treating him and he can't remember routes to and from places. He can read a magazine story over and over, thinking he is reading it for the first time each time. He can't remember what he did yesterday, let alone what he has done for the last 50 years. He doesn't even recognize a current photo of himself, as aging has changed his appearance considerably.

H. M.'s memory losses were originally attributed to the removal of his *hippocampus* (see Figure 7.24),

although theorists now understand that other nearby structures that were removed also contributed to H. M.'s dramatic memory deficits (Delis & Lucas, 1996). Based on decades of additional research, scientists now believe that the entire *hippocampal region* (including the hippocampus, dentate gyrus, subiculum, and entorhinal cortex) and the adjacent *parahippocampal region* are critical for many types of long-term memory (Zola & Squire, 2000). Recent fMRI research by a team of Rotman Institute scientists including Gordon Winocur of Trent University and Morris Moscovitch of the University of Toronto (Gilboa et al., 2004) has shown the importance of the hippocampus in the retrieval of "context-rich" memories. They obtained results suggesting that remote and more recent memories may be associated with different features of the hippocampus. Also consistent with the conclusion linking the hippocampus and memory is research indicating that the hippocampal region is one of the first areas of the brain to sustain significant damage in the course

Figure 7.24

The anatomy of memory. All the brain structures identified here have been implicated in efforts to discover the anatomical structures involved in memory. Although its exact contribution to memory remains the subject of debate, the hippocampus is thought to play an especially central role in memory.

Figure 7.25

Retrograde versus anterograde amnesia. In retrograde amnesia, memory for events that occurred prior to the onset of amnesia is lost. In anterograde amnesia, memory for events that occur subsequent to the onset of amnesia suffers.

Montreal Neurological Institute

Some effects of temporal lobe lesions in man are hard to reconcile with any unitary-process theory of memory.
BRENDA MILNER

McGill researcher Brenda Milner was a co-winner of the 2005 Gairdner Award along with Endel Tulving of the University of Toronto. The Gairdner Award is a prestigious international biomedical award.

of Alzheimer's disease, which produces severe memory impairment in many people, typically after age 65 (Albert & Moss, 2002).

Do these findings mean that memories are stored in the hippocampal region and adjacent areas? Probably not. Many theorists believe that the hippocampal region plays a key role in the *consolidation* of memories (Alvarez & Squire, 1994; Gluck & Myers, 1997; Dudai, 2004). **Consolidation is a hypothetical process involving the gradual conversion of information into durable memory codes stored in long-term memory.** According to this view, memories are consolidated in the hippocampal region and then stored in diverse and widely distributed areas of the cortex (Markowitsch, 2000).

Theorists who have been influenced by parallel distributed processing (PDP) models of memory have come up with a slightly different take on the hippocampal region's contribution to memory. They suggest that the hippocampal area functions to *bind together* the individual elements of a specific memory, which are stored in widely distributed areas of the cortex (Cohen et al., 1999; Nadel & Jacobs, 1998). For example, your memory of attending a baseball game might include a variety of elements—such as when and where it occurred, the final score, certain key plays, the location of your seat, who went with you, and the weather—that are stored in dispersed brain modules. The hippocampal complex may provide a mechanism for bringing these disaggregated elements of a memory together by activating certain ensembles of neurons. In other words, the hippocampal area may play a key role in organizing neural networks that represent specific memories. This analysis is not entirely incompatible with the notion that the hippocampal region handles the consolidation of long-term memories.

Neuroscientists continue to forge ahead in their efforts to identify the anatomical bases of memory. One recent advance has been the demonstration that the *amygdala seems to be critical to the formation of memories for learned fears* (Armony & LeDoux, 2000). This subcortical structure, which is a close neighbour of the hippocampus (see Figure 7.24), may also contribute to other emotional memories (Cahill & McGaugh, 1998; McGaugh, 2004). Investigators are also intrigued by recent evidence regarding the role of the prefrontal cortex in memory (see Figure 7.24). *The prefrontal cortex appears to contribute to memory for temporal sequences and to short-term, working memory* (Gershberg & Shimamura, 1998; Smith, 2000).

As you can see, a host of biochemical processes, neural circuits, and anatomical structures have been implicated as playing a role in memory. Looking for the physiological basis for memory is only slightly less daunting than looking for the physiological basis for thought itself.

REVIEW OF KEY POINTS

- Memory traces may reflect alterations in neurotransmitter release at specific locations. Manipulations of hormone levels and protein synthesis can affect memory.

- Thompson's research suggests that memory traces may consist of localized neural circuits. Memories may also depend on long-term potentiation, which is a durable increase in neural excitability at synapses along a specific neural pathway. Memory formation may also stimulate neural growth.

- In retrograde amnesia, a person loses memory for events prior to the amnesia. In anterograde amnesia, a person shows memory deficits for events subsequent to the onset of the amnesia. Studies of amnesia and other research suggest that the hippocampal complex is involved in the consolidation of memories.

Are There Multiple Memory Systems?

Some theorists believe that evidence on the physiology of memory is confusing because investigators are unwittingly probing into several distinct memory systems that have different physiological bases. A number of research findings inspired this view, foremost among them being the discovery of *implicit memory*. Let's look at this perplexing phenomenon.

Implicit versus Explicit Memory

As noted earlier, patients with anterograde amnesia often appear to have no ability to form long-term memories. If they're shown a list of words and subse-

quently given a test of retention, their performance is miserable. However, different findings emerge when "sneaky" techniques are used to measure their memory indirectly. For instance, they might be asked to work on a word recognition task that is not presented as a measure of retention. In this task, they are shown fragments of words (e.g., _ss_ss_ for assassin) and are asked to complete the fragments with the first appropriate word that comes to mind. The series of word fragments includes ones that correspond to words on a list they saw earlier. In this situation, the amnesiac subjects respond with words that were on the list just as frequently as normal subjects who also saw the initial list (Schacter, Chiu, & Ochsner, 1993). Thus, the amnesiacs *do* remember words from the list. However, when asked, they don't even remember having been shown the list.

The demonstration of long-term retention in amnesiacs who previously appeared to have no long-term memory shocked memory experts when it was first reported by Warrington and Weiskrantz (1970). However, this surprising finding has been replicated in many subsequent studies. This phenomenon has come to be known as implicit memory. ***Implicit memory* is apparent when retention is exhibited on a task that does not require intentional remembering.** Implicit memory is contrasted with *explicit memory,* **which involves intentional recollection of previous experiences.**

Is implicit memory peculiar to people suffering from amnesia? No. When normal subjects are exposed to material and their retention of it is measured indirectly, they, too, show implicit memory (Schacter, 1987, 1989). To draw a parallel with everyday life, implicit memory is simply incidental, unintentional remembering (Mandler, 1989). People frequently remember things that they didn't deliberately store in memory. For example, you might recall the colour of a jacket that your professor wore yesterday. Likewise, people remember things without deliberate retrieval efforts. For instance, you might be telling someone about a restaurant, which somehow reminds you of an unrelated story about a mutual friend.

Research has uncovered many interesting differences between implicit and explicit memory (May, Hasher, & Foong, 2005; Roediger, 1990; Tulving & Schacter, 1990). Explicit memory is conscious, is accessed directly, and can be best assessed with recall or recognition measures of retention. Implicit memory is unconscious, must be accessed indirectly, and can be best assessed with variations on relearning (savings) measures of retention. Implicit memory is largely unaffected by amnesia, age, the administration of certain drugs (such as alcohol), the length of the retention interval, and manipulations of interference. In contrast, explicit memory is affected very much by all these factors.

Some theorists think these differences are found because implicit and explicit memory rely on *different cognitive processes* in encoding and retrieval (Graf & Gallie, 1992; Jacoby, 1988; Roediger, 1990). However, many other theorists argue that the differences exist because implicit and explicit memory are handled by *independent memory systems* (Schacter, 1992, 1994; Squire, 1994). These independent systems are referred to as declarative and procedural memory.

Declarative versus Procedural Memory

 6c

Many theorists have suggested that people have separate memory systems for different kinds of information (see Figure 7.26). The most basic division of memory into distinct systems contrasts *declarative memory* with *nondeclarative* or *procedural memory* (Squire & Zola, 1996; Winograd, 1975). **The *declarative memory system* handles factual information.** It contains recollections of words, definitions, names, dates, faces, events, concepts, and ideas. **The *nondeclarative* or *procedural memory system* houses memory for actions, skills, operations, and conditioned responses.** It contains memories of how to execute such actions as riding a bike, typing, and tying one's shoes. To illustrate the distinction, if you know the rules of tennis (the number of games in a set, scoring, and such), this factual information is stored in declarative memory. If you remember how to hit a serve and swing through a backhand, these perceptual-motor skills are stored in procedural memory.

Some theorists believe that an association exists between implicit memory and the procedural memory system (Squire, Knowlton, & Musen, 1993). Why?

❝*Memory systems constitute the major subdivisions of the overall organization of the memory complex.... An operating component of a system consists of a neural substrate and its behavioral or cognitive correlates.*❞
ENDEL TULVING

University of Toronto researcher Endel Tulving was co-winner of the 2005 Gairdner Award along with Brenda Milner of McGill University.

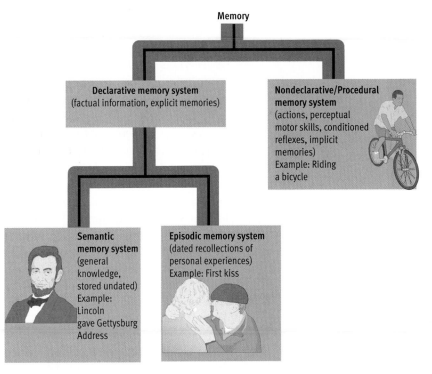

Figure 7.26

Theories of independent memory systems. There is some evidence that different types of information are stored in separate memory systems, which may have distinct physiological bases. The diagram shown here, which blends the ideas of several theorists, is an adaptation of Larry Squire's (1987) scheme. Note that implicit and explicit memory are not memory systems. They are observed behavioural phenomena that appear to be handled by different hypothetical memory systems (the procedural and declarative memory systems), which cannot be observed directly.

Research suggests that memory for perceptual-motor skills, such as the skilled strokes that make Canadian Olympic gold medallist Daniel Nestor a tennis star, are stored in the procedural (nondeclarative) memory system. In contrast, memory for factual information, such as the rules of tennis or game strategies that have worked in the past, are thought to be stored in the declarative memory system.

Because memory for skills is largely unconscious. People execute perceptual-motor tasks such as playing the piano or typing with little conscious awareness of what they're doing. In fact, performance on such tasks often deteriorates if people think too much about what they're doing. Another parallel with implicit memory is that the memory for skills (such as typing and bike riding) doesn't decline much over long retention intervals. Thus, the procedural memory system may handle implicit remembering, while the declarative memory system handles explicit remembering.

Although much remains to be learned, researchers have made some progress toward identifying the neural bases of declarative versus nondeclarative memory. Declarative memory appears to be handled by the hippocampal complex and the far-flung areas of the cortex with which it communicates (Eichenbaum, 2003). It has proven more difficult to pinpoint the neural bases of nondeclarative memory because it consists of more of a hodgepodge of memory func-

tions; however, structures such as the cerebellum and amygdala appear to contribute (Delis & Lucas, 1996; Squire, 2004).

Semantic versus Episodic Memory

As we discussed at the beginning of the chapter, Endel Tulving (1986, 1993, 2002) has further subdivided declarative memory into episodic and semantic memory (see Figure 7.26). Both contain factual information, but episodic memory contains *personal facts* and semantic memory contains *general facts*. **The *episodic memory system* is made up of chronological, or temporally dated, recollections of personal experiences.** Episodic memory is a record of things you've done, seen, and heard. It includes information about *when* you did these things, saw them, or heard them. It contains recollections about being in a ninth-grade play, visiting the Parliament buildings in Ottawa, seeing Sum 41 in concert, or going to see the long-awaited final episode of *Star Wars*.

The *semantic memory system* contains general knowledge that is not tied to the time when the information was learned. Semantic memory contains information such as Christmas is December 25, dogs have four legs, and Saskatoon is located in Saskatchewan. You probably don't remember when you learned these facts. Information like this is usually stored undated. The distinction between episodic and semantic memory can be better appreciated by drawing an analogy to books: Episodic memory is like an autobiography, while semantic memory is like an encyclopedia.

The memory deficits seen in some cases of amnesia suggest that episodic and semantic memory are separate systems. For instance, some amnesiacs forget most personal facts, while their recall of general facts is largely unaffected (Wood, Ebert, & Kinsbourne, 1982). However, debate continues about whether episodic and semantic memory have distinct neural bases (Barba et al., 1998; Wiggs, Weisberg, & Martin, 1999).

Prospective versus Retrospective Memory

A 1984 paper with a clever title, "Remembering to Do Things: A Forgotten Topic" (Harris, 1984), introduced yet another distinction between types of memory: *prospective memory* versus *retrospective memory* (see Figure 7.27). **Prospective memory involves remembering to perform actions in the future.** Examples of prospective memory tasks include remembering to

Figure 7.27

Retrospective versus prospective memory.
Most memory research has explored the dynamics of *retrospective memory*, which focuses on recollections from the past. However, *prospective memory*, which requires people to remember to perform actions in the future, also plays an important role in everyday life.

walk the dog, to call someone, to grab the tickets for the big game, and to turn off your lawn sprinkler. In contrast, **retrospective memory involves remembering events from the past or previously learned information.** Retrospective memory is at work when you try to recall who won the Stanley Cup last year, when you reminisce about your high school days, or when you try to recall what your professor said in a lecture last week. Prospective memory has been a "forgotten" topic in that it has been the subject of relatively little study. But that has begun to change, as research on prospective memory has increased in recent years (Einstein & McDaniel, 1996).

Researchers interested in prospective memory, such as the University of British Columbia's Peter Graf, argue that the topic merits far more study because it plays such a pervasive role in everyday life (Graf & Uttl, 2001). Think about it—a brief trip to attend class at school can be saturated with prospective memory tasks. You may need to remember to pack your notebook, take your umbrella, turn off your coffeemaker, and grab your car keys before you even get out the door. People seem to vary tremendously in their ability to successfully carry out prospective memory tasks (Searleman, 1996), and it is easy to forget these kinds of intentions (Einstein et al., 2003). Individuals who appear deficient in prospective memory are often characterized as "absent-minded."

Much remains to be learned about the factors that influence prospective memory. *Habitual tasks,* such as remembering to pick up your mail, appear to be easier to remember than *infrequent tasks,* such as remembering to stop your mail delivery for an upcoming vacation (Searleman, 1996). Another key factor appears to be whether a prospective memory task is tied to some sort of cue. *Event-based tasks* involve future actions that should be triggered by a specific cue. For example, remembering to give a message to a friend is cued by seeing the friend, or remembering to take medication with one's meal is cued by the meal. *Time-based tasks* require that an action be performed at a certain time or after a certain length of time has elapsed. For example, you might want to start your video recorder at a specific time to tape an interesting show, or you might need to remember to turn off the oven after an hour of baking. Evidence suggests that the cues available in event-based prospective memory tasks make these tasks easier to remember than time-based tasks (Einstein & McDaniel, 1996). Age appears to be another factor that influences the functioning of prospective memory. Older adults seem to be somewhat more vulnerable to problems with prospective memory than younger people are (Einstein et al., 1998; McDaniel et al., 2003).

CONCEPT **CHECK 7.3**

Recognizing Various Types of Memory

Check your understanding of the various types of memory discussed in this chapter by matching the definitions below with the following: (a) declarative memory, (b) episodic memory, (c) explicit memory, (d) implicit memory, (e) long-term memory, (f) procedural memory, (g) prospective memory, (h) retrospective memory, (i) semantic memory, (j) sensory memory, and (k) short-term memory. The answers can be found in Appendix A.

_____ **1.** Memory for factual information.

_____ **2.** An unlimited capacity store that can hold information over lengthy periods of time.

_____ **3.** The preservation of information in its original sensory form for a brief time, usually only a fraction of a second.

_____ **4.** Type of memory apparent when retention is exhibited on a task that does not require intentional remembering.

_____ **5.** Chronological, or temporally dated, recollections of personal experiences.

_____ **6.** The repository of memories for actions, skills, operations, and conditioned responses.

_____ **7.** General knowledge that is not tied to the time when the information was learned.

_____ **8.** Remembering to perform future actions.

_____ **9.** A limited-capacity store that can maintain unrehearsed information for about 20 seconds.

Putting It in Perspective

PREVIEW QUESTIONS
- How did this chapter demonstrate the subjectivity of experience?
- How did this chapter highlight psychology's theoretical diversity and multifactorial causation?

One of our integrative themes—the idea that people's experience of the world is subjective—stood head and shoulders above the rest in this chapter. Let's briefly review how the study of memory has illuminated this idea.

First, our discussion of attention as inherently selective should have shed light on why people's experience of the world is subjective. To a great degree, what you see in the world around you depends on where you focus your attention. This is one of the main reasons that two people can be exposed to the "same" events and walk away with entirely different perceptions. Second, the reconstructive nature of memory should further explain people's tendency to view the world with a subjective slant. When you observe an event, you don't store an exact copy of the event in your memory. Instead, you store a rough, "bare bones" approximation of the event that may be reshaped as time goes by.

A second theme that was apparent in our discussion of memory is psychology's theoretical diversity. We saw illuminating theoretical debates about the nature of memory storage, the causes of forgetting, and the existence of multiple memory systems. Finally, the multifaceted nature of memory demonstrated once again that behaviour is governed by multiple causes. For instance, your memory of a specific event may be influenced by your attention to it, your level of processing, your elaboration, your exposure to interference, how you search your memory store, how you reconstruct the event, and so forth. Given the multifaceted nature of memory, it should come as no surprise that there are many ways to improve memory. We discuss a variety of strategies in the Personal Application section.

REVIEW OF KEY POINTS
- Implicit memory involves unintentional remembering, whereas explicit memory involves intentional recall. Implicit memory is unconscious, must be accessed indirectly, and is largely unaffected by amnesia, age, drugs, and the length of the retention interval.
- Declarative memory is memory for facts, while procedural memory is memory for actions and skills. Theorists suspect that the declarative memory system handles explicit memory, whereas the procedural memory system handles implicit memory.
- Declarative memory can be subdivided into episodic memory for personal facts, and semantic memory for general facts. Theorists have also distinguished between retrospective memory (remembering past events) and prospective memory (remembering to do things in the future).
- Our discussion of memory enhances our understanding of why people's experience of the world is highly subjective. Work in this area also shows that behaviour is governed by multiple causes and that psychology is characterized by theoretical diversity.

Improving
Everyday Memory

Answer the following "true" or "false."

____ 1 Memory strategies were recently invented by psychologists.

____ 2 Imagery can be used to help remember concrete words only.

____ 3 Overlearning of information leads to poor retention.

____ 4 Outlining what you read is not likely to affect retention.

____ 5 Massing practice in one long study session is better than distributing practice across several shorter sessions.

Mnemonic devices **are methods used to increase the recall of information.** They have a long history, so the first statement is false. In fact, one of the mnemonic devices covered in this Application—the method of loci—was described in Greece as early as 86–82 B.C. (Yates, 1966). Actually, mnemonic devices were much more important in ancient times than they are today. In ancient Greece and Rome, for instance, paper and pencils were not readily available for people to write down things they needed to remember, so they had to depend heavily on mnemonic devices.

Are mnemonic devices the key to improving one's everyday memory? No. Mnemonic devices can clearly be helpful in some situations (Wilding & Valentine, 1996), but they are not a panacea. They can be difficult to use and difficult to apply to many everyday situations. Most books and training programs designed to improve memory probably overemphasize mnemonic techniques (Searleman & Herrmann, 1994). Although less exotic strategies such as increasing rehearsal, engaging in deeper processing, and organizing material are more crucial to everyday memory, we will discuss some popular mnemonics as we proceed through this Application. Along the way, you'll learn that all of our opening true-false statements are false.

Engage in Adequate Rehearsal SIM5

Practice makes perfect, or so you've heard. In reality, practice is not likely to guarantee perfection, but it usually leads to improved retention. Studies show that retention improves with increased rehearsal. This improvement presumably occurs because rehearsal helps to transfer information into long-term memory. Although the benefits of practice are well known, people have a curious tendency to overestimate their knowledge of a topic and how well they will perform on a subsequent memory test of this knowledge (Koriat & Bjork, 2005). That's why it is a good idea to informally test yourself on information that you think you have mastered before confronting a real test (for example, by taking the Practice Tests in this text or additional tests available on the Web site for the book).

It even pays to overlearn material (Driskell, Willis, & Copper, 1992). *Overlearning* **refers to continued rehearsal of material after you first appear to have mastered it.** In one study, after subjects had mastered a list of nouns (they recited the list without error), Krueger (1929) required them to continue rehearsing for 50% or 100% more trials. Measuring retention at intervals up to 28 days, Krueger found that greater overlearning was related to better recall of the list. Modern studies have also shown that overlearning can enhance performance on an exam that occurs within a week, although the evidence on its long-term benefits (months later) is inconsistent (Peladeau, Forget, & Gagne, 2003; Rohrer et al., 2005). One other precaution is also worth mentioning. If you are memorizing some type of list, be aware of the serial-position effect, which according to the University of Toronto's Bennet Murdock (2001) is often observed when subjects are tested on their memory of lists. The *serial-position effect*

occurs when subjects show better recall for items at the beginning and end of a list than for items in the middle (see Figure 7.28). The reasons for the serial-position effect are complex and need not concern us, but its pragmatic implications are clear: If you need to learn a list, allocate extra practice trials to items in the middle of the list and check your memorization of those items very carefully.

Schedule Distributed Practice and Minimize Interference

Let's assume that you need to study nine hours for an exam. Should you "cram" all your studying into one nine-hour period (massed practice)? Or is it better to distribute your study among, say, three three-hour periods on successive days (distributed practice)? The evidence indicates that retention tends to be greater after distributed practice than after massed practice (Glenberg, 1992; Payne & Wenger, 1996). For instance, Underwood (1970) studied children (ages 9 to 14) who practised a list of words four times, either in one long session or in four separate sessions. He found that distributed practice led to better recall than a similar amount of massed practice (see Figure 7.29). The superiority of distributed practice suggests that cramming is an ill-advised approach to studying for exams (Dempster, 1996).

Because interference is a major cause of forgetting, you'll probably want to think about how you can minimize it. This issue is especially important for students, because memorizing information for one course can interfere with the retention of information for another course. It may help to allocate study for specific courses to separate days. Thorndyke and Hayes-Roth (1979) found that similar material produced less interference

Although courts give special credence to eyewitness testimony, scientific evidence indicates that eyewitness accounts are less reliable than widely assumed.

The Contribution of Hindsight Bias

The *hindsight bias* is the tendency to mould our interpretation of the past to fit how events actually turned out. When you know the outcome of an event, this knowledge slants your recall of how the event unfolded and what your thinking was at the time (Guilbault et al., 2004). With the luxury of hindsight, there is a curious tendency to say, "I knew it all along" when explaining events that objectively would have been difficult to foresee. With regard to eyewitnesses, their recollections may often be distorted by knowing that a particular person has been arrested and accused of the crime in question. For example, Wells and Bradfield (1998) had simulated eyewitnesses select a perpetrator from a photo line-up. The eyewitnesses' confidence in their identifications tended to be quite modest, which made sense given that the actual perpetrator was not even in the line-up. But when some subjects were told, "Good, you identified the actual suspect," they became highly confident about their identifications, which obviously were incorrect. In another study, participants read identical scenarios about a couple's first date that either had no ending or ended in a rape (described in one additional sentence). The subjects who received the rape ending reconstructed the story to be more consistent with their stereotypes of how rapes occur (Carli, 1999).

The Contribution of Overconfidence

Another flaw in thinking that contributes to inaccuracy in eyewitness accounts is people's tendency to be overconfident about the reliability of their memory. When tested for their memory of general information, people tend to overestimate their accuracy (Lichtenstein, Fischhoff, & Phillips, 1982; Koriat & Bjork, 2005). In studies of eyewitness recall, participants also tend to be overconfident about their recollections. Although jurors tend to be more convinced by eyewitnesses who appear confident, the evidence indicates that there is only a modest correlation between eyewitness confidence and eyewitness accuracy (Bornstein & Zickafoose, 1999).

Strategies to Reduce Overconfidence

Can you learn to make better judgments of the accuracy of your recall of everyday events? Yes, with effort you can get better at making accurate estimates of how likely you are to be correct in the recall of some fact or event. One reason that people tend to be overconfident is that if they can't think of any reasons that they might be wrong, they assume they must be right. Thus, overconfidence is fuelled by yet another common error in thinking—*the failure to seek disconfirming evidence.*

Thus, to make more accurate assessments of what you know and don't know, it helps to engage in a deliberate process of considering why you might be wrong. Here is an example. Based on your reading of Chapter 1, write down the schools of thought associated with the following major theorists: William James, John B. Watson, and Carl Rogers. After you provide your answers, rate your confidence that the information you just provided is correct. Now, write three reasons that your answers might be wrong and three reasons they might be correct. Most people will balk at this exercise, arguing that they cannot think of any reasons that they might be wrong, but after some resistance, they can come up with several. Such reasons might include "I was half asleep when I read that part of the chapter" or "I might be confusing Watson and James." Reasons that you think you're right could include "I distinctly recall discussing this with my friend" or "I really worked on those names in Chapter 1." After listing reasons that you might be right and reasons that you might be wrong, rate your confidence in your accuracy once again. Guess what? Most people are less confident after going through such an exercise than they were before (depending, of course, on the nature of the topic).

The new confidence ratings tend to be more realistic than the original ratings (Koriat, Lichtenstein, & Fischhoff, 1980). Why? Because this exercise forces you to think more deeply about your answers and to search your memory for related information. Most people stop searching their memory as soon as they generate an answer they believe to be correct. Thus, the process of considering reasons that you might be wrong about something—a process that people rarely engage in—is a useful critical thinking skill that can reduce overconfidence effects. Better assessment of what you know and don't know can be an important determinant of the quality of the decisions you make and the way you solve problems and reason from evidence.

Table 7.1 Critical Thinking Skills Discussed in This Application

Skill	Description
Understanding the limitations and fallibility of human memory	The critical thinker appreciates that memory is reconstructive and that even eyewitness accounts may be distorted or inaccurate.
Recognizing the bias in hindsight analysis	The critical thinker understands that knowing the outcome of events biases our recall and interpretation of the events.
Recognizing overconfidence in human cognition	The critical thinker understands that people are frequently overconfident about the accuracy of their projections for the future and their recollections of the past.
Understanding the need to seek disconfirming evidence	The critical thinker understands the value of thinking about how or why one might be wrong about something.

Understanding the Fallibility of Eyewitness Accounts

A number of years ago, the Wilmington, Delaware, area was plagued by a series of armed robberies committed by a perpetrator who was dubbed the "gentleman bandit" by the press because he was an unusually polite and well-groomed thief. The local media published a sketch of the gentleman bandit and eventually an alert resident turned in a suspect who resembled the sketch. Much to everyone's surprise, the accused thief was a Catholic priest named Father Bernard Pagano—who vigorously denied the charges. Unfortunately for Father Pagano, his denials and alibis were unconvincing and he was charged with the crimes. At the trial, *seven* eyewitnesses confidently identified Father Pagano as the gentleman bandit. The prosecution was well on its way to a conviction when there was a stunning turn of events—another man, Ronald Clouser, confessed to the police that he was the gentleman bandit. The authorities dropped the charges against Father Pagano and the relieved priest was able to return to his normal existence (Rodgers, 1982).

This bizarre tale of mistaken identity—which sounds like it was lifted from a movie script—raises some interesting questions about memory. How could seven people "remember" seeing Father Pagano commit armed robberies that he had nothing to do with? How could they mistake him for Ronald Clouser, when the two really didn't look very similar (see the photos to the right)? How could they be so confident when they were so wrong? Perhaps you're thinking that this is just one case and it must be unrepresentative (which would be sound critical thinking). Well, yes, it *is* a rather extreme example of eyewitness fallibility, but researchers have compiled mountains of evidence that eyewitness testimony is not nearly as reliable or as accurate as widely assumed (Cutler & Penrod, 1995; Kassin et al., 2001; Wells & Olson, 2003). This finding is ironic in that people are most confident about their assertions when they can say, "I saw it with my own eyes." Television news shows like to use the title "Eyewitness News" to create the impression that they chronicle events with great clarity and accuracy. And our legal system accords special status to eyewitness testimony because it is considered much more dependable than hearsay or circumstantial evidence. Canadian psychologists such as Daniel Yarmey of the University of Guelph, Rod Lindsay of Queen's, and Regina Schuller of York University have been important contributors to the literature on the accuracy and role of eyewitness testimony and to the literature on psychology and the law more generally (Lindsay et al., in press; Schuller & Ogloff, 2001; Yarmey, 2003).

So, why are eyewitness accounts surprisingly inaccurate? Well, a host of factors and processes contribute to this inaccuracy. Let's briefly review some of the relevant processes that were introduced in the main body of the chapter; then we'll focus on two common errors in thinking that also contribute.

Can you think of any memory phenomena described in the chapter that seem likely to undermine eyewitness accuracy? You could point to the fact that *memory is a reconstructive process,* and eyewitness recall is likely to be distorted by the schemas that people have for various events. A second consideration is that *witnesses sometimes make source-monitoring errors* and get confused about where they saw a face. For example, one rape victim mixed up her assailant with a guest on a TV show that she was watching when she was attacked. Fortunately, the falsely accused suspect had an airtight alibi, as he could demonstrate that he was on live television when the rape occurred (Schacter, 1996). Perhaps the most pervasive factor is the misinformation effect (Loftus, 1993). *Witnesses' recall of events is routinely distorted by information introduced after the event* by police officers, lawyers, news reports, and so forth. In addition to these factors, eyewitness inaccuracy is fuelled by the *hindsight bias* and *overconfidence effects.*

Although he doesn't look that much like the real "gentleman bandit," who is shown on the left, seven eyewitnesses identified Father Pagano (right) as the gentleman bandit, showing just how unreliable eyewitness accounts can be.

Although courts give special credence to eyewitness testimony, scientific evidence indicates that eyewitness accounts are less reliable than widely assumed.

The Contribution of Hindsight Bias

The *hindsight bias* is the tendency to mould our interpretation of the past to fit how events actually turned out. When you know the outcome of an event, this knowledge slants your recall of how the event unfolded and what your thinking was at the time (Guilbault et al., 2004). With the luxury of hindsight, there is a curious tendency to say, "I knew it all along" when explaining events that objectively would have been difficult to foresee. With regard to eyewitnesses, their recollections may often be distorted by knowing that a particular person has been arrested and accused of the crime in question. For example, Wells and Bradfield (1998) had simulated eyewitnesses select a perpetrator from a photo line-up. The eyewitnesses' confidence in their identifications tended to be quite modest, which made sense given that the actual perpetrator was not even in the line-up. But when some subjects were told, "Good, you identified the actual suspect," they became highly confident about their identifications, which obviously were incorrect. In another study, participants read identical scenarios about a couple's first date that either had no ending or ended in a rape (described in one additional sentence). The subjects who received the rape ending reconstructed the story to be more consistent with their stereotypes of how rapes occur (Carli, 1999).

The Contribution of Overconfidence

Another flaw in thinking that contributes to inaccuracy in eyewitness accounts is people's tendency to be overconfident about the reliability of their memory. When tested for their memory of general information, people tend to overestimate their accuracy (Lichtenstein, Fischhoff, & Phillips, 1982; Koriat & Bjork, 2005). In studies of eyewitness recall, participants also tend to be overconfident about their recollections. Although jurors tend to be more convinced by eyewitnesses who appear confident, the evidence indicates that there is only a modest correlation between eyewitness confidence and eyewitness accuracy (Bornstein & Zickafoose, 1999).

Strategies to Reduce Overconfidence

Can you learn to make better judgments of the accuracy of your recall of everyday events? Yes, with effort you can get better at making accurate estimates of how likely you are to be correct in the recall of some fact or event. One reason that people tend to be overconfident is that if they can't think of any reasons that they might be wrong, they assume they must be right. Thus, overconfidence is fuelled by yet another common error in thinking—*the failure to seek disconfirming evidence.*

Thus, to make more accurate assessments of what you know and don't know, it helps to engage in a deliberate process of considering why you might be wrong. Here is an example. Based on your reading of Chapter 1, write down the schools of thought associated with the following major theorists: William James, John B. Watson, and Carl Rogers. After you provide your answers, rate your confidence that the information you just provided is correct. Now, write three reasons that your answers might be wrong and three reasons they might be correct. Most people will balk at this exercise, arguing that they cannot think of any reasons that they might be wrong, but after some resistance, they can come up with several. Such reasons might include "I was half asleep when I read that part of the chapter" or "I might be confusing Watson and James." Reasons that you think you're right could include "I distinctly recall discussing this with my friend" or "I really worked on those names in Chapter 1." After listing reasons that you might be right and reasons that you might be wrong, rate your confidence in your accuracy once again. Guess what? Most people are less confident after going through such an exercise than they were before (depending, of course, on the nature of the topic).

The new confidence ratings tend to be more realistic than the original ratings (Koriat, Lichtenstein, & Fischhoff, 1980). Why? Because this exercise forces you to think more deeply about your answers and to search your memory for related information. Most people stop searching their memory as soon as they generate an answer they believe to be correct. Thus, the process of considering reasons that you might be wrong about something—a process that people rarely engage in—is a useful critical thinking skill that can reduce overconfidence effects. Better assessment of what you know and don't know can be an important determinant of the quality of the decisions you make and the way you solve problems and reason from evidence.

Table 7.1 Critical Thinking Skills Discussed in This Application	
Skill	**Description**
Understanding the limitations and fallibility of human memory	The critical thinker appreciates that memory is reconstructive and that even eyewitness accounts may be distorted or inaccurate.
Recognizing the bias in hindsight analysis	The critical thinker understands that knowing the outcome of events biases our recall and interpretation of the events.
Recognizing overconfidence in human cognition	The critical thinker understands that people are frequently overconfident about the accuracy of their projections for the future and their recollections of the past.
Understanding the need to seek disconfirming evidence	The critical thinker understands the value of thinking about how or why one might be wrong about something.

Figure 7.31

The method of loci. In this example from Bower (1970), a person about to go shopping pairs items to remember with familiar places (loci) arranged in a natural sequence: (1) hot dogs/driveway; (2) cat food/garage interior; (3) tomatoes/front door; (4) bananas/coat closet shelf; (5) whiskey/kitchen sink. The shopper then uses imagery to associate the items on the shopping list with the loci, as shown in the drawing: (1) giant hot dog rolls down a driveway; (2) a cat noisily devours cat food in the garage; (3) ripe tomatoes are splattered on the front door; (4) bunches of bananas are hung from the closet shelf; (5) the contents of a bottle of whiskey gurgle down the kitchen sink. As the last panel shows, the shopper recalls the items by mentally touring the loci associated with them.

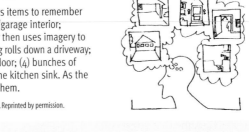

SOURCE: From Bower, G. H. (1970). Analysis of a mnemonic device. *American Scientist, 58,* 496–499. Copyright © 1970 by Scientific Research Society. Reprinted by permission.

should sound like the name that's being learned. For example, you might use Garden as a keyword for *Gordon.* And *debtor man* might be a good keyword for Detterman, if you form an image of Mr. Detterman dressed in ragged clothes. Research suggests that the keyword method can enhance the retention of foreign language and other types of educational material (Bellezza, 1996; Gruneberg, Sykes, & Gillett, 1994).

Levin and Levin (1990) trained students to apply the keyword method to unfamiliar terms in a plant classification system. They coupled this approach with the link method, which was used to group terms that belonged together in categories. The researchers found that these methods enhanced students' memory of the classification system (see Figure 7.32).

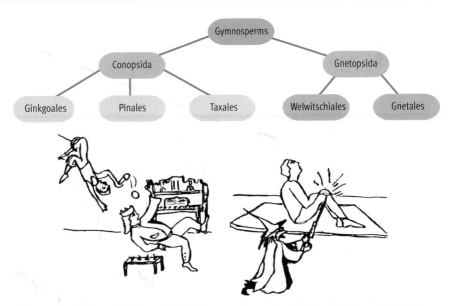

To remember that the subdivision *gymnosperms* includes the class *conopsida,* which in turn includes the three orders *ginkgoales, pinales,* and *taxales,* study the picture of the swinging gymnast with the ice cream cone in his hand. The ice cream is about to splat in the face of the king who is leaping from the bench of his royal piano after sitting on some tacks.

To remember that the subdivision *gymnosperms* includes the class *gnetopsida,* which in turn includes the two orders *welwitschiales* and *gnetales,* study the picture of the fallen gymnast holding his sore knee tops. He is being treated (or tricked!) by a witch doctor who is sticking a very long needle into his injured knee.

Figure 7.32

Combining the keyword and link methods to aid recall. Levin and Levin (1990) set out to help students memorize a difficult plant classification system (a portion of the system is shown in the top part of the figure). They taught students to use a technique that essentially combines the keyword and link methods. Students were trained to generate keywords for the abstract terms in the hierarchy and to form images that linked the keywords that corresponded to portions of the classification system (two examples are shown in the bottom part of the figure). This creative use of visual imagery enhanced students' recall of the plant classification system.

SOURCE: Adapted from Levin, M. E., & Levin, J. R. (1990). Scientific mnemonomies: Methods for maximizing more than memory. *American Educational Research Journal, 27* (2), 301–321. Copyright © 1990 by American Educational Research Association. Adapted by permission.

REVIEW OF KEY POINTS

- Mnemonic devices are methods used to increase the recall of information. Rehearsal, even when it involves overlearning, facilitates retention, although one should be wary of the serial-position effect. Distributed practice tends to be more efficient than massed practice.

- It is wise to plan study sessions so as to minimize interference and maximize deep processing. Evidence also suggests that organization enhances retention, so outlining texts may be valuable.

- Meaningfulness can be enhanced through the use of verbal mnemonics such as acrostics, acronyms, and narrative methods. The link method, the method of loci, and the keyword method are mnemonic devices that depend on the value of visual imagery.

store the name "Roy G. Biv" to remember red, orange, yellow, green, blue, indigo, and violet. Notice that this acronym takes advantage of the principle of chunking.

Narrative Methods

Another useful way to remember a list of words is to create a story that includes the words in the appropriate order. The narrative both increases the meaningfulness of the words and links them in a specific order. Examples of this technique can be seen in Figure 7.30. Bower and Clark (1969) found that this procedure greatly enhanced subjects' recall of lists of unrelated words (as shown in Figure 7.30).

Why—and how—would you use the narrative method? Let's assume that you always manage to forget to put one item in your gym bag on your way to the pool. Short of pasting a list on the inside of the bag, how can you remember everything you need? You could make up a story like the following that includes the items you need:

The wind and rain in COMBINATION nearly LOCKed out the rescue efforts. CAP, the flying ace, TOWELed the soap from his eyes, pulled his GOGGLES from his SUIT pocket, and COMBed the BRUSH for survivors.

Rhymes

Another verbal mnemonic that people often rely on is rhyming. You've probably repeated, "I before E except after C …" thousands of times. Perhaps you also remember the number of days in each month with the old standby, "Thirty days hath September …." Rhyming something to remember it is an old and useful trick.

Enrich Encoding with Visual Mnemonics

Memory can be enhanced by the use of visual imagery. As you may recall, Allan Paivio (1986) believes that visual images create a second memory code and that two codes are better than one for enhancing recall. Many popular mnemonic devices depend on visual imagery, including the link method, method of loci, and keyword method.

Link Method

The *link method* involves forming a mental image of items to be remembered in a way that links them together. For instance, suppose you need to remember some items to pick up at the drugstore: a news magazine, shaving cream, film, and pens. To remember these items, you might visualize a public figure on the magazine cover shaving with a pen while being photographed. There is some evidence that the more bizarre you make your image, the more helpful it is likely to be (McDaniel & Einstein, 1986).

Method of Loci

The *method of loci* involves taking an imaginary walk along a familiar path where images of items to be remembered are associated with certain locations. The first step is to commit to memory a series of loci, or places along a path. Usually these loci are specific locations in your home or neighbourhood. Then envision each thing you want to remember in one of these locations. Try to form distinctive, vivid images. When you need to remember the items, imagine yourself walking along the path. The various loci on your path should serve as cues for the retrieval of the images that you formed (see Figure 7.31). Evidence suggests that the method of loci can be effective in increasing retention (Cornoldi & De Beni, 1996; Moe & De Beni, 2004). Moreover, this method ensures that items are remembered in their *correct order* because the order is determined by the sequence of locations along the pathway.

Keyword Method

Visual images are also useful when you need to form an association between a pair of items, such as a person's name and face or a foreign word and its English translation. However, there is a potential problem that you may recall from our earlier discussion of visual imagery. It's difficult to generate images to represent abstract words (Paivio, 1969). A way to avoid this problem is to use **the *keyword method*, in which you associate a concrete word with an abstract word and generate an image to represent the concrete word.**

A practical use of this method is to help you remember the names of people you meet (Morris, Jones, & Hampson, 1978). Just associate a concrete word with the name and then form an image of the associated word. The associated word, which is the *keyword*,

Figure 7.30

Narrative methods of remembering. Bower and Clark (1969) presented participants with 12 lists of words. Subjects in the "narrative group" were asked to recall the words by constructing a story out of them (like the two stories shown here). Subjects in the control group were given no special instructions. Recoding the material in story form dramatically improved recall, as the graph clearly shows.

Source: Adapted from Bower, G. H., & Clark, M. C. (1969). Narrative stories as mediators of serial learning. *Psychonomic Science, 14*, 181–182. Copyright © 1969 by the Psychonomic Society. Adapted by permission of the Psychonomic Society.

Word lists	Stories
Bird Costume Mailbox Head River Nurse Theatre Wax Eyelid Furnace	A man dressed in a *Bird Costume* and wearing a *Mailbox* on his *Head* was seen leaping into the *River*. A *Nurse* ran out of a nearby *Theatre* and applied *Wax* to his *Eyelids*, but her efforts were in vain. He died and was tossed into the *Furnace*.
Rustler Penthouse Mountain Sloth Tavern Fuzz Gland Antler Pencil Vitamin	A *Rustler* lived in a *Penthouse* on top of a *Mountain*. His specialty was the three-toed *Sloth*. He would take his captive animals to a *Tavern* where he would remove *Fuzz* from their *Glands*. Unfortunately, all this exposure to sloth fuzz caused him to grow *Antlers*. So he gave up his profession and went to work in a *Pencil* factory. As a precaution he also took a lot of *Vitamin* E.

Human Memory   **303**

Improving
Everyday Memory

Answer the following "true" or "false."

_____ 1 Memory strategies were recently invented by psychologists.

_____ 2 Imagery can be used to help remember concrete words only.

_____ 3 Overlearning of information leads to poor retention.

_____ 4 Outlining what you read is not likely to affect retention.

_____ 5 Massing practice in one long study session is better than distributing practice across several shorter sessions.

Mnemonic devices **are methods used to increase the recall of information.** They have a long history, so the first statement is false. In fact, one of the mnemonic devices covered in this Application—the method of loci—was described in Greece as early as 86–82 B.C. (Yates, 1966). Actually, mnemonic devices were much more important in ancient times than they are today. In ancient Greece and Rome, for instance, paper and pencils were not readily available for people to write down things they needed to remember, so they had to depend heavily on mnemonic devices.

Are mnemonic devices the key to improving one's everyday memory? No. Mnemonic devices can clearly be helpful in some situations (Wilding & Valentine, 1996), but they are not a panacea. They can be difficult to use and difficult to apply to many everyday situations. Most books and training programs designed to improve memory probably overemphasize mnemonic techniques (Searleman & Herrmann, 1994). Although less exotic strategies such as increasing rehearsal, engaging in deeper processing, and organizing material are more crucial to everyday memory, we will discuss some popular mnemonics as we proceed through this Application. Along the way, you'll learn that all of our opening true-false statements are false.

Engage in Adequate Rehearsal

Practice makes perfect, or so you've heard. In reality, practice is not likely to guarantee perfection, but it usually leads to improved retention. Studies show that retention improves with increased rehearsal. This improvement presumably occurs because rehearsal helps to transfer information into long-term memory. Although the benefits of practice are well known, people have a curious tendency to overestimate their knowledge of a topic and how well they will perform on a subsequent memory test of this knowledge (Koriat & Bjork, 2005). That's why it is a good idea to informally test yourself on information that you think you have mastered before confronting a real test (for example, by taking the Practice Tests in this text or additional tests available on the Web site for the book).

It even pays to overlearn material (Driskell, Willis, & Copper, 1992). **Overlearning refers to continued rehearsal of material after you first appear to have mastered it.** In one study, after subjects had mastered a list of nouns (they recited the list without error), Krueger (1929) required them to continue rehearsing for 50% or 100% more trials. Measuring retention at intervals up to 28 days, Krueger found that greater overlearning was related to better recall of the list. Modern studies have also shown that overlearning can enhance performance on an exam that occurs within a week, although the evidence on its long-term benefits (months later) is inconsistent (Peladeau, Forget, & Gagne, 2003; Rohrer et al., 2005). One other precaution is also worth mentioning. If you are memorizing some type of list, be aware of the serial-position effect, which according to the University of Toronto's Bennet Murdock (2001) is often observed when subjects are tested on their memory of lists. **The *serial-position effect***

occurs when subjects show better recall for items at the beginning and end of a list than for items in the middle (see Figure 7.28). The reasons for the serial-position effect are complex and need not concern us, but its pragmatic implications are clear: If you need to learn a list, allocate extra practice trials to items in the middle of the list and check your memorization of those items very carefully.

Schedule Distributed Practice and Minimize Interference

Let's assume that you need to study nine hours for an exam. Should you "cram" all your studying into one nine-hour period (massed practice)? Or is it better to distribute your study among, say, three three-hour periods on successive days (distributed practice)? The evidence indicates that retention tends to be greater after distributed practice than after massed practice (Glenberg, 1992; Payne & Wenger, 1996). For instance, Underwood (1970) studied children (ages 9 to 14) who practised a list of words four times, either in one long session or in four separate sessions. He found that distributed practice led to better recall than a similar amount of massed practice (see Figure 7.29). The superiority of distributed practice suggests that cramming is an ill-advised approach to studying for exams (Dempster, 1996).

Because interference is a major cause of forgetting, you'll probably want to think about how you can minimize it. This issue is especially important for students, because memorizing information for one course can interfere with the retention of information for another course. It may help to allocate study for specific courses to separate days. Thorndyke and Hayes-Roth (1979) found that similar material produced less interference

Figure 7.28

The serial-position effect. After learning a list of items to remember, people tend to recall more of the items from the beginning and the end of the list than from the middle, producing the characteristic U-shaped curve shown here. This phenomenon is called the serial-position effect.

SOURCE: Adapted from Rundus, D. (1971). Analysis of rehearsal processes in free recall. *Journal of Experimental Psychology, 89*, 63–77. Copyright © 1971 by the American Psychological Association. Adapted by permission of the author.

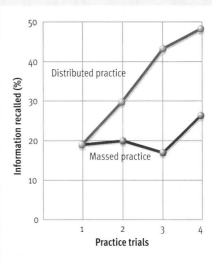

Figure 7.29

Effects of massed versus distributed practice on retention. Children in the Underwood (1970) study showed better recall of information when practice sessions were distributed over time as opposed to being massed together in one session.

SOURCE: Adapted from Underwood, B. J. (1970). A breakdown of the total-time law in free-recall learning. *Journal of Verbal Learning and Verbal Behavior, 9*, 573–580. Copyright © 1970 Elsevier Science USA, reproduced with permission from the publisher.

when it was learned on different days. Thus, the day before an exam in a course, you should study for that course only—if possible. If demands in other courses make that plan impossible, you should study the test material last.

Emphasize Deep Processing and Organize Information

Research on levels of processing suggests that how *often* you go over material is less critical than the *depth* of processing that you engage in (Craik & Tulving, 1975). Thus, if you expect to remember what you read, you have to wrestle fully with its meaning. Many students could probably benefit if they spent less time on rote repetition and devoted more effort to actually paying attention to and analyzing the meaning of their reading assignments. In particular, it is useful to make material *personally* meaningful. When you read your textbooks, try to relate information to your own life and experience. For example, when

you read about classical conditioning, try to think of responses that you display that are attributable to classical conditioning.

Retention tends to be greater when information is well organized. The value of organization has been apparent in studies of people who exhibit remarkable memory capability. For example, Ericsson and Polson (1988) have studied a waiter, known as J. C., who can remember up to 20 complicated dinner orders without taking notes. They found that control subjects tried to memorize dinner requests in the order in which the requests were presented, whereas J. C. reorganized information by dinner element (salad dressings, vegetables, and so on).

Gordon Bower (1970) has shown that hierarchical organization is particularly helpful when it is applicable. Thus, it may be a good idea to *outline* reading assignments for school. Consistent with this reasoning, there is some empirical evidence that outlining material from textbooks can enhance retention of the material (McDaniel, Waddill, & Shakesby, 1996).

Enrich Encoding with Verbal Mnemonics

When you memorize abstract information, it helps to make the information personally meaningful, but it's not always easy to do so. For instance, when you study chemistry you may have a hard time relating to polymers at a personal level. Thus, many mnemonic devices—such as acrostics, acronyms, and narrative methods—are designed to make abstract material more meaningful.

Acrostics and Acronyms

Acrostics are phrases (or poems) in which the first letter of each word (or line) functions as a cue to help you recall information to be remembered (Herrmann et al., 2002). For instance, you may remember the order of musical notes with the saying "Every good boy does fine" (or "deserves favour"). A slight variation on acrostics is the *acronym*— a word formed out of the first letters of a series of words. Students memorizing the order of colours in the light spectrum often

RECAP

Key Ideas

Encoding: Getting Information into Memory

● The multifaceted process of memory begins with encoding. Attention, which facilitates encoding, is inherently selective and has been compared to a filter.

● According to levels-of-processing theory, the kinds of memory codes people create depend on which aspects of a stimulus are emphasized; deeper processing (i.e., semantic encoding) results in better recall of information. Structural, phonemic, and semantic encoding represent progressively deeper and more effective levels of processing.

● Elaboration enriches encoding by linking a stimulus to other information. Visual imagery may work in much the same way, creating two memory codes rather than just one. Encoding that emphasizes personal self-reference may be especially useful in facilitating retention.

Storage: Maintaining Information in Memory

● Sensory memory preserves information in its original form, for only a fraction of a second. Short-term memory has a limited capacity (capable of holding about seven chunks of information) and can maintain unrehearsed information for up to about 20 seconds. Short-term memory is working memory and appears to involve more than a simple rehearsal loop.

● Long-term memory is an unlimited capacity store that may hold information indefinitely. Certain lines of evidence suggest that LTM storage may be permanent, but the evidence is not convincing. Some theorists have raised doubts about whether short-term and long-term memory are really separate.

● Information in LTM can be organized in simple clusters, conceptual hierarchies, or semantic networks. A schema is an organized cluster of knowledge about a particular object or sequence of events. PDP models of memory assert that specific memories correspond to particular patterns of activation in connectionist networks.

Retrieval: Getting Information Out of Memory

● Reinstating the context of an event can facilitate recall. This factor may account for cases in which hypnosis appears to aid recall. Memories are not exact replicas of past experiences. Memory is partially reconstructive.

● Research on the misinformation effect shows that information learned after an event can alter one's memory of it. Source-monitoring and reality-monitoring errors may explain why people sometimes "recall" something that was only suggested to them or something they only imagined.

Forgetting: When Memory Lapses

● Ebbinghaus's early studies of nonsense syllables suggested that people forget very rapidly. Subsequent research showed that Ebbinghaus's forgetting curve was exceptionally steep. Forgetting can be measured by asking people to recall, recognize, or relearn information.

● Decay theory proposes that forgetting occurs spontaneously with the passage of time. It has proven difficult to show that decay occurs in long-term memory. Interference theory proposes that people forget information because of competition from other material.

● Repression involves the motivated forgetting of painful or unpleasant memories. Recent years have seen a surge of reports of repressed memories of sexual abuse in childhood. The authenticity of these recovered memories is the subject of controversy.

In Search of the Memory Trace: The Physiology of Memory

● Memory traces may reflect alterations in neurotransmitter release at specific locations. Memory traces may also consist of localized neural circuits that undergo long-term potentiation. The study of amnesia and other research has implicated the hippocampal region as a key player in memory processes. The hippocampal region may be responsible for the consolidation of memories, but its exact role remains the subject of debate.

Are There Multiple Memory Systems?

● Differences between implicit and explicit memory suggest that people may have several separate memory systems. Declarative memory is memory for facts, whereas nondeclarative or procedural memory is memory for actions and skills. Declarative memory can be subdivided into episodic memory for personal facts, and semantic memory for general facts. Theorists have also distinguished between retrospective and prospective memory.

Putting It in Perspective

● Our discussion of attention and memory enhances understanding of why people's experience of the world is highly subjective. Work in this area also highlights the field's theoretical diversity and shows that behaviour is governed by multiple causes.

Personal Application • Improving Everyday Memory

● Rehearsal, even when it involves overlearning, facilitates retention, although one should be wary of the serial-position effect. Distributed practice tends to be more efficient than massed practice. It is wise to plan study sessions so as to minimize interference. Processing during rehearsal should be deep.

● Meaningfulness can be enhanced with verbal mnemonics such as acrostics, acronyms, and narrative methods. The link method, the method of loci, and the keyword method are mnemonic devices that depend on visual imagery.

Critical Thinking Application • Understanding the Fallibility of Eyewitness Accounts

● Research indicates that eyewitness memory is not nearly as reliable or as accurate as widely believed. Two common errors in thinking that contribute to this situation are the hindsight bias and overconfidence effects. The hindsight bias is the tendency to reshape one's interpretation of the past to fit with known outcomes.

Key Terms

Anterograde amnesia, 295
Attention, 269
Chunk, 275
Clustering, 279
Conceptual hierarchy, 280
Connectionist models, 282
Consolidation, 296
Decay theory, 288
Declarative memory system, 297
Dual-coding theory, 272
Elaboration, 271
Encoding, 268
Encoding specificity principle, 289
Episodic memory system, 298
Explicit memory, 297
Flashbulb memories, 277
Forgetting curve, 286
Hindsight bias, 306
Implicit memory, 297
Interference theory, 288
Keyword method, 303

Levels-of-processing theory, 271
Link method, 303
Long-term memory (LTM), 276
Long-term potentiation (LTP), 294
Method of loci, 303
Mnemonic devices, 301
Nondeclarative memory system, 297
Overlearning, 301
Parallel distributed processing (PDP) models, 282
Proactive interference, 288
Procedural memory system, 297
Prospective memory, 298
Reality monitoring, 285
Recall, 286
Recognition, 286
Rehearsal, 275
Relearning, 287
Repression, 289
Retention, 286
Retrieval, 268

Retroactive interference, 288

Retrograde amnesia, 295

Retrospective memory, 299

Schema, 280

Self-referent encoding, 272

Semantic memory system, 298

Semantic network, 281

Sensory memory, 273

Serial-position effect, 301

Short-term memory (STM), 275

Source monitoring, 285

Source-monitoring error, 285

Storage, 268

Tip-of-the-tongue phenomenon, 282

Transfer-appropriate processing, 289

Key People

Richard Atkinson, 273

Fergus Craik, 270

Hermann Ebbinghaus, 287

Marcia Johnson, 285

Robert Lockhart, 270

Elizabeth Loftus, 284

George Miller, 276

Brenda Milner, 296

Richard Shiffrin, 273

Endel Tulving, 297

PRACTICE TEST

1. Getting information into memory is called _____; getting information out of memory is called _____.
   A. storage; retrieval
   B. encoding; storage
   C. encoding; retrieval
   D. storage; encoding

2. The word *big* is flashed on a screen. A mental picture of the word big represents a _____ code; the definition "large in size" represents a _____ code; "sounds like pig" represents a _____ code.
   A. structural; phonemic; semantic
   B. phonemic; semantic; structural
   C. structural; semantic; phonemic
   D. phonemic; structural; semantic

3. Miles is listening as his mother rattles through a list of 15 or so things that he needs to remember to pack for an upcoming trip. According to George Miller, if Miles doesn't write the items down as he hears them, he will probably remember:
   A. fewer than 5 items from the list.
   B. about 10 to 12 items from the list.
   C. all the items from the list.
   D. 5 to 9 items from the list.

4. Which statement best represents current evidence on the durability of long-term storage?
   A. All forgetting involves breakdowns in retrieval.
   B. LTM is like a barrel of marbles in which none of the marbles ever leak out.
   C. There is no convincing evidence that all one's memories are stored away permanently.
   D. All long-term memories gradually decay at a constant rate.

5. An organized cluster of knowledge about a particular object or event is called a:
   A. semantic network.
   B. conceptual hierarchy.
   C. schema.
   D. retrieval cue.

6. The tip-of-the-tongue phenomenon:
   A. is a temporary inability to remember something you know, accompanied by a feeling that it's just out of reach.
   B. is clearly due to a failure in retrieval.
   C. reflects a permanent loss of information from LTM.
   D. is both a and b.

7. Roberto is telling Rachel about some juicy gossip when she stops him and informs him that she is the one who passed this gossip on to him about a week ago. In this example, Roberto has:
   A. been fooled by the misinformation effect.
   B. made a reality-monitoring error.
   C. made a source-monitoring error.
   D. made a prospective memory error.

8. If decay theory is correct:
   A. information can never be permanently lost from long-term memory.
   B. forgetting is simply a case of retrieval failure.
   C. the principal cause of forgetting should be the passage of time.
   D. all of the above.

9. Bulldog McRae was recently traded to a new football team. He is struggling to remember the plays for his new team because he keeps mixing them up with the plays from his previous team. Bulldog's problem illustrates the operation of:
   A. retroactive interference.

B. proactive interference.
   C. transfer-inappropriate processing.
   D. parallel distributed processing.

10. Many amnesiacs demonstrate _____ memory, even though their _____ memory is extremely impaired.
    A. declarative; procedural
    B. conscious; unconscious
    C. implicit; explicit
    D. semantic; episodic

11. Your memory of how to brush your teeth is contained in your _____ memory.
    A. declarative
    B. procedural
    C. structural
    D. episodic

12. Your knowledge that birds fly, that the sun rises in the east, and that 2 + 2 = 4 is contained in your _____ memory.
    A. structural
    B. procedural
    C. implicit
    D. semantic

13. Dorothy memorized her shopping list. When she got to the store, however, she found she had forgotten many of the items from the middle of the list. This is an example of:
    A. inappropriate encoding.
    B. retrograde amnesia.
    C. proactive interference.
    D. the serial-position effect.

14. Overlearning:
    A. refers to continued rehearsal of material after the point of apparent mastery.
    B. promotes improved recall.
    C. should not be done, since it leads to increased interference.
    D. both a and b.

15. The tendency to mould one's interpretation of the past to fit how events actually turned out is called:
    A. the overconfidence effect.
    B. selective amnesia.
    C. retroactive interference.
    D. the hindsight bias.

See Appendix A for answers to this Practice Test.

CHAPTER 8

Latchezar Boyadjiev, *Conversation,* L.B. Glass Studios

Language: Turning Thoughts into Words
What Is Language?
The Structure of Language
Milestones in Language Development
Featured Study • Babbling in the Manual Mode
Learning More Than One Language: Bilingualism
Can Animals Develop Language?
Language in Evolutionary Context
Theories of Language Acquisition
Culture, Language, and Thought

Problem Solving: In Search of Solutions
Types of Problems
Barriers to Effective Problem Solving
Approaches to Problem Solving
Culture, Cognitive Style, and Problem Solving

Decision Making: Choices and Chances
Making Choices: Selecting an Alternative
Taking Chances: Factors Weighed in Risky Decisions
Heuristics in Judging Probabilities
The Tendency to Ignore Base Rates
The Conjunction Fallacy
Evolutionary Analyses of Flaws in Human Decision Making

Putting It in Perspective

***Personal Application* • Understanding Pitfalls in Reasoning about Decisions**
The Gambler's Fallacy
The Law of Small Numbers
Overestimating the Improbable
Confirmation Bias and Belief Perseverance
The Overconfidence Effect
The Effects of Framing

***Critical Thinking Application* • Shaping Thought with Language: "Only a Naïve Moron Would Believe That"**
Semantic Slanting
Name-Calling

Recap

Practice Test

Language and Thought

On October 17, 1968, Prime Minister Pierre Elliott Trudeau introduced legislation, the Official Languages Bill, which he believed reflected the reality of the Canadian experience and that he hoped would promote Canadian unity in the context of its diversity. He suggested that both French and English should be official languages of Canada. This was essential, he argued, because both language groups were "strong enough in numbers and in material and intellectual resources to resist the forces of assimilation ... this underlying reality of our country has not been adequately reflected in many of our public institutions" (Library and Archives Canada, 2002). The bill became law in July 1969. It manifested the recommendations of an earlier Royal Commission on Bilingualism and Biculturalism (1963) established by then–prime minister and Nobel Prize winner Lester B. Pearson (McRae, 1998). On becoming officially bilingual, Canada joined a small set of countries around the world such as Finland, Sweden, Belgium, South Africa, and Afghanistan that have more than one official language. The themes begun in the Official Languages Bill were continued in the later Canadian Charter of Rights and Freedoms (1982) and the more recent Official Languages Act (1988). The implications of the bill were far reaching—socially, culturally, economically, politically, and educationally.

The opportunity to be educated in either or both of Canada's official languages is now well established. For example, many English-speaking students begin their primary school years not in English but in French, in the context of French immersion programs. Other students are exposed to French through core courses in which the second language is taught as a course for a period during the school day like any other subject. Recent years have seen a slight decline in core French enrollments and an increase in immersion enrollments (Canadian Parents for French, 2004). In the 2002–2003 school year there were 357 000 students in French immersion programs, 1 570 000 students in core French programs, and 560 000 French-speaking children taking English as a second language (Office of the Commissioner of Official Languages, 2004). Interestingly, French immersion

began in Quebec in 1965 when a group of anglophone parents, concerned with the inadequate French language instruction their children were receiving, recommended a program of instruction that formed the basis for current immersion programs (Genesee, 1998). They had sociocultural and economic benefits in mind for their children and Canada.

The motivations underlying and challenges encountered in enrolling children in French immersion are varied and considerable—one of us knows this first-hand, having had children in immersion. While immersion programs will not make you completely bilingual—you are not living full-time in both languages—there are advantages to be derived from bilingualism and immersion education in a second language. Few of us anticipated some of the other potential benefits that might be derived from such experiences. Recent Canadian research by developmental psychologist Ellen Bialystok and

Pierre Elliott Trudeau, prime minister of Canada (1968–1979 and 1980–1984), was a champion of bilingualism.

others suggests that there may be additional cognitive benefits. In addition, a recent Statistics Canada study revealed that French-immersion students outperformed English-only students on literacy scores (Statistics Canada, 2004d). In this chapter we will look more closely at the potential cognitive benefits of bilingualism but before that we will consider the nature of language and language development in children in general. We will have to place the learning of two languages in the context of what we know about how children acquire language more generally.

Of course, bilingualism refers to more than just proficiency in English and French. Many students in Canada also have access to other heritage languages. Overall, however, Canadians are predominantly monolingual. As of 2001, 66% of Canadians knew only one language, 28% knew two, and 6% knew three or more. After English and French, the languages most frequently spoken in Canada are Spanish, German, Italian, Hindi, Arabic, Chinese, Russian, and Hebrew (Office of Commissioner of Official Languages, 2004).

We will also consider the nature of cognition itself, a task we began in Chapter 7. Cognition and language are closely linked, as we will discuss later in the chapter. **Cognition refers to the mental processes involved in acquiring knowledge.** In other words, cognition involves thinking. As we discussed in Chapter 1, the study of cognition has seen peaks and valleys in psychology. When psychology first emerged, it focused on the mind and the research method of choice was *introspection*. But the limitations of that method and the rise of behaviourism, with its focus on observables (have you ever seen a thought?), led to the demise of cognition as a serious scientific topic. It was not until the 1950s that study of cognition came back, an era often referred to as the "cognitive revolution" (Baars, 1986).

Besides memory, which we discussed in Chapter 7, cognitive psychologists investigate the complexities of language, problem solving, decision making, and reasoning. We look at all of these topics in this chapter. Of course, this will not finish our consideration of cognition since it overlaps with many other topics we will deal with later in the book, including developmental psychology (Chapter 11), clinical psychology (Chapter 14), and social psychology (Chapter 16).

Language: Turning Thoughts into Words

PREVIEW QUESTIONS
- What are the four key properties of language?
- How is language structured?
- How do children progress in their use of words and sentences?
- What types of mistakes do they tend to make?
- Does learning two languages at the same time affect language or cognitive development?
- What age is best for learning a second language?

Language obviously plays a fundamental role in human behaviour. Indeed, if you were to ask people, "What characteristic most distinguishes humans from other living creatures?" a great many would reply, "Language." In this section, we'll discuss the nature, structure, and development of language and related topics, such as bilingualism and whether animals can learn language.

What Is Language?

A *language* **consists of symbols that convey meaning, plus rules for combining those symbols, that can be used to generate an infinite variety of messages.** Language systems include a number of critical properties.

First, language is *symbolic*. People use spoken sounds and written words to represent objects, actions, events, and ideas. The word *lamp*, for instance, refers to a class of objects that have certain properties. The symbolic nature of language greatly expands what people can communicate about. Symbols allow one to refer to objects that may be in another place and to events that happened at another time (e.g., a lamp broken at work yesterday). Language symbols are flexible in that a variety of somewhat different objects may be called by the same name (consider the diversity of lamps, for example).

Second, language is *semantic*, or meaningful. The symbols used in a language are arbitrary in that no built-in relationship exists between the look or sound of words and the objects they stand for. Take, for instance, the writing object that you may have in your hand right now. It's represented by the word *pen* in English, *stylo* in French, and *pluma* in Spanish. Although these words are arbitrary (others could have been chosen), they have *shared meanings* for people who speak English, French, and Spanish.

Third, language is *generative*. A limited number of symbols can be combined in an infinite variety of ways to *generate* an endless array of novel messages. Everyone has some "stock sayings," but every day you create sentences that you have never spoken before. You also comprehend many sentences that you have never encountered before (like this one).

Fourth, language is *structured*. Although people can generate an infinite variety of sentences, these sentences must be structured in a limited number of ways. Rules govern the arrangement of words into phrases and sentences; some arrangements are acceptable and some are not. For example, you might say, "The swimmer jumped into the pool," but you would never recombine the same words to say, "Pool the into the jumped swimmer." The structure of language allows people to be inventive with words and still understand each other. Let's take a closer look at the structural properties of language.

The Structure of Language

Human languages have a hierarchical structure (Ratner, Gleason, & Narasimhan, 1998). As Figure 8.1 shows, basic sounds are combined into units with meaning, which are combined into words. Words are combined into phrases, which are combined into sentences.

Phonemes

At the base of the language hierarchy are *phonemes*, **the smallest speech units in a language that can be distinguished perceptually.** Considering that an unabridged English dictionary contains more than 450 000 words, you might imagine that there must be a huge number of phonemes. In fact, linguists estimate that humans are capable of recognizing only about 100 such basic sounds. Moreover, no one language uses all of these phonemes. Different languages use different groups of about 20 to 80 phonemes.

For all its rich vocabulary, the English language is composed of about 40 phonemes, corresponding roughly to the 26 letters of the alphabet plus several variations (see Table 8.1). A letter in the alphabet can represent more than one phoneme if it has more than one pronunciation. For example, the letter *a* is

pronounced differently in the words *father, had, call,* and *take.* Each of these pronunciations corresponds to a different phoneme. In addition, some phonemes are represented by combinations of letters, such as *ch* and *th*. Working with this handful of basic sounds, people can understand and generate all the words in the English language—and invent new ones besides.

Morphemes and Semantics

Morphemes are the smallest units of meaning in a language. There are approximately 50 000 English morphemes, which include root words as well as prefixes and suffixes. Many words, such as *fire, guard,* and *friend,* consist of a single morpheme. Many others represent combinations of morphemes. For example, the word *unfriendly* consists of three morphemes: the root word *friend,* the prefix *un,* and the

Table 8.1 Phonemic Symbols for the Sounds of English

Consonants						Vowels			
/p/	pill	/t/	toe	/g/	gill	/i/	beet	/i/	bit
/b/	bill	/d/	doe	/ŋ/	ring	/e/	bait	/∈/	bet
/m/	mill	/n/	no	/h/	hot	/u/	boot	/ʊ/	foot
/f/	fine	/s/	sink	/?/	uh-oh	/o/	boat	/ɔ/	caught
/v/	vine	/z/	zinc	/l/	low	/æ/	bat	/a/	pot
/θ/	thigh	/č/	choke	/r/	row	/ʌ/	but	/ə/	sofa
/ð/	thy	/ǰ/	joke	/y/	you	/ar/	bite	/au/	out
/š/	shoe	/k/	kill	/w/	win	/ɔɪ/	boy		
/ž/	treasure								

SOURCE: Hoff, E. (2001). *Language development.* Belmont, CA: Wadsworth. Reprinted by permission.

Figure 8.1

An analysis of a simple English sentence. As this example shows, verbal language has a hierarchical structure. At the base of the hierarchy are the *phonemes,* which are units of vocal sound that do not, in themselves, have meaning. The smallest units of meaning in a language are *morphemes,* which include not only root words but also such meaning-carrying units as the past-tense suffix *ed* and the plural *s*. Complex rules of syntax govern how the words constructed from morphemes may be combined into phrases, and phrases into meaningful statements, or sentences.

SOURCE: Clarke-Stewart, A., Friedman, S., & Koch, J. (1985). *Child development: A topical approach* (p. 417). New York: Wiley. Reprinted by permission of John Wiley & Sons, Inc.

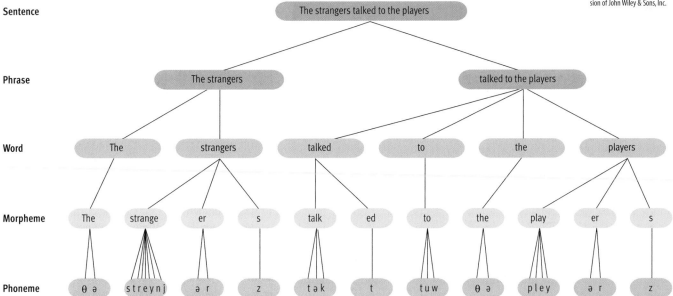

SOURCE: Clarke-Stewart, A., Friedman, S., & Koch, J. (1985). *Child development: A topical approach* (p. 417). New York: Wiley.

suffix *ly*. Each of the morphemes contributes to the meaning of the entire word. **Semantics is the area of language concerned with understanding the meaning of words and word combinations.** Learning about semantics entails learning about the infinite variety of objects and actions that words refer to. A word's meaning may consist of both its *denotation*, which is its dictionary definition, and its *connotation*, which includes its emotional overtones and secondary implications.

Syntax

Of course, most utterances consist of more than a single word. As we've already noted, people don't combine words randomly. ***Syntax* is a system of rules that specify how words can be arranged into sentences.** A simple rule of syntax is that a sentence must have both a *noun phrase* and a *verb phrase*. Thus, "The sound of cars is annoying" is a sentence. However, "The sound of cars" is not a sentence, because it lacks a verb phrase.

Rules of syntax underlie all language use, even though you may not be aware of them. Thus, although they may not be able to verbalize the rule, virtually all

English speakers know that an *article* (such as *the*) comes before the word it modifies. For example, you would never say *swimmer the* instead of *the swimmer*. How children learn the complicated rules of syntax is one of the major puzzles investigated by psychologists interested in language. Like other aspects of language development, children's acquisition of syntax seems to progress at an amazingly rapid pace. Let's look at how this remarkable development unfolds.

Milestones in Language Development

Learning to use language requires learning a number of skills that become important at various points in a child's development (Siegler, 1998). We'll examine this developmental sequence by looking first at how children learn to pronounce words, then at their use of single words, and finally at their ability to combine words to form sentences (see Table 8.2).

Moving toward Producing Words

Three-month-old infants display a surprising language-related talent: They can distinguish phonemes from all the world's languages, including phonemes that they do not hear in their environment. In contrast, adults cannot readily discriminate phonemes that are not used in their native language. Actually, neither can one-year-old children, as this curious ability gradually disappears between four months and 12 months of age (Werker & Desjardins, 1995). The exact mechanisms responsible for this transition are not understood, but it is clear that long before infants utter their first words, they are making remarkable progress in learning the sound structure of their native language. Janet Werker, a senior scientist at the University of British Columbia, has done pioneering work in the development of language in infants. She argues that human infants are well prepared to learn language and that babies have perceptual biases that facilitate and guide the "acquisition of phonology" (Werker, 2003). For example, even at two months they show a tendency to selectively attend more to speech sounds than to complex non-speech analogue sounds (Vouloumanos & Werker, 2004). Some of these perceptual biases that facilitate language acquisition may be derived from listening to speech *in utero*.

Werker argues that there are *optimal periods* for the different subsystems involved in language acquisition but that they are not as rigidly absolute as is sometimes thought (she prefers the term *optimal period* to terms such as *critical period* or *sensitive period*

Table 8.2 Overview of Typical Language Development

Age	General Characteristics
Months	
1–5	*Reflexive communication:* Vocalizes randomly, coos, laughs, cries, engages in vocal play, discriminates language from nonlanguage sounds
6–18	*Babbling:* Verbalizes in response to speech of others; responses increasingly approximate human speech patterns
10–13	*First words:* Uses words; typically to refer to objects
12–18	*One-word sentence stage:* Vocabulary grows slowly; uses nouns primarily; overextensions begin
18–24	*Vocabulary spurt:* Fast mapping facilitates rapid acquisition of new words
Years	
2	*Two-word sentence stage:* Uses telegraphic speech; uses more pronouns and verbs
2.5	*Three-word sentence stage:* Modifies speech to take listener into account; overregularizations begin
3	Uses complete simple active sentence structure; uses sentences to tell stories that are understood by others; uses plurals
3.5	*Expanded grammatical forms:* Expresses concepts with words; uses four-word sentences
4	Uses imaginary speech; uses five-word sentences
5	*Well-developed and complex syntax:* Uses more complex syntax; uses more complex forms to tell stories
6	Displays metalinguistic awareness

NOTE: Children often show individual differences in the exact ages at which they display the various developmental achievements outlined here.

because the latter imply more invariance in the onset and offset of the periods; Werker & Tees, 2005). Thus, while very young infants can discriminate even phonemes not inherent in their language context, without exposure, this facility disappears. As they develop through the first year of life, the language acquisition systems of the infant become tuned to the speech properties of their native language. Recently Werker has developed a model of infant speech processing called PRIMIR (Processing Rich Information from Multidimensional Interactive Representations; Werker & Curtin, 2005).

Progress toward understanding words also occurs during the first year. By 7.5 months, infants begin to recognize common word forms (Jusczyk & Hohne, 1997), and by eight months many infants show the first signs of understanding the meanings of familiar words (Fenson et al., 1994).

During the first six months of life, a baby's vocalizations are dominated by crying, cooing, and laughter, which have limited value as a means of communication. Soon, infants are *babbling,* producing a wide variety of sounds that correspond to phonemes and, eventually, many repetitive consonant–vowel combinations, such as "lalalalalala." Babbling gradually becomes more complex and increasingly resembles the language spoken by parents and others in the child's environment (De Boysson-Bardies & Vihman, 1991). These trends probably reflect ongoing neural development and the maturation of the infant's vocal apparatus (Sachs, 1985), as well as the impact of experience (Kuhl & Meltzoff, 1997). Babbling lasts until around 18 months, continuing even after children utter their first words. According to Laura-Ann Petitto, who worked on babbling and language acquisition while she was at McGill University, babbling is considered to be one of the monumental milestones in language acquisition (Pettito et al., 2004). Interestingly, Petitto began her scientific work on language working with chimps. She lived with a chimpanzee while trying to teach it American Sign Language (National Institute on Deafness, 2004).

Janet Werker, Canada Research Chair in Psychology at the University of British Columbia, examines early processes involved in the acquisition of languages in infants. She was elected as a fellow of the Royal Society of Canada in 2001.

© Photo by: Christiane Dietrich. Photo courtesy of Janet Werker.

While most agree that babbling is a universal stage in language acquisition, there is considerable disagreement about its origins. One view is that babbling is a motor achievement in which the babbling reflects the brain's maturation in controlling the motor operations needed to eventually produce speech—in essence, developing and practising the mechanics of speech. Here, the babbling is a byproduct of the development of the brain and its control over motor operations. An alternative view is that it is a key linguistic achievement, a mechanism that affords the infant the opportunity to both discover and produce the "patterned structure of natural language" (Petitto et al., 2004, p. 44). Thus, babbling allows the infant to acquire the basics of language. Petitto and her colleagues have conducted a series of studies that support the latter interpretation. Some of these studies were conducted in Montreal with normal and deaf babies. Pettito found that the deaf babies exhibited "manual babbling"—babbling with their hands in a manner similar to the verbal babbling of hearing babies (Petitto & Marentette, 1991). She also found that the deaf babies' first "signed words" were continuous with their babbling—much like a baby who verbally babbles "bababa" and whose first word is "baby" (Vihman, 1985). This study is the focus of our Featured Study.

Babbling in the Manual Mode

FEATURED STUDY

The authors begin by reviewing the importance of babbling in the infant's language development and the prevailing view that babbling is a function of the continuing maturation of both the vocal tract and the neurophysiological mechanisms that are related to the mechanical production of speech. The authors support an alternative view; one that sees babbling as a function of the developing language capacity of the infant. Thus,

babbling doesn't reflect so much the developing motor portions of the brain but rather reflects the maturation of the language capacity controlled by the brain. They note that it is difficult to test which view is the more correct one. They offered an innovative solution: There are complex and sophisticated language forms that don't depend on speech, such as American Sign Language, a language form used by the deaf. Their hypothesis was

Investigators: Laura-Ann Petitto (McGill University) and Paula F. Marentette (McGill University)

Source: Babbling in the manual mode: Evidence for the ontogeny of language. *Science*, 1991, *251*, pp. 1493–1496.

"If babbling is due to the maturation of a language capacity and the articulatory mechanisms responsible for speech production, then it should be specific to speech. However, if babbling is due to the maturation of a brain-based language capacity and an expressive capacity capable of processing different types of signals, then it should occur in spoken and signed language modalities" (p. 1493).

Method. The participants in this research consisted of five infants: two profoundly deaf infants of deaf parents acquiring American Sign Language as a first language, and three hearing infants acquiring spoken language. Each was tested and videotaped at 10, 12, and 14 months. All acoustic forms and sounds (for the hearing children) and manual activities (for the deaf children) were transcribed/videotaped and analyzed. To count as babbling, the same criteria were applied to the hearing and deaf children's utterances. For example, all utterances (vocal/hearing, manual/deaf) that were not words were examined for systematic organization. If this was found, further analysis was conducted to determine if the organization had phonetic and syllabic features common to spoken languages.

Results. The analysis of the babbling of the infants was clear. While all infants moved their arms and hands and gestured about, only the deaf infants showed evidence of manual babbling. The results for manual babbling are shown in Figure 8.2. The manual babbling accounted for 32% to 71% of the manual activity of the deaf infants but only 4% to 15% of the hearing children. The manual babbling of the deaf infants demonstrated most of the other properties demonstrated by the hearing children in their babbling. For example, the deaf infants progressed through a similar set of babbling

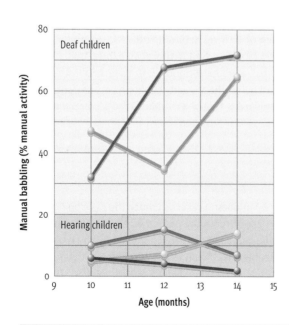

Figure 8.3

Handshape primes The 13 handshape primes produced by the deaf children in their manual babbling. The handshape A4 does not occur in adult ASL; it is a possible but nonexistent phrase.

Source: Petitto, L.-A., and Marentette, P. F., Babbling in the manual mode: Evidence for the ontogeny of language. *Science*, 1991, *251*, p. 1494. Reprinted with permission from *Science*, Babbling in the Manual Mode: Evidence for the Ontogeny of Language, Vol. 251, p. 1496. Copyright © 1991 AAAS.

stages as was observed for hearing babies and at the same time course. As with hearing babies, the babbling used by the deaf infants used only a subset of the possible phonetic units available in the language (American Sign Language). These are shown in Figure 8.3.

Discussion

The results of the study were quite convincing and clear. Deaf infants who are exposed to sign language babble like hearing babies, but they babble manually in their own language form. This suggests the conclusion that babbling is not simply a function of development of motor mechanisms but is instead tied to the developing language capacity of the infant.

Comment

This research was featured because it provides an interesting and convincing demonstration of one of the milestones of language development, babbling. It is a highly innovative study using a novel procedure to test some of the ideas underlying the nature and meaning of babbling. It is a very significant study in the area and was published in the highly prestigious journal *Science*. ■

Figure 8.2

Manual babbling Manual babbling as a percentage of manual activity [manual babbling/(manual babbling + gesture)]. The required ratio is 20% (line) syllabic to total vocal utterances for children to be classed in the syllabic vocal babbling stage of language acquisition (7). The deaf children met and surpassed this ratio in their manual babbling, but the hearing children did not. Each line represents the manual babbling of one child in the study.

Source: Petitto, L.-A., and Marentette, P.F., Babbling in the manual mode: Evidence for the ontogeny of language. *Science*, 1991, *251*, p. 1494.

Recently, Petitto has been examining what she refers to as an "island of tissue" in the brain that may trigger language development in children and the parts of the brain responsible for processing activities related to signed languages (Petitto, 1994) in the brain (American Psychological Association, 1998; Petitto et al., 2000). Petitto is now chair of the Department of Education at Dartmouth College and Professor of psychological and brain sciences.

At around 10 to 13 months of age, most children begin to utter sounds that correspond to words. Most infants' first words are similar in phonetic form and meaning—even in different languages (Gleason & Ratner, 1998). The initial words resemble the syllables that infants most often babble spontaneously. For example, words such as *dada, mama,* and *papa* are names for parents in many languages because they consist of sounds that are easy to produce.

Using Words

After children utter their first words, their vocabulary grows slowly for the next few months (Barrett, 1995). Toddlers typically can say between 3 and 50 words by 18 months. However, their *receptive vocabulary* is larger than their *productive vocabulary*. That is, they can comprehend more words spoken by others than they can actually produce to express themselves (Dan & Gleason, 2001). Thus, toddlers can *understand* 50 words months before they can *say* 50 words. Toddlers' early words tend to refer most often to *objects* and secondarily to familiar *actions* (Menyuk, Liebergott, & Schultz, 1995). Children generally acquire nouns before verbs because the meanings of nouns, which often refer to distinct, concrete objects, tend to be easier to encode than the meanings of verbs, which often refer to more abstract relationships (Gentner & Rattermann, 1991). However, this generalization may not apply to all languages (Bates, Devescovi, & Wulfeck, 2001).

Youngsters' vocabularies soon begin to grow at a dizzying pace, as a *vocabulary spurt* often begins at around 18–24 months (Bates & Carnevale, 1993; see Figure 8.4). By the first grade, the average child has a vocabulary of approximately 10 000 words, which builds to an astonishing 40 000 words by the fifth grade (Anglin, 1993; see Figure 8.5). In building these impressive vocabularies, some two-year-olds learn as many as 20 new words every week. *Fast mapping* appears to be one factor underlying this rapid growth of vocabulary (Markman, Wasow, & Hansen, 2003). **Fast mapping is the process by which children map a word onto an underlying concept after only one exposure.** Thus, children often add words like *tank, board,* and *tape* to their vocabularies

after their first encounter with objects that illustrate these concepts. The vocabulary spurt may be attributable to children's improved articulation skills, improved understanding of syntax, underlying cognitive development, or some combination of these factors (MacWhinney, 1998).

Of course, these efforts to learn new words are not flawless. Toddlers often make errors, such as overextensions and underextensions (Dan & Gleason, 2001). **An *overextension* occurs when a child incorrectly uses a word to describe a wider set of objects or actions than it is meant to.** For example, a child might use the word *ball* for anything round—oranges, apples, even the moon. Overextensions usually appear in children's speech between ages one and two-and-a-half. Specific overextensions typically last up to several months. Toddlers also tend to be guilty of *underextensions,* which occur when a child

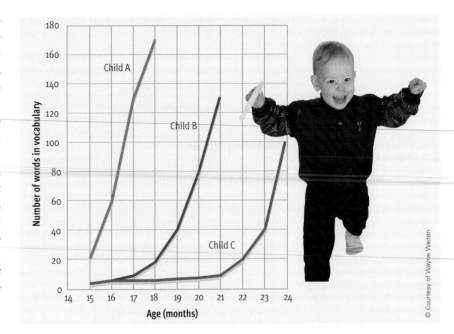

Figure 8.4

The vocabulary spurt.
Children typically acquire their first 10–15 words very slowly, but they soon go through a vocabulary spurt—a period during which they rapidly acquire many new words. The vocabulary spurt usually begins at around 18–24 months, but children vary, as these graphs of three toddlers' vocabulary growth show.

SOURCE: Adapted from Goldfield, B. A., & Resnick, J. S. (1990). Early lexical acquisition: Rate, content, and the vocabulary spurt. *Journal of Child Language, 17,* 171–183. Copyright © 1990 by Cambridge University Press. Adapted by permission. Photo: Courtesy of Wayne Weiten

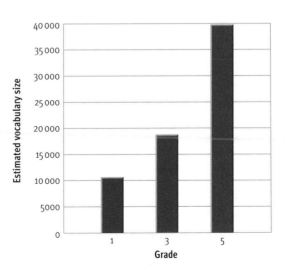

Figure 8.5

The growth of school children's vocabulary.
Vocabulary growth is rapid during the early years of grade school. Youngsters' estimated vocabulary doubles about every two years between grade 1 and grade 5.

SOURCE: Anglin, J. M. (1993). Vocabulary development: A morphological analysis. *Child Development, 58,* Serial 238. Copyright © 1993 The Society for Research in Child Development. Reprinted by permission.

incorrectly uses a word to describe a narrower set of objects or actions than it is meant to. For example, a child might use the word *doll* to refer only to a single, favourite doll. Overextensions and underextensions show that toddlers are actively trying to learn the rules of language—albeit with mixed success.

Combining Words

Children typically begin to combine words into sentences near the end of their second year. Early sentences are characterized as "telegraphic" because they resemble telegrams. *Telegraphic speech consists mainly of content words; articles, prepositions, and other less critical words are omitted.* Thus, a child might say "Give doll" rather than "Please give me the doll." Although not unique to the English language, telegraphic speech is not cross-culturally universal, as once thought (de Villiers & de Villiers, 1992).

Researchers sometimes track language development by keeping tabs on subjects' *mean length of utterance (MLU)—the average length of youngsters' spoken statements (measured in morphemes).* After children grow and begin to combine words, their vocal expressions gradually become longer (Hoff, 2005).

By the end of their third year, most children can express complex ideas such as the plural or the past tense. However, their efforts to learn the rules of language continue to generate revealing mistakes. *Overregularizations occur when grammatical rules are incorrectly generalized to irregular cases where they do not apply.* For example, children will say things like "The girl goed home" or "I hitted the ball." Cross-cultural research suggests that these overregularizations occur in all languages (Slobin, 1985). Most theorists believe that overregularizations demonstrate that children are working actively

to master the *rules* of language (Marcus, 1996). Children don't learn the fine points of grammar and usage in a single leap but gradually acquire them in small steps.

Refining Language Skills

Youngsters make their largest strides in language development in their first four to five years. However, they continue to refine their language skills during their school-age years. They generate longer and more complicated sentences as they receive formal training in written language.

As their language skills develop, school-age children begin to appreciate ambiguities in language. They can, for instance, recognize two possible meanings in sentences such as "Visiting relatives can be bothersome." This interest in ambiguities indicates that they're developing *metalinguistic awareness— the ability to reflect on the use of language.* As metalinguistic awareness grows, children begin to "play" with language, coming up with puns and jokes. They begin to make more frequent and sophisticated use of metaphors, such as "We were packed in the room like sardines" (Gentner, 1988). They also learn to recognize hidden meanings often found in everyday discourse, such as sarcastic comments (Capelli, Nakagawa, & Madden, 1990; Katz, Blasko, & Kazmerski, 2004).

Learning More Than One Language: Bilingualism

Given the complexities involved in acquiring one language, you may be wondering about the ramifications of being asked to learn *two* languages. *Bilingualism is the acquisition of two languages that use different speech sounds, vocabulary, and grammatical rules.* Although not the norm in North America, bilingualism is quite common in Europe and many other regions, and nearly half of the world's population grows up bilingual (Hakuta, 1986; Snow, 1998). One assumption that some people have is that bilingualism hampers language development and has a negative impact on youngsters' educational progress. But does the empirical evidence support this assumption? Let's take a look at the research on bilingualism.

Does Learning Two Languages in Childhood Slow Down Language Development?

If youngsters are learning two languages simultaneously, does one language interfere with the other so that the acquisition of both is impeded? Given the

Web Link 8.1

John Lawler's Homepage (Linguistics & Language)

http://www-personal.umich.edu/~jlawler/index.html

University of Michigan linguistics professor John Lawler has constructed a seemingly endless guide to Internet resources for the study of linguistics and language, a field allied with psychology. His homepage is a goldmine of references and guides.

CONCEPT **CHECK 8.1**

Tracking Language Development

Check your understanding of how language skills progress in youngsters. Number the utterances below to indicate the developmental sequence in which they would probably occur. The answers can be found in Appendix A in the back of the book.

_____ **1.** "Doggie," while pointing to a cow.

_____ **2.** "The dogs runned away."

_____ **3.** "Doggie run."

_____ **4.** "The dogs ran away."

_____ **5.** "Doggie," while pointing to a dog.

_____ **6.** "Tommy thinks like his head is full of mashed potatoes."

far-reaching sociopolitical implications of this question, you might guess that many relevant studies have been conducted, but in reality there is only a modest body of research. Some studies *have* found that bilingual children have smaller vocabularies in each of their languages than monolingual children have in their one language (Umbel et al., 1992). But when their two overlapping vocabularies are added, their total vocabulary is similar or slightly superior to that of children learning a single language (Oller & Pearson, 2002). Laura Petitto, whose research we looked at in our discussion of babbling, has studied children acquiring English and French and children acquiring French and the sign language "Langues des Signes Québécoise" (Petitto et al., 2001). She concluded that there was little evidence of language disadvantage. The bilingual children followed the normal pacing of language milestones, except in this case it was accomplished in *both* languages. Children seem to be adept at differentiating between the two languages before their first words appear (Petitto & Kovelman, 2003). Taken as a whole, the available evidence suggests that bilingual and monolingual children are largely similar in the course and rate of their language development (de Houwer, 1995; Nicoladis & Genesee, 1997). Thus, although more research is needed, so far there is little empirical support for the assumption that bilingualism has a negative effect on language development (Hoff, 2005).

Does Bilingualism Affect Cognitive Processes and Skills?

Does knowing two languages make thinking more difficult, or could bilingualism enhance thought processes? Once again the evidence is mixed, depending on the variables measured and the exact nature of the subject populations that are compared. On some types of tasks, bilinguals may have a slight disadvantage in terms of raw language-processing *speed* (Taylor & Taylor, 1990). When middle-class bilingual subjects who are fluent in both languages are studied, they tend to score somewhat *higher* than monolingual subjects on measures of cognitive flexibility, analytical reasoning, selective attention, and metalinguistic awareness (Bialystok, 1999; Campbell & Sais, 1995; Lambert, 1990). Ellen Bialystok of York University has been examining the effects of bilingualism on children's cognition for many years. She suggests that there are some cognitive advantages to bilingualism. At the beginning of this chapter, we reported on a recent study by Statistics Canada linking enrollment in French immersion with enhanced literacy scores. Bialystok has found that bilingualism is asso-

ciated with higher levels of controlled processing (Bialystok, 2001) on tasks that require control of attention. That is, bilingual children demonstrate greater facility at tasks where there is some type of misleading/distracting information and where response choice is involved. According to Bialystok, some of the processes implicated in these differences between bilingual and monolingual children are those involving selective attention, attentional inhibition to distracting/misleading information, and switching among competing alternatives. Bilingual children don't have an advantage on all tasks; they show an advantage on some aspects of metalinguistic awareness but not for phonemic awareness (Bialystok, Majunder, & Martin, 2003). Bilingual and monolingual children perform similarly on tasks involving representational processes such as encoding problems in sufficient detail and gaining access to relevant information (Bialystok, 1991).

Overall, this research suggests that while bilingualism may not confer an advantage in all aspects of cognitive and linguistic processing, it is important to note that there are some documented advantages and few demonstrated disadvantages—even for children with some specific language impairments, as was found in a recent study by Johanne Paradis from the University of Alberta (Paradis et al., 2003), or those with more general below-average ability levels (Genesee, 2004). Another consideration is derived from the results of some of Bialystok's most recent work on bilingualism and aging conducted with a team of psychologists from York University, Dalhousie University, and the University of Toronto (Bialystok et al., 2004). Here Bialystok and her colleagues found that the advantage conferred by bilingualism on controlled processing persists into adulthood and old age, suggesting that bilingualism may help attenuate age-related losses in certain aspects of cognition. She notes that one of the objectives of the research was to determine if bilingualism "would provide a defense against the decline of these executive processes that occurs with normal cognitive aging…. the present results suggest that it does" (Bialystok et al., 2004, p. 301).

Bilingualism and the processes of second language acquisition continue to be important research topics in Canada. One of the centres of research on this topic continues to be McGill University. McGill scholars, for example, were involved from the beginning in the development of French immersion in Canada. McGill psychologist Wallace Lambert worked closely with the parent group in St. Lambert, a suburb of Montreal, that we discussed at the beginning of the chapter. The project also secured the support and encouragement of Wilder Penfield, the internationally known neuroscientist we discussed in Chapter 3. The program that was developed began on an experimental basis in the South Shore Protestant Regional School Board in 1965. The initial experimental project followed two classes of English-speaking children from kindergarten to grade 1. You can find a fascinating account of the project in Lambert and Tucker's (1969) book *Bilingual Education in Canada*. Lambert was awarded the Donald O. Hebb Award from the Canadian Psychological Association in 1984 and is one of the most influential scholars in the social psychology of language in the world (Reynolds, 1991). McGill University has recently established a new and innovative interdisciplinary Ph.D. program in language acquisition (*McGill Reporter*, 2001). The current director is Fred Genessee, who was a Ph.D. student of one of Lambert's early Ph.D. students.

It is important to note that literacy and cognitive flexibility are not the only benefits to be derived from second language immersion. As Bialystok states, "The development of two languages in childhood turns out to be a profound event that ripples through the life of that individual" (Bialystok, 2001, p. 248). While there are many potential positive benefits to an educational experience in which the child is immersed in a second language, some cautions are also notable in certain circumstances, especially in the case of minority students. Research by Stephen Wright of Simon Fraser University and his colleagues with Inuit, white, and mixed-heritage children living in the sub-Arctic has shown that education of minority children exclusively in the majority language (i.e., English) may undermine both self-esteem and heritage language (i.e., Inuktitut) proficiency (Wright & Taylor, 1995; Wright, Taylor, & Macarthur, 2000). Exposure to the heritage language in an education setting can serve to reverse these effects.

What Factors Influence the Acquisition of a Second Language?

A great many bilingual individuals do not learn their two languages simultaneously. Rather, they learn their native language first and then learn a second language later. Do any key considerations influence the learning of a second language? Yes, the evidence clearly indicates that *age* is a significant correlate of how effectively people can acquire a second language—and younger is better. For example, Figure 8.6, from a study by Johnson and Newport (1989), maps out the relationship between immigrants' age of arrival in the United States and their subsequent mastery of English

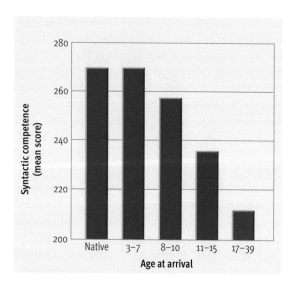

Figure 8.6

Age and second language learning. In a study of how well immigrants to the United States master English as a second language, Johnson and Newport (1989) examined the relationship between the subjects' age of arrival and their mastery of syntax. As you can see, it was advantageous to start learning English at an earlier age, up through about age 15. After that, age of arrival did not make a difference. For example, those who started at 20 were no better off than those who started at 30. (Data from Johnson & Newport, 1989)

grammar. As you can see, people who started learning English at an early age achieved greater mastery than those who began later. For reasons that are not well understood, language learning unfolds more effectively when initiated prior to age seven, and younger continues to be better up through age 15. Older children and adults can certainly become proficient in a second language, but only a small minority become as proficient as native speakers are (Birdsong, 1999; Hakuta, Bialystok, & Wiley, 2003).

A second factor that influences the acquisition of a second language is *acculturation*—**the degree to which a person is socially and psychologically integrated into a new culture.** As you might guess, greater acculturation facilitates more rapid acquisition of the new culture's language (Schumann, 1978, 1993). This finding highlights the fact that language learning is more than a purely cognitive process. Language is a communication tool that is used in varied social contexts. Moreover, language lies at the very core of a nation's culture, which is probably why the debate about bilingualism has been so vigorous.

A third set of factors affecting second language learning relates to the learner's motivation and attitude toward the other group that uses the language to be learned. Wallace Lambert (1967) and his colleagues and students, including Robert Gardner of the University of Western Ontario, Donald Taylor of McGill, Richard Clément of the University of Ottawa, and Richard Lalonde of York University, have examined the role played by these factors in the learning of, among other things, both French and English (and even statistics) as a second language. In this research begun in 1956 with Gardner's master's thesis, they found that second language learning—in this case French—was associated both with language aptitude and what they termed *integrative motivation*, defined as a "willingness to be like valued members of the language community" (Gardner & Lambert, 1959). Subsequent research suggests that second language learning depends on factors other than just an aptitude for language learning—social psychological factors such as a positive attitude toward the learning situation and an interest in the other language group (i.e., integrativeness) serve to promote the learner's motivation to acquire the second language and facilitate language acquisition (Clément, 1987; Gardner, 2000; Lambert, 1967; Lalonde & Gardner, 1984, 1993). These "social psychological" factors that have been found to affect second language acquisition are particularly important considerations in Canada given the history of French–English relations over the past few decades.

In any event, we turn next to another vigorous debate about language acquisition—the debate over whether animals can learn language.

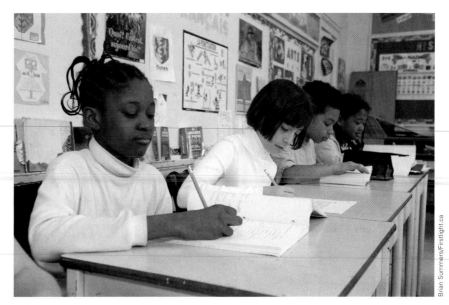

The utility of bilingual education programs has been a hotly debated issue across Canada. Critics argue that bilingualism has a negative effect on children's language and cognitive development, but there is relatively little empirical support for this assertion. Recent research suggests that bilingualism may have some cognitive benefits.

REVIEW OF KEY POINTS

- Languages are symbolic, semantic, generative, and structured. Human languages are structured hierarchically. At the bottom of the hierarchy are the basic sound units, called phonemes. At the next level are morphemes, the smallest units of meaning.

- The initial vocalizations by infants are similar across languages, but their babbling gradually begins to resemble the sounds from their surrounding language. Children typically utter their first words around their first birthday. Vocabulary growth is slow at first, but a vocabulary spurt often begins at around 18–24 months.

- Most children begin to combine words by the end of their second year. Their early sentences are telegraphic, in that they omit many nonessential words. Over the next several years, children gradually learn the complexities of syntax.

- Research does not support the assumption that bilingualism has a negative effect on language development or on cognitive development. The learning of a second language is facilitated by starting at a younger age and by acculturation.

Can Animals Develop Language?

Can other species besides humans develop language? Although this issue does not have the practical, sociopolitical repercussions of the debate about bilingualism, it has intrigued researchers for many decades and led to some fascinating research. Scientists have taught some language-like skills to a number of species, including dolphins (Herman, Kuczaj, & Holder, 1993), sea lions (Schusterman & Gisiner, 1988), and an African gray parrot (Pepperberg, 1993, 2002), but their greatest success has come with the chimpanzee, an intelligent primate widely regarded as humans' closest cousin.

In early studies, researchers tried to teach chimps to *speak* (Hayes & Hayes, 1951). However, investigators quickly concluded that chimps simply didn't have the appropriate vocal apparatus to acquire human speech. But is speech the only way to use language? Of course not. At this moment you're reading a written expression of language.

Like speech, writing may not be a realistic form of communication for chimps, but researchers have tried training chimps to use a nonoral human language: American Sign Language (ASL). ASL is a complex language of hand gestures and facial expressions used by thousands of deaf people. The first effort of this sort was begun by Allen and Beatrice Gardner (1967), who worked with a chimp named Washoe. The Gardners approached the task as if Washoe were a deaf child. They signed to her regularly, rewarded her imitations, and taught her complex signs by

PREVIEW QUESTIONS
- What kind of progress has been made in teaching animals language?
- What is the evolutionary significance of language?
- Do humans have an innate facility for learning language?
- Does language shape thought?

Brian Summers/Firstlight.ca

"What Kanzi tells us is that humans are not the only species that can acquire language if exposed to it at an early age."

SUE SAVAGE-RUMBAUGH

physically moving her hands through the required motions. In four years, Washoe acquired a sign vocabulary of roughly 160 words. She learned to combine these words into simple sentences, such as "Washoe sorry," "Gimme flower," and "More fruit."

Although these accomplishments were impressive, critics expressed doubts about whether Washoe and the other chimps that learned ASL had really acquired language skills. For example, Herbert Terrace (1986) argued that these chimps showed little evidence of mastering *rules* of language. According to Terrace, the chimps' sentences were the products of imitation and operant conditioning, rather than spontaneous generations based on linguistic rules.

In more recent years, Sue Savage-Rumbaugh and her colleagues have reported some striking advances with *bonobo pygmy chimpanzees* that have fuelled additional debate (Lyn & Savage-Rumbaugh, 2000; Savage-Rumbaugh, 1991; Savage-Rumbaugh, Shanker, & Taylor, 1998). In this line of research, the bonobos have been trained to communicate with their caretakers by touching geometric symbols that represent words on a computer-monitored keyboard. Savage-Rumbaugh's star pupil has been a chimp named Kanzi, although many of his feats have been duplicated by his younger sister, Panbanisha. Kanzi has acquired hundreds of words and has used them in thousands of combinations. Many of these combinations were spontaneous and seemed to follow rules of language. For example, to specify whether he wanted to chase or be chased, Kanzi had to differentiate

between symbol combinations in a way that appeared to involve the use of grammatical rules.

As the years went by, Kanzi's trainers noticed that he often seemed to understand the normal utterances that they exchanged with each other. Hence, they began to systematically evaluate his comprehension of spoken English. At age nine, they tested his understanding of 660 sentences that directed Kanzi to execute simple actions, such as "Put the collar in the water." To make sure that he really *understood* the sentences, they included many novel constructions in which the actions were not obvious given the objects involved, such as "Put the raisins in the shoe," or "Go get the balloon that's in the microwave." Kanzi correctly carried out 72% of the 660 requests. Moreover, he demonstrated remarkable understanding of sentence structure, as he could reliably distinguish the actions requested by "Pour the Coke in the lemonade," as opposed to "Pour the lemonade in the Coke."

How have the linguistics experts reacted to Kanzi's surprising progress in language development? Many remain skeptical (Budiansky, 2004; Wynne, 2004) about whether Kanzi's communications demonstrate all the basic properties of a language (Kako, 1999; Seidenberg & Petitto, 1987; Wallman, 1992). Yet, even *critics* such as Kako (1999) acknowledge that "Kanzi clearly comprehends more than just the words in these sentences: He comprehends both the words *and* their relations to one another, as specified by the structure" (p. 10). Overall, it seems reasonable to conclude that the ability to use language may *not* be unique to humans, as has been widely assumed.

However, even if language is *not* unique to humans, they do appear to be exceptionally well suited for learning language. There's no comparison between human linguistic abilities and those of apes or other animals. As remarkable as the language studies with apes are, they should make us marvel even more at the fluency, flexibility, and complexity of human language. A normal human toddler quickly surpasses even the most successfully trained chimps. In mastering language, children outstrip chimps the way jet airplanes outrace horse-drawn buggies. Why are humans so well suited for learning language? According to some theorists, this talent for language is a product of evolution. Let's look at their thinking.

Language in Evolutionary Context

All human societies depend on complex language systems. Even primitive cultures employ languages that are just as complicated as those used in modern

Kanzi, a pygmy chimpanzee, has learned to communicate with his caretakers in surprisingly sophisticated ways via computer-controlled symbol boards, thus raising some doubt about whether language is unique to humans.

societies. The universal nature of language suggests that it is an innate human characteristic. Consistent with this view, Steven Pinker argues that humans' special talent for language is a species-specific trait that is the product of natural selection (Pinker, 1994, 2004; Pinker & Jackendoff, 2005). Pinker, who was born in Montreal and obtained his undergraduate degree in psychology from McGill University, is one of the world's foremost authorities on language and language acquisition. According to Pinker, language is a valuable means of communication that has enormous adaptive value. As Pinker and Bloom (1992) point out, "There is an obvious advantage in being able to acquire information about the world secondhand … one can avoid having to duplicate the possibly time-consuming and dangerous trial-and-error process that won that knowledge" (p. 460). Dunbar (1996) argues that language evolved as a device to build and maintain social coalitions in increasingly larger groups. Although the impetus for the evolution of language remains a matter of speculation, it does not take much imagination to envision how more-effective communication among our ancient ancestors could have aided hunting, gathering, fighting, mating, and the avoidance of poisons, predators, and other dangers.

Although the adaptive value of language seems obvious, some scholars take issue with the assertion that human language is the product of evolution. For example, David Premack (1985) has expressed skepticism that small differences in language skill would influence reproductive fitness in primitive societies where all one had to communicate about was the location of the closest mastodon herd. In an effort to refute this argument, Pinker and Bloom (1992) point out that very small adaptive disparities are sufficient to fuel evolutionary change. For example, they cite an estimate that a 1% difference in mortality rates among overlapping Neanderthal and human populations could have led to the extinction of Neanderthals in just 30 generations. They also note that a trait variation that produces on average just 1% more offspring than its alternative genetic expression would increase in prevalence from 0.1% to 99.9% of the population in 4000 generations. Four thousand generations may seem like an eternity, but in the context of evolution, it is a modest amount of time. Recently, Pinker (2003) has argued that it is likely that there are many genes for language and he suggests that new genes will be discovered that account for language disorders and individual variation in language. He suggests language may represent an adaptation for the "communication of knowledge and intentions" (Pinker & Jackendoff, 2005).

Whether or not evolution gets the credit, language acquisition in humans seems remarkably rapid. As you will see in the next section, this reality looms large in theories of language acquisition.

Theories of Language Acquisition

Since the 1950s, a great debate has raged about the key processes involved in language acquisition. As with arguments we have seen in other areas of psychology, this one centres on the *nature versus nurture* issue. The debate was stimulated by the influential behaviourist B. F. Skinner (1957), who argued that environmental factors govern language development. His provocative analysis brought a rejoinder from Noam Chomsky (1959), who emphasized biological determinism. Let's examine their views and subsequent theories that stake out a middle ground.

Behaviourist Theories

The behaviourist approach to language was first outlined by Skinner in his book *Verbal Behavior* (1957). He argued that children learn language the same way they learn everything else: through imitation, reinforcement, and other established principles of conditioning. According to Skinner, vocalizations that are not reinforced gradually decline in frequency. The remaining vocalizations are shaped with reinforcers until they are correct. Behaviourists assert that by controlling reinforcement, parents encourage their children to learn the correct meaning and pronunciation of words (Staats & Staats, 1963). For example, as children grow older, parents may insist on closer and closer approximations of the word *water* before supplying the requested drink.

Behavioural theorists also use the principles of imitation and reinforcement to explain how children learn syntax. According to the behaviourists' view, children learn how to construct sentences by imitating the sentences of adults and older children. If children's imitative statements are understood, parents are able to answer their questions or respond to their requests, thus reinforcing their verbal behaviour.

Nativist Theories

Skinner's explanation of language acquisition soon inspired a critique and rival explanation from Noam Chomsky (1959, 1965). Chomsky pointed out that there are an infinite number of sentences in a language. It's therefore unreasonable to expect that children learn language by imitation. For example, in English, we add *ed* to the end of a verb to construct past tense. Children routinely overregularize this rule, producing incorrect verbs such as *goed*,

"*If human language is unique in the modern animal kingdom, as it appears to be, the implications for a Darwinian account of its evolution would be as follows: none. A language instinct unique to modern humans poses no more of a paradox than a trunk unique to modern elephants.*"
STEVEN PINKER

Even at low levels of intelligence, at pathological levels, we find a command of language that is totally unattainable by an ape.
NOAM CHOMSKY

eated, and *thinked.* Mistakes such as these are inconsistent with Skinner's emphasis on imitation, because most adult speakers don't use ungrammatical words like *goed.* Children can't imitate things they don't hear. According to Chomsky, children learn *the rules of language,* not specific verbal responses, as Skinner proposed.

Critics have also challenged the behaviourist position that children learn to construct correct sentences through reinforcement. An influential study by Brown and Hanlon (1970) indicated that parents typically respond to meaning and factual accuracy in their youngsters' speech rather than to grammar. Thus, a mother curling her daughter's hair probably won't correct the ungrammatical statement "Her curl my hair," because it is factually accurate. In other words, parents may not engage in much of the language shaping that is critical to the behavioural explanation of language development (Maratsos, 1983; Pinker, 1990).

An alternative theory favoured by Chomsky and others is that humans have an inborn or "native" propensity to develop language (Chomsky, 1975, 1986; Crain, 1991; McNeill, 1970). In this sense, *native* is a variation on the word *nature* as it's used in the nature versus nurture debate. *Nativist theory* proposes that humans are equipped with a **language acquisition device (LAD)—an innate mechanism or process that facilitates the learning of language.** According to this view, humans learn language for the same reason that birds learn to fly—because they're biologically equipped for it. The exact nature of the LAD has not been spelled out in nativist theories. It presumably consists of brain structures and neural wiring that leave humans well prepared to discriminate among phonemes, to fast-map morphemes, to acquire rules of syntax, and so on.

Why does Chomsky believe that children have an innate capacity for learning language? One reason is that children seem to acquire language quickly and effortlessly. How could they develop so complex a skill in such a short time unless they have a built-in capacity for it? Another reason is that language development tends to unfold at roughly the same pace for most children, even though children obviously are reared in diverse home environments. This finding suggests that language development is determined by biological maturation more than personal experience. The nativists also cite evidence that the early course of language development is similar across very different cultures (Gleitman & Newport, 1996; Slobin, 1992). They interpret this to mean that children all over the world are guided by the same innate capabilities.

Interactionist Theories

Like Skinner, Chomsky has his critics (Bohannon & Bonvillian, 2001). They ask: What exactly is a language acquisition device? How does the LAD work? What are the neural mechanisms involved? They argue that the LAD concept is terribly vague. Other critics question whether the rapidity of early language development is as exceptional as nativists assume. They assert that it isn't fair to compare the rapid progress of toddlers, who are immersed in their native language, against the struggles of older students, who may devote only 10–15 hours per week to their foreign language course. Nativist theories have also been undermined by evidence that parents *do* provide their children with subtle corrective feedback about grammar (Bohannon, MacWhinney, & Snow, 1990; Saxton et al., 1998).

The problems apparent in Skinner's and Chomsky's explanations of language development have led some psychologists to outline *interactionist theories* of language acquisition. These theories assert that biology and experience *both* make important contributions to the development of language. Interactionist theories come in at least three flavours. *Cognitive theories* assert that language development is simply an important aspect of more general cognitive development—which depends on both maturation and experience (Meltzoff & Gopnik, 1989; Piaget, 1983). *Social communication theories* emphasize the functional value of interpersonal communication and the social context in which language evolves (Bohannon & Warren-Leubecker, 1989; Farrar, 1990). *Emergentist theories* argue that the neural circuits supporting language are not prewired but *emerge* gradually in response to language learning experiences (Bates, 1999; MacWhinney, 2001, 2004). These theories tend to assume that incremental changes in connectionist networks (see Chapter 7) underlie children's gradual acquisition of various language skills (Elman, 1999). Practically speaking, emergentist models emphasize the importance of children's learning experiences and their information processing. In recent years, these models have guided some interesting research that has shown infants to have a surprising capacity to draw sophisticated inferences about the workings of language from their linguistic environments (Aslin, Saffran, & Newport, 1999).

Like the nativists, interactionists believe that the human organism is biologically well equipped for learning language. They also agree that much of this learning involves the acquisition of rules. However, like the behaviourists, they believe that social exchanges with parents and others play a critical role in moulding language skills. Thus, interactionist theories maintain that a biological predisposition *and* a supportive environment both contribute to language development (see Figure 8.7).

Culture, Language, and Thought

Another long-running controversy in the study of language concerns the relations among culture, language, and thought. Obviously, people from different cultures generally speak different languages. But does your training in English lead you to think about certain things differently than someone who was raised to speak Chinese or French? In other words, does a cultural group's language determine their thought? Or does thought determine language?

Benjamin Lee Whorf (1956) has been the most prominent advocate of **linguistic relativity, the hypothesis that one's language determines the nature of one's thought.** Whorf speculated that different languages lead people to view the world differently. His classic example compared English and Inuit views of snow. He asserted that the English language has just one word for snow, whereas the Inuit language has many words that distinguish among falling snow, wet snow, and so on. Because of this language gap, Whorf argued that Inuit perceive snow differently than English-speaking people do. However, Whorf's conclusion about these perceptual differences was based on casual observation rather than systematic cross-cultural comparisons of perceptual processes. Moreover, critics subsequently noted that advocates of the linguistic relativity hypothesis had carelessly overestimated the number of Inuit words for snow, while conveniently ignoring the variety of English words that refer to snow, such as slush and blizzard (Martin, 1986; Pullum, 1991).

Nonetheless, Whorf's hypothesis has been the subject of spirited debate (Gleitman & Papafragou, 2005). Many studies have focused on cross-cultural comparisons of how people perceive colours, because substantial variations exist among cultures in how colours are categorized with names. For example, some languages have a single colour name that includes both blue and green, whereas other languages view light blue and dark blue as fundamentally different colours (Davies, 1998). If a language doesn't distinguish between blue and green, do people who speak that language think about colours differently than people in other cultures do? Early efforts to answer this question suggested that the colour categories in a language have relatively little influence on how people perceive and think about colours (Berlin & Kay, 1969; Rosch, 1973). However, a flurry of recent studies have provided new evidence favouring

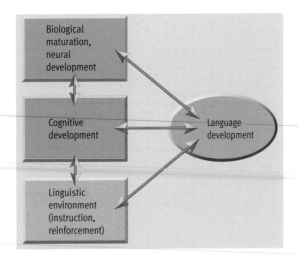

Figure 8.7

Interactionist theories of language acquisition. The interactionist view is that nature and nurture are both important to language acquisition. Maturation is thought to drive language development directly and to influence it indirectly by fostering cognitive development. Meanwhile, verbal exchanges with parents and others are also thought to play a critical role in moulding language skills. The complex bidirectional relations depicted here shed some light on why there is room for extensive debate about the crucial factors in language acquisition.

the linguistic relativity hypothesis (Davidoff, 2001, 2004; Roberson et al., 2005). For example, studies of subjects who speak African languages that do not have a boundary between blue and green have found that language affects their colour perception, as they have more trouble making quick discriminations between blue and green colours than English-speaking subjects do (Ozgen, 2004). Additional studies using a variety of methods have found that a culture's colour categories shape subjects' similarity judgments and groupings of colours (Pilling & Davies, 2004; Roberson, Davies, & Davidoff, 2000). These findings have led Ozgen (2004) to conclude that "it is just possible that what you see when you look at the rainbow depends on the language you speak" (p. 98). Moreover, the new support for linguistic relativity is not limited to the study of colour perception. Other studies have found that language also has some impact on how people think about motion (Gennari et al., 2002), time (Boroditsky, 2001), and shapes (Roberson, Davidoff, & Shapiro, 2002).

Does the language you speak determine how you think? Yes, said Benjamin Lee Whorf, who argued that the Inuit language, which has numerous words for snow, leads Inuit to perceive snow differently from English speakers. However, the overall evidence provides little support for the strong version of Whorf's hypothesis.

Problem Solving: In Search of Solutions

Look at the two problems below. Can you solve them?

In the Thompson family there are five brothers, and each brother has one sister. If you count Mrs. Thompson, how many females are there in the Thompson family?

Fifteen percent of the people in Topeka have unlisted telephone numbers. You select 200 names at random from the Topeka phone book. How many of these people can be expected to have unlisted phone numbers?

These problems, borrowed from Sternberg (1986, p. 214), are exceptionally simple, but many people fail to solve them. The answer to the first problem is *two:* The only females in the family are Mrs. Thompson and her one daughter, who is a sister to each of her brothers. The answer to the second problem is *none*—you won't find any people with *unlisted* phone numbers in the phone book.

Why do many people fail to solve these simple problems? You'll learn why in a moment, when we discuss barriers to effective problem solving. But first, let's examine a scheme for classifying problems into a few basic types.

Types of Problems SIM7, 6D

Problem solving **refers to active efforts to discover what must be done to achieve a goal that is not readily attainable.** Obviously, if a goal is readily attainable, there isn't a problem. But in problem-solving situations, one must go beyond the information given to overcome obstacles and reach a goal. Jim Greeno (1978) has proposed that problems can be categorized into three basic classes:

1. *Problems of inducing structure* require people to discover the relations among numbers, words, symbols, or ideas. The *series completion problems* and the *analogy problems* in Figure 8.8 are examples of problems of inducing structure.

2. *Problems of arrangement* require people to arrange the parts of a problem in a way that satisfies some criterion. The parts can usually be arranged in many ways, but only one or a few of the arrangements form a solution. The *string problem* and the *anagrams* in Figure 8.8 fit in this category. Arrangement problems are often solved with a burst of insight. **Insight is the sudden discovery of the correct solution following incorrect attempts based primarily on trial and error** (Mayer, 1995).

3. *Problems of transformation* require people to carry out a sequence of transformations in order to reach a specific goal. The *hobbits and orcs problem* and the *water jar problem* in Figure 8.8 are examples of transformation problems. Transformation problems can be challenging. Even though you know exactly what the goal is, it's often not obvious how the goal can be achieved.

Greeno's list is not an exhaustive scheme for classifying problems, but it provides a useful system for understanding some of the variety seen in everyday problems.

Barriers to Effective Problem Solving 6D

On the basis of their studies of problem solving, psychologists have identified a number of barriers that frequently impede subjects' efforts to arrive at solutions. Common obstacles to effective problem solving include a focus on irrelevant information, functional fixedness, mental set, and the imposition of unnecessary constraints.

A. Analogy

What word completes the analogy?

Merchant : Sell : : Customer : _____

Lawyer : Client : : Doctor : _____

B. String problem

Two strings hang from the ceiling but are too far apart to allow a person to hold one and walk to the other. On the table are a book of matches, a screwdriver, and a few pieces of cotton. How could the strings be tied together?

C. Hobbits and orcs problem

Three hobbits and three orcs arrive at a river bank, and they all wish to cross onto the other side. Fortunately, there is a boat, but unfortunately, the boat can hold only two creatures at one time. Also, there is another problem. Orcs are vicious creatures, and whenever there are more orcs than hobbits on one side of the river, the orcs will immediately attack the hobbits and eat them up. Consequently, you should be certain that you never leave more orcs than hobbits on either river bank. How should the problem be solved? It must be added that the orcs, though vicious, can be trusted to bring the boat back! (From Matlin, 1989, p. 319)

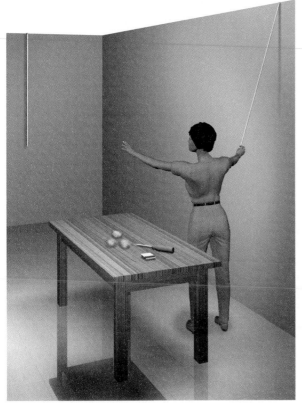

D. Water jar problem

Suppose that you have a 21-cup jar, a 127-cup jar, and a 3-cup jar. Drawing and discarding as much water as you like, you need to measure out exactly 100 cups of water. How can this be done?

E. Anagram

Rearrange the letters in each row to make an English word.

RWAET

KEROJ

F. Series completion

What number or letter completes each series?

1 2 8 3 4 6 5 6 _____

A B M C D M _____

Irrelevant Information

 6D

We began our discussion of problem solving with two simple problems that people routinely fail to solve (see page 326). The catch is that these problems contain *irrelevant information* that leads people astray. In the first problem, the number of brothers is irrelevant in determining the number of females in the Thompson family. In the second problem, subjects tend to focus on the figures of 15% and 200 names. But this numerical information is irrelevant, since all the names came out of the phone book.

Sternberg (1986) points out that people often incorrectly assume that all the numerical information in a problem is necessary to solve it. They therefore try to figure out how to use quantitative information before they even consider whether it's

relevant. Focusing on irrelevant information can have adverse effects on reasoning and problem solving (Gaeth & Shanteau, 2000). Hence, effective problem solving requires that you attempt to figure out what information is relevant and what is irrelevant before proceeding.

Figure 8.8

Six standard problems used in studies of problem solving. Try solving the problems and identifying which class each belongs to before reading further. The problems can be classified as follows. The *analogy problems* and *series completion problems* are problems of inducing structure. The solutions for the analogy problems are *Buy* and *Patient*. The solutions for the series completion problems are *4* and *E*. The *string problem* and the *anagram problems* are problems of arrangement. To solve the string problem, attach the screwdriver to one string and set it swinging as a pendulum. Hold the other string and catch the swinging screwdriver. Then you need only untie the screwdriver and tie the strings together. The solutions for the anagram problems are *WATER* and *JOKER*. The *hobbits and orcs problem* and the *water jar problem* are problems of transformation. The solutions for these problems are outlined in Figures 8.9 and 8.10.

Figure 8.9

Solution to the hobbits and orcs problem. This problem is difficult because it is necessary to temporarily work "away" from the goal.

Figure 8.10

The method for solving the water jar problem. As explained in the text, the correct formula is B – A – 2C.

Functional Fixedness

Another common barrier to successful problem solving, identified by Gestalt psychologists, is *functional fixedness—the tendency to perceive an item only in terms of its most common use.* Functional fixedness has been seen in the difficulties that people have with the string problem (Maier, 1931). Solving this problem requires finding a novel use for one of the objects: the screwdriver. Subjects tend to think of the screwdriver in terms of its usual functions—

turning screws and perhaps prying things open. They have a hard time viewing the screwdriver as a weight. Their rigid way of thinking about the screwdriver illustrates functional fixedness (Dominowski & Bourne, 1994). Ironically, young children appear to be less vulnerable to functional fixedness than older children or adults because they have less knowledge about the conventional uses of various objects (Defeyter & German, 2003).

Mental Set

Rigid thinking is also at work when a mental set interferes with effective problem solving. A *mental set exists when people persist in using problem-solving strategies that have worked in the past.* The effects of mental set were seen in a classic study by Gestalt psychologist Abraham Luchins (1942). He asked subjects to work a series of water jar problems, like the one introduced earlier. Six such problems are outlined in Figure 8.11, which shows the capacities of the three jars and the amounts of water to be measured out. Try solving these problems.

Were you able to develop a formula for solving these problems? The first four all require the same strategy, which was described in Figure 8.10. You have to fill jar B, draw off the amount that jar A holds once, and draw off the amount that jar C holds twice. Thus, the formula for your solution is B – A – 2C. Although there is an obvious and much simpler solution (A – C) for the fifth problem (see Figure 8.15 on page 331), Luchins found that most subjects stuck with the more cumbersome strategy that they had used in problems 1–4. Moreover, most subjects couldn't solve the sixth problem in the allotted time, because they kept trying to use their proven strategy, which does *not* work for this problem. The subjects' reliance on their "tried and true" strategy is an illustration of mental set in problem solving. This tendency to let one's thinking get into a rut is a common barrier to successful problem solving (Smith, 1995). Mental set may explain why having expertise in an area sometimes backfires and in fact hampers problem-solving efforts (Leighton & Sternberg, 2003).

Unnecessary Constraints

Effective problem solving requires specifying all the constraints governing a problem *without assuming any constraints that don't exist.* An example of a problem in which people place an unnecessary constraint on the solution is shown in Figure 8.12 (Adams, 1980). Without lifting your pencil from the paper, try to draw four straight lines that will cross through all nine dots. Most people will not draw lines outside the imaginary boundary that surrounds

| | Capacity of empty jars | | | Desired amount of water |
Problem	A	B	C	
1	14	163	25	99
2	18	43	10	5
3	9	42	6	21
4	20	59	4	31
5	23	49	3	20
6	28	76	3	25

Figure 8.11

Additional water jar problems. Using jars A, B, and C, with the capacities indicated in each row, figure out how to measure out the desired amount of water specified on the far right. The solutions are shown in Figure 8.15. (Based on Luchins, 1942)

Figure 8.12

The nine-dot problem. Without lifting your pencil from the paper, draw no more than four lines that will cross through all nine dots. For possible solutions, see Figure 8.16.

SOURCE: Adams, J. L. (1980). *Conceptual block-busting: A guide to better ideas.* New York: W. H. Freeman. Copyright © 1980 by James L. Adams. Reprinted by permission of W. H. Freeman & Co.

the dots. Notice that this constraint is not part of the problem statement. It's imposed only by the problem solver. Correct solutions, two of which are shown in Figure 8.16 on page 331, extend outside the imaginary boundary. People often make assumptions that impose unnecessary constraints on problem-solving efforts. A recent model and analysis of insight by James MacGregor of the University of Victoria and his colleagues (MacGregor, Ormerod, and Chronicle, 2001) suggests that failure in such problems results from both constraint and from some type of drive or dynamic that "steers activity into the constraint" (Ormerod et al., 2002, pp. 798).

Approaches to Problem Solving

In their classic treatise on problem solving, Allen Newell and Herbert Simon (1972) use a spatial metaphor to describe the process of problem solving. They use the term **problem space to refer to the set of possible pathways to a solution considered by the problem solver.** Thus, they see problem solving as a search in space. The problem solver's task is to find a solution path among the potential pathways that could lead from the problem's initial state to its goal state. The problem space metaphor highlights the fact that people must choose from among a variety of conceivable pathways or strategies in attempting to solve problems (Hunt, 1994). In this section, we'll examine some general strategies.

Using Algorithms and Heuristics

Trial and error is a common approach to solving problems. **Trial and error involves trying possible** solutions and discarding those that are in error until one works. Trial and error is often applied haphazardly, but people sometimes try to be systematic. An **algorithm is a methodical, step-by-step procedure for trying all possible alternatives in searching for a solution to a problem.** For instance, to solve the anagram IHCRA, you could write out all the possible arrangements of these letters until you eventually reached an answer (CHAIR). If an algorithm is available for a problem, it guarantees that one can eventually find a solution.

Algorithms can be effective when there are relatively few possible solutions to be tried out. However, algorithms do not exist for many problems, and they can become impractical when the problem space is large. Consider, for instance, the problem shown in Figure 8.13. The challenge is to move just two matches to create a pattern containing four equal squares. Sure, you could follow an algorithm in moving pairs of matches about. But you'd better allocate plenty of time to this effort, as there are over 60 000 possible rearrangements to check out (see Figure 8.17 on page 331 for the solution).

Because algorithms are inefficient, people often use shortcuts called *heuristics* in problem solving. A **heuristic is a guiding principle or "rule of thumb" used in solving problems or making decisions.** In solving problems, a heuristic allows you to discard some alternatives while pursuing selected alternatives that appear more likely to lead to a solution (Holyoak, 1995). Heuristics can be useful because they selectively narrow the problem space, but they don't guarantee success. Helpful heuristics in problem solving include forming subgoals, working backward, searching for analogies, and changing the representation of a problem.

Figure 8.13

The matchstick problem. Move two matches to form four equal squares. A solution can be found in Figure 8.17.

SOURCE: Kendler, H. H. (1974). *Basic psychology.* Menlo Park, CA: Benjamin-Cummings. Copyright © 1974 The Benjamin-Cummings Publishing Co. Adapted by permission of Howard H. Kendler.

Forming Subgoals

A useful strategy for many problems is to formulate *subgoals,* intermediate steps toward a solution. When you reach a subgoal, you've solved part of the problem. Some problems have fairly obvious subgoals, and research has shown that people take advantage of them. For instance, in analogy problems, the first subgoal usually is to figure out the possible relations between the first two parts of the analogy. In a study by Simon and Reed (1976), subjects working on complex problems were given subgoals that weren't obvious. Providing subgoals helped the subjects solve the problems much more quickly.

The wisdom of formulating subgoals can be seen in the *tower of Hanoi problem,* depicted in Figure 8.14. The terminal goal for this problem is to move all three rings on peg A to peg C, while abiding by two restrictions: only the top ring on a peg can be moved, and a ring must never be placed above a smaller ring. See whether you can solve the problem before continuing.

Dividing this problem into subgoals facilitates a solution (Kotovsky, Hayes, & Simon, 1985). If you think in terms of subgoals, your first task is to get ring 3 to the bottom of peg C. Breaking this task into sub-subgoals, subjects can figure out that they should move ring 1 to peg C, ring 2 to peg B, and ring 1 from peg C to peg B. These manoeuvres allow you to place ring 3 at the bottom of peg C, thus meeting your first subgoal. Your next subgoal—getting ring 2 over to peg C—can be accomplished in just two steps: move ring 1 to peg A and ring 2 to peg C. It should then be obvious how to achieve your final subgoal—getting ring 1 over to peg C.

Working Backward

Try to work the *lily pond problem* described below:

The water lilies on the surface of a small pond double in area every 24 hours. From the time the first water lily appears until the pond is completely covered takes 60 days. On what day is half of the pond covered with lilies?

If you're working on a problem that has a well-specified end point, you may find the solution more readily if you begin at the end and work backward. This strategy is the key to solving the lily pond problem (Davidson, 2003). If the entire pond is covered on the 60th day, and the area covered doubles every day, how much is covered on the 59th day? One-half of the pond will be covered, and that happens to be the exact point you were trying to reach. The lily pond problem is remarkably simple when you work backward. In contrast, if you move forward from the starting point, you wrestle with questions about the area of the pond and the size of the lilies, and you find the problem riddled with ambiguities.

Searching for Analogies

Searching for analogies is another of the major heuristics for solving problems (Holyoak, 2005). If you can spot an analogy between problems, you may be able to use the solution to a previous problem to solve a current one. Of course, using this strategy depends on recognizing the similarity between two problems, which may itself be a challenging problem. People often are unable to recognize that two problems are similar (Gilhooly, 1996). One prominent reason that people have difficulty recognizing analogies between problems is that they tend to focus on superficial, surface features of problems rather than their underlying structure (Bassok, 2003). Nonetheless, analogies can be a powerful tool in efforts to solve problems. Try to make use of analogies to solve the following two problems:

A teacher had 23 pupils in his class. All but seven of them went on a museum trip and thus were away for the day. How many students remained in class that day?

Susan gets in her car in Edmonton and drives toward Lethbridge, averaging 100 kilometres per hour. Twenty minutes later, Ellen gets in her car in Lethbridge and starts driving toward Edmonton, averaging 120 kilometres per hour. Both women take the same route, which extends a total of 440 kilometres between the two cities. Which car is nearer to Edmonton when they meet?

These problems, adapted from Sternberg (1986, pp. 213 and 215), resemble the ones that opened our discussion of problem solving. Each has an obvious solution that's hidden in irrelevant quantitative information. If you recognized this similarity, you probably solved the problems easily. If not, take another look now that you know what the analogy is. Neither problem requires any calculation whatsoever. The answer to the first problem is *seven.* As for

Figure 8.14

The tower of Hanoi problem. Your mission is to move the rings from peg A to peg C. You can move only the top ring on a peg and can't place a larger ring above a smaller one. The solution is explained in the text.

Figure 8.15

Solutions to the additional water jar problems. The solution for problems 1–4 is the same (B – A – 2C) as the solution shown in Figure 8.10. This method will work for problem 5, but there also is a simpler solution (A – C), which is the only solution for problem 6. Many subjects exhibit a mental set on these problems, as they fail to notice the simpler solution for problem 5.

Figure 8.16

Two solutions to the nine-dot problem. The key to solving the problem is to recognize that nothing in the problem statement forbids going outside the imaginary boundary surrounding the dots.

SOURCE: Adams, J. L. (1980). *Conceptual blockbusting: A guide to better ideas*. New York: W. H. Freeman. Copyright © 1980 by James L. Adams. Reprinted by permission of W. H. Freeman & Co.

Figure 8.17

Solution to the matchstick problem. The key to solving this problem is to "open up" the figure, something many subjects are reluctant to do because they impose unnecessary constraints on the problem.

SOURCE: Kendler, H. H. (1974). *Basic psychology*. Menlo Park, CA: Benjamin-Cummings. Copyright © 1974 The Benjamin-Cummings Publishing Co. Adapted by permission of Howard H. Kendler.

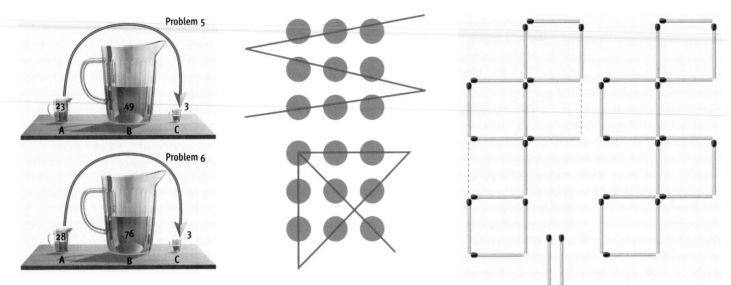

the second problem, when the two cars meet they're in the same place. Obviously, they have to be the same distance from Edmonton.

Changing the Representation of the Problem

Whether you solve a problem often hinges on how you envision it—your *representation of the problem*. Many problems can be represented in a variety of ways, such as verbally, mathematically, or spatially. You might represent a problem with a list, a table, an equation, a graph, a matrix of facts or numbers, a hierarchical tree diagram, or a sequential flowchart (Halpern, 2003). Some studies have shown that diagrams can facilitate reasoning on some types of problems by making it easier to find crucial information and by making alternative possibilities more salient (Bauer & Johnson-Laird, 1993). There isn't one ideal way to represent problems. The best representation will depend on the nature of the problem. But when you fail to make progress with your initial representation, changing your representation is often a good strategy (Novick & Bassok, 2005). As an illustration, see whether you can solve the *bird and train problem* (adapted from Bransford & Stein, 1993, p. 11):

Two train stations are 50 kilometres apart. At 1 P.M. on Sunday a train pulls out from each of the stations and the trains start toward each other. Just as the trains pull out from the stations, a bird flies into the air in front of the first train and flies ahead to the front of the second train. When the bird reaches the second train, it turns around and flies toward the first train. The bird continues in this way until the trains meet. Assume that both trains travel at the speed of 25 kilometres per hour and the bird flies at a constant speed of 100 kilometres per hour. How many kilometres will the bird have flown when the trains meet?

This problem asks about the *distance* the bird will fly, so people tend to represent the problem spatially, as shown in Figure 8.18. Represented this way, the problem can be solved, but the steps are tedious and difficult. But consider another angle. The problem asks how far the bird will fly in the time it takes the trains to meet. Since we know how fast the bird flies, all we really need to know is how much *time* it takes for the trains to meet. Changing the representation of the problem from a question of *distance* to a question of *time* makes for an easier solution, as follows: The train stations are 50 kilometres apart. Since the trains are travelling toward each other at the same speed, they will meet midway and each will have travelled 25 kilometres. The trains are moving at 25 kilometres per hour. Hence, the time it takes them to meet 25 kilometres from each station is one hour. Since the

Web Link 8.2

Critical Thinking Consortium
http://www.criticalthinking.org/

The many resources at the Critical Thinking Consortium are directed primarily toward teachers at every level to help them develop their students' critical thinking skills. Visitors will find many online pamphlets on critical thinking and active learning.

bird flies at 100 kilometres per hour, it will fly 100 kilometres in the hour it takes the trains to meet.

Let's consider one more problem in which representation plays a crucial role. See whether you can solve the *Buddhist monk problem*:

At sunrise, a Buddhist monk sets out to climb a tall mountain. He follows a narrow path that winds around the mountain and up to a temple. He stops frequently to rest and climbs at varying speeds, arriving around sunset. After staying a few days, he begins his return journey. As before, he starts at sunrise, rests often, walks at varying speeds, and arrives around sunset. Prove that there must be a spot along the path that the monk will pass on both trips at precisely the same time of day.

Why should there be such a spot? The monk's walking speed varies. Shouldn't it all be a matter of coincidence if he reaches a spot at the same time each day? Moreover, if there is such a spot, how would you prove it? Subjects who represent this problem in terms of verbal, mathematical, or spatial information struggle. Subjects who work with a graphic representation fare much better. The best way to represent the problem is to envision the monk (or two different monks) ascending and descending the mountain at the same time. The two monks must meet at some point. If you construct a graph (see Figure 8.19) you can vary the speed of the monk's descent in endless ways, but you can see that there's always a place where they meet. The location of this place and the time of day can vary, but there will always be a crossing point where the monk(s) is (are) in the same place at the same time.

Culture, Cognitive Style, and Problem Solving

Do the varied experiences of people from different cultures lead to cross-cultural variations in problem solving? Yes, at least to some degree, as researchers have found cultural differences in the cognitive style that people exhibit in solving problems.

Back in the 1940s, Herman Witkin was intrigued by the observation that some airplane pilots would fly into a cloudbank upright but exit it upside down without realizing that they had turned over. Witkin's efforts to explain this aviation problem led to the discovery of an interesting dimension of cognitive style (Witkin, 1950; Witkin et al., 1962). **Field dependence–independence refers to individuals' tendency to rely primarily on external versus internal frames of reference when orienting themselves in space.** People who are *field dependent* rely on external frames of reference and tend to accept the physical environment as a given instead of trying to analyze or restructure it. People who are *field independent* rely on internal frames of reference and tend to analyze and try to restructure the physical environment rather than accepting it as is. In solving problems, field-dependent people tend to focus on the total context of a problem instead of zeroing in on specific aspects or breaking it into component parts. In contrast, field-independent people are more likely to focus on specific features of a problem and to reorganize the component parts.

Research has shown that field dependence–independence is related to diverse aspects of cognitive, emotional, and social functioning (Witkin &

Figure 8.18

Representing the bird and train problem. The typical inclination is to envision this problem spatially, as shown here. However, as the text explains, this representation makes the problem much more difficult than it really is.

100 km/h

25 km/h

25 km/h

50 km

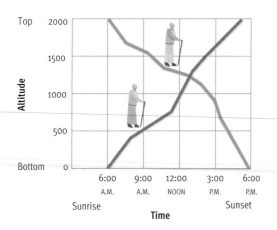

Figure 8.19

Solution to the Buddhist monk problem. If you represent this problem graphically and think in terms of two monks, it is readily apparent that the monk does pass a single spot at the same time each day.

Goodenough, 1981). Each style has its strengths and weaknesses, but studies have shown that field-independent subjects outperform field-dependent subjects on a variety of classic laboratory problems, including the string problem, matchstick problem, candle problem, and water jar problem (Witkin et al., 1962). Field-independent subjects' superiority on

these types of problems has been attributed to their propensity to analyze and rearrange the elements of a problem and their ability to overcome the context in which problems are presented.

An extensive body of research suggests that some cultures encourage a field-dependent cognitive style, whereas others foster a field-independent style (Berry, 1990; Mishra, 2001). The educational practices in modern Western societies seem to nourish field independence. A field-independent style is also more likely to be predominant in nomadic societies that depend on hunting and gathering for subsistence and in societies that encourage personal autonomy. In contrast, a field-dependent style is found more in sedentary agricultural societies and in societies that stress conformity.

In research published while he was at the University of Western Ontario, Tory Higgins showed that if participants were given an earlier memory test in a supposedly unrelated experiment before the candle problem (Concept Check 8.2) consisting of items such as "a tray *and* tomatoes," they solved the candle problem more quickly than participants who were given highly similar memory items, such as "a tray *of* tomatoes" (Higgins & Chaires, 1980). Higgins suggests that being exposed to items such as "a tray and tomatoes" affected how participants later encoded

CONCEPT **CHECK 8.2**

Thinking about Problem Solving

Check your understanding of problem solving by answering some questions about the following problem. Begin by trying to solve the problem.

The candle problem. Using the objects shown—candles, a box of matches, string, and some tacks—figure out how you could mount a candle on a wall so that it could be used as a light.

Work on the problem for a while, then turn to page 334 to see the solution. After you've seen the solution, respond to the following questions. The answers are in Appendix A.

1. If it didn't occur to you that the matchbox could be converted from a container to a platform, this illustrates _____ _____.

2. While working on the problem, if you thought to yourself, "How can I create a platform attached to the wall?" you used the heuristic of _____ _____.

3. If it occurred to you suddenly that the matchbox could be used as a platform, this realization would be an example of _____.

4. If you had a hunch that there might be some similarity between this problem and the string problem in Figure 8.8 (the similarity is the novel use of an object), your hunch would illustrate the heuristic of _____ ___ _____.

5. In terms of Greeno's three types of problems, the candle problem is a(n) _____ problem.

Language and Thought 333

The solution to the candle problem in Concept Check 8.2.

the items given to them in the candle problem, thus affecting their solution to the problem. Being exposed to "and" led them to differentiate the items.

Richard Nisbett and his colleagues (2001) have argued that people from East Asian cultures (such as China, Japan, and Korea) display a *holistic cognitive style* that focuses on context and relationships among elements in a field, whereas people from Western cultures (North America and Europe) exhibit an *analytic cognitive style* that focuses on objects and their properties rather than context. To put it simply, Easterners see wholes where Westerners see parts. Nisbett et al. (2001) trace Eastern societies' holistic style of thinking back to ancient Chinese philosophies, while they trace Western societies' analytic style of thinking back to ancient Greek philosophies. Although these contrasting cognitive styles are rooted in ancient traditions, Nisbett and his colleagues argue that these styles continue to influence reasoning and problem solving in our contemporary world.

To demonstrate this influence, Masuda and Nisbett (2001) presented computer-animated scenes of fish and other underwater objects to Japanese and American participants and asked them to report what they had seen. The initial comments of American subjects typically referred to the focal fish, whereas the initial comments of Japanese subjects usually referred to background elements (see Figure 8.20). Furthermore, compared to the Americans, the Japanese participants made about 70% more statements about context or background and about twice as many statements about relationships between elements in

the scenes. Other studies have shown that cultural variations in analytic versus holistic thinking influence subjects' patterns of logical reasoning, their vulnerability to hindsight bias (see Chapter 7), and their tolerance of contradictions (Nisbett, 2003; Nisbett et al., 2001). Research also suggests that people from Eastern cultures tend to be more field-dependent than their Western counterparts (Ji, Peng, & Nisbett, 2000), but Nisbett and his colleagues view field dependence–independence as just one facet of a broader preference for holistic versus analytic thinking. Based on these and many other findings, Nisbett et al. (2001) conclude that cultural disparities in cognitive style are substantial and that "literally different cognitive processes are often invoked by East Asians and Westerners dealing with the same problem" (p. 305).

Problems are not the only kind of cognitive challenge that people grapple with on a regular basis. Life also seems to constantly demand decisions. As you might expect, cognitive psychologists have shown great interest in the process of decision making, which is our next subject.

REVIEW OF KEY POINTS

● In studying problem solving, psychologists have differentiated among several types of problems. In problems that require inducing structure, the problem solver must discover the relations among the parts of a problem. Transformation problems require that the problem solver carry out a sequence of transformations (moves) in order to reach a specific goal. Arrangement problems require the problem solver to arrange the parts in a way that satisfies a general goal.

● Common barriers to problem solving include functional fixedness, mental set, getting bogged down in irrelevant information, and placing unnecessary constraints on one's solutions. An algorithm is a procedure for trying all possible alternatives in searching for a solution to a problem.

● A variety of strategies, or heuristics, are used for solving problems. When people form subgoals, they try breaking the problem into several parts. Sometimes it is useful to start at the goal state and work backward toward the initial state. Other general strategies include searching for analogies between new problems and old problems, and changing the representation of problems.

● Some cultures encourage a field-dependent cognitive style, whereas others foster more field independence. People who are field independent tend to analyze and restructure problems more than those who are field dependent. Research suggests that Eastern cultures exhibit a more holistic cognitive style, whereas Western cultures display a more analytic cognitive style.

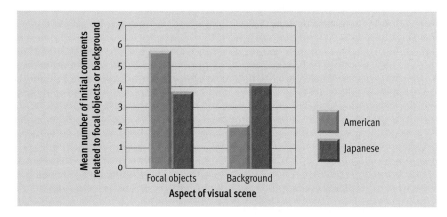

Figure 8.20

Cultural disparities in cognitive style. In one of the studies conducted by Masuda and Nisbett (2001), the participants were asked to describe computer-animated visual scenes. As you can see, the initial comments made by American subjects referred more to focal objects in the scenes, whereas the initial comments made by Japanese subjects referred more to background elements in the scenes. These findings are consistent with the hypothesis that Easterners see wholes (a holistic cognitive style) where Westerners see parts (an analytic cognitive style). (Data from Masuda & Nisbett, 2001)

Decision Making: Choices and Chances

Decisions, decisions. Life is full of them. You decided to read this book today. Earlier today you decided when to get up, whether to eat breakfast, and if so, what to eat. Usually you make routine decisions like these with little effort. But on occasion you need to make important decisions that require more thought. Big decisions—such as selecting a car, a home, or a job—tend to be difficult. The alternatives usually have a number of attributes that need to be weighed. For instance, in choosing among several cars, you may want to compare their costs, roominess, fuel economy, handling, acceleration, stylishness, reliability, safety features, and warranties.

Decision making **involves evaluating alternatives and making choices among them.** Most people try to be systematic and rational in their decision making. However, the work that earned Herbert Simon the 1978 Nobel Prize in economics showed that people don't always live up to these goals. Before Simon's work, most traditional theories in economics assumed that people make rational choices to maximize their economic gains. Simon (1957) demonstrated that people have a limited ability to process and evaluate information on numerous facets of possible alternatives. Thus, Simon's **theory of bounded rationality asserts that people tend to use simple strategies in decision making that focus on only a few facets of available options and often result in "irrational" decisions that are less than optimal.**

Spurred by Simon's analysis, psychologists have devoted several decades to the study of how cognitive biases distort people's decision making. The results of this research have sometimes been disturbing, leading some theorists to conclude that "normal adult human subjects do a singularly bad job at the business of reasoning, even when they are calm, clearheaded, and under no pressure to perform quickly" (Stich, 1990, pp. 173–174). Researchers' focus on *biases and mistakes* in making decisions may seem a little peculiar, but as Kahneman (1991) has pointed out, the study of people's misguided decisions has illuminated the process of decision making, just as the study of illusions and forgetting has enhanced our understanding of visual perception and memory, respectively.

Making Choices: Selecting an Alternative

Many decisions involve choices about *preferences,* which can be made using a variety of strategies (Hogarth, 1987). For instance, imagine that Boris has found two reasonably attractive apartments and is trying to decide between them. How should he go about selecting between his alternatives? Let's look at some strategies Boris might use in trying to make his decision.

If Boris wanted to use an *additive strategy,* he would list the attributes that influence his decision. Then he would rate the desirability of each apartment on each attribute. For example, let's say that Boris wants to consider four attributes: rent, noise level, distance to campus, and cleanliness. He might make ratings from –3 to +3, like those shown in Table 8.3, add up the ratings for each alternative, and select the one with the largest total. Given the ratings in Table 8.3, Boris should select apartment B.

To make an additive strategy more useful, you can *weight* attributes differently, based on their importance (Shafir & LeBoeuf, 2004). For example, if Boris considers distance to campus to be twice as important as the other considerations, he could multiply his ratings of this attribute by 2. The distance rating would then be +6 for apartment A and –2 for apartment B, and apartment A would become the preferred choice.

People also make choices by gradually eliminating less attractive alternatives (Slovic, 1990; Tversky, 1972). This strategy is called *elimination by aspects* because it assumes that alternatives are eliminated by evaluating them on each attribute or aspect in turn. Whenever any alternative fails to satisfy some minimum criterion for an attribute, it is eliminated from further consideration.

To illustrate, suppose Juanita is looking for a new car. She may begin by eliminating all cars that cost over $18 000. Then she may eliminate cars that use more than 10 litres of gas for every 100 kilometres. By continuing to reject choices that don't satisfy some minimum criterion on selected attributes, she can gradually eliminate alternatives until only a single car remains.

Table 8.3 Application of the Additive Model to Choosing an Apartment

Attribute	Apartment A	B
Rent	+1	+2
Noise level	–2	+3
Distance to campus	+3	–1
Cleanliness	+2	+2
Total	**+4**	**+6**

PREVIEW QUESTIONS
- How do people make choices about preferences?
- What factors are important in risky decision making?
- What shortcuts do people use in judging probabilities?
- What do evolutionary psychologists have to say about error and bias in human decision making?

Carnegie Mellon University

"The capacity of the human mind for formulating and solving complex problems is very small compared with the size of the problems whose solution is required for objectively rational behavior in the real world ..."
HERBERT SIMON

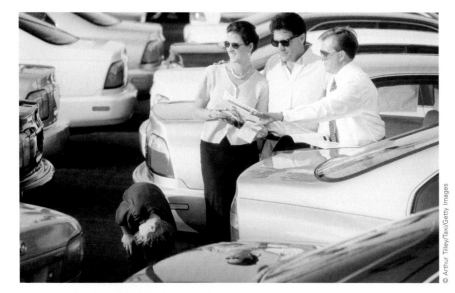
People often have to decide between alternative products, such as computers, cars, refrigerators, and so forth, that are not all that different. They often struggle with the abundant choices and delay making a decision. Extra deliberation does not necessarily lead to better decisions.

The final choice in elimination by aspects depends on the order in which attributes are evaluated. For example, if cost was the last attribute Juanita evaluated, she could have previously eliminated all cars that cost under $18 000. If she has only $18 000 to spend, her decision-making strategy would not have brought her very far. Thus, when using elimination by aspects, it's best to evaluate attributes in the order of their importance.

Both the additive and the elimination-by-aspects strategies have advantages, but which strategy do people actually tend to use? Research by John Payne (1976) suggests that when decisions involve relatively few options that need to be evaluated on only a few attributes, people tend to use additive strategies. However, as more options and factors are added to a decision task, people tend to shift to elimination by aspects. Thus, people adapt their approach to the demands of the task. When their choices become very complex, they shift toward simpler decision strategies (Payne & Bettman, 2004). Difficulties in choosing between alternatives can also lead people to delay their decisions. Tversky and Shafir (1992) note that "the experience of conflict is the price one pays for the freedom to choose" (p. 358). They argue that when alternatives are not dramatically different in attractiveness, people struggle with conflict and often defer decisions, taking additional time to look for a new car, apartment, or whatever.

Taking Chances: Factors Weighed in Risky Decisions

Suppose you have the chance to play a dice game in which you might win some money. You must decide whether it would be to your advantage to play. You're going to roll a fair die. If the number 6 appears, you win $5. If one of the other five numbers appears, you win nothing. It costs you $1 every time you play. Should you participate?

This problem calls for a type of decision making that is somewhat different from making choices about preferences. In selecting alternatives that reflect preferences, people generally weigh known outcomes (apartment A will require a long commute to campus, car B will get better mileage, and so forth). In contrast, *risky decision making* involves **making choices under conditions of uncertainty.** Uncertainty exists when people don't know what will happen. At best, they know the probability that a particular event will occur.

One way to decide whether to play the dice game would be to figure out the *expected value* of participation in the game. To do so, you would need to calculate the average amount of money you could expect to win or lose each time you play. The value of a win is $4 ($5 minus the $1 entry fee). The value of a loss is –$1. To calculate expected value, you also need to know the probability of a win or loss. Since a die has six faces, the probability of a win is one out of six, and the probability of a loss is five out of six. Thus, on five out of every six trials, you lose $1. On one out of six, you win $4. The game is beginning to sound unattractive, isn't it? We can figure out the precise expected value as follows:

$$\text{Expected value} = (^1\!/_6 \times 4) + (^5\!/_6 \times -1)$$
$$= {}^4\!/_6 + (-^5\!/_6) = -^1\!/_6$$

The expected value of this game is –1/6 of a dollar, which means that you lose an average of about 17 cents per turn. Now that you know the expected value, surely you won't agree to play. Or will you?

If we want to understand why people make the decisions they do, the concept of expected value is not enough. People frequently behave in ways that are inconsistent with expected value (Slovic, Lichtenstein, & Fischhoff, 1988). Anytime the expected value is negative, a gambler should expect to lose money. Yet a great many people gamble at racetracks and casinos and buy lottery tickets. Although they realize that the odds are against them, they continue to gamble. Even people who don't gamble buy homeowner's insurance, which has a negative expected value. After all, when you buy insurance, your expectation (and hope!) is that you will lose money on the deal.

To explain decisions that violate expected value, some theories replace the objective value of an outcome with its *subjective utility* (Fischhoff, 1988). Subjective utility represents what an outcome is personally worth to an individual. For example, buying a few lottery tickets may allow you to dream about becoming wealthy. Buying insurance may give you a sense of security. Subjective utilities like these vary from one person to another. If we know an individual's subjective utilities, we can better understand that person's risky decision making.

Another way to improve our understanding of risky decision making is to consider individuals' estimates of the *subjective probability* of events (Shafer & Tversky, 1988). If people don't know actual probabilities, they must rely on their personal estimates of probabilities. These estimates can have interesting effects on the perceived utility of various outcomes.

Heuristics in Judging Probabilities

6E

- What are your chances of passing your next psychology test if you study only three hours?
- How likely is a major downturn in the stock market during the upcoming year?
- What are the odds of your getting into graduate school in the field of your choice?

These questions ask you to make probability estimates. Amos Tversky and Daniel Kahneman (1974, 1982; Kahneman & Tversky, 2000) have conducted extensive research on the *heuristics,* or mental shortcuts, that people use in grappling with probabilities. This research on heuristics earned Kahneman the Nobel Prize in Economics in 2002 (unfortunately, his collaborator, Amos Tversky, died in 1996).

Availability is one such heuristic. The ***availability heuristic* involves basing the estimated probability of an event on the ease with which relevant instances come to mind.** For example, you may estimate the divorce rate by recalling the number of divorces among your friends' parents. Recalling specific instances of an event is a reasonable strategy to use in estimating the event's probability. However, if instances occur frequently but you have difficulty retrieving them from memory, your estimate will be biased. For instance, it's easier to think of words that begin with a certain letter than words that contain that letter at some other position. Hence, people should tend to respond that there are more words starting with the letter *K* than words having a *K* in the third position. To test this hypothesis, Tversky and Kahneman (1973) selected five consonants (*K, L, N, R, V*) that occur more frequently in the third position of a word than in the first. Subjects were asked whether each of the letters appears more often in the first or third position. Most of the subjects erroneously believed that all five letters were

much more frequent in the first than in the third position, confirming the hypothesis.

Representativeness is another guide in estimating probabilities identified by Kahneman and Tversky (1982). **The *representativeness heuristic* involves basing the estimated probability of an event on how similar it is to the typical prototype of that event.** To illustrate, imagine that you flip a coin six times and keep track of how often the result is heads (H) or tails (T). Which of the following sequences is more likely?

1. T T T T T T
2. H T T H H T

People generally believe that the second sequence is more likely. After all, coin tossing is a random affair, and the second sequence looks much more representative of a random process than the first. In reality, the probability of each exact *sequence* is precisely the same ($1/2 \times 1/2 \times 1/2 \times 1/2 \times 1/2 \times 1/2 = 1/64$). Let's look at another phenomenon in which the representativeness heuristic plays a key role.

The Tendency to Ignore Base Rates

6E

Steve is very shy and withdrawn, invariably helpful, but with little interest in people or in the world of reality. A meek and tidy soul, he has a need for order and structure and a passion for detail. Do you think Steve is a salesperson or a librarian? (Adapted from Tversky & Kahneman, 1974, p. 1124)

Using the *representativeness heuristic,* subjects tend to guess that Steve is a librarian because he resembles their prototype of a librarian (Tversky & Kahneman, 1982). In reality, this is not a very wise guess, because it *ignores the base rates* of librarians and salespeople in the population. Virtually everyone knows that salespeople outnumber librarians by a wide margin (roughly 75 to 1 in North America). This fact makes it much more likely that Steve is in sales. But in estimating probabilities, people often ignore information on base rates.

Although people do not *always* neglect base rate information, it is a persistent phenomenon (Birnbaum, 2004; Koehler, 1996). Moreover, people are particularly bad about applying base rates to themselves. For instance, Weinstein (1984; Weinstein & Klein, 1995) has found that people underestimate the risks of their own health-impairing habits while viewing others' risks much more accurately. Thus, smokers are realistic in estimating the degree to which smoking

Courtesy of Daniel Kahneman

❝*The human mind suppresses uncertainty. We're not only convinced that we know more about our politics, our businesses, and our spouses than we really do, but also that what we don't know must be unimportant.*❞
DANIEL KAHNEMAN

Stanford University News and Publication Service

❝*People treat their own cases as if they were unique, rather than part of a huge lottery. You hear this silly argument that 'The odds don't apply to me.' Why should God, or whoever runs this lottery, give you special treatment?*❞
AMOS TVERSKY

Web Link 8.4

Has Natural Selection Shaped How Humans Reason?
http://online.itp.ucsb.edu/online/colloq/cosmides1/

This link will take you to a recorded talk by Leda Cosmides and John Tooby (University of California, Santa Barbara) in which they discuss their evolutionary perspective on human decision making.

Courtesy of Leda Cosmides

Courtesy of John Tooby

❝*The problems our cognitive devices are designed to solve do not reflect the problems our modern life experiences lead us to see as normal.... Instead, they are the ancient and seemingly esoteric problems that our hunter-gatherer ancestors encountered generation after generation over hominid evolution.*❞

LEDA COSMIDES AND
JOHN TOOBY

increases someone else's risk of heart attack but underestimate the risk for themselves. Similarly, people starting new companies ignore the high failure rate for new businesses, and burglars underestimate the likelihood that they will end up in jail. Thus, in risky decision making, people often think that they can beat the odds. As Amos Tversky put it, "People treat their own cases as if they were unique, rather than part of a huge lottery. You hear this silly argument that 'The odds don't apply to me.' Why should God, or whoever runs this lottery, give you special treatment?" (McKean, 1985, p. 27).

The Conjunction Fallacy

Imagine that you're going to meet a man who is an articulate, ambitious, power-hungry wheeler-dealer. Do you think it's more likely that he's a university professor or a university professor who's also a politician?

People tend to guess that the man is a "university professor who's a politician" because the description fits with the typical prototype of politicians. But stop and think for a moment. The broader category of university professors completely includes the smaller subcategory of university professors who are politicians (see Figure 8.21). The probability of being in the subcategory cannot be higher than the probability of being in the broader category. It's a logical impossibility!

Tversky and Kahneman (1983) call this error the *conjunction fallacy*. **The *conjunction fallacy* occurs when people estimate that the odds of two uncertain events happening together are greater than the odds of either event happening alone.** The

University professors

University professors
who are also
politicians

Figure 8.21

The conjunction fallacy. People routinely fall victim to the conjunction fallacy, but as this diagram makes obvious, the probability of being in a subcategory (university professors who are politicians) cannot be higher than the probability of being in the broader category (university professors). As this case illustrates, it often helps to represent a problem in a diagram.

conjunction fallacy has been observed in a number of studies and has generally been attributed to the powerful influence of the representativeness heuristic (Epstein, Donovan, & Denes-Raj, 1999), although some doubts have been raised about this interpretation (Fisk, 2004).

Evolutionary Analyses of Flaws in Human Decision Making

A central conclusion of the last 25 years of research on decision making has been that human decision-making strategies are riddled with errors and biases that yield surprisingly irrational results (Goldstein & Hogarth, 1997; Shafir & LeBoeuf, 2002). Theorists have discovered that people have "mental limitations" and have concluded that people are not as bright and rational as they think they are. Conversely, over the same period of time, researchers studying the behaviour of animals in their natural environments have been increasingly impressed by how the animals tend to make sound choices that approximate optimal decision making (see Chapter 6) consistent with elaborate mathematical models of optimality (Real, 1991; Shettleworth, 1998). So, we have quite a

CONCEPT CHECK 8.3

Recognizing Heuristics in Decision Making

Check your understanding of heuristics in decision making by trying to identify the heuristics used in the following example. Each numbered element in the anecdote below illustrates a problem-solving heuristic. Write the relevant heuristic in the space on the left. You can find the answers in Appendix A.

_____ **1.** Marsha can't decide on a major. She evaluates all the majors available at her university on the attributes of how much she would enjoy them (likability), how challenging they are (difficulty), and how good the job opportunities are in the field (employability). She drops from consideration any major that she regards as "poor" on any of these three attributes.

_____ **2.** When she considers history as a major, she thinks to herself, "Gee, I know four history graduates who are still looking for work," and concludes that the probability of getting a job using a history degree is very low.

_____ **3.** She finds that every major gets a "poor" rating on at least one attribute, so she eliminates everything. Because this is unacceptable, she decides she has to switch to another strategy. Marsha finally focuses her consideration on five majors that received just one "poor" rating. She uses a 4-point scale to rate each of these majors on each of the three attributes she values. She adds up the ratings and selects the major with the highest total as her leading candidate.

paradox: How can humans appear so dumb, when animals appear so bright? This paradox has led some evolutionary psychologists to reconsider the work on human decision making, and their take on the matter is quite interesting. First, they argue that traditional decision research has imposed an invalid and unrealistic standard of rationality, which assumes that people should be impeccable in applying the laws of deductive logic and statistical probability while objectively and precisely weighing multiple factors in arriving at decisions (Gigerenzer, 2000). Second, they argue that humans only *seem* irrational because cognitive psychologists have been asking the wrong questions and formulating problems in the wrong ways—ways that have nothing to

do with the adaptive problems that the human mind has evolved to solve (Cosmides & Tooby, 1996).

According to Leda Cosmides and John Tooby (1994, 1996), the human mind consists of a large number of specialized cognitive mechanisms that have emerged over the course of evolution to solve specific adaptive problems, such as finding food, shelter, and mates and dealing with allies and enemies. Thus, human decision and problem-solving strategies have been tailored to handle real-world adaptive problems. Participants perform poorly in cognitive research, say Cosmides and Tooby, because it confronts them with contrived, artificial problems that do not involve natural categories and have no adaptive significance.

Putting It in Perspective

Four of our unifying themes have been especially prominent in this chapter. The first is the continuing question about the relative influences of heredity and environment. The controversy about how children acquire language skills replays the nature versus nurture debate. The behaviourist theory, that children learn language through imitation and reinforcement, emphasizes the importance of the environment. The nativist theory, that children come equipped with an innate language acquisition device, argues for the importance of biology. The debate is far from settled, but the accumulating evidence suggests that language development depends on both nature and nurture, as more recent interactionist theories have proposed.

The second pertinent theme is the empirical nature of psychology. For many decades, psychologists paid little attention to cognitive processes, because most of them assumed that thinking is too private to be studied scientifically. During the 1950s and 1960s, however, psychologists began to devise creative new ways to measure mental processes. These innovations fuelled the cognitive revolution that put the *psyche* (the mind) back in psychology. Thus, once again, we see how empirical methods are the lifeblood of the scientific enterprise.

Third, the study of cognitive processes shows how there are both similarities and differences across cultures in behaviour. On the one hand, we saw that language development unfolds in much the same way in widely disparate cultures and that thought processes are largely invariant in spite of sharp differences in cultures' linguistic heritage. On the other hand, we learned that there are interesting cultural variations in cognitive style.

The fourth theme is the subjective nature of human experience. We have seen that decision making is a highly subjective process. For example, probabilities weighed in decisions that are objectively identical can subjectively seem very different. The subjectivity of decision processes will continue to be prominent in the upcoming Personal Application, which discusses some more common pitfalls in reasoning about decisions.

REVIEW OF KEY POINTS

- Simon's theory of bounded rationality suggests that human decision strategies are simplistic and often yield irrational results. An additive decision model is used when people make decisions by rating the attributes of each alternative and selecting the alternative that has the highest sum of ratings.

- When elimination by aspects is used, people gradually eliminate alternatives whose attributes fail to satisfy some minimum criterion. To some extent, people adapt their decision-making strategy to the situation, moving toward simpler strategies when choices become complex. In making decisions, people have a curious tendency to pursue information that is not likely to alter their decisions.

- Models of how people make risky decisions focus on the expected value or subjective utility of various outcomes and the objective or subjective probability that these outcomes will occur.

- People use the representativeness and availability heuristics in estimating probabilities. These heuristics can lead people to ignore base rates and to fall prey to the conjunction fallacy.

- Evolutionary psychologists maintain that many errors and biases in human reasoning are greatly reduced when problems are presented in ways that resemble the type of input humans would have processed in ancestral times.

- Four of our unifying themes surfaced in the chapter. Our discussion of language acquisition revealed once again that all aspects of behaviour are shaped by both nature and nurture. The recent progress in the study of cognitive processes showed how science depends on empirical methods. Research on decision making illustrated the importance of subjective perceptions, and we saw that cognitive processes are moderated—to a limited degree—by cultural factors.

PREVIEW QUESTIONS

- Where did the nature versus nurture debate surface in this chapter?
- How did this chapter highlight the importance of research methods?
- How did this chapter illustrate both cultural variance and invariance?
- How did this chapter demonstrate the subjectivity of experience?

Understanding Pitfalls in Reasoning about Decisions

Consider the following scenario:

Laura is in a casino watching people play roulette. The 38 slots in the roulette wheel include 18 black numbers, 18 red numbers, and 2 green numbers. Hence, on any one spin, the probability of red or black is slightly less than 50-50 (0.474 to be exact). Although Laura hasn't been betting, she has been following the pattern of results in the game very carefully. The ball has landed in red seven times in a row. Laura concludes that black is long overdue and she jumps into the game, betting heavily on black.

Has Laura made a good bet? Do you agree with Laura's reasoning? Or do you think that Laura misunderstands the laws of probability? You'll find out momentarily, as we discuss how people reason their way to decisions—and how their reasoning can go awry.

The pioneering work of Amos Tversky and Daniel Kahneman (1974, 1982) led to an explosion of research on risky decision making. In their efforts to identify the heuristics that people use in decision making, investigators stumbled onto quite a few misconceptions, oversights, and biases. It turns out that people deviate in predictable ways from optimal decision strategies—with surprising regularity (Goldstein & Hogarth, 1997). As explained in the chapter, recent evolutionary research on decision making has offered a new explanation for *why* our decision making appears to be muddled. And evolutionary theorists argue that our decision strategies actually are rational—when viewed as evolved mechanisms designed to solve the adaptive problems faced in ancestral times (Cosmides & Tooby, 1996).

But, while the evolutionary explanations for our foibles in reasoning *may* be on target, the fact remains that *we do not live in ancestral times.* We live in the information

age and we have to deal with base rates, probabilities, and percentages on a routine basis. In our modern world, reproductive fitness surely depends more on school success than on counting berries. So, mainstream cognitive research on flaws in human reasoning about decisions remains relevant (Stanovich, 2003). Fortunately, there is evidence that increased awareness of common shortcomings in reasoning about decisions can lead to improved decision making (Agnoli & Krantz, 1989; Fischhoff, 1982; Keren, 1990). With this goal in mind, let's look at some common pitfalls in decision making.

The Gambler's Fallacy

As you may have guessed by now, Laura's reasoning in our opening scenario is flawed. A great many people tend to believe that Laura has made a good bet (Stanovich, 2003; Tversky & Kahneman, 1982). However, they're wrong. Laura's behaviour illustrates the *gambler's fallacy*—**the belief that the odds of a chance event increase if the event hasn't occurred recently.** People believe that the laws of probability should yield fair results and that a random process must be self-correcting (Barns & Corpus, 2004). These aren't bad assumptions in the long run. However, they don't apply to individual, independent events.

The roulette wheel does not remember its recent results and make adjustments for them. Each spin of the wheel is an independent event. The probability of black on each spin remains at 0.474, even if red comes up 100 times in a row! The gambler's fallacy reflects the pervasive influence of the *representativeness heuristic.* In betting on black, Laura is predicting that future results will be more representative of a random process. This logic can be used to estimate

the probability of black across a *string of spins.* But it doesn't apply to a *specific spin* of the roulette wheel.

The Law of Small Numbers

Envision a small urn filled with a mixture of red and green beads. You know that two-thirds of the beads are one colour and one-third are the other colour. However, you don't know whether red or green predominates. A blindfolded person reaches into the urn and comes up with 3 red beads and 1 green bead. These beads are put back in the urn and a second person scoops up 14 red beads and 10 green beads. Both samplings suggest that red beads outnumber green beads in the urn. But which sample provides better evidence? (Adapted from McKean, 1985, p. 25)

Many subjects report that the first sampling is more convincing, because of the greater preponderance of red over green. What are the actual odds that each sampling accurately reflects the dominant colour in the urn? The odds for the first sampling are 4 to 1. These aren't bad odds, but the odds that the second sampling is accurate are much higher—16 to 1. Why? Because the second sample is substantially larger than the first. The likelihood of misleading results is much greater in a small sample than a large one. For example, in flipping a fair coin, the odds of getting all heads in a sample of five coin flips dwarfs the odds of getting all heads in a sample of 100 coin flips.

Most people appreciate the value of a large sample as an abstract principle, but they don't fully understand that results based on small samples are more variable and more likely to be a fluke (Well, Pollatsek, & Boyce, 1990). Hence, they frequently assume that results based on small samples are representative of the population (Poulton, 1994). Tversky and Kahneman (1971) call this the *belief in the law of small numbers*. This misplaced faith in small numbers explains why people are often willing to draw general conclusions based on a few individual cases.

Overestimating the Improbable

Various causes of death are paired up below. In each pairing, which is the more likely cause of death?

> *Asthma or tornadoes?*
> *Accidental fall or firearms accident?*
> *Tuberculosis or floods?*
> *Suicide or murder?*

Table 8.4 shows the actual mortality rates for each of the causes of death just listed. As you can see, the first choice in each pair is the more common cause of death. If you guessed wrong for several pairings, don't feel bad. Like many other people, you may be a victim of the tendency to *overestimate the improbable*. People tend to greatly overestimate the likelihood of dramatic, vivid—but infrequent—events that receive heavy media coverage. Thus, the number of fatalities due to tornadoes, firearms accidents, floods, and murders is usually overestimated (Slovic, Fischhoff, & Lichtenstein, 1982). Fatalities due to asthma and other common diseases, which receive less media coverage, tend to be underestimated. For instance, a majority of subjects estimate that tornadoes kill more people than asthma, even though asthma fatalities outnumber tornado fatalities by a ratio of 80 to 1. This tendency to exaggerate the improbable reflects the operation of the *availability heuristic* (Reber, 2004). Instances of floods, tornadoes, and such are readily available in memory because people are exposed to a great deal of publicity about such events.

Confirmation Bias and Belief Perseverance

Imagine a young physician examining a sick patient. The patient is complaining of a high

The availability heuristic can be dramatized by juxtaposing the unrelated phenomena of floods and asthma. Many people are killed by floods, but far more die from asthma (see Table 8.4). However, since the news media report flood fatalities frequently and prominently, but rarely focus on deaths from asthma, people tend to assume that flood-related deaths are more common. Even in 2005, when Hurricane Katrina (whose devastation is shown in this photo) killed more than 1200 people, the death rate from floods was still below typical death rates for asthma.

fever and a sore throat. The physician must decide on a diagnosis from among a myriad of possible diseases. The physician thinks that it may be the flu. She asks the patient if he feels "achey all over." The answer is "yes." The physician asks if the symptoms began a few days ago. Again, the response is "yes." The physician concludes that the patient has the flu. (Adapted from Halpern, 1984, pp. 215–216)

Do you see any flaws in the physician's reasoning? Has she probed into the causes of the patient's malady effectively? No, she has asked about symptoms that would be consistent with her preliminary diagnosis, but she has not inquired about symptoms that

could rule it out. Her questioning of the patient illustrates *confirmation bias*—**the tendency to seek information that supports one's decisions and beliefs while ignoring disconfirming information** (see Figure 8.22). This bias is common in medical diagnosis and other forms of decision making (Nickerson, 1998). There's nothing wrong with searching for confirming evidence to support one's decisions. However, people should also seek disconfirming evidence—which they often neglect to do.

Confirmation bias contributes to another, related problem called *belief perseverance*—**the tendency to hang on to beliefs in the face of contradictory evidence** (Gorman,

Table 8.4 Actual U.S. Mortality Rates for Selected Causes of Death

Cause of Death	Rate	Cause of Death	Rate
Asthma	2 000	Tornadoes	25
Accidental falls	6 021	Firearms accidents	320
Tuberculosis	400	Floods	44
Suicide	11 300	Homicide	6 800

NOTE: Mortality rates are per 100 million people and are based on the *Statistical Abstract of the United States, 2001*.

Figure 8.22

Confirmation bias and belief perseverance. Confirmation bias exists when people seek out and react favourably to information that supports their beliefs. Belief perseverance is the tendency to cling to beliefs despite exposure to contradictory evidence.

1989). It is difficult to dislodge an idea after having embraced it. To investigate this phenomenon, researchers have given subjects evidence to establish a belief (e.g., high risk takers make better firefighters) and later exposed the subjects to information discrediting the idea. These studies have shown that the disconfirming evidence tends to fall on deaf ears (Ross & Anderson, 1982). Thus, once people arrive at a decision, they are prone to accept supportive evidence at face value while subjecting contradictory evidence to tough, skeptical scrutiny.

The Overconfidence Effect

Make high and low estimates of the total Canadian Defence Department spending budgeted for the year 2005. Choose estimates far enough apart to be 98% confident that the actual figure lies between them. In other words, you should feel that there is only a 2% chance that the correct figure is lower than your low estimate or higher than your high estimate. Write your estimates in the spaces provided, before reading further.

High estimate: _____

Low estimate: _____

When working on problems like this one, people reason their way to their best estimate and then create a confidence interval around it. For instance, let's say that you arrived at $8 billion as your best estimate of the defence budget. You would then expand a range around that estimate—say $6 billion to $10 billion—that you're sure will contain the correct figure. The answer in this case is $13 billion. If the answer falls outside your estimated range, you are not unusual. In making this type of estimate, people consistently tend to make their confidence intervals too narrow (Lichtenstein, Fischhoff, & Phillips, 1982; Soll & Klayman, 2004). For example, subjects' 98% confidence intervals should include the correct answer 98% of the time, but they actually do so only about 60% of the time.

The crux of the problem is that people tend to put too much faith in their estimates, beliefs, and decisions, even when they should know better, a principle called the *overconfidence effect*. People vary considerably in their tendency to be overconfident (Stanovich, 1999), but overconfidence effects have been seen in perceptual judgments, predictions of sports results, and economic forecasts, among many other

things (West & Stanovich, 1997). The overconfidence effect is seen even when people make probability predictions about themselves. For instance, in one study (Vallone et al., 1990), students were asked to make predictions about personal matters for the upcoming fall quarter and the entire academic year. Their predictions concerned such things as whether they would drop any courses, whether they would vote in an upcoming election, or whether they would break up with their boyfriend or girlfriend. The subjects were also asked to rate their confidence in each of their predictions, from 50% confidence to 100% confidence (the predictions were either–or propositions, making 50% a chance level of accuracy and the lowest possible level of confidence). The accuracy of the subjects' predictions was assessed at the end of the year. The analyses of thousands of predictions revealed that the students were more confident than accurate. Moreover, the more confident subjects were about their predictions, the more likely it was that they were overconfident (see Figure 8.23).

The overconfidence effect is also seen among experts in many walks of life (Fischhoff, 1988). Studies have shown that physicians, weather forecasters, military leaders, gamblers, investors, and scientists tend to be overconfident about their predictions. As Daniel Kahneman puts it, "The human mind suppresses uncertainty. We're not only convinced that we know more about our politics, our businesses, and our spouses than we really do, but also that what we don't know must be unimportant" (McKean, 1985, p. 27).

The Effects of Framing

Another consideration in making decisions involving risks is the framing of questions (Tversky & Kahneman, 1988, 1991). *Framing* **refers to how decision issues are posed or how choices are structured.** People often allow a decision to be shaped by the language or context in which it's presented, rather than explore it from different perspectives. Consider the following scenario, which is adapted from Kahneman and Tversky (1984, p. 343):

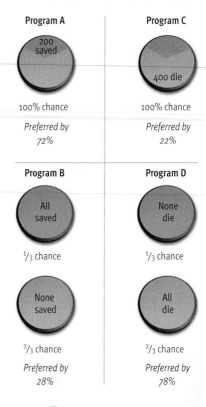

Figure 8.23

Results of the Vallone et al. (1990) study. The subjects in this study (sample 1) made 3776 predictions about personal matters. Their mean confidence level for all these predictions was 82.3%, but their mean accuracy was only 68.2%. When the predictions were divided into low-, medium-, and high-confidence predictions, an interesting pattern emerged. As subjects' confidence level went up, the gap between their confidence and their accuracy increased. This finding suggests that the more confident you are about a personal prediction, the more likely it is that you are overconfident. (Data from Vallone at al., 1990)

Imagine that a country is preparing for the outbreak of a dangerous disease, which is expected to kill 600 people. Two alternative programs to combat the disease have been proposed. Assume that the exact scientific estimates of the consequences of the programs are as follows:

- *If Program A is adopted, 200 people will be saved.*
- *If Program B is adopted, there is a one-third probability that all 600 people will be saved and a two-thirds probability that no people will be saved.*

Kahneman and Tversky found that 72% of their subjects chose the "sure thing" (Program A) over the "risky gamble" (Program B). However, they obtained different results when the alternatives were reframed as follows:

- *If Program C is adopted, 400 people will die.*
- *If Program D is adopted, there is a one-third probability that nobody will die and a two-thirds probability that all 600 people will die.*

Although framed differently, Programs A and B represent exactly the same probability situation as Programs C and D (see Figure 8.24). In spite of this equivalence, 78% of the subjects chose Program D. Thus, subjects chose the sure thing when the decision was framed in terms of lives saved, but they went with the risky gamble when the decision was framed in terms of lives lost. Additional experiments have shown that these results reflect a general trend in thinking about decisions. *When seeking to obtain gains, people tend to avoid risky options. However, when seeking to cut their losses, people are much more likely to take risks.*

Obviously, sound decision making should yield consistent decisions that are not altered dramatically by superficial changes in how options are presented, so framing effects once again highlight the foibles of human decision making. Fortunately, however, there are some limiting conditions that reduce the likelihood of framing effects (Mellers, Schwartz, & Cooke, 1998).

Nonetheless, research shows that framing is a factor in many of the choices people face in everyday life, including medical decisions (Gurm & Litaker, 2000) and consumer choices (Park, Jun, & Macinnis, 2000). For instance, some oil companies charge gas station patrons more when they pay with a credit card. This fee clearly is a credit surcharge that results in a small financial loss. However, the oil companies never explicitly label it as a surcharge. Instead, they assert that they offer a discount for cash. Thus, they frame the decision as a choice between the normal price or an opportunity for a gain. They understand that it's easier for customers to forsake a gain than it is to absorb a loss.

Figure 8.24

The framing of questions. This chart shows that Programs A and C involve an identical probability situation, as do Programs B and D. When choices are framed in terms of possible gains, people prefer the safer plan. However, when choices are framed in terms of losses, people are more willing to take a gamble.

REVIEW OF KEY POINTS

- The heuristics that people use in decision making can lead to various flaws in reasoning. For instance, the use of the representativeness heuristic contributes to the gambler's fallacy and faith in small numbers.

- The availability heuristic underlies the tendency to overestimate the improbable. People tend to cling to their beliefs in spite of contradictory evidence, in part because they exhibit confirmation bias—the tendency to only seek information that supports one's view.

- People generally fail to appreciate these shortcomings, which leads to the overconfidence effect. Evidence suggests that the more confident you feel about a prediction, the more likely it is that you are overconfident. In evaluating choices, it is wise to understand that decisions can be influenced by the language in which they are framed.

Shaping Thought with Language: "Only a Naïve Moron Would Believe That"

As explained in the chapter, the strong version of the *linguistic relativity hypothesis*—the idea that people's language determines how they think about things—has *not* been supported by research (Hunt & Agnoli, 1991). But research does show that carefully chosen words can exert subtle influence on people's feelings about various issues (Calvert, 1997; Johnson & Dowling-Guyer, 1996; Pohl, 2004; Weatherall, 1992). In everyday life, many people clearly recognize that language can tilt thought along certain lines. This possibility is the basis for some of the concerns that have been expressed about sexist language. Women who object to being called "girls," "chicks," and "babes" believe that these terms influence the way people think about and interact with women. In a similar vein, used car dealers that sell "pre-owned cars" and airlines that outline precautions for "water landings" are manipulating language to influence thought. Indeed, bureaucrats, politicians, advertisers, and big business have refined the art of shaping thought by tinkering with language, and to a lesser degree the same techniques are used by many people in everyday interactions. Let's look at two of these techniques: semantic slanting and name-calling.

Semantic Slanting

Semantic slanting refers to deliberately choosing words to create specific emotional responses. For example, consider the crafty word choices made in the incendiary debate about abortion (Halpern, 1996). The anti-abortion movement recognized that it is better to be *for* something than to be *against* something and then decided to characterize its stance as "pro-life" rather than "anti-choice." Likewise, the faction that favoured abortion did not like the connotation of an "anti-life" or "pro-abortion" campaign, so they characterized their position as "pro-choice." The position advocated is exactly the same either way, but the label clearly influences how people respond. Thinking along similar lines, some "pro-life" advocates have asserted that the best way to win the debate about abortion is to frequently use the words *kill* and *baby* in the same sentence (Kahane, 1992). Obviously, these are words that push people's buttons and trigger powerful emotional responses.

In his fascinating book *Doublespeak,* William Lutz (1989) describes an endless series of examples of how government, business, and advertisers manipulate language to bias people's thoughts and feelings. For example, in the language of the military, an invasion is a "pre-emptive counterattack," bombing the enemy is providing "air support," a retreat is a "back-loading of augmentation personnel," civilians accidentally killed or wounded by military strikes are "collateral damage," and troops killed by their own troops are "friendly casualties." In the world of business, layoffs and firings become "headcount reductions," "work-force adjustments," or "career alternative enhancement programs," whereas bad debts become "non-performing assets." And in the language of

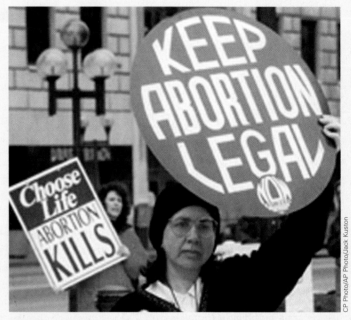

Semantic slanting, which consists of carefully choosing words to create specific emotional reactions, has been used extensively by both sides in the debate about abortion.

CP Photo/AP Photo/Jack Kuston

bureaucrats, hospital deaths become "negative patient care outcomes" and tax increases become "revenue enhancement initiatives," leading Lutz to quip that "Nothing in life is certain except negative patient care outcome and revenue enhancement." You can't really appreciate how absurd this process can become until you go shopping for "genuine imitation leather" or "real counterfeit diamonds."

Of course, you don't have to be a bureaucrat or military spokesperson to use semantic slanting. For example, if a friend of yours is annoyed at her 60-year-old professor for giving a tough exam and describes him as an "old geezer," she would be using semantic slanting. She would have communicated that the professor's age is a negative factor—one that is associated with a host of unflattering stereotypes about older people. And she would have implied that he gave an inappropriate exam because of his antiquated

Briefings on the status of military actions are renowned for their creative but unintelligible manipulation of language, which is often necessary to obscure the unpleasant realities of war.

expectations or senile incompetence—all with a couple of well-chosen words. We are all the recipients of many such messages containing emotionally laden words and content. An important skill of critical thinking is to recognize when semantic slanting is being used to influence how you think so you can resist this subtle technique.

In becoming sensitive to semantic slanting, notice how the people around you and those whom you see on television and read about in the newspapers refer to people from other racial and ethnic groups. You can probably determine a politician's attitudes toward immigration, for example, by considering the words he or she uses when speaking about people from other countries. Are the students on your campus who come from other countries referred to as "international students" or "foreign students"? The term "international" seems to convey a more positive image, with associations of being cosmopolitan and worldly. On the other hand, the term "foreign" suggests someone who is strange. Clearly, it pays to be careful when selecting the words you use in your own communication.

Name-Calling

Another way that word choice influences thinking is in the way people tend to label and categorize others through the strategy of *name-calling*. People often attempt to neutralize or combat views they don't like by attributing such views to "radical feminists," "knee-jerk liberals," "right-wingers," "religious zealots," or "extremists." In everyday interactions, someone who inspires our wrath may be labelled as a "bitch," a "moron," or a "cheapskate." In these examples, the name-calling is not subtle and is easy to recognize. But name-calling can also be used with more cunning and finesse. Sometimes, there is an

implied threat that if you make an unpopular decision or arrive at a conclusion that is not favoured, a negative label will be applied to you. For example, someone might say, "Only a naïve moron would believe that" to influence your attitude on an issue. This strategy of *anticipatory name-calling* makes it difficult for you to declare that you favour the negatively valued belief because it means that you make yourself look like a "naïve moron." Anticipatory name-calling can also invoke positive group memberships, such as asserting that "all good Canadians will agree …" or "people in the know think that …" Anticipatory name-calling is a shrewd tactic that can be effective in shaping people's thinking.

Regardless of your position on these issues, how would you respond to someone who says, "Only a knee-jerk liberal would support racial quotas or affirmative action programs that give unfair advantages to minorities." Or "Only a stupid bigot would oppose affirmative action programs that rectify the unfair discrimination that minorities face." Can you identify the anticipatory name-calling and the attempts at semantic slanting in each of these examples? More important, can you resist attempts like these to influence how you think about a host of complicated social issues?

Table 8.5 Critical Thinking Skills Discussed in This Application

Skill	Description
Understanding the way language can influence thought	The critical thinker appreciates that when you want to influence how people think, you should choose your words carefully.
Recognizing semantic slanting	The critical thinker is vigilant about how people deliberately choose certain words to elicit specific emotional responses.
Recognizing name-calling and anticipatory name-calling	The critical thinker is on the lookout for name-calling and the implied threats used in anticipatory name-calling.

CHAPTER 9

Latchezar Boyadjiev, *Energy*, L.B. Glass Studios

Key Concepts in Psychological Testing
Principal Types of Tests
Standardization and Norms
Reliability
Validity

The Evolution of Intelligence Testing
Galton's Studies of Hereditary Genius
Binet's Breakthrough
Terman and the Stanford-Binet
Wechsler's Innovations
Intelligence Testing Today

Basic Questions about Intelligence Testing
What Kinds of Questions Are on Intelligence Tests?
What Do Modern IQ Scores Mean?
Do Intelligence Tests Measure Potential or Knowledge?
Do Intelligence Tests Have Adequate Reliability?
Do Intelligence Tests Have Adequate Validity?
Do Intelligence Tests Predict Vocational Success?
Are IQ Tests Widely Used in Other Cultures?

Extremes of Intelligence
Mental Retardation
Giftedness

Heredity and Environment as Determinants of Intelligence
Evidence for Hereditary Influence
Evidence for Environmental Influence
The Interaction of Heredity and Environment
Cultural Differences in IQ Scores
Featured Study • Racial Stereotypes and Test Performance

New Directions in the Assessment and Study of Intelligence
Increasing Emphasis on Specific Abilities
Exploring Biological Indexes of Intelligence
Investigating Cognitive Processes in Intelligent Behaviour
Expanding the Concept of Intelligence
Measuring Emotional Intelligence

Putting It in Perspective

Personal Application • **Understanding Creativity**
The Nature of Creativity
Measuring Creativity
Correlates of Creativity

Critical Thinking Application • **The Intelligence Debate, Appeals to Ignorance, and Reification**
Appeal to Ignorance
Reification

Recap

Practice Test

PRACTICE TEST

1. The two-year-old child who refers to every four-legged animal as "doggie" is making which of the following errors?
   A. underextension
   B. overextension
   C. overregularization
   D. underregularization

2. Research suggests that bilingualism has a negative effect on:
   A. language development.
   B. cognitive development.
   C. metalinguistic awareness.
   D. none of the above.

3. Based on the work with Kanzi, which statement best summarizes the current status of the research on whether chimps can learn language?
   A. Chimps can acquire the use of symbols but cannot combine them into sentences or learn rules of language.
   B. Chimps are as well suited for learning and using language as humans.
   C. Chimps are incapable even of learning the symbols of a language.
   D. Chimps can learn some genuine language skills, including the use of rules, but the linguistic capacities of humans are far superior.

4. Chomsky proposed that children learn a language:
   A. because they possess an innate language acquisition device.
   B. through imitation, reinforcement, and shaping.
   C. as the quality of their thought improves with age.
   D. because they need to in order to get their increasingly complex needs met.

5. The linguistic relativity hypothesis is the notion that:
   A. one's language determines the nature of one's thought.
   B. one's thought determines the nature of one's language.
   C. language and thought are separate and independent processes.
   D. language and thought interact, with each influencing the other.

6. Arrangement problems are often solved:
   A. suddenly in a burst of insight.
   B. gradually in small, incremental steps.
   C. through fast mapping.
   D. by maximizing mental set.

7. Problems that require a common object to be used in an unusual way may be difficult to solve because of:
   A. mental set.
   B. irrelevant information.
   C. unnecessary constraints.
   D. functional fixedness.

8. A heuristic is:
   A. a flash of insight.
   B. a guiding principle or "rule of thumb" used in problem solving.
   C. a methodical procedure for trying all possible solutions to a problem.
   D. a way of making a compensatory decision.

9. In solving problems, people who are field dependent:
   A. rely on external frames of reference.
   B. tend to accept the physical environment as a given.
   C. tend to focus on specific features of a problem.
   D. all of the above.
   E. a and b.

10. According to Nisbett, Eastern cultures tend to favour a(n) _____ cognitive style, whereas Western cultures tend to display a(n) _____ cognitive style.
    A. analytic; holistic
    B. holistic; analytic
    C. holistic; field dependent
    D. field independent; field dependent

11. According to John Payne (1976), when do people use additive strategies?
    A. when decisions involve relatively few options
    B. when decisions involve many options
    C. when decisions involve familiar material and issues
    D. when decisions involve novel issues

12. When you estimate the probability of an event by judging the ease with which relevant instances come to mind, you are relying on:
    A. an additive decision-making model.
    B. the representativeness heuristic.
    C. the availability heuristic.
    D. a noncompensatory model.

13. The belief that the probability of heads is higher after a long string of tails:
    A. is rational and accurate.
    B. is an example of the "gambler's fallacy."
    C. reflects the influence of the representativeness heuristic.
    D. b and c.

14. The more confident you are about your predictions of upcoming events in your life:
    A. the less likely it is that your predictions are accurate.
    B. the less likely it is that your predictions are overconfident.
    C. the more likely it is that your predictions are overconfident.
    D. a and b.

15. If someone says, "Only a congenital pinhead would make that choice," this use of language would represent:
    A. confirmation bias.
    B. syntactic slanting.
    C. anticipatory name-calling.
    D. telegraphic speech.

   See Appendix A for answers to this Practice Test.

 ON THE WEB

For additional resources on the topics covered in this chapter, visit the *Psychology: Themes and Variations* Web site, where you will find practice quizzes, tutorials, Web links, simulations, critical thinking activities, flash cards, interactive exercises, and suggested readings available through INFOTRAC.

http://www.themesandvariations.nelson.com

  http://hed.nelson.com

Go to this site for the link to ThomsonNOW™, your one-stop study shop. Take a Pretest for this chapter and ThomsonNOW™ will generate a personalized Study Plan based on your test results! The Study Plan will identify the topics you need to review and direct you to online resources to help you master those topics. You can then take a Posttest to help you determine the concepts you have mastered and what you still need work on.

Latchezar Boyadjiev, *Energy,* L.B. Glass Studios

Key Concepts in Psychological Testing
Principal Types of Tests
Standardization and Norms
Reliability
Validity

The Evolution of Intelligence Testing
Galton's Studies of Hereditary Genius
Binet's Breakthrough
Terman and the Stanford-Binet
Wechsler's Innovations
Intelligence Testing Today

Basic Questions about Intelligence Testing
What Kinds of Questions Are on Intelligence Tests?
What Do Modern IQ Scores Mean?
Do Intelligence Tests Measure Potential or Knowledge?
Do Intelligence Tests Have Adequate Reliability?
Do Intelligence Tests Have Adequate Validity?
Do Intelligence Tests Predict Vocational Success?
Are IQ Tests Widely Used in Other Cultures?

Extremes of Intelligence
Mental Retardation
Giftedness

Heredity and Environment as Determinants of Intelligence
Evidence for Hereditary Influence
Evidence for Environmental Influence
The Interaction of Heredity and Environment
Cultural Differences in IQ Scores
Featured Study • Racial Stereotypes and Test Performance

New Directions in the Assessment and Study of Intelligence
Increasing Emphasis on Specific Abilities
Exploring Biological Indexes of Intelligence
Investigating Cognitive Processes in Intelligent Behaviour
Expanding the Concept of Intelligence
Measuring Emotional Intelligence

Putting It in Perspective

Personal Application • **Understanding Creativity**
The Nature of Creativity
Measuring Creativity
Correlates of Creativity

Critical Thinking Application • **The Intelligence Debate, Appeals to Ignorance, and Reification**
Appeal to Ignorance
Reification

Recap

Practice Test

Briefings on the status of military actions are renowned for their creative but unintelligible manipulation of language, which is often necessary to obscure the unpleasant realities of war.

expectations or senile incompetence—all with a couple of well-chosen words. We are all the recipients of many such messages containing emotionally laden words and content. An important skill of critical thinking is to recognize when semantic slanting is being used to influence how you think so you can resist this subtle technique.

In becoming sensitive to semantic slanting, notice how the people around you and those whom you see on television and read about in the newspapers refer to people from other racial and ethnic groups. You can probably determine a politician's attitudes toward immigration, for example, by considering the words he or she uses when speaking about people from other countries. Are the students on your campus who come from other countries referred to as "international students" or "foreign students"? The term "international" seems to convey a more positive image, with associations of being cosmopolitan and worldly. On the other hand, the term "foreign" suggests someone who is strange. Clearly, it pays to be careful when selecting the words you use in your own communication.

Name-Calling

Another way that word choice influences thinking is in the way people tend to label and categorize others through the strategy of *name-calling*. People often attempt to neutralize or combat views they don't like by attributing such views to "radical feminists," "knee-jerk liberals," "right-wingers," "religious zealots," or "extremists." In everyday interactions, someone who inspires our wrath may be labelled as a "bitch," a "moron," or a "cheapskate." In these examples, the name-calling is not subtle and is easy to recognize. But name-calling can also be used with more cunning and finesse. Sometimes, there is an *implied threat* that if you make an unpopular decision or arrive at a conclusion that is not favoured, a negative label will be applied to you. For example, someone might say, "Only a naïve moron would believe that" to influence your attitude on an issue. This strategy of *anticipatory name-calling* makes it difficult for you to declare that you favour the negatively valued belief because it means that you make yourself look like a "naïve moron." Anticipatory name-calling can also invoke positive group memberships, such as asserting that "all good Canadians will agree ..." or "people in the know think that ..." Anticipatory name-calling is a shrewd tactic that can be effective in shaping people's thinking.

Regardless of your position on these issues, how would you respond to someone who says, "Only a knee-jerk liberal would support racial quotas or affirmative action programs that give unfair advantages to minorities." Or "Only a stupid bigot would oppose affirmative action programs that rectify the unfair discrimination that minorities face." Can you identify the anticipatory name-calling and the attempts at semantic slanting in each of these examples? More important, can you resist attempts like these to influence how you think about a host of complicated social issues?

Table 8.5 Critical Thinking Skills Discussed in This Application

Skill	Description
Understanding the way language can influence thought	The critical thinker appreciates that when you want to influence how people think, you should choose your words carefully.
Recognizing semantic slanting	The critical thinker is vigilant about how people deliberately choose certain words to elicit specific emotional responses.
Recognizing name-calling and anticipatory name-calling	The critical thinker is on the lookout for name-calling and the implied threats used in anticipatory name-calling.

RECAP

Key Ideas

Language: Turning Thoughts into Words

● Languages are symbolic, semantic, generative, and structured. Human languages are structured hierarchically. At the bottom of the hierarchy are the basic sound units, called phonemes. At the next level are morphemes, the smallest units of meaning.

● Children typically utter their first words around their first birthday. Vocabulary growth is slow at first, but a vocabulary spurt often begins at around 18–24 months. Children begin to combine words by the end of their second year. Their early sentences are telegraphic, in that they omit many nonessential words. Over the next several years, children gradually learn the complexities of syntax.

● Research does not support the assumption that bilingualism has a negative effect on language development or on cognitive development. The learning of a second language is facilitated by starting at a younger age and by acculturation.

● Sue Savage-Rumbaugh's work with Kanzi suggests that some animals are capable of some genuine language acquisition. Many theorists believe that humans' special talent for language is the product of natural selection.

● According to Skinner and other behaviourists, children acquire a language through imitation and reinforcement. Nativist theories assert that humans have an innate capacity to learn language rules. Today, theorists are moving toward interactionist perspectives, which emphasize the role of both biology and experience. The evidence supports only a weak version of the linguistic relativity hypothesis.

Problem Solving: In Search of Solutions

● Psychologists have differentiated among several types of problems, including problems of inducing structure, problems of transformation, and problems of arrangement. Common barriers to problem solving include functional fixedness, mental set, getting bogged down in irrelevant information, and placing unnecessary constraints on one's solutions.

● A variety of strategies, or heuristics, are used for solving problems, including trial and error, forming subgoals, working backward, searching for analogies, and changing the representation of a problem.

● Some cultures encourage a field-dependent cognitive style, whereas others foster more field independence. People who are field independent tend to analyze and restructure problems more than those who are field dependent. Research suggests that Eastern cultures exhibit a more holistic cognitive style, whereas Western cultures display a more analytic cognitive style.

Decision Making: Choices and Chances

● Simon's theory of bounded rationality suggests that human decision strategies are simplistic and often yield irrational results. An additive decision model is used when people make decisions by rating the attributes of each alternative and selecting the alternative that has the highest sum of ratings.

● When elimination by aspects is used, people gradually eliminate alternatives if their attributes fail to satisfy some minimum criterion. To some extent, people adapt their decision-making strategy to the situation, moving toward simpler strategies when choices become complex.

● Models of how people make risky decisions focus on the expected value or subjective utility of various outcomes and the objective or subjective probability that these outcomes will occur.

● People use the representativeness and availability heuristics in estimating probabilities. These heuristics can lead people to ignore base rates and to fall for the conjunction fallacy.

● Evolutionary psychologists maintain that many errors and biases in human reasoning are greatly reduced when problems are presented in ways that resemble the type of input humans would have processed in ancestral times.

Putting It in Perspective

● Four of our unifying themes surfaced in the chapter. Our discussion of language acquisition revealed once again that all aspects of behaviour are shaped by both nature and nurture. The recent progress in the study of cognitive processes showed how science depends on empirical methods. Research on decision making illustrated the importance of subjective perceptions. We also saw that cognitive processes are moderated—to a limited degree—by cultural factors.

Personal Application • Understanding Pitfalls in Reasoning about Decisions

● The heuristics that people use in decision making lead to various flaws in reasoning. For instance, the use of the representativeness heuristic contributes to the gambler's fallacy and faith in small numbers. The availability heuristic underlies the tendency to overestimate the improbable.

● People tend to cling to their beliefs in spite of contradictory evidence, in part because they exhibit confirmation bias. People generally fail to appreciate these shortcomings, which leads to the overconfidence effect. In evaluating choices, it is wise to understand that decisions can be influenced by the language in which they are framed.

Critical Thinking Application • Shaping Thought with Language: "Only a Naïve Moron Would Believe That"

● Language can exert subtle influence over how people feel about various issues. Semantic slanting refers to the deliberate choice of words to create specific emotional responses, as has been apparent in the debate about abortion. In anticipatory name-calling, there is an implied threat that a negative label will apply to you if you express certain views.

Key Terms

Acculturation, 320
Algorithm, 329
Availability heuristic, 337
Belief perseverance, 341
Bilingualism, 318
Cognition, 312
Confirmation bias, 341
Conjunction fallacy, 338
Decision making, 335
Fast mapping, 317
Field dependence–independence, 332
Framing, 342
Functional fixedness, 328
Gambler's fallacy, 340
Heuristic, 329
Insight, 326
Language, 312
Language acquisition device (LAD), 324
Linguistic relativity, 325
Mean length of utterance (MLU), 318
Mental set, 328
Metalinguistic awareness, 318
Morphemes, 313
Overextension, 317
Overregularization, 318
Phonemes, 313
Problem solving, 326
Problem space, 329
Representativeness heuristic, 337
Risky decision making, 336
Semantics, 314
Syntax, 314
Telegraphic speech, 318
Theory of bounded rationality, 335
Trial and error, 329
Underextensions, 317

Key People

Ellen Bialystok, 319
Noam Chomsky, 324
Leda Cosmides, 338
Daniel Kahneman, 337
Wallace Lambert, 319
Laura-Ann Petitto, 315
Steven Pinker, 323
Sue Savage-Rumbaugh, 322
Herbert Simon, 335
B. F. Skinner, 325
John Tooby, 338
Amos Tversky, 337
Janet Werker, 315

Intelligence and Psychological Testing

As we suggested in Chapter 3, people seem to be endlessly fascinated with the brain. The research and theory we discussed in that chapter revealed the many important functions that the brain serves and the abilities it affords us. Among these, of course—and this may be part of the reason for our fascination—is the notion of intelligence. When we think of highly intelligent people we often apply the label "genius" to someone like Albert Einstein, who made critical contributions to our understanding of the universe, or Gerhard Herzberg, a Canadian who won the Nobel Prize for Chemistry in 1971. Herzberg's main contributions were to the field of atomic and molecular spectroscopy (Stoicheff, 2002). Incidentally, his son Paul is a psychologist.

Some have also applied the term genius to another well-known Canadian—golfer Moe Norman. Many think of him as the greatest golfer that ever lived and as a man possessing the "perfect swing." Norman was also a math prodigy and a high school dropout (CBC, n.d.). Interestingly, like Einstein, Norman was considered an eccentric. You may be wondering right now what success in academia has to do with athletic success. While one seems a natural fit with the topic of intelligence, the other seems to be out of place. Before we suggest an answer, let us introduce you to two other Canadians, this time young Canadians about whom you may hear more in the future.

Fourteen-year-old Chen Kupperman is now in his second year of studies at York University in Toronto. Chen began his studies in 2004 in mathematics and says he has been trying to make a career out of math since the age of six ("14-Year-Old," 2005). Charlotte Petrick is a seven-year-old tennis prodigy from Ontario. She regularly travels to study at the world-famous Bollettieri Tennis Academy in Florida. Her goal, she says, is to be number one by the time she is 17 (Starkman, 2005). What these two kids have in common, and what Herzberg and Norman have in common, is exceptional ability. But, each is demonstrating exceptional ability in quite different spheres. It may surprise you, but according to some recent

theories of intelligence (e.g., Gardner, 1993), both sets of abilities may reflect different facets of high intelligence. The nature of intelligence is just one of the issues we will discuss in this chapter.

We will also deal with the social and sometimes very personal implications of differences in intelligence. As we will see later in the chapter, some have suggested that differences in intelligence are directly tied to social class and race, a concept with important social implications. Variation in intelligence, especially assumed low intelligence, has had important personal consequences for many Canadians. Consider, for example, the story of Leilani Muir, who was sterilized in 1959 at the age of 14 in Alberta (Pringle, 1997). She had tested low on one IQ test and was considered a "mental defective." Before the operation, she was told she was having surgery on her appendix. She was a resident of Alberta's Provincial Training School for Mental Defectives and was one of many who suffered a similar fate. Muir successfully sued the Alberta government in 1996. University of Alberta psychologist Douglas Wahlsten has written extensively about this case and related issues (Wahlsten, 1997a, 1999). Leilani's story is documented

Gerhard Herzberg won the Nobel Prize for Chemistry in 1971. He worked at the University of Saskatchewan and the National Research Council.

CP Photo/Ottawa Citizen

Canadian golfer Moe Norman was thought to possess the "perfect swing."

Most children become familiar with standardized psychological tests—intelligence, achievement, and aptitude tests—in school settings.

in the 1996 National Film Board production titled *The Sterilization of Leilani Muir.*

The vast enterprise of modern testing evolved from psychologists' pioneering efforts to measure *general intelligence*. The first useful intelligence tests, which were created soon after the turn of the twentieth century, left a great many "descendants." Today, there are over 2600 published psychological tests that measure a diverse array of mental abilities and other behavioural traits. Indeed, psychological testing has become a big business that annually generates millions of dollars of revenues.

Clearly, North American society has embraced psychological testing (Hanson, 1993). Each year in Canada alone, people take *millions* of intelligence and achievement tests. Scholarships, degrees, jobs, and self-concepts are on the line as Canadians attempt to hurdle a seemingly endless succession of tests. Because your life is so strongly affected by how you perform on psychological tests, it pays to be aware of their strengths and limitations. In this chapter we'll explore many questions about testing, including the following:

- How did psychological testing become so prevalent in modern society?
- How do psychologists judge the validity of their tests?
- What exactly do intelligence tests measure?
- Is intelligence inherited? If so, to what extent?
- How do psychological tests measure creativity?

We'll begin by introducing some basic concepts in psychological testing. Then we'll explore the history of intelligence tests, because they provided the model for subsequent psychological tests. Next we'll address practical questions about how intelligence tests work. After examining the nature versus nurture debate as it relates to intelligence, we'll explore some new directions in the study of intelligence. In the Personal Application, we'll discuss efforts to measure and understand another type of mental ability: creativity. In the Critical Thinking Application, we will critique some of the reasoning used in the vigorous debate about the roots of intelligence.

Key Concepts in Psychological Testing

A *psychological test* is a standardized measure of a sample of a person's behaviour. Psychological tests are measurement instruments. They're used to measure the *individual differences* that exist among people in abilities, aptitudes, interests, and aspects of personality.

Your responses to a psychological test represent a *sample* of your behaviour. The word *sample* should alert you to one of the key limitations of psychological tests: A particular behaviour sample may not be representative of your characteristic behaviour. Everyone has bad days. A stomachache, a fight with a friend, a problem with your car—all might affect your responses to a particular test on a particular day. Because of the limitations of the sampling process, test scores should always be interpreted *cautiously*.

Principal Types of Tests

Psychological tests are used extensively in research, but most of them were developed to serve a practical purpose outside of the laboratory. Most tests can be placed in one of two broad categories: mental ability tests and personality tests.

Mental Ability Tests

Psychological testing originated with efforts to measure general mental ability. Today, tests of mental abilities remain the most common kind of psychological test. This broad class of tests includes three principal subcategories: intelligence tests, aptitude tests, and achievement tests.

Intelligence tests measure general mental ability. They're intended to assess intellectual potential rather than previous learning or accumulated knowledge. *Aptitude tests* are also designed to measure potential more than knowledge, but they break mental ability into separate components. Thus, *aptitude tests assess specific types of mental abilities.* For example, the Differential Aptitude Tests assess verbal reasoning, numerical ability, abstract reasoning, perceptual speed and accuracy, mechanical reasoning, space relations, spelling, and language usage (see Figure 9.1). Like aptitude tests, *achievement tests* have a specific focus, but they're supposed to measure previous learning instead of potential. Thus, *achievement tests gauge a person's mastery and knowledge of various subjects* (such as reading, English, or history).

Personality Tests

If you had to describe yourself in a few words, what words would you use? Are you introverted? Independent? Ambitious? Enterprising? Conventional? Assertive? Domineering? Words such as these refer to personality traits. These *traits* can be assessed systematically with personality tests, of which there are more than 500. *Personality tests measure various aspects of personality, including motives, interests, values, and attitudes.* Many psychologists prefer to call these tests personality *scales* because, unlike tests of mental abilities, the questions do not have right and wrong answers. We'll look at the various types of personality scales in Chapter 12.

Standardization and Norms

Both personality scales and tests of mental abilities are *standardized* measures of behaviour. *Standardization refers to the uniform procedures used in the administration and scoring of a test.* All subjects get the same instructions, the same questions, and the same time limits so that their scores can be compared meaningfully. This means, for instance, that a person taking the Differential Aptitude Tests (DAT) in Madoc, Ontario, in 1984, another taking the DAT in Powell River, British Columbia, in 1994, and another taking it in 2005 in Bedford, Nova Scotia, all confront exactly the same test-taking task.

The standardization of a test's scoring system includes the development of test norms. *Test norms provide information about where a score on a psychological test ranks in relation to other scores on that test.* Why are test norms needed? Because in psychological testing, everything is relative. Psychological tests tell you how you score *relative to other people*. They tell you, for instance, that you are average in creativity or slightly above average in clerical ability. These interpretations are derived from the test norms that help you understand what your test score means.

Usually, test norms allow you to convert your "raw score" on a test into a *percentile*. A *percentile score indicates the percentage of people who score at or below the score one has obtained.* For example, imagine that you take a 40-item assertiveness scale and obtain a raw score of 26. In other words, you indicate a preference for the assertive option on 26 of the questions. Your score of 26 has little meaning until you consult the test norms and find out that it places

PREVIEW QUESTIONS

- Why is it wise to be cautious when interpreting test results?
- What are the two main categories of psychological tests?
- What makes a test standardized?
- What are test norms and percentile scores?
- What is reliability, and how can it be measured?
- What are the three types of test validity?

Web Link 9.1

The ETS Test Collection
http://www.ets.org/testcoll/

Educational Testing Service (ETS) has made available online the ETS Test Collection database listing more than 25 000 tests and research instruments. Users can search the database to discover basic information about each test and its availability.

Figure 9.1

Examples of aptitude tests.
Aptitude tests measure specific mental abilities instead of general mental ability. The questions shown here illustrate the specific types of abilities assessed by the Differential Aptitude Tests.

Verbal reasoning
Choose the correct pair of words to fill the blanks. The first word of the pair goes in the blank space at the beginning of the sentence; the second word of the pair goes in the blank at the end of the sentence.

_____ is to fin as bird is to _____

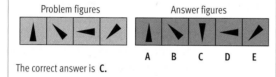

A water–feather   **C** fish–wing
B shark–nest   **D** flipper–fly
      E fish–sky

The correct answer is **C.**

Numerical reasoning
Choose the correct answer for the problem.

    18
    10
  +17

A 13
B 11
C 7
D 6
E none of these

The correct answer is **E.**

Abstract reasoning
The four "problem figures" make a series. Find the one among the "answer figures" that would be next in the series.

Problem figures   Answer figures

                                       A   **B**   **C**   **D**   **E**

The correct answer is **C.**

Perceptual speed and accuracy
In each test item, one of the five combinations is underlined. Find the same combination on the answer sheet and mark it.

Test items   Sample of answer sheet

1.	XY	Xy	XX	_YX_	Yy		1	Xy	Yy	YX	XX	XY
2.	6g	_6G_	G6	Gg	g6		2	g6	Gg	6g	G6	6G
3.	_nm_	mn	mm	nn	nv		3	nn	mn	nv	nm	mm

Mechanical reasoning

A   B   C

Which load will be easier to pull through soft sand?

The correct answer is **C.**

Space relations
Which one of the following figures could be made by folding the pattern at the left? The pattern always shows the outside of the figure.

                           A   **B**   **C**   **D**

The correct answer is **C.**

Spelling
Decide which word is not spelled correctly.

     A   numeral
     B   interest
     C   desloyal
     D   salary

The correct answer is **C.**

Language usage
Decide which of the lettered parts of the sentence contains an error and mark the corresponding letter on the answer sheet. If there is no error, mark *No Error.*

Jane and Tom / is going / to the office / this morning.
      A   **B**   **C**   **D**

The correct answer is **B.**

Web Link 9.2

ERIC Clearinghouse on Assessment and Evaluation
http://ericae.net/

This site assembles the most comprehensive set of links regarding psychological testing and assessment on the Web. A recent addition is the full-text library of more than 250 scholarly and professional books and articles regarding assessment.

Web Link 9.3

Finding Information about Psychological Tests
http://www.apa.org/science/faq-findtests.html

Maintained by the American Psychological Association, this FAQ site answers all sorts of questions about the availability of various kinds of tests. It explains how to find specific tests, how to get information on tests, and outlines information on the proper use of tests.

---

you at the 82nd percentile. This normative information would indicate that you appear to be as assertive as or more assertive than 82% of the sample of people who provided the basis for the test norms.

The sample of people that the norms are based on is called a test's *standardization group.* Ideally, test norms are based on a large sample of people who were carefully selected to be representative of the broader population. For example, the American norms for most intelligence tests are based on samples of 2000–6000 people whose demographic characteristics closely match the overall demographics of the United States (Woodcock, 1994). Separate norms are developed for the use and interpretation of many intelligence tests, such as the WAIS-III in Canada

(Psychological Corporation, 2001). University of Saskatchewan psychologist Donald Saklofske and his colleagues recently published Canadian norms for a general ability index for the WAIS-III (Saklofske et al., 2005). Even though Canadian and American societies are similar in many ways, there are also many important differences in culture, language, and educational systems that might be important considerations when evaluating an individual's performance on a test. Thus, for many tests, the most appropriate comparison group is other Canadians of similar age and status. Although intelligence tests have been standardized pretty carefully, the representativeness of standardization groups for other types of tests varies considerably from one test to another.

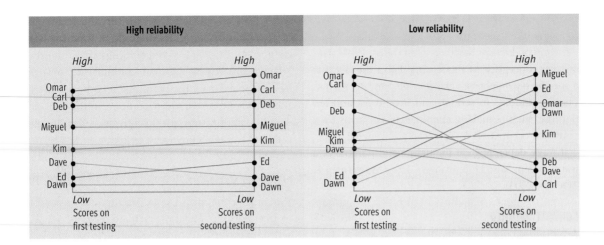

High reliability		Low reliability	

Figure 9.2

Test–retest reliability. In each panel, subjects' scores on the first administration of an assertiveness test are represented on the left, and their scores on a second administration of the same test a few weeks later are shown on the right. If participants obtain similar scores on both administrations, as in the left panel, the test measures assertiveness consistently and has high test–retest reliability. If they get very different scores on the second administration, as in the right panel, the test has low reliability.

Reliability

 SIM 8, 7D

Any kind of measuring device, whether it's a tire gauge, a stopwatch, or a psychological test, should be reasonably consistent. That is, repeated measurements should yield reasonably similar results. Psychologists call this quality *reliability*. Consistency in measurement is essential to accuracy in measurement.

Reliability refers to the measurement consistency of a test (or of other kinds of measurement techniques). Like most other types of measuring devices, psychological tests are not perfectly reliable. A test's reliability can be estimated in several ways. One widely used approach is to check *test–retest reliability*, which is estimated by comparing subjects' scores on two administrations of a test. If we wanted to check the test–retest reliability of a newly developed test of assertiveness, we would ask a group of subjects to take the test on two occasions, probably a few weeks apart (see Figure 9.2). The underlying assumption is that assertiveness is a fairly stable aspect of personality that won't change in a matter of a few weeks. Thus, changes in participants' scores across the two administrations of the test would presumably reflect inconsistency in measurement.

Reliability estimates require the computation of correlation coefficients, which we introduced in Chapter 2 (see Figure 9.3 for a brief recapitulation). *A correlation coefficient is a numerical index of the degree of relationship between two variables.* In estimating test–retest reliability, the two variables that must be correlated are the two sets of scores from the two administrations of the test. If people get fairly similar scores on the two administrations of our hypothetical assertiveness test, this consistency yields a substantial positive correlation. The magnitude of the correlation gives us a precise indication of the test's consistency. The closer the correlation comes to +1.00, the more reliable the test is.

There are no absolute guidelines about acceptable levels of reliability. What's acceptable depends to some extent on the nature and purpose of the test (Reynolds, 1994). The reliability estimates for most psychological tests are above 0.70. Many exceed 0.90. The higher the reliability coefficient, the more consistent the test is. As reliability goes down, concern about measurement error increases.

Validity

 SIM 8, 7D

Even if a test is quite reliable, we still need to be concerned about its validity. **Validity refers to the ability of a test to measure what it was designed to measure.** If we develop a new test of assertiveness, we have to provide some evidence that it really

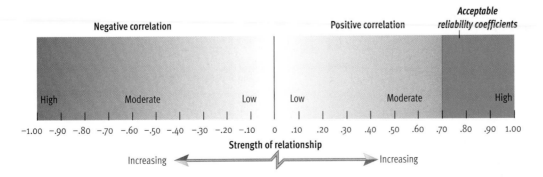

Figure 9.3

Correlation and reliability. As explained in Chapter 2, a positive correlation means that two variables co-vary in the *same* direction; a negative correlation means that two variables co-vary in *opposite* directions. The closer the correlation coefficient gets to either −1.00 or +1.00, the stronger the relationship. At a minimum, reliability estimates for psychological tests must be moderately high positive correlations. Most reliability coefficients fall between 0.70 and 0.95.

measures assertiveness. Increasingly, the term *validity* is also used to refer to the accuracy or usefulness of the *inferences* or *decisions* based on a test (Moss, 1994). This broader conception of validity highlights the fact that a specific test might be valid for one purpose, such as placing students in school, and invalid for another purpose, such as making employment decisions for a particular occupation. Validity can be estimated in several ways, depending on the nature and purpose of a test (Golden, Sawicki, & Franzen, 1990; Wasserman & Bracken, 2003).

Content Validity

Achievement tests and educational tests such as classroom exams should have adequate content validity. ***Content validity* refers to the degree to which the content of a test is representative of the domain it's supposed to cover.** Imagine a poorly prepared psychology exam that includes questions on material that was not covered in class or in assigned reading. The professor has compromised the content validity of the exam. Content validity is evaluated with logic more than with statistics.

Criterion-Related Validity

Psychological tests are often used to make predictions about specific aspects of individuals' behaviour. They are used to predict performance in university, job capability, and suitability for training programs, as just a few examples. Criterion-related validity is a central concern in such cases. ***Criterion-related validity* is estimated by correlating subjects' scores on a test with their scores on an independent criterion (another measure) of the trait assessed by the test.** For example, let's say you developed a test to measure aptitude for becoming an airplane pilot. You could check its validity by correlating subjects'

scores on your aptitude test with subsequent ratings of their performance in their pilot training (see Figure 9.4). The performance ratings would be the independent criterion of pilot aptitude. If your test has reasonable validity, there ought to be a reasonably strong positive correlation between the test and the criterion measure. Such a correlation would help validate your test's predictive ability.

Construct Validity

Many psychological tests attempt to measure abstract personal qualities, such as creativity, intelligence, extraversion, or independence. No obvious criterion measures exist for these abstract qualities, which are called *hypothetical constructs*. In measuring abstract qualities, psychologists are concerned about ***construct validity*—the extent to which there is evidence that a test measures a particular hypothetical construct.**

The process of demonstrating construct validity can be complicated. It usually requires a series of studies that examine the correlations between the test and various measures *related* to the trait in question. A thorough demonstration of construct validity requires looking at the relations between a test and many other measures. For example, some of the evidence on the construct validity of a measure of extraversion (the Expression scale from the Psychological Screening Inventory) is summarized in Figure 9.5. This network of correlation coefficients shows that the Expression scale correlates negatively, positively, or not at all with various measures, much as one would expect if the scale is really assessing extraversion. Ultimately, it's the overall pattern of correlations that provides convincing (or unconvincing) evidence of a test's construct validity.

Figure 9.4

Criterion-related validity. To evaluate the criterion-related validity of a pilot aptitude test, a psychologist would correlate subjects' test scores with a criterion measure of their aptitude, such as ratings of their performance in a pilot training program. The validity of the test is supported if the people who score high on the test also score high on the criterion measure (as shown in the left panel), yielding a substantial correlation between the two measures. If little or no relationship exists between the two sets of scores (as shown in the right panel), the data do not provide support for the validity of the test.

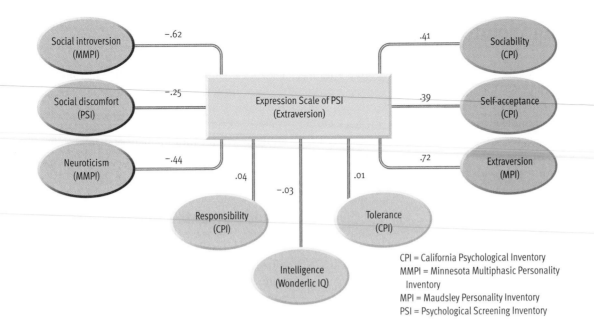

Figure 9.5

Construct validity. Some of the evidence on the construct validity of the Expression Scale from the Psychological Screening Inventory is summarized here. This scale is supposed to measure the personality trait of *extraversion*. As you can see on the left side of this network of correlations, the scale correlates negatively with measures of social introversion, social discomfort, and neuroticism, just as one would expect if the scale is really tapping extraversion. On the right, you can see that the scale is correlated positively with measures of sociability and self-acceptance and another index of extraversion, as one would anticipate. At the bottom, you can see that the scale does not correlate with several traits that should be unrelated to extraversion. Thus, the network of correlations depicted here supports the idea that the Expression scale measures the construct of extraversion.

Douglas Jackson of the University of Western Ontario is a well-known proponent of the importance of construct validity in test development (Jackson & Paunonen, 1980). The systematic application of construct validation principles to his test development work has resulted in his tests being viewed as some of the best in their area of application. We will learn more about these types of tests in later chapters.

The complexities involved in demonstrating construct validity will be apparent in our upcoming discussion of intelligence testing. The ongoing debate about the construct validity of intelligence tests is one of the oldest debates in psychology. We'll look first at the origins of intelligence tests; this historical review will help you appreciate the current controversies about intelligence testing.

REVIEW OF KEY POINTS

- Psychological tests are standardized measures of behaviour—usually mental abilities or aspects of personality. Test scores are interpreted by consulting test norms to find out what represents a high or low score.

- As measuring devices, psychological tests should produce consistent results, a quality called reliability. Test–retest reliability is estimated by comparing subjects' scores on two administrations of a test. Reliability estimates should yield fairly high positive correlations.

- Validity refers to the degree to which there is evidence that a test measures what it was designed to measure. Content validity is crucial on classroom tests. Criterion-related validity is critical when tests are used to predict performance. Construct validity is critical when a test is designed to measure a hypothetical construct.

CONCEPT CHECK 9.1

Recognizing Basic Concepts in Testing

Check your understanding of basic concepts in psychological testing by answering the questions below. Select your responses from the following concepts. The answers are in Appendix A.

Test norms Split-half reliability Construct validity
Test–retest reliability Criterion-related validity Content validity

1. At the request of the HiTechnoLand computer store chain, Professor Charlz develops a test to measure aptitude for selling computers. Two hundred applicants for sales jobs at HiTechnoLand stores are asked to take the test on two occasions, a few weeks apart. A correlation of +0.82 is found between applicants' scores on the two administrations of the test. Thus, the test appears to possess reasonable _____.

2. All 200 of these applicants are hired and put to work selling computers. After six months Professor Charlz correlates the new workers' aptitude test scores with the dollar value of the computers that each sold during the first six months on the job. This correlation turns out to be −0.21. This finding suggests that the test may lack _____.

3. Back at the university, Professor Charlz is teaching a course in theories of personality. He decides to use the same midterm exam that he gave last year, even though the exam includes questions about theorists that he did not cover or assign reading on this year. There are reasons to doubt the _____ of Professor Charlz's midterm exam.

PREVIEW QUESTIONS

- When and how did intelligence testing begin?
- What were Binet's contributions to the progress of intelligence testing?
- What is an IQ score, and with what test did it originate?
- How did Wechsler improve intelligence testing?

> "There is no escape from the conclusion that nature prevails enormously over nurture when the differences in nurture do not exceed what is commonly to be found among persons of the same rank of society and in the same country."
>
> SIR FRANCIS GALTON

> "The intelligence of anyone is susceptible of development. With practice, enthusiasm, and especially with method one can succeed in increasing one's attention, memory, judgment, and in becoming literally more intelligent than one was before."
>
> ALFRED BINET

Psychological tests may play a prominent role in contemporary society, but this wasn't always so. The first psychological tests were invented only a little over a hundred years ago. Since then, the reliance on psychological tests has grown gradually. In this section, we discuss the pioneers who launched psychological testing with their efforts to measure general intelligence.

Galton's Studies of Hereditary Genius

It all began with the work of a British scholar, Sir Francis Galton, in the later part of the 19th century. Galton studied family trees and found that success and eminence appeared consistently in some families over generations. For the most part, these families were much like Galton's: well-bred, upper-class families with access to superior schooling and social connections that pave the way to success. Yet Galton discounted the advantages of such an upbringing. In his book *Hereditary Genius,* Galton (1869) concluded that success runs in families because great intelligence is passed from generation to generation through genetic inheritance. Galton himself was an example—his half-cousin was Charles Darwin. According to York University's Ray Fancher (1979), while Galton and Darwin were never really close, Darwin's evolutionary ideas did impact Galton's research and theories.

To better demonstrate that intelligence is governed by heredity, Galton needed an objective measure of intelligence. His approach to this problem was guided by the theoretical views of his day. Thus, he assumed that the contents of the mind are built out of elementary *sensations,* and he hypothesized that exceptionally bright people should exhibit exceptional sensory acuity. Working from this premise, he tried to assess innate mental ability by measuring simple sensory processes. Among other things, he measured sensitivity to high-pitched sounds, colour perception, and reaction time (the speed of one's response to a stimulus). His efforts met with little success. Research eventually showed that the sensory processes that he measured were largely unrelated to other criteria of mental ability that he was trying to predict, such as success in school or in professional life (Kaufman, 2000).

In pursuing this line of investigation, Galton coined the phrase *nature versus nurture* to refer to the heredity–environment issue (Hilgard, 1989). Along the way, he also invented the concepts of *correlation* and *percentile test scores* (Roberts et al., 2005). Although Galton's mental tests were a failure, his work created an interest in the measurement of mental ability, setting the stage for a subsequent breakthrough by Alfred Binet, a prominent French psychologist.

Binet's Breakthrough

In 1904 a commission on education in France asked Alfred Binet to devise a test to identify mentally subnormal children. The commission was motivated by admirable goals: It wanted to single out youngsters in need of special training. It also wanted to avoid complete reliance on teachers' evaluations, which might often be subjective and biased.

In response to this need, Binet and a colleague, Theodore Simon, published the first useful test of general mental ability in 1905. They had the insight to load it with items that required abstract reasoning skills, rather than the sensory skills Galton had measured (Brody, 2000). Their scale was a success because it was inexpensive, easy to administer, objective, and capable of predicting children's performance in school fairly well (Siegler, 1992). Thanks to these qualities, its use spread across Europe and North America.

The Binet-Simon scale expressed a child's score in terms of "mental level" or "mental age." A child's **mental age indicated that he or she displayed the mental ability typical of a child of that chronological (actual) age.** Thus, a child with a mental age of six performed like the average six-year-old on the test. Binet realized that his scale was a somewhat crude initial effort at measuring mental ability. He revised it in 1908 and again in 1911. Unfortunately, his revising came to an abrupt end with his death in 1911. However, other psychologists continued to build on Binet's work.

Terman and the Stanford-Binet

In the United States, Lewis Terman and his colleagues at Stanford University soon went to work on a major expansion and revision of Binet's test. Their work led to the 1916 publication of the Stanford-Binet Intelligence Scale (Terman, 1916). Although this revision was quite loyal to Binet's original con-

Table 9.1 Calculating the Intelligence Quotient

Measure	Child 1	Child 2	Child 3	Child 4
Mental age (MA)	6 years	6 years	9 years	12 years
Chronological age (CA)	6 years	9 years	12 years	9 years
$IQ = \dfrac{MA}{CA} \times 100$	$\dfrac{6}{6} \times 100 = 100$	$\dfrac{6}{9} \times 100 = 67$	$\dfrac{9}{12} \times 100 = 75$	$\dfrac{12}{9} \times 100 = 133$

Web Link 9.4

Human Intelligence
http://www.indiana.edu/%7Eintell/

A graphic approach to the history of intelligence testing is taken at this site, which uses coloured arrows to show academic lineage and connections among various theorists. Maintained by Jonathan Plucker of Indiana University, this site covers all the major intelligence theorists and there are excellent discussions of contemporary topics.

ceptions, it incorporated a new scoring scheme based on the "intelligence quotient" suggested by William Stern (1914). **An *intelligence quotient (IQ)* is a child's mental age divided by chronological age, multiplied by 100.** As you can see, IQ scores originally involved actual quotients:

$$IQ = \frac{\text{Mental age}}{\text{Chronological age}} \times 100$$

The ratio of mental age to chronological age made it possible to compare children of different ages. In Binet's system, such comparisons were awkward. The IQ ratio placed all children (regardless of age) on the same scale, which was centred at 100 if their mental age corresponded to their chronological age (see Table 9.1 for examples of IQ calculations).

The Stanford-Binet quickly became the world's foremost intelligence test and the standard of comparison for virtually all intelligence tests that followed (White, 2000). Since its publication in 1916, the Stanford-Binet has been updated periodically—in 1937, 1960, 1973, 1986, and 2003. Although the most recent (1986) revision introduced some major changes in the organizational structure of the test (see pages 377–378), the modern Stanford-Binet remains loyal to the conception of intelligence originally formulated by Binet and Terman.

Wechsler's Innovations

 7E

As chief psychologist at New York's massive Bellevue Hospital, David Wechsler was charged with overseeing the psychological assessment of thousands of adult patients. He found the Stanford-Binet somewhat unsatisfactory for this purpose. Thus, Wechsler set out to improve on the measurement of intelligence *in adults*. In 1939 he published the first high-quality IQ test designed specifically for adults, which came to be known as the Wechsler Adult Intelligence Scale (WAIS) (Wechsler, 1955, 1981). Ironically, Wechsler (1949, 1967, 1991, 2003) eventually devised downward extensions of his scale for children.

The Wechsler scales were characterized by at least two major innovations (Prifitera, 1994). First, Wechsler

made his scales less dependent on subjects' verbal ability than the Stanford-Binet. He included many items that required nonverbal reasoning. To highlight the distinction between verbal and nonverbal ability, he formalized the computation of separate scores for verbal IQ, performance (nonverbal) IQ, and full-scale (total) IQ.

Second, Wechsler discarded the intelligence quotient in favour of a new scoring scheme based on the *normal distribution*. This scoring system has since been adopted by most other IQ tests, including the Stanford-Binet. Although the term *intelligence quotient* lingers on in our vocabulary, scores on intelligence tests are no longer based on an actual quotient. We'll take a close look at the modern scoring system for IQ tests a little later.

Intelligence Testing Today

Today, psychologists and educators have many IQ tests available for their use. Basically, these tests fall

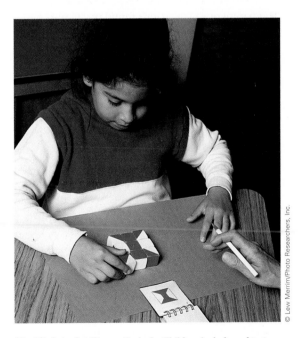

The Wechsler Intelligence Scale for Children includes subtests that measure verbal and performance abilities. This block design task is one of the performance subtests.

Archives of the History of American Psychology, University of Akron, Akron, Ohio

"It is the method of tests that has brought psychology down from the clouds and made it useful to men; that has transformed the 'science of trivialities' into the 'science of human engineering.'"
LEWIS TERMAN

Archives of the History of American Psychology, University of Akron, Akron, Ohio

"The subtests [of the WAIS] are different measures of intelligence, not measures of different kinds of intelligence."
DAVID WECHSLER

into two categories: *individual tests* and *group tests*. Individual IQ tests are administered only by psychologists who have special training for this purpose. A psychologist works face to face with a single examinee at a time. The Stanford-Binet and the Wechsler scales are both individual IQ tests.

The problem with individual IQ tests is that they're expensive and time-consuming to administer. Therefore, researchers have developed a number of IQ tests that can be administered to large groups of people at once (Kaufman, 2000). Because of their cost-effectiveness, group tests such as the Otis-Lennon School Ability Test and the Cognitive Abilities Test enjoy wide usage at all educational levels. Indeed, if you've taken an IQ test, chances are that it was a group test (Cianciolo & Sternberg, 2004). As you'll see in the next section, many school districts routinely administer group IQ tests.

Basic Questions about Intelligence Testing

Misconceptions abound when it comes to intelligence tests. In this section we'll use a question-and-answer format to explain the basic principles underlying intelligence testing.

What Kinds of Questions Are on Intelligence Tests?

The nature of the questions found on IQ tests varies somewhat from test to test. These variations depend on whether the test is intended for children or adults (or both) and whether the test is designed for individuals or groups. Overall, the questions are fairly diverse in format. The Wechsler scales, with their numerous subtests, provide a representative example of the kinds of items that appear on most IQ tests. As you can see in Figure 9.6, the items in the Wechsler subtests require subjects to furnish information, recognize vocabulary, and demonstrate basic memory. Generally speaking, examinees are required to manipulate words, numbers, and images through abstract reasoning.

What Do Modern IQ Scores Mean?

 7E

As we've discussed, scores on intelligence tests once represented a ratio of mental age to chronological age. However, this system has given way to one based on the normal distribution and the standard

deviation (see Chapter 2). **The *normal distribution* is a symmetric, bell-shaped curve that represents the pattern in which many characteristics are dispersed in the population.** When a trait is normally distributed, most cases fall near the centre of the distribution (an average score) and the number of cases gradually declines as one moves away from the centre in either direction (see Figure 9.7).

The normal distribution was first discovered by 18th-century astronomers. They found that their measurement errors were distributed in a predictable way that resembled a bell-shaped curve. Since then, research has shown that many human traits, ranging from height to running speed to spatial ability, also follow a normal distribution. Psychologists eventually recognized that intelligence scores also fall into a normal distribution. This insight permitted David Wechsler to devise a more sophisticated scoring system for his tests that has been adopted by virtually all subsequent IQ tests. In this system, raw scores are translated into *deviation IQ scores* that **locate subjects precisely within the normal distribution, using the standard deviation as the unit of measurement.**

For most IQ tests, the mean of the distribution is set at 100 and the standard deviation (SD) is set at 15. These choices were made to provide continuity with the original IQ ratio (mental age to chronological age) that was centred at 100. In this system, which is depicted in Figure 9.7, a score of 115 means

Wechsler Adult Intelligence Scale (WAIS)		
Test	Description	Example
Verbal scale		
Information	Taps general range of information	On what continent is France?
Comprehension	Tests understanding of social conventions and ability to evaluate past experience	Why are children required to go to school?
Arithmetic	Tests arithmetic reasoning through verbal problems	How many hours will it take to drive 150 kilometres at 50 kilometres per hour?
Similarities	Asks in what way certain objects or concepts are similar; measures abstract thinking	How are a calculator and a typewriter alike?
Digit span	Tests attention and rote memory by orally presenting series of digits to be repeated forward or backward	Repeat the following numbers backward: 2 4 3 5 1 8 6
Vocabulary	Tests ability to define increasingly difficult words	What does audacity mean?
Performance scale		
Digit symbol	Tests speed of learning through timed coding tasks in which numbers must be associated with marks of various shapes	
Picture completion	Tests visual alertness and visual memory through presentation of an incompletely drawn figure; the missing part must be discovered and named	
Block design	Tests ability to perceive and analyze patterns by presenting designs that must be copied with blocks	
Picture arrangement	Tests understanding of social situations through a series of comic-strip-type pictures that must be arranged in the right sequence to tell a story	
Object assembly	Tests ability to deal with part/whole relationships by presenting puzzle pieces that must be assembled to form a complete object	

Figure 9.6

Subtests on the Wechsler Adult Intelligence Scale (WAIS). The WAIS is divided into scales that yield separate verbal and performance (nonverbal) IQ scores. The verbal scale consists of six subtests and the performance scale is made up of five subtests. Examples of low-level (easy) test items that closely resemble those on the WAIS are shown on the right.

that a person scored exactly one SD (15 points) above the mean. A score of 85 means that a person scored one SD below the mean. A score of 100 means that a person showed average performance. You don't really need to know how to work with standard deviations to understand this system (but if you're interested, consult Appendix B). *The key point is that modern IQ scores indicate exactly where you fall in the normal distribution of intelligence.* Thus, a score of 120 does not indicate that you answered 120 questions

Figure 9.7

The normal distribution.
Many characteristics are distributed in a pattern represented by this bell-shaped curve. The horizontal axis shows how far above or below the mean a score is (measured in plus or minus standard deviations). The vertical axis is used to graph the number of cases obtaining each score. In a normal distribution, the cases are distributed in a fixed pattern. For instance, 68.26% of the cases fall between +1 and −1 standard deviation. Modern IQ scores indicate where a person's measured intelligence falls in the normal distribution. On most IQ tests, the mean is set at an IQ of 100 and the standard deviation at 15. Any deviation IQ score can be converted into a percentile score. The mental classifications at the bottom of the figure are descriptive labels that roughly correspond to ranges of IQ scores.

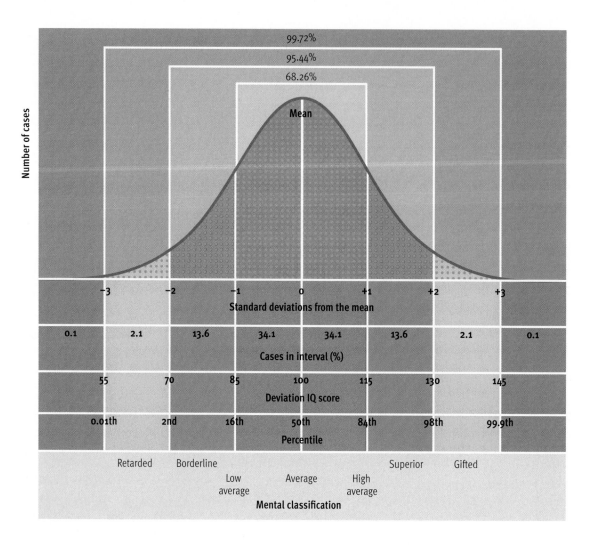

correctly. Nor does it mean that you have 120 "units" of intelligence. A deviation IQ score places you at a specific point in the normal distribution of intelligence.

Deviation IQ scores can be converted into percentile scores (see Figure 9.7). In fact, a major advantage of this scoring system is that a specific score on a specific test always translates into exactly the same percentile score, regardless of the person's age group. The old system of IQ ratio scores lacked this consistency.

Do Intelligence Tests Measure Potential or Knowledge?

Intelligence tests are intended to measure intellectual potential. They do so by presenting novel questions that require test takers to think on their feet, rather than questions that simply tap factual knowledge. However, because people's backgrounds differ, it's not easy to devise items that are completely unaffected by differences in knowledge. Test developers try to circumvent this problem by requiring subjects to *apply* relatively *common* knowledge. Nevertheless, IQ tests unavoidably contain items that are influenced by the test taker's previous learning. *Hence, IQ tests measure a blend of potential and knowledge.* Test developers try to tilt the balance toward the assessment of potential as much as possible, but factual knowledge clearly has an impact on intelligence test scores (Ackerman & Beier, 2005; Cianciolo & Sternberg, 2004; Glaser, 1991; Zigler & Seitz, 1982).

Do Intelligence Tests Have Adequate Reliability?

Do IQ tests produce consistent results when people are retested? Yes. Most IQ tests report commendable reliability estimates. The correlations generally range into the 0.90s (Kaufman, 2000). In comparison to most other types of psychological tests, IQ tests are exceptionally reliable. However, like other tests, they *sample* behaviour, and a specific testing may yield an unrepresentative score.

Variations in examinees' motivation to take an IQ test or in their anxiety about the test can sometimes produce misleading scores (Hopko et al., 2005; Spielberger & Sydeman, 1994; Zimmerman & Woo-Sam, 1984). The most common problem is that low motivation or high anxiety may drag a person's score down on a particular occasion. Although the reliability of IQ tests is excellent, caution is always in order in interpreting test scores.

Do Intelligence Tests Have Adequate Validity?

Do intelligence tests measure what they're supposed to measure? Yes, but this answer has to be qualified very carefully. IQ tests are valid measures of the kind of intelligence that's necessary to do well in academic work. But if the purpose is to assess intelligence in a broader sense, the validity of IQ tests is questionable.

As you may recall, intelligence tests were originally designed with a relatively limited purpose in mind: to predict school performance. This has continued to be the principal purpose of IQ testing. Efforts to document the validity of IQ tests have usually concentrated on their relationship to grades in school. Typically, positive correlations in the 0.40s and 0.50s are found between IQ scores and school grades (Kline, 1991). Even higher correlations (between 0.60 and 0.80) are found between IQ scores and the number of years of school that people complete (Ceci, 1991).

However, the meaning of this finding is complicated by the fact that the causal links between IQ and schooling are bidirectional. Although high IQ clearly fosters success in school, schooling also has a positive effect on IQ (Ceci & Williams, 1997).

In any event, these correlations are about as high as one could expect, given that many factors besides a person's intelligence are likely to affect grades and school progress. For example, school grades may be influenced by a student's motivation, diligence, or personality, not to mention teachers' subjective biases. Thus, IQ tests are reasonably valid indexes of school-related intellectual ability, or academic intelligence.

However, over the years people have mistakenly come to believe that IQ tests measure mental ability in a truly general sense. In reality, IQ tests have always focused on the abstract reasoning and verbal fluency that are essential to academic success. The tests do not tap social competence, practical problem solving, creativity, mechanical ingenuity, or artistic talent.

When Robert Sternberg and his colleagues (1981) asked people to list examples of intelligent behaviour, they found that the examples fell into three categories: (1) *verbal intelligence,* (2) *practical intelligence,* and (3) *social intelligence* (see Figure 9.8). Thus, people generally recognize three basic components of intelligence. For the most part, IQ tests assess only the first of these three components. Although IQ tests are billed as measures of *general* mental ability, they actually focus somewhat narrowly on a specific type of intelligence: academic/verbal intelligence (Sternberg, 1998, 2003).

Figure 9.8

Laypersons' conceptions of intelligence. Robert Sternberg and his colleagues (1981) asked participants to list examples of behaviours characteristic of intelligence. The examples tended to sort into three groups that represent the three types of intelligence recognized by the average person: verbal intelligence, practical intelligence, and social intelligence. The three well-known individuals shown here are prototype examples of verbal intelligence (former governor general Adrienne Clarkson), practical intelligence (scientist and broadcaster David Suzuki), and social intelligence (singer/songwriter/activist Bono).

Source: Adapted from Sternberg, R. J., Conway, B. E., Keton, J. L., & Bernstein, M. (1981). People's conceptions of intelligence. *Journal of Personality and Social Psychology, 41* (1), 37–55. Copyright © 1981 by the American Psychological Association. Adapted by permission of the author.

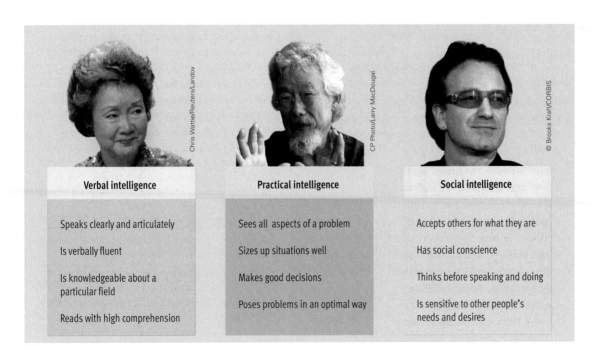

Verbal intelligence	Practical intelligence	Social intelligence
Speaks clearly and articulately	Sees all aspects of a problem	Accepts others for what they are
Is verbally fluent	Sizes up situations well	Has social conscience
Is knowledgeable about a particular field	Makes good decisions	Thinks before speaking and doing
Reads with high comprehension	Poses problems in an optimal way	Is sensitive to other people's needs and desires

Do Intelligence Tests Predict Vocational Success?

Vocational success is a vague, value-laden concept that's difficult to quantify. Nonetheless, researchers have attacked this question by examining correlations between IQ scores and specific indicators of vocational success, such as the prestige of subjects' occupations or ratings of subjects' job performance. On the positive side of the ledger, it's clear that IQ is related to occupational attainment. *People who score high on IQ tests are more likely than those who score low to end up in high-status jobs* (Austin & Hanisch, 1990; Gottfredson, 2003; Herrnstein & Murray, 1994; Ree & Earles, 1992). Because IQ tests measure school ability fairly well and school performance is important in reaching certain occupations, this link between IQ scores and job status makes sense.

On the negative side of the ledger, there is considerable debate about whether IQ scores are effective predictors of performance within a particular occupation (Hunter & Schmidt, 1996; McClelland, 1993; Sternberg & Wagner, 1993; Wagner, 1997). Because of this and various legal challenges to this use of IQ tests, companies are increasingly turning to personality tests to select employees who are conscientious, calm under pressure, persistent, reliable, and so forth (Hogan, Hogan, & Roberts, 1996). Psychologists are also trying to develop tests of practical intelligence to aid employers in their hiring decisions (Sternberg et al., 1995). Thus, psychological tests that measure abilities relevant to specific jobs continue to be valuable tools in selecting employees (Landy, Shankster, & Kohler, 1994).

Are IQ Tests Widely Used in Other Cultures?

In other Western cultures with European roots, the answer to this question is yes. In most non-Western cultures, the answer is only very little. IQ testing has a long history and continues to be a major enterprise in many Western countries, such as Britain, France, Norway, and Australia, as well as the United States and Canada (Irvine & Berry, 1988). However, efforts to export IQ tests to non-Western societies have met with mixed results. The tests have been well received in some non-Western cultures, such as Japan, where the Binet-Simon scales were introduced as early as 1908 (Iwawaki & Vernon, 1988), but they have been met with indifference or resistance in other cultures, such as China and India (Chan & Vernon, 1988; Sinha, 1983).

According to Queen's University's John Berry, a cross-cultural psychologist, the bottom line is that Western IQ tests do not translate well into the language and cognitive frameworks of many non-Western cultures (Berry, 1994; Sternberg, 2004). Berry (1984) asserts that this approach assumes that the cultural life of the two cultures differs only in language and that the cognitive abilities characteristic of the two cultures differ only in level. Using an intelligence test with a cultural group other than the one for which it was originally designed can be problematic. The entire process of test administration, with its emphasis on rapid information processing, decisive responding, and the notion that ability can be quantified, is foreign to some cultures. Moreover, different cultures have different conceptions of what intelligence is and value different mental skills (Das, 1994; Sternberg & Kaufman, 1998). In a landmark treatise on culture and cognition, Cole and his colleagues (1971) concluded that "people will be good at doing things that are important to them and that they have occasion to do often" (p. xi). *In other words, the ingredients of intelligence are culture-specific.* Even when a non-Western culture is largely in agreement with Western views about the ingredients of intelligent behaviour, it can be difficult to construct equivalent tests that measure these ingredients with equal reliability and validity in both cultural contexts (Greenfield, 1997).

REVIEW OF KEY POINTS

- Intelligence tests contain a diverse mixture of questions. In the modern scoring system, deviation IQ scores indicate where people fall in the normal distribution of intelligence for their age group. On most tests, the mean is set at 100 and the standard deviation is set at 15.

- Although they are intended to measure potential for learning, IQ tests inevitably assess a blend of potential and knowledge. IQ tests are exceptionally reliable, with reliability coefficients typically ranging into the 0.90s.

- IQ tests are reasonably valid measures of academic intelligence in that they predict school grades and the number of years of school that people complete. However, they do not tap social or practical intelligence, and they do not measure intelligence in a truly general sense.

- IQ scores are correlated with occupational attainment. However, there is active debate about whether they predict performance within an occupation very well.

- Intelligence testing is largely a Western enterprise and IQ tests are not widely used in most non-Western cultures. One reason is that different cultures have different conceptions of intelligence.

Extremes of Intelligence

What are the cut-off scores for extremes in intelligence that lead children to be designated as retarded or gifted? On the low end, IQ scores roughly two standard deviations or more below the mean are regarded as subnormal. On the high end, children who score more than two or three standard deviations above the mean are regarded as gifted. However, designations of mental retardation and giftedness should not be based exclusively on IQ test results. Let's look more closely at the concepts of mental retardation and intellectual giftedness.

Mental Retardation

According to the American Association on Mental Retardation (AAMR), **mental retardation refers to subaverage general mental ability accompanied by deficiencies in adaptive skills, originating before age 18**. Adaptive skills consist of everyday living skills in ten domains, including communication (e.g., writing a letter), self-care (dressing oneself), home living (preparing meals), social interaction (coping with others' demands), community use (shopping), and health/safety (recognizing illness).

There are two noteworthy aspects to this definition. First, the IQ criterion of subnormality is arbitrary. In the 1992 and 2002 releases of its manual on mental retardation, the AAMR set a flexible cut-off line, which is an IQ score of 70 to 75 or below. This cut-off line could be drawn elsewhere. Indeed, the AAMR has changed the cut-off four times in the last four decades (Ramey & Ramey, 2000). Second, the requirement of deficits in everyday living skills is included because experts feel that retardation should not be determined solely on the basis of individuals' test ability (Bunch, 1994). This requirement acknowledges that "school learning" is not the only important kind of learning. Unfortunately, there are no objective methods of measuring everyday living skills, so this assessment is necessarily subjective (Detterman, Gabriel, & Ruthsatz, 2000).

Levels of Retardation

Approximately 2%–3% of the school-age population is diagnosed as mentally retarded (Frazier, 1999). Mental retardation has traditionally been classified into four levels characterized as mild, moderate, severe, or profound. Table 9.2 lists the IQ range for each level and the typical behavioural and educational characteristics of individuals at each level.

As Figure 9.9 shows, the vast majority of retarded people fall in the *mildly retarded* category. Only about 15% of retarded people exhibit the obvious mental deficiencies that most people envision when they think of retardation. Many mildly retarded individuals are not all that easily distinguished from the rest of the population. The mental deficiency of children in the mildly retarded category often is not noticed until they have been in school a few years. Outside of school, many are considered normal. Furthermore, many of these children manage to shed the label of retardation when they reach adulthood and leave the educational system (Popper et al., 2003). A significant portion of them become self-supporting and are integrated into the community.

Origins of Retardation

Many organic conditions can cause mental retardation (Szymanski & Wilska, 2003). *Down syndrome* is a condition marked by distinctive physical characteristics (such as slanted eyes, stubby limbs, and thin hair) that is associated with mild to severe retardation.

PREVIEW QUESTIONS
- What are the different levels of retardation and how common are they?
- How often is retardation due to a known biological cause?
- How are children typically selected for gifted programs?
- Are most gifted children lonely and maladjusted?
- Do most gifted children achieve eminence as adults?
- Which contributes more to extraordinary achievement: innate talent or hard work?

Web Link 9.6

The ARC
http://www.thearc.org/

The ARC is a U.S. "organization of and for people with mental retardation and related developmental disabilities and their families." Materials available here include overviews of the causes of mental retardation, education and employment of the mentally retarded, and many other resources.

Table 9.2 Categories of Mental Retardation

Category of Retardation	IQ Range	Education Possible	Life Adaptation Possible
Mild	51–70	Sixth grade (maximum) by late teens; special education helpful	Can be self-supporting in nearly normal fashion if environment is stable and supportive; may need help with stress
Moderate	36–50	Second to fourth grade by late teens; special education necessary	Can be semi-independent in sheltered environment; needs help with even mild stress
Severe	20–35	Limited speech, toilet habits, and so forth with systematic training	Can help contribute to self-support under total supervision
Profound	below 20	Little or no speech; not toilet-trained; relatively unresponsive to training	Requires total care

NOTE: As explained in the text, diagnoses of retardation should not be made on the basis of IQ scores alone.

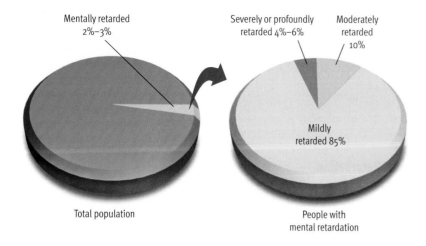

Mentally retarded 2%–3%

Severely or profoundly retarded 4%–6%

Moderately retarded 10%

Mildly retarded 85%

Total population

People with mental retardation

Figure 9.9

The prevalence and severity of mental retardation. The overall prevalence of mental retardation is 2%–3% of the general population. The vast majority (85%) of the retarded population falls in the mildly retarded category (IQ: 51–70). Only about 15% of the retarded population falls into the subcategories of moderate, severe, or profound retardation.

Most children exhibiting this syndrome carry an extra chromosome. The FRM 1 gene contributes to the development of *Fragile X syndrome* (FXS), a common cause of hereditary mental retardation (Cornish, Sudhalter & Turk, 2004). In FXS there is a mutation in the inherited gene. According to Kim Cornish, Canada Research Chair in Neuropsychology at McGill University, FXS is characterized by, among other things, an inhibitory control deficit. This deficit may lead to activation of neural connections irrelevant to the context or task facing the individual. *Phenylketonuria* is a metabolic disorder (due to an inherited enzyme deficiency) that can lead to retardation if it is not caught and treated in infancy. In *hydrocephaly,* an excessive accumulation of cerebrospinal fluid in the skull destroys brain tissue and causes retardation. Although over 350 such organic syndromes are known to cause retardation (King, Hodapp, & Dykens, 2000), diagnosticians are able to pin down an organic cause for retardation in fewer than 25% of cases (Popper & West, 1999). However, this percentage appears to be increasing as scientists unravel more of the genetic bases for various kinds of disorders (Simonoff, Bolton, & Rutter, 1998).

The cases of unknown origin tend to involve milder forms of retardation. A number of theories attempt to identify the factors that underlie retardation in the absence of a known organic pathology (Hodapp, 1994). Some theorists believe that subtle, difficult-to-detect physiological defects contribute to many of these cases. However, the predominant view is that the cases not involving obvious organic pathology are mainly caused by a variety of unfavourable environmental factors. Consistent with this hypothesis, the vast majority of mildly retarded children come from the lower socioeconomic classes (see Figure 9.10), where a host of factors—such as greater marital instability and parental neglect, inadequate nutrition and

medical care, and lower-quality schooling—may contribute to children's poor intellectual development (Popper et al., 2003).

Giftedness

Like mental retardation, giftedness is widely misunderstood. This misunderstanding is a result, in part, of television and movies inaccurately portraying gifted children as social misfits and "nerds."

Identifying Gifted Children

Some curious discrepancies exist between ideals and practice in how gifted children are identified. The experts who shape government policy consistently assert that giftedness should not be equated with high intelligence and they recommend that schools not rely too heavily on IQ tests to select gifted children (Gallagher & Courtright, 1986; Robinson & Clinkenbeard, 1998). In practice, however, efforts to identify gifted children focus almost exclusively on IQ scores and rarely consider qualities such as

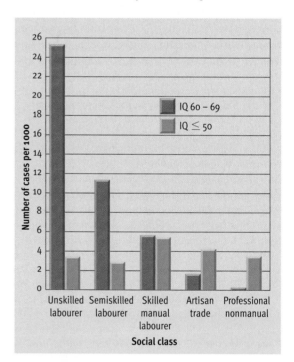

Figure 9.10

Social class and mental retardation. This graph charts the prevalence of mild retardation (IQ 60 to 69) and more severe forms of retardation (IQ below 50) in relation to social class. Severe forms of retardation are distributed pretty evenly across the social classes, a finding that is consistent with the notion that they are the product of biological aberrations that are equally likely to strike anyone. In contrast, the prevalence of mild retardation is greatly elevated in the lower social classes, a finding that meshes with the notion that mild retardation is largely a product of unfavourable environmental factors. (Data from Popper and Steingard, 1994) creativity, leadership, or special talent (Callahan, 2000). Most school districts consider children who fall in the upper 2%–3% of the IQ distribution to be gifted. Thus, the minimum IQ score for gifted programs usually falls somewhere around 130.

Personal Qualities of the Gifted

Gifted children have long been stereotyped as weak, sickly, socially inept "bookworms" who are often emotionally troubled. The empirical evidence *largely* contradicts this view. The best evidence comes from a major longitudinal study of gifted children begun by Lewis Terman in 1921 (Terman, 1925; Terman & Oden, 1959). Other investigators have continued to study this group through the present (Cronbach, 1992; Holahan & Sears, 1995). This project represents psychology's longest-running study.

Terman's original subject pool consisted of around 1500 youngsters who had an average IQ of 150. In comparison to normal subjects, Terman's gifted children were found to be above average in height, weight, strength, physical health, emotional adjustment, mental health, and social maturity. As a group, Terman's subjects continued to exhibit better-than-average physical health, emotional stability, and social satisfaction throughout their adult years. A variety of other studies have also found that samples of high-IQ children are either average or above average in social and emotional development (Garland & Zigler, 1999; Robinson & Clinkenbeard, 1998).

However, some other lines of research raise some questions about this conclusion. For instance, Ellen Winner (1997, 1998) asserts that moderately gifted children (those with an IQ of 130–150) are very different from profoundly gifted children (those with an IQ above 180). She asserts that profoundly gifted children are often introverted and socially isolated. She also estimates that the incidence of interpersonal and emotional problems in this group is about twice as high as in other children. Another line of research, which is discussed in more detail in the Personal Application, has focused on samples of people who have displayed truly exceptional creative achievement. Contrary to the findings of the Terman study, investigators have found elevated rates of mental illness in these samples (Ludwig, 1995). Thus, the psychosocial adjustment of gifted individuals may depend in part on their level of giftedness.

Giftedness and Achievement in Life

Terman's gifted children grew up to be very successful by conventional standards. By midlife they had produced 92 books, 235 patents, and nearly 2200 scientific articles. Although Terman's gifted

Young Nirav Gathani made exam history in England when he became the youngest student to pass the General Certificate of Secondary Education at age seven. As amazing as this feat was, it is hard to say whether Nirav will go on to achieve eminence, which typically requires a combination of exceptional intelligence, motivation, and creativity.

children accomplished a great deal, no one in the group achieved recognition for genius-level contributions. In retrospect, this finding may not be surprising. The concept of giftedness is applied to two very different groups. One consists of high-IQ children who are the cream of the crop in school. The other consists of eminent adults who make enduring contributions in their fields. According to Siegler and Kotovsky (1986), a sizable gap exists between these two groups. The accomplishments of the latter group involve a much higher level of giftedness. Joseph Renzulli (1986, 1999, 2002) theorizes that this rarer form of giftedness depends on the intersection of three factors: high intelligence, high creativity, and high motivation (see Figure 9.11). He emphasizes that high intelligence alone does not usually foster genuine greatness. Thus, the vast majority of children selected for gifted school programs do not achieve eminence as adults or make genius-like contributions to society (Callahan, 2000; Richert, 1997; Winner, 2003).

Even in school itself, not all gifted children succeed. University of Alberta psychologist Judy Lupart and the University of Calgary's Michael Pyryt (1996) argue that specific subgroups of gifted children exist, including one they refer to as the "hidden gifted." These are gifted children who for a variety of reasons (e.g., learning disabled/gifted, cultural minority gifted, gifted females) may not be properly identified

"*Moderately gifted children are very different from profoundly gifted children.... Most gifted children do not grow into eminent adults.*"
ELLEN WINNER

Figure **9.11**

A three-ring conception of eminent giftedness.
According to Renzulli (1986), high intelligence is only one of three requirements for achieving eminence. He proposes that a combination of exceptional ability, creativity, and motivation leads some people to make enduring contributions in their fields.

Source: Adapted from Renzulli, J. S. (1986). The three-ring conception of giftedness: A developmental model for creative productivity. In R. J. Sternberg & J. E. Davidson (Eds.), *Conceptions of Giftedness* (pp. 53–92). New York: Cambridge University Press. Copyright © 1986 Cambridge University Press. Adapted by permission.

as gifted as they are underperforming academically. As a result, these hidden gifted students are not afforded the opportunities offered by educational programs designed to help gifted students meet their potential. These students often remain hidden because they underachieve in school—perhaps, in part, as a result of their attitudes toward school itself or because of the expectations of others. In their study, Lupart and Pyryt compared the expected performance of gifted students based on their IQ scores with their academic performance in school. In their sample, they found that 21% of their gifted students were underachieving in school.

In addition to her continuing research on giftedness (Lupart, 2004), Lupart and her colleagues have gone on to examine the reasons for women's underrepresentation in science, and she has been involved in a mentoring program for girls called "SCiberMentor," in which girls are mentored in science and mathematics via computer by women in those fields (Lupart & Cannon, 2003).

Another hot issue in the study of giftedness concerns the degree to which extraordinary achievement depends on innate talent as opposed to intensive training and hard work. In recent years, the emphasis has been on what Simonton (2001) calls the "drudge theory" of exceptional achievement. According to this view, eminence primarily or entirely depends on dogged determination; endless, tedious practice; and outstanding mentoring and training (Bloom, 1985; Ericsson & Lehman, 1996; Howe, 1999). This conclusion is based on studies of eminent scientists, artists, writers, musicians, and athletes, which show that they push themselves much harder and engage in far more deliberate practice than their less successful counterparts. The essence of the drudge theory is captured by the reaction of one

violin virtuoso after a critic hailed him as a genius: "A genius! For 37 years I've practiced fourteen hours a day, and now they call me a genius!" (quoted in Simonton, 1999). Chen Kupperman, whom we introduced at the beginning of the chapter, would seem to agree. When asked to comment on his success, he said, "I am just learning harder—that's all" ("14-Year-Old," n.d.). While hard work is clearly not the whole story, it is a critical component.

Although the evidence linking strenuous training and prodigious effort to world-class achievement is convincing, Winner (2000) points out that obsessive hard work and inborn ability may be confounded in retrospective analyses of eminent individuals. The youngsters who work the hardest may be those with the greatest innate talent, who are likely to find their efforts more rewarding than others. In other words, innate ability may be the key factor fostering the single-minded commitment that seems to be crucial to greatness. Simonton (1999) has devised an elaborate theory of talent development that allocates a significant role to both innate ability and a host of supportive environmental factors. In sum, recent research has clearly demonstrated that quality training, monumental effort, and perseverance are crucial factors in greatness, but many experts on giftedness maintain that extraordinary achievement also requires rare, innate talent.

Judy Lupart, Canada Research Chair in Special Education at the University of Alberta, has done research on gifted education and the underrepresentation of female students in science. She has helped develop a mentoring program for girls in science and has won an award from the Women in Engineering Programs and Advocate Network for her work in this area.

Heredity and Environment as Determinants of Intelligence

Most early pioneers of intelligence testing maintained that intelligence is inherited (Cravens, 1992). Small wonder, then, that this view lingers on among many people. Gradually, however, it has become clear that both heredity and environment influence intelligence (Locurto, 1991; Plomin, 2003; Scarr, 1997). Does this mean that the nature versus nurture debate has been settled with respect to intelligence? Absolutely not. Theorists and researchers continue to argue vigorously about which of the two is more important, in part because the issue has such far-reaching sociopolitical implications.

Theorists who believe that intelligence is largely inherited downplay the value of special educational programs for underprivileged groups (Herrnstein & Murray, 1994; Jensen, 1980; Rushton & Jensen, 2005). They assert that a child's intelligence cannot be increased noticeably, because a child's genetic destiny cannot be altered. Other theorists take issue with this point, asserting that inherited characteristics are not necessarily unchangeable (Sternberg, Grigorenko, & Kidd, 2005; Wahlsten, 1997b). The people in this camp tend to maintain that even more funds should be allocated for remedial education programs, improved schooling in lower-class neighbourhoods, and postsecondary financial aid for the underprivileged. Because the debate over the role of heredity in intelligence has direct relevance to important social issues and political decisions, we'll take a detailed look at this complex controversy.

Evidence for Hereditary Influence

Galton's observation that intelligence runs in families was quite accurate. However, *family studies* can determine only whether genetic influence on a trait is

plausible, not whether it is certain (see Chapter 3). Family members share not just genes, but similar environments. If high intelligence (or low intelligence) appears in a family over several generations, this consistency could reflect the influence of either shared genes or shared environment. Because of this problem, researchers must turn to *twin studies* and *adoption studies* to obtain more definitive evidence on whether heredity affects intelligence.

Twin Studies

The best evidence regarding the role of genetic factors in intelligence comes from studies that compare identical and fraternal twins. The rationale for twin studies is that both identical and fraternal twins normally develop under similar environmental conditions. However, identical twins share more genetic kinship than fraternal twins. Hence, if pairs of identical twins are more similar in intelligence than pairs of fraternal twins, it's presumably because of their greater genetic similarity. (See Chapter 3 for a more detailed explanation of the logic underlying twin studies.)

What are the findings of twin studies regarding intelligence? The data from over 100 studies of intellectual similarity for various kinds of kinship relations and childrearing arrangements are summarized in Figure 9.12. This figure plots the average correlation observed for various types of relationships. As you can see, the average correlation reported for identical twins (0.86) is very high, indicating that identical twins tend to be quite similar in intelligence. The average correlation for fraternal twins (0.60) is significantly lower. This correlation indicates that fraternal twins also tend to be similar in intelligence, but noticeably less so than identical twins. These results support the notion that IQ is inherited to a considerable degree (Bouchard, 1998; Plomin & Spinath, 2004).

PREVIEW QUESTIONS

● What types of evidence suggest that intelligence is inherited?

● What is heritability, and what are some limitations of heritability estimates?

● How has research demonstrated that environment influences IQ?

● How is the concept of reaction range used to explain the interaction of heredity and environment?

● How have Jensen and Herrnstein and Murray explained cultural disparities in average IQ scores?

● What are some alternative explanations for ethnic differences in average IQ scores?

Of course, critics have tried to poke holes in this line of reasoning. They argue that identical twins are more alike in IQ because parents and others treat them more similarly than they treat fraternal twins. This environmental explanation of the findings has some merit. After all, identical twins are always the same sex, and gender influences how a child is raised. However, this explanation seems unlikely in light of the evidence on identical twins reared apart because of family break-ups or adoption (Bouchard, 1997; Bouchard et al., 1990). *Although reared in different environments, these identical twins still display greater similarity in IQ (average correlation: 0.72) than fraternal twins reared together (average correlation: 0.60).* Moreover, the gap in IQ similarity between identical twins reared apart and fraternal twins reared together appears to widen in middle and late adulthood, suggesting paradoxically that the influence of heredity increases with age (Pedersen et al., 1992).

Adoption Studies 7F

Research on adopted children also provides evidence about the effects of heredity (and of environment, as we shall see). If adopted children resemble their biological parents in intelligence even though they were not reared by these parents, this finding supports the genetic hypothesis. The relevant studies indicate that there is indeed more than chance similarity between adopted children and their biological parents (Plomin et al., 2001; refer again to Figure 9.12).

Heritability Estimates 7F

Various experts have sifted through mountains of correlational evidence to estimate the *heritability* of intelligence. A **heritability ratio is an estimate of the proportion of trait variability in a population that is determined by variations in genetic inheritance**. Heritability can be estimated for any trait. For example, the heritability of height is estimated to be around 90% (Plomin, 1994). Heritability can be estimated in a variety of ways that appear logically and mathematically defensible (Loehlin, 1994; Schonemann, 1994). Given the variety of methods available and the strong views that experts bring to the IQ debate, it should come as no surprise that heritability estimates for intelligence vary considerably (see Figure 9.13).

At the high end, a few theorists, such as Arthur Jensen (1980, 1998), maintain that the heritability of IQ ranges as high as 80%. That is, they believe that only about 20% of the variation in intelligence is attributable to environmental factors. In recent years, the consensus estimates of the experts tend to hover around 50% (Petrill, 2005; Plomin & Spinath, 2004).

However, it's important to understand that heritability estimates have certain limitations (Ceci et al., 1997; Grigorenko, 2000; Reeve & Hakel, 2002). First, a heritability estimate is a *group statistic* based on studies of trait variability within a specific group. A heritability estimate cannot be applied meaningfully to *individuals*. In other words, even if the heritability

Figure 9.12

Studies of IQ similarity. The graph shows the mean correlations of IQ scores for people of various types of relationships, as obtained in studies of IQ similarity. Higher correlations indicate greater similarity. The results show that greater genetic similarity is associated with greater similarity in IQ, suggesting that intelligence is partly inherited (compare, for example, the correlations for identical and fraternal twins). However, the results also show that living together is associated with greater IQ similarity, suggesting that intelligence is partly governed by environment (compare, for example, the scores of siblings reared together and reared apart). (Data from McGue et al., 1993)

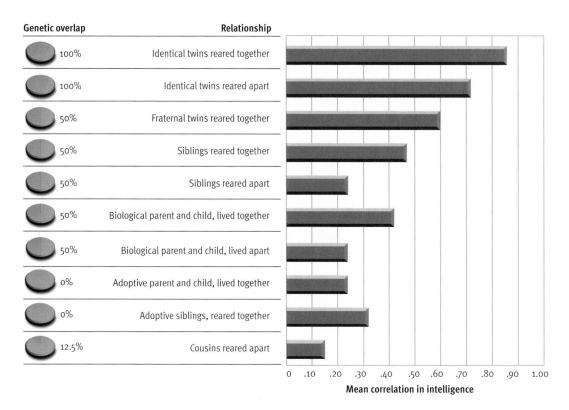

Heritability estimates for intelligence

"High" estimate

"Low" estimate

30% of variation in intelligence determined by environment

70% of variation in intelligence determined by heredity

50% of variation in intelligence determined by heredity

50% of variation in intelligence determined by environment

Figure 9.13

The concept of heritability.
A heritability ratio is an estimate of the portion of variation in a trait determined by heredity—with the remainder presumably determined by environment—as these pie charts illustrate. Typical heritability estimates for intelligence range between a high of 70% and a low of 50%, although some estimates have fallen outside this range. Bear in mind that heritability ratios are *estimates* and have certain limitations that are discussed in the text.

of intelligence is 60%, this does not mean that each individual's intelligence is 60% inherited. Second, the heritability of a specific trait may vary from one group to another depending on a variety of factors. For instance, in a group with a given gene pool, heritability will increase if there's a shift toward rearing group members in more similar circumstances. Why? Because the extent of environmental differences will be reduced. To date, heritability estimates for intelligence have been based largely on research with white, middle-class subjects. Hence, they should be applied only to such groups.

Evidence for Environmental Influence

 7F

Heredity unquestionably influences intelligence, but a great deal of evidence indicates that upbringing also affects mental ability. In this section, we'll examine various approaches to research that show how life experiences shape intelligence.

Adoption Studies

 7F

Research with adopted children provides useful evidence about the impact of experience as well as heredity (Dickens & Flynn, 2001; Locurto, 1990; Loehlin, Horn, & Willerman, 1997). Many of the correlations in Figure 9.12 reflect the influence of the environment. For example, adopted children show some resemblance to their adoptive parents in IQ. This similarity is usually attributed to the fact that their adoptive parents shape their environment. Adoption studies also indicate that siblings reared together are more similar in IQ than siblings reared apart. This is true even for identical twins, who have the same genetic endowment. Moreover, entirely unrelated children who are raised in the same home also show a significant resemblance in IQ. All of these findings indicate that environment influences intelligence.

Environmental Deprivation and Enrichment

If environment affects intelligence, children who are raised in substandard circumstances should experience a gradual decline in IQ as they grow older (since other children will be progressing more rapidly). This *cumulative deprivation hypothesis* was tested decades ago. Researchers studied children consigned to understaffed orphanages and children raised in the poverty and isolation of the back hills of Appalachia (Sherman & Key, 1932; Stoddard, 1943). Generally, investigators *did* find that environmental deprivation led to the predicted erosion in IQ scores.

Conversely, children who are removed from a deprived environment and placed in circumstances more conducive to learning should benefit from their environmental enrichment. Their IQ scores should gradually increase. This hypothesis has been tested by studying children who have been moved from disadvantaged homes into middle- and upper-class adoptive homes (Scarr & Weinberg, 1977, 1983; Schiff & Lewontin, 1986; Skodak & Skeels, 1947). Although there are limits on the improvements seen, the IQs of these children tend to increase noticeably (typically 10–12 points). These findings also show that environment influences IQ.

Home Environment and Schooling Effects

Researchers have detected the influence of environment on intelligence in still other ways. One approach involves going into intact homes (mother and father living together with their children) to make an elaborate, systematic assessment of the quality of the intellectual environment there. If environment shapes intelligence, these assessments

Courtesy of Sandra Scarr

"My research has been aimed at asking in what kind of environments genetic differences shine through and when do they remain hidden."

SANDRA SCARR

of home environments should correlate with youngsters' IQ scores, which they do (Okagaki, 1994). Schooling effects also demonstrate the impact of environment. Ceci and Williams (1997) have reviewed seven lines of evidence that show that school attendance has a positive impact on measured IQ.

Generational Changes: The Flynn Effect

The most interesting, albeit perplexing, evidence showcasing the importance of the environment is the finding that performance on IQ tests has steadily increased over generations. This trend was not widely appreciated until recently because the tests are renormed periodically with new standardization groups, so that the mean IQ always remains at 100. However, in a study of the IQ tests used by the U.S. military, James Flynn noticed that the level of performance required to earn a score of 100 jumped upward every time the tests were renormed. Curious about this unexpected finding, he eventually gathered extensive data from 20 nations and demonstrated that IQ performance has been rising steadily all over the industrialized world since the 1930s (Flynn, 1987, 1994, 1998, 1999, 2003). Thus, the performance that today would earn you an average score of 100 would have earned you an IQ score of about 120 back in the 1930s (see Figure 9.14). Researchers who study intelligence are now scrambling to explain this trend, which has been dubbed the "Flynn effect." About the only thing they mostly agree on is that the

Flynn effect has to be attributed to environmental factors, as the modern world's gene pool could not have changed overnight (in evolutionary terms, 70 years is more like a fraction of a second) (Dickens & Flynn, 2001; Neisser, 1998; Sternberg et al., 2005). At this point, the proposed explanations for the Flynn effect are conjectural.

The Interaction of Heredity and Environment 7F

Clearly, heredity and environment both influence intelligence to a significant degree. Indeed, many theorists now assert that the question of which is more important ought to take a back seat to the question of *how they interact* (Petrill, 2005) to govern IQ.

The current thinking, perhaps championed most prominently by Sandra Scarr (1991), is that heredity may set certain limits on intelligence and that environmental factors determine where individuals fall within these limits (Bouchard, 1997; Weinberg, 1989). According to this idea, genetic makeup places an upper limit on a person's IQ that can't be exceeded even when environment is ideal. Heredity is also thought to place a lower limit on an individual's IQ, although extreme circumstances (e.g., being locked in an attic until age ten) could drag a person's IQ beneath this boundary. Theorists use the term **reaction range to refer to these genetically determined limits on IQ (or other traits).**

According to the reaction-range model, children reared in high-quality environments that promote the development of intelligence should score near the top of their potential IQ range (see Figure 9.15). Children reared under less ideal circumstances should score lower in their reaction range. The reaction range for most people is *estimated* to be around 20–25 points on the IQ scale (Weinberg, 1989).

The concept of a reaction range can explain why high-IQ children sometimes come from poor environments. It can also explain why low-IQ children sometimes come from very good environments. Moreover, it can explain these apparent paradoxes without discounting the role that environment undeniably plays. But how can the genetic boundaries on a person's intelligence be measured? That's the problem with the reaction-range concept. There is no readily apparent way to measure the range, which makes it difficult to test the reaction-range model empirically. The impossibility of measuring individuals' genetically determined intellectual potential also makes it difficult to resolve the debate about the causes of ethnic differences in IQ scores. We'll try to sort through this complex issue in the next section.

Figure 9.14

Generational increases in measured IQ. IQ tests are renormed periodically so that the mean score remains at 100. However, research by James Flynn has demonstrated that performance on IQ tests around the world has been increasing throughout most of the last century. This graph traces the estimated increases in IQ in the United States from 1918 to 1995. In relation to the axis on the right, the graph shows how average IQ would have increased if IQ tests had continued to use 1918 norms. In relation to the axis on the left, the graph shows how much lower the average IQ score would have been in earlier years if 1995 norms had been used. The causes of the "Flynn effect" are unknown, but they have to involve environmental factors.

SOURCE: Adapted from Flynn, J. R. (1998). IQ gains over time: Toward finding the causes. In U. Neisser (Ed.), *The rising curve: Long-term gains in IQ and related measures* (p. 37). Washington, DC: American Psychological Association. Copyright © 1998 by the American Psychological Association. Reprinted by permission of the author.

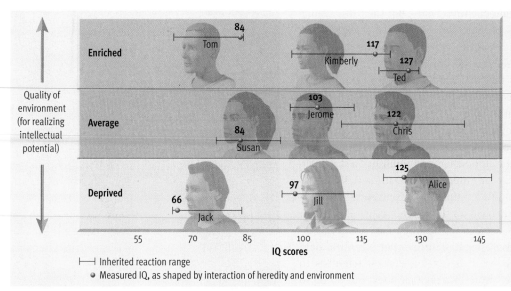

Figure 9.15

Reaction range. The concept of reaction range posits that heredity sets limits on one's intellectual potential (represented by the horizontal bars), while the quality of one's environment influences where one scores within this range (represented by the dots on the bars). People raised in enriched environments should score near the top of their reaction range, whereas people raised in poor-quality environments should score near the bottom of their range. Genetic limits on IQ can be inferred only indirectly, so theorists aren't sure whether reaction ranges are narrow (like Ted's) or wide (like Chris's). The concept of reaction range can explain how two people with similar genetic potential can be quite different in intelligence (compare Tom and Jack) and how two people reared in environments of similar quality can score quite differently (compare Alice and Jack).

Enriched — Tom 84, Kimberly 117, Ted 127

Average — Jerome 103, Susan 84, Chris 122

Deprived — Jack 66, Jill 97, Alice 125

Quality of environment (for realizing intellectual potential)

IQ scores — 55 70 85 100 115 130 145

|—| Inherited reaction range
• Measured IQ, as shaped by interaction of heredity and environment

Cultural Differences in IQ Scores

The age-old nature versus nurture debate lies at the core of the current controversy about ethnic differences in average IQ. Although the full range of IQ scores is seen in all ethnic groups, the average IQ for many of the larger minority groups in the United States (such as blacks, Native Americans, and Hispanics) is somewhat lower than the average for whites. The disparity ranges from 3 to 15 points, depending on the group tested and the IQ scale used (Loehlin, 2000; Nisbett, 2005; Perlman & Kaufman, 1990; Suzuki & Vraniak, 1994). There is little argument about the existence of these group differences, variously referred to as racial, ethnic, or cultural differences in intelligence. The controversy concerns *why* the differences are found. A vigorous debate continues as to whether cultural differences in intelligence are mainly due to the influence of heredity or of environment.

Heritability as an Explanation

In 1969 Arthur Jensen sparked a heated war of words by arguing that cultural differences in IQ are largely due to heredity. The cornerstone for Jensen's argument was his analysis suggesting that the heritability of intelligence is about 80%. Essentially, he asserted that (1) intelligence is largely genetic in origin, and (2) therefore, genetic factors are "strongly implicated" as the cause of ethnic differences in intelligence. Jensen's article triggered outrage, bitter criticism, and even death threats, as well as a flurry of research that shed additional light on the determinants of intelligence.

Twenty-five years later, Richard Herrnstein and Charles Murray (1994) reignited the same controversy with the publication of their widely discussed book *The Bell Curve*. Their main thesis is that in recent decades intellectual ability, which they believe is largely inherited, has become the primary determinant of individuals' success in life. They go on to argue that ethnic and cultural differences in average intelligence are substantial and not easily reduced and that these differences have profound and disturbing implications. Perhaps having learned from Jensen's nightmarish experiences, they try to tiptoe around the incendiary issue of whether ethnic differences in

CONCEPT **CHECK 9.2**

Understanding Correlational Evidence on the Heredity–Environment Question

Check your understanding of how correlational findings relate to the nature versus nurture issue by indicating how you would interpret the meaning of each "piece" of evidence described below. The numbers inside the parentheses are the mean IQ correlations observed for the relationships described (based on McGue et al., 1993), which are shown in Figure 9.12 (p. 368). In the spaces on the left, enter the letter H if the findings suggest that intelligence is shaped by heredity, enter the letter E if the findings suggest that intelligence is shaped by the environment, and enter the letter B if the findings suggest that intelligence is shaped by both (or either) heredity and environment. The answers can be found in Appendix A.

_____ **1.** Identical twins reared apart are more similar (0.72) than fraternal twins reared together (0.60).

_____ **2.** Identical twins reared together are more similar (0.86) than identical twins reared apart (0.72).

_____ **3.** Siblings reared together are more similar (0.47) than siblings reared apart (0.24).

_____ **4.** Biological parents and the children they rear are more similar (0.42) than unrelated persons who are reared apart (no correlation if sampled randomly).

_____ **5.** Adopted children show similarity to their biological parents (0.24) and to their adoptive parents (0.24).

"Despite more than half a century of repeated efforts by psychologists to improve the intelligence of children, particularly those in the lower quarter of the IQ distribution relative to those in the upper half of the distribution, strong evidence is still lacking as to whether or not it can be done."

ARTHUR JENSEN

Courtesy of Arthur R. Jensen

W(W)W

Web Link 9.7

Upstream-Issues:
The Bell Curve
http://www.mugu.com/cgi-bin/
Upstream/Issues/bell-curve/
index.html

The editors of Upstream, champions of "politically incorrect" conversation, have assembled perhaps the broadest collection of commentaries on the Internet regarding Herrnstein and Murray's *The Bell Curve*. Despite the marked political conservatism of this site, it contains a full range of opinion and analyses of the book.

W(W)W

Web Link 9.8

The Rushton–Suzuki Debate
http://archives.cbc.ca/IDC-1-74-663-3727/people/david_suzuki/clip5
Videos of Phillipe Rushton's debate with David Suzuki can be viewed at the archives of the CBC Web site.

average IQ are due to heredity. But their discussions of "dysgenic pressures" in ethnic groups clearly imply that these disparities are at least partly genetic in origin. Moreover, the implicit message throughout the book is that disadvantaged groups cannot avoid their fate because it is their genetic destiny.

The central idea of *The Bell Curve*, that we are evolving toward a meritocracy based on intellect, may have some merit. Nonetheless, it is curious that neither of the authors has ever published a single scientific article on intelligence (Dorfman, 1995). By choosing to present their data exclusively in a popular book intended for the general reader, Herrnstein and Murray avoided having their data analyses subjected to the critical scrutiny that scientific data must withstand. It is not unusual for scientists to describe their work in a popular book, but doing so normally occurs *after* the scientists have published many technical articles on a topic, which they then attempt to summarize for the layperson. Herrnstein and Murray did not have any work of their own on intelligence to summarize.

Canadian psychologist J. Phillipe Rushton of the University of Western Ontario also created a great deal of controversy with his views concerning race and intelligence. Rushton (1994, 1995) argued from the nature perspective that the races could be ranked in terms of inherited intelligence, social behaviour, and physical attributes. He asserted that Asians are the most intelligent, most law abiding, hardest working, least sexually promiscuous, and have the largest brain size of the races. Blacks rank on the opposite ends of these dimensions, with whites in the middle. Rushton's views on racial hierarchies were condemned not only because of the social harm they might cause, but because his conclusions were based on bad science, sloppy reasoning, and inaccuracies. For example, one review of his 1995 book concluded "the low standards of scholarship evident in this book render it largely irrelevant for modern science" ("Race, Evolution & Behaviour," 1995, p. 129). Commenting on his work, Canadian psychologists Weizmann, Wiener, Wiesenthal, and Ziegler stated that "the collecting and cataloguing of *ad hoc* racial differences in behaviour says nothing about any evolutionary, genetic, or environmental origins and causes of such differences. It also betrays a naïve and outdated inductivist view of science" (1990, p. 11).

Rushton debated his views with David Suzuki on CBC television ("The Rushton-Suzuki Debate," n.d.) in 1989. Although his job was protected by the principle of academic freedom, Rushton was investigated by the police and a provincial human rights board.

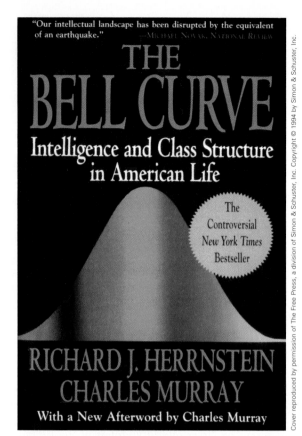

"Our intellectual landscape has been disrupted by the equivalent of an earthquake." —MICHAEL NOVAK, NATIONAL REVIEW

THE BELL CURVE
Intelligence and Class Structure in American Life

The Controversial New York Times Bestseller

RICHARD J. HERRNSTEIN
CHARLES MURRAY

With a New Afterword by Charles Murray

Cover reproduced by permission of The Free Press, a division of Simon & Schuster, Inc. Copyright © 1994 by Simon & Schuster, Inc.

In their 1994 bestseller, Herrnstein and Murray added fuel to the fire of the race–intelligence controversy.

David Peterson, then the premier of Ontario, said he would fire Rushton if he could, and the University of Western Ontario prohibited Rushton from using the undergraduate psychology participant pool for a period of time, cancelled some of his lectures, promised to monitor some of his future lectures, and apologized for any pain caused by his views (Helwig, 1989; Platiel & Struass, 1989; Tenszen, 1989).

In addition to the specific criticisms of Rushton's work, in general, heritability explanations for ethnic differences in IQ have a variety of flaws and weaknesses (Devlin et al., 2002; Horn, 2002; Myerson et al., 1998; Sternberg, 1995). For example, a heritability estimate applies only to the specific group on which the estimate is based. Heritability estimates for intelligence have been based on studies dominated almost entirely by white subjects (Brody, 1992). Hence, there is doubt about the validity of applying this estimate to other cultural groups (Grigorenko, 2000).

Moreover, even if one accepts the assumption that the heritability of IQ is very high, it does not follow logically that differences in *group averages* must be due largely to heredity. Leon Kamin has presented a compelling analogy that highlights the logical fallacy in this reasoning (see Figure 9.16):

We fill a white sack and a black sack with a mixture of different genetic varieties of corn seed. We make certain that the proportions of each variety of seed are identical in each sack. We then plant the seed from the white sack in fertile Field A, while that from the black sack is planted in barren Field B. We will observe that within Field A, as within Field B, there is considerable variation in the height of individual corn plants. This variation will be due largely to genetic factors (seed differences). We will also observe, however, that the average height of plants in Field A is greater than that in Field B. That difference will be entirely due to environmental factors (the soil). The same is true of IQs: differences in the average IQ of various human populations could be entirely due to environmental differences, even if within each population all variation were due to genetic differences! (Eysenck & Kamin, 1981, p. 97)

Kamin's analogy shows that even if the heritability of intelligence is high, group differences in average IQ *could* still be caused entirely (or in part) by environmental factors, a reality acknowledged by Arthur Jensen (1994b) and the authors of *The Bell Curve*.

The available evidence certainly does not allow us to rule out the possibility that ethnic and cultural disparities in average intelligence are partly genetic. And the hypothesis should not be dismissed without study simply because many people find it offensive or distasteful. However, there are several alternative explanations for the culture gap in intelligence that seem more plausible. Let's look at them.

Socioeconomic Disadvantage as an Explanation

Some theorists have approached the issue by trying to show that socioeconomic disadvantages are the main cause of ethnic differences in average IQ. Many social scientists argue that minority students' IQ scores are depressed because these children tend to grow up in deprived environments that create a disadvantage—both in school and on IQ tests. Obviously, living circumstances vary greatly within ethnic groups, but there is no question that, on the average, whites and minorities tend to be raised in very different circumstances. Most minority groups have endured a long history of economic discrimination and are greatly overrepresented in the lower social classes. A lower-class upbringing tends to carry a number of disadvantages that work against the development of a youngster's full intellectual potential (Evans, 2004; Lott, 2002; McLoyd, 1998; Seifer, 2001). In comparison to the middle and upper classes, lower-class children are more likely to come from large families and from single-parent homes, factors that may often limit the parental attention they receive. Lower-class children also tend to be exposed

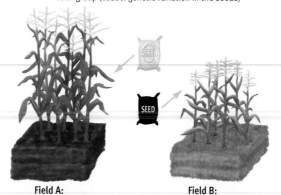

Individual variation in corn plant heights within each group (cause: genetic variation in the seeds)

Field A:
More fertile soil

Field B:
Less fertile soil

Differences in average corn plant height between groups (cause: the soils in which the plants were grown)

Figure 9.16

Genetics and between-group differences on a trait. Leon Kamin's analogy (see text) shows how between-group differences on a trait (the average height of corn plants) could be due to environment, even if the trait is largely inherited. The same reasoning presumably applies to ethnic-group differences in average intelligence.

to fewer books, to have fewer learning supplies, to have less privacy for concentrated study, and to get less parental assistance in learning. Typically, they also have poorer role models for language development, experience less pressure to work hard on intellectual pursuits, and attend poorer-quality schools that are underfunded and understaffed. Many of these children grow up in crime-, drug-, and gang-infested neighbourhoods where it is far more important to develop street intelligence than school intelligence. Some theorists also argue that children in the lower classes are more likely to suffer from malnutrition or to be exposed to environmental toxins (Brody, 1992). Either of these circumstances could interfere with youngsters' intellectual development (Bellinger & Adams, 2001; Grantham-McGregor, Ani, & Fernald, 2001).

In light of these disadvantages, it's not surprising that average IQ scores among children from lower social classes tend to run about 15 points below the average scores obtained by children from middle and upper class homes (Seifer, 2001; Williams & Ceci, 1997). This is the case even if race is factored out of the picture by studying whites exclusively. Admittedly, there is room for argument about the direction of the causal relationships underlying this association between social class and intelligence (Turkheimer, 1998). Nonetheless, given the overrepresentation of minorities in the lower classes, many researchers argue that ethnic differences in intelligence are really social class differences in disguise.

Racial Stereotype Vulnerability as an Explanation

Socioeconomic disadvantages probably are a major factor in various minority groups' poor performance on IQ and other standardized tests, but some theorists maintain that other factors and processes are

Intelligence and Psychological Testing

❝I believe that in significant part the crisis in black Americans' education stems from the power of this vulnerability to undercut identification with schooling.❞
CLAUDE STEELE

also at work. For example, Claude Steele (1992, 1997), a social psychologist at Stanford University, has argued that derogatory stereotypes of stigmatized groups' intellectual capabilities create unique feelings of vulnerability in the educational arena. These feelings of *stereotype vulnerability* can undermine group members' performance on tests, as well as other measures of academic achievement.

Steele points out that demeaning stereotypes of stigmatized groups are widely disseminated, creating a subtle climate of prejudice, even in the absence of overt discrimination. He further notes that members of minority groups are keenly aware of any negative stereotypes that exist regarding their intellect. Hence, when a minority student does poorly on a test, he or she must confront a disturbing possibility: *that others will attribute the failure to racial inferiority.* Steele maintains that females face the same problem when they venture into academic domains where stereotypes suggest that they are inferior to males, such as mathematics, engineering, and the physical sciences. That is, *they worry about people blaming their failures on their sex.* According to Steele, minorities and women in male-dominated fields are in a no-win situation. When they do well and contradict stereotypes, people tend to view their success with suspicion, but when they do poorly, people readily view their failure as vindication of the stereotypes.

Steele maintains that stigmatized groups' apprehension about "confirming" people's negative stereotypes can contribute to academic underachievement in at least two ways. First, it can undermine their emotional investment in academic work. As Steele notes, "Doing well in school requires a belief that school achievement can be a promising basis of self-esteem, and that belief needs constant reaffirmation even for advantaged students" (1992, p. 72). When this belief is relentlessly undercut instead of frequently reaffirmed, students tend to "disidentify" with school and write off academic pursuits as a source of self-worth. Their academic motivation declines and their performance suffers as a result. Second, standardized tests such as IQ tests may be especially anxiety arousing for members of stigmatized groups because the importance attributed to the tests makes one's stereotype vulnerability particularly salient. This anxiety may impair students' test performance by temporarily disrupting their cognitive functioning. We'll look at how Steele tested his theory in our Featured Study.

FEATURED STUDY

Racial Stereotypes and Test Performance

Investigators: Claude M. Steele (Stanford University) and Joshua Aronson (University of Texas, Austin)

Source: Stereotype threat and the intellectual test performance of African Americans. *Journal of Personality and Social Psychology,* 1995, *69,* 797–811.

In this article, Steele and Aronson report on a series of four studies that tested various aspects of Steele's theory about the ramifications of stereotype vulnerability. We will examine their first study in some detail and then discuss the remaining studies more briefly. The purpose of the first study was to test the hypothesis that raising the threat of stereotype vulnerability would have a negative impact on black students' performance on a mental ability test.

Method

Participants. The participants were 114 black and white undergraduates attending Stanford University who were recruited through campus advertisements. As expected, given Stanford's highly selective admissions, both groups of students were well above average in academic ability, as evidenced by their mean scores on the verbal subtest of the Scholastic Aptitude Test (SAT). The study compared black and white students with high and roughly equal ability and preparation (based on their SAT scores) to rule out cultural disadvantage as a factor.

Procedure. The participants were asked to take a challenging, 30-minute test of verbal ability comprised of items from the verbal subtest of the Graduate Record Exam (GRE). In one condition, the issue of stereotype vulnerability was not made salient, as the test was presented to subjects as a device to permit the researchers to analyze participants' problem-solving strategies. In another condition, the spectre of stereotype vulnerability was raised, as the test was presented as an excellent index of one's general verbal ability. The principal dependent variable was subjects' performance on the verbal test.

Results

When the black students' stereotype vulnerability was not made salient, the performance of the black and white students did not differ, as you can see in Figure 9.17. However, when the same test was presented in a way that increased blacks' stereotype vulnerability, the black students scored significantly lower than their white counterparts (see Figure 9.17).

Discussion

Based on their initial study, the authors inferred that stereotype vulnerability does appear to impair minority group members' test performance. They went on to replicate their finding in a second study of 40 black and white female students. In a third study, they demonstrated that their manipulations of stereotype vulnerability were indeed activating thoughts about negative stereotypes, ability-related self-doubts, and performance apprehension in their black participants. Their fourth study showed that stereotype vulnerability can be activated even when a test is not explicitly presented as an index of one's ability.

Comment

More evidence is clearly needed on the effects of stereotype vulnerability, but Steele's theory has been supported in a number of additional studies (Aronson et al., 1999; Croizet et al., 2004; Spencer, Steele, & Quinn, 2002). The concept of stereotype vulnerability has the potential to clear up some of the confusion surrounding the controversial issue of racial disparities in IQ scores. It seems likely that socioeconomic disadvantage makes a substantial contribution to cultural differences in average IQ, but various lines of evidence suggest that this factor cannot account for the culture gap by itself (Neisser et al., 1996). For years, many theorists have argued that test bias accounts for the rest of the culture gap, but as we will discuss momentarily, recent research suggests otherwise. Thus, Steele's groundbreaking research gives scientists an entirely new explanatory tool for understanding the vexing cultural disparities in average IQ. ■

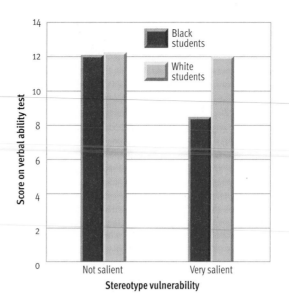

Figure 9.17

Stereotype vulnerability and test performance. Steele and Aronson (1995) compared the performance of black and white students of equal ability on a 30-item verbal ability test constructed from difficult GRE questions. When the black students' stereotype vulnerability was not salient, their performance did not differ from that of the white students; but when the spectre of stereotype vulnerability was raised, the black students performed significantly worse than the white students.

SOURCE: Adapted from Steele, C. M., & Aronson, J. (1995). Stereotype threat and the intellectual test performance of African Americans. *Journal of Personality and Social Psychology, 69,* 797–811. Copyright © 1995 by the American Psychological Association. Reprinted by permission of the author.

Cultural Bias on IQ Tests as an Explanation

Some critics of IQ tests have argued that cultural differences in IQ scores are partly due to a cultural bias built into IQ tests. They argue that because IQ tests are constructed by white, middle-class psychologists, they naturally draw on experience and knowledge typical of white, middle-class lifestyles and use language and vocabulary that reflect the white, middle-class origins of their developers (Cohen, 2002; Helms, 1992; Hilliard, 1984; Williams et al., 1980). Given these concerns, many testing experts assert that minority students' IQ scores should be interpreted with extra caution (Puente, 1990). However, the balance of evidence suggests that the cultural slant on IQ tests is modest to negligible. The charges of bias stimulated a great deal of research on the issue in the 1970s and 1980s. *As a whole, the accumulated evidence suggests that cultural bias produces only weak and inconsistent effects on the IQ scores of minority examinees* (Hunter & Schmidt, 2000; Kaplan, 1985; Reynolds, 2000). However, Suzuki and Valencia (1997) express some caution about this conclusion, noting that the studies of test bias may use culturally biased criteria of academic success to evaluate the tests. They also assert that little research has been done on some widely used tests and with some minority populations.

Taken as a whole, the various alternative explanations for cultural and ethnic disparities in average IQ provide serious challenges to genetic explanations, which appear weak at best—and suspiciously racist at worst. Unfortunately, since the earliest days of IQ testing some people have used IQ tests to further elitist goals. The current controversy about ethnic differences in IQ is just another replay of a record that has been heard before. For instance, beginning in 1913, Henry Goddard tested a great many immigrants to the United States at Ellis Island in New York. Goddard reported that the vast majority of Italian, Hungarian, and Jewish immigrants tested out as *feeble-minded* (Kamin, 1974). As you can see, claims about ethnic deficits in intelligence are nothing new—only the victims have changed.

The debate about ethnic differences in intelligence illustrates how IQ tests have often become entangled in thorny social conflicts. This is unfortunate, because it brings politics to the testing enterprise. Intelligence testing has many legitimate and valuable uses. However, the controversy associated with intelligence tests has undermined their value, leading to some of the new trends that we discuss in the next section.

New Directions in the Assessment and Study of Intelligence

PREVIEW QUESTIONS

- Do modern IQ tests emphasize general ability or specific talents?
- Do measures of mental speed correlate with intelligence?
- What are the key features of Sternberg's theory of successful intelligence?
- What is Gardner's thesis about the nature of intelligence?
- What is emotional intelligence and can it be measured?

Intelligence testing has been through a period of turmoil, and changes are on the horizon. In fact, many changes have occurred already. Let's discuss some of the major new trends and projections for the future.

Increasing Emphasis on Specific Abilities

Although the pendulum may be starting to swing back the other way, recent years have brought an increased emphasis on the measurement of *specific mental abilities* as opposed to *general mental ability* (Daniel, 1997; Das, 1992; Gardner, 1993). Intelligence testing grew out of a particular theoretical climate in the first few decades of the last century. At that time, Charles Spearman's (1904, 1923) ideas about the structure of intellect were dominant. Spearman developed an advanced statistical procedure called factor analysis. In *factor analysis*, **correlations among many variables are analyzed to identify closely related clusters of variables.** If a number of variables correlate highly with one another, the assumption is that a single factor is influencing all of them. Factor analysis attempts to identify these hidden factors.

Spearman used factor analysis to examine the correlations among tests of many specific mental abilities. He concluded that all cognitive abilities share an important core factor, which he labelled *g* for general mental ability. Spearman recognized that people also have "special" abilities (such as numerical reasoning or memory). However, he thought that individuals' ability in these specific areas is largely determined by their general mental ability (see Figure 9.18). Thus, test developers came to see *g* as the Holy Grail in their quest to measure mental ability. Since then, intelligence tests have usually been designed to tap as much of *g* as possible.

A very different view of the structure of intellect began to emerge in the 1940s. Using a somewhat different approach to factor analysis, L. L. Thurstone (1938, 1955) concluded that intelligence involves multiple abilities. Thurstone argued that Spearman and his followers placed far too much emphasis on *g*. In contrast, Thurstone found that he could carve intelligence into seven distinct factors called *primary mental abilities:* word fluency, verbal comprehension, spatial ability, perceptual speed, numerical ability, inductive reasoning, and memory. Following in this tradition, J. P. Guilford (1959, 1985) upped the ante. His theory divided intelligence into *150* separate abilities—and did away with *g* entirely (see Figure 9.19). Thurstone's and Guilford's theories attracted favourable attention, but their ideas had relatively little effect on the day-to-day enterprise of intelligence testing (Horn, 1979).

However, another approach to carving up intelligence *has* had some impact. This approach was originally proposed by Raymond Cattell (1963) and was further developed by John Horn (1985). They suggest that *g* should be divided into *fluid intelligence* and *crystallized intelligence*. **Fluid intelligence involves reasoning ability, memory capacity, and speed of information processing.** *Crystallized intelligence* **involves ability to apply acquired knowledge and skills in problem solving.** Cattell originally assumed

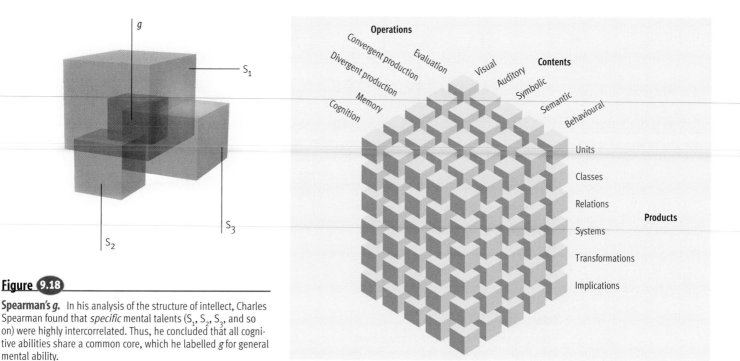

Figure 9.18

Spearman's *g*. In his analysis of the structure of intellect, Charles Spearman found that *specific* mental talents (S_1, S_2, S_3, and so on) were highly intercorrelated. Thus, he concluded that all cognitive abilities share a common core, which he labelled *g* for general mental ability.

Figure 9.19

Guilford's model of mental abilities. In contrast to Spearman (see Figure 9.18), J. P. Guilford concluded that intelligence is made up of many separate abilities. According to his analysis, we may have as many as 150 distinct mental abilities that can be characterized in terms of the operations, contents, and products of intellectual activity.

that fluid intelligence is largely determined by biological factors, and crystallized intelligence by education and experience. However, not all theorists who use the fluid–crystallized distinction assume that fluid intelligence has a stronger biological basis (Lohman, 1989).

The distinction between fluid and crystallized intelligence is central to the hierarchical model of intelligence that guided the most recent revision of the Stanford-Binet IQ test (Thorndike, Hagen, & Sattler, 1986). For the first 70 years of its existence, the Stanford-Binet yielded just one score, which was widely viewed as the ultimate index of general intelligence. However, the Stanford-Binet was broken into subtests for the first time in its long history in the 1986 revision. As Figure 9.20 shows, the modern Stanford-Binet includes 15 subtests. This major change in the structure of the Stanford-Binet seems to reflect a general trend toward devising tests of mental ability that assess specific abilities.

Exploring Biological Indexes of Intelligence

Although specific abilities are increasingly emphasized in the world of education, in the world of research some investigators continue to stalk *g* with single-minded determination. In particular, biologically oriented theorists, such as Arthur Jensen (1987, 1993, 1998) and Hans Eysenck (1988, 1989), have attempted to find raw physiological indicators of gen-

eral intelligence. Their search for a "culture-free" measure of intelligence has led them to focus on sensory processes, much as Sir Francis Galton did over a century ago. Armed with much more sophisticated equipment, they hope to succeed where Galton failed.

Jensen's (1982, 1987, 1992) studies of mental speed are representative of this line of inquiry. In his studies, Jensen measures *reaction time* (RT), using a panel of paired buttons and lights. On each trial, the subject rests a hand on a "home button." When one of the lights is activated, the subject is supposed to push the button for that light as quickly as possible. RT is typically averaged over a number of trials involving varied numbers of lights. Modest correlations (0.20s to 0.30s) have been found between faster RTs and higher scores on conventional IQ tests.

Jensen's findings suggest an association between raw mental speed and intelligence, as Galton originally suggested. This correlation is theoretically interesting and, in retrospect, not all that surprising. Many conventional IQ tests have imposed demanding time limits on examinees, working under the assumption that "fast is smart." However, the correlation between RT and IQ appears to be too weak to give RT any practical value as an index of intelligence.

However, another approach to measuring mental speed may have more practical potential. Measures of *inspection time* assess how long it takes participants to make simple perceptual discriminations that meet a certain criterion of accuracy (Deary & Stough, 1996). For example, in a series of trials, participants may be

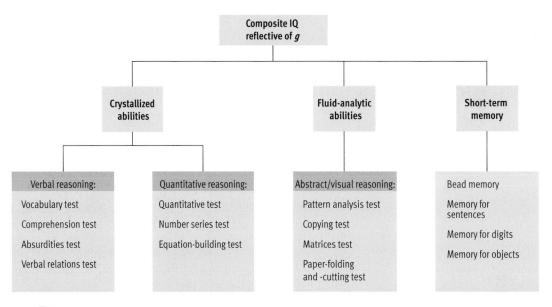

Figure 9.20

The organization of the modern Stanford-Binet. The 1986 edition of the classic Stanford-Binet Intelligence Test is based on the hierarchical model of intelligence diagrammed here, which is built around the distinction between fluid and crystallized intelligence. The modern Stanford-Binet yields a composite score that presumably reflects *g*, four second-order scores for broad types of mental ability (verbal reasoning, quantitative reasoning, abstract/visual reasoning, and short-term memory), and scores on 15 subtests that measure specific mental abilities.

SOURCE: Adapted from Thorndike, R. L., Hagen, E. P., & Sattler, J. M. (1986). *Stanford-Binet Intelligence Scale: Guide for administering and scoring* (4th Ed.). Chicago: Riverside Publishing Company. Reprinted with permission of The Riverside Publishing Company, Copyright © 1986.

asked repeatedly to indicate which of two lines is shorter. The pairs of lines are presented for very brief exposures and participants are told to concentrate on making *accurate* judgments. A person's inspection time is the exposure duration required for that person to achieve a specific level of accuracy, such as 85% correct judgments (see Figure 9.21). Correlations in the 0.40s have been found between participants' inspection time scores and their scores on measures of fluid intelligence (Deary, 2000). These correlations are high enough to have some practical potential,

although a great deal of work remains to be done to standardize inspection time measures and to figure out why they are associated with intelligence.

Psychologist Tony Vernon of the University of Western Ontario and his colleagues suggest that while there have been some replicable biological correlates of intelligence, work in this area is limited by the lack of a systematic theory that can account for the findings in an integrative fashion (Vernon et al., 2000). As we pointed out in Chapter 1, scientific advance is often dependent upon the development

Figure 9.21

Research on inspection time as a biological index of intelligence. (Left) In studies of inspection time, participants are shown stimuli for very brief durations and are asked to make accurate judgments about them (such as whether the longer line is on the right or the left). (Right) Each participant's accuracy in making these perceptual discriminations is graphed as a function of exposure duration. A subject's inspection time for a particular task is the exposure duration required to achieve a certain level of accuracy. In this case, 85% accuracy is the criterion and the participant's inspection time for the task is 14 milliseconds.

SOURCE: Graph adapted from Deary, I. J., Caryl, P. G., & Gibson, G. J. (1993). Nonstationarity and the measurement of psychophysical response in a visual inspection time task. *Perception, 22,* 1245–1256. Copyright © 1993 by Pion Ltd. Adapted by permission.

of a good theory that can both account for current findings and generate novel predictions.

Investigating Cognitive Processes in Intelligent Behaviour

As noted in Chapters 1 and 8, psychologists are increasingly taking a cognitive perspective in their efforts to study many topics. For over a century, the investigation of intelligence has been approached primarily from a *testing perspective*. This perspective emphasizes measuring the *amount* of intelligence people have and figuring out why some have more than others. In contrast, the *cognitive perspective* focuses on how people *use* their intelligence. The interest is in process rather than amount. In particular, cognitive psychologists focus on the information-processing strategies that underlie intelligence.

The application of the cognitive perspective to intelligence has been spearheaded by Robert Sternberg (1985, 1988b, 1991). His *triarchic theory of human intelligence* consists of three parts: the contextual, experiential, and componential subtheories. In his *contextual subtheory*, Sternberg argues that intelligence is a culturally defined concept. He asserts that different manifestations of intelligent behaviour are valued in different contexts. For example, the verbal skills emphasized in North American culture may take a back seat to hunting skills in another culture.

In his *experiential subtheory,* Sternberg explores the relationships between experience and intelligence. He emphasizes two factors as the hallmarks of intelligent behaviour. The first is the ability to deal effectively with novelty—new tasks, demands, and situations. The second factor is the ability to learn how to handle familiar tasks automatically and effortlessly. Sternberg's *componential subtheory* describes three types of mental

processes that intelligent thought depends on: meta-components, performance components, and knowledge-acquisition components (see Figure 9.22). This part of the theory has guided extensive research on the specific thinking strategies that contribute to intelligent problem solving. Investigations of cognitive processes in intelligent behaviour have some interesting implications for intelligence testing. Cognitive research has shown that more-intelligent subjects spend more time figuring out how to best represent problems and planning how to solve them than less-intelligent subjects do. Because planning takes time, Sternberg (1985) argues that traditional IQ tests place too much emphasis on speed.

In more recent extensions of his theory, Sternberg (1999, 2000b, 2003) has asserted that there are three aspects or facets of what he calls "successful intelligence": analytical intelligence, creative intelligence, and practical intelligence. *Analytical intelligence* involves abstract reasoning, evaluation, and judgment. It is the type of intelligence that is crucial to most schoolwork and that is assessed by conventional IQ tests. *Creative intelligence* involves the ability to generate new ideas and to be inventive in dealing with novel problems. *Practical intelligence* involves the ability to deal effectively with the kinds of problems that people encounter in everyday life, such as on the job or at home. A big part of practical intelligence involves learning what one needs to know to work

❝To understand intelligent behavior, we need to move beyond the fairly restrictive tasks that have been used both in experimental laboratories and in psychometric tests of intelligence.❞
ROBERT STERNBERG

Figure 9.22

Sternberg's triarchic theory of intelligence. Sternberg's model of intelligence consists of three parts: the contextual subtheory, the experiential subtheory, and the componential subtheory. Much of Sternberg's research has been devoted to the componential subtheory, as he has attempted to identify the cognitive processes that contribute to intelligence. He believes that these processes fall into three groups: metacomponents, performance components, and knowledge-acquisition components. All three component processes contribute to each of three aspects or types of intelligence: analytical intelligence, practical intelligence, and creative intelligence.

Intelligence and Psychological Testing

Courtesy of Howard Gardner, photo © Jay Gardner

❝*It is high time that the view of intelligence be widened to incorporate a range of human computational capacities…. But where is it written that intelligence needs to be determined on the basis of tests?*❞

HOWARD GARDNER

efficiently in an environment that is not explicitly taught and that often is not even verbalized.

According to Sternberg, all three of the component processes underlying intelligence (metacomponents, performance components, and knowledge-acquisition components) contribute to each of the three facets of intelligence (analytical, creative, and practical intelligence). In a series of studies, Sternberg and his colleagues have gathered data suggesting that (1) all three facets of intelligence can be measured reliably, (2) the three facets of intelligence are relatively independent (uncorrelated), and (3) the assessment of all three aspects of intelligence can improve the prediction of intelligent behaviour in the real world (Grigorenko & Sternberg, 2001; Henry, Sternberg, & Grigorenko, 2005; Sternberg et al., 1999, 2001). A great deal of additional research will be needed to explore the predictive validity and value of Sternberg's new measures of analytical, creative, and practical intelligence. Nonetheless, he certainly has been an articulate voice arguing for a broader, expanded concept of intelligence, which is a theme that has been echoed by others.

Expanding the Concept of Intelligence

In recent years, a number of theorists besides Sternberg have concluded that the focus of tradi-

tional IQ tests is too narrow (Ceci, 1990; Greenspan & Driscoll, 1997). These theorists argue that to assess intelligence in a truly general sense, tests should sample from a wider range of tasks. The most prominent proponent of this view has been Howard Gardner (1983, 1993, 1998, 2004).

According to Gardner, IQ tests have generally emphasized verbal and mathematical skills, to the exclusion of other important skills. He suggests the existence of a number of relatively autonomous *human intelligences,* which are listed in Table 9.3. To build his list of separate intelligences, Gardner reviewed the evidence on cognitive capacities in normal individuals, people suffering from brain damage, and special populations, such as prodigies and idiot savants. He concluded that humans exhibit eight intelligences: logical–mathematical, linguistic, musical, spatial, bodily–kinesthetic, interpersonal, intrapersonal, and naturalist. Recently, Gardner (1999) has suggested the possibility that other intelligences may be identified, including that of an existential intelligence, which he describes as the "intelligence of big questions" (Gardner, 2003, p. 7). But to date, according to Gardner, the evidence is most supportive of the eight listed in Table 9.3. Some of the different facets described by Gardner certainly correspond with the different types of exceptional ability that we referred to in the beginning of the chapter in our discussion of Albert Einstein and Moe Norman,

Table 9.3 Gardner's Eight Intelligences

Intelligence	End-States	Core Components
Logical–mathematical	Scientist Mathematician	Sensitivity to, and capacity to discern, logical or numerical patterns; ability to handle long chains of reasoning
Linguistic	Poet Journalist	Sensitivity to sounds, rhythms, and meanings of words; sensitivity to the different functions of language
Musical	Composer Violinist	Abilities to produce and appreciate rhythm, pitch, and timbre; appreciation of the forms of musical expressiveness
Spatial	Navigator Sculptor	Capacities to perceive the visual–spatial world accurately and to perform transformations on one's initial perceptions
Bodily–kinesthetic	Dancer Athlete	Abilities to control one's body movements and to handle objects skillfully
Interpersonal	Therapist Salesperson	Capacities to discern and respond appropriately to the moods, temperaments, motivations, and desires of other people
Intrapersonal	Person with detailed, accurate self-knowledge	Access to one's own feelings and the ability to discriminate among them and draw upon them to guide behaviour; knowledge of one's own strengths, weaknesses, desires, and intelligences
Naturalist	Biologist Naturalist	Abilities to recognize and categorize objects and processes in nature

SOURCE: Adapted from Gardner, H., & Hatch, T. (1989). Multiple intelligences go to school: Educational implications of the theory of multiple intelligences. *Educational Researcher, 18* (8), 4–10. American Educational Research Association. Additional information from Gardner, 1998.

and Chen Kupperman and Charlotte Petrick. These intelligences obviously include quite a variety of talents that are not assessed by conventional IQ tests. Gardner is investigating the extent to which these intelligences are largely independent, as his theory asserts. For the most part, he has found that people tend to display a mixture of strong, intermediate, and weak abilities, which is consistent with the idea that the various types of intelligence are independent.

Gardner's books have been very popular and his theory clearly resonates with many people (Shearer, 2004). His ideas have had an impact on educators around the world (Cuban, 2004; Kornhaber, 2004). He has done a superb job of synthesizing research from neuropsychology, developmental psychology, cognitive psychology, and other areas to arrive at fascinating speculations about the structure of human abilities. He has raised thought-provoking questions about what abilities should be included under the rubric of intelligence. However, he has his critics (Hunt, 2001; Klein, 1997; Morgan, 1996). Some argue that his use of the term *intelligence* is so broad, encompassing virtually any valued human ability, it makes the term almost meaningless. These critics wonder whether there is any advantage to relabelling talents such as musical ability and motor coordination as forms of intelligence. Critics also note that Gardner's theory has not generated much research on the predictive value of measuring individual differences in the eight intelligences he has described. This research would require the development of tests to measure the eight intelligences, but Gardner is not particularly interested in the matter of assessment and he loathes conventional testing. This reality makes it difficult to predict where Gardner's theory will lead, as research is crucial to the evolution of a theory.

Measuring Emotional Intelligence

In yet another highly publicized effort to expand the concept of intelligence, a variety of theorists have argued that the measurement of *emotional intelligence* can enhance the prediction of success at school, at work, and in interpersonal relationships. The concept of emotional intelligence was originally developed by Peter Salovey and John Mayer (1990). Their concept languished in relative obscurity until Daniel Goleman (1995) wrote a compelling book titled *Emotional Intelligence,* which made the best-seller lists. Since then, empirical research on the measurement of emotional intelligence has increased dramatically.

Emotional intelligence consists of the ability to perceive and express emotion, assimilate emotion in thought, understand and reason with emotion, **and regulate emotion.** Emotional intelligence includes four essential components (Salovey, Mayer, & Caruso, 2002). First, people need to be able to accurately perceive emotions in themselves and others and have the ability to express their own emotions effectively. Second, people need to be aware of how their emotions shape their thinking, decision making, and coping with stress. Third, people need to be able to understand and analyze their emotions, which may often be complex and contradictory. Fourth, people need to be able to regulate their emotions so that they can dampen negative emotions and make effective use of positive emotions.

Several tests of emotional intelligence have already been developed. The test that has the strongest empirical foundation is the Multifactor Emotional Intelligence Scale (MEIS) devised by Mayer, Caruso, and Salovey (1999). More recently, James Parker of Trent University along with his colleague Reuven Bar-On has developed a youth version of an emotional intelligence measure to assess children and adolescents (Bar-On & Parker, 2000a). Parker, a Canada Research Chair in Emotion and Health, is an active researcher in the area of emotional intelligence (Bar-On & Parker, 2000b; Parker et al., 2004). He has suggested that emotional intelligence may be particularly important in difficult transitional phases, such as moving from high school to university. He found that under certain conditions there was an association between emotional intelligence and academic success for first-year university students (Parker et al., 2004). While not all researchers

CONCEPT CHECK 9.3

Recognizing Theories of Intelligence

Check your understanding of various theories on the nature of intelligence by matching the names of their originators with the brief descriptions of the theories' main themes that appear below. Choose from the following theorists: (a) Sir Francis Galton, (b) Howard Gardner, (c) Arthur Jensen, (d) Sandra Scarr, (e) Robert Sternberg, (f) Alfred Binet, and (g) David Wechsler. The answers are in Appendix A.

_____ **1.** This theorist posited eight human intelligences: logical–mathematical, linguistic, musical, spatial, bodily–kinesthetic, interpersonal, intrapersonal, and naturalist.

_____ **2.** On the basis of a study of eminence and success in families, this theorist concluded that intelligence is inherited.

_____ **3.** This theorist stated that the heritability of intelligence is about 80% and that IQ differences between ethnic groups are mainly due to genetics.

_____ **4.** This theorist stated that heredity sets certain limits on intelligence and that environmental factors determine where one falls within those limits.

_____ **5.** This person's theory of intelligence is divided into contextual, experiential, and componential subtheories and posits three facets of intelligence: analytical, practical, and creative intelligence.

have similar findings, Parker's research certainly suggests the importance of emotional intelligence in dealing with stressful events.

Skeptics have questioned whether sophistication about emotion should be viewed as a form of intelligence, and they have correctly pointed out that a great deal of additional research will be needed to fully validate the MEIS and to fully document the adaptive significance of emotional intelligence (Izard, 2001; Matthews, Zeidner, & Roberts, 2005). However, advocates for the concept of emotional intelligence—unlike advocates for the concept of multiple intelligences—seem to relish that challenge, and serious research on emotional intelligence is flourishing. It will be interesting to see where this research leads over the next decade.

Putting It in Perspective

PREVIEW QUESTIONS
- What did this chapter reveal about the importance of cultural factors and the nature versus nurture debate?
- How did this chapter illustrate the connections between psychology and the world at large?

As you probably noticed, three of our integrative themes surfaced in this chapter. Our discussions illustrated that cultural factors shape behaviour, that psychology evolves in a sociohistorical context, and that heredity and environment jointly influence behaviour.

Pervasive psychological testing is largely a Western phenomenon. The concept of general intelligence also has a special, Western flavour to it. Many non-Western cultures have very different ideas about the nature of intelligence. Within Western societies, the observed ethnic differences in average intelligence also illustrate the importance of cultural factors, as these disparities appear to be due in large part to cultural disadvantage and other culture-related considerations. Thus, we see once again that if we hope to achieve a sound understanding of behaviour, we need to appreciate the cultural contexts in which behaviour unfolds.

Human intelligence is shaped by a complex interaction of hereditary and environmental factors. We've drawn similar conclusions before in other chapters where we examined other aspects of behaviour. However, this chapter should have enhanced your appreciation of this idea in at least two ways. First, we examined more of the details of how scientists arrive at the conclusion that heredity and environment jointly shape behaviour. Second, we encountered dramatic illustrations of the immense importance attached to the nature versus nurture debate. For example, Arthur Jensen has been the target of savage criticism. After his controversial 1969 article, he was widely characterized as a racist. When he gave speeches, he was often greeted by protestors carrying signs, such as "Kill Jensen" and "Jensen Must Perish." J. Phillipe Rushton had similar experiences in Canada. As you can see, the debate about the inheritance of intelligence inspires passionate feelings in many people. In part, this is because the debate has far-reaching social and political implications, which brings us to another prominent theme in the chapter.

There may be no other area in psychology where the connections between psychology and society at large are so obvious. Prevailing social attitudes have always exerted some influence on testing practices and the interpretation of test results. In the first half of the 20th century, a strong current of racial and class prejudice was apparent in North America and Britain. This prejudice supported the idea that IQ tests measured innate ability and that "undesirable" groups scored poorly because of their genetic inferiority. Although these beliefs did not go unchallenged within psychology, their widespread acceptance in the field reflected the social values of the time. It's ironic that IQ tests have sometimes been associated with social prejudice. When used properly, intelligence tests provide relatively objective measures of mental ability that are less prone to bias than the subjective judgments of teachers or employers.

Today, psychological tests serve many diverse purposes. In the upcoming Personal Application, we focus on creativity tests and on the nature of creative thinking and creative people.

REVIEW OF KEY POINTS
- Modern intelligence tests place a greater emphasis on the measurement of specific mental abilities and less emphasis on tapping Spearman's g than their predecessors. The distinction between fluid and crystallized intelligence is the basis for the most recent revision of the Stanford-Binet IQ test.
- Although reaction-time indexes of intelligence are being explored, they seem to have little practical utility. Measures of inspection time may prove more useful, although additional research is needed.
- Research on intelligence increasingly uses a cognitive perspective, which emphasizes the need to understand how people use their intelligence. Many modern theorists, such as Robert Sternberg and Howard Gardner, argue that the concept of intelligence should be expanded to encompass a greater variety of skills. Researchers have made some progress in their efforts to measure emotional intelligence.
- Three of our integrative themes stood out in the chapter. Our discussions of intelligence showed how heredity and environment interact to shape behaviour, how psychology evolves in a sociohistorical context, and how one has to consider cultural contexts to fully understand behaviour.

Understanding Creativity

Answer the following "true" or "false."

_____**1.** Creative ideas often come out of nowhere.

_____**2.** Creativity usually occurs in a burst of insight.

_____**3.** Creativity depends on inspiration far more than on perspiration.

Intelligence is not the only type of mental ability that psychologists have studied. They have devised tests to explore a variety of mental abilities. Among these, creativity is certainly one of the most interesting. People tend to view creativity as an essential trait for artists, musicians, and writers, but it is important in *many* walks of life. In this Application, we'll discuss psychologists' efforts to measure and understand creativity. As we progress, you'll learn that all the statements above are false.

The Nature of Creativity

What makes thought creative? *Creativity involves the generation of ideas that are original, novel, and useful.* Creative thinking is fresh, innovative, and inventive. But novelty by itself is not enough. In addition to being unusual, creative thinking must be adaptive. It must be appropriate to the situation and problem.

Does Creativity Occur in a Burst of Insight?

It is widely believed that creativity usually involves sudden flashes of insight and great leaps of imagination. Robert Weisberg (1986) calls this belief the "aha! myth." Undeniably, creative bursts of insight do occur (Feldman, 1988). However, the evidence suggests that major creative achievements generally are logical extensions of existing ideas, involving long, hard work and many small, faltering steps forward (Weisberg, 1993). Creative ideas do not come out of nowhere. Creative ideas come from a deep well of experience and training in a specific area, whether it's music, painting, business, or science (Weisberg, 1999). As Snow (1986) puts it, "Creativity is not a light bulb in the mind, as most cartoons depict it. It is an accomplishment born of intensive study, long reflection, persistence, and interest" (p. 1033).

Does Creativity Depend on Unconscious Thought Processes?

Some fascinating reports have attributed creative breakthroughs to unconscious thought processes (Ghiselin, 1952). For example, creative giants such as Mozart, Dostoyevsky, and Coleridge reported that dazzling insights came to them while sleeping or daydreaming. These stories have led some theorists to conclude that creativity depends on the unconscious, which is not constrained by normal logic and rationality (Kris, 1952).

As a whole, however, reports of unconscious breakthroughs are few and of dubious accuracy. In at least some cases, it appears that artists have fabricated stories of unconscious breakthroughs to attract publicity, to confound rivals, or to enhance the legend of their genius (Weisberg, 1993). Most cognitive psychologists have concluded that creativity emerges out of normal problem-solving efforts that depend on conscious thought processes (Hayes, 1989; Klahr & Simon, 1999) and that creativity can be learned or enhanced, at least to some degree (Nickerson, 1999).

Does Creativity Depend on Divergent Thinking?

According to many theorists, the key to creativity lies in *divergent thinking*—thinking "that goes off in different directions," as J. P. Guilford (1959) put it. In his model of mental abilities (see Figure 9.19 on page 377), Guilford distinguished between convergent thinking and divergent thinking. **In *convergent thinking* one tries to narrow down a list of alternatives to converge on a single correct answer.** For example, when you take a multiple-choice exam, you try to eliminate incorrect options until you hit on the correct response. Most training in school encourages convergent thinking. **In *divergent thinking* one tries to expand the range of alternatives by generating many possible solutions.** Imagine that you work for an advertising agency. To come up with as many slogans as possible for a client's product, you must use divergent thinking. Some of your slogans may be clear losers, and eventually you will have to engage in convergent thinking to pick the best, but coming up with the range of new possibilities depends on divergent thinking.

Thirty years of research on divergent thinking has yielded mixed results. As a whole, the evidence suggests that divergent thinking contributes to creativity, but it clearly does not represent the essence of creativity, as originally proposed (Brown, 1989; Plucker & Renzulli, 1999). In retrospect, it was probably unrealistic to expect creativity to depend on a single cognitive skill. According to Sternberg (1988a), the cognitive processes that underlie creativity are multifaceted.

Measuring Creativity SIM8

Although its nature may be elusive, creativity clearly is important in today's world. Creative masterpieces in the arts and literature enrich human existence. Creative insights in the sciences illuminate people's understanding of the world. Creative inventions fuel technological progress. Thus, it is understandable that psychologists have been interested in measuring creativity with psychological tests.

CHAPTER 10

Latchezar Boyadjiev, *Joy,* L.B. Glass Studios

Motivational Theories and Concepts
Drive Theories
Incentive Theories
Evolutionary Theories
The Range and Diversity of Human Motives

The Motivation of Hunger and Eating
Biological Factors in the Regulation of Hunger
Environmental Factors in the Regulation of Hunger
Eating and Weight: The Roots of Obesity

Sexual Motivation and Behaviour
Determinants of Sexual Desire
Evolutionary Analyses of Human Sexual Behaviour
Featured Study • Evolution, Culture, and Mating Priorities
The Mystery of Sexual Orientation
The Human Sexual Response

Affiliation: In Search of Belongingness

Achievement: In Search of Excellence
Individual Differences in the Need for Achievement
Situational Determinants of Achievement Behaviour

The Elements of Emotional Experience
The Cognitive Component: Subjective Feelings
The Physiological Component: Diffuse and Multifaceted
The Behavioural Component: Nonverbal Expressiveness
Culture and the Elements of Emotion

Theories of Emotion
James-Lange Theory
Cannon-Bard Theory
Schachter's Two-Factor Theory
Evolutionary Theories of Emotion

Putting It in Perspective

Personal Application • **Exploring the Ingredients of Happiness**
How Happy Are People?
Factors That Do Not Predict Happiness
Moderately Good Predictors of Happiness
Strong Predictors of Happiness
Conclusions about Subjective Well-Being

Critical Thinking Application • **Analyzing Arguments: Making Sense out of Controversy**
The Anatomy of an Argument
Common Fallacies
Evaluating the Strength of Arguments

Recap

Practice Test

PRACTICE TEST

1. Which of the following does not belong with the others?
- A. aptitude tests
- B. personality tests
- C. intelligence tests
- D. achievement tests

2. If you score at the 75th percentile on a standardized test, this means that:
- A. 75% of those who took the test scored better than you did.
- B. 25% of those who took the test scored less than you did.
- C. 75% of those who took the test scored the same or less than you did.
- D. you answered 75% of the questions correctly.

3. If a test has good test–retest reliability:
- A. there is a strong correlation between items on the test.
- B. it accurately measures what it says it measures.
- C. it can be used to predict future performance.
- D. the test yields similar scores if taken at two different times.

4. Which of the following is a true statement regarding Francis Galton?
- A. He took the position that intelligence is largely determined by heredity.
- B. He advocated the development of special programs to tap the intellectual potential of the culturally disadvantaged.
- C. He developed tests that identified those children who were unable to profit from a normal education.
- D. He took the position that intelligence is more a matter of environment than heredity.

5. On most modern IQ tests, a score of 115 would be:
- A. about normal.
- B. about 15% higher than the average of one's age mates.
- C. an indication of genius.
- D. one standard deviation above the mean.

6. IQ tests have proven to be good predictors of:
- A. social intelligence.
- B. practical problem-solving intelligence.
- C. school performance.
- D. all of the above.

7. Mr. and Mrs. Proudparent are beaming because their son, little Newton, has been selected for a gifted children program at school. They think Newton is a genius. What sort of advice do they need to hear?
- A. Youngsters with a 130–140 IQ tend to be very maladjusted.
- B. Most gifted children do not go on to make genius-level, major contributions to society that earn them eminence.
- C. They should prepare to be famous, based on their parentage of Newton.
- D. They should be warned that gifted children often have deficits in fluid intelligence.

8. Which of the following is a true statement about mental retardation?
- A. Most retarded people are unable to live normal lives because of their mental deficiencies.
- B. With special tutoring, a mentally retarded person can attain average intelligence.
- C. The majority of mentally retarded people fall in the mildly retarded category.
- D. Diagnoses of mental retardation should be based exclusively on IQ scores.

9. Most school districts consider children who _____ to be gifted.
- A. have IQ scores above 115
- B. score in the upper 2%–3% of the IQ distribution
- C. have parents in professional careers
- D. demonstrate high levels of leadership and creativity

10. In which of the following cases would you expect to find the greatest similarity in IQ?
- A. between fraternal twins
- B. between identical twins
- C. between nontwin siblings
- D. between parent and child

11. Evidence indicating that upbringing affects one's mental ability is provided by which of the following findings?
- A. that identical twins are more similar in IQ than fraternal twins
- B. that there is more than a chance similarity between adopted children and their biological parents
- C. that siblings reared together are more similar in IQ than siblings reared apart
- D. that identical twins reared apart are more similar in IQ than siblings reared together

12. Which of the following is a likely consequence of stereotype vulnerability for members of minority groups?
- A. Academic motivation declines.
- B. Academic performance often suffers.
- C. Standardized tests may be especially anxiety arousing.
- D. All of the above are likely consequences.

13. Which of the following is a current trend in the assessment of intelligence?
- A. using biological indexes of intelligence in the schools
- B. narrowing the concept of intelligence
- C. greater emphasis on measuring *g* rather than specific abilities
- D. greater emphasis on measuring specific abilities rather than *g*

14. When you try to narrow down a list of alternatives to arrive at a single correct answer, you engage in:
- A. convergent thinking.
- B. divergent thinking.
- C. creativity.
- D. insight.

15. Nora has a blind date with Nick who, she's been told, is considered a true genius by the faculty in the art department. Now she's having second thoughts, because she's always heard that geniuses are a little off their rocker. Does she have reason to be concerned?
- A. Yes. It's been well documented that the stress of creative achievement often leads to schizophrenic symptoms.
- B. No. Extensive research on creativity and psychological disorders shows no evidence for any connection.
- C. Perhaps. There is evidence of a correlation between major creative achievement and vulnerability to mood disorders.
- D. Of course not. The stereotype of the genius who's mentally ill is purely a product of the jealousy of untalented people.

See Appendix A for answers to this Practice Test.

  ON THE WEB

For additional resources on the topics covered in this chapter, visit the *Psychology: Themes and Variations* Web site, where you will find practice quizzes, tutorials, Web links, simulations, critical thinking activities, flash cards, interactive exercises, and suggested readings available through INFOTRAC.

http://www.themesandvariations.nelson.com

 Thomson NOW! http://hed.nelson.com

Go to this site for the link to ThomsonNOW™, your one-stop study shop. Take a Pretest for this chapter and ThomsonNOW™ will generate a personalized Study Plan based on your test results! The Study Plan will identify the topics you need to review and direct you to online resources to help you master those topics. You can then take a Posttest to help you determine the concepts you have mastered and what you still need work on.

CHAPTER 10

Latchezar Boyadjiev, *Joy*, L.B. Glass Studios

Motivational Theories and Concepts
Drive Theories
Incentive Theories
Evolutionary Theories
The Range and Diversity of Human Motives

The Motivation of Hunger and Eating
Biological Factors in the Regulation of Hunger
Environmental Factors in the Regulation of Hunger
Eating and Weight: The Roots of Obesity

Sexual Motivation and Behaviour
Determinants of Sexual Desire
Evolutionary Analyses of Human Sexual Behaviour
Featured Study • Evolution, Culture, and Mating Priorities
The Mystery of Sexual Orientation
The Human Sexual Response

Affiliation: In Search of Belongingness

Achievement: In Search of Excellence
Individual Differences in the Need for Achievement
Situational Determinants of Achievement Behaviour

The Elements of Emotional Experience
The Cognitive Component: Subjective Feelings
The Physiological Component: Diffuse and Multifaceted
The Behavioural Component: Nonverbal Expressiveness
Culture and the Elements of Emotion

Theories of Emotion
James-Lange Theory
Cannon-Bard Theory
Schachter's Two-Factor Theory
Evolutionary Theories of Emotion

Putting It in Perspective

Personal Application • **Exploring the Ingredients of Happiness**
How Happy Are People?
Factors That Do Not Predict Happiness
Moderately Good Predictors of Happiness
Strong Predictors of Happiness
Conclusions about Subjective Well-Being

Critical Thinking Application • **Analyzing Arguments: Making Sense out of Controversy**
The Anatomy of an Argument
Common Fallacies
Evaluating the Strength of Arguments

Recap

Practice Test

RECAP

Key Ideas

Key Concepts in Psychological Testing

● Psychological tests are standardized measures of behaviour—usually mental abilities or aspects of personality. Test scores are interpreted by consulting test norms to find out what represents a high or low score. Psychological tests should produce consistent results, a quality called reliability.

● Validity refers to the degree to which there is evidence that a test measures what it was designed to measure. Content validity is crucial on classroom tests. Criterion-related validity is critical when tests are used to predict performance. Construct validity is critical when a test is designed to measure a hypothetical construct.

The Evolution of Intelligence Testing

● The first crude efforts to devise intelligence tests were made by Sir Francis Galton, who wanted to show that intelligence is inherited. Modern intelligence testing began with the work of Alfred Binet, who devised a scale to measure a child's mental age.

● Lewis Terman revised the original Binet scale to produce the Stanford-Binet in 1916. It introduced the intelligence quotient and became the standard of comparison for subsequent tests. David Wechsler devised an improved measure of intelligence for adults and a new scoring system based on the normal distribution.

Basic Questions about Intelligence Testing

● In the modern scoring system, deviation IQ scores indicate where people fall in the normal distribution of intelligence for their age group. Although they are intended to measure potential for learning, IQ tests inevitably assess a blend of potential and knowledge.

● IQ tests are exceptionally reliable. They are reasonably valid measures of academic intelligence, but they do not tap social or practical intelligence.

● IQ scores are correlated with occupational attainment, but their ability to predict performance within occupations is the subject of debate. Intelligence testing is largely a Western enterprise; IQ tests are not widely used in most non-Western cultures.

Extremes of Intelligence

● IQ scores below 70–75 are usually diagnostic of mental retardation, but these diagnoses should not be based solely on test results. Four levels of retardation have been distinguished. Most of the retarded population falls in the mildly retarded category. Although many biological conditions can cause retardation, biological causes can be pinpointed in only about 25% of cases.

● Children who obtain IQ scores above 130 may be viewed as gifted, but cut-offs for accelerated programs vary. Research by Terman showed that gifted children tend to be socially mature and well adjusted, although Winner has raised concerns about the adjustment of profoundly gifted individuals. Extraordinary achievement seems to depend on intensive training and hard work, but innate talent may also contribute.

Heredity and Environment as Determinants of Intelligence

● Twin studies show that identical twins are more similar in IQ than fraternal twins, suggesting that intelligence is inherited, at least in part. Estimates of the heritability of intelligence mostly range from 50% to 70%, but heritability ratios have certain limitations.

● Many lines of evidence indicate that environment is also an important determinant of intelligence. Of particular interest is the recent discovery of generational increases in measured IQ. The concept of reaction range posits that heredity places limits on one's intellectual potential while the environment determines where one falls within these limits.

● Genetic explanations for cultural differences in IQ have been challenged on a variety of grounds. Even if the heritability of IQ is great, group differences in average intelligence may not be due to heredity. Moreover, ethnicity varies with social class, so socioeconomic disadvantage may account for low IQ scores among minority students. Stereotype vulnerability and cultural bias on IQ tests may also contribute to ethnic differences in average IQ.

New Directions in the Assessment and Study of Intelligence

● In contemporary testing, there is a greater emphasis on the measurement of specific mental abilities and less emphasis on tapping Spearman's g. The distinction between fluid and crystallized intelligence is the basis for the most recent revision of the Stanford-Binet IQ test.

● Biological indexes of intelligence are being explored; however, they seem to have little practical utility, although the inspection time measure appears to have potential. Research on intelligence increasingly takes a cognitive perspective, which emphasizes the need to understand how people use their intelligence. Many modern theorists, such as Robert Sternberg and Howard Gardner, argue that the concept of intelligence should be expanded to encompass a greater variety of skills.

Putting It in Perspective

● Three of our integrative themes stood out in the chapter. Our discussions of intelligence showed how heredity and environment interact to shape behaviour, how psychology evolves in a sociohistorical context, and how one has to consider cultural contexts to fully understand behaviour.

Personal Application • Understanding Creativity

● Creativity involves the generation of original, novel, and useful ideas. Creativity does not usually involve sudden insight, and it consists of more than divergent thinking. Creativity tests are mediocre predictors of creative productivity in the real world.

● Creativity is only weakly related to intelligence. The correlations are modest, but some personality traits are associated with creativity. Recent evidence suggests that creative geniuses may exhibit heightened vulnerability to psychological disorders, especially mood disorders.

Critical Thinking Application • The Intelligence Debate, Appeals to Ignorance, and Reification

● The appeal to ignorance involves misusing the general lack of knowledge or information on an issue to support an argument. This fallacy has surfaced in the debate about intelligence, wherein it has been argued that because we have little or no evidence that intelligence can be increased by environmental interventions, intelligence must be mostly inherited.

● Reification occurs when a hypothetical construct is treated as though it were a tangible object. The concepts of intelligence and heritability have both been subject to reification.

Key Terms

Achievement tests, 351
Aptitude tests, 351
Construct validity, 354
Content validity, 354
Convergent thinking, 383
Correlation coefficient, 353
Creativity, 383
Criterion-related validity, 354
Crystallized intelligence, 376
Deviation IQ scores, 358
Divergent thinking, 383
Emotional intelligence, 381
Factor analysis, 376
Fluid intelligence, 376
Heritability ratio, 368
Intelligence quotient (IQ), 357
Intelligence tests, 351

Mental age, 356
Mental retardation, 363
Normal distribution, 358
Percentile score, 351
Personality tests, 351
Psychological test, 351
Reaction range, 370
Reification, 387
Reliability, 353
Standardization, 351
Test norms, 351
Validity, 353

Key People

Alfred Binet, 356
Sir Francis Galton, 356
Howard Gardner, 380
Arthur Jensen, 372
Sandra Scarr, 370
Claude Steele, 374
Robert Sternberg, 379
Lewis Terman, 357
David Wechsler, 357
Ellen Winner, 365

scores?" Yes, one could argue that the programs failed to yield the expected increments in IQ scores because they were poorly planned, poorly executed, too brief, or underfunded (Ramey, 1999; Siegel, 2004). The inability of the enrichment programs to produce enduring increases in IQ does not necessarily imply that intelligence is unchangeable because it is largely a product of heredity.

You may also be wondering, "Aren't there contradictory data?" Once again, the answer is yes. Some lesser-known educational enrichment programs attempted with smaller groups of children *have* yielded durable gains in IQ scores or other measures of academic achievement (Barnett, 1995; Ramey, Ramey, & Lanzi, 2001; Reynolds et al., 2001). Moreover, completely different approaches to gauging the impact of environmental enrichment—such as studies of children adopted from underprivileged homes into middle-class homes—have demonstrated that an improved environment can lead to meaningful increases in IQ (Scarr & Weinberg, 1983).

But we're supposed to be discussing appeals to ignorance, and there was another notable example of this fallacy in the chapter. Can you identify where this slippery logic was used? It surfaced in the discussion of the causes of mental retardation. As you may recall, roughly 25% of the time diagnosticians can pinpoint a biological cause for retardation. The remaining 75% of the cases are of unknown origin, but they are typically assumed to be due to environmental factors. In other words, the reasoning goes, *we don't have any evidence that these cases are due to biological anomalies, so they must be environmental in origin.* This is an appeal to ignorance, and the assertion that most cases of retardation must be due to environmental factors is open to some questioning.

Reification

The dialogue on intelligence has also been marred by the tendency to engage in reification. **Reification occurs when a hypothetical, abstract concept is given a name and then treated as though it were a concrete, tangible object.** Some hypothetical constructs just become so familiar and so taken for granted that we begin to think about them as if they were real. People often fall into this trap with the Freudian personality concepts of id, ego, and superego (see Chapter 12). They begin to think of the *ego*, for instance, as a genuine entity that can be strengthened or controlled, when the ego is really nothing more than a hypothetical abstraction. The concept of intelligence has also been reified in many quarters. Like the ego, intelligence is nothing more than a useful abstraction—a hypothetical construct that is estimated, rather arbitrarily, by a collection of paper-and-pencil measures called IQ tests. Yet people routinely act as if intelligence is a tangible commodity, fighting vitriolic battles over whether it can be measured precisely, whether it can be changed, and whether it can ensure job success. This reification clearly contributes to the tendency for people to attribute excessive importance to the concept of intelligence. It would be wise to remember that intelligence is no more real than the concept of "the environment" or "cyberspace."

Reification has also occurred in the debate about the *degree* to which intelligence is inherited. Arguments about the heritability coefficient for intelligence often imply that there is a single, true number lurking somewhere "out there" waiting to be discovered. In reality, heritability is a hypothetical construct that can be legitimately estimated in several ways that can lead to somewhat different results. Moreover, heritability ratios will vary from

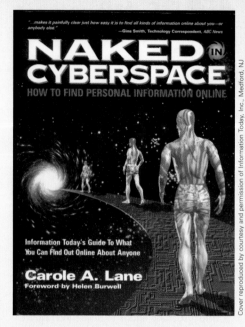

Reification occurs when we think of hypothetical constructs as if they were real. Like intelligence, the concept of cyberspace has been subject to reification. The fact that cyberspace is merely an abstraction becomes readily apparent when artists are asked to "draw" cyberspace for conference posters or book covers.

one population to the next, depending on the amount of genetic variability and the extent of environmental variability in the populations. No exactly accurate number that corresponds to "true heritability" awaits discovery. Thus, it is important to understand that hypothetical constructs have great heuristic value in the study of complex phenomena such as human thought and behaviour, but they do not actually exist in the world—at least not in the same way that a table or a person exists.

Table 9.4 Critical Thinking Skills Discussed in This Application

Skill	Description
Recognizing and avoiding appeals to ignorance	The critical thinker understands that the lack of information on an issue cannot be used to support an argument.
Recognizing and avoiding reification	The critical thinker is vigilant about the tendency to treat hypothetical constructs as if they were concrete things.
Looking for alternative explanations for findings and events	In evaluating explanations, the critical thinker explores whether there are other explanations that could also account for the findings or events under scrutiny.
Looking for contradictory evidence	In evaluating the evidence presented on an issue, the critical thinker attempts to look for contradictory evidence that may have been left out of the debate.

The Intelligence Debate, Appeals to Ignorance, and Reification

A *fallacy* is a mistake or error in the process of reasoning. Cognitive scientists who study how people think have developed long lists of common errors that people make in their reasoning processes. One of these fallacies has a curious name, which is the *appeal to ignorance*. It involves misusing the general lack of knowledge or information on an issue (a lack of knowledge is a kind of ignorance) to support an argument. This fallacy often surfaces in the debate about the relative influence of heredity and environment on intelligence. Before we tackle the more difficult issue of how this fallacy shows up in the debate about intelligence, let's start with a simpler example.

Appeal to Ignorance

Do ghosts exist? This is probably not the kind of question you expected to find in your psychology textbook, but it can clarify the appeal to ignorance. Those who assert that ghosts *do* exist will often support their conclusion by arguing that no one can prove that ghosts do *not* exist; therefore ghosts must exist. The lack of evidence or inability to show that ghosts do not exist is used to conclude the opposite. Conversely, those who assert that ghosts *do not* exist often rely on the same logic. They argue that no one can prove that ghosts exist; therefore, they must not exist. Can you see what is wrong with these appeals to ignorance? The lack of information on an issue cannot be used to support any conclusion—other than the conclusion that we are too ignorant to draw a conclusion.

One interesting aspect of the appeal to ignorance is that the same appeal can be used to support two conclusions that are diametrically opposed to each other. This paradox is a telltale clue that appeals to ignorance involve flawed reasoning. It is easy to see what is wrong with appeals to ignorance when the opposite arguments (ghosts exist—ghosts do not exist) are presented together and the lack of evidence on the issue under discussion is obvious. However, when the same fallacy surfaces in more complex debates and the appeal to ignorance is not as blatant, the strategy can be more difficult to recognize. Let's look at how the appeal to ignorance has been used in the debate about intelligence.

As you saw in the main body of the chapter, the debate about the relative contributions of nature and nurture to intelligence is one of psychology's longest-running controversies. This complex and multifaceted debate is exceptionally bitter and acrimonious because it has far-reaching sociopolitical repercussions. In this debate, one argument that has frequently been made is that we have little or no evidence that intelligence can be increased by environmental (educational) interventions; therefore, intelligence must be mostly inherited. In other words, the argument runs: No one has demonstrated that intelligence is largely shaped by environment, so it must be largely inherited. This argument was part of Jensen's (1969) landmark treatise that greatly intensified the debate about intelligence, and it was one of the arguments made by Herrnstein and Murray (1994) in their controversial book *The Bell Curve*. What the argument refers to is the evidence that educational enrichment programs, which have been designed to enhance the intellectual development of underprivileged children, generally have not produced substantial, long-term gains in IQ (Bentler & Woodward, 1978; Neisser et al., 1996). These findings may have some important implications for government policy in the educational arena, but the way in which they have been applied to the nature–nurture debate regarding intelligence has resulted in an appeal to ignorance. In its simplest form, the absence of evidence showing that environmental changes can increase intelligence is used to support the conclusion that intelligence is mostly determined by genetic inheritance. But the absence of evidence (ignorance) cannot be used to argue for or against a position.

By the way, if you have assimilated some of the critical thinking skills discussed in earlier chapters, you may be thinking, "Wait a minute. Aren't there alternative explanations for the failure of educational enrichment programs to increase IQ

For the most part, educational enrichment programs for underprivileged children have not produced durable increases in participants' IQ scores. However, as the text explains, this finding does not provide logically sound support for the notion that intelligence is largely inherited.

represent different types of mental ability. Thus, it's not surprising that correlations between measures of creativity and measures of intelligence are generally weak (Sternberg & O'Hara, 1999). Creativity and intelligence are not entirely unrelated, however, as creative achievements in most fields require a minimum level of intelligence. Hence, most highly creative people are probably well above average in intelligence (Simonton, 1999).

Is There a Connection between Creativity and Mental Illness?

There may be a connection between truly exceptional creativity and mental illness. The list of creative geniuses who suffered from psychological disorders is endless (Prentky, 1989). Kafka, Hemingway, Rembrandt, Van Gogh, Chopin, Tchaikovsky, Descartes, and Newton are but a few examples (see Figure 9.25). Of course, a statistical association cannot be demonstrated by citing a handful of examples.

In this case, however, some statistical data are available. And these data *do* suggest a correlation between creative genius and maladjustment—in particular, mood disorders such as depression. When Andreasen (1987) studied 30 accomplished writers who had been invited as visiting faculty to the prestigious Iowa Writers Workshop, she found that 80% of her sample had suffered a mood disorder at some point in their lives. In a similar study of 59 female writers from another writers' conference, Ludwig (1994) found that 56% had experienced depression. These figures are far above the base rate (roughly 15%) for mood disorders in the general population. Other studies have also found an association between creativity and mood disorders, as well as other kinds of psychological disorders (Frantom &

Sherman, 1999; Jamison, 1988; Ludwig, 1998; Post, 1996; Schildkraut, Hirshfeld, & Murphy, 1994). Perhaps the most ambitious examination of the issue has been Arnold Ludwig's (1995) analyses of the biographies of 1004 people who achieved eminence in 18 fields. He found greatly elevated rates of depression and other disorders among eminent writers, artists, and composers.

Thus, accumulating empirical data tentatively suggest that there may be a correlation between major creative achievement and vulnerability to mood disorders. According to Andreasen (1996), creativity and maladjustment probably are *not* causally related. Instead, she speculates that certain cognitive styles may both foster creativity and predispose people to psychological disorders. Another, more mundane possibility is that creative individuals' elevated pathology may simply reflect all the difficulty and frustration they experience as they struggle to get their ideas or works accepted in artistic fields that enjoy relatively little public support (Csikszentmihalyi, 1994, 1999).

REVIEW OF KEY POINTS

- Creativity involves the generation of original, novel, and useful ideas. Creativity does not usually involve sudden insight and it does not depend on unconscious thought processes. Divergent thinking contributes to creativity but does not represent its essence.

- Creativity tests are mediocre predictors of creative productivity in the real world. One problem is that creativity is specific to particular domains of expertise. Another problem is that creative achievement depends on a host of factors besides one's creativity.

- Creative people are more likely than others to exhibit certain personality traits, but the correlations between creativity and personality are weak. The association between creativity and intelligence is also modest, although creativity probably requires above-average intelligence. Recent evidence suggests that creative geniuses may exhibit heightened vulnerability to mood disorders.

Figure 9.25

Examples of people who achieved creative eminence and suffered from psychological disorders. As these brief lists show, it is easy to compile rosters of great artists, scientists, composers, and writers who struggled with mental illness. However, while interesting, anecdotal evidence such as this cannot demonstrate that there is an association between creative eminence and mental disorder. [Based on information from Prentky (1980) and Rothenberg (1990).]

Artists	Scientists	Composers	Writers
Bosch	Copernicus	Beethoven	Blake
Durer	Descartes	Berlioz	Coleridge
Goya	Kepler	Chopin	Dostoyevsky
Kandinsky	Linnaeus	Handel	Hemingway
Raphael	Mendel	Saint-Saens	Kafka
Rembrandt	Newton	Schubert	Poe
Van Gogh	Pascal	Tchaikovsky	Plath

Rembrandt
Rembrandt, Harmensz, van Rijn, *Self-Portrait with Beard*. Museu de Arte, Sao Paulo, Brazil. Giraudon/Art Resource, NY.

Chopin
Delacroix, Eugene, *Portrait of Chopin*, Louvre, Paris: Giraudon/Art Resource, NY.

Copernicus
Pomerian, 16th cent. *Portrait of Nicolas Copernicus*. Museum, Torun, Poland. Erich Lessing/Art Resource, NY.

Figure 9.24

Answers to the remote associates items.

Source: Matlin, M. W. (1994). *Cognition* (3rd Ed.). Fort Worth, TX: Harcourt Brace. Reprinted by permission of the author.

1. PRINCE	6. BOAT
2. DOG	7. DEFENCE
3. COLD	8. BLACK
4. GLASSES	9. PIT
5. CLUB	10. WRITER

Understanding Creativity

Answer the following "true" or "false."

_____ **1.** Creative ideas often come out of nowhere.

_____ **2.** Creativity usually occurs in a burst of insight.

_____ **3.** Creativity depends on inspiration far more than on perspiration.

Intelligence is not the only type of mental ability that psychologists have studied. They have devised tests to explore a variety of mental abilities. Among these, creativity is certainly one of the most interesting. People tend to view creativity as an essential trait for artists, musicians, and writers, but it is important in *many* walks of life. In this Application, we'll discuss psychologists' efforts to measure and understand creativity. As we progress, you'll learn that all the statements above are false.

The Nature of Creativity

What makes thought creative? *Creativity* **involves the generation of ideas that are original, novel, and useful.** Creative thinking is fresh, innovative, and inventive. But novelty by itself is not enough. In addition to being unusual, creative thinking must be adaptive. It must be appropriate to the situation and problem.

Does Creativity Occur in a Burst of Insight?

It is widely believed that creativity usually involves sudden flashes of insight and great leaps of imagination. Robert Weisberg (1986) calls this belief the "aha! myth." Undeniably, creative bursts of insight do occur (Feldman, 1988). However, the evidence suggests that major creative achievements generally are logical extensions of existing ideas, involving long, hard work and many small, faltering steps forward (Weisberg, 1993). Creative ideas do not

come out of nowhere. Creative ideas come from a deep well of experience and training in a specific area, whether it's music, painting, business, or science (Weisberg, 1999). As Snow (1986) puts it, "Creativity is not a light bulb in the mind, as most cartoons depict it. It is an accomplishment born of intensive study, long reflection, persistence, and interest" (p. 1033).

Does Creativity Depend on Unconscious Thought Processes?

Some fascinating reports have attributed creative breakthroughs to unconscious thought processes (Ghiselin, 1952). For example, creative giants such as Mozart, Dostoyevsky, and Coleridge reported that dazzling insights came to them while sleeping or daydreaming. These stories have led some theorists to conclude that creativity depends on the unconscious, which is not constrained by normal logic and rationality (Kris, 1952).

As a whole, however, reports of unconscious breakthroughs are few and of dubious accuracy. In at least some cases, it appears that artists have fabricated stories of unconscious breakthroughs to attract publicity, to confound rivals, or to enhance the legend of their genius (Weisberg, 1993). Most cognitive psychologists have concluded that creativity emerges out of normal problem-solving efforts that depend on conscious thought processes (Hayes, 1989; Klahr & Simon, 1999) and that creativity can be learned or enhanced, at least to some degree (Nickerson, 1999).

Does Creativity Depend on Divergent Thinking?

According to many theorists, the key to creativity lies in *divergent thinking*—thinking "that goes off in different directions," as J. P. Guilford (1959) put it. In his model of mental abilities (see Figure 9.19 on page 377),

Guilford distinguished between convergent thinking and divergent thinking. **In *convergent thinking* one tries to narrow down a list of alternatives to converge on a single correct answer.** For example, when you take a multiple-choice exam, you try to eliminate incorrect options until you hit on the correct response. Most training in school encourages convergent thinking. **In *divergent thinking* one tries to expand the range of alternatives by generating many possible solutions.** Imagine that you work for an advertising agency. To come up with as many slogans as possible for a client's product, you must use divergent thinking. Some of your slogans may be clear losers, and eventually you will have to engage in convergent thinking to pick the best, but coming up with the range of new possibilities depends on divergent thinking.

Thirty years of research on divergent thinking has yielded mixed results. As a whole, the evidence suggests that divergent thinking contributes to creativity, but it clearly does not represent the essence of creativity, as originally proposed (Brown, 1989; Plucker & Renzulli, 1999). In retrospect, it was probably unrealistic to expect creativity to depend on a single cognitive skill. According to Sternberg (1988a), the cognitive processes that underlie creativity are multifaceted.

Measuring Creativity

Although its nature may be elusive, creativity clearly is important in today's world. Creative masterpieces in the arts and literature enrich human existence. Creative insights in the sciences illuminate people's understanding of the world. Creative inventions fuel technological progress. Thus, it is understandable that psychologists have been interested in measuring creativity with psychological tests.

How Do Psychological Tests Measure Creativity?

 SIM8

A diverse array of psychological tests have been devised to measure individuals' creativity (Cooper, 1991). Usually, the items on creativity tests assess divergent thinking by giving respondents a specific starting point and then requiring them to generate as many possibilities as they can in a short period of time. Typical items on a creativity test might include the following: (1) List as many uses as you can for a newspaper. (2) Think of as many fluids that burn as you can. (3) Imagine that people no longer need sleep and think of as many consequences as you can. Subjects' scores on these tests depend on the *number* of alternatives they generate and on the *originality* and *usefulness* of the alternatives.

One seminal test of creativity is the Remote Associates Test (RAT) developed by Sarnoff and Martha Mednick (1968). This test is based on the assumption that creative people see unusual relationships and make nonobvious connections between ideas. Items on the test require subjects to figure out the obscure links (the remote associations) among three words by coming up with a fourth word that is related to the three stimulus words. Examples of items similar to those found on the RAT are shown in Figure 9.23.

How Well Do Tests Predict Creative Productivity?

In general, studies indicate that creativity tests are mediocre predictors of creative achievement in the real world (Hocevar & Bachelor, 1989; Plucker & Renzulli, 1999). Why? One reason is that these tests measure creativity in the abstract, as a *general trait.* However, the accumulation of evidence suggests that *creativity is specific to particular domains* (Amabile, 1990, 1996; Baer, 1994). Despite some rare exceptions, creative people usually excel in a single field, in which they typically have considerable training and expertise (Policastro & Gardner, 1999). A remarkably innovative physicist might have no potential to be a creative poet or an inventive advertising executive. Measuring this person's creativity outside of physics

may be meaningless. Thus, creativity tests may have limited value because they measure creativity out of context.

Why Is Creative Achievement So Difficult to Predict?

Even if better tests of creativity were devised, predicting creative achievement would probably still prove difficult. Why? Because creative achievement depends on many factors besides creativity (Cropley, 2000). Creative productivity over the course of an individual's career will depend on his or her motivation, personality, and intelligence, as well as situational factors, including training, mentoring, and good fortune (Amabile, 1983; Feldman, 1999).

Motivational factors may be particularly important. People who make creative breakthroughs tend to have a single-minded, "workaholic," commitment to their endeavours and show great perseverance in the face of obstacles and setbacks (Simonton, 1999). Although their ideas are often attacked or dismissed, they do not give up easily. To underscore this point, Sternberg (2000a, 2001) asserts that creativity appears to be in large part a *decision.* By this he means that highly creative people often have to make a choice to defy conventional thinking.

Correlates of Creativity

What are creative people like? Are they brighter, or more open minded, or less well adjusted than average? A great deal of research has been conducted on the correlates of creativity.

Is There a Creative Personality?

Creative people exhibit the full range of personality traits, but investigators have found modest correlations between certain personality characteristics and creativity (Ochse, 1990). Based on a meta-analysis of over 80 studies, Feist (1998) concludes that highly creative people "are more autonomous, introverted, open to new experiences, norm-doubting, self-confident, self-accepting, driven, ambitious, dominant, hostile, and impulsive" (p. 299). At the core of this set of personality characteristics are the related traits of independence and nonconformity. Creative people tend to think for themselves and are less easily influenced by the opinions of others than the average person is. Sternberg and Lubart (1992) also suggest that creative people are willing to grow and change and willing to take risks.

Are Creativity and Intelligence Related?

Are creative people exceptionally smart? Conceptually, creativity and intelligence

Instructions: For each set of three words, try to think of a fourth word that is related to all three words. For example, the words ROUGH, RESISTANCE, and BEER suggest the word DRAFT because of the phrases ROUGH DRAFT, DRAFT RESISTANCE, and DRAFT BEER.

1.	CHARMING	STUDENT	VALIANT
2.	FOOD	CATCHER	HOT
3.	HEARTED	FEET	BITTER
4.	DARK	SHOT	SUN
5.	CANADIAN	GOLF	SANDWICH
6.	TUG	GRAVY	SHOW
7.	ATTORNEY	SELF	SPENDING
8.	MAGIC	PITCH	POWER
9.	ARM	COAL	PEACH
10.	TYPE	GHOST	STORY

Figure 9.23

Remote associates as an index of creativity. One groundbreaking creativity test is the Remote Associates Test (RAT) developed by Sarnoff and Martha Mednick (1967). The items shown here are similar to those on the RAT. See whether you can identify the remote associations between the three stimulus words by coming up with a fourth word that is related to all three. The answers can be found in Figure 9.24.

Source: Matlin, M. W. (1994). *Cognition* (3rd Ed.). Fort Worth, TX: Harcourt Brace. Reprinted by permission of the author.

Motivation and Emotion

Motivation and emotion are two important topics in psychology that are often discussed in the same chapter. While there are distinct literatures and theories in each of these areas, they are clearly linked. In the first part of the chapter we discuss research and theory in the study of motivation. Motivation relates to the study of the processes involved in goal-directed behaviour. Our goal-directed behaviour, of course, is often associated with specific emotions. For example, think back to the goal you set for yourself on the first test in this course. You may have set a goal of getting an A on the first test and then studied hard to achieve it. Then think about your reaction when you found out your grade on that test. Your reaction would have been very different if you received an A than if you got a lower grade. Motivation and emotion, then, are often linked. Consider for a moment a different type of goal setting, setting a goal of winning an Olympic medal.

In 2004, Athens, Greece, played host to the summer Olympic Games and then the Paralympic Games in the fall. The Olympics were viewed by as many as 4 billion people worldwide, and you may have spent some time watching the performance of your favourite Canadian athlete or team. In the summer Olympics, Canada finished with 12 medals—three gold, six silver, and three bronze—and tied for 19th place with Bulgaria (Athens, 2004). One of Canada's top medal hopes was hurdler Perdita Felicien. In the Paralympic games, Canada finished with 72 medals (28 gold, 19 silver, and 25 bronze), finishing in third place behind China and Great Britain. Chantal Petitclerc dominated the women's wheelchair racing events in the Paralympics. She won five gold medals and was later named 2004 female athlete of the year at the Canadian Sports Awards (Ewing, 2005).

For most of us, we can only begin to imagine the dedication and motivation that bring an athlete to these levels. What drives or motivates an individual such as Edmonton's Danielle Peers, a member of the 2004 women's wheelchair basketball team, to begin training each day at 5:00 A.M. for two-and-a-half hours before going to a full day's work (Danielle Peers, 2004)? Some Olympic athletes have provided

some insight. Myriam Bedard, biathlete and winner of two gold medals, states that "What drives me most is the passion I have for the sport. That's why I do it" (Canadian Olympic Committee, 2005). Whatever their individual reasons, Olympic athletes must be highly motivated to continue to prepare for and compete in their chosen sports. In this chapter we will discuss the topic of motivation, looking at topics ranging from hunger motivation and eating to achievement motivation, the type of motivation that may have brought you to the study of psychology in the first place.

The other topic considered in this chapter is the study of emotion. Our lives are filled with emotions. Your reaction after obtaining your grade in the first test in this course would have been only one of many emotionally relevant experiences you had that day. In some cases, the explanation for our emotion is clear. Consider Perdita Felicien's reaction after the Olympic gold medal race in the 100-metre hurdles was over. Perdita was expected to win, and why not? She was the reigning world champion. Unfortunately for her, the race did not end, or even begin, as it was expected to—she hit the first hurdle and fell. The race was won by American Joanna Hayes in a new

Paralympic wheelchair racer Chantal Petitclerc was just one of the highly motivated athletes who represented Canada in 2004.

© Reuters/CORBIS

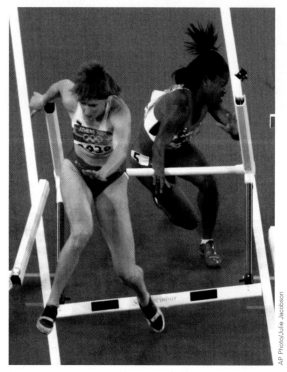

Olympic athletes such as Perdita Felicien experience the full range of emotions over the course of their athletic career. Perdita was expected to win the 100-metre hurdles in the 2004 Olympics, but was unable to finish because of a fall. She regained her form in 2005.

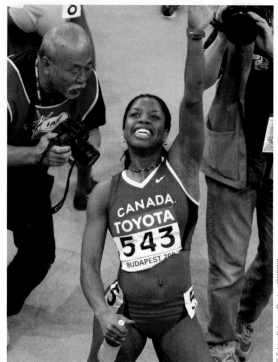

Olympic record time. Perdita's reaction after the race was "This is my worst nightmare come true" (CBC, 2004). The look on her face after the fall tells you all you need to know about what she was feeling. As we will learn in this chapter, there is a close connection between what you are feeling and the expression on your face.

Perdita won her first comeback race in 2005 and was shown in media reports smiling broadly at the finish line. Just imagine how motivated she must have been to come back after her Olympic experience. While the eliciting events and emotions experienced in her case seem quite obvious, it is not always so clear why we are feeling the way that we are or, indeed, what caused us to feel that way. In this chapter we will discuss some of the theories and research examining our emotional experiences. You may be surprised at what some of the research tells us about our emotions. Think back to the Featured Study in Chapter 2 (see page 46), in which males crossed high or low bridges spanning the Capilano River in British Columbia. Did you expect that their emotions could have been so easily manipulated by the experimenters? In the last part of this chapter we will learn more about what factors affect our subjective feeling states.

Motivational Theories and Concepts

PREVIEW QUESTIONS

- What is the distinction between drive and incentive theories of motivation?
- How do evolutionary theories explain various motives?
- What are the two major categories of human motives?

Motives are the needs, wants, interests, and desires that propel people in certain directions. In short, **motivation involves goal-directed behaviour.** Motivation to achieve relevant goals can be an important determinant of adjustment. Street kids, for example, in research conducted by Donald Taylor of McGill University, are often characterized by little motivation to reach *definable and coherent* goals (Taylor et al., 2004). Goals and our motivation to achieve them are often important characteristics of successful adjustment. There are a number of theoretical approaches to motivation. Let's look at some of these theories and the concepts they employ.

Drive Theories

Many theories view motivational forces in terms of *drives*. The drive concept appears in a diverse array of theories that otherwise have little in common, such as psychoanalytic (Freud, 1915) and behaviourist formulations (Hull, 1943). This approach to understanding motivation was explored most fully by Clark Hull in the 1940s and 1950s.

Hull's concept of drive was derived from Walter Cannon's (1932) observation that organisms seek to maintain **homeostasis, a state of physiological equilibrium or stability.** The body maintains homeostasis in various ways. For example, human body temperature normally fluctuates around 37 degrees Celsius (see Figure 10.1). If your body temperature rises or drops noticeably, automatic responses occur: If your temperature goes up, you'll perspire; if your temperature goes down, you'll shiver. These reactions are designed to move your temperature back toward 37 degrees. Thus, your body reacts to many disturbances in physiological stability by trying to restore equilibrium.

Drive theories apply the concept of homeostasis to behaviour. A *drive* **is an internal state of tension that motivates an organism to engage in activities that should reduce this tension.** These unpleasant states of tension are viewed as disruptions of the preferred equilibrium. According to drive theories, when individuals experience a drive, they're motivated to pursue actions that will lead to *drive reduction*. For example, the hunger motive has usually been conceptualized as a drive system. If you go without food for a while, you begin to experience some discomfort. This internal tension (the drive) motivates you to obtain food. Eating reduces the drive and restores physiological equilibrium.

Drive theories have been very influential, and the drive concept continues to be widely used in modern psychology. *However, drive theories cannot explain all motivation* (Berridge, 2004). Homeostasis appears irrelevant to some human motives, such as a "thirst for knowledge." Also, motivation may exist without drive arousal. You may stop for some ice cream after seeing an advertisement even though you are not hungry. Because drive theories assume that people always try to reduce internal tension, they can't explain this behaviour very well. Incentive theories, which represent a different approach to motivation, can account for this behaviour more readily.

Incentive Theories

Incentive theories propose that external stimuli regulate motivational states (Bolles, 1975; McClelland, 1975; Skinner, 1953). **An** *incentive* **is an external goal that has the capacity to motivate behaviour.** Ice cream, a juicy steak, a monetary prize, approval from friends, an A on an exam, and a promotion at work are all incentives. Some of these incentives may reduce drives, but others may not.

Drive and incentive models of motivation are often contrasted as *push versus pull* theories. Drive theories emphasize how *internal* states of tension *push* people in certain directions. Incentive theories emphasize how *external* stimuli *pull* people in certain

Blood vessels in skin dilate to remove heat
Person sweats

Turn down furnace
Remove sweater

Restore equilibrium

Temperature too high

Comfortable range for body temperature centred around 37°C

Temperature too low

Restore equilibrium

Blood vessels in skin constrict to conserve heat
Person shivers

Turn up furnace
Put on sweater

Figure 10.1

Temperature regulation as an example of homeostasis. The regulation of body temperature provides a simple example of how organisms often seek to maintain homeostasis, or a state of physiological equilibrium. When your temperature moves out of an acceptable range, automatic bodily reactions (such as sweating or shivering) occur that help restore equilibrium. Of course, these automatic reactions may not be sufficient by themselves, so you may have to take other actions (such as turning a furnace up or down) to bring your body temperature back into its comfort zone.

directions. According to drive theories, the source of motivation lies *within* the organism. According to incentive theories, the source of motivation lies *outside* the organism, in the environment. This means that incentive models don't operate according to the principle of homeostasis, which hinges on internal changes in the organism. Thus, in comparison to drive theories, incentive theories emphasize environmental factors and downplay the biological bases of human motivation.

As you're painfully aware, people can't always obtain the goals they desire, such as good grades or choice promotions. *Expectancy-value models* of motivation are incentive theories that take this reality into account (Atkinson & Birch, 1978). According to expectancy-value models, one's motivation to pursue a particular course of action will depend on two factors: (1) *expectancy* about one's chances of attaining the incentive and (2) the *value* of the desired incentive. Thus, your motivation to pursue a promotion at work will depend on your estimate of the likelihood

Motivation and Emotion

Examples of Biological Motives in Humans	Examples of Social Motives in Humans
Hunger motive	Achievement motive (need to excel)
Thirst motive	Affiliation motive (need for social bonds)
Sex motive	Autonomy motive (need for independence)
Temperature motive (need for appropriate body temperature)	Nurturance motive (need to nourish and protect others)
Excretory motive (need to eliminate bodily wastes)	Dominance motive (need to influence or control others)
Sleep and rest motive	Exhibition motive (need to make an impression on others)
Activity motive (need for optimal level of stimulation and arousal)	Order motive (need for orderliness, tidiness, organization)
Aggression motive	Play motive (need for fun, relaxation, amusement)

Figure 10.2

The diversity of human motives. People are motivated by a wide range of needs, which can be divided into two broad classes: biological motives and social motives. The list on the left (adapted from Madsen, 1973) shows some important biological motives in humans. The list on the right (adapted from Murray, 1938) provides examples of prominent social motives in humans. The distinction between biological and social motives is not absolute.

that you can snare the promotion (expectancy) and on how appealing the promotion is to you (value).

Evolutionary Theories

Psychologists who take an evolutionary perspective assert that human motives and those of other species are the products of evolution, just as anatomical characteristics are (Durrant & Ellis, 2003). They argue that natural selection favours behaviours that maximize reproductive success—that is, passing on genes to the next generation. Thus, they explain motives such as affiliation, achievement, dominance, aggression, and sex drive in terms of their adaptive value. If dominance is a crucial motive for a species, they say, it's because dominance provides a reproductive or survival advantage.

Evolutionary analyses of motivation are based on the premise that motives can best be understood in terms of the adaptive problems they have solved for our hunter-gatherer ancestors (Tooby & Cosmides, 2005). For example, the need for dominance is thought to be greater in men than women because it could facilitate males' reproductive success in a variety of ways including (1) females may prefer mating with dominant males, (2) dominant males may poach females from subordinate males, (3) dominant males may intimidate male rivals in competition for sexual access, and (4) dominant males may acquire more material resources, which may increase

mating opportunities (Buss, 1999). Consider, also, the *affiliation motive,* or need for belongingness. As we will discuss later, the adaptive benefits of affiliation for our ancestors probably included help with offspring, collaboration in hunting or defence, opportunities for sexual interaction, and so forth (Baumeister & Leary, 1995). David Buss (1995) points out that it is not by accident that achievement, power (dominance), and intimacy are among the most heavily studied social motives, as the satisfaction of each of these motives is likely to affect one's reproductive success.

The Range and Diversity of Human Motives

Motivational theorists of all persuasions agree on one point: Humans display an enormous diversity of motives. Most theories (evolutionary theories being a notable exception) distinguish between *biological motives* that originate in bodily needs, such as hunger, and *social motives* that originate in social experiences, such as the need for achievement.

People have a limited number of biological needs. According to K. B. Madsen (1968, 1973), most theories identify 10 to 15 such needs, some of which are listed on the left side of Figure 10.2. People all share the same biological motives, most of which are based on needs essential to survival, but their social motives vary depending on their experiences. For example, we all need to eat, but not everyone acquires a need for orderliness. Although people have a limited number of biological motives, they can acquire an unlimited number of social motives through learning and socialization. Some examples of social motives—from an influential list compiled by Henry Murray (1938)—are shown on the right side of Figure 10.2. He theorized that most people have needs for achievement, autonomy, affiliation, dominance, exhibition, and order, among other things. Of course, the strength of these motives varies from person to person, depending on personal history.

Given the range and diversity of human motives, we can examine only a handful in depth. To a large degree, our choices reflect the motives psychologists have studied the most. Specifically, we'll draw two examples each from the two broad classes of human needs, biological and social. We'll focus on hunger and sexual motivation to show how researchers have dissected biological needs. Then we'll examine affiliation and achievement to illustrate how psychologists have analyzed social motives.

The Motivation of Hunger and Eating

Why do people eat? Because they're hungry. What makes them hungry? A lack of food. Any grade-school child can explain these basic facts. So hunger is a simple motivational system, right? Wrong! Hunger is deceptive. It only looks simple. Actually, it's a puzzling and complex motivational system. Despite extensive studies of hunger, scientists are still struggling to understand the factors that regulate eating behaviour. Let's examine a few of these factors.

Biological Factors in the Regulation of Hunger

You have probably had embarrassing occasions when your stomach growled loudly at an inopportune moment. Someone may have commented, "You must be starving!" Most people equate a rumbling stomach with hunger, and, in fact, the first scientific theories of hunger were based on this simple equation. In an elaborate 1912 study, Walter Cannon and A. L. Washburn verified what most people have noticed based on casual observation: There is an association between stomach contractions and the experience of hunger.

Based on this correlation, Cannon theorized that stomach contractions *cause* hunger. However, as we've seen before, correlation is no assurance of causation, and his theory was eventually discredited. Stomach contractions often accompany hunger, but they don't cause it. How do we know? Because later research showed that people continue to experience hunger even after their stomachs have been removed out of medical necessity (Wangensteen & Carlson, 1931). If hunger can occur without a stomach, then stomach contractions can't be the cause of hunger. This realization led to more elaborate theories of hunger that focus on (1) the role of the brain, (2) blood sugar level, and (3) hormones.

Brain Regulation

Research with laboratory animals eventually suggested that the experience of hunger is controlled in the brain—specifically, in two centres located in the hypothalamus. As we have noted before, the *hypothalamus* is a tiny structure involved in the regulation of a variety of biological needs related to survival (see Figure 10.3). Investigators found that when they lesioned animals' *lateral hypothalamus (LH)*, the animals showed little or no interest in eating, as if their hunger centre had been destroyed (Anand & Brobeck, 1951). In contrast, when researchers

lesioned animals' *ventromedial nucleus of the hypothalamus (VMH)*, the animals ate excessively and gained weight rapidly, as if their ability to recognize satiety (fullness) had been destroyed (Brobeck, Tepperman, & Long, 1943). Given these results, investigators concluded that the LH and VMH were the brain's on–off switches for the control of hunger (Stellar, 1954). However, over the course of several decades, a host of empirical findings complicated this simple picture and undermined the dual-centres model of hunger (Valenstein, 1973; Winn, 1995). The current thinking is that the lateral and ventromedial areas of the hypothalamus are elements in the neural circuitry that regulates hunger but are not the key elements

PREVIEW QUESTIONS
- Which brain centres appear to control the experience of hunger?
- How do fluctuations in blood glucose and hormones contribute to hunger?
- How is eating influenced by the availability of food, learned habits, and stress?
- How common and how dangerous is obesity?
- What have scientists learned about the causes of obesity?

Figure 10.3

The hypothalamus. This small structure at the base of the forebrain plays a role in regulating a variety of human biological needs, including hunger. The detailed blow-up shows that the hypothalamus is made up of a variety of discrete areas. Scientists used to believe that the lateral and ventromedial areas were the brain's on–off centres for eating. However, more recent research suggests that the paraventricular nucleus may be more crucial to the regulation of hunger, and that it makes more sense to think in terms of neural circuits than anatomical centres.

The rat in front has had its ventromedial hypothalamus lesioned, resulting in a dramatic increase in weight.

"People's metabolic machinery is constituted in such a way that the fatter they are, the fatter they are primed to become."
JUDITH RODIN

and not simple on–off centres. Today, scientists believe that another area of the hypothalamus—the *paraventricular nucleus (PVN)*—plays a larger role in the modulation of hunger (Woods et al., 2000) (see Figure 10.3).

Contemporary theories of hunger focus more on *neural circuits* that pass through the hypothalamus, rather than on *anatomical centres* in the brain. These circuits depend on a variety of neurotransmitters, with neuropeptide Y and serotonin playing particularly prominent roles (Halford & Blundell, 2000; Seeley & Schwartz, 1997). Accumulating evidence suggests that the hypothalamus contains a confluence of interacting systems that regulate eating by monitoring a diverse array of physiological processes. Let's look at some other physiological processes that appear to provide input to these systems.

Glucose and Digestive Regulation

Much of the food taken into the body is converted into *glucose,* which circulates in the blood. **Glucose is a simple sugar that is an important source of energy.** Manipulations that decrease blood glucose level can increase hunger. Manipulations that increase glucose level can make people feel satiated. Based on these findings, Jean Mayer (1955, 1968) proposed that hunger is regulated by the rise and fall of blood glucose levels. *Glucostatic theory* proposed that fluctuations in blood glucose level are monitored in the brain by *glucostats*—**neurons sensitive to glucose in the surrounding fluid.** Like the dual-centres theory, the glucostatic theory of hunger gradually ran into a host of complications, not the least of which was that glucose levels in the blood really don't fluctuate all that much or all that fast (LeMagnen, 1981). Nonetheless, some researchers continue to believe that glucostatic mechanisms *contribute* to the modulation of eating (Smith & Campfield, 1993).

The digestive system also includes other mechanisms that influence hunger (Ritter, 2004). It turns out that Walter Cannon was not entirely wrong in hypothesizing that the stomach regulates hunger. After you have consumed food, cells in the stomach can send signals to the brain that inhibit further eating (Deutsch, 1990). For example, the vagus nerve carries information about the stretching of the stomach walls that indicates when the stomach is full. Other nerves carry satiety messages that depend on how rich in nutrients the contents of the stomach are.

Hormonal Regulation

A variety of hormones circulating in the bloodstream also appear to contribute to the regulation of hunger. *Insulin* is a hormone secreted by the pancreas. It must be present for cells to extract glucose from the blood. Indeed, an inadequate supply of insulin is what causes diabetes. The secretion of insulin is associated with increased hunger. And, in landmark research that blurred the distinction between biological and environmental determinants of hunger, Judith Rodin (1985) demonstrated that the mere sight and smell of enticing food can stimulate the secretion of insulin. Moreover, insulin levels appear to be sensitive to fluctuations in the body's fat stores (Seeley et al., 1996). These findings suggest that insulin secretions play a role in the fluctuation of hunger.

Finally, the recent discovery of a previously undetected hormone, since christened *leptin,* has shed new light on the hormonal regulation of hunger as well as the regulation of numerous other bodily functions (Ahima & Osei, 2004). Leptin is produced by fat cells throughout the body and released into the bloodstream. Higher levels of fat generate higher levels of leptin (Schwartz et al., 1996). Leptin circulates through the bloodstream and ultimately provides the hypothalamus with information about the body's fat

University of Toronto researchers Peter Herman and Janet Polivy are well known in the area of the psychology of eating. Their recent research has examined the effects of social cues on eating behaviour.

stores (Campfield, 2002). When leptin levels are high, the propensity to feel hungry diminishes. Leptin apparently activates receptors in the brain that inhibit the release of neuropeptide Y, which leads to activity in the paraventricular nucleus of the hypothalamus, which inhibits eating (Schwartz et al., 2000; Stephens et al., 1995). Researchers are currently exploring whether leptin itself, or drugs that affect leptin levels, might be helpful to people trying to lose weight (Heshka & Heymsfield, 2002).

If all this sounds confusing, it is, and we haven't even mentioned *all* the physiological processes involved in the regulation of hunger and eating. Frankly, researchers are still struggling to figure out exactly how all these processes work together, as hunger depends on complex interactions between neural circuits, neurotransmitter systems, digestive processes, and hormonal fluctuations.

Environmental Factors in the Regulation of Hunger

Hunger clearly is a biological need, but eating is not regulated by biological factors alone. Studies show that social and environmental factors govern eating to a considerable extent. Three key environmental factors are (1) the availability of food, (2) learned preferences and habits, and (3) stress.

Food Availability and Related Cues

Most of the research on the physiological regulation of hunger has been based on the assumption that hunger operates as a drive system in which homeostatic mechanisms are at work. However, some theorists emphasize the incentive value of food and argue that humans and other animals are often motivated to eat not by the need to compensate for energy deficits but by the anticipated pleasure of eating (Hetherington & Rolls, 1996; Ramsay et al., 1996). According to this perspective, the availability and palatability of food are the key factors regulating hunger. This view is bolstered by the observation made earlier that the presence of tasty food often leads people to eat even though they are already quite full from recently consumed food. Consistent with the incentive view, research shows that hunger is influenced by food availability and palatability (Mrdjenovic & Levitsky, 2005; Pinel, Assanand, & Lehman, 2000; Schachter & Rodin, 1974).

Hunger can also be triggered by exposure to environmental cues that have been associated with eating. You have no doubt had your hunger aroused by television commercials for delicious-looking food or by seductive odours coming from the kitchen.

According to incentive models of hunger, the availability and palatability of food are key factors regulating hunger. An abundance of diverse foods tends to lead to increased eating.

Consistent with this observation, studies by researchers such as Peter Herman and Janet Polivy of the University of Toronto and others have shown that hunger can be increased by exposure to pictures, written descriptions, and video depictions of attractive foods (Halford et al., 2004; Herman, Ostovich, & Polivy, 1999; Marcelino et al., 2001; Oakes & Slotterback, 2000).

It is also clear that eating is often a social action. Herman, Polivy, and their colleagues have considered the effects of the presence of others on one's intake of food (Herman, Roth, & Polivy, 2003). They suggest that social cues based on the behaviour of others are some of the most important determinants of food intake. They have integrated a variety of ideas about the effects of the presence of others on our eating in developing their inhibitory norm model of social influence on eating. They suggest that the presence of others generally inhibits eating. But, under certain specific conditions, eating may increase. In essence, they suggest that our eating is influenced by extant social norms determined by the behaviour of the others around us at the time. Thus, while it's clear that hunger and eating are governed in part by the availability of food and the presence of a variety of food-related cues, other social factors also play an important role.

Learned Preferences and Habits

Are you fond of eating calves' brains? How about eels or snakes? Could we interest you in a grasshopper or some dog meat? Probably not, but these are delicacies in some regions of the world. Inuit in the Arctic like to eat maggots! You probably prefer chicken, apples, eggs, lettuce, potato chips, pizza, cornflakes, or ice cream. These preferences are acquired through learning. People from different cultures display very different patterns of food consumption (Kittler &

Sucher, 1998). If you doubt this fact, just visit a grocery store in an ethnic neighbourhood (not your own, of course). As Paul Rozin (1996) points out, immigrant groups "seem to retain their ethnic identity through food long after they have become assimilated in most other ways" (p. 20).

Humans do have some innate taste preferences of a general sort. For example, a preference for sweet tastes is present at birth (Menella & Beauchamp, 1996), and humans' preference for high-fat foods appears to be at least partly genetic in origin (Schiffman et al., 1998). Evidence also suggests that an unlearned preference for salt emerges at around four months of age in humans (Birch & Fisher, 1996). Nonetheless, learning wields a great deal of influence over what people prefer to eat (Booth, 1994). Taste preferences are partly a function of learned associations formed through classical conditioning (Capaldi, 1996). For example, youngsters can be conditioned to prefer flavours paired with high caloric intake or other pleasant events. Conditioning also likely plays a role in one of our own experiences. When one of us goes to a Toronto Maple Leafs hockey game, he always heads for the hotdog stand—that's what he thinks of first when he gets hungry. His 14-year-old son orders sushi. When the adult was growing up and attending hockey games, hotdogs were about all you could get to eat at a hockey game, and that is the type of food he associates with hockey games. Of course, as we learned in Chapter 6, taste aversions can also be acquired through conditioning when foods are followed by nausea (Schafe & Bernstein, 1996). As you might expect based on our discussion of learning in Chapter 6, eating habits are also shaped by observational learning. Young children are more likely to taste an unfamiliar food if an adult tries it first. Repeated exposures to a new food may often lead to increased liking.

Stress and Eating 8A

You may behave like we sometimes do after an exceptionally stressful day, and head for the refrigerator, a grocery store, or a restaurant—usually in pursuit of something chocolate. This response is not particularly unusual. Studies have shown that stress leads to increased eating in a substantial portion of people (Greeno & Wing, 1994; Laitinen, Ek, & Sovio, 2002). Some studies suggest that stress-induced eating may be especially common among chronic dieters (Heatherton, Striepe, & Wittenberg, 1998). Some theorists believe that it is stress-induced *physiological arousal* rather than stress itself that stimulates eating (Striegel-Moore & Rodin, 1986). Other researchers suspect that it is the *negative emotions* often evoked by stress that promote additional eating (Macht & Simons, 2000). Some people respond to emotional distress by eating tasty foods because they expect the enjoyable treats to make them feel better

The fact that culture influences food preferences is evident in these photos, in which you can see delicacies such as grilled bat (left) and crocodile soup (right).

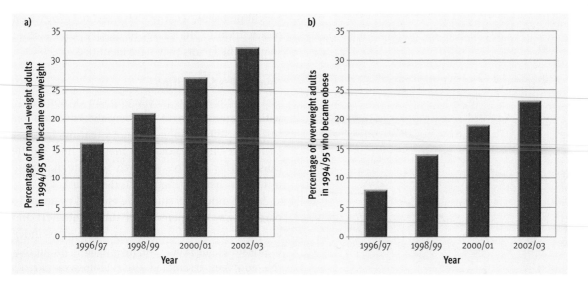

Figure 10.4

Change in obesity and overweight rates for Canadian males and females.

a) Percentage of adults of normal weight in 1994–95 who became overweight by 2002–03.

b) Percentage of overweight adults in 1994–95 who became obese by 2002–03.

Source: Christel Le Petit & Jean-Marie Berthelot (2005). Obesity: A growing issue. Statistics Canada. Retrieved May 9, 2005, from http://www.statcan.english/research/82-168-MIE/82-168). Adapted from the Statistics Canada publication, "Healthy today, healthy tomorrow? Findings from the National Population Health Survey." *Obesity: A Growing Issue, 1994-1995 to 2002-2003*, no. 03, catalogue 82-618, April 7, 2005.

(Tice, Bratslavsky, & Baumeister, 2001). Unfortunately, this strategy of emotional regulation does not appear to be very effective, as eating does not usually lead to lasting mood changes (Thayer, 1996). In any event, stress is another environmental factor that can influence hunger, although it's not clear whether the effects are direct or indirect.

Eating and Weight: The Roots of Obesity

We just saw that hunger is regulated by a complex interaction of biological and psychological factors. The same kinds of complexities emerge when investigators explore the roots of *obesity,* **the condition of being overweight.** Recent results from the Canadian Community Health Survey released by Statistics Canada (Statistics Canada, 2004a, 2005a) reveal the extent of the problem in Canada (see Figure 10.4). In this survey, definitions of overweight and obese are based on the *body mass index (BMI)*, **which is an individual's weight (in kilograms) divided by height (in metres) squared.** A BMI over 30 is considered obese, while BMIs between 25 and 29.9 are considered overweight. The survey revealed a number of important findings. There is good news and bad news. The good news is that the overall rate of obesity in Canada of 15% is lower than that in the United States. In the U.S., one out of every five adults is obese (Le Petit & Berthelot, 2005). The bad news is that we may be headed toward the same statistic since obesity rates in Canada have doubled in the last two decades. Data derived from the United States indicate that obesity lowers life expectancy considerably, 7.1 years for females and 5.8 years for males (Le Petit & Berthelot, 2005). While men were more likely to go from normal to overweight than women, women were more likely to go from overweight to obese. Since 1981, the prevalence of overweight and obese children has increased dramatically (Public Health Agency of Canada, n.d). Over one-third of Canadian children 2 to 11 years of age were considered overweight in 1998–99, with about one-half of those considered obese (Statistics Canada, 2002a). Having obese parents increases the odds of obesity in children (Statistics Canada, 2003b), and it was found that once people are overweight they are more likely than not to put on more weight (Statistics Canada, 2005a).

If obesity merely frustrated people's vanity, there would be little cause for concern. Unfortunately, obesity is a significant health problem that elevates one's mortality risk (Allison et al., 1999; Bender et al., 1999; Flegal et al., 2005; Fontaine et al., 2003). Overweight people are more vulnerable than others to cardiovascular diseases, diabetes, hypertension, respiratory problems, gallbladder disease, stroke, arthritis, muscle and skeletal pain, and some types of cancer (Manson, Skerrett, & Willet, 2002; Pi-Sunyer, 2002). For example, Figure 10.5 shows how the prevalence of diabetes, hypertension, coronary disease, and musculoskeletal pain are elevated as BMI increases.

Evolutionary-oriented researchers such as University of British Columbia psychologist John Pinel and his colleagues have a plausible explanation for the dramatic increase in the prevalence of obesity (Pinel et al., 2000). They point out that over the course of history, most animals and humans have lived in environments in which there was fierce competition for limited, unreliable food resources and where starvation was a very real threat. Hence, warm-blooded, foraging animals evolved a propensity to consume more food than immediately necessary when the opportunity presented itself because food might not be available later. Excess calories were stored in the

Figure 10.5

Weight and the prevalence of various diseases. This graph shows how obesity, as indexed by BMI, is related to the prevalence of four common types of illness. The prevalence of diabetes, heart disease, muscle pain, and hypertension all increase as BMI goes up. Clearly, obesity is a significant health risk. (Based on data in Brownell & Wadden, 2000)

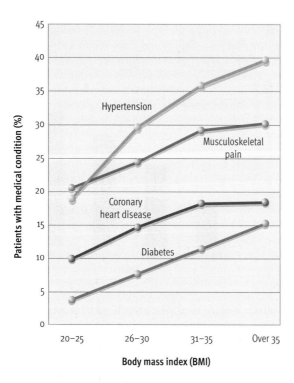

Web Link 10.1

American Obesity Association

http://www.obesity.org

This nonprofit U.S. organization's Web site provides in-depth information on the causes, consequences, and treatments of obesity.

body (as fat) to prepare for future food shortages. This approach to eating remains adaptive for most species of animals that continue to struggle with the ebb and flow of unpredictable food supplies. However, in today's modern, industrialized societies, the vast majority of humans live in environments that provide an abundant, reliable supply of tasty, high-calorie food. In these environments, humans' evolved tendency to overeat when food is plentiful leads most people down a pathway of chronic, excessive food consumption. According to this line of thinking, most people in food-replete environments tend to overeat in relation to their physiological needs, but because of variations in genetics, metabolism, and other factors only some become overweight.

Cognizant of the health problems associated with obesity, many people attempt to lose weight. At any given time, about 21% of men and 39% of women are dieting (Hill, 2002). A recent Council of Ministers of Education in Canada survey of children in grades 7, 9, and 11 revealed that about 12% of grade 9 and 11 girls and 3%–4% of boys are actively dieting. The rates for grade 7 boys are about the same as grade 9 and 11 boys (4%), and the rate for grade 7 girls is about 7% (Council of Ministers of Education, 2003). Although concerns have been raised that dieting carries its own risks, the evidence clearly indicates that weight loss efforts involving moderate changes in eating and exercise are more beneficial than harmful to people's health (Devlin, Yanovski, & Wilson, 2000). Given the health concerns associated with

weight problems, scientists have devoted a great deal of attention to the causes of obesity. Let's look at some of the factors they have identified.

Genetic Predisposition

You may know some people who can eat constantly without gaining weight. You may also know less fortunate people who get chubby eating far less. Differences in physiological makeup must be the cause of this paradox. Research suggests that these differences have a genetic basis (Bouchard, 2002).

In one influential study, adults raised by adoptive parents were compared with their biological and adoptive parents in regard to body mass index (Stunkard et al., 1986). The investigators found that the adoptees resembled their biological parents much more than their adoptive parents. In a subsequent *twin study,* Stunkard and colleagues (1990) found that identical twins reared apart were far more similar in BMI than fraternal twins reared together (see Figure 10.6). In another study of over 4000 twins, Allison and colleagues (1994) estimated that genetic factors account for 61% of the variation in weight among men, and 73% among women. Thus, it appears that some people inherit a genetic *vulnerability* to obesity (Cope, Fernandez, & Allison, 2004; Schwartz & Seeley, 1997).

Excessive Eating and Inadequate Exercise

The bottom line for overweight people is that their energy intake from food consumption chronically exceeds their energy expenditure from physical activities and resting metabolic processes. In other words, they eat too much in relation to their level of exercise (Wing & Polley, 2001). In modern North America, the tendency to overeat is easy to understand (Henderson & Brownell, 2004). Tasty, caloric, high-fat foods in ever-increasing portions are readily available nearly everywhere, not just in restaurants and grocery stores but in shopping malls, airports, gas stations, schools, and factories (Brownell, 2002). Unfortunately, the increased availability of highly caloric food in North America has been paralleled by declining physical activity (Hill & Peters, 1998). Modern conveniences, such as cars and elevators, and changes in the world of work, such as the shift to more desk jobs, have conspired to make our lifestyles more sedentary than ever before. This is of special concern in children. Recent statistics reported by the Public Health Agency of Canada revealed that over half of Canadian children and youth between the ages of 5 and 17 are considered not active enough for "optimal growth and development" (Public Health Agency of Canada, n.d.).

The Concept of Set Point

People who lose weight on a diet have a rather strong (and depressing) tendency to gain back all the weight they lose. The reverse is also true. People who have to work to put weight on often have trouble keeping it on. According to Richard Keesey (1995), these observations suggest that your body may have a *set point,* or a natural point of stability in body weight. **Set-point theory proposes that the body monitors fat-cell levels to keep them (and weight) fairly stable.** When fat stores slip below a crucial set point, the body supposedly begins to compensate for this change (Keesey, 1993). This compensation apparently leads to increased hunger and decreased metabolism.

Studies have raised some doubts about various details of set-point theory, leading John Pinel and his colleagues to propose an alternative called *settling-point theory* (Pinel et al., 2000). **Settling-point theory proposes that weight tends to drift around the level at which the constellation of factors that determine food consumption and energy expenditure achieves an equilibrium.** According to this view, weight tends to remain stable as long as there are no durable changes in any of the factors that influence it. Settling-point theory casts a much wider net than set-point theory, which attributes weight stability to very specific physiological processes. Another difference is that set-point theory asserts that an obese person's body will initiate processes that actively defend an excessive weight, whereas settling-point theory suggests that if an obese person makes long-term changes in eating or exercise that person's settling point will drift downward without active resistance. Thus, settling-point theory is a little more encouraging to those who hope to lose weight.

Dietary Restraint

Some investigators have proposed that vacillations in *dietary restraint* contribute to obesity (Polivy & Herman, 1995; Wardle et al., 2000). According to this theory, chronic dieters are *restrained eaters*—people who consciously work overtime to control their eating impulses and who feel guilty when they fail. To lose weight, restrained eaters go hungry much of the time, but they are constantly thinking about food. However, when their cognitive control is disrupted, they become *disinhibited* and eat to excess (Lowe, 2002). The crux of the problem is that restrained eaters assume, "Either I am on a diet, or I am out of control." A variety of events, such as drinking alcohol or experiencing emotional distress, can disrupt restrained eaters' control (Federoff, Polivy, & Herman, 2003; Lattimore & Caswell, 2004). But for many, the most common source of disinhibition is simply the percep-

tion that they have cheated on their diet. "I've already blown it," they think to themselves after perhaps just one high-calorie appetizer, "so I might as well enjoy as much as I want." They then proceed to consume a large meal or to go on an eating binge for the remainder of the day. Paradoxically, then, dietary restraint is thought to lead to frequent overeating and thus contribute to obesity.

Dietary restraint also contributes to the tendency to overeat just before beginning a diet, as shown in a recent study conducted by University of Toronto researchers (Urbszat, Herman, & Polivy, 2002). Thus, it would appear that restrained eaters show a tendency to fall off the wagon before getting on—anticipation of food deprivation seems to act as another

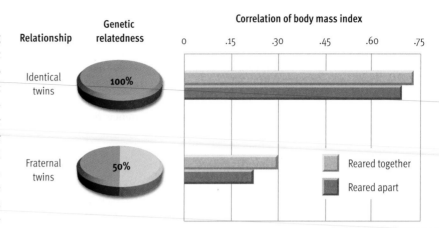

Figure 10.6

The heritability of weight. These data from a twin study by Stunkard et al. (1990) reveal that identical twins are much more similar in body mass index than fraternal twins, suggesting that genetic factors account for much of the variation among people in the propensity to become overweight. (Data from Stunkard et al., 1990)

CONCEPT CHECK 10.1

Understanding Factors in the Regulation of Hunger

Check your understanding of the effects of the various factors that influence hunger by indicating whether hunger would tend to increase or decrease in each of the situations described below. Indicate your choice by marking an I (increase), a D (decrease), or a ? (can't be determined without more information) next to each situation. You'll find the answers in Appendix A at the back of the book.

_____ **1.** The ventromedial nucleus of a rat's brain is destroyed by lesioning.

_____ **2.** The glucose level in Marlene's bloodstream decreases.

_____ **3.** Norman just ate, but his roommate just brought home his favourite food—a pizza that smells great.

_____ **4.** You're offered an exotic, strange-looking food from another culture and told that everyone in that culture loves it.

_____ **5.** You are participating in an experiment on the effects of leptin and have just been given an injection of leptin.

_____ **6.** Elton has been going crazy all day. It seems like everything's happening at once, and he feels totally stressed out. Finally he's been able to break away for a few minutes so he can catch a bite to eat.

_____ **7.** You have been on a successful diet, but you just broke down and ate some appetizers at a party.

disinhibitor. Restrained eaters also seem to be particularly sensitive to the media's portrayal of idealized thin body types. York University psychologist Jennifer Mills (Mills et al., 2002) has shown that after viewing such idealized images, restrained eaters tend to report a thinner ideal body size than do unrestrained eaters, and they show a tendency to report being thinner than they actually are.

Eating Disorders

We have just been considering some of the factors that affect eating behaviour, in particular, factors contributing to overeating. Of course, that is only one side of the problem that some people encounter in eating. While the topic of eating disorders will be considered more fully in Chapter 14, we want to introduce some of the concepts and issues here. According to Polivy and Herman (2002; Polivy et al., 2003), the late 1960s saw the increased prevalence of what was considered previously to be a very rare disorder, *anorexia nervosa*—a disorder in which (mostly) young women literally starve themselves, sometimes to death. A related disorder, *bulimia nervosa*, in which (mostly) young women alternate between binge eating and purging, increased in profile in the 1970s. This disorder in particular became salient to Canadians when it was revealed that one of Canada's best female tennis players and athletes of the 1980s, Carling Bassett-Seguso, suffered from bulimia (Nunes, 2002). At 13 she was the best women's tennis player in Canada and at 14 the best under-18 in the world. At 15 she joined the professional tour and was shown by another tour player how to vomit to maintain her weight. Her binging and purging contributed to an early end to her career.

A recent Health Canada study reveals the extent of the problem (Health Canada, 2002b). Eating disorders are more prevalent in women than men, affecting approximately 3% of Canadian women sometime in their lifetime. In Canada, since 1987, the rate of hospitalization for eating disorders has increased dramatically for young (under 15) and older (15–24 years) females alike (up 34% and 29%, respectively). As we will detail in Chapter 14, a variety of factors have been implicated in the occurrence of eating disorders, including biological, psychological, developmental, and social factors such as the overemphasis on idealized thin images (Polivy et al., 2003) and the pressure to be thin associated with various sports and professions.

University of Alberta researchers David Pierce and Frank Epling suggest in their work on *activity anorexia* (Epling & Pierce, 1992; Pierce & Epling, 1997) that because of some of these social prescriptions for thinness, some individuals may engage in a combination of severe dieting and excessive exercise that elicits a biochemical process resulting in starvation and even death. In their approach to activity anorexia, they argue that excessive physical activity, rather than just being a secondary symptom of anorexia as is commonly believed, is really central to understanding the nature of anorexia and that physical activity actually decreases rather than increases appetite. In Chapter 14 we will consider the topic of eating disorders in more detail. There are a variety of public and private treatment programs and support groups available in Canada. You can visit some of these through their Web sites, including the British Columbia Children's Hospital Eating Disorders Program (**http://www2.vpl.vancouver.bc.ca/dbs/redbook/ orgpgs/1/168.html**) and the National Eating Disorder Information Centre (**http://www.nedic.ca/**).

REVIEW OF KEY POINTS

- Drive theories apply a homeostatic model to motivation. They assume that organisms seek to reduce unpleasant states of tension called drives. In contrast, incentive theories emphasize how external goals energize behaviour.

- Evolutionary theorists explain motives in terms of their adaptive value. Madsen's list of biological needs and Murray's list of social needs illustrate that a diverse array of motives govern human behaviour.

- Eating is regulated by a complex interaction of biological and environmental factors. In the brain, the lateral and ventromedial areas of the hypothalamus were once viewed as on–off centres for the control of hunger, but their exact role is now unclear. Recent research suggests that hunger is regulated by neural circuits rather than anatomical centres in the brain.

- Fluctuations in blood glucose also seem to play a role in hunger, but the exact location of the "glucostats" and their mode of functioning are yet to be determined. Hormonal regulation of hunger depends primarily on insulin and leptin.

- Incentive-oriented models assert that eating is regulated by the availability and palatability of food. Learning processes, such as classical conditioning and observational learning, exert a great deal of influence over both what people eat and how much they eat. Cultural traditions also shape food preferences. Stress can stimulate eating.

- Obesity is a serious health problem that elevates the risk of many diseases. Evidence indicates that there is a genetic predisposition to obesity.

- Weight problems occur when people eat too much in relation to their exercise level. According to set-point theory, the body monitors fat stores to keep them fairly stable. Settling-point theory suggests that a multitude of factors contribute to weight stability. Vacillations in dietary restraint resulting in disinhibition may contribute to obesity in some people.

- Weight problems may also be manifested as eating disorders such as anorexia nervosa and bulimia nervosa. These disorders, which are more prevalent in women than in men, have a variety of causes.

Sexual Motivation and Behaviour

How does sex resemble food? Sometimes it seems that people are obsessed with both. People joke and gossip about sex constantly. Magazines, novels, movies, and television shows are saturated with sexual activity and innuendo. The advertising industry uses sex to sell everything from mouthwash to designer jeans to automobiles. This intense interest in sex reflects the importance of sexual motivation. In this portion of the chapter, we'll examine the factors that influence sexual desire and sexual orientation, and we'll describe the physiology of the human sexual response.

Doing research in this area is difficult and the recruitment of participants has its own problems. Brock University's Anthony Bogaert (1996) suggests that individuals who volunteer to take part in human sexuality research, filling out surveys about their sexuality and sexual behaviour, for example, may differ from those who do not volunteer for such research. As you learned in Chapter 2, the representativeness of your sample is of concern in all research. If your sample is biased, it may limit the generalizability of some of the findings of your research.

Determinants of Sexual Desire

Sex is essential for the survival of a species, but it's not essential to an *individual's* survival. Sexual motivation is not driven by deprivation to the extent that hunger is—you can live out a long life without sex, but without food your life will be very short.

Nonetheless, sex is clearly on people's minds. Children begin to experiment with sex as they enter their teens. Recent surveys and reports by the Canadian Council of Ministers of Education (2003), the Public Health Agency of Canada (2003a, 2003b), and Statistics Canada (2005f) give us some insight into the sexual activities of Canadian teens and young adults. Approximately 28% of 15–17-year-olds report engaging in sexual intercourse, with the rate increasing to 80% for Canadians 20–24 years of age. In that age range, one-third of those who are sexually active report having more than one sexual partner in the previous year. Those who first have sexual intercourse by age 13 are more likely to have multiple sex partners than those who begin later. Girls with weak self-concepts at 13 are more likely than those with strong self-concepts to engage in sex early. Strikingly, sex without a condom is still common. Approximately 30% of those who had multiple partners did not use a condom the last time they engaged in sex, and sex without a condom

appears to increase with age such that 44% of sexually active Canadians aged 20–24 reported having sex without a condom, compared to 22% of those aged 15–17. Young Canadians appear to be relatively sexually active, but do not always practise safe sex. We will consider such health-related behaviours more fully in Chapter 13. For now, we will consider some of the factors that influence our sexual behaviour. Like hunger, sexual desire is influenced by a complicated network of biological and social factors.

Hormonal Regulation

Hormones secreted by the *gonads*—the ovaries in females and the testes in males—can influence sexual motivation (consult Figure 3.23 on page 106). **Estrogens are the principal class of gonadal hormones in females. Androgens are the principal class of gonadal hormones in males.** Actually, both classes of hormones are produced in both sexes, but the relative balance is much different. The hypothalamus and the pituitary gland regulate these hormonal secretions.

The influence of hormones on sexual desire can be seen quite vividly in the animal kingdom (Hull & Dominguez, 2003). In many species, females are sexually receptive only just prior to ovulation, coinciding with an elevation in circulating levels of gonadal hormones. Hormones also influence sexual desire in males. For instance, if a male rat's testes are removed, the lack of a key androgen (testosterone) results in a lack of sexual interest. Testosterone injections can revive sexual desire in such castrated animals. Thus, it's clear that gonadal hormones regulate the sex drive in many animals.

Moving up the phylogenetic scale from rats to primates, hormones exert less and less influence over sexual behaviour (Wallen & Zehr, 2004). However, several lines of evidence suggest that they do *contribute* to the modulation of sexual desire in humans. For example, males who develop an endocrine disorder called *hypogonadism* during adulthood exhibit abnormally low levels of androgens and reduced sexual motivation, which can be revived by hormone replacement therapy (Rabkin, Wagner, & Rabkin, 2000). Experiments with male sex offenders suggest that drugs that drastically lower testosterone levels can be used to reduce sexual interest, although they certainly do not preclude further sexual assaults (Prentky, 1997). Curiously, *androgen* levels seem related to sexual motivation in *both* sexes. Higher levels of testosterone correlate with higher rates of sexual activity in both males (Schiavi et al., 1997) and

PREVIEW QUESTIONS
- How much do hormones influence sexual desire in humans?
- How do erotic materials affect sexual behaviour?
- What has evolutionary-oriented research revealed about gender differences in sexual activity and mating preferences?

females (Davis, 2000). And rising testosterone levels predict the onset of sexual activity in adolescent females (Halpern, Udry, & Suchindran, 1997).

The links between hormone levels and sexual activity in humans are interesting, but the correlations are modest, and much of the evidence comes from abnormal syndromes that may tell us little about normal sexual functioning. Furthermore, it is difficult to sort out the causal relations, as sexual activity can increase testosterone levels (Stoleru et al., 1993). At present, we can only conclude that hormonal fluctuations probably have a small impact on sexual desire in humans.

Erotic Materials

Erotic reading material, photographs, and films can stimulate sexual desire in many people. According to William Fisher of the University of Western Ontario, people don't all respond favourably to sexually explicit media (Fisher et al., 1988). Men are more likely than women to report that they find erotic materials enjoyable and arousing (Gardos & Mosher, 1999; Koukounas & McCabe, 1997). However, this finding may simply reflect the fact that the vast majority of erotic materials are scripted to appeal to males and often portray women in degrading roles that elicit negative reactions from female viewers (Mosher & MacIan, 1994; Pearson & Pollack, 1997). Access to pornographic material has become much easier with the development of the Internet, and Fisher argues for accelerated research on the nature and effects of Internet pornography (Fisher & Barak, 2001).

How much impact does erotic material have on actual sexual behaviour? The empirical data on this hotly debated question are inconsistent and are open to varied interpretations (Seto, Maric, & Barbaree, 2001). The balance of evidence suggests that exposure to erotic material elevates the likelihood of overt sexual activity for a few hours immediately after the exposure (Both et al., 2004; Donnerstein, Linz, & Penrod, 1987). This relatively modest effect may explain why attempts to find a link between the availability of erotica and sex crime rates have largely yielded negative results. For the most part, researchers have not found correlations between greater availability of pornography and elevated rates of sex crimes (Kimmel & Linders, 1996; Kutchinsky, 1991; Nemes, 1992; Winick & Evans, 1996). Although most sex offenders admit to an extensive history of using pornographic materials, a review of the relevant research indicated that sex offenders typically do not have earlier or more extensive exposure to pornography in childhood or adolescence than do other people (Bauserman, 1996).

Although erotic materials don't appear to incite overpowering sexual urges, they may alter *attitudes* in ways that eventually influence sexual behaviour. Zillmann and Bryant (1984) found that male and female undergraduates exposed to a large dose of pornography (three or six films per week for six weeks) developed more liberal attitudes about sexual practices. For example, they came to view premarital and extramarital sex as more acceptable. Another study by Zillmann and Bryant (1988) suggests that viewing sexually explicit films may make some people dissatisfied with their own sexual interactions. In comparison to control subjects, the subjects exposed to a steady diet of pornography reported less satisfaction with their partners' physical appearance, sexual curiosity, and sexual performance. Thus, pornography may create unrealistic expectations about sexual relations.

Moreover, research on *aggressive pornography* has raised some serious concerns about its effects. Aggressive pornography typically depicts violence against women. Many films show women who gradually give in to and enjoy rape and other sexually degrading acts after some initial resistance. Some studies indicate that this type of material increases male subjects' aggressive behaviour toward women, at least in the context of the research laboratory (Donnerstein & Malamuth, 1997; Zillmann & Weaver, 1989). In the typical study, male subjects work on a laboratory task and are led to believe (falsely) that they are delivering electric shocks to other subjects. In this situation, their aggression toward females tends to be elevated after exposure to aggressive pornography. Exposure to aggressive pornography may also make sexual coercion seem less offensive and may desensitize males to the horror of sexual violence (Mullin & Linz, 1995). In particular, it helps perpetuate the myth that women enjoy being raped and ravaged (Allen et al., 1995). This effect is not limited to sexually explicit media. Mainstream (R-rated) movies suggesting that women enjoy rape can also influence males' attitudes about sexual coercion (Milburn, Mather, & Conrad, 2000).

The effects of aggressive pornography are especially worrisome in light of evidence about rape. It is difficult to obtain accurate information about the prevalence of rape because fewer than 4% of victims make reports to authorities (Fisher et al., 2003). Despite extensive rape prevention efforts, the incidence of rape appears to be unchanged (Rozee & Koss, 2001). Estimates suggest that as many as one-quarter of young women in the United States may be victims of rape or attempted rape (Campbell & Wasco, 2004; Koss, 1993). In Canada, recent statistics indicate that sexual assaults are declining somewhat but that the numbers are still frightening; in 1999, there were approximately 24 000 sexual assaults reported to police in Canada (Statistics Canada, 1999a). Only a minority of reported rapes are committed by strangers (see Figure 10.7). Particularly common is *date rape,* which occurs when a woman is forced to have sex in the context of dating. Research suggests that date rape is a serious problem on university and college campuses (Banyard et al., 2005). In one survey of students at 32 American colleges, one in seven women reported having been victimized by date rape or an attempted date rape (Koss, Gidycz, & Wisniewski, 1987). Moreover, one in 12 men admitted either to having forced a date into sex or to having tried to do so. However, *none* of these men identified himself as a rapist. While acknowledging that statistics in Canada are difficult to obtain, the Public Health Agency of Canada suggests that between 16% and 35% of women surveyed reported at least one physical assault by a dating partner (Public Health Agency of Canada, n.d.). Although other factors are surely at work, many theorists, such as Neil Malamuth, who conducted much of his research at the University of Manitoba, believe that aggressive pornography has contributed to this failure to see sexual coercion for what it is (Malamuth, Addison, & Koss, 2000).

Evolutionary Analyses of Human Sexual Behaviour

As you have already seen in previous chapters, the relatively new evolutionary perspective in psychology has generated intriguing hypotheses related to a host of topics, including perception, learning, language, and problem solving. However, evolutionary theorists' analyses of sexual behaviour have drawn the most attention. Obviously, the task of explaining sexual behaviour is crucial to the evolutionary perspective, given its fundamental thesis that natural selection is fuelled by variations in reproductive success. The thinking in this area has been guided by Robert Trivers's (1972) *parental investment theory,* which maintains that a species' mating patterns depend on what each sex has to invest—in terms of time, energy, and survival risk—to produce and nurture offspring. According to Trivers, *the sex that makes the smaller investment will compete for mating opportunities with the sex that makes the larger investment, and the sex with the larger investment will tend to be more discriminating in selecting its partners.* Let's look at how this analysis applies to humans.

Like many mammalian species, human males are *required* to invest little in the production of offspring

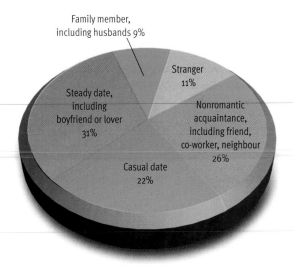

Figure 10.7

Rape victim–offender relationships. Based on a national survey of 3187 U.S. college women, Mary Koss and her colleagues (1988) identified a sample of 468 women who indicated that they had been a victim of rape and who provided information on their relationship to the offender. Contrary to the prevailing stereotype, only a small minority (11%) of these women were raped by a stranger. As you can see, many of the women were raped by men they were dating. (Based on data from Koss et al., 1988)

beyond the act of copulation, so their reproductive potential is maximized by mating with as many females as possible. The situation for females is quite different. Females have to invest nine months in pregnancy, and our female ancestors typically had to devote at least several additional years to nourishing offspring through breastfeeding. These realities place a ceiling on the number of offspring women can produce, regardless of how many males they mate with. Hence, females have little or no incentive for mating with many males. Instead, females can optimize their reproductive potential by being selective in mating. Thus, in humans, males are thought to compete with other males for the relatively scarce and valuable "commodity" of reproductive opportunities. Parental investment theory predicts that in comparison to women, men will show more interest in sexual activity, more desire for variety in sexual partners, and more willingness to engage in uncommitted sex (see Figure 10.8). In contrast, females are thought to be the conservative, discriminating sex that is highly selective in choosing partners. This selectivity supposedly entails seeking partners who have the greatest ability to contribute toward feeding and caring for offspring. Why? Because in the world of our ancient ancestors, males' greater strength and agility would have been crucial assets in the never-ending struggle to find food and shelter and defend one's territory. A female who chose a mate who was

Web Link 10.2

The Evolutionary Psychology FAQ

http://www.anth.ucsb.edu/projects/human/evpsychfaq.html

Maintained by Edward Hagen (Institute for Theoretical Biology, Humboldt University, Berlin), this site provides answers to a host of controversial questions on the subject of evolutionary psychology. Covered questions include: What is an adaptation? How can we identify psychological adaptations? Is evolutionary psychology sexist? If my genes made me do it, am I still responsible? Why do some people hate evolutionary psychology?

Figure 10.8

Parental investment theory and mating preferences.
Parental investment theory suggests that basic differences between males and females in parental investment have great adaptive significance and lead to gender differences in mating propensities and preferences, as outlined here.

Sex	Biological reality	Evolutionary significance	Behavioural outcomes
Males	Reproduction involves minimal investment of time, energy, and risk	Maximize reproductive success by seeking more sexual partners with high reproductive potential	More interest in uncommitted sex, greater number of sex partners over lifetime; look for youth and attractiveness in partners
Females	Reproduction involves substantial investment of time, energy, and risk	Maximize reproductive success by seeking partners willing to invest material resources in your offspring	Less interest in uncommitted sex, smaller number of sex partners over lifetime; look for income, status, and ambition in partners

Figure 10.9

The gender gap in how much people think about sex.
This graph summarizes data on how often males and females think about sex, based on a large-scale survey by Laumann, Gagnon, and Michaels (1994). As evolutionary theorists would predict, based on parental investment theory, males seem to manifest more interest in sexual activity than their female counterparts do. (Data from Laumann et al., 1994)

lazy or unreliable or who had no hunting, fighting, building, farming, or other useful economic skills would have suffered a substantial disadvantage in her efforts to raise her children and pass on her genes.

Gender Differences in Patterns of Sexual Activity

Consistent with evolutionary theory, males generally show a greater interest in sex than females do (Peplau, 2003). Men think about sex more often than women (see Figure 10.9), they initiate sex more frequently (Morokoff et al., 1997), and they are more interested in sex for its own sake (Whitley, 1988). Some theorists also argue that men's greater liking of pornography reflects the influence of evolutionary forces that have made males more interested in sex (Malamuth, 1996).

Men also are more motivated than women to pursue sex with a variety of partners. Buss and Schmitt (1993) found that college men indicate that they would ideally like to have 18 sex partners across their lives, whereas college women report that they would prefer only five partners (see Figure 10.10). Surveys inquiring about adults' actual sexual histories also indicate that men engage in sex with a larger

number of partners than women do, on the average (Janus & Janus, 1993; Laumann et al., 1994).

Clear gender disparities are also seen in regard to people's willingness to engage in casual or uncommitted sex. For example, Buss and Schmitt (1993) asked undergraduates about the likelihood that they would consent to sex with someone they found desirable whom they had known for one hour, one day, one week, one month, or longer periods. Men were much more likely than women to have sex with someone they had known for only a brief period.

In a definitive review of the empirical evidence, Roy Baumeister and colleagues (2001) conclude, "Across many different studies and measures, men have been shown to have more frequent and more intense sexual desires than women, as reflected in spontaneous

Figure 10.10

The gender gap in desire for a variety of sexual partners.
Buss and Schmitt (1993) asked college students about how many sexual partners they ideally would like to have for various time intervals ranging up to one's entire lifetime. As evolutionary theorists would predict, males are interested in having considerably more partners than females are.

SOURCE: Buss, D. M., & Schmitt, D. P. (1993). Sexual strategies theory: An evolutionary perspective on human mating. *Psychological Review, 100,* 204–232. Copyright © 1993 by the American Psychological Association. Reprinted by permission of the authors.

thoughts about sex, frequency and variety of sexual fantasies, desired frequency of intercourse, desired number of partners, masturbation, liking for various sexual practices, willingness to forgo sex, and other measures. No contrary findings (indicating stronger sexual motivation among women) were found" (p. 242). That said, evidence suggests that the sexual disparities between males and females may be exaggerated a little by reliance on subjects' self-reports (Alexander & Fisher, 2003). Because of the "double standard" regarding sexuality, women worry more than men about being viewed as sexually permissive, which may lead them to underestimate or downplay their sexual motivation (Crawford & Popp, 2003).

Gender Differences in Mate Preferences

According to evolutionary theorists, if males had been left to their own devices over the course of history, they probably would have shown little interest in long-term mating commitments, but females have generally demanded long-term commitments from males before consenting to sex (Buss, 1994a). Hence, long-term mating commitments are a normal part of the social landscape in human societies. However, parental investment theory suggests that there should be some glaring disparities between men and women in what they look for in a long-term mate (consult Figure 10.8 again).

The adaptive problem for our male ancestors was to find a female with good reproductive potential who would be sexually faithful and effective in nurturing children. Given these needs, evolutionary theory predicts that men should place more emphasis than women on partner characteristics such as youthfulness (which allows for more reproductive years) and attractiveness (which is assumed to be correlated with health and fertility). In contrast, the adaptive problem for our female ancestors was to find a male who could provide material resources and protect his family and who was dependable and willing to invest his resources in his family. Given these needs, evolutionary theory predicts that women should place more emphasis than men on partner characteristics such as intelligence, ambition, income, and social status (which are associated with the ability to provide more material resources). Evolutionary theorists are quick to point out that these differing priorities *do not reflect conscious strategies*. For the most part, people do not think about sex in terms of maximizing their reproductive potential. Instead, these different priorities are viewed as subconscious preferences that have been hardwired into the human brain by evolutionary forces. In any event, gender differences in mating preferences have been the subject of much research, including our Featured Study for this chapter.

Evolution, Culture, and Mating Priorities

FEATURED STUDY

According to evolutionary theories, human females enhance their chances of passing on their genes by seeking male partners who possess or are likely to acquire more material resources that can be invested in children. Thus, women should emphasize education, income, status, ambition, and industriousness in potential partners. Men, on the other hand, are assumed to maximize their reproductive outlook by seeking female partners with good breeding potential. Thus, men are thought to look for youth, attractiveness, good health, and other characteristics presumed to be associated with higher fertility. If these evolutionary analyses of sexual motivation are on the mark, gender differences in mating preferences should be virtually universal and thus transcend culture.

Method

To test this hypothesis, David Buss coordinated the efforts of 50 scientists from around the world, who collected data on what people want in a mate. They surveyed more than 10 000 people from 37 cultures distributed across six continents and five islands. Subjects responded to two

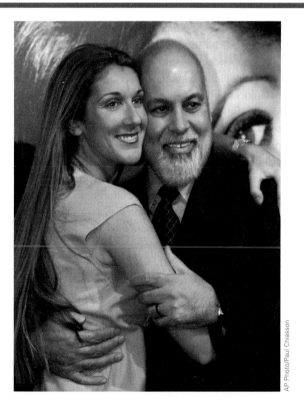

Investigator: David M. Buss (University of Michigan)

Source: Sex differences in human mate preferences: Evolutionary hypotheses tested in 37 cultures. *Behavioral and Brain Sciences,* 1989, 12, 1–49.

Evolutionary theory posits that men can maximize their reproductive fitness by seeking youthful partners, whereas women can maximize their reproductive success by searching for mates that are rich in material resources that can be invested in children. Obviously, this theory can explain why attractive young women often become romantically involved with much older men who happen to be wealthy.

Singer Elton John recently married his partner of 11 years, David Furnish, after England's same-sex marriage law went into effect in December 2005.

© Joanna Hunt/Reuters/CORBIS

upheld a lower court ruling that Everett Klippert be labelled a "dangerous offender" and imprisoned after he admitted to being gay and having sex with other males. He was finally released in 1971. In 1967, Pierre Elliott Trudeau, then the federal justice minister, proposed an amendment to the Criminal Code that would relax the laws against homosexuality. It was passed in 1969 and began the process of the decriminalization of homosexuality (CBC News Online, 2005). Today Canada is on the verge of legalizing same-sex marriage. In 2005, the Liberal government of Paul Martin tabled legislation that would make it legal for same-sex couples to marry (Department of Justice, 2005). The legislation was passed on June 28, 2005 and became law on July 20, 2005. One high profile same-sex marriage in England involves a Canadian, David Furnish, who married singer Elton John.

England's same-sex marriage law went into effect in December 2005 ("Elton John," 2005). Of course, not everyone supports this social trend or agrees on the factors affecting sexual orientation.

People tend to view heterosexuality and homosexuality as an all-or-none distinction. However, in a large-scale survey of sexual behaviour, Alfred Kinsey and his colleagues (1948, 1953) discovered that many people who define themselves as heterosexuals have had homosexual experiences—and vice versa. Thus, Kinsey and others have concluded that it is more accurate to view heterosexuality and homosexuality as end points on a continuum (Haslam, 1997). Indeed, Kinsey devised a seven-point scale, shown in Figure 10.13, that can be used to characterize individuals' sexual orientation.

How common is homosexuality? No one knows for sure. Part of the problem is that this question is vastly more complex than it appears at first glance (LeVay, 1996). Given that sexual orientation is best represented as a continuum, where do you draw the lines between heterosexuality, bisexuality, and homosexuality? And how do you handle the distinction between overt behaviour and desire? Where, for instance, do you put a person who is married and has never engaged in homosexual behaviour but who reports homosexual fantasies and acknowledges being strongly drawn to members of the same sex? The other part of the problem is that many people have extremely prejudicial attitudes about homosexuality, which makes gays cautious and reluctant to give candid information about their sexuality (Herek, 1996, 2000). Small wonder then that estimates of the portion of the population that is homosexual vary pretty widely. A frequently cited estimate of the number of people who are gay is 10%, but recent surveys suggest that this percentage may be an

Figure 10.13

Homosexuality and heterosexuality as endpoints on a continuum. Sex researchers view heterosexuality and homosexuality as falling on a continuum rather than make an all-or-none distinction. Kinsey and his associates (1948, 1953) created this seven-point scale (from 0 to 6) to describe people's sexual orientation. They used the term *ambisexual* to describe those who fall in the middle of the scale, but such people are commonly called *bisexual* today.

0	1	2	3	4	5	6
Heterosexual		**Ambisexual or bisexual**			**Homosexual**	
Exclusively heterosexual behaviour	Incidental homosexual behaviour	More than incidental homosexual behaviour	Equal amount of heterosexual and homosexual behaviour	More than incidental heterosexual behaviour	Incidental heterosexual behaviour	Exclusively homosexual behaviour

Subsequent studies have provided additional support for the existence of gender disparities in mating preferences. For example, Sprecher, Sullivan, and Hatfield (1994) examined a large, representative sample of adults in the United States and replicated the findings that men look for youth and attractiveness in partners, whereas women are more concerned about potential partners' education and income potential. In a study of personal ads placed in newspapers and magazines, Wiederman (1993) found that female advertisers explicitly sought financial resources in potential partners 11 times as often as male advertisers did. Numerous studies, using diverse samples and a variety of research methods, have replicated the disparities between males and females in mating priorities and preferences (Okami & Shackelford, 2001; Schmitt, 2005).

Criticism and Alternative Explanations

So, the findings on gender differences in sexual behaviour mesh very nicely with predictions derived from evolutionary theory. But, in the world of science, everyone is a critic—so you may be wondering: What types of criticism has this line of research generated? One set of concerns centres on the fact that the findings do not paint a very flattering picture of human nature. Men end up looking like sordid sexual predators; women come across as cynical, greedy materialists; and evolutionary theory appears to endorse these ideas as the inevitable outcome of natural selection. As Buss (1998) acknowledges, "Much of what I discovered about human mating is not nice" (p. 408). This controversy demonstrates once again that psychological theories can have far-reaching social and political ramifications, but the sociopolitical fallout has no bearing on evolutionary theory's scientific validity or utility.

However, some critics *have* expressed doubts about the validity of evolutionary explanations of gender differences in sexual behaviour. They note that one can posit alternative explanations for the findings. For example, women's emphasis on males' material resources could be a byproduct of cultural and economic forces rather than the result of biological imperatives (Wallen, 1989). Women may have learned to value males' economic clout because their own economic potential has been severely limited in virtually all cultures by a long history of discrimination (Hrdy, 1997; Kasser & Sharma, 1999). In a similar vein, Roy Baumeister, who has convincingly documented that men have stronger sexual motivation than women (Baumeister et al., 2001), has argued that this disparity may be largely due to extensive cultural processes that serve to suppress female sexuality

(Baumeister & Twenge, 2002). Evolutionary theorists counter these arguments by pointing out that the cultural and economic processes at work may themselves be products of evolution. At present, evolutionary theory appears to provide a more complete account for gender disparities in sexual behaviour than the alternative explanations (Archer, 1996). But more research is needed—and given the controversial nature of the findings, you can rest assured more research will be conducted.

REVIEW OF KEY POINTS

- Hormones exert considerable influence over sexual motivation in many animals. Some interesting correlations between testosterone fluctuations and sexual activity in humans suggest that hormonal swings may have a small impact on human sexual desire.

- People respond to a variety of erotic materials, which may elevate sexual desire for only a few hours but may have an enduring impact on attitudes about sex. Aggressive pornography may make sexual coercion seem less offensive and may contribute to date rape. Attraction to a potential partner is a critical determinant of sexual interest in both animals and humans.

- According to parental investment theory, males are thought to compete with other males for reproductive opportunities and females are assumed to be the discriminating sex that is selective in choosing partners. Consistent with evolutionary theory, males tend to think about and initiate sex more than females do and to have more sexual partners and more interest in casual sex than do females.

- The Featured Study by Buss demonstrated that there are gender differences in mating preferences that largely transcend cultural boundaries. Males emphasize potential partners' youthfulness and attractiveness, whereas females emphasize potential partners' status and financial prospects.

The Mystery of Sexual Orientation

Sex must be a contentious topic, as the controversy swirling around evolutionary explanations of gender differences in sexuality is easily equalled by the controversy surrounding the determinants of *sexual orientation*. **Sexual orientation refers to a person's preference for emotional and sexual relationships with individuals of the same sex, the other sex, or either sex. *Heterosexuals* seek emotional-sexual relationships with members of the other sex, *bisexuals* with members of either sex, and *homosexuals* with members of the same sex.** In recent years, the terms *gay* and *straight* have become widely used to refer to homosexuals and heterosexuals, respectively. Although *gay* can refer to homosexuals of either sex, most homosexual women prefer to call themselves *lesbians*.

The controversy surrounding sexual orientation is particularly current in Canada. It was not so long ago, 1965 in fact, that the Supreme Court of Canada

PREVIEW QUESTIONS

- Is sexual orientation an either-or distinction?
- How common is homosexuality?
- How have theorists explained the development of homosexuality?
- What are the four phases of the human sexual response?

Singer Elton John recently married his partner of 11 years, David Furnish, after England's same-sex marriage law went into effect in December 2005.

upheld a lower court ruling that Everett Klippert be labelled a "dangerous offender" and imprisoned after he admitted to being gay and having sex with other males. He was finally released in 1971. In 1967, Pierre Elliott Trudeau, then the federal justice minister, proposed an amendment to the Criminal Code that would relax the laws against homosexuality. It was passed in 1969 and began the process of the decriminalization of homosexuality (CBC News Online, 2005). Today Canada is on the verge of legalizing same-sex marriage. In 2005, the Liberal government of Paul Martin tabled legislation that would make it legal for same-sex couples to marry (Department of Justice, 2005). The legislation was passed on June 28, 2005 and became law on July 20, 2005. One high profile same-sex marriage in England involves a Canadian, David Furnish, who married singer Elton John.

England's same-sex marriage law went into effect in December 2005 ("Elton John," 2005). Of course, not everyone supports this social trend or agrees on the factors affecting sexual orientation.

People tend to view heterosexuality and homosexuality as an all-or-none distinction. However, in a large-scale survey of sexual behaviour, Alfred Kinsey and his colleagues (1948, 1953) discovered that many people who define themselves as heterosexuals have had homosexual experiences—and vice versa. Thus, Kinsey and others have concluded that it is more accurate to view heterosexuality and homosexuality as end points on a continuum (Haslam, 1997). Indeed, Kinsey devised a seven-point scale, shown in Figure 10.13, that can be used to characterize individuals' sexual orientation.

How common is homosexuality? No one knows for sure. Part of the problem is that this question is vastly more complex than it appears at first glance (LeVay, 1996). Given that sexual orientation is best represented as a continuum, where do you draw the lines between heterosexuality, bisexuality, and homosexuality? And how do you handle the distinction between overt behaviour and desire? Where, for instance, do you put a person who is married and has never engaged in homosexual behaviour but who reports homosexual fantasies and acknowledges being strongly drawn to members of the same sex? The other part of the problem is that many people have extremely prejudicial attitudes about homosexuality, which makes gays cautious and reluctant to give candid information about their sexuality (Herek, 1996, 2000). Small wonder then that estimates of the portion of the population that is homosexual vary pretty widely. A frequently cited estimate of the number of people who are gay is 10%, but recent surveys suggest that this percentage may be an

Figure 10.13

Homosexuality and heterosexuality as endpoints on a continuum. Sex researchers view heterosexuality and homosexuality as falling on a continuum rather than make an all-or-none distinction. Kinsey and his associates (1948, 1953) created this seven-point scale (from 0 to 6) to describe people's sexual orientation. They used the term *ambisexual* to describe those who fall in the middle of the scale, but such people are commonly called *bisexual* today.

thoughts about sex, frequency and variety of sexual fantasies, desired frequency of intercourse, desired number of partners, masturbation, liking for various sexual practices, willingness to forgo sex, and other measures. No contrary findings (indicating stronger sexual motivation among women) were found" (p. 242). That said, evidence suggests that the sexual disparities between males and females may be exaggerated a little by reliance on subjects' self-reports (Alexander & Fisher, 2003). Because of the "double standard" regarding sexuality, women worry more than men about being viewed as sexually permissive, which may lead them to underestimate or downplay their sexual motivation (Crawford & Popp, 2003).

Gender Differences in Mate Preferences

According to evolutionary theorists, if males had been left to their own devices over the course of history, they probably would have shown little interest in long-term mating commitments, but females have generally demanded long-term commitments from males before consenting to sex (Buss, 1994a). Hence, long-term mating commitments are a normal part of the social landscape in human societies. However, parental investment theory suggests that there should be some glaring disparities between men and women in what they look for in a long-term mate (consult Figure 10.8 again).

The adaptive problem for our male ancestors was to find a female with good reproductive potential who would be sexually faithful and effective in nurturing children. Given these needs, evolutionary theory predicts that men should place more emphasis than women on partner characteristics such as youthfulness (which allows for more reproductive years) and attractiveness (which is assumed to be correlated with health and fertility). In contrast, the adaptive problem for our female ancestors was to find a male who could provide material resources and protect his family and who was dependable and willing to invest his resources in his family. Given these needs, evolutionary theory predicts that women should place more emphasis than men on partner characteristics such as intelligence, ambition, income, and social status (which are associated with the ability to provide more material resources). Evolutionary theorists are quick to point out that these differing priorities *do not reflect conscious strategies*. For the most part, people do not think about sex in terms of maximizing their reproductive potential. Instead, these different priorities are viewed as subconscious preferences that have been hardwired into the human brain by evolutionary forces. In any event, gender differences in mating preferences have been the subject of much research, including our Featured Study for this chapter.

Web Link 10.3
Go Ask Alice!
http://www.alice.columbia.edu/
One of the longest-standing and most popular sources of frank information on the Internet has been *Alice!* from Columbia University's Health Education Program. Geared especially to the needs of undergraduate students, the site offers direct answers to questions about relationships, sexuality and sexual health, alcohol and drug consumption, emotional health, and general health.

Evolution, Culture, and Mating Priorities

FEATURED STUDY

According to evolutionary theories, human females enhance their chances of passing on their genes by seeking male partners who possess or are likely to acquire more material resources that can be invested in children. Thus, women should emphasize education, income, status, ambition, and industriousness in potential partners. Men, on the other hand, are assumed to maximize their reproductive outlook by seeking female partners with good breeding potential. Thus, men are thought to look for youth, attractiveness, good health, and other characteristics presumed to be associated with higher fertility. If these evolutionary analyses of sexual motivation are on the mark, gender differences in mating preferences should be virtually universal and thus transcend culture.

Method

To test this hypothesis, David Buss coordinated the efforts of 50 scientists from around the world, who collected data on what people want in a mate. They surveyed more than 10 000 people from 37 cultures distributed across six continents and five islands. Subjects responded to two

AP Photo/Paul Chiasson

Investigator: David M. Buss (University of Michigan)

Source: Sex differences in human mate preferences: Evolutionary hypotheses tested in 37 cultures. *Behavioral and Brain Sciences*, 1989, 12, 1–49.

Evolutionary theory posits that men can maximize their reproductive fitness by seeking youthful partners, whereas women can maximize their reproductive success by searching for mates that are rich in material resources that can be invested in children. Obviously, this theory can explain why attractive young women often become romantically involved with much older men who happen to be wealthy.

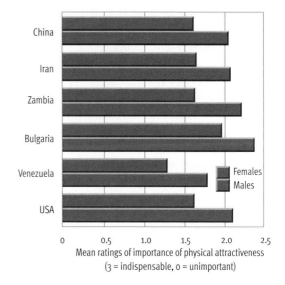

Figure 10.11

Gender and potential mates' financial prospects. Consistent with evolutionary theory, Buss (1989) found that females place more emphasis on potential partners' financial prospects than males do. Moreover, he found that this trend transcended culture. The specific results for 6 of the 37 cultures studied by Buss are shown here. (Based on data from Buss, 1989)

Figure 10.12

Gender and potential mates' physical attractiveness. Consistent with evolutionary theory, Buss (1989) found that all over the world males place more emphasis on potential partners' good looks than females do. The specific results for 6 of the 37 cultures studied by Buss are shown here. (Based on data from Buss, 1989)

Courtesy of David M. Buss

"*Evolutionary psychologists develop hypotheses about the psychological mechanisms that have evolved in humans to solve particular adaptive problems that humans have faced under ancestral conditions.*"
DAVID BUSS

questionnaires, which asked them to rate the importance of 32 characteristics in potential mates.

Results

The findings revealed that males and females exhibit both similarities and differences in mating preferences. Many characteristics, such as kindness, emotional stability, dependability, and a pleasant disposition, were rated very highly by both sexes. However, a few crucial differences between males' and females' priorities were found, and these differences were universal across cultures. As a group, women placed a higher value than men on potential partners' status, ambition, and financial prospects (see Figure 10.11). These priorities were not limited to industrialized or capitalist countries; they were apparent in third-world cultures, socialist countries, and all varieties of economic systems. In contrast, men consistently showed more interest than women in potential partners' youthfulness and physical attractiveness (see Figure 10.12). Cross-cultural variations in mate preferences were relatively modest. The most prominent variation was in the emphasis placed on female chastity—a woman's lack of previous sexual intercourse. Chastity was highly valued in some societies but viewed with indifference in others.

Discussion

According to Buss, social scientists have traditionally assumed that mating preferences are shaped by learning and that they vary considerably from culture to culture. His findings suggest that culture matters, but only in a limited way. He also concludes that his data provide striking support for evolutionary theories of sexual motivation. As predicted, women emphasized males' prospects for acquisition of material resources, whereas men emphasized females' reproductive capacity.

Comment

Besides supporting evolutionary theories of sexual motivation, this study exemplifies the rich potential of psychology's new commitment to cross-cultural research (see Chapter 1). Interestingly, though, Buss (1994b) notes that his data "were extraordinarily difficult to obtain." Authorities in some countries tried to sabotage the study, while others banned it completely. These nightmares and the logistical difficulties inherent in gathering data from 37 disparate cultures illustrate the extra-challenging nature of cross-cultural research. Of course, sexual behaviour is a particularly sensitive topic of study, as we'll see throughout this section. ■

Both biological and environmental factors appear to contribute to homosexuality, although its precise developmental roots remain obscure.

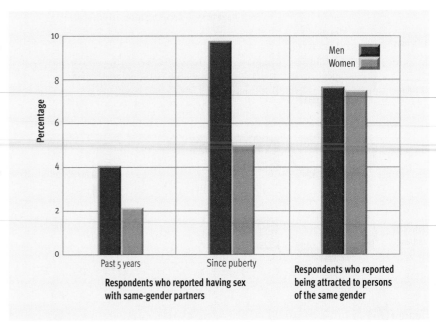

Figure 10.14

How common is homosexuality? The answer to this question is both complex and controversial. Michaels (1996) brought together data from two large-scale surveys to arrive at the estimates shown here. If you look at how many people have actually had a same-sex partner in the last five years, the figures are relatively low, but if you count those who have had a same-sex partner since puberty the figures more than double. Still another way to look at it is to ask people whether they are attracted to people of the same sex (regardless of their actual behaviour). This approach suggests that about 8% of the population could be characterized as homosexual. (Data from Michaels, 1996)

overestimate. Michaels (1996) has combined data from two of the better large-scale surveys in recent years to arrive at the estimates shown in Figure 10.14. As you can see, the numbers are open to varying interpretations, but as a whole they suggest that about 5%–8% of the population could reasonably be characterized as homosexual.

Environmental Theories

Over the years many environmental theories have been floated to explain the origins of homosexuality, but when tested empirically, these theories have garnered remarkably little support. For example, psychoanalytic and behavioural theorists, who usually agree on very little, both proposed environmental explanations for the development of homosexuality. The Freudian theorists argued that a male is likely to become gay when raised by a weak, detached, ineffectual father who is a poor heterosexual role model and by an overprotective, close-binding mother, with whom the boy identifies. Behavioural theorists argued that homosexuality is a learned preference acquired when same-sex stimuli have been paired with sexual arousal, perhaps through chance seductions by adult homosexuals. Extensive research on homosexuals' upbringing and childhood experiences have failed to support either of these theories (Bell, Weinberg, & Hammersmith, 1981).

However, efforts to research homosexuals' personal histories have yielded a number of interesting insights. Extremely feminine behaviour in young boys or masculine behaviour in young girls does predict the subsequent development of homosexuality (Bailey & Zucker, 1995). For example, 75%–90% of highly feminine young boys eventually turn out to be gay (Blanchard et al., 1995). Consistent with this finding, most gay men and women report that they can trace their homosexual leanings back to their early childhood, even before they understood what

sex was really about (Bailey, 2003). Most also report that because of negative parental and societal attitudes about homosexuality, they initially struggled to deny their sexual orientation. Hence, they felt that their homosexuality was not a matter of choice and not something that they could readily change (Breedlove, 1994). These findings obviously suggest that the roots of homosexuality are more biological than environmental.

Biological Theories

Nonetheless, initial efforts to find a biological basis for homosexuality met with little success. Most theorists originally assumed that hormonal differences between heterosexuals and homosexuals must underlie a person's sexual orientation (Doerr et al., 1976; Dorner, 1988). However, studies comparing circulating hormone levels in gays and straights found only small, inconsistent differences that could not be linked to sexual orientation in any convincing way (Garnets & Kimmel, 1991; Gladue, 1988).

Thus, like environmental theorists, biological theorists were stymied for quite a while in their efforts to explain the roots of homosexuality. However, that picture changed in the 1990s when a pair of behavioural genetics studies reported findings

Motivation and Emotion   **411**

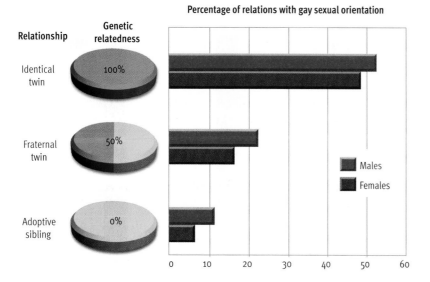

Percentage of relations with gay sexual orientation

Relationship	Genetic relatedness
Identical twin	100%
Fraternal twin	50%
Adoptive sibling	0%

Males
Females

0 10 20 30 40 50 60

Figure 10.15

Genetics and sexual orientation. If relatives who share more genetic relatedness show greater similarity on a trait than relatives who share less genetic overlap, this evidence suggests a genetic predisposition to the characteristic. Studies of both gay men and lesbian women have found a higher prevalence of homosexuality among their identical twins than their fraternal twins, who, in turn, are more likely to be homosexual than their adoptive siblings. These findings suggest that genetic factors influence sexual orientation. (Data from Bailey & Pillard, 1991; Bailey et al., 1993)

suggesting that homosexuality has a hereditary basis. In the first study, conducted by Bailey and Pillard (1991), the subjects were gay men who had either a twin brother or an adopted brother. They found that 52% of the subjects' identical twins were gay, that 22% of their fraternal twins were gay, and that 11% of their adoptive brothers were gay. A companion study (Bailey et al., 1993) of lesbians yielded a similar pattern of results (see Figure 10.15). Given that identical twins share more genetic overlap than fraternal twins, who share more genes than unrelated adoptive siblings, these results suggest that there is a genetic predisposition to homosexuality (see Chapter 3 for an explanation of the logic underlying twin and adoption studies). More recent twin studies, with larger and more representative samples, have provided further support for the conclusion that heredity influences sexual orientation (Bailey, Dunne, & Martin, 2000; Kendler et al., 2000). However, these newer studies have yielded smaller estimates of genetic influence, which have been attributed to improved sampling. The sampling method used in the earlier studies—although appropriate for exploratory investigations—probably led to somewhat inflated estimates of genetic influence.

In another line of research, LeVay (1991, 1993) has reported anatomical differences between gay and straight men in a region of the brain thought to

influence sexual behaviour. He focused on a tiny cluster of neurons in the anterior hypothalamus that is known to be larger in men than in women. Because the structure is too small to be measured effectively in the living brain, it is studied posthumously. LeVay compared the autopsied brains of 19 homosexual and 16 heterosexual men and found that the targeted structure tended to be about half as large in the gay men. LeVay (1996) stresses that his findings on brain structure should be interpreted with caution, as most of his subjects had died of AIDS, which clearly can wreak havoc in the brain. Although the data on disparities in brain structure are preliminary, they point to a biological basis for sexual orientation.

Many theorists suspect that disparities between heterosexuals and homosexuals in brain structure may reflect the organizing effects of prenatal hormones on neurological development. Several lines of research suggest that hormonal secretions during critical periods of prenatal development may shape sexual development, organize the brain in a lasting manner, and influence subsequent sexual orientation (Berenbaum & Snyder, 1995). For example, researchers have found elevated rates of homosexuality among women exposed prenatally to a synthetic hormone (DES) that was formerly used to reduce the risk of miscarriage (by their mothers) and among women who have an adrenal disorder that results in abnormally high androgen levels during prenatal development (Breedlove, 1994; Meyer-Bahlburg et al., 1995).

Despite the recent breakthroughs, much remains to be learned about the determinants of sexual orientation. The pathways to homosexuality appear to be somewhat different for males as opposed to females (Gladue, 1994). The behavioural genetics data suggest that the hereditary predisposition to homosexuality is not overpowering. Environmental influences of some kind probably contribute to the development of homosexuality, but the nature of these environmental factors remains a mystery.

Once again, though, we can see that the nature versus nurture debate can have far-reaching social and political implications. Homosexuals have long been victims of extensive—and in many instances *legal*—discrimination. However, if research were to show that being gay is largely a matter of biological destiny, much like being female, or short, many of the arguments against equal rights for gays would disintegrate. Why ban gays from teaching, for instance, if their sexual preference cannot "rub off" on their students? Although we would argue that discrimination against gays should be brought to an end either way, many individuals' opinions about gay rights may be swayed by the outcome of the nature–nurture debate on the roots of homosexuality.

The Human Sexual Response

Assuming people are motivated to engage in sexual activity, exactly what happens to them physically? This may sound like a simple question. But scientists really knew very little about the physiology of the human sexual response before William Masters and Virginia Johnson did groundbreaking research in the 1960s. Although our society seems obsessed with sex, until relatively recently (the 1980s) it did not encourage scientists to study sex. At first Masters and Johnson even had difficulty finding journals that were willing to publish their studies.

Masters and Johnson used physiological recording devices to monitor the bodily changes of volunteers engaging in sexual activities. They even equipped an artificial penile device with a camera to study physiological reactions inside the vagina! Their observations of and interviews with subjects yielded a detailed description of the human sexual response and won them widespread acclaim.

Masters and Johnson (1966, 1970) divide the sexual response cycle into four stages: excitement, plateau, orgasm, and resolution. Figure 10.16 shows how the intensity of sexual arousal changes as women and men progress through these stages. Let's take a closer look at these phases in the human sexual response.

Excitement Phase

During the initial phase of excitement, the level of physical arousal usually escalates rapidly. In both sexes, muscle tension, respiration rate, heart rate, and blood pressure increase quickly. **Vasocongestion—engorgement of blood vessels—**produces penile erection and swollen testes in males. In females, vasocongestion leads to a swelling and hardening of the clitoris, expansion of the vaginal lips, and vaginal lubrication.

Plateau Phase

During the plateau phase, physiological arousal usually continues to build, but at a much slower pace. In women, further vasocongestion produces a tightening of the vaginal entrance, as the clitoris withdraws under the clitoral hood. Many men secrete a bit of fluid at the tip of the penis. This is not ejaculate, but it may contain sperm. When foreplay is lengthy, fluctuation in arousal is normal for both sexes. This fluctuation is more apparent in men;

erections may increase and decrease noticeably. In women, this fluctuation may be reflected in changes in vaginal lubrication.

Orgasm Phase

Orgasm **occurs when sexual arousal reaches its peak intensity and is discharged in a series of muscular contractions that pulsate through the pelvic area.** Heart rate, respiration rate, and blood pressure increase sharply during this exceedingly pleasant spasmodic response. In males, orgasm is accompanied by ejaculation of the seminal fluid. The subjective experience of orgasm appears to be very similar for men and women.

However, there *are* some interesting gender differences in the orgasm phase of the sexual response cycle. On the one hand, women are more likely than men to be *multi-orgasmic*. A woman is said to be multi-orgasmic if she experiences more than one climax in a very brief time period (pattern C in Figure 10.16). On the other hand, women are more likely than men to engage in intercourse without experiencing an orgasm (see Figure 10.17; Laumann et al., 1994). Whether these differences reflect attitudes and sexual practices versus physiological processes is

❝*The conviction has grown that the most effective treatment of sexual incompatibility involves the technique of working with both members of the family unit.*❞
WILLIAM MASTERS AND VIRGINIA JOHNSON

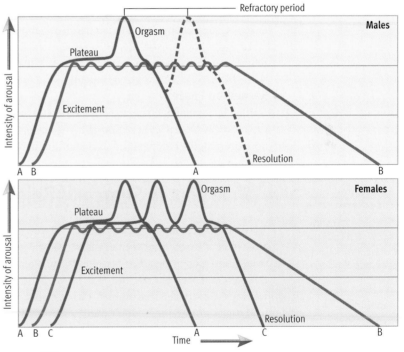

Figure 10.16

The human sexual response cycle. There are similarities and differences between men and women in patterns of sexual arousal. Pattern A, which culminates in orgasm and resolution, is the ideal sequence for both sexes but not something one can count on. Pattern B, which involves sexual arousal without orgasm followed by a slow resolution, is seen in both sexes but is more common among women (see Figure 10.17). Pattern C, which involves multiple orgasms, is seen almost exclusively in women, as men go through a refractory period before they are capable of another orgasm.

Source: Based on Masters, W. H., & Johnson, V. E. (1966). *Human sexual response.* Boston: Little, Brown. Copyright ©1966 Little, Brown and Company.

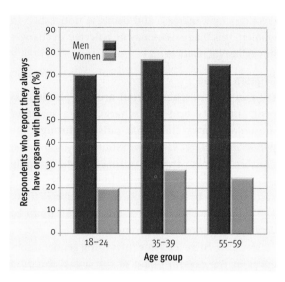

Figure 10.17

The gender gap in orgasm consistency. In their sexual interactions, men seem to reach orgasm more reliably than women. The data shown here suggest that the gender gap in orgasmic consistency is pretty sizable. Both biological and sociocultural factors may contribute to this gender gap. (Data from Laumann et al., 1994)

open to debate. On the one hand, it is easy to argue that males' greater orgasmic consistency must be a product of evolution, as it would have obvious adaptive significance for men's reproductive fitness. On the other hand, over the years theorists have come up with a variety of plausible environmental explanations for this disparity, such as gender differences in the socialization of guilt feelings about sex, and sexual scripts and practices that are less than optimal for women (Lott, 1987). Consistent with this view, evidence suggests that lesbian women reach orgasm more easily and consistently in sexual interactions than heterosexual women do (Peplau et al., 2004).

Resolution Phase

During the resolution phase, the physiological changes produced by sexual arousal subside. If orgasm has not occurred, the reduction in sexual tension may be relatively slow and sometimes unpleasant. After orgasm, men experience a *refractory period*, a time following orgasm during which males are largely unresponsive to further stimulation. The length of the refractory period varies from a few minutes to a few hours and increases with age.

Masters and Johnson's exploration of the human sexual response led to major insights into the nature and causes of sexual problems. Ironically, although Masters and Johnson broke new ground in studying the *physiology* of sexual arousal, their research demonstrated that sexual problems are typically caused by *psychological* factors. Their conclusion shows once again that human sexuality involves a fascinating blend of biological and social processes. We turn next to the related motive of affiliation, which is more social in origin.

REVIEW OF KEY POINTS

- Modern theorists view heterosexuality and homosexuality not as an all-or-none distinction but as endpoints on a continuum. Recent data on the prevalence of homosexuality suggest that 5%–8% of the population may be gay. Although most gays can trace their homosexual leanings back to early childhood, research has not supported Freudian or behavioural theories of sexual orientation.

- Recent studies suggest that there is a genetic predisposition to homosexuality and that some subtle disparities in brain structure may be associated with homosexuality. Idiosyncrasies in prenatal hormonal secretions may also contribute to the development of homosexuality.

- The human sexual response cycle can be divided into four stages: excitement, plateau, orgasm, and resolution. The subjective experience of orgasm is fairly similar for both sexes. Intercourse leads to orgasm in women less consistently than in men, but women are much more likely to be multi-orgasmic.

Affiliation: In Search of Belongingness

PREVIEW QUESTIONS

- What is the evolutionary significance of affiliation?
- What is the affiliation motive? How is it measured?
- How do those who score high in the need for affiliation differ from those who score low?

How would you like to spend the rest of your life alone on a pleasant but deserted island? Most people would find this to be a terrible fate. Why? Because the fundamental human need to be with others would be thwarted. Some animals (bears, tigers, and bald eagles, for example) don't mind going it alone. Humans, however, react badly to prolonged periods of social isolation. Humans are social animals and have to have meaningful contact with others. **The affiliation motive is the need to associate with others and maintain social bonds.** Affiliation encompasses one's needs for companionship, friendship, and love. People need more than mere interpersonal contact; they need enduring social bonds marked by mutual concern for one another.

In an overview of research on affiliation, Roy Baumeister and Mark Leary (1995) argued that it has a strong evolutionary basis, as social bonds offer a host of survival and reproductive benefits. They noted that by joining together, our ancestors could share food, provide better care for their offspring, engage in more effective hunting or gathering, enhance their defence against predators, defuse risks, and provide more opportunities for mating. Small wonder, then, that humans seem to form bonds readily and go to great lengths to preserve their interpersonal attachments. In discussing the significance of affiliation, Baumeister and Leary described evidence that the quality of people's personal relationships is a major determinant of their happiness. They

Affiliation arousal

George is an engineer who is working late. He is *worried that his wife will be annoyed* with him for neglecting her. She has been *objecting* that he cares more about his work than his wife and family. He seems *unable to satisfy* both his boss and his wife, but he *loves her* very much and will do his best to *finish up* fast and get home to her.

Achievement arousal

George is an engineer who *wants to win* a competition in which the man with the *most practicable drawing* will be awarded the contract to build a bridge. He is taking a moment to think *how happy he will be* if he wins. He has been *baffled by how to make such a long span strong*, but he remembers to *specify a new steel alloy* of great strength, submits his entry, but does not win, and is *very unhappy.*

Figure 10.18

Measuring motives with the Thematic Apperception Test (TAT). Subjects taking the TAT tell or write stories about what is happening in a scene, such as this one showing a man at work. The two stories shown here illustrate strong affiliation motivation and strong achievement motivation. The italicized parts of the stories are thematic ideas that would be identified by a TAT scorer.

Source: Stories reprinted by permission of Dr. David McClelland.

also discussed the strong link between affiliation issues and negative emotions—how the threat of rejection triggers anxiety, how concern about losing a partner evokes jealousy, and how loneliness is associated with depression. While we all need to belong and to affiliate with others, dependency may not be adaptive. According to York University psychologists Doug McCann and Toru Sato (McCann & Sato, 2000), overinvestment in dependent relations may be linked to the experience of depressive episodes. In sum, Baumeister and Leary (1995) made an eloquent case for the pervasive importance of affiliation, asserting that "much of what human beings do is done in the service of belongingness" (p. 498).

Although virtually everyone exhibits the need for belongingness, some people have stronger affiliation needs than others. Much of the research on affiliation has looked into these individual differences. In this research, investigators usually measure subjects' need for affiliation with some variant of Henry Murray's Thematic Apperception Test (Morgan & Murray, 1935; Murray, 1943). The Thematic Apperception Test (TAT) is a *projective test,* a test that requires subjects to respond to vague, ambiguous stimuli in ways that may reveal personal motives and

traits (see Chapter 12). The stimulus materials for the TAT are pictures of people in ambiguous scenes open to interpretation. Examples include a man working at a desk and a woman seated in a chair staring off into space. Subjects are asked to write or tell stories about what's happening in the scenes and what the characters are feeling. The themes of these stories are then scored to measure the strength of various needs. Figure 10.18 shows examples of stories dominated by affiliation and achievement themes.

How do people who score high in the need for affiliation differ from those who score low? First, *they devote more time to interpersonal activities*. For example, they join more social groups such as clubs and church organizations (Smart, 1965). They make more phone calls and visits to friends (McClelland & Winter, 1969), and they tend to devote more time to conversations and letter writing than others do (McAdams & Constantian, 1983). Second, *people with strong affiliation needs worry more about acceptance than those with a low affiliation drive do* (Koestner & McClelland, 1992). For example, they experience greater anxiety when they're being evaluated socially by peers. They also go out of their way to avoid being argumentative in groups, because they fear rejection.

Achievement: In Search of Excellence

At the beginning of this chapter, we profiled some of Canada's recent Olympians. They have endured extraordinary hardships to achieve their goal. What motivates people to push themselves so hard? In all likelihood, it's a strong need for achievement. **The *achievement motive* is the need to master difficult challenges, to outperform others, and to meet high standards of excellence.** Above all else, the need for achievement involves the desire to excel, especially in competition with others.

David McClelland and his colleagues (McClelland et al., 1953; McClelland, 1985) have been studying the achievement motive for about 40 years. McClelland believes that achievement motivation is of the utmost importance. He has estimated the average achievement motivation for *entire societies* by using TAT-like scoring procedures to assess the themes in representative examples of literature from those societies (rather than individuals' stories). These estimates of entire societies' need for achievement at specific times corre-

PREVIEW QUESTIONS

- What is the achievement motive, and how is it measured?
- How do those who score high in the need for achievement behave?
- What are some situational factors that can influence achievement strivings?

Canadian Steve Nash, who plays for the Phoenix Suns, was named the NBA's MVP in May 2005. Early on he was never considered a top player. He is known for his hard work and dedication to the game. But the contribution of his extremely high need for achievement should not be underestimated. He is known for having pushed himself in order to achieve his goals.

❝*People with a high need for achievement are not gamblers; they are challenged to win by personal effort, not by luck.*❞

DAVID MCCLELLAND

late with progress and productivity in those societies (Winter, 1992). For example, estimates of changes in achievement motivation in ancient Greece relate closely to the rise and fall of Greek civilization (McClelland, 1961). Also, estimates of achievement need in the United States have fluctuated in tandem with inventive activity as measured by the U.S. Patent Index (deCharms & Moeller, 1962).

McClelland sees the need for achievement as the spark that ignites economic growth, scientific progress, inspirational leadership, and masterpieces in the creative arts. It's difficult to argue with his assertion about the immense importance of achievement motivation. Consider how much poorer our culture would be if people such as Charles Darwin, Thomas Edison, Alexander Graham Bell, Pablo Picasso, Marie Curie, Abraham Lincoln, Mother Teresa, Martin Luther King, and David Suzuki hadn't had a fire burning in their hearts.

Individual Differences in the Need for Achievement

 8B

In May 2005, Steve Nash achieved what no Canadian before him had ever achieved; he was named the "Most Valuable Player" in the National Basketball Association (NBA). He was an undersized player

(about 190 cm) in a sport often dominated by much taller players. He struggled to find a college willing to offer him a scholarship so he could refine his skill. He is only the sixth guard in NBA history to win this prize. In his first game after being named MVP, he led his team to a dramatic playoff win over his former team, the Dallas Mavericks, while the crowd chanted "M-V-P" (Smith, 2005). While he is clearly a talented player, other factors were needed to bring him to the top. High among these was his desire to achieve.

The need for achievement is a fairly stable aspect of personality. Hence, research in this area has focused mostly on individual differences in achievement motivation. Subjects' need for achievement can be measured effectively with the Thematic Apperception Test (C. Smith, 1992; Spangler, 1992).

The research on individual differences in achievement motivation has yielded interesting findings on the characteristics of people who score high in the need for achievement. They tend to work harder and more persistently on tasks than people low in the need for achievement (Brown, 1974). And they handle negative feedback about task performance more effectively than others (Fodor & Carver, 2000). They also are more future oriented than others and more likely to delay gratification in order to pursue long-term goals (Mischel, 1961; Raynor & Entin, 1982). In terms of careers, they typically go into competitive, entrepreneurial occupations that provide them with an opportunity to excel (McClelland, 1987). Apparently, their persistence and hard work often pay off. High achievement motivation correlates positively with measures of career success and with upward social mobility among lower-class men (Crockett, 1962; McClelland & Boyatzis, 1982).

Do people high in achievement need always tackle the biggest challenges available? Not necessarily. A curious finding has emerged in laboratory studies in which subjects have been asked to choose how difficult a task they want to work on. Subjects high in the need for achievement tend to select tasks of intermediate difficulty (McClelland & Koestner, 1992). For instance, in one study, where subjects playing a ring-tossing game were allowed to stand as close to or far away from the target peg as they wanted, high achievers tended to prefer a moderate degree of challenge (Atkinson & Litwin, 1960).

Situational Determinants of Achievement Behaviour

 8B

Your achievement drive is not the only determinant of how hard you work. Situational factors can also influence achievement strivings. John Atkinson

Figure 10.19

Determinants of achievement behaviour. According to John Atkinson, a person's pursuit of achievement in a particular situation depends on several factors. Some of these factors, such as need for achievement or fear of failure, are relatively stable motives that are part of the person's personality. Many other factors, such as the likelihood and value of success or failure, vary from one situation to another, depending on the circumstances.

(1974, 1981, 1992) has elaborated extensively on McClelland's original theory of achievement motivation and has identified some important situational determinants of achievement behaviour. Atkinson theorizes that the tendency to pursue achievement in a particular situation depends on the following factors:

- The strength of one's *motivation* to *achieve success*. This is viewed as a stable aspect of personality.
- One's estimate of the *probability of success* for the task at hand. This varies from task to task.
- The *incentive value of success*. This depends on the tangible and intangible rewards for success on the specific task.

The last two variables are situational determinants of achievement behaviour (see Figure 10.19). That is, they vary from one situation to another. According to Atkinson, the pursuit of achievement increases as the probability and incentive value of success go up.

Let's apply Atkinson's model to a simple example. According to his theory, your tendency to pursue a good grade in calculus should depend on your general motivation to achieve success, your estimate of the probability of getting a good grade in the class, and the value you place on getting a good grade in calculus. Thus, given a certain motivation to achieve success, you will pursue a good grade in calculus less vigorously if your professor gives impossible exams (thus lowering your expectancy of success) or if a good grade in calculus is not required for your major (lowering the incentive value of success).

The joint influence of these situational factors may explain why high achievers prefer tasks of intermediate difficulty. Atkinson notes that the probability of success and the incentive value of success on tasks are interdependent to some degree. As tasks get easier, success becomes less satisfying. As tasks get harder, success becomes more satisfying, but its likelihood obviously

declines. When the probability and incentive value of success are weighed together, moderately challenging tasks seem to offer the best overall value in terms of maximizing one's sense of accomplishment.

According to Atkinson, a person's fear of failure must also be considered to understand achievement behaviour (Atkinson & Birch, 1978). He maintains that people vary in their *motivation to avoid failure*. This motive is considered a stable aspect of personality. Together with situational factors such as the probability of failure and the negative value placed on failure, it influences achievement strivings. Figure 10.19 diagrams all the factors in Atkinson's model that are thought to govern achievement behaviour. Approach and avoidance are key concepts in Atkinson's approach to motivation. Atkinson's emphasis on distinguishing between approach and avoidance tendencies in the study of motivation has influenced more recent motivation theories, such as the theory of uncertainty orientation, which was developed by Richard Sorrentino of the University of Western Ontario (Sorrentino & Roney, 2000).

Fear is one of the most fundamental emotions. Thus, the relationship between achievement behaviour and *fear* of failure illustrates how motivation and emotion are often intertwined. On the one hand, *emotion can cause motivation*. For example, *anger* about your work schedule may motivate you to look for a new job. *Jealousy* of an ex-girlfriend may motivate you to ask out her roommate. On the other hand, *motivation can cause emotion*. For example, your motivation to win a photography contest may lead to great *anxiety* during the judging and either great *joy* if you win or great *gloom* if you don't. There may even be individual differences in the motivation to approach or avoid emotions. University of Western Ontario researcher Victoria Esses and her colleague Gregory Maio have developed a measure of individual differences in the

Understanding the Determinants of Achievement Behaviour

According to John Atkinson, one's pursuit of achievement in a particular situation depends on several factors. Check your understanding of these factors by identifying each of the following vignettes as an example of one of the following four determinants of achievement behaviour: (a) need for achievement, (b) perceived probability of success, (c) incentive value of success, (d) fear of failure. The answers can be found in Appendix A.

_____ **1.** Donna has just received a B in biology. Her reaction is typical of the way she responds to many situations involving achievement: "I didn't get an A, it's true, but at least I didn't flunk; that's what I was really worried about."

_____ **2.** Belinda is nervously awaiting the start of the finals of the 200-metre dash in the last meet of her high school career. "I've gotta win this race! This is the most important race of my life!"

_____ **3.** Corey grins as he considers the easy time he's going to have this semester. "This class is supposed to be a snap. I hear the professor gives an A to nearly everyone."

_____ **4.** Diana's just as hard-charging as ever. She's gotten the highest grade on every test throughout the semester, yet she's still up all night studying for the final. "I know I've got an A in the bag, but I want to be the best student Dr. McClelland's ever had!"

need for affect. They suggest that there are differences in people's motivation to approach or avoid emotion-inducing situations (Maio & Esses, 2001). Thus, motivation and emotion are closely related, but that does not mean they're the same thing. We'll analyze the nature of emotion in the next section.

REVIEW OF KEY POINTS

● Affiliation encompasses various needs for social bonds. Affiliation probably had many adaptive benefits for our ancestors. Individual differences in the need for affiliation are usually measured with the TAT. People who are relatively high in the need for affiliation tend to devote more time to interpersonal activities and to worry more about acceptance than others do.

● Achievement involves the need to excel, especially in competition with others. The need for achievement is usually measured with the TAT. People who are relatively high in the need for achievement work harder and more persistently than others. They delay gratification well and pursue competitive careers.

● Situational factors also influence achievement behaviour. The pursuit of achievement tends to increase when the probability of success and the incentive value of success are high.

The Elements of Emotional Experience

PREVIEW QUESTIONS
● How do emotions affect autonomic activity?
● How does a lie detector device work?
● Which brain centres contribute to the experience of emotions?
● What is the connection between emotion and body language?
● Are there cultural differences in how people recognize, describe, or express their emotions?

The most profound and important experiences in life are saturated with emotion. Think of the *joy* that people feel at weddings, the *grief* they feel at funerals, the *ecstasy* they feel when they fall in love. Emotions also colour everyday experiences. For instance, you might experience *anger* when a professor treats you rudely, *dismay* when you learn that your car needs expensive repairs, and *happiness* when you see that you aced your economics exam. In some respects, emotions lie at the core of mental health. The two most common complaints that lead people to seek psychotherapy are *depression* and *anxiety*. Clearly, emotions play a pervasive role in people's lives. Reflecting this reality, modern psychologists have increased their research on emotion in recent decades (Cacioppo & Gardner, 1999).

But exactly what is an emotion? Everyone has plenty of personal experience with emotion, but it's an elusive concept to define (LeDoux, 1995). Emotion includes cognitive, physiological, and behavioural components, which are summarized in the following definition: *Emotion* involves (1) **a subjective conscious experience (the cognitive component) accompanied by (2) bodily arousal (the physiological component) and by (3) characteristic overt expressions (the behavioural component)**. That's a

pretty complex definition. Let's take a closer look at each of these three components of emotion.

The Cognitive Component: Subjective Feelings

 8c

Over 550 words in the English language refer to emotions (Averill, 1980). Ironically, however, people often have difficulty describing their emotions to others (Zajonc, 1980). Emotion is a highly personal, subjective experience. In studying the cognitive component of emotions, psychologists generally rely on subjects' verbal reports of what they're experiencing. Their reports indicate that emotions are potentially intense internal feelings that sometimes seem to have a life of their own. People can't click their emotions on and off like a bedroom light. If it were as simple as that, you could choose to be happy whenever you wanted. As Joseph LeDoux puts it, "Emotions are things that happen to us rather than things we will to occur" (1996, p. 19). Actually, some degree of emotional control is possible (Thayer, 1996), but emotions tend to involve automatic reactions that are difficult to regulate (Ohman & Wiens, 2003) (see Chapter 13).

People's cognitive appraisals of events in their lives are key determinants of the emotions they experience

(Ellsworth & Scherer, 2003; R. Lazarus, 1995). A specific event, such as giving a speech, may be highly threatening and thus anxiety arousing for one person but a "ho-hum," routine matter for another. The conscious experience of emotion includes an *evaluative* aspect. People characterize their emotions as pleasant or unpleasant (Lang, 1995; Schlosberg, 1954). Of course, individuals often experience "mixed emotions" that include both pleasant and unpleasant qualities (Cacioppo & Berntson, 1999). For example, an executive just given a promotion with challenging new responsibilities may experience both happiness and anxiety. A young man who has just lost his virginity may experience a mixture of apprehension, guilt, and delight.

For the most part, researchers have paid more attention to negative emotions than positive ones (Fredrickson, 1998). Why have positive emotions been neglected? Fredrickson and Branigan (2001) and Rozin (2003) note that there appear to be fewer positive emotions than negative ones and that positive emotions are less clearly differentiated from each other than negative emotions. Another consideration is that negative emotions appear to have more powerful effects than positive emotions (Baumeister et al., 2001). Although these factors probably have contributed, the neglect of positive emotions is symptomatic of a broad and deeply rooted bias in the field of psychology, which has historically focused on pathology, weaknesses, and suffering (and how to heal these conditions) rather than health, strengths, and resilience (Fredrickson, 2002). In recent years, the architects of the "positive psychology movement" have set out to shift the field's focus away from negative experiences (Seligman, 2002; Seligman & Csikszentmihalyi, 2000). The advocates of *positive psychology* argue for increased research on contentment, well-being, human strengths, and positive emotions. One outgrowth of this movement has been increased interest in the dynamics of happiness. We will discuss this research in the Personal Application at the end of this chapter.

The Physiological Component: Diffuse and Multifaceted

Emotional processes are closely tied to physiological processes, but the interconnections are enormously complex. The biological bases of emotions are diffuse, involving many areas in the brain and many neurotransmitter systems, as well as the autonomic nervous system and the endocrine system.

Emotions involve automatic reactions that can be difficult to control.

© Bob Dammerich/The Image Works

Autonomic Arousal

Imagine your reaction as your car spins out of control on an icy highway. Your fear is accompanied by a variety of physiological changes. Your heart rate and breathing accelerate. Your blood pressure surges, and your pupils dilate. The hairs on your skin stand erect, giving you "goose bumps," and you start to perspire. Although the physical reactions may not always be as obvious as in this scenario, *emotions are accompanied by visceral arousal* (Cacioppo et al., 1993). Surely you've experienced a "knot in your stomach" or a "lump in your throat"—thanks to anxiety.

Much of the discernible physiological arousal associated with emotion occurs through the actions of the *autonomic nervous system* (Janig, 2003), which regulates the activity of glands, smooth muscles, and blood vessels (see Figure 10.20). As you may recall from Chapter 3, the autonomic nervous system is responsible for the highly emotional *fight-or-flight response,* which is largely modulated by the release of adrenal *hormones* that radiate throughout the body. Hormonal changes clearly play a crucial role in emotional responses to stress and may contribute to many other emotions as well (McEwen & Seeman, 2003).

One prominent part of emotional arousal is the *galvanic skin response (GSR),* **an increase in the electrical conductivity of the skin that occurs when sweat glands increase their activity.** GSR is a convenient and sensitive index of autonomic arousal that has been used as a measure of emotion in many laboratory studies.

The connection between emotion and autonomic arousal provides the basis for the *polygraph,* **or** *lie detector,* **a device that records autonomic fluctuations while a subject is questioned.** A polygraph can't actually detect lies. It's really an emotion detector. It monitors key indicators of autonomic arousal, typically heart rate, blood pressure, respiration rate, and GSR. The assumption is that when subjects lie, they experience emotion (presumably

Figure 10.20

Emotion and autonomic arousal. The autonomic nervous system (ANS) is composed of the nerves that connect to the heart, blood vessels, smooth muscles, and glands (consult Figure 3.8 on page 89 for a more detailed view). The ANS is divided into the *sympathetic system*, which mobilizes bodily resources in response to stress, and the *parasympathetic system*, which conserves bodily resources. Emotions are frequently accompanied by sympathetic ANS activation, which leads to goose bumps, sweaty palms, and the other physical responses listed on the left side of the diagram.

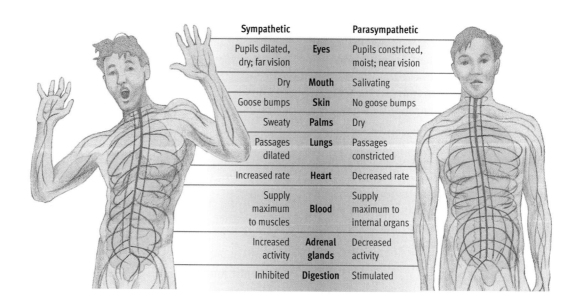

Sympathetic		Parasympathetic
Pupils dilated, dry; far vision	**Eyes**	Pupils constricted, moist; near vision
Dry	**Mouth**	Salivating
Goose bumps	**Skin**	No goose bumps
Sweaty	**Palms**	Dry
Passages dilated	**Lungs**	Passages constricted
Increased rate	**Heart**	Decreased rate
Supply maximum to muscles	**Blood**	Supply maximum to internal organs
Increased activity	**Adrenal glands**	Decreased activity
Inhibited	**Digestion**	Stimulated

Figure 10.21

Emotion and the polygraph. A lie detector device measures the autonomic arousal that most people experience when they tell a lie. After using nonthreatening questions to establish a baseline, a polygraph examiner looks for signs of arousal (such as the sharp change in GSR shown here) on incriminating questions. Unfortunately, the polygraph is not a very dependable index of whether people are lying.

anxiety) that produces noticeable changes in these physiological indicators (see Figure 10.21). The polygraph examiner asks a subject a number of nonthreatening questions to establish the subject's baseline on these autonomic indicators. Then the examiner asks the critical questions (e.g., "Where were you on the night of the burglary?") and observes whether the subject's autonomic arousal changes.

Polygraph advocates claim that lie detector tests are about 85%–90% accurate and that the validity of polygraph testing has been demonstrated in empirical studies, but these claims clearly are not supported by the evidence (Iacono & Patrick, 1999; Iacono & Lykken, 1997). Methodologically sound research on the validity of polygraph testing is surprisingly sparse (largely because it is difficult research to do), and the limited evidence available is not very impressive (Branaman & Gallagher, 2005; Fielder, Schmid, & Stahl, 2002; Saxe

& Ben-Shakhar, 1999). Part of the problem is that people who are telling the truth may experience emotional arousal when they respond to incriminating questions. Thus, polygraph tests sometimes lead to accusations of lying against people who are innocent. Another problem is that some people can lie without experiencing anxiety or autonomic arousal. The crux of the problem, as Leonard Saxe (1994) notes, is that "there is no evidence of a unique physiological reaction to deceit" (p. 71). The polygraph *is* a potentially useful tool that can help police check out leads and alibis. However, polygraph results are not reliable enough to be submitted as evidence in most types of courtrooms.

Neural Circuits 8c

The autonomic responses that accompany emotions are ultimately controlled in the brain. The hypothalamus,

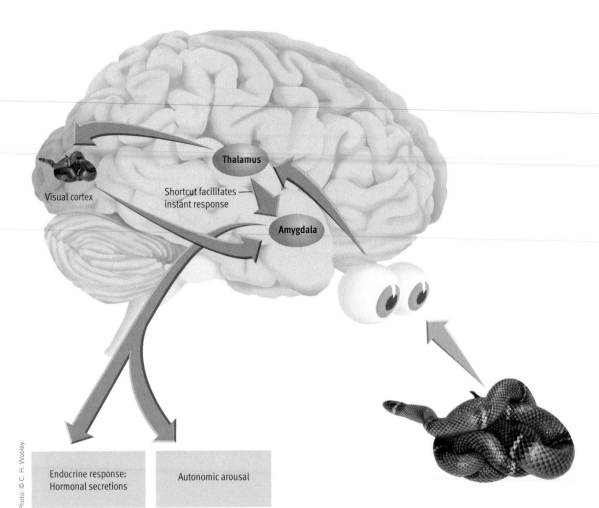

Photo: © C. H. Wooley.

Figure 10.22

The amygdala and fear.
Emotions are controlled by a constellation of interacting brain systems, but the amygdala appears to play a particularly crucial role. According to LeDoux (1996), sensory inputs that can trigger fear (such as seeing a snake while out walking) arrive in the thalamus and then are routed along a fast pathway (shown in red) directly to the amygdala, and along a slow pathway (shown in blue) that allows the cortex time to think about the situation. Activity in the fast pathway also elicits the autonomic arousal and hormonal responses that are part of the physiological component of emotion. (Adapted from LeDoux, 1994)

amygdala, and adjacent structures in the *limbic system* have long been viewed as the seat of emotions in the brain (Izard & Saxton, 1988; MacLean, 1993). Recent evidence suggests that the *amygdala* (see Figure 10.22) plays a particularly central role in the modulation of emotion. Joseph LeDoux (1986, 1993, 1996) and his colleagues have conducted extensive research on the classical conditioning of fear responses in animals. They have demonstrated that if an animal's amygdala is destroyed, the animal is unable to learn conditioned fear responses. Moreover, brain-imaging studies with human participants indicate that the amygdala is activated when subjects are shown emotion-arousing stimuli, such as pictures of mutilated bodies (Irwin et al., 1996) and when subjects are shown pictures depicting facial expressions of fear (Morris et al., 1996). That's *not* to say that the amygdala processes emotion by itself, as it appears to modulate activity in the cortex (Kapp, Supple, & Whalen, 1994). Recent studies suggest that areas in the *prefrontal cortex* make important contributions to the processing of emotional events (Davidson, Jackson, & Kalin, 2000; Teasdale et al., 1999).

According to LeDoux (1996, 2000), the amygdala lies at the core of a complex set of neural circuits that process emotion. He believes that sensory inputs capable of eliciting emotions arrive in the thalamus, which simultaneously routes the information along two separate pathways: a fast pathway to the nearby amygdala and a slower pathway to areas in the cortex (see Figure 10.22). The amygdala processes the information quickly, and if it detects a threat it almost instantly triggers neural activity that leads to the autonomic arousal and endocrine (hormonal) responses associated with emotion. The processing in this pathway is extremely fast, so that emotions may be triggered even before the brain has had a chance to really "think" about the input. Meanwhile, the information shuttled along the other pathway is subjected to a more "leisurely" cognitive appraisal in the cortex. This slower system, which can encode more details about a potential threat and evaluate the threat more thoroughly, then sends additional information to the amygdala, which is the "hub" of the system. LeDoux believes that the rapid-response pathway evolved because it is a highly adaptive warning system that can "be the difference between life and death." Although the amygdala has been widely characterized as a brain centre for emotion in

Courtesy of Joseph LeDoux, New York University

❝*In situations of danger, it is very useful to be able to respond quickly. The time saved by the amygdala in acting on the thalamic information, rather than waiting for the cortical input, may be the difference between life and death.*❞
JOSEPH LEDOUX

general, the research has mainly focused on the single emotion of fear. Hence, Whalen (1998) suggests that it might be more accurate to characterize the amygdala as the hub of a "vigilance" system.

The Behavioural Component: Nonverbal Expressiveness

 8c

At the behavioural level, people reveal their emotions through characteristic overt expressions such as smiles, frowns, furrowed brows, clenched fists, and slumped shoulders. In other words, *emotions are expressed in "body language," or nonverbal behaviour.*

Facial expressions reveal a variety of basic emotions. In an extensive research project, Paul Ekman and Wallace Friesen have asked subjects to identify what emotion a person was experiencing on the basis of facial cues in photographs. They have found that subjects are generally successful in identifying six fundamental emotions: happiness, sadness, anger, fear, surprise, and disgust (Ekman & Friesen, 1975, 1984). These studies have been criticized on the grounds that they have used a rather small set of artificial, highly posed photographs that don't do justice to the variety of facial expressions that can accompany specific emotions (Carroll & Russell, 1997). Still, the overall evidence indicates that people are reasonably skilled at deciphering emotions from others' facial expressions (Galati, Scherer, & Ricci-Bitti, 1997).

Some theorists believe that muscular feedback from one's own facial expressions contributes to one's conscious experience of emotions (Izard, 1990; Tomkins, 1991). Proponents of the *facial-feedback hypothesis* assert that facial muscles send signals to the brain and that these signals help the brain recognize the emotion that one is experiencing (see Figure 10.23). According to this view, smiles, frowns, and furrowed brows help create the subjective experience of various emotions. Consistent with this idea, studies show that if subjects are instructed to contract their facial muscles to mimic facial expressions associated with certain emotions, they tend to report that they actually experience these emotions to some degree (Kleinke, Peterson, & Rutledge, 1998; Levenson, 1992).

The facial expressions that go with various emotions may be largely innate (Eibl-Ebesfeldt, 1975). For the most part, people who have been blind since birth smile and frown much like everyone else, even though they've never seen a smile or frown (Galati et al., 1997). The idea that facial expressions of emotion might be biologically built in has led to extensive cross-cultural research on the dynamics of emotion. Let's look at what investigators have learned about culture and the elements of emotional experience.

Culture and the Elements of Emotion

Are emotions innate reactions that are universal across cultures? Or are they socially learned reactions that are culturally variable? The voluminous research on this lingering question has not yielded a simple answer. Investigators have found both remarkable similarities and dramatic differences between cultures in the experience of emotion.

Cross-Cultural Similarities in Emotional Experience

After demonstrating that Western subjects could discern specific emotions from facial expressions, Ekman and Friesen (1975) took their facial-cue photographs on the road to other societies to see whether nonverbal expressions of emotion transcend cultural boundaries. Testing subjects in Argentina, Spain, Japan, and other countries, they found considerable cross-cultural agreement in the identification of happiness, sadness, anger, fear, surprise, and disgust based on facial expressions (see Figure 10.24). Still, Ekman and Friesen wondered whether this agreement might be the result of learning rather than biology, given that people in different cultures often share considerable exposure to Western mass media (magazines, newspapers, television, and so forth), which provide many visual depictions of people's emotional reactions. To rule out this possibility, they took their photos to a remote area in New Guinea and showed them to a group of natives (the Fore) who had had virtually no contact with Western culture. Even the people from this preliterate culture did a fair job of identifying the emotions portrayed in the pictures (see the data in the bottom row of Figure 10.24). Subsequent comparisons of many other societies have also shown considerable cross-cultural congruence in the judgment of facial expressions (Biehl et al., 1997; Ekman, 1992, 1993). Although some theorists disagree (Russell, 1994, 1995), there is reasonably convincing evidence that people in widely disparate cultures express their emotions and interpret those expressions in much the same way (Izard, 1994; Keltner et al., 2003; Matsumoto, 2001).

Cross-cultural similarities have also been found in the cognitive and physiological elements of emotional experience (Scherer & Wallbott, 1994). For example, in making cognitive appraisals of events that might elicit emotional reactions, people from different cultures generally think along the same lines (Mauro, Sato, & Tucker, 1992; Mesquita & Frijda, 1992). That is, they evaluate situations along the same dimensions (pleasant versus unpleasant, expected versus unexpected, fair

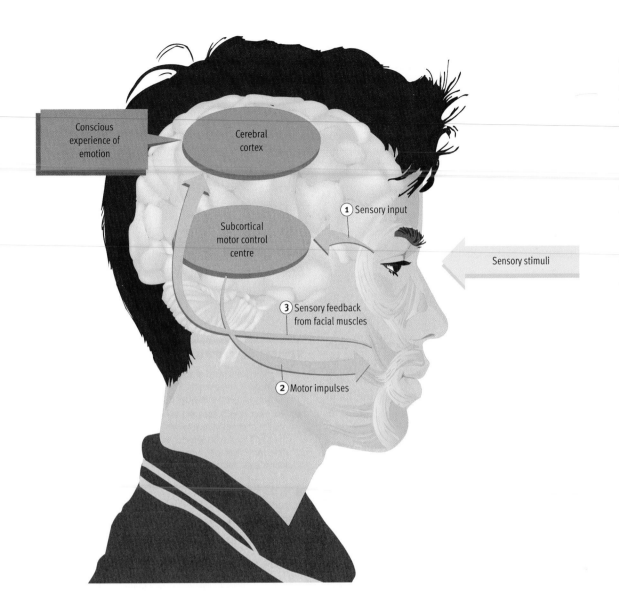

Figure 10.23

The facial feedback hypothesis. According to the facial feedback hypothesis, inputs to subcortical centres automatically evoke facial expressions associated with certain emotions, and the facial muscles then feed signals to the cortex that help it to recognize the emotion that one is experiencing. According to this view, facial expressions help create the subjective experience of various emotions.

SOURCE: Smith, R. E. (1993). *Psychology.* St. Paul, MN: West Publishing. Copyright © 1993 by West Publishing. Reprinted by permission of Wadsworth Publishing.

Conscious experience of emotion

Cerebral cortex

Subcortical motor control centre

1 Sensory input

Sensory stimuli

3 Sensory feedback from facial muscles

2 Motor impulses

versus unfair, and so on). Understandably, then, the types of events that trigger specific emotions are fairly similar across cultures (Frijda, 1999; Scherer, 1997). Around the globe, achievements lead to joy, injustices lead to anger, and risky situations lead to fear. Finally, as one might expect, the physiological arousal that accompanies emotion also appears to be largely invariant across cultures (Wallbott & Scherer, 1988). Thus, researchers have found a great deal of cross-cultural continuity and uniformity in the cognitive, physiological, and behavioural (expressive) elements of emotional experience.

Cross-Cultural Differences in Emotional Experience

The cross-cultural similarities in emotional experience are impressive, but researchers have also found many cultural disparities in how people think about and express their emotions (Mesquita, 2001, 2003). Foremost among these disparities are the fascinating variations in how cultures categorize emotions. Some basic categories of emotion that are universally understood in Western cultures appear to go unrecognized—or at least unnamed—in some non-Western cultures. James Russell (1991) has compiled numerous examples of English words for emotions that have no equivalent in other languages. For example, Tahitians have no word that corresponds to *sadness*. Many non-Western groups, including the Yoruba of Nigeria, the Kaluli of New Guinea, and the Chinese, lack a word for *depression*. The concept of *anxiety* seems to go unrecognized among Inuit, and the Quichua of Ecuador lack a word for *remorse*.

Cultural disparities have also been found in regard to nonverbal expressions of emotion. Although the natural facial expressions associated with basic emotions appear to be pancultural, people can and do learn to control and modify these expressions. **Display rules** are norms that regulate the appropriate expression of emotions. They prescribe when,

Figure 10.24

Cross-cultural comparisons of people's ability to recognize emotions from facial expressions. Ekman and Friesen (1975) found that people in highly disparate cultures showed fair agreement on the emotions portrayed in these photos. This consensus across cultures suggests that facial expressions of emotions may be universal and that they have a strong biological basis.

Source: Data from Ekman, P., & Friesen, W. V. (1975). *Unmasking the face.* Englewood Cliffs, NJ: Prentice-Hall. © 1975 by Paul Ekman, photographs courtesy of Paul Ekman. © Ekman 1975–2004.

Country	Fear	Disgust	Happiness	Anger
		Agreement in judging photos (%)		
United States	85	92	97	67
Brazil	67	97	95	90
Chile	68	92	95	94
Argentina	54	92	98	90
Japan	66	90	100	90
New Guinea	54	44	82	50

how, and to whom people can show various emotions. These norms vary from one culture to another (Ekman, 1992), as do attitudes about specific emotions (Eid & Diener, 2001). For instance, the Ifaluk (a Pacific Island culture) severely restrict expressions of happiness because they believe that this emotion often leads people to neglect their duties (Lutz, 1987). Japanese culture emphasizes the suppression of negative emotions in public. More so than in other cultures, the Japanese are socialized to mask emotions such as anger, sadness, and disgust with stoic facial expressions or polite smiling. Thus, nonverbal expressions of emotions vary somewhat across cultures because of culture-specific attitudes and display rules.

REVIEW OF KEY POINTS

- Emotion is made up of cognitive, physiological, and behavioural components. The cognitive component involves subjective feelings that have an evaluative aspect.

- The most readily apparent aspect of the physiological component of emotion is autonomic arousal. This arousal is the basis for the lie detector, which is really an emotion detector. Polygraphs are not all that accurate in assessing individuals' veracity. The amygdala appears to be the hub of an emotion-processing system in the brain.

- At the behavioural level, emotions are expressed through body language, with facial expressions being particularly prominent. Ekman and Friesen have found considerable cross-cultural agreement in the identification of emotions based on facial expressions.

- Cross-cultural similarities have also been found in the cognitive and physiological components of emotion. However, there are some striking cultural variations in how people categorize and display their emotions.

Theories of Emotion

PREVIEW QUESTIONS

- What are the differences between the James–Lange and Cannon–Bard theories of emotion?

- How did the two-factor theory of emotion try to reconcile these differences?

- How do evolutionary theorists explain emotions?

How do psychologists explain the experience of emotion? A variety of theories and conflicting models exist. Some have been vigorously debated for over a century. As we describe these theories, you'll recognize a familiar bone of contention. Like so many other types of theories, theories of emotion differ in their emphasis on the innate biological basis of emotion versus the social, environmental basis.

James–Lange Theory

 8D

As we noted in Chapter 1, William James was a prominent early theorist who urged psychologists to explore the functions of consciousness. James (1884) developed a theory of emotion over 100 years

ago that remains influential today. At about the same time, he and Carl Lange (1885) independently proposed that *the conscious experience of emotion results from one's perception of autonomic arousal.* Their theory stood common sense on its head. Everyday logic suggests that when you stumble onto a rattle-snake in the woods, the conscious experience of fear leads to visceral arousal (the fight-or-flight response). The James–Lange theory of emotion asserts the opposite: that the perception of visceral arousal leads to the conscious experience of fear (see Figure 10.25). In other words, while you might assume that your pulse is racing because you're fearful, James and Lange argued that you're fearful because your pulse is racing.

The James–Lange theory emphasizes the physiological determinants of emotion. According to this view, *different patterns of autonomic activation lead to the experience of different emotions*. Hence, people supposedly distinguish emotions such as fear, joy, and anger on the basis of the exact configuration of physical reactions they experience.

Cannon–Bard Theory 8D

Walter Cannon (1927) found the James–Lange theory unconvincing. Cannon pointed out that physiological arousal may occur without the experience of emotion (if one exercises vigorously, for instance). He also argued that visceral changes are too slow to precede the conscious experience of emotion. Finally, he argued that people experiencing very different emotions, such as fear, joy, and anger, exhibit almost identical patterns of autonomic arousal.

Thus, Cannon espoused a different explanation of emotion. Later, Philip Bard (1934) elaborated on it. The resulting Cannon–Bard theory argues that emotion occurs when the thalamus sends signals *simultaneously* to the cortex (creating the conscious experience of emotion) and to the autonomic nervous system (creating visceral arousal). The Cannon–Bard model is compared to the James–Lange model in Figure 10.25. Cannon

and Bard were off the mark a bit in pinpointing the thalamus as the neural centre for emotion. However, many modern theorists agree with the Cannon–Bard view that emotions originate in subcortical brain structures (LeDoux, 1996; Panksepp, 1991; Rolls, 1990) and with the assertion that people do not discern their emotions from different patterns of autonomic activation (Frijda, 1999; Wagner, 1989).

Schachter's Two-Factor Theory 8D

In another influential analysis, Stanley Schachter asserted that people look at situational cues to differentiate among alternative emotions. According to Schachter (1964; Schachter & Singer, 1962, 1979), the experience of emotion depends on two factors: (1) autonomic arousal and (2) cognitive interpretation of that arousal. Schachter proposed that when you experience visceral arousal, you search your environment for an explanation (see Figure 10.25 again). If you're stuck in a traffic jam, you'll probably label your arousal as anger. If you're taking an important exam, you'll probably label it as anxiety. If you're celebrating your birthday, you'll probably label it as happiness. You may recall that we used Schachter's theory in understanding the results of the Featured Study in Chapter 2 (see page 46). In the Dutton and

" *Cognitive factors play a major role in determining how a subject interprets his bodily feelings.* "
STANLEY SCHACHTER

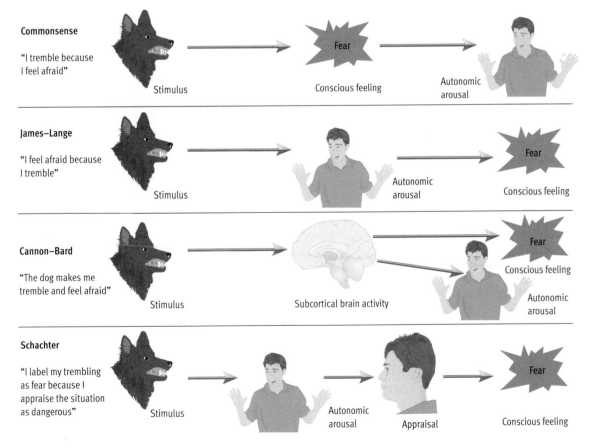

Figure 10.25

Theories of emotion.
Three influential theories of emotion are contrasted with one another and with the commonsense view. The James–Lange theory was the first to suggest that feelings of arousal cause emotion, rather than vice versa. Schachter built on this idea by adding a second factor—interpretation (appraisal and labelling) of arousal.

Commonsense

"I tremble because I feel afraid"

Stimulus → Fear (Conscious feeling) → Autonomic arousal

James–Lange

"I feel afraid because I tremble"

Stimulus → Autonomic arousal → Fear (Conscious feeling)

Cannon–Bard

"The dog makes me tremble and feel afraid"

Stimulus → Subcortical brain activity → Fear (Conscious feeling) / Autonomic arousal

Schachter

"I label my trembling as fear because I appraise the situation as dangerous"

Stimulus → Autonomic arousal → Appraisal → Fear (Conscious feeling)

Motivation and Emotion

Silvan Tomkins	Carroll Izard	Robert Plutchik
Fear	Fear	Fear
Anger	Anger	Anger
Enjoyment	Joy	Joy
Disgust	Disgust	Disgust
Interest	Interest	Anticipation
Surprise	Surprise	Surprise
Contempt	Contempt	
Shame	Shame	
	Sadness	Sadness
Distress		
	Guilt	
		Acceptance

Figure 10.26

Primary emotions.

Evolutionary theories of emotion attempt to identify primary emotions. Three leading theorists—Silvan Tomkins, Carroll Izard, and Robert Plutchik—have compiled different lists of primary emotions, but this chart shows great overlap among the basic emotions identified by these theorists. (Based on Mandler, 1984)

Aron (1974) study, participants who crossed the high, arousal-producing bridge over the Capilano River and who were met by an attractive female confederate were found to be more sexually attracted to her than participants who were met by the same female confederate but after crossing a lower, solid, nonarousing bridge. In this case, arousal and salient cue (i.e., the female confederate) combined in influencing the emotional state of the participants.

Schachter agreed with the James–Lange view that emotion is inferred from arousal. However, he also agreed with the Cannon–Bard position that different emotions yield indistinguishable patterns of arousal. He reconciled these views by arguing that people look to external rather than internal cues to differentiate and label their specific emotions. In essence, Schachter suggested that people think along the following lines: "If I'm aroused and you're obnoxious, I must be angry."

Although the two-factor theory has received support, studies have revealed some limitations as well (Leventhal & Tomarken, 1986). Situations can't mould emotions in just any way at any time. And in searching to explain arousal, subjects don't limit themselves to the immediate situation (Sinclair et al., 1994). Thus, emotions are not as pliable as the two-factor theory initially suggested.

Evolutionary Theories of Emotion

As the limitations of the two-factor theory were exposed, theorists began returning to ideas espoused by Charles Darwin over a century ago. Darwin (1872) believed that emotions developed because of their adaptive value. Fear, for instance, would help an organism avoid danger and thus would aid in survival. Hence, Darwin viewed human emotions as a product of evolution. This premise serves as the

foundation for several prominent theories of emotion developed independently by S. S. Tomkins (1980, 1991), Carroll Izard (1984, 1991), and Robert Plutchik (1984, 1993).

These *evolutionary theories* consider emotions to be largely innate reactions to certain stimuli. As such, emotions should be immediately recognizable under most conditions without much thought. After all, primitive animals that are incapable of complex thought seem to have little difficulty in recognizing their emotions. Evolutionary theorists believe that emotion evolved before thought. They assert that thought plays a relatively small role in emotion, although they admit that learning and cognition may have some influence on human emotions. Evolutionary theories generally assume that emotions originate in subcortical brain structures that evolved before the higher brain areas in the cortex associated with complex thought.

Evolutionary theories also assume that evolution has equipped humans with a small number of innate emotions with proven adaptive value. Hence, the principal question that evolutionary theories of emotion wrestle with is, *What are the fundamental emotions?* Figure 10.26 summarizes the conclusions of the leading theorists in this area. As you can see, Tomkins, Izard, and Plutchik have not come up with

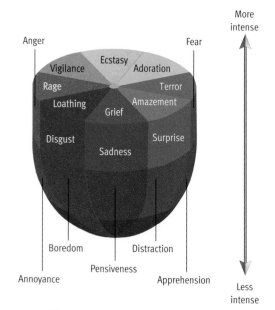

Figure 10.27

Emotional intensity in Plutchik's model. According to Plutchik, diversity in human emotion is a product of variations in emotional intensity, as well as blendings of primary emotions. Each vertical slice in the diagram is a primary emotion that can be subdivided into emotional expressions of varied intensity, ranging from most intense (top) to least intense (bottom).

SOURCE: Based on art in Plutchik, R. (1980). A language for emotions. *Psychology Today, 13* (9), 68–78. Reprinted with permission from Psychology Today Magazine. Copyright © 1980 by Sussex Publishers.

identical lists, but there is considerable agreement. All three conclude that people exhibit eight to ten primary emotions. Moreover, six of these emotions appear on all three lists: fear, anger, joy, disgust, interest, and surprise.

Of course, people experience more than just eight to ten emotions. How do evolutionary theories account for this variety? They propose that the many emotions that people experience are produced by (1) blends of primary emotions and (2) variations in intensity. For example, Robert Plutchik (1980, 1993) has devised an elegant model of how primary emotions such as fear and surprise may blend into secondary emotions such as awe. Plutchik's model also posits that various emotions, such as apprehension, fear, and terror, involve one primary emotion experienced at different levels of intensity (see Figure 10.27).

CONCEPT **CHECK 10.3**

Understanding Theories of Emotion

Check your understanding of theories of emotion by matching the theories we discussed with the statements below. Let's borrow William James's classic example: Assume that you just stumbled upon a bear in the woods. The first statement expresses the common-sense explanation of your fear. Each of the remaining statements expresses the essence of a different theory; indicate which theory in the spaces provided. The answers are provided in Appendix A.

1. You tremble because you're afraid.

Common sense

2. You're afraid because you're trembling.

3. You're afraid because situational cues (the bear) suggest that's why you're trembling.

4. You're afraid because the bear has elicited an innate primary emotion.

Putting It in Perspective

Five of our organizing themes were particularly prominent in this chapter: the influence of cultural contexts, the dense connections between psychology and society at large, psychology's theoretical diversity, the interplay of heredity and environment, and the multiple causes of behaviour.

Our discussion of motivation and emotion demonstrated once again that there are both similarities and differences across cultures in behaviour. The neural, biochemical, genetic, and hormonal processes underlying hunger and eating, for instance, are universal. But cultural factors influence what people prefer to eat, how much they eat, and whether they worry about dieting. In a similar vein, researchers have found a great deal of cross-cultural congruence in the cognitive, physiological, and expressive elements of emotional experience, but they have also found cultural variations in how people think about and express their emotions. Thus, as we have seen in previous chapters, psychological processes are characterized by both cultural variance and invariance.

Our discussion of the controversies surrounding evolutionary theory, aggressive pornography, and the determinants of sexual orientation show once again that psychology is not an ivory tower enterprise. It evolves in a sociohistorical context that helps to shape the debates in the field, and these debates often have far-reaching social and political ramifications for society at large. We ended the chapter with a discussion of various theories of emotion, which showed once again that psychology is characterized by great theoretical diversity.

Finally, we repeatedly saw that biological and environmental factors jointly govern behaviour. For example, we learned that eating behaviour, sexual desire, and the experience of emotion all depend on complicated interactions between biological and environmental determinants. Indeed, complicated interactions permeated the entire chapter, demonstrating that if we want to fully understand behaviour, we have to take multiple causes into account. In the upcoming Personal Application, we will continue our discussion of emotion, looking at recent research on the correlates of happiness. In the Critical Thinking Application that follows, we discuss how to carefully analyze the types of arguments that permeated this chapter.

REVIEW OF KEY POINTS

- The James–Lange theory asserts that emotion results from one's perception of autonomic arousal. The Cannon–Bard theory counters with the proposal that emotions originate in subcortical areas of the brain.

- According to Schachter's two-factor theory, people infer emotion from arousal and then label the emotion in accordance with their cognitive explanation for the arousal. Evolutionary theories of emotion maintain that emotions are innate reactions that require little cognitive interpretation.

- Our look at motivation and emotion showed once again that psychology is characterized by theoretical diversity, that biology and environment shape behaviour interactively, that behaviour is governed by multiple causes, that psychological processes are characterized by both cultural variance and invariance, and that psychology evolves in a sociohistorical context.

PREVIEW QUESTIONS

- How did this chapter demonstrate the influence of cultural factors and the dense connections between psychology and society?

- How did this chapter illustrate psychology's theoretical diversity, the interplay of heredity and environment, and the multifactorial causation of behaviour?

PERSONAL APPLICATION

Exploring the Ingredients of Happiness

Answer the following "true" or "false."

____ **1.** The empirical evidence indicates that most people are relatively unhappy.

____ **2.** Although wealth doesn't *guarantee* happiness, wealthy people are much more likely to be happy than the rest of the population.

____ **3.** People who have children are happier than people without children.

____ **4.** Good health is an essential requirement for happiness.

____ **5.** Good-looking people are happier than those who are unattractive.

The answer to all these questions is "false." These assertions are all reasonable and widely believed hypotheses about the correlates of happiness, but they have *not* been supported by empirical research. Recent years have brought a surge of interest in the correlates of *subjective well-being—individuals' personal perceptions of their overall happiness and life satisfaction.* The findings of these studies are quite interesting. As you have already seen from our true–false questions, many commonsense notions about happiness appear to be inaccurate.

How Happy Are People?

One of these inaccuracies is the apparently widespread assumption that most people are relatively unhappy. Writers, social scientists, and the general public seem to believe that people around the world are predominantly dissatisfied and unhappy, yet empirical surveys consistently find that the vast majority of respondents—even those who are poor or disabled—characterize themselves as fairly happy (Diener & Diener, 1996; Myers & Diener, 1995). When people are asked to rate their happiness, only a small minority place themselves below the neutral point on the various scales used (see Figure 10.28). When the average subjective well-being of entire nations is computed, based on almost 1000 surveys, the means cluster toward the positive end of the scale, as shown in Figure 10.29 (Veenhoven, 1993). That's not to say that everyone is equally happy. Researchers find substantial and thought-provoking disparities among people in subjective well-being, which we will analyze momentarily, but the overall picture seems rosier than anticipated.

Factors That Do Not Predict Happiness

Let us begin our discussion of individual differences in happiness by highlighting those things that turn out to be relatively unimportant determinants of subjective well-being. Quite a number of factors that you might expect to be influential appear to bear little or no relationship to general happiness.

Money There *is* a positive correlation between income and subjective feelings of happiness, but in modern, affluent cultures the association is surprisingly weak (Diener & Seligman, 2004; Myers & Diener, 1995). For example, one study found a correlation of just 0.12 between income and happiness in the United States (Diener et al., 1993). Admittedly, being very poor can make people unhappy, but once people ascend above the poverty level, little relation is seen between income and happiness. On the average, even wealthy people are only marginally happier than those in the middle classes. The problem with money is that in this era of voracious consumption, most of us find a way to spend all our money and come out short no matter how much we make. Complaints about not having enough money are routine even among people who earn six-figure incomes. Interestingly, there is some evidence that people who place an especially strong emphasis on the pursuit of wealth and materialistic goals tend to be somewhat less happy than others (Kasser, 2002; Ryan & Deci, 2001).

Figure 10.28

Measuring happiness with a nonverbal scale. Researchers have used a variety of methods to estimate the distribution of happiness. For example, in one study in the United States, respondents were asked to examine the seven facial expressions shown and select the one that "comes closest to expressing how you feel about your life as a whole." As you can see, the vast majority of participants chose happy faces. (Data adapted from Myers, 1992)

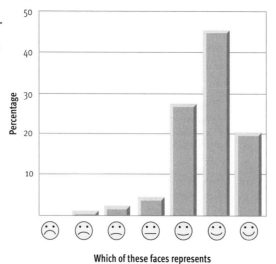

Which of these faces represents the way you feel about life as a whole?

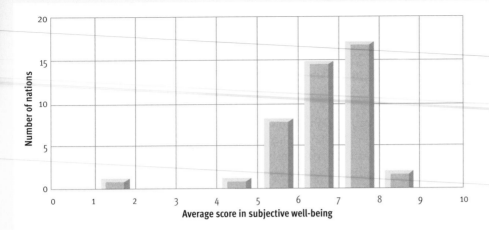

Figure (10.29)

The subjective well-being of nations. Veenhoven (1993) combined the results of almost 1000 surveys to calculate the average subjective well-being reported by representative samples from 43 nations. The mean happiness scores clearly pile up at the positive end of the distribution, with only two scores falling below the neutral point of 5. (Data adapted from Diener and Diener, 1996)

Age Age and happiness are consistently found to be unrelated. Age accounts for less than 1 percent of the variation in people's happiness (Inglehart, 1990; Myers & Diener, 1997). The key factors influencing subjective well-being may shift some as people grow older—work becomes less important, health more so—but people's average level of happiness tends to remain remarkably stable over the life span.

Parenthood Children can be a tremendous source of joy and fulfillment, but they can also be a tremendous source of headaches and hassles. Compared to childless couples, parents worry more and experience more marital problems (Argyle, 1987). Apparently, the good and bad aspects of parenthood balance each other out, because the evidence indicates that people who have children are neither more nor less happy than people without children (Argyle, 2001).

Intelligence Intelligence is a highly valued trait in modern society, but researchers have not found an association between IQ scores and happiness (Diener, 1984). Educational attainment also appears to be unrelated to life satisfaction (Ross & Van Willigen, 1997).

Physical Attractiveness Good-looking people enjoy a variety of advantages in comparison to unattractive people (see Chapter 16). Given that physical attractiveness is an important resource, we might expect that attractive people would be happier than others, but the available

data indicate that the correlation between attractiveness and happiness is negligible (Diener, Wolsic, & Fujita, 1995).

Moderately Good Predictors of Happiness

Research has identified four facets of life that appear to have a *moderate* association with subjective well-being: health, social activity, religious belief, and culture.

Health Good physical health would seem to be an essential requirement for happiness, but people adapt to health problems. Research reveals that individuals who develop serious, disabling health conditions aren't as unhappy as one might guess (Myers, 1992; Riis et al., 2005). Furthermore, Freedman (1978) argues that good health does not, by itself, produce happiness, because people tend to take good health for granted. Considerations such as these may help to explain why researchers find only a moderate positive correlation (average = 0.32) between health status and subjective well-being (Argyle, 1999).

Social Activity Humans are social animals, and interpersonal relations *do* appear to contribute to people's happiness. Those who are satisfied with their social support and friendship networks and those who are socially active report above-average levels of happiness (Diener & Seligman, 2004; Myers, 1999). And people who are exceptionally happy tend to report greater satis-

faction with their social relations than those who are average or low in subjective well-being (Diener & Seligman, 2002).

Religion The link between religiosity and subjective well-being is modest, but a number of large-scale surveys suggest that people with heartfelt religious convictions are more likely to be happy than people who characterize themselves as nonreligious (Argyle, 1999; Ferris, 2002). Researchers aren't sure how religious faith fosters happiness, but Myers (1992) offers some interesting

© Carlos Alvarez/Getty Images

If beauty, wealth, fame, and success bring happiness, then actress Halle Berry should be as happy as they come, but her past struggles with depression demonstrate that the ingredients of happiness are more subjective and complex than one might guess.

conjectures. Among other things, he discusses how religion can give people a sense of purpose and meaning in their lives, help them accept their setbacks gracefully, connect them to a caring, supportive community, and comfort them by putting their ultimate mortality in perspective.

Culture Researchers have found some modest cultural variations in average subjective well-being and in the key sources of happiness (Diener, Diener, & Diener, 1995; Suh et al., 1998). These variations have mostly been related to cultural differences in *individualism versus collectivism*. **Individualism involves putting personal goals ahead of group goals and defining one's identity in terms of personal attributes rather than group memberships.** In contrast, *collectivism* **involves putting group goals ahead of personal goals and defining one's identity in terms of the groups one belongs to** (such as one's family, tribe, work group, social class, caste, and so on). In comparison to individualistic cultures, collectivist cultures place a higher priority on shared values and resources, cooperation, mutual interdependence, and concern for how one's actions will affect other group members. Consistent with these realities, *relationship harmony* appears to be a more important determinant of happiness in collectivist cultures than in individualistic cultures (Kwan, Bond, & Singelis, 1997).

Strong Predictors of Happiness

The list of factors that turn out to have fairly strong associations with happiness is surprisingly short. The key ingredients of happiness appear to involve love, work, and personality.

Love and Marriage Romantic relationships can be stressful, but people consistently rate being in love as one of the most critical ingredients of happiness (Myers, 1999). Furthermore, although people complain a lot about their marriages, the evidence indicates that marital status is a key correlate of happiness. Among both men and women, married people are happier

than people who are single or divorced (see Figure 10.30; Myers & Diener, 1995), and this relationship holds around the world in widely different cultures (Diener et al., 2000). However, the causal relations underlying this correlation are unclear. It may be that happiness causes marital satisfaction more than marital satisfaction promotes happiness. Perhaps people who are happy tend to have better intimate relationships and more stable marriages, while people who are unhappy have more difficulty finding and keeping mates.

Work Given the way people often complain about their jobs, one might not expect work to be a key source of happiness, but it is. Although less critical than love and marriage, job satisfaction has a substantial association with general happiness (Warr, 1999). Studies also show that unemployment has strong negative effects on subjective well-being (Argyle, 1999; Lucas et al., 2004). It is difficult to sort out whether job satisfaction causes happiness or vice versa, but evidence suggests that causation flows both ways (Argyle, 1987, 2001).

Personality The best predictor of individuals' future happiness is their past happiness (Diener & Lucas, 1999). Some people seem destined to be happy and others unhappy, regardless of their triumphs or setbacks. The limited influence of life events was apparent in a stunning study that found only marginal differences in overall happiness between recent lottery winners and recent accident victims who became quadriplegics (Brickman, Coates, & Janoff-Bulman, 1978). Investigators were amazed that extremely fortuitous and horrible events like these didn't have a dramatic impact on happiness. Actually, *several* lines of evidence suggest that happiness does not depend on external circumstances—buying a nice house, getting promoted—so much as internal factors, such as one's outlook on life (Lykken & Tellegen, 1996). With this fact in mind, researchers have begun to look for links between personality and subjective well-being, and they have found some intriguing correlations. For example, *extraversion* is one of the better predictors of happiness. People who are outgoing, upbeat, and sociable tend to be

Figure 10.30

Happiness and marital status. This graph shows the percentage of adults characterizing themselves as "very happy" as a function of marital status (Myers, 1999). Among both women and men, happiness shows up more in those who are married as opposed to those who are separated, are divorced, or have never married. These data and many others suggest that marital satisfaction is a key ingredient of happiness.

Source: Myers, D. G. (1999). Close relationships and quality of life. In D. Kahneman, E. Diener, & N. Schwarz (Eds.), *Well-being: The foundations of hedonic psychology.* New York: Russell Sage Foundation. Copyright © 1999. Reprinted by permission of the Russell Sage Foundation.

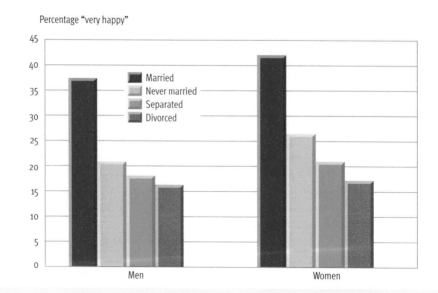

happier than others. Additional positive correlates of happiness include self-esteem and optimism (Lucas, Diener, & Suh, 1996).

Conclusions about Subjective Well-Being

We must be cautious in drawing inferences about the causes of happiness because the available data are correlational (see Figure 10.31). Nonetheless, the empirical evidence suggests that many popular beliefs about the sources of happiness are unfounded. The data also demonstrate that happiness is shaped by a complex constellation of variables. In spite of this complexity, however, a number of worthwhile insights about the ingredients of happiness can be gleaned from the recent flurry of research.

First, research on happiness demonstrates that the determinants of subjective well-being are precisely that: subjective. *Objective realities are not as important as subjective feelings.* In other words, your health, your wealth, and your job are not as influential as how you *feel* about your health, wealth, and job (Schwarz & Strack, 1999). These feelings are likely to be influenced by what your *expectations* were. Research suggests that bad outcomes feel worse when unexpected than when expected and good outcomes feel better when unexpected than when expected (Shepperd & McNulty, 2002). Thus, the same objective event, such as a pay raise of $2000 annually, may generate positive feelings in someone who wasn't expecting a raise and negative feelings in someone expecting a much larger increase in salary.

Second, *when it comes to happiness everything is relative* (Argyle, 1999; Hagerty, 2000). In other words, you evaluate what you have relative to what the people around you have. Generally, we compare ourselves with others who are similar to us. Thus, people who are wealthy assess what they have by comparing themselves with their wealthy friends and neighbours. This is one reason that there is little correlation between wealth and happiness. You might have a lovely home, but if it sits next door to a neighbour's palatial mansion, it might be a source of more dissatisfaction than happiness.

Third, *research on subjective well-being indicates that people often adapt to their circumstances.* This adaptation effect is one reason why increases in income don't necessarily bring increases in happiness. Thus **hedonic adaptation occurs when the mental scale that people use to judge the pleasantness–unpleasantness of their experiences shifts so that their neutral point, or baseline for comparison, changes.** Unfortunately, when people's experiences improve, hedonic adaptation may *sometimes* put them on a *hedonic treadmill*—their neutral point moves upward, so that the improvements yield no real benefits (Kahneman, 1999). However, when people have to grapple with major setbacks, hedonic adaptation probably helps protect their mental and physical health. For example, people who are sent to prison and people who develop debilitating diseases are not as unhappy as one might assume, because they adapt to their changed situations and evaluate events from a new perspective (Frederick & Loewenstein, 1999).

This effect is probably related to the fourth conclusion we can draw about subjective well-being: *Research shows that the quest for happiness is never hopeless* (Freedman, 1978; Myers, 1992). Although there are no simple recipes for happiness, the evidence indicates that some people find happiness in spite of seemingly insurmountable problems. There is nothing, short of terminal illness—no setback, shortcoming, difficulty, or inadequacy—that makes happiness impossible.

REVIEW OF KEY POINTS

- Research on happiness reveals that many commonsense notions about the roots of happiness appear to be incorrect, including the notion that most people are unhappy. Factors such as income, age, parenthood, intelligence, and attractiveness are largely uncorrelated with subjective well-being.

- Physical health, good social relationships, religious faith, and culture appear to have a modest impact on feelings of happiness. The only factors that are good predictors of happiness are love and marriage, work satisfaction, and personality.

- Research on happiness indicates that objective realities are not as important as subjective feelings and that subjective well-being is a relative concept. The evidence also indicates that people adapt to their circumstances and that the quest for happiness is almost never hopeless.

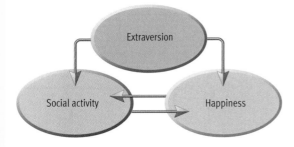

Figure 10.31

Possible causal relations among the correlates of happiness. Although we have considerable data on the correlates of happiness, it is difficult to untangle the possible causal relationships. For example, we know that a moderate positive correlation exists between social activity and happiness, but we can't say for sure whether high social activity causes happiness or whether happiness causes people to be more socially active. Moreover, in light of the research showing that a third variable—extraversion—correlates with both variables, we have to consider the possibility that extraversion causes both greater social activity and greater happiness.

Analyzing Arguments: Making Sense out of Controversy

Consider the following argument. "Dieting is harmful to your health because the tendency to be obese is largely inherited." What is your reaction to this reasoning? Do you find it convincing? We hope not, as this argument is seriously flawed. Can you see what's wrong? There is no relationship between the conclusion that "dieting is harmful to your health" and the reason given that "the tendency to be obese is largely inherited." The argument is initially seductive because you know from reading this chapter that obesity *is* largely inherited, so the reason provided represents a true statement. But the reason is unrelated to the conclusion advocated. This scenario may strike you as odd, but if you start listening carefully to discussions about controversial issues, you will probably notice that people often cite irrelevant considerations in support of their favoured conclusions.

This chapter was loaded with controversial issues that sincere, well-meaning people could argue about for weeks. Does the availability of pornography increase the prevalence of sex crimes? Are gender differences in mating preferences a product of evolution or of modern economic realities? Is there a biological basis for homosexuality?

Unfortunately, arguments about issues such as these typically are unproductive in terms of moving toward resolution or agreement because most people know little about the rules of argumentation. In this application, we will explore what makes arguments sound or unsound in the hope of improving your ability to analyze and think critically about arguments.

The Anatomy of an Argument

In everyday usage, the word *argument* is used to refer to a dispute or disagreement between two or more people, but in the technical language of rhetoric, **an *argument* consists of one or more premises that are used to provide support for a conclusion.** *Premises* **are the reasons that are presented to persuade someone that a conclusion is true or probably true.** *Assumptions* **are premises for which no proof or evidence is offered.** Assumptions are often left unstated. For example, suppose that your doctor tells you that you should exercise regularly because regular exercise is good for your heart. In this simple argument, the conclusion is "You should exercise regularly." The premise that leads to this conclusion is the idea that "exercise is good for your heart." An unstated assumption is that everyone wants a healthy heart.

In the language of argument analysis, premises are said to support (or not support) conclusions. A conclusion may be supported by one reason or by many reasons. One way to visualize these possibilities is to draw an analogy between the reasons that support a conclusion and the legs that support a table (Halpern, 1996, 2003). As shown in Figure 10.32, a table top (conclusion) could be supported by one strong leg (a single strong reason) or many thin legs (lots of weaker reasons). Of course, the reasons provided for a conclusion may fail to support the conclusion. Returning to our table analogy, the table top might not be supported because the legs are too thin (very weak reasons) or because the legs are not attached (irrelevant reasons).

Arguments can get pretty complicated, as they usually have more parts than just reasons and conclusions. In addition, there often are *counterarguments,* which are reasons that take support away from a conclusion. And sometimes the most important part of an argument is a part that is not there—reasons that have been omitted, either

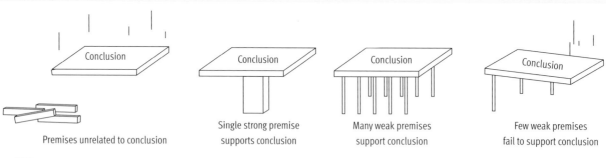

Premises unrelated to conclusion

Single strong premise supports conclusion

Many weak premises support conclusion

Few weak premises fail to support conclusion

Figure 10.32

An analogy for understanding the strength of arguments. Halpern (1996) draws an analogy between the reasons that support a conclusion and the legs that support a table. She points out that a conclusion may be supported effectively by one strong premise or many weak premises. Of course, the reasons provided for a conclusion may also *fail* to provide adequate support.

Source: Halpern, D. F. (1996). *Thought & knowledge: An introduction to critical thinking.* Mahwah, NJ: Erlbaum. Copyright © 1996 Lawrence Erlbaum Associates. Reprinted by permission.

deliberately or not, that would lead to a different conclusion if they were supplied. Given all the complex variations that are possible in arguments, it is impossible to give you simple rules for judging arguments, but we can highlight some common fallacies and then provide some criteria that you can apply in thinking critically about arguments.

Common Fallacies

As noted in previous chapters, cognitive scientists have compiled lengthy lists of fallacies that people frequently display in their reasoning. These fallacies often show up in arguments. In this section we will describe five common fallacies. To illustrate each one, we will assume the role of someone arguing that pornographic material on the Internet (cyberporn) should be banned or heavily regulated.

Irrelevant Reasons Reasons cannot provide support for an argument unless they are relevant to the conclusion. Arguments that depend on irrelevant reasons—either intentionally or inadvertently—are quite common. You already saw one example at the beginning of this application. The Latin term for this fallacy is *non sequitur,* which literally translates to "it doesn't follow." In other words, the conclusion does not follow from the premise. For example, in the debate about Internet pornography, you might hear the following *non sequitur:* "We need to regulate cyberporn because research has shown that most date rapes go unreported."

Circular Reasoning In *circular reasoning* the premise and conclusion are simply restatements of each other. People vary their wording a little so it isn't obvious, but when you look closely, the conclusion *is* the premise. For example, in arguments about Internet pornography you might hear someone assert, "We need to control cyberporn because it currently is unregulated."

Slippery Slope The concept of *slippery slope* argumentation takes its name from the notion that if you are on a slippery slope and you don't dig your heels in, you will slide and slide until you reach the bottom. A slippery slope argument typically asserts that if you allow X to happen, things will spin out of control and far worse events will follow. The trick is that there is no inherent connection between X and the events that are predicted to follow. For example, in the debate about medical marijuana, opponents have argued, "If you legalize medical marijuana, the next thing you know cocaine and heroin will be legal." In the debate about cyberporn, a slippery slope argument might go, "If we don't ban cyberporn, the next thing you know, grade-school children will be watching smut all day long in their school libraries."

Weak Analogies An *analogy* asserts that two concepts or events are similar in some way. Hence, you can draw conclusions about event B because of its similarity to event A. Analogies are useful in thinking about complex issues, but some analogies are weak or inappropriate because the similarity between A and B is superficial, minimal, or irrelevant to the issue at hand. For example, in the debate about Internet erotica, someone might argue, "Cyberporn is morally offensive, just like child molestation. We wouldn't tolerate child molestation, so we shouldn't permit cyberporn."

False Dichotomy A *false dichotomy* creates an either–or choice between two outcomes: the outcome advocated and some obviously horrible outcome that any sensible person would want to avoid. These outcomes are presented as the only two possibilities, when in reality there could be other outcomes, including ones that lie somewhere between the extremes depicted in the false dichotomy. In the debate about Internet pornography, someone might argue, "We can ban cyberporn, or we can hasten the moral decay of modern society."

Evaluating the Strength of Arguments

In everyday life, you may frequently need to assess the strength of arguments made by friends, family, co-workers, politicians, media pundits, and so forth. You may also want to evaluate your own arguments when you write papers or speeches for school or prepare presentations for your work. The following questions can help you make systematic evaluations of arguments (adapted from Halpern, 1996, 2003):

- What is the conclusion?
- What are the premises provided to support the conclusion? Are the premises valid?
- Does the conclusion follow from the premises? Are there any fallacies in the chain of reasoning?
- What assumptions have been made? Are they valid assumptions? Should they be stated explicitly?
- What are the counterarguments? Do they weaken the argument?
- Is there anything that has been omitted from the argument?

Table 10.1 Critical Thinking Skills Discussed in This Application

Skill	Description
Understanding the elements of an argument	The critical thinker understands that an argument consists of premises and assumptions that are used to support a conclusion.
Recognizing and avoiding common fallacies, such as irrelevant reasons, circular reasoning, slippery slope reasoning, weak analogies, and false dichotomies	The critical thinker is vigilant about conclusions based on unrelated premises, conclusions that are rewordings of premises, superficial analogies, and contrived dichotomies.
Evaluating arguments systematically	The critical thinker carefully assesses the validity of the premises, assumptions, and conclusions in an argument, and considers counterarguments and missing elements.

RECAP

Key Ideas

Motivational Theories and Concepts

● Drive theories apply a homeostatic model to motivation. They assume that organisms seek to reduce unpleasant states of tension called drives. In contrast, incentive theories emphasize how external goals energize behaviour.

● Evolutionary theorists explain motives in terms of their adaptive value. Madsen's list of biological needs and Murray's list of social needs illustrate that a diverse array of motives govern human behaviour.

The Motivation of Hunger and Eating

● Eating is regulated by a complex interaction of biological and environmental factors. In the brain, the lateral, ventromedial, and paraventricular areas of the hypothalamus appear to be involved in the control of hunger, but their exact role is unclear.

● Fluctuations in blood glucose also seem to play a role in hunger. The stomach can send two types of satiety signals to the brain. Hormonal regulation of hunger depends primarily on insulin and leptin secretions.

● Incentive-oriented models assert that eating is regulated by the availability and palatability of food. Learning processes, such as classical conditioning and observational learning, exert a great deal of influence over both what people eat and how much they eat. Cultural traditions also shape food preferences. Stress can stimulate eating.

● Evidence indicates that there is a genetic predisposition to obesity. According to set-point theory, the body monitors fat stores to keep them fairly stable. Settling-point theory suggests that a multitude of factors contribute to weight stability. Vacillations in dietary restraint resulting in disinhibition may contribute to obesity in some people.

Sexual Motivation and Behaviour

● Scientists are not sure, but hormonal swings appear to have a modest impact on human sexual desire. People respond to a variety of erotic materials, which may elevate sexual desire for only a few hours but may have an enduring impact on attitudes about sex. Aggressive pornography may make sexual coercion seem less offensive and may contribute to date rape.

● Consistent with evolutionary theory, males tend to think about and initiate sex more than females and to have more sexual partners and more interest in casual sex than females. The Featured Study by Buss demonstrated that there are gender differences in mating preferences that largely transcend cultural boundaries. Males emphasize potential partners' youthfulness and attractiveness, whereas females emphasize potential partners' financial prospects.

● The determinants of sexual orientation are not well understood. Recent studies suggest that there may be a genetic predisposition to homosexuality and that idiosyncrasies in prenatal hormonal secretions may contribute, but much remains to be learned. The human sexual response cycle can be divided into four stages: excitement, plateau, orgasm, and resolution.

Affiliation: In Search of Belongingness

● Affiliation probably had many adaptive benefits for our ancestors. Individual differences in the need for affiliation are usually measured with the TAT. People who are relatively high in the need for affiliation tend to devote more time to interpersonal activities and to worry more about acceptance than others do.

Achievement: In Search of Excellence

● McClelland pioneered the use of the TAT to measure achievement motivation. People who are high in the need for achievement work harder and more persistently than others, although they often choose to tackle challenges of intermediate difficulty. The pursuit of achievement tends to increase when the probability of success and the incentive value of success are high.

The Elements of Emotional Experience

● Emotion is made up of cognitive, physiological, and behavioural components. The cognitive component involves subjective feelings that have an evaluative aspect. In the peripheral nervous system, the physiological component is dominated by autonomic arousal. In the brain, the amygdala seems to be the hub of the neural circuits that process emotion. At the behavioural level, emotions are expressed through body language, with facial expressions being particularly prominent.

● Ekman and Friesen have found considerable cross-cultural agreement in the identification of emotions based on facial expressions. Cross-cultural similarities have also been found in the cognitive and physiological components of emotion. However, there are cultural variations in how people categorize and display their emotions.

Theories of Emotion

● The James–Lange theory asserts that emotion results from one's perception of autonomic arousal. The Cannon–Bard theory counters with the proposal that emotions originate in subcortical areas of the brain. According to Schachter's two-factor theory, people infer emotion from arousal and then label the emotion in accordance with their cognitive explanation for the arousal. Evolutionary theories of emotion maintain that emotions are innate reactions that require little cognitive interpretation.

Putting It in Perspective

● Our look at motivation and emotion showed once again that psychology is characterized by theoretical diversity, that biology and environment shape behaviour interactively, that behaviour is governed by multiple causes, that psychological processes are characterized by both cultural variance and invariance, and that psychology evolves in a sociohistorical context.

Personal Application • Exploring the Ingredients of Happiness

● Factors such as income, age, parenthood, intelligence, and attractiveness are largely uncorrelated with subjective well-being. Physical health, good social relationships, religious faith, and culture appear to have a modest impact on feelings of happiness. Strong predictors of happiness include love and marriage, work satisfaction, and personality.

● Research on happiness indicates that objective realities are not that important, that happiness is relative, that people adapt to their circumstances, and that the quest for happiness is almost never hopeless.

Critical Thinking Application • Analyzing Arguments: Making Sense out of Controversy

● An argument consists of one or more premises used to provide support for a conclusion. Arguments are often marred by fallacies in reasoning, such as irrelevant reasons, circular reasoning, slippery slope scenarios, weak analogies, and false dichotomies. Arguments can be evaluated more effectively by applying systematic criteria.

Key Terms

Achievement motive, 415
Affiliation motive, 414
Androgens, 403
Argument, 432
Assumptions, 432
Bisexuals, 409
Body mass index (BMI), 399
Collectivism, 430
Display rules, 423
Drive, 393
Emotion, 418
Estrogens, 403
Galvanic skin response (GSR), 419
Glucose, 396
Glucostats, 396
Hedonic adaptation, 431
Heterosexuals, 409
Homeostasis, 392
Homosexuals, 409
Incentive, 393
Individualism, 430
Lie detector, 419
Motivation, 392
Obesity, 399
Orgasm, 413
Polygraph, 419
Premises, 432
Refractory period, 414
Set-point theory, 401
Settling-point theory, 401
Sexual orientation, 409
Subjective well-being, 428
Vasocongestion, 413

Key People

John Atkinson, 416
David Buss, 408
Walter Cannon, 395
Paul Ekman, 422
Wallace Friesen, 422
William James, 424
Virginia Johnson, 413
Joseph LeDoux, 421
William Masters, 413
David McClelland, 416
Henry Murray, 415
Judith Rodin, 396
Stanley Schachter, 425

PRACTICE TEST

1. Jackson had a huge breakfast this morning and is still feeling stuffed when he arrives at work. However, one of his colleagues has brought some delicious-looking doughnuts to the morning staff meeting and Jackson just can't resist. Although he feels full, he eats three doughnuts. His behaviour is inconsistent with:
   A. incentive theories of motivation.
   B. drive theories of motivation.
   C. evolutionary theories of motivation.
   D. the Cannon–Bard theory of motivation.

2. The heritability of weight appears to be:
   A. virtually impossible to demonstrate.
   B. very low.
   C. in the range of 60%–70%
   D. irrelevant to the understanding of obesity.

3. Which of the following is the most common source of disinhibition for restrained eaters?
   A. emotional distress
   B. the fear of becoming too thin
   C. drinking alcohol in small quantities
   D. the perception that they have cheated on their diet

4. Some recent studies suggest that exposure to aggressive pornography:
   A. may increase males' aggressive behaviour toward women.
   B. may perpetuate the myth that women enjoy being raped.
   C. both a and b.
   D. neither a nor b.

5. Which of the following has *not* been found in research on gender differences in sexual interest?
   A. Men think about sex more than women.
   B. Men initiate sex more frequently than women.
   C. Women are more interested in having many partners than men are.
   D. Women are less interested in uncommitted sex.

6. Kinsey maintained that sexual orientation:
   A. depends on early classical conditioning experiences.
   B. should be viewed as a continuum.
   C. depends on normalities and abnormalities in the amygdala.
   D. should be viewed as an either–or distinction.

7. In research on affiliation, individual differences in affiliation are usually measured:
   A. by observing subjects' actual social behaviour.
   B. by asking subjects about their affiliation needs.
   C. with the Thematic Apperception Test.
   D. with the Minnesota Multiphasic Personality Inventory.

8. The determinant of achievement behaviour that increases when a college student enrolls in a class that is *required* for graduation is:
   A. the probability of success.
   B. the need to avoid failure.
   C. the incentive value of success.
   D. the fear of success.

9. A polygraph (lie detector) device works by:
   A. monitoring physiological indices of autonomic arousal.
   B. directly assessing the truthfulness of a person's statements.
   C. monitoring the person's facial expressions.
   D. all of the above.

10. Which of the following statements about cross-cultural comparisons of emotional experience is *not* true?
    A. The types of events that trigger specific emotions are fairly similar across cultures.
    B. The physiological reactions that accompany emotions tend to be similar across cultures.
    C. People of different cultures tend to categorize emotions somewhat differently.
    D. All of the above statements are true.

11. According to the James–Lange theory of emotion:
    A. the experience of emotion depends on autonomic arousal and on one's cognitive interpretation of that arousal.
    B. different patterns of autonomic activation lead to the experience of different emotions.
    C. emotion occurs when the thalamus sends signals simultaneously to the cortex and to the autonomic nervous system.
    D. emotions develop because of their adaptive value.

12. Which theory of emotion implies that people can change their emotions simply by changing the way they label their arousal?
    A. the James–Lange theory
    B. the Cannon–Bard theory
    C. Schachter's two-factor theory
    D. opponent-process theory

13. The fact that eating behaviour, sexual desire, and the experience of emotion all depend on interactions between biological and environmental determinants lends evidence to which of your text's organizing themes?
    A. psychology's theoretical diversity
    B. psychology's empiricism
    C. people's experience of the world is subjective
    D. the joint influence of biology and environment

14. Which of the following statements is (are) true?
    A. For the most part, people are pretty happy.
    B. Age is unrelated to happiness.
    C. Income is largely unrelated to happiness.
    D. All of the above.

15. The sales pitch "We're the best dealership in town because the other dealerships just don't stack up against us" is an example of:
    A. a false dichotomy.
    B. semantic slanting.
    C. circular reasoning.
    D. slippery slope.

   See Appendix A for answers to this Practice Test.

 ON THE WEB

For additional resources on the topics covered in this chapter, visit the *Psychology: Themes and Variations* Web site, where you will find practice quizzes, tutorials, Web links, simulations, critical thinking activities, flash cards, interactive exercises, and suggested readings available through INFOTRAC.

   http://www.themesandvariations.nelson.com

 http://hed.nelson.com

Go to this site for the link to ThomsonNOW™, your one-stop study shop. Take a Pretest for this chapter and ThomsonNOW™ will generate a personalized Study Plan based on your test results! The Study Plan will identify the topics you need to review and direct you to online resources to help you master those topics. You can then take a Posttest to help you determine the concepts you have mastered and what you still need work on.

CHAPTER 11

Latchezar Boyadjiev, *Transition*, L.B. Glass Studios

Progress before Birth: Prenatal Development
The Course of Prenatal Development
Environmental Factors and Prenatal Development

The Wondrous Years of Childhood
Exploring the World: Motor Development
Easy and Difficult Babies: Differences in Temperament
Early Emotional Development: Attachment
Becoming Unique: Personality Development
The Growth of Thought: Cognitive Development
The Development of Moral Reasoning

The Transition of Adolescence
Puberty and the Growth Spurt
Time of Turmoil?
Featured Study • Youth Suicide in Canada's First Nations
The Search for Identity

The Expanse of Adulthood
Personality Development
Transitions in Family Life
Aging and Physical Changes
Aging and Cognitive Changes

Putting It in Perspective

Personal Application • **Understanding Gender Differences**
How Do the Sexes Differ in Behaviour?
Biological Origins of Gender Differences
Environmental Origins of Gender Differences
Conclusion

Critical Thinking Application • **Are Fathers Essential to Children's Well-Being?**
The Basic Argument
Evaluating the Argument

Recap

Practice Test

Human Development across the Life Span

If you think about yourself now and compare yourself to how you looked and behaved ten years ago, and if you then add what has happened to you in the years in between, you would be able to generate a rather long list of the many ways in which you have changed. Most of these changes have been positive and exciting. For example, do you remember counting down the days and hours until you metamorphosed into that higher life form—the teenager? You were convinced that life would be different after the clock struck midnight on that special day.

Some of the challenges you faced were likely quite difficult and you may have been able to talk about them with—and receive reassurance and support from—your parents or caregivers. While there are many things that you shared with your parents in conversation over the years, there is one thing that your parents should have told you, or talked to you about, before you found out on your own. No, we aren't referring to *that* talk but rather to another one. They should have confessed that, like most parents, they have talked and continue to talk about you all the time to all sorts of other people and that they have done so since the moment of your birth. That's why family, friends, and indeed even people you haven't met seem to know so much about you. If you are like our own children you may not always appreciate this sharing. However, you may also have discovered that parents are not easily dissuaded from such activity.

Why do parents spend so much of their time talking about their children? This is likely a multi-determined behaviour, but a couple of the reasons are relevant to the issues discussed in this chapter. In part, this reflects the level of their engagement with you and their belief that a high level of engagement is important for your development. Their degree of involvement and parenting style affects many things, including your level of attachment. Attachment between a child and caregivers and its effects on later development are among the issues we will discuss in this chapter. You may recall in Chapter 1 that we introduced you to Mary Ainsworth, one of the major contributors to the scientific literature on attachment and related issues.

Another reason why your parents talk about you so much may be that they are continually amazed at the changes you have evidenced as you have grown and developed from a newborn to an infant, child, adolescent, young adult, and beyond. Once you have the opportunity to be around a child on a continuous basis for a lengthy time period you too will be amazed at how much they change and at how differently they behave and think at different stages of development. Cognitive and social–emotional development will also be a focus in this chapter. While children change dramatically in the way they think about themselves and the world, sometimes even very young children can show an amazing grasp of things. One of us had to pull his car over to the side

Craig Kielburger (left) founded Free the Children, an international organization dedicated to the empowerment and enrichment of children all over the world. He was 12 in 1995 when he started the organization, after reading of the murder of Iqbal Masih. Iqbal is pictured on the right. To date, Free the Children has helped to build 400 schools worldwide and continues to advocate for the abolishment of child labour. While still a teenager, Craig was nominated for the Nobel Peace Prize.

of the road one day when his four-year-old son asked from the back seat, "Dad, what makes life possible?" Or consider another example, the definition recounted in a speech given in 1930 by famed Canadian artist Emily Carr when a young girl was asked about the process of creative art. When asked to describe how it's done, the young child responded, "I think, and then I draw a line round my think" (Carr, 1972, p. 8). Carr, herself a world-renowned artist, could not think of a better description of the creative process and she believed that children often grasp such things much more quickly and adequately than adults. On the other hand, young children frequently show the most amazing misunderstanding of even simple logic. What do we know about the young child's developing sense of the world around her or him? Research in psychology has taken us some distance toward understanding this developing theory of the world and how it works and specific characteristics of children at different ages.

Much of a child's development is the result of relatively predetermined physiological changes. We will discuss some of these in this chapter—standing, crawling, walking, and so on. The physical challenges and accomplishments facing the typical developing child are enormous. Some children, of course, face special circumstances. These challenges are even more pronounced for children born prematurely, such as Noella Brescacin, born on April 13, 2000, in Victoria, B.C. (Lunman, 2001). She was born four months premature and was given a 5 percent chance of survival. She was one of the smallest babies ever born who survived, at birth weighing 450 grams or about the same as a can of pop. Her foot at birth was the size of her father's thumbnail and her skin was so fragile that it tore wherever she was touched. Although she faced some serious complications in the beginning, today she is thriving and developing.

Although important, physical changes are only part of the story we focus on in this chapter. Children and their development are also affected by cultural and social forces, forces that today may differ from those experienced by children in the past. Consider the experiences and accomplishments of Craig Kielburger, who was born in Thornhill, Ontario, in 1982. Until the age of 12 he was just like most other Canadian children.

On April 19, 1995, all that changed (Kielburger, 1998). That morning over breakfast he was looking through the newspaper for some of his favourite comics to read while eating his cereal before heading off to school. He was stopped by a story on the front page detailing the murder of a child in India named Iqbal Masih. Iqbal had been given into slavery at the age of four in order to pay off a family debt of $16.

Iqbal toiled for years as a child labourer before escaping and becoming a champion of children's rights while still a young teen. Iqbal had been threatened in an attempt to silence him and then was murdered. Craig decided to carry on Iqbal's work crusading against child labour. He started that morning by requesting class time from his teacher in order to ask his classmates for volunteers to help. With a small group of volunteers, Craig started to work for children. Later that year he travelled to Asia by himself to investigate child labour conditions and to visit the grave of Iqbal. He was met by an adult mentor once he arrived. Since then, Free the Children (**http://www.freethe children.org**) has grown to be an international organization dedicated to children's rights. Craig has met with and been endorsed by prime ministers, monarchs, Pope John Paul II, and Mother Teresa, and international celebrities such as Oprah Winfrey. He believes that children are a critically important resource, that the developing child needs more than exposure to facts in school, that childhood is a critical time of formation, and that we should focus on "helping them to better understand themselves and the world around them, including their talents and what they have to offer…" (Terry & Woonteiler, 2000).

It is not only children who are affected by changing social conditions. While it has been traditional for people like your parents to think of working to the age of 65 and then retiring, recently this idea has been challenged. While many adults look forward to retiring at 65, not all do. In previous chapters we have described the pioneering work of McGill neuropsychologist Brenda Milner, who in 2005, at age 86, continues to teach and do research; if she had been forced to retire at 65 because of age, she said, it would have been terrible (Won, 2005). She must agree with Canadian humorist Stephen Leacock, who said, "But as to this retirement business, let me give you a word of advice … Have nothing to do with it" (Leacock, 1939, p. 175). By the way, Leacock also had amusing views on the nature and proper place of psychology; he referred to it as the "Black Art" (Leacock, 1939).

Life for many older Canadians may be different in the next few years compared to what would have happened just a few years ago. Mandatory retirement at age 65 has been retired itself in many parts of Canada, including Quebec, Manitoba, Prince Edward Island, Nunavut, the Northwest Territories, and the Yukon. Ontario is the most recent province to propose outlawing mandatory retirement at age 65 (Ferguson, 2005). These types of social changes are also of interest to us in this chapter because the topic of development spans prenatal issues to adolescence, adulthood, and old age. As we see it, *development* is the sequence of age-related changes that occur as a person progresses from conception to death. It is a reasonably orderly, cumulative process that includes both the biological and behavioural changes that take place as people grow older. An infant's newfound ability to grasp objects, a child's gradual mastery of grammar, an adolescent's spurt in physical growth, a young adult's increasing commitment to a vocation, and an older adult's transition into the role of grandparent all represent development. These transitions are predictable changes that are related to age.

Traditionally, psychologists have been most interested in development during childhood. Our coverage reflects this emphasis. However, decades of research have clearly demonstrated that development is a lifelong process. We'll divide the life span into four broad periods: (1) the prenatal period, between conception and birth, (2) childhood, (3) adolescence, and (4) adulthood. We'll examine aspects of development that are especially dynamic during each period. Let's begin by looking at events that occur before birth, during prenatal development.

Progress before Birth: Prenatal Development

Development begins with conception. Conception occurs when fertilization creates a *zygote*, **a one-celled organism formed by the union of a sperm and an egg.** All the other cells in your body developed from this single cell. Each of your cells contains enduring messages from your parents carried on the *chromosomes* that lie within its nucleus. Each chromosome houses many *genes*, the functional units in hereditary transmission. Genes carry the details of your hereditary blueprints, which are revealed gradually throughout life (see Chapter 3 for more information on genetic transmission).

The *prenatal period* extends from conception to birth, usually encompassing nine months of pregnancy. A great deal of important development occurs before birth. In fact, development during the prenatal period is remarkably rapid. If you were an average-sized newborn and your physical growth had continued during the first year of your life at a prenatal pace, by your first birthday you would have weighed nearly 100 kilograms! Fortunately, you didn't grow at that rate—and no human does—because in the final weeks before birth the frenzied pace of prenatal development tapers off dramatically. In this section, we'll examine the usual course of prenatal development and discuss how environmental events can leave their mark on development even before birth exposes the newborn to the outside world.

The Course of Prenatal Development

The prenatal period is divided into three phases: (1) the germinal stage (the first two weeks), (2) the embryonic stage (two weeks to two months), and (3) the fetal stage (two months to birth). Some key developments in these phases are outlined here.

Germinal Stage

The *germinal stage* is the first phase of prenatal development, encompassing the first two weeks after conception. This brief stage begins when a zygote is created through fertilization. Within 36 hours, rapid cell division begins and the zygote becomes a microscopic mass of multiplying cells. This mass of cells slowly migrates along the mother's fallopian tube to the uterine cavity. On about the seventh day, the cell mass begins to implant itself in the uterine wall. This process takes about a week and is far from automatic. Many zygotes are rejected at this point. As many as one in five pregnancies end with the woman never being aware that conception has occurred (Simpson, 2002).

During the implantation process, the placenta begins to form (Buster & Carson, 2002). **The *placenta* is a structure that allows oxygen and nutrients to pass into the fetus from the mother's bloodstream, and bodily wastes to pass out to the mother.** This critical exchange takes place across thin membranes that block the passage of blood cells, keeping the fetal and maternal bloodstreams separate.

Embryonic Stage

The *embryonic stage* is the second stage of prenatal development, lasting from two weeks until the end of the second month. During this stage, most of the vital organs and bodily systems begin to form in the developing organism, which is now called an *embryo*. Structures such as the heart, spine, and brain emerge gradually as cell division becomes more specialized. Although the embryo is typically only about 2.5 cm long at the end of this stage, it's already beginning to look human. Arms, legs, hands, feet, fingers, toes, eyes, and ears are already discernible.

Prenatal development is remarkably rapid. (top left) This 30-day-old embryo is just 6 mm in length. (bottom left) At 14 weeks, the fetus is approximately 5 cm long. Note the well-developed fingers. The fetus can already move its legs, feet, hands, and head and displays a variety of basic reflexes. (right) After four months of prenatal development, facial features are beginning to emerge.

The embryonic stage is a period of great vulnerability because virtually all the basic physiological structures are being formed. If anything interferes with normal development during the embryonic phase, the effects can be devastating. Most miscarriages occur during this period (Simpson, 2002). Most major structural birth defects are also due to problems that occur during the embryonic stage (Mortensen, Sever, & Oakley, 1991; Simpson & Niebyl, 2002).

Fetal Stage

 9A

The *fetal stage* **is the third stage of prenatal development, lasting from two months through birth.** Some highlights of fetal development are summarized in Figure 11.1. The first two months of the fetal stage bring rapid bodily growth, as muscles and bones begin to form (Moore & Persaud, 2003). The developing organism, now called a *fetus,* becomes capable of physical movements as skeletal structures harden. Organs formed in the embryonic stage continue to grow and gradually begin to function. Sex organs start to develop during the third month.

During the final three months of the prenatal period, brain cells multiply at a brisk pace. A layer of fat is deposited under the skin to provide insulation, and the respiratory and digestive systems mature. All of these changes ready the fetus for life outside the cozy, supportive environment of its mother's womb. Sometime between 22 weeks and 26 weeks the fetus reaches **the *age of viability*—the age at which a baby can survive in the event of a premature birth.** The probability of survival is still pretty slim at 22 or 23 weeks, but it climbs steadily over the next month to an 85% survival rate at 26 to 28 weeks (Hack & Fanaroff, 1999; Iams, 2002).

Environmental Factors and Prenatal Development

Although the fetus develops in the protective buffer of the womb, events in the external environment can affect it indirectly through the mother. Because the developing organism and its mother are linked through the placenta, a mother's eating habits, drug use, and physical health, among other things, can affect prenatal development and have long-term health consequences (Hampton, 2004). Figure 11.2 shows the periods of prenatal development during which various structures are most vulnerable to damage.

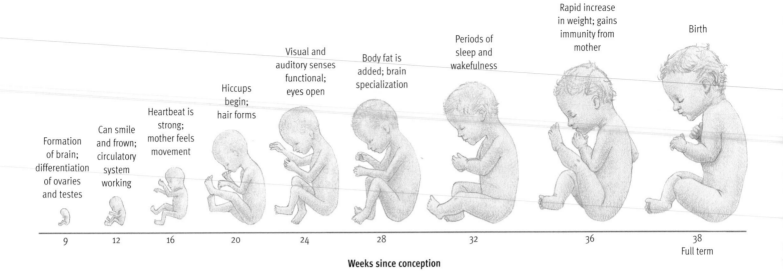

Formation of brain; differentiation of ovaries and testes

Can smile and frown; circulatory system working

Heartbeat is strong; mother feels movement

Hiccups begin; hair forms

Visual and auditory senses functional; eyes open

Body fat is added; brain specialization

Periods of sleep and wakefulness

Rapid increase in weight; gains immunity from mother

Birth

9   12   16   20   24   28   32   36   38
                                                Full term

Weeks since conception

Maternal Nutrition

Guidelines are available from Health Canada regarding eating habits designed to promote healthy maternal nutrition and for material weight gain during pregnancy (Health Canada, 2002a). Too much or too little weight gain during gestation is associated with a variety of birth complications, and guidelines for maternal weight gain are based on pre-pregnancy body mass index. Health Canada suggests that if expectant mothers follow Canada's Food Guide to Healthy Eating (available at **http://www.hc-sc.gc.ca/fn-an/food-guide-aliment/index_e.html**) and maintain a relatively active lifestyle, they should encounter few difficulties regarding weight and nutrition.

The developing fetus needs a variety of essential nutrients. Thus, it's not surprising that severe maternal malnutrition increases the risk of birth complications and neurological defects for the newborn (Coutts, 2000; Fifer, Monk, & Grose-Fifer, 2001). The effects of severe malnutrition are a major problem in underdeveloped nations where food shortages are common. The impact of moderate malnutrition, which is more common in modern societies, is more difficult to gauge, in part because maternal malnutrition is often confounded with other risk factors associated with poverty, such as drug abuse and limited access to health care (Worthington-Roberts & Klerman, 1990). Recent research suggests that prenatal malnutrition may have negative effects decades after a child's birth. For example, prenatal malnutrition has been linked to vulnerability to schizophrenia and other psychiatric disorders in adolescence and early adulthood (Susser, Brown, & Matte, 1999). And low birth weight is associated with an increased risk of heart disease and diabetes in middle adulthood (Forsen et al., 2000; Rich-Edwards et al., 1997). Although birth

weight is influenced by factors besides maternal nutrition (Osrin & Costello, 2000), these findings are alarming.

Maternal Drug Use

A major source of concern about fetal and infant well-being is the mother's consumption of drugs, including such widely used substances as tobacco and alcohol as well as prescription and recreational drugs. Unfortunately, most drugs consumed by a pregnant woman can pass through the membranes of the placenta.

Virtually all "recreational" drugs (see Chapter 5) can be harmful, with sedatives, narcotics, and cocaine being particularly dangerous. Babies of heroin users are born addicted to narcotics and have an increased

Figure 11.1

Overview of fetal development. This chart outlines some of the highlights of development during the fetal stage.

CONCEPT **CHECK 11.1**

Understanding the Stages of Prenatal Development

Check your understanding of the stages of prenatal development by filling in the blanks in the chart below. The first column contains descriptions of a main event from each of the three stages. In the second column, write the name of the stage; in the third column, write the term used to refer to the developing organism during that stage; and in the fourth column, write the time span (in terms of weeks or months) covered by the stage. The answers are in Appendix A at the back of the book.

Event	Stage	Term for organism	Time span
1. Uterine implantation	_____	_____	_____
2. Muscle and bone begin to form	_____	_____	_____
3. Vital organs and body systems begin to form	_____	_____	_____

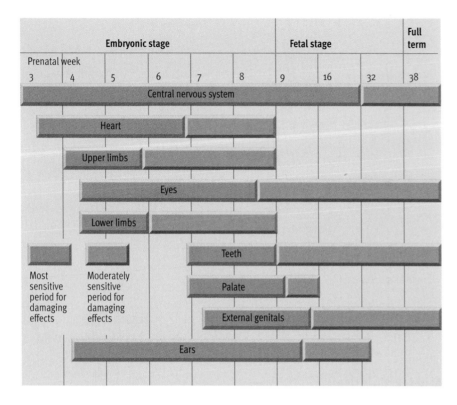

	Embryonic stage						Fetal stage		Full term

Prenatal week

3 | 4 | 5 | 6 | 7 | 8 | 9 | 16 | 32 | 38

Central nervous system

Heart

Upper limbs

Eyes

Lower limbs

Teeth

Palate

External genitals

Ears

Most sensitive period for damaging effects

Moderately sensitive period for damaging effects

Figure 11.2

Periods of vulnerability in prenatal development.

Generally, structures are most susceptible to damage when they are undergoing rapid development. The red regions of the bars indicate the most sensitive periods for various organs and structures, while the purple regions indicate periods of continued, but lessened, vulnerability. As a whole, sensitivity is greatest in the embryonic stage, but some structures remain vulnerable throughout prenatal development.

SOURCE: Adapted from Moore, K. L., & Persaud, T. V. N. (1998). *Before we are born: Essentials of embryology and birth defects.* Philadelphia: W. B. Saunders. Copyright © 1998 Elsevier Science (USA). All rights reserved. Reprinted by permission.

risk of early death due to prematurity, birth defects, respiratory difficulties, and problems associated with their addiction (Finnegan & Kandall, 2005). Prenatal exposure to cocaine is associated with increased risk of birth complications (Bendersky & Lewis, 1999) and a variety of cognitive deficits that are apparent in childhood (Singer et al., 2002, 2004). Peter Fried from Carleton University has conducted a program of research examining the effects of prenatal exposure to marijuana and other substances (Fried & Smith, 2001). He has found such exposure is associated with a variety of physical and cognitive effects. In a recent review of the available literature, he suggested that although the data is limited, it seems that prenatal marijuana exposure may be linked to disturbances in executive functioning associated with the prefrontal part of the brain at age three. These functions have been implicated in disturbances in attention/impulsivity and problem-solving domains.

Problems can also be caused by a great variety of drugs prescribed for legitimate medical reasons, and even some over-the-counter drugs (Niebyl, 2002). The impact of drugs on the embryo or fetus varies greatly depending on the drug, the dose, and the phase of prenatal development.

Alcohol consumption during pregnancy also carries risks. It has long been clear that heavy drinking by a mother can be hazardous to a fetus. *Fetal alcohol syndrome* is a collection of congenital (inborn)

problems associated with excessive alcohol use during pregnancy. Typical problems include microcephaly (a small head), heart defects, irritability, hyperactivity, and delayed mental and motor development (Hannigan & Armant, 2000). Fetal alcohol syndrome is one of the leading causes of mental retardation (Kaemingk & Paquette, 1999), and it is related to an increased incidence of depression, suicide, and criminal behaviour in adulthood (Kelly, Day, & Streissguth, 2000). Furthermore, there are many children who fall short of the criteria for fetal alcohol syndrome but still show serious impairments attributable to their mothers' drinking during pregnancy (Abel, 1998). Even normal social drinking during pregnancy can have enduring negative effects on children, including deficits in IQ, reaction time, motor skills, attention span, and math skills, and increased impulsive, antisocial, and delinquent behaviour (Hunt et al., 1995; Streissguth et al., 1989; Streissguth et al., 1999). There appears to be a correlation between the amount of alcohol that pregnant women consume and the severity of the damage inflicted on their offspring (Ott, Tarter, & Ammerman, 1999).

Tobacco use during pregnancy is also hazardous to prenatal development. Smoking produces a number of subtle physiological changes in the mother that appear to reduce the flow of oxygen and nutrients to the fetus. Pregnant women who smoke have an increased risk for miscarriage, stillbirth, prematurity, and other birth complications (Andres & Day, 2000). Maternal smoking may also increase a child's risk for sudden infant death syndrome (Fullilove & Dieudonne, 1997), slower than average cognitive development (Trasti et al., 1999), and attention deficit disorder (Linnet et al., 2003). Even maternal exposure to second-hand smoke may be dangerous to a fetus (Windham, Eaton, & Hopkins, 1999).

Maternal Illness

The fetus is largely defenceless against infections because its immune system matures relatively late in the prenatal period. The placenta screens out quite a number of infectious agents, but not all. Thus, many maternal illnesses can interfere with prenatal development. Diseases such as rubella (German measles), syphilis, cholera, smallpox, mumps, and even severe cases of the flu can be hazardous to the fetus (Duff, 2002). The nature of any damage depends, in part, on when the mother contracts the illness.

Genital herpes and acquired immune deficiency syndrome (AIDS) are two very deadly diseases that pregnant women can also transmit to their offspring. Genital herpes is typically transmitted during the birth process itself when newborns come into contact

Premature births and infant deaths are much more common than most people realize. Shown here is Wayne Weiten's son, born prematurely in September 1992, receiving postnatal treatment in a hospital intensive care unit. Although prematurity is associated with a variety of developmental problems, T. J., like a great many premature infants, has matured into a robust, healthy child (see page 317 for a picture of him at age 15 months).

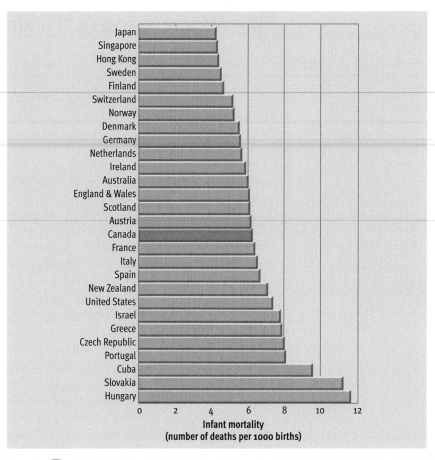

Figure 11.3

Cross-cultural comparisons of infant mortality. Infant mortality is the death rate per 1000 births during the first year of life. Canada ranks 16th in the prevention of infant mortality.

SOURCE: Adapted from Berk, L. E. (2002). *Infants, children, and adolescents.* Boston: Allyn & Bacon. Reprinted by permission.

with their mothers' genital lesions (Gosden, Nicolaides, & Whitting, 1994). Herpes can cause microcephaly, paralysis, deafness, blindness, and brain damage in infants and is fatal for many newborns (Ismail, 1993). The transmission of AIDS may occur prenatally through the placenta, during birth, or through breast-feeding (Eldred & Chaisson, 1996). About 20%–30% of pregnant women who carry the virus for AIDS pass the disease on to their babies (Nourse & Butler, 1998), although improved antiviral drugs can reduce this percentage considerably (Culnane et al., 1999).

Many of the prenatal dangers that we have discussed are preventable if pregnant women receive adequate care and guidance from health professionals. Good quality medical care that begins early in pregnancy is associated with reduced prematurity and higher survival rates for infants (Malloy, Kao, & Lee, 1992). Canada ranks 16th in the prevention of infant mortality (see Figure 11.3).

Science has a long way to go before it uncovers all the factors that shape development before birth. For example, the prenatal effects of fluctuations in maternal emotions are not well understood. Nonetheless, it's clear that critical developments unfold quickly during the prenatal period. In the next section, you'll learn that development continues at a fast pace during the early years of childhood. Of course, attention to maternal factors affecting the child's health continues after birth. For example, maternal nutrition continues to affect the newborn during the breast-feeding period. Currently, Health Canada recommends that exclusive breast-feeding be maintained up to six months, at which point the infant can be introduced

to nutrient-rich, solid foods. It is recommended that breast-feeding continue up to at least two years (Health Canada, 2004b).

REVIEW OF KEY POINTS

- Prenatal development proceeds through the germinal, embryonic, and fetal stages as the zygote is differentiated into a human organism. The embryonic stage is a period of great vulnerability, as most physiological structures are being formed.

- Maternal malnutrition during the prenatal period has been linked to birth complications and other subsequent problems. Maternal drug use can be very dangerous, although the risks depend on the drug used, the dose, and the phase of prenatal development.

- Fetal alcohol syndrome is a collection of congenital problems caused by a mother's excessive alcohol use during pregnancy. A variety of maternal illnesses can interfere with prenatal development.

- Genital herpes and AIDS can be transmitted to offspring during the birth process. Many problems can be avoided if expectant mothers have access to good health care.

The Wondrous Years of Childhood

PREVIEW QUESTIONS

- How uneven is physical growth during infancy?
- How important is maturation to motor development?
- How much does culture influence motor development?
- What is the difference between cross-sectional and longitudinal research?
- What kinds of temperaments have been observed in infancy?

A certain magic is associated with childhood. Young children have an extraordinary ability to captivate adults' attention, especially their parents'. Legions of parents apologize repeatedly to friends and strangers alike as they talk on and on about the cute things their kids do. Most wondrous of all are the rapid and momentous developmental changes of the childhood years. Helpless infants become curious toddlers almost overnight. Before parents can catch their breath, these toddlers are schoolchildren engaged in spirited play with young friends. Then, suddenly, they're insecure adolescents, worrying about dates, part-time jobs, cars, and university. The whirlwind transitions of childhood often seem miraculous.

Miraculous they are, but they should not be taken for granted. Developmental research not only allows us to map developmental trends and processes but also affords us the opportunity to provide supports for that development whenever possible. For example, one of the objectives of the well-known *Early Years Report*, produced under government mandate by Margaret Norrie McCain (New Brunswick's former lieutenant-governor) and McMaster University's Fred Mustard, was to review what we know about neuroscience and early child development and to make recommendations about how we can provide conditions in the home and in school settings that promote success for Canadian children (McCain & Mustard, 1999).

While the transformations that occur in childhood *seem* magical, they actually reflect an orderly, predictable, gradual progression. In this section you'll see what psychologists have learned about this progression. We'll examine various aspects of development that are especially dynamic during childhood. Language development is omitted from this section because we covered it in the chapter on language and thought (see Chapter 8). Let's begin by looking at motor development.

Exploring the World: Motor Development

One of the earliest topics studied by developmental psychologists was motor development. *Motor development* **refers to the progression of muscular coordination required for physical activities.** Basic motor skills include grasping and reaching for objects, manipulating objects, sitting up, crawling, walking, and running.

Basic Principles

A number of principles are apparent in motor development. One is **the *cephalocaudal trend*—the head-to-foot direction of motor development.** Children tend to gain control over the upper part of their bodies before the lower part. You've seen this trend in action if you've seen an infant learn to crawl. Infants gradually shift from using their arms for propelling themselves to using their legs. **The *proximodistal trend* is the centre-outward direction of motor development.** Children gain control over their torso before their extremities. Thus, infants initially reach for things by twisting their entire body, but gradually they learn to extend just their arms.

Early motor development depends in part on physical growth, which is not only rapid during infancy but apparently more uneven than previously appreciated. Infants typically grow to roughly triple their birth weight during the first year, while height increases by about 45% (Needlman, 2004). Until recently, it was assumed that this physical growth involved a gradual, steady process that yielded smooth, continuous growth curves. But improved research methods have demonstrated that early growth is actually very irregular. In a study of infants from birth to 21 months, Lampl, Veldhuis, and Johnson (1992) found that lengthy periods of no growth were punctuated by sudden bursts of growth. These growth spurts tended to be accompanied by restlessness and irritability. More research is needed to determine whether this pattern of episodic growth continues beyond infancy, but parents who sometimes feel that their children are changing overnight may not be imagining it!

Early progress in motor skills has traditionally been attributed almost entirely to the process of maturation. **Maturation is development that reflects the gradual unfolding of one's genetic blueprint.** It is a product of genetically programmed physical changes that come with age—as opposed to experience and learning. However, recent research that has taken a closer look at the *process* of motor development suggests that infants are active agents rather than passive organisms waiting for their brain and limbs to mature (Thelen, 1995). According to the new view, the driving force behind motor development is infants' ongoing exploration of their world and their need to master specific tasks (such as grasping a larger toy or looking out a window). Progress in motor development is attributed to infants' experimentation and their learning and

Web Link 11.1

PBS: The Whole Child

http://www.pbs.org/wholechild/

Coordinated with the videotape series of the same name, this Public Broadcasting System site assembles a broad collection of information for parents, caregivers, and others about the developing child from birth through age five. Resources include an interactive timeline of developmental milestones, reading lists, and a guide to other online sites dealing with child development.

Age (months)

remembering of the consequences of their activities. Although modern researchers acknowledge that maturation facilitates motor development, they argue that its contribution has been oversimplified and overestimated (Bertenthal & Clifton, 1998).

Understanding Developmental Norms

Parents often pay close attention to early motor development, comparing their child's progress with developmental norms. ***Developmental norms*** **indicate the median age at which individuals display various behaviours and abilities** (see Chapter 2 for a discussion of the median). For example, the generalizations that "average children" say their first word at about 12 months and start combining words into sentences at around 24 months are developmental norms. Developmental norms are useful benchmarks as long as parents don't expect their children to progress exactly at the pace specified in the norms.

Some parents get unnecessarily alarmed when their children fall behind developmental norms, but variations from the typical age of accomplishment are entirely normal. This normal variation stands out

in Figure 11.4, which shows norms for many basic motor skills. The left side, interior mark, and right side of the bars in the diagram indicate the ages at which 25%, 50%, and 90% of youngsters can demonstrate each motor skill. Typically, information on developmental norms includes only the median age of attainment indicated by the interior (50%) mark in each bar. This exclusive focus on the central tendency or typical progress fails to convey the immense variability seen in youngsters' development. As Figure 11.4 shows, a substantial portion of normal, healthy children often don't achieve a particular milestone until long after the median time cited in norms.

Cultural Variations and Their Significance

Cross-cultural research has highlighted the dynamic interplay between experience and maturation in motor development. Relatively rapid motor development has been observed in some cultures that provide special practice in basic motor skills. For example, the Kipsigis people of Kenya begin active efforts to train their infants to sit up, stand, and walk soon after birth. Thanks to this training, Kipsigis children achieve these developmental milestones (but not

Figure 11.4

Landmarks in motor development. The left edge, interior mark, and right edge of each bar indicate the age at which 25%, 50%, and 90% of infants have mastered each motor skill shown. Developmental norms typically report only the median age of mastery (the interior mark), which can be misleading in light of the variability in age of mastery apparent in this chart.

Tribes across the world use a variety of methods to foster rapid development of motor abilities in their children. The Kung San of the Kalahari, Botswana, teach their young to dance quite early, using poles to develop the kinesthetic sense of balance.

Web Link 11.2

Early Childhood Care and Development
http://www.ecdgroup.com/

This site's subtitle, International Resources for Early Childhood Development, emphasizes the focus of resources provided: the world-wide (not just North American) challenge of caring for children from birth through age six and fulfilling the needs of their families.

others) about a month earlier than babies in North America (Super, 1976). West Indian children in Jamaica also exhibit advanced motor development that has been linked to a special regimen of motor exercises practised in early infancy (Hopkins & Westra, 1988, 1990). In contrast, relatively slow motor development has been found in some cultures that discourage motor exploration. For example, among the Ache, a nomadic people living in the rain forests of Paraguay, safety concerns dictate that children under three rarely venture more than a metre from their mothers, who carry them virtually everywhere. As a result of these constraints, Ache children are delayed in acquiring a variety of motor skills and typically begin walking about a year later than other children (Kaplan & Dove, 1987).

Cultural variations in the emergence of basic motor skills demonstrate that environmental factors can accelerate or slow early motor development. Nonetheless, the similarities across cultures in the sequence and timing of early motor development outweigh the differences. This fact suggests that *early* motor development depends to a considerable extent on maturation. *Later* motor development is another matter, however. As children in any culture grow older, they acquire more specialized motor skills, some of which may be unique to their culture. Maturation becomes less influential and experience becomes more critical. Obviously, maturation by itself will never lead to the development of ballet or football skills, for example, without exposure to appropriate training.

Easy and Difficult Babies: Differences in Temperament

Infants show considerable variability in temperament. *Temperament* **refers to characteristic mood, activity level, and emotional reactivity.** From the very beginning, some babies seem animated and cheerful while others seem sluggish and ornery. Infants show consistent differences in emotional tone, tempo of activity, and sensitivity to environmental stimuli very early in life (Rothbart & Bates, 1998).

Alexander Thomas and Stella Chess have conducted a major *longitudinal* study of the development of temperament (Thomas & Chess, 1977, 1989; Thomas, Chess, & Birch, 1970). **In a** *longitudinal design* **investigators observe one group of participants repeatedly over a period of time.** This approach to the study of development is often contrasted with the cross-sectional approach (the logic of both approaches is diagrammed in Figure 11.5). **In a** *cross-sectional design* **investigators compare groups of participants of differing age at a single point in time.** For example, in a cross-sectional study an investigator tracing the growth of children's vocabulary might compare 50 six-year-olds, 50 eight-year-olds, and 50 ten-year-olds. In contrast, an investigator using the longitudinal method would assemble one group of 50 six-year-olds and measure their vocabulary at age six, again at age eight, and once more at age ten.

Each method has its advantages and disadvantages. Cross-sectional studies can be completed more quickly, easily, and cheaply than longitudinal studies, which often extend over many years. And when a longitudinal study takes years to complete, participants often drop out because they move away or lose interest. However, longitudinal designs tend to be more sensitive to developmental influences and changes than cross-sectional designs (Magnusson & Stattin, 1998).

To some extent, the choice of a research design to investigate development depends on what the investigators want to learn about. Thomas and Chess wanted to learn about the long-term stability of children's temperaments. Given this goal, they needed to follow the same children in a longitudinal study to assess their temperamental stability over time. They began their study in 1956 with a group of 141 middle-class children. In 1961 they added a second group of 95 children of working-class parents. They have tracked the development of most of these subjects into adolescence and adulthood.

Thomas and Chess found that "temperamental individuality is well established by the time the

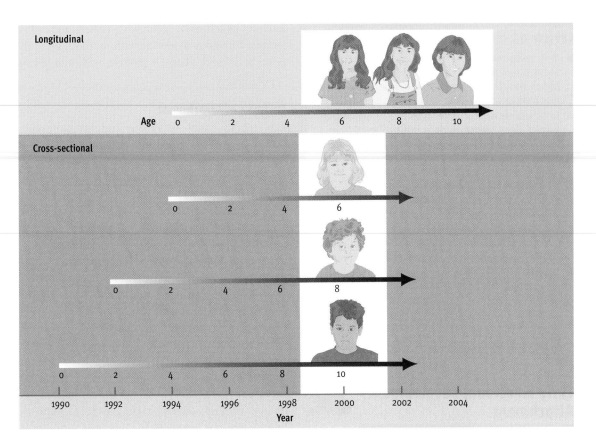

Figure 11.5

Longitudinal versus cross-sectional research. In a longitudinal study of development between ages six and ten, the same children would be observed at six, again at eight, and again at ten. In a cross-sectional study of the same age span, a group of six-year-olds, a group of eight-year-olds, and a group of ten-year-olds would be compared simultaneously. Note that data collection could be completed immediately in the cross-sectional study, whereas the longitudinal study would require four years to complete.

infant is two to three months old" (Thomas & Chess, 1977, p. 153). They identified three basic styles of temperament that were apparent in most of the children. About 40% of the youngsters were *easy children* who tended to be happy, regular in sleep and eating, adaptable, and not readily upset. Another 15% were *slow-to-warm-up children* who tended to be less cheery, less regular in their sleep and eating, and slower in adapting to change. These children were wary of new experiences, and their emotional reactivity was moderate. *Difficult children* constituted 10% of the group. They tended to be glum, erratic in sleep and eating, resistant to change, and relatively irritable. The remaining 35% of the children showed mixtures of these three temperaments.

A child's temperament at three months was a fair predictor of the child's temperament at age ten. Infants categorized as "difficult" developed more emotional problems requiring counselling than other children did. Although basic changes in temperament were seen in some children, temperament was generally stable over time (Chess & Thomas, 1996).

Some critics have expressed concern because Thomas and Chess's data were based on parents' highly subjective ratings of their children's temperament (Mebert, 1991). But other investigators, who

have used a variety of methods to assess infant temperament, have also found it to be fairly stable (Rothbart, Ahadi, & Evans, 2000; Sanson, Hemphill, & Smart, 2002), although the evidence indicates that temperament tends to stabilize a little later (around age one or two) than Thomas and Chess suggested (Lemery et al., 1999).

One prominent example of contemporary research on temperament is the work of Jerome Kagan and his colleagues, who have relied on direct observations of children in their studies of temperament (Kagan & Snidman, 1991; Kagan, Snidman, & Arcus, 1992). They have found that about 15%–20% of infants display an *inhibited temperament* characterized by shyness, timidity, and wariness of unfamiliar people, objects, and events. In contrast, about 25%–30% of infants exhibit an *uninhibited temperament*. These children are less restrained, approaching unfamiliar people, objects, and events with little trepidation. Evidence suggests that these temperamental styles have a genetic basis and that they are reasonably stable into middle childhood (Kagan, 2004; Kagan, Reznick, & Snidman, 1999). Research also indicates that about one-third of those who exhibit an inhibited temperament in their second year of life develop problems with anxiety during their adolescent years (Kagan & Snidman, 1999).

Erik Hesse

"Where familial security is lacking, the individual is handicapped by the lack of what might be called a secure base from which to work."
MARY SALTER AINSWORTH

PREVIEW QUESTIONS

- What are the three patterns of attachment seen in infants?
- Does daycare disrupt attachment processes?
- What kinds of cultural variations have been observed in attachment patterns?
- What is the evolutionary significance of attachment patterns?
- What do stage theories have in common?
- How did Erikson explain personality development?
- What are the strengths and weaknesses of Erikson's theory?

REVIEW OF KEY POINTS

- Motor development follows cephalocaudal (head-to-foot) and proximodistal (centre-outward) trends and depends in part on physical growth, which appears to be more uneven than previously appreciated.

- Early motor development depends on both maturation and learning. Developmental norms for motor skills and other types of development are only group averages, and parents should not be alarmed if their children's progress does not match these norms exactly. Cultural variations in the pacing of motor development demonstrate the importance of learning.

- Cross-sectional and longitudinal studies are both well suited to developmental research. Cross-sectional studies are quicker, easier, and less expensive to conduct. Longitudinal studies are more sensitive to developmental changes.

- Temperamental differences among children are apparent during the first few months of life. Thomas and Chess found that most infants could be classified as easy, slow-to-warm-up, or difficult children. These differences in temperament are fairly stable and probably have a genetic basis.

Early Emotional Development: Attachment 9B

Do mothers and infants forge lasting emotional bonds in the first few hours after birth? Do early emotional bonds affect later development? These are just some of the questions investigated by psychologists interested in attachment. **Attachment refers to the close, emotional bonds of affection that develop between infants and their caregivers.** Researchers have shown a keen interest in how infant–mother attachments are formed early in life. Children eventually may form attachments to many people, including their fathers, grandparents, and others (Cassidy, 1999). However, a child's first important attachment usually occurs with his or her mother because in most cultures she is the principal caregiver, especially in the early years of life (Lamb et al., 1999).

Contrary to popular belief, infants' attachment to their mothers is *not* instantaneous. Initially, babies show little in the way of a special preference for their mothers. They can be handed over to strangers such as babysitters with relatively little difficulty. This situation typically changes at around six to eight months of age, when infants begin to show a preference for their mother's company and often protest when separated from her (Lamb, Ketterlinus, & Fracasso, 1992). This is the first manifestation of *separation anxiety*—emotional distress seen in many infants when they are separated from people with whom they have formed an attachment. Separation anxiety, which may occur with fathers and other familiar caregivers as well as with mothers, typically peaks at around 14 to 18 months and then begins to decline.

Patterns of Attachment

Research by Mary Ainsworth and her colleagues (Ainsworth, 1979; Ainsworth et al., 1978) suggests that attachment emerges out of a complex interplay between infant and mother. (You may recall that Mary Ainsworth was one of the three women pioneers in Canadian psychology profiled in Chapter 1.) Studies reveal that mothers who are sensitive and responsive to their children's needs tend to evoke more secure attachments than mothers who are relatively insensitive or inconsistent in their responding (Isabella, 1995; van den Boom, 1994). However, the correlation between maternal sensitivity and attachment security is modest, so other factors must also be involved (de Wolff & van IJzendoorn, 1997). One obvious factor is that infants are not passive bystanders as this process unfolds. They are active participants who influence the process with their crying, smiling, fussing, and babbling. Difficult infants who are prone to distress, spit up most of their food, make bathing a major battle, refuse to go to sleep, and rarely smile may sometimes undermine a mother's responsiveness (Mangelsdorf et al., 1990).

Infant–mother attachments vary in quality. Ainsworth and her colleagues (1978) found that these attachments follow three patterns (see Figure 11.6). Fortunately, most infants develop a *secure attachment*. They play and explore comfortably with their mother present, become visibly upset when she leaves, and are quickly calmed by her return. However, some children display a pattern called *anxious-ambivalent attachment*. They appear anxious even when their mother is near and protest excessively when she leaves, but they are not particularly comforted when she returns. Children in the third category seek little contact with their mother and often are not distressed when she leaves, a condition labelled *avoidant attachment*. The type of attachment that emerges between an infant and mother may depend in part on the infant's temperament (Seifer et al., 1996). Although the correlations between infant temperament and attachment security are modest, the evidence suggests that insecure (ambivalent or avoidant) attachments occur more often with temperamentally difficult infants who are fussy, fretful, and irritable (Vaughn & Bost, 1999). Some interesting (albeit modest) correlations have also been noted between parents' marital quality and infants' attachment security. Secure attachments are somewhat more

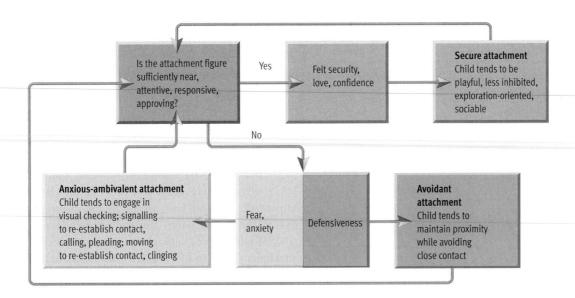

| Is the attachment figure sufficiently near, attentive, responsive, approving? | Yes → | Felt security, love, confidence | → | **Secure attachment** Child tends to be playful, less inhibited, exploration-oriented, sociable |

No

| **Anxious-ambivalent attachment** Child tends to engage in visual checking; signalling to re-establish contact, calling, pleading; moving to re-establish contact, clinging | ← | Fear, anxiety | Defensiveness | **Avoidant attachment** Child tends to maintain proximity while avoiding close contact |

Figure 11.6

Overview of the attachment process. The unfolding of attachment depends on the interaction between a mother (or other caregiver) and an infant. Research by Mary Ainsworth and others suggests that attachment relations fall into three categories—secure, avoidant, and anxious-ambivalent—which depend on how sensitive and responsive caregivers are to their children's needs. The feedback loops shown in the diagram reflect the fact that babies are not passive bystanders in the attachment drama; their reactions to caregivers can affect the caregivers' behaviour.

SOURCE: From Weber, A. & Harvey, J.H. *Perspectives on Close Relationships*. Published by Allyn and Bacon, Boston, MA. Copyright © 1994 by Pearson Education. Adapted by permission of the publisher.

likely in homes where parents are happy with each other, probably because marital satisfaction fosters maternal sensitivity (Belsky, 1990, 1999a).

Effects of Secure Attachment

 9B

Clearly, some children have stronger attachments to their mothers than other children do. Evidence suggests that the quality of these attachment relationships can have important consequences for children. Infants with a relatively secure attachment tend to become resilient, competent toddlers with high self-esteem (Goldsmith & Harman, 1994). In their preschool years, they exhibit more persistence, curiosity, self-reliance, and leadership and have better peer relations (Weinfeld et al., 1999), while experiencing fewer negative emotions and more positive emotions (Kochanska, 2001). In middle childhood they display better social skills and have richer friendship networks than youngsters who lacked a

Infant–mother attachments vary in strength and quality and these variations in attachment relations may have long-lasting repercussions. In this picture, Doug McCann's son Harry is seen interacting with his mother.

secure attachment during infancy (Elicker, Englund, & Sroufe, 1992; Schneider, Atkinson, & Tardif, 2001). Furthermore, research suggests that children who have a secure attachment to *both* their parents are better off than those who have a secure attachment to only one parent (Cabrera et al., 2000). However, it is worth noting that all the relevant data on attachment effects are correlational (experimenters cannot manipulate caregiver–infant attachments), so we cannot assume that secure attachment *causes* all these favourable outcomes. Secure attachment could co-vary with other important factors that contribute to high self-esteem, self-reliance, and so forth.

The repercussions of attachment patterns in infancy appear to even reach into adulthood. In Chapter 16 we'll discuss thought-provoking evidence that infant attachment patterns set the tone for people's romantic relationships in adulthood, not to mention their gender roles, religious beliefs, and patterns of self-disclosure (Feeney, 1999; Kirkpatrick, 1999; Shaver & Hazan, 1993, 1994; Shaver & Mikulincer, 2005).

Daycare and Attachment

The impact of daycare on attachment is the subject of heated debate. The crucial question is whether frequent infant–mother separations might disrupt the attachment process. The issue is an important one, given that over 50% of children under age five receive some nonmaternal child-care, and the rate increased significantly between 1994 (42%) and 2001 (53%) (Statistics Canada, 2005g). Table 11.1 shows that the average number of hours spent in daycare varies across the country. In 2004, the federal government promised to institute a national daycare strategy and to commit future funding to this effort.

Table 11.1 Daycare in Canada

	1994–95	2000–01
Canada	27.0	27.3
Newfoundland and Labrador	26.3	27.5
Prince Edward Island	30.0	31.5
Nova Scotia	29.3	26.7
New Brunswick	27.6	29.1
Quebec	28.5	30.6
Ontario	27.3	27.1
Manitoba	24.9	26.0
Saskatchewan	25.2	25.5
Alberta	25.9	24.9
British Columbia	23.7	22.3

Source: Statistics Canada. Child Care. *The Daily*, February 7, 2005, http://www.statcan.ca/Daily/English/050207/d050207b.htm, Retrieved October 4, 2005. Adapted from the Statistics Canada publication, *The Daily*, Child care, catalogue 11-001, Monday February 7, 2005.

What does the research tell us about the effects of such child-care experiences? Jay Belsky (1988, 1992) suggests that babies who receive nonmaternal care for more than 20 hours per week have an increased risk of developing insecure attachments to their mothers. Belsky's findings have raised many eyebrows, but they need to be put in perspective. First, even the most "alarming" data suggest that the proportion of daycare infants who exhibit insecure attachments is only slightly higher than the norm in North American society and even lower than the norm in some other societies (Lamb, Sternberg, & Prodromidis, 1992). Second, the preponderance of evidence suggests that daycare is *not* harmful to children's attachment relationships (Booth et al., 2002; Lamb, 1998), including the evidence from a recent ten-site U.S. study that has been characterized as the "most rigorous, and most systematic evaluation of day care ever undertaken" (Rutter & O'Connor, 1999, p. 828). Third, given the deprived childrearing conditions found in many homes, there is evidence that daycare can have *beneficial effects* on some youngsters' social development (Andersson, 1992; Egeland & Hiester, 1995).

Table 11.2 Patterns of Attachment (%) from Three Different Cultures

Country (Study)	Avoidant	Secure	Anxious-Ambivalent
United States (Ainsworth et al., 1978)	21	67	12
Germany (Grossmann et al., 1981)	52	35	13
Japan (Takahashi, 1986)	0	68	32

Source: Cole, M. (1999). Culture in development. In M. H. Bornstein & M. E. Lamb (Eds.), *Developmental psychology: An advanced textbook*. Mahwah, NJ: Erlbaum. Copyright © 1999 Lawrence Erlbaum Associates. Reprinted by permission.

Culture and Attachment

Separation anxiety emerges in children at about six to eight months and peaks at about 14 to 18 months in cultures around the world (Grossmann & Grossmann, 1990). These findings, which have been replicated in quite a variety of non-Western cultures, suggest that attachment is a universal feature of human development (van IJzendoorn & Sagi, 1999). However, studies have found some interesting cultural variations in the proportion of infants who fall into the three attachment categories described by Ainsworth. Working with white, middle-class subjects in the United States, Ainsworth and colleagues (1978) found that 67% of infants displayed a secure attachment, 12% an anxious-ambivalent attachment, and 21% an avoidant attachment. As Table 11.2 shows, studies in Germany and Japan have yielded very different figures (Cole, 1999). Avoidant attachments were far more common in the German sample but were nonexistent in the Japanese sample, which yielded more anxious-ambivalent attachments than the U.S. sample.

Researchers have attributed these disparities in attachment patterns to cultural variations in child-rearing practices (Greenfield & Suzuki, 1998). Some critics have argued that cultural disparities in attachment processes have been underestimated by Western researchers who have exhibited an ethnocentric slant in their cross-cultural investigations (Rothbaum et al., 2000). These critics assert that there are significant cultural variations in what represents a secure parent–child attachment and in the effects of secure attachment. The validity of this criticism is currently the subject of vigorous debate (Chao, 2001; Kondo-Ikemura, 2001; Posada & Jacobs, 2001).

Evolutionary Perspectives on Attachment

Attachment theory has had an evolutionary slant from its very beginning, long before evolutionary theory became influential in psychology. John Bowlby (1969, 1973, 1980), who originated the concept of attachment, analyzed attachment in terms of its *survival value* for infants. In contrast, contemporary evolutionary theorists emphasize how attachment contributes to parents' and children's *reproductive fitness* (Belsky, Steinberg, & Draper, 1991; Chisholm, 1996; Simpson, 1999). For example, contemporary theorists point out that if parents expect to pass their genes on to future generations, they need to raise their offspring to reproductive age and help them develop the social maturity required for successful mating. Parent–child attachments make crucial contributions to these outcomes by fostering social and emotional development in children (Kobak, 1999).

Becoming Unique: Personality Development

How do individuals develop their unique constellations of personality traits over time? Many theories have addressed this question. The first major theory of personality development was put together by Sigmund Freud back around 1900. As we'll discuss in Chapter 12, he claimed that the basic foundation of an individual's personality is firmly laid down by age five. Half a century later, Erik Erikson (1963) proposed a sweeping revision of Freud's theory that has proven influential. Like Freud, Erikson concluded that events in early childhood leave a permanent stamp on adult personality. However, unlike Freud, Erikson theorized that personality continues to evolve over the entire life span.

Building on Freud's earlier work, Erikson devised a stage theory of personality development. As you'll see in reading this chapter, many theories describe development in terms of stages. **A *stage* is a developmental period during which characteristic patterns of behaviour are exhibited and certain capacities become established.** Stage theories assume that (1) individuals must progress through specified stages in a particular order because each stage builds on the previous stage, (2) progress through these stages is strongly related to age, and (3) development is marked by major discontinuities that usher in dramatic transitions in behaviour (see Figure 11.7).

Erikson's Stage Theory

Erikson partitioned the life span into eight stages, each of which brings a *psychosocial crisis* involving transitions in important social relationships. According to Erikson, personality is shaped by how individuals deal with these psychosocial crises. Each crisis involves a struggle between two opposing tendencies, such as trust versus mistrust or initiative versus guilt, both of which are experienced by the person. Erikson described the stages in terms of these antagonistic tendencies, which represent personality traits that people display in varying degrees over the remainder of their lives. Although the names for Erikson's stages suggest either–or outcomes, he viewed each stage as a tug of war that determined the subsequent *balance* between opposing polarities in personality. All eight stages in Erikson's theory are charted in Figure 11.8. We describe the first four childhood

(a) Continuous development   **(b) Discontinuous development (stages)**

Figure 11.7

Stage theories of development. Some theories view development as a relatively continuous process, albeit not as smooth and perfectly linear as depicted on the left. In contrast, stage theories assume that development is marked by major discontinuities (as shown on the right) that bring fundamental, qualitative changes in capabilities or characteristic behaviour.

Figure 11.8

Erikson's stage theory. Erikson's theory of personality development posits that people evolve through eight stages over the life span. Each stage is marked by a *psychosocial crisis* that involves confronting a fundamental question, such as "Who am I and where am I going?" The stages are described in terms of alternative traits that are potential outcomes from the crises. Development is enhanced when a crisis is resolved in favour of the healthier alternative (which is listed first for each stage).

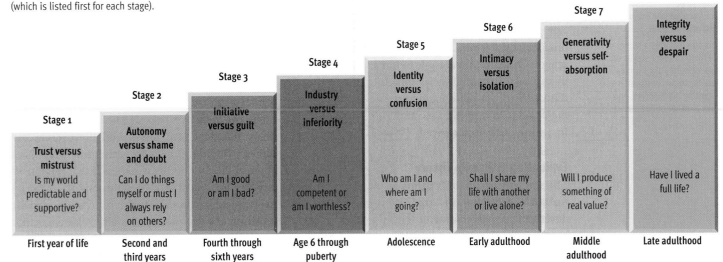

Stage	Crisis	Question	Age
Stage 1	Trust versus mistrust	Is my world predictable and supportive?	First year of life
Stage 2	Autonomy versus shame and doubt	Can I do things myself or must I always rely on others?	Second and third years
Stage 3	Initiative versus guilt	Am I good or am I bad?	Fourth through sixth years
Stage 4	Industry versus inferiority	Am I competent or am I worthless?	Age 6 through puberty
Stage 5	Identity versus confusion	Who am I and where am I going?	Adolescence
Stage 6	Intimacy versus isolation	Shall I share my life with another or live alone?	Early adulthood
Stage 7	Generativity versus self-absorption	Will I produce something of real value?	Middle adulthood
Stage 8	Integrity versus despair	Have I lived a full life?	Late adulthood

that transitional ages may vary, but he was convinced that all children progress through the stages of cognitive development in the same order.

Noting that children actively explore the world around them, Piaget asserted that interaction with the environment and maturation gradually alter the way children think. According to Piaget, children progress in their thinking through the complementary processes of assimilation and accommodation. *Assimilation involves interpreting new experiences in terms of existing mental structures without changing them.* In contrast, *accommodation* **involves changing existing mental structures to explain new experiences.** Accommodation and assimilation often occur interactively. For instance, a child who has learned to call four-legged pets "puppies" may apply this scheme the first time she encounters a cat (assimilation), but she will eventually discover that puppies and cats are different types of animals and make adjustments to her mental schemes (accommodation). With the companion processes of assimilation and accommodation in mind, let's turn now to the four stages in Piaget's theory.

Sensorimotor Period One of Piaget's foremost contributions was to greatly enhance our understanding of mental development in the earliest months of life. The first stage in his theory is the *sensorimotor period*, which lasts from birth to about age two. Piaget called this stage *sensorimotor* because infants are developing the ability to coordinate their sensory input with their motor actions.

The major development during the sensorimotor stage is the gradual appearance of symbolic thought. At the beginning of this stage, a child's behaviour is dominated by innate reflexes. But by the end of the stage, the child can use mental symbols to represent objects (e.g., a mental image of a favourite toy). The key to this transition is the acquisition of the concept of object permanence.

Object permanence **develops when a child recognizes that objects continue to exist even when they are no longer visible.** Although you surely take the permanence of objects for granted, infants aren't aware of this permanence at first. If you show a four-month-old an eye-catching toy and then cover the toy with a pillow, the child will not attempt to search for the toy. Piaget inferred from this observation that the child does not understand that the toy continues to exist under the pillow. The notion of object permanence does not dawn on children overnight. The first signs of this insight usually appear between four and eight months of age, when children will often pursue an object that is *partially* covered in their presence. Progress is gradual, and Piaget believed that children typically don't master the concept of object permanence until they're about 18 months old.

Preoperational Period During the *preoperational period*, which extends roughly from age two to age seven, children gradually improve in their use of mental images. Although progress in symbolic thought continues, Piaget emphasized the *shortcomings* in preoperational thought.

Consider a simple problem that Piaget presented to youngsters. He would take two identical beakers and fill each with the same amount of water. After a child had agreed that the two beakers contained the same amount of water, he would pour the water from one of the beakers into a much taller and thinner beaker (see Figure 11.10). He would then ask the child whether the two differently shaped beakers still contained the same amount of water. Confronted with a problem like this, children in the preoperational period generally said no. They typically focused on the higher water line in the taller beaker and insisted that there was more water in the slender beaker. They had not yet mastered the principle of conservation. *Conservation* **is Piaget's term for the awareness that physical quantities remain constant in spite of changes in their shape or appearance.**

Why are preoperational children unable to solve conservation problems? According to Piaget, their inability to understand conservation is due to some basic flaws in preoperational thinking. These flaws include centration, irreversibility, and egocentrism.

Centration **is the tendency to focus on just one feature of a problem, neglecting other important aspects.** When working on the conservation problem with water, preoperational children tend to concentrate on the height of the water while ignoring the width. They have difficulty focusing on several aspects of a problem at once.

"It is virtually impossible to draw a clear line between innate and acquired behavior patterns."
JEAN PIAGET

Figure 11.10

Piaget's conservation task.
After watching the transformation shown, a preoperational child will usually answer that the taller beaker contains more water. In contrast, the child in the concrete operational period tends to respond correctly, recognizing that the amount of water in beaker C remains the same as the amount in beaker A.

Step 1
The child agrees that beakers A and B contain the same amount of water.

B

Step 2
The child observes as the water from beaker B is poured into beaker C, which is shaped differently.

Step 3
The child is asked: "Do beakers A and C contain the same amount of water?"

A   B   C   A   C

theories of development. This shortcoming surfaces again in the next section, where we'll examine Jean Piaget's stage theory of cognitive development.

- Infants' attachments to their caregivers develop gradually. Separation anxiety usually appears around six to eight months of age. Research shows that attachment emerges out of an interplay between infant and mother. Infant–mother attachments fall into three categories: secure, anxious-ambivalent, and avoidant. A secure attachment fosters self-esteem, persistence, curiosity, and self-reliance, among other desirable traits.

- Bonding during the first few hours after birth does not appear to be crucial to secure attachment. The effects of daycare on attachment are a source of concern, but the evidence is hotly debated. Cultural variations in childrearing can affect the patterns of attachment seen in a society.

- A stage is a developmental period during which characteristic patterns of behaviour are exhibited. Stage theories assume that individuals must progress through a series of specified stages in a particular order and that development is marked by major discontinuities.

- Erik Erikson's theory of personality development proposes that individuals evolve through eight stages over the life span. In each stage the person wrestles with two opposing tendencies evoked by that stage's psychosocial crisis.

Figure 11.9

Piaget's stage theory. Piaget's theory of cognitive development identifies four stages marked by fundamentally different modes of thinking through which youngsters evolve. The approximate age norms and some key characteristics of thought at each stage are summarized here.

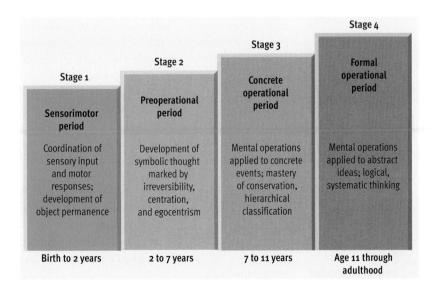

The Growth of Thought: Cognitive Development 9D

***Cognitive development* refers to transitions in youngsters' patterns of thinking, including reasoning, remembering, and problem solving.** The investigation of cognitive development was dominated in most of the second half of the 20th century by the theory of Jean Piaget (Kessen, 1996). Much of our discussion of cognitive development is devoted to Piaget's theory and the research it generated, although we'll also delve into other approaches to cognitive development.

Overview of Piaget's Stage Theory 9D

Jean Piaget (1929, 1952, 1983) was an interdisciplinary scholar whose own cognitive development was exceptionally rapid. In his early 20s, after he had earned a doctorate in natural science and published a novel, Piaget's interest turned to psychology. He met Theodore Simon, who had collaborated with Alfred Binet in devising the first useful intelligence tests (see Chapter 9). Working in Simon's Paris laboratory, Piaget administered intelligence tests to many children to develop better test norms. In doing this testing, Piaget became intrigued by the reasoning underlying the children's *wrong* answers. He decided that measuring children's intelligence was less interesting than studying how children *use* their intelligence. In 1921 he moved to Geneva, where he spent the rest of his life studying cognitive development. Many of his ideas were based on insights gleaned from careful observations of his own three children during their infancy.

Like Erikson's theory, Piaget's model is a *stage theory* of development. Piaget proposed that youngsters progress through four major stages of cognitive development, which are characterized by fundamentally different thought processes: (1) the *sensorimotor period* (birth to age two), (2) the *preoperational period* (ages two to seven), (3) the *concrete operational period* (ages seven to 11), and (4) the *formal operational period* (age 11 onward). Figure 11.9 provides an overview of each of these periods. Piaget regarded his age norms as approximations and acknowledged

PREVIEW QUESTIONS

- What are Piaget's four major stages of cognitive development?
- What are the chief developments in each stage?
- What are the strengths and weaknesses of Piaget's theory?
- Why do some theorists believe that infants have innate cognitive abilities?
- How does children's understanding of mental states progress?
- What are Kohlberg's stages of moral development?
- What are the strengths and weaknesses of Kohlberg's theory?

that transitional ages may vary, but he was convinced that all children progress through the stages of cognitive development in the same order.

Noting that children actively explore the world around them, Piaget asserted that interaction with the environment and maturation gradually alter the way children think. According to Piaget, children progress in their thinking through the complementary processes of assimilation and accommodation. **Assimilation involves interpreting new experiences in terms of existing mental structures without changing them.** In contrast, **accommodation involves changing existing mental structures to explain new experiences.** Accommodation and assimilation often occur interactively. For instance, a child who has learned to call four-legged pets "puppies" may apply this scheme the first time she encounters a cat (assimilation), but she will eventually discover that puppies and cats are different types of animals and make adjustments to her mental schemes (accommodation). With the companion processes of assimilation and accommodation in mind, let's turn now to the four stages in Piaget's theory.

Sensorimotor Period One of Piaget's foremost contributions was to greatly enhance our understanding of mental development in the earliest months of life. The first stage in his theory is the *sensorimotor period*, which lasts from birth to about age two. Piaget called this stage *sensorimotor* because infants are developing the ability to coordinate their sensory input with their motor actions.

The major development during the sensorimotor stage is the gradual appearance of symbolic thought. At the beginning of this stage, a child's behaviour is dominated by innate reflexes. But by the end of the stage, the child can use mental symbols to represent objects (e.g., a mental image of a favourite toy). The key to this transition is the acquisition of the concept of object permanence.

Object permanence develops when a child recognizes that objects continue to exist even when they are no longer visible. Although you surely take the permanence of objects for granted, infants aren't aware of this permanence at first. If you show a four-month-old an eye-catching toy and then cover the toy with a pillow, the child will not attempt to search for the toy. Piaget inferred from this observation that the child does not understand that the toy continues to exist under the pillow. The notion of object permanence does not dawn on children overnight. The first signs of this insight usually appear between four and eight months of age, when children will often pursue an object that is *partially* covered in their presence. Progress is gradual, and Piaget believed that children typically don't master the concept of object permanence until they're about 18 months old.

Preoperational Period During the *preoperational period*, which extends roughly from age two to age seven, children gradually improve in their use of mental images. Although progress in symbolic thought continues, Piaget emphasized the *shortcomings* in preoperational thought.

Consider a simple problem that Piaget presented to youngsters. He would take two identical beakers and fill each with the same amount of water. After a child had agreed that the two beakers contained the same amount of water, he would pour the water from one of the beakers into a much taller and thinner beaker (see Figure 11.10). He would then ask the child whether the two differently shaped beakers still contained the same amount of water. Confronted with a problem like this, children in the preoperational period generally said no. They typically focused on the higher water line in the taller beaker and insisted that there was more water in the slender beaker. They had not yet mastered the principle of conservation. **Conservation is Piaget's term for the awareness that physical quantities remain constant in spite of changes in their shape or appearance.**

Why are preoperational children unable to solve conservation problems? According to Piaget, their inability to understand conservation is due to some basic flaws in preoperational thinking. These flaws include centration, irreversibility, and egocentrism.

Centration is the tendency to focus on just one feature of a problem, neglecting other important aspects. When working on the conservation problem with water, preoperational children tend to concentrate on the height of the water while ignoring the width. They have difficulty focusing on several aspects of a problem at once.

"It is virtually impossible to draw a clear line between innate and acquired behavior patterns."
JEAN PIAGET

Figure 11.10

Piaget's conservation task.
After watching the transformation shown, a preoperational child will usually answer that the taller beaker contains more water. In contrast, the child in the concrete operational period tends to respond correctly, recognizing that the amount of water in beaker C remains the same as the amount in beaker A.

Step 1
The child agrees that beakers A and B contain the same amount of water.

Step 2
The child observes as the water from beaker B is poured into beaker C, which is shaped differently.

Step 3
The child is asked: "Do beakers A and C contain the same amount of water?"

Becoming Unique: Personality Development

How do individuals develop their unique constellations of personality traits over time? Many theories have addressed this question. The first major theory of personality development was put together by Sigmund Freud back around 1900. As we'll discuss in Chapter 12, he claimed that the basic foundation of an individual's personality is firmly laid down by age five. Half a century later, Erik Erikson (1963) proposed a sweeping revision of Freud's theory that has proven influential. Like Freud, Erikson concluded that events in early childhood leave a permanent stamp on adult personality. However, unlike Freud, Erikson theorized that personality continues to evolve over the entire life span.

Building on Freud's earlier work, Erikson devised a stage theory of personality development. As you'll see in reading this chapter, many theories describe development in terms of stages. **A *stage* is a developmental period during which characteristic patterns of behaviour are exhibited and certain capacities become established.** Stage theories assume that (1) individuals must progress through specified stages in a particular order because each stage builds on the previous stage, (2) progress through these stages is strongly related to age, and (3) development is marked by major discontinuities that usher in dramatic transitions in behaviour (see Figure 11.7).

Erikson's Stage Theory

Erikson partitioned the life span into eight stages, each of which brings a *psychosocial crisis* involving transitions in important social relationships. According to Erikson, personality is shaped by how individuals deal with these psychosocial crises. Each crisis involves a struggle between two opposing tendencies, such as trust versus mistrust or initiative versus guilt, both of which are experienced by the person. Erikson described the stages in terms of these antagonistic tendencies, which represent personality traits that people display in varying degrees over the remainder of their lives. Although the names for Erikson's stages suggest either–or outcomes, he viewed each stage as a tug of war that determined the subsequent *balance* between opposing polarities in personality. All eight stages in Erikson's theory are charted in Figure 11.8. We describe the first four childhood

(a) Continuous development   (b) Discontinuous development (stages)

Figure 11.7

Stage theories of development. Some theories view development as a relatively continuous process, albeit not as smooth and perfectly linear as depicted on the left. In contrast, stage theories assume that development is marked by major discontinuities (as shown on the right) that bring fundamental, qualitative changes in capabilities or characteristic behaviour.

Figure 11.8

Erikson's stage theory. Erikson's theory of personality development posits that people evolve through eight stages over the life span. Each stage is marked by a *psychosocial crisis* that involves confronting a fundamental question, such as "Who am I and where am I going?" The stages are described in terms of alternative traits that are potential outcomes from the crises. Development is enhanced when a crisis is resolved in favour of the healthier alternative (which is listed first for each stage).

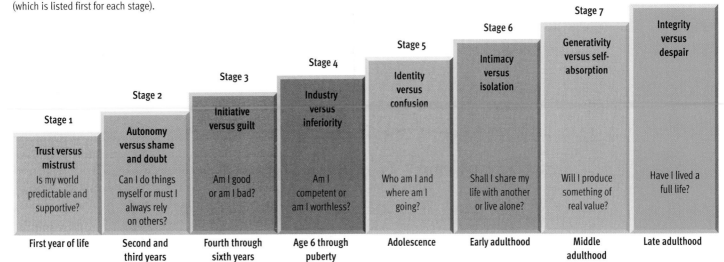

Stage 1	Stage 2	Stage 3	Stage 4	Stage 5	Stage 6	Stage 7	Stage 8
Trust versus mistrust	Autonomy versus shame and doubt	Initiative versus guilt	Industry versus inferiority	Identity versus confusion	Intimacy versus isolation	Generativity versus self-absorption	Integrity versus despair
Is my world predictable and supportive?	Can I do things myself or must I always rely on others?	Am I good or am I bad?	Am I competent or am I worthless?	Who am I and where am I going?	Shall I share my life with another or live alone?	Will I produce something of real value?	Have I lived a full life?
First year of life	Second and third years	Fourth through sixth years	Age 6 through puberty	Adolescence	Early adulthood	Middle adulthood	Late adulthood

stages here and discuss the remaining stages in the upcoming sections on adolescence and adulthood.

Trust versus Mistrust Erikson's first stage encompasses the first year of life, when an infant has to depend completely on adults to take care of its basic needs for such necessities as food, a warm blanket, and changed diapers. If an infant's basic biological needs are adequately met by his or her caregivers and sound attachments are formed, the child should develop an optimistic, trusting attitude toward the world. However, if the infant's basic needs are taken care of poorly, a more distrusting, pessimistic personality may result.

Autonomy versus Shame and Doubt Erikson's second stage unfolds during the second and third years of life, when parents begin toilet training and other efforts to regulate the child's behaviour. The child must begin to take some personal responsibility for feeding, dressing, and bathing. If all goes well, he or she acquires a sense of self-sufficiency. But, if parents are never satisfied with the child's efforts and there are constant parent–child conflicts, the child may develop a sense of personal shame and self-doubt.

Initiative versus Guilt In Erikson's third stage, lasting roughly from ages three to six, children experiment and take initiatives that may sometimes conflict with their parents' rules. Overcontrolling parents may begin to instill feelings of guilt, and self-esteem may suffer. Parents need to support their children's emerging independence while maintaining appropriate controls. In the ideal situation, children will retain their sense of initiative while learning to respect the rights and privileges of other family members.

Industry versus Inferiority In the fourth stage (age six through puberty), the challenge of learning to function socially is extended beyond the family to the broader social realm of the neighbourhood and school. Children who are able to function effectively in this less nurturant social sphere where productivity is highly valued should learn to value achievement and to take pride in accomplishment, resulting in a sense of competence.

Evaluating Erikson's Theory

The strength of Erikson's theory is that it accounts for both continuity and transition in personality development. It accounts for transition by showing how new challenges in social relations stimulate personality development throughout life. It accounts

"Human personality in principle develops according to steps predetermined in the growing person's readiness to be driven toward, to be aware of, and to interact with a widening social radius."

ERIK ERIKSON

Web Link 11.3

Erik Erikson Tutorial Homepage
http://web.cortland.edu/andersmd/ ERIK/welcome.HTML

This site includes a summary of Erikson's eight stages of development, biographical details, some controversies regarding his theories, and links to other online sources.

According to Erik Erikson, school-age children face the challenge of learning how to function in social situations outside of their family, especially with peers and at school. If they succeed, they will develop a sense of competence; if they fail, they may feel inferior.

for continuity by drawing connections between early childhood experiences and aspects of adult personality. One measure of a theory's value is how much research it generates, and Erikson's theory continues to guide a fair amount of research (Thomas, 2005).

On the negative side of the ledger, Erikson's theory has depended heavily on illustrative case studies, which are open to varied interpretations (Thomas, 2005). Another weakness is that the theory provides an "idealized" description of "typical" developmental patterns. Thus, it's not well suited for explaining the enormous personality differences that exist among people. Inadequate explanation of individual differences is a common problem with stage

Irreversibility **is the inability to envision reversing an action.** Preoperational children can't mentally "undo" something. For instance, in grappling with the conservation of water, they don't think about what would happen if the water were poured back from the tall beaker into the original beaker.

Egocentrism **in thinking is characterized by a limited ability to share another person's viewpoint.** Indeed, Piaget felt that preoperational children fail to appreciate that there are points of view other than their own. For instance, if you ask a preoperational girl whether her sister has a sister, she'll probably say no if they are the only two girls in the family. She's unable to view sisterhood from her sister's perspective (this also shows irreversibility).

A notable feature of egocentrism is *animism*—**the belief that all things are living**, just like oneself. Thus, youngsters attribute lifelike, human qualities to inanimate objects, asking questions such as, "When does the ocean stop to rest?" or "Why does the wind get so mad?"

As you can see, Piaget emphasized the weaknesses apparent in preoperational thought. Indeed, that is why he called this stage *pre*operational. The ability to perform *operations*—internal transformations, manipulations, and reorganizations of mental structures—emerges in the next stage.

Concrete Operational Period The development of mental operations marks the beginning of the *concrete operational period*, which usually lasts from about age seven to age 11. Piaget called this stage *concrete* operations because children can perform operations only on images of tangible objects and actual events.

Among the operations that children master during this stage are reversibility and decentration. *Reversibility* permits a child to mentally undo an action. *Decentration* allows the child to focus on more than one feature of a problem simultaneously. The newfound ability to coordinate several aspects of a problem helps the child appreciate that there are several ways to look at things. This ability in turn leads to a *decline in egocentrism* and *gradual mastery of conservation* as it applies to liquid, mass, number, volume, area, and length (see Figure 11.11).

Typical tasks used to measure conservation		Typical age of mastery
	Conservation of number Two equivalent rows of objects are shown to the child, who agrees that they have the same number of objects.	6–7
	One row is lengthened, and the child is asked whether one row has more objects.	
	Conservation of mass The child acknowledges that two clay balls have equal amounts of clay.	7–8
	The experimenter changes the shape of one of the balls and asks the child whether they still contain equal amounts of clay.	
	Conservation of length The child agrees that two sticks aligned with each other are the same length.	7–8
	After moving one stick to the left or right, the experimenter asks the child whether the sticks are of equal length.	
	Conservation of area Two identical sheets of cardboard have wooden blocks placed on them in identical positions; the child confirms that the same amount of space is left on each piece of cardboard.	8–9
	The experimenter scatters the blocks on one piece of cardboard and again asks the child whether the two pieces have the same amount of unoccupied space.	

Figure 11.11

The gradual mastery of conservation. Children master conservation during the concrete operational period, but their mastery is gradual. As outlined here, children usually master the conservation of number at age six or seven, but they may not understand the conservation of area until age eight or nine.

As children master concrete operations, they develop a variety of new problem-solving capacities. Let's examine another problem studied by Piaget. Give a preoperational child seven carnations and three daisies. Tell the child the names for the two types of flowers and ask the child to sort them into carnations and daisies. That should be no problem. Now ask the child whether there are more carnations or more daisies. Most children will correctly respond that there are more carnations. Now ask the child whether there are more carnations or more flowers. At this point, most preoperational children will stumble and respond incorrectly that there are more carnations than flowers. Generally, preoperational children can't handle *hierarchical classification* problems that require them to focus simultaneously on two levels of classification. However, the child who has advanced to the concrete operational stage is not as limited by centration and can work successfully with hierarchical classification problems.

Formal Operational Period The final stage in Piaget's theory is the *formal operational period,* which typically begins around 11 years of age. In this stage, children begin to apply their operations to *abstract* concepts in addition to concrete objects. Indeed, during this stage, youngsters come to *enjoy* the heady contemplation of abstract concepts. Many adolescents spend hours mulling over hypothetical possibilities related to abstractions such as justice, love, and free will.

According to Piaget, youngsters graduate to relatively adult modes of thinking in the formal operations stage. He did *not* mean to suggest that no further cognitive development occurs once children reach this stage. However, he believed that after children achieve formal operations, further developments in thinking are changes in *degree* rather than fundamental changes in the *nature* of thinking.

Adolescents in the formal operational period become more *systematic* in their problem-solving efforts. Children in earlier developmental stages tend to attack problems quickly, with a trial-and-error approach. In contrast, children who have achieved formal operations are more likely to think things through. They envision possible courses of action and try to use logic to reason out the likely consequences of each possible solution before they act. Thus, thought processes in the formal operational period can be characterized as abstract, systematic, logical, and reflective.

Evaluating Piaget's Theory

Jean Piaget made a landmark contribution to psychology's understanding of children in general and

their cognitive development in particular (Beilin, 1992). He founded the field of cognitive development and fostered a new view of children that saw them as active agents constructing their own worlds (Fischer & Hencke, 1996). Above all else, he sought answers to new questions. As he acknowledged in a 1970 interview, "It's just that no adult ever had the idea of asking children about conservation. It was so obvious that if you change the shape of an object, the quantity will be conserved. Why ask a child? The novelty lay in asking the question" (Hall, 1987, p. 56). Piaget's theory guided an enormous volume of productive research that continues through today (Brainerd, 1996; Feldman, 2003). This research has supported many of Piaget's central propositions (Flavell, 1996). In such a far-reaching theory, however, there are bound to be some weak or controversial spots. For example, Piaget's theory views infant development as a relatively discontinuous process composed, as we have seen, of a series of discrete stages. A great deal of research has been conducted to examine this discontinuity assumption. While acknowledging that more research evidence is necessary, some developmental psychologists, such as Memorial University's Mary Courage and Lakehead University's Mark Howe (Courage & Howe, 2002), suggest that there is evidence suggestive of continuity at the end of the second year, a point at which it is assumed that discontinuity would be in evidence. These are difficult issues to examine empirically, but there does not seem to be any slowdown in researchers' attempts to learn more about Piaget's ideas about cognitive development. Let's briefly examine some other criticisms of Piaget's theory:

1. In many areas, Piaget appears to have underestimated young children's cognitive development (Lutz & Sternberg, 1999). For example, researchers have found evidence that children begin to develop object permanence much earlier than Piaget thought, perhaps as early as three to four months of age (Baillargeon, 1987, 1994). Others have marshalled evidence that preoperational children exhibit less egocentrism and animism than Piaget believed (Newcombe & Huttenlocher, 1992).

2. Piaget's model suffers from problems that plague most stage theories. Like Erikson, Piaget had little to say about individual differences in development (Siegler, 1994). Also, people often simultaneously display patterns of thinking that are characteristic of several stages. This "mixing" of stages calls into question the value of organizing development in terms of stages (Bjorklund, 2005; Courage & Howe, 2002; Siegler & Ellis, 1996).

3. Piaget believed that his theory described universal processes that should lead children everywhere to progress through uniform stages of thinking at roughly the same ages. Subsequent research has shown that the *sequence* of stages is largely invariant, but the *timetable* that children follow in passing through these stages varies considerably across cultures (Dasen, 1994; Rogoff, 1990). Thus, Piaget underestimated the influence of cultural factors on cognitive development.

As with any theory, Piaget's is not flawless. However, without Piaget's theory to guide research, many crucial questions about children's development might not have been confronted until decades later (if at all). By some measures, the direct influence of Piaget's theories themselves may be declining (Bjorklund, 1997), but ironically, even many of the new directions in the study of cognitive development grew out of efforts to test, revise, or discredit Piaget's theory (Flavell, 1996). Let's look at some of these new directions.

Neo-Piagetian Theories

There is no doubt that Piaget was one of the most influential developmental psychologists in the history of psychology. Many years after his death, his ideas continue to influence research. One group of scholars, known as neo-Piagetians, have extended some of his ideas, integrating them with current perspectives on the nature of information processing. As you may recall, we first introduced the perspective known as information processing in Chapters 7 and 8. Two Canadian psychologists, Juan Pascual-Leone and Robbie Case, have been particularly influential in this area.

Pascual-Leone of York University introduced the term *neo-Piagetian* to the literature in 1969 (Pascual-Leone & Smith, 1969). When Pascual-Leone went to study with Piaget as a Ph.D. student, Pascual-Leone was already a physician and neuropsychiatrist (Cardellini & Pascual-Leone, 2004), and this training allowed him to view some of Piaget's formulations in a novel way. Pascual-Leone analyzed the typical performances of children of different ages in the data collected by Piaget and suggested that one feature that changed was the complexity of the tasks, or the number of essential aspects, elements, and relations that children must consider simultaneously to perform adequately at each age-appropriate task. By structurally analyzing the tasks, Pascual-Leone found that the complexity that children could deal with varied positively across age. This led Pascual-Leone to reinterpret Piaget's developmental stages and to implicate information-processing concepts in under-

standing cognitive development. One of his developments was the concept of M-capacity, a concept that predates but overlaps with a concept we discussed in Chapter 7, that of working memory. He suggests that an increase in information-processing capacity is one of the attributes that forms the basis of cognitive development. Progressive mental tasks increase the mental demand imposed on the child, and children are successful only if they possess the required mental power (Pascual-Leone, 2000). M-capacity relates to the maximum number of mental concepts that an individual can keep in mind at one time. Gifted students have been found to have a higher M-capacity than their mainstream peers (Johnson, Im-Boulter, & Pascual-Leone, 2003).

Robbie Case, working at the Ontario Institute for Studies in Education at the University of Toronto, developed a complementary neo-Piagetian view of cognitive development that, while based in Piaget's ideas, served to modify and extend them. He is best known for his *Staircase* model of development and the concept of central processing structures (Case, 1991a, 1998). Case suggests that one of the fundamental issues in developmental psychology is whether development can be conceptualized in terms of the development of one rather general intellectual attribute or factor, *or* a set of more discrete aspects (i.e., a more modular approach). Piaget is considered a proponent of the former. Case's view, building on the work of Piaget and other neo-Piagetians such as Pascual-Leone, is that there are four major stages of cognitive development but that each stage is assumed to have its own distinct structure and cognitive operation (Case, 1991b). He argues that, while cognitive development proceeds in line with Piaget's stage view of progression, there is a distinct set of cognitive skills involved that may show uneven development—children may show higher levels of development in some domains than others. Case acknowledges the important role played by culture in cognitive development and that age-related increases in central processing working memory capacity form an important basis of cognitive development.

Are Some Cognitive Abilities Innate?

The frequent finding that Piaget underestimated infants' cognitive abilities has led to a rash of research suggesting that infants have a surprising grasp of many complex concepts. The new findings have been made possible by some innovative research methods that permit investigators to draw inferences about the abilities of very young children. Many studies have made use of the *habituation–dishabituation paradigm*. **Habituation is a gradual reduction in the strength of a response when a stimulus event is presented repeatedly.** If you show infants the same event over and over (such as an object dropping onto a platform), they habituate to it—their heart and respiration rates decline and they spend less time looking at the stimulus. **Dishabituation occurs if a new stimulus elicits an increase in the strength of a habituated response.** Patterns of dishabituation can give researchers insights into what types of events infants can tell apart, which events surprise or interest them, and which events violate their expectations.

Working mostly with the habituation–dishabituation paradigm, researchers have discovered that infants understand basic properties of objects and some of the rules that govern them (Baillargeon, 2002, 2004). At three to four months of age, infants understand that objects are distinct entities with boundaries, that objects move in continuous paths, that one solid object cannot pass through another, that an object cannot pass through an opening that is smaller than the object, and that objects on slopes roll down rather than up (Kim & Spelke, 1992; Spelke & Newport, 1998). Other research has shown that infants' ability to categorize objects is much more advanced than previously appreciated. At 9 to 12 months of age, infants can recognize whether common objects belong to sensible categories, such as foods, animals, and vehicles (Quinn & Eimas, 1996, 1998).

In this line of research, perhaps the most stunning discovery has been the finding that *infants seem to be able to add and subtract small numbers* (Bremner, 2001). If five-month-old infants are shown a sequence of events in which one object is added to another behind a screen, they expect to see two objects when the screen is removed, and they exhibit surprise when their expectation is violated (see Figure 11.12). This expectation suggests that they understand that $1 + 1 = 2$ (Wynn, 1992, 1996). Similar manipulations suggest that infants also understand that $2 - 1 = 1$, that $2 + 1 = 3$, and that $3 - 1 = 2$ (Hauser & Carey, 1998; Wynn, 1998).

Again and again in recent years, research has shown that infants appear to understand surprisingly complex concepts that they have had virtually no opportunity to learn about. These findings have led some theorists to conclude that certain basic cognitive abilities are biologically built into humans' neural architecture. The theorists who have reached this conclusion tend to fall into two camps: nativists and evolutionary theorists. The *nativists* simply assert that humans are prewired to readily understand certain concepts without making any assumptions about *why* humans are prewired in these ways (Spelke, 1994; Spelke & Newport, 1998). Their principal interest is to sort out the complex matter of what is prewired and what isn't.

Evolutionary theorists agree with the nativists that humans are prewired for certain cognitive abilities, but they are keenly interested in *why*. As you might expect, they maintain that this wiring is a product of natural selection, and they strive to understand its adaptive significance (Hauser & Carey, 1998; Wynn, 1998). For example, evolutionary theorists are interested in how basic addition–subtraction abilities may have enhanced our hominid ancestors' success

Figure 11.12

The procedure used to test infants' understanding of number. To see if five-month-old infants have some appreciation of addition and subtraction, Wynn (1992, 1996) showed them sequences of events like those depicted here. If children express surprise (primarily assessed by time spent looking) when the screen drops and they see only one object, this result suggests that they understand that $1 + 1 = 2$. Wynn and others have found that infants seem to have some primitive grasp of simple addition and subtraction.

SOURCE: Adapted from Wynn, K. (1992). Addition and subtraction by human infants. *Nature, 358*, 749–750. Copyright © 1992 Macmillan Magazines, Ltd. Reprinted with permission.

in hunting, foraging, and social bargaining. The evolutionary theorists also argue that the findings on infants' surprising abilities *demonstrate that the human mind is modular*—that it is made up of domain-specific modules that have been crafted by natural selection to solve specific adaptive problems, such as recognizing faces, discriminating simple speech sounds, and understanding basic properties of objects (Gelman & Williams, 1998; Leslie, 1994).

We hasten to add that the question about whether some cognitive abilities are hardwired is much more complicated than it may appear at first glance. Critics assert that infants' dishabituation responses to various events can be interpreted and explained in a variety of ways without assuming that infants possess innate knowledge of objects, categories, and number (Fischer & Bidell, 1991; Haith & Benson, 1998). For example, infants may spend more time looking at novel events simply because these events require more time for perceptual processing and memory encoding (Bogartz & Shinskey, 1998). Thus, the newly emerging debate about whether infants have some innate knowledge of the world around them promises to be very interesting.

What Do Children Understand about the Mind?

Another red-hot topic in the area of cognitive development has been the question of how children's understanding of the mind and mental states progresses over time (Bjorklund, 2000; Lalonde & Chandler, 2002). Researchers exploring this aspect of cognitive development study when and how children come to understand that other people have knowledge, beliefs, and desires that may be quite different from their own. Consider the following scenario. An experimenter shows a five-year-old child a candy box and asks her what she thinks it contains. She answers, "candy." The child is then allowed to look inside the box and discovers that it really contains crayons. Then the experimenter asks the girl what another child who has *not* seen the contents of the box will think it contains. "Candy," she replies, showing her understanding of the planned deception. Now imagine the same experiment with a three-year-old boy. Events unfold in the same way until the experimenter asks what another child will think the candy box contains. The three-year-old typically will say "crayons," thinking that the other child will know what he knows about the hidden contents of the box. More perplexing yet, if questioned further, the three-year-old will probably insist that he originally thought and said that there were crayons in the candy box (Flavell, 1999). Why does the three-year-old respond in this way? Because

most children under age four do not yet appreciate that people can hold *false beliefs* that do not accurately reflect reality.

Researchers have mapped out some milestones in the development of children's understanding of mental states (Bartsch & Wellman, 1995; Flavell & Miller, 1998). Around age two children begin to distinguish between mental states and overt behaviour. The first mental states they understand are *desires* and *emotions*. By age three, children are talking about others' *beliefs* and *thoughts,* as well as their desires. It is not until about age four, however, that children consistently make the connection between mental states and behaviour. That is, they begin to understand how people's beliefs, thoughts, and desires motivate and direct their behaviour. Thus, they can appreciate that Darius *wants* to get some Pokémon cards, which would make him very *happy,* that he *believes* they will be available at the mall, and that these mental states will *motivate* Darius to ask his dad to take him to the mall.

Children's understanding of the mind seems to turn a corner between ages three and four, so that four-year-olds typically begin to grasp the fact that people may hold false beliefs (Wellman & Gelman, 1998). After age four, youngsters' reasoning about mental states continues to improve. For example, four-year-olds are relatively poor at introspection, as they struggle when asked to reconstruct their recent thoughts about something, but their capacity for introspection gradually increases over the next several years (Flavell, 1999). An understanding of the concept of false belief is often seen as the developmental achievement that marks the child's progression to a more mature theory of mind. Christopher Lalonde from the University of Victoria and the University of British Columbia's Michael Chandler, however, argue that there are two developments that mark this progression (Lalonde & Chandler, 2002). They suggest that there is a later developmental milestone, typically arrived at in the early school years, that reflects the development of an *interpretive theory of mind.* According to this view, children initially develop a *copy* view of the mind in which they assume the mind operates like a recording device that may produce accurate or inaccurate representations. The progressively more mature theory of mind is referred to as the interpretive theory of mind, in which children understand that minds "creatively construct and uniquely interpret reality" (Lalonde & Chandler, 2002, p. 192). An understanding of false belief is considered a necessary but not sufficient condition for this more mature theory of mind.

The Development of Moral Reasoning

9E

In Europe, a woman was near death from cancer. One drug might save her, a form of radium that a druggist in the same town had recently discovered. The druggist was charging $2,000, ten times what the drug cost him to make. The sick woman's husband, Heinz, went to everyone he knew to borrow the money, but he could only get together about half of what it cost. He told the druggist that his wife was dying and asked him to sell it cheaper or let him pay later. But the druggist said, "No." The husband got desperate and broke into the man's store to steal the drug for his wife. Should the husband have done that? Why? (Kohlberg, 1969, p. 379)

What's your answer to Heinz's dilemma? Would you have answered the same way three years ago? In the fifth grade? Can you guess what you might have said at age six?

By presenting similar dilemmas to subjects and studying their responses, Lawrence Kohlberg (1976, 1984; Colby & Kohlberg, 1987) devised a model of how moral reasoning develops. What is morality? That's a complicated question that philosophers have debated for centuries. For our purposes, it will suffice to say that *morality* involves the ability to discern right from wrong and to behave accordingly.

Kohlberg's Stage Theory

9E

Kohlberg's model is the most influential of a number of competing theories that attempt to explain how youngsters develop a sense of right and wrong. His work was derived from much earlier work by Jean Piaget (1932), who theorized that moral development is determined by cognitive development. By this he meant that the way individuals think out moral issues depends on their level of cognitive development. This assumption provided the springboard for Kohlberg's research.

Kohlberg's theory focuses on moral *reasoning* rather than overt *behaviour*. This point is best illustrated by describing Kohlberg's method of investigation. He presented his subjects with thorny moral questions such as Heinz's dilemma. He then asked them what the actor in the dilemma should do, and more important, why. It was the *why* that interested Kohlberg. He examined the nature and progression of subjects' moral reasoning.

The result of this work is the stage theory of moral reasoning outlined in Figure 11.13. Kohlberg found that individuals progress through a series of three levels of moral development, each of which can be broken into two sublevels, yielding a total of six stages. Each stage represents a different approach to thinking about right and wrong.

Younger children at the *preconventional level* think in terms of external authority. Acts are wrong because they are punished or right because they lead to positive consequences. Older children who have reached the *conventional level* of moral reasoning see rules as necessary for maintaining social order. They therefore accept these rules as their own. They "internalize" these rules not to avoid punishment but to be virtuous and win approval from others. Moral thinking at this stage is relatively inflexible. Rules are viewed as absolute guidelines that should be enforced rigidly.

"Children are almost as likely to reject moral reasoning beneath their level as to fail to assimilate reasoning too far above their level."

LAWRENCE KOHLBERG

Figure 11.13

Kohlberg's stage theory.
Kohlberg's model posits three levels of moral reasoning, each of which can be divided into two stages. This chart summarizes some of the key facets in how individuals think about right and wrong at each stage.

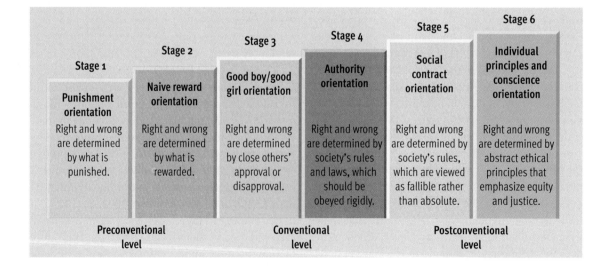

Stage 1	Stage 2	Stage 3	Stage 4	Stage 5	Stage 6
Punishment orientation	Naive reward orientation	Good boy/good girl orientation	Authority orientation	Social contract orientation	Individual principles and conscience orientation
Right and wrong are determined by what is punished.	Right and wrong are determined by what is rewarded.	Right and wrong are determined by close others' approval or disapproval.	Right and wrong are determined by society's rules and laws, which should be obeyed rigidly.	Right and wrong are determined by society's rules, which are viewed as fallible rather than absolute.	Right and wrong are determined by abstract ethical principles that emphasize equity and justice.
Preconventional level		Conventional level		Postconventional level	

During adolescence, some youngsters move on to the *postconventional level,* which involves working out a personal code of ethics. Acceptance of rules is less rigid, and moral thinking shows some flexibility. Subjects at the postconventional level allow for the possibility that someone might not comply with some of society's rules if they conflict with personal ethics. For example, subjects at this level might applaud a newspaper reporter who goes to jail rather than reveal a source of information who was promised anonymity.

Evaluating Kohlberg's Theory

How has Kohlberg's theory fared in research? The central ideas have received reasonable support. Progress in moral reasoning is indeed closely tied to cognitive development (Walker, 1988). Studies also show that youngsters generally do progress through Kohlberg's stages of moral reasoning in the order that he proposed (Walker & Taylor, 1991). Furthermore, relations between age and level of moral reasoning are in the predicted directions (Rest, 1986; Walker, 1989). Representative age trends are shown in Figure 11.14. As children get older, stage 1 and stage 2 reasoning declines, while stage 3 and stage 4 reasoning increases. However, there is great variation in the age at which people reach specific stages. Finally, evidence suggests that moral *reasoning* is predictive of moral *behaviour,* although the association is modest (Bruggerman & Hart, 1996). That is, youngsters who are at higher stages of moral development are somewhat more likely to be altruistic, conscientious, and honest than youngsters at lower stages (Fabes et al., 1999; Taylor & Walker, 1997). Although these findings support the utility of Kohlberg's model, like all influential theorists, he has his critics. They have raised the following issues:

1. It's not unusual to find that a person shows signs of several adjacent levels of moral reasoning at a particular point in development (Walker & Taylor, 1991). As we noted in the critique of Piaget, this mixing of stages is a problem for virtually all stage theories.

2. Researchers have focused too heavily on how people reason about the specific dilemmas devised by Kohlberg. As Wark and Krebs (1996) put it, "It is somewhat disconcerting to consider how much we have learned about people's judgments about Heinz and his dilemma, and how little we have learned about real-life moral judgment" (pp. 220–221).

3. Sizable cultural disparities have been found in people's progress through Kohlberg's stages (Miller,

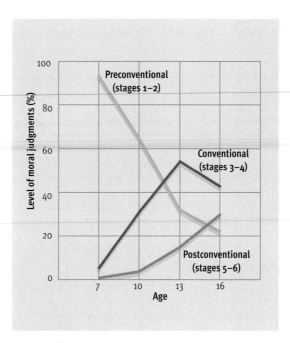

Figure 11.14

Age and moral reasoning. The percentages of different types of moral judgments made by subjects at various ages are graphed here (based on Kohlberg, 1963, 1969). As predicted, preconventional reasoning declines as children mature, conventional reasoning increases during middle childhood, and postconventional reasoning begins to emerge during adolescence. But at each age, children display a mixture of various levels of moral reasoning.

Source: Adapted from Kohlberg, L.J., (1963). The development of children's orientations toward a moral order: I: Sequence in the development of moral thought. *Vita Humana, 6,* 11–33. Copyright © 1963 by S. Karger AG. Reprinted by permission.

2001). Some critics believe that the value judgments built into Kohlberg's theory reflect a liberal, individualistic ideology characteristic of modern Western nations that is much more culture-specific than Kohlberg appreciated (Shweder, Mahapatra, & Miller, 1990). Kohlberg's dilemmas may not be valid indicators of moral development in some cultures (Nucci, 2002).

4. Other critics have argued that Kohlberg's theory was based primarily on male participants' responses and is biased against the equally principled moral reasoning of females. Carol Gilligan, who was initially a research assistant for Kohlberg, published her criticisms in her well-known 1982 book, *In a Different Voice: Psychological Theory and Women's Development.* She argues that males and females are socialized differently, a difference that promotes a focus on individualism reflected in what she terms a morality of justice in males and a focus on relationships reflected in a morality of care in females. In Kohlberg's system, these are equated with stage 4 and stage 3 reasoning, respectively. She suggests that these two orientations are equally principled but that Kohlberg's system is biased in favour of males.

Analyzing Moral Reasoning

Check your understanding of Kohlberg's theory of moral development by analyzing hypothetical responses to the following moral dilemma:

A biologist has conducted numerous studies demonstrating that simple organisms such as worms and paramecia can learn through conditioning. It occurs to her that perhaps she could condition fertilized human ova, to provide a dramatic demonstration that abortions destroy adaptable, living human organisms. This possibility appeals to her, as she is ardently opposed to abortion. However, there is no way to conduct the necessary research on human ova without sacrificing the lives of potential human beings. She desperately wants to conduct the research, but obviously, the sacrifice of human ova is fundamentally incompatible with her belief in the sanctity of human life. What should she do? Why? [Submitted by a student (age 13) to Professor Barbara Banas at Monroe Community College]

In the spaces on the left of each numbered response, indicate the level of moral reasoning shown, choosing from the following: (a) preconventional level, (b) conventional level, or (c) postconventional level. The answers are in Appendix A.

_____ 1. She should do the research. Although it's wrong to kill, there's a greater good that can be realized through the research.

_____ 2. She shouldn't do the research because people will think that she's a hypocrite and condemn her.

_____ 3. She should do the research because she may become rich and famous as a result.

REVIEW OF KEY POINTS

- According to Piaget's theory of cognitive development, the key advance during the sensorimotor period is the child's gradual recognition of the permanence of objects. The preoperational period is marked by certain deficiencies in thinking—notably, centration, irreversibility, and egocentrism.

- During the concrete operations period, children develop the ability to perform operations on mental representations, making them capable of conservation and hierarchical classification. The stage of formal operations ushers in more abstract, systematic, and logical thought.

- Piaget may have underestimated some aspects of children's cognitive development and his theory, like other stage theories, does not explain individual differences very well. Nonetheless, his work has greatly improved psychology's understanding of cognitive development. Neo-Piagetian theories have extended Piaget's formulations by emphasizing the role of information processing concepts.

- Recent research has shown that infants appear to understand surprisingly complex concepts that they have had virtually no opportunity to learn about, leading some theorists to conclude that basic cognitive abilities are biologically built into humans' neural architecture. Children's understanding of the mind seems to turn a corner between ages three and four.

- According to Kohlberg, moral reasoning progresses through six stages that are related to age and determined by cognitive development. Age-related progress in moral reasoning has been found in research, although a great deal of overlap occurs between adjacent stages.

The Transition of Adolescence

PREVIEW QUESTIONS
- When do children reach pubescence and puberty?
- What changes do these landmarks bring?
- How do early attachment relations appear to be related to the timing of sexual maturation?
- Does the empirical evidence support the notion that adolescence is a time of great turmoil?
- What is the chief challenge of adolescence, according to Erikson?
- What are Marcia's four identity statuses?

Adolescence is a transitional period between childhood and adulthood. Its age boundaries are not exact, but in our society adolescence begins at around age 13 and ends at about age 22. As we will discuss, adolescence is a period of development in which individuals are presented with a series of challenges, new experiences, and new demands, and adolescents' sense of self may undergo critical changes. According to Simon Fraser psychologist Marlene Moretti, changes in interpersonal roles and relationships and dramatic changes in capacity for self-reflection and cognition are important influences on the transformation of sense of self during adolescence (Moretti & Holland, 2003).

Although most societies have at least a brief period of adolescence, it is *not* universal across cultures (Larson & Wilson, 2004; Schlegel & Barry, 1991; Whiting, Burbank, & Ratner, 1986). In some cultures, young people move directly from childhood to adulthood. A protracted period of adolescence is seen primarily in industrialized nations. In these societies, rapid technological progress has made lengthy education, and therefore prolonged

The timing of sexual maturation can have important implications for adolescents. Youngsters who mature unusually early or unusually late often feel uneasy about this transition.

Acne

Beard

Voice change

Underarm hair,
chest hair,
muscle
development

Pubic hair

Enlargement
of penis,
scrotum, testes

Ejaculation

Pituitary

Adrenal
glands

Testes

Ovaries

Androgen,
estrogen,
testosterone

Androgen,
estrogen,
progesterone

Acne

Underarm
hair

Breast
development

Pubic hair

Rounded
body contours

Enlargement
of uterus,
clitoris, labia

Menstruation

Figure 11.15

Physical development at puberty. Hormonal changes during puberty lead not only to a growth spurt but also to the development of secondary sex characteristics. The pituitary gland sends signals to the adrenal glands and gonads (ovaries and testes), which secrete hormones responsible for various physical changes that differentiate males and females.

economic dependence, the norm. Thus, in our own culture junior high school, high school, and university students often have a "marginal" status. They are capable of reproduction and so are physiologically mature. Yet they have not achieved the emotional and economic independence from their parents that are the hallmarks of adulthood. Let's begin our discussion of adolescent development with its most visible aspect: the physical changes that transform the body of a child into that of an adult.

Puberty and the Growth Spurt

Recall for a moment your junior high school days. Didn't it seem that your body grew so fast about this time that your clothes just couldn't "keep up"? This phase of rapid growth in height and weight is called the *adolescent growth spurt*. Brought on by hormonal changes, it typically starts at about 11 years of age in girls and about two years later in boys (Archibald,

Graber, & Brooks-Dunn, 2003; Malina, 1990). Scientists are not sure about what triggers the hormonal changes that underlie the adolescent growth spurt, but recent evidence suggests that rising levels of *leptin*, the recently discovered hormone that reflects the body's fat cell storage (see Chapter 10), may provide the crucial signals (Spear, 2000).

The term *pubescence* is used to describe the two-year span preceding puberty during which the changes leading to physical and sexual maturity take place. In addition to growing taller and heavier during pubescence, children begin to develop the physical features that characterize adults of their respective sexes. These features are termed *secondary sex characteristics*—physical features that distinguish one sex from the other but that are not essential for reproduction. For example, males go through a voice change, develop facial hair, and experience greater skeletal and muscle growth in the upper torso, leading to broader shoulders (see Figure 11.15).

Females experience breast growth and a widening of the pelvic bones plus increased fat deposits in this area, resulting in wider hips (Susman & Rogol, 2004).

Note, however, that the capacity to reproduce is not attained in pubescence. This comes later. **Puberty is the stage during which sexual functions reach maturity, which marks the beginning of adolescence.** It is during puberty that the **primary sex characteristics**—the structures necessary for reproduction—develop fully. In the male these include the testes, penis, and related internal structures. In the female they include the ovaries, vagina, uterus, and other internal structures.

In females, the onset of puberty is typically signalled by **menarche**—**the first occurrence of menstruation,** which reflects the culmination of a series of hormonal changes (Dorn et al., 1999). North American girls typically reach menarche at about age 12-and-a-half, with further sexual maturation continuing until approximately 16 (Susman, Dorn, & Schiefelbein, 2003). Most North American boys begin to produce sperm by age 14, with complete sexual maturation occurring around 18 (Archibald et al., 2003). Interestingly, there have been *generational* changes in the timing of puberty. Today's adolescents begin puberty at a younger age, and complete it more rapidly, than did their counterparts in earlier generations (Anderson, Dallal, & Must, 2003; Fredriks et al., 2000). This trend apparently reflects improvements in nutrition and medical care (Brooks-Gunn, 1991). The timing of puberty varies from one adolescent to the next over a range of about five years (10–15 for girls, 11–16 for boys). Much of this variability is governed by hereditary differences (Kaprio et al., 1995), but other factors also are influential, including the quality of a person's family relationships during early childhood (Ellis et al., 1999).

Although the determinants of the timing of puberty remain open to debate, more is known about the *consequences* of variation in the onset of puberty. Generally, *girls who mature early and boys who mature late seem to have more emotional difficulties with the transition to adolescence* (Ge, Conger, & Elder, 1996; Graber et al., 1997). However, in both males and females, early maturation is associated with greater use of alcohol and drugs, more high-risk behaviour, and more trouble with the law (Steinberg & Morris, 2001). Among females, early maturation is also correlated with poorer school performance, earlier experience of intercourse, more unwanted pregnancies, and greater risk for eating problems and disorders (Graber et al., 1994; Stattin & Magnusson, 1990). Thus, we might speculate that early maturation often thrusts both sexes (but especially females) toward the adult world too soon.

Time of Turmoil?

Back around the turn of the last century, G. Stanley Hall (1904), one of psychology's great pioneers (see Chapter 1), proposed that the adolescent years are characterized by convulsive instability and disturbing inner turmoil. Hall attributed this turmoil to adolescents' erratic physical changes and resultant confusion about self-image. There is no doubt that adolescence is a time of change and transition. What do we know about this period? The picture is uneven. Recent results in Canada from the National Longitudinal Survey of Children and Youth (Statistics Canada, 1999c) reveal that most 12- and 13-year-olds are relatively happy with their lives. Ninety-three percent say they are happy with the way things are, and 95% suggest their future looks good. In the same survey, however, many participants reported that they have engaged in dysfunctional behaviours in the last year, including theft (31%), threatening others (41%), and fights (55% for males and 27% for females). For most, however, the absolute frequency was low. For example, only 10% of those who reported engaging in theft did so more than three times in the previous year. While most of the 12- and 13-year-olds surveyed reported being happy, it was also found that about 7% reported contemplating suicide, with the rate for boys about double that of girls.

Statistics on adolescent suicide would seem to support the idea that adolescence is a time marked by turmoil, but the figures can be interpreted in various ways. On the one hand, suicide rates among teens have increased alarmingly over the past few decades. The Canadian Task Force on Preventive Health Care (2003) reported a four-fold increase in suicides for 15- to 19-year-old males and a three-fold increase for females in that age group from 1960 to 1991; this was the greatest increase of any age group. On the other hand, even with this increase, the rates for this age group, according to data from Statistics Canada (Langlois & Morrison, 2003), are lower than for older age groups (see Figure 11.16). Actually, the suicide crisis among teenagers in North America involves *attempted* suicide more than *completed* suicide. As is evident in Figure 11.16(b), attempted suicides are much higher for Canadian females, especially for adolescent girls. Overall, the ratio of attempted to completed suicides is higher for adolescents than for other age groups (Maris, Berman, & Silverman, 2000). A study of adolescent suicide notes by a team of University of Windsor psychologists (Leenaars et al., 2001) revealed that, compared to the suicide notes of other age groups, those of adolescents more frequently give evidence of cognitive

Figure 11.16

Adolescent suicide. **(a)** The suicide rate for Canadian adolescents (15–19) has increased dramatically since 1960. Nonetheless, suicide rates for this age group remain lower than suicide rates for older age groups. **(b)** While teen males are more likely to commit suicide, hospitalization rates for attempted suicide are higher for adolescent females.

SOURCE: Langlois, S., & Morrison, P. (2002). Suicide deaths and suicide attempts. *Health Reports, 13,* No. 2, 9–23. Statistics Canada, Catalogue 82-003, http://www.statcan.ca/english/studies/82-003/feature/hrar2002013002s0a01.pdf. Chart 2, p. 13, and Chart 4, p. 15. Adapted from the Statistics Canada publication, *Health Reports,* catalogue 82-003, Vol. 13, No. 2, January 2002.

constriction (e.g., rigidity in thinking, tunnel vision, concrete thinking), indirect expression (e.g., ambivalent feelings toward a person or life), rejection, and identification with a lost ideal or rejecting person.

An especially vulnerable group are First Nations Canadians. The Canadian Task Force on Preventive Health Care (2003) reports that the suicide rates in this segment of Canadian society are twice the sex-specific rates and three times the age-specific rates reported for the general Canadian population. The particularly high suicide rate among teens is of special concern. Canadian psychologists Chandler and Lalonde have been conducting research in this area for many years (Chandler, 2000; Chandler & Lalonde, 2004; Chandler et al., 2003). They suggest that the increased rate of suicide among First Nations Canadians is specific to certain contexts rather than being true across that population. In some communities the rate is as high as 800 times the national average, while in other communities suicide is virtually unknown. They believe that *cultural continuity factors* differentiate the

settings where suicide rates are high. They argue that a sense of personal and cultural continuity is necessary, especially in times of change, to serve as a critical foundation for personal and cultural identity. While acknowledging the inevitability and importance of change, Chandler and Lalonde argue that a sense of personal continuity or personal persistence is fundamental to psychological health. Two important sets of circumstances may combine to cause the high suicide levels among First Nations teens. One is the set of changes that most adolescents experience. The other arises "whenever one's culture, out of which the particulars of one's identity are necessarily composed, is also thrown into serious disarray. In either case, the grounds upon which a sense of self is ordinarily made to rest are cut away, life is made cheap, and the prospect of one's own death becomes a matter of indifference" (Chandler & Lalonde, 1998, p. 193). The Featured Study for this chapter links suicide rates of First Nations youth to contexts in which cultural continuity has or has not been emphasized.

Youth Suicide in Canada's First Nations

FEATURED STUDY

Chandler and Lalonde began with the disturbing observation that the suicide rate among Canada's First Nations youth is among the highest in any culturally identifiable group in the *world.* They also note, however, that there is incredible variation across Aboriginal communities (or bands) in the local suicide rate, ranging from many times the national average to zero. Their interest was in explicating the factors that might differentiate contexts where high and low youth suicide rates are in evidence.

They used their earlier research on non-Native youth as a starting point. Chandler and Lalonde assert that all of us have a need for belief in self-continuity or self-preservation and that this is a fundamental aspect of healthy self-concept. Adolescence is a time of change, and challenges are presented to this sense of self-continuity. The results of their earlier work suggest a distinction between those adolescents who are and are not actively suicidal. For the healthy youth, they found that "with exceptionless

Investigators: Michael Chandler (University of British Columbia) and Christopher Lalonde (University of Victoria)

Source: Cultural continuity as a hedge against suicide in Canada's First Nations. *Transcultural Psychiatry,* 1998, *35,* 191–219.

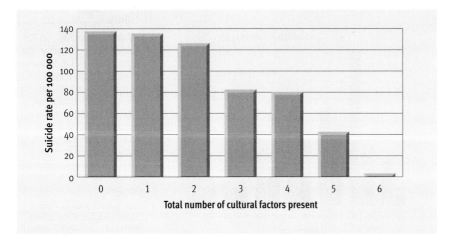

Figure 11.17

British Columbia youth suicide rates by the number of cultural factors present in the community.

SOURCE: Chandler, M. J. & Lalonde, C. (1998). Cultural continuity as a hedge against suicide in Canada's First Nations. *Transcultural Psychiatry*, 35, 191–219. Reprinted by permission of Sage Publications.

Web link 11.5

Youth Suicide

http://www.cmha.ca/bins/content_page.asp?cid=3-101-104

The Canadian Mental Health Association maintains a useful Web site devoted to youth suicide. Some of the warning signs listed include sudden changes in behaviour, apathy, change in eating patterns, unusual preoccupation with death, signs of depression and moodiness, previous suicide attempts, and a recent attempt or death by suicide of a friend or family member.

regularity, all of these young subjects were committed to the necessary importance of, and found some conceptual means of succeeding at, the task of weaving a continuous thread through the various episodes of their own and others' lives" (p. 196). Suicidal youth were typically those who "distinguished themselves by utterly failing in their efforts to find any personally persuasive means of warranting their own self-continuity in time" (pp. 196–197). Of course, culture is another source of continuity.

Chandler and Lalonde applied this reasoning to the variation in suicide rates found among First Nations bands in British Columbia. They then developed measures of *cultural continuity* that could be used to differentiate the bands. The extent to which a band provides markers for cultural continuity should facilitate an individual's process of searching for personal continuity, thereby reducing suicide rates.

Method

Procedure. All identifiable acts of suicide in the province are recorded by the Office of the Chief Coroner of British Columbia. These records also include demographic information, which permitted the suicide to be categorized as Native or non-Native. Population statistics to allow for the calculation of suicide rates were obtained from federal and provincial government databases. A set of markers of cultural continuity were developed and used to categorize each First Nations community. These included:

- *Land claims* (whether the band was actively pursuing claims to traditional lands)
- *Self-government* (whether the band was establishing rights in law to relative independence and self-government)
- *Education services* (whether the band had secured some independence in education by having the majority of students attend a band school)

- *Police and fire services* (whether the band had substantial control over these services)
- *Health services* (whether the band had control over the provision of these services)
- *Cultural facilities* (number of communal facilities located in the community)

A summary cultural factors score counted the number of these markers present and assigned a score to the band of 0 to 6.

Results

The results revealed that the cultural markers did differentiate between the suicide rates of bands that did and did not show evidence of the markers. The differences were greatest for self-government, land claims, and education. When all the cultural factors were summed and related to suicide rates, the analysis revealed a strong linear relationship between suicide rates and cultural factors, with lower suicide rates in bands whose cultural practices worked to help preserve and restore Native culture (see Figure 11.17).

Discussion

The investigators concluded that the risk of suicide in First Nations youth is strongly connected to their developing sense of self-continuity in a period of personal and cultural change. They argue that the extent to which a community has mechanisms in place that preserve cultural continuity positively affects personal identity, which reflects itself in a reduced suicide rate for youth in that community. Adolescent youth are in a period of transition and change, which if combined with the challenges facing First Nations communities, serves to undermine their sense of personal continuity and ability to inhibit self-destructive thoughts and actions.

Comment

We featured this study for several reasons. First, it relates to some of the formulations presented in this chapter that highlight the importance of self-identity issues, especially in the period of adolescence. Second, it illustrates the interplay between basic research and its potential application to society. What began as a program of research by Chandler and Lalonde on the nature of self and identity in development has been shown to be relevant to an important social issue. Finally, the study serves to illustrate the range of methods and data that can be used to examine psychological theories. In this study, archival data were used to test and substantiate the authors' hypotheses about important concepts in human development. It is also important to note that this is a correlational study, which does not allow us any basis for causal statements. ∎

In recent years, the highly publicized problem of adolescent violence has led many people to conclude that adolescence is indeed a time of turmoil. The tragic 1999 shootings at Columbine High School in Littleton, Colorado, and W. R. Myers High School in Taber, Alberta, are examples. In both cases, the shooters were often described as alienated loners who were frequently bullied (Aronson, 2000; Faircairn, 2004; O'Malley, 1999). You may also have heard about the 2005 case of an alleged massacre plot in a high school in Saint John, New Brunswick, planned for the anniversary of the Columbine tragedy. The boys arrested were all air-cadets, and police found pipe-bomb materials at their homes (CBC News, 2005).

In Chapter 1, we introduced you to some of the Canadian research on bullying in schools (Craig & Pepler, 1997; Pepler & Craig, 1995; Pepler et al., 1993). Bullying is a reality in our schools and often involves more than one individual participating in the bullying episode (Pepler et al., 1993). Pepler has helped establish the Teen Relationship Project at the LaMarsh Centre for Research in Toronto. Bullying here is viewed as a relationship problem in which there is a misuse and imbalance of power. One current focus in this area by scholars such as Marlene Moretti of Simon Fraser University is the increasing involvement of girls in interpersonal violence (Moretti, Odgers, & Jackson, 2004).

Returning to our original question, does the weight of evidence support the idea that adolescence is usually a period of turmoil and turbulence? Overall, recent consensus of the experts has been that adolescence is *not* an exceptionally difficult period (Petersen et al., 1993; Steinberg & Levine, 1997). However, in a recent reanalysis of the evidence, Jerry Arnett (1999) has argued convincingly that "not all adolescents experience storm and stress, but storm and stress is more likely during adolescence than at other ages" (p. 317). Arnett is quick to emphasize that turmoil in adolescence is far from universal, but he maintains that, on average, adolescence is somewhat more stressful than other developmental periods.

Although turbulence and turmoil are not *universal* features of adolescence, challenging adaptations *do* have to be made during this period. In particular, most adolescents struggle to some extent in their effort to achieve a sound sense of identity.

The Search for Identity

Erik Erikson was especially interested in personality development during adolescence, which is the fifth of the eight major life stages he described. The psychosocial crisis during this stage pits *identity* against *confu-*

sion. According to Erikson (1968), the premiere challenge of adolescence is the struggle to form a clear sense of identity. This struggle involves working out a stable concept of oneself as a unique individual and embracing an ideology or system of values that provides a sense of direction. In Erikson's view, adolescents grapple with questions such as "Who am I, and where am I going in life?"

Erikson recognized that the process of identity formation begins before adolescence and often extends beyond it, as his own life illustrates (Coles, 1970; Roazen, 1976). Erikson's mother, who was Jewish, was abandoned by her Danish father before Erik's birth in 1902 in Germany. Within a few years, his mother married a Jewish doctor and the two of them raised Erik in the Jewish faith as Erik Homburger. Erik was viewed as a Jew by his schoolmates, but he was viewed as a gentile at his temple because of his decidedly Scandinavian appearance. Thus, Erikson struggled with identity confusion early in life.

During adolescence Erikson began to resist family pressures to study medicine. Instead, he wandered about Europe until he was 25, trying to "find himself" as an artist. His interest in psychoanalysis was sparked by an introduction to Sigmund Freud's youngest daughter, Anna, a pioneer of child psychoanalysis. After his psychoanalytic training, he moved to the United States. When he became a naturalized U.S. citizen in 1939, he changed his surname from Homburger to Erikson. Clearly, Erikson was struggling with the question of "Who am I?" well into adulthood. Small wonder, then, that he focused a great deal of attention on identity formation.

Although the struggle for a sense of identity is a lifelong process (Waterman & Archer, 1990), it does tend to be especially intense during adolescence. Adolescents deal with identity formation in a variety of ways. According to Simon Fraser University's James Marcia (1966, 1980, 1994), the presence or absence of a sense of commitment (to life goals and values) and a sense of crisis (active questioning and exploration) can combine to produce four different *identity statuses* (see Figure 11.18). These are not stages

Web Link 11.6

Teen Relationship Project
http://www.arts.yorku.ca/lamarsh/projects/trp/

More information on bullying and its prevention can be obtained from this useful Web site.

Web Link 11.7

Gender and Aggression Project
http://www.sfu.ca/gap/

Find out more about gender and bullying at this site maintained at Simon Fraser University.

Figure 11.18

Marcia's four identity statuses. According to Canadian psychologist James Marcia (1980), the occurrence of identity crisis and exploration and the development of personal commitments can combine into four possible identity statuses, as shown in this diagram. The progressively darker shades of blue signify progressively more mature identity statuses.

Source: Adapted from Marcia, J. E. (1980). Identity in adolescence. In J. Adelson (Ed.), *Handbook of adolescent psychology* (pp. 159–210). New York: John Wiley. Copyright © 1980 by John Wiley. Adapted by permission.

		Crisis	
		Present	**Absent**
Commitment	**Present**	**Identity achievement** (successful achievement of a sense of identity)	**Identity foreclosure** (unquestioning adoption of parental or societal values)
	Absent	**Identity moratorium** (active struggling for a sense of identity)	**Identity diffusion** (absence of struggle for identity, with no obvious concern about it)

that people pass through, but orientations that may occur at a particular time. In order of increasing maturity, Marcia's four identity statuses are as follows (Meeus, 1996):

- *Identity diffusion* is a state of rudderless apathy. Some people simply refuse to confront the challenge of charting a life course and committing to an ideology. Although this stance allows them to evade the crisis of identity, the lack of direction can become problematic, as people in this status exhibit more social and psychological problems than others (Adams, Gullotta, & Montemayor, 1992).
- *Identity foreclosure* is a premature commitment to visions, values, and roles—typically those prescribed by one's parents. This path allows a person to circumvent much of the struggle for an identity. However, it may backfire and cause problems later (Kroger, 2003).
- An *identity moratorium* involves delaying commitment for a while to experiment with alternative ideologies and careers. Such experimentation can be valuable. Unfortunately, some people remain indefinitely in what should be a temporary phase. Identity moratorium is associated with self-doubt and confusion (Flum, 1994).

- *Identity achievement* involves arriving at a sense of self and direction after some consideration of alternative possibilities. Commitments have the strength of some conviction, although they're not absolutely irrevocable. Identity achievement is associated with higher self-esteem, greater security, and a variety of other healthy traits (Marcia et al., 1993).

Age trends in identity status are depicted in Figure 11.19. Consistent with Marcia's theory, identity moratorium and achievement increase with age while identity diffusion and foreclosure decline (Meeus et al., 1999). Although the age trends seen in Figure 11.19 make sense, they mask the extent to which a sizable majority of adolescents shift back and forth among the four identity statuses (Berzonsky & Adams, 1999). Moreover, people tend to reach identity achievement at later ages than originally envisioned by Marcia. By late adolescence, only a small minority of individuals have reached identity achievement, so the struggle for a sense of identity routinely extends into young adulthood. Actually, even after people reach identity achievement, the process of identity formation continues (Kroger, 1996).

Erikson, Marcia, and many other theorists believe that adequate identity formation is a cornerstone of sound psychological health. Identity confusion can interfere with important developmental transitions that should unfold during the adult years, as you'll see in the next section, which takes a look at developmental trends during adulthood.

Figure 11.19

Age and identity status.

These data from Meilman (1979) summarize the relationship between age and Marcia's (1980) identity statuses. The less mature statuses (diffusion and foreclosure) become less common as people move into young adulthood and the more mature statuses (moratorium and identity achievement) become more common. As you can see, at age 18, relatively few people have reached identity achievement.

SOURCE: Adapted from Meilman, P. W. (1979). Cross-sectional age changes in ego identity status during adolescence. *Developmental Psychology, 15*, 230–231. Copyright © 1979 by the American Psychological Association. Reprinted by permission of the author.

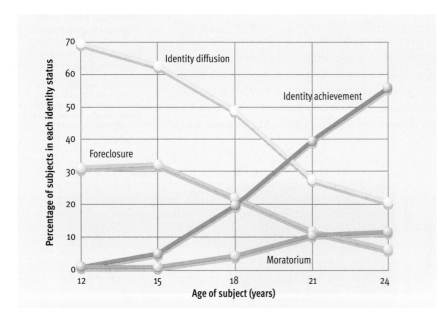

REVIEW OF KEY POINTS

- The growth spurt at puberty is a prominent event involving the development of reproductive maturity and secondary sex characteristics.
- Adolescent suicide rates have climbed dramatically in recent decades, and attempted suicides have increased even more. Although school shootings remain rare, there is an association between adolescence and the prevalence of violent crime. Most theorists do not view adolescence as a time of turmoil, but Arnett argues that adolescence is slightly more stressful than other periods of life.
- According to Erikson, the key challenge of adolescence is to make some progress toward a sense of identity. Marcia identified four patterns of identity formation: identity diffusion, identity foreclosure, identity moratorium, and identity achievement.

The Expanse of Adulthood

The concept of development was once associated almost exclusively with childhood and adolescence, but today it is widely appreciated that development is a life-long journey. The life-span approach to development assumes that important changes occur throughout the life cycle. Recent years have also brought increasing recognition that the historical context people live in can have profound impact on their developmental trajectories. As Stewart and Ostrove (1998) put it, "It makes sense that generations raised with different expectations and in different historical circumstances may age differently" (p. 1185). Events such as the Great Depression, World Wars I and II, the women's movement, the AIDS epidemic, the emergence of television, and the rise of the Internet can leave a lasting mark on the people exposed to them. Complicating the picture further, developmental patterns are becoming increasingly diverse. The boundaries between young, middle, and late adulthood are becoming blurred as more and more people have children later than one is "supposed" to, retire earlier than one is "supposed" to, and so forth. In the upcoming pages we will look at some of the major developmental transitions in adult life, but you should bear in mind that in adulthood (even more so than childhood or adolescence) there are many divergent pathways and timetables.

Personality Development

9c

In recent years, research on adult personality development has been dominated by one key question: How stable is personality over the life span? We'll look at this issue, the question of the midlife crisis, and Erikson's view of adulthood in our discussion of personality development in the adult years.

The Question of Stability

After tracking subjects through adulthood, many researchers have been impressed by the amount of change observed. Roger Gould (1975) studied two samples of men and women and concluded that "the evolution of a personality continues through the fifth decade of life." In a study following women from their college years through their 40s, Helson and Moane (1987) found that "personality does change from youth to middle age in consistent and often predictable ways." After tracking development between the ages of 20 and 42, Whitbourne and her colleagues (1992) found "consistent patterns of personality change."

In contrast, many other researchers have been struck by the stability and durability they have found in personality. The general conclusion that emerged from several longitudinal studies using objective assessments of personality traits was that personality tends to be quite stable over periods of 20 to 40 years (Block, 1981; Caspi & Herbener, 1990; Costa & McCrae, 1994, 1997). Moreover, a recent review of 150 relevant studies, involving almost 50 000 participants, concluded that personality in early adulthood was a good predictor of personality in late adulthood and that the stability of personality increases with age up to about age 50 (Roberts & DelVecchio, 2000).

In sum, researchers assessing the stability of personality in adulthood have reached very different conclusions (Kogan, 1990). How can these contradictory conclusions be reconciled? This appears to be one of those debates in which researchers are eyeing the same findings but from different perspectives. Hence, some conclude that the glass is half full, whereas others conclude that it's half empty. In his discussion of this controversy, Lawrence Pervin (1994) concludes that personality is characterized by *both* stability and change. It appears that some personality traits tend to remain stable, while others tend to change systematically as people grow older. For example, in a recent study of personality functioning between the ages of 18 and 26, the investigators found a great deal of stability, but they also found some interesting changes in the direction of greater maturity (Roberts, Caspi, & Moffitt, 2001). Specifically, the young adults in this study became more controlled and confident and less angry and alienated.

The Question of the Midlife Crisis

There has also been a spirited debate about whether most people go through a *midlife crisis*—**a difficult, turbulent period of doubts and reappraisal of one's life.** The two most influential studies of adult development in the 1970s (Gould, 1978; Levinson et al., 1978) both concluded that a midlife crisis is a normal transition experienced by a majority of people. However, since these landmark studies, a host of subsequent studies have failed to detect an increase in emotional turbulence at midlife (Eisler & Ragsdale, 1992; Roberts & Newton, 1987; Rosenberg, Rosenberg, & Farrell, 1999).

How can we explain this discrepancy? Levinson and Gould both studied samples that were less than

PREVIEW QUESTIONS
- How stable is personality over the life span?
- How did Erikson describe adult development?
- How does marital satisfaction tend to evolve over the life span?
- How difficult are the transitions to parenthood and the empty nest?
- What kinds of physical changes occur in middle and late adulthood?
- What is dementia, and what is its chief cause in old age?
- How well do intelligence and memory hold up in middle and late adulthood?

ideal. Levinson's was unusually small, and Gould's was not very representative. Moreover, both researchers depended primarily on interview and case study methods to gather their data. As we noted in Chapter 2, when knitting together impressionistic case studies, it is easy for investigators to see what they expect to see. Given that the midlife crisis has long been part of developmental folklore, Levinson and Gould may have been prone to interpret their case study data in this light (McCrae & Costa, 1984). In any case, investigators relying on more objective measures of emotional stability have found signs of midlife crises in only a tiny minority (2%–5%) of subjects (Chiriboga, 1989; McCrae & Costa, 1990). Midlife may bring a period of increased reflection as people contemplate the remainder of their lives, but it's clear that the fabled midlife *crisis* is not typical (Lachman, 2004; Lemme, 1999).

Erikson's View of Adulthood 9c

Insofar as personality changes during the adult years, Erik Erikson's (1963) theory offers some clues about the nature of changes people can expect. In his eight-stage model of development over the life span, Erikson divided adulthood into three stages (see again Figure 11.8 on page 451).

Intimacy versus Isolation In early adulthood, the key concern is whether one can develop the capacity to share intimacy with others. Successful resolution of the challenges in this stage should promote empathy and openness, rather than shrewdness and manipulativeness.

Generativity versus Self-Absorption In middle adulthood, the key challenge is to acquire a genuine concern for the welfare of future generations, which results in providing unselfish guidance to younger people and concern with one's legacy. Self-absorption is characterized by self-indulgent concerns with meeting one's own needs and desires.

Integrity versus Despair During the retirement years, the challenge is to avoid the tendency to dwell on the mistakes of the past and on one's imminent death. People need to find meaning and satisfaction in their lives, rather than wallow in bitterness and resentment.

Empirical research on the adult stages in Erikson's theory has been sparse, but generally supportive of the theory. For example, research by Susan Whitbourne and her colleagues (1992) suggests that personality development proceeds in an orderly sequence of stages and that favourable resolutions of psychosocial crises in earlier stages lead to more favourable out-

comes in later stages. And *generativity* has proven to be a measurable trait that increases between young adulthood and middle age as originally envisioned by Erikson (McAdams, de St. Aubin, & Logan, 1993).

Transitions in Family Life

Many of the important transitions in adulthood involve changes in family responsibilities and relationships. Predictable patterns of development can be seen in families, just as they can in individuals (Carter & McGoldrick, 1988, 1999). **The *family life cycle* is a sequence of stages that families tend to progress through.** However, in contemporary North American society, shifting social trends are altering the traditional family life cycle. In the eyes of most people, the typical North American family consists of a husband and wife who have never been married to anyone else, rearing two or more children, with the man serving as the principal breadwinner and the woman filling the homemaker role (Coontz, 2000; McGraw & Walker, 2004). This configuration was never as dominant as widely assumed, and today it is estimated that only a small minority of North American families match this idealized image. The increasing prevalence of people remaining single, cohabitating, getting divorced, being single parents, having stepfamilies, voluntarily remaining childless, or having children out of wedlock, and of wives and mothers working has made the traditional nuclear family a deceptive mirage that does not reflect the diversity of family life.

Diversity aside, everyone emerges from families, and most people go on to form their own family. However, the transitional period during which young adults are "between families" until they form a new family is being prolonged by more and more individuals. According to recent Canadian statistics, the percentage of young adults since the 1970s who are postponing marriage until their late 20s or early 30s has risen dramatically (Wu, 1998; see Figure 11.20). However, if viewed in the context of a longer time period, this upswing represents a return to marriage ages typical of the 1920s. There have also been changes in the structure of committed relationships, with a decline in number of marriages in the 1990s in Canada (Statistics Canada, 2004e). According to an analysis provided by the Canadian Department of Justice (Wichmann, 2005), common-law relationships have increased, going from 5.6% in 1981 to 13.8% in 2001. The trend toward increasing numbers of common-law relationships is particularly strong in Quebec. Also, remaining single is a much more acceptable option today than it was a few decades ago (DeFrain & Olson, 1999). In 2001, there were over 1 million single mature adults and only about one-half of them expected to marry (Statistics Canada, 2005c). The adults who expected not to marry were found to have less conventional views about the importance of love, family, children, and marriage. Nonetheless, most adults—about 90% of Canadians—eventually marry. Recent data also indicate that, once married, fewer Canadians are getting divorced (a decline of 27.1% since the all-time peak in 1997), and when they do divorce, they are doing so at later ages. However, repeat divorces (people divorcing who have been divorced before) are accounting for an increasing percentage of all divorces in Canada (Statistics Canada, 2005e).

Adjusting to Marriage

The newly married couple usually settle into their roles as husband and wife gradually. Difficulties with this transition are more likely when spouses come into a marriage with different expectations about marital roles (Lye & Biblarz, 1993). Unfortunately, substantial differences in role expectations seem particularly likely in this era of transition in gender roles (Brewster & Padavic, 2000).

Women may be especially vulnerable to ambivalence about shifting marital roles. More and more women are aspiring to demanding careers. Yet, research shows that husbands' careers continue to take priority over their wives' vocational ambitions (Haas, 1999). Moreover, many husbands maintain traditional role expectations about housework, child-care, and decision making (Blair, 1993). Men's contribution to housework has increased slightly in recent decades, but studies indicate that wives are still doing the bulk of the household chores, even when they work outside the home (Coltrane, 2001; Robinson & Godbey, 1997). Although married women perform about two-thirds of all housework, only about one-third of wives characterize their division of labour as unfair, because most women don't expect a 50–50 split (Coltrane, 2001). Research shows that women who have nontraditional attitudes about gender roles are more likely to perceive their share of housework as unfair than women with traditional attitudes (Greenstein, 1996). As you might expect, wives who perceive their housework burden to be unfair tend to report lower levels of marital satisfaction (Haas, 1999).

In general, however, the first few years of married life tend to be characterized by great happiness—the proverbial "marital bliss." Numerous studies have measured spouses' overall satisfaction in different stages of the family life cycle and found a U-shaped relationship like that shown in Figure 11.21 (Glenn,

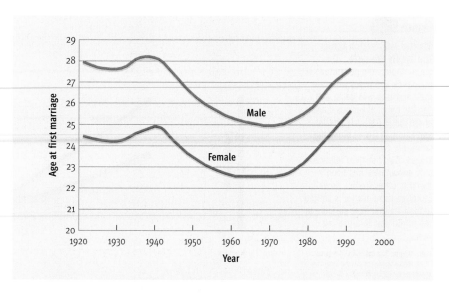

Figure 11.20

Median age at first marriage. The median age at which people in Canada marry for the first time has been creeping up for both males and females since the mid-1970s. This trend indicates that more people are postponing marriage. But, if viewed in historical context since the 1920s, this change reflects a return to previous levels.

SOURCE: Wu, Zheng. (1998). Recent trends in marriage patterns in Canada. *Policy Options, 3*, 3–6. http://www.irpp.org/po/archive/sep98/wu.pdf. Adapted from the Statistics Canada publication, *Selected Marriage Statistics, 1921–1990,* catalogue 82-552, 1992.

1990; Orbuch et al., 1996). This U shape reflects the fact that satisfaction tends to be greatest at the beginning and end of the family life cycle, with a noticeable decline in the middle. The conventional explanation for this pattern is that the burdens of childrearing, and resulting reduction in time spent together, undermine couples' satisfaction, which gradually climbs back up again as children grow up and these burdens ease. However, marital satisfaction tends to decline in the early years of marriage even when there are no children, so other factors and processes may also contribute to this U-shaped pattern (Bradbury, 1998; Glenn, 1998).

The pre-children phase of the family life cycle used to be rather short for most newly married couples. Traditionally, couples just *assumed* that they would proceed to have children. In recent decades, however, ambivalence about the prospect of having children clearly has increased (T. W. Smith, 1999), and the percentage of childless couples has doubled since 1960 (Bulcroft & Teachman, 2004; Groat et al., 1997). Hence, more and more couples are finding themselves struggling to decide *whether* to have children. Interestingly, intentions about having children are not as stable over time as one might expect. In one study that followed adult participants over a span of six years, about one-quarter of the respondents changed their plans (Heaton et al., 1999). These subjects were almost evenly split between

Figure 11.21

Marital satisfaction across the family life cycle. This graph depicts the percentage of husbands and wives who said their marriage was going well "all the time" at various stages of the family life cycle. Rollins and Feldman (1970) broke the family life cycle into eight stages. The U-shaped relationship shown here has been found in other studies as well, although its relevance is limited to families that have children in the traditional childbearing years.

Source: Adapted from Rollins, B. C., & Feldman, H. (1970). Marital satisfaction over the family cycle. *Journal of Marriage and Family, 32*, 20–28. Copyright © 1975 by the National Council on Family Relations. Reprinted by permission.

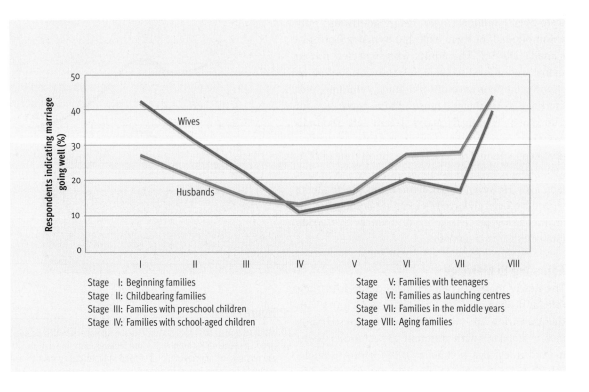

Stage   I: Beginning families
Stage II: Childbearing families
Stage III: Families with preschool children
Stage IV: Families with school-aged children

Stage   V: Families with teenagers
Stage VI: Families as launching centres
Stage VII: Families in the middle years
Stage VIII: Aging families

those who planned to remain childless but subsequently decided they wanted to have children and those who intended to have children but subsequently expressed a preference for remaining child-free.

Adjusting to Parenthood

Although an increasing number of people are choosing to remain childless, the vast majority of married couples continue to have children, and they rate parenthood as a highly positive experience (Demo, 1992). Nonetheless, the arrival of the first child represents a *major* transition, and the disruption of old routines can be extremely stressful (Carter, 1999). The new mother, already physically exhausted by the birth process, is particularly prone to postpartum stress (Hock et al., 1995). Wives are especially vulnerable when they have to shoulder the major burden of infant care (Kalmuss, Davidson, & Cushman, 1992).

Crisis during the transition to first parenthood is far from universal, however (Cox et al., 1999). Couples who have high levels of affection and commitment prior to the first child's birth are likely to maintain a stable level of satisfaction after the birth (Shapiro, Gottman, & Carrere, 2000). The key to making this transition less stressful may be to have *realistic expectations* about parental responsibilities (Belsky & Kelly, 1994). Studies find that stress is greatest in new parents who have overestimated the benefits and underestimated the costs of their new role.

As children grow up, parental influence over them tends to decline, and the early years of parenting—that once seemed so difficult—are often recalled with fondness. When youngsters reach adolescence and seek to establish their own identities, gradual realignments occur in parent–child relationships. On the one hand, parent–adolescent relations generally are not as bitter or contentious as widely assumed (Laursen, Coy, & Collins, 1998). On the other hand, adolescents do spend less time in family activities (Larson et al., 1996) and their closeness to their parents declines while conflicts become more frequent (Grotevant, 1997). The conflicts tend to involve everyday matters (chores and appearance) more than substantive issues (sex and drugs) (Barber, 1994). When conflicts occur, they seem to have more adverse effects on the parents than the children (Steinberg & Steinberg, 1994). Ironically, although research has shown that adolescence is not as turbulent or difficult for youngsters as once believed, their parents *are* stressed out (Steinberg, 2001).

Adjusting to the Empty Nest

When parents do manage to get all their children launched into the adult world, they find themselves faced with an "empty nest." This period was formerly thought to be a difficult transition for many parents, especially mothers who were familiar only with the maternal role. In recent decades, however, more women have experience with other roles outside the home. Hence, recent evidence suggests that most

Although children can be unparalleled sources of joy and satisfaction, the transition to parenthood can be extremely stressful, especially for mothers.

parents adjust effectively to the empty nest transition and are more likely to have problems if their children *return* to the once-empty nest (Blacker, 1999; Dennerstein, Dudley, & Guthrie, 2002).

The postparental period often provides couples with new freedom to devote attention to each other. Many couples take advantage of this opportunity by travelling or developing new leisure interests. However, spouses do have to adapt to spending more time with each other and often need to renegotiate role expectations (Walsh, 1999). Of course, age-related considerations that are independent of the relationship, such as the increased likelihood of physical illness, can make the later years stressful. In general, however, the trend is for couples to report fairly high satisfaction until one of the spouses (usually the husband) dies.

Aging and Physical Changes

People obviously experience many physical changes as they progress through adulthood. In both sexes, hair tends to thin out and become grey, and many males confront receding hairlines and baldness. To the dismay of many, the proportion of body fat tends to increase with age, while the amount of muscle tissue decreases. Overall, weight tends to increase in most adults through the mid-50s, when a gradual decline may begin. These changes have little functional significance, but in our youth-oriented society, they often have an impact on self-concept, leading many people to view themselves as unattractive (Whitbourne, 1999).

In the sensory domain, the key developmental changes occur in vision and hearing. The proportion of people with 20/20 visual acuity declines with age. Farsightedness, difficulty adapting to darkness, and poor recovery from glare are common among older people (Fozard, 1990). Sensitivity to colour and contrast also decline (Fozard & Gordon-Salant, 2001).

Hearing sensitivity begins declining gradually in early adulthood but usually isn't noticeable until after age 50. Hearing loss tends to be greater in men than in women and for high-frequency sounds more than low-frequency sounds (Yost, 2000). These sensory losses could be problematic, but in modern society they can usually be compensated for with eyeglasses, contacts, and hearing aids.

Age-related changes also occur in hormonal functioning during adulthood. Among women, these changes lead to *menopause*. This ending of menstrual periods, accompanied by a loss of fertility, typically occurs at around age 50 (Avis, 1999). Most women experience at least some unpleasant symptoms (such as hot flashes, headaches, night sweats, mood changes), but the amount of discomfort varies considerably. Not long ago, menopause was thought to be almost universally accompanied by severe emotional strain. However, it is now clear that most women experience relatively modest psychological distress (Dennerstein, 1996). Although people sometimes talk about "male menopause," men don't really go through an equivalent experience. Starting in middle age, testosterone levels *do* decline substantially (Morley, 2001), but these decreases are gradual and are not associated with a constellation of symptoms comparable to what women experience (Jacobs, 2001).

The amount of brain tissue and brain weight decline gradually after age 60 (Vinters, 2001). These trends appear to reflect both a decrease in the number of active neurons in some areas of the brain and shrinkage of still-active neurons, with neuron loss perhaps being less important than once believed (Albert & Killiany, 2001). Although this gradual loss of brain tissue sounds alarming, it is a normal part of the aging process. Its functional significance is the subject of some debate, but it doesn't appear to be a key factor in any of the age-related dementias. **A *dementia* is an abnormal condition marked by multiple cognitive deficits that include memory impairment.** Dementia can be caused by quite a variety of diseases, such as Alzheimer's disease, Parkinson's disease, Huntington's disease, and AIDS, to name just a few (Caine & Lyness, 2000). Because many of these diseases are more prevalent in older adults, dementia is seen in about 15%–20% of people over age 75 (Wise, Gray, & Seltzer, 1999). However, it is important to emphasize that dementia and "senility" are not part of the normal aging process. As Cavanaugh (1993) notes, "The term *senility* has no valid medical or psychological meaning, and its continued use simply perpetuates the myth that drastic mental decline is a product of normal aging" (p. 85).

Alzheimer's disease accounts for roughly 70% of all cases of dementia (Fromholt & Bruhn, 1999). Alzheimer's disease is accompanied by major structural deterioration in the brain. Alzheimer's patients exhibit profound and widespread loss of neurons and brain tissue and the accumulation of characteristic neural abnormalities known as neuritic plaques and neurofibrillary tangles (Vinters, 2001). In the early stages of the disease, this damage is largely centred in the hippocampal region, which is known to play a crucial role in many facets of memory, but as the disease advances it spreads throughout much of the brain (Rabins, Lyketsos, & Steele, 1999). The causes that launch this debilitating neural meltdown are not well understood.

Alzheimer's disease is a vicious affliction that can strike during middle age but usually emerges after age 65. The beginnings of Alzheimer's disease are so subtle they are often recognized only after the disease has progressed for a year or two. The hallmark early symptom is the forgetting of newly learned information after surprisingly brief periods of time (Albert & Killiany, 2001). The course of the disease is one of progressive deterioration, typically over a period of eight to ten years, ending in death (Rabins et al., 1999). In the beginning, victims simply lose

the thread of conversations or forget to follow through on tasks they have started. Problems may appear in situations dependent upon selective attention. Research by York University's Susan Murtha and her colleagues (Levinoff et al., 2002) suggests that in the early stages of Alzheimer's, patients show deficits in one particular facet of selective attention—that of inhibition. You may recall our discussion of selective attention in Chapter 7.

Gradually, much more obvious problems begin to emerge, including difficulties in speaking, comprehending, and performing complicated tasks, as well as depression and sleep disturbance. Job performance deteriorates noticeably as victims forget important appointments and suffer indignities such as getting lost while driving and paying the same bill several times. Studies continue to be conducted in attempts to document the specific deficits found in these patients. Research by Jill Rich and her colleagues (Rich et al., 2002), for example, determined that language-based semantic judgments are especially impaired when the memory task is presented to patients with Alzheimer's in unstructured formats as compared to relatively structured, supportive contexts. This suggests that Rich's sample of Alzheimer's patients were showing difficulties in the retrieval stage. Results such as these emphasize the importance of supportive environments for patients suffering from Alzheimer's.

At some point, profound memory loss develops. For example, patients may fail to recognize familiar people, something particularly devastating to family and friends. Many patients become very restless and experience hallucinations, delusions, and paranoid thoughts. Eventually, victims become completely disoriented and are unable to care for themselves. There are some encouraging leads for treatments that might slow the progression of this horrific disease, but a cure does not appear to be on the horizon.

Aging and Cognitive Changes

The evidence indicates that general intelligence is fairly stable throughout most of adulthood, with a small decline in *average* test scores often seen after age 60 (Schaie, 1990, 1994, 1996). However, this seemingly simple assertion masks many complexities and needs to be qualified carefully. First, group averages can be deceptive in that mean scores can be dragged down by a small minority of people who show a decline. For example, when Schaie (1990) calculated the percentage of people who maintain stable performance on various abilities (see Figure 11.22), he found that about 80% showed no decline by age

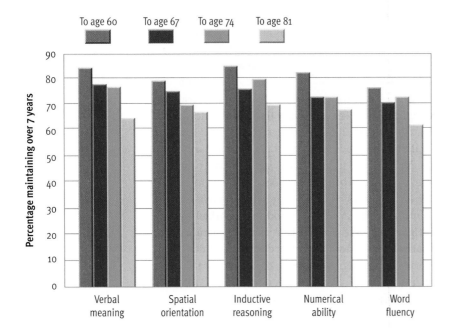

Figure 11.22

Age and the stability of primary mental abilities. In his longitudinal study of cognitive performance begun in 1956, Schaie (1983, 1993) has repeatedly assessed the five basic mental abilities listed along the bottom of this chart. The data graphed here show the percentage of subjects who maintained stable levels of performance on each ability through various ages up to age 81. As you can see, even through the age of 81, the majority of subjects show no significant decline on most abilities. (From Schaie, 1990)

SOURCE: Adapted from Schaie, K. W. (1990). Intellectual development in adulthood. In J. E. Birren and K. W. Schaie (Eds.), *Handbook of the psychology of aging* (pp. 291–309). San Diego: Academic Press. Copyright © 1990 Elsevier Science (USA), reproduced with permission from the publisher.

60 and that about two-thirds were still stable through age 81. Second, even when age-related decreases in intellectual performance are found, they tend to be small in all but a few individuals (Salthouse, 1991). Third, some forms of intelligence are more vulnerable to aging than others. As we noted in Chapter 9, many theorists distinguish between *fluid intelligence,* which refers to basic information-processing skills, and *crystallized intelligence,* which refers to the application of accumulated knowledge. Research suggests that fluid intelligence is much more likely to decline with age, whereas crystallized intelligence tends to remain stable (Baltes, Staudinger, & Lindenberger, 1999; Horn & Hofer, 1992).

What about memory? Numerous studies report decreases in older adults' memory capabilities (Backman et al., 1999). But the memory losses associated with normal aging tend to be moderate and are *not* universal (Shimamura et al., 1995). A major consideration is the type of memory that is assessed (see Chapter 7 for a review of the various types of memory). The most reliable decrements are usually seen in *episodic memory* and *working memory,* with less consistent losses observed on tasks involving *procedural memory* and *semantic memory* (Backman, Small, & Wahlin, 2001; Dixon & Cohen, 2003). According to Salthouse (1994), it is the age-related decline in the capacity of working memory that underlies older adults' poorer performance on a wide range of cognitive tasks. He attributes most of the decline in working memory to age-related decreases in the raw speed of mental processing.

Another important component of memory that is relevant to aging is the concept of meta-memory, or the level of the senior's awareness of the nature of his or her own memory functioning. Recently, Angela Troyer of the Baycrest Centre for Geriatric Care and Jill Rich of York University (Troyer & Rich, 2002) developed a new questionnaire, known as the Multifactorial Memory Questionnaire, designed to assess the dimensions of satisfaction with one's memory ability, perception of everyday memory ability, and the use of everyday memory strategies and aids. This should prove to be a valuable tool in assessing memory functioning in seniors in the future.

In the cognitive domain, aging does seem to take its toll on *speed* first. Many studies indicate that speed in learning, solving problems, and processing information tends to decline with age (Salthouse, 1996). The evidence suggests that the erosion of processing speed may be a gradual, lengthy trend beginning in middle adulthood (Verhaeghen & Salthouse, 1997). The general nature of this trend (across differing

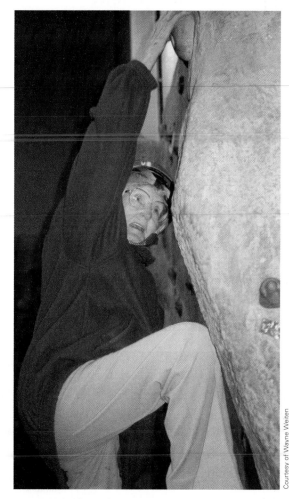

Courtesy of Wayne Weiten

Contrary to widespread stereotypes, many people remain active and productive in their 70s, 80s, and even beyond. Pictured here is Wayne Weiten's Auntie Mildred, at age 99, having a little fun at a child's birthday party held at a rock-climbing facility. Now 102, Mildred still composes poetry and you can't pull her away from her personal computer.

tasks) suggests that it may be the result of age-related changes in neurological functioning (Salthouse, 2000), although doubts have been raised about this conclusion (Bashore, Ridderinkhof, & van der Molen, 1997). Although mental speed declines with age, problem-solving ability remains largely unimpaired if older people are given adequate time to compensate for their reduced speed.

It should be emphasized that many people remain capable of great intellectual accomplishments well into their later years (Simonton, 1990, 1997). This fact was verified in a study of scholarly, scientific, and artistic productivity that examined lifelong patterns of work among 738 men who lived at least through the age of 79. Dennis (1966) found that the 40s decade was the most productive in most professions. However, productivity was remarkably stable through the 60s and even the 70s in many areas.

An Overview of Human Development

Adolescence (12–20)	Young adulthood (20–40)

Adolescence
(12–20)

In boys, growth spurt begins around age 13, bringing dramatic increases in height and weight.

Level of pituitary activity and hormones increases.

Boys' secondary sex characteristics (such as voice change and growth of facial hair) begin to emerge.

In boys, puberty begins around age 14; boys become capable of ejaculation.

Young adulthood
(20–40)

Reaction time and muscular strength peak in early to mid-20s.

Maximum functioning of all body systems, including senses, attained; slow decline begins in 20s.

External signs of aging begin to show in 30s; skin loses elasticity; hair is thinner, more likely to be grey.

Lowered metabolic rate contributes to increased body fat relative to muscle; gain in weight is common.

Formal operational	
Postconventional (if attained)	
Identity vs. confusion	Intimacy vs. isolation
Genital	

Deductive reasoning improves; problem solving becomes more systematic, with alternative possibilities considered before solution is selected.

Thought becomes more abstract and reflective; individual develops ability to mentally manipulate abstract concepts as well as concrete objects.

Individual engages in idealistic contemplation of hypotheticals, "what could be."

Long-term memory continues to improve as elaboration is added to encoding strategies.

Intellectual abilities and speed of information processing are stable.

Greater emphasis is on application, rather than acquisition, of knowledge.

There is some evidence of a trend toward dialectical thought (ideas stimulate opposing ideas), leading to more contemplation of contradictions, pros and cons.

Person experiences increased interactions with opposite-sex peers; dating begins.

Attention is devoted to identity formation, questions such as "Who am I?" and "What do I want out of life?"

Realistic considerations about abilities and training requirements become more influential in thoughts about vocations and jobs.

Energies are focused on intimate relationships, learning to live with marriage partner, starting a family, managing a home.

Trial period is given for occupational choices, followed by stabilization of vocational commitment; emphasis is on self-reliance, becoming one's own person.

For many, close relationship develops with mentor (older person who serves as role model, adviser, and teacher).

© David Young-Wolff/PhotoEdit

PhotoDisc/Getty Images

Early childhood
(2–6)

Connections among neurons continue to increase in density.

Visual acuity reaches 20/20.

Bladder and bowel control is established.

Hand preference is usually solidified by 3–4 years; coordination improves; children learn to dress themselves.

Middle childhood
(6–12)

In girls, growth spurt begins around age 11, bringing dramatic increases in height and weight.

Level of pituitary activity and sex hormones increases.

In girls, puberty begins around age 12; menstruation starts.

Girls' secondary sex characteristics (such as breast development and widening hips) begin to emerge.

Preoperational	Concrete operational
Preconventional	Conventional
Initiative vs. guilt	Industry vs. inferiority
Phallic	Latency

Thought is marked by egocentrism (limited ability to view world from another's perspective).

Thought is marked by centration (inability to focus on more than one aspect of a problem at a time) and irreversibility (inability to mentally undo an action).

Telegraphic speech (omitting nonessential words) appears at 2–3 years; syntax is well developed by age 5; vocabulary increases dramatically.

Short-term memory capacity increases from two items at age 2 to five items around age 6–7; attention span improves.

Conservation (understanding that physical qualities can remain constant in spite of transformations in shape) is gradually mastered.

Child develops decentration (ability to focus on more than one feature of a problem at a time) and reversibility (ability to mentally undo an action).

Metalinguistic awareness (ability to reflect on use of language) leads to play with language, use of puns, riddles, metaphors.

Long-term memory improves with increasing use of encoding strategies of rehearsal and organization.

Child realizes that gender does not change and begins to learn gender roles and form gender identity; social behaviour is influenced by observational learning, resulting in imitation.

Child progresses from parallel (side-by-side, noninteractive) play to cooperative play.

Social world is extended beyond family; first friendships are formed.

Child experiences great increase in social skills, improved understanding of others' feelings; social world is dominated by same-sex peer relationships.

Role-taking skills emerge; fantasy is basis for thoughts about vocations and jobs.

Altruism tends to increase, aggression tends to decrease; aggression tends to become verbal rather than physical, hostile more than instrumental.

An Overview of Human Development

Adolescence
(12–20)

In boys, growth spurt begins around age 13, bringing dramatic increases in height and weight.

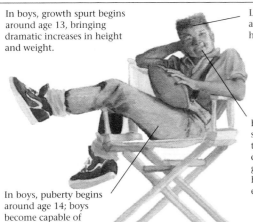

Level of pituitary activity and hormones increases.

Boys' secondary sex characteristics (such as voice change and growth of facial hair) begin to emerge.

In boys, puberty begins around age 14; boys become capable of ejaculation.

Young adulthood
(20–40)

Reaction time and muscular strength peak in early to mid-20s.

External signs of aging begin to show in 30s; skin loses elasticity; hair is thinner, more likely to be grey.

Maximum functioning of all body systems, including senses, attained; slow decline begins in 20s.

Lowered metabolic rate contributes to increased body fat relative to muscle; gain in weight is common.

Formal operational

Postconventional (if attained)

Identity vs. confusion

Intimacy vs. isolation

Genital

Deductive reasoning improves; problem solving becomes more systematic, with alternative possibilities considered before solution is selected.

Thought becomes more abstract and reflective; individual develops ability to mentally manipulate abstract concepts as well as concrete objects.

Individual engages in idealistic contemplation of hypotheticals, "what could be."

Long-term memory continues to improve as elaboration is added to encoding strategies.

Intellectual abilities and speed of information processing are stable.

Greater emphasis is on application, rather than acquisition, of knowledge.

There is some evidence of a trend toward dialectical thought (ideas stimulate opposing ideas), leading to more contemplation of contradictions, pros and cons.

Person experiences increased interactions with opposite-sex peers; dating begins.

Attention is devoted to identity formation, questions such as "Who am I?" and "What do I want out of life?"

Realistic considerations about abilities and training requirements become more influential in thoughts about vocations and jobs.

Energies are focused on intimate relationships, learning to live with marriage partner, starting a family, managing a home.

Trial period is given for occupational choices, followed by stabilization of vocational commitment; emphasis is on self-reliance, becoming one's own person.

For many, close relationship develops with mentor (older person who serves as role model, adviser, and teacher).

60 and that about two-thirds were still stable through age 81. Second, even when age-related decreases in intellectual performance are found, they tend to be small in all but a few individuals (Salthouse, 1991). Third, some forms of intelligence are more vulnerable to aging than others. As we noted in Chapter 9, many theorists distinguish between *fluid intelligence,* which refers to basic information-processing skills, and *crystallized intelligence,* which refers to the application of accumulated knowledge. Research suggests that fluid intelligence is much more likely to decline with age, whereas crystallized intelligence tends to remain stable (Baltes, Staudinger, & Lindenberger, 1999; Horn & Hofer, 1992).

What about memory? Numerous studies report decreases in older adults' memory capabilities (Backman et al., 1999). But the memory losses associated with normal aging tend to be moderate and are *not* universal (Shimamura et al., 1995). A major consideration is the type of memory that is assessed (see Chapter 7 for a review of the various types of memory). The most reliable decrements are usually seen in *episodic memory* and *working memory,* with less consistent losses observed on tasks involving *procedural memory* and *semantic memory* (Backman, Small, & Wahlin, 2001; Dixon & Cohen, 2003). According to Salthouse (1994), it is the age-related decline in the capacity of working memory that underlies older adults' poorer performance on a wide range of cognitive tasks. He attributes most of the decline in working memory to age-related decreases in the raw speed of mental processing.

Another important component of memory that is relevant to aging is the concept of meta-memory, or the level of the senior's awareness of the nature of his or her own memory functioning. Recently, Angela Troyer of the Baycrest Centre for Geriatric Care and Jill Rich of York University (Troyer & Rich, 2002) developed a new questionnaire, known as the Multifactorial Memory Questionnaire, designed to assess the dimensions of satisfaction with one's memory ability, perception of everyday memory ability, and the use of everyday memory strategies and aids. This should prove to be a valuable tool in assessing memory functioning in seniors in the future.

In the cognitive domain, aging does seem to take its toll on *speed* first. Many studies indicate that speed in learning, solving problems, and processing information tends to decline with age (Salthouse, 1996). The evidence suggests that the erosion of processing speed may be a gradual, lengthy trend beginning in middle adulthood (Verhaeghen & Salthouse, 1997). The general nature of this trend (across differing

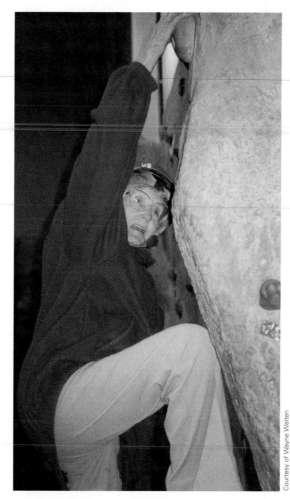

Courtesy of Wayne Weiten

Contrary to widespread stereotypes, many people remain active and productive in their 70s, 80s, and even beyond. Pictured here is Wayne Weiten's Auntie Mildred, at age 99, having a little fun at a child's birthday party held at a rock-climbing facility. Now 102, Mildred still composes poetry and you can't pull her away from her personal computer.

tasks) suggests that it may be the result of age-related changes in neurological functioning (Salthouse, 2000), although doubts have been raised about this conclusion (Bashore, Ridderinkhof, & van der Molen, 1997). Although mental speed declines with age, problem-solving ability remains largely unimpaired if older people are given adequate time to compensate for their reduced speed.

It should be emphasized that many people remain capable of great intellectual accomplishments well into their later years (Simonton, 1990, 1997). This fact was verified in a study of scholarly, scientific, and artistic productivity that examined lifelong patterns of work among 738 men who lived at least through the age of 79. Dennis (1966) found that the 40s decade was the most productive in most professions. However, productivity was remarkably stable through the 60s and even the 70s in many areas.

An Overview of Human Development

Stage of development	Infancy (birth–2)

Physical and sensorimotor development

Rapid brain growth; 75% of adult brain weight is attained by age 2.

Ability to localize sounds is apparent at birth; ability to recognize parent's voice occurs within first week.

Rapid improvement occurs in visual acuity; depth perception is clearly present by 6 months, perhaps earlier.

Landmarks in motor development: Infants sit without support around 6 months, walk around 12–14 months, run freely around 2 years.

Major stage theories

Piaget	Sensorimotor		
Kohlberg	Premoral		
Erikson	Trust vs. mistrust	Autonomy vs. shame	
Freud (see Chapter 12)	Oral	Anal	

Cognitive development

Object permanence gradually develops.

Infant shows orienting response (pupils dilate, head turns) and attention to new stimulus, habituation (reduced orienting response) to repeated stimulus.

Babbling increasingly resembles spoken language.

First word is used around age 1; vocabulary spurt begins around 18 months; frequent overextensions (words applied too broadly) occur.

Social and personality development

Temperamental individuality is established by 2–3 months; infants tend to be easy, difficult, or slow to warm up.

© George Shelley/CORBIS

Attachment to caregiver(s) is usually evident around 6–8 months; secure attachment facilitates exploration.

"Stranger anxiety" often appears around 6–8 months; separation anxiety peaks around 14–18 months.

Information compiled by Barbara Hansen Lemme, College of DuPage

Middle adulthood
(40–65)

Changes occur in vision: increased farsightedness and difficulty recovering from glare; slower dark adaptation.

The amount of brain tissue declines, but significance of this neural loss is unclear.

In women, menopause occurs around age 50; in both sexes, sexual activity declines, although capacity for arousal changes only slightly.

Sensitivity to high-frequency sounds decreases, especially in males after age 55.

Late adulthood
(65 and older)

Height decreases slightly because of changes in vertebral column; decline in weight also common.

Sensitivity of vision, hearing, and taste noticeably decreases.

Chronic diseases, especially heart disease, cancer, and stroke, increase.

Rate of aging is highly individualized.

Generativity vs. self-absorption

There is some evidence for a trend toward improved judgment or "wisdom" based on accumulation of life experiences.

Effectiveness of retrieval from long-term memory begins slow decline, usually not noticeable until after age 55.

Individual experiences gradual decline in speed of learning, problem solving, and information processing.

In spite of decreased speed in cognitive processes, intellectual productivity and problem-solving skills usually remain stable.

Integrity vs. despair

Individual experiences gradual decline in cognitive speed and effectiveness of working memory.

Intellectual productivity depends on factors such as health and lifestyle; many people in 60s and 70s remain quite productive.

Decision making tends to become more cautious.

Fluid intelligence often declines, but crystallized intelligence remains stable or increases.

Midlife transition around age 40 leads to reflection, increased awareness of mortality and passage of time, but usually is not a personal crisis.

"Sandwich generation" is caught between needs of aging parents and children reaching adulthood.

Career development peaks; there is some tendency to shift energy from career concerns to family concerns.

Physical changes associated with aging require adjustments that affect life satisfaction.

Marital satisfaction often increases, but eventually death of spouse presents coping challenge.

Living arrangements are a significant determinant of satisfaction, as 60%–90% of time is spent at home.

Putting It in Perspective

PREVIEW QUESTIONS

● How did this chapter illustrate the interplay of heredity and environment?

● What other unifying themes surfaced in this chapter?

Many of our seven integrative themes surfaced to some degree in our coverage of human development. We saw theoretical diversity in the discussions of attachment, cognitive development, and personality development. We saw that psychology evolves in a sociohistorical context, investigating complex, real-world issues such as the controversy over the effects of daycare. We encountered multifactorial causation of behaviour in the development of temperament and attachment, among other things. We saw cultural invariance and cultural diversity in our examination of attachment, motor development, cognitive development, and moral development.

But above all else, we saw how heredity and environment jointly mould behaviour. We've encountered the dual influence of heredity and environment before, but this theme is rich in complexity, and each chapter draws out different aspects and implications. Our discussion of development amplified the point that genetics and experience work *interactively* to shape behaviour. In the language of science, an interaction means that the effects of one variable depend on the effects of another. In other words, heredity and environment do not operate independently. Children with "difficult" temperaments will elicit different reactions from different parents, depending on the parents' personalities and expectations. Likewise, a particular pair of parents will affect children in different ways, depending on the inborn characteristics of the children. An interplay, or feedback loop, exists between biological and environmental factors. For instance, a temperamentally difficult child may elicit negative reactions from parents, which serve to make the child more difficult, which evokes more negative reactions. If this child develops into an ornery 11-year-old, which do we blame—genetics or experience? Clearly, this outcome is due to the reciprocal effects of both.

All aspects of development are shaped jointly by heredity and experience. We often estimate their relative weight or influence, as if we could cleanly divide behaviour into genetic and environmental components. Although we can't really carve up behaviour that neatly, such comparisons can be of great theoretical interest, as you'll see in our upcoming Personal Application, which discusses the nature and origins of gender differences in behaviour.

REVIEW OF KEY POINTS

● During adulthood, personality is marked by both stability and change. Doubts have surfaced about whether a midlife crisis is a normal developmental transition. Adults who move successfully through the three stages of adulthood posited by Erikson should develop intimacy, generativity, and integrity.

● Many landmarks in adult development involve transitions in family relationships. Difficulty adjusting to marriage is more likely when spouses have different role expectations. Marital satisfaction tends to be highest at the beginning and end of the family life cycle.

● Unrealistic expectations make the adjustment to parenthood more stressful. Parent–adolescent relations are not as contentious as widely assumed. For most parents, the empty nest transition no longer appears to be as stressful as it once was.

● During adulthood, age-related physical transitions include changes in appearance, sensory losses (especially in vision and hearing), and hormonal changes. Menopause is not as problematic as widely suggested. Drastic mental decline is not a part of the normal aging process. However, 15%–20% of adults over age 75 suffer from some form of dementia.

● In the cognitive domain, general intelligence is fairly stable, with a small decline in average test scores seen after the age of 60. Many studies have found decreases in older adults' memory capabilities, but the losses are moderate and variable. Mental speed declines in late adulthood. Nonetheless, many people remain productive well into old age.

● Many of our seven integrative themes stood out in this chapter. But above all else, our discussion of development showed how heredity and environment interactively shape behaviour.

PERSONAL APPLICATION

Understanding Gender Differences

Answer the following "true" or "false."

____ 1 Females are more socially oriented than males.

____ 2 Males outperform females on most spatial tasks.

____ 3 Females are more irrational than males.

____ 4 Males are less sensitive to nonverbal cues than females.

____ 5 Females are more emotional than males.

Are there genuine behavioural differences between the sexes similar to those mentioned above? If so, why do these differences exist? How do they develop? These are the complex and controversial questions that we'll explore in this Application.

Before proceeding further, we need to clarify how some key terms are used, as terminology in this area of research has been evolving and remains a source of confusion (Deaux, 1993; Unger & Crawford, 1993). Although not everyone agrees, we will distinguish between *sex,* **which refers to the biologically based categories of female and male,** and *gender,* **which refers to culturally constructed distinctions between femininity and masculinity.** According to this distinction, individuals are *born* female or male, but they *become* feminine or masculine through complex developmental processes that take years to unfold.

In any event, the statements at the beginning of this Application reflect popular gender stereotypes in our society. *Gender stereotypes* **are widely held beliefs about females' and males' abilities, personality traits, and social behaviour.** Table 11.3 lists some characteristics that are part of the masculine and feminine stereotypes in North American society. The table shows something you may have already noticed on your own. The male stereotype is much more flattering, suggesting that men have virtually cornered the market on competence and rationality. After all, everyone knows that females are more dependent, emotional, irrational, submissive, and talkative than males. Right? Or is that not the case? Let's look at the research.

How Do the Sexes Differ in Behaviour?

Gender differences **are actual disparities between the sexes in typical behaviour or average ability.** Mountains of research, literally thousands of studies, exist on gender differences. It's difficult to sort through this huge body of research, but fortunately, many review articles on gender differences have been published in recent years. As noted in Chapter 2, review articles summarize and reconcile the findings of a large number of studies on a specific issue. Reviews that use meta-analysis have been particularly valuable. *Meta-analysis* **combines the statistical results of many studies of the same question, yielding an estimate of the size and consistency of a variable's effects.**

What does this research show? Are the stereotypes of males and females accurate? Well, the findings are a mixed bag. The research indicates that genuine behavioural differences *do* exist between the sexes and that people's stereotypes are not entirely inaccurate (Halpern, 2000; Eagly, 1995; Swim, 1994). But the differences are fewer in number, smaller in size, and far more complex than stereotypes suggest. As you'll see, only two of the differences mentioned in our opening true–false questions (the even-numbered items) have been largely supported by the research.

Table 11.3 Elements of Traditional Gender Stereotypes

Masculine	Feminine
Active	Aware of others' feelings
Adventurous	Considerate
Aggressive	Creative
Ambitious	Cries easily
Competitive	Devotes self to others
Dominant	Emotional
Independent	Enjoys art and music
Leadership qualities	Excitable in a crisis
Likes math and science	Expresses tender feelings
Makes decisions easily	Feelings hurt
Mechanical aptitude	Gentle
Not easily influenced	Home oriented
Outspoken	Kind
Persistent	Likes children
Self-confident	Neat
Skilled in business	Needs approval
Stands up under pressure	Tactful
Takes a stand	Understanding

SOURCE: Adapted from Ruble, T. L. (1983). Sex stereotypes: Issues of change in the 70s. *Sex Roles, 9,* 397–402. Copyright © 1983 Plenum Publishing Group. Reprinted with kind permission of Springer Science and Business Media.

Cognitive Abilities

In the cognitive domain, it appears that there are three genuine gender differences. First, on the average, females tend to exhibit slightly better *verbal skills* than males. Females tend to start speaking a little earlier, and they have larger vocabularies and better reading scores during the grade-school years (Halpern, 2000). In particular, females seem stronger on tasks that require rapid access to semantic and other information in long-term memory (Halpern, 1997, 2004). Second, starting during high school, males show a slight advantage on tests of *mathematical ability*. When all students are compared, males' advantage is fairly small (Feingold, 1988a; Hyde, Fennema, & Lamon, 1990). However, at the high end of the ability distribution, the gender gap is larger, as far more males than females are found to be mathematically precocious (Stumpf & Stanley, 1996). Third, starting in the grade-school years, males tend to score higher than females on various measures of *visual–spatial ability* (Voyer, Voyer, & Bryden, 1995). The size of these gender differences varies from moderate to small depending on the exact nature of the spatial task. Males appear to be strongest on tasks that require visual transformations in working memory (Halpern, 1997). Some researchers believe that gender disparities in mathematical ability and visual–spatial ability are intimately related, as most advanced topics in math (geometry, trigonometry, calculus) draw on spatial skills.

Social Behaviour and Personality

In regard to social behaviour and personality, research findings support some additional gender differences that are reasonably well documented. First, studies indicate that males tend to be more *aggressive* than females, both verbally and physically (Archer, 2005; Coie & Dodge, 1997; Knight, Fabes, & Higgins, 1996). This disparity shows up early in childhood. Its continuation into adulthood is supported by the fact that men account for a grossly disproportionate number of the violent crimes in our society (Halpern, 2000). However, it is worth noting that females engage in more covert and relational aggression, such as snubbing,

ignoring, and undermining others (Crick, Casas, & Mosher, 1997; Crick & Rose, 2000). Second, there are gender differences in *nonverbal communication*. The evidence indicates that females are more sensitive than males to subtle nonverbal cues (Hall, 1990, 1998; McClure, 2000). Third, males score somewhat higher than females on various assessments of risk taking (Byrnes, Miller, & Schafer, 1999). Fourth, males are more sexually active than females in a variety of ways, and they have more permissive attitudes about casual, premarital, and extramarital sex (Baumeister et al, 2001; Oliver & Hyde, 1993). In regard to personality, the disparities are small but males score a little higher on measures of assertiveness and global self-esteem, whereas females score somewhat higher on measures of anxiety and agreeableness (Costa, Terracciano, & McCrae, 2001; Feingold, 1994; Kling et al., 1999).

Some Qualifications

Although there are some genuine gender differences in behaviour, bear in mind that these are *group* differences that indicate nothing about individuals. Essentially, research results compare the "average man" with the "average woman." However, you are—and every individual is—unique. The average female and male are ultimately figments of our imagination. Furthermore, most of the genuine group differences noted are relatively modest in magnitude. Figure 11.23 shows how scores on a trait, perhaps verbal ability, might be distributed for men and women. Although the group

averages are detectably different, you can see the great variability within each group (sex) and the huge overlap between the two group distributions.

To summarize, the actual behavioural differences between males and females are fewer and smaller than popular stereotypes suggest. Many supposed gender differences have turned out to be more mythical than real (Tavris, 1992). Nonetheless, the few genuine gender differences require explanation, which is the matter we'll attend to next.

Biological Origins of Gender Differences

What accounts for the development of the gender differences that do exist? To what degree are they the product of learning or of biology? This question is yet another manifestation of the nature versus nurture issue. Investigations of the biological origins of gender differences have centred on the evolutionary bases of behaviour, on hormones, and on brain organization.

Evolutionary Explanations

Evolutionary psychologists argue that gender differences in behaviour reflect different natural selection pressures operating on the sexes over the course of human history (Archer, 1996). Evolutionary analyses usually begin by arguing that gender differences in behaviour transcend culture because cultural invariance suggests that biological factors are at work (Kenrick & Trost, 1993). Although

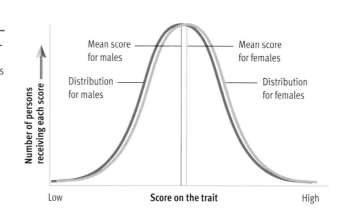

Figure 11.23

The nature of gender differences. Gender differences are group differences that indicate little about individuals because of the great overlap between the groups. For a given trait, one sex may score higher on the average, but far more variation occurs within each sex than between the sexes.

research has turned up some fascinating exceptions, the better-documented gender differences in cognitive abilities, aggression, and sexual behaviour do appear to be pancultural (Beller & Gafni, 1996; Halpern, 1997).

According to evolutionary psychologists, these differences are found around the world because males and females have confronted different adaptive demands (Buss & Kenrick, 1998). For example, as we discussed in Chapter 10, males supposedly are more sexually active and permissive because they invest less than females in the process of procreation and can maximize their reproductive success by seeking many sexual partners (Buss, 1996; Schmitt, 2005). The gender gap in aggression is also explained in terms of reproductive fitness. Because females are more selective about mating than males, males have to engage in more competition for sexual partners than females do. Greater aggressiveness is thought to be adaptive for males in this competition for sexual access because it should foster social dominance over other males and facilitate the acquisition of the material resources emphasized by females when they evaluate potential partners (Campbell, 2005; Cummins, 2005; Kenrick & Trost, 1993). Evolutionary theorists assert that gender differences in spatial ability reflect the division of labour in ancestral hunting and gathering societies in which males typically handled the hunting and females the gathering. Males' superiority on most (but not all) spatial tasks has been attributed to the adaptive demands of hunting versus gathering (Kimura, 1999; Silverman & Choi, 2005; Silverman & Phillips, 1998; see Chapter 1).

Evolutionary analyses of gender differences are interesting, but critics are plentiful. On the one hand, it seems eminently likely that evolutionary forces could have led to some divergence between males and females in typical behaviour. On the other hand, evolutionary hypotheses are highly speculative and difficult to test empirically (Eagly & Wood, 1999; Halpern, 1997, 2000). For example, it is quite a leap to infer that modern paper-and-pencil tests of spatial ability assess a talent that would have made high scorers superior hunters mil-

lions of years ago. But the crux of the problem for some critics is that evolutionary analyses are so "flexible" they can be used to explain almost anything. For example, if the situation regarding spatial ability were reversed—if females scored higher than males—evolutionary theorists might attribute females' superiority to the adaptive demands of gathering food, weaving baskets, and making clothes—and it would be difficult to prove otherwise (Cornell, 1997).

The Role of Hormones

Hormones play a key role in sexual differentiation during prenatal development. The high level of androgens (the principal class of male hormones) in males and the low level of androgens in females appears to be the main factor leading to the differentiation of male and female genital organs. The critical role of prenatal hormones becomes apparent when something interferes with normal prenatal hormonal secretions. About a half-dozen endocrine disorders can cause overproduction or underproduction of specific gonadal hormones during prenatal development. Scientists have also studied children born to mothers who were given an androgen-like drug to prevent miscarriage. The general trend in this research is that females exposed prenatally to abnormally high levels of androgens exhibit more male-typical behaviour than other females do and that males exposed prenatally to abnormally low levels of androgens exhibit more female-typical behaviour than other males (Collaer & Hines, 1995). For example, girls with *congenital adrenal hyperplasia* tend to show "tomboyish" interests in vigorous outdoor activities and in "male" toys and have elevated scores on measures of aggressiveness and spatial ability.

These findings suggest that prenatal hormones contribute to the shaping of gender differences in humans. But there are a few problems with this evidence (Basow, 1992; Fausto-Sterling, 1992). First, the evidence is much stronger for females than for males. Second, it's always dangerous to draw conclusions about the general population based on small samples of people who have abnormal conditions. Third, most of the

endocrine disorders studied have multiple effects (besides altering hormone levels) that create a variety of sometimes worrisome confounds in the research.

A handful of more recent studies have reported associations between circulating levels of male and female hormones and measures of specific traits, such as aggressiveness (Inoff-Germain et al., 1988) and spatial ability (Kimura & Hampson, 1993). For example, testosterone given to normal aging men to enhance their sexual functioning also increases their performance on visual–spatial tests (Janowsky, Oviatt, & Orwoll, 1994). Looking at the evidence as a whole, it does seem likely that hormones contribute to gender differences in behaviour. However, the findings in this line of research have been equivocal and inconsistent, and a great deal remains to be learned.

Disparities in Brain Organization

Interpretive problems have also cropped up in efforts to link gender differences to specialization of the cerebral hemispheres in the brain (see Figure 11.24). As you may recall from Chapter 3, in most people the left hemisphere is more actively involved in verbal processing, whereas the right hemisphere is more active in visual–spatial processing (Sperry, 1982; Springer & Deutsch, 1998). After these findings surfaced, theorists began to wonder whether this division of labour in the brain might be related to gender differences in verbal and spatial skills. Consequently, they began looking for sex-related disparities in brain organization.

Some thought-provoking findings *have* been reported. For instance, some studies have found that *males tend to exhibit more cerebral specialization than females* (Hellige, 1993; Voyer, 1996). In other words, there's a trend for males to depend more heavily than females do on the left hemisphere in verbal processing and more heavily on the right in spatial processing. Some studies also suggest that *females tend to have a larger corpus callosum* (Bigler et al., 1997), which might allow for better transfer of information between hemispheres, which in turn might underlie the more bilateral organization of females' brains (Innocenti, 1994; Steinmetz et al., 1995). Thus, some theorists

Figure 11.24

The cerebral hemispheres and the corpus callosum. In this drawing the cerebral hemispheres have been "pulled apart" to reveal the corpus callosum, the band of fibres that connects the right and left halves of the brain. Research has shown that the right and left hemispheres are specialized to handle different types of cognitive tasks (see Chapter 3), leading some theorists to speculate that patterns of hemispheric specialization might contribute to gender differences in verbal and spatial abilities.

Corpus callosum

have concluded that differences between the sexes in brain organization are responsible for gender differences in verbal and spatial ability (Geschwind & Galaburda, 1987; Kimura & Hampson, 1993).

This idea is intriguing, but psychologists have a long way to go before they can explain gender differences in terms of right brain/left brain specialization. Studies have not been consistent in finding that males have stronger cerebral lateralization than females (Halpern, 1992; Kinsbourne, 1980), and the finding of a larger corpus callosum in females has proven controversial (Bishop & Wahlsten, 1997; Byne & Parsons, 1993). Moreover, it seems peculiar that strong lateralization would produce an advantage for males on one kind of task (spatial) and a disadvantage on another kind of task (verbal). Thus, the theory linking cerebral specialization to gender differences in mental abilities has received some empirical support, but it remains highly speculative.

In summary, researchers have made some intriguing progress in their efforts to document the biological roots of gender differences in behaviour. However, the idea that "anatomy is destiny" has proven difficult to demonstrate. Many theorists remain convinced that gender differences are largely shaped by experience. Let's examine their evidence.

Environmental Origins of Gender Differences

Socialization **is the acquisition of the norms and behaviours expected of people in a particular society.** It includes all the efforts made by a society to ensure that its members learn to behave in a manner that's considered appropriate. The socialization process has traditionally included efforts to train children about gender roles. *Gender roles* **are expectations about what is appropriate behaviour for each sex.** Investigators have identified three key processes involved in the socialization of gender roles: operant conditioning, observational learning, and self-socialization. First we'll examine these processes. Then we'll look at the principal sources of gender-role socialization: families, schools, and the media.

Operant Conditioning

In part, gender roles are shaped by the power of reward and punishment—the key processes in *operant conditioning* (see Chapter 6). Parents, teachers, peers, and others often reinforce (usually with tacit approval) "gender-appropriate" behaviour and respond negatively to "gender-inappropriate" behaviour (Bussey & Bandura, 1999; Fagot, Leinbach, & O'Boyle, 1992). If you're a man, you might recall getting hurt as a young boy and being told that "men don't cry." If you succeeded in inhibiting your crying, you may have earned an approving smile or even something tangible like an ice cream cone. The reinforcement probably strengthened your tendency to "act like a man" and suppress emotional displays. If you're a woman, chances are your crying wasn't dis-couraged as gender-inappropriate. Studies suggest that fathers may encourage and reward gender-appropriate behaviour in their youngsters more than mothers do and that boys experience more pressure to behave in gender-appropriate ways than girls do (Levy, Taylor, & Gelman, 1995). Thus, a ten-year-old boy who enjoys playing with dollhouses is particularly likely to elicit disapproval from his parents, especially his father.

Observational Learning

As a young girl, did you imitate the behaviour of your mother, your aunts, and your older sisters? As a young boy, did you imitate your father and other male role models? Such behaviours reflect *observational learning,* in which behaviour is shaped by the observation of others' behaviour and its consequences (see Chapter 6). In everyday language, observational learning results in *imitation.*

Children imitate both males and females, but most children tend to imitate same-sex role models more than opposite-sex role models (Bussey & Bandura, 1984; Frey & Ruble, 1992). Thus, imitation often leads young girls to play with dolls, dollhouses, and toy stoves. Young boys are more likely to tinker with toy trucks, miniature gas stations, or toolkits. Parents and other adults are not the only role models who contribute to the process of observational learning; same-sex peers may be even more influential than adults (Maccoby, 1998). In fact, one recent study found that the more time children spend playing with same-sex peers, the more gender-typed their behaviour becomes (Martin & Fabes, 2001).

Self-Socialization

Children themselves are active agents in their own gender-role socialization. Several *cognitive theories* of gender-role development emphasize self-socialization (Bem, 1985, 1993; Cross & Markus, 1993; Martin & Ruble, 2004). Self-socialization entails three steps. First, children learn to classify themselves as male or female and to recognize their sex as a permanent quality (around age five or six). Second, this self-categorization motivates them to value those characteristics and behaviours associated with their sex. Third, they strive to bring their behaviour in line with what is considered gender-appropriate in their culture. In other words, children get involved in their own socialization, working diligently to discover the rules that are supposed to govern their behaviour. After gender stereotypes are internalized, they probably continue to influence behaviour throughout life (Geis, 1993).

Sources of Gender-Role Socialization

Three *main* sources influence gender-role socialization: families, schools, and the media. Of course, we are now in an era of transition in gender roles, so the generalizations that follow may say more about how you were socialized than about how children will be socialized in the future.

Families. A great deal of gender-role socialization takes place in the home (McHale, Crouter, & Whiteman, 2003). One review of research (Lytton & Romney, 1991) suggests that parents don't treat girls and boys as differently as one might expect, but there are disparities (Lott & Maluso, 1993; Turner & Gervai, 1995). For example, fathers engage in more "rough-housing" play with their sons than with their daughters, even in infancy (McBride-Chang & Jacklin, 1993). And parents are more likely to explain science concepts to boys than to girls (Crowley et al., 2001). As children grow, boys and girls are encouraged to play with different types of toys (Etaugh & Liss, 1992). Generally, boys have less leeway to play with "feminine" toys than girls do with "masculine" toys.

When children are old enough to help with household chores, the assignments tend to depend on sex (McHale et al., 1990). For example, girls wash dishes and boys mow the lawn. Likewise, the leisure activities that children are encouraged to engage in vary by sex. Johnny plays hockey and Mary practises the piano. Given these patterns, it's not surprising that parents' traditional or nontraditional attitudes about gender roles have been shown to influence the gender roles acquired by their children (Weisner & Wilson-Mitchell, 1990). Older siblings may also influence young-sters' gender-role socialization (Wagner, Schubert, & Schubert, 1993).

Schools. Schools and teachers clearly contribute to the socialization of gender roles. The books that children use in learning to read can influence their ideas about what is suitable behaviour for males and females (Oskamp, Kaufman, & Wolterbeek, 1996). Traditionally, males have been more likely to be portrayed as clever, heroic, and adventurous in these books, while females have been more likely to be shown doing domestic chores. The depiction of stereotypical gender roles in textbooks has declined considerably since the 1970s, but researchers still find subtle differences in how males and females tend to be portrayed (Kortenhaus & Demarest, 1993; Noddings, 1992; Turner-Bowker, 1996).

Preschool and grade-school teachers frequently reward gender-appropriate behaviour in their pupils (Fagot et al., 1985; Ruble & Martin, 1998). Interestingly, teachers tend to pay greater attention to males, helping them, praising them, and scolding them more than females (Sadker & Sadker, 1994). As youngsters progress through the school system, they are often channelled in career directions considered appropriate for their gender (Read, 1991). For example, males have been more likely to be encouraged to study mathematics and to work toward becoming engineers or doctors. Females have often been encouraged to take classes in home economics and to work toward becoming nurses or homemakers.

Media. Television is another source of gender-role socialization (Luecke-Aleksa et al., 1995). There has been some improvement in recent years, but television shows have traditionally depicted men and women in highly stereotypic ways (Galambos, 2004; Signorielli, 2001). Women are often portrayed as submissive, passive, and emotional. Men are more likely to be portrayed as independent, assertive, and competent. Another form of gender bias in television is its inordinate emphasis on physical attractiveness in women. Men on television may or may not be good-looking, but the vast majority of women are young, attractive, and sexy (Davis, 1990). TV commercials are especially likely to portray men and women in stereotypical ways (Bretl & Cantor, 1988; Signorielli, McLeod, & Healy, 1994); women are routinely shown worrying about trivial matters such as the whiteness of their laundry or the shine of their dishes.

Conclusion

As you can see, the findings on gender and behaviour are complex and confusing. Nonetheless, the evidence does permit one very general conclusion—a conclusion that you have seen before and will see again. Taken as a whole, the research in this area suggests that biological factors and environmental factors both contribute to gender differences in behaviour—as they do to all other aspects of development.

REVIEW OF KEY POINTS

- Sex refers to the biological reality of being male or female, whereas gender refers to distinctions between being masculine or feminine. Gender differences in behaviour are fewer in number and smaller in magnitude than gender stereotypes suggest.

- In the cognitive domain, research reviews suggest that there are genuine gender differences in verbal ability, mathematical ability, and spatial ability. In regard to social behaviour and personality, differences have been found in aggression, nonverbal communication, risk taking, sexual behaviour, and a handful of personality traits.

- Evolutionary theorists maintain that gender differences transcend culture because males and females have confronted different adaptive demands over the course of human history. Extensive evidence suggests that prenatal hormones contribute to human gender differences, but the research is marred by interpretive problems. Research linking gender differences to cerebral specialization is intriguing, but much remains to be learned.

- A vast research literature shows that gender differences are shaped by socialization processes. Operant conditioning, observational learning, and self-socialization contribute to the development of gender differences. Families, schools, and the media are among the main sources of gender-role socialization.

Are Fathers Essential to Children's Well-Being?

Are fathers essential for children to experience normal, healthy development? This question is currently the subject of heated debate. While much of this research has been conducted in the United States, it is an important issue for Canadians too, given recent findings on the number of female-headed single-parent families in Canada. According to the 2001 census, of the 8.4 million families in Canada, 15.7% were single-parent families, with 81% of those lone parents being female (Vanier Institute of the Family, 2005). In recent years, a number of social scientists have mounted a thought-provoking argument that father absence is the chief factor underlying a host of modern social ills. For example, David Blankenhorn (1995) argues that "fatherlessness is the most harmful demographic trend of this generation. It is the leading cause of declining child well-being in our society" (p. 1). Expressing a similar view, David Popenoe (1996) maintains that "today's fatherlessness has led to social turmoil-damaged children, unhappy children, aimless children, children who strike back with pathological behavior and violence" (p. 192).

The Basic Argument

What is the evidence for the proposition that fathers are essential to healthy development? Over the last 40 years, the proportion of children growing up without a father in the home has more than doubled (see Figure 11.25). During the same time, we have seen dramatic increases in teenage pregnancy, juvenile delinquency, violent crime, drug abuse, eating disorders, teen suicide, and family dysfunction. Moreover, mountains of studies have demonstrated an association between father absence and an elevated risk for these problems. Summarizing this evidence, Popenoe (1996) asserts that "fatherless children have a risk factor two to three times that of fathered

children for a wide range of negative outcomes, including dropping out of high school, giving birth as a teenager, and becoming a juvenile delinquent" (p. 192), which leads him to infer that "fathers have a unique and irreplaceable role to play in child development" (p. 197). Working from this premise, Popenoe concludes, "If present trends continue, our society could be on the verge of committing social suicide" (p. 192). Echoing this dire conclusion, Blankenhorn (1995) comments that "to tolerate the trend of fatherlessness is to accept the inevitability of continued societal recession" (p. 222).

You might be thinking, "What's all the fuss about?" Surely, proclaiming the importance of fatherhood ought to be no more controversial than advocacy for motherhood or apple pie. But the assertion that a father is essential to a child's well-being has some interesting sociopolitical implications. It suggests that heterosexual marriage is the only appropriate context in

Figure 11.25

Increasing father absence in the United States. Since 1960 the percentage of U.S. children who live in a home without their biological father has risen steadily and probably exceeds 40% today. (Data from Hernandez, 1993)

which to raise children and that other family configurations are fundamentally deficient. Based on this line of reasoning, some people have argued for new laws that would make it more difficult to obtain a divorce and other policies and programs that would favour traditional families over families headed by single mothers, cohabiting parents, and gay and lesbian parents (Silverstein & Auerbach, 1999). Thus, the question about the importance of fathers is creating a great deal of controversy, because it is really a question about alternatives to traditional family structure.

Evaluating the Argument

In light of the far-reaching implications of the view that fathers are essential to normal development, it makes sense to subject this view to critical scrutiny. How could you use critical thinking skills to evaluate this argument? At least three previously discussed ideas seem germane.

First, it is important to recognize that the position that fathers are essential for healthy development rests on a foundation of correlational evidence, and as we have seen repeatedly, *correlation is no assurance of causation.* Yes, there has been an increase in fatherlessness that has been paralleled by increases in teenage pregnancy, drug abuse, eating disorders, and other disturbing social problems. But think of all the other changes that have occurred over the last 40 years, such as the decline of organized religion, the growth of mass media, dramatic shifts in sexual mores, and so forth. Increased fatherlessness has co-varied with a host of other cultural trends. Hence, it is highly speculative to infer that father absence is the chief cause of most modern social maladies.

Second, it always pays to think about whether there are specific, *alternative explanations* for findings that you might have doubts about. What other factors might

Are fathers crucial to children's well-being? This seemingly simple question has sparked heated debate.

account for the association between father absence and children's maladjustment? Think for a moment: What is the most frequent cause of father absence? Obviously, it is divorce. Divorces tend to be highly stressful events that disrupt children's entire lives. Although the evidence suggests that a majority of children seem to survive divorce without lasting, detrimental effects, it is clear that divorce elevates youngsters' risk for a wide range of negative developmental outcomes (Amato, 2001, 2003; Hetherington, 1999, 2003). Given that father absence and divorce are inextricably intertwined, it is possible that the negative effects of divorce account for much of the association between father absence and social problems.

Are there any other alternative explanations for the correlation between fatherlessness and social maladies? Yes, critics point out that the prevalence of father absence co-varies with socioeconomic status. Father absence is much more common in low-income families (Anderson, Kohler, & Letiecq, 2002). Thus, the effects of father absence are entangled to some extent with the many powerful, malignant effects of poverty, which might account for much of the correlation between fatherlessness and negative outcomes (McLoyd, 1998).

A third possible strategy in thinking critically about the effects of father absence would be to look for some of the *fallacies in reasoning* introduced in Chapter 10 (irrelevant reasons, circular reasoning, slippery slope, weak analogies, and false dichotomy). A couple of the quotes from Popenoe and

Blankenhorn were chosen to give you an opportunity to detect two of these fallacies in a new context. Take a look at the quotes once again and see whether you can spot the fallacies.

Popenoe's assertion that "if present trends continue, our society could be on the verge of social suicide" is an example of *slippery slope argumentation,* which involves predictions that if one allows X to happen, things will spin out of control and catastrophic events will follow. "Social suicide" is a little vague, but it sounds as if Popenoe is predicting that father absence will lead to the destruction of modern society. The other fallacy that you might have spotted was the *false dichotomy* apparent in Blankenhorn's assertion that "to tolerate the trend of fatherlessness is to accept the inevitability of continued societal recession." A false dichotomy creates an either–or choice between the position one wants to advocate (in this case, new social policies to reduce father absence) and some obviously horrible outcome that any sensible person would want to avoid (social decay), while ignoring other possible outcomes that might lie between these extremes.

In summary, we can find a number of flaws and weaknesses in the argument that fathers are *essential* to normal development. However, our critical evaluation of this argument *does not mean that fathers are unimportant.* Many types of evidence suggest that fathers generally make significant contributions to their children's development (Phares, 1996; Rohner & Veneziano, 2001). We could argue with merit that fathers typically provide a substantial advan-

tage for children that fatherless children do not have. But there is a crucial distinction between arguing that fathers *promote* normal, healthy development and arguing that fathers are *necessary* for normal, healthy development. If fathers are *necessary,* children who grow up without them could not achieve the same level of well-being as those who have fathers, yet it is clear that a great many children from single-parent homes turn out just fine.

Fathers surely are important, and it seems likely that father absence *contributes* to a variety of social maladies. So, why do Blankenhorn (1995) and Popenoe (1996) argue for the much stronger conclusion—that fathers are *essential?* They appear to prefer the stronger conclusion because it raises much more serious questions about the viability of nontraditional family forms. Thus, they seem to want to advance a *political agenda* that champions traditional family values. They are certainly entitled to do so, but when research findings are used to advance a political agenda—whether conservative or liberal—a special caution alert should go off in your head. When a political agenda is at stake, it pays to scrutinize arguments with extra care, because research findings are more likely to be presented in a slanted fashion. The field of psychology deals with a host of complex questions that have profound implications for a wide range of social issues. The skills and habits of critical thinking can help you find your way through the maze of reasons and evidence that hold up the many sides of these complicated issues.

Table 11.4 Critical Thinking Skills Discussed in This Application

Skill	Description
Understanding the limitations of correlational evidence	The critical thinker understands that a correlation between two variables does not demonstrate that there is a causal link between the variables.
Looking for alternative explanations for findings and events	In evaluating explanations, the critical thinker explores whether there are other explanations that could also account for the findings or events under scrutiny.
Recognizing and avoiding common fallacies, such as irrelevant reasons, circular reasoning, slippery slope reasoning, weak analogies, and false dichotomies	The critical thinker is vigilant about conclusions based on unrelated premises, conclusions that are rewordings of premises, unwarranted predictions that things will spin out of control, superficial analogies, and contrived dichotomies.

RECAP

Key Ideas

Progress before Birth: Prenatal Development

● Prenatal development proceeds through the germinal, embryonic, and fetal stages as the zygote is differentiated into a human organism. During this period, development may be affected by maternal malnutrition, maternal drug use, and some maternal illnesses.

The Wondrous Years of Childhood

● Motor development follows cephalocaudal and proximodistal trends. Early motor development depends on both maturation and learning. Developmental norms for motor skills and other types of development only reflect typical performance.

● Temperamental differences among children are apparent during the first few months of life. These differences are fairly stable and may have far-reaching effects. Research shows that attachment emerges out of an interplay between infant and mother.

● Infant–mother attachments fall into three categories: secure, anxious-ambivalent, and avoidant. The effects of daycare on attachment are a source of concern, but the evidence is hotly debated. Cultural variations in child-rearing can affect the patterns of attachment seen in a society.

● Erik Erikson's theory of personality development proposes that individuals evolve through eight stages over the life span. In each stage the person wrestles with changes (crises) in social relationships.

● According to Piaget's theory of cognitive development, the key advance during the sensorimotor period is the child's gradual recognition of the permanence of objects. The preoperational period is marked by certain deficiencies in thinking—notably, centration, irreversibility, and egocentrism.

● During the concrete operations period, children develop the ability to perform operations on mental representations, making them capable of conservation and hierarchical classification. The stage of formal operations ushers in more abstract, systematic, and logical thought.

● Recent research has shown that infants appear to understand surprisingly complex concepts that they have had virtually no opportunity to learn about, leading some theorists to conclude that basic cognitive abilities are innate. Children's understanding of the mind seems to turn a corner between ages three and four.

● According to Kohlberg, moral reasoning progresses through three levels that are related to age and determined by cognitive development. Age-related progress in moral reasoning has been found in research, although a great deal of overlap occurs between adjacent stages.

The Transition of Adolescence

● The growth spurt at puberty is a prominent event involving the development of reproductive maturity and secondary sex characteristics. Belsky's theory that stress in early family relations might accelerate the process of sexual maturation has received some support, at least for girls.

● Recent decades have brought a surge in attempted suicide by adolescents and there is an association between adolescence and the prevalence of violent crime. Evidence suggests that adolescence may be slightly more stressful than other periods of life. According to Erikson, the key challenge of adolescence is to make some progress toward a sense of identity. Marcia identified four patterns of identity formation.

The Expanse of Adulthood

● During adulthood, personality is marked by both stability and change. Doubts have surfaced about whether a midlife crisis is a normal developmental transition. Many landmarks in adult development involve transitions in family relationships, including adjusting to marriage, parenthood, and the empty nest.

● During adulthood, age-related physical transitions include changes in appearance, sensory losses, and hormonal changes. Drastic mental decline is not a part of the normal aging process. However, 15%–20% of adults over age 75 suffer from some form of dementia. In late adulthood, mental speed declines and working memory suffers, but many people remain productive well into old age.

Putting It in Perspective

● Many of our seven integrative themes stood out in this chapter. But above all else, our discussion of development showed how heredity and environment interactively shape behaviour.

Personal Application • Understanding Gender Differences

● Gender differences in behaviour are fewer in number and smaller in magnitude than gender stereotypes suggest. Research reviews suggest that there are genuine (albeit small) gender differences in verbal ability, mathematical ability, spatial ability, aggression, nonverbal communication, risk taking, sexual behaviour, and several personality traits.

● Evolutionary theorists believe that gender differences reflect the influence of natural selection. Some research does link gender differences in humans to hormones and brain organization, but the research is marred by interpretive problems. Operant conditioning, observational learning, and self-socialization contribute to the development of gender differences.

Critical Thinking Application • Are Fathers Essential to Children's Well-Being?

● Some social scientists have argued that father absence is the chief cause of a host of social problems and that fathers are essential for normal, healthy development. Critics have argued that there are alternative explanations for the association between father absence and negative developmental outcomes.

Key Terms

Accommodation, 454
Age of viability, 440
Animism, 455
Assimilation, 454
Attachment, 448
Centration, 454
Cephalocaudal trend, 444
Cognitive development, 453
Conservation, 454
Cross-sectional design, 446
Dementia, 473
Development, 438
Developmental norms, 445
Dishabituation, 458
Egocentrism, 455
Embryonic stage, 439
Family life cycle, 470
Fetal alcohol syndrome, 442
Fetal stage, 440
Gender, 481
Gender differences, 481
Gender roles, 484
Gender stereotypes, 481
Germinal stage, 439
Habituation, 458
Irreversibility, 455
Longitudinal design, 446
Maturation, 444
Menarche, 464
Meta-analysis, 481
Midlife crisis, 469
Motor development, 444
Object permanence, 454

Placenta, 439
Prenatal period, 439
Primary sex characteristics, 464
Proximodistal trend, 444
Puberty, 464
Pubescence, 463
Secondary sex characteristics, 463
Separation anxiety, 448
Sex, 481
Socialization, 484
Stage, 451
Temperament, 446
Zygote, 439

Key People

Mary Ainsworth, 448
Jay Belsky, 450
John Bowlby, 450
Robbie Case, 457
Stella Chess, 446
Erik Erikson, 452
Lawrence Kohlberg, 460
Juan Pascual-Leone, 457
Jean Piaget, 454
Alexander Thomas, 446

1. The stage of prenatal development during which the developing organism is most vulnerable to injury is the:
A. zygotic stage.
C. fetal stage.
B. germinal stage.
D. embryonic stage.

2. The cephalocaudal trend in the motor development of children can be described simply as a:
A. head-to-foot direction.
B. centre-outward direction.
C. foot-to-head direction.
D. body-appendages direction.

3. Developmental norms:
A. can be used to make extremely precise predictions about the age at which an individual child will reach various developmental milestones.
B. indicate the maximum age at which a child can reach a particular developmental milestone and still be considered "normal."
C. indicate the average age at which individuals reach various developmental milestones.
D. involve both a and b.

4. When the development of the same subjects is studied over a period of time, the study is called a:
A. cross-sectional study.
B. life history study.
C. longitudinal study.
D. sequential study.

5. The quality of infant–caregiver attachment depends:
A. on the quality of bonding in the first few hours of life.
B. exclusively on the infant's temperament.
C. on the interaction between the infant's temperament and the caregiver's responsiveness.
D. on how stranger anxiety is handled.

6. During the second year of life, toddlers begin to take some personal responsibility for feeding, dressing, and bathing themselves in an attempt to establish what Erikson calls a sense of:
A. superiority.
C. generativity.
B. industry.
D. autonomy.

7. Five-year-old David watches as you pour water from a short, wide glass into a tall, narrow one. He says there is now more water than before. This response demonstrates that:
A. David understands the concept of conservation.
B. David does not understand the concept of conservation.
C. David's cognitive development is "behind" for his age.
D. both b and c.

8. Which of the following is *not* one of the criticisms of Piaget's theory of cognitive development?
A. Piaget may have underestimated the cognitive skills of children in some areas.
B. Piaget may have underestimated the influence of cultural factors on cognitive development.
C. The theory does not clearly address the issue of individual differences in development.
D. Evidence for the theory is based on children's answers to questions.

9. If a child's primary reason for not drawing pictures on the living room wall with crayons is to avoid the punishment that would inevitably follow this behaviour, she would be said to be at which level of moral development?
A. conventional
C. preconventional
B. postconventional
D. unconventional

10. The Featured Study on the effects of early family relations on Aboriginal youth suicide found:
A. no association between early stress and youth suicide.
B. that poverty was the major contributor to the high rates of suicide among Canada's Aboriginal youth.
C. that making Aboriginal culture salient was associated with a lower suicide rate.
D. that making Aboriginal culture salient was associated with a higher suicide rate.

11. Girls who mature _____ and boys who mature _____ seem to have more emotional difficulties with the transition to adolescence.
A. early; early
C. late; early
B. early; late
D. late; late

12. Sixteen-year-old Foster wants to spend a few years experimenting with different lifestyles and careers before he settles on who and what he wants to be. Foster's behaviour illustrates the identity status of:
A. identity moratorium.
C. identity achievement.
B. identity foreclosure.
D. identity diffusion.

13. Although women perform about _____ of all housework, about _____ of wives characterize their household division of labour as unfair.
A. one-half; one-half
B. two-thirds; three-quarters
C. two-thirds; one-third
D. three-quarters; one-tenth

14. Males have been found to differ slightly from females in three well-documented areas of mental ability. Which of the following is *not* one of these?
A. verbal ability
B. mathematical ability
C. intelligence
D. visual–spatial ability

15. Research suggests that males exhibit _____ than females and that females have a _____ than males.
A. less cerebral specialization; smaller corpus callosum
B. less cerebral specialization; larger corpus callosum
C. more cerebral specialization; smaller corpus callosum
D. more cerebral specialization; larger corpus callosum

See Appendix A for answers to this Practice Test.

CHAPTER 12

Latchezar Boyadjiev, *Temperament,* L.B. Glass Studios

The Nature of Personality
Defining Personality: Consistency and Distinctiveness
Personality Traits: Dispositions and Dimensions
The Five-Factor Model of Personality Traits

Psychodynamic Perspectives
Freud's Psychoanalytic Theory
Jung's Analytical Psychology
Adler's Individual Psychology
Evaluating Psychodynamic Perspectives

Behavioural Perspectives
Skinner's Ideas Applied to Personality
Bandura's Social Cognitive Theory
Mischel and the Person–Situation Controversy
Evaluating Behavioural Perspectives

Humanistic Perspectives
Rogers's Person-Centred Theory
Featured Study • The Pope Is Watching You: Effects on Self-Concept
Maslow's Theory of Self-Actualization
Evaluating Humanistic Perspectives

Biological Perspectives
Eysenck's Theory
Behavioural Genetics and Personality
The Evolutionary Approach to Personality
Evaluating Biological Perspectives

Contemporary Empirical Approaches to Personality
Sensation Seeking: Life in the Fast Lane
Self-Monitoring: Life as Theatre

Culture and Personality

Putting It in Perspective

Personal Application • **Understanding Personality Assessment**
The Uses of Personality Scales
Self-Report Inventories
Projective Tests

Critical Thinking Application • **Hindsight in Everyday Analyses of Personality**
The Prevalence of Hindsight Bias
Hindsight and Personality
Other Implications of "20/20 Hindsight"

Recap

Practice Test

Personality: Theory, Research, and Assessment

While there are likely a variety of reasons why students take an introductory course in psychology, our own students tell us that a primary reason is the belief that it will better enable them to understand what people are like. Students often search for an explanation for what makes people act in the way that they do. Sometimes the person you are trying to figure out is someone you know well—a best friend, relative, or perhaps even yourself—and sometimes it might be a stranger, someone who did something unique. There certainly is no shortage of people doing unique things, especially in Canada. We have referred to some already—for example, Brenda Milner, Wilder Penfield, Terry Fox, and David Suzuki.

Dan Matthews's accomplishments certainly qualify as extraordinary. Matthews and his fellow Canadian soldier Jason Hamilton were recently nominated for heroism for their actions in Afghanistan (Thorne, 2005). On October 2, 2003, the jeep they were driving blew up as they inadvertently drove onto a mined portion of the road that was supposed to have been already cleared. The two men found each other and then looked for their friends. While bullets and shrapnel fell around them, they put themselves at further risk as they crawled slowly, a centimetre at a time, through the minefield to check on and to help their colleagues. When they reached them, sadly, the soldiers discovered that their friends were dead. Matthews refused to leave their bodies and had to be dragged away from his slain friends. Matthews and Hamilton were later honoured by the governor-general for their conspicuous courage.

Remarkable determination and courage were also evidenced by Nellie McClung and the other members of one of Canada's greatest and most accomplished groups, the "Famous Five." Along with McClung, the Famous Five consisted of Irene Parlby, Emily Murphy, Henrietta Muir Edwards, and Louise Crummy McKinney. They battled social convention and the Supreme Court of Canada in 1927 to have women acknowledged as *persons* (McClung, 1935, 1945). According to the British North America Act, which governed Canada, only qualified persons were allowed to serve in the Senate and, up to that point,

women were not eligible. When the Famous Five lost their Supreme Court petition, they persisted and appealed to the Judicial Committee of the Privy Council in England and won. On October 18, 1929, the term *person* was now seen to include women. The headline that appeared after the victory was "Privy Council Declares that Women are Persons" (Benham, 1975). McClung was a lifelong advocate for women's rights and suffrage and her efforts endured through the obstructionist views of the time. For example, after her meeting with the premier of Manitoba about the possibility of women's voting rights, he told her, "I don't want a hyena in petticoats talking politics to me. I want a nice gentle creature to bring me my slippers" (Benham, 1975, p. 27). You can learn more about the Famous Five by visiting the Library and Archives of Canada's Web site celebrating Canadian women's achievements (**http://www.collectionscanada.ca/women/index-e.html**).

Individuals such as Dan Matthews and Nellie McClung point to the mystery of personality. They

Canadian suffragist and politician Nellie McClung, along with other members of the "Famous Five," had Canadian women declared "persons" in 1929.

are unique individuals who engaged in unique acts. While unusual in many respects, most personality psychologists believe that all individuals can be described in terms of characteristics that make up their personalities. But what exactly is personality and how does it account for the commonplace and the unusual? How does it develop over time? Are we born with a certain personality or is experience critical in shaping the qualities that make us who we are?

Psychologists have approached questions like these from a variety of perspectives. Traditionally, the study of personality has been dominated by "grand theories" that attempt to explain a great many facets of behav-

iour. Our discussion will reflect this emphasis, as we'll devote most of our time to the sweeping theories of Freud, Jung, Skinner, Rogers, and several others. In recent decades, however, the study of personality has shifted toward narrower research programs that examine specific aspects of personality. The last several sections of the chapter will reflect this trend, as we review biological, cultural, and other contemporary empirical approaches to personality. In the Personal Application, we'll discuss how psychological tests are used to measure various aspects of personality. In the Critical Thinking Application, you'll see how hindsight bias can taint people's analyses of personality.

The Nature of Personality

PREVIEW QUESTIONS
- What are the essential features of the concept of personality?
- What are personality traits?
- How many personality traits are necessary to describe personality adequately?

Personality is a complex hypothetical construct that has been defined in a variety of ways. Let's take a closer look at the concepts of personality and personality traits.

Defining Personality: Consistency and Distinctiveness

What does it mean to say that someone has an optimistic personality? This assertion indicates that the person has a fairly *consistent tendency* to behave in a cheerful, hopeful, enthusiastic way, looking at the bright side of things, across a wide variety of situations. Although no one is entirely consistent in behaviour, this quality of *consistency across situations* lies at the core of the concept of personality.

Distinctiveness is also central to the concept of personality. Personality is used to explain why not everyone acts the same way in similar situations. If you were stuck in an elevator with three people, each might react differently. One might crack jokes to relieve the tension. Another might make ominous predictions that "we'll never get out of here." The third might calmly think about how to escape. These varied reactions to the same situation occur because each person has a different personality. Each person has traits that are seen in other people, but each individual has his or her own distinctive *set* of personality traits.

In summary, the concept of personality is used to explain (1) the stability in a person's behaviour over time and across situations (consistency) and (2) the behavioural differences among people reacting to the same situation (distinctiveness). We can combine these ideas into the following definition: *Personality* **refers to an individual's unique constellation of consistent behavioural traits.** Let's look more closely at the concept of *traits*.

Personality Traits: Dispositions and Dimensions

Everyone makes remarks like "Jan is very *conscientious.*" Or you might assert that "Bill is too *timid* to succeed in that job." These descriptive statements refer to personality traits. **A *personality trait* is a durable disposition to behave in a particular way in a variety of situations.** Adjectives such as *honest, dependable, moody, impulsive, suspicious, anxious, excitable, domineering,* and *friendly* describe dispositions that represent personality traits.

Most approaches to personality assume that some traits are more basic than others. According to this notion, a small number of fundamental traits determine other, more superficial traits. For example, a person's tendency to be impulsive, restless, irritable, boisterous, and impatient might all be derived from a more basic tendency to be excitable.

A number of psychologists have taken on the challenge of identifying the basic traits that form the core of personality. For example, Raymond Cattell (1950, 1966, 1990) used the statistical procedure of *factor analysis* to reduce a huge list of personality traits compiled by Gordon Allport (1937) to just 16 basic dimensions of personality. As you may recall from Chapter 9, **in *factor analysis* correlations among many variables are analyzed to identify closely related clusters of variables.** If the measurements of a number of variables (in this case, personality traits) correlate highly with one another, the assumption is that a single factor is influencing all of them. Factor analysis is used to identify these hidden factors. In factor analyses of personality traits, these hidden factors are viewed as very basic, higher-order traits that determine less basic, more specific traits. Based on his factor analytic work, Cattell concluded that an individual's personality can be described completely by measuring just 16 traits. The 16 crucial traits are listed in Figure 12.18 (page 527), which can be found in the Personal Application, where we discuss a personality test that Cattell designed to assess these traits.

The Five-Factor Model of Personality Traits

In recent years, Robert McCrae and Paul Costa (1987, 1997, 1999, 2003) have used factor analysis to arrive at an even simpler, *five-factor model of personality* (see Figure 12.1). McCrae and Costa maintain that most personality traits are derived from just five higher-order traits that have come to be known as the "Big Five": extraversion, neuroticism, openness to experience, agreeableness, and conscientiousness. Let's take a closer look at these traits:

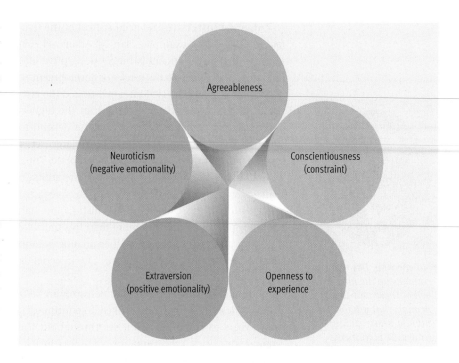

Figure 12.1

The five-factor model of personality. Trait models attempt to analyze personality into its basic dimensions. McCrae and Costa (1985, 1987, 1997) maintain that personality can be described adequately with the five higher-order traits identified here, which are widely referred to as the Big Five.

1. *Extraversion.* People who score high in extraversion are characterized as outgoing, sociable, upbeat, friendly, assertive, and gregarious. Referred to as *positive emotionality* in some trait models, extraversion has been studied extensively in research for many decades (Watson & Clark, 1997).

2. *Neuroticism.* People who score high in neuroticism tend to be anxious, hostile, self-conscious, insecure, and vulnerable. Like extraversion, this trait has been the subject of thousands of studies. Those who score high in neuroticism tend to overreact more in response to stress than others (Mroczek & Almeida, 2004).

3. *Openness to experience.* Openness is associated with curiosity, flexibility, vivid fantasy, imaginativeness, artistic sensitivity, and unconventional attitudes. McCrae (1996) maintains that its importance has been underestimated. Citing evidence that openness fosters liberalism, he argues that this trait is the key determinant of people's political attitudes and ideology.

4. *Agreeableness.* Those who score high in agreeableness tend to be sympathetic, trusting, cooperative, modest, and straightforward. People who score at the opposite end of this personality dimension are characterized as suspicious, antagonistic, and aggressive. Agreeableness may have its roots in childhood temperament and appears to promote altruistic (helping) behaviour in social interactions (Graziano & Eisenberg, 1997).

5. *Conscientiousness.* Conscientious people tend to be diligent, disciplined, well-organized, punctual, and dependable. Referred to as *constraint* in some trait models, conscientiousness is associated with living longer (Bogg & Roberts, 2004).

Like Cattell, McCrae and Costa maintain that personality can be described adequately by measuring the basic traits that they've identified. Their bold claim has been supported in many studies by other researchers, and the five-factor model has become the dominant conception of personality structure in contemporary psychology (John & Srivastava, 1999; McCrae, 2005; Wiggins & Trapnell, 1997). These traits have been characterized as the "latitude and longitude" along which personality should be mapped (Ozer & Reise, 1994, p. 361). Thousands of studies have been conducted, exploring correlations between the Big Five traits and other characteristics such as self-esteem (Watson, Suls, & Haig, 2002), transformational leadership (Judge & Bono, 2000), social status (Anderson et al., 2001), and well-being at midlife (Siegler & Brummett, 2000).

Sampo Paunonen from the University of Western Ontario has been active in examining the nature and implications of the Big Five. Along with colleagues including Douglas Jackson, he developed and tested a nonverbal measure of the Big Five (Paunonen, Ashton, & Jackson, 2001). In Paunonen's other research, while he finds that the Big Five are excellent predictors of complex behaviour, he argues that the prediction can be enhanced by including measures of some of the narrower factors that constitute the Big Five (Paunonen 2003; Paunonen et al., 2003). He concludes that a "judicious selection of such lower-level predictor scales, from both within and beyond the Big Five domain, is a good way to maximize predictive accuracy, and ... increase our understanding of behaviour" (Paunonen et al., 2003, p. 431).

Other theorists have also been critical of the five-factor model. For example, Dan McAdams (1992) points out that the model is purely descriptive and provides no insight into the causes or development of personality. Jack Block (1995) has questioned the generality of the model. He points out that the higher-order traits that emerge in factor analyses depend to some extent on the exact mix of the much larger set of specific traits that are measured in the first place. Thus, he asserts that the five-factor model is more arbitrary than widely appreciated. Other critics of the five-factor model, such as the University of British Columbia's Jerry Wiggins, maintain that more than five traits are necessary to account for most of the variation seen in human personality (Ashton et al., 2004; Benet & Waller, 1995; Paunonen, 1998; Wiggins, 1992).

The debate about how many dimensions are necessary to describe personality is likely to continue for many years to come. As you'll see throughout the chapter, the study of personality is an area in psychology that has a long history of "duelling theories."

We'll divide these diverse personality theories into four broad groups that share certain assumptions, emphases, and interests: (1) psychodynamic perspectives, (2) behavioural perspectives, (3) humanistic perspectives, and (4) biological perspectives. We'll begin our discussion of personality theories by examining the life and work of Sigmund Freud.

National Library of Medicine

"No one who, like me, conjures up the most evil of those half-tamed demons that inhabit the human beast, and seeks to wrestle with them, can expect to come through the struggle unscathed.**"**

SIGMUND FREUD

Psychodynamic Perspectives

Psychodynamic theories **include all the diverse theories descended from the work of Sigmund Freud, which focus on unconscious mental forces**. Freud inspired many brilliant scholars who followed in his intellectual footsteps. Some of these followers simply refined and updated Freud's theory. Others veered off in new directions and established independent, albeit related, schools of thought. Today, the psychodynamic umbrella covers a large collection of loosely related theories that we can only sample from in this text. In this chapter, we'll examine the ideas of Sigmund Freud in some detail. Then we'll take a briefer look at the psychodynamic theories of Carl Jung and Alfred Adler.

Freud's Psychoanalytic Theory 10A

Born in 1856, Sigmund Freud grew up in a middle-class Jewish home in Vienna, Austria. He showed an early interest in intellectual pursuits and became an intense, hardworking young man, driven to achieve fame. He experienced his share of inner turmoil and engaged in regular self-analysis for over 40 years. Freud lived in the Victorian era, which was marked by sexual repression. His life was also affected by World War I, which devastated Europe, and by the growing anti-Semitism of the times. We'll see that the sexual repression and aggressive hostilities that

Freud witnessed left their mark on his view of human nature.

Freud was a physician specializing in neurology when he began his medical practice in Vienna toward the end of the 19th century. Like other neurologists in his era, he often treated people troubled by nervous problems such as irrational fears, obsessions, and anxieties. Eventually he devoted himself to the treatment of mental disorders using an innovative procedure he had developed, called *psychoanalysis,* that required lengthy verbal interactions with patients during which Freud probed deeply into their lives.

Freud's (1901, 1924, 1940) *psychoanalytic theory* grew out of his decades of interactions with his clients in psychoanalysis. Psychoanalytic theory attempts to explain personality, motivation, and psychological disorders by focusing on the influence of early childhood experiences, on unconscious motives and conflicts, and on the methods people use to cope with their sexual and aggressive urges.

Most of Freud's contemporaries were uncomfortable with his theory for at least three reasons. First, in arguing that people's behaviour is governed by unconscious factors of which they are unaware, Freud made the disconcerting suggestion that individuals are not masters of their own minds. Second, in claiming that adult personalities are shaped by childhood experiences and other factors beyond one's control, he suggested that people are not masters of their own destinies. Third, by emphasizing the great importance of how people cope with their sexual urges, he offended those who held the conservative, Victorian values of his time.

Thus, Freud endured a great deal of criticism, condemnation, and outright ridicule, even after his work began to attract more favourable attention. Consider the following recollection from one of Freud's friends: "In those days when one mentioned Freud's name everyone would begin to laugh, as if someone had told a joke. Freud was the queer fellow who wrote a book about dreams … He was the man who saw sex in everything. It was considered bad taste to bring up Freud's name in the presence of ladies" (Donn, 1988, p. 57). Let's examine the ideas that generated so much controversy.

Structure of Personality

Freud divided personality structure into three components: the id, the ego, and the superego (see Figure 12.2). He saw a person's behaviour as the outcome of interactions among these three components.

The *id* is the primitive, instinctive component of personality that operates according to the pleasure principle. Freud referred to the id as the reservoir of psychic energy. By this he meant that the id houses the raw biological urges (to eat, sleep, defecate, copulate, and so on) that energize human behaviour. The id operates according to the *pleasure principle*, which demands immediate gratification of its urges. The id engages in *primary-process thinking*, which is primitive, illogical, irrational, and fantasy oriented.

The *ego* is the decision-making component of personality that operates according to the reality principle. The ego mediates between the id, with its forceful desires for immediate satisfaction, and the external social world, with its expectations and norms regarding suitable behaviour. The ego considers social realities—society's norms, etiquette, rules, and customs—in deciding how to behave. The ego is guided by the *reality principle*, which seeks to delay gratification of the id's urges until appropriate outlets and situations can be found. In short, to stay out of trouble, the ego often works to tame the unbridled desires of the id.

In the long run, the ego wants to maximize gratification, just as the id does. However, the ego engages in *secondary-process thinking*, which is relatively rational, realistic, and oriented toward problem solving. Thus, the ego strives to avoid negative consequences from society and its representatives (e.g., punishment by parents or teachers) by behaving "properly." It also

attempts to achieve long-range goals that sometimes require putting off gratification.

While the ego concerns itself with practical realities, the *superego* is the moral component of personality that incorporates social standards about what represents right and wrong. Throughout their lives, but especially during childhood, people receive training about what constitutes good and bad behaviour. Many social norms regarding morality are eventually internalized. The superego emerges out of the ego at around three to five years of age. In some people, the superego can become irrationally demanding in its striving for moral perfection. Such people are plagued by excessive feelings of guilt. According to Freud, the id, ego, and superego are distributed differently across three levels of awareness, which we'll describe next.

Levels of Awareness

Perhaps Freud's most enduring insight was his recognition of how unconscious forces can influence behaviour. He inferred the existence of the unconscious from a variety of observations that he made with his patients. For example, he noticed that "slips of the tongue" often revealed a person's true feelings. He also realized that his patients' dreams often expressed hidden desires. Most important, through psychoanalysis he often helped patients to discover feelings and conflicts of which they had previously been unaware.

CONSCIOUS:
Contact with outside world

PRECONSCIOUS:
Material just beneath the surface of awareness

EGO
Reality principle
Secondary-process thinking

SUPEREGO
Moral imperatives

UNCONSCIOUS:
Difficult to retrieve material; well below the surface of awareness

ID
Pleasure principle
Primary-process thinking

Figure 12.2

Freud's model of personality structure. Freud theorized that people have three levels of awareness: the conscious, the preconscious, and the unconscious. The enormous size of the unconscious is often dramatized by comparing it to the portion of an iceberg that lies beneath the water's surface. Freud also divided personality structure into three components—id, ego, and superego—which operate according to different principles and exhibit different modes of thinking. In Freud's model, the id is entirely unconscious, but the ego and superego operate at all three levels of awareness.

Web Link 12.1

Victorian Studies Archive
http://www.lang.nagoya-u.ac.jp/~matsuoka/Victorian.html

This site offers numerous links to resources on the Victorian age that will give you an idea of the context within which psychoanalysis developed.

"motivated forgetting." If you forget a dental appointment or the name of someone you don't like, repression may be at work.

Self-deception can also be seen in projection and displacement. **Projection is attributing one's own thoughts, feelings, or motives to another.** Usually, the thoughts one projects onto others are thoughts that would make one feel guilty. For example, if lusting for a co-worker makes you feel guilty, you might attribute any latent sexual tension between the two of you to the *other person's* desire to seduce you. **Displacement is diverting emotional feelings (usually anger) from their original source to a substitute target.** If your boss gives you a hard time at work and you come home and slam the door, kick the dog, and scream at your spouse, you're displacing your anger onto irrelevant targets. Unfortunately, social constraints often force people to hold back their anger, and they end up lashing out at the people they love most.

Other prominent defence mechanisms include reaction formation, regression, and identification. **Reaction formation is behaving in a way that's exactly the opposite of one's true feelings.** Guilt about sexual desires often leads to reaction formation. For example, Freud theorized that many males who ridicule homosexuals are defending against their own latent homosexual impulses. The telltale sign of reaction formation is the exaggerated quality of the opposite behaviour. **Regression is a reversion to immature patterns of behaviour.** When anxious about their self-worth, some adults respond with childish boasting and bragging (as opposed to subtle efforts to impress others). For example, a fired executive having difficulty finding a new job might start making ridiculous

statements about his incomparable talents and achievements. Such bragging is regressive when it's marked by massive exaggerations that virtually anyone can see through. **Identification is bolstering self-esteem by forming an imaginary or real alliance with some person or group.** Youngsters often shore up precarious feelings of self-worth by identifying with rock stars, movie stars, or famous athletes. Adults may join exclusive country clubs or civic organizations as a means of identification.

Recent years have brought a revival of interest in research on defence mechanisms. For example, a series of studies have identified a *repressive coping style* and shown that "repressors" have an impoverished memory for emotional events and negative feedback and that they habitually avoid unpleasant emotions by distracting themselves with pleasant thoughts and memories (Boden & Baumeister, 1997; Weinberger & Davidson, 1994). In another line of research, Newman, Duff, and Baumeister (1997) have shed new light on the cognitive dynamics of *projection.* Newman et al. showed that people actively work to suppress thoughts about the possibility that they might have an undesirable trait (say, dishonesty), but this ongoing effort makes thoughts about the unwanted trait highly accessible, so they chronically use this trait concept to explain others' behaviour and end up routinely attributing the trait to others. Another very interesting study provided support for the Freudian hypothesis that reaction formation underlies homophobia in males. Adams, Wright, and Lohr (1996) found that when homophobic men are shown an erotic videotape depicting homosexual activity, they exhibit sexual arousal not seen in nonhomophobic subjects.

CONCEPT CHECK 12.1

Identifying Defence Mechanisms

Check your understanding of defence mechanisms by identifying specific defences in the story below. Each example of a defence mechanism is underlined, with a number next to it. Write in the defence at work in each case in the numbered spaces after the story. The answers are in Appendix A.

My girlfriend recently broke up with me after we had dated seriously for several years. At first, I cried a great deal and locked myself in my room, where I pouted endlessly. (1.) I was sure that my former girlfriend felt as miserable as I did. I told several friends that she was probably lonely and depressed. (2.) Later, I decided that I hated her. I was happy about the break-up and talked about how much I was going to enjoy my newfound freedom. (3.) I went to parties and socialized a great deal and just forgot about her. It's funny—at one point I couldn't even remember her phone number! (4.) Then I started pining for her again. But eventually I began to look at the situation more objectively. I realized that she had many faults and that we were bound to break up sooner or later, so I was better off without her. (5.)

1. _____
2. _____
3. _____
4. _____
5. _____

you find that you're in a debate with yourself about whether to go to the gym to work out or to the student union to play pool. It's only mid-afternoon—and already you've been through a series of internal conflicts.

Freud believed that conflicts centring on sexual and aggressive impulses are especially likely to have far-reaching consequences. Why did he emphasize sex and aggression? Two reasons were prominent in his thinking. First, he thought that sex and aggression are subject to more complex and ambiguous social controls than other basic motives. The norms governing sexual and aggressive behaviour are subtle, and people often get inconsistent messages about what's appropriate. Thus, Freud believed that these two drives are the source of much confusion. Second, he noted that the sexual and aggressive drives are thwarted more regularly than other basic biological urges. Think about it: If you get hungry or thirsty, you can simply head for a nearby vending machine or a drinking fountain. But if a department store clerk infuriates you, you aren't likely to reach across the counter and slug him or her. Likewise, when you see a person who inspires lustful urges, you don't normally walk up and propose a tryst in a nearby broom closet. There's nothing comparable to vending machines or drinking fountains for the satisfaction of sexual and aggressive urges. Freud ascribed great importance to these needs because social norms dictate that they be routinely frustrated.

Anxiety and Defence Mechanisms 10A

Most internal conflicts are trivial and are quickly resolved one way or the other. Occasionally, however, a conflict will linger for days, months, or even years, creating internal tension. More often than not, such prolonged and troublesome conflicts involve sexual and aggressive impulses that society wants to tame. These conflicts are often played out entirely in the unconscious. Although you may not be aware of these unconscious battles, they can produce *anxiety* that slips to the surface of conscious awareness. The anxiety can be attributed to your ego worrying about (1) the id getting out of control and doing something terrible that leads to severe negative consequences or (2) the superego getting out of control and making you feel guilty about a real or imagined transgression.

The arousal of anxiety is a crucial event in Freud's theory of personality functioning (see Figure 12.3). Anxiety is distressing, so people try to rid themselves of this unpleasant emotion any way they can. This effort to ward off anxiety often involves the use of defence mechanisms. ***Defence mechanisms* are largely**

unconscious reactions that protect a person from unpleasant emotions such as anxiety and guilt (see Table 12.1). Typically, they're mental manoeuvres that work through self-deception. Consider *rationalization,* **which is creating false but plausible excuses to justify unacceptable behaviour.** For example, after cheating someone in a business transaction, you might reduce your guilt by rationalizing that "everyone does it."

According to University of British Columbia psychologist Delroy Paulhus and his colleagues, repression is "the flagship in the psychoanalytic fleet of defense mechanisms" (Paulhus, Fridhandler, & Hayes, 1997); repression is the most basic and widely used defence mechanism. ***Repression* is keeping distressing thoughts and feelings buried in the unconscious.** People tend to repress desires that make them feel guilty, conflicts that make them anxious, and memories that are painful. Repression has been called

Figure 12.3

Freud's model of personality dynamics. According to Freud, unconscious conflicts among the id, ego, and superego sometimes lead to anxiety. This discomfort may lead to the use of defence mechanisms, which may temporarily relieve anxiety.

Table 12.1 Defence Mechanisms, with Examples

Defence Mechanism	Definition	Example
Repression	Keeping distressing thoughts and feelings buried in the unconscious	A traumatized soldier has no recollection of the details of a close brush with death.
Projection	Attributing one's own thoughts, feelings, or motives to another	A woman who dislikes her boss thinks she likes her boss but feels that the boss doesn't like her.
Displacement	Diverting emotional feelings (usually anger) from their original source to a substitute target	After parental scolding, a young girl takes her anger out on her little brother.
Reaction formation	Behaving in a way that is exactly the opposite of one's true feelings	A parent who unconsciously resents a child spoils the child with outlandish gifts.
Regression	A reversion to immature patterns of behaviour	An adult has a temper tantrum when he doesn't get his way.
Rationalization	Creating false but plausible excuses to justify unacceptable behaviour	A student watches TV instead of studying, saying that "additional study wouldn't do any good anyway."
Identification	Bolstering self-esteem by forming an imaginary or real alliance with some person or group	An insecure young man joins a fraternity to boost his self-esteem.

NOTE: See Table 13.2 on page 547 for additional examples of defence mechanisms.

"motivated forgetting." If you forget a dental appointment or the name of someone you don't like, repression may be at work.

Self-deception can also be seen in projection and displacement. *Projection* **is attributing one's own thoughts, feelings, or motives to another.** Usually, the thoughts one projects onto others are thoughts that would make one feel guilty. For example, if lusting for a co-worker makes you feel guilty, you might attribute any latent sexual tension between the two of you to the *other person's* desire to seduce you. *Displacement* **is diverting emotional feelings (usually anger) from their original source to a substitute target.** If your boss gives you a hard time at work and you come home and slam the door, kick the dog, and scream at your spouse, you're displacing your anger onto irrelevant targets. Unfortunately, social constraints often force people to hold back their anger, and they end up lashing out at the people they love most.

Other prominent defence mechanisms include reaction formation, regression, and identification. *Reaction formation* **is behaving in a way that's exactly the opposite of one's true feelings.** Guilt about sexual desires often leads to reaction formation. For example, Freud theorized that many males who ridicule homosexuals are defending against their own latent homosexual impulses. The telltale sign of reaction formation is the exaggerated quality of the opposite behaviour. *Regression* **is a reversion to immature patterns of behaviour.** When anxious about their self-worth, some adults respond with childish boasting and bragging (as opposed to subtle efforts to impress others). For example, a fired executive having difficulty finding a new job might start making ridiculous statements about his incomparable talents and achievements. Such bragging is regressive when it's marked by massive exaggerations that virtually anyone can see through. *Identification* **is bolstering self-esteem by forming an imaginary or real alliance with some person or group.** Youngsters often shore up precarious feelings of self-worth by identifying with rock stars, movie stars, or famous athletes. Adults may join exclusive country clubs or civic organizations as a means of identification.

Recent years have brought a revival of interest in research on defence mechanisms. For example, a series of studies have identified a *repressive coping style* and shown that "repressors" have an impoverished memory for emotional events and negative feedback and that they habitually avoid unpleasant emotions by distracting themselves with pleasant thoughts and memories (Boden & Baumeister, 1997; Weinberger & Davidson, 1994). In another line of research, Newman, Duff, and Baumeister (1997) have shed new light on the cognitive dynamics of *projection*. Newman et al. showed that people actively work to suppress thoughts about the possibility that they might have an undesirable trait (say, dishonesty), but this ongoing effort makes thoughts about the unwanted trait highly accessible, so they chronically use this trait concept to explain others' behaviour and end up routinely attributing the trait to others. Another very interesting study provided support for the Freudian hypothesis that reaction formation underlies homophobia in males. Adams, Wright, and Lohr (1996) found that when homophobic men are shown an erotic videotape depicting homosexual activity, they exhibit sexual arousal not seen in nonhomophobic subjects.

CONCEPT CHECK 12.1

Identifying Defence Mechanisms

Check your understanding of defence mechanisms by identifying specific defences in the story below. Each example of a defence mechanism is underlined, with a number next to it. Write in the defence at work in each case in the numbered spaces after the story. The answers are in Appendix A.

My girlfriend recently broke up with me after we had dated seriously for several years. At first, I cried a great deal and locked myself in my room, where I pouted endlessly. (1.) I was sure that my former girlfriend felt as miserable as I did. I told several friends that she was probably lonely and depressed. (2.) Later, I decided that I hated her. I was happy about the break-up and talked about how much I was going to enjoy my newfound freedom. (3.) I went to parties and socialized a great deal and just forgot about her. It's funny—at one point I couldn't even remember her phone number! (4.) Then I started pining for her again. But eventually I began to look at the situation more objectively. I realized that she had many faults and that we were bound to break up sooner or later, so I was better off without her. (5.)

1. _____   4. _____

2. _____   5. _____

3. _____

childhood experiences and other factors beyond one's control, he suggested that people are not masters of their own destinies. Third, by emphasizing the great importance of how people cope with their sexual urges, he offended those who held the conservative, Victorian values of his time.

Thus, Freud endured a great deal of criticism, condemnation, and outright ridicule, even after his work began to attract more favourable attention. Consider the following recollection from one of Freud's friends: "In those days when one mentioned Freud's name everyone would begin to laugh, as if someone had told a joke. Freud was the queer fellow who wrote a book about dreams ... He was the man who saw sex in everything. It was considered bad taste to bring up Freud's name in the presence of ladies" (Donn, 1988, p. 57). Let's examine the ideas that generated so much controversy.

Structure of Personality

Freud divided personality structure into three components: the id, the ego, and the superego (see Figure 12.2). He saw a person's behaviour as the outcome of interactions among these three components.

The *id* is the primitive, instinctive component of personality that operates according to the pleasure principle. Freud referred to the id as the reservoir of psychic energy. By this he meant that the id houses the raw biological urges (to eat, sleep, defecate, copulate, and so on) that energize human behaviour. The id operates according to the *pleasure principle*, which demands immediate gratification of its urges. The id engages in *primary-process thinking*, which is primitive, illogical, irrational, and fantasy oriented.

The *ego* is the decision-making component of personality that operates according to the reality principle. The ego mediates between the id, with its forceful desires for immediate satisfaction, and the external social world, with its expectations and norms regarding suitable behaviour. The ego considers social realities—society's norms, etiquette, rules, and customs—in deciding how to behave. The ego is guided by the *reality principle*, which seeks to delay gratification of the id's urges until appropriate outlets and situations can be found. In short, to stay out of trouble, the ego often works to tame the unbridled desires of the id.

In the long run, the ego wants to maximize gratification, just as the id does. However, the ego engages in *secondary-process thinking*, which is relatively rational, realistic, and oriented toward problem solving. Thus, the ego strives to avoid negative consequences from society and its representatives (e.g., punishment by parents or teachers) by behaving "properly." It also

attempts to achieve long-range goals that sometimes require putting off gratification.

While the ego concerns itself with practical realities, the *superego* is the moral component of personality that incorporates social standards about what represents right and wrong. Throughout their lives, but especially during childhood, people receive training about what constitutes good and bad behaviour. Many social norms regarding morality are eventually internalized. The superego emerges out of the ego at around three to five years of age. In some people, the superego can become irrationally demanding in its striving for moral perfection. Such people are plagued by excessive feelings of guilt. According to Freud, the id, ego, and superego are distributed differently across three levels of awareness, which we'll describe next.

Levels of Awareness

Perhaps Freud's most enduring insight was his recognition of how unconscious forces can influence behaviour. He inferred the existence of the unconscious from a variety of observations that he made with his patients. For example, he noticed that "slips of the tongue" often revealed a person's true feelings. He also realized that his patients' dreams often expressed hidden desires. Most important, through psychoanalysis he often helped patients to discover feelings and conflicts of which they had previously been unaware.

CONSCIOUS:
Contact with outside world

PRECONSCIOUS:
Material just beneath the surface of awareness

EGO
Reality principle
Secondary-process thinking

SUPEREGO
Moral imperatives

UNCONSCIOUS:
Difficult to retrieve material; well below the surface of awareness

ID
Pleasure principle
Primary-process thinking

Figure 12.2

Freud's model of personality structure. Freud theorized that people have three levels of awareness: the conscious, the preconscious, and the unconscious. The enormous size of the unconscious is often dramatized by comparing it to the portion of an iceberg that lies beneath the water's surface. Freud also divided personality structure into three components—id, ego, and superego—which operate according to different principles and exhibit different modes of thinking. In Freud's model, the id is entirely unconscious, but the ego and superego operate at all three levels of awareness.

Web Link 12.1

Victorian Studies Archive
http://www.lang.nagoya-u.ac.jp/~matsuoka/Victorian.html

This site offers numerous links to resources on the Victorian age that will give you an idea of the context within which psychoanalysis developed.

Freud contrasted the unconscious with the conscious and preconscious, creating three levels of awareness. **The *conscious* consists of whatever one is aware of at a particular point in time.** For example, at this moment your conscious may include the train of thought in this text and a dim awareness in the back of your mind that your eyes are getting tired and you're beginning to get hungry. **The *preconscious* contains material just beneath the surface of awareness that can easily be retrieved.** Examples might include your middle name, what you had for supper last night, or an argument you had with a friend yesterday. **The *unconscious* contains thoughts, memories, and desires that are well below the surface of conscious awareness but that nonetheless exert great influence on behaviour.** Examples of material that might be found in your unconscious include a forgotten trauma from childhood, hidden feelings of hostility toward a parent, and repressed sexual desires.

Freud's conception of the mind is often compared to an iceberg that has most of its mass hidden beneath the water's surface (see Figure 12.2). He believed that the unconscious (the mass below the surface) is much larger than the conscious or preconscious. As you can see in Figure 12.2, he proposed that the ego and superego operate at all three levels of awareness. In contrast, the id is entirely unconscious, expressing its urges at a conscious level through the ego. Of course, the id's desires for immediate satisfaction often trigger internal conflicts with the ego and superego. These conflicts play a key role in Freud's theory.

Web Link 12.2
Sigmund Freud Museum
http://www.freud-museum.at/e/
This online museum offers a detailed chronology of Freud's life and an explanation of the most important concepts of psychoanalysis.

Freud's psychoanalytic theory was based on decades of clinical work. He treated a great many patients in the consulting room pictured here. The room contains numerous artifacts from other cultures—and the original psychoanalytic couch.

© Peter Aprahamian/CORBIS

Conflict and the Tyranny of Sex and Aggression

Freud assumed that behaviour is the outcome of an ongoing series of internal conflicts. He saw internal battles between the id, ego, and superego as routine. Why? Because the id wants to gratify its urges immediately, but the norms of civilized society frequently dictate otherwise. For example, your id might feel an urge to clobber a co-worker who constantly irritates you. However, society frowns on such behaviour, so your ego would try to hold this urge in check. Hence, you would find yourself in conflict. You may be experiencing conflict at this very moment. In Freudian terms, your id may be secretly urging you to abandon reading this chapter so that you can fix a snack and watch some television. Your ego may be weighing this appealing option against your society-induced need to excel in school.

Freud believed that people's lives are dominated by conflict. He asserted that individuals career from one conflict to another. The following scenario provides a concrete illustration of how the three components of personality interact to create constant conflicts:

Imagine lurching across your bed to shut off your alarm clock as it rings obnoxiously. It's 7 A.M. and time to get up for your history class. However, your id (operating according to the pleasure principle) urges you to return to the immediate gratification of additional sleep. Your ego (operating according to the reality principle) points out that you really must go to class since you haven't been able to decipher the textbook on your own. Your id (in its typical unrealistic fashion) smugly assures you that you will get the A grade that you need and suggests lying back to dream about how impressed your roommates will be. Just as you're relaxing, your superego jumps into the fray. It tries to make you feel guilty about all the money your parents paid in tuition for the class that you're about to skip. You haven't even gotten out of bed yet, but there's already a pitched battle in your psyche.

Let's say your ego wins the battle. You pull yourself out of bed and head for class. On the way, you pass a doughnut shop and your id clamours for cinnamon rolls. Your ego reminds you that you're supposed to be on a diet. Your id wins this time. After you've attended your history lecture, your ego reminds you that you need to do some library research for a paper in philosophy. However, your id insists on returning to your apartment to watch some sitcom reruns. As you re-enter your apartment, you're overwhelmed by how messy it is. It's your roommates' mess, and your id suggests that you tell them off. As you're about to lash out, however, your ego convinces you that diplomacy will be more effective. Three sitcoms later

A great variety of theorists have made extensive additions to Freud's original list of defences (Vaillant, 1992). We'll examine some of these additional defence mechanisms in the next chapter, when we discuss the role of defences in coping with stress. For now, however, let's turn our attention to Freud's ideas about the development of personality.

Development: Psychosexual Stages 10A

Freud believed that "the child is father to the man." In fact, he made the rather startling assertion that the basic foundation of an individual's personality has been laid down by the tender age of five. To shed light on these crucial early years, Freud formulated a stage theory of development. He emphasized how young children deal with their immature but powerful sexual urges (he used the term *sexual* in a general way to refer to many urges for physical pleasure). According to Freud, these sexual urges shift in focus as children progress from one stage of development to another. Indeed, the names for the stages (oral, anal, genital, and so on) are based on where children are focusing their erotic energy during that period. Thus, *psychosexual stages* **are developmental periods with a characteristic sexual focus that leave their mark on adult personality.**

Freud theorized that each psychosexual stage has its own, unique developmental challenges or tasks (see Table 12.2). The way these challenges are handled supposedly shapes personality. The process of *fixation* plays an important role in this process. **Fixation is a failure to move forward from one stage to another as expected.** Essentially, the child's development stalls for a while. Fixation can be caused by *excessive gratification* of needs at a particular stage or by *excessive frustration* of those needs. Either way, fixations left over from childhood affect adult personality. Generally, fixation leads to an overemphasis on the psychosexual needs prominent during the fixated stage. Freud described a series of five psychosexual stages. Let's examine some of the highlights in this sequence.

According to Freud, early childhood experiences such as toilet training (a parental attempt to regulate a child's biological urges) can influence an individual's personality, with consequences lasting throughout adulthood.

Oral Stage This stage encompasses the first year of life. During this period, the main source of erotic stimulation is the mouth (in biting, sucking, chewing, and so on). In Freud's view, the handling of the child's feeding experiences is crucial to subsequent development. He attributed considerable importance to the manner in which the child is weaned from the breast or the bottle. According to Freud, fixation at the oral stage could form the basis for obsessive eating or smoking later in life (among many other things).

Anal Stage In their second year, children get their erotic pleasure from their bowel movements, through either the expulsion or retention of feces. The crucial event at this time is toilet training, which represents society's first systematic effort to regulate the child's biological urges. Severely punitive toilet training leads to a variety of possible outcomes. For example,

Table 12.2 Freud's Stages of Psychosexual Development

Stage	Approximate Ages	Erotic Focus	Key Tasks and Experiences
Oral	0–1	Mouth (sucking, biting)	Weaning (from breast or bottle)
Anal	2–3	Anus (expelling or retaining feces)	Toilet training
Phallic	4–5	Genitals (masturbating)	Identifying with adult role models; coping with Oedipal crisis
Latency	6–12	None (sexually repressed)	Expanding social contacts
Genital	Puberty onward	Genitals (being sexually intimate)	Establishing intimate relationships; contributing to society through working

excessive punishment might produce a latent feeling of hostility toward the "trainer," usually the mother. This hostility might generalize to women as a class. Another possibility is that heavy reliance on punitive measures could lead to an association between genital concerns and the anxiety that the punishment arouses. This genital anxiety derived from severe toilet training could evolve into anxiety about sexual activities later in life.

Phallic Stage Around age four, the genitals become the focus for the child's erotic energy, largely through self-stimulation. During this pivotal stage, the *Oedipal complex* emerges. That is, little boys develop an erotically tinged preference for their mother. They also feel hostility toward their father, whom they view as a competitor for mom's affection. Similarly, little girls develop a special attachment to their father; and around the same time, they learn that little boys have very different genitals, and supposedly they develop *penis envy*. According to Freud, young girls feel hostile toward their mother because they blame her for their anatomical "deficiency."

To summarize, **in the *Oedipal complex* children manifest erotically tinged desires for their opposite-sex parent, accompanied by feelings of hostility toward their same-sex parent**. The name for this syndrome was taken from a tragic myth from ancient Greece. In this story, Oedipus was separated from his parents at birth. Not knowing the identity of his real parents, when he grew up he inadvertently killed his father and married his mother. The complex in girls is sometimes referred to as the *Electra complex* but this was not endorsed by Freud himself (Corsini, 1999).

According to Freud, the way parents and children deal with the sexual and aggressive conflicts inherent in the Oedipal complex is of paramount importance. The child has to resolve the Oedipal dilemma by purging the sexual longings for the opposite-sex parent and by crushing the hostility felt toward the same-sex parent. In Freud's view, healthy psychosexual development hinges on the resolution of the Oedipal conflict. Why? Because continued hostility toward the same-sex parent may prevent the child from identifying adequately with that parent. Freudian theory predicts that without such identification, sex typing, conscience, and many other aspects of the child's development won't progress as they should.

Latency and Genital Stages From around age six through puberty, the child's sexuality is largely suppressed—it becomes *latent*. Important events during this *latency stage* centre on expanding social contacts beyond the immediate family. With puberty, the child progresses into the *genital stage*. Sexual urges reappear and focus on the genitals once again. At this point, sexual energy is normally channelled toward peers of the other sex, rather than toward oneself as in the phallic stage.

In arguing that the early years shape personality, Freud did not mean that personality development comes to an abrupt halt in middle childhood. However, he did believe that the foundation for adult personality has been solidly entrenched by this time. He maintained that future developments are rooted in early, formative experiences and that significant conflicts in later years are replays of crises from childhood.

In fact, Freud believed that unconscious sexual conflicts rooted in childhood experiences cause most personality disturbances. His steadfast belief in the psychosexual origins of psychological disorders eventually led to bitter theoretical disputes with two of his most brilliant colleagues: Carl Jung and Alfred Adler. Jung and Adler both argued that Freud overemphasized sexuality. Freud rejected their ideas, and the other two theorists felt compelled to go their own way, developing their own theories of personality.

Jung's Analytical Psychology

Carl Jung was born to middle-class Swiss parents in 1875. The son of a Protestant pastor, he was a deeply introverted, lonely child, but an excellent student. Jung had earned his medical degree and was an established young psychiatrist in Zurich when he began to write to Freud in 1906. When the two men had their first meeting, they were so taken by each other's insights that they talked nonstop for 13 hours! They exchanged 359 letters before their friendship and theoretical alliance were torn apart. Their relationship was ruptured irreparably in 1913 by a variety of theoretical disagreements.

Jung called his new approach *analytical psychology* to differentiate it from Freud's psychoanalytic theory. Jung's analytical psychology eventually attracted many followers. Perhaps because of his conflicts with Freud, Jung claimed to deplore the way schools of thought often become dogmatic, discouraging new ideas. Although many theorists came to characterize themselves as "Jungians," Jung himself often remarked, "I am not a Jungian" and said, "I do not want anybody to be a Jungian. I want people above all to be themselves" (van der Post, 1975).

Like Freud, Jung (1921, 1933) emphasized the unconscious determinants of personality. However, he proposed that the unconscious consists of two layers. The first layer, called the *personal unconscious,* is essentially the same as Freud's version of the unconscious.

© Bettmann/CORBIS

"I am not a Jungian . . . I do not want anybody to be a Jungian. I want people above all to be themselves."
CARL JUNG

The *personal unconscious* houses material that is not within one's conscious awareness because it has been repressed or forgotten. In addition, Jung theorized the existence of a deeper layer he called the collective unconscious. The *collective unconscious* is a storehouse of latent memory traces inherited from people's ancestral past. According to Jung, each person shares the collective unconscious with the entire human race (see Figure 12.4). It contains the "whole spiritual heritage of mankind's evolution, born anew in the brain structure of every individual" (Jung, quoted in Campbell, 1971, p. 45).

Jung called these ancestral memories *archetypes*. They are not memories of actual, personal experiences. Instead, *archetypes* are emotionally charged images and thought forms that have universal meaning. These archetypal images and ideas show up frequently in dreams and are often manifested in a culture's use of symbols in art, literature, and religion. According to Jung, symbols from very different cultures often show striking similarities because they emerge from archetypes that are shared by the whole human race. For instance, Jung found numerous cultures in which the *mandala,* or "magic circle," has served as a symbol of the unified wholeness of the self (see Figure 12.4). Jung felt that an understanding of archetypal symbols helped him make sense of his

patients' dreams. This was of great concern to him, as he thought that dreams contain important messages from the unconscious. Like Freud, he depended extensively on dream analysis in his treatment of patients.

Jung's unusual ideas about the collective unconscious had little impact on the mainstream of thinking in psychology. Their influence was felt more in other fields, such as anthropology, philosophy, art, and religious studies. However, many of Jung's other ideas *have* been incorporated into the mainstream of psychology. For instance, Jung was the first to describe the introverted (inner-directed) and extraverted (outer-directed) personality types. *Introverts* tend to be preoccupied with the internal world of their own thoughts, feelings, and experiences. Like Jung himself, they generally are contemplative and aloof. In contrast, *extraverts* tend to be interested in the external world of people and things. They're more likely to be outgoing, talkative, and friendly, instead of reclusive.

Adler's Individual Psychology

Like Freud, Alfred Adler grew up in Vienna in a middle-class Jewish home. He was a sickly child who struggled to overcome rickets and an almost fatal case of pneumonia. At home, he was overshadowed by an exception-

Figure 12.4

Jung's vision of the collective unconscious. Much like Freud, Jung theorized that each person has conscious and unconscious levels of awareness. However, he also proposed that the entire human race shares a collective unconscious, which exists in the deepest reaches of everyone's awareness. He saw the collective unconscious as a storehouse of hidden ancestral memories, called archetypes. Jung believed that important cultural symbols emerge from these universal archetypes. Thus, he argued that remarkable resemblances among symbols from disparate cultures (such as the mandalas shown here) are evidence of the existence of the collective unconscious.

Source: Images from C. G. Jung Bild Und Wort, © Walter-Verlag AG, Olten, Switzerland, 1977

Mandalas from various cultures

Russia

Navajo Indians

Tibet

Web Link 12.3

C. G. Jung, Analytical Psychology, & Culture
http://www.cgjungpage.org/
Synchronicity, archetypes, collective unconscious, introversion, extraversion—these and many other important concepts arising from analytical psychology and Jung's tremendously influential theorizing are examined at this comprehensive site.

ally bright and successful older brother. Nonetheless, he went on to earn his medical degree, and he practised ophthalmology and general medicine before his interest turned to psychiatry. He was a charter member of Freud's inner circle—the Vienna Psychoanalytic Society. However, he soon began to develop his own theory of personality, perhaps because he didn't want to be dominated once again by an "older brother" (Freud). His theorizing was denounced by Freud in 1911, and Adler was forced to resign from the Psychoanalytic Society. He took 9 of its 23 members with him to form his own organization. Adler's new approach to personality was christened *individual psychology*.

Like Jung, Adler (1917, 1927) argued that Freud had gone overboard in centring his theory on sexual conflicts. According to Adler, the foremost source of human motivation is a striving for superiority. In his view, this striving does not necessarily translate into the pursuit of dominance or high status. Adler saw ***striving for superiority* as a universal drive to adapt, improve oneself, and master life's challenges.** He noted that young children understandably feel weak and helpless in comparison with more competent older children and adults. These early inferiority feelings supposedly motivate them to acquire new skills and develop new talents. Thus, Adler maintained that striving for superiority is the prime goal of life, rather than physical gratification (as suggested by Freud).

Adler asserted that everyone has to work to overcome some feelings of inferiority—a process he called

«*The goal of the human soul is conquest, perfection, security, superiority.*»
ALFRED ADLER

Adler's theory has been used to analyze the tragic life of the legendary actress Marilyn Monroe (Ansbacher, 1970). During her childhood, Monroe suffered from parental neglect that left her with acute feelings of inferiority. Her inferiority feelings led her to overcompensate by flaunting her beauty, marrying celebrities (Joe DiMaggio and Arthur Miller), keeping film crews waiting for hours, and seeking the adoration of her fans.

compensation. ***Compensation* involves efforts to overcome imagined or real inferiorities by developing one's abilities.** Adler believed that compensation is entirely normal. However, in some people inferiority feelings can become excessive, resulting in what is widely known today as an *inferiority complex*—exaggerated feelings of weakness and inadequacy. Adler thought that either parental pampering or parental neglect could cause an inferiority complex. Thus, he agreed with Freud on the importance of early childhood experiences, although he focused on different aspects of parent–child relations.

Adler explained personality disturbances by noting that excessive inferiority feelings can pervert the normal process of striving for superiority. He asserted that some people engage in *overcompensation* to conceal, even from themselves, their feelings of inferiority. Instead of working to master life's challenges, people with an inferiority complex work to achieve status, gain power over others, and acquire the trappings of success (fancy clothes, impressive cars, or whatever looks important to them). They tend to flaunt their success in an effort to cover up their underlying inferiority complex. However, the problem is that such people engage in unconscious self-deception, worrying more about *appearances* than *reality*.

Adler's theory stressed the social context of personality development (Hoffman, 1994). For instance, it was Adler who first focused attention on the possible importance of *birth order* as a factor governing personality. He noted that first-borns, second children, and later-born children enter varied home environments and are treated differently by parents and that these experiences are likely to affect their personality. For example, he hypothesized that only children are often spoiled by excessive attention from parents and that first-borns are often problem children because they become upset when they're "dethroned" by a second child. Adler's theory stimulated hundreds of studies on the effects of birth order, but these studies generally failed to support his hypotheses and did not uncover any reliable correlations between birth order and personality (Ernst & Angst, 1983; Harris, 2000).

In recent years, however, Frank Sulloway (1995, 1996) has argued persuasively that birth order *does* have an impact on personality. Sulloway's reformulated hypotheses focus on how the Big Five traits are shaped by competition among siblings as they struggle to find a "niche" in their family environments. For example, he hypothesizes that first-borns should be more conscientious but less agreeable and open to experience than later-borns. In light of these personality patterns, he further speculates that first-borns tend to be conventional and achievement oriented, whereas later-borns tend to be liberal and rebellious. To evaluate his hypotheses, Sulloway re-examined decades of research on birth order. After eliminating many studies that failed to control for important confounding variables, such as social class and family size, he concluded that the results of the remaining, well-controlled studies provided impressive evidence in favour of his hypotheses. Some subsequent studies have provided additional support for Sulloway's analyses such as that conducted by the University of British Columbia's Delroy Paulhus and the University of Winnipeg's Paul Trapnell (Paulhus, Trapnell, & Chen, 1999), but others have not (Freese, Powell, & Steelman, 1999; Harris, 2000; Skinner, 2003). More studies will be needed, as research on birth order is enjoying a bit of a renaissance.

Evaluating Psychodynamic Perspectives

The psychodynamic approach has provided a number of far-reaching, truly "grand" theories of personality. These theories yielded some bold new insights when they were first presented. Although one might argue about exact details of interpretation, research has demonstrated that (1) unconscious forces can influence behaviour, (2) internal conflict often plays a key role in generating psychological distress, (3) early childhood experiences can have powerful influences on adult personality, and (4) people do use defence mechanisms to reduce their experience of unpleasant emotions (Bornstein, 2003; Westen, 1998; Westen & Gabbard, 1999).

In addition to being praised, psychodynamic formulations have also been criticized on several grounds, including the following (Eysenck, 1990b; Fine, 1990; Macmillan, 1991; Torrey, 1992):

1. *Poor testability.* Scientific investigations require testable hypotheses. Psychodynamic ideas have often been too vague and conjectural to permit a clear scientific test. For instance, how would you prove or disprove the assertion that the id is entirely unconscious?

2. *Inadequate evidence.* The empirical evidence on psychodynamic theories has often been characterized as "inadequate." Psychodynamic theories depend too heavily on clinical case studies in which it's much too easy for clinicians to see what they expect to see. Re-examinations of Freud's own clinical work suggest that he frequently distorted his patients' case histories to make them mesh with his theory (Esterson, 2001; Powell & Boer, 1995). Insofar as researchers have accumulated evidence on psychodynamic theories, the evidence has provided only modest support for many of the central hypotheses (Fisher & Greenberg, 1985, 1996; Westen & Gabbard, 1999).

3. *Sexism.* Many critics have argued that psychodynamic theories are characterized by a sexist bias against women. Freud believed that females' penis envy made them feel inferior to males. He also thought that females tended to develop weaker superegos and to be more prone to neurosis than males. The sex bias in modern psychodynamic theories has been reduced considerably. Nonetheless, the psychodynamic approach has generally provided a rather male-centred point of view (Lerman, 1986; Person, 1990).

It's easy to ridicule Freud for concepts such as penis envy, and it's easy to point to Freudian ideas that have turned out to be wrong. However, you have to remember that Freud, Jung, and Adler began to fashion their theories over a century ago. It's not entirely fair to compare these theories to other models that are only a decade or two old. That's like asking the Wright brothers to race the Concorde. Freud and his colleagues deserve great credit for breaking new ground with their speculations about psychodynamics. In psychology as a whole, no other school of thought has been as influential, with the exception of behaviourism, which we turn to next.

REVIEW OF KEY POINTS

- Psychodynamic approaches include all the theories derived from Freud's insights. Freud described personality structure in terms of three components—the id, ego, and superego—which are routinely involved in an ongoing series of internal conflicts.
- Freud described three levels of awareness: the conscious, the preconscious, and the unconscious. His theory emphasized the importance of unconscious processes. Freud theorized that conflicts centring on sex and aggression are especially likely to lead to significant anxiety. According to Freud, anxiety and other unpleasant emotions such as guilt are often warded off with defence mechanisms.
- Freud believed that the first five years of life are extremely influential in shaping adult personality. He described a series of five psychosexual stages of development: oral, anal, phallic, latency, and genital. Certain experiences during these stages can have lasting effects on adult personality. Resolution of the Oedipal complex is thought to be particularly critical to healthy development.
- Jung's most innovative concept was the collective unconscious, a storehouse of latent memory traces inherited from people's ancestral past. Archetypes are emotionally charged images that have universal meaning. Jung also provided the first description of introversion and extraversion.
- Adler's individual psychology emphasizes how people strive for superiority to compensate for their feelings of inferiority. He explained personality disturbances in terms of overcompensation and inferiority complexes.
- Overall, psychodynamic theories have produced many groundbreaking insights about the unconscious, the role of internal conflict, and the importance of early childhood experiences in personality development. However, psychodynamic theories have been criticized for their poor testability, their inadequate base of empirical evidence, and their male-centred views.

Behavioural Perspectives

PREVIEW QUESTIONS

- How can Skinner's theory explain personality and its development?
- How did Bandura revise the behavioural approach to personality?
- What is self-efficacy, and how does it affect behaviour?
- How did Mischel question the concept of personality?
- What are the strengths and weaknesses of the behavioural approach?

Behaviourism is a theoretical orientation based on the premise that scientific psychology should study only observable behaviour. As we saw in Chapter 1, behaviourism has been a major school of thought in psychology since 1913, when John B. Watson began campaigning for the behavioural point of view. Research in the behavioural tradition has focused largely on learning. For many decades behaviourists devoted relatively little attention to the study of personality. However, their interest in personality began to pick up after John Dollard and Neal Miller (1950) attempted to translate selected Freudian ideas into behavioural terminology. Dollard and Miller showed that behavioural concepts could provide enlightening insights about the complicated subject of personality.

In this section, we'll examine three behavioural views of personality, as we discuss the ideas of B. F. Skinner, Albert Bandura, and Walter Mischel. For the most part, you'll see that behaviourists explain personality the same way they explain everything else—in terms of learning.

Skinner's Ideas Applied to Personality

As we noted in Chapters 1 and 6, modern behaviourism's most prominent theorist has been B. F. Skinner, an American psychologist who lived from 1904 to 1990. After earning his doctorate in 1931, Skinner spent most of his career at Harvard University. There he achieved renown for his research on the principles of learning, which were mostly discovered through

the study of rats and pigeons. Skinner's (1953, 1957) concepts of *operant conditioning* were never meant to be a theory of personality. However, his ideas have affected thinking in all areas of psychology and have been applied to the explanation of personality. Here we'll examine Skinner's views as they relate to personality structure and development.

Personality Structure: A View from the Outside

Skinner made no provision for internal personality structures similar to Freud's id, ego, and superego because such structures can't be observed. Following in the tradition of Watson's radical behaviourism, Skinner showed little interest in what goes on "inside" people. He argued that it's useless to speculate about private, unobservable cognitive processes. Instead, he focused on how the external environment moulds overt behaviour. Indeed, he argued for a strong brand of *determinism,* asserting that behaviour is fully determined by environmental stimuli. He claimed that free will is but an illusion, saying, "There is no place in the scientific position for a self as a true originator or initiator of action" (Skinner, 1974, p. 225).

How can Skinner's theory explain the consistency that can be seen in individuals' behaviour? According to his view, people show some consistent patterns of behaviour because they have some stable *response tendencies* that they have acquired through experience. These response tendencies may change in the future, as a result of new experience, but they're enduring enough to create a certain degree of consistency in a person's behaviour. Implicitly, then, Skinner viewed an individual's personality as a *collection of response tendencies that are tied to various stimulus situations.* A specific situation may be associated with a number of response tendencies that vary in strength, depending on past conditioning (see Figure 12.5).

Personality Development as a Product of Conditioning

Skinner's theory accounts for personality development by explaining how various response tendencies are acquired through learning. He believed that most human responses are shaped by the type of conditioning that he described: operant conditioning. As we discussed in Chapter 6, Skinner maintained that environmental consequences—reinforcement, punishment, and extinction—determine people's patterns of responding. On the one hand, when responses are followed by favourable consequences (reinforce-

Figure 12.5

A behavioural view of personality. Staunch behaviourists devote little attention to the structure of personality because it is unobservable, but they implicitly view personality as an individual's collection of response tendencies. A possible hierarchy of response tendencies for a particular person in a specific stimulus situation (a large party) is shown here.

Operant response tendencies

Stimulus situation

Large party where you know relatively few people

R₁ — Circulate, speaking to others only if they approach you first

R₂ — Stick close to the people you already know

R₃ — Politely withdraw by getting wrapped up in host's book collection

R₄ — Leave at the first opportunity

ment), they are strengthened. For example, if your joking at a party pays off with favourable attention, your tendency to joke at parties will increase (see Figure 12.6). On the other hand, when responses lead to negative consequences (punishment), they are weakened. Thus, if your impulsive decisions always backfire, your tendency to be impulsive will decline.

Because response tendencies are constantly being strengthened or weakened by new experiences, Skinner's theory views personality development as a continuous, lifelong journey. Unlike Freud and many other theorists, Skinner saw no reason to break the developmental process into stages. Nor did he attribute special importance to early childhood experiences.

Skinner believed that conditioning in humans operates much the same as in the rats and pigeons that he studied in his laboratory. Hence, he assumed that conditioning strengthens and weakens response tendencies "mechanically"—that is, without the person's conscious participation. Thus, Skinner was able to explain consistencies in behaviour (personality) without being concerned about individuals' cognitive processes.

Figure (12.6)

Personality development and operant conditioning. According to Skinner, people's characteristic response tendencies are shaped by reinforcers and other consequences that follow behaviour. Thus, if your joking at a party leads to attention and compliments, your tendency to be witty and humorous will be strengthened.

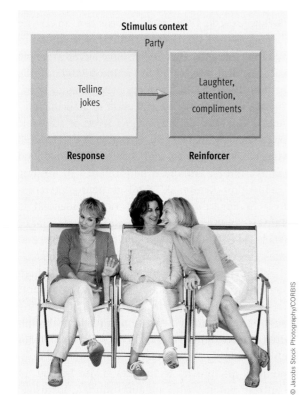

Skinner's ideas continue to be highly influential, but his mechanical, deterministic, noncognitive view of personality has not gone unchallenged by other behaviourists. In recent decades, several theorists have developed somewhat different behavioural models with a more cognitive emphasis.

Bandura's Social Cognitive Theory

Albert Bandura is a modern theorist who has helped reshape the theoretical landscape of behaviourism. As you may recall, in Chapter 6 we highlighted some of Bandura's other contributions to learning theory, notably his groundbreaking research with Waterloo University's Richard Walters on modelling and aggression. Bandura, who was born in Alberta and earned his doctorate in psychology at the University of Iowa, has spent his entire academic career at Stanford University, where he has conducted influential research on behaviour therapy and the determinants of aggression.

Cognitive Processes and Reciprocal Determinism

Bandura is one of several theorists who have added a cognitive flavour to behaviourism since the 1960s. Bandura (1977), Walter Mischel (1973), and Julian Rotter (1982) take issue with Skinner's "pure" behaviourism. They point out that humans obviously are conscious, thinking, feeling beings. Moreover, these theorists argue that in neglecting cognitive processes, Skinner ignored the most distinctive and important feature of human behaviour. Bandura and like-minded theorists originally called their modified brand of behaviourism *social learning theory*. Today, Bandura refers to his model as *social cognitive theory*.

Bandura (1982, 1986) agrees with the fundamental thrust of behaviourism in that he believes that personality is largely shaped through learning. However, he contends that conditioning is not a mechanical process in which people are passive participants. Instead, he maintains that "people are self-organizing, proactive, self-reflecting, and self-regulating, not just reactive organisms shaped and shepherded by external events" (Bandura, 1999, p. 154). Bandura (2001, p. 7) also emphasizes the important role of forward-directed planning, noting that "people set goals for themselves, anticipate the likely consequences of prospective actions, and select and create courses of action likely to produce desired outcomes and avoid detrimental ones."

Comparing his theory to Skinner's highly deterministic view, Bandura advocates a position called *reciprocal*

"The practice of looking inside the organism for an explanation of behavior has tended to obscure the variables which are immediately available for a scientific analysis. These variables lie outside the organism, in its immediate environment and in its environmental history. . . . The objection to inner states is not that they do not exist, but that they are not relevant."
B.F. SKINNER

"Most human behaviour is learned by observation through modeling."
ALBERT BANDURA

determinism. According to this notion, the environment does determine behaviour (as Skinner would argue). However, behaviour also determines the environment (in other words, people can act to alter their environment). Moreover, personal factors (cognitive structures such as beliefs and expectancies) determine and are determined by both behaviour and the environment (see Figure 12.7). Thus, *reciprocal determinism* **is the idea that internal mental events, external environmental events, and overt behaviour all influence one another.** According to Bandura, humans are neither masters of their own destiny nor hapless victims buffeted about by the environment. To some extent, people shape their environments.

Observational Learning

Bandura's foremost theoretical contribution has been his description of observational learning, which we introduced in Chapter 6. *Observational learning* **occurs when an organism's responding is influenced by the observation of others, who are called models.** According to Bandura, both classical and operant conditioning can occur vicariously when one person observes another's conditioning. For example, watching your sister get cheated by someone giving her a bad cheque for her old stereo could strengthen your tendency to be suspicious of others. Although your sister would be the one actually experiencing the negative consequences, they might also influence you—through observational learning.

Bandura maintains that people's characteristic patterns of behaviour are shaped by the *models* that they're exposed to. He isn't referring to the fashion models who dominate the mass media—although they do qualify. In observational learning, **a *model* is a person whose behaviour is observed by another.** At one time or another, everyone serves as a model for others. Bandura's key point is that many response tendencies are the product of imitation.

As research has accumulated, it has become apparent that some models are more influential than others (Bandura, 1986). Both children and adults tend to imitate people they like or respect more than people they don't. People are also especially prone to imitate the behaviour of people whom they consider attractive or powerful (such as rock stars). In addition, imitation is more likely when people see similarity between models and themselves. Thus, children tend to imitate same-sex role models somewhat more than opposite-sex models. Finally, people are more likely to copy a model if they observe that the model's behaviour leads to positive outcomes.

Self-Efficacy

Bandura discusses how a variety of personal factors (aspects of personality) govern behaviour. In recent years, the factor he has emphasized most is self-efficacy (Bandura, 1990, 1993, 1995). *Self-efficacy* **refers to one's belief about one's ability to perform behaviours that should lead to expected outcomes.** When self-efficacy is high, individuals feel confident that they can execute the responses necessary to earn reinforcers. When self-efficacy is low, individuals worry that the necessary responses may be beyond their abilities. Perceptions of self-efficacy are subjective and specific to certain kinds of tasks. For instance, you might feel extremely confident about your ability to handle difficult social situations but doubtful about your ability to handle academic challenges.

Perceptions of self-efficacy can influence which challenges people tackle and how well they perform. Studies have found that feelings of greater self-efficacy are associated with greater success in giving up smoking (Boudreaux et al., 1998), greater adherence to an exercise regimen (Rimal, 2001), better outcomes in substance abuse treatment (Bandura, 1999), more success in coping with medical rehabilitation (Waldrop et al., 2001), better self-care among diabetics (Williams & Bond, 2002), greater persistence and effort in academic pursuits (Zimmerman, 1995), higher levels of academic performance (Chemers, Hu, & Garcia, 2001), reduced vulnerability to anxiety and depression in childhood (Muris, 2002), enhanced performance in athletic competition (Kane et al., 1996), greater receptiveness to technological training (Christoph, Schoenfeld, & Tansky, 1998), higher work-related performance (Stajkovic & Luthans, 1998), and greater resistance to stress (Jex et al., 2001), among many other things.

What are the developmental antecedents of high self-efficacy? Schneewind (1995) asserts that parents can foster self-efficacy by providing a stimulating environment and by being responsive to their children's behaviour. An emphasis on warm support for children, early independence training, and non-punitive disciplinary techniques is also helpful. In contrast, parents who are authoritarian, intrusive,

Figure 12.7

Bandura's reciprocal determinism. Bandura rejects Skinner's highly deterministic view that behaviour is governed by the environment and that freedom is an illusion. Bandura argues that internal mental events, external environmental contingencies, and overt behaviour all influence one another.

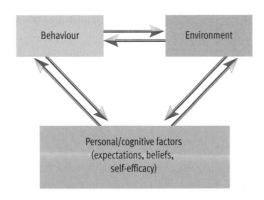

overprotective, or neglectful are likely to undermine self-efficacy in their offspring.

Mischel and the Person–Situation Controversy

Walter Mischel was born in Vienna, not far from Freud's home. His family emigrated to the United States in 1939, when he was nine. After earning his doctorate in psychology, he spent many years on the faculty at Stanford, as a colleague of Bandura's. He has since moved to Columbia University.

Like Bandura, Mischel (1973, 1984) is an advocate of social learning theory. Mischel's chief contribution to personality theory has been to focus attention on the extent to which situational factors govern behaviour. According to social learning theory, people try to gauge the reinforcement contingencies and adjust their behaviour to the circumstances. For example, if you believe that hard work in your job will pay off by leading to raises and promotions, you'll probably be diligent and industrious. But if you think that hard work in your job is unlikely to be rewarded, you may act lazy and irresponsible. Thus, social learning theory predicts that people will often behave differently in different situations.

Mischel (1968, 1973) reviewed decades of research and concluded that, indeed, people exhibit far less consistency across situations than had been widely assumed. For example, studies show that a person who is honest in one situation may be dishonest in another. Someone who wouldn't dream of being dishonest in a business deal might engage in wholesale cheating in filling out tax returns. Similarly, some people are quite shy in one situation and outgoing in another. In light of these realities, Mischel maintains that behaviour is characterized by more *situational specificity* than consistency.

Mischel's position has generated great controversy because it strikes at the heart of the concept of personality itself. As we discussed at the beginning of the chapter, the concept of personality is used to explain consistency in people's behaviour over time and situations. If there isn't much consistency, there isn't much need for the concept of personality.

Mischel's views have attracted many critics who have sought to defend the value of the personality concept. For instance, Epstein (1980, 1986) argued that the methods used in much of the research reviewed by Mischel led to an underestimate of cross-situational consistency. One consideration is that studies have often used young people as subjects, but personality doesn't fully stabilize until middle age (Roberts & Pomerantz, 2004). Critics also noted that it

is unreasonable to expect complete cross-situational consistency, because specific traits are more easily expressed in some situations than others (Kenrick & Funder, 1991). For example, a person's fun-loving, humorous qualities aren't likely to be apparent at a funeral, where everyone is expected to be sombre. Thus, Mischel's provocative theories have sparked a robust debate about the relative importance of the *person* as opposed to the *situation* in determining behaviour. This debate has led to a growing recognition that *both* the person and the situation are important determinants of behaviour (Fleeson, 2004; Funder, 2001; Mischel & Shoda, 1999; Roberts & Pomerantz, 2004).

Mischel's (1968) analysis of the trait construct has proven to be extremely provocative over the intervening years and has led to several extensions of the concept. Norman Endler of York University is a well-known advocate of an *interactional* approach to personality. Along with his colleague David Magnusson, Endler has argued that personality traits *interact* with situational factors to produce behaviour (Endler & Magnusson, 1976). Thus, in order to accurately predict how someone will behave, you not only need to know something about that person's standing on relevant personality traits, but you also need information about the nature of the situational context he or she is facing. Neither factor alone will allow you to accurately predict an individual's behaviour.

Evaluating Behavioural Perspectives

Behavioural theories are firmly rooted in extensive empirical research rather than clinical intuition. Skinner's ideas have shed light on how environmental consequences and conditioning mould people's characteristic behaviour. Bandura's social cognitive theory has expanded the horizons of behaviourism and increased its relevance to the study of personality. Mischel deserves credit for increasing psychology's awareness of how situational factors shape behaviour.

Of course, each theoretical approach has its weaknesses and shortcomings, and the behavioural approach is no exception. Major lines of criticism include the following (Liebert & Liebert, 1998; Maddi, 1989):

1. *Overdependence on animal research.* Many principles in behavioural theories have been discovered through research on rats and other animals. Some critics argue that behaviourists have depended too much on animal research and that they have indiscriminately generalized from animal behaviour to human behaviour.

2. *Dehumanizing nature of radical behaviourism.* Skinner and other radical behaviourists have been

"It seems remarkable how each of us generally manages to reconcile his seemingly diverse behavior into one self-consistent whole."
WALTER MISCHEL

criticized heavily for denying the existence of free will and the importance of cognitive processes. The critics argue that the radical behaviourist viewpoint strips human behaviour of its most uniquely human elements and that it therefore cannot provide an accurate model of human functioning.

3. *Fragmentation of personality.* Behaviourists have also been criticized for providing a fragmented view of personality. The behavioural approach carves personality up into stimulus–response associations. There are no unifying structural concepts (such as Freud's ego) that tie these pieces together. Humanistic theorists, whom we shall cover next, have been particularly vocal in criticizing this piecemeal analysis of personality.

REVIEW OF KEY POINTS

● Behavioural theories explain how personality is shaped through learning. Skinner had little interest in unobservable cognitive processes and embraced a strong determinism.

● Skinner's followers view personality as a collection of response tendencies tied to specific stimulus situations. They assume that personality development is a lifelong process in which response tendencies are shaped and reshaped by learning, especially operant conditioning.

● Social learning theory focuses on how cognitive factors such as expectancies regulate learned behaviour. Bandura's concept of observational learning accounts for the acquisition of responses from models. High self-efficacy has been related to successful health regimens, academic success, and athletic performance, among other things.

● Mischel has questioned the degree to which people display cross-situational consistency in behaviour. Mischel's arguments have increased psychologists' awareness of the situational determinants of behaviour.

● Behavioural approaches to personality are based on rigorous research. They have provided ample insights into how environmental factors and learning mould personalities. The behaviourists have been criticized for their overdependence on animal research, their fragmented analysis of personality, and radical behaviourism's dehumanizing view of human nature.

Humanistic Perspectives

PREVIEW QUESTIONS

● What led to the emergence of humanism, and what are its central assumptions?
● How did Rogers explain the development of the self and defensive behaviour?
● How did Maslow organize motives?
● What was Maslow's view of the healthy personality?
● What are the strengths and weaknesses of the humanistic approach?

Humanistic theory emerged in the 1950s as something of a backlash against the behavioural and psychodynamic theories that we have just discussed (Cassel, 2000; DeCarvalho, 1991). The principal charge hurled at these two models was that they are dehumanizing. Freudian theory was criticized for its belief that behaviour is dominated by primitive, animalistic drives. Behaviourism was criticized for its preoccupation with animal research and for its mechanistic, fragmented view of personality. Critics argued that both schools of thought are too deterministic and that both fail to recognize the unique qualities of human behaviour.

Many of these critics blended into a loose alliance that came to be known as humanism, because of its exclusive focus on human behaviour. **Humanism is a theoretical orientation that emphasizes the unique qualities of humans, especially their freedom and their potential for personal growth.** Humanistic psychologists don't believe that animal research can reveal anything of any significance about the human condition. In contrast to most psychodynamic and behavioural theorists, humanistic theorists take an optimistic view of human nature. They assume that (1) people can rise above their primitive animal heritage and control their biological urges, and (2) people are largely conscious and rational beings who are not dominated by unconscious, irrational needs and conflicts.

Humanistic theorists also maintain that a person's subjective view of the world is more important than objective reality. According to this notion, if you think

that you're homely or bright or sociable, this belief will influence your behaviour more than the realities of how homely, bright, or sociable you actually are. Therefore, the humanists embrace the *phenomenological approach,* **which assumes that one has to appreciate individuals' personal, subjective experiences to truly understand their behaviour.** As Carl Rogers (1951) put it, "The best vantage point for understanding behavior is from the internal frame of reference of the individual himself" (p. 494). Let's look at Rogers's ideas.

Rogers's Person-Centred Theory

Carl Rogers (1951, 1961, 1980) was one of the founders of the human potential movement. This movement emphasizes self-realization through sensitivity training, encounter groups, and other exercises intended to foster personal growth. Rogers grew up in a religious, upper-middle-class home in the suburbs of Chicago. He was a bright student, but he had to rebel against his parents' wishes in order to pursue his graduate study in psychology. While he was working at the University of Chicago in the 1940s, Rogers devised a major new approach to psychotherapy. Like Freud, Rogers based his personality theory on his extensive therapeutic interactions with many clients. Because of its emphasis on a person's subjective point of view, Rogers's approach is called a *person-centred theory.*

The Self

Rogers viewed personality structure in terms of just one construct. He called this construct the *self,* although it's more widely known today as the *self-concept.* A *self-concept* **is a collection of beliefs about one's own nature, unique qualities, and typical behaviour.** Your self-concept is your own mental picture of yourself. It's a collection of self-perceptions. For example, a self-concept might include beliefs such as "I'm easygoing" or "I'm sly and crafty" or "I'm pretty" or "I'm hard-working." According to Rogers, individuals are aware of their self-concept. It's not buried in their unconscious.

Rogers stressed the subjective nature of the self-concept. Your self-concept may not be entirely consistent with your experiences. Most people tend to distort their experiences to some extent to promote a relatively favourable self-concept. For example, you may believe that you're quite bright, but your grade transcript might suggest otherwise. Rogers called the gap between self-concept and reality incongruence. *Incongruence* **is the degree of disparity between one's self-concept and one's actual experience.** In contrast, if a person's self-concept is reasonably accurate, it's said to be *congruent* with reality (see Figure 12.8). Everyone experiences *some* incongruence. The crucial issue is how much. As we'll see, Rogers maintained that too much incongruence undermines one's psychological well-being.

Development of the Self

In terms of personality development, Rogers was concerned with how childhood experiences promote congruence or incongruence between one's self-concept and one's experience. According to Rogers, people have a strong need for affection, love, and acceptance from others. Early in life, parents provide most of this affection. Rogers maintained that some parents make their affection *conditional.* That is, it depends on the child's behaving well and living up to expectations. When parental love seems conditional, children often block out of their self-concept those experiences that make them feel unworthy of love. They do so because they're worried about parental

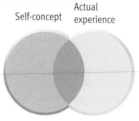

Congruence
Self-concept meshes well with actual experience (some incongruence is probably unavoidable)

Incongruence
Self-concept does not mesh well with actual experience

acceptance, which appears precarious. At the other end of the spectrum, some parents make their affection *unconditional.* Their children have less need to block out unworthy experiences because they've been assured that they're worthy of affection, no matter what they do.

Hence, Rogers believed that unconditional love from parents fosters congruence and that conditional love fosters incongruence. He further theorized that if individuals grow up believing that affection from others is highly conditional, they will go on to distort more and more of their experiences in order to feel worthy of acceptance from a wider and wider array of people (see Figure 12.9).

Anxiety and Defence

According to Rogers, experiences that threaten people's personal views of themselves are the principal cause of troublesome anxiety. The more inaccurate your self-concept, the more likely you are to have experiences that clash with your self-perceptions. Thus, people with highly incongruent self-concepts are especially likely to be plagued by recurrent anxiety (see Figure 12.9).

To ward off this anxiety, individuals often behave defensively in an effort to reinterpret their experience so that it appears consistent with their self-concept. Thus, they ignore, deny, and twist reality to protect and perpetuate their self-concept. Consider a young

Figure 12.8

Rogers's view of personality structure. In Rogers's model, the self-concept is the only important structural construct. However, Rogers acknowledged that one's self-concept may not be consistent with the realities of one's actual experience—a condition called incongruence.

"I have little sympathy with the rather prevalent concept that man is basically irrational, and that his impulses, if not controlled, will lead to destruction of others and self. Man's behavior is exquisitely rational, moving with subtle and ordered complexity toward the goals his organism is endeavoring to achieve."
CARL ROGERS

Figure 12.9

Rogers's view of personality development and dynamics. Rogers's theory of development posits that conditional love leads to a need to distort experiences, which fosters an incongruent self-concept. Incongruence makes one prone to recurrent anxiety, which triggers defensive behaviour, which fuels more incongruence.

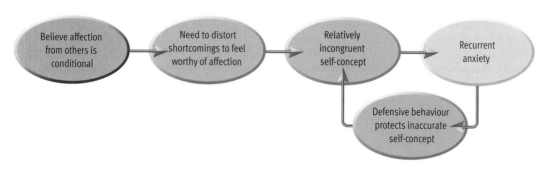

Personality: Theory, Research, and Assessment **509**

woman who, like most people, considers herself a "nice person." Let's suppose that in reality she is rather conceited and selfish. She gets feedback from both boyfriends and girlfriends that she is a "self-centred, snotty brat." How might she react in order to protect her self-concept? She might ignore or block out those occasions when she behaves selfishly. She might attribute her girlfriends' negative comments to their jealousy of her good looks. Perhaps she would blame her boyfriends' negative remarks on their disappointment because she won't get more serious with them. As you can see, people will sometimes go to great lengths to defend their self-concept.

Rogers's work emphasized the importance of the self and has influenced contemporary psychology in terms of its views of the centrality of the self for understanding personality (McCann & Sato, 2000), the implications of incongruence in the self system for dysfunctional emotions (Higgins, 1987), and the importance of others for one's view of the self (Baldwin, 2001). Our Featured Study in this chapter is one of Mark Baldwin's initial demonstrations of the relevance of others for our own views of self. In it, he and his colleagues attempt to determine the effects of priming or activating a cognitive structure representing participants' relationship with a significant other on their self-relevant judgments. One of the interesting aspects of the study is that the cognitive structures relevant to the significant other are primed subliminally.

FEATURED STUDY

The Pope Is Watching You: Effects on Self-Concept

Investigators: Mark W. Baldwin (McGill University), Suzanne Carrell (University of Waterloo), and David Lopez (University of Waterloo).

Source: Priming relationship schemas: My advisor and the Pope are watching me from the back of my mind. *Journal of Experimental Social Psychology, 26,* 1990, 435–454.

Self-theorists such as Carl Rogers and others have suggested that one factor that influences how an individual construes or judges himself or herself is the views of others—what the individual believes others think about him or her. As Baldwin points out, this process of *reflected appraisal* has long been assumed by scholars interested in the self to be one of the most important factors affecting an individual's self-construal or concept. Especially important are signs from others suggesting that they approve or disapprove of you and your actions.

Baldwin wanted to determine the effects of activating cognitive structures that represent well-learned interaction patterns—for example, patterns reflecting your relations with your parents or others with whom you have a significant relationship. In these two studies the specific significant others employed were academic advisors for graduate students (Study 1) and the Pope for Catholic girls (Study 2). What makes the studies really interesting is that cognitive structures representing these two sets of significant others were activated or *primed* subliminally, or without the research participants' awareness. In Study 1 Baldwin examined the effects of priming their advisor on how good graduate students thought their research ideas were, and in Study 2 he examined the effects of priming the Pope on Catholic girls' views of themselves after they had read a sexual prose passage.

Study 1

Method. In this preliminary test of his ideas, Baldwin had 16 graduate students first think about and note three of their current research ideas. They were to rate one of the ideas after each of three types of slides had been presented to them. Then the students were given a task during which they were subliminally presented with four presentations each of a blank slide and then in randomized order the disapproving (i.e., scowling) face of their research supervisor or an approving (i.e., smiling) face of another Ph.D. in psychology they were acquainted with. After each type of slide had been presented and before the next type of slide was presented, they rated the quality and importance of one of their research ideas.

Results and Discussion. The results were just as Baldwin had predicted. After being exposed to the disapproving face of someone of significance to them in an academic context, the graduate students rated their ideas lower than after they had been exposed to an approving face. It is important to keep in mind that these effects on rating one's research ideas were obtained after the faces had been presented without participants being aware of them. While the results confirmed the authors' hypothesis, the study was considered to be preliminary and it had some limitations. It had a very small sample size and there were some inadequacies with the method. But, given the generally supportive findings, the authors decided to do another study in which they were able to have a larger sample size and to clean up some of the problems encountered in Study 1.

Follow-Up Study

A second study with the same general objective was then conducted. In this study, Baldwin and his colleagues wanted to determine the effects on participants' judgments of themselves. They wondered what the effect would be of having Catholic girls read a prose passage containing sexual content and then having them rate themselves after being subliminally exposed either to a scowling, disapproving face of the Pope or a scowling face of someone with whom they had no contact. In fact, the unknown scowling face was the same face used in Study 1.

In this case, however, the Study 1 scowling face was not someone who was significant to the participants.

Method. Forty-six female undergraduate students at the University of Waterloo participated in the study. All of the participants were Catholic. The participants first filled out some questionnaires and then read a prose passage that portrayed a permissive attitude toward sexuality. Participants then were exposed to subliminal presentations of a blank slide, a disapproving picture of the Pope (John Paul II), or the disapproving picture of the face used in Study 1. Participants then completed some questionnaires assessing their views about themselves in the areas of morality, competency, and anxiety. Participants also indicated the degree to which they were practising or nonpractising Catholics. For the Pope to be a significant other, the authors reasoned that the participants must be practising Catholics.

Results and Discussion. Once again the results supported the authors' hypothesis. Catholic girls rated themselves lower (see Table 12.3) after being exposed to the disapproving face of the Pope than they did when exposed to the disapproving face of an unknown other. This effect of the Pope on self-evaluations was observed only for practising Catholics for whom the Pope serves as a truly significant other. Thus, it's not just the disapproving face that affected participants' self-ratings, but disapproval coming from someone with whom one has a personally significant relationship. The authors conclude that the results "are consistent with the hypothesis that a person's momentary sense of self can be shaped by cognitive structures representing significant interpersonal information" (p. 449). The study also shows that one need not even be aware of this influence on your self-relevant judgments.

Comment

This study was featured because it took a creative approach to exploring an interesting phenomenon in a

Table 12.3 Overall Self-Ratings* by High- and Low-Practising Catholics

Stimulus	Low Practising	High Practising
Control (blank)	6.93	7.11
Pope	6.70	6.00
Unknown other	6.64	7.77

*In making their self-ratings, participants were presented with a series of adjective pairs, for example, *dishonest/honest*. Participants were asked to rate themselves in the context of each pair on a scale of 1 to 9. Higher numbers indicate agreement with the more positive member of the pair.

SOURCE: Adapted from Baldwin et al., 1990.

way that implicated processes occurring below the level of our conscious awareness. While scholars such as Rogers had speculated and collected data on the critical effects of our perceptions of others' views of us on our judgments and evaluation of our selves, it had rarely been examined in the context of a subliminal activation of those relationships. Given the important impact of the significant others examined in this research, we can see just how critical the views of our parents can be in laying the groundwork for a child's sense of self. Rogers's views and work on the self helped to make the self an important topic of research and theory in personality psychology. The self was another one of the early casualties of the rise of behaviourism in which speculation of processes of consciousness and self-reflection was viewed as being irrelevant. Baldwin has continued his work on the self and self-esteem and has developed a series of computer games that are designed to raise self-esteem (Baccus, Baldwin, & Packer, 2004). You can play the games and learn more about them by visiting his Web site at http://www.selfesteemgames.mcgill.ca. ■

Maslow's Theory of Self-Actualization

 10c

Abraham Maslow, who grew up in Brooklyn, New York, described his childhood as "unhappy, lonely, [and] isolated." To follow through on his interest in psychology, he had to resist parental pressures to go into law. Maslow spent much of his career at Brandeis University, where he created an influential theory of motivation and provided crucial leadership for the fledgling humanistic movement. Like Rogers, Maslow (1968, 1970) argued that psychology should take an optimistic view of human nature instead of

dwelling on the causes of disorders. "To oversimplify the matter somewhat," he said, "it's as if Freud supplied to us the sick half of psychology and we must now fill it out with the healthy half" (1968, p. 5). Maslow's key contributions were his analysis of how motives are organized hierarchically and his description of the healthy personality.

Hierarchy of Needs

Maslow proposed that human motives are organized into a ***hierarchy of needs***—a systematic arrangement of needs, according to priority, in which basic needs must be met before less basic needs are aroused. This hierarchical arrangement is usually portrayed as

Figure **12.10**

Maslow's hierarchy of needs. According to Maslow, human needs are arranged a hierarchy, and people must satisfy their basic needs before they can satisfy higher needs. In the diagram, higher levels in the pyramid represent progressively less-basic needs. Individuals progress upward in the hierarchy when lower needs are satisfied reasonably well, but they may regress back to lower levels if basic needs are no longer satisfied.

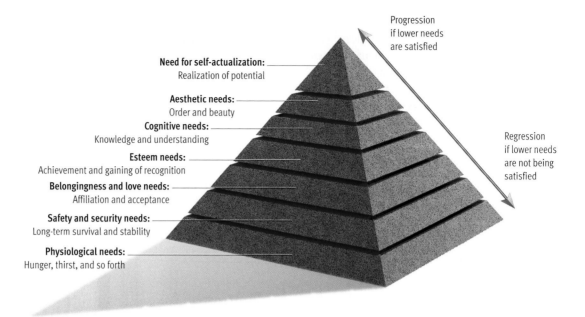

Progression if lower needs are satisfied

Need for self-actualization: Realization of potential

Aesthetic needs: Order and beauty

Cognitive needs: Knowledge and understanding

Esteem needs: Achievement and gaining of recognition

Belongingness and love needs: Affiliation and acceptance

Safety and security needs: Long-term survival and stability

Physiological needs: Hunger, thirst, and so forth

Regression if lower needs are not being satisfied

It is as if Freud supplied to us the sick half of psychology and we must now fill it out with the healthy half.
ABRAHAM MASLOW

a pyramid (see Figure 12.10). The needs toward the bottom of the pyramid, such as physiological or security needs, are the most basic. Higher levels in the pyramid consist of progressively less basic needs. When a person manages to satisfy a level of needs reasonably well (complete satisfaction is not necessary), *this satisfaction activates needs at the next level.*

Like Rogers, Maslow argued that humans have an innate drive toward personal growth—that is, evolution toward a higher state of being. Thus, he described the needs in the uppermost reaches of his hierarchy as *growth needs.* These include the needs for knowledge, understanding, order, and aesthetic beauty. Foremost among them is the *need for self-actualization,* **which is the need to fulfill one's potential; it is the highest need in Maslow's motivational hierarchy.** Maslow summarized this concept with a simple statement: "What a man *can* be, he *must* be." According to Maslow, people will be frustrated if they are unable to fully utilize their talents or pursue their true interests. For example, if you have great musical talent but must work as an accountant, or if you have scholarly interests but must work as a sales clerk, your need for self-actualization will be thwarted.

The Healthy Personality

10c

Because of his interest in self-actualization, Maslow set out to discover the nature of the healthy personality. He tried to identify people of exceptional mental health so that he could investigate their characteristics. In one case, he used psychological tests and interviews to sort out the healthiest 1% of a sizable population of college students. He also studied

admired historical figures (such as Thomas Jefferson and William James) and personal acquaintances characterized by superior adjustment. Over a period of years, he accumulated his case histories and gradually sketched, in broad strokes, a picture of ideal psychological health.

According to Maslow, *self-actualizing persons* **are people with exceptionally healthy personalities, marked by continued personal growth.** Maslow identified various traits characteristic of self-actualizing people. Many of these traits are listed in Figure 12.11. In brief, Maslow found that self-actualizers are accurately tuned in to reality and that they're at peace with themselves. He found that they're open and spontaneous and that they retain a fresh appreciation of the world around them. Socially, they're sensitive to others' needs and enjoy rewarding interpersonal relations. However, they're not dependent on others for approval or uncomfortable with solitude. They thrive on their work, and they enjoy their sense of humour. Maslow also noted that they have "peak experiences" (profound emotional highs) more often than others. Finally, he found that they strike a nice balance between many polarities in personality. For instance, they can be both childlike and mature, both rational and intuitive, both conforming and rebellious.

Evaluating Humanistic Perspectives

The humanists added a refreshing new perspective to the study of personality. Their argument that a person's subjective views may be more important than objective reality has proven compelling. As we noted earlier, even behavioural theorists have begun to take into account subjective personal factors such as beliefs and expectancies. The humanistic approach also deserves some of the credit for making the self-concept an important construct in psychology. Today, theorists of many persuasions use the self-concept in their analyses of personality. Finally, one could argue that the humanists' optimistic, growth- and health-oriented approach laid the foundation for the emergence of the positive psychology movement that is increasingly influential in contemporary psychology (Sheldon & Kasser, 2001; Taylor, 2001).

Of course, there's a negative side to the balance sheet as well. Critics have identified some weaknesses in the humanistic approach to personality, including the following (Burger, 2004):

1. *Poor testability.* Like psychodynamic theorists, the humanists have been criticized for generating hypotheses that are difficult to put to a scientific test. Humanistic concepts such as personal growth and self-actualization are difficult to define and measure.

2. *Unrealistic view of human nature.* Critics also charge that the humanists have been unrealistic in their assumptions about human nature and their descriptions of the healthy personality. For instance, Maslow's self-actualizing people sound nearly perfect. In reality, Maslow had a hard time finding such people. When he searched among the living, the results were so disappointing that he turned to the study of historical figures. Thus, humanistic portraits of psychological health are perhaps a bit too optimistic.

3. *Inadequate evidence.* For the most part, humanistic psychologists haven't been particularly research-oriented. Although Rogers and Maslow both conducted and encouraged empirical research, many of their followers have been scornful of efforts to quantify human experience to test hypotheses. Much more research is needed to catch up with the theorizing in the humanistic camp. This is precisely the opposite of the situation that we'll encounter in the next section, which examines biological approaches to personality.

Characteristics of self-actualizing people	
• Clear, efficient perception of reality and comfortable relations with it	• Mystical and peak experiences
• Spontaneity, simplicity, and naturalness	• Feelings of kinship and identification with the human race
• Problem centring (having something outside themselves they "must" do as a mission)	• Strong friendships, but limited in number
	• Democratic character structure
• Detachment and need for privacy	• Ethical discrimination between good and evil
• Autonomy, independence of culture and environment	• Philosophical, unhostile sense of humour
• Continued freshness of appreciation	• Balance between polarities in personality

Figure 12.11

Maslow's view of the healthy personality.
Humanistic theorists emphasize psychological health instead of maladjustment. Maslow's description of characteristics of self-actualizing people evokes a picture of the healthy personality.

Source: Adapted from Potkay, C. R., & Allen, B. P. (1986). *Personality: Theory, research and application.* Pacific Grove, CA: Brooks/Cole. Copyright © 1986 by C. R. Potkay & B. P. Allen. Adapted by permission of the author.

Web Link 12.5

The Personality Project
http://www.personality-project.org/

William Revelle, director of the graduate program in personality at Northwestern University's Psychology Department, has assembled a directory to many Internet-based resources in the study of personality.

CONCEPT **CHECK 12.2**

Recognizing Key Concepts in Personality Theories

Check your understanding of psychodynamic, behavioural, and humanistic personality theories by identifying key concepts from these theories in the scenarios below. The answers can be found in Appendix A.

1. Thirteen-year-old Sarah watches a TV show in which the leading female character manipulates her boyfriend by acting helpless and purposely losing a tennis match against him. The female lead repeatedly expresses her slogan, "Never let them [men] know you can take care of yourself." Sarah becomes more passive and less competitive around boys her own age.

Concept: _____

2. Yolanda has a secure, enjoyable, reasonably well-paid job as a tenured English professor at a community college. Her friends are dumbfounded when she announces that she's going to resign and give it all up to try writing a novel. She tries to explain, "I need a new challenge, a new mountain to climb. I've had this lid on my writing talents for years, and I've got to break free. It's something I have to try. I won't be happy until I do."

Concept: _____

3. Vladimir, who is four years old, seems to be emotionally distant from and inattentive to his father. He complains whenever he's left with his dad. In contrast, he often cuddles up in bed with his mother and tries very hard to please her by behaving properly.

Concept: _____

Biological Perspectives

PREVIEW QUESTIONS

● How did Eysenck explain variations in extraversion–introversion?

● To what degree is personality heritable?

● Do family environments have much impact on personality?

● What do evolutionary theorists have to say about personality?

● What are the strengths and weaknesses of the biological approach?

Like many identical twins reared apart, Jim Lewis and Jim Springer found they had been leading eerily similar lives. Separated four weeks after birth in 1940, the Jim twins grew up 45 miles apart in Ohio and were reunited in 1979. Eventually, they discovered that both drove the same model blue Chevrolet, chain-smoked Salems, chewed their fingernails, and owned dogs named Toy. Each had spent a good deal of time vacationing at the same three-block strip of beach in Florida. More important, when tested for such personality traits as flexibility, self-control, and sociability, the twins responded almost exactly alike. (Leo, 1987, p. 63)

So began a *Time* magazine summary of a major twin study conducted at the University of Minnesota Center for Twin and Adoption Research. Since 1979 the investigators at this centre have been studying the personality resemblance of identical twins reared apart. Not all the twin pairs have been as similar as Jim Lewis and Jim Springer, but many of the parallels have been uncanny (Lykken et al., 1992). Identical twins Oskar Stohr and Jack Yufe were separated soon after birth. Oskar was sent to a Nazi-run school in Czechoslovakia while Jack was raised in a Jewish home on a Caribbean island. When they were reunited for the first time during middle age, they showed up wearing similar moustaches, haircuts, shirts, and wire-rimmed glasses! A pair

of previously separated female twins both arrived at the Minneapolis airport wearing seven rings on their fingers. One had a son named Richard Andrew and the other had a son named Andrew Richard!

Could personality be largely inherited? These anecdotal reports of striking resemblances between identical twins reared apart certainly raise this possibility. In this section we'll discuss Hans Eysenck's theory, which emphasizes the influence of heredity, look at recent behavioural genetics research on the heritability of personality, and outline the evolutionary perspective on personality.

Eysenck's Theory 10D

Hans Eysenck was born in Germany but fled to London during the era of Nazi rule. He went on to become one of Britain's most prominent psychologists. Eysenck (1967, 1982, 1990a) views personality structure as a hierarchy of traits, in which many superficial traits are derived from a smaller number of more basic traits, which are derived from a handful of fundamental higher-order traits, as shown in Figure 12.12. His studies suggest that all aspects of personality emerge from just three higher-order traits: extraversion, neuroticism, and psychoticism. *Extraversion* involves being

Figure 12.12

Eysenck's model of personality structure. Eysenck described personality structure as a hierarchy of traits. In this scheme, a few higher-order traits, such as extraversion, determine a host of lower-order traits, which determine a person's habitual responses.

SOURCE: Eysenck, H. J. (1976). *The biological basis of personality*. Springfield, IL: Charles C. Thomas. Reprinted by permission of the publisher.

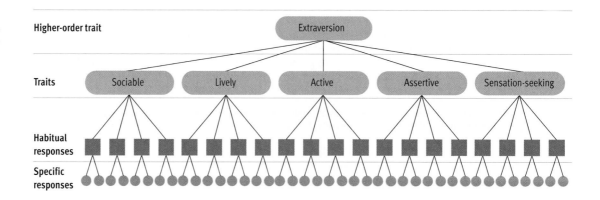

sociable, assertive, active, and lively. *Neuroticism* involves being anxious, tense, moody, and low in self-esteem. *Psychoticism* involves being egocentric, impulsive, cold, and antisocial. Each of these traits is represented in the theory as a bipolar dimension with the endpoints for each dimension as follows: extraversion–introversion, stability–neuroticism (instability), and psychoticism–self-control.

According to Eysenck, "Personality is determined to a large extent by a person's genes" (1967, p. 20). How is heredity linked to personality in Eysenck's model? In part, through conditioning concepts borrowed from behavioural theory. Eysenck theorizes that some people can be conditioned more readily than others because of differences in their physiological functioning. These variations in "conditionability" are assumed to influence the personality traits that people acquire through conditioning processes.

Eysenck has shown a special interest in explaining variations in *extraversion–introversion,* the trait dimension first described years earlier by Carl Jung. He has proposed that introverts tend to have higher levels of physiological arousal, or perhaps higher "arousability," which make them more easily conditioned than extraverts. According to Eysenck, people who condition easily acquire more conditioned inhibitions than others. These inhibitions make them more bashful, tentative, and uneasy in social situations. This social discomfort leads them to turn inward. Hence, they become introverted.

Behavioural Genetics and Personality

Recent research in behavioural genetics has provided impressive support for the idea that many personality traits are largely inherited (Livesley, Jang, & Vernon, 2003; Rowe & van den Oord, 2005). A great deal of work in this area has examined the heritability of the Big Five (Jang, Livesley, & Vernon, 1996; Livesley, Jang, & Vernon, 2002). For instance, Figure 12.13 shows the mean correlations observed for identical and fraternal twins in studies of the Big Five personality traits summarized by Loehlin (1992). Higher correlations are indicative of greater similarity on a trait. On all five traits, identical twins have been found to be much more similar than fraternal twins. Based on these and many other data, Loehlin (1992) and others conclude that genetic factors exert considerable influence over personality (see Chapter 3 for an explanation of the logic of twin studies).

Some skeptics wonder whether identical twins might exhibit more trait similarity than fraternal twins because they're treated more alike. In other words, they wonder whether environmental factors (rather than heredity) could be responsible for identical twins' greater personality resemblance. This nagging question can be answered only by studying identical twins reared apart, which is why the twin study at the University of Minnesota has been so important. The Minnesota study (Tellegen et al., 1988) was the first to

"*Personality is determined to a large extent by a person's genes.***"**
HANS EYSENCK

Figure 12.13

Twin studies of personality.
Loehlin (1992) has summarized the results of twin studies that have examined the Big Five personality traits. The N under each trait indicates the number of twin studies that have examined that trait. The chart plots the average correlations obtained for identical and fraternal twins in these studies. As you can see, identical twins have shown greater resemblance in personality than fraternal twins have, suggesting that personality is partly inherited. (Based on data from Loehlin, 1992)

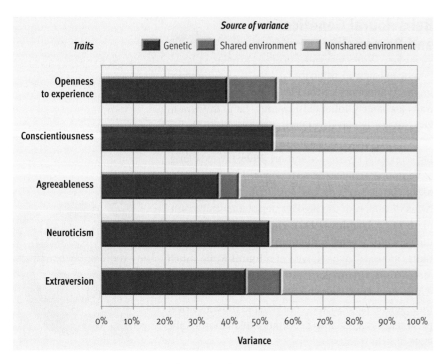

Source of variance

Genetic   Shared environment   Nonshared environment

Traits

Openness to experience

Conscientiousness

Agreeableness

Neuroticism

Extraversion

0% 10% 20% 30% 40% 50% 60% 70% 80% 90% 100%

Variance

Figure 12.14

Heritability and environmental variance for the Big Five traits. Based on the twin study data of Riemann et al. (1997), Plomin and Caspi (1999) estimated the heritability of each of the Big Five traits. The data also allowed them to estimate the amount of variance on each trait attributable to shared environment and nonshared environment. As you can see, the heritability estimates hovered in the vicinity of 40%, with two exceeding 50%. As in other studies, the influence of shared family environment was very modest.

Source: Adapted from Plomin R., & Caspi, A. (1999). Behavioral genetics and personality. In L. A. Pervin & O. P. John (Eds.), *Handbook of personality: Theory and research.* New York: Guilford Press.

administer the same personality test to identical and fraternal twins reared apart, as well as together. Most of the twins reared apart were separated quite early in life (median age of 2.5 months) and remained separated for a long time (median period of almost 34 years).

The results revealed that identical twins reared apart were substantially more similar in personality than fraternal twins reared together. The *heritability estimates* (see Chapter 9) for the traits examined ranged from 40% to 58%. The investigators concluded that their results support the hypothesis that genetic blueprints shape the contours of personality.

Another large-scale twin study of the Big Five traits, conducted in Germany and Poland, yielded similar conclusions (Riemann, Angleitner, & Strelau, 1997). The heritability estimates based on the data from this study are in the same range as the estimates from the Minnesota study (see Figure 12.14). Moreover, a unique feature of this study was that it obtained peer ratings of subjects' personality traits, as well as the usual measures based on participants' responses to personality tests, and these independent ratings yielded roughly similar estimates of heritability. Thus, recent behavioural genetics research suggests that personality is shaped to a considerable degree by hereditary factors.

Research on the heritability of personality has inadvertently turned up an interesting finding that was apparent in the Riemann et al. (1997) study. As you can see in Figure 12.14, *shared family environment* appears to have remarkably little impact on personality. This unexpected finding has been observed quite consistently in behavioural genetics research (Beer, Arnold, & Loehlin, 1998; Rowe & van den Oord, 2005).

It is surprising in that social scientists have long assumed that the family environment shared by children growing up together led to some personality resemblance among them. *These findings have led some theorists to conclude that parents don't matter—that they wield very little influence over how their children develop* (Cohen, 1999; Harris, 1998; Rowe, 1994).

Critics have argued with merit that the methods used in behavioural genetics studies have probably underestimated the impact of shared environment on personality (Collins et al., 2000; Stoolmiller, 1999). They also note that shared experiences—such as being raised with authoritarian discipline—may often have different effects on two siblings, which obscures the impact of environment but is not the same result as having no effect (Turkheimer & Waldron, 2000). And the critics argue that decades of research in developmental psychology have clearly demonstrated that parents have significant influence on their children (Maccoby, 2000).

Although the assertion that "parents don't matter" seems premature and overstated, the perplexing findings in behavioural genetics studies of personality have led researchers to investigate why children from the same family are often so different. Thus far, the evidence suggests that children in the same family experience home environments that are not nearly as homogeneous as previously assumed (Hetherington, Reiss, & Plomin, 1994; Pike et al., 2000). Children in the same home may be treated quite differently, because gender and birth order can influence parents' approaches to childrearing. Temperamental differences between children may also evoke differences in parenting. Focusing on how environmental factors vary *within* families represents a promising new way to explore the determinants of personality.

The Evolutionary Approach to Personality

In the realm of biological perspectives on personality, another recent development has been the emergence of evolutionary theory. Evolutionary theorists assert that personality has a biological basis because natural selection has favoured certain traits over the course of human history (Figueredo et al., 2005). Thus, evolutionary analyses focus on how various personality traits—and the ability to recognize these traits in others—may have contributed to reproductive fitness in ancestral human populations.

For example, David Buss (1991, 1995, 1997) has argued that the Big Five personality traits stand out as important dimensions of personality across a variety of cultures because those traits have had significant adaptive implications. Buss points out that humans historically have depended heavily on groups, which afford protection from predators or enemies, opportunities for sharing food, and a diverse array of other benefits. In the context of these group interactions, people have had to make difficult but crucial judgments about the characteristics of others, asking such questions as: Who will make a good member of my coalition? Who can I depend on when in need? Who will share their resources? Thus, Buss (1995) argues, "those individuals able to accurately discern and act upon these individual differences likely enjoyed a considerable reproductive advantage" (p. 22).

According to Buss, the Big Five emerge as fundamental dimensions of personality because humans have evolved special sensitivity to variations in the ability to bond with others (extraversion), the willingness to cooperate and collaborate (agreeableness), the tendency to be reliable and ethical (conscientiousness), the capacity to be an innovative problem solver (openness to experience), and the ability to handle stress (low neuroticism). In a nutshell, Buss argues that the Big Five reflect the most salient features of others' adaptive behaviour over the course of evolutionary history. MacDonald (1998) takes this line of thinking one step further, asserting that the traits themselves (as opposed to the ability to recognize them) are products of evolution that were adaptive in ancestral environments.

Evaluating Biological Perspectives

Researchers have compiled convincing evidence that biological factors exert considerable influence over personality. Nonetheless, we must take note of some weaknesses in biological approaches to personality:

1. David Funder (2001, p. 207) makes the observation that behavioural genetics researchers exhibit something of an "obsession with establishing the exact magnitude of heritability coefficients." As we discussed in Chapter 9, heritability ratios are ballpark estimates that will vary depending on sampling procedures and other considerations. There is no one magic number awaiting discovery, so the inordinate focus on heritability does seem ill advised.

2. The results of efforts to carve behaviour into genetic and environmental components are ultimately artificial. The effects of nature and nurture are twisted together in complicated interactions that can't be separated cleanly (Brody & Crowley, 1995).

3. At present there's no comprehensive biological theory of personality. Eysenck's model doesn't provide a systematic overview of how biological factors govern personality structure and development (and was never intended to). In regard to personality, evolutionary theory currently is even more limited in scope than Eysenck's theory. Additional theoretical work is needed to catch up with recent empirical findings on the biological basis for personality.

REVIEW OF KEY POINTS

- Contemporary biological theories stress the genetic origins of personality. Eysenck views personality structure as a hierarchy of traits. He believes that heredity influences individual differences in physiological functioning that affect how easily people acquire conditioned inhibitions.
- Twin studies of the Big Five personality traits find that identical twins are more similar in personality than fraternal twins, thus suggesting that personality is partly inherited. Estimates for the heritability of personality hover in the vicinity of 40%. Recent research in behavioural genetics has suggested that shared family environment has surprisingly little impact on personality, although a variety of theorists have been critical of this conclusion.
- Evolutionary analyses of personality suggest that certain traits and the ability to recognize them may have contributed to reproductive fitness. The biological approach has been criticized because of methodological problems with heritability ratios and because it offers no systematic model of how physiology shapes personality.

Courtesy of David M. Buss

" *In sum, the five factors of personality, in this account, represent important dimensions of the social terrain that humans were selected to attend to and act upon.* **"**
DAVID BUSS

Web Link 12.6
Great Ideas in Personality
http://www.personalityresearch.org

Northwestern University personality psychologist G. Scott Acton demonstrates that scientific research programs in personality generate broad and compelling ideas about what it is to be a human being. He charts the contours of 12 research perspectives, including behaviourism, behavioural genetics, and sociobiology, and backs them up with extensive links to published and online resources associated with each perspective.

CONCEPT CHECK 12.3

Understanding the Implications of Major Theories: Who Said This?

Check your understanding of the implications of the personality theories we've discussed by indicating which theorist is likely to have made the statements below. The answers are in Appendix A.

Choose from the following theorists:

Alfred Adler

Albert Bandura

Hans Eysenck

Sigmund Freud

Abraham Maslow

Walter Mischel

Quotes

1. "If you deliberately plan to be less than you are capable of being, then I warn you that you'll be deeply unhappy for the rest of your life." _____

2. "I feel that the major, most fundamental dimensions of personality are likely to be those on which [there is] strong genetic determination of individual differences." _____

3. "People are in general not candid over sexual matters ... they wear a heavy overcoat woven of a tissue of lies, as though the weather were bad in the world of sexuality." _____

Four Views of Personality

Theorist and orientation	Source of data and observations	Key motivational forces

A psychodynamic view

Sigmund Freud

Case studies from clinical practice of psychoanalysis

Sex and aggression; need to reduce tension resulting from internal conflicts

A behavioural view

B. F. Skinner

Laboratory experiments, primarily with animals

Pursuit of primary (unlearned) and secondary (learned) reinforcers; priorities depend on personal history

A humanistic view

Carl Rogers

Case studies from clinical practice of client-centred therapy

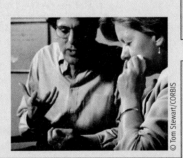

Actualizing tendency (motive to develop capacities and experience personal growth) and self-actualizing tendency (motive to maintain self-concept and behave in ways that are consistent with self-concept)

A biological view

Hans Eysenck

Twin, family, and adoption studies of heritability; factor analysis studies of personality structure

No specific motivational forces singled out

Model of personality structure	View of personality development	Roots of disorders

Three interacting components (id, ego, superego) operating at three levels of consciousness

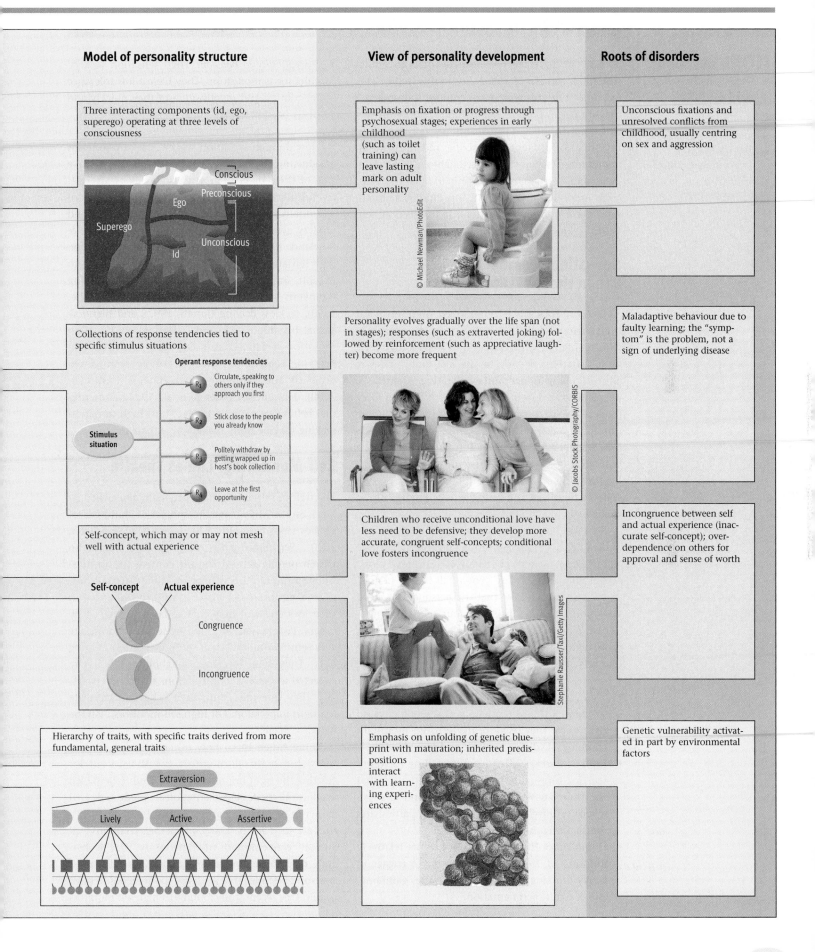

Emphasis on fixation or progress through psychosexual stages; experiences in early childhood (such as toilet training) can leave lasting mark on adult personality

© Michael Newman/PhotoEdit

Unconscious fixations and unresolved conflicts from childhood, usually centring on sex and aggression

---

Collections of response tendencies tied to specific stimulus situations

Operant response tendencies

Stimulus situation
- R₁ Circulate, speaking to others only if they approach you first
- R₂ Stick close to the people you already know
- R₃ Politely withdraw by getting wrapped up in host's book collection
- R₄ Leave at the first opportunity

Personality evolves gradually over the life span (not in stages); responses (such as extraverted joking) followed by reinforcement (such as appreciative laughter) become more frequent

© Jacobs Stock Photography/CORBIS

Maladaptive behaviour due to faulty learning; the "symptom" is the problem, not a sign of underlying disease

---

Self-concept, which may or may not mesh well with actual experience

Self-concept   Actual experience

Congruence

Incongruence

Children who receive unconditional love have less need to be defensive; they develop more accurate, congruent self-concepts; conditional love fosters incongruence

Stephanie Rausser/Taxi/Getty Images

Incongruence between self and actual experience (inaccurate self-concept); over-dependence on others for approval and sense of worth

---

Hierarchy of traits, with specific traits derived from more fundamental, general traits

Extraversion

Lively   Active   Assertive

Emphasis on unfolding of genetic blueprint with maturation; inherited predispositions interact with learning experiences

Genetic vulnerability activated in part by environmental factors

PREVIEW QUESTIONS

- What is sensation seeking?
- How does it influence adjustment and mental health?
- What is self-monitoring?
- What effects does it have on interpersonal behaviour?

So far, our coverage has been devoted to grand, panoramic theories of personality. In this section we'll examine some contemporary empirical approaches that are narrower in scope, tending to focus on specific traits. In modern personality research programs, investigators attempt to describe and measure an important personality trait, shed light on its development, and ascertain its relationship to other traits and behaviours. To get a sense of this kind of research, we'll take a look at two such traits in this section: sensation seeking and self-monitoring.

Sensation Seeking: Life in the Fast Lane

Sensation seeking **is a generalized preference for high or low levels of sensory stimulation.** People who are high in sensation seeking prefer a high level of stimulation, or "life in the fast lane." They're always looking for new and exhilarating experiences. People who are low in sensation seeking prefer more modest levels of stimulation. They tend to choose tranquillity over excitement. Sensation seeking was first described by Marvin Zuckerman (1971, 1979), a biologically oriented theorist influenced by Hans Eysenck's views. Zuckerman (1990, 1991, 1996) believes that there is a strong genetic predisposition to high or low sensation seeking.

Sensation-seeking tendencies are measured by Zuckerman's (1984) Sensation Seeking Scale (see Figure 12.15). Sensation seeking is distributed along a continuum, and many people fall in the middle. Factor analyses indicate that the personality trait of sensation seeking consists of four related components. When compared to low sensation seekers, those high in sensation seeking display the following four sets of characteristics (Zuckerman, 1979, 1994):

- *Thrill and adventure seeking.* They're more willing to engage in activities that may involve a physical risk. Thus, they're more likely to go mountain climbing, skydiving, surfing, and scuba diving.
- *Experience seeking.* They're more willing to volunteer for unusual experiments or activities that they may know little about. They tend to relish extensive travel, provocative art, wild parties, and unusual friends.
- *Disinhibition.* High sensation seekers are relatively uninhibited. Hence, they are prone to engage in heavy drinking, recreational drug use, gambling, and sexual experimentation.

- *Susceptibility to boredom.* High sensation seekers' chief foe is monotony. They have a low tolerance for routine and repetition, and they quickly and easily become bored.

How do high sensation seekers stack up in terms of adjustment and mental health? On the positive side of the ledger, high sensation seekers are relatively tolerant of stress. They find many types of potentially stressful events to be less threatening and anxiety arousing than others (Franken, Gibson, & Rowland, 1992). On the negative side of the ledger, high sensation seekers are more likely than others to exhibit impulsive, last-minute decision making (Franken, 1993), poor health habits (Watanabe, 1998), reckless driving (Jonah, 1997), and high-risk sexual behaviour (McCoul & Haslam, 2001). High sensation seeking is also associated with problem drinking (Parent & Newman, 1999), recreational drug use and gambling (Zuckerman & Kuhlman, 2000), delinquency (Luengo et al., 1994), and criminal behaviour (Arnett, 1996). Thus, high sensation seeking may be more maladaptive than adaptive.

Self-Monitoring: Life as Theatre

The trait of self-monitoring, originally unearthed by Mark Snyder, has been the subject of hundreds of studies since the mid-1970s (Gangestad & Snyder, 2000). *Self-monitoring* **refers to the degree to which people attend to and control the impression they make on others in social interactions.** According to Snyder (1979, 1987), people vary in their awareness of how they're being perceived by others. People who are high in self-monitoring are very sensitive to how their self-presentation is going over. They seek information about how they're expected to behave in a situation, and, when necessary, they shrewdly adjust their behaviour to create the right impression. For high self-monitors, "All the world's a stage."

Being tuned in to how others view you is one thing, but high self-monitors also show a gift for creating the right impression. They tend to be skilled at adjusting their self-presentations to produce desired audience responses (Larkin, 1988). In other words, they are good actors. They control their emotions well and can feign emotions when necessary. They deliberately regulate nonverbal signals (e.g., facial expressions and gestures) that are fairly spontaneous in most people. One recent study found that high self-monitors

Measuring sensation seeking

Answer "true" or "false" to each of the items listed below by circling "T" or "F." A "true" means that the item expresses your preference most of the time. A "false" means that you do not agree that the item is generally true for you. After completing the test, score your responses according to the instructions that follow the test items.

T F 1. I would really enjoy skydiving.
T F 2. I can imagine myself driving a sports car in a race and loving it.
T F 3. My life is very secure and comfortable—the way I like it.
T F 4. I usually like emotionally expressive or artistic people, even if they are sort of wild.
T F 5. I like the idea of seeing many of the same warm, supportive faces in my everyday life.
T F 6. I like doing adventurous things and would have enjoyed being a pioneer in the early days of this country.
T F 7. A good photograph should express peacefulness creatively.
T F 8. The most important thing in living is fully experiencing all emotions.
T F 9. I like creature comforts when I go on a trip or vacation.
T F 10. Doing the same things each day really gets to me.
T F 11. I love snuggling in front of a fire on a wintry day.
T F 12. I would like to try several types of drugs as long as they didn't harm me permanently.
T F 13. Drinking and being rowdy really appeals to me on the weekend.
T F 14. Rational people try to avoid dangerous situations.
T F 15. I prefer Figure A to Figure B.

Give yourself 1 point for answering "true" to the following items: 1, 2, 4, 6, 8, 10, 12, and 13. Also give yourself 1 point for answering "false" to the following items: 3, 5, 7, 9, 11, 14, and 15. Add up your points, and compare your total to the following norms: 11–15, high sensation seeker; 6–10, moderate sensation seeker; 1–5, low sensation seeker. Bear in mind that this is a shortened version of the Sensation Seeking Scale and that it provides only a rough approximation of your status on this personality trait.

Figure 12.15

A brief scale to assess sensation seeking. Follow the instructions for this scale to obtain a rough estimate of your own sensation-seeking tendencies.

Source: Grasha, A. F., & Kirschenbaum, D. S. (1986). *Adjustment and competence: Concepts and applications.* St. Paul, MN: West Publishing. Reprinted by permission of Anthony F. Grasha.

indicated that they would be better than others at feigning romantic interest in someone and that they would enjoy it more than others (Leck & Simpson, 1999). Another by McCann and Hancock (1983) found that high self-monitors tend to modify what they say about a target person known to them and their listener depending upon whether their listener likes or dislikes the target person. In effect, if they were talking to someone who likes the target person, they would emphasize that person's good points, and if they were talking to someone who dislikes the target person, they would emphasize his or her more negative points. People who are high in self-monitoring tend to invest a lot of effort in "reading" and remembering others' self-presentations (Beers, Lassiter, & Flannery, 1997). Ironically, they are good at spotting deceptive impression management *in other people*. For instance, they can tell when others are trying to butter them up. They are also better than low self-monitors at accurately judging others' personalities (Sanz, Sanchez-Bernardos, & Avia, 1996). Like sensation seeking, self-monitoring appears to be determined in part by people's genetic makeup (Gangestad & Simpson, 1993).

Culture and Personality

Are there connections between culture and personality? The investigation of this question dates back to the 1940s and 1950s, when researchers set out to describe various cultures' *modal personality* (Kardiner & Linton, 1945) or *national character* (Kluckhohn & Murray, 1948). These investigations, which were largely guided by Freud's psychoanalytic theory, met with relatively little success (Bruner, 1974). Part of the problem may have been the rather culture-bound, Eurocentric nature of Freudian theory, but the crux of the problem was that it was unrealistic to expect to find a single, dominant personality type in each culture (Draguns, 1979). As we have seen repeatedly,

given the realities of multifactorial causation, behaviour is never that simple. In retrospect, the research on modal personality overestimated the impact of cultural contexts and the uniformity of people within societies.

Studies of the links between culture and personality dwindled after the disappointments of the 1940s and 1950s. However, in recent years psychology's new interest in cultural factors has led to a renaissance of culture–personality research. This research has sought to determine whether Western personality constructs are relevant to other cultures and whether cultural differences can be seen in the prevalence of specific personality traits. As with

PREVIEW QUESTIONS
- Does the five-factor model have any relevance in non-Western cultures?
- How do conceptions of self vary across cultures?
- How does an inter-dependent view of self relate to self-enhancement?

"Most of what psychologists currently know about human nature is based on one particular view—the so-called Western view of the individual as an independent, self-contained, autonomous entity."
HAZEL MARKUS AND
SHINOBU KITAYAMA

cross-cultural research in other areas of psychology, these studies have found evidence of both continuity and variability across cultures.

For the most part, continuity has been apparent in cross-cultural comparisons of the *trait structure* of personality. When English language personality scales have been translated and administered in other cultures, the predicted dimensions of personality have emerged from the factor analyses (Paunonen & Ashton, 1998). For example, when scales that tap the Big Five personality traits have been administered and subjected to factor analysis in other cultures, the usual five traits have typically emerged (Katigbak et al., 2002; McCrae et al., 2005).

The cross-cultural similarities observed thus far seem impressive, but skepticism has been voiced in some quarters. Critics argue that the strategy of "exporting" Western tests to other cultures is slanted in favour of finding cross-cultural compatibility and is unlikely to uncover culture-specific traits (Church & Lonner, 1998). They also note that the non-Western samples studied thus far have not been all that culturally different from Western samples (Triandis & Suh, 2002). Furthermore, even though the Big Five traits are replicated in many cultures, this finding does not demonstrate that the traits have the same predictive meaning in those cultures (Markus & Kitayama, 1998). In other words, the correlates of a high neuroticism score in China may be different from the correlates that have been observed in Western cultures. In sum, preliminary research tentatively suggests that the basic dimensions of personality trait structure may be pancultural, but additional research is needed.

Perhaps the most interesting recent work on culture and personality has been that of Hazel Markus and Shinobu Kitayama (1991, 1994), comparing American and Asian conceptions of the self. According to Markus and Kitayama, American parents teach their children to be self-reliant, to feel good about themselves, and to view themselves as special individuals. Children are encouraged to excel in competitive endeavours and to strive to stand out from the crowd. They are told that "the squeaky wheel gets the grease" and that "you have to stand up for yourself." Thus, Markus and Kitayama argue that *American culture fosters an independent view of the self.* American youngsters learn to define themselves in terms of their personal attributes, abilities, accomplishments, and possessions. Their unique strengths and achievements become the basis for their sense of self-worth. Hence, they are prone to emphasize their uniqueness.

Most North Americans take this individualistic mentality for granted. Indeed, Markus and Kitayama maintain that "most of what psychologists currently know about human nature is based on one particular view—the so-called Western view of the individual as an independent, self-contained, autonomous entity" (1991, p. 224). However, they marshal convincing evidence that this view is *not* universal. They argue that in Asian cultures such as Japan and China, socialization practices foster a more *interdependent view of the self,* which emphasizes the fundamental connectedness of people to each other (see Figure 12.16). In these cultures, parents teach their children that they can rely on family and friends, that they should be modest about their personal accomplishments so they don't diminish others' achievements, and that they should view themselves as part of a larger social matrix. Children are encouraged to fit in with others and to avoid standing out from the crowd. A popular adage in Japan reminds children that "the nail that stands out gets pounded down." Hence, Markus and Kitayama assert that Asian youngsters typically learn to define themselves in terms of the groups they belong to. Their harmonious relations with others and their pride in group achievements become the basis for their sense of self-worth. Because their self-esteem does not hinge so much on personal strengths, they are less likely to emphasize their uniqueness. Consistent with this analysis, Markus and Kitayama report that Asian subjects tend to view themselves as more similar to their peers than American subjects do.

The ramifications of these discrepant views of self are many. For example, these differing self-views lead to cultural disparities in self-enhancement. *Self-enhancement* involves focusing on positive feed-

Culture can shape personality. Children in Asian cultures, for example, grow up with a value system that allows them to view themselves as interconnected parts of larger social units. Hence, they tend to avoid positioning themselves so that they stand out from others.

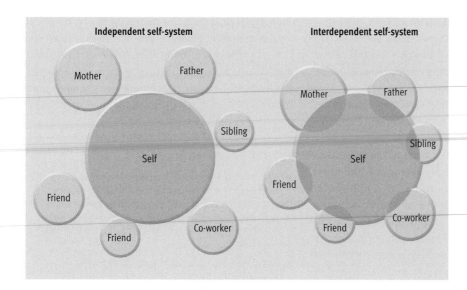

Independent self-system   Interdependent self-system

Figure 12.16

Culture and conceptions of self.

According to Markus and Kitayama (1991), Western cultures foster an independent view of the self as a unique individual who is separate from others, as diagrammed on the left. In contrast, Asian cultures encourage an interdependent view of the self as part of an interconnected social matrix, as diagrammed on the right. The interdependent view leads people to define themselves in terms of their social relationships (e.g., as someone's daughter, employee, colleague, or neighbour).

Source: Adapted from Markus, H. R., & Kitayama, S. (1991). Culture and the self: Implications for cognition, emotion, and motivation. *Psychological Review, 98*, 224–253. Copyright © 1991 by the American Psychological Association. Adapted by permission of the author.

back from others, exaggerating one's strengths, and seeing oneself as above average. These tendencies are pervasive in Western cultures but are quite rare in Asian cultures, where the norm is to be more sensitive to negative feedback, to reflect on one's shortcomings, and to look for avenues of improvement (Cross & Markus, 1999). Recent work by Paulhus and his colleagues suggests that while there is an overall tendency for Chinese participants to engage in less self-enhancement, it does vary by the aspect of the self that is being judged (Yik, Bond, & Paulhus, 1998).

In the hopes of fitting in better and contributing more to the group, people with interdependent self-views seem to be more interested in *self-criticism* than self-enhancement. Does all this self-criticism lead to lower self-esteem, on the average, in some cultures? Preliminary research suggests that the answer may be yes (Heine et al., 1999; Kitayama et al., 1997). But, ironically, low self-esteem may not have the same significance in cultures that encourage interdependent self-views. In Japan, for instance, self-esteem does not correlate with subjective well-being the way it does in Western cultures (Diener & Diener, 1995). This finding demonstrates once again that we cannot assume that Western models of psychological processes will apply equally well in other cultures.

Putting It in Perspective

The preceding discussion of culture and personality obviously highlighted the text's theme that people's behaviour is influenced by their cultural heritage. This chapter has also been ideally suited for embellishing two other unifying themes: psychology's theoretical diversity and the idea that psychology evolves in a sociohistorical context.

No other area of psychology is characterized by as much theoretical diversity as the study of personality, where there are literally dozens of insightful theories. Some of this diversity exists because different theories attempt to explain different facets of behaviour. However, much of this theoretical diversity reflects genuine disagreements on basic questions about personality. These disagreements are apparent on pages 518–519, which present an illustrated comparative overview of the ideas of Freud,

Skinner, Rogers, and Eysenck, as representatives of the psychodynamic, behavioural, humanistic, and biological approaches to personality.

The study of personality also highlights the sociohistorical context in which psychology evolves. Personality theories have left many marks on modern culture; we can mention only a handful as illustrations. The theories of Freud, Adler, and Skinner have had an enormous impact on childrearing practices. The ideas of Freud and Jung have found their way into literature (influencing the portrayal of fictional characters) and the visual arts. For example, Freud's theory helped inspire surrealism's interest in the world of dreams (see Figure 4.59, Salvador Dali's *The Hallucinogenic Toreador*, on page 172). Social learning theory has become embroiled in the public policy debate about whether media violence should be

PREVIEW QUESTIONS

● How did the chapter illustrate psychology's theoretical diversity?

● How did the chapter show that psychology evolves in a sociohistorical context?

controlled, because of its effects on viewers' aggressive behaviour. Maslow's hierarchy of needs and Skinner's affirmation of the value of positive reinforcement have influenced approaches to management in the world of business and industry.

Sociohistorical forces also leave their imprint on psychology. This chapter provided many examples of how personal experiences, prevailing attitudes, and historical events have contributed to the evolution of ideas in psychology. For example, Freud's pessimistic view of human nature and his emphasis on the dark forces of aggression were shaped to some extent by his exposure to the hostilities of World War I and prevailing anti-Semitic sentiments. Freud's emphasis on sexuality was surely influenced by the Victorian climate of sexual repression that existed in his youth. Adler's views also reflected the social context in which he grew up. His interest in inferiority feelings and compensation appear to have sprung from his own sickly childhood and the difficulties he had to overcome. Likewise, it's reasonable to speculate that Jung's childhood loneliness and introversion may have sparked his interest in the introversion–extraversion dimension of personality. In a similar vein, we saw that both Rogers and Maslow had to resist parental pressures in order to pursue their career interests. Their emphasis on the need to achieve personal fulfillment may have originated in these experiences.

Progress in the study of personality has also been influenced by developments in other areas of psy-chology. For instance, the enterprise of psychological testing originally emerged out of efforts to measure general intelligence. Eventually, however, the principles of psychological testing were applied to the challenge of measuring personality. In the upcoming Personal Application we discuss the logic and limitations of personality tests.

REVIEW OF KEY POINTS

- Modern personality research programs have tended to focus on specific personality traits. Sensation seeking is a trait describing the degree to which people seek high or low levels of sensory stimulation. High sensation seekers are willing to take risks, are open to new experiences, and are susceptible to boredom.

- Self-monitoring is the degree to which people attend to and control the impressions they make on others. High self-monitors are skilled at impression management and sensitive to others' self-presentations.

- Some studies suggest that the basic trait structure of personality may be much the same across cultures. However, some critics have voiced doubts about this conclusion.

- Markus and Kitayama assert that Western culture fosters an independent conception of self, whereas Asian cultures foster an interdependent view of the self. These different views of the self lead to cultural disparities in the tendency to engage in self-enhancement.

- The study of personality illustrates how psychology is characterized by great theoretical diversity. The study of personality also demonstrates how ideas in psychology are shaped by sociohistorical forces and how cultural factors influence psychological processes.

Understanding Personality Assessment

Answer the following "true" or "false."

_____ **1** Responses to personality tests are subject to unconscious distortion.

_____ **2** The results of personality tests are often misunderstood.

_____ **3** Personality test scores should be interpreted with caution.

_____ **4** Personality tests serve many important functions.

If you answered "true" to all four questions, you earned a perfect score. Yes, personality tests are subject to distortion. Admittedly, test results are often misunderstood, and they should be interpreted cautiously. In spite of these problems, however, psychological tests can be quite useful.

Everyone engages in efforts to size up his or her own personality as well as that of others. When you think to yourself that "Mary Ann is shrewd and poised," or when you remark to a friend that "Howard is timid and submissive," you're making personality assessments. In a sense, then, personality assessment is an ongoing part of daily life. Given the popular interest in personality assessment, it's not surprising that psychologists have devised formal measures of personality.

The Uses of Personality Scales 7c

Why are psychological tests used to measure personality? They have a variety of purposes. Benjamin Kleinmuntz (1985) lists four principal uses of personality tests:

1. Personality tests are used extensively by mental health professionals in the *clinical diagnosis* of psychological disorders. Although diagnoses are not made on the basis of test results alone, personality scales can be helpful in arriving at diagnostic decisions.

2. Personality measurement may be done for the purpose of *counselling* individuals about a variety of normal, everyday problems. Counsellors often use personality scales to help people chart career plans and make vocational decisions.

3. Formal personality assessment often plays a key role in *personnel selection* in business, industry, government, and the military services. This use of personality testing has become controversial in recent years. Nonetheless, many organizations continue to use personality scales to assess applicants' suitability for various jobs.

4. Personality scales are frequently used in *psychological research*. Empirical studies on a great variety of issues require precise measurement of some aspect of personality. For instance, let's say you want to investigate whether introversion is related to a certain style of childrearing. Your task is simplified greatly if you have a personality test that measures introversion.

Personality tests can be divided into two broad categories: *self-report inventories* and *projective tests*. In this Application, we'll discuss some representative tests from both categories and discuss their strengths and weaknesses.

Self-Report Inventories 7c

Self-report inventories are personality tests that ask individuals to answer a series of questions about their characteristic behaviour. The logic underlying this approach is simple: Who knows you better? Who has known you longer? Who has more access to your private feelings? Some self-report inventories, such as the Sensation Seeking Scale and the Self-Monitoring Scale, are designed to measure one specific per-

sonality trait. Others can be used to measure many dimensions of personality simultaneously. Single-trait scales are used primarily in research. In clinical, counselling, and personnel work, psychologists rely more on multitrait inventories. We'll discuss three examples of multitrait scales: the MMPI, the 16PF, and the NEO Personality Inventory.

The MMPI

The most widely used multitrait scale is the Minnesota Multiphasic Personality Inventory (MMPI). This test was developed in the 1940s (Hathaway & McKinley, 1943) but underwent a major revision and modernization in the 1980s. The authors of MMPI-2 set out to maintain the original character of the scale while replacing obsolete items, eliminating sexist language, and updating the test norms (Graham, 1990).

The MMPI was originally designed to aid clinicians in the diagnosis of psychological disorders. Consequently, it measures mostly aspects of personality that, when manifested to an extreme degree, are thought to be symptoms of disorders. Examples include traits such as paranoia, depression, and hysteria.

The MMPI is a rather lengthy test. The revised version consists of 567 statements to which the subject answers "true," "false," or "cannot say." The MMPI yields scores on the 14 subscales described in Table 12.4. Four of the subscales are *validity scales* that provide indications about whether a subject has been careless or deceptive in taking the test. The remaining ten are *clinical scales* that measure various aspects of personality.

Are the MMPI clinical scales valid? That is, do they measure what they were designed to measure? The validity of the MMPI has been investigated in hundreds of studies (Butcher & Keller, 1984). Originally, it was assumed that the ten clinical subscales

RECAP

Key Ideas

The Nature of Personality

● The concept of personality explains the consistency in people's behaviour over time and situations while also explaining their distinctiveness. There is considerable debate as to how many trait dimensions are necessary to account for the variation in personality, but the Big Five model has become the dominant conception of personality structure.

Psychodynamic Perspectives

● Freud's psychoanalytic theory emphasizes the importance of the unconscious. Freud described personality structure in terms of three components—the id, ego, and superego—which are routinely involved in an ongoing series of internal conflicts.

● Freud theorized that conflicts centring on sex and aggression are especially likely to lead to anxiety. According to Freud, anxiety and other unpleasant emotions such as guilt are often warded off with defence mechanisms.

● Freud described a series of five stages of development: oral, anal, phallic, latency, and genital. Certain experiences during these stages can have lasting effects on adult personality.

● Jung's most innovative and controversial concept was the collective unconscious. Adler's individual psychology emphasizes how people strive for superiority to compensate for their feelings of inferiority.

● Overall, psychodynamic theories have produced many groundbreaking insights about the unconscious, the role of internal conflict, and the importance of early childhood experiences in personality development. However, psychodynamic theories have been criticized for their poor testability, their inadequate base of empirical evidence, and their male-centred views.

Behavioural Perspectives

● Behavioural theories view personality as a collection of response tendencies tied to specific stimulus situations. They assume that personality development is a lifelong process in which response tendencies are shaped and reshaped by learning, especially operant conditioning.

● Social learning theory focuses on how cognitive factors such as expectancies and self-efficacy regulate learned behaviour. Bandura's concept of observational learning accounts for the acquisition of responses from models. Mischel has questioned the degree to which people display cross-situational consistency in behaviour.

● Behavioural approaches to personality are based on rigorous research. They have provided ample insights into how environmental factors and learning mould personalities. The behaviourists have been criticized for their

overdependence on animal research, their fragmented analysis of personality, and radical behaviourism's dehumanizing view of human nature.

Humanistic Perspectives

● Humanistic theories are phenomenological and take an optimistic view of human potential. Rogers focused on the self-concept as the critical aspect of personality. Maslow theorized that psychological health depends on fulfilling one's need for self-actualization.

● Humanistic theories deserve credit for highlighting the importance of subjective views of oneself and for helping to lay the foundation for positive psychology. Humanistic theories lack a firm base of research, are difficult to put to an empirical test, and may be overly optimistic about human nature.

Biological Perspectives

● Contemporary biological theories stress the genetic origins of personality. Eysenck suggests that heredity influences individual differences in physiological functioning that affect how easily people acquire conditioned responses. Research on the personality resemblance of twins provides impressive evidence that genetic factors shape personality.

● Evolutionary theorists argue that the major dimensions of personality reflect humans' adaptive landscape. The biological approach has demonstrated that personality is partly heritable, but it has been criticized for its narrow focus on heritability and because it offers no systematic model of how physiology shapes personality.

Contemporary Empirical Approaches to Personality

● Sensation seeking is a trait describing the degree to which people seek high or low levels of sensory stimulation. Self-monitoring is the degree to which people attend to and control the impressions they make on others.

Culture and Personality

● Some studies suggest that the basic trait structure of personality may be much the same across cultures. However, notable differences have been found when researchers have compared cultural groups' conceptions of self.

Putting It in Perspective

● The study of personality illustrates how psychology is characterized by great theoretical diversity. It also demonstrates how ideas in psychology are shaped by sociohistorical forces and how cultural factors influence psychological processes.

Personal Application • Understanding Personality Assessment

● Personality assessment is useful in clinical diagnosis, counselling, personnel selection, and

research. Self-report measures ask subjects to describe themselves. Self-report inventories are vulnerable to certain sources of error, including deception, the social desirability bias, and response sets.

● Projective tests assume that subjects' responses to ambiguous stimuli reveal something about their personality. While the projective hypothesis seems plausible, projective tests' reliability and validity are disturbingly low.

Critical Thinking Application • Hindsight in Everyday Analyses of Personality

● Hindsight bias often leads people to assert that "I knew it all along" in discussing outcomes that they did not actually predict. Thanks to hindsight, people can almost always come up with plausible-sounding explanations for known personality traits.

Key Terms

Archetypes, 501
Behaviourism, 504
Collective
    unconscious, 501
Compensation, 502
Conscious, 496
Defence mechanisms, 497
Displacement, 498
Ego, 495
Extraverts, 501
Factor analysis, 492
Fixation, 499
Hierarchy of needs, 511
Hindsight bias, 530
Humanism, 508
Id, 495
Identification, 498
Incongruence, 509
Introverts, 501
Model, 506
Need for self-actualization, 512
Observational learning, 506
Oedipal complex, 500
Personal unconscious, 501
Personality, 492
Personality trait, 492
Phenomenological approach, 508
Pleasure principle, 495
Preconscious, 496
Projection, 498
Projective tests, 528
Psychodynamic theories, 494

Psychosexual stages, 499
Rationalization, 497
Reaction formation, 498
Reality principle, 495
Reciprocal determinism, 506
Regression, 498
Repression, 497
Self-actualizing persons, 512
Self-concept, 509
Self-efficacy, 506
Self-enhancement, 522
Self-monitoring, 520
Self-report inventories, 525
Sensation seeking, 520
Striving for superiority, 502
Superego, 495
Unconscious, 496

Key People

Alfred Adler, 502
Albert Bandura, 505
David Buss, 517
Norman Endler, 507
Hans Eysenck, 515
Sigmund Freud, 494
Carl Jung, 500
Abraham Maslow, 512
Walter Mischel, 507
Delroy Paulhus, 503
Carl Rogers, 509
B. F. Skinner, 505

they thought they influenced their children's personalities. However, parents' retrospective analyses of their children's personality development have to be treated with great skepticism, as they are likely to be distorted by hindsight bias (not to mention the selective recall frequently seen in anecdotal reports).

Unfortunately, hindsight bias is so prevalent it also presents a problem for scientific theories of personality. For example, the spectre of hindsight bias has been raised in many critiques of psychoanalytic theory (Torrey, 1992). Freudian theory was originally built mainly on a foundation of case studies of patients in therapy. Obviously, Freudian therapists who knew what their patients' adult personalities were like probably went looking for the types of childhood experiences hypothesized by Freud (oral fixations, punitive toilet training, Oedipal conflicts, and so forth) in their efforts to explain their patients' personalities.

Another problem with hindsight bias is that once researchers know an outcome, more often than not they can fashion some plausible explanation for it. For instance, Torrey (1992) describes a study inspired by Freudian theory that examined breast-size preferences among men. The original hypothesis was that men who scored higher in dependence—thought to be a sign of oral fixation—would manifest a stronger preference for women with large breasts. When the actual results of the study showed just the opposite—that dependence was associated with a preference for smaller breasts—the finding was attributed to reaction formation on the part of the men. Instead of failing to support Freudian theory, the unexpected findings were simply reinterpreted in a way that was consistent with Freudian theory.

Hindsight bias also presents thorny problems for evolutionary theorists, who generally work backward from known outcomes to reason out how adaptive pressures in humans' ancestral past may have led to those outcomes (Cornell, 1997). Consider, for instance, evolutionary theorists' assertion that the Big Five traits are found to be fundamental dimensions of personality around the world because those specific traits have had major adaptive implications over the course of human history (Buss, 1995; MacDonald, 1998). Their explanation makes sense, but what would have happened if some *other traits* had shown up in the Big Five? Would the evolutionary view have been weakened if dominance, or paranoia, or high sensation seeking had turned up in the Big Five? Probably not. With the luxury of hindsight, evolutionary theorists surely could have constructed plausible explanations for how these traits promoted reproductive success in the distant past. Thus, hindsight bias is a fundamental feature of human cognition, and the scientific enterprise is not immune to this problem.

Other Implications of "20/20 Hindsight"

Our discussion of hindsight has focused on its implications for thinking about personality, but there is ample evidence that hindsight can bias thinking in all sorts of domains. For example, consider the practice of obtaining second opinions on medical diagnoses. The doctor providing the second opinion usually is aware of the first physician's diagnosis, which creates a hindsight bias (Arkes et al., 1981). Second opinions would probably be more valuable if the doctors rendering them were not aware of previous diagnoses. Hindsight also has the potential to distort legal decisions in cases involving allegations of negligence. Jurors' natural tendency to think, "How could they have failed to foresee this problem," may exaggerate the appearance of negligence (LaBine & LaBine, 1996).

Hindsight bias is very powerful. The next time you hear of an unfortunate outcome to a decision made by a public official, carefully examine the way news reporters describe the decision. You will probably find that they believe that the disastrous outcome should have been obvious, because they can clearly see what went wrong after the fact. Similarly, if you find yourself thinking, "Only a fool would have failed to anticipate this disaster" or "I would have foreseen this problem," take a deep breath and try to review the decision *using only information that was known at the time the decision was being made*. Sometimes good decisions, based on the best available information, can have terrible outcomes. Unfortunately, the clarity of "20/20 hindsight" makes it difficult for people to learn from their own and others' mistakes.

Table 12.6 Critical Thinking Skill Discussed in This Application

Skill	Description
Recognizing the bias in hindsight analysis	The critical thinker understands that knowing the outcome of events biases our recall and interpretation of the events.

Personality: Theory, Research, and Assessment

RECAP

Key Ideas

The Nature of Personality

● The concept of personality explains the consistency in people's behaviour over time and situations while also explaining their distinctiveness. There is considerable debate as to how many trait dimensions are necessary to account for the variation in personality, but the Big Five model has become the dominant conception of personality structure.

Psychodynamic Perspectives

● Freud's psychoanalytic theory emphasizes the importance of the unconscious. Freud described personality structure in terms of three components—the id, ego, and superego—which are routinely involved in an ongoing series of internal conflicts.

● Freud theorized that conflicts centring on sex and aggression are especially likely to lead to anxiety. According to Freud, anxiety and other unpleasant emotions such as guilt are often warded off with defence mechanisms.

● Freud described a series of five stages of development: oral, anal, phallic, latency, and genital. Certain experiences during these stages can have lasting effects on adult personality.

● Jung's most innovative and controversial concept was the collective unconscious. Adler's individual psychology emphasizes how people strive for superiority to compensate for their feelings of inferiority.

● Overall, psychodynamic theories have produced many groundbreaking insights about the unconscious, the role of internal conflict, and the importance of early childhood experiences in personality development. However, psychodynamic theories have been criticized for their poor testability, their inadequate base of empirical evidence, and their male-centred views.

Behavioural Perspectives

● Behavioural theories view personality as a collection of response tendencies tied to specific stimulus situations. They assume that personality development is a lifelong process in which response tendencies are shaped and reshaped by learning, especially operant conditioning.

● Social learning theory focuses on how cognitive factors such as expectancies and self-efficacy regulate learned behaviour. Bandura's concept of observational learning accounts for the acquisition of responses from models. Mischel has questioned the degree to which people display cross-situational consistency in behaviour.

● Behavioural approaches to personality are based on rigorous research. They have provided ample insights into how environmental factors and learning mould personalities. The behaviourists have been criticized for their

overdependence on animal research, their fragmented analysis of personality, and radical behaviourism's dehumanizing view of human nature.

Humanistic Perspectives

● Humanistic theories are phenomenological and take an optimistic view of human potential. Rogers focused on the self-concept as the critical aspect of personality. Maslow theorized that psychological health depends on fulfilling one's need for self-actualization.

● Humanistic theories deserve credit for highlighting the importance of subjective views of oneself and for helping to lay the foundation for positive psychology. Humanistic theories lack a firm base of research, are difficult to put to an empirical test, and may be overly optimistic about human nature.

Biological Perspectives

● Contemporary biological theories stress the genetic origins of personality. Eysenck suggests that heredity influences individual differences in physiological functioning that affect how easily people acquire conditioned responses. Research on the personality resemblance of twins provides impressive evidence that genetic factors shape personality.

● Evolutionary theorists argue that the major dimensions of personality reflect humans' adaptive landscape. The biological approach has demonstrated that personality is partly heritable, but it has been criticized for its narrow focus on heritability and because it offers no systematic model of how physiology shapes personality.

Contemporary Empirical Approaches to Personality

● Sensation seeking is a trait describing the degree to which people seek high or low levels of sensory stimulation. Self-monitoring is the degree to which people attend to and control the impressions they make on others.

Culture and Personality

● Some studies suggest that the basic trait structure of personality may be much the same across cultures. However, notable differences have been found when researchers have compared cultural groups' conceptions of self.

Putting It in Perspective

● The study of personality illustrates how psychology is characterized by great theoretical diversity. It also demonstrates how ideas in psychology are shaped by sociohistorical forces and how cultural factors influence psychological processes.

Personal Application • Understanding Personality Assessment

● Personality assessment is useful in clinical diagnosis, counselling, personnel selection, and

research. Self-report measures ask subjects to describe themselves. Self-report inventories are vulnerable to certain sources of error, including deception, the social desirability bias, and response sets.

● Projective tests assume that subjects' responses to ambiguous stimuli reveal something about their personality. While the projective hypothesis seems plausible, projective tests' reliability and validity are disturbingly low.

Critical Thinking Application • Hindsight in Everyday Analyses of Personality

● Hindsight bias often leads people to assert that "I knew it all along" in discussing outcomes that they did not actually predict. Thanks to hindsight, people can almost always come up with plausible-sounding explanations for known personality traits.

Key Terms

Archetypes, 501
Behaviourism, 504
Collective
 unconscious, 501
Compensation, 502
Conscious, 496
Defence mechanisms, 497
Displacement, 498
Ego, 495
Extraverts, 501
Factor analysis, 492
Fixation, 499
Hierarchy of needs, 511
Hindsight bias, 530
Humanism, 508
Id, 495
Identification, 498
Incongruence, 509
Introverts, 501
Model, 506
Need for self-actualization, 512
Observational learning, 506
Oedipal complex, 500
Personal unconscious, 501
Personality, 492
Personality trait, 492
Phenomenological approach, 508
Pleasure principle, 495
Preconscious, 496
Projection, 498
Projective tests, 528
Psychodynamic theories, 494

Psychosexual stages, 499
Rationalization, 497
Reaction formation, 498
Reality principle, 495
Reciprocal determinism, 506
Regression, 498
Repression, 497
Self-actualizing persons, 512
Self-concept, 509
Self-efficacy, 506
Self-enhancement, 522
Self-monitoring, 520
Self-report inventories, 525
Sensation seeking, 520
Striving for superiority, 502
Superego, 495
Unconscious, 496

Key People

Alfred Adler, 502
Albert Bandura, 505
David Buss, 517
Norman Endler, 507
Hans Eysenck, 515
Sigmund Freud, 494
Carl Jung, 500
Abraham Maslow, 512
Walter Mischel, 507
Delroy Paulhus, 503
Carl Rogers, 509
B. F. Skinner, 505

Hindsight in Everyday Analyses of Personality

Consider the case of two close sisters who grew up together: Lorena and Christina. Lorena grew into a frugal adult who is careful about spending her money, only shops when there are sales, and saves every penny she can. In contrast, Christina became an extravagant spender who lives to shop and never saves any money. How do the sisters explain their striking personality differences? Lorena attributes her thrifty habits to the fact that her family was so poor when she was a child that she learned the value of being careful with money. Christina attributes her extravagant spending to the fact that her family was so poor that she learned to really enjoy any money that she might have. Now, it *is* possible that two sisters could react to essentially the same circumstances quite differently, but the more likely explanation is that both sisters have been influenced by the **hindsight bias—the tendency to mould one's interpretation of the past to fit how events actually turned out.** We saw how hindsight can distort memory in Chapter 7. Here, we will see how hindsight tends to make everyone feel as if they are personality experts and how it creates interpretive problems even for scientific theories of personality.

The Prevalence of Hindsight Bias

Hindsight bias is *ubiquitous,* which means that it occurs in many different settings, with all sorts of people. Most of the time, people are not aware of the way their explanations are skewed by the fact that the outcome is already known. The experimental literature on hindsight bias offers a rich array of findings on how the knowledge of an outcome biases the way people think about its causes (Hawkins & Hastie,

1990). For example, when university students were told the results of hypothetical experiments, each group of students could "explain" why the studies turned out the way they did, even though different groups were given opposite results to explain (Slovic & Fischhoff, 1977). The students believed that the results of the studies were obvious when they were told what the experimenter found, but when they were given only the information that was available before the outcome was known, it was not obvious at all. This bias is also called the "I knew it all along" effect because that is the typical refrain of people when they have the luxury of hindsight. Indeed, after the fact, people often act as if events that would have been difficult to predict had in fact been virtually *inevitable.* Looking back at the disintegration of the Soviet Union and the end of the Cold War, for instance, many people today act as though these events were bound to happen, but in reality these landmark events were predicted by almost no one.

Hindsight bias shows up in many contexts. For example, when a couple announces that they are splitting up, many people in their social circle will typically claim they "saw it coming." When a football team loses in a huge upset, you will hear many fans claim, "I knew they were overrated and vulnerable." When public officials make a difficult decision that leads to a disastrous outcome—such as the FBI's 1993 attack on the Branch Davidian compound in Waco, Texas—many of the pundits in the press are quick to criticize, often asserting that only incompetent fools could have failed to foresee the catastrophe. Interestingly, people are not much kinder to themselves when they make ill-fated decisions. When individuals make tough calls that lead to negative results—

such as buying a car that turns out to be a lemon, or investing in a stock that plummets—they often say things like, "Why did I ignore the obvious warning signs?" or "How could I be such an idiot?"

Hindsight and Personality

Hindsight bias appears to be pervasive in everyday analyses of personality. Think about it: If you attempt to explain why you are so suspicious, why your mother is so domineering, or why your best friend is so insecure, the starting point in each case will be the personality outcome. It would probably be impossible to reconstruct the past without being swayed by your knowledge of these outcomes. Thus, hindsight makes everybody an expert on personality, as we can all come up with plausible explanations for the personality traits of people we know well. Perhaps this is why Judith Harris (1998) ignited a firestorm of protest when she wrote a widely read book arguing that parents have relatively little effect on their children's personalities beyond the genetic material that they supply.

In her book *The Nurture Assumption,* Harris summarizes behavioural genetics research and other evidence suggesting that family environment has surprisingly little impact on children's personality (see pp. 514–517). As we discussed in the main body of the chapter, there is room for plenty of debate on this complex issue (Kagan, 1998; Tavris, 1998), but our chief interest here is that Harris made a cogent, compelling argument in her book, which attracted extensive coverage in the press that generated an avalanche of commentary from angry parents who argued that *parents do matter.* For example, *Newsweek* magazine received 350 letters, mostly from parents who provided examples of how

Figure 12.19

The Thematic Apperception Test (TAT). In taking the TAT, a respondent is asked to tell stories about scenes such as this one. The themes apparent in each story can be scored to provide insight about the respondent's personality.

Source: Murray. H. A. (1971). *Thematic Apperception Test.* Cambridge, MA: Harvard University Press. Copyright © 1943 by The President and Fellows of Harvard College, Copyright © 1971 by Henry A. Murray. Reprinted by permission of the publisher.

can't be eliminated entirely, these measurement strategies have proven useful in personality assessment. In light of the potential for distortion, however, the results of personality tests should be interpreted with caution. Of course, as we saw in Chapter 9, prudence is always in order when interpreting psychological test results of any kind.

REVIEW OF KEY POINTS

- Personality assessment is useful in clinical diagnosis, counselling, personnel selection, and research. Personality scales can be divided into self-report inventories and projective tests.

- Self-report measures ask subjects to describe themselves. The MMPI is a widely used inventory that measures pathological aspects of personality. The 16PF assesses 16 dimensions of the normal personality. The NEO personality inventory measures the Big Five personality traits.

- Self-report inventories are vulnerable to certain sources of error, including deception, the social desirability bias, and response sets.

- Projective tests, such as the Rorschach and TAT, assume that subjects' responses to ambiguous stimuli reveal something about their personality. While the projective hypothesis seems plausible, projective tests' reliability and validity are disturbingly low.

vides information to the tester. Hence, it's difficult for people to engage in intentional deception (Groth-Marnat, 1997). Second, the indirect approach used in these tests may make them especially sensitive to unconscious, latent features of personality.

Unfortunately, there is inadequate evidence for the reliability (consistency) and validity of projective measures (Lanyon & Goodstein, 1997; Lilienfeld, Wood, & Garb, 2000). In particular, doubts have been raised about the research evidence on the Rorschach test (Garb, Florio, & Grove, 1998; Wood, Nezworski, & Stejskal, 1996). In spite of these problems, projective tests continue to be widely used by clinicians (Watkins et al., 1995). About 40 years ago, a reviewer characterized the critics of projective tests as "doubting statisticians" and the users of projective tests as "enthusiastic clinicians" (Adcock, 1965). Decades of research not withstanding, little has changed since then.

The continued popularity of the Rorschach and other projective techniques suggests that they are effective in eliciting information that is valuable to many clinicians (Groth-Marnat, 1997). Although the subjectivity of the projective tests raises serious concerns about their use in clinical diagnosis, some projective measures have shown adequate reliability

and validity when used for limited, specific purposes, such as the assessment of achievement motivation (Spangler, 1992).

Although the problems associated with self-report inventories and projective tests

When individuals are given the Rorschach test, they are shown a series of ten inkblots and they are asked to describe the forms that they see in these ambiguous stimuli. Evidence on the reliability and validity of the Rorschach is not particularly impressive, but the test is still used by many clinicians.

assertiveness and generates an exact comparison with the typical behaviour reported by many other respondents for the same circumstances.

Although self-report inventories are much more thorough and precise than casual observations, they are only as accurate as the information that respondents provide. They are susceptible to several sources of error (Ben-Porath, 2003; Kline, 1995; Paulhus, 1991; Rosse et al., 1998; Shedler, Mayman, & Manis, 1993), including the following:

1. *Deliberate deception.* Some self-report inventories include many questions whose purpose is easy to figure out. This problem makes it possible for some respondents to intentionally fake particular personality traits (Rees & Metcalfe, 2003).

2. *Social desirability bias.* Without realizing it, some people consistently respond to questions in ways that make them look good. The social desirability bias isn't a matter of deception so much as wishful thinking.

3. *Response sets.* According to Paulhus (1991) and others, a response set or bias is a systematic tendency to respond to test items in a particular way that is unrelated to the content of the items. For instance, some people, called "yea-sayers," tend to agree with virtually every statement on a test. Other people, called "nay-sayers," tend to disagree with nearly every statement.

Test developers have devised a number of strategies to reduce the impact of deliberate deception, social desirability bias, and response sets (Berry, Wetter, & Baer, 1995; Lanyon & Goodstein, 1997; Paulhus, 2002). For instance, it's possible to insert a "lie scale" into a test to assess the likelihood that a respondent is engaging in deception. The MMPI has a lie scale made up of 15 items that ask the subject to acknowledge minor faults that virtually everyone has. Subjects who report themselves to be nearly faultless on these questions are probably being deceptive.

The best way to reduce the impact of social desirability bias is to identify items that are sensitive to this bias and drop them from the test. Problems with response sets can be reduced by systematically varying the way in which test items are worded. The key is to balance the items so that responses of agreement and disagreement are equally likely to be indicative of the trait being measured.

Projective Tests 7c

Projective tests, which all take a rather indirect approach to the assessment of personality, are used extensively in clinical work. **Projective tests ask subjects to respond to vague, ambiguous stimuli in ways that may reveal the subjects' needs, feelings, and personality traits** (see Table 12.5 for examples). The Rorschach test, for instance, consists of a series of ten inkblots. Respondents are asked to describe what they see in the blots (see the photo on page 529). In the Thematic Apperception Test (TAT), a series of pictures of simple scenes are presented to subjects, who are asked to tell stories about what is happening in the scenes and what the characters are feeling. For instance, one TAT card shows a young boy contemplating a violin resting on a table in front of him (see Figure 12.19 for another example). You may recall that the TAT was used in our Featured Study in Chapter 2 by Dutton and Aron.

The Projective Hypothesis 7A

The "projective hypothesis" is that ambiguous materials can serve as a blank screen onto which people project their characteristic concerns, conflicts, and desires (Frank, 1939). Thus, a competitive person who is shown the TAT card of the boy at the table with the violin might concoct a story about how the boy is contemplating an upcoming musical competition at which he hopes to excel. The same card shown to a person high in impulsiveness might elicit a story about how the boy is planning to sneak out the door to go dirt-bike riding with friends.

The scoring and interpretation of projective tests is very complicated. Rorschach responses may be analyzed in terms of content, originality, the feature of the inkblot that determined the response, and the amount of the inkblot used, among other criteria. In fact, five different systems exist for scoring the Rorschach (Edberg, 1990). TAT stories are examined in terms of heroes, needs, themes, and outcomes.

Strengths and Weaknesses of Projective Tests

Proponents of projective tests assert that the tests have two unique strengths. First, they are not transparent to subjects. That is, the subject doesn't know how the test pro-

Table 12.5 Representative Projective Tests

Test	Stimuli Presented	Response Request
Rorschach test (Rorschach, 1942)	10 cards, each with a bilaterally symmetric inkblot	"Tell me what this might be."
Thematic Apperception Test (TAT) (Murray, 1943)	10 to 12 (out of 30 available) cards depicting simple scenes	"Tell me a story about each picture. Tell me what is happening, what the characters are thinking and feeling …"
Menninger Word Association Test (Rapaport, Gill, & Schafer, 1968)	60 nouns	"Tell me the first word that comes to mind."
Rotter Incomplete Sentence Blank (Rotter & Rafferty, 1950)	40 sentence stems such as "My greatest fear is …"	"Finish the sentence in writing as rapidly as possible."
Draw-a-Person Test (Machover, 1949)	Blank sheet of paper	"Draw a whole person." (When finished: "Draw a person of the other sex.")

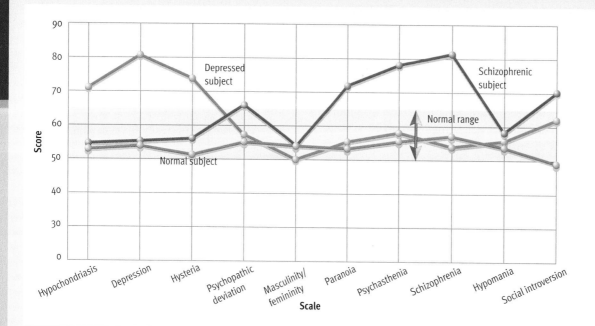

Figure 12.17

MMPI profiles. Scores on the ten clinical scales of the MMPI are often plotted as shown here to create a profile for a client. The normal range for scores on each subscale is 50 to 65. People with disorders frequently exhibit elevated scores on several clinical scales rather than just one.

Strengths and Weaknesses of Self-Report Inventories

To appreciate the strengths of self-report inventories, consider how else you might inquire about an individual's personality. For instance, if you want to know how assertive someone is, why not just ask the person?

Why administer an elaborate 50-item personality inventory that measures assertiveness? The advantage of the personality inventory is that it can provide a more objective and more precise estimate, one that is better grounded in extensive comparative data. Take a moment to consider: How assertive are you? You probably have some vague idea, but to accurately gauge your assertiveness you would need a great deal of comparative information about others' assertiveness, data which you lack. In contrast, a self-report inventory inquires about your typical behaviour in a variety of circumstances requiring

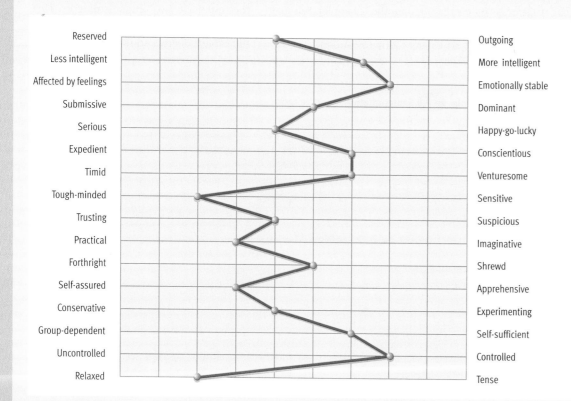

Figure 12.18

The Sixteen Personality Factor Questionnaire (16PF). Unlike the MMPI, Cattell's 16PF is designed to assess normal aspects of personality. The pairs of traits listed across from each other in the figure define the 16 factors measured by this self-report inventory. The profile shown is the average profile seen among a group of airline pilots who took the test.

SOURCE: Cattell, R. B. (1973, July). Personality pinned down. *Psychology Today*, 40–46. Reprinted by permission of Psychology Today Magazine. Copyright © 1973 Sussex Publishers, Inc.

Understanding Personality Assessment

Answer the following "true" or "false."

___ **1** Responses to personality tests are subject to unconscious distortion.

___ **2** The results of personality tests are often misunderstood.

___ **3** Personality test scores should be interpreted with caution.

___ **4** Personality tests serve many important functions.

If you answered "true" to all four questions, you earned a perfect score. Yes, personality tests are subject to distortion. Admittedly, test results are often misunderstood, and they should be interpreted cautiously. In spite of these problems, however, psychological tests can be quite useful.

Everyone engages in efforts to size up his or her own personality as well as that of others. When you think to yourself that "Mary Ann is shrewd and poised," or when you remark to a friend that "Howard is timid and submissive," you're making personality assessments. In a sense, then, personality assessment is an ongoing part of daily life. Given the popular interest in personality assessment, it's not surprising that psychologists have devised formal measures of personality.

The Uses of Personality Scales 7c

Why are psychological tests used to measure personality? They have a variety of purposes. Benjamin Kleinmuntz (1985) lists four principal uses of personality tests:

1. Personality tests are used extensively by mental health professionals in the *clinical diagnosis* of psychological disorders. Although diagnoses are not made on the basis of test results alone, personality scales can be helpful in arriving at diagnostic decisions.

2. Personality measurement may be done for the purpose of *counselling* individuals about a variety of normal, everyday problems. Counsellors often use personality scales to help people chart career plans and make vocational decisions.

3. Formal personality assessment often plays a key role in *personnel selection* in business, industry, government, and the military services. This use of personality testing has become controversial in recent years. Nonetheless, many organizations continue to use personality scales to assess applicants' suitability for various jobs.

4. Personality scales are frequently used in *psychological research*. Empirical studies on a great variety of issues require precise measurement of some aspect of personality. For instance, let's say you want to investigate whether introversion is related to a certain style of childrearing. Your task is simplified greatly if you have a personality test that measures introversion.

Personality tests can be divided into two broad categories: *self-report inventories* and *projective tests*. In this Application, we'll discuss some representative tests from both categories and discuss their strengths and weaknesses.

Self-Report Inventories 7c

Self-report inventories are personality tests that ask individuals to answer a series of questions about their characteristic behaviour. The logic underlying this approach is simple: Who knows you better? Who has known you longer? Who has more access to your private feelings? Some self-report inventories, such as the Sensation Seeking Scale and the Self-Monitoring Scale, are designed to measure one specific per-

sonality trait. Others can be used to measure many dimensions of personality simultaneously. Single-trait scales are used primarily in research. In clinical, counselling, and personnel work, psychologists rely more on multitrait inventories. We'll discuss three examples of multitrait scales: the MMPI, the 16PF, and the NEO Personality Inventory.

The MMPI

The most widely used multitrait scale is the Minnesota Multiphasic Personality Inventory (MMPI). This test was developed in the 1940s (Hathaway & McKinley, 1943) but underwent a major revision and modernization in the 1980s. The authors of MMPI-2 set out to maintain the original character of the scale while replacing obsolete items, eliminating sexist language, and updating the test norms (Graham, 1990).

The MMPI was originally designed to aid clinicians in the diagnosis of psychological disorders. Consequently, it measures mostly aspects of personality that, when manifested to an extreme degree, are thought to be symptoms of disorders. Examples include traits such as paranoia, depression, and hysteria.

The MMPI is a rather lengthy test. The revised version consists of 567 statements to which the subject answers "true," "false," or "cannot say." The MMPI yields scores on the 14 subscales described in Table 12.4. Four of the subscales are *validity scales* that provide indications about whether a subject has been careless or deceptive in taking the test. The remaining ten are *clinical scales* that measure various aspects of personality.

Are the MMPI clinical scales valid? That is, do they measure what they were designed to measure? The validity of the MMPI has been investigated in hundreds of studies (Butcher & Keller, 1984). Originally, it was assumed that the ten clinical subscales

Table 12.4 Personality Characteristics Associated with High MMPI Scores

Scale	Characteristics Associated with Higher Scores
Validity scale Cannot say (?)	May increase evasiveness.
Lie scale (*L*)	Indicates a tendency to present oneself in an overly favourable or highly virtuous light.
Infrequency scale (*F*)	Items on this scale are endorsed very infrequently by most people. Suggests carelessness, confusion, or "faking illness."
Subtle defensiveness (*K*)	Measures defensiveness of a subtle nature.
Clinical scale Hypochondriasis (*Hs*)	Indicates person is preoccupied with self, complaining, hostile, and presenting numerous physical problems that tend to be chronic.
Depression (*D*)	Indicates person is moody, shy, despondent, pessimistic, and distressed; one of the most frequently elevated scales in clinical patients.
Hysteria (*Hy*)	Indicates person tends to rely on neurotic defences such as denial and repression to deal with stress and tends to be dependent, naïve, outgoing, infantile, and narcissistic.
Psychopathic deviation (*Pd*)	May indicate rebelliousness, impulsiveness, hedonism, antisocial behaviour, difficulty in marital or family relationships, and trouble with the law or authority in general.
Masculinity/femininity (*MF*)	Indicates departure from traditional gender roles. High-scoring men are described as sensitive, aesthetic, passive, or feminine. They may show conflicts over sexual identity and low heterosexual drive. Because the direction of scoring is reversed, high-scoring women are seen as masculine, rough, aggressive, self-confident, unemotional, and insensitive.
Paranoia (*Pa*)	Often indicates person is suspicious, aloof, shrewd, guarded, worrisome, and overly sensitive and likely to project or externalize blame.
Psychasthenia (*Pt*)	Indicates person is tense, anxious, ruminative, preoccupied, obsessional, phobic, rigid, and frequently self-condemning and feeling inferior and inadequate.
Schizophrenia (*Sc*)	Often indicates person is withdrawn, shy, unusual, or strange and has peculiar thoughts or ideas, poor reality contact, and perhaps delusions and hallucinations.
Hypomania (*Ma*)	Indicates person is social, outgoing, impulsive, overly energetic, optimistic, and in some cases amoral, flighty, grandiose, and impulsive.
Social introversion (*Sie*)	Indicates person is introverted, shy, withdrawn, socially reserved, submissive, overcontrolled, lethargic, conventional, tense, inflexible, and guilt-prone.

SOURCE: Keller, L. S., Butcher, J. N. & Slutske, W. S. (1990). Objective personality assessment. In G. Goldstein & M. Hersen (Eds.). *Handbook of psychological assessment* (pp. 345–386). New York: Pergamon Press. Copyright © 1990 Pergamon Press, Ltd. Adapted by permission.

would provide direct indexes of specific types of disorders. In other words, a high score on the depression scale would be indicative of depression, a high score on the paranoia scale would be indicative of a paranoid disorder, and so forth. However, research revealed that the relations between MMPI scores and various types of pathology are much more complex than anticipated. People with most types of disorders show elevated scores on *several* MMPI subscales. This means that certain score *profiles* are indicative of specific disorders (see Figure 12.17). Thus, the interpretation of the MMPI is quite complicated. Nonetheless, the MMPI can be a helpful diagnostic tool for the clinician. The fact that the inventory has been translated into more than 115 languages is a testimonial to its usefulness (Butcher, 1990).

The 16PF and NEO Personality Inventory 7c

Raymond Cattell (1957, 1965) set out to identify and measure the *basic dimensions* of the *normal* personality. He started with a previously compiled list of 4504 personality traits. This massive list was reduced to 171 traits by weeding out terms that were virtually synonymous. Cattell then used factor analysis to identify clusters of closely related traits and the factors underlying them. Eventually, he reduced the list of 171 traits to 16 *source traits*. The Sixteen Personality Factor (16PF) Questionnaire is a 187-item scale that assesses these 16 basic dimensions of personality (Cattell, Eber, & Tatsuoka, 1970), which are listed in Figure 12.18.

As we noted in the main body of the chapter, some theorists believe that only five trait dimensions are required to provide a full description of personality. This view has led to the creation of a relatively new test—the NEO Personality Inventory. Developed by Paul Costa and Robert McCrae (1985, 1992), the NEO Inventory is designed to measure the Big Five traits: neuroticism, extraversion, openness to experience, agreeableness, and conscientiousness. In spite of its short life span, the NEO is already widely used in research and clinical work.

PRACTICE TEST

1. Harvey Hedonist has devoted his life to the search for physical pleasure and immediate need gratification. Freud would say that Harvey is dominated by:
   A. his ego.
   B. his superego.
   C. his id.
   D. Bacchus.

2. Furious at her boss for what she considers to be unjust criticism, Tyra turns around and takes out her anger on her subordinates. Tyra may be using the defence mechanism of:
   A. displacement.
   B. reaction formation.
   C. identification.
   D. replacement.

3. Freud believed that most personality disturbances are due to:
   A. the failure of parents to reinforce healthy behaviour.
   B. a poor self-concept resulting from excessive parental demands.
   C. unconscious and unresolved sexual conflicts rooted in childhood experiences.
   D. the exposure of children to unhealthy role models.

4. According to Alfred Adler, the prime motivating force in a person's life is:
   A. physical gratification.
   B. existential anxiety.
   C. striving for superiority.
   D. the need for power.

5. Which of the following learning mechanisms does B. F. Skinner see as being the major means by which behaviour is learned?
   A. classical conditioning
   B. operant conditioning
   C. observational learning
   D. insight learning

6. Always having been a good student, Irving is confident that he will do well in his psychology course. According to Bandura's social cognitive theory, Irving would be said to have:
   A. strong feelings of self-efficacy.
   B. a sense of superiority.
   C. strong feelings of self-esteem.
   D. strong defence mechanisms.

7. Which of the following approaches to personality is least deterministic?
   A. the humanistic approach
   B. the psychoanalytic approach
   C. Skinner's approach
   D. the behavioural approach

8. Which of the following did Carl Rogers believe fosters a congruent self-concept?
   A. conditional love
   B. appropriate role models
   C. immediate-need gratification
   D. unconditional love

9. The strongest support for the theory that personality is heavily influenced by genetics is provided by strong personality similarity between:
   A. identical twins reared together.
   B. identical twins reared apart.
   C. fraternal twins reared together.
   D. nontwins reared together.

10. Which of the following is the best way to regard heritability estimates?
    A. as reliable but not necessarily valid estimates
    B. as ballpark estimates of the influence of genetics
    C. as accurate estimates of the influence of genetics
    D. as relatively useless estimates of the influence of genetics

11. People who are high in self-monitoring:
    A. are sensitive to how their self-presentations go over.
    B. are good judges of others' personality.
    C. readily adjust their self-presentations to create certain impressions.
    D. all of the above.

12. If given a choice between staying home to read a good book and spending the day at an amusement park, Eldridge is likely to stay home. Marvin Zuckerman would say that Eldridge is probably:
    A. a low self-monitor.
    B. an introvert.
    C. relatively low in sensation seeking.
    D. psychologically repressed.

13. In which of the following cultures is an independent view of the self most likely to be the norm?
    A. China
    B. Japan
    C. Africa
    D. United States

14. Which of the following is *not* a shortcoming of self-report personality inventories?
    A. The accuracy of the results is a function of the honesty of the respondent.
    B. Respondents may attempt to answer in a way that makes them look good.
    C. There is sometimes a problem with "yea-sayers" or "nay-sayers."
    D. They are objective measures that are easy to administer and score.

15. In *The Nurture Assumption*, Judith Harris argues that the evidence indicates that family environment has _____ on children's personalities.
    A. largely positive effects
    B. largely negative effects
    C. surprisingly little effect
    D. a powerful effect

See Appendix A for answers to this Practice Test.

WWW   ON THE WEB

For additional resources on the topics covered in this chapter, visit the *Psychology: Themes and Variations* Web site, where you will find practice quizzes,

 tutorials, Web links, simulations, critical thinking activities, flash cards, interactive exercises, and suggested readings available through INFOTRAC.

http://www.themesandvariations.nelson.com

 http://hed.nelson.com

Go to this site for the link to ThomsonNOW™, your one-stop study shop. Take a Pretest for this chapter and ThomsonNOW™ will generate a personalized Study Plan based on your test results! The Study Plan will identify the topics you need to review and direct you to online resources to help you master those topics. You can then take a Posttest to help you determine the concepts you have mastered and what you still need work on.

CHAPTER 13

Latchezar Boyadjiev, *Comfort*, L.B. Glass Studios

The Nature of Stress
Stress as an Everyday Event
Appraisal: Stress Lies in the Eye of the Beholder

Major Types of Stress
Frustration
Conflict
Change
Pressure

Responding to Stress
Emotional Responses
Physiological Responses
Behavioural Responses

The Effects of Stress on Psychological Functioning
Impaired Task Performance
Burnout
Post-Traumatic Stress Disorders
Psychological Problems and Disorders
Positive Effects

The Effects of Stress on Physical Health
Type A Personality, Hostility, and Heart Disease
Emotional Reactions, Depression, and Heart Disease
Stress, Other Diseases, and Immune Functioning
Featured Study • Connecting Stress to the Common Cold
Sizing Up the Link between Stress and Illness

Factors Moderating the Impact of Stress
Social Support
Optimism and Conscientiousness

Health-Impairing Behaviour
Smoking
Poor Nutritional Habits
Lack of Exercise
Alcohol and Drug Use
Behaviour and AIDS
How Does Health-Impairing Behaviour Develop?

Reactions to Illness
Deciding to Seek Treatment
Communicating with Health Providers
Adhering to Medical Advice

Putting It in Perspective

Personal Application • **Improving Coping and Stress Management**
Reappraisal: Ellis's Rational Thinking
Using Humour as a Stress Reducer
Releasing Pent-Up Emotions
Managing Hostility and Forgiving Others
Learning to Relax
Minimizing Physiological Vulnerability

Critical Thinking Application • **Thinking Rationally About Health Statistics and Decisions**
Evaluating Statistics on Health Risks
Thinking Systematically about Health Decisions

Recap

Practice Test

Stress, Coping, and Health

Many circumstances can create stress. It comes in all sorts of packages: big and small, pretty and ugly, simple and complex. All too often, the package comes as a surprise. In this chapter we'll try to sort out these packages. We'll discuss the nature of stress, how people cope with stress, and the potential effects of stress. Stress is more than just an academic topic; it's something we are all experts in, something with which we all have abundant experience. At this point in the academic year all of you who were new to university in September are now veterans. Only a moment's reflection will tell you how much you have changed, how much you have experienced in a few short months. You have experienced the euphoria of being a university student, of being immersed in a novel intellectual and social environment. You have also experienced the tension most students go through as they prepare for their first university midterms or the "all-nighter" experience to get a paper in on time. However, it's not that you haven't experienced stress before. One of us remembers a conversation he had with a second-grade girl who was lined up for class waiting for the bell when all her classmates were out playing in the schoolyard before school. She looked nervous and distressed. When asked why she was lining up so early, she replied that she had "way too much work to do" and that it was "stressing" her out. Although you have had previous experience with academic stress, university may provide increased and more varied stress-provoking situations. Generally, university offers a less structured environment than your high school environment and one in which you may not have the immediacy of a supportive family.

A recent Ipsos-Reid poll of Canadian university students revealed that while many students experience stress in university, 40% reported experiencing *high* stress at exam time (McKenzie, 2005). Some of the students shared their symptoms and advice. Some of these may sound familiar. One Saint Mary's student's symptom is probably typical: "I get really high strung, kind of irritable and tense." What should you do? How do students cope? Here are some of the responses: "I go to the gym"; "I also

might watch TV"; "I usually drink herbal teas"; "I read books other than school-related things"; "I eat and sleep a lot, especially eating sweet stuff"; "I usually eat cakes and chocolate when studying"; "I'll just sleep for 13 hours."

Canadian universities have come to realize the importance of stress reduction for their students. Many universities now schedule *stress buster* events to coincide with exam periods. A quick scan of university Web sites confirmed that this practice is common, including events such as free massages, guided meditations, professional advice on coping with stress, break dancing, carnival games, free video games, martial arts training, and sports competitions. The University of Alberta has interactive software on its Web site titled "Students and Stress: How to Get Your Degree without Losing Your Mind" that provides a stress self-assessment and education regarding stress management (http://www.uofaweb.ualberta.ca/health info/nav02.cfm?nav02=27908&nav01=27613), and the University of Prince Edward Island's Web site has a particularly good section on study hints for students (http://www.upei.ca/healthcentre/html/stress.html).

You bring with yourself to the study of stress and health a wealth of personal experience and likely a personal interest in understanding stress and how to manage it. You will find out that Canadian psychologists such as stress pioneer Hans Selye of McGill

Students attending university get to experience stress first-hand during exam periods.

Figure 13.1

Changing patterns of illness.
Trends in the death rates for various diseases during the 20th century reveal that contagious diseases (shown in blue) have declined as a threat to health. However, the death rates for stress-related chronic diseases (shown in red) have remained quite high. The pie chart (inset) shows the results of these trends: three chronic diseases (heart disease, cancer, and stroke) account for 60.3% of all deaths. (Based on data from the U.S. National Center for Health Statistics)

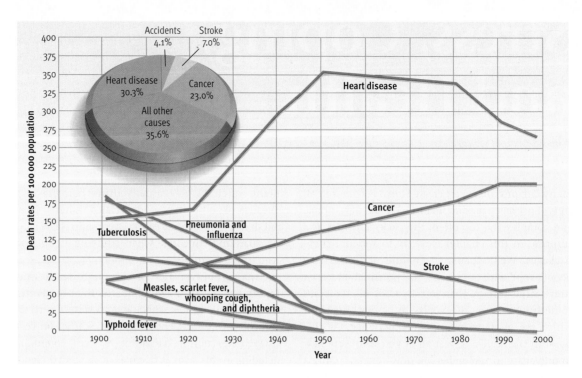

University and Hymie Anisman, Canada Research Chair at Carleton University, have made important contributions to work in this area. According to Anisman and others, exposure to stress is common and may lead to physiological and psychological changes, and some of these responses are adaptive (Anisman & Merali, 1999). If your system is overtaxed, however, there may be negative consequences for your health.

Our examination of the relationship between stress and physical illness will lead us into a broader discussion of the psychology of health. The way people in health professions think about physical illness has changed considerably in the past 20 years. The traditional view of physical illness as a purely biological phenomenon has given way to a biopsychosocial model of illness (Smilkstein, 1990). **The biopsychosocial model holds that physical illness is caused by a complex interaction of biological, psychological, and sociocultural factors.** This model does not suggest that biological factors are unimportant. It simply asserts that these factors operate in a psychosocial context that is also influential.

What has led to this shift in thinking? In part, it's a result of changing patterns of illness. Prior to the 20th century, the principal threats to health were *contagious diseases* caused by infectious agents—diseases such as smallpox, typhoid fever, diphtheria, yellow fever, malaria, cholera, tuberculosis, and polio. Today, none of these diseases is among the leading killers in North America. They were tamed by improvements in nutrition, public hygiene, sanitation, and medical treatment (Grob, 1983). Unfortunately, the void left by contagious diseases has been filled all too quickly by *chronic diseases* that develop gradually, such as heart disease, cancer, and stroke (see Figure 13.1). Psychosocial factors, such as stress and lifestyle, play a large role in the development of these chronic diseases. The growing recognition that psychological factors influence physical health has led to the emergence of a new specialty in psychology. *Health psychology* **is concerned with how psychosocial factors relate to the promotion and maintenance of health and with the causation, prevention, and treatment of illness.** In the second half of this chapter, we'll explore this new domain of psychology. In the Personal Application, we'll focus on strategies for enhancing stress management, and in the Critical Thinking Application we'll discuss strategies for improving health-related decision making.

The Nature of Stress

PREVIEW QUESTIONS
● What is stress?
● How objective are our appraisals of stress?

The word *stress* has been used in different ways by different theorists. We'll define *stress* **as any circumstances that threaten or are perceived to threaten one's well-being and that thereby tax one's coping** abilities. The threat may be to immediate physical safety, long-range security, self-esteem, reputation, peace of mind, or many other things that one values. Stress is a complex concept, so let's explore a little further.

Stress as an Everyday Event

The word *stress* tends to spark images of overwhelming, traumatic crises. People may think of tornadoes, hurricanes, floods, and earthquakes. Undeniably, major disasters such as the tsunami in late 2004 are extremely stressful events. Studies conducted in the aftermath of natural disasters typically find elevated rates of psychological problems and physical illness in the communities affected by these disasters (Brende, 2000; Raphael & Dobson, 2000). However, these unusual events are only a small part of what constitutes stress. Many everyday events, such as waiting in line, having car trouble, shopping for Christmas presents, misplacing your chequebook, and staring at bills you can't pay are also stressful. Researchers such as York University's Paul Kohn have found that everyday problems and the minor nuisances of life are also important forms of stress (Kohn, Lafreniere, & Gurevich, 1991). Of course, major and minor stressors are not entirely independent. A major stressful event, such as going through a divorce, can trigger a cascade of minor stressors, such as looking for a lawyer, changing bank accounts, taking on new household responsibilities, and so forth (Pillow, Zautra, & Sandler, 1996).

According to Anisman and Merali (1999), an individual's response to a stressor is a function of a number of factors including the type of stressor and its controllability, biological factors such as age and gender, and the individual's previous experience with stress.

You might guess that minor stresses would produce minor effects, but that isn't necessarily true. Richard Lazarus and his colleagues developed a scale to measure everyday hassles. Lazarus and his colleagues, including Anita DeLongis from the University of British Columbia, have shown that routine hassles may have significant harmful effects on mental and physical health (DeLongis, Folkman,

& Lazarus, 1988). Why would minor hassles be related to mental health? The answer isn't entirely clear yet, but it may be because of the *cumulative* nature of stress (Seta, Seta, & McElroy, 2002). Stress adds up. Routine stresses at home, at school, and at work might be fairly benign individually, but collectively they could create great strain.

Appraisal: Stress Lies in the Eye of the Beholder

The experience of feeling stressed depends on what events one notices and how one chooses to appraise or interpret them (Lazarus, 1999; Semmer, McGrath & Beehr, 2005). Events that are stressful for one person may be routine for another. For example, many people find flying in an airplane somewhat stressful, but frequent fliers may not be bothered at all. Some people enjoy the excitement of going out on a date with someone new; others find the uncertainty terrifying.

Often, people aren't very objective in their appraisals of potentially stressful events. A study of hospitalized patients awaiting surgery showed only a slight correlation between the objective seriousness of a person's upcoming surgery and the amount of fear experienced by the patients (Janis, 1958). Clearly, some people are more prone than others to feel threatened by life's difficulties. A number of studies have shown that anxious, neurotic people report more stress than others (Watson, David, & Suls, 1999), as do people who are relatively unhappy (Seidlitz & Diener, 1993). Thus, stress lies in the eye (actually, the mind) of the beholder. People's appraisals of stressful events are highly subjective. Questionnaires such as the Stress Appraisal Measure developed by the University of Toronto's Edward Peacock and Trent University's Paul Wong can be used to assess individual differences in such appraisal (Peacock & Wong, 1990).

We developed the Hassle Scale because we think scales that measure major events miss the point. The constant, minor irritants may be much more important than the large, landmark changes.
RICHARD LAZARUS

Major Types of Stress

An enormous variety of events can be stressful for one person or another. Although they're not entirely independent, the four principal types of stress are (1) frustration, (2) conflict, (3) change, and (4) pressure. As you read about each, you'll surely recognize four very familiar adversaries.

Frustration

 11F

I had a wonderful relationship with a nice man for three months. One day when we planned to spend the entire

day together, he called and said he wouldn't be meeting me and that he had decided to stop seeing me. I cried all morning. The grief was like losing someone through death. I still hurt, and I wonder if I'll ever get over him.

This scenario illustrates frustration. As psychologists use the term, **frustration occurs in any situation in which the pursuit of some goal is thwarted.** In essence, you experience frustration when you want something and you can't have it. Everyone has to deal with frustration virtually every day. According

PREVIEW QUESTIONS
- What is frustration?
- What are the three types of conflict?
- Which types of conflict are especially stressful?
- What evidence led to the conclusion that life changes are stressful?
- What is pressure?

Approach–approach

✚ Tennis			✚ Racquetball
✚ Pizza			✚ Spaghetti
✚ Blue sweater			✚ Grey jacket

Avoidance–avoidance

─ Unemployment		─ Degrading job
─ Painful backache		─ Surgery

Approach–avoidance

✚ Date with an attractive person	
─ Rejection	
✚ Investment returns	
─ Loss of capital	

Figure 13.2

Types of conflict.
Psychologists have identified three basic types of conflict. In approach–approach and avoidance–avoidance conflicts, a person is torn between two goals. In an approach–avoidance conflict, there is only one goal under consideration, but it has both positive and negative aspects.

to Canadian psychologists Dwight Hennesy and David Wiesenthal and others, traffic jams, difficult daily commutes, and annoying drivers, for instance, are a routine source of frustration that can elicit anger and aggression (Hennessy & Wiesenthal, 1999, 2004; Rasmussen, Knapp, & Garner, 2000). Fortunately, most frustrations are brief and insignificant. You may be quite upset when you go to a repair shop to pick up your ailing DVD player and find that it hasn't been fixed as promised. However, a week later you'll probably have your DVD player back, and the frustration will be forgotten.

Of course, some frustrations can be sources of significant stress. Failures and losses are two common

kinds of frustration that are often highly stressful. Everyone fails in at least some of his or her endeavours. Losses can be especially frustrating because people are deprived of something that they're accustomed to having. For example, few things are more frustrating than losing a dearly loved boyfriend, girlfriend, spouse, or parent.

Conflict 11F

Should I or shouldn't I? I became engaged at Christmas. My fiancé surprised me with a ring. I knew if I refused the ring he would be terribly hurt and our relationship would suffer. However, I don't really know whether or not I want to marry him. On the other hand, I don't want to lose him either.

Like frustration, conflict is an unavoidable feature of everyday life. The perplexing question "Should I or shouldn't I?" comes up countless times in everyone's life. _Conflict_ **occurs when two or more incompatible motivations or behavioural impulses compete for expression.** As we discussed in Chapter 12, Sigmund Freud proposed over a century ago that internal conflicts generate considerable psychological distress. This link between conflict and distress was measured with new precision in studies by Laura King and Robert Emmons (1990, 1991). They used an elaborate questionnaire to assess the overall amount of internal conflict experienced by subjects. They found that higher levels of conflict were associated with higher levels of anxiety, depression, and physical symptoms.

Conflicts come in three types, which were originally described by Kurt Lewin (1935) and investigated extensively by Neal Miller (1944, 1959). These three basic types of conflict—approach–approach, avoidance–avoidance, and approach–avoidance—are diagrammed in Figure 13.2.

In an _approach–approach conflict_ a choice must be made between two attractive goals. The problem, of course, is that you can choose just one of the two goals. For example: You have a free afternoon; should you play tennis or racquetball?

Among the three kinds of conflict, the approach–approach type tends to be the least stressful. People don't usually stagger out of restaurants exhausted by the stress of choosing which of several appealing entrées to eat. Approach–approach conflicts typically have a reasonably happy ending, whichever way you decide to go. Nonetheless, approach–approach conflicts over important issues may sometimes be troublesome. If you're torn between two appealing majors at university, or two attractive boyfriends, you may find the decision-making process quite stressful, since whichever alternative is not chosen represents a loss of sorts.

In an *avoidance–avoidance conflict* **a choice must be made between two unattractive goals.** Forced to choose between two repelling alternatives, you are, as they say, "caught between a rock and a hard place." For example, should you continue to collect unemployment cheques, or should you take that degrading job at the car wash? Obviously, avoidance–avoidance conflicts are most unpleasant and highly stressful.

In an *approach–avoidance conflict* **a choice must be made about whether to pursue a single goal that has both attractive and unattractive aspects.** For instance, imagine that you're offered a career promotion that will mean a large increase in pay, but you'll have to move to a city where you don't want to live. Approach–avoidance conflicts are common and can be quite stressful. Any time you have to take a risk to pursue some desirable outcome, you're likely to find yourself in an approach–avoidance conflict. Should you risk rejection by asking out a person that you are attracted to? Should you risk your savings by investing in a new business that could fail?

Approach–avoidance conflicts often produce *vacillation*. That is, you go back and forth, beset by indecision. You decide to go ahead, then you decide not to, and then you decide to go ahead again. Humans are not unique in this respect. Many years ago, Neal Miller (1944) observed the same vacillation in his groundbreaking research with rats. He created approach–avoidance conflicts in hungry rats by alternately feeding and shocking them at one end of a runway apparatus. Eventually, these rats tended to hover near the centre of the runway, alternately approaching and retreating from the goal box at the end of the alley.

Change 11F

After my divorce, I lived alone for four years. Six months ago I married a wonderful woman who has two children from her previous marriage. My biggest stress is suddenly having to adapt to living with three people instead of by myself. I was pretty set in my ways. I had certain routines. Now everything is chaos. I love my wife and I'm fond of the kids. They're not really doing anything wrong. But my house and my life just aren't the same, and I'm having trouble dealing with it all.

It has been proposed that life changes, such as a change in marital status, represent a key type of stress. **Life changes** are any noticeable alterations in one's living circumstances that require readjustment.

The importance of life changes was first demonstrated by Thomas Holmes, Richard Rahe, and their colleagues in the 1960s (Holmes & Rahe, 1967; Rahe & Arthur, 1978). Theorizing that stress might make people more vulnerable to illness, they interviewed thousands of tuberculosis patients to find out what kinds of events had preceded the onset of their disease. Surprisingly, the most frequently cited events were not uniformly negative. There were plenty of aversive events, as expected. But there were also many seemingly positive events, such as getting married, having a baby, or getting promoted.

Why would positive events, such as moving to a nicer home, produce stress? According to Holmes and Rahe, it's because they produce *change*. In their view, changes in personal relationships, changes at work, changes in finances, and so forth can be stressful even when the changes are welcomed.

Based on this analysis, Holmes and Rahe (1967) developed the Social Readjustment Rating Scale (SRRS) to measure life change as a form of stress. The scale assigns numerical values to 43 major life events. These values are supposed to reflect the magnitude of the readjustment required by each change (see Table 13.1). In using the scale, respondents are asked to indicate how often they experienced any of these 43 events during a certain time period (typically, the past year). The numbers associated with each event checked are then added. This total is an index of the amount of change-related stress the person has recently experienced.

The SRRS and similar scales based on it have been used in thousands of studies by researchers all over the world. Overall, these studies have shown that people with higher scores on the SRRS tend to be more vulnerable to many kinds of physical illness and to many types of psychological problems as well (Derogatis & Coons, 1993; Gruen, 1993; Scully, Tosi, & Banning, 2000). These results have attracted a great deal of attention, and the SRRS has been reprinted in many popular newspapers and magazines. The attendant publicity has led to the widespread conclusion that life change is inherently stressful.

More recently, however, experts have criticized this research, citing problems with the methods used and raising questions about the meaning of the findings (Hobson & Delunas, 2001; Jones & Kinman, 2001; Wethington, 2000). At this point, it's a key interpretive issue that concerns us. Many critics have argued that the SRRS does not measure *change* exclusively. The main problem is that the list of life changes on the SRRS is dominated by events that are clearly negative or undesirable (death of a spouse, being fired from a job, and so on). These negative

Table 13.1 Social Readjustment Rating Scale

Life Event	Mean Value
Death of a spouse	100
Divorce	73
Marital separation	65
Jail term	63
Death of a close family member	63
Personal injury or illness	53
Marriage	50
Fired at work	47
Marital reconciliation	45
Retirement	45
Change in health of family member	44
Pregnancy	40
Sex difficulties	39
Gain of a new family member	39
Business readjustment	39
Change in financial state	38
Death of a close friend	37
Change to a different line of work	36
Change in number of arguments with spouse	35
Mortgage or loan for major purchase (home, etc.)	31
Foreclosure of mortgage or loan	30
Change in responsibilities at work	29
Son or daughter leaving home	29
Trouble with in-laws	29
Outstanding personal achievement	28
Spouse begins or stops work	26
Begin or end school	26
Change in living conditions	25
Revision of personal habits	24
Trouble with boss	23
Change in work hours or conditions	20
Change in residence	20
Change in school	20
Change in recreation	19
Change in church activities	19
Change in social activities	18
Mortgage or loan for lesser purchase (car, TV, etc.)	17
Change in sleeping habits	16
Change in number of family get-togethers	15
Change in eating habits	15
Vacation	13
Christmas	12
Minor violations of the law	11

SOURCE: Adapted from Holmes, T. H., & Rahe, R. (1967). The Social Readjustment Rating Scale. *Journal of Psychosomatic Research, 11*, 213–218. Copyright © 1967 by Elsevier Science Publishing Co. Reprinted by permission.

events probably generate great frustration. Although there are some positive events on the scale, it turns out that negative life events cause most of the stress tapped by the SRRS (McLean & Link, 1994; Turner & Wheaton, 1995). Thus, it has become apparent that the SRRS assesses a wide range of stressful experiences, not just life change. At present, there's little reason to believe that change is inherently or inevitably stressful. Undoubtedly, some life changes may be quite challenging, but others may be quite benign.

Pressure

My father questioned me at dinner about some things I didn't want to talk about. I know he doesn't want to hear my answers, at least not the truth. My father told me when I was little that I was his favourite because I was "pretty near perfect." I've spent my life trying to keep up that image, even though it's obviously not true. Recently, he has begun to realize this, and it's made our relationship very strained and painful.

At one time or another, most people have remarked that they're "under pressure." What does this mean? Sometimes the pressure comes from a mismatch between what we have to or want to do and the time available. In a recent survey, over half of the Canadians surveyed said they did not have enough time to both work and spend adequate time with their family. In addition, the survey found that the number of people who were identified as severely time-stressed had increased between 1992 and 1998 (Statistics Canada, 1999b). There are many kinds of pressure that we face in our daily lives. More generally, **pressure involves expectations or demands that one behave in a certain way.** You are under pressure to *perform* when you're expected to execute tasks and responsibilities quickly, efficiently, and successfully. For example, salespeople are usually under pressure to move merchandise. Professors at research institutions are often under pressure to publish in prestigious journals. Stand-up comedians are under intense pressure to make people laugh. Pressures to *conform* to others' expectations are also common in our lives. People in the business world are expected to dress in certain ways. Suburban homeowners are expected to keep their lawns well manicured. Teenagers are expected to adhere to their parents' values and rules.

Although widely discussed by the general public, the concept of pressure has received scant attention from researchers. However, Weiten (1988b, 1998) has devised a scale to measure pressure as a form of life stress. It assesses self-imposed pressure, pressure from work and school, and pressure from family relations, peer relations, and intimate relations. In research with this scale, a strong relationship has been found between pressure and a variety of psychological symptoms and problems. In fact, pressure has turned out to be more strongly related to measures of mental health than the SRRS and other established measures of stress are (see Figure 13.3).

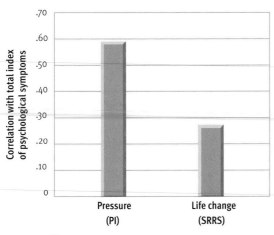

Figure 13.3

Pressure and psychological symptoms. A comparison of pressure and life change as sources of stress suggests that pressure may be more strongly related to mental health than change is. In one study, Weiten (1988b) found a correlation of 0.59 between scores on the Pressure Inventory (PI) and symptoms of psychological distress. In the same sample, the correlation between SRRS scores and psychological symptoms was only 0.28.

CONCEPT CHECK 13.2

Recognizing Sources of Stress

Check your understanding of the major sources of stress by indicating which type or types of stress are at work in each of the examples below. Bear in mind that the four basic types of stress are not mutually exclusive. There's some potential for overlap, so a specific experience might include both change and pressure, for instance. The answers are in Appendix A.

Examples

_____ **1.** Marie is late for an appointment but is stuck in line at the bank.

_____ **2.** Tamika decides that she won't be satisfied unless she gets straight A's this year.

_____ **3.** José has just graduated from business school and has taken an exciting new job.

_____ **4.** Morris has just been fired from his job and needs to find another.

Types of stress

a. frustration

b. conflict

c. change

d. pressure

Responding to Stress

People's response to stress is complex and multidimensional. Stress affects the individual at several levels. Consider the following situation: you're driving home in heavy traffic and thinking about overdue papers, tuition increases, and parental pressures. Let's look at some of the reactions that you might have. When you groan in reaction to the traffic report, you're experiencing an *emotional response* to stress, in this case annoyance and anger. When your pulse quickens and your stomach knots up, you're exhibiting *physiological responses* to stress. When you shout insults at another driver, your verbal aggression is a *behavioural response* to the stress

at hand. Thus, we can analyze a person's reactions to stress at three levels: (1) emotional responses, (2) physiological responses, and (3) behavioural responses. Figure 13.4, which diagrams these three levels of response, provides an overview of the stress process.

Emotional Responses

When people are under stress, they often react emotionally. Studies that have tracked stress and mood on a daily basis have found intimate relationships between the two (Affleck et al., 1994; van Eck, Nicolson, & Berkhof, 1998).

Figure 13.4

Overview of the stress process. A potentially stressful event, such as a major exam, elicits a subjective appraisal of how threatening the event is. If the event is viewed with alarm, the stress may trigger emotional, physiological, and behavioural reactions, as people's response to stress is multidimensional.

Potentially stressful objective events
A major exam, a big date, trouble with one's boss, or a financial setback, which may lead to frustration, conflict, change, or pressure

Subjective cognitive appraisal
Personalized perceptions of threat, which are influenced by familiarity with the event, its controllability, its predictability, and so on

Emotional response
Annoyance, anger, anxiety, fear, dejection, grief

Physiological response
Autonomic arousal, hormonal fluctuations, neurochemical changes, and so on

Behavioural response
Coping efforts, such as lashing out at others, blaming oneself, seeking help, solving problems, and releasing emotions

Emotions Commonly Elicited

No simple one-to-one connections have been found between certain types of stressful events and particular emotions. However, researchers *have* begun to uncover some strong links between *specific cognitive reactions to stress* (appraisals) and specific emotions (Smith & Lazarus, 1993). For example, self-blame tends to lead to guilt, helplessness to sadness, and so forth. Although many emotions can be evoked by stressful events, some are certainly more likely than others. Common emotional responses to stress include (a) annoyance, anger, and rage, (b) apprehension, anxiety, and fear, and (c) dejection, sadness, and grief (Lazarus, 1993; Woolfolk & Richardson, 1978).

Although investigators have tended to focus heavily on the connection between stress and negative emotions, research shows that positive emotions also occur during periods of stress (Folkman, 1997). Although this finding seems counterintuitive, researchers have found that people experience a diverse array of pleasant emotions even while enduring the most dire of circumstances. Consider, for example, the results of a five-year study of coping patterns in 253 caregiving partners of men with AIDS (Folkman et al., 1997). Surprisingly, over the course of the study, the caregivers reported experiencing positive emotions about as often as they experienced negative emotions—except during the time immediately surrounding the death of their partners. Moreover, Susan Folkman and Judith Moskowitz (2000) argue that positive emotions experienced while under duress have important adaptive significance. They review evidence suggesting that positive emotions can promote creativity and flexibility in problem solving, facilitate the processing of important information about oneself, and reduce the adverse physiological effects of stress. Consistent with their analysis, recent research suggests that positive emotions may reduce vulnerability to heart disease in older adults (Ostir et al., 2001).

Effects of Emotional Arousal

Emotional responses are a natural and normal part of life. Even unpleasant emotions serve important purposes. Like physical pain, painful emotions can serve as warnings that one needs to take action. However, strong emotional arousal can also interfere with efforts to cope with stress. For example, there is evidence that high emotional arousal can interfere with attention and memory retrieval and can impair judgment and decision making (Janis, 1993; Mandler, 1993).

Although emotional arousal may hurt coping efforts, that isn't *necessarily* the case. The *inverted-U hypothesis* predicts that task performance should improve with increased emotional arousal—up to a point, after which further increases in arousal become disruptive and performance deteriorates (Anderson, 1990; Mandler, 1993). This idea is referred to as the inverted-U hypothesis because when performance is plotted as a function of arousal, the resulting graphs approximate an upside-down U (see Figure 13.5). In these graphs, the level of arousal at which performance peaks is characterized as the *optimal level of arousal* for a task.

This optimal level of arousal appears to depend in part on the complexity of the task at hand. The conventional wisdom is that *as a task becomes more complex, the optimal level of arousal (for peak performance) tends to decrease.* This relationship is depicted in Figure 13.5. As you can see, a fairly high level of arousal should be optimal on simple tasks (such as driving eight hours to help a friend in a crisis). However, performance should peak at a lower level of arousal on complex tasks (such as making a major decision in which you have to weigh many factors).

The research evidence on the inverted-U hypothesis is inconsistent and subject to varied interpretations

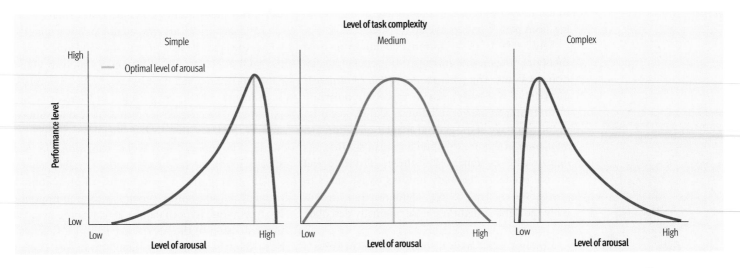

Level of task complexity

Simple   Medium   Complex

Optimal level of arousal

Performance level

High

Low

Low   Level of arousal   High

Figure 13.5

Arousal and performance.
Graphs of the relationship between emotional arousal and task performance tend to resemble an inverted U, as increased arousal is associated with improved performance up to a point, after which higher arousal leads to poorer performance. The optimal level of arousal for a task depends on the complexity of the task. On complex tasks, a relatively low level of arousal tends to be optimal. On simple tasks, however, performance may peak at a much higher level of arousal.

(Neiss, 1988, 1990). Hence, it may be risky to generalize this principle to the complexities of everyday coping efforts. Nonetheless, the inverted-U hypothesis provides a plausible model of how emotional arousal could have either beneficial or disruptive effects on coping, depending on the nature of the stressful demands.

Physiological Responses

As we just discussed, stress frequently elicits strong emotional responses. Now we'll look at the important physiological changes that often accompany these responses.

The Fight-or-Flight Response

Walter Cannon (1932) was one of the first theorists to describe the fight-or-flight response. The *fight-or-flight response* **is a physiological reaction to threat in which the autonomic nervous system mobilizes the organism for attacking (fight) or fleeing (flight) an enemy.** As you may recall from Chapter 3, the *autonomic nervous system (ANS)* controls blood vessels, smooth muscles, and glands. The fight-or-flight response is mediated by the *sympathetic division* of the ANS. In one experiment, Cannon studied the fight-or-flight response in cats by confronting them with dogs. Among other things, he noticed an immediate acceleration in their breathing and heart rate and a reduction in their digestive processes.

The physiological arousal associated with the fight-or-flight response is also seen in humans. In a sense, this automatic reaction is a "leftover" from humanity's evolutionary past. It's clearly an adaptive response in the animal kingdom, where the threat of predators often requires a swift response of fighting or fleeing. But in our modern world, the fight-or-flight response may be less adaptive for human functioning than it was thousands of generations ago (Neese & Young, 2000). Most human stresses can't be handled simply through

fight or flight. Shelley Taylor and her colleagues (2000) have questioned whether the fight-or-flight model applies equally well to both males and females. They note that in most species females have more responsibility for the care of young offspring than males do. Using an evolutionary perspective, they argue that this disparity may make fighting and fleeing less adaptive for females, as both responses may endanger offspring and thus reduce the likelihood of an animal passing on its genes. Taylor et al. (2000) maintain that evolutionary processes have fostered more of a "tend and befriend" response in females. According to this analysis, in reacting to stress, females allocate more effort to the care of offspring and to seeking help and support. More research is needed to evaluate this provocative analysis. Although gender differences may exist in behavioural responses to stress, Taylor and her colleagues are quick to note that the "basic neuroendocrine core of stress responses" is largely the same for males and females.

The General Adaptation Syndrome

The concept of stress was identified and named by Hans Selye (1936, 1956, 1982). Selye was born in Vienna but came to Canada and began his professional career at McGill University in Montreal. He was also professor and director of the Institute of Experimental Medicine and Surgery at the University of Montreal. Beginning in the 1930s, Selye exposed laboratory animals to a diverse array of both physical and psychological stressors (heat, cold, pain, mild shock, restraint, and so on). The patterns of physiological arousal seen in the animals were largely the same, regardless of the type of stress. Thus, Selye concluded that stress reactions are *nonspecific*. In other words, he maintained that the reactions do not vary according to the specific type of stress encountered. Initially, Selye wasn't sure what to call this nonspecific response to a variety of noxious agents.

In the 1940s he decided to call it *stress,* and the word has been part of our vocabulary ever since.

Selye (1956, 1974) formulated an influential theory of stress reactions called the general adaptation syndrome. **The *general adaptation syndrome* is a model of the body's stress response, consisting of three stages: alarm, resistance, and exhaustion.** In the first stage of the general adaptation syndrome, an *alarm reaction* occurs when an organism first recognizes the existence of a threat. Physiological arousal occurs as the body musters its resources to combat the challenge. Selye's alarm reaction is essentially the fight-or-flight response originally described by Cannon.

However, Selye took his investigation of stress a few steps further by exposing laboratory animals to *prolonged* stress, similar to the chronic stress often endured by humans. As stress continues, the organism may progress to the second phase of the general adaptation syndrome, the *stage of resistance.* During this phase, physiological changes stabilize as coping efforts get under way. Typically, physiological arousal continues to be higher than normal, although it may level off somewhat as the organism becomes accustomed to the threat.

If the stress continues over a substantial period of time, the organism may enter the third stage, the *stage of exhaustion.* According to Selye, the body's resources for fighting stress are limited. If the stress can't be overcome, the body's resources may be depleted, and physiological arousal will decrease. Eventually, the organism may collapse from exhaustion. During this phase, the organism's resistance declines. This reduced resistance may lead to what Selye called "diseases of adaptation."

In addition to being an internationally renowned scientist, Selye was a remarkable and accomplished person in other ways. He was fluent in eight languages and could converse in a total of 14 (Rosch, n.d.). Even though he is credited with introducing the term *stress,* he later said that perhaps the term *strain* would have been more appropriate. His work was known beyond the world of science, and the famous Spanish surrealist artist Salvador Dali created a painting for him to commemorate the Second International Symposium on the Management of Stress held in 1979. Selye was awarded the Companion of the Order of Canada in 1968, and in 1997 Hungary issued a Hans Selye stamp. In 1999, Canada Post issued the Hans Selye stamp.

Brain–Body Pathways

Even in cases of moderate stress, you may notice that your heart has started beating faster, you've begun to breathe harder, and you're perspiring more than usual. How does all this (and much more) happen? It appears that there are two major pathways along which the brain sends signals to the endocrine system in response to stress (Tsigos, Kyrou, & Chrousos, 2005; Clow, 2001; Dallman, Bhatnagar, & Viau, 2000; Felker & Hubbard, 1998). As we noted in Chapter 3, the *endocrine system* consists of glands located at various sites in the body that secrete chemicals called hormones. The *hypothalamus* is the brain structure that appears to initiate action along these two pathways.

The first pathway (see Figure 13.6) is routed through the autonomic nervous system. In response to stress, your hypothalamus activates the sympathetic division of the ANS. A key part of this activation involves stimulating the central part of the adrenal glands (the adrenal medulla) to release large amounts of *catecholamines* into the bloodstream. These hormones radiate throughout your body, producing the physiological changes seen in the fight-or-flight response. The net result of catecholamine elevation is that your body is mobilized for action (Lundberg, 2000). Heart rate and blood flow increase, and more blood is pumped to your brain and muscles. Respiration and oxygen consumption speed up, which facilitates alertness. Digestive processes are inhibited to conserve your energy. The pupils of your eyes dilate, increasing visual sensitivity.

The second pathway involves more direct communication between the brain and the endocrine system (see Figure 13.6). The hypothalamus sends signals to the so-called master gland of the endocrine system, the pituitary. In turn, the pituitary secretes a hormone (ACTH) (Anisman & Merali, 1999) that stimulates the outer part of the adrenal glands (the adrenal cortex) to release another important set of hormones—*corticosteroids.* These hormones stimulate the release of chemicals that help increase your energy and help inhibit tissue inflammation in case of injury (Munck, 2000).

Behavioural Responses

Although people respond to stress at several levels, it's clear that *behaviour* is the crucial dimension of their reactions. Most behavioural responses to stress involve coping. ***Coping* refers to active efforts to master, reduce, or tolerate the demands created by stress.** Notice that this definition is neutral as to whether coping efforts are healthful or maladaptive. The popular use of the term often implies that coping is inherently healthful. When people say that someone "coped with her problems," the implication is that she handled them effectively.

"There are two main types of human beings: 'racehorses,' who thrive on stress and are only happy with a vigorous, fast-paced lifestyle; and 'turtles,' who in order to be happy require peace, quiet, and a generally tranquil environment."
HANS SELYE

© Bettmann/CORBIS

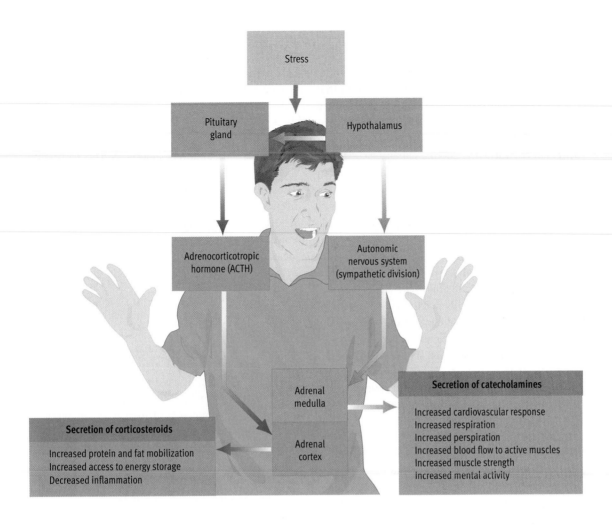

Figure **13.6**

Brain–body pathways in stress. In times of stress, the brain sends signals along two pathways. The pathway through the autonomic nervous system controls the release of catecholamine hormones that help mobilize the body for action. The pathway through the pituitary gland and the endocrine system controls the release of corticosteroid hormones that increase energy and ward off tissue inflammation.

Stress

Pituitary gland

Hypothalamus

Adrenocorticotropic hormone (ACTH)

Autonomic nervous system (sympathetic division)

Adrenal medulla

Adrenal cortex

Secretion of corticosteroids

Increased protein and fat mobilization
Increased access to energy storage
Decreased inflammation

Secretion of catecholamines

Increased cardiovascular response
Increased respiration
Increased perspiration
Increased blood flow to active muscles
Increased muscle strength
Increased mental activity

In reality, however, coping responses may be adaptive or maladaptive (Moos & Schaefer, 1993; Vaillant, 2000). For example, if you were flunking a history course at midterm, you might cope with this stress by (1) increasing your study efforts, (2) seeking help from a tutor, (3) blaming your professor, or (4) giving up on the class without really trying. Clearly, the first two of these coping responses would be more adaptive than the last two.

People cope with stress in many ways, but most individuals exhibit certain styles of coping that are fairly consistent across situations (Carver & Scheier, 1994; Heszen-Niejodek, 1997). York University's Norm S. Endler developed a model of coping based on the formulation that coping is a key aspect of personality, and that as such, it is a stable, dispositional attribute (Endler, 1997). Along with Trent University's James Parker (whom we profiled in Chapter 9 for his work in emotional intelligence), Endler developed a measure designed to assess stable individual differences in coping (Endler & Parker, 1990). The Coping Inventory for Stressful Situations (CISS) measures three stable coping dimensions: task-oriented coping, emotion-oriented coping, and avoidance-oriented

coping. We discussed Endler's views on the interactional nature of personality in Chapter 12. He was influenced in deciding to enter a career in psychology after taking Donald Hebb's course in psychology at McGill University.

Given the immense variety in coping strategies, we can highlight only a few of the more common patterns. In this section we'll focus most of our attention on styles of coping that tend to be less than ideal. We'll discuss a variety of more healthful coping strategies in the Personal Application on stress management.

Giving Up and Blaming Oneself 11G

When confronted with stress, people sometimes simply give up and withdraw from the battle. Some people routinely respond to stress with fatalism and resignation, passively accepting setbacks that might be dealt with effectively. This syndrome is referred to as *learned helplessness* (Seligman, 1974, 1992). ***Learned helplessness* is passive behaviour produced by exposure to unavoidable aversive events.** Learned helplessness seems to occur when individuals come to believe that events are beyond their control. As you might guess, giving up is not a highly regarded method of coping. Carver and his colleagues (1989, 1993) have studied this coping strategy, which they refer to as *behavioural disengagement,* and found that it is associated with increased rather than decreased distress. Furthermore, many studies suggest that learned helplessness can contribute to depression (Seligman & Isaacowitz, 2000).

Blaming oneself is another common response when people are confronted by stressful difficulties. The tendency to become highly self-critical in response to stress has been noted by a number of influential theorists. Albert Ellis (1973, 1987) calls this phenomenon "catastrophic thinking." According to Ellis, catastrophic thinking causes, aggravates, and perpetuates emotional reactions to stress that are often problematic (see the Personal Application for this chapter). In a similar vein, Aaron Beck (1976, 1987) argues that negative self-talk can contribute to the development of depressive disorders (see Chapter 15). Although there is something to be said for recognizing one's weaknesses and taking responsibility for one's failures, Ellis and Beck agree that excessive self-blame can be very unhealthy.

Striking Out at Others

People often respond to stressful events by striking out at others with aggressive behaviour. ***Aggression* is any behaviour that is intended to hurt someone, either physically or verbally.** Many years ago, a team of psychologists (Dollard et al., 1939) proposed the *frustration–aggression hypothesis,* which held that aggression is always caused by frustration. Decades of research have supported this idea of a causal link between frustration and aggression (Berkowitz, 1989). However, this research has also shown that there isn't an inevitable, one-to-one correspondence between frustration and aggression.

Frequently people lash out aggressively at others who had nothing to do with their frustration, apparently because they can't vent their anger at the real source. For example, you'll probably suppress your anger rather than lash out verbally at your boss or at a police officer who's giving you a speeding ticket. Twenty minutes later, however, you might be verbally brutal to a colleague at work. As we discussed in Chapter 12, this diversion of anger to a substitute target was noticed long ago by Sigmund Freud, who called it *displacement.* Unfortunately, research suggests that when people are provoked, displaced aggression is a common response (Marcus-Newhall et al., 2000).

Freud theorized that behaving aggressively could get pent-up emotion out of one's system and thus be adaptive. He coined the term ***catharsis* to refer to**

this release of emotional tension. There is some experimental evidence to support Freud's theory of catharsis (Hokanson & Burgess, 1962). However, the balance of evidence indicates that aggressive behaviour does *not* reliably lead to catharsis (Tavris, 1989). As Carol Tavris notes, "Aggressive catharses are almost impossible to find in continuing relationships because parents, children, spouses, and bosses usually feel obliged to aggress back at you" (1982, p. 131). Thus, the interpersonal conflicts that often emerge from aggressive behaviour may increase rather than relieve stress. For example, if you pick a fight with your spouse after a terrible day at work, you may create new stress for yourself.

Indulging Oneself

Stress sometimes leads to reduced impulse control, or *self-indulgence* (Tice, Bratslavsky, & Baumeister, 2001). When troubled by stress, many people engage in excessive consumption—unwise patterns of eating, drinking, smoking, using drugs, spending money, and so forth. It makes sense that when things are going poorly in one area of their lives, people may try to compensate by pursuing substitute forms of satisfaction. When this happens, self-indulgent responses tend to be relatively easy to execute and highly pleasurable. Thus, it's not surprising that studies have linked stress to increases in eating (Grunberg & Straub, 1992; Laitinen, Ek, & Sovio, 2002), smoking (Cohen & Lichtenstein, 1990; Kassel, Stroud, & Paronis, 2003), and consumption of alcohol and drugs (Colder, 2001; Goeders, 2004; Pihl, 1999).

A new manifestation of this coping strategy that has attracted much attention recently is the tendency to immerse oneself in the online world of the Internet. Kimberly Young (1996, 1998) has described a syndrome called ***Internet addiction,* which consists of spending an inordinate amount of time on the Internet and inability to control online use.**

Defensive Coping

Many people exhibit consistent styles of defensive coping in response to stress (Vaillant, 1994). We noted in Chapter 12 that Sigmund Freud originally developed the concept of the *defence mechanism.* Though rooted in the psychoanalytic tradition, this concept has gained widespread acceptance from psychologists of most persuasions (Cramer, 2000). Building on Freud's initial insights, modern psychologists have broadened the scope of the concept and added to Freud's list of defence mechanisms.

***Defence mechanisms* are largely unconscious reactions that protect a person from unpleasant**

"People largely disturb themselves by thinking in a self-defeating, illogical, and unrealistic manner."
ALBERT ELLIS

emotions such as anxiety and guilt. Many specific defence mechanisms have been identified. For example, Laughlin (1979) lists 49 different defences. We also described seven common defence mechanisms in our discussion of Freud's theory in Chapter 12. Table 13.2 introduces another five defences that people use with some regularity. Although widely discussed in the popular press, defence mechanisms are often misunderstood. To clear up some of the misconceptions, we'll use a question/answer format to elaborate on the nature of defence mechanisms.

What exactly do defence mechanisms defend against? Above all else, defence mechanisms shield the individual from the emotional discomfort that's so often elicited by stress. Their main purpose is to ward off unwelcome emotions or to reduce their intensity. Foremost among the emotions guarded against is *anxiety.* Defences are also used to suppress dangerous feelings of *anger* so that they don't explode into acts of aggression. *Guilt* and *dejection* are two other emotions that people often try to evade through defensive manoeuvres.

How do they work? Through *self-deception.* Defence mechanisms accomplish their goals by distorting reality so that it doesn't appear so threatening. For example, suppose you're not doing well in school and you're in danger of flunking out. Initially you might use *denial* to block awareness of the possibility that you could flunk. This defence might temporarily fend off feelings of anxiety. If it becomes difficult to deny the obvious, you could resort to *fantasy.* You might daydream about how you'll salvage adequate grades by getting spectacular scores on the upcoming final exams, when the objective fact is that you're hopelessly behind in your studies. Thus, defence mechanisms work their magic by bending reality in self-serving ways.

Are they conscious or unconscious? Both. Freudian theory originally assumed that defences operate entirely at an unconscious level. However, the concept of the defence mechanism has been broadened by other theorists to include manoeuvres that people may be aware of. Thus, defence mechanisms may operate at varying levels of awareness, although they're largely unconscious (Cramer, 2001; Erdelyi, 2001).

Are they normal? Definitely. Everyone uses defence mechanisms on a fairly regular basis. They're entirely normal patterns of coping. The notion that only neurotic people use defence mechanisms is inaccurate.

Are they healthy? This is a much more complicated question. More often than not, the answer is "no." Generally, defensive coping is less than optimal for a number of reasons. First, defensive coping is an avoidance strategy, and avoidance rarely provides a genuine solution to problems (Holahan & Moos, 1985, 1990). Second, a repressive coping style has been related to poor health, in part because repression often leads

Experts disagree about whether excessive Internet use should be characterized as an addiction, but the inability to control online activity appears to be an increasingly common syndrome that illustrates the coping strategy of indulging oneself.

Table **13.2** Additional Defence Mechanisms

Mechanism	Description	Example
Denial of reality	Protecting oneself from unpleasant reality by refusing to perceive or face it	A smoker concludes that the evidence linking cigarette use to health problems is scientifically worthless
Fantasy	Gratifying frustrated desires by imaginary achievements	A socially inept and inhibited young man imagines himself chosen by a group of women to provide them with sexual satisfaction
Intellectualization (isolation)	Cutting off emotion from hurtful situations or separating incompatible attitudes so that they appear unrelated	A prisoner on death row awaiting execution resists appeal on his behalf and coldly insists that the letter of the law be followed
Undoing	Atoning for or trying to magically dispel unacceptable desires or acts	A teenager who feels guilty about masturbation ritually touches door knobs a prescribed number of times following each occurrence of the act
Overcompensation	Covering up felt weakness by emphasizing some desirable characteristics, or making up for frustration in one area by overgratification in another	A dangerously overweight woman goes on eating binges when she feels neglected by her husband

SOURCE: Adapted from Carson, R. C., Butcher, J. N., & Coleman, J. C. (1988). *Abnormal psychology and modern life.* Glenview, IL: Scott, Foresman. Copyright © 1988 by Scott, Foresman and Company. Adapted by permission of the publisher.
NOTE: See Table 12.1 on page 497 for another list of defence mechanisms.

Rather than perceiving themselves, the world, and the future accurately, most people regard themselves, their circumstances, and the future as considerably more positive than is objectively likely. . . . These illusions are not merely characteristic of human thought; they appear actually to be adaptive, promoting rather than undermining good mental health.
SHELLEY TAYLOR

people to delay facing up to their problems (Weinberger, 1990). For example, if you were to block out obvious warning signs of cancer or diabetes and fail to obtain needed medical care, your defensive behaviour could be fatal. Third, defences such as denial and fantasy represent wishful thinking, which is likely to accomplish little (Bolger, 1990).

Although defensive behaviour tends to be relatively unhealthful, Shelley Taylor and Jonathon Brown (1988, 1994) have reviewed several lines of evidence suggesting that "positive illusions" may be adaptive for mental health and well-being (Taylor et al., 2003). First, they note that "normal" people tend to have overly favourable self-images. In contrast, depressed subjects exhibit less favourable—but more realistic—self-concepts. Second, normal subjects overestimate the degree to which they control chance events. In comparison, depressed subjects are less prone to this illusion of control. Third, normal individuals are more likely than depressed subjects to display unrealistic optimism in making projections about the future.

The findings on whether positive illusions are healthy are contradictory and controversial (Asendorpf & Ostendorf, 1998; Colvin, Block, & Funder, 1995), so it is hard to make sweeping generalizations about the adaptive value of self-deception. Roy Baumeister (1989) theorizes that it's all a matter of degree and that there is an "optimal margin of illusion." According to Baumeister, extreme distortions of reality are maladaptive, but small illusions are often beneficial.

Constructive Coping 11G

Our discussion thus far has focused on coping strategies that usually are less than ideal. Of course, people also exhibit many healthful strategies for dealing with

stress. We'll use the term *constructive coping* **to refer to relatively healthful efforts that people make to deal with stressful events.** No strategy of coping can *guarantee* a successful outcome. Even the healthiest coping responses may turn out to be ineffective in some circumstances (Folkman & Moskowitz, 2004). Thus, the concept of constructive coping is simply meant to connote a healthful, positive approach, without promising success.

What makes certain coping strategies constructive? Frankly, it's a grey area in which psychologists' opinions vary to some extent. Nonetheless, a consensus about the nature of constructive coping has emerged from the sizable literature on stress management. Key themes in this literature include the following:

1. Constructive coping involves confronting problems directly. It is task relevant and action oriented. It entails a conscious effort to rationally evaluate your options so that you can try to solve your problems.

2. Constructive coping is based on reasonably realistic appraisals of your stress and coping resources. A little self-deception may sometimes be adaptive, but excessive self-deception and highly unrealistic negative thinking are not.

3. Constructive coping involves learning to recognize, and in some cases inhibit, potentially disruptive emotional reactions to stress.

4. Constructive coping includes making efforts to ensure that your body is not especially vulnerable to the possibly damaging effects of stress.

These principles provide a rather general and abstract picture of constructive coping. We'll look at patterns of constructive coping in more detail in the Personal Application, which discusses various stress management strategies that people can use.

CONCEPT CHECK 13.3

Identifying More Defence Mechanisms

In the last chapter you checked your understanding of several defence mechanisms by identifying instances of them in a story. In this chapter, you've learned about five additional defence mechanisms that are sometimes used as ways of coping with stress. Check your understanding of these defence mechanisms by identifying them in the story below. Each example of a defence mechanism is underlined, with a number next to it. Write the name of the defence mechanism exemplified in each case in the numbered spaces after the story. The answers are in Appendix A.

The guys at work have been trying to break it to me gently that they think my job's on the line because I've missed work too many days this year. I don't know how they came up with that idea; I've got nothing to worry about. (1.) Besides, every day I missed, I always did a lot of cleaning up and other chores around the house here. (2.) One of these days the boss will finally recognize how really valuable I am to the company, and I'll be getting a big promotion. (3.) Anyway, since the guys have been dropping these hints about my not missing any more days, I've been trying really hard to make a good impression by saying "Hi" to everyone I see, especially the boss, and telling jokes. (4.) You know, it's really pretty interesting to observe how all these relationships unfold between guys who work together and the people who manage them. (5.)

1. _____   4. _____

2. _____   5. _____

3. _____

The Effects of Stress on Psychological Functioning

People struggle with many stresses every day. Most stresses come and go without leaving any enduring imprint. However, when stress is severe or when many stressful demands pile up, one's psychological functioning may be affected.

Research on the effects of stress has focused mainly on negative outcomes, so our coverage is slanted in that direction. However, it's important to emphasize that stress is not inherently bad. You would probably suffocate from boredom if you lived a stress-free existence. Stress makes life challenging and interesting. Along the way, though, stress can be harrowing, sometimes leading to impairments in performance, to burnout, and to other problems.

Impaired Task Performance

Frequently, stress takes its toll on the ability to perform effectively on a task at hand. For instance, Roy Baumeister's work shows how pressure can interfere with performance. Baumeister's (1984) theory assumes that pressure to perform often makes people self-conscious and that this elevated self-consciousness disrupts their attention. He found support for his theory in a series of laboratory experiments in which he manipulated the pressure to perform well on a simple perceptual-motor task and found that many people tend to "choke" under pressure (Butler & Baumeister, 1998; Baumeister, 1984). His theory has also received some support in studies of the past performance of professional sports teams (Baumeister, 1995; Baumeister & Steinhilber, 1984). Pressure-

induced performance decrements have also been found in studies of mathematical problem-solving and simple sports tasks (Beilock et al., 2002, 2004).

Other research suggests that Baumeister is on the right track in looking to *attention* to explain how stress impairs task performance. In a study of stress and decision making, Keinan (1987) found that stress disrupted two out of the three aspects of attention measured in the study. Stress increased subjects' tendency (1) to jump to a conclusion too quickly without considering all their options and (2) to do an unsystematic, poorly organized review of their available options. In a more recent study, Keinan and colleagues (1999) found that stress impaired performance on cognitive tasks. The results suggested that stress makes it harder for people to suppress competing thoughts. Research also suggests that stress can have detrimental effects on certain memory functions (Beilock & Carr, 2005; Kellog, Hopko, & Ashcraft, 1999; Klein & Boals, 2001; Shors, 2004).

Burnout

Burnout is an overused buzzword that means different things to different people. Nonetheless, a few researchers have described burnout in a systematic way that has facilitated scientific study of the syndrome (Maslach & Leiter, 1997; Pines, 1993). **Burnout involves physical and emotional exhaustion, cynicism, and a lowered sense of self-efficacy that can be brought on gradually by chronic work-related stress.** Exhaustion, which is central to burnout,

Web Link 13.3

National Center for PTSD
http://www.dartmouth.edu/dms/ptsd/Index.html

This site offers numerous resources devoted to post-traumatic stress disorder. Visitors also have access to the PILOTS database, a free searchable guide to the worldwide literature on traumatic stress.

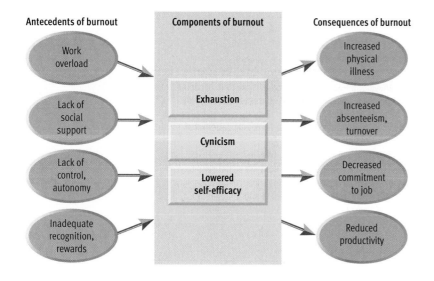

Antecedents of burnout	Components of burnout	Consequences of burnout
Work overload	Exhaustion	Increased physical illness
Lack of social support	Cynicism	Increased absenteeism, turnover
Lack of control, autonomy	Lowered self-efficacy	Decreased commitment to job
Inadequate recognition, rewards		Reduced productivity

Figure 13.7

The antecedents, components, and consequences of burnout. Christina Maslach and Michael Leiter have developed a systematic model of burnout that specifies the antecedents, components, and consequences of burnout. The antecedents on the left in the diagram are the stressful features of the work environment that cause burnout. The burnout syndrome itself consists of the three components shown in the centre of the diagram. Some of the unfortunate results of burnout are listed on the right. (Based on Leiter & Maslach, 2001)

Web Link 13.4

Disaster Psychiatry
http://www.psych.org/disasterpsych/

In light of the traumatic terrorist attacks on 9/11 and their aftermath, the importance of first-rate information about how to respond to disasters is obvious. This site, maintained by the American Psychiatric Association, provides many valuable insights and links related to professional assistance at times of major emergencies.

Web Link 13.5

David Baldwin's Trauma Information Pages
http://www.trauma-pages.com/

This site has long been recognized as the premier repository for Web-based and other resources relating to emotional trauma, traumatic stress, and post-traumatic stress disorder. David Baldwin has assembled more than 1000 links to information about these issues.

includes chronic fatigue, weakness, and low energy. Cynicism is manifested in highly negative attitudes toward oneself, one's work, and life in general. Reduced self-efficacy involves declining feelings of competence at work, which give way to feelings of hopelessness and helplessness.

What causes burnout? Factors in the workplace that appear to promote burnout include work overload, struggling with interpersonal conflicts at work, lack of control over work responsibilities and outcomes, and inadequate recognition for one's work (Leiter & Maslach, 2001; Maslach & Leiter, 2005; see Figure 13.7). A recent study by Statistics Canada (2003c) revealed a set of factors reported by Canadian workers that served as sources of workplace stress. One-third of respondents cited too many demands or work hours as the major source of stress. Other important sources of workplace stress included fear of job loss (13%), poor interpersonal relations at work (15%), and risk of injury (13%). This latter source was especially enhanced among workers who worked rotating shifts (you may recall that we discussed some of the difficulties faced by shift workers in Chapter 5). As you might expect, burnout is associated with increased absenteeism and reduced productivity at work, as well as increased vulnerability to a variety of health problems (Maslach & Leiter, 2000). Burnout is a potential problem in a wide variety of occupations (Lee & Ashforth, 1996).

Post-Traumatic Stress Disorders

Extremely stressful, traumatic incidents can leave a lasting imprint on victims' psychological functioning. The *post-traumatic stress disorder (PTSD)* involves enduring psychological disturbance attributed to the experience of a major traumatic event. Researchers began to appreciate the frequency and severity of post-traumatic stress disorders after the Vietnam War ended in 1975 and a great many psychologically scarred veterans returned home. These veterans displayed a diverse array of psychological problems and symptoms that in many cases lingered much longer than expected (Schlenger et al., 1992).

Although highlighted in the context of the Vietnam War, post-traumatic stress disorders are associated with other types of events including rape, assault, witnessing a death, and so on. Unfortunately, traumatic events such as these appear to be much more common than widely assumed. A survey conducted by Murray Stein and his colleagues (Stein et al, 1997), including University of Manitoba researcher Andrea Hazen, assessed the frequency of experience of various traumatic events (see Figure 13.8). We will discuss PTSD in more detail in Chapter 14.

Psychological Problems and Disorders

Post-traumatic stress disorders are caused by a single episode of extreme stress. Of greater relevance to most of us are the effects of chronic, prolonged, everyday stress. On the basis of clinical impressions, psychologists have long suspected that chronic stress might contribute to many types of psychological problems and mental disorders. Since the late 1960s, advances in the measurement of stress have allowed researchers to verify these suspicions in empirical studies. In the domain of common psychological problems, studies indicate that stress may contribute to poor academic performance (Akgun & Ciarrochi, 2003; Dawod, 1995), insomnia and other sleep disturbances (Vgontzas, Bixler, & Kales, 2000), sexual difficulties (Lemack, Uzzo, & Poppas, 1998), alcohol abuse (Colder, 2001), and drug abuse (Franco, Hubbard, & Martin, 1998; Goeders, 2004).

Above and beyond these everyday problems, research reveals that stress often contributes to the onset of full-fledged psychological disorders, including depression (Kessler, 1997; Rehm, Wagner, & Ivans-Tyndal, 2001), schizophrenia (Fowles, 1992), anxiety disorders (Falsetti & Ballenger, 1998; McGlashan & Hoffman, 2000), and eating disorders (Cooper, 1995). We'll discuss these relations between stress and mental disorders in detail in Chapter 14. Of course, stress is only one of many factors that may contribute to psychological disorders. Nonetheless, it's sobering to realize that stress can have a dramatic impact on one's mental health.

Positive Effects

The effects of stress are not entirely negative. Recent years have brought increased interest in the positive aspects of the stress process, including favourable outcomes that follow in the wake of stress (Folkman & Moskowitz, 2000). To some extent, the new focus on the possible benefits of stress reflects a new emphasis on "positive psychology." As we noted in Chapter 10, some theorists have argued that the field of psychology has historically devoted too much attention to pathology and suffering (Seligman & Csikszentmihalyi, 2000). The advocates of positive psychology argue for increased research on well-being, hope, courage, perseverance, tolerance, and other human strengths and virtues (Seligman, 2003). One of these strengths is resilience in the face of stress.

Recent research on resilience suggests that stress can promote personal growth or self-improvement (Tedeschi, Park, & Calhoun, 1998). For example, studies of people grappling with major health problems show that the majority of respondents report that they derived benefits from their adversity (Tennen & Affleck, 1999). Stressful events sometimes force people to develop new skills, re-evaluate priorities, learn new insights, and acquire new strengths. In other words, the adaptation process initiated by

stress may lead to personal changes that are changes for the better. Confronting and conquering a stressful challenge may lead to improvements in specific coping abilities and to an enhanced self-concept. Moreover, even if people do not conquer stressors, they may be able to learn from their mistakes. Thus, researchers have begun to explore the growth potential of stressful events (Calhoun & Tedeschi, 2001; Park, 1998; Park & Fenster, 2004).

Figure 13.8

The prevalence of traumatic events. We tend to think that traumatic events are relatively unusual and infrequent, but research by Stein et al. (1997) suggests otherwise. They interviewed over 1000 people in Winnipeg, and found that 74.2% of the women and 81.3% of the men reported experiencing at least one highly traumatic event. The percentage of respondents reporting specific types of traumatic events are summarized in this graph. (Based on data from Stein et al., 1997)

REVIEW OF KEY POINTS

- Several lines of research, including Baumeister's work on choking under pressure, suggest that stress can interfere with task performance. Burnout involves exhaustion, cynicism, and lowered self-efficacy as a result of chronic work-related stress.

- Post-traumatic stress disorders are disturbances that surface in the aftermath of a major stressful event. PTSD appears to be fairly common and can be caused by a diverse array of traumatic experiences, ranging from auto accidents to natural disasters.

- Stress can contribute to a host of common problems, such as poor academic performance, insomnia, and sexual difficulties. Stress has also been related to the development of various psychological disorders, including depression, schizophrenia, anxiety disorders, and eating disorders. Research on the effects of stress has concentrated on negative outcomes, but positive effects may also occur.

Major disasters such as the 1998 ice storm in central and eastern Canada are just one of about a half-dozen types of calamitous events that can lead to post-traumatic stress disorder.

Stress, Coping, and Health

The Effects of Stress on Physical Health

PREVIEW QUESTIONS

- What is the Type A personality, and how is hostility related to heart disease?
- Can stress trigger emotional reactions that cause heart attacks?
- How is depression related to heart disease?
- How does stress affect immune function and vulnerability to the common cold?
- How strong is the association between stress and illness?

The effects of stress are not limited to mental health. Stress can also have an impact on one's physical health. This suggestion is reflected in data collected by Statistics Canada (2004d), which found that adults who had suffered high stress in 1994–95 had a higher probability of developing a number of illnesses by 2000–01. Some of the chronic conditions implicated were arthritis, emphysema, ulcers, back problems, heart disease in males, and asthma and migraines in females.

The idea that stress can contribute to physical ailments is not entirely new. Evidence that stress can cause physical illness began to accumulate back in the 1930s. By the 1950s, the concept of *psychosomatic disease* was widely accepted. **Psychosomatic diseases were genuine physical ailments that were thought to be caused in part by stress and other psychological factors.** The classic psychosomatic illnesses were high blood pressure, peptic ulcers, asthma, skin disorders such as eczema and hives, and migraine and tension headaches (Kaplan, 1989; Rogers, Fricchione, & Reich, 1999). Please note, however, these diseases were not regarded as *imagined* physical ailments. The term *psychosomatic* has often been misused to refer to physical ailments that are "all in one's head," but that is an entirely different syndrome (see Chapter 14). Rather, psychosomatic diseases were viewed as *authentic* organic maladies that were heavily stress-related.

Since the 1970s, the concept of psychosomatic disease has gradually fallen into disuse because research has shown that stress can contribute to the development of a diverse array of other diseases previously believed to be purely physiological in origin (Dougall & Baum, 2001; Hubbard & Workman, 1998). Thus, it has become apparent that there is nothing unique about the psychosomatic diseases that requires a special category. Modern evidence continues to demonstrate that the classic psychosomatic diseases are influenced by stress, but as you will see, so are a host of other diseases (Levenson et al., 1999). In this section we'll look at the evidence on the apparent link between stress and physical illness, beginning with heart disease, which is a leading cause of death in North America.

Type A Personality, Hostility, and Heart Disease

Heart disease is one of the leading causes of death in North America. In Canada in 1997 heart disease was second (a very close second) only to cancer (Statistics Canada, n.d.). *Coronary heart disease* involves a reduction in blood flow in the coronary arteries, which supply the heart with blood. This type of heart disease accounts for about 90% of heart-related deaths.

Atherosclerosis is the principal cause of coronary heart disease. This condition is characterized by a gradual narrowing of the coronary arteries. A build-up of fatty deposits and other debris on the inner walls of the arteries is the usual cause of this narrowing. Atherosclerosis progresses slowly over a period of years. However, when a narrowed coronary artery is blocked completely (by a blood clot, for instance), the abrupt interruption of blood flow can produce a heart attack. Atherosclerosis is more prevalent in men than women and tends to increase with age. Other established risk factors for atherosclerosis include smoking, lack of exercise, high cholesterol levels, and high blood pressure (Greenland et al., 2003; Ketterer & Randall, 2000; Khot et al., 2003; Stoney, 2003).

Recently, attention has shifted to the possibility that inflammation may contribute to atherosclerosis and elevated coronary risk (Roivainen et al., 2000). Evidence is mounting that inflammation plays a key role in the initiation and progression of atherosclerosis, as well as the acute complications that trigger heart attacks (Albert et al., 2002; Libby, Ridker, & Maseri, 2002). Fortunately, researchers have found a marker—levels of C-reactive protein (CRP) in the blood—that may help physicians estimate individuals' coronary risk more accurately than was possible previously (Ridker, 2001). Figure 13.9 shows how combined levels of CRP and cholesterol appear to be related to coronary risk.

Research on the relationship between *psychological* factors and heart attacks began in the 1960s and 1970s, when a pair of cardiologists, Meyer Friedman and Ray Rosenman (1974), discovered an apparent connection between coronary risk and a syndrome they called the *Type A personality*, which involves self-imposed stress and intense reactions to stress. **The *Type A personality* includes three elements: (1) a strong competitive orientation, (2) impatience and time urgency, and (3) anger and hostility.** Type A's are ambitious, hard-driving perfectionists who are exceedingly time-conscious. They routinely try to do several things at once. They fidget frantically over the briefest delays. Often they are highly competitive, achievement-oriented workaholics who drive themselves with many deadlines. They are easily irritated and are quick to anger. In contrast, **the *Type B personality* is marked by relatively relaxed, patient, easygoing, amicable behaviour.** Type B's are less hurried, less competitive, and less easily angered than Type A's.

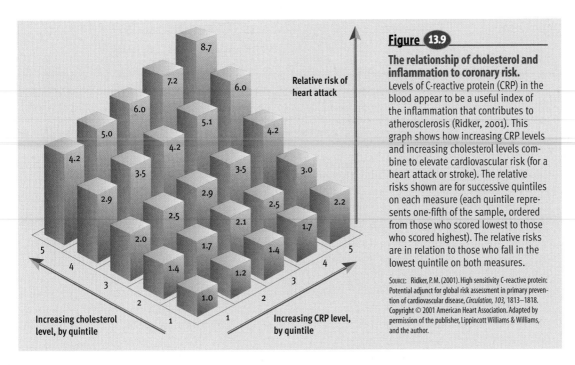

Figure 13.9

The relationship of cholesterol and inflammation to coronary risk.
Levels of C-reactive protein (CRP) in the blood appear to be a useful index of the inflammation that contributes to atherosclerosis (Ridker, 2001). This graph shows how increasing CRP levels and increasing cholesterol levels combine to elevate cardiovascular risk (for a heart attack or stroke). The relative risks shown are for successive quintiles on each measure (each quintile represents one-fifth of the sample, ordered from those who scored lowest to those who scored highest). The relative risks are in relation to those who fall in the lowest quintile on both measures.

SOURCE: Ridker, P.M. (2001). High sensitivity C-reactive protein: Potential adjunct for global risk assessment in primary prevention of cardiovascular disease, *Circulation, 103,* 1813–1818. Copyright © 2001 American Heart Association. Adapted by permission of the publisher, Lippincott Williams & Williams, and the author.

Decades of research uncovered a tantalizingly modest correlation between Type A behaviour and increased coronary risk. More often than not, studies found an association between Type A personality and an elevated incidence of heart disease, but the findings were not as strong or as consistent as expected (Ragland & Brand, 1988; Smith & Gallo, 2001). However, in recent years, researchers have found a stronger link between personality and coronary risk by focusing on a specific component of the Type A personality—*anger and hostility* (Eaker et al., 2004; Niaura et al., 2002; Rozanski, Blumenthal, & Kaplan, 1999). For example, in one study of almost 13 000 men and women who had no prior history of heart disease (Williams et al., 2000), investigators found an elevated incidence of heart attacks among participants who exhibited an angry temperament. The participants, who were followed for a median period of 4.5 years, were classified as being low (37.1%), moderate (55.2%), or high (7.7%) in anger. Among participants with normal blood pressure, the high-anger subjects experienced almost three times as many coronary events as the low-anger subjects (see Figure 13.10). In another study, CT scans were used to look for signs of atherosclerosis in a sample of 374 young men and women whose hostility had been assessed a decade earlier when they were 18 to 30 years old (Irabarren et al., 2000). Participants with above-average hostility scores were twice as likely to exhibit atherosclerosis as participants with below-average hostility scores. Thus, recent research suggests that hostility may be the crucial toxic element in the Type A syndrome.

Emotional Reactions, Depression, and Heart Disease

Although work on personality risk factors has dominated research on how psychological functioning contributes to heart disease, recent studies suggest that emotional reactions may also be critical. *One line of research has supported the hypothesis that transient mental stress and the resulting emotions that people experience can tax the heart.* Based on anecdotal evidence, cardiologists and laypersons have long voiced suspicions that strong emotional reactions might trigger

Figure 13.10

Anger and coronary risk.
Working with a large sample of healthy men and women who were followed for a median of 4.5 years, Williams et al. (2000) found an association between anger and the likelihood of a coronary event. Among subjects who manifested normal blood pressure at the beginning of the study, a moderate anger level was associated with a 36% increase in coronary attacks and a high level of anger nearly tripled participants' risk for coronary disease. (Based on data in Williams et al., 2000)

heart attacks in individuals with coronary disease, but it has been difficult to document this connection. However, advances in cardiac monitoring have facilitated investigation of the issue.

As suspected, laboratory experiments with cardiology patients have shown that brief periods of mental stress can trigger acute symptoms of heart disease (Gottdiener et al., 1994). Overall, the evidence suggests that mental stress can elicit cardiac symptoms in about 30%–70% of patients with stable coronary disease (Kop, Gottdiener, & Krantz, 2001). Moreover, research indicates that these patients have a higher risk for heart attack than the cardiology patients who do not manifest ischemia in response to mental stress (Krantz et al., 2000). In a study that approached the issue from another angle, 660 patients who experienced a nonfatal heart attack were subsequently interviewed about events that occurred in the six hours prior to the onset of their heart attack (Moller et al., 1999). The interviews suggested that episodes of anger were a frequent trigger for the participants' heart attacks. Taken together, these studies suggest that emotional reactions to stressful events may precipitate heart attacks in people with coronary disease (Strike & Steptoe, 2005).

Another line of research has recently implicated depression as a risk factor for heart disease (Krantz & McCeney, 2002). *Depressive disorders,* which are characterized by persistent feelings of sadness and despair, are a fairly common form of mental illness (see Chapter 14). Elevated rates of depression have been found among patients suffering from heart disease in many studies, but most theorists explained this correlation by asserting that being diagnosed with heart disease makes people depressed. Recent evidence, however, suggests that the causal relations may be just the opposite—*that the emotional dysfunction of depression may cause heart disease* (Frasure-Smith & Lesperance, 2005; Thomas, Kalaria, & O'Brien, 2004). For example, Pratt et al. (1996) examined a large sample of people 13 years after they were screened for depression. They found that participants who were depressed at the time of the original study were four times more likely than others to have experienced a heart attack during the intervening 13 years. Since the participants' depressive disorders preceded their heart attacks, we cannot argue that their heart disease caused their depression. Other studies have found that depression roughly doubles one's chances of developing heart disease (Cohen & Alderman, 2001; Ford et al., 1998). Moreover, the predictive link between depression and heart disease remains even after controlling for the effects of smoking (Glassman & Shapiro, 1998).

Stress, Other Diseases, and Immune Functioning

The development of questionnaires to measure life stress has allowed researchers to look for correlations between stress and a variety of diseases. These researchers have uncovered many connections between stress and illness. For example, Zautra and Smith (2001) found an association between life stress and the course of rheumatoid arthritis. Another study found an association between stressful life events and the emergence of lower back pain (Lampe et al., 1998). Other studies have connected stress to the development of diabetes (Landel-Graham, Yount, & Rudnicki, 2003), herpes (Padgett & Sheridan, 2000), and flare-ups of irritable bowel syndrome (Blanchard & Keefer, 2003).

These are just a handful of representative examples of studies relating stress to physical diseases. Table 13.3 provides a longer list of health problems that have been linked to stress. Many of these stress–illness connections are based on tentative or inconsistent findings, but the sheer length and diversity of the list is remarkable. Why should stress increase the

Table 13.3 Health Problems That May Be Linked to Stress

Health Problem	Representative Evidence
AIDS	Ironson et al. (1994)
Appendicitis	Creed (1989)
Asthma	Sriram & Silverman (1998)
Cancer	Holland & Lewis (1993)
Chronic back pain	Lampe et al. (1998)
Common cold	Stone et al. (1992)
Complications of pregnancy	Dunkel-Schetter et al. (2001)
Coronary heart disease	Orth-Gomer et al. (2000)
Diabetes	Riazi & Bradley (2000)
Epileptic seizures	Kelly & Schramke (2000)
Hemophilia	Buxton et al. (1981)
Herpes virus	Padgett & Sheridan (2000)
Hypertension	Pickering et al. (1996)
Hyperthyroidism	Yang, Liu, & Zang (2000)
Inflammatory bowel disease	Searle & Bennett (2001)
Migraine headaches	Ramadan (2000)
Multiple sclerosis	Grant et al. (1989)
Periodontal disease	Marcenes & Sheiham (1992)
Premenstrual distress	Wu-Holt & Boutte (1994)
Rheumatoid arthritis	Huyser & Parker (1998)
Skin disorders	Arnold (2000)
Stroke	Harmsen et al. (1990)
Ulcers	Murison (2001)
Vaginal infections	Williams & Deffenbacher (1983)

risk for so many kinds of illness? A partial answer may lie in immune functioning.

The apparent link between stress and many types of illness raises the possibility that stress may undermine immune functioning. **The *immune response* is the body's defensive reaction to invasion by bacteria, viral agents, or other foreign substances.** The immune response works to protect the body from many forms of disease. Immune reactions are multifaceted, but they depend heavily on actions initiated by specialized white blood cells, called *lymphocytes*.

A wealth of studies indicate that experimentally induced stress can impair immune functioning *in animals* (Moynihan & Ader, 1996). That is, stressors such as crowding, shock, food restriction, and restraint reduce various aspects of immune reactivity in laboratory animals (Chiappelli & Hodgson, 2000).

Studies by Janice Kiecolt-Glaser and her colleagues have also related stress to suppressed immune activity *in humans* (Kiecolt-Glaser & Glaser, 1995). In one study, medical students provided researchers with blood samples so that their immune response could be assessed (Kiecolt-Glaser et al., 1984). The students provided the baseline sample a month before final exams and contributed the "high-stress" sample on the first day of their finals. The subjects also responded to the SRRS as a measure of recent stress. Reduced levels of immune activity were found during the extremely stressful finals week. Reduced immune activity was also correlated with higher scores on the SRRS. Recent research by Canadian psychologists has added to the evidence linking stress with immune functioning. For example, a recent analysis by Suzanne Segerstrom and the University of British Columbia's Gregory Miller found that acute (lasting a few minutes) and chronic or more long-term stressors have different effects on the body's immune system (Segerstrom & Miller, 2004), and a team of researchers from Ottawa found that the lengthy anticipatory phase before some protracted events, such as Ph.D. oral defence that has been scheduled far in advance, produces distinct neuroendocrine and immune alterations (Lacey et al., 2000).

In a thorough review of 30 years of research on stress and immunity, Segerstrom and Miller (2004) conclude that chronic stress can reduce both *cellular immune* responses (which attack intracellular pathogens, such as viruses) and *humoral immune responses* (which attack extracellular pathogens, such as bacteria). They also report that the *duration* of a stressful event is a key factor determining its impact on immune function. Long-lasting stressors, such as caring for a seriously ill spouse or enduring unemployment for months, are associated with greater immune suppression than relatively brief stressors. Underscoring the importance of the link between stress and immune function, a recent study found evidence that chronic stress may produce *premature aging of immune system cells* (Epel et al., 2004). The study revealed that women who were dealing with heavy, long-term stress (caring for a child with a serious, chronic illness, such as cerebral palsy) had immune system cells that appeared to be a decade older than their chronological age, perhaps shedding light for the first time on why people under severe stress often look old and haggard.

Connecting Stress to the Common Cold

Investigators: Sheldon Cohen (Carnegie-Mellon University), David A. J. Tyrrell (Medical Research Council, Salisbury, England), and Andrew P. Smith (University of Wales College of Cardiff)

Source: Negative life events, perceived stress, negative affect, and susceptibility to the common cold. *Journal of Personality and Social Psychology*, 1993, *64*, 131–140.

Researchers have consistently found an association between stress and suppressed immune functioning, but as Sheldon Cohen and his colleagues note, "It is unclear whether the immune changes related to stress in these studies are of the type or magnitude that would influence susceptibility to infection" (p. 131). The handful of studies that have linked stress to actual infections have been plagued by a number of methodological shortcomings (Cohen & Williamson, 1991). For instance, these studies have usually failed to control for variations in subjects' personality, health habits, exposure to infected friends and family, and pre-existing antibodies to the virus used. Hence, Cohen, Tyrrell, and Smith set out to conduct a more carefully controlled study of whether stress elevates vulnerability to infectious disease.

Method

Participants and procedure. The subjects were 154 men and 266 women who volunteered to participate in trials at the Medical Research Council's Common Cold Unit in Salisbury, England, where they were given free accommodations and quarantined for nine days. The volunteers' ages ranged from 18 to 54 (mean = 34). During their first two days on the unit, the participants were given medical exams to verify that they were in good health and were administered a series of questionnaires to assess their recent stress, aspects of their personality, and various health habits. They were then given—with their informed consent—nasal drops that contained either a respiratory virus or a harmless saline solution. A double-blind procedure was used so that neither the subjects nor the investigators knew who received the virus. The subjects were subsequently followed for six days to see whether they developed a viral infection (based on cultures of their nasal secretions) or cold symptoms (based on daily temperature readings for fever and clinical examinations for sore throat, nasal stuffiness, and so on).

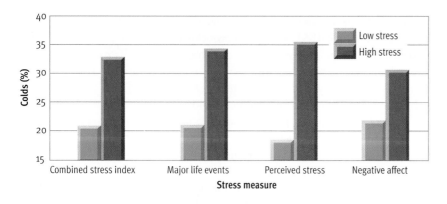

Figure 13.11

Stress and vulnerability to the common cold. After exposing subjects to a respiratory virus, Cohen, Tyrrell, and Smith (1993) compared low-stress and high-stress subjects to see if the latter were more susceptible to colds. The data shown here are for subjects who did *not* have an infected roommate. As you can see, all four measures of stress were predictive of the incidence of colds, with high-stress subjects consistently developing more colds.

SOURCE: Adapted from Cohen, S., Tyrrell, D. A. J., & Smith, A. P. (1993). Negative life events, perceived stress, negative affect, and susceptibility to the common cold. *Journal of Personality and Social Psychology, 64,* 131–140. Copyright © 1993 by the American Psychological Association. Reprinted by permission of the author.

Measurement instruments. Participants provided information about their recent stress by filling out a major life events scale similar to the SRRS, a measure of their subjective, perceived stress, and an assessment of their emotional tone during the previous week. These scales were examined individually and combined into an overall stress index. The subjects also responded to personality scales that measured their self-esteem, self-efficacy, and extraversion. Their health practices were assessed with questionnaires that inquired about their exercise, dietary, sleep, and alcohol consumption habits.

Results

Participants were divided into high-stress and low-stress subjects based on whether they scored above or below the median on each of the stress scales. When the entire sample was analyzed, high-stress subjects were somewhat more likely than low-stress subjects to develop a viral infection and to manifest cold symptoms. However, the results revealed that being housed with a person who became infected (and thus infectious) partly obscured the effects of stress on colds, because these subjects were re-exposed to the virus (from their roommate's sneezing, coughing, and so on). Hence, the most telling comparisons were the analyses of cold rates in the subsample of subjects who did not have an infectious roommate, which are shown in Figure 13.11. In these comparisons, on all the stress measures high-stress subjects were more likely to develop colds than low-stress subjects. The associations between high stress and an increased incidence of colds were still significant even

after the investigators controlled statistically for variations in subjects' personality and health practices.

Discussion

The authors assert that their control procedures eliminated a variety of possible alternative explanations for the apparent link between stress and vulnerability to infection. Hence they conclude that their study demonstrates "what up to now has been somewhat speculative, that psychological stress is associated with increased susceptibility to biologically verified infectious disease processes" (p. 139).

Comment

As you can see in Figure 13.11, the differences between the high-stress and low-stress subjects in the incidence of colds were not particularly large, but as we will discuss momentarily, these results are consistent with other research suggesting that the association between stress and illness is modest in strength. What makes this study outstanding is the enormous effort that the researchers went through to control for possible confounding variables. The quarantine conditions, which were highly unusual, obviously reduced the likelihood that participants would develop colds from other sources besides the virus tested. The monitoring of infections and colds with reliable biological measures (daily temperature readings, nasal cultures, and so on) circumvented the possibility that high-stress subjects might simply report more subjective symptoms of illness than low-stress subjects. By statistically controlling for subjects' health practices, the investigators eliminated the possibility that the stress–illness association might be due to unhealthy habits (smoking, drinking, and so on) that could undermine immune resistance. The investigators neutralized other possible confounds by using a double-blind procedure and by controlling for various demographic variables, pre-existing antibodies, and personality differences. Given the enormous multiplicity of factors that influence behaviour, one can never control for every possible confound and conduct "the perfect study." However, this study illustrates the great lengths that researchers go to in the hopes of coming close. ■

Sizing Up the Link between Stress and Illness

A wealth of evidence shows that stress is related to physical health, and converging lines of evidence suggest that stress contributes to the *causation* of illness. But we have to put this intriguing finding in perspective. Virtually all of the relevant research is correlational, so it can't demonstrate *conclusively* that

stress causes illness (Smith & Gallo, 2001). Subjects' elevated levels of stress and illness could both be due to a third variable, perhaps some aspect of personality (see Figure 13.12). For instance, some evidence suggests that neuroticism may make people overly prone to interpret events as stressful and overly prone to interpret unpleasant sensations as symptoms of illness, thus inflating the correlation between stress and illness (Watson & Pennebaker, 1989).

In spite of methodological problems favouring inflated correlations, the research in this area consistently indicates that the *strength* of the relationship between stress and health is *modest*. The correlations typically fall in the 0.20s and 0.30s (Cohen, Kessler, & Gordon, 1995). Clearly, stress is not an irresistible force that produces inevitable effects on health. Actually, this fact should come as no surprise, as stress is but one factor operating in a complex network of biopsychosocial determinants of health. Other key factors include one's genetic endowment, exposure to infectious agents and environmental toxins, nutrition, exercise, alcohol and drug use, smoking, use of medical care, and cooperation with medical advice. Furthermore, some people handle stress better than others, which is the matter we turn to next.

Figure 13.12

The stress–illness correlation. One or more aspects of personality, physiology, or memory could play the role of a postulated third variable in the relationship between high stress and high incidence of illness. For example, neuroticism may lead some subjects to view more events as stressful and to remember more illness, thus inflating the apparent correlation between stress and illness.

REVIEW OF KEY POINTS

- Stress appears to play a role in many types of illnesses, not just psychosomatic diseases. The Type A personality has been implicated as a contributing cause of coronary heart disease, but hostility may be the most toxic element of the Type A syndrome. Transient, stress-induced emotional reactions and depression have also been identified as cardiovascular risk factors.

- Researchers have found associations between stress and the onset of a great variety of specific diseases, although the evidence on many is highly tentative. Stress may play a role in a host of diseases because it can temporarily suppress the effectiveness of the immune system. The Featured Study provided a well-controlled demonstration of how stress may increase susceptibility to the common cold.

- Although there's little doubt that stress can contribute to the development of physical illness, the link between stress and illness is modest. Stress is only one factor in a complex network of biopsychosocial variables that shape health.

Factors Moderating the Impact of Stress

Some people seem to be able to withstand the ravages of stress better than others (Holohan & Moos, 1994). Why? Because a number of *moderator variables* can lessen the impact of stress on physical and mental health. We'll look at three key moderator variables—social support, optimism, and conscientiousness—to shed light on individual differences in how well people tolerate stress.

Social Support

Friends may be good for your health! This startling conclusion emerges from studies on social support as a moderator of stress. **Social support refers to various types of aid and succour provided by members of one's social networks.** In one study, Jemmott and Magloire (1988) examined the effect of social support on immune functioning in a group of students going through the stress of final exams. They found that students who reported stronger social support had higher levels of an antibody that plays a key role in warding off respiratory infections. Positive correlations between high social support and greater immune functioning have also been found in other studies (Uchino, Uno, & Holt-Lunstad, 1999).

Over the last two decades, a vast body of studies have found evidence that social support is favourably related to physical health (Rutledge et al., 2004; Uchino, 2004; Wills & Fegan, 2001). Social support seems to be good medicine for the mind as well as the body, as most studies also find an association between social support and mental health (Davis, Morris, & Kraus, 1998). It appears that social support serves as a protective buffer during times of high stress, reducing the negative impact of stressful events—and that social support has its own positive effects on health, which may be apparent even when people aren't under great stress (Peirce et al., 1996; Wills & Fegan, 2001). According to research conducted by the University of British Columbia's Anita DeLongis and her colleagues, the positive effects of support from your spouse may not affect emotions as strongly as the negative effects of strain derived from the relationship (DeLongis et al., 2004). It is clear, however, that support from one's spouse does positively affect a sense of well-being. The stress-buffering effects of social support were apparent in a study that found that strong social support was a key factor reducing the likelihood of post-traumatic stress disorders among veterans of the Vietnam War (King et al., 1998).

PREVIEW QUESTIONS
- How does social support influence people's health?
- How is optimism related to health?
- How is conscientiousness related to health?

Optimism and Conscientiousness

Defining **optimism** **as a general tendency to expect good outcomes**, Michael Scheier and Charles Carver (1985) found a correlation between optimism and relatively good physical health in a sample of university students. Another study found optimism to be associated with more effective immune functioning (Segerstrom et al., 1998). Research suggests that optimists cope with stress in more adaptive ways than pessimists (Aspinwall, Richter, & Hoffman, 2001; Carver & Scheier, 1999). Optimists are more likely to engage in action-oriented, problem-focused coping. They are more willing than pessimists to seek social support, and they are more likely to emphasize the positive in their appraisals of stressful events. In comparison, pessimists are more likely to deal with stress by giving up or engaging in denial.

In a related line of research, Christopher Peterson and Martin Seligman have studied how people explain bad events (personal setbacks, mishaps, disappointments, and such). They identified a *pessimistic explanatory style* in which people tend to blame setbacks on their own personal shortcomings versus an *optimistic explanatory style,* which leads people to attribute setbacks to temporary situational factors. In two retrospective studies of people born many decades ago, they found an association between this optimistic explanatory style and relatively good health (Peterson, Seligman, & Vaillant, 1988) and increased longevity (Peterson et al., 1998). Many other studies have linked this optimistic explanatory style to superior physical health (Peterson & Bossio, 2001), as well as higher academic achievement, increased job productivity, enhanced athletic performance, and higher marital satisfaction (Gillham et al., 2001).

Optimism versus pessimism is not the only dimension of personality that has been examined as a possible moderator of physical health. Howard Friedman and his colleagues have found evidence that *conscientiousness,* one of the Big Five personality traits discussed in Chapter 12, may have an impact on physical health. Friedman et al. (1993) related personality measures to longevity in the gifted individuals first studied by Lewis Terman (see Chapter 9), who have been followed closely by researchers since 1921. Data were available on six personality traits, which were measured when the subjects were children. The one trait that predicted greater longevity was conscientiousness. Friedman et al. (1993) reasoned, logically enough, that conscientiousness may simply have fostered better health habits, but a follow-up study (Friedman et al., 1995) found little evidence that this was the case. Hence, the investigators have now turned their attention to how conscientiousness may have affected subjects' coping or stress tolerance.

Individual differences among people in social support, optimism, and conscientiousness explain why stress doesn't have the same impact on everyone. Differences in lifestyle may play an even larger role in determining health. We'll examine some critical aspects of lifestyle in the next section.

REVIEW OF KEY POINTS

- There are individual differences in how much stress people can tolerate without experiencing ill effects. Social support is a key moderator of the relationship between stress and both physical and mental health.

- Optimism may lead to more effective coping with stress, whereas pessimism has been related to passive coping and poor health practices. A recent study of Terman's sample of gifted children suggests that conscientiousness is associated with greater longevity.

> "The concept of explanatory style brings hope into the laboratory, where scientists can dissect it in order to understand how it works."
> MARTIN SELIGMAN

Health-Impairing Behaviour

PREVIEW QUESTIONS

- Why does smoking increase mortality?
- What are some examples of links between nutrition and health?
- What are the health benefits of exercise?
- What are some misconceptions about HIV transmission?
- How do health-impairing habits get started?

Some people seem determined to dig an early grave for themselves. They do precisely those things that are bad for their health. For example, some people drink heavily even though they know that they're damaging their liver. Others eat all the wrong foods even though they know that they're increasing their risk of a second heart attack. Behaviour that's downright *self-destructive* is surprisingly common. In this section we'll discuss how health is affected by smoking, nutrition, exercise, and drug use, and we'll look at behavioural factors in AIDS. We'll also discuss *why* people develop health-impairing lifestyles.

Smoking

The smoking of tobacco is widespread in our culture, but the percentage of people who smoke has declined noticeably since the mid-1980s (see Figure 13.13). Nonetheless, in Canada, as of 2004, about 20% of adult men and 17% of adult women continue to smoke regularly (Health Canada, 2004a).

The evidence clearly shows that smokers face a much greater risk of premature death than non-smokers. For example, the average smoker has an estimated life expectancy *13–14 years shorter* than that of a similar nonsmoker (Schmitz & DeLaune, 2005). The overall risk is positively correlated with the number of cigarettes smoked and their tar and nicotine content. Cigar smoking, which has increased dramatically in recent years, elevates health risks almost as much as cigarette smoking (Baker et al., 2000).

Why are mortality rates higher for smokers? Smoking increases the likelihood of developing a surprisingly large range of diseases (Thun, Apicella, & Henley, 2000; Woloshin, Schwartz, & Welch, 2002). Lung cancer and heart disease kill the largest number of smokers. However, smokers also have an elevated risk for oral, bladder, and kidney cancer, as well as cancers of the larynx, esophagus, and pancreas; for arteriosclerosis, hypertension, stroke, and other cardiovascular diseases; and for bronchitis, emphysema, and other pulmonary diseases. Most smokers know about the risks associated with tobacco use, but they tend to underestimate the actual risks as applied to themselves (Ayanian & Cleary, 1999).

The dangers of smoking are not limited to smokers themselves. Family members and co-workers who spend a lot of time around smokers are exposed to *second-hand smoke* or *environmental tobacco smoke*, which can increase their risk for a variety of illnesses, including lung cancer (Wells, 1998), heart disease (Howard et al., 1998), and breast cancer in women (Lash & Aschengrau, 1999). Young children with asthma are particularly vulnerable to the effects of second-hand smoke (Stoddard & Miller, 1995).

Studies show that if people can give up smoking, their health risks decline reasonably quickly (Samet, 1992; Williams et al., 2002; see Figure 13.14). Evidence suggests that most smokers would like to quit but are reluctant to give up a major source of pleasure, and they worry about craving cigarettes, gaining weight, becoming anxious and irritable, and feeling less able to cope with stress (Grunberg, Faraday, & Rahman, 2001).

Unfortunately, it's difficult to give up cigarettes. People who enroll in formal smoking cessation programs aren't any more successful than people who try to quit on their own (Cohen et al., 1989; Swan, Hudmon, & Kroyan, 2003). Long-term success rates are in the vicinity of only 25%, and some studies report even lower figures. For example, in one study of self-quitters, after six months only 3% had maintained complete abstinence from smoking (Hughes et al., 1992). Relapse rates for quitting smoking are often as bad as those seen in efforts to give up heroin or alcohol (Hunt & Matarazzo, 1982). Interestingly, many people fail several or more times before they eventually succeed. Evidence suggests that the readiness to give up smoking builds gradually as people

cycle through periods of abstinence and relapse (Herzog et al., 1999; Prochaska, 1994).

Poor Nutritional Habits

Evidence is accumulating that patterns of nutrition influence susceptibility to a variety of diseases and health problems. In addition to the problems associated with obesity, which we discussed in Chapter 10, other possible connections between eating patterns and health include the following:

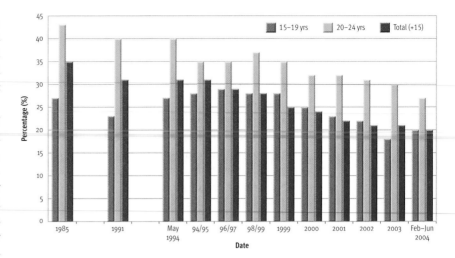

Figure 13.13

The prevalence of smoking in Canada. This graph shows how the percentage of Canadian adults who smoke has declined steadily since the mid-1980s. The figure also illustrates the relatively high incidence of smoking in the 20- to 24-year-old group.

Source: Health Canada (2004a). Canadian Tobacco Use Monitoring Survey (CTUMS). Retrieved June 22, 2005, from http://www.hc-sc.gc.ca/hl-vs/tobac-tabac/research-recherche/stat/ctums-esutc/index_e.html. Data is adapted from the Canadian Tobacco Use Monitoring Survey (CTUMS); Please note: The CTUMS was conducted by Statistics Canada for Health Canada.

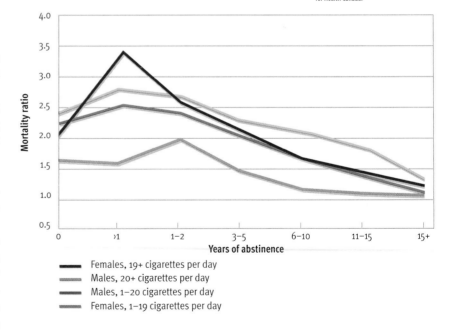

Figure 13.14

Quitting smoking and health risk. Research suggests that various types of health risks associated with smoking decline gradually after people give up tobacco. The data shown here, from the U.S. Surgeon General's (1990) report on smoking, illustrate the overall effects on mortality rates. (Based on data from U.S. Department of Health and Human Services, 1990)

1. Heavy consumption of foods that elevate serum cholesterol level (eggs, cheeses, butter, shellfish, sausage, and the like) appears to increase the risk of cardiovascular disease (Stamler et al., 2000). Eating habits are only one of several factors that influence serum cholesterol level, but they do make an important contribution.

2. Vulnerability to cardiovascular diseases may also be influenced by other dietary factors. For example, low-fibre diets may increase the likelihood of coronary disease (Ludwig et al., 1999; Wolk et al., 1999), and high intake of red and processed meats, sweets, potatoes, and refined grains is associated with increased cardiovascular risk (Hu & Willett, 2002). Recent research indicates that the omega 3 fatty acids found in fish and fish oils offer some protection against coronary disease (Din, Newby, & Flapan, 2004).

3. High salt intake is thought to be a contributing factor in the development of hypertension (Vollmer et al., 2001), although there is still some debate about its exact role.

4. High caffeine consumption may elevate one's risk for hypertension (James, 2004) and for coronary disease (Happonen, Voutilainen, & Salonen, 2004), although the negative effects of caffeine appear relatively modest.

5. High-fat diets have been implicated as possible contributors to some forms of cancer, especially prostate cancer (Rose, 1997), colon and rectal cancer (Shike, 1999), and breast cancer (Wynder et al., 1997). Some studies also suggest that high-fibre diets may reduce one's risk for colon and rectal cancer (Reddy, 1999), but the evidence is not conclusive.

6. Vulnerability to osteoporosis, an abnormal loss of bone mass observed most commonly in postmenopausal women, appears to be elevated by a lifelong pattern of inadequate calcium intake (Kalwarf, Khoury, & Lanphear, 2003).

Of course, nutritional habits interact with other factors—genetics, exercise, environment, and so on—to determine whether one develops a particular disease. Nonetheless, the examples just described indicate that eating habits can influence one's physical health.

Lack of Exercise

There is considerable evidence linking lack of exercise to poor health. Research indicates that regular exercise is associated with increased longevity (Lee, Hsieh, & Paffenbarger, 1995). Why would exercise help people live longer? For one thing, an appropriate exercise program can enhance cardiovascular

fitness and thereby reduce susceptibility to deadly cardiovascular problems (Lee et al., 2001; Phillips, Kiernan, & King, 2001). Second, fitness may indirectly reduce one's risk for a variety of obesity-related health problems, such as diabetes and respiratory difficulties (Epstein et al., 1995). Third, recent studies suggest that physical fitness is also associated with a decreased risk for colon cancer in men and for breast and reproductive cancer in women (Marcus, Bock, & Pinto, 1997; Thune et al., 1997). The apparent link between exercise and reduced cancer risk has been a pleasant surprise for scientists, who are now scrambling to figure out the physiological mechanisms underlying this association. Fourth, exercise can serve as a buffer that reduces the potentially damaging physical effects of stress (Plante, 1999; Plante, Caputo, & Chizmar, 2000). This buffering effect may occur because people high in fitness show less physiological reactivity to stress than those who are less fit. Exercise was one of the most frequently mentioned stress busters when we surveyed Canadian university Web sites. The rates of physical inactivity remain high in Canada (see Figure 13.15). Given its status as a risk factor for many health problems including heart disease and stroke, these figures are a concern for all of us.

Alcohol and Drug Use

Recreational drug use is another common health-impairing habit. The risks associated with the use of various drugs were discussed in detail in Chapter 5. Unlike smoking, poor eating habits, and inactivity, drugs can kill directly and immediately when they are taken in an overdose or when they impair the user enough to cause an accident. In the long run, various recreational drugs may also elevate one's risk for infectious diseases; respiratory, pulmonary, and cardiovascular diseases; liver disease; gastrointestinal problems; cancer; neurological disorders; and pregnancy complications (see Chapter 5). Ironically, the greatest physical damage in the population as a whole is caused by alcohol, the one recreational drug that's legal.

Behaviour and AIDS

At present, some of the most problematic links between behaviour and health may be those related to AIDS. AIDS stands for *acquired immune deficiency syndrome,* a disorder in which the immune system is gradually weakened and eventually disabled by the human immunodeficiency virus (HIV). Being infected with the HIV virus is *not* equivalent to having AIDS. AIDS is the final stage of the HIV infection process, typically manifested about ten years after the original infection (Carey & Vanable, 2003; Treisman, 1999). With the onset of AIDS, one is left virtually defenceless against a host of opportunistic infectious agents. AIDS inflicts its harm indirectly by opening the door to other diseases. The symptoms of AIDS vary widely depending on the specific constellation of diseases that one develops (Cunningham & Selwyn, 2005). Unfortunately, the worldwide prevalence of this deadly disease continues to increase at an alarming rate, especially in certain regions of Africa (De Cock & Janssen, 2002).

Prior to 1996–1997, the average length of survival for people after the onset of the AIDS syndrome was about 18 to 24 months. Encouraging advances in the treatment of AIDS with drug regimens referred to as *highly active antiretroviral therapy* hold out promise for *substantially* longer survival (Kirchner, 2001; Sande & Ronald, 2004). But these drugs have been rushed into service and their long-term efficacy is yet to be determined (Lee et al., 2001; Tang & Glatt, 2001). Medical experts are concerned that the general public has gotten the impression that these treatments have transformed AIDS from a fatal disease to a manageable one, which is a premature conclusion (Mitka, 1999). HIV strains are evolving, and many have developed resistance to the currently available antiretroviral drugs (Tang & Glatt, 2001). Moreover, many patients do not respond well to the new drugs, and many patients who are responsive have difficulty sticking to the complicated drug administration regimens that often require people to take 20–30 pills daily and that often have adverse side effects (Catz & Kelly, 2001; Sorensen, Haug, & Batki, 2005).

Transmission

HIV is transmitted through person-to-person contact involving the exchange of bodily fluids, primarily semen and blood. The two principal modes of transmission in North America have been sexual contact and the sharing of needles by intravenous (IV) drug users. In North America, sexual transmission has occurred primarily among gay and bisexual men, but heterosexual transmission has increased in recent years (Catania et al., 2001; Rosenberg & Biggar, 1998). In the world as a whole, infection through heterosexual relations has been much more common from the beginning (see Figure 13.16). In heterosexual relations, male-to-female transmission is estimated to be about eight times more likely than female-to-male transmission (Ickovics, Thayaparan, & Ethier, 2001). The virus can be found in the tears and saliva of infected individuals, but the concentrations are low

and there is no evidence that the infection can be spread through casual contact. Even most forms of noncasual contact, including kissing, hugging, and sharing food with infected individuals, appear safe (Kalichman, 1995).

Misconceptions

Misconceptions about AIDS are widespread. Ironically, the people who hold these misconceptions fall into two polarized camps. On the one hand, a great many people have unrealistic fears that AIDS can be readily transmitted through casual contact with infected individuals. These people worry unnecessarily about contracting AIDS from a handshake, a sneeze, or an eating utensil. They tend to be paranoid about interacting with homosexuals, thus fuelling discrimination against gays in regard to housing, employment, and so forth. Some people also believe that it is dangerous to donate blood, when in fact blood donors are at no risk whatsoever.

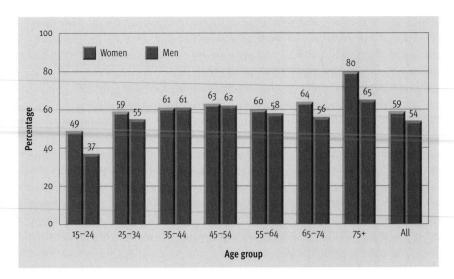

Figure 13.15

Physical inactivity in Canada. Physical inactivity is associated with many health problems. The rates of inactivity remain high in Canada across age groups. In this table we present the proportion of adults who are physically inactive by age and gender.

Source: Public Health Agency of Canada. (2004). The changing face of heart disease and stroke in Canada, 2000. Retrieved June 21, 2005, from http://www.phac-aspc.gc.ca/ccdpc-cpcmc/cvd-mcv/publications/hdsc_2000_e.html. Adapted from Statistics Canada, National Population Health Survey, 1996–97.

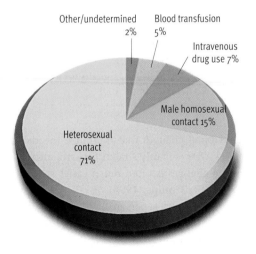

Figure 13.16

HIV transmission worldwide. In North America, most HIV transmission thus far has occurred among gay men or intravenous drug users, perhaps leading to misconceptions about the ease of transmission via heterosexual relations. In the world as a whole, heterosexual relations are the predominant mode of transmission, as these data show.

Source: Mann, J., Tarantola, D. J. M., & Netter, T. W. (1992). *A global report: AIDS in the world.* New York: Oxford University Press.

AIDS Risk Knowledge Test

AIDS Risk Knowledge Test

Answer the following "true" or "false."

T F **1.** The AIDS virus cannot be spread through kissing.

T F **2.** A person can get the AIDS virus by sharing kitchens and bathrooms with someone who has AIDS.

T F **3.** Men can give the AIDS virus to women.

T F **4.** The AIDS virus attacks the body's ability to fight off diseases.

T F **5.** You can get the AIDS virus by someone sneezing, like a cold or the flu.

T F **6.** You can get AIDS by touching a person with AIDS.

T F **7.** Women can give the AIDS virus to men.

T F **8.** A person who got the AIDS virus from shooting up drugs cannot give the virus to someone by having sex.

T F **9.** A pregnant woman can give the AIDS virus to her unborn baby.

T F **10.** Most types of birth control also protect against getting the AIDS virus.

T F **11.** Condoms make intercourse completely safe.

T F **12.** Oral sex is safe if partners "do not swallow."

T F **13.** A person must have many different sexual partners to be at risk for AIDS.

T F **14.** It is more important to take precautions against AIDS in large cities than in small cities.

T F **15.** A positive result on the AIDS virus antibody test often occurs for people who do not even have the virus.

T F **16.** Only receptive (passive) anal intercourse transmits the AIDS virus.

T F **17.** Donating blood carries no AIDS risk for the donor.

T F **18.** Most people who have the AIDS virus look quite ill.

Answers: 1.T 2.F 3.T 4.T 5.F 6.F 7.T 8.F 9.T 10.F 11.F 12.F 13.F 14.F 15.F 16.F 17.T 18.F

Figure 13.17

A quiz on knowledge of AIDS.
Because misconceptions about AIDS abound, it may be wise to take this brief quiz to test your knowledge of AIDS. The answers are shown at the bottom of the figure.

Adapted from Kalichman, S. C. (1995). *Understanding AIDS: A guide for mental health professionals.* Washington, DC: American Psychological Association. Reprinted by permission of the author.

On the other hand, many young heterosexuals who are sexually active with a variety of partners foolishly downplay their risk for HIV, naïvely assuming that they are safe as long as they avoid IV drug use and sexual relations with gay or bisexual men. They greatly underestimate the probability that their sexual partners previously may have used IV drugs or had unprotected sex with an infected individual. They don't understand, for instance, that most bisexual men do not disclose their bisexuality to their female partners (Kalichman et al., 1998). Also, because AIDS is usually accompanied by discernible symptoms, many young people believe that prospective sexual partners who carry the virus will exhibit telltale signs of illness. However, as we have already noted, having AIDS and being infected with HIV are not the same thing, and HIV carriers often remain healthy and symptom-free for many years after they are infected. In sum, many myths about AIDS persist, in spite of extensive efforts to educate the public about this complex and controversial disease. Figure 13.17 contains a short quiz to test your knowledge of the facts about AIDS.

Prevention

The behavioural changes that minimize the risk of developing AIDS are fairly straightforward, although making the changes is often much easier said than done (Coates & Collins, 1998). In all groups, the more sexual partners a person has, the higher the risk that one will be exposed to the virus. Thus, people can reduce their risk by having sexual contacts with fewer partners and by using condoms to control the exchange of semen. It is also important to curtail certain sexual practices (in particular, anal sex) that increase the probability of semen/blood mixing. The 1980s and early 1990s saw considerable progress toward wider use of safe sex practices, but new cohorts of young people appear to be much less concerned about the risk of HIV infection than the generation that witnessed the original emergence of AIDS (Catania et al., 2001). For example, a recent study of 15- to 22-year-old gay men found alarmingly high rates of risky sexual practices, such as unprotected anal sex (Valleroy et al., 2000). Research by Canadian psychologists has examined some of the factors contributing to the tendency not to use condoms and to engage in risky sexual behaviours. Carolyn Hafer from Brock University and her colleagues have found links between an individual's *belief in a just world*, a relatively stable dispositional characteristic, and condom use (Hafer, Bogaert, & McMullen, 2001). Tara McDonald from Queen's University has found links between intentions to engage in risky sexual behaviour and specific conditions of alcohol use, and between such intentions and negative mood combined with low self-esteem (MacDonald & Martineau, 2002; MacDonald et al., 2000). One would like to believe that, given all we know about the spread of AIDS and other sexually transmitted diseases, engaging in risky sexual behaviour would be in general decline. Taken together, these findings do not bode well for efforts to slow the spread of AIDS.

How Does Health-Impairing Behaviour Develop?

It may seem puzzling that people behave in self-destructive ways. How does this happen? Several factors are involved. First, many health-impairing habits creep up on people slowly. For instance, drug use may grow imperceptibly over years, or exercise habits may decline ever so gradually. Second, many health-impairing habits involve activities that are quite pleasant at the time. Actions such as eating favourite foods, smoking cigarettes, or getting "high" are potent reinforcing events. Third, the risks associated with most health-impairing habits are chronic diseases such as cancer that usually lie 10, 20, or 30 years down the road. It's relatively easy to ignore risks that lie in the distant future.

Finally, people have a curious tendency to underestimate the risks that accompany their own health-impairing behaviours while viewing the risks associated with others' self-destructive behaviours much more accurately (Weinstein, 2003; Weinstein & Klein, 1996). Many people are well aware of the dangers associated with certain habits, but when it's time to apply this information to themselves, they often discount it. They figure, for instance, that smoking will lead to cancer or a heart attack in *someone else.*

So far, we've seen that physical health may be affected by stress and by aspects of lifestyle. Next, we'll look at the importance of how people react to physical symptoms, health problems, and health-care efforts.

REVIEW OF KEY POINTS

- People frequently display health-impairing lifestyles. Smokers have much higher mortality rates than nonsmokers because they are more vulnerable to a host of diseases.

Health risks decline reasonably quickly for people who give up smoking, but quitting is difficult and relapse rates are high.

- Poor nutritional habits have been linked to heart disease, hypertension, and cancer, among other things. Lack of exercise elevates one's risk for cardiovascular diseases. Alcohol and drug use carry the immediate risk of overdose and elevate the long-term risk of many diseases.
- Aspects of behaviour influence one's risk of AIDS, which is transmitted through person-to-person contact involving the exchange of bodily fluids, primarily semen and blood. Misconceptions about AIDS are common, and the people who hold these misconceptions tend to fall into polarized camps, either overestimating or underestimating their risk of infection.
- Health-impairing habits tend to develop gradually and often involve pleasant activities. The risks may be easy to ignore because they lie in the distant future and because people tend to underestimate risks that apply to them personally.

Reactions to Illness

Some people respond to physical symptoms and illnesses by ignoring warning signs of developing diseases, while others engage in active coping efforts to conquer their diseases. Let's examine the decision to seek medical treatment, communication with health providers, and compliance with medical advice.

Deciding to Seek Treatment

Have you ever experienced nausea, diarrhea, stiffness, headaches, cramps, chest pains, or sinus problems? Of course you have; we all experience some of these problems periodically. However, whether we view these sensations as *symptoms* is a matter of individual interpretation. When two persons experience the same unpleasant sensations, one may shrug them off as a nuisance while the other may rush to a physician (Martin & Leventhal, 2004). Studies suggest that people who are relatively high in anxiety and neuroticism tend to report more symptoms of illness than others do (Feldman et al., 1999; Leventhal et al., 1996). Those who are extremely attentive to bodily sensations and health concerns also report more symptoms than the average person (Barsky, 1988).

Variations in the perceived seriousness and disruptiveness of symptoms help explain the differences among people in their readiness to seek medical treatment (Cameron, Leventhal, & Leventhal, 1993). The biggest problem in regard to treatment seeking is the tendency of many people to delay the pursuit of

needed professional consultation. Delays can be critical because early diagnosis and quick intervention may facilitate more effective treatment of many health problems (Petrie & Pennebaker, 2004). Unfortunately, procrastination is the norm even when people are faced with a medical emergency, such as a heart attack. Why do people dawdle in the midst of a crisis? Robin DiMatteo (1991), a leading expert on patient behaviour, mentions a number of reasons, noting that people delay because they often (a) misinterpret and downplay the significance of their symptoms, (b) fret about looking silly if the problem turns out to be nothing, (c) worry about "bothering" their physician, (d) are reluctant to disrupt their plans (to go out to dinner, see a movie, and so forth), and (e) waste time on trivial matters (such as taking a shower, gathering personal items, or packing clothes) before going to a hospital emergency room.

Communicating with Health Providers

A large portion of medical patients depart their doctors' offices not understanding what they have been told and what they are supposed to do (DiMatteo, 1991; Johnson & Carlson, 2004). This reality is most unfortunate because good communication is a crucial requirement for sound medical decisions, informed choices about treatment, and appropriate follow-through by patients (Gambone, Reiter, & DiMatteo, 1994).

- What is the biggest problem related to people's decisions to seek medical treatment?
- What are some barriers to effective communication between patients and their health providers?
- What can patients do to improve communication?
- How much of a problem is nonadherence to medical advice?
- What are the causes of nonadherence?

Communication between health-care providers and patients tends to be far from optimal, for a variety of reasons.

Steve Walag, University of California, Riverside

"*A person will not carry out a health behavior if significant barriers stand in the way, or if the steps interfere with favorite or necessary activities.*"
ROBIN DIMATTEO

There are many barriers to effective provider–patient communication (Beisecker, 1990; DiMatteo, 1997; Marteau & Weinman, 2004). Economic realities dictate that medical visits are generally quite brief, allowing little time for discussion. Many providers use too much medical jargon and overestimate their patients' understanding of technical terms. Patients who are upset and worried about their illness may simply forget to report some symptoms or to ask questions they meant to ask. Other patients are evasive about their real concerns because they fear a serious diagnosis. Many patients are reluctant to challenge doctors' authority and are too passive in their interactions with providers.

What can you do to improve your communication with health-care providers? The key is to not be a passive consumer of medical services (Ferguson, 1993; Kane, 1991). Arrive at a medical visit on time, with your questions and concerns prepared in advance. Try to be accurate and candid in replying to your doctor's questions. If you don't understand something the doctor says, don't be embarrassed about asking for clarification. If you have doubts about the suitability or feasibility of your doctor's recommendations, don't be afraid to voice them.

Adhering to Medical Advice

Many patients fail to adhere to the instructions they receive from physicians and other health-care professionals. The evidence suggests that nonadherence to medical advice may occur 30% to 60% of the time (DiMatteo, 1994). Nonadherence takes many forms. Patients may fail to begin a treatment regimen, stop the regimen early, reduce or increase the levels of treatment that were prescribed, or be inconsistent and unreliable in following treatment procedures (Dunbar-Jacob & Schlenk, 2001).

This point is not intended to suggest that you should passively accept all professional advice from medical personnel. However, when you have doubts about a prescribed treatment, you should speak up and ask questions. Passive resistance can backfire. For instance, if a physician sees no improvement in a patient who falsely insists that he has been taking his medicine, the physician may abandon an accurate diagnosis in favour of an inaccurate one. The inaccurate diagnosis could then lead to inappropriate treatments that might be harmful to the patient.

Why don't people comply with the advice that they've sought out from highly regarded health-care professionals? Physicians tend to attribute noncompliance to patients' personality traits, but research indicates that other factors are more important. In many cases, patients simply forget about the requirements of their treatment regimen (Dunbar-Jacob & Schlenk, 2001). Three other considerations are also especially prominent (DiMatteo & Friedman, 1982; Evans & Haynes, 1990; Ley, 1997):

1. Frequently, noncompliance is a result of the patient's failure to understand the instructions as given. Highly trained professionals often forget that what seems obvious and simple to them may be obscure and complicated to many of their patients.

2. Another key factor is how aversive or difficult the instructions are. If the prescribed regimen is unpleasant, compliance will tend to decrease. And the more that following instructions interferes with routine behaviour, the less probable it is that the patient will cooperate successfully.

3. If a patient has a negative attitude toward a physician, the probability of noncompliance will increase. When patients are unhappy with their interactions with the doctor, they're more likely to ignore the medical advice provided.

In response to the noncompliance problem, some health psychologists are exploring ways to increase patients' adherence to medical advice. They've found that the communication process between the practitioner and the patient is of critical importance. Courtesy, encouragement, reassurance, taking time to answer questions, and decreased reliance on medical jargon can improve compliance (DiNicola & DiMatteo, 1984; Hall, Roter, & Katz, 1988). Thus, there's a new emphasis in medicine on enhancing health-care professionals' communication skills.

© Ryan McVay/PhotoDisc/Getty Images

Putting It in Perspective

Which of our themes were prominent in this chapter? As you probably noticed, our discussion of stress and health illustrated multifactorial causation and the subjectivity of experience. As we noted in Chapter 1, people tend to think simplistically, in terms of single causes. In recent years, the highly publicized research linking stress to health has led many people to point automatically to stress as an explanation for illness. In reality, stress has only a modest impact on physical health. Stress can increase the risk for illness, but health is governed by a dense network of factors. Important factors include inherited vulnerabilities, physiological reactivity, exposure to infectious agents, health-impairing habits, reactions to symptoms, treatment-seeking behaviour, compliance with medical advice, personality, and social support. In other words, stress is but one actor on a crowded stage. This should be apparent in Figure 13.18, which shows the multitude of biopsychosocial factors that jointly influence physical health. It illustrates multifactorial causation in all its complexity.

The subjectivity of experience was demonstrated by the frequently repeated point that stress lies in the eye of the beholder. The same job promotion may be stressful for one person and invigorating for another. One person's pressure is another's challenge. When it comes to stress, objective reality is not nearly as important as subjective perceptions. More than anything else, the impact of stressful events seems to depend on how people view them. The critical importance of individual stress appraisals will continue to be apparent in the Personal Application on coping and stress management. Many stress management strategies depend on altering one's appraisals of events.

Figure 13.18

Biopsychosocial factors in health. Physical health can be influenced by a remarkably diverse set of variables, including biological, psychological, and social factors. The host of factors that affect health provide an excellent example of multifactorial causation.

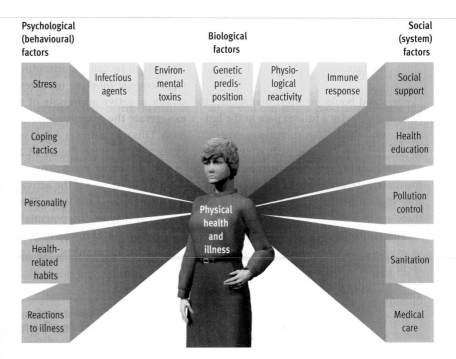

PREVIEW QUESTIONS

- How did this chapter illustrate multifactorial causation?
- How did this chapter highlight the subjectivity of human experience?

REVIEW OF KEY POINTS

- Ignoring physical symptoms may result in the delay of medical treatment. There are many barriers to effective communication between patients and health-care providers.
- Noncompliance with medical advice is a major problem. The likelihood of nonadherence is greater when instructions are difficult to understand, when recommendations are difficult to follow, and when patients are unhappy with their doctor.
- Two of our integrative themes were prominent in this chapter. First, we saw that behaviour and health are influenced by multiple causes. Second, we saw that experience is highly subjective, as stress lies in the eye of the beholder.

Of course, you don't have to be a member of the military to suffer from a psychological disorder. Recently, former British Columbia M.P. Svend Robinson was convicted of stealing an expensive ring in a high-profile court case. His arrest resulted in his resignation from Parliament. Like so many others, he resisted acknowledging his illness in the beginning and refused therapy and his prescribed medication. He was concerned about what others would think: "But like so many others, I think the stigma around mental health stopped me from dealing with it" (Mickleburgh, 2005). What is it about psychological illness that can cause this type of downward spiral? What is it about psychological illness that leads to the stigma attached to it? The potential stigma led some people who knew noted Canadian psychologist Norman Endler to advise him not to tell anyone about his depression. In fact, even his physician advised him to get a psychiatrist out of town so that he would not be *exposed* (Endler, 1982).

What is the basis for judging behaviour as normal versus abnormal? One year one of us (we won't tell you which one) decided to dress completely in exactly the same colour for every class he taught that year. Where would we place that behaviour on the continuum from normal to abnormal? Are people who have psychological disorders dangerous? Are they violent? How common are such disorders? Can they be cured? Have mental disorders always been stigmatized? These are just a few of the questions that we will address in this chapter as we discuss psychological disorders and their complex causes.

Before we begin to discuss psychological disorders, we should let you know that Dallaire received the Order of Canada in 2002 and in 2005 was given the Pearson Peace Medal recognizing his achievements in international service and understanding. Dallaire was appointed to the Canadian Senate in 2005. Interestingly, one man accused of inciting the bloodshed in Rwanda has been hiding in Canada for years. Leon Mugesera faces deportation from Canada to Rwanda for his alleged crimes (*Toronto Star*, 2005).

Abnormal Behaviour: Myths, Realities, and Controversies

PREVIEW QUESTIONS

- What is the medical model?
- What criteria are used to judge abnormality?
- How easy is it to distinguish normality from abnormality?
- What classification system is used to diagnose psychological disorders?
- How common are mental disorders?

Misconceptions about abnormal behaviour are common. Hence, we need to clear up some preliminary issues before we describe the various types of disorders. In this section, we will discuss (1) the medical model of abnormal behaviour, (2) the criteria of abnormal behaviour, (3) stereotypes regarding psychological disorders, (4) the classification of psychological disorders, and (5) how common such disorders are.

The Medical Model Applied to Abnormal Behaviour

The *medical model* proposes that it is useful to think of abnormal behaviour as a disease. This point of view is the basis for many of the terms used to refer to abnormal behaviour, including mental *illness*, psychological *disorder*, and psycho*pathology* (*pathology* refers to manifestations of disease). The medical model gradually became the dominant way of thinking about abnormal behaviour during the 18th and 19th centuries, and its influence remains strong today.

The medical model clearly represented progress over earlier models of abnormal behaviour. Prior to the 18th century, most conceptions of abnormal behaviour were based on superstition. People who behaved strangely were thought to be possessed by demons, to be witches in league with the devil, or to be victims of God's punishment. Their disorders were "treated" with chants, rituals, exorcisms, and such. If the people's behaviour was seen as threatening, they were candidates for chains, dungeons, torture, and death (see Figure 14.1).

The rise of the medical model brought improvements in the treatment of those who exhibited abnormal behaviour. As victims of an illness, they were viewed with more sympathy and less hatred and fear. Although living conditions in early asylums were typically deplorable, gradual progress was made toward more humane care of the mentally ill. It took time, but ineffectual approaches to treatment eventually gave way to scientific investigation of the causes and cures of psychological disorders.

However, in recent decades, some critics have suggested that the medical model may have outlived its usefulness (Kiesler, 1999). A particularly vocal critic has been Thomas Szasz (1974, 1990). He asserts that "strictly speaking, disease or illness can affect only the body; hence there can be no mental illness.... Minds can be 'sick' only in the sense that jokes are 'sick' or economies are 'sick'" (1974, p. 267). He further argues that abnormal behaviour usually involves a deviation from social norms rather than an illness. He contends that such deviations are "problems in living" rather than medical problems. According to Szasz, the medical model's disease analogy converts

Psychological Disorders

The topic of psychological disorders draws many students to an introductory psychology course. Your interest in this topic may stem from your desire to understand the nature, prevalence, and cause of psychological disorders so that you can be better prepared to assist those in need. This is indeed a worthy aspiration and one that we are ourselves familiar with. You may also have been led to the topic because you are already too familiar with the costs that such disorders can exact on the afflicted and their families. Given the rates of occurrence for the various disorders that we will discuss in this chapter, the chances are very good that you know someone, perhaps someone very close to you, who suffers from some type of psychological disturbance. We hope that this chapter on psychological disorders and Chapter 15, which deals with the treatment of psychological disorders, will contribute to your understanding of these important issues. Beyond all the statistics, views on etiology, and varieties of treatment are the very human stories and the real suffering that results from psychological disorders.

One very notable recent story had its beginnings in the mid-1990s, and it has not yet been resolved for the people involved. By all accounts, Roméo Dallaire was at the apex of a long and distinguished career when he was given what all thought was a golden opportunity to put his considerable skills and experience to work for the good of others. As it turned out, however, he was being sent to do an impossible job—with inadequate resources and funding and virtually no support from his superiors. While much of the world was captivated by O. J. Simpson's trial for murder (Pevere, 2005), off-screen, approximately 800 000 Tutsis were slaughtered, many by machetes, by their Hutu neighbours in Rwanda in just 100 days.

Canadian General Roméo Dallaire had been given the command of United Nations Assistance Mission for Rwanda. As he has written in his book *Shake Hands with the Devil: The Failure of Humanity in Rwanda* (Dallaire, 2003) and discussed in the award-winning documentary *Shake Hands with the Devil: The Journey of Roméo Dallaire,* Dallaire was restrained from interfering by the U.N. In addition, he was unable to motivate anyone else in the international community to come to the Tutsis' aid. In fact, he believes he could have prevented the slaughter because of some advance information he had obtained. Dallaire had to stand by and do little but watch during the genocide. The human toll included not only the murdered Tutsis and U.N. peacekeepers from Belgium, but also Dallaire himself. Later, after his return to Canada, he began a much-publicized descent into psychological disturbance and suicide attempts, and at one point was arrested in Ottawa after being found drunk under a park bench. The stress derived from what he saw and his inability to do anything about it led to his diagnosis and treatment for post-traumatic stress disorder (PTSD), a disorder we discussed in Chapter 13 and will examine further in this chapter. The number of Canadian Forces veterans being given pensions because of PTSD has increased astronomically over the last decade (Freeze, 2005). In 2004 over 1100 PTSD pensions were awarded. According to a recent survey of Canadian Forces personnel, the one-year prevalence of PTSD is 2.8%, with a lifetime prevalence of 7.2% (National Defence, 2003).

Retired general Roméo Dallaire was awarded the Pearson Peace Medal in 2005. He suffers from PTSD.

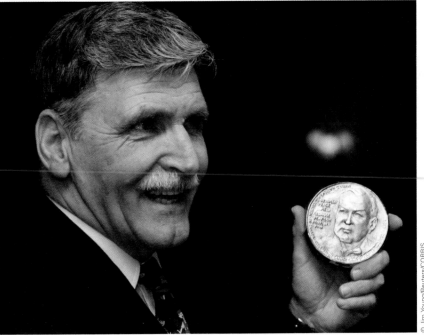

Of course, you don't have to be a member of the military to suffer from a psychological disorder. Recently, former British Columbia M.P. Svend Robinson was convicted of stealing an expensive ring in a high-profile court case. His arrest resulted in his resignation from Parliament. Like so many others, he resisted acknowledging his illness in the beginning and refused therapy and his prescribed medication. He was concerned about what others would think: "But like so many others, I think the stigma around mental health stopped me from dealing with it" (Mickleburgh, 2005). What is it about psychological illness that can cause this type of downward spiral? What is it about psychological illness that leads to the stigma attached to it? The potential stigma led some people who knew noted Canadian psychologist Norman Endler to advise him not to tell anyone about his depression. In fact, even his physician advised him to get a psychiatrist out of town so that he would not be *exposed* (Endler, 1982).

What is the basis for judging behaviour as normal versus abnormal? One year one of us (we won't tell you which one) decided to dress completely in exactly the same colour for every class he taught that year. Where would we place that behaviour on the continuum from normal to abnormal? Are people who have psychological disorders dangerous? Are they violent? How common are such disorders? Can they be cured? Have mental disorders always been stigmatized? These are just a few of the questions that we will address in this chapter as we discuss psychological disorders and their complex causes.

Before we begin to discuss psychological disorders, we should let you know that Dallaire received the Order of Canada in 2002 and in 2005 was given the Pearson Peace Medal recognizing his achievements in international service and understanding. Dallaire was appointed to the Canadian Senate in 2005. Interestingly, one man accused of inciting the bloodshed in Rwanda has been hiding in Canada for years. Leon Mugesera faces deportation from Canada to Rwanda for his alleged crimes (*Toronto Star*, 2005).

Abnormal Behaviour: Myths, Realities, and Controversies

PREVIEW QUESTIONS

- What is the medical model?
- What criteria are used to judge abnormality?
- How easy is it to distinguish normality from abnormality?
- What classification system is used to diagnose psychological disorders?
- How common are mental disorders?

Misconceptions about abnormal behaviour are common. Hence, we need to clear up some preliminary issues before we describe the various types of disorders. In this section, we will discuss (1) the medical model of abnormal behaviour, (2) the criteria of abnormal behaviour, (3) stereotypes regarding psychological disorders, (4) the classification of psychological disorders, and (5) how common such disorders are.

The Medical Model Applied to Abnormal Behaviour

The *medical model* proposes that it is useful to think of abnormal behaviour as a disease. This point of view is the basis for many of the terms used to refer to abnormal behaviour, including mental *illness*, psychological *disorder*, and psycho*pathology* (*pathology* refers to manifestations of disease). The medical model gradually became the dominant way of thinking about abnormal behaviour during the 18th and 19th centuries, and its influence remains strong today.

The medical model clearly represented progress over earlier models of abnormal behaviour. Prior to the 18th century, most conceptions of abnormal behaviour were based on superstition. People who behaved strangely were thought to be possessed by demons, to be witches in league with the devil, or to be victims of God's punishment. Their disorders were "treated" with chants, rituals, exorcisms, and such. If the people's behaviour was seen as threatening, they were candidates for chains, dungeons, torture, and death (see Figure 14.1).

The rise of the medical model brought improvements in the treatment of those who exhibited abnormal behaviour. As victims of an illness, they were viewed with more sympathy and less hatred and fear. Although living conditions in early asylums were typically deplorable, gradual progress was made toward more humane care of the mentally ill. It took time, but ineffectual approaches to treatment eventually gave way to scientific investigation of the causes and cures of psychological disorders.

However, in recent decades, some critics have suggested that the medical model may have outlived its usefulness (Kiesler, 1999). A particularly vocal critic has been Thomas Szasz (1974, 1990). He asserts that "strictly speaking, disease or illness can affect only the body; hence there can be no mental illness.... Minds can be 'sick' only in the sense that jokes are 'sick' or economies are 'sick'" (1974, p. 267). He further argues that abnormal behaviour usually involves a deviation from social norms rather than an illness. He contends that such deviations are "problems in living" rather than medical problems. According to Szasz, the medical model's disease analogy converts

CHAPTER 14

Latchezar Boyadjiev, *Delusion*, L.B. Glass Studios

Abnormal Behaviour: Myths, Realities, and Controversies
The Medical Model Applied to Abnormal Behaviour
Criteria of Abnormal Behaviour
Stereotypes of Psychological Disorders
Psychodiagnosis: The Classification of Disorders
The Prevalence of Psychological Disorders

Anxiety Disorders
Generalized Anxiety Disorder
Phobic Disorder
Panic Disorder and Agoraphobia
Obsessive-Compulsive Disorder
Post-Traumatic Stress Disorder
Etiology of Anxiety Disorders

Somatoform Disorders
Somatization Disorder
Conversion Disorder
Hypochondriasis
Etiology of Somatoform Disorders

Dissociative Disorders
Dissociative Amnesia and Fugue
Dissociative Identity Disorder
Etiology of Dissociative Disorders

Mood Disorders
Major Depressive Disorder
Bipolar Disorder
Etiology of Mood Disorders
Featured Study • Does Negative Thinking *Cause* Depression?

Schizophrenic Disorders
General Symptoms
Subtypes, Course, and Outcome
Etiology of Schizophrenia

Personality Disorders
Diagnostic Problems
Antisocial Personality Disorder

Psychological Disorders and the Law
Insanity

Culture and Pathology
Are Equivalent Disorders Found around the World?
Are Symptom Patterns Culturally Invariant?

Putting It in Perspective

Personal Application • **Understanding Eating Disorders**
Anorexia Nervosa
Bulimia Nervosa
History, Prevalence, and Course
Etiology of Eating Disorders

Critical Thinking Application • **Working with Probabilities in Thinking about Mental Illness**

Recap

Practice Test

PRACTICE TEST

1. It is the weekend before a major psychology exam on Monday, and Janine is experiencing total panic even though she is thoroughly prepared and aced the previous two psychology exams. Janine's panic illustrates that:
   A. high arousal is optimal on complex tasks.
   B. the appraisal of stress is quite objective.
   C. the appraisal of stress is highly subjective.
   D. her adrenal cortex is malfunctioning.

2. The four principal sources of stress are:
   A. frustration, conflict, pressure, and anxiety.
   B. frustration, anger, pressure, and change.
   C. anger, anxiety, depression, and annoyance.
   D. frustration, conflict, pressure, and change.

3. When your boss tells you that a complicated report that you have not yet begun to write must be on her desk by this afternoon, you may experience:
   A. burnout.
   B. pressure.
   C. a double bind.
   D. catharsis.

4. You want very badly to ask someone for a date, but you are afraid to risk rejection. You are experiencing:
   A. an approach–avoidance conflict.
   B. an avoidance–avoidance conflict.
   C. frustration.
   D. self-imposed pressure.

5. Research suggests that a high level of arousal may be most optimal for the performance of a task when:
   A. the task is complex.
   B. the task is simple.
   C. the rewards are high.
   D. an audience is present.

6. The alarm stage of Hans Selye's general adaptation syndrome is essentially the same as:
   A. the fight-or-flight response.
   B. constructive coping.
   C. catharsis.
   D. secondary appraisal.

7. The brain structure responsible for initiating action along the two major pathways through which the brain sends signals to the endocrine system is the:
   A. hypothalamus.
   B. thalamus.
   C. corpus callosum.
   D. medulla.

8. You have been doing poorly in your psychology class and you are in danger of flunking. Which of the following qualifies as a defence mechanism in response to this situation?
   A. You seek the aid of a tutor.
   B. You decide to withdraw from the class and take it another time.
   C. You deny the reality that you are hopelessly behind in the class, convinced that you will somehow ace the final without seeking help.
   D. You consult with the instructor to see what you can do to pass the class.

9. Physical and emotional exhaustion, cynicism, and lowered self-efficacy attributable to chronic work-related stress is referred to as:
   A. learned helplessness.
   B. burnout.

C. fallout.
D. post-traumatic stress disorder.

10. Which personality trait seems to be most strongly related to increased coronary risk?
    A. Type B personality
    B. perfectionism
    C. competitiveness
    D. hostility

11. Many students often develop colds and other minor ailments during final exams. This probably happens because:
    A. stress is associated with the release of corticosteroid hormones.
    B. stress is associated with the release of catecholamine hormones.
    C. burnout causes colds.
    D. stress can suppress immune functioning.

12. Research has found that optimists are more likely than pessimists to:
    A. take their time in confronting problems.
    B. identify the negatives before they identify the positives.
    C. engage in action-oriented, problem-focused coping.
    D. blame others for their personal problems.

13. Which of the following has *not* been found to be a mode of transmission for the HIV virus?
    A. sexual contact among homosexual men
    B. the sharing of needles by intravenous drug users
    C. sexual contact among heterosexuals
    D. sharing food

14. The three phases in Albert Ellis's explanation of emotional reactions are:
    A. alarm, resistance, exhaustion.
    B. id, ego, superego.
    C. activating event, belief system, consequence.
    D. antecedent conditions, behaviour, consequence.

15. In evaluating health statistics, it is useful to:
    A. remember that statistical significance is equivalent to practical significance.
    B. remember that correlation is a reliable indicator of causation.
    C. consider base rates in thinking about probabilities.
    D. all of the above.

See Appendix A for answers to this Practice Test.

 ON THE WEB

For additional resources on the topics covered in this chapter, visit the *Psychology: Themes and Variations* Web site, where you will find practice quizzes, tutorials, Web links, simulations, critical thinking activities, flash cards, interactive exercises, and suggested readings available through INFOTRAC.

http://www.themesandvariations.nelson.com

 http://hed.nelson.com

Go to this site for the link to ThomsonNOW™, your one-stop study shop. Take a Pretest for this chapter and ThomsonNOW™ will generate a personalized Study Plan based on your test results! The Study Plan will identify the topics you need to review and direct you to online resources to help you master those topics. You can then take a Posttest to help you determine the concepts you have mastered and what you still need work on.

RECAP

Key Ideas

The Nature of Stress
● Stress is a common, everyday event, and even seemingly minor stressors or hassles can be problematic. To a large degree, stress lies in the eye of the beholder, as appraisals of stress are highly subjective.

Major Types of Stress
● Major types of stress include frustration, conflict, change, and pressure. Frustration occurs when an obstacle prevents one from attaining some goal. There are three principal types of conflict: approach–approach, avoidance–avoidance, and approach–avoidance.

● A large number of studies with the SRRS suggest that change is stressful. Although this may be true, it is now clear that the SRRS is a measure of general stress rather than just change-related stress. Two kinds of pressure (to perform and conform) also appear to be stressful.

Responding to Stress
● Emotional reactions to stress typically include anger, fear, and sadness, although positive emotions may also occur. Emotional arousal may interfere with coping. The optimal level of arousal on a task depends on the complexity of the task.

● Physiological arousal in response to stress was originally called the fight-or-flight response by Cannon. Selye's general adaptation syndrome describes three stages in physiological reactions to stress: alarm, resistance, and exhaustion.

● There are two major pathways along which the brain sends signals to the endocrine system in response to stress. Actions along these paths release two sets of hormones, catecholamines and corticosteroids, into the bloodstream.

● Some coping responses are less than optimal. Among these are giving up, blaming oneself, and striking out at others with acts of aggression. Indulging oneself is another coping pattern that tends to be of limited value. Defence mechanisms protect against emotional distress through self-deception. Small positive illusions about oneself may sometimes be adaptive.

The Effects of Stress on Psychological Functioning
● Common negative effects of stress in terms of psychological functioning include impaired task performance, burnout, post-traumatic stress disorders, and a variety of other psychological problems and disorders. Stress may also have positive effects, stimulating personal growth and the acquisition of new strengths.

The Effects of Stress on Physical Health
● The Type A personality has been implicated as a contributing cause of coronary heart disease, but hostility may be the toxic element of the Type A syndrome. Transient emotional reactions to stressful events and depression have also been identified as cardiovascular risk factors.

● Stress may play a role in a host of diseases because it can temporarily suppress the effectiveness of the immune system. The Featured Study provided a well-controlled demonstration of how stress may increase susceptibility to the common cold. Although there's little doubt that stress can contribute to the development of physical illness, the link between stress and illness is modest.

Factors Moderating the Impact of Stress
● Social support is a key moderator of the relationship between stress and illness and it is associated with better mental and physical health. Optimism and conscientiousness may lead to more effective coping with stress.

Health-Impairing Behaviour
● People display many forms of health-impairing behaviour. Smokers have much higher mortality rates than nonsmokers because they are more vulnerable to a host of diseases.

● Poor nutritional habits have been linked to heart disease, hypertension, and cancer, among other things. Lack of exercise elevates one's risk for cardiovascular diseases. Alcohol and drug use carry the immediate risk of overdose and elevate the long-term risk of many diseases.

● Aspects of behaviour also influence one's risk of AIDS. Misconceptions about AIDS are common, and the people who hold these misconceptions tend to fall into polarized camps, either overestimating or underestimating their risk of infection. Health-impairing habits tend to develop gradually and often involve pleasant activities.

Reactions to Illness
● Ignoring physical symptoms may result in the delay of needed medical treatment. There are many barriers to effective communication between patients and health-care providers. Noncompliance with medical advice is a major problem.

Putting It in Perspective
● Two of our integrative themes were prominent in this chapter. First, we saw that behaviour and health are influenced by multiple causes. Second, we saw that experience is highly subjective, as stress lies in the eye of the beholder.

Personal Application • Improving Coping and Stress Management
● Action-oriented, realistic, constructive coping can be helpful in managing the stress of daily life. Ellis emphasizes the importance of reappraising stressful events to detect and dispute catastrophic thinking. Humour may be useful in efforts to redefine stressful situations.

● In some cases, it may pay to release pent-up emotions by expressing them. Managing hostility and forgiving others' transgressions can also reduce stress. Relaxation techniques, such as Benson's relaxation response, can be helpful in stress management. Regular exercise can help to make one less vulnerable to the ravages of stress.

Critical Thinking Application • Thinking Rationally about Health Statistics and Decisions
● Evaluations of statistics on health risks can be enhanced by remembering that correlation is no assurance of causation, statistical significance is not equivalent to practical significance, and base rates need to be considered in assessing probabilities. In trying to think systematically about health decisions, one should seek information to reduce uncertainty, make risk–benefit assessments, and consider alternative courses of action.

Key Terms

Acquired immune deficiency syndrome (AIDS), 560
Aggression, 546
Approach–approach conflict, 538
Approach–avoidance conflict, 539
Avoidance–avoidance conflict, 539
Biopsychosocial model, 536
Burnout, 549
Catastrophic thinking, 566
Catharsis, 546
Conflict, 538
Constructive coping, 548
Coping, 544
Defence mechanisms, 546
Fight-or-flight response, 543
Frustration, 537
General adaptation syndrome, 544
Health psychology, 536
Immune response, 555
Internet addiction, 546
Learned helplessness, 545
Life changes, 539
Optimism, 558

Post-traumatic stress disorder (PTSD), 550
Pressure, 540
Psychosomatic diseases, 552
Rational-emotive therapy, 566
Social support, 557
Stress, 536
Type A personality, 552
Type B personality, 552

Key People

Walter Cannon, 543
Robin DiMatteo, 564
Albert Ellis, 546
Meyer Friedman, 552
Thomas Holmes, 539
Janice Kiecolt-Glaser, 555
Richard Lazarus, 537
Neal Miller, 538
Richard Rahe, 539
Martin Seligman, 558
Hans Selye, 544
Shelley Taylor, 548

weighing potential risks and benefits. None of these variables is unique to health decisions—uncertainty, risks, and benefits play prominent roles in economic and political decisions as well as in personal decisions. Let's apply some basic principles of quantitative reasoning to a treatment decision involving whether to prescribe Ritalin for a boy who has been diagnosed with attention deficit disorder (ADD). Keep in mind that the general principles applied in this example can be used for a wide variety of decisions.

Seek Information to Reduce Uncertainty. Gather information and check it carefully for accuracy, completeness, and the presence or absence of conflicting information. For example, is the diagnosis of ADD correct? *Look for conflicting information* that does not fit with this diagnosis. For example, if the child can sit and read for a long period of time, maybe the problem is an undetected hearing loss that makes him appear to be hyperactive in some situations, or perhaps he is just a very active child who prefers physical activity to the sedentary. This is an important first step that is often omitted.

As you consider the additional information, begin *quantifying the degree of uncertainty* or its "flip side," your degree of confidence that the diagnosis is correct. A specific value is usually not possible, but a general approximation along a dimension ranging from "highly confident" to "not at all confident" is useful in helping you think about the next step. If you decide that you are not confident about the diagnosis, you may be trying to solve the wrong problem.

Make Risk–Benefit Assessments. What are the risks and benefits of Ritalin? How likely is this child to benefit from Ritalin, and just how much improvement can be expected? If the child is eight years old and unable to read and is miserable in school and at home, any treatment that could reduce his problems deserves serious consideration. As in the first step, the quantification is at an approximate level. A child who is two years behind at school and has no friends is, in a roughly quantifiable sense, worse off than one who is only six months behind in school and has at least one or two friends.

How likely and how severe are the risks associated with Ritalin? If there is evidence that children do not grow as well when they are on Ritalin, for example, can they be taken off Ritalin over the summer months so that they can catch up?

List Alternative Courses of Action. What are the alternatives to Ritalin? How well do they work? What are the risks associated with the alternatives, including the risk of falling further behind in school? *Consider the pros and cons of each alternative.* A special diet that sometimes works might be a good first step along with the decision to start drug therapy if the child does not show improvement over some time period. What are the relative success rates for different types of treatment for children like the one being considered? To answer these questions, you will need to use probability estimates in your decision making.

As you can see from this example, many parts of the problem are quantified (confidence in the diagnosis, likelihood of improvement, probability of negative outcomes, and so forth). Precise probability values were not used because often the actual numbers are not known. Some of the values that are quantified reflect value judgments, others reflect likelihoods, and others assess the degree of uncertainty. The

decision will have a different outcome depending on the particular child in question, the expected degree of success for alternative modes of treatment, and the associated risks for each. It is important to avoid the (understandable) tendency to give up and do nothing or to just do what the experts say to do, because every course of action has associated risks. It is also important to remember that doing nothing is also a decision, and it may not be the best one.

The decision-making process is not complete even after a decision is made. New decisions are needed as the future unfolds. When new information and new alternatives become available, the decision needs to be reviewed. Decision makers need to adopt deliberate strategies that require them to look for and seriously consider information that conflicts with any decision that was previously made, to avoid the tendency to notice and act only on information that confirms what you already believe to be true.

If you are thinking that the quantification of many unknowns in decision making is a lot of work, you are right. But, it is work worth doing. Whenever there are important decisions to be made about health, the ability to think with numbers will help you reach a better decision. And yes, that assertion is a virtual certainty.

Table 13.4 Critical Thinking Skills Discussed in This Application

Skill	Description
Understanding the limitations of correlational evidence	The critical thinker understands that a correlation between two variables does not demonstrate that there is a causal link between the variables.
Understanding the limitations of statistical significance	The critical thinker understands that weak relationships can be statistically significant when large samples are used in research.
Utilizing base rates in making predictions and evaluating probabilities	The critical thinker appreciates that the initial proportion of some group or event needs to be considered in weighing probabilities.
Seeking information to reduce uncertainty	The critical thinker understands that gathering more information can often decrease uncertainty, and reduced uncertainty can facilitate better decisions.
Making risk–benefit assessments	The critical thinker is aware that most decisions have risks and benefits that need to be weighed carefully.
Generating and evaluating alternative courses of action	In problem solving and decision making, the critical thinker knows the value of generating as many alternatives as possible and assessing their advantages and disadvantages.

Thinking Rationally about Health Statistics and Decisions

With so many conflicting claims about the best ways to prevent or treat diseases, how can anyone ever decide what to do? It seems that every day a report in the media claims that yesterday's health news was wrong.

The inconsistency of health news is only part of the problem. We are also overwhelmed by health-related statistics. As mathematics pundit John Allen Paulos (1995, p. 133) puts it, "Health statistics may be bad for our mental health. Inundated by too many of them, we tend to ignore them completely, to accept them blithely, to disbelieve them closemindedly, or simply to misinterpret their significance."

Perhaps you should just give up or make health decisions based on your own intuitions or the flip of a coin. Is that the right answer? Of course not. Personal decisions about health-related issues can be extremely important, even a matter of life and death. It may not be easy, but it is particularly important to try to think rationally and systematically about health issues. In this Application, we will discuss a few insights that can help you to think critically about statistics on health risks, and then we'll briefly outline a systematic approach to thinking through health decisions.

Evaluating Statistics on Health Risks

News reports seem to suggest that there are links between virtually everything people do, touch, and consume and some type of physical illness. For example, media have reported that coffee consumption is related to hypertension, that sleep loss is related to mortality, and that a high-fat diet is related to heart disease. It's enough to send even the most subdued person into a panic. Fortunately, your evaluation of data on health risks can become more sophisticated by considering the following.

Correlation Is No Assurance of Causation. It is not easy to conduct experiments on health risks, so the vast majority of studies linking lifestyle and demographic factors to diseases are correlational studies. Hence, it pays to remember that there may not be a causal link between two variables that happen to be correlated. Thus, when you hear that a factor is related to some disease, try to dig a little deeper and find out why scientists think this factor is associated with the disease. The suspected causal factor may be something very different from what was measured.

Statistical Significance Is Not Equivalent to Practical Significance. Reports on health statistics often emphasize that the investigators uncovered "statistically significant" findings. As explained in Chapter 2, statistically significant findings are findings that are not likely to be due to chance fluctuations. Statistical significance is a useful concept, but it can sometimes be misleading (Matthey, 1998). Medical studies are often based on rather large samples, because they tend to yield more reliable conclusions than small samples. However, when a large sample is used, weak relationships and small differences between groups can turn out to be statistically significant, and these small differences may not have much practical importance. For example, in one study of sodium (salt) intake and cardiovascular disease, which used a sample of over 14 000 participants, He et al. (1999) found a statistically significant association between high sodium intake and the prevalence of hypertension among normal-weight subjects. However, this statistically significant difference was not particularly large. The prevalence of hypertension among subjects with the lowest sodium intake was 19.1% compared to 21.8% for subjects with the highest sodium intake—not exactly a difference worthy of panic.

Base Rates Should Be Considered in Evaluating Probabilities. In evaluating whether a possible risk factor is associated with some disease, people often fail to consider the base rates of these events and draw far-reaching conclusions based on what may be a matter of sheer coincidence. For example, Paulos (1995) discusses how a handful of cases in which cellular phone users developed brain cancer led to unfounded allegations that cell phones cause brain cancer. Although brain cancer is a rare disease, striking only about six out of 100 000 Americans per year, Paulos points out that with 10 million Americans using cell phones (at that time), one would expect to find 600 new cases of brain cancer annually among cell phone users. Given the paucity of reported cases, he playfully concludes that cellular phones must prevent brain cancer.

It is also useful to consider base rates in evaluating percentage increases in diseases. If the base rate of a disease is relatively low, a small increase can sound quite large if it is reported as a percentage. For example, in the He et al. (1999) study, the prevalence of diabetes among subjects with the lowest sodium intake was 2.1% compared to 3.8% for subjects with the highest sodium intake. Based on this small but statistically significant difference, one could say (the investigators did not) that high sodium intake was associated with an 81% increase (3.8 − 2.1/2.1) in the prevalence of diabetes, an assertion that would exaggerate the role of sodium intake in the development of diabetes.

Thinking Systematically about Health Decisions

Health decisions are oriented toward the future, which means that there are always uncertainties. And they usually involve

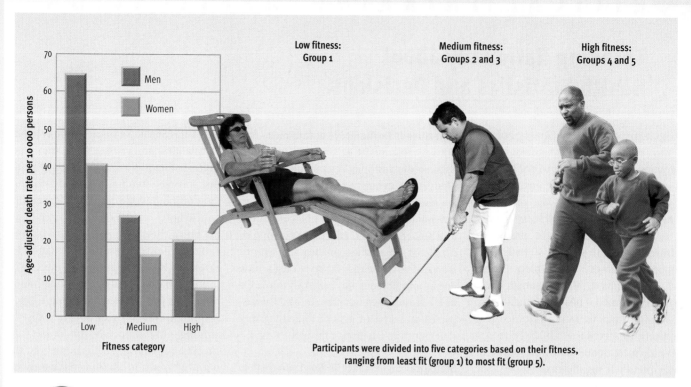

Figure 13.21

Physical fitness and mortality. Blair and colleagues (1989) studied death rates among men and women who exhibited low, medium, or high fitness. As you can see, fitness was associated with lower mortality rates in both sexes.

SOURCE: Adapted from Blair, S. N., Kohl, W. H., Paffenbarger, R. S., Clark, D. G., Cooper, K. H., & Gibbons, L. W. (1989). Physical fitness and all-cause mortality. *Journal of the American Medical Association, 262*, 2395–2401. Copyright © 1989 American Medical Association. Reprinted by permission.

(Photos: left, © C. H. Wooley; middle, © Paul Francis Photo; right, © Michael Newman/PhotoEdit)

(Richardson et al., 2004) (see Figure 13.21). Successful participation in an exercise program can also lead to improvements in your mood and ability to deal with stress (Hays, 1999; Plante, 1999). For example, King, Taylor, and Haskell (1993) found that an exercise regimen led to a decline in depression and anxiety in a study of older adults who also benefited from reductions in perceived stress.

Embarking on an exercise program is difficult for many people. Exercise is time-consuming, and if you're out of shape, your initial attempts may be discouraging. To avoid these problems, it's wise to do the following (Greenberg, 2002; Jackicic & Gallagher, 2002; Phillips et al., 2001):

1. Select an activity that you find enjoyable.
2. Increase your participation gradually.
3. Exercise regularly without overdoing it.
4. Reinforce yourself for your efforts.

If you choose a competitive sport (such as tennis), try to avoid falling into the competition trap. If you become obsessed with winning, you'll put yourself under pressure and *add* to the stress in your life.

REVIEW OF KEY POINTS

- Action-oriented, realistic, constructive coping can be helpful in managing the stress of daily life. Ellis emphasizes the importance of reappraising stressful events to detect and dispute catastrophic thinking. According to Ellis, emotional distress is often due to irrational assumptions that underlie one's thinking.

- Humour may be useful in efforts to redefine stressful situations. In some cases, it may pay to release pent-up emotions. Talking it out may help drain off negative emotions and foster better health. Stress can also be reduced by learning to manage one's hostile feelings more effectively and by learning to be more forgiving toward others.

- Relaxation techniques, such as Benson's relaxation response, can reduce the wear and tear of stress. Physical vulnerability may also be reduced by following a regular exercise regimen.

of divorced or permanently separated women reported by McCullough (2001), the extent to which the women had forgiven their former husbands was positively related to several measures of well-being and inversely related to measures of anxiety and depression. Research also shows that vengefulness is correlated with more rumination and negative emotion and with lower life satisfaction (McCullough et al., 2001). Taken together, these findings suggest that it may be healthful for people to learn to forgive others more readily.

Learning to Relax

Relaxation is a valuable stress management technique that can soothe emotional turmoil and reduce problematic physiological arousal (Lehrer & Woolfolk, 1984, 1993; Smyth et al., 2001). The value of relaxation became apparent to Herbert Benson (1975; Benson & Klipper, 1988) as a result of his research on meditation. Benson, a Harvard Medical School cardiologist, believes that relaxation is the key to the beneficial effects of meditation. According to Benson, the elaborate religious rituals and beliefs associated with meditation are irrelevant to its effects. After "demystifying" meditation, Benson set out to devise a simple, nonreligious procedure that could provide similar benefits. He calls his procedure the *relaxation response*. Although there are several other worthwhile approaches to relaxation training, we'll examine Benson's procedure, as its simplicity makes it especially useful. From his study of a variety of relaxation techniques, Benson concluded that four factors promote effective relaxation:

1. *A quiet environment.* It's easiest to induce the relaxation response in a distraction-free environment. After you become experienced with the relaxation response, you may be able to practise it in a crowded subway. Initially, however, you should practise it in a quiet, calm place.
2. *A mental device.* To shift attention inward and keep it there, you need to focus your attention on a constant stimulus, such as a sound or word recited repetitively.

3. *A passive attitude.* It's important not to get upset when your attention strays to distracting thoughts. You must realize that such distractions are inevitable. Whenever your mind wanders from your attentional focus, calmly redirect attention to your mental device.

4. *A comfortable position.* Reasonable body comfort is essential to avoid a major source of potential distraction. Simply sitting up straight generally works well. Lying down is too conducive to sleep.

Benson's simple relaxation procedure is described in Figure 13.20. For full benefit, it should be practised daily.

Minimizing Physiological Vulnerability

Your body is intimately involved in your response to stress, and the wear and tear of stress can be injurious to your health. To combat this potential problem, it helps to keep your body in relatively sound shape. It's a good idea to consume a nutritionally balanced diet, get adequate sleep, and engage in at least a moderate amount of exercise. It's also a good idea to learn how to control overeating and the use of tobacco, alcohol, and other drugs. Doing these things will not make you immune to the ravages of stress; however, failure to do them may increase your vulnerability to stress-related diseases. We've discussed sleep patterns, drug use, and eating habits in other chapters, so the coverage here will focus exclusively on exercise.

The potential benefits of regular exercise are substantial. Fortunately, evidence indicates that you don't have to be a dedicated athlete to benefit from exercise (Blair et al., 1989). Even a moderate amount of exercise—such as taking a brisk, half-hour walk each day—can reduce your risk of disease

Figure 13.20

Benson's relaxation procedure. Herbert Benson's relaxation procedure is described here. According to Benson, his simple relaxation response can yield benefits similar to meditation. To experience these benefits, you should practise the procedure daily.

Source: Relaxation procedure from THE RELAXATION RESPONSE by Herbert Benson, M.D. with Miriam Z. Klipper. Copyright © 1975 by William Morrow & Company, Inc. Reprinted by permission of HarperCollins Publishers.

1. Sit quietly in a comfortable position.

2. Close your eyes.

3. Deeply relax all your muscles, beginning at your feet and progressing up to your face. Keep them relaxed.

4. Breathe through your nose. Become aware of your breathing. As you breathe out, say the word "one" silently to yourself. For example, breathe in . . . out, "one"; in . . . out, "one"; and so forth. Breathe easily and naturally.

5. Continue for 10 to 20 minutes. You may open your eyes to check the time, but do not use an alarm. When you finish, sit quietly for several minutes, at first with your eyes closed and later with your eyes opened. Do not stand up for a few minutes.

6. Do not worry about whether you are successful in achieving a deep level of relaxation. Maintain a passive attitude and permit relaxation to occur at its own pace. When distracting thoughts occur, try to ignore them by not dwelling on them, and return to repeating "one." With practice, the response should come with little effort. Practise the technique once or twice daily but not within two hours after any meal, since digestive processes seem to interfere with the elicitation of the relaxation response.

© Paul Francis Photo

Ellis asserts that most people don't understand the importance of phase B in this three-stage sequence. They unwittingly believe that the activating event (A) causes the consequent emotional turmoil (C). However, Ellis maintains that A does *not* cause C. It only appears to do so. Instead, Ellis asserts, B causes C. One's emotional distress is actually caused by one's catastrophic thinking.

According to Ellis, it's commonplace for people to turn inconvenience into disaster and to make mountains out of molehills. Ellis theorizes that unrealistic appraisals of stress are derived from irrational assumptions that people hold. He maintains that if you scrutinize your catastrophic thinking, you'll find that your reasoning is based on a logically indefensible premise, such as "I must have approval from everyone" or "I must perform well in all endeavours." These faulty assumptions, which people often hold unconsciously, generate catastrophic thinking and emotional turmoil.

How can you reduce your unrealistic appraisals of stress? Ellis asserts that you must learn (1) how to detect catastrophic thinking and (2) how to dispute the irrational assumptions that cause it. Detection involves acquiring the ability to spot unrealistic pessimism and wild exaggeration in your thinking. Disputing your irrational assumptions requires subjecting your reasoning process to scrutiny. Try to root out the assumptions from which you derive your conclusions. Once the underlying premises are unearthed, their irrationality may be obvious.

Using Humour as a Stress Reducer

A number of years ago, the Chicago area experienced its worst flooding in about a century. Thousands of people saw their homes wrecked when two rivers spilled over their banks. As the waters receded, the flood victims returning to their homes were subjected to the inevitable TV interviews. A remarkable number of victims, surrounded by the ruins of their homes, *joked* about their misfortune. When the going gets tough, it may pay to laugh about it. In a study of

coping styles, McCrae (1984) found that 40% of his subjects used humour to deal with stress.

Empirical evidence showing that humour moderates the impact of stress has been accumulating over the last 25 years (Abel, 1998; Lefcourt, 2001), although Rod Martin from the University of Western Ontario has argued recently that the research to date has some inadequacies and that the area needs more theory-based, rigorous research (Martin, 2001). Martin and his colleagues have developed the Humour Styles Questionnaire that is designed to assess individual differences in humour use. He suggests it may be used to assess types of humour that may be connected to well-being (Martin et al., 2003). University of Waterloo psychologist Herbert Lefcourt and colleagues (1995) argue that high-humour people may benefit from not taking themselves as seriously as low-humour people. As they put it, "If persons do not regard themselves too seriously and do not have an inflated sense of self-importance, then defeats, embarrassments, and even tragedies should have less pervasive emotional consequences for them" (p. 375).

Releasing Pent-Up Emotions

As we discussed in the main body of the chapter, stress often leads to emotional arousal. When this happens, there's merit in the commonsense notion that you should try to release the emotions welling up inside. Why? Because the physiological arousal that accompanies emotions can become problematic. For example, research suggests that people who inhibit the expression of anger and other emotions are somewhat more likely than other people to have elevated blood pressure (Jorgensen et al., 1996). Moreover, research suggests that efforts to actively suppress emotions result in increased autonomic arousal (Gross, 1998, 2001) and decreased immune function (Petrie, Booth, & Pennebaker, 1998).

Although there's no guarantee of it, you can sometimes reduce your physiological arousal by *expressing* your emotions. Evidence is accumulating that writing or talking about life's difficulties can be valuable

in dealing with stress (Hemenover, 2003; Smyth & Pennebaker, 1999). For example, in one study of university students, half the subjects were asked to write three essays about their difficulties in adjusting to university. The other half wrote three essays about superficial topics. The subjects who wrote about their personal problems enjoyed better health in the following months than the other subjects did (Pennebaker, Colder, & Sharp, 1990). Subsequent, similar studies have replicated this finding (Francis & Pennebaker, 1992; Greenberg, Wortman, & Stone, 1996) and shown that emotional disclosure is associated with better immune functioning (Smyth & Pennebaker, 2001). So, if you can find a good listener, you may be able to discharge problematic emotions by letting your secret fears, misgivings, and suspicions spill out in a candid conversation.

Managing Hostility and Forgiving Others

Scientists have compiled quite a bit of evidence that hostility is related to increased risk for heart attacks and other types of illness (Williams, 2001). In light of this reality, many experts assert that people should strive to learn how to manage their feelings of hostility more effectively (Williams & Williams, 2001). The goal of hostility management is not merely to suppress the overt expression of hostility that may continue to seethe beneath the surface, but to actually reduce the frequency and intensity of one's hostile feelings.

We tend to experience hostility and other negative emotions when we feel "wronged"—that is, when we believe that the actions of another person were harmful, immoral, or unjust. When we feel wronged, our natural inclination is either to seek revenge or to avoid further contact with the offender (McCullough, 2001). *Forgiving* someone involves counteracting these natural tendencies and releasing the person from further liability for his or her transgression. Research suggests that forgiving is associated with better adjustment and well-being (McCullough & Witvliet, 2002; Thoresen, Harris, & Luskin, 1999; Worthington & Scherer, 2004). For example, in one study

Putting It in Perspective

Which of our themes were prominent in this chapter? As you probably noticed, our discussion of stress and health illustrated multifactorial causation and the subjectivity of experience. As we noted in Chapter 1, people tend to think simplistically, in terms of single causes. In recent years, the highly publicized research linking stress to health has led many people to point automatically to stress as an explanation for illness. In reality, stress has only a modest impact on physical health. Stress can increase the risk for illness, but health is governed by a dense network of factors. Important factors include inherited vulnerabilities, physiological reactivity, exposure to infectious agents, health-impairing habits, reactions to symptoms, treatment-seeking behaviour, compliance with medical advice, personality, and social support. In other words, stress is but one actor on a crowded stage. This should be apparent in Figure 13.18, which shows the multitude of biopsychosocial factors that jointly influence physical health. It illustrates multifactorial causation in all its complexity.

The subjectivity of experience was demonstrated by the frequently repeated point that stress lies in the eye of the beholder. The same job promotion may be stressful for one person and invigorating for another. One person's pressure is another's challenge. When it comes to stress, objective reality is not nearly as important as subjective perceptions. More than anything else, the impact of stressful events seems to depend on how people view them. The critical importance of individual stress appraisals will continue to be apparent in the Personal Application on coping and stress management. Many stress management strategies depend on altering one's appraisals of events.

Figure 13.18

Biopsychosocial factors in health. Physical health can be influenced by a remarkably diverse set of variables, including biological, psychological, and social factors. The host of factors that affect health provide an excellent example of multifactorial causation.

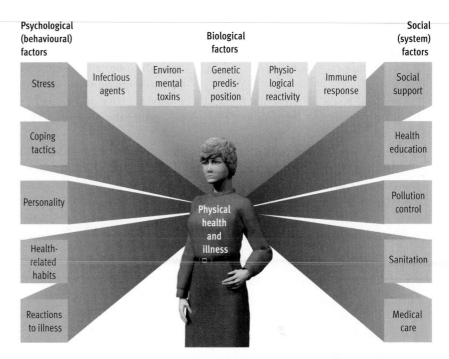

PREVIEW QUESTIONS
- How did this chapter illustrate multifactorial causation?
- How did this chapter highlight the subjectivity of human experience?

REVIEW OF KEY POINTS

- Ignoring physical symptoms may result in the delay of medical treatment. There are many barriers to effective communication between patients and health-care providers.
- Noncompliance with medical advice is a major problem. The likelihood of nonadherence is greater when instructions are difficult to understand, when recommendations are difficult to follow, and when patients are unhappy with their doctor.
- Two of our integrative themes were prominent in this chapter. First, we saw that behaviour and health are influenced by multiple causes. Second, we saw that experience is highly subjective, as stress lies in the eye of the beholder.

Improving Coping and Stress Management

Answer the following "true" or "false."

____ **1.** The key to managing stress is to avoid or circumvent it.

____ **2.** It's best to suppress emotional reactions to stress.

____ **3.** Laughing at one's problems is immature.

Courses and books on stress management have multiplied at a furious pace in the last couple of decades. They summarize experts' advice on how to cope with stress more effectively. How do these experts feel about the three statements above? As you'll see in this Application, most would agree that all three are false.

The key to managing stress does *not* lie in avoiding it. Stress is an inevitable element in the fabric of modern life. As Hans Selye (1973) noted, "Contrary to public opinion, we must not—and indeed can't—avoid stress" (p. 693). Thus, most stress management programs encourage people to confront stress rather than sidestep it. This requires training people to engage in action-oriented, rational, reality-based *constructive coping*.

As we noted earlier, some coping tactics are more healthful than others. In this Application, we'll examine a variety of constructive coping tactics, beginning with Albert Ellis's ideas about changing one's appraisals of stressful events.

Reappraisal: Ellis's Rational Thinking

Albert Ellis (1977, 1985, 1996, 2001) is a prominent theorist who believes that people can short-circuit their emotional reactions to stress by altering their appraisals of stressful events. Ellis's insights about stress appraisal are the foundation for a widely used system of therapy that he devised. *Rational-emotive therapy* is an approach that focuses on altering clients' patterns of irrational thinking to reduce maladaptive emotions and behaviour.

Ellis maintains that *you feel the way you think*. He argues that problematic emotional reactions are caused by negative self-talk, which he calls catastrophic thinking. *Catastrophic thinking* involves unrealistically negative appraisals of stress that exaggerate the magnitude of one's problems. Ellis uses a simple A-B-C sequence to explain his ideas (see Figure 13.19):

• *A: Activating event.* The A in Ellis's system stands for the activating event that produces the stress. The activating event may be any potentially stressful transaction. Examples might include an automobile accident, the cancellation of a date, a delay while waiting in line at the bank, or a failure to get a promotion you were expecting.

• *B: Belief system.* B stands for your belief about the event, or your appraisal of the stress. According to Ellis, people often view minor setbacks as disasters. Thus, they engage in catastrophic thinking: "How awful this is. I can't stand it! Things never turn out fair for me. I'll never get promoted."

• *C: Consequence.* C stands for the consequences of your negative thinking. When your appraisals of stressful events are overly negative, the consequence tends to be emotional distress. Thus, people feel angry, anxious, panic stricken, or dejected.

Figure 13.19

Albert Ellis's A-B-C model of emotional reactions. Although most people attribute their negative emotional reactions directly to negative events that they experience, Ellis argues that events themselves do *not* cause emotional distress—rather, distress is caused by the way people *think* about negative events. According to Ellis, the key to managing stress is to change one's appraisal of stressful events.

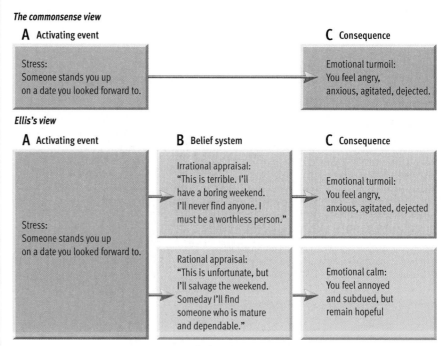

moral and social questions about what is acceptable behaviour into medical questions.

Although Szasz's criticism of the medical model has some merit, we'll take the position that the disease analogy continues to be useful, although one should remember that it is *only* an analogy. Medical concepts such as *diagnosis, etiology,* and *prognosis* have proven valuable in the treatment and study of abnormality. **Diagnosis involves distinguishing one illness from another. Etiology refers to the apparent causation and developmental history of an illness. A prognosis is a forecast about the probable course of an illness.** These medically based concepts have widely shared meanings that permit clinicians, researchers, and the public to communicate more effectively in their discussions of abnormal behaviour.

Criteria of Abnormal Behaviour

If your next-door neighbour scrubs his front porch twice every day and spends virtually all his time cleaning and recleaning his house, is he normal? If your sister-in-law goes to one physician after another seeking treatment for ailments that appear imaginary, is she psychologically healthy? How are we to judge what's normal and what's abnormal? More important, who's to do the judging?

These are complex questions. In making diagnoses, clinicians rely on a variety of criteria, the foremost of which are the following:

1. *Deviance.* As Szasz has pointed out, people are often said to have a disorder because their behaviour deviates from what their society considers acceptable. What constitutes normality varies somewhat from one culture to another, but all cultures have such norms. When people violate these standards and expectations, they may be labelled mentally ill. For example, *transvestic fetishism* is a sexual disorder in which a man achieves sexual arousal by dressing in women's clothing. This behaviour is regarded as disordered because a man who wears a dress, brassiere, and nylons is deviating from our culture's norms. This example illustrates the arbitrary nature of cultural standards regarding normality, as the same overt behaviour (cross-sex dressing) is acceptable for women but deviant for men.

2. *Maladaptive behaviour.* In many cases, people are judged to have a psychological disorder because their everyday adaptive behaviour is impaired. This is the key criterion in the diagnosis of substance use (drug) disorders. In and of itself, alcohol and drug use is not terribly unusual or deviant. However, when the use of cocaine, for instance, begins to

Figure 14.1

Historical conceptions of mental illness. In the Middle Ages people who behaved strangely were sometimes thought to be in league with the devil. The top drawing depicts some of the cruel methods used to extract confessions from suspected witches and warlocks. Some psychological disorders were also thought to be caused by demonic possession. The bottom illustration depicts an exorcism.

SOURCE: (Right) Culver Pictures, Inc. (Below) *St. Catherine of Siena Exorcising a Possessed Woman,* c. 1500–1510. Girolamo Di Benvenuto. Denver Art Museum Collection, Gift of Samuel H. Kress Foundation Collection, 1967.171 © 2001 Denver Art Museum.

interfere with a person's social or occupational functioning, a substance use disorder exists. In such cases, it is the maladaptive quality of the behaviour that makes it disordered.

3. *Personal distress.* Frequently, the diagnosis of a psychological disorder is based on an individual's report of great personal distress. This is usually the criterion met by people who are troubled by depression or anxiety disorders. Depressed people, for instance, may or may not exhibit deviant or maladaptive behaviour. Such people are usually labelled as having a disorder when they describe their subjective pain and suffering to friends, relatives, and mental health professionals.

Although two or three criteria may apply in a particular case, people are often viewed as disordered when only one criterion is met. As you may have already noticed, diagnoses of psychological disorders

"Minds can be 'sick' only in the sense that jokes are 'sick' or economies are 'sick.'"
THOMAS SZASZ

This man clearly exhibits a certain type of deviance, but does that mean that he has a psychological disorder? The criteria of mental illness are more subjective and complicated than most people realize, and to some extent, judgments of mental health represent value judgments.

APWide World Photos

Figure 14.2

Normality and abnormality as a continuum. There isn't a sharp boundary between normal and abnormal behaviour. Behaviour is normal or abnormal in degree, depending on the extent to which one's behaviour is deviant, personally distressing, or maladaptive.

Normal	Deviance	Abnormal
	Personal distress	
	Maladaptive behaviour	

involve *value judgments* about what represents normal or abnormal behaviour (Widiger & Sankis, 2000). The criteria of mental illness are not nearly as value-free as the criteria of physical illness. In evaluating physical diseases, people can usually agree that a malfunctioning heart or kidney is pathological, regardless of their personal values. However, judgments about mental illness reflect prevailing cultural values, social trends, and political forces, as well as scientific knowledge (Kutchins & Kirk, 1997; Mechanic, 1999).

Antonyms such as *normal* versus *abnormal* and *mental health* versus *mental illness* imply that people can be divided neatly into two distinct groups: those who are normal and those who are not. In reality, it is often difficult to draw a line that clearly separates normality from abnormality. On occasion, everybody acts in deviant ways, everyone displays some maladaptive behaviour, and everyone experiences personal distress. People are judged to have psychological disorders only when their behaviour becomes *extremely* deviant, maladaptive, or distressing. Thus, normality and abnormality exist on a continuum. It's a matter of degree, not an either–or proposition (see Figure 14.2).

Stereotypes of Psychological Disorders

We've seen that mental illnesses are not diseases in a strict sense and that judgments of mental health are not value-free. However, still other myths about abnormal behaviour need to be exposed as such. Let's examine three stereotypes about psychological disorders that are largely inaccurate:

1. *Psychological disorders are incurable.* Admittedly, there are mentally ill people for whom treatment is largely a failure. However, they are greatly outnumbered by people who do get better, either spontaneously or through formal treatment (Lambert & Ogles, 2004). The vast majority of people who are diagnosed as mentally ill eventually improve and lead normal, productive lives. Even the most severe psychological disorders can be treated successfully.

2. *People with psychological disorders are often violent and dangerous.* Only a modest association has been found between mental illness and violence-prone tendencies (Monahan, 1997; Tardiff, 1999). This stereotype exists because incidents of violence involving the mentally ill tend to command media attention. A report released by the Public Health Agency of Canada (1996) on mental illness and violence concluded that the strongest predictor of violence was past violence and that there was no *consistent* evidence that psychological disorders uncomplicated by substance abuse are a significant risk factor for violence, once you control for past history of violence.

3. *People with psychological disorders behave in bizarre ways and are very different from normal people.* This is true only in a small minority of cases, usually involving relatively severe disorders. As noted earlier, the line between normal and abnormal behaviour can be difficult to draw. At first glance, people with psychological disorders usually are indistinguishable from those without disorders. A classic study by David Rosenhan (1973) showed that even mental health professionals may have difficulty distinguishing normality from abnormality. To study diagnostic accuracy, Rosenhan arranged for a number of normal people to seek admission to mental hospitals. These "pseudopatients" arrived at the hospitals

complaining of one false symptom—hearing voices. Except for this single symptom, they acted as they normally would and gave accurate information when interviewed about their personal histories. *All* the pseudopatients were admitted, and the average length of their hospitalization was 19 days!

Why is it so hard to distinguish normality from abnormality? The pseudopatients' observations about life on the psychiatric wards offer a clue. They noted that the real patients acted normal most of the time and only infrequently acted in a deviant manner. As you might imagine, Rosenhan's study evoked quite a controversy about our diagnostic system for mental illness. Let's take a look at how this diagnostic system has evolved.

Psychodiagnosis: The Classification of Disorders

Obviously, we cannot lump all psychological disorders together without giving up all hope of understanding them better. A sound taxonomy of mental disorders can facilitate empirical research and enhance communication among scientists and clinicians (Williams, 1999). Hence, a great deal of effort has been invested in devising an elaborate system for classifying psychological disorders (see Figure 14.3).

Guidelines for psychodiagnosis were extremely vague and informal prior to 1952 when the American Psychiatric Association unveiled its *Diagnostic and Statistical Manual of Mental Disorders* (Grob, 1991). This classification scheme described about 100 disorders. Revisions intended to improve the system were incorporated into the second edition (DSM-II) published in 1968, but the diagnostic guidelines were still pretty sketchy. However, the third edition (DSM-III), published in 1980, represented a major advance, as the diagnostic criteria were made much more explicit, concrete, and detailed to facilitate more consistent diagnoses across clinicians (Blacker & Tsuang, 1999). The current, fourth edition (DSM-IV), which was released in 1994, made use of intervening research to refine the criteria introduced in DSM-III. Each revision of the DSM system has expanded the list of disorders covered. The current version describes about three times as many types of psychological disorders as DSM-I (Houts, 2002).

The publication of DSM-III in 1980 introduced a new multiaxial system of classification, which asks for judgments about individuals on five separate dimensions, or "axes." Figure 14.3 provides an overview of the five axes. The diagnoses of disorders are made on Axes I and II. Clinicians record most types of disorders on Axis I. They use Axis II to list long-running personality disorders or mental retardation. People may receive diagnoses on both Axes I and II.

The remaining axes are used to record supplemental information. A patient's physical disorders are listed on Axis III (General Medical Conditions). On Axis IV (Psychosocial and Environmental Problems), the clinician makes notations regarding the types of stress experienced by the individual in the past year. On Axis V (Global Assessment of Functioning), estimates are made of the individual's current level of adaptive functioning (in social and occupational behaviour, viewed as a whole) and of the individual's highest level of functioning in the past year. Figure 14.4 shows an example of a multiaxial evaluation. Most theorists agree that the multiaxial system is a step in the right direction because it recognizes the importance of information besides a traditional diagnostic label.

A great deal of progress had been made in the last two decades in the effort to make psychodiagnosis more reliable, more valid, and more scientific (Blashfield & Livesley, 1999). That said, a host of conceptual headaches and controversial issues remain (Adams, Luscher, & Bernat, 2001; Garfield, 2001). The quest for a scientific system of psychodiagnosis is an ongoing challenge, and there is a great deal of room for further progress (Widiger & Clark, 2000).

The Prevalence of Psychological Disorders

How common are psychological disorders? What percentage of the population is afflicted with mental illness? Is it 10%? Perhaps 25%? Could the figure range as high as 40% or 50%?

Such estimates fall in the domain of *epidemiology—the study of the distribution of mental or physical disorders in a population.* The 1980s and 1990s brought major advances in psychiatric epidemiology, as a host of large-scale investigations provided a huge, new database on the distribution of mental disorders (Murphy, Tohen, & Tsuang, 1999). In epidemiology, *prevalence* **refers to the percentage of a population that exhibits a disorder during a specified time period.** In the case of mental disorders, the most interesting data are the estimates of *lifetime prevalence,* the percentage of people who endure a specific disorder at any time in their lives.

Estimates of lifetime prevalence suggest that psychological disorders are more common than most people realize. Prior to the advent of DSM-III, studies suggested that about *one-fifth* of the population exhibited clear signs of mental illness at some point in their lives (Neugebauer, Dohrenwend, & Dohrenwend,

"How many people, one wonders, are sane but not recognized as such in our psychiatric institutions?"
DAVID ROSENHAN

Web Link 14.2

National Alliance for the Mentally Ill (NAMI)
http://www.nami.org/

NAMI describes itself as "a grassroots, self-help support and advocacy organization of families and friends of people with serious mental illness, and those persons themselves." Its online site responds to their needs with extensive and current information about schizophrenia, bipolar disorder, and other severe disorders.

Figure **14.3**

Overview of the DSM diagnostic system. Published by the American Psychiatric Association, the *Diagnostic and Statistical Manual of Mental Disorders* is the formal classification system used in the diagnosis of psychological disorders. It is a *multiaxial* system, which means that information is recorded on the five axes described here. (Based on American Psychiatric Association, 1994, 2000)

SOURCE: Adapted with permission from the *Diagnostic and Statistical Manual of Mental Disorders, 4th ed. (DSM–TR)*. Copyright © 2000 American Psychiatric Association.

Axis I
Clinical Syndromes

1. **Disorders usually first diagnosed in infancy, childhood, or adolescence**
   This category includes disorders that arise before adolescence, such as attention deficit disorders, autism, enuresis, and stuttering.

2. **Organic mental disorders**
   These disorders are temporary or permanent dysfunctions of brain tissue caused by diseases or chemicals. Examples are delirium, dementia, and amnesia.

3. **Substance-related disorders**
   This category refers to the maladaptive use of drugs and alcohol. This category requires an abnormal pattern of use, as with alcohol abuse and cocaine dependence.

4. **Schizophrenia and other psychotic disorders**
   The schizophrenias are characterized by psychotic symptoms (for example, grossly disorganized behaviour, delusions, and hallucinations) and by over six months of behavioural deterioration. This category also includes delusional disorder and schizoaffective disorder.

5. **Mood disorders**
   The cardinal feature is emotional disturbance. These disorders include major depression, bipolar disorder, dysthymic disorder, and cyclothymic disorder.

6. **Anxiety disorders**
   These disorders are characterized by physiological signs of anxiety (for example, palpitations) and subjective feelings of tension, apprehension, or fear. Anxiety may be acute and focused (panic disorder) or continual and diffuse (generalized anxiety disorder).

7. **Somatoform disorders**
   These disorders are dominated by somatic symptoms that resemble physical illnesses. These symptoms cannot be fully accounted for by organic damage. This category includes somatization and conversion disorders and hypochondriasis.

8. **Dissociative disorders**
   These disorders all feature a sudden, temporary alteration or dysfunction of memory, consciousness, and identity, as in dissociative amnesia and dissociative identity disorder.

9. **Sexual and gender-identity disorders**
   There are three basic types of disorders in this category: gender identity disorders (discomfort with identity as male or female), paraphilias (preference for unusual acts to achieve sexual arousal), and sexual dysfunctions (impairments in sexual functioning).

10. **Eating disorders**
    Eating disorders are severe disturbances in eating behaviour characterized by preoccupation with weight concerns and unhealthy efforts to control weight. Examples include anorexia nervosa and bulimia nervosa.

Axis II
Personality Disorders or Mental Retardation

Personality disorders are longstanding patterns of extreme, inflexible personality traits that are deviant or maladaptive and lead to impaired functioning or subjective distress. *Mental retardation* refers to subnormal general mental ability accompanied by deficiencies in adaptive skills, originating before age 18.

Axis III
General Medical Conditions

Physical disorders or conditions are recorded on this axis. Examples include diabetes, arthritis, and hemophilia.

Axis IV
Psychosocial and Environmental Problems

Axis IV is for reporting psychosocial and environmental problems that may affect the diagnosis, treatment, and prognosis of mental disorders (Axes I and II). A psychosocial or environmental problem may be a negative life event, an environmental difficulty or deficiency, a familial or other interpersonal stress, an inadequacy of social support or personal resources, or another problem that describes the context in which a person's difficulties have developed.

Axis V
Global Assessment of Functioning (GAF) Scale

Code	Symptoms
100	Superior functioning in a wide range of activities
90	Absent or minimal symptoms, good functioning in all areas
80	Symptoms transient and expectable reactions to psychosocial stressors
70	Some mild symptoms or some difficulty in social, occupational, or school functioning, but generally functioning pretty well
60	Moderate symptoms or difficulty in social, occupational, or school functioning
50	Serious symptoms or impairment in social, occupational, or school functioning
40	Some impairment in reality testing or communication or major impairment in family relations, judgment, thinking, or mood
30	Behaviour considerably influenced by delusions or hallucinations, serious impairment in communication or judgment, or inability to function in almost all areas
20	Some danger of hurting self or others, occasional failure to maintain minimal personal hygiene, or gross impairment in communication
10	Persistent danger of severely hurting self or others
1	

1980). However, the older studies did not assess alcohol and drug-related disorders very effectively, because these disorders were vaguely described in DSM-I and DSM-II. Studies published in the 1980s and early 1990s, using the explicit criteria for substance-use disorders in DSM-III, found psychological disorders in roughly *one-third* of the population (Regier & Kaelber, 1995; Robins, Locke, & Regier, 1991). Subsequent research, which has focused on a somewhat younger sample (ages 18–54 instead of over age 18), suggests that about 44% of the adult population will struggle with some sort of psychological disorder at some

A DSM multiaxial evaluation (patient 49-year-old male)	
Axis I	Major depressive disorder Cocaine abuse
Axis II	Borderline personality disorder (provisional, rule out dependent personality disorder)
Axis III	Hypertension
Axis IV	Psychosocial stressors: recent divorce, permitted to see his children only infrequently, job is in jeopardy
Axis V	Current global assessment of functioning (GAF): 46

Figure 14.4

Example of a multiaxial evaluation. A multiaxial evaluation for a depressed man with a cocaine problem might look like this.

point in their lives (Kessler & Zhao, 1999; Regier & Burke, 2000). Obviously, all these figures are *estimates* that depend to some extent on the sampling and assessment techniques used (Wakefield, 1999). Some of the increase in the prevalence of mental illness is more apparent than real, as it is partly attributable to more effective tabulation of certain disorders. However, research also suggests that there has been a genuine increase in the prevalence of mental disorders among more recent age cohorts (Smith & Weissman, 1992).

Recent data from Statistics Canada (2003a) and the Public Health Agency of Canada (2002) give us a snapshot of the prevalence and costs of psychological disorders in Canada. Figure 14.5 presents the reported rates of selected disorders for 2001–02 in Canada (Statistics Canada, 2003a). Overall, one in ten Canadians over 15 years of age reported symptoms consistent with one of the categories of disorder listed. As you can see in Figure 14.5, while the overall rates for males and females are about equal (9.7% and 11.1%), there is gender variation across categories of disorder. Most (68%) of the people who reported symptoms consistent with one of these disorders *did not* seek assistance. The costs of these disorders for the individuals and their families are enormous. In addition, the costs to the health system are also substantial. The report produced by the Public Health Agency of Canada (2002) estimates the 1993 costs of all psychological disorders to be $7.331 billion. In 1999, 1.5 million hospital days were due to admissions for anxiety disorders, major depression, bipolar disorders, schizophrenia, personality disorders, eating disorders, and suicidal behaviour. Hospital admissions for eating disorders increased by 34% between 1987 and 1999 for young women under the age of 15. Eating disorders are discussed in the Personal Application for this chapter on page 614.

In this chapter we cannot discuss in detail all the disorders listed in the DSM-IV. Some of the disorders we have discussed in previous chapters (e.g., see Chapter 5 for a discussion of substance abuse). However, we will introduce you to most of the major categories of disorder to give you an overview of the many forms that psychological disorder can take.

In discussing each set of disorders, we will begin with brief descriptions of the specific syndromes or subtypes that fall in the category. Then we'll focus on the *etiology* of the disorders in that category. Although many paths can lead to specific disorders, some are more common than others. We'll highlight some of the common paths to enhance your understanding of the roots of abnormal behaviour.

	Total		Males		Females	
	Number	%	Number	%	Number	%
Major depression	1 120 000	4.5	420 000	3.4	700 000	5.5
Mania disorder	190 000	0.8	90 000	0.7	100 000	0.8
Any mood	**1 210 000**	**4.9**	**460 000**	**3.8**	**750 000**	**5.9**
Panic disorder	400 000	1.6	130 000	1.1	270 000	2.1
Agoraphobia	180 000	0.7	40 000	0.4	140 000	1.1
Social anxiety disorder (social phobia)	750 000	3.0	310 000	2.6	430 000	3.4
Any anxiety	**1 180 000**	**4.7**	**440 000**	**3.6**	**740 000**	**5.8**
Alcohol dependence	640 000	2.6	470 000	3.8	170 000	1.3
Illicit drugs dependence	170 000	0.7	120 000	1.0	50 000	0.4
Substance dependence	**740 000**	**3.0**	**540 000**	**4.4**	**200 000**	**1.6**
Total – Any measured disorder or substance dependence	**2 600 000**	**10.4**	**1 190 000**	**9.7**	**1 410 000**	**11.1**

Figure 14.5

Reported one-year prevalence of psychological disorders. This figure presents the estimated percentage of people who have suffered from one of a selected set of psychological disorders in the year preceding the survey. The estimates represent people surveyed with symptoms consistent with each type of disorder. The survey targeted Canadians 15 years and older and excluded members of the Armed Forces, First Nations people living on reserves, and people confined to health-care institutions.

SOURCE: Statistics Canada. Canadian community health Survey: Mental health and well-being. *The Daily*, September 3, 2003. Retrieved June 27, 2005, from http://www.statcan.ca/Daily/English/030903/td030903.htm. Adapted from the Statistics Canada publication, "The Daily," Canadian Community Health Survey: Mental health and well-being, Catalogue 11-001, Wednesday, September 3, 2003.

REVIEW OF KEY POINTS

- The medical model assumes that it is useful to view abnormal behaviour as a disease. This view has been criticized on the grounds that it turns questions about deviance into medical questions. Nonetheless, the medical model has proven useful, although one should remember that it is only an analogy.

- Three criteria are used in deciding whether people suffer from psychological disorders: deviance, personal distress, and maladaptive behaviour. Often it is difficult to clearly draw a line between normality and abnormality. Contrary to popular stereotypes, people with psychological disorders are not particularly bizarre or dangerous, and even the most severe disorders are treatable.

- Research by David Rosenhan showed that pseudopatients were routinely admitted to mental hospitals, which were unable to detect the patients' normalcy. His study showed that the distinction between normality and abnormality is not clear-cut.

- DSM-IV is the official psychodiagnostic classification system. This system asks for information about patients on five axes, or dimensions. It is difficult to obtain good data on the prevalence of psychological disorders. Nonetheless, it is clear that they are more common than widely believed.

Psychological Disorders

PREVIEW QUESTIONS

- What are the five major anxiety disorders and what are their chief symptoms?
- Which biological factors have been implicated in anxiety disorders?
- How do conditioning and learning contribute to anxiety disorders?
- How do cognition and stress contribute to anxiety disorders?

Everyone experiences anxiety from time to time. It is a natural and common reaction to many of life's difficulties. For some people, however, anxiety becomes a chronic problem. These people experience high levels of anxiety with disturbing regularity. *Anxiety disorders are a class of disorders marked by feelings of excessive apprehension and anxiety.* We will look at five principal types of anxiety disorders: generalized anxiety disorder, phobic disorder, panic disorder, obsessive-compulsive disorder, and post-traumatic stress disorder. These disorders are not mutually exclusive, as many people who develop one anxiety syndrome often suffer from another at some point in their lives (Hunt & Andrews, 1995).

Generalized Anxiety Disorder 11A

The *generalized anxiety disorder* is marked by a chronic, high level of anxiety that is not tied to any specific threat. This anxiety is sometimes called "free-floating anxiety" because it is nonspecific. People with this disorder worry constantly about yesterday's mistakes and tomorrow's problems. In particular, they worry about minor matters related to family, finances, work, and personal illness (Sanderson & Barlow, 1990). They also worry about how much they worry (Barlow et al., 2003). They often dread decisions and brood over them endlessly. Their anxiety is commonly accompanied by physical symptoms, such as trembling, muscle tension, diarrhea, dizziness, faintness, sweating, and heart palpitations. Generalized anxiety disorder tends to have a gradual onset and is seen more frequently in females than males (Brown, 1999).

Phobic Disorder 11A

In a phobic disorder, an individual's troublesome anxiety has a specific focus. A *phobic disorder is marked by a persistent and irrational fear of an object or situation that presents no realistic danger.* Although mild phobias are extremely common, people are said to have a phobic disorder only when their fears seriously interfere with their everyday behaviour. Phobic reactions tend to be accompanied by physical symptoms of anxiety, such as trembling and palpitations (Rapee & Barlow, 2001).

People can develop phobic responses to virtually anything—even to things you take for granted such as driving. Dr. Martin Antony, an expert on anxiety disorders such as obsessive-compulsive disorder, panic disorder, and phobias (Antony & McCabe, 2003;

Antony et al., in press), is director of the Anxiety Treatment and Research Centre at St. Joseph's Hospital in Hamilton. The centre is affiliated with McMaster University and is one of the leading research and treatment institutions for anxiety disorders. Dr. Antony estimates that 1%–5% of Canadians suffer significant anxiety related to their driving fears (Pooley, 2004), but that those suffering from these disorders are by and large very good drivers.

While people can develop phobias to almost anything, certain types of phobias are more common than others. Particularly common are acrophobia (fear of heights), claustrophobia (fear of small, enclosed places), brontophobia (fear of storms), hydrophobia (fear of water), and various animal and insect phobias (Eaton, Dryman, & Weissman, 1991). People troubled by phobias typically realize that their fears are irrational, but they still are unable to calm themselves when confronted by a phobic object. Among many of them, even *imagining* a phobic object or situation can trigger great anxiety (Thorpe & Salkovskis, 1995).

Panic Disorder and Agoraphobia 11A

A *panic disorder is characterized by recurrent attacks of overwhelming anxiety that usually occur suddenly and unexpectedly.* These paralyzing panic attacks are accompanied by physical symptoms of anxiety. After a number of panic attacks, victims often become apprehensive, wondering when their next panic will occur. Their concern about exhibiting panic in public may escalate to the point where they are afraid to leave home. This creates a condition called *agoraphobia,* which is a common complication of panic disorders.

Several studies have examined the rate of panic attacks in Canadian university students. Questionnaire studies suggest that as many as 34% of undergraduates suffer from this disorder (Norton et al., 1985). Many of these students, however, are likely suffering from *nonclinical* panic, which differs from a diagnosable panic attack. Research by University of Manitoba psychologist Brian Cox suggests that this doesn't mean the problems for the nonclinical group are insignificant. While there are qualitative differences, many symptoms are shared by the two groups, differing only in quantity. Cox suggests that nonclinical and clinical levels of panic attacks may exist on a continuum (Cox, Endler, & Swinson, 1991).

Agoraphobia is a fear of going out to public places (its literal meaning is "fear of the marketplace or open places"). Because of this fear, some people become prisoners confined to their homes, although many will venture out if accompanied by a trusted companion (Hollander & Simeon, 2003). As its name suggests, agoraphobia has traditionally been viewed as a phobic disorder. However, more recent evidence suggests that agoraphobia is mainly a complication of panic disorder. About two-thirds of people who suffer from panic disorder are female (Horwath & Weissman, 2000). The onset of panic disorder typically occurs during late adolescence or early adulthood (Pine, 2000).

Obsessive-Compulsive Disorder 11A

Obsessions are *thoughts* that repeatedly intrude on one's consciousness in a distressing way. Compulsions are *actions* that one feels forced to carry out. Thus, **an obsessive-compulsive disorder (OCD) is marked by persistent, uncontrollable intrusions of unwanted thoughts (obsessions) and urges to engage in senseless rituals (compulsions).** To illustrate, let's examine the bizarre behaviour of a man once reputed to be the wealthiest person in the world:

The famous industrialist Howard Hughes was obsessed with the possibility of being contaminated by germs. This led him to devise extraordinary rituals to minimize the possibility of such contamination. He would spend hours methodically cleaning a single telephone. He once wrote a three-page memo instructing assistants on exactly how to open cans of fruit for him. The following is just a small portion of the instructions that Hughes provided for a driver who delivered films to his bungalow. "Get out of the car on the traffic side. Do not at any time be on the side of the car between the car and the curb.... Carry only one can of film at a time. Step over the gutter opposite the place where the sidewalk dead-ends into the curb from a point as far out into the center of the road as possible. Do not ever walk on the grass at all, also do not step into the gutter at all. Walk to the bungalow keeping as near to the center of the side-walk as possible." (Adapted from Barlett & Steele, 1979, pp. 227–237)

Some of Howard Hughes's obsessions were effectively portrayed in the 2004 film *The Aviator*.

Obsessions often centre on inflicting harm on others, personal failures, suicide, or sexual acts. People troubled by obsessions may feel that they have lost control of their mind. Compulsions usually involve stereotyped rituals that temporarily relieve anxiety. Common examples include constant hand-washing, repetitive cleaning of things that are already clean, and endless

As a young man (shown in the photo), Howard Hughes was a handsome, dashing daredevil pilot and movie producer who appeared to be reasonably well adjusted. However, as the years went by, his behaviour gradually became more and more maladaptive, as obsessions and compulsions came to dominate his life. In his later years (shown in the drawing), he spent most of his time in darkened rooms, naked, unkempt, and dirty, following bizarre rituals to alleviate his anxieties. (The drawing was done by an NBC artist and was based on descriptions from men who had seen Hughes.)

rechecking of locks, faucets, and such (Pato, Eisen, & Phillips, 2003). Specific types of obsessions tend to be associated with specific types of compulsions. For example, obsessions about contamination tend to be paired with cleaning compulsions and obsessions about symmetry tend to be paired with ordering and arranging compulsions (Leckman et al., 1997).

Although many of us can be compulsive at times, full-fledged obsessive-compulsive disorders occur in roughly 2.5% of the population (Turner et al., 2001). The prevalence of obsessive-compulsive disorder seems to be increasing, but this trend may simply reflect changes in clinicians' diagnostic tendencies (Stein et al., 1997). Most cases of OCD emerge before the age of 35 (Kessler et al., 2005; Otto et al., 1999).

While OCD is often seen as a unitary disorder, recent research by Laura Summerfeldt from Trent University, Martin Antony, and their colleagues suggests that it may be a heterogeneous disorder (Summerfeldt et al., 1999). They factor-analyzed the symptom structure of 203 Canadians diagnosed with OCD and found that four factors seemed to underlie the symptoms: obsessions and checking, symmetry and order, cleanliness and washing, and hoarding. They conclude that "Our findings add to the growing body of evidence for the multidimensionality of OCD, but suggest that a comprehensive model of symptom structure has yet to be identified" (p. 309).

Post-Traumatic Stress Disorder (PTSD)

Although we began this chapter with an illustration of PTSD suffered by members of the military, PTSD is not restricted to this context. PTSD is often elicited by any of a variety of traumatic events, including a rape or assault, a severe automobile accident, a natural disaster, or the witnessing of someone's death (Koren, Arnon, & Klein, 1999; Stein et al., 1997; Vernberg et al., 1996). In some instances, PTSD does not surface until many months or years after a person's exposure to severe stress (Holen, 2000).

The proportion of people who develop psychological problems after a traumatic event varies depending on the nature, severity, and duration of the trauma. Averaging over many types of trauma, it is estimated that about 9% of people exposed to a traumatic stressor develop PTSD (Everly, 2000). However, studies suggest that deliberate violence, such as that seen in terrorist attacks, tends to produce more severe negative effects on mental health than accidents or natural disasters. Generally speaking, watching, reading, or listening to media coverage of major disasters does *not* lead to PTSD or other serious psychological problems (Korn, 2001). Some research, however, has demonstrated that indirect exposure to a traumatic event through graphic television coverage *can* lead to PTSD, at least in children (Pfefferbaum et al., 2000). Given the graphic video footage of the destruction of the World Trade Center in 2001, it seems likely that the 9/11 terrorist attacks will lead to the emergence of post-traumatic stress disorder in some people who were not at the scene of the attacks.

Research suggests a variety of factors are predictors of individuals' risk for PTSD (McNally, 1999; Norris et al., 2001; Ursano, Fullerton, & Norwood, 2001). As you might expect, increased vulnerability is associated with greater personal injuries and losses, greater intensity of exposure to the traumatic event, and more exposure to the grotesque aftermath of the event. The likelihood of PTSD is higher among women than men and among people who were already struggling with psychological problems before they were exposed to a traumatic event (Halligan & Yehuda, 2001). Vulnerability to PTSD is not limited to victims, survivors, and witnesses of traumatic events. Rescue workers and cleanup crews who have to grapple with the gruesome carnage of major disasters, dangerous working conditions, and tremendous fatigue also have a highly elevated risk for PTSD (Ursano et al., 1999).

What are the symptoms of post-traumatic stress disorders? Common symptoms include re-experiencing the traumatic event in the form of nightmares and flashbacks, emotional numbing, alienation, problems in social relations, an increased sense of vulnerability, and elevated arousal, anxiety, anger, and guilt (Flannery, 1999; Shalev, 2001). PTSD is also associated with an elevated risk for substance abuse, depression, and suicide attempts (Warshaw et al., 1993), as well as a great variety of physical health problems (Beckham et al., 1998). The frequency and severity of post-traumatic symptoms usually decline gradually over time, but recovery tends to be gradual, and in many cases the symptoms never completely disappear. Many years after his experiences in Rwanda, General Roméo Dallaire is still suffering the aftereffects.

Etiology of Anxiety Disorders

Like most psychological disorders, anxiety disorders develop out of complicated interactions among a variety of biological and psychological factors.

Biological Factors

In studies that assess the impact of heredity on psychological disorders, investigators look at *concordance rates*. A **concordance rate indicates the percentage of twin pairs or other pairs of relatives who exhibit the same disorder.** If relatives who share more genetic similarity show higher concordance rates than relatives who share less genetic overlap, this finding supports the genetic hypothesis. The results of both *twin studies* (see Figure 14.6) and *family studies* (see Chapter 3 for discussions of both methods) suggest that there is a moderate genetic predisposition to anxiety disorders (Fyer, 2000; Hettema, Neale, & Kendler, 2001).

Another line of research suggests that *anxiety sensitivity* may make people vulnerable to anxiety disorders (Reiss, 1991; Weems et al., 2002). According to this notion, some people are highly sensitive to the internal physiological symptoms of anxiety and are

Figure 14.6

Twin studies of anxiety disorders. The concordance rate for anxiety disorders in identical twins is higher than that for fraternal twins, who share less genetic overlap. These results suggest that there is a genetic predisposition to anxiety disorders. (Data based on Noyes et al., 1987; Slater & Shields, 1969; Torgersen, 1979, 1983)

Relationship	Genetic relatedness	Concordance rate (%) (lifetime risk)
Identical twins	100%	(bar to ~37)
Fraternal twins	50%	(bar to ~15)

prone to overreact with fear when they experience these symptoms. Anxiety sensitivity may fuel an inflationary spiral in which anxiety breeds more anxiety, which eventually spins out of control in the form of an anxiety disorder. Cox and his colleagues suggest that some aspects of anxiety sensitivity may serve as vulnerabilities both for panic disorder and depression (Cox et al., 2001).

Recent evidence suggests that a link may exist between anxiety disorders and neurochemical activity in the brain. As you learned in Chapter 3, *neurotransmitters* are chemicals that carry signals from one neuron to another. Therapeutic drugs (such as Valium) that reduce excessive anxiety appear to alter neurotransmitter activity at GABA synapses. This finding and other lines of evidence suggest that disturbances in the neural circuits using GABA may play a role in some types of anxiety disorders (Skolnick, 2003). Abnormalities in neural circuits using serotonin have recently been implicated in panic and obsessive-compulsive disorders (Sullivan & Coplan, 2000). Thus, scientists are beginning to unravel the neurochemical bases for anxiety disorders.

Conditioning and Learning

Many anxiety responses may be *acquired through classical conditioning and maintained through operant conditioning* (see Chapter 6). Imagine, for example, a young child who is buried briefly in the snow by a small avalanche, and who now, as an adult, is afraid of snow. According to Mowrer (1947), an originally neutral stimulus (the snow in this case, for instance) may be paired with a frightening event (the avalanche) so that it becomes a conditioned stimulus eliciting anxiety (see Figure 14.7a). Once a fear is acquired through classical conditioning, the person may start avoiding the anxiety-producing stimulus. The avoidance response is negatively reinforced because it is followed by a reduction in anxiety. This process involves operant conditioning (see Figure 14.7b). Thus, separate conditioning processes may create and then sustain specific anxiety responses (Levis, 1989). Consistent with this view, studies find that a substantial portion of people suffering from phobias can identify a traumatic conditioning experience that probably contributed to their anxiety disorder (Antony & McCabe, 2003; King, Eleonora, & Ollendick, 1998; Stemberger et al., 1995).

The tendency to develop phobias of certain types of objects and situations may be explained by Martin Seligman's (1971) concept of *preparedness*. Like many theorists, Seligman believes that classical conditioning creates most phobic responses. *However, he suggests that people are biologically prepared by their evolutionary history to acquire some fears much more easily than others.*

His theory would explain why people develop phobias of ancient sources of threat (such as snakes and spiders) much more readily than modern sources of threat (such as electrical outlets or hot irons). Some laboratory studies of conditioned fears have yielded evidence that supports Seligman's theory, but the evidence is inconsistent (Rapee & Barlow, 2001).

Critics note a number of problems with conditioning models of phobias (Rachman, 1990). For instance, many people with phobias cannot recall or identify a traumatic conditioning experience that led to their phobia. Conversely, many people endure extremely traumatic experiences that should create a phobia but do not. To provide better explanations for these complexities, conditioning models of anxiety disorders are currently being revised to include a larger role for cognitive factors (de Jong & Merckelbach, 2000), much like conditioning theories in general, as we saw in Chapter 6.

One of these revisions is an increased emphasis on how observational learning can lead to the development of conditioned fears. *Observational learning* occurs when a new response is acquired through watching the behaviour of another (consult Chapter 6). Studies suggest that conditioned fears can be created through observational learning (Fredrikson, Annas, & Wik, 1997; Rachman, 1990). In particular, parents frequently pass on their anxieties to their children. Thus, if a father hides in a closet every time there's a thunderstorm, his children may acquire their father's fear of storms.

Cognitive Factors

Cognitive theorists maintain that certain styles of thinking make some people particularly vulnerable

(a) Classical conditioning: Acquisition of phobic fear

CS
Snow

UCS
Buried in avalanche

CR
Fear
UCR

(b) Operant conditioning: Maintenance of phobic fear (negative reinforcement)

Response

Avoid snow

Aversive stimulus removed

Fear reduced

Web Link 14.3

National Institute of Mental Health: For the Public
http://www.nimh.nih.gov/publicat/index.cfm

A wealth of information on psychological disorders is available at this subpage of the National Institute of Mental Health's massive site. Visitors will find detailed online booklets on generalized anxiety disorder, obsessive-compulsive disorder, panic disorder, depression, bipolar disorder, and other psychological disorders. Brief fact sheets, dense technical reports, and many other resources can also be found here.

Figure 14.7

Conditioning as an explanation for phobias. **(a)** Many phobias appear to be acquired through classical conditioning when a neutral stimulus is paired with an anxiety-arousing stimulus. **(b)** Once acquired, a phobia may be maintained through operant conditioning. Avoidance of the phobic stimulus reduces anxiety, resulting in negative reinforcement.

Figure **14.8**

Cognitive factors in anxiety disorders. Eysenck and his colleagues (1991) compared how subjects with anxiety problems and nonanxious subjects tended to interpret sentences that could be viewed as threatening or non-threatening. Consistent with cognitive models of anxiety disorders, anxious subjects were more likely to interpret the sentences in a threatening light.

Figure **14.9**

Stress and panic disorder. Faravelli and Pallanti (1989) assessed the amount of stress experienced during the 12 months before the onset of panic disorder in a group of 64 patients with this disorder and in a control group drawn from hospital employees and their friends. As you can see, there was a dramatic increase in stress in the month prior to the onset of the patients' panic disorders. These data suggest that stress may contribute to the development of panic disorders.

Source: Adapted from Faravelli, C., & Pallanti, S. (1989). Recent life events and panic disorders. *American Journal of Psychiatry, 146,* 622–626. Reprinted with permission from the *American Journal of Psychiatry,* (copyright 1989). American Psychiatric Association.

one such sentence was "The doctor examined little Emma's growth," which could mean that the doctor checked either her height or the growth of a tumour. As Figure 14.8 shows, the anxious participants interpreted the sentences in a threatening way more often than the nonanxious participants did. Thus, consistent with our theme that human experience is highly subjective, the cognitive view holds that some people are prone to anxiety disorders because they see threat in every corner of their lives (Aikens & Craske, 2001; Riskind, 2005; Williams et al., 1997).

Stress 11A

Finally, studies have supported the long-held suspicion that anxiety disorders are stress related (Sandin et al., 2004; Venturello et al., 2002). For instance, Faravelli and Pallanti (1989) found that patients with panic disorder had experienced a dramatic increase in stress in the month prior to the onset of their disorder (see Figure 14.9). In another study, Brown et al. (1998) found an association between stress and the development of social phobia. Thus, there is reason to believe that high stress often helps to precipitate the onset of anxiety disorders.

REVIEW OF KEY POINTS

● The anxiety disorders include generalized anxiety disorder, phobic disorder, panic disorder, obsessive-compulsive disorder, and post-traumatic stress disorder. Many people who develop one anxiety disorder also suffer from another.

● Twin studies suggest that there is a weak genetic predisposition to anxiety disorders. These disorders may be more likely in people who are especially sensitive to the physiological symptoms of anxiety. Abnormalities in neurotransmitter activity at GABA synapses or serotonin synapses may also play a role in anxiety disorders.

● Many anxiety responses, especially phobias, may be caused by classical conditioning and maintained by operant conditioning. Parents who model anxiety may promote these disorders through observational learning.

● Cognitive theorists maintain that certain styles of thinking—especially a tendency to overinterpret harmless situations as threatening—make some people more vulnerable to anxiety disorders. Stress may also predispose people to anxiety disorders.

to anxiety disorders. According to these theorists, some people are more likely to suffer from problems with anxiety because they tend to (a) misinterpret harmless situations as threatening, (b) focus excessive attention on perceived threats, and (c) selectively recall information that seems threatening (Beck, 1997; McNally, 1994, 1996). In one intriguing test of the cognitive view, anxious and nonanxious subjects were asked to read 32 sentences that could be interpreted in either a threatening or a nonthreatening manner (Eysenck et al., 1991). For instance,

Somatoform Disorders

PREVIEW QUESTIONS

● How do psychosomatic diseases and somatoform disorders differ?

● What are the three major somatoform disorders, and what are their chief symptoms?

● What factors have been implicated in the etiology of somatoform disorders?

Chances are, you have met people who always seem to be complaining about aches, pains, and physical maladies of doubtful authenticity. You may have thought to yourself, "It's all in his head" and concluded that the person exhibited a "psychosomatic" condition. However, as we discussed in Chapter 13, the term *psychosomatic* has been widely misused. *Psychosomatic diseases* involve *genuine* physical ailments caused in part by psychological factors, espe-

cially reactions to stress. These diseases, which include maladies such as ulcers, asthma, and high blood pressure, are not imagined ailments. They are recorded on the DSM axis for physical problems (Axis III). When physical illness appears *largely* psychological in origin, we are dealing with somatoform disorders, which are recorded on Axis I. **Somatoform disorders are physical ailments that cannot be fully explained by organic conditions and are largely**

due to psychological factors. Although their symptoms are more imaginary than real, victims of somatoform disorders are *not* simply faking illness. Deliberate feigning of illness for personal gain is another matter altogether, called *malingering.*

We will discuss three specific types of somatoform disorders: somatization disorder, conversion disorder, and hypochondriasis. Diagnostic difficulties make it hard to obtain sound data on the prevalence of somatoform disorders (Bouman, Eifert, & Lejuez, 1999).

Somatization Disorder

Individuals with somatization disorder are often said to "cling to ill health." **A *somatization disorder* is marked by a history of diverse physical complaints that appear to be psychological in origin.** Somatization disorder occurs mostly in women (Guggenheim, 2000) and often coexists with depression and anxiety disorders (Gureje et al., 1997). Victims report an endless succession of minor physical ailments that seem to wax and wane in response to the stress in their lives (Servan-Schreiber, Kolb, & Tabas, 1999). They usually have a long and complicated history of medical treatment from many doctors.

Conversion Disorder

Conversion disorder **is characterized by a significant loss of physical function (with no apparent organic basis), usually in a single organ system.** Common symptoms include partial or complete loss of vision, partial or complete loss of hearing, partial paralysis, severe laryngitis or mutism, and loss of feeling or function in limbs, such as that seen in the following case:

Mildred was a rancher's daughter who lost the use of both of her legs during adolescence. Mildred was at home alone one afternoon when a male relative attempted to assault her. She screamed for help, and her legs gave way as she slipped to the floor. She was found on the floor a few minutes later when her mother returned home. She could not get up, so she was carried to her bed. Her legs buckled when she made subsequent attempts to walk on her own. Due to her illness, she was waited on hand and foot by her family and friends. Neighbours brought her homemade things to eat or to wear. She became the centre of attention in the household. (Adapted from Cameron, 1963, pp. 312–313)

People with conversion disorder are usually troubled by more severe ailments than people with somatization disorder. In some cases of conversion disorder, telltale clues reveal the psychological origins of the illness because the patient's symptoms are not consistent with medical knowledge about their apparent disease. For instance, the loss of feeling in one hand that is seen in "glove anesthesia" is inconsistent with the known facts of neurological organization (see Figure 14.10).

Hypochondriasis

Hypochondriacs constantly monitor their physical condition, looking for signs of illness. Any tiny alteration from their physical norm leads them to conclude that they have contracted a disease. *Hypochondriasis* **(more widely known as hypochondria) is characterized by excessive preoccupation with health concerns and incessant worry about developing physical illnesses.**

When hypochondriacs are assured by their physician that they do not have any real illness, they often are skeptical and disbelieving (Starcevic, 2001). They frequently assume that the physician must be incompetent, and they go shopping for another doctor. Hypochondriacs don't subjectively suffer from physical distress as much as they *overinterpret* every conceivable sign of illness. Hypochondria frequently appears alongside other psychological disorders, especially anxiety disorders and depression (Iezzi, Duckworth, & Adams, 2001). For example, Howard Hughes's obsessive-compulsive disorder was coupled with profound hypochondria.

(a)   (b)

Figure 14.10

Glove anesthesia. In conversion disorders, the physical complaints are sometimes inconsistent with the known facts of physiology. For instance, given the patterns of nerve distribution in the arm shown in **(a),** it is impossible that a loss of feeling in the hand exclusively, as shown in **(b),** has a physical cause, indicating that the patient's problem is psychological in origin.

Etiology of Somatoform Disorders

Inherited aspects of physiological functioning, such as a highly reactive autonomic nervous system, may predispose some people to somatoform disorders (Weiner, 1992). However, available evidence suggests that these disorders are largely a function of personality and cognitive factors. Let's look at personality factors first.

Personality Factors

People with certain types of personality traits seem to develop somatoform disorders more readily than others. The prime candidates appear to be people with *histrionic* personality characteristics (Nemiah, 1985; Slavney, 1990). The histrionic personality tends to be self-centred, suggestible, excitable, highly emotional, and overly dramatic. Such people thrive on the attention that they get when they become ill. The personality trait of *neuroticism* also seems to elevate individuals' susceptibility to somatoform disorders (Noyes et al., 2005).

Cognitive Factors

In recent years, theorists have devoted increased attention to how cognitive peculiarities might contribute to somatoform disorders. For example, Barsky (2001) asserts that some people focus excessive attention on their internal physiological processes and amplify normal bodily sensations into symptoms of distress, which lead them to pursue unnecessary medical treatment. Recent evidence suggests that people with somatoform disorders tend to draw cat-astrophic conclusions about minor bodily complaints (Salkovskis & Warwick, 2001). They also seem to apply a faulty standard of good health, equating health with a complete absence of symptoms and discomfort, which is unrealistic (Barsky et al., 1993).

The Sick Role

Another consideration is that some people grow fond of the role associated with being sick (Hotopf, 2004). Their complaints of physical symptoms may be reinforced by indirect benefits derived from their illness (Schwartz, Slater, & Birchler, 1994). What are the benefits commonly associated with physical illness? One payoff is that becoming ill is a superb way to avoid having to confront life's challenges. Many people with somatoform disorders are avoiding facing up to marital problems, career frustrations, family responsibilities, and the like. After all, when you're sick, others cannot place great demands on you. Another benefit is that physical problems can provide a convenient excuse when people fail, or worry about failing, in endeavours that are critical to their self-esteem (Organista & Miranda, 1991).

Attention from others is another payoff that may reinforce complaints of physical illness. When people become ill, they command the attention of family, friends, co-workers, neighbours, and doctors. The sympathy that illness often brings may strengthen the person's tendency to feel ill. This clearly occurred in Mildred's case of conversion disorder. Her illness paid handsome dividends in terms of attention, consolation, and kind-hearted assistance from others.

CONCEPT CHECK 14.1

Distinguishing Anxiety and Somatoform Disorders

Check your understanding of the nature of anxiety and somatoform disorders by making preliminary diagnoses for the cases described below. Read each case summary and write your tentative diagnosis in the space provided. The answers are in Appendix A.

1. Malcolm religiously follows an exact schedule every day. His showering and grooming ritual takes two hours. He follows the same path in walking to his classes every day, and he always sits in the same seat in each class. He can't study until his apartment is arranged perfectly. Although he tries not to, he thinks constantly about flunking out of school. Both his grades and his social life are suffering from his rigid routines.

Preliminary diagnosis: _____

2. Jane has been unemployed for the last eight years because of poor health. She has suffered through a bizarre series of illnesses of mysterious origin. Troubles with devastating headaches were followed by months of chronic back pain. Then she developed respiratory problems, frequently gasping for breath. Her current problem is stomach pain. Physicians have been unable to find any physical basis for her maladies.

Preliminary diagnosis: _____

3. Nathan owns a small restaurant that's in deep financial trouble. He dreads facing the possibility that his restaurant will fail. One day, he suddenly loses all feeling in his right arm and the ability to control the arm. He's hospitalized for his condition, but physicians can't find any organic cause for his arm trouble.

Preliminary diagnosis: _____

Dissociative Disorders

Dissociative disorders are among the more unusual syndromes that we will discuss. **Dissociative disorders are a class of disorders in which people lose contact with portions of their consciousness or memory, resulting in disruptions in their sense of identity**. We'll describe three dissociative syndromes—dissociative amnesia, dissociative fugue, and dissociative identity disorder—all of which are relatively uncommon.

Dissociative Amnesia and Fugue

Dissociative amnesia and fugue are overlapping disorders characterized by serious memory deficits. **Dissociative amnesia is a sudden loss of memory for important personal information that is too extensive to be due to normal forgetting**. Memory losses may occur for a single traumatic event (such as an automobile accident or home fire) or for an extended period of time surrounding the event. Cases of amnesia have been observed after people have experienced disasters, accidents, combat stress, physical abuse, and rape, or after they have witnessed the violent death of a parent, among other things (Arrigo & Pezdek, 1997; Loewenstein, 1996). **In *dissociative fugue*, people lose their memory for their entire lives along with their sense of personal identity**. These people forget their name, their family, where they live, and where they work! In spite of this wholesale forgetting, they remember matters unrelated to their identity, such as how to drive a car and how to do math.

Dissociative Identity Disorder

Dissociative identity disorder (DID)* involves the coexistence in one person of two or more largely complete, and usually very different, personalities**. The name for this disorder used to be ***multiple personality disorder, which still enjoys informal use. In dissociative identity disorder, the divergences in behaviour go far beyond those that people normally display in adapting to different roles in life. People with "multiple personalities" feel that they have more than one identity. Each personality has his or her own name, memories, traits, and physical mannerisms. Although rare, this "Dr. Jekyll and Mr. Hyde" syndrome is frequently portrayed in novels, television shows, and movies, such as the *Three Faces of Eve*, a 1957 film starring Joanne Woodward. In popular media portrayals, the syndrome is often mistakenly called *schizophrenia*. As you will see later, schizophrenic disorders are entirely different.

In dissociative identity disorder, the various personalities are often unaware of each other (Eich et al., 1997). In other words, the experiences of a specific personality are recalled only by that personality and not the others. The alternate personalities commonly display traits that are quite foreign to the original personality. For instance, a shy, inhibited person might develop a flamboyant, extraverted alternate personality. Transitions between identities often occur suddenly. The disparities between identities can be bizarre, as different personalities may assert that they are different in age, race, gender, and sexual orientation (Kluft, 1996). Dissociative identity disorder rarely occurs in isolation. Most DID patients also have a history of anxiety, mood, or personality disorders (Ross, 1999).

Starting in the 1970s, there was a dramatic increase in the diagnosis of multiple-personality disorder (Kihlstrom, 2001). Only 79 well-documented cases had accumulated up through 1970, but by the late 1990s about 40 000 cases were estimated to have been reported (Lilienfeld & Lynn, 2003). Some theorists believe that these disorders used to be underdiagnosed—that is, they often went undetected (Maldonado & Spiegel, 2003). However, other theorists argue that a handful of clinicians have begun overdiagnosing the condition and that some clinicians even *encourage and contribute* to the emergence of DID (McHugh, 1995; Powell & Gee, 1999). Consistent with this view, a survey of all the psychiatrists in Switzerland found that 90% of them had never seen a case of dissociative identity disorder, whereas three of the psychiatrists had each seen more than 20 DID patients (Modestin, 1992). The data from this study suggest that 6 psychiatrists (out of 655 surveyed) accounted for two-thirds of the dissociative identity disorder diagnoses in Switzerland.

Etiology of Dissociative Disorders

Psychogenic amnesia and fugue are usually attributed to excessive stress. However, relatively little is known about why this extreme reaction to stress occurs in a tiny minority of people but not in the vast majority who are subjected to similar stress. Some theorists speculate that certain personality traits—fantasy proneness and a tendency to become intensely absorbed in personal experiences—may make some people more susceptible to dissociative

PREVIEW QUESTIONS
- What are the principal types of dissociative disorders, and what are their chief symptoms?
- Why is the dissociative identity disorder controversial?

disorders, but adequate evidence is lacking on this line of thought (Kihlstrom, Glisky, & Angiulo, 1994).

The causes of dissociative identity disorders are particularly obscure. Some skeptical theorists, such as Carleton University psychologist Nicholas Spanos (1994, 1996) and others (Lilienfeld et al., 1999), believe that people with multiple personalities are engaging in intentional role-playing to use mental illness as a face-saving excuse for their personal failings. Spanos also argues that a small minority of therapists help create multiple personalities in their patients by subtly encouraging the emergence of alternate personalities. According to Spanos, dissociative identity disorder is a creation of modern North American culture, much as demonic possession was a creation of early Christianity. To bolster his argument, he discusses how multiple-personality patients' symptom presentations seem to have been influenced by popular media. For example, the typical patient with dissociative identity disorder used to report having two or three personalities, but since the publication of *Sybil* (Schreiber, 1973) and other books describing patients with many personalities, the average number of alternate personalities has climbed to about 15. In a similar vein, there has been a dramatic upsurge in the number of dissociative patients reporting that they were victims of ritual satanic abuse during childhood that dates back to the publication of *Michelle Remembers* (Smith & Pazder, 1980), a book about a multiple-personality patient who purportedly was tortured by a satanic cult.

Despite these concerns, some clinicians are convinced that DID is an authentic disorder (Gleaves, May, & Cardena, 2001). They argue that there is no incentive for either patients or therapists to manufacture cases of multiple personalities, which are often greeted with skepticism and outright hostility. They maintain that most cases of dissociative identity disorder are rooted in severe emotional trauma that occurred during childhood (Draijer & Langeland, 1999). A substantial majority of people with dissociative identity disorder report a childhood history of rejection from parents and physical and sexual abuse (Lewis et al., 1997; Scroppo et al., 1998). However, this abuse typically has not been independently verified (Lilienfeld & Lynn, 2003). Moreover, this link would not be unique to DID, as a history of child abuse elevates the likelihood of *many* disorders, especially among females (MacMillan et al., 2001). In the final analysis, very little is known about the causes of dissociative identity disorder, which remains a controversial diagnosis (Barry-Walsh, 2005). In one survey of American psychiatrists, only one-quarter of the respondents indicated that they felt there was solid evidence for the scientific validity of the DID diagnosis (Pope et al., 1999).

REVIEW OF KEY POINTS

- Somatoform disorders are physical ailments that cannot be fully explained by organic conditions. They are different from psychosomatic diseases, which are genuine physical ailments caused in part by psychological factors.

- Somatoform disorders include somatization disorder, conversion disorder, and hypochondriasis. These disorders often emerge in people with highly suggestible, histrionic personalities and in people who focus excess attention on their internal physiological processes. Somatoform disorders may be a learned avoidance strategy reinforced by attention and sympathy.

- Dissociative disorders include dissociative amnesia, fugue, and dissociative identity disorder (multiple-personality disorder). These disorders are uncommon and their causes are not well understood.

- Some theorists believe that people with dissociative identity disorder are engaging in intentional role-playing to use an exotic mental illness as a face-saving excuse for their personal failings. These disorders may be rooted in emotional trauma that occurred during childhood.

Mood Disorders SIM9

PREVIEW QUESTIONS

- What are the principal mood disorders, and what are their chief symptoms?
- Which biological factors have been implicated in mood disorders?
- How do cognitive processes contribute to depressive disorders?
- How do social skills and stress contribute to depressive disorders?

What do Kurt Cobain, Vincent Van Gogh, Axl Rose, Winston Churchill, Leo Tolstoy, Jim Carrey, Margot Kidder, Sarah McLachlan, and Canadian Olympic figure skater Elizabeth Manley have in common? Yes, they all achieved great prominence, albeit in different ways at different times. But, more pertinent to our interest, they all suffered from severe mood disorders. Although mood disorders can be terribly debilitating, people with mood disorders may still achieve greatness, because such disorders tend to be *episodic*. In other words, mood disturbances often come and go, interspersed among periods of normality. These episodes of disturbance can vary greatly in length, but they typically last 3–12 months (Akiskal, 2000).

Of course, everybody has ups and downs in terms of mood. Life would be dull indeed if people's emotional tone were constant. Everyone experiences depression occasionally. Likewise, everyone has days that he or she sails through on an emotional high. Such emotional fluctuations are natural, but some people are subject to extreme and sustained distortions of mood. **Mood disorders are a class of disorders marked by emotional disturbances of varied kinds that may spill over to disrupt physical, perceptual, social, and thought processes.**

Unipolar mood disorder

Mood state: Manic — Normal — Depressed

Time (years) →

Bipolar mood disorder

Mood state: Manic — Normal — Depressed

Time (years) →

Figure 14.11

Episodic patterns in mood disorders. Time-limited episodes of emotional disturbance come and go unpredictably in mood disorders. People with unipolar disorders suffer from bouts of depression only, whereas people with bipolar disorders experience both manic and depressive episodes. The time between episodes of disturbance varies greatly with the individual and the type of disorder.

There are two basic types of mood disorders: unipolar and bipolar (see Figure 14.11). People with *unipolar disorder* experience emotional extremes at just one end of the mood continuum, as they are troubled only by *depression*. People with *bipolar disorder* are vulnerable to emotional extremes at both ends of the mood continuum, going through periods of both *depression* and *mania* (excitement and elation).

Major Depressive Disorder 11B

The line between normal dejection and unhappiness and abnormal depression can be difficult to draw (Kendler & Gardner, 1998). Ultimately, it requires a subjective judgment. Crucial considerations in this judgment include the duration of the depression and its disruptive effects. When a depression significantly impairs everyday adaptive behaviour for more than a few weeks, there is reason for concern.

In *major depressive disorder* people show persistent feelings of sadness and despair and a loss of interest in previous sources of pleasure. Negative emotions form the heart of the depressive syndrome, but many other symptoms may also appear. The most common symptoms of major depression are summarized and compared with the symptoms of mania in Table 14.1. Depressed people often give up activities that they used to find enjoyable. For example, a depressed person might quit going bowling or might give up a favourite hobby such as photography. Alterations in appetite and sleep patterns are common.

People with depression often lack energy. They tend to move sluggishly and talk slowly. Anxiety, irritability, and brooding are commonly observed. Self-esteem tends to sink as the depressed person begins to feel worthless. Depression plunges people into feelings of hopelessness, dejection, and boundless guilt. To make matters worse, people who suffer from depression often exhibit other disorders as well (Boland & Keller, 2002). Coexisting anxiety disorders and substance use disorders are particularly frequent.

The onset of depression can occur at any point in the life span but a substantial majority of cases emerge before age 40 (Hammen, 2003). The median duration of depressive episodes is five months (Solomon et al.,

Actor Jim Carrey and singer/songwriter Sarah McLachlan are two well-known Canadians who have struggled with mood disorders.

1997). The vast majority (75%–95%) of people who suffer from depression experience more than one episode over the course of their lifetime (Dubovsky, Davies, & Dubovsky, 2003). In one longitudinal study, after recovery from one's first episode of depression, the cumulative probability of recurrence was 25% after one year, 42% after two years, and 60% after five years (Solomon et al., 2000). The severity of depressive disorders varies considerably. When people display relatively mild symptoms of depression, they're given a diagnosis of *dysthymic disorder,* **which consists of chronic depression that is insufficient in severity to justify diagnosis of a major depressive episode.**

How common are depressive disorders? Very common. Research reported by the Canadian Health Agency (2002) suggests that about 8% of Canadians endure a depressive disorder at some time in their lives, with about 1% suffering from a bipolar disorder. Other North American estimates put the lifetime prevalence rate of depression even higher, at 16% (Kessler et al., 1994). Estimates of the prevalence of depression vary quite a bit because of the previously mentioned difficulty in drawing a line between normal dejection and abnormal depression. Hence, different researchers using different procedures and cut-off points obtain varied estimates. Also, the variation in prevalence rates may be due to differences in methodological factors. Moreover, evidence suggests that the prevalence of depression is increasing, as it is higher in more recent age cohorts (Rehm, Wagner, & Ivens-Tyndal, 2001). In particular, age cohorts born since World War II appear to have an elevated risk for depression (Kessler, 2002). The factors underlying this rise in depression are not readily apparent, and researchers are scrambling to collect data that might shed light on this unanticipated trend.

Researchers also find that the prevalence of depression is about twice as high in women as it is in men (Nolen-Hoeksema, 2002). This gender gap in depres-

sion opens up during mid- to late adolescence (Hankin et al., 1998). The many possible explanations for this gender gap are the subject of considerable debate. Simon Fraser psychologist Marlene Moretti suggests that women tend to adopt a self-regulatory style that is relational in nature (Moretti, Rein, & Wiebe, 1998). They are sensitive to discrepancies involving their beliefs about themselves and the ideals they perceive others hold for them. Moretti found that discrepancies were related to elevated levels of dysphoria. The same was not true for the males in her study. Others, such as University of Western Ontario researchers Gillian Kirsch and Nick Kuiper (2002), have linked gender differences in depression to differences in self-schema.

Susan Nolen-Hoeksema (2001) argues that women experience more depression than men because they are far more likely to be victims of sexual abuse and somewhat more likely to endure poverty, harassment, and role constraints. In other words, she attributes the higher prevalence of depression among women to their experience of greater stress and adversity. Nolen-Hoeksema also believes that women have a greater tendency than men to *ruminate* about setbacks and problems. Evidence suggests that this tendency to dwell on one's difficulties elevates vulnerability to depression, as we will discuss momentarily.

Bipolar Disorder 11B

Bipolar disorder **(formerly known as manic-depressive disorder) is characterized by the experience of one or more manic episodes as well as periods of depression.** One manic episode is sufficient to qualify for this diagnosis. The symptoms seen in manic periods generally are the opposite of those seen in depression (see Table 14.1 for a comparison). Canadian psychologist Norman Endler, whom we mentioned at the beginning of this chapter, suffered from bipolar disorder (Endler, 1982). In a manic episode, a person's mood becomes elevated to the point of euphoria. Self-esteem skyrockets as the person bubbles over with optimism, energy, and extravagant plans. He or she becomes hyperactive and may go for days without sleep. The individual talks rapidly and shifts topics wildly, as his or her mind races at breakneck speed. Judgment is often impaired. Some people in manic periods gamble impulsively, spend money frantically, or become sexually reckless. Like depressive disorders, bipolar disorders vary considerably in severity. People are given a diagnosis of *cyclothymic disorder* **when they exhibit chronic but relatively mild symptoms of bipolar disturbance.**

Table 14.1 Comparisons of Common Symptoms in Manic and Depressive Episodes

Characteristics	Manic Episode	Depressive Episode
Emotional	Elated, euphoric, very sociable, impatient at any hindrance	Gloomy, hopeless, socially withdrawn, irritable
Cognitive	Characterized by racing thoughts, flight of ideas, desire for action, and impulsive behaviour; talkative, self-confident; experiencing delusions of grandeur	Characterized by slowness of thought processes, obsessive worrying, inability to make decisions, negative self-image, self-blame, and delusions of guilt and disease
Motor	Hyperactive, tireless, requiring less sleep than usual, showing increased sex drive and fluctuating appetite	Less active, tired, experiencing difficulty in sleeping, showing decreased sex drive and decreased appetite

Source: Sarason, I. G., & Sarason, B. G. (1987). *Abnormal psychology: The problem of maladaptive behavior.* Upper Saddle River, NJ: Prentice-Hall. © 1987 Prentice-Hall, Inc. Reprinted by permission.

You may be thinking that the euphoria in manic episodes sounds appealing. If so, you are not entirely wrong. In their milder forms, manic states can seem attractive. The increases in energy, self-esteem, and optimism can be deceptively seductive. Because of the increase in energy, many bipolar patients report temporary surges of productivity and creativity (Goodwin & Jamison, 1990).

Although manic episodes may have some positive aspects, these periods often have a paradoxical negative undercurrent of irritability and depression (Dilsaver et al., 1999). Moreover, mild manic episodes usually escalate to higher levels that become scary and disturbing. Impaired judgment leads many victims to do things that they greatly regret later, as you'll see in the following case history:

Robert, a dentist, awoke one morning with the idea that he was the most gifted dental surgeon in the area. He decided that he should try to provide services to as many people as possible, so that more people could benefit from his talents. Thus, he decided to remodel his two-chair dental office, installing 20 booths so that he could simultaneously attend to 20 patients. That same day he drew up plans for this arrangement, telephoned a number of remodellers, and invited bids for the work. Later that day, impatient to get rolling on his remodelling, he rolled up his sleeves, got himself a sledgehammer, and began to knock down the walls in his office. Annoyed when that didn't go so well, he smashed his dental tools, washbasins, and X-ray equipment. Later, Robert's wife became concerned about his behaviour and summoned two of her adult daughters for assistance. The daughters responded quickly, arriving at the family home with their husbands. In the ensuing discussion, Robert—after bragging about his sexual prowess—made advances toward his daughters. He had to be subdued by their husbands. (Adapted from Kleinmuntz, 1980, p. 309)

Although not rare, bipolar disorders are much less common than unipolar disorders. Bipolar disorder affects about 1% to 2.5% of the population (Dubovsky et al., 2003). Unlike depressive disorder, bipolar disorder is seen equally often in males and females (Bauer, 2003). As Figure 14.12 shows, the onset of bipolar disorder is age related, with the peak of vulnerability occurring between the ages of 20 and 29 (Goodwin & Jamison, 1990). The mood swings in bipolar disorder can be patterned in many ways. About 20% of bipolar patients exhibit a *rapid-cycling pattern,* which means they go through four or more manic or depressive episodes within a year.

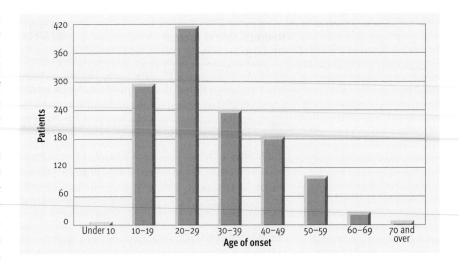

Etiology of Mood Disorders

Quite a bit is known about the etiology of mood disorders, although the puzzle certainly hasn't been assembled completely. There appear to be a number of routes into these disorders, involving intricate interactions between psychological and biological factors.

Genetic Vulnerability

The evidence strongly suggests that genetic factors influence the likelihood of developing major depression or bipolar disorder (Kalidindi & McGuffin, 2003; Sullivan, Neale, & Kendler, 2000). *Twin studies* have found a sizable disparity between identical and fraternal twins in concordance rates for mood disorders (see Figure 14.13). This evidence suggests that heredity can create a *predisposition* to mood disorders. Environmental factors probably determine whether this predisposition is converted into an actual disorder. Research suggests that genetic vulnerability may play a larger role in women's depression than in men's (Bierut et al., 1999). The influence of genetic factors also appears to be stronger for bipolar disorders than for unipolar disorders (Knowles, Kaufmann, & Rieder, 1999).

Figure 14.12

Age of onset for bipolar mood disorder. The onset of bipolar disorder typically occurs in adolescence or early adulthood. The data graphed here, which were combined from 10 studies, show the distribution of age of onset for 1304 bipolar patients. As you can see, bipolar disorder emerges most frequently during the 20s decade.

SOURCE: Goodwin, F. K., & Jamison, K. R. (1990). *Manic-depressive illness* (p. 132). New York: Oxford University Press. Copyright © 1990 Oxford University Press, Inc. Reprinted by permission.

Figure 14.13

Twin studies of mood disorders. The concordance rate for mood disorders in identical twins is much higher than that for fraternal twins, who share less genetic overlap. These results suggest that there must be a genetic predisposition to mood disorders. (Data from Gershon, Berrettini, & Goldin, 1989)

Neurochemical Factors 11B

Heredity may influence susceptibility to mood disorders by creating a predisposition toward certain types of neurochemical abnormalities in the brain. Correlations have been found between mood disorders and abnormal levels of two neurotransmitters in the brain: norepinephrine and serotonin (Rothschild, 1999; Sher & Mann, 2003), although other neurotransmitter disturbances may also contribute (Thase, Jindal, & Howland, 2002). The details remain elusive, but it seems clear that a neurochemical basis exists for at least some mood disorders (Flores et al., 2004). A variety of drug therapies are fairly effective in the treatment of severe mood disorders. Most of these drugs are known to affect the availability (in the brain) of the neurotransmitters that have been related to mood disorders (Garlow, Musselman, & Nemeroff, 1999). Since this effect is unlikely to be a coincidence, it bolsters the plausibility of the idea that neurochemical changes produce mood disturbances.

Studies have also found some interesting correlations between mood disorders and a variety of structural abnormalities in the brain (Flores et al., 2004). Perhaps the best documented correlation is the association between depression and *reduced hippocampal volume* (Campbell et al., 2004). The *hippocampus*, which is known to play a major role in memory consolidation (see Chapter 7), tends to be about 8%–10% smaller in depressed subjects than in normal subjects (Videbech & Ravnkilde, 2004). A fascinating new theory of the biological bases of depression may be able to account for this finding. The springboard for this theory is the recent discovery that the human brain continues to generate new neurons in adulthood, especially in the hippocampal formation (Gage, 2002; see Chapter 3). This process is called *neurogenesis*. Jacobs (2004) has theorized that depression occurs when major life stress causes neurochemical reactions that suppress neurogenesis, resulting in reduced hippocampal volume. According to this view, the suppression of neurogenesis is the central cause of depression. Consistent with this view, Jacobs maintains that antidepressant drugs that elevate serotonin levels relieve depression because serotonin promotes neurogenesis. A great deal of additional research will be required to fully test this innovative new model of the biological bases of depressive disorders.

Dispositional Factors

In the past few years interest in the role of various personality factors in eliciting and maintaining depression has increased. Perfectionism or the setting of excessively high standards has been a charac-

Courtesy of Susan Nolen-Hoeksema

"*By adolescence, girls appear to be more likely than boys to respond to stress and distress with rumination—focusing inward on feelings of distress and personal concerns rather than taking action to relieve their distress.*"
SUSAN NOLEN-HOEKSEMA

teristic long associated with depression (Beck, 1976). Research by the University of British Columbia's Paul Hewitt and his colleague, Canada Research Chair Gordon Flett, has explored the relationship of trait perfectionism to various aspects of depression. They have developed a multidimensional perfectionism scale that assesses three aspects of perfectionism (Hewitt & Flett, 1991): *self-oriented perfectionism*, or the tendency to set high standards for oneself; *other-oriented perfectionism,* which refers to setting high standards for others; and *socially prescribed perfectionism*, which is the tendency to perceive that others are setting high standards for oneself. In an active program of research, Hewitt and Flett have found links between perfectionism and eating disorders (Hewitt & Flett, 1991), symptoms of depression (Hewitt et al., 1998), and problematic interpersonal relations (Flett & Hewitt, 2002).

Two other personality-based models of depression, those proposed by Aaron Beck (1983) and Sidney Blatt (1995), suggest that specific personality variables serve as vulnerability factors for depression. According to Beck, two personality styles, sociotropy and autonomy, are related to depression. Sociotropic individuals are especially invested in interpersonal relations; they are overconcerned with avoiding interpersonal problems and emphasize pleasing others. Autonomous individuals, on the other hand, are primarily oriented toward their own independence and achievement (Sato & McCann, 2002). Research on these personality factors has been conducted by Dennis Pusch and Keith Dobson and their colleagues in Calgary (Pusch et al., 1998). David Clark from the University of New Brunswick has collaborated with Beck in developing a widely used scale to assess these personality dimensions (Clark et al., 1995). Clark (1998) recently edited a special issue of the *Canadian Journal of Behavioural Science* on the topic of Canadian research and theory in depression.

Blatt (1974, 1995) distinguishes between the introjective personality orientation, which involves excessive self-criticism, and the anaclitic orientation involving overdependence on others. Using instruments designed to assess both dependency and self-criticism, McGill University's David Zuroff and York University's Myriam Mongrain have examined some of the facets of these dispositional variables and their relation to depression (Zuroff & Mongrain, 1987). Both Beck's and Blatt's formulations are consistent with a congruency model that suggests that the personality variables operate as vulnerabilities in response to stressors related to that specific disposition. For example, an individual who is high in dependency should suffer depressive symptoms only if he or she experiences difficulties in relationship or interpersonal domains and not if difficulties are experienced in achievement situations. Zuroff and Mongrain (1987) conducted one of the early tests of this type of congruency hypothesis. More recently, Mongrain has conducted a programmatic line of research examining relationship issues and rejection in dependent and self-critical individuals (Mongrain, Lubbers, & Struthers, 2004; Mongrain et al., 1998).

Cognitive Factors 11B

A variety of theories emphasize how cognitive factors contribute to depressive disorders (Abramson et al., 2002). Perhaps the most influential of these theories is that proposed by Aaron Beck (1976, 1987). Since we will discuss his approach and its implications for therapy more fully in Chapter 15, we will only introduce a couple of concepts from his theory here. According to Beck, depressed individuals are characterized by a *negative cognitive triad*, which reflects their tendency to have negative views of themselves, their world, and their future. He suggests that dysfunctional schemas underlie many of the symptoms associated with depression. You may recall our discussion of schemas in Chapter 7. One of the effects of the depressive's negative schemas is the tendency to selectively attend to negative information about the self. Research by Zindel Segal at the Clarke Institute of Psychiatry in Toronto (Rector, Segal, & Gemar, 1998; Segal, 1988) and Scott McCabe at the University of Waterloo (McCabe & Toman, 2000; McCabe, Gotlib, & Martin, 2000) has served to evaluate and largely confirm these aspects of Beck's cognitive theory.

Another important cognitive theory is Martin Seligman's *learned helplessness model* of depression and its most recent descendant, *hopelessness theory*. Based largely on animal research, Seligman (1974) proposed that depression is caused by *learned helplessness*—passive "giving up" behaviour produced by exposure to unavoidable aversive events (such as uncontrollable shock in the laboratory). More recently he has reformulated the theory focusing on more cognitive features such as how people explain their negative experiences (Abramson, Seligman, & Teasdale, 1978). According to Seligman (1990), people who exhibit a *pessimistic explanatory style* are especially vulnerable to depression. These people tend to attribute their setbacks to their personal flaws instead of situational factors, and they tend to draw global, far-reaching conclusions about their personal inadequacies based on these setbacks.

According to *hopelessness theory* (Abramson, Alloy, & Metalsky, 1995), which builds on these insights, a pessimistic explanatory style is just one of several or more factors—along with high stress, low self-esteem, and so forth—that may contribute to hopelessness, and thus depression. Although hopelessness theory casts a wider net than the learned helplessness model, it continues to emphasize the importance of people's *cognitive reactions* to the events in their lives. In a more recent development in this area, Susan Nolen-Hoeksema (1991, 2000) has highlighted the importance of rumination and has found that depressed people who *ruminate* about their depression remain depressed longer than those who try to distract themselves.

F E A T U R E D
S T U D Y

Does Negative Thinking *Cause* Depression?

This article describes a series of studies conducted at Temple University and at the University of Wisconsin, collectively referred to as the Temple–Wisconsin Cognitive Vulnerability to Depression Project. Although the article provides a preliminary report on many facets of the project, we will focus on the study intended to test the hypothesis that a negative cognitive style is predictive of elevated vulnerability to depression.

Method

Participants. Over 5000 first-year students at the two universities responded to two measures of negative thinking. Students who scored in the highest quartile on both measures were characterized as having a *high risk* for depression and those who scored in the lowest quartile on both measures were characterized as having a *low risk* for depression. Randomly selected subsets of these two groups were invited for additional screening

to eliminate anyone who was currently depressed or suffering from any other major psychological disorder. The final sample consisted of 173 students in the high-risk group and 176 students in the low-risk group.

Follow-up assessments. Self-report measures and structured interviews were used to evaluate the mental health of the participants every six weeks for the first two years and then every 16 weeks for an additional three years. The assessments were conducted by interviewers who were blind regarding the subjects' risk group status. The present report summarized the follow-up data for the first 2.5 years of the study.

Results

The data for students who had no prior history of depression showed dramatic differences between the high-risk and low-risk groups in vulnerability to depression. During the relatively brief 2.5-year period, a major depressive disorder

Investigators: Lauren B. Alloy (Temple University), Lyn Y. Abramson (University of Wisconsin), Wayne G. Whitehouse (Temple University), Michael E. Hogan (University of Wisconsin), Nancy A. Tashman (University of Maryland), Dena L. Steinberg (New York State Psychiatric Institute), Donna T. Rose (Counseling Associates of Madison), and Patricia Donovan (University of Wisconsin).

Source: Depressogenic cognitive styles: Predictive validity, information processing and personality characteristics, and developmental origins. *Behavior Research and Therapy*, 1999, *37*, 503–531.

Figure **14.14**

Negative thinking and prediction of depression. Alloy and colleagues (1999) measured the cognitive style of first-year university students and characterized them as high risk or low risk for depression. This graph shows the percentage of these students who experienced major or minor episodes of depression over the next 2.5 years. As you can see, the high-risk students who exhibited a negative thinking style proved to be much more vulnerable to depression. (Data from Alloy et al., 1999)

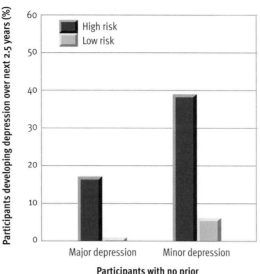

Participants with no prior history of depression

Participants with prior history of depression

emerged in 17% of the high-risk students in comparison to only 1% of the low-risk students. The high-risk subjects also displayed a much greater incidence of minor depressive episodes, as you can see in the left panel of Figure 14.14. The right panel of Figure 14.14 shows the comparisons for participants who had a prior history of depression (but were not depressed or suffering from any other disorder at the beginning of the study). The data show that high-risk subjects were more vulnerable to a recurrence of both major and minor depression during the 2.5-year follow-up.

Discussion

The high-risk participants, who exhibited a negative cognitive style, were consistently found to have an elevated likelihood of developing depressive disorders. Hence, the authors conclude that their results provide strong support for the cognitive vulnerability hypothesis, which asserts that negative thinking makes people more vulnerable to depression.

Comment

Previous studies of the correlation between negative thinking and depression used *retrospective designs,* which look backward in time from known outcomes. For example, investigators might compare depressed

subjects versus nondepressed subjects on some measure of negative thinking. What makes the design retrospective is that the researchers already know which people experienced the outcome of depression. Retrospective designs can yield useful information, but they don't provide much insight about causation. Why? Because if you find an association between depression and negative thinking you can't determine whether the negative thinking preceded the depression or the depression preceded the negative thinking. The present study used a *prospective design,* which moves forward in time, testing hypotheses about future outcomes. Prospective studies are much more difficult and time-consuming to conduct, but they can provide more insight about causation because they can show that one event (in this instance, the development of a negative cognitive style) preceded another (the occurrence of depression). The data are still correlational, so they cannot definitively establish a causal link, but they provide much stronger evidence in favour of causation than retrospective data. Thus, the research by Alloy and her colleagues provides the best evidence to date in support of the hypothesis that negative thinking contributes to the causation of depressive disorders. ∎

In sum, cognitive models of depression maintain that negative thinking is what leads to depression in many people. The principal problem with cognitive theories is their difficulty in separating cause from effect (Rehm, Wagner, & Ivens-Tyndal, 2001). Does negative thinking cause depression? Or does depression cause negative thinking (see Figure 14.15)? A *clear* demonstration of a causal link between nega-

tive thinking and depression is not possible because it would require manipulating people's cognitive style (which is not easy to change) in sufficient degree to produce full-fledged depressive disorders (which would not be ethical). However, the research reported in our Featured Study provided impressive evidence consistent with a causal link between negative thinking and vulnerability to depression.

Interpersonal Roots 11B

Behavioural approaches to understanding depression emphasize how inadequate social skills put people on the road to depressive disorders (see Figure 14.16; Coyne, 1999). According to this notion, depression-prone people lack the social finesse needed to acquire many important kinds of reinforcers, such as good friends, top jobs, and desirable spouses. This paucity of reinforcers could understandably lead to negative emotions and depression. Consistent with this theory, research, such as that conducted at the University of Western Ontario by Ian Gotlib (Gotlib & Robinson, 1982) and others, has found associations between poor social skills and depression (Ingram, Scott, & Siegle, 1999).

Another interpersonal factor is that depressed people tend to be depressing (Joiner & Katz, 1999). Individuals suffering from depression often are irritable and pessimistic. They complain a lot and aren't particularly enjoyable companions. As a consequence, depressed people tend to court rejection from those around them (Joiner & Metalsky, 1995). Depressed people thus have fewer sources of social support than nondepressed people. Social rejection and lack of support may in turn aggravate and deepen a person's depression (Potthoff, Holahan, & Joiner, 1995). To compound these problems, evidence indicates that depressed people may gravitate to partners who view them unfavourably and hence reinforce their negative views of themselves (Joiner, 2002).

Precipitating Stress 11B

Mood disorders sometimes appear mysteriously in people who are leading benign, nonstressful lives. For this reason, experts used to believe that mood disorders are not influenced much by stress. However, advances in the measurement of personal stress have altered this picture. The evidence available today suggests the existence of a moderately strong link between stress and the onset of mood disorders (Kessler, 1997; Kendler, Kuhn, & Prescott, 2004). Stress also appears to affect how people with mood disorders respond to treatment and whether they experience a relapse of their disorder (Monroe & Hadjiyannakis, 2002).

Of course, many people endure great stress without getting depressed. The impact of stress varies, in part, because people vary in their degree of *vulnerability* to mood disorders (Lewinsohn, Joiner, & Rohde, 2001). Similar interactions between stress and vulnerability probably influence the development of many kinds of disorders, including those that are next on our agenda—the schizophrenic disorders.

Figure 14.15

Interpreting the correlation between negative thinking and depression. Cognitive theories of depression assume that consistent patterns of negative thinking cause depression. Although these theories are highly plausible, depression could cause negative thoughts, or both could be caused by a third factor, such as neurochemical changes in the brain.

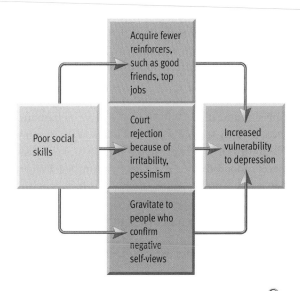

Figure 14.16

Interpersonal factors in depression. Behavioural theories about the etiology of depression emphasize how inadequate social skills may contribute to the development of the disorder through several mechanisms, as diagrammed here.

Web Link 14.4

Dr. Ivan's Depression Central
http://www.psycom.net/depression.central.html

Some might suggest psychiatrist Ivan Goldberg's site would be better titled "Everything You Ever Wanted to Know about Depression." He offers a great depth of resources regarding mood disorders.

REVIEW OF KEY POINTS

- The principal mood disorders are depressive disorder, dysthymic disorder, bipolar disorder, and cyclothymic disorder. Mood disorders are episodic.

- Major depressive disorder is marked by profound sadness, slowed thought processes, low self-esteem, and loss of interest in previous sources of pleasure. Unipolar depression is more common than bipolar disorder, and it appears to be increasing in prevalence.

- Bipolar disorder is marked by the experience of both depressed and manic episodes. Manic episodes are characterized by inflated self-esteem, high energy, grandiose plans, and racing thoughts.

- Evidence indicates that people vary in their genetic vulnerability to mood disorders. These disorders are accompanied by changes in neurochemical activity in the brain. Abnormalities at norepinephrine and serotonin synapses appear particularly critical.

- Cognitive models posit that negative thinking contributes to depression. A pessimistic explanatory style has been implicated, as has a tendency to ruminate about one's problems. Our Featured Study reported impressive new evidence in support of the cognitive vulnerability hypothesis of depression.

- Interpersonal inadequacies may contribute to depressive disorders. Poor social skills may lead to a paucity of life's reinforcers and frequent rejection. The development of mood disorders is also affected by personal stress.

PREVIEW QUESTIONS
- What are the general symptoms of schizophrenia?
- What are the four subtypes of schizophrenic disorders, and what are their chief symptoms?
- What is known about the course and outcome of schizophrenia?
- Which biological factors have been implicated in schizophrenic disorders?
- What is the neurodevelopmental hypothesis of schizophrenia?
- How do family dynamics and stress contribute to schizophrenic disorders?

Literally, *schizophrenia* means "split mind." However, when Eugen Bleuler coined the term in 1911 he was referring to the fragmentation of thought processes seen in the disorder—not to a "split personality." Unfortunately, writers in the popular media often assume that the split-mind notion, and thus schizophrenia, refers to the rare syndrome in which a person manifests two or more personalities. As you have already learned, this syndrome is actually called *dissociative identity disorder* or *multiple-personality disorder*. Schizophrenia is a much more common, and altogether different, type of disorder.

Schizophrenic disorders are a class of disorders marked by delusions, hallucinations, disorganized speech, and deterioration of adaptive behaviour. People with schizophrenic disorders often display some of the same symptoms seen in people with severe mood disorders; however, disturbed *thought* lies at the core of schizophrenic disorders, whereas disturbed *emotion* lies at the core of mood disorders. In fact, scholars such as Canadian schizophrenia expert Walter Heinrichs characterize schizophrenia as a biobehavioural disorder that is manifested first and foremost in cognition. Heinrichs suggests that cognitive assessment techniques are one of the best ways to examine the causes of schizophrenia and that impaired cognition is a primary feature of schizophrenia (Heinrichs, 2005). A recent cognitive analysis of schizophrenia and review of the effectiveness of cognitive behavioural therapy for schizophrenia by Aaron Beck and the University of Toronto's Neil Rector echoes the emphasis that Heinrichs and others place on cognition in schizophrenia (Beck & Rector, 2004; Rector & Beck, 2001). You will recall that Beck is one of the originators of the cognitive approach to depression discussed earlier in this chapter. We will describe the cognitive-behavioural approach to therapy more fully in Chapter 15.

How common is schizophrenia? Prevalence estimates suggest that about 1% of the population may suffer from schizophrenic disorders (Jablensky, 1999). That may not sound like much, but it means that in North America alone there may be several million people troubled by schizophrenic disturbances. Moreover, schizophrenia is an extremely costly illness for society, because it is a severe, debilitating illness that tends to have an early onset and often requires lengthy hospital care (Buchanan & Carpenter, 2000).

General Symptoms 11c

There are a number of distinct schizophrenic syndromes, but they share some general characteristics that we will examine before looking at the subtypes. Many of these characteristics are apparent in the following case history (adapted from Sheehan, 1982).

Sylvia was first given a diagnosis of schizophrenia at age 15. She has been in and out of many types of psychiatric facilities since then. She has never been able to hold a job for any length of time. During severe flare-ups of her disorder, her personal hygiene deteriorates. She rarely washes, she wears clothes that neither fit nor match, she smears makeup on heavily but randomly, and she slops food all over herself. Sylvia occasionally hears voices talking to her. She tends to be argumentative, aggressive, and emotionally volatile. Over the years, she has been involved in innumerable fights with fellow patients, psychiatric staff members, and strangers. Her thoughts can be highly irrational, as is apparent from the following quote, which was recorded while she was a patient in a psychiatric facility called Creedmoor:

"Mick Jagger wants to marry me. If I have Mick Jagger, I don't have to covet Geraldo Rivera. Mick Jagger is St. Nicholas and the Maharishi is Santa Claus. I want to form a gospel rock group called the Thorn Oil, but Geraldo wants me to be the music critic on Eyewitness News, so what can I do? Got to listen to my boyfriend. Teddy Kennedy cured me of my ugliness. I'm pregnant with the son of God. I'm going to marry David Berkowitz and get it over with. Creedmoor is the headquarters of the American Nazi Party. They're eating the patients here. Archie Bunker wants me to play his niece on his TV show. I work for Epic Records. I'm Joan of Arc. I'm Florence Nightingale. The door between the ward and the porch is the dividing line between New York and California. Divorce isn't a piece of paper, it's a feeling. Forget about Zip Codes. I need shock treatments. The body is run by electricity. My wiring is all faulty." (Sheehan, 1982, pp. 104–105)

Sylvia's case clearly shows that schizophrenic thinking can be bizarre and that schizophrenia can be a severe and debilitating disorder. Although no single symptom is inevitably present, the following symptoms are commonly seen in schizophrenia (Black & Andreasen, 1999; Cancro & Lehmann, 2000; Ho, Black, & Andreasen, 2003).

Delusions and Irrational Thought

Disturbed, irrational thought processes are the central feature of schizophrenic disorders (Barch, 2003; Heinrichs, 2005). Various kinds of delusions are common. *Delusions* are false beliefs that are maintained even though they clearly are out of touch with reality. For example, one patient's delusion that he is a tiger (with a deformed body) persisted for more than 15 years (Kulick, Pope, & Keck, 1990). More typically, affected persons believe that their private thoughts are being broadcast to other people, that thoughts are being injected into their mind against their will, or that their thoughts are being controlled by some external force (Maher, 2001). In *delusions of grandeur,* people maintain that they are famous or important. Sylvia expressed an endless array of grandiose delusions, such as thinking that Mick Jagger wanted to marry her, that she had dictated the hobbit stories to J. R. R. Tolkien, and that she was going to win the Nobel Prize for medicine.

Another characteristic of schizophrenia is that the person's train of thought deteriorates. Thinking becomes chaotic rather than logical and linear. There is a "loosening of associations," as people shift topics in disjointed ways. The quotation from Sylvia illustrates this symptom dramatically. The entire quote involves a wild flight of ideas, but at one point (beginning with the sentence "Creedmoor is the headquarters …") she rattles off ten consecutive sentences that have no apparent connection to each other.

Deterioration of Adaptive Behaviour

Schizophrenia usually involves a noticeable deterioration in the quality of the person's routine functioning in work, social relations, and personal care. Friends will often make remarks such as "Hal just isn't himself anymore." This deterioration is readily apparent in Sylvia's inability to get along with others or to function in the work world. It's also apparent in her neglect of personal hygiene.

Hallucinations

A variety of perceptual distortions may occur with schizophrenia, the most common being auditory hallucinations. *Hallucinations* are sensory perceptions that occur in the absence of a real, external stimulus or are gross distortions of perceptual input. People with schizophrenia frequently report that they hear voices of nonexistent or absent people talking to them. Sylvia, for instance, said she heard messages from Paul McCartney. These voices often provide an insulting, running commentary on the person's behaviour ("You're an idiot for shaking his hand").

They may be argumentative ("You don't need a bath"), and they may issue commands ("Prepare your home for visitors from outer space").

Disturbed Emotion

Normal emotional tone can be disrupted in schizophrenia in a variety of ways. Although it may not be an accurate indicator of their underlying emotional experience (Kring, 1999), some victims show little emotional responsiveness, a symptom referred to as "blunted or flat affect." Others show inappropriate emotional responses that don't jibe with the situation or with what they are saying. For instance, a schizophrenic patient might cry over a silly cartoon and then laugh about a news story describing a child's tragic death. People with schizophrenia may also become emotionally volatile. This pattern was displayed by Sylvia, who often overreacted emotionally in erratic, unpredictable ways.

Subtypes, Course, and Outcome

Four subtypes of schizophrenic disorders are recognized, including a category for people who don't fit neatly into any of the first three categories. The major symptoms of each subtype are as follows (Ho et al., 2003).

Paranoid Type

As its name implies, *paranoid schizophrenia* is dominated by delusions of persecution, along with delusions of grandeur. In this common form of schizophrenia, people come to believe that they have many enemies who want to harass and oppress them. They may become suspicious of friends and relatives or they may attribute the persecution to mysterious, unknown persons. They are convinced that they are being watched and manipulated in malicious ways. To make sense of this persecution, they often develop delusions of grandeur. They believe that they must be enormously important people, frequently seeing themselves as great inventors or as famous religious or political leaders.

Catatonic Type

Catatonic schizophrenia is marked by striking motor disturbances, ranging from muscular rigidity to random motor activity. Some patients go into an extreme form of withdrawal known as a catatonic stupor. They may remain virtually motionless and seem oblivious to the environment around them for long periods of time. Others go into a state of catatonic excitement. They become hyperactive and

Disorganized Type

In *disorganized schizophrenia,* **a particularly severe deterioration of adaptive behaviour is seen.** Prominent symptoms include emotional indifference, frequent incoherence, and virtually complete social withdrawal. Aimless babbling and giggling are common. Delusions often centre on bodily functions ("My brain is melting out my ears").

Undifferentiated Type

People who are clearly schizophrenic but who cannot be placed into any of the three previous categories are said to have *undifferentiated schizophrenia,* **which is marked by idiosyncratic mixtures of schizophrenic symptoms.** The undifferentiated subtype is fairly common.

Positive versus Negative Symptoms

Many theorists have raised doubts about the value of dividing schizophrenic disorders into the four subtypes just described (Sanislow & Carson, 2001). Critics note that the catatonic subtype is disappearing and that undifferentiated cases aren't so much a subtype as a hodgepodge of "leftovers." Critics also point out that there aren't meaningful differences between the subtypes in etiology, prognosis, or response to treatment. The absence of such differences casts doubt on the value of the current classification scheme.

Because of such problems, Nancy Andreasen (1990) and others (Carpenter, 1992; McGlashan & Fenton, 1992) have proposed an alternative approach to subtyping. This new scheme divides schizophrenic disorders into just two categories based on the predominance of negative versus positive symptoms. *Negative symptoms* **involve behavioural deficits, such as flattened emotions, social withdrawal, apathy, impaired attention, and poverty of speech.** *Positive symptoms* **involve behavioural excesses or peculiarities, such as hallucinations, delusions, bizarre behaviour, and wild flights of ideas.**

Theorists advocating this scheme hoped to find consistent differences between the two subtypes in etiology, prognosis, and response to treatment, and some progress along these lines *has* been made. For example, a predominance of positive symptoms is associated with better adjustment prior to the onset of schizophrenia and greater responsiveness to treat-

ment (Fenton & McGlashan, 1994; Galderisi et al., 2002). However, the assumption that patients can be placed into discrete categories based on this scheme now seems untenable. Most patients exhibit both types of symptoms and vary only in the *degree* to which positive or negative symptoms dominate (Black & Andreasen, 1999). Moreover, there is some debate about which symptoms should be classified as positive and which should be regarded as negative, and some theorists have proposed a third category of symptoms reflecting *disorganization* of behaviour (Toomey et al., 1997). Although it seems fair to say that the distinction between positive and negative symptoms is enhancing our understanding of schizophrenia, it has not yielded a classification scheme that can replace the traditional subtypes of schizophrenia.

Course and Outcome

Schizophrenic disorders usually emerge during adolescence or early adulthood and only infrequently after age 45 (Howard et al., 1993). The emergence of schizophrenia may be sudden or gradual. Once it clearly emerges, the course of schizophrenia is variable (Norman & Malla, 1995), but patients tend to fall into three broad groups. Some patients, presumably those with milder disorders, are treated successfully and enjoy a full recovery. Other patients experience a partial recovery, but they have frequent relapses and are in and out of treatment facilities for much of the remainder of their lives. Finally, a third group of patients endure chronic illness that sometimes results in permanent hospitalization. Research suggests that perhaps as many as one-half of schizophrenic patients experience a reasonable recovery (Hegarty et al., 1994). For unknown reasons, gender is associated with the course and outcome of schizophrenia. The differences are modest, but in comparison to females, males tend to have an earlier onset of the disease, more hospitalizations, and higher relapse rates (Szymanski et al., 1995).

A number of factors are related to the likelihood of recovery from schizophrenic disorders (Cancro & Lehmann, 2000; Liberman et al., 2002). A patient has a relatively *favourable prognosis* when (1) the onset of the disorder has been sudden rather than gradual, (2) the onset has occurred at a later age, (3) the patient's social and work adjustment were relatively good prior to the onset of the disorder, (4) the proportion of negative symptoms is relatively low, and (5) the patient has a relatively healthy, supportive family situation to return to. Most of these predictors are concerned with the etiology of schizophrenic illness, which is the matter we turn to next.

"*Schizophrenia disfigures the emotional and cognitive faculties of its victims, and sometimes nearly destroys them.*"
NANCY ANDREASEN

Etiology of Schizophrenia

You can probably identify, at least to some extent, with people who suffer from mood disorders, somatoform disorders, and anxiety disorders. You can probably imagine events that could unfold that might leave you struggling with depression, grappling with anxiety, or worrying about your physical health. But what could account for Sylvia's thinking that she was Joan of Arc or that she had dictated the hobbit novels to Tolkien? As mystifying as these delusions may seem, you'll see that the etiology of schizophrenic disorders is not all that different from the etiology of other psychological disorders. We'll begin our discussion by examining the matter of genetic vulnerability.

Genetic Vulnerability

Evidence is plentiful that hereditary factors play a role in the development of schizophrenic disorders (Kendler, 2000; Tsuang, Glatt, & Faraone, 2003). For instance, in twin studies, concordance rates average around 48% for identical twins, in comparison to about 17% for fraternal twins (Gottesman, 1991, 2001). Studies also indicate that a child born to two schizophrenic parents has about a 46% probability of developing a schizophrenic disorder (as compared to the probability in the general population of about 1%). These and other findings that demonstrate the genetic roots of schizophrenia are summarized in Figure 14.17. Overall, the picture is similar to that seen for mood disorders. Several converging lines of evidence indicate that some people inherit a polygenically transmitted *vulnerability* to schizophrenia (Schneider & Deldin, 2001). Although some theorists suspect that genetic factors may account for as much as two-thirds of the variability in susceptibility to schizophrenia, genetic mapping studies have made little progress in identifying the specific genes at work (Levinson et al., 1998; Owen & O'Donovan, 2003).

Neurochemical Factors

Like mood disorders, schizophrenic disorders appear to be accompanied by changes in the activity of one or more neurotransmitters in the brain (Patel, Pinals, & Breier, 2003). Excess *dopamine* activity has been implicated as a possible cause of schizophrenia, as discussed in Figure 14.18 (Abi-Dargham et al., 1998). This hypothesis makes sense because most of the drugs that are useful in the treatment of schizophrenia are known to dampen dopamine activity in the brain (Tamminga & Carlsson, 2003). However, the

John Nash, the Nobel Prize–winning mathematician whose story was told in the film A Beautiful Mind, *has struggled with paranoid schizophrenia since 1959.*

evidence linking schizophrenia to high dopamine levels is riddled with inconsistencies, complexities, and interpretive problems (Abi-Dargham, 2004; Egan & Hyde, 2000). Researchers are currently exploring how interactions between the dopamine and serotonin neurotransmitter systems may contribute to

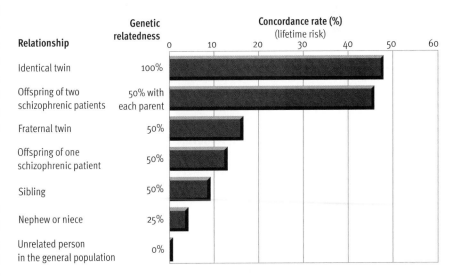

Figure 14.17

Genetic vulnerability to schizophrenic disorders. Relatives of schizophrenic patients have an elevated risk for schizophrenia. This risk is greater among closer relatives. Although environment also plays a role in the etiology of schizophrenia, the concordance rates shown here suggest that there must be a genetic vulnerability to the disorder. These concordance estimates are based on pooled data from 40 studies conducted between 1920 and 1987. (Data from Gottesman, 1991)

Figure 14.18

The dopamine hypothesis as an explanation for schizophrenia. Decades of research have implicated overactivity at dopamine synapses as a key cause of schizophrenic disorders. However, the evidence on the exact mechanisms underlying this overactivity, which is summarized in this graphic, is complex and open to debate. Recent hypotheses about the neurochemical bases of schizophrenia go beyond the simple assumption that dopamine activity is increased. For example, one theory posits that schizophrenia may be accompanied by decreased dopamine activity in one area of the brain (the prefrontal cortex) and increased activity or dysregulation in other areas of the brain (Egan & Hyde, 2000). Moreover, abnormalities in other neurotransmitter systems may also contribute to schizophrenia.

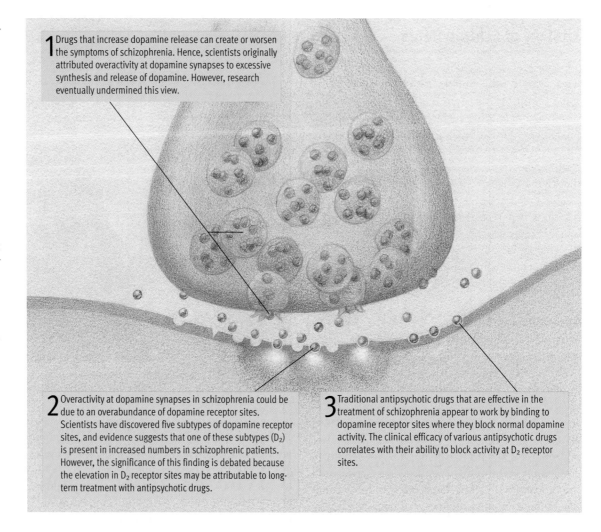

1 Drugs that increase dopamine release can create or worsen the symptoms of schizophrenia. Hence, scientists originally attributed overactivity at dopamine synapses to excessive synthesis and release of dopamine. However, research eventually undermined this view.

2 Overactivity at dopamine synapses in schizophrenia could be due to an overabundance of dopamine receptor sites. Scientists have discovered five subtypes of dopamine receptor sites, and evidence suggests that one of these subtypes (D_2) is present in increased numbers in schizophrenic patients. However, the significance of this finding is debated because the elevation in D_2 receptor sites may be attributable to long-term treatment with antipsychotic drugs.

3 Traditional antipsychotic drugs that are effective in the treatment of schizophrenia appear to work by binding to dopamine receptor sites where they block normal dopamine activity. The clinical efficacy of various antipsychotic drugs correlates with their ability to block activity at D_2 receptor sites.

schizophrenia (Byne et al., 1999). Recent research has also suggested that abnormalities in neural circuits using *glutamate* as a neurotransmitter may play a role in schizophrenic disturbance (Tibbo et al., 2004). Thus, investigators are gradually making progress in their search for the neurochemical bases of schizophrenia.

Structural Abnormalities in the Brain 11c

For decades, studies have suggested that individuals with schizophrenia exhibit a variety of deficits in attention, perception, and information processing (Bellack, Gearon, & Blanchard, 2000). These cognitive deficits suggest that schizophrenic disorders may be caused by neurological defects (Perry & Braff, 1994). Until recent decades this theory was based more on speculation than on actual research. Now, however, advances in brain-imaging technology have yielded mountains of intriguing data. The most reliable finding is that CT scans and MRI scans (see Chapter 3) suggest an association between enlarged brain ventricles (the hollow, fluid-filled cavities in

the brain depicted in Figure 14.19) and schizophrenic disturbance (Egan & Hyde, 2000). Enlarged ventricles are assumed to reflect the degeneration of nearby brain tissue. The significance of enlarged ventricles is hotly debated, however. This structural deterioration (or failure to develop) could be a *consequence* of schizophrenia, or it could be a contributing *cause* of the illness.

Brain-imaging studies have also uncovered structural and metabolic abnormalities in the temporal and frontal lobes of individuals with schizophrenia. Although the research results are not entirely consistent, schizophrenia appears to be associated with reduced metabolic activity in an area of the prefrontal cortex and with increased metabolic activity in an area of the temporal lobe (Egan & Hyde, 2000). Theorists speculate that the frontal lobe dysfunction contributes to positive symptoms and that the temporal lobe dysfunction underlies negative symptoms (Conklin & Iacono, 2002). Scientists are also intrigued by the fact that a major dopamine pathway runs through the area in the prefrontal cortex where metabolic abnormalities have been found. There may be a connection between the abnormal dopamine activity implicated in schizophrenia and the dysfunctional metabolic activity seen in this area of the prefrontal cortex (Conklin & Iacono, 2002).

The Neurodevelopmental Hypothesis

In recent years, several new lines of evidence have led to the emergence of the *neurodevelopmental hypothesis* of schizophrenia, which posits that schizophrenia is caused in part by various disruptions in the normal maturational processes of the brain before or at birth (Brown, 1999). According to this hypothesis, insults to the brain during sensitive phases of prenatal development or during birth can cause subtle neurological damage that elevates individuals' vulnerability to schizophrenia years later in adolescence and early adulthood (see Figure 14.20). What are the sources of these early insults to the brain? Thus far, research has focused on viral infections or malnutrition during prenatal development and obstetrical complications during the birth process.

The evidence on viral infections has been building since Sarnoff Mednick and his colleagues (1988) discovered an elevated incidence of schizophrenia among individuals who were in their second trimester of prenatal development during a 1957 influenza epidemic in Finland. Several subsequent studies in other locations have also found a link between exposure to influenza during the second trimester and increased prevalence of schizophrenia (Brown et al., 2004). Another study, which investigated the possible impact of prenatal malnutrition, found an elevated incidence of schizophrenia in a cohort of people who were prenatally exposed to a severe famine in 1944–45 due to a Nazi blockade of food deliveries in the Netherlands during World War II (Susser et al., 1996). A follow-up study of some schizophrenic patients exposed to this famine found increased brain abnormalities among the patients, as the neurodevelopmental hypothesis would predict (Hulshoff et al., 2000). Other research has shown that schizophrenic patients are more likely than control subjects to have a history of obstetrical complications (Geddes & Lawrie, 1995; Rosso et al., 2000). Finally, research suggests that minor physical anomalies (slight anatomical defects of the head, hands, feet, and face) that would be consistent with prenatal neurological damage are more common among people with schizophrenia than among others (McNeil, Canton-Graae, & Ismail, 2000; Schiffman et al., 2002).

Collectively, these diverse studies argue for a relationship between early neurological trauma and a predisposition to schizophrenia (Mednick et al., 1998).

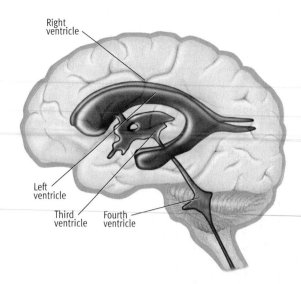

Figure 14.19

Schizophrenia and the ventricles of the brain. Cerebrospinal fluid (CSF) circulates around the brain and spinal cord. The hollow cavities in the brain filled with CSF are called ventricles. The four ventricles in the human brain are depicted here. Recent studies with CT scans and MRI scans suggest that there is an association between enlarged ventricles in the brain and the occurrence of schizophrenic disturbance.

Source: Graphic adapted from Starr, C., & Taggart, R. (1998). *Biology: The unity and diversity of life.* Belmont, CA: Wadsworth. © 1998 Wadsworth Publishing. Reprinted by permission.

However, much remains to be learned. For example, a recent study suggests that early neurological damage may increase vulnerability to *mood disorders,* as well as schizophrenia (Brown et al., 2000). Nonetheless, this new line of inquiry promises to increase our understanding of the etiology of schizophrenia.

Expressed Emotion 11c

Studies of expressed emotion have primarily focused on how this element of family dynamics influences the *course* of schizophrenic illness, after the onset of the disorder (Leff & Vaughn, 1985). *Expressed emotion (EE)* is the degree to which a relative of a schizophrenic patient displays highly critical or emotionally overinvolved attitudes toward the patient. Audiotaped interviews of relatives' communication are carefully evaluated for critical comments, resentment toward the patient, and excessive emotional involvement (overprotective, overconcerned attitudes).

Figure 14.20

The neurodevelopmental hypothesis of schizophrenia. Recent findings have suggested that insults to the brain sustained during prenatal development or at birth may disrupt crucial maturational processes in the brain, resulting in subtle neurological damage that gradually becomes apparent as youngsters develop. This neurological damage is believed to increase both vulnerability to schizophrenia and the incidence of minor physical anomalies (slight anatomical defects of the head, face, hands, and feet).

Two-year relapse rate (%)

Figure 14.21

Expressed emotion and relapse rates in schizophrenia.
Schizophrenic patients who return to a home that is high in expressed emotion have higher relapse rates than those who return to a home low in expressed emotion. Thus, unhealthy family dynamics can influence the course of schizophrenia. (Data adapted from Leff & Vaughn, 1981)

Studies show that a family's expressed emotion is a good predictor of the course of a schizophrenic patient's illness (Hooley & Candela, 1999). After release from a hospital, people with schizophrenia who return to a family high in expressed emotion show relapse

rates about three times that of patients who return to a family low in expressed emotion (see Figure 14.21; Hooley & Hiller, 1998). Part of the problem for patients returning to homes high in expressed emotion is that their families are probably more sources of stress than of social support (Cutting & Docherty, 2000). However, Rosenfarb et al. (1995) caution against placing all the blame on the families high in expressed emotion. They found that patients returning to high-EE homes exhibited more odd and disruptive behaviour than patients returning to low-EE homes. Thus, the more critical, negative attitudes experienced by patients in high-EE homes may be caused in part by their own behaviour.

Precipitating Stress

Most theories of schizophrenia assume that stress plays a key role in triggering schizophrenic disorders (Walker et al., 2004). According to this notion, various biological and psychological factors influence individuals' *vulnerability* to schizophrenia. High stress may then serve to precipitate a schizophrenic disorder in someone who is vulnerable (McGlashan & Hoffman, 2000). Research indicates that high stress can also trigger relapses in patients who have made progress toward recovery (Ventura et al., 1989).

Schizophrenia is the last of the major, Axis I diagnostic categories that we will consider. We'll complete our overview of various types of abnormal behaviour with a brief look at the personality disorders. These disorders are recorded on Axis II in the DSM classification system.

CONCEPT CHECK 14.2

Distinguishing Schizophrenic and Mood Disorders

Check your understanding of the nature of schizophrenic and mood disorders by making preliminary diagnoses for the cases described below. Read each case summary and write your tentative diagnosis in the space provided. The answers are in Appendix A.

1. Max hasn't slept in four days. He's determined to write a great novel before his class reunion, which is a few months away. He expounds eloquently on his novel to anyone who will listen, talking at such a rapid pace that no one can get a word in edgewise. He feels like he's wired with energy and is supremely confident about the novel, even though he's only written 10 to 20 pages. Last week, he charged $8000 worth of new computer software, which is supposed to help him write his book.

Preliminary diagnosis: _____

2. Eduardo maintains that he invented the atomic bomb, even though he was born after its invention. He says he invented it to punish homosexuals, Nazis, and short people. It's short people that he's really afraid of. He's sure that all the short people on TV are talking about him. He thinks that short people are conspiring to make him look like a Conservative. Eduardo frequently gets in arguments with people and is emotionally volatile. His grooming is poor, but he says it's okay because he's the defence minister.

Preliminary diagnosis: _____

3. Margaret has hardly gotten out of bed for weeks, although she's troubled by insomnia. She doesn't feel like eating and has absolutely no energy. She feels dejected, discouraged, spiritless, and apathetic. Friends stop by to try to cheer her up, but she tells them not to waste their time on "pond scum."

Preliminary diagnosis: _____

REVIEW OF KEY POINTS

- Schizophrenic disorders are characterized by deterioration of adaptive behaviour, irrational thought, delusions, hallucinations, and disturbed mood.

- Schizophrenic disorders are classified as paranoid, catatonic, disorganized, or undifferentiated. A new classification scheme based on the predominance of positive versus negative symptoms is under study. Schizophrenic disorders usually emerge during adolescence or young adulthood.

- Research has linked schizophrenia to a genetic vulnerability and changes in neurotransmitter activity at dopamine synapses. Structural abnormalities in the brain, such as enlarged ventricles, are associated with schizophrenia, but their significance is unclear.

- The neurodevelopmental hypothesis of schizophrenia asserts that schizophrenia is attributable to disruptions in the normal maturational processes of the brain before or at birth that are caused by prenatal viral infections, obstetrical complications, and other insults to the brain.

- Precipitating stress and unhealthy family dynamics (high expressed emotion) may also contribute to the development of schizophrenia.

Personality Disorders

We have seen repeatedly that it is often difficult to draw that imaginary line between healthy and disordered behaviour. This is especially true in the case of personality disorders, which are relatively mild disturbances in comparison to most of the Axis I disorders. *Personality disorders* **are a class of disorders marked by extreme, inflexible personality traits that cause subjective distress or impaired social and occupational functioning.** Essentially, people with these disorders display certain personality traits to an excessive degree and in rigid ways that undermine their adjustment. Personality disorders usually emerge during late childhood or adolescence and often continue throughout adulthood. It is difficult to estimate the prevalence of these subtle disorders, but it is clear that they are common (Mattia & Zimmerman, 2001).

DSM-IV lists ten personality disorders. These disorders are described briefly in Table 14.2. If you examine this table, you will find a diverse collection of maladaptive personality syndromes. You may also notice that some personality disorders essentially are mild versions of more severe Axis I disorders. Some of these disorders are more common in men and some in women, as the figures in the far right column of the table indicate.

The ten personality disorders are grouped into three related clusters, as shown in Table 14.2. The three disorders in the *anxious/fearful cluster* are marked by maladaptive efforts to control anxiety and fear about social rejection. People with the three disorders in the *odd/eccentric cluster* are distrustful, socially aloof, and unable to connect with others emotionally. The four personality disorders in the

PREVIEW QUESTIONS
- What are the three clusters of personality disorders?
- What is the major diagnostic challenge with personality disorders?
- What are the symptoms of antisocial personality disorder?
- What factors have been implicated in the etiology of antisocial personality disorders?

Table 14.2 Personality Disorders

Cluster	Disorder	Description	% Male/% Female
Anxious/fearful	Avoidant personality disorder	Excessively sensitive to potential rejection, humiliation, or shame; socially withdrawn in spite of desire for acceptance from others	50/50
	Dependent personality disorder	Excessively lacking in self-reliance and self-esteem; passively allowing others to make all decisions; constantly subordinating own needs to others' needs	31/69
	Obsessive-compulsive personality disorder	Preoccupied with organization, rules, schedules, lists, trivial details; extremely conventional, serious, and formal; unable to express warm emotions	50/50
Odd/eccentric	Schizoid personality disorder	Defective in capacity for forming social relationships; showing absence of warm, tender feelings for others	78/22
	Schizotypal personality disorder	Showing social deficits and oddities of thinking, perception, and communication that resemble schizophrenia	55/45
	Paranoid personality disorder	Showing pervasive and unwarranted suspiciousness and mistrust of people; overly sensitive; prone to jealousy	67/33
Dramatic/ impulsive	Histrionic personality disorder	Overly dramatic; tending to exaggerated expressions of emotion; egocentric, seeking attention	15/85
	Narcissistic personality disorder	Grandiosely self-important; preoccupied with success fantasies; expecting special treatment; lacking interpersonal empathy	70/30
	Borderline personality disorder	Unstable in self-image, mood, and interpersonal relationships; impulsive and unpredictable	38/62
	Antisocial personality disorder	Chronically violating the rights of others; failing to accept social norms, to form attachments to others, or to sustain consistent work behaviour; exploitive and reckless	82/18

SOURCE: Estimated gender ratios from Millon (1981)

dramatic/impulsive cluster have less in common with each other than those grouped in the first two clusters. The histrionic and narcissistic personalities share a flair for overdramatizing everything. Impulsiveness is the common ground shared by the borderline and antisocial personality disorders.

Diagnostic Problems

Many critics have argued that the personality disorders overlap too much with Axis I disorders and with each other (Dolan-Sewell, Krueger, & Shea, 2001). The extent of this problem was documented in a study by Leslie Morey (1988). Morey reviewed the cases of 291 patients who had received a specific personality disorder diagnosis to see how many could have met the criteria for any of the other personality disorders. Morey found massive overlap among the diagnoses. For example, among patients with a diagnosis of histrionic personality disorder, 56% also qualified for a borderline disorder, 54% for a narcissistic disorder, 32% for an avoidant disorder, and 30% for a dependent disorder. Clearly, there are fundamental problems with Axis II as a classification system (Westen & Shedler, 1999). The overlap among the personality disorders makes it extremely difficult to achieve reliable diagnoses. Doubts have also been raised about the decision to place personality disorders on a separate axis, as there does not appear to be any fundamental distinction between personality disorders and Axis I disorders (Livesley, 2001).

In light of these problems, a variety of theorists have questioned the wisdom of the current *categorical approach* to describing personality disorders, which assumes (incorrectly, they argue) that people can reliably be placed in discontinuous (nonoverlapping) diagnostic categories (Trull & McCrae, 1994; Livesley, 2001). These theorists argue instead for a *dimensional approach,* which would describe personality disorders in terms of how people score on a limited number of continuous personality dimensions. The practical logistics of using a dimensional approach to describe personality disorders are formidable. In any event, debate about the classification of personality disorders is likely to continue and changes in the official diagnostic scheme will surely be seen in DSM-V (Widiger, 2001).

The difficulties involved in the diagnosis of personality disorders have clearly hindered research on their etiology and prognosis. The only personality disorder that has a long history of extensive research is the antisocial personality disorder, which we examine next.

Antisocial Personality Disorder

The antisocial personality disorder has a misleading name. The antisocial designation does *not* mean that people with this disorder shun social interaction. In fact, rather than shrinking from social interaction, many are sociable, friendly, and superficially charming. People with this disorder are *antisocial* in that they choose to *reject widely accepted social norms* regarding moral principles and behaviour.

Description

People with antisocial personalities chronically violate the rights of others. They often use their social charm to cultivate others' liking or loyalty for purposes of exploitation. The *antisocial personality disorder* is marked by impulsive, callous, manipulative, aggressive, and irresponsible behaviour that reflects a failure to accept social norms. Since they haven't accepted the social norms they violate, people with antisocial personalities rarely feel guilty about their transgressions. Essentially, they lack an adequate conscience. The antisocial personality disorder occurs much more frequently among males than females. Studies suggest that it is a moderately common disorder, seen in roughly 3%–6% of males and about 1% of females (Widiger & Mullins, 2003).

Many people with antisocial personalities get involved in illegal activities. Moreover, according to University of British Columbia psychologist Robert Hare and his colleagues, antisocial personalities tend to begin their criminal careers at an early age, to commit offences at a relatively high rate, and to be versatile offenders who get involved in many types of criminal activity (Hart & Hare, 1997). However, many people with antisocial personalities keep their exploitive, amoral behaviour channelled within the boundaries of the law. Such people may even enjoy high status in our society. In other words, the concept of the antisocial personality disorder can apply to cutthroat business executives, scheming politicians, unprincipled lawyers, and money-hungry evangelists, as well as to con artists, drug dealers, thugs, burglars, and petty thieves.

Robert Hare is one of the world's leading experts on psychopathy, a term that is often used interchangeably for the term antisocial personality disorder. His influential book *Without Conscience: The Disturbing World of the Psychopaths Among Us* (Hare, 1999) is an important resource for scholars and laypersons alike. Hare (1991) developed an important assessment device for psychopathy, the Psychopathy

Checklist–Revised (PCL–R). For many, this measure is the "single, most important advancement to date toward what will hopefully become our ultimate understanding of psychopathy" (Wormith, 2000, p. 134). Recent research by a team of psychologists from Queen's University and the Mental Health Centre at Penetanguishene (Skilling et al., 2002) supports the validity of the PCL–R.

People with antisocial personalities exhibit quite a variety of maladaptive traits (Hare, Cooke, & Hart, 1999; Sutker & Allain, 2001). Among other things, they rarely experience genuine affection for others. However, they may be skilled at faking affection so they can exploit people. Sexually, they are predatory and promiscuous. Such individuals also tend to be irresponsible and impulsive. They can tolerate little frustration, and they pursue immediate gratification. These characteristics make them unreliable employees, unfaithful spouses, inattentive parents, and undependable friends. Many people with antisocial personalities have a checkered history of divorce, child abuse, and job instability. Paul Bernardo, who was convicted for the 1991 murders of Leslie Mahaffy and Kristen French, has the classic features of someone with antisocial personality disorder.

Etiology

Many theorists believe that biological factors contribute to the development of antisocial personality disorders. Various lines of evidence suggest a genetic predisposition toward these disorders (Moffitt, 2005). Hans Eysenck has noted that people with antisocial personalities lack the inhibitions that most of us have about violating moral standards. Their lack of inhibitions prompted Eysenck (1982) to theorize that such people might inherit relatively sluggish autonomic nervous systems, leading to slow acquisition of inhibitions through classical conditioning. The findings relating to this hypothesis are inconsistent, but the notion that antisocial personalities exhibit underarousal has received a fair amount of support (Raine, 1997). Research also suggests that

subtle neurological damage that occurs during prenatal development or the early years of childhood is associated with an increased prevalence of antisocial behaviour (Brennan & Mednick, 1997). As a whole, the evidence suggests that biological factors may create a genuine but weak predisposition toward antisocial behaviour.

Efforts to relate psychological factors to antisocial behaviour have emphasized inadequate socialization in dysfunctional family systems (Sutker & Allain, 2001). It's easy to envision how antisocial traits could be fostered in homes where parents make haphazard or half-hearted efforts to socialize their children to be respectful, truthful, responsible, unselfish, and so forth. Consistent with this idea, studies find that individuals with antisocial personalities tend to come from homes where discipline is erratic or ineffective, and homes where they experience physical abuse and neglect (Luntz & Widom, 1994; Widom, 1997). Such people are also more likely to emerge from homes where one or both parents exhibit antisocial traits (Black, 2001). These parents presumably model exploitive, amoral behaviour, which their children acquire through observational learning.

REVIEW OF KEY POINTS

- There are ten personality disorders allocated to Axis II in DSM. Personality disorders can be grouped into three clusters: anxious/fearful, odd/eccentric, and dramatic/impulsive.

- Specific personality disorders are poorly defined and there is excessive overlap among them, creating diagnostic problems. Some theorists believe that these problems could be reduced by replacing the current categorical approach to personality disorders with a dimensional approach.

- The antisocial personality disorder involves manipulative, impulsive, exploitive, aggressive behaviour. Research on the etiology of this disorder has implicated genetic vulnerability, autonomic reactivity, inadequate socialization, and observational learning.

Overview of Three Categories of Psychological Disorders

Axis I category	Subtypes	Prevalence/well-known victim

Anxiety disorders

Edvard Munch's *The Scream* expresses overwhelming feelings of anxiety.

Generalized anxiety disorder: Chronic, high level of anxiety not tied to any specific threat

Phobic disorder: Persistent, irrational fear of object or situation that presents no real danger

Panic disorder: Recurrent attacks of overwhelming anxiety that occur suddenly and unexpectedly

Obsessive-compulsive disorder: Persistent, uncontrollable intrusions of unwanted thoughts and urges to engage in senseless rituals

19% Prevalence

The famous industrialist Howard Hughes suffered from obsessive-compulsive disorder.

Mood disorders

Vincent van Gogh's *Portrait of Dr. Gachet* captures the profound dejection experienced in depressive disorders.

Major depressive disorder: Two or more major depressive episodes marked by feelings of sadness, worthlessness, despair

Bipolar disorder: One or more manic episodes marked by inflated self-esteem, grandiosity, and elevated mood and energy, usually accompanied by major depressive episodes

15% Prevalence

Actor Jim Carrey has suffered from depression.

Schizophrenic disorders

The perceptual distortions seen in schizophrenia probably contributed to the bizarre imagery apparent in this portrait of a cat painted by Louis Wain.

Paranoid schizophrenia: Delusions of persecution and delusions of grandeur; frequent auditory hallucinations

Catatonic schizophrenia: Motor disturbances ranging from immobility to excessive, purposeless activity

Disorganized schizophrenia: Flat or inappropriate emotions; disorganized speech and adaptive behaviour

Undifferentiated schizophrenia: Idiosyncratic mixtures of schizophrenic symptoms that cannot be placed into above three categories

1% Prevalence

John Nash, the Nobel Prize–winning mathematician whose story was told in the film *A Beautiful Mind*, has struggled with schizophrenia.

Etiology: Biological factors

Genetic vulnerability: Twin studies and other evidence suggest a mild genetic predisposition to anxiety disorders.

Anxiety sensitivity: Oversensitivity to physical symptoms of anxiety may lead to overreactions to feelings of anxiety, so anxiety breeds more anxiety.

Concordance rate (%)

Neurochemical bases: Disturbances in neural circuits releasing GABA may contribute to some disorders; abnormalities at serotonin synapses have been implicated in panic and obsessive-compulsive disorders.

Genetic vulnerability: Twin studies and other evidence suggest a genetic predisposition to mood disorders.

Sleep disturbances: Disruption of biological rhythms and sleep patterns may lead to neurochemical changes that contribute to mood disorders.

Concordance rate (%)

Neurochemical bases: Disturbances in neural circuits releasing norepinephrine may contribute to some mood disorders; abnormalities at serotonin synapses have also been implicated as a factor in depression.

Genetic vulnerability: Twin studies and other evidence suggest a genetic predispositon to schizophrenic disorders.

Concordance rate (%)

Neurochemical bases: Overactivity in neural circuits releasing dopamine is associated with schizophrenia; but abnormalities in other neurotransmitter systems may also contribute.

Structural abnormalities in brain: Enlarged brain ventricles are associated with schizophrenia, but they may be an effect rather than a cause of the disorder.

Etiology: Psychological factors

Learning: Many anxiety responses may be acquired through classical conditioning or observational learning; phobic responses may be maintained by operant reinforcement.

Stress: High stress may help to precipitate the onset of anxiety disorders.

Cognition: People who misinterpret harmless situations as threatening and who focus excessive attention on perceived threats are more vulnerable to anxiety disorders.

Threatening interpretations endorsed (%)

Interpersonal roots: Behavioural theories emphasize how inadequate social skills can result in a paucity of reinforcers and other effects that make people vulnerable to depression.

Stress: High stress can act as a precipitating factor that triggers depression or bipolar disorder.

Cognition: Negative thinking can contribute to the development of depression; rumination may extend and amplify depression.

Expressed emotion: A family's expressed emotion is a good predictor of the course of a schizophrenic patient's illness.

Stress: High stress can precipitate schizophrenic disorder in people who are vulnerable to schizophrenia.

Two-year relapse rate (%)

The neurodevelopmental hypothesis: Insults to the brain sustained during prenatal development or at birth may disrupt maturational processes in the brain resulting in elevated vulnerability to schizophrenia.

Psychological Disorders and the Law

PREVIEW QUESTIONS
- What is the insanity defence?
- How often is it used?

Societies use laws to enforce their norms regarding appropriate behaviour. Given this function, the law in our society has something to say about many issues related to abnormal behaviour. In this section we examine the concept of insanity.

Insanity

Insanity is *not* a diagnosis; it's a legal concept. **Insanity is a legal status indicating that a person cannot be held responsible for his or her actions because of mental illness.** Why is this an issue in the courtroom? Because criminal acts must be intentional. The law reasons that people who are "out of their mind" may not be able to appreciate the significance of what they're doing. The insanity defence is used in criminal trials by defendants who admit that they committed the crime but claim that they lacked intent.

No simple relationship exists between specific diagnoses of mental disorders and court findings of insanity. Most people with diagnosed psychological disorders would *not* qualify as insane. The people most likely to qualify are those troubled by severe disturbances that display delusional behaviour. The courts apply various rules in making judgments about a defendant's sanity, depending on the jurisdiction. According to one widely used rule, called the *M'Naghten rule,* insanity exists when a mental disorder makes a person unable to distinguish right from wrong. The M'Naghten rule originated in England when a delusional man attempted to kill the prime minister, and shot one of the prime minister's assistants instead. This rule has served as the basis of insanity laws in many countries including Canada. (As you can imagine, evaluating insanity as defined in the M'Naghten rule can be difficult for judges and jurors, not to mention the psychologists and psychiatrists who are called into court as expert witnesses.) According to York University professor Regina Schuller and Simon Fraser's James Ogloff, the "growth in clinical psychology over the first half of the twentieth century resulted in an increased demand from the legal system for clinical evaluations and diagnoses of mental disorders" (Schuller & Ogloff, 2001, p. 6).

Over the years since the establishment of the M'Naghten rule, changes have been made to how psychological disorders are used in court. In Canada, the designation of being found not guilty by reason of insanity (NGRI) was changed in 1991 to the term

Psychologist Regina Schuller is an expert on the interface of psychology and Canadian law. Her research interests include cases involving violence against women.

"not criminally responsible on account of mental disorder" (NCRMD) (Olgoff & Whittemore, 2001). According to Simon Fraser psychologists Jocelyn Lumburner and Ronald Roesch (1999), the use and success of this defence is rarer than most Canadians assume. They suggest that it is rarely successful, and typically only used in cases of the most severely disordered defendants.

According to a team of scholars from Carleton University (Pozzulo, Bennell, & Forth, 2006), issues of fitness, insanity, and automatism are relevant to the two cornerstones of English-Canadian Law—*actus reus* (a wrongful deed) and *mens rea* (criminal intent). Mental health professionals may play an important role at several stages of a trial. Defendants may be found *unfit to stand trial* if they are judged unable to conduct a defence at any point in the legal proceedings because of a psychological disorder such as schizophrenia. This may be due to their inability to understand the proceedings or possible consequences, or an inability to communicate with their lawyers.

Web Link 14.6

David Willshire's Forensic Psychology and Psychiatry Links

http://members.optushome.com.au/dwillsh/

This site's webmaster, a senior psychologist at Australia's Victorian Institute of Forensic Mental Health, has brought together a large set of annotated links on all aspects of forensic matters—that is, how the law and criminal justice system interact with psychology and psychiatry.

Once fitness is restored, a defendant may stand trial. If found fit to stand trial, psychological issues may enter in terms of the insanity defence. If it is found that the defendant was unable to appreciate the quality of the act and the fact that it was wrong, the defendant may be found *not criminally responsible on account of mental disorder*. If found NCRMD, the defendant may be absolutely discharged, given a conditional discharge, or ordered to a psychiatric facility (Pozzulo et al., 2006). A final issue relevant to our discussion is that of *automatism*. Here the idea is that you should not be held responsible if you had no control over your behaviour. The conditions that have been recognized in Canadian courts include physical blows, carbon monoxide poisoning, sleepwalking, and others. You may recall hearing about the successful sleepwalking defence used in the 1988 case of Ken Parks, who drove 23 kilometres and killed his mother-in-law in Ontario. While a defendant may be sent to a psychiatric institution if he or she is judged NCRMD, a "successful (noninsane) automatism verdict means that the defendant is not guilty and is then released without conditions" (Pozzulo et al., 2006, pp. 281).

Culture and Pathology

The legal rules governing insanity and involuntary commitment obviously are culture-specific. And we noted earlier that judgments of normality and abnormality are influenced by cultural norms and values. In light of these realities, would it be reasonable to infer that psychological disorders are culturally variable phenomena? Social scientists are sharply divided on the answer to this question. Some embrace a *relativistic view* of psychological disorders, whereas others subscribe to a *universalistic or pancultural view* (Tanaka-Matsumi, 2001). Theorists who embrace the *relativistic view* argue that the criteria of mental illness vary greatly across cultures and that there are no universal standards of normality and abnormality. According to the relativists, the DSM diagnostic system reflects an ethnocentric, Western, white, urban, middle- and upper-class cultural orientation that has limited relevance in other cultural contexts. In contrast, those who subscribe to the *pancultural view* argue that the criteria of mental illness are much the same around the world and that basic standards of normality and abnormality are universal across cultures. Theorists who accept the pancultural view of psychopathology typically maintain that Western diagnostic concepts have validity and utility in other cultural contexts.

The debate about culture and pathology basically boils down to two specific issues: (1) Are the psychological disorders seen in Western societies found throughout the world? (2) Are the symptom patterns of mental disorders invariant across cultures? Let's briefly examine the evidence on these questions and then reconsider the relativistic and pancultural views of psychological disorders.

Are Equivalent Disorders Found around the World?

Most investigators agree that the principal categories of serious psychological disturbance—schizophrenia, depression, and bipolar illness—are identifiable in all cultures (Tsai et al., 2001). Most behaviours that are regarded as clearly abnormal in Western culture are also viewed as abnormal in other cultures. People who are delusional, hallucinatory, disoriented, or incoherent are thought to be disturbed in all societies, although there are cultural disparities in exactly what is considered delusional or hallucinatory.

Cultural variations are more apparent in the recognition of less severe forms of psychological disturbance (Mezzich, Lewis-Fernandez, & Ruiperez, 2003). Additional research is needed, but relatively mild types of pathology that do not disrupt behaviour in obvious ways appear to go unrecognized in many societies. Thus, syndromes such as generalized anxiety disorder, hypochondria, and narcissistic personality disorder, which are firmly established as diagnostic entities in the DSM, are viewed in some cultures as "run of the mill" difficulties and peculiarities rather than as full-fledged disorders.

Finally, researchers have discovered a small number of *culture-bound disorders* that further illustrate the diversity of abnormal behaviour around the world (Griffith, Gonzalez, & Blue, 2003; Guarnaccia & Rogler, 1999). **Culture-bound disorders are abnormal syndromes found only in a few cultural groups.** For example, *koro*, an obsessive fear that one's penis will withdraw into one's abdomen, is seen only among Chinese males in Malaya and several other regions of

PREVIEW QUESTIONS
● Are the same psychological disorders found in all cultures?
● Are the symptoms of psychological disorders influenced by culture?

southern Asia. *Windigo,* which involves an intense craving for human flesh and fear that one will turn into a cannibal, is seen only among Algonquin cultures, and *Pibloktoq* is a type of Arctic hysteria associated with the Inuit. And until fairly recently, the eating disorder *anorexia nervosa,* discussed in this chapter's Personal Application, was largely seen only in affluent Western cultures.

Are Symptom Patterns Culturally Invariant?

Do the major types of psychological disorders manifest themselves in the same way around the world? For the most part, yes. The constellations of symptoms associated with schizophrenia and bipolar illness are largely the same across widely disparate societies (Draguns, 1980, 1990). However, cultural variations in symptom patterns are also seen. For example, delusions are a common symptom of schizophrenia in all cultures, but the specific delusions that people report are tied to their cultural heritage (Brislin, 1993). In technologically advanced societies, schizophrenic patients report that thoughts are being inserted into their minds through transmissions from electric lines, satellites, or microwave ovens. Victims of schizophrenia in less technological societies experience the same phenomenon but blame

sorcerers or demons. Of the major disorders, symptom patterns are probably most variable for depression. For example, profound feelings of guilt and self-deprecation lie at the core of depression in Western cultures but are far less central to depression in many other societies. In non-Western cultures, depression tends to be expressed in terms of somatic symptoms, such as complaints of fatigue, headaches, and backaches, more than psychological symptoms, such as dejection and low self-esteem (Tsai et al., 2001; Young, 1997). These differences presumably occur because people learn to express symptoms of psychological distress in ways that are acceptable in their culture.

So, what can we conclude about the validity of the relativistic versus pancultural views of psychological disorders? Both views appear to have some merit. As we have seen in other areas of research, psychopathology is characterized by both cultural variance and invariance. Investigators have identified some universal standards of normality and abnormality and found considerable similarity across cultures in the syndromes that are regarded as pathological and in their patterns of symptoms. However, researchers have also discovered many cultural variations in the recognition, definition, and symptoms of various psychological disorders. Given this extensive variability, the relativists' concerns about the ethnocentric nature of the DSM diagnostic system seem well founded.

Putting It in Perspective

PREVIEW QUESTIONS
● How did this chapter illustrate multifactorial causation?
● How did this chapter highlight the interaction of heredity and environment?
● How did this chapter show that psychology evolves in a sociohistorical context?
● How did this chapter illustrate the importance of cultural factors?

Our examination of abnormal behaviour and its roots has highlighted four of our organizing themes: multifactorial causation, the interplay of heredity and environment, the sociohistorical context in which psychology evolves, and the influence of culture on psychological phenomena.

We can safely assert that every disorder described in this chapter has multiple causes. The development of mental disorders involves an interplay among a variety of psychological, biological, and social factors. We also saw that most psychological disorders depend on an interaction of genetics and experience. This interaction shows up most clearly in the *stress-vulnerability models* for mood disorders and schizophrenic disorders (see Figure 14.22). *Vulnerability* to these disorders seems to depend primarily on heredity, whereas stress is largely a function of environment. According to stress-vulnerability theories, disorders emerge when high vulnerability intersects with high stress. A high biological vulnerability may not

be converted into a disorder if a person's stress is low. Similarly, high stress may not lead to a disorder if vulnerability is low. Thus, the impact of heredity depends on the environment, and the effect of environment depends on heredity.

This chapter also demonstrated that psychology evolves in a sociohistorical context. We saw that modern conceptions of normality and abnormality are largely shaped by empirical research, but social trends, economic necessities, and political realities also play a role. Finally, our discussion of psychological disorders showed once again that psychological phenomena are shaped to some degree by cultural parameters. Although some standards of normality and abnormality transcend cultural boundaries, cultural norms influence many aspects of psychopathology. Indeed, the influence of culture will be apparent in our upcoming Personal Application on eating disorders. These disorders are largely a creation of modern, affluent, Western culture.

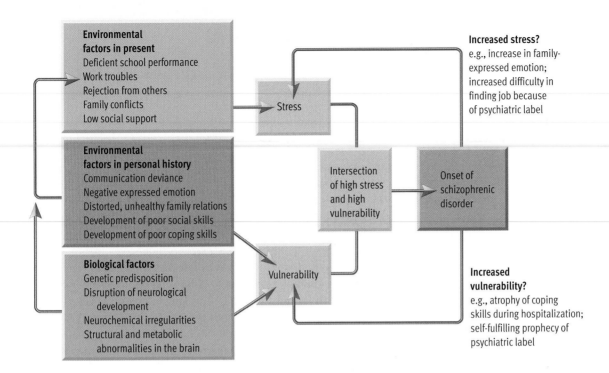

Figure 14.22

The stress-vulnerability model of schizophrenia. Multifactorial causation is readily apparent in current theories about the etiology of schizophrenic disorders. A variety of biological factors and personal history factors influence one's vulnerability to the disorder, which interacts with the amount of stress one experiences. Schizophrenic disorders appear to result from an intersection of high stress and high vulnerability.

REVIEW OF KEY POINTS

- Insanity is a legal concept applied to people who cannot be held responsible for their actions because of mental illness. The insanity defence is used less frequently and less successfully than widely believed.

- The principal categories of psychological disturbance are identifiable in all cultures. But milder disorders may go unrecognized in some societies, and culture-bound disorders further illustrate the diversity of abnormal behaviour around the world. The symptoms associated with specific disorders are largely the same across different cultures, but cultural variations are seen in the details of how these symptoms are expressed.

- This chapter highlighted four of the text's unifying themes, showing that behaviour is governed by multiple causes, that heredity and environment jointly influence mental disorders, that psychology evolves in a sociohistorical context, and that pathology is characterized by both cultural variance and invariance.

PERSONAL APPLICATION

Understanding Eating Disorders

Answer the following "true" or "false."

_____ **1.** Although they have only attracted attention in recent years, eating disorders have a long history and have always been fairly common.

_____ **2.** People with anorexia nervosa are much more likely to recognize that their eating behaviour is pathological than people suffering from bulimia nervosa are.

_____ **3.** The prevalence of eating disorders is twice as high in women as it is in men.

_____ **4.** The binge-and-purge syndrome seen in bulimia nervosa is not common in anorexia nervosa.

All of the above statements are false, as you will see in this Personal Application. The psychological disorders that we discussed in the main body of the chapter have largely been recognized for centuries and most of them are found in one form or another in all cultures and societies. Eating disorders present a sharp contrast to this picture; they have only been recognized in recent decades and they have largely been confined to affluent, Westernized cultures (G. F. M. Russell, 1995; Szmukler & Patton, 1995). In spite of these fascinating differences, eating disorders have much in common with traditional forms of pathology.

Eating disorders **are severe disturbances in eating behaviour characterized by preoccupation with weight concerns and unhealthy efforts to control weight.** The vast majority of cases consist of two sometimes overlapping syndromes: *anorexia nervosa* and *bulimia nervosa.* Although most people don't seem to take eating disorders as seriously as other types of psychological disorders, you will see that they are very dangerous and debilitating (Striegel-Moore & Smolak, 2001).

Anorexia Nervosa

Anorexia nervosa **involves intense fear of gaining weight, disturbed body image, refusal to maintain normal weight, and dangerous measures to lose weight.** Two subtypes have been observed (Herzog & Delinsky, 2001). In *restricting type anorexia nervosa,* people drastically reduce their intake of food, sometimes literally starving themselves. In *binge-eating/purging type anorexia nervosa,* individuals attempt to lose weight by forcing themselves to vomit after meals, by misusing laxatives and diuretics, and by engaging in excessive exercise.

Both types suffer from disturbed body image. No matter how frail and emaciated they become, they insist that they are too fat. Their morbid fear of obesity means that they are never satisfied with their weight. If they gain half a kilogram, they panic. The only thing that makes them happy is to lose more weight. The frequent result is a relentless decline in body weight; people entering treatment for anorexia nervosa are typically 25%–30% below their normal weight (Hsu, 1990). Because of their disturbed body image, people suffering from anorexia generally do *not* appreciate the maladaptive quality of their behaviour and rarely seek treatment on their own. They are typically coaxed or coerced into treatment by friends or family members who are alarmed by their appearance.

Anorexia nervosa eventually leads to a cascade of medical problems, including *amenorrhea* (a loss of menstrual cycles in women), gastrointestinal problems, low blood pressure, *osteoporosis* (a loss of bone density), and metabolic disturbances that can lead to cardiac arrest or circulatory collapse (Herzog & Becker, 1999; Pomeroy & Mitchell, 2002). Anorexia is a very serious illness that leads to death in 5%–10% of patients (Steinhausen, 2002).

Bulimia Nervosa

Bulimia nervosa **involves habitually engaging in out-of-control overeating followed by unhealthy compensatory**

Eating disorders have become common and have been seen in many prominent women, such as Princess Diana (left), and singer Alanis Morissette (right).

efforts, such as self-induced vomiting, fasting, abuse of laxatives and diuretics, and excessive exercise. The eating binges are usually carried out in secret and are followed by intense guilt and concern about gaining weight. These feelings motivate ill-advised strategies to undo the effects of the overeating. However, vomiting only prevents the absorption of about half of recently consumed food, and laxatives and diuretics have negligible impact on caloric intake, so people suffering from bulimia nervosa typically maintain a reasonably normal weight (Beumont, 2002; Kaye et al., 1993). Medical problems associated with bulimia nervosa include cardiac arrhythmias, dental problems, metabolic deficiencies, and gastrointestinal problems (Halmi, 1999, 2002, 2003).

Obviously, bulimia nervosa shares many features with anorexia nervosa, such as a morbid fear of becoming obese, preoccupation with food, and rigid, maladaptive approaches to controlling weight that are grounded in naïve all-or-none thinking. However, the syndromes also differ in crucial ways. First and foremost, bulimia is a much less life-threatening condition. Second, although their appearance is usually more "normal" than that seen in anorexia, people with bulimia are much more likely to recognize that their eating behaviour is pathological and are more prone to cooperate with treatment (Striegel-Moore, Silberstein, & Rodin, 1993).

History, Prevalence, and Course

Historians have been able to track down descriptions of anorexia nervosa that date back centuries, so the disorder is *not* entirely new, but anorexia nervosa did not become a common affliction until the middle part of the 20th century (Vandereycken, 2002). Although binging and purging have a long history in some cultures, they were not part of pathological efforts to control weight, and bulimia nervosa appears to be a new syndrome that emerged gradually in the middle of the 20th century and was first recognized in the 1970s (Parry-Jones & Parry-Jones, 1995; G. F. M. Russell, 1997).

Both disorders are a product of modern, affluent, Western culture, where food is generally plentiful and the desirability of being thin is widely endorsed. Until recently, these disorders were not seen outside of Western cultures (Hoek, 2002). However, in recent years, advances in communication have exported Western culture to far-flung corners of the globe, and eating disorders have started showing up in many non-Western societies, especially affluent Asian countries (Lee & Katzman, 2002).

There is a huge gender gap in the likelihood of developing eating disorders. About 90%–95% of individuals with eating disorders are female (Hoek, 2002). This staggering discrepancy appears to be a result of cultural pressures rather than biological factors (Smolak & Murnen, 2001). Western standards of attractiveness emphasize slenderness more for females than for males, and women generally experience greater pressure to be physically attractive than men do (Sobal, 1995). Eating disorders mostly afflict *young* women. The typical age

of onset for anorexia is 14 to 18 and for bulimia it is 15 to 21 (see Figure 14.23).

How common are eating disorders in Western societies? The prevalence of these disorders has increased substantially in recent decades, although this escalation may be levelling off (Steiger & Seguin, 1999). Studies of young women suggest that about 0.5%–1.5% develop anorexia nervosa (Thompson, 2004) and about 2%–3% develop bulimia nervosa (Romano & Quinn, 2001). These figures may seem small, but they mean that millions of young women wrestle with serious eating problems.

Virtually all of the approaches to treatment that we will discuss in the next chapter—such as insight therapy, group therapy, behaviour therapy, and drug therapy—have been used in the treatment of eating disorders (Halmi, 2000). How successful are these therapeutic interventions? The picture is mixed. About 40%–50% of anorexia patients experience a full recovery, while treatment is largely a failure for about 20%–25% of patients (Steinhausen, 2002).

Figure 14.23

Age of onset for anorexia nervosa. Eating disorders tend to emerge during adolescence, as these data for anorexia nervosa show. This graph shows how age of onset was distributed in a sample of 166 female patients from Minnesota. As you can see, over half the patients experienced the onset of their illness before the age of 20, with vulnerability clearly peaking between the ages of 15 and 19.

Source: Adapted from Lucas, A. R., Beard, C. M., O'Fallon, W. M., & Kurland, L. T. (1991). 50-year trends in the incidence of anorexia nervosa in Rochester, Minn.: A population-based study. *American Journal of Psychiatry, 148,* 917–922. © 1991 American Psychiatric Association.

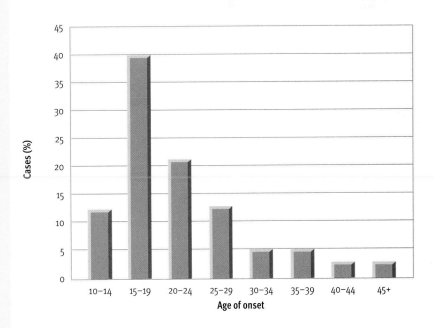

The remaining patients fall somewhere in between, experiencing modest improvement along with continued struggles. The prognosis is better for bulimia nervosa, which has a recovery rate of about 70% (Sullivan, 2002).

Etiology of Eating Disorders

Like other types of psychological disorders, eating disorders are caused by multiple determinants that work interactively. Let's take a brief look at some of the factors that contribute to the development of anorexia nervosa and bulimia nervosa.

Genetic Vulnerability

The evidence is not nearly as strong or complete as it is for many other types of psychopathology (such as anxiety, mood, and schizophrenic disorders), but some people may inherit a genetic vulnerability to eating disorders. Studies show that relatives of patients with eating disorders have elevated rates of anorexia nervosa and bulimia nervosa (Bulik, 2004). And twin studies suggest that a genetic predisposition may be at work (Steiger, Bruce, & Israel, 2003).

Personality Factors

Certain personality traits may increase vulnerability to eating disorders. There are innumerable exceptions, but victims of anorexia nervosa tend to be obsessive, rigid, and emotionally restrained, whereas victims of bulimia nervosa tend to be impulsive, overly sensitive, and low in self-esteem (Wonderlich, 2002). Recent research also suggests that perfectionism is a risk factor for anorexia (Halmi et al., 2000).

Cultural Values

The contribution of cultural values to the increased prevalence of eating disorders can hardly be overestimated (Anderson-Fye & Becker, 2004; Stice, 2001). In Western society, young women are socialized to believe that they must be attractive, and to be attractive they must be as thin as the actresses and fashion models that dominate the media (Lavine, Sweeney, & Wagner, 1999). Thanks to this cultural milieu, many young women are dissatisfied with their weight because the societal ideals promoted by the media are unattainable for most of them (Thompson & Stice, 2001). Unfortunately, in a small portion of these women, the pressure to be thin, in combination with genetic vulnerability, family pathology, and other factors, leads to unhealthful efforts to control weight.

The Role of the Family

Quite a number of theorists emphasize how family dynamics can contribute to the development of anorexia nervosa and bulimia nervosa in young women (Haworth-Hoeppner, 2000). Some theorists suggest that parents who are overly involved in their children's lives turn the normal adolescent push for independence into an unhealthy struggle (Minuchin, Rosman, & Baker, 1978). Needing to assert their autonomy, some adolescent girls seek extreme control over their body, leading to pathological patterns of eating (Bruch, 1978). Other theorists maintain that some mothers contribute to eating disorders simply by endorsing society's message that "you can never be too thin" and by modelling unhealthy dieting behaviours of their own (Pike & Rodin, 1991).

Cognitive Factors

Many theorists emphasize the role of disturbed thinking in the etiology of eating disorders (Williamson et al., 2001). For example, anorexic patients' typical belief that they are fat when they are really wasting away is a dramatic illustration of how thinking goes awry. Patients with eating disorders display rigid, all-or-none thinking and many maladaptive beliefs, such as "I must be thin to be accepted," "If I am not in complete control, I will lose all control," "If I gain 1 kilogram, I'll go on to gain enormous weight." Additional research is needed to determine whether distorted thinking is a *cause* or merely a *symptom* of eating disorders.

REVIEW OF KEY POINTS

- The principal eating disorders are anorexia nervosa and bulimia nervosa. Both disorders reflect a morbid fear of gaining weight. Anorexia and bulimia both lead to a cascade of medical problems. Both disorders appear to be largely a product of modern, affluent, Westernized culture.

- Females account for 90%–95% of eating disorders. The typical age of onset is roughly 15 to 20. There appears to be a genetic vulnerability to eating disorders. Cultural pressures on young women to be thin clearly help to foster eating disorders. Unhealthy family dynamics, certain personality traits, and disturbed thinking can also contribute to the development of eating disorders.

Working with Probabilities in Thinking about Mental Illness

As you read about the various types of psychological disorders, did you think to yourself that you or someone you know was being described? On the one hand, there is no reason to be alarmed. The tendency to see yourself and your friends in descriptions of pathology is a common one, sometimes called the *medical student's disease* because beginning medical students often erroneously believe that they or their friends have whatever diseases they are currently learning about. Consider the statistics in Figure 14.24, which outlines the lifetime prevalence of psychological disorders in the United States. According to the figure, the likelihood of anyone having at least one DSM disorder is estimated to be about 44%.

This estimate strikes most people as surprisingly high. Why is this so? One reason is that when people think about psychological disorders they tend to think of severe disorders, such as bipolar disorder or schizophrenia, which are relatively infrequent, rather than "run of the mill" disturbances, such as anxiety and depressive disorders, which are much more common. When it comes to mental illness, people tend to think of patients in straitjackets or of obviously psychotic homeless people who do not reflect the broad and diverse population of people who suffer from psychological disorders. In other words, their *prototypes* or "best examples" of mental illness consist of severe disorders that are infrequent, so they underestimate the prevalence of mental disorders. This distortion illustrates the influence of the **representativeness heuristic, which is basing the estimated probability of an event on how similar it is to the typical prototype of that event** (see Chapter 8).

Do you still find it hard to believe that the overall prevalence of psychological disorders is about 44%? Another reason this number seems surprisingly high is that many people do not understand that the probability of having *at least one* disorder is much higher than the probability of having the most prevalent disorder by itself. For example, the probability of having a substance-use disorder, the single most common type of disorder, is approximately 24%, but the probability of having a substance-use disorder *or* an anxiety disorder *or* a mood disorder *or* a schizophrenic disorder jumps to 44%. These "or" relationships represent *cumulative probabilities*.

Yet another consideration that makes the prevalence figures seem high is that many people confuse different types of *prevalence rates*. The 44% estimate is for *lifetime prevalence*, which means it is the probability of having *any* disorder *at least once* at any time in one's lifetime. The lifetime prevalence rate is another example of "or" relationships. It is a value that takes into account the probability of having a psychological disorder in childhood *or* adolescence *or* adulthood *or* old age. *Point prevalence rates*, which estimate the percentage of people manifesting various disorders *at a particular*

Figure 14.24

Lifetime prevalence of psychological disorders. The estimated percentage of people who have, at any time in their life, suffered from one of four types of psychological disorders or from a disorder of any kind (top bar) is shown here. Prevalence estimates vary somewhat from one study to the next, depending on the exact methods used in sampling and assessment. The estimates shown here are based on pooling data from Wave 1 and 2 of the Epidemiological Catchment Area Studies and the National Comorbidity Study, as summarized by Reiger and Burke (2000) and Dew, Bromet, and Switzer (2000). These studies, which collectively evaluated over 28 000 subjects, provide the best data to date on the prevalence of mental illness in the United States.

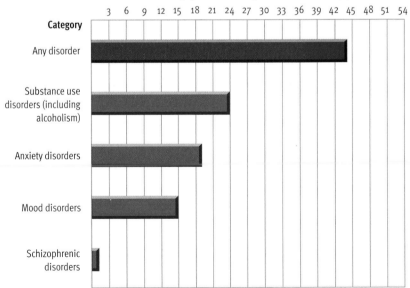

point in time, are much lower because many psychological disorders last only a few months to a few years.

What about "and" relationships—that is, relationships in which we want to know the probability of someone having condition A *and* condition B? For example, given the lifetime prevalence estimates (from Figure 14.24) for each category of disorder, which are shown here in parentheses, what is the probability of someone having a substance-use disorder (24% prevalence) *and* an anxiety disorder (19%) *and* a mood disorder (15%) *and* a schizophrenic disorder (1%) during his or her lifetime? Such "and" relationships represent *conjunctive probabilities.* Stop and think: what must be true about the probability of having all four types of disorders? Will this probability be less than 24%, between 24% and 44%, or over 44%? You may be surprised to learn that this figure is probably well under 1%. You can't have all four disorders unless you have the least frequent disorder (schizophrenia), which has a prevalence of 1%, so the answer *must* be 1% or less. Moreover, of all of the people with schizophrenia, only a tiny subset of them are likely to have all three of the other disorders, so the answer is probably well under 1% (see Figure 14.25). If this type of question strikes you as contrived, think again. Epidemiologists have devoted an enormous amount of research to the estimation of **comorbidity**—the coexis-

tence of two or more disorders—because it greatly complicates treatment issues.

These are two examples of using statistical probabilities as a critical thinking tool. Let's apply this type of thinking to another problem dealing with physical health. Here is a problem used in a study by Tversky and Kahneman (1983, p. 308) that many physicians got wrong:

A health survey was conducted in a sample of adult males in British Columbia, of all ages and occupations. Please give your best estimate of the following values:

What percentage of the men surveyed have had one or more heart attacks? _____

What percentage of the men surveyed both are over 55 years old and have had one or more heart attacks? _____

Fill in the blanks above with your best guesses. Of course, you probably have only a very general idea about the prevalence of heart attacks, but go ahead and fill in the blanks anyway.

The actual values are not as important in this example as the relative values are. Over 65% of the physicians who participated in the experiment by Tversky and Kahneman gave a higher percentage value for the second question than for the first. What is wrong with their answers? The second question is asking about the

Figure 14.25

Conjunctive probabilities. The probability of someone having all four disorders depicted here cannot be greater than the probability of the least common condition by itself, which is 1% for schizophrenia. The intersection of all four disorders (shown in black) has to be a subset of schizophrenic disorders and is probably well under 1%. Efforts to think about probabilities can sometimes be facilitated by creating diagrams that show the relationships and overlap among various events.

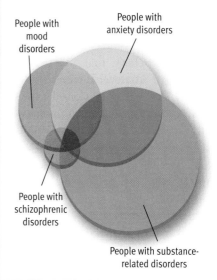

People with mood disorders

People with anxiety disorders

People with schizophrenic disorders

People with substance-related disorders

conjunctive probability of two events. Hopefully, you see why this figure *must* be less than the probability of either one of these events occurring alone. Of all of the men in the survey who had had a heart attack, only some of them are also over 55, so the second number must be smaller than the first. As we saw in Chapter 8, this common error in thinking is called the *conjunction fallacy.* **The conjunction fallacy occurs when people estimate that the odds of two uncertain events happening together are greater than the odds of either event happening alone.**

Why did so many physicians get this problem wrong? They were vulnerable to the conjunction fallacy because they were influenced by the *representativeness heuristic,* or the power of prototypes. When physicians think "heart attack," they tend to envision a man over the age of 55. Hence,

Table 14.3 Critical Thinking Skills Discussed in This Application

Skill	Description
Understanding the limitations of the representativeness heuristic	The critical thinker understands that focusing on prototypes can lead to inaccurate probability estimates.
Understanding cumulative probabilities	The critical thinker understands that the probability of at least one of several events occurring is additive, and increases with time and the number of events.
Understanding conjunctive probabilities	The critical thinker appreciates that the probability of two uncertain events happening together is less than the probability of either event happening alone.
Understanding the limitations of the availability heuristic	The critical thinker understands that the ease with which examples come to mind may not be an accurate guide to the probability of an event.

the second scenario fit so well with their prototype of a heart attack victim, they carelessly overestimated its probability.

Let's consider some additional examples of erroneous reasoning about probabilities involving how people think about psychological disorders. Toward the beginning of the chapter, we discussed the fact that many people tend to stereotypically assume that mentally ill people are likely to be violent. Other research suggests that people tend to wildly overestimate (37-fold in one study) how often the insanity defence is used in criminal trials (Silver et al., 1994). These examples reflect the influence of the *availability heuristic,* **which is basing the estimated probability of an event on the ease with which relevant instances come to mind.** Because of the availability heuristic, people tend to overestimate the probability of dramatic events that receive heavy media coverage, even when these events are rare, because examples of the events are easy to retrieve from memory. Violent acts by former psychiatric patients tend to get lots of attention in the press. And because of the *hindsight bias,* journalists tend to question why authorities couldn't foresee and prevent the violence (see the Critical Thinking Application for Chapter 12), so the mental illness angle tends to be emphasized. In a similar vein, press coverage is usually intense when a defendant in a murder trial mounts an insanity defence.

In sum, the various types of statistics that come up in thinking about psychological disorders demonstrate that we are constantly working with probabilities, even though we may not realize it. Critical thinking requires a good understanding of the laws of probability because there are very few certainties in life.

RECAP

Key Ideas

Abnormal Behaviour: Myths, Realities, and Controversies

● The medical model assumes that it is useful to view abnormal behaviour as a disease. This view has been criticized on the grounds that it turns ethical questions about deviance into medical questions.

● Three criteria are used in deciding whether people suffer from psychological disorders: deviance, personal distress, and maladaptive behaviour. People with psychological disorders are not particularly bizarre or dangerous, and even the most severe disorders are potentially curable.

● DSM-IV is the official psychodiagnostic classification system. This system asks for information about patients on five axes, or dimensions. Psychological disorders are more common than widely believed.

Anxiety Disorders

● The anxiety disorders include generalized anxiety disorder, phobic disorder, panic disorder, obsessive-compulsive disorder, and post-traumatic stress disorder. Heredity, oversensitivity to the physiological symptoms of anxiety, and abnormalities in GABA or serotonin activity may contribute to these disorders.

● Many anxiety responses, especially phobias, may be caused by classical conditioning and maintained by operant conditioning. Cognitive theorists maintain that a tendency to overinterpret harmless situations as threatening may make some people vulnerable to anxiety disorders. Stress may also trigger anxiety disorders.

Somatoform Disorders

● Somatoform disorders include somatization disorder, conversion disorder, and hypochondriasis. These disorders often emerge in people with histrionic personalities and in people who focus excess attention on their internal physiological processes.

Dissociative Disorders

● Dissociative disorders include dissociative amnesia and fugue and dissociative identity disorder. These disorders are uncommon and their causes are not well understood.

Mood Disorders

● The principal mood disorders are major depressive disorder and bipolar disorder. Mood disorders are episodic. Depression is more common in females than males.

● Evidence indicates that people vary in their genetic vulnerability to mood disorders. These disorders are accompanied by changes in neurochemical activity in the brain. Cognitive models posit that negative thinking contributes to depression. Depression is often rooted in interpersonal inadequacies and stress.

Schizophrenic Disorders

● Schizophrenic disorders are characterized by deterioration of adaptive behaviour, delusions, hallucinations, and disturbed mood. Research has linked schizophrenia to genetic vulnerability, changes in neurotransmitter activity, and structural abnormalities in the brain.

● The neurodevelopmental hypothesis asserts that schizophrenia is attributable to disruptions in the normal maturational processes of the brain before or at birth that are caused by prenatal viral infections, obstetrical complications, and other insults to the brain. Precipitating stress and unhealthful family dynamics, including high expressed emotion, may also modulate the course of schizophrenia.

Personality Disorders

● Ten personality disorders are allocated to Axis II in DSM. Personality disorders can be grouped into three clusters: anxious/fearful, odd/eccentric, and dramatic/impulsive.

● The antisocial personality disorder involves manipulative, impulsive, exploitive, aggressive behaviour. Research on the etiology of this disorder has implicated genetic vulnerability, autonomic reactivity, inadequate socialization, and observational learning.

Psychological Disorders and the Law

● Insanity is a legal concept applied to people who cannot be held responsible for their actions because of mental illness.

Culture and Pathology

● The principal categories of psychological disturbance are identifiable in all cultures. But milder disorders may go unrecognized in some societies. The symptoms associated with specific disorders are largely the same across different cultures, but some variability is seen.

Putting It in Perspective

● This chapter highlighted four of our unifying themes, showing that behaviour is governed by multiple causes, that heredity and environment jointly influence mental disorders, that psychology evolves in a sociohistorical context, and that pathology is characterized by both cultural variance and invariance.

Personal Application • Understanding Eating Disorders

● The principal eating disorders are anorexia nervosa and bulimia nervosa. Both disorders reflect a morbid fear of gaining weight and both appear to be largely a product of modern, affluent, Westernized culture. Females account for 90%–95% of eating disorders.

● There appears to be a genetic vulnerability to eating disorders. Cultural pressures on young women to be thin clearly help foster eating disorders. Unhealthful family dynamics and disturbed thinking can also contribute.

Critical Thinking Application • Working with Probabilities in Thinking About Mental Illness

● Probability estimates can be distorted by the representativeness heuristic and the availability heuristic. Cumulative probabilities are additive, whereas conjunctive probabilities are always less than the likelihood of any one of the events happening alone.

Key Terms

Agoraphobia, 583
Anorexia nervosa, 614
Antisocial personality disorder, 606
Anxiety disorders, 582
Availability heuristic, 619
Bipolar disorder, 592
Bulimia nervosa, 614
Catatonic schizophrenia, 599
Comorbidity, 618
Concordance rate, 584
Conjunction fallacy, 618
Conversion disorder, 587
Culture-bound disorders, 611
Cyclothymic disorder, 592
Delusions, 599
Diagnosis, 577
Disorganized schizophrenia, 600
Dissociative amnesia, 589
Dissociative disorders, 589
Dissociative fugue, 589
Dissociative identity disorder (DID), 589
Dysthymic disorder, 592
Eating disorders, 614
Epidemiology, 579
Etiology, 577
Generalized anxiety disorder, 582
Hallucinations, 599
Hypochondriasis, 587

Insanity, 610
Major depressive disorder, 591
Medical model, 576
Mood disorders, 590
Multiple personality disorder, 589
Negative symptoms, 600
Obsessive-compulsive disorder (OCD), 583
Panic disorder, 582
Paranoid schizophrenia, 599
Personality disorders, 605
Phobic disorder, 582
Positive symptoms, 600
Prevalence, 579
Prognosis, 577
Representativeness heuristic, 617
Schizophrenic disorders, 598
Somatization disorder, 587
Somatoform disorders, 586
Undifferentiated schizophrenia, 600

Key People

Nancy Andreasen, 600
Martin Antony, 582
Aaron Beck, 594
Robert Hare, 606
Susan Nolen-Hoeksema, 594
David Rosenhan, 579
Regina Schuller, 610
Thomas Szasz, 577

PRACTICE TEST

1. According to Thomas Szasz, abnormal behaviour usually involves:
   A. behaviour that is statistically unusual.
   B. behaviour that deviates from social norms.
   C. a disease of the mind.
   D. biological imbalance.

2. Although Sue is plagued by a high level of dread, worry, and anxiety, she still manages to meet her daily responsibilities. Sue's behaviour:
   A. should not be considered abnormal, since her adaptive functioning is not impaired.
   B. should not be considered abnormal, since everyone sometimes experiences worry and anxiety.
   C. can still be considered abnormal, since she feels great personal distress.
   D. a and b.

3. The fact that people acquire phobias of ancient sources of threat (such as snakes) much more readily than modern sources of threat (such as electrical outlets) can best be explained by:
   A. classical conditioning.   C. observational learning.
   B. operant conditioning.   D. preparedness.

4. Which of the following statements about dissociative identity disorder is true?
   A. The original personality is always aware of the alternate personalities.
   B. The alternate personalities are usually unaware of the original personality.
   C. The personalities are typically all quite similar to one another.
   D. Starting in the 1970s, there was a dramatic increase in the diagnosis of dissociative identity disorder.

5. People with unipolar disorders experience _____; people with bipolar disorders are vulnerable to _____.
   A. alternating periods of depression and mania; mania only
   B. depression only; alternating periods of depression and mania
   C. mania only; alternating periods of depression and mania
   D. alternating periods of depression and mania; depression and mania simultaneously

6. A concordance rate indicates:
   A. the percentage of relatives who exhibit the same disorder.
   B. the percentage of people with a given disorder who are currently receiving treatment.
   C. the prevalence of a given disorder in the general population.
   D. the rate of cure for a given disorder.

7. People who consistently exhibit _____ thinking are more vulnerable to depression than others.
   A. overly optimistic   C. delusional
   B. negative, pessimistic   D. dysthymic

8. Mary believes that while she sleeps at night, space creatures are attacking her and invading her uterus, where they will multiply until they are ready to take over the world. Mary was chosen for this task, she believes, because she is the only one with the power to help the space creatures succeed. Mary would most likely be diagnosed as _____ schizophrenic.
   A. paranoid   C. disorganized
   B. catatonic   D. undifferentiated

9. As an alternative to the current classification scheme, it has been proposed that schizophrenic disorders be divided into just two categories based on:
   A. whether the prognosis is favourable or unfavourable.
   B. whether the disorder is mild or severe.
   C. the predominance of thought disturbances.
   D. the predominance of negative versus positive symptoms.

10. Most of the drugs that are useful in the treatment of schizophrenia are known to dampen _____ activity in the brain, suggesting that disruptions in the activity of this neurotransmitter may contribute to the development of the disorder.
    A. norepinephrine   C. acetylcholine
    B. serotonin   D. dopamine

11. The main problem with the current classification scheme for personality disorders is that:
    A. it falsely implies that nearly everyone has at least one personality disorder.
    B. the criteria for diagnosis are so detailed and specific that even extremely disturbed people fail to meet them.
    C. the categories often overlap, making diagnosis unreliable.
    D. it contains too few categories to be useful.

12. The diagnosis of antisocial personality disorder would apply to an individual who:
    A. withdraws from social interaction due to an intense fear of rejection or criticism.
    B. withdraws from social interaction due to a lack of interest in interpersonal intimacy.
    C. is emotionally cold, suspicious of everyone, and overly concerned about being slighted by others.
    D. is callous, impulsive, and manipulative.

13. If an individual is found not criminally responsible on account of mental disorder, this means that he or she:
    A. is legally insane.
    B. appears to be a danger to him- or herself or others.
    C. cannot tell the difference between right and wrong.
    D. will experience a lifelong commitment, even if the individual is no longer mentally ill.

14. Those who embrace a relativistic view of psychological disorders would agree that:
    A. the criteria of mental illness vary considerably across cultures.
    B. there are universal standards of normality and abnormality.
    C. Western diagnostic concepts have validity and utility in other cultural contexts.
    D. b and c.

15. About _____ of patients with eating disorders are female.
    A. 40%   C. 75%
    B. 50%–60%   D. 90%–95%

See Appendix A for answers to this Practice Test.

 ON THE WEB

For additional resources on the topics covered in this chapter, visit the *Psychology: Themes and Variations* Web site, where you will find practice quizzes, tutorials, Web links, simulations, critical thinking activities, flash cards, interactive exercises, and suggested readings available through INFOTRAC.

   http://www.themesandvariations.nelson.com

Thomson NOW! http://hed.nelson.com

Go to this site for the link to ThomsonNOW™, your one-stop study shop. Take a Pretest for this chapter and ThomsonNOW™ will generate a personalized Study Plan based on your test results! The Study Plan will identify the topics you need to review and direct you to online resources to help you master those topics. You can then take a Posttest to help you determine the concepts you have mastered and what you still need work on.

CHAPTER 15

Latchezar Boyadjiev, *Passage,* L.B. Glass Studios

The Elements of the Treatment Process
Treatments: How Many Types Are There?
Clients: Who Seeks Therapy?
Therapists: Who Provides Professional Treatment?

Insight Therapies
Psychoanalysis
Client-Centred Therapy
Cognitive Therapy
Group Therapy
Evaluating Insight Therapies

Behaviour Therapies
Systematic Desensitization
Aversion Therapy
Social Skills Training
Evaluating Behaviour Therapies

Biomedical Therapies
Treatment with Drugs
Electroconvulsive Therapy (ECT)

Current Trends and Issues in Treatment
Blending Approaches to Treatment
Featured Study • Combining Insight Therapy and Medication
Increasing Multicultural Sensitivity in Treatment

Institutional Treatment in Transition
Disenchantment with Mental Hospitals
Deinstitutionalization
Mental Illness, the Revolving Door, and Homelessness

Putting It in Perspective

Personal Application • **Looking for a Therapist**
Where Do You Find Therapeutic Services?
Is the Therapist's Profession or Sex Important?
Is Treatment Always Expensive?
Is the Therapist's Theoretical Approach Important?
What Should You Look for in a Prospective Therapist?
What If There Isn't Any Progress?
What Is Therapy Like?

Critical Thinking Application • **From Crisis to Wellness—But Was It the Therapy?**

Recap

Practice Test

Treatment of Psychological Disorders

What do you imagine when you hear the term *psychotherapy?* Unless you've had some personal exposure to therapy, your conception of it has likely been shaped by depictions you've seen on TV or in the movies. This may include a group of people sitting around discussing their problems with one another and a therapist, or you alone with a therapist sitting behind you listening to your dreams. As you will see in this chapter, some of these images are to some degree accurate but they don't exhaust the range of treatment contexts. Contemporary treatments of psychological disorders are varied and reflect a distinct set of theories about human functioning. We have touched on many of these theories in the preceding chapters. The history of treatment for psychological disorders also has its controversial side.

In the 1960s if you were suffering from a psychological disorder in Canada, one therapist you might have been referred to was Dr. D. Ewen Cameron. He was the founder and director of the Allen Institute in Montreal. At the time of Cameron's arrival, McGill was home to two of the most famous behavioural scientists in Canada, Donald Hebb and Wilder Penfield. Cameron was a very famous and significant figure in the treatment of psychological disorders; he had been president of both the Canadian and American Psychiatric Associations and was the author of imposing texts such as *General Psychotherapy: Dynamics and Procedures* (Cameron, 1950) and *Psychotherapy in Action* (Cameron, 1968). He wrote a popular treatise on the nature of living in the mid-20th century with prescriptions for change (Cameron, 1948). In it he suggested that old beliefs and practices were not up to the task of modern living and that they "constitute obstructions over which the torrent of human progress boils up with destructive violence ... that stunts and maims individual lives" (Cameron, 1948, p. v).

During the late 1950s and early '60s, Cameron was engaged in CIA-funded research allegedly designed to examine brainwashing and thought-control techniques. The CIA had been engaged in a secret project known as MKULTRA for years. In Cameron's facility patients were exposed to experimental techniques that included extended drug-induced periods of sleep (sometimes for weeks at a time), massive electroconvulsive (shock) therapy regimens, sensory deprivation, hours upon hours of tape-recorded messages, and LSD treatment. Cameron had earlier developed a technique involving listening to tapes that he thought would speed up psychotherapy. He referred to this technique as automatic psychotherapy, or psychic driving. According to the patients themselves, most of this was done without their knowledge or consent. His objective was to *depattern* the patients and to rid them of old behaviour patterns and replace them with new ones. Cameron's work on this project and the toll it exacted on his patients is detailed in Anne Collins's 1988 compelling book *The Sleep Room: The Story of the CIA Brainwashing Experiments in Canada* and a 1998 CBC miniseries. The *New York Times* exposed the larger CIA project in 1977. Canadian participants subsequently sued, and Minister of Justice Kim Campbell finally agreed to establish a compensation fund in 1992. Ironically, Cameron had testified in the 1940s at the Nuremburg Nazi War Crimes trials. One result of these trials was the Nuremburg Code for ethical human experiments (Endler & Persad, 1988).

The use of LSD in psychotherapy has other, more legitimate connections to Canada. Reports of d-lysergic acid (LSD) began appearing in the scientific literature in the 1940s, and its potential for psychiatric treatment was explored in a series of government-supported studies at the University of Saskatchewan in the 1950s and '60s (Dyck, 2005). Despite some initial optimism,

Dr. D. Ewen Cameron served as director of the Allen Memorial Institute when CIA-funded brainwashing research was conducted there in the late 1950s and early 1960s.

concern about methodological inadequacies and socio-cultural concerns contributed to the end of the project. LSD was also used in treatment on the Social Therapy Unit at Ontario's maximum-security psychiatric institution, the Oak Ridge Division of the Penetanguishene Mental Health Centre. It was used as part of a very innovative treatment program designed by Dr. Elliot Barker for psychopaths in the mid-1960s (Rice & Harris, 1993; Weisman, 1995). Ultimately, the program was considered a failure and some former patients sued, claiming coercion and lack of full consent.

In this chapter, we'll take a down-to-earth look at *psychotherapy,* using the term in its broadest sense, to refer to all the diverse approaches used in the treatment of mental disorders and psychological problems. We'll start by discussing some general questions about the provision of treatment. After considering these issues, we'll examine the goals, techniques, and effectiveness of some of the more widely used approaches to therapy and discuss recent trends and issues in treatment. In the Personal Application, we'll look at practical questions related to finding and choosing a therapist and getting the most out of therapy. And in the Critical Thinking Application we'll address problems involved in determining whether therapy actually helps.

The Elements of the Treatment Process

PREVIEW QUESTIONS

- What are the three major approaches to the treatment of psychological disorders?
- What are the correlates of treatment seeking?
- Why do only a portion of the people who need treatment receive it?
- What professions are involved in the treatment of psychological disorders?

The case of Anna O, whose real name was Bertha Pappenheim, provided the inspiration for Sigmund Freud's invention of psychoanalysis.

Sigmund Freud is widely credited with launching modern psychotherapy. Ironically, the landmark case that inspired Freud was actually treated by one of his colleagues, Josef Breuer. Around 1880, Breuer began to treat a young woman referred to as Anna O (which was a pseudonym—her real name was Bertha Pappenheim). Anna exhibited a variety of physical maladies, including headaches, coughing, and a loss of feeling and movement in her right arm. Much to his surprise, Breuer discovered that Anna's physical symptoms cleared up when he encouraged her to talk about emotionally charged experiences from her past.

When Breuer and Freud discussed the case, they speculated that talking things through had enabled Anna to drain off bottled-up emotions that had caused her symptoms. Breuer found the intense emotional exchange in this treatment not to his liking, so he didn't follow through on his discovery. However, Freud applied Breuer's insight to other patients, and his successes led him to develop a systematic treatment procedure, which he called *psychoanalysis.* Anna O called her treatment "the talking cure." However, as you'll see, psychotherapy isn't always curative, and many modern treatments place little emphasis on talking.

Freud's breakthrough ushered in a century of progress for psychotherapy. Psychoanalysis spawned many offspring as Freud's followers developed their own systems of treatment. Since then, approaches to treatment have steadily grown more numerous, more diverse, and more effective. Today, people can choose from a bewildering array of therapies.

Treatments: How Many Types Are There?

In their efforts to help people, psychotherapists use many treatment methods. They include discussion, advice, emotional support, persuasion, conditioning procedures, relaxation training, role-playing, drug therapy, biofeedback, and group therapy. No one knows exactly how many distinct types of psychotherapy there are. One expert (Kazdin, 1994) estimates that there may be over 400 approaches to treatment. Fortunately, we can impose some order on this chaos. As varied as therapists' procedures are, approaches to treatment can be classified into three major categories:

1. *Insight therapies.* Insight therapy is "talk therapy" in the tradition of Freud's psychoanalysis. In insight therapies, clients engage in complex verbal interactions with their therapists. The goal in these discussions is to pursue increased insight regarding the nature of the client's difficulties and to sort through possible solutions. Insight therapy can be conducted with an individual or with a group. Broadly speaking, family therapy and marital therapy fall in this category.

2. *Behaviour therapies.* Behaviour therapies are based on the principles of learning, which were introduced in Chapter 6. Instead of emphasizing personal insights, behaviour therapists make direct efforts to alter problematic responses (phobias, for instance) and maladaptive habits (drug use, for instance). Behaviour therapists work on changing clients' overt behaviours. They use different procedures for different kinds of problems. Most of their procedures involve classical conditioning, operant conditioning, or observational learning.

3. *Biomedical therapies.* Biomedical approaches to therapy involve interventions into a person's biological functioning. The most widely used procedures are drug therapy and electroconvulsive (shock)

therapy. As the name bio*medical* therapies suggests, these treatments have traditionally been provided only by physicians with a medical degree (usually psychiatrists). This situation may change, however, as psychologists have begun to campaign for prescription privileges (Gutierrez & Silk, 1998; Sammons et al., 2000). They have made some progress toward this goal, even though many psychologists have argued against pursuing the right to prescribe medication (Albee, 1998; Dobson & Dozois, 2001).

Clients: Who Seeks Therapy?

According to a recent poll commissioned by the Canadian Mental Health Association (2005), Canadians are as concerned about their mental health as they are about their physical health, and over 90% report that they make a conscious effort to take care of their mental health on a regular basis. While Canadians seem to have good intentions regarding their mental health, they seem to be less sure what to do about it. The poll also revealed that fewer people were committed to improving their mental health than their physical health over the subsequent six months. If improvements are not forthcoming or if people suffer from unexpected difficulties, they may seek professional assistance.

In the therapeutic triad (therapists, treatments, clients), the greatest diversity of all is seen among the clients. People bring to therapy the full range of human problems: anxiety, depression, unsatisfactory interpersonal relations, troublesome habits, poor self-control, low self-esteem, marital conflicts, self-doubt, a sense of emptiness, and feelings of personal stagnation. The two most common presenting problems are excessive anxiety and depression (Narrow et al., 1993). Interestingly, people often delay for many years before finally seeking treatment for their psychological problems (Kessler, Olfson, & Berglund, 1998). A client in treatment does *not* necessarily have an identifiable psychological disorder. Some people seek professional help for everyday problems (career decisions, for instance) or vague feelings of discontent (Strupp, 1996).

People vary considerably in their willingness to seek psychotherapy. One of the biggest roadblocks is the stigma surrounding the receipt of mental health treatment. You may recall from the beginning of Chapter 14 how some people advised psychologist Norman Endler not to seek psychological treatment in his hometown in case others found out. Unfortunately, many people equate seeking therapy with admitting personal weakness. Of course, nothing could be further from the truth.

Therapists: Who Provides Professional Treatment?

People troubled by personal problems often solicit help from their friends, relatives, clergy, and primary care physicians. These sources of assistance may provide excellent advice, but their counsel does not qualify as therapy. Psychotherapy refers to *professional* treatment by someone with special training. However, a common source of confusion about psychotherapy is the variety of "helping professions" available to offer assistance (Murstein & Fontaine, 1993). Psychology and psychiatry are the principal professions involved in the provision of psychotherapy. However, therapy is increasingly provided by clinical social workers, psychiatric nurses, counsellors, and marriage and family therapists. Let's look at the various mental health professions.

Psychologists

Two types of psychologists may provide therapy. *Clinical psychologists* and *counselling psychologists* specialize in the diagnosis and treatment of psychological disorders and everyday behavioural problems. Clinical psychologists' training emphasizes the treatment of full-fledged disorders. Counselling psychologists' training is slanted toward the treatment of everyday adjustment problems. In practice, however, there is quite a bit of overlap between clinical and counselling psychologists in training, skills, and the clientele that they serve.

Both types of psychologists must earn a doctoral degree (Ph.D., Psy.D., or Ed.D.). A doctorate in psychology requires about five to seven years of training beyond a bachelor's degree. The process of gaining admission to a Ph.D. program in clinical psychology is highly competitive (about as difficult as getting into medical school). Psychologists receive most of their training in universities or independent professional schools. They then serve a one-year internship in a clinical setting, such as a hospital, usually followed by one or two years of postdoctoral fellowship training. Currently, there are approximately 18 000 registered psychologists in Canada (Dobson, 2002).

In providing therapy, psychologists use either insight or behavioural approaches. In comparison to psychiatrists, they are more likely to use behavioural techniques and less likely to use psychoanalytic methods. Clinical and counselling psychologists do psychological testing as well as psychotherapy, and many also conduct research.

For some individuals needing professional assistance for psychological disorders their choice of a health practitioner is limited by the fact that treatment

Web Link 15.1

Canadian Mental Health Association
http://www.cmha.ca/bins/index.asp

It's important to know when to seek help, and the Canadian Mental Health Association Web site contains information concerning psychological disorders and how to seek assistance.

Web Link 15.2

Clinical and Counselling Psychology Programs
http://www.cpa.ca/accredlist.htm

A list of clinical and counselling psychology programs accredited by the Canadian Psychological Association can be obtained from the CPA Web site.

by psychologists is not part of the medicare funding system. According to University of Calgary psychologist Keith Dobson, the current lack of inclusion in the health-care funding system is attributable to several factors, including the relatively recent establishment of the CPA, the pressures by governments to limit health-care funding, divisions within psychology itself, and limited pressure from the profession of psychology (Dobson, 2002). There is also division within the profession of psychology in Canada regarding the advisability of psychologists being granted prescription privileges (Dobson & Dozois, 2001; Walters, 2001). Currently, psychologists in Canada are not allowed to prescribe medication.

Psychiatrists

Psychiatrists **are physicians who specialize in the diagnosis and treatment of psychological disorders.** Many psychiatrists also treat everyday behavioural problems. However, in comparison to psychologists, psychiatrists devote more time to relatively severe disorders (schizophrenia, mood disorders) and less time to everyday marital, family, job, and school problems.

People seeking help for psychological difficulties who access the medical system often begin with their family physician. A team of researchers from the University of British Columbia and the University of Manitoba recently surveyed the use of medical professionals in Manitoba by those seeking medical assistance for psychological difficulties (Watson et al., 2005). They found that 92% of those seeking assistance saw at least one family physician, 42% relied on their family physician and did not see a psychiatrist, 47% saw both, and a little over 2% relied exclusively on a psychiatrist.

Psychiatrists have an M.D. degree. Their graduate training requires four years of coursework in medical school and a four-year apprenticeship in a residency at a hospital. Their psychotherapy training occurs during their residency, since the required coursework in medical school is essentially the same for everyone, whether they are going into surgery, pediatrics, or psychiatry.

In their provision of therapy, psychiatrists increasingly emphasize drug therapies (Olfson, Marcus, & Pincus, 1999), which the other, nonmedical helping professions cannot provide. In comparison to psychologists, psychiatrists are more likely to use psychoanalysis and less likely to use group therapies or behaviour therapies.

Other Mental Health Professionals

Several other mental health professions also provide psychotherapy services, and some of these professions are growing rapidly. In hospitals and other institutions, *clinical social workers* and *psychiatric nurses* often work as part of a treatment team with a psychologist or psychiatrist. Psychiatric nurses, who may have a bachelor's or master's degree in their field, play a large role in hospital inpatient treatment. Clinical social workers generally have a master's degree and typically work with patients and their families to ease the patient's integration back into the community. Although social workers and psychiatric nurses have traditionally worked in institutional settings, they increasingly provide a wide range of therapeutic services as independent practitioners.

Many kinds of *counsellors* also provide therapeutic services. Counsellors are usually found working in schools, colleges, and assorted human service agencies (youth centres, geriatric centres, family planning centres, and so forth). Counsellors typically have a master's degree. They often specialize in particular types of problems, such as vocational counselling, marital counselling, rehabilitation counselling, and drug counselling.

Although there are clear differences among the helping professions in education and training, their roles in the treatment process overlap considerably. In this chapter, we will refer to psychologists or psychiatrists as needed, but otherwise we'll use the terms *clinician, therapist,* and *provider* to refer to mental health professionals of all kinds, regardless of their professional degree.

Now that we have discussed the basic elements in psychotherapy, we can examine specific approaches to treatment in terms of their goals, procedures, and effectiveness. We'll begin with a few representative insight therapies.

REVIEW OF KEY POINTS

- Approaches to treatment are diverse, but they can be grouped into three categories: insight therapies, behaviour therapies, and biomedical therapies.

- Clients bring a wide variety of problems to therapy and do not necessarily have a disorder. People vary in their willingness to seek treatment, and many people who need therapy do not receive it.

- Therapists come from a variety of professional backgrounds. Clinical and counselling psychologists, psychiatrists, clinical social workers, psychiatric nurses, and counsellors are the principal providers of therapeutic services.

- Each of these professions shows different preferences for approaches to treatment. Psychologists typically practise insight or behaviour therapy. Psychiatrists rely more heavily on drug therapies.

Insight Therapies

There are many schools of thought about how to do insight therapy. Therapists with various theoretical orientations use different methods to pursue different kinds of insights. However, what these varied approaches have in common is that *insight therapies* **involve verbal interactions intended to enhance clients' self-knowledge and thus promote healthful changes in personality and behaviour.**

Although there may be hundreds of insight therapies, the leading eight or ten approaches appear to account for the lion's share of treatment. In this section, we'll delve into psychoanalysis, related psychodynamic approaches, client-centred therapy, and cognitive therapy. We'll also discuss how insight therapy can be done with groups as well as individuals.

Psychoanalysis

After the case of Anna O, Sigmund Freud worked as a psychotherapist for almost 50 years in Vienna. Through a painstaking process of trial and error, he developed innovative techniques for the treatment of psychological disorders and distress. His system of *psychoanalysis* came to dominate psychiatry for many decades. Although the dominance of psychoanalysis has eroded in recent years, a diverse collection of psychoanalytic approaches to therapy continues to evolve and to remain influential today (Eagle & Wolitzky, 1992; Ursano & Silberman, 1999).

Psychoanalysis **is an insight therapy that emphasizes the recovery of unconscious conflicts, motives, and defences through techniques such as free association and transference.** To appreciate the logic of psychoanalysis, we have to look at Freud's thinking about the roots of mental disorders. Freud mostly treated anxiety-dominated disturbances, such as phobic, panic, obsessive-compulsive, and conversion disorders, which were then called *neuroses*.

Freud believed that neurotic problems are caused by unconscious conflicts left over from early childhood. As explained in Chapter 12, he thought that these inner conflicts involve battles among the id, ego, and superego, usually over sexual and aggressive impulses. He theorized that people depend on defence mechanisms to avoid confronting these conflicts, which remain hidden in the depths of the unconscious (see Figure 15.1). However, he noted that defensive manoeuvres often lead to self-defeating behaviour. Furthermore, he asserted that defences tend to be only partially successful in alleviating anxiety, guilt, and other distressing emotions. With this model in mind, let's take a look at the therapeutic procedures used in psychoanalysis.

Probing the Unconscious

Given Freud's assumptions, we can see that the logic of psychoanalysis is quite simple. The analyst attempts to probe the murky depths of the unconscious to discover the unresolved conflicts causing the client's neurotic behaviour. In a sense, the analyst functions as a "psychological detective." In this effort to explore the unconscious, the therapist relies on two techniques: free association and dream analysis.

In *free association* **clients spontaneously express their thoughts and feelings exactly as they occur, with as little censorship as possible.** In free associating, clients expound on anything that comes to mind, regardless of how trivial, silly, or embarrassing it might be. Gradually, most clients begin to let everything pour out without conscious censorship. The analyst studies these free associations for clues about what is going on in the client's unconscious.

In *dream analysis* **the therapist interprets the symbolic meaning of the client's dreams.** Freud saw dreams as the "royal road to the unconscious," the most direct means of access to patients' innermost conflicts, wishes, and impulses. Clients are encouraged and trained to remember their dreams, which they describe in therapy. The therapist then analyzes the symbolism in these dreams to interpret their meaning.

To better illustrate these matters, let's look at an actual case treated through psychoanalysis (adapted from Greenson, 1967, pp. 40–41). Mr. N was troubled by an unsatisfactory marriage. He claimed to love his wife, but he preferred sexual relations with prostitutes. Mr. N reported that his parents also endured lifelong marital difficulties. His childhood conflicts about their relationship appeared to be related to his problems. Both dream analysis and free association can be seen in the following description of a session in Mr. N's treatment:

PREVIEW QUESTIONS
- What are the goals and techniques of psychoanalysis?
- What are the goals and techniques of client-centred therapy?
- What are the goals and techniques of cognitive therapy?
- How is group therapy conducted?
- What is the evidence on the efficacy of insight therapy?

"The news that reaches your consciousness is incomplete and often not to be relied on."
SIGMUND FREUD

Figure 15.1

Freud's view of the roots of disorders. According to Freud, unconscious conflicts among the id, ego, and superego sometimes lead to anxiety. This discomfort may lead to pathological reliance on defensive behaviour.

Intrapsychic conflict (among id, ego, and superego) → Anxiety → Reliance on defence mechanisms

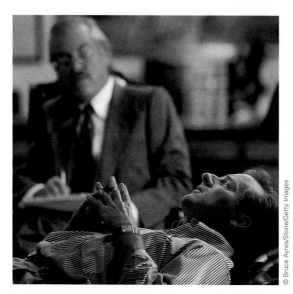

In psychoanalysis, the therapist encourages the client to reveal thoughts, feelings, dreams, and memories, which can then be interpreted in relation to the client's current problems.

Mr. N reported a fragment of a dream. All that he could remember is that he was waiting for a red traffic light to change when he felt that someone had bumped into him from behind.... The associations led to Mr. N's love of cars, especially sports cars. He loved the sensation, in particular, of whizzing by those fat, old expensive cars.... His father always hinted that he had been a great athlete, but he never substantiated it.... Mr. N doubted whether his father could really perform. His father would flirt with a waitress in a café or make sexual remarks about women passing by, but he seemed to be showing off. If he were really sexual, he wouldn't resort to that.

As is characteristic of free association, Mr. N's train of thought meandered about with little direction. Nonetheless, clues about his unconscious conflicts are apparent. What did Mr. N's therapist extract from this session? The therapist saw sexual overtones in the dream fragment, where Mr. N was bumped from behind. The therapist also inferred that Mr. N had a competitive orientation toward his father, based on the free association about whizzing by fat, old expensive cars. As you can see, analysts must *interpret* their clients' dreams and free associations. This is a critical process throughout psychoanalysis.

Interpretation

***Interpretation* refers to the therapist's attempts to explain the inner significance of the client's thoughts, feelings, memories, and behaviours.** Contrary to popular belief, analysts do not interpret everything, and they generally don't try to dazzle clients with startling revelations. Instead, analysts

move forward inch by inch, offering interpretations that should be just out of the client's own reach. Mr. N's therapist eventually offered the following interpretations to his client:

I said to Mr. N near the end of the hour that I felt he was struggling with his feelings about his father's sexual life. He seemed to be saying that his father was sexually not a very potent man.... He also recalls that he once found a packet of condoms under his father's pillow when he was an adolescent and he thought, "My father must be going to prostitutes." I then intervened and pointed out that the condoms under his father's pillow seemed to indicate more obviously that his father used the condoms with his mother, who slept in the same bed. However, Mr. N wanted to believe his wish-fulfilling fantasy: mother doesn't want sex with father and father is not very potent. The patient was silent and the hour ended.

As you may have already guessed, the therapist concluded that Mr. N's difficulties were rooted in an Oedipal complex (see Chapter 12). The man had unresolved sexual feelings toward his mother and hostile feelings about his father. These unconscious conflicts, rooted in Mr. N's childhood, were distorting his intimate relations as an adult.

Resistance

How would you expect Mr. N to respond to the therapist's suggestion that he was in competition with his father for the sexual attention of his mother? Obviously, most clients would have great difficulty accepting such an interpretation. Freud fully expected clients to display some resistance to therapeutic efforts. ***Resistance* refers to largely unconscious defensive manoeuvres intended to hinder the progress of therapy.** Why would clients try to resist the helping process? Because they don't want to face up to the painful, disturbing conflicts that they have buried in their unconscious. Although they have sought help, they are reluctant to confront their real problems.

Resistance can take many forms. Clients may show up late for their sessions, may merely pretend to engage in free association, or may express hostility toward their therapist. For instance, Mr. N's therapist noted that after the session just described, "The next day he [Mr. N] began by telling me that he was furious with me...." Analysts use a variety of strategies to deal with their clients' resistance. Often, a key consideration is the handling of transference, which we consider next.

Transference

***Transference* occurs when clients unconsciously start relating to their therapist in ways that mimic**

critical relationships in their lives. Thus, a client might start relating to a therapist as though the therapist were an overprotective mother, a rejecting brother, or a passive spouse. In a sense, the client *transfers* conflicting feelings about important people onto the therapist. For instance, in his treatment, Mr. N transferred some of the competitive hostility he felt toward his father onto his analyst.

Psychoanalysts often encourage transference so that clients can re-enact relations with crucial people in the context of therapy. These re-enactments can help bring repressed feelings and conflicts to the surface, allowing the client to work through them. The therapist's handling of transference is complicated and difficult, because transference may arouse confusing, highly charged emotions in the client.

Undergoing psychoanalysis is not easy. It can be a slow, painful process of self-examination that routinely requires three to five years of hard work. Ultimately, if resistance and transference can be handled effectively, the therapist's interpretations should lead the client to profound insights. For instance, Mr. N eventually admitted, "The old boy is probably right, it does tickle me to imagine that my mother preferred me and I could beat out my father. Later, I wondered whether this had something to do with my own screwed-up sex life with my wife." According to Freud, once clients recognize the unconscious sources of conflicts, they can resolve these conflicts and discard their neurotic defences.

Modern Psychodynamic Therapies

Though still available, classical psychoanalysis as done by Freud is not widely practised anymore (Kay & Kay, 2003). Freud's psychoanalytic method was geared to a particular kind of clientele that he was seeing in Vienna many years ago. As his followers fanned out across Europe and North America, many found it necessary to adapt psychoanalysis to different cultures, changing times, and new kinds of patients. Thus, many variations on Freud's original approach to psychoanalysis have developed over the years. These descendants of psychoanalysis are collectively known as *psychodynamic approaches* to therapy.

Some of these adaptations, such as those made by Carl Jung (1917) and Alfred Adler (1927), were sweeping revisions based on fundamental differences in theory. Other variations, such as those devised by Melanie Klein (1948) and Heinz Kohut (1971), made substantial changes in theory while retaining certain central ideas. Still other revisions (Alexander, 1954; Stekel, 1950) simply involved efforts to modernize and streamline psychoanalytic techniques. Hence, today we have a rich diversity of psychodynamic approaches to therapy.

Client-Centred Therapy 11D

You may have heard of people going into therapy to "find themselves" or to "get in touch with their real feelings." These now-popular phrases emerged out of the human potential movement, which was stimulated in part by the work of Carl Rogers (1951, 1986). Using a humanistic perspective, Rogers devised client-centred therapy (also known as person-centred therapy) in the 1940s and 1950s.

Client-centred therapy is an insight therapy that emphasizes providing a supportive emotional climate for clients, who play a major role in determining the pace and direction of their therapy. You may wonder why the troubled, untrained client is put in charge of the pace and direction of the therapy. Rogers (1961) provides a compelling justification:

It is the client who knows what hurts, what directions to go, what problems are crucial, what experiences have been deeply buried. It began to occur to me that unless I had a need to demonstrate my own cleverness and learning, I would do better to rely upon the client for the direction of movement in the process. (pp. 11–12)

Rogers's theory about the principal causes of neurotic anxieties is quite different from the Freudian explanation. As discussed in Chapter 12, Rogers maintains that most personal distress is due to inconsistency, or "incongruence," between a person's self-concept and reality (see Figure 15.2). According to his theory, incongruence makes people feel threatened by realistic feedback about themselves from

To my mind, empathy is in itself a healing agent.
CARL ROGERS

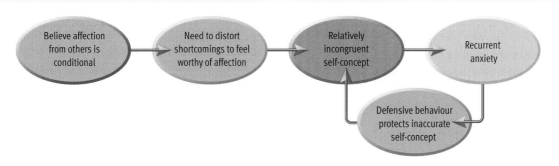

| Believe affection from others is conditional | → | Need to distort shortcomings to feel worthy of affection | → | Relatively incongruent self-concept | → | Recurrent anxiety |

Defensive behaviour protects inaccurate self-concept

Figure 15.2

Rogers's view of the roots of disorders. Rogers's theory posits that anxiety and self-defeating behaviour are rooted in an incongruent self-concept that makes one prone to recurrent anxiety, which triggers defensive behaviour, which fuels more incongruence.

Treatment of Psychological Disorders

others. For example, if you inaccurately viewed yourself as a hard-working, dependable person, you would feel threatened by contradictory feedback from friends or co-workers. According to Rogers, anxiety about such feedback often leads to reliance on defence mechanisms, to distortions of reality, and to stifled personal growth. Excessive incongruence is thought to be rooted in clients' overdependence on others for approval and acceptance.

Given Rogers's theory, client-centred therapists stalk insights that are quite different from the repressed conflicts that psychoanalysts go after. Client-centred therapists help clients to realize that they do not have to worry constantly about pleasing others and winning acceptance. They encourage clients to respect their own feelings and values. They help people restructure their self-concept to correspond better to reality. Ultimately, they try to foster self-acceptance and personal growth.

Therapeutic Climate

According to Rogers, the *process* of therapy is not as important as the emotional *climate* in which the therapy takes place. He believes that it is critical for the therapist to provide a warm, supportive, accepting climate. This creates a safe environment in which clients can confront their shortcomings without feeling threatened. The lack of threat should reduce clients' defensive tendencies and thus help them open up. To create this atmosphere of emotional support, client-centred therapists must provide three conditions:

1. *Genuineness.* The therapist must be genuine with the client, communicating honestly and spontaneously. The therapist should not be phony or defensive.

2. *Unconditional positive regard.* The therapist must also show complete, nonjudgmental acceptance of the client as a person. The therapist should provide warmth and caring for the client, with no strings attached. This does not mean that the therapist must approve of everything that the client says or does. A therapist can disapprove of a particular behaviour while continuing to value the client as a human being.

3. *Empathy.* Finally, the therapist must provide accurate empathy for the client. This means that the therapist must understand the client's world from the client's point of view. Furthermore, the therapist must be articulate enough to communicate this understanding to the client.

Rogers firmly believed that a supportive emotional climate is the critical force promoting healthy changes in therapy. More recently, however, some client-centred therapists, such as Laura Rice and Les Greenberg, have begun to place more emphasis on the therapeutic process (Rice & Greenberg, 1992).

Therapeutic Process

In client-centred therapy, the client and therapist work together as equals. The therapist provides relatively little guidance and keeps interpretation and advice to a minimum. So, just what does the client-centred therapist do, besides creating a supportive climate? Primarily, the therapist provides feedback to help clients sort out their feelings. The therapist's key task is *clarification*. Client-centred therapists try to function like human mirrors, reflecting statements back to their clients, but with enhanced clarity. They help clients become more aware of their true feelings by highlighting themes that may be obscure in the clients' rambling discourse.

By working with clients to clarify their feelings, client-centred therapists hope to gradually build toward more far-reaching insights. In particular, they try to help clients better understand their interpersonal relationships and become more comfortable with their genuine selves. Obviously, these are ambitious goals.

Recently, Canadian psychologists Les Greenberg and Susan Johnson have developed *emotion-focused couples therapy* (Greenberg & Johnson, 1988; Johnson & Greenberg, 1995). One of the assumptions of this approach is that the relationship is not providing for the attachment needs of the relationship partners. In the process of therapy, the nature of the relationship issues and underlying emotions are first identified. The couple are then afforded an opportunity to identify and acknowledge their needs and are encouraged to express these needs and to arrive at solutions to the problems. Acknowledging and working with the underlying emotions are central to this approach. This type of emotion-focused therapy has its roots in earlier client-centred work by Carl Rogers and Fritz Perls and is considered important to any integrative approach to psychotherapy (Greenberg, 2002).

Emotion-focused therapy has been effectively applied in a wide variety of contexts, including University of Windsor psychologist Sandra Paivio's work with child abuse victims (Paivio, Holowaty, & Hall, 2004). Research has attested to the effectiveness of process-experiential approaches. For example, a recent evaluation study by Jeanne Watson and her colleagues from the University of Toronto demonstrated that process-experiential therapy was as effective as cognitive-behavioural therapy and that, additionally, process-experiential therapy resulted in a significant decrease in clients' reports of interpersonal problems (Watson et al., 2003).

Client-centred therapy resembles psychoanalysis in that both seek to achieve a major reconstruction of a client's personality. We'll see more limited and specific goals in cognitive therapy, which we consider next.

Cognitive Therapy

In Chapter 13, we saw that people's cognitive interpretations of events make all the difference in how well they handle stress. In Chapter 14, we learned that cognitive factors play a key role in the development of depression and other disorders. Citing the importance of findings such as these, two former psychoanalysts—Aaron Beck (1976, 1987) and Albert Ellis (1973, 1989)—independently devised cognitive-oriented therapies that became highly influential (Arnkoff & Glass, 1992; Hollon & Beck, 2004). Since we covered the main ideas underlying Ellis's *rational-emotive therapy* in our discussion of coping strategies (see the Personal Application for Chapter 13), we'll focus on Beck's system of *cognitive therapy* here. **Cognitive therapy is an insight therapy that emphasizes recognizing and changing negative thoughts and maladaptive beliefs.**

In recent years cognitive therapy has been applied fruitfully to a wide range of disorders (Beck, 1991; Dobson, 2001; Rush & Beck, 2000), but it was originally devised as a treatment for depression. According to cognitive therapists, depression is caused by "errors" in thinking (see Figure 15.3). They assert that depression-prone people tend to (1) blame their setbacks on personal inadequacies without considering circumstantial explanations, (2) focus selectively on negative events while ignoring positive events, (3) make unduly pessimistic projections about the future, and (4) draw negative conclusions about their worth as a person based on insignificant events. For instance, imagine that you got a low grade on a minor quiz in a class. If you made the kinds of errors in thinking just described, you might blame the grade on your woeful stupidity, dismiss comments from a classmate that it was an unfair test, gloomily predict that you will surely flunk the course, and conclude that you are not genuine university material.

Along with Ellis and Beck, University of Waterloo psychologist Donald Meichenbaum is considered one of the important innovators of cognitive-behavioural therapy. Meichenbaum has applied his techniques in cognitive therapy to a wide variety of issues including post-traumatic stress disorder (Meichenbaum, 1994) and has been consulted in the aftermath of trau-

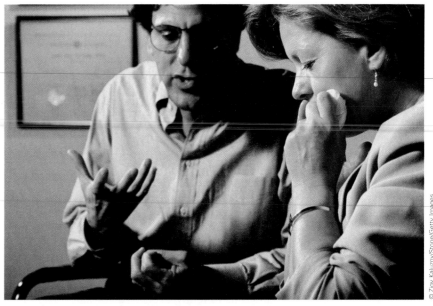

Client-centred therapists emphasize the importance of a supportive emotional climate in therapy. They also work to clarify, rather than interpret, the feelings expressed by their patients.

matic events including the Oklahoma City bombing, the Columbine school shootings, and the 9/11 attacks (Yalom, 2002). In one of his innovations, referred to as *self-instructional training* (Meichenbaum, 1977), clients are taught to develop and use verbal statements that help them cope with difficult contexts. As we discussed in Chapter 13, having readily available coping strategies is critical in dealing with stress. Self-instructional training can help clients deal with current stressors and may serve to inoculate them against future stress. Interestingly, when discussing his self-instructional training method (Yalom, 2002), Meichenbaum sometimes refers to it as his "New York therapy." He grew up in New York City watching all kinds of people talk to themselves on the street. His mother once pointed out the

Web Link 15.4

The Albert Ellis Institute
http://www.rebt.org/

Rational-emotive therapy, developed by Albert Ellis, is an influential cognitive-behavioural approach to treatment (see the Personal Application for Chapter 13). This site demonstrates how rational-emotive therapy has grown over the last 40 years.

Figure 15.3

Beck's view of the roots of disorders. Beck's theory initially focused on the causes of depression, although it was gradually broadened to explain other disorders. According to Beck, depression is caused by the types of negative thinking shown here.

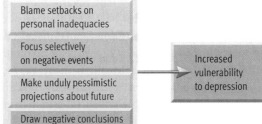

Negative thinking

Blame setbacks on personal inadequacies

Focus selectively on negative events

Make unduly pessimistic projections about future

Draw negative conclusions about personal worth

→ Increased vulnerability to depression

Most people are barely aware of the automatic thoughts which precede unpleasant feelings or automatic inhibitions.
AARON BECK

In the ensuing years, critics pounced on Eysenck's article looking for flaws (Jacobson & Christensen, 1996). They found a variety of shortcomings in his data. For instance, Eysenck used different time frames in comparing the recovery rates of treated and untreated individuals (Strupp & Howard, 1992). Moreover, the treated and untreated groups were not matched in terms of the severity of their disorders, their attitudes and expectations about therapy and recovery, or any other relevant variables that might influence therapeutic outcomes. After re-examining Eysenck's data, Bergin (1971) argued that the data really suggested that the spontaneous remission rate for neurotic problems was in the vicinity of 30% to 40%. Although Eysenck's conclusions were unduly pessimistic, he made an important contribution to the mental health field by sparking debate and research on the effectiveness of insight therapy.

Evaluating the effectiveness of any approach to treatment is a complex challenge (Kendall, Holmbeck, & Verduin, 2004; Hill & Lambert, 2004). This is especially true for insight therapies. If you were to undergo insight therapy, how would you judge its effectiveness? By how you felt? By looking at your behaviour? By asking your therapist? By consulting your friends and family? What would you be looking for? Various schools of thought pursue entirely different goals. And clients' ratings of their progress are likely to be slanted toward a favourable evaluation because they want to justify their effort, their heartache, their expense, and their time. Another problem that crops up in studies of the relative efficacy of different treatments is the *allegiance effect*—researchers comparing different therapies tend to obtain results that favour the therapeutic approach they champion (Luborsky et al., 1999). Allegiance effects are probably due in part to the normal human tendency to see what one wants to see when making subjective evaluations. Allegiance effects may also occur because research teams often have more expertise in supervising and delivering their preferred therapy than the competing approaches under study (Hollon, 1999; Thase, 1999). In any event, allegiance effects further complicate the daunting task of assessing the effectiveness of various insight therapies. In sum, evaluations of therapeutic outcomes tend to be subjective, with little consensus about the best way to assess clients' progress (Lambert & Hill, 1994).

In spite of these difficulties, hundreds of therapy outcome studies have been conducted since Eysenck prodded researchers into action. These studies have examined a broad range of specific clinical problems and used diverse methods to assess therapeutic outcomes, including scores on psychological tests and ratings by family members, as well as therapists' and clients' ratings. These studies consistently indicate that insight therapy *is* superior to no treatment or to placebo treatment and that the effects of therapy are reasonably durable (Kopta et al., 1999; Lambert & Ogles, 2004). In one widely discussed study that focused on patients' self-reports, the vast majority of the respondents subjectively felt that they had derived considerable benefit from their therapy (Seligman, 1995).

Although there is considerable evidence that insight therapy tends to produce positive effects for a sizable majority of clients, there is vigorous debate about the *mechanisms of action* underlying these positive effects. The advocates of various therapies tend to attribute the benefits of therapy to the particular methods and procedures used by each specific approach to therapy (Chambless & Hollon, 1998). In essence, they argue that different therapies achieve similar benefits through different processes. An alternative view espoused by many theorists is that the diverse approaches to therapy share certain *common factors* and that these common factors account for much of the improvement experienced by clients (Frank & Frank, 1991). Evidence supporting the common factors view has mounted in recent years (Ahn & Wampold, 2001; Lambert & Barley, 2001).

What are the common denominators that lie at the core of diverse approaches to therapy? The models proposed to answer to this question vary considerably, but there is some consensus. The most widely cited common factors include (1) the development of a therapeutic alliance with a professional helper, (2) the provision of emotional support and empathic understanding by the therapist, (3) the cultivation of hope and positive expectations in the client, (4) the provision of a rationale for the client's problems and a plausible method for ameliorating them, and (5) the opportunity to express feelings, confront problems, gain new insights, and learn new patterns of behaviour (Grencavage & Norcross, 1990; Weinberger, 1995). How important are the common factors in therapy? Some theorists argue that common factors account for virtually *all* of the progress that clients make in therapy (Wampold, 2001). It seems more likely that the benefits of therapy represent the combined effects of common factors and specific procedures (Beutler & Harwood, 2002). Either way, it is clear that common factors play a significant role in insight therapy.

to be disruptive. Some theorists maintain that judicious selection of participants is crucial to effective group treatment (Salvendy, 1993). There is some debate about whether it is best for the group to be homogeneous—made up of people who are similar in age, sex, and psychological problem. Practical necessities usually dictate that groups are at least somewhat diversified.

In group therapy, participants essentially function as therapists for one another (Stone, 2003). Group members describe their problems, trade viewpoints, share experiences, and discuss coping strategies. Most important, they provide acceptance and emotional support for each other. In this supportive atmosphere, group members work at peeling away the social masks that cover their insecurities. Once their problems are exposed, members work at correcting them. As members come to value one another's opinions, they work hard to display healthy changes to win the group's approval.

In group treatment, the therapist's responsibilities include selecting participants, setting goals for the group, initiating and maintaining the therapeutic process, and protecting clients from harm (Vinogradov et al., 2003). The therapist often plays a relatively subtle role in group therapy, staying in the background and focusing mainly on promoting group cohesiveness (although this strategy will vary depending on the nature of the group). The therapist models supportive behaviours for the participants and tries to promote a healthy climate. He or she always retains a special status, but the therapist and clients are usually on much more equal footing in group therapy than in individual therapy. The leader in group therapy expresses emotions, shares feelings, and copes with challenges from group members.

Advantages of the Group Experience

Group therapies obviously save time and money, which can be critical in understaffed mental hospitals and other institutional settings. Therapists in private practice usually charge less for group than individual therapy, making therapy affordable for more people. However, group therapy is *not* just a less costly substitute for individual therapy. For many types of patients and problems, group therapy can be just as effective as individual treatment (Alonso et al., 2003; Stone, 2003). Moreover, group therapy has unique strengths of its own (Yalom, 1995). For example, in group therapy participants often come to realize that their misery is not unique. They are reassured to learn that many other people have similar or even worse problems. Another

© Bob Daemmrich/The Image Works

advantage is that group therapy provides an opportunity for participants to work on their social skills in a safe environment. Yet another advantage is that certain types of problems and clients respond especially well to the social support that group therapy can provide.

Whether insight therapies are conducted on a group or an individual basis, clients usually invest considerable time, effort, and money. Are these therapies worth the investment? Let's examine the evidence on their effectiveness.

Evaluating Insight Therapies

In 1952 Hans Eysenck shocked mental health professionals by reporting that there was no sound evidence that insight therapy actually helped people. What was the basis for this startling claim? Eysenck reviewed numerous studies of therapeutic outcome for clients suffering from what were then called neurotic disorders (mostly anxiety, somatoform, and mild depressive disorders, in contemporary terminology). He found that about two-thirds of the clients recovered. A two-thirds recovery rate sounds reasonable, except that Eysenck found the same recovery rate among *untreated* neurotics. As we noted in Chapter 14, psychological disorders sometimes clear up on their own. **A *spontaneous remission* is a recovery from a disorder that occurs without formal treatment.** His estimate of the spontaneous remission rate for neurotic disorders led Eysenck to conclude that the therapeutic effects of insight therapy are small or nonexistent.

Group treatments have proven particularly helpful when members share similar problems, such as alcoholism, overeating, or having been sexually abused as a child. Many approaches to insight therapy that were originally designed for individuals—such as cognitive therapy—have been adapted for treatment of groups.

In the ensuing years, critics pounced on Eysenck's article looking for flaws (Jacobson & Christensen, 1996). They found a variety of shortcomings in his data. For instance, Eysenck used different time frames in comparing the recovery rates of treated and untreated individuals (Strupp & Howard, 1992). Moreover, the treated and untreated groups were not matched in terms of the severity of their disorders, their attitudes and expectations about therapy and recovery, or any other relevant variables that might influence therapeutic outcomes. After re-examining Eysenck's data, Bergin (1971) argued that the data really suggested that the spontaneous remission rate for neurotic problems was in the vicinity of 30% to 40%. Although Eysenck's conclusions were unduly pessimistic, he made an important contribution to the mental health field by sparking debate and research on the effectiveness of insight therapy.

Evaluating the effectiveness of any approach to treatment is a complex challenge (Kendall, Holmbeck, & Verduin, 2004; Hill & Lambert, 2004). This is especially true for insight therapies. If you were to undergo insight therapy, how would you judge its effectiveness? By how you felt? By looking at your behaviour? By asking your therapist? By consulting your friends and family? What would you be looking for? Various schools of thought pursue entirely different goals. And clients' ratings of their progress are likely to be slanted toward a favourable evaluation because they want to justify their effort, their heartache, their expense, and their time. Another problem that crops up in studies of the relative efficacy of different treatments is the *allegiance effect*—researchers comparing different therapies tend to obtain results that favour the therapeutic approach they champion (Luborsky et al., 1999). Allegiance effects are probably due in part to the normal human tendency to see what one wants to see when making subjective evaluations. Allegiance effects may also occur because research teams often have more expertise in supervising and delivering their preferred therapy than the competing approaches under study (Hollon, 1999; Thase, 1999). In any event, allegiance effects further complicate the daunting task of assessing the effectiveness of various insight therapies. In sum, evaluations of therapeutic outcomes tend to be subjective, with little consensus about the best way to assess clients' progress (Lambert & Hill, 1994).

In spite of these difficulties, hundreds of therapy outcome studies have been conducted since Eysenck prodded researchers into action. These studies have examined a broad range of specific clinical problems and used diverse methods to assess therapeutic outcomes, including scores on psychological tests and ratings by family members, as well as therapists' and clients' ratings. These studies consistently indicate that insight therapy *is* superior to no treatment or to placebo treatment and that the effects of therapy are reasonably durable (Kopta et al., 1999; Lambert & Ogles, 2004). In one widely discussed study that focused on patients' self-reports, the vast majority of the respondents subjectively felt that they had derived considerable benefit from their therapy (Seligman, 1995).

Although there is considerable evidence that insight therapy tends to produce positive effects for a sizable majority of clients, there is vigorous debate about the *mechanisms of action* underlying these positive effects. The advocates of various therapies tend to attribute the benefits of therapy to the particular methods and procedures used by each specific approach to therapy (Chambless & Hollon, 1998). In essence, they argue that different therapies achieve similar benefits through different processes. An alternative view espoused by many theorists is that the diverse approaches to therapy share certain *common factors* and that these common factors account for much of the improvement experienced by clients (Frank & Frank, 1991). Evidence supporting the common factors view has mounted in recent years (Ahn & Wampold, 2001; Lambert & Barley, 2001).

What are the common denominators that lie at the core of diverse approaches to therapy? The models proposed to answer to this question vary considerably, but there is some consensus. The most widely cited common factors include (1) the development of a therapeutic alliance with a professional helper, (2) the provision of emotional support and empathic understanding by the therapist, (3) the cultivation of hope and positive expectations in the client, (4) the provision of a rationale for the client's problems and a plausible method for ameliorating them, and (5) the opportunity to express feelings, confront problems, gain new insights, and learn new patterns of behaviour (Grencavage & Norcross, 1990; Weinberger, 1995). How important are the common factors in therapy? Some theorists argue that common factors account for virtually *all* of the progress that clients make in therapy (Wampold, 2001). It seems more likely that the benefits of therapy represent the combined effects of common factors and specific procedures (Beutler & Harwood, 2002). Either way, it is clear that common factors play a significant role in insight therapy.

a significant decrease in clients' reports of interpersonal problems (Watson et al., 2003).

Client-centred therapy resembles psychoanalysis in that both seek to achieve a major reconstruction of a client's personality. We'll see more limited and specific goals in cognitive therapy, which we consider next.

Cognitive Therapy

In Chapter 13, we saw that people's cognitive interpretations of events make all the difference in how well they handle stress. In Chapter 14, we learned that cognitive factors play a key role in the development of depression and other disorders. Citing the importance of findings such as these, two former psychoanalysts—Aaron Beck (1976, 1987) and Albert Ellis (1973, 1989)—independently devised cognitive-oriented therapies that became highly influential (Arnkoff & Glass, 1992; Hollon & Beck, 2004). Since we covered the main ideas underlying Ellis's *rational-emotive therapy* in our discussion of coping strategies (see the Personal Application for Chapter 13), we'll focus on Beck's system of *cognitive therapy* here. **Cognitive therapy is an insight therapy that emphasizes recognizing and changing negative thoughts and maladaptive beliefs.**

In recent years cognitive therapy has been applied fruitfully to a wide range of disorders (Beck, 1991; Dobson, 2001; Rush & Beck, 2000), but it was originally devised as a treatment for depression. According to cognitive therapists, depression is caused by "errors" in thinking (see Figure 15.3). They assert that depression-prone people tend to (1) blame their setbacks on personal inadequacies without considering circumstantial explanations, (2) focus selectively on negative events while ignoring positive events, (3) make unduly pessimistic projections about the future, and (4) draw negative conclusions about their worth as a person based on insignificant events. For instance, imagine that you got a low grade on a minor quiz in a class. If you made the kinds of errors in thinking just described, you might blame the grade on your woeful stupidity, dismiss comments from a classmate that it was an unfair test, gloomily predict that you will surely flunk the course, and conclude that you are not genuine university material.

Along with Ellis and Beck, University of Waterloo psychologist Donald Meichenbaum is considered one of the important innovators of cognitive-behavioural therapy. Meichenbaum has applied his techniques in cognitive therapy to a wide variety of issues including post-traumatic stress disorder (Meichenbaum, 1994) and has been consulted in the aftermath of trau-

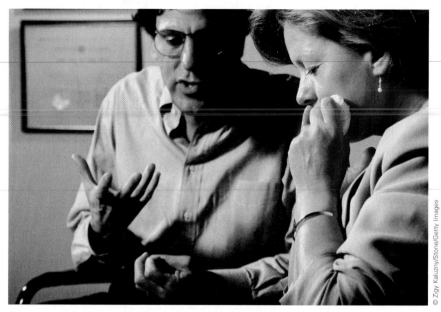

Client-centred therapists emphasize the importance of a supportive emotional climate in therapy. They also work to clarify, rather than interpret, the feelings expressed by their patients.

matic events including the Oklahoma City bombing, the Columbine school shootings, and the 9/11 attacks (Yalom, 2002). In one of his innovations, referred to as *self-instructional training* (Meichenbaum, 1977), clients are taught to develop and use verbal statements that help them cope with difficult contexts. As we discussed in Chapter 13, having readily available coping strategies is critical in dealing with stress. Self-instructional training can help clients deal with current stressors and may serve to inoculate them against future stress. Interestingly, when discussing his self-instructional training method (Yalom, 2002), Meichenbaum sometimes refers to it as his "New York therapy." He grew up in New York City watching all kinds of people talk to themselves on the street. His mother once pointed out the

Web Link 15.4

The Albert Ellis Institute
http://www.rebt.org/

Rational-emotive therapy, developed by Albert Ellis, is an influential cognitive-behavioural approach to treatment (see the Personal Application for Chapter 13). This site demonstrates how rational-emotive therapy has grown over the last 40 years.

Figure 15.3

Beck's view of the roots of disorders. Beck's theory initially focused on the causes of depression, although it was gradually broadened to explain other disorders. According to Beck, depression is caused by the types of negative thinking shown here.

"*Most people are barely aware of the automatic thoughts which precede unpleasant feelings or automatic inhibitions.*"
AARON BECK

University of Waterloo psychologist Donald Meichenbaum is well known for his role in the development of cognitive-behavioural therapy techniques.

similarity between his observations of people talking to themselves in New York and his therapy and asked him, "For this you get paid?" Recently, he developed a set of risk assessment items and guidelines for practice in evaluating suicidal patients (Meichenbaum, 2005). In 1989, Meichenbaum received the CPA Award for Distinguished Contributions to Psychology as a Profession.

Goals and Techniques

The goal of cognitive therapy is to change the way clients think. To begin, clients are taught to detect their automatic negative thoughts—the self-defeating statements they tend to make when analyzing problems. Examples might include "I'm just not smart enough," "No one really likes me," or "It's all my fault." Clients are then trained to subject these automatic thoughts to reality testing. The therapist helps them see how unrealistically negative the thoughts are.

The therapist's goal is not to promote unwarranted optimism but rather to help the client use more reasonable standards of evaluation. For example, a cognitive therapist might point out that a client's failure to get a desired promotion at work can be attributable to many factors and that this setback doesn't mean that the client is incompetent. Gradually, the therapist digs deeper, looking for the unrealistic assumptions that underlie clients' constant negative thinking. These, too, must be changed.

Cognitive therapy tends to be a relatively short-term treatment, typically lasting 4 to 20 sessions (Beck, 1995). Unlike client-centred therapists, cognitive therapists are actively involved in determining the pace and direction of treatment. They usually talk extensively in the therapy sessions. They may even argue openly with clients as they try to persuade them to alter their patterns of thinking.

Kinship with Behaviour Therapy

Cognitive therapy borrows extensively from behavioural approaches to treatment (Wright & Beck, 1999), which we will discuss shortly. Specifically, cognitive therapists often use "homework assignments" that focus on changing clients' overt behaviours. Clients may be instructed to engage in overt responses on their own, outside of the clinician's office. For example, one shy, insecure young man in cognitive therapy was told to go to a singles bar and engage three different women in conversations for up to five minutes each (Rush, 1984). He was instructed to record his thoughts before and after each of the conversations. This assignment elicited various maladaptive patterns of thought that gave the young man and his therapist plenty to talk about in subsequent sessions. As this example illustrates, cognitive therapy is a creative blend of "talk therapy" and behaviour therapy, although it is primarily an insight therapy.

Cognitive therapy was originally designed as a treatment for individuals. However, it has recently been adapted for use with groups (Rose, 1999). Most insight therapies can be conducted on either an individual or a group basis (Kaplan & Sadock, 1993), so let's take a look at the dynamics of group therapy.

Group Therapy

Although it dates back to the early part of the 20th century, group therapy came of age during World War II and its aftermath in the 1950s (Rosenbaum, Lakin, & Roback, 1992). During this period, the expanding demand for therapeutic services forced clinicians to use group techniques (Scheidlinger, 1993). *Group therapy* is the simultaneous treatment of several clients in a group. Most major insight therapies have been adapted for use with groups. In fact, the ideas underlying Rogers's client-centred therapy spawned the much-publicized encounter group movement. Although group therapy can be conducted in a variety of ways, we can provide a general overview of the process as it usually unfolds with outpatient populations (see Alonso, Alonso, & Piper, 2003; Stone, 2003; Vinogradov, Cox, & Yalom, 2003).

Participants' Roles

A therapy group typically consists of 4 to 15 people, with 8 participants regarded as an ideal number (Vinogradov et al., 2003). The therapist usually screens the participants, excluding persons who seem likely

---

- Insight therapies involve verbal interactions intended to enhance self-knowledge. Freudian approaches to therapy assume that neuroses originate from unresolved conflicts lurking in the unconscious. Therefore, in psychoanalysis free association and dream analysis are used to explore the unconscious.

- When an analyst's probing hits sensitive areas, resistance can be expected. The transference relationship may be used to overcome this resistance so that the client can handle interpretations that lead to insight. Classical psychoanalysis is not widely practised anymore, but Freud's legacy lives on in a rich diversity of modern psychodynamic therapies.

- Rogers's client-centred therapy assumes that neurotic anxieties are derived from incongruence between a person's self-concept and reality. Accordingly, the client-centred therapist tries to provide a supportive climate in which clients can restructure their self-concept. The process of client-centred therapy emphasizes clarification of the client's feelings and self-acceptance.

- Beck's cognitive therapy concentrates on changing the way clients think about events in their lives. Cognitive therapists re-educate clients to detect and challenge automatic negative thoughts that cause depression and anxiety.

- Most theoretical approaches to insight therapy have been adapted for use with groups. Participants in group therapy essentially act as therapists for one another, exchanging insights and emotional support. Group therapy has unique advantages in comparison to individual therapy.

- Eysenck's work in the 1950s raised doubts about the effectiveness of insight therapy and stimulated research on its efficacy. Evaluating the effectiveness of any approach to therapy is complex and difficult. Nonetheless, the weight of modern evidence suggests that insight therapies are superior to no treatment or to placebo treatment. Much of the improvement seen in clients in therapy may be attributable to the operation of common factors.

Behaviour Therapies

Behaviour therapy is different from insight therapy in that behaviour therapists make no attempt to help clients achieve grand insights about themselves. Why not? Because behaviour therapists believe that such insights aren't necessary to produce constructive change. For example, consider a client troubled by compulsive gambling. The behaviour therapist doesn't care whether this behaviour is rooted in unconscious conflicts or parental rejection. What the client needs is to get rid of the maladaptive behaviour. Consequently, the therapist simply designs a program to eliminate the compulsive gambling. Actually, behaviour therapists may work with clients to attain some limited insights about how situational factors evoke troublesome behaviours (Franks & Barbrack, 1983). This information can be helpful in designing a behaviour therapy program.

The crux of the difference between insight therapy and behaviour therapy is this: Insight therapists treat pathological symptoms as signs of an underlying problem, whereas behaviour therapists think that the symptoms *are* the problem. Thus, *behaviour therapies* involve the application of learning principles to direct efforts to change clients' maladaptive behaviours.

Behaviourism has been an influential school of thought in psychology since the 1920s. Nevertheless, behaviourists devoted little attention to clinical issues until the 1950s, when behaviour therapy emerged out of three independent lines of research fostered by B. F. Skinner and his colleagues (Skinner, Solomon, & Lindsley, 1953) in the United States; by Hans Eysenck (1959) and his colleagues in Britain; and by Joseph Wolpe (1958) and his colleagues in South Africa (Glass & Arnkoff, 1992). Since then, there has been an explosion of interest in behavioural approaches to psychotherapy.

Behaviour therapies are based on certain assumptions (Berkowitz, 2003). *First, it is assumed that behaviour is a product of learning.* No matter how self-defeating or pathological a client's behaviour might be, the behaviourist believes that it is the result of past learning and conditioning. *Second, it is assumed that what has been learned can be unlearned.* The same learning principles that explain how the maladaptive behaviour was acquired can be used to get rid of it.

PREVIEW QUESTIONS

- What assumptions are behaviour therapies based on?
- How do behaviour therapists treat phobias?
- How does aversion therapy work?
- What are the goals and techniques of social skills training?
- What is the evidence on the efficacy of behaviour therapy?

CONCEPT CHECK 15.2

Understanding Therapists' Goals

Check your understanding of therapists' goals by matching various therapies with the appropriate description. The answers are in Appendix A.

Principal therapeutic goals

_____ **1.** Elimination of maladaptive behaviours or symptoms

_____ **2.** Acceptance of genuine self, personal growth

_____ **3.** Recovery of unconscious conflicts, character reconstruction

_____ **4.** Detection and reduction of negative thinking

Therapy

a. Psychoanalysis

b. Client-centred therapy

c. Cognitive therapy

d. Behaviour therapy

Thus, behaviour therapists attempt to change clients' behaviour by applying the principles of classical conditioning, operant conditioning, and observational learning.

Systematic Desensitization 11E

Devised by Joseph Wolpe (1958), systematic desensitization revolutionized psychotherapy by giving therapists their first useful alternative to traditional "talk therapy" (Fishman & Franks, 1992). *Systematic desensitization* **is a behaviour therapy used to reduce phobic clients' anxiety responses through counterconditioning.** The treatment assumes that most anxiety responses are acquired through classical conditioning (as we discussed in Chapter 14). According to this model, a harmless stimulus (e.g., a bridge) may be paired with a fear-arousing event (lightning striking it), so that it becomes a conditioned stimulus eliciting anxiety. The goal of systematic desensitization is to weaken the association between the conditioned stimulus (the bridge) and the conditioned response of anxiety (see Figure 15.4). Systematic desensitization involves three steps.

First, the therapist helps the client build an anxiety hierarchy. The hierarchy is a list of anxiety-arousing stimuli related to the specific source of anxiety, such as flying, academic tests, or snakes. The client ranks the stimuli from the least anxiety arousing to the most anxiety arousing. This ordered list of stimuli is the *anxiety hierarchy.* An example of an anxiety hierarchy for one woman's fear of heights is shown in Figure 15.5.

The second step involves training the client in deep muscle relaxation. This second phase may begin during early sessions while the therapist and client are still constructing the anxiety hierarchy. Various therapists use different relaxation training procedures. Whatever procedures are used, the client must learn to engage in deep, thorough relaxation on command from the therapist.

In the third step, the client tries to work through the hierarchy, learning to remain relaxed while imagining each stimulus. Starting with the least anxiety-arousing stimulus, the client imagines the situation as vividly as possible while relaxing. If the client experiences strong anxiety, he or she drops the imaginary scene and concentrates on relaxation. The client keeps repeating this process until he or she can imagine a scene with little or no anxiety. Once a particular scene is conquered, the client moves on to the next stimulus situation in the anxiety hierarchy. Gradually, over a number of therapy sessions, the client progresses through the hierarchy, unlearning troublesome anxiety responses.

"*Neurotic anxiety is nothing but a conditioned response.*"
JOSEPH WOLPE

Systematic desensitization is a behavioural treatment for phobias. Early studies of the procedure's efficacy often used people who had snake phobias as research subjects because people with snake phobias were relatively easy to find. This research showed that systematic desensitization is generally an effective treatment.

Figure 15.4

The logic underlying systematic desensitization.
Behaviourists argue that many phobic responses are acquired through classical conditioning, as in the example diagrammed here. Systematic desensitization targets the conditioned associations between phobic stimuli and fear responses.

As clients conquer *imagined* phobic stimuli, they may be encouraged to confront the *real* stimuli. Although desensitization to imagined stimuli *can* be effective by itself, contemporary behaviour therapists usually follow it up with direct exposures to the real anxiety-arousing stimuli (Emmelkamp, 2004). Indeed, behavioural interventions emphasizing direct exposures to anxiety-arousing situations have become behaviour therapists' treatment of choice for phobic and other anxiety disorders (Goldfried, Greenberg, & Marmar, 1990). Usually, these real-life confrontations prove harmless and individuals' anxiety responses decline.

According to Wolpe (1958, 1990), the principle at work in systematic desensitization is simple. Anxiety and relaxation are incompatible responses. The trick is to recondition people so that the conditioned stimulus elicits relaxation instead of anxiety. This is *counterconditioning*—an attempt to reverse the process of classical conditioning by associating the crucial stimulus with a new conditioned response. Although Wolpe's explanation of how systematic desensitization works has been questioned, the technique's effectiveness in eliminating specific anxieties has been well documented (Spiegler & Guevremont, 2003).

Aversion Therapy 11E

Aversion therapy is far and away the most controversial of the behaviour therapies. It's not something that you would sign up for unless you were pretty desperate. Psychologists usually suggest it only as a treatment of last resort, after other interventions have failed. What's so terrible about aversion therapy? The client has to endure decidedly unpleasant stimuli, such as shocks or drug-induced nausea.

Aversion therapy **is a behaviour therapy in which an aversive stimulus is paired with a stimulus that elicits an undesirable response.** For example, alcoholics have had an *emetic drug* (one that causes nausea and vomiting) paired with their favourite drinks during therapy sessions (Landabaso et al., 1999). By pairing the drug with alcohol, the therapist hopes to create a conditioned aversion to alcohol (see Figure 15.6).

Aversion therapy takes advantage of the automatic nature of responses produced through classical conditioning. Admittedly, alcoholics treated with aversion therapy know that they won't be given an emetic outside of their therapy sessions. However, their reflex response to the stimulus of alcohol may be changed so they respond to it with nausea and distaste (remember the "sauce béarnaise syndrome" described in Chapter 6?). Obviously, this response should make it much easier to resist the urge to drink.

Aversion therapy is not a widely used technique, and when it is used it is usually only one element in a larger treatment program. Troublesome behaviours treated successfully with aversion therapy have included drug and alcohol abuse, sexual deviance, gambling, shoplifting, stuttering, cigarette smoking, and overeating (Bordnick et al., 2004; Emmelkamp, 1994; Grossman & Ruiz, 2004; Maletzky, 2002).

Social Skills Training

Many psychological problems grow out of interpersonal difficulties. Behaviour therapists point out that people are not born with social finesse—they acquire social skills through learning. Unfortunately, some people have not learned how to be friendly, how to make conversation, how to express anger appropriately, and so forth. Social ineptitude can contribute to anxiety, feelings of inferiority, and various kinds of disorders. In light of these findings, therapists are increasingly using social skills training in efforts to improve clients' social abilities. This approach to therapy has yielded promising results in the treatment of social anxiety (Shear & Beidel, 1998), autism (Kransny et al., 2003), and schizophrenia (Bellack et al., 2004).

Social skills training **is a behaviour therapy designed to improve interpersonal skills that emphasizes modelling, behavioural rehearsal, and shaping**. This type of behaviour therapy can be conducted with individual clients or in groups. Social skills training depends on the principles of operant conditioning and observational learning. With *modelling*, the client is encouraged to watch socially skilled friends and colleagues in order to acquire appropriate responses (eye contact, active listening, and so on) through observation. In *behavioural rehearsal*, the client tries to practise social techniques

An Anxiety Hierarchy for Systematic Desensitization	
Degree of fear	
5	I'm standing on the balcony of the top floor of an apartment tower.
10	I'm standing on a stepladder in the kitchen to change a light bulb.
15	I'm walking on a ridge. The edge is hidden by shrubs and treetops.
20	I'm sitting on the slope of a mountain, looking out over the horizon.
25	I'm crossing a bridge 2 metres above a creek. The bridge consists of a 45-cm-wide board with a handrail on one side.
30	I'm riding a ski lift 2.5 metres above the ground.
35	I'm crossing a shallow, wide creek on a 45-cm-wide board, 1 metre above water level.
40	I'm climbing a ladder outside the house to reach a second-storey window.
45	I'm pulling myself up a 30-degree wet, slippery slope on a steel cable.
50	I'm scrambling up a rock, 2.5 metres high.
55	I'm walking 3 metres on a resilient, 45-cm-wide board, which spans a 2.5-metre-deep gulch.
60	I'm walking on a wide plateau, 60 cm from the edge of a cliff.
65	I'm skiing an intermediate hill. The snow is packed.
70	I'm walking over a railway trestle.
75	I'm walking on the side of an embankment. The path slopes to the outside.
80	I'm riding a chair lift 5 metres above the ground.
85	I'm walking up a long, steep slope.
90	I'm walking up (or down) a 15-degree slope on a 1-metre-wide trail. On one side of the trail the terrain drops down sharply; on the other side is a steep upward slope.
95	I'm walking on a 1-metre-wide ridge. The slopes on both sides are long and more than 25 degrees steep.
100	I'm walking on a 1-metre-wide ridge. The trail slopes on one side. The drop on either side of the trail is more than 25 degrees.

Figure 15.5

Example of an anxiety hierarchy. Systematic desensitization requires the construction of an anxiety hierarchy like the one shown here, which was developed for a woman who had a fear of heights but wanted to go hiking in the mountains.

Source: Rudestam, K. E. (1980). *Methods of self-change: An ABC primer.* Belmont, CA: Wadsworth. Copyright © 1980 by Wadsworth Publishing. Reprinted by permission of the author.

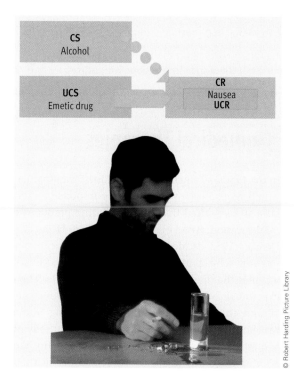

Figure 15.6

Aversion therapy. Aversion therapy uses classical conditioning to create an aversion to a stimulus that has elicited problematic behaviour. For example, in the treatment of drinking problems, alcohol may be paired with a nausea-inducing drug to create an aversion to drinking.

in structured role-playing exercises. The therapist provides corrective feedback and uses approval to reinforce progress. Eventually, of course, clients try their newly acquired skills in real-world interactions. Usually, they are given specific homework assignments. *Shaping* is used in that clients are gradually asked to handle more complicated and delicate social situations. For example, a nonassertive client may begin by working on making requests of friends. Only much later will he be asked to tackle standing up to his boss at work.

Evaluating Behaviour Therapies

Behaviour therapists have historically placed more emphasis on the importance of measuring therapeutic outcomes than insight therapists have. Hence, there is ample evidence attesting to the effectiveness of behaviour therapy (Lambert & Bergin, 1992). Of course, behaviour therapies are not well suited to the treatment of some types of problems (vague feelings of discontent, for instance). Furthermore, it's mis-

leading to make global statements about the effectiveness of behaviour therapies, because they include many types of procedures designed for very different purposes. For example, the value of systematic desensitization for phobias has no bearing on the value of aversion therapy for sexual deviance.

For our purposes, it is sufficient to note that there is favourable evidence on the efficacy of most of the widely used behavioural interventions (Jacob & Pelham, 2000). Behaviour therapies can make important contributions to the treatment of phobias, obsessive-compulsive disorders, sexual dysfunction, schizophrenia, drug-related problems, eating disorders, psychosomatic disorders, hyperactivity, autism, and mental retardation (Berkowitz, 2003; Emmelkamp, 2004).

Many of these problems would not be amenable to treatment with the biomedical therapies, which we consider next. To some extent, the three major approaches to treatment have different strengths. Let's see where the strengths of the biomedical therapies lie.

CONCEPT **CHECK 15.3**

Understanding the Types of Behaviour Therapy

Check your understanding of the varieties of behaviour therapy discussed in the text by matching the therapies with the appropriate description. Choose from the following: (a) systematic desensitization, (b) social skills training, and (c) aversion therapy. The answers are in Appendix A.

_____ **1.** Anxiety is reduced by conditioning the client to respond positively to stimuli that previously aroused anxiety.

_____ **2.** Unwanted behaviours are eliminated by conditioning the client to have an unpleasant response to stimuli that previously triggered the behaviour.

_____ **3.** Behavioural techniques are used to teach the client new behaviours aimed at enhancing the quality of their interactions with others.

REVIEW OF KEY POINTS

- Behaviour therapies use the principles of learning in direct efforts to change specific aspects of behaviour. Wolpe's systematic desensitization, a treatment for phobias, involves the construction of an anxiety hierarchy, relaxation training, and step-by-step movement through the hierarchy, pairing relaxation with each phobic stimulus.

- In aversion therapy, a stimulus associated with an unwanted response is paired with an unpleasant stimulus in an effort to eliminate the maladaptive response. Social skills training can improve clients' interpersonal skills through shaping, modelling, and behavioural rehearsal.

- There is ample evidence that behaviour therapies are effective in the treatment of a wide variety of disorders.

Biomedical Therapies

PREVIEW QUESTIONS

- What are the principal types of psychiatric drugs, and what disorders are they used for?

- How effective are psychiatric drugs, and what are their disadvantages?

- What is ECT and what is it used for?

- How effective is ECT and what are the risks?

In the 1950s, a French surgeon looking for a drug that would reduce patients' autonomic response to surgical stress noticed that chlorpromazine produced a mild sedation. Based on this observation, Delay and Deniker (1952) decided to give chlorpromazine to hospitalized schizophrenic patients. They wanted to see whether the drug would have calming effects. Their experiment was a dramatic success. Chlorpromazine became the first effective antipsychotic drug, and a revolution in psychiatry was begun. Hundreds of thousands of severely disturbed patients who had appeared doomed to spend the remainder of their

lives in mental hospitals were gradually sent home, thanks to the therapeutic effects of antipsychotic drugs. Today, biomedical therapies such as drug treatment lie at the core of psychiatric practice.

***Biomedical therapies* are physiological interventions intended to reduce symptoms associated with psychological disorders.** These therapies assume that psychological disorders are caused, at least in part, by biological malfunctions. As we discussed in the previous chapter, this assumption clearly has merit for many disorders, especially the more severe ones.

When laypersons hear the phrase biomedical therapies, many of them often think of psychosurgery and lobotomies, the type of treatment portrayed in the classic film *One Flew over the Cuckoo's Nest* starring Jack Nicholson. While psychosurgery was performed thousands of times up to the middle part of the 20th century, in the 1950s it went into decline as a treatment and was replaced by the recently developed pharmacological treatments (Ackerknecht, 1968; Alexander & Selesnick, 1966; Millon, 2004), some of which we discuss below.

While a form of psychosurgery, *trephening*, was used by the Greeks and Romans and throughout the medieval period, modern use dates from 1888 when Swiss psychiatrist Gottleib Burckhardt removed portions of the cortex of six psychotic patients as a treatment for hallucinations (Millon, 2004). In the 1930s, Antonio Egas Moniz, a Portuguese psychiatrist, developed the *prefrontal leucotomy*, for which he was awarded the Nobel Prize in 1949. This type of treatment was modified and popularized by the American psychiatrist Walter Freeman in the 1940s. Over 20 000 patients in North America received this treatment. The first lobotomies in Ontario were performed in 1944 by Dr. K. G. McKenzie, who did 19 such surgeries that year at the Toronto Psychiatric Hospital. Between 1944 and 1967, over 1000 lobotomies were done in Ontario. After 1967 the frequency declined, with only 17 performed between 1968 and 1974. The last lobotomies were performed by Dr. Kenneth Livingstone at the Clarke Institute of Psychiatry in 1981. He performed three that year (Simmons, 1987). According to Simmons's archival research, the reasons particular lobotomies were performed were not even always treatment related: "In some cases, psychosurgery was administered to ease staffing problems, for experimental purposes, or simply out of sheer curiosity. Often the consent of the patients or relatives was not obtained" (p. 537). The procedure has largely been abandoned except in a modified form (*cingulotomy*) in extreme situations, such as the treatment-refractory obsessive-compulsive disorders (Dougherty et al., 2002).

In this section we will discuss two current biomedical approaches to psychotherapy: drug therapy and electroconvulsive (shock) therapy.

Treatment with Drugs

Psychopharmacotherapy is the treatment of mental disorders with medication. We will refer to this kind of treatment more simply as *drug therapy*. The three main categories of therapeutic drugs for psychological problems are: (1) antianxiety drugs, (2) antipsychotic drugs, and (3) antidepressant drugs. Of these drugs, the antidepressant drugs have surpassed the antianxiety agents as the most widely prescribed psychiatric drugs (Pincus et al., 1998).

Using data collected for Statistics Canada's National Population Health Survey (1998–1999), the Canadian Centre for Substance Abuse indicated that 2.3% of Canadians 15 years of age and older reported using tranquillizers and 3.9% reported using antidepressants in the preceding month. In both cases, the rate was higher for females than for males (Canadian Centre for Substance Abuse, n.d.). A report by Health Canada (2002c) stated that senior women are prescribed mild tranquillizers and sedatives at a rate that exceeds any other population group in Canada.

Antianxiety Drugs

Most of us know someone who pops pills to relieve anxiety. The drugs involved in this common coping strategy are *antianxiety drugs*, **which relieve tension, apprehension, and nervousness.** The most popular of these drugs are Valium and Xanax. These are the trade names (the proprietary names that pharmaceutical companies use in marketing drugs) for diazepam and alprazolam, respectively.

Valium, Xanax, and other drugs in the *benzodiazepine* family are often called *tranquillizers*. These drugs exert their effects almost immediately, and they can be fairly effective in alleviating feelings of anxiety (Ballenger, 2000). However, their effects are measured in hours, so their impact is relatively short-lived. Antianxiety drugs are routinely prescribed for people with anxiety disorders, but they are also given to millions of people who simply suffer from chronic nervous tension. In the mid-1970s, pharmacists in North America were filling nearly *100 million* prescriptions each year for Valium and similar antianxiety drugs. Many critics characterized this level of use as excessive (Lickey & Gordon, 1991).

All the drugs used to treat psychological problems have potentially troublesome side effects that show up in some patients but not others. The antianxiety drugs are no exception. The most common side effects of Valium and Xanax are listed in Table 15.1. Some of these side effects—such as drowsiness, depression, nausea, and confusion—present serious problems for some patients. These drugs also have potential for abuse, drug dependence, and overdose, although these risks have probably been exaggerated in the press (Ballenger, 2000; Silberman, 1998). Another drawback is that patients who have been on antianxiety drugs for a while often experience withdrawal symptoms when their drug treatment is stopped (Raj & Sheehan, 2004).

Table 15.1 Side Effects of Xanax and Valium

Side Effects	Patients Experiencing Side Effects (%)	
	Xanax	Valium
Drowsiness	36.0	49.4
Light-headedness	18.6	24.0
Dry mouth	14.9	13.0
Depression	11.9	17.0
Nausea, vomiting	9.3	10.0
Constipation	9.3	11.3
Insomnia	9.0	6.7
Confusion	9.3	14.1
Diarrhea	8.5	10.5
Tachycardia, palpitations	8.1	7.2
Nasal congestion	8.1	7.2
Blurred vision	7.0	9.1

SOURCE: Evans, R. L. (1981). New drug evaluations: Alprazolam. *Drug Intelligence and Clinical Pharmacy,* *15*, 633–637. Copyright © 1981 by Harvey Whitney Books Company. Reprinted by permission.

A newer antianxiety drug called Buspar (buspirone), which does not belong to the benzodiazepine family, appears useful in the treatment of generalized anxiety disorder (Brawman-Mintzer, Lydiard, & Ballenger, 2000). Unlike Valium, Buspar is slow acting, exerting its effects in one to three weeks, but with fewer sedative side effects (Ninan & Muntasser, 2004).

Antipsychotic Drugs 11E

Antipsychotic drugs are used primarily in the treatment of schizophrenia. They are also given to people with severe mood disorders who become delusional. The trade names (and generic names) of some classic drugs in this category are Thorazine (chlorpromazine), Mellaril (thioridazine), and Haldol (haloperidol). ***Antipsychotic drugs*** **are used to gradually reduce psychotic symptoms, including hyperactivity, mental confusion, hallucinations, and delusions.** The traditional antipsychotics appear to decrease activity at dopamine synapses, although the exact relationship between their neurochemical effects and their clinical effects remains obscure (Egan & Hyde, 2000).

Studies suggest that antipsychotics reduce psychotic symptoms in about 70% of patients, albeit in varied degrees (Marder, 2000). When antipsychotic drugs are effective, they work their magic gradually, as shown in Figure 15.7. Patients usually begin to respond within two days to a week. Further improvement may occur for several months. Many schizophrenic patients are placed on antipsychotics indefinitely because these drugs can reduce the likelihood of a relapse into an active schizophrenic episode (Marder & van Kammen, 2000).

Antipsychotic drugs undeniably make a huge contribution to the treatment of severe mental disorders, but they are not without problems. They have many unpleasant side effects (Cohen, 1997; Wikaitis, Mulvhill, & Nasrallah, 2004). Drowsiness, constipation, and cottonmouth are common. The drugs may also produce effects that resemble the symptoms of Parkinson's disease, including muscle tremors, muscular rigidity, and impaired motor coordination. After being released from a hospital, many schizophrenic patients, supposedly placed on antipsychotics indefinitely, discontinue their drug regimen because of the disagreeable side effects. Unfortunately, a relapse eventually occurs in most patients after they stop taking antipsychotic medication (Gitlin et al., 2001). In addition to their nuisance side effects, antipsychotics may cause a more severe and lasting problem called *tardive dyskinesia,* which is seen in about 20%–30% of patients who receive long-term treatment with traditional antipsychotics (Marder, 2000). ***Tardive dyskinesia*** **is a neurological disorder marked by involuntary writhing and tic-like movements of the mouth, tongue, face, hands, or feet.** Once this debilitating syndrome emerges, there is no cure, although spontaneous remission sometimes occurs after the discontinuation of antipsychotic medication (Pi & Simpson, 2000).

Psychiatrists are currently enthusiastic about a new class of antipsychotic agents called *atypical antipsychotic drugs* (such as clozapine, olanzapine, and quetiapine). These drugs are roughly as effective as traditional antipsychotics (Fleischhacker, 2002) and they can help some patients who do not respond to

Figure 15.7

The time course of antipsychotic drug effects.
Antipsychotic drugs reduce psychotic symptoms gradually, over a span of weeks, as graphed here. In contrast, patients given placebo medication show little improvement.

SOURCE: Cole, J. O., Goldberg, S. C., & Davis, J. M. (1966). Drugs in the treatment of psychosis. In P. Solomon (Ed.), *Psychiatric drugs.* New York: Grune & Stratton. From data in the NIMH-PSC Collaborative Study I. Reprinted by permission of J. M. Davis.

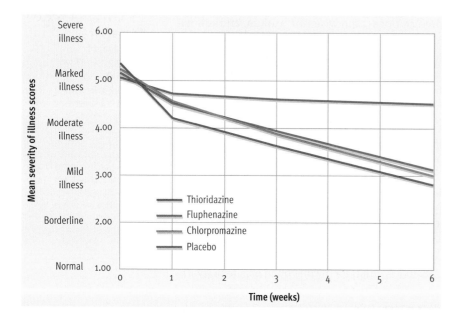

Tricyclic antidepressants inhibit reuptake at serotonin and norepinephrine synapses, which elevates activity at both types of synapses. Tricyclics also block activity at several subtypes of postsynaptic receptors.

Selective serotonin reuptake inhibitors (SSRIs) slow reuptake at serotonin synapses, so activity is increased only at serotonin synapses.

MAO inhibitors work by disabling MAO enzymes that would normally metabolize and inactivate neurotransmitters at dopamine, norepinephrine, and serotonin synapses.

Figure 15.8

Antidepressant drugs' mechanisms of action. The three types of antidepressant drugs all increase activity at serotonin synapses, which is probably the principal basis for their therapeutic effects. However, they increase serotonin activity in different ways, with different spillover effects (Marangell et al., 1999). Tricyclics and MAO inhibitors have effects at a much greater variety of synapses, which presumably explains why they have more side effects. The more recently developed SSRIs are much more specific in targeting serotonin synapses.

conventional antipsychotic medications (Volavka et al., 2002). Moreover, the atypical antipsychotics produce fewer unpleasant side effects and carry less risk for tardive dyskinesia (Pi & Simpson, 2000; Stip, 2000). Of course, like all powerful drugs, they are not without their risks, as they appear to increase patients' vulnerability to diabetes and cardiovascular problems (Meltzer et al., 2002).

Antidepressant Drugs

 11E

As their name suggests, *antidepressant drugs* **gradually elevate mood and help bring people out of a depression.** Prior to 1987, there were two principal classes of antidepressants: *tricyclics* (such as Elavil) and *MAO inhibitors* (such as Nardil). These two sets of drugs affect neurochemical activity in different ways (see Figure 15.8) and tend to work with different patients. Overall, they are beneficial for about two-thirds of depressed patients (Gitlin, 2002), although only about one-third of treated patients experience a *complete resolution* of their symptoms (Shulman, 2001). The tricyclics have fewer problems with side effects and complications than the MAO inhibitors (Rush, 2000). Like antipsychotic drugs, antidepressants exert their effects gradually over a period of weeks.

Today, psychiatrists are more likely to prescribe a newer class of antidepressants, called *selective serotonin reuptake inhibitors (SSRIs)*, which slow the reuptake process at serotonin synapses. The drugs in this class, which include Prozac (fluoxetine), Paxil (paroxetine), and Zoloft (sertraline), seem to yield rapid therapeutic gains in the treatment of depression while producing fewer unpleasant or dangerous side effects (Marangell, Yudofsky, & Silver, 1999). SSRIs have also proven valuable in the treatment of obsessive-compulsive disorders, panic disorders, and other anxiety disorders

(Rivas-Vazquez, 2001). However, Prozac and the other SSRIs are not "miracle drugs," as suggested by some popular magazines. Like all drugs for psychological disorders, the SSRIs have side effects and risks that must be carefully weighed against their benefits (Baldessarini, 2001).

A major concern in recent years has been evidence from a number of studies that SSRIs may increase the risk for suicide (Healy & Whitaker, 2003; Holden, 2004). The challenge of collecting definitive data on this issue is much more daunting than one might guess, in part because suicide rates are already elevated among people who exhibit the disorders for which SSRIs are prescribed (Rihmer, 2003; Wessely & Kerwin, 2004). Some researchers have collected data that suggest that suicide rates have *declined* slightly because of widespread prescription of SSRIs (Olfson et al., 2003), while others have found no association between SSRIs and suicide (Lapierre, 2003; Tardiff, Marzuk, & Leon, 2002). At present, the data are too fragmentary and inconsistent to permit a firm, confident conclusion (Gunnell & Ashby, 2004). That said, the issue should be taken seriously, and patients on SSRIs should be carefully monitored by their physicians and families (Culpepper et al., 2004). Elevated suicide risk appears to mainly be a problem among a small minority of children and adolescents in the first month after starting antidepressants, especially during the first nine days (Jick, Kaye, & Jick, 2004).

Lithium and Other Mood Stabilizers

Lithium **is a chemical used to control mood swings in patients with bipolar mood disorders.** Lithium can help to prevent *future* episodes of both mania and depression in patients with bipolar illness (Maj et al., 1998; Tondo et al., 1998). Lithium can also be used

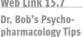

Web Link 15.7

Dr. Bob's Psychopharmacology Tips
http://www.dr-bob.org/tips/

Psychopharmacology is the use of medication to treat psychological disorders. Physician and pharmacology specialist Robert Hsiung (University of Chicago) provides both broad and specific references about the interface of drugs and the human mind, including a searchable archive of professional information.

in efforts to bring patients with bipolar illness out of *current* manic or depressive episodes. However, antipsychotics and antidepressants are more frequently used for these purposes. On the negative side of the ledger, lithium does have some dangerous side effects if its use isn't managed skillfully (Jefferson & Greist, 2000). Lithium levels in the patient's blood must be monitored carefully because high concentrations can be highly toxic and even fatal. Kidney and thyroid gland complications are the major problems associated with lithium therapy.

In recent years a number of alternatives to lithium have been developed. Collectively, these drugs are referred to as *mood stabilizers*. The most popular of these drugs is an anticonvulsant agent called *valproic acid,* which has become about as widely used as lithium in the treatment of bipolar disorders (Blanco et al., 2002). Valproic acid appears to be roughly as effective as lithium in efforts to treat current manic episodes and to prevent future affective disturbances (McElroy, Pope, & Keck, 2000). The advantage provided by valproic acid is that it produces fewer adverse effects than lithium and is better tolerated by patients (Bowden, 2004).

Evaluating Drug Therapies

Drug therapies can produce clear therapeutic gains for many kinds of patients. What's especially impressive is that they can be effective with disorders that otherwise defy therapeutic endeavours. Nonetheless, drug therapies are controversial. Critics of drug therapy have raised a number of issues (Cohen & McCubbin, 1990; Lickey & Gordon, 1991; Whitaker, 2002; Healy, 2004). First, some critics argue that drug therapies are not as effective as advertised and that they often produce superficial, short-lived curative effects (Greenberg & Fisher, 1997). For example, Valium does not really solve problems with anxiety; it merely provides temporary relief from an unpleasant symptom. Moreover, relapse rates are substantial when drug regimens are discontinued. Second, critics charge that many drugs are overprescribed and many patients overmedicated. According to these critics, a number of physicians routinely hand out prescriptions without giving adequate consideration to more complicated and difficult interventions. Third, some critics charge that the damaging side effects of therapeutic drugs are underestimated by psychiatrists and that these side effects are often worse than the illnesses that the drugs are supposed to cure (Breggin, 1990, 1991; Whitaker, 2002). Consistent with this assertion, research suggests that over 2 million people experience serious adverse drug effects (from all types of medications, not just psychiatric

drugs) in the United States each year and that adverse medication effects are responsible for over 100 000 deaths annually, making adverse drug reactions the fourth to sixth leading cause of death in the United States (Lazarou, Pomeranz, & Corey, 1998).

Critics maintain that the negative effects of psychiatric drugs are not fully appreciated because the pharmaceutical industry has managed to gain undue influence over the research enterprise as it relates to drug testing (Angell, 2000; Carpenter, 2002; Healy, 2004). Today, most researchers who investigate the benefits and risks of medications and write treatment guidelines have lucrative financial arrangements with the pharmaceutical industry (Bodenheimer, 2000; Choudhry, Stelfox, & Detsky, 2002). Their studies are funded by drug companies and they often receive substantial consulting fees. These financial arrangements have become so common, the prestigious *New England Journal of Medicine* had to relax its conflict-of-interest rules because it had difficulty finding expert reviewers who did not have financial ties to the drug industry (Drazen & Curfman, 2002). Unfortunately, these financial ties appear to undermine the objectivity required in scientific research, as studies funded by drug companies are far less likely to report unfavourable results than nonprofit-funded studies (Friedberg et al., 1999; Rennie & Luft, 2000). Industry-financed drug trials also tend to be much too brief to detect the long-term risks associated with new drugs (O'Brien, 1996). And research designs are often slanted in a multitude of ways so as to exaggerate the positive effects and minimize the negative effects of the drugs under scrutiny (Carpenter, 2002; Rennie, 1999). The conflicts of interest that appear to be pervasive in contemporary drug research raise grave concerns that require attention from researchers, universities, and governments.

Obviously, drug therapies have stirred up some debate. However, this controversy pales in comparison to the furious debates inspired by electroconvulsive (shock) therapy (ECT). ECT is so controversial that the residents of Berkeley, California, voted in 1982 to outlaw ECT in their city. However, in subsequent lawsuits, the courts ruled that scientific questions cannot be settled through a vote, and they overturned the law. What makes ECT so controversial? You'll see in the next section.

Electroconvulsive Therapy (ECT)

In the 1930s, a Hungarian psychiatrist named Ladislas von Meduna speculated that epilepsy and schizophrenia could not coexist in the same body. On the basis of this observation, which turned out to be inaccurate, von Meduna theorized that it might be useful to induce epileptic-like seizures in schizophrenic patients. Initially, a drug was used to trigger these seizures. However, by 1938 a pair of Italian psychiatrists (Cerletti & Bini, 1938) demonstrated that it was safer to elicit the seizures with electric shock. Thus, modern electroconvulsive therapy was born.

Electroconvulsive therapy (ECT) is a biomedical treatment in which electric shock is used to produce a cortical seizure accompanied by convulsions. In ECT, electrodes are attached to the skull over the temporal lobes of the brain (see the photo at right). A light anesthesia is induced, and the patient is given a variety of drugs to minimize the likelihood of complications. An electric current is then applied either to the right side or to both sides of the brain for about a second. Unilateral shock delivered to the right hemisphere is the preferred method of treatment today (Abrams, 2000). The current triggers a brief (about 30 seconds) convulsive seizure. The patient normally awakens in an hour or two and manifests some confusion, disorientation, and nausea, which usually clear up in a matter of hours. People typically receive between 6 and 20 treatments over a period of a month or so (Glass, 2001).

The clinical use of ECT peaked in the 1940s and 1950s, before effective drug therapies were widely available. ECT has long been controversial, and its use did decline in the 1960s and 1970s. Nonetheless, there has been a resurgence in the use of ECT, and it is not a rare form of therapy. Although only about 8% of psychiatrists administer ECT (Hermann et al., 1998), it is estimated that about 100 000 people receive ECT treatments yearly in the United States (Hermann et al., 1995). Some critics argue that ECT is overused because it is a lucrative procedure that boosts psychiatrists' income while consuming relatively little of their time in comparison to insight therapy (Frank, 1990). Conversely, some ECT advocates argue that ECT is underutilized because the public harbours many misconceptions about its risks and side effects (McDonald et al., 2004).

Controversy about ECT is also fuelled by patients' reports that the treatment is painful, dehumanizing, and terrifying. Substantial improvements in the administration of ECT have made it less disagreeable than it once was (Bernstein et al., 1998). Nonetheless, some patients continue to report that they find the treatment extremely aversive (Johnstone, 1999). Two personal reports by Canadians, one on each side of the controversy, are interesting places to begin your consideration of the use of ECT. One, written by Wendy Funk (1998), addresses concerns she has over her treatment.

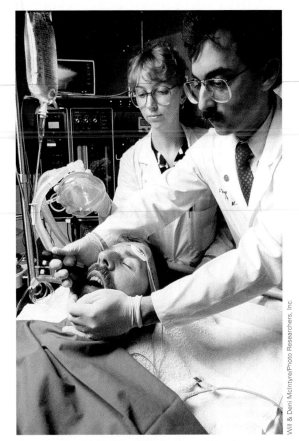

This patient is being prepared for electroconvulsive therapy (ECT). In ECT an electric shock is used to elicit a brief cortical seizure. The shock is delivered through electrodes attached to the patient's skull.

The other, by Canadian psychologist Norman Endler (1982), whom we profiled in Chapter 14, is based on his own ECT treatment and is supportive of its use.

Effectiveness of ECT

The evidence on the therapeutic efficacy of ECT is open to varied interpretations. Proponents of ECT maintain that it is a remarkably effective treatment for major depression (Prudic & Sackeim, 1999; Swartz, 1993). Moreover, they note that many patients who do not benefit from antidepressant medication improve in response to ECT (Isenberg & Zorumski, 2000). However, opponents of ECT argue that the available studies are flawed and inconclusive and that ECT is probably no more effective than a placebo (Breggin, 1991; Friedberg, 1983). Overall, there does seem to be enough favourable evidence to justify *conservative* use of ECT in treating severe mood disorders in patients who have not responded to medication (Metzger, 1999; Rudorfer & Goodwin, 1993). Unfortunately, relapse rates after ECT are distressingly high. Over 50% of patients relapse within 6 to 12 months, although relapse rates can be reduced by giving ECT patients antidepressant drugs (Sackeim et al., 2001).

Curiously, to the extent that ECT may be effective, no one is sure why. The discarded theories about how ECT works could fill several books. Many ECT advocates theorize that the treatment must affect neurotransmitter activity in the brain. However, the evidence supporting this view is fragmentary, inconsistent, and inconclusive (Abrams, 1992; Kapur & Mann, 1993). ECT opponents have a radically different, albeit equally unproven, explanation for why ECT might *appear* to be effective: They maintain that some patients find ECT so aversive that they muster all their willpower to climb out of their depression to avoid further ECT treatments.

Risks Associated with ECT

Even ECT proponents acknowledge that memory losses are common short-term side effects of electroconvulsive therapy (Lisanby et al., 2000; Weiner, 2000). However, ECT proponents assert that these deficits are mild and usually disappear within a month or two (Glass, 2001). A recent American Psychiatric Association (2001) task force concluded that there is no objective evidence that ECT causes structural damage in the brain or that it has any lasting negative effects on the ability to learn and remember information. In contrast, ECT critics maintain that ECT-induced cognitive deficits are often significant and sometimes permanent (Breggin, 1991; Rose et al., 2003), although their evidence seems to be largely anecdotal. Given the doubts that have been raised about the efficacy and risks of ECT, it appears that this treatment will remain controversial for some time to come.

CONCEPT CHECK 15.4

Understanding Biomedical Therapies

Check your understanding of biomedical therapies by matching each treatment with its chief use. The answers are in Appendix A.

Treatment

_____ **1.** Antianxiety drugs

_____ **2.** Antipsychotic drugs

_____ **3.** Antidepressant drugs

_____ **4.** Lithium

_____ **5.** Electroconvulsive therapy (ECT)

Chief purpose

a. To reduce psychotic symptoms

b. To bring a major depression to an end

c. To suppress tension, nervousness, and apprehension

d. To prevent future episodes of mania or depression in bipolar disorders

REVIEW OF KEY POINTS

- Biomedical therapies are physiological interventions for psychological problems. A great variety of disorders are treated with drugs. Antianxiety drugs are used to relieve excessive apprehension.

- Antipsychotic drugs are used primarily in the treatment of schizophrenia. Antidepressants are used to bring people out of episodes of depression. Lithium and other mood stabilizers are used to prevent the recurrence of episodes of disturbance in people with bipolar mood disorders.

- Drug therapies can be quite effective, but they have their drawbacks. All of the drugs produce side effects, and some of these side effects can be very troublesome. Some critics maintain that drugs' curative effects are superficial and that some drugs are overprescribed. Disturbing questions have been raised about the scientific impartiality of contemporary research on therapeutic drugs.

- Electroconvulsive therapy (ECT) is used to trigger a cortical seizure that is believed to have therapeutic value for mood disorders, especially depression. Evidence about the effectiveness and risks of ECT is contradictory, but the overall evidence seems sufficient to justify conservative use of the procedure.

Current Trends and Issues in Treatment

PREVIEW QUESTIONS

- What have researchers found when they have combined insight therapy and drug therapy?
- What is eclecticism in therapy?
- Why is therapy underutilized by some ethnic groups?

The controversy about ECT is only one of many contentious issues and shifting trends in the world of mental health care. In this section, we will discuss the continuing trend toward blending various approaches to therapy and efforts to respond more effectively to increasing cultural diversity in Western societies.

Blending Approaches to Treatment

In this chapter we have reviewed many approaches to treatment. However, there is no rule that a client must be treated with just one approach. Often, a clinician will use several techniques in working with a client. For example, a depressed person might receive cognitive therapy (an insight therapy), social skills training (a behaviour therapy), and antidepressant medication (a biomedical therapy). Multiple approaches are particularly likely when a treatment team provides therapy. Studies suggest that combining approaches to treatment has merit (Glass, 2004; Riba & Miller, 2003), as you will see in our Featured Study for this chapter.

The value of multiple approaches to treatment may explain why a significant trend seems to have crept into the field of psychotherapy: a movement away from strong loyalty to individual schools of thought and a corresponding move toward integrating various approaches to therapy (Norcross & Goldfried, 1992; D. A. Smith, 1999). Most clinicians used to depend exclusively on one system of therapy

Therapeutic Goals

Insights regarding unconscious conflicts and motives; resolution of conflicts; personality reconstruction

Increased congruence between self-concept and experience; acceptance of genuine self; self-determination and personal growth

Reduction of negative thinking; substitution of more realistic thinking

Elimination of maladaptive symptoms; acquisition of more adaptive responses

Elimination or reduction of symptoms; prevention of relapse

Therapeutic Techniques

Free association, dream analysis, interpretation, transference

Genuineness, empathy, unconditional positive regard, clarification, reflecting back to client

Thought stopping, recording of automatic thoughts, refuting of negative thinking, homework assignments

Classical and operant conditioning, systematic desensitization, aversive conditioning, social skills training, reinforcement, shaping, punishment, extinction, biofeedback

PhotoDisc/Getty Images

Antianxiety, antidepressant, and antipsychotic drugs; lithium; electroconvulsive therapy

Curiously, to the extent that ECT may be effective, no one is sure why. The discarded theories about how ECT works could fill several books. Many ECT advocates theorize that the treatment must affect neurotransmitter activity in the brain. However, the evidence supporting this view is fragmentary, inconsistent, and inconclusive (Abrams, 1992; Kapur & Mann, 1993). ECT opponents have a radically different, albeit equally unproven, explanation for why ECT might *appear* to be effective: They maintain that some patients find ECT so aversive that they muster all their willpower to climb out of their depression to avoid further ECT treatments.

Risks Associated with ECT

Even ECT proponents acknowledge that memory losses are common short-term side effects of electroconvulsive therapy (Lisanby et al., 2000; Weiner, 2000). However, ECT proponents assert that these deficits are mild and usually disappear within a month or two (Glass, 2001). A recent American Psychiatric Association (2001) task force concluded that there is no objective evidence that ECT causes structural damage in the brain or that it has any lasting negative effects on the ability to learn and remember information. In contrast, ECT critics maintain that ECT-induced cognitive deficits are often significant and sometimes permanent (Breggin, 1991; Rose et al., 2003), although their evidence seems to be largely anecdotal. Given the doubts that have been raised about the efficacy and risks of ECT, it appears that this treatment will remain controversial for some time to come.

CONCEPT CHECK 15.4

Understanding Biomedical Therapies

Check your understanding of biomedical therapies by matching each treatment with its chief use. The answers are in Appendix A.

Treatment

_____ 1. Antianxiety drugs

_____ 2. Antipsychotic drugs

_____ 3. Antidepressant drugs

_____ 4. Lithium

_____ 5. Electroconvulsive therapy (ECT)

Chief purpose

a. To reduce psychotic symptoms

b. To bring a major depression to an end

c. To suppress tension, nervousness, and apprehension

d. To prevent future episodes of mania or depression in bipolar disorders

Current Trends and Issues in Treatment

The controversy about ECT is only one of many contentious issues and shifting trends in the world of mental health care. In this section, we will discuss the continuing trend toward blending various approaches to therapy and efforts to respond more effectively to increasing cultural diversity in Western societies.

Blending Approaches to Treatment

In this chapter we have reviewed many approaches to treatment. However, there is no rule that a client must be treated with just one approach. Often, a clinician will use several techniques in working with a client. For example, a depressed person might receive cognitive therapy (an insight therapy), social skills training (a behaviour therapy), and antidepressant medication (a biomedical therapy). Multiple approaches are particularly likely when a treatment team provides therapy. Studies suggest that combining approaches to treatment has merit (Glass, 2004; Riba & Miller, 2003), as you will see in our Featured Study for this chapter.

The value of multiple approaches to treatment may explain why a significant trend seems to have crept into the field of psychotherapy: a movement away from strong loyalty to individual schools of thought and a corresponding move toward integrating various approaches to therapy (Norcross & Goldfried, 1992; D. A. Smith, 1999). Most clinicians used to depend exclusively on one system of therapy basis of this observation, which turned out to be inaccurate, von Meduna theorized that it might be useful to induce epileptic-like seizures in schizophrenic patients. Initially, a drug was used to trigger these seizures. However, by 1938 a pair of Italian psychiatrists (Cerletti & Bini, 1938) demonstrated that it was safer to elicit the seizures with electric shock. Thus, modern electroconvulsive therapy was born.

Electroconvulsive therapy **(ECT) is a biomedical treatment in which electric shock is used to produce a cortical seizure accompanied by convulsions.** In ECT, electrodes are attached to the skull over the temporal lobes of the brain (see the photo at right). A light anesthesia is induced, and the patient is given a variety of drugs to minimize the likelihood of complications. An electric current is then applied either to the right side or to both sides of the brain for about a second. Unilateral shock delivered to the right hemisphere is the preferred method of treatment today (Abrams, 2000). The current triggers a brief (about 30 seconds) convulsive seizure. The patient normally awakens in an hour or two and manifests some confusion, disorientation, and nausea, which usually clear up in a matter of hours. People typically receive between 6 and 20 treatments over a period of a month or so (Glass, 2001).

The clinical use of ECT peaked in the 1940s and 1950s, before effective drug therapies were widely available. ECT has long been controversial, and its use did decline in the 1960s and 1970s. Nonetheless, there has been a resurgence in the use of ECT, and it is not a rare form of therapy. Although only about 8% of psychiatrists administer ECT (Hermann et al., 1998), it is estimated that about 100 000 people receive ECT treatments yearly in the United States (Hermann et al., 1995). Some critics argue that ECT is overused because it is a lucrative procedure that boosts psychiatrists' income while consuming relatively little of their time in comparison to insight therapy (Frank, 1990). Conversely, some ECT advocates argue that ECT is underutilized because the public harbours many misconceptions about its risks and side effects (McDonald et al., 2004).

Controversy about ECT is also fuelled by patients' reports that the treatment is painful, dehumanizing, and terrifying. Substantial improvements in the administration of ECT have made it less disagreeable than it once was (Bernstein et al., 1998). Nonetheless, some patients continue to report that they find the treatment extremely aversive (Johnstone, 1999). Two personal reports by Canadians, one on each side of the controversy, are interesting places to begin your consideration of the use of ECT. One, written by Wendy Funk (1998), addresses concerns she has over her treatment.

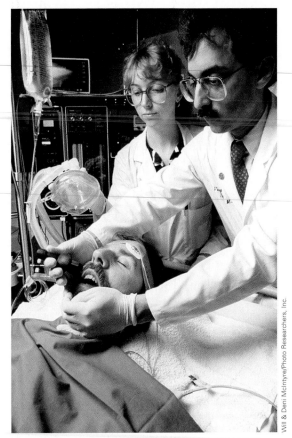

This patient is being prepared for electroconvulsive therapy (ECT). In ECT an electric shock is used to elicit a brief cortical seizure. The shock is delivered through electrodes attached to the patient's skull.

Will & Deni McIntyre/Photo Researchers, Inc.

The other, by Canadian psychologist Norman Endler (1982), whom we profiled in Chapter 14, is based on his own ECT treatment and is supportive of its use.

Effectiveness of ECT

The evidence on the therapeutic efficacy of ECT is open to varied interpretations. Proponents of ECT maintain that it is a remarkably effective treatment for major depression (Prudic & Sackeim, 1999; Swartz, 1993). Moreover, they note that many patients who do not benefit from antidepressant medication improve in response to ECT (Isenberg & Zorumski, 2000). However, opponents of ECT argue that the available studies are flawed and inconclusive and that ECT is probably no more effective than a placebo (Breggin, 1991; Friedberg, 1983). Overall, there does seem to be enough favourable evidence to justify *conservative* use of ECT in treating severe mood disorders in patients who have not responded to medication (Metzger, 1999; Rudorfer & Goodwin, 1993). Unfortunately, relapse rates after ECT are distressingly high. Over 50% of patients relapse within 6 to 12 months, although relapse rates can be reduced by giving ECT patients antidepressant drugs (Sackeim et al., 2001).

Therapy/founder

Roots of Disorders

Psychoanalysis

National Library of Medicine

Developed by Sigmund Freud in Vienna, from the 1890s through the 1930s

Intrapsychic conflict (among id, ego, and superego) → Anxiety → Reliance on defence mechanisms

Unconscious conflicts resulting from fixations in earlier development cause anxiety, which leads to defensive behaviour. The repressed conflicts typically centre on sex and aggression.

Client-centred therapy

Courtesy of Center for Studies of the Person

Created by Carl Rogers at the University of Chicago during the 1940s and 1950s

Need to distort shortcomings to feel worthy of affection → Relatively incongruent self-concept → Recurrent anxiety

Defensive behaviour protects inaccurate self-concept

Overdependence on acceptance from others fosters incongruence, which leads to anxiety and defensive behaviour and thwarts personal growth.

Cognitive therapy

Courtesy of Aaron T. Beck

Devised by Aaron Beck at the University of Pennsylvania in the 1960s and 1970s

Blame setbacks on personal inadequacies

Focus selectively on negative events

Make unduly pessimistic projections about future

Draw negative conclusions about personal worth

→ Increased vulnerability to depression

Pervasive negative thinking about events related to self fosters anxiety and depression.

Behaviour therapy

Courtesy of Dr. Joseph Wolpe

Launched primarily by South African Joseph Wolpe's description of systematic desensitization in 1958

CS
Bridge

UCS
Lightning strikes

CR
Fear
UCR

Maladaptive patterns of behaviour are acquired through learning. For example, many phobias are thought to be created through classical conditioning and maintained by operant conditioning.

Biomedical therapy

Many researchers contributed; key break-throughs in drug treatment made around 1950 by John Cade in Australia, Henri Laborit in France, and Jean Delay and Pierre Deniker, also in France

Overactivity at DA synapses may be caused by excessive release of DA or overabundance of DA receptor sites.

Most disorders are attributed to genetic predisposition and physiological malfunctions, such as abnormal neurotransmitter activity. For example, schizophrenia appears to be associated with overactivity at dopamine synapses.

Combining Insight Therapy and Medication

Depression is common in older people and contributes to physical health problems, chronic disability, and increased mortality among the elderly. Geriatric depression is also a highly recurrent problem. After successful treatment of depression, elderly patients tend to relapse more quickly and more frequently than younger clients. The purpose of this study was to determine whether a combination of insight therapy and antidepressant medication could reduce the recurrence of depression in an elderly population.

Method

Participants. The participants were 107 elderly patients diagnosed with recurrent, unipolar, major depression. The minimum age of the patients was 60 and the mean age at the beginning of the study was 67.6. The subjects had all been successfully treated for a recent episode of depression and had remained stable for four months.

Treatments. The medication employed in the study was *nortriptyline*, a tricyclic antidepressant that appears to be relatively effective and well tolerated in elderly populations. The insight therapy was *interpersonal psychotherapy (IPT)*, an approach to therapy that emphasizes the social roots of depression and focuses on how improved social relations can protect against depression (Klerman & Weissman, 1993). Clients learn how social isolation and unsatisfying interpersonal relationships can provoke depression and how confidants and supportive interactions can decrease vulnerability to depression.

Design. The subjects were randomly assigned to one of four maintenance treatment conditions: (1) monthly interpersonal therapy and medication, (2) medication alone, (3) monthly interpersonal therapy and placebo medication, and (4) placebo medication alone. A *double-blind* procedure was employed, so the clinicians who provided the treatments did not know which subjects were getting genuine medication as opposed to placebo pills. Patients remained in maintenance treatment for three years or until a recurrence of a major depressive episode.

Results

The relapse rates for the four treatment conditions are shown in Figure 15.9. The relapse rate for the combination of interpersonal therapy and medication was significantly less than that for either medication alone or interpersonal therapy alone (with placebo medication). The prophylactic value of the combined therapy proved most valuable to patients over 70 years of age and during the first year of the study, during which most relapses occurred.

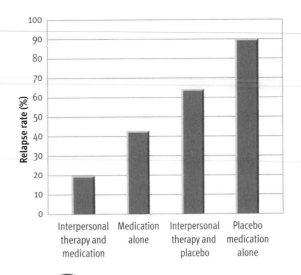

Figure 15.9

Relapse rates in the Reynolds et al. (1999) study. Following up over a period of three years, Reynolds et al. (1999) compared the preventive value of (1) monthly interpersonal therapy and medication, (2) medication alone, (3) monthly interpersonal therapy and placebo medication, and (4) placebo medication alone in a sample of elderly patients prone to recurrent depression. The combined treatment of insight therapy and medication yielded the lowest relapse rates and thus proved superior to either insight therapy or drug therapy alone. (Data from Reynolds et al., 1999)

Discussion

The authors conclude that "the continuation of combined medication and psychotherapy may represent the best long-term treatment strategy for preserving recovery in elderly patients with recurrent major depression" (p. 44). They speculate that the combined treatment may be "best-suited for dealing with both the biological and psychosocial substrates of old-age depression" (p. 45). However, they acknowledge the need for further research and recommend additional studies with newer antidepressant drugs (the SSRIs) that are increasingly popular.

Comment

This study was featured because it illustrated how to conduct a well-controlled experimental evaluation of the efficacy of therapeutic interventions. It also highlighted the value of combining approaches to treatment, which is a laudable trend in the treatment of psychological disorders. The fact that the study was published in the highly prestigious *Journal of the American Medical Association* also demonstrates how prominent and important research on therapeutic efficacy has become. ■

Investigators: Charles F. Reynolds III, Ellen Frank, James F. Perel, Stanley D. Imber, Cleon Cornes, Mark D. Miller, Sati Mazumdar, Patricia R. Houck, Mary Amanda Dew, Jacqueline A. Stack, Bruce G. Pollock, and David J. Kupfer (University of Pittsburgh Medical Center)

Source: Nortriptyline and interpersonal psychotherapy as maintenance therapies for recurrent major depression: A randomized controlled trial in patients older than 59 years. *Journal of the American Medical Association,* 1999, 281, 39–45.

while rejecting the utility of all others. This era of fragmentation may be drawing to a close. In recent surveys of psychologists' theoretical orientations, researchers have been surprised to find that the greatest proportion of respondents describe themselves as *eclectic* in approach (Garfield & Bergin, 1994).

Eclecticism in the practice of therapy involves drawing ideas from two or more systems of therapy instead of committing to just one system. Therapists can be eclectic in a number of ways (Arkowitz, 1992). Two common approaches are theoretical integration and technical eclecticism. In *theoretical integration*, two or more systems of therapy are combined or blended to take advantage of the strengths of each. Paul Wachtel's (1977, 1991) efforts to blend psychodynamic and behavioural therapies are a prominent example. *Technical eclecticism* involves borrowing ideas, insights, and techniques from a variety of sources while tailoring one's intervention strategy to the unique needs of each client. Advocates of technical eclecticism, such as Arnold Lazarus (1989, 1992, 1995), maintain that therapists should ask themselves, "What is the best approach for this specific client, problem, and situation?" and then adjust their strategy accordingly.

Increasing Multicultural Sensitivity in Treatment

Modern psychotherapy emerged during the second half of the 19th century in Europe and North America, spawned in part by a cultural milieu that viewed the self as an independent, reflective, rational being, capable of self-improvement (Cushman, 1992). Psychological disorders were assumed to have natural causes like physical diseases and to be amenable to medical treatments derived from scientific research. But the individualized, medicalized institution of modern psychotherapy reflects Western cultural values that are far from universal (Sue & Sue, 1999). In many nonindustrialized societies, psychological disorders are attributed to supernatural forces (possession, witchcraft, angry gods, and so forth), and victims seek help from priests, shamans, and folk healers, rather than doctors (Wittkower & Warnes, 1984). Thus, efforts to export Western psychotherapies to non-Western cultures have met with mixed success. Indeed, some even argue that the highly culture-bound origins of modern therapies have raised questions about their applicability to ethnic minorities *within* Western culture.

Research on how cultural factors influence the process and outcome of psychotherapy has burgeoned in recent years, motivated in part by the need to improve mental health services for ethnic

minority groups (Lee & Ramirez, 2000). The data are ambiguous for a couple of ethnic groups, but studies suggest that North American minority groups generally underutilize therapeutic services (Mays & Albee, 1992; Vega et al., 1999; Wells et al., 2001). Why? A variety of barriers appear to contribute to this problem, including the following (Sue, Zane, & Young, 1994; Takeuchi, Uehara, & Maramba, 1999; U.S. Department of Health and Human Services, 1999):

1. *Cultural barriers.* In times of psychological distress, some cultural groups are reluctant to turn to formal, professional sources of assistance. Given their socialization, they prefer to rely on informal assistance from family members, the clergy, respected elders, herbalists, acupuncturists, and so forth, who share their cultural heritage. Many members of minority groups have a history of frustrating interactions with bureaucracies and are distrustful of large, intimidating, foreign institutions, such as hospitals and community mental health centres (Pierce, 1992).

2. *Language barriers.* Effective communication is crucial to the provision of psychotherapy, yet most hospitals and mental health agencies are not adequately staffed with therapists who speak the languages used by minority groups in their service areas. The resulting communication problems make it awkward and difficult for many minority group members to explain their problems and to obtain the type of help that they need.

3. *Institutional barriers.* When all is said and done, Stanley Sue and Nolan Zane (1987) argue that the "single most important explanation for the problems in service delivery involves the inability of therapists to provide culturally responsive forms of treatment" (p. 37). The vast majority of therapists have been trained almost exclusively in the treatment of white, middle-class clients and are not familiar with the cultural backgrounds and unique characteristics of various ethnic groups. This culture gap often leads to misunderstandings and ill-advised treatment strategies (Hughes, 1993). Unfortunately, there is a grievous shortage of ethnic therapists to meet the needs of various ethnic groups (Mays & Albee, 1992).

Issues concerning diversity are of clear relevance to the Canadian context. Canada is a true multicultural society in which diversity is highlighted and championed. To get a sense of the extent of diversity in Canada, all you have to do is to look around you in your classroom at the diversity represented by your peers. Nowhere is this diversity more evident than in Toronto. Maxine Wintre and her colleagues recently surveyed 1071 first-year undergraduates in

Web Link 15.8

Aboriginal Mental Health Research Team

http://www.mcgill.ca/amh/

This McGill University–based group brings together community members (e.g., the Native Friendship Centre, the Cree Board of Health and Social Services, the Aboriginal Healing Centre) in partnership with mental health professionals to implement Aboriginal concerns in the mental health system.

Toronto concerning diversity issues and found that they represented 94 countries of origin, 69 languages spoken at home, and personal identifications with an amazing 203 cultural or ethnic groups (Wintre et al., 2000). When immigrant groups come to Canada, they are frequently met by a host of misconceptions and stereotypes such as those chronicled by the University of Toronto's Morton Beiser in his book on the "boat people's" first ten years in Canada (Beiser, 2000).

To treat their clients appropriately and effectively, clinicians need to be sensitive to diverse cultural conventions and sensitivities. This may be especially important with First Nations peoples. We saw in previous chapters that the suicide rate in some Aboriginal communities is extremely high, and these high suicide rates are accompanied by high rates of psychological disorders. In a study of First Nations, Métis, and Inuit peoples of Canada, McGill University's Laurence Kirmayer and his colleagues found elevated levels of many disorders and problems, including substance abuse, depression, violence, and suicide (Kirmayer, Brass, & Tait, 2000). The authors note that indigenous healing practices, often called *pan-Amerindian* healing movements, are increasingly visible and popular in Aboriginal treatment centres. They also note that therapy settings that fail to take into account indigenous experience are not effective: "In most urban areas, mental health services have not adapted well to the needs of Aboriginal clients and this is reflected in low rates of use" (Kirmayer et al., 2000, p. 612).

What can be done to improve mental health services for minority groups? Researchers in this area have offered a variety of suggestions (Hong, Garcia, & Soriano, 2000; Miranda et al., 2005; Pedersen, 1994; Yamamoto et al., 1993). Discussions of possible solutions usually begin with the need to recruit and train more ethnic minority therapists. Studies show that ethnic minorities are more likely to go to mental health facilities that are staffed by a higher proportion of people who share their ethnic background (Snowden & Hu, 1996; Sue et al., 1994). Furthermore, clients' satisfaction with therapy tends to be greater when they are treated by therapists from their own culture. Therapists can also be given special training to work more effectively with people from different cultural backgrounds.

According to the University of Calgary's Meyen Hertzsprung and Keith Dobson, past president of the Canadian Psychological Association, while there are a host of arguments for incorporating diversity issues into clinical psychology training in Canada, the process has been slow and difficult. In a survey examining the extent of diversity training in clinical programs in Canada, Hertzsprung and Dobson (2002) conclude that while clear progress has been made, much more needs to be done in this area: "Indeed, there is a need for further *indigenous* research on diversity issues in Canada, which has a unique history, population composition, and cultural base" (p. 190).

REVIEW OF KEY POINTS

- Combinations of insight, behavioural, and biomedical therapies are often used fruitfully in the treatment of psychological disorders. For example, our Featured Study showed how the tandem of interpersonal therapy and antidepressant medication could be valuable in preventing additional depressive episodes in an elderly population. Many modern therapists are eclectic, using specific ideas, techniques, and strategies gleaned from a number of theoretical approaches.

- The highly culture-bound origins of Western therapies have raised doubts about their applicability to other cultures and even to ethnic groups in Western society. Because of cultural, language, and access barriers, therapeutic services are underutilized by ethnic minorities in Canada.

- More culturally responsive approaches to treatment will require more minority therapists, special training for therapists, and additional investigation of how traditional therapies can be tailored to be more compatible with specific ethnic groups' cultural heritage.

Institutional Treatment in Transition

Traditionally, much of the treatment of mental illness has been carried out in institutional settings, primarily in mental hospitals. A *mental hospital* is a **medical institution specializing in providing inpatient care for psychological disorders.** In the United States, a national network of state-funded mental hospitals started to emerge in the 1840s through the efforts of Dorothea Dix and other reformers (see Figure 15.10). Prior to these reforms, the mentally ill who were poor were housed in jails and poorhouses or were left to wander the countryside. Dorothea Dix also played an important role in the treatment of those suffering from psychological disorders in Canada (Goldman, 1990).

Sable Island is a remote island 300 kilometres offshore from Halifax and was a place where some Nova Scotians sent their relatives—often without their consent—who suffered from psychological disorders. Dorothea Dix often spent her summers in St. John's and Halifax, where she heard about what were referred

PREVIEW QUESTIONS
- What led to the community mental health movement?
- What is deinstitutionalization, and what problems has it been blamed for?
- Is increased homelessness a mental health problem or an economic problem?

Figure 15.10

Dorothea Dix and the advent of mental hospitals in North America. During the 19th century, Dorothea Dix (inset) campaigned tirelessly to obtain funds for building mental hospitals in the United States and in some parts of Canada. Many of these hospitals were extremely large facilities. Although public mental hospitals improved the care of the mentally ill, they had a variety of shortcomings, which eventually prompted the deinstitutionalization movement.

SOURCE: Culver Pictures, Inc. (inset); Detail of painting in Harrisburg State Hospital, photo by Ken Smith/LLR Collection.

to at the time as the "banished lunatics." As soon as she heard about the situation, she set sail for Sable Island to see things for herself (Goldman, 1990). At the time, Nova Scotia was the only Canadian province without a major psychiatric hospital. Dix advocated for a psychiatric hospital before the Nova Scotia Legislature and even selected the site. It opened on December 26, 1857. She was not a woman to leave things unattended to—after noticing the inadequate life-saving resources available on the island to rescue the victims of shipwrecks, she also raised money and purchased lifeboats for Sable Island. Dix was also credited with helping to establish the psychiatric hospital in St. John's, employing there as elsewhere her formidable skills in persuasion and fundraising.

Today, mental hospitals continue to play an important role in the delivery of mental health services. However, since World War II, institutional care for mental illness has undergone a series of major transitions—and the dust hasn't settled yet. Let's look at how institutional care has evolved in recent decades.

Disenchantment with Mental Hospitals

By the 1950s, it had become apparent that public mental hospitals were not fulfilling their goals very well (Mechanic, 1980). Experts began to realize that hospitalization often *contributed* to the development of pathology instead of curing it.

What were the causes of these unexpected negative effects? Part of the problem was that the facilities were usually underfunded (Bloom, 1984). The lack of adequate funding meant that the facilities were overcrowded and understaffed. Hospital personnel were undertrained and overworked, making them hard-pressed to deliver minimal custodial care. Despite gallant efforts at treatment, the demoralizing conditions made most public mental hospitals decidedly nontherapeutic (Scull, 1990). These problems were aggravated by the fact that mental hospitals served large geographic regions, resulting in the fact that many patients were uprooted from their community and isolated from their social support networks.

Disenchantment with the public mental hospital system inspired the *community mental health movement* that emerged in the 1960s (Duckworth & Borus, 1999). The community mental health movement emphasizes (1) local, community-based care, (2) reduced dependence on hospitalization, and (3) the prevention of psychological disorders. Thus, in the 1960s much of the responsibility for the treatment of psychological disorders was turned over to community mental health centres, which supplement mental hospitals with decentralized and more accessible services.

Deinstitutionalization

Mental hospitals continue to care for many people troubled by chronic mental illness, but their role in patient care has diminished. Since the 1960s, a policy of deinstitutionalization has been followed in Canada, the United States, and most other Western countries (Fakhoury & Priebe, 2002). **Deinstitutionalization refers to transferring the treatment of mental illness from inpatient institutions to community-based facilities that emphasize outpatient care.** This shift in responsibility was made possible by two developments: (1) the emergence of effective drug therapies for severe disorders and (2) the deployment of community mental health centres to coordinate local care (Goff & Gudeman, 1999).

The exodus of patients from mental hospitals has been dramatic. In the United States, the average inpatient population in state and county mental hospitals dropped from a peak of nearly 550 000 in the mid-1950s to around 70 000 in the late 1990s, as shown in Figure 15.11. Similar trends have been observed in Canada. In their analysis of 40 years of deinstitutionalization in Canada, Patricia Sealy and Paul Whitehead from the University of Western Ontario note that deinstitutionalization is not just an event that took place in the 1960s—it has been continuous for the past four decades (Sealy & Whitehead, 2004). The number of beds in psychiatric hospitals per 100 000 population fell from four to one between 1964 and 1981, with Alberta and Quebec leading in the closings (Sealy & Whitehead, 2004). These trends, however, do not mean that hospitalization for mental illness has become a thing of the past. A great many people are still hospitalized, but there's been a shift toward placing them in local general hospitals for brief periods instead of distant psychiatric hospitals for long periods (Kiesler, 1992). When people are admitted to psychiatric hospitals or specialized units, they tend to stay for shorter periods of time. In Canada, the length of stay in psychiatric hospitals and on psychiatric units in general hospitals has decreased dramatically since 1985. In keeping with the philosophy of deinstitutionalization, these local facilities try to get patients stabilized and back into the community as swiftly as possible.

How has deinstitutionalization worked out? It gets mixed reviews. On the positive side, many people have benefited by avoiding or shortening disruptive and unnecessary hospitalization. Ample evidence suggests that alternatives to hospitalization can be both as effective as and less costly than inpatient care (McGrew et al., 1999; Reinharz, Lesage, & Contandriopoulos, 2000). Moreover, follow-up studies of discharged patients reveal that a substantial majority prefer the greater freedom provided by community-based treatment (Leff, Trieman, & Gooch, 1996).

Nonetheless, some unanticipated problems have arisen (Elpers, 2000; Munk-Jorgensen, 1999). Many patients suffering from chronic psychological disorders had nowhere to go when they were released. They had no families, friends, or homes to return to. Many had no work skills and were poorly prepared to live on their own. These people were supposed to be absorbed by "halfway houses," sheltered workshops, and other types of intermediate care facilities. Unfortunately, many communities were never able to fund and build the planned facilities (H. Lamb, 1998). Coordination of support services for the chronically

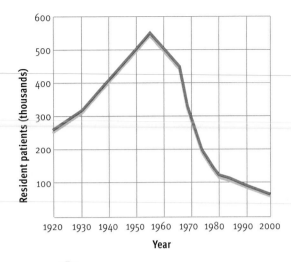

Figure 15.11

Declining inpatient population at U.S. public mental hospitals. The U.S. inpatient population in public mental hospitals has declined dramatically since the late 1950s, as a result of deinstitutionalization and the development of effective antipsychotic medication. (Data from the National Institute of Mental Health)

mentally ill has often been poor, and former patients have not been integrated effectively into their communities (Dewees, Pulice, & McCormick, 1996).

Thus, deinstitutionalization left two major problems in its wake: a "revolving door" population of people who flow in and out of psychiatric facilities, and a sizable population of homeless mentally ill people.

Mental Illness, the Revolving Door, and Homelessness

Although the proportion of hospital days attributable to mental illness has dwindled, admission rates for psychiatric hospitalization have actually climbed. What has happened? Deinstitutionalization and drug therapy have created a revolving door through which many mentally ill people pass again and again (Geller, 1992; Langdon et al., 2001).

Most of the people caught in the mental health system's revolving door suffer from chronic, severe disorders that frequently require hospitalization (Haywood et al., 1995). They respond well to drug therapies in the hospital, but once they're stabilized through drug therapy they no longer qualify for expensive hospital treatment according to the new standards created by deinstitutionalization. Thus, they're sent back out the door, into communities that often aren't prepared to provide adequate outpatient care. Because they lack appropriate care and support, their condition deteriorates and they soon require readmission to a hospital, where the cycle begins once again. Over two-thirds of all psychiatric inpatient admissions involve rehospitalizing a former patient.

Deinstitutionalization has also been blamed for the growing population of homeless people. Studies have consistently found elevated rates of mental illness among the homeless. Taken as a whole, the evidence suggests that roughly one-third of the homeless suffer from severe mental illness (schizophrenic and mood disorders), that another one-third or more are struggling with alcohol and drug problems, and that many qualify for multiple diagnoses (Bassuk et al., 1998; Haugland et al., 1997; Vazquez, Munoz, & Sanz, 1997).

The popular media routinely equate homelessness with mental illness, and it is widely assumed that deinstitutionalization is largely responsible for the rapid growth of homelessness in North America. Although deinstitutionalization probably has *contributed* to the growth of homelessness, many experts in this area maintain that it is misleading to blame the problem of homelessness chiefly on deinstitutionalization (Main, 1998; Sullivan, Burnam, & Koegel, 2000).

Those who criticize the tendency to equate homelessness with mental illness worry that this equation diverts attention from the real causes of the homelessness crisis (Kiesler, 1991). They marshal evidence to show that the sharp increase in the homeless population is due to a variety of economic, social, and political trends, including increased unemployment

and poverty, decreased support for welfare and subsidized housing programs, the loss of much low-income housing to urban renewal, and so forth (Cohen & Thompson, 1992; Mojtabai, 2005; Rossi, 1990). They maintain that homelessness is primarily an economic problem and that it requires economic solutions.

In light of the revolving door problem and homelessness among the mentally ill, what can we conclude about deinstitutionalization? It appears to be a worthwhile idea that has been poorly executed (H. Lamb, 1998). Overall, the policy has probably been a benefit to countless people with milder disorders but a cruel trick on many others with severe, chronic disorders. Ultimately, it's clear that our society is not providing adequate care for a sizable segment of the mentally ill population (Elpers, 2000; Torrey, 1996). That's not a new development. Inadequate care for mental illness has always been the norm. Societies always struggle with the problem of what to do with the mentally ill and how to pay for their care (Duckworth & Borus, 1999).

What's the solution? Virtually no one advocates returning to the era of custodial warehouses. Many do advocate increasing the quality and availability of intermediate care facilities and programs (Lamb, 1999). Research shows that intermediate care initiatives (such as outreach and case management programs) can be effective, but they require significant funding (Rosenheck, 2000). Only time will tell whether our society will be willing to make the financial commitment to follow through on this recommendation.

Putting It in Perspective

PREVIEW QUESTIONS
- How did this chapter illustrate the importance of cultural factors?
- How did this chapter illustrate the value of theoretical diversity?

In our discussion of psychotherapy, one of our unifying themes—the value of theoretical diversity—was particularly prominent, and one other theme—the importance of culture—surfaced briefly. Let's discuss the latter theme first. The approaches to treatment described in this chapter are products of modern, white, middle-class, Western culture. Some of these therapies have proven useful in some other cultures, but many have turned out to be irrelevant or counterproductive when used with different cultural groups, including ethnic minorities in Western

society. Thus, we have seen once again that cultural factors influence psychological processes and that Western psychology cannot assume that its theories and practices have universal applicability.

As for theoretical diversity, its value can be illustrated with a rhetorical question: Can you imagine what the state of modern psychotherapy would be if everyone in psychology and psychiatry had simply accepted Freud's theories about the nature and treatment of psychological disorders? If not for theoretical diversity, psychotherapy might still be in the dark ages. Psychoanalysis can be a useful method of therapy, but it would be a tragic state of affairs if it were the *only* treatment available. Multitudes of people have benefited from alternative approaches to treatment that emerged out of tensions between psychoanalytic theory and other theoretical perspectives. People have diverse problems, rooted in varied origins, that call for the pursuit of different therapeutic goals. Thus, it's fortunate that people can choose from a diverse array of approaches to treatment. The graphic overview on pages 644–645 summarizes and compares the approaches that we've discussed in this chapter. This summary chart shows that the major approaches to treatment each have their own vision of the nature of human discontent and the ideal remedy.

Of course, diversity can be confusing. The range and variety of available treatments in modern psychotherapy leaves many people puzzled about their options. Thus, in our Personal Application we'll sort through the practical issues involved in selecting a therapist.

REVIEW OF KEY POINTS

- Disenchantment with the negative effects of psychiatric hospitals led to the advent of more localized community mental health centres and a policy of deinstitutionalization. Long-term hospitalization for mental disorders is largely a thing of the past.

- Unfortunately, deinstitutionalization has left some unanticipated problems in its wake, including the revolving door problem and increased homelessness, although some theorists argue that homelessness is primarily an economic problem.

- Our discussion of psychotherapy highlighted the value of theoretical diversity. Conflicting theoretical orientations have generated varied approaches to treatment. Our coverage of therapy also showed once again that cultural factors shape psychological processes.

Looking for a Therapist

Answer the following "true" or "false."

___ **1.** Psychotherapy is an art as well as a science.

___ **2.** Psychotherapy can be harmful or damaging to a client.

___ **3.** Psychotherapy does not have to be expensive.

___ **4.** The type of professional degree that a therapist holds is relatively unimportant.

All of these statements are true. Do any of them surprise you? If so, you're in good company. Many people know relatively little about the practicalities of selecting a therapist.

The task of finding an appropriate therapist is complex. Should you see a psychologist or psychiatrist? Should you opt for individual therapy or group therapy? Should you see a client-centred therapist or a behaviour therapist? The unfortunate part of this situation is that people seeking psychotherapy often feel overwhelmed by personal problems. The last thing they need is to be confronted by yet another complex problem.

Nonetheless, the importance of finding a good therapist cannot be overestimated. Treatment can sometimes have harmful rather than helpful effects. We have already discussed how drug therapies and ECT can sometimes be damaging, but problems are not limited to these interventions. Talking about your problems with a therapist may sound pretty harmless, but studies indicate that insight therapies can also backfire (Lambert & Ogles, 2004; Singer & Lalich, 1996). Although a great many talented therapists are available, psychotherapy, like any other profession, has incompetent practitioners as well. Therefore, you should shop for a skilled therapist, just as you would for a good lawyer or a good mechanic.

In this Application, we'll go over some information that should be helpful if you ever have to look for a therapist for yourself or for a friend or family member (based on Beutler, Bongar, & Shurkin, 1998; Bruckner-Gordon, Gangi, & Wallman, 1988; Ehrenberg & Ehrenberg, 1994; Pittman, 1994).

Where Do You Find Therapeutic Services?

Psychotherapy can be found in a variety of settings. Contrary to general belief, most therapists are not in private practice. Many work in institutional settings such as community mental health centres, hospitals, and human service agencies. The principal sources of therapeutic services are described in Table 15.2. The exact configuration of therapeutic services available will vary from one community to another. To find out what your community has to offer, it is a good idea to consult your friends, your local phone book, or your local community mental health centre.

Is the Therapist's Profession or Sex Important?

Psychotherapists may be trained in psychology, psychiatry, social work, counselling, psychiatric nursing, or marriage and family therapy. Researchers have *not* found any reliable associations between therapists' professional background and therapeutic efficacy (Beutler et al., 2004), probably because many talented therapists can be found in all of these professions. Thus, the kind of degree that a therapist

Table 15.2 Principal Sources of Therapeutic Services

Source	Comments
Private practitioners	Self-employed therapists are listed in the Yellow Pages under their professional category, such as psychologists or psychiatrists. Private practitioners tend to be relatively expensive, but they also tend to be highly experienced therapists.
Community mental health centres	Community mental health centres have salaried psychologists, psychiatrists, and social workers on staff. The centres provide a variety of services and often have staff available on weekends and at night to deal with emergencies.
Hospitals	Several kinds of hospitals provide therapeutic services. There are both public and private mental hospitals that specialize in the care of people with psychological disorders. Many general hospitals have a psychiatric ward, and those that do not usually have psychiatrists and psychologists on staff and on call. Although hospitals tend to concentrate on inpatient treatment, many provide outpatient therapy as well.
Human service agencies	Various social service agencies employ therapists to provide short-term counselling. Depending on your community, you may find agencies that deal with family problems, juvenile problems, drug problems, and so forth.
Schools and workplaces	Most high schools and colleges have counselling centres where students can get help with personal problems. Similarly, some large businesses offer in-house counselling to their employees.

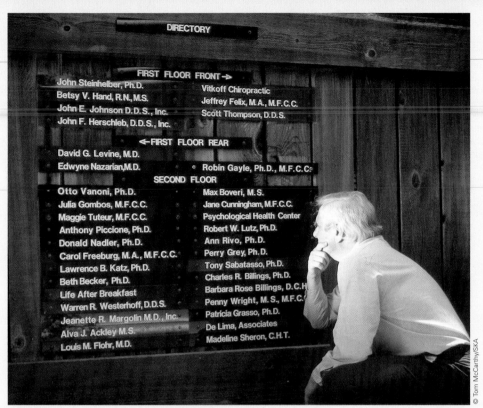

Finding the right therapist is no easy task. You need to take into account the therapist's training and orientation, fees charged, and personality. An initial visit should give you a good idea of what a particular therapist is like.

(Pope, Keith-Spiegel, & Tabachnick, 1986). These incidents almost always involve a male therapist making advances to a female client. The available evidence indicates that these sexual liaisons are usually very harmful to clients (Gabbard, 1994; Williams, 1992). There are absolutely no situations in which therapist–client sexual relations are an ethical therapeutic practice. If a therapist makes sexual advances, a client should terminate treatment.

Is Treatment Always Expensive?

Psychotherapy does not have to be prohibitively expensive. Private practitioners tend to be the most expensive, charging between $75 and $140 per (50-minute) hour. These fees may seem high, but they are in line with those of similar professionals, such as dentists and lawyers. Community mental health centres and social service agencies are usually supported by tax dollars. And as we mentioned earlier, provincial health-care programs often cover the services of a psychiatrist, but the services of psychologists in private practice are not universally covered.

holds doesn't need to be a crucial consideration in your selection process. At the present time, it is true that psychiatrists are the only type of therapist who can prescribe drugs. However, other types of therapists can refer you to a psychiatrist if they think that drug therapy would be helpful.

Whether a therapist's sex is important depends on your attitude. If *you* feel that the therapist's sex is important, then for you it is. The therapeutic relationship must be characterized by trust and rapport. Feeling uncomfortable with a therapist of one sex or the other could inhibit the therapeutic process. Hence, you should feel free to look for a male or female therapist if you prefer to do so. This point is probably most relevant to female clients whose troubles may be related to the extensive sexism in our society (A. Kaplan, 1985). It is entirely reasonable for women to seek a therapist with a feminist perspective if that would make them feel more comfortable.

Speaking of sex, you should be aware that sexual exploitation is an occasional problem in the context of therapy. Studies indicate that a small minority of therapists take advantage of their clients sexually

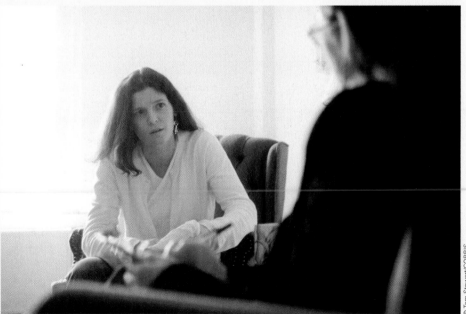

Therapy is both a science and an art. It is scientific in that practitioners are guided in their work by a huge body of empirical research. It is an art in that therapists often have to be creative in adapting their treatment procedures to individual patients and their idiosyncrasies.

Treatment of Psychological Disorders

Figure 15.12

Estimates of the effectiveness of various approaches to psychotherapy. Smith and Glass (1977) reviewed nearly 400 studies in which clients who were treated with a specific type of therapy were compared with a control group made up of individuals with similar problems who went untreated. The bars indicate the percentile rank (on outcome measures) attained by the average client treated with each type of therapy when compared to control subjects. The higher the percentile, the more effective the therapy was. As you can see, the various approaches were fairly similar in their overall effectiveness.

Source: Adapted from Smith, M. L., & Glass, G. V. (1977). Meta-analysis of psychotherapy outcome series. *American Psychologist, 32*, 752–760. Copyright © 1977 by the American Psychological Association. Adapted by permission of the author.

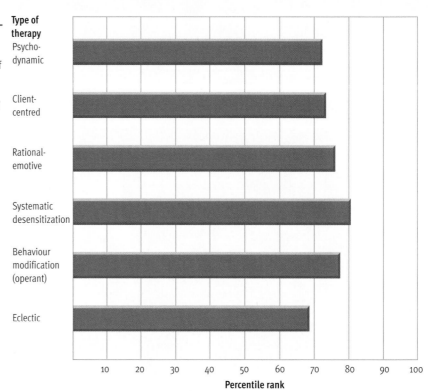

Is the Therapist's Theoretical Approach Important?

Logically, you might expect that the diverse approaches to therapy vary in effectiveness. For the most part, this is *not* what researchers find, however. After reviewing many studies of therapeutic efficacy, Jerome Frank (1961) and Lester Luborsky and his colleagues (1975) both quote the dodo bird who has just judged a race in *Alice in Wonderland*: "*Everybody* has won, and *all* must have prizes." Improvement rates for various theoretical orientations usually come out pretty close in most studies (Lambert, Bergin, & Garfield, 2004; Luborsky et al., 2002; Wampold, 2001; see Figure 15.12).

However, these findings are a little misleading, as the estimates of overall effectiveness have been averaged across many types of patients and many types of problems. Most experts seem to think that *for certain types of problems, some approaches to therapy are more effective than others* (Beutler, 2002; Crits-Christoph, 1997; Norcross, 1995).

For example, Martin Seligman (1995) asserts that panic disorders respond best to cognitive therapy, that specific phobias are most amenable to treatment with systematic desensitization, and that obsessive-compulsive disorders are best treated with behaviour therapy or medication. Thus, for a specific type of problem, a therapist's theoretical approach *may* make a difference.

It is also important to point out that the finding that different approaches to therapy are roughly equal in overall efficacy does not mean that all *therapists* are created equal. Some therapists unquestionably are more effective than others. However, these variations in effectiveness appear to depend on individual therapists' personal skills rather than on their theoretical orientation (Beutler et al., 2004). Good, bad, and mediocre therapists are found within each school of thought.

The key point is that effective therapy requires skill and creativity. Arnold Lazarus, who devised multimodal therapy, emphasizes that therapists "straddle the fence between science and art." Therapy is scientific in that interventions are based on extensive theory and empirical research (Forsyth & Strong, 1986). Ultimately, though, each client is a unique human being, and the therapist has to creatively fashion a treatment program that will help that individual.

What Should You Look for in a Prospective Therapist?

Some clients are timid about asking prospective therapists questions about their training, approach, fees, and so forth. However, these are reasonable questions, and the vast majority of therapists will be most accommodating in providing answers. Usually, you can ask your preliminary questions over the phone. If things seem promising, you may decide to make an appointment for an interview (for which you will probably have to pay). In this interview, the therapist will gather more information to determine the likelihood of helping you, given his or her training and approach to treatment. At the same time, you should be making a similar judgment about whether *you* believe the therapist can help you with your problems.

What should you look for? First, you should look for personal warmth and sincere concern. Try to judge whether you will be able to talk to this person in a candid, nondefensive way. Second, look for empathy and understanding. Is the person capable of appreciating your point of view? Third, look for self-confidence. Self-assured therapists will communicate a sense of competence without trying to intimidate you with jargon or boasting needlessly about what they can do for you. When all is said and done, you should *like* your therapist. Otherwise, it will be difficult to establish the needed rapport.

What If There Isn't Any Progress?

If you feel that your therapy isn't going anywhere, you should probably discuss these feelings with your therapist. Don't be surprised, however, if the therapist suggests that it may be your own fault. The concept of *resistance* originally described by Freud has some validity (Beutler et al., 2001).

Some clients *do* have difficulty facing up to their problems. Thus, if your therapy isn't progressing, you may need to *consider* whether your resistance may be slowing progress. This self-examination isn't easy, as you are not an unbiased observer. Some common signs of resistance identified by Ehrenberg and Ehrenberg (1994) are listed in Figure 15.13.

Given the very real possibility that poor progress may be due to resistance, you should not be too quick to leave therapy when dissatisfied. However, it *is* possible that your therapist isn't sufficiently skilled or that the two of you are incompatible. Thus, after careful and deliberate consideration, you should feel free to terminate your therapy.

What Is Therapy Like?

It is important to have realistic expectations about therapy, or you may be unnecessarily disappointed. Some people expect miracles. They expect to turn their life around quickly with little effort. Others expect their therapist to run their life for them. These are unrealistic expectations.

Therapy is usually a slow process. Your problems are not likely to melt away quickly. Moreover, therapy is hard work, and your therapist is only a facilitator. Ultimately, *you* have to confront the challenge of changing your behaviour, your feelings, or your personality. This process may not be pleasant. You may have to face up to some painful truths about yourself. As Ehrenberg and Ehrenberg (1986) point out, "Psychotherapy takes time, effort, and courage."

REVIEW OF KEY POINTS

- Therapeutic services are available in many settings, and such services need not be expensive. Both excellent and mediocre therapists can be found in all of the mental health professions. Thus, therapists' personal skills are more important than their professional degree.

- The various theoretical approaches to therapy appear to be fairly similar in overall effectiveness. However, for certain types of problems, some approaches are probably more effective than others, and all therapists are not created equal.

- In selecting a therapist, warmth, empathy, confidence, and likability are desirable traits, and it is reasonable to insist on a therapist of one sex or the other. If progress is slow, your own resistance may be the problem.

Figure 15.13

Signs of resistance. Resistance in therapy may be subtle, but Ehrenberg and Ehrenberg (1994) have identified some telltale signs to look for.

Signs of resistance in therapy
If you're dissatisfied with your progress in therapy, resistance may be the problem when:
1 You have nothing specific or concrete to complain about.
2 Your attitude about therapy changes suddenly just as you reach the truly sensitive issues.
3 You've had the same problem with other therapists in the past.
4 Your conflicts with the therapist resemble those that you have with other people.
5 You start hiding things from your therapist.

CRITICAL THINKING APPLICATION

From Crisis to Wellness— But Was It the Therapy?

It often happens this way. Problems seem to go from bad to worse—the trigger could be severe pressures at work, an acrimonious fight with your spouse, or a child's unruly behaviour spiralling out of control. At some point, you recognize that it might be prudent to seek professional assistance from a therapist, but where do you turn? If you are like most people, you will probably hesitate before actively seeking professional help. People hesitate because therapy carries a stigma, because the task of finding a therapist is daunting, and because they hope that their psychological problems will clear up on their own—which *does* happen with some regularity. When people finally decide to pursue mental health care, it is often because they feel like they have reached rock bottom in terms of their functioning and they have no choice. Motivated by their crisis, they enter into treatment, looking for a ray of hope. Will therapy help them feel better?

It may surprise you to learn that the answer *generally* would be "yes," even if professional treatment itself were utterly worthless and totally ineffectual. There are two major reasons that people entering therapy are likely to get better, regardless of whether their treatment is effective. You can probably guess one of these reasons, which has been mentioned repeatedly in the chapter: the power of the *placebo*. **Placebo effects** occur when people's expectations lead them to experience some change even though they receive a fake treatment (like getting a sugar pill instead of a real drug). Clients generally enter therapy with expectations that it will have positive effects, and as we have emphasized throughout this text, *people have a remarkable tendency to see what they expect to see*. Because of this factor, studies of the efficacy of medical drugs always include a placebo condition in which subjects are given fake medication (see Chapter 2). Researchers are often quite surprised by just how much the placebo subjects improve (Fisher & Greenberg, 1997; Walsh et al., 2002). Placebo effects can be very powerful and should be taken into consideration whenever efforts are made to evaluate the efficacy of some approach to treatment.

The other factor at work is the main focus in this Application. It is an interesting statistical phenomenon that we have not discussed previously: *regression toward the mean*. **Regression toward the mean occurs when people who score extremely high or low on some trait are measured a second time and their new scores fall closer to the mean (average).** Regression effects work in both directions: On the second measurement high scorers tend to fall back toward the mean and low scorers tend to creep upward toward the mean. For example, let's say we wanted to evaluate the effectiveness of a one-day coaching program intended to improve performance on a new high-school math test. We reason that coaching is most likely to help students who have performed poorly on the test, so we recruit a sample of participants who have previously scored in the bottom 20% on the test. Thanks to regression toward the mean, most of these students will score higher if they take that test a second time, so our coaching program may *look* effective even if it has no value. By the way, if we set out to see whether our coaching program could increase the performance of high scorers, regression effects would be working *against* us. If we recruited a sample of students who had scored in the upper 20% on the math test, there would be a tendency for their scores to move downward when tested a second time, which could cancel out most or all of the beneficial effects of the coaching program. The processes underlying regression toward the mean are complex matters of probability, but they can be approximated by a simple principle: If you are near the bottom, there's almost nowhere to go but up, and if you are near the top, there's almost nowhere to go but down.

What does all of this have to do with the effects of professional treatment for psychological problems and disorders? Well, chance variations in the ups and downs of life occur for all of us. But recall that most people enter psychotherapy during a time of severe crisis, when they are at a really low point in their lives. If you measure the mental health of a group of people entering therapy, they will mostly get relatively low scores. If you measure their mental health again a few months later, chances are that most of them will score higher—with or without therapy—because of regression toward the mean. This is not a matter of idle speculation. Studies of untreated subjects demonstrate that poor scores on measures of mental health regress toward the mean when participants are assessed a second time (Flett, Vredenburg, & Krames, 1995; Hsu, 1995).

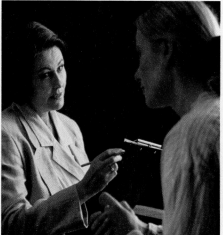

Placebo effects and regression toward the mean are two prominent factors that make it difficult to evaluate the efficacy of various approaches to therapy.

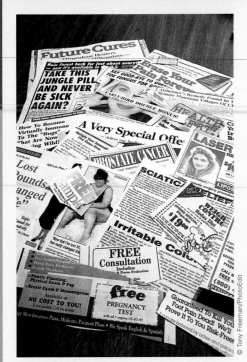

In North American society we are frequently exposed to claims of programs that will improve our wellness. Rigorous and systematic scientific research is the only way to verify these claims.

Does the fact that most people will get better even if there is no therapy mean that there is no sound evidence that psychotherapy works? No, regression effects, along with placebo effects, do create major headaches for researchers evaluating the efficacy of various therapies, but these problems *can* be circumvented. Control groups, random assignment, placebo conditions, and statistical adjustments can be used to control for regression and placebo effects, as well as for other threats to validity. As discussed in the main body of the chapter, researchers have accumulated rigorous evidence that most approaches to therapy have demonstrated efficacy. However, our discussion of placebo and regression effects shows you some of the factors that make this type of research far more complicated and challenging than might be anticipated.

Recognizing how regression toward the mean can occur in a variety of contexts is an important critical thinking skill, so let's look at some additional examples. Think about an outstanding young pro baseball player who has a fabulous first season and is named "Rookie of the Year." What sort of performance would you predict for this athlete for the next year? Before you make your prediction, think about regression toward the mean. Statistically speaking, our Rookie of the Year is likely to perform well above average the next year, but not as well as he did in his first year. If you are a sports fan, you may recognize this pattern as the "sophomore slump." Many sports columnists have written about the sophomore slump, which they typically blame on the athlete's personality or motivation ("He got lazy," "He got cocky," "The money and fame went to his head," and so forth). A simple appeal to regression toward the mean could explain this sort of outcome, with no need to denigrate the personality or motivation of the athlete. Of course, sometimes the Rookie of the Year performs even better during his second year. Thus, our baseball example can be used to emphasize an important point. Regression toward the mean is not an inevitability. It is a statistical tendency that predicts what will happen far more often than not, but it is merely a matter of probability—which means it is a much more reliable principle when applied to groups (say, the top ten rookies in a specific year) rather than to individuals.

Let's return to the world of therapy for one last thought about the significance of both regression and placebo effects. Over the years, a host of quacks, charlatans, con artists, herbalists, and faith healers have marketed and sold an endless array of worthless treatments for both psychological problems and physical maladies. In many instances, people who have been treated with these phony therapies have expressed satisfaction or even praise and gratitude. For instance, you may have heard someone sincerely rave about some herbal remedy or psychic advice that you were pretty sure was really worthless. If so, you were probably puzzled by their glowing testimonials. Well, you now have two highly plausible explanations for why people can honestly believe that they have derived great benefit from harebrained, bogus treatments: placebo effects and regression effects. The people who provide testimonials for worthless treatments may have experienced *genuine* improvements in their conditions, but those improvements were probably the results of placebo effects and regression toward the mean. Placebo and regression effects add to the many reasons that you should always be skeptical about anecdotal evidence. And they help explain why charlatans can be so successful and why unsound, ineffective treatments can have sincere proponents.

Table 15.3 Critical Thinking Skills Discussed in This Application

Skill	Description
Recognizing situations in which placebo effects might occur	The critical thinker understands that if people have expectations that a treatment will produce a certain effect, they may experience that effect even if the treatment was fake or ineffectual.
Recognizing situations in which regression toward the mean may occur	The critical thinker understands that when people are selected for their extremely high or low scores on some trait, their subsequent scores will probably fall closer to the mean.
Recognizing the limitations of anecdotal evidence	The critical thinker is wary of anecdotal evidence, which consists of personal stories used to support one's assertions. Anecdotal evidence tends to be unrepresentative, inaccurate, and unreliable.

RECAP

Key Ideas

The Elements of the Treatment Process

● Approaches to treatment are diverse, but they can be grouped into three categories: insight therapies, behaviour therapies, and biomedical therapies.

● Therapists come from a variety of professional backgrounds. Clinical and counselling psychologists, psychiatrists, clinical social workers, psychiatric nurses, counsellors, and marriage and family therapists are key providers of therapeutic services.

Insight Therapies

● Insight therapies involve verbal interactions intended to enhance self-knowledge. In psychoanalysis, free association and dream analysis are used to explore the unconscious. When an analyst's probing hits sensitive areas, resistance can be expected.

● The transference relationship may be used to overcome this resistance so that the client can handle interpretations that lead to insight. Classical psychoanalysis is not widely practised anymore, but Freud's legacy lives on in a rich diversity of modern psychodynamic therapies.

● The client-centred therapist tries to provide a supportive climate in which clients can restructure their self-concept. The process of therapy emphasizes clarification of the client's feelings and self-acceptance.

● Beck's cognitive therapy concentrates on changing the way clients think about events in their lives. Cognitive therapists re-educate clients to detect and challenge automatic negative thoughts that cause depression and anxiety.

● Most theoretical approaches to insight therapy have been adapted for use with groups. Evaluating the effectiveness of any approach to treatment is complex and difficult. Nonetheless, the weight of the evidence suggests that insight therapies are superior to no treatment or placebo treatment. Studies suggest that common factors make a significant contribution to the benefits of various therapies.

Behaviour Therapies

● Behaviour therapies use the principles of learning in direct efforts to change specific aspects of behaviour. Wolpe's systematic desensitization is a counterconditioning treatment for phobias. In aversion therapy, a stimulus associated with an unwanted response is paired with an unpleasant stimulus in an effort to eliminate the maladaptive response.

● Social skills training can improve clients' interpersonal skills through shaping, modelling, and behavioural rehearsal. There is ample evidence that behaviour therapies are effective in the treatment of a wide variety of disorders.

Biomedical Therapies

● Biomedical therapies are physiological interventions for psychological problems. Antianxiety drugs are used to relieve excessive apprehension. Antipsychotic drugs are used primarily in the treatment of schizophrenia. Antidepressants are used to bring people out of episodes of depression. Bipolar mood disorders are treated with lithium and other mood stabilizers.

● Drug therapies can be quite effective, but they have their drawbacks. All of the drugs produce problematic side effects. The adverse effects of psychiatric drugs may be underestimated because pharmaceutical research is not as impartial as it should be.

● Electroconvulsive therapy (ECT) is used to trigger a cortical seizure that is believed to have therapeutic value for mood disorders, especially depression. There is contradictory evidence about the effectiveness and risks of ECT.

Current Trends and Issues in Treatment

● Combinations of insight, behavioural, and biomedical therapies are often used fruitfully in the treatment of psychological disorders. Many modern therapists are eclectic, using specific ideas, techniques, and strategies gleaned from a number of theoretical approaches.

● Because of cultural, language, and access barriers, therapeutic services are underutilized by ethnic minorities. However, the crux of the problem is the failure of institutions to provide culturally sensitive and responsive forms of treatment for ethnic minorities.

Institutional Treatment in Transition

● Disenchantment with the negative effects of mental hospitals led to the advent of more localized community mental health centres and a policy of deinstitutionalization. Long-term hospitalization for mental disorders is largely a thing of the past.

● Unfortunately, deinstitutionalization has left some unanticipated problems in its wake, such as the revolving door problem and increased homelessness. However, many theorists believe that homelessness is primarily an economic problem.

Putting It in Perspective

● Our discussion of psychotherapy highlighted the value of theoretical diversity. Conflicting theoretical orientations have generated varied approaches to treatment. Our coverage of therapy also showed once again that cultural factors shape psychological processes.

Personal Application • **Looking for a Therapist**

● Therapeutic services are available in many settings, and such services need not be expensive. Excellent therapists and mediocre therapists can be found in all of the mental health professions, using the full range of therapeutic approaches.

● In selecting a therapist, warmth, empathy, confidence, and likability are desirable traits, and it is reasonable to insist on a therapist of one sex or the other. If progress is slow, your own resistance may be the problem.

Critical Thinking Application • **From Crisis to Wellness—But Was It the Therapy?**

● People entering therapy are likely to get better even if their treatment is ineffective because of placebo effects and regression toward the mean.

● Regression toward the mean occurs when people selected for their extremely high or low scores on some trait are measured a second time and their new scores fall closer to the mean. Regression and placebo effects may also help explain why people can often be deceived by phony, ineffectual treatments.

Key Terms

Antianxiety drugs, 639
Antidepressant drugs, 641
Antipsychotic drugs, 640
Aversion therapy, 636
Behaviour therapies, 635
Biomedical therapies, 638
Client-centred therapy, 629
Cognitive therapy, 631
Deinstitutionalization, 650
Dream analysis, 627
Eclecticism, 648
Electroconvulsive therapy (ECT), 643
Free association, 627
Group therapy, 632
Insight therapies, 627
Interpretation, 628
Lithium, 641
Mental hospital, 649
Placebo effects, 658
Psychiatrists, 626
Psychoanalysis, 627
Psychopharmacotherapy, 639
Regression toward the mean, 658
Resistance, 628
Social skills training, 637
Spontaneous remission, 633
Systematic desensitization, 636
Tardive dyskinesia, 640
Transference, 628

Key People

Aaron Beck, 631
Dorothea Dix, 649
Keith Dobson, 626
Hans Eysenck, 633
Sigmund Freud, 627
Les Greenberg, 630
Donald Meichenbaum, 631
Carl Rogers, 629
Joseph Wolpe, 636

PRACTICE TEST

1. The goal of behaviour therapy is to:
   A. identify the early childhood unconscious conflicts that are the source of the client's symptoms.
   B. change the client's thought patterns so that negative emotions can be controlled.
   C. alter the frequency of specific problematic responses by using conditioning techniques.
   D. alter the client's brain chemistry by prescribing specific drugs.

2. After undergoing psychoanalysis for several months, Karen has suddenly started "forgetting" to attend her therapy sessions. Karen's behaviour is most likely a form of:
   A. resistance.   C. insight.
   B. transference.   D. catharsis.

3. Because Suzanne has an unconscious sexual attraction to her father, she behaves seductively toward her therapist. Suzanne's behaviour is most likely a form of:
   A. resistance.   C. misinterpretation.
   B. transference.   D. an unconscious defence mechanism.

4. The key task of the client-centred therapist is:
   A. interpretation of the client's thoughts, feelings, memories, and behaviours.
   B. clarification of the client's feelings.
   C. confrontation of the client's irrational thoughts.
   D. modification of the client's problematic behaviours.

5. A therapist openly challenges a client's statement that she is a failure as a woman because her boyfriend left her, insisting that she justify it with evidence. Which type of therapy is probably being used?
   A. psychodynamic therapy   C. behaviour therapy
   B. client-centred therapy   D. cognitive therapy

6. Based on a review of numerous studies of therapeutic outcome, Eysenck (1952) concluded that the recovery rate for neurotics treated with:
   A. insight therapy was about the same as the spontaneous remission rate for neurotic disorders.
   B. insight therapy was significantly higher than the spontaneous remission rate for neurotic disorders.
   C. group therapy was significantly higher than the recovery rate for neurotics treated with individual therapy.
   D. individual therapy was significantly higher than the recovery rate for neurotics treated with group therapy.

7. Systematic desensitization is particularly effective for the treatment of _____ disorders.
   A. generalized anxiety   C. obsessive-compulsive
   B. panic   D. phobic

8. Linda's therapist has her practise active listening skills in structured role-playing exercises. Later, Linda is gradually asked to practise these skills with family members, friends, and finally, her boss. Linda is undergoing:
   A. systematic desensitization.   C. a token economy procedure.
   B. biofeedback.   D. social skills training.

9. After being released from a hospital, many schizophrenic patients stop taking their antipsychotic medication because:
   A. their mental impairment causes them to forget.
   B. of the unpleasant side effects.
   C. most schizophrenics don't believe they are ill.
   D. all of the above.

10. Selective serotonin reuptake inhibitors (SSRIs) can be effective in the treatment of _____ disorders.
    A. depressive   C. obsessive-compulsive
    B. schizophrenic   D. both a and c

11. Modern psychotherapy:
    A. was spawned by a cultural milieu that viewed the self as an independent, rational being.
    B. embraces universal cultural values.
    C. has been successfully exported to many non-Western cultures.
    D. both b and c.

12. The community mental health movement emphasizes:
    A. segregation of the mentally ill from the general population.
    B. increased dependence on long-term inpatient care.
    C. local care and the prevention of psychological disorders.
    D. all of the above.

13. Many people repeatedly go in and out of mental hospitals. Typically, such people are released because _____; they are eventually readmitted because _____.
    A. they have been stabilized through drug therapy; their condition deteriorates once again because of inadequate outpatient care
    B. they run out of funds to pay for hospitalization; they once again can afford it
    C. they have been cured of their disorder; they develop another disorder
    D. they no longer want to be hospitalized; they voluntarily recommit themselves

14. The type of professional training a therapist has:
    A. is the most important indicator of his or her competence.
    B. should be the major consideration in choosing a therapist.
    C. is not all that important, since talented therapists can be found in all of the mental health professions.
    D. both a and b.

15. Which of the following could be explained by regression toward the mean?
    A. You get an average bowling score in one game and a superb score in the next game.
    B. You get an average bowling score in one game and a very low score in the next game.
    C. You get an average bowling score in one game and another average score in the next game.
    D. You get a terrible bowling score in one game and an average score in the next game.

See Appendix A for answers to this Practice Test.

 ON THE WEB

For additional resources on the topics covered in this chapter, visit the *Psychology: Themes and Variations* Web site, where you will find practice quizzes, tutorials, Web links, simulations, critical thinking activities, flash cards, interactive exercises, and suggested readings available through INFOTRAC.

http://www.themesandvariations.nelson.com

 Thomson NOW!   http://hed.nelson.com

Go to this site for the link to ThomsonNOW™, your one-stop study shop. Take a Pretest for this chapter and ThomsonNOW™ will generate a personalized Study Plan based on your test results! The Study Plan will identify the topics you need to review and direct you to online resources to help you master those topics. You can then take a Posttest to help you determine the concepts you have mastered and what you still need work on.

CHAPTER 16

Latchezar Boyadjiev, *Dance,* L.B. Glass Studios

Person Perception: Forming Impressions of Others
Effects of Physical Appearance
Cognitive Schemas
Stereotypes
Subjectivity in Person Perception
An Evolutionary Perspective on Bias in Person Perception

Attribution Processes: Explaining Behaviour
Internal versus External Attributions
Attributions for Success and Failure
Bias in Attribution
Culture and Attributional Tendencies

Close Relationships: Liking and Loving
Key Factors in Attraction
Perspectives on the Mystery of Love
Culture and Close Relationships
An Evolutionary Perspective on Attraction

Attitudes: Making Social Judgments
Components and Dimensions of Attitudes
Attitudes and Behaviour
Trying to Change Attitudes: Factors in Persuasion
Theories of Attitude Formation and Change

Conformity and Obedience: Yielding to Others
Conformity
Obedience
Featured Study • "I Was Just Following Orders"
Cultural Variations in Conformity and Obedience

Behaviour in Groups: Joining with Others
Behaviour Alone and in Groups: The Case of the Bystander Effect
Group Productivity and Social Loafing
Decision Making in Groups

Putting It in Perspective

Personal Application • **Understanding Prejudice**
Stereotyping and Subjectivity in Person Perception
Biases in Attribution
Forming and Preserving Prejudicial Attitudes
Dividing the World into Ingroups and Outgroups

Critical Thinking Application • **Whom Can You Trust?**
Analyzing Credibility and Social Influence Tactics
Evaluating Credibility
Recognizing Social Influence Strategies

Recap

Practice Test

Social Behaviour

The Canadian Charter of Rights and Freedoms (1982) establishes equality before and under the law and equal protection and benefits of the law. It acts as a standard for the treatment of persons in Canada. This is of critical importance when considering racism, stereotyping, and prejudice, which exist at all levels within Canada. Consider the complaint brought against a Quebec firm early in the 21st century.

The Centre Maraîcher Eugène Guinois Jr. is located outside of Montreal and is one of Canada's largest commercial vegetable farms, comprising about 530 hectares. At the centre of the complaint were allegations made by four black farm workers that the working conditions at the farm included segregation, racism, and neglect. They alleged that there were two cafeterias—one for the whites and one for the black workers. The blacks' cafeteria was unheated and lacked running water, proper toilets, and refrigeration facilities (Patriquin, 2005). The black farm workers stated that they were the victims of verbal and physical abuse and racist graffiti. During harvest time, black farm workers were bussed in from Longueuil, and they were referred to as the "workers from Longueuil." One full-time black employee, Celissa Michel, reported that when he tried to heat his food in the whites' cafeteria, he was pushed out. Another black worker who tried to sit at the picnic tables near the cafeteria was told by the owner's wife that those tables were only for *Quebecers*. Michel commented on the experience, "It's frustrating and it hurts, but I had to stay there and just take it" (Patriquin, 2005, p. A9).

The circumstances considered by the Human Rights Tribunal in Quebec seemed more the stuff of fiction, or events that might have transpired in the southern United States in the early to middle part of the last century—not in Canada and surely not now. The presiding judge, Michèle Pauze, felt compelled to contextualize her decision with the following: "The events you are going to read happened here, in Quebec, during the years 2000 and 2001" (Patriquin, 2005, p. A1).

While it may not be consistent with Canadians' views of themselves or their country, stereotyping, prejudice, and discrimination can be found here, as in other countries. In a poll conducted by Ipsos-Reid in March 2005, one in six Canadians reported that they had been the victim of racism (*Globe and Mail*, 2005). A recent study by a University of Toronto criminologist on racial profiling found that black motorists and pedestrians in Kingston, Ontario, were four times more likely to be stopped than were whites (Appleby, 2005). The Toronto Police Services annual report on hate crimes indicated that, although 2004 was a good year on average since the number of hate crimes reported was below the 12-year average, the number of hate crimes in 2004 increased 12% over 2003 levels. The most frequent victims of reported hate crimes were Jews.

Racism is an important issue in Canada. Historically, we can see this in the marginalization of Asian immigrants. This was reflected in the treatment of the Chinese immigrants who helped build the Canadian Pacific Railway and the internment and loss of rights and property of Japanese Canadians during World War II. Aboriginal peoples have often been the targets of racism and stereotyping, and the effects of the residential school policy are still being felt.

Canada is a country of diversity and, according to University of Western Ontario psychologists Victoria

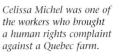
Image by John Morstad

Celissa Michel was one of the workers who brought a human rights complaint against a Quebec farm.

NEL

Social Behaviour **663**

Saba Safdar from the University of Guelph conducts research in the area of cross-cultural psychology.

Esses and Bob Gardner (Esses & Gardner, 1996), the ethnic composition of Canada is changing with an increase in the proportion of visible minorities. By 2017, it is projected that 20% of Canadians will be members of a visible minority (Statistics Canada, 2005b). The increase in visible minorities is fuelled by immigration, with about 70% of those identifying themselves as members of a visible minority in 2001 being born outside of Canada. Members of visible minorities are often the targets of racism and, according to research by the University of Guelph's Saba Safdar, they have specific stressors that are tied to their status (Safdar & Lay, 2003). In addition, emigrating from another country may challenge immigrants to weigh traditional values against the new values they find. Social psychologists such as Richard Lalonde have studied the effects of cultural identity and family cultural influence on relationship partner choice (Lalonde et al., 2004).

How are we to make sense of stereotyping, prejudice, and discrimination? What factors lead to such negative attitudes toward others? How do these attitudes affect our behaviour? Is there anything we can do to change such negative outcomes? These are just some of the issues we will be concerned with in this chapter, in which we examine social psychology. **Social psychology is the branch of psychology concerned with the way individuals' thoughts, feelings, and behaviours are influenced by others.** Our coverage of social psychology will focus on six broad topics:

- *Person perception.* How do we formulate our ideas about what others are like? To what extent do people's expectations colour their impressions of others?

- *Attribution processes.* Whenever we observe the behaviour of others or reflect on our own behaviour, we often make attributions about that behaviour. How do people use attributions to explain social behaviour?
- *Interpersonal attraction.* What factors affect our attraction to other people? Why do we wish to have relationships with some people and not others? What role do things such as similarity play in our attraction toward specific other people?
- *Attitudes.* How are attitudes formed? What leads to attitude change? How do attitudes affect people's behaviour?
- *Conformity and obedience.* What factors influence conformity? Can people be coaxed into doing things that contradict their values?
- *Behaviour in groups.* We all belong to various groups. Do people behave differently when they are in groups as opposed to when they are alone? Why do people in groups often think alike?

Social psychologists study how people are affected by the actual, imagined, or implied presence of others. Their interest is not limited to individuals' interactions with others, as people can engage in social behaviour even when they're alone. For instance, if you were driving by yourself on a deserted highway and tossed your trash out your car window, your littering would be a social action. It would defy social norms, reflect your socialization and attitudes, and have repercussions (albeit small) for other people in your society. Social psychologists often study individual behaviour in a social context. This interest in understanding individual behaviour should be readily apparent in our first section, on person perception.

Person Perception: Forming Impressions of Others

PREVIEW QUESTIONS

- How do aspects of physical appearance sway impressions of others?
- What are social schemas and stereotypes?
- How do illusory correlations and other phenomena illustrate subjectivity in person perception?
- How do evolutionary psychologists explain biases in person perception?

Can you remember the first meeting of your introductory psychology class? What impression did your professor make on you that day? Did your instructor appear to be confident? Easygoing? Pompous? Open-minded? Cynical? Friendly? Were your first impressions supported or undermined by subsequent observations? Our impressions of others are affected by a variety of factors including physical appearance. Take a moment to look at the man pictured on page 665. What do you think he is like? What does he do? What are his interests?

No matter whether you are correct or not, you probably found it easy to generate some idea of what he is like. We seem to be almost automatically drawn

to trying to figure others out, to getting an impression of them.

While we often gather many pieces of information about another person, our final impressions can often be dramatically affected by just one piece of information. In some of the classic research in impression formation, Solomon Asch (1946) demonstrated the importance that what he called central traits can have on the impressions we form of others. When you interact with people, you're constantly engaged in ***person perception,*** **the process of forming impressions of others.** People show considerable ingenuity in piecing together clues about others' characteristics. However, impressions are often inaccurate

Our impressions of others are affected by physical appearance. What do you think this man is like?

because of the many biases and fallacies that occur in person perception. In this section we consider some of the factors that influence, and often distort, people's perceptions of others.

Effects of Physical Appearance

 SIM10

"You shouldn't judge a book by its cover." "Beauty is only skin deep." People know better than to let physical attractiveness determine their perceptions of others' personal qualities. Or do they? Studies have shown that judgments of others' personality are often swayed by their appearance, especially their physical attractiveness. People tend to ascribe desirable personality characteristics to those who are good looking, seeing them as more sociable, friendly, poised, warm, and well adjusted than those who are less attractive (Eagly et al., 1991; Wheeler & Kim, 1997). Karen Dion of the University of Toronto (Dion, Berscheid, & Walster, 1972), in a study conducted with University of Toronto undergraduates, found that not only were the attractive targets ascribed all those positive characteristics, but they were also expected to have better lives, to be better spouses, and to be more successful in their chosen careers. In another study Dion (1973) showed that linking the *beautiful* with the *good* starts early. In that study, three- to six-and-a-half-year-old children were shown pictures of attractive and unattractive kids, and were asked to make a series of judgments. As you can see in Table 16.1, the attractive kids were

viewed more positively on a variety of dimensions. Unattractive kids are scarier and hit you without a good reason, while attractive kids won't hit you back even if you hit them first. In reality, research findings suggest that there is little correlation between attractiveness and personality traits (Feingold, 1992). Why do we inaccurately assume that a connection exists between good looks and personality? One reason is that extremely attractive people are vastly over-represented in the entertainment media, where they are mostly portrayed in a highly favourable light (Smith, McIntosh, & Bazzini, 1999).

You might guess that physical attractiveness would influence perceptions of competence less than perceptions of personality, but the data suggest otherwise. A recent review of the relevant research found that people have a surprisingly strong tendency to view good-looking individuals as more competent than less attractive individuals (Langlois et al., 2000). This bias literally pays off for good-looking people, as they tend to secure better jobs and earn higher salaries than less attractive individuals (Collins & Zebrowitz, 1995; Engemann & Owyang, 2005; Frieze, Olson, & Russell, 1991). Good looks seem to have relatively little impact on perceptions of honesty and integrity (Eagly et al., 1991). However, people tend to view those with *baby-faced features*—such as large eyes, smooth skin, and a rounded chin—as more honest and trustworthy (Zebrowitz, Voinescu, & Collins, 1996). Baby-faced individuals are also seen as relatively warm, submissive, helpless, and naïve (Zebrowitz, 1996), although evidence suggests that there is no association between baby-faced features and these traits (Zebrowitz, Collins, & Dutta, 1998).

Table 16.1 Frequency of Assignment of Behavioural Descriptions to Attractive versus Unattractive Children

| | Attractiveness of Child Chosen | |
Behavioural item	Unattractive	Attractive
1. Fights a lot	37	24
2. Hits without a good reason	42	19*
3. Says angry things	37	24
4. Scares you	42	18*
5. Might hurt you	40	21*
6. Very friendly to other children	16	45*
7. Helps children when they're hurt or sad	28	33
8. Doesn't like fighting or shouting	18	43*
9. Doesn't hit, even if someone else hits first	21	40*

* The items marked with an asterisk reflect significant differences.

SOURCE: Adapted from Dion, K. (1973). Young children's stereotyping of facial attractiveness. *Journal of Personality and Social Psychology, 9*, 187. Copyright © 1973 by the American Psychological Association. Adapted with permission.

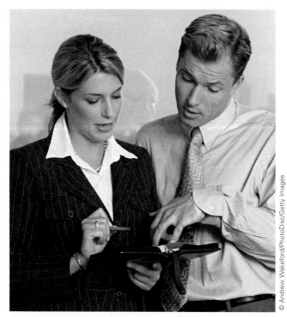

In general, people have a bias toward viewing good-looking men and women as bright, competent, and talented. However, people sometimes downplay the talent of successful women who happen to be attractive, attributing their success to their good looks instead of to their competence.

Figure 16.1

Examples of social schemas. Everyone has social schemas for various "types" of people, such as sophisticated professionals or working-class stiffs. Social schemas are clusters of beliefs that guide information processing.

Sophisticated professional

- Drinks fine wine
- Hobby is travel
- Patron of the arts
- Health-conscious
- Reads books often

Working-class stiff

- Drinks beer
- Hobby is bowling
- Sports fan
- Smokes
- Watches TV often

Observers are also quick to draw inferences about people based on how they move, talk, and gesture—that is, their style of nonverbal expressiveness—and these inferences tend to be fairly accurate (Ambady & Rosenthal, 1993; Borkenau et al., 2004). For example, based on a mere ten seconds of videotape, participants can guess strangers' sexual orientation (heterosexual–homosexual) with decent accuracy (Ambady, Hallahan, & Conner, 1999). It is also widely believed that it is reasonable to draw inferences about someone's personality based on their handshake. Surprisingly little research has been conducted on handshaking and person perception, but preliminary evidence suggests that a firm, vigorous handshake is associated with relatively favourable first impressions (Chaplin et al., 2000).

Cognitive Schemas

Even though every individual is unique, people tend to categorize one another. Such labels reflect the use of cognitive schemas in person perception. As we discussed in Chapter 7, *schemas* are cognitive structures that guide information processing. Individuals use schemas to organize the world around them—including their social world. **Social schemas are organized clusters of ideas about categories of social events and people.** People have social schemas for events such as dates, picnics, committee meetings, and family reunions, as well as for certain categories of people, such as "dumb jocks," "social climbers," "frat rats," and "wimps" (see Figure 16.1). Individuals depend on social schemas because the schemas help them to efficiently process and store the wealth of information that they take in about others in their interactions. Hence, people routinely place one another in categories, and these categories influence the process of person perception (Macrae & Bodenhausen, 2000).

Sometimes we have more than one schema that might apply to a specific person or situation. What determines which schema will be used? One factor is the level of activation of a schema. In a series of studies, Tory Higgins has shown that *priming* specific schemas can affect how information is interpreted and remembered (Higgins, Rholes, & Jones, 1977). Schemas can be primed or made *accessible* in a variety of ways, including through subliminal activation (as we saw in the Featured Study in Chapter 12).

Stereotypes

Some of the schemas that individuals apply to people are unique products of their personal experiences, while other schemas may be part of their shared cultural background. *Stereotypes* are special types of schemas that fall into the latter category. **Stereotypes are widely held beliefs that people have certain characteristics because of their membership in a particular group.**

The most common stereotypes in our society are those based on sex, age, and membership in ethnic or occupational groups. People who subscribe to traditional *gender stereotypes* tend to assume that women are emotional, submissive, illogical, and passive, while men are unemotional, dominant, logical, and aggressive. *Age stereotypes* suggest that elderly people are slow, feeble, rigid, forgetful, and asexual.

Notions that Jews are mercenary, Germans are methodical, and Italians are passionate are examples of common *ethnic stereotypes. Occupational stereotypes* suggest that lawyers are manipulative, accountants are conforming, artists are moody, and so forth.

Stereotyping is a normal cognitive process that is frequently automatic and that saves on the time and effort required to get a handle on people individually (Devine & Monteith, 1999; Operario & Fiske, 2001). Stereotypes save energy by simplifying our social world. However, this conservation of energy often comes at some cost in terms of accuracy (Wigboldus, Dijksterhuis, & van Knippenberg, 2003). Stereotypes frequently are broad overgeneralizations that ignore the diversity within social groups and foster inaccurate perceptions of people (Hilton & von Hippel, 1996). Obviously, not all males, Jews, and lawyers behave alike. Most people who subscribe to stereotypes realize that not all members of a group are identical. For instance, they may admit that some men aren't competitive, some Jews aren't mercenary, and some lawyers aren't manipulative. However, they may still tend to assume that males, Jews, and lawyers are *more likely* than others to have these characteristics. Even if stereotypes mean only that people think in terms of slanted *probabilities*, their expectations may lead them to misperceive individuals with whom they interact. As we've noted in previous chapters, perception is subjective, and people often see what they expect to see.

Our perception of others is also subject to self-fulfilling prophecy. This was clearly demonstrated in a classic study by Word, Zanna, & Cooper (1974). (Mark Zanna, a professor of psychology at the University of Waterloo, received the CPA's Donald O. Hebb Award in 1993.) The research had two studies. In the first study, researchers had white undergraduate males interview either a black or white job applicant. The applicant was, in fact, an experimental accomplice or confederate. It was found that when the job applicant was black, the interviewers tended to sit farther away, end the interview more quickly, and make more speech errors (e.g., stuttering, stammering). Clearly, then, the white interviewers changed how they acted depending on the race of the interviewee. In interviewing a white accomplice, they adopted what was referred to as an *immediate* style (i.e., sitting closer, more eye contact), but when they interviewed a black accomplice they used a *nonimmediate style* (i.e., sitting farther away, making more speech errors, looking away). In the second study, Word, Zanna, and Cooper attempted to find out how it would feel to have someone behave toward you in a nonimmediate style. In the study, white experimental accomplices interviewed other white students while adopting either the immediate or nonimmediate style. Students who had been interviewed in the nonimmediate style seemed more anxious and did not perform as well in the interview.

The study was designed to show the operation of self-fulfilling prophecy. If you hold strong beliefs about the characteristics of another group, you may behave in such a way so as to bring these characteristics about. If you believe, for example, that all professors do is read books, the next time you sit next to a professor on a bus, all you might ask her about is the books she has read. If she is like most people, she can report back to you on the latest book of fiction she has read. If things go like this, then you may leave the situation believing that, yes indeed, professors only read books. However, because of your stereotypes, you may have failed to find out how much she likes rap music.

Subjectivity in Person Perception

Stereotypes and other schemas create biases in person perception that frequently lead to confirmation of people's expectations about others. According to University of Western Ontario social psychologist James Olson, if someone's behaviour is ambiguous, people are likely to interpret what they see in a way that's consistent with their expectations (Olson, Roese, & Zanna, 1996). Thus, after dealing with a pushy female customer, a salesman who holds traditional gender stereotypes might characterize the woman as "emotional." In contrast, he might characterize a male who exhibits the same pushy behaviour as "aggressive."

People not only see what they expect to see, but also tend to overestimate how often they see it (Johnson & Mullen, 1994; Shavitt et al., 1999). *Illusory correlation* **occurs when people estimate that they have encountered more confirmations of an association between social traits than they have actually seen.** People also tend to underestimate the number of disconfirmations they have encountered, as illustrated by statements like "I've never met an honest lawyer."

Memory processes can contribute to confirmatory biases in person perception in a variety of ways. Often, individuals selectively recall facts that fit with their schemas and stereotypes (Fiske, 1998). Evidence for such a tendency was found in a study by Cohen (1981). In this experiment, participants watched a videotape of a woman, described as either a waitress or a librarian, who engaged in a variety of activities, including listening to classical music, drinking beer, and watching TV. When asked to recall what the woman did during the filmed sequence, participants tended to remember activities consistent with their stereotypes of waitresses and librarians. For instance, subjects who thought the woman was a waitress tended to recall her beer drinking, while subjects who thought she was a librarian tended to recall her listening to classical music.

Further evidence for the subjectivity of social perception comes from a phenomenon called the *spotlight effect*—people's tendency to assume that the social spotlight shines more brightly on them than it actually does (Gilovich & Savitsky, 1999). Recent studies show that people frequently overestimate the degree to which others pay attention to their appearance and behaviour. For example, in one study some college students were induced to wear an embarrassing T-shirt depicting the face of a singer only someone their parents' age would like in interactions with other participants and were subsequently asked to estimate the percentage of the other subjects who had noticed the shirt. Their estimates were over twice as high as the actual percentage of subjects who noticed the embarrassing T-shirt (see Figure 16.2; Gilovich, Medvec, & Savitsky, 2000). The bad news about the spotlight effect is that it occurs in moments

of triumph as well as moments of embarrassment, so our successes and accomplishments often garner less attention from others than we believe they do. The good news is that our blunders and failures are less salient to others than we think they are and that people's inferences about us based on these blunders are not as harsh as widely assumed (Savitsky, Epley, & Gilovich, 2001).

A similar type of subjective perception is apparent in research on the *illusion of asymmetric insight*—the finding that people tend to think that their knowledge of their peers is greater than their peers' knowledge of them (Pronin et al., 2001). For example, in a study of college roommates the participants tended to believe that they knew their roommates better than their roommates knew them. Additional research is needed to pinpoint the processes underlying this phenomenon. Pronin and her colleagues (2001) speculate that most of us have had many experiences where we feel that our behaviour has been misinterpreted or our motives misunderstood, so we develop doubts that anyone can really know us, but most of us fail to appreciate that this insight also applies to our perceptions of others. Consistent with this analysis, a subsequent study found that people tend to recognize biased social perception in others much more readily than in themselves (Pronin, Lin, & Ross, 2002).

An Evolutionary Perspective on Bias in Person Perception

Why is the process of person perception riddled with bias? Evolutionary psychologists like Simon Fraser University's Dennis Krebs argue that many of the biases seen in social perception were adaptive in humans' ancestral environment (Krebs & Denton, 1997). For example, they argue that person perception is swayed by physical attractiveness because attractiveness was associated with reproductive potential in women and with health, vigour, and the accumulation of material resources in men. What about baby-faced features? Evolutionary theorists assert that the tendency to view babies as helpless creatures requiring nurture would be highly adaptive and has probably been preprogrammed in humans by natural selection (Springer & Berry, 1997). The tendency to view baby-faced adults as naïve, submissive, and honest may simply be a spillover effect from humans' evolutionary heritage.

What about the human tendency to automatically categorize others? Evolutionary theorists attribute this behaviour to our distant ancestors' need to quickly separate friend from foe. They assert that humans are programmed by evolution to immedi-

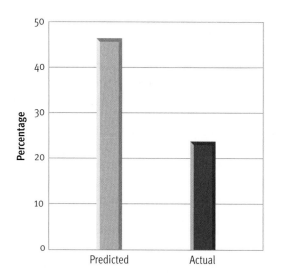

Figure 16.2

The spotlight effect. In a study of the spotlight effect, Gilovich, Medvec, and Savitsky (2000) induced college students to wear an embarrassing T-shirt while interacting with other participants. The shirt depicted Barry Manilow, a singer who was characterized by the authors as "not terribly popular among college students." The subjects who wore the Manilow shirt were asked to predict what percentage of the other participants would notice the shirt. As you can see, their predictions far exceeded the actual number of participants who noticed the embarrassing shirt.

SOURCE: Adapted from Gilovich, T., Medvec, V. H., & Savitsky, K. (2000). The spotlight effect in social judgment: An egocentric bias in estimates of the salience of one's own actions and appearance. *Journal of Personality and Social Psychology, 78*, 211–222. Copyright © 2000 by the American Psychological Association. Used by permission of the author.

ately classify people as members of an *ingroup*—a **group that one belongs to and identifies with**, or as members of an *outgroup*—**a group that one does not belong to or identify with.** This crucial categorization is thought to structure subsequent perceptions. As Krebs and Denton (1997) put it, "It is as though the act of classifying others as ingroup or outgroup members activates two quite different brain circuits" (p. 27). Ingroup members tend to be viewed in a favourable light, whereas outgroup members tend to be viewed in terms of various negative stereotypes. According to Krebs and Denton, these negative stereotypes ("They are inferior; they are all alike; they will exploit us") move outgroups out of our domain of empathy, so we feel justified in not liking them or discriminating against them.

Thus, evolutionary psychologists ascribe much of the bias in person perception to cognitive mechanisms that have been shaped by natural selection. Their speculation is thought provoking, but empirical work is needed to test their hypotheses.

REVIEW OF KEY POINTS

● People's perceptions of others can be distorted by a variety of factors, including physical appearance. People tend to attribute desirable characteristics, such as intelligence, competence, warmth, and friendliness, to those who are good looking.

● Baby-faced people are viewed as honest. Perceptions of people are also influenced by their style of nonverbal expressiveness. People use social schemas to categorize others into types. Stereotypes are widely held social schemas that lead people to expect that others will have certain characteristics because of their membership in a specific group.

● Gender, age, ethnic, and occupational stereotypes are common. In interacting with others, stereotypes may lead people to see what they expect to see and to overestimate how often they see it. The spotlight effect and the illusion of asymmetric insight illustrate the subjective nature of social perception.

● Evolutionary psychologists argue that many biases in person perception were adaptive in humans' ancestral past. The human tendency to automatically categorize others may reflect the primitive need to quickly separate friend from foe.

Attribution Processes: Explaining Behaviour

It's Friday evening and you're sitting around at home feeling bored. You call a few friends to see whether they'd like to go out. They all say that they'd love to go, but they have other commitments and can't. Their commitments sound vague, and you feel that their reasons for not going out with you are rather flimsy. How do you explain these rejections? Do your friends really have commitments? Are they worn out by school and work? When they said that they'd love to go, were they being sincere? Or do they find you boring? Could they be right? Are you boring? These questions illustrate a process that people engage in routinely: the explanation of behaviour. Not only do *attributions* play a key role in these explanatory efforts, but they also have significant effects on social relations. For example, consider a situation in which a friend of yours claims credit for your work. Perhaps, eventually, the friend may feel guilty and apologize to you, asking for your forgiveness. Research by Canadian psychologist Ward Struthers has shown that your attributions for the apology can dramatically affect whether your forgiveness is forthcoming (Struthers, Dupuis, & Eaton, 2005). Even though everyone involved in a specific incident is motivated to explain the event, they do not always agree on those explanations. There may often be bias in our search for explanations. Imagine being questioned by your parents after fighting with your brother. What would your answer be if you were asked who started the fight? Wilfrid Laurier University

researcher Anne Wilson and her colleagues found that siblings, even when questioned by strangers, tended to blame each other, especially when the incidents were more serious (Wilson et al., 2004).

What are attributions? ***Attributions*** **are inferences that people draw about the causes of events, others' behaviour, and their own behaviour.** If you conclude that a friend turned down your invitation because she's overworked, you have made an attribution about the cause of her behaviour (and, implicitly, have rejected other possible explanations). If you conclude that you're stuck at home with nothing to do because you failed to plan ahead, you've made an attribution about the cause of an event (being stuck at home). If you conclude that you failed to plan ahead because you're a procrastinator, you've made an attribution about the cause of your own behaviour. People make attributions mainly because they have a strong need to understand their experiences. They want to make sense out of their own behaviour, others' actions, and the events in their lives. In this section, we'll take a look at some of the patterns seen when people make attributions.

Internal versus External Attributions

12A

Fritz Heider (1958) was the first to describe how people make attributions. He asserted that people

PREVIEW QUESTIONS

● What are attributions, and how do internal and external attributions differ?

● What types of factors influence the likelihood of internal versus external attributions?

● How do actors and observers differ in their patterns of attribution?

● What are defensive attribution and the self-serving bias?

● How do individualism and collectivism influence attribution bias?

University of Kansas

"Often the momentary situation which, at least in part, determines the behavior of a person is disregarded and the behavior is taken as a manifestation of personal characteristics."
FRITZ HEIDER

Figure 16.3

Weiner's model of attributions for success and failure.
Weiner's model assumes that people's explanations for success and failure emphasize internal versus external causes and stable versus unstable causes. Examples of causal factors that fit into each of the four cells in Weiner's model are shown in the diagram.

SOURCE: Weiner, B., Friese, I., Kukla, A., Reed, L., & Rosenbaum, R. M. (1972). Perceiving the causes of success and failure. In E. E. Jones, D. E. Kanouse, H. H. Kelley, R. E. Nisbett, S. Valins, & B. Weiner (Eds.), *Perceiving the causes of behavior*. Morristown, NJ: General Learning Press. Used by permission of Bernard Weiner.

tend to locate the cause of behaviour either *within a person,* attributing it to personal factors, or *outside a person,* attributing it to environmental factors.

Elaborating on Heider's insight, various theorists have agreed that explanations of behaviour and events can be categorized as internal or external attributions (Jones & Davis, 1965; Kelley, 1967; Weiner, 1974). *Internal attributions* **ascribe the causes of behaviour to personal dispositions, traits, abilities, and feelings.** *External attributions* **ascribe the causes of behaviour to situational demands and environmental constraints.** For example, if a friend's business fails, you might attribute it to his or her lack of business acumen (an internal, personal factor) or to negative trends in the nation's economic climate (an external, situational explanation). Parents who find out that their teenage son has just banged up the car may blame it on his carelessness (a personal disposition) or on slippery road conditions (a situational factor).

Internal and external attributions can have a tremendous impact on everyday interpersonal interactions. Blaming a friend's business failure on poor business acumen as opposed to a poor economy will have a great impact on how you view your friend. Likewise, if parents attribute their son's automobile accident to slippery road conditions, they're likely to deal with the event very differently than if they attribute it to his carelessness.

Attributions for Success and Failure

 12A

Some psychologists have sought to discover additional dimensions of attributional thinking besides the internal–external dimension. After studying the attributions that people make in explaining success and failure, Bernard Weiner (1980, 1986, 1994) concluded that people often focus on the *stability* of the causes underlying behaviour. According to Weiner, the stable–unstable dimension in attribution cuts

across the internal–external dimension, creating four types of attributions for success and failure, as shown in Figure 16.3.

Let's apply Weiner's model to a concrete event. Imagine that you're contemplating why you failed to get a job that you wanted. You might attribute your setback to internal factors that are stable (lack of ability) or unstable (inadequate effort to put together an eye-catching résumé). Or you might attribute your setback to external factors that are stable (too much outstanding competition) or unstable (bad luck). If you got the job, your explanations for your success would fall into the same four categories: internal–stable (your excellent ability), internal–unstable (your hard work to assemble a superb résumé), external–stable (lack of top-flight competition), and external–unstable (good luck).

Bias in Attribution

 12A

Attributions are only inferences. Your attributions may not be the correct explanations for events. Paradoxical as it may seem, people often arrive at inaccurate explanations even when they contemplate the causes of *their own behaviour.* Attributions ultimately represent *guesswork* about the causes of events, and these guesses tend to be slanted in certain directions. Let's look at the principal biases seen in attribution.

Actor-Observer Bias

 12A

Your view of your own behaviour can be quite different from the view of someone else observing you. When an actor and an observer draw inferences about the causes of the actor's behaviour, they often make different attributions. A common form of bias seen in observers is the *fundamental attribution error,* **which refers to observers' bias in favour of internal attributions in explaining others' behaviour.** Of course, in many instances, an internal attribution may not be an "error." However, observers have a curious tendency to overestimate the likelihood that an actor's behaviour reflects personal qualities rather than situational factors (Krull, 2001). Why? One reason is that situational pressures may not be readily apparent to an observer. As Gilbert and Malone (1995) put it, "When one tries to point to a situation, one often stabs empty air" (p. 25). Another reason is that attributing others' behaviour to their dispositions is a relatively simple, effortless process that borders on automatic (Trope & Liberman, 1993). In contrast, explaining people's behaviour in terms of situational factors is a more complex process that requires more thought and effort (see Figure 16.4; Krull & Erickson, 1995).

	Stability dimension	
	Unstable cause (temporary)	Stable cause (permanent)
Internal cause	Effort Mood Fatigue	Ability Intelligence
External cause	Luck Chance Opportunity	Task difficulty

Internal–external dimension

To illustrate the gap that often exists between actors' and observers' attributions, imagine that you're visiting your bank and you fly into a rage over a mistake made on your account. Observers who witness your rage are likely to make an internal attribution and infer that you are surly, temperamental, and quarrelsome. They may be right, but if asked, you'd probably attribute your rage to the frustrating situation. Perhaps you're normally a calm, easygoing person, but today you've been in line for 20 minutes, you just straightened out a similar error by the same bank last week, and you're being treated rudely by the teller. Observers are often unaware of historical and situational considerations such as these, so they tend to make internal attributions for another's behaviour (Gilbert, 1998).

In contrast, the circumstances that have influenced an actor's behaviour tend to be more salient to the actor. Hence, actors are more likely than observers to locate the cause of their behaviour in the situation. In general, then, *actors favour external attributions for their behaviour, whereas observers are more likely to explain the same behaviour with internal attributions* (Jones & Nisbett, 1971; Krueger, Ham, & Linford, 1996).

Defensive Attribution

 12A

In attempting to explain the calamities and setbacks that befall other people, an observer's tendency to make internal attributions may become even stronger than normal. Let's say that a friend gets mugged and severely beaten. You may attribute the mugging to

your friend's carelessness or stupidity ("He should have known better than to be in that neighbourhood at that time") rather than to bad luck. Why? Because if you attribute your friend's misfortune to bad luck,

Traditional model of attribution

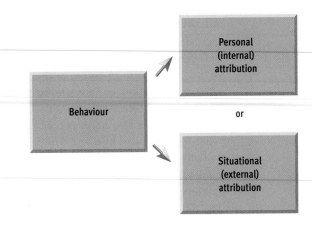

Alternative two-step model of attribution

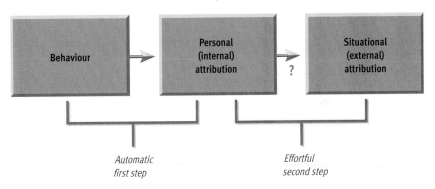

Figure 16.4

An alternative view of the fundamental attribution error. According to Gilbert (1989) and others, the nature of attribution processes favours the *fundamental attribution error*. Traditional models of attribution assume that internal and external attributions are an either–or proposition requiring equal amounts of effort. In contrast, Gilbert posits that people tend to automatically make internal attributions with little effort, and then they *may* expend additional effort to adjust for the influence of situational factors, which can lead to an external attribution. Thus, external attributions for others' behaviour require more thought and effort, which makes them less frequent than personal attributions.

CONCEPT CHECK 16.1

Analyzing Attributions

Check your understanding of attribution processes by analyzing possible explanations for an athletic team's success. Imagine that the women's track team at your school has just won a provincial championship that qualifies it for the national tournament. Around the campus, you hear people attribute the team's success to a variety of factors. Examine the attributions shown below and place each of them in one of the cells of Weiner's model of attribution (just record the letter inside the cell). The answers are in Appendix A.

a. "They won only because the best two athletes on Ottawa's team were out with injuries—talk about good fortune!"
b. "They won because they have some of the best talent in the country."
c. "Anybody could win in this province; the competition is far below average in comparison to the rest of the country."
d. "They won because they put in a great deal of last-minute effort and practice, and they were incredibly fired up for the regional tourney after last year's near miss."

you have to face the ugly reality that it could just as easily happen to you. To avoid disturbing thoughts such as these, people often attribute mishaps to victims' negligence (Salminen, 1992; Thornton, 1984, 1992).

***Defensive attribution* is a tendency to blame victims for their misfortune, so that one feels less likely to be victimized in a similar way.** *Hindsight bias* probably contributes to this tendency, but blaming victims also helps people maintain their belief that they live in a just world, where they're unlikely to experience similar troubles (Lerner & Goldberg, 1999). *Belief in a just world* theory was developed by University of Waterloo social psychologist Melvin Lerner (1980). He suggested that evidence we get telling us that the world is not a just place is threatening and that we feel compelled to restore this belief. One way in which we can restore this belief is to see victims as deserving their consequences. Carolyn Hafer of Brock University recently reviewed research on this theory and suggests that, while the results have been largely supportive, there are some inadequacies that should be addressed (Hafer & Begue, 2005).

The bias toward making defensive attributions can have unfortunate consequences. Blaming victims for their setbacks causes them to be seen in a negative light, and undesirable traits are unfairly attributed to them. Thus, it is assumed that burglary victims must be careless, that people who get fired must be incompetent, that poor people must be lazy, that rape victims must be seductive ("She probably asked for it"), and so on. As you can see, defensive attribution can lead to unwarranted derogation of victims of misfortune.

Self-Serving Bias
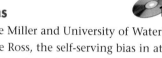 **12A**

According to Dale Miller and University of Waterloo psychologist Mike Ross, the self-serving bias in attribution comes into play when people attempt to explain success and failure (Miller & Ross, 1975). This bias may either strengthen or weaken one's normal attributional tendencies, depending on whether one is trying to explain positive or negative outcomes (Campbell & Sedikides, 1999; Mezulis et al., 2004). The *self-serving bias* is the tendency to attribute one's successes to personal factors and one's failures to situational factors. Interestingly, this bias grows stronger as time passes after an event, so that people tend to take progressively more credit for their successes and less responsibility for their failures (Burger, 1986).

In explaining *failure*, the usual actor-observer biases are apparent. Actors tend to make external attributions, blaming their failures on unfavourable

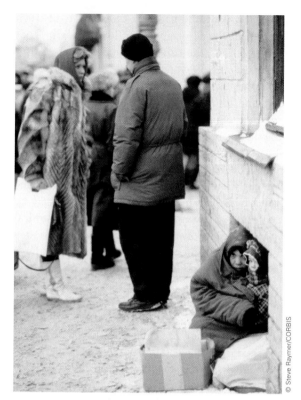

A common example of defensive attribution is the tendency to blame the homeless for their plight.

© Steve Raymer/CORBIS

situational factors, while observers attribute the same failures to the actors' personal shortcomings. Thus, if you fail an exam, you may place the blame on the poorly constructed test items, lousy teaching, distractions in the hallway, or a bad week at work (all external attributions). However, an observer is more likely to attribute your failure to your lack of ability or lack of study (both internal attributions). In explaining success, the usual actor-observer differences are reversed to some degree. Thus, if you get a high exam score, you'll probably make an internal attribution and point to your ability or your hard work (Forsyth & McMillan, 1981).

Culture and Attributional Tendencies

Do the patterns of attribution observed in subjects from Western societies transcend culture? More research is needed, but the preliminary evidence suggests not. Some interesting cultural disparities have emerged in research on attribution processes.

According to Harry Triandis (1989, 1994, 2001), cultural differences in *individualism* versus *collectivism* influence attributional tendencies as well as other aspects of social behaviour. **Individualism involves putting personal goals ahead of group goals and defining one's identity in terms of** personal attributes rather than group member-ships. In contrast, *collectivism* involves putting group goals ahead of personal goals and defining one's identity in terms of the groups one belongs to (such as one's family, tribe, work group, social class, caste, and so on). In comparison to individualistic cultures, collectivist cultures place a higher priority on shared values and resources, cooperation, mutual inter-dependence, and concern for how one's actions will affect other group members. Childrearing patterns in collectivist cultures emphasize the importance of obe-dience, reliability, and proper behaviour, whereas individualistic cultures emphasize the development of independence, self-esteem, and self-reliance.

A variety of factors influence whether societies cherish individualism as opposed to collectivism. Among other things, increases in a culture's afflu-ence, education, urbanization, and social mobility tend to foster more individualism (Triandis, 1994). Many contemporary societies are in transition, but generally speaking, North American and Western European cultures tend to be individualistic, whereas Asian, African, and Latin American cultures tend to be higher in collectivism (Hofstede, 1980, 1983, 2001). Canada ranks fourth in individualism (tied with the Netherlands), behind the U.S., Australia, and Great Britain (see Figure 16.5).

How does individualism versus collectivism relate to patterns of attribution? The evidence suggests that collectivist cultures may promote different attri-butional biases than individualistic cultures. For example, people from collectivist societies appear to

Hofstede's rankings of national cultures' individualism		
Individualistic cultures	**Intermediate cultures**	**Collectivist cultures**
1. United States	19. Israel	37. Hong Kong
2. Australia	20. Spain	38. Chile
3. Great Britain	21. India	40. Singapore
4. Canada	22. Argentina	40. Thailand
4. Netherlands	23. Japan	40. West Africa region
6. New Zealand	24. Iran	42. El Salvador
7. Italy	25. Jamaica	43. South Korea
8. Belgium	26. Arab region	44. Taiwan
9. Denmark	27. Brazil	45. Peru
10. France	28. Turkey	46. Costa Rica
11. Sweden	29. Uruguay	47. Indonesia
12. Ireland	30. Greece	47. Pakistan
13. Norway	31. Philippines	49. Colombia
14. Switzerland	32. Mexico	50. Venezuela
15. West Germany	34. East Africa region	51. Panama
16. South Africa	34. Portugal	52. Ecuador
17. Finland	34. Yugoslavia	53. Guatemala
18. Austria	36. Malaysia	

Figure 16.5

Individualism versus collectivism around the world. Hofstede (1980, 1983, 2001) used survey data from over 100 000 employees of a large, multinational corporation to estimate the emphasis on individ-ualism versus collectivism in 50 nations and three regions. His large, diverse international sample remains unequalled to date. In the figure, cultures are ranked in terms of how strongly they embraced the values of individualism. As you can see, Hofstede's estimates suggest that North American and Western European nations tend to be relatively individualistic, whereas more collectivism is found in Asian, African, and Latin American countries.

SOURCE: Adapted from Hofstede, G. (2001). *Culture's consequences* (2nd Ed., p. 215). Thousand Oaks, CA: Sage. Copyright © 2001 Sage Publications. Adapted by permis-sion of Dr. Geert Hofstede.

be less prone to the *fundamental attribution error* than those from individualistic societies (Choi, Nisbett, & Norenzayan, 1999; Triandis, 2001). In Western cul-tures, people are viewed as autonomous individuals

CONCEPT CHECK 16.2

Recognizing Bias in Social Cognition

Check your understanding of bias in social cognition by identifying various types of errors that are common in person perception and attribu-tion. Imagine that you're a nonvoting student member of a committee that is hiring a new political science professor at your university. As you listen to the committee's discussion, you hear examples of (a) the illusory correlation effect, (b) stereotyping, (c) the fundamental attribution error, and (d) defensive attribution. Indicate which of these is at work in the excerpts from committee members' deliberations below. The answers are in Appendix A.

_____ 1. "I absolutely won't consider the fellow who arrived 30 minutes late for his interview. Anybody who can't make a job interview on time is either irresponsible or hopelessly disorganized. I don't care what he says about the airline messing up his reservations."

_____ 2. "You know, I was very, very impressed with the young female applicant, and I would love to hire her, but every time we add a young woman to the faculty in liberal arts, she gets pregnant within the first year." The committee chairperson, who has heard this line from this professor before replies, "You always say that, so I finally did a systematic check of what's happened in the past. Of the last 14 women hired in liberal arts, only one has become pregnant within a year."

_____ 3. "The first one I want to rule out is the guy who's been practising law for the last ten years. Although he has an excellent back-ground in political science, I just don't trust lawyers. They're all ambitious, power-hungry, manipulative cutthroats. He'll be a divi-sive force in the department."

_____ 4. "I say we forget about the two candidates who lost their faculty slots in the massive financial crisis at Western Polytechnic last year. I know it sounds cruel, but they brought it on themselves with their fiscal irresponsibility over at Western. Thank goodness we'll never let any-thing like that happen around here. As far as I'm concerned, if these guys couldn't see that crisis coming, they must be pretty dense."

Social Behaviour

who are responsible for their actions. Endorsing beliefs such as "You can do anything you put your mind to" or "You have no one to blame but yourself," Westerners typically explain behaviour in terms of people's personality traits and unique abilities. In contrast, collectivists, who value interdependence and obedience, are more likely to assume that one's behaviour reflects adherence to group norms.

Although the *self-serving bias* has been documented in a variety of cultures (Fletcher & Ward, 1988), it may be particularly prevalent in individualistic, Western societies, where an emphasis on competition and high self-esteem motivates people to try to impress others, as well as themselves (Mezulis et al., 2004). In contrast, Japanese subjects exhibit a *self-effacing bias* in explaining success (Akimoto & Sanbonmatsu, 1999; Markus & Kitayama, 1991), as they tend to attribute their successes to help they receive from others or to the ease of the task, while downplaying the importance of their ability. When they fail, Japanese subjects tend to be more self-critical than subjects from individualistic cultures, according to research conducted by the University of British Columbia's Steve Heine (Heine & Renshaw, 2002). Japanese subjects are more likely to accept responsibility for their failures and to use their setbacks as an impetus for self-improvement (Heine et al., 2001).

Studies have also failed to find the usual self-serving bias in Nepalese and Chinese samples (Lee & Seligman, 1997; Smith & Bond, 1994). A great deal of additional research is needed before any broad conclusions can be drawn, but collectivism may put a different spin on attributional bias.

REVIEW OF KEY POINTS

- Attributions are inferences about the causes of events and behaviour. Individuals make attributions to understand their social world. Attributions can be classified as internal or external. Internal attributions ascribe behaviour to personal dispositions and traits, whereas external attributions locate the cause of behaviour in the environment.

- Weiner's model proposes that attributions for success and failure should be analyzed in terms of the stability of causes, as well as along the internal–external dimension. Observers favour internal attributions to explain another's behaviour (the fundamental attribution error), while actors favour external attributions to explain their own behaviour.

- In defensive attribution, people unfairly blame victims for their misfortune (with internal attributions) to reduce their own feelings of vulnerability. The self-serving bias is the tendency to attribute one's good outcomes to personal factors and one's bad outcomes to situational factors.

- Cultures vary in their emphasis on individualism as opposed to collectivism, and these differences appear to influence attributional tendencies. The fundamental attribution error and the self-serving bias in attribution may be byproducts of Western cultures' individualism.

Close Relationships: Liking and Loving

PREVIEW QUESTIONS

- To what extent are good looks, similarity, reciprocity, and ideals important in interpersonal attraction?

- How do theorists distinguish among different types of love?

- How are attachment patterns related to intimate relations?

- How does culture influence patterns of mating?

- How have mating strategies been shaped by evolution?

"I just don't know what she sees in him. She could do so much better for herself. I suppose he's a nice guy, but they're just not right for each other." You've probably heard similar remarks on many occasions. These comments illustrate people's interest in analyzing the dynamics of attraction. *Interpersonal attraction* **refers to positive feelings toward another.** Social psychologists use this term broadly to encompass a variety of experiences, including liking, friendship, admiration, lust, and love. In this section, we'll analyze key factors that influence attraction and examine some theoretical perspectives on the mystery of love.

Key Factors in Attraction

Many factors influence who is attracted to whom. Here we'll discuss factors that promote the development of liking, friendship, and love. Although these are different types of attraction, the interpersonal dynamics at work in each are largely similar.

Physical Attractiveness

Although people often say that "beauty is only skin deep," the empirical evidence suggests that most people don't really believe that homily. The importance of physical attractiveness was demonstrated in a study of college students in which unacquainted men and women were sent off on a "get-acquainted" date (Sprecher & Duck, 1994). The investigators were mainly interested in how communication might affect the process of attraction, but to put this factor in context they also measured subjects' perceptions of their date's physical attractiveness and similarity to themselves. They found that the quality of communication during the date did have some effect on females' interest in friendship, but the key determinant of romantic attraction for both sexes was the physical attractiveness of the other person. Many other studies have demonstrated the singular prominence of physical attractiveness in the initial stage of dating and have shown that it continues to influence the course of commitment as dating relationships evolve (Hendrick & Hendrick, 1992). In the realm of romance, being physically attractive appears to be more important for females than males (Regan, 2003). For example, in a study of college students (Speed & Gangestad, 1997), the correlation between romantic popularity (assessed by peer ratings) and physical attractiveness was higher for females (0.76) than for males (0.47).

Although people prefer physically attractive partners in romantic relationships, they may consider their own level of attractiveness in pursuing dates. What people want in a partner may be different from what they are willing to settle for (Regan, 1998). The *matching hypothesis* proposes that males and females of approximately equal physical attractiveness are likely to select each other as partners. The matching hypothesis is supported by evidence that married couples tend to be very similar in level of physical attractiveness (Feingold, 1988b). Interestingly, people expect that individuals who are similar in attractiveness will be more satisfied as couples and less likely to break up (Garcia & Khersonsky, 1996).

Similarity Effects

Is it true that "birds of a feather flock together," or do "opposites attract"? Research provides far more support for the former than the latter. Married and dating couples tend to be similar in age, race, religion, social class, personality, education, intelligence, physical attractiveness, and attitudes (Kalmijn, 1998; Watson et al., 2004). In married couples, personality similarity appears to be associated with greater marital happiness (Caspi & Herbener, 1990). Similarity is also seen among friends. For instance, adult friends tend to be relatively similar in terms of income, education, occupational status, ethnicity, and religion (Blieszner & Adams, 1992).

The most obvious explanation for these correlations is that similarity causes attraction. Laboratory experiments on *attitude similarity*, conducted by Donn Byrne and his colleagues, suggest that similarity *does* cause attraction (Byrne, 1997; Byrne, Clore, & Smeaton, 1986). However, research also suggests that attraction can foster similarity, as Davis and Rusbult (2001) found that dating partners gradually modify their attitudes in ways that make them more congruent, a phenomenon they called *attitude alignment*. Moreover, people in stable, satisfying intimate relationships tend to subjectively overestimate how similar they and their partners are (Murray et al., 2002). Wanting to believe that they have found a kindred spirit, they tend to assume that their partners are mirrors of themselves.

Reciprocity Effects

In his book *How to Win Friends and Influence People*, Dale Carnegie (1936) suggested that people can gain others' liking by showering them with praise and flattery. However, we've all heard that "flattery will get you nowhere." Which advice is right? The evidence suggests that flattery will get you somewhere, with some people, some of the time.

In interpersonal attraction, *reciprocity* involves liking those who show that they like you. In general, research indicates that we tend to like those who show that they like us and that we tend to see others as liking us more if we like them. Thus, it appears that liking breeds liking and loving promotes loving (Sprecher, 1998). Reciprocating attraction generally entails providing friends and intimate partners with positive feedback that results in a *self-enhancement* effect—in other words, you help them feel good about themselves (Sedikides & Strube, 1997). However, studies suggest that people are also interested in *self-verification*—that is, they seek feedback that matches and supports their self-concepts (Bosson & Swann, 2001).

Romantic Ideals

In the realm of romance, people want their partner to measure up to their ideals. These ideals spell out the personal qualities that one hopes to find in a partner, such as warmth, good looks, loyalty, high status, a sense of humour, and so forth. According to Simpson, Fletcher, and Campbell (2001), people routinely evaluate how close their intimate partners come to matching these ideal standards, and these evaluations influence how relationships progress. Consistent with this theory, research shows that the more closely individuals' perceptions of their partners

According to the matching hypothesis, males and females who are similar in physical attractiveness are likely to be drawn together. This type of matching may also influence the formation of friendships.

Courtesy of Elaine Hatfield

"Passionate love is like any other form of excitement. By its very nature, excitement involves a continuous interplay between elation and despair, thrills and terror."
ELAINE HATFIELD

Figure **16.6**

Sternberg's view of love over time. In his theory of love, Robert Sternberg (1988a) hypothesizes that the various elements of love progress in different ways over the course of time. According to Sternberg, passion peaks early in a relationship, whereas intimacy and commitment typically continue to build gradually. (Graphs adapted from Trotter, 1986)

match their ideals, the more satisfied they tend to be with their relationship—both in the early stages of dating (Fletcher, Simpson, & Thomas, 2000) and in stable, long-term relationships (Fletcher et al., 1999). Moreover, the size of the discrepancy between ideals and perceptions predicts whether a dating relationship will continue or dissolve (Fletcher et al., 2000).

Of course, these evaluations of how our partners compare to our ideals are subjective, leaving room for distortion. When people are highly invested in a relationship, they can reduce the discrepancy between their ideals and their perceptions either by lowering their standards or by making charitable evaluations of their partners. Research suggests that the latter strategy is more common. For example, in a study of 180 couples, University of Waterloo psychologist John Holmes and his colleagues found that most participants viewed their partners more favourably than the partners viewed themselves (Murray, Holmes, and Griffin 1996a). Individuals' perceptions of their romantic partners seemed to reflect their ideals for a partner more than reality. Moreover, the data showed that people were happier in their relationship when they idealized their partners and when their partners idealized them. A follow-up study found that relationships were more likely to persist—even in the face of conflicts and doubts—when partners idealized each other (Murray, Holmes, & Griffin, 1996b). Another study found that individuals who are satisfied with their romantic relationships tend to focus on their partners' virtues, and to minimize and rationalize their partners' faults (Murray & Holmes, 1999). This line of research suggests that small, positive illusions about one's partner may foster happier and more resilient romantic relationships (Murray, 2001).

Perspectives on the Mystery of Love

Love has proven to be an elusive subject of study. It's difficult to define, difficult to measure, and frequently difficult to understand. Nonetheless, psychologists have begun to make some progress in their study of love. Let's look at their theories and research.

Passionate and Companionate Love **12**B

Two early pioneers in research on love were Elaine Hatfield (formerly Walster) and Ellen Berscheid (Berscheid, 1988; Berscheid & Walster, 1978; Hatfield & Rapson, 1993). They have proposed that romantic relationships are characterized by two kinds of love: passionate love and companionate love. **Passionate love is a complete absorption in another that includes tender sexual feelings and the agony and ecstasy of intense emotion.** **Companionate love is warm, trusting, tolerant affection for another whose life is deeply intertwined with one's own.** Passionate and companionate love *may* coexist, but they don't necessarily go hand in hand.

The distinction between passionate and companionate love has been further refined by Robert Sternberg (1988a), who suggests that love has three facets rather than just two. He subdivides companionate love into intimacy and commitment. **Intimacy refers to warmth, closeness, and sharing in a relationship. Commitment is an intent to maintain a relationship in spite of the difficulties and costs that may arise.** Sternberg has mapped out the probable relations between the passage of time and the three components of love, as shown in Figure 16.6. Like Hatfield and Berscheid, he suspects that passion reaches its zenith in the early phases of love and then erodes. He believes that intimacy and commitment increase with time, although at different rates.

Love as Attachment **12**B

In another groundbreaking analysis of love, Cindy Hazan and Phillip Shaver (1987) have looked not at the components of love but at similarities between love and *attachment relationships* in infancy. We noted in our chapter on human development (Chapter 11) that infant–caretaker bonding, or attachment, emerges in the first year of life. Early attachments vary in quality, and infants tend to fall into one of three groups, which depend in part on parents' caregiving styles (Ainsworth et al., 1978). Most infants develop a *secure attachment*. However, some are very anxious when separated from their caretaker, a syndrome called *anxious-ambivalent attachment*. A third group of infants, characterized by *avoidant attachment,* never bond very well with their caretaker (see Figure 16.7).

Level

Commitment

Intimacy

Passion

Time

According to Hazan and Shaver, romantic love is an attachment process, and people's intimate relationships in adulthood follow the same form as their attachments in infancy. According to their theory, a person who had an anxious-ambivalent attachment in infancy will tend to have romantic relations marked by anxiety and ambivalence in adulthood. In other words, people relive their early bonding with their parents in their adult romantic relationships.

Hazan and Shaver's (1987) initial survey study provided striking support for their theory. They found that adults' love relationships could be sorted into groups that paralleled the three patterns of attachment seen in infants. *Secure adults* (56% of the subjects) found it relatively easy to get close to others, described their love relations as trusting, rarely worried about being abandoned, and reported the fewest divorces. *Anxious-ambivalent adults* (20% of the subjects) reported a preoccupation with love accompanied by expectations of rejection and described their love relations as volatile and marked by jealousy. *Avoidant adults* (24% of the subjects) found it difficult to get close to others and described their love relations as lacking intimacy and trust. Consistent with their theory, Hazan and Shaver (1987) found that the percentage of adults falling into each category was roughly the same as the percentage of infants in each comparable category—a finding that was subsequently replicated with a nationally representative sample of American adults (Mickelson, Kessler, & Shaver, 1997).

Also, subjects' recollections of their childhood relations with their parents were consistent with the idea that people relive their infant attachment experiences in adulthood.

Understandably, Hazan and Shaver's theory has attracted considerable interest. In fact, it has generated thousands of studies on the effects of attachment style. For example, research has shown that securely attached individuals have more committed, satisfying, interdependent, well-adjusted, and longer-lasting relationships compared to people with either anxious-ambivalent or avoidant attachment styles (Feeney, 1999). Moreover, studies have shown attachment patterns are reasonably stable over time (Fraley, 2002) and that people with different attachment styles are predisposed to think, feel, and behave differently in their relationships (Collins & Allard, 2001). For example, anxious-ambivalent people tend to report more intense emotional highs and lows in their romantic relationships. They also report having more conflicts with their partners, that these conflicts are especially stressful, and that these conflicts often have a negative impact on how they feel about their relationship (Campbell et al., 2005). In a similar vein, attachment anxiety promotes *excessive reassurance seeking*—the tendency to persistently ask for assurances from partners that one is worthy of love (Shaver, Schachner, & Mikulincer, 2005).

Attachment style is also related to the motivations that underlie people's sexual interactions.

Courtesy of Ellen Berscheid

The emotion of romantic love seems to be distressingly fragile. As a 16th-century sage poignantly observed, 'the history of a love affair is the drama of its fight against time.'
ELLEN BERSCHEID

Parents' caregiving style	Infant attachment	Adult attachment style
Warm–responsive She/he was generally warm and responsive; she/he was good at knowing when to be supportive and when to let me operate on my own; our relationship was almost always comfortable, and I have no major reservations or complaints about it.	**Secure attachment** An infant–caregiver bond in which the child welcomes contact with a close companion and uses this person as a secure base from which to explore the environment	**Secure** I find it relatively easy to get close to others and am comfortable depending on them and having them depend on me. I don't often worry about being abandoned or about someone getting too close to me.
Cold–rejecting She/he was fairly cold and distant, or rejecting, not very responsive; I wasn't her/his highest priority, her/his concerns were often elsewhere; it's possible that she/he would just as soon not have had me.	**Avoidant attachment** An insecure infant–caregiver bond, characterized by little separation protest and a tendency of the child to avoid or ignore the caregiver	**Avoidant** I am somewhat uncomfortable being close to others; I find it difficult to trust them, difficult to allow myself to depend on them. I am nervous when anyone gets too close, and often love partners who want me to be more intimate than I feel comfortable being.
Ambivalent–inconsistent She/he was noticeably inconsistent in her/his reactions to me, sometimes warm and sometimes not; she/he had her/his own agenda, which sometimes got in the way of her/his receptiveness and responsiveness to my needs; she/he definitely loved me but didn't always show it in the best way.	**Anxious–ambivalent attachment** An insecure infant–caregiver bond, characterized by strong separation protest and a tendency of the child to resist contact initiated by the caregiver, particularly after a separation	**Anxious–ambivalent** I find that others are reluctant to get as close as I would like. I often worry that my partner doesn't really love me or won't want to stay with me. I want to merge completely with another person, and this desire sometimes scares people away.

Figure 16.7

Infant attachment and romantic relationships.
According to Hazan and Shaver (1987), people's romantic relationships in adulthood are similar in form to their attachment patterns in infancy, which are determined in part by parental caregiving styles. The theorized relations between parental styles, attachment patterns, and intimate relations are outlined here. (Data for parental caregiving styles and adult attachment styles based on Hazan and Shaver, 1986, 1987; infant attachment patterns adapted from Shaffer, 1985)

Social Behaviour

People high in attachment anxiety report that they tend to have sex to reduce their feelings of insecurity and to enhance the closeness in their relationships, whereas avoidant individuals tend to engage in more casual sex in an effort to impress their peer group (Schachner & Shaver, 2004). Reactions to romantic breakups also tend to vary depending on attachment style. People who are high in attachment anxiety have much more difficulty than others in dealing with the dissolution of romantic relationships. They report greater emotional and physical distress, greater preoccupation with the former partner, more attempts to regain the lost partner, more angry and vengeful behaviour, and more maladaptive coping responses, such as using alcohol and drugs to cope with the loss (Davis, Shaver, & Vernon, 2003).

Studies have further suggested that attachment patterns may have far-reaching repercussions that extend into many aspects of people's lives besides their romantic relationships. For instance, people with secure attachments tend to have high self-esteem and to be relatively well adjusted. In contrast, people with avoidant or anxious-ambivalent attachments tend to be overrepresented in groups suffering from depression, eating disorders, and other types of psychopathology (Crowell, Fraley, & Shaver, 1999). Attachment security promotes compassionate feelings and values and more helping behaviour when people are in need (Mikulincer & Shaver, 2005). Researchers have also found correlations between attachment styles and gender roles (Schwartz, Waldo, & Higgins, 2004), religious beliefs (Kirkpatrick, 2005), attitudes about work (Shaver & Hazan, 1993, 1994), health habits (Huntsinger & Luecken, 2004), styles of coping with stress (Howard & Medway, 2004), and vulnerability to burnout (Pines, 2004). Thus, Hazan and Shaver's innovative ideas about the long-term effects of infant attachment experiences have triggered an avalanche of thought-provoking research.

Culture and Close Relationships

Relatively little cross-cultural research has been conducted on the dynamics of close relationships. The limited evidence suggests both similarities and differences between cultures in romantic relationships (Hendrick & Hendrick, 2000; Schmitt, 2005). Psychologists such as the University of Toronto's Karen and Ken Dion suggest that cultures vary considerably in terms of how they understand and conceptualize love and relationships (Dion & Dion, 1996). They suggest that some of this variability is attributable to differences in societal and psychological differences in individualism and collectivism.

Marriages based on romantic love are the norm in Western cultures, whereas arranged marriages prevail in collectivist cultures.

For the most part, similarities have been seen when research has focused on what people look for in prospective mates. As we discussed in Chapter 10, David Buss (1989, 1994a) has collected data on mate preferences in 37 divergent cultures and found that people all over the world value mutual attraction, kindness, intelligence, emotional stability, dependability, and good health in a mate. Buss also found that gender differences in mating priorities were nearly universal, with males placing more emphasis on physical attractiveness and females putting a higher priority on social status and financial resources.

Cultures vary, however, in their emphasis on love—especially passionate love—as a prerequisite for marriage. Love as the basis for marriage is an 18th-century invention of Western culture (Stone, 1977). As Hatfield and Rapson (1993) note, "Marriage-for-love represents an ultimate expression of individualism" (p. 2). In contrast, marriages arranged by families and other go-betweens remain common in cultures high in collectivism, including India (Gupta, 1992), Japan (Iwao, 1993), and China (Xiaghe & Whyte, 1990). This practice is declining in some societies as a result of Westernization, but in collectivist societies people contemplating marriage still tend to think in terms of "What will my parents and other people say?" rather than "What does my heart say?" (Triandis, 1994). Studies show that attitudes about love in collectivist societies reflect these cultural priorities. For example, in comparison to Western participants, subjects from Eastern countries report that romantic love is less important for marriage (Levine et al., 1995; Medora et al., 2002). Sometimes the clash of cultural values can have tragic consequences. For example, in July 2003, Rajinder Atwal of New Westminster, British Columbia, allegedly killed his 17-year-old-daughter, Amandeep, because she was in a relationship with Todd McIsaac. Rajinder Atwal is currently on trial for the second-degree murder of his child (Bharandari, 2005).

An Evolutionary Perspective on Attraction

Evolutionary psychologists have a great deal to say about heterosexual attraction. For example, they assert that physical appearance is an influential determinant of attraction because certain aspects of good looks can be indicators of sound health, good genes, and high fertility, all of which can contribute to reproductive potential (Soler et al., 2003; Sugiyama, 2005). Consistent with this analysis, recent research has found that some standards of attractiveness are more consistent across cultures than previously believed (Cunningham, Druen, & Barbee, 1997). For example, *facial symmetry* seems to be a key element of attractiveness in highly diverse cultures (Cunningham et al., 1995; Fink & Penton-Voak, 2002). Facial symmetry is thought to be valued because a host of environmental insults and developmental abnormalities are associated with physical asymmetries, which may serve as markers of relatively poor genes or health (Jones et al., 2001). Another facet of appearance that may transcend culture is *women's waist-to-hip ratio*. Around the world, men seem to prefer women with a waist-to-hip ratio around 0.70–0.80, which appears to be a meaningful correlate of females' reproductive potential (Hughes & Gallup, 2003; Sugiyama, 2005).

Evolutionary theorists also maintain that the unexpected correlations between infants' attachment patterns and adults' romantic relationships can be explained in terms of adaptive pressures. As discussed in Chapter 11, in ancestral societies infant attachment patterns may have reflected how safe and rich in resources local environments were and fostered mindsets about interpersonal relations and reproductive strategies that were adaptive, given the conditions in the local environments (Belsky, 1999b). Thus, the fascinating connections between attachment and intimate relations may reflect the influence of evolutionary processes (Zeifman & Hazan, 1997).

The most thoroughly documented findings on the evolutionary bases of heterosexual attraction are the findings on gender differences in humans' mating preferences. Consistent with the notion that humans are programmed by evolution to behave in ways that enhance their reproductive fitness, evidence indicates that men generally are more interested than women in seeking youthfulness and physical attractiveness in their mates because these traits should be associated with greater reproductive potential (see Chapter 10). On the other hand, research shows that women place a greater premium on prospective mates' ambition, social status, and financial potential because these traits should be associated with the ability to invest material resources in children (Buss & Kenrick, 1998; Li et al., 2002).

REVIEW OF KEY POINTS

● People tend to like and love others who are physically attractive. The matching hypothesis asserts that people who are similar in physical attractiveness are more likely to be drawn together than those who are not.

● Byrne's research suggests that similarity causes attraction, although attitude alignment may also be at work. Reciprocity involves liking those who show that they like you. In intimate relationships, romantic ideals influence the progress of relationships. Romantic partners often idealize each other.

● Berscheid and Hatfield have distinguished between passionate and companionate love. Sternberg builds on their distinction by dividing companionate love into intimacy and commitment.

● Hazan and Shaver's theory suggests that love relationships in adulthood mimic attachment patterns in infancy. People tend to be secure, avoidant, or anxious-ambivalent in their romantic relationships. Those who are secure tend to have more committed, satisfying relationships.

● The characteristics that people seek in prospective mates are much the same around the world. The gender differences in mating preferences seen in Western societies also appear to transcend culture. However, cultures vary considerably in their emphasis on passionate love as a prerequisite for marriage.

● According to evolutionary psychologists, certain aspects of good looks influence attraction because they are indicators of reproductive fitness. Consistent with evolutionary theory, men tend to seek youthfulness and attractiveness in their mates, whereas women emphasize prospective mates' financial potential and willingness to invest material resources in children.

Web Link 16.3

Y? The National Forum on People's Differences

http://www.yforum.com/index.html

Did you ever want to ask a sensitive question of someone who was different from you—another race or religion or sexual orientation—but were too embarrassed or shy? In a cyberforum with clear rules for courteous and respectful dialogue, newspaper writer and editor Philip J. Milano allows visitors to share differences openly and frankly and to learn about topics that are frequently kept quiet.

Attitudes: Making Social Judgments

Social psychology's interest in attitudes has a much longer history than its interest in attraction. Indeed, in its early days social psychology was defined as the study of attitudes. In this section we'll discuss the nature of attitudes, efforts to change attitudes through persuasion, and theories of attitude change.

What are attitudes? **Attitudes are positive or negative evaluations of objects of thought.** "Objects of thought" may include social issues (capital punishment or gun control, for example), groups (liberals, farmers), institutions (the Lutheran church, the Supreme Court), consumer products (yogurt, computers), and people (the prime minister, your next-door neighbour).

Components and Dimensions of Attitudes

Social psychologists have traditionally viewed attitudes as being made up of three components: a cognitive component, an affective component, and a behav-

PREVIEW QUESTIONS

● What are the key components and dimensions of attitudes?

● What factors influence the effectiveness of persuasive efforts?

● How do various theories explain attitude change?

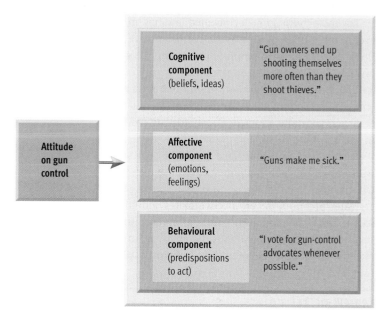

Figure **16.8**

The possible components of attitudes. Attitudes may include cognitive, affective, and behavioural components, as illustrated here for a hypothetical person's attitude about gun control.

ioural component. However, it gradually became apparent that many attitudes do not include all three components (Fazio & Olson, 2003), so it is more accurate to say that *attitudes may include up to three types of components*. The *cognitive component* of an attitude is made up of the beliefs that people hold about the object of an attitude. The *affective component* of an attitude consists of the *emotional feelings* stimulated by an object of thought. The *behavioural component* of an attitude consists of *predispositions to act* in certain ways toward an attitude object. Figure 16.8 provides concrete examples of how someone's attitude about gun control might be divided into its components.

According to the University of Western Ontario's Jim Olson and the University of Waterloo's Mark Zanna, attitudes vary along several crucial dimensions, including their *strength, accessibility,* and *ambivalence* (Olson & Zanna, 1993). Definitions of *attitude strength* differ, but they generally view strong attitudes as ones that are firmly held (resistant to change), durable over time, and that have a powerful impact on behaviour (Krosnick & Petty, 1995). The *accessibility* of an attitude refers to how often one thinks about it and how quickly it comes to mind. Highly accessible attitudes are quickly and readily available (Fazio, 1995). Attitude accessibility is correlated with attitude strength, as highly accessible attitudes *tend* to be strong, but the concepts are distinct and there is no one-to-one correspondence. *Ambivalent attitudes* are conflicted evaluations that include both positive and negative feelings about an object of thought (Thompson, Zanna, & Griffin, 1995). Like attitude strength, attitude ambivalence has been measured in different ways (Priester & Petty, 2001). Generally speaking, ambivalence increases as the ratio of positive to

negative evaluations gets closer to being equal. When ambivalence is low, an attitude tends to be more predictive of behaviour and less pliable in the face of persuasion (Armitage & Conner, 2000).

Recent years have brought a great deal of research on the determinants and correlates of attitude strength. One determinant is *importance*—the subjective sense of caring and significance that a person attaches to an attitude. Attitudes that are important to people tend to be relatively strong (Boninger et al., 1995). Another factor is whether a person has a *vested interest* in an attitude. A vested interest exists when an attitude relates to an issue that can affect an individual's personal outcomes. For example, university students tend to have a vested interest in whether the province in which they are attending university decides to raise tuition levels. A vested interest in an attitude tends to make it stronger (Crano, 1995). Yet another consideration is one's knowledge of an attitude object. The more *knowledge and information* one has about an object of thought, the stronger one's attitude about it tends to be (Wood, Rhodes, & Biek, 1995). Perhaps this is true because thinking carefully about an attitude object can increase attitude strength (Petty, Haugtvedt, & Smith, 1995).

Attitudes and Behaviour

In the early 1930s, when prejudice against Asians was common in North America, Richard LaPiere journeyed across the United States with a Chinese couple. He was more than a little surprised when they weren't turned away from any of the restaurants they visited in their travels—184 restaurants in all. About six months after his trip, LaPiere surveyed the same restaurants and asked whether they would serve Chinese customers. Roughly half of the restaurants replied to the survey, and over 90% of them indicated that they would not seat Chinese patrons. Thus, LaPiere (1934) found that people who voice prejudicial attitudes may not behave in discriminatory ways. Since then, theorists have often asked: Why don't attitudes predict behaviour better?

Admittedly, LaPiere's study had a fundamental flaw that you may already have detected. The person who seated LaPiere and his Chinese friends may not have been the same person who responded to the mail survey sent later. Nonetheless, numerous follow-up studies, using more sophisticated methods, have shown that attitudes are mediocre predictors of people's behaviour (Ajzen & Fishbein, 2005; McGuire, 1985). That's not to say that they are irrelevant or meaningless. Kraus (1995) reviewed 88 attitude–behaviour studies and found that the average correlation between attitudes and behaviour was 0.38. That figure is high enough to justify Eagly's (1992) conclusion that researchers have identified "many conditions under which attitudes are substantial predictors of behavior" (p. 697). But on the whole, social psychologists have been surprised by how often a favourable attitude toward a candidate or product does not translate into a vote or a purchase.

Why aren't attitude–behaviour relations more consistent? One consideration is that until recently researchers had failed to take variations in *attitude strength* into account. Accumulating evidence indicates that attitude strength influences the connection between attitudes and behaviour. Stronger attitudes are more predictive of behaviour (Eagly & Chaiken, 1998), but this factor has been left uncontrolled in decades of research on attitudes.

Another reason for the inconsistent relations between attitudes and behaviour is that behaviour depends on situational constraints—especially your subjective perceptions of how people expect you to behave. Thus, Icek Ajzen (1985, 1991) maintains that attitudes interact with situational norms to shape people's intentions, which then determine their behaviour. Although you may be strongly opposed to marijuana use, you may not say anything when friends start passing a joint around at a party because you don't want to turn the party into an argument. However, in another situation governed by different norms, such as a class discussion, you may speak out forcefully against marijuana use. If so, you may be trying to change others' attitudes, the process we'll discuss next.

Trying to Change Attitudes: Factors in Persuasion

The fact that attitudes aren't always good predictors of a person's behaviour doesn't stop others from trying to change those attitudes. Indeed, every day you're bombarded by efforts to alter your attitudes. To illustrate, let's trace the events of an imaginary morning. You may not even be out of bed before you start hearing radio advertisements intended to influence your attitudes about specific mouthwashes, computers, athletic shoes, and telephone companies. When you unfurl your newspaper, you find not only more ads but quotes from government officials and special interest groups, carefully crafted to shape your opinions. When you arrive at school, you encounter a group passing out leaflets that urge you to repent your sins and join them in worship. In class, your economics professor champions the wisdom of free markets in international trade. At lunch, the person you've been dating argues about the merits of an "open relationship." Your discussion is interrupted by someone who wants both of you to sign a petition. "Doesn't it ever let up?" you wonder. When it comes to persuasion, the answer is "no." As Anthony Pratkanis and Elliot Aronson (2000) put it, we live in the "age of propaganda." In light of this reality, let's examine some of the factors that determine whether persuasion works.

The process of persuasion includes four basic elements: source, receiver, message, and channel (see Figure 16.9). **The *source* is the person who sends a communication, and the *receiver* is the person to whom the message is sent.** Thus, if you watch a political news conference on TV, the politician is the source, and you and millions of other viewers are the receivers. **The *message* is the information transmitted by the source, and the *channel* is the medium through which the message is sent.** Although the research on communication channels is interesting, we'll confine our discussion to source, message, and receiver variables, which are most applicable to persuasion.

Source Factors

Occasional exceptions to the general rule are seen, but persuasion tends to be more successful when the source has high *credibility* (Pornpitakpan, 2004). What gives a person credibility? Either expertise or trustworthiness. *Expertise* tends to be more influential when

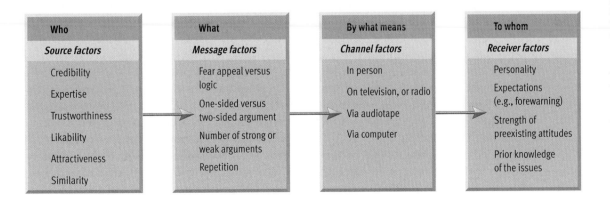

Who	What	By what means	To whom
Source factors	**Message factors**	**Channel factors**	**Receiver factors**
Credibility	Fear appeal versus logic	In person	Personality
Expertise	One-sided versus two-sided argument	On television, or radio	Expectations (e.g., forewarning)
Trustworthiness	Number of strong or weak arguments	Via audiotape	Strength of preexisting attitudes
Likability	Repetition	Via computer	Prior knowledge of the issues
Attractiveness			
Similarity			

Figure 16.9

Overview of the persuasion process. The process of persuasion essentially boils down to *who* (the source) communicates *what* (the message) *by what means* (the channel) *to whom* (the receiver). Thus, there are four sets of variables that influence the process of persuasion: source, message, channel, and receiver factors. The diagram lists some of the more important factors in each category (including some that are not discussed in the text due to space limitations). (Adapted from Lippa, 1994)

Sidney Crosby, who plays for the Pittsburgh Penguins, is considered the next potential superstar in the NHL and is highly sought after by advertisers. If he doesn't fulfill predictions that he'll be the next hockey superstar, he'll lose his value to advertisers seeking to profit from his very positive image.

arguments are ambiguous (Chaiken & Maheswaran, 1994). People try to convey their expertise by mentioning their degrees, their training, and their experience or by showing an impressive grasp of the issue at hand.

Expertise is a plus, but *trustworthiness* can be even more important. Many people tend to accept messages from trustworthy sources with little scrutiny (Priester & Petty, 1995, 2003). If you were told that your province needs to reduce corporate taxes to stimulate its economy, would you be more likely to believe it from the president of a huge corporation in your province or from an economics professor from another province? Probably the latter. Trustworthiness is undermined when a source, such as the corporation president, appears to have something to gain. In contrast, trustworthiness is enhanced when people appear to argue against their own interests (Hunt, Smith, & Kernan, 1985). This effect explains why salespeople often make remarks like, "Frankly, my snowblower isn't the best. They have a better brand down the street. Of course, you'll have to spend quite a bit more...."

Likability also increases the effectiveness of a persuasive source (Johnson, Maio, & Smith-McLallen, 2005), and some of the factors at work in attraction

therefore have an impact on persuasion. Thus, the favourable effect of *physical attractiveness* on likability can make persuasion more effective (Shavitt et al., 1994). We also respond better to sources who share *similarity* with us in ways that are relevant to the issue at hand (Mackie, Worth, & Asuncion, 1990).

The importance of source variables can be seen in advertising. Many companies spend a fortune to obtain an ideal spokesperson. Right now one of the most sought-after spokespersons in Canada is Sidney Crosby. Crosby, although only 18, is being billed as the next superstar of the NHL. Companies quickly abandon spokespersons when their likability declines. If Crosby doesn't fulfill people's expectations for him, he will be dropped as advertisers look for the next superstar.

Message Factors

If you were going to give a speech to a local community group advocating a reduction in taxes on corporations, you'd probably wrestle with a number of questions about how to structure your message. Should you look at both sides of the issue, or should you present just your side? Should you use all of the arguments at your disposal, or should you concentrate on the stronger arguments? Should you deliver a low-key, logical speech? Or should you try to strike fear into the hearts of your listeners? These questions are concerned with message factors in persuasion.

Let's assume that you're aware that there are two sides to the taxation issue. On the one hand, you're convinced that lower corporate taxes will bring new companies to your city and stimulate economic growth. On the other hand, you realize that reduced tax revenues may hurt the quality of education and roads in your province (but you think the benefits will outweigh the costs). Should you present a *one-sided argument* that ignores the possible problems for education and road quality? Or should you present a *two-sided argument* that acknowledges concern about education and road quality and then downplays the probable magnitude of these problems? The optimal strategy depends on a variety of considerations, but overall, two-sided arguments tend to be more effective (Petty & Wegener, 1998). Just mentioning that there are two sides to an issue can increase your credibility with an audience.

In presenting your side, should you use every argument you can think of, or should you focus on the stronger points? One study suggests that it is wise to concentrate on your strong arguments (Friedrich et al., 1996). The investigators exposed students to a variety of weak and strong arguments advocating a new senior comprehensive exam at their school. They found that adding strong arguments paid off, but adding weak arguments hurt rather than helped (see Figure 16.10). It appears that weak arguments may actually raise doubts rather than add to your case.

On the other hand, raw repetition of a message does seem to be an effective strategy. The *validity effect* refers to the finding that simply repeating a statement causes it to be perceived as more valid or true. It doesn't matter whether the statement is true, false, or clearly just an opinion; if you repeat something often enough, some people come to believe it (Boehm, 1994).

Persuasive messages frequently attempt to arouse fear. Opponents of nuclear power scare us with visions of meltdowns. Anti-smoking campaigns emphasize the threat of cancer, and deodorant ads highlight the risk of embarrassment. You could follow their lead and argue that if corporate taxes aren't reduced, your province will be headed toward economic ruin and massive unemployment. *Do appeals to fear work?* Yes—if they are successful in arousing fear. Research reveals that many messages intended to induce fear fail to do so. However, studies involving a wide range of issues (nuclear policy, auto safety, dental hygiene, and so on) have shown that messages that are effective in arousing fear tend to increase persuasion (Block & Keller, 1997; Witte & Allen, 2000). Fear appeals are most likely to work when your listeners view the dire consequences

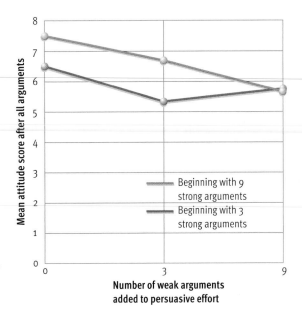

Figure 16.10

The effect of adding weak arguments to one's case. Friedrich et al. (1996) exposed students to various arguments in favour of requiring a new comprehensive exam for seniors at their school. This graph shows the effects of adding zero, three, or nine weak arguments to three or nine strong arguments. As you can see, in this instance, adding weak arguments generally had a negative effect on overall persuasion. (Data from Friedrich et al., 1996)

that you describe as exceedingly unpleasant, fairly probable if they don't take your advice, and avoidable if they do (Das, de Wit, & Stroebe, 2003).

Receiver Factors

What about the receiver of the persuasive message? Are some people easier to persuade than others? Undoubtedly, but researchers have not found any

CONCEPT CHECK 16.3

Understanding Attitudes and Persuasion

Check your understanding of the possible components of attitudes and the elements of persuasion by analyzing hypothetical political strategies. Imagine you're working on a political campaign and you're invited to join the candidate's inner circle in strategy sessions, as staff members prepare the candidate for upcoming campaign stops. During the meetings, you hear various strategies discussed. For each strategy below, indicate which component of voters' attitudes (cognitive, affective, or behavioural) is being targeted for change, and indicate which element in persuasion (source, message, or receiver factors) is being manipulated. The answers are in Appendix A.

1. "You need to convince this crowd that your program for regulating nursing homes is sound. Whatever you do, don't acknowledge the two weaknesses in the program that we've been playing down. I don't care if you're asked point blank. Just slide by the question and keep harping on the program's advantages."

2. "You haven't been smiling enough lately, especially when the TV cameras are rolling. Remember, you can have the best ideas in the world, but if you don't seem likable, you're not gonna get elected. By the way, I think I've lined up some photo opportunities that should help us create an image of sincerity and compassion."

3. "This crowd is already behind you. You don't have to alter their opinions on any issue. Get right to work convincing them to contribute to the campaign. I want them lining up to give money."

personality traits that are reliably associated with susceptibility to persuasion (Petty & Wegener, 1998). Other factors, such as the forewarning a receiver gets about a persuasive effort and the receiver's initial position on an issue, generally seem to be more influential than the receiver's personality.

An old saying suggests that "to be forewarned is to be forearmed." The value of *forewarning* applies to targets of persuasive efforts (Wood & Quinn, 2003). When you shop for a new TV, you *expect* salespeople to work at persuading you, and to some extent this forewarning reduces the impact of their arguments. Considerations that stimulate counterarguing in the receiver tend to increase resistance to persuasion (Jain, Buchanan, & Maheswaran, 2000).

A receiver's resistance to persuasion will depend in part on the nature of the attitude or belief that the source is trying to change. Obviously, resistance is greater when you have to advocate a position that is incompatible with the receiver's existing attitudes or beliefs. In general, people display a *disconfirmation bias* in evaluating arguments (Edwards & Smith, 1996). Arguments that are in conflict with one's prior attitudes are scrutinized longer and subjected to more skeptical analysis than arguments that are consistent with one's prior beliefs.

Furthermore, studies show that *stronger attitudes are more resistant to change* (Eagly & Chaiken, 1998). Strong attitudes may be tougher to alter because they tend to be embedded in networks of beliefs and values that might also require change (Erber, Hodges, & Wilson, 1995). Strong attitudes may also generate more biased and selective processing of persuasive arguments. *Prior knowledge about the issue* at hand also affects the difficulty experienced in trying to change someone's attitude. People who have more issue-relevant knowledge tend to scrutinize arguments more carefully and be more resistant to persuasion (Tormala & Petty, 2002, 2004).

Our review of source, message, and receiver variables has shown that attempting to change attitudes through persuasion involves a complex interplay of factors—and we haven't even looked beneath the surface yet. How do people acquire attitudes in the first place? What dynamic processes within people produce attitude change? We turn to these theoretical issues next.

Theories of Attitude Formation and Change

Many theories have been proposed to explain the mechanisms at work in attitude change (Kruglanski & Stroebe, 2005), whether or not it occurs in response to persuasion. We'll look at four theoretical perspectives: learning theory, dissonance theory, self-perception theory, and the elaboration likelihood model.

Learning Theory

We've seen repeatedly that *learning theory* can help explain a wide range of phenomena, from conditioned fears to the acquisition of sex roles to the development of personality traits. Now we can add attitude formation and change to our list.

The affective, or emotional, component in an attitude can be created through *classical conditioning,* just as other emotional responses can (Olson & Fazio, 2001, 2002). As we discussed in Chapter 6, advertisers routinely try to take advantage of classical conditioning by pairing their products with stimuli that elicit pleasant emotional responses, such as extremely attractive models, highly likable spokespersons, and cherished events, such as the Olympics (Till & Priluck, 2000; Grossman & Till, 1998). This conditioning process is diagrammed in Figure 16.11.

Operant conditioning may come into play when you openly express an attitude, such as "I believe that husbands should do more housework." Some people may endorse your view, while others may jump down your throat. Agreement from other people generally functions as a reinforcer, strengthening your tendency to express a specific attitude (Bohner & Schwarz, 2001). Disagreement often func-

Figure 16.11

Classical conditioning of attitudes in advertising.
Advertisers routinely pair their products with likable celebrities in the hope that their products will come to elicit pleasant emotional responses. See the Critical Thinking Application in Chapter 6 for a more in-depth discussion of this practice.

CS
Products
(e.g., autos, foods)

UCS
Likable
celebrity

CR
Pleasant emotional
response
UCR

tions as a form of punishment, which may gradually weaken your commitment to your viewpoint.

Another person's attitudes may rub off on you through *observational learning* (Oskamp, 1991). If you hear your uncle say, "Conservatives are nothing but puppets of big business" and your mother heartily agrees, your exposure to your uncle's attitude and your mother's reinforcement of your uncle may influence your attitude toward the Conservative Party. Studies show that parents and their children tend to have similar political attitudes (Sears, 1975). Observational learning presumably accounts for much of this similarity. The opinions of teachers, coaches, co-workers, talk-show hosts, rock stars, and so forth are also likely to sway people's attitudes through observational learning.

Dissonance Theory

Leon Festinger's *dissonance theory* assumes that inconsistency among attitudes propels people in the direction of attitude change. Dissonance theory burst into prominence in 1959 when Festinger and J. Merrill Carlsmith published a famous study of counterattitudinal behaviour. Let's look at their findings and at how dissonance theory explains them.

Festinger and Carlsmith (1959) had male college students come to a laboratory, where they worked on excruciatingly dull tasks such as turning pegs repeatedly. When a subject's hour was over, the experimenter confided that some participants' motivation was being manipulated by telling them that the task was interesting and enjoyable before they started it. Then, after a moment's hesitation, the experimenter asked if the subject could help him out of a jam. His usual helper was delayed and he needed someone to testify to the next "subject" (really an accomplice) that the experimental task was interesting. He offered to pay the subject if he would tell the person in the adjoining waiting room that the task was enjoyable and involving.

This entire scenario was enacted to coax participants into doing something that was inconsistent with their true feelings—that is, to engage in *counterattitudinal behaviour*. Some participants received a token payment of $1 for their effort, while others received a more substantial payment of $20 (an amount equivalent to about $80–$90 today, in light of inflation). Later, a second experimenter inquired about the subjects' true feelings regarding the dull experimental task. Figure 16.12 summarizes the design of the Festinger and Carlsmith study.

Who do you think rated the task more favourably—the subjects who were paid $1 or those who were paid $20? Both common sense and learning theory would

predict that the subjects who received the greater reward ($20) should come to like the task more. In reality, however, the subjects who were paid $1 exhibited more favourable attitude change—just as Festinger and Carlsmith had predicted. Why? Dissonance theory provides an explanation.

According to Festinger (1957), **cognitive dissonance exists when related cognitions are inconsistent—that is, when they contradict each other.** Cognitive dissonance is thought to create an unpleasant state of tension that motivates people to reduce their dissonance—usually by altering their cognitions. In the study by Festinger and Carlsmith, the subjects' contradictory cognitions were "The task is boring" and "I told someone the task was enjoyable." The subjects who were paid $20 for lying had an obvious reason for behaving inconsistently with their true attitudes, so these subjects experienced little dissonance. In contrast, the subjects paid $1 had

➤*Cognitive dissonance is a motivating state of affairs. Just as hunger impels a person to eat, so does dissonance impel a person to change his opinions or his behavior.*➤
LEON FESTINGER

Figure 16.12

Design of the Festinger and Carlsmith (1959) study. The sequence of events in this landmark study of counterattitudinal behaviour and attitude change is outlined here. The diagram omits a third condition (no dissonance), in which subjects were not induced to lie. The results in the nondissonance condition were similar to those found in the low-dissonance condition.

Hypothesis:
High dissonance about counterattitudinal behaviour will cause attitude change

Random assignment
Subjects randomly assigned to experimental and control groups

Manipulation of independent variable

Experimental group
Subjects paid $1 for saying task is fun (high dissonance)

Control group
Subjects paid $20 for saying task is fun (low dissonance)

Measurement of dependent variable
Dull task is rated more enjoyable by the high-dissonance subjects

Conclusion:
Dissonance about counterattitudinal behaviour does cause attitude change

Social Behaviour

no readily apparent justification for their lie and experienced high dissonance. To reduce it, they tended to persuade themselves that the task was more enjoyable than they had originally thought. Thus, dissonance theory sheds light on why people sometimes come to believe their own lies.

Cognitive dissonance is also at work when people turn attitudinal somersaults to justify efforts that haven't panned out, a syndrome called *effort justification*. Aronson and Mills (1959) studied effort justification by putting college women through a "severe initiation" before they could qualify to participate in what promised to be an interesting discussion of sexuality. In the initiation, the women had to read obscene passages out loud to a male experimenter. After all that, the highly touted discussion of sexuality turned out to be a boring, taped lecture on reproduction in lower animals. Subjects in the severe initiation condition experienced highly dissonant cognitions ("I went through a lot to get here" and "This discussion is terrible"). How did they reduce their dissonance? Apparently by changing their attitude about the discussion, since they rated it more favourably than subjects in two control conditions. Effort justification may be at work in many facets of everyday life. For example, people who wait in line for an hour or more to get into an exclusive restaurant often praise the restaurant afterward even if they have been served a mediocre meal.

Dissonance theory has been tested in hundreds of studies with mixed, but largely favourable, results. The dynamics of dissonance appear to underlie many important types of attitude changes (Draycott & Dabbs, 1998; Hosseini, 1997; Keller & Block, 1999). Research has supported Festinger's claim that dissonance involves genuine psychological discomfort and even physiological arousal (Croyle & Cooper, 1983; Devine et al., 1999). However, dissonance effects are not among the most reliable phenomena in social psychology, perhaps because people vary in the need for cognitive consistency (Cialdini, Trost, & Newsom, 1995). Moreover, even

when people exhibit a clear preference for consistency, it's difficult to predict when dissonance will occur, and it has become apparent that people can reduce their dissonance in quite a variety of ways besides changing their attitudes (Olson & Stone, 2005; Visser & Cooper, 2003).

Self-Perception Theory 12c

After taking a close look at studies of counterattitudinal behaviour, Daryl Bem (1967) concluded that self-perception, rather than dissonance, explains why people sometimes come to believe their own lies. According to Bem's *self-perception theory*, people often *infer* their attitudes from their behaviour. Thus, Bem argued that in the study by Festinger and Carlsmith (1959), the subjects paid $1 probably thought to themselves, "A dollar isn't enough money to get me to lie, so I must have found the task enjoyable."

This thinking isn't much different from what dissonance theory would predict. Both theories suggest that people often think, "If I said it, it must be true." But the two theories propose that similar patterns of thought unfold for entirely different reasons. According to dissonance theory, subjects think along these lines because they're struggling to reduce tension caused by inconsistency among their cognitions. Research by Zanna and his colleagues (Zanna & Cooper, 1974) demonstrated that arousal was central to the attitude change produced in dissonance-arousing situations. According to self-perception theory, subjects are engaged in normal attributional efforts to better understand their own behaviour. Bem originally believed that most findings explained by dissonance were really due to self-perception. However, studies eventually showed that self-perception is at work primarily when subjects do not have well-defined attitudes regarding the issue at hand (Olson & Roese, 1995). Although self-perception theory did not replace dissonance theory, Bem's work demonstrated that attitudes are sometimes inferred from one's own behaviour (Olson & Stone, 2005) (see Figure 16.13).

Elaboration Likelihood Model 12c

The *elaboration likelihood model* of attitude change, originally proposed by Richard Petty and John Cacioppo (1986), asserts that there are two basic "routes" to persuasion (Petty & Wegener, 1999). The *central route* is taken when people carefully ponder the content and logic of persuasive messages. The *peripheral route* is taken when persuasion depends on nonmessage factors, such as the attractiveness and credibility of the source, or on conditioned emotional responses (see Figure 16.14). For example, a politician who campaigns by delivering carefully

Figure 16.13

Bem's self-perception theory. The traditional view is that attitudes determine behaviour. However, Bem stood conventional logic on its head when he proposed that behaviour often determines (or causes people to draw inferences about) their attitudes. Subsequent research on attribution has shown that sometimes people *do* infer their attitudes from their behaviour.

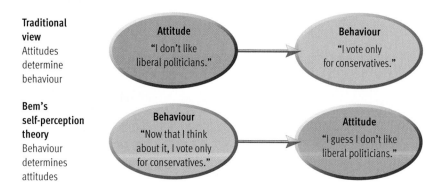

Traditional view
Attitudes determine behaviour

Bem's self-perception theory
Behaviour determines attitudes

Figure **16.14**

The elaboration likelihood model. According to the elaboration likelihood model (Petty & Cacioppo, 1986), the central route to persuasion leads to more elaboration of message content and more enduring attitude change than the peripheral route to persuasion.

researched speeches that thoughtfully analyze complex issues is following the central route to persuasion. In contrast, a politician who depends on marching bands, flag waving, celebrity endorsements, and emotional slogans is following the peripheral route.

Both routes can lead to persuasion. However, according to the elaboration likelihood model, the durability of attitude change depends on the extent to which people elaborate on (think about) the contents of persuasive communications. Studies suggest that the central route to persuasion leads to more enduring attitude change than the peripheral route (Petty & Wegener, 1998). Research also suggests that attitudes changed through central processes predict behaviour better than attitudes changed through peripheral processes (Kruglanski & Stroebe, 2005; Petty, Wegener, & Fabrigar, 1997).

REVIEW OF KEY POINTS

- Attitudes may be made up of cognitive, affective, and behavioural components. Attitudes and behaviour aren't as consistent as one might assume, in part because attitude strength varies and in part because attitudes only create predispositions to behave in certain ways.

- A source of persuasion who is credible, expert, trustworthy, likable, and physically attractive tends to be relatively effective in stimulating attitude change.

- Although there are some situational limitations, two-sided arguments and fear arousal are effective elements in persuasive messages. Repetition is helpful, but adding weak arguments to one's case may hurt more than help.

- Persuasion is undermined when a receiver is forewarned, when the sender advocates a position that is incompatible with the receiver's existing attitudes, or when strong attitudes are targeted.

- Attitudes may be shaped through classical conditioning, operant conditioning, and observational learning. Festinger's dissonance theory asserts that inconsistent attitudes cause tension and that people alter their attitudes to reduce cognitive dissonance.

- Dissonance theory has been used to explain attitude change following counterattitudinal behaviour and efforts that haven't panned out. Some of these results can be explained by self-perception theory, which posits that people may infer their attitudes from their behaviour.

- The elaboration likelihood model of persuasion holds that the central route to persuasion tends to yield longer-lasting attitude change than the peripheral route.

Conformity and Obedience: Yielding to Others 12E

Social influence can take many forms. Sometimes we change our behaviour as a result of adopting a new social role. This was shown dramatically by psychologist Philip Zimbardo in his famous Stanford prison experiment conducted in 1971. He recruited average male undergraduates to take part in a simulation of a prison setting. Students were randomly assigned to play the role of a prisoner or a guard. As the simulation progressed, guards and prisoners appeared to get caught up in playing their roles, with the guards becoming increasingly aggressive. Eventually, the simulation had to be stopped for the safety of all concerned. Similar processes have been invoked in attempts to understand the behaviour of American military personnel in their treatment of Iraqi prisoners at Abu Ghraib. In a similar setting, atrocities (including the murder of a 16-year-old Somali boy) were carried out by members of the Canadian Airborne Regiment while they were on a peacekeeping mission in Somalia in 1993 (Cheney, 2004). While role-playing may explain such behaviour in part (Haney & Zimbardo, 1998), what sometimes also happens in these situations is that once people begin behaving in a certain way, others become caught up in the pressure to conform.

We all have had experiences when we've had to decide between doing what we believe is right or just going along with the crowd or with someone perceived to be in authority. These situations are very difficult, and most people find themselves sometimes

PREVIEW QUESTIONS

- How did Asch study conformity, and what did he learn?
- How did Milgram study obedience, and what did he learn?
- Why were Milgram's findings so controversial?
- How well do North American findings on conformity and obedience generalize to other cultures?

Web Link 16.5

The Stanford Prison Experiment

http://www.prisonexp.org/

View slides of Philip Zimbardo's experiment and learn how it parallels more recent examples of conformity, such as the Abu Ghraib abuse scandal.

❝*That we have found the tendency to conformity in our society so strong that reasonably intelligent and well-meaning young people are willing to call white black is a matter of concern.*❞
SOLOMON ASCH

going with the crowd or obeying the authority figure even though they know it isn't right. What are the factors that influence our decisions in such contexts? In this section, we'll analyze the dynamics of social influence at work in conformity and obedience.

Conformity

If you keep a well-manicured lawn, are you exhibiting conformity? According to social psychologists, it depends on whether your behaviour is the result of group pressure. *Conformity* **occurs when people yield to real or imagined social pressure.** For example, if you maintain a well-groomed lawn only to avoid complaints from your neighbours, you're conforming to social pressure. However, if you maintain a nice lawn because you genuinely prefer a nice lawn, that's *not* conformity.

In the 1950s, Solomon Asch (1951, 1955, 1956) devised a clever procedure that reduced ambiguity about whether subjects were conforming, allowing him to investigate the variables that govern conformity. Let's re-create one of Asch's (1955) classic experiments, which have become the most widely replicated studies in the history of social psychology (Markus, Kitayama, & Heiman, 1996). The subjects are male undergraduates recruited for a study of visual perception. A group of seven subjects are shown a large card with a vertical line on it and are then asked to indicate which of three lines on a second card matches the original "standard line" in length (see Figure 16.15). All seven subjects are given a turn at the task, and they announce their choice to the group. The subject in the sixth chair doesn't know it, but everyone else in the group is an accomplice of the experimenter, and they're about to make him wonder whether he has taken leave of his senses.

The accomplices give accurate responses on the first two trials. On the third trial, line number 2 clearly is the correct response, but the first five "subjects" all say that line number 3 matches the standard line. The genuine subject is bewildered and can't believe his ears. Over the course of the next 15 trials, the accomplices all give the same incorrect response on 11 of them. How does the real subject respond? The line judgments are easy and unambiguous. So, if the participant consistently agrees with the accomplices, he isn't making honest mistakes—he's conforming.

Averaging across all 50 participants, Asch (1955) found that the young men conformed on 37% of the trials. The subjects varied considerably in their tendency to conform, however. Of the 50 participants, 13 never caved in to the group, while 14 conformed on more than half the trials. One could argue that the results show that people confronting a unanimous majority generally tend to *resist* the pressure to conform, but given how clear and easy the line judgments were, most social scientists viewed the findings as a dramatic demonstration of humans' propensity to conform (Levine, 1999).

In subsequent studies, Asch (1956) found that *group size* and *group unanimity* are key determinants of conformity. To examine the impact of group size, Asch repeated his procedure with groups that included from 1 to 15 accomplices. Little conformity was seen when a subject was pitted against just one person, but conformity increased rapidly as group size went from two to four, and then levelled off (see Figure 16.16). Thus, Asch reasoned that as groups grow larger, conformity increases—up to a point, a conclusion that has been echoed by other researchers (Cialdini & Trost, 1998).

However, group size made little difference if just one accomplice "broke" with the others, wrecking their unanimous agreement. The presence of another dissenter lowered conformity to about one-quarter of its peak, even when the dissenter made *inaccurate* judgments that happened to conflict with the majority view. Apparently, the subjects just needed to hear someone else question the accuracy of the group's perplexing responses. The importance of unanimity in fostering conformity has been replicated in subsequent research (Nemeth & Chiles, 1988).

What additional factors influence the likelihood of conformity? Among other things, people are more likely to conform when they are in ambiguous situations or when they have reasons to doubt their own judgments (Campbell, Tesser, & Fairey, 1986). Interestingly, if the situation is ambiguous, increasing the importance of the judgment—that is, the incentives for being accurate—only serves to heighten partici-

Figure **16.15**

Stimuli used in Asch's conformity studies. Subjects were asked to match a standard line (top) with one of three other lines displayed on another card (bottom). The task was easy—until experimental accomplices started responding with obviously incorrect answers, creating a situation in which Asch evaluated subjects' conformity.

SOURCE: Adapted from Asch, S. (1955). Opinion and social pressure. *Scientific American, 193* (5), 31–35. Based on illustrations by Sara Love. Copyright © 1955 by Scientific American, Inc. All rights reserved.

1   2   3

pants' tendency to conform (Baron, Vandello, & Brunsman, 1996). In other words, when the pressure is on, people tend to follow the leader.

While the majority typically rules the day, there are some circumstances under which the minority opinion may win out. For example, the more consistent the minority is in its opposition, the more influence it may have in swaying the opinion of the majority (Moscovici, 1976). Not only may the minority prevail, but its members may also be viewed quite positively by observers. The University of Toronto's John Bassili found that observers often rated a consistent minority positively in terms of strength, conviction, consistency, and integrity (Bassili & Provencal, 1988).

Obedience 12E

***Obedience* is a form of compliance that occurs when people follow direct commands, usually from someone in a position of authority**. To a surprising extent, when an authority figure says, "Jump!" many people simply ask, "How high?" For most people, willingness to obey someone in authority is the rule, not the exception.

Milgram's Studies

Stanley Milgram wanted to study this tendency to obey authority figures. Like many other people after World War II, he was troubled by how readily the citizens of Germany had followed the orders of dictator Adolf Hitler, even when the orders required morally

repugnant actions, such as the slaughter of millions of Jews. Milgram, who had worked with Solomon Asch, set out to design a standard laboratory procedure for the study of obedience, much like Asch's procedure for studying conformity. The clever experiment that Milgram devised became one of the most famous and controversial studies in the annals of psychology. It has been hailed as a "monumental contribution" to science and condemned as "dangerous, dehumanizing, and unethical research" (Ross, 1988). Decades after the research was conducted, it still generates spirited debate (Berkowitz, 1999; Lutsky, 1995). Because of its importance, it's our Featured Study for this chapter.

Figure 16.16

Conformity and group size. This graph shows the percentage of trials on which participants conformed as a function of group size in Asch's research. Asch found that conformity became more frequent as group size increased up to about four, and then conformity levelled off. (Data from Asch, 1955)

SOURCE: Adapted from Asch, S. (1955). Opinion and social pressure. *Scientific American, 193* (5), 31–35. Based on illustrations by Sara Love. Copyright © 1955 by Scientific American, Inc. All rights reserved.

FEATURED STUDY

"I Was Just Following Orders"

"I was just following orders." That was the essence of Adolf Eichmann's defence when he was tried for his war crimes, which included masterminding the Nazis' attempted extermination of European Jews. Milgram wanted to determine the extent to which people are willing to follow authorities' orders. In particular, he wanted to identify the factors that lead people to follow commands that violate their ethics, such as commands to harm an innocent stranger.

Method

The participants were a diverse collection of 40 men from the local community, recruited through advertisements to participate in a study at Yale University. When a subject arrived at the lab, he met the experimenter and another subject, a likable, 47-year-old accountant, who was actually an accomplice of the experimenter. The "subjects" were told that the study would concern

the effects of punishment on learning. They drew slips of paper from a hat to get their assignments, but the drawing was fixed so that the real subject always became the "teacher" and the accomplice the "learner."

The participant then watched as the learner was strapped into an electrified chair through which a shock could be delivered to the learner whenever he made a mistake on the task (left photo in Figure 16.17). The subject was told that the shocks would be painful but "would not cause tissue damage," and he was then taken to an adjoining room that housed the shock generator that he would control in his role as the teacher. This elaborate apparatus (right photo in Figure 16.17) had 30 switches designed to administer shocks varying from 15 to 450 volts, with labels ranging from "Slight shock" to "Danger: severe shock" and "XXX." Although the apparatus looked and sounded realistic, it was a fake, and the learner was never shocked.

Investigator: Stanley Milgram (Yale University)

Source: Behavioral study of obedience. *Journal of Abnormal and Social Psychology,* 1963, *67,* 371–378.

Figure 16.17

Milgram's experiment on obedience. The photo on the left shows the "learner" being connected to the shock generator during one of Milgram's experimental sessions. The photo on the right shows the fake shock generator used in the study. The surprising results of the Milgram (1963) study are summarized in the bar graph. Although subjects frequently protested, the vast majority (65%) delivered the entire series of shocks to the learner.

SOURCE: Photos copyright © 1965 by Stanley Milgram. From the film *Obedience*, distributed by The Pennsylvania State University. Reprinted by permission of Alexandra Milgram.

Level of shock (as labelled on Milgram's shock machine)

| Slight shock | Moderate shock | Strong shock | Very strong shock | Intense shock | Extreme intensity shock | Danger: severe shock | XXX |

As the "learning experiment" proceeded, the accomplice made many mistakes that necessitated shocks from the teacher, who was instructed to increase the shock level after each wrong answer. At "300 volts," the learner began to pound on the wall between the two rooms in protest and soon stopped responding to the teacher's questions. At this point, participants ordinarily turned to the experimenter for guidance. The experimenter, a 31-year-old male in a grey lab coat, firmly indicated that no response was the same as a wrong answer and that the teacher should continue to give stronger and stronger shocks to the now silent learner. If the participant expressed unwillingness to continue, the experimenter responded sternly with one of four prearranged prods, such as, "It is absolutely essential that you continue."

When a participant refused to obey the experimenter, the session came to an end. The dependent variable was the maximum shock the participant was willing to administer before refusing to cooperate. After each session, the true purpose of the study was explained to the subject, who was reassured that the shock was fake and the learner was unharmed.

Results

No participant stopped cooperating before the learner reached the point of pounding on the wall, but five quit at that point. As the graph in Figure 16.17 shows, only 14 out of 40 subjects defied the experimenter before the full series of shocks was completed. Thus, 26 of the 40 subjects (65%) administered all 30 levels of shock. Although they

tended to obey the experimenter, many participants voiced and displayed considerable distress about harming the learner. The horrified subjects groaned, bit their lips, stuttered, trembled, and broke into a sweat, but they continued administering the shocks.

Discussion

Based on these results, Milgram concluded that obedience to authority is even more common than he or others had anticipated. Before the study was conducted, Milgram had described it to 40 psychiatrists and had asked them to predict how much shock subjects would be willing to administer to their innocent victims. Most of the psychiatrists had predicted that fewer than 1% of the subjects would continue to the end of the series of shocks!

In interpreting his results, Milgram argued that strong pressure from an authority figure can make decent people do indecent things to others. Applying this insight to Nazi war crimes and other travesties, Milgram asserted that some sinister actions may not be due to actors' evil character so much as to situational pressures that can lead normal people to engage in acts of treachery and violence. Thus, he arrived at the disturbing conclusion that given the right circumstances, anyone might obey orders to inflict harm on innocent strangers.

Comment

In itself, obedience is not necessarily bad or wrong. Social groups of any size depend on obedience to function smoothly. Life would be chaotic if orders from police, parents, physicians, bosses, generals, and government officials were routinely ignored. However, Milgram's study suggests that many people are overly willing to submit to the orders of someone in command.

If you're like most people, you're probably confident that you wouldn't follow an experimenter's demands to inflict harm on a helpless victim. But the empirical findings indicate that you're probably wrong. After many replications, the results are deplorable, but clear: Most people can be coerced into engaging in actions that violate their morals and values. This finding is disheartening, but it sharpens our understanding of moral atrocities, such as the Nazi persecutions of Jews. ■

After his initial demonstration, Milgram (1974) tried about 20 variations on his experimental procedure, looking for factors that influence participants' obedience. In one variation, Milgram moved the study away from Yale's campus to see if the prestige of the university was contributing to the subjects' obedience. When the study was run in a seedy office building by the "Research Associates of Bridgeport," only a small decrease in obedience was observed (48% of the subjects gave all the shocks).

In another version of the study, Milgram borrowed a trick from Asch's conformity experiments and set up teams of three teachers that included two more accomplices. When they drew lots, the real subject was always selected to run the shock apparatus in consultation with his fellow teachers. When both accomplices accepted the experimenter's orders to continue shocking the learner, the pressure increased obedience a bit. However, if an accomplice defied the experimenter and supported the subject's objections, obedience declined dramatically (only 10% of the subjects gave all the shocks), just as conformity had dropped rapidly when dissent surfaced in Asch's conformity studies. Dissent from another "teacher" turned out to be one of the few variations that reduced participants' obedience appreciably. As a whole, Milgram was surprised at how high subjects' obedience remained as he changed various aspects of his experiment.

The Ensuing Controversy

Milgram's study evoked a controversy that continues through today. Some critics argued that Milgram's results couldn't be generalized to apply to the real world (Baumrind, 1964; Orne & Holland, 1968). They maintained that participants went along only because they knew it was an experiment and "everything must be okay." Or they argued that subjects who agree to participate in a scientific study *expect to obey* orders from an experimenter. Milgram (1964, 1968) replied by arguing that if subjects had thought, "everything must be okay," they wouldn't have experienced the enormous distress that they clearly showed.

As for the idea that research participants expect to follow an experimenter's commands, Milgram pointed out that so do real-world soldiers and bureaucrats who are accused of villainous acts performed in obedience to authority. "I reject Baumrind's argument that the observed obedience doesn't count because it occurred where it is appropriate," said Milgram (1964). "That is precisely why it *does* count." Overall, the evidence supports the generalizability of Milgram's results, which were consistently replicated for many years, in diverse settings, with a variety of subjects and procedural variations (Blass, 1999; Miller, 1986).

Critics also questioned the ethics of Milgram's procedure (Baumrind, 1964; Kelman, 1967). They noted that without prior consent, subjects were exposed to extensive deception that could undermine their trust in people and to severe stress that could leave emotional scars. Moreover, most participants also had to confront the disturbing fact that they caved in to the experimenter's commands to inflict harm on an innocent victim.

Milgram's defenders argued that the brief distress experienced by his subjects was a small price to pay for the insights that emerged from his obedience studies. Looking back, however, many psychologists seem to share the critics' concerns about the ethical implications of Milgram's work. His procedure is questionable by contemporary standards of research ethics, and no replications of his obedience study have been conducted in the United States since the mid-1970s (Blass, 1991)—a bizarre epitaph for what may be psychology's best-known experiment.

Cultural Variations in Conformity and Obedience 12E

Are conformity and obedience unique to American or Western culture? By no means. The Asch and Milgram experiments have been repeated in many societies, where they have yielded results roughly

The essence of obedience is that a person comes to view himself as the instrument for carrying out another person's wishes, and he therefore no longer regards himself as responsible for his actions.
STANLEY MILGRAM

similar to those seen in the United States. Thus, the phenomena of conformity and obedience seem to transcend culture.

The replications of Milgram's obedience study have largely been limited to industrialized nations similar to the United States. Comparisons of the results of these studies must be made with caution because the composition of the samples and the experimental procedures have varied somewhat. But many of the studies have reported even higher obedience rates than those seen in Milgram's American samples. For example, obedience rates of over 80% have been reported for samples from Italy, Germany, Austria, Spain, and Holland (Smith & Bond, 1994). Thus, the surprisingly high level of obedience observed by Milgram does not appear to be peculiar to the United States.

The Asch experiment has been repeated in a more diverse range of societies than the Milgram experiment. Like many other cultural differences in social behaviour, variations in conformity appear to be related to the degree of *individualism versus collectivism* seen in a society. Various theorists have argued that collectivistic cultures, which emphasize respect for group norms, cooperation, and harmony, probably encourage more conformity than individualistic cultures (Schwartz, 1990) and have a more positive view of conformity (Kim & Markus, 1999). As Matsumoto (1994, p. 162) puts it, "To conform in American culture

is to be weak or deficient somehow. But this is not true in other cultures. Many cultures foster more collective, group-oriented values, and concepts of conformity, obedience, and compliance enjoy much higher status." Consistent with this analysis, studies *have* found higher levels of conformity in collectivistic cultures than in individualistic cultures (Bond & Smith, 1996; Smith, 2001).

REVIEW OF KEY POINTS

● Conformity involves yielding to social pressure. Asch found that subjects often conform to the group, even when the group reports inaccurate judgments on a simple line-judging task. Conformity becomes more likely as group size increases, up to a group size of four, and then levels off. If a small group isn't unanimous, conformity declines rapidly.

● In Milgram's landmark study of obedience to authority, adult men drawn from the community showed a remarkable tendency, in spite of their misgivings, to follow orders to shock an innocent stranger. Milgram concluded that situational pressures can make decent people do indecent things.

● Critics asserted that Milgram's results were not generalizable to the real world and that his methods were unethical. The generalizability of Milgram's findings has stood the test of time, but his work also helped to stimulate stricter ethical standards for research.

● The Asch and Milgram experiments have been replicated in many cultures. These replications have uncovered modest cultural variations in the propensity to conform or to obey an authority figure.

Behaviour in Groups: Joining with Others

12E

PREVIEW QUESTIONS

● What is the bystander effect?

● What processes contribute to reduced individual productivity in larger groups?

● What is group polarization?

● What are the antecedent conditions and symptoms of groupthink?

Social psychologists study groups as well as individuals, but exactly what is a group? Are all the divorced fathers living in Saskatoon a group? Are three strangers moving skyward in an elevator a group? What if the elevator gets stuck? How about four students from your psychology class who study together regularly? A jury deciding a trial? The Vancouver Canucks? The Canadian Parliament? Some of these collections of people are groups and others aren't. Let's examine the concept of a group to find out which of these collections qualify.

In social psychologists' eyes, **a *group* consists of two or more individuals who interact and are interdependent.** The divorced fathers in Saskatoon aren't likely to qualify on either count. Strangers sharing an elevator might interact briefly, but they're not interdependent. However, if the elevator got stuck and they had to deal with an emergency together, they could suddenly become a group. Your

psychology classmates who study together are a group, as they interact and depend on each other to achieve shared goals. So do the members of a jury, a sports team such as the Vancouver Canucks, and a large organization such as the Canadian Parliament. Historically, most groups have interacted on a face-to-face basis, but advances in telecommunications are changing that reality. In the era of the Internet, people can interact, become interdependent, and develop a group identity, without ever meeting in person (Bargh & McKenna, 2004; McKenna & Bargh, 1998).

Groups vary in many ways. Obviously, a study group, the Canucks, and Parliament are very different in terms of size, purpose, formality, longevity, similarity of members, and diversity of activities. Can anything meaningful be said about groups if they're so diverse? Yes. In spite of their immense variability, groups share certain features that affect their functioning. Among other things, most groups have *roles* that allocate special responsibilities to some members, *norms* about suitable behaviour, a *communication structure* that reflects who talks to whom, and a *power structure* that determines which members wield the most influence (Forsyth, 1999).

Thus, when people join together in a group, they create a social organism with unique characteristics and dynamics that can take on a life of its own. One of social psychology's enduring insights is that in a given situation you may behave quite differently when you're in a group than when you're alone. To illustrate this point, let's look at some interesting research on helping behaviour.

Behaviour Alone and in Groups: The Case of the Bystander Effect

Imagine that while waiting for the subway at Bloor Station in downtown Toronto, you lose your balance and find yourself lying on the tracks with a train speeding toward you. Would you be better off if there were lots of people on the subway platform? It certainly makes sense since, after all, there's "safety in numbers." Logically, as group size increases, the probability of having a "good Samaritan" on the scene increases. Or does it?

Kaur-Hayer Harbajan, a 58-year-old mother, found herself facing a situation exactly like that on September 15, 2003 (Freed, 2003). As she was waiting for the subway train, she lost her balance and fell onto the tracks. She could see the train fast approaching her. Fortunately for her, 22-year-old Petru George Ciorau jumped down and, seeing that he could not get her back onto the platform in time, carried her across the tracks and squeezed them both against the tunnel wall as the train made its arrival. Mrs. Harbajan was lucky, because some classic research in social psychology tells us that the more people there are around, the less likely it is that help will be forthcoming. Ciorau was stunned by the inaction of others. He said, "I was wondering why most people wouldn't do that. If that's my mom down there and some people are watching I would want someone to jump in" (Freed, 2003, p. B5).

We've seen before that human behaviour isn't necessarily logical. When it comes to helping behaviour, many studies have uncovered an apparent paradox called the **bystander effect:** **People are less likely to provide needed help when they are in groups than when they are alone.** Evidence that your probability of getting help *declines* as group size increases was first described by John Darley and Bibb Latané (1968), who were conducting research on the determinants of helping behaviour. In the Darley

and Latané study, students in individual cubicles connected by an intercom participated in discussion groups of three sizes. (The separate cubicles allowed the researchers to examine each individual's behaviour in a group context, a technique that minimizes confounded variables in individual–group comparisons.) Early in the discussion, a student who was an experimental accomplice hesitantly mentioned that he was prone to seizures. Later in the discussion, the same accomplice feigned a severe seizure and cried out for help. Although a majority of subjects sought assistance for the student, the tendency to seek help *declined* with increasing group size.

Similar trends have been seen in many other experiments, in which over 6000 subjects have had opportunities to respond to apparent emergencies, including fires, asthma attacks, faintings, crashes, and flat tires, as well as less pressing needs to answer a door or to pick up objects dropped by a stranger (Latané & Nida, 1981). Many of the experiments have been highly realistic studies conducted in subways, stores, and shopping malls, and many have compared individuals against groups in face-to-face interaction. Pooling the results of this research, Latané and Nida (1981) estimated that subjects who were alone provided help 75% of the time, whereas subjects in the presence of others provided help only 53% of the time. They concluded that the only significant limiting condition on the bystander effect is that it is less likely to occur when the need for help is not ambiguous.

What accounts for the bystander effect? A number of factors may be at work. Bystander effects are most likely in ambiguous situations because people look around to see whether others think there's an emergency. If everyone hesitates, their inaction suggests that there's no real need for help. The *diffusion of responsibility* that occurs in a group is also important. If you're by yourself when you encounter someone in need of help, the responsibility to provide help rests squarely on your shoulders. However, if other people are present, the responsibility is divided among you, and you may all say to yourselves, "Someone else will help." A reduced sense of responsibility may contribute to other aspects of behaviour in groups, as we'll see in the next section.

Group Productivity and Social Loafing

Have you ever driven through a road construction project—at a snail's pace, of course—and become irritated because so many workers seem to be just standing around? Maybe the irony of the posted sign

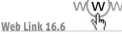

Web Link 16.6

The Psychology of Cyberspace
http://www.rider.edu/users/suler/psycyber/psycyber.html

As the Internet continues to develop into an ever more important part of our lives, a number of social scientists have begun to examine human behaviour in the computer-mediated environment called cyberspace. John Suler's site at Rider University presents a major overview of the research being carried out in this new field.

"Your tax dollars at work" made you imagine that they were all dawdling. And then again, perhaps not. Individuals' productivity often *does* decline in larger groups (Karau & Williams, 1993). This fact is unfortunate, as many important tasks can only be accomplished in groups. Group productivity is crucial to committees, sports teams, firefighting crews, sororities, study groups, symphonies, and work teams of all kinds, from the morning crew in a little diner to the board of directors of a major company.

Two factors appear to contribute to reduced individual productivity in larger groups. One factor is *reduced efficiency* resulting from the *loss of coordination* among workers' efforts. As you put more people on a yearbook staff, for instance, you'll probably create more and more duplication of effort and increase how often group members end up working at cross purposes.

The second factor contributing to low productivity in groups involves *effort* rather than efficiency. **Social loafing is a reduction in effort by individuals when they work in groups as compared to when they work by themselves.** To investigate social loafing, Latané and his colleagues (1979) measured the sound output produced by subjects who were asked to cheer or clap as loud as they could. So they couldn't see or hear other group members, subjects were told that the study concerned the importance of sensory feedback and were asked to don blindfolds and put on headphones through which loud noise was played. This manoeuvre permitted a simple deception: Subjects were *led to believe* that they were working alone or in a group of two or six, when in fact *individual* output was actually measured.

When participants *thought* that they were working in larger groups, their individual output declined. Since lack of coordination could not affect individual output, the subjects' decreased sound production had to be due to reduced effort. Latané and his colleagues also had the same subjects clap and shout in genuine groups of two and six and found an additional decrease in production that was attributed to loss of coordination. Figure 16.18 shows how social loafing and loss of coordination combined to reduce productivity as group size increased.

The social-loafing effect has been replicated in numerous studies in which subjects have worked on a variety of tasks, including cheering, pumping air, swimming in a relay race, solving mazes, evaluating editorials, and brainstorming for new ideas (Karau & Williams, 1995; Levine & Moreland, 1998). Social loafing and the bystander effect appear to share a common cause: diffusion of responsibility in groups (Comer, 1995; Latané, 1981). As group size increases, the responsibility for getting a job done is divided among more people, and many group members ease up because their individual contribution is less recognizable. Thus, social loafing occurs in situations where individuals can "hide in the crowd" (Karau & Williams, 1993).

Social loafing is *not* inevitable. Social loafing is less likely when group members are convinced that individual performance is crucial to group performance and that excellent group performance will lead to valued outcomes (Shepperd & Taylor, 1999). And social loafing is reduced when people work in cohesive, close-knit, committed groups (Karau & Hart, 1998). Cultural factors may also influence the likelihood of social loafing. Studies with subjects from Japan, China, and Taiwan suggest that social loafing may be less prevalent in collectivistic cultures, which place a high priority on meeting group goals and contributing to one's ingroups (Karau & Williams, 1995; Smith, 2001).

Decision Making in Groups

Productivity is not the only issue that commonly concerns groups. When people join together in groups, they often have to make decisions about what the group will do and how it will use its resources. Whether it's your study group deciding

Figure 16.18

The effect of loss of coordination and social loafing on group productivity. The amount of sound produced per person declined noticeably when people worked in actual groups of two or six (orange line). This decrease in productivity reflects both loss of coordination and social loafing. Sound per person also declined when subjects merely thought they were working in groups of two or six (purple line). This smaller decrease in productivity is due to social loafing.

SOURCE: Adapted from Latané, B., Williams, K., & Harkins, S. (1979). Many hands make light the work: The causes and consequences of social loafing. *Journal of Personality and Social Psychology, 37,* 822–832. Copyright © 1979 by the American Psychological Association. Adapted by permission of the author.

what type of pizza to order, a jury deciding on a verdict, or Parliament deciding on whether to pass a bill, groups make decisions. There is good evidence that decision making in groups may sometimes display or accentuate important biases when compared to individual decision making. These biases may be reflected in a variety of decision-making contexts, such as the common chore of making predictions regarding completion of one of the group's tasks. For example, research by Wilfrid Laurier University's Roger Buehler and his colleagues has shown that the tendency of individuals to make optimistic predictions regarding how long it will take to complete a task is accentuated as a result of group discussion (Buehler, Messervey, & Griffin, 2005).

Evaluating decision making is often more complicated than evaluating productivity. In many cases, the "right" decision may not be readily apparent. Who can say whether your study group ordered the right pizza or whether Parliament passed the right bills? Nonetheless, social psychologists have discovered some interesting tendencies in group decision making. We'll take a brief look at *group polarization* and *groupthink*.

Group Polarization

Who leans toward more cautious decisions: individuals or groups? Common sense suggests that groups will work out compromises that cancel out members' extreme views. Hence, the collective wisdom of the group should yield relatively conservative choices. Is common sense correct? To investigate this question, Stoner (1961) asked individual subjects to give their recommendations on tough decisions and then asked the same subjects to engage in group discussion to arrive at joint recommendations. When Stoner compared individuals' average recommendation against their group decision generated through discussion, he found that groups arrived at *riskier* decisions than individuals did. Stoner's finding was replicated in other studies (e.g., Pruitt, 1971), and the phenomenon acquired the name *risky shift*.

However, investigators eventually determined that groups can shift either way, toward risk or caution, depending on which way the group is leaning to begin with (Friedkin, 1999; Myers & Lamm, 1976). A shift toward a more extreme position, an effect called *polarization,* is often the result of group discussion (Tindale, Kameda, & Hinsz, 2003). Thus, **group polarization occurs when group discussion strengthens a group's dominant point of view and produces a shift toward a more extreme decision in that direction** (see Figure 16.19). Group polarization does *not* involve widening the gap between factions in a group, as its name might suggest. In fact, group polarization can contribute to consensus in a group, as we'll see in our upcoming discussion of groupthink.

Why does group polarization occur? One reason is that group discussion often exposes group members to persuasive arguments that they had not thought about previously (Stasser, 1991). Another reason is that when people discover that their views are shared by others, they tend to express even stronger views because they want to be liked by their ingroups (Hogg, Turner, & Davidson, 1990).

Groupthink

In contrast to group polarization, which is a normal process in group dynamics, groupthink is more like a "disease" that can infect decision making in groups. *Groupthink* **occurs when members of a cohesive group emphasize concurrence at the expense of critical thinking in arriving at a decision.** As you might imagine, groupthink doesn't produce very effective decision making. Indeed, groupthink can lead to major blunders that may look incomprehensible after the fact. Irving Janis (1972) first described groupthink in his effort to explain how former U.S. president John F. Kennedy and his advisers could have miscalculated so badly in deciding to invade Cuba at the Bay of Pigs in 1961. The attempted invasion failed miserably and, in retrospect, seemed remarkably ill-conceived.

Figure 16.19

Group polarization. Two examples of group polarization are diagrammed here. In the first example (top) a group starts out mildly opposed to an idea, but after discussion sentiment against the idea is stronger. In the second example (bottom), a group starts out with a favourable disposition toward an idea, and this disposition is strengthened by group discussion.

Overview of Janis's model of groupthink. The antecedent conditions, symptoms, and resultant effects of groupthink postulated by Janis (1972) are outlined here. His model of groupthink has been very influential, but practical difficulties have limited research on the theory.

SOURCE: Adapted with the permission of The Free Press, a Division of Simon & Schuster Adult Publishing Group, from *DECISION MAKING: A Psychological Analysis of Conflict, Choice, and Commitment* by Irving L. Janis and Leon Mann. Copyright © 1977 by The Free Press. All rights reserved.

Antecedent conditions
1. High cohesiveness
2. Insulation of the group
3. Lack of methodical procedures for search and appraisal
4. Directive leadership
5. High stress with low degree of hope for finding better solution than the one favoured by the leader or other influential persons

↓

Concurrence-seeking tendency

↓

Symptoms of groupthink
1. Illusion of invulnerability
2. Collective rationalization
3. Belief in inherent morality of the group
4. Stereotypes of outgroups
5. Direct pressure on dissenters
6. Self-censorship
7. Illusion of unanimity
8. Self-appointed mind guards

↓

Symptoms of defective decision making
1. Incomplete survey of alternatives
2. Incomplete survey of objectives
3. Failure to examine risks of preferred choice
4. Poor information search
5. Selective bias in processing information at hand
6. Failure to reappraise alternatives
7. Failure to work out contingency plans

Applying his many years of research and theory on group dynamics to the Bay of Pigs fiasco, Janis developed a model of groupthink, which is summarized in Figure 16.20. When groups get caught up in groupthink, members suspend their critical judgment and the group starts censoring dissent as the pressure to conform increases. Soon, everyone begins to think alike. Moreover, "mind guards" try to shield the group from information that contradicts the group's view.

If the group's view is challenged from outside, victims of groupthink tend to think in simplistic "us versus them" terms. Members begin to overestimate the ingroup's unanimity, and they begin to view the outgroup as the enemy. Groupthink also promotes incomplete gathering of information. Like individuals, groups often display a confirmation bias, as they tend to seek and focus on information that supports their initial views (Schulz-Hardt et al., 2000).

Recent research has uncovered another factor that may contribute to groupthink—individual members often fail to share information that is unique to them (Postmes, Spears, & Cihangir, 2001). Sound decision making depends on group members combining their information effectively (Winquist & Larson, 1998). However, when groups discuss issues, they have an interesting tendency to focus mainly on the information that the members already share as opposed to encouraging offers of information unique to individual members (Stasser, Vaughn, & Stewart, 2000). Additional research is needed to determine why groups are mediocre at pooling members' information.

What causes groupthink? According to Janis, a key precondition is high group cohesiveness. **Group cohesiveness refers to the strength of the liking relationships linking group members to each other and to the group itself.** Members of cohesive groups are close-knit, are committed, have "team spirit," and are very loyal to the group. Cohesiveness itself isn't bad. It can facilitate group productivity (Mullen & Copper, 1994) and help groups achieve great things. But Janis maintains that the danger of groupthink is greater when groups are highly cohesive. Groupthink is also more likely when a group works in relative isolation, when the group's power structure is dominated by a strong, directive leader, and when the group is under stress to make a major decision (see Figure 16.20). Under these conditions, group discussions can easily lead to group polarization, strengthening the group's dominant view.

A relatively small number of experiments have been conducted to test Janis's theory, because the antecedent conditions thought to foster groupthink—such as high decision stress, strong group cohesiveness, and dominating leadership—are difficult to create effectively in laboratory settings (Aldag & Fuller, 1993). The evidence on groupthink consists mostly of retrospective case studies of major decision-making fiascos (Eaton, 2001). Thus, Janis's model of groupthink should probably be characterized as an innovative, sophisticated, intuitively appealing theory that needs to be subjected to much more empirical study (Esser, 1998).

CONCEPT **CHECK 16.4**

Scrutinizing Common Sense

Check your understanding of the implications of research in social psychology by indicating whether the commonsense assertions listed below have been supported by empirical findings. Do the trends in research summarized in this chapter indicate that the following statements are true or false? The answers are in Appendix A.

_____ **1.** Generally, in forming their impressions of others, people don't judge a book by its cover.

_____ **2.** When it comes to attraction, birds of a feather flock together.

_____ **3.** In the realm of love, opposites attract.

_____ **4.** If you're the target of persuasion, to be forewarned is to be forearmed.

_____ **5.** When you need help, there's safety in numbers.

Our discussion of social psychology has provided a final embellishment on three of our seven unifying themes. One of these is the value of psychology's commitment to empiricism—that is, its reliance on systematic observation through research to arrive at conclusions. The second theme that stands out is the importance of cultural factors in shaping behaviour, and the third is the extent to which people's experience of the world is highly subjective. Let's consider the virtues of empiricism first.

It's easy to question the need to do scientific research on social behaviour, because studies in social psychology often seem to verify common sense. While most people wouldn't presume to devise their own theory of colour vision, question the significance of REM sleep, or quibble about the principal causes of schizophrenia, everyone has beliefs about the nature of love, how to persuade others, and people's willingness to help in times of need. Thus, when studies demonstrate that credibility enhances persuasion, or that good looks facilitate attraction, it's tempting to conclude that social psychologists go to great lengths to document the obvious, and some critics say, "Why bother?"

You saw why in this chapter. Research in social psychology has repeatedly shown that the predictions of logic and common sense are often wrong. Consider just a few examples. Even psychiatric experts failed to predict the remarkable obedience to authority uncovered in Milgram's research. The bystander effect in helping behaviour violates cold-blooded mathematical logic. Dissonance research has shown that after a severe initiation, the bigger the letdown, the more favourable people's feelings are. These principles defy common sense. Thus, research on social behaviour provides dramatic illustrations of why psychologists put their faith in empiricism.

Our coverage of social psychology also demonstrated once again that, cross-culturally, behaviour is characterized by both variance and invariance. Thus, we saw substantial cultural differences in patterns of attribution, the role of love in mating relationships, attitudes about conformity, the tendency to obey authority figures, and the likelihood of social loafing. Although basic social phenomena such as stereotyping, attraction, obedience, and conformity probably occur all over the world, cross-cultural studies of social behaviour show that research findings based on North American samples may not generalize precisely to other cultures.

Research in social psychology is also uniquely well suited for making the point that people's view of the world is highly personal and subjective. In this chapter we saw how physical appearance can colour perception of a person's ability or personality, how social schemas can lead people to see what they expect to see in their interactions with others, how pressure to conform can make people begin to doubt their senses, and how groupthink can lead group members down a perilous path of shared illusions.

The subjectivity of social perception will surface once again in our Applications for the chapter. The Personal Application focuses on prejudice, a practical problem that social psychologists have shown great interest in, whereas the Critical Thinking Application examines aspects of social influence.

PREVIEW QUESTIONS

- How did this chapter illustrate the value of empiricism?
- How did this chapter highlight the importance of cultural factors?
- How did this chapter demonstrate that human experience is highly subjective?

REVIEW OF KEY POINTS

- People who help someone in need when they are alone are less likely to provide help when a group is present. This phenomenon, called the bystander effect, occurs primarily because a group creates diffusion of responsibility.

- Individuals' productivity often declines in larger groups because of loss of coordination and because of social loafing. Social loafing seems to be due mostly to diffusion of responsibility and may be less prevalent in collectivist cultures.

- Group polarization occurs when discussion leads a group to shift toward a more extreme decision in the direction the group was already leaning. In groupthink, a cohesive group suspends critical judgment in a misguided effort to promote agreement in decision making.

- Social psychology illustrates the value of empiricism because research in this area often proves that common sense is wrong. Cross-cultural research on social behaviour illustrates that findings based on Western samples may not generalize precisely to other cultures. Additionally, several lines of research on social perception demonstrate that people's experience of the world is highly subjective.

PRACTICE TEST

1. Stereotypes are:
   A. special types of schemas that are part of people's shared cultural background.
   B. widely held beliefs that people have certain characteristics because of their membership in a particular group.
   C. equivalent to prejudice.
   D. both a and b.

2. You believe that short men have a tendency to be insecure. The concept of illusory correlation implies that you will:
   A. overestimate how often short men are insecure.
   B. underestimate how often short men are insecure.
   C. overestimate the frequency of short men in the population.
   D. falsely assume that shortness in men causes insecurity.

3. A father suggests that his son's low marks in school are due to the child's laziness. The father has made a (an) _____ attribution.
   A. external   C. situational
   B. internal   D. high consensus

4. Bob explains his failing grade on a term paper by saying that he really didn't work very hard at it. According to Weiner's model, Bob is making an _____ attribution about his failure.
   A. internal-stable   C. external-stable
   B. internal-unstable   D. external-unstable

5. The fundamental attribution error refers to the tendency of:
   A. observers to favour external attributions in explaining the behaviour of others.
   B. observers to favour internal attributions in explaining the behaviour of others.
   C. actors to favour external attributions in explaining the behaviour of others.
   D. actors to favour situational attributions in explaining the behaviour of others.

6. According to Hazan and Shaver (1987):
   A. romantic relationships in adulthood follow the same form as attachment relationships in infancy.
   B. those who had ambivalent attachments in infancy are doomed never to fall in love as adults.
   C. those who had avoidant attachments in infancy often overcompensate by becoming excessively intimate in their adult love relationships.
   D. all of the above.

7. Cross-cultural similarities are most likely to be found in which of the following areas?
   A. what people look for in prospective mates
   B. the overall value of romantic love
   C. passionate love as a prerequisite for marriage
   D. the tradition of prearranged marriages

8. Cognitive dissonance theory predicts that after people engage in counterattitudinal behaviour, they will:
   A. convince themselves they really didn't perform the behaviour.
   B. change their attitude to make it more consistent with their behaviour.
   C. change their attitude to make it less consistent with their behaviour.
   D. do nothing.

9. "I always choose romance novels rather than biographies. I guess I must like romance novels better." This thought process illustrates the premise of _____ theory.
   A. cognitive dissonance   C. evolutionary
   B. learning   D. self-perception

10. The elaboration likelihood model of attitude change suggests that:
    A. the peripheral route results in more enduring attitude change.
    B. the central route results in more enduring attitude change.
    C. only the central route to persuasion can be effective.
    D. only the peripheral route to persuasion can be effective.

11. The results of Milgram's (1963) study imply that:
    A. in the real world, most people will refuse to follow orders to inflict harm on a stranger.
    B. many people will obey an authority figure even if innocent people get hurt.
    C. most people are willing to give obviously wrong answers when ordered to do so.
    D. most people stick to their own judgment, even when group members unanimously disagree.

12. According to Latané (1981), social loafing is due to:
    A. social norms that stress the importance of positive interactions among group members.
    B. duplication of effort among group members.
    C. diffusion of responsibility in groups.
    D. a bias toward making internal attributions about the behaviour of others.

13. Groupthink occurs when members of a cohesive group:
    A. are initially unanimous about an issue.
    B. stress the importance of caution in group decision making.
    C. emphasize concurrence at the expense of critical thinking in arriving at a decision.
    D. shift toward a less extreme position after group discussion.

14. Discrimination:
    A. refers to a negative attitude toward the members of a group.
    B. refers to unfair behaviour toward the members of a group.
    C. is the same thing as prejudice.
    D. is all of the above.

15. The foot-in-the-door technique involves asking people to agree to a _____ request first to increase the likelihood that they will comply with a _____ request later.
    A. large; small
    B. small; large
    C. large; large
    D. large; larger

See Appendix A for answers to this Practice Test.

WWW   ON THE WEB

For additional resources on the topics covered in this chapter, visit the *Psychology: Themes and Variations* Web site, where you will find practice quizzes, tutorials, Web links, simulations, critical thinking activities, flash cards, interactive exercises, and suggested readings available through INFOTRAC.

http://www.themesandvariations.nelson.com

Thomson
NOW!   http://hed.nelson.com

Go to this site for the link to ThomsonNOW™, your one-stop study shop. Take a Pretest for this chapter and ThomsonNOW™ will generate a personalized Study Plan based on your test results! The Study Plan will identify the topics you need to review and direct you to online resources to help you master those topics. You can then take a Posttest to help you determine the concepts you have mastered and what you still need work on.

RECAP

Key Ideas

Person Perception: Forming Impressions of Others

● People tend to attribute desirable characteristics to those who are good looking. Perceptions of people are also influenced by their style of nonverbal expressiveness.

● Stereotypes are widely held social schemas that lead people to expect that others will have certain characteristics because of their membership in a specific group. In interacting with others, stereotypes may lead people to see what they expect to see and to overestimate how often they see it.

Attribution Processes: Explaining Behaviour

● Internal attributions ascribe behaviour to personal traits, whereas external attributions locate the cause of behaviour in the environment. Weiner's model proposes that attributions for success and failure should be analyzed in terms of the stability of causes, as well as along the internal–external dimension.

● Observers favour internal attributions to explain another's behaviour (the fundamental attribution error), while actors favour external attributions to explain their own behaviour. Cultures vary in their emphasis on individualism as opposed to collectivism, and these differences appear to influence attributional tendencies.

Close Relationships: Liking and Loving

● People tend to like and love others who are similar, who reciprocate expressions of affection, and who are physically attractive. In intimate relationships, romantic ideals influence the progress of relationships.

● Berscheid and Hatfield have distinguished between passionate and companionate love. Sternberg builds on their distinction by dividing companionate love into intimacy and commitment. Hazan and Shaver's theory suggests that love relationships in adulthood mimic attachment patterns in infancy.

● The characteristics that people seek in prospective mates are much the same around the world. However, cultures vary considerably in their emphasis on passionate love as a prerequisite for marriage.

● According to evolutionary psychologists, certain aspects of good looks influence attraction because they are indicators of reproductive fitness. Consistent with evolutionary theory, gender differences in mating preferences appear to transcend culture.

Attitudes: Making Social Judgments

● Attitudes may be made up of cognitive, affective, and behavioural components.

Attitudes vary in strength, accessibility, and ambivalence. Attitudes and behaviour aren't as consistent as one might assume.

● A source of persuasion who is credible, expert, trustworthy, likable, and physically attractive tends to be relatively effective. Two-sided arguments and fear arousal are effective elements in persuasive messages.

● Attitudes may be shaped through classical conditioning, operant conditioning, and observational learning. Festinger's dissonance theory asserts that inconsistent attitudes cause tension and that people alter their attitudes to reduce cognitive dissonance.

● Self-perception theory posits that people may infer their attitudes from their behaviour. The elaboration likelihood model of persuasion holds that the central route to persuasion tends to yield longer-lasting attitude change than the peripheral route.

Conformity and Obedience: Yielding to Others

● Asch found that conformity becomes more likely as group size increases, up to a group size of four, and then levels off. If a small group isn't unanimous, conformity declines rapidly.

● In Milgram's study of obedience, subjects showed a remarkable tendency to follow orders to shock an innocent stranger. The generalizability of Milgram's findings has stood the test of time, but his work also helped to stimulate stricter ethical standards for research.

● The Asch and Milgram experiments have been replicated in many cultures. These replications have uncovered modest cultural variations in the propensity to conform or to obey an authority figure.

Behaviour in Groups: Joining with Others

● The bystander effect occurs primarily because a group creates diffusion of responsibility. Individuals' productivity often declines in larger groups because of loss of coordination and because of social loafing.

● Group polarization occurs when discussion leads a group to shift toward a more extreme decision in the direction the group was already leaning. In groupthink, a cohesive group suspends critical judgment in a misguided effort to promote agreement in decision making.

Putting It in Perspective

● Our study of social psychology illustrated the value of empiricism, the cultural limits of research based on North American samples, and the subjectivity of perception.

Personal Application • Understanding Prejudice

● Prejudice is supported by selectivity and memory biases in person perception and stereotyping. Attributional biases, such as the ten-

dency to assume that others' behaviour reflects their dispositions, can contribute to prejudice.

● The tendency to attribute others' failures to personal factors and the tendency to derogate victims can also foster prejudice. The tendency to favour one's ingroups promotes ethnocentrism. The propensity to see outgroups as homogenous serves to strengthen prejudice.

Critical Thinking Application • Whom Can You Trust? Analyzing Credibility and Social Influence Tactics

● Useful criteria in judging credibility include whether a source has vested interests or appropriate credentials. One should also consider the method of analysis used in reaching conclusions and why information might not coincide with conventional wisdom.

● To resist manipulative efforts, it helps to be aware of social influence tactics, such as the foot-in-the-door technique, misuse of the reciprocity norm, the lowball technique, and feigned scarcity.

Key Terms

Attitudes, 679
Attributions, 669
Bystander effect, 693
Channel, 681
Cognitive dissonance, 685
Collectivism, 673
Commitment, 676
Companionate love, 676
Conformity, 688
Defensive attribution, 672
Discrimination, 698
Ethnocentrism, 700
External attributions, 670
Foot-in-the-door technique, 703
Fundamental attribution error, 670
Group, 692
Group cohesiveness, 696
Group polarization, 695
Groupthink, 695
Illusory correlation, 667
Individualism, 672
Ingroup, 669
Internal attributions, 670
Interpersonal attraction, 674
Intimacy, 676
Lowball technique, 703
Matching hypothesis, 675
Message, 681
Obedience, 689
Outgroup, 669
Passionate love, 676
Person perception, 664
Prejudice, 698
Receiver, 681
Reciprocity, 675
Reciprocity norm, 703
Self-serving bias, 672
Social loafing, 694
Social psychology, 664
Social schemas, 666
Source, 681
Stereotypes, 666

Key People

Solomon Asch, 688
Ellen Berscheid, 677
David Buss, 678
Leon Festinger, 685
Elaine Hatfield, 676
Cindy Hazan, 676
Fritz Heider, 670
Irving Janis, 695
Stanley Milgram, 691
Phillip Shaver, 676
Bernard Weiner, 670
Mark Zanna, 680

in a specific week, or the number of bodies that could be disposed of in a single day (Shermer, 1997). Some inconsistencies are exactly what one should expect based on piecing together multiple accounts from sources working with different portions of incomplete information. But the strategy of focusing on trivial inconsistencies is a standard method for raising doubts about credible information. For example, this strategy was employed brilliantly by the defence lawyers in the O. J. Simpson murder trial.

Recognizing Social Influence Strategies

It pays to understand social influence strategies because advertisers, salespeople, and fundraisers—not to mention our friends and neighbours—frequently rely on them to manipulate our behaviour. Let's look at four basic strategies: the foot-in-the-door technique, misuse of the reciprocity norm, the lowball technique, and feigned scarcity.

Door-to-door salespeople have long recognized the importance of gaining a *little* cooperation from sales targets (getting a "foot in the door") before hitting them with the real sales pitch. **The *foot-in-the-door* technique involves getting people to agree to a small request to increase the chances that they will agree to a larger request later.** This technique is widely used in all walks of life. For example, groups seeking donations often ask people to simply sign a petition first.

In an early study of the foot-in-the-door technique (Freedman & Fraser, 1966), the large request involved asking homemakers whether a team of six men doing consumer research could come into their home to classify *all* their household products. Only 22% of the control subjects agreed to this outlandish request. However, when the same request was made three days after a small request (to answer a few questions about soap preferences), 53% of the participants agreed to the large request. Why does the foot-in-the-door technique work? According to Burger (1999), quite a variety of processes contribute to its effectiveness,

including people's tendency to try to behave consistently (with their initial response) and their reluctance to renege on their sense of commitment to the person who made the initial request.

Most of us have been socialized to believe in the *reciprocity norm*—the rule that we should pay back in kind what we receive from others. Robert Cialdini (2001) has written extensively about how the reciprocity norm is used in social influence efforts. For example, groups seeking donations routinely send address labels, key rings, and other small gifts with their pleas. Salespeople using the reciprocity principle distribute free samples to prospective customers. When they return a few days later, most of the customers feel obligated to buy some of their products. The reciprocity rule is meant to promote fair exchanges in social interactions. However, when people manipulate the reciprocity norm, they usually give something of minimal value in the hopes of getting far more in return (Howard, 1995).

The lowball technique is even more deceptive. The name for this technique derives from a common practice in automobile sales, in which a customer is offered a terrific bargain on a car. The bargain price gets the customer to commit to buying the car. Soon after this commitment is made, however, the dealer starts revealing some hidden costs. Typically, the customer learns that options assumed to be included in the original price are actually going to cost extra. Once they have committed to buying a car, most customers are unlikely to cancel the deal. Thus, **the *lowball* technique involves getting someone to commit to an attractive proposition before its hidden costs are revealed.** Car dealers aren't the only ones who use this technique. For instance, a friend might ask whether you want to spend a week with him at his charming backwoods cabin. After you accept this seemingly generous proposition, he may add, "Of course there's some work for us to do. We need to repair the pier, paint the exterior, and...." Lowballing is a surprisingly effective strategy (Cialdini & Trost, 1998).

A number of years ago, Jack Brehm (1966) demonstrated that telling people they can't have something only makes them want it more. This phenomenon helps explain why companies often try to create the impression that their products are in scarce supply. Scarcity threatens your freedom to choose a product, thus creating an increased desire for the scarce commodity. Advertisers frequently feign scarcity to drive up the demand for products. Thus, we constantly see ads that scream "limited supply available," "for a limited time only," "while they last," and "time is running out." Like genuine scarcity, feigned scarcity *can* enhance the desirability of a commodity (Highhouse et al., 1998; Lynn, 1992).

Table 16.2 Critical Thinking Skills Discussed in This Application	
Skill	**Description**
Judging the credibility of an information source	The critical thinker understands that credibility and bias are central to determining the quality of information and looks at factors such as vested interests, credentials, and appropriate expertise.
Recognizing social influence strategies	The critical thinker is aware of manipulative tactics such as the foot-in-the-door and lowball techniques, misuse of the reciprocity norm, and feigned scarcity.

Whom Can You Trust? Analyzing Credibility and Social Influence Tactics

You can run, but you cannot hide. This statement aptly sums up the situation that exists when it comes to persuasion and social influence. There is no way to successfully evade the constant, pervasive, omnipresent efforts of others to shape your attitudes and behaviour. In this Application we will discuss two topics that can enhance your resistance to manipulation. First, we will outline some ideas that can be useful in evaluating the credibility of a persuasive source. Second, we will describe some widely used social influence strategies that it pays to know about.

Evaluating Credibility

The salesperson at your local health food store swears that a specific herb combination improves memory and helps people stay healthy. A popular singer touts a psychic hotline, where the operators can "really help" with the important questions in life. Speakers at a "historical society" meeting claim that the Holocaust never happened. These are just a few real-life examples of how people are always attempting to persuade the public to believe something. In these examples, the "something" people are expected to believe runs counter to the conventional or scientific view, but who is to say who is right? After all, people are entitled to their own opinions, aren't they?

Yes, people *are* entitled to their own opinions, but that does not mean that all opinions are equally valid. Some opinions are just plain wrong, and others are highly dubious. Every person is not equally believable. In deciding what to believe, it is important to carefully examine the evidence presented and the logic of the argument that supports the conclusion (see the Critical Thinking Application for Chapter 10). In deciding what to believe, you also need

to decide *whom* to believe, a task that requires assessing the *credibility* of the source of the information. Let's look at some questions that can provide guidance in this decision-making process.

Does the source have a vested interest in the issue at hand? If the source is likely to benefit in some way from convincing you of something, you need to take a skeptical attitude. In the examples provided here, it is easy to see how the sales clerk and popular singer will benefit if you buy the products they are selling, but what about the so-called historical society? How would members benefit by convincing large numbers of people that the Holocaust never happened? Like the sales clerk and singer, they are also selling something, in this case a particular view of history that they hope will influence future events in certain ways. Someone does *not* have to have a financial gain at stake to have a vested interest in an issue. Of course, the fact that these sources have a vested interest does not necessarily mean that the information they are providing is false or that their arguments are invalid. But a source's credibility needs to be evaluated with extra caution when the person or group has something to gain.

What are the source's credentials? Does the person have any special training, an advanced degree, or any other basis for claiming special knowledge about the topic? The usual training for a sales clerk or singer does not include how to assess research results in medical journals or claims of psychic powers. The Holocaust deniers are more difficult to evaluate. Some of them have studied history and written books on the topic, but the books are mostly self-published and few of these "experts" hold positions at reputable universities where scholars are subject to peer evaluation. That's *not* to say that legitimate

credentials ensure a source's credibility. A number of popular diets that are widely regarded by nutritional experts as worthless, if not hazardous (Drewnewski, 1995; Dwyer, 1995), were created and marketed by genuine physicians. Of course, these physicians have a *vested interest* in the diets, as they have made millions of dollars from them.

Is the information grossly inconsistent with the conventional view on the issue? Just being different from the mainstream view certainly does *not* make a conclusion wrong. But claims that vary radically from most other information on a subject should raise a red flag that leads to careful scrutiny. Bear in mind that charlatans and hucksters are often successful because they typically try to persuade people to believe things that they want to believe. Wouldn't it be great if we could effortlessly enhance our memory, foretell the future, eat all we *want* and still lose weight, and earn hundreds of dollars per hour working at home? And wouldn't it be nice if the Holocaust had never happened? It pays to be wary of wishful thinking.

What was the method of analysis used in reaching the conclusion? The purveyors of miracle cures and psychic advice inevitably rely on anecdotal evidence. But you have already learned about the perils and unreliability of anecdotal evidence (see Chapter 2). One method frequently used by charlatans is to undermine the credibility of conventional information by focusing on trivial inconsistencies. This is one of the many strategies used by the people who argue that the Holocaust never occurred. They question the credibility of thousands of historical documents, photographs, and artifacts, and the testimony of countless people, by highlighting small inconsistencies among historical records relating to trivial matters, such as the number of people transported to a concentration camp

"They all look alike." The illusion of homogeneity in the outgroup makes it easier to sustain stereotypic beliefs about its members (Ryan, Park, Judd, 1996). This point disposes of our last unanswered question from the list that opened the Application. Just in case you missed one of the answers, the statements were all false.

In modern societies that endorse egalitarian attitudes, the prejudices that most people harbour tend to be subtle, unconscious, automatic, covert biases that mostly result in ingroup favouritism. Only a small minority of people (perhaps 10%) appear to be extremists who harbour blatant, conscious, overt, prejudices against outgroups that lead to hatred and aggression (Fiske, 2002). Still, 10% of the population adds up to an enormous number of people who can inflict great harm. Moreover, even subtle prejudices can foster a hostile, stressful environment for outgroup members (Fiske, 2002).

Our discussion has shown that a plethora of processes conspire to create and maintain personal prejudices against a diverse array of outgroups. Most of the factors at work reflect normal, routine processes in social behaviour. Thus, it is understandable that most people—whether privileged or underprivileged, minority members or majority members—probably harbour some prejudicial attitudes. Our analysis of the causes of prejudice may have permitted you to identify prejudices of your own or their sources. Perhaps it's wishful thinking on our part, but an enhanced awareness of your personal prejudices may help you become a little more tolerant of the endless diversity seen in human behaviour. If so, that alone would mean that our efforts in writing this book have been amply rewarded.

REVIEW OF KEY POINTS

- Prejudice is supported by selectivity and memory biases in person perception and stereotyping. Stereotypes are highly resistant to change.

- Attributional biases, such as the tendency to assume that others' behaviour reflects their dispositions, can contribute to prejudice. The tendency to attribute others' failures to personal factors and the tendency to derogate victims can also foster prejudice.

- Negative attitudes about groups are often acquired through observational learning and strengthened through operant conditioning. The tendency to favour one's ingroups promotes ethnocentrism. The propensity to see outgroups as homogenous serves to strengthen prejudice.

attribution help sustain the stereotype that men are more competent than women. Similar patterns of bias have been seen in attributional explanations of ethnic minorities' successes and failures (Jackson, Sullivan, & Hodge, 1993; Kluegel, 1990). Generally, when minorities experience stereotype-inconsistent success, it is discounted by attributing it to external factors or to unstable, internal causes.

Recall that the *fundamental attribution error* is a bias toward explaining events by pointing to the personal characteristics of the actors as causes (internal attributions). Research suggests that people are particularly likely to make this error when evaluating targets of prejudice (Hewstone, 1990). Thus, when people take note of ethnic neighbourhoods dominated by crime and poverty, the personal qualities of the residents are blamed for these problems, while other explanations emphasizing situational factors (job discrimination, poor police service, and so on) are downplayed or ignored. The old saying "They should be able to pull themselves up by their bootstraps" is a blanket dismissal of how situational factors may make it especially difficult for minorities to achieve upward mobility.

Defensive attribution, which involves unjustly blaming victims of misfortune for their adversity, can also contribute to prejudice. A prominent example in recent years has been the assertion by some people that homosexuals brought the AIDS crisis on themselves and so deserve their fate (Anderson, 1992). By blaming AIDS on gays' alleged character flaws, heterosexuals may be unknowingly seeking to reassure themselves that they're immune to a similar fate.

Forming and Preserving Prejudicial Attitudes

If prejudice is an attitude, where does it come from? Many prejudices appear to be handed down as a legacy from parents (Ponterotto & Pedersen, 1993). Research by McGill University's Frances Aboud shows that prejudicial attitudes can be found in children as young as ages four or five (Aboud & Amato, 2001). This transmission of prejudice across generations presumably depends to some extent on *observational learning.* For example, if a young boy hears his father ridicule homosexuals, his exposure to his father's attitude is likely to affect his attitude about gays. If the young boy then goes to school and makes disparaging remarks about gays that are reinforced by approval from peers, his prejudice will be strengthened through *operant conditioning.* Consistent with this analysis, one study found that university students' opinions on racial issues were swayed by overhearing others voice racist or antiracist sentiments (Blanchard, Lilly, & Vaughn, 1991). Of course, prejudicial attitudes are not acquired only through direct experience. Stereotypic portrayals of various groups in the media can also foster prejudicial attitudes (Herrett-Skjellum & Allen, 1996; Williams & Giles, 1998).

Another problem is that when people meet individuals who behave in ways that conform to prejudicial expectations, they are all too willing to generalize from the individual to the group. For example, one study showed that encountering a single black person who performs a negative or stereotypical action can reaffirm whites' stereotypes of blacks (Henderson-King & Nisbett, 1996). The investigators attribute the inordinately large influence of a single person to a common pitfall in reasoning—*belief in the law of small numbers* (see the Personal Application for Chapter 8).

Another characteristic of modern prejudice or racism that serves to make it intractable is that it has moved underground. Most people are well aware that it is inappropriate, and sometimes even illegal, to display overt racism. In some cases, people may not even be aware that they are carrying around this prejudice—this is often referred to as *implicit prejudice* (Dividio, Kawakami, & Gaertner, 2002). If the racism is hidden, it may even be more difficult to change. Research by University of Guelph psychologist Leanne Son Hing has shown that inducing feelings of hypocrisy (being reminded that you are not behaving in a manner that is consistent with your attitudes) in people high in implicit racism may serve to induce them to behave in a nondiscriminatory manner (Son Hing, Li, & Zanna, 2002).

Dividing the World into Ingroups and Outgroups

As noted in the main body of the chapter, when people join together in groups, they sometimes divide the social world into "us versus them," or *ingroups versus outgroups* (Taylor & Moghaddam, 1994; Lalonde & Gardner, 1989). These social dichotomies can promote **ethnocentrism—a tendency to view one's own group as superior to others and as the standard for judging the worth of foreign ways.**

As you might anticipate, people tend to evaluate outgroup members less favourably than ingroup members (Krueger, 1996; Reynolds, Turner, & Haslam, 2000). One reason is that when people derogate an outgroup, they tend to feel superior as a result, and this feeling helps to affirm their self-worth (Fein & Spencer, 1997). The more strongly one identifies with an ingroup, the more one tends to note outgroup membership, and the more one tends to be prejudiced toward competing outgroups (Blascovich et al., 1997; Perreault & Bourhis, 1999). People also tend to think simplistically about outgroups. They tend to see diversity among the members of their ingroup but to overestimate the homogeneity of the outgroup (Oakes, 2001; Ostrom & Sedikides, 1992). At a simple, concrete level, the essence of this process is captured by the statement

Leanne S. Son Hing is a social psychologist at the University of Guelph. She conducts research in social cognition.

Figure 16.22

Relationship between prejudice and discrimination. As these examples show, prejudice can exist without discrimination and discrimination without prejudice. In the green cells, there is a disparity between attitude and behaviour.

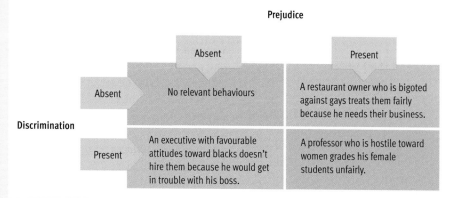

		Prejudice	
		Absent	**Present**
Discrimination	**Absent**	No relevant behaviours	A restaurant owner who is bigoted against gays treats them fairly because he needs their business.
	Present	An executive with favourable attitudes toward blacks doesn't hire them because he would get in trouble with his boss.	A professor who is hostile toward women grades his female students unfairly.

& Gaertner, 1999). Many people carefully avoid overt expressions of prejudicial attitudes but covertly continue to harbour negative views of racial minorities. These people endorse racial equality as an abstract principle but often oppose concrete programs intended to promote equality, on the grounds that discrimination is no longer a problem. Recent studies suggest that modern sexism has become subtle in much the same way as racism (Swim & Campbell, 2001).

Research indicates that stereotypes are so pervasive and insidious they are often activated automatically (Bargh, 1999; Fiske, 2000). According to Devine and Monteith (1999), prejudicial stereotypes are highly accessible cognitive schemas that can be activated automatically, even in people who truly renounce prejudice. Thus, a man who rejects prejudice against homosexuals may still feel uncomfortable sitting next to a gay male on a bus, even though he regards his reaction as inappropriate.

Unfortunately, stereotypes are highly resistant to change. Research by University of Waterloo psychologist Ziva Kunda has found that when people encounter members of a group that they view with prejudice who deviate from the stereotype of that group, they often discount this evidence by assuming that the atypical group members constitute a distinct subtype of that group, such as wealthy blacks or conservative homosexuals (Kunda & Oleson, 1995, 1997). Consigning deviants to a sub-

type that is viewed as unrepresentative of the group allows people to preserve their stereotype of the group.

Stereotypes also persist because the *subjectivity* of person perception makes it likely that people will see what they expect to see when they actually come into contact with groups that they view with prejudice (Dunning & Sherman, 1997). For example, Duncan (1976) had white subjects watch and evaluate interaction on a TV monitor that was supposedly live (actually it was a videotape) and varied the race of a person who gets into an argument and gives another person a slight shove. The shove was coded as "violent behaviour" by 73% of the sub-

jects when the actor was black but by only 13% of the subjects when the actor was white. As we've noted before, people's perceptions are highly subjective. Because of stereotypes, even "violence" may lie in the eye of the beholder.

Memory biases are also tilted in favour of confirming people's prejudices (Ybarra, Stephan, Schaberg, 2000). For example, if a man believes that "women are not cut out for leadership roles," he may dwell with delight on his female supervisor's mistakes and quickly forget about her achievements. Thus, the *illusory correlation effect* can contribute to the maintenance of prejudicial stereotypes (Berndsen et al., 2002; McConnell, Leibold, & Sherman, 1997).

Biases in Attribution

Attribution processes can also help perpetuate stereotypes and prejudice. Research taking its cue from Weiner's (1980) model of attribution has shown that people often make *biased attributions for success and failure*. For example, men and women don't get equal credit for their successes (Swim & Sanna, 1996). Observers often discount a woman's success by attributing it to good luck, sheer effort, or the ease of the task (except on traditional feminine tasks). In comparison, a man's success is more likely to be attributed to his outstanding ability (see Figure 16.23). These biased patterns of

Figure 16.23

Bias in the attributions used to explain success and failure by men and women. Attributions about the two sexes often differ. For example, men's successes tend to be attributed to their ability and intelligence (blue cell), whereas women's successes tend to be attributed to hard work, good luck, or low task difficulty (green cells). These attributional biases help to perpetuate the belief that men are more competent than women.

		Stability dimension	
		Unstable cause (temporary)	**Stable cause (permanent)**
Internal–external dimension	**Internal cause**	Effort Mood Fatigue	Ability Intelligence
	External cause	Luck Chance Opportunity	Task difficulty

Putting It in Perspective

Our discussion of social psychology has provided a final embellishment on three of our seven unifying themes. One of these is the value of psychology's commitment to empiricism—that is, its reliance on systematic observation through research to arrive at conclusions. The second theme that stands out is the importance of cultural factors in shaping behaviour, and the third is the extent to which people's experience of the world is highly subjective. Let's consider the virtues of empiricism first.

It's easy to question the need to do scientific research on social behaviour, because studies in social psychology often seem to verify common sense. While most people wouldn't presume to devise their own theory of colour vision, question the significance of REM sleep, or quibble about the principal causes of schizophrenia, everyone has beliefs about the nature of love, how to persuade others, and people's willingness to help in times of need. Thus, when studies demonstrate that credibility enhances persuasion, or that good looks facilitate attraction, it's tempting to conclude that social psychologists go to great lengths to document the obvious, and some critics say, "Why bother?"

You saw why in this chapter. Research in social psychology has repeatedly shown that the predictions of logic and common sense are often wrong. Consider just a few examples. Even psychiatric experts failed to predict the remarkable obedience to authority uncovered in Milgram's research. The bystander effect in helping behaviour violates cold-blooded mathematical logic. Dissonance research has shown that after a severe initiation, the bigger the letdown, the more favourable people's feelings are. These principles defy common sense. Thus, research on social behaviour provides dramatic illustrations of why psychologists put their faith in empiricism.

Our coverage of social psychology also demonstrated once again that, cross-culturally, behaviour is characterized by both variance and invariance. Thus, we saw substantial cultural differences in patterns of attribution, the role of love in mating relationships, attitudes about conformity, the tendency to obey authority figures, and the likelihood of social loafing. Although basic social phenomena such as stereotyping, attraction, obedience, and conformity probably occur all over the world, cross-cultural studies of social behaviour show that research findings based on North American samples may not generalize precisely to other cultures.

Research in social psychology is also uniquely well suited for making the point that people's view of the world is highly personal and subjective. In this chapter we saw how physical appearance can colour perception of a person's ability or personality, how social schemas can lead people to see what they expect to see in their interactions with others, how pressure to conform can make people begin to doubt their senses, and how groupthink can lead group members down a perilous path of shared illusions.

The subjectivity of social perception will surface once again in our Applications for the chapter. The Personal Application focuses on prejudice, a practical problem that social psychologists have shown great interest in, whereas the Critical Thinking Application examines aspects of social influence.

PREVIEW QUESTIONS

- How did this chapter illustrate the value of empiricism?
- How did this chapter highlight the importance of cultural factors?
- How did this chapter demonstrate that human experience is highly subjective?

REVIEW OF KEY POINTS

- People who help someone in need when they are alone are less likely to provide help when a group is present. This phenomenon, called the bystander effect, occurs primarily because a group creates diffusion of responsibility.

- Individuals' productivity often declines in larger groups because of loss of coordination and because of social loafing. Social loafing seems to be due mostly to diffusion of responsibility and may be less prevalent in collectivist cultures.

- Group polarization occurs when discussion leads a group to shift toward a more extreme decision in the direction the group was already leaning. In groupthink, a cohesive group suspends critical judgment in a misguided effort to promote agreement in decision making.

- Social psychology illustrates the value of empiricism because research in this area often proves that common sense is wrong. Cross-cultural research on social behaviour illustrates that findings based on Western samples may not generalize precisely to other cultures. Additionally, several lines of research on social perception demonstrate that people's experience of the world is highly subjective.

PERSONAL APPLICATION

Understanding Prejudice

Answer the following "true" or "false."

___ **1.** Prejudice and discrimination amount to the same thing.

___ **2.** Stereotypes are always negative or unflattering.

___ **3.** Ethnic and racial groups are the only widespread targets of prejudice in modern society.

___ **4.** People see members of their own ingroup as being more alike than the members of outgroups.

Prejudice is a major social problem. It harms victims' self-concepts, suppresses human potential, creates tension and strife between groups (Dion, 2003), and even instigates wars. The first step toward reducing prejudice is to understand its roots. Hence, in this Application, we'll try to achieve a better understanding of why prejudice is so common. Along the way, you'll learn the answers to the true–false questions above.

Prejudice and discrimination are closely related concepts, and the terms have become nearly interchangeable in popular use. Social scientists, however, prefer to define their terms precisely, so let's clarify which is which. *Prejudice* **is a negative attitude held toward members of a group.** Like many other attitudes, prejudice can include three components (see Figure 16.21): beliefs ("Indians are mostly alcoholics"), emotions ("I despise Jews"), and behavioural dispositions ("I wouldn't hire a Mexican"). Racial prejudice receives the lion's share of publicity, but prejudice is *not* limited to ethnic groups. Women, homosexuals, the aged, the handicapped, and the mentally ill are also targets of widespread prejudice. Thus, many people hold prejudicial attitudes toward one group or another, and many have been victims of prejudice.

Prejudice may lead to *discrimination*, **which involves behaving differently, usually unfairly, toward the members of** **a group.** Prejudice and discrimination tend to go hand in hand, but as LaPiere's (1934) pioneering study of discrimination in restaurant seating showed, attitudes and behaviour do not necessarily correspond (see Figure 16.22). In our discussion, we'll concentrate primarily on the attitude of prejudice. Let's begin by looking at processes in person perception that promote prejudice.

Stereotyping and Subjectivity in Person Perception

 12D

While some traditional models of prejudice have almost equated prejudice with stereotype, more recent analyses have viewed prejudice as being a function of cognitive, behavioural, and affective factors (Zanna, 1994). There is no doubt, however, that stereotypes play a large role in prejudice. That's not to say that stereotypes are inevitably negative. Although it's an overgeneralization, it's hardly insulting to assert that Americans are ambitious or that the Japanese are industrious. Unfortunately, many people do subscribe to derogatory stereotypes of various ethnic groups. Although studies suggest that negative racial stereotypes have diminished over the last 50 years, they're not a thing of the past (Gaertner et al., 1999; Madon et al., 2001). According to a variety of investigators, modern racism has merely become more subtle (Devine, Plant, & Blair, 2001; Dovidio

Figure 16.21

The three potential components of prejudice as an attitude. Attitudes can consist of up to three components. The tricomponent model of attitudes, applied to prejudice against women, would view sexism as negative beliefs about women (cognitive component) that lead to a feeling of dislike (affective component), which in turn leads to a readiness to discriminate against women (behavioural component).

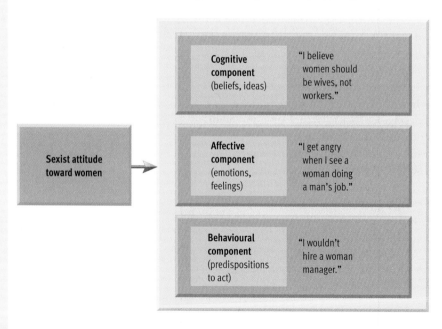

Appendix A   Answers to Concept Checks and Practice Tests

The answers to the Concept Checks and Practice Tests for each chapter are provided below on a chapter-by-chapter basis.

Chapter 1

Concept Check 1.1

1. c. John B. Watson (1930, p. 103), dismissing the importance of genetic inheritance while arguing that traits are shaped entirely by experience.

2. a. Wilhelm Wundt (1874/1904, p. v), campaigning for a new, independent science of psychology.

3. b. William James (1890), commenting negatively on the structuralists' efforts to break consciousness into its elements and his view of consciousness as a continuously flowing stream.

Concept Check 1.2

1. b. B. F. Skinner (1971, p. 17), explaining why he believes that freedom is an illusion.

2. a. Sigmund Freud (1905, pp. 77–78), arguing that it is possible to probe into the unconscious depths of the mind.

3. c. Carl Rogers (1961, p. 27), commenting on others' assertion that he had an overly optimistic (Pollyannaish) view of human potential and discussing humans' basic drive toward personal growth.

Concept Check 1.3

a. 2. Psychology is theoretically diverse.

b. 6. Heredity and environment jointly influence behaviour.

c. 4. Behaviour is determined by multiple causes.

d. 7. Our experience of the world is highly subjective.

Practice Test

1. A p. 4	7. A p. 11	13. C p. 29
2. D p. 5	8. C p. 14	14. A p. 34
3. A p. 5	9. B p. 19	15. D p. 36
4. B p. 6	10. B p. 24	16. C p. 17
5. A p. 8	11. A p. 16	
6. D p. 10	12. B p. 28	

Chapter 2

Concept Check 2.1

1. IV: Film violence (present versus absent)

   DV: Heart rate and blood pressure (there are two DVs)

2. IV: Courtesy training (training versus no training)

   DV: Number of customer complaints

3. IV: Stimulus complexity (high versus low) and stimulus contrast (high versus low) (there are two IVs)

   DV: Length of time spent staring at the stimuli

4. IV: Group size (large versus small)

   DV: Conformity

Concept Check 2.2

1. d. Survey. You would distribute a survey to obtain information on subjects' social class, education, and attitudes about nuclear disarmament.

2. c. Case study. Using a case study approach, you could interview people with anxiety disorders, interview their parents, and examine their school records to look for similarities in childhood experiences. As a second choice, you might have people with anxiety disorders fill out a survey about their childhood experiences.

3. b. Naturalistic observation. To answer this question properly, you would want to observe baboons in their natural environment, without interference.

4. a. Experiment. To demonstrate a causal relationship, you would have to conduct an experiment. You would manipulate the presence or absence of food-related cues in controlled circumstances where subjects had an opportunity to eat some food, and monitor the amount eaten.

Concept Check 2.3

1. b and e. The other three conclusions all equate correlation with causation.

2. a. Negative. As age increases, more people tend to have visual problems and acuity tends to decrease.

   b. Positive. Studies show that highly educated people tend to earn higher incomes and that people with less education tend to earn lower incomes.

   c. Negative. As shyness increases, the size of one's friendship network should decrease. However, research suggests that this inverse association may be weaker than widely believed.

Practice Test

1. D p. 42	6. C p. 49	11. B p. 62
2. A p. 44	7. B p. 52	12. C p. 64
3. B p. 48	8. B p. 52	13. B p. 66
4. D p. 48	9. C p. 58	14. B p. 70
5. C p. 49	10. C p. 61	15. D p. 72

Chapter 3

Concept Check 3.1

1. d. Dendrite

2. f. Myelin

3. b. Neuron

4. e. Axon

5. a. Glia

6. g. Terminal button

7. h. Synapse

Concept Check 3.2

1. d. Serotonin

2. b. and d. Serotonin and norepinephrine

3. e. Endorphins

4. c. Dopamine

5. a. Acetylcholine

Concept Check 3.3

1. Left hemisphere damage, probably to Wernicke's area

2. Deficit in dopamine synthesis in an area of the midbrain

3. Degeneration of myelin sheaths surrounding axons

4. Disturbance in dopamine activity, possibly associated with enlarged ventricles in the brain

Please note that neuropsychological assessment is not as simple as this introductory exercise may suggest. There are many possible causes of most disorders, and we discussed only a handful of leading causes for each.

Concept Check 3.4

1. Closer relatives; more distant relatives

2. Identical twins; fraternal twins

3. Biological parents; adoptive parents

4. Genetic overlap or closeness; trait similarity

Practice Test

1. A p. 80	**6.** C p. 97	**11.** C p. 106
2. C p. 85	**7.** B p. 99	**12.** B p. 108
3. B p. 85	**8.** C p. 102	**13.** A p. 110
4. D p. 88	**9.** D p. 102	**14.** D p. 114
5. D p. 95	**10.** B p. 105	**15.** A p. 119

Chapter 4

Concept Check 4.1

1.

Dimension	Rods	Cones
Physical shape	Elongated	Stubby
Number in the retina	125 million	6.4 million
Area of the retina in which they are dominant receptor	Periphery	Centre/fovea
Critical to colour vision	No	Yes
Critical to peripheral vision	Yes	No
Sensitivity to dim light	Strong	Weak
Speed of dark adaptation	Slow	Rapid

2. Consider the responses of two ganglion cells in the retina whose firing is affected by light falling in centre-surround receptive fields, like those drawn onto the grid in the lower right corner. An identical amount of light falls in the centre of each receptive field. However, more light is falling in the surround of the receptive field on the left. Hence, the cell for this receptive field responds at a lower level than its neighbour because of greater inhibition by the surround (thanks to lateral antagonism). This reduced responding translates into the dark spots that you see. Why don't you see a dark spot at the intersection you are staring at? Because when you stare directly at a point, the image falls on the fovea, where receptive fields are much smaller, like the

one drawn in the lower left corner. This receptive field does not produce a reduced response because an equal amount of light is falling in the centre and the surround.

Concept Check 4.2

_✓_ **1.** Interposition. The arches in front cut off part of the corridor behind them.

_✓_ **2.** Height in plane. The back of the corridor is higher on the horizontal plane than the front of the corridor is.

_✓_ **3.** Texture gradient. The more distant portions of the hallway are painted in less detail than the closer portions are.

_✓_ **4.** Relative size. The arches in the distance are smaller than those in the foreground.

_✓_ **5.** Light and shadow. Light shining in from the crossing corridor (it's coming from the left) contrasts with shadow elsewhere.

_✓_ **6.** Linear perspective. The lines of the corridor converge in the distance.

Concept Check 4.3

Dimension	Vision	Hearing
1. Stimulus	Light waves	Sound waves
2. Elements of stimulus and related perceptions	Wavelength/hue Amplitude/brightness Purity/saturation	Frequency/pitch Amplitude/loudness Purity/timbre
3. Receptors	Rods and cones	Hair cells
4. Location of receptors	Retina	Basilar membrane
5. Main location of processing in brain	Occipital lobe, visual cortex	Temporal lobe, auditory cortex
6. Spatial aspect of perception	Depth perception	Auditory localization

Concept Check 4.4

Dimension	Taste	Smell	Touch
1. Stimulus	Soluble chemicals in saliva	Volatile chemicals in air	Mechanical, thermal, and chemical energy due to external contact
2. Receptors	Clusters of taste cells	Olfactory cilia (hairlike structures)	Many (at least 6) types
3. Location of receptors	Taste buds on tongue	Upper area of nasal passages	Skin
4. Basic elements of perception	Sweet, sour, salty, bitter	No satisfactory classification scheme	Pressure, hot, cold, pain

Practice Test

1. B	p. 127	**6.** B	p. 136	**11.** D	p. 150
2. A	p. 129	**7.** B	p. 141	**12.** C	p. 157
3. D	p. 130	**8.** D	p. 145	**13.** C	p. 164
4. B	p. 133	**9.** D	p. 149	**14.** D	p. 170
5. D	p. 135	**10.** C	p. 145	**15.** C	p. 176

Chapter 5

Concept Check 5.1

Characteristic	REM sleep	NREM sleep
1. Type of EEG activity	"Wide awake" brain waves, mostly beta	Varied, lots of delta waves
2. Eye movements	Rapid, lateral	Slow or absent
3. Dreaming	Frequent, vivid	Less frequent
4. Depth (difficulty in awakening)	Varied, generally difficult to awaken	Varied, generally easier to awaken
5. Percentage of total sleep (in adults)	About 20%	About 80%
6. Increases or decreases (as percentage of sleep) during childhood	Percentage decreases	Percentage increases
7. Timing in sleep (dominates early or late)	Dominates late in cycle	Dominates early in cycle

Concept Check 5.2

1. Beta. Video games require alert information processing, which is associated with beta waves.

2. Alpha. Meditation involves relaxation, which is associated with alpha waves, and studies show increased alpha in meditators.

3. Theta. In stage 1 sleep, theta waves tend to be prevalent.

4. Delta. Sleepwalking usually occurs in deep NREM sleep, which is dominated by delta activity.

5. Beta. Nightmares are dreams, so you're probably in REM sleep, which paradoxically produces "wide awake" beta waves.

Practice Test

1. B	p. 182	**6.** C	p. 193	**11.** A	p. 208
2. C	p. 185	**7.** D	p. 196	**12.** D	p. 208
3. C	p. 186	**8.** A	p. 199	**13.** D	p. 212
4. A	p. 188	**9.** A	p. 200	**14.** C	p. 217
5. B	p. 188	**10.** B	p. 204	**15.** D	p. 220

Chapter 6

Concept Check 6.1

1. CS: Fire in fireplace
   UCS: Pain from burn   CR/UCR: Fear

2. CS: Brake lights in rain
   UCS: Car accident   CR/UCR: Tensing up

3. CS: Sight of cat
   UCS: Cat dander   CR/UCR: Wheezing

Concept Check 6.2

1. FR. Each sale is a response and every third response earns reinforcement.

2. VI. A varied amount of time elapses before the response of doing yard work can earn reinforcement.

3. VR. Reinforcement occurs after a varied number of unreinforced casts (time is irrelevant; the more casts Martha makes, the more reinforcers she will receive).

4. CR. The designated response (reading a book) is reinforced (with a gold star) every time.

5. FI. A fixed time interval (three years) has to elapse before Skip can earn a salary increase (the reinforcer).

Concept Check 6.3

1. Positive punishment.

2. Positive reinforcement.

3. Negative punishment.

4. Negative reinforcement (for Audrey); the dog is positively reinforced for its whining.

5. Negative reinforcement.

6. Extinction. When Sharma's co-workers start to ignore her complaints, they are trying to extinguish the behaviour (which had been positively reinforced when it won sympathy).

Concept Check 6.4

1. Classical conditioning. Midori's blue windbreaker is a CS eliciting excitement in her dog.

2. Operant conditioning. Playing new songs leads to negative consequences (punishment), which weaken the tendency to play new songs. Playing old songs leads to positive reinforcement, which gradually strengthens the tendency to play old songs.

3. Classical conditioning. The song was paired with the passion of new love so that it became a CS eliciting emotional, romantic feelings.

4. Both. Ralph's workplace is paired with criticism so that his workplace becomes a CS eliciting anxiety. Calling in sick is operant behaviour that is strengthened through negative reinforcement (because it reduces anxiety).

Practice Test

1. D p. 228	**6.** A p. 238	**11.** D p. 251
2. C p. 228	**7.** A p. 242	**12.** C p. 252
3. B p. 247	**8.** B p. 243	**13.** C p. 254
4. D p. 235	**9.** C p. 245	**14.** A p. 255
5. C p. 236	**10.** A p. 250	**15.** C p. 258

Chapter 7

Concept Check 7.1

Feature	Sensory memory	Short-term memory	Long-term memory
Main encoding format	Copy of input	Largely phonemic	Largely semantic
Storage capacity	Limited	Small (7 ± 2 chunks)	No known limit
Storage duration	About 1/4 second	Up to 20 seconds	Minutes to years

Concept Check 7.2

1. Ineffective encoding due to lack of attention

2. Retrieval failure due to motivated forgetting

3. Proactive interference (previous learning of Joe Cocker's name interferes with new learning)

4. Retroactive interference (new learning of sociology interferes with older learning of history)

Concept Check 7.3

1. a. Declarative memory

2. e. Long-term memory

3. j. Sensory memory

4. d. Implicit memory

5. b. Episodic memory

6. f. Procedural memory

7. i. Semantic memory

8. g. Prospective memory

9. k. Short-term memory

Practice Test

1. C p. 268	**6.** D p. 282	**11.** B p. 297
2. C p. 270	**7.** C p. 285	**12.** D p. 298
3. D p. 275	**8.** C p. 288	**13.** D p. 301
4. C p. 275	**9.** B p. 288	**14.** D p. 301
5. C p. 280	**10.** C p. 296	**15.** D p. 305

Chapter 8

Concept Check 8.1

1. 1. One-word utterance in which the word is overextended to refer to a similar object.

2. 4. Words are combined into a sentence, but the rule for past tense is overregularized.

3. 3. Telegraphic sentence.

4. 5. Words are combined into a sentence, and past tense is used correctly.

5. 2. One-word utterance without overextension.

6. 6. "Longer" sentence with metaphor.

Concept Check 8.2

1. Functional fixedness

2. Forming subgoals

3. Insight

4. Searching for analogies

5. Arrangement problem

Concept Check 8.3

1. Elimination by aspects

2. Availability heuristic

3. Shift to additive strategy

Practice Test

1. B p. 317	**6.** A p. 326	**11.** A p. 336
2. D p. 318	**7.** D p. 326	**12.** C p. 337
3. D p. 322	**8.** B p. 329	**13.** D p. 337
4. A p. 324	**9.** E p. 332	**14.** C p. 342
5. A p. 325	**10.** B p. 334	**15.** C p. 345

Chapter 9

Concept Check 9.1

1. Test–retest reliability

2. Criterion-related validity

3. Content validity

Concept Check 9.2

1. H. Given that the identical twins were reared apart, their greater similarity in comparison to fraternals reared together can only be due to heredity. This comparison is probably the most important piece of evidence supporting the genetic determination of IQ.

2. E. We tend to associate identical twins with evidence supporting heredity, but in this comparison genetic similarity is held constant since both sets of twins are identical. The only logical explanation for the greater similarity in identicals reared together is the effect of their being reared together (environment).

3. E. This comparison is similar to the previous one. Genetic similarity is held constant and a shared environment produces greater similarity than being reared apart.

4. B. This is nothing more than a quantification of Galton's original observation that intelligence runs in families. Since families share both genes and environment, either or both could be responsible for the observed correlation.

5. B. The similarity of adopted children to their biological parents can only be due to shared genes, and the similarity of adopted children to their adoptive parents can only be due to shared environment, so these correlations show the influence of both heredity and environment.

Concept Check 9.3

1. b. Gardner

2. a. Galton

3. c. Jensen

4. d. Scarr

5. e. Sternberg

Practice Test

1. B p. 351	**6.** C p. 361	**11.** C p. 369
2. C p. 351	**7.** B p. 365	**12.** D p. 374
3. D p. 353	**8.** C p. 363	**13.** D p. 376
4. A p. 356	**9.** B p. 365	**14.** A p. 383
5. D p. 358	**10.** B p. 367	**15.** C p. 385

Chapter 10

Concept Check 10.1

1. I. Early studies indicated that lesioning the ventromedial nucleus of the hypothalamus leads to overeating (although it is an oversimplification to characterize the VMH as the brain's "stop eating" centre).

2. I. According to Mayer, hunger increases when the amount of glucose in the blood decreases.

3. I or ?. Food cues generally trigger hunger and eating, but reactions vary among individuals.

4. D. Food preferences are mostly learned, and we tend to like what we are accustomed to eating. Most people will not be eager to eat a strange-looking food.

5. D. When leptin levels are increased, hunger tends to decrease.

6. I. Reactions vary, but stress generally tends to increase eating.

7. I. Research on dietary restraint suggests that when people feel that they have cheated on their diet, they tend to become disinhibited and eat to excess.

Concept Check 10.2

1. d. Fear of failure

2. c. Incentive value of success

3. b. Perceived probability of success

4. a. Need for achievement

Concept Check 10.3

2. James–Lange theory

3. Schachter's two-factor theory

4. Evolutionary theories

Practice Test

1. B p. 392	**6.** B p. 410	**11.** B p. 424
2. C p. 401	**7.** C p. 415	**12.** C p. 425
3. D p. 401	**8.** C p. 417	**13.** D p. 427
4. C p. 404	**9.** A p. 419	**14.** D p. 428
5. C p. 406	**10.** D p. 423	**15.** C p. 433

Chapter 11

Concept Check 11.1

	Event	Stage	Organism	Time span
1.	Uterine implantation	Germinal	Zygote	0–2 weeks
2.	Muscle and bone begin to form	Fetal	Fetus	2 months to birth
3.	Vital organs and body systems begin to form	Embryonic	Embryo	2 weeks to 2 months

Concept Check 11.2

1. b. Animism is characteristic of the preoperational period.

2. c. Mastery of hierarchical classification occurs during the concrete operational period.

3. a. Lack of object permanence is characteristic of the sensorimotor period.

Concept Check 11.3

1. c. Commitment to personal ethics is characteristic of postconventional reasoning.

2. b. Concern about approval of others is characteristic of conventional reasoning.

3. a. Emphasis on positive or negative consequences is characteristic of preconventional reasoning.

Practice Test

1. D p. 439	**6.** D p. 451	**11.** B p. 464
2. A p. 444	**7.** B p. 452	**12.** A p. 468
3. C p. 445	**8.** D p. 453	**13.** C p. 471
4. C p. 446	**9.** C p. 460	**14.** C p. 481
5. C p. 449	**10.** C p. 465	**15.** D p. 484

Chapter 12

Concept Check 12.1

1. Regression

2. Projection

3. Reaction formation

4. Repression

5. Rationalization

Concept Check 12.2

1. Bandura's observational learning. Sarah imitates a role model from television.

2. Maslow's need for self-actualization. Yolanda is striving to realize her fullest potential.

3. Freud's Oedipal complex. Vladimir shows preference for his opposite-sex parent and emotional distance from his same-sex parent.

Concept Check 12.3

1. Maslow (1971, p. 36), commenting on the need for self-actualization.

2. Eysenck (1977, pp. 407–408), commenting on the biological roots of personality.

3. Freud (in Malcolm, 1980), commenting on the repression of sexuality.

Practice Test

1. C p. 495	**6.** A p. 506	**11.** D p. 520
2. A p. 498	**7.** A p. 508	**12.** C p. 520
3. C p. 500	**8.** D p. 509	**13.** D p. 522
4. C p. 501	**9.** B p. 515	**14.** D p. 528
5. B p. 504	**10.** B p. 517	**15.** C p. 530

Chapter 13

Concept Check 13.1

1. b. A choice between two unattractive options

2. c. Weighing the positive and negative aspects of a single goal

3. a. A choice between two attractive options

Concept Check 13.2

1. a. Frustration due to delay

2. d. Pressure to perform

3. c. Change associated with leaving school and taking a new job

4. a. Frustration due to loss of job

  c. Change in life circumstances

  d. Pressure to perform (in quickly obtaining new job)

Concept Check 13.3

1. Denial of reality

2. Undoing

3. Fantasy

4. Overcompensation

5. Intellectualization

Practice Test

1. C p. 537	**9.** B p. 549
2. D p. 537	**10.** D p. 553
3. B p. 540	**11.** D p. 554
4. A p. 539	**12.** C p. 558
5. B p. 542	**13.** D p. 561
6. A p. 543	**14.** C p. 566
7. A p. 544	**15.** C p. 570
8. C p. 547	

Chapter 14

Concept Check 14.1

1. Obsessive-compulsive disorder (key symptoms: frequent rituals, ruminations about school)

2. Somatization disorder (key symptoms: history of physical complaints involving many different organ systems)

3. Conversion disorder (key symptoms: loss of function in single organ system)

Concept Check 14.2

1. Bipolar disorder, manic episode (key symptoms: extravagant plans, hyperactivity, reckless spending)

2. Paranoid schizophrenia (key symptoms: delusions of persecution and grandeur, along with deterioration of adaptive behaviour)

3. Major depression (key symptoms: feelings of despair, low self-esteem, lack of energy)

Practice Test

1. B p. 576	**6.** A p. 584	**11.** C p. 606
2. C p. 582	**7.** B p. 595	**12.** D p. 606
3. D p. 585	**8.** A p. 599	**13.** C p. 610
4. D p. 589	**9.** D p. 600	**14.** A p. 611
5. B p. 591	**10.** D p. 601	**15.** D p. 615

Chapter 15

Concept Check 15.1

1. c   **2.** a   **3.** b

Concept Check 15.2

1. d   **2.** b   **3.** a   **4.** c

Concept Check 15.3

1. a. Systematic desensitization

2. c. Aversion therapy

3. b. Social skills training

Concept Check 15.4

1. c   **2.** a   **3.** b   **4.** d   **5.** b

Practice Test

1. C p. 624	**6.** A p. 633	**11.** A p. 648
2. A p. 628	**7.** D p. 636	**12.** C p. 650
3. B p. 628	**8.** D p. 637	**13.** A p. 651
4. B p. 629	**9.** B p. 640	**14.** C p. 654
5. D p. 631	**10.** D p. 641	**15.** D p. 658

Chapter 16

Concept Check 16.1

	Unstable	Stable
Internal	d	b
External	a	c

Concept Check 16.2

1. c. Fundamental attribution error (assuming that arriving late reflects personal qualities)

2. a. Illusory correlation effect (overestimating how often one has seen confirmations of the assertion that young, female professors get pregnant soon after being hired)

3. b. Stereotyping (assuming that all lawyers have certain traits)

4. d. Defensive attribution (derogating the victims of misfortune to minimize the apparent likelihood of a similar mishap)

Concept Check 16.3

1. *Target:* Cognitive component of attitudes (beliefs about program for regulating nursing homes)

  Persuasion: Message factor (advice to use one-sided instead of two-sided arguments)

2. *Target:* Affective component of attitudes (feelings about candidate)

Persuasion: Source factor (advice on appearing likable, sincere, and compassionate)

3. *Target:* Behavioural component of attitudes (making contributions)

Persuasion: Receiver factor (considering audience's initial position regarding the candidate)

Concept Check 16.4

1. False **2.** True **3.** False **4.** True **5.** False

Practice Test

1. D p. 666	**6.** A p. 676	**11.** B p. 689
2. A p. 667	**7.** A p. 678	**12.** C p. 693
3. B p. 669	**8.** B p. 685	**13.** C p. 695
4. B p. 670	**9.** D p. 684	**14.** B p. 698
5. B p. 670	**10.** B p. 684	**15.** B p. 703

Appendix B Statistical Methods

Empiricism depends on observation; precise observation depends on measurement; and measurement requires numbers. Thus, scientists routinely analyze numerical data to arrive at their conclusions. Over 3000 empirical studies are cited in this text, and all but a few of the simplest ones required a statistical analysis. **Statistics is the use of mathematics to organize, summarize, and interpret numerical data.** We discussed statistics briefly in Chapter 2, but in this Appendix we take a closer look.

To illustrate statistics in action, imagine a group of students who want to test a hypothesis that has generated quite an argument in their psychology class. The hypothesis is that university students who watch a great deal of television aren't as bright as those who watch TV infrequently. For the fun of it, the class decides to conduct a correlational study of itself, collecting survey and psychological test data. All the classmates agree to respond to a short survey on their TV viewing habits. Because everyone at that school has had to take the Scholastic Aptitude Test (SAT), the class decides to use scores on the SAT verbal subtest as an index of how bright students are. The SAT is one of a set of tests that high school students in the United States take before applying to college or university. Universities frequently use test scores like these, along with the students' high school grades and other relevant information, when considering admitting students to university. In this class, all of the students agree to allow the records office at the university to furnish their SAT scores to the professor, who replaces each student's name with a subject number (to protect students' right to privacy). Let's see how they could use statistics to analyze the data collected in their pilot study (a small, preliminary investigation).

Graphing Data 1c

After collecting the data, the next step is to organize the data to get a quick overview of our numerical results. Let's assume that there are 20 students in the class, and when they estimate how many hours they spend per day watching TV, the results are as follows:

3	2	0	3	1
3	4	0	5	1
2	3	4	5	2
4	5	3	4	6

One of the simpler things that they can do to organize data is to create a *frequency distribution*—**an orderly arrangement of scores indicating the frequency of each score or group of scores.** Figure B.1(a) shows a frequency distribution for the data on TV viewing. The column on the left lists the possible scores (estimated hours of TV viewing) in order, and the column on the right lists the number of subjects or participants with each score. Graphs can provide an even better overview of the data. One approach is to portray the data in a *histogram*, **which is a bar graph that presents data from a frequency distribution.** Such a histogram, summarizing our TV viewing data, is presented in Figure B.1(b).

Another widely used method of portraying data graphically is the *frequency polygon*—**a line figure used to present data from a frequency distribution.** Figures B.1(c) and B.1(d) show how the TV viewing data can be converted from a histogram to a frequency polygon. In both the bar graph and the line figure, the horizontal axis lists the possible scores and the vertical axis is used to indicate the frequency

Figure B.1

Graphing data. (**a**) The raw data are tallied into a frequency distribution. (**b**) The same data are portrayed in a bar graph called a histogram. (**c**) A frequency polygon is plotted over the histogram. (**d**) The resultant frequency polygon is shown by itself.

Score	Tallies	Frequency
6	I	1
5	III	3
4	IIII	4
3	ʅʯʯ	5
2	III	3
1	II	2
0	II	2

(a) Frequency distribution

(b) Histogram

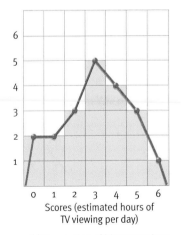

(c) Conversion of histogram into frequency polygon

(d) Frequency polygon

Measures of central tendency. Although the mean, median, and mode sometimes yield different results, they usually converge, as in the case of the TV viewing data.

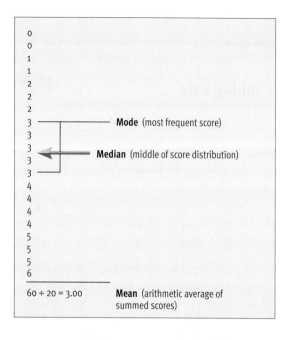

```
0
0
1
1
2
2
2
3  ─────────── Mode (most frequent score)
3
3
3  ◄───────── Median (middle of score distribution)
3
3
4
4
4
4
5
5
5
6
─────────────────────────
60 ÷ 20 = 3.00    Mean (arithmetic average of
                        summed scores)
```

Measures of central tendency in skewed distributions. In a symmetrical distribution (**a**), the three measures of central tendency converge. However, in a negatively skewed distribution (**b**) or in a positively skewed distribution (**c**), the mean, median, and mode are pulled apart as shown here. Typically, in these situations the median provides the best index of central tendency.

of each score. This use of the axes is nearly universal for frequency polygons, although sometimes it is reversed in histograms (the vertical axis lists possible scores, so the bars become horizontal).

The graphs improve on the jumbled collection of scores that they started with, but *descriptive statistics*, **which are used to organize and summarize data**, provide some additional advantages. Let's see what the three measures of central tendency tell us about the data.

Measuring Central Tendency 1c

In examining a set of data, it's routine to ask, "What is a typical score in the distribution?" For instance, in this case we might compare the average amount of TV watching in the sample to national estimates, to determine whether the subjects appear to be rep-

resentative of the population. The three measures of central tendency—the median, the mean, and the mode—give us indications regarding the typical score in a data set. As explained in Chapter 2, **the *median* is the score that falls in the centre of a distribution, the *mean* is the arithmetic average of the scores,** and **the *mode* is the score that occurs most frequently.**

All three measures of central tendency are calculated for the TV viewing data in Figure B.2. As you can see, in this set of data, the mean, median, and mode all turn out to be the same score, which is 3. Although our example in Chapter 2 emphasized that the mean, median, and mode can yield different estimates of central tendency, the correspondence among them seen in the TV viewing data is quite common. Lack of agreement usually occurs when a few extreme scores pull the mean away from the centre of the distribution, as shown in Figure B.3. The curves plotted in Figure B.3 are simply "smoothed out" frequency polygons based on data from many subjects. They show that when a distribution is symmetric, the measures of central tendency fall together, but this is not true in skewed or unbalanced distributions.

Figure B.3(b) shows a *negatively skewed distribution,* **in which most scores pile up at the high end of the scale** (the negative skew refers to the direction in which the curve's "tail" points). A *positively skewed distribution,* **in which scores pile up at the low end of the scale**, is shown in Figure B.3(c). In both types of skewed distributions, a few extreme scores at one end pull the mean, and to a lesser degree the median, away from the mode. In these situations, the mean may be misleading and the median usually provides the best index of central tendency.

In any case, the measures of central tendency for the TV viewing data are reassuring, since they all

(a) Symmetrical distribution

(b) Negatively skewed distribution

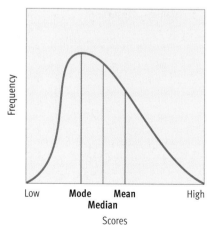

(c) Positively skewed distribution

agree and they fall reasonably close to national estimates regarding how much young adults watch TV (Nielsen Media Research, 1998). Given the small size of the student group, this agreement with national norms doesn't *prove* that the sample is representative of the population, but at least there's no obvious reason to believe that it is unrepresentative.

Measuring Variability

Of course, the subjects in the sample did not report identical TV viewing habits. Virtually all data sets are characterized by some variability. **Variability refers to how much the scores tend to vary or depart from the mean score.** For example, the distribution of golf scores for a mediocre, erratic golfer would be characterized by high variability, while scores for an equally mediocre but consistent golfer would show less variability.

The *standard deviation* is an index of the amount of variability in a set of data. It reflects the dispersion of scores in a distribution. This principle is portrayed graphically in Figure B.4, where the two distributions of golf scores have the same mean but the upper one has less variability because the scores are "bunched up" in the centre (for the consistent golfer). The distribution in Figure B.4(b) is characterized by more variability, as the erratic golfer's scores are more spread out. This distribution will yield a higher standard deviation than the distribution in Figure B.4(a).

The formula for calculating the standard deviation is shown in Figure B.5, where d stands for each score's deviation from the mean and Σ stands for summation. A step-by-step application of this formula to our TV viewing data, shown in Figure B.5, reveals that the standard deviation for our TV viewing data is 1.64. The standard deviation has a variety of uses. One of these uses will surface in the next section, where we discuss the normal distribution.

The Normal Distribution

The hypothesis in the study was that brighter students watch less TV than relatively dull students. To test this hypothesis, the students decided to correlate TV

Figure B.4

The standard deviation and dispersion of data. Although both these distributions of golf scores have the same mean, their standard deviations will be different. In (a) the scores are bunched together and there is less variability than in (b), yielding a lower standard deviation for the data in distribution (a).

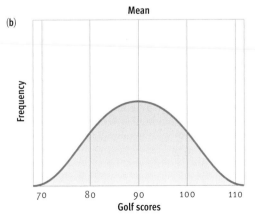

TV viewing score (X)	Deviation from mean (d)	Deviation squared (d^2)
0	−3	9
0	−3	9
1	−2	4
1	−2	4
2	−1	1
2	−1	1
2	−1	1
3	0	0
3	0	0
3	0	0
3	0	0
3	0	0
4	+1	1
4	+1	1
4	+1	1
4	+1	1
5	+2	4
5	+2	4
5	+2	4
6	+3	9

$N = 20$

$\Sigma X = 60$ $\Sigma d^2 = 54$

$$\text{Mean} = \frac{\Sigma X}{N} = \frac{60}{20} = 3.0$$

$$\text{Standard deviation} = \sqrt{\frac{\Sigma d^2}{N}} = \sqrt{\frac{54}{20}}$$

$$= \sqrt{2.70} = 1.64$$

Figure B.5

Steps in calculating the standard deviation. (1) Add the scores (ΣX) and divide by the number of scores (N) to calculate the mean (which comes out to 3.0 in this case). (2) Calculate each score's deviation from the mean by subtracting the mean from each score (the results are shown in the second column). (3) Square these deviations from the mean and total the results to obtain (Σd^2) as shown in the third column. (4) Insert the numbers for N and Σd^2 into the formula for the standard deviation and compute the results.

viewing with SAT scores. But to make effective use of the SAT data, they need to understand what SAT scores mean, which brings us to the normal distribution.

The *normal distribution* **is a symmetric, bell-shaped curve that represents the pattern in which many human characteristics are dispersed in the population.** A great many physical qualities (e.g., height, nose length, and running speed) and psychological traits (intelligence, spatial reasoning ability, introversion) are distributed in a manner that closely resembles this bell-shaped curve. When a trait is normally distributed, most scores fall near the centre of the distribution (the mean), and the number of scores gradually declines as one moves away from the centre in either direction. The normal distribution is *not* a law of nature. It's a mathematical function, or theoretical curve, that approximates the way nature seems to operate.

The normal distribution is the bedrock of the scoring system for most psychological tests, including the SAT. As we discuss in Chapter 9, psychological tests are *relative measures;* they assess how people score on a trait in comparison to other people. The normal distribution gives us a precise way to measure how people stack up in comparison to each other. The scores under the normal curve are dispersed in a fixed pattern, with the standard deviation serving as the unit of measurement, as shown in Figure B.6. About 68% of the scores in the distribution fall within plus or minus 1 standard deviation of the mean, while 95% of the scores fall within plus or minus 2 standard deviations of the mean. Given this fixed pattern, if you know the mean and standard deviation of a normally distributed trait, you can tell where any score falls in the distribution for the trait.

Although you may not have realized it, you probably have taken many tests in which the scoring system is based on the normal distribution, such as IQ tests. On the SAT, for instance, raw scores (the number of items correct on each subtest) are converted into standard scores that indicate where a student falls in the normal distribution for the trait measured. In this conversion, the mean is set arbitrarily at 500 and the standard deviation at 100, as shown in Figure B.7. Therefore, a score of 400 on the SAT verbal subtest means that the student scored 1 standard deviation below the mean, while an SAT score of 600 indicates that the student scored 1 standard deviation above the mean. Thus, SAT scores tell us how many standard deviations above or below the mean a specific student's score was. This system also provides the metric for IQ scales and many other types of psychological tests (see Chapter 9).

Figure B.6

The normal distribution.
Many characteristics are distributed in a pattern represented by this bell-shaped curve (each dot represents a case). The horizontal axis shows how far above or below the mean a score is (measured in plus or minus standard deviations). The vertical axis shows the number of cases obtaining each score. In a normal distribution, most cases fall near the centre of the distribution, so that 68.26% of the cases fall within plus or minus 1 standard deviation of the mean. The number of cases gradually declines as one moves away from the mean in either direction, so that only 13.59% of the cases fall between 1 and 2 standard deviations above or below the mean, and even fewer cases (2.14%) fall between 2 and 3 standard deviations above or below the mean.

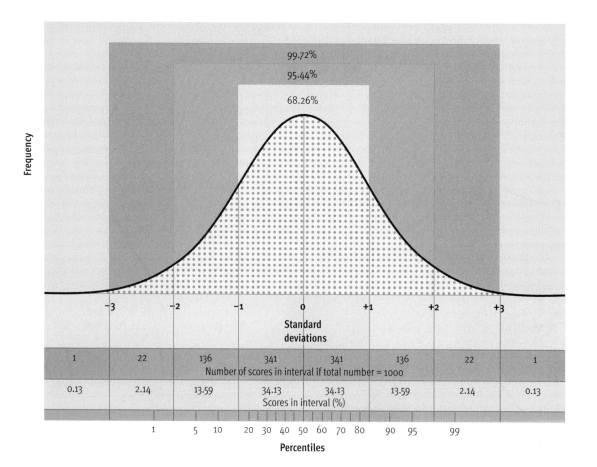

Test scores that place examinees in the normal distribution can always be converted to percentile scores, which are a little easier to interpret. A **percentile score indicates the percentage of people who score at or below a particular score.** For example, if you score at the 60th percentile on an IQ test, 60% of the people who take the test score the same or below you, while the remaining 40% score above you. There are tables available that permit us to convert any standard deviation placement in a normal distribution into a precise percentile score. Figure B.6 gives some percentile conversions for the normal curve.

Of course, not all distributions are normal. As we saw in Figure B.3, some distributions are skewed in one direction or the other. As an example, consider what would happen if a classroom exam were much too easy or much too hard. If the test were too easy, scores would be bunched up at the high end of the scale, as in Figure B.3(b). If the test were too hard, scores would be bunched up at the low end, as in Figure B.3(c).

Measuring Correlation

To determine whether TV viewing is related to SAT scores, the students have to compute a **correlation coefficient—a numerical index of the degree of relationship between two variables.** As discussed in Chapter 2, a *positive* correlation means that two variables—say X and Y—co-vary in the *same* direction. This means that high scores on variable X are associated with high scores on variable Y and that low scores on X are associated with low scores on Y. A *negative* correlation indicates that two variables co-vary in the *opposite* direction. This means that people who score high on variable X tend to score low on

variable Y, whereas those who score low on X tend to score high on Y. In their study, the psychology students hypothesized that as TV viewing increases, SAT scores will decrease, so they should expect a negative correlation between TV viewing and SAT scores.

The *magnitude* of a correlation coefficient indicates the *strength* of the association between two variables. This coefficient can vary between 0 and ±1.00. The coefficient is usually represented by the letter r (e.g., r = 0.45). A coefficient near 0 tells us that there is no relationship between two variables. A coefficient of +1.00 or −1.00 indicates that there is a perfect, one-to-one correspondence between two variables. A perfect correlation is found only rarely when working with real data. The closer the coefficient is to either −1.00 or +1.00, the stronger the relationship is.

The direction and strength of correlations can be illustrated graphically in scatter diagrams (see Figure B.8). A **scatter diagram is a graph in which paired X and Y scores for each subject are plotted as single**

Figure B.7

The normal distribution and SAT scores. The normal distribution is the basis for the scoring system on many standardized tests. For example, on the SAT, the mean is set at 500 and the standard deviation at 100. Hence, an SAT score tells you how many standard deviations above or below the mean a student scored. For example, a score of 700 means that person scored 2 standard deviations above the mean.

Figure B.8

Scatter diagrams of positive and negative correlations. Scatter diagrams plot paired X and Y scores as single points. Score plots slanted in the opposite direction result from positive (top row) as opposed to negative (bottom row) correlations. Moving across both rows (to the right), you can see that progressively weaker correlations result in more and more scattered plots of data points.

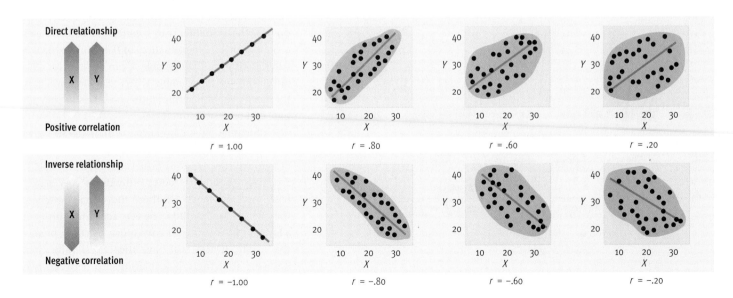

Figure B.9

Scatter diagram of the correlation between TV viewing and SAT scores. The hypothetical data relating TV viewing to SAT scores are plotted in this scatter diagram. Compare it to the scatter diagrams shown in Figure B.8 and see whether you can estimate the correlation between TV viewing and SAT scores in the students' data (see the text for the answer).

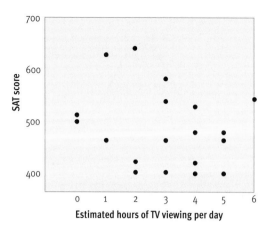

Figure B.10

Computing a correlation coefficient. The calculations required to compute the Pearson product-moment coefficient of correlation are shown here. The formula looks intimidating, but it's just a matter of filling in the figures taken from the sums of the columns shown above the formula.

Subject number	TV viewing score (X)	X^2	SAT score (Y)	Y^2	XY
1	0	0	500	250 000	0
2	0	0	515	265 225	0
3	1	1	450	202 500	450
4	1	1	650	422 500	650
5	2	4	400	160 000	800
6	2	4	675	455 625	1350
7	2	4	425	180 625	850
8	3	9	400	160 000	1200
9	3	9	450	202 500	1350
10	3	9	500	250 000	1500
11	3	9	550	302 500	1650
12	3	9	600	360 000	1800
13	4	16	400	160 000	1600
14	4	16	425	180 625	1700
15	4	16	475	225 625	1900
16	4	16	525	275 625	2100
17	5	25	400	160 000	2000
18	5	25	450	202 500	2250
19	5	25	475	225 625	2375
20	6	36	550	302 500	3300
$N = 20$	$\Sigma X = 60$	$\Sigma X^2 = 234$	$\Sigma Y = 9815$	$\Sigma Y^2 = 4\,943\,975$	$\Sigma XY = 28\,825$

Formula for Pearson product-moment correlation coefficient

$$r = \frac{(N)\,\Sigma XY \; - \; (\Sigma X)(\Sigma Y)}{\sqrt{[(N)\,\Sigma X^2 - (\Sigma X)^2]\,[(N)\,\Sigma Y^2 - (\Sigma Y)^2]}}$$

$$= \frac{(20)\,(28\,825) \; - \; (60)\,(9815)}{\sqrt{[(20)\,(234) - (60)^2]\,[(20)\,(4\,943\,975) - (9815)^2]}}$$

$$= \frac{-12\,400}{\sqrt{[1080]\,[2\,545\,275]}}$$

$$= -.237$$

points. Figure B.8 shows scatter diagrams for positive correlations in the upper half and for negative correlations in the bottom half. A perfect positive correlation and a perfect negative correlation are shown on the far left. When a correlation is perfect, the data points in the scatter diagram fall exactly in a straight line. However, positive and negative correlations yield lines slanted in the opposite direction because the lines map out opposite types of associations. Moving to the right in Figure B.8, you can see what happens when the magnitude of a correlation decreases. The data points scatter farther and farther from the straight line that would represent a perfect relationship.

What about the data relating TV viewing to SAT scores? Figure B.9 shows a scatter diagram of these data. Having just learned about scatter diagrams, perhaps you can estimate the magnitude of the correlation between TV viewing and SAT scores. The scatter diagram of our data looks a lot like the one shown in the bottom right corner of Figure B.8, suggesting that the correlation will be in the vicinity of –0.20.

The formula for computing the most widely used measure of correlation—the Pearson product-moment correlation—is shown in Figure B.10, along with the calculations for the data on TV viewing and SAT scores. The data yield a correlation of $r = -0.24$. This coefficient of correlation reveals that there is a weak inverse association between TV viewing and performance on the SAT. Among the sample of participants, as TV viewing increases, SAT scores decrease, but the trend isn't very strong. We can get a better idea of how strong this correlation is by examining its predictive power.

Correlation and Prediction

As the magnitude of a correlation increases (gets closer to either –1.00 or +1.00), our ability to predict one variable based on knowledge of the other variable steadily increases. This relationship between the magnitude of a correlation and predictability can be quantified precisely. All we have to do is square the correlation coefficient (multiply it by itself) and this gives us the *coefficient of determination,* **the percentage of variation in one variable that can be predicted based on the other variable.** Thus, a correlation of 0.70 yields a coefficient of determination of 0.49 ($0.70 \times 0.70 = 0.49$), indicating that variable X can account for 49% of the variation in variable Y. Figure B.11 shows how the coefficient of determination goes up as the magnitude of a correlation increases.

Unfortunately, a correlation of 0.24 doesn't give us much predictive power. The students can account only for a little over 6% of the variation in variable Y. So, if they tried to predict individuals' SAT scores based on how much TV those individuals watched, their predictions wouldn't be very accurate. Although a low correlation doesn't have much practical, predictive utility, it may still have theoretical value. Just knowing that there is a relationship between two variables can be theoretically interesting. However,

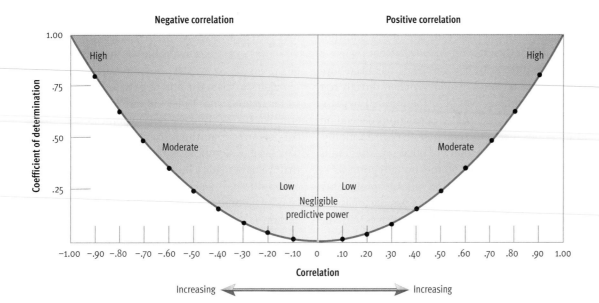

Correlation and the coefficient of determination.
The coefficient of determination is an index of a correlation's predictive power. As you can see, whether positive or negative, stronger correlations yield greater predictive power.

we haven't yet addressed the question of whether the observed correlation is strong enough to support the hypothesis that there is a relationship between TV viewing and SAT scores. To make this judgment, we have to turn to *inferential statistics* and the process of hypothesis testing.

Hypothesis Testing

Inferential statistics go beyond the mere description of data. ***Inferential statistics*** **are used to interpret data and draw conclusions.** They permit researchers to decide whether their data support their hypotheses.

In Chapter 2, we showed how inferential statistics can be used to evaluate the results of an experiment; the same process can be applied to correlational data. In the study of TV viewing, the students hypothesized that they would find an inverse relationship between amount of TV watched and SAT scores. Sure enough, that's what they found. However, a critical question remains: Is this observed correlation large enough to support the hypothesis, or might a correlation of this size have occurred by chance?

We have to ask a similar question nearly every time we conduct a study. Why? Because we are working only with a sample. In research, we observe a limited *sample* (in this case, 20 participants) to draw conclusions about a much larger *population* (students in general). In any study, there's always a possibility that if we drew a different sample from the population, the results might be different. Perhaps our results are unique to our sample and not generalizable to the larger population. If we were able to collect data on the entire population, we

would not have to wrestle with this problem, but our dependence on a sample necessitates the use of inferential statistics to precisely evaluate the likelihood that our results are due to chance factors in sampling. Thus, inferential statistics are the key to making the inferential leap from the sample to the population (see Figure B.12).

Although it may seem backward, in hypothesis testing we formally test the *null hypothesis*. As applied to correlational data, the **null hypothesis is the assumption that there is no true relationship between the variables observed.** In the students' study, the null hypothesis is that there is no genuine association between TV viewing and SAT scores.

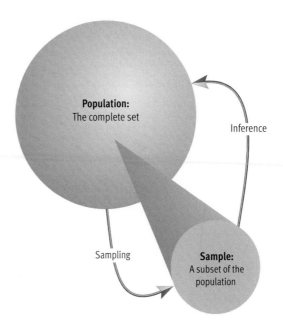

The relationship between the population and the sample. In research, we are usually interested in a broad population, but we can observe only a small sample from the population. After making observations of our sample, we draw inferences about the population, based on the sample. This inferential process works well as long as the sample is reasonably representative of the population.

They want to determine whether their results will permit them to *reject* the null hypothesis and thus conclude that their *research hypothesis* (that there *is* a relationship between the variables) has been supported. In such cases why do researchers directly test the null hypothesis instead of the research hypothesis? Because our probability calculations depend on assumptions tied to the null hypothesis. Specifically, we compute the probability of obtaining the results that we have observed if the null hypothesis is indeed true. The calculation of this probability hinges on a number of factors. A key factor is the amount of variability in the data, which is why the standard deviation is an important statistic.

Statistical Significance

When we reject the null hypothesis, we conclude that we have found *statistically significant* results. **Statistical significance is said to exist when the probability that the observed findings are due to chance is very low, usually fewer than 5 chances in 100.** This means that if the null hypothesis is correct and we conduct our study 100 times, drawing a new sample from the population each time, we will get results such as those observed only 5 times out of 100. If our calculations allow us to reject the null hypothesis, we conclude that our results support our research hypothesis. Thus, statistically significant results typically are findings that *support* a research hypothesis.

The requirement that there be fewer than 5 chances in 100 that research results are due to chance is the *minimum* requirement for statistical significance. When this requirement is met, we say the results are significant at the 0.05 level. If researchers calculate that there is less than 1 chance in 100 that their results are due to chance factors in sampling, the results are significant at the 0.01 level. If there is less than a 1 in 1000 chance that findings are attributable to sampling error, the results are significant at the 0.001 level. Thus, there are several *levels* of significance that you may see cited in scientific articles.

Because we are only dealing in matters of probability, there is always the possibility that our decision to accept or reject the null hypothesis is wrong. The various significance levels indicate the probability of erroneously rejecting the null hypothesis (and inaccurately accepting the research hypothesis). At the 0.05 level of significance, there are 5 chances in 100 that we have made a mistake when we conclude that our results support our hypothesis, and at the 0.01 level of significance the chance of an erroneous conclusion is 1 in 100. Although researchers hold the probability of this type of error quite low, the probability is never zero. This is one of the reasons that competently executed studies of the same question can yield contradictory findings. The differences may be due to chance variations in sampling that can't be prevented.

What do we find when we evaluate the data linking TV viewing to students' SAT scores? The calculations indicate that, given the sample size and the variability in the data, the probability of obtaining a correlation of –0.24 by chance is greater than 20%. That's not a high probability, but it's *not* low enough to reject the null hypothesis. Thus, the findings are not strong enough to allow us to conclude that the students have supported their hypothesis.

Statistics and Empiricism

In summary, conclusions based on empirical research are a matter of probability, and there's always a possibility that the conclusions are wrong. However, two major strengths of the empirical approach are its precision and its intolerance of error. Scientists can give you precise estimates of the likelihood that their conclusions are wrong, and because they're intolerant of error, they hold this probability extremely low. It's their reliance on statistics that allows them to accomplish these goals.

Appendix C Industrial/Organizational Psychology

By Paul M. Muchinsky (University of North Carolina at Greensboro) and Victor M. Catano
(Saint Mary's University, Halifax)

Throughout this book we have seen many examples of how psychology has been applied to practical problems in a wide variety of settings. But we have yet to discuss in earnest one setting that has received a great deal of attention from the earliest beginnings of psychology—the work setting. **Industrial and organizational (I/O) psychology is the branch of psychology concerned with the application of psychological principles in the workplace.** I/O psychology is studied throughout the world, although its name varies some from one locale to the next. For example, in the United Kingdom it is called *occupational psychology,* in many European countries *work and organizational psychology,* and in Australia *organisational psychology.* The Canadian Society for Industrial and Organizational Psychology (CSIOP; see http://www.ssc.uwo.ca/psychology/csiop/) is the major professional organization for I/O psychologists. The number of I/O psychologists has more than doubled in recent years, and it appears that this growth will continue. I/O psychologists are mostly found in four work settings: industry, universities, government, and consulting firms (see Figure C.1).

People devote an enormous part of their lives to occupational activities. Thus, I/O psychology is devoted to understanding one of the major domains of human behaviour. In broad terms, I/O psychology is concerned with behaviour in work situations. There are two sides of I/O psychology: science and practice. On the one hand, I/O psychology is a productive, fascinating area of scientific inquiry, concerned with advancing knowledge about behaviour in the workplace. In this respect, I/O psychology is an academic discipline that seeks to test hypotheses, gather data, and make generalizations about work-related behaviour. On the other hand, I/O psychology is a profession concerned with the application of knowledge to solve real problems in the world of work. I/O psychologists strive to help organizations hire better employees, reduce absenteeism, improve communication at work, increase job satisfaction, and solve countless other problems. Accordingly, the education of I/O psychologists is founded on the *scientist-practitioner model,* which trains them in both scientific inquiry and practical applications.

I/O psychology was originally called *industrial psychology.* During its early years (roughly the first half of the 20th century), the field focused primarily on

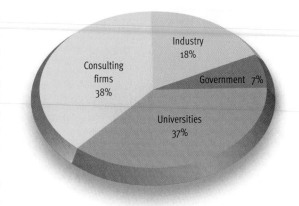

Figure C.1

Principal work settings of industrial/organizational psychologists. I/O psychologists are mainly found in the four work settings identified here. As the pie chart shows, about three-quarters of I/O psychologists work either in universities or at consulting firms. (Based on Society for Industrial and Organizational Psychology 2001 member database)

SOURCE: Muchinsky, P. M. (2003). *Psychology applied to work.* Belmont, CA: Wadsworth. Reprinted by permission.

recruiting and selecting employees, training, evaluating job performance, and leadership in the workplace. In the 1950s and 1960s psychologists in this area became more concerned with the organizational context in which work occurs. This shift in emphasis was also fuelled by changes in the economy, which gradually moved from a predominantly manufacturing base to more of a service economy. Because of these trends, the field's name was officially changed to industrial/organizational psychology in 1970. This name change is not merely cosmetic, as it captures the essence of the field. The topics of interest to contemporary I/O psychology generally fall into the traditional domain of *industrial psychology* or the more recently emerging domain of *organizational psychology.* Our coverage will reflect this reality, as we begin by discussing topics in industrial psychology and then turn to topics in organizational psychology.

Industrial Psychology

Industrial psychology focuses on topics associated with personnel matters. It is concerned with picking the right people for the right jobs and cultivating a productive work force. We will discuss five topics of interest in the field of industrial psychology: recruitment, selection, employment discrimination, training, and performance appraisal.

Recruitment

Recruitment is the process of attracting people to apply for a job. Organizations can select from only those candidates who apply for their positions. If few people apply for a job, the odds of finding a strong

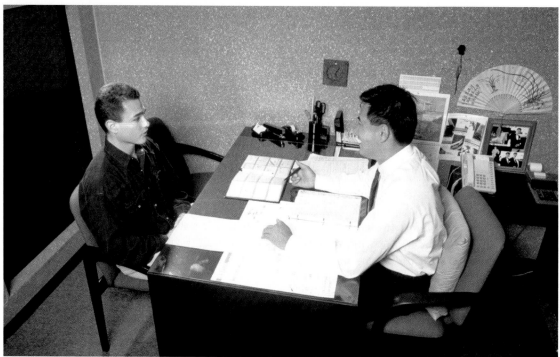

candidate are lower than if many candidates apply. With the growing acceptability of conducting business via the Internet, organizations are now developing Web sites to attract job applicants. Online recruiting is the fastest-growing medium for attracting job applicants and is particularly popular for candidates in their 20s and 30s (Catano et al., 2005; Graham, 2000).

There is a relationship between the recruitment of job applicants and broad-based economic conditions. When the economy is stagnating or contracting, jobs are generally scarce and typically there will be many applicants for each opening. In contrast, when the economy is growing, competition among employers for qualified job applicants can be intense. Rynes (1993) noted that most of the emphasis on personnel decisions from an I/O psychology perspective centres on how employers can make better decisions in assessing applicants. However, as Rynes observed, the process can be viewed from the opposite perspective—that is, the extent to which applicants consider the company to be a desirable employer. Specifically, what impressions of the company are generated by the company's recruitment and assessment practices? Applicant reactions to assessment procedures are often vivid and highly emotional, as the following examples from Rynes (1993) illustrate:

A married graduate student with a 3.9 grade point average reported that the first three questions in a company's psychological assessment procedure involved inquiries about her personal relationship with her husband and children. Although the company asked her what she thought of the procedure before she left, she lied because she was afraid that telling the truth would eliminate her from future consideration. Because of dual-career constraints, she continued to pursue an offer, but noted that if she got one, her first on-the-job priority would be to try to get the assessor fired.

The first interview question asked of a female student was, "We're a pretty macho organization … Does that bother you?" Unfortunately it did, and she simply wrote the company out of her future interviewing plans. (p. 242)

These examples show that job applicants are not merely passive recipients of personnel selection procedures. Rather, applicants react to what they are asked to do or say to get a job. Sometimes a negative experience results in withdrawal from the application process. Companies and applicants should realize that the recruitment process is *mutual*—both parties are engaged in assessing the degree of fit with each other. L. Harris (2000) asserts that it might be wise for organizations to explain to rejected candidates why they were denied employment in a way that reduces negative feelings and damage to self-esteem rather than to provide explanations that are designed to protect the companies from potential litigation.

Selection

The process of personnel selection consists of deciding which of the job applicants will be extended an offer of employment. The selection process should be based on careful consideration of the knowledge, skills, and abilities possessed by each applicant. The goal is to get a good match or fit between the work demands of the job and the personal attributes of the applicant.

Schmitt and Chan (1998) identified five major changes in modern society that have affected the ways personnel selection decisions are made in many organizations. The first is the *speed of technological change*. With computer-based technology, work today is often conducted in ways that people couldn't even imagine 25 years ago. This rapid rate of change compels companies to hire workers who can adapt to ever-evolving work conditions. Emphasis is thus placed on a person's willingness and capacity to learn new job skills on a continuous basis. Second is the growing reliance on the *use of teams to accomplish work*. More and more work tasks require coordinated efforts by teams of employees as opposed to individual workers and their supervisors. Traditionally, however, personnel selection methods have been geared toward the selection of individuals based on their achievements. Today, organizations increasingly need to select employees who can fit well into the team concept. The third factor consists of *changes in communication technology*. Faxes, e-mail, and hand-held electronic devices permit workers to communicate with others instantaneously around the world. It is no longer necessary to meet face to face or even communicate by telephone. These new, impersonal methods of communication have implications for classic organizational issues, such as the bond between co-workers, worker morale, and employee commitment. The fourth change is that *most large corporations are now global*. Many employees now work outside of Canada. The products of many Canadian companies are sold and serviced throughout the world. Hence, companies need to select employees who are adaptable and open to cultures other than their own. Finally, the Canadian economy is continuing its long-running *transition from a manufacturing orientation to a service orientation*. Organizations that provide services must strive to hire employees who are likely to be sensitive to the customers' needs and adept at satisfying them. This objective has increased the emphasis on applicants' interpersonal skills.

These trends are likely to lead companies in the 21st century to select employees with somewhat different qualities than the companies sought in the past. If jobs are constantly changing, organizations will probably increase their emphasis on hiring candidates with high intelligence. Teaching them the specific knowledge or skills required on the job can be left to post-hiring training. If jobs are increasingly service oriented, companies will want to hire people who are conscientious and interpersonally flexible. However, as Behling (1998) has noted, these skills are most appropriate when new employees will have to do a lot of problem solving, will have a lot of autonomy, will learn skills on the job that are more important than those brought to the job, and will need to adapt rapidly. Of course, many jobs in modern society do not fit this description. In some jobs it is still critical to pursue a match between the specific skills applicants already have and specific job requirements. Thus, in a rapidly changing work environment the desired match is more between the *person* and the *organization*, whereas in a stable work environment the desired match is more between the *person* and the *job*.

I/O psychologists use a diverse array of personnel selection tools, including personality and intelligence tests, performance tests (e.g., a typing test), interviews, tests of physical ability, letters of recommendation, and drug tests. These techniques are all designed to gauge candidates' suitability for employment. I/O psychologists strive to devise selection methods that are accurate predictors of future job performance, legally defensible, appropriate for the job, and cost-efficient. Obviously, selection decisions can have profound effects on job candidates' lives. These decisions can also be critical to the success of organizations. Catano et al. (2005) provide more information on these selection tools and techniques.

Employment Discrimination

The tasks of employee recruitment and selection are intimately intertwined with the sometimes-controversial issue of employment discrimination. Understanding this topic necessitates an awareness of the cultural and social changes taking place in Canada. Until the 1970s most immigrants to Canada were from the United States and Western Europe and reflected the culture and values of the English and French settlers. Today's immigrants are from various nations, cultures, races, and religions. However, over the course of history, some groups have been treated less equitably than others. The injustice of discrimination became a prominent concern in the 1970s. Up until that time it was acceptable, for example, to pay a woman less money than a man even though they had equal job performance and seniority. In response to changing values and mounting political pressures, the federal Parliament and the provincial legislatures have passed human rights legislation that prohibits discrimination in many areas of life, including the world of work. While there is variation among the different pieces of legislation, all Canadian jurisdictions prohibit discrimination on the basis of race or colour, religion or creed, age, sex, marital status, and physical/mental handicap or disability. In addition, the federal employment equity legislation is intended to promote the entry and retention of people from designated groups, including women, visible minorities, Aboriginal peoples, and people with disabilities, into the workplace.

These legislative efforts have had a dramatic impact on the field of industrial psychology, making it accountable to many new legal standards. In addition to ensuring that their employee recruitment and selection methods represent sound science and sound business practice, contemporary I/O psychologists must strive to ensure that their practices are legally sound.

Training

Organizations select employees on the basis of their predicted likelihood of succeeding on the job. Although some employees are expected to perform their jobs well immediately, the vast majority of employees are given some time to grow into their jobs. This growth process is expedited by formal organizational training processes. Training is designed to help new employees acquire the skills, rules, concepts, or attitudes that result in improved job performance.

Training is important because the knowledge and skill demands of work are continually escalating. Martocchio and Baldwin (1997) expressed this perspective clearly: "In an age of technological innovation in which robots, telecommunications, artificial intelligence, software, and lasers perform routine tasks, worker skills soon become obsolete. Put bluntly, today's jobs require new and different skills at all levels of an organization" (p. 6). One major reason for the increased emphasis on training is the growing reliance on computers in the conduct of work. Computer-assisted manufacturing and computer-assisted design are two major technological innovations in production. Manufacturing employees are now often expected to have some fluency in computer-based operations. The acquisition of such skills often depends on post-hire training programs.

In 2000, Canadian business and labour leaders identified "skills shortages" among their top 10 concerns (Sangster & Wortsman, 2001). Competition for skilled workers is becoming fierce. In addition, many people seeking to enter the work force lack essential skills needed for success. Human Resources and Skills Development Canada (HRSDC) initiated an essential skills development and literacy program in 2003 to ensure that Canadians have the right skills for changing work and life demands. Essential skills are those skills that make it possible to learn all others

and enable people to participate fully in the workplace. These include reading text, document use, numeracy, writing, oral communication, working with others, thinking skills, computer use, and continuous learning. The HRSDC Web site (http://www.hrsdc.gc.ca/en/home.shtml) provides access to over 200 occupational profiles together with the most important skills, and the level of the skill, needed to pursue entry into the occupation. The profiles are also used to determine occupational training needs and priorities. HRSDC provides, in partnership with both private- and public-sector organizations, many skills development and training programs designed to enhance both the essential and advanced skills of both young and older workers.

Pressures are growing in all areas of work to operate more efficiently and to enhance the overall quality of goods and services. Such changes require enhanced organizational performance in increasingly competitive markets. Training, therefore, is a process to improve the fit between job demands and employee attributes. Training needs to occur in virtually all organizations on a continuous basis. Thus, it might be advisable to think of your college and university years as "learning through education" and of your working years as "learning through training."

Obviously, training programs vary in their effectiveness. Successful training initiatives depend on four main considerations. First, the organization must value training, encourage employees to participate in training, and then design work so the training can be used back on the job. Second, there must be a clear understanding about what kind of training needs to occur, how it will benefit the organization, and which employees should receive the training. Third, there should be an approximate match between training methods and training needs. Some training methods are more geared to technical skill enhancement, while others are more suited for enhancing interpersonal skills. Fourth, there must be clear support systems in place to ensure that what is learned in training generalizes back to the job. The extent to which training actually improves job performance is the ultimate test of training effectiveness.

Performance Appraisal

With or without the input of I/O psychologists, employees continually have their job performance evaluated. Informal appraisals may be made from haphazard observations, memory, hearsay, or intuition. I/O psychologists endeavour to design performance appraisal methods that are formal, rational, systematic, accurate, fair, and useful to all concerned.

Performance appraisals serve many purposes for both employers and employees, as outlined in Figure C.2. Murphy and Cleveland (1995) maintain that effective performance appraisals can help organizations in several ways. First, they can enhance the quality of organizational decisions, ranging from pay raises to promotions to discharge. The purpose of the human resource function in an organization is to maximize the contributions of employees to the goals of the organization, and assessments of employee job performance can play a major role in accomplishing that function.

Second, performance appraisals can improve the quality of individual decisions, ranging from career choices to the development of future strengths. Accurate performance feedback is an important component of effective training and provides critical input for realistic self-assessments by employees. Performance feedback is also a key factor in promoting high levels of motivation in the work force.

Third, performance appraisals can affect employees' views of, and attachment to, their organization. A fair and effective appraisal system can help build employee morale and satisfaction. In contrast, employees who believe that an organization's performance appraisals are irrational or unfair are unlikely to develop a strong commitment to that organization.

Finally, formal performance appraisals provide a legally defensible basis for personnel decisions, which cannot be capricious. Organizations must have reasonable explanations for why some employees are promoted, discharged, or receive differential pay raises compared to others.

Performance appraisal often requires evaluations of many aspects of job performance. At the lower level of complexity, jobs typically require employees to show up for work on time, cooperate with co-workers, and so forth. At higher levels of complexity, jobs may require the demonstration of technical expertise or leadership capability. I/O psychologists assist in deciding which aspects of job performance should be appraised and in designing the appraisal methods. They also try to find ways to deal with the fact that many employees don't like to be appraised and some supervisors don't like to evaluate their colleagues. The challenge for I/O psychologists is to help foster an atmosphere within the organization that recognizes the legitimate need for all parties to provide honest and accurate performance appraisals.

Organizational Psychology

Organizational psychology is the branch of I/O psychology concerned with how the collective social

---

Employer and employee reasons for conducting appraisals

Employer perspective

1. Despite imperfect measurement, individual differences in performance make a difference.
2. Documentation of performance appraisal and feedback may be needed for legal defence.
3. Appraisal provides a rational basis for constructing a bonus or merit system.
4. Appraisal dimensions and standards can operationalize strategic goals and clarify performance expectations.
5. Providing individual feedback is part of a performance management process.
6. Despite the traditional individual focus, appraisal criteria can include teamwork and teams can be the focus of appraisal.

Employee perspective

1. Performance feedback is needed and desired.
2. Improvement in performance requires assessment.
3. Fairness requires that differences in performance levels across workers be measured and have an impact on outcomes.
4. Assessment and recognition of performance levels can motivate improved performance.

---

context of the work environment affects workers' behaviour and attitudes. We will examine five topics that are important in contemporary organizational psychology: organizational culture, work teams, the psychological contract between employers and their employees, work motivation, and leadership.

Organizational Culture

The concept of *culture* has long been used to describe the customs, values, and norms of *societies,* but I/O psychologists have also found the concept useful in the description of *organizations.* An *organizational culture* consists of the language, values, attitudes, beliefs, and customs shared by the employees of a company. An organization's culture gives it its unique "flavour" or "personality." Several definitions of organizational culture have been proposed, but the most succinct was offered by Deal and Kennedy (1982): "The way we do things around here."

Furnham and Gunter (1993) proposed three features of organizational culture. First, an organization's culture can often be traced to its founders. These people often possess dynamic personalities, strong values, and a clear vision of what the organization should look like. They play a big role in the initial hiring of employees, and their ideas and values are readily transmitted to new employees. Second, culture often develops out of an organization's experience with the external environment. Every organization must establish its own identity in its industry and in the marketplace where it operates. As it struggles to do so, it may find that some values and practices are more effective than others. Third, an organizational culture develops from the need to maintain effective working relationships among

Figure C.2

Employer and employee perspectives on performance appraisals. I/O psychologists often play an important role in designing performance appraisal systems. Although sometimes awkward for the people involved, performance appraisals serve many important purposes for both employers and employees. Some of the reasons that both organizations and workers desire fair and accurate appraisals are outlined here.

SOURCE: Cardy, R. L. (1998). Performance appraisal in a quality context: A new look at an old problem. In J. W. Smither (Ed.), *Performance appraisal.* San Francisco: Jossey-Bass. Reprinted by permission.

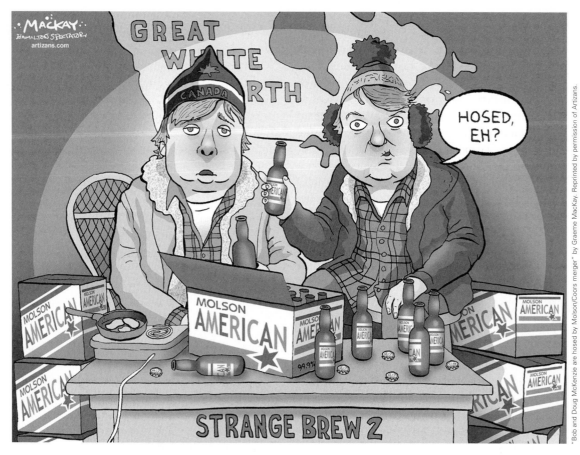

employees. Depending on the nature of the organization's business and the characteristics of the people it hires, different expectations and values develop.

Deeply ingrained within organizational culture are communication processes, for it is through communication that culture is transmitted. Interactions with long-time organizational members ensure that new recruits are enculturated. New employees learn the language and appropriate behaviour of the group, hear its stories and legends, and observe the organization's rites and rituals. The culture of an organization can best be understood by analyzing its tangible and visible rites, including rites of passage (hiring and basic training), degradation (dismissal), conflict reduction (grievance committees), and integration (office holiday party). New members must determine what is appropriate dress, how to arrange their office, and how much latitude they have in being on time for appointments and in making deadlines. Culture may also be communicated through other channels, such as in-house memos, official policies, statements of corporate philosophy, and any other means of expressing values. Schein (1996) asserted that understanding the culture of an organization is critical to making sense of the behaviour observed in the organization. A description of behaviour divorced from the cultural context in which it occurs is of limited value.

Schneider (1996) emphasizes that it is the people who populate the organization who most define its culture. That is, employees are not actors who fill predetermined roles in an established culture, but rather their personalities, values, and interests make the organization what it is. Schneider (1987) proposed what he calls the *attraction-selection-attrition (ASA) cycle.* In this cycle, people with similar personalities and values are recruited by (*attraction*) and hired into certain organizations (*selection*); those who don't fit into the pattern of shared values eventually leave the organization (*attrition*). The ASA cycle is assumed to unfold gradually over time. It is often difficult to bring about a change in organizational culture because that would necessitate altering underlying values and beliefs that may be deeply entrenched. It is not surprising that many mergers between organizations with different cultures, such as Molson and Coors, encounter problems in their early stages. In any event, a full understanding of an organization requires some appreciation of its culture.

Work Teams

Historically, I/O psychologists have focused their attention on *individuals*—finding the right person for a job, training the person, and subsequently monitoring the individual's performance. However, recent years have seen an upsurge of interest in *work groups*.

Teams are bounded social units that work within a larger social system—the organization. A team has identifiable members (i.e., members and nonmembers know who is a member and who is not) and an identifiable task or set of tasks to perform. The team's work requires that members interact by exchanging information, sharing resources, and coordinating activities, so there is always some degree of interdependence among the members of a team. Organizations tend to give teams more decision authority than comparable employees working individually. The team members often must decide among themselves who will do what, where, when, and how.

What underlies the new emphasis on teams? Three factors are critical. The first is the burgeoning amount of information and knowledge available. Huge amounts of information from multiple sources often have to be absorbed to respond to complex business issues. Because no one person can have technical expertise in all areas of knowledge, a team approach, representing a pooling of mental resources, becomes more tenable. Second, the working population is becoming better educated and trained. When the traditional organizational structures of 100 years ago were created, the work force was relatively uneducated. The members of the traditional working class were monitored by members of "management," who often possessed much more education or training than their subordinates. However, the workers of today are more highly qualified and better able to serve in the types of leadership roles called for in work teams. As an employee who now works in a production team in a manufacturing organization stated, "I'm no longer expected to check my brain at the front gate when I enter the factory." The third factor is the rate of change in work activities and responsibilities. For many years workers tended to have well-defined job responsibilities that rarely changed. In the current work world, there are pressures to make new products, modify services, alter processes to improve quality, and in general be in a continual state of transformation. Work teams are thought to be more adaptable to these ever-changing conditions of work.

The evolution of teams and teamwork has compelled I/O psychology to address a host of new issues (Ilgen, 1999). Some of what we have learned about individuals in the workplace generalizes to teams, but other issues are more specific to teams. However, teams are *not* universally superior to individuals for conducting work across all relevant performance indices. For example, teams do not necessarily produce better decisions than some individuals do.

There is nothing magical about transforming individuals into work teams. Teams are merely one means of performing work.

I/O psychologists are concerned with the structure of teams, including their size, roles filled by various members, and the planned length of their existence. Issues relating to team processes include how older team members socialize new members, as well as matters of team communication, conflict, cohesion, and trust. Some teams have members that have never met face to face. They interact only electronically and belong to "virtual teams." Some of what I/O psychologists have learned regarding the selection, training, and appraisal of individuals also applies to teams, but some aspects of team functioning require new concepts, insights, and research.

The Psychological Contract between Employers and Employees

Rousseau (1995) has noted that employers and their employees enter into a *psychological contract*. It is not a formal written contract between the two parties but an implied relationship based on perceptions of mutual contributions and reciprocal obligations. Employees have beliefs about the organization's obligations to them as well as their obligations to the organization. Thus, employees may believe that the organization has agreed to provide job security and promotion opportunities in exchange for hard work and loyalty from the employee. The psychological contract is oriented toward the future. Without the promise of future exchange, neither party has incentive to contribute anything to the other, and the relationship may not endure.

The psychological contract is composed of a belief that some form of a promise has been made and that the terms and conditions of the contract have been accepted by both parties. However, this belief does not necessarily mean that both parties share a common understanding of all contract terms. The psychological contract is revised throughout the employee's tenure in the organization. The longer the relationship endures and the two parties interact, the broader the array of contributions that might be included in the contract. Rousseau and Parks (1993) found that employment itself is perceived as a promise (the implied contract of continued future employment) and that an employee's performance is perceived as a contribution (a way of paying for the promise). Robinson, Kraatz, and Rousseau (1994) examined how psychological contracts change over time. They found that during the first two years of employment, employees came to perceive that they owed less to their employer while the employers in turn owed them more.

There is an element of power in all contracts. Unequal power is most common in employment relationships. Power inequities affect the perceived voluntariness of the exchange relationship, dividing the two parties into contract makers (relatively powerful) and contract takers (relatively powerless). As contract takers, employees cannot easily exit the employment relationship. This situation may result in a perceived loss of control in the relationship, which is likely to intensify feelings of mistreatment and injustice when violations are perceived. Because the employer is the more powerful party, the terms of the contract can be dictated to the less powerful employee, who must either accept them or exit the relationship.

The psychological contract is violated when one party in a relationship perceives the other as failing to fulfill promised obligations. The failure of one party to meet its obligations to another can be expected to undermine their mutual relationship. Violations by an employer may affect not only what an employee feels he or she is owed by the employer but also what an employee feels obligated to offer in return. Violation of a psychological contract undermines the very factors (such as trust) that led to emergence of a relationship. If the employer reneges on an implied promise, the employer's integrity is questioned. A violation signals that the employer's original motives to build and maintain a mutually beneficial relationship have changed or were false from the beginning. The psychological contract binds the employee and the employer—a form of guarantee that if each does his or her part, then the relationship will be mutually beneficial. Thus, violations weaken this bond.

In recent decades, the changing nature of the psychological contract between employers and employees has required employees to assume greater responsibility for their own career development. Organizations are now far less likely to offer the implicit promise to provide career-advancing opportunities. Consider the following message found posted on the bulletin board of a plant experiencing widespread layoffs (as reported by Hall & Mirvis, 1995, p. 326):

We can't promise you how long we'll be in business.
We can't promise you that we won't be bought by another company.
We can't promise that there'll be room for promotion.
We can't promise that your job will exist until you reach retirement age.
We can't promise that the money will be available for your pension.
We can't expect your undying loyalty and we aren't sure we want it.

Based on a multinational study, Rousseau and Schalk (2000) concluded that the psychological contract as a promise-based exchange is widely generalizable to a variety of societies. Given the rise of global business, it is likely that the nature of cultural differences in the psychological contract will continue to evolve. For example, people from Asian cultures generally prefer to first establish a relationship between parties and then carry out business transactions. In contrast, people from Western cultures generally prefer to create a relationship through repeated business transactions. In the future it is likely both styles will manifest themselves in new and varied forms.

Work Motivation

Have you ever observed a person who appears driven to perform well or succeed? Perhaps you would describe yourself in that way. Such people may or may not have more ability than others, but it appears they are willing to work harder or expend more effort than their peers. Psychologists refer to this attribute or trait as *ambition* or *motivation*. Motivation is not directly observable; it must be inferred from patterns of behaviour.

According to Pinder (1998), *work motivation* refers to the set of forces that initiate work-related behaviour and determine its direction, intensity, and duration. There are three noteworthy components to this definition. First, *direction* addresses the choice of activities people make in expending effort. That is, people may choose to work diligently at some tasks and not at others. Second, *intensity* implies people have the potential to exert various levels of effort, depending on how much is needed. Third, *duration* reflects persistence of motivation over time. Motivation can thus be conceptualized along three dimensions: direction, intensity, and persistence. Each dimension has its associated issues that are relevant to both the organization and the individual. Direction pertains to those activities you focus your energy on. Organizations want employees who will direct themselves to their work responsibilities, and many employees want jobs that will inspire their motivation and commitment. Intensity pertains to the amount of motivation that is expended in pursuit of an activity. Organizations want employees who will exhibit high levels of energy. Such people are often referred to as "self-starters," implying they do not require organizational inducements to work hard. Likewise, many employees hope to find jobs that are sufficiently appealing to invite large commitments of energy. The third dimension, persistence, pertains to sustained energy over time. Researchers know the least about this dimension, but it is the focus of more recent motivational theories. You can think of a career as an interrelated series of jobs through which individuals manifest their energies over a working lifetime. Organizations want employees who will persevere through good times and bad. Likewise, employees want jobs that will sustain their interests over the long haul. Each of the three dimensions of motivation has direct implications for both organizations and individuals.

Work motivation depends on a constellation of factors, which can often become blurred. Chief among these factors are the following:

- *Behaviour.* The overt actions from which motivation can be inferred. The behaviour in question may be typing, preparing a meal, organizing a stockroom, communicating with customers, or engaging in an endless array of other work-related activities.
- *Performance.* Evaluation of behaviour. The basic unit of observation is behaviour, but it is coupled with an assessment of the behaviour as judged against some standard. Thus, if the behaviour is typing, a judgment can be made as to whether a person's typing speed and accuracy are adequate to hold a job. The level of performance that is adequate for one job may be inadequate for another job. Most organizational theories tend to be concerned with performance, not just behaviour.
- *Ability.* One of three determinants of behaviour and performance. It is generally regarded as fairly stable within an individual and may be represented by a broad construct such as intelligence or a more specific construct such as physical coordination.
- *Situational constraints.* The second determinant of behaviour. These are environmental factors and opportunities that facilitate or undermine performance. Examples include tools, equipment, procedures, and the like, which may enhance or hinder performance.
- *Motivation.* The third determinant of behaviour. You can think of ability as reflecting what you *can* do, motivation as what you *will* do (given your ability), and the situational constraints as what you are *allowed* to do.

Each of the three components is critical to the manifestation of behaviour and performance. Maximum performance is observed when a person has high ability, exhibits high motivation, and is in a supportive environment. The judgment of "poor performance" could be attributed to four factors. First, the organization in which the behaviour occurs may have high standards, which in another organization might result in a more positive evaluation of performance. Second, the individual may lack the ability required for the desired behaviour. Third, the individual may lack the motivation to exhibit the desired behaviour. Fourth, the individual may lack needed equipment or other crucial elements of support.

Motivation is one of the most complex concepts that I/O psychologists study. People can be motivated by different factors, and the same person can be motivated by different factors during different stages of his or her career. Most organizations believe it is critical to their success to have a highly motivated work force.

Leadership

When you think of *leadership,* many ideas may come to mind. Your thoughts might relate to power, authority, or influence. Maybe you think of actual people, such as Pierre Trudeau, Winston Churchill, or Nelson Mandela. In short, leadership is a multidimensional concept.

I/O psychologists have tried to grapple with the multifaceted concept of leadership as it relates to behaviour in the world of work. Investigators have approached the concept from various perspectives. Some research has examined what strong leaders are like as people by looking at demographic variables, personality traits, special skills, and so on. Without followers, there can be no leaders; accordingly, some research has examined leader–follower relationships. Presumably strong leaders accomplish things that weak leaders do not. Thus, other research has examined the effects of leadership. An interesting question concerns how contextual factors affect leadership—for example, is leadership of a prison more demanding than leadership of a business organization? Thus, the situation in which leadership occurs has attracted much attention. Other areas of interest within the domain of leadership research have also been investigated. While such diversity of interest expands our understanding, it also creates ambiguity as to exactly what leadership is all about. Table C.1 identifies research topics of interest to I/O psychologists in studying leadership.

Despite the diversity of approaches used in exploring leadership, Yukl (1994) noted that there is some convergence in the empirical findings. Yukl identified three consistent themes in leadership research. First, influence is the essence of leadership. Much of the activity of leaders involves attempts to influence the attitudes and behaviours of people, including subordinates, peers, and outsiders. Motivating behaviour includes a variety of social influence techniques for developing commitment to organizational objectives and compliance with requests. Much of the influence behaviour of charismatic

Table C.1 Research Topics and Associated Issues in Leadership Research

Research Topic	Unit of Analysis	Variables of Interest	Research Questions
Positional power	Organizational roles and positions	Influence tactics; use of power	Under what conditions will organizations resort to strong influence attempts?
The leader	Individual leaders	Personality characteristics; leader behaviours	What traits and behaviours differentiate effective and ineffective leaders?
The led	Work groups and subordinates	Group size; experience of subordinates	What types of subordinates desire close supervision?
Influence process	Superior–subordinate interface	Receptivity to influence; nature of influence attempts	Under what conditions are leaders most susceptible to subordinate influence attempts?
The situation	Environment or context in which leadership occurs	Situational effects on leader behaviour; factors defining favourable situations	How do various situations modify behaviour?
Leader emergence versus effectiveness	Individual and/or groups	Group dynamics and individual characteristics	How do individuals become recognized as leaders?

Source: Muchinsky, P. M. (2003). *Psychology applied to work.* Belmont, CA: Wadsworth. Reprinted by permission.

leaders falls into the motivating category, including inspiring commitment to new objectives and strategies, modelling exemplary behaviour for followers to imitate, and appealing to values and aspirations. Some of the traits and skills that predict leader effectiveness relate to the use of power. Leaders with high need for power and high self-confidence make more influence attempts. Self-confidence, persuasive ability, relevant expertise, and political insight facilitate the effectiveness of influence attempts. Interpersonal skills are necessary to articulate an appealing vision and persuade people of the need for change.

Second, effective leaders establish cooperative relationships characterized by high levels of mutual trust and loyalty. Research has shown that subordinates are usually more satisfied with a leader who is friendly and helpful, shows trust and respect, and demonstrates concern for their needs and feelings. Several of the traits and skills predictive of leadership effectiveness appear important for developing favourable relationships with subordinates, peers, and superiors. Relevant interpersonal talents include tact and diplomacy, listening skills, and social sensitivity. A leader with a positive regard for others is more likely to develop friendly relationships with people. Leaders who are preoccupied with personal ambition tend to do things that jeopardize relationships with people, such as betraying a trust or reneging on a promise.

Third, much of the activity of leaders involves decision making, but leaders seldom make important decisions at a single point in time, except for problem solving in immediate crises. In dealing with day-to-day decisions, effective leaders are guided by their long-term objectives and strategies. People who effectively solve problems or develop successful strategies gain in status and power as a result. The reputation for expertise gained from successful decisions made in the past gives a person greater influence over subsequent decisions. Several of the traits and skills predictive of leadership effectiveness are relevant for decision making. Leaders with extensive technical knowledge and cognitive skills are more likely to make high-quality decisions. These skills are important for analyzing problems, identifying causal patterns and trends, and forecasting likely outcomes of different strategies for attaining objectives. Self-confidence and tolerance for ambiguity and stress help leaders cope with the responsibility for making major decisions on the basis of incomplete information.

Putting It All Together: A Case Study

Let's take a look at a recent, very real, and extremely important problem to see how the diverse aspects of I/O psychology are relevant to the world of work. The problem involves how to improve the screening of airport passengers and their baggage. You will see how many of the topics discussed in this appendix are germane to this daunting problem.

The Problem: Improving Airport Screening

The terrorist attacks of September 11, 2001 on the World Trade Center in New York and the Pentagon in Washington, D.C. focused attention on airport security personnel and their performance. These employees are entrusted with the responsibility of screening all passengers and their luggage in order to detect any objects that might be a security risk to the flight personnel or passengers. Such objects include guns and knives but also everyday objects that potentially could be used as a weapon, such as scissors, cigarette lighters, or corkscrews. There are typically four jobs that contribute to the screening process—two devoted to passengers and two devoted to luggage. One person is responsible for ensuring that each passenger goes through the metal detector. If a passenger activates the metal detector, the passenger must step aside and be rescreened with a portable, hand-held metal detector, called a "wand." A second employee is in charge of conducting this screening. The usual items that activate the metal detector are jewellery, metal belt buckles, and metal supports in shoes. The second employee's job is to identify the reason the metal detector was activated and to ensure that the cause is benign.

The third employee is responsible for examining the contents of passengers' luggage via an X-ray machine. As hand-carried items pass through the X-ray machine on a conveyor belt, the third employee peers at a monitor. If the employee sees an object that looks suspicious, that piece of luggage is subject to a manual search of its contents. A fourth employee is in charge of this manual search and verifying that the contents of the luggage are harmless; this manual search may also involve "sweeping" the hand luggage and electronics for the presence of certain chemicals.

Of these four jobs, one in particular is the source of errors: visually examining the monitor of the X-ray machine. Luggage moves along the conveyor belt quickly, about six pieces per minute, 360 pieces per hour—almost 3000 pieces in an eight-hour workday. The examiner has but a few seconds to visually inspect the contents of each bag. The overwhelming majority of passengers do not pack dangerous items in their luggage. Occasionally there will be a suspicious-looking object, but it usually turns out (on manual inspection) to be harmless. If a potentially dangerous object is spotted, it is confiscated by airport security personnel. Because passengers know that potentially dangerous objects will not be allowed on the airplane, the vast majority pack only items that are not potentially harmful to others. The consequence of this pattern of behaviour is that the X-ray machine screener is looking for a rare object. With hundreds of pieces of luggage passing through the machine every hour, it is difficult for screeners to remain vigilant and focused. Their attention begins to wander after viewing so many pieces of luggage that look alike. Hence, it is not surprising that dangerous objects sometimes make it through the

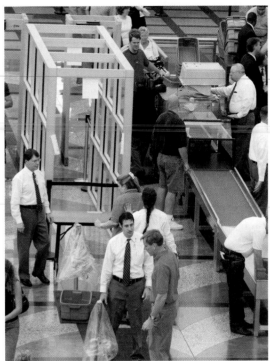

The task of improving airport screening of passengers and their baggage illustrates how problems in the workplace are often multifaceted. As the text explains, a host of strategies may be relevant to this extremely complicated and important challenge.

© 2002 AP/Wide World Photos

screening process. In some cases airport authorities have intentionally "planted" knives in luggage just to see whether they would be detected. Most are, but some are not. Given the enormous importance of this screening task, even a small error rate of, for example, 0.01% (i.e., one potentially dangerous object per 10 000 cases), is considered unacceptable. In other words, if 99.99% of all luggage is screened properly, the error rate (0.01%) is still too high to meet desired safety standards! Thus, our question is: What types of solutions might an I/O psychologist propose to help improve the performance of airport security inspectors?

Possible Solutions

The topics discussed in this appendix are all potentially relevant to this problem. Let's begin with the process of recruitment. Perhaps if the airports attracted a higher quality of applicant pool from which to draw their employees, fewer errors would be made by the inspectors. If the wage level for airport security personnel were raised, perhaps more skilled individuals would be attracted to the jobs. Alternatively, it is possible the quality of the applicant pool is satisfactory, but what is needed are better personnel selection methods to identify the best candidates. Perhaps special types of visual acuity tests could be used, or tests that measure the capacity for sustained mental alertness. Perhaps the solution lies not so much with how the employees are chosen as how they are trained. It is possible that current training methods are insufficient or fail to capture the need for sustained vigilance over an eight-hour workday. Finally, little is known about the degree to which airports reward security officers for effective performance. Perhaps if supervisors appraised the job performance of their security officers and acknowledged their successes, their failures would decline. There are also legal issues to consider. Passengers of certain nationalities or races cannot indiscriminately be singled out for closer scrutiny without just cause. Engaging in such a practice would be an example of "racial profiling," which is frowned upon.

There is a rich organizational component to this problem that must also be considered before a solution becomes evident. The organizational culture of airport security operations tells us something about the nature of flying, passengers, and safety precautions. Many airports around the world are now staffed with uniformed military personnel carrying exposed weapons. Passengers see these military figures and their weapons and realize they are entering a potentially dangerous environment. Although passengers accept the need for airport security, no one likes to be hassled and intimidated. Airport security personnel are "just doing their job," but what they do can produce stress for passengers. If passengers become sufficiently dissatisfied with the emotional experiences associated with flying, some of them will either stop flying altogether or fly far less frequently. A reduction in the number of passengers can (and has) led some airlines to lose so much money they have had to declare bankruptcy. The decline in air passenger traffic following 9/11 was one factor leading to Air Canada seeking protection from its creditors under the Bankruptcy Act. While it is possible that different methods of recruitment, personnel selection, training, and performance appraisal may help alleviate the problem encountered in this situation, it is also true that staring into a monitor over a prolonged time period is boring. Perhaps what needs to be done is lessen the time period of visual inspection from eight hours to two hours. Since four jobs are involved in passenger and baggage screening, perhaps the four employees could be viewed as a team, and the team members could rotate assignments every two hours to break the tedium. Such a solution would presume that all four team members are equally suited to perform each of the four jobs. This approach attempts to solve the problem of boredom and fatigue by limiting the length of time an employee is exposed to the conditions that produce them.

The psychological contract between the airport and its security personnel must also be considered. The flying passengers, our society, and governments demand a "zero-tolerance" policy for errors in screening passengers and luggage. The consequence of making errors in airport security can be extremely tragic. However, there are few jobs where a 99.99% success rate is judged to be not good enough. The airport security personnel are under stress from two sources. One source is the need to remain highly vigilant and attentive in what is a repetitive and boring job. The second is that they know they are responsible for the safety and welfare of the flying public. The airport as an organization must walk a fine line between demanding very high standards of performance yet being sensitive to the conditions under which their security personnel operate. If such sensitivity and support are not shown, the security personnel would probably exhibit little loyalty to an employer that demands so much of its employees. The needed support for the security personnel can come in the form of encouraging motivation and leadership. Supervisors who are present at the security area (or nearby) can provide attention, encouragement, and recognition to the security personnel. The supervisors can serve to break the tedium of the security jobs by establishing their presence, asking questions, acknowledging the contributions of the security officers, and in general providing recognition for employees performing highly stressful work. Finally, all of these actions must be taken within yet a broader context, that of increasing security without unduly inconveniencing the flying public.

There is no reason to believe there is *one* correct solution to the problem facing airport security personnel. In reality an I/O psychologist would probably invoke many of the possible solutions to this case, not just one. It is also possible that a solution lies in more sophisticated X-ray technology that reduces the role of human judgment in assessing potential risk. Such equipment is currently being developed, but it is extremely expensive and thus unlikely to be used in all airports. While such technology may reduce the human element, it will never eliminate it.

Conclusion

I/O psychologists must be prepared to use the full complement of their skills to solve problems in the workplace that are increasing in complexity. I/O psychology is a most rewarding and useful field that endeavours to improve the quality of work life. Students interested in learning more about this field are encouraged to read P. M. Muchinsky's *Psychology Applied to Work* (2003) and to visit the Canadian Society for Industrial and Organizational Psychology's Web site (http://www.ssc.uwo.ca/psychology/csiop/) to learn about career opportunities.

Appendix D Evaluating the Quality of Web-Based Resources

By Vincent W. Hevern (Le Moyne College)

Toward the end of every semester in my abnormal psychology course, my students conduct a public policy forum about an important but controversial topic in psychology. To prepare for the forum, I give students a research assignment. They must gather information from various types of sources: scholarly articles in journals, professional books, popular magazines, and sites on the Internet ("the Net"). However, to complete the Net part of the assignment, students must hand in two types of information: Some material must come from a "good" or "excellent" Web site, while other material must be from a "terrible" or "poor" Web site. Further, students must also tell me *why* these sites are either excellent or poor. Students regularly tell me later on that they had never paid attention before to whether a Web page might be "good" or "bad." Many students actually say they appreciate learning how to recognize the difference between sites of high versus low quality.

What students tell me supports the comments that I hear from many college professors: They wish students would realize that research done with Internet-based resources can be both dangerous and misleading unless students recognize the issue of quality. Further, as psychology teachers across the California State University system recently noted, an important educational goal for student learning is developing the competence to "locate appropriate sources by searching electronic and traditional databases and providing evidence of the search" (Allen et al., 2000, p. 4). The important phrase is "appropriate sources." Which resources online are appropriate, and which should you avoid? Students and all other researchers need to think carefully about the quality of data or reference sources found online. Your teachers will expect it, and in the emerging Information Economy, so will many employers.

Criteria for Quality on the Net

So, what are the standards or criteria by which you can judge the quality of a Web page or resource? What can you actually *do* to increase the chances that the material you take from the Net is worth your effort? In recent years, information specialists have researched how people browsing the Internet can tell the difference. For example, University of Georgia Professor Gene Wilkinson and two doctoral students, Kevin Oliver and Lisa Bennett, conducted an intensive study of 125 criteria by polling the Webmasters of highly regarded online resource sites, while reference librarians Janet E. Alexander and Marsha Ann Tate at Widener University's Wolfgram Memorial Library consulted intensively with their colleagues across the world (Alexander & Tate, 1999). Although these and other specialists have gathered standards in slightly different ways, they are in substantial agreement about what characteristics are associated with quality on the Web. I've summarized their findings and my own experience in Figure D.1, and I elaborate on each criterion in this appendix. Some of these standards relate to an entire Web site from which material may be drawn, while others relate to a specific document in which the researcher may be interested. Users of the Net must weigh both kinds of criteria. In simplest terms, the key to finding quality resources online will always be a researcher's *active exercise of judgment and critical thinking.*

Identity and Qualifications of the Authors

The Internet is a kind of worldwide democracy. Pretty much anyone can construct a Web page and put online what they want to say. With so few restrictions on Net publishing, the range and quality of online resources is bound to vary, from invaluable to completely worthless. So, researchers who turn to the Net need to ask two related questions: *Who has written this material?* and *What are their qualifications for so doing?* The answers to these questions are probably the two most important guides to quality among online resources.

Sometimes you will find no clue to the identity of the author of a particular site or resource—no name, no organizational affiliation, nothing that reveals the authorship of the material. In such cases, you should be skeptical about relying on the information. It's hard to defend the quality of a work when "Anonymous" is the author. One exception may be some "first person" accounts dealing with sensitive personal issues such as sexuality, child abuse, and the like. Some authors understandably prefer to use pseudonyms to protect themselves. In such cases, researchers must look for other clues to quality.

Suppose one or more authors are listed by name. The next task is to discover the *qualifications* of these

1. Identity and qualifications of the author(s)

- Who is the author of the material? Is the author identified or anonymous?
- What is the author's academic or professional background and experience?
- Is the author writing within or outside his/her area of expertise and skill?
- If the material is the product of a group (a committee, governmental agency, or the like), what is that group's qualifications or expertise regarding this subject?

2. Publisher or sponsor of the Web site

- Is the material self-published by the author or is there some recognized organization (university, medical centre, government agency, nonprofit foundation, and so forth) that sponsors the Web site for the material?
- Does the site's sponsor or publisher have a positive reputation?

3. Balance, objectivity, and independence

- Does the material or Web site strive for balance and objectivity rather than use extreme, inflammatory, or highly subjective language or opinions?
- Is more than one point of view evident at the site?
- If the material takes a strong stand on one side of a controversial issue, does the author or site acknowledge there may be another side to the matter?
- Is the Web site sponsored by any commercial or political organization that advocates for a particular point of view?
- Does the author have any financial or commercial interest that might conflict with a fair or objective presentation of the topic?
- Is the material drawn from a site that sells a product or solicits customers for a service?

4. Quality of online presentation

- Is the site well organized or designed so that browsers can easily visit and retrieve information?
- Does the site or online material show care in its preparation, such as proper spelling and good grammar in all posted materials?
- Does the site work effectively, so that the links to subpages and external sites are accurate and helpful?
- How recently has the site been updated? Does the site show evidence that someone regularly attends to it with corrections, new materials, and so forth?

5. Other cues to quality

- Does the material contain clear and useful references to other scholarship from journals, professional books, and recognized research studies?
- Have supporting references in the material been published in recent years, or do they include mostly out-of-date, or possibly obsolete, sources?
- Have any editors or external reviewers judged the quality of the material at the site?

Figure D.1

Evaluating online resources. The questions listed here, which draw heavily on the work of Alexander and Tate (1999), can help you to evaluate the quality and reliability of resource materials found on the Internet.

in reputable, peer-reviewed journals or belongs to professional or scholarly organizations concerned with the subject.

There are other cautions for researchers to keep in mind. Some authors may be qualified to comment on one topic but go beyond their area of expertise into other domains of knowledge. For example, a physician may comment on economics or a biologist may pontificate on educational methods. Researchers need to be cautious about writers who move too far away from their fields of specialization. Another consideration is whether authors may also have a financial stake or commercial interest in the issue that might compromise their objectivity.

Finally, suppose the "author" of a Web-based publication is a corporation or an organization, such as a professional association, a government agency, or a nonprofit organization. How should qualifications be weighed in such cases? Certainly the overall reputation of the corporate author should be recognized. For example, a consensus statement on a treatment approach produced by the National Institute of Mental Health or a report on the employment characteristics of psychologists issued by the American Psychological Association would probably be an excellent reference source. Most such reports include a list of individual contributors or committee members who worked to produce the material released under the name of an organization. It is important to inquire whether these persons may also have the credentials or professional status to render their work trustworthy. Alternatively, you might look for a broad corporate board of editors or advisers associated with an institutional voice on the Net. Beware of fancy-sounding "Institutes" or "Commissions" or "Associations" that may in fact be the product of a single person or a handful of individuals and serve only to artificially embellish the opinions of their creators.

Publisher or Sponsor of the Web Site

Book authors traditionally use print publishers to promote and distribute their writings. In turn, publishers place their reputations on the line by issuing new books. Discerning readers rely on a publisher's overall standing when they consider whether to acquire new works. Especially in academic publishing, readers know that an editorial and review process usually precedes publication, in an effort to ensure a high level of quality for the published material. Indeed, the essence of academic scholarship lies in a willingness to submit scholarly work to the early critiques of knowledgeable colleagues. Occasionally, though, an author circumvents the editorial and

authors. Do they have some type of expertise to justify writing the online material or constructing the site? You should look for a statement of an author's academic credentials (such as a Ph.D. or an M.D. degree) or appropriate work experience (such as "director of personnel" at a company or "senior researcher" at a laboratory). If the data appear on a personal home page, you can discover other evidence of expertise elsewhere at the site, such as a bibliography of past writings or a résumé that demonstrates the author's competence to write about the topic under review. You should also try to determine whether the author has published on a similar topic peer review process and pays to have his or her book published. This practice, called "vanity publishing," is usually looked down on by other scholars.

In a practice reminiscent of vanity publishing, many Web authors post materials online directly through commercial or free Internet service providers. Because these writings have not been edited or evaluated prior to their publication, you must be cautious in judging their quality. This is not to disparage all self-published resources on the Web. Clearly, there are valuable resources that experts have laboured to bring to cyberspace. But, in the absence of a clear process of scholarly peer review, you must look for other indicators of quality. For this reason, the overall qualifications of an author as an expert may be crucial in determining whether to use a resource.

Sites sponsored by academic institutions, government agencies, and nonprofit or scholarly organizations have URLs that end with the designation *.edu*, *.gov*, or *.org* rather than *.com* or *.net*. For example, if you were interested in obtaining health statistics for Ontario or British Columbia, you might visit the Ontario Ministry of Health Web site (http://www.health.gov.on.ca/) or the British Columbia Web site (http://www.gov.bc.ca/). A particularly useful site is that of Canada's national statistical agency, Statistics Canada (http://www.statcan.ca/). Many of the statistics in this book are drawn from that site. Such sites would be expected to offer some assurance of higher quality for data posted there.

A particular clue to quality at corporate sites may be a copyright notice by a sponsoring organization rather than a single individual. Often located at the bottom of a Web page, this notice may signal that the organization is willing to put its reputation behind the resource. For example, online health information centres range in quality from the dismal to the superb. One excellent site, *Go Ask Alice! Columbia University's Health Education Program* (http://www.alice.columbia.edu/; Web Link 10.3), is maintained by Columbia University, one of the top universities in the world. The sponsor in this case is clearly identified.

Balance, Objectivity, and Independence

At the checkout line in a supermarket, shoppers often face a set of tabloid newspapers with outrageous headlines and the promise of lurid stories inside. Many people pick up a copy of their favourite tabloid as entertainment, something to be read purely for relaxation and enjoyment but not as an objective or reliable source of information or reporting about the world. Although tabloid papers are an extreme example, other sources of informa-

tion should arouse similar suspicions because of their subjective, unbalanced, and biased style of presentation. Certainly, the presence of language, graphic images, or opinions that are extreme, inflammatory, or highly subjective on a Web site suggests that the material should be treated with some skepticism. The more extreme, vulgar, or intemperate the manner of presentation, the less likely that the resource is reliable and trustworthy.

A more difficult case arises from material found on sites clearly advocating a particular point of view, such as those for a lobbying group, political movement, or professional advocacy or commercial trade association. Researchers should expect that resources available at these sites will support the point of view of the group. This fact does not necessarily disqualify the importance of materials found there. The sponsoring organization may provide valuable information for visitors to their sites. Greater reliance can probably be given to resources found on a site that acknowledges there is more than one side to a controversial issue. Some sites even offer links to the opposing side of a disputed topic. This openness should inspire confidence by users because it suggests fairness.

A challenge to researchers of psychological topics comes from commercial sites that stand to make money or gain new customers on the basis of what they post online. These sites may be businesses (with a *.com* Net address) or may be allied with the professional office or practice of individuals such as psychotherapists or physicians. Sometimes these sites offer a "Resource Centre" or similar area filled with articles relating to the product or service of the site's sponsor. These articles may include scientific-sounding titles, and many come from magazines, journals, or books that seem to be similarly professional. Most evaluators warn researchers to be careful when using materials from any site that has a direct financial motivation in sharing information. A close examination of the actual reference sources cited in online articles may give a clue as to how much credence a researcher should put in them. For example, are the references only for the author's own works, or do they include reputable journal articles written by a range of other scholars? Finding quality in online materials is always a judgment call, and the more you know about a topic from other sources, the better you can make that call at commercial sites.

Quality of Online Presentation

Another important index of quality is the care with which sites and materials have been organized and maintained. You should consider how easily you can use a site. Do the hypertext links within the site work, or do they point to empty or missing pages? Can browsers easily find the information they are looking for? Is there evidence that the design of the site was carefully considered and executed? Similarly, the actual text of materials retrieved from the Net should be free from any gross errors. Poor grammar and improper spelling usually indicate that something is amiss. Frankly, reputable scholars are fanatical about eliminating sloppiness or careless mistakes in what they write. They believe any such errors would suggest a parallel sloppiness in their thinking. Thus, the presence of mechanical and stylistic mistakes at a Web site or in a document should raise doubts about how reputable the actual content of the resource may be. Finally, more credibility can be assigned to materials retrieved from sites that are frequently updated and carefully corrected. You should look for clear dates on pages containing important information. Ideally, one date will indicate when the page was first posted online and another when it was last changed or revised.

Other Cues to Quality

When I use the Net for research purposes, I use at least three further cues to evaluate the quality of the material or sites I find. First, in articles or papers online, I look at the references used by the author and consider whether they include scholarly materials from journals, professional books, or other recognized research sources. Second, I examine the dates of the supporting references. How recent are they? Do they include sources published in the last several years? Or do they include only older and possibly out-of-date materials? Finally, I look for evidence that the site itself has been recognized by an outside reviewer as possessing significant quality. For example, evaluation sites such as the Argus Clearinghouse (http://www.clearinghouse.net) provide an estimate of the overall quality of Internet subject guides. If a site is listed with high ratings, I am more likely to value the materials posted there. You should be alert to any designation by a Web site that it has received a favourable review by such an evaluation source.

A Final Note of Advice

I hope the suggestions summarized here make it clear that any researcher must actively exercise judgment and critical thinking skills in evaluating online resources. Such skills are enormously enhanced when the researcher chooses a balanced overall research strategy. It is one thing to seek a quick fact or a simple definition through a Web site; it is another to rely on the Internet as the sole data source for a major paper or research project. Yes, for many people, the Net is an easily "surfable" medium, one that can quickly lead to information of varying levels of quality. The very ease of conducting research online often seduces student researchers to skip more difficult, but crucially important steps offline.

The most important strategy a student can bring to any research project is to develop an overall perspective, or a broad vantage point, regarding the topic of the project. And that means using sources of different types—scholarly books, journal and magazine articles, and printed research reports—*in addition to* materials retrieved from the Internet. It is both easy to understand, but embarrassing in the long run, when a student hands in a paper with only Internet-based sources and later discovers, in a professor's grading, that the Net provided a biased or slanted view of the topic. Without the counterbalance of non-Net sources, a student risks seriously misjudging how psychologists, medical researchers, and other scientists actually approach an issue. So, my final suggestion about research is a simple rule of thumb: The longer and more important the research project or paper, the broader the kinds of references you must use to answer the research question.

For Further Reference and Reading

To further explore the question of identifying quality in online materials and sites, consider the outstanding text by Janet Alexander and Marsha Tate: *Web Wisdom: How to Evaluate and Create Information Quality on the Web* (Mahwah, NJ: Erlbaum, 1999).

Two other excellent Web-based resources on this topic are:

Engle, M. (1999). Evaluating web sites: Criteria and tools [online document]. Ithaca, NY: Cornell University, Olin-Kroch-Uris Libraries, Reference Division. Available on the World Wide Web at http://www.library.cornell.edu/okuref/research/webeval.html.

Grassian, E. (1999). Thinking critically about world wide web resources [online document]. Los Angeles, CA: UCLA College Library Instruction. Available on the World Wide Web at http://www.library.ucla.edu/college/help/critical/index.htm.

Many Canadian university libraries maintain Web site information for evaluating Web resources. For example, take a look at the guidelines suggested by the Queen's University Library Web site (http://library.queensu.ca/inforef/tutorials/qcat/evalint.htm).

A

Absolute refractory period The minimum length of time after an action potential during which another action potential cannot begin.

Absolute threshold The minimum amount of stimulation that an organism can detect for a specific type of sensory input.

Accommodation Changing existing mental structures to explain new experiences.

Acculturation The degree to which a person is socially and psychologically integrated into a new culture.

Achievement motive The need to master difficult challenges, to outperform others, and to meet high standards of excellence.

Achievement tests Tests that gauge a person's mastery and knowledge of various subjects.

Acquired immune deficiency syndrome (AIDS) A disorder in which the immune system is gradually weakened and eventually disabled by the human immunodeficiency virus (HIV).

Acquisition The formation of a new conditioned response tendency.

Action potential A brief change in a neuron's electrical charge.

Adaptation An inherited characteristic that increased in a population (through natural selection) because it helped solve a problem of survival or reproduction during the time it emerged.

Additive colour mixing Formation of colours by superimposing lights, putting more light in the mixture than exists in any one light by itself.

Adoption studies Research studies that assess hereditary influence by examining the resemblance between adopted children and both their biological and their adoptive parents.

Afferent nerve fibres Axons that carry information inward to the central nervous system from the periphery of the body.

Affiliation motive The need to associate with others and maintain social bonds.

Afterimage A visual image that persists after a stimulus is removed.

Age of viability The age at which a baby can survive in the event of a premature birth.

Aggression Any behaviour that is intended to hurt someone, either physically or verbally.

Agonist A chemical that mimics the action of a neurotransmitter.

Agoraphobia A fear of going out to public places.

Alcohol A variety of beverages containing ethyl alcohol.

Algorithm A methodical, step-by-step procedure for trying all possible alternatives in searching for a solution to a problem.

Amnesia A significant memory loss that is too extensive to be due to normal forgetting. See also *Anterograde amnesia, Retrograde amnesia.*

Androgens The principal class of gonadal hormones in males.

Anecdotal evidence Personal stories about specific incidents and experiences.

Animism The belief that all things are living.

Anorexia nervosa Eating disorder characterized by intense fear of gaining weight, disturbed body image, refusal to maintain normal weight, and dangerous measures to lose weight.

Antagonist A chemical that opposes the action of a neurotransmitter.

Antecedents In behaviour modification, events that typically precede the target response.

Anterograde amnesia Loss of memories for events that occur after a head injury.

Antianxiety drugs Medications that relieve tension, apprehension, and nervousness.

Antidepressant drugs Medications that gradually elevate mood and help bring people out of a depression.

Antipsychotic drugs Medications used to gradually reduce psychotic symptoms, including hyperactivity, mental confusion, hallucinations, and delusions.

Antisocial personality disorder A type of personality disorder marked by impulsive, callous, manipulative, aggressive, and irresponsible behaviour that reflects a failure to accept social norms.

Anxiety disorders A class of disorders marked by feelings of excessive apprehension and anxiety.

Applied psychology The branch of psychology concerned with everyday, practical problems.

Approach–approach conflict A conflict situation in which a choice must be made between two attractive goals.

Approach–avoidance conflict A conflict situation in which a choice must be made about whether to pursue a single goal that has both attractive and unattractive aspects.

Aptitude tests Psychological tests used to assess talent for specific types of mental ability.

Archetypes According to Jung, emotionally charged images and thought forms that have universal meaning.

Argument One or more premises used to provide support for a conclusion.

Ascending reticular activating system (ARAS) The afferent fibres running through the reticular formation that influence physiological arousal.

Assimilation Interpreting new experiences in terms of existing mental structures without changing them.

Assumptions Premises for which no proof or evidence is offered.

Attachment A close, emotional bond of affection between infants and their caregivers.

Attention Focusing awareness on a narrowed range of stimuli or events.

Attitudes Orientations that locate objects of thought on dimensions of judgment.

Attributions Inferences that people draw about the causes of events, others' behaviour, and their own behaviour.

Auditory localization Locating the source of a sound in space.

Autonomic nervous system (ANS) The system of nerves that connect to the heart, blood vessels, smooth muscles, and glands.

Availability heuristic Basing the estimated probability of an event on the ease with which relevant instances come to mind.

Aversion therapy A behaviour therapy in which an aversive stimulus is paired with a stimulus that elicits an undesirable response.

Avoidance learning Learning that has occurred when an organism engages in a response that prevents aversive stimulation from occurring.

Avoidance–avoidance conflict A conflict situation in which a choice must be made between two unattractive goals.

Axon A long, thin fibre that transmits signals away from the neuron cell body to other neurons, or to muscles or glands.

B

Basilar membrane A structure that runs the length of the cochlea in the inner ear and holds the auditory receptors, called hair cells.

Behaviour Any overt (observable) response or activity by an organism.

Behaviour modification A systematic approach to changing behaviour through the application of the principles of conditioning.

Behaviour therapies Application of the principles of learning to direct efforts to change clients' maladaptive behaviours.

Behavioural contract A written agreement outlining a promise to adhere to the contingencies of a behaviour modification program.

Behavioural genetics An interdisciplinary field that studies the influence of genetic factors on behavioural traits.

Behaviourism A theoretical orientation based on the premise that scientific psychology should study only observable behaviour.

Belief perseverance The tendency to hang on to beliefs in the face of contradictory evidence.

Bilingualism The acquisition of two languages that use different speech sounds, vocabularies, and grammatical rules.

Binocular depth cues Clues about distance based on the differing views of the two eyes.

Biological rhythms Periodic fluctuations in physiological functioning.

Biomedical therapies Physiological interventions intended to reduce symptoms associated with psychological disorders.

Biopsychosocial model A model of illness that holds that physical illness is caused by a complex interaction of biological, psychological, and sociocultural factors.

Bipolar disorder (formerly known as manic-depressive disorder) Mood disorder marked by the experience of both depressed and manic periods.

Bisexuals Persons who seek emotional–sexual relationships with members of either sex.

Body mass index (BMI) Weight (in kilograms) divided by height (in metres) squared (kg/m^2).

Bottom-up processing In form perception, progression from individual elements to the whole.

Bulimia nervosa Eating disorder characterized by habitually engaging in out-of-control overeating followed by unhealthy compensatory efforts, such as self-induced vomiting, fasting, abuse of laxatives and diuretics, and excessive exercise.

Burnout Physical, mental, and emotional exhaustion that is attributable to work-related stress.

Bystander effect A paradoxical social phenomenon in which people are less likely to provide needed help when they are in groups than when they are alone.

C

Cannabis The hemp plant from which marijuana, hashish, and THC are derived.

Case study An in-depth investigation of an individual subject.

Catastrophic thinking Unrealistically pessimistic appraisals of stress that exaggerate the magnitude of one's problems.

Catatonic schizophrenia A type of schizophrenia marked by striking motor disturbances, ranging from muscular rigidity to random motor activity.

Catharsis The release of emotional tension.

Central nervous system (CNS) The brain and the spinal cord.

Centration The tendency to focus on just one feature of a problem, neglecting other important aspects.

Cephalocaudal trend The head-to-foot direction of motor development.

Cerebral cortex The convoluted outer layer of the cerebrum.

Cerebral hemispheres The right and left halves of the cerebrum.

Cerebrospinal fluid (CSF) A solution that fills the hollow cavities (ventricles) of the brain and circulates around the brain and spinal cord.

Channel The medium through which a message is sent.

Chromosomes Threadlike strands of DNA (deoxyribonucleic acid) molecules that carry genetic information.

Chunk A group of familiar stimuli stored as a single unit.

Circadian rhythms The 24-hour biological cycles found in humans and many other species.

Classical conditioning A type of learning in which a neutral stimulus acquires the ability to evoke a response that was originally evoked by another stimulus.

Client-centred therapy An insight therapy that emphasizes providing a supportive emotional climate for clients, who play a major role in determining the pace and direction of their therapy.

Clinical psychologists Psychologists who specialize in the diagnosis and treatment of psychological disorders and everyday behavioural problems.

Clinical psychology The branch of psychology concerned with the diagnosis and treatment of psychological problems and disorders.

Clustering The tendency to remember similar or related items in groups.

Cochlea The fluid-filled, coiled tunnel in the inner ear that contains the receptors for hearing.

Coefficient of determination The percentage of variation in one variable that can be predicted based on the other variable.

Cognition The mental processes involved in acquiring knowledge.

Cognitive development Transitions in youngsters' patterns of thinking, including reasoning, remembering, and problem solving.

Cognitive dissonance A psychological state that exists when related cognitions are inconsistent.

Cognitive therapy An insight therapy that emphasizes recognizing and changing negative thoughts and maladaptive beliefs.

Collective unconscious According to Jung, a storehouse of latent memory traces inherited from people's ancestral past.

Collectivism Putting group goals ahead of personal goals and defining one's identity in terms of the groups one belongs to.

Colour blindness Deficiency in the ability to distinguish among colours.

Commitment An intent to maintain a relationship in spite of the difficulties and costs that may arise.

Comorbidity The coexistence of two or more disorders.

Companionate love Warm, trusting, tolerant affection for another whose life is deeply intertwined with one's own.

Comparitors People, objects, events, and other standards that are used as a baseline for comparisons in making judgments.

Compensation According to Adler, efforts to overcome imagined or real inferiorities by developing one's abilities.

Complementary colours Pairs of colours that produce grey tones when added together.

Conceptual hierarchy A multilevel classification system based on common properties among items.

Concordance rate The percentage of twin pairs or other pairs of relatives that exhibit the same disorder.

Conditioned reinforcers. See *Secondary reinforcers*.

Conditioned response (CR) A learned reaction to a conditioned stimulus that occurs because of previous conditioning.

Conditioned stimulus (CS) A previously neutral stimulus that has, through conditioning, acquired the capacity to evoke a conditioned response.

Cones Specialized visual receptors that play a key role in daylight vision and colour vision.

Confirmation bias The tendency to seek information that supports one's decisions and beliefs while ignoring disconfirming information.

Conflict A state that occurs when two or more incompatible motivations or behavioural impulses compete for expression.

Conformity The tendency for people to yield to real or imagined social pressure.

Confounding of variables A condition that exists whenever two variables are linked together in a way that makes it difficult to sort out their independent effects.

Conjunction fallacy An error that occurs when people estimate that the odds of two uncertain events happening together are greater than the odds of either event happening alone.

Connectionist models. See *Parallel distributed processing (PDP) models*.

Conscious Whatever one is aware of at a particular point in time.

Conservation Piaget's term for the awareness that physical quantities remain constant in spite of changes in their shape or appearance.

Consolidation A hypothetical process involving the gradual conversion of information into durable memory codes stored in long-term memory.

Construct validity The extent to which there is evidence that a test measures a particular hypothetical construct.

Constructive coping Relatively healthful efforts that people make to deal with stressful events.

Content validity The degree to which the content of a test is representative of the domain it's supposed to cover.

Continuous reinforcement Reinforcing every instance of a designated response.

Control group Subjects in a study who do not receive the special treatment given to the experimental group.

Convergence A cue to depth that involves sensing the eyes converging toward each other as they focus on closer objects.

Convergent thinking Narrowing down a list of alternatives to converge on a single correct answer.

Conversion disorder A somatoform disorder characterized by a significant loss of physical function (with no apparent organic basis), usually in a single organ system.

Coping Active efforts to master, reduce, or tolerate the demands created by stress.

Corpus callosum The structure that connects the two cerebral hemispheres.

Correlation The extent to which two variables are related to each other.

Correlation coefficient A numerical index of the degree of relationship between two variables.

Counselling psychologists Psychologists who specialize in the treatment of everyday adjustment problems.

Creativity The generation of ideas that are original, novel, and useful.

Criterion-related validity Test validity that is estimated by correlating subjects' scores on a test with their scores on an independent criterion (another measure) of the trait assessed by the test.

Critical period A limited time span in the development of an organism when it is optimal for certain capacities to emerge because the organism is especially responsive to certain experiences.

Critical thinking The use of cognitive skills and strategies that increase the probability of a desired outcome.

Cross-sectional design A research design in which investigators compare groups of subjects of differing age who are observed at a single point in time.

Crystallized intelligence One's ability to apply acquired skills and knowledge in problem solving.

Culture The widely shared customs, beliefs, values, norms, institutions, and other products of a community that are transmitted socially across generations.

Culture-bound disorders Abnormal syndromes found in only a few cultural groups.

Cumulative recorder A graphic record of reinforcement and responding in a Skinner box as a function of time.

Cyclothymic disorder Exhibiting chronic but relatively mild symptoms of bipolar disturbance.

D

Dark adaptation The process in which the eyes become more sensitive to light in low illumination.

Data collection techniques Procedures for making empirical observations and measurements.

Decay theory The idea that forgetting occurs because memory traces fade with time.

Decision making The process of evaluating alternatives and making choices among them.

Declarative memory system Memory for factual information.

Defence mechanisms Largely unconscious reactions that protect a person from unpleasant emotions such as anxiety and guilt.

Defensive attribution The tendency to blame victims for their misfortune, so that one feels less likely to be victimized in a similar way.

Deinstitutionalization Transferring the treatment of mental illness from inpatient institutions to community-based facilities that emphasize outpatient care.

Delusions False beliefs that are maintained even though they are clearly out of touch with reality.

Dementia An abnormal condition marked by multiple cognitive defects that include memory impairment.

Dendrites Branchlike parts of a neuron that are specialized to receive information.

Dependent variable In an experiment, the variable that is thought to be affected by the manipulation of the independent variable.

Depth perception Interpretation of visual cues that indicate how near or far away objects are.

Descriptive statistics Statistics that are used to organize and summarize data.

Development The sequence of age-related changes that occur as a person progresses from conception to death.

Developmental norms The average age at which individuals display various behaviours and abilities.

Deviation IQ scores Scores that locate subjects precisely within the normal distribution, using the standard deviation as the unit of measurement.

Diagnosis Distinguishing one illness from another.

Discrimination Behaving differently, usually unfairly, toward the members of a group.

Discriminative stimuli Cues that influence operant behaviour by indicating the probable consequences (reinforcement or nonreinforcement) of a response.

Dishabituation An increase in the strength of a habituated response elicited by a new stimulus.

Disorganized schizophrenia A type of schizophrenia in which particularly severe deterioration of adaptive behaviour is seen.

Displacement Diverting emotional feelings (usually anger) from their original source to a substitute target.

Display rules Cultural norms that regulate the appropriate expressions of emotions.

Dissociation A splitting off of mental processes into two separate, simultaneous streams of awareness.

Dissociative amnesia A sudden loss of memory for important personal information that is too extensive to be due to normal forgetting.

Dissociative disorders A class of disorders in which people lose contact with portions of their consciousness or memory, resulting in disruptions in their sense of identity.

Dissociative fugue A disorder in which people lose their memory for their entire lives along with their sense of personal identity.

Dissociative identity disorder (DID) A type of dissociative disorder characterized by the coexistence in one person of two or more largely complete, and usually very different, personalities. Also called multiple-personality disorder.

Distal stimuli Stimuli that lie in the distance (that is, in the world outside the body).

Divergent thinking Trying to expand the range of alternatives by generating many possible solutions.

Dominant gene A gene that is expressed when paired genes are heterozygous (different).

Door-in-the-face technique Making a large request that is likely to be turned down as a way to increase the chances that people will agree to a smaller request later.

Double-blind procedure A research strategy in which neither subjects nor experimenters know which subjects are in the experimental or control groups.

Dream analysis A psychoanalytic technique in which the therapist interprets the symbolic meaning of the client's dreams.

Drive An internal state of tension that motivates an organism to engage in activities that should reduce the tension.

Dual-coding theory Paivio's theory that memory is enhanced by forming semantic and visual codes, since either can lead to recall.

Dysthymic disorder A chronic depression that is insufficient in severity to merit diagnosis of a major depressive episode.

E

Eating disorders Severe disturbances in eating behaviour characterized by preoccupation with weight concerns and unhealthy efforts to control weight.

Eclecticism In psychotherapy, drawing ideas from two or more systems of therapy instead of committing to just one system.

Efferent nerve fibres Axons that carry information outward from the central nervous system to the periphery of the body.

Ego According to Freud, the decision-making component of personality that operates according to the reality principle.

Egocentrism A limited ability to share another person's viewpoint.

Elaboration Linking a stimulus to other information at the time of encoding.

Electrical stimulation of the brain (ESB) Sending a weak electric current into a brain structure to stimulate (activate) it.

Electroconvulsive therapy (ECT) A biomedical treatment in which electric shock is used to produce a cortical seizure accompanied by convulsions.

Electroencephalograph (EEG) A device that monitors the electrical activity of the brain over time by means of recording electrodes attached to the surface of the scalp.

Electromyograph (EMG) A device that records muscular activity and tension.

Electro-oculograph (EOG) A device that records eye movements.

Elicit To draw out or bring forth.

Embryonic stage The second stage of prenatal development, lasting from two weeks until the end of the second month.

Emit To send forth.

Emotion A subjective conscious experience (the cognitive component) accompanied by bodily arousal (the physiological component) and by characteristic overt expressions (the behavioural component).

Emotional intelligence The ability to perceive and express emotion, assimilate emotion in thought, understand and reason with emotion, and regulate emotion.

Empiricism The premise that knowledge should be acquired through observation.

Encoding Forming a memory code.

Encoding specificity principle The idea that the value of a retrieval cue depends on how well it corresponds to the memory code.

Endocrine system A group of glands that secrete chemicals into the bloodstream that help control bodily functioning.

Endorphins The entire family of internally produced chemicals that resemble opiates in structure and effects.

Epidemiology The study of the distribution of mental or physical disorders in a population.

Episodic memory system Chronological, or temporally dated, recollections of personal experiences.

Escape learning A type of learning in which an organism acquires a response that decreases or ends some aversive stimulation.

Estrogens The principal class of gonadal hormones in females.

Ethnocentrism The tendency to view one's own group as superior to others and as the standard for judging the worth of foreign ways.

Etiology The apparent causation and developmental history of an illness.

Evolutionary psychology Theoretical perspective that examines behavioural processes in terms of their adaptive value for a species over the course of many generations.

Excitatory PSP An electric potential that increases the likelihood that a postsynaptic neuron will fire action potentials.

Experiment A research method in which the investigator manipulates a variable under carefully controlled conditions and observes whether any changes occur in a second variable as a result.

Experimental group The subjects in a study who receive some special treatment in regard to the independent variable.

Experimenter bias A phenomenon that occurs when a researcher's expectations or preferences about the outcome of a study influence the results obtained.

Explicit memory Intentional recollection of previous experiences.

External attributions Ascribing the causes of behaviour to situational demands and environmental constraints.

Extinction The gradual weakening and disappearance of a conditioned response tendency.

Extraneous variables Any variables other than the independent variable that seem likely to influence the dependent variable in a specific study.

Extraverts People who tend to be interested in the external world of people and things.

F

Factor analysis Statistical analysis of correlations among many variables to identify closely related clusters of variables.

Family life cycle A sequence of stages that families tend to progress through.

Family studies Scientific studies in which researchers assess hereditary influence by examining blood relatives to see how much they resemble each other on a specific trait.

Farsightedness A vision deficiency in which distant objects are seen clearly but close objects appear blurry.

Fast mapping The process by which children map a word onto an underlying concept after only one exposure to the word.

Feature analysis The process of detecting specific elements in visual input and assembling them into a more complex form.

Feature detectors Neurons that respond selectively to very specific features of more complex stimuli.

Fechner's law A psychophysical law stating that larger and larger increases in stimulus intensity are required to produce perceptible increments in the magnitude of sensation.

Fetal alcohol syndrome A collection of congenital (inborn) problems associated with excessive alcohol use during pregnancy.

Fetal stage The third stage of prenatal development, lasting from two months through birth.

Field dependence–independence Individuals' tendency to rely primarily on external versus internal frames of reference when orienting themselves in space.

Fight-or-flight response A physiological reaction to threat in which the autonomic nervous system mobilizes the organism for attacking (fight) or fleeing (flight) an enemy.

Fitness The reproductive success (number of descendants) of an individual organism relative to the average reproductive success of the population.

Fixation According to Freud, failure to move forward from one psychosexual stage to another as expected.

Fixed-interval (FI) schedule A reinforcement schedule in which the reinforcer is given for the first response that occurs after a fixed time interval has elapsed.

Fixed-ratio (FR) schedule A reinforcement schedule in which the reinforcer is given after a fixed number of nonreinforced responses.

Flashbulb memories Unusually vivid and detailed recollections of momentous events.

Fluid intelligence One's reasoning ability, memory capacity, and speed of information processing.

Foot-in-the-door technique Getting people to agree to a small request to increase the chances that they will agree to a larger request later.

Forebrain The largest and most complicated region of the brain, encompassing a variety of structures, including the thalamus, hypothalamus, limbic system, and cerebrum.

Forgetting curve A graph showing retention and forgetting over time.

Fovea A tiny spot in the centre of the retina that contains only cones; visual acuity is greatest at this spot.

Framing How issues are posed or how choices are structured.

Fraternal twins Twins that result when two eggs are fertilized simultaneously by different sperm cells, forming two separate zygotes. Also called *dizygotic twins*.

Free association A psychoanalytic technique in which clients spontaneously express their thoughts and feelings exactly as they occur, with as little censorship as possible.

Frequency distribution An orderly arrangement of scores indicating the frequency of each score or group of scores.

Frequency polygon A line figure used to present data from a frequency distribution.

Frequency theory The theory that perception of pitch corresponds to the rate, or frequency, at which the entire basilar membrane vibrates.

Frustration The feeling that people experience in any situation in which their pursuit of some goal is thwarted.

Functional fixedness The tendency to perceive an item only in terms of its most common use.

Functionalism A school of psychology based on the belief that psychology should investigate the function or purpose of consciousness, rather than its structure.

Fundamental attribution error Observers' bias in favour of internal attributions in explaining others' behaviour.

G

Galvanic skin response (GSR) An increase in the electrical conductivity of the skin that occurs when sweat glands increase their activity.

Gambler's fallacy The belief that the odds of a chance event increase if the event hasn't occurred recently.

Gate-control theory The idea that incoming pain sensations must pass through a "gate" in the spinal cord that can be closed, thus blocking pain signals.

Gender Culturally constructed distinctions between masculinity and femininity.

Gender differences Actual disparities between the sexes in typical behaviour or average ability.

Gender roles Expectations about what is appropriate behaviour for each sex.

Gender stereotypes Widely held beliefs about males' and females' abilities, personality traits, and behaviour.

General adaptation syndrome Selye's model of the body's stress response, consisting of three stages: alarm, resistance, and exhaustion.

Generalized anxiety disorder A psychological disorder marked by a chronic, high level of anxiety that is not tied to any specific threat.

Genes DNA segments that serve as the key functional units in hereditary transmission.

Genetic mapping The process of determining the location and chemical sequence of specific genes on specific chromosomes.

Genotype A person's genetic makeup.

Germinal stage The first phase of prenatal development, encompassing the first two weeks after conception.

Gestalt psychology A theoretical orientation based on the idea that the whole is greater than the sum of its parts.

Glucose A simple sugar that is an important source of energy.

Glucostats Neurons sensitive to glucose in the surrounding fluid.

Group Two or more individuals who interact and are interdependent.

Group cohesiveness The strength of the liking relationships linking group members to each other and to the group itself.

Group polarization A phenomenon that occurs when group discussion strengthens a group's dominant point of view and produces a shift toward a more extreme decision in that direction.

Group therapy The simultaneous treatment of several clients in a group.

Groupthink A process in which members of a cohesive group emphasize concurrence at the expense of critical thinking in arriving at a decision.

Gustatory system The sensory system for taste.

H

Habituation A gradual reduction in the strength of a response when a stimulus event is presented repeatedly.

Hallucinations Sensory perceptions that occur in the absence of a real, external stimulus, or gross distortions of perceptual input.

Hallucinogens A diverse group of drugs that have powerful effects on mental and emotional functioning, marked most prominently by distortions in sensory and perceptual experience.

Health psychology The subfield of psychology concerned with how psychosocial factors relate to the promotion and maintenance of health and with the causation, prevention, and treatment of illness.

Hedonic adaptation An effect that occurs when the mental scale that people use to judge the pleasantness/unpleasantness of their experiences shifts so that their neutral point, or baseline for comparison, changes.

Heritability ratio An estimate of the proportion of trait variability in a population that is determined by variations in genetic inheritance.

Heterosexuals Persons who seek emotional–sexual relationships with members of the other sex.

Heterozygous condition The situation that occurs when two genes in a specific pair are different.

Heuristic A strategy, guiding principle, or rule of thumb used in solving problems or making decisions.

Hierarchy of needs Maslow's systematic arrangement of needs according to priority, which assumes that basic needs must be met before less basic needs are aroused.

Higher-order conditioning A type of conditioning in which a conditioned stimulus functions as if it were an unconditioned stimulus.

Hindbrain The part of the brain that includes the cerebellum and two structures found in the lower part of the brainstem: the medulla and the pons.

Hindsight bias The tendency to mould one's interpretation of the past to fit how events actually turned out.

Histogram A bar graph that presents data from a frequency distribution.

Homeostasis A state of physiological equilibrium or stability.

Homosexuals Persons who seek emotional–sexual relationships with members of the same sex.

Homozygous condition The situation that occurs when two genes in a specific pair are the same.

Hormones The chemical substances released by the endocrine glands.

Humanism A theoretical orientation that emphasizes the unique qualities of humans, especially their freedom and their potential for personal growth.

Hypnosis A systematic procedure that typically produces a heightened state of suggestibility.

Hypochondriasis A somatoform disorder characterized by excessive preoccupation with health concerns and incessant worry about developing physical illnesses.

Hypothalamus A structure found near the base of the forebrain that is involved in the regulation of basic biological needs.

Hypothesis A tentative statement about the relationship between two or more variables.

I

Id According to Freud, the primitive, instinctive component of personality that operates according to the pleasure principle.

Identical twins Twins that emerge from one zygote that splits for unknown reasons. Also called *monozygotic twins*.

Identification Bolstering self-esteem by forming an imaginary or real alliance with some person or group.

Illusory correlation A misperception that occurs when people estimate that they have encountered more confirmations of an association between social traits than they have actually seen.

Immune response The body's defensive reaction to invasion by bacteria, viral agents, or other foreign substances.

Implicit memory Type of memory apparent when retention is exhibited on a task that does not require intentional remembering.

Impossible figures Objects that can be represented in two-dimensional pictures but cannot exist in three-dimensional space.

Incentive An external goal that has the capacity to motivate behaviour.

Inclusive fitness The sum of an individual's own reproductive success plus the effects the organism has on the reproductive success of related others.

Incongruence The degree of disparity between one's self-concept and one's actual experience.

Independent variable In an experiment, a condition or event that an experimenter varies in order to see its impact on another variable.

Individualism Putting personal goals ahead of group goals and defining one's identity in terms of personal attributes rather than group memberships.

Industrial and organizational (I/O) psychology The branch of psychology concerned with the application of psychological principles to the workplace.

Inferential statistics Statistics that are used to interpret data and draw conclusions.

Ingroup The group that people belong to and identify with.

Inhibitory PSP An electric potential that decreases the likelihood that a postsynaptic neuron will fire action potentials.

Insanity A legal status indicating that a person cannot be held responsible for his or her actions because of mental illness.

Insight In problem solving, the sudden discovery of the correct solution following incorrect attempts based primarily on trial and error.

Insight therapies Psychotherapy methods characterized by verbal interactions intended to enhance clients' self-knowledge and thus promote healthful changes in personality and behaviour.

Insomnia Chronic problems in getting adequate sleep.

Instinctive drift The tendency for an animal's innate responses to interfere with conditioning processes.

Instrumental learning. See *Operant conditioning*.

Intelligence quotient (IQ) A child's mental age divided by chronological age, multiplied by 100.

Intelligence tests Psychological tests that measure general mental ability.

Interference theory The idea that people forget information because of competition from other material.

Intermittent reinforcement A reinforcement schedule in which a designated response is reinforced only some of the time.

Internal attributions Ascribing the causes of behaviour to personal dispositions, traits, abilities, and feelings.

Internet addiction Spending an inordinate amount of time on the Internet and being unable to control online use.

Interpersonal attraction Positive feelings toward another.

Interpretation In psychoanalysis, the therapist's attempts to explain the inner significance of the client's thoughts, feelings, memories, and behaviours.

Intimacy Warmth, closeness, and sharing in a relationship.

Introspection Careful, systematic observation of one's own conscious experience.

Introverts People who tend to be preoccupied with the internal world of their own thoughts, feelings, and experiences.

Irreversibility The inability to envision reversing an action.

J

Journal A periodical that publishes technical and scholarly material, usually in a narrowly defined area of inquiry.

Just noticeable difference (JND) The smallest difference in the amount of stimulation that a specific sense can detect.

K

Keyword method A mnemonic technique in which one associates a concrete word with an abstract word and generates an image to represent the concrete word.

Kinesthetic system The sensory system that monitors the positions of the various parts of one's body.

L

Language A set of symbols that convey meaning, and rules for combining those symbols, that can be used to generate an infinite variety of messages.

Language acquisition device (LAD) An innate mechanism or process that facilitates the learning of language.

Latent content According to Freud, the hidden or disguised meaning of the events in a dream.

Lateral antagonism A process in the retina that occurs when neural activity in a cell opposes activity in surrounding cells.

Law of effect The principle that if a response in the presence of a stimulus leads to satisfying effects, the association between the stimulus and the response is strengthened.

Learned helplessness Passive behaviour produced by exposure to unavoidable aversive events.

Learning A relatively durable change in behaviour or knowledge that is due to experience.

Lens The transparent eye structure that focuses the light rays falling on the retina.

Lesioning Destroying a piece of the brain.

Levels-of-processing theory The theory holding that deeper levels of mental processing result in longer-lasting memory codes.

Lie detector See *Polygraph.*

Life changes Any noticeable alterations in one's living circumstances that require readjustment.

Light adaptation The process whereby the eyes become less sensitive to light in high illumination.

Limbic system A densely connected network of structures roughly located along the border between the cerebral cortex and deeper subcortical areas.

Linguistic relativity The theory that one's language determines the nature of one's thought.

Link method Forming a mental image of items to be remembered in a way that links them together.

Lithium A chemical used to control mood swings in patients with bipolar mood disorders.

Long-term memory (LTM) An unlimited-capacity store that can hold information over lengthy periods of time.

Long-term potentiation (LTP) A long-lasting increase in neural excitability in synapses along a specific neural pathway.

Longitudinal design A research design in which investigators observe one group of subjects repeatedly over a period of time.

Lowball technique Getting someone to commit to an attractive proposition before revealing the hidden costs.

Lucid dreams Dreams in which people can think clearly about the circumstances of waking life and the fact that they are dreaming, yet they remain asleep in the midst of a vivid dream.

M

Major depressive disorder Mood disorder characterized by persistent feelings of sadness and despair and a loss of interest in previous sources of pleasure.

Manifest content According to Freud, the plot of a dream at a surface level.

Matching hypothesis The idea that males and females of approximately equal physical attractiveness are likely to select each other as partners.

Maturation Development that reflects the gradual unfolding of one's genetic blueprint.

MDMA A compound drug related to both amphetamines and hallucinogens, especially mescaline; commonly called "ecstasy."

Mean The arithmetic average of the scores in a distribution.

Mean length of utterance (MLU) The average length of children's spoken statements (measured in phonemes).

Median The score that falls exactly in the centre of a distribution of scores.

Medical model The view that it is useful to think of abnormal behaviour as a disease.

Meditation A family of mental exercises in which a conscious attempt is made to focus attention in a nonanalytical way.

Menarche The first occurrence of menstruation.

Mental age In intelligence testing, a score that indicates that a child displays the mental ability typical of a child of that chronological (actual) age.

Mental hospital A medical institution specializing in providing inpatient care for psychological disorders.

Mental retardation Subnormal general mental ability accompanied by deficiencies in everyday living skills originating prior to age 18.

Mental set Persisting in using problem-solving strategies that have worked in the past.

Message The information transmitted by a source.

Meta-analysis Combining the statistical results of many studies of the same question, yielding an estimate of the size and consistency of a variable's effects.

Metalinguistic awareness The ability to reflect on the use of language.

Method of loci A mnemonic device that involves taking an imaginary walk along a familiar path where images of items to be remembered are associated with certain locations.

Midbrain The segment of the brain stem that lies between the hindbrain and the forebrain.

Midlife crisis A difficult, turbulent period of doubts and reappraisal of one's life.

Mnemonic devices Strategies for enhancing memory.

Mode The score that occurs most frequently in a distribution.

Model A person whose behaviour is observed by another.

Monocular depth cues Clues about distance based on the image from either eye alone.

Mood disorders A class of disorders marked by emotional disturbances of varied kinds that may spill over to disrupt physical, perceptual, social, and thought processes.

Morphemes The smallest units of meaning in a language.

Motion parallax Cue to depth that involves images of objects at different distances moving across the retina at different rates.

Motivated forgetting Purposeful suppression of memories.

Motivation Goal-directed behaviour.

Motor development The progression of muscular coordination required for physical activities.

Multiple-personality disorder See *Dissociative identity disorder.*

Mutation A spontaneous, heritable change in a piece of DNA that occurs in the individual organism.

Myelin sheath Insulating material, derived from glial cells, that encases some axons of neurons.

N

Narcolepsy A disease marked by sudden and irresistible onsets of sleep during normal waking periods.

Narcotics (opiates) Drugs derived from opium that are capable of relieving pain.

Natural selection Principle stating that heritable characteristics that provide a survival reproductive advantage are more likely than alternative characteristics to be passed on to subsequent generations and thus come to be "selected" over time.

Naturalistic observation A descriptive research method in which the researcher engages in careful, usually prolonged, observation of behaviour without intervening directly with the subjects.

Nearsightedness A vision deficiency in which close objects are seen clearly but distant objects appear blurry.

Need for self-actualization The need to fulfill one's potential.

Negative punishment The removal of a rewarding stimulus.

Negative reinforcement The strengthening of a response because it is followed by the removal of an aversive (unpleasant) stimulus.

Negative symptoms Schizophrenic symptoms that involve behavioural deficits, such as flattened emotions, social withdrawal, apathy, impaired attention, and poverty of speech.

Negatively skewed distribution A distribution in which most scores pile up at the high end of the scale.

Nerves Bundles of neuron fibres (axons) that are routed together in the peripheral nervous system.

Neurons Individual cells in the nervous system that receive, integrate, and transmit information.

Neurotransmitters Chemicals that transmit information from one neuron to another.

Night terrors Abrupt awakenings from NREM sleep accompanied by intense autonomic arousal and feelings of panic.

Nightmares Anxiety-arousing dreams that lead to awakening, usually from REM sleep.

Non-REM (NREM) sleep Sleep stages 1 through 4, which are marked by an absence of rapid eye movements, relatively little dreaming, and varied EEG activity.

Nondeclarative memory system Memory for actions, skills, and operations.

Normal distribution A symmetric, bell-shaped curve that represents the pattern in which many characteristics are dispersed in the population.

Null hypothesis In inferential statistics, the assumption that there is no true relationship between the variables being observed.

O

Obedience A form of compliance that occurs when people follow direct commands, usually from someone in a position of authority.

Obesity The condition of being overweight.

Object permanence Recognizing that objects continue to exist even when they are no longer visible.

Observational learning A type of learning that occurs when an organism's responding is influenced by the observation of others, who are called models.

Obsessive-compulsive disorder (OCD) A type of anxiety disorder marked by persistent, uncontrollable intrusions of unwanted thoughts (obsessions) and urges to engage in senseless rituals (compulsions).

Oedipal complex According to Freud, children's manifestation of erotically tinged desires for their opposite-sex parent, accompanied by feelings of hostility toward their same-sex parent.

Olfactory system The sensory system for smell.

Operant chamber See *Skinner box.*

Operant conditioning A form of learning in which voluntary responses come to be controlled by their consequences.

Operational definition A definition that describes the actions or operations that will be made to measure or control a variable.

Opiates See *Narcotics.*

Opponent process theory The theory that colour perception depends on receptors that make antagonistic responses to three pairs of colours.

Optic chiasm The point at which the optic nerves from the inside half of each eye cross over and then project to the opposite half of the brain.

Optic disk A hole in the retina where the optic nerve fibres exit the eye.

Optical illusion An apparently inexplicable discrepancy between the appearance of a visual stimulus and its physical reality.

Optimism A general tendency to expect good outcomes.

Orgasm The release of sexual tension that occurs when arousal reaches its peak intensity and is discharged in a series of muscular contractions that pulsate through the pelvic area.

Outgroup People who are not part of the ingroup.

Overextension Using a word incorrectly to describe a wider set of objects or actions than it is meant to.

Overlearning Continued rehearsal of material after one first appears to have mastered it.

Overregularization In children, incorrect generalization of grammatical rules to irregular cases where they do not apply.

P

Panic disorder A type of anxiety disorder characterized by recurrent attacks of overwhelming anxiety that usually occur suddenly and unexpectedly.

Parallel distributed processing (PDP) models Models of memory that assume cognitive processes depend on patterns of activation in highly interconnected computational networks that resemble neural networks. Also called *connectionist models.*

Parallel processing Simultaneously extracting different kinds of information from the same input.

Paranoid schizophrenia A type of schizophrenia that is dominated by delusions of persecution along with delusions of grandeur.

Parasympathetic division The branch of the autonomic nervous system that generally conserves bodily resources.

Partial reinforcement See *Intermittent reinforcement.*

Participants See *Subjects.*

Passionate love A complete absorption in another that includes tender sexual feelings and the agony and ecstasy of intense emotion.

Pavlovian conditioning. See *Classical conditioning.*

Percentile score A figure that indicates the percentage of people who score below the score one has obtained.

Perception The selection, organization, and interpretation of sensory input.

Perceptual asymmetries Left–right imbalances between the cerebral hemispheres in the speed of visual or auditory processing.

Perceptual constancy A tendency to experience a stable perception in the face of continually changing sensory input.

Perceptual hypothesis An inference about which distal stimuli could be responsible for the proximal stimuli sensed.

Perceptual set A readiness to perceive a stimulus in a particular way.

Peripheral nervous system All those nerves that lie outside the brain and spinal cord.

Person perception The process of forming impressions of others.

Personal unconscious According to Jung, the level of awareness that houses material that is not within one's conscious awareness because it has been repressed or forgotten.

Personality An individual's unique constellation of consistent behavioural traits.

Personality disorders A class of psychological disorders marked by extreme, inflexible personality traits that cause subjective distress or impaired social and occupational functioning.

Personality tests Psychological tests that measure various aspects of personality, including motives, interests, values, and attitudes.

Personality trait A durable disposition to behave in a particular way in a variety of situations.

Phenomenological approach The assumption that one must appreciate individuals' personal, subjective experiences to truly understand their behaviour.

Phenotype The ways in which a person's genotype is manifested in observable characteristics.

Phi phenomenon The illusion of movement created by presenting visual stimuli in rapid succession.

Phobias Irrational fears of specific objects or situations.

Phobic disorder A type of anxiety disorder marked by a persistent and irrational fear of an object or situation that presents no realistic danger.

Phonemes The smallest units of sound in a spoken language.

Physical dependence The condition that exists when a person must continue to take a drug to avoid withdrawal illness.

Pictorial depth cues Clues about distance that can be given in a flat picture.

Pituitary gland The "master gland" of the endocrine system; it releases a great variety of hormones that fan out through the body, stimulating actions in the other endocrine glands.

Place theory The idea that perception of pitch corresponds to the vibration of different portions, or places, along the basilar membrane.

Placebo effects The fact that subjects' expectations can lead them to experience some change even though they receive an empty, fake, or ineffectual treatment.

Placenta A structure that allows oxygen and nutrients to pass into the fetus from the mother's bloodstream and bodily wastes to pass out to the mother.

Pleasure principle According to Freud, the principle upon which the id operates, demanding immediate gratification of its urges.

Polygenic traits Characteristics that are influenced by more than one pair of genes.

Polygraph A device that records autonomic fluctuations while a subject is questioned, in an effort to determine whether the subject is telling the truth.

Population The larger collection of animals or people from which a sample is drawn and that researchers want to generalize about.

Positive punishment The presentation of an aversive stimulus.

Positive reinforcement Reinforcement that occurs when a response is strengthened because it is followed by the presentation of a rewarding stimulus.

Positive symptoms Schizophrenic symptoms that involve behavioural excesses or peculiarities, such as hallucinations, delusions, bizarre behaviour, and wild flights of ideas.

Positively skewed distribution A distribution in which scores pile up at the low end of the scale.

Postsynaptic potential (PSP) A voltage change at the receptor site on a postsynaptic cell membrane.

Post-traumatic stress disorder (PTSD) Disturbed behaviour that is attributed to a major stressful event but that emerges after the stress is over.

Preconscious According to Freud, the level of awareness that contains material just beneath the surface of conscious awareness that can easily be retrieved.

Prejudice A negative attitude held toward members of a group.

Premises The reasons presented to persuade someone that a conclusion is true or probably true.

Prenatal period The period from conception to birth, usually encompassing nine months of pregnancy.

Preparedness A species-specific predisposition to be conditioned in certain ways and not others.

Pressure Expectations or demands that one behave in a certain way.

Prevalence The percentage of a population that exhibits a disorder during a specified time period.

Primary reinforcers Events that are inherently reinforcing because they satisfy biological needs.

Primary sex characteristics The sexual structures necessary for reproduction.

Proactive interference A memory problem that occurs when previously learned information interferes with the retention of new information.

Problem solving Active efforts to discover what must be done to achieve a goal that is not readily available.

Problem space The set of possible pathways to a solution considered by the problem solver.

Procedural memory system The repository of memories for actions, skills, and operations.

Prognosis A forecast about the probable course of an illness.

Projection Attributing one's own thoughts, feelings, or motives to another.

Projective tests Psychological tests that ask subjects to respond to vague, ambiguous stimuli in ways that may reveal the subjects' needs, feelings, and personality traits.

Prospective memory The ability to remember to perform actions in the future.

Proximal stimuli The stimulus energies that impinge directly on sensory receptors.

Proximodistal trend The centre-outward direction of motor development.

Psychiatrists Physicians who specialize in the diagnosis and treatment of psychological disorders.

Psychiatry A branch of medicine concerned with the diagnosis and treatment of psychological problems and disorders.

Psychoactive drugs Chemical substances that modify mental, emotional, or behavioural functioning.

Psychoanalysis An insight therapy that emphasizes the recovery of unconscious conflicts, motives, and defences through techniques such as free association and transference.

Psychoanalytic theory A theory developed by Freud that attempts to explain personality, motivation, and mental disorders by focusing on unconscious determinants of behaviour.

Psychodynamic theories All the diverse theories descended from the work of Sigmund Freud that focus on unconscious mental forces.

Psychological dependence The condition that exists when a person must continue to take a drug in order to satisfy intense mental and emotional craving for the drug.

Psychological test A standardized measure of a sample of a person's behaviour.

Psychology The science that studies behaviour and the physiological and cognitive processes that underlie it, and the profession that applies the accumulated knowledge of this science to practical problems.

Psychopharmacotherapy The treatment of mental disorders with medication.

Psychophysics The study of how physical stimuli are translated into psychological experience.

Psychosexual stages According to Freud, developmental periods with a characteristic sexual focus that leave their mark on adult personality.

Psychosomatic diseases Physical ailments with a genuine organic basis that are caused in part by psychological factors, especially emotional distress.

Puberty The period of early adolescence marked by rapid physical growth and the development of sexual (reproductive) maturity.

Pubescence The two-year span preceding puberty during which the changes leading to physical and sexual maturity take place.

Punishment An event that follows a response that weakens or suppresses the tendency to make that response.

Pupil The opening in the centre of the iris that helps regulate the amount of light passing into the rear chamber of the eye.

R

Random assignment The constitution of groups in a study such that all subjects have an equal chance of being assigned to any group or condition.

Rational-emotive therapy An approach to therapy that focuses on altering clients' patterns of irrational thinking to reduce maladaptive emotions and behaviour.

Rationalization Creating false but plausible excuses to justify unacceptable behaviour.

Reaction formation Behaving in a way that's exactly the opposite of one's true feelings.

Reaction range Genetically determined limits on IQ or other traits.

Reality monitoring The process of deciding whether memories are based on external sources (our perceptions of actual events) or internal sources (our thoughts and imaginations).

Reality principle According to Freud, the principle on which the ego operates, which seeks to delay gratification of the id's urges until appropriate outlets and situations can be found.

Recall A memory test that requires subjects to reproduce information on their own without any cues.

Receiver The person to whom a message is sent.

Receptive field of a visual cell The retinal area that, when stimulated, affects the firing of that cell.

Recessive gene A gene whose influence is masked when paired genes are different (heterozygous).

Reciprocal determinism The assumption that internal mental events, external environmental events, and overt behaviour all influence each other.

Reciprocity Liking those who show that they like you.

Reciprocity norm The rule that people should pay back in kind what they receive from others.

Recognition A memory test that requires subjects to select previously learned information from an array of options.

Refractory period A time following orgasm during which males are largely unresponsive to further stimulation.

Regression A reversion to immature patterns of behaviour.

Regression toward the mean Effect that occurs when people who score extremely high or low on some trait are measured a second time and their new score falls closer to the mean (average).

Rehearsal The process of repetitively verbalizing or thinking about information to be stored in memory.

Reification Giving an abstract concept a name and then treating it as though it were a concrete, tangible object.

Reinforcement An event following a response that strengthens the tendency to make that response.

Reinforcement contingencies The circumstances or rules that determine whether responses lead to the presentation of reinforcers.

Relearning A memory test that requires a subject to memorize information a second time to determine how much time or effort is saved by having learned it before.

Reliability The measurement consistency of a test (or of other kinds of measurement techniques).

REM sleep A deep stage of sleep marked by rapid eye movements, high-frequency brain waves, and dreaming.

Replication The repetition of a study to see whether the earlier results are duplicated.

Representativeness heuristic Basing the estimated probability of an event on how similar it is to the typical prototype of that event.

Repression Keeping distressing thoughts and feelings buried in the unconscious.

Research methods Differing approaches to the manipulation and control of variables in empirical studies.

Resistance Largely unconscious defensive manoeuvres a client uses to hinder the progress of therapy.

Resistance to extinction In operant conditioning, the phenomenon that occurs when an organism continues to make a response after delivery of the reinforcer for it has been terminated.

Respondent conditioning See *Classical conditioning*.

Response set A tendency to respond to questions in a particular way that is unrelated to the content of the questions.

Resting potential The stable, negative charge of a neuron when it is inactive.

Retention The proportion of material retained (remembered).

Retina The neural tissue lining the inside back surface of the eye; it absorbs light, processes images, and sends visual information to the brain.

Retinal disparity A cue to depth based on the fact that objects project images to slightly different locations on the right and left retinas, so the right and left eyes see slightly different views of the object.

Retrieval Recovering information from memory stores.

Retroactive interference A memory problem that occurs when new information impairs the retention of previously learned information.

Retrograde amnesia Loss of memories for events that occurred prior to a head injury.

Retrospective memory The ability to remember events from the past or previously learned information.

Reuptake A process in which neurotransmitters are sponged up from the synaptic cleft by the presynaptic membrane.

Reversible figure A drawing that is compatible with two different interpretations that can shift back and forth.

Risky decision making Making choices under conditions of uncertainty.

Rods Specialized visual receptors that play a key role in night vision and peripheral vision.

S

Sample The collection of subjects selected for observation in an empirical study.

Sampling bias A problem that occurs when a sample is not representative of the population from which it is drawn.

Scatter diagram A graph in which paired X and Y scores for each subject are plotted as single points.

Schedule of reinforcement A specific presentation of reinforcers over time.

Schema An organized cluster of knowledge about a particular object or sequence of events.

Schizophrenic disorders A class of psychological disorders marked by disturbances in thought that spill over to affect perceptual, social, and emotional processes.

Secondary (conditioned) reinforcers Stimulus events that acquire reinforcing qualities by being associated with primary reinforcers.

Secondary sex characteristics Physical features that are associated with gender but that are not directly involved in reproduction.

Sedatives Sleep-inducing drugs that tend to decrease central nervous system activation and behavioural activity.

Self-actualizing persons People with exceptionally healthy personalities, marked by continued personal growth.

Self-concept A collection of beliefs about one's own nature, unique qualities, and typical behaviour.

Self-efficacy One's belief about one's ability to perform behaviours that should lead to expected outcomes.

Self-enhancement Focusing on positive feedback from others, exaggerating one's strengths, and seeing oneself as above average.

Self-esteem A person's overall assessment of her or his personal adequacy or worth.

Self-monitoring The degree to which people attend to and control the impression they make on others in social interactions.

Self-referent encoding Deciding how or whether information is personally relevant.

Self-report inventories Personality tests that ask individuals to answer a series of questions about their characteristic behaviour.

Self-serving bias The tendency to attribute one's successes to personal factors and one's failures to situational factors.

Semantic memory system General knowledge that is not tied to the time when the information was learned.

Semantic network Concepts joined together by links that show how the concepts are related.

Semantics The area of language concerned with understanding the meaning of words and word combinations.

Sensation The stimulation of sense organs.

Sensation seeking A generalized preference for high or low levels of sensory stimulation.

Sensory adaptation A gradual decline in sensitivity to prolonged stimulation.

Sensory memory The preservation of information in its original sensory form for a brief time, usually only a fraction of a second.

Separation anxiety Emotional distress seen in many infants when they are separated from people with whom they have formed an attachment.

Serial-position effect In memory tests, the fact that subjects show better recall for items at the beginning and end of a list than for items in the middle.

Set-point theory The idea that the body monitors fat-cell levels to keep them (and weight) fairly stable.

Settling-point theory The idea that weight tends to drift around a level at which the constellation of factors that determine food consumption and energy expenditure achieve an equilibrium.

Sex The biologically based categories of male and female.

Sexual orientation A person's preference for emotional and sexual relationships with individuals of the same sex, the other sex, or either sex.

Shaping The reinforcement of closer and closer approximations of a desired response.

Short-term memory (STM) A limited-capacity store that can maintain unrehearsed information for about 20 to 30 seconds.

Signal-detection theory A psychophysiological theory proposing that the detection of stimuli involves decision processes as well as sensory processes, which are influenced by a variety of factors besides the physical intensity of a stimulus.

Skinner box A small enclosure in which an animal can make a specific response that is systematically recorded while the consequences of the response are controlled.

Sleep apnea A sleep disorder characterized by frequent reflexive gasping for air that awakens a person and disrupts sleep.

Slow-wave sleep (SWS) Sleep stages 3 and 4, during which low-frequency delta waves become prominent in EEG recordings.

Social desirability bias A tendency to give socially approved answers to questions about oneself.

Social loafing A reduction in effort by individuals when they work in groups as compared to when they work by themselves.

Social psychology The branch of psychology concerned with the way individuals' thoughts, feelings, and behaviours are influenced by others.

Social schemas Organized clusters of ideas about categories of social events and people.

Social skills training A behaviour therapy designed to improve interpersonal skills that emphasizes shaping, modelling, and behavioural rehearsal.

Social support Various types of aid and succour provided by members of one's social networks.

Socialization The acquisition of the norms, roles, and behaviours expected of people in a particular society.

Soma The cell body of a neuron; it contains the nucleus and much of the chemical machinery common to most cells.

Somatic nervous system The system of nerves that connect to voluntary skeletal muscles and to sensory receptors.

Somatization disorder A type of somatoform disorder marked by a history of diverse physical complaints that appear to be psychological in origin.

Somatoform disorders A class of psychological disorders involving physical ailments with no authentic organic basis that are due to psychological factors.

Somnambulism (sleepwalking) Arising and wandering about while remaining asleep.

Source The person who sends a communication.

Source monitoring The process of making attributions about the origins of memories.

Source-monitoring error An error that occurs when a memory derived from one source is misattributed to another source.

Split-brain surgery A procedure in which the bundle of fibres that connects the cerebral hemispheres (the corpus callosum) is cut to reduce the severity of epileptic seizures.

Spontaneous recovery In classical conditioning, the reappearance of an extinguished response after a period of nonexposure to the conditioned stimulus.

Spontaneous remission Recovery from a disorder without formal treatment.

SQ3R A study system designed to promote effective reading by means of five steps: survey, question, read, recite, and review.

Stage A developmental period during which characteristic patterns of behaviour are exhibited and certain capacities become established.

Standard deviation An index of the amount of variability in a set of data.

Standardization The uniform procedures used in the administration and scoring of a test.

Statistical significance The condition that exists when the probability that the observed findings are due to chance is very low.

Statistics The use of mathematics to organize, summarize, and interpret numerical data. See also *Descriptive statistics, Inferential statistics.*

Stereotypes Widely held beliefs that people have certain characteristics because of their membership in a particular group.

Stimulants Drugs that tend to increase central nervous system activation and behavioural activity.

Stimulus Any detectable input from the environment.

Stimulus discrimination The phenomenon that occurs when an organism that has learned a response to a specific stimulus does not respond in the same way to stimuli that are similar to the original stimulus.

Aldag, R. J., & Fuller, S. R. (1993). Beyond fiasco: A reappraisal of the groupthink phenomenon and a new model of group decision processes. *Psychological Bulletin, 113,* 533–552.

Aldrich, M. S. (2000). Cardinal manifestations of sleep disorders. In M. H. Kryger, T. Roth & W. C. Dement (Eds.), *Principles and practice of sleep medicine.* Philadelphia: Saunders.

Alexander, C. N., Davies, J. L., Dixon, C. A., Dillbeck, M. C., Druker, S. M., Oetzel, R. M., Muehlman, J. M., & Orme-Johnson, D. W. (1990). Growth of higher states of consciousness: The Vedic psychology of human development. In C. N. Alexander & E. J. Langer (Eds.), *Higher stages of human development: Perspectives on adult growth.* New York: Oxford University Press.

Alexander, C. N., Robinson, P., Orme-Johnson, D. W., Schneider, R. H., et al. (1994). The effects of transcendental meditation compared with other methods of relaxation and meditation in reducing risk factors, morbidity, and mortality. *Homeostasis in Health & Disease, 35,* 243–263.

Alexander, F. (1954). Psychoanalysis and psychotherapy. *Journal of the American Psychoanalytic Association, 2,* 722–733.

Alexander, F. G., & Selesnick, S. T. (1966). *The history of psychiatry: An evaluation of psychiatric thought and practice from prehistoric times to the present.* New York: Harper and Row.

Alexander, M. G., & Fisher, T. D. (2003). Truth and consequences: Using the bogus pipeline to examine sex differences in self-reported sexuality. *Journal of Sex Research, 40(1),* 27–35.

Alexander, J., & Tate, M. (1999). *Web wisdom: How to evaluate and create information quality on the web.* Mahwah, NJ: Erlbaum.

Allan, R. W. (1998). Operant-respondent interactions. In W. O'Donohue (Ed.), *Learning and behavior therapy.* Boston: Allyn & Bacon.

Allen, C. T., & Shimp, T. A. (1990). On using classical conditioning methods for researching the impact of ad-evoked feelings. In S. J. Agres, J. A. Edell, & T. M. Dubitsky (Eds.), *Emotion in advertising: Theoretical and practical explorations.* New York: Quorum Books.

Allen, M. J., Noel, R., Degan, J., Halpern, D. F., & Crawford, C. (2000). *Goals and objectives for the undergraduate psychology major: Recommendations from a meeting of the California State University psychology faculty.* Distributed by the Office of Teaching Resources in Psychology, Society for the Teaching of Psychology, http://www.lemoyne.edu/OTRP/otrpresources/otrpoutcomes.html.

Allen, M., Emmers, T., Gebhardt, L., & Giery, M. A. (1995). Exposure to pornography and acceptance of rape myths. *Journal of Communication, 45,* 5–26.

Allgood, W. P., Risko, V. J., Alvarez, M. C., & Fairbanks, M. M. (2000). Factors that influence study. In R. F. Flippo & D. C. Caverly (Eds.), *Handbook of college reading and study strategy research.* Mahwah, NJ: Erlbaum.

Allison, D. B., Fontaine, K. R., Manson, J. E., Stevens, J., & VanItallie, T. B. (1999). Annual deaths attributable to obesity in the United States. *Journal of the American Medical Association, 282,* 1530–1538.

Allison, D. B., Heshka, S., Neale, M. C., Lykken, D. T., & Heymsfield, S. B. (1994). A genetic analysis of relative weight among 4,020 twin pairs, with an emphasis on sex effects. *Health Psychology, 13,* 362–365.

Alloy, L. B., Abramson, L. Y., Whitehouse, W. G., Hogan, M. E., Tashman, N. A., Steinberg, D. L., Rose, D. T., & Donovan, P. (1999). Depressogenic cognitive styles: Predictive validity, information processing and personality characteristics, and developmental origins. *Behavioral Research and Therapy, 37,* 503–531.

Allport, G. W. (1937). *Personality: A psychological interpretation.* New York: Holt.

Alonso, A., Alonso, S., & Piper, W. (2003). Group psychotherapy. In G. Stricker & T. A. Widiger (Eds.), *Handbook of psychology, Vol. 8: Clinical psychology.* New York: Wiley.

Altman, I. (1990). Centripetal and centrifugal trends in psychology. In L. Brickman & H. Ellis (Eds.), *Preparing psychologists for the 21st century: Proceedings of the National Conference on Graduate Education in Psychology.* Hillsdale, NJ: Erlbaum.

Alvarez, P., & Squire, L. (1994). Memory consolidation and the medial temporal lobe: A simple network model. *Proceedings of the National Academy of Sciences, USA, 91,* 7041–7045.

Amabile, T. M. (1983). *The social psychology of creativity.* New York: Springer-Verlag.

Amabile, T. M. (1990). Within you, without you: The social psychology of creativity, and beyond. In M. A. Runco & R. S. Albert (Eds.), *Theories of creativity.* Newbury Park, CA: Sage.

Amabile, T. M. (1996). *Creativity in context.* Boulder, CO: Westview.

Amato, P. R. (2001). The consequences of divorce for adults and children. In R. M. Milardo (Ed.), *Understanding families into the new millenium: A decade in review.* Minneapolis: National Council on Family Relations.

Amato, P. R. (2003). Reconciling divergent perspectives: Judith Wallerstein, quantitative family research and children of divorce. *Family Relations: Interdisciplinary Journal of Applied Family Studies, 52,* 332–339.

Amato, P. R., & Keith, B. (1991). Parental divorce and adult well-being: A meta-analysis. *Journal of Marriage and the Family, 53,* 43–58.

Ambady, N., & Rosenthal, R. (1993). Half a minute: Predicting teacher evaluations from thin slices of nonverbal behavior and physical attractiveness. *Journal of Personality and Social Psychology, 64,* 431–441.

Ambady, N., Hallahan, M., & Conner, B. (1999). Accuracy of judgments of sexual orientation from thin slices of behavior. *Journal of Personality and Social Psychology, 77,* 538–547.

American Association on Mental Retardation. (1992). *Mental retardation: Definition, classification, and systems of supports.* Washington, DC: Author.

American Psychiatric Association Task Force on Electroconvulsive Therapy. (2001). *The practice of electroconvulsive therapy: Recommendations for treatment* (2nd ed.). Washington, DC: American Psychiatric Association.

American Psychiatric Association. (1994). *Diagnostic and statistical manual of mental disorders* (4th ed.). Washington, DC: Author.

American Psychiatric Association. (2000). *Diagnostic and statistical manual of mental disorders* (4th ed. Text revision). Washington, DC: Author.

American Psychological Association. (1998). Psychologists among Guggenheim winners. *APA Monitor, 29,* June 6, 1998. Retrieved May 13, 2005, from http://www.apa.org/monitor/jun98/gugg.html.

Anand, B. K., & Brobeck, J. R. (1951). Hypothalamic control of food intake in rats and cats. *Yale Journal of Biology and Medicine, 24,* 123–140.

Anch, A. M., Browman, C. P., Mitler, M. M., & Walsh, J. K. (1988). *Sleep: A scientific perspective.* Englewood Cliffs, NJ: Prentice-Hall.

Anderson, C., John, O. P., Keltner, D., & Kring, A. M. (2001). Who attains social status? Effects of personality and physical attractiveness in social groups. *Journal of Personality and Social Psychology, 81(1),* 116–132.

Anderson, E. A., Kohler, J. K., & Letiecq, B. L. (2002). Low-income fathers and "Responsible Fatherhood" programs: A qualitative investigation of participants' experiences. *Family Relations, 51,* 148–155.

Anderson, K. J. (1990). Arousal and the inverted-U hypothesis: A critique of Neiss's "reconceptualizing arousal." *Psychological Bulletin, 107,* 96–100.

Anderson, M. C., & Neely, J. H. (1996). Interference and inhibition in memory retrieval. In E. L. Bjork & R. A. Bjork (Eds.), *Memory.* San Diego: Academic Press.

Anderson, S. E., Dallal, G. E., & Must, A. (2003). Relative weight and race influence average age at menarche: Results from two nationally representative surveys of U.S. girls studied 25 years apart. *Pediatrics, 111,* 844–850.

Anderson, V. L., Levinson, E. M., Barker, W., & Kiewra, K. R. (1999). The effects of meditation on teacher perceived occupational stress, state and trait anxiety and burnout. *School Psychology Quarterly, 14,* 3–25.

Anderson, V. N. (1992). For whom is this world just? Sexual orientation and AIDS. *Journal of Applied Social Psychology, 22(3),* 248–259.

Anderson-Fye, E. P., & Becker, A. E. (2004). Sociocultural aspects of eating disorders and obesity. In J. K. Thompson (Ed.), *Handbook of eating disorders and obesity.* New York: Wiley.

Andersson, B. E. (1992). Effects of day-care on cognitive and socio-emotional competence of thirteen-year-old Swedish schoolchildren. *Child Development, 63,* 20–36.

Andreasen, N. C. (1987). Creativity and mental illness: Prevalence rates in writers and their first-degree relatives. *American Journal of Psychiatry, 144,* 1288–1292.

Andreasen, N. C. (1990). Positive and negative symptoms: Historical and conceptual aspects. In N. C. Andreasen (Ed.), *Modern problems of pharmacopsychiatry: Positive and negative symptoms and syndromes.* Basel: Karger.

Andreasen, N. C. (1996). Creativity and mental illness: A conceptual and historical overview. In J. J. Schildkraut & A. Otero (Eds.),

References

Abel, E. L. (1998). *Fetal alcohol abuse syndrome*. New York: Plenum.

Abel, M. H. (1998). Interaction of humor and gender in moderating relationships between stress and outcomes. *Journal of Psychology, 132,* 267–276.

Abi-Dargham, A. (2004). Do we still believe in the dopamine hypothesis? New data bring new evidence. *International Journal of Neuropsychopharmacology, 7*(Supplement 1), S1–S5.

Abi-Dargham, A., Gil, R., Krystal, J., Baldwin, R. M., Seibyl, J. P., Bowers, M., van Dyck, C. H., Charney, D. S., Innis, R. B., & Laruelle, M. (1998). Increased striatal dopamine transmission in schizophrenia: Confirmation in a second cohort. *American Journal of Psychiatry, 155,* 761–767.

Aboud, F. E., & Amato, M. (2001). Developmental and socialization influences on intergroup bias. In R. Brown & S. L. Gaertner (Eds.), *Blackwell handbook of social psychology: Intergroup processes.* Malden, MA: Blackwell.

Abraham, C. (2002). *Possessing genius*. New York, NY: St. Martin's Press.

Abramowitz, A. J., & O'Leary, S. G. (1990). Effectiveness of delayed punishment in an applied setting. *Behavior Therapy, 21,* 231–239.

Abrams, R. (1992). *Electroconvulsive therapy*. New York: Oxford University Press.

Abrams, R. (2000). Electroconvulsive therapy requires higher dosage levels: Food and Drug Administration action is required. *General Psychiatry, 57,* 445–446.

Abrams, R. L., Klinger, M. R., & Greenwald, A. G. (2002). Subliminal words activate semantic categories (not automated motor responses). *Psychonomic Bulletin & Review, 9*(1), 100–106.

Abramson, L. Y., Alloy, L. B., & Metalsky, J. I. (1995). Hopelessness depression. In J. N. Buchanan & M. E. P. Seligman (Eds.), *Explanatory style.* Hillsdale, NJ: Erlbaum.

Abramson, L. Y., Alloy, L. B., Hankin, B. L., Haeffel, G. J., MacCoon, D. G., & Gibb, B. E. (2002). Cognitive vulnerability-stress models of depression in a self-regulatory and pychobiological context. In I. H. Gotlib & C. L. Hammen (Eds.), *Handbook of depression.* New York: Guilford.

Abramson, L. Y., Seligman, M. E. P., & Teasdale, J. (1978). Learned helplessness in humans: Critique and reformulation. *Journal of Abnormal Psychology, 87,* 32–48.

Acker, M. M., & O'Leary, S. G. (1996). Inconsistency of mothers' feedback and toddlers' misbehavior and negative affect. *Journal of Abnormal Child Psychology, 24,* 703–714.

Ackerknecht, E. H. (1968). *A short history of psychiatry*. New York: Hafner Publishing Company.

Ackerman, P. L., & Beier, M. E. (2005). Knowledge and intelligence. In O. Wilhelm & R. W. Engle (Eds.), *Handbook of understanding and measuring intelligence.* Thousand Oaks, CA: Sage.

Adair, J. G. (2001). Ethics of psychological research: New policies; continuing issues; new concerns. *Canadian Psychology, 42,* 25–35.

Adamopoulos, J., & Lonner, W. J. (2001). Culture and psychology at a crossroad: Historical perspective and theoretical analysis. In D. Matsumoto (Ed.), *The handbook of culture and psychology.* New York: Oxford University Press.

Adams, G., Gullotta, T., & Montemayor, R. (1992). *Adolescent identity formation.* Newbury Park, CA: Sage.

Adams, H. E., Luscher, K. A., & Bernat, J. A. (2001). The classification of abnormal behavior: An overview. In P. B. Sutker & H. E. Adams (Eds.), *Comprehensive handbook of psychopathology.* New York: Kluwer Academic/Plenum.

Adams, H. E., Wright, L. W., Jr., & Lohr, B. A. (1996). Is homophobia associated with homosexual arousal? *Journal of Abnormal Psychology, 105,* 440–445.

Adams, J. L. (1980). *Conceptual blockbusting.* San Francisco: W. H. Freeman.

Adcock, C. J. (1965). Thematic Apperception Test. In O. K. Buros (Ed.), *Sixth Mental Measurements Yearbook.* Highland Park, NY: Gryphon Press.

Ader, R. (2001). Psychoneuroimmunology. *Current Directions in Psychological Science, 10*(3), 94–98.

Ader, R., & Cohen, N. (1984). Behavior and the immune system. In W. D. Gentry (Ed.), *Handbook of behavioral medicine.* New York: Guilford.

Ader, R., & Cohen, N. (1993). Psychoneuroimmunology: Conditioning and stress. *Annual Review of Psychology, 44,* 53–85.

Adler, A. (1917). *Study of organ inferiority and its psychical compensation.* New York: Nervous and Mental Diseases Publishing Co.

Adler, A. (1927). *Practice and theory of individual psychology.* New York: Harcourt, Brace & World.

Adler, L. L. (Ed.). (1993). *International handbook on gender roles.* Westport, CT: Greenwood.

Affleck, G., Tennen, H., Urrows, S., & Higgins, P. (1994). Person and contextual features of daily stress reactivity: Individual differences in relations of undesirable daily events with mood disturbance and chronic pain intensity. *Journal of Personality and Social Psychology, 66,* 329–340.

Agnoli, F., & Krantz, D. H. (1989). Suppressing natural heuristics by formal instruction: The case of the conjunction fallacy. *Cognitive Psychology, 21,* 515–550.

Agras, W. S., & Berkowitz, R. I. (1999). Behavior therapies. In R. E. Hales, S. C. Yudofsky, & J. A. Talbott (Eds.), *American Psychiatric Press textbook of psychiatry.* Washington, DC: American Psychiatric Press.

Ahima, R. S., & Osei, S. Y. (2004). Leptin signaling. *Physiology & Behavior, 81,* 223–241.

Ahn, H., & Wampold, B. E. (2001). Where oh where are the specific ingredients? A meta-analysis of component studies in counseling and psychotherapy. *Journal of Counseling Psychology, 48,* 251–257.

Aikins, D. E., & Craske, M. G. (2001). Cognitive theories of generalized anxiety disorder. *Psychiatric Clinics of North America, 24*(1), 57–74.

Ainsworth, M. D. S. (1979). Attachment as related to mother-infant interaction. In J. S. Rosenblatt, R. A. Hinde, C. Beer, & M. Busnel (Eds.), *Advances in the study of behavior* (Vol. 9). New York: Academic Press.

Ainsworth, M. D. S., Blehar, M. C., Waters, E., & Wall, S. (1978). *Patterns of attachment: A psychological study of the strange situation.* Hillsdale, NJ: Erlbaum.

Ajzen, I. (1985). From intentions to actions: A theory of planned behavior. In J. Kuhl & J. Beckman (Eds.), *Action-control: From cognition to behavior.* Heidelberg: Springer.

Ajzen, I. (1991). The theory of planned behavior. *Organizational Behavior and Human Decision Processes, 50,* 179–211.

Ajzen, I., & Fishbein, M. (2005). The influence of attitudes on behavior. In D. Albarracin, B. T. Johnson, & M. P. Zanna (Eds.), *The handbook of attitudes.* Mahwah, NJ: Erlbaum.

Akerstedt, T., Hume, K., Minors, D., & Waterhouse, J. (1997). Good sleep—its timing and physiological sleep characteristics. *Journal of Sleep Research, 6,* 221–229.

Akgun, S., & Ciarrochi, J. (2003). Learned resourcefulness moderates the relationship between academic stress and academic performance. *Educational Psychology, 23,* 287–294.

Akimoto, S. A., & Sanbonmatsu, D. M. (1999). Differences in self-effacing behavior between European and Japanese Americans: Effect on competence evaluations. *Journal of Cross-Cultural Psychology, 30,* 159–177.

Akiskal, H. S. (2000). Mood disorders: Clinical features. In B. J. Sadock & V. A. Sadock (Eds.), *Kaplan and Sadock's comprehensive textbook of psychiatry* (7th ed., Vol. 1, pp. 1338–1376). Philadelphia: Lippincott/Williams & Wilkins.

Albee, G. W. (1998). Fifty years of clinical psychology: Selling our soul to the devil. *Applied and Preventive Psychology, 7*(3), 189–194.

Albert, C. M., Ma, J., Rifai, N., Stampfer, M. J., & Ridker, P. M. (2002). Prospective study of C-reactive protein, homocysteine, and plasma lipid levels as predictors of sudden cardiac death. *Circulation, 105,* 2595–2599.

Albert, M. S., & Killiany, R. J. (2001). Age-related cognitive change and brain-behavior relationships. In J. E. Birren & K. W. Schaie (Eds.), *Handbook of the psychology of aging* (5th ed., pp. 160–184). San Diego, CA: Academic Press.

Albert, M. S., & Moss, M. B. (2002). Neuropsychological approaches to preclinical indentification of Alzheimers disease. In L. R. Squire & D. L. Schacter (Eds.), *Neuropsychology of memory.* New York: Guilford.

Albert, R. D. (1988). The place of culture in modern psychology. In P. Bronstein & K. Quina (Eds.), *Teaching a psychology of people: Resources for gender and sociocultural awareness.* Washington, DC: American Psychological Association.

Alcock, J. (1998). *Animal behavior: An evolutionary approach.* Sunderland, MA: Sinauer Associates.

Aldag, R. J., & Fuller, S. R. (1993). Beyond fiasco: A reappraisal of the groupthink phenomenon and a new model of group decision processes. *Psychological Bulletin, 113*, 533–552.

Aldrich, M. S. (2000). Cardinal manifestations of sleep disorders. In M. H. Kryger, T. Roth & W. C. Dement (Eds.), *Principles and practice of sleep medicine*. Philadelphia: Saunders.

Alexander, C. N., Davies, J. L., Dixon, C. A., Dillbeck, M. C., Druker, S. M., Oetzel, R. M., Muehlman, J. M., & Orme-Johnson, D. W. (1990). Growth of higher states of consciousness: The Vedic psychology of human development. In C. N. Alexander & E. J. Langer (Eds.), *Higher stages of human development: Perspectives on adult growth*. New York: Oxford University Press.

Alexander, C. N., Robinson, P., Orme-Johnson, D. W., Schneider, R. H., et al. (1994). The effects of transcendental meditation compared with other methods of relaxation and meditation in reducing risk factors, morbidity, and mortality. *Homeostasis in Health & Disease, 35*, 243–263.

Alexander, F. (1954). Psychoanalysis and psychotherapy. *Journal of the American Psychoanalytic Association, 2*, 722–733.

Alexander, F. G., & Selesnick, S. T. (1966). *The history of psychiatry: An evaluation of psychiatric thought and practice from prehistoric times to the present*. New York: Harper and Row.

Alexander, M. G., & Fisher, T. D. (2003). Truth and consequences: Using the bogus pipeline to examine sex differences in self-reported sexuality. *Journal of Sex Research, 40*(1), 27–35.

Alexander, J., & Tate, M. (1999). *Web wisdom: How to evaluate and create information quality on the web*. Mahwah, NJ: Erlbaum.

Allan, R. W. (1998). Operant-respondent interactions. In W. O'Donohue (Ed.), *Learning and behavior therapy*. Boston: Allyn & Bacon.

Allen, C. T., & Shimp, T. A. (1990). On using classical conditioning methods for researching the impact of ad-evoked feelings. In S. J. Agres, J. A. Edell, & T. M. Dubitsky (Eds.), *Emotion in advertising: Theoretical and practical explorations*. New York: Quorum Books.

Allen, M. J., Noel, R., Degan, J., Halpern, D. F., & Crawford, C. (2000). *Goals and objectives for the undergraduate psychology major: Recommendations from a meeting of the California State University psychology faculty*. Distributed by the Office of Teaching Resources in Psychology, Society for the Teaching of Psychology, http://www.lemoyne.edu/OTRP/otrpresources/otrpoutcomes.html.

Allen, M., Emmers, T., Gebhardt, L., & Giery, M. A. (1995). Exposure to pornography and acceptance of rape myths. *Journal of Communication, 45*, 5–26.

Allgood, W. P., Risko, V. J., Alvarez, M. C., & Fairbanks, M. M. (2000). Factors that influence study. In R. F. Flippo & D. C. Caverly (Eds.), *Handbook of college reading and study strategy research*. Mahwah, NJ: Erlbaum.

Allison, D. B., Fontaine, K. R., Manson, J. E., Stevens, J., & VanItallie, T. B. (1999). Annual deaths attributable to obesity in the United States. *Journal of the American Medical Association, 282*, 1530–1538.

Allison, D. B., Heshka, S., Neale, M. C., Lykken, D. T., & Heymsfield, S. B. (1994). A genetic analysis of relative weight among 4,020 twin pairs, with an emphasis on sex effects. *Health Psychology, 13*, 362–365.

Alloy, L. B., Abramson, L. Y., Whitehouse, W. G., Hogan, M. E., Tashman, N. A., Steinberg, D. L., Rose, D. T., & Donovan, P. (1999). Depressogenic cognitive styles: Predictive validity, information processing and personality characteristics, and developmental origins. *Behavioral Research and Therapy, 37*, 503–531.

Allport, G. W. (1937). *Personality: A psychological interpretation*. New York: Holt.

Alonso, A., Alonso, S., & Piper, W. (2003). Group psychotherapy. In G. Stricker & T. A. Widiger (Eds.), *Handbook of psychology, Vol. 8: Clinical psychology*. New York: Wiley.

Altman, I. (1990). Centripetal and centrifugal trends in psychology. In L. Brickman & H. Ellis (Eds.), *Preparing psychologists for the 21st century: Proceedings of the National Conference on Graduate Education in Psychology*. Hillsdale, NJ: Erlbaum.

Alvarez, P., & Squire, L. (1994). Memory consolidation and the medial temporal lobe: A simple network model. *Proceedings of the National Academy of Sciences, USA, 91*, 7041–7045.

Amabile, T. M. (1983). *The social psychology of creativity*. New York: Springer-Verlag.

Amabile, T. M. (1990). Within you, without you: The social psychology of creativity, and beyond. In M. A. Runco & R. S. Albert (Eds.), *Theories of creativity*. Newbury Park, CA: Sage.

Amabile, T. M. (1996). *Creativity in context*. Boulder, CO: Westview.

Amato, P. R. (2001). The consequences of divorce for adults and children. In R. M. Milardo (Ed.), *Understanding families into the new millenium: A decade in review*. Minneapolis: National Council on Family Relations.

Amato, P. R. (2003). Reconciling divergent perspectives: Judith Wallerstein, quantitative family research and children of divorce. *Family Relations: Interdisciplinary Journal of Applied Family Studies, 52*, 332–339.

Amato, P. R., & Keith, B. (1991). Parental divorce and adult well-being: A meta-analysis. *Journal of Marriage and the Family, 53*, 43–58.

Ambady, N., & Rosenthal, R. (1993). Half a minute: Predicting teacher evaluations from thin slices of nonverbal behavior and physical attractiveness. *Journal of Personality and Social Psychology, 64*, 431–441.

Ambady, N., Hallahan, M., & Conner, B. (1999). Accuracy of judgments of sexual orientation from thin slices of behavior. *Journal of Personality and Social Psychology, 77*, 538–547.

American Association on Mental Retardation. (1992). *Mental retardation: Definition, classification, and systems of supports*. Washington, DC: Author.

American Psychiatric Association Task Force on Electroconvulsive Therapy. (2001). *The practice of electroconvulsive therapy: Recommendations for treatment* (2nd ed.). Washington, DC: American Psychiatric Association.

American Psychiatric Association. (1994). *Diagnostic and statistical manual of mental disorders* (4th ed.). Washington, DC: Author.

American Psychiatric Association. (2000). *Diagnostic and statistical manual of mental disorders* (4th ed. Text revision). Washington, DC: Author.

American Psychological Association. (1998). Psychologists among Guggenheim winners. *APA Monitor, 29*, June 6, 1998. Retrieved May 13, 2005, from http://www.apa.org/monitor/jun98/gugg.html.

Anand, B. K., & Brobeck, J. R. (1951). Hypothalamic control of food intake in rats and cats. *Yale Journal of Biology and Medicine, 24*, 123–140.

Anch, A. M., Browman, C. P., Mitler, M. M., & Walsh, J. K. (1988). *Sleep: A scientific perspective*. Englewood Cliffs, NJ: Prentice-Hall.

Anderson, C., John, O. P., Keltner, D., & Kring, A. M. (2001). Who attains social status? Effects of personality and physical attractiveness in social groups. *Journal of Personality and Social Psychology, 81*(1), 116–132.

Anderson, E. A., Kohler, J. K., & Letiecq, B. L. (2002). Low-income fathers and "Responsible Fatherhood" programs: A qualitative investigation of participants' experiences. *Family Relations, 51*, 148–155.

Anderson, K. J. (1990). Arousal and the inverted-U hypothesis: A critique of Neiss's "reconceptualizing arousal." *Psychological Bulletin, 107*, 96–100.

Anderson, M. C., & Neely, J. H. (1996). Interference and inhibition in memory retrieval. In E. L. Bjork & R. A. Bjork (Eds.), *Memory*. San Diego: Academic Press.

Anderson, S. E., Dallal, G. E., & Must, A. (2003). Relative weight and race influence average age at menarche: Results from two nationally representative surveys of U.S. girls studied 25 years apart. *Pediatrics, 111*, 844–850.

Anderson, V. L., Levinson, E. M., Barker, W., & Kiewra, K. R. (1999). The effects of meditation on teacher perceived occupational stress, state and trait anxiety and burnout. *School Psychology Quarterly, 14*, 3–25.

Anderson, V. N. (1992). For whom is this world just? Sexual orientation and AIDS. *Journal of Applied Social Psychology, 22*(3), 248–259.

Anderson-Fye, E. P., & Becker, A. E. (2004). Sociocultural aspects of eating disorders and obesity. In J. K. Thompson (Ed.), *Handbook of eating disorders and obesity*. New York: Wiley.

Andersson, B. E. (1992). Effects of day-care on cognitive and socio-emotional competence of thirteen-year-old Swedish schoolchildren. *Child Development, 63*, 20–36.

Andreasen, N. C. (1987). Creativity and mental illness: Prevalence rates in writers and their first-degree relatives. *American Journal of Psychiatry, 144*, 1288–1292.

Andreasen, N. C. (1990). Positive and negative symptoms: Historical and conceptual aspects. In N. C. Andreasen (Ed.), *Modern problems of pharmacopsychiatry: Positive and negative symptoms and syndromes*. Basel: Karger.

Andreasen, N. C. (1996). Creativity and mental illness: A conceptual and historical overview. In J. J. Schildkraut & A. Otero (Eds.),

Reuptake A process in which neurotransmitters are sponged up from the synaptic cleft by the presynaptic membrane.

Reversible figure A drawing that is compatible with two different interpretations that can shift back and forth.

Risky decision making Making choices under conditions of uncertainty.

Rods Specialized visual receptors that play a key role in night vision and peripheral vision.

S

Sample The collection of subjects selected for observation in an empirical study.

Sampling bias A problem that occurs when a sample is not representative of the population from which it is drawn.

Scatter diagram A graph in which paired *X* and *Y* scores for each subject are plotted as single points.

Schedule of reinforcement A specific presentation of reinforcers over time.

Schema An organized cluster of knowledge about a particular object or sequence of events.

Schizophrenic disorders A class of psychological disorders marked by disturbances in thought that spill over to affect perceptual, social, and emotional processes.

Secondary (conditioned) reinforcers Stimulus events that acquire reinforcing qualities by being associated with primary reinforcers.

Secondary sex characteristics Physical features that are associated with gender but that are not directly involved in reproduction.

Sedatives Sleep-inducing drugs that tend to decrease central nervous system activation and behavioural activity.

Self-actualizing persons People with exceptionally healthy personalities, marked by continued personal growth.

Self-concept A collection of beliefs about one's own nature, unique qualities, and typical behaviour.

Self-efficacy One's belief about one's ability to perform behaviours that should lead to expected outcomes.

Self-enhancement Focusing on positive feedback from others, exaggerating one's strengths, and seeing oneself as above average.

Self-esteem A person's overall assessment of her or his personal adequacy or worth.

Self-monitoring The degree to which people attend to and control the impression they make on others in social interactions.

Self-referent encoding Deciding how or whether information is personally relevant.

Self-report inventories Personality tests that ask individuals to answer a series of questions about their characteristic behaviour.

Self-serving bias The tendency to attribute one's successes to personal factors and one's failures to situational factors.

Semantic memory system General knowledge that is not tied to the time when the information was learned.

Semantic network Concepts joined together by links that show how the concepts are related.

Semantics The area of language concerned with understanding the meaning of words and word combinations.

Sensation The stimulation of sense organs.

Sensation seeking A generalized preference for high or low levels of sensory stimulation.

Sensory adaptation A gradual decline in sensitivity to prolonged stimulation.

Sensory memory The preservation of information in its original sensory form for a brief time, usually only a fraction of a second.

Separation anxiety Emotional distress seen in many infants when they are separated from people with whom they have formed an attachment.

Serial-position effect In memory tests, the fact that subjects show better recall for items at the beginning and end of a list than for items in the middle.

Set-point theory The idea that the body monitors fat-cell levels to keep them (and weight) fairly stable.

Settling-point theory The idea that weight tends to drift around a level at which the constellation of factors that determine food consumption and energy expenditure achieve an equilibrium.

Sex The biologically based categories of male and female.

Sexual orientation A person's preference for emotional and sexual relationships with individuals of the same sex, the other sex, or either sex.

Shaping The reinforcement of closer and closer approximations of a desired response.

Short-term memory (STM) A limited-capacity store that can maintain unrehearsed information for about 20 to 30 seconds.

Signal-detection theory A psychophysiological theory proposing that the detection of stimuli involves decision processes as well as sensory processes, which are influenced by a variety of factors besides the physical intensity of a stimulus.

Skinner box A small enclosure in which an animal can make a specific response that is systematically recorded while the consequences of the response are controlled.

Sleep apnea A sleep disorder characterized by frequent reflexive gasping for air that awakens a person and disrupts sleep.

Slow-wave sleep (SWS) Sleep stages 3 and 4, during which low-frequency delta waves become prominent in EEG recordings.

Social desirability bias A tendency to give socially approved answers to questions about oneself.

Social loafing A reduction in effort by individuals when they work in groups as compared to when they work by themselves.

Social psychology The branch of psychology concerned with the way individuals' thoughts, feelings, and behaviours are influenced by others.

Social schemas Organized clusters of ideas about categories of social events and people.

Social skills training A behaviour therapy designed to improve interpersonal skills that emphasizes shaping, modelling, and behavioural rehearsal.

Social support Various types of aid and succour provided by members of one's social networks.

Socialization The acquisition of the norms, roles, and behaviours expected of people in a particular society.

Soma The cell body of a neuron; it contains the nucleus and much of the chemical machinery common to most cells.

Somatic nervous system The system of nerves that connect to voluntary skeletal muscles and to sensory receptors.

Somatization disorder A type of somatoform disorder marked by a history of diverse physical complaints that appear to be psychological in origin.

Somatoform disorders A class of psychological disorders involving physical ailments with no authentic organic basis that are due to psychological factors.

Somnambulism (sleepwalking) Arising and wandering about while remaining asleep.

Source The person who sends a communication.

Source monitoring The process of making attributions about the origins of memories.

Source-monitoring error An error that occurs when a memory derived from one source is misattributed to another source.

Split-brain surgery A procedure in which the bundle of fibres that connects the cerebral hemispheres (the corpus callosum) is cut to reduce the severity of epileptic seizures.

Spontaneous recovery In classical conditioning, the reappearance of an extinguished response after a period of nonexposure to the conditioned stimulus.

Spontaneous remission Recovery from a disorder without formal treatment.

SQ3R A study system designed to promote effective reading by means of five steps: survey, question, read, recite, and review.

Stage A developmental period during which characteristic patterns of behaviour are exhibited and certain capacities become established.

Standard deviation An index of the amount of variability in a set of data.

Standardization The uniform procedures used in the administration and scoring of a test.

Statistical significance The condition that exists when the probability that the observed findings are due to chance is very low.

Statistics The use of mathematics to organize, summarize, and interpret numerical data. See also *Descriptive statistics, Inferential statistics*.

Stereotypes Widely held beliefs that people have certain characteristics because of their membership in a particular group.

Stimulants Drugs that tend to increase central nervous system activation and behavioural activity.

Stimulus Any detectable input from the environment.

Stimulus discrimination The phenomenon that occurs when an organism that has learned a response to a specific stimulus does not respond in the same way to stimuli that are similar to the original stimulus.

Stimulus generalization The phenomenon that occurs when an organism that has learned a response to a specific stimulus responds in the same way to new stimuli that are similar to the original stimulus.

Storage Maintaining encoded information in memory over time.

Stress Any circumstances that threaten or are perceived to threaten one's well-being and that thereby tax one's coping abilities.

Striving for superiority According to Adler, the universal drive to adapt, improve oneself, and master life's challenges.

Structuralism A school of psychology based on the notion that the task of psychology is to analyze consciousness into its basic elements and to investigate how these elements are related.

Subjective contours The perception of contours where none actually exist.

Subjective well-being Individuals' perceptions of their overall happiness and life satisfaction.

Subjects The persons or animals whose behaviour is systematically observed in a study.

Subliminal perception The registration of sensory input without conscious awareness.

Subtractive colour mixing Formation of colours by removing some wavelengths of light, leaving less light than was originally there.

Superego According to Freud, the moral component of personality that incorporates social standards about what represents right and wrong.

Survey A descriptive research method in which researchers use questionnaires or interviews to gather information about specific aspects of subjects' behaviour.

Sympathetic division The branch of the autonomic nervous system that mobilizes the body's resources for emergencies.

Synapse A junction where information is transmitted from one neuron to the next.

Synaptic cleft A microscopic gap between the terminal button of a neuron and the cell membrane of another neuron.

Syntax A system of rules that specify how words can be combined into phrases and sentences.

Systematic desensitization A behaviour therapy used to reduce clients' anxiety responses through counterconditioning.

T

Tactile system The sensory system for touch.

Tardive dyskinesia A neurological disorder marked by chronic tremors and involuntary spastic movements.

Telegraphic speech Speech that consists mainly of content words; articles, prepositions, and other less critical words are omitted.

Temperament An individual's characteristic mood, activity level, and emotional reactivity.

Terminal buttons Small knobs at the end of axons that secrete chemicals called neurotransmitters.

Test norms Standards that provide information about where a score on a psychological test ranks in relation to other scores on that test.

Testwiseness The ability to use the characteristics and format of a cognitive test to maximize one's score.

Thalamus A structure in the forebrain through which all sensory information (except smell) must pass to get to the cerebral cortex.

Theory A system of interrelated ideas that is used to explain a set of observations.

Theory of bounded rationality Simon's assertion that people tend to use simple strategies in decision making that focus on only a few facets of available options and often result in "irrational" decisions that are less than optimal.

Threshold A dividing point between energy levels that do and do not have a detectable effect.

Tip-of-the-tongue phenomenon A temporary inability to remember something accompanied by a feeling that it's just out of reach.

Token economy A system for doling out symbolic reinforcers that are exchanged later for a variety of genuine reinforcers.

Tolerance A progressive decrease in a person's responsiveness to a drug.

Top-down processing In form perception, a progression from the whole to the elements.

Transfer-appropriate processing The situation that occurs when the initial processing of information is similar to the type of processing required by the subsequent measures of attention.

Transference In therapy, the phenomenon that occurs when clients start relating to their therapists in ways that mimic critical relationships in their lives.

Trial In classical conditioning, any presentation of a stimulus or pair of stimuli.

Trial and error Trying possible solutions sequentially and discarding those that are in error until one works.

Trichromatic theory The theory of colour vision holding that the human eye has three types of receptors with differing sensitivities to different wavelengths.

Twin studies A research design in which hereditary influence is assessed by comparing the resemblance of identical twins and fraternal twins with respect to a trait.

Type A personality Personality characterized by (1) a strong competitive orientation, (2) impatience and time urgency, and (3) anger and hostility.

Type B personality Personality characterized by relatively relaxed, patient, easygoing, amicable behaviour.

U

Unconditioned response (UCR) An unlearned reaction to an unconditioned stimulus that occurs without previous conditioning.

Unconditioned stimulus (UCS) A stimulus that evokes an unconditioned response without previous conditioning.

Unconscious According to Freud, thoughts, memories, and desires that are well below the surface of conscious awareness but that nonetheless exert great influence on behaviour.

Underextensions Errors that occur when a child incorrectly uses a word to describe a narrower set of objects or actions than it is meant to.

Undifferentiated schizophrenia A type of schizophrenia marked by idiosyncratic mixtures of schizophrenic symptoms.

V

Validity The ability of a test to measure what it was designed to measure.

Variability The extent to which the scores in a data set tend to vary from each other and from the mean.

Variable-interval (VI) schedule A reinforcement schedule in which the reinforcer is given for the first response after a variable time interval has elapsed.

Variable-ratio (VR) schedule A reinforcement schedule in which the reinforcer is given after a variable number of nonreinforced responses.

Variables Any measurable conditions, events, characteristics, or behaviours that are controlled or observed in a study.

Vasocongestion Engorgement of blood vessels.

Vestibular system The sensory system that responds to gravity and keeps people informed of their body's location in space.

Visual agnosia An inability to recognize objects.

Volley principle The theory holding that groups of auditory nerve fibres fire neural impulses in rapid succession, creating volleys of impulses.

W

Weber's law The theory stating that the size of a just noticeable difference is a constant proportion of the size of the initial stimulus.

Z

Zygote A one-celled organism formed by the union of a sperm and an egg.

Depression and the spiritual in modern art: Homage to Miro. New York: Wiley.

Andreasen, N. C. (2001). *Brave new brain: Conquering mental illness in the era of the human genome.* New York: Oxford University Press.

Andres, R. L., & Day, M.-C. (2000). Perinatal complications associated with maternal tobacco use. *Seminars in Neonatology, 5,* 231–241.

Angell, M. (2000). Is academic medicine for sale? *New England Journal of Medicine, 342,* 1516–1518.

Anglin, J. M. (1993). Vocabulary development: A morphological analysis. *Monographs of the Society for Research in Child Development, 58.*

Angoff, W. H. (1988). The nature-nurture debate, aptitudes, and group differences. *American Psychologist, 43*(9), 713–720.

Anisman, H, & Merali, Z. (1999). Understanding stress: Characteristics and caveats. *Alcohol Research and Health, 23,* 241–249.

Ansbacher, H. (1970, February). Alfred Adler, individual psychology. *Psychology Today,* pp. 42–44, 66.

Anthenelli, R. M., & Schuckit, M. A. (1997). Genetics. In J. H. Lowinson, P. Ruiz, R. B. Millman, & J. G. Langrod (Eds.), *Substance abuse: A comprehensive textbook.* Baltimore: Williams & Wilkins.

Antony, M. M. & Swinson, R. P. (1996). *Anxiety disorders: Future directions for research and treatment (A discussion paper).* Retrieved April 27, 2005, from http://www.phac-aspc.gc.ca/mh-sm/mentalhealth/pubs/anxiety/index.html.

Antony, M. M., & McCabe, R. E. (2003). Anxiety disorders: Social and specific phobias. In A. Tasman, J. Kay, & J. A. Lieberman (Eds.), *Psychiatry.* New York: Wiley.

Antony, M. M., Ledley, D. R., Liss, A., & Swinson, R. P. (in press). Responses to symptom induction exercises in panic disorder. *Behavior Research and Therapy.*

Antrobus, J. (1993). Characteristics of dreams. In M. A. Carskadon (Ed.), *Encyclopedia of sleep and dreaming.* New York: Macmillan.

Antrobus, J. (2000). Theories of dreaming. In M. H. Kryger, T. Roth & W. C. Dement (Eds.), *Principles and practice of sleep medicine.* Philadelphia: Saunders.

Appleby, T. (2005). Kingston police more likely to stop blacks, study finds. *Toronto Star,* May 27, 2005, p. A12.

Archer, J. (1996). Sex differences in social behavior: Are the social role

and evolutionary explanations compatible? *American Psychologist, 51,* 909–917.

Archer, J. (2005). Are women or men the more aggressive sex? In S. Fein, G. R. Goethals, & M. J. Sansdtrom (Eds.), *Gender and aggression: Interdisciplinary perspectives.* Mahwah, NJ: Erlbaum.

Archibald, A. B., Graber, J. A., & Brooks–Gunn, J. (2003). Pubertal processes and physiological growth in adolescence. In G. R. Adams & M. D. Berzonsky (Eds.), *Blackwell handbook of adolescence.* Malden, MA: Blackwell Publishing.

Arendt, J., & Skene, D. J. (2005). Melatonin as a chronobiotic. *Sleep Medicine Review, 9*(1), 25–39.

Arendt, J., Stone, B., & Skene, D. (2000). Jet lag and sleep disruption. In M. H. Kryger, T. Roth & W. C. Dement (Eds.), *Principles and practice of sleep medicine.* Philadelphia: Saunders.

Arendt, J., Stone, B., & Skene, D. J. (2005). Sleep disruption in jet lag and other circadian rhythm-related disorders. In M. H. Kryger, T. Roth, & W. C. Dement (Eds.). *Principles and practice of sleep medicine.* Philadelphia: Elsevier Saunders.

Argyle, M. (1987). *The psychology of happiness.* London: Metheun.

Argyle, M. (1999). Causes and correlates of happiness. In D. Kahneman, E. Diener & N. Schwarz (Eds.), *Well-being: The foundations of hedonic psychology.* New York: Russell Sage Foundation.

Argyle, M. (2001). *The psychology of happiness.* New York: Routledge.

Arkes, H. R., Wortmann, R. L., Saville, P. D., & Harkness, A. R. (1981). Hindsight bias among physicians weighing the likelihood of diagnoses. *Journal of Applied Psychology, 66,* 252–254.

Arkowitz, H. (1992). Integrative theories of therapy. In D. K. Freedheim (Ed.), *History of psychotherapy: A century of change.* Washington, DC: American Psychological Association.

Armbruster, B. B. (2000). Taking notes from lectures. In R. F. Flippo & D. C. Caverly (Eds.), *Handbook of college reading and study strategy research.* Mahwah, NJ: Erlbaum.

Armitage, C. J., & Conner, M. (2000). Attitudinal ambivalence: A test of three key hypotheses. *Personality and Social Psychology Bulletin, 26,* 1421–1432.

Armony, J. L., & LeDoux, J. E. (2000). How danger is encoded: Toward a systems, cellular, and computational understanding of cognitive-emotional interactions in fear. In M. S. Gazzaniga (Ed.), *The*

new cognitive neurosciences (2nd ed., pp. 1067–1080). Cambridge, MA: MIT Press.

Arnett, J. J. (1996). Sensation seeking, aggressiveness, and adolescent reckless behavior. *Personality & Individual Differences, 20,* 693–702.

Arnett, J. J. (1999). Adolescent storm and stress, reconsidered. *American Psychologist, 54,* 317–326.

Arnkoff, D. B., & Glass, C. R. (1992). Cognitive therapy and psychotherapy. In D. K. Freedheim (Ed.), *History of psychotherapy: A century of change.* Washington, DC: American Psychological Association.

Arnold, L. M. (2000). Psychocutaneous disorders. In B. J. Sadock & V. A. Sadock (Eds.), *Kaplan and Sadock's comprehensive textbook of psychiatry* (7th ed., pp. 1818–1827). Philadelphia: Lippincott/Williams & Wilkins.

Aron, A. (1970). Relationship variables in human heterosexual attraction. Microfilm of typescript: Canadian theses on microfilm, no. 8501. Ottawa, National Library of Canada.

Aronson, E. (2000). *Nobody left to hate: Teaching compassion after Columbine.* New York: W. H. Freeman.

Aronson, E., & Mills, J. (1959). The effect of severity of initiation on liking for a group. *Journal of Abnormal and Social Psychology, 59,* 177–181.

Aronson, J., Lustina, M. J., Good, C., Keough, K., Steele, C. M., & Brown, J. (1999). When white men can't do math: Necessary and sufficient factors in stereotype threat. *Journal of Experimental Social Psychology, 35,* 29–46.

Arrigo, J. M., & Pezdek, K. (1997). Lessons from the study of psychogenic amnesia. *Current Directions in Psychological Science, 6,* 148–152.

Asch, S. (1946). Forming impressions on personality. *Journal of Abnormal and Social Psychology, 41,* 258–290.

Asch, S. (1951). Effects of group pressure upon the modification and distortion of judgments. In H. Guetzkow (Ed.), *Groups, leadership and men: Research in human relations* (pp. 177–190). Oxford, England: Carnegie Press.

Asch, S. E. (1955). Opinions and social pressures. *Scientific American, 193*(5), 31–35.

Asch, S. E. (1956). Studies of independence and conformity: A minority of one against a unanimous majority. *Psychological Monographs, 70*(9, Whole No. 416).

Asendorpf, J. B., & Ostendorf, F. (1998). Is self-enhancement healthy? Conceptual, psychometric, and empirical analysis. *Journal of Personality and Social Psychology, 74,* 955–966.

Aserinsky, E., & Kleitman, N. (1953). Regularly occurring periods of eye mobility and concomitant phenomena during sleep. *Science, 118,* 273–274.

Ashford, J. W., Mattson, M., & Kumar, V. (1998). Neurobiological systems disrupted by Alzheimer's disease and molecular biological theories of vulnerability. In V. Kumar & C. Eisdorfer (Eds.), *Advances in the diagnosis and treatment of Alzheimer's disease.* New York: Springer Publishing Company.

Ashton, M. C., Lee, K., Perugini, M. , Szarota, P., de Vries, R. E., Di Blas, L., Boies, K., & De Raad, B. (2004). A six-factor structure of personality descriptive adjectives: Solutions from psycholexical studies in seven languages. *Journal of Personality and Social Psychology, 86*(2), 356–366.

Aslin, R. N., Saffran, J. R., & Newport, E. L. (1999). Statistical learning in linguistic and nonlinguistic domains. In B. MacWhinney (Ed.), *The emergence of language* (pp. 359–380). Mahwah, NJ: Erlbaum.

Aspinwall, L. G., Richter, L., & Hoffman R. R., III. (2001). Understanding how optimism works: An examination of optimists' adaptive moderation of belief and behavior. In E. C. Chang (Ed.), *Optimism and pessimism: Implications for theory, research, and practice* (pp. 217–238). Washington, DC: American Psychological Association.

Athens 2004: The Official Website of the Athens 2004 Olympic Games. (2004). Retrieved May 2, 2005, from http://www.athens2004.com/en/OlympicMedals/medals

Atkinson, J. W. (1974). The mainsprings of achievement-oriented activity. In J. W. Atkinson & J. O. Raynor (Eds.), *Motivation and achievement.* New York: Wiley.

Atkinson, J. W. (1981). Studying personality in the context of an advanced motivational psychology. *American Psychologist, 36,* 117–128.

Atkinson, J. W. (1992). Motivational determinants of thematic apperception. In C. P. Smith (Ed.), *Motivation and personality: Handbook of thematic content analysis.* New York: Cambridge University Press.

Atkinson, J. W., & Birch, D. (1978). *Introduction to motivation.* New York: Van Nostrand.

Atkinson, J. W., & Litwin, G. H. (1960). Achievement motive and test anxiety conceived as motive to approach success and to avoid failure. *Journal of Abnormal and Social Psychology, 60,* 52–63.

Atkinson, R. C., & Shiffrin, R. M. (1968). Human memory: A proposed system and its control processes. In K. W. Spence & J. T. Spence (Eds.), *The psychology of learning and motivation* (Vol. 2). New York: Academic Press.

Atkinson, R. C., & Shiffrin, R. M. (1971). The control of short-term memory. *Scientific American, 225,* 82–90.

Austin, J. T., & Hanisch, K. A. (1990). Occupational attainment as a function of abilities and interests: A longitudinal analysis using Project TALENT data. *Journal of Applied Psychology, 75,* 77–86.

Averill, J. A. (1980). A constructivist view of emotion. In R. Plutchik & H. Kellerman (Eds.), *Emotion: Theory, research, and experience: Vol. 1. Theories of emotion.* New York: Academic Press.

Avis, N. E. (1999). Women's health at midlife. In S. L. Willis & J. D. Reid (Eds.), *Life in the middle: Psychological and social development in middle age* (pp. 105–146). San Diego, CA: Academic Press.

Axel, R. (1995, April). The molecular logic of smell. *Scientific American, 273,* 154–159.

Ayanian, J. Z., & Cleary, P. D. (1999). Perceived risks of heart disease and cancer among cigarette smokers. *Journal of the American Medical Association, 281,* 1019–1021.

Ayers, M. S., & Reder, L. M. (1998). A theoretical review of the misinformation effect: Predictions from an activation-based memory model. *Psychonomic Bulletin & Review, 5,* 1–21.

Ayres, J. J. B. (1998). Fear conditioning and avoidance. In W. O'Donohue (Ed.), *Learning and behavior therapy.* Boston: Allyn & Bacon.

Baars, B. J. (1986). *The cognitive revolution in psychology.* New York: Guilford.

Baccus, J. R., Baldwin, M. W., & Packer, D. J. (2004). Increasing implicit self-esteem through classical conditioning. *Psychological Science, 15,* 498–505.

Bäckman, L., Small, B. J., & Wahlin, Å. (2001). Aging and memory: Cognitive and biological perspectives. In J. E. Birren & K. W. Schaie (Eds.), *Handbook of the psychology of aging* (5th ed.,

pp. 348–376). San Diego, CA: Academic Press.

Bäckman, L., Small, B. J., Wahlin, Å., & Larsson, M. (1999). Cognitive functioning in very old age. In F. I. M. Craik & T. A. Salthouse (Eds.), *Handbook of cognitive aging* (Vol. 2, pp. 499–558). Mahwah, NJ: Erlbaum.

Baddeley, A. D. (1986). *Working memory.* New York: Oxford University Press.

Baddeley, A. D. (1989). The uses of working memory. In P. R. Soloman, G. R. Goethals, C. M. Kelley, & B. R. Stephens (Eds.), *Memory: Interdisciplinary approaches.* New York: Springer-Verlag.

Baddeley, A. D. (1992). Working memory. *Science, 255,* 556–559.

Baddeley, A. D. (2001). Is working memory still working? *American Psychologist, 56,* 851–864.

Baddeley, A. D., & Hitch, G. (1974). Working memory. In G. H. Bower (Ed.), *The psychology of learning and motivation* (Vol. 8). New York: Academic Press.

Badia, P. (1990). Memories in sleep: Old and new. In R. R. Bootzin, J. F. Kihlstrom, & D. L. Schacter (Eds.), *Sleep and cognition.* Washington, DC: American Psychological Association.

Baenninger, M., & Newcombe, N. (1995). Environmental input to the development of sex-related differences in spatial and mathematical ability. *Learning & Individual Differences, 7,* 363–379.

Baenninger, R. (1997). On yawning and its functions. *Psychonomic Bulletin & Review, 4,* 198–207.

Baer, J. (1994). Divergent thinking is not a general trait: A multidomain training experiment. *Creativity Research Journal, 7,* 35–36.

Bahrick, H. P. (2000). Long-term maintenance of knowledge. In E. Tulving & F. I. M. Craik (Eds.), *The Oxford handbook of memory* (pp. 347–362). New York: Oxford University Press.

Bailey, J. M. (2003). Biological perspectives on sexual orientation. In L. D. Garnets & D. C. Kimmel (Eds.), *Psychological perspectives on lesbian, gay, and bisexual experiences.* New York: Columbia University Press.

Bailey, J. M., & Pillard, R. C. (1991). A genetic study of male homosexual orientation. *Archives of General Psychology, 48,* 1089–1097.

Bailey, J. M., & Zucker, K. J. (1995). Childhood sex-typed behavior and sexual orientation: A conceptual analysis and quantitative review. *Developmental Psychology, 31,* 43–55.

Bailey, J. M., Dunne, M. P., & Martin, N. G. (2000). Genetic and environmental influences on sexual orientation and its correlates in an Australian twin sample. *Journal of Personality and Social Psychology, 78,* 524–536.

Bailey, J. M., Pillard, R. C., Neale, M. C. I., & Agyei, Y. (1993). Heritable factors influence sexual orientation in women. *Archives of General Psychiatry, 50,* 217–223.

Baillargeon, R. (1987). Object permanence in 3.5- and 4.5-month-old infants. *Developmental Psychology, 23,* 655–664.

Baillargeon, R. (1994). How do infants learn about the physical world? *Current Directions in Psychological Science, 3,* 133–140.

Baillargeon, R. (2002). The acquisition of physical knowledge in infancy: A summary in eight lessons. In U. Goswami (Ed.), *Blackwell handbook of childhood cognitive development.* Malden, MA: Blackwell Publishing.

Baillargeon, R. (2004). Infants' physical world. *Current Directions in Psychological Science, 13*(3), 89–94.

Bakan, P. (1971, August). The eyes have it. *Psychology Today,* pp. 64–69.

Baker, F., Ainsworth, S. R., Dye, J. T., Crammer, C., Thun, M. J., Hoffmann, D., Repace, J. L., Henningfield, J. E., Slade, J., Pinney, J., Shanks, T., Burns, D. M., Connolly, G. N., & Shopland, D. R. (2000). Health risks associated with cigar smoking. *Journal of the American Medical Association, 284,* 735–740.

Baldessarini, R. J. (2001). Drugs and the treatment of psychiatric disorders: Depression and the anxiety disorders. In J. G. Hardman & L. E. Limbird (Eds.), *Goodman & Gilman's the pharmacological basis of therapeutics.* New York: McGraw-Hill.

Baldwin, M. (2001). Does Bob Zajonc ever scowl at you from the back of your mind? In J. Bargh & D. Apsley (Eds.), *Unravelling the complexities of social life: A festschrift in honor of Robert B. Zajonc* (pp. 55–67). Washington, DC: American Psychological Association.

Baldwin, M. W. (1992). Relational schemas and the processing of social information. *Psychological Bulletin, 112,* 461–484.

Baldwin, M. W., & Main, K. J. (2001). The cued activation of relational schemas in social anxiety. *Personality and Social Psychology Bulletin, 27,* 1637–1647.

Baldwin, M. W., Baccus, J. R., & Fitzsimons, G. M. (2004). Self-

esteem and the dual processing of interpersonal contingencies. *Self and Identity, 3,* 81–93.

Baldwin, M. W., Carrell, S. E., & Lopez, D. F. (1990). Priming relationship schemas: My advisor and the Pope are watching me from the back of my mind. *Journal of Experimental Social Psychology, 26,* 435–454.

Baldwin, W. (2000). Information no one else knows: The value of self-report. In A. A. Stone, J. S. Turkkan, C. A. Bachrach, J. B. Jobe, H. S. Kurtzman & V. Cain (Eds.), *The science of self-report: Implications for research and practice.* Mahwah, NJ: Erlbaum.

Ball, H. L., Hooker, E., & Kelly, P. J. (2000). Parent-infant co-sleeping: Father's roles and perspectives. *Infant and Child Development, 9*(2), 67–74.

Ballenger, J. C. (2000). Benzodiazepine receptor agonists and antagonists. In B. J. Sadock & V. A. Sadock (Eds.), *Kaplan and Sadock's comprehensive textbook of psychiatry.* Philadelphia: Lippincott/Williams & Wilkins.

Balsam, P. D. (1988). Selection, representation, and equivalence of controlling stimuli. In R. C. Atkinson, R. J. Herrnstein, G. Lindzey, & R. D. Luce (Eds.), *Stevens' handbook of experimental psychology.* New York: Wiley.

Baltes, P. B., Staudinger, U. M., & Lindenberger, U. (1999). Lifespan psychology: Theory and application to intellectual functioning. *Annual Review of Psychology, 50,* 471–507.

Bandura, A. (1965). Influence of model's reinforcement contingencies on the acquisition of imitated responses. *Journal of Personality and Social Psychology, 1,* 589–595.

Bandura, A. (1977). *Social learning theory.* Englewood Cliffs, NJ: Prentice-Hall.

Bandura, A. (1982). The psychology of chance encounters and life paths. *American Psychologist, 37,* 747–755.

Bandura, A. (1986). *Social foundations of thought and action: A social-cognitive theory.* Englewood Cliffs, NJ: Prentice-Hall.

Bandura, A. (1990). Perceived self-efficacy in the exercise of personal agency. *Journal of Applied Sport Psychology, 2*(2), 128–163.

Bandura, A. (1993). Perceived self-efficacy in cognitive development and functioning. *Educational Psychologist, 28*(2), 117–148.

Bandura, A. (1995). Exercise of personal and collective efficacy in changing societies. In A. Bandura (Ed.), *Self-efficacy in changing soci-*

eties. New York: Cambridge University Press.

Bandura, A. (1999a). Social cognitive theory of personality. In L. A. Pervin, & O. P. John (Eds.), *Handbook of personality: Theory and research*. New York: Guilford.

Bandura, A. (1999b). A sociocognitive analysis of substance abuse: An agentic perspective. *Psychological Science, 10*(3), 214–217.

Bandura, A. (2001). Social cognitive theory: An agentic perspective. *Annual Review of Psychology, 52,* 1–26.

Bandura, A. (2001). The changing face of psychology at the dawning of a globalization era. *Canadian Psychology, 42,* 12–25.

Bandura, A., & Walters, R. H. (1959). *Adolescent aggression: A study of the influence of child-training practices and family interrelationships.* New York: The Ronald Press Company.

Bandura, A., & Walters, R. H. (1963). *Social learning and personality development.* New York: Holt, Rinehart & Winston, Inc.

Bandura, A., Ross, D., & Ross, S. A. (1961). Transmission of aggression through imitation of aggressive models. *Journal of Abnormal and Social Psychology, 63,* 575–582.

Bandura, A., Ross, D., & Ross, S. A. (1963a). Imitation of film-mediated aggressive models. *Journal of Abnormal and Social Psychology, 66*(1), 3–11.

Bandura, A., Ross, D., & Ross, S. A. (1963b). Vicarious reinforcement and imitative learning. *Journal of Abnormal and Social Psychology, 67*(6), 601–607.

Banich, M. T., & Heller, W. (1998). Evolving perspectives on lateralization of function. *Current Directions in Psychological Science, 7,* 1.

Banks, W. P., & Krajicek, D. (1991). Perception. *Annual Review of Psychology, 42,* 305–331.

Banyard, V. L., & Williams, L. M. (1999). Memories for child sexual abuse and mental health functioning: Findings on a sample of women and implications for future research. In L. M. Williams & V. L. Banyard (Eds.), *Trauma & memory.* Thousand Oaks, CA: Sage Publications.

Banyard, V. L., Plante, E. G., Cohn, E. S., Moorhead, C., Ward, S., & Walsh, W. (2005). Revisiting unwanted sexual experiences on campus: A 12-year follow-up. *Violence Against Women, 11,* 426–446.

Barba, G. D., Parlato, V., Jobert, A., Samson, Y., & Pappata, S. (1998). Cortical networks implicated in semantic and episodic memory: Common or unique. *Cortex, 34,* 547–561.

Barber, B. K. (1994). Cultural, family, and personal contexts of parent-adolescent conflict. *Journal of Marriage and the Family, 56,* 375–386.

Barber, T. X. (1979). Suggested ("hypnotic") behavior: The trance paradigm versus an alternative paradigm. In E. Fromm & R. E. Shor (Eds.), *Hypnosis: Developments in research and new perspectives.* New York: Aldine.

Barber, T. X. (1986). Realities of stage hypnosis. In B. Zilbergeld, M. G. Edelstien, & D. L. Araoz (Eds.), *Hypnosis: Questions and answers.* New York: Norton.

Barch, D. M. (2003). Cognition in schizophrenia: Does working memory work? *Current Directions in Psychological Science, 12*(4), 146–150.

Bard, P. (1934). On emotional experience after decortication with some remarks on theoretical views. *Psychological Review, 41,* 309–329.

Bargh, J. A. (1999). The cognitive monster: The case against the controllability of automatic stereotype effects. In S. Chaiken & Y. Trope (Eds.), *Dual-process theories in social psychology.* New York: Guilford.

Bargh, J. A., & McKenna, K. Y. A. (2004). The Internet and social life. *Annual Review of Psychology, 55,* 573–590.

Barlett, D. L., & Steele, J. B. (1979). *Empire: The life, legend and madness of Howard Hughes.* New York: Norton.

Barlow, D. H., Pincus, D. B., Heinrichs, N., & Choate, M. L. (2003). Anxiety disorders. In G. Stricker & T. A. Widiger (Eds.), *Handbook of psychology, Vol. 8: Clinical psychology.* New York: Wiley.

Barnes, V. A., Treiber, F., & Davis, H. (2001). The impact of Transcendental Meditation on cardiovascular function at rest and during acute stress in adolescents with high normal blood pressure. *Journal of Psychosomatic Research, 51,* 597–605.

Barnett, W. S. (1995). Long-term effects of early childhood programs on cognitive and school outcomes. *Future of Children, 5,* 25–50.

Barnier, A. J. (2002). Posthypnotic amnesia for autobiographical episodes: A laboratory model of functional amnesia. *Psychological Science, 13,* 232–237.

Barnier, A. J., & McConkey, K. M. (1998). Posthypnotic responding away from the hypnotic setting. *Psychological Science, 9,* 256–262.

Baron, R. S., Vandello, J. A., & Brunsman, B. (1996). The forgotten variable in conformity research: Impact of task importance on social influence. *Journal of Personality and Social Psychology, 71,* 915–927.

Bar-On, R., & Parker, J. D. A. (2000a). *Bar-On Emotional Quotient Inventory (Youth Version): Technical manual.* Toronto: Multi-Health Systems.

Bar-On, R., & Parker, J. D. A. (2000b). *Handbook of emotional intelligence: Theory, development, assessment, and application at home, school, and in the workplace.* San Francisco, CA: Jossey-Bass.

Barrett, D. (1988–1989). Dreams of death. *Omega, 19*(2), 95–101.

Barrett, M. (1995). Early lexical development. In P. Fletcher & B. MacWhinney (Eds.), *The handbook of child language.* Cambridge, MA: Blackwell.

Barry-Walsh, J. (2005). Dissociative identity disorder. *Australian & New Zealand Journal of Psychiatry, 39*(1–2), 109–110.

Barsky, A. J. (1988). The paradox of health. *New England Journal of Medicine, 318,* 414–418.

Barsky, A. J. (2001). Somatosensory amplification and hypochondriasis. In V. Starcevic & D. R. Lipsitt (Eds.), *Hypochondriasis: Modern perspectives on an ancient malady.* New York: Oxford University Press.

Barsky, A. J., Coeytaux, R. R., Sarnie, M. K., & Cleary, P. D. (1993). Hypochondriacal patients' beliefs about good health. *American Journal of Psychiatry, 150,* 1085–1090.

Bartlett, F. C. (1932). *Remembering: A study in experimental and social psychology.* New York: Macmillan.

Bartoshuk, L. M. (1993a). Genetic and pathological taste variation: What can we learn from animal models and human disease? In D. Chadwick, J. Marsh, & J. Goode (Eds.), *The molecular basis of smell and taste transduction.* New York: Wiley.

Bartoshuk, L. M. (1993b). The biological basis of food perception and acceptance. *Food Quality and Preference, 4,* 21–32.

Bartoshuk, L. M., & Beauchamp, G. K. (1994). Chemical senses. *Annual Review of Psychology, 45,* 419–449.

Bartoshuk, L. M., Duffy, V. B., & Miller, I. J. (1994). PTC/PROP taste: Anatomy, psychophysics, and sex effects. *Physiology & Behavior, 56,* 1165–1171.

Bartsch, K., & Wellman, H. M. (1995). *Children talk about the mind.* New York: Oxford University Press.

Basbaum, A. I., & Jessel, T. M. (2000). The perception of pain. In E. R. Kandel, J. H. Schwartz, & T. M. Jessell (Eds.), *Principles of neural science.* New York: McGraw-Hill.

Bashore, T. R., Ridderinkhof, K. R., & van der Molen, M. W. (1997). The decline of cognitive processing speed in old age. *Current Directions in Psychological Science, 6,* 163–169.

Basow, S. A. (1992). *Gender: Stereotypes and roles.* Pacific Grove, CA: Brooks/Cole.

Bassili, J. N., & Provencal, A. (1988). Perceiving minorities: A factor-analytic approach. *Personality and Social Psychology Bulletin, 14,* 5–15.

Bassiri, A. B., & Guilleminault, C. (2000). Clinical features and evaluation of obstructive sleep apnea-hypopnea syndrome. In M. H. Kryger, T. Roth & W. C. Dement (Eds.), *Principles and practice of sleep medicine.* Philadelphia: Saunders.

Bassok, M. (2003). Analogical transfer in problem solving. In J. E. Davidson & R. J. Sternberg (Eds.), *The psychology of problem solving.* New York: Cambridge University Press.

Bassuk, E. L., Buckner, J. C., Perloff, J. N., & Bassuk, S. S. (1998). Prevalence of mental health and substance use disorders among homeless and low-income housed mothers. *American Journal of Psychiatry, 155,* 1561–1564.

Bates, E. (1999). Plasticity, localization, and language development. In S. H. Broman & J. M. Fletcher (Eds.), *The changing nervous system: Neurobehavioral consequences of early brain disorders* (pp. 214–247). New York: Oxford University Press.

Bates, E., & Carnevale, G. (1993). New directions in research on language development. *Developmental Review, 13,* 436–70.

Bates, E., Devescovi, A., & Wulfeck, B. (2001). Psycholinguistics: A cross-language perspective. *Annual Review of Psychology, 52,* 369–396.

Bates, M. S., Edwards, W. T., & Anderson, K. O. (1993). Ethnocultural influences on variation in chronic pain perception. *Pain, 52*(1), 101–112.

Bauer, M. I., & Johnson-Laird, P. N. (1993). How diagrams can improve reasoning. *Psychological Science, 4,* 372–378.

Bauer, M. S. (2003). Mood disorders: Bipolar (manic-depressive) disorders. In A. Tasman, J. Kay, & J. A.

Lieberman (Eds.), *Psychiatry*. New York: Wiley.

Baum, A., Grunberg, N. E., & Singer, J. E. (1992). Biochemical measurements in the study of emotion. *Psychological Science, 3,* 56–60.

Baumeister, R. F. (1984). Choking under pressure: Self-consciousness and paradoxical effects of incentives on skillful performance. *Journal of Personality and Social Psychology, 46,* 610–620.

Baumeister, R. F. (1989). The optimal margin of illusion. *Journal of Social and Clinical Psychology, 8,* 176–189.

Baumeister, R. F. (1995). Disputing the effects of championship pressures and home audiences. *Journal of Personality and Social Psychology, 68,* 644–648.

Baumeister, R. F., & Steinhilber, A. (1984). Paradoxical effects of supportive audiences on performance under pressure: The home field disadvantage in sports championships. *Journal of Personality and Social Psychology, 47,* 85–93.

Baumeister, R. F., & Twenge, J. M. (2002). Cultural suppression of female sexuality. *Review of General Psychology, 6,* 166–203.

Baumeister, R. F., Bratslavsky, E., Finkenauer, C., & Vohs, K. D. (2001). Bad is stronger than good. *Review of General Psychology, 5,* 323–370.

Baumeister, R. F., Catanese, K. R., & Vohs, K. D. (2001). Is there a gender difference in strength of sex drive? Theoretical views, conceptual distinctions and a review of relevant evidence. *Personality and Social Psychology Review, 5,* 242–273.

Baumeister, R. J., & Leary, M. R. (1995). The need to belong: Desire for interpersonal attachments as a fundamental human motivation. *Psychological Bulletin, 117,* 497–529.

Baumrind, D. (1964). Some thoughts on the ethics of reading Milgram's "Behavioral study of obedience." *American Psychologist, 19,* 421–423.

Baumrind, D. (1985). Research using intentional deception: Ethical issues revisited. *American Psychologist, 40,* 165–174.

Baumrind, D., Larzelere, R. E., & Cowan, P. A. (2002). Ordinary physical punishment: Is it harmful? Comment on Gershoff. *Psychological Bulletin, 128,* 580–589.

Bauserman, R. (1996). Sexual aggression and pornography: A review of correlational research. *Basic and Applied Social Psychology, 18,* 405–427.

Baycrest Centre for Geriatric Care. (2004). *Memory-link program.*

Retrieved May 18, 2005 from http://www.baycrest.org/psychology/psychology/program_mem_link.htm.

Baylis, G. C., & Driver, J. (1995). One-sided edge assignment in vision: 1. Figure-ground segmentation and attention to objects. *Current Directions in Psychological Science, 4,* 140–146.

Beahrs, J. O. (1983). Co-consciousness: A common denominator in hypnosis, multiple personality and normalcy. *American Journal of Clinical Hypnosis, 26*(2), 100–113.

Beck, A. T. (1976). *Cognitive therapy and the emotional disorders.* New York: International Universities Press.

Beck, A. T. (1983). Cognitive therapy of depression: New perspectives. In P. J. Clayton & J. E. Barrett (Eds.), *Treatment of depression: Old controversies and new approaches* (pp. 265–290). New York: Raven Press.

Beck, A. T. (1987). Cognitive therapy. In J. K. Zeig (Ed.), *The evolution of psychotherapy.* New York: Brunner/Mazel.

Beck, A. T. (1991). Cognitive therapy: A 30-year retrospective. *American Psychologist, 46,* 368–375.

Beck, A. T. (1997). Cognitive therapy: Reflections. In J. K. Zeig (Ed.), *The evolution of psychotherapy: The third conference.* New York: Brunner/Mazel.

Beck, A. T., Rector, N. A. (2004). Cognitive approaches to schizophrenia: Theory and therapy. *Annual Review of Clinical Psychology, 1,* 577–606.

Beck, J. (1995). *Cognitive therapy: Basics and beyond.* New York: Guilford.

Beckham, J. C., Moore, S. D., Feldman, M. E., Hertzberg, M. A., Kirby, A. C., & Fairbank, J. A. (1998). Health status, somatization, and severity of posttraumatic stress disorder in Vietnam combat veterans with posttraumatic stress disorder. *American Journal of Psychiatry, 155,* 1565–1569.

Beeman, M. J., & Chiarello, C. (1998). Complementary right and left hemisphere language comprehension. *Current Directions in Psychological Science, 7,* 2–7.

Beer, J. M., Arnold, R. D., & Loehlin, J. C. (1998). Genetic and environmental influences on MMPI Factor Scales: Joint model fitting to twin and adoption data. *Journal of Personality and Social Psychology, 74,* 818–827.

Beers, M., Lassiter, G. D., & Flannery, B. C. (1997). Individual differences in person memory: Self-

monitoring and the recall of consistent and inconsistent behavior. *Journal of Social Behavior and Personality, 12,* 811–820.

Behling, O. (1998). Employee selection: Will intelligence and conscientiousness do the job? *Academy of Management, 12,* 77–86.

Beilin, H. (1992). Piaget's enduring contribution to developmental psychology. *Developmental Psychology, 28,* 191–204.

Beilock, S. L., & Carr, T. H. (2005). When high-powered people fail: Working memory and "choking under pressure" in math. *Psychological Science, 16,* 101–105.

Beilock, S. L., Carr, T. H., MacMahon, C., & Starkes, J. L. (2002). When paying attention becomes counterproductive: Impact of divided versus skill-focused attention on novice and experienced performance of sensorimotor skills. *Journal of Experimental Psychology: Applied, 8*(1), 6–16.

Beilock, S. L., Kulp, C. A., Holt, L. E., & Carr, T. H. (2004). More on the fragility of performance: Choking under pressure in mathematical problem solving. *Journal of Experimental Psychology: General, 133,* 584–600.

Beisecker, A. E. (1990). Patient power in doctor-patient communication: What do we know? *Health Communication, 2,* 105–122.

Beiser, M. (1999). *Strangers at the gate: The "Boat People's" first ten years in Canada.* Toronto: University of Toronto Press.

Békésy, G. von. (1947). The variation of phase along the basilar membrane with sinusoidal vibrations. *Journal of the Acoustical Society of America, 19,* 452–460.

Bell, A. P., Weinberg, M. S., & Hammersmith, S. K. (1981). *Sexual preference: Its development in men and women.* Bloomington: Indiana University Press.

Bellack, A. S., Gearon, J. S., & Blanchard, J. J. (2000). Schizophrenia: Psychopathology. In M. Hersen & A. S. Bellack (Eds.), *Psychopathology in adulthood.* Boston: Allyn & Bacon.

Bellack, A. S., Mueser, K. T., & Gingerich, J. A. (2004). *Social skills training for schizophrenia: A step-by-step guide.* New York: Guilford.

Beller, M., & Gafni, N. (1996). The 1991 international assessment of educational progress in mathematics and sciences: The gender differences perspective. *Journal of Educational Psychology, 88,* 365–377.

Bellezza, F. S. (1996). Mnemonic methods to enhance storage and retrieval. In E. L. Bjork & R. A.

Bjork (Eds.), *Memory.* San Diego: Academic Press.

Belli, R. F., Winkielman, P., Read, J. D., Schwarz, N., & Lynn, S. J. (1998). Recalling more childhood events leads to judgments of poorer memory: Implications for the recovered/false memory debate. *Psychonomic Bulletin & Review, 5,* 318–323.

Bellinger, D. C., & Adams, H. F. (2001). Environmental pollutant exposures and children's cognitive abilities. In R. J. Sternberg & E. L. Grigorenko (Eds.), *Environmental effects on cognitive abilities.* Mahwah, NJ: Erlbaum.

Belsky, J. (1988). The "effects" of infant day care reconsidered. *Early Childhood Research Quarterly, 3,* 235–272.

Belsky, J. (1990). Children and marriage. In F. D. Fincham & T. N. Bradbury (Eds.), *The psychology of marriage: Basic issues and applications.* New York: Guilford.

Belsky, J. (1992). Consequences of child care for children's development: A deconstructionist view. In A. Booth (Ed.), *Child care in the 1990s.* Hillsdale, NJ: Erlbaum.

Belsky, J. (1999a). Interactional and contextual determinants of attachment security. In J. Cassidy & P. R. Shaver (Eds.), *Handbook of attachment: Theory, research and clinical applications.* New York: Guilford.

Belsky, J. (1999b). Modern evolutionary theory and patterns of attachment. In J. Cassidy & P. R. Shaver (Eds.), *Handbook of attachment: Theory, research and clinical applications.* New York: Guilford.

Belsky, J., & Kelly, J. (1994). *The transition to parenthood.* New York: Dell.

Belsky, J., Steinberg, L., & Draper, P. (1991). Childhood experience, interpersonal development, and reproductive strategy: An evolutionary theory of socialization. *Child Development, 62,* 647–670.

Bem, D. J. (1967). Self-perception: An alternative interpretation of cognitive dissonance phenomena. *Psychological Review, 74,* 183–200.

Bem, S. L. (1985). Androgyny and gender schema theory: A conceptual and empirical integration. In T. B. Sonderegger (Ed.), *Nebraska symposium on motivation, 1984: Psychology and gender* (Vol. 32). Lincoln: University of Nebraska Press.

Bem, S. L. (1993). *The lenses of gender: Transforming the debate on sexual inequality.* New Haven: Yale University Press.

Benca, R. M. (2001). Consequences of insomnia and its therapies. *Journal of Clinical Psychiatry, 62* (suppl 10), 33–38.

Bender, R., Jockel, K. H., Trautner, C., Spraul, M., & Berger, M. (1999). Effect of age on excess mortality in obesity. *Journal of the American Medical Association, 281,* 1498–1504.

Bendersky, M., & Lewis, M. (1999). Prenatal cocaine exposure and neonatal condition. *Infant Behavior & Development, 22,* 353–366.

Benet, V., & Waller, N. G. (1995). The big seven factor model of personality description: Evidence for its cross-cultural generality in a Spanish sample. *Journal of Personality and Social Psychology, 69,* 701–718.

Benham, M. L. (1975). *Nellie McClung.* Toronto: Fitzhenry & Whiteside, Ltd.

Benjamin, L. T., Jr. (2000). The psychology laboratory at the turn of the 20th century. *American Psychologist, 55,* 318–321.

Benjamin, L. T., Jr., Cavell, T. A., & Shallenberger, W. R., III. (1984). Staying with initial answers on objective tests: Is it a myth? *Teaching of Psychology, 11,* 133–141.

Benjamin, L. T., Jr., DeLeon, P. H., Freedheim, D. K., & VandenBos, G. R. (2003). Psychology as a profession. In D. K. Freedheim (Ed.), *Handbook of psychology, Vol. 1: History of psychology.* New York: Wiley.

Bennett, H. L. (1993). The mind during surgery: The uncertain effects of anesthesia. *Advances, 9*(1), 5–16.

Ben-Porath, Y. S. (2003). Assessing personality and psychopathology with self-report inventories. In J. R. Graham & J. A. Naglieri (Eds.), *Handbook of psychology, Volume 10: Assessment psychology.* New York: Wiley.

Benson, H. (1975). *The relaxation response.* New York: Morrow.

Benson, H., & Klipper, M. Z. (1988). *The relaxation response.* New York: Avon.

Bentler, P. M., & Woodward, J. A. (1978). A Head Start reevaluation: Positive effects are not yet demonstrable. *Evaluation Quarterly, 2,* 493–510.

Bereczkei, T. (2000). Evolutionary psychology: A new perspective in the behavioral sciences. *European Psychologist, 5*(3), 175–190.

Berenbaum, S. A., & Snyder, E. (1995). Early hormonal influences on childhood sex-typed activity and playmate preferences: Implications for the development of sexual orientation. *Developmental Psychology, 31,* 31–42.

Bergin, A. E. (1971). The evaluation of therapeutic outcomes. In A. E. Bergin & S. L. Garfield (Eds.), *Handbook of psychotherapy and behavior change: An empirical analysis.* New York: Wiley.

Berkowitz, L. (1989). Frustration-aggression hypothesis: Examination and reformulation. *Psychological Bulletin, 106,* 59–73.

Berkowitz, L. (1999). Evil is more than banal: Situationism and concept of evil. *Personality and Social Psychology Review, 3,* 246–253.

Berkowitz, R. I. (2003). Behavior therapies. In R. E. Hales & S. C. Yudofsky (Eds.), *Textbook of Clinical Psychiatry.* Washington, DC: American Psychiatric Publishing.

Berlin, B., & Kay, P. (1969). *Basic color terms: Their universality and evolution.* Berkeley, CA: University of California Press.

Berliner, L., & Briere, J. (1999). Trauma, memory, and clinical practice. In L. M. Williams & V. L. Banyard (Eds.), *Trauma & memory.* Thousand Oaks, CA: Sage Publications.

Berman, R. F. (1991). Electrical brain stimulation used to study mechanisms and models of memory. In J. L. Martinez Jr. & R. P. Kesner (Eds.), *Learning and memory: A biological view.* San Diego: Academic Press.

Berndsen, M., Spears, R., van der Plight, J., & McGarty, C. (2002). Illusory correlation and stereotype formation: Making sense of group differences and cognitive biases. In C. McGarty, V. Y. Yzerbyt, & R. Spears (Eds.), *Stereotypes as explanations: The formation of meaningful beliefs about social groups.* New York: Cambridge University Press.

Bernhardt, P. C. (1997). Influences of serotonin and testosterone in aggression and dominance: Convergence with social psychology. *Current Directions in Psychological Science, 6,* 44–48.

Bernstein, H. J., Beale, M. D., Burns, C., & Kellner, C. H. (1998). Patient attitudes about ECT after treatment. *Psychiatric Annuals,* 524–527.

Berridge, K. C. (2004). Motivation concepts in behavioral neuroscience. *Physiology and Behavior, 81*(2), 179–209.

Berridge, K. C., & Robinson, T. E. (1998). What is the role of dopamine in reward: Hedonic impact, reward learning, or incentive salience? *Brain Research Reviews, 28,* 309–369.

Berry, D. T. R., Wetter, M. W., & Baer, R. A. (1995). Assessment of malingering. In J. N. Butcher (Ed.), *Clinical personality assessment: Practical approaches.* New York: Oxford University Press.

Berry, J. W. (1984). Towards a universal psychology of cognitive competence. In P. S. Fry (Ed.), *Changing conceptions of intelligence and intellectual functioning* (pp. 35–61). Amsterdam: Elsevier Science Publishers.

Berry, J. W. (1990). Cultural variations in cognitive style. In S. P. Wapner (Ed.), *Bio-psycho-social factors in cognitive style.* Hillsdale, NJ: Erlbaum.

Berry, J. W. (1994). Cross-cultural variations in intelligence. In R. J. Sternberg (Ed.), *Encyclopedia of human intelligence.* New York: Macmillan.

Berry, J. W., Poortinga, Y., Segall, M., & Dasen, P. (1992). *Cross-cultural psychology.* New York: Cambridge University Press.

Berscheid, E. (1988). Some comments on love's anatomy: Or, whatever happened to old-fashioned lust. In R. J. Sternberg & M. L. Barnes (Eds.), *The psychology of love.* New Haven: Yale University Press.

Berscheid, E., & Walster, E. (1978). *Interpersonal attraction.* Reading, MA: Addison-Wesley.

Bertenthal, B. I., & Clifton, R. K. (1998). Perception and action. In W. Damon (Ed.), *Handbook of child psychology (Vol. 2): Cognition, perception, and language.* New York: Wiley.

Berzonsky, M., & Adams, G. (1999). Commentary: Reevaluating the identity status paradigm: Still useful after 35 years. *Developmental Review, 19,* 557–590.

Beumont, P. J. V. (2002). Clinical presentation of anorexia nervosa and bulimia nervosa. In C. G. Fairburn & K. D. Brownell (Eds.), *Eating disorders and obesity: A comprehensive handbook.* New York: Guilford.

Beutler, L. E. (2002). The dodo bird is extinct. *Clinical Psychology: Science & Practice, 9*(1), 30–34.

Beutler, L. E., & Harwood, T. M. (2002). What is and can be attributed to the therapeutic relationship? *Journal of Contemporary Psychotherapy, 32*(1), 25–33.

Beutler, L. E., Bongar, B., & Shurkin, J. N. (1998). *Am I crazy, or is it my shrink?* New York: Oxford University Press.

Beutler, L. E., Machado, P. P. P., & Neufeldt, S. A. (1994). Therapist variables. In A. E. Bergin & S. L. Garfield (Eds.), *Handbook of psychotherapy and behavior change* (4th ed.). New York: Wiley.

Beutler, L. E., Malik, M., Alimohamed, S., Harwood, T. M., Talebi, H., Noble, S., & Wong, E. (2004). Therapist variables. In M. J. Lambert (Ed.), *Bergin and Garfield's handbook of psychotherapy and behavior change.* New York: Wiley.

Beutler, L. E., Rocco, F., Moleiro, C. M., & Talebi, H. (2001). Resistance. *Psychotherapy: Theory, Research, Practice, Training, 38,* 431–436.

Bhandari, A. (2005). Guess who's coming to dinner? *The Globe and Mail,* March 12, 2005, p. F7.

Bhattachary, S., & Powell, J. H. (2001). Recreational use of 3,4-methylenedioxymethamphetamine (MDMA) or "ecstasy": Evidence for cognitive impairment. *Psychological Medicine, 31,* 647–658.

Bialystok, E. (1991). Metalinguistic dimensions of bilingual language proficiency. In E. Bialystok (Ed.), *Language processing in bilingual children* (pp. 113–140). New York, NY: Cambridge University Press.

Bialystok, E. (1999). Cognitive complexity and attentional control in the bilingual mind. *Child Development, 70,* 636–644.

Bialystok, E. (2001). *Bilingualism in development: Language, literacy and cognition.* Cambridge, UK: Cambridge University Press.

Bialystok, E., Craik, F. I. M., Klein, R., & Viswanathan, M. (2004). Bilingualism, aging, and cognitive control: Evidence from the Simon task. *Cognition and Aging, 19,* 290–303.

Bialystok, E., Majumder, S., & Martin, M. (2003). Developing phonological awareness: Is there a bilingual advantage? *Applied Psycholinguistics, 24,* 27–44.

Biederman, I., Hilton, H. J., & Hummel, J. E. (1991). Pattern goodness and pattern recognition. In G. R. Lockhead & J. R. Pomerantz (Eds.), *The perception of structure.* Washington, DC: American Psychological Association.

Biehl, M., Matsumoto, D., Ekman, P., Hearn, V., Heider, K., Kudoh, T., & Ton, V. (1997). Matsumoto and Ekman's Japanese and Caucasian Facial Expressions of Emotion (JACFEE): Reliability data and cross-national differences. *Journal of Nonverbal Behavior, 21,* 3–21.

Bierut, L. J., Heath, A. C., Bucholz, K. K., Dinwiddie, S. H., Madden, P. A. F., Statham, D. J., Dunne, M. P., & Martin, N. G. (1999). Major depressive disorder in a community-based twin sample. *Archives of General Psychiatry, 56,* 557–563.

Bigler, E. D., Blatter, D. D., Anderson, C. V., Johnson, S. C., Gale, S. D., Hopkins, R. O., & Burnett, B. (1997). Hippocampal volume in normal aging and traumatic brain injury. *American Journal of Neuroradiology, 18,* 11–23.

Binet, A. (1911). Nouvelle recherches sur la mesure du niveau intellectuel chez les enfants d'école. *L'Année Psychologique, 17,* 145–201.

Binet, A., & Simon, T. (1905). Méthodes nouvelles pour le diagnostic du niveau intellectuel des anormaux. *L'Année Psychologique, 11,* 191–244.

Binet, A., & Simon, T. (1908). Le développement de l'intelligence chez les enfants. *L'Année Psychologique, 14,* 1–94.

Birch, L. L., & Fisher, J. A. (1996). The role of experience in the development of children's eating behavior. In E. D. Capaldi (Ed.), *Why we eat what we eat: The psychology of eating* (pp. 113–143). Washington, DC: American Psychological Association.

Birdsong, D. (1999). Introduction: Whys and why nots of the critical period hypothesis for second language acquisition. In D. Birdsong (Ed.), *Second language acquisition and the critical period hypothesis* (pp. 1–22). Mahwah, NJ: Erlbaum.

Birnbaum, M. H. (2004). Base rates in Bayesian inference. In F. P. Rudiger (Ed.), *Cognitive illusions.* New York: Psychology Press.

Bishop, K. M., & Wahlsten, D. (1997). Sex differences in the human corpus callosum: Myth or reality? *Neuroscience and Biobehavioral Reviews, 12,* 581–601.

Bishop, S. R. (2002). What do we really know about mindfulness-based stress reduction? *Psychosomatic Medicine, 64*(1), 71–83.

Bjork, R. A. (1992). Interference and forgetting. In L. R. Squire (Ed.), *Encyclopedia of learning and memory.* New York: Macmillan.

Bjorklund, D. F. (1997). In search of a metatheory for cognitive development (or, Piaget is dead and I don't feel so good myself). *Child Development, 68,* 144–148.

Bjorklund, D. F. (2000). *Children's thinking: Developmental function and individual differences.* Belmont, CA: Wadsworth.

Bjorklund, D. F. (2005). *Children's thinking: Cognitive development and individual differences.* Belmont, CA: Wadsworth.

Black, D. W. (2001). Antisocial personality disorder: The forgotten patients of psychiatry. *Primary Psychiatry, 8*(1), 30–81.

Black, D. W., & Andreasen, N. C. (1999). Schizophrenia, schizophreniform disorder, and delusional (paranoid) disorders. In R. E. Hales, S. C. Yudofsky, & J. A. Talbott (Eds.), *American Psychiatric Press textbook of psychiatry* (3rd ed.). Washington, DC: American Psychiatric Press.

Blacker, D., & Tsuang, M. T. (1999). Classification and DSM-IV. In A. M. Nicholi (Ed.), *The Harvard guide to psychiatry.* Cambridge, MA: Harvard University Press.

Blacker, L. (1999). The launching phase of the life cycle. In B. Carter & M. McGoldrick (Eds.), *The expanded family life cycle: Individual, family, and social perspectives* (3rd ed., pp. 287–306). Boston: Allyn & Bacon.

Blagrove, M. (1992). Dreams as a reflection of our waking concerns and abilities: A critique of the problem-solving paradigm in dream research. *Dreaming, 2,* 205–220.

Blagrove, M. (1996). Problems with the cognitive psychological modeling of dreaming. *Journal of Mind and Behavior, 17,* 99–134.

Blair, S. L. (1993). Employment, family, and perceptions of marital quality among husbands and wives. *Journal of Family Issues, 14,* 189–212.

Blair, S. N., Kohl, H. W., Paffenbarger, R. S., Clark, D. G., Cooper, K. H., & Gibbons, L. W. (1989). Physical fitness and all-cause mortality: A prospective study of healthy men and women. *Journal of the American Medical Association, 262,* 2395–2401.

Blakeslee, T. R. (1980). *The right brain.* Garden City, NY: Doubleday/Anchor.

Blanchard, E. B., & Keefer, L. (2003). Irritable bowel syndrome. In A. M. Nezu, C. M. Nezu, & P. A. Geller (Eds.), *Handbook of psychology, Vol. 9: Health psychology.* New York: Wiley.

Blanchard, F. A., Lilly, T., & Vaughn, L. A. (1991). Reducing the expression of racial prejudice. *Psychological Science, 2,* 101–105.

Blanchard, R., Zucker, K. J., Bradley, S. J., & Hume, C. S. (1995). Birth order and siblings sex ratio in homosexual male adolescents and probably prehomosexual feminine boys. *Developmental Psychology, 31,* 22–30.

Blanco, C., Laje, G., Olfson, M., Marcus, S. C., & Pincus, H. A. (2002). Trends in the treatment of bipolar disorder by outpatient psychiatrists. *American Journal of Psychiatry, 159,* 1005–1010.

Blankenhorn, D. (1995). *Fatherless America: Confronting our most urgent social problem.* New York: Basic Books.

Blascovich, J., Wyer, N. A., Swart, L. A., & Kibler, J. L. (1997). Racism and racial categorization. *Journal of Personality and Social Psychology, 72,* 1364–1372.

Blashfield, R. K., & Livesley, W. J. (1999). Classification. In T. Millon, P. H. Blaney, & R. D. Davis (Eds.), *Oxford textbook of psychopathology.* New York: Oxford University Press.

Blass, T. (1991). Understanding behavior in the Milgram obedience experiment: The role of personality, situations, and their interactions. *Journal of Personality and Social Psychology, 60,* 398–413.

Blass, T. (1999). The Milgram Paradigm after 35 years: Some things we now know about obedience to authority. *Journal of Applied Social Psychology, 29,* 955–978.

Blatt, S. J. (1974). Levels of object representation in anaclitic and introjective depression. *Psychoanalytic Study of the Child, 29* (10), 7–157.

Blatt, S. J. (1995). Interpersonal relatedness and self-definition: Two personality configurations and their implications for psychopathology and psychotherapy, In J. L. Singer (Ed.), *Repression and dissociation: Implications for personality theory, psychopathology, and health* (pp. 299–335). Chicago: University of Chicago Press.

Blau, Z. S. (1981). *Black children/white children: Competence, socialization and social structure.* New York: Free Press.

Bleuler, E. (1911). *Dementia praecox or the group F schizophrenias.* New York: International Universities Press.

Blieszner, R., & Adams, R. G. (1992). *Adult friendship.* Newbury Park, CA: Sage.

Bliwise, D. L. (2000). Normal aging. In M. H. Kryger, T. Roth, & W. C. Dement (Eds.), *Principles and practice of sleep medicine.* Philadelphia: Saunders.

Bliwise, D. L. (2005). Normal aging. In M. H. Kryger, T. Roth, & W. C. Dement (Eds.), *Principles and practice of sleep medicine.* Philadelphia: Elsevier Saunders.

Block, J. (1981). Some enduring and consequential structures of personality. In A. I. Rabins, J. Aronoff, A. Barclay, & R. Zucker (Eds.), *Further explorations in personality.* New York: Wiley.

Block, J. (1995). A contrarian view of the five-factor approach to personality description. *Psychological Bulletin, 117,* 187–215.

Block, J. R., & Yuker, H. E. (1992). *Can you believe your eyes?: Over 250 illusions and other visual oddities.* New York: Brunner/Mazel.

Block, L. G., & Keller, P. A. (1997). Effects of self-efficacy and vividness on the persuasiveness of health communication. *Journal of Consumer Psychology, 6,* 31–54.

Bloodworth, R. C. (1987). Major problems associated with marijuana abuse. *Psychiatric Medicine, 3*(3), 173–184.

Bloom, B. L. (1984). *Community mental health: A general introduction.* Pacific Grove, CA: Brooks/Cole.

Bloom, B. S. (Ed.). (1985). *Developing talent in young people.* New York: Ballantine.

Bloomfield, H. H., & Kory, R. B. (1976). *Happiness: The TM program, psychiatry, and enlightenment.* New York: Simon & Schuster.

Blundell, J. E., & Halford, J. C. G. (1998). Serotonin and appetite regulation: Implications for the pharmacological treatment of obesity. *CNS Drugs, 9,* 473–495.

Boatswain, S., Brown, N., Fiksenbaum, L., Goldstein, L., Greenglass, E. R., Nadler, E., & Pyke, S. (2001). Canadian feminist psychology: Where are they now? *Canadian Psychology, 42,* 276–286.

Bock, G. R., & Goode, J. A. (Eds.). (1996). *Genetics of criminal and antisocial behavior.* Chichester, England: Wiley.

Boden, J. M., & Baumeister, R. F. (1997). Repressive coping: Distraction using pleasant thoughts and memories. *Journal of Personality and Social Psychology, 73,* 45–62.

Bodenheimer, T. (2000). Uneasy alliance: Clinical investigators and the pharmaceutical industry. *New England Journal of Medicine, 342,* 1539–1544.

Boehm, L. E. (1994). The validity effect: A search for mediating variables. *Personality and Social Psychology Bulletin, 20,* 285–293.

Bogaert, A. F. (1996). Volunteer bias in human sexuality research: Evidence for both sexuality and personality differences in males. *Archives of Sexual Behavior, 25,* 125–142.

Bogartz, R. S., & Shinskey, J. L. (1998). On perception of a partially occluded object in 6-month-olds. *Cognitive Development, 13,* 141–163.

Bogen, J. E. (1985). The dual brain: Some historical and methodological aspects. In D. F. Benson & E. Zaidel

(Eds.), *The dual brain: Hemispheric specialization in humans.* New York: Guilford.

Bogen, J. E. (1990). Partial hemispheric independence with the neocommissures intact. In C. Trevarthen (Ed.), *Brain circuits and functions of the mind. Essays in honor of Roger W. Sperry.* Cambridge, MA: Cambridge University Press.

Bogen, J. E. (2000). Split-brain basics: Relevance for the concept of one's other mind. *Journal of the American Academy of Psychoanalysis & Dynamic Psychiatry, 28,* 341–369.

Bogg, T., & Roberts, B. W. (2004). Conscientiousness and health-related behaviors: A meta-analysis of the leading behavioral contributors to mortality. *Psychological Bulletin, 130,* 887–919.

Bohannon, J. N., III, & Bonvillian, J. D. (2001). Theoretical approaches to language acquisition. In J. B. Gleason (Ed.), *The development of language* (5th ed., pp. 254–314). Boston: Allyn & Bacon.

Bohannon, J. N., III, & Warren-Leubecker, A. (1989). Theoretical approaches to language acquisition. In J. Berko Gleason (Ed.), *The development of language.* Columbus, OH: Merrill.

Bohannon, J. N., III, MacWhinney, B., & Snow, C. (1990). No negative evidence revisited: Beyond learnability or who has to prove what to whom. *Developmental Psychology, 26,* 221–226.

Bohner, G., & Schwarz, N. (2001). Attitudes, persuasion, and behavior. In A. Tesser & N. Schwarz (Eds.), *Blackwell handbook of social psychology: Intraindividual processes.* Malden, MA: Blackwell.

Bohning, D. E., Lorberbaum, J. P., Shastri, A., Nahas, Z., & George, M. S. (1998). Structural brain imaging (CT and MRI) in primary psychiatry. *Primary Psychiatry, 5,* 46–51.

Boland, R. J., & Keller, M. B. (2002). Course and outcome of depression. In I. H. Gotlib & C. L. Hammen (Eds.), *Handbook of depression.* New York: Guilford.

Bolger, N. (1990). Coping as a personality process: A prospective study. *Journal of Personality and Social Psychology, 59,* 525–537.

Bolles, R. C. (1975). *Theory of motivation.* New York: Harper & Row.

Bolles, R. C. (1990). A functionalistic approach to feeding. In E. D. Capaldi & T. L. Powley (Eds.), *Taste, experience, and feeding* (pp. 3–13). Washington, DC: American Psychological Association.

Bolles, R. C., & Fanselow, M. S. (1980). A perceptual-defensive-recuperative model of fear and pain. *Behavioral and Brain Sciences, 3,* 291–323.

Bond, C. F., Jr., Pitre, U., & Van Leeuwen, M. D. (1991). Encoding operations and the next-in-line effect. *Personality and Social Psychology Bulletin, 17,* 435–441.

Bond, R., & Smith, P. B. (1996). Culture and conformity: A meta-analysis of studies using Asch's line judgment task. *Psychological Bulletin, 119,* 111–137.

Boninger, D. S., Krosnick, J. A., Berent, M. K., & Fabrigar, L. R. (1995). The causes and consequences of attitude importance. In R. E. Petty & J. A. Krosnick (Eds.), *Attitude strength: Antecedents and consequences.* Mahwah, NJ: Erlbaum.

Bonnet, M. H. (1991). Sleep deprivation. In M. Kryger, T. Roth, & W. C. Dement (Eds.), *Principles and practice of sleep medicine* (2nd ed.). Philadelphia: Saunders.

Bonnet, M. H. (2000). Sleep deprivation. In M. H. Kryger, T. Roth, & W. C. Dement (Eds.), *Principles and practice of sleep medicine.* Philadelphia: Saunders.

Bonnet, M. H. (2005). Acute sleep deprivation. In M. H. Kryger, T. Roth, & W. C. Dement (Eds.), *Principles and practice of sleep medicine.* Philadelphia: Elsevier Saunders.

Booth, C. L., Clarke-Stewart, K. A., Vandell, D. L., McCartney, K., & Owen, M. T. (2002). Child-care usage and mother-infant "quality time." *Journal of Marriage and Family, 64,* 16–26.

Booth, D. (1994). Palatability and the intake of food and drinks. In M. S. Westerterp-Plantenga, E. W. H. M. Frederix, & A. B. Steffens (Eds.), *Food intake and energy expenditure.* Boca Raton, FL: CRC Press.

Bootzin, R. R., Manber, R., Loewy, D. H., Kuo, T. F., & Franzen, P. L. (2001). Sleep disorders. In P. B. Sutker & H. E. Adams (Eds.), *Comprehensive handbook of psychopathology.* New York: Kluwer Academic/Plenum.

Borbely, A. A. (1986). *Secrets of sleep.* New York: Basic Books.

Borbely, A. A. (1994). Sleep homeostasis and models of sleep regulation. In M. H. Kryger, T. Roth, & W. C. Dement (Eds.), *Principles and practice of sleep medicine* (2nd ed.). Philadelphia: Saunders.

Borbely, A. A., & Achermann, P. (2000). Sleep homeostasis and models of sleep regulation. In M. H. Kryger, T. Roth & W. C. Dement

(Eds.), *Principles and practice of sleep medicine.* Philadelphia: Saunders.

Borbely, A. A., & Achermann, P. (2005). Sleep homeostasis and models of sleep regulation. In M. H. Kryger, T. Roth, & W. C. Dement (Eds.), *Principles and practice of sleep medicine.* Philadelphia: Elsevier Saunders.

Bordnick, P. S., Elkins, R. L., Orr, T. E., Walters, P., & Thyer, B. A. (2004). Evaluating the relative effectiveness of three aversion therapies designed to reduce craving among cocaine abusers. *Behavioral Interventions, 19*(1), 1–24.

Borgida, E., & Nisbett, R. E. (1977). The differential impact of abstract vs. concrete information on decisions. *Journal of Applied Social Psychology, 7,* 258–271.

Boring, E. G. (1966). A note on the origin of the word *psychology. Journal of the History of the Behavioral Sciences, 2,* 167.

Borkenau, P., Mauer, N., Rieman, R., Spinath, F. M., & Angleitner, A. (2004). Thin slices of behavior as cues of personality and intelligence. *Journal of Personality and Social Psychology, 86,* 599–614.

Bornstein, B. H., & Zickafoose, D. J. (1999). "I know I know it, I know I saw it": The stability of the confidence-accuracy relationship across domains. *Journal of Experimental Psychology: Applied, 5,* 76–88.

Bornstein, R. F. (2003). Psychodynamic models of personality. In T. Millon & M. J. Lerner (Eds.), *Handbook of psychology, Vol. 5: Personality and social psychology.* New York: Wiley.

Boroditsky, L. (2001). Does language shape thought? Mandarin and English speakers' conceptions of time. *Cognitive Psychology, 43*(1), 1–22.

Bosson, J. K., & Swann, W. B. (2001). The paradox of the sincere chameleon: Strategic self-verification in close relationships. In J. H. Harvey & A. Wenzel (Eds.), *Close romantic relationships: Maintenance and enhancement.* Mahwah, N.J.: Erlbaum.

Both, S., Spiering, M., Everaerd, W., & Laan, E. (2004). Sexual behavior and responsiveness to sexual stimuli following laboratory-induced sexual arousal. *Journal of Sex Research, 41,* 242–258.

Bouchard, C. (2002). Genetic influences on body weight. In C. G. Fairburn & K. D. Brownell (Eds.), *Eating disorders and obesity: A comprehensive handbook* (pp. 16–21). New York: Guilford.

Bouchard, T. J., Jr. (1997). IQ similarity in twins reared apart:

Findings and responses to critics. In R. J. Sternberg, & E. L. Grigorenko (Eds.), *Intelligence, heredity, and environment.* New York: Cambridge University Press.

Bouchard, T. J., Jr. (1998). Genetic and environmental influences on adult intelligence and special mental abilities. *Human Biology, 70,* 257–279.

Bouchard, T. J., Jr., Lykken, D. T., McGue, M., Segal, N. L., & Tellegen, A. (1990). Sources of human psychological differences: The Minnesota study of twins reared apart. *Science, 250,* 223–228.

Boudreaux, E., Carmack, C. L., Scarinci, I. C., & Brantley, P. J. (1998). Predicting smoking stage of change among a sample of low socioeconomic status, primary care outpatients: Replication and extension using decisional balance and self-efficacy theories. *International Journal of Behavioral Medicine, 5,* 148–165.

Bouman, T. K., Eifert, G. H., & Lejeuz, C. W. (1999). Somatoform disorders. In T. Millon, P. H. Blaney, & R. D. Davis (Eds.), *Oxford textbook of psychopathology* (pp. 444–465). New York: Oxford University Press.

Bousfield, W. A. (1953). The occurrence of clustering in the recall of randomly arranged associates. *Journal of General Psychology, 49,* 229–240.

Bouton, M. E. (1994). Context, ambiguity, and classical conditioning. *Current Directions in Psychological Science, 3,* 49–53.

Bouton, M. E., & Nelson, J. B. (1998). The role of context in classical conditioning: Some implications for cognitive behavior therapy. In W. O'Donohue (Ed.), *Learning and behavior therapy.* Boston: Allyn & Bacon.

Bowden, C. L. (2004). Valproate. In A. F. Schatzberg & C. B. Nemeroff (Eds.), *Textbook of psychopharmacology.* Washington, DC: American Psychiatric Publishing.

Bower, G. H. (1970). Organizational factors in memory. *Cognitive Psychology, 1,* 18–46.

Bower, G. H. (2000). A brief history of memory research. In E. Tulving & F. I. M. Craik (Eds.), *The Oxford handbook of memory* (pp. 3–32). New York: Oxford University Press.

Bower, G. H., & Clark, M. C. (1969). Narrative stories as mediators of serial learning. *Psychonomic Science, 14,* 181–182.

Bower, G. H., & Springston, F. (1970). Pauses as recoding points in letter series. *Journal of Experimental Psychology, 83,* 421–430.

Bower, G. H., Clark, M. C., Lesgold, A. M., & Winzenz, D. (1969). Hierarchical retrieval schemes in recall of categorized word lists. *Journal of Verbal Learning and Verbal Behavior, 8,* 323–343.

Bowlby, J. (1969). *Attachment and loss: Vol. 1. Attachment.* New York: Basic Books.

Bowlby, J. (1973). *Attachment and loss: Vol. 2. Separation, anxiety and anger.* New York: Basic Books.

Bowlby, J. (1980). *Attachment and loss: Vol. 3. Sadness and depression.* New York: Basic Books.

Boynton, R. M. (1990). Human color perception. In K. N. Leibovic (Ed.), *Science of vision.* New York: Springer-Verlag.

Bozarth, M. A., & Wise, R. A. (1985). Toxicity associated with long-term intravenous heroin and cocaine self-administration in the rat. *Journal of the American Medical Association, 254*(1), 81–83.

Bradbury, T. N. (1998). *The developmental course of marital dysfunction.* New York: Cambridge University Press.

Bradshaw, J. L. (1981). In two minds. *Behavioral and Brain Sciences, 4,* 101–102.

Bradshaw, J. L. (1989). *Hemispheric specialization and psychological function.* New York: Wiley.

Brady, K. T., Myrick, H., & Malcolm, R. (1999). Sedative-hypnotic and anxiolytic agents. In B. S. McCrady & E. E. Epstein (Eds.), *Addictions: A comprehensive guidebook.* New York: Oxford University Press.

Braffman, W., & Kirsch, I. (1999). Imaginative suggestibility and hypnotizability: An empirical analysis. *Journal of Personality and Social Psychology, 77,* 578–587.

Braginsky, D. D. (1985). Psychology: Handmaiden to society. In S. Koch & D. E. Leary (Eds.), *A century of psychology as science.* New York: McGraw-Hill.

Brainerd, C. J. (1996). Piaget: A centennial celebration. *Psychological Science, 7,* 191–195.

Branaman, T. F., & Gallagher, S. N. (2005). Polygraph testing in sex offender treatment: A review of limitations. *American Journal of Forensic Psychology, 23*(1), 45–64.

Bransford, J. D., & Stein, B. S. (1993). *The IDEAL problem solver.* New York: W. H. Freeman.

Brawman-Mintzer, O., Lydiard, R. B., & Ballenger, J. C. (2000). Buspirone. In B. J. Sadock & V. A. Sadock (Eds.), *Kaplan and Sadock's comprehensive textbook of psychiatry* (7th ed., Vol. 1, pp. 2329–2333).

Philadelphia: Lippincott/Williams & Wilkins.

Bredart, S., Lampinen, J. M., & Defeldre, A. C. (2003). Phenomenal characteristics of cryptomnesia. *Memory, 11*(1), 1–11.

Breedlove, S. M. (1992). Sexual differentiation of the brain and behavior. In J. B. Becker, S. M. Breedlove, & D. Crews (Eds.), *Behavioral endocrinology.* Cambridge, MA: MIT Press.

Breedlove, S. M. (1994). Sexual differentiation of the human nervous system. *Annual Review of Psychology, 45,* 389–418.

Breggin, P. R. (1990). Brain damage, dementia and persistent cognitive dysfunction associated with neuroleptic drugs: Evidence, etiology, implications. *The Journal of Mind and Behavior, 11*(3/4), 425–464.

Breggin, P. R. (1991). *Toxic psychiatry.* New York: St. Martin's Press.

Brehm, J. W. (1966). *A theory of psychological reactance.* New York: Academic Press.

Breland, K., & Breland, M. (1961). The misbehavior of organisms. *American Psychologist, 16,* 681–684.

Breland, K., & Breland, M. (1966). *Animal behavior.* New York: Macmillan.

Bremner, J. G. (2001). Cognitive development: Knowledge of the physical world. In G. Bremner & A. Fogel (Eds.), *Blackwell handbook of infant development* (pp. 99–138). Malden, MA: Blackwell.

Brende, J. O. (2000). Stress effects of floods. In G. Fink (Ed.), *Encyclopedia of stress* (Vol. 2, pp. 153–157). San Diego: Academic Press.

Brennan, K. A., & Shaver, P. R. (1995). Dimensions of adult attachment, affect regulation, and romantic relationship functioning. *Personality and Social Psychology Bulletin, 21,* 267–283.

Brennan, P. A., & Mednick, S. A. (1997). Medical histories of antisocial individuals. In D. M. Stoff, J. Breiling & J. D. Maser (Eds.), *Handbook of antisocial behavior.* New York: Wiley.

Breslau, N., Kilbey, M. M., & Andreski, P. (1991). Nicotine dependence, major depression, and anxiety in young adults. *Archives of General Psychiatry, 48,* 1069–1074.

Breslau, N., Kilbey, M. M., & Andreski, P. (1993). Nicotine dependence and major depression: New evidence from a prospective investigation. *Archives of General Psychiatry, 50,* 31–35.

Bretherton, I. & Main, M. (2000). Mary Dinsmore Salter Ainsworth (1913–1999). *American Psychologist, 55,* 1148–1149.

Bretl, D. J., & Cantor, J. (1988). The portrayal of men and women in U.S. television commercials: A recent content analysis and trend over 15 years. *Sex Roles, 18,* 595–609.

Brewer, W. F., & Treyens, J. C. (1981). Role of schemata in memory for places. *Cognitive Psychology, 13,* 207–230.

Brewin, C. R. (2003). *Posttraumatic stress disorder: Malady or myth.* New Haven: Yale University Press.

Brewster, K. L., & Padavic, I. (2000). Change in gender-ideology, 1977–1996: The contributions of intracohort change and population turnover. *Journal of Marriage and the Family, 62,* 477–487.

Brickman, P., Coates, D., & Janoff-Bulman, R. (1978). Lottery winners and accident victims: Is happiness relative? *Journal of Personality and Social Psychology, 36,* 917–927.

Briere, J., & Conte, J. R. (1993). Self-reported amnesia for abuse in adults molested as children. *Journal of Traumatic Stress, 6*(1), 21–31.

Bringmann, W. G., & Balk, M. M. (1992). Another look at Wilhelm Wundt's publication record. *History of Psychology Newsletter, 24*(3/4), 50–66.

Brislin, R. (1993). *Understanding culture's influence on behavior.* Fort Worth: Harcourt Brace College Publishers.

Brislin, R. (2000). *Understanding culture's influence on behavior.* Belmont, CA: Wadsworth.

Broadbent, D. E. (1958). *Perception and communication.* New York: Pergamon Press.

Brobeck, J. R., Tepperman, T., & Long, C. N. (1943). Experimental hypothalamic hyperphagia in the albino rat. *Yale Journal of Biology and Medicine, 15,* 831–853.

Bröder, A. (1998). Deception can be acceptable. *American Psychologist, 53,* 805–806.

Brody, N. (1992). *Intelligence.* San Diego: Academic Press.

Brody, N. (2000). History of theories and measurements of intelligence. In R. J. Sternberg (Ed.), *Handbook of intelligence* (pp. 16–33). New York: Cambridge University Press.

Brody, N., & Crowley, M. J. (1995). Environmental (and genetic) influences on personality and intelligence. In D. H. Saklofske & M. Zeidner (Eds.), *International hand-book of personality and intelligence.* New York: Plenum.

Bromage, B. K., & Mayer, R. E. (1986). Quantitative and qualitative effects of repetition on learning from technical text. *Journal of Educational Psychology, 78,* 271–278.

Bronstein, P., & Quina, K. (1988). Perspectives on gender balance and cultural diversity in the teaching of psychology. In P. Bronstein & K. Quina (Eds.), *Teaching a psychology of people: Resources for gender and sociocultural awareness.* Washington, DC: American Psychological Association.

Brooks-Gunn, J. (1991). Maturational timing variations in adolescent girls, antecedents of. In R. M. Lerner, A. C. Petersen, & J. Brooks-Gunn (Eds.), *Encyclopedia of adolescence.* New York: Garland.

Brooks-Gunn, J., & Reiter, E. O. (1990). The role of pubertal process. In S. S. Feldman & G. R. Elliot (Eds.), *At the threshold: The developing adolescent.* Cambridge, MA: Harvard University Press.

Broughton, R. (1994). Important underemphasized aspects of sleep onset. In R. D. Ogilvie & J. R. Harsh (Eds.), *Sleep onset: Normal and abnormal processes.* Washington, DC: American Psychological Association.

Brown, A. S. (1991). A review of the tip-of-the-tongue experience. *Psychological Bulletin, 109,* 204–223.

Brown, A. S. (1999). New perspectives on the neurodevelopmental hypothesis of schizophrenia. *Psychiatric Annals, 29*(3), 128–130.

Brown, A. S., Begg, M. D., Gravenstein, S., Schaefer, C. S., Wyatt, R. J., Bresnahan, M., Babulas, V. P., & Susser, E. S. (2004). Serologic evidence of prenatal influenza in the etiology of schizophrenia. *Archives of General Psychiatry, 61,* 774–780.

Brown, A. S., van Os, J., Driessens, C., Hoek, H. W., & Susser, E. S. (2000). Further evidence of relation between prenatal famine and major affective disorder. *American Journal of Psychiatry, 157,* 190–195.

Brown, D., Scheflin, A. W., & Hammond, D. C. (1998). *Memory, trauma treatment, and the law.* New York: Norton.

Brown, D., Scheflin, A. W., & Whitfield, C. L. (1999). Recovered memories: The current weight of the evidence in science and in the courts. *Journal of Psychiatry & Law, 27,* 5–156.

Brown, E. J., Juster, H. R., Heimberg, R. G., & Winning, C. D. (1998). Stressful life events and personality styles: Relation to impairment and treatment outcome in patients with social phobia. *Journal of Anxiety Disorders, 12,* 233–251.

Brown, H. D., & Kosslyn, S. M. (1993). Cerebral lateralization. *Current Opinion in Neurobiology, 3,* 183–186.

Brown, J. D., & Rogers, R. J. (1991). Self-serving attributions: The role of physiological arousal. *Personality and Social Psychology Bulletin, 17,* 501–506.

Brown, L. Women left unprotected by law. *Toronto Star,* February 21, 2005, pp. A3.

Brown, M. (1974). Some determinants of persistence and initiation of achievement-related activities. In J. W. Atkinson & J. O. Raynor (Eds.), *Motivation and achievement.* Washington, DC: Halsted.

Brown, R. D., Goldstein, E., & Bjorklund, D. F. (2000). The history and zeitgeist of the repressed–false-memory debate: Scientific and sociological perspectives on suggestibility and childhood memory. In D. F. Bjorklund (Ed.), *False-memory creation in children and adults* (pp. 1–30). Mahwah, NJ: Erlbaum.

Brown, R. T. (1989). Creativity: What are we to measure? In J. A. Glover, R. R. Ronning, & C. R. Reynolds (Eds.), *Handbook of creativity.* New York: Plenum.

Brown, R., & Hanlon, C. (1970). Derivational complexity and order of acquisition. In J. R. Hayes (Ed.), *Cognition and the development of language.* New York: Wiley.

Brown, R., & Kulik, J. (1977). Flashbulb memories. *Cognition, 5,* 73–79.

Brown, R., & McNeill, D. (1966). The "tip-of-the-tongue" phenomenon. *Journal of Verbal Learning and Verbal Behavior, 5*(4), 325–337.

Brown, S. C., & Craik, F. I. M. (2000). Encoding and retrieval of information. In E. Tulving & F. I. M. Craik (Eds.), *The Oxford handbook of memory* (pp. 93–108). New York: Oxford University Press.

Brownell, H. H., & Gardner, H. (1981). Hemisphere specialization: Definitions not incantations. *Behavioral and Brain Sciences, 4,* 64–65.

Brownell, K. D. (2002). The environment and obesity. In C. G. Fairburn & K. D. Brownell (Eds.), *Eating disorders and obesity: A comprehensive handbook* (pp. 433–438). New York: Guilford.

Brownell, K. D., & Wadden, T. A. (2000). Obesity. In B. J. Sadock & V. A. Sadock (Eds.), *Kaplan and Sadock's comprehensive textbook of psychiatry* (7th ed., Vol. 2, pp. 1787–1796). Philadelphia: Lippincott Williams & Wilkins.

Bruce, D., Dolan, A., & Phillips-Grant, K. (2000). On the transition from childhood amnesia to the recall of personal memories. *Psychological Science, 11,* 360–364.

Bruch, H. (1978). *The golden cage: The enigma of anorexia nervosa.* Cambridge, MA: Harvard University Press.

Bruckner-Gordon, F., Gangi, B. K., & Wallman, G. U. (1988). *Making therapy work: Your guide to choosing, using, and ending therapy.* New York: Harper & Row.

Bruer, J. T. (2002). Avoiding the pediatricians error: How neuroscientists can help educators (and themselves). *Nature Neuroscience, 5,* 1031–1033.

Bruggerman, E. L., & Hart, K. J. (1996). Cheating, lying, and moral reasoning by religious and secular high school students. *Journal of Educational Research, 89,* 340–344.

Bruner, J. S. (1974). Concluding comments and summary of conference. In J. L. M. Dawson & W. J. Lonner (Eds.), *Readings in cross-cultural psychology.* Hong Kong: University of Hong Kong Press.

Bryden, M. P. (1982). *Laterality: Functional asymmetry in the intact brain.* New York: Academic Press.

Buchanan, R. W., & Carpenter, W. T. (2000). Schizophrenia: Introduction and overview. In B. J. Sadock & V. A. Sadock (Eds.), *Kaplan and Sadock's comprehensive textbook of psychiatry* (7th ed., Vol. 1). Philadelphia: Lippincott/Williams & Wilkins.

Buck, L. B. (2000). Smell and taste: The chemical senses. In E. R. Kandel, J. H. Schwartz, & T. M. Jessell (Eds.), *Principles of neural science.* New York: McGraw-Hill.

Buck, L., & Axel, R. (1991). A novel multigene family may encode ordorant receptors: A molecular basis for odour recognition. *Cell, 65,* 175–187.

Buckman, R. (2002). Communications and emotions: Skills and effort are key. *British Medical Journal, 325,* 672.

Budiansky, S. (2004). Human and animal intelligence: The gap is a chasm. *Cerebrum, 6*(2), 85–95.

Buehler, R., Messervey, D., & Griffin, D. (2005). Collaborative planning and prediction: Does group discussion affect optimistic biases in time estimation? *Organizational Behavior and Human Decision Processes, 97,* 47–63.

Bühler, C., & Allen, M. (1972). *Introduction to humanistic psychology.* Pacific Grove, CA: Brooks/Cole.

Bulcroft, R., & Teachman, J. (2004). Ambiguous constructions: Development of a childless or child-free life course. In M. Coleman & L. H. Ganong (Eds.), *Handbook of contemporary families: Considering the past, contemplating the future.* Thousand Oaks, CA: Sage.

Bulik, C. M. (2004). Genetic and biological risk factors. In J. K. Thompson (Ed.), *Handbook of eating disorders and obesity.* New York: Wiley.

Bull, D. L. (1999). A verified case of recovered memories of sexual abuse. *American Journal of Psychotherapy, 53,* 221–224.

Bunce, S. C., Bernat, E., Wong, P. S., & Shevrin, H. (1999). Further evidence for unconscious learning: Preliminary support for the conditioning of facial EMG to subliminal stimuli. *Journal of Psychiatric Research, 33,* 341–347.

Bunch, B. (1994). Mainstreaming. In R. J. Sternberg (Ed.), *Encyclopedia of human intelligence.* New York: Macmillan.

Burger, J. M. (1986). Temporal effects on attributions: Actor and observer differences. *Social Cognition, 4,* 377–387.

Burger, J. M. (1997). *Personality.* Pacific Grove: Brooks/Cole.

Burger, J. M. (1999). The foot-in-the-door compliance procedure: A multiple process analysis review. *Personality and Social Psychology Review, 3,* 303–325.

Burger, J. M. (2004). *Personality.* Belmont, CA: Wadsworth.

Burgess, C., O'Donohoe, A., & Gill, M. (2000). Agony and ecstasy: A review of MDMA effects and toxicity. *European Psychiatry, 15,* 287–294.

Burke, D. M., & Shafto, M. A. (2004). Aging and language production. *Current Directions in Psychological Science, 13*(1), 21–24.

Burns, B. D., & Corpus, B. (2004). Randomness and inductions from streaks: "Gambler's fallacy" versus "hot hand." *Psychonomic Bulletin & Review, 11*(1), 179–184.

Burnstein, E., Crandall, C., & Kitayama, S. (1994). Some neo-Darwinian decision rules for altruism: Weighing cues for inclusive fitness as a function of the biological importance of the decision. *Journal of Personality and Social Psychology, 67,* 773–789.

Buss, D. M. (1985). Human mate selection. *American Scientist, 73,* 47–51.

Buss, D. M. (1988). The evolution of human intrasexual competition: Tactics of mate attraction. *Journal of Personality and Social Psychology, 54,* 616–628.

Buss, D. M. (1989). Sex differences in human mate preferences: Evolutionary hypotheses tested in 37 cultures. *Behavioral and Brain Sciences, 12,* 1–49.

Buss, D. M. (1991). Evolutionary personality psychology. *Annual Review of Psychology, 42,* 459–491.

Buss, D. M. (1994a). *The evolution of desire: Strategies of human mating.* New York: Basic Books.

Buss, D. M. (1994b). Mate preferences in 37 cultures. In W. J. Lonner & R. S. Malpass (Eds.), *Psychology and culture.* Boston: Allyn & Bacon.

Buss, D. M. (1995). Evolutionary psychology: A new paradigm for psychological science. *Psychological Inquiry, 6,* 1–30.

Buss, D. M. (1996). The evolutionary psychology of human social strategies. In E. T. Higgins & A. W. Kruglanski (Eds.), *Social psychology: Handbook of basic principles.* New York: Guilford.

Buss, D. M. (1997). Evolutionary foundation of personality. In R. Hogan, J. Johnson, & S. Briggs (Eds.), *Handbook of personality psychology.* San Diego: Academic Press.

Buss, D. M. (1998). The psychology of human mate selection: Exploring the complexity of the strategic repertoire. In C. Crawford, & D. L. Krebs (Eds.), *Handbook of evolutionary psychology: Ideas, issues, and applications.* Mahwah, NJ: Erlbaum.

Buss, D. M. (1999). *Evolutionary psychology: The new science of the mind.* Boston: Allyn & Bacon.

Buss, D. M., & Kenrick, D. T. (1998). Evolutionary social psychology. In D. T. Gilbert, S. T. Fiske, & G. Lindzey (Eds.), *The handbook of social psychology.* New York: McGraw-Hill.

Buss, D. M., & Reeve, H. K. (2003). Evolutionary psychology and developmental dynamics: Comment on Lickliter and Honeycutt (2003). *Psychological Bulletin, 129,* 848–853.

Buss, D. M., & Schmitt, D. P. (1993). Sexual strategies theory: A contextual evolutionary analysis of human mating. *Psychological Review, 100,* 204–232.

Bussey, K., & Bandura, A. (1984). Influence of gender constancy and social power on sex-linked modeling. *Journal of Personality and Social Psychology, 47,* 1292–1302.

Bussey, K., & Bandura, A. (1999). Social cognitive theory of gender development and differentiation. *Psychological Review, 106,* 676–713.

Buster, J. E., & Carson, S. A. (2002). Endocrinology and diagnosis of pregnancy. In S. G. Gabbe, J. R. Niebyl, & J. L. Simpson (Eds.), *Obstetrics: Normal and problem pregnancies.* New York: Churchill Livingstone.

Butcher, J. N. (1990). *The MMPI-2 in psychological treatment.* New York: Oxford University Press.

Butcher, J. N., & Keller, L. S. (1984). Objective personality assessment. In G. Goldstein & M. Hersen (Eds.), *Handbook of psychological assessment.* New York: Pergamon Press.

Butler, J. L., & Baumeister, R. F. (1998). The trouble with friendly faces: Skilled performance with a supportive audience. *Journal of Personality and Social Psychology, 75,* 1213–1230.

Buxton, M. N., Arkey, Y., Lagos, J., Deposito, F., Lowenthal, F., & Simring, S. (1981). Stress and platelet aggregation in hemophiliac children and their family members. *Research Communications in Psychology, Psychiatry and Behavior, 6*(1), 21–48.

Byne, W., & Parsons, B. (1993). Human sexual orientation: The biological theories reappraised. *Archives of General Psychiatry, 50,* 228–239.

Byne, W., Kemether, E., Jones, L., Haroutunian, V., & Davis, K. L. (1999). The neurochemistry of schizophrenia. In D. S. Charney, E. J. Nestler & B. S. Bunney (Eds.), *Neurobiology of mental illness* (pp. 236–245). New York: Oxford University Press.

Byrne, D. (1997). An overview (and underview) of research and theory within the attraction paradigm. *Journal of Social and Personal Relationships, 14,* 417–431.

Byrne, D., Clore, G. L., & Smeaton, G. (1986). The attraction hypothesis: Do similar attitudes affect anything? *Journal of Personality and Social Psychology, 51,* 1167–1170.

Byrnes, J. P., Miller, D. C., & Schafer, W. D. (1999). Gender differences in risk taking: A meta-analysis. *Psychological Bulletin, 125,* 367–383.

Cabral, G. A., & Petitt, D. A. D. (1998). Drugs and immunity: Cannabinoids and their role in decreased resistance to infectious disease. *Journal of Neuroimmunology, 83,* 116–123.

Cabrera, N. J., Tamis-LeMonda, C. S., Bradley, R. H., Hofferth, S., & Lamb, M. E. (2000). Fatherhood in the twenty-first century. *Child Development, 71,* 127–136.

Cacioppo, J. T., & Berntson, G. G. (1999). The affect system: Architecture and operating characteristics. *Current Directions in Psychological Science, 8,* 133–137.

Cacioppo, J. T., & Gardner, W. L. (1999). Emotion. *Annual Review of Psychology, 50,* 191–214.

Cacioppo, J. T., Klein, D. J., Berntson, G. G., & Hatfield, E. (1993). The psychophysiology of emotions. In M. Lewis & J. M. Haviland (Eds.), *Handbook of emotions.* New York: Guilford.

Cahill, L., & McGaugh, J. L. (1998). Mechanisms of emotional arousal and lasting declarative memory. *Trends in Neurosciences, 21,* 294–299.

Cain, W. S. (1988). Olfaction. In R. C. Atkinson, R. J. Herrnstein, G. Lindzey, & R. D. Luce (Eds.), *Stevens' handbook of experimental psychology: Perception and motivation* (Vol. 1). New York: Wiley.

Caine, E. D., & Lyness, J. M. (2000). Delirium, dementia, and amnestic and other cognitive disorders. In B. J. Sadock & V. A. Sadock (Eds.), *Kaplan and Sadock's comprehensive textbook of psychiatry.* Philadelphia: Lippincott/Williams & Wilkins.

Calhoun, L. G., & Tedeschi, R. G. (2001). Posttraumatic growth: The positive lessons of loss. In R. A. Neimeyer (Ed.), *Meaning reconstruction and the experience of loss* (pp. 157–172). Washington, DC: American Psychological Association.

Calkins, S. D., Fox, N. A., & Marshall, T. R. (1996). Behavioral and physiological antecedents of inhibited and uninhibited behavior. *Child Development, 67,* 523–540.

Callahan, C. M. (2000). Intelligence and giftedness. In R. J. Sternberg (Ed.), *Handbook of intelligence* (pp. 159–175). New York: Cambridge University Press.

Calof, D. (1998). Facing the truth about false memory. In R. A. Baker (Ed.), *Child sexual abuse and false memory syndrome.* Amherst, NY: Prometheus Books.

Calvert, C. (1997). Hate speech and its harms: A communication theory perspective. *Journal of Communication, 47,* 4–19.

Cameron, D. E. (1948). *Life is for living.* New York: MacMillan.

Cameron, D. E. (1950). *General psychotherapy: Dynamics and procedures.* New York: Grune & Stratton.

Cameron, D. E. (1968). *Psychotherapy in action.* New York: Grune & Stratton.

Cameron, L., Leventhal, E. A., & Leventhal, H. (1993). Symptom representations and affect as determinants of care seeking in a community-dwelling, adult sample population. *Health Psychology, 12,* 171–179.

Cameron, N. (1963). *Personality development and psychopathology.* Boston: Houghton Mifflin.

Cami, J., & Farre, M. (2003). Mechanisms of disease: Drug addiction. *New England Journal of Medicine, 349,* 975–986.

Campbell, A. (2005). Aggression. In D. M. Buss (Ed.), *The handbook of evolutionary psychology.* New York: Wiley.

Campbell, J. (1971). *Hero with a thousand faces.* New York: Harcourt Brace Jovanovich.

Campbell, J. D., Tesser, A., & Fairey, P. J. (1986). Conformity and attention to stimulus: Some temporal and contextual dynamics. *Journal of Personality and Social Psychology, 51,* 315–324.

Campbell, K. B. (2000). Introduction to the special section: Information processing during sleep onset and sleep. *Canadian Journal of Experimental Psychology, 54*(4), 209–218.

Campbell, L., Simpson, J. A., Boldry, J., & Kashy, D. A. (2005). Perceptions of conflict and support in romantic relationships: The role of attachment anxiety. *Journal of Personality and Social Psychology, 88,* 510–531.

Campbell, R. J. (2000). Managed care. In B. J. Sadock & V. A. Sadock (Eds.), *Kaplan and Sadock's comprehensive textbook of psychiatry* (7th ed., Vol. 2). Philadelphia: Lippincott/Williams & Wilkins.

Campbell, R., & Sais, E. (1995). Accelerated metalinguistic (phonological) awareness in bilingual children. *British Journal of Developmental Psychology, 13,* 61–68.

Campbell, R., & Wasco, S. M. (2005). Understanding rape and sexual assault: 20 years of progress and future decisions. *Journal of Interpersonal Violence, 20*(1), 127–131.

Campbell, S., Marriott, M., Nahmias, C., & MacQueen, G. M. (2004). Lower hippocampal volume in patients suffering from depression: A meta-analysis. *American Journal of Psychiatry, 161,* 598–607.

Campbell, W. K., & Sedikides, C. (1999). Self-threat magnifies the self-serving bias: A meta-analytic integration. *Review of General Psychology, 3,* 23–43.

Campfield, L. A. (2002). Leptin and body weight regulation. In C. G. Fairburn & K. D. Brownell (Eds.), *Eating disorders and obesity: A comprehensive handbook* (pp. 32–36). New York: Guilford.

Canadian Broadcasting Corporation Online. (2005). *Indepth: Same Sex rights Canada timeline.* Retrieved May 10, 2005, from http://www.cbc.ca/news/background/samesexrights/timeline.

Canadian Broadcasting Corporation. (n.d.). *Life and times: Moe Norman: The king of swing.* Retrieved April 21, 2005, from http://www.cbc.ca/Lifeandtimes/norman.html.

Canadian Broadcasting Corporation: Athens 2004. (2004). Retrieved May 2, 2005, from http://www.cbc.ca/story/olympics/national/2004/08/24/Sports/perdita.

Canadian Centre for Substance Abuse. (n.d.). National Population Health Survey, 1998–1999. Retrieved July 4, 2005, from http://www.ccsa.ca/ccendu/pdf/nphs_ca_1998.

Canadian Community Health Survey: Mental Health and Well-Being. (2002). Retrieved April 13, 2005, from http://www.statcan.ca/Daily/English/030903/d030903a.htm.

Canadian Government tries anew to decriminalize marijuana. (2004, November 2). *The Washington Post.* Retrieved March 4, 2005, from http://www.washingtonpost.com.

Canadian Mental Health Association. (2005). *Physical and mental health equally important to Canadians.* Retrieved July 3, 2005, from http://www.cmha.ca/bins/content_page.asp?cid=6-20-21-386.

Canadian Olympic Committee: Athletes. (2005). Retrieved May 2, 2005, from http://www.olympic.ca/EN/athletes/index.shtml.

Canadian Parents for French. (2004). *The State of French second language education in Canada 2004.* Retrieved May 11, 2005, from http://www.cpf.ca/english/Resources/FSL2004/2004%.

Canadian Psychological Association (2004). Annual report (2004). Retrieved February 21, 2005, from http://www.cpa.ca.

Canadian Psychological Association. (n.d.). *CPA Awards.* Retrieved February 21, 2005, from http://www.cpa.ca/recip.html.

Canadian Space Agency. (n.d., a). Canadian Space Milestones. Retrieved March 22, 2005, from http://www.space.gc.ca/asc/eng/about/cms_complete.asp.

Canadian Space Agency. (n.d., b). Interview with Douglas G.D. Watt. Retrieved March 22, 2005, from http://www.space.gc.ca/asc/eng/sciences/interview_0406.asp.

Canadian Space Agency. (n.d., c). Role of visual cues in spatial orientation (VISO). Retrieved March 22, 2005, from http://www.space.gc.ca/asc/eng/missions/sts-090-neurola.

Canadian Task Force on Preventive Health Care. (2003). *Prevention of suicide.* Retrieved June 19, 2005, from http://www.canadiancrc.com/Can_Preventive_Care_suicide.htm.

Cancro, R., & Lehmann, H. E. (2000). Schizophrenia: Clinical features. In B. J. Sadock & V. A. Sadock (Eds.), *Kaplan and Sadock's comprehensive textbook of psychiatry* (7th ed., Vol. 1, pp. 1169–1198). Philadelphia: Lippincott/Williams & Wilkins.

Cannon, W. B. (1927). The James-Lange theory of emotions: A critical examination and an alternate theory. *American Journal of Psychology, 39,* 106–124.

Cannon, W. B. (1932). *The wisdom of the body.* New York: Norton.

Cannon, W. B., & Washburn, A. L. (1912). An explanation of hunger. *American Journal of Physiology, 29,* 444–454.

Canter, P. H. (2003). The therapeutic effects of meditation. *British Medical Journal, 326,* 1049–1050.

Cao, Y., Vikingstad, E. M., Huttenlocher, P. R., Towle, V. L., & Levin, D. N. (1994). Functional magnetic resonance imaging studies of the reorganization of the human head sensorimotor area after unilateral brain injury. *Proceeding of the National Academy of Sciences of the United States of America, 91,* 9612–9616.

Capaldi, E. D. (1996). Conditioned food preferences. In E. D. Capaldi (Ed.), *Why we eat what we eat: The psychology of eating* (pp. 53–81). Washington, DC: American Psychological Association.

Capaldi, E. D., & VandenBos, G. R. (1991). Taste, food exposure, and eating behavior. *Hospital and Community Psychiatry, 42*(8), 787–789.

Capelli, C. A., Nakagawa, N., & Madden, C. M. (1990). How children understand sarcasm: The role of context and intonation. *Child Development, 61,* 1824–1841.

Caporael, L. R., & Brewer, M. B. (1995). Hierarchical evolutionary theory: There is an alternative, and it's not creationism. *Psychological Inquiry, 6,* 31–34.

Cardellini, L, & Pascual-Leone, J. (2004). On mentors, cognitive development, education, and constructivism: An interview with Juan Pascual-Leone. *Journal of Cognitive Education and Psychology, 4,* 199–219.

Carey, G., & Goldman, D. (1997). The genetics of antisocial behavior. In D. M. Stoff, J. Breiling, & J. D. Maser (Eds.), *Handbook of antisocial behavior.* New York: Wiley.

Carey, M. P., & Vanable, P. A. (2003). AIDS/HIV. In A. M. Nezu, C. M. Nezu, & P. A. Geller (Eds.), *Handbook of psychology, Vol. 9: Health psychology.* New York: Wiley.

Carli, L. L. (1999). Cognitive, reconstruction, hindsight, and reactions to victims and perpetrators. *Personality & Social Psychology Bulletin, 25,* 966–979.

Carmichael, A. (2005). Ellard gets life sentence for role in Rena Virk's slaying. *Toronto Star,* July 8, 2005, p. A17.

Carnegie, D. (1936). *How to win friends and influence people.* New York: Simon & Schuster.

Caro, R. M. (1986). The functions of stotting in Thomson's gazelles: Some tests of the predictions. *Animal Behavior, 34,* 663–684.

Carpenter, W. T. (1992). The negative symptom challenge. *Archives of General Psychiatry, 49,* 236–237.

Carpenter, W. T. (2002). From clinical trial to prescription. *Archives of General Psychology, 59,* 282–285.

Carr, E. (1972). *Fresh Seeing: Two addresses by Emily Carr.* Toronto: Clarke, Irwin & Co.

Carrington, P. (1987). Managing meditation in clinical practice. In M. A. West (Ed.), *The psychology of meditation.* Oxford: Clarendon Press.

Carroll, J. M., & Russell, J. A. (1997). Facial expressions in Hollywood's portrayal of emotion. *Journal of Personality and Social Psychology, 72,* 164–176.

Carskadon, M. A., & Dement, W. C. (2000). Normal human sleep: An overview. In M. H. Kryger, T. Roth, & W. C. Dement (Eds.), *Principles and practice of sleep medicine.* Philadelphia: Saunders.

Carskadon, M. A., & Dement, W. C. (2005). Normal human sleep: An overview. In M. H. Kryger, T. Roth, & W. C. Dement (Eds.), *Principles and practice of sleep medicine.* Philadelphia: Elsevier Saunders.

Carskadon, M. A., & Rechtschaffen, A. (2000). Monitoring and staging human sleep. In M. H. Kryger, T. Roth, & W. C. Dement (Eds.), *Principles and practice of sleep medicine.* Philadelphia: Saunders.

Carskadon, M. A., & Rechtschaffen, A. (2005). Monitoring and staging human sleep. In M. H. Kryger, T. Roth, & W. C. Dement (Eds.). *Principles and practice of sleep medicine.* Philadelphia: Elsevier Saunders.

Carskadon, M., & Dement, W. C. (1994). Normal human sleep: An overview. In M. Kryger, T. Roth, and W. Dement (Eds.). *Principles and practice of sleep medicine* (pp. 3–15). Philadelphia: WB Saunders.

Carson, R. C., & Butcher, C. N., & Coleman, J. C. (1988). *Abnormal psychology and modern life.* Glenview, IL: Scott, Foresman.

Carter, B. (1999). Becoming parents: The family with young children. In B. Carter & M. McGoldrick (Eds.), *The expanded family life cycle: Individual, family, and social perspectives* (3rd ed., pp. 249–273). Boston: Allyn & Bacon.

Carter, B., & McGoldrick, M. (1999). Overview: The expanded family life cycle: Individual, family, and social perspectives. In B. Carter & M. McGoldrick (Eds.), *The expanded family life cycle: Individual, family, and social perspectives* (3rd ed., pp. 1–26). Boston: Allyn & Bacon.

Carter, E. A., & McGoldrick, M. (1988). Overview: The changing family life cycle—A framework for family therapy. In E. A. Carter & M. McGoldrick (Eds.), *The changing family cycle: A framework for family therapy* (2nd ed.). New York: Gardner Press.

Carter, P. J., & Russell, K. (2001). *Workout for a balanced brain: Exercises, puzzles & games to sharpen both sides of your brain.* Readers Digest Association.

Carter, R. (1998). *Mapping the mind.* Berkeley: University of California Press.

Cartwright, R. D. (1977). *Night life: Explorations in dreaming.* Englewood Cliffs, NJ: Prentice-Hall.

Cartwright, R. D. (1991). Dreams that work: The relation of dream incorporation to adaptation to stressful events. *Dreaming, 1,* 3–9.

Cartwright, R. D. (1994). Dreams and their meaning. In M. H. Kryger, T. Roth, & W. C. Dement (Eds.), *Principles and practice of sleep medicine* (2nd ed.). Philadelphia: Saunders.

Cartwright, R. D. (2004). The role of sleep in changing our minds: A psychologist's discussion of papers on memory reactivation and consolidation in sleep. *Learning & Memory, 11,* 660–663.

Cartwright, R. D., & Lamberg, L. (1992). *Crisis dreaming.* New York: HarperCollins.

Carver, C. S., & Scheier, M. F. (1994). Situational coping and coping dispositions in a stressful transaction. *Journal of Personality and Social Psychology, 66,* 184–195.

Carver, C. S., & Scheier, M. F. (1999). Optimism. In C. R. Snyder (Ed.), *Coping: The psychology of what works.* New York: Oxford University Press.

Carver, C. S., Pozo, C., Harris, S. D., Noriega, V., Scheier, M. F., Robinson, D. S., Ketcham, A. S., Moffat, F. L., Jr., & Clark, K. C. (1993). How coping mediates the effect of optimism on distress: A study of women with early stage breast cancer. *Journal of Personality and Social Psychology, 65,* 375–390.

Carver, C. S., Scheier, M. F., & Weintraub, J. K. (1989). Assessing coping strategies: A theoretically based approach. *Journal of Personality and Social Psychology, 56,* 267–283.

Casanova, C., Merabet, L., Desautels, A., & Minville, K. (2001). Higher-order motion processing in the pulvinar. *Progress in Brain Research, 134,* 71–82.

Case, D. A., Fantino, E., & Goodie, A. S. (1999). Base-rate training without case cues reduces base-rate neglect. *Psychonomic Bulletin & Review, 6,* 310–327.

Case, R. (1991a). *The mind's staircase: Exploring the conceptual underpinnings of children's thought and knowledge.* Hillsdale, NJ: Lawrence Erlbaum & Associates.

Case, R. (1991b). A neo-Piagetian approach to the issues of cognitive generality and specificity. In R. Case (Ed.), *The mind's staircase: Exploring the conceptual underpinnings of children's thought and knowledge.* Hillsdale, NJ: Lawrence Erlbaum & Associates.

Case, R. (1998). The development of conceptual structures. In W. Damon (Series Editor) D. Kuhn & R. S. Seigler (Volume Editors.), *Handbook of child psychology, Vol. 2. Cognition, perception and language* (5th ed., pp. 128–162). New York: Wiley.

Casey, R., & Rozin, P. (1989). Changing children's food preferences: Parent opinions. *Appetite, 12,* 171–182.

Caspi, A., & Herbener, E. S. (1990). Continuity and change: Assortative marriage and the consistency of personality in adulthood. *Journal of Personality and Social Psychology, 58*(2), 250–258.

Caspi, O., & Burleson, K. O. (2005). Methodological challenges in meditation research. *Advances in Mind-Body Medicine, 21*(1), 4–11.

Cassel, R. N. (2000). Third force psychology and person-centered theory: From ego-status to ego-ideal. *Psychology: A Journal of Human Behavior, 37*(3), 44–48.

Cassidy, J. (1999). The nature of the child's ties. In J. Cassidy & P. R. Shaver (Eds.), *Handbook of attachment: Theory, research, and clinical applications.* New York: Guilford.

Catalano, E. M. (1990). *Getting to sleep.* Oakland, CA: New Harbinger.

Catania, A. C. (1992). Reinforcement. In L. R. Squire (Ed.), *Encyclopedia of learning and memory.* New York: Macmillan.

Catania, J. A., Binson, D., Dolcini, M. M., Moskowitz, J. T., & van der Straten, A. (2001). In A. Baum, T. A. Revenson, & J. E. Singer (Eds.), *Handbook of health psychology.* Mahwah, NJ: Erlbaum.

Catania, J. A., Binson, D., Dolcini, M. M., Moskowitz, J. T., & van der Straten, A. (2001). In A. Baum, T. A. Revenson, & J. E. Singer (Eds.), *Handbook of health psychology.* Mahwah, NJ: Erlbaum.

Catano, V. M., Wiesner, W. H., Hackett, R. D., & Methot, L. (2005). *Recruitment and selection in Canada*, 3rd ed. Toronto. Nelson.

Cattell, R. B. (1950). *Personality: A systematic, theoretical and factual study.* New York: McGraw-Hill.

Cattell, R. B. (1957). *Personality and motivation: Structure and measurement.* New York: Harcourt, Brace & World.

Cattell, R. B. (1963). Theory of fluid and crystallized intelligence: A critical experiment. *Journal of Educational Psychology, 54,* 1–22.

Cattell, R. B. (1965). *The scientific analysis of personality.* Baltimore: Penguin.

Cattell, R. B. (1966). *The scientific analysis of personality.* Chicago: Aldine.

Cattell, R. B. (1990). Advances in Cattellian personality theory. In L. A. Pervin (Ed.), *Handbook of personality: Theory and research.* New York: Guilford.

Cattell, R. B., Eber, H. W., & Tatsuoka, M. M. (1970). *Handbook of the Sixteen Personality Factor Questionnaire (16PF).* Champaign, IL: Institute for Personality and Ability Testing.

Catz, S. L., & Kelly, J. A. (2001). Living with HIV disease. In A. Baum, T. A. Revenson, & J. E. Singer (Eds.), *Handbook of health psychology* (pp. 841–850). Mahwah, NJ: Erlbaum.

Cavanaugh, J. C. (1993). *Adult development and aging* (2nd ed.). Pacific Grove, CA: Brooks/Cole.

Caverly, D. C., Orlando, V. P., & Mullen, J. L. (2000). Textbook study reading. In R. F. Flippo & D. C. Caverly (Eds.), *Handbook of college reading and study strategy research.* Mahwah, NJ: Erlbaum.

CBC News. (2005). High school attack foiled: police. March 17, 2005. Retrieved June 29, 2005, from http://www.cbc.ca/cgi-bin/newsworld/viewer.cgi?FILE=NL2005 0318.html&TEMPLATE=newsreal_archive.ssi&SC=NL.

Ceci, S. J. (1990). *On intelligence . . . more or less: A bio-ecological treatise on intellectual development.* Englewood Cliffs, NJ: Prentice-Hall.

Ceci, S. J. (1991). How much does schooling influence general intelligence and its cognitive components? A reassessment of the evidence. *Developmental Psychology, 27,* 703–722.

Ceci, S. J., & Bruck, M. (1993). Suggestibility of the child witness: A historical review and synthesis. *Psychological Bulletin, 113,* 403–439.

Ceci, S. J., & Williams, W. M. (1997). Schooling, intelligence, and income. *American Psychologist, 52,* 1051–1058.

Ceci, S. J., Rosenblum, T., de Bruyn, E., & Lee, D. Y. (1997). A bio-ecological model of intellectual development: Moving beyond *h*2. In R. J. Sternberg & E. L. Grigorenko (Eds.), *Intelligence, heredity, and environment.* New York: Cambridge University Press.

Cerletti, U., & Bini, L. (1938). Un nuevo metodo di shockterapie "L'elettro-shock". *Boll. Acad. Med. Roma, 64,* 136–138.

Chaiken, S., & Maheswaran, D. (1994). Heuristic processing can bias systematic processing: Effects of source credibility, argument ambiguity, and task importance on attitude judgment. *Journal of Personality and Social Psychology, 66,* 460–473.

Chambers, K. C., & Phoenix, C. H. (1987). Differences among ovariectomized female rhesus macaques in the display of sexual behavior without and with estradiol treatment. *Behavioral Neuroscience, 101,* 303–308.

Chambless, D. L., & Hollon, S. D. (1998). Defining empirically supported therapies. *Journal of Consulting & Clinical Psychology, 66,* 7–18.

Chan, J. W. C., & Vernon, P. E. (1988). Individual differences among the peoples of China. In S. H. Irvine & J. W. Berry (Eds.), *Human abilities in cultural context.* New York: Cambridge University Press.

Chance, P. (1999). Thorndike's puzzle boxes and the origins of the experimental analysis of behavior. *Journal of the Experimental Analysis of Behavior, 72,* 433–440.

Chance, P. (2001, September/October). The brain goes to school: Why neuroscience research is going to the head of the class. *Psychology Today,* p. 72.

Chandler, C. C. (1991). How memory for an event is influenced by related events: Interference in modified recognition tests. *Journal of Experimental Psychology: Learning, Memory, & Cognition, 17,* 115–125.

Chandler, C. C., & Fisher, R. P. (1996). Retrieval processes and witness memory. In E. L. Bjork & R. A. Bjork (Eds.), *Memory.* San Diego: Academic Press.

Chandler, M. (2000). Surviving time: The persistence of identity in this culture and that. *Culture and Psychology, 6,* 209–231.

Chandler, M. J., & Lalonde, C. (1998). Cultural continuity as a hedge against suicide in Canada's First Nations. *Transcultural Psychiatry, 35,* 191–219.

Chandler, M. J., & Lalonde, C. E. (2004). Culture, selves, and time: Theories of personal persistence in native and non-native youth. In C. Lightfoot, C. Lalonde, & M. Chandler (Eds.), *Changing conceptions of psychological life* (pp. 207–229). Mahwah, NJ: Lawrence Erlbaum & Associates.

Chandler, M., Lalonde, C.E., Sokol, B., & Hallett, D. (2003). Personal persistence, identity development, and suicide: A study of native and non-native North American adolescents. *Monographs of the Society for Research in Child Development, 68,* 2, Serial No. 273.

Chao, R. (2001). Integrating culture and attachment. *American Psychologist, 56,* 822–823.

Chaplin, W. F., Phillips, J. B., Brown, J. D., Clanton, N. R., & Stein, J. L. (2000). Handshaking, gender, personality, and first impressions. *Journal of Personality and Social Psychology, 79*(1), 110–117.

Chard, J., & Badets, J. (2004). The Ethnic Diversity Survey (EDS): Content and data availability. A paper presented at the 2004 Congress & RDC Symposium of the Canadian Population Society. Retrieved March 15, 2005, from http://www.canpopsoc.org/2004. secure/chardCPS.ppt.

Charney, D. S., Nagy, L. M., Bremer, J. D., Goddard, A. W., Yehuda, R., & Southwich, S. M. (1996). Neurobiological mechanisms of human anxiety. In B. S.

Fogel, R. B. Schiffer, & S. M. Rao (Eds.), *Neuropsychiatry.* Baltimore: Williams & Wilkins.

Chemers, M. M., Hu, L., & Garcia, B. F. (2001). Academic self-efficacy and first year college student performance and adjustment. *Journal of Educational Psychology, 93*(1), 55–64.

Cheney, P. (2004). Our Abu Ghraib. *The Globe and Mail,* May 15, 2004, pp. F1, F5.

Chess, S., & Thomas, A. (1996). *Temperament: Theory and practice.* New York: Brunner/Mazel.

Chiappelli, F., & Hodgson, D. (2000). Immune suppression. In G. Fink (Ed.), *Encyclopedia of stress* (Vol. 2, pp. 531–535). San Diego: Academic Press.

Chiriboga, D. A. (1989). Mental health at the midpoint: Crisis, challenge, or relief? In S. Hunter & M. Sundel (Eds.), *Mid life myths: Issues, findings, and practice implications.* Newbury Park, CA: Sage.

Chisholm, J. S. (1996). The evolutionary ecology of attachment organization. *Human Nature, 7,* 1–38.

Cho, K., Ennaceur, A., Cole, J. C., & Kook Suh, C. (2000). Chronic jet lag produces cognitive deficits. *Journal of Neuroscience, 20*(6), RC66.

Choi, I., Nisbett, R. E., & Norenzayan, A. (1999). Causal attribution across cultures: Variation and universality. *Psychological Bulletin, 125,* 47–63.

Chomsky, N. (1957). *Syntactic structures.* The Hague: Mouton.

Chomsky, N. (1959). A review of B. F. Skinner's "Verbal Behavior." *Language, 35,* 26–58.

Chomsky, N. (1965). *Aspects of theory of syntax.* Cambridge, MA: MIT Press.

Chomsky, N. (1975). *Reflections on language.* New York: Pantheon.

Chomsky, N. (1986). *Knowledge of language: Its nature, origins, and use.* New York: Praeger.

Choudhry, N. K., Stelfox, H. T., & Detsky, A. S. (2002). Relationships between authors of clinical practice guidelines and the pharmaceutical industry. *Journal of the American Medical Association, 287*(5), 612–617.

Christoph, R. T., Schoenfeld, G. A., & Tansky, J. W. (1998). Overcoming barriers to training utilizing technology: The influence of self-efficacy factors on multimedia-based training receptiveness. *Human Resource Development Quarterly, 9,* 25–38.

Chu, J. A., Frey, L. M., Ganzel, B. L., & Matthews, J. A. (1999).

Memories of childhood abuse: Dissociation, amnesia, and corroboration. *American Journal of Psychiatry, 156,* 749–755.

Chun, M. M., & Wolfe, J. M. (2001). Visual attention. In E. B. Goldstein (Ed.), *Blackwell handbook of perception.* Malden, MA: Blackwell.

Church, A. T. (1994). Relating to Tellegen and five-factor models of personality structure. *Journal of Personality and Social Psychology, 67,* 898–909.

Church, A. T., & Lonner, W. J. (1998). The cross-cultural perspective in the study of personality: Rationale and current research. *Journal of Cross-Cultural Psychology, 29,* 32–62.

Church, R. M. (1989). Theories of timing behavior. In S. P. Klein & R. R. Mowrer (Eds.), *Contemporary learning theories: Instrumental conditioning theory and the impact of biological constraints on learning.* Hillsdale, NJ: Erlbaum.

Cialdini, R. B. (1993). *Influence: Science and practice.* Glenview, IL: HarperCollins.

Cialdini, R. B. (2001). *Influence: Science and practice.* Boston: Allyn & Bacon.

Cialdini, R. B., & Trost, M. R. (1998). Social influence: Social norms, conformity, and compliance. In D. T. Gilbert, S. T. Fiske, & G. Lindzey (Eds.), *The handbook of social psychology.* New York: McGraw-Hill.

Cialdini, R. B., Trost, M. R., & Newsom, J. T. (1995). Preference for consistency: The development of a valid measure and the discovery of surprising behavioral implications. *Journal of Personality and Social Psychology, 69,* 318–328.

Cianciolo, A. T., & Sternberg, R. J. (2004). *Intelligence: A brief history.* Malden, MA: Blackwell Publishing.

Clancy, S. A., Schacter, D. L., McNally, R. J., & Pitman, R. K. (2000). False recognition in women reporting recovered memories of sexual abuse. *Psychological Science, 11,* 26–31.

Clark, C., & Freeze, C. (2005, March 4). Ottawa aims to get tough on marijuana gro-ops. *Globe and Mail,* pp. A1, A6.

Clark, D. A., Steer, R. A., Beck, A. T., & Ross, L. (1995). Psychometric characteristics of revised sociotropy and autonomy scales in college students. *Behaviour Research and Therapy, 33,* 325–334.

Clark, D.A. (1998). Canadian perspectives on research in depression. *Canadian Journal of Behavioural Science, 30,* 2107–212.

Clark, L. F. (1993). Stress and the cognitive-conversational benefits of social interaction. *Journal of Social and Clinical Psychology, 12,* 25–55.

Clément, R. (1987). Second language proficiency and acculturation: An investigation of the effects of language status and individual characteristics. *Journal of Language and Social Psychology, 5,* 271–290.

Clow, A. (2001). The physiology of stress. In F. Jones & J. Bright (Eds.), *Stress: Myth, theory, and research.* Harlow, UK: Pearson, Education.

Coates, T. J., & Collins, C. (1998). Preventing HIV infection. *Scientific American, 279*(1), 96–97.

Coenen, A. (1998). Neuronal phenomena associated with vigilance and consciousness: From cellular mechanisms to electroencephalographic patterns. *Consciousness & Cognition: An International Journal, 7,* 42–53.

Cohen, C. E. (1981). Person categories and social perception: Testing some boundaries of the processing effects of prior knowledge. *Journal of Personality and Social Psychology, 40,* 441–452.

Cohen, C. I., & Thompson, K. S. (1992). Homeless mentally ill or mentally ill homeless? *American Journal of Psychiatry, 149,* 816–823.

Cohen, D. (1997). A critique of the use of neuroleptic drugs in psychiatry. In S. Fisher & R. P. Greenberg (Eds.), *From placebo to panacea: Putting psychiatric drugs to the test.* New York: Wiley.

Cohen, D. B. (1999). *Stranger in the nest: Do parents really shape their child's personality, intelligence, or character?* New York: Wiley.

Cohen, D., & McCubbin, M. (1990). The political economy of tardive dyskinesia: Asymmetries in power and responsibility. *The Journal of Mind and Behavior, 11*(3/4), 465–488.

Cohen, H. W., & Alderman, M. H. (2001). The association between depression and cardiovascular disease in patients with hypertension. *Primary Psychiatry, 8*(7), 39–54.

Cohen, M. N. (2002). An anthropologist looks at "race" and IQ testing. In J. M. Fish (Ed.), *Race and intelligence: Separating science from myth* (pp. 201–224). Mahwah, NJ: Erlbaum.

Cohen, N. J., Ryan, J., Hunt, C., Romine, L., Wszalek, T., & Nash, C. (1999). Hippocampal system and declarative (relational) memory: Summarizing the data from functional neuroimaging studies. *Hippocampus, 9,* 83–98.

Cohen, S., & Lichtenstein, E. (1990). Perceived stress, quitting smoking, and smoking relapse. *Health Psychology, 9,* 466–478.

Cohen, S., & Williamson, G. M. (1991). Stress and infectious disease in humans. *Psychological Bulletin, 109*(1), 5–24.

Cohen, S., Kessler, R. C., & Gordon, L. U. (1995). Strategies for measuring stress in studies of psychiatric and physical disorders. In S. Cohen, R. C. Kessler, & L. U. Gordon (Eds.), *Measuring stress: A guide for health and social scientists* (pp. 3–28). New York: Oxford University Press.

Cohen, S., Lichtenstein, E., Prochaska, J. O., Rossi, J. S., Gritz, E. R., Carr, C. R., Orleans, C. T., Schoenbach, V. J., Biener, L., Abrams, D., DiClemente, C., Curry, S., Marlatt, G. A., Cummings, K. M., Emont, S. L., Giovino, A., & Ossip-Klien, D. (1989). Debunking myths about self-quitting: Evidence from 10 prospective studies of persons who attempt to quit smoking by themselves. *American Psychologist, 44,* 1355–1365.

Cohen, S., Tyrrell, D. A. J., & Smith, A. P. (1993). Negative life events, perceived stress, negative affect, and susceptibility to the common cold. *Journal of Personality and Social Psychology, 64,* 131–140.

Cohn, E., Cohn, S., & Bradley, J. (1995). Notetaking, working memory, and learning principles of economics. *Journal of Economics Education, 26,* 291–307.

Coie, J. D., & Dodge, K. A. (1997) Aggression and antisocial behavior. In W. Damon & N. Eisenberg (Eds.), *Handbook of child psychology* (Vol. 3). New York: Wiley.

Colby, A., & Kohlberg, L. (1987). *The measurement of moral judgment* (Vols. 1–2). New York: Cambridge University Press.

Colder, C. R. (2001). Life stress, physiological and subjective indexes of negative emotionality and coping reasons for drinking: Is there evidence for a self-medication model of alcohol use? *Psychology of Addictive Behaviors, 15,* 237–245.

Cole, J. O., Goldberg, S. C., & Davis, J. M. (1966). Drugs in the treatment of psychosis. In P. Solomon (Ed.), *Psychiatric drugs.* New York: Grune & Stratton.

Cole, M. (1999). Culture in development. In M. H. Bornstein & M. E. Lamb (Eds.), *Developmental psychology: An advanced textbook* (4th ed.). Hillsdale, NJ: Erlbaum.

Cole, M., Gay, J., Glick, J. A., Sharp, D. W. (1971). *The cultural context of learning and thinking: An exploration in experimental anthropology.* New York: Basic Books.

Coles, R. (1970). *Erik H. Erikson: The growth of his work.* Boston: Little, Brown.

Collaer, M. L., & Hines, M. (1995). Human behavioral sex differences: A role for gonadal hormones during early development? *Psychological Bulletin, 118,* 55–107.

Collins, A. (1988). *In the sleep room: The story of the CIA brainwashing experiments in Canada.* Toronto: Lester & Orpen Dennys.

Collins, A. M., & Loftus, E. F. (1975). A spreading activation theory of semantic processing. *Psychological Review, 82,* 407–428.

Collins, F. S., & McKusick, V. A. (2001). Implications of the human genome project for medical science. *Journal of the American Medical Association, 285,* 540–544.

Collins, M. A., & Zebrowitz, L. A. (1995). The contributions of appearance to occupational outcomes in civilian and military settings. *Journal of Applied Social Psychology, 25,* 129–163.

Collins, N. L., & Allard, L. M. (2001). Cognitive representations of attachment: The content and function of working models. In G. J. O. Fletcher & M. S. Clark (Eds.), *Blackwell handbook of social psychology: Interpersonal processes.* Malden, MA: Blackwell.

Collins, N. L., & Allard, L. M. (2001). Cognitive representations of attachment: The content and function of working models. In G. J. O. Fletcher & M. S. Clark (Eds.), *Blackwell handbook of social psychology: Interpersonal processes.* Malden, MA: Blackwell.

Collins, W. A., Maccoby, E. E., Steinberg, L., Hetherington, E. M., & Bornstein, M. H. (2000). Contemporary research in parenting: The case for nature and nurture. *American Psychologist, 55,* 218–232.

Coltrane, S. (2001). Research on household labor: Modeling and measuring the social embeddedness of routine family work. In R. M. Milardo (Ed.), *Understanding families into the new millennium: A decade in review* (pp. 427–452). Minneapolis, MN: National Council on Family Relations.

Colvin, C. R., Block, J., & Funder, D. C. (1995). Overly positive self-evaluations and personality: Negative implications for mental health. *Journal of Personality and Social Psychology, 68,* 1152–1162.

Colwill, R. M. (1993). An associative analysis of instrumental learning. *Current Directions in Psychological Science, 2*(4), 111–116.

Comer, D. R. (1995). A model of social loafing in real work groups. *Human Relations, 48,* 647–667.

Conklin, H. M., & Iacono, W. G. (2002). Schizophrenia: A neurodevelopmental perspective. *Current Directions in Psychological Science, 11,* 33–37.

Connolly, J. F., & D'Arcy, R. C. N. (2000). Innovations in neuropsychological assessment using event-related brain potentials. *International Journal of Psychophysiology, 37,* 31–47.

Connolly, J. F., Mate-Kole, C. C., & Joyce, B. (1999). Global aphasia: An innovative assessment approach. *Archives of Physical Medicine and Rehabilitation, 80,* 1309–1315.

Conway, L. C., & Schaller, M. (2002). On the verifiability of evolutionary psychological theories: An analysis of the psychology of scientific persuasion. *Personality and Social Psychology Review, 6,* 152–166.

Coontz, S. (2000). *The way we never were: American families and the nostalgia trap.* New York: Basic Books.

Cooper, E. (1991). A critique of six measures for assessing creativity. *Journal of Creative Behavior, 25*(3), 194–204.

Cooper, H., Okamura, L., & Gurka, V. (1992). Social activity and subjective well-being. *Personality and Individual Differences, 13,* 573–583.

Cooper, J. R., Bloom, F. E., & Roth, R. H. (1996). *The biochemical basis of neuropharmacology.* New York: Oxford University Press.

Cooper, Z. (1995). The development and maintenance of eating disorders. In K. D. Brownell & C. G. Fairburn (Eds.), *Eating disorders and obesity: A comprehensive handbook.* New York: Guilford.

Cope, M. B., Fernandez, J. R., & Allison, D. B. (2004). Genetic and biological risk factors. In J. K. Thompson (Ed.), *Handbook of eating disorders and obesity.* New York: Wiley.

Corballis, M. C. (1991). *The lopsided ape.* New York: Oxford University Press.

Corballis, P. M. (2003). Visuospatial processing and the right-hemisphere interpreter. *Brain & Cognition, 53*(2), 171–176.

Coren, S. (1992). *The left-hander syndrome: The causes and consequences of left-handedness.* New York: Free Press.

Coren, S. (1996). Accidental Death and the shift to Daylight Savings Time. *Perceptual and Motor Skills, 83,* 921–922.

Coren, S. (1996). *Sleep thieves: An eye-opening exploration into the science and mysteries of sleep.* New York: Free Press.

Coren, S., & Aks, D. J. (1990). Moon illusion in pictures: A multi-mechanism approach. *Journal of Experimental Psychology: Human Perception and Performance, 16,* 365–380.

Coren, S., & Girgus, J. S. (1978). *Seeing is deceiving: The psychology of visual illusions.* Hillsdale, NJ: Erlbaum.

Corkin, S. (1984). Lasting consequences of bilateral medial temporal lobectomy: Clinical course and experimental findings in H. M. *Seminars in Neurology, 4,* 249–259.

Cornell, D. G. (1997). Post hoc explanation is not prediction. *American Psychologist, 52,* 1380.

Cornish, K., Sudhalter, V., & Turk, J. (2004). Attention and language in Fragile X. *Mental Retardation and Developmental Disabilities Research Reviews, 10,* 11–16.

Cornoldi, C., & De Beni, R. (1996). Mnemonics and metacognition. In D. J. Herrmann, C. McEvoy, C. Hertzog, P. Hertel, & M. K. Johnson (Eds.), *Basic and applied memory research: Practical applications.* Mahwah, NJ: Erlbaum.

Corsini, R. J. (1999). *The dictionary of psychology.* Philadelphia: Brunner/Mazel.

Cosmides, L. L., & Tooby, J. (1989). Evolutionary psychology and the generation of culture. Part II. Case study: A computational theory of social exchange. *Ethology and Sociobiology, 10,* 51–97.

Cosmides, L., & Tooby, J. (1994). Beyond intuition and instinct blindness: Toward an evolutionarily rigorous cognitive science. *Cognition, 50,* 41–77.

Cosmides, L., & Tooby, J. (1996). Are humans good intuitive statisticians after all? Rethinking some conclusions from the literature on judgment under uncertainty. *Cognition, 58,* 1–73.

Costa, G. (1996). The impact of shift and night work on health. *Applied Ergonomics, 27,* 9–16.

Costa, P. T., Jr., & McCrae, R. R. (1985). *NEO Personality Inventory.* Odessa, FL: Psychological Assessment Resources.

Costa, P. T., Jr., & McCrae, R. R. (1992). *Revised NEO Personality Inventory: NEO PI and NEO Five-Factor Inventory* (Professional Manual). Odessa, FL: Psychological Assessment Resources.

Costa, P. T., Jr., & McCrae, R. R. (1994). Set like plaster? Evidence for the stability of adult personality. In T. F. Heatherton & J. L. Weinberger (Eds.), *Can personality change?* Washington, DC: American Psychological Association.

Costa, P. T., Jr., & McCrae, R. R. (1997). Longitudinal stability of adult personality. In R. Hogan, J. Johnson, & S. Briggs (Eds.), *Handbook of personality psychology.* San Diego: Academic Press.

Costa, P. T., Jr., Terracciano, A., & McCrae, R. R. (2001). Gender differences in personality traits across cultures: Robust and surprising findings. *Journal of Personality and Social Psychology, 81,* 322–331.

Council of Ministers of Education. (2003). *Canadian youth, sexual health and HIV/AIDS Study.* Retrieved May 3, 2005, from http://www.cmec.ca/publications/aids/.

Courage, M. L., & Howe, M. L. (2002). From infant to child: The dynamics of cognitive change in the second year of life. *Psychological Bulletin, 128*(2), 250–277.

Courage, M. L., & Howe, M. L. (2002). From infant to child: The dynamics of cognitive change in the second year of life. *Psychological Bulletin, 128,* 250–277.

Coutts, A. (2000). Nutrition and the life cycle. 1: Maternal nutrition and pregnancy. *British Journal of Nursing, 9,* 1133–1138.

Cowan, N. (1988). Evolving conceptions of memory storage, selective attention, and their mutual constraints within the human information-processing system. *Psychological Bulletin, 104,* 163–191.

Cowan, N. (1995). *Attention and memory: An integrated framework.* New York: Oxford University Press.

Cowan, N. (1999). An embedded-processes model of working memory. In A. Miyake & P. Shah (Eds.), *Models of working memory: Mechanisms of active maintenance and executive control.* New York: Cambridge University Press.

Cowan, N., Wood, N. L., Nugent, L. D., & Treisman, M. (1997). There are two word-length effects in verbal short-term memory: Opposed effects on duration and complexity. *Psychological Science, 8,* 290–295.

Cowan, W. M., Kopinski, K. L., & Hyman, S. E. (2002). The human genome project and its impact on psychiatry. *Annual Review of Neuroscience, 25,* 1–50.

Cowart, B. J., & Rawson, N. E. (2001). Olfaction. In E. B. Goldstein (Ed.), *Blackwell handbook of perception.* Malden, MA: Blackwell.

Cowey, A. (1994). Cortical visual areas and the neurobiology of higher visual processes. In M. J. Farah & G. Ratcliff (Eds.), *The neuropsychology of high-level vision: Collected tutorial essays.* Hillsdale, NJ: Erlbaum.

Cox, B. J., Endler, N. S., & Swinson, R. P. (1991). Clinical and nonclinical panic attacks: An empirical test of a panic attack continuum. *Journal of Anxiety Disorders, 5,* 21–34.

Cox, B. J., Enns, M. W., Walker, J. R., Kjernisted, K., & Pidlubny, S. R. (2001). Psychological vulnerabilities in patients with major depression vs. panic disorder. *Behaviour Research and Therapy, 39,* 567–573.

Cox, M. J., Paley, B., Burchinal, M., & Payne, C. (1999). Marital perceptions and interactions across the transition to parenthood. *Journal of Marriage and the Family, 61,* 611–625.

Coyne, J. C. (1999). Thinking interactionally about depression: A radical restatement. In T. E. Joiner & J. C. Coyne (Eds.), *Interpersonal processes in depression* (pp. 369–392). Washington, DC: American Psychological Association.

Craig, J. C., & Rollman, G. B. (1999). Somesthesis. *Annual Review of Psychology, 50,* 305–331.

Craig, W. & Pepler, D. J. (1997). Observations of bullying and victimization in the schoolyard. *Canadian Journal of School Psychology, 13,* 41–60.

Craik, F. I. M. (2001). Effects of dividing attention on encoding and retrieval processes. In H. L. Roediger III, J. S. Nairne, I. Neath, & A. M. Surprenant (Eds.), *The nature of remembering: Essays in honor of Robert G. Crowder* (pp. 55–68). Washington, DC: American Psychological Association.

Craik, F. I. M. (2002). Levels of processing: Past, present ... and future? *Memory, 10*(5–6), 305–318.

Craik, F. I. M., & Bialystok, E. (2005). Intelligence and executive control: Evidence from aging and bilingualism. *Cortex, 41,* 222–224.

Craik, F. I. M., & Kester, J. D. (2000). Divided attention and memory: Impairment of processing or consolidation? In E. Tulving (Ed.), *Memory, consciousness, and the brain: The Tallinn conference* (pp. 38–51). Philadelphia: Psychology Press.

Craik, F. I. M., & Tulving, E. (1975). Depth of processing and the retention of words in episodic memory. *Journal of Experimental Psychology: General, 104,* 268–294.

Craik, F. I. M., Govoni, R., Naveh-Benjamin, M., & Anderson, N. D. (1996). The effects of divided attention on encoding and retrieval processes in human memory. *Journal of Experimental Psychology: General, 125,* 159–180.

Craik, F. I. M., Moroz, T. M., Moscovitch, M., Stuss, D. T., Winocur, G., Tulving, E., & Kapur, S. (1999). In search of the self: A positron emission tomography study. *Psychological Science, 10,* 26–34.

Craik, F. I. M., & Lockhart, R. S. (1972). Levels of processing: A framework for memory research. *Journal of Verbal Learning and Verbal Behavior, 11,* 671–684.

Crain, S. (1991). Language acquisition in the absence of experience. *Behavioral and Brain Sciences, 14,* 597–650.

Cramer, P. (2000). Defense mechanisms in psychology today: Further processes for adaptation. *American Psychologist, 55*(6), 637–646.

Cramer, P. (2001). The unconscious status of defense mechanisms. *American Psychologist, 56,* 762–763.

Crano, W. D. (1995). Attitude strength and vested interest. In R. E. Petty & J. A. Krosnick (Eds.), *Attitude strength: Antecedents and consequences.* Mahwah, NJ: Erlbaum.

Cravens, H. (1992). A scientific project locked in time: The Terman Genetic Studies of Genius, 1920s–1950s. *American Psychologist, 47,* 183–189.

Crawford, J. D., Medendorp, W. P., & Marotta, J. J. (2004). Spatial transformations for eye-hand coordination. *Journal of Neurophysiology, 92,* 10–19.

Crawford, M., & Popp, D. (2003). Sexual double standards: A review and methodological critique of two decades of research. *Journal of Sex Research, 40*(1), 13–26.

Creed, F. (1989). Appendectomy. In G. W. Brown & T. O. Harris (Eds.), *Life events and illness.* New York: Guilford.

Creed, T. L. (1987). Subliminal deception: Pseudoscience on the college lecture circuit. *The Skeptical Inquirer, 11,* 358–366.

Crick, N. R., & Rose, A. J. (2000). Toward a gender-balanced approach to the study of social-emotional development: A look at relational aggression. In R. G. Geen & E. Donnerstein (Eds.), *Human aggression: Theories, research, and implications for social policy* (pp. 153–168). San Diego, CA: Academic Press.

Crick, N. R., Casas, J. F., & Mosher, M. (1997). Relational and overt aggression in preschool. *Developmental Psychology, 33,* 579–588.

Critelli, J. W., & Ee, J. S. (1996). Stress and physical illness: Development of an integrative model. In T. W. Miller (Ed.), *Theory and assessment of stressful life events.* Madison, CT: International Universities Press.

Crits-Christoph, P. (1997). Limitations of the dodo bird verdict and the role of clinical trials in psychotherapy research: Comment on Wampold et al (1997). *Psychological Bulletin, 122,* 216–220.

Crockett, H. (1962). The achievement motive and differential occupational mobility in the United States. *American Sociological Review, 27,* 191–204.

Croizet, J., & Claire, T. (1998). Extending the concept of stereotype threat to social class: The intellectual underperformance of students from low socioeconomic backgrounds. *Personality and Social Psychology Bulletin, 24,* 588–594.

Croizet, J., Despres, G., Gauzins, M. E., Huguet, P., Leyens, J., & Meot, A. (2004). Stereotype threat undermines intellectual performance by triggering a disruptive mental load. *Personality and Social Psychology Bulletin, 30,* 721–731.

Cronbach, L. J. (1992). *Acceleration among the Terman males: Correlates in midlife and after.* Paper presented at the Symposium in Honor of Julian Stanley, San Francisco.

Cropley, A. J. (2000). Defining and measuring creativity: Are creativity tests worth using? *Roeper Review, 23,* 72–79.

Cross, S. E., & Markus, H. R. (1993). Gender in thought, belief, and action: A cognitive approach. In A. E. Beall & R. J. Sternberg (Eds.), *The psychology of gender.* New York: Guilford.

Cross, S. E., & Markus, H. R. (1999). The cultural constitution of personality. In L. A. Pervin & O. P. John (Eds.), *Handbook of personality: Theory and research.* New York: Guilford.

Crowder, R. G. (1993). Short-term memory: Where do we stand? *Memory & Cognition, 21,* 142–145.

Crowder, R. G., & Greene, R. L. (2000). Serial learning: Cognition and behavior. In E. Tulving & F. I. M. Craik (Eds.), *The Oxford handbook of memory* (pp. 125–136). New York: Oxford University Press.

Crowell, J. A., Fraley, R. C., & Shaver, P. R. (1999). Measurement of individual differences in adolescent and adult attachment. In J. Cassidy & P. R. Shaver (Eds.), *Handbook of attachment: Theory, research, and clinical applications.* New York: Guilford.

Crowell, J. A., Fraley, R. C., & Shaver, P. R. (1999). Measurement of individual differences in adolescent and adult attachment. In J. Cassidy & P. R. Shaver (Eds.), *Handbook of attachment: Theory, research, and clinical applications.* New York: Guilford.

Crowley, K., Callanan, M. A., Tenenbaum, H. R., & Allen, E. (2001). Parents explain more often to boys than to girls during shared scientific thinking. *Psychological Science, 12,* 258–261.

Croyle, R. T., & Cooper, J. (1983). Dissonance arousal: Physiological evidence. *Journal of Personality and Social Psychology, 45,* 782–791.

Cruz, C., della Rocco, P., & Hackworth, C. (2000). Effects of quick rotating schedules on the health and adjustment of air traffic controllers. *Aviation, Space, & Environmental Medicine, 71,* 400–407.

Csikszentmihalyi, M. (1994). Creativity. In R. J. Sternberg (Ed.), *Encyclopedia of human intelligence.* New York: Macmillan.

Csikszentmihalyi, M. (1999). Implications of a systems perspective for the study of creativity. In R. J. Sternberg (Ed.), *Handbook of creativity.* New York: Cambridge University Press.

Cuban, L. (2004). Assessing the 20-year impact of multiple intelligences on schooling. *Teachers College Record, 106*(1), 140–146.

Cuesta, M. J., Peralta, B., & DeLeon, J. (1994). Schizophrenic syndromes associated with treatment response. *Progress in Neurology, Psychopharmacology, and Biological Psychiatry, 18,* 87–99.

Culnane, M., Fowler, M. G., Lee, S. S., McSherry, G., Brady, M., & O'Donnell, K. (1999). Lack of long-term effects of in utero exposure to zidovudine among uninfected children born to HIV-infected women. *Journal of the American Medical Association, 281,* 151–157.

Culpepper, L., Davidson, J. R. T., Dietrich, A. J., Goodman, W. K., Kroenke, K., & Schwenk, T. L. (2004). Suicidality as a possible effect of antidepressant treatment. *Journal of Clinical Psychiatry, 65,* 742–749.

Cummins, D. (2005). Dominance, status, and social hierarchies. In D. M. Buss (Ed.), *The handbook of evolutionary psychology.* New York: Wiley.

Cunningham, C. O., & Selwyn, P. A. (2005). HIV-related medical complications and treatment. In J. H. Lowinson, P. Ruiz, R. B. Millman, & J. G. Langrod (Eds.), *Substance abuse: A comprehensive textbook.* Philadelphia: Lippincott/Williams & Williams.

Cunningham, M. R., Druen, P. B., & Barbee, A. P. (1997). Angels, mentors, and friends: Trade-offs among evolutionary, social, and individual variables in physical appearance. In J. A. Simpson & D. T. Kenrick (Eds.), *Evolutionary social psychology.* Mahwah, NJ: Erlbaum.

Cunningham, M. R., Roberts, A. R., Barbee, A. P., Druen, P. B., & Wu, C. (1995). "Their ideas of beauty are, on the whole, the same as ours": Consistency and variability in the cross-cultural perception of female physical attractiveness. *Journal of Personality and Social Psychology, 68,* 261–279.

Cushman, P. (1992). Psychotherapy to 1992: A historically situated interpretation. In D. K. Freedheim (Ed.), *History of psychotherapy: A century of change.* Washington, DC: American Psychological Association.

Cutler, B. L., & Penrod, S. D. (1995). *Mistaken identification: The eyewitness, psychology, and the law.* New York: Cambridge University Press.

Cutting, L. P., & Docherty, N. M. (2000). Schizophrenia outpatients' perceptions of their parents: Is expressed emotion a factor? *Journal of Abnormal Psychology, 109,* 266–272.

Czeisler, C. A., & Khalsa, S. B. S. (2000). The human circadian timing system and sleep-wake regulation. In M. H. Kryger, T. Roth, & W. C. Dement (Eds.), *Principles and practice of sleep medicine.* Philadelphia: Saunders.

Czeisler, C. A., Buxton, O. M., & Khalsa, S. (2005). The human circadian timing system and sleep-wake regulation. In M. H. Kryger, T. Roth, & W. C. Dement (Eds.), *Principles and practice of sleep medicine.* Philadelphia: Elsevier Saunders.

Czeisler, C. A., Cajochen, C., & Turek, F. W. (2000). Melatonin in the regulation of sleep and circadian rhythms. In M. H. Kryger, T. Roth, & W. C. Dement (Eds.), *Principles and practice of sleep medicine.* Philadelphia: Saunders.

Dallaire, R. A. (2003). *Shake hands with the devil: The failure of humanity in Rwanda.* Toronto: Random House.

Dallman, M. F., Bhatnagar, S., & Viau, V. (2000). Hypothalamo-pituitary-adrenal axis. In G. Fink (Ed.), *Encyclopedia of stress* (Vol. 2, pp. 468–476). San Diego: Academic Press.

Daly, M., & Wilson, M. (1985). Child abuse and other risks of not living with both parents. *Ethology and Sociobiology, 6*, 197–210.

Daly, M., & Wilson, M. (1988). *Homicide.* Hawthorne, NY: Aldine.

Dan, B. A., & Gleason, J. B. (2001). Semantic development: Learning the meanings of words. In J. B. Gleason (Ed.), *The development of language* (5th ed., pp. 125–161). Boston: Allyn & Bacon.

D'Andrade, R. G. (1961). Anthropological studies of dreams. In F. Hsu (Ed.), *Psychological anthropology: Approaches to culture and personality.* Homewood, IL: Dorsey Press.

Daniel, M. H. (1997). Intelligence testing: Status and trends. *American Psychologist, 52*, 1038–1045.

Danielle Peers: Featured Athlete (2004). Retrieved May 2, 2005, from http://www.paralympic.ca/ english/athens2004/featured_ athlete.

Danton, W. G., & Antonuccio, D. O. (1997). A focused empirical analysis of treatments for panic and anxiety. In S. Fisher & R. P. Greenberg (Eds.), *From placebo to panacea: Putting psychiatric drugs to the test.* New York: Wiley.

Danziger, K. (1990). *Constructing the subject: Historical origins of psychological research.* Cambridge, England: Cambridge University Press.

Darley, J. M., & Latané, B. (1968). Bystander intervention in emergencies: Diffusion of responsibility. *Journal of Personality and Social Psychology, 8*, 377–383.

Darwin, C. (1859). *On the origin of species.* London: Murray.

Darwin, C. (1871). *Descent of man.* London: Murray.

Darwin, C. (1872). *The expression of emotions in man and animals.* New York: Philosophical Library.

Das, H. H. J., de Wit, J. B. F., & Stroebe, W. (2005). Fear appeals motivate acceptance of action recommendations: Evidence for a positive bias in the processing of persuasive messages. *Personality and Social Psychology Bulletin, 29*, 650–664.

Das, J. P. (1992). Beyond a unidimensional scale of merit. *Intelligence, 16*(2), 137–149.

Das, J. P. (1994). Eastern views of intelligence. In R. J. Sternberg (Ed.), *Encyclopedia of human intelligence.* New York: Macmillan.

Dasen, P. R. (1994). Culture and cognitive development from a Piagetian perspective. In W. J. Lonner & R. Malpass (Eds.), *Psychology and culture.* Boston: Allyn & Bacon.

Davidoff, J. (2001). Language and perceptual categorization. *Trends in Cognitive Sciences, 5*, 382–387.

Davidoff, J. (2004). Coloured thinking. *Psychologist, 17*, 570–572.

Davidson, J. E. (2003). Insights about insightful problem solving. In J. E. Davidson & R. J. Sternberg (Eds.), *The psychology of problem solving.* New York: Cambridge University Press.

Davidson, R. J., Jackson, D. C., & Kalin, N. H. (2000). Emotion, plasticity, context, and regulation: Perspectives from affective neuroscience. *Psychological Bulletin, 126*, 890–909.

Davidson, R. J., Kabat-Zinn, J., Schumacher, J., Rosenkranz, M., Muller, D., Santorelli, S. F., Urbanowski, F., Harrington, A., Bonus, K., & Sheridan, J. F. (2003a). Alterations in brain and immune function produced by mindfulness meditation. *Psychosomatic Medicine, 65*, 564–570.

Davidson, R. J., Pizzagalli, D., Nitschke, J. B., & Kalin, N. H. (2003b). Parsing the subcomponents of emotion and disorders of emotion: Perspectives from affective neuroscience. In R. J. Davidson, K. R. Scherer, & H. H. Goldsmith (Eds.), *Handbook of affective sciences.* New York: Oxford University Press.

Davies, I. R. L. (1998). A study of colour in three languages: A test of linguistic relativity hypothesis. *British Journal of Psychology, 89*, 433–452.

Davis, D. M. (1990). Portrayals of women in prime-time network television: Some demographic characteristics. *Sex Roles, 23*, 325–332.

Davis, D., Shaver, P. R., & Vernon, M. L. (2003). Physical, emotional, and behavioral reactions to breaking up: The roles of gender, age, emotional involvement, and attachment style. *Personality and Social Psychology Bulletin, 29*, 871–884.

Davis, H. (1996). Underestimating the rat's intelligence. *Cognitive Brain Research, 3*, 291–298.

Davis, J. L., & Rusbult, C. E. (2001). Attitude alignment in close relationships. *Journal of Personality and Social Psychology, 81*(1), 65–84.

Davis, M. H., Morris, M. M., & Kraus, L. A. (1998). Relationship-specific and global perceptions of social support: Associations with well-being and attachment. *Journal of Personality and Social Psychology, 74*, 468–481.

Davis, S. (2000). Testosterone and sexual desire in women. *Journal of Sex Education & Therapy, 25*, 25–32.

Dawod, N. (1995). Stressors encountered by junior high school students and their relation to grade point average, sex and grade. *Dirasat, 22A (Supplement)*, 3671–3706.

Dawson, W. A. (1993). Aboriginal dreaming. In M. A. Carskadon (Ed.), *Encyclopedia of sleep and dreaming.* New York: Macmillan.

Day, R. H. (1965). Inappropriate constancy explanation of spatial distortions. *Nature, 207*, 891–893.

Deal, T., & Kennedy, A. (1982). *Corporate cultures.* Reading, MA: Addison-Wesley.

Deary, I. J. (2000). Simple information processing and intelligence. In R. J. Sternberg (Ed.), *Handbook of intelligence* (pp. 267–284). New York: Cambridge University Press.

Deary, I. J., & Stough, C. (1996). Intelligence and inspection time: Achievements, prospects, and problems. *American Psychologist, 51*, 599–608.

Deary, I. J., Caryl, P. G., & Gibson, G. J. (1993). Nonstationarity and the measurement of psychological response in a visual inspection time task. *Perception, 22*, 1245–1256.

Deaux, K. (1993). Commentary: Sorry, wrong number—A reply to Gentile's call. *Psychological Science, 4*, 125–126.

De Boysson-Bardies, B., & Vihman, M. (1991). Adaptation to language: Evidence from babbling and early words in four languages. *Language, 61*, 297–319.

DeCarvalho, R. J. (1991). *The founders of humanistic psychology.* New York: Praeger.

deCharms, R., & Moeller, G. H. (1962). Values expressed in American children's readers: 1800–1950. *Journal of Abnormal and Social Psychology, 64*, 136–142.

De Cock, K. M., & Janssen, R. S. (2002). An unequal epidemic in an unequal world. *Journal of the American Medical Association, 288*, 236–238.

Defeyter, M. A., & German, T. P. (2003). Acquiring an understanding of design: Evidence from children's insight problem solving. *Cognition, 89*(2), 133–155.

DeFrain, J., & Olson, D. H. (1999). Contemporary family patterns and relationships. In M. B. Sussman, S. K. Steinmetz & G. W. Peterson (Eds.), *Handbook of marriage and the family* (pp. 309–326). New York: Plenum.

De Guise, E. & Lassonde, M. (2001). Callosal contribution to procedural learning in children. *Developmental Neuropsychology, 19*, 253–272.

De Guise, E., Del Pesce, M., Foschi, N., Quattrini, A., Papo, I., & Lassonde, M. (1999). Callosal and cortical contribution to procedural learning. *Brain, 122*, 1049–1062.

de Houwer, A. (1995). Bilingual language acquisition. In P. Fletcher & B. MacWhinney (Eds.), *The handbook of child language.* Oxford, OH: Basil Blackwell.

De Houwer, J. (2001). Contingency awareness and evaluative conditioning: When will it be enough? *Consciousness & Cognition: An International Journal, 10*, 550–558.

de Houwer, J., Hendrickx, H., & Baeyens, F. (1997). Evaluative learning with "subliminally" presented stimuli. *Consciousness & Cognition: An International Journal, 6*, 87–107.

de Jong, P. J., & Merckelbach, H. (2000). Phobia-relevant illusory correlations: The role of phobic responsivity. *Journal of Abnormal Psychology, 109*, 597–601.

De Koninck, J. (1997). Sleep, the common denominator for psychological adaptation. *Canadian Psychology, 38*, 191–195.

De Koninck, J. (2000). Waking experiences and dreaming. In M. H. Kryger, T. Roth, & W. C. Dement (Eds.), *Principles and practice of sleep medicine.* Philadelphia: Saunders.

Delay, J., & Deniker, P. (1952). *Trente-huit cas de psychoses traitees par la cure prolongee et continue de 4560 RP.* Paris: Masson et Cie.

Delis, D. C., & Lucas, J. A. (1996). Memory. In B. S. Fogel, R. B. Schiffer, & S. M. Rao (Eds.), *Neuropsychiatry.* Baltimore: Williams & Wilkins.

DelMonte, M. M. (2000). Retrieved memories of childhood sexual abuse. *British Journal of Medical Psychology, 73*, 1–13.

DeLong, M. R. (2000). The basal ganglia. In E. R. Kandel, J. H. Schwartz, & T. M. Jessell (Eds.), *Principles of neural science* (pp. 853–872). New York: McGraw-Hill.

DeLongis, A., Capreol, M., Holtzman, S., O'Brien, T., & Campbell, J. (2004). Social support and social strain among husbands and wives: A multilevel analysis. *Journal of Family Psychology, 18*, 470–479.

DeLongis, A., Folkman, S., & Lazarus, R. S. (1988). The impact of daily stress on health and mood: Psychological and social resources as mediators. *Journal of Personality and Social Psychology, 54,* 486–495.

Delorme, M.-A., Lortie-Lussie, M., & De Koninck, J. (2002). Stress and coping in the waking and dreaming states during an examination period. *Dreaming, 12,* 171–183.

Delprato, D. J., & Midgley, B. D. (1992). Some fundamentals of B. F. Skinner's behaviorism. *American Psychologist, 47,* 1507–1520.

DeMaio, T. J. (1984). Social desirability and survey measurement: A review. In C. F. Turner & E. Martin (Eds.), *Surveying subjective phenomena* (Vol. 2). New York: Russell Sage Foundation.

Dement, W. C. (1978). *Some must watch while some must sleep.* New York: Norton.

Dement, W. C. (1992). *The sleepwatchers.* Stanford, CA: Stanford Alumni Association.

Dement, W. C. (1997). The perils of drowsy driving. *New England Journal Medicine, 337,* 783–784.

Dement, W. C. (2000). History of sleep physiology and medicine. In M. H. Kryger, T. Roth, & W. C. Dement (Eds.), *Principles and practice of sleep medicine.* Philadelphia: Saunders.

Dement, W. C. (2003). Knocking on Kleitman's door: The view from 50 years later. *Sleep Medicine Reviews, 7*(4), 289–292.

Dement, W. C. (2005). History of sleep psychology. In M. H. Kryger, T. Roth, & W. C. Dement (Eds.), *Principles and practice of sleep medicine.* Philadelphia: Elsevier Saunders.

Dement, W. C., & Vaughan, C. (1999). *The promise of sleep.* New York: Delacorte Press.

Dement, W. C., & Wolpert, E. (1958). The relation of eye movements, bodily motility, and external stimuli to dream content. *Journal of Experimental Psychology, 53,* 543–553.

Demo, D. H. (1992). Parent-child relations: Assessing recent changes. *Journal of Marriage and the Family, 54,* 104–117.

Dempster, F. N. (1996). Distributing and managing the conditions of encoding and practice. In E. L. Bjork & R. A. Bjork (Eds.), *Memory.* San Diego: Academic Press.

Dennerstein, L. (1996). Well-being, symptoms and the menopausal transition. *Maturitas, 23,* 147–157.

Dennerstein, L., Dudley, E., & Guthrie, J. (2002). Empty nest or revolving door? A prospective study of women's quality of life in midlife during the phase of children leaving and re-entering the home. *Psychological Medicine, 32,* 545–550.

Dennis, W. (1966). Age and creative productivity. *Journal of Gerontology, 21*(1), 1–8.

Derogatis, L. R., & Coons, H. L. (1993). Self-report measures of stress. In L. Goldberger & S. Breznitz (Eds.), *Handbook of stress: Theoretical and clinical aspects* (2nd ed.). New York: Free Press.

Desimone, R. (1991). Face selective cells in the temporal cortex of monkeys. *Journal of Cognitive Neuroscience, 3,* 1–8.

Des Jarlais, D. C., Hagan, H., & Friedman, S. R. (1997). Epidemiology and emerging public health perspectives. In J. H. Lowinson, P. Ruiz, R. B. Millman, & J. G. Langrod (Eds.), *Substance abuse: A comprehensive textbook.* Baltimore: Williams & Wilkins.

Des Jarlais, D. C., Hagan, H., & Friedman, S. R. (2005). Epidemiology and emerging public health perspectives. In J. H. Lowinson, P. Ruiz, R. B. Millman, & J. G. Langrod (Eds.), *Substance abuse: A comprehensive textbook.* Philadelphia: Lippincott/Williams & Wilkins.

Detterman, L. T., Gabriel, L. T., & Ruthsatz, J. M. (2000). Intelligence and mental retardation. In R. J. Sternberg (Ed.), *Handbook of intelligence* (pp. 141–158). New York: Cambridge University Press.

Deutch, J. A. (1990). Food intake: Gastric factors. In E. M. Stricker (Ed), *Handbook of behavioral neurobiology: Vol 10. Neurobiology of food and fluid intake.* New York: Plenum.

DeValois, R. L., & Jacobs, G. H. (1984). Neural mechanisms of color vision. In I. Darian-Smith (Ed.), *The nervous system* (Vol. 3). Baltimore: Williams & Wilkins.

De Villiers, P. (1977). Choice in concurrent schedules and a quantitative formulation of the law of effect. In W. K. Honig & J. E. R. Staddon (Eds.), *Handbook of operant behavior.* Englewood Cliffs, NJ: Prentice-Hall.

de Villiers, P. A. & de Villiers, J. G. (1992). Language development. In M. H. Bornstein & M. E. Lamb (Eds.), *Developmental psychology: An advanced textbook* (3rd ed.). Hillsdale, NJ: Erlbaum.

Devine, P. G., & Monteith, M. J. (1999). Automaticity and control in stereotyping. In S. Chaiken & Y. Trope (Eds.), *Dual-process theories in social psychology.* New York: Guilford.

Devine, P. G., Plant, E. A., & Blair, I. V. (2001). Classic and contemporary analysis of racial prejudice. In R. Brown & S. L. Gaertner (Eds.), *Blackwell handbook of social psychology: Intergroup processes.* Malden, MA: Blackwell.

Devine, P. G., Tauer, J. M., Barron, K. E., Elliot, A. J., & Vance, K. M. (1999). Moving beyond attitude change in the study of dissonance-related processes. In E. Harmon-Jones & J. Mills (Eds.), *Cognitive dissonance: Progress on a pivotal theory in social psychology.* Washington, DC: American Psychological Association.

Devlin, B., Daniels, M., & Roeder, K. (1997). The heritability of IQ. *Nature, 388,* 468–471.

Devlin, B., Fienberg, S. E., Resnick, D. P., & Roeder, K. (2002). Intelligence and success: Is it all in the genes? In J. M. Fish (Ed.), *Race and intelligence: Separating science from myth* (pp. 355–368). Mahwah, NJ: Erlbaum.

Devlin, M. J., Yanovski, S. Z., & Wilson, G. T. (2000). Obesity: What mental health professionals need to know. *American Journal of Psychiatry, 157,* 854–866.

Dew, M. A., Bromet, E. J., & Switzer, G. E. (2000). Epidemiology. In M. Hersen & A. S. Bellack (Eds.), *Psychopathology in adulthood.* Boston: Allyn & Bacon.

Dewees, M., Pulice, R. T., & McCormick, L. L. (1996). Community integration of former state hospital patients: Outcomes of a policy shift in Vermont. *Psychiatric Services, 47,* 1088–1092.

de Wijk, R. A., Schab, F. R., & Cain, W. S. (1995). Odor identification. In F. R. Schab & R. G. Crowder (Eds.), *Memory for odors.* Mahwah, NJ: Erlbaum.

de Wolff, M. S., & van IJzendoorn, M. H. (1997). Sensitivity and attachment: A meta-analysis on parental antecedents of infant attachment. *Child Development, 68,* 571–591.

Deyoub, P. L. (1984). Hypnotic stimulation of antisocial behavior: A case report. *International Journal of Clinical and Experimental Hypnosis, 32*(3), 301–306.

Di Chiara, G. (1999). Drug addiction as a dopamine-dependent associative learning disorder. *European Journal of Pharmacology, 375,* 13–30.

Dick, D. M., & Rose, R. J. (2002). Behavior genetics: What's new? What's next? *Current Directions in Psychological Science, 11*(2), 70–74.

Dickens, W. T., & Flynn, J. R. (2001). Heritability estimates versus large environmental effects: The IQ paradox resolved. *Psychological Review, 108,* 346–369.

Dickens, W. T., & Flynn, J. R. (2001). Heritability estimates versus large environmental effects: The IQ paradox resolved. *Psychological Review, 108,* 346–369.

Diebel, L. & Roy, C. (2004). You made me do this. *Toronto Star,* August 27, 2004, pp. A1.

Diener, E. (1984). Subjective well-being. *Psychological Bulletin, 93,* 542–575.

Diener, E., & Diener, C. (1996). Most people are happy. *Psyhological Science, 7,* 181–185.

Diener, E., & Diener, M. (1995). Cross-cultural correlates of life satisfaction and self-esteem. *Journal of Personality and Social Psychology, 68,* 653–663.

Diener, E., & Lucas, R. E. (1999). Personality and subjective well-being. In D. Kahneman, E. Diener, & N. Schwarz (Eds.), *Well-being: The foundations of hedonic psychology.* New York: Russell Sage Foundation.

Diener, E., & Seligman, E. P. (2002). Very happy people. *Psychological Science, 13,* 81–84.

Diener, E., & Seligman, M. E. P. (2004). Beyond money: Toward an economy of well-being. *Psychological Science in the Public Interest, 5*(1), 1–31.

Diener, E., Diener, M., & Diener, C. (1995). Factors predicting the subjective well-being of nations. *Journal of Personality and Social Psychology, 69,* 851–864.

Diener, E., Gohm, C. L., Suh, E., & Oishi, S. (2000). Similarity of the relations between marital status and subjective well-being across cultures. *Journal of Cross-Cultural Psychology, 31,* 419–436.

Diener, E., Sandvik, E., Seidlitz, L., & Diener, M. (1993). The relationship between income and subjective well-being. Relative or absolute? *Social Indicators Research, 28,* 195–223.

Diener, E., Wolsic, B., & Fujita, F. (1995). Physical attractiveness and subjective well-being. *Journal of Personality and Social Psychology, 69,* 120–129.

Dijksterhuis, A. (2004). I like myself but I don't know why: Enhancing implicit self-esteem by subliminal evaluative conditioning. *Journal of Personality and Social Psychology, 86,* 345–355.

Dillbeck, M. C., & Orme-Johnson, D. W. (1987). Physiological differences between transcendental meditation and rest. *American Psychologist, 42,* 879–881.

Di Lorenzo, P. M., & Youngentob, S. L. (2003). Olfaction and taste. In M. Gallagher & R. J. Nelson (Eds.), *Handbook of psychology, Vol. 3: Biological psychology*. New York: Wiley.

Dilsaver, S. C., Chen, Y. R., Shoaib, A. M., & Swann, A. C. (1999). Phenomenology of mania: Evidence for distinct depressed, dysphoric, and euphoric presentations. *American Journal of Psychiatry, 156*, 426–430.

DiMatteo, M. R. (1991). *The psychology of health, illness, and medical care: An individual perspective*. Pacific Grove, CA: Brooks/Cole.

DiMatteo, M. R. (1994). Enhancing patient adherence to medical recommendations. *Journal of the American Medical Association, 271*, 79–83.

DiMatteo, M. R. (1997). Health behaviors and care decisions: An overview of professional-patient communication. In D. S. Gochman (Ed.), *Handbook of health behavior research II: Provider determinants*. New York: Plenum.

DiMatteo, M. R., & Friedman, H. S. (1982). *Social psychology and medicine*. Cambridge, MA: Oelgeschlager, Gunn & Hain.

Din, J. N., Newby, D. E., & Flapan, A. D. (2004). Omega 3 fatty acids and cardiovascular disease—fishing for a natural treatment. *British Medical Journal, 328*, 30–35.

Dinges, D. F. (1989). Napping patterns and effects in human adults. In D. F. Dinges & R. J. Broughton (Eds.), *Sleep and alertness: Chronobiological, behavioral, and medical aspects of napping*. New York: Raven.

Dinges, D. F. (1993). Napping. In M.A. Carskadon (Ed.), *Encyclopedia of sleep and dreaming*. New York: Macmillan.

Dinges, D. F. (1995). Overview of sleepiness and accidents. *Journal of Sleep Research, 4*, 4–14.

Dinges, D. F., Rogers, N. L., & Baynard, M. D. (2005). Chronic sleep deprivation. In M. H. Kryger, T. Roth, & W. C. Dement (Eds.), *Principles and practice of sleep medicine*. Philadelphia: Elsevier Saunders.

DiNicola, D. D., & DiMatteo, M. R. (1984). Practitioners, patients, and compliance with medical regimens: A social psychological perspective. In A. Baum, S. E. Taylor, & J. E. Singer (Eds.), *Handbook of psychology and health: Vol. 4. Social psychological aspects of health*. Hillsdale, NJ: Erlbaum.

Dinsmoor, J. A. (1992). Setting the record straight: The social views of B. F. Skinner. *American Psychologist, 47*, 1454–1463.

Dinsmoor, J. A. (1998). Punishment. In W. O'Donohue (Ed.), *Learning and behavior therapy*. Boston: Allyn & Bacon.

Dion, K. (1973). Young children's stereotyping of facial attractiveness. *Developmental Psychology, 9*, 183–188.

Dion, K. K., & Dion, K. L. (1996). Cultural perspectives on romantic love. *Personal Relationships, 3*, 5–17.

Dion, K. L. (2003). Prejudice, racism, and discrimination. In T. Millon & M. J. Lerner (Eds.), *Handbook of Psychology, Vol. 5: Personality and social psychology*. New York: Wiley.

Dion, K., Berscheid, E., & Walster, E. (1972). What is beautiful is good. *Journal of Personality and Social Psychology, 24*, 285–290.

Dixon, M., & Laurence, J. R. (1992). Two hundred years of hypnosis research: Questions resolved? Questions unanswered! In E. Fromm & M. R. Nash (Eds.), *Contemporary hypnosis research*. New York: Guilford.

Dixon, R. A., & Cohen, A. (2003). Cognitive development in adulthood. In R. M. Lerner, M. A. Easterbrooks, & J. Mistry (Eds.), *Handbook of psychology, Vol. 6: Developmental psychology*. New York: Wiley.

Dobson, K. S. (2002). A national imperative: Public funding of psychological services. *Canadian Psychology, 43*, 65–76.

Dobson, K. S. (Ed.). (2001). *Handbook of cognitive-behavioral therapies*. New York: Guilford Press.

Dobson, K. S., & Dozois, D. J. A. (2001). Professional psychology and the prescription debate: Still not ready to go to the altar. *Canadian Psychology, 42*, 131–135.

Dobzhansky, T. (1937). *Genetics and the origin of species*. New York: Columbia University Press.

Dodwell, P. C. & Humphrey, G. K. (1990). A functional theory of the McCollough Effect. *Psychological Review, 97*, 78–89.

Doerr, P., Pirke, K. M., Kockott, G., & Dittmor, F. (1976). Further studies on sex hormones in male homosexuals. *Archives of General Psychiatry, 33*, 611–614.

Doghramji, P. P. (2001). Detection of insomnia in primary care. *Journal of Clinical Psychiatry, 62* (suppl 10), 18–26.

Dolan, M., Anderson, I. M., & Deakin, J. F. W. (2001). Relationship between 5-HT function and impulsivity and aggression in male offenders with personality disorders. *British Journal of Psychiatry, 178*, 352–359.

Dolan-Sewell, R. T., Krueger, R. F., & Shea, M. T. (2001). Co-occurrence with syndrome disorders. In W. J. Livesley (Ed.), *Handbook of personality disorders: Theory, research, and treatment*. New York: Guilford.

Dollard, J., & Miller, N. E. (1950). *Personality and psychotherapy: An analysis in terms of learning, thinking and culture*. New York: McGraw-Hill.

Dollard, J., Doob, L. W., Miller, N. E., Mowrer, O. H., & Sears, R. R. (1939). *Frustration and aggression*. New Haven: Yale University Press.

Domhoff, G. W. (2000). Methods and measures for the study of dream content. In M. H. Kryger, T. Roth, & W. C. Dement (Eds.), *Principles and practice of sleep medicine*. Philadelphia: Saunders.

Domhoff, G. W. (2001). A new neurocognitive theory of dreams. *Dreaming, 11*, 13–33.

Domhoff, G. W. (2005a). The content of dreams: Methodologic and theoretical implications. In M. H. Kryger, T. Roth, & W. C. Dement (Eds.), *Principles and practice of sleep medicine*. Philadelphia: Elsevier Saunders.

Domhoff, G. W. (2005b). Refocusing the neurocognitive approach to dreams: A critique of the Hobson versus Solms debate. *Dreaming, 15*(1), 3–20.

Dominowski, R. L., & Bourne, L. E., Jr. (1994). History of research on thinking and problem solving. In R. J. Sternberg (Ed.), *Thinking and problem solving*. San Diego: Academic Press.

Domjan, M. (1992). Adult learning and mate choice: Possibilities and experimental evidence. *American Zoologist, 32*, 48–61.

Domjan, M. (1994). Formulation of a behavior system for sexual conditioning. *Psychonomic Bulletin & Review, 1*, 421–428.

Domjan, M. (1998). *The principles of learning and behavior*. Pacific Grove: Brooks/Cole.

Domjan, M., Blesbois, E., & Williams, J. (1998). The adaptive significance of sexual conditioning: Pavlovian control of sperm release. *Psychological Science, 9*, 411–415.

Donahoe, J. W., & Vegas, R. (2004). Pavlovian conditioning: The CS-UR relation. *Journal of Experimental Psychology: Animal Behavior Processes, 30*(1), 17–33.

Donn, L. (1988). *Freud and Jung: Years of friendship, years of loss*. New York: Scribner's.

Donnerstein, E., & Malamuth, N. (1997). Pornography: Its consequences on the observer. In L. B. Schlesinger & E. Revitch (Eds.), *Sexual dynamics of anti-social behavior*. Springfield, IL: Charles C. Thomas.

Donnerstein, E., Linz, D., & Penrod, S. (1987). *The question of pornography: Research findings and policy implications*. New York: Free Press.

Dorfman, D. D. (1995). Soft science with a neoconservative agenda. *Contemporary Psychology, 40*, 418–421.

Dorn, L. D., Nottelmann, E. D., Susman, E. J., Inoff-Germain, G., Cutler, G. B., & Chrousos, G. P. (1999). Variability in hormone concentrations and self-reported menstrual histories in young adolescents: Menarche as an integral part of a developmental process. *Journal of Youth and Adolescence, 28*, 283–304.

Dorner, G. (1988). Neuroendocrine response to estrogen and brain differentiation. *Archives of Sexual Behavior, 17*(1), 57–75.

Doty, R. L. (1991). Olfactory system. In T. V. Getchell, R. L. Doty, L. M. Bartoshuk, & J. B. Snow, Jr. (Eds.), *Smell and taste in health and disease*. New York: Raven.

Doty, R. L. (2001). Olfaction. *Annual Review of Psychology, 52*, 423–452.

Dougall, A. L., & Baum, A. (2001). Stress, health, and illness. In A. Baum, T. A. Revenson & J. E. Singer (Eds.), *Handbook of health psychology* (pp. 321–338). Mahwah, NJ: Erlbaum.

Dougherty, D. D., & Rauch, S. L. (2003). Brain imaging in psychiatry. In A. Tasman, J. Kay, & J. A. Lieberman (Eds.), *Psychiatry*. New York: Wiley.

Dougherty, D. D., Baer, L., Cosgrove, G. R., Cassem, E. H., Price, B.H., Nierenberg, A. A., Jenike, M. A., & Rauch, S. L. (2002). Prospective long-term follow-up of 44 patients who received cingulotomy for treatment-refractory obsessive-compulsive disorder. *American Journal of Psychiatry, 159*, 269–275.

Douzenis, A., Tsirka, Z., Vassilopoulou, C., & Christodoulou, G. N. (2004). The role of serotonin in neurobiology of aggression. *Psychiatriki, 15*(2), 169–179.

Dovidio, J. F., & Gaertner, S. L. (1999). Reducing prejudice: Combating intergroup biases. *Current Directions in Psychological Science, 8*, 101–105.

Dovidio, J. F., Kawakami, K., & Gaertner, S. L. (2002). Implicit and explicit prejudice and interracial interaction. *Journal of Personality and Social Psychology, 82,* 62–82.

Draguns, J. G. (1979). Culture and personality. In A. J. Marsella, R. G. Tharp, & T. J. Ciborowski (Eds.), *Perspectives on cross-cultural psychology.* New York: Academic Press.

Draguns, J. G. (1980). Psychological disorders of clinical severity. In H. C. Triandis & J. Draguns (Eds.), *Handbook of cross-cultural psychology* (Vol. 6). Boston: Allyn & Bacon.

Draguns, J. G. (1990). Applications of cross-cultural psychology in the field of mental health. In R. Brislin (Ed.), *Applied cross-cultural psychology.* Newbury Park, CA: Sage.

Draijer, N., & Langeland, W. (1999). Childhood trauma and perceived parental dysfunction in the etiology of dissociative symptoms in psychiatric inpatients. *American Journal of Psychiatry, 156,* 379–385.

Draijer, N., & Langeland, W. (1999). Childhood trauma and perceived parental dysfunction in the etiology of dissociative symptoms in psychiatric inpatients. *American Journal of Psychiatry, 156,* 379–385.

Draine, S. C., & Greenwald, A. G. (1998). Replicable unconscious semantic processing. *Journal of Experimental Psychology: General, 127,* 286–303.

Draycott, S., & Dabbs, A. (1998). Cognitive dissonance 1: An overview of the literature and its integration into theory and practice of clinical psychology. *British Journal of Clinical Psychology, 37,* 341–353.

Drazen, J. M., & Curfman, G. D. (2002). Financial associations of authors. *New England Journal of Medicine, 346,* 1901–1902.

Drewnowski, A. (1995). Standards for the treatment of obesity. In K. D. Brownell, & C. G. Fairburn (Eds.), *Eating disorders and obesity: A comprehensive handbook.* New York: Guilford.

Driskell, J. E., Willis, R. P., & Copper, C. (1992). Effect of overlearning on retention. *Journal of Applied Psychology, 77*(5), 615–622.

Dubovsky, S. L., & Buzan, R. (1999). Mood disorders. In R. E. Hales, S. C. Yudofsky, & J. A. Talbott (Eds.), *American Psychiatric Press Textbook of Psychiatry.* Washington, DC: American Psychiatric Press.

Dubovsky, S. L., Davies, R., & Dubovsky, A. N. (2003). Mood disorders. In R. E. Hales & S. C. Yudofsky (Eds.), *Textbook of clinical psychiatry.* Washington, DC: American Psychiatric Publishing.

Duckworth, K., & Borus, J. F. (1999). Population-based psychiatry in the public sector and managed care. In A. M. Nicholi (Ed.), *The Harvard guide to psychiatry.* Cambridge, MA: Harvard University Press.

Dudai, Y. (2004). The neurobiology of consolidation, or, how stable is the engram? *Annual Review of Psychology, 55,* 51–86.

Duff, P. (2002). Maternal and perinatal infection. In S. G. Gabbe, J. R. Niebyl, & J. L. Simpson (Eds.), *Obstetrics: Normal and problem pregnancies.* New York: Churchill Livingstone.

Duggal, S., & Sroufe, L. A. (1998). Recovered memory of childhood sexual trauma: A documented case from a longitudinal study. *Journal of Traumatic Stress, 11,* 301–321.

Dunbar, R. (1996). *Grooming, gossip, and the evolution of language.* Cambridge, MA: Harvard University Press.

Dunbar-Jacob, J., & Schlenk, E. (2001). Patient adherence to treatment regimen. In A. Baum, T. A. Revenson, & J. E. Singer (Eds.), *Handbook of health psychology* (pp. 571–580). Mahwah, NJ: Erlbaum.

Duncan, B. L. (1976). Differential social perception and attribution of intergroup violence: Testing the lower limits of stereotyping of blacks. *Journal of Personality and Social Psychology, 34,* 590–598.

Dunkel-Schetter, C., Gurung, R. A. R., Lobel, M., & Wadhwa, P. D. (2001). Stress processes in pregnancy and birth: Psychological, biological, and sociocultural influences. In A. Baum, T. A. Revenson, & J. E. Singer (Eds.), *Handbook of health psychology* (pp. 495–518). Mahwah, NJ: Erlbaum.

Dunning, D., & Sherman, D. A. (1997). Stereotypes and tacit inference. *Journal of Personality and Social Psychology, 73,* 459–471.

Durlach, N. I., & Colburn, H. S. (1978). Binaural phenomenon. In E. C. Carterette & M. P. Friedman (Eds.), *Handbook of perception* (Vol. 4). New York: Academic Press.

Durrant, R., & Ellis, B. J. (2003). Evolutionary psychology. In M. Gallagher & R. J. Nelson (Eds.), *Handbook of Psychology, Vol. 3: Biological psychology.* New York: Wiley.

Dutton, D. G., & Aron, A. P. (1974). Some evidence for heightened sexual attraction under conditions of high anxiety. *Journal of Personality and Social Psychology, 30,* 510–517.

Dwyer, J. (1995). Popular diets. In K. D. Brownell & C. G. Fairburn (Eds.), *Eating disorders and obesity.* New York: Guilford.

Dyck, E. (2005). Flashback: Psychiatric experimentation with LSD in historical perspective. *Canadian Journal of Law and Psychiatry, 50,* 381–388.

Eacott, M. J., & Crawley, R. A. (1998). The offset of childhood amnesia: Memory for events that occurred before age three. *Journal of Experimental Psychology: General, 127,* 22–23.

Eagle, M. N., & Wolitzky, D. L. (1992). Psychoanalytic theories of psychotherapy. In D. K. Freedheim (Ed.), *History of psychotherapy: A century of change.* Washington, DC: American Psychological Association.

Eagly, A. H. (1992). Uneven progress: Social psychology and the study of attitudes. *Journal of Personality and Social Psychology, 63,* 693–710.

Eagly, A. H. (1995). The science and politics of comparing women and men. *American Psychologist, 50,* 145–158.

Eagly, A. H., & Chaiken, S. (1998). Attitude structure and function. In D. T. Gilbert, S. T. Fiske, & G. Lindzey (Eds.), *The handbook of social psychology.* New York: McGraw-Hill.

Eagly, A. H., & Wood, W. (1999). The origins of sex differences in human behavior: Evolved dispositions versus social roles. *American Psychologist, 54,* 408–423.

Eagly, A. H., Ashmore, R. D., Makhijani, M. G., & Longo, L. C. (1991). What is beautiful is good, but . . .: A meta-analytic review of research on the physical attractiveness stereotype. *Psychological Bulletin, 110,* 109–128.

Eaker, E. D., Sullivan, L. M., Kelly-Hayes, M., D'Agostino, R. B., & Benjamin, E. J. (2004). Anger and hostility predict the development of atrial fibrillation in men in the Framingham Offspring Study. *Circulation, 109,* 1267–1271.

Easterlin, B. L., & Cardena, E. (1999). Cognitive and emotional differences between short- and long-term Vipassana meditators. *Imagination, Cognition and Personality, 18*(1), 68–81.

Eastman, R. (2004). The EEG in psychiatry. *South African Psychiatry Review, 7*(2), 29.

Eaton, J. (2001). Management communication: The threat of groupthink. *Corporate Communications, 6,* 183–192.

Eaton, W. W., Dryman, A., & Weissman, M. M. (1991). Panic and phobia. In L. N. Robins & D. A. Regier (Eds.), *Psychiatric disorders in America: The epidemiologic catchment area study.* New York: Free Press.

Ebbinghaus, H. (1885/1964). *Memory: A contribution to experimental psychology* (H. A. Ruger & E. R. Bussemius, Trans.). New York: Dover. (Original work published 1885).

Edberg, P. (1990). Rorschach assessment. In A. Goldstein & M. Hersen (Eds.), *Handbook of psychological assessment.* New York: Pergamon Press.

Edinger, J. D., & Krystal, A. D. (2003). Subtyping primary insomnia: Is sleep state misperception a distinct clinical entity? *Sleep Medicine Reviews, 7*(3), 203–214.

Edinger, J. D., & Means, M. K. (2005). Overview of insomnia: Definitions, epidemiology, differential diagnosis, and assessment. In M. H. Kryger, T. Roth, & W. C. Dement (Eds.), *Principles and practice of sleep medicine.* Philadelphia: Elsevier Saunders.

Edlin, G., & Golanty, E. (1992). *Health and wellness: A holistic approach.* Boston: Jones and Bartlett.

Edwards, K., & Smith, E. E. (1996). A disconfirmation bias in the evaluation of arguments. *Journal of Personality and Social Psychology, 71,* 5–24.

Efron, R. (1990). *The decline and fall of hemispheric specialization.* Hillsdale, NJ: Erlbaum.

Egan, J. P. (1975). *Signal detection theory and ROC-analysis.* New York: Academic Press.

Egan, M. F., & Hyde, T. M. (2000). Schizophrenia: Neurobiology. In B. J. Sadock & V. A. Sadock (Eds.), *Kaplan and Sadock's comprehensive textbook of psychiatry* (7th ed., Vol. 1, pp. 1129–1146). Philadelphia: Lippincott/Williams & Wilkins.

Egeland, B., & Hiester, M. (1995). The long-term consequences of infant day-care and mother-infant attachment. *Child Development, 66,* 474–485.

Ehrenberg, O., & Ehrenberg, M. (1986). *The psychotherapy maze.* Northvale, NJ: Aronson.

Ehrenberg, O., & Ehrenberg, M. (1994). *The psychotherapy maze: A consumer's guide to getting in and out of therapy.* Northvale, NJ: Jason Aronson.

Ehrenreich, H., Rinn, T., Kunert, H. J., Moeller, M. R., Poser, W., Schilling, L., Gigerenzer, G., &

Hoehe, M. R. (1999). Specific attentional dysfunction in adults following early start of cannabis use. *Psychopharmacology, 142*, 295–301.

Eibl-Eibesfeldt, I. (1975). *Ethology: The biology of behavior.* New York: Holt, Rinehart & Winston.

Eich, E. (1990). Learning during sleep. In R. R. Bootzin, J. F. Kihlstrom, & D. L. Schacter (Eds.), *Sleep and cognition.* Washington, DC: American Psychological Association.

Eich, E., Macaulay, D., Loewenstein, R. J., & Dihle, P. H. (1997). Memory, amnesia, and dissociative identity disorder. *Psychological Science, 8*, 417–422.

Eich, J. E. (1980). The cue-dependent nature of state-dependent retrieval. *Memory and Cognition, 8*, 157–173.

Eich, J. E., & Metcalfe, J. (1989). Mood-dependent memory for internal versus external events. *Journal of Experimental Psychology: Learning, Memory and Cognition, 15*, 443–455.

Eichenbaum, H. (1997). Declarative memory: Insights from cognitive neurobiology. *Annual Review of Psychology, 48*, 547–572.

Eichenbaum, H. (2003). Memory systems. In M. Gallagher & R. J. Nelson (Eds.), *Handbook of psychology, Vol. 3: Biological psychology.* New York: Wiley.

Eid, M., & Diener, E. (2001). Norms for experiencing emotions in different cultures: Inter- and intranational differences. *Journal of Personality and Social Psychology, 81*, 869–885.

Einstein, G. O., & McDaniel, M. A. (1996). Remembering to do things: Remembering a forgotten topic. In D. J. Herrmann, C. McEvoy, C. Hertzog, P. Hertel, & M. K. Johnson (Eds.), *Basic and applied memory research: Practical applications* (Vol. 2). Mahwah, NJ: Erlbaum.

Einstein, G. O., McDaniel, M. A., Smith, R. E., & Shaw, P. (1998). Habitual prospective memory and aging: Remembering intentions and forgetting actions. *Psychological Science, 9*, 284–288.

Einstein, G. O., McDaniel, M. A., Williford, C. L., Pagan, J. L., & Dismukes, R. K. (2003). Forgetting of intentions in demanding situations is rapid. *Journal of Experimental Psychology: Applied, 9*(3), 147–162.

Eisler, R. M., & Ragsdale, K. (1992). Masculine gender role and midlife transition in men. In V. B. Van Hasselt & M. Hersen (Eds.), *Handbook of social development: A lifespan perspective.* New York: Plenum.

Ekman, P. (1992). Facial expressions of emotion: New findings, new questions. *Psychological Science, 3*, 34–38.

Ekman, P. (1993). Facial expression and emotion. *American Psychologist, 48*, 384–392.

Ekman, P., & Friesen, W. V. (1975). *Unmasking the face.* Englewood Cliffs, NJ: Prentice-Hall.

Ekman, P., & Friesen, W. V. (1984). *Unmasking the face.* Palo Alto: Consulting Psychologists Press.

Elbert, T., Pantev, C., Weinbruch, C., Rockstroh, B., & Taub, E. (1995). Increased cortical representation of the fingers of the left hand in string players. *Science, 270*, 305–307.

Eldred, L., & Chaisson, R. (1996). The clinical course of HIV infection in women. In R. R. Faden & N. E. Kass (Eds.), *HIV, AIDS, and childbearing.* New York: Oxford University Press.

Elicker, J., Englund, M., & Sroufe, L. A. (1992). Predicting peer competence and peer relationships in childhood from early parent-child relationships. In R. D. Parke & G. W. Ladd (Eds.), *Family-peer relationships: Modes of linkage.* Hillsdale, NJ: Erlbaum.

Ellis, A. (1973). *Humanistic psychotherapy: The rational-emotive approach.* New York: Julian Press.

Ellis, A. (1977). *Reason and emotion in psychotherapy.* Seacaucus, NJ: Lyle Stuart.

Ellis, A. (1985). *How to live with and without anger.* New York: Citadel Press.

Ellis, A. (1987). The evolution of rational-emotive therapy (RET) and cognitive behavior therapy (CBT). In J. K. Zeig (Ed.), *The evolution of psychotherapy.* New York: Brunner/Mazel.

Ellis, A. (1989). Rational-emotive therapy. In R. J. Corsini & D. Wedding (Eds.), *Current Psychotherapies.* Itasca, IL: F. E. Peacock.

Ellis, A. (1996). How I learned to help clients feel better and get better. *Psychotherapy, 33*, 149–151.

Ellis, A. (2001). *Feeling better, getting better, staying better: Profound self-help therapy for your emotions.* Atascadero, CA: Impact Publishers.

Ellis, B. J., McFadyen-Ketchum, S., Dodge, K. A., Pettit, G. S., & Bates, J. E. (1999). Quality of early family relationships and individual differences in the timing of pubertal maturation in girls: A longitudinal test of an evolutionary model. *Journal of Personality and Social Psychology, 77*, 387–401.

Ellsworth, P. C., & Scherer, K. R. (2003). Appraisal processes in emotion. In R. J. Davidson, K. R. Scherer, & H. H. Goldsmith (Ed.), *Handbook of affective sciences.* New York: Oxford University Press.

Elman, J. L. (1999). The emergence of language: A conspiracy theory. In B. MacWhinney (Ed.), *The emergence of language* (pp. 1–28). Mahwah, NJ: Erlbaum.

Elpers, J. R. (2001). Public psychiatry. In B. J. Sadock & V. A. Sadock (Eds.), *Kaplan and Sadock's comprehensive textbook of psychiatry* (7th ed., Vol. 2). Philadelphia: Lippincott/Williams & Wilkins.

Elton John to wed T.O. partner. (2005) *Toronto Star.* April 26, 2005, A3.

Emavardhana, T., & Tori, C. D. (1997). Changes in self-concept, ego defense mechanisms, and religiosity following seven-day Vipassana meditation retreats. *Journal for the Scientific Study of Religion, 36*, 194–206.

Emmelkamp, P. M. G. (1994). Behavior therapy with adults. In A. E. Bergin & S. L. Garfield (Eds.), *Handbook of psychotherapy and behavior change* (4th ed.). New York: Wiley.

Emmelkamp, P. M. G. (2004). In M. J. Lambert (Ed.), *Bergin and Garfield's handbook of psychotherapy and behavior change.* New York: Wiley.

Emmelkamp, P. M. G., & Scholing, A. (1990). Behavioral treatment for simple and social phobias. In R. Noyes, Jr., M. Roth, & G. D. Burrows (Eds.), *Handbook of anxiety: The treatment of anxiety* (Vol. 4). Amsterdam: Elsevier.

Endler, N. S. & Parker, J. D. A. (1990). *The coping inventory for stressful situations (CISS): Manual.* Toronto: Multi-Health Systems.

Endler, N. S. (1982). *Holiday of darkness: A psychologist's personal journey out of his depression.* New York: John Wiley and Sons.

Endler, N. S. (1997). Stress, anxiety and coping: The Multidimensional interaction model. *Canadian Psychology, 38*, 136–153.

Endler, N. S., & Magnusson, D. (1976). Toward an interactional psychology of personality. *Psychological Bulletin, 83*, 956–979.

Endler, N. S., & Persad, E. (1988). *Electroconvulsive therapy: The myths and realities.* Toronto: Hans Huber Publishers.

Engemann, K. M., & Owyang, M. T. (2005, April). So much for that merit raise: The link between wages and appearance. *The Regional Economist*, pp. 10–11.

Epel, E. S., Blackburn, E. H., Lin, J., Dhabhar, F. S., Adler, N. E., Morrow, J. D., & Cawthon, R. M. (2004). Accelerated telomere shortening in response to life stress. *Proceedings of the National Academy of Science, 101*, 17312–17315.

Epley, N., & Huff, C. (1998). Suspicion, affective response, and educational benefit as a result of deception in psychology research. *Personality and Social Psychology Bulletin, 24*, 759–768.

Epling, W. F., & Pierce, W. D. (1992). *Solving the anorexia puzzle: A scientific approach.* Toronto: Hogrefe & Huber Publishers.

Epstein, L. H., Valoski, A. M., Vara, L. S., McCurley, J., Wisniewski, L., Kalarchian, M. A., Klein, K. R., & Shrager, L. R. (1995). Effects of decreasing sedentary behavior and increasing activity on weight change in obese children. *Health Psychology, 14*, 109–115.

Epstein, S. P. (1980). The stability of confusion: A reply to Mischel and Peake. *Psychological Review, 90*, 179–184.

Epstein, S. P. (1986). Does aggregation produce spuriously high estimates of behavior stability? *Journal of Personality and Social Psychology, 50*, 1199–1210.

Epstein, S., Donovan, S., & Denes-Raj, V. (1999). The missing link in the paradox of the Linda conjunction problem: Beyond knowing and thinking of the conjunction rule, the intrinsic appeal of heuristic processing. *Personality and Social Psychology Bulletin, 25*, 204–214.

Erber, M. W., Hodges, S. D., & Wilson, T. D. (1995). Attitude strength, attitude stability, and the effects of analyzing reasons. In R. E. Petty & J. A. Krosnick (Eds.), *Attitude strength: Antecedents and consequences.* Mahwah, NJ: Erlbaum.

Erdelyi, M. H. (2001). Defense processes can be conscious or unconscious. *American Psychologist, 56*, 761–762.

Erickson, R. P., DiLorenzo, P. M., & Woodbury, M. A. (1994). Classification of taste responses in brain stem: Membership in fuzzy sets. *Journal of Neurophysiology, 71*, 2139–2150.

Ericsson, K. A., & Lehman, A. C. (1996). Expert and exceptional performance: Evidence of maximal adaptation to task constraints. *Annual Review of Psychology, 47*, 273–305.

Ericsson, K. A., & Polson, P. G. (1988). An experimental analysis of the mechanisms of a memory skill. *Journal of Experimental Psychology: Learning, Memory and Cognition, 14*, 305–316.

Erikson, E. (1963). *Childhood and society.* New York: Norton.

Erikson, E. (1968). *Identity: Youth and crisis.* New York: Norton.

Eriksson, P. S., Perfilieva, E., Bjork-Eriksson, T., Alborn, A. M., Nordborg, C., Peterson, D. A., & Gage, F. H. (1998). Neurogenesis in the adult human hippocampus. *Nature Medicine, 4*, 1313–1317.

Ernst, C., & Angst, J. (1983). Birth order: Its influence on personality. *Behavioral and Brain Sciences, 10*(1), 55.

Esposito, M. J., Nielsen, T. A., & Paquette, Y. (2004). Reduced Alpha power associated with the recall of mentation from Stage 2 and Stage REM sleep. *Psychophysiology, 41*, 288–297.

Esposito's turtleneck. (n.d.). Retrieved April 27, 2005, from http://www. anecdotage.com/ index.php?aid=15970.

Esser, J. K. (1998). Alive and well after twenty-five years: A review of groupthink research. *Organizational Behavior & Human Decision Processes, 73*, 116–141.

Esses, V. M., & Gardner, R. C. (1996). Multiculturalism in Canada: Context and current status. *Canadian Journal of Behavioural Science, 28*, 145–152.

Esterson, A. (1993). *Seductive mirage: An exploration of the work of Sigmund Freud.* Chicago: Open Court.

Esterson, A. (2001). The mythologizing of psychoanalytic history: Deception and self-deception in Freud's accounts of the seduction theory episode. *History of Psychiatry, 7*, 329–352.

Estes, R. E., Coston, M. L., & Fournet, G. P. (1990). *Rankings of the most notable psychologists by department chairpersons.* Unpublished manuscript.

Estes, W. K. (1999). Models of human memory: A 30-year retrospective. In C. Izawa (Ed.), *On human memory: Evolution, progress, and reflections on the 30th anniversary of the Atkinson-Shiffrin model.* Mahwah, NJ: Erlbaum.

Etaugh, C., & Liss, M. B. (1992). Home, school, and playroom: Training grounds for adult gender roles. *Sex Roles, 26*, 129–147.

Evan, R. I. (1989). *Albert Bandura: The man and his ideas—a dialogue.* New York: Praeger.

Evans, C. E., & Haynes, R. B. (1990). Patient compliance. In R. E. Rakel (Ed.), *Textbook of family practice.* Philadelphia: Saunders.

Evans, F. J. (1990). Behavioral responses during sleep. In R. R. Bootzin, J. F. Kihlstrom, & D. L. Schacter (Eds.), *Sleep and cognition.* Washington, DC: American Psychological Association.

Evans, G. W. (2004). The environment of childhood poverty. *American Psychologist, 59*(2), 77–92.

Evans, R. I. (1980). *The making of social psychology: Discussions with creative contributors.* New York: Gardner Press, Inc.

Evans, R. L. (1981). New drug evaluations: Alprazolam. *Drug Intelligence and Clinical Pharmacy, 15*, 633–637.

Everly, G. S., Jr. (2000). Five principles of crisis intervention: Reducing the risk of premature crisis intervention. *International Journal of Emergency Mental Health, 2*, 1–4.

Ewing, L. (2005). Wheelchair racer Petitclerc wins female athlete, gymnast Shewfelt wins men's. Retrieved May 2, 2005, from http://news.h=yahoo.com/news?tmpl=story&u=cpress/20050330/ca_pr.

Eysenck, H. J. (1952). The effects of psychotherapy: An evaluation. *Journal of Consulting Psychology, 16*, 319–324.

Eysenck, H. J. (1959). Learning theory and behaviour therapy. *Journal of Mental Science, 195*, 61–75.

Eysenck, H. J. (1967). *The biological basis of personality.* Springfield, IL: Charles C. Thomas.

Eysenck, H. J. (1982). *Personality, genetics and behavior: Selected papers.* New York: Praeger.

Eysenck, H. J. (1988). The concept of "intelligence": Useful or useless? *Intelligence, 12*(1), 1–16.

Eysenck, H. J. (1989). Discrimination reaction time and "g": A reply to Humphreys. *Intelligence, 13*(4), 325–326.

Eysenck, H. J. (1990a). Biological dimensions of personality. In L. A. Pervin (Ed.), *Handbook of personality: Theory and research.* New York: Guilford.

Eysenck, H. J. (1990b). *Decline and fall of the Freudian empire.* Washington, DC: Scott-Townsend.

Eysenck, H. J., & Kamin, L. (1981). *The intelligence controversy.* New York: Wiley.

Eysenck, M. W. (1984). *A handbook of cognitive psychology.* Hillsdale, NJ: Erlbaum.

Eysenck, M. W., Mogg, K., May, J., Richards, A., & Mathews, A. (1991). Bias in interpretation of ambiguous sentences related to threat in anxiety. *Journal of Abnormal Psychology, 100*, 144–150.

Fabes, R. A., Carlo, G., Kupanoff, K., & Laible, D. (1999). Early adolescence and prosocial/moral behavior I: The role of individual processes. *Journal of Early Adolescence, 19*, 5–16.

Fagot, B. I., Hagan, R., Leinbach, M. D., & Kronsberg, S. (1985). Differential reactions to assertive and communicative acts of toddler boys and girls. *Child Development, 56*, 1499–1505.

Fagot, B. I., Leinbach, M. D., & O'Boyle, C. (1992). Gender labeling, gender stereotyping, and parenting behaviors. *Developmental Psychology, 28*, 225–230.

Fahey, P. J., & Gallagher-Allred, C. (1990). Nutrition. In R. E. Rakel (Ed.), *Textbook of family practice* (4th ed.). Philadelphia: Saunders.

Fairburn, S. (2004). Teen who killed at Taber school kept in prison. *Globe and Mail,* February 21, 2004, p. A7.

Fakhoury, W., & Priebe, S. (2002). The process of deinstitutionalization: An international overview. *Current Opinion in Psychiatry, 15*(2), 187–192.

Falls, W. A. (1998). Extinction: A review of therapy and the evidence suggesting that memories are not erased with nonreinforcement. In W. O'Donohue (Ed.), *Learning and behavior therapy.* Boston: Allyn & Bacon.

Falsetti, S. A., & Ballenger, J. C. (1998). Stress and anxiety disorders. In J. R. Hubbard & E. A. Workman (Eds.), *Handbook of stress medicine: An organ system approach.* New York: CRC Press.

Fancher, R. (1979). *Pioneers of psychology.* New York, NY: W. W. Norton and Company.

Fancher, R. E. (1979). *Pioneers of psychology.* New York: Norton.

Fancher, R. E. (2000). Snapshot of Freud in America, 1899–1999. *American Psychologist, 55*, 1025–1028.

Faraday, A. (1974). *The dream game.* New York: Harper & Row.

Farah, A. (1997). An overview of ECT. *Primary Psychiatry, 4*, 58–62.

Faravelli, C., & Pallanti, S. (1989). Recent life events and panic disorders. *American Journal of Psychiatry, 146*, 622–626.

Farrar, M. J. (1990). Discourse and the acquisition of grammatical morphemes. *Journal of Child Language, 17*, 607–624.

Fausto-Sterling, A. (1992). *Myths of gender.* New York: Basic Books.

Fazio, R. H. (1995). Attitudes as object-evaluation associations: Determinants, consequences, and correlates of attitude accessibility. In R. E. Petty & J. A. Krosnick (Eds.), *Attitude strength: Antecedents and consequences.* Mahwah, NJ: Erlbaum.

Fazio, R. H., & Olson, M. A. (2003). Attitudes: Foundations, functions, and consequences. In M. A. Hogg & J. Cooper (Eds.), *The Sage handbook of social psychology.* Thousand Oaks, CA: Sage.

Fechner, G. T. (1860). *Elemente der psychophysik* (Vol. 1). Leipzig: Breitkopf & Harterl.

Feder, H. (1984). Hormones and sexual behavior. *Annual Review of Psychology, 35*, 165–200.

Federoff, I., Polivy, J., & Herman, C. P. (2003). The specificity of restrained versus unrestrained eaters' responses to food cues: General desire to eat, or crazing for the cued food. *Appetite, 41*(1), 7–13.

Feeney, D. M. (1987). Human rights and animal welfare. *American Psychologist, 42*, 593–599.

Feeney, J. A. (1999). Adult romantic attachment and couple relationships. In J. Cassidy & P. R. Shaver (Eds.), *Handbook of attachment: Theory, research, and clinical applications.* New York: Guilford.

Feeney, J. A. (1999). Adult romantic attachment and couple relationships. In J. Cassidy & P. R. Shaver (Eds.), *Handbook of attachment: Theory, research, and clinical applications.* New York: Guilford.

Fein, S., & Spencer, S. J. (1997). Prejudice as self-image maintenance: Affirming the self through derogating others. *Journal of Personality and Social Psychology, 73*, 31–44.

Feingold, A. (1988a). Cognitive gender differences are disappearing. *American Psychologist, 43*, 95–103.

Feingold, A. (1988b). Matching for attractiveness in romantic partners and same-sex friends: A meta-analysis and theoretical critique. *Psychological Bulletin, 104*, 226–235.

Feingold, A. (1990). Gender differences in effects of physical attractiveness on romantic attraction: A comparison across five research paradigms. *Journal of Personality and Social Psychology, 59*, 981–993.

Feingold, A. (1992). Good-looking people are not what we think. *Psychological Bulletin, 111*, 304–341.

Feingold, A. (1994). Gender differences in personality: A meta-analysis. *Psychological Bulletin, 116*, 429–456.

Feist, G. J. (1998). A meta-analysis of personality in scientific and artistic creativity. *Personality and Social Psychology Review, 2*, 290–309.

Feldman, D. H. (1988). Creativity: Dreams, insights, and transformations. In R. J. Sternberg (Ed.), *The nature of creativity: Contemporary psychological perspectives.* Cambridge: Cambridge University Press.

Feldman, D. H. (1999). The development of creativity. In R. J. Sternberg (Ed.), *Handbook of creativity.* New York: Cambridge University Press.

Feldman, D. H. (2003). Cognitive development in childhood. In R. M. Lerner, M. A. Easterbrooks, & J. Mistry (Eds.), *Handbook of psychology, Vol. 6: Developmental psychology.* New York: Wiley.

Feldman, P. J., Cohen, S., Doyle, W. J., Skoner, D. P., & Gwaltney, J. M., Jr. (1999). The impact of personality on the reporting of unfounded symptoms and illness. *Journal of Personality and Social Psychology, 77*, 370–378.

Felker, B., & Hubbard, J. R. (1998). Influence of mental stress on the endocrine system. In J. R. Hubbard & E. A. Workman (Eds.), *Handbook of stress medicine: An organ system approach.* New York: CRC Press.

Fenson, L., Dale, P., Reznick, J., Bates, E., Thal, D., & Pethick, S. (1994). Variability in early communicative development. *Monographs of the Society for Research in Child Development, 59*(5, Serial No. 242), 1–173.

Fenton, W. S., & McGlashan, T. H. (1994). Antecedents, symptom progression, and long-term outcome of the deficit syndrome in schizophrenia. *American Journal of Psychiatry, 151*, 351–356.

Fenwick, P. (1987). Meditation and the EEG. In M. A. West (Ed.), *The psychology of meditation.* Oxford: Clarendon Press.

Ferguson, J. M. (2001). SSRI antidepressant medications: Adverse effects and tolerability. *Primary Care Companion Journal of Clinical Psychiatry, 3*, 22–27.

Ferguson, R. (2005). Ontario set to scrap mandatory retirement. *Toronto Star,* June 7, 2005, pp. A1, A7.

Ferguson, T. (1993). Working with your doctor. In D. Goleman & J. Gurin (Eds.), *Mind-body medicine: How to use your mind for better health.* Yonkers, NY: Consumer Reports Books.

Ferris, A. L. (2002). Religion and the quality of life. *Journal of Happiness Studies, 3*, 199–215.

Ferster, C. S., & Skinner, B. F. (1957). *Schedules of reinforcement.* New York: Appleton-Century-Crofts.

Festinger, L. (1957). *A theory of cognitive dissonance.* Stanford, CA: Stanford University Press.

Festinger, L., & Carlsmith, J. M. (1959). Cognitive consequences of forced compliance. *Journal of Abnormal and Social Psychology, 58*, 203–210.

Fielder, K., Schmid, J., & Stahl, T. (2002). What is the current truth about polygraph lie detection? *Basic & Applied Social Psychology, 24*, 313–324.

Fields, H. L., & Levine, J. D. (1984). Placebo analgesia: A role for endorphins. *Trends in Neuroscience, 7*, 271–273.

Fifer, W. P., Monk, C. E., & Grose-Fifer, J. (2001). Prenatal development and risk. In G. Bremner & A. Fogel (Eds.), *Blackwell handbook of infant development* (pp. 505–542). Malden, MA: Blackwell.

50 Goals in 50 games. (n.d.). *CBC Archives.* Retrieved April 27, 2005, from http://archives.cbc.ca/400i.asp?IDCat=41&IDDos=1093&IDCli=6056.

Figueredo, A. J., Sefcek, J. A., Vasquez, G., Brumbach, B. H., King, J. E., & Jacobs, W. J. (2005). Evolutionary personality psychology. In D. M. Buss (Ed.), *The handbook of evolutionary psychology.* New York: Wiley.

Fine, R. (1990). *The history of psychoanalysis.* New York: Continuum.

Finer, B. (1980). Hypnosis and anaesthesia. In G. D. Burrows & L. Dennerstein (Eds.), *Handbook of hypnosis and psychosomatic medicine.* Amsterdam: Elsevier/North Holland Biomedical Press.

Fink, B., & Penton-Voak, I. (2002). Evolutionary psychology of facial attractiveness. *Current Directions in Psychological Science, 11*(5), 154–158.

Fink, M. (1992). Electroconvulsive therapy. In E. S. Paykel (Ed.), *Handbook of affective disorders* (2nd ed.). New York: Guilford.

Finnegan, L. P., & Kandall, S. R. (1997). Maternal and neonatal effects of alcohol and drugs. In J. H. Lowinson, P. Ruiz, R. B. Millman, & J. G. Langrod (Eds.), *Substance abuse: A comprehensive textbook.* Baltimore: Williams & Wilkins.

Fischer, K. W., & Bidell, T. (1991). Constraining nativist inferences about cognitive capacities. In S. Carey & R. Gelman (Eds.), *The epigenesis of mind: Essays on biology and cognition.* Hillsdale, NJ: Erlbaum.

Fischer, K. W., & Hencke, R. W. (1996). Infants' construction of actions in context: Piaget's contribution to research on early development. *Psychological Science, 7*, 204–210.

Fischhoff, B. (1982). Debiasing. In D. Kahneman, P. Slovic, & A. Tversky (Eds.), *Judgment under uncertainty: Heuristics and biases.* Cambridge, MA: Cambridge University Press.

Fischhoff, B. (1988). Judgment and decision making. In R. J. Sternberg & E. E. Smith (Eds.), *The psychology of human thought.* Cambridge: Cambridge University Press.

Fisher, B. S., Daigle, L. E., Cullen, F. T., & Turner, M. G. (2003). Reporting sexual victimization to the police and others: Results from a national-level study of college women. *Criminal Justice & Behavior, 30*(1), 6–38.

Fisher, S., & Greenberg, R. P. (1985). *The scientific credibility of Freud's theories and therapy.* New York: Columbia University Press.

Fisher, S., & Greenberg, R. P. (1996). *Freud scientifically reappraised: Testing the theories and therapy.* New York: Wiley.

Fisher, S., & Greenberg, R. P. (1997). The curse of the placebo: Fanciful pursuit of a pure biological therapy. In S. Fisher & R. P. Greenberg (Eds.), *From placebo to panacea: Putting psychiatric drugs to the test.* New York: Wiley.

Fisher, W. A., & Barak, A. (2001). Internet pornography: A social psychological perspective on internet sexuality. *The Journal of Sex Research, 38*, 312–323.

Fisher, W. A., Byrne, D., White, L. A., & Kelley, K. (1988). Erotophobia-erotophilia as a dimension of personality. *Journal of Sex Research, 25*(1), 123–151.

Fishman, D. B., & Franks, C. M. (1992). Evolution and differentiation within behavior therapy: A theoretical epistemological review. In D. K. Freedheim (Ed.), *History of psychotherapy: A century of change.* Washington, DC: American Psychological Association.

Fisk, J. E. (2004). Conjunction fallacy. In F. P. Rudiger (Ed.), *Cognitive illusions.* New York: Psychology Press.

Fiske, S. T. (1998). Stereotyping, prejudice, and discrimination. In D. T. Gilbert, S. T. Fiske, & G. Lindzey (Eds.), *The handbook of social psychology.* New York: McGraw-Hill.

Fiske, S. T. (2000). Stereotyping, prejudice, and discrimination at the seam between the centuries: Evolution, culture, mind and brain. *European Journal of Social Psychology, 30*, 299–322.

Fiske, S. T. (2002). What we know now about bias and intergroup conflict, the problem of the century. *Current Directions in Psychological Science, 11*(4), 123–128.

Flannery, R. B., Jr. (1999). Psychological trauma and posttraumatic stress disorder: A review. *International Journal of Mental Health, 1*, 135–140.

Flavell, J. H. (1996). Piaget's legacy. *Psychological Science, 7*, 200–203.

Flavell, J. H. (1999). Cognitive development: Children's knowledge about the mind. *Annual Review of Psychology, 50*, 21–45.

Flavell, J. H., & Miller, P. H. (1998). Social cognition. In W. Damon (Ed.), *Handbook of child psychology (Vol. 2): Cognition, perception, and language.* New York: Wiley.

Fleeson, W. (2004). Moving personality beyond the person-situation debate: The challenge and the opportunity of within-person variability. *Current Directions in Psychological Science, 13*(2), 83–87.

Flegal, K. M., Graubard, B. I., Williamson, D. F., & Gail, M. H. (2005). Excess deaths associated with underweight, overweight, and obesity. *Journal of the American Medical Association, 293*, 1861–1861.

Fleischhacker, W. W. (2002). Second generation antipsychotics. *Psychopharmacology, 162*(1), 90–91.

Fletcher, G. J. O., & Ward, C. (1988). Attribution theory and processes: A cross-cultural perspective. In M. H. Bond (Ed.), *The cross-cultural challenge to social psychology.* Newbury Park, CA: Sage.

Fletcher, G. J. O., Simpson, J. A., & Thomas, G. (2000). Ideals, perceptions, and evaluations in early relationship development. *Journal of Personality and Social Psychology, 79*, 933–940.

Fletcher, G. J. O., Simpson, J. A., Thomas, G., & Giles, L. (1999). Ideals in intimate relationships. *Journal of Personality and Social Psychology, 76*, 72–89.

Flett, G. L., & Hewitt, P. L. (2002). (Eds.). *Perfectionism: Theory, research, and treatment.* Washington, DC: American Psychological Association.

Flett, G. L., Vredenburg, K., & Krames, L. (1995). The stability of depressive symptoms in college students: An empirical demonstration of regression to the mean. *Journal of Psychopathology & Behavioral Assessment, 17*, 403–415.

Flippo, R. F. (2000). *Testwise: Strategies for success in taking tests*. Torrance, CA: Good Apple.

Flippo, R. F., Becker, M. J., & Wark, D. M. (2000). Preparing for and taking tests. In R. F. Flippo & D. C. Caverly (Eds.), *Handbook of college reading and study strategy research*. Mahwah, NJ: Erlbaum.

Flores, B. H., Musselman, D. L., DeBattista, C., Garlow, S. J., Schatzberg, A. F., & Nemeroff, C. B. (2004). Biology of mood disorders. In A. F. Schatzberg & C. B. Nemeroff (Eds.), *Textbook of psychopharmacology*. Washington, DC: American Psychiatric Publishing.

Flum, H. (1994). Styles of identity formation in early and middle adolescence. *Genetic, Social, and General Psychology Monographs, 120*, 435–467.

Flynn, J. R. (1987). Massive IQ gains in 14 nations: What IQ tests really measure. *Psychological Bulletin, 101*, 171–191.

Flynn, J. R. (1994). IQ gains over time. In R. J. Sternberg (Ed.), *The encyclopedia of human intelligence*. New York: Macmillan.

Flynn, J. R. (1998). IQ gains over time: Toward finding the causes. In U. Neisser (Ed.), *The rising curve: Long-term gains in IQ and related measures*. Washington, DC: American Psychological Association.

Flynn, J. R. (1999). Searching for justice: The discovery of IQ gains over time. *American Psychologist, 54*, 5–20.

Flynn, J. R. (2003). Movies about intelligence: The limitations of g. *Current Directions in Psychological Science, 12*(3), 95–99.

Foa, E. B., & Kozak, M. J. (1995). DSM-IV field trial: Obsessive-compulsive disorder. *American Journal of Psychiatry, 152*, 90–96.

Fodor, E. M., & Carver, R. A. (2000). Achievement and power motives, performance feedback, and creativity. *Journal of Research in Personality, 34*, 380–396.

Folkman, S. (1997). Positive psychological states and coping with severe stress. *Social Science and Medicine, 45*, 1207–1221.

Folkman, S., & Moskowitz, J. T. (2000). Positive affect and the other side of coping. *American Psychologist, 55*, 647–654.

Folkman, S., & Moskowitz, J. T. (2004). Coping: Pitfalls and promise. *Annual Review of Psychology, 55*, 745–774.

Folkman, S., Moskowitz, J. T., Ozer, E. M., & Park, C. L. (1997). Positive meaningful events and coping in the context of HIV/AIDS.

In B. H. Gottlieb (Ed.), *Coping with chronic stress* (pp. 293–314). New York: Plenum.

Fontaine, K. R., Redden, D. T., Wang, C., Westfall, A. O., & Allison, D. B. (2003). Years of life lost due to Obesity. *Journal of the American Medical Association, 289*, 187–193.

Ford, D. E., Mead, L. A., Chang, P. P., Cooper-Patrick, L., Wang, N. Y., & Klag, M. J. (1998). Depression is a risk factor for coronary artery disease in men: The precursors study. *Archives of Internal Medicine, 158*, 1422–1426.

Forsén, T., Eriksson, J., Tuomilehto, J., Reunanen, A., Osmond, C., & Barker, D. (2000). The fetal and childhood growth of persons who develop type 2 diabetes. *Annals of Internal Medicine, 133*, 176–182.

Forsyth, D. R. (1999). *An introduction to group dynamics*. Belmont, CA: Wadsworth.

Forsyth, D. R., & McMillan, J. H. (1981). Attributions, affect, and expectations: A test of Weiner's three-dimensional model. *Journal of Educational Psychology, 73*, 393–403.

Forsyth, D. R., & Strong, S. R. (1986). The scientific study of counseling and psychotherapy: A unificationist view. *American Psychologist, 41*, 113–119.

Foster, R. G. (2004). Are we trying to banish biological time? *Cerebrum, 6*, 7–26.

Foulkes, D. (1982). *Children's dreams*. New York: Wiley.

Foulkes, D. (1985). *Dreaming: A cognitive-psychological analysis*. Hillsdale, NJ: Erlbaum.

Foulkes, D. (1996). Dream research: 1953–1993. *Sleep, 19*, 609–624.

Foulkes, D. (1999). *Children's dreaming and the development of consciousness*. Cambridge: Harvard University Press.

14-year-old York U Student proves age is no barrier. (n.d.). York University Media Release Archive. Retrieved April 21, 2005, from http://www.yorku.ca/mediar/archive/Release/asp?Releas=852.

Fowers, B. J., & Richardson, F. C. (1996). Why is multiculturalism good? *American Psychologist, 51*, 609–621.

Fowles, D. C. (1992). Schizophrenia: Diathesis-stress revisited. *Annual Review of Psychology, 43*, 303–336.

Fozard, J. L. (1990). Vision and hearing in aging. In J. E. Birren & K.W. Schaie (Eds.), *Handbook of the psychology of aging* (3rd ed.). San Diego: Academic Press.

Fozard, J. L., & Gordon-Salant, S. (2001). Changes in vision and hearing with aging. In J. E. Birren & K. W. Schaie (Eds.), *Handbook of the psychology of aging* (5th ed., pp. 240–265). San Diego, CA: Academic Press.

Fraley, R. C. (2002). Attachment stability from infancy to adulthood: Meta-analysis and dynamic modeling of developmental mechanisms. *Personality and Social Psychology Review, 6*, 123–151.

Fraley, R. C. (2002). Attachment stability from infancy to adulthood: Meta-analysis and dynamic modeling of developmental mechanisms. *Personality and Social Psychology Review, 6*, 123–151.

Francis, M. E., & Pennebaker, J. W. (1992). Putting stress into words: The impact of writing on psychological, absentee and self-reported emotional well-being measures. *American Journal of Health Promotion, 6*, 280–287.

Franco, S. E., Hubbard, J. R., & Martin, P. R. (1998). Stress and addiction. In J. R. Hubbard & E. A. Workman (Eds.), *Handbook of stress medicine: An organ system approach*. New York: CRC Press.

Frank, J. D. (1961). *Persuasion and healing*. Baltimore: Johns Hopkins University Press.

Frank, J. D., & Frank, J. B. (1991). *Persuasion and healing: A comparison study of psychotherapy*. Baltimore: Johns Hopkins University Press.

Frank, L. K. (1939). Projective methods for the study of personality. *Journal of Psychology, 8*, 343–389.

Frank, L. R. (1990). Electroshock: Death, brain damage, memory loss, and brainwashing. *The Journal of Mind and Behavior, 11*(3/4), 489–512.

Franken, R. E. (1993). Sensation seeking and keeping your options open. *Personality and Individual Differences, 14*, 247–249.

Franken, R. E., Gibson, K. J., & Rowland, G. L. (1992). Sensation seeking and the tendency to view the world as threatening. *Personality and Individual Differences, 13*(1), 31–38.

Franks, C. M., & Barbrack, C. R. (1983). Behavior therapy with adults: An integrative perspective. In M. Hersen, A. E. Kazdin, & A. S. Bellack (Eds.), *The clinical psychology handbook*. New York: Pergamon Press.

Frantom, C., & Sherman, M. F. (1999). At what price art? Affective instability within a visual art population. *Creativity Research Journal, 12*, 15–23.

Frasure-Smith, N., & Lesperance, F. (2005). Depression and coronary heart disease: Complex synergism of mind, body, and environment. *Current Directions in Psychological Science, 14*(1), 39–43.

Frazer, A., Daws, L. C., Duncan, G. E., & Morilak, D. A. (2003). Basic mechanisms of neurotransmitter action. In A. Tasman, J. Kay, & J. A. Lieberman (Eds.), *Psychiatry*. New York: Wiley.

Frazier, J. A. (1999). The person with mental retardation. In A. M. Nicholi (Ed.), *The Harvard guide to psychiatry* (3rd ed., pp. 660–671). Cambridge, MA: Harvard University Press.

Frederick, S., & Loewenstein, G. (1999). Hedonic adaptation. In D. Kahneman, E. Diener, & N. Schwarz (Eds.), *Well-being: The foundations of hedonic psychology*. New York: Russell Sage Foundation.

Frederickson, B. L. (1998). What good are positive emotions? *Review of General Psychology, 2*, 300–319.

Fredrickson, B. L. (2002). Positive emotions. In C. R. Snyder & S. J. Lopez (Eds.), *Handbook of positive psychology* (pp. 120–134). New York: Oxford University Press.

Fredrickson, B. L., & Branigan, C. (2001). Positive emotions. In T. J. Mayne & G. A. Bonanno (Eds.), *Emotions: Current issues and future directions* (pp. 123–151). New York: Guilford.

Fredriks, A. M., Van Buren, S., Burgmeijer, R. J. F., Muelmeester, J. F., Roelien, J., Brugman, E., Roede, M. J., Verloove-Vanhorick, S. P., & Wit, J. M. (2000). Continuing positive secular growth change in the Netherlands, 1955–1997. *Pediatric Research, 47*, 316–323.

Fredrikson, M., Annas, P., & Wik, G. (1997). Parental history, aversive exposure and the development of snake and spider phobia in women. *Behavioral Research and Therapy, 35*, 23–28.

Freed, D. A. (2003). Man leaps to subway tracks, saves life: Hundreds stand by and merely watch. *Toronto Star*, September 20, p. B5.

Freedman, J. L. (1978). *Happy people*. New York: Harcourt Brace Jovanovich.

Freedman, J. L. (2002). *Media violence and its effect on aggression*. Toronto: University of Toronto Press.

Freedman, J. L., & Fraser, S. C. (1966). Compliance without pressure: The foot-in-the-door technique. *Journal of Personality and Social Psychology, 4*, 195–202.

Freese, J., Powell, B., & Steelman, L. C. (1999). Rebel without a cause or effect: Birth order and social attitudes. *American Sociological Review, 64*, 207–231.

Freeze, C. (2005). Pensions for stress disorder skyrocket. *The Globe and Mail*, May 14, 2005, p. A1.

Freud, S. (1900/1953). *The interpretation of dreams*. In J. Strachey (Ed.), *The standard edition of the complete psychological works of Sigmund Freud* (Vols. 4 and 5). London: Hogarth.

Freud, S. (1901/1960). *The psychopathology of everyday life*. In J. Strachey (Ed.), *The standard edition of the complete psychological works of Sigmund Freud* (Vol. 6). London: Hogarth.

Freud, S. (1915/1959). Instincts and their vicissitudes. In E. Jones (Ed.), *The collected papers of Sigmund Freud* (Vol. 4). New York: Basic Books.

Freud, S. (1924). *A general introduction to psychoanalysis*. New York: Boni & Liveright.

Freud, S. (1933/1964). *New introductory lectures on psychoanalysis*. In J. Strachey (Ed.), *The standard edition of the complete psychological works of Sigmund Freud* (Vol. 22). London: Hogarth.

Freud, S. (1940). An outline of psychoanalysis. *International Journal of Psychoanalysis, 21*, 27–84.

Frey, K. S., & Ruble, D. N. (1992). Gender constancy and the cost of sex-typed behavior: A test of the conflict hypothesis. *Developmental Psychology, 28*, 714–721.

Freyd, J. J. (1996). *Betrayal trauma: The logic of forgetting childhood abuse*. Cambridge, MA: Harvard University Press.

Fried, P. A., & Smith, A. M. (2001). A literature review of the consequences of prenatal marihuana exposure: An emerging theme of a deficiency in aspects of executive functioning. *Neurotoxicology and Teratology, 23*, 1–11.

Friedberg, J. M. (1983). Shock treatment II: Resistance in the 1970's. In R. F. Morgan (Ed.), *The iatrogenics handbook: A critical look at research and practice in the helping professions*. Fair Oaks, CA: Morgan Foundation Publishers.

Friedberg, M., Saffron, B., Stinson, T. J., Nelson, W., & Bennett, C. L. (1999). Evaluation of conflict of interest in economic analyses of new drugs used in oncology. *Journal of the American Medical Association, 282*, 1453–1457.

Friedkin, N. E. (1999). Choice shift and group polarization. *American Sociological Review, 64*, 856–875.

Friedman, H. S., Tucker, J. S., Schwartz, J. E., Martin, L. R., Tomlinson-Keasey, C., Wingard, D. L., & Criqui, M. H. (1995). Childhood conscientiousness and longevity: Health behaviors and cause of death. *Journal of Personality and Social Psychology, 68*, 696–703.

Friedman, H. S., Tucker, J. S., Tomlinson-Keasey, C., Schwartz, J. E., Wingard, D. L., & Criqui, M. H. (1993). Does childhood personality predict longevity? *Journal of Personality and Social Psychology, 65*, 176–185.

Friedman, M., & Rosenman, R. F. (1974). *Type A behavior and your heart*. New York: Knopf.

Friedrich, J., Fetherstonhaugh, D., Casey, S., & Gallagher, D. (1996). Argument integration and attitude change: Suppression effects in the integration of one-sided arguments that vary in persuasiveness. *Personality and Social Psychology Bulletin, 22*, 179–191.

Frieze, I. H., Olson, J. E., & Russell, J. (1991). Attractiveness and income for men and women in management. *Journal of Applied Social Psychology, 21*, 1039–1057.

Frijda, N. H. (1999). Emotions and hedonic experience. In D. Kahneman, E. Diener, & N. Schwarz (Eds.), *Well-being: The foundations of hedonic psychology*. New York: Russell Sage Foundation.

Frishman, L. J. (2001). Basic visual processes. In E. B. Goldstein (Ed.), *Blackwell handbook of perception*. Malden, MA: Blackwell.

Fromholt, P., & Bruhn, P. (1999). Cognitive dysfunction and dementia. In I. H. Nordhus, G. R. VandenBos, S. Berg & P. Fromholt (Eds.), *Clinical geropsychology* (pp. 183–188). Washington, DC: American Psychological Association.

Fromm, E. (1979). The nature of hypnosis and other altered states of consciousness: An ego-psychological theory. In E. Fromm & R. E. Shor (Eds.), *Hypnosis: Developments in research and new perspectives*. New York: Aldine.

Fromm, E. (1992). An ego-psychological theory of hypnosis. In E. Fromm & M. R. Nash (Eds.), *Contemporary hypnosis research*. New York: Guilford.

Frumkes, T. E. (1990). Classical and modern psychophysical studies of dark and light adaptation and their relationship to underlying retinal function. In K. N. Leibovic (Ed.), *Science of vision*. New York: Springer-Verlag.

Fullilove, M., & Dieudonne, I. (1996). Substance abuse in pregnancy. In *The Hatherleigh guide to treating substance abuse* (pp. 93–117). New York: Hatherleigh Press.

Funder, D. C. (2001). Personality. *Annual Review of Psychology, 52*, 197–221.

Funk, W. (1998). *What difference does it make? The journey of a soul survivor*. Cranbrook, BC: Wild Flower Publisher.

Furnham, A., & Gunter, B. (1993). Corporate culture: Definition, diagnosis, and change. In C. L. Cooper & I. T. Robertson (Eds.), *International review of industrial and organizational psychology* (Vol. 8, pp. 234–261). London: Wiley.

Fuster, J. M. (1996). Frontal lobe lesions. In B. S. Fogel, R. B. Schiffer, & S. M. Rao (Eds.), *Neuropsychiatry*. Baltimore: Williams & Wilkins.

Fyer, A. J. (2000). Anxiety disorders: Genetics. In B. J. Sadock & V. A. Sadock (Eds.), *Kaplan and Sadock's comprehensive textbook of psychiatry* (7th ed., Vol. 1, pp. 1457–1463). Philadelphia: Lippincott/Williams & Wilkins.

Gabbard, G. O. (1994). Reconsidering the American Psychological Association's policy on sex with former patients: Is it justifiable? *Professional Psychology: Research and Practice, 25*, 329–335.

Gaertner, S. L., Dovidio, J. F., Nier, J. A., Ward, C. M., & Banker, B. S. (1999). Across cultural divides: The value of a superordinate identity. In D. A. Prentice & D. T. Miller (Eds.), *Cultural divides: Understanding and overcoming group conflict*. New York: Russell Sage Foundation.

Gaeth, G. J., & Shanteau, J. (2000). Reducing the influence of irrelevant information on experienced decision makers. In T. Connolly, H. R. Arkes, & K. R. Hammond (Eds.), *Judgment and decision making: An interdisciplinary reader* (2nd ed., pp. 305–323). New York: Cambridge University Press.

Gage, F. H. (2002). Neurogenesis in the adult brain. *Journal of Neuroscience, 22*, 612–613.

Galambos, N. L. (2004). Gender and gender role development in adolescence. In R. M. Lerner & L. Steinberg (Eds.), *Handbook of adolescent psychology*. New York: Wiley.

Galanter, E. (1962). Contemporary psychophysics. In R. Brown (Ed.), *New directions in psychology*. New York: Holt, Rinehart & Winston.

Galati, D., Scherer, K. R., & Ricci-Bitti, P. E. (1997). Voluntary facial expression of emotion: Comparing congenitally blind with normally sighted encoders. *Journal of Personality and Social Psychology, 73*, 1363–1379.

Galderisi, S., Maj, M., Mucci, A., Cassano, G. B., Invernizzi, G., Rossi, A., Vita, A., Dell'Osso, L., Daneluzzo, E., & Pini, S. (2002). Historical, psychopathological, neurological, and neuropsychological, aspects of deficit schizophrenia: A multicenter study. *American Journal of Psychiatry, 159*, 983–990.

Gallagher, J. J., & Courtright, R. D. (1986). The educational definition of giftedness and its policy implications. In R. J. Sternberg & J. E. Davidson (Eds.), *Conceptions of giftedness*. Cambridge: Cambridge University Press.

Gallistel, C. R. (2000). The replacement of general-purpose learning models with adaptively specialized learning modules. In M. S. Gazzaniga (Ed.), *The new cognitive neurosciences* (2nd ed., pp. 1179–1192). Cambridge, MA: MIT Press.

Galton, F. (1869). *Hereditary genius: An inquiry into its laws and consequences*. New York: Appleton.

Gambone, J. C., Reiter, R. C., & DiMatteo, M. R. (1994). *The PREPARED provider: A guide for improved patient communication*. Beaverton, OR: Mosybl Great Performance.

Gangestad, S. W., & Simpson, J. A. (1993). Development of a scale measuring genetic variation related to expressive control. *Journal of Personality, 61*(2), 133–158.

Gangestad, S. W., & Snyder, M. (2000). Self-monitoring: Appraisal and reappraisal. *Psychological Bulletin, 126*, 530–555.

Gantt, W. H. (1975, April 25). Unpublished lecture, Ohio State University. Cited in D. Hothersall, (1984), *History of psychology*. New York: Random House.

Garb, H. N., Florio, C. M., & Grove, W. M. (1998). The validity of the Rorschach and the Minnesota Multiphasic Personality Inventory: Results form meta-analysis. *Psychological Science, 9*, 402–404.

Garcia, J. (1989). Food for Tolman: Cognition and cathexis in concert. In T. Archer & L. G. Nilsson (Eds.), *Aversion, avoidance, and anxiety: Perspectives on aversively motivated behavior*. Hillsdale, NJ: Erlbaum.

Garcia, J., & Koelling, R. A. (1966). Learning with prolonged delay of reinforcement. *Psychonomic Science, 5*, 121–122.

Garcia, J., & Rusiniak, K. W. (1980). What the nose learns from the mouth. In D. Muller-Schwarze & R. M. Silverstein (Eds.), *Chemical signals*. New York: Plenum.

Garcia, J., Clarke, J. C., & Hankins, W. G. (1973). Natural responses to scheduled rewards. In

P. P. G. Bateson & P. Klopfer (Eds.), *Perspectives in ethology*. New York: Plenum.

Garcia, S. D., & Khersonsky, D. (1996). "They make a lovely couple": Perceptions of couple attractiveness. *Journal of Social Behavior and Personality, 11*, 667–682.

Gardner, B. T., & Gardner, R. A. (1967). Teaching sign language to a chimpanzee: II. Demonstrations. Psychonomic Bulletin, *1*(2), 36.

Gardner, E. L. (1997). Brain reward mechanisms. In J. H. Lowinson, P. Ruiz, R. B. Millman, & J. G. Langrod (Eds.), *Substance abuse: A comprehensive textbook*. Baltimore: Williams & Wilkins.

Gardner, E. P., & Kandel, E. R. (2000). Touch. In E. R. Kandel, J. H. Schwartz, & T. M. Jessell (Eds.), *Principles of neural science*. New York: McGraw-Hill.

Gardner, H. (1983). *Frames of mind: The theory of multiple intelligences*. New York: Basic Books.

Gardner, H. (1985). *The mind's new science: A history of the cognitive revolution*. New York: Basic Books.

Gardner, H. (1993). *Multiple intelligences: The theory in practice*. New York: Basic Books.

Gardner, H. (1998). A multiplicity of intelligences. *Scientific American Presents Exploring Intelligence, 9*, 18–23.

Gardner, H. (1999). *Intelligence reframed: Multiple intelligences for the 21st century*. New York: Basic Books Inc.

Gardner, H. (2003). Three distinct meanings of intelligence. In R. Sternberg, J. Lautrey, & T. I. Lubart (Eds.), *Models of intelligence: International perspectives* (pp. 43–54). Washington, DC: American Psychological Association.

Gardner, H. (2004). Audiences for the theory of multiple intelligences. *Teachers College Record, 106*(1), 212–220.

Gardner, R. A., & Gardner, B. T. (1967). Teaching sign language to a chimpanzee: I. Methodology and preliminary results. Psychonomic Bulletin, *1*(2), 36.

Gardner, R. C. (2000). Correlation, causation, motivation and second language acquisition. *Canadian Psychology, 41*, 10–22.

Gardner, R. C., & Lambert, W. E. (1959). Motivational variables in second-language acquisition. *Canadian Journal of Psychology, 13*, 266–272.

Gardos, P. S., & Mosher, D. L. (1999). Gender differences in reactions to viewing pornographic vignettes: Essential or interpretive? *Journal of Psychology & Human Sexuality, 11*, 65–83.

Garfield, S. L. (2001). Methodological issues in clinical diagnosis. In P. B. Sutker & H. E. Adams (Eds.), *Comprehensive handbook of psychopathology*. New York: Kluwer Academic/Plenum.

Garfield, S. L., & Bergin, A. E. (1994). Introduction and historical overview. In A. E. Bergin & S. L. Garfield (Eds.), *Handbook of psychotherapy and behavior change* (4th ed.). New York: Wiley.

Garland, A. F., & Zigler, E. (1999). Emotional and behavioral problems among highly intellectually gifted youth. *Roeper Review, 22*, 41–44.

Garlow, S. J., Musselman, D. L., & Nemeroff, C. B. (1999). The neurochemistry of mood disorders: Clinical studies. In D. S. Charney, E. J. Nestler & B. S. Bunney (Eds.), *Neurobiology of mental illness*. New York: Oxford University Press.

Garnets, L., & Kimmel, D. (1991). Lesbian and gay male dimensions in the psychological study of human diversity. In J. D. Goodchilds (Ed.), *Psychological perspectives on human diversity in America*. Washington, DC: American Psychological Association.

Garvey, C. R. (1929). List of American psychology laboratories. *Psychological Bulletin, 26*, 652–660.

Gatchel, R. J., & Maddrey, A. M. (2004). The biopsychosocial perspective of pain. In J. M. Raczynski & L. C. Leviton (Eds.), *Handbook of clinical health psychology Vol. 2: Disorders of behavior and health*. Washington, DC: American Psychological Association.

Gazzaniga, M. S. (1970). *The bisected brain*. New York: Appleton-Century-Crofts.

Gazzaniga, M. S. (2000). Cerebral specialization and interhemispheric communication. *Brain, 123*, 1293–1326.

Gazzaniga, M. S., Bogen, J. E., & Sperry, R. W. (1965). Observations on visual perception after disconnection of the cerebral hemispheres in man. *Brain, 88*, 221–236.

Ge, X., Conger, R. D., & Elder, G. H. Jr. (1996). Coming of age too early: Pubertal influences on girls' vulnerability to psychological distress. *Child Development, 67*, 3386–3400.

Geddes, J. R., & Lawrie, S. M. (1995). Obstetrical complications and schizophrenia: A meta-analysis. *British Journal of Psychiatry, 167*, 786–793.

Geiger, M. A. (1997). An examination of the relationship between answer changing, testwiseness and examination performance. *Journal of Experimental Education, 66*, 49–60.

Geis, F. L. (1993). Self-fulfilling prophecies: A social psychological view of gender. In A. E. Beall & R. J. Sternberg (Eds.), *The psychology of gender*. New York: Guilford.

Geller, J. L. (1992). A historical perspective on the role of state hospitals viewed from the era of the "revolving door." *American Journal of Psychiatry, 149*, 1526–1533.

Geller, L. (1982). The failure of self-actualization theory: A critique of Carl Rogers and Abraham Maslow. *Journal of Humanistic Psychology, 22*, 56–73.

Gelman, R., & Williams, E. M. (1998). Enabling constraints for cognitive development and learning: Domain-specificity and epigenesis. In W. Damon (Ed.), *Handbook of child psychology (Vol. 2): Cognition, perception, and language*. New York: Wiley.

Genesee, F. (1998). French immersion in Canada. In J. Edwards (Ed.), *Language in Canada* (pp. 305–326). Cambridge, UK: Cambridge University Press.

Genesee, F. (2004). What do we know about bilingual education for majority-language students? In T. K. Bhatia & W. C. Ritchie (Eds.), *The handbook of bilingualism* (pp. 547–576). Oxford, UK: Blackwell Publishing Ltd.

Gennari, S. P., Sloman, S. A., Malt, B. C., & Fitch, W. T. (2002). Motion events in language and cognition. *Cognition, 83*(1), 49–79.

Gentner, D. (1988). Metaphor as structure mapping: The relational shift. *Child Development, 59*, 47–59.

Gentner, D., & Rattermann, M. J. (1991). Language and the career of similarity. In S. A. Gelman & J. P. Byrnes (Eds.), *Perspectives on language and thought: Interrelations in development*. Cambridge, MA: Cambridge University Press.

Gergen, K. J., Gulerce, A., Lock, A., & Misra, G. (1996). Psychological science in cultural context. *American Psychologist, 51*, 496–503.

German, T. P., & Defeyter, M. A. (2000). Immunity to functional fixedness in young children. *Psychonomic Bulletin & Review, 7*, 707–712.

Gershberg, F. B., & Shimamura, A. P. (1998). The neuropsychology of human learning and memory. In J. L. Martinez, Jr. & R. P. Kesner (Eds.), *Neurobiology of learning and memory*. San Diego: Academic Press.

Gershoff, E. T. (2002). Parental corporal punishment and associated child behaviors and experiences: A meta-analytic and theoretical review. *Psychological Bulletin, 128*, 539–579.

Gershon, E. S., Berrettini, W. H., & Goldin, L. R. (1989). Mood disorders: Genetic aspects. In H. I. Kaplan & B. J. Sadock (Eds.), *Comprehensive textbook of psychiatry/V*. Baltimore: Williams & Wilkins.

Geschwind, N., & Galaburda, A. M. (1987). *Cerebral lateralization: Biological mechanisms, associations, and pathology*. Cambridge, MA: MIT Press.

Gest, S. D. (1997). Behavioral inhibition: Stability and associations with adaptation from childhood to early adulthood. *Journal of Personality and Social Psychology, 72*, 467–475.

Ghez, C., & Thach, W. T. (2000). The cerebellum. In E. R. Kandel, J. H. Schwartz & T. M. Jessell (Eds.), *Principles of neural science* (pp. 832–852). New York: McGraw-Hill.

Ghiselin, B. (Ed.). (1952). *The creative process*. New York: Mentor.

Gibson, H. B., & Heap, M. (1991). *Hypnosis in therapy*. Hillsdale, NJ: Erlbaum.

Gigerenzer, G. (2000). *Adaptive thinking: Rationality in the real world*. New York: Oxford University Press.

Gilbert, C. D. (1993). Rapid dynamic changes in adult cerebral cortex. *Current Opinion in Neurobiology, 3*, 100–103.

Gilbert, D. T. (1989). Thinking lightly about others: Automatic components of the social inference process. In J. S. Uleman & J. A. Bargh (Eds.), *Unintended thought: Limits of awareness, intention, and control*. New York: Guilford.

Gilbert, D. T. (1998). Speeding with Ned: A personal view of the correspondence bias. In J. M. Darley & J. Cooper (Ed.), *Attribution and social interaction: The legacy of Edward E. Jones*. Washington, DC: American Psychological Association.

Gilbert, D. T., & Malone, P. S. (1995). The correspondence bias. *Psychological Bulletin, 117*, 21–38.

Gilboa, A., Winocur, G., Grady, C. L., Hevenor, S. J., Moscovitch, M. (2004). Remembering our past: Functional neuroanatomy of recollection of recent and very remote personal events. *Cerebral Cortex, 14*(11), 1214–1225.

Gilgen, A. R. (1982). *American psychology since World War II: A profile of the discipline.* Westport, CT: Greenwood Press.

Gilhooly, K. J. (1996). Thinking: Directed, undirected and creative. London: Academic Press.

Gillberg, M., & Akerstedt, T. (1998). Sleep loss and performance: No "safe" duration of a monotonous task. *Physiology & Behavior, 64,* 599–604.

Gillberg, M., Kecklund, G., Axelsson, J., & Akerstedt, T. (1996). The effects of a short daytime nap after restricted night sleep. *Sleep, 19,* 570–575.

Gillham, J. E., Shatté, A. J., Reivich, K. J., & Seligman, M. E. P. (2001). Optimism, pessimism, and explanatory style. In E. C. Chang (Ed.), *Optimism & pessimism: Implications for theory, research, and practice* (pp. 53–76). Washington, DC: American Psychological Association.

Gilligan, C. (1982). *In a different voice: Psychological theory and women's development.* Cambridge, MA: Harvard University Press.

Gilovich, T., & Savitsky, K. (1999). The spotlight effect and the illusion of transparency: Egocentric assessments of how we're seen by others. *Current Directions in Psychological Science, 8,* 165–168.

Gilovich, T., Medvec, V. H., & Savitsky, K. (2000). The spotlight effect in social judgment: An egocentric bias in estimates of the salience of one's own actions and appearance. *Journal of Personality and Social Psychology, 78,* 211–222.

Gitlin, M. (2002). Pharmacological treatment of depression. In I. H. Gotlib & C. L. Hammen (Eds.), *Handbook of depression.* New York: Guilford.

Gitlin, M., Nuechterlein, K., Subotnik, K. L., Ventura, J., Mintz, J., Fogelson, D. L., Bartzokis, G., & Aravagiri, M. (2001). Clinical outcome following neuroleptic discontinuation in patients with remitted recent-onset schizophrenia. *American Journal of Psychiatry, 158,* 1835–1842.

Gladue, B. A. (1988). Hormones in relationship to homosexual/bisexual/heterosexual gender orientation. In J. M. A. Sitesen (Ed.), *Handbook of sexology: The pharmacology and endocrinology of sexual function* (Vol. 6). Amsterdam: Elsevier.

Gladue, B. A. (1994). The biopsychology of sexual orientation. *Current Directions in Psychological Science, 3,* 150–154.

Glaser, R. (1991). Intelligence as an expression of acquired knowledge. In H. A. H. Rowe (Ed.), *Intelligence: Reconceptualization and measurement.* Hillsdale, NJ: Erlbaum.

Glass, C. R., & Arnkoff, D. B. (1992). Behavior therapy. In D. K. Freedheim (Ed.), *History of psychotherapy: A century of change.* Washington, DC: American Psychological Association.

Glass, R. M. (2001). Electroconvulsive therapy. *Journal of the American Medical Association, 285,* 1346–1348.

Glass, R. M. (2004). Treatment of adolescents with major depression: Contributions of a major trial. *Journal of the American Medical Association, 292,* 861–863.

Glassman, A. H., & Shapiro, P. A. (1998). Depression and the course of coronary artery disease. *American Journal of Psychiatry, 155,* 4–11.

Gleason, J. B., & Ratner, N. B. (1998). Language acquisition. In J. B. Gleason & N. B. Ratner (Eds.), *Psycholinguistics.* Fort Worth, TX: Harcourt College Publishers.

Gleaves, D. H. (1994). On "The reality of repressed memories." *American Psychologist, 49,* 440–441.

Gleaves, D. H., May, M. C., & Cardena, E. (2001). An examination of the diagnostic validity of dissociative identity disorders. *Clinical Psychology Review, 21,* 577–608.

Gleaves, D. H., May, M. C., & Cardena, E. (2001). An examination of the diagnostic validity of dissociative identity disorders. *Clinical Psychology Review, 21,* 577–608.

Gleaves, D. H., Smith, S. M., Butler, L. D., & Spiegel, D. (2004). False and recovered memories in the laboratory and clinic: A review of experimental and clinical evidence. *Clinical Psychology: Science & Practice, 11*(1), 3–28.

Gleitman, L. R., & Newport, E. (1996). *The invention of language by children.* Cambridge, MA: MIT Press.

Gleitman, L., & Papafragou. (2005). Language and thought. In K. J. Holyoak & R. G. Morrison (Eds.), *The Cambridge handbook of thinking and reasoning.* New York: Cambridge University Press.

Glenberg, A. M. (1992). Distributed practice effects. In L. R. Squire (Ed.), *Encyclopedia of learning and memory.* New York: Macmillan.

Glenn, N. D. (1990). Quantitative research on marital quality in the 1980s: A critical review. *Journal of Marriage and the Family, 52,* 818–831.

Glenn, N. D. (1998). The course of marital success and failure in five American 10-year marriage cohorts. *Journal of Marriage and the Family, 60,* 569–576.

Globe and Mail. (2005). One in six people report being victims of racism. March 21, 2005, p. A7.

Gluck, M. A., & Myers, C. E. (1997). Psychobiological models of hippocampal function in learning and memory. *Annual Review of Psychology, 48,* 481–514.

Goddard, H. H. (1917). Mental tests and the immigrant. *Journal of Delinquency, 2,* 243–277.

Godden, D. R., & Baddeley, A. D. (1975). Context-dependent memory in two natural environments: On land and underwater. *British Journal of Psychology, 66*(3), 325–331.

Goeders, N. E. (2004). Stress, motivation, and drug addiction. *Current Directions in Psychological Science, 13*(1), 33–35.

Goff, D. C., & Coyle, J. T. (2001). The emerging role of glutamate in the pathophysiology and treatment of schizophrenia. *American Journal of Psychiatry, 158,* 1367–1377.

Goff, D. C., & Gudeman, J. E. (1999). The person with chronic mental illness. In A.M. Nicholi (Ed.), *The Harvard guide to psychiatry.* Cambridge, MA: Harvard University Press.

Gold, M. S. (1997). Cocaine (and crack): Clinical aspects. In J. H. Lowinson, P. Ruiz, R. B. Millman, & J. G. Langrod (Eds.), *Substance abuse: A comprehensive textbook.* Baltimore: Williams & Wilkins.

Gold, M. S., & Miller, N. S. (1997). Cocaine (and crack): Neurobiology. In J. H. Lowinson, P. Ruiz, R. B. Millman, & J. G. Langrod (Eds.), *Substance abuse: A comprehensive textbook.* Baltimore: Williams & Wilkins.

Goldberg, M. E., & Hudspeth, A. J. (2000). The vestibular system. In E. R. Kandel, J. H. Schwartz, & T. M. Jessell (Eds.), *Principles of neural science.* New York: McGraw-Hill.

Golden, C. J., Sawicki, R. F., & Franzen, M. D. (1990). Test construction. In G. Goldstein & M. Hersen (Eds.), *Handbook of psychological assessment.* New York: Pergamon Press.

Goldenberg, H. (1983). *Contemporary clinical psychology.* Pacific Grove, CA: Brooks/Cole.

Goldfield, B. A., & Reznick, J. S. (1990). Early lexical acquisition: Rate, content, and the vocabulary spurt. *Journal of Child Language, 17,* 171–183.

Goldfried, M. R., Greenberg, L. S., & Marmar, C. (1990). Individual psychotherapy: Process and outcome. *Annual Review of Psychology, 41,* 659–688.

Goldman, D. L. (1990). Dorothea Dix and her two missions of mercy in Nova Scotia. *Canadian Journal of Psychiatry, 35,* 139–142.

Goldman-Rakic, P. S. (1993). Working memory and the mind. In *Mind and brain: Readings from Scientific American magazine.* New York: W. H. Freeman.

Goldman-Rakic, P. S. (1998). The prefrontal landscape: Implications of functional architecture for understanding human mentation and the central executive. In A. C. Roberts, T. W. Robbins, & L. Weiskrantz (Eds.), *The prefrontal cortex: Executive and cognitive functions.* New York: Oxford University Press.

Goldsmith, H. H., & Harman, C. (1994). Temperament and attachment; individuals and relationships. *Current Directions in Psychological Science, 3,* 53–57.

Goldstein, E. B. (1996). *Sensation and perception* (4th ed.). Pacific Grove, CA: Brooks/Cole.

Goldstein, E. B. (2001). Pictorial perception and art. In E. B. Goldstein (Ed.), *Blackwell handbook of perception.* Malden, MA: Blackwell.

Goldstein, E., & Farmer, K. (Eds.) (1993). *True stories of false memories.* Boca Raton, FL: Sir Publishing.

Goldstein, W. M. (1990). Judgments of relative importance in decision making: Global vs. local interpretations of subjective weight. *Organizational Behavior and Human Decision Processes, 47,* 313–336.

Goldstein, W. M., & Hogarth, R. M. (1997). Judgement and decision research: Some historical context. In W. M. Goldstein, & R. M. Hogarth (Eds.), *Research on judgement and decision making.* New York: Cambridge University Press.

Goleman, D. (1995). *Emotional intelligence.* New York: Bantam Books.

Gonzalez-Lopez, A., & Kamps, D. M. (1997). Social skills training to increase social interactions between children with autism and their typical peers. *Focus on Autism & Other Developmental Disabilities, 12,* 2–14.

Goodale, M. A., & Humphrey, G. K. (2001). Separate visual systems for action and perception. In E.B. Goldstein (Ed.), *Blackwell handbook of perception* (pp. 309–343). Oxford UK: Blackwell Publishers Ltd.

Goodale, M. A., & Milner, A. D. (1992). Separate visual pathways for perception and action. *Trends in Neuroscience, 15,* 20–25.

Goodale, M. A., & Milner, A. D. (2004). *Sight unseen: An exploration of conscious and unconscious vision.* Oxford UK: Oxford University Press.

Goodale, M. A., & Westwood, D. A. (2004). An evolving view of duplex vision: Separate but interacting cortical pathways for perception and action. *Current Opinion in Neurobiology, 14,* 203–211.

Goodenough, D. R. (1991). Dream recall: History and current status of the field. In S. J. Ellman & J. S. Antrobus (Eds.), *The mind in sleep: Psychology and psychophysiology* (2nd ed.). New York: Wiley.

Goodwin, C. J. (1991). Misportraying Pavlov's apparatus. *American Journal of Psychology, 104*(1), 135–141.

Goodwin, D. W., & Gabrielli, W. F. (1997). Alcohol: Clinical aspects. In J. H. Lowinson, P. Ruiz, R. B. Millman, & J. G. Langrod (Eds.), *Substance abuse: A comprehensive textbook.* Baltimore: Williams & Wilkins.

Goodwin, F. K., & Jamison, K. R. (1990). *Manic-depressive illness.* New York: Oxford University Press.

Gooley, J. J., & Saper, C. B. (2005). Anatomy of the mammalian circadian system. In M. H. Kryger, T. Roth, & W. C. Dement (Eds.), *Principles and practice of sleep medicine.* Philadelphia: Elsevier Saunders.

Gopnik, A., Meltzoff, A. N., & Kuhl, P. K. (1999). *The scientist in the crib: Minds, brains, and how children learn.* New York: Morrow.

Gordon, H. W. (1990). The neurobiological basis of hemisphericity. In C. Trevarthen (Ed.), *Brain circuits and functions of the mind. Essays in honor of Roger W. Sperry.* Cambridge, MA: Cambridge University Press.

Gordon, J., & Abramov, I. (2001). Color vision. In E. B. Goldstein (Ed.), *Blackwell handbook of perception.* Malden, MA: Blackwell.

Gorman, M. E. (1989). Error, falsification and scientific inference: An experimental investigation. *Quarterly Journal of Experimental Psychology, 41*(2–A), 385–412.

Gosden, C., Nicolaides, K., & Whitting, V. (1994). *Is my baby all right? A guide for expectant parents.* Oxford, England: Oxford University Press.

Gotlib, I. H., & Robinson, L. A. (1982). Responses to depressed individuals: Discrepancies between self-reports and observer-rated behavior. *Journal of Abnormal Psychology, 91,* 231–240.

Gottdiener, J. S., Krantz, D. S., Howell, R. H., Hecht, G. M., Klein, J., Falconer, J. J., & Rozanski, A. (1994). Induction of silent myocardial ischemia with mental stress testing: Relationship to the triggers of ischemia during daily life activities and to ischemic functional severity. *Journal of the American College of Cardiology, 24,* 1645–1651.

Gottesman, I. I. (1991). *Schizophrenia genesis: The origins of madness.* New York: W. H. Freeman.

Gottesman, I. I. (1993). Origins of schizophrenia: Past as prologue. In R. Plomin & G. E. McClearn (Eds.), *Nature, nurture and psychology.* Washington, DC: American Psychological Association.

Gottesman, I. I. (2001). Psychopathology through a life span-genetic prism. *American Psychologist, 56,* 867–878.

Gottesman, I. I., & Hanson, D. R. (2005). Human development: Biological and genetic processes. *Annual Review of Psychology, 56,* 263–286.

Gottesman, I. I., & Moldin, S. O. (1998). Genotypes, genes, genesis, and pathogenesis in schizophrenia. In M. F. Lenzenweger & R. H. Dworkin (Eds.), *Origins and development of schizophrenia: Advances in experimental psychopathology.* Washington, DC: American Psychological Association.

Gottesman, I. I., & Moldin, S. O. (1998). Genotypes, genes, genesis, and pathogenesis in schizophrenia. In M. F. Lenzenweger & R. H. Dworkin (Eds.), *Origins and development of schizophrenia: Advances in experimental psychopathology.* Washington, DC: American Psychological Association.

Gottfredson, L. S. (2003a). Dissecting practical intelligence theory: Its claims and evidence. *Intelligence, 31,* 343–397.

Gottfredson, L. S. (2003b). *G,* jobs and life. In H. Nyborg (Ed.), *The scientific study of general intelligence: Tribute to Arthur R. Jensen.* Oxford, UK: Pergamon.

Gould, E., & Gross, C. G. (2002). Neurogenesis in adult mammals: Some progress and problems. *Journal of Neuroscience, 22,* 619–623.

Gould, E., Reeves, A. J., Graziano, M. S. A., & Gross, C. G. (1999). Neurogenesis in the neocortex of adult primates. *Science, 286,* 548–552.

Gould, R. L. (1975, February). Adult life stages: Growth toward self-tolerance. *Psychology Today,* pp. 74–78.

Gould, R. L. (1978). *Transformations: Growth and change in adult life.* New York: Simon & Schuster.

Gould, S. J. (1993). The sexual politics of classification. *Natural History,* 20–29.

Gouras, P. (1991). Color vision. In E. R. Kandel, J. H. Schwartz, & T. M. Jessell (Eds.), *Principles of neural science* (3rd ed.). New York: Elsevier.

Gourevitch, M. N., & Arnsten, J. H. (2005). Medical complications of drug use. In J. H. Lowinson, P. Ruiz, R. B. Millman, & J. G. Langrod (Eds.), *Substance abuse: A comprehensive textbook.* Philadelphia: Lippincott/Williams & Wilkins.

Gouzoulis-Mayfrank, E., Daumann, J., Tuchtenhagen, F., Pelz, S., Becker, S., Kunert, H. J., Fimm, B., & Sass, H. (2000). Impaired cognition in drug free users of recreational ecstasy (MDMA). *Journal of Neurology, Neurosurgery, & Psychiatry, 68,* 719–725.

Gow, K. M. (1999). Recovered memories of abuse: Real, fabricated, or both? *Australian Journal of Clinical & Experimental Hypnosis, 27*(2), 81–97.

Graber, J. A., Brooks-Gunn, J., Paikoff, R. L., & Warren, M. P. (1994). Prediction of eating problems: An 8-year study of adolescent girls. *Developmental Psychology, 30,* 823–834.

Graber, J. A., Lewinsohn, P. M., Seeley, J. R., & Brooks-Gunn, J. (1997). Is psychopathology associated with the timing of pubertal development? *Journal of the American Academy of Child & Adolescent Psychiatry, 36,* 1768–1776.

Graf, P., & Gallie, K. A. (1992). A transfer-appropriate processing account for memory and amnesia. In L. R. Squire & N. Butters (Eds.), *Neuropsychology of memory* (2nd ed.). New York: Guilford.

Graf, P., & Uttl, B. (2001). Prospective memory: A new focus for research. *Consciousness & Cognition: An International Journal, 10,* 437–450.

Graham, D. (2000). *Online recruiting.* Palo Alto, CA: Davies-Black.

Graham, J. R. (1990). *MMPI-2: Assessing personality and psychopathology.* New York: Oxford University Press.

Graham, S. A., Kilbreath, C. S., & Welder, A. N. (2004). 13-month-olds rely on shared labels and shape similarity for inductive inferences. *Child Development,75,* 409–427.

Granberg, G., & Holmberg, S. (1991). Self-reported turnout and voter validation. *American Journal of Political Science, 35,* 448–459.

Grant, I., McDonald, W. I., Patterson, T., & Trimble, M. R. (1989). Multiple sclerosis. In G. W. Brown & T. O. Harris (Eds.), *Life events and illness.* New York: Guilford.

Grantham-McGregor, S., Ani, C., & Fernald, L. (2001). The role of nutrition in intellectual development. In R. J. Sternberg & E. L. Grigorenko (Eds.), *Environmental effects on cognitive abilities* (pp. 119–156). Mahwah, NJ: Erlbaum.

Gratton, A. (1996). In vivo analysis of the role of dopamine in stimulant and opiate self-administration. *Journal of Psychiatry & Neuroscience, 21,* 264–279.

Graziano, W. G. (1995). Evolutionary psychology: Old music, but now on CDs? *Psychological Inquiry, 6,* 41–44.

Graziano, W. G., & Eisenberg, N. H. (1997). Agreeableness: A dimension of personality. In R. Hogan, J. Johnson, & S. Briggs (Eds.), *Handbook of personality psychology.* San Diego: Academic Press.

Green, C. D. (2002). Toronto's "other" original APA member: James Gibson Hume. *Canadian Psychology, 43,* 35–45.

Green, C. D. (2004). The hiring of James Mark Baldwin and James Gibson Hume at the University of Toronto in 1889. *History of Psychology, 7,* 130–153.

Green, J. P. (1999). Hypnosis, context effects, and recall of early autobiographical memories. *International Journal of Clinical & Experimental Hypnosis, 47,* 284–300.

Green, L. W., Tryon W. W., Marks, B., & Huryn, J. (1986). Periodontal disease as a function of life events stress. *Journal of Human Stress, 12*(1), 32–36.

Greenberg, J. S. (1993). *Comprehensive stress management.* Dubuque, IA: William C. Brown.

Greenberg, J. S. (2002). *Comprehensive stress management: Health and human performance.* New York: McGraw-Hill.

Greenberg, L. S. (2002). Integrating an emotion-focused approach to treatment into psychotherapy integration. *Journal of Psychotherapy Integration, 12,* 111–125.

Greenberg, L. S., & Johnson, S. M. (1988). *Emotion focussed couples therapy.* New York: Guilford Press.

Greenberg, M. A., Wortman, C. B., & Stone, A. A. (1996). Emotional expression and physical health:

Revising traumatic memories or fostering self-regulation? *Journal of Personality and Social Psychology, 71,* 588–602.

Greenberg, R. P., & Fisher, S. (1997). Mood-mending medicines: Probing drug, psychotherapy and placebo solutions. In S. Fisher & R. P. Greenberg (Eds.), *From placebo to panacea: Putting psychiatric drugs to the test.* New York: Wiley.

Greenfield, P. M. (1997). You can't take it with you: Why ability assessments don't cross cultures. *American Psychologist, 52,* 1115–1124.

Greenfield, P. M., & Suzuki, L. K. (1998). Culture and human development: implications for parenting, education, pediatrics, and mental health. In W. Damon (Ed.), *Handbook of child psychology (Vol. 4): Child psychology in practice.* New York: Wiley.

Greenland, P., Knoll, M. D., Stamler, J., Neaton, J. D., Dyer, A. R., Garside, D. B., & Wilson, P. W. (2003). Major risk factors as antecedents of fatal and nonfatal coronary heart disease events. *Journal of the American Medical Association, 290,* 891–897.

Greeno, C. G., & Wing, R. R. (1994). Stress-induced eating. *Psychological Bulletin, 115,* 444–464.

Greeno, J. G. (1978). Nature of problem-solving abilities. In W. K. Estes (Ed.), *Handbook of learning and cognitive processes* (Vol. 5). Hillsdale, NJ: Erlbaum.

Greenough, W. T. (1975). Experiential modification of the developing brain. *American Scientist, 63,* 37–46.

Greenough, W. T. (1985). The possible role of experience-dependent synaptogenesis, or synapses on demand in the memory process. In N. M. Weinberger, J. L. McGaugh, & G. Lynch (Eds.), *Memory systems of the brain.* New York: Guilford.

Greenough, W. T., & Volkmar, F. R. (1973). Pattern of dendritic branching in occipital cortex of rats reared in complex environments. *Experimental Neurology, 40,* 491–504.

Greenson, R. R. (1967). *The technique and practice of psychoanalysis* (Vol. 1). New York: International Universities Press.

Greenspan, S., & Driscoll, J. (1997). The role of intelligence in a broad model of personal competence. In D. P. Flanagan, J. L. Genshaft, & P. L. Harrison (Eds.), *Contemporary intellectual assessment: Theories, tests, and issues.* New York: Guilford.

Greenstein, T. N. (1996). Husbands' participation in domestic labor: Interactive effects of wives' and husbands' gender ideologies. *Journal of Marriage and the Family, 58,* 535–595.

Greenwald, A. G. (1992). New look 3: Unconscious cognition reclaimed. *American Psychologist, 47,* 766–779.

Gregory, R. J. (1996). *Psychological testing: History, principles, and applications* (2nd ed.). Boston: Allyn & Bacon.

Gregory, R. L. (1973). *Eye and brain.* New York: McGraw-Hill.

Gregory, R. L. (1978). *Eye and brain* (2nd ed.). New York: McGraw-Hill.

Grencavage, L. M., & Norcross, J. C. (1990). Where are the commonalities among the therapeutic factors? *Professional Psychology: Research and Practice, 21,* 372–378.

Gretzky, W. & Reilly, R. (1990). *Gretzky: An autobiography.* Toronto: HarperCollins.

Griffith, E. E. H., González, C. A., & Blue, H. C. (1999). The basics of cultural psychiatry. In R. E. Hales, S. C. Yudofsky, & J. A. Talbott (Eds.), *The American Psychiatric Press textbook of psychiatry.* Washington, DC: American Psychiatric Press.

Griffith, E. E., Gonzales, C. A., & Blue, H. C. (2003). Introduction to cultural psychiatry. In R. E. Hales & S. C. Yudofsky (Eds.), *Textbook of clinical psychiatry.* Washington, DC: American Psychiatric Publishing.

Grigorenko, E. L. (2000). Heritability and intelligence. In R. J. Sternberg (Ed.), *Handbook of intelligence* (pp. 53–91). New York: Cambridge University Press.

Grigorenko, E. L., & Sternberg, R. J. (2001). Analytical, creative, and practical intelligence as predictors of self-reported adaptive functioning: A case study in Russia. *Intelligence, 29,* 57–73.

Grigorenko, E. L., & Sternberg, R. J. (2003). The nature-nurture issue. In A. Slater & G. Bremner (Eds.), *An introduction to development psychology.* Malden, MA: Blackwell Publishers.

Grinspoon, L., & Bakalar, J. B. (1997). Marihuana. In J. H. Lowinson, P. Ruiz, R. B. Millman, & J. G. Langrod (Eds.), *Substance abuse: A comprehensive textbook.* Baltimore: Williams & Wilkins.

Groat, H. T., Giordano, P. C., Cernkovich, S. A., Pugh, M. D., & Swinford, S. P. (1997). Attitudes toward childbearing among young parents. *Journal of Marriage and the Family, 59,* 568–581.

Grob, C. S., & Poland, R. E. (1997). MDMA. In J. H. Lowinson, P. Ruiz, R. B. Millman, & J. G. Langrod (Eds.), *Substance abuse: A comprehensive textbook.* Baltimore: Williams & Wilkins.

Grob, C. S., & Poland, R. E. (2005). MDMA. In J. H. Lowinson, P. Ruiz, R. B. Millman, & J. G. Langrod (Eds.), *Substance abuse: A comprehensive textbook.* Philadelphia: Lippincott/Williams & Wilkins.

Grob, G. N. (1983). Disease and environment in American history. In D. Mechanic (Ed.), *Handbook of health, health care, and the health professions.* New York: Free Press.

Grob, G. N. (1991). Origins of DSM-I: A study in appearance and reality. *American Journal of Psychiatry, 148,* 421–431.

Grobbee, D. E., Rimm, E. B., Giovannucci, E., Colditz, G., Stampfer, M., & Willett, W. (1990). Coffee, caffeine, and cardiovascular disease in men. *New England Journal of Medicine, 323,* 1026–1032.

Gross, J. J. (1998). Antecedent and response focused emotion regulation: Divergent consequences for experience, expression, and physiology. *Journal of Personality and Social Psychology, 74,* 224–237.

Gross, J. J. (2001). Emotion regulation in adulthood: Timing is everything. *Current Directions in Psychological Science, 10,* 214–219.

Grossarth-Maticek, R., & Eysenck, H. J. (1991). Coffee-drinking and personality as factors in the genesis of cancer and coronary heart disease. *Neuropsychobiology, 23,* 153–159.

Grossman, J. B., & Ruiz, P. (2004). Shall we make a leap-of-faith to disulfiram (Antabuse)? *Addictive Disorders & Their Treatment, 3*(3), 129–132.

Grossman, R. P., & Till, B. D. (1998). The persistence of classically conditioned brand attitudes. *Journal of Advertising, 27,* 23–31.

Grossman, S. P., Dacey, D., Halaris, A. E., Collier, T., & Routtenberg, A. (1978). Aphagia and adipsia after preferential desruction of nerve cell bodies in hypothalamus. *Science, 202,* 537–539.

Grossmann, K. E., & Grossmann, K. (1990). The wider concept of attachment in cross-cultural research. *Human Development, 33,* 31–47.

Grossmann, K. E., Grossmann, K., Huber, F., & Wartner, U. (1981). Children's behavior towards their mothers at 12 months and their fathers at 18 months in Ainsworth's Strange Situation. *International Journal of Behavioral Development, 4,* 157–181.

Grotevant, H. (1997). Adolescent development in family contexts. In N. Eisenberg (Ed.), *Handbook of child psychology. Vol. 3: Social, emotional, and personality development* (5th ed., pp. 1097–1149). New York: Wiley.

Groth-Marnat, G. (1997). *Handbook of psychological assessment.* New York: Wiley.

Gruen, R. J. (1993). Stress and depression: Toward the development of integrative models. In L. Goldberger & S. Breznitz (Eds.), *Handbook of stress: Theoretical and clinical aspects.* New York: Free Press.

Grunberg, N. E., & Straub, R. O. (1992). The role of gender and taste class in the effects of stress on eating. *Health Psychology, 11,* 97–100.

Grunberg, N. E., Faraday, M. M., & Rahman, M. A. (2001). The psychobiology of nicotine self-administration. In A. Baum, T. A. Revenson, & J. E. Singer (Eds.), *Handbook of health psychology* (pp. 249–262). Mahwah, NJ: Erlbaum.

Gruneberg, M. M., Sykes, R. N., & Gillett, E. (1994). The facilitating effects of mnemonic strategies on two learning disabled adults. *Neuropsychological Rehabilitation, 4,* 241–254.

Guarnaccia, P. J., & Rogler, L. H. (1999). Research on culture-bound syndromes: New directions. *American Journal of Psychiatry, 156,* 1322–1327.

Gudjonsson, G. H. (2001). Recovered memories: Effects upon the family and community. In G. M. Davies & T. Dalgleish (Eds.), *Recovered memories: Seeking the middle ground.* Chichester, England: Wiley.

Guenther, K. (1988). Mood and memory. In G. M. Davies & D. M. Thomson (Eds.), *Memory in context: Context in memory.* New York: Wiley.

Guggenheim, F. G. (2000). Somatoform disorders. In B. J. Sadock & V. A. Sadock (Eds.), *Kaplan and Sadock's comprehensive textbook of psychiatry* (7th ed., Vol. 1, pp. 1504–1532). Philadelphia: Lippincott/Williams & Wilkins.

Guilbault, R. L., Bryant, F. B., Brockway, J. H., & Posavac, E. J. (2004). A meta-analysis of research on hindsight bias. *Basic & Applied Social Psychology, 26*(2–3), 103–117.

Guilford, J. P. (1959). Three faces of intellect. *American Psychologist, 14,* 469–479.

Guilford, J. P. (1985). The structure-of-intellect model. In B. B. Wolman (Ed.), *Handbook of intelli-*

gence: Theories, measurements and applications. New York: Wiley.

Guilleminault, C., & Anagnos, A. (2000). Narcolepsy. In M. H. Kryger, T. Roth, & W. C. Dement (Eds.), *Principles and practice of sleep medicine*. Philadelphia: Saunders.

Guilleminault, C., & Fromherz, S. (2005). Narcolepsy: Diagnosis and management. In M. H. Kryger, T. Roth, & W. C. Dement (Eds.), *Principles and practice of sleep medicine*. Philadelphia: Elsevier Saunders.

Gunn, D. V., Warm, J. S., Dember, W. N., & Temple, J. N. (2000). Subjective organization and the visibility of illusory contours. *American Journal of Psychology, 113,* 553–568.

Gunnell, D., & Ashby, D. (2004). Antidepressents and suicide: What is the balance of benefit and harm? *British Medical Journal, 329*(7456), 34–38.

Gupta, G. R. (1992). Love, arranged marriage, and the Indian social structure. In J. J. Macionis & N. V. Benokraitis (Eds.), *Seeing ourselves: Classic, contemporary and cross-cultural reading in sociology.* Englewood Cliffs, NJ: Prentice-Hall.

Gureje, O., Simon, G. E., Ustun, T. B., & Goldberg, D. P. (1997). Somatization in cross-cultural perspective: A world health organization study in primary care. *American Journal of Psychiatry, 154,* 989–995.

Gurm, H., & Litaker, D. G. (2000). Framing procedural risks to patients: Is 99% safe the same as a risk of 1 in 100? *Academic Medicine, 75,* 840–842.

Gutierrez, P. M., & Silk, K. R. (1998). Prescription privileges for psychologists: A review of the psychological literature. *Professional Psychology: Research and Practice, 29,* 213–222.

Guyton, A. C. (1991). *Textbook of medical physiology.* Philadelphia: Saunders.

Güzeldere, G., Flanagan, O., & Hardcastle, V. G. (2000). The nature and function of consciousness: Lessons from blindsight. In M. S. Gazzaniga (Ed.), *The new cognitive neurosciences.* Cambridge, MA: The MIT Press.

Haas, L. (1999). Families and work. In M. B. Sussman, S. K. Steinmetz, & G. W. Peterson (Eds.), *Handbook of marriage and the family* (pp. 571–612). New York: Plenum.

Hack, M., & Fanaroff, A. A. (1999). Outcomes of children of extremely low birthweight and gestational age in the 1990's. *Early Human Development, 53,* 193–218.

Hadjistavropoulous, T., Malloy, D. C., Sharpe, D., Green, S. M., & Fuchs-Lacelle, S. (2002). The relative importance of the ethical principles adopted by the American Psychological Association. *Canadian Psychology, 43,* 254–260.

Hafer, C. L., & Begue, L. (2005). Experimental research on just-world theory: Problems, developments, and future challenges. *Psychological Bulletin, 131,* 128–167.

Hafer, C., Bogaert, A. F., & McMullen, S-L. (2001). Belief in a just world and condom use in a sample of gay and bisexual men. *Journal of Applied Social Psychology, 31,* 1892–1910.

Hagerty, M. R. (2000). Social comparisons of income in one's community: Evidence from national surveys of income and happiness. *Journal of Personality and Social Psychology, 78,* 764–771.

Hagman, M. (1999). John Clark Murray on the emancipation of women: A comparison with John Stuart Mill. *History and Philosophy of Psychology Bulletin, 11,* 11–16.

Haith, M. M., & Benson, J. B. (1998). Infant cognition. In W. Damon (Ed.), *Handbook of child psychology (Vol. 2): Cognition, perception, and language.* New York: Wiley.

Hakuta, K. (1986). *Mirror of language.* New York: Basic Books.

Hakuta, K., Bialystok, E., & Wiley, E. (2003). Critical evidence: A test of the critical-period hypothesis for second-language acquisition. *Psychological Science, 14,* 31–38.

Halaas, J. L., Gajiwala, K. S., Maffel, M., Cohen, S. L., Chait, B. T., Rabinowitz, D., Lallone, R. L., Burley, S. K., & Friedman, J. M. (1995). Weight-reducing effects of the plasma protein encoded by the obese gene. *Science, 269,* 543–546.

Hales, D. (1987). *How to sleep like a baby.* New York: Ballantine.

Halford, J. C. G., & Blundell, J. E. (2000). Separate systems for serotonin and leptin in appetite control. *Annals of Medicine, 32,* 222–232.

Halford, J. C. G., Gillespie, J., Brown, V., Pontin, E. E., & Dovey, T. M. (2004). Effect of television advertisements for foods on food consumption in children. *Appetite, 42*(2), 221–225.

Hall, C. C. I. (1997). Cultural malpractice: The growing obsolescence of psychology with the changing U.S. population. *American Psychologist, 52,* 642–651.

Hall, C. S. (1966). *The meaning of dreams.* New York: McGraw-Hill.

Hall, C. S. (1979). The meaning of dreams. In D. Goleman & R. J.

Davidson (Eds.), *Consciousness: Brain, states of awareness, and mysticism.* New York: Harper & Row.

Hall, C. S., & Nordby, V. J. (1972). *The individual and his dreams.* New York: Mentor.

Hall, D. T., & Mirvis, P. H. (1995). Careers as lifelong learning. In A. Howard (Ed.), *The changing nature of work* (pp. 323–381). San Francisco: Jossey-Bass.

Hall, E. (1987). *Growing and changing: What the experts say.* New York: Random House.

Hall, G. S. (1904). *Adolescence.* New York: Appleton.

Hall, J. A. (1990). *Nonverbal sex differences: Communication accuracy and expressive style* (2nd ed.). Baltimore: Johns Hopkins University Press.

Hall, J. A. (1998). How big are nonverbal sex differences? The case of smiling and sensitivity to nonverbal cues. In D. J. Canary & K. Dindia (Eds.), *Sex differences and similarities in communication: Critical essays and empirical investigations of sex and gender in interaction* (pp. 155–177). Mahwah, NJ: Erlbaum.

Hall, J. A., Roter, D. L., & Katz, N. R. (1988). Meta-analysis of correlates of provider behavior in medical encounters. *Medical Care, 26,* 1–19.

Hall, W., Solowij, N., & Lemon, J. (1994). *The health and psychological consequences of cannabis use.* Canberra, Australia: Australian Government Publishing Service.

Halligan, S. L., & Yehuda, R. (2001). Cognitive and biologic components involved in the development of posttraumatic stress disorder. *Primary Psychiatry, 8*(10), 50–60.

Halmi, K. A. (1999). Eating disorders: Anorexia nervosa, bulimia nervosa, and obesity. In R. E. Hales, S. C. Yudofsky, & J. A. Talbott (Eds.), *American Psychiatric Press Textbook of Psychiatry.* Washington, DC: American Psychiatric Press.

Halmi, K. A. (2000). Eating disorders. In B. J. Sadock & V. A. Sadock (Eds.), *Kaplan and Sadock's comprehensive textbook of psychiatry* (7th ed., Vol. 1, pp. 1663–1676). Philadelphia: Lippincott/Williams & Wilkins.

Halmi, K. A. (2002). Physiology of anorexia nervosa and bulimia nervosa. In C. G. Fairburn & K. D. Brownell (Eds.), *Eating disorders and obesity: A comprehensive handbook.* New York: Guilford.

Halmi, K. A. (2003). Eating disorders: Anorexia nervosa, bulimia nervosa, and obesity. In R. E. Hales

& S. C. Yudofsky (Eds.), *Textbook of Clinical Psychiatry.* Washington, DC: American Psychiatric Publishing.

Halmi, K. A., Sunday, S. R., Strober, M., Kaplan, A., Woodside, D. B., Fichter, M., Treasure, J., Berrettini, W. H., & Kaye, W. H. (2000). Perfectionism in anorexia nervosa: Variation by clinical subtype, obsessionality, and pathological eating behavior. *American Journal of Psychiatry, 157,* 1799–1805.

Halpern, C. T., Udry, J. R., & Suchindran, C. (1997). Testosterone predicts initiation of coitus in adolescent females. *Psychosomatic Medicine, 59,* 161–171.

Halpern, D. F. (1984). *Thought and knowledge: An introduction to critical thinking.* Hillsdale, NJ: Erlbaum.

Halpern, D. F. (1992). *Sex differences in cognitive abilities.* Hillsdale, NJ: Erlbaum.

Halpern, D. F. (1996). *Thought and knowledge: An introduction to critical thinking.* Mahwah, NJ: Erlbaum.

Halpern, D. F. (1997). Sex differences in intelligence: Implications for education. *American Psychologist, 52,* 1091–1102.

Halpern, D. F. (1998). Teaching critical thinking for transfer across domains: Dispositions, skills, structure training, and metacognitive monitoring. *American Psychologist, 53,* 449–455.

Halpern, D. F. (2000). *Sex differences in cognitive abilities.* Mahwah, NJ: Erlbaum.

Halpern, D. F. (2003). *Thought and knowledge: An introduction to critical thinking.* Mahwah, NJ: Erlbaum.

Halpern, D. F. (2004). A cognitive-process taxonomy for sex differences in cognitive abilities. *Current Directions in Psychological Science, 13*(4), 135–139.

Halverson, C. F., Jr., & Wampler, K. S. (1997). Family influences on personality development. In R. Hogan, J. Johnson, & S. Briggs (Eds.), *Handbook of personality psychology.* San Diego: Academic Press.

Hamill, R., Wilson T. D., & Nisbett, R. E. (1980). Insensitivity to sample bias: Generalizing from atypical cases. *Journal of Personality and Social Psychology, 39,* 578–589.

Hamilton, W. D. (1964). The evolution of social behavior. *Journal of Theoretical Biology, 7,* 1–52.

Hammen, C. (2003). Mood disorders. In G. Stricker & T. A. Widiger (Eds.), *Handbook of psychology, Vol. 8: Clinical psychology.* New York: Wiley.

Hampton, T. (2004). Fetal environment may have profound long-term consequences for health. *Journal of the American Medical Association, 292,* 1285–1286.

Haney, C., & Zimbardo, P. G. (1998). The past and future of U.S. prison policy: Twenty-five years after the Stanford Prison Experiment. *American Psychologist, 53,* 709–727.

Hankin, B. L., Abramson, L. Y., Moffitt, T. E., Silva, P. A., McGee, R., & Angell, K. E. (1998). Development of depression from preadolescence to young adulthood: Emerging gender differences in a 10-year longitudinal study. *Journal of Abnormal Psychology, 107,* 128–140.

Hannigan, J. H., & Armant, D. R. (2000). Alcohol in pregnancy and neonatal outcome. *Seminars in Neonatology, 5,* 243–254.

Hanson, F. A. (1993). *Testing testing: Social consequences of the examined life.* Berkeley: University of California Press.

Happonen, P., Voutilainen, S., & Salonen, J. T. (2004). Coffee drinking is dose dependently related to the risk of acute coronary events in middle-aged men. *Journal of Nutrition, 134,* 2381–2386.

Harding, K, & Walton, D. (2005, March 4). In the line of duty. *Globe and Mail,* pp. A1, A6.

Hare, R. D. (1991). *The Hare psychopathy checklist-revised.* Toronto: Multihealth Systems.

Hare, R. D. (1999). *The disturbing world of the psychopaths among us.* New York: Guilford Press.

Hare, R. D., Cooke, D. J., & Hart, S. D. (1999). Psychopathy and sadistic personality disorder. In T. Millon, P. H. Blaney, & R. D. Davis (Eds.), *Oxford textbook of psychopathology.* New York: Oxford University Press.

Harmsen, P., Rosengren, A., Tsipogianni, A., & Wilhelmsen, L. (1990). Risk factors for stroke in middle-aged men in Goteborg, Sweden. *Stroke, 21,* 23–29.

Harrington, M. E., & Mistlberger, R. E. (2000). Anatomy and physiology of the mammalian circadian system. In M. H. Kryger, T. Roth, & W. C. Dement (Eds.), *Principles and practice of sleep medicine.* Philadelphia: Saunders.

Harris, J. E. (1984). Remembering to do things: A forgotten topic. In J. E. Harris & P. E. Morris (Eds.), *Everyday memory, actions, and absent-mindedness.* New York: Academic Press.

Harris, J. R. (1998). *The nurture assumption: Why children turn out the way they do.* New York: Free Press.

Harris, J. R. (2000). Context-specific learning, personality, and birth order. *Current Directions in Psychological Science, 9*(5), 174–177.

Harris, L. (2000). Procedural justice and perceptions of fairness in selection practice. *International Journal of Selection and Assessment, 8,* 148–157.

Hart, S. D., & Hare, R. D. (1997). Psychopathology: Assessment and association with criminal conduct. In D. M. Stoff, J. Breiling, & J. D. Maser (Eds.), *Handbook of antisocial behavior.* New York: Wiley.

Harvey, M. H. (1999). Memory research and clinical practice: A critique of three paradigms and a framework for psychotherapy with trauma survivors. In L. M. Williams & V. L. Banyard (Eds.), *Trauma & memory.* Thousand Oaks, CA: Sage Publications.

Hasher, L. & Zacks, R. (1974). Automatic processing of fundamental information: The case of frequency of occurrence. *American Psychologist, 39,* 1372–1388.

Haslam, N. (1997). Evidence that male sexual orientation is a matter of degree. *Journal of Personality and Social Psychology, 73,* 862–870.

Hastorf, A., & Cantril, H. (1954). They saw a game: A case study. *Journal of Abnormal and Social Psychology, 49,* 129–134.

Hatfield, E., & Rapson, R. L. (1993). *Love, sex, and intimacy: Their psychology, biology, and history.* New York: HarperCollins.

Hathaway, S. R., & McKinley, J. C. (1943). *Manual for the Minnesota Multiphasic Personality Inventory.* New York: Psychological Corporation.

Haugland, G., Siegel, C., Hopper, K., & Alexander, M. J. (1997). Mental illness among homeless individuals in a suburban county. *Psychiatric Services, 48,* 504–509.

Hauri, P. J. (2000). Primary insomnia. In M. H. Kryger, T. Roth, & W. C. Dement (Eds.), *Principles and practice of sleep medicine.* Philadelphia: Saunders.

Hauri, P. J. (2002). Psychological and psychiatric issues in the etiopathogenesis of insomnia. *Journal of Clinical Psychiatry, 4*(suppl. 1), 17–20.

Hauser, M., & Carey, S. (1998). Building a cognitive creature from a set of primitives: Evolutionary and developmental insights. In D. D. Cummins & C. Allen (Eds.), *The evolution of mind.* New York: Oxford University Press.

Hawkins, S. A., & Hastie, R. (1990). Hindsight: Biased judgments of past events after the outcomes are known. *Psychological Bulletin, 107,* 311–327.

Haworth-Hoeppner, S. (2000). The critical shapes of body image: The role of culture and family in the production of eating disorders. *Journal of Marriage and the Family, 62,* 212–227.

Hayashi, M., Watanabe, M., & Hori, T. (1999). The effects of a 20-minute nap in the mid-afternoon on mood, performance and EEG activity. *Clinical Neurophysiology, 110,* 272–279.

Hayes, J. R. (1989). Cognitive processes in creativity. In J. A. Glover, R. R. Ronning, & C. R. Reynolds (Eds.), *Handbook of creativity.* New York: Plenum.

Hayes, K. J., & Hayes, C. (1951). The intellectual development of a home-raised chimpanzee. *Proceedings of the American Philosophical Society, 95,* 105–109.

Hayman-Abello, B. A., Hayman-Abello, S. E., & Rourke, B. P. (2003). Human neuropsychology in Canada: The 1990s (a review of research by Canadian neuropsychologists conducted over the past decade). *Canadian Psychology, 44*(2), 100–138.

Hays, K. F. (1999). *Working it out: Using exercise in psychotherapy.* Washington, DC: American Psychological Association.

Haywood, T. W., Kravitz, H. M., Grossman, L. S., Cavanaugh, J. L., Jr., Davis, J. M., & Lewis, D. A. (1995). Predicting the "revolving door" phenomenon among patients with schizophrenic, schizoaffective, and affective disorders. *American Journal of Psychiatry, 152,* 861–956.

Hazan, C., & Shaver, P. (1986). *Parental caregiving style questionnaire.* Unpublished questionnaire.

Hazan, C., & Shaver, P. (1987). Romantic love conceptualized as an attachment process. *Journal of Personality and Social Psychology, 52,* 511–524.

He, J., Ogden, L. G., Vupputuri, S., Bazzano, L. A., Loria, C., & Whelton, P. K. (1999). Dietary sodium intake and subsequent risk of cardiovascular disease in overweight adults. *Journal of the American Medical Association, 282,* 2027–2034.

Health Canada. (2002a). Nutrition for a healthy pregnancy—National guidelines for the childbearing years. Retrieved June 17, 2005, from http://www.hc-sc.gc.ca/ hpfb-dgpsa/onpp-bppn/national_ guidelines.

Health Canada. (2002b). A report on mental illnesses in Canada. Retrieved May 9, 2005, from http://www.phac-aspc.gc.ca/ publicat/miic-mmac/.

Health Canada. (2002c). The health of senior women. Retrieved July 4, 2005, from http://www. hc-sc.gc.ca/english/women/facts_ issues/facts_seniors.htm.

Health Canada. (2004a). Canadian Tobacco Use Monitoring Survey (CTUMS). Retrieved June 22, 2005, from http://www.hc-sc.gc.ca/hl-vs/ tobac-tabac/research-recherche/stat/ ctums-esutc/index_e.html.

Health Canada. (2004b). Exclusive breastfeeding duration—2004 Health Canada Recommendation. Retrieved from http://www.hc-sc. gc.ca/hpfb-dgpsa/onpp-bppn/ exclusive_breastfeeding_duration_ e.html.

Healy, A. F., & McNamara, D. S. (1996). Verbal learning and memory: Does the modal model still work? *Annual Review of Psychology, 47,* 143–172.

Healy, D. (2004). *Let them eat Prozac: The unhealthy relationship between the pharmaceutical industry and depression.* New York: NYU Press.

Healy, D., & Whitaker, C. (2003). Antidepressants and suicide: Risk-benefit conundrums. *Journal of Psychiatry & Neuroscience, 28*(5), 28.

Hearst, E. (1988). Fundamentals of learning and conditioning. In R. C. Atkinson, R. J. Herrnstein, G. Lindzey, & R. D. Luce (Eds.), *Stevens' handbook of experimental psychology.* New York: Wiley.

Heatherton, T. F., Striepe, M., & Wittenberg, L. (1998). Emotional distress and disinhibited eating: The role of self. *Personality and Social Psychology Bulletin, 24,* 301–313.

Heaton, T. B., Jacobson, C. K., & Holland, K. (1999). Persistence and change in decisions to remain childless. *Journal of Marriage and the Family, 61,* 531–539.

Hebb, D. O. (1949). *The organization of behavior: A neuropsycholgical theory.* New York, NY: John Wiley & Sons, Inc.

Hebb, D. O. (2002). *The organization of behavior: A neuropsychological theory.* Mahwah, NJ: Lawrence Erlbaum Associates.

Hegarty, J. D., Balderssarini, R. J., Tohen, M., Waternaux, C., & Oepen, G. (1994). One hundred years of schizophrenia: A meta-analysis of the outcome literature. *American Journal of Psychiatry, 151,* 1409–1416.

Heider, F. (1958). *The psychology of interpersonal relations*. New York: Wiley.

Heine, S. H., Lehman, D. R., Markus, H. R., & Kitayama, S. (1999). Is there a universal need for positive self-regard? *Psychological Review, 106*(4), 766–794.

Heine, S. J., & Renshaw, K. (2002). Interjudge agreement, self-enhancement, and liking: Cross-cultural divergences. *Personality and Social Psychology Bulletin, 28*(5), 578–587.

Heine, S. J., Kitayama, S., Lehman, D. R., Takata, T., Ide, E., Leung, C., & Matsumoto, H. (2001). Divergent consequences of success and failure in Japan and North America: An investigation of self-improving motivations and malleable selves. *Journal of Personality and Social Psychology, 81*, 599–615.

Heinrichs, R. W. (2005). The primacy of cognition in schizophrenia. *American Psychologist, 60*, 229–242.

Heller, W., Nitschke, J. B., Etienne, M. A., & Miller, G. A. (1997). Patterns of regional brain activity differentiate types of anxiety. *Journal of Abnormal Psychology, 106*, 376–385.

Hellige, J. B. (1990). Hemispheric asymmetry. *Annual Review of Psychology, 41*, 55–80.

Hellige, J. B. (1993a). Unity of thought and action: Varieties of interaction between left and right cerebral hemispheres. *Current Directions in Psychological Science, 2*(1), 21–25.

Hellige, J. B. (1993b). *Hemispheric asymmetry: What's right and what's left.* Cambridge, MA: Harvard University Press.

Helmholtz, H. von. (1852). On the theory of compound colors. *Philosophical Magazine, 4*, 519–534.

Helmholtz, H. von. (1863). *On the sensations of tone as a physiological basis for the theory of music* (A. J. Ellis, Trans.). New York: Dover.

Helms, J. E. (1992). Why is there no study of cultural equivalence in standard cognitive ability testing? *American Psychologist, 47*, 1083–1101.

Helson, R., & Moane, G. (1987). Personality change in women from college to midlife. *Journal of Personality and Social Psychology, 53*, 176–186.

Helwig, D. (1989). UWO apologizes in Rushton affair. *Globe and Mail*, March 3, 1989, p. A14.

Hemenover, S. H. (2003). The good, the bad, and the healthy: Impacts of emotional disclosure of trauma on resilient self-concept and psychological distress. *Personality and Social Psychology Bulletin, 29*, 1236–1244.

Henderson, K. E., & Brownell, K. D. (2004). The toxic environment and obesity: Contribution and cure. In J. K. Thompson (Ed.), *Handbook of eating disorders and obesity*. New York: Wiley.

Henderson-King, E. I., & Nisbett, R. E. (1996). Anti-black prejudice as a function of exposure to the negative behavior of a single black person. *Journal of Personality and Social Psychology, 71*, 654–664.

Hendrick, S. S., & Hendrick, C. (1992). *Liking, loving, and relating* (2nd ed.). Pacific Grove, CA: Brooks/Cole.

Hendrick, S. S., & Hendrick, C. (2000). Romantic love. In S. S. Hendrick & C. Hendrick (Eds.), *Close relationships*. Thousand Oaks, CA: Sage.

Hennessy, D. A. & Wiesenthal, D. L. (Eds.). (2004). *Contemporary issues in road user behavior and traffic safety*. Hauppauge, NY: Nova Science Publishers.

Hennessy, D. A., & Wiesenthal, D. L. (1999). Traffic congestion, driver stress, and driver aggression. *Aggressive Behavior, 25*, 409–423.

Henriksson, M. M., Aro, H. M., Marttunen, M. J., Heikkinen, M. E., Isometsa, E. T., Kuoppasalmi, K. I., & Lonnqvist, J. K. (1993). Mental disorders and commorbidity of suicide. *American Journal of Psychiatry, 150*, 935–940.

Henry, K. R. (1984). Cochlear damage resulting from exposure to four different octave bands of noise at three different ages. *Behavioral Neuroscience, 1*, 107–117.

Henry, P. J., Sternberg, R. J., & Grigorenko, E. L. (2005). Capturing successful intelligence through measures of analytic, creative, and practical skills. In O. Wilhelm & R. W. Engle (Eds.), *Handbook of understanding and measuring intelligence*. Thousand Oaks, CA: Sage.

Herek, G. M. (1996). Heterosexism and homophobia. In R. P. Cabaj & T. S. Stein (Eds.), *Textbook of homosexuality and mental health*. Washington, DC: American Psychiatric Press.

Herek, G. M. (2000). The psychology of sexual prejudice. *Current Directions in Psychological Science, 9*, 19–22.

Hering, E. (1878). *Zür lehre vom lichtsinne*. Vienna: Gerold.

Herman, C. P., Ostovich, J. M., & Polivy, J. (1999). Effects of attentional focus on subjective hunger ratings. *Appetite, 33*, 181–193.

Herman, C. P., Roth, D., & Polivy, J. (2003). Effects of the presence of others on food intake: A normative interpretation. *Psychological Bulletin, 129*, 873–886.

Herman, J. L. (1992). *Trauma and recovery*. New York: Basic Books.

Herman, J. L. (1994). Presuming to know the truth. *Nieman Reports, 48*, 43–45.

Herman, L. M., Kuczaj, S. A., & Holder, M. D. (1993). Responses to anomalous gestural sequences by a language-trained dolphin: Evidence for processing of semantic relations and syntactic information. *Journal of Experimental Psychology: General, 122*, 184–194.

Hermann, R. C., Dorwart, R. A., Hoover, C. W., & Brody, J. (1995). Variation in ECT use in the United States. *American Journal of Psychiatry, 152*, 869–875.

Hermann, R. C., Ettner, S. L., Dorwart, R. A., Hoover, C. W., & Yeung, E. (1998). Characteristics of psychiatrists who perform ECT. *American Journal of Psychiatry, 155*, 889–894.

Hernandez, D. J. (1993). *America's children: Resources from family, government, and the economy*. New York: Russell Sage Foundation.

Herrett-Skjellum, J., & Allen, M. (1996). Television programming and sex stereotyping: A meta-analysis. In B. R. Burleson (Ed.), *Communication yearbook 19* (pp. 157–185). Thousand Oaks, CA: Sage.

Herrmann, D., Raybeck, D., & Gruneberg, M. (2002). *Improving memory and study skills: Advances in theory and practice*. Ashland, OH: Hogrefe & Huber.

Herrnstein, R. J., & Murray, C. (1994). *The bell curve: Intelligence and class structure in American life*. New York: Free Press.

Hertzsrung, E. A. M., & Dobson, K. S. (2000). Diversity training: Conceptual issues and practices for Canadian clinical psychology programs. *Canadian Psychology, 41*, 184–191.

Herzog, D. B., & Becker, A. E. (1999). Eating disorders. In A. M. Nicholi (Ed.), *The Harvard guide to psychiatry*. Cambridge, MA: Harvard University Press.

Herzog, D. B., & Delinski, S. S. (2001). Classification of eating disorders. In R. H. Striegel-Moore & L. Smolak (Eds.), *Eating disorders* (pp. 31–50). Washington, DC: American Psychological Association.

Herzog, T. A., Abrams, D. B., Emmons, K. M., Linnan, L. A., & Shadel, W. G. (1999). Do processes of change predict smoking stage movements? A prospective analysis of the transtheoretical model. *Health Psychology, 18*, 369–375.

Heshka, S., & Heymsfield, S. B. (2002). Pharmacological treatments on the horizon. In C. G. Fairburn & K. D. Brownell (Eds.), *Eating disorders and obesity: A comprehensive handbook* (pp. 557–561). New York: Guilford.

Heszen-Niejodek, I. (1997). Coping style and its role in coping with stressful encounters. *European Psychologist, 2*, 342–351.

Hetherington, E. M. (1999). Should we stay together for the sake of the children? In E. M. Hetherington (Ed.), *Coping with divorce, single parenting, and remarriage*. Mahwah, NJ: Erlbaum.

Hetherington, E. M. (2003). Intimate pathways: Changing patterns in close personal relationships across time. *Family Relations: Interdisciplinary Journal of Applied Family Studies, 52*, 318–331.

Hetherington, E. M., Bridges, M., & Insabella, G. M. (1998). What matters? What does not? Five perspectives on the association between marital transitions and children's adjustments. *American Psychologist, 53*, 167–184.

Hetherington, E. M., Reiss, D., & Plomin, R. (1994). *Separate social worlds of siblings: The impact of nonshared environment on development*. Hillsdale, NJ: Erlbaum.

Hetherington, M. M., & Rolls, B. J. (1996). Sensory-specific satiety: Theoretical frameworks and central characteristics. In E. D. Capaldi (Ed.), *Why we eat what we eat: The psychology of eating* (267–290). Washington, DC: American Psychological Association.

Hettema, J. M., Neale, M. C., & Kendler, K. S. (2001). A review and meta-analysis of the genetic epidemiology of anxiety disorders. *American Journal of Psychiatry, 158*, 1568–1578.

Hettich, P. I. (1998). *Learning skills for college and career*. Pacific Grove, CA: Brooks/Cole.

Hewitt, P. L., & Flett, G. L. (1991). Perfectionism in the self and social contexts: Conceptualization, assessment, and association with psychopathology. *Journal of Personality and Social Psychology, 60*, 456–470.

Hewitt, P. L., Flett, G. L., Ediger, E., Norton, G. R., & Flynn, C. A. (1998). Perfectionism in chronic and state symptoms of depression. *Canadian Journal of Behavioural Science, 30*, 234–242.

Hewstone, M. (1990). The "ultimate attribution error"? A review of the literature on intergroup causal attribution. *European Journal of Social Psychology, 20,* 311–335.

Higgins, E. T. (1987). Self-discrepancy theory. *Psychological Review, 94,* 319–340.

Higgins, E. T. (2004). Making a theory useful: Lessons handed down. *Personality and Social Psychology Review, 8*(2), 138–145.

Higgins, E. T., & Chaires, W. M. (1980). Accessibility of interrelational constructs: Implications for stimulus encoding and creativity. *Journal of Experimental Social Psychology, 16,* 348–361.

Higgins, E. T., Rholes, W. S., & Jones, C. R. (1977). Category accessibility and impression formation. *Journal of Experimental Social Psychology, 13,* 141–154.

Highhouse, S., Beadle, D., Gallo, A., & Miller, L. (1998). Get 'em while they last! Effects of scarcity information in job advertisements. *Journal of Applied Social Psychology, 28,* 779–795.

Hilgard, E. R. (1965). *Hypnotic susceptibility.* New York: Harcourt, Brace & World.

Hilgard, E. R. (1986). *Divided consciousness: Multiple controls in human thought and action.* New York: Wiley.

Hilgard, E. R. (1987). *Psychology in America: A historical survey.* San Diego: Harcourt Brace Jovanovich.

Hilgard, E. R. (1989). The early years of intelligence measurement. In R. L. Linn (Ed.), *Intelligence: Measurement, theory, and public policy.* Urbana: University of Illinois Press.

Hilgard, E. R. (1992). Dissociation and theories of hypnosis. In E. Fromm & M. R. Nash (Eds.), *Contemporary hypnosis research.* New York: Guilford.

Hill, A. J. (2002). Prevalence and demographics of dieting. In C. G. Fairburn & K. D. Brownell (Eds.), *Eating disorders and obesity: A comprehensive handbook* (pp. 80–83). New York: Guilford.

Hill, C. E., & Lambert, M. J. (2004). Methodological issues in studying psychotherapy processes and outcomes. In M. J. Lambert (Ed.), *Bergin and Garfield's handbook of psychotherapy and behavior change.* New York: Wiley.

Hill, J. O., & Peters, J. C. (1998). Environmental contributions to the obesity epidemic. *Science, 280,* 1371–1374.

Hilliard, A. G., III. (1984). IQ testing as the emperor's new clothes: A critique of Jensen's *Bias in Mental Testing.* In C. R. Reynolds & R. T. Brown (Eds.), *Perspectives on bias in mental testing.* New York: Plenum.

Hilton, J. L., & von Hippel, W. (1996). Stereotypes. *Annual Review of Psychology, 47,* 237–271.

Hineline, P. N. (1981). The several roles of stimuli in negative reinforcement. In P. Harzem & M. D. Zeiler (Eds.), *Predictability, correlation and continuity.* Chichester, England: Wiley.

Hinton, G. (2003). The ups and downs of Hebb synapses. *Canadian Psychology, 44,* 21–26.

Hirsh, I. J., & Watson, C. S. (1996). Auditory psychophysics and perception. *Annual Review of Psychology, 47,* 461–484.

Hirt, E. R., McDonald, H. E., & Markman, K. D. (1998). Expectancy effects in reconstructive memory: When the past is just what we expected. In S. J. Lynn & K. M. McConkey (Eds.), *Truth in memory.* New York: Guilford.

Ho, B. C., Nopoulos, P., Flaum, M., Arndt, S., & Andreasen, N. C. (1998). Two-year outcome in first-episode schizophrenia: Predictive value of symptoms for quality of life. *American Journal of Psychiatry, 155,* 1196–1201.

Ho, B., Black, D. W., & Andreasen, N. C. (2003). Schizophrenia and other psychotic disorders. In R. E. Hales & S. C. Yudofsky (Eds.), *Textbook of clinical psychiatry.* Washington, DC: American Psychiatric Publishing.

Hobson, C. J., & Delunas, L. (2001). National norms and life-event frequencies for the revised Social Readjustment Rating Scale. *International Journal of Stress Management, 8*(4), 299–314.

Hobson, J. A. (1988). *The dreaming brain.* New York: Basic Books.

Hobson, J. A. (1989). *Sleep.* New York: Scientific American Library.

Hobson, J. A. (1995). *Sleep.* New York: Scientific American Library.

Hobson, J. A. (2002). *Dreaming: An introduction to the science of sleep.* New York: Oxford University Press.

Hobson, J. A., & McCarley, R. W. (1977). The brain as a dream state generator: An activation-synthesis hypothesis of the dream process. *American Journal of Psychiatry, 134,* 1335–1348.

Hobson, J. A., Pace-Schott, E. F., & Stickgold, R. (2000). Dreaming and the brain: Toward a cognitive neuroscience of conscious states. *Behavioral and Brain Sciences, 23,* 793–842; 904–1018; 1083–1121.

Hocevar, D., & Bachelor, P. (1989). A taxonomy and critique of measurements used in the study of creativity. In J. A. Glover, R. R. Ronning, & C. R. Reynolds (Eds.), *Handbook of creativity.* New York: Plenum.

Hochberg, J. (1988). Visual perception. In R. C. Atkinson, R. J. Herrnstein, G. Lindzey, & R. D. Luce (Eds.), *Stevens' handbook of experimental psychology* (2nd ed., Vol. 1). New York: Wiley.

Hock, E., Schirtzinger, M. B., Lutz, W. J., & Widaman, K. (1995). Maternal depressive symptomatology over the transition to parenthood: Assessing the influence of marital satisfaction and marital sex role traditionalism. *Journal of Family Psychology, 9,* 79–88.

Hodapp, R. M. (1994). Cultural-familial mental retardation. In R. J. Sternberg (Ed.), *Encyclopedia of human intelligence.* New York: Macmillan.

Hodgkin, A. L., & Huxley, A. F. (1952). Currents carried by sodium and potassium ions through the membrane of the giant axon of Loligo. *Journal of Physiology, 116,* 449–472.

Hoek, H. W. (2002). Distribution of eating disorders. In C. G. Fairburn & K. D. Brownell (Eds.), *Eating disorders and obesity: A comprehensive handbook.* New York: Guilford.

Hofbauer, R. K., Rainville, P., Duncan, G. H., & Bushnell, M. C. (2001). Cortical representation of the sensory dimension of pain. *Journal of Neurophysiology, 86,* 402–411.

Hoff, E. (2001). *Language development.* Belmont, CA: Wadsworth.

Hoff, E. (2005). *Language development.* Belmont, CA: Wadsworth.

Hoff, T. L. (1992). Psychology in Canada one hundred years ago: James Mark Baldwin at the University of Toronto. *Canadian Psychology, 33,* 683–694.

Hoffman, E. (1994). *The drive for self: Alfred Adler and the founding of individual psychology.* Reading, MA: Addison-Wesley.

Hoffstein, V. (2005). Snoring and upper airway resistance. In M. H. Kryger, T. Roth, & W. C. Dement (Eds.). *Principles and practice of sleep medicine.* Philadelphia: Elsevier Saunders.

Hofstede, G. (1980). *Culture's consequences: International differences in work-related values.* Beverly Hills, CA: Sage.

Hofstede, G. (1983). Dimensions of national cultures in fifty countries and three regions. In J. Deregowski, S. Dziurawiec, & R. Annis (Eds.), *Explications in cross-cultural psychology.* Lisse: Swets and Zeitlinger.

Hofstede, G. (2001). *Culture's consequences: Comparing values, behaviors, institutions, and organizations across nations.* Thousand Oaks, CA: Sage.

Hogan, J., & Ones, D. S. (1997). Conscientiousness and integrity at work. In R. Hogan, J. Johnson, & S. Briggs (Eds.), *Handbook of personality psychology.* San Diego: Academic Press.

Hogan, R., Hogan, J., & Roberts, B. W. (1996). Personality measurement and employment decisions. *American Psychologist, 51,* 469–477.

Hogarth, R. M. (1987). *Judgement and choice.* New York: Wiley.

Hogg, M. A., Turner, J. C., & Davidson, B. (1990). Polarized norms and social frames of reference: A test of the self-categorization theory of group polarization. *Basic and Applied Social Psychology, 11,* 77–100.

Hokanson, J. E., & Burgess, M. (1962). The effects of three types of aggression on vascular processes. *Journal of Abnormal and Social Psychology, 65,* 446–449.

Holahan, C. J., & Moos, R. H. (1985). Life stress and health: Personality, coping, and family support in stress resistance. *Journal of Personality and Social Psychology, 49,* 739–747.

Holahan, C. J., & Moos, R. H. (1990). Life stressors, resistance factors, and improved psychological functioning: An extension of the stress resistance paradigm. *Journal of Personality and Social Psychology, 58,* 909–917.

Holahan, C. J., & Moos, R. H. (1994). Life stressors and mental health: Advances in conceptualizing stress resistance. In W. R. Avison & J. H. Gotlib (Eds.), *Stress and mental health: Contemporary issues and prospects for the future.* New York: Plenum.

Holahan, C., & Sears, R. (1995). *The gifted group in later maturity.* Stanford, CA: Stanford University Press.

Holden, C. (2004). FDA weighs suicide risk in children on antidepressants. *Science, 303,* 745.

Holen, A. (2000). Posttraumatic stress disorder, delayed. In G. Fink (Ed.), *Encyclopedia of stress* (Vol. 3, pp. 179–180). San Diego: Academic Press.

Hollan, D. (1989). The personal use of dream beliefs in the Toraja Highlands. *Ethos, 17,* 166–186.

Holland, J. C., & Lewis, S. (1993). Emotions and cancer: What do we really know? In D. Goleman & J. Gurin (Eds.), *Mind/body medicine: How to use your mind for better* *health*. Yonkers, NY: Consumer Reports Books.

Hollander, E., & Simeon, D. (2003). Anxiety disorders. In R. E. Hales & S. C. Yudofsky (Eds.), *Textbook of clinical psychiatry*. Washington, DC: American Psychiatric Publishing.

Hollander, E., Simeon, D., & Gorman, J. M. (1999). Anxiety disorders. In R. E. Hales, S. C. Yudofsky, & J. A. Talbott (Eds.), *American Psychiatric Press Textbook of Psychiatry*. Washington, DC: American Psychiatric Press.

Hollingworth, L. S. (1914). *Functional periodicity: An experimental study of the mental and motor abilities of women during menstruation*. New York: Teachers College, Columbia University.

Hollingworth, L. S. (1916). Sex differences in mental tests. *Psychological Bulletin, 13*, 377–383.

Hollis, K. L. (1997). Contemporary research on Pavlovian conditioning: A "new" functional analysis. *American Psychologist, 52*, 956–965.

Hollister, L. E. (1988). Marijuana and immunity. *Journal of Psychoactive Drugs, 20*, 3–7.

Hollon, S. D. (1999). Allegiance effects in treatment research: A commentary. *Clinical Psychology: Science & Practice, 6*, 107–112.

Hollon, S. D., & Beck, A. T. (2004). Cognitive and cognitive behavioral therapies. In M. J. Lambert (Ed.), *Bergin and Garfields handbook of psychotherapy and behavior change*. New York: Wiley.

Holmes, D. S. (1990). The evidence for repression: An examination of sixty years of research. In J. Singer (Ed.), *Repression and dissociation: Implications for personality, theory, psychopathology, and health*. Chicago: University of Chicago Press.

Holmes, T. H., & Rahe, R. H. (1967). The Social Readjustment Rating Scale. *Journal of Psychosomatic Research, 11*, 213–218.

Holtgraves, T. (2004). Social desirability and self-reports: Testing models of socially desirable responding. *Personality and Social Psychology Bulletin, 30*, 161–172.

Holyoak, K. J. (1995). Problem solving. In E. E. Smith & D. N. Osherson (Eds.), *Thinking* (2nd ed., pp. 267–295). Cambridge, MA: MIT Press.

Holyoak, K. J. (2005). Analogy. In K. J. Holyoak & R. G. Morrison (Eds.), *The Cambridge handbook of thinking and reasoning*. New York: Cambridge University Press.

Holyoak, K. J., & Thagard, P. (1997). The analogical mind. *American Psychologist, 52*, 35–44.

Homma-True, R., Greene, B., Lopez, S. R., & Trimble, J. E. (1993). Ethnocultural diversity in clinical psychology. *The Clinical Psychologist, 46*(2), 50–63.

Hong, G. K., Garcia, M., & Soriano, M. (2000). Responding to the challenge: Preparing mental health professionals for the new millennium. In I. Cuellar & F. A. Paniagua (Eds.), *Handbook of multicultural mental health: Assessment and treatment of diverse populations*. San Diego: Academic Press.

Honig, W. K., & Alsop, B. (1992). Operant behavior. In L. R. Squire (Ed.), *Encyclopedia of learning and memory*. New York: Macmillan.

Hooley, J. M., & Candela, S. F. (1999). Interpersonal functioning in schizophrenia. In T. Millon, P. H. Blaney, & R. D. Davis (Eds.), *Oxford textbook of psychopathology* (pp. 311–338). New York: Oxford University Press.

Hooley, J. M., & Hiller, J. B. (1998). Expressed emotion and the pathogenesis of relapse in schizophrenia. In M. F. Lenzenweger & R. H. Dworkin (Eds.), *Origins and development of schizophrenia: Advances in experimental psychopathology*. Washington DC: American Psychological Association.

Hooper, J., & Teresi, D. (1986). *The 3-pound universe—The brain*. New York: Laurel.

Hopkins, B., & Westra, T. (1988). Maternal handling and motor development: An intracultural study. *Genetic, Social and General Psychology Monographs, 14*, 377–420.

Hopkins, B., & Westra, T. (1990). Motor development, maternal expectations, and the role of handling. *Infant Behavior and Development, 13*, 117–122.

Hopko, D. R., Crittendon, J. A., Grant, E., & Wilson, S. A. (2005). The impact of anxiety on performance IQ. *Anxiety, Stress, & Coping: An International Journal, 18*(1), 17–35.

Horn, J. L. (1979). Trends in the measurement of intelligence. In R. J. Sternberg & D. K. Detterman (Eds.), *Human intelligence: Perspectives on its theory and measurement*. Norwood, NJ: Ablex.

Horn, J. L. (1985). Remodeling old models of intelligence. In B. B. Wolman (Ed.), *Handbook of intelligence*. New York: Wiley.

Horn, J. L. (2002). Selections of evidence, misleading assumptions, and oversimplifications: The political message of *The Bell Curve*.

In J. M. Fish (Ed.), *Race and intelligence: Separating science from myth* (pp. 297–326). Mahwah, NJ: Erlbaum.

Horn, J. L., & Hofer, S. M. (1992). Major abilities and development in the adult period. In R. J. Sternberg & C. A. Berg (Eds.), *Intellectual development*. Cambridge: Cambridge University Press.

Hornstein, G. A. (1992). The return of the repressed: Psychology's problematic relations with psychoanalysis, 1909–1960. *American Psychologist, 47*, 254–263.

Horowitz, F. D. (1992). John B. Watson's legacy: Learning and environment. *Developmental Psychology, 28*, 360–367.

Horwath, E., & Weissman, M. M. (2000). Anxiety disorders: Epidemiology. In B. J. Sadock & V. A. Sadock (Eds.), *Kaplan and Sadock's comprehensive textbook of psychiatry* (7th ed., Vol. 1, pp. 1441–1449). Philadelphia: Lippincott/Williams & Wilkins.

Hossain, J. L., & Shapiro, C. M. (1999). Considerations and possible consequences of shift work. *Journal of Psychosomatic Research, 47*, 293–296.

Hosseini, H. (1997). Cognitive dissonance as a means of explaining economics of irrationality and uncertainty. *Journal of Socio-Economics, 26*, 181–189.

Hotopf, M. (2004). Preventing somatization. *Psychological Medicine, 34*(2), 195–198.

Houts, A. C. (2002). Discovery, invention, and the expansion of the modern *Diagnostic and Statistical Manuals of Mental Disorders*. In L. E. Beutler & M. L. Malik (Eds.), *Rethinking the DSM*. Washington, DC: American Psychological Association.

Howard, D. J. (1995). "Chaining" the use of influence strategies for producing compliance behavior. *Journal of Social Behavior and Personality, 10*, 169–185.

Howard, G., Wagenknecht, L. E., Burke, G. L., Diez-Roux, A., Evans, G. W., McGovern, P., Nieto, J., & Tell, G. S. (1998). Cigarette smoking and progression of atherosclerosis: The atherosclerosis risk in communities (ARIC) study. *Journal of the American Medical Association, 279*, 119–124.

Howard, I. P., & Rogers, B. J. (1995). *Binocular vision and stereopsis*. New York: Oxford University Press.

Howard, I. P., & Templeton, W. B. (1966). *Human spatial orientation*. New York: Wiley.

Howard, K. I., Krasner, R. F., & Saunders, S. M. (2000). Evaluation of psychotherapy. In B. J. Sadock & V. A. Sadock (Eds.), *Kaplan and Sadock's comprehensive textbook of psychiatry* (7th ed., Vol. 1, pp. 2217–2224). Philadelphia: Lippincott/Williams & Wilkins.

Howard, M. S., & Medway, F. J. (2004). Adolescents' attachment and coping with stress. *Psychology in Schools, 41*, 391–402.

Howard, R., Castle, D., Wessely, S., & Murray, R. (1993). A comparative study of 470 cases of early-onset and late-onset schizophrenia. *British Journal of Psychiatry, 163*, 352–357.

Howe, M. J. A. (1999). *The psychology of high abilities*. New York: New York University Press.

Hrdy, S. B. (1997). Raising Darwin's consciouness: Female sexuality and the prehominid origins of patriarchy. *Human Nature: An Interdiciplinary Biosocial Perspective, 8*, 1–49.

Hsu, L. K. G. (1990). *Eating disorders*. New York: Guilford.

Hsu, L. K. G. (1995). Outcome of bulimia nervosa. In K. D. Brownell, & C. G. Fairburn (Eds.), *Eating disorders and obesity: A comprehensive handbook*. New York: Guilford.

Hsu, L. M. (1995). Regression toward the mean associated with measurement error and identification of improvement and deterioration in psychotheray. *Journal of Consulting & Clinical Psychology, 63*, 141–144.

Hu, F. B., & Willett, W. C. (2002). Optimal diets for prevention of coronary heart disease. *Journal of the American Medical Association, 288*, 2569–2578.

Hua, J. Y., & Smith, S. J. (2004). Neural activity and the dynamics of central nervous system development. *Nature Neuroscience, 7*, 327–332.

Hubbard, J. R., & Workman, E. A. (1998). *Handbook of stress medicine: An organ system approach*. New York: CRC Press.

Hubel, D. H., & Wiesel, T. N. (1962). Receptive fields, binocular interaction and functional architecture in the cat's visual cortex. *Journal of Physiology, 160*, 106–154.

Hubel, D. H., & Wiesel, T. N. (1963). Receptive fields of cells in striate cortex of very young visually inexperienced kittens. *Journal of Neurophysiology, 26*, 994–1002.

Hubel, D. H., & Wiesel, T. N. (1979). Brain mechanisms of vision. In Scientific American (Eds.), *The brain*. San Franciso: W. H. Freeman.

Hublin, C. G. M., & Partinen, M. M. (2002). The extent and impact of insomnia as a public health problem. *Journal of Clinical Psychiatry, 4*(suppl. 1), 8–12.

Hudson, W. (1960). Pictorial depth perception in sub-cultural groups in Africa. *Journal of Social Psychology, 52,* 183–208.

Hudspeth, A. J. (2000). Sensory transduction in the ear. In E. R. Kandel, J. H. Schwartz, & T. M. Jessell (Eds.), *Principles of neural science.* New York: McGraw-Hill.

Huettel, S. A., Mack, P. B., McCarthy, G., Hua, J. Y., & Smith, S. J. (2002). Perceiving patterns in random series: Dynamic processing of sequence in prefrontal cortex. *Nature Neuroscience, 5,* 485–490.

Hughes, C. C. (1993). Culture in clinical psychiatry. In A. C. Gaw (Ed.), *Culture, ethnicity, and mental illness.* Washington, DC: American Psychiatric Press.

Hughes, J. R., Gulliver, S. B., Fenwick, J. W., Valliere, W. A., Cruser, K., Pepper, S., Shea, P., Solomon, L. J., & Flynn, B. S. (1992). Smoking cessation among self-quitters. *Health Psychology, 11,* 331–334.

Hughes, J., Smith, T. W., Kosterlitz, H. W., Fothergill, L. A., Morgan, B. A., & Morris, H. R. (1975). Identification of two related pentapeptides from the brain with the potent opiate agonist activity. *Nature, 258,* 577–579.

Hughes, R. J., & Badia, P. (1997). Sleep-promoting and hypothermic effects of daytime melatonin administration in humans. *Sleep, 20,* 124–131.

Hughes, S. M., & Gallup, G. G. (2003). Sex differences in morphological predictors of sexual behavior. *Evolution and Human Behavior, 24,* 173–178.

Hull, C. L. (1943). *Principles of behavior.* New York: Appleton.

Hull, E. M., & Dominguez, J. M. (2003). Sex behavior. In M. Gallagher & R. J. Nelson (Eds.), *Handbook of psychology, Vol. 3: Biological psychology.* New York: Wiley.

Hulshoff, H. E., Hoek, H. W., Susser, E., Brown, A. S., Dingemans, A., Schnack, H. G., van Haren, N. E. M., Ramos, L. M. P., Gispen-de Wied, C. C., & Kahn, R. S. (2000). Prenatal exposure to famine and brain morphology in schizophrenia. *American Journal of Psychiatry, 157,* 1170–1172.

Humphrey, G. K., & Goodale, M. A. (1998). Probing unconscious visual processing with the McCollough Effect. *Consciousness and Cognition, 7,* 494–519.

Humphrey, G. K., James, T. W., Gati, J. S., Menon, R. S., & Goodale, M. A. (1999). Perception of the McCollough Effect correlates with activity in extrastriate cortex: A functional magnetic resonance imaging study. *Psychological Science, 10,* 444–448.

Hunt, C., & Andrews, G. (1995). Comorbidity in the anxiety disorders: The use of a life-chart approach. *Journal of Psychiatric Research, 29,* 467–480.

Hunt, E. (1994). Problem solving. In R. J. Sternberg (Ed.), *Thinking and problem solving.* San Diego: Academic Press.

Hunt, E. (2001). Multiple views of multiple intelligence [Review of the book *Intelligence reframed: Multiple intelligence in the 21st century*]. *Contemporary Psychology, 46,* 5–7.

Hunt, E., & Agnoli, F. (1991). The Whorfian hypothesis: A cognitive psychology perspective. *Psychological Review, 98,* 377–389.

Hunt, E., Streissguth, A. P., Kerr, B., & Olsen, H. C. (1995). Mothers' alcohol consumption during pregnancy: Effects on spatial-visual reasoning in 14-year-old children. *Psychological Science, 6,* 339–342.

Hunt, H. (1989). *The multiplicity of dreams: Memory, imagination and consciousness.* New Haven: Yale University Press.

Hunt, J. M., Smith, M. F., & Kernan, J. B. (1985). The effects of expectancy disconfirmation and argument strength on message processing level: An application to personal selling. In E. C. Hirschman & M. B. Holbrook (Eds.), *Advances in consumer research* (Vol. 12). Provo, UT: Association for Consumer Research.

Hunt, W. A., & Matarazzo, J. D. (1982). Changing smoking behavior: A critique. In R. J. Gatchel, A. Baum, & J. E. Singer (Eds.), *Handbook of psychology and health: Vol. 1. Clinical psychology and behavioral medicine, overlapping disciplines.* Hillsdale, NJ: Erlbaum.

Hunter, J. E., & Schmidt, F. L. (1996). Intelligence and job performance: Economic and social implications. *Psychology, Public Policy, & Law, 2,* 447–472.

Hunter, J. E., & Schmidt, F. L. (2000). Racial and gender bias in ability and achievement tests: Resolving the apparent paradox. *Psychology, Public Policy, and Law, 6,* 151–158.

Huntsinger, E. T., & Luecken, L. J. (2004). Attachment relationships and health behavior: The media-tional role of self-esteem. *Psychology & Health, 19,* 515–526.

Hurvich, L. M. (1981). *Color vision.* Sunderland, MA: Sinnauer Associates.

Huston, A. C., & Wright, J. C. (1982). Effects of communications media on children. In C. B. Kopp & J. B. Krakow (Eds.), *The child: Development in a social context.* Reading, MA: Addison-Wesley.

Huttenlocher, P. R. (1979). Synaptic density in human frontal cortex: Developmental changes of aging. *Brain Research, 163,* 195–205.

Huttenlocher, P. R. (1994). Synaptogenesis in human cerebral cortex. In G. Dawson & K. W. Fischer (Eds.), *Human behavior and the developing brain.* New York: Guilford.

Huyser, B., & Parker, J. C. (1998). Stress and rheumatoid arthritis: An integrative review. *Arthritis Care and Research, 11,* 135–145.

Hyde, J. S., Fennema, E., & Lamon, S. J. (1990). Gender differences in mathematics performance: A meta-analysis. *Psychological Bulletin, 107,* 139–155.

Hyman, I. A. (1996). Using research to change policy: Reflections on 20 years of effort to eliminate corporal punishment in the schools. *Pediatrics, 98,* 818–821.

Hyman, I. E., Jr., & Kleinknecht, E. E. (1999). False childhood memories: Research, theory, and applications. In L. M. Williams & V. L. Banyard (Eds.), *Trauma & memory.* Thousand Oaks, CA: Sage Publications.

Hyman, I. E., Jr., Husband, T. H., & Billings, J. F. (1995). False memories of childhood experiences. *Applied Cognitive Psychology, 9,* 181–197.

Iacono, W. G., & Lykken, D. T. (1997). The validity of the lie detector: Two surveys of scientific opinion. *Journal of Applied Psychology, 82,* 426–433.

Iacono, W. G., & Patrick, C. J. (1999). Polygraph ("lie detector") testing: The state of the art. In A. K. Hess & I. B. Weiner (Eds.), *The handbook of forensic psychology* (pp. 440–473). New York: Wiley.

Iams, J. D. (2002). Preterm birth. In S. G. Gabbe, J. R. Niebyl, & J. L. Simpson (Eds.), *Obstetrics: Normal and problem pregnancies.* New York: Churchill Livingstone.

Ickovics, J. R., Thayaparan, B., & Ethier, K. A. (2001). Women and AIDS: A contextual analysis. In A. Baum, T. A. Revenson, & J. E. Singer (Eds.), *Handbook of health psychology* (pp. 817–840). Mahwah, NJ: Erlbaum.

Iezzi, T., Duckworth, M. P., & Adams, H. E. (2001). Somatoform and factitious disorders. In P. B. Sutker & H. E. Adams (Eds.), *Comprehensive handbook of psychopathology* (3rd ed., pp. 211–258). New York: Kluwer Academic/ Plenum Publishers.

Ilgen, D. R. (1999). Teams embedded in organizations: Some implications. *American Psychologist, 54,* 129–139.

Infante, J. R., Torres-Avisbal, M., Pinel, P., Vallejo, J. A., Peran, F., Gonzalez, F., Contreras, P., Pacheco, C., Roldan, A., & Latre, J. M. (2001). Catecholamine levels in practitioners of the transcendental meditation technique. *Physiology & Behavior, 72*(1–2), 141–146.

Inglehart, R. (1990). *Culture shift in advanced industrial society.* Princeton, NJ: Princeton University Press.

Ingram, R. E., Scott, W., & Siegle, G. (1999). Depression: Social and cognitive aspects. In T. Millon, P. H. Blaney, & R. D. Davis (Eds.), *Oxford textbook of psychopathology* (pp. 203–226). New York: Oxford University Press.

Innocenti, G. M. (1994). Some new trends in the study of the corpus callosum. *Behavioral and Brain Research, 64,* 1–8.

Inoff-Germain, G., Arnold, G. S., Nottelman, E. D., Susman, E. J., Cutler, G. B., Jr., & Chrousos, G. P. (1988). Relations between hormone levels and observational measures of aggressive behavior of young adolescents in family interactions. *Developmental Psychology, 24,* 129–139.

Iribarren, C., Sidney, S., Bild, D. E., Liu, K., Markovitz, J. H., Roseman, J. M., & Matthews, K. (2000). Association of hostility with coronary artery calcification in young adults: The CARDIA study. *Journal of the American Medical Association, 283,* 2546–2551.

Ironson, G., Klimas, N. G., Antoni, M., Friedman, A., Simoneau, J., LaPerriere, A., Baggett, L., August, S., Arevalo, F., Schneiderman, N., & Fletcher, M. A. (1994). Distress, denial, and low adherence to behavioral interventions predict faster disease progression in gay men infected with human immunodeficiency virus. *International Journal of Behavioral Medicine, 1,* 90–98.

Ironson, G., Wynings, C., Schneiderman, N., Baum, A., Rodriguez, M., Greenwood, D., Benight, C., Antoni, M., LaPerriere, A., Huang, H. S., Klimas, N., & Fletcher, M. A.

(1997). Post-traumatic stress symptoms, intrusive thoughts, loss, and immune function after Hurricane Andrew. *Psychosomatic Medicine, 59,* 128–141.

Irvine, S. H., & Berry, J. W. (1988). *Human abilities in cultural context.* New York: Cambridge University Press.

Irwin, W., Davidson, R. J., Lowe, M. J., Mock, B. J., Sorenson, J. A., & Turski, P. A. (1996). Human amygdala activation detected with echoplanar functional magnetic resonance imaging. *NeuroReport, 7,* 1765–1769.

Isabella, R. A. (1995). The origins of infant-mother attachment: Maternal behavior and infant development. In R. Vasta (Ed.), *Annals of child development.* London: Jessica Kingsley.

Isada, N. B., & Grossman, J. H., III. (1991). Perinatal infections. In S. G. Gabbe, J. R. Niebyl, & J. L. Simpson (Eds.), *Obstetrics: Normal and problem pregnancies.* New York: Churchill Livingstone.

Isenberg, K. E., & Zorumski, C. F. (2000). Electroconvulsive therapy. In B. J. Sadock & V. A. Sadock (Eds.), *Kaplan and Sadock's Comprehensive textbook of psychiatry* (7th ed., Vol. 1, pp. 2503–2515). Philadelphia: Lippincott/Williams & Wilkins.

Ismail, M. A. (1993). Maternal-fetal infections. In C. Lin, M. S. Verp, & R. E. Sabbagha (Eds.), *The high-risk fetus: Pathophysiology, diagnosis, management.* New York: Springer-Verlag.

Isometsa, E. T., Heikkinen, M. E., Marttunen, M. J., Henriksson, M. M., Aro, H. M., & Lonnqvist, J. K. (1995). The last appointment before suicide: Is suicide intent communicated? *American Journal of Psychiatry, 152,* 919–922.

Iversen, S., Iversen, L., & Saper, C. B. (2000). The autonomic nervous system and the hypothalamus. In E. R. Kandel, J. H. Schwartz, & T. M. Jessell (Eds.), *Principles of neural science* (pp. 960–981). New York: McGraw-Hill.

Iwao, S. (1993). *The Japanese woman: Traditional image and changing reality.* New York: Free Press.

Iwawaki, S., & Vernon, P. E. (1988). Japanese abilities and achievements. In S. H. Irvine & J. W. Berry (Eds.), *Human abilities in cultural context.* New York: Cambridge University Press.

Izard, C. E. (1984). Emotion-cognition relationships and human development. In C. E. Izard, J. Kagan, & R. B. Zajonc (Eds.), *Emotions, cognition and behavior.*

Cambridge, England: Cambridge University Press.

Izard, C. E. (1990). Facial expressions and the regulation of emotions. *Journal of Personality and Social Psychology, 58,* 487–498.

Izard, C. E. (1991). *The psychology of emotions.* New York: Plenum.

Izard, C. E. (1994). Innate and universal facial expressions: Evidence from developmental and cross-cultural research. *Psychological Bulletin, 115,* 288–299.

Izard, C. E. (2001). Emotional intelligence or adaptive emotions? *Emotion, 1,* 249–257.

Izard, C. E., & Saxton, P. M. (1988). Emotions. In R. C. Atkinson, R. J. Herrnstein, G. Lindzey, & R. D. Luce (Eds.), *Stevens' handbook of experimental psychology* (Vol. 1). New York: Wiley.

Jablensky, A. (1999). The 100-year epidemiology of schizophrenia. *Schizophrenia Research, 28,* 111–125.

Jackicic, J., & Gallagher, K. I. (2002). Physical activity considerations for management of body weight. In D. H. Bessesen & R. Kushner (2002), *Evaluation and management of obesity.* Philadelphia: Hanley & Belfus.

Jackson, D. N., & Paunonen, S. V. (1980). Personality structure and assessment. *Annual Review of Psychology, 31,* 77–95.

Jackson, L. A., Sullivan, L. A., & Hodge, C. N. (1993). Stereotype effects on attributions, predictions, and evaluations: No two social judgments are quite alike. *Journal of Personality and Social Psychology, 65,* 69–84.

Jacob, R. G., & Pelham, W. H. (2000). Behavior therapy. In B. J. Sadock & V. A. Sadock (Eds.), *Kaplan and Sadock's comprehensive textbook of psychiatry* (7th ed., Vol. 1, pp. 2080–2127). Philadelphia: Lippincott/Williams & Wilkins.

Jacobs, B. L. (2004). Depression: The brain finally gets into the act. *Current Directions in Psychological Science, 13*(3), 103–106.

Jacobs, H. S. (2001). Idea of male menopause is not useful. *Medical Crossfire, 3,* 52–55.

Jacobson, E. (1938). *Progressive relaxation.* Chicago: University of Chicago Press.

Jacobson, J. W., & Mulick, J. A. (1992). A new definition of mental retardation or a new definition of practice? *Psychology in Mental Retardation and Developmental Disabilities, 18,* 9–14.

Jacobson, N. S., & Christensen, A. (1996). Studying the effectiveness

of psychotherapy: How well can clinical trials do the job? *American Psychologist, 51,* 1031–1039.

Jacoby, L. L. (1988). Memory observed and memory unobserved. In U. Neisser & E. Winograd (Eds.), *Remembering reconsidered: Ecological and traditional approaches to the study of memory.* Cambridge: Cambridge University Press.

Jacoby, L. L., Hessels, S., & Bopp, K. (2001). Proactive and retroactive effects in memory performance: Dissociating recollection and accessibility bias. In H. L. Roediger, J. S. Nairne, I. Neath, & A. M. Surprenant (Eds.), *The nature of remembering: Essays in honor of Robert G. Crowder* (pp. 35–54). Washington, DC: American Psychological Association.

Jain, S. P., Buchanan, B., & Maheswaran, D. (2000). Comparative versus noncomparative advertising. *Journal of Consumer Psychology, 9,* 201–211.

James, J. E. (2004). Critical review of dietary caffeine and blood pressure: A relationship that should be taken more seriously. *Psychosomatic Medicine, 66*(1), 63–71.

James, W. (1884). What is emotion? *Mind, 19,* 188–205.

James, W. (1890). *The principles of psychology.* New York: Holt.

James, W. (1902). *The varieties of religious experience.* New York: Modern Library.

Jamison, K. R. (1988). Manic-depressive illness and accomplishment: Creativity, leadership, and social class. In F. K. Goodwin & K. R. Jamison (Eds.), *Manic-depressive illness.* Oxford, England: Oxford University Press.

Jang, K. L., Livesley, W. J., & Vernon, P. A. (1996). Heritability of the Big Five personality dimensions and their facets: A twin study. *Journal of Personality, 64,* 577–591.

Janig, W. (2003). The autonomic nervous system and its coordination by the brain. In R. J. Davidson, K. R. Scherer, & H. H. Goldsmith (Eds.), *Handbook of affective sciences.* New York: Oxford University Press.

Janis, I. L. (1958). *Psychological stress.* New York: Wiley.

Janis, I. L. (1972). *Victims of group-think.* Boston: Houghton Mifflin.

Janis, I. L. (1993). Decision making under stress. In L. Goldberger & S. Breznitz (Eds.), *Handbook of stress: Theoretical and clinical aspects* (2nd ed.). New York: Free Press.

Janis, I. L., & Mann, L. (1977). *Decision making: A psychological analysis of conflict, choice, and commitment.* New York: Free Press.

Janowsky, J. S., Oviatt, S. K., & Orwoll, E. S. (1994). Testosterone influences spatial cognition in older men. *Behavioral Neuroscience, 108,* 325–332.

Janus, S. S., & Janus, C. L. (1993). *The Janus report on sexual behavior.* New York: Wiley.

Jaroff, L. (1993, November 29). Lies of the mind. *Time,* pp. 52–59.

Jarvik, M. E., & Schneider, N. G. (1992). Nicotine. In J. H. Lowinson, P. Ruiz, & R. B. Millman (Eds.), *Substance abuse: A comprehensive text-book* (2nd ed.). Baltimore: Williams & Wilkins.

Jefferson, J. W., & Greist, J. H. (2000). Lithium. In B. J. Sadock & V. A. Sadock (Eds.), *Kaplan and Sadock's comprehensive textbook of psychiatry* (7th ed., Vol. 1, pp. 2377–2389). Philadelphia: Lippincott/Williams & Wilkins.

Jemmott, J. B., III, & Magloire, K. (1988). Academic stress, social support, and secretory immunoglobin A. *Journal of Personality and Social Psychology, 55,* 803–810.

Jenkin, H. L., Dyde, R. T., Jenkin, M. R., Howard, I. P., & Harris, L. R. (2003). Relative role of visual and non-visual cues in determining the direction of "up": Experiments in the York tilted room facility. *Journal of Vestibular Research, 13,* 287–293.

Jenkin, H. L., Dyde, R. T., Zacher, J. E., Zikovitz, D. C., Jenkin, M. R., Allison, R. S., Howard, I. P., & Harris, L. R. (in press). The relative role of visual and non-visual cues in determining the perceived direction of "up": Experiments in parabolic flight. *Acta Astronautica.*

Jensen, A. R. (1969). How much can we boost IQ and scholastic achievement? *Harvard Educational Review, 39,* 1–23.

Jensen, A. R. (1980). *Bias in mental testing.* New York: Free Press.

Jensen, A. R. (1982). Reaction time and psychometric g. In H. J. Eysenck (Ed.), *A model for intelligence.* New York: Springer-Verlag.

Jensen, A. R. (1987). Process differences and individual difference in some cognitive tasks. *Intelligence, 11,* 107–136.

Jensen, A. R. (1992a). The Cyril Burt scandal, research taboos, and the media. *The General Psychologist, 28*(3), 16–21.

Jensen, A. R. (1992b). The importance of intraindividual variation in reaction time. *Personality and Individual Differences, 13,* 869–881.

Jensen, A. R. (1993). Why is reaction time correlated with psychometric g? *Current Directions in Psychological Science, 2*(2), 53–56.

Jensen, A. R. (1994). Race and IQ scores. In R. J. Sternberg (Ed.), *Encyclopedia of human intelligence*. New York: Macmillan.

Jensen, A. R. (1998). *The g factor: The science of mental ability*. Westport, CT: Praeger.

Jensen, A. R. (2000). Testing: The dilemma of group differences. *Psychology, Public Policy, and Law, 6*, 121–127.

Jensen, E. (2000). *Brain-based learning*. San Diego: Brain Store.

Jessell, T. M., & Kelly, D. D. (1991). Pain and analgesia. In E. R. Kandel, J. H. Schwartz & T. M. Jessell (Eds.), *Principles of neural science* (3rd ed.). New York: Elsevier.

Jex, S. M., Bliese, P. D., Buzzell, S., & Primeau, J. (2001). The impact of self-efficacy on stressor-strain relations: Coping style as an explanatory mechanism. *Journal of Applied Psychology, 86*, 401–409.

Ji, L.-J., Peng, K., & Nisbett, R. E. (2000). Culture, control, and perception of relationships in the environment. *Journal of Personality and Social Psychology, 78*, 943–955.

Jick, H., Kaye, J. A., & Jick, S. S. (2004). Antidepressants and the risk of suicidal behaviors. *Journal of The American Medical Association, 292*, 338–343.

John, O. P., & Srivastava, S. (1999). The big five trait taxonomy: History, measurement, and theoretical perspectives. In L. A. Pervin & O. P. John (Eds.), *Handbook of personality: Theory and research*. New York: Guilford.

Johnson, B. A., & Ait-Daoud, N. (2005). Alcohol: Clinical aspects. In J. H. Lowinson, P. Ruiz, R. B. Millman, & J. G. Langrod (Eds.), *Substance abuse: A comprehensive textbook*. Philadelphia: Lippincott/Williams & Wilkins.

Johnson, B. T. (1994). Effects of outcome-relevant involvement and prior information on persuasion. *Journal of Experimental Social Psychology, 30*, 556–579.

Johnson, B. T., Maio, G. R., & Smith-McLallen, A. (2005). Communication and attitude change: Causes, processes, and effects. In D. Albarracin, B. T. Johnson, & M. P. Zanna (Eds.), *The handbook of attitudes*. Mahwah, NJ: Erlbaum.

Johnson, C., & Mullen, B. (1994). Evidence for the accessibility of paired distinctiveness in distinctiveness-based illusory correlation in stereotyping. *Personality and Social Psychology Bulletin, 20*, 65–70.

Johnson, D. F. (2000). Cultivating the field of psychology. *American Psychologist, 55*, 1144–1147.

Johnson, J. S., & Newport, E. L. (1989). Critical period effects in second language learning: The influence of maturational state on the acquisition of English as a second language. *Cognitive Psychology, 21*, 60–99.

Johnson, J., Im-Boulter, N., & Pascual-Leone, J. (2003). Development of mental attention in gifted and mainstream children: The role of mental capacity, inhibition, and speed of processing. *Child Development, 74*, 1594–1614.

Johnson, M. E., & Dowling-Guyer, S. (1996). Effects of inclusive vs. exclusive language on evaluations of the counselor. *Sex Roles, 34*, 407–418.

Johnson, M. K. (1996). Fact, fantasy, and public policy. In D. J. Herrmann, C. McEvoy, C. Hertzog, P. Hertel, & M. K. Johnson (Eds.), *Basic and applied memory research: Theory in context* (Vol. 1). Mahwah, NJ: Erlbaum.

Johnson, M. K., Hashtroudi, S., & Lindsay, D. S. (1993). Source monitoring. *Psychological Bulletin, 114*, 3–28.

Johnson, S. B., & Carlson, D. N. (2004). Medical regimen adherence: Concepts assessment, and interventions. In J. M. Raczynski & L. C. Leviton (Eds.), *Handbook of clinical health psychology: Vol 2. Disorders of behavior and health*. Washington, DC: American Psychological Association.

Johnson, S. M., & Greenberg, L. S. (1995). The emotion focussed approach to problems of adult attachment. In N. S. Jacobson & A. S. Gurman (Eds.), *Clinical handbook of couples therapy* (pp. 124–144). New York: Guilford.

Johnston, J. C., & McClelland, J. L. (1974). Perception of letters in words: Seek not and ye shall find. *Science, 184*, 1192–1194.

Johnston, L. D., O'Malley, P. M., & Bachman, J. G. (2001). *Monitoring the Future national survey results on drug use, 1975–2000*. Bethesda MD: National Institute of Drug Abuse.

Johnstone, L. (1999). Adverse psychological effects of ECT. *Journal of Mental Health (UK), 8*, 69–85.

Joiner, T. E. (2002). Depression in its interpersonal context. In I. H. Gotlib & C. L. Hammen (Eds.), *Handbook of depression*. New York: Guilford.

Joiner, T. E., & Katz, J. (1999). Contagion of depressive symptoms and mood: Meta-analytic review and explanations from cognitive, behavioral, and interpersonal viewpoints. *Clinical Psychology: Science and Practice, 6*, 149–164.

Joiner, T. E., Jr., & Metalsky, G. I. (1995). A prospective test of an integrative interpersonal theory of depression: A naturalistic study of college students. *Journal of Personality and Social Psychology, 69*, 778–788.

Jonah, B. A. (1997). Sensation seeking and risky driving: A review and synthesis of the literature. *Accident Analysis & Prevention, 29*, 651–665.

Jones, B. C., Little, A. C., Penton-Voak, I. S., Tiddeman, B. P., Burt, D. M., & Perrett, D. I. (2001). Facial symmetry and judgments of apparent health: Support for a "good genes" explanation of the attractiveness-symmetry relationship. *Evolution and Human Behavior, 22*, 417–429.

Jones, B. E. (2000). Basic mechanisms of sleep-wake states. In M. H. Kryger, T. Roth, & W. C. Dement (Eds.), *Principles and practice of sleep medicine*. Philadelphia: Saunders.

Jones, B. E. (2005). Basic mechanisms of sleep-wake states. In M. H. Kryger, T. Roth, & W. C. Dement (Eds.). *Principles and practice of sleep medicine*. Philadelphia: Elsevier Saunders.

Jones, E. E., & Davis, K. E. (1965). From acts to dispositions: The attribution process in person perception. In L. Berkowitz (Ed.), *Advances in experimental social psychology* (Vol. 2). New York: Academic Press.

Jones, E. E., & Nisbett, R. E. (1971). The actor and the observer: Divergent perceptions of the causes of behavior. In E. E. Jones, D. E. Kanouse, H. H. Kelley, R. E. Nisbett, S. Valins, & B. Weiner (Eds.), *Attribution: Perceiving the causes of behavior*. Morristown, NJ: General Learning Press.

Jones, F., & Kinman, G. (2001). Approaches to studying stress. In F. Jones & J. Bright (Eds.), *Stress: Myth, theory, and research*. Harlow, UK: Pearson Education.

Jordan, B. (1983). *Birth in four cultures*. Quebec: Eden Press.

Jordon, C. H., & Zanna, M. P. (1999). How to read a journal article in social psychology. In R.F. Baumeister (Ed.), *The self in social psychology* (pp. 461–470). Philadelphia: Psychology Press.

Jorgensen, R. S., Johnson, B. T., Kolodziej, M. E., & Schreer, G. E. (1996). Elevated blood pressure and personality: A meta-analytic review. *Psychological Bulletin, 120*, 293–320.

Joseph, R. (1992). *The right brain and the unconscious*. New York: Plenum.

Joshipura, K. J., Ascherio, A., Manson, J. E., Stampfer, M. J.,

Rimm, E. B., Speizer, F. E., Hennekens, C. H., Speigelman, D., & Willett, W. C. (1999). Fruit and vegetable intake in relation to risk of ischemic stroke. *Journal of the American Medical Association, 282*, 1233–1239.

Josse, G., & Tzourio-Mazoyer, N. (2004). Hemispheric specialization for language. *Brain Research Reviews, 44*, 1–12.

Judge, T. A., & Bono, J. E. (2000). Five-factor model of personality and transformational leadership. *Journal of Applied Psychology, 85*, 751–765.

Julien, R. M. (2001). *A primer of drug action*. New York: Freeman.

Jung, C. G. (1917/1953). *On the psychology of the unconscious*. In H. Read, M. Fordham, & G. Adler (Eds.), *Collected works of C. G. Jung* (Vol. 7). Princeton, NJ: Princeton University Press.

Jung, C. G. (1921/1960). *Psychological types*. In H. Read, M. Fordham, & G. Adler (Eds.), *Collected works of C. G. Jung* (Vol. 6). Princeton, NJ: Princeton University Press.

Jung, C. G. (1933). *Modern man in search of a soul*. New York: Harcourt, Brace & World.

Jung, K. (1999). John Watson on authority and truth: Psychology as a moral science. *History and Philosophy of Psychology Bulletin, 11*, 17–21.

Jusczyk, P., & Hohne, E. (1997). Infants' memory for spoken words. *Science, 277*, 1984–1986.

Kaas, J. H. (2000). The reorganization of sensory and motor maps after injury in adult mammals. In M. S. Gazzaniga (Ed.), *The new cognitive neurosciences*. Cambridge, MA: The MIT Press.

Kaemingk, K., & Paquette, A. (1999). Effects of prenatal alcohol exposure on neuropsychological functioning. *Developmental Neuropsychology, 15*, 111–140.

Kagan, J. (1998, November/December). A parent's influence is peerless. *Harvard Education Letter*.

Kagan, J. (2004). New insights into temperament. *Cerebrum, 6(1)*, 51–66.

Kagan, J., & Snidman, N. (1991). Temperamental factors in human development. *American Psychologist, 46*, 856–862.

Kagan, J., & Snidman, N. (1999). Early childhood predictors of adult anxiety disorders. *Biological Psychiatry, 46*, 1536–1541.

Kagan, J., Reznik, J. S., & Snidman, N. (1999). Biological basis of childhood shyness. In A.

Slater & D. Muir (Eds.), *The Blackwell reader in developmental psychology* (pp. 65–78). Malden, MA: Blackwell.

Kagan, J., Snidman, N., & Arcus, D. M. (1992). Initial reactions to unfamiliarity. *Current Directions in Psychological Science, 1*(6), 171–174.

Kahan, T. L., & Johnson, M. K. (1992). Self-effects in memory for person information. *Social Cognition, 10*(1), 30–50.

Kahan, T. L., & LaBerge, S. (1994). Lucid dreaming as metacognition: Implications for cognitive science. *Consciousness and Cognition, 3,* 246–264.

Kahan, T. L., & LaBerge, S. (1996). Cognition and metacognition in dreaming and waking: Comparisons of first- and third-person ratings. *Dreaming, 6,* 235–249.

Kahane, H. (1992). *Logic and contemporary rhetoric: The use of reason in everyday life.* Belmont, CA: Wadsworth.

Kahneman, D. (1991). Judgment and decision making: A personal view. *Psychological Science, 2,* 142–145.

Kahneman, D. (1999). Objective happiness. In D. Kahneman, E. Diener, & N. Schwarz (Eds.), *Well-being: The foundations of hedonic psychology.* New York: Russell Sage Foundation.

Kahneman, D., & Tversky, A. (1982). Subjective probability: A judgment of representativeness. In D. Kahneman, P. Slovic, & A. Tversky (Eds.), *Judgment under uncertainty: Heuristics and biases.* Cambridge: Cambridge University Press.

Kahneman, D., & Tversky, A. (1984). Choices, values, and frames. *American Psychologist, 39,* 341–350.

Kahneman, D., & Tversky, A. (2000). *Choices, values, and frames.* New York: Cambridge University Press.

Kako, E. (1999). Elements of syntax in the systems of three language-trained animals. *Animal Learning and Behavior, 27,* 1–14.

Kalat, J. W. (2001). *Biological psychology.* Belmont, CA: Wadsworth.

Kales, J. D., Kales, A., Bixler, E. O., Soldatos, C. R., Cadieux, R. J., Kashurba, G. J., & Vela-Bueno, A. (1984). Biopsychobehavioral correlates of insomnia: V. Clinical characteristics and behavioral correlates. *American Journal of Psychiatry, 141,* 1371–1376.

Kalichman, S. C. (1995). *Understanding AIDS: A guide for mental health professionals.*

Washington, DC: American Psychological Association.

Kalichman, S. C., Roffman, R. A., Picciano, J. F., & Bolan, M. (1998). Risk for HIV infection among bisexual men seeking HIV-prevention services and risks posed to their female partners. *Health Psychology, 17,* 320–327.

Kalidindi, S., & McGuffin, P. (2003). The genetics of affective disorders: Present and future. In R. Plomin, J. C. Defries, I. W. Craig, & P. McGuffin (Eds.), *Behavioral genetics in the postgenomic era.* Washington, DC: American Psychological Association.

Kalmijn, M. (1998). Intermarriage and homogamy: Causes, patterns, trends. *Annual Review of Sociology, 24,* 395–421.

Kalmuss, D., Davidson, A., & Cushman, L. (1992). Parenting expectations, experiences, and adjustment to parenthood: A test of the violated expectations framework. *Journal of Marriage and the Family, 52,* 516–526.

Kalwarf, H. J., Khoury, J. C., & Lanphear, B. P. (2003). Milk intake during childhood and adolescence, adult bone density, and osteoporotic fractures in US women. *American Journal of Clinical Nutrition, 77,* 257–265.

Kamin, L. J. (1974). *The science and politics of IQ.* Hillsdale, NJ: Erlbaum.

Kandel, E. R. (2000). Nerve cells and behavior. In E. R. Kandel, J. H. Schwartz, & T. M. Jessell (Eds.), *Principles of neural science* (pp. 19–35). New York: McGraw-Hill.

Kandel, E. R. (2001). The molecular biology of memory storage: A dialogue between genes and synapses. *Science, 294,* 1030–1038.

Kandel, E. R., & Jessell, T. M. (1991). Touch. In E. R. Kandel, J. H. Schwartz, & T. M. Jessell (Eds.), *Principles of neural science* (3rd ed.). New York: Elsevier.

Kandel, E. R., & Schwartz, J. H. (1982). Molecular biology of learning: Modification of transmitter release. *Science, 218,* 433–442.

Kandel, E. R., & Siegelbaum, S. A. (2000). Synaptic integration. In E. R. Kandel, J. H. Schwartz & T. M. Jessell (Eds.), *Principles of neural science* (pp. 207–228). New York: McGraw-Hill.

Kane, J. (1991). *Be sick well: A healthy approach to chronic illness.* Oakland, CA: New Harbinger Publications.

Kane, T. D., Marks, M. A., Zaccaro, S. J., & Blair, V. (1996). Self-efficacy, personal goals, and wrestlers' self-regulation. *Journal of*

Sport & Exercise Psychology, 18, 36–48.

Kaplan, A. G. (1985). Female or male therapists for women patients: New formulations. *Psychiatry, 48,* 111–121.

Kaplan, H. I. (1989). History of psychosomatic medicine. In H. I. Kaplan & B. J. Sadock (Eds.), *Comprehensive textbook of psychiatry* (5th ed.). Baltimore: Williams & Wilkins.

Kaplan, H. I., & Sadock, B. J. (Eds.). (1993). *Comprehensive group psychotherapy.* Baltimore: Williams & Wilkins.

Kaplan, H., & Dove, H. (1987). Infant development among the Ache of Eastern Paraguay. *Developmental Psychology, 23,* 190–198.

Kaplan, R. M. (1985). The controversy related to the use of psychological tests. In B. B. Wolman (Ed.), *Handbook of intelligence: Theories, measurements, and applications.* New York: Wiley.

Kapp, B. S., Supple, W. F., & Whalen, P. J. (1994). Effects of electrical stimulation of the amygdaloid central nucleus on neocortical arousal in the rabbit. *Behavioral Neuroscience, 108,* 81–93.

Kaprio, J., Rimpela, A., Winter, T., Viken, R. J., Rimpela, M., & Rose, R. J. (1995). Common genetic influence on BMI and age at menarche. *Human Biology, 67,* 739–753.

Kapur, S., & Mann, J. J. (1993). Antidepressant action and the neurobiologic effects of ECT: Human studies. In C. E. Coffey (Ed.), *The clinical science of electroconvulsive therapy.* Washington, DC: American Psychiatric Press.

Karau, S. J., & Hart, J. W. (1998). Group cohesiveness and social loafing: Effects of a social interaction manipulation on individual motivation within groups. *Group Dynamics, 2,* 185–191.

Karau, S. J., & Williams, K. D. (1993). Social loafing: A meta-analytic review and theoretical integration. *Journal of Personality and Social Psychology, 65,* 681–706.

Karau, S. J., & Williams, K. D. (1995). Social loafing: Research findings, implications, and future directions. *Current Directions in Psychological Science, 4,* 134–140.

Kardiner, A., & Linton, R. (1945). *The individual and his society.* New York: Columbia University Press.

Karon, B. P., & Widener, A. J. (1997). Repressed memories and World War II: Lest we forget! *Professional Psychology: Research & Practice, 28,* 338–340.

Kassel, J. D., Stroud, L. R., & Paronis, C. A. (2003). Smoking, stress, and negative affect: Correlation, causation, and context across stages of smoking. *Psychological Bulletin, 129,* 270–304.

Kasser, T. (2002). *The high prices of materialism.* Cambridge, MA: MIT Press.

Kasser, T., & Sharma, Y. S. (1999). Reproductive freedom, educational equality, and females' preference for resource-aquisition characteristics in mates. *Psychological Science, 10,* 374–377.

Kassin, S. M., Tubb, V. A., Hosch, H. M., & Memon, A. (2001). On the "general acceptance" of eyewitness testimony research: A new survey of the experts. *American Psychologist, 56,* 405–416.

Katigbak, M. S., Church, A. T., Guanzon-Lapena, M. A., Carlota, A. J. & del Pilar, G. H. (2002). Are indigenous personality dimensions culture specific? Philippine inventories and the five-factor model. *Journal of Personality and Social Psychology, 82,* 89–101.

Katz, A. N., Blasko, D. G., & Kazmerski, V. A. (2004). Saying what you don't mean: Social influences on sarcastic language processing. *Current Directions in Psychological Science, 13*(5), 186–189.

Kaufman, A. S. (2000). Tests of intelligence. In R. J. Sternberg (Ed.), *Handbook of intelligence* (pp. 445–476). New York: Cambridge University Press.

Kaufman, L., & Rock, I. (1962). The moon illusion I. *Science, 136,* 953–961.

Kay, J., & Kay, R. I. (2003). Individual psychoanalytic psychotherapy. In A. Tasman, J. Kay, & J. A. Lieberman (Eds.), *Psychiatry.* New York: Wiley.

Kaye, W. H., Weltzin, T. E., Hsu L. K. G., McConaha, C. W., & Bolton, B. (1993). Amount of calories retained after binge eating and vomiting. *American Journal of Psychiatry, 150,* 969–971.

Kazdin, A. (2001). *Behavior modification in applied settings.* Belmont: Wadsworth.

Kazdin, A. E. (1982). History of behavior modification. In A. S. Bellack, M. Hersen, & A. E. Kazdin (Eds.), *International handbook of behavior modification and behavior therapy.* New York: Plenum.

Kazdin, A. E. (1994). Methodology, design, and evaluation in psychotherapy research. In A. E. Bergin & S. L. Garfield (Eds.), *Handbook of psychotherapy and behavior change* (4th ed.). New York: Wiley.

Kazdin, A., & Benjet, C. (2003). Spanking children: Evidence and issues. *Current Directions in Psychological Science, 12*(3), 99–103.

Keefauver, S. P., & Guilleminault, C. (1994). Sleep terrors and sleep-walking. In M. H. Kryger, T. Roth, & W. C. Dement (Eds.), *Principles and practice of sleep medicine* (2nd ed.). Philadelphia: Saunders.

Keesey, R. E. (1993). Physiological regulation of body energy: Implications for obesity. In A. J. Stunkard & T. A. Wadden (Eds.), *Obesity theory and therapy.* New York: Raven.

Keesey, R. E. (1995). A set point model of body weight regulation. In K. D. Brownell & C. G. Fairburn (Eds.), *Eating disorders and obesity: A comprehensive handbook.* New York: Guilford.

Keesey, R. E., & Powley, T. L. (1975). Hypothalamic regulation of body weight. *American Scientist, 63,* 558–565.

Kehoe, E. J., & Macrae, M. (1998). Classical conditioning. In W. O'Donohue (Ed.), *Learning and behavior therapy.* Boston, Allyn & Bacon.

Keinan, G. (1987). Decision making under stress: Scanning of alternatives under controllable and uncontrollable threats. *Journal of Personality and Social Psychology, 52,* 639–644.

Keinan, G., Friedland, N., Kahneman, D., & Roth, D. (1999). The effect of stress on the suppression of erroneous competing responses. *Anxiety, Stress & Coping: An International Journal, 12,* 455–476.

Keller, L. S., Butcher, J. N., & Slutske, W. S. (1990). Objective personality assessment. In G. Goldstein & M. Hersen (Eds.), *Handbook of psychological assessment.* New York: Pergamon Press.

Keller, P. A., & Block, L. G. (1999). The effect of affect-based dissonance versus cognition-based dissonance on motivated reasoning and health-related persuasion. *Journal of Experimental Psychology: Applied, 5,* 302–313.

Kelley, H. H. (1950). The warm-cold variable in first impressions of persons. *Journal of Personality, 18,* 431–439.

Kelley, H. H. (1967). Attributional theory in social psychology. *Nebraska Symposium on Motivation, 15,* 192–241.

Kelley, W. M., Macrae, C. N., Wyland, C. L., Caglar, S., Inati, S., & Heatherton, T. F. (2002). Finding the self? An event-related

fMRI Study. *Journal of Cognitive Neuroscience, 14,* 785–794.

Kellogg, J. S., Hopko, D. R., & Ashcraft, M. H. (1999). The effects of time pressure on arithmetic performance. *Journal of Anxiety Disorders, 13,* 591–600.

Kelly, J. P. (1991). The sense of balance. In E. R. Kandel, J. H. Schwartz, & T. M. Jessell (Eds.), *Principles of neural science* (3rd ed.). New York: Elsevier.

Kelly, K. M., & Schramke, C. J. (2000). Epilepsy. In G. Fink (Ed.), *Encyclopedia of stress* (pp. 66–70). San Diego: Academic Press.

Kelly, S. J., Day, N., & Streissguth, A. P. (2000). Effects of prenatal alcohol exposure on social behavior in humans and other species. *Neurotoxicology & Teratology, 22,* 143–149.

Kelman, H. C. (1967). Human use of human subjects: The problem of deception in social psychological experiments. *Psychological Bulletin, 67,* 1–11.

Kelman, H. C. (1982). Ethical issues in different social science methods. In T. L. Beauchamp, R. R. Faden, R. J. Wallace, Jr., & L. Walters (Eds.), *Ethical issues in social science research.* Baltimore: Johns Hopkins University Press.

Kelsoe, J. R. (2004). Genomics and the human genome project: Implications for psychiatry. *International Review of Psychiatry, 16*(4), 294–300.

Keltner, D., Ekman, P., Gonzaga, G. C., & Beer, J. (2003). Facial expression of emotion. In R. J. Davidson, K. R. Scherer, & H. H. Goldsmith (Eds.), *Handbook of affective sciences.* New York: Oxford University Press.

Kendall, P. C., Holmbeck, G., & Verduin, T. (2004). Methodology, design, and evaluation in psychotherapy research. In M. J. Lambert (Ed.), *Bergin and Garfield's handbook of psychotherapy and behavior change.* New York: Wiley.

Kendler, K. S. (2000). Schizophrenia: Genetics. In B. J. Sadock & V. A. Sadock (Eds.), *Kaplan and Sadock's comprehensive textbook of psychiatry* (7th ed., Vol. 1, pp. 1147–1158). Philadelphia: Lippincott/Williams & Wilkins.

Kendler, K. S., & Gardner, C. O., Jr. (1998). Boundaries of major depression: An evaluation of DSM-IV criteria. *American Journal of Psychiatry, 155,* 172–177.

Kendler, K. S., Karkowski, L. M., & Prescott, C. A. (1999). Causal relationship between stressful life events and the onset of major

depression. *American Journal of Psychiatry, 156,* 837–841.

Kendler, K. S., Kuhn, J., & Prescott, C. A. (2004). The interrelationship of neuroticism, sex, and stressful life events in the prediction of episodes of major depression. *American Journal of Psychiatry, 161,* 631–636.

Kendler, K. S., Thornton, L. M., Gilman, S. E., & Kessler, R. C. (2000). Sexual orientation in a U.S. national sample of twin and non-twin sibling pairs. *American Journal of Psychiatry, 157,* 1843–1846.

Kennedy, T. E., Hawkins, R. D., & Kandel, E. R. (1992). Molecular interrelationships between short- and long-term memory. In L. R. Squire & N. Butters (Eds.), *Neuropsychology of Memory* (2nd ed.). New York: Wiley.

Kenrick, D. T. (1995). Evolutionary theory versus the confederacy of dunces. *Psychological Inquiry, 6,* 56–62.

Kenrick, D. T., & Funder, D. C. (1991). The person-situation debate: Do personality traits really exist? In N. J. Derlega, B. A. Winstead, & W. H. Jones (Eds.), *Personality: Contemporary theory and research.* Chicago: Nelson-Hall.

Kenrick, D. T., & Gutierres, S. E. (1980). Contrast effects and judgments of physical attractiveness: When beauty becomes a social problem. *Journal of Personality and Social Psychology, 38,* 131–140.

Kenrick, D. T., & Trost, M. R. (1993). The evolutionary perspective. In A. E. Beall & R. J. Sternberg (Eds.), *The psychology of gender.* New York: Guilford.

Kenwood, C. (1999). The anti-sceptical psychology of George Paxton Young. *History and Philosophy of Psychology Bulletin, 11,* 4–10.

Keren, G. (1990). Cognitive aids and debiasing methods: Can cognitive pills cure cognitive ills? In J. P. Caverni, J. M. Fabre, & M. Gonzalez (Eds.), *Cognitive biases.* Amsterdam: North-Holland.

Kerfoot, P., Sakoulas, G., & Hyman, S. E. (1996). Cocaine. In L. S. Friedman, N. F. Fleming, D. H. Roberts, & S. E. Hyman (Eds.), *Source book of substance abuse and addiction.* Baltimore: Williams & Wilkins.

Kesner, R. P. (1998). Neural mediation of memory for time: Role of the hippocampus and medial prefrontal cortex. *Pscyhonomic Bulletin & Review, 5,* 585–596.

Kessen, W. (1996). American psychology just before Piaget. *Psychological Science, 7,* 196–199.

Kessler, R. C. (1997). The effects of stressful life events on depression. *Annual Review of Psychology, 48,* 191–214.

Kessler, R. C. (2002). Epidemiology of depression. In I. H. Gotlib & C. L. Hammen (Eds.), *Handbook of depression.* New York: Guilford.

Kessler, R. C., & Zhao, S. (1999). The prevalence of mental illness. In A. V. Horvitz & T. L. Scheid (Eds.), *A handbook for the study of mental health: Social contexts, theories, and systems.* New York: Cambridge University Press.

Kessler, R. C., Berglund, P., Demler, O., Jin, R., & Walters, E. E. (2005a). Lifetime prevalence and age-of-onset distributions of DSM-IV disorders in the national comorbidity survey replication. *Archives of General Psychiatry, 62,* 593–602.

Kessler, R. C., Demier, O., Frank, R. G., Olfson, M., Pincus, H. A., Walters, E. E., Wang, P., Wells, K. B., & Zaslavsky, A. M. (2005b). Prevalence and treatment of mental disorders: 1990–2003. *New England Journal of Medicine, 352,* 2515–2523.

Kessler, R. C., McGonagle, K. A., Zhao, S., Nelson, C. B., Hughes, M., Eshleman, S., Wittchen, H. U., & Kendler, K. S. (1994). Lifetime and 12–month prevalence of DSM-III-R psychiatric disorders in the United States: Results from the National Comorbidity Survey. *Archives of General Psychiatry, 51,* 8–19.

Kessler, R. C., Olfson, M., & Berglund, P. A. (1998). Patterns and predictors of treatment contact after first onset of psychiatric disorders. *American Journal of Psychiatry, 155,* 62–69.

Ketterer, M. W., & Randall, M. (2000). Atherosclerosis. In G. Fink (Ed.), *Encyclopedia of stress* (pp. 258–261). San Diego: Academic Press.

Key, W. B. (1973). *Subliminal seduction.* Englewood Cliffs, NJ: Prentice-Hall.

Key, W. B. (1976). *Media sexploitation.* Englewood Cliffs, NJ: Prentice-Hall.

Key, W. B. (1980). *The clam-plate orgy and other subliminal techniques for manipulating your behavior.* Englewood Cliffs, NJ: Prentice-Hall.

Khot, U. N., Khot, M. B., Bajzer, C. T., Sapp, S. K., Ohman, E. M., Brener, S. J., Ellis, S. G., Lincoff, M. A., & Topol, E. J. (2003). Prevalence of conventional risk factors in patients with coronary heart disease. *Journal of the American Medical Association, 290,* 898–904.

Kiecolt-Glaser, J. K., & Glaser, R. (1995). Measurement of immune response. In S. Cohen, R. C. Kessler, & L. U. Gordon (Eds.), *Measuring stress: A guide for health and social scientists.* New York: Oxford University Press.

Kiecolt-Glaser, J. K., Garner, W., Speicher, C., Penn, G. M., Holliday, J., & Glaser, R. (1984). Psychosocial modifiers of immunocompetence in medical students. *Psychosomatic Medicine, 46*(1), 7–14.

Kiecolt-Glaser, J. K., Kennedy, S., Malkoff, S., Fisher, L., Speicher, C. E., & Glaser, R. (1988). Marital discord and immunity in males. *Psychosomatic Medicine, 50,* 213–229.

Kiecolt-Glaser, J. K., McGuire, L., Robles, T. F., & Glaser, R. (2002). Emotions, morbidity, and mortality: New perspectives from psychoneuroimmunology. *Annual Review of Psychology, 53,* 83–107.

Kielburger, C. (with Kevin Major). (1998). *Free the children: A young man's personal crusade against child labor.* New York, NY: HarperCollins Publishers, Inc.

Kiesler, C. A. (1991). Homelessness and public policy priorities. *American Psychologist, 46,* 1245–1252.

Kiesler, C. A. (1992). U.S. mental health policy: Doomed to fail. *American Psychologist, 47,* 1077–1082.

Kiesler, D. J. (1999). *Beyond the disease model of mental disorders.* New York: Praeger Publishers.

Kihlstrom, J. F. (1985). Hypnosis. *Annual Review of Psychology, 36,* 385–418.

Kihlstrom, J. F. (1998a). Dissociations and dissociation theory in hypnosis: Comment on Kirsch and Lynn (1998). *Psychological Bulletin, 123,* 186–191.

Kihlstrom, J. F. (1998b). Exhumed memory. In S. J. Lynn, & K. M. McConkey (Eds.), *Truth in memory.* New York: Guilford.

Kihlstrom, J. F. (2001). Dissociative disorders. In P. B. Sutker & H. E. Adams (Eds.), *Comprehensive handbook of psychopathology* (3rd ed., pp. 259–276). New York: Kluwer Academic/Plenum Publishers.

Kihlstrom, J. F. (2004). An unbalanced balancing act: Blocked, recovered, and false memories in the laboratory and clinic. *Clinical Psychology: Science & Practice, 11*(1), 34–41.

Kihlstrom, J. F., Barnhardt, T. M., & Tataryn, D. J. (1992). Implicit perception. In R. F. Bornstein & T. S. Pittman (Eds.), *Perception without awareness: Cognitive, clinical, and social perspectives.* New York: Guilford.

Kihlstrom, J. F., Glisky, M. L., & Angiulo, M. J. (1994). Dissociative tendencies and dissociative disorders. *Journal of Abnormal Psychology, 103,* 117–124.

Kihlstrom, J. F., Schacter, D. L., Cork, R. C., Hurt, C. A., & Behr, S. E. (1990). Implicit and explicit memory following surgical anesthesia. *Psychological Science, 1,* 303–306.

Kihlstrom, J. F., Tataryn, D. J., & Hoyt, I. P. (1993). Dissociative disorders. In P. B. Sutker & H. E. Adams (Eds.), *Comprehensive handbook of psychopathology* (2nd ed.). New York: Plenum.

Killeen, P. R. (1981). Learning as causal inference. In M. L. Commons & J. A. Nevin (Eds.), *Quantitative analyses of behavior: Vol. 1. Discriminative properties of reinforcement schedules.* Cambridge, MA: Ballinger.

Kilpatrick, D. G., Edmunds, C. N., & Seymour, A. (1992). *Rape in America.* Arlington, VA: National Victim Center.

Kim, H., & Markus, H. R. (1999). Deviance or uniqueness, harmony or conformity? A cultural analysis. *Journal of Personality and Social Psychology, 77,* 785–800.

Kim, K., & Spelke, E. S. (1992). Infants' sensitivity to effects of gravity on visible object motion. *Journal of Experimental Psychology: Human Perception and Performance, 18,* 385–393.

Kimberg, D. Y., D'Esposito, M., & Farah, M. J. (1997). Cognitive functions in the prefrontal cortex—Working memory and executive control. *Current Directions in Psychological Science, 6,* 185–192.

Kimmel, M. S., & Linders, A. (1996). Does censorship make a difference? An aggregate empirical analysis of pornography and rape. *Journal of Psychology and Human Sexuality, 8,* 1–20.

Kimura, D. (1973). The asymmetry of the human brain. *Scientific American, 228,* 70–78.

Kimura, D. (1992). Sex Differences in the brain. *Scientific American,* (September), 119–125.

Kimura, D. (1999). *Sex and cognition.* Cambridge, MA: MIT Press.

Kimura, D. (2004). Human sex differences in cognition: Fact not predicament. *Sexualities, Evolution and Gender, 6,* 45–53.

Kimura, D., & Hampson, E. (1993). Neural and hormonal mechanisms mediating sex differences in cognition. In P. A. Vernon (Ed.), *Biological approaches to the study of human intelligence.* Norwood, NJ: Ablex.

King, A. C., Oman, R. F., Brassington, G. S., Bliwise, D. L., & Haskell, W. L. (1997). Moderate-intensity exercise and self-rated quality of sleep in older adults: A randomized controlled trial. *Journal of the American Medical Association, 277,* 32–37.

King, A. C., Taylor, C. B., & Haskell, W. L. (1993). Effects of differing intensities and formats of 12 months of exercise training on psychological outcomes in older adults. *Health Psychology, 12,* 292–300.

King, B. H., Hodapp, R. M., & Dykens, E. M. (2000). Mental retardation. In B. J. Sadock & V. A. Sadock (Eds.), *Kaplan and Sadock's comprehensive textbook of psychiatry* (7th ed., pp. 2587–2613). Philadelphia: Lippincott/Williams & Wilkins.

King, G. R., & Ellinwood Jr., E. H. (2005). Amphetamines and other stimulants. In J. H. Lowinson, P. Ruiz, R. B. Millman, & J. G. Langrod (Eds.), *Substance abuse: A comprehensive textbook.* Philadelphia: Lippincott/Williams & Wilkins.

King, G. R., & Ellinwood, E. H., Jr. (1997). Amphetamines and other stimulants. In J. H. Lowinson, P. Ruiz, R. B. Millman, & J. G. Langrod (Eds.), *Substance abuse: A comprehensive textbook.* Baltimore: Williams & Willkins.

King, L. A., & Emmons, R. A. (1990). Conflict over emotional expression: Psychological and physical correlates. *Journal of Personality and Social Psychology, 58,* 864–877.

King, L. A., & Emmons, R. A. (1991). Psychological, physical, and interpersonal correlates of emotional expressiveness, conflict and control. *European Journal of Personality, 5,* 131–150.

King, L. A., King, D. W., Fairbank, J. A., Keane, T. M., & Adams, G. A. (1998). Resilience-recovery factors in post-traumatic stress disorder among female and male Vietnam veterans: Hardiness, postwar social support, and additional stressful life events. *Journal of Personality and Social Psychology, 74,* 420–434.

King, N. J., Eleonora, G., & Ollendick, T. H. (1998). Etiology of childhood phobias: Current status of Rachman's three pathways theory. *Behaviour Research and Therapy, 36,* 297–309.

Kinsbourne, M. (1980). If sex differences in brain lateralization exist, they have yet to be discovered. *Behavioral and Brain Sciences, 3,* 241–242.

Kinsbourne, M. (1997). What qualifies a representation for a role in consciousness? In J. D. Cohen & J. W. Schooler (Eds.), *Scientific approaches to consciousness.* Mahwah, NJ: Erlbaum.

Kinsey, A. C., Pomeroy, W. B., & Martin, C. E. (1948). *Sexual behavior in the human male.* Philadelphia: Saunders.

Kinsey, A. C., Pomeroy, W. B., Martin, C. E., & Gebhard, P. H. (1953). *Sexual behavior in the human female.* Philadelphia: Saunders.

Kirchner, J. T. (2001, September). Ten things primary care physicians should know about HIV/AIDS. *Medical Aspects of Human Sexuality,* 7–9.

Kirkpatrick, L. A. (1999). Attachment and religious representations and behavior. In J. Cassidy & P. R. Shaver (Eds.), *Handbook of attachment: Theory, research and clinical applications.* New York: Guilford.

Kirkpatrick, L. A. (2005). *Attachment, evolution, and the psychology of religion.* New York: Guilford.

Kirkpatrick, L. A., & Davis, K. E. (1994). Attachment style, gender, and relationship stability: A longitudinal study. *Journal of Personality and Social Psychology, 66,* 502–512.

Kirmayer, L. J., Brass, G. M., & Tait, C. L. (2000). The mental health of aboriginal peoples: Transformations of identity and community. *Canadian Journal of Psychiatry, 45,* 607–612.

Kirmayer, L. J., Robbins, J. M., & Paris, J. (1994). Somatoform disorders: Personality and the social matrix of somatic distress. *Journal of Abnormal Psychology, 103,* 125–136.

Kirsch, I. (1997). Response expectancy theory and application: A decennial review. *Applied and Preventive Psychology, 6,* 69–79.

Kirsch, I., & Braffman, W. (2001). Imaginative suggestibility and hypnotizability. *Current Directions in Psychological Science, 10*(2), 57–61.

Kirsch, I., & Lynn, S. J. (1998). Dissociation theories of hypnosis. *Psychological Bulletin, 123,* 100–115.

Kirsh, G. A., & Kuiper, N. A. (2002). Individualism and relatedness themes in the context of depression, gender, and a self-schema model of emotion. *Canadian Psychology, 43,* 76–91.

Kitayama, S., Markus, H. R., Matsumoto, H., & Norasakkunkit, V. (1997). Individual and collective processes in the construction of the self: Self-enhancement in the United States and self-criticism in Japan. *Journal of Personality and Social Psychology, 72,* 1245–1267.

Kitchens, A. (1991). Left brain/right brain theory: Implications for developmental math instruction. *Review of Research in Developmental Education, 8,* 20–23.

Kittler, P. G., & Sucher, K. P. (1998). *Food and culture in America: A nutrition handbook.* St. Paul: West.

Klahr, D., & Simon, H. A. (1999). Studies of scientific discovery: Complementary approaches and convergent findings. *Psychological Bulletin, 125,* 524–543.

Klein, K., & Boals, A. (2001). The relationship of life event stress and working memory capacity. *Applied Cognitive Psychology, 15,* 565–579.

Klein, M. (1948). *Contributions to psychoanalysis.* London: Hogarth.

Klein, P. D. (1997). Multiplying the problems of intelligence by eight: A critique of Gardner's theory. *Canadian Journal of Education, 22,* 377–394.

Klein, R. M. (1999). The Hebb legacy. *Canadian Journal of Behavioural Science, 53,* 1–20.

Kleinke, C. L., Peterson, T. R., & Rutledge, T. R. (1998). Effects of self-generated facial expressions on mood. *Journal of Personality and Social Psychology, 74,* 272–279.

Kleinmuntz, B. (1980). *Essentials of abnormal psychology.* San Francisco: Harper & Row.

Kleinmuntz, B. (1985). *Personality and psychological assessment.* Malabar, FL: Robert E. Krieger.

Klerman, E. B. (1993). Deprivation, selective: NREM sleep. In M. A. Carskadon (Ed.), *Encyclopedia of sleep and dreaming.* New York: Macmillan.

Klerman, G. L., & Weissman, M. M. E. (1993). *New applications of interpersonal therapy.* Washington, DC: American Psychiatric Press.

Kline, P. (1991). *Intelligence: The psychometric view.* New York: Routledge, Chapman, & Hall.

Kline, P. (1995). A critical review of the measurement of personality and intelligence. In D. H. Saklofske & M. Zeidner (Eds.), *International handbook of personality and intelligence.* New York: Plenum.

Kling, K. C., Hyde, J. S., Showers, C. J., & Buswell, B. N. (1999). Gender differences in self-esteem: A meta-analysis. *Psychological Bulletin, 125,* 470–500.

Klosch, G., & Kraft, U. (2005). Sweet dreams are made of this. *Scientific American Mind, 16*(2), 38–45.

Kluckhohn, C., & Murray, H. A. (1948). *Personality in nature, society and culture.* New York: Knopf.

Kluegel, J. R. (1990). Trends in whites' explanations of the black-white gap in socioeconomic status. *American Sociological Review, 55,* 512–525.

Kluft, R. P. (1996). Dissociative identity disorder. In L. K. Michelson & W. J. Ray (Eds.), *Handbook of dissociation: Theoretical, empirical, and clinical perspectives.* New York: Plenum.

Kluft, R. P. (1999). True lies, false truths, and naturalistic raw data: Applying clinical research findings to the false memory debate. In L. M. Williams & V. L. Banyard (Eds.), *Trauma & memory.* Thousand Oaks, CA: Sage Publications.

Knable, M. B., Kleinman, J. E., & Weinberger, D. R. (1995). Neurobiology of schizophrenia. In A. F. Schatzberg & C. B. Nemeroff (Eds.), *The American Psychiatric Press textbook of psychopharmacology.* Washington, DC: American Psychiatric Press.

Knight, G. P., Fabes, R. A., & Higgins, D. A. (1996). Concerns about drawing causal inference from meta-analysis: An example in the study of gender differences in aggression. *Psychological Bulletin, 119,* 410–421.

Knowles, J. A., Kaufmann, C. A., & Rieder, R. O. (1999). Genetics. In R. E. Hales, S. C. Yudofsky, & J. A. Talbott (Eds.), *American Psychiatric Press textbook of Psychiatry.* Washington, DC: American Psychiatric Press.

Knox, D., Zusman, M., & Nieves, W. (1997). College students' homogamous preferences for a date and mate. *College Student Journal, 31,* 445–448.

Kobak, R. (1999). The emotional dynamics of disruptions in attachment relationships: Implications for theory, research, and clinical intervention. In J. Cassidy & P. R. Shaver (Eds.), *Handbook of attachment.* New York: Guilford.

Kochanska, G. (2001). Emotional development in children with different attachment histories: The first three years. *Child Development, 72,* 474–490.

Koehler, J. J. (1996). The base rate fallacy reconsidered: Descriptive, normative, and methodological challenges. *Behavioral Brain Sciences, 19,* 1–53.

Koester, J., & Siegelbaum, S. A. (2000). Propagated signaling: The action potential. In E. R. Kandel, J. H. Schwartz, & T. M. Jessell (Eds.), *Principles of neural science* (pp. 150–174). New York: McGraw-Hill.

Koestner, R., & McClelland, D. C. (1992). The affiliation motive. In C. P. Smith (Ed.), *Motivation and personality: Handbook of thematic content analysis.* New York: Cambridge University Press.

Kogan, N. (1990). Personality and aging. In J. E. Birren & K. W. Schaie (Eds.), *Handbook of the psychology of aging.* San Diego: Academic Press.

Kohlberg, L. (1963). The development of children's orientations toward a moral order: I. Sequence in the development of moral thought. *Vita Humana, 6,* 11–33.

Kohlberg, L. (1969). Stage and sequence: The cognitive-developmental approach to socialization. In D. A. Goslin (Ed.), *Handbook of socialization theory and research.* Chicago: Rand McNally.

Kohlberg, L. (1976). Moral stages and moralization: Cognitive-developmental approach. In T. Lickona (Ed.), *Moral development and behavior: Theory, research and social issues.* New York: Holt, Rinehart & Winston.

Kohlberg, L. (1984). *Essays on moral development: Vol. 2. The psychology of moral development.* San Francisco: Harper & Row.

Kohn, P. M., Lafreniere, K., & Gurevich, M. (1991). Hassles, health, and personality. *Journal of Personality and Social Psychology, 61,* 478–482.

Kohut, H. (1971). *Analysis of the self.* New York: International Universities Press.

Kolb, B., & Whishaw, I. Q. (1998). Brain plasticity and behavior. *Annual Review of Psychology, 49,* 43–64.

Kolb, B., Gibb, R., & Robinson, T. E. (2003). Brain plasticity and behavior. *Current Directions in Psychological Science, 12,* 1–5.

Kondo-Ikemura, K. (2001). Insufficient evidence. *American Psychologist, 56,* 825–826.

Koob, G. F. (1997). Neurochemical explanations for addiction. *Hospital Practice, April,* 12–14.

Koob, G. F., & Bloom, F. E. (1988). Cellular and molecular mechanisms of drug dependence. *Science, 242,* 715–723.

Kop, W. J., Gottdiener, J. S., & Krantz, D. S. (2001). Stress and silent ischemia. In A. Baum, T. A. Revenson, & J. E. Singer (Eds.), *Handbook of health psychology* (pp. 669–682). Mahwah, NJ: Erlbaum.

Kopta, S. M., Lueger, R. J., Saunders, S. M., & Howard, K. I. (1999). Individual psychotherapy outcome and process research: Challenges leading to greater turmoil or a positive transition? *Annual Review of Psychology, 50,* 441–469.

Koren, D., Arnon, I., & Klein, E. (1999). Acute stress response and posttraumatic stress disorder in traffic accident victims: A one-year prospective, follow-up study. *American Journal of Psychiatry, 156,* 367–373.

Koriat, A., & Bjork, R. A. (2005). Illusions of competence in monitoring one's knowledge during study. *Journal of Experimental Psychology: Learning, Memory, and Cognition, 31*(2), 187–194.

Koriat, A., & Melkman, R. (1987). Depth of processing and memory organization. *Psychological Research, 49,* 183–188.

Koriat, A., Goldsmith, M., & Pansky, A. (2000). Toward a psychology of memory accuracy. *Annual Review of Psychology, 51,* 481–537.

Koriat, A., Goldsmith, M., & Pansky, A. (2000). Toward a psychology of memory accuracy. *Annual Review of Psychology, 51,* 481–537.

Koriat, A., Lichtenstein, S., & Fischhoff, B. (1980). Reasons for confidence. *Journal of Experimental Psychology, 6,* 107–118.

Korn, J. H. (1997). *Illusions of reality: A history of deception in social psychology.* Albany: State University of New York Press.

Korn, J. H., Davis, R., & Davis, S. F. (1991). Historians' and chairpersons' judgements of eminence among psychologists. *American Psychologist, 46,* 789–792.

Korn, M. L. (2001). Trauma related disorders: Conversations with the experts—Posttraumatic stress disorder: An interview with Marilyn Bowman. Retrieved November 20, 2001, from Medscape Mental Health Web site: http://www.medscape.com/Medscape/psychiatry/journal/2001/v06.n06.n05/myh5/mh1002.01.yehu/mh1002.01.yehu.html. *Medscape Mental Health, 6*(5).

Kornhaber, M. L. (2004). Multiple intelligences: From the ivory tower to the dusty classroom—But why? *Teachers College Record, 106*(1), 57–76.

Kortenhaus, C. M., & Demarest, J. (1993). Gender role stereotyping in children's literature: An update. *Sex Roles, 3,* 219–232.

Koss, M. P. (1993). Rape: Scope, impact, interventions, and public policy responses. *American Psychologist, 48,* 1062–1069.

Koss, M. P., Gidycz, C. A., & Wisniewski, N. (1987). The scope of rape: Incidence and prevalence of sexual aggression and victimization in a national sample of higher education students. *Journal of*

Consulting and Clinical Psychology, 55(2), 162–170.

Kotovsky, K., Hayes, J. R., & Simon, H. A. (1985). Why are some problems hard? Evidence from Tower of Hanoi. *Cognitive Psychology, 17,* 248–294.

Kotulak, R. (1996). *Inside the brain: Revolutionary discoveries of how the mind works.* Kansas City, MO: Andrews McMeel.

Koukounas, E., & McCabe, M. (1997). Sexual and emotional variables influencing sexual response to erotica. *Behaviour Research and Therpy, 35,* 221–230.

Kracke, W. (1991). Myths in dreams, thought in images: An Amazonian contribution to the psychoanalytic theory of primary process. In B. Tedlock (Ed.), *Dreaming: Anthropological and psychological interpretations.* Santa Fe, NM: School of American Research Press.

Kramer, M. (1994). The scientific study of dreaming. In M. H. Kryger, T. Roth, & W. C. Dement (Eds.), *Principles and practice of sleep medicine* (2nd ed.). Philadelphia: Saunders.

Kransny, L., Williams, B. J., Provencal, S., & Ozonoff, S. (2003). Social skills interventions for the autism spectrum: Essential ingredients and a model curriculum. *Child and Adolescent Psychiatric Clinics of North America, 12*(1), 107–122.

Krantz, D. S., & McCeney, M. K. (2002). Effects of psychological and social factors on organic disease: A critical assessment of research on coronary heart disease. *Annual Review of Psychology, 53,* 341–369.

Krantz, D. S., Sheps, D. S., Carney, R. M., & Natelson, B. H. (2000). Effects of mental stress in patients with coronary artery disease. *Journal of the American Medical Association, 283,* 1800–1802.

Kraus, S. J. (1995). Attitudes and the prediction of behavior: A meta-analysis of the empirical literature. *Personality and Social Psychology Bulletin, 21,* 58–75.

Krebs, D. L., & Denton, K. (1997). Social illusions and self-deception: The evolution of biases in person perception. In J. A. Simpson & D. T. Kenrick (Eds.), *Evolutionary social psychology.* Mahwah, NJ: Erlbaum.

Kring, A. M. (1999). Emotion in schizophrenia: Old mystery, new understanding. *Current Directions in Psychological Science, 8,* 160–163.

Kris, E. (1952). *Psychoanalytic explorations in art.* New York: International Universities Press.

Kroger, J. (1995). The differentiation of "firm" and "developmental" foreclosure identity statuses: A longitudinal study. *Journal of Adolescent Research, 10,* 317–337.

Kroger, J. (1996). Identity, regression, and development. *Journal of Adolescence, 19,* 203–222.

Kroger, J. (2003). Identity development during adolescence. In G. R. Adams & M. D. Berzonsky (Eds.), *Blackwell handbook of adolescence.* Malden, MA: Blackwell Publishing.

Krosnick, J. A. (1999). Survey research. *Annual Review Psychology, 50,* 537–567.

Krosnick, J. A., & Fabrigar, L. R. (1998). *Designing good questionnaires: Insights from psychology.* New York: Oxford University Press.

Krosnick, J. A., & Petty, R. E. (1995). Attitude strength: An overview. In R. E. Petty & J. A. Krosnick (Eds.), *Attitude strength: Antecedents and consequences.* Mahwah, NJ: Erlbaum.

Krosnick, J. A., Betz, A. L., Jussim, L. J., & Lynn, A. R. (1992). Subliminal conditioning of attitudes. *Personality and Social Psychology Bulletin, 18,* 152–162.

Krueger, J. (1996). Personal beliefs and cultural stereotypes about racial characteristics. *Journal of Personality and Social Psychology, 71,* 536–548.

Krueger, J., Ham, J. J., & Linford, K. M. (1996). Perceptions of behavioral consistency: Are people aware of the actor-observer effect? *Psychological Science, 7,* 259–264.

Krueger, W. C. F. (1929). The effect of overlearning on retention. *Journal of Experimental Psychology, 12,* 71–78.

Kruglanski, A. W., & Stroebe, W. (2005). The influence of beliefs and goals on attitudes: Issues of structure, function, and dynamics. In D. Albarracin, B. T. Johnson, & M. P. Zanna (Eds.), *The handbook of attitudes.* Mahwah, NJ: Erlbaum.

Krull, D. S. (2001). On partitioning the fundamental attribution error: Dispositionalism and the correspondence bias. In G. B. Moskowitz (Ed.), *Cognitive social psychology: The Princeton Symposium on the legacy and future of social cognition.* Mahwah, NJ: Erlbaum.

Krull, D. S., & Erickson, D. J. (1995). Inferential hopscotch: How people draw social inferences from behavior. *Current Directions in Psychological Science, 4,* 35–38.

Kryger, M. H. (1993). Snoring. In M. A. Carskadon (Ed.), *Encyclopedia of sleep and dreaming.* New York: Macmillan.

Kryger, M. H., Roth, T., & Dement, W. C. (2000). *Principles and practice of sleep medicine.* Philadelphia: Saunders.

Kubovy, M., Epstein, W., & Gepshtein, S. (2003). Foundations of visual perception. In A. F. Healy & R. W. Proctor (Eds.), *Handbook of psychology.* New York: Wiley.

Kuhl, P. K., & Meltzoff, A. N. (1997). Evolution, nativism and learning in the development of language and speech. In M. Gopnik (Ed.), *The inheritance and innateness of grammars* (pp. 7–44). New York: Oxford University Press.

Kuiper, N. A., & Derry, P. (1981). The self as a cognitive prototype: An application to person perception and depression. In N. Cantor & J. F. Kihlstrom (Eds.), *Personality, cognition, and social interaction* (pp. 215–232). Hillsdale, NJ: Erlbaum.

Kuiper, N. A., & Rogers, T. B. (1979). Encoding of personal information: Self-other differences. *Journal of Personality and Social Psychology, 37,* 499–514.

Kulick, A. R., Pope, H. G., & Keck, P. E. (1990). Lycanthropy and self-identification. *Journal of Nervous & Mental Disease, 178*(2), 134–137.

Kumar, V. M. (2004). Body temperature and sleep: Are they controlled by the same mechanism? *Sleep & Biological Rhythms, 2*(2), 103–125.

Kunda, Z., & Oleson, K. C. (1995). Maintaining stereotypes in the face of disconfirmation: Constructing grounds for subtyping deviants. *Journal of Personality and Social Psychology, 68,* 565–579.

Kunda, Z., & Oleson, K. C. (1997). When exceptions prove the rule: How extremity of deviance determines the impact of deviant examples on stereotypes. *Journal of Personality and Social Psychology, 72,* 965–979.

Kupfermann, I., Kandel, E. R., & Iversen, S. (2000). Motivational and addictive states. In E. R. Kandel, J. H. Schwartz, & T. M. Jessell (Eds.), *Principles of neural science.* New York: McGraw-Hill.

Kutchins, H., & Kirk, S. A. (1997). *Making us crazy: DSM—The psychiatric Bible and the creation of mental disorders.* New York: Free Press.

Kutchinsky, B. (1991). Pornography and rape: Theory and practice? Evidence from crime data in four countries where pornography is easily available. *International Journal of Law and Psychiatry, 14,* 47–64.

Kwan, V. S. Y., Bond, M. H., & Singelis, T. M. (1997). Pancultural explanations for life satisfaction: Adding relationship harmony to self-esteem. *Journal of Personality and Social Psychology, 73,* 1038–1051.

La Cerra, P., & Kurzban, R. (1995). The structure of scientific revolutions and the nature of the adapted mind. *Psychological Inquiry, 6,* 62–65.

LaBerge, S. (1988). Lucid dreaming in Western literature. In J. Gackenbach & S. LaBerge (Eds.), *Conscious mind, sleeping brain: Perspectives on lucid dreaming.* New York: Plenum.

LaBerge, S. (1990). Lucid dreaming: Psychophysiological studies of consciousness during REM sleep. In R. R. Bootzin, J. F. Kihlstrom, & D. L. Schacter (Eds.), *Sleep and cognition.* Washington, DC: American Psychological Association.

LaBerge, S., Nagel, L., Dement, W. C., & Zarcone, V., Jr. (1981). Lucid dreaming verified by volitional communication during REM sleep. *Perceptual and Motor Skills, 52,* 727–732.

LaBine, S. J., & LaBine, G. (1996). Determinations of negligence and the hindsight bias. *Law & Human Behavior, 20,* 501–516.

Lacey, K., Zaharian, M.D., Griffiths, J., Ravindran, A.V., Merali, Z., & Anisman, H. (2000). A prospective study of neuroendocrine and immune alterations associated with the stress of an oral academic examination among graduate students. *Psychoneuroendocrinology, 25,* 339–356.

Lachman, M. E. (2004). Development in midlife. *Annual Review of Psychology, 55,* 305–331.

Lachman, S. J. (1996). Processes in perception: Psychological transformations of highly structured stimulus material. *Perceptual and Motor Skills, 83,* 411–418.

Lachter, J., Forster, K. I., & Ruthruff, E. (2004). Forty-five years after Broadbent (1958): Still no identification without attention. *Psychological Review, 111,* 880–913.

Lader, M. H. (2002). Managing dependence and withdrawal with newer hypnotic medications in the treatment of insomnia. *Journal of Clinical Psychiatry, 4*(suppl. 1), 33–37.

Lahey, B. B., Piancentini, J. C., McBurnett, K., Stone, P., Hartdagen, S., & Hynd, G. (1988). Psychopathology in the parents of children with conduct disorder and hyperactivity. *Journal of the American Academy of Child and Adolescent Psychiatry, 27,* 163–170.

Laitinen, J., Ek, E., & Sovio, U. (2002). Stress-related eating and drinking behavior and body mass index and predictors of this behavior. *Preventive Medicine: An International Journal Devoted to Practice & Theory, 34,* 29–39.

Lakein, A. (1996). *How to get control of your time and your life.* New York: New American Library.

Lalonde, C. E., & Chandler, M. J. (2002). Children's understanding of interpretation. *New Ideas in Psychology: Special Issue on Folk Epistemology, 20,* 163–198.

Lalonde, R. N., & Gardner, R. C. (1984). Investigating a causal model of second language acquisition: Where does personality fit in? *Canadian Journal of Behavioural Science, 16,* 224–237.

Lalonde, R. N., & Gardner, R. C. (1989). An intergroup perspective on stereotype organization and processing. *British Journal of Social Psychology, 28,* 289–303.

Lalonde, R. N., & Gardner, R. C. (1993). Statistics as a second language? A model for predicting performance in psychology students. *Canadian Journal of Behavioural Science, 25,* 108–125.

Lalonde, R. N., Hynie, M., Pannu, M., & Tatla, S. (2004). The role of culture in interpersonal relationships: Do second generation South Asian Canadians want a traditional partner? *Journal of Cross-Cultural Psychology, 35,* 503–524.

Lamb, H. R. (1998). Deinstitutionalization at the beginning of the new millenium. *Harvard Review of Psychiatry, 6,* 1–10.

Lamb, H. R. (1999). Public psychiatry and prevention. In R. E. Hales, S. C. Yudofsky, & J. A. Talbott (Eds.), *American Psychiatric Press textbook of psychiatry.* Washington, DC: American Psychiatric Press.

Lamb, M. E. (1998). Nonparental child care: context, quality, correlates, and consequences. In W. Damon (Ed.), *Handbook of child psychology (Vol. 4): Child psychology in practice.* New York: Wiley.

Lamb, M. E., Hwang, C. P., Ketterlinus, R. D., & Fracasso, M. P. (1999). Parent-child relationships: Development in the context of the family. In M. H. Bornstein & M. E. Lamb (Eds.), *Developmental psychology and advanced textbook.* Mahwah, NJ: Erlbaum.

Lamb, M. E., Ketterlinus, R. D., & Fracasso, M. P. (1992). Parent-child relationships. In M. H. Bornstein & M. E. Lamb (Eds.), *Developmental psychology: An advanced textbook* (3rd ed.). Hillsdale, NJ: Erlbaum.

Lamb, M. E., Sternberg, K. J., & Prodromidis, M. (1992). Nonmaternal care and the security of infant-mother attachment: A reanalysis of the data. *Infant Behavior and Development, 15,* 71–83.

Lambert, M. J., & Barley, D. E. (2001). Research summary on the therapeutic relationship and psychotherapy outcome. *Psychotherapy: Theory, Research, Practice, Training, 38,* 357–361.

Lambert, M. J., & Bergin, A. E. (1992). Achievements and limitations of psychotherapy research. In D. K. Freedheim (Ed.), *History of psychotherapy: A century of change.* Washington, DC: American Psychological Association.

Lambert, M. J., & Bergin, A. E. (1994). The effectiveness of psychotherapy. In A. E. Bergin & S. L. Garfield (Eds.), *Handbook of psychotherapy and behavior change* (4th ed.). New York: Wiley.

Lambert, M. J., & Hill, C. E. (1994). Assessing psychotherapy outcomes and processes. In A. E. Bergin & S. L. Garfield (Eds.), *Handbook of psychotherapy and behavior change* (4th ed.). New York: Wiley.

Lambert, M. J., & Ogles, B. M. (2004). The efficacy and effectiveness of psychotherapy. In M. J. Lambert (Ed.), *Bergin and Garfield's handbook of psychotherapy and behavior change.* New York: Wiley.

Lambert, M. J., Bergin, A. E., & Garfield, S. L. (2004). Introduction and historical overview. In M. J. Lambert (Ed.), *Bergin and Garfield's handbook of psychotherapy and behavior change.* New York: Wiley.

Lambert, W. E. (1967). A social psychology of bilingualism. *Journal of Social Issues, 23,* 91–109.

Lambert, W. E. (1990). Persistent issues in bilingualism. In B. Harley, P. Allen, J. Cummins, & M. Swain (Eds.), *The development of second language proficiency.* Cambridge, England: Cambridge University Press.

Lambert, W. E., & Tucker, G. R. (1969). *Bilingual education in Canada: The St. Lambert experiment.* Rowley, MA: Newbury House.

Lampe, A., Soellner, W., Krismer, M., Rumpold, G., Kantner-Rumplmair, W., Ogon, M., & Rathner, G. (1998). The impact of stressful life events on exacerbation of chronic low-back pain. *Journal of Psychosomatic Research, 44,* 555–563.

Lampe, A., Soellner, W., Krismer, M., Rumpold, G., Kantner-Rumplmair, W., Ogon, M., & Rathner, G. (1998). The impact of stressful life events on exacerbation of chronic low-back pain. *Journal of Psychosomatic Research, 44,* 555–563.

Lampinen, J. M., Neuschatz, J. S., & Payne, D. G. (1999). Source attributions and false memories: A test of the demand characteristics account. *Psychonomic Bulletin & Review, 6,* 130–135.

Lampl, M., Veldhuis, J. D., & Johnson, M. L. (1992). Saltation and stasis: A model of human growth. *Science, 258,* 801–803.

Landabaso, M. A., Iraurgi, I., Sanz, J., Calle, R., Ruiz de Apodaka, J., Jimenez-Lerma, J. M., & Gutierrez-Fraile, M. (1999). Naltrexone in the treatment of alcoholism. Two-year follow up results. *European Journal of Psychiatry, 13,* 97–105.

Landau, J. D., & Marsh, R. L. (1997). Monitoring source in an unconscious plagiarism paradigm. *Psychonomic Bulletin & Review, 4,* 265–270.

Landel-Graham, J., Yount, S. E., & Rudnicki, S. R. (2003). Diabetes mellitus. In A. M. Nezu, C. M. Nezu, & P. A. Geller (Eds.), *Handbook of psychology, Vol. 9: Health psychology.* New York: Wiley.

Landesman, S., & Ramey, C. (1989). Developmental psychology and mental retardation: Integrating scientific principles with treatment practices. *American Psychologist, 44,* 409–415.

Landy, F. J., Shankster, L. J., & Kohler, S. S. (1994). Personnel selection and placement. *Annual Review of Psychology, 45,* 261–296.

Lang, P. J. (1995). The emotion probe: Studies of motivation and attention. *American Psychologist, 50,* 372–385.

Langdon, P. E., Yagueez, L., Brown, J., & Hope, A. (2001). Who walks through the "revolving door" of a British psychiatric hospital? *Journal of Mental Health (UK), 10,* 525–533.

Lange, C. (1885). One leuds beveegelser. In K. Dunlap (Ed.), *The emotions.* Baltimore: Williams & Wilkins.

Langlois, J. H., Kalakanis, L., Rubenstein, A. J., Larson, A., Hallam, M., & Smoot, M. (2000). Maxims or myths of beauty? A meta-analytic and theoretical review. *Psychological Bulletin, 126,* 390–423.

Langlois, S., & Morrison, P. (2002). Suicide deaths and suicide attempts. *Health Reports, 13,* No. 2, 9–23. Statistics Canada, Catalogue 82-003, http://www.statcan.ca/english/studies/82-003/feature/hrar2002013002s0a01.pdf.

Lanyon, R. I., & Goodstein, L. D. (1997). *Personality assessment.* New York: Wiley.

LaPiere, R. T. (1934). Attitude and actions. *Social Forces, 13,* 230–237.

Lapierre, Y. D. (2003). Suicidality with selective serotonin reuptake inhibitors: Valid claim? *Journal of Psychiatry & Neuroscience, 28,* 340–347.

Larkin, J. A. (1988). Are good teachers perceived as high self-monitors? *Personality and Social Psychology Bulletin, 13,* 64–72.

Larson, R., & Wilson, S. (2004). Adolescence across place and time: Globalization and the changing pathways to adulthood. In R. M. Lerner & L. Steinberg (Eds.), *Handbook of adolescent psychology.* New York: Wiley.

Larson, R., Richards, M., Moneta, G. , Holmbeck, G., & Duckett, E. (1996). Changes in adolescents' daily interactions with their families from ages 10 to 18: Disengagement and transformation. *Developmental Psychology, 32,* 744–754.

Larzelere, R. E., Schneider, W. N., Larson, D. B., & Pike, P. L. (1996). The effects of discipline responses in delaying toddler misbehavior recurrences. *Child and Family Behavior Therapy, 18,* 35–37.

Lash, T. L., & Aschengrau, A. (1999). Active and passive cigarette smoking and the occurrence of breast cancer. *American Journal of Epidemiology, 149,* 5–12.

Latané, B. (1981). The psychology of social impact. *American Psychologist, 36,* 343–356.

Latané, B., & Nida, S. A. (1981). Ten years of research on group size and helping. *Psychological Bulletin, 89,* 308–324.

Latané, B., Williams, K., & Harkins, S. (1979). Many hands make light the work: The causes and consequences of social loafing. *Journal of Personality and Social Psychology, 37,* 822–832.

Lattal, K. A. (1992). B. F. Skinner and psychology [Introduction to the Special Issue]. *American Psychologist, 27,* 1269–1272.

Lattimore, P., & Caswell, N. (2004). Differential effects of active and passive stress on food intake in restrained and unrestrained eaters. *Appetite, 42,* 167–173.

Latz, S., Wolf, A. W., & Lozoff, B. (1999). Cosleeping in context: Sleep practices and problems in young children in Japan and United States. *Archives of Pediatrics*

& *Adolescent Medicine, 153*, 339–346.

Laughlin, H. (1979). *The ego and its defenses.* New York: Aronson.

Laumann, E. O., Gagnon, J. H., Michael, R. T., & Michaels, S. (1994). *The social organization of sexuality: Sexual practices in the United States.* Chicago: University of Chicago Press.

Laursen, B., Coy, K. C., & Collins, W. A. (1998). Reconsidering changes in parent-child conflict across adolescence: A meta-analysis. *Child Development, 69,* 817–832.

Lavie, P. (1997). Melatonin: Role in gating nocturnal rise in sleep propensity. *Journal of Biological Rhythms, 12,* 657–665.

Lavie, P. (2001). Sleep-wake as a biological rhythm. *Annual Review of Psychology, 52,* 277–303.

Lavine, H., Sweeney, D., & Wagner, S. H. (1999). Depicting women as sex objects in television advertising: Effects on body dissatisfaction. *Personality and Social Psychology Bulletin, 25,* 1049–1058.

Lawless, H. T. (2001). Taste. In E. B. Goldstein (Ed.), *Blackwell handbook of perception.* Malden, MA: Blackwell.

Lazarou, J., Pomeranz, B. H., & Corey, P. N. (1998). Incidence of adverse drug reactions in hospitalized patients: A meta-analysis of prospective studies. *Journal of the American Medical Association, 279,* 1200–1205.

Lazarus, A. A. (1989). Multimodal therapy. In R. J. Corsini & D. Wedding (Eds.), *Current Psychotherapies.* Itasca, IL: F. E. Peacock.

Lazarus, A. A. (1992). Multimodal therapy: Technical eclecticism with minimal integration. In J. C. Norcross & M. R. Goldfried (Eds.), *Handbook of psychotherapy integration.* New York: Basic Books.

Lazarus, A. A. (1995). Different types of eclecticism and integration: Let's be aware of the dangers. *Journal of Psychotherapy Integration, 5,* 27–39.

Lazarus, R. S. (1991). *Emotion and adaptation.* New York: Oxford University Press.

Lazarus, R. S. (1993). Why we should think of stress as a subset of emotion. In L. Goldberger & S. Breznitz (Eds.), *Handbook of stress: Theoretical and clinical aspects* (2nd ed.). New York: Free Press.

Lazarus, R. S. (1995). Vexing research problems inherent in cognitive-mediational theories of emotion—and some solutions. *Psychological Inquiry, 6,* 183–196.

Lazarus, R. S. (1999). *Stress and emotion: A new synthesis.* New York: Springer Publishing Company.

Le Petit, D., & Berthelot, J.-M. (2005). Obesity: A growing issue. Statistics Canada. Retrieved May 9, 2005, from http://www.statcan.ca/english/research/82-168-MIE/168.

Leacock, S. (1939). *Too much college; or, Education eating up life: with kindred essays in education and humour.* New York: Dodd, Mead & Company.

Leahey, T. H. (1992). The mythical revolutions of American psychology. *American Psychologist, 47,* 308–318.

Leavitt, F. (1995). *Drugs and behavior* (3rd ed.). Thousand Oaks, CA: Sage.

Leavitt, F. (2001). Iatrogenic recovered memories: Examining the empirical evidence. *American Journal of Forensic Psychology, 19*(2), 21–32.

LeBoeuf, M. (1980, February). Managing time means managing yourself. *Business Horizons,* 41–46.

Leck, K., & Simpson, J. (1999). Feigning romantic interest: The role of self-monitoring. *Journal of Research in Personality, 33,* 69–91.

Leckman, J. F., Grice, D. E., Boardman, J., Zhang, H., Vitale, A., Bondi, C., Alsobrook, J., Peterson, B. S., Cohen, D. J., Rasmussen, S. A., Goodman, W. K., McDougle, C. J., & Pauls, D. (1997). Symptoms of obsessive-compulsive disorder. *American Journal of Psychiatry, 154,* 911–917.

LeDoux, J. E. (1986). The neurobiology of emotion. In J. E. LeDoux & W. Hirst (Eds.), *Mind and brain: Dialogues in cognitive neuroscience.* Cambridge, England: Cambridge University Press.

LeDoux, J. E. (1993). Emotional networks in the brain. In M. Lewis & J. M. Haviland (Eds.), *Handbook of emotions.* New York: Guilford.

LeDoux, J. E. (1994). Emotion, memory and the brain. *Scientific American, 270,* 50–57.

LeDoux, J. E. (1995). Emotion: Clues from the brain. *Annual Review of Psychology, 46,* 209–235.

LeDoux, J. E. (1996). *The emotional brain.* New York: Simon & Schuster.

LeDoux, J. E. (2000). Emotion circuits in the brain. *Annual Review of Neuroscience, 23,* 155–184.

Lee, I.-M., Hsieh, C., & Paffenbarger, R. S. Jr. (1995). Exercise intensity and longevity in men. *Journal of the American Medical Association, 273,* 1179–1184.

Lee, I.-M., Karon, J. M., Selik, R., Neal, J. J., & Fleming, P. L. (2001). Survival after AIDS diagnosis in adolescents and adults during the treatment era, United States, 1984–1997. *Journal of the American Medical Association, 285,* 1308–1315.

Lee, I.-M., Rexrode, K. M., Cook, N. R., Manson, J. E., & Buring, J. E. (2001). Physical activity and coronary heart disease in women: Is "no pain, no gain" passé? *Journal of the American Medical Association, 285,* 1447–1454.

Lee, P. J., & Brown, N. R. (2003). Delay related changes in personal memories for September 11, 2001. *Applied Cognitive Psychology, 17,* 1007–1015.

Lee, R. M., & Ramirez, M. (2000). The history, current status, and future of multicultural psychotherapy. In I. Cuellar & F. A. Paniagua (Eds.), *Handbook of multicultural mental health: Assessment and treatment of diverse populations.* San Diego: Academic Press.

Lee, R. T., & Ashforth, B. E. (1996). A meta-analytic examination of the correlates of the three dimensions of job burnout. *Journal of Applied Psychology, 81,* 123–133.

Lee, S., & Katzman, M. A. (2002). Cross-cultural perspectives on eating disorders. In C. G. Fairburn & K. D. Brownell (Eds.), *Eating disorders and obesity: A comprehensive handbook.* New York: Guilford.

Lee, Y. T., & Seligman, M. E. P. (1997). Are Americans more optimistic than the Chinese? *Personality and Social Psychology Bulletin, 23,* 32–40.

Leenaars, A. A., De Wilde, E. J., Wenckstern, S., & Kral, M. (2002). Suicide notes of adolescents: A lifespan comparison. *Canadian Journal of Behavioural Science, 33,* 47–57.

Leeper, R. W. (1935). A study of a neglected portion of the field of learning: The development of sensory organization. *Journal of Genetic Psychology, 46,* 41–75.

Lefcourt, H. M. (2001). The humor solution. In C. R. Snyder (Ed.), *Coping with stress: Effective people and processes* (pp. 68–92). New York: Oxford University Press.

Lefcourt, H. M., Davidson, K., Shepherd, R., Phillips, M., Prkachin, K., & Mills, D. (1995). Perspective-taking humor: Accounting for stress moderation. *Journal of Social and Clinical Psychology, 14,* 373–391.

Leff, J. P., & Vaughn, C. E. (1981). The role of maintenance therapy and relatives' expressed emotion in relapse of schizophrenia: A two-year follow-up. *British Journal of Psychiatry, 139,* 102–104.

Leff, J., & Vaughn, C. (1985). *Expressed emotion in families.* New York: Guilford.

Leff, J., Trieman, N., & Gooch, C. (1996). Team for the Assessment of Psychiatric Services (TAPS) Project 33: Prospective follow-up study of long-stay patients discharged from two psychiatric hospitals. *American Journal of Psychiatry, 153,* 1318–1324.

Lehman, D. R., Chiu, C., & Schaller, M. (2004). Psychology and culture. *Annual Review of Psychology, 55,* 689–714.

Lehrer, P. M., & Woolfolk, R. L. (1984). Are stress reduction techniques interchangeable, or do they have specific effects? A review of the comparative empirical literature. In R. L. Woolfolk & P. M. Lehrer (Eds.), *Principles and practice of stress management.* New York: Guilford.

Lehrer, P. M., & Woolfolk, R. L. (1993). Specific effects of stress management techniques. In P. M. Lehrer & R. L. Woolfolk (Eds.), *Principles and practice of stress management* (2nd ed.). New York: Guilford.

Leibovic, K. N. (1990). Vertebrate photoreceptors. In K. N. Leibovic (Ed.), *Science of vision.* New York: Springer-Verlag.

Leighton, J. P., & Sternberg, R. J. (2003). Reasoning and problem solving. In A. F. Healy & R. W. Proctor (Eds.), *Handbook of psychology, Vol. 4: Experimental psychology.* New York: Wiley.

Leiter, M. P., & Maslach, C. (2001). Burnout and health. In A. Baum, T. A. Revenson, & J. E. Singer (Eds.), *Handbook of health psychology* (pp. 415–426). Mahwah, NJ: Erlbaum.

Lemack, G. E., Uzzo, R. G., & Poppas, D. P. (1998). Effects of stress on male reproductive function. In J. R. Hubbard & E. A. Workman (Eds.), *Handbook of stress medicine: An organ system approach.* New York: CRC Press.

LeMagnen, J. (1981). The metabolic basis of dual periodicity of feeding in rats. *Behavioral and Brain Sciences, 4,* 561–607.

Lemery, K. S., Goldsmith, H. H., Klinnert, M. D., & Mrazek, D. A. (1999). Developmental models of infant and childhood temperament. *Developmental Psychology, 35,* 189–204.

Lemme, B. H. (1999). *Development in adulthood.* Boston: Allyn & Bacon.

Lennie, P. (2000). Color vision. In E. R. Kandel, J. H. Schwartz, & T. M. Jessell (Eds.), *Principles of neural science*. New York: McGraw-Hill.

Leo, J. (1987, January). Exploring the traits of twins. *Time*, p. 63.

Lerman, H. (1986). *A mote in Freud's eye: From psychoanalysis to the psychology of women*. New York: Springer.

Lerner, M. J. (1980). *The belief in a just world: A fundamental delusion*. New York: Plenum Press.

Lerner, M. J., & Goldberg, J. H. (1999). When do decent people blame victims? The differing effects of the explicit/rational and implicit/experiential cognitive systems. In S. Chaiken & Y. Trope (Eds.), *Dual-process theories in social psychology*. New York: Guilford.

Lesher, G. W. (1995). Illusory contours: Toward a neurally based perceptual theory. *Psychonomic Bulletin & Review, 2*, 279–321.

Leslie, A. M. (1994). ToMM, ToBy, and agency: Core architecture and domain specificity in cognition and culture. In L. A. Hirschfeld & S. A. Gelman (Eds.), *Mapping the mind: Domain specificity in cognition and culture*. New York: Cambridge University Press.

LeVay, S. (1991). A difference in hypothalamic structure between heterosexual and homosexual men. *Science, 253*, 1034–1037.

LeVay, S. (1993). *The sexual brain*. Cambridge, MA: MIT Press.

LeVay, S. (1996). *Queer science: The use and abuse of research into homosexuality*. Cambridge, MA: MIT Press.

Levenson, J. L., McDaniel, J. S., Moran, M. G., & Stoudemire, A. (1999). Psychological factors affecting medical conditions. In R. E. Hales, S. C. Yudofsky & J. A. Talbott (Eds.), *Textbook of psychiatry* (3rd ed., pp. 635–662). Washington, DC: American Psychiatric Press, Inc.

Levenson, R. W. (1992). Autonomic nervous system differences among emotions. *Psychological Science, 3*, 23–27.

Leventhal, E. A., Hansell, S., Diefenbach, M., Leventhal, H., & Glass, D. C. (1996). Negative affect and self-report of physical symptoms: Two longitudinal studies of older adults. *Health Psychology, 15*, 193–199.

Leventhal, H., & Tomarken, A. J. (1986). Emotion: Today's problems. *Annual Review of Psychology, 37*, 565–610.

Levin, M. E., & Levin, J. R. (1990). Scientific mnemonomies: Methods for maximizing more than

memory. *American Educational Research Journal, 27*(2), 301–321.

Levine, J. M. (1999). Solomon Asch's legacy for group research. *Personality and Social Psychology Review, 3*, 358–364.

Levine, J. M., & Moreland, R. L. (1998). Small groups. In D. T. Gilbert, S. T. Fiske, & G. Lindzey (Eds.), *The handbook of social psychology*. New York: McGraw-Hill.

Levine, M. W. (2001). Principles of neural processing. In E. B. Goldstein (Ed.), *Blackwell handbook of perception*. Malden, MA: Blackwell.

Levine, R., & Norenzayan, A. (1999). The pace of life in 31 countries. *Journal of Cross-Cultural Psychology, 30*, 178–205.

Levine, R., Sata, S., Hashimoto, T., & Verma, J. (1995). Love and marriage in eleven cultures. *Journal of Cross-Cultural Psychology, 26*, 554–571.

Levinoff, E. J., Li, K. Z. H., Murtha, S., & Chertkow, J. (2002). Selective attention impairments in Alzheimer's disease: Evidence for dissociable components. *Neuropsychology, 18*, 580–588.

Levinson, D. F., Mahtani, M. M., Nancarrow, D. J., Brown, D. M., Kruglyak, L., Kirby, A., Hayward, N. K., Crowe, R. R., Andreasen, N. C., Black, D. W., Silverman, J. M., Endicott, J., Sharpe, I., Mohs, R. C., Siever, L. J., Walters, M. K., Lennon, D. P., Jones, H. L., Nurs, B., Nertney, D. A., Daly, M. J., Gladis, M., & Mowry, B. J. (1998). Genome scan of schizophrenia. *American Journal of Psychiatry, 155*, 741–750.

Levinson, D. J., with Darrow, C. M., Klein, E. G., Levinson, M. H., & McKee, B. (1978). *The seasons of a man's life*. New York: Knopf.

Levinthal, C. F. (1999). *Drugs, behavior, and modern society*. Boston: Allyn & Bacon.

Levinthal, C. F. (2002). *Drugs, behavior, and modern society*. Boston: Allyn & Bacon.

Levis, D. J. (1989). The case for a return to a two-factor theory of avoidance: The failure of non-fear interpretations. In S. B. Klein & R. R. Bowrer (Eds.), *Contemporary learning theories: Pavlovian conditioning and the status of traditional learning theory*. Hillsdale NJ: Erlbaum.

Levy, G. D., Taylor, M. G., & Gelman, S. A. (1995). Traditional and evaluative aspects of flexibility in gender roles, social conventions, moral rules, and physical laws. *Child Development, 66*, 515–531.

Levy, J. (1985, May). Right brain, left brain: Fact or fiction. *Psychology Today*, 38–44.

Levy, J., Trevarthen, C., & Sperry, R. W. (1972). Perception of bilateral chimeric figures following hemispheric disconnection. *Brain, 95*, 61–78.

Levy, S. M., Herberman, R. B., Simons, A., Whiteside, T., Lee, J., McDonald, R., & Beadle, M. (1989). Persistently low natural killer cell activity in normal adults: Immunological, hormonal and mood correlates. *Natural Immune Cell Growth Regulation, 8*, 173–186.

Lewandowsky, S., Duncan, M., & Brown, G. D. A. (2004). Time does not cause forgetting in short-term serial recall. *Psychonomic Bulletin & Review, 11*(5), 771–790.

Lewin, K. (1935). *A dynamic theory of personality*. New York: McGraw-Hill.

Lewinsohn, P. M., Joiner, T. E., Jr., & Rohde, P. (2001). Evaluation of cognitive diathesis-stress models in predicting major depressive disorder in adolescents. *Journal of Abnormal Psychology, 110*, 203–215.

Lewis, D. O., Yeager, C. A., Swica, Y., Pincus, J. H., & Lewis, M. (1997). Objective documentation of child abuse and dissociation in 12 murderers with dissociative identity disorder. *American Journal of Psychiatry, 154*, 1703–1710.

Lewis, D. O., Yeager, C. A., Swica, Y., Pincus, J. H., & Lewis, M. (1997). Objective documentation of child abuse and dissociation in 12 murderers with dissociative identity disorder. *American Journal of Psychiatry, 154*, 1703–1710.

Ley, P. (1997). Compliance among patients. In A. Baum, S. Newman, J. Weiman, R. West, & C. McManus (Eds.), *Cambridge handbook of psychology, health, and medicine*. Cambridge, England: Cambridge University Press.

Li, N. P., Bailey, J. M., Kenrick, D. T., & Linsenmeier, J. A. W. (2002). The necessities and luxuries of mate preferences: Testing the trade-offs. *Journal of Personality and Social Psychology, 82*, 947–955.

Libby, P., Ridker, P. M., & Maseri, A. (2002). Inflammation and atherosclerosis. *Circulation, 105*, 1135–1143.

Liberman, R. P., Kopelowicz, A., Ventura, J., & Gutkind, D. (2002). Operational criteria and factors related to recovery from schizophrenia. *International Review of Psychiatry, 14*(4), 256–272.

Library and Archives Canada. (2001). Statement on the introduction of the Official Languages

Bill, October 17, 1968. Retrieved May 11, 2005, from http://www.collectionscanada.ca/primeministers/h4-4066-e.html.

Lichtenstein, S., Fischhoff, B., & Phillips, L. (1982). Calibration of probabilities: The state of the art to 1980. In D. Kahneman, P. Slovic, & A. Tversky (Eds.), *Judgment under uncertainty: Heuristics and biases*. Cambridge, England: Cambridge University Press.

Lickey, M. E., & Gordon, B. (1991). *Medicine and mental illness: The use of drugs in psychiatry*. New York: W. H. Freeman.

Lickliter, R., & Honeycutt, H. (2003). Developmental dynamics: Toward a biologically plausible evolutionary psychology. *Psychological Bulletin, 129*, 819–835.

Liebert, R. M., & Liebert, L. L. (1998). *Liebert & Spiegler's personality strategies and issues*. Pacific Grove: Brooks/Cole.

Liebert, R. M., & Sprafkin, J. (1988). *The early window: Effects of television on children and youth*. Oxford, England: Pergamon Press.

Lilienfeld, S. O., & Lynn, S. J. (2003). Dissociative identity disorder: Multiple personalities, multiple controversies. In S. O. Lilienfeld, S. J. Lynn, & J. M. Lohr (Eds.), *Science and pseudoscience in clinical psychology*. New York: Guilford.

Lilienfeld, S. O., Lynn, S. J., Kirsch, I., Chaves, J. F., Sarbin, T. R., Ganaway, G. K., & Powell, R. A. (1999). Dissociative identity disorder and the sociocognitive model: Recalling the lessons of the past. *Psychological Bulletin, 125*, 507–523.

Lilienfeld, S. O., Wood, J. M., & Garb, H. N. (2000). The scientific status of projective tests. *Psychological Science in the Public Interest, 1*(2), 27–66.

Lin, S. W., & Anthenelli, R. M. (2005). Genetic factors in the risk for substance use disorders. In J. H. Lowinson, P. Ruiz, R. B. Millman, & J. G. Langrod (Eds.), *Substance abuse: A comprehensive textbook*. Philadelphia: Lippincott/Williams & Wilkins.

Lindgren, H. C. (1969). *The psychology of college success: A dynamic approach*. New York: Wiley.

Lindsay, D. S. (1993). Eyewitness suggestibility. *Current Directions in Psychological Science, 2*(3), 86–89.

Lindsay, D. S. (1998). Depolarizing views on recovered memory experiences. In S. J. Lynn & K. M. McConkey (Eds.), *Truth in memory*. New York: Guilford.

Lindsay, D. S., & Johnson, M. K. (1989). The eyewitness suggestibility effects and memory for source. *Memory & Cognition, 17,* 349–358.

Lindsay, D. S., & Poole, D. A. (1995). Remembering childhood sexual abuse in therapy: Psychotherapists' self-reported beliefs, practices, and experiences. *Journal of Psychiatry & Law,* 461–476.

Lindsay, D. S., & Read, J. D. (1994). Psychotherapy and memories of childhood sexual abuse: A cognitive perspective. *Applied Cognitive Psychology, 8,* 281–338.

Lindsay, P. H., & Norman, D. A. (1977). *Human information processing.* New York: Academic Press.

Lindsay, R. C. L., Ross, D. F., Read, J. D., & Toglia, M. (Eds.) (in press). *Handbook of eyewitness psychology: Memory for people,* Lawrence Erlbaum and Associates.

Lindsay, S. D., & Read, J. D. (2001). The recovered memories controversy: Where do we go from here? In G. M. Davies & T. Dalgleish (Eds.), *Recovered memories: Seeking the middle ground.* Chichester, England: Wiley.

Lindsay, S. D., Allen, B. P., Chan, J. C. K., & Dahl, L. C. (2004). Eyewitness suggestibility and source similarity: Intrusions of details from one event into memory reports of another event. *Journal of Memory & Language, 50*(1), 96–111.

Linnet, K. M., Dalsgaard, S., Obel, C., Wisborg, K., Henriksen, T. B., Rodriguez, A., Kotimaa, A., Moilanen, I., Thomsen, P. H., Olsen, J., & Jarvelin, M. (2003). Maternal lifestyle factors in pregnancy risk of attention deficit hyperactivity disorder and associated behaviors: Review of the current evidence. *American Journal of Psychiatry, 160,* 1028–1040.

Lippa, R. A. (1994). *Introduction to social psychology.* Pacific Grove, CA: Brooks/Cole.

Lipsey, M. W., & Wilson, D. B. (1993). The efficacy of psychological, educational, and behavioral treatment: Confirmation from meta-analysis. *American Psychologist, 48,* 1181–1209.

Lipsitt, L. P., & Behl, G. (1990). Taste-mediated differences in the sucking behavior of human newborns. In E. D. Capaldi & T. L. Powley (Eds.), *Taste, experience, and feeding.* Washington, DC: American Psychological Association.

Lisanby, S. H., Maddox, J. H., Prudic, J., Devanand, D. P., & Sackeim, H. A. (2000). The effects of electroconvulsive therapy on

memory of autobiographical and public events. *General Psychiatry, 57,* 581–590.

Litt, I. F., & Vaughan, V. C., III. (1992). Adolescence. In R. E. Behrman (Ed.), *Nelson textbook of pediatrics.* Philadelphia: Saunders.

Liu, S., Siegel, P. Z., Brewer, R. D., Mokdad, A. H., Sleet, D. A., & Serdula, M. (1997). Prevalence of alcohol-impaired driving: Results from a national self-reported survey of health behaviors. *Journal of the American Medical Association, 277,* 122–125.

Livesley, W. J. (2001). Conceptual and taxonomic issues. In W. J. Livesley (Ed.), *Handbook of personality disorders: Theory, research, and treatment.* New York: Guilford.

Livesley, W. J., Jang, K. L., & Vernon, P. A. (2002). The genetic basis of personality structure. In T. Million & M. J. Lerner (Eds.), *The handbook of psychology* (pp. 34–56). New York: Wiley.

Livesley, W. J., Jang, K. L., & Vernon, P. A. (2003). Genetic basis of personality structure. In T. Million & M. J. Lerner (Eds.), *Handbook of psychology, Vol. 5: Personality and social psychology.* New York: Wiley.

Lizarraga, M. L. S., & Ganuza, J. M. G. (2003). Improvement of mental rotation in girls and boys. *Sex Roles, 40,* 277–286.

Lockhart, R. S. (1992). Measurement of memory. In L. R. Squire (Ed.), *Encyclopedia of learning and memory.* New York: Macmillan.

Lockhart, R. S. (2000). Methods of memory research. In E. Tulving & F. I. M. Craik (Eds.), *The Oxford handbook of memory* (pp. 45–58). New York: Oxford University Press.

Lockhart, R. S., & Craik, F. I. (1990). Levels of processing: A retrospective commentary on a framework for memory research. *Canadian Journal of Psychology, 44*(1), 87–112.

Lockhart, R. S., & Craik, F. I. (1990). Levels of processing: A retrospective commentary on a framework for memory research. *Canadian Journal of Psychology, 44*(1), 87–112.

Locurto, C. (1990). The malleability of IQ as judged from adoption studies. *Intelligence, 14,* 275–292.

Locurto, C. (1991). *Sense and nonsense about IQ: The case for uniqueness.* New York: Praeger.

Loehlin, J. C. (1989). Partitioning environmental and genetic contributions to behavioral development. *American Psychologist, 44,* 1285–1292.

Loehlin, J. C. (1992). *Genes and environment in personality development.* Newbury Park, CA: Sage.

Loehlin, J. C. (1994). Behavior genetics. In R. J. Sternberg (Ed.), *Encyclopedia of human intelligence.* New York: Macmillan.

Loehlin, J. C. (2000). Group differences in intelligence. In R. J. Sternberg (Ed.), *Handbook of intelligence* (pp. 176–195). New York: Cambridge University Press.

Loehlin, J. C., Horn, J. M., & Willerman, L. (1997). Heredity, environment, and IQ in the Texas Adoption Project. In R. J. Sternberg & E. L. Grigorenko (Eds.), *Intelligence, heredity, and environment.* New York: Cambridge University Press.

Loewenstein, R. J. (1996). Dissociative amnesia and dissociative fugue. In L. K. Michelson & W. J. Ray (Eds.), *Handbook of dissociation: Theoretical, empirical, and clinical perspectives.* New York: Plenum.

Loftus, E. F. (1979). *Eyewitness testimony.* Cambridge, MA: Harvard University Press.

Loftus, E. F. (1992). When a lie becomes memory's truth: Memory distortion after exposure to misinformation. *Current Directions in Psychological Science, 1,* 121–123.

Loftus, E. F. (1993a). Psychologist in the eyewitness world. *American Psychologist, 48,* 550–552.

Loftus, E. F. (1993b). The reality of repressed memories. *American Psychologist, 48,* 518–537.

Loftus, E. F. (1994). The repressed memory controversy. *American Psychologist, 49,* 443–445.

Loftus, E. F. (1997, September). Creating false memories. *Scientific American,* 71–75.

Loftus, E. F. (1998). Remembering dangerously. In R. A. Baker (Ed.), *Child sexual abuse and false memory syndrome.* Amherst, NY: Prometheus Books.

Loftus, E. F. (1998). Remembering dangerously. In R. A. Baker (Ed.), *Child sexual abuse and false memory syndrome.* Amherst, NY: Prometheus Books.

Loftus, E. F. (2000). Remembering what never happened. In E. Tulving (Ed.), *Memory, consciousness, and the brain: The Tallinn conference* (pp. 106–118). Philadelphia: Psychology Press.

Loftus, E. F. (2003). Make believe memories. *American Psychologist, 58,* 864–873.

Loftus, E. F. (2004). Memories of things unseen. *Current Directions in Psychological Science, 13*(4), 145–147.

Loftus, E. F., & Ketcham, K. (1994). *The myth of repressed memory: False memories and allegations of sexual abuse.* New York: St. Martin's Press.

Loftus, E. F., & Klinger, M. R. (1992). Is the unconscious smart or dumb? *American Psychologist, 47,* 761–765.

Loftus, E. F., & Mazzoni, G. A. L. (1998). Using imagination and personalized suggestion to change people. *Behavior Therapy, 29,* 691–706.

Loftus, E. F., & Palmer, J. C. (1974). Reconstruction of automobile destruction: An example of the interaction between language and memory. *Journal of Verbal Learning and Verbal Behavior, 13,* 585–589.

Loftus, E. F., Garry, M., & Feldman, J. (1998). Forgetting sexual trauma: What does it mean when 38% forget? In R. A. Baker (Ed.), *Child sexual abuse and false memory syndrome.* Amherst, NY: Prometheus Books.

Lohman, D. F. (1989). Human intelligence: An introduction to advances in theory and research. *Review of Educational Research, 59*(4), 333–373.

LoLordo, V. (2001). Learned helplessness and depression. In M. E. Carroll & J. B. Overmier (Eds.), *Animal research and human health: Advancing human welfare through behavioral science* (pp. 63–77). Washington, DC: American Psychological Association.

LoLordo, V. M., & Droungas, A. (1989). Selective associations and adaptive specializations: Taste aversions and phobias. In S. B. Klein & R. R. Mower (Eds.), *Contemporary learning theories: Instrumental conditioning theory and the impact of biological constraints on learning.* Hillsdale, NJ: Erlbaum.

Longman, D. G., & Atkinson, R. H. (2002). *College learning and study skills.* Belmont, CA: Wadsworth.

Longo, L. P. (1998). Anxiety: Neurobiologic underpinnings. *Psychiatric Annals, 28,* 130–138.

Lorberbaum, J. P., Bohning, D. E., Shastri, A., Nahas, Z., & George, M. S. (1998). Functional magnetic resonance imaging (fMRI) for the psychiatrist. *Primary Psychiatry, 5,* 60–71.

Lott, B. (1987). *Women's lives.* Pacific Grove, CA: Brooks/Cole.

Lott, B. (2002). Cognitive and behavioral distancing from the poor. *American Psychologist, 57,* 100–110.

Lott, B., & Maluso, D. (1993). The social learning of gender. In A. E. Beall & R. J. Sternberg (Eds.), *The psychology of gender*. New York: Guilford.

Lovallo, W. R., a'Absi, M., Pincomb, G. A., Everson, S. A., Sung, B. E., Passey, R. B., & Wilson, M. F. (1996). Caffeine and behavioral stress effects on blood pressure in borderline hypertensive caucasian men. *Health Psychology, 15*, 11–17.

Lowe, M. R. (2002). Dietary restraint and overeating. In C. G. Fairburn & K. D. Brownell (Eds.), *Eating disorders and obesity: A comprehensive handbook* (pp. 88–92). New York: Guilford.

Lowinson, J. H., Ruiz, P., Millman, R. B., & Langrod, J. G. (2005). *Substance abuse: A comprehensive textbook*. Philadelphia: Lippincott/Williams & Wilkins.

Lowinson, J. H., Ruiz, P., Millman, R. B., & Langrod, J. G. (Eds.). (1997). *Substance abuse: A comprehensive textbook*. Baltimore: Williams & Wilkins.

Luborsky, L., Diguer, L., Seligman, D. A., Rosenthal, R., Krause, E. D., Johnson, S., Halperin, G., Bishop, M., Berman, J. S., & Schweizer, E. (1999). The researcher's own therapy allegiance: A "wild card" in comparisons of treatment efficacy. *Clinical Psychology: Science & Practice, 6*(1), 95–106.

Luborsky, L., Rosenthal, R., Diguer, L., Andrusyna, T. P., Berman, J. S., Levitt, J. T., Seligman, D. A., & Krause, E. D. (2002). The dodo bird verdict is alive and well—mostly. *Clinical Psychology: Science & Practice, 9*, 2–12.

Luborsky, L., Singer, B., & Luborsky, L. (1975). Comparative studies of psychotherapies: Is it true that everyone has won and all must have prizes? *Archives of General Psychiatry, 32*, 995–1008.

Lucas, A. R., Beard, C. M., O'Fallon, W. M., & Kurland, L. T. (1991). 50-year trends in the incidence of anorexia nervosa in Rochester, Minn.: A population-based study. *American Journal of Psychiatry, 148*, 917–922.

Lucas, R. E., Clark, A. E., Georgellis, Y., & Diener, E. (2004). Unemployment alters the set point for life satisfaction. *Psychological Science, 15*(1), 8–13.

Lucas, R. E., Diener, E., & Suh, E. (1996). Discriminant validity of well-being measures. *Journal of Personality and Social Psychology, 71*, 616–628.

Luchins, A. S. (1942). Mechanization in problem solving. *Psychological Monographs, 54*(6, Whole No. 248).

Lucid Dreaming. Retrieved March 11, 2005, from http://www.crhsc.umontreal.ca/dreams.ld.htm.

Ludwig, A. M. (1994). Mental illness and creative activity in female writers. *American Journal of Psychiatry, 151*, 1650–1656.

Ludwig, A. M. (1995). *The price of greatness: Resolving the creativity and madness controversy*. New York: Guilford.

Ludwig, A. M. (1998). Method and madness in the arts and sciences. *Creativity Research Journal, 11*, 93–101.

Ludwig, D. S., Pereira, M. A., Kroenke, C. H., Hilner, J. E., Van Horn, L., Slattery, M. L., & Jacobs, D. R., Jr. (1999). Dietary fiber, weight gain, and cardiovascular disease risk factors in young adults. *Journal of the American Medical Association, 282*, 1539–1546.

Ludwig, D. S., Pereira, M. A., Kroenke, C. H., Hilner, J. E., Van Horn, L., Slattery, M. L., & Jacobs, D. R., Jr. (1999). Dietary fiber, weight gain, and cardiovascular disease risk factors in young adults. *Journal of the American Medical Association, 282*, 1539–1546.

Luecke-Aleksa, D., Anderson, D. R., Collins, P. A., & Schmitt, K. L. (1995). Gender constancy and television viewing. *Developmental Psychology, 31*, 773–780.

Luengo, M. A., Otero, J. M., Carillo-de-la-Pena, M. T., & Miron, L. (1994). Dimensions of antisocial behaviour in juvenile delinquency: A study of personality variables. *Psychology, Crime & Law, 1*(1), 27–37.

Luft, A. R., Buitrago, M. M., Ringer, T., Schulz, J. B., & Dichgans, J. (2004). Motor skill learning depends on protein synthesis in motor cortex after training. *Journal of Neuroscience, 24*, 6515–6520.

Lugaresi, E., Cirignotta, F., Montagna, P., & Sforza, E. (1994). Snoring: Pathogenic, clinical, and therapeutic aspects. In M. H. Kryger, T. Roth, & W. C. Dement (Eds.), *Principles and practice of sleep medicine* (2nd ed.). Philadelphia: Saunders.

Luh, C. W. (1922). The conditions of retention. *Psychological Monographs, 31*.

Lundberg, U. (2000). Catecholamines. In G. Fink (Ed.), *Encyclopedia of stress* (Vol. 1, pp. 408–413). San Diego: Academic Press.

Lunman, K. (2001). Born fighting, baby Noella weighted in at one pound. *Globe and Mail*, November 10, 2001, pp. A1, A3.

Luntz, B. K., & Widom, C. S. (1994). Antisocial personality disorder in abused and neglected children grown up. *Journal of Psychiatry, 151*, 670–674.

Lupart, J. L. (2004). Unravelling the mysteries of G/LD: Toward the application of cognitive theory to assessment. In T. Newman & R. Sternberg (Eds.), *Students with both gifts and learning disabilities: Identification, assessment and outcomes* (pp. 49–72). Boston, MA: Kluwer.

Lupart, J. L., & Cannon, E. (2003). SCiberMENTOR: Connecting young girls and adult mentors in science. In F. J. Monks & H. Wagner (Eds.), *Development of human potential: Investment into our future. Proceedings of the 8th conference of the European Council For High Ability (ECHA)* (pp. 230–232). Bad Honnef, Germany: K.H. Bock.

Lupart, J. L., & Pyryt, M. C. (1996). Identifying the hidden gifted. *Journal for the Education of the Gifted, 20*, 36–53.

Lutsky, N. (1995). When is "obedience" obedience? Conceptual and historical commentary. *Journal of Social Issues, 51*, 55–65.

Lutz, C. (1987). Goals, events and understanding in Ifaluk emotion theory. In N. Quinn & D. Holland (Eds.), *Cultural models in language and thought*. Cambridge, England: Cambridge University Press.

Lutz, D. J., & Sternberg, R. J. (1999). Cognitive development. In M. H. Bornstein & M. E. Lamb (Eds.), *Developmental psychology an advanced textbook*. Mahwah, NJ: Erlbaum.

Lutz, W. (1989). *Doublespeak*. New York: Harper Perennial.

Lye, D. N., & Biblarz, T. J. (1993). The effects of attitudes toward family life and gender roles on marital satisfaction. *Journal of Family Issues, 14*, 157–188.

Lykken, D. T. (1998). *A tremor in the blood: Uses and abuses of the lie detector*. New York: Plenum Press.

Lykken, D. T., McGue, M., Tellegen, A., & Bouchard, T. J., Jr. (1992). Emergenesis: Genetic traits that may not run in families. *American Psychologist, 47*, 1565–1577.

Lykken, D., & Tellegen, A. (1996). Happiness is a stochastic phenomenon. *Psychological Science, 7*, 186–189.

Lymburner, J. A., & Roesch, R. (1999). The insanity defense: Five years of research (1993–1997). *International Journal of Law and Psychiatry, 22*, 213–240.

Lyn, H., & Savage-Rumbaugh, E. S. (2000). Observational word learning in two bonobos (*Pan paniscus*): Ostensive and nonostensive contexts. *Language & Communication, 20*, 255–273.

Lynn, M. (1992). Scarcity's enhancement of desirability: The role of naive economic theories. *Basic & Applied Social Psychology, 13*, 67–78.

Lynn, S. J., & Nash, M. (1994). Truth in memory: Ramifications for psychotherapy and hypnotherapy. *Journal of Clinical Hypnosis, 36*, 194–208.

Lynn, S. J., & Nash, M. (1994). Truth in memory: Ramifications for psychotherapy and hypnotherapy. *Journal of Clinical Hypnosis, 36*, 194–208.

Lynn, S. J., Kirsch, I., Barabasz, A., Cardena, E., & Patterson, D. (2000). Hypnosis as an empirically supported clinical intervention: The state of the evidence and a look to the future. *International Journal of Clinical & Experimental Hypnosis, 48*, 239–259.

Lynn, S. J., Lock, T. G., Myers, B., & Payne D. G. (1997). Recalling the unrecallable: Should hypnosis be used to recover memories in psychotherapy? *Current Directions in Psychological Science, 6*, 79–83.

Lynn, S. J., Lock, T., Loftus, E. F., Krackow, E., & Lilienfeld, S. O. (2003). The remembrance of things past: Problematic memory recovery techniques in psychotherapy. In S. O. Lilienfeld, S. J. Lynn, & J. M. Lohr (Eds.), *Science and pseudoscience in clinical psychology*. New York: Guilford.

Lynn, S. J., Neuschatz, J., & Fite, R. (2002). Hypnosis and memory: Implications for the courtroom and psychotherapy. In M. L. Eisen (Ed.), *Memory and suggestibility in the forensic interview*. Mahwah, NJ: Erlbaum.

Lytton, H. (1997). Physical punishment is a problem, whether conduct disorder is endogenous or not. *Psychological Inquiry, 8*, 211–214.

Lytton, H., & Romney, D. M. (1991). Parents' differential socialization of boys and girls: A meta-analysis. *Psychological Bulletin, 109*, 267–296.

Lyznicki, J. M., Doege, T. C., Davis, R. M., & Williams, M. A. (1998). Sleepiness, driving, and motor vehicle crashes. *Journal of the American Medical Association, 279*, 1908–1913.

Maas, J. B. (1998). *Power sleep*. New York: Harper Perennial.

Maccoby, E. E. (1998). *The two sexes: Growing up apart, coming together.* Cambridge, MA: Belknap Press.

Maccoby, E. E. (2000). Parenting and its effects on children: On reading and misreading behavior genetics. *Annual Review of Psychology, 51,* 1–27.

MacCoun, R. J. (1998). Biases in the interpretation and use of research results. *Annual Review Psychology, 49,* 259–287.

MacDonald, G., Zanna, M. P., & Holmes, J. G. (2000). An experimental test of the role of alcohol in relationship conflict. *Journal of Experimental Social Psychology, 36,* 182–193.

MacDonald, K. (1998). Evolution, culture, and the five-factor model. *Journal of Cross-Cultural Psychology, 29,* 119–149.

MacDonald, T. K., MacDonald, G., Zanna, M. P., & Fong, G. (2000). Alcohol, sexual arousal, and intentions to use condoms in young men: Applying alcohol myopia theory to risky sexual behavior. *Health Psychology, 19*(3), 290–298.

MacDonald, T., & Martineau, A. M. (2002). Self-esteem, mood, and intentions to use condoms: When does low self-esteem lead to risky health behaviors? *Journal of Experimental Social Psychology, 38,* 299–306.

MacDonald, T., Fong, G. T., Zanna, M. P., & Martineau, A. M. (2000). Alcohol myopia and condom use: Can alcohol intoxication be associated with more prudent behavior? *Journal of Personality and Social Psychology, 78,* 605–619.

MacGregor, J. N., Ormerod, T. C., & Chronicle, E. P. (2001). Information processing and insight: A process model of performance on the nine-dot and related problems. *Journal of Experimental Psychology: Learning, Memory and Cognition, 27,* 176–201.

Machover, K. (1949). *Personality projection in the drawing of the human figure.* Springfield, IL: Charles C Thomas.

Macht, M., & Simons, G. (2000). Emotions and eating in everyday life. *Appetite, 35,* 65–71.

Mack, A. H., Franklin, J. E., Jr., & Frances, R. J. (2003). Substance use disorders. In R. E. Hales & S. C. Yudofsky (Eds.), *Textbook of clinical psychiatry.* Washington, DC: American Psychiatric Publishing.

Mackie, D. M., Worth, L. T., & Asuncion, A. G. (1990). Processing of persuasive in-group messages. *Journal of Personality and Social Psychology, 58,* 812–822.

Maclean, A. W., Davies, D. R. T., & Thiele, K. (2003). The hazards and prevention of driving while sleepy. *Sleep Medicine Reviews, 7,* 507–521.

MacLean, P. D. (1954). Studies on limbic system ("viosceal brain") and their bearing on psychosomatic problems. In E. D. Wittkower & R. A. Cleghorn (Eds.), *Recent developments in psychosomatic medicine.* Philadelphia: Lippincott.

MacLean, P. D. (1993). Cerebral evolution of emotion. In M. Lewis & J. M. Haviland (Eds.), *Handbook of emotions.* New York: Guilford.

MacMillan, H. L., Fleming, J. E., Streiner, D. L., Lin, E., Boyle, M. H., Jamieson, E., Duku, E. K., Walsh, C. A., Wong, M. Y. Y., & Beardslee, W. R. (2001). Childhood abuse and lifetime psychopathology in a community sample. *American Journal of Psychiatry, 158,* 1878–1883.

MacMillan, H. L., Fleming, J. E., Trocme, N., Boyle, M. H., Wong, M., Racine, Y. A., Beardslee, W. R., & Offord, D. R. (1997). Prevalence of child physical and sexual abuse in the community: Results from the Ontario health supplement. *Journal of the American Medical Association, 278,* 131–135.

Macmillan, M. (1991). *Freud evaluated: The completed arc.* Amsterdam: North-Holland.

MacQueen, G., Marshall, J., Perdue, M., Siegel, S., & Bienenstock, J. (1989). Pavlovian conditioning of rat mucosal mast cells to secrete rat mast cell protease II. *Science, 243,* 83–86.

Macrae, C. N., & Bodenhausen, G. V. (2000). Social cognition: Thinking categorically about others. *Annual Review of Psychology, 51,* 93–120.

MacWhinney, B. (1998). Models of the emergence of language. *Annual Review of Psychology, 49,* 199–227.

MacWhinney, B. (1999). The emergence of language from embodiment. In B. MacWhinney (Ed.), *The emergence of language* (pp. 213–256). Mahwah, NJ: Erlbaum.

MacWhinney, B. (2001). Emergentist approaches to language. In J. Bybee & P. Hooper (Eds.), *Frequency and the emergence of linguistic structure.* Amsterdam: John Benjamins Publishing.

MacWhinney, B. (2004). A multiple process solution to the logical problem of language acquisition. *Journal of Child Language, 31,* 883–914.

Maddi, S. R. (1989). *Personality theories: A comparative analysis.* Chicago, IL: Dorsey Press.

Madon, S., Guyll, M., Aboufadel, K., Montiel, E., Smith, A., Palumbo, P., & Jussim, L. (2001). Ethnic and national stereotypes: The Princeton trilogy revisited and revised. *Personality and Social Psychology Bulletin, 27,* 996–1010.

Madsen, K. B. (1968). *Theories of motivation.* Copenhagen: Munksgaard.

Madsen, K. B. (1973). Theories of motivation. In B. B. Wolman (Ed.), *Handbook of general psychology.* Englewood Cliffs, NJ: Prentice-Hall.

Magnusson, D., & Stattin, H. (1998). Person-context interaction theories. In W. Damon (Ed.), *Handbook of child psychology (Vol. 1): Theoretical models of human development.* New York: Wiley.

Maguire, W., Weisstein, N., & Klymenko, V. (1990). From visual structure to perceptual function. In K. N. Leibovic (Ed.), *Science of vision.* New York: Springer-Verlag.

Maher, B. A. (2001). Delusions. In P. B. Sutker & H. E. Adams (Eds.), *Comprehensive handbook of psychopathology* (3rd ed., pp. 309–370). New York: Kluwer Academic/Plenum Publishers.

Mahowald, M. W. (1993). Sleepwalking. In M. A. Carskadon (Ed.), *Encyclopedia of sleep and dreaming.* New York: Macmillan.

Maier, N. R. F. (1931). Reasoning and learning. *Psychological Review, 38,* 332–346.

Main, D. M., & Main, E. K. (1991). Preterm birth. In S. G. Gabbe, J. R. Niebyl, & J. L. Simpson (Eds.), *Obstetrics: Normal and problem pregnancies.* New York: Churchill Livingstone.

Main, T. (1998). How to think about homelessness: Balancing structural and individual causes. *Journal of Social Distress & the Homeless, 7,* 41–54.

Maio, G. R., & Esses, V. M. (2001). The need for affect: Individual differences in the motivation to approach or avoid emotions. *Journal of Personality, 69,* 883–619.

Maj, M., Pirozzi, R., Magliano, L., & Bartoli, L. (1998). Long-term outcome of lithium prophylaxis in bipolar disorder: A 5-year prospective study on 402 patients at a lithium clinic. *American Journal of Psychiatry, 155,* 30–35.

Malamuth, N. M. (1996). Sexually explicit media, gender differences, and evolutionary theory. *Journal of Communication, 46,* 8–31.

Malamuth, N. M., Addison, T., & Koss, M. (2000). Pornography and sexual aggression: Are there reliable effects and can we understand them? *Annual Review of Sex Research, 11,* 26–91.

Maldonado, J. R., & Spiegel, D. (2003). Dissociative disorders. In R. E. Hales & S. C. Yudofsky (Eds.), *Textbook of clinical psychiatry.* Washington, DC: American Psychiatric Publishing.

Maletzky, B. M. (2002). The paraphilias: Research and treatment. In P. E. Nathan & J. M. Gorman (Eds.), *A guide to treatments that work.* London: Oxford University Press.

Malhotra, A. K., & Goldman, D. (1999). Benefits and pitfalls encountered in psychiatric genetic association studies. *Biological Psychiatry, 45,* 541–550.

Malina, R. M. (1990). Physical growth and performance during the transitional years (9–16). In G. R. Adams & T. P. Gullota (Eds.), *From childhood to adolescence: A transitional period?* Newbury Park, CA: Sage.

Malloy, M. H., Kao, T., & Lee, Y. J. (1992). Analyzing the effect of prenatal care on pregnancy outcome: A conditional approach. *American Journal of Public Health, 82,* 448–453.

Maltzman, I. (1994). Why alcoholism is a disease. *Journal of Psychoactive Drugs, 26,* 13–31.

Mandler, G. (1984). *Mind and body.* New York: Norton.

Mandler, G. (1989). Memory: Conscious and unconscious. In P. R. Soloman, G. R. Goethals, C. M. Kelley, & B. R. Stephens (Eds.), *Memory: Interdisciplinary approaches.* New York: Springer-Verlag.

Mandler, G. (1993). Thought, memory, and learning: Effects of emotional stress. In L. Goldberger & S. Breznitz (Eds.), *Handbook of stress: Theoretical and clinical aspects* (2nd ed.). New York: Free Press.

Mangelsdorf, S., Gunnar, M., Kestenbaum, R., Lang, S., & Andreas, D. (1990). Infant proneness-to-distress temperament, maternal personality, and mother-infant attachment: Associations and goodness of fit. *Child Development, 61,* 830–831.

Manson, J. E., Skerrett, P. J., & Willett, W. C. (2002). Epidemiology of health risks associated with obesity. In C. G. Fairburn & K. D. Brownell (Eds.), *Eating disorders and obesity: A comprehensive handbook* (pp. 422–428). New York: Guilford.

Marangell, L. B., Silver, J. M., & Yudofsky, S. C. (1999). Psychopharmocology and electroconvulsive therapy. In R. E. Hales, S. C. Yudofsky, & J. A. Talbott (Eds.), *American Psychiatric Press* textbook of psychiatry. Washington, DC: American Psychiatric Press.

Maratsos, M. (1983). Some current issues in the study of the acquisition of grammar. In J. H. Flavell & E. M. Markman (Eds.), Handbook of child psychology (Vol. 3). New York: Wiley.

Marcelino, A. S., Adam, A. S., Couronne, T., Koester, E. P., & Sieffermann, J. M. (2001). Internal and external determinants of eating initiation in humans. Appetite, 36, 9–14.

Marcenes, W. G., & Sheiham, A. (1992). The relationship between work stress and oral health status. Social Science and Medicine, 35, 1511.

Marcia, J. E. (1966). Development and validation of ego identity status. Journal of Personality and Social Psychology, 3, 551–558.

Marcia, J. E. (1980). Identity in adolescence. In J. Adelson (Ed.), Handbook of adolescent psychology. New York: Wiley.

Marcia, J. E. (1994). The empirical study of ego identity. In H. A. Bosma, T. L. G. Graafsma, H. D. Grotevant, & D. J. de Levita (Eds.), Identity and development: An interdisciplinary approach. Thousand Oaks, CA: Sage.

Marcia, J. E., Waterman, A. S., Matteson, D. R., Archer, S. L., & Orlofsky, J. L. (1993). Ego identity: A handbook for psychosocial research. New York: Springer-Verlag.

Marcus, B. H., Bock, B. C., & Pinto, B. M. (1997). Initiation and maintenance of exercise behavior. In D. S. Gochman (Ed.), Handbook of health behavior research II: Provider determinants. New York: Plenum.

Marcus, G. F. (1996). Why do children say "breaked"? Current Directions in Psychological Science, 5, 81–85.

Marcus-Newhall, A., Pedersen, W. C., Carlson, M., & Miller, N. (2000). Displaced aggression is alive and well: A meta-analytic review. Journal of Personality and Social Psychology, 78, 670–689.

Marder, S. R. (2000). Schizophrenia: Somatic treatment. In B. J. Sadock & V. A. Sadock (Eds.), Kaplan and Sadock's comprehensive textbook of psychiatry (7th ed., Vol. 1, pp. 1199–1209). Philadelphia: Lippincott/Williams & Wilkins.

Marder, S. R., & van Kammen, D. P. (2000). Dopamine receptor antagonists (typical antipsychotics). In B. J. Sadock & V. A. Sadock (Eds.), Kaplan and Sadock's comprehensive textbook of psychiatry (7th ed., Vol. 1, pp. 2356–2376).

Philadelphia: Lippincott/Williams & Wilkins.

Maris, R. W., Berman, A. L., & Silverman, M. M. (2000). Comprehensive textbook of suicidology. New York: Guilford.

Mark, V. (1996). Conflicting communicative behavior in a split-brain patient: Support for dual consciousness. In S. R. Hameroff, A. W. Kaszniak, & A. C. Scott (Eds.), Toward a science of consciousness. The first Tucson discussions and debates. Cambridge, MA: MIT Press.

Markman, E. M., Wasow, J. L., & Hansen, M. B. (2003). Use of the mutual exclusivity assumption by young word learners. Cognitive Psycology, 47, 241–275.

Markowitsch, H. J. (2000). Neuroanatomy of memory. In E. Tulving & F. I. M. Craik (Eds.), The Oxford handbook of memory (pp. 465–484). New York: Oxford University Press.

Markus, H. R., & Kitayama, S. (1991). Culture and the self: Implications for cognition, emotion, and motivation. Psychological Review, 98, 224–253.

Markus, H. R., & Kitayama, S. (1994). The cultural construction of self and emotion: Implications for social behavior. In S. Kitayama & H. R. Markus (Eds.), Emotions and culture: Empirical studies of mutual influence. Washington, DC: American Psychological Association.

Markus, H. R., & Kitayama, S. (1998). The cultural psychology of personality. Journal of Cross-Cultural Psychology, 29, 63–87.

Markus, H. R., Kitayama, S., & Heiman, R. J. (1996). Culture and "basic" psychological principles. In E. T. Higgins, & A. W. Kruglanski (Eds.), Social Psychology: Handbook of basic principles. New York: Guilford.

Marschark, M. (1992). Coding processes: Imagery. In L. R. Squire (Ed.), Encyclopedia of learning and memory. New York: Macmillan.

Marsh, E. J., Meade, M. L., & Roediger, H. L. (2003). Learning facts from fiction. Journal of Memory & Language, 49, 519–536.

Marteau, T. M., & Weinman, J. (2004). Communicating about health threats and treatments. In S. Sutton, A. Baum, & M. Johnston (Ed.), The Sage handbook of health psychology. Thousand Oaks, CA: Sage.

Martin, C. L., & Fabes, R. A. (2001). The stability and consequences of young children's same-sex peer interactions. Developmental Psychology, 37, 431–446.

Martin, C. L., & Ruble, D. (2004). Children's search for gender cues: Cognitive perspectives on gender development. Current Directions in Psychological Science, 13(2), 67–70.

Martin, J. H. (1991). The collective electrical behavior of cortical neurons: The electroencephalogram and the mechanisms of epilepsy. In E. R. Kandel, J. H. Schwartz, & T. M. Jessell (Eds.), Principles of neural science (3rd ed.). New York: Elsevier.

Martin, L. (1986). "Eskimo words for snow": A case study in the genesis and decay of an anthropological example. American Psychologist, 88, 418–423.

Martin, R. (2001). Humor, laughter, and physical health: Methodological issues and research findings. Psychological Bulletin, 127, 504–519.

Martin, R., & Leventhal, H. (2004). Symptom perception and health care-seeking behavior. In J. M. Raczynski & L. C. Leviton (Eds.), Handbook of clinical health psychology, Vol. 2: Disorders of behavior and health. Washington, DC: American Psychological Association.

Martin, R., Puhlik-Doris, P., Larsen, G., Gray, J., & Weir, K. (2003). Individual differences in uses of humor and their relation to psychological well-being: Development of the Humor Styles Questionnaire. Journal of Research in Personality, 37, 48–75.

Martinez, J. L., Jr., Barea-Rodriguez, E. J., & Derrick, B. E. (1998). Long-term potentiation, long-term depression, and learning. In J. L. Martinez, Jr., & R. P. Kesner (Eds.), Neurobiology of learning and memory. San Diego: Academic Press.

Martocchio, J. J., & Baldwin, T. T. (1997). The evolution of strategic organizational training: New objectives and research agenda. In G. R. Ferris (Ed.), Research in personnel and human resources management (Vol. 11, pp. 259–329). Greenwich, CT: JAI Press.

Maslach, C., & Leiter, M. P. (1997). The truth about burnout. San Francisco: Jossey-Bass.

Maslach, C., & Leiter, M. P. (2000). Burnout. In G. Fink (Ed.), Encyclopedia of stress (Vol. 1, pp. 358–362). San Diego: Academic Press.

Maslach, C., & Leiter, M. P. (2005). Stress and burnout: The critical research. In C. L. Cooper (Ed.), Handbook of stress medicine and health. Boca Raton, FL: CRC Press.

Maslow, A. H. (1954). Motivation and personality. New York: Harper & Row.

Maslow, A. H. (1968). Toward a psychology of being. New York: Van Nostrand.

Maslow, A. H. (1970). Motivation and personality. New York: Harper & Row.

Massaro, D. W., & Loftus, G. R. (1996). Sensory and perceptual storage: Data and theory. In E. L. Bjork & R. A. Bjork (Eds.), Memory. San Diego: Academic Press.

Masters, R. D. (1995). Mechanism and function in evolutionary psychology: Emotion, cognitive neuroscience, and personality. Psychological Inquiry, 6, 65–68.

Masters, W. H., & Johnson, V. E. (1966). Human sexual response. Boston: Little, Brown.

Masters, W. H., & Johnson, V. E. (1970). Human sexual inadequacy. Boston: Little, Brown.

Masuda, T., & Nisbett, R. E. (2001). Attending holistically versus analytically: Comparing the context sensitivity of Japanese and Americans. Journal of Personality and Social Psychology, 81, 922–934.

Matsumoto, D. (1994). People: Psychology from a cultural perspective. Pacific Grove, CA: Brooks/Cole.

Matsumoto, D. (2001). Culture and emotion. In D. Matsumoto (Ed.), The handbook of culture and psychology (pp. 171–194). New York: Oxford University Press.

Matsumoto, D. (2003). Cross-cultural research. In S. F. Davis (Ed.), Handbook of research methods in experimental psychology. Malden, MA: Blackwell Publishers.

Matthews, G., Zeidner, M., & Roberts, R. D. (2005). Emotional intelligence: An elusive ability? In O. Wilhelm & R. W. Engle (Eds.), Handbook of understanding and measuring intelligence. Thousand Oaks, CA: Sage.

Matthey, S. (1998). P<.05—But is it clinically significant?: Practical examples for clinicians. Behaviour Change, 15, 140–146.

Mattia, J. I., & Zimmerman, M. (2001). Epidemiology. In W. J. Livesley (Ed.), Handbook of personality disorders: Theory, research, and treatment. New York: Guilford.

Matute, H., & Miller, R. R. (1998). Detecting causal relations. In W. O'Donohue (Ed.), Learning and behavior therapy. Boston, Allyn & Bacon.

Mauro, R., Sato, K., & Tucker, J. (1992). The role of appraisal in human emotions: A cross-cultural study. Journal of Personality and Social Psychology, 62, 301–317.

May, C. P., Hasher, L., & Foong, N. (2005). Implicit memory, age, and time of day. *Psychological Science, 16*, 96–100.

Mayer, J. (1955). Regulation of energy intake and the body weight: The glucostatic theory and the lipostatic hypothesis. *Annals of the New York Academy of Science, 63*, 15–43.

Mayer, J. (1968). *Overweight: Causes and control.* Englewood Cliffs, NJ: Prentice-Hall.

Mayer, J. D., & Salovey, P. (1997). What is emotional intelligence? In P. Salovey & D. Sluyter (Eds.), *Emotional development and emotional intelligence: Educational implications.* New York: Basic Books.

Mayer, J. D., Caruso, D. R., & Salovey, P. (1999). Emotional intelligence meets traditional standards for an intelligence. *Intelligence, 27*, 267–298.

Mayer, R. E. (1995). The search for insight: Grappling with Gestalt psychology's unanswered questions. In R. J. Sternberg, & J. E. Davidson (Eds.), *The nature of insight.* Cambridge, MA: The MIT Press.

Mayes, A. (1992). Brain damage and memory disorders. In M. M. Gruneberg, & P. E. Morris (Eds.), *Aspects of memory, Vol. 1: The practical aspects* (2nd ed., pp. 86-123). Florence, KY: Taylor & Frances/Routledge.

Mays, V. M., & Albee, G. W. (1992). Psychotherapy and ethnic minorities. In D. K. Freedheim (Ed.), *History of psychotherapy: A century of change.* Washington, DC: American Psychological Association.

Mazur, J. E. (1993). Predicting the strength of a conditioned reinforcer: Effects of delay and uncertainty. *Current Directions in Psychological Science, 2*(3), 70–74.

McAdams, D. P. (1992). The five-factor model in personality: A critical appraisal. *Journal of Personality, 60*, 329–361.

McAdams, D. P., & Constantian, C. A. (1983). Intimacy and affiliation motives in daily living: An experience sampling analysis. *Journal of Personality and Social Psychology, 45*, 851–861.

McAdams, D. P., de St. Aubin, E., & Logan, R. (1993). Generativity in young, midlife, and older adults. *Psychology and Aging, 8*, 221–230.

McAllister, W. R., & McAllister, D. E. (1995). Two-factor fear theory: Implications from understanding anxiety-based clinical phenomena. In W. O'Donohue & L. Krasner (Eds.), *Theories of behavior therapy: Exploring behavior change.* Washington, DC: American Psychological Association.

McBride-Chang, C., & Jacklin, C. N. (1993). Early play arousal, sex-typed play, and activity level as precursors to later rough-and-tumble play. *Early Education & Development, 4*, 99–108.

McCabe, S. B., & Toman, P. E. (2000). Stimulus exposure duration in a deployment-of-attention task: Effects on dysphoric, recently dysphoric and nondysphoric individuals. *Cognition and Emotion, 14*, 125–142.

McCabe, S. B., & Toman, P. E. (2002). Stimulus exposure duration in a deployment-of-attention task: Effects on dysphoric, recently dysphoric, and nondysphoric individuals. *Cognition and Emotion, 14*, 125–142.

McCabe, S. B., Gotlib, I. H., & Martin, R. A. (2000). Cognitive vulnerability for depression: Deployment of attention as a function of history of depression and current mood state. *Cognitive Therapy and Research, 24*, 427–444.

McCain, M. N., & Mustard, J. F. (1999). *Reversing the real brain drain: Early Years study—Final report.* Toronto: Canadian Institute for Advanced Research

McCann, C. D. (1990). Interpersonal factors in depression. In C. D. McCann & N. S. Endler (Eds.), *Depression: New directions in theory, research and practice* (pp. 27–47). Toronto: Wall & Emerson.

McCann, C. D., & Hancock, R. D. (1983). Self-monitoring in communicative interactions: Social cognitive consequences of goal-directed message modification. *Journal of Experimental Social Psychology, 19*, 109–121.

McCann, D., & Sato, T. (2000). Personality, cognition and the self. *European Journal of Personality, 14*, 449–462.

McCarley, R. W. (1994). Dreams and the biology of sleep. In M. H. Kryger, T. Roth, & W. C. Dement (Eds.), *Principles and practice of sleep medicine* (2nd ed.). Philadelphia: Saunders.

McCartt, A. T., Ribner, S. A., Pack, A. I., & Hammer, M. C. (1996). The scope and nature of the drowsy driving problem in New York State. *Accident Analysis and Prevention, 28*, 511–517.

McCarty, D., Argeriou, M., Huebner, R. B., & Lubran, B. (1991). Alcoholism, drug abuse, and the homeless. *American Psychologist, 46*, 1139–1148.

McCauley, M. E., Eskes, G., & Moscovitch, M. (1996). The effect of imagery on explicit and implicit tests of memory in young and old people: A double dissociation.

Canadian Journal of Experimental Psychology, 50, 34–41.

McClelland, D. C. (1961). *The achieving society.* Princeton, NJ: Van Nostrand.

McClelland, D. C. (1975). *Power: The inner experience.* New York: Irvington.

McClelland, D. C. (1985). How motives, skills and values determine what people do. *American Psychologist, 40*, 812–825.

McClelland, D. C. (1987). Characteristics of successful entrepreneurs. *Journal of Creative Behavior, 3*, 219–233.

McClelland, D. C. (1993). Intelligence is not the best predictor of job performance. *Current Directions in Psychological Science, 2*(1), 5–6.

McClelland, D. C., & Boyatzis, R. E. (1982). The leadership motive pattern and long-term success in management. *Journal of Applied Psychology, 67*, 737–743.

McClelland, D. C., & Koestner, R. (1992). The achievement motive. In C. P. Smith (Ed.), *Motivation and personality: Handbook of thematic content analysis.* New York: Cambridge University Press.

McClelland, D. C., & Winter, D. G. (1969). *Motivating economic achievement.* New York: Free Press.

McClelland, D. C., Atkinson, J. W., Clark, R. A., & Lowell, E. L. (1953). *The achievement motive.* New York: Appleton-Century-Crofts.

McClelland, J. L. (1992). Parallel-distributed processing models of memory. In L. R. Squire (Ed.), *Encyclopedia of learning and memory.* New York: Macmillan.

McClelland, J. L. (2000). Connectionist models of memory. In E. Tulving & F. I. M. Craik (Eds.), *The Oxford handbook of memory* (pp. 583–596). New York: Oxford University Press.

McClelland, J. L., & Rogers, T. T. (2003). The parallel distributed processing approach to semantic cognition. *Nature Reviews Neuroscience, 4*, 310–322.

McClelland, J. L., & Rumelhart, D. E. (1985). Distributed memory and the representation of general and specific information. *Journal of Experimental Psychology: General, 114*, 159–188.

McCloskey, M. (1992). Special versus ordinary memory mechanisms in the genesis of flashbulb memories. In E. Winograd & U. Neisser (Eds.), *Affect and accuracy in recall: Studies of "flashbulb" memories.* New York: Cambridge University Press.

McClung, N. L. (1935). *Clearing in the west: My own story.* Toronto: Thomas Allen.

McClung, N. L. (1945). *The stream runs fast.* Toronto: Thomas Allen.

McClure, E. B. (2000). A meta-analytic review of sex differences in facial expression processing and their development in infants, children, and adolescents. *Psychological Bulletin, 126*, 424–453.

McConkey, K. M. (1992). The effects of hypnotic procedures on remembering: The experimental findings and their implications for forensic hypnosis. In E. Fromm & M. R. Nash (Eds.), *Contemporary hypnosis research.* New York: Guilford.

McConkey, K. M., Barnier, A. J., & Sheehan, P. W. (1998). Hypnosis and pseudomemory: Understanding the findings and their implications. In S. J. Lynn & K. M. McConkey (Eds.), *Truth in memory.* New York: Guilford.

McConnell, A. R., Leibold, J. M., & Sherman, S. J. (1997). Within-target illusory correlations and the formation of context-dependent attitudes. *Journal of Personality and Social Psychology, 73*, 675–686.

McConnell, J. V. (1962). Memory transfer through cannibalism in planarians. *Journal of Neuropsychiatry, 3*(Suppl. 1), 542–548.

McConnell, J. V., Cutler, R. L., & McNeil, E. B. (1958). Subliminal stimulation: An overview. *American Psychologist, 13*, 229–242.

McCoul, M. D., & Haslam, N. (2001). Predicting high-risk sexual behaviour in heterosexual and homosexual men: The roles of impulsivity and sensation seeking. *Personality & Individual Differences, 31*, 1303–1310.

McCrae, K. (1998). Official bilingualism: from the 1960's to the 1990's. In J. Edwards (Ed.), *Language in Canada* (pp. 61–83). Cambridge, UK: Cambridge University Press.

McCrae, R. R. (1984). Situational determinants of coping responses: Loss, threat and challenge. *Journal of Personality and Social Psychology, 46*, 919–928.

McCrae, R. R. (1996). Social consequences of experimental openness. *Psychological Bulletin, 120*, 323–337.

McCrae, R. R. (2001). Trait psychology and culture: Exploring intercultural comparisons. *Journal of Personality, 69*, 819–846.

McCrae, R. R. (2005). Personality structure. In V. A. Derlega, B. A. Winstead, & W. H. Jones (Eds.), *Personality: Contemporary theory and research.* Belmont, CA: Wadsworth.

McCrae, R. R., & Costa, P. T., Jr. (1984). *Emerging lives, enduring dispositions: Personality in adulthood.* Boston: Little, Brown.

McCrae, R. R., & Costa, P. T., Jr. (1987). Validation of the five-factor model of personality across instruments and observers. *Journal of Personality and Social Psychology, 52,* 81–90.

McCrae, R. R., & Costa, P. T., Jr. (1990). *Personality in adulthood.* New York: Guilford.

McCrae, R. R., & Costa, P. T., Jr. (1997). Personality trait structure as a human universal. *American Psychologist, 52,* 509–516.

McCrae, R. R., & Costa, P. T., Jr. (1999). A five-factor theory of personality. In L. A. Pervin & O. P. John (Eds.), *Handbook of personality: Theory and research.* New York: Guilford.

McCrae, R. R., & Costa, P. T., Jr. (2003). *Personality in adulthood: A five factor theory perspective.* New York: Guilford.

McCrae, R. R., & Costa., P. T., Jr. (1985). Updating Norman's "adequate taxonomy": Intelligence and personality dimensions in natural language and in questionnaires. *Journal of Personality and Social Psychology, 49,* 710–721.

McCrae, R. R., Terracciano, A., & 78 members of the Personality Profiles of Cultures Project. (2005). Universal features of personality traits from the observer's perspective: Data from 50 cultures. *Journal of Personality and Social Psychology, 88,* 547–561.

McCullough, M. E. (2001). Forgiving. In C. R. Snyder (Ed.), *Coping with stress: Effective people and processes* (pp. 93–113). New York: Oxford University Press.

McCullough, M. E., & Witvliet, C. V. (2002). The psychology of forgiveness. In C. R. Synder & S. J. Lopez (Eds.), *Handbook of positive psychology.* New York: Oxford University Press.

McCullough, M. E., Bellah, C. G., Kilpatrick, S. D., & Johnson, J. L. (2001). Vengefulness: Relationships with forgiveness, rumination, well-being, and the Big Five. *Personality and Social Psychology Bulletin, 27,* 601–610.

McDaniel, M. A., & Einstein, G. O. (1986). Bizarre imagery as an effective memory aid: The importance of distinctiveness. *Journal of Experimental Psychology: Learning, Memory & Cognition, 12,* 54–65.

McDaniel, M. A., Einstein, G. O., Stout, A. C., & Morgan, Z. (2003). Aging and maintaining intentions over delays: Do it or lose it. *Psychology and Aging, 18,* 823–835.

McDaniel, M. A., Waddill, P. J., & Shakesby, P. S. (1996). Study strategies, interest, and learning from text: The application of material appropriate processing. In D. J. Herrmann, C. McEvoy, C. Hertzog, P. Hertel, & M. K. Johnson (Eds.), *Basic and applied memory research: Theory in context* (Vol. 1). Mahwah, NJ: Erlbaum.

McDonald, C., & Murphy, K. C. (2003). The new genetics of schizophrenia. *Psychiatric Clinics of North America, 26*(1), 41–63.

McDonald, R. V. & Siegel, S. (2004). Intra-administration associations and withdrawal symptoms: Morphine-elicited morphine withdrawal. *Experimental and Clinical Psychopharmacology, 12,* 3–11.

McDonald, R. V., & Siegel, S. (2004). Intra-administration associations and withdrawal symptoms: Morphine-elicited morphine withdrawal. *Experimental & Clinical Psychopharmacology, 12*(1), 3–11.

McDonald, W. M., Thompson, T. R., McCall W. V., & Zormuski, C. F. (2004). Electroconvulsive therapy. In A. F. Schatzberg & C. B. Nemeroff (Eds.), *Textbook of psychopharmacology.* Washington, DC: American Psychiatric Publishing.

McElroy, S. L., Pope, H. G., & Keck, P. E. (2001). Valproate. In B. J. Sadock & V. A. Sadock (Eds.), *Kaplan and Sadock's comprehensive textbook of psychiatry* (7th ed., Vol. 2). Philadelphia: Lippincott/Williams & Wilkins.

McGaugh, J. L. (1995). Emotional activation, neuromodulatory systems, and memory. In D. L. Schacter, J. T. Coyle, G. D. Fischbach, M. Mesulam, & L. E. Sullivan (Eds.), *Memory distortion.* Cambridge, MA: Harvard University Press.

McGaugh, J. L. (2000). Memory: A century of consolidation. *Science, 287,* 248–251.

McGaugh, J. L. (2002). The amygdala regulates memory consolidation. In L. R. Squire & D. L. Schacter (Eds.), *Neuropsychology of memory.* New York: Guilford.

McGaugh, J. L. (2004). The amygdala modulates the consolidation of memories of emotionally arousing experiences. *Annual Review of Neuroscience, 27,* 1–28.

McGaugh, J. L., & Roozendaal, B. (2002). Role of adrenal stress hormones in forming lasting memories in the brain. *Current Opinions in Neurobiology, 12,* 205–210.

McGaugh, J. L., Roozendaal, B., & Cahill, L. (2000). Modulation of memory storage by stress hormones and the amygdaloid complex. In M. S. Gazzaniga (Ed.), *The new cognitive neurosciences* (2nd ed., pp. 1081–1098). Cambridge, MA: MIT Press.

McGeoch, J. A., & McDonald, W. T. (1931). Meaningful relation and retroactive inhibition. *American Journal of Psychology, 43,* 579–588.

McGill Reporter. (2001). Talking the talk: McGill a force in language studies. *McGill Reporter,* January 25, 2001. Retrieved May 10, 2005, from http://www.mcgill.ca/reporter/33/09/language/.

McGinty, D. (1993). Thermoregulation. In M. A. Carskadon (Ed.), *Encyclopedia of sleep and dreaming.* New York: Macmillan.

McGlashan, T. H., & Fenton, W. S. (1992). The positive-negative distinction in schizophrenia: Review of natural history validators. *Archives of General Psychiatry, 49,* 63–72.

McGlashan, T. H., & Hoffman, R. E. (2000). Schizophrenia: Psychodynamic to neurodynamic theories. In B. J. Sadock & V. A. Sadock (Eds.), *Kaplan and Sadock's comprehensive textbook of psychiatry* (7th ed., Vol. 1, pp. 1159–1168). Philadelphia: Lippincott/Williams & Wilkins.

McGraw, L. A., & Walker, A. J. (2004). The more things change, the more they stay the same. In M. Coleman, & L. J. Ganong (Eds.), *Handbook of contemporary families: Considering the past, contemplating the future.* Thousand Oaks, CA: Sage.

McGrew, J. H., Wright, E. R., Pescosolido, B. A., & McDonel, E. C. (1999). The closing of Central State Hospital: Long-term outcomes for persons with severe mental illness. *Journal of Behavioral Health Services & Research, 26,* 246–261.

McGue, M., Bouchard, T. J., Jr., Iacono, W. G., & Lykken, D. T. (1993). Behavioral genetics of cognitive ability: A life-span perspective. In R. Plomin & G. E. McClearn (Eds.), *Nature, nurture and psychology.* Washington, DC: American Psychological Association.

McGuire, W. J. (1985). Attitudes and attitude change. In G. Lindzey & E. Aronson (Eds.), *Handbook of social psychology* (Vol. 2). New York: Random House.

McHale, S. M., Bartko, W. T., Crouter, A. C., & Perry-Jenkins, M. (1990). Children's housework and psychosocial functioning: The mediating effects of parents' sex-role behaviors and attitudes. *Child Development, 61,* 1413–1426.

McHale, S. M., Crouter, A. C., & Whiteman, S. D. (2003). The family contexts of gender development in childhood and adolescence. *Social Development, 12,* 125–148.

McHugh, P. R. (1995). Dissociative identity disorder as a socially constructed artifact. *Journal of Practical Psychiatry and Behavioral Health, 1,* 158–166.

McKean, K. (1985, June). Decisions, decisions. *Discover,* pp. 22–31.

McKelvie, P., & Low, J. (2002). Listening to Mozart does not improve children's spatial ability: Final curtains for the Mozart effect. *British Journal of Development Psychology, 20,* 241–258.

McKenna, J. J. (1993). Co-sleeping. In M. A. Carskadon (Ed.), *Encyclopedia of sleep and dreaming.* New York: Macmillan.

McKenna, K. Y. A., & Bargh, J. A. (1998). Coming out in the age of the Internet: Identity "demarginalization" through virtual group participation. *Journal of Personality and Social Psychology, 75,* 681–694.

McKenzie, D. (2005). Students feeling stress at exam time cope in several different ways. *Canadian Press,* April 23, 2005. Retrieved June 22, 2005, from http://www.mediresource.sympatico.ca/channel_health_news_detail.asp?channel_id=11&menu_item_id=4&news_id=6518.

McLean, D. E., & Link, B. G. (1994). Unraveling complexity: Strategies to refine concepts, measures, and research designs in the study of life events and mental health. In W. R. Avison & I. H. Gotlib (Eds.), *Stress and mental health: Contemporary issues and prospects for the future.* New York: Plenum.

McLellan, A. T., Lewis, D. C., O'Brien, C. P., & Kleber, H. D. (2000). Drug dependence, a chronic mental illness: Implications for treatment, insurance, and outcome evaluation. *Journal of the American Medical Association, 284,* 1689–1695.

McLoyd, V. C. (1998). Socioeconomic disadvantage and child development. *American Psychologist, 53,* 185–204.

McNally, R. J. (1994). Cognitive bias in panic disorder. *Current Directions in Psychological Science, 3,* 129–132.

McNally, R. J. (1996). *Panic disorder: A critical analysis.* New York: Guilford.

McNally, R. J. (1999). Posttraumatic stress disorder. In T.

Millon, P. H. Blaney, & R. D. Davis (Eds.), *Oxford textbook of psychopathology* (pp. 144–165). New York: Oxford University Press.

McNally, R. J. (2003). *Remembering trauma*. Cambridge, MA: Belknap Press/Harvard University Press.

McNeil, T. F., Cantor-Graae, E., & Ismail, B. (2000). Obstetrics complications and congenital malformation in schizophrenia. *Brain Research Reviews, 31*, 166–178.

McNeill, D. (1970). *The acquisition of language: The study of developmental psycholinguistics*. New York: Harper & Row.

Mebert, C. J. (1991). Dimensions of subjectivity in parents' ratings of infant temperament. *Child Development, 62*, 352–361.

Mechanic, D. (1980). *Mental health and social policy*. Englewood Cliffs, NJ: Prentice-Hall.

Mechanic, D. (1999). Mental health and mental illness. In A. V. Horvitz & T. L. Scheid (Eds.), *A handbook for the study of mental health: Social contexts, theories, and systems*. New York: Cambridge University Press.

Mednick, S. A. (1968). The Remote Associates Test. *Journal of Creative Behavior, 2*(3), 213–214.

Mednick, S. A., Machon, R. A., Huttunen, M. O., & Bonett, D. (1988). Adult schizophrenia following prenatal exposure to an influenza epidemic. *Archives of General Psychiatry, 45*, 189–192.

Mednick, S. A., Watson, J. B., Huttunen, M., Cannon, T. D., Katila, H., Machon, R., Mednick, B., Hollister, M., Parnas, J., Schulsinger, F., Sajaniemi, N., Voldsgaard, P., Pyhala, R., Gutkind, D., & Wang, X. (1998). A two-hit working model of the etiology of schizophrenia. In M. F. Lenzenweger & R. H. Dworkin (Eds.), *Origins and development of schizophrenia: Advances in experimental psychopathology*. Washington DC: American Psychological Association.

Medora, N. P., Larson, J. H., Hortacsu, N., & Dave, P. (2002). Perceived attitudes towards romanticism: A cross-cultural study of American, Asian-Indian, and Turkish young adults. *Journal of Comparative Family Studies, 33*, 155–178.

Meegan, D. V., Glazebrook, C. M., Dhillon, V. P., Tremblay, L., Welsh, T. N., & Elliot, D. (2004). The Müller-Lyer illusion affects the planning and control of manual aiming movements. *Experimental Brain Research, 155*, 37–47.

Meeus, W. (1996). Studies on identity development in adolescence: An overview of research and some new data. *Journal of Youth & Adolescence, 25*, 569–598.

Meeus, W., Iedema, J., Helsen, M., & Vollebergh, W. (1999). Patterns of adolescent identity development: Review of literature and longitudinal analysis. *Developmental Review, 19*, 419–461.

Mega, M. S., Cummings, J. L., Salloway, S., & Malloy, P. (1997). The limbic system: An anatomic, phylogenetic, and clinical perspective. *Journal of Neuropsychiatry & Clinical Neurosciences, 9*, 315–330.

Meichenbaum, D. (1977). *Cognitive-behavior modification*. New York: Plenum Press.

Meichenbaum, D. (2005). 35 years of working with suicidal patients: Lessons learned. *Canadian Psychology, 46*, 64–72.

Meichenbaum, D. A. (1994). *Clinical handbook/practical therapist manual for assessing and treating adults with post-traumatic stress disorder (PTSD)*. Waterloo, ON: Institute Press.

Meilman, P. W. (1979). Cross-sectional age changes in ego identity status during adolescence. *Developmental Psychology, 15*, 230–231.

Meiser, T., & Klauer, K. C. (1999). Working memory and changing-state hypothesis. *Journal of Experimental Psychology: Learning, Memory, & Cognition, 25*, 1272–1299.

Mellers, B. A., Schwartz, A. & Cooke, A. D. J. (1998). Judgment and decision making. *Annual Review of Psychology, 49*, 447–477.

Meltzer, H. Y., Davidson, M., Glassman, A. H., & Vieweg, V. R. (2002). Assessing cardiovascular risks versus clinical benefits of atypical antipsychotic drug treatment. *Journal of Clinical Psychiatry, 63*(9), 25–29.

Meltzoff, A. N., & Gopnik, A. (1989). On linking nonverbal imitation, representation, and language learning in the first two years of life. In G. E. Speidel & K. E. Nelson (Eds.), *The many faces of imitation in language learning*. New York: Springer-Verlag.

Melzack, R. (1975). The McGill pain questionnaire: Major properties and scoring methods. *Pain, 1*, 277–299.

Melzack, R. (2001). Pain and the neuromatrix in the brain. *Journal of Dental Education, 65*, 1378–1382.

Melzack, R., & Katz, J. (2004). The gate control theory: Reaching for the brain. In T. Hadjistavropoulos

& K. D. Craig (Eds.), *Pain: Psychological perspectives* (pp. 13–34). Mahwah, NJ: Lawrence Erlbaum Associates, Publishers.

Melzack, R., & Wall, P. D. (1965). Pain mechanisms: A new theory. *Science, 150*, 971–979.

Melzack, R., & Wall, P. D. (1982). *The challenge of pain*. New York: Basic Books.

Mendelson, W. B. (2000). Hypnotics: Basic mechanisms and pharmacology. In M. H. Kryger, T. Roth & W. C. Dement (Eds.), *Principles and practice of sleep medicine*. Philadelphia: Saunders.

Mendelson, W. B. (2001). Neurotransmitters and sleep. *Journal of Clinical Psychiatry, 62*(suppl 10), 5–8.

Mennella, J. A., & Beauchamp, G. K. (1996). The early development of human flavor preferences. In E. D. Capaldi (Ed.), *Why we eat what we eat: The psychology of eating* (pp. 83–112). Washington, DC: American Psychological Association.

Mentzer, R. L. (1982). Response biases in multiple-choice test item files. *Educational and Psychological Measurement, 42*, 437–448.

Menyuk, P., Liebergott, J. W., & Schultz, M. C. (1995). *Early language development in full-term and premature infants*. Hillsdale, NJ: Erlbaum.

Merikle, P. M., & Daneman, M. (1996). Memory for unconsciously perceived events: Evidence from anesthetized patients. *Conciousness & Cognition: An International Journal, 5*, 525–541.

Merikle, P. M., & Daneman, M. (1998). Psychological investigations of unconscious perception. *Journal of Consciousness Studies, 5*, 5–18.

Mervis, C. B., & Bertrand, J. (1994). Acquisition of the novel name-nameless category principle. *Child Development, 65*, 1646–1662.

Mesquita, B. (2001). Culture and emotion: Different approaches to the question. In T. J. Mayne & G. A. Bonanno (Eds.), *Emotions: Current issues and future directions*. New York: Guilford.

Mesquita, B., & Frijda, N. H. (1992). Cultural variations in emotions: A review. *Psychological Bulletin, 112*, 179–204.

Messerli, F. H., Schmieder, R. E., & Weir, M. R. (1997). Salt: A perpetrator of hypertensive target organ disease? *Archive of Internal Medicine, 157*, 2449–2452.

Metzger, E. D. (1999). Electroconvulsive therapy. In A. M. Nicholi (Ed.), *The Harvard guide to*

psychiatry. Cambridge, MA: Harvard University Press.

Meyer, D. E., & Schvaneveldt, R. W. (1976). Meaning, memory structure, and mental processes. *Science, 192*, 27–33.

Meyer, R. E. (1996). The disease called addiction: Emerging evidence in a 200-year debate. *The Lancet, 347*, 162–166.

Meyer, R. G. (1992). *Practical clinical hypnosis: Techniques and applications*. New York: Lexington Books.

Meyer-Bahlburg, H. F. L., Ehrhardt, A. A., Rosen, L. R., Gruen, R. S., Veridiano, N. P., Vann, F. H., & Neuwalder, H. F. (1995). Prenatal estrogens and the development of homosexual orientation. *Developmental Psychology, 31*, 12–21.

Mezulis, A. H., Abramson, L. Y., Hyde, J. S., & Hankin, B. L. (2004). Is there a universal positivity bias in attributions? A meta-analytic review of individual, developmental and cultural differences in the self-serving attributional bias. *Psychological Bulletin, 130*, 711–747.

Mezzich, J. E., Lewis-Fernandez, R., & Ruiperez, M. A. (2003). The cultural framework of psychiatric disorders. In A. Tasman, J. Kay, & J. A. Lieberman (Eds.), *Psychiatry*. New York: Wiley.

Michaels, S. (1996). The prevelance of homosexuality in the United States. In R. P. Cabaj & T. S. Stein (Eds.), *Textbook of homosexuality and mental health*. Washington, DC: American Psychiatric Press.

Mickelson, K. D., Kessler, R. C., & Shaver, P. R. (1997). Adult attachment in a nationally representative sample. *Journal of Personality and Social Psychology, 73*, 1092–1106.

Mickleburgh, R. (2005). Robinson acknowledges having mental illness. *Globe and Mail*, May 7, 2005, p. A9.

Mignot, E. (2000). Pathophysiology of narcolepsy. In M. H. Kryger, T. Roth, & W. C. Dement (Eds.), *Principles and practice of sleep medicine*. Philadelphia: Saunders.

Mignot, E. (2005). Narcolepsy: Diagnosis and management. In M. H. Kryger, T. Roth, & W. C. Dement (Eds.), *Principles and practice of sleep medicine*. Philadelphia: Elsevier Saunders.

Mikulincer, M., & Shaver, P. R. (2005). Attachment security, compassion, and altruism. *Current Directions in Psychological Science, 14*(1), 34–38.

Milberger, S., Biederman, J., Faraone, S. V., & Jones, J. (1998). Further evidence of an association between maternal smoking during pregnancy and attention-deficit hyperactivity disorder: Findings from a high-risk sample of siblings. *Journal of Clinical Child Psychology, 27,* 352–358.

Milgram, S. (1963). Behavioral study of obedience. *Journal of Abnormal and Social Psychology, 67,* 371–378.

Milgram, S. (1964). Issues in the study of obedience. *American Psychologist, 19,* 848–852.

Milgram, S. (1968). Reply to the critics. *International Journal of Psychiatry, 6,* 294–295.

Milgram, S. (1974). *Obedience to authority.* New York: Harper & Row.

Millburn, M. A., Mather, R., & Conrad, S. D. (2000). The effects of viewing R-rated movie scenes that objectify women on perceptions of date rape. *Sex Roles, 43,* 645–664.

Miller, A. G. (1986). *The obedience experiments: A case study of controversy in social science.* New York: Praeger.

Miller, D. T., & Ross, M. (1975). Self-serving biases in the attribution of causality: Fact or fiction. *Psychological Bulletin, 82,* 213–225.

Miller, G. A. (1956). The magical number seven, plus or minus two: Some limits on our capacity for processing information. *Psychological Review, 63,* 81–97.

Miller, G. A. (2003). The cognitive revolution: A historical perspective. *Trends in Cognitive Sciences, 7*(3), 141–144.

Miller, G. F. (1998). How mate choice shaped human nature: A review of sexual selection and human evolution. In C. Crawford & D. L. Krebs (Eds.), *Handbook of evolutionary psychology: Ideas, issues, and applications.* Mahwah, NJ: Erlbaum.

Miller, I. J., & Reedy, F. E., Jr. (1990). Variations in human taste-bud density and taste intensity perception. *Physiological Behavior, 47,* 1213–1219.

Miller, J. G. (1999). Cultural psychology: Implications for basic psychological theory. *Psychological Science, 10,* 85–91.

Miller, J. G. (2001). Culture and moral development. In D. Matsumoto (Ed.), *The handbook of culture and psychology* (pp. 151–170). New York: Oxford University Press.

Miller, N. E. (1944). Experimental studies of conflict. In J. M. Hunt (Ed.), *Personality and the behavior disorders* (Vol. 1). New York: Ronald.

Miller, N. E. (1951). Learnable drives and rewards. In S. S. Stevens (Ed.), *Handbook of experimental psychology.* New York: Wiley.

Miller, N. E. (1959). Liberalization of basic S-R concepts: Extension to conflict behavior, motivation, and social learning. In S. Koch (Ed.), *Psychology: A study of a science* (Vol. 2). New York: McGraw-Hill.

Miller, R. R., & Grace, R. C. (2003). Conditioning and learning. In A. F. Healy & R. W. Proctor (Eds.), *Handbook of psychology, Vol. 4: Experimental psychology.* New York: Wiley.

Millman, J., Bishop, C. H., & Ebel, R. (1965). An analysis of test-wiseness. *Educational and Psychological Measurement, 25,* 707–726.

Millon, T. (1981). *Disorders of personality: DSM-III, axis II.* New York: Wiley.

Millon, T. (2004). *Masters of the Mind: Exploring the story of mental illness from ancient times to the new millennium.* New York: John Wiley & Sons.

Mills, J. S., Polivy, J., Herman, C. P., & Tiggemann, M. (2002). Effects of exposure to thin media images: Evidence of self-enhancement among restrained eaters. *Personality and Social Psychology Bulletin, 28,* 1687–1699.

Milner, B. (1965). Memory disturbance after bilateral hippocampal lesions. In P. Milner & S. E. Glickman (Eds.), *Cognitive processes and the brain: An enduring problem in psychology* (pp. 97–111). Princeton, NJ: D. Van Nostrand Co., Inc.

Milner, B., Corkin, S., & Teuber, H. (1968). Further analysis of the hippocampal amnesic syndrome: 14-year follow-up study of H. M. *Neuropsychologia, 6,* 215–234.

Milner, P. (2003). A brief history of the Hebbian learning rule. *Canadian Psychology, 44,* 5–9.

Milstone, C. (1997). Sybil minds. *Saturday Night, 112,* 35–42.

Mineka, S., & Hamida, S. (1998). Observational and nonconscious learning. In W. O'Donohue (Ed.), *Learning and behavior therapy.* Boston: Allyn & Bacon.

Minuchin, S., Rosman, B. L., & Baker, L. (1978). *Psychosomatic families: Anorexia nervosa in context.* Cambridge, MA: Harvard University Press.

Miranda, J., Bernal, G., Lau, A., Kohn, L., Hwang, W., & LaFromboise, T. (2005). State of the science on psychosocial interventions for ethnic minorities. *Annual Review of Clinical Psychology, 1,* 113–42.

Mischel, W. (1961). Delay of gratification, need for achievement, and acquiescence in another culture.

Journal of Abnormal and Social Psychology, 62, 543–552.

Mischel, W. (1968). *Personality and assessment.* New York: Wiley.

Mischel, W. (1973). Toward a cognitive social learning conceptualization of personality. *Psychological Review, 80,* 252–283.

Mischel, W. (1984). Convergences and challenges in the search for consistency. *American Psychologist, 39,* 351–364.

Mischel, W., & Shoda, Y. (1999). Integrating dispositions and processing dynamics within a unified theory of personality: The cognitive-affective personality system. In L. A. Pervin & O. P. John (Eds.), *Handbook of personality: Theory and research.* New York: Guilford.

Mishra, R. C. (2001). Cognition across cultures. In D. Matsumoto (Ed.), *The handbook of culture and psychology* (pp. 119–136). New York: Oxford University Press.

Mitchell, B. (2005). Alcohol-related collisions jump dramatically in 2004. *Globe and Mail,* January 25, 2005.

Mitchell, K. J., & Johnson, M. K. (2000). Source monitoring: Attributing mental experiences. In E. Tulving & F. I. M. Craik (Eds.), *The Oxford handbook of memory* (pp. 179–196). New York: Oxford University Press.

Mitka, M. (1999). Slowing decline in AIDS deaths prompts concern. *Journal of the American Medical Association, 282,* 1216–1217.

Mitler, M. M. (1993). Public safety in the workplace. In M. A. Carskadon (Ed.), *Encyclopedia of sleep and dreaming.* New York: Macmillan.

Mitler, M. M., Dement, W. C., & Dinges, D. F. (2000). Sleep medicine, public policy, and public health. In M. H. Kryger, T. Roth, & W. C. Dement (Eds.), *Principles and practice of sleep medicine.* Philadelphia: Saunders.

Moak, D. H., & Anton, R. F. (1999). Alcohol. In B. S. McCrady & E. E. Epstein (Eds.), *Addictions: A comprehensive guidebook.* New York: Oxford University Press.

Modestin, J. (1992). Multiple personality disorder in Switzerland. *American Journal of Psychiatry, 149,* 88–92.

Modestin, J. (1992). Multiple personality disorder in Switzerland. *American Journal of Psychiatry, 149,* 88–92.

Moe, A., & De Beni, R. (2004). Studying passages with the loci method: Are subject-generated more effective than experimenter-

supplied loci pathways? *Journal of Mental Imagery, 28*(3–4), 75–86.

Moffitt, T. E. (2005). The new look of behavioral genetics in developmental psychopathology: Gene-environment interplay in antisocial behaviors. *Psychological Bulletin, 131,* 533–554.

Moghaddam, F. M., Taylor, D. M., & Wright, S. C. (1993). *Social psychology in cross-cultural perspective.* New York: W. H. Freeman.

Mojtabai, R. (2005). Perceived reasons for loss of housing and continued homelessness among homeless persons with mental illness. *Psychiatric Services, 56*(2), 172–178.

Moline, M. L. (1993). Jet lag. In M. A. Carskadon (Ed.), *Encyclopedia of sleep and dreaming.* New York: Macmillan.

Möller, J., Hallqvist, J., Diderichsen, F., Theorell, T., Reuterwall, C., & Ahlbom, A. (1999). Do episodes of anger trigger myocardial infarction? A case-crossover analysis in the Stockholm heart epidemiology program (SHEEP). *Psychosomatic Medicine, 61,* 842–849.

Mollon, J. D. (1989). "Tho' she kneel'd in that place where they grew …" *Journal of Experimental Biology, 146,* 21–38.

Monahan, J. (1997). Major mental disorders and violence to others. In D. M. Stoff, J. Breiling, & J. D. Maser (Eds.), *Handbook of antisocial behavior.* New York: Wiley.

Monahan, J. L., Murphy, S. T., & Zajonc, R. B. (2000). Subliminal mere exposure: Specific, general, and diffuse effects. *Psychological Science, 11,* 462–466.

Mongrain, M., Vettese, L.C., Shuster, B., & Kendal, N. (1998). Perceptual biases, affect, and behavior in the relationships of dependents and self-critics. *Journal of Personality and Social Psychology, 75,* 230–241.

Monroe, S. M., & Hadjiyannakis, K. (2002). The social environment and depression: Focusing on severe life stress. In I. H. Gotlib & C. L. Hammen (Eds.), *Handbook of depression.* New York: Guilford.

Monroe, S. M., & McQuaid, J. R. (1994). Measuring life stress and assessing its impact on mental health. In W. R. Avison & I. H. Gotlib (Eds.), *Stress and mental health: Contemporary issues and prospects for the future.* New York: Plenum.

Montgomery, G. H., DuHamel, K. N., & Redd, W. H. (2000). A meta-analysis of hypnotically induced analgesia: How effective is hypnosis? *International Journal of Clinical & Experimental Hypnosis, 48*, 138–153.

Moore, B. C. J. (2001). Basic auditory processes. In E. B. Goldstein (Ed.), *Blackwell handbook of perception*. Malden, MA: Blackwell.

Moore, K. L., & Persaud, T. V. N. (1998). *Before we are born*. Philadelphia: Saunders.

Moore, K. L., & Persaud, T. V. N. (2003). *Before we are born*. Philadelphia: Saunders.

Moos, R. H., & Schaefer, J. A. (1993). Coping resources and processes: Current concepts and measures. In L. Goldberger & S. Breznitz (Eds.), *Handbook of stress: Theoretical and clinical aspects* (2nd ed.). New York: Free Press.

Moretti, M. M., & Odgers, C. (2002). Aggressive and violent girls: Prevalence, profiles, and contributing factors. In R. Corrado, R. Roesch, S. Hart & J. Gierowski (Eds.), *Multi-problem and violent youth: A foundation for comparative research* (pp. 116–129). Amsterdam, Netherlands Antilles: IOS Press.

Moretti, M. M., Odgers, C., & Jackson, M. (Eds.). (2004). *Girls and aggression: Contributing factors and intervention principles*. New York: Kluwer Academic Press/Plenum Publishers.

Moretti, M. M., Rein, A. S., & Wiebe, V. J. (1998). Relational self-regulation: Gender differences in risk for dysphporia. *Canadian Journal of Behavioural Science, 30*, 243–252.

Moretti, M., & Holland, R. (2003). The journey of adolescence: Transitions in self within the context of attachment relationships. In S. Johnson & V. Whiffen (Eds.), *Attachment processes in couple and family therapy* (pp. 234–257). New York: Guilford Press.

Morey, L. C. (1988). Personality disorders in DSM-III and DSM-III-R: Convergence, coverage, and internal consistency. *American Journal of Psychiatry, 145*, 573–577.

Morgan, C. D., & Murray, H. A. (1935). A method for investigating fantasies: The Thematic Apperception Test. *Archives of Neurology and Psychiatry, 34*, 289–306.

Morgan, H. (1996). An analysis of Gardner's theory of multiple intelligence. *Roeper Review, 18*, 263–269.

Morgan, M. J. (2000). Ecstacy (MDMA): A review of its possible persistent psychological effects. *Psychopharmacology, 152*, 230–248.

Mori, E., Ikeda, M., Hirono, N., Kitagaki, H., Imamura, T., & Shimomura, T. (1999). Amygdalar volume and emotional memory in Alzheimer's disease. *American Journal of Psychiatry, 156*, 216–222.

Moriarity, J. L., Boatman, D., Krauss, G. L., Storm, P. B., & Lenz, F. A. (2001). Human "memories" can be evoked by stimulation of the lateral temporal cortex after ipsilateral medical temporal lobe resection. *Journal of Neurology, Neurosurgery & Psychiatry, 71*, 549–551.

Morin, C. M. (2002). Contributions of cognitive-behavioral approaches to the clinical management of insomnia. *Journal of Clinical Psychiatry, 4*(suppl. 1), 21–26.

Morin, C. M., Colecchi, C., Stone, J., Sood, R., & Brink, D. (1999). Behavioral and pharmacological therapies for late-life insomnia: A randomized controlled trial. *Journal of the American Medical Association, 281*, 991–999.

Morin, C.M., Bastien, C., & Savard, J. (2003). Current status of cognitive-behavior therapy for insomnia: Evidence for treatment effectiveness and feasibility. In M. L. Perlis & K. L. Lichstein (Eds.), *Treating sleep disorders: Principles and practice of behavioral sleep medicine* (pp. 262–285). Hoboken, NJ: John Wiley & Sons.

Morley, J. E. (2001). Male menopause is underdiagnosed and undertreated. *Medical Crossfire, 3*(1), 46–47, 51.

Morokoff, P. J., Quina, K., Harlow, L. L., Whitmire, L., Grimley, D. M., Gibson, P. R., & Burkholder, G. J. (1997). Sexual assertivenes scale (SAS) for women: Development and validation. *Journal of Personality and Social Psychology, 73*, 790–804.

Morris, C. D., Bransford, J. D., & Franks, J. J. (1977). Levels of processing versus transfer appropriate processing. *Journal of Verbal Learning and Verbal Behavior, 16*, 519–533.

Morris, J. S., Frith, C. D., Perrett, D. I., Rowland, D., Young, A. W., Calder, A. J., & Dolan, R. J. (1996). A differential neural response in the human amygdala to fearful and happy facial expressions. *Nature, 383*, 812–815.

Morris, P. E., Jones, S., & Hampson, P. (1978). An imagery mnemonic for the learning of people's names. *British Journal of Psychology, 69*, 335–336.

Mortensen, M. E., Sever, L. E., & Oakley, G. P., Jr. (1991). Teratology and the epidemiology of birth defects. In S. G. Gabbe, J. R. Niebyl, & J. L. Simpson (Eds.), *Obstetrics: Normal and problem pregnancies*. New York: Churchill Livingstone.

Moruzzi, G. (1964). Reticular influences on the EEG. *Electroencephalography and Clinical Neurophysiology, 16*, 2–17.

Moscovici, S. (1976). *Social influence and social change*. London: Academic Press.

Mosher, D., & Maclan, P. (1994). College men and women respond to X-rated videos intended for male or female audiences: Gender and sexual scripts. *Journal of Sex Research, 31*, 99–113.

Moss, P. (1994). Validity. In R. J. Sternberg (Ed.), *Encyclopedia of human intelligence*. New York: Macmillan.

Most, S. B., Simons, D. J., Scholl, B. J., Jimenez, R., Clifford, E., & Chabris, C. F. (2001). How not to be seen: The contribution of similarity and selective ignoring to sustained inattentional blindness. *Psychological Science, 12*(1), 9–17.

Mowrer, O. H. (1947). On the dual nature of learning: A reinterpretation of "conditioning" and "problem-solving." *Harvard Educational Review, 17*, 102–150.

Moynihan, J. A., & Ader, R. (1996). Psychoneuroimmunology: Animal models of disease. *Psychosomatic Medicine, 58*, 546–558.

Mrdjenovic, G., & Levitsky, D. A. (1944). Children eat what they are served: The imprecise regulation of energy intake. *Appetite, 3*, 273–282.

Mroczek, D. K., & Almeida, D. M. (2004). The effect of daily stress, personality, and age on daily negative effect. *Journal of Personality, 72*, 355–378.

Muchinsky, P. M. (2003). *Psychology applied to work* (7th ed.). Belmont, CA: Wadsworth.

Muir, D., & Mitchell, D. E. (1975). Behavioral deficits in cats following early selected visual exposure to contours of a single orientation. *Brain Research, 85*, 459–471.

Mullen, B., & Copper, C. (1994). The relation between group cohesiveness and performance: An integration. *Psychological Bulletin, 115*, 210–227.

Mulligan, N. W. (1998). The role of attention during encoding in implicit and explicit memory. *Journal of Experimental Psychology: Learning, Memory, & Cognition, 24*, 27–47.

Mullin, C. R., & Linz, D. (1995). Desensitization and resensitization to violence against women: Effects of exposure to sexually violent films on judgments of domestic violence victims. *Journal of Personality and Social Psychology, 69*, 449–459.

Munck, A. (2000). Corticosteroids and stress. In G. Fink (Ed.), *Encyclopedia of stress* (Vol. 1, pp. 570–577). San Diego: Academic Press.

Munk-Jorgensen, P. (1999). Has deinstitutionalization gone too far? *European Archives of Psychiatry & Clinical Neuroscience, 249*(3), 136–143.

Murdock, B. (2001). Analysis of the serial position curve. In H. L. Roediger III, J. S. Nairne, I. Neath, & A. M. Surprenant (Eds.), *The nature of remembering: Essays in honor of Robert G. Crowder* (pp. 151–170). Washington, DC: American Psychological Association.

Muris, P. (2002). Relationships between self-efficacy and symptoms of anxiety disorders and depression in a normal adolescent sample. *Personality and Individual Differences, 32*, 337–348.

Murison, R. (2001). Is there a role for psychology in ulcer disease? *Integrative Physiological and Behavioral Science, 36*(1), 75–83.

Murphy, J. M., Tohen, M., & Tsuang, M. T. (1999). Psychiatric epidemiology. In A. M. Nicholi (Ed.), *The Harvard guide to psychiatry*. Cambridge, MA: Harvard University Press.

Murphy, K. R., & Cleveland, J. N. (1995). *Understanding performance appraisal: Social, organizational, and goal-based perspectives*. Thousand Oaks, CA: Sage.

Murray, H. A. (1938). *Explorations in personality*. New York: Oxford University Press.

Murray, H. A. (1943). *Thematic Apperception Test—Manual*. Cambridge, MA: Harvard University Press.

Murray, J. B. (1995). Evidence for acupuncture's analgesic effectiveness and proposals for the physiological mechanisms involved. *Journal of Psychology, 129*, 443–461.

Murray, S. L. (2001). Seeking a sense of conviction: Motivated cognition in close relationships. In G. J. O. Fletcher & M. S. Clark (Eds.), *Blackwell handbook of social psychology: Interpersonal processes*. Malden, MA: Blackwell.

Murray, S. L., & Holmes, J. G. (1999). The (mental) ties that bind: Cognitive structures that predict relationship resilience. *Journal of Personality and Social Psychology, 77*, 1228–1244.

Murray, S. L., Holmes, J. G., & Griffin, D. W. (1996a). The benefits of positive illusions: Idealization and the construction of satisfaction in close relationships. *Journal of*

Personality and Social Psychology, 70, 79–98.

Murray, S. L., Holmes, J. G., & Griffin, D. W. (1996b). The self-fulfilling nature of positive illusions in romantic relationships: Love is not blind, but prescient. *Journal of Personality and Social Psychology, 71,* 1155–1180.

Murray, S. L., Holmes, J. G., Bellavia, G., Griffin, D. W., & Dolderman, D. (2002). Kindred spirits? The benefits of egocentrism in close relationships. *Journal of Personality and Social Psychology, 82,* 563–581.

Murstein, B. I., & Fontaine, P. A. (1993). The public's knowledge about psychologists and other mental health professionals. *American Psychologist, 48,* 839–845.

Myers, C. R. (1982). Psychology at Toronto. In M.J. Wright & C.R. Myers (Eds.), *History of academic psychology in Canada.* Toronto, ON: C. J. Hogrefe, Inc.

Myers, D. G. (1992). *The pursuit of happiness: Who is happy—and why.* New York: Morrow.

Myers, D. G. (1999). Close relationships and quality of life. In D. Kahneman, E. Diener, & N. Schwarz (Eds.), *Well-being: The foundations of hedonic psychology.* New York: Russell Sage Foundation.

Myers, D. G., & Diener, E. (1995). Who is happy? *Psychological Science, 6,* 10–19.

Myers, D. G., & Diener, E. (1997). The pursuit of happiness. *Scientific American Special Issue, 7,* 40–43.

Myers, D. G., & Lamm, H. (1976). The group polarization phenomenon. *Psychological Bulletin, 83,* 602–627.

Myerson, J., Rank, M. R., Raines, F. Q., & Schnitzler, M. A. (1998). Race and general cognitive ability: The myth of diminishing returns to education. *Psychological Science, 9,* 139–142.

Nadel, L., & Jacobs, W. J. (1998). Traumatic memory in special. *Current Directions in Psychological Science, 7 ,* 154–157.

Nader, R., & Smith, C. (2003). A role for stage 2 sleep in memory processing. In Maquet, P., Smith, C., & Stickgold, R. (Eds.), *Sleep and brain plasticity* (pp. 87–98). Oxford, UK: Oxford University Press.

Nahas, Z., George, M. S., Lorberbaum, J. P., Risch, S. C., & Spicer, K. M. (1998). SPECT and PET in neuropsychiatry. *Primary Psychiatry, 5,* 52–59.

Nairne, J. S. (1996). Short-term/working memory. In E. L. Bjork & R. A. Bjork (Eds.), *Memory.* San Diego: Academic Press.

Nairne, J. S. (2001). A functional analysis of primary memory. In H. L. I. Roediger III, J. S. Nairne, I. Neath, & A. M. Surprenant (Eds.), *The nature of remembering: Essays in honor of Robert G. Crowder* (pp. 283–296). Washington, DC: American Psychological Association.

Nairne, J. S. (2002). Remembering over the short-term: The case against the standard model. *Annual Review of Psychology, 53,* 53–81.

Nairne, J. S. (2003). Sensory and working memory. In A. F. Healy & R. W. Proctor (Eds.), *Handbook of psychology, Vol. 4: Experimental psychology.* New York: Wiley.

Nairne, J. S., Neath, I., & Serra, M. (1997). Proactive interference plays a role in the word-length effect. *Psychonomic Bulletin & Review, 4,* 541–545.

Nakajima, S., & Patterson, R. L. (1997). The involvement of dopamine D2 receptors, but not D3 or D4 receptors, in the rewarding effect of brain stimulation in the rat. *Brain Research, 760,* 74–79.

Narrow, W. E., Regier, D. A., Rae, D. S., Manderscheid, R. W., & Locke, B. Z. (1993). Use of services by persons with mental and addictive disorders: Findings from the National Institute of Mental Health Epidemiologic Catchment Area Program. *Archives of General Psychiatry, 50,* 95–107.

Nash, M. R. (2001, July). The truth and hype of hypnosis. *Scientific American, 285,* 36–43.

Nathan, P. E., Stuart, S. P., & Dolan, S. L. (2000). Research on psychotherapy efficacy and effectiveness: Between Scylla and Charybdis? *Psychological Bulletin, 126,* 964–981.

National Defence. (2003). Statistics Canada CF mental health survey: A "Milestone." Retrieved June 27, 2005, from http://www.forces.gc.ca/health/information/op_health/stats_can/engraph/MH_Survey_e.asp.

National Institute on Deafness and Other Communication Disorders. (2002). Neural and behavioral aspects of early language development: Presenter: Laura-Ann Pettito. Retrieved May 10, 2005, from http://www.nidcd.nih.gov/news/meetings/02/earlylanguage/petitto.asp.

Needlman, R. D. (2004). Growth and development. In R. E. Behrman, R. M. Kliegman, & H. B. Jenson (Eds.), *Nelson textbook of pediatrics.* Philadelphia: Saunders.

Neiss, R. (1988). Reconceptualizing arousal: Psychobiological states in motor performance. *Psychological Bulletin, 103,* 345–366.

Neiss, R. (1990). Ending arousal's reign of error: A reply to Anderson. *Psychological Bulletin, 107,* 101–105.

Neisser, U. (1967). *Cognitive psychology.* New York: Appleton-Century-Crofts.

Neisser, U. (1998). Introduction: Rising test scores and what they mean. In U. Neisser (Ed.), *The rising curve: Long-term gains in IQ and related measures.* Washington, DC: American Psychological Association.

Neisser, U., & Harsch, N. (1992). Phantom flashbulbs: False recollections of hearing the news about *Challenger.* In E. Winograd & U. Neisser (Eds.), *Affect and accuracy in recall: Studies of "flashbulb" memories.* New York: Cambridge University Press.

Neisser, U., Boodoo, G., Bouchard, T. J., Jr., Boykin, A. W., Brody, N., Ceci, S. J., Halpern, D. F., Loehlin, J. C., Perloff, R., Sternberg, R. J., & Urbina, S. (1996). Intelligence: Knowns and unknowns. *American Psychologist, 51,* 77–101.

Nelson, R. J., & Chiavegatto, S. (2001). Molecular basis of aggression. *Trends in Neuroscience, 24,* 713–719.

Nemeroff, C. B. (1998). The neurobiology of depression. *Scientific American, June,* 42–49.

Nemes, I. (1992). The relationship between pornography and sex crimes. *Journal of Psychiatry and Law, 20,* 459–481.

Nemeth, C., & Chiles, C. (1988). Modelling courage: The role of dissent in fostering independence. *European Journal of Social Psychology, 18,* 275–280.

Nemiah, J. C. (1985). Somatoform disorders. In H. I. Kaplan & B. J. Sadock (Eds.), *Comprehensive textbook of psychiatry* (4th ed.). Baltimore: Williams & Wilkins.

Nesse, R. M., & Young, E. A. (2000). Evolutionary origins and functions of the stress response. In G. Fink (Ed.), *Encyclopedia of stress* (Vol. 2, pp. 79–83). San Diego: Academic Press.

Nestler, E. J., & Malenka, R. C. (2004). The addicted brain. *Scientific American, 290*(3), 78–85.

Neugebauer, R., Dohrenwend, B. P., & Dohrenwend, B. S. (1980). Formulation of hypotheses about the true prevalence of functional psychiatric disorders among adults in the United States. In B. P. Dohrenwend, B. S. Dohrenwend, M. S. Gould, B. Link, R. Neugebauer, & R. Wunsch-Hitzig (Eds.), *Mental illness in the United States: Epidemiological estimates.* New York: Praeger.

Newberg, A., Alavi, A., Baime, M., Pourdehnad, M., Santanna, J., & D'Aquili, E. (2001). The measurement of regional cerebral blood flow during the complex cognitive task of meditation: A preliminary SPECT study. *Psychiatry Research: Neuroimaging, 106*(2), 113–122.

Newcombe, N., & Huttenlocher, J. (1992). Children's early ability to solve perspective-taking problems. *Developmental Psychology, 28,* 635–643.

Newell, A., & Simon, H. A. (1972). *Human problem solving.* Englewood Cliffs, NJ: Prentice-Hall.

Newell, A., Shaw, J. C., & Simon, H. A. (1958). Elements of a theory of human problem solving. *Psychological Review, 65,* 151–166.

Newman, L. S., Duff, K. J., & Baumeister, R. F. (1997). A new look at defensive projection: Thought suppression, accessibility, and biased person perception. *Journal of Personality and Social Psychology, 72,* 980–1001.

Newsom, C., Favell, J. E., & Rincover, A. (1983). Side effects of punishment. In S. Axelrod & J. Apsche (Eds.), *The effects of punishment on human behavior.* New York: Academic Press.

Niaura, R., Todaro, J. F., Stroud, L., Spiro, A., Ward, K. D., & Weiss, S. (2002). Hostility, the metabolic syndrome, and incident coronary heart disease. *Health Psychology, 21,* 588–593.

Nickerson, R. S. (1998). Confirmation bias: A ubiquitous phenomenon in many guises. *Review of General Psychology, 2,* 175–220.

Nickerson, R. S. (1999). Enhancing creativity. In R. J. Sternberg (Ed.), *Handbook of creativity.* New York: Cambridge University Press.

Nicoladis, E., & Genesee, F. (1997). Language development in preschool bilingual children. *Journal of Speech-Language Pathology & Audiology, 21,* 258–270.

Niebyl, J. R. (1991). Drugs in pregnancy and lactation. In S. G. Gabbe, J. R. Niebyl, & J. L. Simpson (Eds.), *Obstetrics: Normal and problem pregnancies.* New York: Churchill Livingstone.

Niebyl, J. R. (2002). Drugs in pregnancy and lactation. In S. G. Gabbe, J. R. Niebyl, & J. L. Simpson (Eds.), *Obstetrics: Normal and problem pregnancies.* New York: Churchill Livingstone.

Nielsen Media Research. (1998). *Report on television: 1998.* New York: Author.

Nielsen, T. A., & Zadra, A. (2000). Dreaming disorders. In M. H.

Kryger, T. Roth, & W. C. Dement (Eds.), *Principles and practice of sleep medicine.* Philadelphia: Saunders.

Nielsen, T. A., Zadra, A. L., Simard, V., Saucier, S., Stenstrom, P., Smith, C., & Kuiken, D. (2003). The typical dreams of Canadian university students. *Dreaming, 13* (4), 211–235.

Nielsen, T.A. (2000). A review of mentation in REM and NREM sleep: "Covert" REM sleep as a possible reconciliation of two opposing models. *Behavior and Brain Sciences, 23,* 793–1121.

Nikelly, A. G. (1994). Alcoholism: Social as well as psycho-medical problem—The missing "big picture." *Journal of Alcohol & Drug Education, 39,* 1–12.

Nikles, C. D., Brecht, D. L., Klinger, E., & Bursell, A. L. (1998). The effects of current concern- and nonconcern-related waking suggestions on nocturnal dream content. *Journal of Personality and Social Psychology, 75,* 242–255.

Ninan, P. T., & Muntasser, S. (2004). Buspiron and gepirone. In A. F. Schatzberg & C. B. Nemeroff (Eds.), *Textbook of psychopharmacology.* Washington, DC: American Psychiatric Publishing.

Nisbett, R. E. (2003). *The geography of thought: How Asians and Westerners think differently … and why.* New York: Free Press.

Nisbett, R. E. (2005). Heredity, environment, and race differences in IQ: A commentary on Rushton and Jensen. *Psychology, Public Policy, and the Law, 11,* 302–310.

Nisbett, R. E. (Ed.). (1993). *Rules for reasoning.* Hillsdale, NJ: Erlbaum.

Nisbett, R. E., Peng, K., Choi, I., & Norenzayan, A. (2001). Culture and systems of thought: Holistic versus analytic cognition. *Psychological Review, 108,* 291–310.

Nishino, S., Mignot, E., & Dement, W. C. (1995). Sedative-hypnotics. In A. F. Schatzberg & C. B. Nemeroff (Eds.), *American Psychiatric Press textbook of psychopharmacology.* Washington, D.C.: American Psychiatric Press.

Nist, S. L., & Holschuh, J. L. (2000). Comprehension strategies at the college level. In R. F. Flippo & D. C. Caverly (Eds.), *Handbook of college reading and study strategy research.* Mahwah, NJ: Erlbaum.

Nobel Prize. (n.d.). David H. Hubel—Autobiography. Retrieved March 22, 2005, from http://www.nobelprize.org/medicine/laureates/1981/hubel-autob.

Nobel Prize. (n.d.). The Nobel Prize in Physiology or Medicine 2004. Retrieved March 25, 2005, from http://nobelprize.org/medicine/laureates/2004/.

Noddings, N. (1992). Gender and the curriculum. In P. W. Jackson (Ed.), *Handbook of research on curriculum.* New York: Macmillan.

Nolen-Hoeksema, S. (1991). Responses to depression and their effects on the duration of depressive episodes. *Journal of Abnormal Psychology, 100,* 569–582.

Nolen-Hoeksema, S. (2000). The role of rumination in depressive disorders and mixed anxiety/depressive symptoms. *Journal of Abnormal Psychology, 109,* 504–511.

Nolen-Hoeksema, S. (2001). Gender differences in depression. *Current Directions in Psychological Science, 10,* 173–176.

Nolen-Hoeksema, S. (2002). Gender differences in depression. In I. H. Gotlib & C. L. Hammen (Eds.), *Handbook of depression.* New York: Guilford.

Norcross, J. C. (1995). Dispelling the dodo bird verdict and the exclusivity myth in psychotherapy. *Psychotherapy, 32,* 500–504.

Norcross, J. C., & Goldfried, M. R. (Eds.). (1992). *Handbook of psychotherapy integration.* New York: Basic Books.

Norman, R. M. G., & Malla, A. K. (1995). Prodromal symptoms of relapse in schizophrenia: A review. *Schizophrenia Bulletin, 21,* 527–539.

Norris, F. H., with Byrne, C. M., Diaz, E., & Kaniasty, K. (2001). *Risk factors for adverse outcomes in natural and human-caused disasters: A review of the empirical literature.* Retrieved November 21, 2001 from U.S. Department of Veterans Affairs National Center for PTSD Website: http://www.ncptsd.org/facts/disasters/fs_riskfactors.html.

Norton, G. R., Harrison, B., Haunch, J., & Rhodes, L. (1985). Characteristics of people with infrequent panic attacks. *Journal of Abnormal Psychology, 94,* 216–221.

Nourse, C. B., & Butler, K. M. (1998). Perinatal transmission of HIV and diagnosis of HIV infection in infants: A review. *Irish Journal of Medical Science, 167,* 28–32.

Novick, L. R., & Bassok, M. (2005). Problem solving. In K. J. Holyoak & R. G. Morrison (Eds.), *The Cambridge handbook of thinking and reasoning.* New York: Cambridge University Press.

Noyes, R. Jr., Clarkson, C., Crowe, R. R., Yates, W. R. & McChesney, C. M. (1987). A family study of generalized anxiety disorder. *American Journal of Psychiatry, 144*(8), 1019–1024.

Noyes, R., Jr., Watson, D. B., Letuchy, E. M., Longley, S. L., Black, D. W., Carney, C. P., & Doebbeling, B. N. (2005). Relationship between hypochondriacal concerns and personality dimensions and traits in a military population. *Journal of Nervous and Mental Disease, 193*(2), 110–118.

Nucci, L. P. (2002). The development of moral reasoning. In U. Goswami (Eds.), *Blackwell handbook of childhood cognitive development.* Malden, MA: Blackwell Publishing.

Nunes, J. (2002). *Beyond Crazy: Journeys through mental illness.* Toronto: McClelland & Stewart Ltd.

Nurnberger, J. I., & Zimmerman, J. (1970). Applied analysis of human behavior: An alternative to conventional motivational inferences and unconscious determination in therapeutic programming. *Behavior Therapy, 1,* 59–69.

Oakes, M. E., & Slotterback, C. S. (2000). Self-reported measures of appetite in relation to verbal cues about many foods. *Current Psychology: Developmental, Learning, Personality, Social, 19,* 137–142.

Oakes, P. (2001). The root of all evil in intergroup relations? Unearthing the categorization process. In R. Brown & S. L. Gaertner (Eds.), *Blackwell handbook of social psychology: Intergroup processes.* Malden, MA: Blackwell.

O'Brien, B. (1996). Economic evaluation of pharmaceuticals. *Medical Care, 34,* 99–108.

Ochse, R. (1990). *Before the gates of excellence: The determinants of creative genius.* Cambridge, England: Cambridge University Press.

O'Donnell, A., & Dansereau, D. F. (1993). Learning from lectures: Effects of cooperative review. *Journal of Experimental Education, 61,* 116–125.

O'Donohue, W. (1998). Conditioning and third generation behavior therapy. In W. O'Donohue (Ed.), *Learning and behavior therapy.* Boston: Allyn & Bacon.

Office of the Commissioner of Official Languages. (2004). *A look at bilingualism.* Retrieved May 11, 2005, from http://www.ocol-clo.gc.ca/symposium/documents/brochure/brochure_e.htm.

Ogilvie, R. D., Wilkinson, R.T., & Allison, S. (1989). The detection of sleep onset: Behavioral, physiological, and subjective convergence. *Sleep, 12*(5), 458–474.

Ogloff, J. R. P., & Whittemore, K. E. (2001). Fitness to stand trial and criminal responsibility in Canada. In R. A. Schuller & J. R. P. Ogloff (Eds.), *Introduction to psychology and law: Canadian perspectives* (pp. 283–313). Toronto: University of Toronto Press.

Ohayon, M. M., Carskadon, M. A., Guilleminault, C., & Vitiello, M. V. (2004). Meta-analysis of quantitative sleep parameters from childhood to old age in healthy individuals: Developing normative sleep values across the human lifespan. *Sleep: Journal of Sleep & Sleep Disorders Research, 27,* 1255–1273.

Ohman, A., & Wiens, S. (2003). On the automaticity of autonomic responses in emotion: An evolutionary perspective. In R. J. Davidson, K. R. Scherer, & H. H. Goldsmith (Eds.), *Handbook of affective sciences.* New York: Oxford University Press.

Okagaki, L. (1994). Socialization of intelligence. In R. J. Sternberg (Ed.), *Encyclopedia of human intelligence.* New York: Macmillan.

Okami, P., & Shackelford, T. K. (2001). Human sex differences in sexual psychology and behavior. *Annual Review of Sex Research, 12,* 186–241.

Olden, K. W. (1998). Stress and the gastrointestinal tract. In J. R. Hubbard, & E. A. Workman (Eds.), *Handbook of stress medicine: An organ system approach.* New York: CRC Press.

Olds, J. (1956). Pleasure centers in the brain. *Scientific American, 193,* 105–116.

Olds, J., & Milner, P. (1954). Positive reinforcement produced by electrical stimulation of the septal area and other regions of the rat brain. *Journal of Comparative and Physiological Psychology, 47,* 419–427.

Olds, M. E., & Fobes, J. L. (1981). The central basis of motivation: Intracranial self-stimulation studies. *Annual Review of Psychology, 32,* 523–574.

O'Leary, K. D., Kent, R. N., & Kanowitz, J. (1975). Shaping data collection congruent with experimental hypotheses. *Journal of Applied Behavior Analysis, 8,* 43–51.

Olfson, M., Marcus, S. C., & Pincus, H. A. (1999). Trends in office-based psychiatric practice. *American Journal of Psychiatry, 156,* 451–457.

Olfson, M., Shaffer, D., Marcus, S. C., & Greenberg, T. (2003). Relationship between antidepressant medication treatment and suicide in adolescents. *Archives of General Psychiatry, 60,* 978–982.

Olio, K. (1994). Truth in memory. *American Psychologist, 49,* 442–443.

Oliver, M. B., & Hyde, J. S. (1993). Gender differences in sexuality: A meta-analysis. *Psychological Bulletin, 114,* 29–51.

Oller, K., & Pearson, B. Z. (2002). Assessing the effects of bilingualism: D. K. D. Oller & R. E. Eilers (Eds.), *Language and literacy in bilingual children.* Clevedon, UK: Multilingual Matters.

Olson, J. M., & Roese, N. J. (1995). The perceived funniness of humorous stimuli. *Personality and Social Psychology Bulletin, 21,* 908–913.

Olson, J. M., & Stone, J. (2005). The influence of behavior on attitudes. In D. Albarracin, B. T. Johnson, & M. P. Zanna (Eds.), *The handbook of attitudes.* Mahwah, NJ: Erlbaum.

Olson, J. M., & Zanna, M. P. (1993). Attitudes and attitude change. *Annual Review of Psychology, 44,* 117–154.

Olson, J. M., Roese, N. J., & Zanna, M. P. (1996). Expectancies. In E. T. Higgins & A. W. Kruglanski (Eds.), *Social psychology: Handbook of basic principles.* New York: Guilford.

Olson, M. A., & Fazio, R. H. (2001). Implicit attitude formation through classical conditioning. *Psychological Science, 12,* 413–417.

Olson, M. A., & Fazio, R. H. (2002). Implicit acquisition and manifestation of classically conditioned attitudes. *Social Cognition, 20*(2), 89–104.

O'Malley, M. (1999). Taber shooting: Questions will be answered. *CBC News Online.* Retrieved June 19, 2005, from http://www.cbc.ca/news/background/taber/omalley2.html.

Operario, D., & Fiske, S. T. (2001). Stereotypes: Content, structures, processes, and context. In R. Brown & S. L. Gaertner (Eds.), *Blackwell handbook of social psychology: Interpersonal processes.* Malden, MA: Blackwell.

Orbuch, T. L., House, J. S., Mero, R. P., & Webster, P. S. (1996). Marital quality over the life course. *Social Psychology Quarterly, 59,* 162–171.

Organista, P. B., & Miranda, J. (1991). Psychosomatic symptoms in medical outpatients: An investigation of self-handicapping theory. *Health Psychology, 10,* 427–431.

Ormerod, T. C., MacGregor, J. N., & Chronicle, E. P. (2002). Dynamics and constraints in insight problem solving. *Journal of Experimental Psychology: Learning, Memory and Cognition, 28,* 791–799.

Orne, M. T. (1951). The mechanisms of hypnotic age regression: An experimental study. *Journal of Abnormal and Social Psychology, 46,* 213–225.

Orne, M. T., & Dinges, D. F. (1989). Hypnosis. In H. I. Kaplan & B. J. Sadock (Eds.), *Comprehensive textbook of psychiatry* (5th ed., Vol. 2). Baltimore: Williams & Wilkins.

Orne, M. T., & Holland, C. C. (1968). On the ecological validity of laboratory deceptions. *International Journal of Psychiatry, 6,* 282–293.

Ornstein, R. E. (1977). *The psychology of consciousness.* New York: Harcourt Brace Jovanovich.

Ornstein, R. E. (1997). *The right mind: Making sense of the hemispheres.* San Diego: Harcourt.

Ornstein, R. E., & Dewan, T. (1991). *The evolution of consciousness: Of Darwin, Freud, and cranial fire—The origins of the way we think.* New York: Prentice-Hall.

Orth-Gomer, K., Wamala, S. P., Horsten, M., Schenck-Gustafsson, K., Schneiderman, N., & Mittleman, M. A. (2000). Marital stress worsens prognosis in women with coronary heart disease: The Stockholm female coronary risk study. *Journal of the American Medical Association, 284,* 3008–3014.

Ortmann, A., & Hertwig, R. (1997). Is deception acceptable? *American Psychologist, 52,* 746–747.

Oskamp, S. (1991). *Attitudes and opinions.* Englewood Cliffs, NJ: Prentice-Hall.

Oskamp, S., Kaufman, K., & Wolterbeek, L. A. (1996). Gender role portrayals in preschool picture books. *Journal of Social Behavior and Personality, 11,* 27–39.

Osrin, D., & de L. Costello, A. M. (2000). Maternal nutrition and fetal growth: Practical issues in international health. *Seminars in Neonatology, 5,* 209–219.

Ostir, G. V., Peek, M. K., Markides, K. S., & Goodwin, J. S. (2001). The association between emotional well being and future risk of myocardial infarction in older adults. *Primary Psychiatry, 8*(7), 34–38.

Ostrom, T. M., & Sedikides, C. (1992). Outgroup homogeneity effects in natural and minimal groups. *Psychological Bulletin, 112,* 536–552.

Oswald, I., & Adam, K. (1980). The man who had not slept for ten years. *British Medical Journal, 281,* 1684–1685.

Oswald, L. M., Wong, D. F., McCaul, M., Zhou, Y., Kuwabara, H., Choi, L., Brasic, J., & Wand, G. S. (2005). Relationships among ventral striatal dopamine release, cortisol secretion, and subjective responses to amphetamine. *Neuropsychopharmacology, 30,* 821–832.

Ott, P. J., Tarter, R. E., & Ammerman, R. T. (1999). *Sourcebook on substance abuse: Etiology, epidemiology, assessment, and treatment.* Boston: Allyn & Bacon.

Otto, M. W., Pollack, M. H., Jenike, M. A., & Rosenbaum, J. F. (1999). Anxiety disorders and their treatment. In A. M. Nicholi (Ed.), *The Harvard guide to psychiatry* (3rd ed., pp. 220–239). Cambridge, MA: Harvard University Press.

Owen, M. J., & O'Donovan, M. C. (2003). Schizophrenia and genetics. In R. Plomin, J. C. Defries, I. W. Craig & P. McGuffin (Eds.), *Behavioral genetics in the postgenomic era.* Washington, DC: American Psychological Association.

Ozer, D. J., & Reise, S. P. (1994). Personality assessment. *Annual Review of Psychology, 45,* 357–388.

Ozgen, E. (2004). Language, learning, and color perception. *Current Directions in Psychological Science, 13*(3), 95–98.

Pace-Schott, E. F. (2005). The neurobiology of dreaming. In M. H. Kryger, T. Roth, & W. C. Dement (Eds.). *Principles and practice of sleep medicine.* Philadelphia: Elsevier Saunders.

Padgett, D. A., & Sheridan, J. F. (2000). Herpesviruses. In G. Fink (Ed.), *Encyclopedia of stress* (pp. 357–363). San Diego: Academic Press.

Pagel, J. F., Blagrove, M., Levin, R., States, B., Stickgold, B., & White, S. (2001). Definitions of dream: A paradigm for comparing field descriptive specific studies of dream. *Dreaming: Journal of the Association for the Study of Dreams, 11,* 195–202.

Paivio, A. (1969). Mental imagery in associative learning and memory. *Psychological Review, 76,* 241–263.

Paivio, A. (1986). *Mental representations: A dual coding approach.* New York: Oxford University Press.

Paivio, A., Khan, M., & Begg, I. (2000). Concreteness of relational effects on recall of adjective-noun pairs. *Canadian Journal of Experimental Psychology, 54*(3), 149–160.

Paivio, A., Smythe, P. E., & Yuille, J. C. (1968). Imagery versus meaningfulness of nouns in paired-associate learning. *Canadian Journal of Psychology, 22,* 427–441.

Paivio, S. C., Holowaty, K. A. M., & Imogen, E. (2004). The influence of therapist adherence and competence on client reprocessing of child abuse memories. *Psychotherapy: Theory, Research, Practice, Training, 41,* 14–34.

Palladino, J. J., & Carducci, B. J. (1984). Students' knowledge of sleep and dreams. *Teaching of Psychology, 11,* 189–191.

Palmer, S. E. (2003). Visual perception of objects. In A. F. Healy & R. W. Proctor (Eds.), *Handbook of psychology, Vol. 4: Experimental psychology.* New York: Wiley.

Palmere, M., Benton, S. L., Glover, J. A., & Ronning, R. (1983). Elaboration and recall of main ideas in prose. *Journal of Educational Psychology, 75,* 898–907.

Panksepp, J. (1991). Affective neuroscience: A conceptual framework for the neurobiological study of emotions. In K. T. Strongman (Ed.), *International review of studies on emotion.* Chichester, England: Wiley.

Paradis, J., Crago, J., Genesee, F., & Rice, M. (2003). French-English bilingual children with SLI: How do they compare with their monolingual peers? *Journal of Speech, Language and Hearing Research, 46,* 113–127.

Paradiso, S. P., Robinson, R. G., Andreasen, N. C., Downhill, J. E., Davidson, R. J., Kirchner, P. T., Watkins, G. L., Boles Ponto, L. L., & Hichwa, R. D. (1997). Emotional activation of limbic circuitry in elderly normal subjects in a PET study. *American Journal of Psychiatry, 154,* 384–389.

Parent, E. C., & Newman, D. L. (1999). The role of sensation-seeking in alcohol use and risk-taking behavior among college women. *Journal of Alcohol & Drug Education, 44*(2), 12–28.

Paris, J. (1999). *Genetics and psychopathology: Predisposition-stress interactions.* Washington, DC: American Psychiatric Press.

Park, C. L. (1998). Stress-related growth and thriving through coping: The roles of personality and cognitive processes. *Journal of Social Issues, 54,* 267–277.

Park, C. L., & Fenster, J. R. (2004). Stress-related growth: Predictors of occurrence and correlates with psychological adjustment. *Journal of Social and Clinical Psychology, 23,* 195–215.

Park, C. W., Jun, S. Y., & Macinnis, D. J. (2000). Choosing what I want versus rejecting what I do not want: An application of decision framing to product option choice decisions. *Journal of Marketing Research, 37,* 187–202.

Parke, R. D. (2002). Punishment revisited—science, values, and the right question: Comment on Gershoff. *Psychological Bulletin, 128,* 596–601.

Parke, R. D., & Slaby, R. G. (1983). The development of aggression. In E. M. Hetherington (Ed.), *Handbook of child psychology: Socialization, personality, and social development* (Vol. 4). New York: Wiley.

Parker, J. D. A., Summerfeldt, L. J., Hogan, M. J., & Majeski, S. A. (2004). Emotional intelligence and academic success: Examining the transition from high school to university. *Personality and Individual Differences, 36,* 163–172.

Parkinson, B. (1997). Untangling the appraisal-emotion connection. *Personality and Social Psychology Review, 1,* 62–79.

Parrot, A. C. (2000). Human research on MDMA (3,4-Methylenedioxymethamphetamine) neurotoxicity: Cognitive and behavioral indices of change. *Neuropsychobiology, 42*(1), 17–24.

Parrot, A., & Bechhofer, L. (1991). *Acquaintance rape: The hidden crime.* New York: Wiley.

Parry-Jones, B., & Parry-Jones, W. L. (1995). History of bulimia and bulimia nervosa. In K. D. Brownell & C. G. Fairburn (Eds.), *Eating disorders and obesity: A comprehensive handbook.* New York: Guilford.

Partinen, M., & Hublin, C. (2000). Epidemiology of sleep disorders. In M. H. Kryger, T. Roth, & W. C. Dement (Eds.), *Principles and practice of sleep medicine.* Philadelphia: Saunders.

Partinen, M., & Hublin, C. (2005). Epidemiology of sleep disorders. In M. H. Kryger, T. Roth, & W. C. Dement (Eds.), *Principles and practice of sleep medicine.* Philadelphia: Elsevier Saunders.

Pascual-Leone, J. & Smith, J. (1969). The encoding and decoding of symbols by children: A new experimental paradigm and a neo-Piagetian model. *Journal of Experimental Child Psychology, 8,* 328–355.

Pascual-Leone, J. (2000). Reflections on working memory: Are the two models complementary? *Journal of Experimental Child Psychology, 77,* 138–154.

Pashler, H., & Carrier, M. (1996). Stuctures, processes, and the flow of information. In E. L. Bjork & R. A. Bjork (Eds.), *Memory.* San Diego: Academic Press.

Pashler, H., Johnston, J. C., & Ruthruff, E. (2001). Attention and performance. *Annual Review of Psychology, 52,* 629–651.

Patel, J. K., Pinals, D. A., & Breier, A. (2003). Schizophrenia and other psychoses. In A. Tasman, J. Kay, & J. A. Lieberman (Eds.), *Psychiatry.* New York: Wiley.

Pato, M. T., Eisen, J. L., & Phillips, K. A. (2003). Obsessive-compulsive disorder. In A Tasman, J. Kay, & J. A. Lieberman (Eds.), *Psychiatry.* New York: Wiley.

Patrick, H., Nicklas, T. A., Hughes, S. O., & Morales, M. (2005). The benefits of authoritative feeding style: Caregiver feeding styles and children's food consumption patterns. *Appetite, 44,* 243–249.

Patriquin, M. (2005). Quebec farm segregated black workers. *The Globe and Mail,* April 30, 2005, p. A1, A2.

Patterson, D. R. (2004). Treating pain with hypnosis. *Current Directions in Psychological Science, 13*(6), 252–255.

Patterson, D. R., & Jensen, M. P. (2003). Hypnosis and clinical pain. *Psychological Bulletin, 129,* 495–521.

Pauk, W. (1990). *How to study in college.* Boston: Houghton Mifflin.

Paulhus, D. L. (1991). Measurement and control of response bias. In J. P. Robinson, P. Shaver, & L. S. Wrightsman (Eds.), *Measures of personality and social psychological attitudes.* San Diego: Academic Press.

Paulhus, D. L. (2002). Social desirability responding: The evolution of a construct. In H. Braun, D. N. Jackson & D. E. Wiley (Eds.), *The role of constructs in psychological and educational measurement* (pp. 67–88). Hillsdale, NJ: Erlbaum.

Paulhus, D. L., Fridhandler, B., & Hayes, S. (1997). Psychological defense: Contemporary theory and research. In R. Hogan, J. Johnson, & S. Briggs (Eds.), *Handbook of personality psychology.* San Diego: Academic Press.

Paulhus, D. L., Trapnell, P. D., & Chen, D. (1999). Birth order effects on personality and achievement within families. *Psychological Science, 10,* 482–488.

Paulos, J. A. (1995). *A mathematician reads the newspaper.* New York: Doubleday.

Paunonen, S. V. (1998). Hierarchical organization of personality and prediction of behavior. *Journal of Personality and Social Psychology, 74,* 538–556.

Paunonen, S. V. (2003). Big Five factors of personality and replicated predictions of behavior. *Journal of Personality and Social Psychology, 84,* 411–424.

Paunonen, S. V., & Ashton, M. C. (1998). The structured assessment of personality across cultures. *Journal of Cross-Cultural Psychology, 29,* 150–170.

Paunonen, S. V., Ashton, M. C., & Jackson, D. N. (2001). Nonverbal assessment of the Big Five personality factors. *European Journal of Personality, 15,* 3–18.

Paunonen, S. V., Haddock, G., Forsterling, F., & Keinonen, M. (2003). Broad versus narrow personality measures and the prediction of behavior across cultures. *European Journal of Personality, 17,* 413–433.

Pavlov, I. P. (1906). The scientific investigation of psychical faculties or processes in the higher animals. *Science, 24,* 613–619.

Pavlov, I. P. (1927). *Conditioned reflexes* (G. V. Anrep, Trans.). London: Oxford University Press.

Payne, D. G., & Blackwell, J. M. (1998). Truth in memory: Caveat emptor. In S. J. Lynn & K. M. McConkey (Eds.), *Truth in memory.* New York: Guilford.

Payne, D. G., & Wenger, M. J. (1996). Practice effects in memory: Data, theory, and unanswered questions. In D. J. Herrmann, C. McEvoy, C. Hertzog, P. Hertel, & M. K. Johnson (Eds.), *Basic and applied memory research: Practical applications* (Vol. 2). Mahwah, NJ: Erlbaum.

Payne, J. W. (1976). Task complexity and contingent processing in decision making: An information search and protocol analysis. *Organizational Behavior and Human Performance, 16,* 366–387.

Payne, J. W., & Bettman, J. R. (2004). Walking with the scarecrow: The information-processing approach to decision research. In D. J. Koehler & N. Harvey (Ed.), *Blackwell Handbook of judgment and decision making.* Malden, MA: Blackwell Publishing.

Payne, J. W., Bettman, J. R., & Johnson, E. J. (1992). Behavioral decision research: A constructive processing perspective. *Annual Review of Psychology, 43,* 87–131.

Peacock, E. J., & Wong, P. (1990). The stress appraisal measure (SAM): A multidimensional approach to cognitive appraisal. *Stress Medicine, 6,* 227–236.

Pearson, B. Z., Fernandez, S. C., & Oller, D. K. (1993). Lexical development in bilingual infants and toddler: Comparison to monolingual norms. *Language Learning, 43,* 93–120.

Pearson, S. E., & Pollack, R. H. (1997). Female response to sexually explicit films. *Journal of Psychology and Human Sexuality, 9,* 73–88.

Pedersen, N. L., Plomin, R., Nesselroade, J. R., & McClearn, G. E. (1992). A quantitative genetic analysis of cognitive abilities during the second half of the life span. *Psychological Science, 3,* 346–353.

Pedersen, P. (1994). A culture-centered approach to counseling. In W. J. Lonner & R. Malpass (Eds.), *Psychology and culture.* Boston: Allyn & Bacon.

Peele, S. (1989). *Diseasing of America: Addiction treatment out of control.* Lexington, MA: Lexington Books.

Peele, S. (2000). What addiction is and is not: The impact of mistaken notions of addiction. *Addiction Research, 8,* 599–607.

Peirce, R. S., Frone, M. R., Russell, M., & Cooper, M. L. (1996). Financial stress, social support, and alcohol involvement: A longitudinal test of the buffering hypothesis in a general population survey. *Health Psychology, 15,* 38–47.

Peladeau, N., Forget, J., & Gagne, F. (2003). Effect of paced and unpaced practice on skill application and retention: How much is enough? *American Educational Research Journal, 40,* 769–801.

Penfield, W. W., & Jasper, H. (1954). *Epilepsy and the functional anatomy of the Human Brain.* Boston, MA: Little, Brown and Company.

Penfield, W., & Perot, P. (1963). The brain's record of auditory and visual experience. *Brain, 86,* 595–696.

Penfield. W. (1977). *No man alone: A neurosurgeon's life.* Boston, MA: Little, Brown and Company.

Pennebaker, J. W., Colder, M., & Sharp, L. K. (1990). Accelerating the coping process. *Journal of Personality and Social Psychology, 58,* 528–537.

Pennisi, E. (2001). The human genome. *Science, 291,* 1177–1180.

Peplau, L. A. (2003). Human sexuality: How do men and women differ? *Current Directions in Psychological Science, 12*(2), 37–40.

Peplau, L. A., Fingerhut, A., & Beals, K. P. (2004). Sexuality in the relationships of lesbians and gay men. In J. H. Harvey, A. Wenzel, & S. Sprecher (Eds.), *The handbook of sexuality in close relationships.* Mahwah, NJ: Erlbaum.

Pepler, D., & Craig, W. (1995). A peek behind the fence: Naturalistic observations of aggressive children with remote audiovisual recording. *Developmental Psychology, 31,* 548–553.

Pepler, D., Craig, W., Zeigler, S., & Charach, A. (1993). A school-based antibullying intervention: Preliminary evaluation. In D. Tatum (Ed.), *Understanding and managing bullying* (pp. 70–96). New York: Heinemann Books.

Pepperberg, I. M. (1990). Cognition in an African gray parrot (*Psittacus erithacus*): Further evidence for comprehension of categories and labels. *Journal of Comparative Psychology, 104,* 41–52.

Pepperberg, I. M. (1993). Cognition and communication in an African Grey parrot (*Psittacus erithacus*): Studies on a nonhuman, nonprimate, nonmammalian subject. In H. L. Roitblat, L. H. Herman, & P. E. Nachtigall (Eds.), *Language and communication: Comparative perspectives*. Hillsdale, NJ: Erlbaum.

Pepperberg, I. M. (2002). Cognitive and communicative abilities of grey parrots. *Current Directions in Psychological Science, 11*(3), 83–87.

Peretz, I., & Zatorre, R. J. (2005). Brain organization for music processing. *Annual Review of Psychology, 56,* 89–114.

Perlman, M. D., & Kaufman, A. S. (1990). Assessment of child intelligence. In G. Goldstein & M. Hersen (Eds.), *Handbook of psychological assessment*. New York: Pergamon Press.

Perone, M., Galizio, M., & Baron, A. (1988). The relevance of animal-based principles in the laboratory study of human operant conditioning. In G. Davey & C. Cullen (Eds.), *Human operant conditioning and behavior modification*. New York: Wiley.

Perreault, S., & Bourhis, R. Y. (1999). Ethnocentrism, social identification, and discrimination. *Personality and Social Psychology Bulletin, 25,* 92–103.

Perry, C., Nadon, R., & Button, J. (1992). The measurement of hypnotic ability. In E. Fromm & M. R. Nash (Eds.), *Contemporary hypnosis research*. New York: Guilford.

Perry, D. G., Kusel, S. J., & Perry, L. C. (1988). Victims of peer aggression. *Developmental Psychology, 24,* 807–814.

Perry, W., & Braff, D. L. (1994). Information-processing deficits and thought disorder in schizophrenia. *American Journal of Psychiatry, 151,* 363–367.

Person, E. S. (1990). The influence of values in psychoanalysis: The case of female psychology. In C. Zanardi (Ed.), *Essential papers in psychoanalysis*. New York: New York University Press.

Pert, C. B., & Snyder, S. H. (1973). Opiate receptor: Demonstration in the nervous tissue. *Science, 179,* 1011–1014.

Perugini, E. M., Kirsch, I., Allen, S. T., Coldwell, E., Meredith, J. M., Montgomery, G. H., & Sheehan, J. (1998). Surreptitious observation of response to hypnotically suggested hallucinations: A test of the compliance hypothesis. *International Journal of Clinical & Experimental Hypnosis, 46,* 191–203.

Pervin, L. A. (1994). Personality stability, personality change, and the question of process. In T. F. Heatherton & J. L. Weinberger (Eds.), *Can personality change?* Washington, DC: American Psychological Association.

Peterhans, E., & Von Der Heydt, R. (1991). Elements of form perception in monkey prestriate cortex. In A. Gorea, Y. Fregnac, Z. Kapoula, & J. Findlay (Eds.), *Representations of vision—Trends and tacit assumptions in vision research*. Cambridge, MA: Cambridge University Press.

Petersen, A. C., Compas, B. E., Brooks-Gunn, J., Stemmler, M., Ey, S., & Grant, K. E. (1993). Depression in adolescence. *American Psychologist, 48,* 155–168.

Peterson, C., & Bossio, L. M. (2001). Optimism and physical well-being. In E. C. Chang (Ed.), *Optimism and pessimism: Implications for theory, research, and practice* (pp. 127–146). Washington, DC: American Psychological Association.

Peterson, C., Seligman, M. E. P., & Vaillant, G. E. (1988). Pessimistic explanatory style is a risk factor for physical illness: A thirty-five-year longitudinal study. *Journal of Personality and Social Psychology, 55,* 23–27.

Peterson, C., Seligman, M. E. P., Yurko, K. H., Martin, L. R., & Friedman, H. S. (1998). Catastrophizing and untimely death. *Psychological Science, 9,* 127–130.

Peterson, L. R., & Peterson, M. J. (1959). Short-term retention of individual verbal items. *Journal of Experimental Psychology, 58,* 193–198.

Petitto, L. A. & Marentette, P. (1991). Babbling in the manual mode: Evidence for the ontogeny of language. *Science, 251,* 1483–1496.

Petitto, L. A. (1994). Are signed languages "real" languages? Evidence from American Sign Language and Langue des Signes Québécoise. *Signpost (International Journal of the Sign Linguistics Association), 7*(3), 1–10.

Petitto, L. A., & Kovelman, I. (2003). The bilingual paradox: How signing-speaking bilingual children help us to resolve it and teach us about the brain's mechanisms underlying all language acquisition. *Learning Languages, 8,* 5–18.

Petitto, L. A., Holowka, S., Sergio, L. E., Levy, B., & Ostry, D. J. (2004). Baby hands that move to the rhythm of language: Hearing babies acquiring sign languages babble silently on the hands. *Cognition, 93,* 43–73.

Petitto, L. A., Katerelos, M., Levy, B. G., Gauna, K., Tetreault, K., & Ferraro, V. (2001). Bilingual signed and spoken language acquisition from birth: Implications for the mechanisms underlying early bilingual language acquisition. *Journal of Child Language, 28,* 453–496.

Petitto, L. A., Zatorre, R. J., Gauna, K., Nikelski, E. J., Dostie, D., & Evans, A. C. (2000). Speech-like cerebral activity in profoundly deaf people processing signed languages: Implications for the neural basis of human language. *Proceedings of the National Academy of Science USA, 97,* 13961–13966.

Petrie, K. J., & Pennebaker, J. W. (2004). Health-related cognitions. In S. Sutton, A. Baum, & M. Johnston (Eds.), *The Sage handbook of health psychology*. Thousand Oaks, CA: Sage.

Petrie, K. J., Booth, R. J., & Pennebaker, J. W. (1998). The immunological effects of thought suppression. *Journal of Personality and Social Psychology, 75,* 1264–1272.

Petrill, S. A. (2005). Behavioral genetics and intelligence. In O. Wilhelm & R. W. Engle (Eds.), *Handbook of understanding and measuring intelligence*. Thousand Oaks, CA: Sage.

Petty, R. E., & Cacioppo, J. T. (1986). *Communication and persuasion: Central and peripheral routes to attitude change*. New York: Springer-Verlag.

Petty, R. E., & Wegener, D. T. (1998). Attitude change: Multiple roles for persuasion variables. In D. T. Gilbert, S. T. Fiske, & G. Lindzey (Eds.), *The handbook of social psychology*. New York: McGraw-Hill.

Petty, R. E., & Wegener, D. T. (1999). The elaboration likelihood model: Current status and controversies. In S. Chaiken & Y. Trope (Eds.), *Dual-process theories in social psychology*. New York: Guilford.

Petty, R. E., Haugtvedt, C. P., & Smith, S. M. (1995). Elaboration as a determinant of attitude strength: Creating attitudes that are persistent, resistant, and predictive of behavior. In R. E. Petty & J. A. Krosnick (Eds.), *Attitude strength: Antecedents and consequences*. Mahwah, NJ: Erlbaum.

Petty, R. E., Wegener, D. T., & Fabrigar, L. R. (1997). Attitudes and attitude change. *Annual Review of Psychology, 48,* 609–647.

Pevere, G. (2005). Dallaire a hero for all reasons. *Globe and Mail,* January 7, 2005, pp. D1, D8.

Pfau, M., Kenski, H. C., Nitz, M., & Sorenson, J. (1990). Efficacy of inoculation strategies in promoting resistance to political attack messages: Application to direct mail. *Communication Monographs, 57,* 25–43.

Pfau, M., Kenski, H. C., Nitz, M., & Sorenson, J. (1990). Efficacy of inoculation strategies in promoting resistance to political attack messages: Application to direct mail. *Communication Monographs, 57,* 25–43.

Pfaus, J. G., Kippin, T. E., & Centeno, S. (2001). Conditioning and sexual behavior: A review. *Hormones & Behavior, 40,* 291–321.

Pfefferbaum, B., Seale, T. W., McDonald, N. B., Brandt, E. N., Rainwater, S. M., Maynard, B. T., Meierhoefer, B., & Miller, P. D. (2000). Posttraumatic stress two years after the Oklahoma City bombing in youths geographically distant from the explosion. *Psychiatry, 63,* 358–370.

Phares, V. (1996). *Fathers and developmental psychopathology*. New York: Wiley.

Phillips, W. T., Kiernan, M., & King, A. C. (2001). The effects of physical activity on physical and psychological health. In A. Baum, T. A. Revenson, & J. E. Singer (Eds.), *Handbook of health psychology* (pp. 627–660). Mahwah, NJ: Erlbaum.

Phillips, W. T., Kiernan, M., & King, A. C. (2001). The effects of physical activity on physical and psychological health. In A. Baum, T. A. Revenson, & J. E. Singer (Eds.), *Handbook of health psychology* (pp. 627–660). Mahwah, NJ: Erlbaum.

Pi, E. H., & Simpson, G. M. (2001). Medication-induced movement disorders. In B. J. Sadock & V. A. Sadock (Eds.), *Kaplan and Sadock's comprehensive textbook of psychiatry* (7th ed., Vol. 2). Philadelphia: Lippincott/Williams & Wilkins.

Piaget, J. (1929). *The child's conception of the world*. New York: Harcourt, Brace.

Piaget, J. (1932). *The moral judgment of the child*. Glencoe, IL: Free Press.

Piaget, J. (1952). *The origins of intelligence in children*. New York: International Universities Press.

Piaget, J. (1954). *The construction of reality in the child*. New York: Basic Books.

Piaget, J. (1983). Piaget's theory. In P. H. Mussen (Ed.), *Handbook of child psychology* (Vol. 1). New York: Wiley.

Pickering, T. G., Devereux, R. B., James, G. D., Gerin, W., Landsbergis, P., Schnall, P. L., & Schwartz, J. E. (1996). Environmental influences on blood pressure and the role of job strain. *Journal of Hypertension, 14*, S179–S185.

Pickles, J. O. (1988). *An introduction to the physiology of hearing* (2nd ed.). London: Academic Press.

Pierce, C. M. (1992). Contemporary psychiatry: Racial perspectives on the past and future. In A. Kales, C. M. Pierce, & M. Greenblatt (Eds.), *The mosaic of contemporary psychiatry in perspective*. New York: Springer-Verlag.

Pierce, W. D., & Epling, W. F. (1997). Activity anorexia: The interplay of culture, behavior and biology. In P. A. Lamal (Ed.), *Cultural contingencies: Behavioral analytic perspectives on cultural practices* (pp. 53–86). Westport, CT: Praeger.

Pihl, R. O. (1999). Substance abuse: Etiological considerations. In T. Millon, P. H. Blaney, & R. D. Davis (Eds.), *Oxford textbook of psychopathology*. New York: Oxford University Press.

Pihl, R. O., Assaad, J.M., & Hoaken, P. N. S. (2003). The alcohol-aggression relationship and differential sensitivity to alcohol. *Aggressive Behavior, 29*, 302–315.

Pike, A., Manke, B., Reiss, D., & Plomin, R. (2000). A genetic analysis of differential experiences of adolescent siblings across three years. *Social Development, 9*, 96–114.

Pike, K. M., & Rodin, J. (1991). Mothers, daughters, and disordered eating. *Journal of Abnormal Psychology, 100*, 198–294.

Pilcher, J. J., & Huffcutt, A. I. (1996). Effects of sleep deprivation on performance: A meta-analysis. *Sleep, 19*, 318–326.

Pilcher, J. J., & Walters, A. S. (1997). How sleep deprivation affects psychological variables related to college students' cognitive performance. *Journal of American College Health, 46*, 121–126.

Pilcher, J. J., Ginter, D. R., & Sadowsky, B. (1997). Sleep quality versus sleep quantity: Relationships between sleep and measures of health, well-being and sleepiness in college students. *Journal of Psychosomatic Research, 42*, 583–596.

Pilling, M., & Davies, I. R. L. (2004). Linguistic relativism and colour cognition. *British Journal of Psychology, 95*, 429–455.

Pillow, D. R., Zautra, A. J., & Sandler, I. (1996). Major life events and minor stressors: Identifying mediational links in the stress process. *Journal of Personality and Social Psychology, 70*, 381–394.

Pilowsky, I. (1993). Aspects of abnormal illness behaviour. *Psychotherapy and Psychosomatics, 60*, 62–74.

Pincus, H. A., Tanielian, T. L., Marcus, S. C., Olfson, M., Zarin, D. A., Thompson, J., & Zito, J. M. (1998). Prescribing trends in psychotropic medications: Primary care, psychiatry, and other medical specialties. *Journal of the American Medical Association, 279*, 526–531.

Pinder, C. C. (1998). *Work motivation in organizational behavior*. Upper Saddle River, NJ: Prentice-Hall.

Pine, D. S. (2000). Anxiety disorders: Clinical features. In B. J. Sadock & V. A. Sadock (Eds.), *Kaplan and Sadock's comprehensive textbook of psychiatry* (7th ed., Vol. 1, pp. 1476–1489). Philadelphia: Lippincott/Williams & Wilkins.

Pinel, J. P. J., Assanand, S., & Lehman, D. R. (2000). Hunger, eating, and ill health. *American Psychologist, 55*, 1105–1116.

Pines, A. M. (1993). Burnout. In L. Goldberger & S. Breznitz (Eds.), *Handbook of stress: Theoretical and clinical aspects*. New York: Free Press.

Pines, A. M. (2004). Adult attachment styles and their relationship to burnout: A preliminary, cross-cultural investigation. *Work & Stress, 18*(1), 66–80.

Pinker, S. & Jackendoff, R. (2004). The faculty of language: What's special about it? *Cognition, 95*, 201–236.

Pinker, S. (1990). Language acquisition. In D. N. Osherson & H. Lasnik (Eds.), *Language: An invitation to cognitive science* (Vol. 1). Cambridge, MA: MIT Press.

Pinker, S. (1994). *Language is to us as flying is to geese*. New York: Morrow.

Pinker, S. (2003). Language as an adaptation to the cognitive niche. In M. Christiansen & S. Kirby (Eds.), *Language evolution: States of the Art*. New York: Oxford University Press.

Pinker, S. (2004). Language as an adaptation to the cognitive niche. In D. T. Kenrick & C. L. Luce (Eds.), *The functional mind: Readings in evolutionary psychology*. Essex, England: Pearson Education Limited.

Pinker, S., & Bloom, P. (1992). Natural language and natural selection. In J. H. Barkow, L. Cosmides, & J. Tooby (Eds.), *The adapted mind: Evolutionary psychology and the generation of culture*. New York: Oxford University Press.

Pinker, S., & Jackendoff, R. (2005). The faculty of language: What's special about it? *Cognition, 95*, 201–236.

Piomelli, D. (2004). The endogenous cannabinoid system and the treatment of marijuana dependence. *Neuropharmacology, 47*, 359–367.

Piper, W. E. (1993). Group psychotherapy research. In H. I. Kaplan & B. J. Sadock (Eds.), *Comprehensive group psychotherapy*. Baltimore: Williams & Wilkins.

Pi-Sunyer, F. X. (2002). Medical complications of obesity in adults. In C. G. Fairburn & K. D. Brownell (Eds.), *Eating disorders and obesity: A comprehensive handbook* (pp. 467–472). New York: Guilford.

Pittman, F., III. (1994, January/February). A buyer's guide to psychotherapy. *Psychology Today, 50–53*, 74–81.

Pivik, R. T. (2000). Psychophysiology of dreams. In M. H. Kryger, T. Roth, & W. C. Dement (Eds.), *Principles and practice of sleep medicine*. Philadelphia: Saunders.

Plante, T. G. (1999a). *Contemporary clinical psychology*. New York: Wiley & Sons, Inc.

Plante, T. G. (1999b). Could the perception of fitness account for many of the mental and physical health benefits of exercise? *Advances in Mind-Body Medicine, 15*, 291–295.

Plante, T. G., Caputo, D., & Chizmar, L. (2000). Perceived fitness and responses to laboratory-induced stress. *International Journal of Stress Management, 7*(1), 61–73.

Platiel, R., & Strauss, S. (1989) University chief defends professor's right to voice racial theory. *Globe and Mail*, February 4, 1989, p. A6.

Plomin, R. (1993). Nature and nurture: Perspective and prospective. In R. Plomin & G. E. McClearn (Eds.), *Nature, nurture and psychology*. Washington, DC: American Psychological Association.

Plomin, R. (1994). Nature, nurture, and development. In R. J. Sternberg (Ed.), *Encyclopedia of human intelligence*. New York: Macmillan.

Plomin, R. (2003). General cognitive ability. In R. Plomin & J. C. DeFries (Eds.), *Behavioral genetics in the postgenomic era*. Washinton, DC: American Psychological Association.

Plomin, R. (2004). Genetics and developmental psychology. *Merrill-Palmer Quarterly, 50*, 341–352.

Plomin, R., & Caspi, A. (1999). Behavioral genetics and personality. In L. A. Pervin & O. P. John (Eds.), *Handbook of personality: Theory and research*. New York: Guilford.

Plomin, R., & Crabbe, J. (2000). DNA. *Psychological Bulletin, 126*, 806–828.

Plomin, R., & McGuffin, P. (2003). Psychopathology in the postgenomic era. *Annual Review of Psychology, 54*, 205–228.

Plomin, R., & Petrill, S. A. (1997). Genetics and intelligence: What's new? *Intelligence, 24*, 53–77.

Plomin, R., & Rende, R. (1991). Human behavioral genetics. *Annual Review of Psychology, 42*, 161–190.

Plomin, R., & Spinath, F. M. (2004). Intelligence: Genetics, genes, and genomics. *Journal of Personality & Social Psychology, 86*, 112–129.

Plomin, R., DeFries, J. C., McClearn, G. E., & McGuffin, P. (2001). *Behavioral genetics*. New York: Freeman.

Plotkin, H. (2004). *Evolutionary thought in psychology: A brief history*. Malden, MA: Blackwell Publishing.

Plucker, J. A., & Renzulli, J. S. (1999). Psychometric approaches to the study of human creativity. In R. J. Sternberg (Ed.), *Handbook of creativity*. New York: Cambridge University Press.

Plutchik, R. (1980, February). A language for the emotions. *Psychology Today*, pp. 68–78.

Plutchik, R. (1984). Emotions: A general psychoevolutionary theory. In K. R. Scherer & P. Ekman (Eds.), *Approaches to emotion*. Hillsdale, NJ: Erlbaum.

Plutchik, R. (1993). Emotions and their vicissitudes: Emotions and psychopathology. In M. Lewis & J. M. Haviland (Eds.), *Handbook of emotions*. New York: Guilford.

Pohl, R. F. (2004). Effects of labeling. In F. P. Rudiger (Ed.), *Cognitive illusions*. New York: Psychology Press.

Policastro, E., & Gardner, H. (1999). From case studies to robust generalizations: An approach to the study of creativity. In R. J. Sternberg (Ed.), *Handbook of creativity*. New York: Cambridge University Press.

Polivy, J., & Herman, C. P. (1995). Dieting and its relation to eating disorders. In K. D. Brownell & C. G. Fairburn (Eds.), *Eating disorders and obesity: A comprehensive handbook*. New York: Guilford.

Polivy, J., & Herman, C. P. (2002). Causes of eating disorders. *Annual Review of Psychology, 53*, 187–213.

Polivy, J., Herman, C. P., Mills, J. S., & Wheeler, H. B. (2003). Eating disorders. In G. R. Adams & M. D. Berzonsky (Eds.), *Blackwell handbook of adolescence* (pp. 522–549). Oxford, UK: Blackwell Publishing.

Poloma, M., & Pendleton, B. F. (1990). Religious domains and general well-being. *Social Indicators Research, 22*, 255–276.

Pols, H. (2002). Between the laboratory and life: Child development research in Toronto, 1919–1956. *History of Psychology, 5*, 135–162.

Pomeroy, C., & Mitchell, J. E. (2002). Medical complications of anorexia nervosa and bulimia nervosa. In C. G. Fairburn & K. D. Brownell (Eds.), *Eating disorders and obesity: A comprehensive handbook*. New York: Guilford.

Ponterotto, J. G., & Pedersen, P. B. (1993). *Preventing prejudice: A guide for counselors and educators*. Newbury Park, CA: Sage.

Pooley, E. (2004). The road not taken. *Globe and Mail*, June 25, 2004, p. A19.

Pope, H. G., Gruber, A. J., & Yurgelun-Todd, D. (2001). Residual neuropsychologic effects of cannabis. *Current Psychiatry Report, 3*, 507–512.

Pope, H. G., Gruber, A. J., Hudson, J. I., Huestis, M. A., & Yurgelun-Todd, D. (2001). Neuropsychological performance in long-term cannabis users. *Archives of General Psychiatry, 58*, 909–915.

Pope, H. G., Jr., & Hudson, J. I. (1998). Can memories of childhood sexual abuse be repressed? In R. A. Baker (Ed.), *Child sexual abuse and false memory syndrome*. Amherst, NY: Prometheus Books.

Pope, H. G., Jr., Oliva, P. S., Hudson, J. I., Bodkin, J. A., & Gruber, A. J. (1999). Attitudes toward DSM-IV dissociative disorders diagnoses among board-certified American psychiatrists. *American Journal of Psychiatry, 156*, 321–323.

Pope, K. S. (1996). Memory, abuse, and science: Questioning claims about the false memory syndrome epidemic. *American Psychologist, 51*, 957–974.

Pope, K. S., & Brown, L. (1996). *Recovered memories of abuse: Assessment, therapy, forensics*.

Washington, D.C.: American Psychological Association.

Pope, K. S., Keith-Spiegel, P., & Tabachnick, B. G. (1986). Sexual attraction to clients. *American Psychologist, 41*, 147–158.

Popenoe, D. (1996). *Life without father*. New York: Pressler Press.

Popper, C. W., & Steingard, R. J. (1994). Disorders usually first diagnosed in infancy, childhood, or adolescence. In R. E. Hales, S. C. Yudofsky, & J. A. Talbott (Eds.), *The American Psychiatric Press textbook of psychiatry*. Washington, DC: American Psychiatric Press.

Popper, C. W., & West, S. A. (1999). Disorders usually first diagnosed in infancy, childhood, or adolescence. In R. E. Hales, S. C. Yudofsky, & J. A. Talbott (Eds.), *The American Psychiatric Press textbook of psychiatry* (3rd ed., pp. 825–954). Washington, DC: American Psychiatric Press.

Popper, C. W., Gammon, G. D., West, S. A., & Bailey, C. E. (2003). Disorders usually first diagnosed in infancy, childhood, and adolescence. In Robert E. Hales & Stuart C. Yudofsky (Eds.), *Textbook of clinical psychiatry*. Washington, DC: American Psychiatric Publishing.

Pornpitakpan, C. (2004). The persuasiveness of source credibility: A critical review of five decades' evidence. *Journal of Applied Social Psychology, 34*, 243–281.

Porter, S., Spencer, L. & Birt, A. (2003). Blinded by emotion? Effect of the emotionality of a scene on susceptibility to false memories. *Canadian Journal of Behavioural Science, 35*, 165–175.

Posada, G., & Jacobs, A. (2001). Child-mother attachment relationships and culture. *American Psychologist, 56*, 821–822.

Posner, M. I., & DiGirolamo, G. J. (2000). Attention in cognitive neuroscience: An overview. In M. S. Gazzaniga (Ed.), *The new cognitive neurosciences* (2nd ed., pp. 623–632). Cambridge, MA: MIT Press.

Posner, M. I., & Rothbart, M. K. (2004). Hebb's neural networks support the integration of psychological science. *Canadian Psychology, 45*, 265–278.

Post, F. (1996). Verbal creativity, depression and alcoholism: An investigation of one hundred American and British writers. *British Journal of Psychiatry, 168*, 545–555.

Postman, L. (1985). Human learning and memory. In G. A. Kimble & K. Schlesinger (Eds.), *Topics in the history of psychology*. Hillsdale, NJ: Erlbaum.

Postmes, T., Spears, R., & Cihangir, S. (2001). Quality of decision making and group norms. *Journal of Personality and Social Psychology, 80*, 918–930.

Potthoff, J. G., Holahan, C. J., & Joiner, T. E., Jr. (1995). Reassurance-seeking, stress generation, and depressive symptoms: An integrative model. *Journal of Personality and Social Psychology, 68*, 664–670.

Poulton, E. C. (1994). *Behavioral decision theory: A new approach*. Cambridge, England: Cambridge University Press.

Powell, R. A., & Boer, D. P. (1995). Did Freud misinterpret reported memories of sexual abuse as fantasies? *Psychological Reports, 77*, 563–570.

Powell, R. A., & Gee, T. L. (1999). The effects of hypnosis on dissociative identity disorder: A reexamination of the evidence. *Canadian Journal of Psychiatry, 44*, 914–916.

Powell, R. A., Symbaluk, D. G., & MacDonald, S. E. (2002). *Introduction to learning and behavior*. Belmont, CA: Wadsworth.

Pozzulo, J., Bennell, C., & Forth, A. (2006). *Forensic psychology*. Toronto: Pearson Education Inc.

Pratkanis, A. R., & Aronson, E. (2000). *Age of propaganda: The everyday use and abuse of persuasion*. New York: Freeman.

Pratt, L. A., Ford, D. E., Crum, R. M., Armenian, H. K., Gallo, J. J., & Eaton, W. W. (1996). Depression, psychotropic medication, and risk of myocardinal infarction: Prospective data from Baltimore ECA follow-up. *Archives of Internal Medicine, 94*, 3123–3129.

Premack, D. (1985). "Gavagai!" or the future history of the animal language controversy. *Cognition, 19*, 207–296.

Prentky, R. (1989). Creativity and psychopathology: Gamboling at the seat of madness. In J. A. Glover, R. R. Ronning, & C. R. Reynolds (Eds.), *Handbook of creativity*. New York: Plenum.

Prentky, R. A. (1980). *Creativity and psychopathology: A neurocognitive perspective*. New York: Praeger.

Prentky, R. A. (1997). Arousal reduction in sexual offenders: A review of antiandrogen interventions. *Sexual Abuse: Journal of Research and Treatment, 9*, 335–347.

Priester, J. R., & Petty, R. E. (1995). Source attributions and persuasion; Perceived honesty as a determinant of message scrutiny. *Personality and Social Psychology Bulletin, 21*, 637–654.

Priester, J. R., & Petty, R. E. (2001). Extending the bases of subjective attitudinal ambivalence: Interpersonal and intrapersonal antecedents of evaluative tension. *Journal of Personality and Social Psychology, 80*, 19–34.

Priester, J. R., & Petty, R. E. (2003). The influence of spokesperson trustworthiness on message elaboration, attitude strength, and advertising. *Journal of Consumer Psychology, 13*, 408–421.

Prifitera, A. (1994). Wechsler scales of intelligence. In R. J. Sternberg (Ed.), *Encyclopedia of human intelligence*. New York: Macmillan.

Prince, G. (1978). Putting the other half to work. *Training: The Magazine of Human Resources Development, 15*, 57–61.

Pringle, H. (1997). Alberta barren. *Saturday Night*, June 1997, pp. 30–74.

Prochaska, J. O. (1994). Strong and weak principles for progressing from precontemplation to action on the basis of twelve problem behaviors. *Health Psychology, 13*, 47–51.

Proffitt, D. R., & Caudek, C. (2003). Depth perception and the perception of events. In A. F. Healy & R. W. Proctor (Eds.), *Handbook of psychology, Vol. 4: Experimental psychology*. New York: Wiley.

Pronin, E., Gilovich, T., & Ross, L. (2004). Objectivity in the eye of the beholder: Divergent perceptions of bias in self versus others. *Psychological Review, 111*, 781–799.

Pronin, E., Kruger, J., Savitsky, K., & Ross, L. (2001). You don't know me, but I know you: The illusion of asymmetric insight. *Journal of Personality and Social Psychology, 81*, 639–656.

Pronin, E., Lin, D. Y., & Ross, L. (2002). The bias blind spot: Perceptions of bias in self versus others. *Personality and Social Psychology Bulletin, 28*, 369–381.

Provine, R. R. (1989). Faces as releasers of contagious yawning: An approach to face detection using normal human subjects. *Bulletin of the Psychonomic Society, 27*, 211–214.

Provine, R. R. (1993). Yawning. In M. A. Carskadon (Ed.), *Encyclopedia of sleep and dreaming*. New York: Macmillan.

Prudic, J., & Sackeim, H. A. (1999). Electroconvulsive therapy and suicide risk. *Journal of Clinical Psychiatry, 60*, 104–110.

Pruitt, D. G. (1971). Choice shifts in group discussion: An introductory review. *Journal of Personality and Social Psychology, 20*, 339–360.

Psychological Corporation. (2001). *WAIS-III Canadian technical manual.* San Antonio, TX: Author.

Public Health Agency of Canada. (1996). *Mental Illness and violence: Proof or stereotype?* Retrieved June 27, 2005, from http://www.phac-aspc.gc.ca/mh-sm/mentalhealth/pubs/mental_illness/.

Public Health Agency of Canada. (2002). *A report on mental illnesses in Canada.* Retrieved June 25, 2005, from http://www.phac-aspc.gc.ca/publicat/miic-mmac/app_b_e.html.

Public Health Agency of Canada. (2003a). Canadian youth, sexual behavior and HIV/AIDS Study. Retrieved May 9, 2005, from http://www.phac-aspc.gc.ca/aids-sida/hiv-aids/federal_initiative/publications/cmec.html.

Public Health Agency of Canada. (2003b). HIV/AIDS Communique. Retrieved May 9, 2005, from http://www.phac-aspc.gc.ca/aids-sida/hiv_aids/federal_initiative/communique_sept.html.

Public Health Agency of Canada. (2004). The Changing face of heart disease and stroke in Canada 2000. Retrieved June 21, 2005, from http://www.phac-aspc.gc.ca/ccdpc-cpcmc/cvd-mcv/publications/pdf/card2ke.pdf.

Public Health Agency of Canada. (n.d.). Dating Violence. Retrieved May 9, 2005, from http://www.phac-aspc.gc.ca/ncfv-cnivf/familyviolence/html/femdatfreq_e.html.

Public Heath Agency of Canada. (n.d.). Physical activity statistics: Canadian physical activity levels for children and youth. Retrieved May 3, 2005, from http://www.phac-aspc.gc.ca/pau-uap/paguide/child_youth/children/.

Pucetti, R. (1981). The case for mental duality: Evidence from split brain data and other considerations. *Behavioral and Brain Sciences, 4,* 93–123.

Puente, A. E. (1990). Psychological assessment of minority group members. In G. Goldstein & M. Hersen (Eds.), *Handbook of psychological assessment.* New York: Pergamon Press.

Pullum, G. K. (1991). *The Great Eskimo vocabulary hoax.* Chicago: University of Chicago Press.

Pusch, D., Dobson, K., Ardo, K, & Murphy, T. (1998). The relationship between sociotropic and autonomous personality styles and depressive realism in dysphoric and nondysphoric university students. *Canadian Journal of Behavioural Science, 30,* 253–265.

Quinn, P. C., & Eimas, P. D. (1996). Perceptual cues that permit categorical differentiation of animal species by infants. *Journal of Experimental Child Psychology, 63,* 189–211.

Quinn, P. C., & Eimas, P. D. (1998). Evidence for a global categorical representation of humans by young infants. *Journal of Experimental Child Psychology, 69,* 151–174.

Quitkin, F. M. (1999). Placebos, drug effects, and study design: A clinician's guide. *American Journal of Psychiatry, 156,* 829–836.

Rabins, P. V., Lyketsos, C. G., & Steele, C. D. (1999). *Practical dementia care.* New York: Oxford University Press.

Rabkin, J. G., Wagner, G. J., & Rabkin, R. (2000). A double-blind, placebo-controlled trial of testosterone therapy for HIV-positive men with hypogonadal symptoms. *Archives of General Psychiatry, 57,* 141–147.

Race, evolution & behavior: A life history perspective—Review. *Canadian Journal of Sociology, 20,* p. 129.

Rachman, S. J. (1990). *Fear and courage.* New York: W. H. Freeman.

Rachman, S. J. (1992). Behavior therapy. In L. R. Squire (Ed.), *Encyclopedia of learning and memory.* New York: Macmillan.

Racine, R. J., & deJonge, M. (1988). Short-term and long-term potentiation in projection pathways and local circuits. In P. W. Landfield & S. A. Deadwyler (Eds.), *Long-term potentiation: From biophysics to behavior.* New York: Liss.

Ragland, D. R., & Brand, R. J. (1988). Type A behavior and mortality from coronary heart disease. *The New England Journal of Medicine, 318*(2), 65–69.

Rahe, R. H., & Arthur, R. H. (1978). Life change and illness studies. *Journal of Human Stress, 4*(1), 3–15.

Raichle, M. E. (1994). Images of the mind: Studies with modern imaging techniques. *Annual Review of Psychology, 45,* 333–356.

Raine, A. (1997). Antisocial behavior and psychophysiology: A biosocial perspective and a prefrontal dysfunction hypothesis. In D. M. Stoff, J. Breiling, & J. D. Maser (Eds.), *Handbook of antisocial behavior.* New York: Wiley.

Rains, G. D. (2002). *Principles of human neuropsychology.* New York: McGraw-Hill.

Rainville, P., Duncan, G. H., Price, D. D., Carrier, B., & Bushnell, M. C. (1997). Pain affect encoded in human anterior cingulate but not somatosensory cortex. *Science, 277,* 968–971.

Raj, A., & Sheehan, D. (2004). Benzodiazepines. In A. F. Schatzberg & C. B. Nemeroff (Eds.), *Textbook of psychopharmacology.* Washington, DC: American Psychiatric Publishing.

Rakic, P., Bourgeois, J. P., & Goldman-Rakic, P. S. (1994). Synaptic development of the cerebral cortex: Implications for learning, memory, and mental illness. *Progress in brain research.*

Ramadan, N. M. (2000). Migraine. In G. Fink (Ed.), *Encyclopedia of stress* (pp. 757–770). San Diego: Academic Press.

Ramaekers, J. G., Robbe, H. W. J., & O'Hanlon, J. F. (2000). Marijuana, alcohol and actual driving performance. *Human Psychopharmacology: Clinical & Experimental, 15,* 551–558.

Ramey, C. T., & Ramey, S. L. (2000). Intelligence and public policy. In R. J. Sternberg (Ed.), *Handbook of intelligence* (pp. 534–548). New York: Cambridge University Press.

Ramey, C. T., Ramey, S. L., & Lanzi, R. G. (2001). Intelligence and experience. In R. J. Sternberg & E. L. Grigorenko (Eds.), *Environmental effects on cognitive abilities* (pp. 83–116). Mahwah, NJ: Erlbaum.

Ramey, S. L. (1999). Head Start and preschool education: Toward continued improvement. *American Psychologist, 54,* 344–346.

Ramsay, D. S., Seeley, R. J., Bolles, R. C., & Woods, S. C. (1996). Ingestive homeostasis: The primacy of learning. In E. D. Capaldi (Ed.), *Why we eat what we eat: The psychology of eating* (pp. 11–29). Washington, DC: American Psychological Association.

Rapaport, D., Gill, M., & Schafer, R. (1968). *Diagnostic psychological testing.* New York: International Universities Press.

Rapee, R. M., & Barlow, D. H. (2001). Generalized anxiety disorders, panic disorders, and phobias. In P. B. Sutker & H. E. Adams (Eds.), *Comprehensive handbook of psychopathology* (3rd ed., pp. 131–154). New York: Kluwer Academic/Plenum Publishers.

Raphael, B., & Dobson, M. (2000). Effects of public disasters. In G. Fink (Ed.), *Encyclopedia of stress* (Vol. 1, pp. 699–705). San Diego: Academic Press.

Rasmussen, C., Knapp, T. J., & Garner, L. (2000). Driving-induced stress in urban college students. *Perceptual & Motor Skills, 90,* 437–443.

Rasmussen, T., & Milner, B. (1977). The role of early left brain injury in determining lateralization of cerebral speech functions. *Annals of the New York Academy of Sciences, 299,* 355–369.

Ratner, N. B., Gleason, J. B., & Narasimhan, B. (1998). An introduction to psycholinguistics: What do language users know? In J. B. Gleason & N. B. Ratner (Eds.), *Psycholinguistics* (2nd ed., pp. 1–40). Fort Worth, TX: Harcourt College Publishers.

Rauscher, F. H., Shaw, G. L., & Ky, K. N. (1993). Music and spatial task performance. *Nature, 365,* 611.

Rauscher, F. H., Shaw, G. L., & Ky, K. N. (1995). Listening to Mozart enhances spatial-temporal reasoning: Towards a neurophysiological basis. *Neuroscience Letters, 185,* 44–47.

Rayner, B. (2005). Celebrity care package. *Globe and Mail,* January 14, 2005, p. A8.

Raynor, J. O., & Entin, E. E. (1982). Future orientation and achievement motivation. In J. O. Raynor & E. E. Entin (Eds.), *Motivation, career striving, and aging.* New York: Hemisphere.

Read, C. R. (1991). Achievement and career choices: Comparisons of males and females. *Roeper Review, 13,* 188–193.

Real, L. (1991). Animal choice behavior and the evolution of cognitive architecture. *Science, 253,* 980–986.

Reber, R. (2004). Availability. In F. P. Rudiger (Ed.), *Cognitive illusions.* New York: Psychology Press.

Recanzone, G. H. (2000). Cerebral cortical plasticity: Perception and skill acquisition. In M. S. Gazzaniga (Ed.), *The new cognitive neurosciences.* Cambridge, MA: The MIT Press.

Recht, L. D., Lew, R. A., & Schwartz, W. J. (1995). Baseball teams beaten by jet lag. *Nature, 377,* 583.

Rechtschaffen, A. (1994). Sleep onset: Conceptual issues. In R. D. Ogilvie & J. R. Harsh (Eds.), *Sleep onset: Normal and abnormal processes.* Washington, DC: American Psychological Association.

Rector, N. A., & Beck, A. T. (2001). Cognitive behavioral therapy for schizophrenia. An empirical review. *Journal of Nervous and Mental Disorders, 189,* 278–287.

Rector, N. A., Segal, Z., & Gemar, M. (1998). Schema research in depression: A Canadian Perspective.

Canadian Journal of Behavioural Science, 30, 213–224.

Reddy, B. S. (1999). Role of dietary fiber in colon cancer: An overview. *American Journal of Medicine, 106*(1A), 16S–19S.

Ree, M. J., & Earles, J. A. (1992). Intelligence is the best predictor of job performance. *Current Directions in Psychological Science, 1,* 86–89.

Reed, J. G., & Baxter P. M. (1992). *Library use: A handbook for psychology.* Washington, DC: American Psychological Association.

Reed, J. G., & Baxter, P. M. (2003). *Library use: A handbook for psychology.* Washington, DC: American Psychological Association.

Rees, C. J., & Metcalfe, B. (2003). The faking of personality question-naire results: Who's kidding whom? *Journal of Managerial Psychology, 18*(2), 156–165.

Reeve, C. L., & Hakel, M. D. (2002). Asking the right questions about *g. Human Performance, 15,* 47–74.

Regan, P. C. (1998). What if you can't get what you want? Willingness to compromise ideal mate selection standards as a function of sex, mate value, and relationship context. *Personality and Social Psychology Bulletin, 24,* 1294–1303.

Regan, P. C. (2003). *The mating game: A primer on love, sex, and marriage.* Thousand Oaks, CA: Sage.

Regier, D. A., & Burke, J. D. (2000). Epidemiology. In B. J. Sadock & V. A. Sadock (Eds.), *Kaplan and Sadock's comprehensive textbook of psychiatry.* Philadelphia: Lippincott/Williams & Wilkins.

Regier, D. A., & Kaelber, C. T. (1995). The Epidemiologic Catchment Area (ECA) program: Studying the prevalence and incidence of psychopathology. In M. T. Tsuang, M. Tohen, & G. E. P. Zahner (Eds.), *Textbook in psychiatric epidemiology.* New York: Wiley.

Rehm, L. P., Wagner, A., & Ivens-Tyndal, Co. (2001). Mood disorders: Unipolar and bipolar. In P. B. Sutker & H. E. Adams (Eds.), *Comprehensive handbook of psychopathology.* New York: Kluwer Academic/Plenum.

Rehm, L. P., Wagner, A., & Ivens-Tyndal, Co. (2001). Mood disorders: Unipolar and bipolar. In P. B. Sutker & H. E. Adams (Eds.), *Comprehensive handbook of psychopathology* (pp. 277–308). New York: Kluwer Academic/Plenum.

Reibel, D. K., Greeson, J. M., Brainard, G. C., & Rosenzweig, S. (2001). Mindfulness-based stress reduction and health-related

quality of life in a heterogeneous patient population. *General Hospital Psychiatry, 23*(4), 183–192.

Reichert, T. (2003). The prevalence of sexual imagery in ads targeted to young adults. *Journal of Consumer Affairs, 37,* 403–412.

Reichert, T., & Lambiase, J. (2003). How to get "kissably close": Examining how advertisers appeal to consumers' sexual needs and desires. *Sexuality & Culture: An Interdisciplinary Quarterly, 7*(3), 120–136.

Reinharz, D., Lesage, A. D., & Contandriopoulos, A. P. (2000). Cost-effectiveness analysis of psychiatric deinstitutionalization. *Canadian Journal of Psychiatry, 45,* 533–538.

Reisner, A. D. (1998). Repressed memories: True and false. In R. A. Baker (Ed.), *Child sexual abuse and false memory syndrome.* Amherst, NY: Prometheus Books.

Reiss, S. (1991). Expectancy model of fear, anxiety and panic. *Clinical Psychology Review, 11,* 141–154.

Rennie, D. (1999). Fair conduct and fair reporting of clinical trials. *Journal of the American Medical Association, 282,* 1766–1768.

Rennie, D., & Luft, H. S. (2000). Making them transparent, making them credible. *Journal of the American Medical Association, 283,* 2516–2521.

Renzulli, J. S. (1986). The three-ring conception of giftedness: A developmental model for creative productivity. In R. J. Sternberg & J. E. Davidson (Eds.), *Conceptions of giftedness.* Cambridge: Cambridge University Press.

Renzulli, J. S. (1999). What is this thing called giftedness, and how do we develop it? A twenty-five year perspective. *Journal for the Education of the Gifted, 23,* 3–54.

Renzulli, J. S. (2002). Emerging conceptions of giftedness: Building a bridge to the new century. *Exceptionality, 10,* 67–75.

Repetto, M., & Gold, M. S. (2005). Cocaine and crack: Neurobiology. In J. H. Lowinson, P. Ruiz, R. B. Millman, & J. G. Langrod (Eds.), *Substance abuse: A comprehensive textbook.* Philadelphia: Lippincott/Williams & Wilkins.

Rescorla, R. A. (1978). Some implications of a cognitive perspective on Pavlovian conditioning. In S. H. Hulse, H. Fowler, & W. K. Honig (Eds.), *Cognitive processes in animal behavior.* Hillsdale, NJ: Erlbaum.

Rescorla, R. A. (1980). *Pavlovian second-order conditioning.* Hillsdale, NJ: Erlbaum.

Rescorla, R. A., & Solomon, R. L. (1967). Two-process learning theory: Relationships between Pavlovian conditioning and instrumental learning. *Psychological Review, 74,* 151–182.

Rescorla, R. A., & Wagner, A. R. (1972). A theory of Pavlovian conditioning: Variations in the effectiveness of reinforcement and nonreinforcement. In A. H. Black & W. F. Prokasky (Eds.), *Classical conditioning: II. Current research and theory.* New York: Appleton-Century-Crofts.

Rest, J. R. (1986). *Moral development: Advances in research and theory.* New York: Praeger.

Reuter-Lorenz, P. A., & Miller, A. C. (1998). The cognitive neuroscience of human laterality: Lessons from the bisected brain. *Current Directions in Psychological Science, 7,* 15–20.

Reynolds, A. G. (1991). *Bilingualism, multiculturalism, and second language learning: The McGill conference in honour of Wallace E. Lambert.* Hillsdale, NJ: Lawrence Erlbaum and Associates.

Reynolds, A. J., Temple, J. T., Robertson, D. L., & Mann, E. A. (2001). Long-term effects of an early childhood intervention on educational achievement and juvenile arrest: A 15-year follow-up of low-income children in public schools. *Journal of the American Medical Association, 285,* 2339–2346.

Reynolds, C. F., III, Frank, E., Perel, J. M., Imber, S. D., Cornes, C., Miller, M. D., Mazumdar, S., Houck, P. R., Dew, M. A., Stack, J. A., Pollock, B. G., & Kupfer, D. J. (1999). Nortriptyline and interpersonal psychotherapy as maintenance therapies for recurrent major depression: A randomized controlled trial in patients older than 50 years. *Journal of the American Medical Association, 28,* 39–45.

Reynolds, C. F., III, Kupfer, D. J., Buysse, D. J., Coble, P. A., & Yeager, A. (1991). Subtyping DSM-III-R primary insomnia: A literature review by the DSM-IV work group on sleep disorders. *American Journal of Psychiatry, 148,* 432–438.

Reynolds, C. R. (1994). Reliability. In R. J. Sternberg (Ed.), *Encyclopedia of human intelligence.* New York: Macmillan.

Reynolds, C. R. (2000). Why is psychometric research on bias in mental testing so often ignored? *Psychology, Public Policy, and Law, 6,* 144–150.

Reynolds, K. J., Turner, J. C., & Haslam, S. A. (2000). When are we better than them and they worse

than us? A closer look at social discrimination in positive and negative domains. *Journal of Personality and Social Psychology, 78,* 64–80.

Riazi, A., & Bradley, C. (2000). Diabetes, Type I. In G. Fink (Ed.), *Encyclopedia of stress* (pp. 688–693). San Diego: Academic Press.

Riba, M. B., & Miller, R. R. (2003). Combined therapies: Psychotherapy and pharmacotherapy. In A. Tasman, J. Kay, & J. A. Lieberman (Eds.), *Psychiatry.* New York: Wiley.

Rice, L. N., & Greenberg, L. S. (1992). Humanistic approaches to psychotherapy. In D. K. Freedheim (Ed.), *History of psychotherapy: A century of change.* Washington, DC: American Psychological Association.

Rice, M., & Harris, G. T. (1993). Ontario's maximum security hospital at Penetanguishene. *International Journal of Law and Psychiatry, 16,* 195–215.

Rich, J. B., Park, N. W., Dopkins, S., & Brandt, J. (2002). What do Alzheimer's disease patients know about animals? It depends on task structure and presentation format. *Journal of the International Neuropsychological Society, 8,* 83–94.

Richardson, C. R., Kriska, A. M., Lantz, P. M., & Hayword, R. A. (2004). Physical activity and mortality across cardiovascular disease risk groups. *Medicine and Science in Sports and Exercise, 36,* 1923–1929.

Richardson, G. S. (1993). Circadian rhythms. In M. A. Carskadon (Ed.), *Encyclopedia of sleep and dreaming.* New York: Macmillan.

Rich-Edwards, J. W., Stampfer, M. J., Manson, J. E., Rosner, B., Hankinson, S. E., Colditz, G. A., Willett, W. C., & Hennekens, C. H. (1997). Birth weight and risk of cardiovascular disease in a cohort of women followed up since 1976. *British Medical Journal, 315,* 396–400.

Richert, E. S. (1997). Excellence with equity in identification and programming. In N. Colangelo, & G. A. Davis (Eds.), *Handbook of gifted education.* Boston: Allyn & Bacon.

Ridker, P. M. (2001). High-sensitivity C-reactive protein: Potential adjunct for global risk assessment in the primary prevention of cardiovascular disease. *Circulation, 103,* 1813–1818.

Rieber, R. W. (1998). The assimilation of psychoanalysis in America: From popularization to vulgarization. In R. W. Rieber & K. D. Salzinger (Eds.), *Psychology: Theoretical-historical perspectives.*

Washington, DC: American Psychological Association.

Riemann, R., Angleitner, A., & Strelau, J. (1997). Genetic and environmental influences on personality: A study of twins reared together using the self- and peer report NEO-FFI scales. *Journal of Personality, 65,* 449–476.

Rihmer, Z. (2003). Do SSRI's increase the risk of suicide among depressives even if they are only taking placebo? *Psychotherapy & Psychosomatics, 72,* 357–358.

Riis, J., Loewenstein, G., Baron, J., Jepson, C., Fagerlin, A., & Ubel, P. A. (2005). Ignorance of hedonic adaptation to hemodialysis: A study using ecological momentary assessment. *Journal of Experimental Psychology: General, 134*(1), 3–9.

Rilling, M. (1996). The mystery of the vanished citations: James McConnell's forgotten 1960s quest for planarian learning, a biochemical engram, and celebrity. *American Psychologist, 51,* 589–598.

Rimal R. N. (2001). Longitudinal influences of knowledge and self-efficacy on exercise behavior: Tests of a mutual reinforcement model. *Journal of Health Psychology, 6,* 31–46.

Riskind, J. H. (2005). Cognitive mechanisms in generalized anxiety disorder: A second generation of theoretical perspectives. *Cognitive Therapy & Research, 29*(1), 1–5.

Ritter, R. C. (2004). Gastrointestinal mechanisms of satiation for food. *Physiology & Behavior, 81,* 249–273.

Rivas-Vazquez, R. A. (2001). Antidepressants as first-line agents in the current pharmacotherapy of anxiety disorders. *Professional Psychology: Research & Practice, 32*(1), 101–104.

Roazen, P. (1976). *Erik H. Erikson: The power and limits of a vision.* New York: Free Press.

Roberson, D., Davidoff, J., & Shapiro, L. (2002). Squaring the circle: The cultural relativity of good shape. *Journal of Cognition & Culture, 2*(1), 29–51.

Roberson, D., Davidoff, J., Davies, I. R. L., & Shapiro, L. R. (2005). Color categories: Evidence for the cultural relativity hypothesis. *Cognitive Psychology, 50,* 378–411.

Roberson, D., Davies, I., & Davidoff, J. (2000). Color categories are not universal: Replications and new evidence from a stone-age culture. *Journal of Experimental Psychology: General, 129,* 369–398.

Roberts, B. W., & DelVecchio, W. F. (2000). The rank-order consistency of personality traits from childhood to old age: A quantitative review of longitudinal studies. *Psychological Bulletin, 126,* 3–25.

Roberts, B. W., & Pomerantz, E. M. (2004). On traits, situations, and their integration: A developmental perspective. *Personality and Social Psychology Review, 8,* 402–416.

Roberts, B. W., Caspi, A., & Moffitt, T. E. (2001). The kids are alright: Growth and stability in personality development from adolescence to adulthood. *Journal of Personality and Social Psychology, 81,* 670–683.

Roberts, B. W., Walton, K. E., & Bogg, T. (2005). Conscientiousness and health across the life course. *Review of General Psychology, 9*(2), 156–168.

Roberts, L. (2001). Controversial from the start. *Science, 291,* 1182–1188.

Roberts, P., & Newton, P. M. (1987). Levinsonian studies of women's adult development. *Psychology and Aging, 2*(2), 154–163.

Roberts, R. D., Markham, P. M., Matthews, G., & Zeidner, M. (2005). Assessing intelligence: Past, present, and future. In O. Wilhelm & R. W. Engle (Eds.), *Handbook of understanding and measuring intelligence.* Thousand Oaks, CA: Sage.

Roberts, R. D., Zeidner, M., & Matthews, G. (2001). Does emotional intelligence meet traditional standards for an intelligence? Some new data and conclusions. *Emotion, 1,* 196–231.

Roberts, W. A. (2002). Are animals stuck in time? *Psychological Bulletin, 128,* 473–489.

Robins, L. N., Locke, B. Z., & Regier, D. A. (1991). An overview of psychiatric disorders in America. In L. N. Robins & D. A. Regier (Eds.), *Psychiatric disorders in America: The epidemiologic catchment area study.* New York: Free Press.

Robins, R. W., Gosling, S. D., & Craik, K. H. (1999). An empirical analysis of trends in psychology. *American Psychologist, 54,* 117–128.

Robinson, A., & Clinkenbeard, P. R. (1998). Giftedness: An exceptionality examined. *Annual Review of Psychology, 49,* 117–139.

Robinson, F. P. (1970). *Effective study* (4th ed.). New York: Harper & Row.

Robinson, J. P., & Godbey, G. (1997). *Time for life: The surprising ways Americans use their time.* University Park: Pennsylvania State University Press.

Robinson, S. L., Kraatz, M. S., & Rousseau, D. M. (1994). Changing obligations and the psychological contract: A longitudinal study. *Academy of Management Journal, 37,* 137–152.

Rock, I. (1986). The description and analysis of object and event perception. In K. R. Boff, L. Kaufman, & J. P. Thomas (Eds.), *Handbook of perception and human performance* (Vol. 2). New York: Wiley.

Rodgers, J. E. (1982). The malleable memory of eyewitnesses. *Science Digest, 3,* 32–35.

Rodgers, J., Buchanan, T., Scholey, A. B., Heffernan, T. M., Ling, J., & Parrott, A. C. (2003). Patterns of drug use and the influence of gender on self-reports of memory ability in ecstasy users: A web-based study. *Journal of Psychopharmacology, 17,* 389–396.

Rodin, J. (1985). Insulin levels, hunger, and food intake: An example of feedback loops in body weight regulation. *Health Psychology, 4,* 1–24.

Roediger, H. L., III, & Guynn, M. J. (1996). Retrieval processes. In E. L. Bjork & R. A. Bjork (Eds.), *Memory.* San Diego: Academic Press.

Roediger, H. L., III, & McDermott, K. B. (1995). Creating false memories: Remembering words not presented in lists. *Journal of Experimental Psychology: Learning, Memory, and Cognition, 21,* 803–814.

Roediger, H. L., III, & McDermott, K. B. (2000). Tricks of memory. *Current Directions in Psychological Science, 9,* 123–127.

Roediger, H. L., III, Wheeler, M. A., & Rajaram, S. (1993). Remembering, knowing, and reconstructing the past. In D. L. Medin (Ed.), *The psychology of learning and motivation: Advances in research and theory.* San Diego: Academic Press.

Roediger, H. L., III. (1980). Memory metaphors in cognitive psychology. *Memory & Cognition, 8,* 231–246.

Roediger, H. L., III. (1990). Implicit memory: Retention without remembering. *American Psychologist, 45,* 1043–1056.

Roediger, H. L., III. (2000). Why retrieval is the key process in understanding human memory. In E. Tulving (Ed.), *Memory, consciousness, and the brain: The Tallinn conference* (pp. 52–75). Philadelphia: Psychology Press.

Roehrs, T., & Roth, T. (2000). Hypnotics: Efficacy and adverse effects. In M. H. Kryger, T. Roth, & W. C. Dement (Eds.), *Principles and practice of sleep medicine.* Philadelphia: Saunders.

Roehrs, T., Carskadon, M. A., Dement, W. C., & Roth, T. (2000). Daytime sleepiness and alertness. In M. H. Kryger, T. Roth, & W. C. Dement (Eds.), *Principles and practice of sleep medicine.* Philadelphia: Saunders.

Roehrs, T., Carskadon, M. A., Dement, W. C., & Roth, T. (2005). Daytime sleepiness and alertness. In M. H. Kryger, T. Roth, & W. C. Dement (Eds.). *Principles and practice of sleep medicine.* Philadelphia: Elsevier Saunders.

Roehrs, T., Zorick, F. J., & Roth, T. (2000). Transient and short term insomnias. In M. H. Kryger, T. Roth, & W. C. Dement (Eds.), *Principles and practice of sleep medicine.* Philadelphia: Saunders.

Roffwarg, H. P., Muzio, J. N., & Dement, W. C. (1966). Ontogenetic development of the human sleep-dream cycle. *Science, 152,* 604–619.

Rogers, C. R. (1951). *Client-centered therapy: Its current practice, implications, and theory.* Boston: Houghton Mifflin.

Rogers, C. R. (1961). *On becoming a person: A therapist's view of psychotherapy.* Boston: Houghton Mifflin.

Rogers, C. R. (1980). *A way of being.* Boston: Houghton Mifflin.

Rogers, C. R. (1986). Client-centered therapy. In I. L. Kutash & A. Wolf (Eds.), *Psychotherapist's casebook.* San Francisco: Jossey-Bass.

Rogers, M. P., Fricchione, G., & Reich, P. (1999). Psychosomatic medicine and consultation-liaison psychiatry. In A. M. Nicholi (Ed.), *The Harvard guide to psychiatry* (3rd ed., pp. 362–389). Cambridge, MA: Harvard University Press.

Rogers, P. (1998). The cognitive psychology of lottery gambling: A theoretical review. *Journal of Gambling Studies, 14,* 111–134.

Rogers, R. W. (1983). Cognitive and physiological processes in fear appeals and attitude change: A revised theory of protection motivation. In J. Cacioppo & R. Petty (Eds.), *Social psychophysiology.* New York: Guilford.

Rogers, T. B., Kuiper, N. A., & Kirker, W. S. (1977). Self-reference and the encoding of personal information. *Journal of Personality and Social Psychology, 35,* 677–688.

Rogers, W. T., & Yang, P. (1996). Test-wiseness: Its nature and application. *European Journal of Psychological Assessment, 12,* 247–259.

Rogoff, B. (1990). *Apprenticeship in thinking.* New York: Oxford University Press.

Rohner, R. P., & Veneziano, R. A. (2001). The importance of father love: History and contemporary evidence. *Review of General Psychology, 5,* 382–405.

Rohrer, D., Taylor, K., Pashler, H., Wixted, J. T., & Capeda, N. J. (2005). The effect of overlearning on long-term retention. *Applied Cognitive Psychology, 19,* 361–374.

Roivainen, M., Viik-Kajander, M., Palosuo, T., Toivanen, P., Leinonen, M., Saikku, P., Tenkanen, L., Manninen, V., Hovi, T., & Mänttäri, M. (2000). Infections, inflammation, and the risk of coronary heart disease. *Circulation, 101,* 252–257.

Rojahn, K., & Pettigrew, T. F. (1992). Memory for schema-relevant information: A meta-analytic resolution. *British Journal of Social Psychology, 31,* 81–109.

Rollins, B., & Feldman, H. (1970). Marital satisfaction over the family life cycle. *Journal of Marriage and the Family, 32,* 20–28.

Rollman, G. B. (1992). Cognitive effects in pain and pain judgements. In D. Algom (Ed.), *Psychophysical approaches to cognition.* Amsterdam: North Holland.

Rolls, E. T. (1990). A theory of emotion, and its application to understanding the neural basis of emotion. *Cognitive and Emotion, 4,* 161–190.

Rolls, E. T., & Tovee, M. T. (1995). Sparseness of the neuronal representation of stimuli in the primate temporal visual cortex. *Journal of Neurophysiology, 73,* 713–726.

Romano, S. J., & Quinn, L. (2001). Evaluation and treatment of bulimia nervosa. *Primary Psychiatry, 8*(2), 57–62.

Rorschach, H. (1942). *Psychodiagnostics: A diagnostic test based on perception.* Berne: Huber.

Rosch, E. H. (1973). Natural categories. *Cognitive Psychology, 4,* 328–350.

Rosch, P. J. (n.d.). Reminiscences of Hans Selye, and the birth of "Stress." Retrieved June 22, 2005, from http://www.stress.org/mementos.htm.

Rose, D. P. (1997). Dietary fatty acids and cancer. *American Journal of Clinical Nutrition, 66,* 998S–1003S.

Rose, D., Wykes, T., Leese, M., Bindman, J., & Fleischmann, P. (2003). Patient's perspectives on electroconvulsive therapy: Systematic review. *British Medical Journal, 326,* 1363–1365.

Rose, H., & Rose, S. E. (2000). *Alas, poor Darwin: Arguments against evolutionary psychology.* New York: Harmony Books.

Rose, R. J. (1995). Genes and human behavior. *Annual Review of Psychology, 46,* 625–654.

Rose, S. D. (1999). Group therapy: A cognitive-behavioral approach. In J. R. Price & D. R. Hescheles (Ed.), *A guide to starting psychotherapy groups.* San Diego: Academic Press.

Rose, S. P. R. (1992). Protein synthesis in long-term memory in vertebrates. In L. R. Squire (Ed.), *Encyclopedia of learning and memory.* New York: Macmillan.

Rosenbaum, M., Lakin, M., & Roback, H. B. (1992). Psychotherapy in groups. In D. K. Freedheim (Ed.), *History of psychotherapy: A century of change.* Washington, DC: American Psychological Association.

Rosenberg, P. S., & Biggar, R. J. (1998). Trends in HIV incidence among young adults in the United States. *Journal of the American Medical Association, 279,* 1894–1899.

Rosenberg, S. D., Rosenberg, H. J., & Farrell, M. P. (1999). Midlife crisis revisited. In S. L. Willis & J. D. Reid (Eds.), *Life in the middle: Psychological and social development in middle age* (pp. 47–70). San Diego, CA: Academic Press.

Rosenfarb, I. S., Goldstein, M. J., Mintz, J., & Nuechterlein, K. H. (1995). Expressed emotion and subclinical psychopathology observable within the transactions between schizophrenic patients and their family members. *Journal of Abnormal Psychology, 104,* 259–267.

Rosenhan, D. L. (1973). On being sane in insane places. *Science, 179,* 250–258.

Rosenheck, R. (2000). Cost-effectiveness of services for mentally ill homeless people: The application of research to policy and practice. *American Journal of Psychiatry, 157,* 1563–1570.

Rosenthal, R. (1976). *Experimenter effects in behavioral research.* New York: Halsted.

Rosenthal, R. (1994). Interpersonal expectancy effects: A 30–year perspective. *Current Directions in Psychological Science, 3,* 176–179.

Rosenthal, R. (2002). Experimenter and clinical effects in scientific inquiry and clinical practice. *Prevention & Treatment, 5*(38), no pagination specified.

Rosenthal, R., & Fode, K. L. (1963). Three experiments in experimenter bias. *Psychological Reports, 12,* 491–511.

Rosenzweig, M. R. (1996). Aspects of the search for neural mechanisms of memory. *Annual Review of Psychology, 47,* 1–32.

Rosenzweig, M. R., & Bennet, E. L. (1996). Psychobiology of plasticity: Effects of training and experience on brain and behavior. *Behavioural Brain Research, 78*(5), 57–65.

Rosenzweig, M. R., Krech, D., & Bennett, E. L. (1961). Heredity, environment, brain biochemistry, and learning. In *Current trends in psychological theory.* Pittsburgh: University of Pittsburgh Press.

Rosenzweig, M., Krech, D., Bennett, E. L., & Diamond, M. (1962). Effects of environmental complexity and training on brain chemistry and anatomy: A replication and extension. *Journal of Comparative and Physiological Psychology, 55,* 429–437.

Rosenzweig, S. (1985). Freud and experimental psychology: The emergence of idiodynamics. In S. Koch & D. E. Leary (Eds.), *A century of psychology as a science.* New York: McGraw-Hill.

Roskos-Ewoldsen, D. R., & Fazio, R. H. (1992). The accessibility of source likability as a determinant of persuasion. *Personality and Social Psychology Bulletin, 18,* 19–25.

Rosler, F. (2005). From single-channel recordings to brain-mapping devices: The impact of electroencephalography on experimental psychology. *History of Psychology, 8*(1), 95–117.

Ross, B. (1991). William James: Spoiled child of American psychology. In G. A. Kimble, M. Wertheimer, & C. White (Eds.), *Portraits of pioneers in psychology.* Hillsdale, NJ: Erlbaum.

Ross, C. A. (1999). Dissociative disorders. In T. Millon, P. H. Blaney, & R. D. Davis (Eds.), *Oxford textbook of psychopathology* (pp. 466–484). New York: Oxford University Press.

Ross, C. E., & Van Willigen, M. (1997). Education and the subjective quality of life. *Journal of Health and Social Behavior, 38,* 275–297.

Ross, L. D. (1988). The obedience experiments: A case study of controversy. *Contemporary Psychology, 33,* 101–104.

Ross, L. D., & Anderson, C. A. (1982). Shortcomings in the attribution process: On the origins and maintenance of erroneous social assessments. In D. Kahneman, P. Slovic, & A. Tversky (Eds.), *Judgement under uncertainty: Heuristics and biases.* Cambridge: Cambridge University Press.

Rosse, J. G., Stecher, M. D., Miller, J. L., & Levin, R. A. (1998). The impact of response distortion on preemployment personality testing and hiring decisions. *Journal of Applied Psychology, 83,* 634–644.

Rossi, P. H. (1990). The old homeless and the new homelessness in historical perspective. *American Psychologist, 45*(8), 954–959.

Rosso, I. M., Cannon, T. D., Huttunen, T., Huttunen, M. O., Lönnqvist, J., & Gasperoni, T. L. (2000). Obstetric risk factors for early-onset schizophrenia in a Finnish birth cohort. *American Journal of Psychiatry, 157,* 801–807.

Roth, T., & Drake, C. (2004). Evolution of insomnia: Current status and future direction. *Sleep Medicine, 5*(Supplemental 1), S23–S30.

Rothbart, M. K., & Bates, J. E. (1998).Temperament. In W. Damon (Ed.), *Handbook of child psychology (Vol. 3): Social, emotional, and personality development.* New York: Wiley.

Rothbart, M. K., Ahadi, S. A., & Evans, D. E. (2000). Temperament and personality: Origins and outcomes. *Journal of Personality and Social Psychology, 78,* 122–135.

Rothbaum, F., Weisz, J., Pott, M., Miyake, K., & Morelli, G. (2000). Attachment and culture: Security in the United States and Japan. *American Psychologist, 55,* 1093–1104.

Rothenberg, A. (1990). *Creativity and madness.* Baltimore: John Hopkins University Press.

Rothschild, A. J. (1999). Mood disorders. In A. M. Nicholi, Jr. (Ed.), *The Harvard guide to psychiatry* (3rd ed., pp. 281–307). Cambridge, MA: Harvard University Press.

Rotter, J. B. (1982). *The development and application of social learning theory.* New York: Praeger.

Rotter, J. B., & Rafferty, J. E. (1950). *Manual: The Rotter incomplete sentence blank.* New York: Psychological Corporation.

Rouiller, E. M. (1997). Functional organization of the auditory pathways. In G. Ehret & R. Romand (Eds.), *The central auditory system.* Oxford, England: Oxford University Press.

Rousseau, D. M. (1995). *Psychological contracts in organizations.* Thousand Oaks, CA: Sage.

Rousseau, D. M., & Parks, J. M. (1993). The contracts of individuals and organizations. In B. M. Staw & L. L. Cummings (Eds.), *Research in organizational behavior* (Vol. 15, pp. 1–43). Greenwich, CT: JAI Press.

Rousseau, D. M., & Schalk, R. (2000). Learning from cross-national perspectives on psychological contracts. In D. M. Rousseau &

R. Schalk (Eds.), *Psychological contracts in employment: Cross-national perspectives* (pp. 283–403). Thousand Oaks, CA: Sage.

Rowe, D. (1994). *The limits of family influence: Genes, experience, and behavior.* New York: Guilford.

Rowe, D. C. (1997). Genetics, temperament, and personality. In R. Hogan, J. Johnson, & S. Briggs (Eds.), *Handbook of personality psychology.* San Diego: Academic Press.

Rowe, D., & van den Oord, E. J. C. G. (2005). Genetic and environmental influences. In V. A. Derlega, B. A. Winstead, & W. H. Jones (Eds.), *Personality: Contemporary theory and research.* Belmont, CA: Wadsworth.

Rozanski, A., Blumenthal, J. A., & Kaplan, J. (1999). Impact of psychological factors on the pathogenesis of cardiovascular disease and implications for therapy. *Circulation, 99,* 2192–2197.

Rozee, P. D., & Koss, M. P. (2001). Rape: A century of resistance. *Psychology of Women Quarterly, 25* (4), 295–311.

Rozin, P. (1990). The importance of social factors in understanding the acquisition of food habits. In E. D. Capaldi & T. L. Powley (Eds.), *Taste, experience, and feeding.* Washington, DC: American Psychological Association.

Rozin, P. (1996). Towards a psychology of food and eating: From motivation to module to model to marker, morality, meaning, and metaphor. *Current Directions in Psychological Science, 5,* 18–24.

Rozin, P. (2003). Introduction: Evolutionary and cultural perspectives on affect. In R. J. Davidson, K. R. Scherer, & H. H. Goldsmith (Eds.), *Handbook of affective sciences.* New York: Oxford University Press.

Ruble, D. N., & Martin, C. L. (1998). Gender development. In W. Damon (Ed.), *Handbook of child psychology (Vol. 3): Social, emotional, and personality development.* New York: Wiley.

Ruble, T. L. (1983). Sex stereotypes: Issues of change in the 70s. *Sex Roles, 9,* 397–402.

Rudorfer, M. V., & Goodwin, F. K. (1993). Introduction. In C. E. Coffey (Ed.), *The clinical science of electroconvulsive therapy.* Washington, DC: American Psychiatric Press.

Rusak, B. (1990). Biological Rhythms: From Physiology to behavior. In J. Montplaisir & R. Bodbout (Eds.), *Sleep and biological rhythms: Basic mechanism and applications to psychiatry* (pp. 11–24). New York: Oxford University Press.

Rusak, B., & Zucker, I. (1979). Neural regulation of circadian rhythms. *Physiological Review, 59,* 449–526.

Ruscio, J. (2002). *Clear thinking with psychology: Separating sense from nonsense.* Belmont, CA: Wadsworth.

Rush, A. J. (1984). Cognitive therapy. In T. B. Karasu (Ed.), *The psychiatric therapies.* Washington, DC: American Psychiatric Press.

Rush, A. J. (2000). Mood disorders: Treatment of depression. In B. J. Sadock & V. A. Sadock (Eds.), *Kaplan and Sadock's comprehensive textbook of psychiatry* (7th ed., Vol. 1, pp. 1377–1384). Philadelphia: Lippincott/Williams and Wilkins.

Rush, A. J., & Beck, A. T. (2000). Cognitive therapy. In B. J. Sadock & V. A. Sadock (Eds.), *Kaplan and Sadock's comprehensive textbook of psychiatry* (7th ed., Vol. 1, pp. 2167–2177). Philadelphia: Lippincott/Williams & Wilkins.

Rushton, J. P. (1994). Sex and race differences in cranial capacity from International Labour Office data. *Intelligence, 19,* 281–294.

Rushton, J. P. (1995). *Race, evolution, and behavior. A life-history perspective.* New Brunswick, NJ: Transaction.

Rushton, J. P., & Jensen, A. R. (2005). Thirty years of research on race differences in cognitive ability. *Psychology, Public Policy, and Law, 11,* 235–294.

Rushton–Suzuki Debate. (n.d.). http://archives.cbc.ca/IDC-1-74-663-3727/people/david_suzuki/clip5.

Russell, G. F. M. (1995). Anorexia nervosa through time. In G. Szmukler, C. Dare, & J. Treasure (Eds.), *Handbook of eating disorders: Theory, treatment, and research.* New York: Wiley.

Russell, G. F. M. (1997). The history of bulimia nervosa. In D. M. Garner, & P. E. Garfinkel (Eds.), *Handbook of treatment for eating disorders.* New York: Guilford.

Russell, J. A. (1991). Culture and the categorization of emotions. *Psychological Bulletin, 110,* 426–450.

Russell, J. A. (1994). Is there universal recognition of emotion from facial expression? A review of the cross-cultural studies. *Psychological Bulletin, 115,* 102–141.

Russell, J. A. (1995). Facial expressions of emotion: What lies beyond minimal universality? *Psychological Bulletin, 118,* 379–391.

Rutherford, A. (2000). Radical behaviorism and psychology's public: B. F. Skinner in the popular press, 1934–1990. *History of Psychology, 3,* 371–395.

Rutherford, A. (2003). B. F. Skinner's technology of behavior in American life: From consumer culture to counterculture. *Journal of History of the Behavioral Sciences, 39,* 1–23.

Rutherford, A. (in press). B. F. Skinner. In R. Wozniak (Psychology Ed.), *Dictionary of modern American philosophers.* Bristol, England: Thoemmes Press.

Rutherford, W. (1886). A new theory of hearing. *Journal of Anatomy and Physiology, 21,* 166–168.

Rutledge, T., Reis, S. E., Olson, M., Owens, J., Kelsey, S. F., Pepine, C. J., Mankad, S., Rogers, W. J., Merz, C. N. B., Sopko, G., Cornell, C. E., Sharaf, B., & Matthews, K. A. (2004). Social networks are associated with lower mortality rates among women with suspected coronary disease: The National Heart Lung, and Blood Institute–sponsored women's ischemia syndrome evaluation study. *Psychosomatic Medicine, 66,* 882–888.

Rutter, M. L. (1997). Nature-nurture intergration: The example of antisocial behavior. *American Psychologist, 52,* 390–398.

Rutter, M., & O'Connor, T. G. (1999). Implications of attachment theory for child care policies. In J. Cassidy & P. R. Shaver (Eds.), *Handbook of attachment: Theory, research and clinical applications.* New York: Guilford.

Rutter, M., & Silberg, J. (2002). Gene-environment interplay relation to emotional and behavioral disturbance. *Annual Review of Psychology, 53,* 463–490.

Ryan, C. S., Park, B., & Judd, C. M. (1996). Assessing stereotype accuracy: Implications for understanding the stereotyping process. In C. N. Macrae, C. Stangor, & M. Hewstone (Eds.), *Stereotypes and stereotyping.* New York: Guilford.

Ryan, R. M., & Deci, E. L. (2001). On happiness and human potentials: A review of research on hedonic and eudaimonic well-being. *Annual Review of Psychology, 52,* 141–166.

Rynes, S. S. (1993). Who's selecting whom? Effects of selection practices on applicant attitudes and behavior. In N. Schmitt & W. C. Borman (Eds.), *Personnel selection in organizations* (pp. 240–274). San Francisco: Jossey-Bass.

Sachs, J. (1985). Prelinguistic development. In J. B. Gleason (Ed.), *The development of language.* Columbus: Charles E. Merrill.

Sackeim, H. A., Haskett, R. F., Mulsant, B. H., Thase, M. E., Mann, J. J., Pettinati, H. M., Greenberg, R. M., Crowe, R. R., Cooper, T. B., & Prudic, J. (2001). Continuation pharmacotherapy in the prevention of relapse following electroconvulsive therapy: A randomized controlled trial. *Journal of the American Medical Association, 285,* 1299–1307.

Sadker, M., & Sadker, D. (1994). *Failing at fairness: How America's schools cheat girls.* New York: Scribners.

Safdar, S., & Lay, C. (2003). The relations of immigrant-specific and non-specific daily hassles to distress controlling for psychological adjustment and cultural competence. *Journal of Applied Social Psychology, 33,* 299–320.

Saklofske, D. H., Gorsuch, R. L., Weiss, L. G., Zhu, J., & Peterson, C. A. (2005). General ability index for the WAIS-III: Canadian Norms. *Canadian Journal of Behavioural Science, 37,* 44–48.

Salkovskis, P. M., & Warwick, H. M. C. (2001). Meaning, misinterpretations, and medicine: A cognitive-behavioral approach to understanding health anxiety and hypochondriasis. In V. Starcevic & D. R. Lipsitt (Eds.), *Hypochondriasis: Modern perspectives on an ancient malady.* New York: Oxford University Press.

Sallot, J. (2005). U.S. authorities fear influx of Canadian ecstasy. *Globe and Mail,* March 10, p. A18.

Salminen, S. (1992). Defensive attribution hypothesis and serious occupational accidents. *Psychological Reports, 70,* 1195–1199.

Salovey, P., & Mayer, J. D. (1990). Emotional intelligence. *Imagination, Cognition, and Personality, 9,* 185–211.

Salovey, P., Mayer, J. D., & Caruso, D. (2002). The positive psychology of emotional intelligence. In C. R. Synder & J. Lopez (Eds.), *Handbook of positive psychology.* New York: Oxford University Press.

Salthouse, T. A. (1991). Mediation of adult age differences in cognition by reductions in working memory and speed of processing. *Psychological Science, 2,* 179–183.

Salthouse, T. A. (1994). The nature of the influence of speed on adult age differences in cognition. *Developmental Psychology, 30,* 240–259.

Salthouse, T. A. (1996). The processing-speed theory of adult age differences in cognition. *Psychological Review, 103,* 403–428.

Salthouse, T. A. (2000). Aging and measures of processing speed. *Biological Psychology, 54*, 35–54.

Salvendy, J. T. (1993). Selection and preparation of patients and organization of the group. In H. I. Kaplan & B. J. Sadock (Eds.), *Comprehensive group psychotherapy.* Baltimore: Williams & Wilkins.

Samelson, F. (1981). Struggle for scientific authority: The reception of Watson's behaviorism, 1913–1920. *Journal of the History of the Behavioral Sciences, 17*, 399–425.

Samelson, F. (1994). John B. Watson in 1913: Rhetoric and practice. In J. T. Todd & E. K. Morris (Eds.), *Modern perspectives on John B. Watson and classical behaviorism.* Westport, CT: Greenwood Press.

Samet, J. M. (1992). The health benefits of smoking cessation. *Medical Clinics of North America, 76*, 399–414.

Sammons, M. T., Gorny, S. W., Zinner, E. S., & Allen, R. P. (2000). Prescriptive authority for psychologists: A consensus of support. *Professsional Psychology: Research and Practice, 31*, 604–609.

Sande, M. A., & Ronald, A. (2004). Treatment of HIV/AIDS: Do the dilemmas only increase? *Journal of the American Medical Association, 292*, 224–236.

Sanderson, W. C., & Barlow, D. H. (1990). A description of patients diagnosed with DSM-III-R generalized anxiety disorder. *Journal of Nervous and Mental Disease, 178*, 588–591.

Sandin, B., Chorot, P., Santed, M. A., & Valiente, R. M. (2004). Differences in negative life events between patients with anxiety disorders, depression and hypochondriasis. *Anxiety, Stress & Coping: An International Journal, 17*(1), 37–47.

Sandler, J. (1975). Aversion methods. In F. H. Kanfer & A. P. Goldstein (Eds.), *Helping people change: A textbook of methods.* New York: Pergamon Press.

Sangster, D. & Wortsman, A. (2001) Labour and business perspectives on Canada's skills challenge. *Workplace Gazette, 4*(3): 46–53.

Sanislow, C. A., & Carson, R. C. (2001). Schizophrenia: A critical examination. In P. B. Sutker & H. E. Adams (Eds.), *Comprehensive handbook of psychopathology* (3rd ed., pp. 403–444). New York: Kluwer Academic/Plenum.

Sanson, A., Hemphill, S. A., & Smart, D. (2002). Temperament and social development. In P. K. Smith & C. H. Hart (Eds.), *Blackwell handbook of childhood social development.* Malden, MA: Blackwell Publishing.

Sanz, J., Sanchez-Bernardos, M. L., & Avia, M. D. (1996). Self-monitoring and the prediction of one's own and others' personality test scores. *European Journal of Personality, 10*, 173–184.

Saper, C. B. (2000). Brain stem, reflexive behavior, and the cranial nerves. In E. R. Kandel, J. H. Schwartz, & T. M. Jessell (Eds.), *Principles of neural science* (pp. 873–888). New York: McGraw-Hill.

Sapolsky, R. M. (1992). Neuroendocrinology and the stress-response. In J. B. Becker, S. M. Breedlove, & D. Crews (Eds.), *Behavioral endocrinology.* Cambridge, MA: MIT Press.

Sarason, I. G., & Sarason, B. G. (1987). *Abnormal psychology: The problem of maladaptive behavior.* Englewood Cliffs, NJ: Prentice-Hall.

Sato, T., & McCann, D. (2002). Advances in the study of sociotropy-autonomy and depression. *Advances in Psychology Research, 15*, pp. 35–54.

Savage-Rumbaugh, E. S. (1991). Language learning in the bonobo: How and why they learn. In N. A. Krasnegor, D. M. Rumbaugh, & R. L. Schiefelbusch/M. Studdert-Kennedy (Eds.), *Biological and behavioral determinants of language development.* Hillsdale, NJ: Erlbaum.

Savage-Rumbaugh, S., McDonald, K., Sevcik, R. A., Hopkins, W. D., & Rupert, E. (1986). Spontaneous symbol acquisition and communication use by pygmy chimpanzees (*Pan paniscus*). *Journal of Experimental Psychology: General, 115*, 211–235.

Savage-Rumbaugh, S., Shanker, S. G., & Taylor, T. J. (1998). *Apes, language, and the human mind.* New York: Oxford University Press.

Savitsky, K., Epley, N., & Gilovich, T. (2001). Do others judge us as harshly as we think? Overestimating the impact of our failures, shortcomings, and mishaps. *Journal of Personality and Social Psychology, 81*, 44–56.

Saxe, G. N., van der Kolk, B. A., Berkowitz, R., Chinman, G., Hall, K., Lieberg, G., & Schwartz, J. (1993). Dissociative disorders in psychiatric inpatients. *American Journal of Psychiatry, 150*, 1037–1042.

Saxe, L. (1994). Detection of deception: Polygraph and integrity tests. *Current Directions in Psychological Science, 3*, 69–73.

Saxe, L., & Ben-Shakhar, G. (1999). Admissibility of polygraph tests: The application of scientific standards post-Daubert. *Psychology, Public Policy, and Law, 5*, 203–223.

Saxton, M., Kulcsar, B., Marshall, G., & Rupra, M. (1998). Longer-term effects of corrective input: An experimental approach. *Journal of Child Language, 25*, 701–721.

Scarr, S. (1991). *Theoretical issues in investigating intellectual plasticity.* S. E. Brauth, W. S. Hall, & R. Dooling (Eds.), *Plasticity of development.* Cambridge, MA: MIT Press.

Scarr, S. (1997). Behavior-genetic and socialization theories of intelligence: Truce and reconciliation. In R. J. Sternberg & E. L. Grigorenko (Eds.), *Intelligence, heredity, and environment.* New York: Cambridge University Press.

Scarr, S., & Weinberg, R. A. (1977). Intellectual similarities within families of both adopted and biological children. *Intelligence, 32*, 170–190.

Scarr, S., & Weinberg, R. A. (1983). The Minnesota adoption studies: Genetic differences and malleability. *Child Development, 54*, 260–267.

Schachner, D. A., & Shaver, P. R. (2004). Attachment dimensions and sexual motives. *Personal Relationships, 11*(2), 179–195.

Schachter, S. (1964). The interaction of cognitive and physiological determinants of emotional state. In L. Berkowitz (Ed.), *Advances in experimental social psychology* (Vol. 1). New York: Academic Press.

Schachter, S., & Rodin, J. (1974). *Obese humans and rats.* Hillsdale, NJ: Erlbaum.

Schachter, S., & Singer, J. E. (1962). Cognitive, social and physiological determinants of emotional state. *Psychological Review, 69*, 379–399.

Schachter, S., & Singer, J. E. (1979). Comments on the Maslach and Marshall-Zimbardo experiments. *Journal of Personality and Social Psychology, 37*, 989–995.

Schacter, D. L. (1987). Implicit memory: History and current status. *Journal of Experimental Psychology: Learning, Memory and Cognition, 14*, 501–518.

Schacter, D. L. (1989). On the relation between memory and consciousness: Dissociable interactions and conscious experience. In H. L. Roediger III & F. I. M. Craik (Eds.), *Varieties of memory and consciousness.* Hillsdale, NJ: Erlbaum.

Schacter, D. L. (1992). Understanding implicit memory: A cognitive neuroscience approach. *American Psychologist, 47*, 559–569.

Schacter, D. L. (1994). Priming and multiple memory systems: Perceptual mechanisms of implicit memory. In D. L. Schacter & E. Tulving (Eds.), *Memory systems.* Cambridge, MA: MIT Press.

Schacter, D. L. (1996). *Searching for memory: The brain, the mind, and the past.* New York: Basic Books.

Schacter, D. L. (1999). The seven sins of memory: Insights from psychology and cognitive neuroscience. *American Psychologist, 54*, 182–203.

Schacter, D. L. (2001). *The seven sins of memory: How the mind forgets and remembers.* Boston, MA: Houghton Mifflin.

Schacter, D. L., Chiu, C. Y. P., & Ochsner, K. N. (1993). Implicit memory: A selective review. *Annual Review of Neuroscience, 16*, 159–182.

Schaeffer, N. C. (2000). Asking questions about threatening topics: A selective overview. In A. A. Stone, J. S. Turkkan, C. A. Bachrach, J. B. Jobe, H. S. Kurtzman, & V. Cain (Eds.), *The science of self-report: Implications for research and practice.* Mahwah, NJ: Erlbaum.

Schafe, G. E., & Bernstein, I. E. (1996). Taste aversion learning. In E. D. Capaldi (Ed.), *Why we eat what we eat: The psychology of eating* (pp. 31–52). Washington, DC: American Psychological Association.

Schaie, K. W. (1983). The Seattle longitudinal study: A twenty-one year exploration of psychometric intelligence in adulthood. In K. W. Schaie (Ed.), *Longitudinal studies of adult psychological development.* New York: Guilford.

Schaie, K. W. (1990). Intellectual development in adulthood. In J. E. Birren & K. W. Schaie (Eds.), *Handbook of the psychology of aging* (3rd ed.). San Diego: Academic Press.

Schaie, K. W. (1993). The Seattle longitudinal studies of adult intelligence. *Current Directions, 2*, 171–175.

Schaie, K. W. (1994). The course of adult intellectual development. *American Psychologist, 49*, 304–313.

Schaie, K. W. (1996). *Adult intellectual development: The Seattle longitudinal study.* New York: Cambridge University Press.

Scheidlinger, S. (1993). History of group psychotherapy. In H. I. Kaplan & B. J. Sadock (Eds.), *Comprehensive group psychotherapy.* Baltimore: Williams & Wilkins.

Scheier, M. F., & Carver, C. S. (1985). Optimism, coping and health: Assessment and implications of generalized expectancies. *Health Psychology, 4*, 219–247.

Schein, E. H. (1996). Culture: The missing concept in organizational studies. *Administrative Science Quarterly, 41*, 229–240.

Scherer, K. R. (1997). The role of culture in emotion-antecedent appraisal. *Journal of Personality and Social Psychology, 73*, 902–922.

Scherer, K. R., & Wallbott, H. G. (1994). Evidence for universality and cultural variation of differential emotion response patterning. *Journal of Personality and Social Psychology, 66*, 310–328.

Schiavi, R. C., White, D., Mandeli, J., & Levine, A. C. (1997). Effect of testosterone administration on sexual behavior and mood in men with erectile dysfunction. *Archives of Sexual Behavior, 26*, 231–241.

Schiff, M., & Lewontin, R. (1986). *Education and class: The irrelevance of IQ genetic studies.* Oxford: Clarendon Press.

Schiffman, J., Ekstrom, M., LaBrie, J., Schulsinger, F., Sorenson, H., & Mednick, S. (2002). Minor physical anomalies and schizophrenia spectrum disorders: A prospective investigation. *American Journal of Psychiatry, 159*, 238–243.

Schiffman, S. S., Graham, B. G., Sattely-Miller, E. A., & Warwick, Z. S. (1998). Orosensory perception of dietary fat. *Current Directions in Psychological Science, 7*, 137–143.

Schildkraut, J. J., Hirshfeld, A. J., & Murphy, J. M. (1994). Mind and mood in modern art, II: Depressive disorders, spirituality, and early deaths in the abstract expressionist artists of the New York School. *American Journal of Psychiatry, 151*, 482–488.

Schlaadt, R. G., & Shannon, P. T. (1994). *Drugs: Use, misuse, and abuse* (4th ed.). Englewood Cliffs, NJ: Prentice-Hall.

Schlaepfer, T. E., Pearlson, G. D., Wong, D. F., Marenco, S., & Dannals, R. F. (1997). PET study of competition between intravenous cocaine and [11C] raclopride at dopamine receptors in human subjects. *American Journal of Psychiatry, 154*, 1209–1213.

Schlegel, A., & Barry, H., III. (1991). *Adolescence: An anthropological inquiry.* New York: Free Press.

Schlenger, W. E., Kulka, R. A., Fairbank, J. A., Hough, R. L., Jordan, B. K., Marmar, C. R., & Weiss, D. S. (1992). The prevalence of post-traumatic stress disorder in the Vietnam generation: A multimethod, multisource assessment of psychiatric disorder. *Journal of Traumatic Stress, 5*(3), 333–363.

Schlosberg, H. (1954). Three dimensions of emotion. *Psychological Review, 61*, 81–88.

Schmitt, D. P. (2005). Fundamentals of human mating strategies. In D. M. Buss (Ed.), *The handbook of evolutionary psychology.* New York: Wiley.

Schmitt, N., & Chan, D. (1998). *Personnel selection: A theoretical approach.* Thousand Oaks, CA: Sage.

Schmitz, J. M., & DeLaune, K. A. (2005). Nicotine. In J. H. Lowinson, P. Ruiz, R. B. Millman, & J. G. Langrod (Eds.), *Substance abuse: A comprehensive textbook.* Philadelphia: Lippincott/Williams & Williams.

Schmitz, J. M., Jarvik, M. E., & Schneider, N. G. (1997). Nicotine. In J. H. Lowinson, P. Ruiz, R. B. Millman, & J. G. Langrod (Eds.), *Substance abuse: A comprehensive textbook.* Baltimore: Williams & Wilkins.

Schmolck, H., Buffalo, E. A., & Squire, L. R. (2000). Memory distortions develop over time: Recollections of the O. J. Simpson trial verdict after 15 and 32 months. *Psychological Science, 11*, 39–45.

Schmolck, H., Buffalo, E. A., & Squire, L. R. (2000). Memory distortions develop over time: Recollections of the O. J. Simpson trial verdict after 15 and 32 months. *Psychological Science, 11*, 39–45.

Schneewind, K. A. (1995). Impact of family processes on control beliefs. In A. Bandura (Ed.), *Self-efficacy in changing societies.* New York: Cambridge University Press.

Schneider, B. (1987). The people make the place. *Personnel Psychology, 40*, 437–454.

Schneider, B. (1996). When individual differences aren't. In K. R. Murphy (Ed.), *Individual differences and behaviors in organizations* (pp. 548–572). San Francisco: Jossey-Bass.

Schneider, B. H., Atkinson, L., & Tardif, C. (2001). Child-parent attachment and children's peer relations: A quantitative review. *Developmental Psychology, 37*, 86–100.

Schneider, F., & Deldin, P. J. (2001). Genetics and schizophrenia. In P. B. Sutker & H. E. Adams (Eds.), *Comprehensive handbook of psychopathology* (3rd ed., pp. 371–402). New York: Kluwer Academic/Plenum.

Scholey, A. B., Parrott, A. C., Buchanan, T., Heffernan, T. M., Ling, J., & Rodgers, J. (2004). Increased intensity of Ecstasy and polydrug usage in the more experienced recreational Ecstasy/MDMA users: A WWW study. *Addictive Behaviors, 29*, 743–752.

Schonemann, P. H. (1994). Heritability. In R. J. Sternberg (Ed.), *Encyclopedia of human intelligence.* New York: Macmillan.

Schooler, J. W. (1999). Seeking the core: The issues and evidence surrounding recovered accounts of sexual trauma. In L. M. Williams & V. L. Banyard (Eds.), *Trauma & memory.* Thousand Oaks, CA: Sage Publications.

Schooler, J. W., & Eich, E. (2000). Memory for emotional events. In E. Tulving & F. I. M. Craik, (Eds.), *The Oxford handbook of memory* (pp. 379–397). Oxford, UK: Oxford University Press.

Schreiber, F. R. (1973). *Sybil.* New York: Warner.

Schuller, R. A. & Ogloff, J. R. P. (2001) (Eds.). *An introduction to law and psychology: Canadian perspectives.* Toronto: University of Toronto Press.

Schuller, R. A., & Ogloff, J. R. P. (2001). An introduction to psychology and the law. In R. A. Schuller & J. R. P. Ogloff (Eds.), *Introduction to psychology and the law: Canadian perspectives* (pp. 3–28). Toronto: University of Toronto Press.

Schultz, J. H., & Luthe, W. (1959). *Autogenic training.* New York: Grune & Stratton.

Schulz-Hardt, S., Frey, D., Luethgens, C., & Moscovici, S. (2000). Biased information search in group decision making. *Journal of Personality & Social Psychology, 78*, 655–669.

Schuman, H., & Kalton, G. (1985). Survey methods. In G. Lindzey & E. Aronson (Eds.), *Handbook of social psychology* (3rd ed.). New York: Random House.

Schumann, J. (1978). The acculturation model for second language acquisition. In R. C. Gingras (Ed.), *Second-language acquisition and foreign language teaching.* Washington, DC: Center for Applied Linguistics.

Schumann, J. (1993). Some problems with falsification: An illustration from SLA research. *Applied Linguistics, 14*, 295–306.

Schusterman, R. J., & Gisiner, R. (1988). Artificial language comprehension in dolphins and sea lions: The essential cognitive skills. *Psychological Record, 38*, 311–348.

Schwartz, B. L. (1999). Sparkling at the end of the tongue: The etiology of tip-of-the-tongue phenomenology. *Psychonomic Bulletin & Review, 6*, 379–393.

Schwartz, B., & Robbins, S. J. (1995). *Psychology of learning and behavior* (4th ed.). New York: Norton.

Schwartz, J. H. (2000). Neurotransmitters. In E. R. Kandel, J. H. Schwartz, & T. M. Jessell (Eds.), *Principles of neural science.* New York: McGraw-Hill.

Schwartz, J. H., & Westbrook, G. L. (2000). The cytology of neurons. In E. R. Kandel, J. H. Schwartz, & T. M. Jessell (Eds.), *Principles of neural science* (pp. 67–104). New York: McGraw-Hill.

Schwartz, J. P., Waldo, M., & Higgins, A. J. (2004). Attachment styles: Relationship to masculine gender role conflict in college men. *Psychology of Men & Masculinity, 5*(2), 143–146.

Schwartz, L., Slater, M. A., & Birchler, G. R. (1994). Interpersonal stress and pain behaviors in patients with chronic pain. *Journal of Consulting and Clinical Psychology, 62*, 861–864.

Schwartz, M. W., & Seeley, R. J. (1997). The new biology of body weight regulation. *Journal of the American Dietetic Association, 97*, 54–58.

Schwartz, M. W., Peskind, E., Raskind, M., Nicolson, M., Moore, J., Morawiecki, A., Boyko, E. J., & Porte, D. J. (1996). Cerebrospinal fluid leptin levels: Relationship to plasma levels and to adiposity in humans. *Nature Medicine, 2*, 589–593.

Schwartz, M. W., Woods, S. C., Porte, D., Seeley, R. J., & Baskin, D. G. (2000). Central nervous system control of food intake. *Nature, 404*, 661–671.

Schwartz, N., & Strack, F. (1999). Reports of subjective well-being: Judgmental processes and their methodological implications. In D. Kahneman, E. Diener, & N. Schwarz (Eds.), *Well-being: The foundations of hedonic psychology.* New York: Russell Sage Foundation.

Schwartz, S. H. (1990). Individualism-collectivism: Critique and proposed refinements. *Journal of Cross-Cultural Psychology, 21*, 139–157.

Schwartz, W. J. (1996). Internal timekeeping. *Science & Medicine, 3*, 44–53.

Schwarz, N. (1999). Self-reports: How the questions shape the answers. *American Psychologist, 54*, 93–105.

Scoboria, A., Mazzoni, G., Kirsch, I., & Milling, L. S. (2002). Immediate and persisting effects of misleading questions and hypnosis on memory reports. *Journal of Experimental Psychology: Applied, 8*(1), 26–32.

Scott, T. R. (1990). The effect of physiological need on taste. In E.

D. Capaldi & T. L. Powley (Eds.), *Taste, experience, and feeding.* Washington, DC: American Psychological Association.

Scoville, W. B., & Milner, B. (1957). Loss of recent memory after bilateral hippocampal lesions. *Journal of Neurology, Neurosurgery & Psychiatry, 20,* 11–21.

Scroppo, J. C., Drob, S. L., Weinberger, J. L., & Eagle, P. (1998). Identifying dissociative identity disorder: A self-report and projective study. *Journal of Abnormal Psychology, 107,* 272–284.

Scull, A. (1990). Deinstitution-alization: Cycles of despair. *The Journal of Mind and Behavior, 11*(3/4), 301–312.

Scully, J. A., Tosi, H., & Banning, K. (2000). Life event checklists: Revisiting the social readjustment rating scale after 30 years. *Educational & Psychological Measurement, 60,* 864–876.

Seabrook, R., Brown, G. D. A., & Solity, J. E. (2005). Distributed and massed practice: From laboratory to classroom. *Applied Cognitive Psychology, 19*(1), 107–122.

Sealy, P., & Whitehead, P. C. (2004). Forty years of deinstitution-alization of psychiatric services in Canada: An empirical assessment. *Canadian Journal of Psychiatry, 49,* 249–257.

Searle, A., & Bennett, P. (2001). Psychological factors and inflam-matory bowel disease: A review of a decade of literature. *Psychology, Health and Medicine, 6,* 121–135.

Searleman, A. (1996). Personality variables and prospective memory performance. In D. J. Herrmann, C. McEvoy, C. Hertzog, P. Hertel, & M. K. Johnson (Eds.), *Basic and applied memory research: Practical applica-tions* (Vol. 2). Mahwah, NJ: Erlbaum.

Searleman, A., & Herrmann, D. (1994). *Memory from a broader per-spective.* New York: McGraw-Hill.

Sears, D. O. (1975). Political social-ization. In F. I. Greenstein & N. W. Polsby (Eds.), *Handbook of political science* (Vol. 2). Reading, MA: Addison-Wesley.

Sears, D. O. (1986). College sopho-mores in the laboratory: Influences of a narrow database on social psy-chology's view of human nature. *Journal of Personality and Social Psychology, 51,* 515–530.

Sedikides, C., & Strube, M. J. (1997). Self-evaluation: To thine own self be good, to thine own self be sure, to thine own self be true, and to thine own self be better. In M. P. Zanna (Ed.), *Advances in exper-imental social psychology.* New York: Academic Press.

Seeley, R. J., & Schwartz, M. W. (1997). Regulation of energy bal-ance: Peripheral endocrine signals and hypothalamic neuropeptides. *Current Directions in Psychological Science, 6,* 39–44.

Seeley, R. J., Matson, C. A., Chavez, M., Woods, S. C., & Schwartz, M. W. (1996). Behavioral, endocrine and hypo-thalamic responses to involuntary overfeeding. *American Journal of Physiology, 271,* R819–R823.

Segal, Z. (1988). Appraisal of the self-schema construct in cognitive models of depression. *Psychological Bulletin, 103,* 147–161.

Segall, M. H., Campbell, D. T., Herskovits, M. J. (1966). *The influ-ence of culture on visual perception.* Indianapolis: Bobbs-Merrill.

Segall, M. H., Dasen, P. R., Berry, J. W., & Poortinga, Y. H. (1990). *Human behavior in global perspective: An introduction to cross-cultural psy-chology.* New York: Pergamon Press.

Segall, M. H., Lonner, W. J., & Berry, J. W. (1998). Cross-cultural psychology as a scholarly disci-pline: On the flowering of culture in behavioral research. *American Psychologist, 53,* 1101–1110.

Segerstrom, S. C., & Miller, G. E. (2004). Psychological stress and the human immune system: A meta-analytic study of 30 years of inquiry. *Psychological Bulletin, 130,* 601–630.

Segerstrom, S. C., Taylor, S. E., Kemeny, M. E., & Fahey, J. L. (1998). Optimism is associated with mood, coping and immune change in response to stress. *Journal of Personality and Social Psychology, 74,* 1646–1655.

Segerstrom, S., & Miller, G.E. (2004). Psychological stress and the human immune system: A meta-analytic study of 30 years of inquiry. *Psychological Bulletin, 130,* 601–630.

Seibyl, J. P., Scanley, E., Krystal, J. H., & Innis, R. B. (1999). Neuroimaging methodologies. In D. S. Charney, E. J. Nestler, & B. S. Bunney (Eds.), *Neurobiology of mental illness.* New York: Oxford University Press.

Seidenberg, M. S., & Petitto, L. A. (1986). Communication, symbolic communication, and language: Comment on Savage-Rumbaugh, McDonald, Sevcik, Hopkins, and Rupert (1986). *Journal of Experimental Psychology, 116,* 279–287.

Seidlitz, L., & Diener, E. (1993). Memory for positive versus nega-tive life events: Theories for the dif-ferences between happy and unhappy persons. *Journal of Personality and Social Psychology, 64,* 654–664.

Seifer, R. (2001). Socioeconomic status, multiple risks, and develop-ment of intelligence. In R. J. Sternberg & E. L. Grigorenko (Eds.), *Environmental effects on cognitive abilities* (pp. 59–82). Mahwah, NJ: Erlbaum.

Seifer, R., Schiller, M., Sameroff, A. J., Resnick, S., & Riordan, K. (1996). Attachment, maternal sensi-tivity, and infant temperament during the first year of life. *Developmental Psychology, 32,* 12–25.

Sejnowski, T. J. (2003). The once and future Hebb synapse. *Canadian Psychology, 44,* 17–20.

Self, D. W. (1997). Neurobiological adaptations to drug use. *Hospital Practice, April,* 5–9.

Seligman, M. E. P. (1971). Phobias and preparedness. *Behavior Therapy, 2,* 307–321.

Seligman, M. E. P. (1974). Depression and learned helpless-ness. In R. J. Friedman & M. M. Katz (Eds.), *The psychology of depres-sion: Contemporary theory and research.* New York: Wiley.

Seligman, M. E. P. (1990). *Learned optimism.* New York: Pocket Books.

Seligman, M. E. P. (1992). *Helplessness: On depression, develop-ment, and death.* New York: Freeman.

Seligman, M. E. P. (1995). The effectiveness of psychotherapy. *American Psychologist, 50,* 965–974.

Seligman, M. E. P. (2002). Positive psychology, positive prevention, and positive therapy. In C. R. Snyder & S. J. Lopez (Eds.), *Handbook of positive psychology* (pp. 3–11). New York: Oxford University Press.

Seligman, M. E. P. (2003). The past and future of positive psychology. In C. L. M. Keyes & J. Haidt (Eds.), *Flourishing: Positive psychology and the life well-lived.* Washington, DC: American Psychological Association.

Seligman, M. E. P., & Csikszentmihalyi, M. (2000). Positive psychology: An introduc-tion. *American Psychologist, 55,* 5–14.

Seligman, M. E. P., & Hager, J. L. (1972, August). Biological bound-aries of learning (The sauce béar-naise syndrome). *Psychology Today,* pp. 59–61, 84–87.

Seligman, M. E. P., & Isaacowitz, D. M. (2000). Learned helplessness. In G. Fink (Ed.), *Encyclopedia of stress* (Vol. 2, pp. 599–602). San Diego: Academic Press.

Selye, H. (1936). A syndrome pro-duced by diverse nocuous agents. *Nature, 138,* 32.

Selye, H. (1956). *The stress of life.* New York: McGraw-Hill.

Selye, H. (1973). The evolution of the stress concept. *American Scientist, 61*(6), 672–699.

Selye, H. (1974). *Stress without dis-tress.* New York: Lippincott.

Selye, H. (1982). History and present status of the stress concept. In L. Goldberger & S. Breznitz (Eds.), *Handbook of stress: Theoretical and clinical aspects.* New York: Free Press.

Semmer, N. K., McGrath, J. E., & Beehr, T. A. (2005). Conceptual issues in research on stress and health. In C. L. Cooper (Ed.), *Handbook of stress medicine and health.* Boca Raton, FL: CRC Press.

Serbin, L. A., Powlishta, K. K., & Gulko, J. (1993). *The development of sex typing in middle childhood.* Chicago: University of Chicago Press.

Servan-Schreiber, D., Kolb, R., & Tabas, G. (1999). The somatizing patient. *Primary Care, 26,* 225–242.

Seta, J. J., Seta, C. E., & McElroy, T. (2002). Strategies for reducing the stress of negative life experi-ences: An average/summation analysis. *Personality and Social Psychology Bulletin, 28,* 1574–1585.

Seta, J. J., Seta, C. E., & Wang, M. A. (1991). Feelings of negativity and stress: An averaging-summation analysis of impressions of negative life experiences. *Personality and Social Psychology Bulletin, 17,* 376–384.

Seto, M. C., Maric, A., & Barbaree, H. E. (2001). The role of pornog-raphy in the etiology of sexual aggression. *Aggression & Violent Behavior, 6,* 35–53.

Shafer, G., & Tversky, A. (1988). Languages and designs for proba-bility judgement. In D. E. Bell, H. Raiffa, & A. Tversky (Eds.), *Decision making: Descriptive, normative, and prescriptive interactions.* New York: Cambridge University Press.

Shaffer, D. R. (1985). *Developmental psychology: Theory, research, and applications.* Pacific Grove, CA: Brooks/Cole.

Shafir, E., & LeBoeuf, R. A. (2002). Rationality. *Annual Review of Psychology, 53,* 491–517.

Shafir, E., & LeBoeuf, R. A. (2004). Context and conflict in multi-tribute choice. In D. J. Koehler & N. Harvey (Ed), *Blackwell handbook of judgment and decision making.* Malden, MA: Blackwell Publishing.

Shalev, A. Y. (2001). Posttraumatic stress disorder. *Primary Psychiatry, 8*(10), 41–46.

Shank, R. P., Smith-Swintosky, V. L., & Twyman, R. E. (2000). Amino acid neurotransmitters. In B. J. Sadock & V. A. Sadock (Eds), *Comprehensive textbook of psychiatry* (Vol. 1). New York: Lippincott/Williams & Wilkins.

Shapiro, A. F., Gottman, J. M., & Carrère. (2000). The baby and marriage: Identifying factors that buffer against decline in marital satisfaction after the first baby arrives. *Journal of Family Psychology, 14,* 59–70.

Shapiro, D. H., Jr. (1984). Overview: Clinical and physiological comparison of meditation with other self-control strategies. In D. H. Shapiro, Jr., & R. N. Walsh (Eds.), *Meditation: Classic and contemporary perspectives.* New York: Aldine.

Shapiro, D. H., Jr. (1987). Implications of psychotherapy research for the study of meditation. In M. A. West (Ed.), *The psychology of meditation.* Oxford: Clarendon Press.

Shapiro, S. L., Schwartz, G. E. R., & Santerre, C. (2002). Meditation and positive psychology. In C. R. Snyder & S. J. Lopez (Eds.), *Handbook of positive psychology.* New York: Oxford University Press.

Sharps, M. J., & Wertheimer, M. (2000). Gestalt perspectives on cognitive science and on experimental psychology. *Review of General Psychology, 4,* 315–336.

Shatz, C. J. (1992, September). The developing brain. *Scientific American,* 60–67.

Shaver P. R., & Hazan, C. (1993). Adult attachment: Theory and research. In W. Jones & D. Perlman (Eds.), *Advances in personal relationships* (Vol. 4). London: Jessica Kingsley.

Shaver, P. R., & Hazan, C. (1994). Attachment. In A. L. Weber & J. H. Harvey (Eds.), *Perspectives on close relationships.* Boston: Allyn & Bacon.

Shaver, P. R., & Mikulincer, M. (2005). Attachment theory and research: Resurrection of the psychodynamic approach to personality. *Journal of Research in Personality, 39*(1), 22–45.

Shaver, P. R., Schachner, D. A., & Mikulincer, M. (2005). Attachment style, excessive reassurance seeking, relationship processes, and depression. *Personality and Social Psychology Bulletin, 31*(3), 343–359.

Shavitt, S., Sanbonmatsu, D. M., Smittipatana, S., & Posavac, S. S. (1999). Broadening the conditions for illusory correlation formation: Implications for judging minority groups. *Basic & Applied Social Psychology, 21,* 263–279.

Shavitt, S., Swan, S., Lowery, T. M., & Wanke, M. (1994). The interaction of endorser attractiveness and involvement in persuasion depends on the goal that guides message processing. *Journal of Consumer Psychology, 3,* 137–162.

Shear, J., & Jevning, R. (1999). Pure consciousness: Scientific exploration of meditation techniques. *Journal of Consciousness Studies, 6,* 189–209.

Shear, M. K., & Beidel, D. C. (1998). Psychotherapy in the overall management strategy for social anxiety disorder. *Journal of Clinical Psychiatry, 59,* 39–46.

Shearer, B. (2004). Multiple intelligences theory after 20 years. *Teachers College Record, 106*(1), 2–16.

Shedler, J., Mayman, M., & Manis, M. (1993). The illusion of mental health. *American Psychologist, 48,* 1117–1131.

Sheehan, S. (1982). *Is there no place on earth for me?* Boston: Houghton Mifflin.

Sheldon, K. M., & Kasser, T. (2001). Goals, congruence, and positive well-being: New empirical support for humanistic theories. *Journal of Humanistic Psychology, 41*(1), 30–50.

Shepard, R. N. (1990). *Mind sights.* New York: W. H. Freeman.

Shepperd, J. A., & McNulty, J. K. (2002). The affective consequences of expected and unexpected outcomes. *Psychological Science, 13,* 85–88.

Shepperd, J. A., & Taylor, K. M. (1999). Social loafing and expectancy-value theory. *Personality and Social Psychology Bulletin, 25,* 1147–1158.

Sher, L., & Mann, J. J. (2003). Psychiatric pathophysiology: Mood disorders. In A. Tasman, J. Kay, & J. A. Lieberman (Eds.), *Psychiatry.* New York: Wiley.

Sherman, M., & Key, C. B. (1932). The intelligence of isolated mountain children. *Child Development, 3,* 279–290.

Sherman, P. W. (1981). Reproductive competition and infanticide in Belding's ground squirrels and other animals. In R. D. Alexander & D. W. Tinkle (Eds.), *Natural selection and social behavior: Recent Research and new theory*

(pp. 311–331). New York: Chiron Press.

Shermer, M. (1997). *Why people believe weird things: Pseudoscience, superstition, and other confusions of our time.* New York: W. H. Freeman.

Shermer, M. (2004, March). None so blind. *Scientific American,* p. 42.

Sherry, D. F. (1992). Evolution and learning. In L. R. Squire (Ed.), *Encyclopedia of learning and memory.* New York: Macmillan.

Shettleworth, S. J. (1998). *Cognition, evolution, and behavior.* New York: Oxford University Press.

Shiffrin, R. M. (1988). Attention. In R. C. Atkinson, R. J. Herrnstein, G. Lindzey, & R. D. Luce (Eds.), *Stevens' handbook of experimental psychology* (Vol. 2). New York: Wiley.

Shike, M. (1999). Diet and lifestyle in the prevention of colorectal cancer: An overview. *American Journal of Medicine, 106*(1A), 11S–15S, 50S–51S.

Shike, M. (1999). Diet and lifestyle in the prevention of colorectal cancer: An overview. *American Journal of Medicine, 106*(1A), 11S–15S, 50S–51S.

Shimamura, A. P. (1995). Memory and the prefrontal cortex. In J. Grafman, K. J. Holyoak, & F. Boller (Eds), *Structure and functions of the human prefrontal cortex.* New York: New York Academy of Sciences.

Shimamura, A. P. (1996). Unraveling the mystery of the frontal lobes: Explorations in cognitive neuroscience. *Psychological Science Agenda, September-October,* 8–9.

Shimamura, A. P., Berry, J. M., Mangels, J. A., Rusting, C. L., & Jurica, P. J. (1995). Memory and cognitive abilities in university professors: Evidence for successful aging. *Psychological Science, 6,* 271–277.

Shobe, K. K., & Schooler, J. W. (2001). Discovering fact and fiction: Case-based analyses of authentic and fabricated discovered memories of abuse. In G. M. Davies & T. Dalgleish (Eds.), *Recovered memories: Seeking the middle ground.* Chichester, England: Wiley.

Shors, T. J. (2004). Learning during stressful times. *Learning and Memory, 11*(2), 137–144.

Shulman, R. B. (2001). Response versus remission in the treatment of depression: Understanding residual symptoms. *Primary Psychiatry, 8*(5), 28–30, 34.

Shweder, R. A., Mahapatra, M., & Miller, J. G. (1990). Culture and moral development. In J. W. Stigler,

R. A. Shweder, & G. Herdt (Eds.), *Cultural psychology.* New York: Cambridge University Press.

Siebert, A. (1995). *Student success: How to succeed in college and still have time for your friends.* Fort Worth: Harcourt Brace Jovanovich.

Siegel, J. M. (2000). Brainstem mechanisms generating REM sleep. In M. H. Kryger, T. Roth, & W. C. Dement (Eds.), *Principles and practice of sleep medicine.* Philadelphia: Saunders.

Siegel, J. M. (2004). The neurotransmitters of sleep. *Journal of Clinical Psychiatry, 65*(Suppl16), 4–7.

Siegel, J. M. (2005). REM sleep. In M. H. Kryger, T. Roth, & W. C. Dement (Eds.). *Principles and practice of sleep medicine.* Philadelphia: Elsevier Saunders.

Siegel, S. (1976). Morphine analgesic tolerance: Its situational specificity supports a Pavlovian conditioning model. *Science, 193,* 323–325.

Siegel, S. (2001). Pavlovian conditioning and drug overdose: When tolerance fails. *Addiction Research & Theory, 9,* 503–513.

Siegel, S. (2002). The ghost in the addict: Drug anticipation and drug addiction. *Proceedings of the Royal Society of Canada.* http://www.http://www.rsc.ca/files/publications/transactions/2002/siegel.pdfrsc.ca/files/publications/transactions/2002/siegel.pdf.

Siegel, S., & Allan, L. G. (1998). Learning and homeostasis: Drug addiction and the McCollough effect. *Psychological Bulletin, 124,* 230–239.

Siegler, I. C., & Brummett, B. H. (2000). Associations among NEO personality assessments and well-being at mid-life: Facet-level analyses. *Psychology & Aging, 15,* 710–714.

Siegler, R. S. (1992). The other Alfred Binet. *Developmental Psychology, 28,* 179–190.

Siegler, R. S. (1994). Cognitive variability: A key to understanding cognitive development. *Current Directions in Psychological Science, 3*(1), 1–5.

Siegler, R. S. (1998). *Children's thinking.* Upper Saddle River, NJ: Prentice-Hall.

Siegler, R. S., & Ellis, S. (1996). Piaget on childhood. *Psychological Science, 7,* 211–215.

Siegler, R. S., & Kotovsky, K. (1986). Two levels of giftedness: Shall ever the twain meet? In R. J. Sternberg & J. E. Davidson (Eds.), *Conceptions of giftedness.* Cambridge: Cambridge University Press.

Signorielli, N. (2001). Television's gender role images and contribution to stereotyping: Past present future. In D. G. Singer & J. L. Singer (Eds.), *Handbook of children and the media*. Thousand Oaks, CA: Sage.

Signorielli, N., & Bacue, A. (1999). Recognition and respect: A content analysis of prime-time television characters across three decades. *Sex Roles, 40*, 527–544.

Signorielli, N., McLeod, D., & Healy, E. (1994). Gender stereotypes in MTV commercials: The beat goes on. *Journal of Broadcasting & Electronic Media, 38*, 91–101.

Silberman, E. K. (1998). Psychiatrists' and internists' beliefs. *Primary Psychiatry, 5*, 65–71.

Silver, E., Cirincion, C., & Steadman, H. J. (1994). Demythologizing inaccurate perceptions of the insanity defense. *Law & Human Behavior, 18*, 63–70.

Silverman, I., & Choi, J. (2005). Locating places. In D. M. Buss (Ed.), *The handbook of evolutionary psychology*. New York: Wiley.

Silverman, I., & Eals, M. (1992). Sex differences in spatial ability: Evolutionary theory and data. In J. Barkow, L. Cosmides, & J. Tooby (Eds.), *The adapted mind*. New York: Oxford University Press.

Silverman, I., & Phillips, K. (1998). The evolutionary psychology of spatial sex differences. In C. Crawford & D.L. Krebs (Eds.), *Handbook of evolutionary psychology: Ideas, issues, and applications*. Mahwah, NJ: Erlbaum.

Silverman, I., Choi, J., Mackewn, A., Fisher, M., Moro, J., & Olshansky, E. (2000). Evolved mechanisms underlying wayfinding: Further studies on the hunter-gatherer theory of spatial sex differences. *Evolution and Human Behavior, 21*, 201–213.

Silverstein, L. B., & Auerbach, C. F. (1999). Deconstructing the essential father. *American Psychologist, 54*, 397–407.

Simmons, H. G. (1987). Psychosurgery and the abuse of psychiatric authority in Ontario. *Journal of Health Politics, Policy, and Law, 12*, 537–550.

Simon, G. E., & VonKorff, M. (1997). Prevalence, burden, and treatment of insomnia in primary care. *American Journal Psychiatry, 154*, 1417–1423.

Simon, H. A. (1957). *Models of man*. New York: Wiley.

Simon, H. A. (1974). How big is a chunk? *Science, 183*, 482–488.

Simon, H. A., & Reed, S. K. (1976). Modeling strategy shifts in a problem-solving task. *Cognitive Psychology, 8*, 86–97.

Simonoff, E., Bolton, P., & Rutter, M. (1998). Genetic perspectives on mental retardation: A short introduction. In J. A. Burack, R. M. Hodapp, & E. Zigler (Eds.), *Handbook of mental retardation and development*. New York: Cambridge University Press.

Simons, D. K., & Chabris, C. F. (1999). Gorillas in our midst: Sustained inattentional blindness for dynamic events. *Perception, 28*, 1059–1074.

Simonton, D. K. (1990). Creativity and wisdom in aging. In J. E. Birren & K. W. Schaie (Eds.), *Handbook of the psychology of aging*. San Diego: Academic Press.

Simonton, D. K. (1997). Creative productivity: A predictive and explanatory model of career trajectories and landmarks. *Psychological Review, 104*, 66–89.

Simonton, D. K. (1999a). Creativity and genius. In L. A. Pervin & O. John (Eds.), *Handbook of personality theory and research*. New York: Guilford.

Simonton, D. K. (1999b). Talent and its development: An emergenic and epigenetic model. *Psychological Review, 106*, 435–457.

Simonton, D. K. (2001). Totally made, not at all born [Review of the book *The psychology of high abilities*]. *Contemporary Psychology, 46*, 176–179.

Simpson, J. A. (1990). Influence of attachment styles on romantic relationships. *Journal of Personality and Social Psychology, 59*, 971–980.

Simpson, J. A. (1999). Attachment theory in modern evolutionary perspective. In J. Cassidy & P. R. Shaver (Eds.), *Handbook of attachment: Theory, research, and clinical applications*. New York: Guilford.

Simpson, J. A., Fletcher, G. J. O., & Campbell, L. (2001). The structure and function of ideal standards in close relationships. In G. J. O. Fletcher & M. S. Clark (Eds.), *Blackwell handbook of social psychology: Interpersonal processes*. Malden, MA: Blackwell.

Simpson, J. A., Rholes, W. S., & Phillips, D. (1996). Conflict in close relationships: An attachment perspective. *Journal of Personality and Social Psychology, 71*, 899–914.

Simpson, J. L. (2002). Fetal wastage. In S. G. Gabbe, J. R. Niebyl, & J. L. Simpson (Eds.), *Obstetrics: Normal and problem pregnancies*. New York: Churchill Livingstone.

Simpson, J. L., & Niebyl, J. R. (2002). Occupational and environmental perspectives on birth defects. In S. G. Gabbe, J. R. Niebyl, & J. L. Simpson (Eds.), *Obstetrics: Normal and problem pregnancies*. New York: Churchill Livingstone.

Sinclair, D. (1981). *Mechanisms of cutaneous stimulation*. Oxford, England: Oxford University Press.

Sinclair, R. C., Hoffman, C., Mark, M. M., Martin, L. L., & Pickering, T. L. (1994). Construct accessibility and the misattribution of arousal: Schachter and Singer revisited. *Psychological Science, 5*, 15–19.

Singer, L. T., Arendt, R., Minnes, S., Farkas, K., Salvator, A., Kirchner, H. L., & Kliegman, R. (2002). Cognitive and motor outcomes of cocaine-exposed infants. *Journal of the American Medical Association, 287*, 1952–1960.

Singer, L. T., Minnes, S., Short, E., Arendt, R., Farkas, K., Lewis, B., Klein, N., Russ, S., Min, M. O., & Kirchner, H. L. (2004). Cognitive outcomes of preschool children with prenatal cocaine exposure. *Journal of the American Medical Association, 291*, 2448–2456.

Singer, M. T., & Lalich, J. (1996). *Crazy therapies: What are they? Do they work?* San Francisco: Jossey-Bass.

Singh, D. (1993). Adaptive significance of female physical attractiveness: Role of waist-to-hip ratio. *Journal of Personality and Social Psychology, 65*, 293–307.

Sinha, D. (1983). Human assessment in the Indian context. In S. H. Irvine & J. W. Berry (Eds.), *Human assessment and cultural factors*. New York: Plenum.

Skilling, T. A., Harris, G. T., Rice, M. E., & Quinsey, V. L. (2002). Identifying persistently antisocial offenders using the Hare Psychopathy Checklist and the DSM antisocial personality disorder criteria. *Psychological Assessment, 14*, 27–38.

Skinner, A. E. G. (2001). Recovered memories of abuse: Effects on the individual. In G. M. Davies, & T. Dalgleish (Eds.), *Recovered memories: Seeking the middle ground*. Chichester, England: Wiley & Sons.

Skinner, B. F. (1938). *The behavior of organisms*. New York: Appleton-Century-Crofts.

Skinner, B. F. (1953). *Science and human behavior*. New York: Macmillan.

Skinner, B. F. (1957). *Verbal behavior*. New York: Appleton-Century-Crofts.

Skinner, B. F. (1967). Autobiography. In E. G. Boring & G. Lindzey (Eds.), *A history of psychology in autobiography* (Vol. 5). New York: Appleton-Century-Crofts.

Skinner, B. F. (1969). *Contingencies of reinforcement*. New York: Appleton-Century-Crofts.

Skinner, B. F. (1971). *Beyond freedom and dignity*. New York: Knopf.

Skinner, B. F. (1974). *About behaviorism*. New York: Knopf.

Skinner, B. F. (1984). Selection by consequences. *Behavioral and Brain Sciences, 7*(4), 477–510.

Skinner, B. F. (2003). Birth order effects in dominance: Failure to support Sulloway's view. *Psychological Reports, 92*, 387–388.

Skinner, B. F., Solomon, H. C., & Lindsley, O. R. (1953). *Studies in behavior therapy: Status report I*. Waltham, MA: Unpublished report, Metropolitan State Hospital.

Skodak, M., & Skeels, H. M. (1947). A follow-up study of one hundred adopted children in Iowa. *American Psychologist, 2*, 278.

Skolnick, P. (2003). Psychiatric pathophysiology: Anxiety disorders. In A. Tasman, J. Kay, & J. A. Lieberman (Eds.), *Psychiatry*. New York: Wiley.

Slaby, A. E. (1997). Beyond reasonable doubt: The case for SSRI's. *Primary Psychiatry, 4*, 26–27.

Slamecka, N. J. (1985). Ebbinghaus: Some associations. *Journal of Experimental Psychology: Learning, Memory and Cognition, 11*, 414–435.

Slamecka, N. J. (1992). Forgetting. In L. R. Squire (Ed.), *Encyclopedia of learning and memory*. New York: Macmillan.

Slater, E., & Shields, J. (1969). Genetical aspects of anxiety. In M. H. Lader (Ed.), *Studies of anxiety*. Ashford, England: Headley Brothers.

Slaughter, M. (1990). The vertebrate retina. In K. N. Leibovic (Ed.), *Science of vision*. New York: Springer-Verlag.

Slavney, P. R. (1990). *Perspectives on hysteria*. Baltimore: Johns Hopkins University Press.

Slobin, D. I. (1985). *A cross-linguistic study of language acquisition*. Hillsdale, NJ: Erlbaum.

Slobin, D. I. (1992). *The cross-linguistic study of language acquisition*. Hillsdale, NJ: Erlbaum.

Slovic, P. (1990). Choice. In D. N. Osherson & E. E. Smith (Eds.), *Thinking: An invitation to cognitive science* (Vol. 3). Cambridge, MA: MIT Press.

Slovic, P., & Fischhoff, B. (1977). On the psychology of experimental surprises. *Journal of Experimental Psychology: Human Perception and Performance, 3*, 544–551.

Slovic, P., Fischhoff, B., & Lichtenstein, S. (1982). Facts versus fears: Understanding perceived risk. In D. Kahneman, P. Slovic, & A. Tversky (Eds.), *Judgment under uncertainty: Heuristics and biases*. Cambridge, England: Cambridge University Press.

Slovic, P., Lichtenstein, S., & Fischhoff, B. (1988). Decision making. In R. C. Atkinson, R. J. Herrnstein, G. Lindzey, & R. D. Luce (Eds.), *Stevens' handbook of experimental psychology* (Vol. 2). New York: Wiley.

Smail, B. (1983). Spatial visualization skills and technical crafts education. *Educational Research, 25*, 230–231.

Smart, R. (1965). Social-group membership, leadership and birth order. *Journal of Social Psychology, 67*, 221–225.

Smedley, S. R., & Eisner, T. (1996). Sodium: A male moth's gift to its offspring. *Proceedings of the National Academy of Sciences, 93*, 809–813.

Smilkstein, G. (1990). Psychosocial influences on health. In R. E. Rakel (Ed.), *Textbook of family practice*. Philadelphia: Saunders.

Smith, A. L., & Weissman, M. M. (1992). Epidemiology. In E. S. Paykel (Ed.), *Handbook of affective disorders* (2nd ed.). New York: Guilford.

Smith, C. (1996). Sleep states, memory processes and synaptic plasticity. *Behavioural Brain Research, 78*, 49–56.

Smith, C. (2003). The REM sleep window and memory processing. In Maquet, P., Smith, C., & Stickgold, R. (Eds.), *Sleep and brain plasticity* (pp. 116-133). Oxford, UK: Oxford University Press.

Smith, C. A., & Lazarus, R. S. (1993). Appraisal components, core relational themes, and the emotions. *Cognition and Emotion, 7*, 233–269.

Smith, C. P. (1992). Reliability issues. In C. P. Smith (Ed.), *Motivation and personality: Handbook of thematic content analysis*. New York: Cambridge University Press.

Smith, C., & Fazekas, A. (1997). Amounts of REM sleep and stage 2 required for efficient learning. Poster presented at the annual meeting of the Associated Professional Sleep Societies.

Smith, D. (2005). Hot Nash burns Mavs. *Toronto Star*, May 10, 2005. E1, E4.

Smith, D. A. (1999). The end of theoretical orientations? *Applied & Preventative Psychology, 8*, 269–280.

Smith, E. E. (2000). Neural bases of human working memory. *Current Directions in Psychological Science, 9*, 45–49.

Smith, F. J., & Campfield, L. A. (1993). Meal initiation occurs after experimental induction of transient declines in blood glucose. *American Journal of Physiology, 265*, 1423–1429.

Smith, G. N., Flynn, S. W., Kopala, L. C., Bassett, A. S., Lapointe, J. S., Falkai, P., & Honer, W. G. (1997). A comprehensive method of assessing routine CT scans in schizophrenia. *Acta Psychiatrica Scandinavica, 96*, 395–401.

Smith, G. S., Dewey, S. L., Brodie, J. D., Logan, J., Vitkun, S. A., Simkowitz, P., Schloesser, R., Alexoff, D. A., Hurley, A., Cooper, T., & Volkow, N. D. (1997). Serotonergic modulation of dopamine measured with [11C] raclopride and PET in normal human subjects. *American Journal of Psychiatry, 154*, 490–496.

Smith, J. C. (1975). Meditation and psychotherapy: A review of the literature. *Psychological Bulletin, 32*, 553–564.

Smith, J. W., Frawley, P. J., & Polissar, N. L. (1997). Six- and twelve-month abstinence rates in inpatient alcoholics treated with either faradic aversion or chemical aversion compared with matched inpatients from a treatment registry. *Journal of Addictive Diseases, 16*, 5–24.

Smith, M. L., & Glass, G. V. (1977). Meta-analysis of psychotherapy outcome studies. *American Psychologist, 32*, 752–760.

Smith, M. T., Perlis, M. L., Park, A., Smith, M. S., Pennington, J., Giles, D. E., & Buysse, D. J. (2002). Comparative meta-analysis of pharmacotherapy and behavior therapy for persistent insomnia. *American Journal of Psychiatry, 159*, 5–11.

Smith, M., & Pazder, L. (1980). *Michelle remembers*. New York: Pocket Books.

Smith, N. A., & Schmuckler, M. A. (2004). The perception of tonal structure through the differentiation and organization of pitches. *Journal of Experimental Psychology: Human Perception and Performance, 30*, 268–286.

Smith, P. B. (2001). Cross-cultural studies of social influence. In D. Matsumoto (Ed.), *The handbook of culture and psychology*. New York: Oxford University Press.

Smith, P. B., & Bond, M. H. (1994). *Social psychology across cultures: Analysis and perspectives*. Boston: Allyn & Bacon.

Smith, S. (1988). Environmental context-dependent memory. In G. M. Davies & D. M. Thomson (Eds.), *Memory in context: Context in memory*. New York: Wiley.

Smith, S. B. (2000). *Diana in search of herself: Portrait of a troubled princess*. New York: Signet.

Smith, S. M. (1995). Getting into and out of mental ruts: A theory of fixation, incubation, and insight. In R. J. Sternberg & J. E. Davidson (Eds.), *The nature of insight* (pp. 229–251). Cambridge, MA: MIT Press.

Smith, S. M., McIntosh, W. D., & Bazzini, D. G. (1999). Are the beautiful good in Hollywood? An investigation of the beauty-and-goodness stereotype on film. *Basic & Applied Social Psychology, 21*, 69–80.

Smith, T. W. (1999). *The emerging 21st century American family*. Chicago: University of Chicago, National Opinion Research Center.

Smith, T. W., & Gallo, L. C. (2001). Personality traits as risk factors for physical illness. In A. Baum, T. A. Revenson, & J. E. Singer (Eds.), *Handbook of health psychology* (pp. 139–174). Mahwah, NJ: Erlbaum.

Smith, W. P., Compton, W. C., & West, W. B. (1995). Meditation as an adjunct to a happiness enhancement program. *Journal of Clinical Psychology, 51*, 269–273.

Smolak, L., & Murnen, S. K. (2001). Gender and eating problems. In R. H. Striegel-Moore & L. Smolak (Eds.), *Eating disorders: Innovative directions in research and practice* (pp. 91–110). Washington, DC: American Psychological Association.

Smolensky, P. (1995). On the proper treatment of connectionism. In C. Macdonald, & G. Macdonald (Eds.), *Connectionism: Debates on psychological explanation*. Cambridge, USA: Blackwell.

Smyth, J. M., & Pennebaker, J. W. (1999). Sharing one's story: Translating emotional experiences into words as a coping tool. In C. R. Snyder (Ed.), *Coping: The psychology of what works*. New York: Oxford University Press.

Smyth, J. M., & Pennebaker, J. W. (2001). What are the health effects of disclosure? In A. Baum, T. A. Revenson & J. E. Singer (Eds.), *Handbook of health psychology* (pp. 339–348). Mahwah, NJ: Erlbaum.

Smyth, J., Litcher, L., Hurewitz, A., & Stone, A. (2001). Relaxation training and cortisol secretion in adult asthmatics. *Journal of Health Psychology, 6*, 217–227.

Snow, C. E. (1998). Bilingualism and second language acquisition. In J. B. Gleason & N. B. Ratner (Eds.), *Psycholinguistics*. Fort Worth, TX: Harcourt College Publishers.

Snow, R. E. (1986). Individual differences in the design of educational programs. *American Psychologist, 41*, 1029–1039.

Snowden, L. R., & Hu, T. W. (1996). Outpatient service use in minority-serving mental health programs. *Administration and Policy in Mental Health, 24*, 149–159.

Snyder, A. (1989). *Relationship excellence: Right brain relationship skills for left brain personalities*. Seattle: Gresham Publishing.

Snyder, M. (1979). Self-monitoring processes. In L. Berkowitz (Ed.), *Advances in experimental social psychology* (Vol. 12). New York: Academic Press.

Snyder, M. (1987). *Public appearances/Private realities: The psychology of self-monitoring*. New York: W. H. Freeman.

Snyder, S. H. (1996). *Drugs and the brain*. New York: Scientific American Library.

Snyder, S. H. (2002). Forty years of neurotransmitters: A personal account. *Archives of General Psychiatry, 59*, 983–994.

Snyder, S. H., & Ferris, C. D. (2000). Novel neurotransmitters and their neuropsychiatric relevance. *American Journal of Psychiatry, 157*, 1738–1751.

Snyderman, M., & Rothman, S. (1987). Survey of expert opinion on intelligence and aptitude testing. *American Psychologist, 42*, 137–144.

So, K. T., & Orme-Johnson, D. W. (2001). Three randomized experiments on the longitudinal effects of the Transcendental Meditation technique on cognition. *Intelligence, 29*, 419–440.

Sobal, J. (1995). Social influences on body weight. In K. D. Brownell & C. G. Fairburn (Eds.), *Eating disorders and obesity: A comprehensive handbook*. New York: Guilford.

Soler, C., Nunez, M., Gutierrez, R., Nunez, J., Medina, P., Sancho, M., Alvarez, J., & Nunez, A. (2003). Facial attractiveness in men provides clues to semen quality. *Evolution and Human Behavior, 24*, 199–207.

Soll, J. B., & Klayman, J. (2004). Overconfidence in interval estimates. *Journal of Experimental*

Psychology: Learning, Memory, & Cognition, 30, 299–314.

Solomon, D. A., Keller, M. B., Leon, A. C., Mueller, T. I., Lavori, P. W., Shea, M. T., Coryell, W., Warshaw, M., Turvey, C., Maser, J. D., & Endicott, J. (2000). Multiple recurrences of major depressive disorder. American Journal of Psychiatry, 157, 229–233.

Solomon, D. A., Keller, M. B., Leon, A. C., Mueller, T. I., Shea, M. T., Warshaw, M., Maser, J. D., Coryell, W., & Endicott, J. (1997). Recovery from major depression: A 10-year prospective follow-up across multiple episodes. Archives of General Psychiatry, 54, 1001–1006.

Solowij, N., Stephens, R. S., Roffman, R. A., Babor, T., Kadden, R., Miller, M., Christiansen. K., McRee, B., & Vendetti, J. (2002). Cognitive functioning of long-term heavy cannabis users seeking treatment. Journal of the American Medical Association, 287, 1123–1131.

Solso, R. L. (1994). Cognition and the visual arts. Cambridge, MA: MIT Press.

Sommer, B. (1987). Not another diet book: A right-brain program for successful weight management. Alameda, CA: Hunter House.

Son Hing, L. S., Li, W., & Zanna, M. P. (2002). Inducing hypocrisy to reduce prejudicial responses among aversive racists. Journal of Experimental Social Psychology, 38(1), 71–78.

Song, S., Sjostrom, P. J., Reigl, M., Nelson, S., & Chklovskii, D. B. (2005). Highly nonrandom features of synaptic connectivity in local cortical circuits. PLoS Biol, 3(3), 1–13.

Sorensen, J. L., Haug, N. A., & Batki, S. L. (2005). Psychosocial issues of HIV/AIDS among drug users in treatment. In J. H. Lowinson, P. Ruiz, R. B. Millman, & J. G. Langrod (Eds.), Substance abuse: A comprehensive textbook. Philadelphia: Lippincott/Williams & Williams.

Sorrentino, R. M., & Roney, C. J. R. (2000). The uncertain mind. Philadelphia, PA: Psychology Press.

Sotiriou, P. E. (2002). Integrating college study skills: Reasoning in reading, listening, and writing. Belmont, CA: Wadsworth.

Sousa, D. A. (2000). How the brain learns: A classroom teacher's guide. Thousand Oaks, CA: Corwin Press.

Spangler, W. D. (1992). Validity of questionnaire and TAT measures of need for achievement: Two meta-analyses. Psychological Bulletin, 112, 140–154.

Spanos, N. P. (1986). Hypnotic behavior: A social-psychological interpretation of amnesia, analgesia, and "trance logic." Behavioral & Brain Sciences, 9(3), 449–467.

Spanos, N. P. (1994). Multiple identity enactments and multiple personality disorder: A sociocognitive perspective. Psychological Bulletin, 116, 143–165.

Spanos, N. P. (1996). Multiple identities and false memories. Washington, DC: American Psychological Association.

Spanos, N. P., & Chaves, J. F. (1991). History and hisiotiography of hypnosis. In S. J. Lynn & J. W. Rhue (Eds.), Theories of hypnosis: Current models and perspectives (pp. 43–78). New York, NY: The Guilford Press.

Spanos, N. P., & Coe, W. C. (1992). A social-psychological approach to hypnosis. In E. Fromm & M. R. Nash (Eds.), Contemporary hypnosis research. New York: Guilford.

Spear, P. (2000). The adolescent brain and age-related behavioral manifestations. Neuroscience and Biobehavioral Reviews, 24, 417–463.

Spearman, C. (1904). "General intelligence" objectively determined and measured. American Journal of Psychology, 15, 201–293.

Spearman, C. (1923). The nature of "intelligence" and the principles of cognition. London: Macmillan.

Speed, A., & Gangestad, S. W. (1997). Romantic popularity and mate preferences: A peer-nomination study. Personality and Social Psychology Bulletin, 23, 928–936.

Spelke, E. S. (1994). Initial knowledge: Six suggestions. Cognition, 50, 431–455.

Spelke, E. S., & Newport, E. L. (1998). Nativism, empiricism, and the development of knowledge. In W. Damon (Ed.), Handbook of child psychology (Vol. 1): Theoretical models of human development. New York: Wiley.

Spencer, S. J., Steele, C. M., & Quinn, D. M. (1999). Stereotype threat and women's math performance. Journal of Experimental Social Psychology, 35, 4–28.

Sperling, G. (1960). The information available in brief visual presentations. Psychological Monographs, 74(11, Whole No. 498).

Sperry, R. W. (1982). Some effects of disconnecting the cerebral hemispheres. Science, 217, 1223–1226, 1250.

Spiegel, D. (1995). Hypnosis, dissociation, and trauma: Hidden and overt observers. In J. L. Singer (Ed.), Repression and dissociation:

Implications for personality theory, psychopathology, and health. Chicago: University of Chicago Press.

Spiegel, D. (2003a). Hypnosis and traumatic dissociation: Therapeutic opportunities. Journal of Trauma & Dissociation, 4(3), 73–90.

Spiegel, D. (2003b). Negative and positive visual hypnotic hallucinations: Attending inside and out. International Journal of Clinical & Experimental Hypnosis, 51(2), 130–146.

Spiegel, D., & Maldonado, J. R. (1999). Dissociative disorders. In R. E. Hales, S. C. Yudofsky, & J. A. Talbott (Eds.), American Psychiatric Press Textbook of Psychiatry, (3rd ed.). Washington, DC: American Psychiatric Press.

Spiegel, D., Cutcomb, S., Ren, C., & Pribram, K. (1985). Hypnotic hallucination alters evoked potentials. Journal of Abnormal Psychology, 94, 249–255.

Spiegel, H., Greenleaf, M., & Spiegel, D. (2000). Hypnosis. In B. J. Sadock & V. A. Sadock (Eds.), Kaplan and Sadock's comprehensive textbook of psychiatry. Philadelphia: Lippincott/Williams & Wilkins.

Spiegler, M. D., & Guevremont, D. C. (1998). Contemporary behavior therapy. Pacific Grove, CA: Brooks/Cole.

Spiegler, M. D., & Guevremont, D. C. (2003). Contemporary behavior therapy. Belmont, CA: Wadsworth.

Spielberger, C. D., & Sydeman, S. J. (1994). Anxiety. In R. J. Sternberg (Ed.), Encyclopedia of human intelligence. New York: Macmillan.

Spitzer, R. L., Terman, M., Williams, J. B. W., Terman, J. S., Malt, U. F., Singer, F., & Lewy, A. J. (1999). Jet lag: Clinical features, validation of a new syndrome-specific scale, and lack of response to melatonin in a randomized, double-blind trial. American Journal Psychiatry, 156, 1392–1396.

Sprecher, S. (1998). Insiders' perspectives on reasons for attraction to a close other. Social Psychology Quarterly, 61, 287–300.

Sprecher, S., & Duck, S. (1994). Sweet talk: The importance of perceived communication for romantic and friendship attraction experienced during a get-acquainted date. Personality and Social Psychology Bulletin, 20, 391–400.

Sprecher, S., Sullivan, Q., & Hatfield, E. (1994). Mate selection preferences: Gender differences examined in a national sample. Journal of Personality and Social Psychology, 66, 1074–1080.

Sprenger, M. (2001). Becoming a "wiz" at brain-based teaching: From translation to application. Thousand Oaks, CA: Corwin Press.

Springer, K., & Berry, D. S. (1997). Rethinking the role of evolution in the ecological model of social perception. In J. A. Simpson & D. T. Kenrick (Eds.), Evolutionary psychology. Mahwah, NJ: Erlbaum.

Springer, S. P., & Deutsch, G. (1998). Left brain, right brain. New York: W. H. Freeman.

Squire, L. R. (1987). Memory and brain. New York: Oxford University Press.

Squire, L. R. (1994). Declarative and nondeclarative memory: Multiple brain systems supporting learning and memory. In D. L. Schacter & E. Tulving (Eds.), Memory systems. Cambridge, MA: MIT Press.

Squire, L. R. (2004). Memory systems of the brain: A brief history and current perspective. Neurobiology of Learning & Memory, 82(3), 171–177.

Squire, L. R., & Knowlton, B. J. (2000). The medial temporal lobe, the hippocampus, and the memory systems of the brain. In M. S. Gazzaniga (Ed.), The new cognitive neurosciences (2nd ed., pp. 765–780). Cambridge, MA: MIT Press.

Squire, L. R., & Zola, S. M. (1996). Structure and function of declarative and nondeclarative memory systems. Proceedings of the National Academy of Sciences, USA, 93, 13515–13522.

Squire, L. R., Knowlton, B., & Musen, G. (1993). The structure and organization of memory. Annual Review of Psychology, 44, 453–495.

Sriram, T. G., & Silverman, J. J. (1998). The effects of stress on the respiratory system. In J. R. Hubbard & E. A. Workman (Eds.), Handbook of stress medicine: An organ system approach. New York: CRC Press.

Staats, A. W., & Staats, C. K. (1963). Complex human behavior. New York: Holt, Rinehart & Winston.

Stahl, S. M. (1998). Getting stoned without inhaling: Anandamide is the brain's natural marijuana. Journal of Clinical Psychiatry, 59, 566–567.

Stajkovic, A. D., & Luthans, F. (1998). Self-efficacy and work-related performance: A meta-analysis. Psychological Bulletin, 124, 240–261.

Stalling, R. B. (1992). Mood and pain: The influence of positive and negative affect on reported body aches. *Journal of Social Behavior and Personality, 7*(2), 323–334.

Stamler, J., Daviglus, M. L., Garside, D. B., Dyer, A. R., Greenland, P., & Neaton, J. D. (2000). Relationship of baseline serum cholesterol levels in three large cohorts of younger men to long-term coronary, cardiovascular, and all-cause mortality and to longevity. *Journal of the American Medical Association, 284,* 311–318.

Stamler, J., Daviglus, M. L., Garside, D. B., Dyer, A. R., Greenland, P., & Neaton, J. D. (2000). Relationship of baseline serum cholesterol levels in three large cohorts of younger men to long-term coronary, cardiovascular, and all-cause mortality and to longevity. *Journal of the American Medical Association, 284,* 311–318.

Stanovich, K. E. (1999). *Who is rational? Studies of individual differences in reasoning.* Mahwah, NJ: Erlbaum.

Stanovich, K. E. (2003). The fundamental computational biases of human cognition: Heuristics that (sometimes) impair decision making and problem solving. In J. E. Davidson & R. J. Sternberg (Eds.), *The psychology of problem solving.* New York: Cambridge University Press.

Stanovich, K. E. (2004). *How to think straight about psychology.* Boston: Allyn & Bacon.

Starcevic, V. (2001). Clinical features and diagnosis of hypochondriasis. In V. Starcevic & D. R. Lipsitt (Eds.), *Hypochondriasis: Modern perspectives on an ancient malady.* New York: Oxford University Press.

Starkman, R. (2005). Serving notice. *Toronto Star,* January 12, 2005, pp. E1, E7.

Stasser, G. (1991). Pooling of unshared information during group discussion. In S. Worchel, W. Wood, & J. Simpson (Eds.), *Group process and productivity.* Beverly Hills, CA: Sage.

Stasser, G., Vaughan, S. I., & Stewart, D. D. (2000). Pooling unshared information: The benefits of knowing how access to information is distributed among group members. *Organizational Behavior and Human Decision Processes, 82,* 102–116.

Statistics Canada. (1999a). Crime statistics. *The Daily,* July 18, 1999. Retrieved May 9, 2005, from http://statcan.ca/Daily/English/000718/d000718a.htm.

Statistics Canada. (1999b). General social survey: Time use. *The Daily,* November 9, 1999. Retrieved June 21, 2005, from http://www.statcan.ca/Daily/English/991109/d991109a.htm.

Statistics Canada. (1999c). National longitudinal survey of children and youth: Transition into adolescence. *The Daily,* July 6, 1999. Retrieved June 1, 2005, from http://www.statcan.ca/Daily/English/990706/d990706a.htm.

Statistics Canada. (2002a). National longitudinal survey of children and youth: Childhood obesity. *The Daily,* October 18, 2002. Retrieved April 30, 2005, from http://www.statcan.ca/Daily/English/021018/d021018b.htm.

Statistics Canada. (2002b). Participation and activity limitation survey: A profile of disability in Canada. *The Daily,* Tuesday, December 3, 2002. Retrieved May 17, 2005, from http://www.statcan.ca/Daily/English/021203/td021203.htm.

Statistics Canada. (2002c). Shift work and health. *The Daily,* July 25, 2002 (Retrieved from http://www.statcan.ca/Daily/English/020725/d020725b.htm, March 9, 2005).

Statistics Canada. (2003a). Canadian community health survey: Mental health and well-being. *The Daily,* September 3, 2003. Retrieved June 27, 2005, from http://www.statcan.ca/Daily/English/030903/td030903.htm.

Statistics Canada. (2003b). Parent and child factors associated with youth obesity. *The Daily,* November 3, 2003. Retrieved April 30, 2005, from http://www.statcan.ca/Daily/English/031103/d031103a.htm.

Statistics Canada. (2003c). Sources of workplace stress. *The Daily,* June 25, 2003. Retrieved June 21, 2005, from http://www.statcan.ca/Daily/English/030625/d030625c.htm.

Statistics Canada. (2004a). Canadian community health survey. *The Daily,* June 15, 2004. Retrieved April 30, 2005, from http://www.statcan.ca/Daily/English/040615/d040615b.htm.

Statistics Canada. (2004b). Child Care. *The Daily,* February 7, 2005. Retrieved June 17, 2005, from http://dissemination.statcan.ca/Daily/English/050207/d050207b.htm.

Statistics Canada. (2004c). Heath reports: Stress and chronic conditions, excess weight and arthritis. *The Daily,* January 21, 2004. Retrieved June 21, 2005, from http://www.statcan.ca/Daily/English/040121/d040121b.htm.

Statistics Canada. (2004d). Study: Student reading performance in minority-language school. *The Daily,* March 22, 2004. Retrieved May 11, 2005, from http://www.statcan.ca/Daily/English/040322/d040322a.htm.

Statistics Canada. (2004e). Divorces. *The Daily,* May 4, 2004. Retrieved June 1, 2005, from http://www.statcan.ca/Daily/English/040504/d040504a.htm.

Statistics Canada. (2005a). National Population Health Survey—Obesity: a growing issue. *The Daily,* April 7, 2005. Retrieved April 11, 2005 from http://www.statcan.ca/Daily/English/050407/d050407a.htm.

Statistics Canada. (2005b). Study: Canada's visible minority population in 2017. *The Daily,* March 22, 2005. Retrieved July 7, 2005, from http://www.statcan.ca/Daily/English/050322/d050322b.htm.

Statistics Canada. (2005c). Study: Mature singles who don't expect to marry. *The Daily,* June 7, 2005. Retrieved June 7, 2005, from http://www.statcan.ca/Daily/English/050607/d050607a.htm.

Statistics Canada. (2005d). Study: The rising profile of women academics. *The Daily,* Thursday, February 24, 2005.

Statistics Canada. (2005e). Divorces. *The Daily,* March 9, 2005. Retrieved June 20, 2005, from http://www.statcan.ca/Daily/English/050309/d050309b.htm.

Statistics Canada. (2005f). Early sexual intercourse, condom use and sexually transmitted diseases. *The Daily,* May 3, 2005. Retrieved May 9, 2005 from http://www.statcan.ca/Daily/English/050503/d050503a.htm.

Statistics Canada. (2005g). Child Care. *The Daily,* February 7, 2005. Retrieved October 4, 2005, from http://www.statcan.ca/Daily/English/050207/d050207b.htm.

Statistics Canada. (n.d.). Selected leading causes of death, by sex. Retrieved June 22, 2005, from http://www40.statcan.ca/101/cst01/health36.htm.

Stattin, H., & Magnusson, D. (1990). *Pubertal maturation in female development.* Hillsdale, NJ: Erlbaum.

Steele, C. M. (1992, April). Race and the schooling of black Americans. *The Atlantic Monthly,* pp. 68–78.

Steele, C. M. (1997). A threat in the air: How stereotypes shape intellectual identity and performance. *American Psychologist, 52,* 613–629.

Steele, C. M., & Aronson, J. (1995). Stereotype threat and the intellectual test performance of African Americans. *Journal of Personality and Social Psychology, 69,* 797–811.

Steele, K. M. (2003). Do rats show a Mozart effect? *Music Perception, 21,* 251–265.

Steele, K. M., Bass, K. E., & Crook, M. D. (1999). The mystery of the Mozart Effect: Failure to replicate. *Psychological Science, 10,* 366–369.

Steiger, H., & Seguin, J. R. (1999). Eating disorders: Anorexia nervosa and bulimia nervosa. In T. Millon, P. H. Blaney, & R. D. Davis (Eds.), *Oxford textbook of psychopathology* (pp. 365–389). New York: Oxford University Press.

Steiger, H., Bruce, K. R., & Israel, M. (2003). Eating disorders. In G. Stricker & T. A. Widiger (Eds.), *Handbook of psychology, Vol. 8: Clinical psychology.* New York: Wiley.

Stein, B. E., & Meredith, M. A. (1993). *Vision, touch, and audition: Making sense of it all.* Cambridge, MA: MIT Press.

Stein, B. E., Wallace, M. T., & Stanford, T. R. (2000). Merging sensory signals in the brain: The development of multisensory integration in the superior colliculus. In M. S. Gazzaniga (Ed.), *The new cognitive neurosciences.* Cambridge, MA: The MIT Press.

Stein, B. E., Wallace, M. T., & Stanford, T. R. (2001). Brain mechanisms for synthesizing information from different sensory modalities. In E. B. Goldstein (Ed.), *Blackwell handbook of perception.* Malden, MA: Blackwell.

Stein, M. B., Forde, D. R., Anderson, G., & Walker, J. R. (1997a). Obsessive-compulsive disorder in the community: An epidemiologic survey with clinical reappraisal. *American Journal of Psychiatry, 154,* 1120–1126.

Stein, M. B., Walker, J. R., Hazen, A. L., & Forde, D. R. (1997b). Full and partial posttraumatic stress disorder: Findings from a community survey. *American Journal of Psychiatry, 154,* 1114–1119.

Steinberg, L. (2001). We know some things: Adolescent-parent relationships in retrospect and prospect. *Journal of Research on Adolescence, 11,* 1–20.

Steinberg, L., & Levine, A. (1997). *You and your adolescent: A parents' guide for ages 10 to 20.* New York: Harper Perennial.

Steinberg, L., & Morris, A. S. (2001). Adolescent development. *Annual Review of Psychology, 52,* 83–110.

Steinberg, L., & Steinberg, W. (1994). *Crossing paths: How your child's adolescence triggers your own crisis.* New York: Simon & Schuster.

Steinhausen, H. (2002). The outcome of anorexia nervosa in the 20th century. *American Journal of Psychiatry, 159*, 1284–1293.

Steinmetz, H., Staiger, J. F., Schluag, G., Huang, Y., & Jancke, L. (1995). Corpus callosum and brain volume in women and men. *Neuroreport, 6*, 1002–1004.

Steinmetz, J. E. (1998). The localization of a simple type of learning and memory: The cerebellum and classical eyeblink conditioning. *Current Directions in Psychological Science, 7*, 72–77.

Stekel, W. (1950). *Techniques of analytical psychotherapy*. New York: Liveright.

Stellar, E. (1954). The physiology of motivation. *Psychological Review, 61*, 5–22.

Stemberger, R. T., Turner, S. M., Beidel, D. C., & Calhoun, K. S. (1995). Social phobia: An analysis of possible developmental factors. *Journal of Abnormal Psychology, 104*, 526–531.

Stepanski, E. J. (2000). Behavioral therapy for insomnia. In M. H. Kryger, T. Roth, & W. C. Dement (Eds.), *Principles and practice of sleep medicine*. Philadelphia: Saunders.

Stepanski, E. J., & Wyatt, J. K. (2003). Use of sleep hygiene in the treatment of insomnia. *Sleep Medicine Reviews, 7*(3), 215–225.

Stephens, R. S. (1999). Cannabis and hallucinogens. In B. S. McCrady & E. E. Epstein (Eds.), *Addictions: A comprehensive guidebook*. New York: Oxford University Press.

Stephens, T. W., Basinski, M., Bristow, P. K., Bue-Valleskey, J. M., Burgett, S. G., Craft, L., Hale, J., Hoffman, J., Hsiung, H. M., Kriauciunas, A., MacKellar, W., Rosteck, P. R., Jr., Schoner, B., Smith, D., Tinsley, F. C., Zhang, W. Y., & Heiman, M. (1995). The role of neuropeptide Y in the antiobesity action of the obese gene product. *Nature, 377*, 530–532.

Steraide, M. (2000). Brain electrical activity and sensory processing during waking and sleep states. In M. H. Kryger, T. Roth, & W. C. Dement (Eds.), *Principles and practice of sleep medicine*. Philadelphia: Saunders.

Steriade, M. (2005). Brain electrical activity and sensory processing during waking and sleep states. In M. H. Kryger, T. Roth, & W. C. Dement (Eds.), *Principles and practice of sleep medicine*. Philadelphia: Elsevier Saunders.

Stern, W. (1914). *The psychological method of testing intelligence*. Baltimore: Warwick & York.

Sternberg, R. J. (1985). *Beyond IQ: A triarchic theory of human intelligence*. New York: Cambridge University Press.

Sternberg, R. J. (1986). *Intelligence applied: Understanding and increasing your intellectual skills*. New York: Harcourt Brace Jovanovich.

Sternberg, R. J. (1988a). A three-facet model of creativity. In R. J. Sternberg (Ed.), *The nature of creativity: Contemporary psychological perspectives*. Cambridge, England: Cambridge University Press.

Sternberg, R. J. (1988b). *The triarchic mind: A new theory of human intelligence*. New York: Viking.

Sternberg, R. J. (1991). Theory-based testing of intellectual abilities: Rationale for the triarchic abilities test. In H. A. H. Rowe (Ed.), *Intelligence: Reconceptualization and measurement*. Hillsdale, NJ: Erlbaum.

Sternberg, R. J. (1995). For whom *The Bell Curve* tolls: A review of *The Bell Curve*. *Psychological Science, 6*, 257–261.

Sternberg, R. J. (1998). How intelligent is intelligence testing? *Scientific American Presents Exploring Intelligence, 9*, 12–17.

Sternberg, R. J. (1999). The theory of successful intelligence. *Review of General Psychology, 3*, 292–316.

Sternberg, R. J. (2000a). Creativity is a decision. In A. L. Costa (Ed.), *Teaching for intelligence II* (pp. 85–106). Arlington Heights, IL: Skylight Training.

Sternberg, R. J. (2000b). Successful intelligence: A unified view of giftedness. In C. F. M. van Lieshout & P. G. Heymans (Eds.), *Developing talent across the life span* (pp. 43–65). Philadelphia: Psychology Press.

Sternberg, R. J. (2001). What is the common thread of creativity? Its dialectical relation to intelligence and wisdom. *American Psychologist, 56*, 360–362.

Sternberg, R. J. (2003a). Construct validity of the theory of successful intelligence. In R. J. Sternberg, J. Lautrey, & T. I. Lubart (Eds.), *Models of intelligence: International perspectives*. Washington, DC: American Psychological Association.

Sternberg, R. J. (2003b). My house is a very, very, very fine house—But it is not the only house. In H. Nyborg (Ed.), *The scientific study of general intelligence: Tribute to Arthur R. Jensen*. Oxford, UK: Pergamon.

Sternberg, R. J. (2004). Culture and Intelligence. *American Psychologist, 59*, 325–338.

Sternberg, R. J., & Kaufman, J. C. (1998). Human abilities. *Annual Review of Psychology, 49*, 479–502.

Sternberg, R. J., & Lubart, T. I. (1992). Buy low and sell high: An investment approach to creativity. *Current Directions in Psychological Science, 1*(1), 1–5.

Sternberg, R. J., & O'Hara, L. A. (1999). Creativity and intelligence. In R. J. Sternberg (Ed.), *Handbook of creativity*. New York: Cambridge University Press.

Sternberg, R. J., & Wagner, R. K. (1993). The *g*-ocentric view of intelligence and job performance is wrong. *Current Directions in Psychological Science, 2*(1), 1–5.

Sternberg, R. J., Castejon, J. L., Prieto, M. D., Hautamaeki, J., & Grigorenko, E. L. (2001). Confirmatory factor analysis of the Sternberg Triarchic Abilities Test in three international samples: An empirical test of the triarchic theory of intelligence. *European Journal of Psychological Assessment, 17*, 1–16.

Sternberg, R. J., Conway, B. E., Ketron, J. L., & Bernstein, M. (1981). People's conceptions of intelligence. *Journal of Personality and Social Psychology, 41*, 37–55.

Sternberg, R. J., Grigorenko, E. L., & Kidd, K. K. (2005). Intelligence, race, and genetics. *American Psychologist, 60*, 45–69.

Sternberg, R. J., Grigorenko, E. L., Ferrari, M., & Clinkenbeard, P. (1999). A triarchic analysis of an aptitude interaction. *European Journal of Psychological Assessment, 15*, 1–11.

Sternberg, R. J., Wagner, R. K., Williams, W. M., & Horvath, J. A. (1995). Testing common sense. *American Psychologist, 50*, 912–927.

Stevens, S. S. (1955). The measurement of loudness. *Journal of the Acoustical Society of America, 27*, 815–819.

Stewart, A. J., & Ostrove, J. M. (1998). Women's personality in middle age: Gender, history, and midcourse corrections. *American Psychologist, 53*, 1185–1194.

Stewart-Williams, S. (2004). The placebo puzzle: Putting the pieces together. *Health Psychology, 23*, 198–206.

Stice, E. (2001). Risk factors for eating pathology: Recent advances and future directions. In R. H. Striegel-Moore & L. Smolak (Eds.), *Eating disorders: Innovative directions in research and practice* (pp. 51–74). Washington, DC: American Psychological Association.

Stich, S. P. (1990). Rationality. In D. N. Osherson & E. E. Smith (Eds.), *Thinking: An invitation to cognitive science* (Vol. 3). Cambridge, MA: MIT Press.

Stickgold, R. (2005). Why we dream. In M. H. Kryger, T. Roth, & W. C. Dement (Eds.). *Principles and practice of sleep medicine*. Philadelphia: Elsevier Saunders.

Stickgold, R., James, L., & Hobson, J. A. (2000). Visual discrimination learning requires sleep after training. *Nature Neuoroscience, 3*, 1237–1238.

Stickgold, R., Whidbee, D., Schirmer, B., Patel, V., & Hobson, J. A. (2000). Visual discrimination task improvement: A multi-step process occurring during sleep. *Journal of Cognitive Neuroscience, 12*, 246–254.

Stine, S. M., & Kosten, T. R. (1999). Opioids. In B. S. McCrady, & E. E. Epstein (Eds.), *Addictions: A comprehensive guidebook*. New York: Oxford University Press.

Stip, E. (2000). Novel antipsychotics: Issues and controversies. Typicality of atypical antipsychotics. *Journal of Psychiatry & Neuroscience, 25*, 137–153.

Stoddard, G. (1943). *The meaning of intelligence*. New York: Macmillan.

Stoddard, J. J., & Miller, T. (1995). Impact of parental smoking on the prevalence of wheezing respiratory illness in children. *American Journal of Epidemiology, 141*, 96–102.

Stoicheff, B. (2002). Gerhard Herzberg: An illustrious life in science. Ottawa, ON: NRC Press, McGill-Queens Press.

Stoleru, S., Ennaji, A., Cournot, A., & Spira, A. (1993). LH pulsatile secretion and testosterone blood levels are influenced by sexual arousal in human males. *Psychoneuroendocrinology, 18*, 205–218.

Stone, A. A., Bovbjerg, D. H., Neale, J. M., Napoli, A., Valdimarsdottir, H., Cox, D., Hayden, F. G., & Gwaltney, J. M. (1992). Development of the common cold symptoms following experimental rhinovirus infection is related to prior stressful events. *Behavioral Medicine, 18*, 115–120.

Stone, L. (1977). *The family, sex and marriage in England 1500–1800*. New York: Harper & Row.

Stone, W. N. (2003). Group psychotherapy. In A. Tasman, J. Kay, & J. A. Lieberman (Eds.), *Psychiatry*. New York: Wiley.

Stoner, J. A. F. (1961). *A comparison of individual and group decisions involving risk*. Unpublished master's thesis, Massachusetts Institute of Technology.

Stoney, C. M. (2003). Gender and cardiovascular disease: A psychobiological and integrative approach.

Current Directions in Psychological Science, 12(4), 129–133.

Stoohs, R. A., Blum, H. C., Haselhorst, M., Duchna, H. W., Guilleminault, C., & Dement, W. C. (1998). Normative data on snoring: A comparison between younger and older adults. *European Respiratory Journal, 11,* 451–457.

Stoolmiller, M. (1999). Implications of the restricted range of family environments for estimates of heritability and nonshared environment in behavior-genetic adoption studies. *Psychological Bulletin, 125,* 392–409.

Storm, C., & Gurevich, M. (2001). Looking forward, looking back: Women in psychology. *Canadian Psychology, 42*(4), 245–248.

Stormshak, E. A., Bierman, K. L., McMahon, R. J., & Lengua, L. J. (2000). Parenting practices and child disruptive behavior problems in early elementary school. *Journal of Clinical Child Psychology, 29*(1), 17–29.

Straus, M. A. (2000). Corporal punishment and primary prevention of physical abuse. *Child Abuse & Neglect, 24,* 1109–1114.

Straus, M. A., & Kantor, G. K. (1994). Corporal punishment of adolescents by parents: A risk factor in the epidemiology of depression, suicide, alcohol abuse, child abuse, and wife beating. *Adolescence, 29,* 543–561.

Straus, M. A., & Stewart, J. H. (1999). Corporal punishment by American parents: National data on prevalence, chronicity, severity, and duration, in relation to child family characteristics. *Clinical Child & Family Psychology Review, 2*(2), 55–70.

Strayer, D. L., & Johnston, W. A. (2001). Driven to distraction: Dual-task studies of simulated driving and conversing on a cellular telephone. *Psychological Science, 12,* 462–466.

Streissguth, A. P., Barr, H. M., Bookstein, F. L., Sampson, P. D., & Olson, H. C. (1999). The long-term neurocognitive consequences of prenatal alcohol exposure: A 14-year study. *Psychological Science, 10,* 186–190.

Streissguth, A. P., Barr, H. M., Sampson, P. D., Darby, B. L., & Martin, D. C. (1989). IQ at age 4 in relation to maternal alcohol use and smoking during pregnancy. *Developmental Psychology, 25,* 3–11.

Striegel-Moore, R. H., & Rodin, J. (1986). The influence of psychological variables in obesity. In K. D. Brownell & J. P. Foreyt (Eds.), *Handbook of eating disorders: Physiology, psychology, and treatment of obesity, anorexia and bulimia.* New York: Basic Books.

Striegel-Moore, R. H., & Smolak, L. (2001). Introduction. In R. H. Striegel-Moore & L. Smolak (Eds.), *Eating disorders: Innovative directions in research and practice* (pp. 3–8). Washington, DC: American Psychological Association.

Striegel-Moore, R. H., Silberstein, L. R., & Rodin, J. (1993). The social self in bulimia nervosa: Public self-consciousness, social anxiety, and perceived fraudulence. *Journal of Abnormal Psychology, 102.*

Strike, P. C., & Steptoe, A. (2005). Behavioral and emotional triggers of acute coronary syndromes: A systematic review and critique. *Psychosomatic Medicine, 67*(2), 179–186.

Strober, M., Freeman, R., Lampert, C., Diamond, J., & Kaye, W. (2000). Controlled family study of anorexia nervosa and bulimia nervosa: Evidence of shared liability and transmission of partial syndromes. *American Journal of Psychiatry, 157,* 393–401.

Strupp, H. H. (1996). The tripartite model and the *Consumer Reports* study. *American Psychologist, 51,* 1017–1024.

Strupp, H. H., & Howard, K. I. (1992). A brief history of psychotherapy research. In D. K. Freedheim (Ed.), *History of psychotherapy: A century of change.* Washington, DC: American Psychological Association.

Struthers, C. W., Dupuis, R., & Eaton, J. (2005). Promoting forgiveness among coworkers following a workplace transgression: The effects of social motivation training. *Canadian Journal of Behavioural Sciences* (Special Issue on Creating a Healthy Workplace) *37*(4), 299–308.

Stuart, E. W., Shimp, T. A., & Engle, R. W. (1987). Classical conditioning of consumer attitudes: Four experiments in an advertising context. *Journal of Consumer Research, 14,* 334–349.

Stuart, E. W., Shimp, T. A., & Engle, R. W. (1991). A program of classical conditioning experiments testing variations in the conditioned stimulus and context. *Journal of Consumer Research, 18,* 1–12.

Stumpf, H., & Stanley, J. C. (1996). Gender-related differences on the College Board's Advanced Placement and Achievement Tests, 1982–1992. *Journal of Educational Psychology, 88,* 353–364.

Stunkard, A. J., Harris, J. R., Pederson, N. L., & McClearn, G. E. (1990). The body-mass index of twins who have been reared apart. *New England Journal of Medicine, 322,* 1483–1487.

Stunkard, A. J., Sorensen, T., Hanis, C., Teasdale, T. W., Chakraborty, R., Schull, W. J., & Schulsinger, F. (1986). An adoption study of human obesity. *New England Journal of Medicine, 314,* 193–198.

Subrahmanyam, K., & Greenfield, P. M. (1996). Effect of video game practice on spatial skills in girls and boys. In P. M. Greenfield, & R. R. Cocking (Eds.), *Interacting with video.* Norwood, NJ: Ablex Publishing Corp.

Sue, D. W., & Sue, D. (1999). *Counseling the culturally different: Theory and practice.* New York: Wiley.

Sue, D. W., Bingham, R. P., Porche-Burke, L., & Vasquez, M. (1999). The diversification of psychology: A multicultural revolution. *American Psychologist, 54,* 1061–1069.

Sue, S. (2003). In defense of cultural competency in psychotherapy and treatment. *American Psychologist, 58,* 964–970.

Sue, S., & Zane, N. (1987). The role of culture and cultural techniques in psychotherapy: A critique and reformulation. *American Psychologist, 42,* 37–45.

Sue, S., Zane, N., & Young, K. (1994). Research on psychotherapy with culturally diverse populations. In A. E. Bergin & S. L. Garfield (Eds.), *Handbook of psychotherapy and behavior change* (4th ed.). New York: Wiley.

Suedfeld, P. (2003). Canadian space psychology: The future may be almost here. *Canadian Psychology, 44,* 85–92.

Sugiyama, L. S. (2005). Physical attractiveness in adaptionist perspective. In D. M. Buss (Ed.), *The handbook of evolutionary psychology.* New York: Wiley.

Suh, E., Diener, E., Oishi, S., & Triandis, H. C. (1998). The shifting basis of life satisfaction judgments across cultures: Emotions versus norms. *Journal of Personality and Social Psychology, 74,* 482–493.

Sullivan, G. M., & Coplan, J. D. (2000). Anxiety disorders: Biochemical aspects. In B. J. Sadock & V. A. Sadock (Eds.), *Kaplan and Sadock's comprehensive textbook of psychiatry* (7th ed., Vol. 1). Philadelphia: Lippincott/Williams & Wilkins.

Sullivan, G., Burnam, A., & Koegel, P. (2000). Pathways to homelessness among the mentally ill. *Social Psychiatry & Psychiatric Epidemiology, 35,* 444–450.

Sullivan, P. F. (2002). Course and outcome of anorexia nervosa and bulimia nervosa. In C. G. Fairburn & K. D. Brownell (Eds.), *Eating disorders and obesity: A comprehensive handbook.* New York: Guilford.

Sullivan, P. F., Neale, M. C., & Kendler, K. S. (2000). Genetic epidemiology of major depression: Review and meta-analysis. *American Journal of Psychiatry, 157,* 1552–1562.

Sulloway, F. J. (1995). Birth order and evolutionary psychology: A meta-analytic overview. *Psychological Inquiry, 6,* 75–80.

Sulloway, F. J. (1996). *Born to rebel: Birth order, family dynamics, and creative lives.* New York: Pantheon Books.

Summerfeldt, L. J., Richter, M. A., Antony, M. M., & Swinson, R. P. (1999). Symptom structure in obsessive-compulsive disorder: A confirmatory factor-analytic study. *Behaviour Research and Therapy, 37,* 297–311.

Super, C. M. (1976). Environmental effects on motor development: A case of African infant precocity. *Developmental Medicine and Child Neurology, 18,* 561–567.

Susman, E. J., & Rogol, A. (2004). Puberty and psychological development. In R. M. Lerner & L. Steinberg (Eds.), *Handbook of adolescent psychology.* New York: Wiley.

Susman, E. J., Dorn, L. D., & Schiefelbein, V. L. (2003). Puberty, sexuality, and health. In R. M. Lerner, M. A. Easterbrooks, & J. Mistry (Eds.), *Handbook of psychology, Vol. 6: Developmental psychology.* New York: Wiley.

Susser, E. B., Brown, A., & Matte, T. D. (1999). Prenatal factors and adult mental and physical health. *Canadian Journal of Psychiatry, 44,* 326–334.

Susser, E. B., Neugebauer, R., Hoek, H. W., Brown, A. S., Lin, S., Labovitz, D., & Gorman, J. M. (1996). Schizophrenia after prenatal famine: Further evidence. *Archives of General Psychiatry, 53,* 25–31.

Sutker, P. B., & Allain, A. N. (2001). Antisocial personality disorder. In P. B. Sutker & H. E. Adams (Eds.), *Comprehensive handbook of psychopathology.* New York: Kluwer Academic/Plenum.

Sutker, P. B., Bugg, F. & West, J. A. (1993). Antisocial personality disorder. In P. B. Sutker & H. E. Adams (Eds.), *Comprehensive handbook of psychopathology* (2nd ed.). New York: Plenum.

Weiner, R. D. (2000). Retrograde amnesia with eletroconvulsive therapy: Characteristics and implications. *General Psychiatry, 57,* 591–592.

Weinfield, N. S., Sroufe, L. A., Egeland, B., & Carlson, E. A. (1999). The nature of individual differences in infant-caregiver attachment. In J. Cassidy & P. R. Shaver (Eds.), *Handbook of attachment: Theory, research, and clinical applications.* New York: Guilford.

Weinger, M. B., & Ancoli-Israel, S. (2002). Sleep deprivation and clinical performance. *Journal of the American Medical Association, 287,* 955–957.

Weinstein, L. N., Schwartz, D. G., & Arkin, A. M. (1991). Qualitative aspects of sleep mentation. In S. J. Ellman & J. S. Antrobus (Eds.), *The mind in sleep: Psychology and psychophysiology* (2nd ed.). New York: Wiley.

Weinstein, N. D. (1984). Why it won't happen to me: Perceptions of risk factors and susceptibility. *Health Psychology, 3,* 431–458.

Weinstein, N. D. (2003). Exploring the links between risk perceptions and preventative health behavior. In J. Suls & K. A. Wallston (Eds.), *Social psychological foundations of health and illness.* Malden, MA: Blackwell Publishing.

Weinstein, N. D., & Klein, W. M. (1995). Resistance of personal risk perceptions to debiasing interventions. *Health Psychology, 14,* 132–140.

Weinstein, N. D., & Klein, W. M. (1996). Unrealistic optimism: Present and future. *Journal of Social and Clinical Psychology, 15,* 1–8.

Weisberg, R. W. (1986). *Creativity: Genius and other myths.* New York: W. H. Freeman.

Weisberg, R. W. (1993). *Creativity: Beyond the myth of genius.* New York: W. H. Freeman.

Weisberg, R. W. (1999). Creativity and knowledge: A challenge to theories. In R. J. Sternberg (Ed.), *Handbook of creativity.* New York: Cambridge University Press.

Weisman, R. (1995). Reflections on the Oak Ridge experiment with mentally disordered offenders, 1965–1968. *International Journal of Law and Psychiatry, 18,* 265–290.

Weisner, T. S., & Wilson-Mitchell, J. E. (1990). Nonconventional family life-styles and sex typing in six-year-olds. *Child Development, 61,* 1915–1933.

Weiten, W. (1984). Violation of selected item-construction principles in educational measurement.

Journal of Experimental Education, 51, 46–50.

Weiten, W. (1988b). Pressure as a form of stress and its relationship to psychological symptomatology. *Journal of Social and Clinical Psychology, 6*(1), 127–139.

Weiten, W. (1998). Pressure, major life events, and psychological symptoms. *Journal of Social Behavior and Personality, 13,* 51–68.

Weiten, W., & Diamond, S. S. (1979). A critical review of the jury-simulation paradigm: The case of defendant characteristics. *Law and Human Behavior, 3,* 71–93.

Weiten, W., & Wight, R. D. (1992). Portraits of a discipline: An examination of introductory psychology textbooks in America. In A. E. Puente, J. R. Matthews, & C. L. Brewer (Eds.), *Teaching psychology in America: A history.* Washington, DC: American Psychological Association.

Weizmann, F., Wiener, N. I., Wiesenthal, D. L., & Ziegler, M. (1990). *Canadian Psychology, 31,* 1–13.

Well, A. D., Pollatsek, A., & Boyce, S. J. (1990). Understanding the effects of sample size on the variability of the mean. *Organizational Behavior and Human Decision Processes, 47,* 289–312.

Wellman, H. M., & Gelman, S. A. (1998). Knowledge acquisition in foundational domians. In W. Damon (Ed.), *Handbook of child psychology (Vol. 2): Cognition, perception, and language.* New York: Wiley.

Wells, A. J. (1998). Lung cancer from passive smoking at work. *American Journal of Public Health, 88,* 1025–1029.

Wells, C. G. (1991). *Right-brain sex: How to reach the heights of sensual pleasure by releasing the erotic power of your mind.* New York: Avon.

Wells, G. L., & Bradfield, A. L. (1998). "Good, you identified the suspect": Feedback to eyewitnesses disorts their reports of the witnessing experience. *Journal of Applied Psychology, 83,* 360–376.

Wells, G. L., & Olson, E. A. (2003). Eyewitness testimony. *Annual Review of Psychology, 54,* 277–295.

Wells, H. G. (1895/1995). *The time machine.* New York: Dover Publications.

Wells, K., Klap, R., Koike, A., & Sherbourne, C. (2001). Ethnic disparities in unmet need for alcoholism, drug abuse, and mental health care. *American Journal of Psychiatry, 158,* 2027–2032.

Werbach, M. R. (1988). *Nutritional influences on illness: A sourcebook of*

clinical research. Tarzana, CA: Third Line Press.

Werker, J. (2003). Baby steps to learning language. *Journal of Pediatrics, 143* (Supplement), 62–69.

Werker, J. F., & Desjardins, R. N. (1995). Listening to speech in the 1st year of life: Experiential influences on phoneme perception. *Current Directions in Psychological Science, 4,* 76–81.

Werker, J., & Curtin, S. (2005). PRIMIR: A developmental framework of infant speech processing. *Language and Learning Development, 1,* 197–234.

Werker, J., & Tees, R. C. (2005). Speech perception as a window for understanding plasticity and commitment in language systems of the brain. *Developmental Psychobiology, 46,* 233–251.

Wertheimer, M. (1912). Experiment-elle studien über das sehen von bewegung. *Zeitschrift für Psychologie, 60,* 312–378.

Wertz, F. J. (1998). The role of the humanistic movement in the history of psychology. *Journal of Humanistic Psychology, 38,* 42–70.

Wessely, S., & Kerwin, R. (2004). Suicide risk and the SSRI's. *Journal of the American Medical Association, 292,* 379–381.

Wesson, D. R., Smith, D. E., Ling, W., & Seymour, R. B. (1997). Sedative-hypnotics and tricyclics. In J. H. Lowinson, P. Ruiz, R. B. Millman, & J. G. Langrod (Eds.), *Substance abuse: A comprehensive textbook.* Baltimore: Williams & Wilkin.

West, R. F., & Stanovich, K. E. (1997). The domain specificity and generality of overconfidence: Individual differences in performance estimation bias. *Psychonomic Bulletin & Review, 4,* 387–392.

Westbrook, G. L. (2000). Seizures and epilepsy. In E. R. Kandel, J. H. Schwartz, & T. M. Jessell (Eds.), *Principles of neural science.* New York: McGraw-Hill.

Westen, D. (1998). The scientific legacy of Sigmund Freud: Toward a psychodynamically informed psychological science. *Psychological Bulletin, 124,* 333–371.

Westen, D., & Gabbard, G. O. (1999). Psychoanalytic approaches to personality. In L. A. Pervin & O. P. John (Eds.), *Handbook of personality: Theory and research.* New York: Guilford.

Westen, D., & Shedler, J. (1999). Revising and assessing Axis II, Part II: Toward an empirically based and clinically useful classification of personality disorders. *American Journal of Psychiatry, 156,* 273–285.

Wethington, E. (2000). Life events scale. In G. Fink (Ed.), *Encyclopedia of stress* (Vol. 1, pp. 618–622). San Diego: Academic Press.

Wever, E. G., & Bray, C. W. (1937). The perception of low tones and the resonance-volley theory. *Journal of Psychology, 3,* 101–114.

Wexler, B. E., Gottschalk, C. H., Fulbright, R. K., Prohovnik, I., Lacadie, C. M., Rounsaville, B. J., & Gore, J. C. (2001). Functional magnetic resonance imaging of cocaine craving. *American Journal of Psychiatry, 158,* 86–95.

Whalen, P. J. (1998). Fear, vigilance, and ambiguity: Initial neuroimaging studies of the human amygdala. *Current Directions in Psychological Science, 7,* 177–188.

Wheeler, L., & Kim, Y. (1997). What is beautiful is culturally good: The physical attractiveness stereotype has different content in collectivistic cultures. *Personality and Social Psychology Bulletin, 23,* 795–800.

Whitaker, R. (2002). *Mad in America: Bad science, bad medicine, and the enduring mistreatment of the mentally ill.* New York: Perseus Publishing.

Whitbourne, S. K. (1999). Physical changes. In J. C. Cavanaugh & S. K. Whitbourne (Eds.), *Gerontology: Interdisciplinary perspectives* (pp. 91–122). New York: Oxford University Press.

Whitbourne, S. K., Zuschlag, M. K., Elliot, L. B., & Waterman, A. S. (1992). Psychosocial development in adulthood: A 22-year sequential study. *Journal of Personality and Social Psychology, 63,* 260–271.

White, S. H. (2000). Conceptual foundations of IQ testing. *Psychology, Public Policy, and Law, 6,* 33–43.

Whitehouse, W. G., & Dinges, D. F., Orne, E. C., & Orne, M. T. (1988). Hypnotic hyperamnesia: Enhanced memory accessibility or report bias? *Journal of Abnormal Psychology, 97,* 298–295.

Whitfield, C. L. (1995). *Memory and abuse: Remembering and healing the effects of trauma.* Deerfield Beach, FL: Health Communications.

Whiting, J. W. M., Burbank, V. K., & Ratner, M. S. (1986). The duration of maidenhood. In J. B. Lancaster & B. A. Hamburg (Eds.), *School age pregnancy and parenthood.* Hawthorne, NY: Aldine de Gruyter.

Whitley, B. E., Jr. (1988). *College students' reasons for sexual intercourse: A sex role perspective.* Paper presented at the 96th Annual Meeting of the American Psychological Association, Atlanta.

macological treatment of insomnia. *Sleep: Journal of Sleep Research & Sleep Medicine, 22*, 371–375.

Walsh, J. K., Dement, W. C., & Dinges, D. F. (2005). Sleep medicine, public policy, and public health. In M. H. Kryger, T. Roth, & W. C. Dement (Eds.). *Principles and practice of sleep medicine*. Philadelphia: Elsevier Saunders.

Walter, T., & Siebert, A. (1990). *Student success: How to succeed in college and still have time for your friends*. Fort Worth: Holt, Rinehart & Winston.

Walters, E. E., & Kendler, K. S. (1995). Anorexia nervosa and anorexic-like syndromes in a population-based female twin sample. *American Journal of Psychiatry, 152*, 64–71.

Walters, G. D. (2001). A meta-analysis of opinion data on the prescription privilege debate. *Canadian Psychology, 42*, 119–126.

Walther, E., & Grigoriadis, S. (2003). Why sad people like shoes better: The influence of mood on the evaluative conditioning of consumer attitudes. *Psychology & Marketing, 10*, 755–775.

Walther, E., Nagengast, B., & Trasselli, C. (2005). Evaluative conditioning in social psychology: Facts and speculations. *Cognition and Emotion, 19*(2), 175–196.

Waltz, J. A., Knowlton, B. J., Holyoak, K. J., Boone, K. B., Mishkin, F. S., de Menezes Santos, M., Thomas, C. R., & Miller, B. L. (1999). A system for relational reasoning in human prefrontal cortex. *Psychological Science, 10*, 119–125.

Wampold, B. E. (2001). *The great psychotherapy debate*. Mahwah, NJ: Erlbaum.

Wangensteen, O. H., & Carlson, A. J. (1931). Hunger sensation after total gastrectomy. *Proceedings of the Society for Experimental Biology, 28*, 545–547.

Wardle, J., Steptoe, A., Oliver, G., & Lipsey, Z. (2000). Stress, dietary restraint and food intake. *Journal of Psychosomatic Research, 48*, 195–202.

Wark, G. R., & Krebs, D. L. (1996). Gender and dilemma differences in real-life moral judgment. *Developmental Psychology, 32*, 220–230.

Warr, P. (1999). Well-being and the workplace. In D. Kahneman, E. Diener, & N. Schwarz (Eds.), *Well-being: The foundations of hedonic psychology*. New York: Russell Sage Foundation.

Warrington, E. K., & Weiskrantz, L. (1970). Amnesic syndrome:

Consolidation or retrieval? *Nature, 228*, 629–630.

Warshaw, M. G., Fierman, E., Pratt, L., Hunt, M., Yonkers, K. A., Massion, A. O., & Keller, M. B. (1993). Quality of life and dissociation in anxiety disorder patients with histories of trauma or PTSD. *American Journal of Psychiatry, 150*, 1512–1516.

Washburn, M. F. (1908). *The animal mind*. New York: Macmillan.

Wasserman, J. D., & Bracken, B. A. (2003). Psychometric characteristics of assessment procedures. In J. R. Graham & J. A. Naglieri (Eds.), *Handbook of psychology, Vol. 10: Assessment psychology*. New York: Wiley.

Watanabe, M. (1998). The relationship between sensation seeking and health risk behavior: A survey on traffic-related risk behavior, cigarette smoking and alcohol drinking among university students. *Japanese Journal of Health Psychology, 11*, 28–38.

Waterman, A., & Archer, S. (1990). A life-span perspective on identity formation: Development in form, function, and process. In P. B. Baltes, D. L. Featherman, & R. M. Lerner (Eds.), *Life-span development and behavior* (Vol. 10). Hillsdale, NJ: Erlbaum.

Watkins, C. E., Campbell, V. L., Nieberding, R., & Hallmark, R. (1995). Contemporary practice of psychological assessment by clinical psychologists. *Professional Psychology: Research and Practice, 26*, 54–60.

Watson, D. E., Heppner, P., Roos, N. D., Reid, R. J., & Katz, A. (2005). Population-based use of mental health services and patterns of delivery among family physicians. *Canadian Journal of Psychiatry, 50*, 398–406.

Watson, D. L., & Tharp, R. G. (1997). *Self-directed behavior: Self-modification for personal adjustment* (6th ed.). Pacific Grove, CA: Brooks/Cole.

Watson, D. L., & Tharp, R. G. (2002). *Self-directed behavior: Self-modification for personal adjustment*. Belmont, CA: Wadsworth.

Watson, D., & Clark, L. A. (1997). Extraversion and its positive emotional core. In R. Hogan, J. Johnson, & S. Briggs (Eds.), *Handbook of personality psychology*. San Diego: Academic Press.

Watson, D., & Pennebaker, J. W. (1989). Health complaints, stress, and distress: Exploring the central role of negative affectivity. *Psychological Review, 96*, 234–254.

Watson, D., David, J. P., & Suls, J. (1999). Personality, affectivity, and coping. In C. R. Snyder (Ed.), *Coping: The psychology of what works*. New York: Oxford University Press.

Watson, D., Klohen, E. C., Casillas, A., Nus Simms, E., Haig, J., & Berry, D. S. (2004). Match makers and deal breakers: Analyses of assortative mating in newlywed couples. *Journal of Personality, 72*, 1029–1068.

Watson, D., Suls, J., & Haig, J. (2002). Global self-esteem in relation to structural models of personality and affectivity. *Journal of Personality and Social Psychology, 83*, 185–197.

Watson, J. B. (1913). Psychology as the behaviorist views it. *Psychological Review, 20*, 158–177.

Watson, J. B. (1919). *Psychology from the standpoint of a behaviorist*. Philadelphia: Lippincott.

Watson, J. B. (1924). *Behaviorism*. New York: Norton.

Watson, J. C., Gordon, L. B., Stermac, L., Steckley, P., & Kalogerakos, F. (2003). Comparing the effectiveness of process-experiential with cognitive-behavioral psychotherapy in the treatment of depression. *Journal of Consulting and Clinical Psychology, 71*(4), 773–781.

Waugh, N. C., & Norman, D. A. (1965). Primary memory. *Psychological Review, 72*, 89–104.

Weatherall, A. (1992). Gender and languages: Research in progress. *Feminism & Psychology, 2*, 177–181.

Weaver, C. A., III. (1993). Do you need a "flash" to form a flashbulb memory? *Journal of Experimental Psychology: General, 122*, 39–46.

Weaver, M. F., & Schnoll, S. H. (1999). Stimulants: Amphetamines and cocaine. In B. S. McCrady & E. E. Epstein (Eds.), *Addictions: A comprehensive guidebook*. New York: Oxford University Press.

Webb, W. B. (1992a). Developmental aspects and a behavioral model of human sleep. In C. Stampi (Ed.), *Why we nap: Evolution, chronobiology, and functions of polyphasic and ultrashort sleep*. Boston: Birkhaeuser.

Webb, W. B. (1992b). *Sleep: The gentle tyrant*. Bolton, MA: Anker.

Webb, W. B., & Dinges, D. F. (1989). Cultural perspectives on napping and the siesta. In D. F. Dinges & R. J. Broughton (Eds.), *Sleep and alertness: Chronobiological, behavioral, and medical aspects of napping*. New York: Raven.

Wechsler, D. (1939). *The measurement of adult intelligence*. Baltimore: Williams & Wilkins.

Wechsler, D. (1949). *Wechsler intelligence scale for children*. New York: Psychological Corporation.

Wechsler, D. (1955). *Manual, Wechsler adult intelligence scale*. New York: Psychological Corporation.

Wechsler, D. (1967). *Manual for the Wechsler preschool and primary scale of intelligence*. New York: Psychological Corporation.

Wechsler, D. (1981). *Manual for the Wechsler adult intelligence scale—revised*. New York: Psychological Corporation.

Wechsler, D. (1991). *WISC-III manual*. San Antonio: Psychological Corporation.

Wechsler, D. (2003). *Wechsler Intelligence Scale for Children-Fourth Edition (WISC IV)*. San Antonio, TX: Psychological Corporation.

Weems, C. F., Hayward, C., Killen, J., & Taylor, C. B. (2002). A longitudinal investigation of anxiety sensitivity in adolescence. *Journal of Abnormal Psychology, 111*, 471–477.

Weinberg, R. A. (1989). Intelligence and IQ: Landmark issues and great debates. *American Psychologist, 44*, 98–104.

Weinberger, D. A. (1990). The construct validity of the repressive coping style. In J. L. Singer (Ed.), *Repression and dissociation*. Chicago: University of Chicago Press.

Weinberger, D. A., & Davidson, M. A. (1994). Styles of inhibiting emotional expression: Distinguishing repressive coping from impression management. *Journal of Personality, 62*, 589–611.

Weinberger, J. (1995). Common factors aren't so common: The common factors dilemma. *Clinical Psychology: Science and Practice, 2*, 45–69.

Weiner, B. (1980). *Human motivation*. New York: Holt, Rinehart & Winston.

Weiner, B. (1986). *An attributional theory of motivation and emotion*. New York: Springer-Verlag.

Weiner, B. (1994). Integrating social and personal theories of achievement striving. *Review of Educational Research, 64*, 557–573.

Weiner, B. (Ed.). (1974). *Achievement motivation and attribution theory*. Morristown, NJ: General Learning Press.

Weiner, H. (1992). *Perturbing the organism: The biology of stressful experience*. Chicago: University of Chicago Press.

Weiner, M. F. (1993). Role of the leader in group psychotherapy. In H. I. Kaplan & B. J. Sadock (Eds.), *Comprehensive group psychotherapy*. Baltimore: Williams & Wilkins.

Weiner, R. D. (2000). Retrograde amnesia with eletroconvulsive therapy: Characteristics and implications. *General Psychiatry, 57,* 591–592.

Weinfield, N. S., Sroufe, L. A., Egeland, B., & Carlson, E. A. (1999). The nature of individual differences in infant-caregiver attachment. In J. Cassidy & P. R. Shaver (Eds.), *Handbook of attachment: Theory, research, and clinical applications.* New York: Guilford.

Weinger, M. B., & Ancoli-Israel, S. (2002). Sleep deprivation and clinical performance. *Journal of the American Medical Association, 287,* 955–957.

Weinstein, L. N., Schwartz, D. G., & Arkin, A. M. (1991). Qualitative aspects of sleep mentation. In S. J. Ellman & J. S. Antrobus (Eds.), *The mind in sleep: Psychology and psychophysiology* (2nd ed.). New York: Wiley.

Weinstein, N. D. (1984). Why it won't happen to me: Perceptions of risk factors and susceptibility. *Health Psychology, 3,* 431–458.

Weinstein, N. D. (2003). Exploring the links between risk perceptions and preventative health behavior. In J. Suls & K. A. Wallston (Eds.), *Social psychological foundations of health and illness.* Malden, MA: Blackwell Publishing.

Weinstein, N. D., & Klein, W. M. (1995). Resistance of personal risk perceptions to debiasing interventions. *Health Psychology, 14,* 132–140.

Weinstein, N. D., & Klein, W. M. (1996). Unrealistic optimism: Present and future. *Journal of Social and Clinical Psychology, 15,* 1–8.

Weisberg, R. W. (1986). *Creativity: Genius and other myths.* New York: W. H. Freeman.

Weisberg, R. W. (1993). *Creativity: Beyond the myth of genius.* New York: W. H. Freeman.

Weisberg, R. W. (1999). Creativity and knowledge: A challenge to theories. In R. J. Sternberg (Ed.), *Handbook of creativity.* New York: Cambridge University Press.

Weisman, R. (1995). Reflections on the Oak Ridge experiment with mentally disordered offenders, 1965–1968. *International Journal of Law and Psychiatry, 18,* 265–290.

Weisner, T. S., & Wilson-Mitchell, J. E. (1990). Nonconventional family life-styles and sex typing in six-year-olds. *Child Development, 61,* 1915–1933.

Weiten, W. (1984). Violation of selected item-construction principles in educational measurement. *Journal of Experimental Education, 51,* 46–50.

Weiten, W. (1988b). Pressure as a form of stress and its relationship to psychological symptomatology. *Journal of Social and Clinical Psychology, 6*(1), 127–139.

Weiten, W. (1998). Pressure, major life events, and psychological symptoms. *Journal of Social Behavior and Personality, 13,* 51–68.

Weiten, W., & Diamond, S. S. (1979). A critical review of the jury-simulation paradigm: The case of defendant characteristics. *Law and Human Behavior, 3,* 71–93.

Weiten, W., & Wight, R. D. (1992). Portraits of a discipline: An examination of introductory psychology textbooks in America. In A. E. Puente, J. R. Matthews, & C. L. Brewer (Eds.), *Teaching psychology in America: A history.* Washington, DC: American Psychological Association.

Weizmann, F., Wiener, N. I., Wiesenthal, D. L., & Ziegler, M. (1990). *Canadian Psychology, 31,* 1–13.

Well, A. D., Pollatsek, A., & Boyce, S. J. (1990). Understanding the effects of sample size on the variability of the mean. *Organizational Behavior and Human Decision Processes, 47,* 289–312.

Wellman, H. M., & Gelman, S. A. (1998). Knowledge acquisition in foundational domians. In W. Damon (Ed.), *Handbook of child psychology (Vol. 2): Cognition, perception, and language.* New York: Wiley.

Wells, A. J. (1998). Lung cancer from passive smoking at work. *American Journal of Public Health, 88,* 1025–1029.

Wells, C. G. (1991). *Right-brain sex: How to reach the heights of sensual pleasure by releasing the erotic power of your mind.* New York: Avon.

Wells, G. L., & Bradfield, A. L. (1998). "Good, you identified the suspect": Feedback to eyewitnesses disorts their reports of the witnessing experience. *Journal of Applied Psychology, 83,* 360–376.

Wells, G. L., & Olson, E. A. (2003). Eyewitness testimony. *Annual Review of Psychology, 54,* 277–295.

Wells, H. G. (1895/1995). *The time machine.* New York: Dover Publications.

Wells, K., Klap, R., Koike, A., & Sherbourne, C. (2001). Ethnic disparities in unmet need for alcoholism, drug abuse, and mental health care. *American Journal of Psychiatry, 158,* 2027–2032.

Werbach, M. R. (1988). *Nutritional influences on illness: A sourcebook of clinical research.* Tarzana, CA: Third Line Press.

Werker, J. (2003). Baby steps to learning language. *Journal of Pediatrics, 143* (Supplement), 62–69.

Werker, J. F., & Desjardins, R. N. (1995). Listening to speech in the 1st year of life: Experiential influences on phoneme perception. *Current Directions in Psychological Science, 4,* 76–81.

Werker, J., & Curtin, S. (2005). PRIMIR: A developmental framework of infant speech processing. *Language and Learning Development, 1,* 197–234.

Werker, J., & Tees, R. C. (2005). Speech perception as a window for understanding plasticity and commitment in language systems of the brain. *Developmental Psychobiology, 46,* 233–251.

Wertheimer, M. (1912). Experiment-elle studien über das sehen von bewegung. *Zeitschrift für Psychologie, 60,* 312–378.

Wertz, F. J. (1998). The role of the humanistic movement in the history of psychology. *Journal of Humanistic Psychology, 38,* 42–70.

Wessely, S., & Kerwin, R. (2004). Suicide risk and the SSRI's. *Journal of the American Medical Association, 292,* 379–381.

Wesson, D. R., Smith, D. E., Ling, W., & Seymour, R. B. (1997). Sedative-hypnotics and tricyclics. In J. H. Lowinson, P. Ruiz, R. B. Millman, & J. G. Langrod (Eds.), *Substance abuse: A comprehensive textbook.* Baltimore: Williams & Wilkin.

West, R. F., & Stanovich, K. E. (1997). The domain specificity and generality of overconfidence: Individual differences in performance estimation bias. *Psychonomic Bulletin & Review, 4,* 387–392.

Westbrook, G. L. (2000). Seizures and epilepsy. In E. R. Kandel, J. H. Schwartz, & T. M. Jessell (Eds.), *Principles of neural science.* New York: McGraw-Hill.

Westen, D. (1998). The scientific legacy of Sigmund Freud: Toward a psychodynamically informed psychological science. *Psychological Bulletin, 124,* 333–371.

Westen, D., & Gabbard, G. O. (1999). Psychoanalytic approaches to personality. In L. A. Pervin & O. P. John (Eds.), *Handbook of personality: Theory and research.* New York: Guilford.

Westen, D., & Shedler, J. (1999). Revising and assessing Axis II, Part II: Toward an empirically based and clinically useful classification of personality disorders. *American Journal of Psychiatry, 156,* 273–285.

Wethington, E. (2000). Life events scale. In G. Fink (Ed.), *Encyclopedia of stress* (Vol. 1, pp. 618–622). San Diego: Academic Press.

Wever, E. G., & Bray, C. W. (1937). The perception of low tones and the resonance-volley theory. *Journal of Psychology, 3,* 101–114.

Wexler, B. E., Gottschalk, C. H., Fulbright, R. K., Prohovnik, I., Lacadie, C. M., Rounsaville, B. J., & Gore, J. C. (2001). Functional magnetic resonance imaging of cocaine craving. *American Journal of Psychiatry, 158,* 86–95.

Whalen, P. J. (1998). Fear, vigilance, and ambiguity: Initial neuroimaging studies of the human amygdala. *Current Directions in Psychological Science, 7,* 177–188.

Wheeler, L., & Kim, Y. (1997). What is beautiful is culturally good: The physical attractiveness stereotype has different content in collectivistic cultures. *Personality and Social Psychology Bulletin, 23,* 795–800.

Whitaker, R. (2002). *Mad in America: Bad science, bad medicine, and the enduring mistreatment of the mentally ill.* New York: Perseus Publishing.

Whitbourne, S. K. (1999). Physical changes. In J. C. Cavanaugh & S. K. Whitbourne (Eds.), *Gerontology: Interdisciplinary perspectives* (pp. 91–122). New York: Oxford University Press.

Whitbourne, S. K., Zuschlag, M. K., Elliot, L. B., & Waterman, A. S. (1992). Psychosocial development in adulthood: A 22-year sequential study. *Journal of Personality and Social Psychology, 63,* 260–271.

White, S. H. (2000). Conceptual foundations of IQ testing. *Psychology, Public Policy, and Law, 6,* 33–43.

Whitehouse, W. G., & Dinges, D. F., Orne, E. C., & Orne, M. T. (1988). Hypnotic hyperamnesia: Enhanced memory accessibility or report bias? *Journal of Abnormal Psychology, 97,* 298–295.

Whitfield, C. L. (1995). *Memory and abuse: Remembering and healing the effects of trauma.* Deerfield Beach, FL: Health Communications.

Whiting, J. W. M., Burbank, V. K., & Ratner, M. S. (1986). The duration of maidenhood. In J. B. Lancaster & B. A. Hamburg (Eds.), *School age pregnancy and parenthood.* Hawthorne, NY: Aldine de Gruyter.

Whitley, B. E., Jr. (1988). *College students' reasons for sexual intercourse: A sex role perspective.* Paper presented at the 96th Annual Meeting of the American Psychological Association, Atlanta.

Vernon, P. A., Wickett, J. C., Bazana, P. G., & Stelmack, R. M. (2000). The neuropsychology and psychophysiology of human intelligence. In R. J. Sternberg (Ed.), *Handbook of intelligence* (pp. 245–266). Cambridge, MA: Cambridge University Press.

Vgontzas, A. N., Bixler, E. O., & Kales, A. K. (2000). Sleep, sleep disorders, and stress. In G. Fink (Ed.), *Encyclopedia of stress* (Vol. 3, p. 449–457). San Diego: Academic Press.

Videbech, P., & Ravnkilde, B. (2004). Hippocampal volume and depression: A meta-analysis of MRI studies. *American Journal of Psychiatry, 161,* 1957–1966.

Vierck, C. (1978). Somatosensory system. In R. B. Masterston (Ed.), *Handbook of sensory neurobiology.* New York: Plenum.

Vihman, M. M. (1985). Language differentiation by the bilingual infant. *Journal of Child Language, 12,* 297–324.

Vinogradov, S., Cox, P. D., & Yalom, I. D. (1999). Group therapy. In R. E. Hales, S. C. Yudofsky, & J. A. Talbott (Eds.), *American Psychiatric Press textbook of psychiatry.* Washington, DC: American Psychiatric Press.

Vinogradov, S., Cox. P. D., & Yalom, I. D. (2003). Group therapy. In R. E. Hales & S. C. Yudofsky (Eds.), *Textbook of clinical psychiatry.* Washington, DC: American Psychiatric Publishing.

Vinters, H. V. (2001). Aging and the human nervous system. In J. E. Birren & K. W. Schaie (Eds.), *Handbook of the psychology of aging* (5th ed., pp. 134–159). San Diego, CA: Academic Press.

Visser, P. S., & Cooper, J. (2003). Attitude change. In M. A. Hogg & J. Cooper (Eds.), *The Sage handbook of social psychology.* Thousand Oaks, CA: Sage.

Vodelholzer, U., Homyak, M., Thiel, B., Huwig-Poppe, C., Kiemen, A., Konig, A., Backhaus, J., Reimann, D., Berger, M., & Hohagen, R. (1998). Impact of experimentally induced serotonin deficiency by tryphophan depletion on sleep EEG in healthy subjects. *Neuropsychopharmacology, 18,* 112–124.

Vokey, J. R., & Read, J. D. (1985). Subliminal messages: Between the devil and the media. *American Psychologist, 40,* 1231–1239.

Volavka, J., Czobor, P., Sheitman, B., Lindenmayer, J. P., Citrome, L., McEvoy, J. P., Cooper, T. B., Chakos, M., & Lieberman, J. A. (2002). Clozapine, olanzapine, risperidone, haloperidol in the treatment of patients with chronic schizophrenia and schizoaffective disorder. *American Journal of Psychiatry, 159,* 255–262.

Volkow, N. D., Fowler, J. S., & Wang, G. J. (2004). The addicted human brain viewed in the light of imaging studies: Brain circuits and treatment strategies. *Neuropharmacology, 47,* 3–13.

Volkow, N. D., Fowler, J. S., Wang, G. J., & Swanson, J. M. (2004). Dopamine in drug abuse and addiction: Results from imaging studies and treatment implications. *Molecular Psychiatry, 9,* 557–569.

Vollmer, W. M., Sacks, F. M., Ard, J., Appel, L. J., Bray, G. A., Simons-Morton, D. G., Conlin, P. R., Svetkey, L. P., Erlinger, T. P., Moore, T. J., & Karanja, N. (2001). Effects of diet and sodium intake on blood pressure: Subgroup analysis of the DASH-sodium trial. *Annals of Internal Medicine, 18,* 1019–1028.

Vouloumanos, A., & Werker, J. (2004). Tuned to signal: The privileged status of speech for young infants. *Developmental Science, 7,* 270–276.

Voyer, D. (1996). On the magnitude of laterality effects and sex differences in functional lateralities. *Laterality, 1,* 51–83.

Voyer, D., Nolan, C., & Voyer, S. (2000). The relation between experience and spatial performance in men and women. *Sex Roles, 43,* 891–915.

Voyer, D., Voyer, S., & Bryden, M. P. (1995). Magnitude of sex differences in spatial abilities: A meta-analysis and consideration of critical variables. *Psychological Bulletin, 117,* 250–270.

Wachtel, P. L. (1977). *Psychoanalysis and behavior therapy: Toward an integration.* New York: Basic Books.

Wachtel, P. L. (1991). From eclectism to synthesis: Toward a more seamless psychotherapeutic integration. *Journal of Psychotherapy Integration, 1,* 43–54.

Wagner, H. (1989). The physiological differentiation of emotions. In H. Wagner & A. Manstead (Eds.), *Handbook of social psychophysiology.* New York: Wiley.

Wagner, M. E., Schubert, H. J. P., & Schubert, D. S. P. (1993). Sex-of-sibling effects: Part 1. Gender role, intelligence, achievement, and creativity. In H. W. Reese (Ed.), *Advances in child development and behavior* (Vol. 24). San Diego: Academic Press.

Wagner, R. K. (1997). Intelligence, training, and employment. *American Psychologist, 52,* 1059–1069.

Wahlsten, D. (1997a). Leilani Muir versus the Philosopher King: Eugenics on trial in Alberta. *Genetica, 20,* 185–198.

Wahlsten, D. (1997b). The malleability of intelligence is not constrained by heritability. In B. Devlin, S. E. Fienberg, D. P. Resnick, & K. Roeder (Eds.), *Intelligence, genes, and success: Scientists respond to The Bell Curve.* New York: Springer-Verlag.

Wahlsten, D. (1999). The eugenics of John. M. MacEachran warrant revocation of honours. *History of Psychology and Philosophy Bulletin, 10,* 22–25.

Wakefield, J. C. (1999). The measurement of mental disorder. In A. V. Horvitz & T. L. Scheid (Eds.), *A handbook for the study of mental health: Social contexts, theories, and systems.* New York: Cambridge University Press.

Wald, G. (1964). The receptors of human color vision. *Science, 145,* 1007–1017.

Waldman, I. D. (1997). Unresolved questions and future directions in behavior-genetic studies of intelligence. In R. J. Sternberg, & E. L. Grigorenko (Eds.), *Intelligence, heredity, and environment.* New York: Cambridge University Press.

Waldrop, D., Lightsey, O. R., Ethington, C. A., Woemmel, C. A., & Coke, A. L. (2001). Self-efficacy, optimism, health competence, and recovery from orthopedic surgery. *Journal of Counseling Psychology, 48,* 233–238.

Walker, E. F., Baum, K. M., & Diforio, D. (1998). Developmental changes in behavioral expression and vulnerability for schizophrenia. In M. F. Lenzenweger & R. H. Dworkin (Eds.), *Origins and development of schizophrenia: Advances in experimental psychopathology.* Washington DC: American Psychological Association.

Walker, E., Kestler, L., Bollini, A., & Hochman, K. M. (2004). Schizophrenia: Etiology and course. *Annual Review of Psychology, 55,* 401–430.

Walker, I., & Hulme, C. (1999). Concrete words are easier to recall than abstract words: Evidence for a semantic contribution to short-term serial recall. *Journal of Experimental Psychology: Learning, Memory, & Cognition, 25,* 1256–1271.

Walker, L. J. (1988). The development of moral reasoning. In R. Vasta (Ed.), *Annals of child development* (Vol. 5). Greenwich, CT: JAI Press.

Walker, L. J. (1989). A longitudinal study of moral reasoning. *Child Development, 60,* 157–166.

Walker, L. J., & Taylor, J. H. (1991). Strange transitions in moral reasoning: A longitudinal study of developmental processes. *Developmental Psychology, 27,* 330–337.

Walker, M. P., & Stickgold, R. (2004). Sleep-dependent learning and memory consolidation. *Neuron, 44,* 121–133.

Wall, P. D. (1993). Pain and the placebo response. In G. R. Bock & J. Marsh (Eds.), *Experimental and theoretical studies of consciousness.* Chichester, England: Wiley.

Wallace, B., & Fisher, L. E. (1999). *Consciousness and behavior.* Boston: Allyn & Bacon.

Wallace, C. J. (1998). Social skills training in psychiatric rehabilitation: Recent findings. *International Review of Psychiatry, 10,* 9–10.

Wallace, R. K., & Benson, H. (1972). The physiology of meditation. *Scientific American, 226,* 84–90.

Wallbott, H. G., & Scherer, K. R. (1988). How universal and specific is emotional experience? Evidence from 27 countries. In K. R. Scherer (Ed.), *Facets of emotions.* Hillsdale, NJ: Erlbaum.

Wallen, K. (1989). Mate selection: Economics and affection. *Behavioral and Brain Sciences, 12,* 37–38.

Wallen, K., & Zehr, J. L. (2004). Hormones and history: The evolution and development of primate female sexuality. *Journal of Sex Research, 41*(1), 101–112.

Wallman, J. (1992). *Aping language.* Cambridge, England: Cambridge University Press.

Walraven, J., Enroth-Cugell, C., Hood, D. C., MacLeod, D. I. A., & Schnapf, J. L. (1990). The control of visual sensitivity: Receptoral and postreceptoral processes. In L. Spillmann & J. S. Werner (Eds.), *Visual perception: The neurophysiological foundations.* San Diego: Academic Press.

Walsh, B. T., Seidman, S. N., Sysko, R., & Gould, M. (2002). Placebo response studies of major depression: Variable, substantial and growing. *Journal of the American Medical Association, 287,* 1840–1847.

Walsh, F. (1999). Families in later life: Challenges and opportunities. In B. Carter & M. McGoldrick (Eds.), *The expanded family life cycle: Individual, family, and social perspectives* (3rd ed., pp. 307–326). Boston: Allyn & Bacon.

Walsh, J. K., & Scweitzer, P. K. (1999). Ten-year trends in the pharnumbers. *Psychological Bulletin, 76,* 105–110.

Tversky, A., & Kahneman, D. (1973). Availability: A heuristic for judging frequency and probability. *Cognitive Psychology, 5,* 207–232.

Tversky, A., & Kahneman, D. (1974). Judgments under uncertainty: Heuristics and biases. *Science, 185,* 1124–1131.

Tversky, A., & Kahneman, D. (1982). Judgment under uncertainty: Heuristics and biases. In D. Kahneman, P. Slovic, & A. Tversky (Eds.), *Judgment under uncertainty: Heuristics and biases.* New York: Cambridge University Press.

Tversky, A., & Kahneman, D. (1983). Extensional versus intuitive reasoning: The conjunction fallacy in probability judgment. *Psychological Review, 90,* 283–315.

Tversky, A., & Kahneman, D. (1988). Rational choice and the framing of decisions. In D. E. Bell, H. Raiffa, & A. Tversky (Eds.), *Decision making: Descriptive, normative, and prescriptive interactions.* New York: Cambridge University Press.

Tversky, A., & Kahneman, D. (1991). Loss aversion in riskless choice: A reference-dependent model. *Quarterly Journal of Economics, 106,* 1039–1061.

Tversky, A., & Shafir, E. (1992). Choice under conflict: The dynamics of deferred decision. *Psychological Science, 3,* 358–361.

U.S. Department of Health and Human Services. (1990). *The health benefits of smoking cessation: A report of the surgeon general.* Washington, DC: U.S. Government Printing Office.

U.S. Department of Health and Human Services. (1999). *Mental health: A report of the Surgeon General.* Washington, DC: U.S. Government Printing Office.

Uchino, B. N. (2004). *Social support and physical health outcomes: Understanding the health consequences of our relationships.* New Haven, CT: University Press.

Uchino, B. N., Uno, D., & Holt-Lunstad, J. (1999). Social support, physiological processes, and health. *Current Directions in Psychological Science, 8,* 145–148.

Umbel, V. M., Pearson, B. Z., Fernandez, S. C., & Oller, D. K. (1992). Measuring bilingual children's receptive vocabularies. *Child Development, 63,* 1012–1020.

Underwood, B. J. (1961). Ten years of massed practice on distributed practice. *Psychological Review, 68,* 229–247.

Underwood, B. J. (1970). A breakdown of the total-time law in free-recall learning. *Journal of Verbal Learning and Verbal Behavior, 9,* 573–580.

Unger, R. K., & Crawford, M. (1992). *Women and gender: A feminist psychology.* New York: McGraw-Hill.

Ungerleider, L. G., & Mishkin, N. (1982). Two cortical systems. In D. J. Ingle, M. A. Goodale, & R. J. W. Mansfield (Eds.), *Analysis of visual behavior* (pp. 549–586). Cambridge MA: MIT Press.

Urbszat, D., & Herman, C. P., & Polivy, J. (2002). Eat. Drink, and be merry for tomorrow we diet: Effects of anticipated deprivation on food intake in restrained and unrestrained eaters. *Journal of Abnormal Psychology, 111,* 396–401.

Ursano, R. J., & Silberman, E. K. (1999). Psychoanalysis, psychoanalytic psychotherapy, and supportive psychotherapy. In R. E. Hales, S. C. Yudofsky, & J. A. Talbott (Eds.), *American Psychiatric Press textbook of psychiatry.* Washington, DC: American Psychiatric Press.

Ursano, R. J., Fullerton, C. S., & Norwood, A. E. (2001). *Psychiatric dimensions of disaster: Patient care, community consultation, and preventive medicine.* Retrieved November 20, 2001 from American Psychiatric Association Web site: http:www.psych.org/pract_of_psych/disaster.cfm.

Ursano, R. J., Fullerton, C. S., Vance, K., & Kao, T. C. (1999). Posttraumatic stress disorder and identification in disaster workers. *American Journal of Psychiatry, 156,* 353–359.

Vaillant, G. E. (1992). *Ego mechanisms of defense: A guide for clinicians and researchers.* Washington, DC: American Psychiatric Press.

Vaillant, G. E. (1994). Ego mechanisms of defense and personality psychopathology. *Journal of Abnormal Psychology, 103,* 44–50.

Vaillant, G. E. (2000). Adaptive mental mechanisms: Their role in a positive psychology. *American Psychologist, 55,* 89–98.

Valenstein, E. S. (1973). *Brain control.* New York: Wiley.

Valleroy, L. A., MacKellar, D. A., Karon, J. M., Rosen, D. H., McFarland, W., Shehan, D. A., Stoyanoff, S. R., LaLota, M., Celentano, D. D., Koblin, B. A., Thiede, H., Katz, M. H., Torian, L. V., & Janssen, R. S. (2000). HIV prevalence and associated risks in young men who have sex with men. *Journal of the American Medical Association, 284,* 198–204.

Vallone, R. P., Griffin, D. W., Lin, S., & Ross, L. (1990). Overconfident prediction of future actions and outcomes by self and others. *Journal of Personality and Social Psychology, 58,* 582–592.

Van Cauter, E., Leproult, R., & Plat, L. (2000). Age-related changes in slow wave sleep and REM sleep and relationship with growth hormone and cortisol levels in healthy men. *Journal of the American Medical Association, 284,* 861–868.

Van de Castle, R. L. (1994). *Our dreaming mind.* New York: Ballantine Books.

van den Boom, D. C. (1994). The influence of temperament and mothering on attachment and exploration: An experimental manipulation of sensitive responsiveness among lower-class mothers and irritable infants. *Child Development, 65,* 1457–1477.

van der Post, L. (1975). *Jung and the story of our time.* New York: Vintage Books.

Van Dongen, H. P. A., & Dinges, D. F. (2000). Circadian rhythms in fatigue, alertness and performance. In M. H. Kryger, T. Roth, & W. C. Dement (Eds.), *Principles and practice of sleep medicine.* Philadelphia: Saunders.

van Eck, M., Nicolson, N. A., & Berkhof, J. (1998). Effects of stressful daily events on mood states: Relationship to global perceived stress. *Journal of Personality and Social Psychology, 75,* 1572–1585.

Van Hoesen, G. W., Morecraft, R. J., & Semendeferi, K. (1996). Functional neuroanatomy of the limbic system and prefrontal cortex. In B. S. Fogel, R. B. Schiffer, & S. M. Rao (Eds), *Neuropsychiatry.* Baltimore: Williams & Wilkins.

Van Houten, R. (1983). Punishment: From the animal laboratory to the applied setting. In S. Axelrod & J. Apsche (Eds.), *The effects of punishment on human behavior.* New York: Academic Press.

van IJzendoorn, M. H., & Sagi, A. (1999). Cross-cultural patterns of attachment: Universal and contextual dimensions. In J. Cassidy & P. R. Shaver (Eds.), *Handbook of attachment: Theory, research, and clinical applications.* New York: Guilford.

Vandereycken, W. (2002). History of anorexia nervosa and bulimia nervosa. In C. G. Fairburn, & K. D. Brownell (Eds.), *Eating disorders and obesity.* New York: Guilford.

VanderPlate, C., Aral, S. O., & Magder, L. (1988). The relationship among genital herpes simplex virus, stress, and social support. *Health Psychology, 7,* 159–168.

VanderStoep, S. W., & Seifert, C. M. (1994). Problem solving, transfer, and thinking. In P. R. Pintrich, D. R. Brown, & C. E. Weinstein (Eds.), *Student motivation, cognition, and learning: Essays in honor of Wilbert J. McKeachie* (pp. 27–49). Hillsdale, NJ: Erlbaum.

Vanier Institute of the Family. (2005). Family Facts. Retrieved June 20, 2005, from http://www.vifamily.ca/library/facts/facts/html.

Vase, L. R. I. J., & Price, D. (2002). A comparison of placebo effects in clinical analgesic trials versus studies of placebo analgesia. *Pain, 99,* 443–452.

Vaughn, B. E., & Bost, K. K. (1999). Attachment and temperament: Redundant, independent, or interacting influences on interpersonal adaptation and personality development? In J. Cassidy & P. R. Shaver (Eds.), *Handbook of attachment: Theory, research, and clinical applications.* New York: Guilford.

Vazquez, C., Munoz, M., & Sanz, J. (1997). Lifetime and 12-month prevalence of DSM-III-R mental disorders among the homeless in Madrid: A European study using the CIDI. *Acta Psychiatrica Scandinavica, 95,* 523–530.

Veenhoven, R. (1993). *Happiness in nations.* Rotterdam, Netherlands: Risbo.

Vega, W. A., Kolody, B., Aguilar-Gaxiola, S., & Catalano, R. (1999). Gaps in service utilization by Mexican Americans with mental health problems. *American Journal of Psychiatry, 156,* 928–934.

Ventura, J., Nuechterlein, K. H., Lukoff, D., & Hardesty, J. P. (1989). A prospective study of stressful life events and schizophrenic relapse. *Journal of Abnormal Psychology, 98,* 407–411.

Venturello, S., Barzega, G., Maina, G., & Bogetto, F. (2002). Premorbid conditions and precipitating events in early-onset panic disorder. *Comprehensive Psychiatry, 43*(1), 28–36.

Verdone, P. (1993). Psychophysiology of dreaming. In M. A. Carskadon (Ed.), *Encyclopedia of dreaming.* New York: Macmillan.

Verhaeghen, P., & Salthouse, T. A. (1997). Meta-analyses of age-cognition relations in adulthood: Estimates of linear and nonlinear age effects and structural models. *Psychological Bulletin, 122,* 231–249.

Vernberg, E. M., La Greca, A. M., Silverman, W. K., & Prinstein, M. J. (1996). Prediction of posttraumatic stress symptoms in children after Hurricane Andrew. *Journal of Abnormal Psychology, 105,* 237–248.

Tolman, E. C. (1932). *Purposive behavior in animals and men.* New York: Appleton-Century-Crofts.

Tolman, E. C. (1938). The determiners of behavior at a choice point. *Psychological Review, 45,* 1–41.

Tomkins, S. S. (1980). Affect as amplification: Some modifications in theory. In R. Plutchik & H. Kellerman (Eds.), *Emotion: Theory, research and experience* (Vol. 1). New York: Academic Press.

Tomkins, S. S. (1991). *Affect, imagery, consciousness: 3. Anger and fear.* New York: Springer-Verlag.

Tondo, L., Baldessarini, R. J., Hennen, J., & Floris, G. (1998). Lithium maintenance treatment of depression and mania in bipolar I and bipolar II disorders. *American Journal of Psychiatry, 155,* 638–645.

Tooby, J., & Cosmides, L. (1989). Evolutionary psychology and the generation of culture: Part 1. Theoretical considerations. *Ethology and Sociobiology, 10,* 29–49.

Tooby, J., & Cosmides, L. (2005). Conceptual foundations of evolutionary psychology. In D. M. Buss (Ed.), *The handbook of evolutionary psychology.* New York: Wiley.

Toomey, R., Kremen, W. S., Simpson, J. C., Samson, J. A., Seidman, L. J., Lyons, M. J., Faraone, S. V., & Tsuang, M. T. (1997). Revisiting the factor structure for positive and negative symptoms: Evidence from a large heterogeneous group of psychiatric patients. *American Journal of Psychiatry, 154,* 371–377.

Torgersen, S. (1979). The nature and origin of common phobic fears. *British Journal of Psychiatry, 119,* 343–351.

Torgersen, S. (1983). Genetic factors in anxiety disorders. *Archives of General Psychiatry, 40,* 1085–1089.

Tormala, Z. L., & Petty, R. E. (2002). What doesn't kill me makes me stronger: The effects of resisting persuasion on attitude certainty. *Journal of Personality and Social Psychology, 83,* 1298–1313.

Tormala, Z. L., & Petty, R. E. (2004). Resistance to persuasion and attitude certainty: The moderating role of elaboration. *Personality and Social Psychology Bulletin, 30,* 1446–1457.

Toronto Star. (2005). Rwandan wants war crimes trial. *Toronto Star,* June 27, 2005, p. A21.

Torrey, E. F. (1992). *Freudian fraud: The malignant effect of Freud's theory on American thought and culture.* New York: Harper Perennial.

Torrey, E. F. (1996). *Out of the shadows.* New York: Wiley.

Torrey, E. F., Bowler, A. E., Taylor, E. H., & Gottesman, I. I. (1994). *Schizophrenia and manic-depressive disorder.* New York: Basic Books.

Toufexis, A. (1990, December 17). Drowsy America. *Time,* pp. 78–85.

Trasti, N., Vik, T., Jacobson, G., & Bakketeig, L. S. (1999). Smoking in pregnancy and children's mental and motor development at age 1 and 5 years. *Early Human Development, 55,* 137–147.

Travis, F. (2001). Autonomic and EEG patterns distinguish transcending from other experiences during Transcendental Meditation practice. *International Journal of Psychophysiology, 42,* 1–9.

Travis, F., & Pearson, C. (2000). Pure consciousness: Distinct phenomenological and physiological correlates of "consciousness itself." *International Journal of Neuroscience, 100*(14), 77–89.

Treisman, G. J. (1999). AIDS education for psychiatrists. *Primary Psychiatry, 6*(5), 71–73.

Trent University Sleep Specialist Receives $48K Grant. Retrieved March 9, 2005, from http://www.trentu.ca/news/pressreleases/o40318csmith2.html.

Triandis, H. C. (1989). Self and social behavior in differing cultural contexts. *Psychological Review, 96,* 269–289.

Triandis, H. C. (1994). *Culture and social behavior.* New York: McGraw-Hill.

Triandis, H. C. (2001). Individualism and collectivism: Past, present, and future. In D. Matsumoto (Ed.), *The handbook of culture and psychology.* New York: Oxford University Press.

Triandis, H. C., & Suh, E. M. (2002). Cultural influences on personality. *Annual Review of Psychology, 53,* 133–160.

Trivers, R. L. (1971). The evolution of reciprocal altruism. *Quarterly Review of Biology, 46,* 35–57.

Trivers, R. L. (1972). Parental investment and sexual selection. In B. Campbell (Ed.), *Sexual selection and the descent of man.* Chicago: Aldine.

Trope, Y., & Liberman, A. (1993). The use of trait conceptions to identify other people's behavior and to draw inferences about their personalities. *Personality and Social Psychology Bulletin, 19,* 553–562.

Trotter, R. J. (1986, September). The three faces of love. *Psychology Today,* pp. 46–54.

Troyer, A. K., & Rich, J. B. (2002). Psychometric properties of a new metamemory questionnaire for older adults. *The Journals of Gerontology Series B: Psychological Sciences and Social Sciences, 57,* 19–27.

Trull, T. J., & McCrae, R. R. (1994). A five-factor perspective on personality disorder research. In P. T. Costa, Jr. & T. A. Widiger (Eds.), *Personality disorders and the five-factor model of personality.* Washington, DC: American Psychological Association.

Tsai, J. L., Butcher, J. N., Muñoz, R. F., & Vitousek, K. (2001). Culture, ethnicity, and psychopathology. In P. B. Sutker & H. E. Adams (Eds.), *Comprehensive handbook of psychopathology.* New York: Kluwer Academic/Plenum.

Tseng, W. S. et al., (1986). Diagnostic pattern for neuroses in China, Japan, and the United States. *American Journal of Psychiatry, 143*(8), 1010–1014.

Tsigos, C., Kyrou, I., & Chrousos, G. P. (2005). Stress, endocrine manifestations and diseases. In C. L. Cooper (Ed.), *Handbook of stress medicine and health.* Boca Raton, FL: CRC Press.

Tsuang, M. T., Glatt, S. J., & Faraone, S. V. (2003). Genetics and genomics in schizophrenia. *Primary Psychiatry, 10*(3), 37–40, 50.

Tulving, E. (1972). Episodic and semantic memory. In E. Tulving & W. Donaldson (Eds.), *Organization of memory* (pp. 381–403). New York: Academic Press.

Tulving, E. (1983). *Elements of episodic memory.* Oxford, UK: Oxford University Press.

Tulving, E. (1986). What kind of a hypothesis is the distinction between episodic and semantic memory? *Journal of Experimental Psychology: Learning, Memory and Cognition, 12,* 307–311.

Tulving, E. (1993). What is episodic memory? *Current Directions in Psychological Science, 2*(3), 67–70.

Tulving, E. (2001). Origin of autonoesis in episodic memory. In H. L. Roediger III, J. S. Nairne, I. Neath, & A. M. Surprenant (Eds.), *The nature of remembering: Essays in honor of Robert G. Crowder* (pp. 17–34). Washington, DC: American Psychological Association.

Tulving, E. (2002). Episodic memory: From mind to brain. *Annual Review of Psychology, 53,* 1–25.

Tulving, E., & Pearlstone, Z. (1966). Availability and accessibility of information in memory for words. *Journal of Verbal Learning and Verbal Behavior, 5,* 381–391.

Tulving, E., & Schacter, D. L. (1990). Priming and human memory systems. *Science, 247,* 301–306.

Tulving, E., & Thomson, D. M. (1973). Encoding specificity and retrieval processes in episodic memory. *Psychological Review, 80,* 352–373.

Turk, D. C. (1994). Perspectives on chronic pain: The role of psychological factors. *Current Directions in Psychological Science, 3,* 45–48.

Turk, D. C., & Okifuji, A. (2003). Pain management. In A. M. Nezu, C. M. Nezu, & P. A. Geller (Eds.), *Handbook of psychology, Vol. 9: Health psychology.* New York: Wiley.

Turkheimer, E. (1991). Individual and group differences in adoption studies of IQ. *Psychological Bulletin, 110,* 392–405.

Turkheimer, E. (1998). Heritability and biological explanation. *Psychological Review, 105,* 782–791

Turkheimer, E. (2000). Three laws of behavior genetics and what they mean. *Current Directions in Psychological Science, 9*(5), 160–164.

Turkheimer, E., & Waldron, M. (2000). Nonshared environment: A theoretical, methodological, and quantitative review. *Psychological Bulletin, 126,* 78–108.

Turkkan, J. S. (1989). Classical conditioning: The new hegemony. *Behavioral and Brain Sciences, 12,* 121–179.

Turner, J. R., & Wheaton, B. (1995). Checklist measurement of stressful life events. In S. Cohen, R. C. Kessler, & L. U. Gordon (Eds.), *Measuring stress: A guide for health and social scientists.* New York: Oxford University Press.

Turner, P. J., & Gervai, J. (1995). A multidimensional study of gender typing in preschool children and their parents: Personality, attitudes, preferences, behavior, and cultural differences. *Developmental Psychology, 31,* 759–772.

Turner, S. M., Beidel, D. C., Stanley, M. A., & Heiser, N. (2001). Obsessive-compulsive disorder. In P. B. Sutker & H. E. Adams (Eds.), *Comprehensive textbook of psychiatry* (3rd ed., pp. 155–182). New York: Kluwer Academic/Plenum.

Turner-Bowker, D. M. (1996). Gender stereotyped descriptions in children's picture books: Does "curious Jane" exist in the literature? *Sex Roles, 35,* 461–488.

Tversky, A. (1972). Elimination by aspects: A theory of choice. *Psychological Review, 79,* 281–299.

Tversky, A., & Kahneman, D. (1971). Belief in the law of small taster status. *Physiology & Behavior, 61*, 949–954.

Terman, L. M. (1916). *The measurement of intelligence.* Boston: Houghton Mifflin.

Terman, L. M. (1925). *Genetic studies of genius: Vol. 1. Mental and physical traits of a thousand gifted children.* Stanford, CA: Stanford University Press.

Terman, L. M., & Oden, M. H. (1959). *Genetic studies of genius: Vol. 5. The gifted group at mid-life.* Stanford, CA: Stanford University Press.

Terr, L. (1994). *Unchained memories.* New York: Basic Books.

Terrace, H. S. (1986). *Nim: A chimpanzee who learned sign language.* New York: Columbia University Press.

Terry, J., & Woonteiler, D. (2000). An interview with Craig Kielburger, founder of Free the Children. *Community Youth Development Journal.* Retrieved June 7, 2005, from http://www.cydjournal.org/2000Winter/kielburger.html.

Tessier-Lavigne, M. (2000). Visual processing by the retina. In E. R. Kandel, J. H. Schwartz, & T. M. Jessell (Eds.), *Principles of neural science.* New York: McGraw-Hill.

Testa, K. (1996). Church to pay $1 million in false-memory case. *San Jose Mercury News,* 8A.

Teuber, M. (1974). Sources of ambiguity in the prints of Maurits C. Escher. *Scientific American, 231,* 90–104.

Thase, M. E. (1999). What is the investigator allegiance effect and what should we do about it? *Clinical Psychology: Science & Practice, 6*(1), 113–115.

Thase, M. E., Jindal, R., & Howland, R. H. (2002). Biological aspects of depression. In I. H. Gotlib & C. L. Hammen (Eds.), *Handbook of depression.* New York: Guilford.

Thayer, R. E. (1996). *The origin of everyday moods.* New York: Oxford University Press.

Thelen, E. (1995). Motor development: A new synthesis. *American Psychologist, 50,* 79–95.

Thomas, A. J., Kalaria, R. N., & O'Brien, J. T. (2004). Depression and vascular disease: What is the relationship? *Journal of Affective Disorders, 79*(1–3), 81–95.

Thomas, A., & Chess, S. (1977). *Temperament and development.* New York: Brunner/Mazel.

Thomas, A., & Chess, S. (1989). Temperament and personality. In G. A. Kohnstamm, J. E. Bates, & M.

K. Rothbart (Eds.), *Temperament in childhood.* New York: Wiley.

Thomas, A., Chess, S., & Birch, H. G. (1970). The origin of personality. *Scientific American, 223*(2), 102–109.

Thomas, D. R. (1992). Discrimination and generalization. In L. R. Squire (Ed.), *Encyclopedia of learning and memory.* New York: Macmillan.

Thomas, R. M. (2000). *Comparing theories of child development.* Belmont, CA: Wadsworth.

Thomas, R. M. (2005). *Comparing theories of child development.* Belmont, CA: Wadsworth.

Thomason, B. T., Brantkey, P. J., Jones, G. N., Dyer, H. R., & Morris, J. L. (1992). The relation between stress and disease activity in rheumatoid arthritis. *Journal of Behavioral Medicine, 15,* 215–220.

Thompson, J. K. (2004). Eating disorders and obesity: Definitions, prevalence, and associated features. In J. K. Thompson (Ed.), *Handbook of eating disorders and obesity.* New York: Wiley.

Thompson, J. K., & Stice, E. (2001). Thin-ideal internalization: Mounting evidence for a new risk factor for body-image disturbance and eating pathology. *Current Directions in Psychological Science, 10*(5), 181–183.

Thompson, M. M., Zanna, M. P., & Griffin, D. W. (1995). Let's not be indifferent about (attitudinal) ambivalence. In R. E. Petty & J. A. Krosnick (Eds.), *Attitude strength: Antecedents and consequences.* Mahwah, NJ: Erlbaum.

Thompson, R. A., & Nelson, C. A. (2001). Developmental science and the media: Early brain development. *American Psychologist, 56,* 5–15.

Thompson, R. F. (1989). A model system approach to memory. In P. R. Solomon, G. R. Goethals, C. M. Kelley, & B. R. Stephens (Eds.), *Memory: Interdisciplinary approaches.* New York: Springer-Verlag.

Thompson, R. F. (1992). Memory. *Current Opinion in Neurobiology, 2,* 203–208.

Thompson, R. F. (2005). In search of memory traces. *Annual Review of Psychology, 56,* 1–23.

Thompson, R. F., & Zola, S. M. (2003). In D. K. Freedheim (Ed.), *Handbook of psychology* (Vol. 2): New York: Wiley.

Thompson, W. F., Schellenberg, E. G., & Husain, G. (2001). Arousal, mood and the Mozart effect. *Psychological Science, 12,* 248–251.

Thompson, W. F., Schellenberg, E. G., & Husain, G. (2004). Decoding

speech prosody: Do music lessons help? *Emotion, 4,* 46–64.

Thoresen, C. E., Harris, A. H. S., & Luskin, F. (1999). Forgiveness and health: An unanswered question. In M. E. McCullough, K. I. Pargament & C. E. Thoresen (Eds.), *Forgiveness: Theory, research, and practice* (pp. 254–280). New York: Guilford.

Thorndike, E. L. (1913). *Educational psychology: The psychology of learning* (Vol. 2). New York: Teachers College.

Thorndike, R. L., Hagen, E. P., & Sattler, J. M. (1986). *The Stanford-Binet intelligence scale: Fourth edition technical manual.* Chicago: Riverside.

Thorndyke, P. W., & Hayes-Roth, B. (1979). The use of schemata in the acquisition and transfer of knowledge. *Cognitive Psychology, 11,* 83–106.

Thorne, B. M., & Henley, T. B. (1997). *Connections in the history and systems of psychology.* Boston: Houghton Mifflin.

Thorne, S. (2005). Canadians' bravery saluted. *Toronto Star,* February 4, 2005, p. A12.

Thornhill, R. (1976). Sexual selection and nuptial feeding behavior in *Bittacus apicalis* (Insecta: Mecoptera). *American Naturalist, 110,* 529–548.

Thornton, B. (1984). Defensive attribution of responsibility: Evidence for an arousal-based motivational bias. *Journal of Personality and Social Psychology, 46,* 721–734.

Thornton, B. (1992). Repression and its mediating influence on the defensive attribution of responsibility. *Journal of Research in Personality, 26,* 44–57.

Thornton, B., & Moore, S. (1993). Physical attractiveness contrast effect: Implications for self-esteem and evaluations of the social self. *Personality and Social Psychology Bulletin, 19,* 474–480.

Thorpe, S. J., & Salkozskis, P. M. (1995). Phobia beliefs: Do cognitive factors play a role in specific phobias? *Behavioral Research and Therapy, 33,* 805–816.

Thorpy, M., & Yager, J. (2001). *Sleeping well: The sourcebook for sleep and sleep disorders.* New York: Checkmark Books.

Thun, M. J., Apicella, L. F., & Henley, S. J. (2000). Smoking vs. other risk factors as the cause of smoking-attributable deaths: Confounding in the courtroom. *Journal of the American Medical Association, 284,* 706–712.

Thune, I., Brenn, T., Lund, E., & Gaard, M. (1997). Physical activity and the risk of breast cancer. *New*

England Journal of Medicine, 336, 1269–1275.

Thurstone, L. L. (1938). *Primary mental abilities* (Psychometric Monographs No. 1). Chicago: University of Chicago Press.

Thurstone, L. L. (1955). *The differential growth of mental abilities* (Psychometric Laboratory Rep. No. 14). Chapel Hill: University of North Carolina.

Tibbo, P., Hanstock, C., Valiakalayil, A., & Allen, P. (2004). 3-T proton MRS investigation and glutamine in adolescents at high genetic risk for schizophrenia. *American Journal of Psychiatry, 161,* 1116–1118.

Tice, D. M., Bratslavsky, E., & Baumeister, R. F. (2001). Emotional distress regulation takes precedence over impulse control: If you feel bad, do it! *Journal of Personality and Social Psychology, 80,* 53–67.

Till, B. D., & Priluck, R. L. (2000). Stimulus generalization in classical conditioning: An initial investigation and extension. *Psychology and Marketing, 17,* 55–72.

Tindale, R. S., Kameda, T., & Hinsz, V. B. (2003). Group decision making. In M. A. Hogg & J. Cooper (Eds.), *The Sage handbook of social psychology.* Thousand Oaks, CA: Sage.

Titsworth, B. S., & Kiewra, K. A. (2004). Spoken organizational lecture cues and student notetaking as facilitators of student learning. *Contemporary Educational Psychology, 29,* 447–461.

Todd, J. T., & Morris, E. K. (1992). Case histories in the great power of steady misrepresentation. *American Psychologist, 47,* 1441–1453.

Todd, M. (2003). Characteristics associated with superstitious behavior in track and field athletes: Are there NCAA divisional differences? *Journal of Sport Behavior, 26,* 168–178.

Todes, D. P. (1997). From the machine to the ghost within: Pavlov's transition from digestive physiology to conditional reflexes. *American Psychologist, 52,* 947–955.

Tohen, M., & Goodwin, F. K. (1995). Epidemiology of bipolar disorder. In M. T. Tsuang, M. Tohen, & G. E. P. Zahner (Eds.), *Textbook in psychiatric epidemiology.* New York: Wiley.

Tolman, C. (1999). Introduction. *History and Philosophy of Psychology Bulletin, 11,* 3.

Tolman, E. C. (1922). A new formula for behaviorism. *Psychological Review, 29,* 44–53.

Current Directions in Psychological Science, 12(4), 129–133.

Stoohs, R. A., Blum, H. C., Haselhorst, M., Duchna, H. W., Guilleminault, C., & Dement, W. C. (1998). Normative data on snoring: A comparison between younger and older adults. *European Respiratory Journal, 11,* 451–457.

Stoolmiller, M. (1999). Implications of the restricted range of family environments for estimates of heritability and nonshared environment in behavior-genetic adoption studies. *Psychological Bulletin, 125,* 392–409.

Storm, C., & Gurevich, M. (2001). Looking forward, looking back: Women in psychology. *Canadian Psychology, 42*(4), 245–248.

Stormshak, E. A., Bierman, K. L., McMahon, R. J., & Lengua, L. J. (2000). Parenting practices and child disruptive behavior problems in early elementary school. *Journal of Clinical Child Psychology, 29*(1), 17–29.

Straus, M. A. (2000). Corporal punishment and primary prevention of physical abuse. *Child Abuse & Neglect, 24,* 1109–1114.

Straus, M. A., & Kantor, G. K. (1994). Corporal punishment of adolescents by parents: A risk factor in the epidemiology of depression, suicide, alcohol abuse, child abuse, and wife beating. *Adolescence, 29,* 543–561.

Straus, M. A., & Stewart, J. H. (1999). Corporal punishment by American parents: National data on prevalence, chronicity, severity, and duration, in relation to child family characteristics. *Clinical Child & Family Psychology Review, 2*(2), 55–70.

Strayer, D. L., & Johnston, W. A. (2001). Driven to distraction: Dual-task studies of simulated driving and conversing on a cellular telephone. *Psychological Science, 12,* 462–466.

Streissguth, A. P., Barr, H. M., Bookstein, F. L., Sampson, P. D., & Olson, H. C. (1999). The long-term neurocognitive consequences of prenatal alcohol exposure: A 14-year study. *Psychological Science, 10,* 186–190.

Streissguth, A. P., Barr, H. M., Sampson, P. D., Darby, B. L., & Martin, D. C. (1989). IQ at age 4 in relation to maternal alcohol use and smoking during pregnancy. *Developmental Psychology, 25,* 3–11.

Striegel-Moore, R. H., & Rodin, J. (1986). The influence of psychological variables in obesity. In K. D. Brownell & J. P. Foreyt (Eds.), *Handbook of eating disorders: Physiology, psychology, and treatment of obesity, anorexia and bulimia.* New York: Basic Books.

Striegel-Moore, R. H., & Smolak, L. (2001). Introduction. In R. H. Striegel-Moore & L. Smolak (Eds.), *Eating disorders: Innovative directions in research and practice* (pp. 3–8). Washington, DC: American Psychological Association.

Striegel-Moore, R. H., Silberstein, L. R., & Rodin, J. (1993). The social self in bulimia nervosa: Public self-consciousness, social anxiety, and perceived fraudulence. *Journal of Abnormal Psychology, 102.*

Strike, P. C., & Steptoe, A. (2005). Behavioral and emotional triggers of acute coronary syndromes: A systematic review and critique. *Psychosomatic Medicine, 67*(2), 179–186.

Strober, M., Freeman, R., Lampert, C., Diamond, J., & Kaye, W. (2000). Controlled family study of anorexia nervosa and bulimia nervosa: Evidence of shared liability and transmission of partial syndromes. *American Journal of Psychiatry, 157,* 393–401.

Strupp, H. H. (1996). The tripartite model and the *Consumer Reports* study. *American Psychologist, 51,* 1017–1024.

Strupp, H. H., & Howard, K. I. (1992). A brief history of psychotherapy research. In D. K. Freedheim (Ed.), *History of psychotherapy: A century of change.* Washington, DC: American Psychological Association.

Struthers, C. W., Dupuis, R., & Eaton, J. (2005). Promoting forgiveness among coworkers following a workplace transgression: The effects of social motivation training. *Canadian Journal of Behavioural Sciences* (Special Issue on Creating a Healthy Workplace) *37*(4), 299–308.

Stuart, E. W., Shimp, T. A., & Engle, R. W. (1987). Classical conditioning of consumer attitudes: Four experiments in an advertising context. *Journal of Consumer Research, 14,* 334–349.

Stuart, E. W., Shimp, T. A., & Engle, R. W. (1991). A program of classical conditioning experiments testing variations in the conditioned stimulus and context. *Journal of Consumer Research, 18,* 1–12.

Stumpf, H., & Stanley, J. C. (1996). Gender-related differences on the College Board's Advanced Placement and Achievement Tests, 1982–1992. *Journal of Educational Psychology, 88,* 353–364.

Stunkard, A. J., Harris, J. R., Pederson, N. L., & McClearn, G. E. (1990). The body-mass index of twins who have been reared apart. *New England Journal of Medicine, 322,* 1483–1487.

Stunkard, A. J., Sorensen, T., Hanis, C., Teasdale, T. W., Chakraborty, R., Schull, W. J., & Schulsinger, F. (1986). An adoption study of human obesity. *New England Journal of Medicine, 314,* 193–198.

Subrahmanyam, K., & Greenfield, P. M. (1996). Effect of video game practice on spatial skills in girls and boys. In P. M. Greenfield, & R. R. Cocking (Eds.), *Interacting with video.* Norwood, NJ: Ablex Publishing Corp.

Sue, D. W., & Sue, D. (1999). *Counseling the culturally different: Theory and practice.* New York: Wiley.

Sue, D. W., Bingham, R. P., Porche-Burke, L., & Vasquez, M. (1999). The diversification of psychology: A multicultural revolution. *American Psychologist, 54,* 1061–1069.

Sue, S. (2003). In defense of cultural competency in psychotherapy and treatment. *American Psychologist, 58,* 964–970.

Sue, S., & Zane, N. (1987). The role of culture and cultural techniques in psychotherapy: A critique and reformulation. *American Psychologist, 42,* 37–45.

Sue, S., Zane, N., & Young, K. (1994). Research on psychotherapy with culturally diverse populations. In A. E. Bergin & S. L. Garfield (Eds.), *Handbook of psychotherapy and behavior change* (4th ed.). New York: Wiley.

Suedfeld, P. (2003). Canadian space psychology: The future may be almost here. *Canadian Psychology, 44,* 85–92.

Sugiyama, L. S. (2005). Physical attractiveness in adaptionist perspective. In D. M. Buss (Ed.), *The handbook of evolutionary psychology.* New York: Wiley.

Suh, E., Diener, E., Oishi, S., & Triandis, H. C. (1998). The shifting basis of life satisfaction judgments across cultures: Emotions versus norms. *Journal of Personality and Social Psychology, 74,* 482–493.

Sullivan, G. M., & Coplan, J. D. (2000). Anxiety disorders: Biochemical aspects. In B. J. Sadock & V. A. Sadock (Eds.), *Kaplan and Sadock's comprehensive textbook of psychiatry* (7th ed., Vol. 1). Philadelphia: Lippincott/Williams & Wilkins.

Sullivan, G., Burnam, A., & Koegel, P. (2000). Pathways to homelessness among the mentally ill. *Social Psychiatry & Psychiatric Epidemiology, 35,* 444–450.

Sullivan, P. F. (2002). Course and outcome of anorexia nervosa and bulimia nervosa. In C. G. Fairburn & K. D. Brownell (Eds.), *Eating disorders and obesity: A comprehensive handbook.* New York: Guilford.

Sullivan, P. F., Neale, M. C., & Kendler, K. S. (2000). Genetic epidemiology of major depression: Review and meta-analysis. *American Journal of Psychiatry, 157,* 1552–1562.

Sulloway, F. J. (1995). Birth order and evolutionary psychology: A meta-analytic overview. *Psychological Inquiry, 6,* 75–80.

Sulloway, F. J. (1996). *Born to rebel: Birth order, family dynamics, and creative lives.* New York: Pantheon Books.

Summerfeldt, L. J., Richter, M. A., Antony, M. M., & Swinson, R. P. (1999). Symptom structure in obsessive-compulsive disorder: A confirmatory factor-analytic study. *Behaviour Research and Therapy, 37,* 297–311.

Super, C. M. (1976). Environmental effects on motor development: A case of African infant precocity. *Developmental Medicine and Child Neurology, 18,* 561–567.

Susman, E. J., & Rogol, A. (2004). Puberty and psychological development. In R. M. Lerner & L. Steinberg (Eds.), *Handbook of adolescent psychology.* New York: Wiley.

Susman, E. J., Dorn, L. D., & Schiefelbein, V. L. (2003). Puberty, sexuality, and health. In R. M. Lerner, M. A. Easterbrooks, & J. Mistry (Eds.), *Handbook of psychology, Vol. 6: Developmental psychology.* New York: Wiley.

Susser, E. B., Brown, A., & Matte, T. D. (1999). Prenatal factors and adult mental and physical health. *Canadian Journal of Psychiatry, 44,* 326–334.

Susser, E. B., Neugebauer, R., Hoek, H. W., Brown, A. S., Lin, S., Labovitz, D., & Gorman, J. M. (1996). Schizophrenia after prenatal famine: Further evidence. *Archives of General Psychiatry, 53,* 25–31.

Sutker, P. B., & Allain, A. N. (2001). Antisocial personality disorder. In P. B. Sutker & H. E. Adams (Eds.), *Comprehensive handbook of psychopathology.* New York: Kluwer Academic/Plenum.

Sutker, P. B., & Bugg, F. & West, J. A. (1993). Antisocial personality disorder. In P. B. Sutker & H. E. Adams (Eds.), *Comprehensive handbook of psychopathology* (2nd ed.). New York: Plenum.

Suzuki, L. A., & Valencia, R. R. (1997). Race-ethnicity and measured intelligence: Educational implications. *American Psychologist, 52,* 1103–1114.

Suzuki, L. A., & Vraniak, D. A. (1994). Ethnicity, race, and measured intelligence. In R. J. Sternberg (Ed.), *Encyclopedia of human intelligence.* New York: Macmillan.

Swan, G. E., Hudmon, K. S., & Kroyan, T. V. (2003). Tobacco dependence. In A. M. Nezu, C. M. Nezu, & P. A. Geller (Eds.), *Handbook of psychology, Vol. 9: Health Psychology.* New York: Wiley.

Swartz, C. M. (1993). Clinical and laboratory predictors of ECT response. In C. E. Coffey (Ed.), *The clinical science of electroconvulsive therapy.* Washington, DC: American Psychiatric Press.

Swets, J. A., Tanner, W. P., & Birdsall, T. G. (1961). Decision processes in perception. *Psychological Review, 68,* 301–340.

Swihart, G., Yuille, J., & Porter, S. (1999). The role of state-dependent memory in Red-outs. *International Journal of Law and Psychiatry, 22,* 199–212.

Swim, J. K. (1994). Perceived versus meta-analytic effect sizes: An assessment of the accuracy of gender stereotypes. *Journal of Personality and Social Psychology, 66,* 21–36.

Swim, J. K., & Campbell, B. (2001). Sexism: Attitudes, beliefs, and behaviors. In R. Brown & S. L. Gaertner (Eds.), *Blackwell handbook of social psychology: Intergroup processes.* Malden, MA: Blackwell.

Swim, J. K., & Sanna, L. J. (1996). He's skilled, she's lucky: A meta-analysis of observers' attributions for women's and men's successes and failures. *Personality and Social Psychology Bulletin, 22,* 507–519.

Symons, C. S., & Johnson, B. T. (1997). The self-reference effect in memory: A meta-analysis. *Psychological Bulletin, 121,* 371–394.

Szasz, T. (1974). *The myth of mental illness.* New York: Harper & Row.

Szasz, T. (1990). Law and psychiatry: The problems that will not go away. *The Journal of Mind and Behavior, 11*(3/4), 557–564.

Szechtman, H., Woody, E., Bowers, K. S., & Nahmias, C. (1998). Where the imaginal appears real: A positron emission tomography study of auditory hallucinations. *Proceedings of the National Academy of Sciences, 95,* 1956–1960.

Szmukler, G. I., & Patton, G. (1995). Sociocultural models of eating disorders. In G. Szmukler, C. Dare, & J. Treasure (Eds.), *Handbook of eating disorders: Theory, treatment, and research.* New York: Wiley.

Szymanski, L. S., & Wilska, M. (2003). Childhood disorders: Mental retardation. In A. Tasman, J. Kay, & J. A. Lieberman (Eds.), *Psychiatry.* New York, NY: Wiley.

Szymanski, S., Lieberman, J. A., Alvir, J. M., Mayerhoff, D., Loebel, A., Geisler, S., Chakos, M., Koreen, A., Jody, D., Kane, J., Woerner, M., & Cooper, T. (1995). Gender differences in onset of illness, treatment response, course, and biologic indexes in first-episode schizophrenic patients. *American Journal of Psychiatry, 152,* 698–703.

Takahashi, K. (1986). Examining the Strange Situation procedure with Japanese mothers and 12-month-old infants. *Developmental Psychology, 19,* 184–191.

Takahashi, M., Nakata, A., Haratani, T., Ogawa, Y., & Arito, H. (2004). Post-lunch nap as a worksite intervention to promote alertness on the job. *Ergonomics, 47,* 1003–1013.

Takahashi, T., Sasaki, M., Itoh, H., Yamadera, W., Ozone, M., Obuchi, K., Hayashida, K., Matsunaga, N., & Sano, H. (2002). Melatonin alleviates jet lag symptoms caused by an 11-hour eastward flight. *Psychiatry & Clinical Neurosciences, 56,* 301–302.

Takeuchi, D. T., Uehara, E., & Maramba, G. (1999). Cultural diversity and mental health treatment. A. V. Horwitz & T. L. Scheid (Eds.), *A handbook for the study of mental health.* New York: Cambridge University Press.

Talarico, J. M., & Rubin, D. C. (2003). Confidence, not consistency, characterizes flashbulb memories. *Psychological Science, 14,* 455–461.

Tamminga, C. A. (1999). Principles of the pharmacotherapy of schizophrenia. In D. S. Charney, E. J. Nestler, & B. S. Bunney (Eds.), *Neurobiology of mental illness* (pp. 272–290). New York: Oxford University Press.

Tamminga, C. A., & Carlsson A. (2003). Psychiatric pathophysiology: Schizophrenia. In A. Tasman, J. Kay, & J. A. Lieberman (Eds.), *Psychiatry.* New York: Wiley.

Tanaka-Matsumi, J. (2001). Abnormal psychology and culture. In D. Matsumoto (Ed.), *The handbook of culture & psychology.* New York: Oxford University Press.

Tang, I. T., & Glatt, A. E. (2001, September). The new approach to antiretroviral therapy. *Medical Aspects of Human Sexuality,* 27–33.

Tardiff, K. (1999). Violence. In R. E. Hales, S. C. Yudofsky, & J. A. Talbott (Eds.), *American Psychiatric Press textbook of psychiatry.* Washington, DC: American Psychiatric Press.

Tardiff, K., Marzuk, P. M., & Leon, A. C. (2002). Role of anitdepressants in murder and suicide. *American Journal of Psychiatry, 159,* 1248–1249.

Tart, C. T. (1988). From spontaneous event to lucidity: A review of attempts to consciously control nocturnal dreaming. In J. Gackenbach & S. LaBerge (Eds.), *Conscious mind, sleeping brain: Perspectives on lucid dreaming.* New York: Plenum.

Tart, C. T. (1990). Toward the experimental control of dreaming: A review of the literature. In C. T. Tart (Ed.), *Altered states of consciousness* (3rd ed.). San Francisco: Harper.

Tashkin, D. P., Baldwin, G. C., Sarafian, T., Dubinett, S., & Roth, M. D. (2002). Respiratory and immunologic consequences of marijuana smoking. *Journal of Clinical Pharmacology, 42,* 71S–81S.

Tavris, C. (1982). *Anger: the misunderstood emotion.* New York: Simon & Schuster.

Tavris, C. (1989). *Anger: The misunderstood emotion* (2nd ed.). New York: Simon & Schuster.

Tavris, C. (1992). *The mismeasure of woman.* New York: Simon & Schuster.

Tavris, C. (1998, September 13). Peer pressure (Review of *The Nurture Assumption*). *The New York Times Book Review, 103,* p. 14.

Taylor, D. M., & Moghaddam, F. M. (1994) *Theories of intergroup relations: International, social psychological perspectives.* New York: Praeger Publications.

Taylor, D. M., Lydon, J. E., Bougie, E., & Johannsen, K. (2004). "Street kids": Towards an understanding of their motivational context. *Canadian Journal of Behavioural Science, 36,* 1–16.

Taylor, E. (1999). An intellectual renaissance of humanistic psychology. *Journal of Humanistic Psychology, 39,* 7–25.

Taylor, E. (2001). Positive psychology and humanistic psychology: A reply to Seligman. *Journal of Humanistic Psychology, 41*(1), 13–29.

Taylor, I., & Taylor, M. M. (1990). *Psycholinguistics: Learning and using language.* Englewood Cliffs, NJ: Prentice-Hall.

Taylor, J. H., & Walker, L. J. (1997). Moral climate and the development of moral reasoning: The effects of dyadic discussions between young offenders. *Journal of Moral Education, 26,* 21–43.

Taylor, S. E., & Brown, J. D. (1988). Illusion and well-being: A social psychological perspective on mental health. *Psychological Bulletin, 103,* 193–210.

Taylor, S. E., & Brown, J. D. (1994). Positive illusions and well-being revisited: Separating fact from fiction. *Psychological Bulletin, 116,* 21–27.

Taylor, S. E., Klein, L. C., Lewis, B. P., Gruenewald, T. L., Gurung, R. A. R., & Updegraff, J. A. (2000). Biobehavioral responses to stress in females: Tend and befriend, not fight or flight. *Psychological Review, 107,* 411–429.

Taylor, S. E., Lerner, J. S., Sherman, D. K., Sage, R. M., & McDowell, N. K. (2003). Are self-enhancing cognitions associated with healthy or unhealthy biological profiles? *Journal of Personality and Social Psychology, 85,* 605–615.

Teasdale, J. D., Howard, R. J., Cox, S. G., Ha, Y., Brammer, M. J., Williams, S. C. R., & Checkley, S. A. (1999). Functional MRI study of the cognitive generation of affect. *American Journal of Psychiatry, 156,* 209–215.

Tedeschi, R. G., Park, C. L., & Calhoun, L. G. (1998). Posttraumatic growth: Conceptual issues. In R. G. Tedeschi, C. L. Park, & L. G. Calhoun (Eds.), *Posttraumatic growth: Positive changes in the aftermath of crisis* (pp. 1–22). Mahwah, NJ: Erlbaum.

Tees, R. (2003). A book review of Donald O. Hebb's (1949) *The Organization of Behavior: A Neuropsychological theory, Canadian Psychology, 44*(1), 74–76.

Tellegen, A., Lykken, D. T., Bouchard, T. J., Jr., Wilcox, K. J., Segal, N. L., & Rich, S. (1988). Personality similarity in twins reared apart and together. *Journal of Personality and Social Psychology, 54,* 1031–1039.

Tennen, H., & Affleck, G. (1999). Finding benefits in adversity. In C. R. Snyder (Ed.), *Coping: The psychology of what works.* New York: Oxford University Press.

Tenszen, M. (1989). Rushton ready to teach race theories: Psychology department to monitor lectures, chairman promises. *Toronto Star,* February 22, p. A8.

Tepper, B. J., & Nurse, R. J. (1997). Fat perception is related to PROP

Whorf, B. L. (1956). Science and linguistics. In J. B. Carroll (Ed.), *Language, thought and reality: Selected writings of Benjamin Lee Whorf*. Cambridge, MA: MIT Press.

Wichmann, C. (2005). Profile of families and children. *JustResearh No. 12*. Retrieved June 1, 2005, from http://www.canada.justice.gc.ca/en/ps/rs/rep/jr12/jr12_005a.htm.

Wickelgren, W. (1999). Webs, cell assemblies, and chunking in neural nets: Introduction. *Canadian Journal of Experimental Psychology, 53*, 118–131.

Wickens, T. D. (1999). Measuring the time course of retention. In C. Izawa (Ed.), *On human memory: Evolution, progress, and reflections on the 30th anniversary of the Atkinson-Shiffrin model*. Mahwah, NJ: Erlbaum.

Widiger, T. A. (2001). Official classification systems. In W. J. Livesley (Ed.), *Handbook of personality disorders: Theory, research, and treatment*. New York: Guilford.

Widiger, T. A., & Clark, L. A. (2000). Toward DSM-V and the classification of psychopathology. *Psychological Bulletin, 126*, 946–963.

Widiger, T. A., & Mullins, S. (2003). Personality disorders. In A. Tasman, J. Kay, & J. A. Lieberman (Eds.), *Psychiatry*. New York: Wiley.

Widiger, T. A., & Sankis, L. M. (2000). Adult psychopathology: Issues and controversies. *Annual Review of Psychology, 51*, 377–404.

Widom, C. S. (1997). Child abuse, neglect, and witnessing violence. In D. M. Stoff, J. Breiling, & J. D. Maser (Eds.), *Handbook of antisocial behavior*. New York: Wiley.

Wiederman, M. W. (1993). Evolved gender differences in mate preferences: Evidence from personal advertisements. *Ethology and Sociobiology, 14*, 331–352.

Wiesel, T. N., & Hubel, D. H. (1963). Single-cell responses in striate cortex of kittens deprived of vision in one eye. *Journal of Neurophysiology, 26*, 1003–1017.

Wiesel, T. N., & Hubel, D. H. (1965). Extent of recovery from the effects of visual deprivation in kittens. *Journal of Neurophysiology, 28*, 1060–1072.

Wigboldus, D. H. J., Dijksterhuis, A., & van Knippenberg, A. (2003). When stereotypes get in the way: Stereotypes obstruct stereotype-inconsistent trait inferences. *Journal of Personality and Social Psychology, 84*, 470–484.

Wiggins, J. S. (1992). Have model, will travel. *Journal of Personality, 60*, 527–532.

Wiggins, J. S., & Trapnell, P. D. (1997). Personality structure: The return of the big five. In R. Hogan, J. Johnson, & S. Briggs (Eds.), *Handbook of personality psychology*. San Diego, CA: Academic Press.

Wiggs, C. L., Weisberg, J., & Martin, A. (1999). Neural correlates of semantic and episodic memory retreival. *Neuropsychologia, 37*, 103–118.

Wikaitis, J., Mulvhill, T., & Nasrallah, H. A. (2004). Classic antipsychotic medications. In A. F. Schatzberg & C. B. Nemeroff (Eds.), *Textbook of psychopharmacology*. Washington, DC: American Psychiatric Publishing.

Wilcox, A. J., Weinberg, C. R., O'Connor, J. F., Baurd, D. D., Schlatterer, J. P., Canfield, R. E., Armstrong, E. G., & Nisula, B. C. (1988). Incidence of early loss of pregnancy. *New England Journal of Medicine, 319*, 189–194.

Wilding, J., & Valentine, E. (1996). Memory expertise. In D. J. Herrmann, C. McEvoy, C. Hertzog, P. Hertel, & M. K. Johnson (Eds.), *Basic and applied memory research: Theory in context* (Vol. 1). Mahwah, NJ: Erlbaum.

Wiley, J. L. (1999). Cannabis: Discrimination of "internal bliss"? *Pharmacology, Biochemistry & Behavior, 64*, 257–260.

Williams, A., & Giles, H. (1998). Communication of ageism. In M. C. Hecht (Ed.), *Communicating prejudice* (pp. 136–160). Thousand Oaks, CA: Sage.

Williams, B. A. (1988). Reinforcement, choice, and response strength. In R. C. Atkinson, R. J. Herrnstein, G. Lindzey, & R. D. Luce (Eds.), *Stevens' handbook of experimental psychology*. New York: Wiley.

Williams, B. A. (1994). Conditioned reinforcement: Neglected or outmoded explanatory construct? *Psychonomic Bulletin & Review, 1*, 457–475.

Williams, C. (2001). You snooze, you lose? Sleep patterns in Canada. Retrieved March 4, 2005, from http://www.statcan.ca.

Williams, C. G., Gagne, M., Ryan, R. M., & Deci, E. L. (2002). Facilitating autonomous motivation for smoking cessation. *Health Psychology, 21*, 40–50.

Williams, G. C. (1966). *Adaptation and natural selection*. Princeton, NJ: Princeton University Press.

Williams, J. B. W. (1999). Psychiatric classification. In R.E. Hales, S. C. Yudofsky, & J. A. Talbott (Eds.), *American Psychiatric Press textbook of psychiatry* (3rd ed.). Washington, DC: American Psychiatric Press.

Williams, J. E., Paton, C. C., Siegler, I. C., Eigenbrodt, M. L., Neito, F. J., & Tyroler, H. A. (2000). Anger proneness predicts coronary heart disease risk. *Circulation, 101*, 2034–2039.

Williams, J. M. G., Watts, F. N., MacLeod, C., & Mathews, A. (1997). *Cognitive psychology and emotional disorders*. Chichester, England: Wiley.

Williams, K. E., & Bond, M. J. (2002). The roles of self-efficacy, outcome expectancies and social support in the self-care behaviors of diabetics. *Psychology, Health & Medicine, 7*(2), 127–141.

Williams, L. M. (1994). Recall of childhood trauma: A prospective study of women's memories of child sexual abuse. *Journal of Consulting and Clinical Psychology, 62*, 1167–1176.

Williams, L. V. (1986). *Teaching for the two-sided mind: A guide to right brain–left brain education*. New York: Simon & Schuster.

Williams, M. H. (1992). Exploitation and inference: Mapping the damage from therapist-patient sexual involvement. *American Psychologist, 47*, 412–421.

Williams, N. A., & Deffenbacher, J. L. (1983). Life stress and chronic yeast infections. *Journal of Human Stress, 9*(1), 26–31.

Williams, R. B. (2001). Hostility (and other psychosocial risk factors): Effects on health and the potential for successful behavioral approaches to prevention and treatment. In A. Baum, T. A. Revenson, & J. E. Singer (Eds.), *Handbook of health psychology* (pp. 661–668). Mahwah, NJ: Erlbaum.

Williams, R. B., & Williams, V. P. (2001). Managing hostile thoughts, feelings, and actions: The lifeskills approach. In C. R. Snyder (Ed.), *Coping with stress: Effective people and processes* (pp. 137–153). New York: Oxford University Press.

Williams, R. L., & Eggert, A. (2002). Notetaking predictors of test performance. *Teaching of Psychology, 29*(3), 234–237.

Williams, R. L., Dotson, W., Dow, P., & Williams, W. S. (1980). The war against testing: A current status report. *Journal of Negro Education, 49*, 263–273.

Williams, R., & Stockmyer, J. (1987). *Unleashing the right side of the brain: The LARC creativity program*. New York: Viking Penguin.

Williams, W. M., & Ceci, S. J. (1997). Are Americans becoming more or less alike?: Trends in race, class, and ability differences in intelligence. *American Psychologist, 52*, 1226–1235.

Williamson, D. A., Zucker, N. L., Martin, C. K., & Smeets, M. A. M. (2001). Etiology and management of eating disorders. In P. B. Sutker & H. E. Adams (Eds.), *Comprehensive handbook of psychopathology*. New York: Kluwer Academic/Plenum.

Willis, W. D. (1985). *The pain system. The neural basis of nococeptive transmission in the mammalian nervous system*. Basel: Karger.

Willoughby, T., Motz, M., & Wood, E. (1997). The impact of interest and strategy use on memory performance for child, adolescent, and adult learners. *Alberta Journal of Educational Research, 43*, 127–141.

Wills, T. A., & Fegan, M. (2001). Social networks and social support. In A. Baum, T. A. Revenson, & J. E. Singer (Eds.), *Handbook of health psychology* (pp. 209–234). Mahwah, NJ: Erlbaum.

Wilsnack, S. C., Wonderlich, S. A., Kristjanson, A. F., Vogeltanz-Holm, N. D., & Wilsnack, R. W. (2002). Self-reports of forgetting and remembering childhood sexual abuse in a nationally representative sample of U.S. women. *Child Abuse and Neglect, 26*(2), 139–147.

Wilson, A. E., Smith, M. D., Ross, H. S., & Ross, M. (2004). Young children's personal accounts of their sibling disputes. *Merrill-Palmer Quarterly, 50*, 39–60.

Wilson, G. T. (1982). Alcohol and anxiety: Recent evidence on the tension reduction theory of alcohol use and abuse. In K. R. Blankstein & J. Polivy (Eds.), *Self-control and self-modification of emotional behavior*. New York: Plenum.

Windham, G. C., Eaton, A., & Hopkins, B. (1999). Evidence for an association between environmental tobacco smoke exposure and birthweight: A meta-analysis and new data. *Paediatrics and Perinatal Epidemiology, 13*, 35–37.

Windholz, G. (1997). Ivan P. Pavlov: An overview of his life and psychological work. *American Psychologist, 52*, 941–946.

Wing, R. R., & Polley, B. A. (2001). Obesity. In A Baum, T. A. Revenson, & J. E. Singer (Eds.), *Handbook of health psychology*. Mahwah, NJ: Erlbaum.

Winick, C., & Evans, J. T. (1996). The relationship between nonenforcement of state pornography laws and rates of sex crime arrests. *Archives of Sexual Behavior, 25*, 439–453.

Winick, C., & Norman, R. L. (2005). Epidemiology. In J. H. Lowinson, P. Ruiz, R. B. Millman, & J. G. Langrod (Eds.), *Substance abuse: A comprehensive textbook*. Philadelphia: Lippincott/Williams & Wilkins.

Winn, P. (1995). The lateral hypothalamus and motivated behavior: An old syndrome reassessed and a new perspective gained. *Current Directions in Psychological Science, 4,* 182–187.

Winner, E. (1997). Exceptionally high intelligence and schooling. *American Psychologist, 52,* 1070–1081.

Winner, E. (1998). Uncommon talents: Gifted children, prodigies and savants. *Scientific American Presents Exploring Intelligence, 9,* 32–37.

Winner, E. (2000). The origins and ends of giftedness. *American Psychologist, 55,* 159–169.

Winner, E. (2003). Creativity and talent. In M. H. Bornstein & L. Davidson (Eds.), *Well-being: Positive development across the life course*. Mahwah, NJ: Erlbaum.

Winograd, T. (1975). Frame representations and the declarative-procedural controversy. In D. Bobrow & A. Collins (Eds.), *Representation and understanding: Studies in cognitive science*. New York: Academic Press.

Winquist, J. R., & Larson, J. R. Jr. (1998). Information pooling: When it impacts group decision making. *Journal of Personality and Social Psychology, 74,* 371–377.

Winter, D. G. (1992). Content analysis of archival materials, personal documents, and everyday verbal productions. In C. P. Smith (Ed.), *Motivation and personality: Handbook of thematic content analysis*. New York: Cambridge University Press.

Wintre, M. G., North, C., & Sugar, L. A. (2001). Psychologists' response to criticisms about research based on undergraduate participants: A developmental perspective. *Canadian Psychology, 42,* 216–226.

Wintre, M. G., Sugar, L. A., Yaffe, M., & Costin, D. (2000). Generational Status: A Canadian response to the editors' consortium statement with regard to race/ethnicity. *Canadian Psychology, 41,* 244–257.

Winzelberg, A. J., & Luskin, F. M. (1999). The effect of a meditation training in stress levels in secondary school teachers. *Stress Medicine, 15,* 69–77.

Wise, M. G., Gray, K. F., & Seltzer, B. (1999). Delirium, dementia, and amnestic disorders. In R. E. Hales, S. C. Yudofsky, & J. A. Talbott (Eds.), *The American Psychiatric Press textbook of psychiatry* (3rd ed., pp. 317–362). Washington, DC: American Psychiatric Press.

Wise, R. A. (1999). Animal models of addiction. In D. S. Charney, E. J. Nestler, & B. S. Bunney (Eds.), *Neurobiology of mental illness*. New York: Oxford University Press.

Witelson, S. F., Kigar, D. L., & Harvey, T. (1999). The exceptional brain of Albert Einstein. *The Lancet, 353,* 2149–2153.

Witkin, H. A. (1950). Individual differences in ease of perception of embedded figures. *Journal of Personality, 19,* 1–15.

Witkin, H. A., & Goodenough, D. (1981). *Cognitive styles: Essence and origins*. New York: International Universities Press.

Witkin, H. A., Dyk, R. B., Paterson, H. F., Goodenough, D. R., & Karp, S. (1962). *Psychological differentiation*. New York: Wiley.

Witte, K., & Allen, M. (2000). A meta-analysis of fear appeals: Implications for effective public health campaigns. *Health Education & Behavior, 27,* 591–615.

Witte, K., Berkowitz, J. M., Cameron, K. A., & McKeon, J. K. (1998). Preventing the spread of genital warts: Using fear appeals to promote self-protective behaviors. *Health Education & Behavior, 25,* 571–585.

Wittkower, E. D., & Warnes, H. (1984). Cultural aspects of psychotherapy. In J. E. Mezzich & C. E. Berganza (Eds.), *Culture and psychopathology*. New York: Columbia University Press.

Wolfe D. A., Wekerle C., Scott K., Straatman A. L., Grasley C., Reitzel-Jaffe D. (2003). Dating violence prevention with at-risk youth: A controlled outcome evaluation. *Journal of Consulting and Clinical Psychology. 71,* 279–291.

Wolk, A., Manson, J. E., Stampfer, M. J., Colditz, G. A., Hu, F. B., Speizer, F. E., Hennekens, C. H., & Willett, W. C. (1999). Long-term intake of dietary fiber and decreased risk of coronary heart disease among women. *Journal of the American Medical Association, 281,* 1998–2004.

Wolk, A., Manson, J. E., Stampfer, M. J., Colditz, G. A., Hu, F. B., Speizer, F. E., Hennekens, C. H., & Willett, W. C. (1999). Long-term intake of dietary fiber and decreased risk of coronary heart disease among women. *Journal of the American Medical Association, 281,* 1998–2004.

Woloshin, S., Schwartz, L. M., & Welch, H. G. (2002). Risk charts: Putting cancer in context. *Journal of the National Cancer Institute, 94,* 799–804.

Wolpe, J. (1958). *Psychotherapy by reciprocal inhibition*. Stanford, CA: Stanford University Press.

Wolpe, J. (1990). *The practice of behavior therapy*. Elmsford, NY: Pergamon Press.

Won, S. (2005, March 16). At 86, a professor who is still going strong. *Globe and Mail*, p. C2.

Wonder, J. (1992). *Whole brain thinking: Working both sides of the brain to achieve peak job performance*. New York: Morrow.

Wonderlich, S. A. (2002). Personality and eating disorders. In C. G. Fairburn & K. D. Brownell (Eds.), *Eating disorders and obesity: A comprehensive handbook*. New York: Guilford.

Wood, F., Ebert, V., & Kinsbourne, M. (1982). The episodic-semantic memory distinction in memory and amnesia: Clinical and experimental observations. In L. Cermak (Ed.), *Human memory and amnesia*. Hillsdale, NJ: Erlbaum.

Wood, J. M., Nezworski, M. T., & Stejskal, W. J. (1996). The comprehensive system for the Rorschach: A critical examination. *Psychological Science, 7,* 3–10.

Wood, N. L., & Cowan, N. (1995). The cocktail party phenomenon revisited: Attention and memory in the classic selective listening procedure of Cherry (1953). *Journal of Experimental Psychology: Learning, Memory, & Cognition, 21,* 255–260.

Wood, W., & Quinn, J. M. (2003). Forewarned and forearmed? Two meta-analytic syntheses of forewarnings of influence appeals. *Psychological Bulletin, 129,* 119–138.

Wood, W., Rhodes, N., & Biek, M. (1995). Working knowledge and attitude strength: An information-processing analysis. In R. E. Petty & J. A. Krosnick (Eds.), *Attitude strength: Antecedents and consequences*. Mahwah, NJ: Erlbaum.

Woodcock, R. W. (1994). Norms. In R. J. Sternberg (Ed.), *Encyclopedia of human intelligence*. New York: Macmillan.

Woods, S. C., Schwartz, M. W., Baskin, D. G., & Seeley, R. J. (2000). Food intake and the regulation of body weight. *Annual Review of Psychology, 51,* 255–277.

Woolfolk, R. L., & Richardson, F. C. (1978). *Stress, sanity and survival*. New York: Sovereign/Monarch.

Word, D. H., Zanna, M. P., & Cooper, J. (1974). The nonverbal mediation of self-fulfilling prophesies in interracial interaction. *Journal of Experimental Social Psychology, 10,* 109–120.

Wormith, S. (2000). Without conscience: The disturbing world of the psychopaths among us. *Canadian Psychology, 41,* 134–137.

Worthen, J. B., & Wade, C. E. (1999). Direction of travel and visiting team athletic performance: Support for a circadian dysrhythmia hypothesis. *Journal of Sport Behavior, 22,* 279–287.

Worthington, E. L., Jr., & Scherer, M. (2004). Forgiveness is an emotion-focused coping strategy that can reduce health risks and promote health resilience: Theory, review, and hypotheses. *Psychology and Health, 19,* 385–405.

Worthington-Roberts, B. S., & Klerman, L. V. (1990). Maternal nutrition. In I. R. Merkatz & J. E. Thompson (Eds.), *New perspectives on prenatal care*. New York: Elsevier.

Wright, J. H., & Beck, A. T. (1999). Cognitive therapies. In R. E. Hales, S. C. Yudofsky, & J. A. Talbott (Eds.), *American Psychiatric Press textbook of psychiatry*. Washington, DC: American Psychiatric Press.

Wright, M. J. (1992a). The golden anniversary symposium: CPA's first 50 years. *Canadian Psychology, 33,* 695–698.

Wright, M. J. (1992b). The golden anniversary symposium: CPA's first 50 years. *Canadian Psychology, 33,* 1–3.

Wright, M. J. (1992c). Women groundbreakers in Canadian psychology: World War II and its aftermath. *Canadian Psychology, 33,* 675–685.

Wright, M. J., & Myers, C. R. (1982). *History of academic psychology in Canada*. Toronto: C. J. Hogrefe, Inc.

Wright, S. C., & Taylor, D. M. (1995). Identity and the language of the classroom: Investigating the impact of heritage versus second language instruction on personal and collective self-esteem. *Journal of Educational Psychology, 87,* 241–252.

Wright, S. C., Taylor, D. M., & Macarthur, J. (2000). Subtractive bilingualism and the survival of the Inuit language: Heritage- versus second-language education. *Journal of Educational Psychology, 92,* 63–84.

Wu, Z. (1998). Recent trends in marriage patterns in Canada. *Policy Options, 3,* 3–6.

Wu-Holt, P., & Boutte, J. (1994). The relationship between daily hassles, ways of coping, and menstrual cycle symptomatology. *International*

Journal of Stress Management, 1, 173–183.

Wundt, W. (1874/1904). *Principles of physiological psychology*. Leipzig: Engelmann.

Wurtz, R. H., & Kandel, E. R. (2000). Central visual pathways. In E. R. Kandel, J. H. Schwartz, & T. M. Jessell (Eds.), *Principles of neural science*. New York: McGraw-Hill.

Wylie, M. S. (1998). The shadow of a doubt. In R. A. Baker (Ed.), *Child sexual abuse and false memory syndrome*. Amherst, NY: Prometheus Books.

Wynder, E. L., Cohen, L. A., Muscat, J. E., Winters, B., Dwyer, J. T., & Blackburn, G. (1997). Breast cancer: Weighing the evidence for a promoting role of dietary fat. *Journal of the National Cancer Institute, 89*, 766–775.

Wynder, E. L., Cohen, L. A., Muscat, J. E., Winters, B., Dwyer, J. T., & Blackburn, G. (1997). Breast cancer: Weighing the evidence for a promoting role of dietary fat. *Journal of the National Cancer Institute, 89*, 766–775.

Wynn, K. (1992). Addition and subtraction by human infants. *Nature, 358*, 749–750.

Wynn, K. (1996). Infants' individuation and enumeration of sequential actions. *Psychological Science, 7*, 164–169.

Wynn, K. (1998). An evolved capacity for number. In D. D. Cummins & C. Allen (Eds.), *The evolution of mind*. New York: Oxford University Press.

Wynne, C. D. L. (2004). *Do animals think?* Princeton, NJ: Princeton University Press.

Xiaghe, X., & Whyte, M. K. (1990). Love matches and arranged marriages: A Chinese replication. *Journal of Marriage and the Family, 52*, 709–722.

Yalom, I. D. (1995). *The theory and practice of group psychotherapy* (4th ed.). New York: Basic Books.

Yalom, V. (2002). Interview with Donald Meichenbaum, Ph.D. Retrieved July 4, 2005, from http://www.psychotherapy.net/totm/meichenbaum.shtml.

Yamamoto, J., Silva, J. A., Justice, L. R., Chang, C. Y., & Leong, G. B. (1993). Cross-cultural psychotherapy. In A. C. Gaw (Ed.), *Culture, ethnicity, and mental illness*. Washington, DC: American Psychiatric Press.

Yang, H., Liu, T., & Zang, D. (2000). A study of stressful life events before the onset of hypothyroidism. *Chinese Mental Health Journal, 14*, 201–202.

Yapko, M. D. (1994). *Suggestions of abuse: True and false memories of childhood sexual trauma*. New York: Simon & Schuster.

Yarmey, A. D. (2003). Eyewitness identification: Guidelines and recommendations for identification procedures in the United States and in Canada. *Canadian Psychology, 44*(3), 181–189.

Yates, F. A. (1966). *The art of memory*. London: Routledge & Kegan Paul.

Ybarra, O., Stephan, W. G., & Schaberg, L. (2000). Misanthropic memory for the behavior of group members. *Personality and Social Psychology Bulletin, 26*, 1515–1525.

Yerkes, R. M., & Morgulis, S. (1909). The method of Pavlov in animal psychology. *Psychological Bulletin, 6*, 257–273.

Yik, M. S. M., Bond, M., & Paulhus, D. L. (1998). Do Chinese self-enhance or self-efface?: It's a matter of domain. *Personality and Social Psychology Bulletin, 24*, 399–406.

Yost, W. A. (2000). *Fundamentals of hearing: An introduction*. San Diego, CA: Academic Press.

Yost, W. A. (2001). Auditory, localization, and scene perception. In E. B. Goldstein (Ed.), *Blackwell handbook of perception*. Malden, MA: Blackwell.

Young, D. M. (1997). Depression. In W. S. Tseng & J. Streltzer (Eds.), *Culture and psychopathology: A guide to clinical assessment*. New York: Brunner/Mazel.

Young, K. S. (1996, August). *Internet addiction: The emergence of a new clinical disorder*. Paper presented at the meeting of the American Psychological Association: Toronto, Ontario.

Young, K. S. (1998). *Caught in the net: How to recognize the signs of Internet addiction—and a winning strategy for recovery*. New York: Wiley.

Yudofsky, S. C. (1999). Parkinson's disease, depression, and electrical stimulation of the brain. *New England Journal of Medicine, 340*, 1500–1502.

Yukl, G. A. (1994). *Leadership in organizations* (3rd ed.). Englewood Cliffs, NJ: Prentice-Hall.

Zadra, A. L., & Donderi, D. C. (2000). Nightmares and Bad Dreams: Their prevalence and relationship to well-being. *Journal of Abnormal Psychology, 109*, 273–281.

Zadra, A. L., Donderi, D. C., & Pihl, R. O. (1992). Efficacy of lucid dream induction for lucid and non-lucid dreamers. *Dreaming, 2*, 85–89.

Zajonc, R. B. (1980). Feeling and thinking: Preferences need no inferences. *American Psychologist, 35*, 151–175.

Zakzanis, K. K., & Young, D. A. (2001). Memory impairment in abstinent MDMA ("Ecstasy") users: A longitudinal investigation. *Neurology, 56*, 966–969.

Zanna, M. P. (1994). On the nature of prejudice. *Canadian Psychology, 35*, 11–23.

Zanna, M. P., & Cooper, J. (1974). Dissonance and the pill: An attributional approach to studying the arousal properties of dissonance. *Journal of Personality and Social Psychology, 29*, 703–709.

Zarcone, V. P., Jr. (2000). Sleep hygiene. In M. H. Kryger, T. Roth, & W. C. Dement (Eds.), *Principles and practice of sleep medicine*. Philadelphia: Saunders.

Zatzick, D. F., & Dimsdale, J. E. (1990). Cultural variations in response to painful stimuli. *Psychosomatic Medicine, 52*(5), 544–557.

Zautra, A. J., & Smith, B. W. (2001). Depression and reactivity to stress in older women with rheumatoid arthritis and osteoarthritis. *Psychosomatic Medicine, 63*, 687–696.

Zebrowitz, L. A. (1996). *Reading faces*. Boulder, CO: Westview Press.

Zebrowitz, L. A., Collins, M. A., & Dutta, R. (1998). The relationship between appearance and personality across the life span. *Personality and Social Psychology Bulletin, 24*, 736–749.

Zebrowitz, L. A., Voinescu, L., & Collins, M. A. (1996). "Wide-eyed" and "crooked-face": Determinants of perceived and real honesty across the life span. *Personality and Social Psychology Bulletin, 22*, 1258–1269.

Zechmeister, E. B., & Nyberg, S. E. (1982). *Human memory: An introduction to research and theory*. Pacific Grove, CA: Brooks/Cole.

Zeifman, D., & Hazan, C. (1997). Attachment: The bond in pairbonds. In J. A. Simpson & D. T. Kenrick (Eds.), *Evolutionary social psychology*. Mahwah, NJ: Erlbaum.

Zeiler, M. (1977). Schedules of reinforcement: The controlling variables. In W. K. Honig & J. E. R. Staddon (Eds.), *Handbook of operant behavior*. Englewood Cliffs, NJ: Prentice-Hall.

Zeki, S. (1993). The visual association cortex. *Current Opinion in Neurobiology, 3*, 155–159.

Zellner, D. A. (1991). How foods get to be liked: Some general mechanisms and some special cases. In

R. C. Bolles (Ed.), *The hedonics of taste*. Hillsdale, NJ: Erlbaum.

Zenhausen, R. (1978). Imagery, cerebral dominance and style of thinking: A unified field model. *Bulletin of the Psychonomic Society, 12*, 381–384.

Zepelin, H. (1993). Internal alarm clock. In M. A. Carskadon (Ed.), *Encyclopedia of sleep and dreaming*. New York: Macmillan.

Zigler, E., & Seitz, V. (1982). Social policy and intelligence. In R. J. Sternberg (Ed.), *Handbook of human intelligence*. Cambridge, MA: Cambridge University Press.

Zigler, E., & Styfco, S. J. (1994). Head Start: Criticisms in a constructive context. *American Psychologist, 49*, 127–132.

Zillmann, D., & Bryant, J. (1984). Effects of massive exposure to pornography. In N. M. Malamuth & E. Donnerstein (Eds.), *Pornography and sexual aggression*. New York: Academic Press.

Zillmann, D., & Bryant, J. (1988). Pornography's impact on sexual satisfaction. *Journal of Applied Social Psychology, 18*, 438–453.

Zillmann, D., & Weaver, J. B. (1989). Pornography and men's sexual callousness toward women. In D. Zillmann & J. Bryant (Eds.), *Pornography: Research advances and policy considerations*. Hillsdale, NJ: Erlbaum.

Zillmann, D., Bryant, J., & Huston, A. C. (1994). *Media, family, and children*. Hillsdale, NJ: Erlbaum.

Zillmer, E. A., & Spiers, M. V. (2001). *Principles of neuropsychology*. Belmont, CA: Wadsworth.

Zimmerman, B. J. (1995). Self-efficacy and educational development. In A. Bandura (Ed.), *Self-efficacy in changing societies*. New York: Cambridge University Press.

Zimmerman, I. L., & Woo-Sam, J. M. (1984). Intellectual assessment of children. In G. Goldstein & M. Hersen (Eds.), *Handbook of psychological assessment*. New York: Pergamon Press.

Zoellner, L. A., Foa, E. B., Brigidi, B. D., & Przeworski, A. (2000). Are trauma victims susceptible to "false memories"? *Journal of Abnormal Psychology, 109*, 517–524.

Zola, S. M., & Squire, L. R. (2000). The medial temporal lobe and the hippocampus. In E. Tulving & F. I. M. Craik (Eds.), *The Oxford handbook of memory* (pp. 485–500). New York: Oxford University Press.

Zorick, F. J., & Walsh, J. K. (2000). Evaluation and management of insomnia: An overview. In M. H. Kryger, T. Roth, & W. C. Dement

(Eds.), *Principles and practice of sleep medicine*. Philadelphia: Saunders.

Zrenner, E., Abramov, I., Akita, M., Cowey, A., Livingstone, M., & Valberg, A. (1990). Color perception: Retina to cortex. In L. Spillman & J. S. Werner (Eds.), *Visual perception: The neurophysiological foundations*. San Diego: Academic Press.

Zubieta, J., Smith, Y. R., Bueller, J. A., Xu, Y., Kilbourn, M. R., Jewett, D. M., Meyer, C. R., Loeppe, R. A., & Stohler, C. S. (2001). Regional mu opioid receptor regulation of sensory and affective dimensions of pain. *Science, 293,* 311–315.

Zuckerman, M. (1971). Dimensions of sensation seeking. *Journal of Consulting and Clinical Psychology, 36,* 45–52.

Zuckerman, M. (1979). *Sensation seeking: Beyond the optimal level of arousal.* Hillsdale, NJ: Erlbaum.

Zuckerman, M. (1984). Experience and desire: A new format for sensation seeking scales. *Journal of Behavioral Assessment, 6,* 101–114.

Zuckerman, M. (1990). The psychophysiology of sensation seeking. *Journal of Personality, 58*(1), 313–345.

Zuckerman, M. (1991). *Psychobiology of personality.* New York: Cambridge University Press.

Zuckerman, M. (1994). *Behavioral expressions and biosocial bases of sensation seeking.* New York: Cambridge University Press.

Zuckerman, M. (1996). The psychobiological model for impulsive unsocialized sensation seeking: A comparative approach. *Neuropsychobiology, 34,* 125–129.

Zuckerman, M., & Kuhlman, D. M. (2000). Personality and risk-taking: Common biosocial factors. *Journal of Personality, 68,* 999–1029.

Zuroff, D. C., & Mongrain, M. (1987). Dependency and self-criticism: Vulnerability factors for depressive affective states. *Journal of Abnormal Psychology, 96,* 14–22.

Zwislocki, J. J. (1981). Sound analysis in the ear: A history of discoveries. *American Scientist, 69,* 184–192.

Name Index

A

Abel, E.L., 442
Abel, M.H., 567
Abi-Dargham, A., 601
Aboud, F.E., 700
Abraham, C., 77
Abramov, I., 141
Abramowitz, A.J., 248
Abrams, R., 130, 643, 646
Abramson, L.Y., 595
Achermann, P., 193
Acker, M.M., 248
Ackerknecht, E.H., 639
Ackerman, P.L., 360
Adair, J., 66
Adam, K., 194
Adamopoulos, J., 19
Adams, G., 468
Adams, H.E., 498, 579, 587
Adams, H.F., 373
Adams, J.L., 328, 329
Adams, R.G., 675
Adcock, C.J., 529
Addison, T., 405
Ader, R., 231, 555
Adler, A., 9, 11, 37, 494, 502, 524, 629
Affleck, G., 541, 551
Agnoli, F., 340, 344
Ahadi, S.A., 447
Ahima, R.S., 396
Ahn, H., 634
Aikins, D.E., 586
Ainsworth, M.D.S., 13, 448, 676
Ait-Daoud, N., 220
Ajzen, I., 680, 681
Akerstedt, T., 184, 191
Akgun, S., 550
Akimoto, S.A., 674
Akiskal, H.S., 590
Aks, D.J., 152
Alavi, A., 205
Albee, G.W., 625, 648
Albers, J., 175, 176
Albert, C.M., 552
Albert, M.S., 296, 473, 474
Albert, R.D., 18
Alcock, J., 115
Aldag, R.J., 696
Alderman, M.H., 554
Aldrich, M.S., 196
Alexander, C.N., 63, 205
Alexander, F., 629
Alexander, F.G., 639
Alexander, M.G., 407
Allain, A.N., 607
Allan, R.W., 229, 236
Allard, L.M., 677
Allen, B.P., 513
Allen, M., 11, 404, 683, 700
Allgood, W.P., 31
Allison, D.B., 399, 400
Allison, R.S., 126
Allison, S., 216
Alloy, L.B., 595, 596
Allport, G., 492
Almeida, D.M., 493
Alonso, A., 632, 633
Alonso, S., 632
Alsop, B., 240
Altman, I., 27
Alvarez, P., 296
Amabile, T.M., 384
Amato, M., 700

Amato, P.R., 487
Ambady, N., 666
Ames, A., 151
Ammerman, R.T., 442
Anand, B.K., 395
Anch, A.M., 191
Ancoli-Israel, S., 191
Anderson, C.A., 342, 493
Anderson, E.A., 487
Anderson, I.M., 85
Anderson, K.J., 542
Anderson, K.O., 165
Anderson, M.C., 288
Anderson, V.N., 700
Anderson-Fye, E.P., 616
Andersson, B.E., 450
Andreasen, N.C., 93, 109, 385, 598, 600
Andres, R.L., 442
Andreski, P., 60
Andrews, G., 582
Angell, M., 642
Angiulo, M.J., 590
Angleitner, A., 516
Anglin, J.M., 317
Angst, J., 502
Ani, C., 373
Anisman, H., 536, 537, 544
Annas, P., 585
Anthenelli, R.M., 220
Anton, R.F., 210, 213
Antony, M., 639
Antony, M.M., 226, 227, 582, 585
Antrobus, J., 197
Apicella, L.F., 559
Appleby, T., 663
Archer, J., 482
Archibald, A.B., 463, 464
Arcus, D.M., 447
Arendt, J., 184, 185
Argyle, M., 429, 430, 431
Arkes, H.R., 531
Arkin, A.M., 219
Arkowitz, H., 648
Armant, D.R., 442
Armbruster, B.B., 33
Armitage, C.J., 680
Armony, J.L., 97, 296
Arnett, J., 467
Arnett, J.J., 520
Arnkoff, D.B., 631, 635
Arnold, L.M., 554
Arnold, R.D., 516
Arnon, I., 584
Arnsten, J.H., 213
Aron, A.P., 42, 44, 45, 46, 47, 48, 49, 50, 426
Aronson, E., 467, 681, 686
Aronson, J., 374, 375
Arrigo, J.M., 589
Arthur, R.H., 539
Asch, S., 664, 688, 689, 692
Aschengrau, A., 559
Asendorpf, J.B., 548
Aserinsky, E., 187
Ashby, D., 641
Ashcraft, M.H., 549
Ashforth, B.E., 550
Ashton, M.C., 493, 494, 522
Aslin, R.N., 324
Aspinwall, L.G., 558
Assaad, J.M., 213

Assanand, S., 397
Asuncion, A.G., 682
Atkinson, J., 416
Atkinson, J.W., 393, 417, 418
Atkinson, L., 449
Atkinson, R.C., 157, 273, 274
Atkinson, R.H., 34
Atkinson, R.L., 157
Auerbach, C.F., 486
Austin, J.T., 362
Averill, J.A., 418
Avis, N.E., 473
Axel, R., 164
Ayanian, J.Z., 559
Ayers, M.S., 284, 285
Ayres, J.J.B., 229

B

Baars, B.J., 312
Baccus, J.R., 281, 511
Bachelor, P., 384
Bäckman, L., 475
Baddely, A.D., 275, 276, 283
Badets, J., 19
Badia, P., 185, 216
Baenninger, R., 217
Baer, J., 384
Baer, R.A., 528
Baeyens, F., 130
Bahrick, H.P., 286
Bailey, J.M., 411, 412
Baillargeon, R., 456, 458
Baime, M., 205
Bakalar, J.B., 213
Bakan, P., 118
Baker, F., 559
Baker, L., 616
Baldessarini, R.J., 641
Baldwin, D., 550
Baldwin, J.M., 4, 12, 14, 22
Baldwin, M.W., 281, 510, 511
Baldwin, W., 64
Balk, M.M., 3
Ball, H.L., 189
Ballenger, J.C., 195, 550, 639, 640
Baltes, P.B., 475
Bandura, A., 253, 254, 255, 256, 484, 504, 505, 506, 507
Banich, M.T., 117
Banks, W.P., 146
Banning, K., 539
Banyard, V.L., 290, 405
Bar-On, R., 381
Barak, A., 404
Barba, G.D., 298
Barbaree, H.E., 404
Barbee, A.P., 679
Barber, B.K., 472
Barber, T., 203
Barber, T.X., 203
Barbrack, C.R., 635
Barch, D.M., 599
Bard, P., 425
Barea-Rodriguez, E.J., 295
Bargh, J.A., 692, 699
Barlett, D.L., 583
Barley, D.E., 634
Barlow, D.H., 582, 585

Barnes, V.A., 205
Barnett, W.S., 387
Barnhardt, T.M., 130
Barnier, A.J., 203, 283
Baron, A., 244
Baron, R.S., 689
Barrett, D., 219
Barrett, M., 317
Barry, H., III, 462
Barry-Walsh, J., 590
Barsky, A.J., 563, 588
Bartlett, F.C., 284
Bartoshuk, L.M., 162, 163, 164
Bartsch, K., 459
Basbaum, A.I., 86, 166
Basow, S.A., 483
Bassili, J.N., 689
Bassiri, A.B., 196
Bassok, M., 330, 331
Bassuk, E.L., 652
Bastien, C., 195
Bates, E., 317, 324
Bates, J.E., 446
Bates, M.S., 165
Batki, S.L., 561
Bauer, M.I., 331
Bauer, M.S., 593
Baum, A., 552
Baumeister, R.F., 406, 409, 414, 482, 498, 546, 548, 549
Baumeister, R.J., 394, 399, 415
Baumrind, D., 65, 248
Bauserman, R., 404
Baxter, P.M., 69
Baylis, G.C., 145
Baynard, M.D., 191
Bazzini, D.G., 665
Beahrs, J.O., 204
Beard, C.M., 615
Beauchamp, G.K., 164, 398
Beck, A., 546, 586, 594, 595, 598, 631, 632, 644
Becker, A.E., 614, 616
Becker, M.J., 34
Beckham, J.C., 584
Beehr, T.A., 537
Beeman, M.J., 118
Beer, J.M., 516
Beers, M., 521
Begg, I., 272
Begue, L., 672
Behl, G., 162
Beidel, D.C., 637
Beier, M.E., 360
Beilin, H., 456
Beilock, S.L., 549
Beisecker, A.E., 564
Beiser, M., 649
Békésy, G. von, 158
Bell, A.P., 411
Bellack, A.S., 602, 637
Beller, M., 483
Bellezza, F.S., 304
Belli, R.F., 291
Bellinger, D.C., 373
Bellini, G., 169, 170
Belsky, J., 449, 450, 472, 679
Bem, D., 686
Bem, S.L., 484

Ben-Porath, Y.S., 528
Ben-Shakhar, G., 420
Benca, R.M., 194
Bender, R., 399
Bendersky, M., 442
Benet, V., 494
Benham, M.L., 491
Benjamin, L.T. Jr., 4, 14, 34
Benjet, C., 248
Bennell, C., 610
Bennet, E.L., 101
Bennett, H.L., 182
Bennett, P., 554
Benson, H., 205, 218, 568
Benson, J.B., 459
Bentler, P.M., 386
Bereczkei, T., 20
Berenbaum, S.A., 412
Berger, H., 90
Bergin, A.E., 634, 638, 648, 656
Berglund, P.A., 625
Berk, L.E., 443
Berkhof, J., 541
Berkowitz, L., 546, 635, 689
Berkowitz, R.I., 638
Berlin, B., 325
Berliner, L., 293
Berman, A.L., 464
Berman, R.F., 92
Bernat, J.A., 579
Berndsen, M., 699
Bernhardt, P.C., 85
Bernstein, H.J., 643
Bernstein, I.E., 398
Bernstein, M., 361
Berntson, G.G., 419
Berrettini, W.H., 593
Berridge, K.C., 98, 393
Berry, D.S., 668
Berry, D.T.R., 528
Berry, J.W., 18, 149, 333, 362
Berscheid, E., 665, 676, 677, 679
Bertenthal, B.I., 445
Berthelot, J.-M., 399
Berzonsky, M., 468
Bettman, J.R., 336
Beumont, P.J.V., 615
Beutler, L.E., 634, 654, 656, 657
Bharandari, 678
Bhatnagar, S., 544
Bhattachary, S., 214
Bialystok, E., 270, 311, 319, 320
Biblarz, T.J., 471
Bidell, T., 459
Biederman, I., 146
Biehl, M., 422
Biek, M., 680
Bierut, L.J., 593
Biggar, R.J., 561
Bigler, E.D., 483
Billings, J.F., 291
Binet, A., 22, 356, 358, 388, 453
Bini, L., 643
Birch, D., 393, 417
Birch, H.G., 446
Birch, L.L., 398
Birchler, G.R., 588
Birdsall, T.G., 128

Birdsong, D., 320
Birnbaum, M.H., 336, 337
Birt, A., 283
Bishop, C.H., 35
Bishop, K.M., 484
Bishop, S.R., 205
Bixler, E.O., 550
Bjork, R.A., 288, 301, 306
Bjorklund, D.F., 291, 456, 457, 459
Black, D.W., 109, 598, 600, 607
Blacker, D., 579
Blackwell, J.M., 278
Blagrove, M., 200
Blair, I.V., 698
Blair, S.L., 471, 568
Blair, S.N., 569
Blakeslee, T., 118
Blanchard, E.B., 554
Blanchard, F.A., 700
Blanchard, J.J., 602
Blanchard, R., 411
Blanco, C., 642
Blankenhorn, D., 486, 487
Blascovich, J., 700
Blashfield, R.K., 579
Blasko, D.G., 318
Blass, T., 691
Blatt, S., 594
Blesbois, E., 232
Bleuler, E., 598
Blieszner, R., 675
Bliwise, D.L., 189
Block, J., 469, 494, 548
Block, L.G., 683, 686
Bloodworth, R.C., 213
Bloom, B.L., 650
Bloom, B.S., 366
Bloom, P., 323
Bloomfield, H.H., 205
Blue, H.C., 611
Blumenthal, J.A., 553
Blundell, J.E., 85, 396
Boals, A., 549
Boatswain, S., 13
Bock, B.C., 560
Boden, J.M., 498
Bodenhausen, G.V., 666
Bodenheimer, T., 642
Boehm, L.E., 683
Boer, D.P., 503
Bogaert, A., 403
Bogaert, A.F., 562
Bogartz, R.S., 459
Bogen, J.E., 16, 102, 117, 119
Bogg, T., 493
Bohannon, J.N., III, 324
Bohner, G., 684
Bohning, D.E., 93
Boland, R.J., 591
Bolger, N., 548
Bolles, R.C., 246, 393
Bolton, P., 364
Bond, C.F., Jr., 269
Bond, M., 523
Bond, M.H., 430, 674, 692
Bond, M.J., 506
Bondar, R., 125
Bongar, B., 654
Boninger, D.S., 680
Bonnet, M.H., 191, 193
Bono, J.E., 493
Bonvillain, J.D., 324
Booth, C.L., 450
Booth, D., 398
Booth, R.J., 567

Bootzin, R.R., 188, 195
Bopp, K., 288
Borbely, A., 194
Borbely, A.A., 193
Bordnick, P.S., 637
Borgida, E., 72
Boring, E.G., 3
Borkenau, P., 666
Bornstein, B.H., 306
Bornstein, R.F., 503
Boroditsky, L., 325
Borus, J.F., 650, 652
Bossio, L.M., 558
Bosson, J.K., 675
Bost, K.K., 448
Both, S., 404
Bouchard, C., 400
Bouchard, T.J., Jr., 367, 368, 370
Boudreaux, E., 506
Bouman, T.K., 587
Bourgeois, J.P., 121
Bourhis, R.Y., 700
Bourne, L.E., Jr., 328
Bousfield, W.A., 279
Bouton, M.E., 234
Boutte, J., 554
Bowden, C.L., 642
Bower, G.H., 280, 288, 302, 303, 304
Bowlby, J., 450
Boyatzis, R.E., 416
Boyce, S.J., 340
Bozarth, M.A., 212
Bracken, B.A., 354
Bradbury, T.N., 471
Bradfield, A.L., 306
Bradley, C., 554
Bradshaw, J.L., 105, 119
Brady, K.T., 210
Braff, D.L., 602
Braffman, W., 202
Braginsky, D.D., 27
Braid, J., 201
Brainerd, C.J., 456
Branaman, T.F., 420
Brand, R.J., 553
Branigan, C., 419
Bransford, J.D., 289
Brass, G.M., 649
Bratslavsky, E., 399, 546
Brawman-Mintzer, O., 640
Bray, C.W., 159
Bredart, S., 285
Breedlove, S.M., 106, 411, 412
Breggin, P.R., 642, 643, 646
Bregman, A.S., 18
Brehm, J., 703
Breier, A., 601
Breland, K., 240, 241, 249
Breland, M., 240, 241, 249
Bremner, J.G., 458
Brende, J.O., 537
Brennan, P.A., 607
Breslau, N., 60
Bretherton, I., 13
Bretl, D.J., 485
Breuer, J., 624
Brewer, M.B., 20
Brewer, W.F., 280
Brewin, C.R., 290
Brewster, K.L., 471
Brickman, P., 430
Briere, J., 290, 293
Brill, A., 8
Bringmann, W.G., 3
Brislin, R., 28, 29, 612

Broadbent, D.E., 273
Brobeck, J.R., 395
Broca, P., 102
Broder, 66
Brody, N., 356, 372, 373, 517
Bromet, E.J., 617
Bronstein, P., 19
Brooks-Gunn, J., 463, 464
Broughton, R., 186
Brown, A., 283, 441
Brown, A.S., 582, 603
Brown, D., 293
Brown, E.J., 586
Brown, G.D.A., 275
Brown, H.D., 118
Brown, J., 548
Brown, L., 41, 293
Brown, M., 416
Brown, N., 13, 276
Brown, P.K., 142
Brown, R., 278, 283, 324
Brown, R.D., 291
Brown, R.T., 383
Brown, S.C., 283, 287
Browndyke, J., 80
Brownell, H.H., 119
Brownell, K.D., 400
Bruce, D., 293
Bruce, K.R., 616
Bruch, H., 616
Bruckner-Gordon, F., 654
Bruer, J.T., 121
Bruner, J.S., 521
Brunsman, B., 689
Bryant, J., 404
Bryden, M.P., 105, 482
Bryden, P., 18
Buchanan, B., 684
Buchanan, R.W., 598
Buck, L.B., 162, 164
Budiansky, S., 322
Buehler, R., 695
Buffalo, E.A., 276, 278
Bühler, C., 11
Bulcroft, R., 471
Bulik, C.M., 616
Bull, D.L., 290
Bunch, B., 363
Burbank, V.K., 462
Burckhardt, G., 639
Burger, J.M., 513, 672, 703
Burgess, M., 546
Burke, D.M., 283
Burke, J.D., 581, 617
Burleson, K.O., 205
Burnam, A., 652
Burns, B.D., 340
Burnstein, E., 115
Busis, N., 84, 85
Buss, D., 11, 20, 408, 516, 517, 678
Buss, D.M., 20, 394, 406, 407, 409, 483, 531, 679
Bussey, K., 484
Buster, J.E., 439
Butcher, J.N., 525, 526, 547
Butler, J.L., 549
Butler, K.M., 443
Button, J., 202
Buxton, M.N., 554
Byne, W., 484, 602
Byrne, D., 675, 679

C

Cabral, G.A., 213
Cabrera, N.J., 449

Cacioppo, J., 686
Cacioppo, J.T., 418, 419, 687
Cade, J., 644
Caglar, S., 95
Cahill, L., 294
Cain, W.S., 164
Caine, E.D., 473
Calhoun, L.G., 551
Calkins, M.W., 5, 6
Callahan, C.M., 365
Calof, D., 293
Calvert, C., 344
Cameron, D.E., 623
Cameron, L., 563
Cameron, N., 587
Cami, J., 210, 211
Campbell, A., 483
Campbell, B., 699
Campbell, D.T., 152
Campbell, J., 501
Campbell, J.D., 688
Campbell, K.B., 182
Campbell, L., 675, 677
Campbell, R., 319, 404
Campbell, S., 594
Campbell, W.K., 672
Campfield, L.A., 396, 397
Cancro, R., 598, 600
Candela, S.F., 604
Cannon, E., 366
Cannon, W., 88, 392, 395, 425, 543
Cantor, J., 485
Cantor-Graae, E., 603
Cantril, H., 29
Cao, Y., 101
Capaldi, E.D., 163, 398
Capelli, C.A., 318
Caporael, L.R., 20
Caputo, D., 560
Carballis, 105
Cardellini, L., 457
Cardena, E., 205, 590
Carducci, B.J., 216
Carey, M.P., 561
Carey, S., 458
Carli, L.L., 306
Carlsmith, J.M., 685, 686
Carlson, A.J., 395
Carlson, D.N., 563
Carlsson, A., 85, 601
Carmichael, A., 1
Carnegie, D., 675
Carnevale, G., 317
Caro, R.M., 116
Carpenter, W.T., 598, 600, 642
Carr, E., 438
Carr, T.H., 549
Carrell, S., 510
Carrère, 472
Carrier, M., 273
Carroll, J.M., 422
Carskadon, M.A., 186, 216
Carson, R.C., 547, 600
Carson, S.A., 439
Carter, 205
Carter, B., 470, 472
Carter, E.A., 470
Carter, P.J., 118
Carter, R., 82
Cartwright, R.D., 197, 200, 201
Caruso, D., 381
Carver, C.S., 545, 546, 558
Carver, R.A., 416
Caryl, P.G., 378

Casanova, C., 136
Case, R., 457
Caspi, A., 469, 516, 675
Caspi, O., 205
Cassel, R.N., 508
Cassidy, J., 448
Caswell, N., 401
Catania, A.C., 242
Catania, J.A., 561, 562
Cattell, H., 376
Cattell, J.M., 5
Cattell, R., 492
Cattell, R.B., 526, 527
Catz, S.L., 561
Caudek, C., 148
Cavanaugh, J.C., 473
Cavell, T.A., 34
Caverly, D.C., 33
Ceci, S.J., 284, 361, 368, 370, 373, 380
Centeno, S., 231
Cerletti, U., 643
Chabris, C.F., 143
Chaiken, S., 681, 682, 684
Chaires, W.M., 333
Chaisson, R., 443
Chambless, D.L., 634
Chan, J.W.C., 362
Chance, P., 120, 237
Chandler, C.C., 283, 284
Chandler, M.J., 459, 465, 466
Chao, R., 450
Chaplin, W.F., 666
Chapman, L., 293
Chard, J., 19
Chaves, J.F., 201
Chemers, M.M., 506
Chen, D., 503
Cheney, P., 687
Chess, S., 446, 447
Chiappelli, F., 555
Chiarello, C., 118
Chiavegatto, S., 85
Chiles, C., 688
Chiriboga, D.A., 470
Chisholm, J.S., 450
Chiu, C., 19
Chiu, C.Y.P., 297
Chizmar, L., 560
Cho, K., 184
Choi, I., 673
Choi, J., 483
Chomsky, N., 11, 16, 23, 323, 324
Choudhry, N.K., 642
Christensen, A., 634
Christoph, R.T., 506
Chronicle, E.P., 329
Chrousos, G.P., 544
Chu, J.A., 291
Chun, M.M., 143
Church, A.T., 522
Church, R.M., 242
Cialdini, R.B., 175, 263, 686, 688, 703
Ciarrochi, J., 550
Cihangir, S., 696
Clancy, S.A., 292
Clark, C., 181
Clark, D., 594
Clark, K., 23
Clark, L.A., 493, 579
Clark, M., 23
Clark, M.C., 303
Clarke, J.C., 250
Clarke-Stewart, A., 313

Cleary, P.D., 559
Clément, R., 321
Clifton, R.K., 445
Clinkenbeard, P.R., 364, 365
Clore, G.L., 675
Clow, A., 106, 544
Coates, D., 430
Coates, T.J., 562
Coe, W.C., 203
Coenen, A., 97
Cohen, A., 475
Cohen, C.E., 667
Cohen, C.I., 652
Cohen, D., 640, 642
Cohen, D.B., 516
Cohen, H.W., 554
Cohen, M.N., 375
Cohen, N., 231
Cohen, N.J., 296
Cohen, S., 546, 555, 556, 557, 559
Coie, J.D., 482
Colburn, H.S., 159
Colby, A., 460
Colder, C.R., 546, 550
Colder, M., 567
Cole, J.O., 640
Cole, M., 362, 450
Coleman, J.C., 547
Coleman, R., 184
Coles, R., 467
Collaer, M.L., 483
Collins, A.M., 281
Collins, C., 562
Collins, F.S., 112
Collins, M.A., 665
Collins, N.L., 677
Collins, W.A., 472, 516
Coltrane, S., 471
Colvin, C.R., 548
Colwill, R.M., 240
Comer, D.R., 694
Compton, W.C., 205
Conger, R.D., 464
Conklin, H.M., 602, 603
Conner, B., 666
Conner, M., 680
Connolly, J., 77
Connolly, J.F., 78
Conrad, S.D., 404
Constantian, C.A., 415
Contandriopoulos, A.P., 651
Conte, J.R., 290
Conway, B.E., 361
Conway, L.C., 20
Cooke, A.D.J., 343
Cooke, D.J., 607
Coons, H.L., 539
Coontz, S., 470
Cooper, E., 384
Cooper, J., 667, 686
Cooper, K.H., 569
Cooper, Z., 550
Cope, M.B., 400
Coplan, J.D., 585
Copper, C., 301, 696
Corballis, M.C., 117
Corballis, P.M., 118
Coren, S., 119, 150, 152, 185, 192
Corey, P.N., 642
Corkin, S., 53, 295
Cornell, D.G., 483, 531
Cornes, C., 647
Cornish, K., 364
Cornoldi, C., 303

Corpus, B., 340
Corsini, R.J., 500
Cosmides, L., 11, 20, 338, 339, 340, 394
Costa, P.T., Jr., 469, 470, 482, 493, 526
Costello, A.M., 441
Coston, M.L., 10
Courage, M.L., 456
Courtright, R.D., 364
Coutts, A., 441
Cowan, N., 269, 270, 279
Cowan, P.A., 248
Cowan, W.M., 112
Cowart, B.J., 164
Cox, B.J., 582, 585
Cox, M.J., 472
Cox, P.D., 632
Coy, K.C., 472
Coyne, J.C., 597
Crabbe, J., 112
Craig, J.C., 166
Craig, K.D., 18
Craig, W., 1, 15, 467
Craik, F.I.M., 18, 93, 94, 268, 269, 270, 271, 272, 283, 287, 302
Craik, K.H., 16
Crain, S., 324
Cramer, P., 546, 547
Crandall, C., 115
Crano, W.D., 680
Craske, M.G., 586
Cravens, H., 367
Crawford, J.D., 99
Crawford, M., 407, 481
Creed, F., 554
Creed, T., 129
Crick, N.R., 482
Crits-Christoph, P., 656
Crockett, H., 416
Croizet, J., 375
Cronbach, L.J., 365
Cropley, A.J., 384
Cross, S.E., 484, 523
Crouter, A.C., 485
Crowder, R.G., 279, 287
Crowell, J.A., 678
Crowley, K., 485
Crowley, M.J., 517
Crummy, L., 491
Cruz, C., 185
Csikszentmihalyi, M., 385, 419, 551
Cuban, L., 381
Culnane, M., 443
Culpepper, L., 641
Cummins, D., 483
Cunningham, C.O., 561
Cunningham, M.R., 679
Curfman, G.D., 642
Curtin, S., 315
Cushman, L., 472
Cushman, P., 648
Cutler, B.L., 305
Cutler, R.L., 129
Cutting, L.P., 604
Czeisler, C.A., 183, 184, 185

D
D'Andrade, R.G., 199
D'Aquili, E., 205
D'Arcy, R.C.N., 78
D'Esposito, M., 101
Dabbs, J., 686
Dalhousie, 12
Dali, S., 172, 523

Dallaire, R.A., 575, 576
Dallman, M.F., 544
Daly, M., 11, 20
Dan, B.A., 317
Daneman, M., 130, 182
Daniel, M.H., 376
Danziger, K., 27
Darley, J., 692
Darwin, C., 5, 19, 20, 113, 114, 115, 356, 426
Das, H.H.J., 362, 683
Das, J.P., 376
Dasen, P.R., 457
David, J.P., 537
Davidoff, J., 325
Davidson, A., 472
Davidson, B., 695
Davidson, J.E., 330, 366
Davidson, M.A., 498
Davidson, R.J., 205, 421
Davies, D.R.T., 192
Davies, I.R.L., 325
Davies, R., 592
Davis, D., 678
Davis, D.M., 485
Davis, H., 205, 237, 238
Davis, J.L., 675
Davis, J.M., 640
Davis, K.E., 670
Davis, M.H., 557
Davis, R., 10
Davis, S., 404
Davis, S.F., 10
Dawod, N., 550
Dawson, G., 84
Dawson, W.A., 199
Day, M.-C., 442
Day, N., 442
Day, R.H., 150
De Beni, R., 303
De Boysson-Bardies, B., 315
De Cock, K.M., 561
De Guise, E., 104, 105
De Houwer, A., 319
De Houwer, J., 130
de Jong, P.J., 585
De Koninck, J., 183, 197, 198
de Villiers, J.G., 318
De Villiers, P., 244
de Villiers, P.A., 318
De Wijk, R.A., 164
de Wit, J.B.F., 683
de Wolff, M.S., 448
Deakin, J.F.W., 85
Deary, I.J., 377, 378
Deaux, K., 481
DeCarvalho, R.J., 508
Deci, E.L., 428
Defeldre, A.C., 285
Defeyter, M.A., 328
Deffenbacher, J.L., 554
DeFrain, J., 470
deJonge, M., 294
Del Monte, M.M., 290
Del Pesce, M., 104
DeLaune, K.A., 559
Delay, J., 638, 644
Deldin, P.J., 601
Delinski, S.S., 614
Delis, D.C., 295, 298
della Rocco, P., 185
DeLong, M.R., 85, 97
DeLongis, A., 537, 557
Delorme, M.-A., 198
Delprato, D.J., 9
Delunas, L., 539
DelVecchio, W.F., 469

Demarest, J., 485
Dement, W., 181, 189
Dement, W.C., 186, 187, 188, 190, 191, 195, 198, 216, 217
Demo, D.H., 472
Dempster, F.N., 301
Denes-Raj, V., 338
Deniker, P., 638, 644
Dennerstein, L., 473
Dennis, W., 475
Denton, K., 668, 669
Derogatis, L.R., 539
Derrick, B.E., 295
Derry, P., 273
Des Jarlais, D.C., 213
Desimone, R., 138
Desjardins, R.N., 314
Detsky, A.S., 642
Detterman, L.T., 363
Deutch, J.A., 396
Deutsch, G., 105, 118, 119, 484
DeValois, R.L., 142
Devescovi, A., 317
Devine, P.G., 667, 698, 699
Devlin, B., 372
Devlin, M.J., 400
Dew, M.A., 617, 647
Dewan, T., 182
Dewees, M., 651
Dewey, J., 5
Dewey, R., 203
Deyoub, P.L., 203
Dhillon, V.P., 150
Di Chara, 212
Di Lorenzo, P.M., 162
Diamond, S.S., 51
Dick, D., 112
Dickens, W.T., 369, 370
Diebel, L., 42
Diener, C., 428, 430
Diener, E., 424, 428, 429, 430, 431, 523, 537
Diener, M., 430, 523
Dieudonne, I., 442
DiGirolamo, G.J., 270
Dijksterhuis, A., 130, 667
Dillbeck, M.C., 205
DiMatteo, M.R., 563, 564
Dimsdale, J.E., 166
Din, J.N., 560
Dinges, D.F., 183, 189, 191, 203, 216
DiNicola, D.D., 564
Dinsmoor, J.A., 10, 247
Dion, K., 18, 665
Dion, K.K., 678
Dion, K.L., 678, 698
Dixon, M., 203
Dixon, R.A., 475
Dobson, K., 594, 649
Dobson, K.S., 625, 626, 631
Dobson, M., 537
Dobzhansky, T., 114
Docherty, N.M., 604
Dodge, K.A., 482
Dodwell, P., 18
Dodwell, P.C., 139
Doerr, P., 411
Doghramji, P.P., 192
Dohrenwend, B.P., 579
Dohrenwend, B.S., 579
Dolan, A., 293
Dolan, M., 85
Dolan-Sewell, R.T., 606
Dollard, J., 546

Domhoff, G.W., 198, 199, 200
Dominguez, J.M., 403
Dominowski, R.L., 328
Domjan, M., 232, 246
Donahoe, J.W., 236
Donderi, D.C., 196, 199
Donn, L., 495
Donnerstein, E., 404
Donovan, P., 595
Donovan, S., 338
Dorfman, D.D., 372
Dorn, L.D., 106, 464
Dorner, G., 411
Doty, R.L., 164
Dougall, A.L., 552
Dougherty, D.D., 92, 639
Dove, H., 446
Dovidio, J.F., 698, 700
Dowling-Guyer, S., 344
Dozois, D.J.A., 625, 626
Draguns, J.G., 521, 612
Draijer, N., 590
Drake, C., 194
Draper, P., 450
Draycott, S., 686
Drazen, J.M., 642
Drewnewski, 702
Driscoll, J., 380
Driskell, J.E., 301
Driver, J., 145
Droungas, A., 250
Druen, P.B., 679
Dryman, A., 227, 582
Dubovsky, A.N., 592
Dubovsky, S.L., 592, 593
Duchamp, M., 171, 172
Duck, S., 674
Duckworth, K., 650, 652
Duckworth, M.P., 587
Dudai, Y., 294, 296
Dudley, E., 473
Duff, K.J., 498
Duff, P., 442
Duffy, V.B., 163
Duggal, S., 290
Dunbar, R., 323
Dunbar-Jacob, J., 564
Duncan, B.L., 699
Duncan, M., 275
Dunkel-Schetter, C., 554
Dunne, M.P., 412
Dunning, D., 699
Dupuis, R., 669
Durlach, N.I., 159
Durrant, R., 394
Dutta, R., 665
Dutton, D.G., 42, 44, 45, 46, 47, 48, 49, 50, 425
Dwyer, 702
Dyck, E., 623
Dyde, R.T., 126
Dykens, E.M., 364

E
Eagle, M.N., 627
Eagly, A.H., 481, 483, 665, 681, 684
Eaker, E.D., 553
Eals, M., 20, 37
Easterlin, B.L., 205
Eastman, R., 90
Eaton, A., 442
Eaton, J., 669, 696
Eaton, W.W., 227, 582
Ebbinghaus, H., 286, 287
Ebel, R., 35

Eber, H.W., 526
Ebert, V., 298
Edberg, P., 528
Edinger, J.D., 194
Edlin, G., 221
Edmunds, C.N., 404
Edwards, H.M., 491
Edwards, K., 684
Edwards, W.T., 165
Efron, R., 118
Egan, J.P., 128
Egan, M.F., 601, 602, 640
Egeland, B., 450
Eggert, A., 33
Ehrenberg, M., 657
Ehrenberg, O., 657
Ehrenreich, H., 214
Eibl-Ebesfeldt, I., 422
Eich, E., 216, 283, 589
Eich, J.E., 283
Eichenbaum, H., 298
Eid, M., 424
Eifert, G.H., 587
Eimas, P.D., 458
Einstein, G.O., 299, 303
Eisen, J.L., 583
Eisenberg, N.H., 493
Eisler, R.M., 469
Eisner, T., 116
Ek, E., 398, 546
Ekman, P., 422, 424
Elbert, T., 101
Elder, G.H., Jr., 464
Eldred, L., 443
Eleonora, G., 585
Elicker, J., 449
Ellinwood, E.H., Jr., 86
Elliot, D., 150
Ellis, A., 546, 566, 631
Ellis, B.J., 394, 464
Ellis, S., 456
Ellsworth, P.C., 419
Elpers, J.R., 651, 652
Emavardhana, T., 205
Emmelkamp, P.M.G., 636, 637, 638
Emmons, R., 538
Endler, N.S., 18, 507, 545, 576, 582, 592, 623, 643
Engemann, K.M., 665
Engle, R.W., 263
Englund, M., 449
Entin, E.E., 416
Epel, E.S., 555
Epley, N., 65, 668
Epling, W.F., 402
Epstein, L.H., 560
Epstein, S., 338
Epstein, S.P., 507
Epstein, W., 129
Erber, M.W., 684
Erdelyi, M.H., 547
Erickson, D.J., 670
Erickson, R.P., 162
Ericsson, K.A., 302, 366
Erikson, E., 23, 451, 452, 453, 456, 467, 468
Eriksson, P.S., 101
Ernst, C., 502
Escher, M.C., 172, 173, 174
Eskes, G., 272
Esposito, M.J., 187
Esser, J.K., 696
Esses, V.M., 417, 663, 664
Esterson, A., 503
Estes, R.E., 10
Estes, W.K., 273
Etaugh, C., 485

Ethier, K.A., 561
Evans, 253, 255
Evans, C.E., 564
Evans, D.E., 447
Evans, F.J., 182
Evans, G.W., 373
Evans, J.T., 404
Evans, R.L., 640
Everly, G.S., Jr., 584
Ewing, L., 391
Eysenck, H.J., 373, 377, 503, 514, 515, 517, 518, 520, 523, 586, 607, 633, 634, 635

F
Fabes, R.A., 461, 482, 484
Fabrigar, L.R., 64, 687
Fagot, B.I., 484, 485
Faircairn, 467
Fairey, P.J., 688
Fakhoury, W., 650
Falls, W.A., 243
Falsetti, S.A., 550
Fanaroff, A.A., 440
Fancher, R., 227, 356
Fancher, R.E., 9
Fanselow, M.S., 246
Faraday, A., 219
Faraday, M.M., 559
Farah, M.J., 101
Faraone, S.V., 601
Faravelli, C., 586
Farrar, M.J., 324
Farre, M., 210, 211
Farrell, M.P., 469
Fausto-Sterling, A., 483
Fazekas, A., 188
Fazio, R.H., 262, 680, 684
Fechner, G., 127, 128
Federoff, I., 401
Feeney, J.A., 449, 677
Fegan, M., 557
Fein, S., 700
Feingold, A., 482, 665, 675
Feist, G.J., 384
Feldman, D.H., 383, 384, 456, 563
Feldman, H., 472
Feldman, J., 291
Felker, B., 544
Fenichel, M., 468
Fennema, E., 482
Fenson, L., 315
Fenster, J.R., 551
Fenton, W.S., 600
Fenwick, P., 205
Ferenczi, S., 8
Ferguson, R., 438
Ferguson, T., 13, 564
Fernald, L., 373
Fernandez, J.R., 400
Ferris, A.L., 429
Ferris, C.D., 84
Ferster, C.S., 242
Festinger, L., 685, 686
Fielder, K., 420
Fields, H.L., 166
Fifer, W.P., 441
Figueredo, A.J., 516
Fiksenbaum, L., 13
Fine, R., 503
Fink, B., 679
Finnegan, L.P., 442
Fischer, K.W., 84, 456, 459
Fischhoff, B., 306, 336, 340, 341, 342, 530
Fishbein, M., 680

Fisher, J.A., 398
Fisher, L.E., 182
Fisher, R.P., 283
Fisher, S., 200, 503, 642, 658
Fisher, T.D., 407
Fisher, W.A., 404
Fishman, D.B., 636
Fisk, J.E., 338
Fiske, S.T., 667, 699, 701
Fite, R., 283
Fitzsimons, G.M., 281
Flanagan, O., 182
Flannery, B.C., 521
Flannery, R.B., Jr., 584
Flapan, A.D., 560
Flavell, J.H., 456, 457, 459
Fleeson, W., 507
Flegal, K.M., 399
Fleischhacker, W.W., 640
Fletcher, G.J.O., 674, 675, 676
Flett, G.L., 594, 658
Flippo, R.F., 34, 35
Flores, B.H., 594
Florio, C.M., 529
Flum, H., 468
Flynn, J.R., 369, 370
Fobes, J.L., 98
Fodor, E.M., 416
Folkman, S., 537, 542, 548, 551
Fong, G.T., 213
Fontaine, K.R., 399
Fontaine, P.A., 625
Foong, N., 270, 297
Ford, D.E., 554
Forget, J., 301
Forsén, T., 441
Forster, K.I., 269
Forsyth, D., 695
Forsyth, D.R., 656, 672, 692
Forth, A., 610
Foschi, N., 104
Foster, R.G., 183, 184
Foulkes, D., 197, 200, 219
Fournet, G.P., 10
Fowler, J.S., 211
Fowles, D.C., 550
Fozard, J.L., 473
Fracasso, M.P., 448
Fraley, R.C., 677, 678
Frances, R.J., 213
Francesco, S., 169
Francis, M.E., 567
Franco, S.E., 550
Frank, E., 647
Frank, J., 656
Frank, J.B., 634
Frank, J.D., 634
Frank, L.K., 269
Frank, L.R., 643
Franken, R.E., 520
Franklin, J.E., Jr., 213
Franks, C.M., 635, 636
Franks, J.J., 289
Frantom, C., 385
Franzen, M.D., 354
Fraser, S.C., 703
Frasure-Smith, N., 554
Frazer, A., 86
Frazier, J.A., 363
Frederick, S., 431
Frederickson, B.L., 419
Fredrikson, M., 585
Freed, D.A., 692
Freedman, J.L., 254, 431, 703

Freeman, W., 639
Freese, J., 503
Freeze, C., 181, 575
Freud, S., 7, 8, 10, 11, 12, 14, 22, 23, 26, 27, 28, 172, 182, 199, 201, 289, 392, 492, 494, 495, 496, 497, 500, 501, 502, 505, 518, 523, 524, 532, 546, 624, 627, 629, 644
Frey, D., 696
Frey, K.S., 484
Freyd, J.J., 291
Fricchione, G., 552
Fridhandler, B., 497
Fried, P.A., 442
Friedberg, J.M., 643
Friedberg, M., 642
Friedkin, N.E., 695
Friedman, H.S., 558, 564
Friedman, M., 552
Friedman, S., 313
Friedman, S.R., 213
Friedrich, J., 682, 683
Friese, I., 670
Friesen, W.V., 422, 424
Frieze, I.H., 665
Frijda, N.H., 422, 423, 425
Frishman, L.J., 134
Fromherz, S., 196
Fromm, E., 204
Frumkes, T.E., 134
Fuchs-Lacelle, S., 66
Fujita, F., 429
Fuller, S.R., 696
Fullerton, C.S., 584
Fullilove, M., 442
Funder, D., 517
Funder, D.C., 507, 548
Funk, W., 643
Fuster, J.M., 101
Fyer, A.J., 584

G
Gabbard, G.O., 503, 655
Gabriel, L.T., 363
Gaertner, S.L., 698, 699, 700
Gaeth, G.J., 327
Gafni, N., 483
Gage, F.H., 101, 594
Gagne, F., 301
Gagnon, J.H., 406
Galaburda, A.M., 484
Galambos, N.L., 485
Galanter, E., 128
Galati, D., 422
Galderisi, S., 600
Galizio, M., 244
Gallagher, J.J., 364
Gallagher, K.I., 569
Gallagher, S.N., 420
Gallie, K.A., 297
Gallistel, C.R., 251
Gallo, L.C., 553, 556
Gallup, G.G., 679
Galton, F., 356, 358, 377, 388
Gambone, J.C., 563
Gangestad, S.W., 520, 521, 675
Gangi, B.K., 654
Gantt, W.H., 227
Ganuza, J.M.G., 37
Garb, H.N., 529
Garcia, B.F., 506
Garcia, J., 250
Garcia, M., 649

Garcia, S.D., 675
Gardner, A., 321
Gardner, B., 321
Gardner, C.O., Jr., 591
Gardner, E.P., 165
Gardner, H., 16, 119, 349, 376, 380, 381, 384
Gardner, R.C., 321, 664, 700
Gardner, W.L., 418
Gardos, P.S., 404
Garfield, S.L., 579, 648, 656
Garland, A.F., 365
Garlow, S.J., 594
Garneau, M., 125
Garner, L., 538
Garnets, L., 411
Garry, M., 291
Garvey, C.R., 4
Gatchel, R.J., 165
Gati, J.S., 139
Gazzaniga, M.S., 16, 102, 103, 105
Ge, X., 464
Gearon, J.S., 602
Geddes, J.R., 603
Gee, T.L., 589
Geiger, M.A., 34
Geller, J.L., 651
Gelman, R., 459
Gelman, S.A., 484
Gemar, M., 595
Genesee, F., 311, 319
Gennari, S.P., 325
Gentner, D., 317, 318
Gepshtein, S., 129
Gergen, K.J., 18
German, T.P., 328
Gershberg, F.B., 296
Gershoff, E.T., 247, 248
Gershon, E.S., 593
Gervai, J., 485
Geschwind, N., 484
Ghez, C., 95
Ghiselin, B., 383
Gibb, R., 101
Gibbons, L.W., 569
Gibson, G.J., 378
Gibson, H.B., 203
Gibson, K.J., 520
Gidycz, C.A., 405
Gigerenzer, G., 339
Gilbert, C.D., 101
Gilbert, D.T., 670, 671
Gilboa, A., 295
Giles, H., 700
Gilgen, A., 237
Gilgen, A.R., 10
Gilhooly, K.J., 330
Gillberg, M., 191
Gillette, 195
Gillett, E., 304
Gillham, J.E., 558
Gilligan, C., 461
Gilovich, T., 30, 668
Ginter, D.R., 184
Girgus, J.S., 150
Gisiner, R., 321
Gitlin, M., 640, 641
Gladue, B.A., 411, 412
Glaser, R., 360, 555
Glass, C.R., 631, 635
Glass, G.V., 656
Glass, R.M., 643, 646
Glassman, A.H., 554
Glassman, W.E., 26
Glatt, A.E., 561
Glatt, S.J., 601

Glazebrook, C.M., 150
Glazier, L., 1
Gleason, J.B., 313, 317
Gleaves, D.H., 293, 590
Gleitman, L., 325
Gleitman, L.R., 324
Glenberg, A.M., 301
Glenn, N.D., 471
Glisky, M.L., 590
Gluck, M.A., 97, 296
Godbey, G., 471
Goddard, H., 375
Godden, D.R., 283
Goeders, N.E., 546, 550
Goff, D.C., 650
Golanty, E., 221
Gold, M.S., 86, 213
Goldberg, I., 597
Goldberg, J.H., 672
Goldberg, M.E., 167
Goldberg, S.C., 640
Golden, C.J., 354
Goldenberg, H., 14
Goldfield, B.A., 317
Goldfried, M.R., 636, 646
Goldin, L.R., 593
Goldman, D.L., 649, 650
Goldman-Rakic, P.S., 101, 121
Goldsmith, H.H., 449
Goldsmith, M., 280, 284
Goldstein, E., 291
Goldstein, E.B., 169
Goldstein, L., 13
Goldstein, W.M., 338, 340
Goleman, D., 381
Gonzales, C.A., 611
Gooch, C., 651
Goodale, M.A., 139, 153, 154, 155
Goodenough, D., 333
Goodenough, D.R., 218, 219
Goodstein, L.D., 528, 529
Goodwin, F.K., 593, 643
Gooley, J.J., 184
Gopnik, A., 121, 324
Gordon, B., 639, 642
Gordon, H.W., 119
Gordon, J., 141
Gordon, L.U., 557
Gordon-Salant, S., 473
Gorman, M.E., 341
Gosden, C., 443
Gosling, S.D., 16
Gotlib, I.H., 595, 597
Gottdiener, J.S., 554
Gottesman, I.I., 109, 110, 112, 601
Gottfredson, L.S., 362
Gottman, J.M., 472
Gould, 470
Gould, E., 101
Gould, R., 469
Gould, R.L., 469
Gould, S.J., 20
Gouras, P., 141
Gourevitch, M.N., 213
Gouzoulis-Mayfrank, E., 214
Gow, K.M., 293
Graber, J.A., 463, 464
Grace, R.C., 233
Graf, P., 297, 299
Graham, J.R., 525
Graham, S.A., 43
Granberg, G., 64
Grant, I., 554

Grantham-McGregor, S., 373
Grasha, A.F., 521
Grasley, C., 48
Gratton, A., 98
Gray, K.F., 473
Graziano, W.G., 20, 493
Green, 552
Green, C., 6, 12
Green, C.D., 4
Green, J.P., 204
Green, S.M., 66
Greenberg, L.S., 630, 636
Greenberg, M.A., 567
Greenberg, R.P., 200, 503, 642, 658
Greene, R.L., 287
Greenfield, D., 54
Greenfield, P.M., 362, 450
Greenglass, E.R., 13
Greenleaf, M., 201
Greeno, C.G., 398
Greeno, J.G., 326
Greenough, W.T., 120
Greenson, R.R., 627
Greenspan, S., 380
Greenstein, T.N., 471
Greenwald, A.G., 130
Gregory, R.J., 59
Gregory, R.L., 147, 150
Greist, J.H., 642
Grencavage, L.M., 634
Gretzky, W., 225, 226, 229
Griffin, D., 695
Griffin, D.W., 676, 680
Griffith, E.E., 611
Grigorenko, E.L., 29, 110, 367, 368, 372, 380
Grinspoon, L., 213
Groat, H.T., 471
Grob, C.S., 214
Grob, G.N., 536, 579
Grohol, J., 639
Grose-Fifer, J., 441
Gross, J.J., 567
Grossman, J.B., 637
Grossman, R.P., 263
Grossman, S.P., 97
Grossmann, K., 450
Grossmann, K.E., 450
Grotevant, H., 472
Groth-Marnat, G., 529
Grove, W.M., 529
Gruber, A.J., 214
Gruen, R.J., 539
Grunberg, N.E., 546, 559
Gruneberg, M.M., 304
Guarnaccia, P.J., 611
Gudeman, J.E., 650
Gudjonsson, G.H., 290
Guenther, K., 289
Guevremont, D.C., 636
Guggenheim, F.G., 587
Guilbault, R.L., 306
Guilford, J.P., 376, 377, 383
Guilleminault, C., 196
Gullikson, H., 37
Gullotta, T., 468
Gunn, D.V., 145
Gunnell, D., 641
Gupta, G.R., 678
Gureje, O., 587
Gurevich, M., 537
Gurm, H., 343
Guthrie, J., 473
Gutierres, S.E., 176
Gutierrez, P.M., 625
Guynn, M.J., 289

Guyton, A.C., 132
Güzeldere, G., 182

H

Haas, L., 471
Hack, M., 440
Hackworth, C., 185
Hadjistavropoulos, T., 66
Hadjiyannakis, K., 597
Hafer, C., 562
Hafer, C.L., 672
Hagan, H., 213
Hagen, E.P., 377, 378
Hager, J.L., 249
Hagerty, M.R., 431
Hagman, M., 12
Haig, J., 493
Haith, M.M., 459
Hakel, M.D., 368
Hakuta, K., 318, 320
Hales, D., 218
Halford, J.C.G., 85, 396, 397
Hall, C., 197
Hall, C.C.I., 18
Hall, C.S., 219
Hall, E., 456
Hall, G.S., 4, 7, 8, 9, 10, 12, 22, 464
Hall, J.A., 482, 564
Hall, W., 213
Hallahan, M., 666
Halligan, S.L., 584
Halmi, K.A., 615, 616
Halpern, D.F., 20, 36, 37, 331, 341, 344, 432, 433, 481, 482, 483, 484
Ham, J.J., 671
Hamida, S., 250
Hamill, R., 73
Hamilton, W.D., 20, 115
Hammen, C., 591
Hammersmith, S.K., 411
Hammond, D.C., 293
Hampson, E., 483, 484
Hampson, P., 303
Hampton, T., 440
Hancock, R.D., 521
Haney, C., 687
Hanisch, K.A., 362
Hankin, B.L., 592
Hankins, W.G., 250
Hanlon, C., 324
Hannigan, J.H., 442
Hansen, M.B., 317
Hanson, D.R., 112
Hanson, F.A., 350
Happonen, P., 560
Hardcastle, V.G., 182
Harding, K., 181
Hare, R.D., 606, 607
Harkins, S., 694
Harman, C., 449
Harmsen, P., 554
Harrington, M.E., 184
Harris, A.H.S., 567
Harris, G.T., 624
Harris, J., 530
Harris, J.E., 298
Harris, J.R., 503, 516
Harris, L., 502
Harris, L.R., 126
Harsch, N., 276
Hart, J.W., 694
Hart, S.D., 606, 607
Harvey, M.H., 293
Harvey, T., 77
Harwood, T.M., 634

Hasher, L., 268, 270, 297
Hashtroudi, S., 285
Haskell, W.L., 569
Haslam, N., 410, 520
Haslam, S.A., 700
Hastie, R., 530
Hastorf, A., 29
Hatch, T., 380
Hatfield, E., 409, 676, 678, 679
Hathaway, S.R., 525
Haug, N.A., 561
Haugland, G., 652
Haugtvedt, C.P., 680
Haupt, E.J., 9
Hauri, P., 91, 187
Hauri, P.J., 194
Hauser, M., 458
Hawkins, R.D., 294
Hawkins, S.A., 530
Haworth-Hoeppner, S., 616
Hayes, C., 321
Hayes, J.R., 383
Hayes, K.J., 321
Hayes, S., 497
Hayes-Roth, B., 301
Hayman-Abello, B.A., 77
Hayman-Abello, S.E., 77
Haynes, R.B., 564
Hays, K.F., 569
Haywood, T.W., 651
Hazan, C., 449, 676, 677, 678, 679
He, J., 570
Healy, A.F., 279
Healy, D., 641, 642
Healy, E., 485
Heap, M., 203
Hearst, E., 233
Heatherton, T.F., 95, 398
Heaton, T.B., 471
Hebb, D., 545, 623
Hebb, D.O., 17, 18, 23, 77, 83, 91, 98
Hegarty, J.D., 600
Heider, F., 669, 670
Heiman, R.J., 688
Heine, S.H., 523
Heine, S.J., 674
Heinrichs, R.W., 598, 599
Heller, W., 90, 117
Hellige, J.B., 118, 119, 483
Helmholtz, H. von, 140, 158
Helms, J.E., 375
Helson, R., 469
Helwig, D., 372
Hemenover, S.H., 567
Hemphill, S.A., 447
Hencke, R.W., 456
Henderson, K.E., 400
Henderson-King, E.I., 700
Hendrick, C., 675, 678
Hendrick, S.S., 675, 678
Hendrickx, H., 130
Henley, S.J., 559
Henley, T.B., 5
Hennessy, D.A., 538
Henriksson, M.M., 52, 53
Henry, K.R., 156
Herbener, E.S., 469, 675
Herek, G.M., 410
Hering, E., 141
Herman, C.P., 397, 401, 402
Herman, J.L., 290
Herman, L.M., 321
Herman, P., 396

Hermann, R.C., 643
Hernandez, D.J., 486
Herrett-Skjellum, J., 700
Herrmann, D., 301, 302
Herrnstein, R.J., 362, 367, 372, 386
Herskovits, M.J., 152
Hertwig, R., 65
Hertzsprung, M., 649
Herzberg, G., 349
Herzog, D.B., 614
Herzog, T.A., 559
Heshka, S., 397
Hessels, S., 288
Heszen-Niejodek, I., 545
Hetherington, E.M., 487, 516
Hetherington, M.M., 397
Hettema, J.M., 584
Hettich, P.I., 31
Hewitt, P.L., 594
Hewstone, M., 700
Heymsfield, S.B., 397
Hiester, M., 450
Higgins, A.J., 678
Higgins, D.A., 482
Higgins, E.T., 43, 333, 666
Highhouse, S., 703
Hilgard, E., 201, 202, 204
Hilgard, E.R., 4, 5, 27, 157
Hilgard, J., 201
Hill, A.J., 400
Hill, C.E., 634
Hill, J.O., 400
Hiller, J.B., 604
Hilliard, A.G., III, 375
Hilton, H.J., 146
Hilton, J.L., 667
Himeline, M.J., 25
Hineline, P.N., 246
Hines, M., 483
Hinsz, V.B., 695
Hinton, G., 84
Hirsh, I.J., 155
Hirshfeld, A.J., 385
Hirt, E.R., 284
Hitch, G., 275
Ho, B., 109, 598, 599
Hoaken, P.N.S., 213
Hobson, C.J., 539
Hobson, J.A., 190, 193, 200, 201, 218
Hocevar, D., 384
Hochberg, J., 146, 148
Hock, E., 472
Hodapp, R.M., 364
Hodge, C.N., 700
Hodges, S.D., 684
Hodgkin, A.L., 79, 80, 90
Hodgson, D., 555
Hoek, H.W., 615
Hofbauer, R.K., 204
Hofer, S.M., 475
Hoff, E., 318, 319
Hoff, T.L., 4, 12
Hoffman, E., 502
Hoffman, R.E., 550, 604
Hoffman, R.R., III, 558
Hoffstein, V., 217
Hofstede, G., 673
Hogan, J., 362
Hogan, M.E., 595
Hogan, R., 362
Hogarth, R.M., 335, 338, 340
Hogg, M.A., 695
Hohne, E., 315
Hokanson, J.E., 546

Holahan, C., 365
Holahan, C.J., 547, 557, 597
Holden, C., 641
Holder, M.D., 321
Holen, A., 584
Hollan, D., 199
Holland, C.C., 691
Holland, J.C., 554
Holland, R., 462
Hollander, E., 583
Hollingworth, L., 5, 22
Hollis, K.L., 233, 251
Hollister, L.E., 213
Hollon, S.D., 631, 634
Holmbeck, G., 634
Holmberg, S., 64
Holmes, D.S., 289
Holmes, J.G., 213, 676
Holmes, T.H., 539, 540
Holowaty, K.A.M., 630
Holschuh, J.L., 33
Holt-Lunstad, J., 557
Holyoak, K.J., 329, 330
Honeycutt, H., 20
Hong, G.K., 649
Honig, W.K., 240
Hooker, E., 189
Hooley, J.M., 604
Hooper, J., 117, 119
Hopkins, B., 442, 446
Hopko, D.R., 361, 549
Hopper, C., 282
Horn, J.L., 372, 376, 475
Horn, J.M., 369
Hornstein, G.A., 9
Horowitz, F.D., 6
Horwath, E., 583
Hossain, J.L., 185
Hosseini, H., 686
Hotopf, M., 588
Houck, P.R., 647
Houts, A.C., 579
Howard, D.J., 703
Howard, G., 559
Howard, I., 125
Howard, I.P., 126
Howard, K.I., 634
Howard, M.S., 678
Howard, R., 600
Howe, M.J.A., 366
Howe, M.L., 456
Howland, R.H., 85, 594
Hrdy, S.B., 409
Hsieh, C., 560
Hsiung, R., 641
Hsu, L.K.G., 614, 658
Hu, F.B., 560
Hu, L., 506
Hu, T.W., 649
Hua, J.Y., 83
Hubbard, J.R., 544, 550, 552
Hubel, D., 11, 16, 23, 120, 137
Hubel, D.H., 98
Hublin, C., 194, 196
Hublin, C.G.M., 193, 195
Hudmon, K.S., 559
Hudson, J.I., 291
Hudson, W., 149
Hudspeth, A.J., 157, 167
Huettel, S.A., 101
Huff, C., 65
Huffcut, A.I., 191
Hughes, C.C., 648
Hughes, H., 583, 587, 608
Hughes, J., 86

Hughes, J.R., 559
Hughes, R.J., 185
Hughes, S.M., 679
Huitt, W., 362
Hull, C., 23, 392
Hull, E.M., 403
Hulme, C., 279
Hulshoff, H.E., 603
Hume, J.G., 4, 12
Hummel, J.E., 146
Humphrey, G.K., 139, 153, 154
Hunt, C., 582
Hunt, E., 329, 344, 381, 442
Hunt, H., 199
Hunt, J.M., 682
Hunt, W.A., 559
Hunter, J.E., 362, 375
Hurvich, L.M., 142
Husain, G., 121, 160, 161
Husband, T.H., 291
Huston, A.C., 254
Huttenlocher, J., 456
Huttenlocher, P.R., 83, 84, 121
Huxley, A.F., 79, 80, 90
Huyser, B., 554
Hyde, J.S., 482
Hyde, T.M., 601, 602, 640
Hyman, I.E., 247
Hyman, I.E., Jr., 291
Hyman, S.E., 112

I

Iacono, W.G., 420, 602, 603
Iams, J.D., 440
Ickovics, J.R., 561
Iezzi, T., 587
Im-Boulter, N., 457
Imber, S.D., 647
Imogen, E., 630
Inati, S., 95
Infante, J.R., 205
Inglehart, R., 429
Ingram, R.E., 597
Innocenti, G.M., 483
Inoff-Germain, G., 483
Iribarren, C., 553
Ironson, G., 554
Irvine, S.H., 362
Irwin, W., 421
Isaacowitz, D.M., 546
Isabella, R.A., 448
Isenberg, K.E., 643
Ismail, B., 603
Ismail, M.A., 443
Isometsa, E.T., 52, 53
Israel, M., 616
Ivens-Tyndal, Co., 550, 592, 596
Iversen, L., 97
Iversen, S., 97
Iwao, S., 678
Iwawaki, S., 362
Izard, C., 426
Izard, C.E., 382, 421, 422

J

Jablensky, A., 598
Jackendoff, R., 323
Jackicic, J., 569
Jacklin, C., 23
Jacklin, C.N., 485
Jackson, D.C., 421
Jackson, D.N., 355, 493
Jackson, L.A., 700

Jackson, M., 467
Jacob, R.G., 638
Jacobs, A., 450
Jacobs, B.L., 594
Jacobs, G.H., 142
Jacobs, H.S., 473
Jacobs, W.J., 296
Jacobson, E., 218
Jacobson, N.S., 634
Jacoby, L.L., 288, 297
Jain, S.P., 684
James, H., 5
James, J.E., 560
James, L., 193
James, T.W., 139
James, W., 4, 5, 6, 7, 10, 19, 20, 22, 182, 183, 424
Jamison, K.R., 385, 593
Jang, K.L., 515
Janig, W., 419
Janis, I., 695
Janis, I.L., 537, 542, 696
Janoff-Bulman, R., 430
Janowsky, J.S., 483
Janssen, R.S., 561
Janus, C.L., 406
Janus, S.S., 406
Jaroff, L., 292
Jasper, H., 92, 137
Jefferson, J.W., 642
Jemmott, J.B., III, 557
Jenkin, H.L., 126
Jenkin, M.R., 126
Jensen, A., 368, 372, 373, 376, 377
Jensen, A.R., 367, 386
Jensen, E., 120
Jensen, M.P., 203
Jessel, T.M., 86, 166
Jessell, 165
Jevning, R., 205
Jex, S.M., 506
Ji, L.-J., 334
Jick, H., 641
Jick, S.S., 641
Jindal, R., 85, 594
John, O.P., 493
Johnson, B.A., 220
Johnson, B.T., 273, 682, 684
Johnson, C., 667
Johnson, D.F., 12
Johnson, J., 457
Johnson, J.S., 320
Johnson, M.E., 344
Johnson, M.K., 272, 284, 285
Johnson, M.L., 444
Johnson, S.B., 563
Johnson, S.M., 630
Johnson, V.E., 413
Johnson-Laird, P.N., 331
Johnston, J.C., 144, 270
Johnston, W.A., 270
Johnstone, L., 643
Joiner, T.E., 597
Joiner, T.E., Jr., 597
Jonah, B.A., 520
Jones, B.C., 679
Jones, B.E., 190
Jones, C.R., 666
Jones, E., 8
Jones, E.E., 670, 671
Jones, F., 539
Jones, S., 303
Jordan, B., 165
Jordan, C., 71
Jorgensen, R.S., 567

Joseph, R., 117
Josse, G., 118
Joyce, B., 78
Judd, C.M., 701
Judge, T.A., 493
Julien, R.M., 207, 210
Jun, S.Y., 343
Jung, C., 8, 9, 11, 12, 492, 494, 500, 501, 502, 515, 532, 629
Jusczyk, P., 315

K

Kaas, J.H., 101
Kaelber, C.T., 580
Kaemingk, K., 442
Kagan, J., 447, 530
Kahan, T.L., 197, 219, 272
Kahane, H., 344
Kahneman, D., 335, 337, 338, 340, 341, 342, 431, 618
Kako, E., 322
Kalaria, R.N., 554
Kalat, J.W., 185, 211
Kales, A., 218
Kales, A.K., 550
Kales, J.D., 218
Kalichman, S.C., 561, 562
Kalidindi, S., 593
Kalin, N.H., 421
Kalmijn, M., 675
Kalmuss, D., 472
Kalton, G., 64
Kalwarf, H.J., 560
Kameda, T., 695
Kamin, L., 372, 373
Kamin, L.J., 375
Kandall, S.R., 442
Kandel, E.R., 78, 80, 82, 84, 87, 97, 136, 165, 294
Kane, J., 564
Kane, T.D., 506
Kanowitz, J., 64
Kao, T., 443
Kaplan, A., 655
Kaplan, A.G., 375
Kaplan, H., 446
Kaplan, H.I., 552, 632
Kaplan, J., 553
Kapp, B.S., 421
Kaprio, J., 464
Kapur, S., 94, 646
Karau, S.J., 694
Kardiner, A., 521
Karon, B.P., 290
Kassel, J.D., 546
Kasser, T., 409, 428, 513
Kassin, S.M., 305
Katigbak, M.S., 522
Katz, A.N., 318
Katz, J., 166, 597
Katz, N.R., 564
Katzman, M.A., 615
Kaufman, A.S., 356, 358, 360, 371
Kaufman, J.C., 362
Kaufman, K., 485
Kaufman, L., 152
Kaufmann, C.A., 593
Kawakami, K., 700
Kay, J., 629
Kay, P., 325
Kay, R.I., 629
Kaye, J.A., 641
Kaye, W.H., 615
Kazdin, A., 248
Kazdin, A.E., 258, 624

Kazmerski, V.A., 318
Keck, P.E., 599, 642
Keefauver, S.P., 196
Keefer, L., 554
Keesey, R.E., 97, 401
Kehoe, E.J., 233
Keinan, G., 549
Keith-Spiegel, P., 655
Keller, L.S., 525, 526
Keller, M.B., 591
Keller, P.A., 683, 686
Kelley, H.H., 29, 30, 670
Kelley, W.M., 95
Kellogg, J.S., 549
Kelly, D.D., 166
Kelly, J., 472
Kelly, J.A., 561
Kelly, J.P., 167
Kelly, K.M., 554
Kelly, P.J., 189
Kelly, S.J., 442
Kelman, H.C., 65, 691
Kelsoe, J.R., 111
Keltner, D., 422
Kendall, P.C., 634
Kendler, H.H., 329
Kendler, K.S., 412, 584, 591, 593, 597, 601
Kennedy, T.E., 294
Kenrick, D.T., 176, 482, 483, 507, 679
Kent, R.N., 64
Kenwood, C., 12
Keren, G., 340
Kernan, J.B., 682
Kerwin, R., 641
Kessen, W., 453
Kessler, R.C., 550, 557, 581, 583, 592, 597, 625, 677
Kester, J.D., 270
Keton, J.L., 361
Ketterer, M.W., 552
Ketterlinus, R.D., 448
Key, C.B., 369
Key, W.B., 129
Khalsa, S.B.S., 183
Khan, M., 272
Khersonsky, D., 675
Khot, U.N., 552
Khoury, J.C., 560
Kidd, K.K., 367
Kiecolt-Glaser, J.K., 555
Kielburger, C., 438
Kiernan, M., 560
Kiesler, C.A., 651
Kiesler, D.J., 576
Kiewra, K.A., 33
Kigar, D.L., 77
Kihlstrom, J.F., 204, 291, 589, 590
Kilbey, M.M., 60
Kilbreath, C.S., 43
Kilhlstrom, J.F., 130
Killeen, P.R., 252
Killiany, R.J., 473, 474
Kilpatrick, D.G., 404
Kim, H., 692
Kim, K., 458
Kim, Y., 665
Kimberg, D.Y., 101
Kimmel, D., 411
Kimmel, M.S., 404
Kimura, D., 13, 18, 106, 118, 483, 484
King, A.C., 217, 560, 569
King, B.H., 364
King, G.R., 86
King, L., 538

King, L.A., 557
King, N.J., 585
Kinman, G., 539
Kinsbourne, M., 182, 298, 484
Kinsey, A., 410
Kippin, T.E., 231
Kirchner, J.T., 561
Kirk, S.A., 578
Kirker, W.S., 272
Kirkpatrick, L.A., 449, 678
Kirmayer, L.J., 649
Kirsch, G., 592
Kirsch, I., 202, 203, 204
Kirschenbaum, D.S., 521
Kitayama, S., 115, 522, 523, 688
Kitchens, A., 118
Kittler, P.G., 163, 397
Klahr, D., 383
Klauer, K.C., 279
Klayman, J., 342
Klein, E., 584
Klein, K., 549
Klein, M., 629
Klein, P.D., 381
Klein, R.M., 17
Klein, W.M., 337, 563
Kleinke, C.L., 422
Kleinknecht, E.E., 291
Kleinmuntz, B., 525, 593
Kleitman, N., 187
Klerman, E.B., 193
Klerman, G.L., 647
Klerman, L.V., 441
Kline, P., 361, 528
Kling, K.C., 482
Klinger, M.R., 130
Klipper, M.Z., 218, 568
Klosch, G., 218
Kluckhohn, C., 521
Kluegel, J.R., 700
Kluft, R.P., 293, 589
Klymenko, V., 138
Knapp, T.J., 538
Knight, G.P., 482
Knowles, J.A., 593
Knowlton, B., 297
Knowlton, B.J., 97
Kobak, R., 450
Koch, J., 313
Kochanska, G., 449
Koegel, P., 652
Koelling, R.A., 250
Koester, J., 80
Koestner, R., 415, 416
Kogan, N., 469
Kohlberg, L., 460, 462
Kohlberg, L.J., 461
Kohler, J.K., 487
Kohler, S.S., 362
Kohn, P.M., 537
Kohut, H., 629
Kolb, B., 18, 84, 101
Kolb, R., 587
Kondo-Ikemura, K., 450
Kop, W.J., 554
Kopinski, K.L., 112
Kopta, S.M., 634
Koren, D., 584
Koriat, A., 271, 280, 284, 301, 306
Korn, J.H., 10, 65
Korn, M.L., 584
Kornhaber, M.L., 381
Kortenhaus, C.M., 485
Kory, R.B., 205
Koss, M., 405

Koss, M.P., 404, 405
Kosslyn, S.M., 118
Kosslyn, K., 365
Kotulak, R., 120
Koukounas, E., 404
Kovelman, I., 319
Kracke, W., 199
Kraft, U., 218
Krajicek, D., 146
Kramer, M., 198
Krames, L., 658
Kransny, L., 637
Krantz, D.H., 340
Krantz, D.S., 554
Krantz, J., 143
Kraus, L.A., 557
Kraus, S.J., 680
Krebs, D.L., 668, 669
Kresner, 101
Kring, A.M., 599
Kris, E., 383
Kroger, J., 468
Krosnick, J.A., 54, 64, 130, 680
Kroyan, T.V., 559
Krueger, J., 671, 700
Krueger, R.F., 606
Krueger, W.C.F., 301
Kruglanski, A.W., 684, 687
Krull, D.S., 670
Kryger, M.H., 195, 217
Krystal, A.D., 194
Kubovy, M., 129
Kuczaj, S.A., 321
Kuhl, P.K., 121, 315
Kuhlman, D.M., 520
Kuhn, J., 597
Kuiken, D., 198
Kuiper, N., 592
Kuiper, N.A., 272, 273
Kukla, A., 670
Kulick, A.R., 599
Kulik, J., 278
Kumar, V.M., 183
Kunda, Z., 699
Kupfer, D.J., 647
Kupfermann, I., 97
Kurland, L.T., 615
Kurzban, R., 20
Kusel, S.J., 204
Kutchins, H., 578
Kutchinsky, B., 404
Kwan, V.S.Y., 430
Ky, K.N., 121, 160
Kyrou, I., 544

L

La Cerra, P., 20
LaBerge, S., 197, 219
LaBine, G., 531
LaBine, S.J., 531
Laborit, H., 644
Lacey, K., 555
Lachman, M.E., 470
Lachter, J., 269
Lader, M.H., 195
Lafreniere, K., 537
Laitinen, J., 398, 546
Lakein, A., 31
Lakin, M., 632
Lalich, J., 654
Lalonde, C., 466
Lalonde, C.E., 459, 465
Lalonde, R.N., 321, 664, 700
Lamb, H., 652
Lamb, M.E., 448, 450
Lamberg, L., 200

Lambert, M.J., 578, 634, 638, 654, 656
Lambert, W., 18, 319
Lambert, W.E., 319, 320, 321
Lambiase, J., 262
Lamm, H., 695
Lamon, S.J., 482
Lampe, A., 554
Lampinen, J.M., 285
Lampl, M., 444
Landabaso, M.A., 637
Landel-Graham, J., 554
Landy, F.J., 362
Lang, P.J., 419
Langdon, P.E., 651
Lange, C., 424
Langeland, W., 590
Langlois, J.H., 665
Langlois, S., 464, 465
Lanphear, B.P., 560
Lanyon, R.I., 528, 529
Lanzi, R.G., 387
LaPierre, R.T., 680, 698
Lapierre, Y.D., 641
Larkin, J.A., 520
Larson, R., 462, 472
Larzelere, R.E., 248
Lash, T.L., 559
Lassiter, G.D., 521
Lassonde, M., 104, 105
Latané, B., 692, 693
Lattal, K.A., 237
Lattimore, P., 401
Latz, S., 189
Laughlin, H., 547
Laumann, E.O., 406, 413, 414
Laurence, J.R., 203
Laursen, B., 472
Lavie, P., 183, 185
Lavine, H., 616
Lawler, J., 318
Lawless, H.T., 163
Lawrie, S.M., 603
Lay, C., 664
Lazarou, J., 642
Lazarus, A., 648
Lazarus, R.S., 537, 542
Le Petit, D., 399
Leacock, S., 438
Leahey, T.H., 7
Leary, M., 414
Leary, M.R., 394, 415
Leavitt, F., 206, 209, 293
LeBoeuf, M., 31
LeBoeuf, R.A., 335, 338
Leck, K., 521
Leckman, J.F., 583
LeDoux, J.E., 97, 296, 418, 421, 425
Lee, I.-M., 560, 561
Lee, R.M., 648
Lee, R.T., 550
Lee, S., 615
Lee, Y.J., 443
Lee, Y.T., 674
Leenaars, A.A., 464
Lefcourt, H.M., 567
Leff, J., 651
Leff, J.P., 603, 604
Lehman, A.C., 366
Lehman, D.R., 19, 397
Lehmann, H.E., 598, 600
Lehrer, P.M., 568
Leibold, J.M., 699
Leibovic, K.N., 134
Leighton, J.P., 328

Leinbach, M.D., 484
Leiter, M.P., 549, 550
Lejeuz, C.W., 587
Lemack, G.E., 550
LeMagnen, J., 396
Lemery, K.S., 447
Lemme, B.H., 470, 476
Lemon, J., 213
Lennie, P., 142
Leo, J., 514
Leon, A.C., 641
Lepore, F., 18
Lerman, H., 503
Lerner, M.J., 672
Lesage, A.D., 651
Lesher, G.W., 145
Leslie, A.M., 459
Lesperance, F., 554
Letiecq, B.L., 487
LeVay, S., 410, 412
Levenson, J.L., 552
Levenson, R.W., 422
Leventhal, E.A., 563
Leventhal, H., 426, 563
Levin, J.R., 304
Levin, M.E., 304
Levine, A., 467
Levine, J.D., 166
Levine, J.M., 688, 694
Levine, M.W., 138
Levine, R., 678
Levine, R.V., 52, 53, 56, 59
Levinson, 470
Levinson, D.F., 601
Levinson, D.J., 469
Levinthal, C.F., 207
Levis, D.J., 246, 585
Levitsky, D.A., 397
Levy, G.D., 484
Levy, J., 102, 119
Lew, R.A., 185
Lewandowsky, S., 275
Lewin, K., 538
Lewinsohn, P.M., 597
Lewis, D.O., 590
Lewis, M., 442
Lewis, S., 554
Lewis-Fernandez, R., 611
Lewontin, R., 369
Ley, P., 564
Li, N.P., 679
Li, W., 700
Libby, P., 552
Liberman, A., 670
Liberman, R.P., 600
Lichtenstein, E., 546
Lichtenstein, S., 306, 336, 341, 342
Lickey, M.E., 639, 642
Licklider, R., 20
Liebergott, J.W., 317
Liebert, L.L., 507
Liebert, R.M., 254, 507
Lilienfeld, S.O., 529, 589, 590
Lilly, T., 700
Lin, D.Y., 30, 668
Lin, S.W., 220
Lindenberger, U., 475
Linders, A., 404
Lindgren, H.C., 34
Lindsay, D.S., 284, 285, 291, 293
Lindsay, P.H., 143
Lindsay, R., 305
Lindsley, O.R., 635
Linford, K.M., 671

Link, B.G., 540
Linnet, K.M., 442
Linton, R., 521
Linz, D., 404
Lippa, R.A., 681
Lipsitt, L.P., 162
Lisanby, S.H., 646
Liss, M.B., 485
Litaker, D.G., 343
Liu, S., 213
Liu, T., 554
Livesley, W.J., 515, 579, 606
Livingstone, K., 639
Lizarraga, M.L.S., 37
Lloyd, M., 25
Locke, B.Z., 580
Lockhart, R., 270
Lockhart, R.S., 94, 271, 286, 287
Locurto, C., 367, 369
Loehlin, J.C., 110, 111, 368, 369, 371, 515, 516
Loewenstein, G., 431
Loewenstein, R.J., 589
Loftus, E.F., 130, 281, 284, 291, 292, 305
Loftus, G.R., 274
Lohman, D.F., 377
Lohr, B.A., 498
LoLordo, V.M., 250
Long, C.N., 395
Longman, D.G., 34
Lonner, W.J., 18, 19, 522
Lopez, D., 510
Lortie-Lussie, M., 198
Lott, B., 373, 414, 485
Low, J., 121
Lowe, M.R., 401
Lowinson, J.H., 207
Lubart, T.I., 384
Lubbers, 595
Luborsky, L., 634, 656
Lucas, A.R., 615
Lucas, J.A., 295, 298
Lucas, R.E., 430, 431
Luchins, A., 328
Luchins, A.S., 329
Ludwig, A.M., 365, 385
Ludwig, D.S., 560
Luecke-Aleksa, D., 485
Luecken, L.J., 678
Luengo, M.A., 520
Luft, A.R., 294
Luft, H.S., 642
Lugaresi, E., 217
Luh, C.W., 287
Lumburner, J., 610
Lundberg, U., 544
Lunman, K., 438
Luntz, B.K., 607
Lupart, J.L., 366
Luscher, K.A., 579
Luskin, F., 567
Luskin, F.M., 205
Luthans, F., 506
Luthe, W., 218
Lutsky, N., 689
Lutz, C., 424
Lutz, D.J., 456
Lutz, W., 344
Lydiard, R.B., 640
Lye, D.N., 471
Lyketsos, C.G., 474
Lykken, D.T., 420, 514
Lyn, H., 322
Lyness, J.M., 473
Lynn, M., 703

Lynn, S.J., 201, 203, 204, 283, 291, 292, 589, 590
Lytton, H., 247, 485
Lyznicki, J.M., 192

M

Maas, J.B., 216, 217
Macarthur, J., 320
Maccoby, E., 23
Maccoby, E.E., 484, 516
MacCoun, R.J., 62, 64
MacDonald, G., 213
MacDonald, K., 517, 531
MacDonald, S.E., 248
MacDonald, T., 213, 562
MacGregor, J.N., 329
Macht, M., 398
Macinnis, D.J., 343
Mack, A.H., 213
Mack, P.B., 101
Mackie, D.M., 682
Maclan, P., 404
Maclean, A.W., 192
MacLean, P., 97
MacMillan, H.L., 290, 590
Macmillan, M., 503
MacQueen, G., 231
Macrae, C.N., 95, 666
Macrae, M., 233
MacWhinney, B., 317, 324
Madden, C.M., 318
Maddi, S.R., 507
Maddrey, A.M., 165
Madon, S., 698
Madsen, K.B., 394
Magloire, K., 557
Magnusson, D., 446, 464, 507
Magritte, R., 174
Maguire, W., 138, 143
Mahapatra, M., 461
Maher, B.A., 599
Maheswaran, D., 684
Mahowald, M.W., 196
Mahsewaran, D., 682
Maier, N.R.F., 328
Main, K.J., 281
Main, M., 13
Main, T., 652
Maio, G., 417
Maio, G.R., 682
Maj, M., 641
Majumder, S., 319
Malamuth, N., 404, 405
Malamuth, N.M., 406
Malcolm, R., 210
Maldonado, J.R., 589
Malenka, R.C., 211, 212
Maletzky, B.M., 637
Malina, R.M., 463
Malla, A.K., 600
Malloy, D.C., 66
Malloy, M.H., 443
Malone, P.S., 670
Maltzman, I., 220
Maluso, D., 485
Mandler, G., 297, 426, 542
Mangelsdorf, S., 448
Manis, M., 528
Mann, J., 561
Mann, J.J., 85, 646
Mann, L., 696
Manson, J.E., 399
Maramba, G., 648
Marangell, L.B., 641
Marcelino, A.S., 397
Marcenes, W.G., 554

Marcia, J.E., 467, 468
Marcus, B.H., 560
Marcus, G.F., 318
Marcus, S.C., 652
Marcus-Newhall, A., 546
Marder, S.R., 640
Marentette, P., 315, 316
Maric, A., 404
Maris, R.W., 464
Mark, V., 119
Markman, E.M., 317
Markman, K.D., 284
Markowitsch, H.J., 296
Markus, H.R., 484, 522, 523, 688, 692
Marmar, C., 636
Marotta, J.J., 99
Marschark, M., 272
Marsh, E.J., 285
Marteau, T.M., 564
Martin, A., 298
Martin, C.L., 484, 485
Martin, J.H., 90
Martin, L., 325
Martin, M., 319
Martin, M.W., 384
Martin, N.G., 412
Martin, P.R., 550
Martin, R., 567
Martin, R.A., 595
Martineau, A.M., 213, 562
Martinez, J.L. Jr., 295
Marzuk, P.M., 641
Maseri, A., 552
Maslach, C., 549, 550
Maslow, A., 11, 14, 23, 524
Maslow, A.H., 511, 512
Massaro, D.W., 274
Masters, R.D., 20
Masters, W.H., 413
Masuda, T., 334
Matarazzo, J.D., 559
Mate-Kole, C.C., 78
Mather, R., 404
Matsumoto, D., 19, 422, 692
Matte, T.D., 441
Matthews, G., 382
Matthey, S., 570
Mattia, J.I., 605
Matute, H., 252
Maudler, 16
Mauro, R., 422
May, C.P., 270, 297
May, M.C., 590
Mayer, J., 396
Mayer, J.D., 381
Mayer, R.E., 326
Mayes, A., 295
Mayman, M., 528
Mays, V.M., 648
Mazumdar, S., 647
Mazur, J.E., 242
Mazzoni, G.A.L., 292
McAdams, D.P., 415, 494
McAllister, D.E., 229
McAllister, W.R., 229
McBride-Chang, C., 485
McCabe, M., 404
McCabe, R.E., 227, 582, 585
McCabe, S.B., 595
McCain, M.N., 444
McCann, C.D., 281, 521
McCann, D., 415, 510, 594
McCarley, R.W., 187, 200, 201
McCarthy, G., 101

McCauley, M.E., 272
McCeney, M.K., 554
McClelland, D.C., 362, 393, 415, 416, 417, 434
McClelland, J.L., 144, 282
McCloskey, M., 276
McClung, N.L., 491
McClure, E.B., 482
McCollough, 567, 568
McConkey, K.M., 203, 283
McConnell, A.R., 699
McConnell, J.V., 129, 294
McCormick, L.L., 651
McCoul, M.D., 520
McCrae, R.R., 469, 470, 482, 493, 522, 526, 567, 606
McCubbin, M., 642
McDaniel, M.A., 299, 302, 303
McDermott, K.B., 292
McDonald, C., 112
McDonald, H.E., 284
McDonald, R.V., 212, 231
McDonald, W.M., 643
McDonald, W.T., 288
McElroy, S.L., 642
McElroy, T., 537
McEwen, 419
McGaugh, J.L., 294, 296
McGeoch, J.A., 288
McGlashan, T.H., 550, 600, 604
McGoldrick, M., 470
McGrath, J.E., 537
McGraw, L.A., 470
McGrew, J.H., 651
McGue, M., 110, 111, 368, 371
McGuffin, P., 593
McGuire, W.J., 680
McHale, S.M., 485
McHugh, P.R., 589
McIntosh, W.D., 665
McKean, K., 338, 340, 342
McKelvie, P., 121
McKenna, J.J., 189
McKenna, K.Y.A., 692
McKenzie, D., 535
McKenzie, K.G., 639
McKinley, J.C., 525
McKusick, V.A., 112
McLean, D.E., 540
McLellan, A.T., 220
McLeod, D., 485
McLoyd, V.C., 373, 487
McMillan, J.H., 672
McMullen, S.-L., 562
McNally, R.J., 291, 584, 586
McNamara, D.S., 279
McNeil, E.B., 129
McNeil, T.F., 603
McNeill, D., 283, 324
McNulty, J.K., 431
McRae, 311
Meade, M.L., 285
Means, M.K., 194
Mebert, C.J., 447
Mechanic, D., 578, 650
Medendorp, W.P., 99
Mednick, M., 384
Mednick, S., 384, 603
Mednick, S.A., 607
Medora, N.P., 678
Medvec, V.H., 668
Medway, F.J., 678
Meegan, D.V., 150
Meeus, W., 468

Mega, M.S., 97
Meichenbaum, D., 631, 632
Meilman, P.W., 468
Meiser, T., 279
Melkman, R., 271
Mellers, B.A., 343
Meltzer, H.Y., 641
Meltzoff, A.N., 121, 315, 324
Melzack, R., 18, 165, 166
Mendel, G., 114
Mendelson, W.B., 190, 195
Menon, R.S., 139
Mennella, J.A., 398
Mentzer, R.L., 35
Menyuk, P., 317
Merali, Z., 536, 537, 544
Merckelbach, H., 585
Meredith, M.A., 136
Merikle, P.M., 130, 182
Mesmer, F.A., 201
Mesquita, B., 422, 423
Messervey, D., 695
Metalsky, G.I., 597
Metalsky, J.I., 595
Metcalfe, B., 528
Metcalfe, J., 283
Metzger, E.D., 643
Meyer, D.E., 281
Meyer, R.E., 220
Meyer, R.G., 201, 283
Meyer-Bahlburg, H.F.L., 412
Mezulis, A.H., 672, 674
Mezzich, J.E., 611
Michaels, S., 406, 411
Mickelson, K.D., 677
Mickleburgh, R., 576
Midgley, B.D., 9
Mignot, E., 195, 196
Mikulincer, M., 449, 677, 678
Milano, P.J., 679
Milgram, S., 23, 689, 690, 691, 692
Millburn, M.A., 404
Miller, A.C., 105, 119
Miller, A.G., 691
Miller, D.T., 672
Miller, G., 23, 276
Miller, G.A., 275
Miller, G.E., 555
Miller, I.J., 163
Miller, J.G., 19, 461
Miller, M.D., 647
Miller, N., 66, 504, 538, 539
Miller, N.E., 246
Miller, P.H., 459
Miller, R.R., 233, 252, 646
Miller, T., 559
Millman, J., 35
Millon, T., 639
Mills, J., 686
Mills, J.S., 402
Milner, A.D., 153, 154
Milner, B., 13, 18, 53, 77, 84, 90, 91, 118, 119, 267, 295, 296
Milner, P., 98
Mineka, S., 250
Minuchin, S., 616
Miranda, J., 588, 649
Mischel, W., 416, 504, 505, 507
Mishkin, N., 155
Mishra, R.C., 333
Mistlberger, R.E., 184
Mitchell, B., 213

Mitchell, D.E., 138
Mitchell, J.E., 614
Mitchell, K.J., 285
Mitka, M., 561
Moak, D.H., 210, 213
Moane, G., 469
Modestin, J., 589
Moffitt, T.E., 469, 607
Moghaddam, F.M., 29, 700
Mojtabai, R., 652
Moldin, S.O., 109
Moldofsky, H., 125
Möller, J., 554
Mollon, J.D., 140
Monahan, J., 578
Monahan, J.L., 130
Monet, C., 169, 170
Mongrain, M., 594, 595
Moniz, A.E., 639
Monk, C.E., 441
Monroe, S.M., 597
Monteith, M.J., 667, 699
Montemayor, R., 468
Moore, B.C.J., 156
Moore, K.L., 440, 442
Moore, S., 176
Moos, R.H., 545, 547, 557
Morecraft, R.J., 97
Moreland, R.L., 694
Moretti, M., 462
Moretti, M.M., 15, 467, 592
Morey, L., 606
Morgan, C.D., 415
Morgan, H., 381
Morgan, M.J., 214
Morgulis, S., 228
Mori, E., 97
Morin, C.M., 195
Morley, J.E., 473
Morokoff, P.J., 406
Moroz, T.M., 94
Morris, A.S., 464
Morris, C.D., 289
Morris, E.K., 6
Morris, J.S., 421
Morris, M.M., 557
Morris, P.E., 303
Morrison, P., 464, 465
Mortensen, M.E., 440
Moruzzi, G., 190
Moscovici, S., 689
Moscovitch, M., 94, 272, 295
Mosher, D.L., 404
Moskowitz, J.T., 542, 548, 551
Moss, M.B., 296
Moss, P., 354
Most, S.B., 143
Motz, M., 271
Mowat, O., 12
Mowrer, O.H., 246, 585
Moynihan, J.A., 555
Mrdjevic, G., 397
Mroczek, D.K., 493
Muir, D., 138
Mullen, B., 667, 696
Mullen, J.L., 33
Mulligan, N.W., 269
Mullin, C.R., 404
Mullins, S., 606
Mulvhill, T., 640
Munck, A., 544
Munk-Jorgensen, P., 651
Munoz, M., 652
Murdock, B., 301
Muris, P., 506
Murison, R., 554

Murnen, S.K., 615
Murphy, E., 491
Murphy, J.M., 385, 579
Murphy, K.C., 112
Murphy, S.T., 130
Murray, C., 362, 367, 371, 372, 386
Murray, H., 394
Murray, H.A., 394, 415, 521, 529
Murray, J.B., 166
Murray, S.L., 675, 676
Murstein, B.I., 625
Murtha, S., 474
Musen, G., 297
Musselman, D.L., 594
Mustard, J.F., 444
Muzio, J.N., 188, 190
Myers, C.E., 97, 296
Myers, C.R., 12
Myers, D.G., 428, 429, 430, 431, 695
Myerson, J., 372
Myrick, H., 210

N

Nadel, L., 296
Nader, R., 188
Nadler, E., 13
Nadon, R., 202
Nagengast, B., 262
Nahas, Z., 93
Naime, J., 88
Nairne, J.S., 275, 279
Nakagawa, N., 318
Nakajima, S., 98
Narasimhan, B., 313
Narrow, W.E., 625
Nash, J., 601, 608
Nash, M., 291
Nash, M.R., 202
Nasrallah, H.A., 640
Neale, M.C., 584, 593
Needlman, R.D., 444
Neely, J.H., 288
Neiss, R., 543
Neisser, U., 16, 276, 370, 375, 386
Nelson, C.A., 120, 121
Nelson, J.B., 234
Nelson, R.J., 85
Nemeroff, C.B., 594
Nemes, I., 404
Nemeth, C., 688
Nemiah, J.C., 588
Nesse, R.M., 543
Nestler, E.J., 211, 212
Netter, T.W., 561
Neugebauer, R., 579
Neuschatz, J., 283
Neuschatz, J.S., 285
Newberg, A., 205
Newby, D.E., 560
Newcombe, N., 456
Newell, A., 16, 329
Newman, D.L., 520
Newman, L.S., 498
Newport, E., 324
Newport, E.L., 320, 324, 458
Newsom, J.T., 686
Newton, P.M., 469
Nezworski, M.T., 529
Niaura, R., 553
Nickerson, R.S., 341, 383
Nicoladis, E., 319
Nicolaides, K., 443
Nicolson, N.A., 541

Nida, S.A., 692
Niebyl, J.R., 440, 442
Nielsen, T.A., 187, 196, 198
Nikelly, A.G., 220
Nikles, C.D., 219
Nisbett, R.E., 36, 72, 73, 334, 371, 671, 673, 700
Nishino, S., 195
Nist, S.L., 33
Noddings, N., 485
Nolan, C., 37
Nolen-Hoeksema, S., 592, 594, 595
Norcross, J.C., 634, 646, 656
Norenzayan, A., 52, 53, 56, 59, 673
Norman, D.A., 143, 273
Norman, R.L., 206
Norman, R.M.G., 600
Norris, F.H., 584
North, C., 46
Norton, G.R., 582
Norwood, A.E., 584
Nourse, C.B., 443
Novick, L.R., 331
Noyes, R., Jr., 584, 588
Nucci, L.P., 461
Nunes, J., 402
Nurnberger, J.I., 261
Nurse, R.J., 163
Nyberg, S.E., 31

O

O'Boyle, C., 484
O'Brien, B., 642
O'Brien, J.T., 554
O'Connor, T.G., 450
O'Donohue, W., 258
O'Donovan, M.C., 601
O'Fallon, W.M., 615
O'Hanlon, J.F., 213
O'Hara, L.A., 385
O'Leary, K.D., 64
O'Leary, S.G., 248
O'Malley, M., 467
Oakes, M.E., 397
Oakes, P., 700
Oakley, G.P., Jr., 440
Ochse, R., 384
Ochsner, K.N., 297
Oden, M.H., 365
Odgers, C., 15, 467
Ogilvie, R.D., 216
Ogles, B.M., 578, 634, 654
Ogloff, J.R.P., 305, 610
Ohayon, M.M., 189
Ohman, A., 418
Okagaki, L., 370
Okami, P., 409
Okifuji, A., 165
Olds, J., 11, 16, 98
Olds, M.E., 98
Oleson, K.C., 699
Olfson, M., 625, 626, 641
Olio, K., 293
Oliver, M.B., 482
Ollendick, T.H., 585
Oller, K., 319
Olson, D.H., 470
Olson, E.A., 305
Olson, J.E., 665
Olson, J.M., 667, 686
Olson, M.A., 262, 680, 684
Oman, C., 125
Operario, D., 667
Orbuch, T.L., 471
Organista, P.B., 588

Orlando, V.P., 33
Orme-Johnson, D.W., 205
Ormerod, T.C., 329
Orne, M.T., 203, 691
Ornstein, R., 118
Ornstein, R.E., 117, 118, 182
Orth-Gomer, K., 554
Ortmann, A., 65
Orwoll, E.S., 483
Osei, S.Y., 396
Oskamp, S., 485, 685
Osrin, D., 441
Ostendorf, F., 548
Ostir, G.V., 542
Ostovich, J.M., 397
Ostrom, T.M., 700
Ostrove, J.M., 469
Oswald, I., 194
Oswald, L.M., 93
Ott, P.J., 442
Otto, M.W., 583
Oviatt, S.K., 483
Owen, M.J., 601
Owyang, M.T., 665
Ozer, D.J., 493
Ozgen, E., 325

P

Pace-Schott, E.F., 187, 200
Packer, D.J., 511
Padavic, I., 471
Padgett, D.A., 554
Pagel, J.F., 197
Paivio, A., 272, 303
Paivio, A.U., 18
Paivio, S.C., 630
Palladino, J.J., 216
Pallanti, S., 586
Palmer, J.C., 284
Palmer, S.E., 145
Palmere, M., 271, 272
Panksepp, J., 425
Pansky, A., 280, 284
Papafragou, 325
Papo, I., 104
Paquette, A., 442
Paquette, Y., 187
Paradis, J., 319
Paradiso, S.P., 97
Parent, E.C., 520
Park, B., 701
Park, C.L., 551
Park, C.W., 343
Parke, R.D., 248
Parker, J.C., 554
Parker, J.D.A., 381, 545
Parlby, I., 491
Paronis, C.A., 546
Parrot, A.C., 214
Parry-Jones, B., 615
Parry-Jones, W.L., 615
Parsons, B., 484
Partinen, M., 194, 196
Partinen, M.M., 193, 195
Pascual-Leone, J., 457
Pashler, H., 270, 273
Patel, J.K., 601
Pato, M.T., 583
Patrick, C.J., 420
Patrick, H., 163
Patriquin, M., 663
Patterson, D.R., 202, 203
Patterson, R.L., 98
Patton, G., 614
Pauk, W., 35

Paulhus, D.L., 497, 503, 523, 528
Paulos, J.A., 570
Paunonen, S.V., 355, 493, 494, 522
Pavlov, I., 7, 9, 10, 11, 22, 227, 228, 234, 237, 256
Payne, D.G., 278, 285, 301
Payne, J.W., 336
Pazder, L., 590
Peacock, E.J., 537
Pearlstone, Z., 282
Pearson, B.Z., 319
Pearson, C., 205
Pearson, S.E., 404
Pedersen, N.L., 368
Pedersen, P., 649
Pedersen, P.B., 700
Peele, S., 220
Peers, D., 391
Peirce, R.S., 557
Peladeau, N., 301
Pelham, W.H., 638
Peng, K., 334
Pennebaker, J.W., 556, 563, 567
Penrod, S., 404
Penrod, S.D., 305
Penton-Voak, I., 679
Penfield, W., 77, 90, 91, 137, 276, 294, 320, 623
Penfield, W.W., 92
Peplau, L.A., 406, 414
Pepler, D., 1, 15
Pepler, D.J., 467
Perel, J.F., 647
Perera, T., 9
Peretz, I., 160
Perlman, M.D., 371
Perone, M., 244
Perot, P., 276, 294
Perreault, S., 700
Perry, C., 202
Perry, D.G., 204
Perry, L.C., 204
Perry, W., 602
Persad, E., 623
Persaud, T.V.N., 440, 442
Person, E.S., 503
Pert, C.B., 86
Perugini, E.M., 204
Pervin, L., 469
Peterhans, E., 145
Peters, J.C., 400
Petersen, A.C., 467
Peterson, C., 558
Peterson, L.R., 275
Peterson, M.J., 275
Peterson, T.R., 422
Petitt, D.A.D., 213
Petitto, L.A., 315, 316, 317, 319, 322
Petrie, K.J., 563, 567
Petrill, S.A., 368, 370
Pettigrew, T.F., 280
Petty, R., 686
Petty, R.E., 680, 682, 684, 687
Pevere, G., 575
Pezdek, K., 589
Pfau, M., 263
Pfaus, J.G., 231
Pfefferbaum, B., 584
Phares, V., 487
Phillips, A., 18
Phillips, K., 20, 37, 483
Phillips, K.A., 583
Phillips, L., 306, 342

Phillips, W.T., 560, 569
Phillips-Grant, K., 293
Pi, E.H., 640, 641
Pi-Sunyer, F.X., 399
Piaget, J., 10, 11, 16, 324, 453, 454, 455, 456, 460, 461, 462
Picasso, P., 170, 171
Pickering, T.G., 554
Pickles, J.O., 157
Pierce, C.M., 648
Pierce, W.D., 402
Pihl, R.O., 199, 213, 546
Pike, A., 516
Pike, K.M., 616
Pilcher, J.J., 184, 191, 192
Pillard, R.C., 412
Pilling, M., 325
Pillow, D.R., 537
Pinals, D.A., 601
Pinard, A., 18
Pincus, H.A., 626
Pine, D.S., 583
Pinel, J.P.J., 397, 399, 401
Pines, A.M., 549, 678
Pinker, S., 323, 324
Pinto, B.M., 560
Piomelli, D., 211
Piper, W., 632
Pitre, U., 269
Plant, E.A., 698
Plante, T.G., 560, 569
Platiel, R., 372
Plomin, R., 29, 109, 112, 367, 368, 516
Plotkin, H., 20
Plucker, J.A., 383, 384
Plutchik, R., 426, 427
Pohl, R.F., 344
Poland, R.E., 214
Policastro, E., 384
Polivy, J., 396, 397, 401, 402
Pollack, R.H., 404
Pollatsek, A., 340
Polley, B.A., 400
Pollock, B.G., 647
Pols, H., 12, 13
Polson, P.G., 302
Pomerantz, E.M., 507
Pomeranz, B.H., 642
Pomeroy, C., 614
Ponterotto, J.G., 700
Pooley, E., 582
Pope, H.G., 214, 590, 599, 642
Pope, H.G., Jr., 291
Pope, K.S., 293, 655
Popenoe, D., 486, 487
Popp, D., 407
Poppas, D.P., 550
Popper, C.W., 363, 364
Porter, S., 283
Posada, G., 450
Posner, M.I., 17, 84, 270
Post, F., 385
Postman, L., 286
Postmes, T., 696
Potkay, C.R., 513
Potthoff, J.G., 597
Poulton, E.C., 341
Pourdehnad, M., 205
Powell, B., 503
Powell, J.H., 214
Powell, R.A., 248, 589
Powley, T.L., 97
Pozzulo, J., 610, 611
Pratkanis, A., 681

Premack, D., 323
Prentky, R., 385
Prentky, R.A., 403
Prescott, C.A., 597
Price, D., 165
Priebe, S., 650
Priester, J.R., 680, 682
Prifitera, A., 357
Priluck, R.L., 230, 262, 684
Prince, G., 118
Pringle, H., 349
Prochaska, J.O., 559
Prodromidis, M., 450
Proffitt, D.R., 148
Pronin, E., 30, 668
Provencal, A., 689
Provine, R.R., 217
Prudic, J., 643
Pruitt, D.G., 695
Pucetti, R., 117
Puente, A.E., 375
Pulice, R.T., 651
Pullum, G.K., 325
Pusch, D., 594
Pyke, S., 13
Pylyshyn, Z., 18
Pyryt, M., 365
Pyryt, M.C., 366

Q

Quattrini, A., 104
Quina, K., 19
Quinn, D.M., 375
Quinn, L., 615
Quinn, P.C., 458
Quitkin, F.M., 63

R

Rabins, P.V., 474
Rabkin, J.G., 403
Rabkin, R., 403
Rachman, S.J., 258, 585
Racine, R.J., 294
Ragland, D.R., 553
Ragsdale, K., 469
Rahe, R., 540
Rahe, R.H., 539
Rahman, M.A., 559
Raichle, M.E., 93
Raine, A., 607
Rains, G.D., 101
Raj, A., 639
Rajaram, S., 73, 284
Rakic, P., 121
Ramadan, N.M., 554
Ramaekers, J.G., 213
Ramey, C.T., 363, 387
Ramey, S.L., 363, 387
Ramirez, M., 648
Ramsay, D.S., 397
Randall, M., 552
Randolfi, E., 540
Rapee, R.M., 585
Raphael, B., 537
Rapson, R.L., 676, 678
Rasmussen, C., 538
Rasmussen, T., 118, 119
Ratner, M.S., 462
Ratner, N.B., 313, 317
Ratterman, M.J., 317
Rauch, S.L., 93
Rauscher, F.H., 121, 160
Ravnkilde, B., 594
Rawson, N.E., 164
Rayner, B., 41
Raynor, J.O., 416
Read, C.R., 485
Read, J.D., 129, 291, 293

Real, L., 338
Reber, R., 341
Recht, L.D., 185
Rechtschaffen, A., 186
Rector, N.A., 595, 598
Reddy, B.S., 560
Reder, L.M., 284, 285
Ree, M.J., 362
Reed, J.G., 69
Reed, L., 670
Reed, S.K., 330
Reedy, F.E., Jr., 163
Rees, C.J., 528
Reeve, C.L., 368
Reeve, H.K., 20
Regan, D., 18
Regan, P.C., 675
Regier, D.A., 580, 581, 617
Rehm, L.P., 550, 592, 596
Reibel, D.K., 63, 205
Reich, P., 552
Reichert, T., 262
Reilly, R., 226, 229
Rein, A.S., 592
Reinharz, D., 651
Reise, S.P., 493
Reisner, A.D., 289, 290
Reiss, D., 516
Reiss, S., 584
Reiter, R.C., 563
Reitzel-Jaffe, D., 48
Rennie, D., 642
Renshaw, K., 674
Renzulli, J., 365
Renzulli, J.S., 366, 383, 384
Repetto, M., 86, 213
Rescorla, R.A., 235, 246, 251, 252
Resnick, J.S., 317
Rest, J.R., 461
Reuter-Lorenz, P.A., 105, 119
Revelle, W., 513
Reynolds, A.G., 320, 387
Reynolds, C.F., 194
Reynolds, C.F., III, 647
Reynolds, C.R., 353, 375
Reynolds, K.J., 700
Reznik, J.S., 447
Rhodes, N., 680
Rholes, W.S., 666
Riazi, A., 554
Riba, M.B., 646
Ricci-Bitti, P.E., 422
Rice, L.N., 630
Rice, M., 624
Rich, J.B., 474, 475
Rich-Edwards, J.W., 441
Richard, R., 225
Richardson, C.R., 569
Richardson, F.C., 542
Richardson, G.S., 183
Richert, E.S., 365
Richter, L., 558
Ridderinkhof, K.R., 475
Ridker, P.M., 552, 553
Rieber, R.W., 8, 9
Rieder, R.O., 593
Riemann, R., 516
Rihmer, Z., 641
Riis, J., 429
Riley, I.J., 165
Rilling, M., 294
Rimal, R.N., 506
Ritter, R.C., 396
Rivas-Vazquez, R.A., 641
Roazen, P., 467
Roback, H.B., 632

Robbe, H.W.J., 213
Robbins, S.J., 243
Roberson, D., 325
Roberts, B.W., 362, 469, 493, 507
Roberts, P., 469
Roberts, R.D., 382
Roberts, W.A., 267
Robins, L.N., 580
Robins, R.W., 16
Robinson, A., 364, 365
Robinson, F.P., 33
Robinson, J.P., 471
Robinson, L.A., 597
Robinson, T.E., 98, 101
Rock, I., 145, 152
Rodgers, J.E., 305
Rodin, J., 396, 397, 398, 615, 616
Roedeger, H.L., III, 73, 273, 282, 284, 285, 289, 292, 297
Roehrs, T., 192, 194, 195
Roesch, R., 610
Roese, N.J., 667, 686
Roffwarg, H.P., 188, 190
Rogers, 214
Rogers, C., 10, 11, 12, 14, 23, 28, 492, 508, 509, 510, 511, 512, 518, 523, 524, 629, 630, 644
Rogers, M.P., 552
Rogers, N.L., 191
Rogers, T.B., 272, 273
Rogers, T.T., 282
Rogers, W.T., 34
Rogler, L.H., 611
Rogoff, B., 457
Rogol, A., 464
Rohde, P., 597
Rohner, R.P., 487
Roivainen, M., 552
Rojahn, K., 280
Rollins, B.C., 472
Rollman, G.B., 165, 166
Rolls, B.J., 397
Rolls, E.T., 138, 425
Romano, S.J., 615
Romney, D.M., 485
Ronald, A., 561
Roney, C.J.R., 417
Roozendaal, B., 294
Rosch, E.H., 325
Rosch, P.J., 544
Rose, A.J., 482
Rose, D., 646
Rose, D.P., 560
Rose, D.T., 595
Rose, H., 20
Rose, R., 112
Rose, S.D., 632
Rose, S.E., 20
Rose, S.P.R., 294
Rosenbaum, M., 632
Rosenbaum, R.M., 670
Rosenberg, H.J., 469
Rosenberg, P.S., 561
Rosenberg, S.D., 469
Rosenfarb, I.S., 604
Rosenhan, D., 578
Rosenheck, R., 652
Rosenman, R., 552
Rosenthal, R., 64, 666
Rosenzweig, M.R., 101, 120, 121, 294, 295
Rosenzweig, S., 9
Rosler, F., 90
Rosman, B.L., 616

Ross, C.A., 589
Ross, D., 254
Ross, L., 30, 668
Ross, L.D., 342, 689
Ross, M., 672
Ross, S.A., 254
Rosse, J.G., 528
Rossi, P.H., 652
Rosso, I.M., 603
Roter, D.L., 564
Roth, D., 397
Roth, T., 194, 195
Rothbart, M.K., 17, 84, 446, 447
Rothbaum, F., 450
Rothenberg, A., 385
Rothschild, A.J., 594
Rotter, J., 505
Rouiller, E.M., 157
Rourke, B.P., 18, 77
Rowe, D., 515, 516
Rowland, G.L., 520
Roy, C., 42
Rozanski, A., 553
Rozee, P.D., 404
Rozin, P., 163, 398
Rubin, D.C., 276, 278
Ruble, D.N., 484, 485
Ruble, T.L., 485
Rudestam, K.E., 637
Rudnicki, S.R., 554
Rudorfer, M.V., 643
Ruiperez, M.A., 611
Ruiz, P., 637
Rumelhart, D.E., 282
Rundus, D., 302
Rusak, B., 184
Rusbult, C.E., 675
Ruscio, J., 73
Rush, A.J., 631, 632, 641
Rushton, J.P., 367, 372, 382
Rusiniak, K.W., 250
Russell, G.F.M., 614, 615
Russell, J., 423, 665
Russell, J.A., 422
Russell, K., 118
Rutherford, A., 9, 10
Rutherford, W., 158
Ruthruff, E., 269, 270
Ruthsatz, J.M., 363
Rutledge, T., 557
Rutledge, T.R., 422
Rutter, M., 112, 364, 450
Rutter, M.L., 112
Ryan, C.S., 701
Ryan, R.M., 428

S

Sachs, J., 315
Sackeim, H.A., 643
Sadker, D., 485
Sadker, M., 485
Sadock, B.J., 632
Sadowsky, B., 184
Safdar, S., 664
Saffran, J.R., 324
Sagi, A., 450
Sais, E., 319
Saklofske, D.H., 352
Salkovskis, P.M., 582, 588
Sallot, J., 214
Salminen, S., 672
Salonen, J.T., 560
Salovey, P., 381
Salthouse, T.A., 475
Salvendy, J.T., 633
Samelson, F., 7
Samet, J.M., 559

Sammons, M.T., 625
Sanbonmatsu, D.M., 674
Sande, M.A., 561
Sanderson, W.C., 582
Sandin, B., 586
Sandler, I., 537
Sanger, 195
Sanislow, C.A., 600
Sankis, L.M., 578
Sanna, L.J., 699
Sanson, A., 447
Santanna, J., 205
Santerre, C., 205
Sanz, J., 652
Saper, C.B., 97, 184
Sarason, B.G., 592
Sarason, I.G., 592
Sato, K., 422
Sato, T., 415, 510, 594
Sattler, J.M., 377, 378
Saucier, S., 198
Savage-Rumbaugh, E.S., 322
Savage-Rumbaugh, S., 322, 346
Savard, J., 195
Savitsky, K., 668
Sawicki, R.F., 354
Saxe, L., 420
Saxton, M., 324
Saxton, P.M., 421
Scarr, S., 367, 369, 370, 387
Schab, F.R., 164
Schaberg, L., 699
Schachner, D.A., 677, 678
Schachter, D.L., 293, 297
Schachter, S., 44, 46, 397, 425, 426
Schacter, D.L., 278, 305
Schaefer, J.A., 545
Schaeffer, N.C., 64
Schafe, G.E., 398
Schaie, K.W., 474
Schaller, M., 19, 20
Scheflin, A.W., 293
Scheidlinger, S., 632
Scheier, M.F., 545, 558
Schellenberg, E.G., 121, 160, 161
Scherer, K.R., 419, 422, 423
Scherer, M., 567
Schiavi, R.C., 403
Schiefelbein, V.L., 106, 464
Schiff, M., 369
Schiffman, J., 603
Schiffman, S.S., 398
Schildkraut, J.J., 385
Schlegel, A., 462
Schlenger, W.E., 550
Schlenk, E., 564
Schmid, J., 420
Schmidt, F.L., 362, 375
Schmitt, D.P., 406, 409, 678
Schmitz, J.M., 559
Schmolck, H., 276, 278
Schmuckler, M.A., 160
Schneewind, K.A., 506
Schneider, B.H., 449
Schneider, F., 601
Schoenfeld, G.A., 506
Scholey, A.B., 214
Schonemann, P.H., 368
Schooler, J.W., 283, 291
Schramke, C.J., 554
Schreiber, F.R., 590
Schubert, D.S.P., 485
Schubert, H.J.P., 485
Schuller, R.A., 305, 610
Schultz, J.H., 218

Schultz, M.C., 317
Schulz-Hardt, S., 696
Schuman, H., 64
Schumann, J., 320
Schusterman, R.J., 321
Schvaneveldt, R.W., 281
Schwartz, A., 343
Schwartz, B., 243
Schwartz, B.L., 283
Schwartz, D.G., 219
Schwartz, G.E.R., 205
Schwartz, J.H., 79, 294
Schwartz, J.P., 678
Schwartz, L., 588
Schwartz, L.M., 559
Schwartz, M.W., 396, 397, 400
Schwartz, N., 431
Schwartz, S.H., 692
Schwartz, W.J., 185
Schwarz, N., 64, 684
Scoboria, A., 203
Scott, K., 48
Scott, T.R., 163
Scott, W., 597
Scoville, W.B., 91, 295
Scroppo, J.C., 590
Scully, J.A., 539
Scweitzer, P.K., 195
Sealy, P., 651
Searle, A., 554
Searleman, A., 299, 301
Sears, D.O., 63, 685
Sears, R., 365
Sedikides, C., 672, 675, 700
Seeley, R.J., 396, 400
Seeman, 419
Segal, Z., 595
Segall, M.H., 18, 152, 153
Segerstrom, S.C., 555, 558
Seguin, J.R., 615
Seidenberg, M.S., 322
Seidlitz, L., 537
Seifer, R., 373, 448
Seitz, V., 360
Sejnowkski, T.J., 84
Selesnick, S.T., 639
Self, D.W., 212
Seligman, M.E.P., 249, 250, 419, 428, 429, 545, 546, 551, 558, 585, 595, 634, 656, 674
Seltzer, B., 473
Selwyn, P.A., 561
Selye, H., 23, 88, 535, 543, 544, 566
Semendeferi, K., 97
Semmer, N.K., 537
Servan-Schreiber, D., 587
Seta, C.E., 537
Seta, J.J., 537
Seto, M.C., 404
Seudfeld, P., 125
Seurat, G., 170, 171, 173
Sever, L.E., 440
Seymour, A., 404
Shackelford, T.K., 409
Shafer, G., 337
Shaffer, D.R., 677
Shafir, E., 335, 336, 338
Shafto, M.A., 283
Shakesby, P.S., 302
Shalev, A.Y., 584
Shallenberger, W.R., III, 34
Shank, R.P., 86
Shanker, S.G., 322
Shankster, L.J., 362
Shanteau, J., 327

Shapiro, A.F., 472
Shapiro, C.M., 185
Shapiro, D.H., Jr., 63, 205
Shapiro, L., 325
Shapiro, P.A., 554
Shapiro, S.L., 205
Sharma, Y.S., 409
Sharp, L.K., 567
Sharpe, D., 66
Sharps, M.J., 146
Shatz, C.J., 121
Shaver, P., 676, 677, 679
Shaver, P.R., 449, 677, 678
Shavitt, S., 667, 682
Shaw, G.L., 121, 160
Shaw, J.C., 16
Shea, M.T., 606
Shear, J., 205
Shear, M.K., 637
Shearer, B., 381
Shedler, J., 528, 606
Sheehan, D., 639
Sheehan, P.W., 283
Sheehan, S., 598
Sheiham, A., 554
Sheldon, K.M., 513
Shepard, R.N., 151, 153
Shepperd, J.A., 431, 694
Sher, L., 85
Sheridan, J.F., 554
Sherman, D.A., 699
Sherman, M., 369
Sherman, M.F., 385
Sherman, P.W., 115
Sherman, S.J., 699
Shermer, M., 143, 703
Sherry, D.F., 251
Shettleworth, S.J., 251, 338
Shields, J., 584
Shiffrin, R.M., 273, 274
Shike, M., 560
Shimamura, A.P., 99, 101, 296
Shimp, T.A., 263
Shinskey, J.L., 459
Shoda, Y., 507
Shors, T.J., 549
Shulman, R.B., 641
Shurkin, J.N., 654
Shweder, R.A., 461
Siebert, A., 31, 35
Siegel, J.M., 190, 387
Siegel, S., 212, 231
Siegelbaum, S.A., 80, 82, 84
Siegle, G., 597
Siegler, R.S., 314, 356, 365, 456
Signorielli, N., 485
Silberg, J., 112
Silberman, E.K., 627, 639
Silberstein, L.R., 615
Silk, K.R., 625
Silver, E., 619
Silver, J.M., 641
Silverman, I., 20, 37, 483
Silverman, J.J., 554
Silverman, M.M., 464
Silverstein, L.B., 486
Simard, V., 198
Sime, W.E., 542
Simeon, D., 583
Simmons, H.G., 639
Simon, H., 11, 23, 329, 346
Simon, H.A., 16, 275, 330, 335, 383
Simon, T., 356, 453
Simonoff, E., 364
Simons, D.K., 143

Simons, G., 398
Simonton, D.K., 366, 384, 385, 475
Simpson, G.M., 640, 641
Simpson, J., 521
Simpson, J.A., 450, 675, 676
Simpson, J.L., 439, 440
Sinclair, D., 165
Sinclair, R.C., 426
Singelis, T.M., 430
Singer, J.E., 425
Singer, L.T., 442
Singer, M.T., 654
Sinha, D., 362
Skeels, H.M., 369
Skene, D.J., 184, 185
Skerrett, P.J., 399
Skilling, T.A., 607
Skinner, B.F., 6, 8, 9, 10, 11, 12, 14, 23, 28, 32, 236, 237, 238, 242, 256, 290, 323, 346, 393, 492, 503, 504, 505, 508, 518, 523, 524, 635
Skodak, M., 369
Skolnick, P., 86, 585
Slamecka, N.J., 286, 288
Slater, E., 584
Slater, M.A., 588
Slaughter, M., 135
Slavney, P.R., 588
Slobin, D.I., 324
Slotterback, C.S., 397
Slovic, P., 335, 336, 341, 530
Slutske, W.S., 526
Small, B.J., 475
Smart, D., 447
Smart, A., 415
Smeaton, G., 675
Smedley, S.R., 116
Smilkstein, G., 536
Smith, A.L., 581
Smith, A.M., 442
Smith, A.P., 555, 556
Smith, B.W., 554
Smith, C., 188, 193, 198, 416
Smith, C.A., 542
Smith, D., 416
Smith, D.A., 646
Smith, E.E., 296, 684
Smith, E.F., 157
Smith, E.R., 672
Smith, F.J., 396
Smith, G.N., 93
Smith, J., 457
Smith, J.C., 205
Smith, M., 590
Smith, M.F., 682
Smith, M.L., 656
Smith, M.T., 195
Smith, N.A., 160
Smith, P.B., 674, 692, 694
Smith, R.E., 423
Smith, S., 283
Smith, S.J., 83
Smith, S.M., 328, 665, 680
Smith, T.W., 471, 553, 556
Smith, W.P., 205
Smith-McLallen, A., 682
Smith-Swintosky, V.L., 86
Smolak, L., 614, 615
Smolensky, P., 282
Smyth, J., 568
Smyth, J.M., 567
Smythe, P.E., 272

Snidman, N., 447
Snow, C., 324
Snow, C.E., 318
Snow, R.E., 383
Snowden, L.R., 649
Snyder, A., 119
Snyder, E., 412
Snyder, M., 520
Snyder, S.H., 84, 86
So, K.T., 205
Sobal, J., 615
Soler, C., 679
Soll, J.B., 342
Solomon, D.A., 591
Solomon, H.C., 635
Solomon, R.L., 246
Solowij, N., 213, 214
Solso, R.L., 169
Sommer, B., 119
Son Hing, L.S., 700
Song, S., 83
Sorenson, J.L., 561
Soriano, M., 649
Sorrentino, R.M., 417
Sousa, D.A., 120
Sovio, U., 398, 546
Spangler, W.D., 416, 529
Spanos, N.P., 201, 203, 291, 590
Spear, P., 463
Spearman, C., 376, 377, 388
Spears, R., 696
Speed, A., 675
Spelke, E.S., 458
Spencer, L., 283
Spencer, S.J., 375, 700
Sperling, G., 274
Sperry, R., 11, 16, 23
Sperry, R.W., 16, 102, 103, 483
Spiegel, D., 201, 203, 204, 589
Spiegel, H., 201
Spiegler, M.D., 636
Spielberger, C.D., 361
Spiers, M.V., 101
Spinath, F.M., 367, 368
Sprafkin, J., 254
Sprecher, S., 409, 674, 675
Sprenger, M., 120
Springer, K., 668
Springer, S.P., 105, 118, 119, 483
Squire, L., 296
Squire, L.R., 97, 276, 278, 295, 297, 298
Sriram, T.G., 554
Srivastava, S., 493
Sroufe, L.A., 290, 449
Staats, A.W., 323
Staats, C.K., 323
Stack, J.A., 647
Stafford, R.E., 37
Stahl, T., 420
Stajkovic, A.D., 506
Stalling, R.B., 165
Stamler, J., 560
Stanford, T.R., 95, 167
Stanley, J.C., 482
Stanovich, K.E., 73, 340, 342
Starcevic, V., 587
Starkman, R., 349
Starr, C., 89, 106, 603
Stasser, G., 695, 696
Stattin, H., 446, 464
Staudinger, U.M., 475

Steele, C., 376
Steele, C.D., 474
Steele, C.M., 374, 375
Steele, J.B., 583
Steele, K.M., 121
Steele, M., 374
Steelman, L.C., 503
Steiger, H., 615, 616
Stein, B.E., 95, 136, 167
Stein, M.B., 550, 551, 583, 584
Steinberg, D.L., 595
Steinberg, L., 450, 464, 467, 472
Steinberg, W., 472
Steingard, R.J., 364
Steinhausen, H., 614, 615
Steinhilber, A., 549
Steinmetz, H., 483
Steinmetz, J.E., 294
Stejskal, W.J., 529
Stekel, W., 629
Stelfox, H.T., 642
Stellar, E., 395
Stemberger, R.T., 585
Stenstorm, P., 198
Stepanski, E.J., 195, 217
Stephan, W.G., 699
Stephens, R.S., 211
Stephens, T.W., 397
Steptoe, A., 554
Steriade, M., 190
Stern, W., 357
Sternberg, K.J., 450
Sternberg, R., 676
Sternberg, R.J., 29, 100, 326, 327, 328, 330, 358, 360, 361, 362, 366, 367, 370, 372, 379, 380, 384, 385, 456
Stevens, S.S., 156
Stewart, A.J., 469
Stewart, D.D., 696
Stewart, J.H., 247
Stewart-Williams, S., 63, 165
Stice, E., 616
Stich, S.P., 335
Stickgold, R., 193, 200
Stip, E., 641
Stockmyer, J., 118
Stoddard, G., 369
Stoddard, J.J., 559
Stoicheff, B., 349
Stoleru, S., 404
Stone, A.A., 554, 567
Stone, B., 184
Stone, J., 686
Stone, L., 678
Stone, W.N., 632, 633
Stoner, J.A.F., 695
Stoney, C.M., 552
Stoohs, R.A., 217
Stoolmiller, M., 516
Stough, C., 377
Straatman, A.L., 48
Strack, F., 431
Straub, R.O., 546
Straus, M.A., 247
Strauss, S., 372
Strayer, D.L., 270
Streissguth, A.P., 442
Strelau, J., 516
Striegel-Moore, R.H., 398, 614, 615
Striepe, M., 398
Strike, P.C., 554
Stroebe, W., 683, 684, 687

Strong, S.R., 656
Stroud, L.R., 546
Strube, M.J., 675
Strupp, H.H., 625, 634
Struss, D., 94
Struthers, 595
Struthers, C.W., 669
Stuart, E.W., 263
Stumpf, H., 482
Stunkard, A.J., 400, 401
Sucher, K.P., 163, 398
Sudhalter, V., 364
Sue, D., 648
Sue, D.W., 648
Sue, S., 19, 648, 649
Suedfeld, P., 18
Sugar, L.A., 46
Sugiyama, L.S., 679
Suh, E., 430, 431
Suh, E.M., 522
Suler, J., 692
Sullivan, G., 652
Sullivan, G.M., 585
Sullivan, L.A., 700
Sullivan, P.F., 593, 616
Sullivan, Q., 409
Sulloway, F., 502
Suls, J., 493, 537
Summerfeldt, L.J., 583
Super, C.M., 446
Supple, W.F., 421
Susman, E.J., 106, 464
Susser, E.B., 441, 603
Sutker, P.B., 607
Suzuki, D., 2, 285, 372
Suzuki, L.A., 371, 375
Suzuki, L.K., 450
Swan, G.E., 559
Swann, W.B., 675
Swartz, C.M., 643
Sweeney, D., 616
Swets, J.A., 128
Swihart, G., 283
Swim, J.K., 481, 699
Swinson, R.P., 226, 582
Switzer, G.E., 617
Sydeman, S.J., 361
Sykes, R.N., 304
Symbaluk, D.G., 248
Symons, C.S., 273
Szasz, T., 576, 577
Szmukler, G.I., 614
Szymanski, L.S., 363
Szymanski, S., 600

T
Tabachnick, B.G., 655
Tabas, G., 587
Taggart, R., 89, 106, 603
Tait, C.L., 649
Takahashi, M., 216
Takahashi, T., 185
Takeuchi, D.T., 648
Talarico, J.M., 276, 278
Tamminga, C.A., 85, 601
Tanaka-Matsumi, J., 611
Tang, I.T., 561
Tanner, W.P., 128
Tansky, J.W., 506
Tarantola, D.J.M., 561
Tardif, C., 449
Tardiff, K., 578, 641
Tart, C.T., 199, 219
Tarter, R.E., 442
Tashkin, D.P., 213
Tashman, N.A., 595
Tataryn, D.J., 130
Tatsuoka, M.M., 526

Tavris, C., 482, 530, 546
Taylor, C.B., 569
Taylor, D., 321
Taylor, D.M., 29, 320, 392, 700
Taylor, E., 12
Taylor, I., 319
Taylor, J.H., 461
Taylor, K.M., 694
Taylor, M.G., 484
Taylor, M.M., 319
Taylor, S., 543
Taylor, S.E., 548
Taylor, T.J., 322
Teachman, J., 471
Teasdale, J., 595
Teasdale, J.D., 421
Tedeschi, R.G., 551
Tees, R.C., 315
Tellegen, A., 515
Tennen, H., 551
Tenszen, M., 372
Tepper, B.J., 163
Tepperman, T., 395
Teresi, D., 117, 119
Terman, L., 22, 357
Terman, L.M., 356, 365
Terr, L., 290
Terracciano, A., 482
Terrace, H., 322
Terry, J., 438
Tesser, A., 688
Tessier-Lavigne, M., 135, 136
Testa, K., 291
Teuber, H., 53, 295
Teuber, M., 172
Thach, W.T., 95
Tharp, R., 258
Tharp, R.G., 260
Thase, M.E., 85, 594, 634
Thayaparan, B., 561
Thayer, R.E., 399, 418
Thelen, E., 444
Thiele, K., 192
Thomas, A., 446, 447
Thomas, A.J., 554
Thomas, D.R., 234, 235
Thomas, G., 676
Thomas, R.M., 452
Thompson, D.M., 283
Thompson, J.K., 615, 616
Thompson, K.S., 652
Thompson, M.M., 680
Thompson, R.A., 120, 121
Thompson, R.F., 16, 294
Thompson, W.F., 121, 160, 161
Thomson, D.M., 289
Thoresen, C.E., 567
Thorndike, E.L., 10, 237
Thorndike, R.L., 377, 378
Thorndyke, P.W., 301
Thorne, B.M., 5
Thorne, S., 491
Thornhill, R., 116
Thornton, B., 176, 672
Thorpe, S.J., 582
Thorpy, M., 216, 217
Thun, M.J., 559
Thune, I., 560
Thurstone, L.L., 376
Tibbo, P., 602
Tice, D.M., 399, 546
Till, B.D., 230, 262, 263, 684
Tindale, R.S., 695
Titchener, E., 5, 7

Titsworth, B.S., 33
Todd, J.T., 6
Todd, M., 226
Todes, D.P., 228
Tohen, M., 579
Tolman, C., 12
Tolman, E.C., 251
Toman, P.E., 595
Tomarken, A.J., 426
Tomkins, S.S., 422, 426
Tondo, L., 641
Tooby, J., 11, 20, 338, 339, 340, 394
Toomey, R., 600
Torgersen, S., 584
Tori, C.D., 205
Tormala, Z.L., 684
Torrey, E.F., 503, 531, 652
Tosi, H., 539
Toufexis, A., 191
Tovee, M.T., 138
Trapnell, P.D., 493, 503
Trasselli, C., 262
Travis, F., 205
Treiber, F., 205
Treisman, G.J., 561
Tremblay, L., 150
Trevarthen, C., 102
Treyens, J.C., 280
Triandis, H.C., 522, 672, 673, 678
Trieman, N., 651
Trivers, R., 405
Trivers, R.L., 20
Trope, Y., 670
Trost, M.R., 482, 483, 686, 688, 703
Trotter, R.J., 676
Troyer, A.K., 475
Trudeau, P.E., 311
Trull, T.J., 606
Tsai, J.L., 611, 612
Tsigos, C., 544
Tsuang, M.T., 579, 601
Tuck, 195
Tucker, G.R., 320
Tucker, J., 422
Tulving, E., 18, 94, 267, 271, 272, 282, 283, 287, 289, 297, 302
Turk, D.C., 165
Turk, J., 364
Turkheimer, E., 373, 516
Turkkan, J.S., 236
Turner, J.C., 695, 700
Turner, J.R., 540
Turner, P.J., 485
Turner, S.M., 583
Turner-Bowker, D.M., 485
Tversky, A., 335, 336, 337, 338, 340, 341, 342, 618
Twenge, J.M., 409
Twyman, R.E., 86
Tyrrel, D.A.J., 555, 556
Tzourio-Mazoyer, N., 118

U
Uchino, B.N., 557
Uehara, E., 648
Umbel, V.M., 319
Underwood, B.J., 31, 301
Unger, R.K., 481
Ungerleider, L.G., 155
Uno, D., 557
Urbszat, D., 401
Ursano, R.J., 584, 627
Uttl, B., 299
Uzzo, R.G., 550

V
Vaillancourt, T., 1
Vaillant, G.E., 499, 545, 546, 558
Valencia, R.R., 375
Valenstein, E.S., 395
Valentine, E., 301
Valleroy, L.A., 562
Vallone, R.P., 342, 343
Van de Castle, R.L., 197
van den Boom, D.C., 448
van den Oord, E.J.C.G., 515, 516
van der Molen, M.W., 475
van der Post, L., 500
Van Dongen, H.P.A., 183
van Eck, M., 541
Van Gogh, V., 150, 608
Van Hoesen, G.W., 97
van IJzendoorn, M.H., 448, 450
van Kammen, D.P., 640
van Knippenberg, A., 667
Van Leeuwen, M.D., 269
Vanable, P.A., 561
Vandello, J.A., 689
VandenBos, G.R., 163
Vandereycken, W., 615
Vanderplas, V., 173, 174
Vase, L.R., 165
Vasarely, V., 173, 174
Vase, L.R., 165
Vaughan, C., 217
Vaughan, S.I., 696
Vaughn, B.E., 448
Vaughn, C.E., 603, 604
Vaughn, L.A., 700
Vazquez, C., 652
Veenhoven, R., 428
Vega, W.A., 648
Vegas, R., 236
Veldhuis, J.D., 444
Veneziano, R.A., 487
Ventura, J., 604
Venturello, S., 586
Verdone, P., 197
Verduin, T., 634
Verhaeghen, P., 475
Vernberg, E.M., 584
Vernon, M.L., 678
Vernon, P.A., 378, 515
Vernon, P.E., 362
Vgontzas, A.N., 550
Viau, V., 544
Videbech, P., 594
Vierck, C., 167
Vihman, M., 315
Vinogradov, S., 632, 633
Vinters, H.V., 473, 474
Visser, P.S., 686
Vodelholzer, U., 85
Voinescu, L., 665
Vokey, J.R., 129
Volavka, J., 641
Volkmar, F.R., 120
Volkow, N.D., 210, 211
Vollmer, W.M., 560
Von Der Heydt, R., 145
von Hippel, W., 667
von Meduna, L., 642, 643
Vouloumanos, A., 314
Voutilainen, S., 560
Voyer, D., 37, 482, 483
Voyer, S., 37, 482
Vraniak, D.A., 371
Vredenburg, K., 658

W
Wachtel, P., 648
Wadden, T.A., 400

Waddill, P.J., 302
Wade, C.E., 185
Wagner, A., 550, 592, 596
Wagner, A.R., 252
Wagner, G.J., 403
Wagner, H., 425
Wagner, M.E., 485
Wagner, R.K., 362
Wagner, S.H., 616
Wahlin, Å., 475
Wahlsten, D., 349, 367, 484
Wain, L., 608
Wakefield, J.C., 581
Wald, G., 142
Waldo, M., 678
Waldron, M., 516
Waldrop, D., 506
Walker, A.J., 470
Walker, E., 604
Walker, I., 279
Walker, L.J., 461
Walker, M.P., 200
Wall, P.D., 165, 166
Wallace, B., 182
Wallace, M.T., 95, 167
Wallace, R.K., 205
Wallbott, H.G., 422, 423
Wallen, K., 403, 409
Waller, N.G., 494
Wallman, G.U., 654
Wallman, J., 322
Walraven, J., 134
Walsh, B.T., 658
Walsh, F., 473
Walsh, J.K., 191, 194, 195
Walster, E., 665, 676
Walter, T., 35
Walters, A.S., 192
Walters, R., 505
Walters, R.H., 254
Walther, E., 262, 263
Walton, D., 181
Waltz, J.A., 101
Wampold, B.E., 634, 656
Wang, G.J., 211
Wangensteen, O.H., 395
Ward, C., 674
Wardle, J., 401
Wark, D.M., 34
Warnes, H., 648
Warr, P., 430
Warren-Leubecker, A., 324
Warrington, E.K., 297
Warshaw, M.G., 584
Warwick, H.M.C., 588
Wasco, S.M., 404
Washburn, A.L., 395
Washburn, M., 5, 22
Washburn, M.F., 6
Wasow, J.L., 317
Wasserman, J.D., 354
Watanabe, M., 520
Watkins, C.E., 529
Watson, C.S., 155
Watson, D., 258, 493, 537, 556, 675
Watson, D.E., 626
Watson, D.L., 260
Watson, J., 630
Watson, J.B., 6, 7, 9, 10, 11, 14, 22, 28, 504
Watson, J.C., 631
Watt, D., 125
Waugh, N.C., 273
Weaver, C.A., III, 276
Weaver, J.B., 404
Webb, W.B., 189, 216
Wechsler, D., 357, 358, 388

Weems, C.F., 584
Wegener, D.T., 682, 684, 687
Weinberg, M.S., 411
Weinberg, R.A., 369, 370, 387
Weinberger, D.A., 498, 548
Weinberger, J., 634
Weiner, B., 670
Weiner, H., 588
Weiner, R.D., 646
Weinfeld, N.S., 449
Weinger, M.B., 191
Weinman, J., 564
Weinstein, L.N., 219
Weinstein, N.D., 337, 563
Weisberg, J., 298
Weisberg, R.W., 383
Weiskrantz, L., 297
Weisman, R., 624
Weissman, M.M., 227, 581, 582, 583
Weissman, M.M.E., 647
Weisstein, N., 138
Weiten, W., 5, 35, 51, 540, 541
Weizmann, F., 372
Wekerle, C., 48
Welch, H.G., 559
Welder, A.N., 43
Well, A.D., 340
Wellman, H.M., 459
Wells, A.J., 559
Wells, C.G., 119
Wells, G.L., 305, 306
Wells, H.G., 267
Wells, K., 648
Welsh, T.N., 150
Wenger, M.J., 301
Werker, J., 314, 315
Werker, J.F., 314
Wertheimer, M., 145, 146
Wertz, F.J., 12
Wessely, S., 641
Wesson, D.R., 195
West, R.F., 342
West, S.A., 364
West, W.B., 205
Westbrook, G.L., 79, 90
Westen, D., 9, 503, 606
Westra, T., 446
Westwood, D.A., 155
Wetter, M.W., 528
Wever, E.G., 159
Wexler, B.E., 93
Whalen, P.J., 421, 422
Wheaton, B., 540
Wheeler, L., 665

Wheeler, M.A., 73, 284
Whishaw, I.Q., 84, 101
Whitaker, C., 641
Whitaker, R., 642
Whitbourne, S., 470
Whitbourne, S.K., 469, 473
Whitehead, P.C., 651
Whitehouse, W.G., 292, 595
Whiteman, S.D., 485
Whitfield, C.L., 290, 293
Whiting, J.W.M., 462
Whittemore, K.E., 610
Whitting, V., 443
Whorf, B.L., 325
Whyte, M.K., 678
Wichmann, C., 470
Wickelgren, W., 17
Wickens, T.D., 275
Widener, A.J., 290
Widiger, T.A., 578, 579, 606
Widom, C.S., 607
Wiebe, V.J., 592
Wiederman, M.W., 409
Wiener, N.I., 372
Wiens, S., 418
Wiesel, T., 11, 16, 23, 120, 137
Wiesel, T.N., 98
Wiesenthal, D.L., 372, 538
Wigboldus, D.H.J., 667
Wiggins, J.S., 493, 494
Wiggs, C.L., 298
Wight, R.D., 5
Wik, G., 585
Wikaitis, J., 640
Wilding, J., 301
Wiley, E., 320
Wiley, J.L., 211
Wilkinson, R.T., 216
Willerman, L., 369
Willet, W.C., 399
Willett, W.C., 560
Williams, A., 700
Williams, B.A., 243, 291
Williams, C., 181, 185
Williams, C.G., 559
Williams, E.M., 459
Williams, J., 232
Williams, J.B.W., 579
Williams, J.E., 553
Williams, K., 694
Williams, K.D., 694
Williams, K.E., 506
Williams, L.M., 290
Williams, M.H., 655
Williams, N.A., 554
Williams, R., 118

Williams, R.B., 567
Williams, R.L., 33, 375
Williams, V.P., 567
Williams, W.M., 361, 370, 373
Williamson, D.A., 616
Williamson, G.M., 555
Willis, R.P., 301
Willis, W.D., 165
Willoughby, T., 271
Wills, T.A., 557
Willshire, D., 610
Wilsnack, S.C., 290, 293
Wilson, A.E., 669
Wilson, G.T., 209, 400
Wilson, M., 11, 20
Wilson, S., 462
Wilson, T.D., 73, 684
Windham, G.C., 442
Windholz, G., 228
Wing, R.R., 398, 400
Winick, C., 206, 404
Winn, P., 395
Winner, E., 365, 366
Winocur, G., 94, 268, 295
Winograd, T., 297
Winter, D.G., 415, 416
Wintre, M.G., 46, 47, 648, 649
Winzelberg, A.J., 205
Wise, M.G., 473
Wise, R.A., 212
Wisniewski, N., 405
Witelson, S.F., 77
Witkin, H.A., 332, 333
Witrliet, 567
Witte, K., 683
Wittenberg, L., 398
Wittkower, E.D., 648
Wolfe, D., 18, 50
Wolfe, D.A., 48
Wolfe, J.M., 143
Wolitzky, D.L., 627
Wolk, A., 560
Woloshin, S., 559
Wolpe, J., 635, 636, 644
Wolpert, E., 198
Wolsic, B., 429
Wolterbeek, L.A., 485
Won, S., 438
Wonder, J., 118
Wonderlich, S.A., 616
Wong, P., 537
Woo-Sam, J.M., 361
Wood, E., 271
Wood, F., 298
Wood, J.M., 529

Wood, N.L., 269
Wood, W., 483, 680
Woodbury, M.A., 162
Woodcock, R.W., 352
Woods, S.C., 396
Woodward, J.A., 386
Woolfolk, R.L., 542, 568
Woonteiler, D., 438
Word, D.H., 667
Workman, E.A., 552
Wormith, S., 607
Worth, L.T., 682
Worthen, J.B., 185
Worthington, E.L., 567
Worthington-Roberts, B.S., 441
Wortman, C.B., 567
Wright, J.C., 254
Wright, J.H., 632
Wright, L.W., Jr., 498
Wright, M.J., 12, 13
Wright, S.C., 29, 320
Wu, S., 683
Wu, Z., 471
Wu-Holt, P., 554
Wulfeck, B., 317
Wundt, W., 3, 4, 5, 7, 10, 12, 21, 22, 36, 127
Wurtz, R.H., 136
Wyatt, J.K., 217
Wyland, C.L., 95
Wylie, M.S., 290
Wynder, E.L., 560
Wynn, K., 458
Wynne, C.D.L., 322

X

Xiaghe, X., 678

Y

Yager, J., 216, 217
Yalom, I.D., 632, 633
Yalom, V., 631
Yamamoto, J., 649
Yang, H., 554
Yang, P., 34
Yanovski, S.Z., 400
Yapko, M.D., 291
Yarmey, D., 305
Yates, F.A., 301
Ybarra, O., 699
Yehuda, R., 584
Yerkes, R.M., 228
Yik, M.S.M., 523
Yost, W.A., 473
Young, D.M., 612
Young, E.A., 543
Young, K., 546, 648

Youngentob, S.L., 162
Yount, S.E., 554
Yudofsky, S.C., 92, 641
Yuille, J., 283
Yuille, J.C., 272
Yurgelun-Todd, D., 214

Z

Zacher, J.E., 126
Zacks, R., 270
Zadra, A., 196, 198, 199
Zadra, A.L., 196
Zajonc, R.B., 130, 418
Zane, N., 648
Zang, D., 554
Zanna, M., 18, 71, 698
Zanna, M.P., 213, 667, 680, 686, 700
Zarcone, V.P., Jr., 217
Zatorre, R.J., 160
Zatzick, D.F., 166
Zautra, A.J., 537, 554
Zebrowitz, L.A., 665
Zechmeister, E.B., 31
Zehr, J.L., 403
Zeidner, M., 382
Zeifman, D., 679
Zeiler, M., 243
Zeki, S., 138
Zellner, D.A., 163
Zenhausen, R., 118
Zepelin, H., 217
Zhao, S., 581
Zickafoose, D.J., 306
Ziegler, M., 372
Zigler, E., 360, 365
Zikovitz, D.C., 126
Zillman, D., 404
Zillmer, E.A., 101
Zimbardo, P., 688
Zimbardo, P.G., 687
Zimmerman, B.J., 506
Zimmerman, I.L., 361
Zimmerman, J., 261
Zimmerman, M., 605
Zoellner, L.A., 292
Zola, S.M., 16, 295, 297
Zorick, F.J., 194
Zorumski, C.F., 643
Zrenner, E., 142
Zubieta, J., 166
Zucker, I., 184
Zucker, K.J., 411
Zuckerman, M., 520
Zuroff, D.C., 594, 595
Zwislocki, J.J., 159

A

A-delta fibres, 165
abnormal behaviour
  see also psychological
    disorders
  criteria of, 577–578
  and deviance, 577
  historical conceptions of
    mental illness, 577f
  maladaptive behaviour, 577
  medical model and,
    576–577
  misconceptions, 576
  personal distress, 577
  value judgments, 578
Abramson, Lyn Y., 595
absolute refractory period, 80
absolute threshold, 127,
  127f, 128t
academic performance,
  improvement of,
  31–35
accommodation, 132, 454
acculturation, 320
acetylcholine (ACh), 84–85
achievement motive
  defined, 415
  individual differences, 416
  situational determinants,
    416–417, 417f
  societal, 415
achievement tests, 351
acoustics, 302–303
acquired immune defi-
  ciency syndrome
  (AIDS), 442–443,
  560–562
acquisition, 233, 238–240,
  254
acronyms, 302–303
action potential, 80
activation-synthesis model,
  200
activity anorexia, 402
actor-observer bias,
  670–671
actus reus, 610
adaptations, 114
adaptive traits, 115–116
additive colour mixing, 140
additive strategy, 335, 335f
Adler, Alfred, 501–503
adolescence
  described, 462–463
  formal operational
    period, 456
  growth spurt, 463–464
  personality development,
    467–468
  puberty, 463–464, 463f
  search for identity,
    467–468
  suicide, 464–466
  turmoil and, 464–465
adoption studies
  described, 110
  intelligence, environmental
    influence on, 369
  intelligence, hereditary
    influence on, 368
adulthood
  aging, 473–475
  empty nest, 472–473

Erikson's view, 470
family life transitions,
  470–473
marriage, 471–472
midlife crisis, 469–470
parenthood, 472
personality development,
  469–470
stability, 469
adventure seeking, 520
advertising, and classical
  conditioning, 230,
  231f, 262
afferent nerve fibres, 88
affiliation motive, 414–415
afterimage, 141, 274
age
  happiness, 429
  and identity status, 468,
    468f
  median age at first
    marriage, 471f
  mental age, 356
  and prospective memory,
    299
  second language learning,
    320, 320f
  and sleep, 188–189
  stereotypes, 666–667
age of viability, 440
aggression
  defined, 546
  psychoanalytic theory
    and, 496–497
  and psychological
    disorders, 578
  and stress, 546
  worries about, 41–42
aggressive pornography,
  404–405
aging
  cognitive changes,
    474–475
  dementia, 473–474
  and memory, 475
  menopause, 473
  physical changes,
    473–474
  primary mental
    abilities, 474f
agonist, 84
agoraphobia, 582, 583
agreeableness, 493
Ainsworth, Mary Salter,
  13f, 448
alarm reaction, 544
alcohol, 209, 210–211,
  216, 560
alcoholism, 220–221, 221f
algorithms, 329
Allan Memorial Institute,
  65
allergic reactions, 231
Alloy, Lauren B., 595
alpha, 182
altered states of
  consciousness
  drugs. *See* drugs
  hypnosis, 201–204
  meditation, 204–205
alternative, selection of,
  335–336
alternative courses of
  action, 571

Alzheimer's disease, 474
ambisexual, 410f
amenorrhea, 614
American Association on
  Mental Retardation
  (AAMR), 363
American Psychological
  Association, 6, 14, 24
American Psychological
  Society, 14
American Sign Language
  (ASL), 321–322
Ames room, 151, 152f
amino acids, 86
amnesia
  anterograde amnesia,
    295, 295f
  H.M. case, 295
  and hypnosis, 203
  red-outs, 283
  retrograde amnesia, 295,
    295f
amphetamines, 208, 210,
  211f
amplitude, 131, 155, 182
amygdala, 97, 296,
  421–422, 421f
anagrams, 326, 327f
anal stage, 499–500
analogies, 330–331, 433
analogy problems, 326, 327f
analytic cognitive style,
  334
analytical intelligence, 379
analytical psychology,
  500–501
anandamide, 211
anatomical centres, 396
anatomy of memory,
  295–296, 295f
Andreasen, Nancy, 600
androgens, 403–404
anecdotal evidence, 72–73
anesthesia, 202–203
anger, 417, 553
animals
  and language, 321–322
  research on, and behav-
    ioural theories, 507
animism, 455
Anna O, 624
anorexia nervosa, 402, 612,
  614, 615f
antagonist, 85
antecedents, 259, 261
anterograde amnesia, 295,
  295f
antianxiety drugs, 639–640
antibodies, 230
anticipatory name-calling,
  345
antidepressant drugs, 641
antipsychotic drugs,
  640–641, 640f
antisocial personality
  disorder, 606–607
Antony, Martin, 582
anxiety
  arousal of, 497
  and defence, 509–510
  and defence mechanisms,
    497–499
  free-floating anxiety, 582
  separation anxiety, 448

anxiety disorders
  agoraphobia, 582, 583
  biological factors, 584–585
  cognitive factors,
    585–586, 586f
  and conditioning, 585
  defined, 582
  generalized anxiety
    disorder, 582
  and learning, 585
  obsessive-compulsive
    disorder (OCD),
    583–584
  panic disorder, 582, 586f
  phobias, 585f
  phobic disorder, 582
  post-traumatic stress
    disorder (PTSD),
    550, 575, 584
  stress, 586
anxiety hierarchy, 637f
anxious-ambivalent adults,
  677
anxious-ambivalent
  attachment, 448, 676
appeal to ignorance,
  386–387
appeals, 683
appearances, 502
application, 42
applied psychology, 14
approach-approach
  conflict, 538
approach-avoidance
  conflict, 539
aptitude tests, 351, 352f
archetypes, 501
arguments, 432–433
Aron, Arthur, 74
Aronson, Joshua, 374
arrangement problems, 326
art, and illusion, 169–174
ascending reticular acti-
  vating system (ARAS),
  190, 191f
Asch, Solomon, 688
assimilation, 454
assumptions, 432
asymmetric insight, 668
atherosclerosis, 552
Atkinson, John, 416
Atkinson, Richard, 273
attachment
  anxious-ambivalent
    attachment, 448,
    676
  avoidant attachment,
    448, 676
  and culture, 450
  daycare and, 449–450
  defined, 448
  evolutionary perspectives,
    450
  love as attachment,
    676–678, 677f
  overview, 449f
  patterns, 448–449
  secure attachment, 448,
    449, 676
  separation anxiety, 448
attention, 253, 269–270, 549
attitude similarity, 675
attitudes
  and behaviour, 680–681

components of, 679–680,
  680f
counter-attitudinal
  behaviour, 685
defined, 679
dimensions of, 679–680
dissonance theory,
  685–686
effort justification, 686
elaboration likelihood
  model, 686–687
learning theory, 684–685
persuasion, 681–684
prejudice, 698–701
self-perception theory,
  686, 686f
strength of, 681, 684
theories, 684–687
attraction. *See* interpersonal
  attraction
attributions
  actor-observer bias,
    670–671
  bias, 670–672
  culture and attributional
    tendencies, 672–674
  defensive attributions,
    671–672
  defined, 669
  external attributions,
    669–670
  failure, 670, 670f
  fundamental attribution
    error, 670–671, 671f,
    673
  internal attributions,
    669–670
  self-serving bias,
    672, 674
  and social relations, 669
  success, 670, 670f
atypical antipsychotic
  drugs, 640–641
auditory localization,
  159, 160f
auditory perception
  frequency theory, 158
  place theory, 158
  reconciling theories,
    158–159
  volley principle, 159
auditory system
  auditory localization,
    159, 160f
  auditory perception,
    157–159
  basilar membrane, 157,
    159f
  cochlea, 156–157
  the ear, 156–157, 158f
  human hearing capacities,
    156
  music, 159–160
  sound, 155, 156f
  sound pressure, 157f
  theories of hearing,
    157–159
autogenic training, 218
automatic psychotherapy,
  623
autonomic arousal,
  419–420, 420f
autonomic nervous system,
  87, 88, 89f, 419, 543

autonomy *versus* shame and doubt, 452
availability, 337
availability heuristic, 337, 341, 619
aversion therapy, 636–637, 637*f*
avoidance, 245–246
avoidance-avoidance conflict, 539
avoidance learning, 246
avoidant adults, 677
avoidant attachment, 448, 676
awareness level, 495–496
axon, 79

B

babbling, 315
bad trip, 209
Baldwin, James Mark, 12
Baldwin, Mark W., 510
Bandura, Albert, 253, 505–507
Barber, Theodore, 203
Bartoshuk, Linda, 163
base rates, 337–338
baseline data, 258–259
basilar membrane, 157, 159*f*
Beck, Aaron, 594, 631, 644
behaviour
    as adaptive traits, 115–116
    and attitudes, 680–681
    and the brain, 95–101
    cultural heritage, 28–29
    defined, 6
    environment, influence of, 29
    health-impairing behaviour, 558–564
    and heredity, 107–112
    heredity, influence of, 29
    multiple causes, 28
    and neurotransmitters, 84–87
    questions about behaviour, 41–42
    scientific approach, 42–47
    sexual behaviour. *See* sexual behaviour
    situational specificity, 507
behaviour modification
    behavioural contract, 261
    defined, 258
    self-control, 258–261
    and studying, 33
behaviour therapies
    assumptions of, 635–636
    aversion therapy, 636–637, 637*f*
    cognitive behavioural therapy (CBT), 195
    and cognitive therapy, 632
    defined, 635
    described, 624
    evaluation of, 638
    insomnia, 195
    social skills training, 637–638
    systematic desensitization, 636, 636*f*, 637*f*
behavioural contract, 261
behavioural disengagement, 546

behavioural genetics, 107
    see also genetics
behavioural interventions. *See* behaviour therapies
behavioural manoeuvres, 115
behavioural responses to stress, 544–548
behavioural traits, 115
behaviourism
    debut of, 6–7
    defined, 6, 504
    dehumanizing nature of radical behaviourism, 507–508
    evaluation of, 507–508
    fragmentation of personality, 508
    language acquisition, 323
    overdependence on animal research, 507
    person-situation controversy, 507
    personality, 504–508
    radical behaviourism, 9
    Skinner's contributions, 9–10, 504–505
    social cognitive theory (Bandura), 505–507
    social learning theory, 505
belief in a just world, 672
belief in the law of small numbers, 340–341, 700
belief perseverance, 341–342, 342*f*
The Bell Curve (Herrnstein and Murray), 371–372
Belsky, Jay, 450
Benson's relaxation procedure, 568*f*
benzodiazepine medications, 194–195, 639
Berscheid, Ellen, 677
beta, 182
Bialystok, Ellen, 319
bias
    actor-observer bias, 670–671
    in attribution, 670–672, 699–700
    belief in a just world, 672
    confirmation bias, 341–342, 342*f*
    cultural bias, 375
    defensive attributions, 671–672, 700
    disconfirmation bias, 684
    experimenter bias, 64–65
    fundamental attribution error, 670–671, 671*f*, 673, 700
    hindsight bias, 306, 530–531, 672
    memory biases, 699
    in person perception, 667–668
    and prejudice, 699–700
    sampling bias, 62–63, 73
    self-serving bias, 672, 674
    social desirability bias, 64, 73, 528
bilingualism, 318–321
Binet, Alfred, 356
Binet-Simon scale, 356
binge-eating/purging type anorexia nervosa, 614
binocular depth cues, 148

biochemistry of memory, 294
biological clocks, 184
biological constraints on conditioning
    conditioned taste aversion, 249–250
    instinctive drift, 249
    "sauce béarnaise syndrome," 249–250
biological factors
    anxiety disorders, 584–585
    eating disorders, 616
    mood disorders, 593–594
    schizophrenic disorders, 601–603
biological indexes of intelligence, 377–379
biological perspectives
    see also evolutionary psychology; genetics; heredity
    evaluation of, 517
    Eysenck's theory, 514–515, 514*f*
    gender differences, 482–484
    homosexuality, 411–413
    hunger, 395–397
    on personality, 514–517
    sexual orientation, 411–413
biological rhythms, 183–185
biomedical therapies
    defined, 638
    described, 624–625
    drug therapy, 639–642
    electroconvulsive therapy (ECT), 642–646
    lobotomies, 639
    psychosurgery, 639
biopsychosocial model, 536
bipolar disorder, 592–593
bird and train problem, 331, 332*f*
birth order, 502
bisexuals, 409, 410*f*
blaming oneself, 546
Blesbois, Elisabeth, 232
blind spot, 134
blunted affect, 599
Bobo doll, 254, 254*f*
body language, 422
body mass index (BMI), 399
bonobo pygmy chimpanzees, 322
boredom, susceptibility to, 520
bottom-up processing, 144, 144*f*
Bowlby, John, 450
the brain
    see also nervous system
    areas in, 96*f*
    and behaviour, 95–101
    brain-imaging procedures, 92–93
    brainstem, 95
    Broca's area, 102
    cerebellum, 95, 294
    cerebral cortex, 97, 98, 100*f*
    cerebral hemispheres, 99, 99*f*
    cerebral laterality, 102–105, 117–119

cerebral specialization, 117–118
cerebrum, 97, 98–101
    and consciousness, 182–183, 182*t*
corpus callosum, 99, 99*f*
CT (computerized tomography) scan, 92*f*, 93
    described, 89
DF case, 154–155
electrical recordings, 90
electrical stimulation of the brain (ESB), 91–92
electroencephalograph (EEG), 90, 91*f*
forebrain, 97–101
frontal lobe, 99
functional magnetic resonance imaging (fMRI), 93, 93*f*
    and gender differences, 484
hemispheric specialization, 104–105
hindbrain, 95
H.M. case, 91, 295
    and hunger, 395–396
hypothalamus, 97
language processing in, 102*f*
lesioning, 91
limbic system, 97–98
lobes, 99
localized neural circuits, and memory, 294–295
medial forebrain bundle, 98
medulla, 95
midbrain, 95–97
    and mood disorders, 594
MRI (magnetic resonance imaging) scan, 93, 93*f*
neural development, 120
occipital lobe, 99
parietal lobe, 99
perceptual asymmetries, 105
PET (positron emission tomography) scanning, 93, 93*f*
plasticity of, 101
pons, 95
prefrontal cortex, 99–101
primary auditory cortex, 99
primary motor cortex, 99, 100*f*
regions of, 95
research methods, 90–95
reticular formation, 97
reward pathway, 211, 211*f*
right brain/left brain, 102–105
    and schizophrenic disorders, 602–603
    and the self, 94–95
self-stimulation centres, 98
split-brain surgery, 102–104
stress, and brain-body pathways, 544, 545*f*
structures in, 96*f*

temporal lobes, 99
thalamus, 97
"two minds in one" concept, 117–119
    and vision, 136–139
    visual pathways, 136, 137*f*
Wernicke's area, 102*f*
brain-imaging procedures, 92–93
brain plasticity, 101
brain waves, 182–183
brainstem, 95
Breuer, Josef, 624
Broca's area, 102
Buddhist monk problem, 332, 333*f*
Buffalo, E.A., 277
bulimia nervosa, 402, 614–615
bullying, 15
burnout, 549–550, 550*f*
business negotiations, 262–263
Buss, David M., 407, 408, 517, 678
bystander effect, 693

C

C fibres, 165
Cade, John, 644
Calkins, Mary Whiton, 5
Cameron, D. Ewen, 623
Canada Research Chair program, 43, 43*t*
Canadian Addiction Survey (CAS), 206–207, 207*t*
Canadian Charter of Rights and Freedoms, 663
Canadian Code of Ethics for Psychologists, 66
Canadian Psychological Association, 13, 14, 17, 66
Canadian Society for Brain, Behaviour and Cognitive Science (CSBBCS), 14
Canadian Space Agency, 125
candle problem, 333, 334*f*
cannabinoid receptors, 211
cannabis, 209
Cannon, Walter, 395
Cannon-Bard theory of emotion, 425
capacity of storage, 275–276
Carrell, Suzanne, 510
Cartwright, Rosalind, 200
Case, Robbie, 457
case studies, 52–54, 54*f*
catastrophic thinking, 566–567
catatonic schizophrenia, 599–600
catecholamines, 544
catharsis, 546
causation
    and correlation, 60
    multifactorial causation, 28, 209
    stress, and illness, 556–557
causes
    insomnia, 194
    mental retardation, 363–364
cell assemblies, 83

central nervous system, 87,
    88–89
central route, 686
centration, 454
cephalocaudal trend, 444
cerebellum, 95, 294
cerebral cortex, 97, 98, 100*f*
cerebral hemispheres,
    99, 99*f*
cerebral laterality, 102–105,
    117–119
cerebral specialization,
    117–118, 484
cerebrospinal fluid (CSF),
    88–89
cerebrum, 97, 98–101
Chandler, Michael, 465
change, 539–540
channel, 681
chemical senses, 162–164
Chess, Stella, 446
child abuse, 290*f*
child custody, 72
childhood development
    attachment, 448–450
    cognitive development,
        453–459
    early emotional develop-
        ment, 448–450
    moral reasoning, 460–461
    motor development,
        444–446
    personality development,
        451–452
    temperament, 446–447
children
    child abuse, 290*f*
    fathers, and children's
        well-being, 486–487
    giftedness, 364–366
    language development,
        314–318
    mental age, 356
    and the mind, 459
    separation anxiety, 448
    sudden infant death
        syndrome, 442
    temperament, 446–447
Chomsky, Noam, 16,
    323–324
chromosomes, 107, 439
chunks, 275–276
cingulotomy, 639
circadian rhythms
    defined, 183
    examples of, 184*f*
    ignoring, effect of,
        184–185
    and melatonin, 185
    role of, 183–184
circular reasoning, 433
classical conditioning
    see also conditioning
    acquisition, 233
    advertising, 230, 231*f*,
        262
    allergic reactions, 231
    anxiety disorders, 585
    apparatus, 228*f*
    attitude formation and
        change, 684
    awareness of processes,
        263
    basic processes, 233–235
    business negotiations,
        262–263
    conditioned fears,
        229–230

conditioned reflex,
    228–229
conditioned response
    (CR), 228
conditioned stimulus
    (CS), 228
defined, 227
drug tolerance, 231
elicited reflexes, 229
emotional responses, 230
everyday life, 229–231
extinction, 234
fear response, 230*f*
generalization gradients,
    235, 235*f*
higher-order condi-
    tioning, 235, 236*f*
immunosuppression,
    231, 231*f*
vs. operant conditioning,
    241*t*
persuasion, 262–263
physiological responses,
    230–231
in politics, 263
procedures, 228–229
process of, 229*f*
psychic reflexes, 227–228,
    228–229
renewal effect, 234
and romance, 230*f*
signal relations, 251–252
spontaneous recovery,
    234
stimulus contiguity, 233
stimulus discrimination,
    235
stimulus generalization,
    234–235
terminology, 228–229
trial, 229
unconditioned response
    (UCR), 228
unconditioned stimulus
    (UCS), 228
client-centred therapy,
    629–631
clinical psychologists, 625
clinical psychology
    described, 14, 24, 25*f*
    vs. psychiatry, 25
clinical scales, 525
clinical social workers, 626
close relationships. *See*
    interpersonal attrac-
    tion; love
closure, 145
clustering, 279–280
co-sleeping, 189
cocaine, 208, 211*f*, 213
cochlea, 156–157
cocktail party phenom-
    enon, 269
cognition
    and cerebral specializa-
        tion, 117–118
    defined, 16
    and gender differences,
        482
    renewed interest in,
        16–17
cognitive appraisals,
    418–419
cognitive behavioural
    therapy (CBT), 195
cognitive development
    in childhood, 453–459
    defined, 453

dishabituation, 458
habituation, 458
innate cognitive abilities,
    458–459
neo-Piagetian theories,
    457–458
Piaget's stage theory,
    453–457
Staircase model, 457
cognitive dissonance,
    685–686
cognitive factors
    anxiety disorders,
        585–586, 586*f*
    eating disorders, 616
    mood disorders, 595
    somatoform disorders, 588
cognitive perspective, 17
cognitive processes
    and bilingualism,
        319–320
    in conditioning, 251–252
    in intelligent behaviour,
        379–380
    and reciprocal deter-
        minism, 505–507
cognitive reactions, 595
cognitive schemas, 666
cognitive style
    analytic cognitive style,
        334
    and brain hemispheres,
        119
    cultural differences in,
        332–333, 334*f*
    field dependence-
        independence,
        332–333
    field-dependent cognitive
        style, 333
    holistic cognitive style,
        334
    and problem solving,
        332–333
cognitive theories of lan-
    guage acquisition, 324
cognitive therapy, 631–632
Cohen, Sheldon, 555
collective unconscious,
    501, 501*f*
collectivism, 430, 673, 692
colour blindness, 141
colour circle, 141, 141*f*
colour solid, 140
colour vision
    additive colour mixing, 140
    afterimage, 141
    colour blindness, 141
    complementary colours,
        141, 141*f*
    opponent process theory,
        141–142
    reconciling theories of,
        142, 142*f*
    stimulus for colour, 140
    subtractive colour mixing,
        140
    trichromatic theory,
        140–141
Comes, Cleon, 647
commitment, 676
common cold, 555–556
commonsense notions, 47
communication in the
    nervous system. *See*
    nervous system
community mental health
    movement, 650

comorbidity, 618
companionate love, 676
comparitors, 176
compensation, 502
complementary colours,
    141, 141*f*
complete sleep deprivation,
    191
complex cells, 137–138
conceptual hierarchy,
    280, 280*f*
conclusions, 45
concordance rate, 584
concrete operational
    period, 455–456
conditional love, 509
conditioned fears, 229–230
conditioned reflex,
    228–229
conditioned reinforcement,
    242
conditioned reinforcers, 242
conditioned response (CR),
    228
conditioned stimulus (CS),
    228
conditioned taste aversion,
    249–250, 250*f*
conditioning
    see also learning
    and anxiety disorders, 585
    biological constraints,
        249–251
    changing directions in
        study of, 249–252
    classical conditioning,
        227–236
    cognitive processes,
        251–252
    described, 226
    instinctive drift, 249
    operant conditioning,
        236–248
    response-outcome rela-
        tions, and reinforce-
        ment, 252
    "sauce béarnaise syn-
        drome," 249–250
    signal relations, 251–252
cones, 134, 142
confirmation bias,
    341–342, 342*f*
conflict
    approach-approach con-
        flict, 538
    approach-avoidance con-
        flict, 539
    avoidance-avoidance con-
        flict, 539
    defined, 538
    and psychoanalytic
        theory, 496–497
    types of, 538*f*
conformity
    Asch's experiment, 688
    cultural variations in,
        691–692
    defined, 688
    and group size, 688, 689*f*
confounding of variables,
    49–50
congenital adrenal
    hyperplasia, 483
conjunction fallacy, 338,
    338*f*, 618
conjunctive probabilities,
    618
connectionist models, 282

conscientiousness, 493, 558
conscious, 496
consciousness
    biological rhythms,
        183–185
    and brain activity,
        182–183, 182*t*
    described, 182
    dissociation, 204
    divided consciousness, 204
    dreams, 197–200
    drugs. *See* drugs
    hypnosis, 201–204
    levels of awareness, 182
    meditation, 204–205
    nature of, 182–183
    sleep. *See* sleep
    stream of consciousness,
        182
    structure of, 5
    variations in, 182
conservation, 454, 455*f*
consistent tendency, 492
consolidation, 296
constraint, 493
construct validity, 354–355,
    355*f*
constructive coping, 548, 566
contemporary psychology,
    21–25
content validity, 354
context, 148, 174
context cues, 283
contingencies, 252, 260
continuity, 146
continuous reinforcement,
    243
contrast effects, 175–176,
    176*f*
control, 42
control group, 48–49
conventional level, 460
convergence, 148
convergent thinking, 383
conversion disorder, 587
coping
    aggression, 546
    blaming oneself, 546
    catastrophic thinking,
        566–567
    catharsis, 546
    constructive coping, 548,
        566
    defensive coping,
        546–548
    defined, 544
    forgiving others, 567–568
    hostility management,
        567–568
    humour, 567
    improvement of, 566–569
    learned helplessness,
        545–546
    minimization of physio-
        logical vulnerability,
        568–569
    rational-emotive therapy,
        566–567
    relaxation, 568
    releasing pent-up emotions,
        567
    self-indulgence, 546
    styles of, 545
coronary heart disease, 552
corpus callosum, 99, 99*f*
correlation
    and causation, 60, 486,
        570

correlation coefficient, 58, 59f
defined, 58
and intelligence testing, 356
negative correlation, 58, 59f
positive correlation, 58, 59f
and prediction, 59–60
strength of, 58–59
stress-illness correlation, 556–557, 557f
correlation coefficient, 58, 59f, 353
correlational research. See descriptive/correlational research
corticosteroids, 544
Cosmides, Leda, 338
counselling psychologists, 625
counselling psychology, 24, 25f
counsellors, 626
counter-attitudinal behaviour, 685
counterarguments, 432–433
CPA Donald O. Hebb Award, 17, 18t
Craig, Wendy M., 15
Craik, Fergus I.M., 94, 270
crank, 208
Crawford, Doug, 99
creative intelligence, 379
creative personality, 384
creativity
    correlates of, 384–385
    creative productivity, prediction of, 384
    defined, 383
    difficulty of prediction, 384
    and divergent thinking, 383
    and insight, 383
    and intelligence, 384–385
    measurement of, 383–384
    and mental illness, 385, 385f
    nature of, 383
    and particular domains, 384
    and psychological tests, 384
    and unconscious thought processes, 383
credibility, 681, 702–703
criterion-related validity, 354
critical period, 120
critical thinking
    alcoholism, 220–221
    alternative courses of action, 571
    anecdotal evidence, 72–73
    appeal to ignorance, 386–387
    arguments, 432–433
    contrast effects, 175–176
    credibility, 702–703
    defined, 36
    efficacy of treatment, 658–659
    eyewitness accounts, 305–306
    fathers, and children's well-being, 486–487

health risks and decisions, 570–571
hindsight bias, 530–531
intelligence debate, 386–387
overextrapolation, dangers of, 120–121
persuasion, 262–263
probabilities, 617–619
psychological disorders, 617–619
reification, 387
risk-benefit assessments, 571
shaping thought with language, 344–345
skills, development of, 36–37
social influence strategies, 703
uncertainty, 571
cross-cultural variations. See cultural differences
cross-sectional design, 446, 447f
cryptomnesia, 285
crystallized intelligence, 376–377, 475
CT (computerized tomography) scan, 92f, 93
Cubism, 170–171
cultural bias, 375
cultural differences
    see also culture
    co-sleeping, 189
    cognitive styles, and problem solving, 332–334, 334f
    conformity, 691–692
    dreams, 199
    emotional experiences, 423–424
    increased interest in cultural diversity, 18–19
    infant mortality, 443f
    in IQ scores, 371–374
    learned preferences and habits, 397–398
    motor development, 445–446
    obedience, 691–692
    optical illusions, 152–153
    perceptual inferences, 152–153
    sleep, 189
    taste preferences, 163
cultural heritage, 28–29
culture
    see also cultural differences
    and attachment, 450
    and attributional tendencies, 672–674
    and close relationships, 678
    collectivism, 430, 673, 692
    conceptions of self, 523f
    defined, 28
    and eating disorders, 616
    and emotion, 422–425
    and happiness, 430
    individualism, 430, 672–673, 692
    and intelligence testing, 362
    linguistic relativity, 325
    and mating priorities, 407–408
    model personality, 521

multicultural sensitivity in treatment, 648–649
national character, 521
and personality, 521–523
and problem solving, 332–334
culture-bound disorders, 611–612
cumulative deprivation hypothesis, 369
cumulative probabilities, 617
cumulative recorder, 238, 239f
cyclothymic disorder, 592

D

dark adaptation, 134, 134f
Darwin, Charles, 5, 113–114
data analysis, 45
data collection techniques, 45, 45t
date rape, 405
dating abuse, 48
day residue, 198
daycare, and attachment, 449–450
decay, 279
decay theory, 288
decentration, 455
deception, 65–66, 528
decibels (dB), 156
decision making
    additive strategy, 335, 335f
    availability, 337
    belief perseverance, 341–342, 342f
    confirmation bias, 341–342, 342f
    conjunction fallacy, 338, 338f
    defined, 335
    elimination by aspects, 335–336
    evolutionary analyses of flaws, 338–339
    framing, 342–343, 343f
    gambler's fallacy, 340
    groups, 694–696
    heuristics in judging probabilities, 337
    ignoring base rates, 337–338
    law of small numbers, 340–341
    overconfidence effect, 342
    overestimation of the improbable, 341
    pitfalls, understanding, 340–343
    representativeness, 337
    risky decisions, 336–337
    selection of alternative, 335–336
    subjective probability, 337
    subjective utility, 336–337
    taking chances, 336–337
    theory of bounded rationality, 335
    weight attributes, 335
declarative memory system, 297–298
deep processing, 302
defence mechanisms
    defensive coping, 546–548

defined, 497, 546–547
displacement, 498
identification, 498
projection, 498
rationalization, 497
reaction formation, 498
regression, 498
repression, 497–498
table of, with examples, 497t
table of additional defence mechanisms, 547t
defensive attributions, 671–672, 700
deinstitutionalization, 650–652
Delay, Jean, 644
delayed reinforcement, 242
delta, 182
delusions, 599
delusions of grandeur, 599
Dement, William, 188
dementia, 473–474
dendrites, 79
dendritic trees, 79
Deniker, Pierre, 644
dependent variables, 48, 50
depression, 553–554, 591, 592, 595–596
    see also mood disorders
depressive disorders, 554
depressive episodes, 592t
depth perception, 148–149
description, 42
descriptive/correlational research
    advantages, 55–56
    case studies, 52–54, 54f
    described, 52
    disadvantages, 56–57
    naturalistic observation, 52
    surveys, 54–55
descriptive statistics
    central tendency, 57
    correlation, 58–60
    correlation coefficient, 58, 59f
    defined, 57
    mean, 57
    median, 57
    mode, 57
    standard deviation, 57–58
    variability, 57–58
deterioration of adaptive behaviour, 599
determinism, 504
development
    adolescence, 462–468
    adulthood, 469–475
    aging, 473–475
    childhood. See childhood development
    defined, 438–439
    overview, 476–479
    prenatal development, 439–443
    psychosexual stages of development, 499–500
developmental norms, 445
deviance, 577
deviation IQ scores, 358
Dew, Mary Amanda, 647
diagnosis, 577
Diagnostic and Statistical Manual of Mental

Disorders (DSM-IV), 579, 580f
dichromats, 141
dietary restraint, 401–402
Differential Aptitude Tests (DAT), 351
difficult children, 447
diffusion of responsibility, 693
digestive regulation, 396
DiMatteo, Robin, 564
disciplinary procedures, 247
disconfirmation bias, 684
discrimination, 698, 699f
discriminative stimuli, 240–241
dishabituation, 458
disinhibition, 203, 520
disorganized schizophrenia, 600
displacement, 498, 546
display rules, 423–424
dissociation, 204
dissociative amnesia, 589
dissociative disorders
    defined, 589
    dissociative amnesia, 589
    dissociative fugue, 589
    dissociative identity disorder (DID), 589, 598
    etiology, 589–590
dissociative fugue, 589
dissociative identity disorder (DID), 589, 598
dissonance theory, 685–686
distal stimuli, 146, 147f
distinctiveness, 492
distortions in self-report data, 64
distributed practice, 301–302, 302f
disturbed emotion, 599
divergent thinking, 383
divided attention, 270
divided consciousness, 204
Dix, Dorothea, 649–650
dizygotic twins, 109–110, 111f
DNA, 111
Dobson, Keith, 626
dominant gene, 107–108
Domjan, Michael, 232
Donald O. Hebb Award, 17, 18t
Donovan, Patricia, 595
door-in-the-face technique, 175
dopamine circuits, 210
dopamine (DA), 85
dopamine hypothesis, 601–602
double-blind procedure, 64–65
Down syndrome, 363–364
dream analysis, 627
dreams
    activation-synthesis model, 200
    cognitive, problem-solving view, 200
    common questions about, 218–219
    contents of, 197
    and culture, 199
    day residue, 198
    described, 197
    fatal dream, 219

interpretation, 219
latent content, 219
lucid dreams, 198–199, 219
manifest content, 219
remembering dreams, 218–219
theories of dreaming, 199–200
the Toraja of Indonesia, 199, 199t
typical dreams, Canadian university students, 198f
and waking life, 198–199
wish fulfillment, 199–200
drive, 393
drive theories, 392–393
drudge theory, 366
drug therapy
    antianxiety drugs, 639–640
    antidepressant drugs, 641
    antipsychotic drugs, 640–641, 640f
    combined with insight therapy, 647
    evaluation of, 642
    lithium, 641–642
    mood stabilizers, 642
drugs
    alcohol, 209
    Canadian Addiction Survey (CAS), 206–207, 207t
    cannabis, 209
    commonly abused drugs, 206–209, 208t
    dependence, 212
    direct effects, 213
    factors influencing drug effects, 209
    hallucinogens, 208–209
    and health, 212–214
    health risks of, 560
    indirect effects, 213
    marijuana, 181, 209, 213–214
    maternal drug use, 441–442
    MDMA ("ecstasy"), 207, 209, 214
    mechanisms of drug action, 210–211
    mesolimbic dopamine pathway, 211, 211f
    multifactorial causation, 209
    narcotics, 207–208
    opiates, 207–208
    overdose, 212–213
    physical dependence, 212
    psychoactive drugs, 206
    psychological dependence, 212
    reward pathway, 211, 211f
    sedatives, 208
    and sleep, 216
    stimulants, 196, 210f
    subjectivity of experience, 209
    tolerance, 209, 210f, 231
dual-code theory, 272
Dutton, Donald, 46
dysthymic disorder, 592

E
the ear, 156–157, 158f
eardrum, 156
early research laboratories, 4f
easy children, 447
eating
    see also hunger
    excessive eating, 400
    learned preferences and habits, 397–398
    motivation of, 395–402
    and negative emotions, 398–399
    and obesity, 399–401
    physiological arousal, 398
    as social action, 397
    social influence on, 397
    and stress, 398–399
eating disorders
    age of onset, 615f
    anorexia nervosa, 402, 612, 614, 615f
    bulimia nervosa, 402, 614–615
    cognitive factors, 616
    course of, 615–616
    and culture, 616
    etiology, 616
    family, role of, 616
    genetic vulnerability, 616
    history of, 615–616
    personality factors, 616
    prevalence, 615–616
Ebbinghaus, Hermann, 286, 287
Ebbinghaus' forgetting curve, 286, 286f
eclecticism, 648
ecstasy. See MDMA ("ecstasy")
educational and school psychology, 24, 25f
efferent nerve fibres, 88
effort justification, 686
effortful processing, 270
ego, 495
egocentrism, 455
Einstein, Albert, 77
Ekman, Paul, 422
elaboration, 271
elaboration likelihood model, 686–687
election campaign ads, 263
electrical recordings of the brain, 90
electrical stimulation of the brain (ESB), 91–92
electroconvulsive therapy (ECT), 642–646
electroencephalograph (EEG), 90, 91f, 182, 182f, 186
electromyograph (EMG), 186
electrooculograph (EOG), 186
elicited responses, 229
elimination by aspects, 335–336
Ellis, Albert, 546, 631
embryonic stage, 439–440
emergentist theories of language acquisition, 324
emitted responses, 238
emotion
    autonomic arousal, 419–420, 420f

behavioural component, 422
Cannon-Bard theory of emotion, 425
cognitive component, 418–419
conditioned emotional responses, 230
and culture, 422–425
defined, 418
and eating, 398–399
evolutionary theories, 426–427
facial-feedback hypothesis, 422, 423f
galvanic skin response (GSR), 419
happiness, 428–431
inverted-U hypothesis, 542–543
James-Lange theory of emotion, 424–425
and limbic system, 97–98
and motivation, 417
neural circuits, 420–422
nonverbal expressiveness, 422
physiological component, 419–422
polygraph, 419–420, 420f
primary emotions, 426f
releasing pent-up emotions, 567
Schachter's two-factor theory, 425–426
subjective feelings, 418–419
theories of, 424–427, 425f
emotion-focused couples therapy, 630
emotional arousal, 542–543
emotional development
    attachment, 448–450
    early emotional development, 448–450
emotional intelligence, 381–382
emotional responses to stress, 541–543, 553–554
empathy, 630
empirical approaches to personality, 520–521
empirical nature of psychology, 26
empiricism, 26
empty nest, 472–473
encoding
    attention, 269–270
    defined, 268
    dual-code theory, 272
    elaboration, 271
    enriching, 271–273
    examples, effects of, 272f
    ineffective encoding, 287–288
    internal state, 283
    levels-of-processing theory, 270–271, 270f, 271f
    next-in-line effect, 269
    phonemic encoding, 271, 279
    selective attention models, 269f
    self-referent encoding, 272–273

semantic encoding, 271, 279
and verbal mnemonics, 302–304
visual imagery, 271–272
visual mnemonics, 303–304
encoding specificity principle, 283, 289
Endler, Norman, 507
endocrine system, 105–107, 106f, 544
endorphins, 86, 211
environment
    contingencies, 252
    gender differences, 484–485
    and heredity, 112
    and homosexuality, 411
    and hunger, 397–399
    influence of, 29
    and intelligence, 369–370
    and prenatal development, 440–443
    sexual orientation and, 411
environmental deprivation and enrichment, 369
environmental tobacco smoke, 559
epidemiology, 579
episodic buffer, 276
episodic memory system, 298, 475
Erikson, Erik, 451–452, 470
erotic materials, 404–405
escape learning, 245
essay exam tips, 35
estrogens, 403
ethics in research, 65–67, 66t
ethnic ancestry by generational status, 19f
ethnic stereotypes, 667
ethnocentrism, 19, 700
etiology
    antisocial personality disorder, 607
    of anxiety disorders, 584–586
    defined, 577
    of dissociative disorders, 589–590
    eating disorders, 616
    of mood disorders, 593–595
    schizophrenia, 601–604
    of somatoform disorders, 588
evaluation of research, 62–65
event-based tasks, 299
evolution of language, 322–323
evolutionary analyses of flaws, 338–339
evolutionary psychology
    adaptations, 114
    adaptive traits, 115–116
    attachment, 450
    critics of, 20
    Darwin's insights, 113–114
    described, 19–20
    emergence of, 19–21
    fitness, 113
    gender differences, 482–483

inclusive fitness, 115
innate cognitive abilities, 458–459
interpersonal attraction, 679
learning, 251
mating priorities, 407–408
mutation, 114
natural selection, 5, 113
person perception, bias in, 668–669
personality, 516–517
refinements to evolutionary theory, 114–115
sexual behaviour, 405–409
evolutionary theories of emotion, 426–427
evolutionary theories of motivation, 394
examples, 272f
excessive frustration, 499
excessive gratification, 499
excitatory PSP, 82
excitement phase, 413
executive control system, 276
exercise, 560, 561f
exhaustion stage, 544
expectancy-value models, 393–394
expectations, 431
experience seeking, 520
experiment, 48
experimental group, 48–49
experimental psychology, 12
experimental research
    advantages, 51
    confounding of variables, 49–50
    control group, 48–49
    dependent variables, 48, 50
    disadvantages, 51
    experiment, 48
    experimental group, 48–49
    extraneous variables, 49–50
    independent variables, 48
    manipulation of independent variables, 50
    random assignment, 49
    variations in design of experiments, 50
experimenter bias, 64–65
expertise, 681–682
explicit memory, 296–297
expressed emotion, 603–604, 604f
expression of emotions, 567
external attributions, 669–670
external ear, 156
extinction, 234, 240
extraneous variables, 49–50
extrapolation, 120–121
extraversion, 430–431, 493, 514–515
extraversion-introversion, 515
extraverts, 501
the eye, 132–133, 132f

eyewitness accounts, 305–306
Eysenck, Hans, 514–515, 633
Eysenck's theory, 514–515

F

facial-feedback hypothesis, 422, 423f
facial symmetry, 679
factor analysis, 376, 492–493
fallacies
  circular reasoning, 433
  conjunction fallacy, 338, 338f, 618
  false dichotomy, 433
  gambler's fallacy, 340
  irrelevant reasons, 433
  nominal fallacy, 221
  slippery slope, 433
  weak analogies, 433
false dichotomy, 433, 487
false memories, 290–293
families, and gender-role socialization, 485
family life cycle, 470
family life transitions
  described, 470–471
  empty nest, 472–473
  marriage, 471–472
  parenthood, 472
family studies, 109, 110f, 367
farsightedness, 133, 133f
fast mapping, 317
fatal dream, 219
fathers, and children's well-being, 486–487
fear, and sexual attraction, 46–47, 50, 50t
feature analysis, 143–145, 144f
feature detectors, 138
featured research studies. See research studies (featured studies)
Fechner, Gustav, 127, 128
Fechner's law, 128
Festinger, Leon, 685
fetal alcohol syndrome, 442
field dependence-independence, 332–333
field-dependent cognitive style, 333
field independent, 332
fight-or-flight response, 88, 419, 543
figure and ground, 145, 145f
First Nations, and youth suicide, 465–466
fitness, 113
five-factor model of personality, 493–494
fixation, 499
fixed-interval (FI) schedule, 243
fixed-ratio (FR) schedule, 243
flashbulb memories, 277–278
flat affect, 599
flavour, 163
fluid intelligence, 376–377
Flynn effect, 370, 370f
food availability, 397
foot-in-the-door technique, 703

forebrain, 97–101
forewarning, 684
forgetting
  anterograde amnesia, 295, 295f
  decay theory, 288
  encoding specificity principle, 289
  forgetting curve, 286, 286f
  ineffective encoding, 287–288
  interference theory, 288
  measures of, 286–287
  motivated forgetting, 289
  proactive interference, 288, 289f
  pseudoforgetting, 287–288
  reasons for, 287–289
  recall, 286
  recognition, 286–287
  relearning, 287
  repressed memories controversy, 290–293
  repression, 289
  retention, 286
  retrieval failure, 289
  retroactive interference, 288, 289f
  retrograde amnesia, 295, 295f
  transfer-appropriate processing, 289
forgetting curve, 286, 286f
forgiving others, 567–568
form perception. See visual perception
formal operational period, 456
fovea, 134
Fragile X syndrome (FXS), 364
framing, 342–343, 343f
Frank, Ellen, 647
fraternal twins, 109–110, 111f
free association, 627
free-floating anxiety, 582
free will, 10
frequency, 156, 182
frequency theory, 158
Freud, Sigmund, 7, 8–9, 199–200, 494–500, 627, 644
Friesen, Wallace, 422
frontal lobe, 99
frustration, 537–538
frustration-aggression hypothesis, 546
functional fixedness, 328
functional magnetic resonance imaging (fMRI), 93, 93f
functionalism
  described, 5
  vs. structuralism, 4–6
fundamental attribution error, 670–671, 671f, 673, 700

G

GABA (gamma-aminobutyric acid), 86
Galton, Sir Francis, 29, 356
galvanic skin response (GSR), 419

gambler's fallacy, 340
Garcia, John, 250
Gardner, Howard, 380–381
gate-control theory, 166
gay, 409
Gazzaniga, Michael, 102
gender, 481
gender differences
  biological origins, 482–484
  brain organization, disparities in, 484
  cerebral specialization, 484
  cognitive abilities, 482
  defined, 481
  environmental origins, 484–485
  evolutionary explanations, 482–483
  gender-role socialization, 485
  hormones, role of, 483
  mate preferences, 407
  and observational learning, 484
  and operant conditioning, 484
  personality, 482
  puberty, timing of, 464
  self-socialization, 484–485
  sexual activity patterns, 406–407
  social behaviour, 482
  thinking about sex, 406f
  understanding, 481–485
  variety of sexual partners, 406f
gender-role socialization, 485
gender roles, 484
gender stereotypes, 481, 481f, 666
general adaptation syndrome, 543–544
general mental ability, 376
generalization gradients, 235, 235f
generalized anxiety disorder, 582
generativity versus self-absorption, 470
genes, 107, 439
genetic drift, 114
genetic mapping, 110–112
genetic relatedness, 108
genetics
  see also heredity
  adoption studies, 110
  basic principles, 107–109
  chromosomes, 107
  dominant gene, 107–108
  eating disorders, 616
  family studies, 109
  genotype, 108–109
  heterozygous condition, 107, 108f
  homozygous condition, 107, 108f
  mood disorders, vulnerability to, 593
  mutation, 114
  and personality, 515–516, 515f
  phenotype, 108–109
  polygenic traits, 109
  research methods, 109–112

and schizophrenic disorders, 601
  selective breeding, 109
  twin studies, 109–110
genital herpes, 442
genital stage, 500
genotype, 108–109
genuineness, 630
germinal stage, 439
Gestalt principles, 146f
  closure, 145
  continuity, 146
  figure and ground, 145, 145f
  in paintings, 171
  phi phenomenon, 145
  proximity, 145
  similarity, 145
  simplicity, 145–146
Gestalt psychology, 7
giftedness
  drudge theory, 366
  hidden gifted, 365–366
  identification of gifted children, 364–365
  and life achievements, 365–366
  personal qualities of, 365
  three-ring conception of eminent giftedness, 366f
glia, 78
gloom, 417
glucose, 396
glucostats, 396
glycine, 86
gonadotropins, 106
gonads, 106
Goodale, Mel, 154, 154f
Greenberg, Les, 630
group cohesiveness, 696
group polarization, 695
group tests, 358
group therapy, 632–633
group unanimity, 688
groups
  bystander effect, 693
  common features, 692–693
  decision making, 694–696
  defined, 692
  group polarization, 695
  groupthink, 695–696
  productivity, 693–694
  size, and conformity, 688
  social loafing, 694
groupthink, 695–696, 696f
growth needs, 512
growth spurt, 463–464
gustatory system, 162–164, 162f

H

habitual tasks, 299
habituation, 458
hair cells, 157
Hall, Calvin, 197
Hall, G. Stanley, 4, 12
hallucinations, 599
hallucinogens, 208–209
happiness
  age, 429
  and culture, 430
  health, 429
  hedonic adaptation, 431
  intelligence, 429
  love and marriage, 430

moderately good predictors of happiness, 429–430
  and money, 428
  non-predictive factors, 428–429
  parenthood, 429
  physical attractiveness, 429
  possible causal relations among correlates, 431f
  and religion, 429–430
  social activity, 429
  strong predictors of happiness, 430–431
  subjective well-being, 428, 431
  work, 430
Hare, Robert, 606–607
hashish, 209
Hatfield, Elaine, 676
Hazen, Cindy, 676
health
  biopsychosocial model, 536
  and drugs, 212–214
  and happiness, 429
  health-impairing behaviour, 558–564
  heart disease, 552–554
  illness, changing patterns of, 536f
  and obesity, 399–400, 400f
  rational thinking about risks and decisions, 570–571
  stress, effects of, 552–557
  stress-illness correlation, 556–557, 557f
health-impairing behaviour
  and AIDS, 560–562
  alcohol and drug use, 560
  development of, 562–563
  lack of exercise, 560, 561f
  poor nutritional habits, 559–560
  smoking, 558–559
healthy personality, 512, 513f
hearing. See auditory system
heart disease, 552–553
Hebb, Donald, 17, 17f, 83
Hebbian Learning Rule, 83–84
hedonic adaptation, 431
Heider, Fritz, 669–670
height in plane, 149
hemispheric specialization, 104–105
hereditary genius, 356
heredity
  see also genetics
  and behaviour, 107–112
  and the environment, 112
  and hunger, 395–397
  influence of, 29
  and intelligence, 367–369, 370
  polygenic traits, 109
  research methods, 109–112
  and sexual orientation, 411–413

heritability estimates, 368–369, 369f, 516
heritability ratio, 368–369
Hermann grid, 136f
hertz (Hz), 156
heterosexuals, 409
heterozygous condition, 107, 108f
heuristics
  availability heuristic, 337, 341, 619
  in decision making, 337
  defined, 329
  representation of the problem, 331–332
  representativeness heuristic, 337, 617
  searching for analogies, 330–331
  subgoals, 330
  working backward, 330
hidden gifted, 365–366
hierarchical classification problems, 456
hierarchy of needs, 511–512, 512f
higher-order conditioning, 235, 236f
highly active antiretroviral therapy, 561
highway hypnosis, 204
Hilgard, Ernest, 204
hindbrain, 95
hindsight bias, 306, 530–531, 672
hippocampal region, 295
hippocampal volume, 594
hippocampus, 97, 594
history of psychology (overview), 22–23
hobbits and orcs problem, 326, 327f, 328f
Hobson, J. Alan, 200
Hodgkin, Alan, 79
Hogan, Michael E., 595
holistic cognitive style, 334
Hollingworth, Leta, 5
homelessness, 651–652
homeostasis, 392–393, 393f
homosexuality
  biological theories, 411–413
  discrimination, 412–413
  environmental theories, 411
  statistics, 410–411
homosexuals, 409
homozygous condition, 107, 108f
hopelessness theory, 595
hormonal regulation. See hormones
hormones
  androgens, 403–404
  defined, 105
  developmental effects, 106–107
  estrogens, 403
  and gender differences, 483
  and hunger, 396–397
  negative feedback systems, 106
  and sexual desire, 403–404
hostility, and stress, 552–553, 567–568
Houck, Patricia R., 647

Hubel, David, 16, 137
human development. See development
Human Genome Project, 111
human hearing capacities, 156
human subjectivity, 29–30
humanism
  defined, 508
  described, 11–12
  evaluation of, 512–513
  inadequate evidence, 513
  person-centred theory (Rogers), 508–510
  phenomenological approach, 508
  poor testability, 513
  self-actualization theory (Maslow), 511–512
  view of human nature, 513
Hume, James Gibson, 12
humour, 567
hunger
  see also eating
  biological factors, 395–397
  brain regulation, 395–396
  digestive regulation, 396
  environmental factors, 397–399
  and food availability, 397
  glucose, 396
  hormonal regulation, 396–397
  hypothalamus, 395, 395f
  motivation of, 395–402
hunger centre, 97
Husain, Gabriela, 161
Huxley, Andrew, 79
hydrocephaly, 364
hypnic jerks, 186
hypnosis
  as altered state of consciousness, 204
  and amnesia, 203
  anesthesia, 202–203
  brain-imaging studies, 204
  defined, 201
  disinhibition, 203
  dissociation, 204
  highway hypnosis, 204
  hypnotic phenomena, 202–203
  hypnotic susceptibility, 201–202, 202f
  myth vs. reality, 202f
  posthypnotic suggestions, 203
  as role playing, 203–204
  sensory distortions and hallucinations, 203
  theories of hypnosis, 203–204
hypnotic induction, 201
hypnotic susceptibility, 201–202, 202f
hypnotism, 201
hypochondriasis, 587
hypogonadism, 4.3
hypothalamus, 97, 106, 395, 395f, 544
hypothesis
  defined, 42
  formulation of, 44
hypothetical constructs, 354

I
"I have a friend who" syndrome, 72–73
ice, 208
id, 495
identical twins, 109, 111f
identification, 498
identity, 467–468
identity achievement, 468
identity diffusion, 468
identity foreclosure, 468
identity moratorium, 468
identity statuses, 467–468, 467f, 468f
ignoring base rates, 337–338
illness
  biopsychosocial model, 536
  changing patterns of, 536f
  communication with health providers, 563–564
  decision to seek treatment, 563
  health-impairing behaviour, 558–564
  heart disease, 552–554
  medical advice, adherence to, 564
  reactions to, 563–564
  stress, effects of, 552–557
  stress-illness correlation, 556–557, 557f
  symptoms, 563
illusion, and art, 169–174
illusion of asymmetric insight, 668
illusory correlation, 667, 699
imagery, 271–272
imaginative suggestibility, 202
Imber, Stanley D., 647
imitation, 484
immediate style, 667
immune response, 555
immune system, 230
immunosuppression, 231, 231f
impaired task performance, 549
implicit memory, 296–297
impossible figures, 151, 152f, 153f
Impressionists, 169
improbable, overestimation of, 341
inattentional blindness, 143
incentive, 393
incentive theories, 393–394
inclusive fitness, 115
incongruence, 509
independent memory systems, 296–299, 297f
independent variables, 48, 50
independent view of self, 522
individual psychology, 501–503
individual tests, 358
individualism, 430, 672–673, 692
inducing structure problems, 326

industrial and organizational psychology, 24, 25f
industry versus inferiority, 452
ineffective encoding, 287–288
infant mortality, 443f
infants, and babbling, 315
inferential statistics, 60–61
inferiority complex, 502
information processing
  in retina, 134–136
  in visual cortex, 136–138
information-processing theories, 273
infrared spectrum, 132
infrequent tasks, 299
ingroup, 669, 700–701
inhibited temperament, 447
inhibitory PSP, 82
initiative versus guilt, 452
innate cognitive abilities, 458–459
inner ear, 156–157
insanity, 610–611
insight, 326
insight therapies
  client-centred therapy, 629–631
  cognitive therapy, 631–632
  combined with medication, 647
  defined, 627
  described, 624
  evaluation of, 633–634
  group therapy, 632–633
  psychoanalysis, 8, 494, 624, 627–629
insomnia, 193–195, 218, 218f
inspection time, 377–378
instinctive drift, 249
institutional treatment, 649–652
instrumental response, 237
insulin, 396
integrative motivation, 321
integrity versus despair, 470
intelligence
  adoption studies, 368, 369
  analytical intelligence, 379
  biological indexes of intelligence, 377–379
  cognitive processes, 379–380
  creative intelligence, 379
  and creativity, 384–385
  crystallized intelligence, 376–377, 475
  cultural bias on IQ tests, 375
  cultural differences in IQ scores, 371–374
  culture-specific nature of, 362
  cumulative deprivation hypothesis, 369
  emotional intelligence, 381–382
  and environment, 369–370
  extremes of, 363–366
  factor analysis, 376

  family studies, 367
  fluid intelligence, 376–377, 475
  Flynn effect, 370, 370f
  Gardner's eight intelligences, 380–381, 380f
  generational changes, 370, 370f
  giftedness, 364–366
  group averages, differences in, 372–373
  Guilford's model of mental abilities, 377f
  and happiness, 429
  heredity and, 367–369, 370
  heritability, and cultural differences, 371–373
  heritability estimates, 368–369, 369f
  home environment, effects of, 369–370
  intelligence debate, 386–387
  IQ similarity, studies of, 368f
  laypersons' conceptions of, 361f
  mental retardation, 363, 363t
  multiple intelligences, 380–381
  new directions in study of, 376–381
  practical intelligence, 361, 379–380
  and racial stereotype vulnerability, 373–375
  reaction range, 370
  schooling effects, 369–370
  social intelligence, 361
  and socioeconomic disadvantage, 373
  Spearman's g, 377f
  specific mental abilities, increased emphasis on, 376–377
  testing perspective, 379
  triarchic theory of human intelligence, 379, 379f
  twin studies, 111f, 367–368
  verbal intelligence, 361
intelligence quotient (IQ), 357, 357t
intelligence testing
  basic questions about, 358–363
  Binet's breakthrough, 356
  correlation and, 356
  cultural bias, 375
  deviation IQ scores, 358
  emotional intelligence tests, 381
  evolution of, 356–357
  Galton's studies of hereditary genius, 356
  group tests, 358
  individual tests, 358
  intelligence quotient (IQ), 357, 357t
  IQ scores, 358–360
  knowledge, measurement of, 360
  normal distribution, 358, 360f

in other cultures, 362
percentile score, 356
potential, measurement
of, 360
questions, kinds of, 358
reliability of, 360–361
Terman and the Stanford-
Binet, 356–357
today, 357–358
validity, 361
vocational success, pre-
diction of, 362
Wechsler's innovations,
357
intelligence tests, 351
see also intelligence
testing
interactionist theories of
language acquisition,
324–325, 325*f*
interdependent view of self,
522
interference, 279, 301–302
interference theory, 288
intermittent reinforcement,
243
internal attributions,
669–670
Internet addiction, 546
interpersonal attraction
attachment, 676–678,
677*f*
culture, and close rela-
tionships, 678
defined, 674
evolutionary perspective,
679
key factors, 674–676
love, 676–678
matching hypothesis, 675
physical attractiveness,
674–675
reciprocity, 675
romantic ideals, 675–677
similarity effects, 675
interpersonal factors, and
mood disorders, 597,
597*f*
interposition, 149
interpretation, 628
interpretive theory of
mind, 459
interval schedules, 243
intimacy, 676
intimacy *versus* isolation,
470
introspection, 5
introverts, 501
inverted-U hypothesis,
542–543
IQ scores, 358–360
iris, 133
irrational thought, 599
irrelevant information, 327
irrelevant reasons, 433
irreversibility, 455

J

James, William, 5, 182, 424
James-Lange theory of
emotion, 424–425
Janis, Irving, 695
jealousy, 417
Jensen, Arthur, 371, 372
jet lag, 184–185
Johnson, Marcia K., 285
Johnson, Virginia, 413
joint custody, 72

journal, 45
journal articles, 69–71
joy, 417
Jung, Carl, 500–501
just noticeable difference
(JND), 128

K

Kahneman, Daniel, 337
Kapur, Shitij, 94
keyword method, 303, 304*f*
Kimura, Doreen, 13*f*, 106
kinesthetic system, 167
Kinetic Art, 173
knowledge, 279–282
Kohlberg, Lawrence,
460–461
Kohlberg's stage theory,
460–461, 460*f*
Kolb, Bryan, 101
koro, 611
Kupfer, David J., 647

L

Laborit, Henri, 644
lack of attention, 287
lack of exercise, 560
Lalonde, Christopher, 465
Lambert, Wallace, 319
language
acquisition of. *See* language acquisition
animals and, 321–322
anticipatory name-
calling, 345
bilingualism, 318–321
and the brain, 102*f*
defined, 312
described, 312–314
development of. *See* language development
in evolutionary
context, 322–323
generative nature
of, 312
linguistic relativity, 325
morphemes, 313–314
name-calling, 345
phonemes, 313, 313*t*
semantic nature of, 312
semantics, 313–314
shaping thought with
language, 344–345
structure of, 313–314
structured nature of,
312–313
symbolic nature of, 312
syntax, 314
language acquisition
behaviourist theories, 323
cognitive theories, 324
emergentist theories, 324
interactionist theories,
324–325, 325*f*
language acquisition
device (LAD), 324
nativist theories, 323–324
semantic slanting,
344–345
social communication
theories, 324
language acquisition device
(LAD), 324
language development
babbling, 315
bilingualism, effect of,
318–319
combining words, 318

fast mapping, 317
manual babbling,
315–316
mean length of utterance
(MLU), 318
metalinguistic awareness,
318
milestones, 314–318
optimal periods, 314–315
overextension, 317
overregularizations, 318
overview of, 314*t*
productive vocabulary,
317
receptive vocabulary, 317
telegraphic speech, 318
using words, 317
vocabulary spurt, 317,
317*f*
word production,
314–315
language tasks, 118
Lassonde, Maryse, 104
latency stage, 500
latent content, 219
lateral antagonism,
135–136
lateral geniculate nucleus
(LGN), 136
lateral hypothalamus, 395
the law, and personality
disorders, 610–611
law of effect, 237
law of small numbers,
340–341
Lazarus, Richard, 537
learned helplessness,
545–546, 595
learned preferences and
habits, 397–398
learning
and anxiety disorders,
585
and attitude formation
and change,
684–685
avoidance learning, 246
and behaviour modifica-
tion, 258–261
classical conditioning,
227–236
conditioning, 226,
249–252
defined, 226
escape learning, 245
evolutionary perspectives,
251
observational learning,
253–255
operant conditioning,
236–248
overlearning, 301
types of, 256–257
lectures, 33–34
LeDoux, Joseph, 421
left hemisphere, 102–105,
117–119
lens, 132
leptin, 396–397
lesbian, 409
levels of awareness, 182
levels-of-processing theory,
270–271, 270*f*, 271*f*
lie detector, 419–420
life changes, 539–540
lifetime prevalence, 579,
617, 617*f*
light, 131–132, 131*f*, 149

light adaptation, 134
likability, 682
lily pond problem, 330
limbic system, 97–98, 421
linear perspective, 149
linguistic relativity, 325
linguistic relativity hypothesis, 344–345
link method, 303, 304*f*
lithium, 641–642
lobes, 99
lobotomies, 639
Lockhart, Robert, 270
Loftus, Elizabeth, 284
long-term memory (LTM)
defined, 276
flashbulb memories,
277–278
permanency of storage,
276–277
vs. short-term memory,
278–279
long-term potentiation,
294–295
longitudinal design, 446, 447*f*
Lopez, David, 510
love
as attachment, 676–678,
677*f*
commitment, 676
companionate love, 676
and happiness, 430
intimacy, 676
passionate love, 676
lowball technique, 703
LSD, 209, 623–624
lucid dreams, 198–199, 219

M

magnocellular channels,
136
major depressive disorder,
591–592
maladaptive behaviour, 577
male menopause, 473
malingering, 587
mania, 591, 592
see also mood disorders
manic episodes, 592*t*
manifest content, 219
mantra, 205
manual babbling, 315–316
MAO inhibitors, 641
Marentette, Paula F., 315
marijuana, 181, 209,
213–214
marital satisfaction, 472*f*
marriage, and happiness,
430, 471–472
Maslow, Abraham, 11,
511–512
Masters, William, 413
matching hypothesis, 675
matchstick problem, 329*f*,
331*f*
mate preferences, 407
maternal drug use, 441–442
maternal illness, 442–443
maternal nutrition, 441
mathematical ability, 482
mating priorities, 407–408
maturation, 444–445
Mazumdar, Sati, 647
McClelland, David,
415–416
McCollough effect, 139, 139*f*
MDMA ("ecstasy"), 207,
209, 214

mean, 57
mean length of utterance
(MLU), 318
measurement, 42
media, and gender-role
socialization, 485
medial forebrain bundle, 98
median, 57
medical advice, adherence
to, 564
medical model, 576–577
meditation
brain-imaging technolo-
gies, 205
defined, 204
long-term benefits, 205
mantra, 205
physiological correlates,
205
medulla, 95
Meichenbaum, Donald,
631–632
melatonin, 184, 185
Melzack, Ronald, 166
memory
and aging, 475
anatomy of memory,
295–296, 295*f*
biochemistry of memory,
294
chunks, 275–276
clustering, 279–280
conceptual hierarchy,
280, 280*f*
and confirmatory biases,
667
connectionist models,
282
consolidation, 296
deep processing, 302
distributed practice,
301–302, 302*f*
divided attention, 270
dual-code theory, 272
encoding, 268, 269–273
explicit memory, 296–297
eyewitness accounts,
305–306
false memories, 290–293
flashbulb memories,
277–278
forgetting, 286–293
hindsight bias, 306
implicit memory,
296–297
improvement of, 301–304
interference, 301–302
key processes in, 268*f*
knowledge, representa-
tion and organiza-
tion of, 279–282
localized neural circuits,
294–295
long-term memory (LTM),
276–279
long-term potentiation,
294–295
memory traces, 294–296
mnemonic devices,
301–304
neural circuitry, 294–295
next-in-line effect, 269
organization of informa-
tion, 302
parallel distributed pro-
cessing (PDP)
models, 282
physiology of, 294–296

prospective memory, 298–299, 299f
reconstructions, 284–285
rehearsal, 275, 301
retrieval, 268, 282–285
retrospective memory, 299, 299f
schema, 280–281
semantic networks, 281–282, 281f
sensory memory, 273–274, 274f
serial-position effect, 301, 302f
short-term memory (STM), 275–276
storage, 268, 273–282
systems. See memory systems
working memory, 276, 276f, 475
memory biases, 699
memory consolidation, 193
memory systems
  declarative memory system, 297–298
  episodic memory system, 298, 475
  multiple memory systems, 296–299
  non-declarative memory system, 297–298
  procedural memory system, 297–298, 475
  semantic memory system, 298, 475
  theories of independent memory systems, 296–299, 297f
memory traces, 294–296
menarche, 464
meninges, 88
meningitis, 88
menopause, 473
mens rea, 610
mental ability tests, 351
mental age, 356
mental health professionals, 626
mental hospital, 649–650
mental illness. See psychological disorders
mental retardation
  categories of, 363t
  defined, 363
  levels of retardation, 363
  mildly retarded category, 363
  origins of, 363–364
  prevalence, 364f
  severity, 364f
  and social class, 364f
mental set, 328
mescaline, 209
Mesmer, Franz Anton, 201
mesolimbic dopamine pathway, 211, 211f
message, 681
meta-analysis, 481
metalinguistic awareness, 318
method of loci, 303, 304f
microelectrodes, 79
midbrain, 95–97
middle ear, 156
midlife crisis, 469–470
Milgram, Stanley, 689–691

Miller, George, 275–276
Miller, Mark D., 647
Miller, Neal, 66
Milner, Brenda, 13, 90, 90f, 91, 296
minimization of physiological vulnerability, 568–569
Minnesota Multiphasic Personality Inventory (MMPI), 525–526, 526t, 527f
Mischel, Walter, 507
misinformation effect, 284–285, 285f, 305
M'Naghten rule, 610
mnemonic devices
  acoustics, 302–303
  acronyms, 302–303
  defined, 301
  keyword method, 303, 304f
  link method, 303, 304f
  method of loci, 303, 304f
  narrative methods, 303, 303f
  rhymes, 303
  verbal mnemonics, 302–304
  visual mnemonics, 303–304
mode, 57
model, 506
model personality, 521
molecular geneticists, 110–111
money, and happiness, 428
monoamines, 85–86, 210
monocular cues, 148–149
monozygotic twins, 109, 111f
Montreal Neurological Institute, 92
mood disorders
  basic types of, 591
  bipolar disorder, 592–593
  cognitive factors, 595
  cyclothymic disorder, 592
  defined, 590
  depression, 553–554, 591, 592, 595–596
  depressive episodes, 592t
  dispositional factors, 594–596
  dysthymic disorder, 592
  etiology, 593–595
  genetic vulnerability, 593
  hippocampal volume, 594
  hopelessness theory, 595
  interpersonal factors, 597, 597f
  learned helplessness model, 595
  major depressive disorder, 591–592
  mania, 591, 592
  manic episodes, 592t
  negative thinking, 597f
  and negative thinking, 595–596
  neurochemical factors, 594
  predisposition to, 593
  and stress, 597
mood stabilizers, 642
moon illusion, 152, 153f
moral reasoning, 460–461
Moroz, Tara M., 94

morphemes, 313–314
morphine, 86
mortality rates, 341t
Moscovitch, Morris, 94
motion parallax, 149
motivated forgetting, 289, 498
motivation
  see also motivational theories
  achievement, 415–417
  affiliation, 414–415
  to avoid failure, 417
  described, 392
  diversity of human motives, 394, 394f
  and emotion, 417
  of hunger and eating, 395–402
  integrative motivation, 321
  and observational learning, 254
  sexual motivation. See sexual behaviour
motivational theories
  drive theories, 392–393
  evolutionary theories, 394
  expectancy-value models, 393–394
  incentive theories, 393–394
motor development
  basic principles, 444–445
  cephalocaudal trend, 444
  cultural differences, 445–446
  defined, 444
  developmental norms, 445
  maturation, 444–445
  proximodistal trend, 444
Mozart effect, 121, 160
MRI (magnetic resonance imaging) scan, 93, 93f
Müller-Lyer illusion, 150, 150f, 152–153
multi-orgasmic, 413
multiaxial evaluation, 581f
multicultural sensitivity in treatment, 648–649
Multifactor Emotional Intelligence Scale (MEIS), 381
multifactorial causation, 209
multiple causes, 28
multiple-choice exam tips, 35
multiple memory systems, 296–299
multiple personality disorder, 589
multiple sclerosis, 79
Murray, Henry, 415
music, 159–160, 161
mutation, 114
myelin sheath, 79

N
name-calling, 345
napping, 189
naps, 216
narcolepsy, 195–196
narcotics, 207–208
narrative methods, 303, 303f
national character, 521

nativist theories of language acquisition, 323–324
natural selection, 5, 113
naturalistic observation, 52
nature versus nurture, 356
nearsightedness, 132–133, 133f
Necker cube, 147, 147f, 172–173
need for self-actualization, 512
negative correlation, 58, 59f
negative feedback systems, 106
negative punishment, 247
negative reinforcement
  and avoidant behaviour, 245–246
  defined, 245
  vs. positive reinforcement, 244–245, 245f
  vs. punishment, 247, 247f
negative symptoms, 600
negative thinking, 595–596, 597f
negotiations, 262–263
NEO Personality Inventory, 526
neo-Piagetian theories, 457–458
nerves, 87
nervous system
  see also the brain; neurons; neurotransmitters
  autonomic nervous system, 87, 88, 89f, 419
  axon, 79
  central nervous system, 87, 88–89
  communication in, 78–86
  dendrites, 79
  dendritic trees, 79
  glia, 78
  myelin sheath, 79
  neural impulse, 79–80, 81f
  neural networks, 82–83
  neurons, 78–79, 79f
  organization of, 87–89, 87f
  parasympathetic division, 88
  peripheral nervous system, 87–88
  soma, 79
  somatic nervous system, 87, 88
  spinal cord, 89
  sympathetic division, 88
  synapses, 79, 82f
  synaptic cleft, 80–82
  synaptic pruning, 83, 84f
  synaptic transmission, 83f
  terminal buttons, 79
neural circuits, 294–295, 396, 420–422
neural development, 120
neural impulse, 79–80, 81f
neural networks, 82–83
neuro-scientists, 90
neurodevelopmental hypothesis, 603, 603f
neurons
  see also nervous system

absolute refractory period, 80
action potential, 80
defined, 78
dendritic trees, 79
described, 78–79
glia cells, 78
Hebbian Learning Rule, 83–84
and neural impulse, 79–80
postsynaptic neuron, 80
presynaptic neuron, 80
relative refractory period, 80
resting potential, 80
structure of, 79f
synapses, 80–84, 82f
neuroticism, 493, 515
neurotransmitters
  see also nervous system
  acetylcholine (ACh), 84–85
  and agonists, 84
  and antagonists, 85
  and behaviour, 84–87
  defined, 80
  endorphins, 86
  excitatory PSP, 82
  functions of common neurotransmitters, 85f
  GABA (gamma-aminobutyric acid), 86
  inhibitory PSP, 82
  monoamines, 85–86
  nervous system, 79
  postsynaptic potential (PSP), 82
  reuptake, 82
  schizophrenic disorders, 601–602
  and stimulants, 210–211, 210f
  synaptic transmission, 83f
New York therapy, 631–632
next-in-line effect, 269
night terrors, 196
nightmares, 196
nine-dot problem, 329f, 331f
noise, 129
Nolen-Hoeksema, Susan, 594
nominal fallacy, 221
non-declarative memory system, 297–298
non-REM (NREM) sleep, 188
non sequitur, 433
non-verbal communication, 482
noncorporal punishment, 248
nonimmediate style, 667
nontasters, 163
nonverbal expressiveness, 422
norepinephrine, 85
normal distribution, 357, 358, 360f
not criminally responsible on account of mental disorder, 610, 611
not guilty by reason of insanity (NGR), 610
nucleus accumbens, 211
nutritional habits, 559–560

O

obedience
cultural variations in, 691–692
defined, 689
Milgram's studies, 689–691
obesity
defined, 399
dietary restraint, 401–402
excessive eating, 400
genetic predisposition, 400
heritability of weight, 401f
inadequate exercise, 400
prevalence of, 399–400
set-point theory, 401
settling-point theory, 401
weight, and various diseases, 400f
object perception. See visual perception
object permanence, 454
observational learning
acquisition, 254
applications, 254–255
attention, 253
attitude formation and change, 685
basic processes, 253–254
Bobo doll, 254, 254f
defined, 506
described, 253
and gender differences, 484
motivation, 254
performance, 254
reproduction, 253–254
retention, 253
obsessive-compulsive disorder (OCD), 583–584
occipital lobe, 99
occupational stereotypes, 667
odours, 164
Oedipal complex, 500
Official Languages Act, 311
Olds, James, 98
olfactory cilia, 164
olfactory system, 164, 164f
one-sided argument, 682
openness to experience, 493
operant chamber, 238
operant conditioning
see also conditioning
acquisition, 238–240
anxiety disorders, 585
attitude formation and change, 684–685
basic processes, 238–241
vs. classical conditioning, 241t
cumulative recorder, 238, 239f
defined, 236
discriminative stimuli, 240–241
emitted responses, 238
extinction, 240
and gender differences, 484
law of effect, 237
operant chamber, 238
and personality, 504–506
prejudice, preservation of, 700

procedures, 237–238
punishment, 246–248
reinforcement, 237, 242–246
reinforcement contingencies, 238
resistance to extinction, 240
schedule of reinforcement, 240, 242–244
shaping, 238–240, 241f
Skinner box, 238, 239f
stimulus control, 240–241
stimulus discrimination, 241
stimulus generalization, 241
terminology, 237–238
operational definition, 44
opiates, 207–208
opponent process theory, 141–142
optic chiasm, 136
optic disk, 134
optical illusions, 150–153
optimism, 558
optimistic explanatory style, 558
oral stage, 499
organization of information, 302
orgasm, 413–414
osteoporosis, 614
other-oriented perfectionism, 594
outgroup, 669, 700–701
overcompensation, 502
overconfidence, 306
overconfidence effect, 342
overdose, 212–213
overestimation of the improbable, 341
overextension, 317
overextrapolations, 120–121
overlearning, 301
overregularizations, 318

P

pain perception, 165–167
pancultural view, 611
panic disorder, 582, 586f
Pappenheim, Bertha, 624
parahippocampal region, 295
parallel distributed processing (PDP) models, 282
parallel processing, 136
paranoid schizophrenia, 599
parasympathetic division, 88
paraventricular nucleus (PVN), 396
parental investment theory, 405, 406f
parenthood
adjustments to, 472
and happiness, 429
parietal lobe, 99
Parkinsonism, 85
partial reinforcement, 243
partial sleep deprivation, 191–192
participants, 45
parvocellular channels, 136
Pascual-Leone, Juan, 457

passionate love, 676
pattern perception. See visual perception
patterns of neural activity, 83
Paulhus, Delroy, 503
Pavlov, Ivan, 7, 227
Pavlovian conditioning, 227
see also classical conditioning
Penfield, Wilder, 90, 90f, 92
penis envy, 500
Pepler, Debra J., 15
percentile score, 351–352, 356
perception
see also senses
art, and illusion, 169–174
auditory perception, 157–159
defined, 126
of flavour, 163
manipulation of person perception, 30f
pain perception, 165–167
person perception, 664–669
vs. sensation, 126f
subliminal perception, 129–130
vision for perception, 153–155
visual perception. See visual perception
perceptual ambiguity, 172
perceptual asymmetries, 105, 118f
perceptual constancies, 149–150
perceptual hypothesis, 146–148
perceptual organization. See visual perception
perceptual set, 143
Perel, James F., 647
perfectionism, 594
performance of response, 254
periaqueductal gray (PAG), 166
peripheral nervous system, 87–88
peripheral route, 686
persistent nightmares, 196
person-centred theory
anxiety and defence, 509–510
described, 508
development of the self, 509
incongruence, 509
personality development and dynamics, 509f
personality structure, 509f
self-concept, 509
person perception
bias in, 667–668
cognitive schemas, 666
defined, 664
evolutionary perspective, 668–669
illusion of asymmetric insight, 668
ingroup, 669
outgroup, 669
physical appearance, effects of, 665–666

prejudice and, 698–699
social schemas, 666, 666f
spotlight effect, 668
stereotypes, 666–667
subjectivity, 667–668
person-situation controversy, 507
personal distress, 577
personal unconscious, 501
personality
analytical psychology (Jung), 500–501
and behavioural genetics, 515–516, 515f
behaviourism, 504–508
biological perspectives, 514–517
consistency, 492
contemporary empirical approaches, 520–521
creative personality, 384
and culture, 521–523
defined, 492
distinctiveness, 492
and eating disorders, 616
evolutionary approach, 516–517
Eysenck's theory, 514–515, 514f
five-factor model of personality traits, 493–494
fragmented view of, 508
gender differences, 482
and happiness, 430–431
healthy personality, 512, 513f
hindsight bias, 530–531
humanism, 508–513
individual psychology (Adler), 501–503
major views of, 518–519
mood disorders, 594–596
nature of, 492–494
operant conditioning, 504–506
person-centred theory (Rogers), 508–510
person-situation controversy, 507
psychoanalytic theory (Freud), 494–500
psychodynamic perspectives, 494–503
self-actualization theory (Maslow), 511–512
self-monitoring, 520–521
sensation seeking, 520, 521f
Skinner's ideas, 504–505
social cognitive theory (Bandura), 505–507
and somatoform disorders, 588
structure of, 495, 504, 509f
twin studies, 111f
Type A personality, 552–553
Type B personality, 552–553
personality assessment
Minnesota Multiphasic Personality Inventory (MMPI), 525–526, 526t, 527f
NEO Personality Inventory, 526

personality scales, 525
projective test, 528t
projective tests, 528–529
self-report inventories, 525–528
Sixteen Personality Factor (16PF) Questionnaire, 526, 527f
personality development
adolescence, 467–468
adulthood, 469–470
childhood development, 451–452
Erikson's stage theory, 451–452, 451f
midlife crisis, 469–470
stability, 469
personality disorders
antisocial personality disorder, 606–607
clusters, 605–606
defined, 605
diagnostic problems, 606
overview of, 605t
personality scales, 525
personality tests, 351
personality traits
defined, 492
factor analysis, 492–493
persuasion
appeals, 683
channel, 681
classical conditioning, 262–263
message, 681
message factors, 682–683
overview of process, 681f
receiver factors, 683–684
source, 681
source factors, 681–682
validity effect, 683
Pert, Candace, 86
pessimistic explanatory style, 558, 595
PET (positron emission tomography) scanning, 93, 93f
Petitto, Laura-Anne, 315
phallic stage, 500
phenomenological approach, 508
phenotype, 108–109
phenylketonuria, 364
phi phenomenon, 145
phobias, 227, 229–230, 585f
phobic disorder, 582
phonemes, 313, 313t
phonemic encoding, 271, 279
phonological rehearsal loop, 276
physical appearance, 665–666
physical attractiveness, 176f, 429, 674–675
physical characteristics, 115
physical dependence, 212
physical fitness, and mortality, 569f
physical inactivity, 560, 561f
physiological arousal, 398
physiological responses to stress, 543–544
physiology, 16–17
Piaget, Jean, 16, 453–457

Piaget's stage theory
accommodation, 454
animism, 455
assimilation, 454
centration, 454
concrete operational period, 455–456
conservation, 454, 455f
decentration, 455
described, 453–454
egocentrism, 455
evaluation of, 456–457
formal operational period, 456
irreversibility, 455
object permanence, 454
preoperational period, 454–455
reversibility, 455
sensorimotor period, 454
Pibloktoq, 612
pictorial depth cues, 149
Pilcher, June J., 192
pineal gland, 184
Pinker, Steven, 323
pinna, 156
pitfalls, 340–343
pituitary gland, 106
place theory, 158
placebo, 63
placebo effects, 63, 658
placenta, 439
plateau phase, 413
pleasure principle, 495
Plomin, Robert, 112
Poggendorff illusion, 151f
point prevalence rates, 617
pointillism, 170
political agenda, 487
politics, and classical conditioning, 263
Pollock, Bruce G., 647
polygenic traits, 109
polygraph, 419–420, 420f
pons, 95
Ponzo illusion, 150–151, 151f
poor nutritional habits, 559–560
population, 62, 62f
pornography, 404–405
positive correlation, 58, 59f
positive emotionality, 493
positive psychology, 419
positive punishment, 247
positive reinforcement, 244–245, 245f
positive symptoms, 600
post-traumatic stress disorder (PTSD), 550, 575, 584
postconventional level, 461
posthypnotic suggestions, 203
postsynaptic potential (PSP), 82
practical intelligence, 361, 379–380
Pragnanz, 145
preconscious, 496
preconventional level, 460
prediction, 42, 59–60, 362
predictive value, 252
preferences, 335
prefrontal cortex, 99–101, 296, 421
prefrontal leucotomy, 639

prejudice
biases in attribution, 699–700
defined, 698
discrimination, 698, 699f
ethnocentrism, 700
formation of, 700
ingroups, 700–701
outgroups, 700–701
potential components of, 698f
preservation of, 700
stereotypes, 698–699
subjectivity in person perception, 698–699
premises, 432
prenatal development
age of viability, 440
course of, 439–440
embryonic stage, 439–440
environmental factors, 440–443
fetal stage, 440
germinal stage, 439
maternal drug use, 441–442
maternal illness, 442–443
maternal nutrition, 441
overview of fetal development, 441f
placenta, 439
vulnerability periods, 442f
zygote, 439
prenatal period, 439
preoperational period, 454–455
preparedness, 250–251, 585
pressure, 165, 540, 541f
presynaptic neuron, 80
prevalence
childhood abuse, 290f
defined, 579
depression, 592
eating disorders, 615–616
false memories, 292f
insomnia, 194
lifetime prevalence, 579
mental retardation, 364f
obesity, 399–400
psychological disorders, 55t, 579–581, 581f
schizophrenic disorders, 598
smoking in Canada, 559f
of traumatic events, 551f
weight, and various diseases, 400f
primary auditory cortex, 99
primary emotions, 426f
primary mental abilities, 376
primary motor cortex, 99, 100f
primary-process thinking, 495
primary reinforcers, 242
primary sex characteristics, 464
primary somatosensory cortex, 99
primary tastes, 162
primary visual cortex, 99, 136
proactive interference, 288, 289f
probabilities, 617–619
problem solving
algorithms, 329
approaches, 329–332

barriers, 326–329
and culture, 332–334
defined, 326
field dependence-independence, 332–333
functional fixedness, 328
heuristics, 329–332
irrelevant information, 327
mental set, 328
problem space, 329
representation of the problem, 331–332
searching for analogies, 330–331
standard problems, 326, 327f
subgoals, 330
trial and error, 329
types of problems, 326
unnecessary constraints, 328–329
working backward, 330
problem-solving view, 200
problem space, 329
procedural memory system, 297–298, 475
productive vocabulary, 317
professional specialties in psychology, 25–26
professionalization of psychology, 14–16
prognosis, 577
progressive relaxation, 218
projection, 498
projective hypothesis, 528
projective test, 415, 528t
projective tests, 528–529
prospective memory, 298–299, 299f
proximal stimuli, 146–147, 147f
proximity, 145
proximodistal trend, 444
pseudo-insomnia, 194
pseudoforgetting, 287–288
psilocybin, 209
psychiatric nurses, 626
psychiatrists, 626
psychiatry, 25
psychic driving, 623
psychic reflexes, 227–228, 228–229
psychoactive drugs, 206
see also drugs
psychoanalysis
defined, 627
described, 8, 494
development of, 624
dream analysis, 627
free association, 627
interpretation, 628
modern psychodynamic therapies, 629
resistance, 628
transference, 628–629
psychoanalytic theory
anxiety, 497–499
conflict, 496–497
conscious, 496
defence mechanisms, 497–499
described, 8, 494–495
ego, 495
id, 495
influence of, 9

levels of awareness, 495–496
personality dynamics model, 497f
pleasure principle, 495
preconscious, 496
psychosexual stages of development, 499–500
reality principle, 495
resistance to, 9
sex and aggression, conflict and tyranny of, 496–497
structure of personality, 495
superego, 495
unconscious, 496
psychodynamic theories
analytical psychology (Jung), 500–501
defined, 494
evaluation of, 503
inadequate evidence, 503
individual psychology (Adler), 501–503
poor testability, 503
psychoanalytic theory (Freud), 494–500
sexism in, 503
psychodynamic therapies, 629
psychological autopsies, 53
psychological dependence, 212
psychological disorders
see also abnormal behaviour
anxiety disorders, 582–586
classification of, 579, 580f
comorbidity, 618
and creativity, 385, 385f
critical thinking about, 617–619
and culture, 611–612
culture-bound disorders, 611–612
diagnosis, 577
dissociative disorders, 589–590
eating disorders, 614–616
epidemiology, 579
etiology, 577
and the law, 610–611
lifetime prevalence, 617, 617f
mood disorders, 590–597
multiaxial evaluation, 581f
overview of three categories of, 608–609
pancultural view, 611
personality disorders, 605–607
post-traumatic stress disorders (PTSD), 550, 575
prevalence, 55t, 579–581, 581f
prognosis, 577
relativistic view, 611
and revolving door, 651–652
schizophrenic disorders, 598–604
somatoform disorders, 586–588

stereotypes of, 578–579
stress, 550–551
treatment. See treatment
universalistic view, 611
violence and, 578
vulnerability, 112
Psychological Screening Inventory, 354
psychological tests
achievement tests, 351
aptitude tests, 351, 352f
correlation coefficient, 353
and creativity, 384
defined, 351
intelligence tests, 351
see also intelligence testing
mental ability tests, 351
percentile score, 351–352
personality tests, 351
reliability, 353
standardization, 351–352
standardization group, 352
test norms, 351–352
types of, 351
validity, 353–355
psychological themes
cultural heritage, effect of, 28–29
empirical nature of psychology, 26
heredity and environment, 29
multiple causes of behaviour, 28
sociohistorical context, 27–28
study of psychology, 26–28
subject matter of psychology, 28–30
subjective nature of experiences, 29–30
theoretical diversity, 26–27
psychologists, 21f, 625–626
psychology
applied psychology, 14
behaviourism, debut of, 6–7
in Canada, 13–14
clinical psychology, 14
cognition, renewed interest in, 16–17
contemporary psychology, 21–25
and cultural diversity, 18–19
defined, 21
development of, 3–21
early research laboratories, 4f
and ethnocentrism, 19
evolutionary psychology, 19–21
Freud's contributions, 8–9
functionalism, 4–6
Hall's contributions, 4
humanism, 11–12
important figures in, 10t
major research areas, 24, 24f
origins of word, 3
overview of history, 22–23

physiology, renewed interest in, 16–17
professional specialties, 25–26
professionalization of, 14–16
Skinner's contributions, 9–10
structuralism, 4–6
themes. *See* psychological themes
Watson's contribution, 6–7
women in, 13, 13*f*
Wundt's contributions, 3–4
Psychopathy Checklist— Revised (PCL-R), 606–607
psychopharmacotherapy, 639
see also drug therapy
psychophysical scaling, 128
psychophysics
see also senses
absolute threshold, 127, 127*f*, 128*t*
defined, 127
Fechner's law, 128
just noticeable difference (JND), 128
psychophysical scaling, 128
sensory adaptation, 130
signal-detection theory, 128–129
subliminal perception, 129–130
thresholds, 127
Weber's law, 128
psychosexual stages
anal stage, 499–500
defined, 499
described, 499*t*
fixation, 499
genital stage, 500
latency stage, 500
Oedipal complex, 500
oral stage, 499
phallic stage, 500
psychosocial crisis, 451
psychosomatic, 586
psychosomatic diseases, 552, 586
psychosurgery, 639
psychotherapy
see also treatment
described, 624
psychoticism, 515
PsycINFO, 69–70
puberty, 463–464, 463*f*
pubescence, 463
pull theories, 393
punishment
defined, 247
negative punishment, 247
vs. negative reinforcement, 247, 247*f*
noncorporal punishment, 248
positive punishment, 247
and self-modification programs, 261
side effects of physical punishment, 247–248

pupil, 133
purity, 131, 155
push theories, 393

Q

quails, and sex, 232

R

racial stereotype vulnerability, 373–375
racism, 663
radical behaviourism, 9
random assignment, 49
rape victim-offender relationships, 405*f*
rapid response rate, 238
ratio schedules, 243
rational-emotive therapy, 566–567
rationalization, 497
reaction formation, 498
reaction range, 370, 371*f*
reaction time (RT), 377
reading, 33
reading journal articles, 69–71
reality monitoring, 285, 502
reality principle, 495
reappraisal, 566–567
recall, 286
receptive field, 135, 135*f*, 165, 165*f*
receptive vocabulary, 317
receptor sites, 82
reciprocal determinism, 505–507
reciprocity, 675
reciprocity norm, 263, 703
recognition, 286–287
reconstructions, 284–285
recreational drug use. *See* drugs
red-outs, 283
refractory period, 414
regression, 498
regression toward the mean, 658
rehearsal, 275, 301
reification, 387
reinforcement
conditioned reinforcement, 242
conditioned reinforcers, 242
continuous reinforcement, 243
defined, 237
delayed reinforcement, 242
effect of, 242
intermittent reinforcement, 242–244, 243
negative reinforcement, 244–246
partial reinforcement, 243
positive reinforcement, 244–245
primary reinforcers, 242
and response-outcome relations, 252
schedules. *See* schedules of reinforcement
secondary reinforcers, 242
and self-modification programs, 260
reinforcement contingencies, 238

reinstating the context of an event, 282–283
relational schemas, 281
relationship harmony, 430
relative refractory period, 80
relative size, 149
relativistic view, 611
relaxation, 568
relaxation procedures, 195
relaxation response, 218, 568
relearning, 287
reliability, 353, 353*f*, 360–361
religion, and happiness, 429–430
REM deprivation, 192–193
REM sleep, 187–188
Remote Associates Test (RAT), 384, 384*f*
renewal effect, 234
replication, 62
reporting on findings, 45
representation of the problem, 331–332
representativeness, 337
representativeness heuristic, 337, 617
repressed memories controversy, 290–293
repression, 289, 497–498
reproduction, 253–254
Rescorla, Robert, 264
research
see also research methods
conclusions, 57–61
double-blind procedure, 64–65
ethics, 65–67, 66*f*
evaluation of, 62–65
experimenter bias, 64–65
major research areas, 24, 24*f*
placebo effects, 63
replication, 62
response set, 64
sampling bias, 62–63
self-report data, distortions in, 64
social desirability bias, 64
statistics, 57–61
research ethics, 65–67
research methods
brain research, 90–95
case studies, 52–54, 54*f*
defined, 47
descriptive/correlational research, 52–57
experimental research, 48–51
hereditary influence, investigation of, 109–112
naturalistic observation, 52
overview of key methods, 56*f*
selection of, 44–45
surveys, 54–55
vision research, 138–139
research studies
design of, 44–45
participants, 45
replication, 62
subjects, 45
research studies (featured studies)

the brain, and the self, 94–95
bullying in Canadian schoolyards, 15
combining insight therapy and medication, 647
fear, and sexual attraction, 46–47, 50, 50*t*
flashbulb memories, accuracy of, 277–278
insight therapy and medication, combined, 647
manual babbling, 315–316
mating priorities, 407–408
Milgram's obedience studies, 689–691
negative thinking, and depression, 595–596
quails, and sex, 232–233
racial stereotypes and test performance, 374–375
self-concept, effects on, 510–511
sleep deprivation, 192–193
speech prosody, and music, 161
stress, and the common cold, 555–556
youth suicide in Canada's First Nations, 465–466
resistance, 628, 657*f*
resistance stage, 544
resistance to extinction, 240
resolution phase, 414
response-outcome relations, and reinforcement, 252
response rate, 238
response set, 64, 528
response tendencies, 504
restrained eaters, 401
restricting type anorexia nervosa, 614
retention, 253, 286
reticular formation, 97, 190
retina, 132, 133–136, 133*f*
retinal disparity, 148
retrieval
context cues, 283
defined, 268
encoding specificity principle, 283
failure of, 289
misinformation effect, 284–285, 285*f*
reality monitoring, 285
reconstructions, 284–285
reinstating the context of an event, 282–283
retrieval cues, 282–283
source monitoring, 285
tip-of-the-tongue phenomenon, 282–283
retrieval cues, 282–283
retroactive interference, 288, 289*f*
retrograde amnesia, 295, 295*f*
retrospective memory, 299, 299*f*
reuptake, 82

reversibility, 455
reversible figure, 143, 147, 147*f*, 148*f*
reward pathway, 211, 211*f*
Reynolds, Charles F. III, 647
rhymes, 303
right hemisphere, 102–105, 117–119
risk-benefit assessments, 571
risky decision making, 336
risky decisions, 336–337
Rodin, Judith, 396
rods, 134
Rogers, Carl, 11, 508–510, 629, 644
romance, 230*f*
romantic ideals, 675–677
Rose, Donna T., 595
Rosenhan, David, 578–579
Rosenthal, Robert, 64

S

sample, 62, 62*f*, 351
sampling bias, 62–63, 73
saturation, 131*f*
"sauce béarnaise syndrome," 249–250
Savage-Rambaugh, Sue, 322
savings scores, 287
Scarr, Sandra, 370
Schachter, Stanley, 425–426
Schachter's two-factor theory, 425–426
schedules of reinforcement
described, 240, 242–243
fixed-interval (FI) schedule, 243
fixed-ratio (FR) schedule, 243
interval schedules, 243
and patterns of response, 244*f*
ratio schedules, 243
research on, 244
variable-interval (VI) schedule, 243
variable-ratio (VR) schedule, 243
Schellenberg, E. Glenn, 161
schema, 280–281
schizophrenia
see also schizophrenic disorders
and dopamine synapses, 85
etiology, 601–604
family studies, 110*f*
meaning of term, 598
stress-vulnerability model, 613*f*
schizophrenic disorders
see also schizophrenia
catatonic schizophrenia, 599–600
course of, 600
defined, 598
delusions, 599
deterioration of adaptive behaviour, 599
disorganized schizophrenia, 600
disturbed emotion, 599
dopamine hypothesis, 601–602
etiology, 601–604
expressed emotion, 603–604, 604*f*

general symptoms, 598–599
genetic vulnerability, 601
hallucinations, 599
irrational thought, 599
negative symptoms, 600
neurochemical factors, 601–602
neurodevelopmental hypothesis, 603, 603f
outcome, 600
paranoid schizophrenia, 599
positive symptoms, 600
prevalence, 598
stress, 604
structural brain abnormalities, 602–603
subtypes, 599–600
undifferentiated schizophrenia, 600
Schmolck, H., 277
schools, and gender-role socialization, 485
Schuller, Regina, 610
science of behaviour, 6
scientific approach
see also research
application and control, 42
conclusions, 45
data analysis, 45
data collection, 45, 45t
description, 42
descriptive/correlational research, 52–57
design of study, 44–45
experimental research, 48–51
formulation of hypothesis, 44
goals of, 42–44
measurement, 42
operational definition, 44
prediction, 42
reporting on findings, 45
selection of research method, 44–45
steps in scientific investigation, 44–47
understanding, as goal, 42
search for identity, 467–468
searching for analogies, 330–331
second-hand smoke, 559
second language learning, 318–321, 320f
secondary-process thinking, 495
secondary reinforcers, 242
secondary sex characteristics, 463–464
secure adults, 677
secure attachment, 448, 449, 676
sedatives, 194–195, 208
seeing. See visual system
selection of alternative, 335–336
selective attention models, 269f
selective breeding, 109
selective deprivation, 192–193
selective serotonin reuptake inhibitors (SSRIs), 641

the self
and the brain, 94–95
culture, and conceptions of self, 523f
development of, 509
independent view of self, 522
interdependent view of self, 522
self-actualization theory
healthy personality, 512, 513f
hierarchy of needs, 511–512, 512f
need for self-actualization, 512
self-actualizing persons, 512
self-concept, 509, 510–511
self-control, 258–261
self-criticism, 523
self-deception, 498, 547
self-efficacy, 506–507
self-enhancement, 522–523, 675
self-indulgence, 546
self-instructional training, 631
self-monitoring, 520–521
self-oriented perfectionism, 594
self-perception theory, 686, 686f
self-referent encoding, 272–273
self-report data, 64, 73
self-report inventories, 525–528
self-sacrifice, 115
self-serving bias, 672, 674
self-socialization, 484–485
self-stimulation centres, 98
Seligman, Martin, 249, 558
semantic encoding, 271, 279
semantic memory system, 298, 475
semantic networks, 281–282, 281f
semantic slanting, 344–345
semantics, 313–314
semicircular canals, 167
sensation
see also senses; specific senses
defined, 126
vs. perception, 126f
sensation seeking, 520, 521f
senses
hearing. See auditory system
kinesthetic system, 167
smell, 164, 164f
taste, 162–164, 162f
touch, 165–166
vestibular system, 167
vision. See visual system
sensorimotor period, 454
sensory adaptation, 130
sensory integration, 167
sensory memory, 273–274, 274f
sensory scaling, 128
sensory systems. See senses
separation anxiety, 448
serial-position effect, 301, 302f
series completion problems, 326, 327f

serotonin, 85
set-point theory, 401
settling-point theory, 401
sex
defined, 481
psychoanalytic theory and, 496–497
sexual arousal, 413–414
sexual attraction, and fear, 46–47, 50, 50t
sexual behaviour
determinants of sexual desire, 403–405
evolutionary analyses, 405–409
gender differences in sexual activity patterns, 406–407
parental investment theory, 405
sexual arousal, 413–414
sexual orientation, 409–413
sexual response, 413–414
sexual desire, 403–405
sexual orientation
biological theories, 411–413
continuum, 410f
controversy, 409–410
defined, 409
environmental theories, 411
homosexuality, statistics, 410–411
sexual response, 413–414
shadow, 149
shaping, 238–240, 241f
shared family environment, 516
Shaver, Philip, 676
Shiffrin, Richard, 273
shift work, 185
short-term memory
capacity of storage, 275–276
chunks, 275–276
defined, 275
durability of storage, 275
vs. long-term memory, 278–279
Peterson and Peterson study, 275f
rehearsal, 275
vs. working memory, 276, 276f
shuttle box, 245
sick role, 588
Siegel, Shepard, 212
siesta cultures, 189
signal-detection theory, 128–129
signal relations, 251–252
similarity, 145, 682
similarity effects, 675
Simon, Herbert, 16, 335
Simon, Theodore, 356
simple cells, 137
simplicity, 145–146
situational specificity, 507
Sixteen Personality Factor (16PF) Questionnaire, 526, 527f
skin, 165–166
Skinner, B.F., 9–10, 236, 237, 238, 325, 504–505
Skinner box, 238, 239f

sleep
age trends, 188–189
and alcohol, 216
ascending reticular activating system (ARAS), 190, 191f
and biological rhythms, 183–185
changes in patterns, over life span, 190f
and circadian rhythms, 183–185
co-sleeping, 189
common questions about, 216–218
and culture, 189
cycles of, 186–188, 188f, 196f
deprivation, 191–193
and drugs, 216
electroencephalograph (EEG), 186
electromyograph (EMG), 186
electrooculograph (EOG), 186
hypnic jerks, 186
neural bases of, 190
non-REM (NREM) sleep, 188
quality of, 184
REM sleep, 187–188
repeating the cycle, 188
siesta cultures, 189
sleep needs, 216, 216f
sleep spindles, 186
slow-wave sleep (SWS), 186, 193
snoring, 217
stages 1-4, 186
yawning, 217
sleep apnea, 196
sleep deprivation
complete sleep deprivation, 191
impact of, 192–193
partial sleep deprivation, 191–192
REM deprivation, 192–193, 194f
selective deprivation, 192–193
sleep disorders
avoidance of, 217–218, 217f
and cycle of sleep, 196f
insomnia, 193–195, 218, 218f
narcolepsy, 195–196
night terrors, 196
nightmares, 196
pseudo-insomnia, 194
sleep apnea, 196
somnambulism, 196
sleep learning, 216
sleep restriction, 191–192
sleep spindles, 186
sleep state misperception, 194
sleep terrors, 196
sleepwalking, 196
slippery slope, 433
slotting behaviour, 115–116
slow response rate, 238
slow-to-warm-up children, 447
slow-wave sleep (SWS), 186, 193

smell, 164, 164f
Smith, Andrew P., 555
smoking, 558–559
snoring, 217
Snyder, Solomon, 86
social activity, and happiness, 429
social behaviour, 482
social class, and mental retardation, 364f
social cognitive theory
cognitive processes and reciprocal determinism, 505–506
observational learning, 506
self-efficacy, 506–507
social communication theories of language acquisition, 324
social desirability bias, 64, 73, 528
social influence strategies, 703
social intelligence, 361
social learning theory, 505
social loafing, 694
social perception. See person perception
social policy, 181
social psychology
attitudes, 679–687
attribution processes, 669–674
conformity, 688–689
defined, 664
groups, 692–696
interpersonal attraction, 674–679
obedience, 689–691
person perception, 664–669
prejudice, 698–701
Social Readjustment Rating Scale, 539, 540t
social schemas, 666, 666f
social skills training, 637–638
social support, 557
socialization, 484
socially prescribed perfectionism, 594
socioeconomic disadvantage, 373
sociohistorical context, 27–28
soma, 79
somatic nervous system, 87, 88
somatization disorder, 587
somatoform disorders
cognitive factors, 588
conversion disorder, 587
defined, 586–587
etiology, 588
hypochondriasis, 587
personality factors, 588
sick role, 588
somatization disorder, 587
somnambulism, 196
sound, 155, 156f
sound pressure, 157f
source, 681
source monitoring, 285
source-monitoring error, 285
sources of sound, 159

spanking, 247–248
Spanos, Nicholas, 201
spatial tasks, 118
specific mental abilities, 376–377
speech localization, 119f
speech prosody, 161
Sperry, Roger, 16, 102, 103
spinal cord, 89
split-brain patients, 119
split-brain surgery, 102–104
spontaneous recovery, 234
spontaneous remission, 633
spotlight effect, 668
SQ3R, 33
Squire, L.R., 277
Stack, Jacqueline A., 647
stage, 451
standard deviation, 57–58
standardization, 351–352
standardization group, 352
Stanford-Binet Intelligence Scale, 356–357, 378f
statistical significance, 61, 570
statistics
    central tendency, 57
    correlation, 58–60
    correlation coefficient, 58, 59f
    for data analysis, 45
    defined, 57
    descriptive statistics, 57–60
    on health risks, 570
    inferential statistics, 60–61
    mean, 57
    median, 57
    mode, 57
    standard deviation, 57–58
    statistical significance, 61, 570
    variability, 57–58
Steele, Claude, 374
Steele, C.M., 374
Steinberg, Dena L., 595
stereotype vulnerability, 373–375
stereotypes, 666–667, 698–699
Sternberg, Robert, 379–380
stimulants, 196, 210f
stimulus, 6
stimulus contiguity, 233
stimulus control, 240–241
stimulus discrimination, 235, 241
stimulus generalization, 234–235, 241
stimulus-response (S-R) psychology, 6
storage
    Atkinson and Shiffrin model, 274f
    capacity of, 275–276
    defined, 268
    durability of, 275
    knowledge, representation and organization of, 279–282
    long-term memory (LTM), 276–279
    sensory memory, 273–274, 274f
    short-term memory (STM), 275–276

stream of consciousness, 182
stress
    aggression, 546
    and anxiety disorders, 586
    behavioural responses, 544–548
    blaming oneself, 546
    and brain-body pathways, 544, 545f
    burnout, 549–550, 550f
    catharsis, 546
    and common cold, 555–556
    common emotions, 542
    conflict, 538–539
    conscientiousness, 558
    coping. See coping
    defined, 536
    and depression, 553–554
    and eating, 398–399
    emotional arousal, 542–543
    emotional responses, 541–543
    as everyday event, 537
    fight-or-flight response, 543
    frustration, 537–538
    general adaptation syndrome, 543–544
    heart disease, 552–554
    hostility, 552–553
    and immune functioning, 554–555
    impaired task performance, 549
    inverted-U hypothesis, 542–543
    learned helplessness, 545–546
    life changes, 539–540
    moderator variables, 557–558
    and mood disorders, 597
    nature of, 536–537
    and optimism, 558
    and other health problems, 554–555, 554t
    overview of stress process, 542f
    and panic disorder, 586f
    physical health, effects on, 552–557
    physiological responses, 543–544
    positive effects of, 551
    post-traumatic stress disorders (PTSD), 550
    pressure, 540, 541f
    psychological functioning, effects on, 549–551
    psychological problems and disorders, 550–551
    psychosomatic diseases, 552
    responses to, 541–548
    schizophrenic disorders, 604
    self-indulgence, 546
    and social support, 557
    stress-illness correlation, 556–557, 557f

subjective appraisal of, 537
    Type A personality, 552–553
    types of, 537–541
stress-illness correlation, 556–557, 557f
stress management, 566–569
    see also coping
stress-vulnerability model of schizophrenia, 613f
string problem, 326, 327f
striving for superiority, 502
structuralism
    described, 5
    vs. functionalism, 4–6
Struss, Donald, 94
studies. See research studies
study habits, 31–33
subgoals, 330
subjective contours, 144–145, 144f
subjective feelings, 418–419
subjective probability, 337
subjective utility, 336–337
subjective well-being, 428, 431
subjectivity of experience, 29–30, 209
subjects, 45
subliminal perception, 129–130
subtractive colour mixing, 140
sudden infant death syndrome, 442
suicide
    adolescent suicide, 464–466
    First Nations youths, 465–466
    psychological autopsies, 53
superego, 495
superior colliculus, 136
superstitions, 225–226
supertasters, 163
suprachiasmatic nucleus (SCN), 184
Surrealists, 172
surveys, 54–55
survival of the fittest, 113
susceptibility to boredom, 520
sympathetic division, 88, 543
symptoms, 563
synapses, 79, 80–84, 82f, 210
synaptic cleft, 80–82
synaptic pruning, 83, 84f
synaptic transmission, 83f
synaptic vesicles, 80–81
syntax, 314
systematic desensitization, 636, 636f, 637f
Szasz, Thomas, 577

T

taking chances, 336–337
talking cure, 624
tardive dyskinesia, 640
Tashman, Nancy A., 595
taste, 162–164, 162f
taste buds, 162
Taylor, Shelley, 548
technical eclecticism, 648
technical journals, 69

telegraphic speech, 318
temperament, 446–447
temporal lobes, 99
Terman, Lewis, 356–357
terminal buttons, 79
test norms, 351–352
test-retest reliability, 353, 353f
test-taking strategies, 34–35
testing perspective, 379
testwiseness, 34
texture gradients, 149
thalamus, 97
THC, 209
Thematic Apperception Test (TAT), 415, 415f, 528, 529f
theoretical integration, 648
theoretical perspectives
    see also specific theoretical perspectives
    behaviourism, 6–7
    evolutionary psychology, 19–21
    functionalism, 4–6
    humanism, 11–12
    overview of, 11t
    psychoanalytic theory, 8–9
    relative prominence of major schools of thought, 16f
    structuralism, 4–6
theory
    construction, 44f
    defined, 26, 42
    testable nature of, 43–44
theory of bounded rationality, 335
therapeutic services, 654–657
therapists, 654–657
theta, 182
Thomas, Alexander, 446
Thompson, William Forde, 161
Thorndike, E.L., 237
Thorndike's law of effect, 237
three-ring conception of eminent giftedness, 366f
thresholds, 127
thrill, 520
time-based tasks, 299
time management, 32f
tip-of-the-tongue phenomenon, 282–283
Titchener, Edward, 5
token economy, 260
tolerance, 209, 210f
tongue, 162f
Tooby, John, 338
top-down processing, 144, 144f
the Toraja of Indonesia, 199, 199t
touch
    pain, 165–167
    pressure, 165
    receptive field, 165, 165f
tower of Hanoi problem, 330, 330f
tranquilizers, 639
transcendental meditation (TM), 204–205
transfer-appropriate processing, 289

transference, 628–629
transformation problems, 326
transvestic fetishism, 577
traumatic events, 551f
treatment
    behaviour therapies, 624, 635–638
    biomedical therapies, 624–625, 638–643
    blending approaches, 646–648
    clients, 625
    critical thinking about, 658–659
    cultural barriers, 648
    current trends and issues, 646–649
    deinstitutionalization, 650–652
    eclecticism, 648
    elements of treatment process, 624–626
    expense of, 655
    insight therapies, 624, 627–634
    insomnia, 194–195
    institutional barriers, 648
    institutional treatment, 649–652
    language barriers, 648
    multicultural sensitivity, 648–649
    other mental health professionals, 626
    overview of major approaches, 644–645
    psychiatrists, 626
    psychologists, 625–626
    therapist, finding a, 654–657
    therapists, 625–626
    types of, 624–625
trephening, 639
Tri-Council, 67
trial, 229
trial and error, 329
triarchic theory of human intelligence, 379, 379f
trichromatic theory of colour vision, 140–141
tricyclics, 641
trivial memory illusions, 292
trust versus mistrust, 452
trustworthiness, 682
tsunami, 41
Tulving, Endel, 94, 297
Tuskegee Syphilis Study, 65
Tversky, Amos, 337
twin studies
    anxiety disorders, 584f
    described, 109–110
    intelligence, hereditary influence on, 367–368
    intelligence and personality, 111f
    mood disorders, 593, 593f
    obesity, 400
    personality, 515–516, 515f
two-process theory of avoidance, 246
two-sided argument, 682
Type A personality, 552–553
Type B personality, 552–553
Tyrrell, David A. J., 555

U

ultraviolet spectrum, 132
uncertainty, 571
unconditional love, 509
unconditional positive regard, 630
unconditioned response (UCR), 228
unconditioned stimulus (UCS), 228
unconscious, 8, 496
underextensions, 317–318
undifferentiated schizophrenia, 600
unfit to stand trial, 610
uninhibited temperament, 447
universalistic view, 611
unnecessary constraints, 328–329
upside-down T illusion, 151f

V

vacillation, 539
validity
  construct validity, 354–355, 355f
  content validity, 354
  criterion-related validity, 354
  defined, 353
  intelligence tests, 361
validity effect, 683
validity scales, 525
value judgments, 578
variable-interval (VI) schedule, 243
variable-ratio (VR) schedule, 243
variables
  confounding of variables, 49–50

defined, 42
dependent variables, 48, 50
extraneous variables, 49–50
independent variables, 48, 50
manipulation of independent variables, 50
variations in design of experiments, 50
vasocongestion, 413
ventricles, 89, 89f
ventromedial nucleus of the hypothalamus (VMH), 395
verbal intelligence, 361
verbal mnemonics, 302–304
vestibular system, 167
Veterans Administration (VA) hospitals, 14
violence. See aggression
visceral arousal, 419
vision for action, 153–155
vision for perception, 153–155
visual acuity, 134
visual agnosia, 138
visual imagery, 271–272
visual mnemonics, 303–304
visual perception
  binocular depth cues, 148
  bottom-up processing, 144, 144f
  context, 148
  contrast effects, 176f
  depth perception, 148–149
  distal stimuli, 146, 147f
  feature analysis, 143–145, 144f

Gestalt principles, 145–146
inattentional blindness, 143
linear perspective, 149
monocular cues, 148–149
motion parallax, 149
optical illusions, 150–153
perceptual constancies, 149–150
perceptual hypothesis, formulation of, 146–148
perceptual set, 143
pictorial depth cues, 149
proximal stimuli, 146–147, 147f
reversible figure, 143
subjective contours, 144–145, 144f
top-down processing, 144, 144f
vision for perception, 153–155
visual receptors, 134
visual-spatial ability, 20, 482
visual system
  see also visual perception
  blind spot, 134
  and the brain, 136–139
  colour vision, 140–142
  cones, 134, 142
  dark adaptation, 134, 134f
  the eye, 132–133, 132f
  farsightedness, 133, 133f
  feature detectors, 138
  fovea, 134
  Hermann grid, 136f
  information processing in visual cortex, 136–138
  iris, 133
  lateral antagonism, 135–136

lens, 132
light, 131–132
light adaptation, 134
McCollough effect, 139, 139f
nearsightedness, 132–133, 133f
optic chiasm, 136
optic disk, 134
parallel processing, 136
pupil, 133
receptive field, 135, 135f
research methods, 138–139
retina, 132, 133–136, 133f
rods, 134
visual agnosia, 138
visual pathways through the brain, 136, 137f
visual receptors, 134
visuospatial sketchpad, 276
vocabulary spurt, 317, 317f
vocational success, 362
volley principle, 159
von Helmholtz, Hermann, 158, 159
vulnerability, 112

W

WAIS-III, 352
wakefulness. See sleep
Wall, Patrick, 166
Walters, Amy S., 192
Washburn, Mary, 5
water jar problem, 326, 327f, 328f, 329f, 331f
Watson, John B., 6–7, 29
wavelength, 131, 155
weak analogies, 433
Weber, Ernst, 128
Weber fraction, 128
Weber's law, 128
Wechsler, David, 357

Wechsler Adult Intelligence Scale (WAIS), 359f
Wechsler scales, 357, 358
weight, and various diseases, 400f
weight attributes, 335
Weiner, Bernard, 670
Werker, Janet, 315
Wernicke's area, 102f
Wertheimer, Max, 145
Whitehouse, Wayne G., 595
Wiesel, Torsten, 16, 137
Williams, John, 232
windigo, 612
Winner, Ellen, 365
Winocur, Gordon, 94
wish fulfillment, 199–200
Wolfe, David, 48
Wolpe, Joseph, 636, 644
women
  biased patterns of attribution, 699–700
  menarche, 464
  menopause, 473
  in psychology, 13, 13f
work, and happiness, 430
working backward, 330
working memory, 276, 276f, 475
Wright, Mary, 13f
Wundt, Wilhelm, 3–4

Y

yawning, 217

Z

Zanna, Mark, 667
Zollner illusion, 151f
zygote, 107, 439